Concise
Critical
Comments
of the
Old Testament

Concise
Critical
Comments
of the
Old Testament

Robert Young, LL. D.

Sovereign Grace Publishers, Inc.
P.O. Box 4998
Lafayette, IN 47903
2001

Printed In the United States of America
By Lightning Source, Inc.

PREFACE

No BOOK in the world has called forth such an amount of literature as the Bible; it has been translated into nearly two hundred dialects; it has afforded mental study to millions of the human race now living, and to millions more now in glory. It is computed that upwards of *fifty thousand* works on separate portions of it have been published in the English language alone; of these, about twenty-five hundred relate to the Pentateuch, five thousand to the Psalms, two thousand to Isaiah, six thousand to the four Gospels, three thousand to Romans, and two thousand to Revelation, besides those on the whole Bible! Daily the number is increasing, and doubtless will increase.

In spite of this extraordinary amount of Biblical Literature, it is doubtful whether the Church has increased much in her knowledge of the Bible beyond what was possessed a century ago. And the chief reason is conceived to be, that few of these commentators really thought, to any extent, for themselves; they compared, enlarged, or condensed the writings of the authors who lived before them, quoted this father and that father, supported their theories by one council and another council; so that, in fact, the reader gets something like a *history* of the interpretation of the text, what the Calvinists thought, and what the Arminians thought, and what the Papists thought, and what the Unitarians thought, rather than the *interpretation itself*. 'Poli Synopsis Criticorum,' was the great source from which they drew their inspiration, and with a few odds and ends gathered from other quarters, a great many practical remarks, which were often good but far from being textual, their work was complete; all run in the same beaten path—elaborate explanations and reflections are given when none is necessary, and almost none at all when they are really indispensable to the enquiring reader.

Yet the Bible is not a difficult book; the subjects it treats of are, in some respects, 'hard to be understood,' but the language in which they are expressed is *generally*—it might be said *uniformly*—simple. The danger lies in attaching to the simple words of Scripture meanings which they *might, could, would, or should have*, and of straining the meaning to the utmost extent of which the words are capable. Starting with pre-conceived notions, formed it may be insensibly, the words are tortured to support them: for example, most translators or expositors of the Bible, starting with the notion that the narrative in the first chapter of Genesis describes the original creation of the matter of the universe, use and understand the words *beginning, created, made, &c.*, in the highest sense of which the words are capable; but if one were to start with the conviction that it is not so, that the narrative describes rather a reconstruction or reorganization of a previously existing state of things, he would find no difficulty in maintaining his views from the more ordinary use of the original words. Round the plainest Scripture language there is such a cluster of traditions which have not the shadow of a foundation to rest on, that the Jewish and Mohammedan legends regarding Adam, Cain, Nimrod, David, Solomon, &c., are only grosser representations of them.

The plain grammatical and historical interpretation is the only clue out of this labyrinth. It is the only certain plan, as it is the easiest. The question is not—what *may* this teach? but—what does it teach? not—does it agree with what is called the analogy of faith? but—*is it the truth of the text?* However startling a translation be, if it be only certain that it is the *literal* and *idiomatic* rendering of the passage in question, it *must be* in accordance with every other part of God's will—whether we see it or not.

The present work is more especially designed as a Companion to the 'New Translation of the Bible,' its primary object being to illustrate the principal passages in which—

I. The New Version differs from the Common one, or where
II. The meaning of either or both Versions is obscure

No difficult passage is left unnoticed, and should the reader think otherwise, he may rest assured, the omission is unintentional. The object is not to say all that could be said on any given subject, but only what is thought strictly necessary. All the works of the commentators and critics (as well as the chief ancient and modern Versions) within reach, have been consulted occasionally, but the desire has been to present chiefly what had previously passed through the writer's own mind in the work of translation.

One peculiar feature of this Commentary will commend itself to the approval of every intelligent mind, viz. that the meaning attached to every word or phrase discussed is supported by references to those passages only in which the same term is employed in the original, by which means a kind of *positive certainty* is attained, very different from the confusion and inconsistency arising from the use of Cruden's Concordance, and of all other works based on a mere translation, however perfect. To carry this principle out still further, parallel passages are *primarily* taken from the other portions of the same writer's compositions, e.g. those in 'Genesis' from the other four books attributed to Moses; those in 'Romans' from the other acknowledged writings of Paul, and so on.

GENESIS

GENESIS is, by the almost unanimous consent of the Jewish and Christian Churches, ascribed to Moses. The book itself does not, however, say so; nor can it be with certainty inferred from any passage in the Old or New Testaments; neither is it essential, provided its author's inspiration be admitted. With the exception, perhaps, of the book of Job, it may be regarded as the oldest of the Scripture Books. There is reason to believe that *writing*, as well as *speech*, was a divine gift, and that Adam or the other patriarchs left records behind them of what had occurred to them. Moses, or the author of Genesis, prompted by the Divine Spirit, collected and embodied these into a regular narrative as an introduction to Exodus, &c.

I. 1. IN THE BEGINNING OF.] The Hebrew word thus rendered occurs *fifty-one* times in the Old Testament. In *forty-five* of these, it occurs in the *construct state*, being followed by a noun or pronoun. The remaining instances are Le. 2. 12, De. 33. 21, Ne. 12. 44, (in all of which it appears to be a technical name—first-fruits, i.e. of the land, &c.); Pr. 4. 7, *the first thing* is wisdom ;' Is. 46. 10, ' declaring the end from *the beginning.*' This last is the only passage in the Old Testament in which the word is used *absolutely* in reference to *time*, and whether it is sufficient to overrule the *forty-five*, is much more than doubtful. Accordingly, the ancient Jewish commentator Rashi, as well as the modern German critics, Bunsen, Ewald, &c., have preferred understanding the next Hebrew word as a noun, not as a verb. Viewed in this light, the passage reads thus : ' In the beginning of God's preparing the heavens and the earth, the earth then has existed waste and void,' and has no reference to the original creation of matter, but to a subsequent formation, probably referred to also in Pr. 8. 26, ' while He hath not made the earth, or the outplaces, or the *highest part* of the dusts of the (habitable *or* fruit-bearing) world.' See also v. 23, of the same chapter: ' of old I have been set up (*or* anointed, see Ps. 2. 6,) from the beginning, from former states of the earth.' Contrary to all Hebrew idiom is the translation of some, ' first of all, *or* in the first place, God,' &c.

GOD.] Heb. ELOHIM, a plural noun, the singular form of which is *Eloah*, meaning 'The Worshipful One ;' it seems to point out a superabundance of *qualities* in the Divine Being rather than ᴀ plurality ot *persons*, as it is applied alike to Jehovah and to the false gods of the nations. It is found almost invariably accompanied by a verb in the singular number.

PREPARING.] This is preferable to ' *creating*,' which is now so closely connected with the idea of production *from nothing*, that it is much too strong for the real significance of the Hebrew word, which is applied in Ge. 1. 21, to the formation of seamonsters; in v. 27, to the formation of man; in Ex. 34. 10, to performing marvels; in Ps. 51. 10, to the formation or creation of a clean heart; in 89. 12, to the appointment of the north and the south ; in 102. 18, to the formation of a people; in Is. 4. 5, to the production of a cloud and smoke; in 45. 7, to the producing or bringing to pass of darkness and evil; in 57. 19 to the producing of the fruit of the lips; in 65. 18 to making or appointing Jerusalem a rejoicing; in 48. 7 to the producing or bringing forth of hidden things; in Je. 31. 22 to producing or bringing to pass a new thing; in Ez. 21. 30 to the formation of a nation; in 28. 13 to a person being born *or* being appointed king; in Amos 4. 13 to producing the wind. Compare also Ez. 23. 47, Jos. 17. 15, 18. To limit it to creation *from nothing*, ME-AYIN would require to be added to the verb. Very childish is the objection of some that if this word *bara* does not express creation proper, the Hebrews had no other verb to do so. ' To create from nothing,' is a phrase, and no language on earth, it is believed, can express it, save by a phrase, any more than Hebrew, in which *asah meayin*, *hotzia me-ayin*, *paal me-ayin*, &c., are equally suitable with *bara me-ayin*.

2. EXISTED.] This rendering is, perhaps, preferable to that of the Common Version ' *was*;' the Hebrew verb is not simply the logical nexus *is*, *was*, &c., but the real verb of existence. The thought is, that, at the beginning here referred to, the earth was, and has been existing in a certain state described as—

WASTE AND VOID.] Two Hebrew words almost if not entirely synonymous. Compare Je. 4. 23, where they are repeated, also Is. 34. 11; 41. 19, Job 26. 7; 45. 18, &c. The words combined form a phrase: ' utterly void,' i.e. of light and life.

DARKNESS.] The original word denotes the *natural darkness of night*, which may

A

imply the existence of daylight at a former period.

DEEP.] In Ge. 7. 11, Is. 51. 10, Amos 7. 4, it is called 'the *great* deep.' Perhaps 'the humming thing, the waves, the ocean;' once in Ps. 71. 20, 'the depths of earth.' Comp. Ps. 36. 6, Pr. 8. 24.

SPIRIT OF GOD.] This phrase always means in the Pentateuch the Holy Spirit; never a great wind,' as some have conjectured.

FLUTTERING.] The original word only occurs in two other Scripture passages, viz. De. 32. 11, 'As an eagle .. over its young ones fluttereth,' and Je. 23. 9, 'fluttered have all my bones.'

3. AND GOD SAITH.] The present tense 'saith' expresses the beautiful and striking peculiarity of the Hebrew and Eastern writers, who, in narrating or describing *past* or *future scenes*, invariably place themselves in the position of *eye-witnesses* and *contemporaries*. The same thing is often done by lively writers in all languages.

Once for all, it may be remarked, that when *speaking*, *resting*, *repenting*, &c., are used of God, it is after the manner of men. We understand anything of *the Unknown* only by figures derived from the *known*.

LET LIGHT BE.] This does not necessarily imply that light did not before exist in the universe (see note on v. 2 above), but that it was now to take possession of a spot which, at the time the command was given, was in darkness. In numerous cases it is translated, 'It cometh to pass, happeneth,' &c. More literally still, it might be rendered simply, 'There is light !' which heightens our idea of the Divine Majesty—which spake and it was done.

4. SEPARATETH.] This is preferable to '*divide*,' we divide *one* thing ; we separate *two*.

5. DAY.] This Hebrew word, which occurs twice in this v. is derived from a root, 'to hum, make a noise,' or from another, 'to be hot.' It thus denotes the busy time of day, i.e. daylight, a period of about twelve hours ; in the last clause, however, it appears to be extended so as to include day and night, a period of twenty-four hours. In Ge. 2. 4 it is applied to the whole period of the formation of the heavens and the earth described by Moses. In the plural it occurs, Ge. 4. 3 ; 24. 55, in the sense of seven days or a week. In Ge. 39. 11, and 1 Sa. 3. 2, it evidently means *time* in *general*; and in Le. 25. 29 it apparently means *a year*.

EVENING,] 'a mixture,' or 'darkness,' the period between sunset and night.

MORNING,] 'a breaking forth' 'daybreak,' the period between night and sunrise.

DAY ONE.] The inspired Seer, viewing the day's work as complete in itself, and without reference to future operations declares it to be *day one*, which proves eventually to be the *first* of a series.

6. AN EXPANSE.] Heb. *rakia*, i.e. the atmosphere, surrounding the earth, which bears up the waters of the clouds. Most commentators, following the Latin and Greek versions, have rendered the word

'firmament ;' but this is now abandoned by critics.

7. MAKETH.] The original word has a great latitude of meaning and application. In v. 11 it means to *make* or *yield* fruit; in 8. 6, to *build* a ship; in 18. 7, to *make ready* food ; in Ex. 5. 9, to *work* in general ; in 29. 36, to *make* a sacrifice; in 12. 48, to *observe* a festival ; in De. 21. 12, to *dress* the nails ; in Job 15. 27, to *make* fat on the loins ; in Isa. 7. 22, to *yield* milk ; in 19, 10, to *earn* wages ; in 2 Sa. 19. 24, to *dress* the beard ; in 1 K. 12. 31, 1 Sa. 12. 6, to *appoint* a person to an office.

AND IT IS SO.] The original word (which occurs also in v. 9, 11, 15. 24, 30) is derived from a root signifying 'right, erect, honest, upright.' See Ge. 42. 11, 19, 31, Is. 16. 6, Ex. 10. 29, Nu. 27. 7 ; 36. 5, Ec. 8. 10, 2. K. 7. 9.

8. HEAVENS.] The original word is always in the old plural number, never in the *singular*. It is commonly derived from an Arabic word signifying 'high,' in opposition to the earth, the 'low' place. Some explain it as the place 'where there are waters.' It might perhaps with great propriety always be rendered '*skies*.'

9. COLLECTED] or WAIT. The original word is elsewhere only in Je. 3. 17, and seems to be connected with another term signifying 'a rope or cord' for girding or binding.

10. EARTH.] The original word, as stated above, is commonly derived from an Arabic root signifying a 'low' place, in opposition to 'heavens,' the high or heaved-up things. It is often translated 'land, country,' and ought perhaps to be so rendered throughout this chapter.

SEAS.] The Hebrew word may signify 'noisy, tumultuous,' and is a fitting appellation for the 'restless sea.'

11. TENDER GRASS.] From a root signifying 'to sprout, to be green,' (Joel 2. 22), hence first sprouts, differing from the next word translated—

HERB,] which is the more mature herbage, fully grown and in seed, intended for the use of man and beast. See v. 29, 30.

14. LUMINARIES.] This word is different from that translated 'light' in v. 3. That signifies light itself, this the 'light-givers,' or 'places of light.'

16. AND THE STARS.] There is no reference to the creation or formation of the stars, but to their (apparent) offices in reference to this earth. Compare Ps. 136. 9, 'The moon and stars for the rule of the night.' Also Je. 31. 35. To think otherwise arises from ignorance of Hebrew and Greek idiom, which allows a verb to have a nominative preceding it, and another succeeding it, e.g. Is. 48. 16, 'And now, the Lord Jehovah hath sent me—and His Spirit ;' the idiom is too common to be doubtful; yet what is to be thought of the Biblical Critics who coolly suppose the stars to be made 6000 years ago, and risk the credibility of the Bible on the truth of this notion ?

17. GIVETH.] The original word has a great latitude of meaning. See its use in Ex. 30. 16, Nu. 35. 6, Jos. 20. 2, 8, Ezra 8.

20, Is. 61. 8, Je. 1. 5, Ez. 4. 6; 36. 5, 2 Sa. 11. 16, 2 K. 8. 6, 1 Ch. 6. 48; 16. 4, Ez. 45. 6, Ge. 17. 5, Ps. 89. 27; 78. 66; 119. 110.

IN,] or 'through' the expanse of the heavens, as the Heb. particle often signifies.

20. TEEM.] The original word is expressive of fecundity. Ge. 7. 21; 8. 17; 9. 7, Ex. 1. 7; 8. 3, Le. 11. 29, 41, 42, 43, Ps. 105. 30.

AND LET FOWL FLY]. The Common Version implies that the waters were to bring forth fowl, which is in opposition to ch. 2. 19, where it is said, 'and Jehovah God formeth from the ground every beast of the field, and every fowl of the heavens.'

21. PREPARETH THE GREAT MONSTERS.] On the word 'prepare' see remarks on v. 1 above. The common translation 'whale' is too definite, the idea of the original word being simply that of a *long extended animal*, belonging either to the *sea* (Job 7. 12, Is. 27. 1), or to the *land* (Ex. 7. 9, 10, 12, De. 32. 33, Ps. 74. 13; 91. 13). See also Ps 14. 27, Is. 51. 9, &c.

26. LET US.] This can only reasonably be understood of the *Three in One*. Compare similar expressions in ch. 3. 22; 11. 7. Only twice in the Old Testament, and these in later times, (Ezra and Daniel), do any instances occur of single individuals using the plural form, but these exceptions only support the general rule, and the consequent inference. On no principle of language can one person say 'one of us,' when speaking of himself alone.

27. PREPARETH.] See note on v. 1 above.

29. HERB SOWING SEED,] as in v. 11, 12.

FOR FOOD.] Most critics prefer the word 'food' to 'meat,' as the latter is often used now for *flesh*.

30. BREATH OF LIFE.] The same original phrase is in v. 20, 21, 24; 2, 19, translated 'living creature.'

31. THAT HE HATH DONE.] Comp. Ge. 3. 14; 6.22; 8.21; 9.24; 12.18; 20.5; 21.26; Ps. 115.3.

II. 1. COMPLETED.] The idea is not only that the work was finished or ended, but that it was perfected and adorned.

HOST.] Applied to any regularly constituted body or company or assembly of *persons (soldiers*, Nu. 31. 53, *Levites*, Nu. 4. 23, 35, 39, 43, *women*, Ex. 38. 8, 1 Sa. 2. 22) or *things (sun, moon*, and *stars*, Is. 34. 4; 40. 26; 45. 12, Je. 33. 22, Da. 8. 10). It is applied to God's servants, whether *angelic* (1 K. 22. 19, 2 Ch. 18. 18, Ps. 148. 2) or *human* (Ex. 12. 41, &c.)

The first chapter properly ends with the third verse of the second chapter.

4. BIRTHS.] Highly expressive of the various stages of the earth's progress, from a root signifying 'to yield, bring forth.'

5. SHRUB.] The following are all the places in which the original word occurs, viz. Ge. 21. 15, Job 30. 4, 7.

NO SHRUB IS YET....NO HERB YET SPROUTETH.] The Common Version of this verse implies that the shrubs and herbs were *made* before they *grew*, contrary to v. 9.

6. MIST,] or '*vapour*,' as it is translated in Job 36. 27, the only other passage where the same original word occurs.

7. JEHOVAH,] i.e. He (who) is; the Existing One; the personal name of the God of Israel.

FORMETH] man. The same original word occurs also in v. 8, 19, below. It is applied to the formation of man, beasts, leviathan (Ps. 104. 26), idols (Is. 44. 10), the world (Is. 45. 18), summer and winter (Ps. 74. 17) the heart (Ps. 33. 15), the eye (Ps. 94. 9), mischief (Ps. 94. 20), light (Is. 45. 7), the earth (Is. 45. 18), the mountains (Amos 4. 13), grasshoppers (Amos 7. 1), the spirit of man (Ze. 12. 1), weapons (Is. 54. 17).

LIVING CREATURE.] The same phrase occurs in ch. 1. 20, 24, 30; 2. 19; 9. 10, 12, 15; Le. 11. 10. It does not denote the immortal part of man, but his animal life.

8. EDEN,] i.e. delight, pleasure. Variously supposed to have been in Armenia, Syria, &c.

9. THE TREE OF LIFE.] As the fruit of this tree was not forbidden to our first parents, they doubtless partook of it as well as of the other trees of the garden: now, if Adam possessed a bodily frame incapable of dissolution, of what use could this tree be to him? The probability is that his bodily frame was originally liable to decay, but having unlimited use of the tree of life, that liability was preternaturally arrested; the sacred tree being always within his reach, had he continued faithful, he would never have tasted of death.

THE TREE OF KNOWLEDGE OF GOOD AND EVIL.] From the true translation of ch. 3. 22, (which see), it would seem that man before he sinned had a knowledge of good and evil, that is, he knew evil as God did, viz. as a matter of fact in the history of God's creatures. The tempter deceived man at first (as he has often done since) by holding out hopes of blessings which man was already is possession of.

11. PISON.] Josephus considered this to be the 'Ganges,' Reland the 'Phasis,' Gesenius the 'Indus.' The Samaritan Version has the 'Nile.' The Deluge doubtless destroyed the possibility of our now being able to distinguish these antediluvian rivers.

HAVILAH] Gesenius conjectures to be India.

12. BDOLAH.] The Common Version, after the Septuagint, Aquila, Symmachus, Jerome, and Josephus, understands by this word a kind of gem called 'bdellium.' Bochart argues for 'pearls,' Lee for 'crystal or beryl.' Nu. 11. 7 is the only other place where the same original word occurs.

SHOHAM,] which is only mentioned elsewhere in Ex. 25. 7; 28. 9, 20; 35. 9, 27; 39. 6, 13, 1 Ch. 29. 2, Job 28. 16, and Ez. 28. 13, is commonly translated *onyx*.

13. GIHON.] The Septuagint, Josephus, Apocrypha, and Gesenius suppose this to be the 'Nile,' others the 'Araxes.'

CUSH.] There appears to have been two or more localities with this name, one in *Asia*, the other in *Africa*.

14. HIDDEKEL.] This is generally agreed to be the Tigris.

PHRAT,] agreed to be the Euphrates, rising in Armenia.

15. CAUSETH HIM TO REST.] The original conveys the idea of depositing a thing for safe keeping. See Ez. 37. 14; 44. 10.

TO KEEP IT.] Properly 'to watch, guard, preserve it.'

17. IN THE DAY.] As our first parents did not die immediately after sinning, it is probable the death threatened here was primarily spiritual death, except we suppose that the meaning was simply that they were then to become *liable* to temporal death. The latter interpretation, however, does not seem so natural as the former.

DYING THOU DOST DIE.] This form of expression is very common in Hebrew, and denotes either (1) the *certainty* of a thing, or (2) its *intensity*. The first is the more common.

18. NOT GOOD FOR THE MAN TO BE ALONE.] Lit. 'the existence of the man by himself is not good.'

AS HIS COUNTERPART.] Lit. 'as *one* over against him,' corresponding to him.

21. DEEP SLEEP.] Ge. 15. 12, 1 Sa. 26. 12, Job 4. 13; 33. 15, Pr. 19. 15, Is. 29. 10, are all the other passages where the same original word occurs. In a *verbal* form it is applied to the sleep of Sisera, Jonah, and Daniel. The word is *radam*, from which come probably the Latin *dormio*. and the English *dream*. Ps. 76. 6, Pr. 10. 5.

22. BUILDETH UP.] The original word is applied in Scripture to the building of a temple, palace, altar, house, &c., and denotes the care and attention bestowed.

23. STEP] or 'movement.' As a *verb* the original word occurs only in Ge. 41. 8, Jud. 13. 25, Ps. 77. 4, Da. 2. 1, 3. As a *noun* it occurs in Gen. 33. 3, Ex. 8. 32, Jud. 5. 28, 2 K. 19. 24, 1 Ch. 11. 11, Ps. 17, 5; 57. 6; 85. 13; 119. 133; 40. 4; Is. 26. 6, &c. translated by such words as *time, wheel, foot, going*, &c. The phrase *de* notes the man's approbation, and his recognition of her as his counterpart.

ON THIS ACCOUNT.] This appears to be the language of the inspired historian, not of Adam. See Mat. 19. 4, 5.

25. ASHAMED OF THEMSELVES.] The form of the original word here occurring is found only in this place.

III. 1. THE SERPENT] is called in the Hebrew *Nahash*, from its hissing sound. According to Lee, it is the generic name of the *serpent* tribe, for (1) the *Nahash* is the form into which the rod of Moses was changed, Ex. 4. 3. (2) It is said to be crooked, Is. 27. 1. (3) It is said to bite, Pr. 23. 32. Ec. 10. 8, 11, Amos 5. 19; 9. 3. (4) It is poisonous, Ps. 58. 4. (5) it has a divided tongue, Ps. 140. 3. (6) It has a gliding motion, Pr. 30. 19. (7) It conceals itself in fences and the holes of walls, Ec. 10. 8, Amos 5. 19. (8) Its threatening sound is mentioned, Je. 46. 22. Compare in addition the following passages, Ge. 49. 17, Nu. 21. 6, 7, 9, Is. 14. 29; 65. 25, Je. 8. 17, Mi. 7. 17. Four kinds of serpents are mentioned in the Old Testament. The supposition of Dr A. Clarke that the original word means '*a monkey*' is quite untenable.

SUBTILE.] The Hebrew word here used never really occurs in a bad sense. It is found eight times in Proverbs (viz. ch. 12 16, 23; 13. 16; 14, 8, 15, 18; 22. 3; 27. 12), in all of which it is translated *prudent*. The only other places where it occurs are Job 5. 12; 15. 5, where some have rendered it *crafty*, but it should be '*subtile*.'

3. NOR TOUCH IT.] This is an *addition* of the woman's to the command of God, see 2. 17.

LEST YE DIE.] This is an *alteration* of God's words: His language is express—'dying thou dost die.' As the command appears to have been originally given to the man alone, before the formation of the woman, she may have known it only through the man. This would illustrate the importance of avoiding second-hand authority in matters of religion.

5. YOUR EYES HAVE BEEN OPENED.] The verb in the original is in the past tense; the meaning is, that God will then see that your eyes have been opened to see your true interest.

AS GOD.] It is improbable that, at such an early period of the world's history, there was any knowledge of false gods; it is better therefore to consider the allusion to be to God himself.

8. AT THE BREEZE.] Lit. the 'wind' of the day, which is so refreshing in eastern countries, at sunset.

WALKING UP AND DOWN.] The form of the original verb denotes repetition, as in Job 1. 7; 2. 2; 1 Sa. 30. 31, Ez. 28. 14, &c.

13. CAUSED ME TO FORGET] by command. Or it may be rendered, 'the serpent *lifted me up* (with pride.)'

14. CURSED ART THOU ABOVE ALL THE CATTLE.] This does not necessarily imply that all the cattle are cursed, any more than the expression in ver. 1 ('and the serpent hath been more subtile than any beast of the field') implies that every beast of the field is subtile.

ON THY BELLY DOST THOU GO.] This does not necessarily imply that the serpent before this had feet, or that it had ever any other mode of progress than that which it has at present, but that it shall continue in this state, and never rise above it.

AND DUST THOU DOST EAT.] In Is. 65. 25, when mention is made of the recovery of the wolf and the lion, it is added, 'as to the serpent, dust *is* its food.' This is its fate, unalterably fixed. But it is necessary to look beyond the serpent to him who moved it. As applied to the Tempter, the curse is—deep degradation and abasement.

15. ENMITY.] The original word occurs elsewhere only in Nu. 35. 21, 22, Ez. 25. 15; 35. 5.

HE DOTH BRUISE THEE—THE HEAD.] 'He,' refers to the Seed of the woman, primarily the Saviour, but generally the human race, of whom He is head. The word in the original translated '*bruise*,' occurs only elsewhere in Ps. 139. 11, 'And if I say, Surely darkness shall *bruise* me, then the night is light for me;' and in Job 9. 17,

'For with a tempestuous shower he *bruis-eth* me.' The *head* is a vital part—the *heel* is not.

16. THY SORROW AND THY CONCEPTION.] Some understand this—'thy sorrow, even thy conception,' others 'the sorrow of thy conception ;' the plain literal sense is preferable. In the latter half of the verse the thought appears to be—'notwithstanding this multiplied sorrow and multiplied conception, thy desire is still towards thy husband for more sons, and in the midst of all this he is thy master.'

18. THOU HAST EATEN THE HERB OF THE FIELD.] In ch. 1. 29, we find that *herbs* were given to man for food from the beginning, so that this verse assigns him nothing new in the way of food. But the *quality* of the land is changed ; it is to bring forth thorns and brambles, if not for the first time, at least in greater abundance than it did before, and only by the sweat of his face (that is labour, physical or mental) doth he 'eat bread,' or receive support for his bodily frame ; in sorrow (the same word as in v. 16) he doth eat it all the days of his life.

19. BY THE SWEAT.] The original word occurs nowhere else in Scripture ; in the Hebrew of Ez. 44. 18, there is one nearly related to it.

20. EVE,] properly *Havvah*, i.e. 'life.'

21. COATS.] The same original word occurs in Ge. 27. 3, 23, (Joseph's coat,) Ex. 28. 4, 'the priest's coat,) 2 Sa. 13 . 18, (Tamar's coat,) 2 Sa. 15. 32, (Hushai's coat,) Job 30. 18, (Job's coat,) Song 5. 3, (the bride's coat,) Is. 22. 21, (Shebna, the steward or treasurer's coat).

OF SKIN.] Most probably that of animals offered in sacrifice, which must have been by divine appointment. In Ge. 27. 16, we read of Rebekah putting the *skins* of the kids of the goats upon Jacob's neck, and in 2 K. 1. 8, of Elijah having a girdle of *skin* about his loins.

22. WAS AS ONE OF US.] This refers to ch. 1. 26, 'Let Us make man in Our image,' &c. Man *did* not and *could* not 'become' like God by sinning; the verb in the original is simply 'was,' *not* 'become,' as the Common Version has rendered it.

AS TO THE KNOWLEDGE OF GOOD AND EVIL.] As remarked above (on chap. 2. 9,) man, before he sinned, may be supposed to have been acquainted with 'evil' as a *fact* in the history of God's creation. It is only as such that God can he said 'to know evil,' and man, before he fell, could know it only in the same way.

24. CASTETH OUT.] The original word here occurs also in Ge. 4. 14 ; 21. 10 ; Ex. 2. 17 ; 6. 1 ; 10. 11 ; Ps. 34. 1 ; Ho. 9. 15, applied to the expulsion of Cain, Hagar, daughters of Jethro, Moses, Aaron, David, Ephraim, &c.

CAUSETH TO TABERNACLE.] Compare Ps. 78. 55, Job 11. 14, Ez. 32. 4, Jo. 18. 1, Ps. 7. 5.

CHERUBS.] Beings (as described by Ezekiel ch. 10) in figure a compound of a man, an ox, a lion, and an eagle. They are represented as guarding the way of the tree of

life ; also as a means of conveyance adopted by God (2 Sa. 22. 11, Ps. 18. 11) ; as His dwelling-place (Nu. 7, 89, 1 Sa. 4. 4, 2 Sa. 6. 2, 2 K. 19. 15, 1 Ch. 13. 6, Ps. 80. 1 ; 99. 1, Ez. 9. 3 ; 10. 4). They had representations in the inner part of the tabernacle (Ex. 25. 18), of the temple built by Solomon (1 K. 6. 23), and in the spiritual temple described by Ezekiel.

THE FLAME OF THE SWORD.] This expression is found nowhere else in Scripture.

WHICH TURNETH ITSELF ROUND.] The same original word occurs again in Job 37. 12 ; 38. 14, Ju. 7. 13.

IV 1. I HAVE GOTTEN,] or 'gained, acquired, obtained.' Compare Ge. 14. 19, 22 ; 25. 10, De. 32. 6, Ps. 139. 13, Pr. 1. 5 ; 4. 5, 7 ; 8. 22 ; 16. 16.

BY THE LORD.] The Hebrew particle here translated 'by' occurs in Ps. 21. 6 : 'For thou makest him blessings for ever, thou causest him to rejoice with joy *by* thy countenance.' The plain meaning is—by the help or aid of the Lord. Comp. Ju. 8. 7.

2. AND SHE CONTINUETH TO BEAR HIS BROTHER, EVEN ABEL.] No mention being made of any interval of time between the births, or of a *second* conception, it has been inferred that Abel was a twin-brother of Cain.

ABEL FEEDETH A .FLOCK.] The primary idea perhaps is—'he enjoyeth *or* taketh delight in' a flock, and secondarily, 'he feedeth' it. The Hebrew word translated 'flock' includes sheep and goats, but not larger cattle. Abel's is a new occupation, Cain's is that of his father.

3. AT THE END OF DAYS.] The word in the original here rendered *days* occurs in Ge. 24. 55, in the sense of a week or seven days, 'And her brother and her mother say, Let the young person remain with us *days or ten*,' clearly meaning 'seven or ten days.' Compare also Ge. 40. 4. It may be naturally inferred from this that it was on a sabbath that Cain and Abel brought their

OFFERING, OR PRESENT.] Heb. *mincha*, generally derived from an Arabic root signifying 'to give, distribute,' but perhaps from a Hebrew one signifying 'to rest, give rest, quiet.' Both Cain and Abel's offerings are called by the same word, so that Cain's offering was not rejected (as some suppose) because it was not a bloody sacrifice, but because of his want of faith, or of its being offered in an improper spirit.

4. HATH LOOKED TOWARDS]—Abel's offering, and probably by so doing consumed it, in token of acceptance.

7. A SIN-OFFERING.] The same original word occurs with this meaning in Le. 6. 25, 30, Ex. 29. 14, 36, Nu. 8. 8.

CROUCHETH.] Applied to the lying down of a lion (Ge. 49. 9,) of wild beasts (Is. 13. 21,) of flocks (Is. 17. 2,) of an ass (Nu. 22. 27,) of a leopard (Is.11. 6,) of sheep (Ge. 29. 2,) of Issachar (Ge. 49. 14,) of the deep (Ge. 49. 25,) of curses (De. 29. 20,) of a bird (De. 22. 6,) of a person (Song 1. 7).

THOU RULEST OVER IT.] That is, thou hast power over the animal to keep alive or to offer in sacrifice; its desire is towards thee—it is not afraid of thee.

8. CAIN SAITH UNTO ABEL.] This is the exact literal translation of the Hebrew verb used here, which, wherever it occurs in the Old Testament, is invariably followed by the words spoken, except in this passage and in Job 9. 7, 'who commandeth (*lit.* who saith to) the sun and it riseth not.' The Samaritan Text and Version, the Septuagint, the Syriac, and the Latin Vulgate Versions, all agree in supplying the words, 'Let us go into the field,' as the words made use of by Cain. The only difficulty is that in no Hebrew MSS. have these or similar words been found as yet. The probability is in favour of their genuineness; the reader, however, will observe that they are printed in *italics*, as the translators of the Common Version have done in somewhat similar circumstances with 1 John 2. 23, &c.

12. A WANDERER.] Compare La. 4. 14, 15, Amos 4. 8; 8. 12, Je. 14. 10.

A TREMBLING ONE.] The literal meaning of the original verb here is 'to nod,' hence 'a nodding one;' compare Ps. 56. 8, Je. 18. 16, 1 K. 14. 15, &c.

13. MY PUNISHMENT.] The original word denotes primarily *perversity, iniquity*; secondarily, the *guilt* or *punishment* it entails on the offender.

14. THE GROUND.] Not 'the earth,' as in the Common Version, but the ground—the ground which I have cultivated.

15. GIVETH A TOKEN TO CAIN.] Exhibits some sign which satisfies Cain's mind that he shall not be slain.

16. MOVING ABOUT.] The original word (*Nod*) does not occur elsewhere in Scripture as the name of a place; it is therefore, perhaps, better to translate it.

17. ENOCH.] That is, 'initiated, trained. A CITY.] The primary idea of the original word is thought to be 'stir, bustle.'

19. TWO WIVES.] This was probably the first instance of polygamy. Even in Hindu and Mohammedan countries, though permitted by law, not one man in fifty has more than one wife.

ADAH,] i.e. an ornament, beauty.

ZILLAH,] i.e., a shade.

20. JABAL,] i.e., a river, stream. The chief of those who dwelt in tents and in purchased possessions.

21. JUBAL,] i.e., joyful.

22. TUBAL-CAIN,] i.e., a flowing of gain. INSTRUCTOR,] i.e. a sharpener.

NAAMAH,] i.e., pleasantness.

23. FOR MY WOUND—FOR MY HURT.] The reasoning seems to be—If the murder of Cain who *without provocation* slew his brother be avenged, how much more mine who have been wounded and hurt.

25. SETH,] i.e. an appointed person or thing.

26. ENOS,] i.e. mortal, sick, incurable.

PREACHING IN THE NAME OF JEHOVAH.] *lit.* 'cry.' It cannot mean ' calling on the name,' for surely Adam, Eve, Abel, Cain, Seth, &c. had done so before.

V 1. LIST,] or enumeration, from a verb signifying 'to number,' Ge. 15. 5, Le. 15. 13, 28.

3. IN HIS LIKENESS.] It is not said 'God's likeness;' that was lost.

22. WALKETH HABITUALLY.] The form of the Hebrew word implies *repetition*. Compare Job 1. 7; 2. 2, Zec. 1. 10, Ez. 19. 6; 1. 13, Ge. 3. 8; 6. 9; 24. 40; 48. 15; 13. 17; 17. 1.

24. AND HE IS NOT,] that is—he does not exist any more *in this world*.

FOR GOD HATH TAKEN HIM,] that is, to himself, to heaven, as the New Testament tells us, clearly teaching the immortality of the soul.

32. A SON OF 500 YEARS.] A striking Hebrew idiom, denoting the length of his existence.

VI. 2. SONS OF GOD.] Two opinions are entertained as to whom these were. The *first* is, that they were angels (especially the *fallen* ones, see v. 4), as these are supposed to be thus denominated in Job 1. 6; 2. 1; 38. 7, (comp. Ps. 29. 1; 89. 7). The *second* is that they mean *men*, the pious descendants of Seth, worshippers of God, compare De. 14. 1, Ps. 73. 15, Pr. 14. 26.

DAUGHTERS OF MEN.] This appellation occurs nowhere else in Scripture. As ' sons of men' does not necessarily signify impious men, neither does 'daughters of men' necessarily signify ungodly women.

3. MY SPIRIT.] That is, the Holy Spirit.

STRIVE IN MAN.] The original word only occurs here. The Septuagint, Syriac, and Vulgate read ' *dwell* ;' others render i' 'judge;' 'be humbled.'

IN THEIR ERRING THEY ARE FLESH. The Common Version: 'for that he also is flesh,' supposes the original phrase to be a Chaldaism, of which there is no other example in the Pentateuch.

4. THE FALLEN ONES.]Heb. 'the Nephilim,' supposed by some to be apostate spirits, by others, simply ungodly men; see note on v. 2; there does not appear to be any authority for the translation 'giants.'

5, 6. SEETH—REPENTETH—GRIEVETH.]See note on Ge. 1. 3.

7. WIPE AWAY.] For the use of this word compare 7. 4, 23, Ex. 17. 4; 32. 33, Nu. 5. 23, De. 9. 14; 25. 6. 19; 29. 20, 2 K. 21. 13.

9. RIGHTEOUS.] Heb. *tzadik*, 'right,' in what he does, in opposition to *rasha*, one 'wrong' in his cause, actions, &c.; the term 'right' or 'righteous' is used both of God and man.

PERFECT,] i.e., sound, complete, entire: used of Abraham, of the passover lamb, of God's work, way, law, &c.

14. AN ARK.] The original word is only applied to this vessel prepared by Noah, and to that in which Moses was put, Ex. 2. 3, 5.

GOPHER WOOD.] Perhaps simply 'cypress wood,' as the original word here occurring is found no where else.

ROOMS,] *lit.* 'nests,' from a root signifying 'to prepare or acquire;' the use of the word is quite characteristic of the simple modes of expression used in ancient times.

COVERED WITH CYPRESS.] The word certainly never means 'pitch,' but *lit.* 'a covering,' it is evidently a scribe's error: *kophar* for *gophar.*

16. WINDOW,] *lit.* 'a bright or shining thing.' In the old plural form it occurs in 23 passages of the Old Testament, where it is always translated 'noon.'

18. COVENANT.] This is the first instance in which the word occurs in the Holy Writings, and it properly means 'an eating,' because eating was indispensable to the ratifying of any agreement among the parties contracting.

VII. 1. HOUSE,] i.e. household.

3. TO KEEP ALIVE SEED.] God could easily have destroyed the animal creation, and formed them anew, but he never performs miracles unnecessarily.

4. AFTER OTHER SEVEN DAYS.] Another opportunity is thus held out for Noah's preaching and man's repentance.

FORTY.] This number occurs often in Scripture . compare the period of the mourning for Jacob, the search of the spies, the stay of Moses in the mount, the fasting of Elijah, the preaching of Jonah, the temptation of Christ, his sojourn after the resurrection, &c., see also v. 17; 8. 6; 25. 20; 26. 34; 32. 15, Nu. 14. 34; 33. 38, De. 25. 3, Jo. 14. 7, Ju. 3. 11; 5. 31; 8. 28; 13. 1, 1 Sa. 4. 18; 17. 16, 2 Sa. 2. 10; 5. 4, 1 K. 2. 11; 11. 42, &c.

WIPED AWAY.] See note on 6. 7; the word is used of tears, sin, filth, a name, a city, a writing, &c.

SUBSTANCE.] The original word is only found elsewhere in v. 23, and in De. 11. 6.

11. FOUNTAINS.] Compare 8. 2, Pr. 8. 24, Le. 11. 36.

GREAT DEEP.] Compare Ps. 36. 6; 78. 15, Is. 51. 10, Amos 7. 4.

NET-WORK.] Compare 8. 2; 2 K. 7. 2, 19, Ec. 12. 3, Is. 24. 18; 60. 8, Ho. 13. 3, Ma. 3. 10; these are all the passages where this word occurs.

BROKEN UP.] Compare Job 26. 8, Pr. 3. 20, Is. 35. 6, Ex. 14. 21.

12. SHOWER.] Compare 8. 2, Le. 26. 4, Ez. 13. 11; 34. 26.

19. ALL...THE WHOLE.] These words, at first sight, seem to express an entire universality; we ought not to be too positive however, terms such as 'all, whole, every,' must frequently be understood in connection with limiting circumstances; e.g. Acts 2. 5, 'out of every nation under heaven;' Rom. 1. 8. 'throughout the whole world,' Luke 2. 1, 'all the world;' John 21. 25, 'the world itself would not contain,' &c.

VIII. 1. SUBSIDE,] i.e. become low *or* pacified; compare Nu. 17. 5, Je. 5. 26, Est. 2. 1; 7. 10; applied to the putting down of murmurings, wrath, and snares.

2. CLOSED,] or 'secured;' compare Ps. 63. 11, Is. 19. 4, Ezra 4. 5.

3. GOING AND TURNING BACK,] i.e. to and fro, backwards and forwards.

4. ARARAT,] mentioned again in 2 K. 19. 37, Is. 37. 38, Je. 51. 27, and by universal tradition considered to be Armenia.

6. WINDOW.] The original word here is different from that used in 6. 16; it occurs other 30 times in the Old Testament, in which it is always rendered 'window.'

7. THE RAVEN.] The male one, as the gender of the original word shows.

8. THE DOVE,] the female, for the same reason.

11. TORN OFF.] Not one found floating on the waters, but one which the dove had plucked from a tree, indicating to Noah that the waters were lessening.

12. SEVEN DAYS.] It is worthy of remark how often this phrase occurs; it appears to show that the division of time by weeks (and sabbaths) was a common and well-understood thing.

20. ALTAR....BURNT-OFFERINGS.] This is the first time these words occur, though in Ge. 4. 4, Abel is said to have brought to the Lord from the female firstlings of his flock an offering or present, *lit.* a minchah.

21. DISESTEEM,] i.e. think or speak lightly of or about any thing or person; it never means 'to curse,' as some have supposed.

IMAGINATION.] *lit.* 'frame' or 'formation,' hence the thing framed by the heart: it is found only in Ge. 6. 5; 8. 21, De. 31. 21, 1 Ch. 28. 9; 29. 18, Ps. 103. 14, Is. 26. 3; 29. 16, Hab. 2 18, Job 17. 7.

IX. 1. BE FRUITFUL.] A renewal of the blessing given to Adam, see Ge. 1. 28.

2. YOUR FEAR.] 'Dominion' over the creatures was originally given to man, but now, only his 'fear and dread.'

3. EVERY CREEPING THING.] Animal food, which was not at first given to man (at least by express mention,) is now sanctioned, without distinction of any kind, any more than there is in reference to

THE GREEN HERB.] More *lit.* 'the green thing of the herb.'

4. FLESH in its life—its blood—ye do not eat.] From Acts 15. 29, it appears that the apostles considered the injunction as binding on the believers at Antioch.

5. AND ONLY YOUR BLOOD, &c.] This and the succeeding verse is omitted in some of Kennicott's Hebrew MSS.

EVERY LIVING THING,] or 'every beast,' which seems supported by the Mosaic laws which enjoined the death of an animal killing a human being.

12. TOKEN,] or sign; see same word in Ge. 1. 14; 4. 15; 9. 12, 13, 17; 17. 11, Ex. 3. 12, &c.

13. I HAVE GIVEN.] The rainbow, being a natural phenomenon, most probably existed from the beginning, but it is now appointed by God to serve a more specific purpose.

20. REMAINETH.] It was no new occupation; same word in 8. 10, 12.

VINEYARD.] This is the first time such a thing is mentioned, but the expression 'planteth' seems to imply design and previous acquaintance with it.

21. DRUNKEN.] Compare, however, the use of the original word in 43. 34, Song 5. 1, Is. 51. 21.

22. HAM,] here said to be 'father of

Canaan,' to point out the party on whom the punishment would be particularly visible.

23. THE GARMENT.] Probably that belonging to Noah, who had cast it aside thoughtlessly.

25. CURSED IS CANAAN.] This is a prophecy (not an imprecation) of what should hereafter be the lot of Noah's son; it was not to be developed in the offender himself, but in his younger son Canaan, and this perhaps in order that Ham might experience the anguish arising from a knowledge of his child's fortunes, that Noah had experienced through his misconduct.

SERVANT OF SERVANTS,] i.e. the most humble servant; it can never, however, justify the unchristian and antichristian practice of keeping in involuntary bondage any portion of the Hamitic race; a practice which is, and always has been man-stealing —a crime punished with death by the law of Moses.

26. BLESSED...IS SHEM.] In the Common Version, Shem has no blessing at all, and Noah is represented as blessing God instead. The parallelism is now restored, which has been obscured by the Masoretic punctuation of the seventh or eighth century.

27. GIVETH BEAUTY TO JAPHETH.] There is in the original a kind of play upon words, as if one were to say in English, 'God beautifies the beauteous one.' The name of Japheth is commonly derived from a root signifying 'to enlarge or persuade,' but more probably from one signifying 'to be fair'; hence the word 'mopheth,' which denotes any 'wonderful thing,' causing admiration. In this view it is descriptive of the fair Japhetic race, whereas Ham, is descriptive of the hot=black race, and Shem of the 'renowned' race.

X 4. DODANIM.] Some Hebrew MSS. read 'Rodanim,' meaning probably the Rhodians.

5. ISLES,] or perhaps simply 'countries,' especially those bordering on the sea.

8. NIMROD] probably acquired power over his fellows by his skill or strength in hunting and destroying wild beasts; there is no reason to suppose him to have been an ungodly man. He is the first mentioned as having 'a kingdom,' but it ought to be remembered that in ancient times, a small village or district was so designated, just as in India, even at the present day, there are hundreds of persons called Rajah, which literally means a 'king.'

21. SHEM] is here described as 'father of all sons of Eber,' and 'brother of Japheth the elder.' Some have rendered the last phrase, 'elder brother of Japheth;' the original is perhaps capable of both renderings, but the first is, on the whole, preferable.

XI. 1. PRONUNCIATION,] more lit. 'lip.'

2. VALLEY.] As places of this kind are often of considerable extent, the word has sometimes been rendered 'a plain,' but it seems preferable to express the radical idea of the word, which is 'a cleft place:' com-

pare De. 8. 7; 11. 11, Jo. 11..17; 12. 7, Ps. 104. 8, Is. 41. 18.

SHINAR.] A district around Babylon.

4. ITS HEAD IN THE HEAVENS.] An oriental figure of speech, meaning simply 'very high.'

A NAME,] or renown.

6. DREAMED.] They had, as it were, 'day-dreams,' unsubstantial projects which could never be realized.

RESTRAINED.] No person of wisdom or piety had stayed their progress.

7. LET US GO DOWN.] Comp. Ge. 1. 26; 3. 22.

MINGLE.] Compare the meaning of the same original word in v. 9, and in Ex. 29. 2, 40, Le. 2. 4, 5, Ju. 19. 21, Ho. 7. 8.

UNDERSTAND,] lit. 'hear.'

COMPANION,] or, 'friend, neighbour.'

9. BABEL.] Its site is now scarcely known; such is the vanity of earthly ambition.

26. ABRAM, NAHOR, AND HARAN.] Abram is mentioned first, though younger than Haran (comp. v. 32; 12. 4), because more conspicuous, as in the parallel case of Shem. the preference of the younger over the elder is remarkable likewise in the case of Abel, Isaac, Jacob, Judah, Joseph, Ephraim, Moses, David, &c.

28. UR OF THE CHALDEES.] Now called Orpha, i.e. light, a city in Upper Mesopotamia, supposed to be the same place afterwards called Edessa, famous for its early Christian history, and still said to contain 50,000 inhabitants.

XII. 1. THE LAND,] which was not yet definitely named, for the trial of his faith, see Heb. 11. 8.

2. BE THOU A BLESSING.] The original is imperative; not merely a promise, but a charge.

3. THOSE BLESSING THEE.] The plural is here used, while in the next clause it is the singular, implying that his friends would be more numerous than his foes.

DISESTEEMING,] as in 8. 21, same Hebrew word.

FAMILIES OF THE GROUND.] The same phrase occurs in 28. 14, and Amos 3. 2.

5. GAINED.] The original verb only occurs elsewhere in 31. 18; 36. 6; 46. 6.

PERSONS,] Heb. NEPHESH, from a verb signifying 'to take breath;' used in a variety of ways, and translated 'breath, soul, mind, body,' &c; properly 'a breathing creature,' either rational or irrational; it is even applied to a corpse, see Le. 22. 4, Nu. 5. 2; 9. 6, 7, 10; 19. 13, &c.

OBTAINED,] lit. made; see note on Ge. 1. 7.

6. OAK,] or, terebinth tree; the Orientals always select the shelter of a large tree before fixing their tents, to protect them from the scorching rays of the sun; the tree of Moreh is referred to again in 35. 4, 8, Jo. 24. 26, Ju. 9. 6.

CANAANITE IS THEN.] This tribe, which eventually succeeded in giving a name to the land, was not one of the aboriginal tribes, but intruders, who were afterwards justly expelled for their vices.

7. ALTAR.] By this Abram shewed himself heir to the patriarch Noah, see Ge. 8. 20.

8. PREACHETH,] or, 'calleth,' in the divine name; the subject of his preaching is not mentioned, but he who rejoiced to see the day of Christ, could scarcely fail to speak of it to others.

10. EGYPT,] in Hebrew 'Mitzraim,' (the name of the second son of Cush, see 10. 6,) a well-known country in Africa, but forming probably only a very small portion of what is comprehended under the general name of 'Egypt,'—the fertility of which is proverbial.

12. SEE THEE.] The corrupt practices of the Egyptians, as well as Abram's shortsightedness, are here strikingly displayed.

13. MY SISTER.] The truth, but not the whole truth, as it was intended to convey the impression that she was nothing more than his sister.

15. PHARAOH.] A common name of the rulers of Egypt, signifying the ruler of that country 'a king;' and in Hebrew 'a freeman, head, chief man,' compare De. 32. 42, Ju. 5. 2, Ex. 5. 4, &c.

TAKEN,] without leave asked or obtained, as the absolute power of eastern rulers was rarely resisted; as a kind of purchasemoney, Pharaoh loaded Abram with gifts which apparently he had no need of.

18. PHARAOH CALLETH.] It is not said how he came to associate the plagues with their proper cause; probably by a dream or vision, as in a later case mentioned in ch. 20. 3. Being warned, he calls for, and reproves Abram for his duplicity, restores Sarai, and sends them away in peace.

XIII. 3. BETH-EL,] i.e. House of God, so named by Jacob (Ge. 28. 19), and here used by the historian in anticipation : its former name was Luz. Jacob also built an altar here (Ge. 35. 7),— Samuel came here yearly to judge the people (1 Sa. 7. 16), here Jeroboam put one of his golden calves (1 K. 12. 29—33), king Josiah destroyed its altars and idols (2 Ch. 13. 19, 2 K. 23. 15—18); but after the Babylonian captivity it was rebuilt, (Ezra 2. 28, Ne. 7. 32; 11. 31).

HAI,] called Ai, in the book of Joshua.

6. SUBSTANCE...MUCH.] The flocks and herds of wealthy eastern sheiks are occasionally numbered by tens and hundreds of thousands,

7. PERIZZITE,] lit. villager, living in the hill-country of Judea; see also 15. 20; 34. 30, Ex. 3. 8, 17; 23. 23; 33. 2; 34. 11, De. 7. 1; 20. 17, Jo. 3. 10; 9. 1; 11. 3; 12. 8; 17. 15; 24. 11, Ju. 1. 4, 5; 3. 5, 1 K. 9. 20, 2 Ch. 8. 7, Ezra 9. 1, Ne. 9. 8.

8. FOR WE ARE MEN..BRETHREN,] both by nature, and blood, and religious profession.

9. BE PARTED, I PRAY THEE.] The Orientals are remarkable for their politeness and civility of language and deportment to each other, irrespective of their different positions; Abram, though the elder, yields gracefully to the younger his choice of the pasturage.

10. AS THE GARDEN OF JEHOVAH,] referring doubtless to Ge. 2. 8; see also Is. 51. 3, Ez. 28. 13; 31. 8, 9; 36. 35, Joel 2. 3.

11. THE JORDAN] is sometimes called pre-eminently, 'the river,' being the principal one in the whole land, and rises about three miles from Banias;. running through the lake of Tiberias, it flows into the Dead Sea, (a circuitous course of about 150 miles in all,) from which there is no outlet save by evaporation.

14. AFTER LOT'S BEING PARTED.] The design of God from the beginning evidently was to separate Abram so completely from his merely fleshly ties and connexions that he should always have his mind set on the divine promise.

18. ALTAR.] See Ge. 12. 7, 8; 13. 4, 18; 22. 9.

XIV 1. SHINAR...ELAM.] These are generally supposed to be Babylonia and Persia, but it is scarcely credible that the rulers of these distant regions should have come so far to attack five paltry cities on the borders of the Salt Sea, and that they should have been combined with two other kings, whose very realms—Ellaser and Goyim—are unknown; more likely they are the names of districts near Damascus.

GOYIM,] lit. nations, but more probably the name of a tribe or district of that name, compare Nu. 24. 20.

2. MADE WAR.] The first of which we have any account in sacred or profane history.

ADMAH...ZEBOIM.] Two cities on the border of the Salt Sea, which were destroyed with Sodom and Gomorrah, while Bela only was spared at the request of Lot.

5. REPHAIM.] One of the tribes of the Canaanites, see Ge. 15. 20. The word is somewhat unaccountably rendered by the Septuagint, Onkelos, Syriac, and Samaritan Versions, by 'giant;' the etymology of the original is ambiguous : 'those healing,' or 'those feeble;' the first is perhaps preferable.

ZUZIM,] also rendered by the preceding versions 'strong ones;' according to Gesenius they were the aborigines of the land of the Ammonites, and dispossessed by the posterity of Lot afterwards.

IN HAM.] The Septuagint, Samaritan. and Syriac Versions, read 'with them;' but Onkelos and Jonathan consider it the name of a place.

EMIM,] who are compared in De. 2. 10, 11, with the Anakim, for stature, &c.

SHAVEH KIRIATHAIM.] A plain taken from Sihon, and afterwards in possession of the tribe of Reuben, Nu. 13. 9.

6. HORITES.] Afterwards driven out from Mount Seir by the sons of Esau, Ge. 36. 20 —30, De. 2. 12, 22.

7. FIELD,] that is, the cultivated part of the land, and perhaps here, (as elsewhere,) put for the whole territory.

EN-MISHPAT,] lit. 'the fountain of judgment.'

KADESH,] on the border of the land of Edom, Nu. 20. 1, 12, 13, 16, where Moses struck the rock.

HAZEZON-TAMAR.] Perhaps the same as Engedi, near the Salt Sea, 300 furlongs from Jerusalem.

9. WITH THE FIVE] kings who all dwelt

on the border of the Salt Sea, and whose united territories did not, probably, exceed the circumference of London.

10. BITUMEN-PITS.] So that the place was almost naturally prepared for what it afterward became—a bituminous lake.

12. THEY TAKE LOT,] though a neutral party.

AND HIS SUBSTANCE,] for which he had given up his spiritual comforts.

13. ABRAM THE HEBREW.] So called either from his being a descendant of Eber, or from his being one who had 'passed over' into the land.

ALLIES,] *lit.* 'masters of a covenant,' compare the similar phrase Ne. 6. 18, 'masters of an oath.'

14. DRAWETH OUT.] Compare the use of the same original word in Ex. 15. 9, Le. 26. 33, Ge. 42. 35.

TRAINED,] i.e. instructed, initiated.

DOMESTICS,] more *lit.* 'children or born ones of his house:' the household of Abram could not contain less than twelve hundred persons, which was probably as many as belonged to any one of the nine kings engaged in the warfare.

DAN,] probably some place near the source of the river Jor-dan ; another Dan is mentioned in 2 Sa. 24. 6.

15. BY NIGHT,] showing his sagacity as a warrior, and conscious of the riotous hilarity of the retreating freebooters.

16. BRINGETH BACK....LOT,] who, strange to say, apparently unwarned by his dangerous escape, settled again among the Sodomites.

18. MELCHI-ZEDEK,] which means 'king of righteousness,' was one of the few who had remained attached to the true God, and at once a priest and king, in which character, as well as in his lack of official genealogy, he was a type of the Saviour, see Heb. 7. 1.

SALEM,] a place between Damascus and Sodom, and probably the same as Salim where John baptized, or Shalem, mentioned in Ge. 33. 18, though most commentators prefer Jerusalem.

BREAD AND WINE] to nourish the weary though victorious band.

19. POSSESSING.] Not a few critics have rendered this 'creating or creator,' but the word never has this signification ; it denoting simply one who has possession of a thing, independently of the manner in which it becomes his, whether by purchase or otherwise; see Le. 25. 28, 30, 50, De. 28. 68, Pr. 15. 32 ; 19. 8 ; 20. 14.

20. A TENTH OF ALL] the spoils of the enemies, as explained in He. 7. 4.

22. LIFTED UP MY HAND,] the common form of an appeal to Heaven.

JEHOVAH.] The addition of this name was doubtless designed to point out more significantly the object he worshipped—not pantheism nor polytheism, but the Living One—Jehovah.

23. THREAD....SHOE-LATCHET,] i.e. the most insignificant thing.

I HAVE MADE ABRAM RICH,] preferring that his riches should be attributed to the true source—the blessing of Jehovah.

24. SAVE ONLY.] Abram had no wish to bind others to do as he did ; his allies were entitled to reward for their fidelity and assistance, and 'they take their portion.'

XV 1. AFTER THESE THINGS,] to prevent him from being afraid of the return of the enemies he had defeated.

THE WORD OF JEHOVAH.] This is the first instance in which this phrase occurs, and there is a diversity of opinion regarding its import ; was it simply a revelation of the will of God, or of the personal Logos, afterwards more fully revealed ? The question is very difficult, but on fuller reconsideration, the first hypothesis appears, on the whole, preferable.

IN A VISION] by night, see v. 5.

SHIELD,] from a root signifying 'to cover over, protect.'

THY REWARD IS.] So Rosenmuller, Geddes, &c.

2. AN ACQUIRED SON,] *lit.* a son of acquisition, i.e. a son whom I have acquired, and adopted.

DEMMESEK ELIEZER.] So Septuagint and Jerome, and as the order of the words in Hebrew imperatively requires.

LORD JEHOVAH.] This is the first instance of the title being used in SS.

3. SEED,] i.e. posterity, according to Hebrew idiom.

A DOMESTIC.] See note on 14. 14 ; adoption of children is a very old and common eastern custom.

5. LOOK ATTENTIVELY.] Same word as in 19. 17, 26, Ex. 3. 6 ; 33. 8, Nu. 12. 8 ; 21. 9 ; 23. 21, Zec. 12. 10.

6. BELIEVED IN,] *or* 'remained steadfast in' his belief of the divine promises.

RECKONETH,] i.e. counteth, imputeth.

RIGHTEOUSNESS,] i.e. a state of rightness, in reference either to God or to man.

7. This probably commences a new vision, at a different time from the preceding.

9. A YOUNG BIRD.] Not necessarily 'a pigeon,' as the Common Version has rendered it; the original word only occurs elsewhere in De. 32. 11, 'as an eagle..over its *young ones* fluttereth.'

12. DEEP SLEEP.] See note on Ge. 2. 21.

13. A LAND NOT THEIRS,] i.e. not given to them, like the land of Canaan.

FOUR HUNDRED YEARS,] more definitely stated as 430 in Ex. 12. 40; it is possible that the 400 years are to be dated from the time of this vision, but more probably from the descent of Jacob into Egypt.

14. I JUDGE,] as he did by the ten plagues.

GREAT SUBSTANCE.] Compare Ex. 11. 2, 3 ; 12. 35, 36, Ps. 105. 37.

15. UNTO THY FATHERS.] This must refer to his soul, not his body, which was not interred with his fathers, but in Canaan.

BURIED.] The practice of burying the dead is the oldest known way of disposing of the mortal remains of man ; only in later ages did the Parsees or Zoroastrians or Fire-worshippers ever think of the revolting practice of exposing them as food to the ravenous birds, or the Hindus of burning them; some of the lower classes of Hindus do indeed bury them, as do also the Mohammedans.

16. COMPLETE.] This shows the justice of God, and his mercy, for though the Amorites, &c. were very vile, they are not cut off till their course of iniquity had come to the full.

17. A FURNACE OF SMOKE,] indicating, perhaps, the fiery trials awaiting his posterity, while A LAMP OF FIRE] may point out the purifying, sanctifying influence accompanying them.

18. THIS LAND,] as in 12. 7; 13. 15, but now more fully defined as follows.

RIVER OF EGYPT.] Not the Nile, but that branch of it called 'the river of the wilderness,' in Amos 6. 14, running between Egypt and Palestine.

PHRAT.] Compare 2 Sa. 8. 3, and 1 K. 4. 21. This noble river is about 1400 miles long.

19. An enumeration of the several tribes then inhabiting the land.

XVI. 1. HANDMAID,] see 12. 16, probably one of those given by Pharaoh.

2. RESTRAINED.] The Scripture worthies were more alive to the direct superintending agency of God than men are now; in Scripture nothing is left to chance or second causes.

HEARKENETH.] Perhaps he thought this might be, after all, the real plan by which God would fulfil his promise, but, like the Israelites in the case of Gibeon, he forgot to ask counsel from the Lord.

3. TO HIM FOR A WIFE.] Polygamy had not been expressly prohibited, as it was afterwards, (Le. 18. 18,) and we are not entitled to try Abram by the more perfectly developed law of God which we now have; his example is not commended, and the evil fruits of it soon became apparent.

4. LIGHTLY ESTEEMED.] The mother of a child would likely soon expect to be preferred to a barren wife.

5. VIOLENCE.] So the word always signifies; Sarah had probably chastised her, and now reproves Abram by asserting it was for his benefit, and on his account she did so.

6. IN THY HAND,] i.e. under thy power: too timidly yielding perhaps to her will.

7. MESSENGER.] The first time this word occurs in the SS.; it denotes the 'office,' not the 'nature,' of the being so called, hence it ought never to be rendered 'angel,' which is now exclusively applied to heavenly messengers, whereas the Hebrew word (as well as the corresponding Greek one) is applied also to earthly ones.

MESSENGER OF JEHOVAH.] This name is always singular—we nowhere read of 'Messengers of Jehovah;' when the plural is used it is always 'Messengers of God.' Hence it is inferred that there is only one being having the name 'Messenger of Jehovah,' i.e. the Messenger of the Covenant; and certainly in this case he speaks as a Divine Being, see v. 10, 'I will multiply thy seed;' which is surely the prerogative of God alone; he is also expressly called

'Jehovah' in v. 13, by the historian. Mere names, however, are of little real importance, as the same is afterwards given to Haggai (1. 13); more important is the argument from his works and words.

SHUR,] on her way to Egypt.

8. SARAI'S HANDMAID.] Reminding her of her real position.

12. WILD-ASS MAN,] i.e. free as the wild-ass, so graphically described in Job 39. 5.

AGAINST EVERY ONE.] A prophecy which is a perpetual living witness to the truth of God.

BEFORE THE FACE OF] Keturah's children, the Midianites, Edomites, Moabites, Ammonites, Israelites, &c.

13. EVEN HERE I HAVE LOOKED.] There is no propriety in making this a question; it is an affirmation.

14. ISHMAEL,] i.e. God heareth; Hagar had doubtless recounted the whole of her story to Abraham, who thus acquiesced in the revelation made to her.

XVII. 1. GOD ALMIGHTY.] The first time this title occurs in SS.; it is also very frequent in the book of Job. It does not, however, properly mean All-mighty, but simply 'he who is sufficient.'

WALK HABITUALLY,] as the form of the original verb denotes.

BE THOU PERFECT.] Man's inability to be perfect does not weaken the propriety of the injunction.

2. MY COVENANT,] i.e. of circumcision.

4. THOU HAST BECOME,] i.e. in the determinate counsel and foreknowledge of God. A MULTITUDE OF NATIONS,] such as Judah, Israel, Edom, Ishmael, &c., and more especially of all those believing.

5. ABRAM...ABRAHAM,] first, 'an exalted father,' now 'father of a multitude of nations.'

7. AGE-DURING.] This is the literal and proper meaning of the word, which is applied to hills, generations, possessions, priesthood, ceremonial laws, a heap of stones, hatred, desolation, love, &c. &c.

10. CIRCUMCISED.] This rite was practised by the ancient Egyptians, Ethiopians, Colchi, Phenicians, Syrians, and others; the Spaniards found it in the 16th century among the idolatrous inhabitants of Jucatana, Sancta Crux, &c. In the case of Abraham, however, it is distinctly set apart as a religious duty and symbol for a special end.

14. CUT OFF FROM HIS PEOPLE,] i.e. from all the religious privileges they enjoy in consequence of this covenant, which the person who neglects this rite shows he despises.

15. SARAI...SARAH,] first 'my lady,' now 'the lady.'

16. KINGS,] as it had been promised to Abraham in v. 6 above.

18. O THAT ISHMAEL.] The promise of a son by Sarah does not lead him to neglect Ishmael.

19. ISAAC,] i.e. he laughs; generally implying the idea of derision, though not universally. Ishmael and Isaac are the two first who are mentioned in SS. as having names given to them before their birth.

20. I HAVE HEARD THEE,] and by inference 'answered' thy prayer.

1 HAVE BLESSED HIM.] The past tense in Hebrew is a very common form of expressing the *certainty* of the thing.

TWELVE PRINCES,] whose names are found in 25. 13—15.

23—27.] These verses show the ready and complete obedience of Abraham to the Divine will—a feature for which he is remarkable from the beginning to the end of his life, so far as narrated in SS.

XVIII. 1. APPEARETH] about 3 months after the institution of circumcision.

2. THREE MEN,] i.e. in outward appearance, one of whom is expressly called Jehovah, the other two are, in 19. 1, called 'messengers,' doubtless created beings, accompanying him to do his will.

TOWARDS THE EARTH.] None but those who have seen it can appreciate the exquisite gracefulness of an Eastern salutation.

3. MY LORD,] addressing him who appeared the chief.

4. WASH YOUR FEET,] a grateful proposal to a weary Eastern traveller, and the neglect of which shows great inhospitality ; comp. (Lu. 7. 44,) Ge. 19. 2 ; 24. 32 ; 43. 24, Ju. 19. 21, &c.

TREE,] for shelter from the heat.

5. A PIECE OF BREAD,] compare the same word in Le. 2. 6; 6. 21 (14), Ju. 19. 5, Ruth 2. 14; 1 Sa. 2. 36 ; 28. 22; 2 Sa. 12. 3; 1 K. 17. 11; Job 31. 17; Ps. 147. 17; Pr. 17. 1 ; 23. 8 ; 28. 21.

SUPPORT,] as in Pr. 20. 28; Is. 9. 7 (6); Ps. 18. 35 (36) ; 20. 2 (3) ; 41. 3 (4) ; 94. 18 ; 104. 15 ; 119. 117; Ju. 19. 5, 8; 1 K. 13. 7.

6. MAKE CAKES,] by herself or servants.

8. SETTETH BEFORE THEM.] In warm countries animal flesh does not keep till the second day, hence the necessity for fresh food daily, which is prepared in an almost incredibly short space of time.

STANDETH BY THEM,] as a token of respect.

9. THY WIFE.] This, apparently the first question they asked, is the *last* asked now-a-days, the Orientals being very reserved about their females.

10. ABOUT THE TIME OF LIFE,] i.e. nine months, so in v. 14.

12. ENTERING INTO DAYS,] a common but beautiful figure of speech, expressive of advance in age.

13. The original text has nothing to point out this expression as being spoken interrogatively : it is an exclamation of surprise.

14. JEHOVAH SAITH.] This shows the historian's belief in the divinity of the being who had promised a son to Sarah ; it also shows omniscience in discerning her heart.

WONDERFUL,] as the word always signifies.

16. SEND THEM AWAY,] as a matter of courtesy.

17. AM I CONCEALING.] A sort of inward meditation regarding the propriety of acquainting Abraham—his friend—with his designs.

19. COMMANDETH,] i.e. chargeth, or exhorteth.

SONS..HOUSEHOLD,] these are generally, but not always distinguished from each other in SS.

20. SAITH,] that is, to Abraham, revealing his purpose.

21. GO DOWN,] to the plain on which Sodom and Gomorrah stood, or the shore of the Salt Sea.

ITS CRY] of oppression and violence.

22. THE MEN,] i.e. two of them.

23. DUST THOU.] Observe the boldness of faith.

CONSUME,] i.e. finish, end.

24. BEAR WITH,] *lit.* lift up to.

25. FAR BE IT,] *lit.* profane to thee !

JUSTICE,] discriminating between righteous and wicked.

26. FOR THEIR SAKE.] the Scriptures are full with illustrations of this principle of God's actings towards men.

I HAVE WILLED,] so v. 31. Compare the use of the word in Ex. 2. 21; De. 1. 5; Jo. 7. 7 ; 17. 12; Ju. 1. 27, 35 ; 17. 11; 19. 6; 1 Sa. 12. 22 ; 17. 39 ; 2 Sa. 7. 29 ; 2 K. 5. 23 ; 6. 3 ; 1 Ch. 17. 27 ; Job 6. 9, 28 ; Ho. 5. 11, being all the passages where the word occurs.

DUST AND ASHES.] Same phrase occurs in Job 30. 39, expressive of great abasement.

28. FOR FIVE.] The Common Version unnecessarily supplies ' for *lack of* five.'

32. TEN.] Ought not these six gracious answers to have strengthened the faith of the suppliant rather than exhausted it ? Who can tell whether if he had asked that the cities should be spared even for Lot's sake—the request would not have been granted ? But the father of the faithful was faithless—he had not, because he asked not.

XIX 1. TWO OF THE MESSENGERS] already mentioned.

SITTING AT THE GATE,] the place of public concourse, and public justice, to guide and invite any weary traveller. Hospitality is, and has always been a cardinal virtue in the East.

2. THE BROAD PLACE,] where travellers could pitch their tents, and pass the night under the mild influence of Eastern moonlight.

3. A BANQUET,] *lit.* a drinking, wine being the principal feature and ingredient in it.

UNLEAVENED THINGS.] Food being sooner prepared without leaven than with it; this is the first occurrence of what became a matter of ritual observance in Israel.

4. BOTH YOUNG AND OLD.] Nothing could give a more shocking idea of their iniquity.

8. DO...AS IS GOOD IN YOUR EYES.] The safety of a guest is to an Oriental a primary duty, to which even a desire of vengeance gives way for the time.

9. COME NIGH HITHER.] The Common Version translates this strangely enough, ' stand back !'

TO SOJOURN,] i.e. for a little time, but now—

HE DOTH CERTAINLY JUDGE,] *lit.* judging he doth judge.

11. BLINDNESS,] *lit.* blindnesses, i.e. very

dense, as in the case of Elisha and the Syrians.

12. BRING OUT.] A good man brings blessings, and gives blessings.

14. THOSE TAKING,] they were betrothed to them, but did not yet live with them.

16. LINGERETH,] loath to leave his substance, his sons-in-law, his neighbours, &c.

17. LOOK NOT EXPECTINGLY,] as in 15. 5; 19. 26.

MOUNTAIN.] The same to which the kings of Sodom and Gomorrah with their followers had fled, according to 14. 10.

21. I HAVE ACCEPTED.] Another instance of the long-suffering grace of God.

22 ZOAR,] i.e. little.

24. SODOM....GOMORRAH,] to which must be added Admah and Zeboim, see De. 29. 23.

JEHOVAH...JEHOVAH,] i.e. from Himself.

25. OVERTHROWETH,] and thereby maketh them (Jude 7) 'an example of fire age-during, justice suffering;' comp. De. 29. 23 (22); 32. 32; Is. 1. 9, 10; 3. 9; 13. 19; Je. 23. 14; 49. 18; 50. 40, La. 4. 6; Ez. 16. 46, 48, 49, 53, 55, 56; Am. 4. 11; Zep. 2. 9, in all of which reference is made to their fate.

26. LOOKETH EXPECTINGLY,] though directly forbidden in v. 17.

AND SHE IS,] This singular expression points out, not the manner of the change, but the fact itself.

A PILLAR.] The original word occurs nowhere else in the Pentateuch; it is found in 1 Sa. 10. 5; 13. 3, 41; 2 Sa. 8. 6, 14; 1 Ch. 11. 16; 18. 13; 2 Ch. 17. 2, in all of which it is translated 'garrison,' in 1 K. 4. 19 and 2 Ch. 8. 10, it is rendered 'officer.' It evidently means anything 'set up.'

27. RISETH EARLY,] impatient to know the fate of the city, and of Lot his nephew.

29. REMEMBERETH ABRAHAM.] This was often a ground of pleading with God adopted by his posterity, see Ex. 32. 13, De. 9. 27, &c.

30. ZOAR,] which lay in the plain; glad at last to take the advice recorded in v. 17.

CAVE,] probably that in which David with 600 men lodged (1 Sa. 24. 3) in Engedi.

31. OLD.] About 65 years of age, according to Usher and the Jewish chronologists.

ALL THE EARTH,] or perhaps simply, 'all the land.'

32—36.] This whole transaction can only be explained by remembering the intense desire of Eastern females for children, the want of them being considered a positive curse; with the members of the Abrahamic family there was the additional hope of the coming Saviour; if this latter consideration was in the view of the parties here mentioned—strange to say, it was realized, for He came through Ruth the Moabitess.

37. MOAB,] i.e. 'waters of a father,' or simply, 'from a father.'

BEN-AMMI,] i.e. 'son of my people.'

XX. 1. FROM THENCE,] i.e. the oaks of Mamre, to

GERAR,] about six miles distant, and supposed to be the same as Ashkelon, one of the five lordships of the Philistines.

2. SISTER,] as in 12. 13, strangely neglectful of his former danger and deliverance.

ABIMELECH,] i.e. father of the king; a common name of the rulers of Gerar, as Pharaoh, Cæsar, &c. were of other rulers.

MARRIED TO A HUSBAND,] lit. 'the lady of a lord.'

7. INSPIRED.] 'Prophet' of the Common Version does not at all give the meaning of the Hebrew word 'Nabi;' the one is now used in English invariably to express the individual who foretells future events; the Hebrew word rarely, if ever, expresses this, but simply the recipient of a divine influence, which may or may not concern future circumstances.

8. RISETH EARLY,] anxious to avoid the threatened evil, by complying with the Divine command.

9. CALLETH FOR ABRAHAM.] How humiliating for a man of God to be reproved by a heathen!

13. GOD CAUSED ME TO WANDER.] Both the nominative and the verb are in the plural number, hence some have supposed that the reference is not to the true God, but to the false gods, whose worship he forsook, and for which, according to Jewish tradition, he was exposed to danger and death.

15. DWELL.] This language contrasts favourably with the hasty dismissal he received from Pharaoh, as recorded in 12. 19.

16. THY BROTHER,] said doubtless in a kind of pleasantry, for conciliation.

IT IS TO THEE,] i.e. the gift of the silver is a peace-offering to thee and those with thee.

REASONED WITH.] The original word only occurs elsewhere in Is. 1. 18, Job 23. 7, and there can be no doubt of its true meaning.

XXI 1. LOOKED AFTER.] The original word always expresses the idea of inspection and supervision, being descriptive of the conduct of a superior to an inferior, never vice versa; it never signifies 'to visit, come to see,' though often so rendered in the Common Version.

3. ISAAC,] as had been directed in 17. 19.

6. LAUGHTER FOR ME,] i.e. a cause of laughter.

LAUGHETH FOR ME,] i.e. on my account and behalf.

7. WHO HATH SAID,] i.e. at any time.

8. BANQUET.] See note on 19. 3.

WEANED.] In the East weaning is often delayed till a much later period than it is in the West.

9. THE SON OF HAGAR,] i.e. Ishmael.

MOCKING,] which the apostle Paul explains as persecuting, Gal. 4. 29.

11. WRONG,] i.e. evil; Heb. rang, doubtless the origin of the word 'wrong.'

13. A NATION,] as the Ishmaelites soon became.

14. RISETH EARLY,] again manifesting his ready and complete submission to the Divine will.

A BOTTLE OF WATER,] doubtless made of skin, as is still customary in the East.

LAD,] who was now about 16 or 17 years of age.

GOETH ASTRAY,] i.e. unintentionally, in the wilderness of Beer-Sheba, which shows her intention was to return to Egypt, her native land.

15. WATER IS CONSUMED.] Only those who have experienced the heat of an Eastern sun can conceive fully the horrors of her condition.

17. THE YOUTH,] his dying cries entered into the heart of the Lord of Sabaoth, and were graciously and immediately answered.

MESSENGER OF GOD.] Evidently the same being just called 'God,' as in the very next verse he says, 'I will make him become a great nation.'

19. OPENED HER EYES,] which were blinded with sorrow, and tears, and dust, and fatigue; her energies being aroused, she saw a well of water, which in her distress she had not previously observed. Many instances are on record of persons in Arabia lying dying of thirst within a very short distance of a well of water, which the dimness of eyes caused by excessive thirst, had prevented their seeing.

20. GOD IS WITH THE YOUTH,] so that like David he could say, (Ps. 27. 10,) 'When my father and my mother have forsaken me, then Jehovah doth gather me.'

AN ARCHER,] lit. a shooter with the bow.

21. EGYPT,] her native place; marriages in the East are always arranged by the parents, the young people rarely ever objecting to their parents' choice for them.

23. CONTINUATOR.] this Hebrew word NEEN, only occurs elsewhere in Job 18. 19, and Is. 14. 22; it is evidently derived from nun, 'to be continued,' found in Ps. 72. 17.

SUCCESSOR.] This word only occurs elsewhere in the above passages in connection with the preceding word.

24. I SWEAR,] promptly and unhesitatingly, as an honest man.

25. REASONED WITH,] not necessarily 'reproved,' as in the Common Version.

31. BEER-SHEBA,] i.e. 'well of the oath.'

33. TAMARISK,] most unwarrantably rendered by the Common Version 'a grove.'

PREACHETH IN,] see note on 12. 8; 13. 4.

GOD AGE-DURING.] see note on 17. 7.

XXII. 1. TRIED] his faith and endurance; God often 'tries,' but cannot 'tempt' any one, as Jas. 1. 13.

I PRAY THEE.] The Hebrew particle NA here occurring, is never any thing else than a respectful mark of supplication, and is badly translated by the 'now' of the Common Version.

2. Quite remarkable is the number of epithets here used, 'son—only son—whom thou hast loved—Isaac;' all tending to excite Abraham's paternal love, rendering the trial more severe.

LAND OF MORIAH,] so called by anticipation, on one of the mountains of which the temple was afterwards built. Moriah, means 'shown of Jehovah,' not 'provided of Jehovah,' as Gesenius asserts.

3. RISETH EARLY,] see note on 19. 27.

4. THIRD DAY.] Travelling in the East is very slow, twenty miles a day being thought a great feat, and the distance from Beer-sheba (where Abraham was dwelling) to

Moriah was about 42 miles. This delay was a sore trial doubtless to Abraham's faith, as he had thus time to consider the whole circumstances of the case, and any mere enthusiasm must have all passed away on the long and weary journey.

5. WE TURN BACK.] Spoken, perhaps, under an unconscious spirit of prophecy.

9. BINDETH ISAAC,] which only could have been with his own consent, for he was now 25, or as some say, 37 years of age, and quite able to have resisted his father, who was a hundred years older than he.

10. TO SLAUGHTER HIS SON.] the term used for putting sacrificed animals to death.

11. MESSENGER OF JEHOVAH.] See note on 16. 7.

12. FROM ME.] This identifies the speaker with the God who 'tried' Abraham.

14. JIREH,] i.e. 'he doth provide,' agreeably to v. 8; the Common Version, 'it shall be seen,' is altogether inappropriate and wrong.

16. THE AFFIRMATION OF JEHOVAH,] i.e. his solemn protestation.

18. BLESSED THEMSELVES,] as the reflexive form of the verb denotes; compare also 26. 4; De. 29. 19; Ps. 72. 17; Is. 65. 16; Je. 4. 2.

21. HUZ,] or rather Uz, supposed by some to have given his name to the land where Job dwelt, which seems to derive countenance from Elihu being said (in Job 32. 2) to be son of Barachel the Buzite, one of the kindred perhaps of the Buz mentioned in this verse.

XXIII. 2. KIRJATH-ARBA,] i.e. the city of Arba, afterwards called Hebron, in the land of Canaan.

GOETH IN,] i.e. unto her tent.

4. A SOJOURNER.] So the word literally means; an entirely different word is used when 'a stranger' is intended; so also in the next clause the word 'settler' (or squatter) is the true meaning, not 'sojourner' merely. The idea is: he is sojourning with them, and has settled in the land, without the intention of leaving.

6. A PRINCE OF GOD,] commonly explained as 'a mighty prince,' but decidedly to be understood literally: 'a prince set up by God,' or 'a godly prince.'

8. MIND,] or, desire, lit. soul.

MEET FOR ME WITH,] i.e. open up a communication on my behalf with Ephron, &c.

9. FULL MONEY,] i.e. full value.

10. SITTING,] or 'dwelling,' but the former seems preferable, as it is the more literal; he happened to be present at the meeting.

IN THE EARS,] i.e. in the hearing of all those then coming in at the gate of the city, where public business was commonly transacted.

11. I HAVE GIVEN.] The verb is in the past tense, and is repeated thrice, for the purpose of giving greater force and certainty to what he says, and to save further words.

13. I HAVE GIVEN.] Abraham here also uses the past tense for precisely the same object as Ephron.

16. WEIGHETH.] Money in the East, even at the present day, is generally weighed, not counted.

17. The wording of this agreement shows that legal phraseology in those early days was not far behind the verbage of the present.

XXIV 2. PUT THY HAND UNDER MY THIGH.] An ancient attitude adopted in swearing, which Jacob also required of Joseph, see 47. 29.

3. CANAANITE.] Doubtless because they were idolators.

FOR MY SON.] Parents in the East invariably choose their children's partners in life, e. g. Hagar, Hamor, Manoah, Caleb, &c.

7. SWARE,] see 15. 18, and 22. 16, 17.

10. ARAM-NAHARAIM,] *lit.* Aram of the two rivers. i.e. Mesopotamia, mentioned again in De. 23. 4, Ju. 3. 8, 1 Ch. 19. 6, Ps. 60. 1.

CITY OF NAHOR,] i.e. where he resided; compare 'the city of Andrew and Peter,' Jno. 1. 44. From Hebron (where Abraham was residing) to Haran, is about 468 miles, a journey of about 24 days.

11. AT THE WELL,] i.e. some particular one without the gate; at the watering place he was most likely to hear all the news, and obtain any information required, as these are the chief places where the inhabitants of Eastern countries meet in the evenings.

WOMEN WHO DRAW WATER.] At the present day also, this work is performed by females.

12. CAUSE TO MEET BEFORE ME.] The original verb cannot, by any possibility, be rendered, 'send me good speed;' it occurs only in 27. 20, Nu. 35. 11, in the causitive form; in its simple form it occurs in 42. 29; 44. 29, Nu. 11. 23, De. 25. 18, Ruth 2. 3, 1 Sa. 28. 10, Ec. 2. 14, 15; 9. 11, Is. 41. 22, Da. 10. 14, Est. 4. 7; 6. 13.

13. FOUNTAIN,] a different word from that used in v. 11 ; so again in v. 42, 43, 45.

14. DECIDED.] The original word occurs in v. 44; 31. 37, 42; 21. 25, Job 9. 33, Is. 2. 4; 11. 3, 4, Ge. 21. 25.

15. BEFORE HE HATH FINISHED SPEAKING,] his prayer was answered, agreeably to the promise in Is. 65. 24.

HER SHOULDER,] It is also very commonly borne on the head.

16. A VIRGIN.] The Hebrew word in itself does not necessarily denote strict virginity, otherwise the next clause would be superfluous; compare also Joel 1. 8, where one so named is spoken of as having a husband.

21. WONDERING] at her affability and courtesy, her humility and condescension, her readiness and diligence.

22. A RING,] not necessarily 'an earring,' (see v. 47, and Ez. 16. 12,) the word occurs also in v. 30, 47; 35. 4, Ex. 32. 2, 3; 35. 22, Ju. 8. 24, 25, 26, Job 42. 11, Pr. 11. 22; 25. 12; Is. 3. 21, Ho. 2. 13.

BEKAH,] i.e. half a shekel, equal to eighty barley corns.

26. OBEISANCE.] The Hebrew word denotes a kind of prostration and reverence given alike to God and to man, (compare especially 1 Ch. 29. 20), see Ge. 18. 2; 19. 1; 22. 5; 23. 7, 12; 24. 26, 48, 52; 27. 29; 33. 3, 6, 7; 37. 7, 10; 42. 6; 43. 26, 28; 47. 31; 48. 12; 49. 8.

28. HER MOTHER'S HOUSE,] i.e. to her elder female relatives.

32. HIS FEET.] The Vulgate strangely enough reads, 'the feet of the camels.'

34—49.] This passage exhibits at once the simplicity and honesty of Abraham's servant; his plain unvarnished tale carries conviction to the heart of his hearers ; and they agree in acknowledging the Lord's hand to be appparent in it all, and leave it in His hand, which is the very obvious meaning of the latter clause of v. 50, otherwise unintelligible.

50. LABAN AND BETHUEL.] The latter, though father, is mentioned last, being probably too aged or infirm to take a leading part; from beginning to end, Laban was the active leading personage.

53. GIVETH TO REBEKAH] as proofs of her future husband's wealth ; he gave also to her brother and her mother, as a kind of purchase-money, for the general practice in the East has always been for the husband to buy the wife, either by giving money or cattle, or *labour*, as in the case of Jacob.

54. AND THEY EAT AND DRINK,] not only to refresh themselves, but as settling the engagement.

55. DAYS OR TEN.] See note on 1. 5; 4. 3; they were very naturally indisposed for such an abrupt departure.

57. ASK AT HER MOUTH,] i.e. hear it from her own lips, what she says to the hasty journey, for they never seemed to think it possible for her to have refused the offer.

59. HER NURSE,] whose name was Deborah, according to 35. 8. According to v. 61 other females also attended her.

60. POSSESS THE GATE,] i.e. occupy the cities, and rule over them, as in Ge. 22. 7 ; Ju. 5. 8, 11. Am. 5. 15.

61. CAMELS.] Perhaps the most useful animal in the East ; its power of subsisting on the poorest fare, of enduring the extremest thirst, and the suitability of its foot for the barren land, renders its services invaluable.

62. LAHAI-ROI,] i.e. 'well of the Living One, my beholder,' where the messenger of Jehovah met Hagar, see 16. 7, 14.

LAND OF THE SOUTH,] at Beer-Sheba, see 22. 19.

63. CAMELS.] Not 'the camels ;' he did not as yet know whose they were.

64. FALLETH FROM OFF THE CAMEL.] A common mark of respect paid in eastern lands to a superior by an inferior when meeting him.

XXV 1. KETURAH,] i.e. 'perfume or incense.' This second wife of Abraham is (in 1 Ch. 1. 32.) called a 'concubine,' which seems to imply that she was so during Sarah's life-time. In v. 6. 'concubines' are mentioned, these were Hagar and Keturah, whose descendants are enumerated in this chapter. Others are of opinion that it was three years after the death of Sarai before he took Keturah, after Isaac was married, and when Abraham was 140 years of age.

2. ZIMRAN,] hence perhaps the Zamareni, a people in Arabia Felix, mentioned by Pliny, Nat. Hist. l. 6, c. 28.

JOKSHAN,] ancestor of the Shebæans and Dedanites.

MEDAN AND MIDIAN,] from whom sprung the Midianites, see Ge. 37. 28, 36.

SHUAH,] from whom were the Shuachites; Bildad (Job 2. 11) was perhaps one of his descendants.

3. SHEBA,] whence were the Sabæans who carried off Job's cattle.

DEDAN,] whose posterity is perhaps spoken of in Is. 21. 13; Je. 25. 23, 24; 49. 8; Ez. 27. 15, 20; 38. 15. Bochart mentions a city in Idumea named 'Dedan.'

EPHAH,] is noticed along with Midian in Is. 60. 6.

5. TO ISAAC,] who had been specially designated by God as his heir, see 15. 4.

GIFTS.] Though they were not the seed specially promised, they were nevertheless dear to him, as his prayer testified : 'O that Ishmael may live before thee.'

SENDETH THEM AWAY,] to prevent any disturbance to Isaac, and his own settled arrangements.

8. EXPIRETH,] in the 175th year of his age, when Isaac was 75, and Esau and Jacob about 15 years old.

SATISFIED] with life, seeing his sons settled, and his grandchildren growing.

GATHERED UNTO HIS PEOPLE.] This is the first occurrence of this phrase, which (as remarked on 15. 15) cannot be understood of the body but of the soul, for his people were buried in Chaldee, and he in Canaan ; it is also generally (perhaps exclusively) used of the righteous, see v. 17; 35. 29; 49. 29, 33; Nu. 20. 24, 26; 27. 13; 31. 2, De. 32. 50; Ju. 2. 10; 2 K. 22. 20; 2 Ch. 34. 28; Job 27. 19; Je. 8. 2; 25. 33; Is. 57. 1.

9. HIS SONS BURY HIM.] It is pleasant to think that his sons united together to show him the last tokens of respect and love, though their characters and fates were different.

MACHPELAH,] i.e. a double cave, see 23. 9, 18, 19.

11. DOTH BLESS ISAAC,] owning him as the heir of promise.

13. NEBAJOTH,] mentioned in Is. 60. 7.

KEDAR] whose posterity and possessions are reckoned by Isaiah (21. 13) as part of Arabia ; the tents of Kedar are alluded to in Song 1. 6.

14. DUMAH.] A country of this name is mentioned in Is. 21. 11, and Ptolemy makes mention of a place in Arabia called 'Dumaetha.'

15. TEMA,] whose passengers are mentioned in Job 6. 19, and whose inhabitants are said to be Arabians in Is. 21. 13, 14.

JETUR, NAPHISH,] are both reckoned among the Hagarites, as the Ishmaelites were sometimes called, 1 Ch 5. 19; from Jetur sprung the Itureans.

KEDEMAH,] from whom perhaps arose the 'men or sons of the east,' or 'men of Kedem,' Je. 49. 28.

16. TWELVE PRINCES.] Agreeably to the prophecy, recorded in 17. 20.

HATH IT FALLEN,] i.e. his dwelling-place; some, however, apply it to his death, as having taken place peaceably, in the midst of his brethren.

20. PADAN-ARAM,] i.e. the plain of Aram, a district of Aram-Naharaim, on which see 24. 10. Compare Ge. 28. 2, 6, 7; 31. 8; 33. 18. In Ge. 48. 7, it is simply called 'Padan;' in Ho. 14, 3, it is denominated 'the field of Aram.' Compare also Nu. 23. 7, with De. 23. 4.

21. FOR HIS WIFE,] lit. 'over against his wife,' hence it has been supposed to have been a mutual or social prayer.

BARREN,] twenty years having now elapsed since their marriage.

22. RIGHT,] i.e. if all be right, why am I so pained ?

GOETH TO SEEK.] Perhaps this is only an idiom that she sought Jehovah, otherwise it may imply that there was some special place when God's presence and guidance was sought for by all those fearing Him, as in after times they resorted to Shiloh and the temple ; and she sought not in vain.

23. TWO NATIONS,] i.e. two persons, from whose loins do spring two nations and peoples.

THE LESS,] or the younger, which was fulfilled in the Edomites becoming David's tributaries, as 2 K. 8. 14, and also when in the days of Hircanus they became Jews; compare Rom. 9. 11, 12.

24. TWINS.] A double blessing granted— more than was either asked or expected.

25. ESAU,] i.e. 'prepared,' already clothed, as it were, with a natural garment.

26. JACOB,] i.e. one who retards or keeps back by laying hold on another, compare 27. 36, Ho. 12. 3, Je. 9. 4, Job 37. 4.

27. ACQUAINTED WITH HUNTING.] Compare this idiom with Is. 53. 3, 'acquainted with sickness.'

PLAIN MAN.] Compare the use of the same original word in Job 1. 1, 8; 2. 3; 8. 20; 9. 20, 21, 22; Ps. 37. 37; 64. 4; Pr. 29. 10; Song 5. 2; 6. 9.

28. FOR HIS HUNTING IS IN HIS MOUTH,] that is, from the produce of his skill in archery were made the tasteful dishes alluded to in 27. 4, 9, 14.

29. POTTAGE] of lentiles or small beans, as noticed in v. 34; see 2 Sa. 17. 28; 23. 11. Ez. 4. 9.

30. RED RED THING.] Ignorant or forgetful of its proper name, he speaks of it by its colour, 'ADOM,' hence his own name, vulgarly spelled Edom.

31. BIRTHRIGHT,] which in those early days had special prerogatives, e.g. a double portion, (De. 21. 17,) authority over his brethren, (Ge. 27. 29; 49. 3,) a type of Christ and the Church, (Ex. 4. 22) : for despising and under-valuing these, Esau is (in Heb. 12. 16) justly called 'profane.'

XXVI. 1. DAYS OF ABRAHAM,] mentioned

in 12. 10, a hundred years before this, when he went down to Egypt.

AHIMELECH,] son or grandson of the ruler of the same name mentioned in 20. 2; it was perhaps a common name, like Pharaoh, &c. From Beer-Sheba to Gerar was about eight miles.

PHILISTINES,] first mentioned in Ge. 10. 14; and again in 21. 32, 34; Ex. 13. 17, &c., they were of Semitic descent, as their names show; they came originally from Egypt, and kept such a hold of a part of Canaan that their name is applied often to the whole; their territory extended from Ekron to the brook of Egypt, along the shore of the Great Sea—the Mediterranean.

2. EGYPT.] Probably the famine was in Gerar likewise, and Isaac was meditating a journey to Egypt, as his father had done before him, owing to its great fertility, but Jehovah directly prohibited it.

4. BLESSED THEMSELVES,] as the reflexive form of the verb denotes; see note on 22. 8.

THY SEED,] thy posterity generally—the Messiah especially; see 22. 18.

5. The will of God is strongly denoted by the epithets here employed; 'voice—charge—commands—statutes—laws.'

6. IN GERAR,] according to the command given him.

7. The language and feelings of Isaac are almost identical with those of Abraham, and with less plausibility—Rebekah being only his cousin.

8. PLAYING,] a euphemism; compare Ge. 39. 14, 17; Ex. 32. 6.

10. AS A LITTLE THING,] thinking it no great offence, supposing her unmarried; which language, nevertheless, indicates a very corrupt state of morality, the knowledge of which had worked so much on the mind of the patriarch as to make him distrust the providence and promise (v. 3) of God.

11. SURELY DIE,] lit. dying doth die; this is the first mention made of the sovereign power of a king to put to death, apparently at his own pleasure.

12. AN HUNDRED FOLD,] lit. 'an hundred barleys,' pointing out the kind of grain sown. Pliny speaks of 100 and 150 fold being not uncommon in Byzacium, and Herodotus gives 200 and even 300 as the increase on the banks of the Euphrates; see also Mat. 13. 23.

13. GREAT..GREAT..VERY GREAT,] a reduplication expressive of great superiority, over even the king himself, according to his own confession in v. 16.

14. SERVICE,] for his household and followers.

15. STOPPED THEM.] Wells are the most valued possessions of the East, constructed at great expense, and to fill them up is the greatest cruelty and injustice that could be invented, compare 2 K. 3. 19, 25; 2 Ch. 32. 4. So much were they valued that (in Le. 11. 36) they were exempt from being considered unclean by any polluted thing falling into them. Among the Hindus the

digging of a well is considered an act meriting salvation, and thousands of rupees are lavished on them to secure stability, and extent, and suitability.

DUST,] not 'earth,' as in Common Version.

16. MIGHTIER.] Abraham had more than 318 trained male followers, probably Isaac may have had double that number, so that he was the head of a numerous clan, all probably bearing his name, and bound to him by religion, birth, and servitude.

17. VALLEY OF GERAR,] at some small distance from the town, to avoid quarrels.

18. HAD CALLED THEM,] manifesting reverence and affection for his father.

19. RUNNING,] lit. 'living' water, see Le. 14. 6, 51, 52; 15. 13; Nu. 19. 17.

20. EZEK,] i.e. 'strife or contention,' a word occurring nowhere else; when the water is scarce, and the labour and expense of digging for it great, the ownership of a well is a matter of supreme importance.

21. SITNAH,] i.e. 'hatred;' compare the cognate word 'Satan,' an adversary, Nu. 22. 22, 32.

22. REHOBOTH,] i.e. 'broad places;' see its use in Ge. 10. 11; 36. 37; 6, 15; 13. 17; 19. 2; 34. 21, &c.

25. ALTAR.] See note on 8. 20; 12. 7.

PREACHETH,] lit. 'calleth.'

26. PHICHOL,] probably an official name like his master's, as one of that name and office is mentioned in 21. 22.

AHUZZOTH.] Jarchi and Jonathan, strangely enough, take this name as an appellative, denoting a 'company' of friends.

28. AN OATH,] or 'execration;' see the use of the original word in Ge. 24. 41; Le. 5. 1; Nu. 5. 21, 23, 27; De. 29. 12, 14, 19, 20, 21; 30. 7; Ju. 17. 2, &c.

30. A BANQUET,] lit. a drinking, see Ge. 19. 3; 21. 8, as was customary at the making of covenants.

33. SHEBAH,] i.e. 'swearing,' as in v. 31.

BEER-SHEBA,] i.e. 'well of swearing.'

34. FORTY YEARS,] the same age as his father when he married, see 25. 20.

JUDITH....BASHEMATH.] In ch. 36. 2, 3, among the wives of Esau, no mention is made of Judith; Bashemath also is said to have been daughter of Ishmael, but probably he may have had two wives of the same name. These two especially were married against the will, or at least, without the consent of his parents, and were what is emphatically called—'a bitterness of spirit' to them.

XXVII. 1. AGED,] being about 137 years of age, the age of his brother Ishmael when he died, which probably happening at that time, reminded Isaac of the propriety of setting his house in order.

SON,] now 77 years of age, but whose residence was still with his parents.

3. INSTRUMENTS,] that is, of hunting.

4. DOTH BLESS THEE.] Isaac, unmindful of the promise, 'The elder doth serve the younger,' wished still to constitute the first born 'heir of the promises.'

7—10.] It was, without doubt, the spiritual blessings of the first-born which Rebekah and Jacob so earnestly desired, but a faithful reliance on the word of God, revealed to her at his birth, ought to have persuaded her to leave the whole in the hands of Him who worketh all things according to the counsel of His own will.

12. IT MAY BE.] Jacob evidently fears detection rather than sin.

DISESTEEM,] see note on Ge. 8. 21; compare also De. 27. 18.

13. ON BE THY DISESTEEM.] The curse causeless does not come, but Rebekah—like those who in after-times cried, 'His blood be on us and on our children,'—found it a heavy burden indeed.

16. SKINS...HANDS...NECK.] The hairy character of Esau's skin must have been very remarkable, when the skin of a kid was not distinguished from it.

18. MY FATHER,] in Hebrew ABI, a word of two short syllables: he was afraid his very voice might reveal him.

20. CAUSED TO COME BEFORE ME,] attributing his success to God.

21. WHETHER THOU ART HE.] His eyes being dim, his hearing imperfect, he desires to *feel* him, to make certain.

22. THE VOICE OF JACOB.] There is no means by which one person can distinguish another so well, very often, as by the voice.

24. ART THOU HE?] again anxious to be sure.

27. FIELD...BLESSED,] i.e. a very fruitful one.

28. DEW OF THE HEAVENS,] so free, so abundant, and so fertilizing.

CORN AND WINE,] every thing needful for sustenance.

29. PEOPLES....NATIONS,] however diversified, great, and mighty, as the Canaanites, Philistines, Moabites, Syrians, &c.

BRETHREN,] here used, as often elsewhere, of relatives generally; he had only one brother, strictly speaking.

30. ONLY JUST GOING OUT.] How narrow an escape from the eye of man! he thought not of the all-seeing eye of Jehovah.

33. YEA, BLESSED IS HE.] Though trembling excessively from the first surprise, he feels he cannot revoke his blessing, and therefore declares his firm belief in its realization.

35. TAKETH,] *or*, 'receiveth,' as the word often means, see Ge. 4. 11; 33. 10; 38. 20; Ex. 22. 11.

SUBTILITY.] See same word in 34.13; 2 K. 9. 23; Job 15. 35; 31. 5.

36. BIRTHRIGHT..TAKEN.] In his passion he forgot that he had despised and sold his birthright.

38 WEEPETH.] As remarked in Heb. 12. 17, he found no room for a reformation or change in his father's blessings; there could be no revocation.

39. FATNESS...DEW,] the same kind of temporal blessings which were bestowed on Jacob, see v. 28.

40. BY THY SWORD,] in constant warfare, with the surrounding tribes and wild beasts.

BROTHER THOU DOST SERVE,] as previously declared in 25. 23.

RULEST,] *or*, 'goest down,' *or*, 'goest free,' *or* 'mournest,' according to the various (defective) roots from which it is derived; all of these yield a suitable sense.

BREAK OFF,] as is narrated in 2 K. 8. 20–22.

41. HATETH,] as Cain did Abel, as Ishmael did Isaac, as the ten sons of Jacob did Joseph.

MOURNING FOR MY FATHER.] He coolly contemplates his father's death, and could almost long for it, that he might gratify his vengeance.

I DO SLAY.] Hatred does not long dwell in the heart before it leads to worse—even premeditated murder.

42. COMFORT HIMSELF.] A strange feeling is the love of vengeance; the very thought of it gives comfort, but the realization of it breaks the enchantment—'every one finding me doth slay me!'

44. SOME DAYS.] How shortsighted is man! the 'some days' were twenty years; see 31. 38.

45. BEREAVED OF YOU BOTH.] Her punishment has begun: Esau may slay Jacob: the law of retaliation may follow Esau, and render her childless.

46. DISGUSTED WITH MY LIFE,] because of Esau's threatened violence, and of his heathenish wives.

XXVIII. 1. THOU DOST NOT TAKE A WIFE.] The same prohibition that was laid on himself, see Ge. 24. 3; Jacob was now 77 years of age, and being the heir of the promised covenant-blessing, must not be connected with the corrupt race of Canaan.

2. DAUGHTERS OF LABAN.] Possibly some communication was kept up with Rebekah's brother's family, by means of which Isaac knew that Laban had daughters.

4. BLESSING OF ABRAHAM,] i.e. the one promised to Abraham, (see 12. 2) transmitted to Isaac, and now to Jacob, and to his seed.

9. TAKETH UNTO HIS WIVES] two other wives, with the view of pleasing his aged parents, but apparently without enquiring at the Lord; at the same time, it is possible one or both of his wives may have recently died.

12. LADDER.] This original word occurs nowhere else.

TOUCHING THE HEAVENS,] and thus connecting heaven and earth, its base being on the latter.

MESSENGERS OF GOD,] whose number is innumerable, and whose occupation is incessant.

13. JEHOVAH...UPON IT,] *or* above it; the messages come from and go to Him. Having first revealed Himself as the God of Jacob's fathers, He renews the grant of the land (formerly expressly given to them) to Jacob and his seed, whom He promises to bless abundantly, and to make the means of blessing others, and assures him of his continued protection. The obvious design of the vision was to assure Jacob that he was indeed the inheritor of his father's blessings.

17. FEARFUL,] as in Ex. 15. 11; 34. 10; De. 1. 19; 7. 21; 8. 15; 10. 17, 21; 28. 58.

HOUSE OF GOD,] i.e. the place where God is, and where he reveals Himself; the name is never applied to heaven in the O. T.; it is the New Testament alone which reveals heaven as our Father's house.

18. A STANDING PILLAR,] that he might mark it out for future time, as in Jo. 4. 3—9; see Le. 26. 1; De. 7. 5; 12. 3.

POURETH OIL ON IT,] to anoint it as sacred to God; travellers in the East almost always carry oil about with them, especially on a journey; compare Lu. 10. 34; Jas. 5. 14. 'It appears from this that oil was used in the ceremony of consecration, before the law of Moses. We learn from Clemens Alexandrinus, (Strom. lib. vii. p. 713,) that the Greeks worshipped these rude altars or stones, which had been distinguished and rendered sacred by the affusion of oil.'—*Hewlett.*

19. LUZ,] i.e. an almond tree. Luz or Beth-El is 12 miles distant from Jerusalem.

20. JACOB VOWETH.] The original word denotes 'to separate, set apart;' this is the first instance of its occurrence. For other instances, see Nu. 21. 2; Ju. 11. 30; 1 Sa. 1. 11, 21; 2 Sa. 15. 7, 8; Jon. 1. 16.

SEEING,] as the Hebrew particle often signifies; compare Job 14. 5; Je. 23. 38; Ez. 35. 6. The vow has been greatly misunderstood by its mistranslation; the true meaning is: 'When I have turned back in peace to the house of my father, and Jehovah hath become my God—then this stone which I have made a standing pillar is the house of God, and all that Thou dost give to me, I do certainly tithe to Thee.'

XXIX. 1. LIFTETH UP HIS FEET,] expressive of his joyful progress henceforth.

SONS OF THE EAST,] or, 'sons of Kedem,' i.e. Mesopotamia. Same phrase occurs in Ju. 6. 3, 33; 7. 12; 8. 10, 11; 1 K. 4. 30; Job 1. 3; Je. 49. 28; Ez. 25. 4, 10.

2. STONE..WELL'S MOUTH.] Chardin writes: 'In Arabia and other places, they cover up their wells of water, lest the sand, which is put into motion by the winds, should fill, and quite stop them up;' and Harmer adds : 'So great was their care not to leave the well open any length of time, that they waited till the flocks were all gathered together before they began to draw water, and when they had finished, the well was immediately closed again.'

4. MY BRETHREN,] a courteous and common mode of addressing any one in the East.

5. SON OF NAHOR,] more correctly, his grandson.

6. HATH HE PEACE?] The language of a people is always strikingly characteristic of that people; the character of a people is not affected by its language, but the language by the character of the people who speak it. 'Peace, quietness, undisturbed repose,' is the primary idea of happiness in the minds of most Oriental nations, and therefore their first salutation is 'Peace;' the more active Briton aims after abundance of trade and business operations, and salutes his friend with 'How do you do?' which is, we suppose, 'How are you doing?

—prosperous?' while the spirited Frenchman aims at a good deportment, *lit.* 'How do you carry yourself?'

HIS DAUGHTER IS COMING.] Females of the highest position in the East even still (and much more in ancient times) are engaged in such occupations.

7. DELIGHT YOURSELVES.] See note on Ge. 4. 2, and compare the use of the word in Pr. 13. 20; 22. 24; 28. 7; 29. 3; Ju. 14. 20; Ps. 37. 3; Is. 14. 30; 11. 7; 27. 10; 30. 23; 49. 9; 65. 25; 44. 20; Song 2. 6; 6. 3; Je. 6. 3; Mic. 5. 4; Ho. 12. 1; Na. 3. 18.

9. SHE IS SHEPHERDESS,] having, perhaps, others under her, if the flock was large.

11. KISSETH.] Most nations of the East, and even of the continent of Europe, are more liberal of their courtesies and salutations than the Anglo-Saxon race.

AND WEEPETH.] Tears are often the accompaniment of deep joy; see Ge. 45. 14, 15; 46. 29, &c.

12. HER FATHER'S BROTHER,] properly 'nephew,' but the word 'brother' is used with the common latitude.

13. ALL THESE THINGS,] the cause of his journey, and its events, his meeting with Rachel, &c.

14. ONLY,] i.e. nothing else; expressive of confidence and acknowledgement, as in Ge. 2. 23.

16. LEAH,] *lit.* 'wearied.'

RACHEL,] *lit.* 'a lamb.'

17. TENDER.] See the use of the same word in Ge. 18. 7; 33. 13; De. 20. 8; 28. 54, 56; 2 Sa. 3. 39; 1 Ch. 22. 5; 29. 1; 2 Ch. 13. 7; Job 41. 3; Pr. 4. 3; 15. 1; 25. 15; Is. 47. 1; Ez. 17. 22.

18. I SERVE THEE,] having no dowry to give, he offers his services; like David, 1 Sa. 18. 25.

19. BETTER...TO THEE,] as a relative, a known friend.

22. BANQUET,] *lit.* drinking, in honour of the marriage, which often lasted for a considerable time, the guests invited going home and returning again, as long as the entertainment lasted.

24. ZILPAH,] i.e. 'a dropping.'

25. IT IS LEAH.] Ockley relates that in Barbary the bride is obliged, in modesty, not to speak or answer on any account; if such a practice prevailed in Haran, the imposition on Jacob is easily accounted for; Hartley relates a similar fact as occurring in Smyrna.

26. IT IS NOT DONE SO.] This was no excuse; if it were true, he ought to have communicated the fact to Jacob, who found when too late that the stratagem practised upon an aged parent and unsuspecting brother was not to go unpunished. Halhed's Code of Gentoo Laws proves that there really was an enactment in India of a precisely similar character.

27. FULFIL THE WEEK] of the marriage festival; when the bride was a widow, it only lasted three days.

WE GIVE ALSO THIS ONE.] Polygamy appears to have been considered no sin in those days.

29. BILHAH,] *lit.* 'fear *or* modesty.'
31. THE HATED ONE,] i.e. less esteemed, as in De. 21. 15-17 ; Ma. 1. 3, compared with Rom. 9. 13 ; Luke 14. 6, &c.
32. REUBEN,] i.e. 'see a son.'
LOVE ME,] knowing the double claim a mother, especially the mother of a *son*, has over a barren wife.
33. SIMEON,] i.e. 'hearing.'
34. LEVI,] i.e. 'joined.'
35. JUDAH,] i.e. 'praised one.' Compare also Ge. 49. 8.
CEASETH,] *lit.* 'standeth,' that is, for a time, for she afterwards bore two sons and a daughter, see Ge. 30. 17-19.
XXX. 1. AND IF THERE IS NONE—I DIE.] Strange but true, the granting of her desire was the very cause of her death.
2. WITHHELD,] reverently acknowledging that children are the heritage of the Lord, Ps. 127. 3.
3. LO, MY HANDMAID.] Perhaps she had heard of Sarah's doing so with Hagar, see 16. 2.
4. JACOB GOETH IN,] as did Abraham to Hagar.
6. DECIDED FOR ME.] Compare the use of the same word in Je. 5. 28 ; 22. 16 ; Ps. 54. 1 ; 110. 6.
DAN,] i.e. 'a judge.'
8. NAPHTALI,] i.e. 'my wrestling;' compare the use of the verb in Job 5. 13 ; Pr. 8. 8 ; 2 Sa. 22. 27 ; Ps. 18. 26.
11. GAD,] i.e. 'a troop,' or 'an assaulter ;' see Ge. 49. 17.
13. HAPPY.] the word never means 'blessed,' but simply 'happy,' as in Ma. 3. 12, 15 ; Job 29. 11 ; Ps. 41. 2 ; 72. 17 ; Pr. 3. 18 ; 4. 14 ; 9. 6 ; 23. 19 ; 31. 28 ; Song 6. 9 ; Is. 1. 17 ; 3. 12 ; 9. 16.
ASHER,] i.e. 'happy,' never 'blessed.'
14. LOVE-APPLES,] in Hebrew DUDAIM, found again in v. 15, 16 ; Song 7. 13 ; Je. 24. 1, from a root signifying to love ; the word 'mandrake' is a corruption from 'mandragora,' the word used by the Septuagint, and understood by most of the ancient Versions. This fruit is thought by the Orientals to excite love. It is found wild in the field, and is of the size of a small apple.
15. THOU HAST TAKEN.] The past tense would seem to point out the eagerness and greedy desire with which they were coveted ; compare similar form of expression in Mat. 5. 28.
16. UNTO ME,] i.e. unto my tent, which was separate from Rachel's.
18. ISSACHAR,] i.e. 'there is a hire, *or* reward.'
20. ENDOWED....DOWRY.] The original words found here occur nowhere else in SS.
ZEBULUN,] i.e. 'dwelling, habitation.'
21. DINAH,] i.e. 'judged, decided,' the feminine form of Dan, the first son of Rachel by Bilhah, as a counterpart to whom Leah probably gave her daughter this name. Daughters are but little esteemed in the East in comparison with sons.
22. REMEMBERED,] as he had done Noah, 8. 1,) in kindness and love.

23. GATHERED UP,] i.e. removed my reproach and shame of barrenness ; compare the use of the same word in 6. 21 ; 29. 22 ; 42. 17 ; 49. 33.
24. JOSEPH,] i.e. 'He doth add,' spoken in high hope and confident anticipation, which was afterwards realized.
25. JOSEPH,] at the end of his 14 years of servitude for his two wives to Laban.
PLACE,] to Beer-Sheba, where Isaac was residing, whom he longed to see again.
27. OBSERVED DILIGENTLY.] Same original word occurs in 44. 5, 15 ; Le. 19. 26 ; De. 18. 10 ; 1 K. 20. 33 ; 2 K. 21. 6 ; 17. 17 ; 2 Ch. 33. 6.
28. DEFINE.] Same word as in Nu. 1. 17 ; Am. 6. 1 ; 1 Ch. 12. 31 ; 16. 41 ; 2 Ch. 28. 15 ; 31. 19 ; Ezra 8. 20 ; Le. 24. 11, 16 ; Nu. 23. 8, 25.
30. DO I MAKE,] i.e. earn, prepare, acquire anything for my own household.
BEFORE MY COMING,] *lit.* 'at my face *or* presence.'
BREAKETH FORTH,] as in v. 43 ; 28. 14 ; 38. 29 ; Ex. 1. 12 ; 19. 22, 24, &c.
32. SPECKLED....SPOTTED.] Such sheep must always be comparatively rare ; it was therefore apparently very favourable for Laban.
AT MY COMING,] *lit.* 'at my feet,' perhaps meaning 'wherever I go.'
33. RIGHTEOUSNESS,] i.e. right, character, or state.
37. TAKETH,] according to Divine direction ; see 31. 12.
FRESH POPLAR,] not 'green,' describing its moisture, not its colour.
HAZEL,] which the Jewish Commentator and Translator, Saadias Gaon, takes for the almond tree, while the 'chesnut' is thought by Ainsworth and others to have been the plantane or plane-tree.
MAKING BARE,] as in Ps. 29. 9 ; Is. 20. 4 ; 30. 14 ; 47. 2 ; 52. 10 ; Je. 13. 26 ; 49. 10 ; Ez. 4. 7 ; Joel 1. 7 ; Hag. 2. 16.
38. CONCEIVE,] through the power of imagination ; but Shuckford writes : 'It cannot be proved that the method which Jacob here used is a natural and effectual way to produce variegated cattle. The ancient naturalists indeed have carried their thoughts on these subjects much too far. The effect of impressions on the imagination must be very accidental, because the objects that should cause them may, or may not be noticed, as any one will find who tries Jacob's peeled rods as a means to variegate his cattle. But whether this effect were owing to natural causes, or to those which we call preternatural and miraculous, it is equally agreeable to the Scripture style and true wisdom, to ascribe it to God, as Jacob does, chap. 31. 9.'
39. BRINGETH FORTH] such as was Jacob's hire or reward.
XXXI. 1. TAKEN ALL.] This exaggeration was very natural in their excited state of feeling ; compare John 4. 29, 'who told me all.'
HONOUR,] *lit.* 'weight, heaviness,' i.e.

wealth and riches in money, or in cattle and substance.

2. AS HERETOFORE,] *lit.* 'as yesterday—third day;' so again in v. 5; Ex. 4. 10; 5. 7, 8, 14; 21. 29, 36; De. 4. 42; 19. 4, 6.

4. TO THE FIELD,] that he might have more unrestrained conversation with them, without fear of being overheard by the spies of Laban.

6. YE HAVE KNOWN,] appealing to their own knowledge of his behaviour.

7. TEN TIMES,] many times, expressed by a round number (see Le. 26. 26,) which he repeats again to Laban himself in v. 41, showing thereby his consciousness of being right.

TO DO EVIL,] that is, any real evil.

10-13. These verses explain how God had 'taken away' Laban's substance, and 'given' it to Jacob, by showing how he was directed to proceed for the increase of his hire.

15. SOLD US,] for fourteen years service; seeking his own profit, not our comfort.

16. ALL THAT GOD..DO,] implying thereby their entire acquiescence in his plans; illustrating Ge. 2. 24.

17. SONS...WIVES,] ten sons, one daughter, two wives, and two handmaids.

CAMELS,] being the usual means of conveyance apparently in those days, (compare Ge. 24. 10, 61, &c.) horses being almost unknown in that region.

19. TERAPHIM,] mentioned also in 31. 34, 35; Ju. 17. 5; 18. 14; 17, 18, 20; 1 Sa. 15. 23; 19. 13, 16; 2 K. 23. 24; Ez. 21. 21; Ho. 3. 4. Zec. 10. 2; supposed to have been domestic gods or idols, of the human form and size, (1 Sa. 19. 13, 16,) from which responses were sought; perhaps *lit.* 'tearers,' destructive demons; Rachel took them away, with the view doubtless of preventing her father doing her any evil by their (supposed) power.

20. DECEIVETH,] *lit.* 'stealeth' the heart of Laban; compare similar passages, in v. 26, 27; 2 Sa. 15. 6.

21. THE RIVER,] i.e. the Euphrates, which separates the plain of Aram from Syria; its greatest breadth is about 200 paces.

GILEAD.] A ridge of mountains, stretching from Lebanon to Moab, east of Jordan, so called here by anticipation, (see v. 45,) about 380 miles from Haran, on the borders of Canaan, noted for its balm, Je. 8. 21; 46. 11.

23. BRETHREN,] i.e. relatives and neighbours.

24. DREAM.] Supernatural revelations of the Divine will were not confined to the children of God, but were often afforded to worldly men, such as Balaam, Pharaoh, Abimelech, &c.; the power of working miracles was no doubt enjoyed and exercised by Judas as well as by his fellow-apostles.

27. WITH JOY...HARP,] which it was customary to have on setting out on long journeys, but mere pretence on the part of Laban.

29. MY HAND IS TO GOD,] raised in a vow to the Most High, threatening vengeance on thee.

GOD OF YOUR FATHER.] Laban was without

doubt an idolator, and feared (without worshipping) Jehovah, as did the Samaritans of a later age, see 2 K. 17. 33.

30. VERY DESIROUS.] It is a common but true saying, that *home* is never so dear to any as to those who have been involuntarily taken away from it for a length of time.

STOLEN MY GODS.] Were it not from habit and early prepossessions, the notion of any intelligent man worshipping the work of his own hands, would be deemed an absurdity too great to be believed; compare the graphic irony of the prophet, Is. 44. 16; and in Ju. 6. 31, 32.

34. FURNITURE,] i.e. the cushions and drapery on the camel's back for riding.

38. TWENTY YEARS,] so that Jacob was now 97 years of age.

NOT EATEN,] as a worthless shepherd would have done, see Ez. 34. 3.

39. DECEIVED,] same word in v. 20, 26, 27.

40. DROUGHT.] The average of the thermometer in Palestine by day is about 75 degrees.

FROST.] The cold dews and frosts in summer during the nights are said often to be as severe in Syria as in Paris in the month of March.

WANDERETH.] From incessant watchfulness against freebooters, and wild beasts, and ravenous fowls; an Eastern shepherd's life was no childish amusement, but required a man of undaunted courage and iron perseverance.

41. TEN TIMES.] See note on v. 7.

42. FEAR, i.e. the object of the fear of Isaac; He whom he worshipped.

YESTERNIGHT.] It is impossible not to be struck with the bold, honest, manly tone adopted by Jacob towards Laban; he had borne long with his injustice and selfishness for the sake of his wives and family, but the restraint having been broken by a false accusation, he pours out a torrent of resistless eloquence, before which Laban has to succumb immediately.

43. THE DAUGHTERS ARE MY DAUGHTERS.] This was true of course, but his manner of dealing with them had not been such as became a father alive to his duties and responsibilities.

44. MAKE A COVENANT,] forgetting and forgiving past causes of difference, and beginning, as it were, a new friendship.

46. EAT THERE ON THE HEAP,] eating being with the Orientals a token of friendship, and the heap being thus, as it were, sanctified.

47. JEGAR-SAHADUTHA,] i.e. 'a heap of testimony,' in his own vernacular tongue the Aramæan, while Jacob called it GALEED,] a Hebrew word of precisely the same meaning as the former.

49. MIZPAH,] i.e. 'a watch-tower,' as appears from next clause; in Ju. 11. 29. more fully 'Mizpah of Gilead.' To this place Joshua's troops pursued such of Jabin's army as fled eastward, Jos. 11. 3, 8; here Jephthah dwelt, and mustered his army against the Ammonites, Ju. 11. 3, 11.

29. There was another Mizpeh, about 18
miles east of Jerusalem, (Jo. 15. 38,) where
Israel met regarding the Levite's concubine,
(Ju. 20. 1;) there Samuel dwelt, (1 K. 7.
5, 6,) and Saul was anointed, (1 Sa. 10. 17;)
it was rebuilt by Asa, (1 K. 15. 22,) and inhabited by Gedaliah, (Je. 40. 41) : its inhabitants helped to build the walls of Jerusalem, Neh. 3. 7, 15, 19.

HIDDEN] by distance ; compare the use
of the same word in Ge. 4. 14, Nu. 5. 13,
De. 7. 20; 29. 29; 1 Sa. 20. 5, 19, 24; 1 K. 17.
3 ; Job 3. 23 ; 13. 20 ; 28. 21 ; 34. 22.

50. TAKE WIVES.] Yet he himself was the
means of compelling Jacob to have more
than one ; in both cases selfishness was his
prevailing motive.

GOD IS WITNESS.] Ungodly men are always
the readiest to appeal to God when it suits
their purpose.

53. THE GOD OF THEIR FATHER,] who
was probably all his days an idolator ; this
combination of deities arose from a desire
to render the covenant more binding.

FEAR,] see note on v. 42 ; thus serving
himself heir to his father, and affording to
Laban the best pledge he could give of his
sincerity and fidelity.

54. A SACRIFICE,] any thing offered to
God. There are a few passages in which
this word is supposed to denote merely an
animal slaughtered for food, but the common idea of a sacrifice offered to God will
suit every instance of its occurrence.

EAT BREAD,] a common phrase, signifying, ' to dine, take food.'

55. PLACE,] after which we hear no more
of him ; he had been the means of protecting Jacob for a time, of trying his
patience, and fortitude, and faithfulness, of
furnishing to the church those two who
did build the house of Israel, and now he
turns to his gods and his gold.

XXXII. 1. MESSENGERS OF GOD,] as at the
commencement of his outward journey he
had been encouraged by a vision of the
messengers of God going up and coming
down by a ladder from heaven, so now as
he wends his way homeward they come
again to him, compare Ps. 34. 7 ; 91. 11, 12 ;
1 K. 6. 17 ; Luke 2. 13.

2. MAHANAIM,] i. e. ' two camps,' referred
to again in Song 7. 1. (6.13.) This place was
in the land of Gilead, and (afterwards) in
the possession of the tribe of Dan, 44 miles
from Jerusalem.

3. SEIR,] so named from Seir the Horite,
(but anciently Hor) and coming partly into
the hand of Esau, through his marriage,
he and his sons drove out the remant of
the Horites, and possessed it.

4. MY LORD,] a title of respect as an elder
brother, and as a chieftain, and as both
courtesy and expediency suggested.

THY SERVANT.] A soft answer turneth
away wrath ; yet in 27. 29, he had been
made lord over him.

6. 400 MEN WITH HIM,] which was more
than Abraham could muster on a very important occasion ; so greatly had the
branches spread, and the promises ripened.

7. DISTRESSED,] at his ignorance of Esau's
real sentiments, the danger to himself, his
wives, and family, the thought of his never
seeing his aged parent again.

8. ESCAPE,] from the sword of Esau.

9. O GOD.] Jacob having made such
arrangement as worldly prudence suggested, turns to the Rock higher than he,
and was saved from that which he feared :
this is the first recorded prayer of any
extent in Scripture.

ABRAHAM...ISAAC.] These had served him
in their day and generation; their memorial
was dear is His sight, and their descendant
was in danger, which He who doth kindness to thousands of generations could not
overlook.

WHO SAITH.] This is another powerful
argument ; Jacob's return homeward was
in obedience to God's express command,
(31. 13;) by this journey he is brought into
unforeseen danger : may not Jacob reasonably expect deliverance ? to have returned
home of himself might have been a tempting
of God, but the command was express.

10. MY STAFF,] i.e. alone and a fugitive.

TWO CAMPS.] The little one had become
a chief, the small one a great nation.

12. THOU HAST SAID.] It is thine own
word of promise, save me then from this
hour.

13. A PRESENT,] consisting in all of 550
head of cattle, such as would be most
prized by Esau, and most exquisitely arranged for value and appearance; suckling
camels were of a very great price, and the
whole would have appeased the wrath of a
more relentless adversary than Esau.

20. LIFTETH UP MY FACE,] accepting my
present, he will discard resentment, and
unite in friendship.

22. JABBOK,] a stream near mount Gilead,
on the northern border of the Ammonites,
flowing into Jordan on the east, 3 or 4
miles south of the sea of Tiberias : it divided
the kingdom of Sihon from that of Og, De.
32. 22 ; Nu. 21. 24 ; De. 2. 37 ; 3. 16 ; Jo. 2. 2 ;
Ju. 11. 13, 22.

24. ONE,] lit. 'a man, person, individual ;'
in Ho. 12. 4. called 'a messenger.'

WRESTLETH,] lit. 'maketh dust,' as
wrestlers do with their feet. Warburton
observes, (Divine Legation of Moses,) that
'Information by action was at this time a
very familiar mode of instruction, and the
difficulties of language were supplied by
significant signs. If we turn back to Jacob's
prayer, and consider the circumstances he
was in when it pleased God to wrestle with
him, we may perceive that God's intention
was to inform him of the happy issue of his
adventure, and that his petition was granted,
by a significant action. This mode of information concerning only the actor, who little
needed to be told the meaning of what was
at that time in vulgar use, hath now an
obscurity, which the Scripture relations of
the same mode of information to the prophets are free from, by reason of their being
given for the use of the people to whom
they were to be explained.'

26. EXCEPT THOU HAST BLESSED ME.] Compare Ex. 32. 10: Is. 62. 7; Ja. 5. 16. 17.

28. ISRAEL,] i.e. 'he is a prince with God.'

29. DECLARE THY NAME.] Compare Ex. 3. 13; Ju. 13. 17.

30. PENIEL,] i.e. 'face of God;' it was 4 miles from Mahanaim; see also Ju. 8. 8; 1 K. 12. 25; in v. 31, Penuel.

DELIVERED.] The common opinion very naturally was, that the sight of God would cause death; see Ex. 20. 19; 33. 18; De. 5. 25; Ju. 13. 22; Ge. 16. 13.

31. THE SUN RISETH ON HIM,] an emblem of prosperity, and a figure of the Sun of righteousness, Mal. 4. 1.

32. UNTO THIS DAY,] when the historian was writing.

XXXIII 1. DIVIDETH] into three divisions, according to the regard he bore them severally.

3. HIMSELF PASSED OVER] at their head, to meet and avert the coming danger; he had this grace from on high; 'as thy day so is thy strength.'

SEVEN TIMES,] in token of profound submission; perhaps 'seven' here is a perfect number.

5. HATH GRACIOUSLY GIVEN,] or 'hath graced' thy servant, i.e. favoured and adorned him.

7. JOSEPH,] who was about six years of age.

8. TO FIND GRACE.] Presents are invariably presented to superiors in the East, compare 1 Sa. 9. 8; and to decline to receive one is considered very suspicious, as ominous of evil consequences, hence Jacob's anxiety for Esau's acceptance of his present.

10. AS THE SEEING OF THE FACE OF GOD,] which I did not expect to see, and value greatly as an honour and privilege.

11. BLESSING,] i.e. expression of my desire for thy welfare.

I HAVE ALL] good things, temporal and spiritual, for the life that now is, and for the life that is to come. Compare the language of New Testament saints, 1 Cor. 3. 22; Phil. 4. 18.

13. CHILDREN ARE TENDER,] Reuben being 13, and Joseph only 6 years of age.

BEATEN THEM.] Same word in Ju. 19. 22; Song. 5. 2, which are all the instances of its occurrence.

14. TO SEIR,] whither, however, he does not appear to have ever gone, so far as the narrative is concerned, from some cause left unexplained.

15. LET ME PLACE,] as a guard, and protection, and honour to him.

17. SUCCOTH.] So called by anticipation, as the last clause of the verse shows. It was situated in the territory of Gad, on the east of Jordan, south of the sea of Galilee, Jo. 13. 27; Ju. 8. 5; 1 K. 7. 46; Ps. 60. 6. Succoth was also the name of a station of the Israelites in the wilderness, Ex. 12. 37: 13. 20.

18. SHALEM,] i.e. Salim, near Ænon, (Jno. 3. 23;) but some Jewish writers translate it 'in peace.'

SHECHEM.] built by Hamor, and called after his son, the same with Sychar (Jno. 4. 5,) on this side of Jordan, about eight miles from Succoth; a city in Mount Ephraim, between Ebal and Gerizim, now called Nablus, see Ge. 12. 6; 34. 2; Jo. 20. 7; 21. 20, 21; Ps. 60. 8; 1 K. 12. 25; Ho. 6. 9. Acts 7. 16;

19. BUYETH.] Though 'heir' of the whole land, he had only at this time the burying place of Machpelah for a possession, he now adds the 'portion of the field where he had stretched out his tent.'

HUNDRED KESITAH.] This word only occurs elsewhere in Job 42. 11; the Septuagint, Onkelos, Samaritan, Syriac, and Arabic Versions, render it 'a hundred lambs,' cattle being used in those days as a means of barter; in Acts 7. 16, it is said to have been 'money,' perhaps with the stamp of a lamb upon them.

20. AN ALTAR,] serving himself thereby heir to Isaac, see 26. 25.

XXXIV. 1. DINAH,] now about 14 or 15 years of age.

LOOK ON,] as was natural, having no sister or person, it may be, of her own age, to pass her time with.

2. HAMOR, i.e. an ass.

3. HIS SOUL CLEAVETH.] It was not a mere temporary passion, but real affection.

UNTO THE HEART,] in such a tender loving manner, as to excite her love in return, a very common phrase in SS.

4. TAKE FOR ME.] The very language of Samson to his parents, (Ju. 14. 2,) for a similar object, showing how much in the East marriages were contracted for by the parents, with or without the young people's consent.

5. TILL THEIR COMING.] Their age and number, along with the forward spirit of several of them, constrained Jacob to take no steps in the matter till they had decided; brothers also more than fathers, are considered in the East as the guardians of their sisters.

7. GRIEVE THEMSELVES,] as the reflective form of the verb shows.

FOLLY,] which in SS. is generally regarded as sin, iniquity.

AGAINST ISRAEL.] The Common Version 'in Israel,' could only have been used when Israel became a nation.

8. YOUR DAUGHTER.] The plural pronoun shows that he wished the consent of her brothers, as well as of her father, as was customary, see 24. 50, 51, 55, 59.

9. JOIN YE IN MARRIAGE WITH US,] which neither Jacob nor Isaac had been allowed to do by their parents, (24, 3; 28. 1,) and which was afterwards expressly prohibited in De. 7. 3.

11. SHECHEM SAITH.] His father having stated the advantages of the proposed alliance, he himself states his desire to make every satisfaction which he had in his power for the wrong done, manifesting his love to Dinah: 'I give as ye say unto me, without hesitation or limitation.

14. WE ARE NOT ABLE TO DO.] There was no positive law against it, (it could only be

by inference from 17. 12,) but they answered deceitfully, as the historian tells us.

15. IF YE BE AS WE,] in religious profession, as commanded in 17. 10.

20. GATE OF THEIR CITY,] where all public business was transacted.

24. HEARKEN,] i.e. obey, either because the will of their prince was absolute, or because they considered it would tend to strengthen their community.

25. THE THIRD DAY,] when the pain of circumcision is said to be greatest.

DINAH'S BRETHREN,] by the mother's side as well as the father's; they were Leah's children, and so most provoked at their only sister's dishonour.

EVERY MALE] grown up; the little ones were spared, according to v. 29.

27. THE SONS OF JACOB,] it is not easy to say whether these were the whole ten sons, or only Simeon and Levi.

28. FLOCK..HERD..THEY HAVE TAKEN,] which was perhaps in some measure a fit recompense for the covetous hopes of the Shechemites in v. 33.

30. TROUBLED ME.] Compare the same word in Jo. 6. 18; 7. 25; Ju. 11. 35; 1 Sa. 14. 29; 1 K. 18. 17, 18; 1 Ch. 2. 7; Ps. 39. 2; Pr. 11. 17, 29; 15. 6, 27.

CAUSING ME TO STINK,] as in Ex. 5. 21; 16. 24; 1 Sa. 27. 12; Ps. 38. 5; Pr. 13. 5; Ec. 10. 1; this feeling never left Jacob, and at his death (see Ge. 49. 5, 7) he marked his abhorrence of it.

FEW,] lit. 'men of number,' i.e. who could easily be numbered.

31. HARLOT,] boldly preferring danger and death rather than family dishonour; yet were not deceit, hypocrisy, and the murder of so many unoffending helpless men greater sins?

XXXV 1. JACOB,] when in distress and alarm, seeking, it may be, divine guidance and help, either by a dream or vision.

BETH-EL,] 30 miles south of Shechem.

MAKE THERE AN ALTAR,] which he appears hitherto to have neglected to have done, though he had now been nine or ten years in the land of Canaan, after his return from Laban; might not the affair of Dinah have been permitted as a punishment for his unfulfilled vow?

2. THE GODS OF THE STRANGER.] This charge probably was not needed by the more intimate part of his relatives, but by his numerous followers, and may have had reference to the 'gods' taken among the spoils of Shechem.

CHANGE YOUR GARMENTS,] for your journey; but some suppose it was for a religious or ceremonial purpose, in which case it is the first instance of such in the Bible.

HIDETH..OAK.] The gods may have been of wood or stone, and the rings of ivory; had they been of silver or gold, they would probably have been melted, and applied to better purposes, as Napoleon Bonaparte is said to have done with a silver statue of some Roman saint. The oak was chosen, being a kind of sacred tree in ancient times, and not likely to be cut down.

5. TERROR OF GOD,] inspired by Him, to protect his servant; compare Ex. 34. 24, where the promise is, that while the people are absent from their dwellings keeping the feasts of the Lord, no man should desire their land.

6. LUZ,] here said to be in 'the land of Canaan;' another place of the same name was in 'the land of the Hittites,' see Ju. 1. 26.

8. DEBORAH,] i.e. 'a bee,' mentioned before in 24. 59.

OAK OF WEEPING,] in Heb. Allon-Bachuth.

9. AGAIN,] in addition to the appearances at Penuel and at Shechem.

PADAN-ARAM.] See note on 25. 20.

10. ISRAEL IS THY NAME.] See 32. 28.

11. GOD SAITH.] Compare similar language in 28. 13; 26. 3, 4, 24; 22. 17, 18; 17. 1-8, 16, &c., to Jacob, to Isaac, and to Abraham.

13. GOETH UP FROM HIM.] Constant communion with God is not the portion even of believers; they walk by faith, not by sight.

14. OBLATION..OIL,] see note on Ge. 28. 18. The oblation was generally of oil.

15. BETH-EL,] as he had done before; see 28. 19.

16. KIBRATH.] This word probably means 'length, space,' and occurs again only in 48. 7; 2 K. 5. 19.

EPHRATHA,] afterwards called in 48. 7, Bethlehem, and more fully, Bethlehem Ephratah, (Mic. 5. 2,) a town in the tribe of Judah, twelve miles from Bethel, on the way to Hebron.

17. SHARPLY PAINED.] Compare Ge. 3. 16.

SAID..A SON,] who had been long and confidently hoped for, as noted in 30. 24.

18. SHE DIED,] by the realization of that for lack of which she had said she would die, see 30. 1.

BEN-ONI,] i.e. 'son of my sorrow,' or 'iniquity,' or 'strength,' for the word is used in all these significations; see Nu. 23. 21; De. 26. 14; 1 Sa. 15. 23; Job 4. 8. (Compare also Ge. 49. 3; De. 21. 17.)

BENJAMIN,] i.e. 'son of the right hand,' or 'son of days,' i.e. son of his old age, as in 44. 20.

19. BETH-LEHEM,] i.e. 'house of bread.'

20. UNTO THIS DAY] when the historian was writing, and even till the time of Samuel, see 1 Sa. 10. 2.

21. ISRAEL.] This is the first instance in which the historian himself calls Jacob by this name.

TOWER OF EDAR,] i.e. 'tower of the herd,' a place about a mile to the south of Bethlehem; the name occurs again in Mic. 4. 8, where the Targum of Jonathan translates it, 'O king Messiah!'

22. IN THAT LAND,] i.e. of Judah, near Bethlehem.

CONCUBINE,] i.e. a secondary wife, Rachel's handmaid, given to her by Laban her father.

HEARETH.] The Septuagint unnecessarily adds, 'and it was evil in his eyes;' this was doubtless one of the things which compelled him to say in 47. 9, 'few and evil have been the days of the years of my life.'

23—26. Only the sons of Jacob are enu

merated; the daughter Dinah is passed over unnoticed, while Benjamin is classed among those born in Padan-Aram, the historian taking for granted that the reader will bear in mind the preceding statements in v. 16-18. To suppose that there is an error in this and similar genealogical tables, (as Colenso, Davidson, and others do,) is to refuse to grant the popular use of language to the inspired historian.

27. HIS FATHER.] No mention being made of his mother, it is probable she was already dead, (see note on 27. 44.) Jacob had now been about ten years in Canaan, yet this is the first mention made of his visiting his father.

MAMRE.] See 13. 18; 14. 13.

CITY OF ARBA,] or Kirjath-Arba, as in 23. 2.

HEBRON,] i.e. 'junction,' name of a city 22 miles south of Jerusalem, built on a hill, seven years before Zoan in Egypt, (Nu. 13. 22); inhabited by Anak and his sons, who were expelled by Caleb, after whose son Hebron it was named, (Jos. 14. 13, 14); also a city of refuge given to the priests, (Ju. 21. 13,) where David reigned 7 years, (2 Sa. 2. 11,) and Absalom set up for king, (2 Sa. 15. 10); repaired by Rehoboam it was held by the Edomites; see Ge. 13. 18; 23. 2.

28. 180 YEARS,] which was 5 years older than his father, and forty years after he thought he was dying (27. 2.) Jacob was now 120 years of age, and Joseph 28, so that Isaac died 12 years after Joseph was sold into Egypt.

29. Compare the similar language used of Abraham in 25. 8.

BURY HIM,] it is not said where, but from 49. 31, we learn that it was in the cave of Machpelah.

ESAU AND JACOB.] It is pleasant to think that the two brothers united together in this filial act, and that in their father's grave they may have buried for ever their envy and selfishness.

XXXVI. 1. ESAU..EDOM,] see on 25. 30.

2. DAUGHTERS OF CANAAN,] who were a bitterness of spirit to Isaac and Rebekah, see 26. 35.

4. ELIPHAZ,] whom Jerome and the Targum of Jonathan assert to have been the Eliphaz of the book of Job; but as he is called the 'Temanite,' he may have been his grandson, see v. 11.

6. INTO THE COUNTRY,] i.e. of Seir, where he had been before, see 32.3; 33.16, and from which he had come to bury his father, whose possessions having been divided into their respective shares, Esau took off his with him to Seir, as the land of Judah did not afford sufficient nourishment for the united flocks of himself and Jacob, as happened in the parallel case of Abraham and Lot, recorded in 13. 6.

8. SEIR,] i.e. 'hairy,' woody, a mountainous region, extending from the Salt Sea to the Elanic Gulf, originally inhabited by the Horites, (Ge. 14. 6; De. 2. 12,) then by Esau, (32. 4; 33. 16,) and his descendants, (De. 2. 4; 2 Ch. 20. 10.)

11. TEMAN,] whose name is given to a city in Idumea; see Je. 49. 7; Am. 1. 11; Job 2. 11.

ZEPHO,] in 1 Ch. 1. 36, called Zephi.

12. TIMNATH,] said in 1 Ch. 1. 36 to have been sister of Lotan, eldest son of Seir the Horite.

14. DAUGHTER,] the Samaritan, Syriac, and Septuagint Versions read son, 'son' of Zibeon.

15. CHIEFS,] or 'leaders.'

20. INHABITANTS,] i.e. the first, those 'before Esau,' as the Targum of Jonathan adds.

23. ALVAN] is in 1 Ch. 1. 40 called Alian, and Sheppo is Shephi.

24. IMIM,] variously translated: the Vulgate has 'hot baths;' so Geddes, Boothroyd, Rosenmuller, Gesenius, Schumann; Syriac, simply 'waters;' Wagenseil thinks it a plant; Arabic has 'mules;' the Samaritan text has 'the Emin,' i.e. giants; so Pool, Horsley, Onkelos, and Jonathan; the Septuagint has preserved the Hebrew word, which apparently was not known about 270 years B.C., and is not likely to be discovered now.

26. DISHON,] i.e. son of Seir, v. 21.

HEMDAN,] called in 1 Ch. 1. 41, Amram, or Chamram.

27. EZER,] another son of Seir, v. 21.

ZAAVAN AND AKAN,] in 1 Ch. 1. 42, called Zavan and Jakan.

28. DISHAN,] the last mentioned son of Seir, v. 21.

UZ,] who gave his name to a portion of the land of Idumea, Lam. 4. 21, which some suppose to have been the same Uz as that in which Job dwelt.

31. There being no king in Israel till long after the death of Moses, it has been questioned whether the last clause of the verse is not a later addition of Ezra's; that out of Israel kings were to come, is quite evident from Ge. 17. 6; 35. 11; with these prophecies in view, Moses lay down (in De. 17. 14-20) explicit directions regarding the office; there can therefore, be no real or solid objection to maintaining that the clause was really written by Moses, notwithstanding the objections of Colenso, Davidson, Paine, &c.

32. BELA,] supposed by Bedford (in his Scripture Chronology, p. 315,) to have reigned A.M. 2002.

33. JOBAB,] mentioned again in Is. 34. 6; 63. 1; Je. 48. 24; 49. 13, 22; Amos 1. 12; Mic. 2. 12.

34. TEMANITE,] or, 'of the south,' as the Targum of Jonathan has it.

37. REHOBOTH BY THE RIVER,] i.e. of Euphrates according to Jonathan, but Jerome speaks of a village so named in Idumea, by a river.

39. HADAR,] the last of the Horite kings, succeeded by Esau, from whom came the following chiefs.

41. AHOLIBAMAH] is the name of a woman in v. 25; here of a man.

XXXVII 1. JACOB DWELLETH,] said in opposition to Esau's forsaking the promised land, and thereby virtually renouncing the covenant-blessings; this verse is properly the last of the preceding chapter.

2. ENJOYING HIMSELF,] see note on Ge. 4. 2.

SONS OF BILHAH..ZILPAH,] viz. Dan and Naphtali, and Gad and Asher.

3. A LONG COAT.] *lit.* 'a coat for the extremities,' (reaching to his ancles, and to his wrists,) as the word means in Da. 6. 5, 25, the only instances of its occurrence.

5. DREAM.] This mode of receiving a divine communication had already been enjoyed by Abimelech (20. 3, 6,) Jacob (31. 10, 11,) Laban, (31. 24,) and afterwards by the two servants of Pharaoh, (40. 5, 8, 9, 16,) and Pharaoh himself, (41. 7, 8, 15, 17, 22, &c.) It is expressly mentioned as such by God, (Nu. 12. 6,) and claimed by false prophets, (De. 13. 1, 3, 5.) Compare also Ju. 7. 13, 15; 1 Sa. 28. 6, 15; 1 K. 3. 5, 15; Job 7. 14; 20. 8; 33. 15; Ec. 5. 2, 7; Ps. 73. 20; Is. 29. 7; Je. 23. 27, 28. 32; 27. 9; 29. 8; Da. 1. 17; 2. 1; 2. 2, 3; Joel 2. 28; Zec. 10. 2.

7. BINDING BUNDLES,] i.e. of corn, after it had been cut down, implying that Jacob's sons were husbandmen as well as shepherds.

MY BUNDLE,] or sheaf, which an ancient Jewish writer, (Raya Mehimna, in Zohar, fol. 82, 2,) interprets of Messiah, son of Ephraim, a fanciful creation of Jewish antichristian theology.

BOW THEMSELVES.] See the fulfilment in 42. 6.

8. HIS WORDS,] which Jarchi refers to the evil report he took to their father, but more naturally referring to his repeating his dream.

9. SUN....MOON....STARS,] emblems of principalities and powers in a state; see Ex. 32. 7; Ps. 84. 11; Song 6. 10; Job 30. 28; Is. 60. 20; Je. 15. 9; Am. 8. 9; Mal. 4. 2; compare also Mat. 13. 46; 24. 29; Acts 2. 20; Rev. 6. 12; 8. 12; 9. 2; 21. 23. The special mention of eleven stars appears to confine its application to his own family.

10. PUSHETH AGAINST HIM.] The original word GAAR, is evidently the root of the English word *gore;* compare all the passages where it occurs; Ruth 2. 6; Ps. 9. 5; 68. 30; 106. 9; 119. 21; Is. 17. 13; 54. 9; Je. 29. 27; Na. 1. 4; Zec. 3. 2; Ma. 2. 3; 3. 11; the Common Version in all passages (save Ma. 2. 3) translate it by 'rebuke,' which leaves the particle 'against' untranslated.

11. JEALOUS OF,] or zealous against him; the idea is more one of 'zeal' than of 'envy.'

MATTER] of the two dreams. Compare Da. 7. 28; Lu. 2. 51.

12. SHECHEM,] about 60 miles distant from Hebron, where they were now residing; a considerable time must have elapsed before they could have ventured back to the place where they had committed so great an outrage; perhaps their numbers were now so great that they did not fear the Canaanite or the Perizzite dwelling there; but there still remaining some degree of anxiety on their father's mind, he bethought himself of sending Joseph to see about them, and so the Targum of Jonathan explains it.

15. WANDERING IN THE FIELD,] perhaps the one Jacob had purchased, (33. 19,) where he expected naturally to meet with his brethren.

17. DOTHAN,] a town 12 miles north of Samaria, (mentioned again in 2 K. 6. 13,) in the tribe of Manasseh, 44 miles north of Jerusalem, and 6 west of Tiberias.

19. MAN OF THE DREAMS,] *or* 'possessor, lord, owner, master of dreams;' one addicted to them, a title of derision.

20. PITS,] dug for the collection of water.

21. DELIVERETH] for the present time, but only for a time.

SMITE THE LIFE,] i.e. put to death; compare Pr. 19. 18.

22. SHED NO BLOOD,] in accordance with Ge. 9. 6.

FATHER.] Some explain Reuben's conduct as not flowing from any love to Joseph, or fear of guilt, but from a desire to propitiate his father, whom he had so grievously offended, (35. 22.)

25. EAT BREAD,] the common phrase for taking food, bread being used for every kind of nourishment, as in Mat. 6. 11.

ISHMAELITES,] called in v. 28 'Midianites,' and in v. 36 'Midianites.' The Jewish Targumists, Onkelos and Jonathan, call them by the general name 'Arabians,' and the Jerusalem Targum 'Saracens.'

GILEAD,] where they had got the spices and 'balm,' for which it was famed, to carry down to Egypt, for embalming, &c.

SPICES...MYRRH,] both of these are only mentioned elsewhere in 43. 11.

26. GAIN.] Compare Ps. 30. 9; Job 22. 3.

28. TWENTY SILVERINGS,] only two-thirds of the price of a slave, Ex. 21. 32.

29. RENDETH HIS GARMENTS.] The most ancient mode of testifying grief, and the first mention of it in SS.; see again v. 34; 44. 13; Nu. 14. 6; Jos. 7. 6; Ju. 11. 35, &c.

30. LAD IS NOT,] not the 'child;' he was now 17 years of age.

31. KID OF THE GOATS,] whose blood, accordingly to Jonathan and Jarchi, is most like human blood.

32. THEY SEND...BRING] by the hand of their servants.

34. SACKCLOTH,] which though now men- tioned for the first time, is very frequently hereafter; see Job 16. 15; 2 Sa. 3. 31; 21. 10; 1 K. 20. 31, 32; 21. 27; 2 K. 6. 30; 19. 1, 2; 1 Ch. 21. 16; Neh. 9. 1; Est. 4. 1, 2, 3, 4, &c. The Hebrew word is SACK, which has been transferred into about 20 different languages, with the signification of 'bag, sack,' in which sense it is found in every other instance of its occurrence in the Pentateuch, viz. Ge. 42. 25, 27, 35; Le. 11. 32, and in Jo. 9. 8.

35. TO COMFORT HIMSELF,] as the re- flexive form of the verb denotes.

TO SHEOL,] i.e. the place of departed spirits; it occurs 65 times in the Old Testa- ment, and is translated in the Common Version 31 times by *grave,* 3 times by *pit,* and 32 times by *hell.* It occurs 7 times in the Pentateuch, viz. Ge. 37. 35; 42. 38; 44. 29, 31; Nu. 16. 30, 33; De. 32. 22. Compare the N. T. use of 'Hades,' the unseen world, to which good and bad alike go.

HIS FATHER BEWAILETH HIM,] apparently Jacob; but Jonathan, Jarchi, Aben Ezra, and Abendana understand it of Isaac, who lived twelve years after this occurrence.

36. MEDANITES,] according to the Hebrew text, (not Midianites,) supposed to have sprung from Medan, brother of Midian, and son of Keturah, Ge. 24. 2.

POTIPHAR,] i.e. according to Gesenius, one 'who belongs to the sun.'

EUNUCH,] as indicated by the literal meaning of the word, (compare Is. 56. 3, 4,) his having a wife is no objection to this, as it was doubtless from show and vanity, aiming to appear as other men. The only other places where the word occurs in the Pentateuch are 39. 1; 40. 2, 7.

EXECUTIONERS,] or still more literally, 'slaughterers;' Septuagint, 'cooks;' they were doubtless the king's body-guard, employed not only to defend him, but to put his orders into execution.

XXXVIII. 1. AT THAT TIME,] not very definitely stated, but probably about the time of the death of Rachel, a year or two before the selling of Joseph.

GOETH DOWN,] probably from Hebron to Adullam, a city 8 miles south-west of Jerusalem, where was a famous cave in David's time; compare Jo. 12. 15; 15. 35; 1 Sa. 22. 1; 2 Sa. 23. 13; 1 Ch. 11. 15; 2 Ch. 11. 7; Ne. 11. 30; Mic. 1. 15.

2. CANAANITE,] or 'merchant,' as Onkelos, Jonathan, Jarchi, and Ben Gerson interpret the word, as in Job 41. 6; Pr. 31. 24; Zec. 14. 21; Is. 23. 8; Ez. 17. 4; Ho. 12. 7, Zep. 1. 11.

SHUAH] is the name of the father, not of the daughter; see v. 12.

3. ER,] i.e. 'a watchman,' or 'enemy.'

4. ONAN,] i.e. 'strength, sorrow, iniquity.'

5. SHELAH,] i.e. 'safety, rest,' or 'error.'

CHEZIB,] probably the same as Achzib, (see Mic. 1. 13,) a city in the tribe of Judah.

6. TAKETH,] as was customary, see note on 21. 21.

TAMAR,] i.e. 'a palm tree.'

8. MARRY.] The original word here used is only applied to the marrying of a brother's wife; it appears to have been a custom at this time, and afterwards became an express statute law, (De. 25. 5,) if the deceased brother left no male children. It existed also among the Egyptians.

BROTHER,] to bear his name, and enjoy his inheritance.

10. EVIL,] showing want of fraternal affection, and a breach (probably) of divine law.

12. TIMNATH,] a city in the tribe of Judah, (Jo. 15. 10, 57,) then of the Danites, (Jo. 19. 43,) long subject to the Philistines, Ju. 14.) 1; 2 Ch. 28. 18,) six miles from Adullam.

14. GARMENTS OF HER WIDOWHOOD,] hence we learn that widows had special articles of dress to distinguish them then as now.

VAIL,] to disguise herself.

ENAYIM.] Septuagint reads Gates of Ænan.

WIFE,] as she expected, and as Judah had promised.

15. HARLOT,] by her dress, posture, manner, or place.

16. COME IN UNTO THEE,] a common euphemism; compare Ge. 6. 4; 16. 4.

WHAT DOST THOU GIVE TO ME.] Compare 30. 16. &c.

17. I SEND] from Timnath or Adullam.

21. SEPARATED ONE.] Such is the literal meaning of the word, and which is commonly rendered 'holy one;' prostitutes were so called, either by way of irony, or because in some cases, they were dedicated to vile heathen temples.

24. AND SHE IS BURNT.] She was legally the espoused wife of Shelah, and as adultery was punished with death even among heathens, (Je. 29. 22, 23,) Judah, who stood in the position of her father, had the power of ordering it to be put into execution; such was the absolute power possessed by parents in those days, no investigation or explanation was asked or sought for. The phrase is strikingly expressive of the decisiveness of the sentence.

25. BROUGHT OUT] to death, by the servants of her father-in-law.

26. MORE RIGHTEOUS.] Had he said 'less wicked,' he would have been nearer the truth.

27. TWINS,] as in the case of Rebekah.

28. BINDETH,] to distinguish the first born, who had peculiar privileges above the other children; see note on 25. 31.

29. PHAREZ,] i.e. 'breaker forth,' from whom came Jesus, Mat. 1. 3.

30. ZARAH,] i.e. 'a rising' (of the sun.)

XXXIX. 1. EGYPT,] by the Ishmaelites. as recorded in 37. 28; probably to Memphis or Heliopolis.

2. WITH JOSEPH,] as in v. 21, and as he had been with Ishmael, (21. 20,) with Isaac, (26. 3,) with Jacob, (28. 15,) and afterwards with Moses, (Ex. 3. 12,) &c.

PROSPEROUS.] See the use of the same word in 24. 21, 40, 42, 56; 39. 2, 3, 23; Nu 14. 41; De. 28. 29; Ps. 37. 7.

3. SEETH,] as Abimelech saw in the case of Isaac, (26. 28,) and Laban in that of Jacob, (30. 27.)

4. HIS HAND,] i.e. his power, according to the common Hebrew idiom; see Ge. 9. 2; 14. 20; 16. 6, 9; 24. 10; 30. 35; 35. 4, &c.

5. FOR JOSEPH'S SAKE.] There is no fact more distinctly stated, and more fully illustrated, in SS. than this, that God does good to some men for the sake of others: had there been ten righteous men in Sodom, the whole of that city would have been saved. 'Ye are the salt of the earth.'

6. FAIR FORM.....FAIR APPEARANCE.] Similar expressions are used in 24. 16 of Rebekah his grandmother, and in 29. 17 of Rachel his mother; it is here noticed for the purpose of explaining the following circumstances narrated.

7. HIS LORD'S WIFE,] of whom there are numerous Jewish and Mohammedan traditions still extant.

9. EVIL.] Adultery has always been treated as a great evil even in countries where whoredom was not so reckoned, and the

punishment proportionably severe; but the feeling of Joseph was of a different kind—sin against God.

13. LEFT HIS GARMENT...FLEETH,] like the young man mentioned in Mark 14. 51.

14. HE HATH BROUGHT,] meaning her husband; compare the expression in Pr. 7. 19.

TO PLAY,] compare Ge. 26. 18; Ex. 32. 6; her love is now changed into hatred, as was Amon's, (2 Sa. 13. 15).

20. TAKETH HIM,] without apparently examining him, or hearing him in his own defence, by which he lost the services of a faithful servant, did injustice to an innocent man, and suffered the guilty to escape.

ROUND-HOUSE.] This word occurs nowhere else, save in Song 7. 2, a 'round' goblet; the next clause describes its character.

21. STRETCHETH OUT.] Compare the use of the same word in Ge. 12. 8; 26. 25; 33. 19; 35. 21; 38. 1, 16; 49. 15; Ex. 6. 6; 7. 5, 19; 8. 5, 6, 16, 17; 9. 22, 23; 10. 12, 13, 21, 22; 14. 16, 21, 26, 27; 15. 12; 23. 2; 33. 7, &c. applied to the stretching out of an arm, hand, tent, rod, kindness, &c.

PUTTETH HIS GRACE,] i.e. exhibited his good qualities before the eyes of his master; see the promise in 1 Sa. 2. 30, 'He who is honouring me, I do honour.'

22. DOER,] i.e. the cause of everything being done; Scripture and common sense concur in attributing the credit or discredit of any work, not merely to the instrumentality by which it has been done, but to the directing or superintending power, as in Ge. 3. 20, &c.

23. IS CAUSING TO PROSPER.] See Ps. 1. 3.

XL. 1. BUTLER,] or 'cup-bearer,' who, with the 'baker,' had not improbably been accused of tampering,more or less seriously, with the royal provisions; in the next verse, they are specially mentioned as 'heads' or 'chiefs' of their several departments: very often the highest nobles were selected for these occupations, 1 Sa. 9. 11.

3. GIVETH THEM IN CHARGE,] that the matter may be investigated; very different from the hasty conduct of Judah, (38. 24,) but the one was a leader in a wandering clan, the other a ruler in a highly civilized land.

4. DAYS.] See note on Ge. 1. 5; 4. 3, &c.

5. ACCORDING TO THE INTERPRETATION] which Joseph afterwards gave.

6. MOROSE.] See the use of the same word in Da. 1. 10; Pr. 19. 3, 12; 1 K. 20. 43; 21. 4; Is. 30. 30; Jo. 1. 15, Mi. 7. 9, 2 Ch. 16. 10; 26. 19; 28. 9, which are all the instances in which it occurs.

8. NO INTERPRETER] in the prison; there were many out of it who were thought to be able, see 41 8.

WITH GOD, as in 41. 15, 16; Ps. 25. 14; Is. 8. 20; Da. 2 11, 28, 47; 4. 8; 5. 11.

9. RECOUNTETH,] being glad to disburden his mind of its load.

A VINE IS BEFORE ME.] 'The dream cometh by the abundance of business,' according to E. 5. 3, but they were often overruled by the hand of the Most High to

fulfil his own ends, and naturally enough, both of the dreamers here are occupied with their respective callings. Egyptian paintings are full of illustration regarding the vines of Egypt, and their writers claim for (their) Osiris the honour of being the first vine cultivator: vines are also common in modern Egypt.

11. TAKE THE GRAPES,] i.e. from off the vine-tree, and 'press' their juice into the cup. The rapidity of the narrative renders it somewhat obscure; it is hardly creditable that it was ever customary to drink such new wine, if wine it could be called at all. Gill suggests 'it is more probable, that the grapes were poured into another vessel, and so made wine of, and then poured into Pharaoh's cup, or mixed in it, though this circumstance is omitted.' It is not at all likely that this took place in Pharaoh's presence.

PHARAOH'S HAND,] as formerly he had been in the habit of doing.

12. SAITH] without hesitation or ambiguity, being divinely inspired, (v. 8.)

13. LIFT UP THY HEAD.] Compare the use of the same phrase in Ex. 30. 12; Nu. 1. 2, 49; 4. 2, 22; 25. 4; 26. 2; 31. 26, 49, meaning to number, inspect, reckon with, not necessarily favourably, for the same expression is used in v. 20 regarding the baker.

STATION.] Compare Ge. 41. 43; Da. 11. 7, 20, 21, 38; in Ex. 30. 18, 28; 31. 9; 35. 16; 38. 8; 39. 39; 40. 11; Le. 8. 11; 1 K. 7. 29, 31 it denotes a 'base or pedestal.'

14. WELL WITH THEE,] As Moses wished to do with his father-in-law, (Nu. 10. 29,) and David with the family of Jonathan, (2 Sa. 9. 1,) and with the king of Ammon, (2 Sa. 10. 2.)

15. STOLEN.] lit. 'Stolen I have been stolen,' i.e. without his father's consent, or his own; he does not, however, indicate by whom, unwilling probably to cast reproach upon his family; their character was dear to him, not merely as brethren of the same blood, but as fellow-members of the same 'assembly of God.'

LAND OF THE HEBREWS.] This language is justified by the numerous promises made to Abraham, to Isaac, and to Jacob, that the land was given to them and to their seed.

DONE NOTHING] worthy of bonds or imprisonment, like Paul (Acts 23. 29,) and David (1 Sa. 24. 11,) and Daniel (6. 22;) here again it is to be noticed he does not accuse others, as Adam did, (Ge. 3. 12,) while defending himself.

PIT,] i.e. prison; see the same word in Ge. 37. 20, 22, 24, 28, 29; 40. 15; 41. 14; Ex. 12. 29; 21. 33, 34; Le. 11. 36; De. 6. 11, &c. also in Ps. 7. 15; 28. 1; 30. 3; 40. 2; 88. 4, 6; 143. 7, &c.

16. BASKETS OF WHITE BREAD.] So Saadiah Gaon and Jonathan; three baskets, one above the other.

19. FROM OFF THEE,] by decapitation, which was a very common mode of punishment in the East. either when the criminal is alive, or after he has been put to death

in some other way, as here, by hanging on a tree.

HANGED.] This mode of punishment was thought very disgraceful compared to decapitation, it is referred to again in v. 22; 41. 13; De. 21. 22, 23; Jo. 8. 29; 10. 26; 2 Sa. 4. 12; 18. 10; 21. 12; La. 5. 12; Es. 2. 23; 5. 14; 6. 4; 7. 9, 10; 8. 7. 9. 13, 14. 15. The only remaining passages where the word occurs are Job 26. 7; Song. 4. 41, Is. 22. 24, Ez. 15. 3; 27. 10. 11; Ps. 137. 2.

BIRDS HAVE EATEN THY FLESH,] as in v. 17; 1 Sa. 17. 44, 46; 2 Sa. 21. 10; Ez. 39. 4; Ge. 15. 11.

23. HATH NOT REMEMBERED,] selfishness and indolence prevailing as in the case of Job (10. 14,) Jerubbaal (Ju. 8. 24,) Jehoiada (2 Ch. 24. 22,) the poor wise man, (Ec. 9. 15,) &c.

XLI. 1. TWO YEARS OF DAYS,] i.e. two complete years from the release of the butler; hope deferred was doubtless making Joseph's heart sick.

2. THE RIVER,] i.e. the Nile, by some of its canals or branches. This river has its origin in Upper Ethiopia: it is about 2500 miles in length; it has seven cataracts or rapids: its seven streams referred to in Is. 11. 15. are now reduced to two, viz. Damietta and Rosetta; in June, July, and August the river rises to an overflow from the rain in Ethiopia; its water is esteemed as a sweet drink by the natives, but the sight of it was sufficient in the writer's case to drive away his thirst.

THE REEDS,] in Hebrew, ACHU, the meaning of which was unknown to the Septuagint translators, (B.C. 270,) as they have retained the Hebrew term untranslated; it only occurs elsewhere in Job 8. 11: it is evidently an herb, not a place, as the Common Version has rendered it.

4. AWAKETH,] through surprise and agitation.

5. A SECOND TIME.] See v. 32; also Job 33. 14.

6. EAST WIND.] So v. 23, 27; the most violent in western Asia and the adjoining seas, Ex. 10. 13; 14. 21; Job 15. 2; 27. 21; 38. 24; Ps. 48. 7; 78. 26; Is. 27. 8; Je. 18. 17; Ho. 12. 1; 13. 15; Jon. 4. 8; Hab. 1. 9. All the other places where it is mentioned are in Ezekiel.

8. MOVED.] See the same word in Ju. 13. 25; Ps. 77. 4; Da. 2. 1, 2; it is found nowhere else in SS.

SCRIBES.] See v. 24; Ex. 7. 11, 22; 8. 7, 18, 19; 9. 11; Da. 1. 20; 2. 2, 10, 27; 4. 7, 9; 5. 11. They were one of the numerous classes into which the Egyptian priesthood was divided, probably that one which devoted itself not so much to religious observances as to the pursuit of the occult sciences, the 'sacred scribes' spoken of by Tacitus Hist. iv. c. 72. 73.

NO INTERPRETER,] as in 40. 8.

9. I MENTION,] not 'remember' as the C. V. has rendered it.

10. PHARAOH] being an official title, was not offensive, which would have been the case had it been simply a personal name;

this ruler is supposed to have been the same as Aphophis, one of the Memphite kings, whose capital was On or Heliopolis.

13. HE PUT BACK...HIM HE HANGED.] What Joseph only foretold he is here said to do, according to the language of SS. and of common life; this illustrates the real meaning of Ex. 7. 3, compared with Ex. 3. 19, &c.

14. CAUSE HIM TO RUN,] the king's command being hasty.

SHAVETH.] This is incidentally a striking proof of the author's accuracy, as the Egyptians were perhaps the only nation in ancient times who preferred a smooth chin to a long flowing beard.

16. WITHOUT ME.] Same phrase occurs in v. 44; 2 K. 18. 25; Is. 36. 10; Je. 44. 19; compare also Ge. 14. 24; Nu. 5. 29; Jo. 22. 19; 2 Sa. 22. 32; Job 34. 32; Ps. 18. 31; Is. 43. 11; 44. 6, 8; 45. 6, 21. He disclaims all merit or power of his own, but assures Pharaoh that God doth answer him with peace; it is not a prayer properly, but a pledge or promise. Compare the language of Daniel to Nebuchadnezzar.

18. OUT OF THE RIVER COMING UP,] as in v. 2. above; cattle are proverbially fond of water, and these had been sporting and enjoying themselves in the river. By a strange inconsideration one commentator thinks they were the hippopotamuses, or river-horses.

21. COME IN UNTO THEIR MIDST,] i.e. they have been entirely swallowed up, yet the lean ones are apparently no fatter than before; kine to devour kine was the most startling thing of the whole.

22. SEVEN EARS.] Compare v. 47; Jowett says, from personal knowledge, that, in modern Egypt, three, seven, fourteen, and eighteen ears are often found on one stalk.

24. THERE IS NONE,] confessing, like Nebuchadnezzar and Belshazzar, that vain is the wisdom of men.

25. ONE,] i.e. both dreams represent the same thing in different aspects.

32. REPEATING...TWICE.] See note on v. 5 above.

IS HASTENING,] as the original word always denotes; see Ge. 18. 6, 7; 19. 22; 24. 18, 20, 46; 43. 20; 44. 11, 45. 9, 13; Ex. 2. 18; 10. 16; 12. 33; 34. 8; Jo. 4. 10; Pr 6. 18; Mal. 3. 5, &c.

35. HEAP UP,] as in v. 49; Ex. 8. 14; Job 27. 16; Ps. 39. 6; Hab. 1. 10; Zec. 9. 3; (2 K. 10. 8.)

36. CUT OFF,] as in Ge. 9. 11; 17. 14; Ex. 4. 25; 8. 9; 12. 15, 19; 30. 33, 38; 31. 14; Le.-7. 20, 21, 25, 27, &c.

38. THE SPIRIT OF GOD,] i.e. a Divine Spirit.

39. CAUSING THEE TO KNOW,] as in De. 8. 3.

AT THY MOUTH....KISS.] Compare 1 K. 19. 18; Job 31. 27; Ho. 13. 2; Ps. 2. 12; a phrase denoting affection and submission.

41. I HAVE PUT THEE.] This sudden elevation of a stranger and a prisoner to almost regal power, is too common in Eastern history to excite surprise; and of all ancient countries, Egypt is most remarkable for its frequency.

42. SEAL-RING.] See Nu. 31. 50 ; Est. 3. 10, 12 ; 8. 2, 8, 10 ; Is. 30. 21 ; in the book of Exodus this word occurs 38 times, and appears to be used exclusively in the general signification of a 'ring.' The seal-ring was committed only to the second in the kingdom—as Joseph, Haman, Mordecai, and it conferred great power on its possessor.

GARMENTS OF FINE LINEN,] i.e. byssus, so called from its whiteness ; compare Ex. 39. 2, 3, 5, 8, 27, 28, 29 ; Pr. 31. 22 ; Ez. 16. 10, 13 ; 27. 7 ; 'royal garments' were among the things coveted by Haman, Est. 6. 8, 9 ; and garments are mentioned as customary gifts in 88., e.g. to Joseph, Benjamin, his brethren, his father, Samson, Daniel, Rebekah, Naaman, Joshua the high priest, &c.

CHAIN OF GOLD.] The word here rendered 'chain' is only found elsewhere in Ez. 16. 11 ; compare this investiture with Da. 5. 7, 29.

43. BOW THE KNEE,] or 'tender father,' or 'native prince,' or 'father of the king ;' the common rendering is preferable.

44. PHARAOH,] i.e. 'king,' or 'sun.'

LIFT UP HAND OR FOOT,] i.e. do any thing of importance.

45. ZAPHNATH-PAANEAH,] i.e. 'revealer of secrets,' or 'saviour of the world.'

ASENATH,] i.e. 'she who is of Neth,' according to Gesenius.

POTI-PHERAH,] i.e. 'one who belongs to the sun,' or 'to the king.'

PRIEST OF ON,] or 'prince, minister,' of Heliopolis, Aven or Beth-Shemesh, 'house of the sun,' in Egypt, 22 miles from Memphis, west from north point of the Red Sea, eastward from the Nile ; Nebuchadnezzar captured it, see Ez. 30. 17 ; Je. 43. 13.

JOSEPH GOETH OUT,] impatient to carry out his plans for the safety and happiness of his adopted people.

46. THIRTY YEARS,] having been 13 years in Egypt already, seeing he was 17 years when sold thither, (37. 2.)

47. BY HANDFULS,] alluding to the practice of Eastern reapers of seizing the head of corn alone, and cutting it off.

48. HE GATHERETH ALL THE FOOD] which was superfluous and over-abundant, which he doubtless bought from the inhabitants, and afterwards resold to them.

51. MANASSEH,] i.e. 'forgetfulness.'

52. EPHRAIM,] i.e. 'fruitfulness.'

54. ALL THE LANDS,] i.e. the countries surrounding Egypt.

BREAD,] i.e. food.

XLII. 1. SEETH,] i.e. perceiveth from the reports of others.

CORN.] This word occurs in v. 2, 19, 26 ; 43. 2 ; 44. 2 ; 47. 14 ; Ne. 10. 31 ; Am. 8. 5 ; it properly means 'a breaking, the thing broken, ground corn.'

AT EACH OTHER,] not knowing next what to say or do.

2. GO DOWN.] This is the uniform Scripture way of speaking regarding the locality of Egypt, e.g. Ge. 12. 10 ; 26. 2 ; 42. 3 ; 43. 20 ; 44. 26 ; 45. 9 ; 46. 3, &c., on the other hand, a traveller from Egypt to Canaan is said 'to go up,' e.g. Ex. 12. 38 ; 13. 18 ; 1 K. 9. 16, 24 ; 14. 25, &c.

5. THOSE COMING] into Egypt from the land of Canaan, &c.

CANAAN,] as it had previously been in the days of Abraham (12. 10,) and of Isaac (26. 1.)

6. RULER,] as noted in 41. 40-44.

SELLING,] as in 41. 56.

BOW THEMSELVES,] and thus unwittingly fulfilling the dreams of Joseph, in 37. 7, 9.

FACE TO THE EARTH,] i.e. in the most humble and respectful manner.

7. DISCERNETH THEM,] from their number, their dress, their language, and probably from their features, though a considerable number of years had elapsed since he had last seen them.

MAKETH HIMSELF STRANGE,] like the wife of Jeroboam, 1 K. 14. 5, where the same Hebrew word occurs ; in the only other place where it is found, (Pr. 20. 11,) it is commonly rendered the reverse of the present, viz. 'Also by his actions a youth maketh himself known,' but it is possible the word there also may really mean 'strange, or unknown.'

SHARP THINGS.] This was done partly to keep up appearances, and partly to awaken their consciences, in both of which it succeeded. See the use of the same word in v. 30 ; Ex. 18. 26 ; 32. 9 ; 1 Sa. 20. 10 ; 25, 3 ; 2 Sa. 3. 39 ; 1 K. 12. 4, 13 ; 14. 6 ; 2 Ch. 10. 13 ; Ps. 60. 3, &c.

8. NOT DISCERNED HIM,] he being but a youth when they sold him, but now a full-grown man ; his dress and position were also so different from formerly, that it is not wonderful they did not recognize him.

9. SPIES.] 'footmen,' pedestrians ; but the word is always used in a bad sense, compare v. 11, 14, 16, 30, 31, 34 ; Jo. 2. 1 ; 6. 22, 23 ; 1 Sa. 26. 4 ; 2 Sa. 15. 14. The original verbal form occurs in Ps. 15. 3 ; 2 Sa. 19. 27, and rendered 'slander or backbite ;' also in Nu. 21. 32 ; De. 1. 24 ; Jo. 6. 25 ; 7. 2 ; 14. 7 ; Ju. 18. 2, 14, 17 ; 2 Sa. 10. 3 ; 1 Ch. 19. 3.

11. ALL OF US SONS OF ONE MAN.] It was not likely that one man would send all his sons on such a dangerous expedition, or that ten members of one family would accept such a risk.

RIGHT MEN,] i.e. upright, erect, honest, as in v. 19. 31, 33, 34. Compare note on Ge. 1. 7.

12. NAKEDNESS,] or exposed state ; see the same word in Ge. 9. 22, 23 ; 42, 9, 12 ; Ex. 20. 26 ; 28. 42 ; Le. 18. 6—19 ; 20. 11—21 ; De. 23. 14 ; 24. 1 ; 1 Sa. 20. 30 ; Is. 20. 4 ; 47. 3 ; La. 1. 8 ; Ez. 16. 8, 36, 37 ; 22. 10 ; 23. 10, 18, 29 ; Ho. 2. 9 ; Ez. 4. 14.

13. ONE IS NOT.] See note on Ge. 5. 24 ; this was not consistent with their own belief, but in accordance with what they had led their father to believe.

15. PROVED.] This word is applied to the testing of metals, &c., see v. 16, Job 7. 18 ; 12. 11 ; 23. 10 ; 34. 3, 36 · Ps. 7. 9 ; 11. 4, 5 ; 17. 3 ; 26. 2 ; 66. 10 ; 81. 7 ; 95. 9 ; 139. 23 ; Pr. 17. 3 ; Je. 6. 27 ; 9. 7 ; 11. 20 ; 12. 3 ; 17. 10 ; 20. 12 ; Ez. 21. 13 ; Zec. 13. 19 ; Ma. 3. 10, 15 ; 1 Ch. 29. 17. Compare Is. 28. 16 · 32. 14.

PHARAOH LIVETH,] a phrase of the same import as 'Jehovah liveth,' in Ju. 8. 19; 'thy soul liveth,' in 1 Sa. 1. 26; 'God liveth,' 2 Sa. 2. 27; 'Jehovah thy God liveth,' 1 K. 17. 12; a solemn asseveration.

17. THREE DAYS.] What their feelings were during this time is not said ; like the apostles during the interval between Christ's burial and rising again? or Jonah's in the fish's belly? it is to be feared more like the former than the latter, as they showed no signs of reformation.

18. GOD I FEAR.] By using the general title 'God,' instead of the more definite one 'Jehovah,' he keeps up his appearance as a stranger to them. 'Fear' in SS. often means 'reverence,' as here ; the same thing is said of Abraham, (22. 12,) of Obadiah, (1 K. 18. 3,) of Job, (1. 1, 8,) of Jonah, (1. 9,) &c. Compare also Ge. 32. 11; Ex. 1. 21; 3. 6; 9. 20; 18. 21; De. 25. 18; Le. 19. 14. 32; 25. 17, 36, 43; Nu. 12. 8. &c.

19. FOR THE FAMINE OF YOUR HOUSES,] i.e. a very little, which accounts for its rapid consumption, (see 43. 2.)

21. DISTRESS OF HIS SOUL,] alluded to in Ps. 105. 18. The word rendered 'distress' occurs in Ge. 35. 3; De. 31. 17, 21; Ju. 10. 14; 1 Sa. 10. 19; 26. 24; 2 Sa. 4. 9; 1 K. 1. 29; 2 K. 19. 3; 2 Ch. 15. 6; 20. 9; Ne. 9. 27, 37; Job 5. 19; 27. 9; Ps. 9. 9, &c., and again in the last clause of this verse.

MAKING SUPPLICATION,] as in De. 3. 23; Job 8. 5; 9. 15; 19. 16; Ps. 30. 8; 142. 1; Ho. 12. 4; 1 K. 8. 33, 47, 59; 9. 3; 2 Ch. 6. 24. 37; 2 K. 1. 18; Es. 4. 8; 8. 3: the idea is not of asking justice, but grace, unmerited kindness.

22. HEARKENED NOT.] From 37. 21—24, it appears they did agree to Reuben's proposal to spare Joseph's life, but probably he now refers to some effort of his (not recorded) to prevent them selling Joseph, which they did not comply with, and which they carried out during Reuben's absence.

IT IS REQUIRED,] as stated in Ge. 9. 5, 6.

23. INTERPRETER,] as in Job 16. 20 ; 33. 23; Is. 43. 27; 2 Ch. 32. 31, being all the passages in which the word occurs: it comes from a root signifying 'to make sweet,' (Ps. 119. 103; compare also Pr. 1. 6; Hab. 2. 6;) the duty of such an one being not merely to convey the sentiments of persons speaking different dialects to one another, but to conciliate both parties.

24. SIMEON.] Perhaps Joseph detained Simeon because he was one of the cruelest (34. 25; 49. 5,) of his brethren, or the most obstinate and inpenitent.

BINDETH HIM BEFORE THEIR EYES,] that they might be the more readily induced to bring down Benjamin to effect the liberation of Simeon.

25. THEY FILL,] i.e. Joseph's servants.

DOTH TO THEM SO,] i.e. Joseph's steward does as his master commanded

26. ASSES,] which, with camels, were the principal beasts of burden in Palestine at that time ; the ass there was a very different animal in appearance, spirit, and character, from those in Europe; compare 22. 3; 30.

43; 32. 5; 45. 23; 49. 14; Ex. 4. 20; Jo. 15. 18; 1 Sa. 8. 16; 25. 20; 2 Sa. 16. 2; 17. 23; 19. 26; 1 K. 2. 40; 13. 13; 2 Ch. 28. 15; compare also Ge. 32. 15; 49. 11; Ju. 10. 4; 12. 14; Job 11. 12; Is. 30. 6, 24; Zec. 9. 9.

27. LODGING-PLACE,] which in the East is very little different from a mere shed, affording a slight shelter from rain or heat; travellers carry their own servants and provisions with them, as the place affords nothing but a temporary covering.

28. HEART GOETH OUT,] with alarm and astonishment; compare similar phrases in Song 5. 6; 2 K. 5. 26; Ge. 45. 26; 35. 18, &c.

29. MEETING THEM,] as in 44. 29; Ex. 3. 18; Nu. 11. 23; 23. 3, 4, 15, 16; De. 25. 18; Ruth 2. 3; 1 Sa. 28. 10, &c.

30. THE MAN.] This is not spoken disrespectfully, as might appear at first sight, as it is immediately added, 'the lord of the land.'

MAKETH,] lit. 'giveth' or 'committeth' us to ward, as spies.

35. BUNDLE.] Compare the use of this word in 1 Sa. 25. 29; 2 Sa. 17. 13; Job 14. 17 ; Pr. 7. 20; 26. 8; Song 1. 13; Amos 9. 9; Hag. 1. 6.

36. BEREAVED,] same word as in Ge. 27. 45; 31. 38; 42. 36; 43. 14; Ex. 23. 26; Le. 26. 22; De. 32. 25; Job 21. 10; 1 Sa. 15. 33; 2 K. 2. 19, 21; Is. 49. 21; Je. 15. 7; 50. 9; La. 1. 20; Ez. 5. 17; 14. 15; 36. 12—14; Ho. 9. 12, 14; Ma. 3. 11.

AGAINST ME.] Here spake the language of unbelief; he knew not and felt not that all these were for him, in reality : Joseph's absence was to preserve him a seed, Simeon's to bring him back his son.

37. Reuben's proposal shows his earnestness more than his discretion ; as the eldest son he felt himself in a dilemma, and yet compelled to speak, which he does rashly and unadvisedly with his lips.

38. Jacob's answer is simply a repetition of the old objections, and his want of faith in the superintending providence of God is suffered to keep him a little longer from happiness and his long-lost son.

MISCHIEF,] as in v. 4.

GREY HAIRS,] or old age; compare Ge. 15. 15; 25. 8; 42. 38; 44. 29, 31; Le. 9. 32; De. 32. 25; Ju. 8. 32; Ruth 4. 15; 1 K. 2. 6; 1 Ch. 29. 28; Job 41. 32; Ps. 71. 18; 92. 14; Pr. 16. 31; 20. 29; Is. 46. 4; Ho. 7. 9; 1 K. 14. 4; 1 Sa. 12. 2; Job 15. 10; Ezra 5. 5, 9; 6. 7, 8, 14.

IN SORROW,] as in 44. 31; Es. 9. 22; Ps. 13. 2; 31. 10; 107. 39; 116. 3; Is. 35. 10; 51. 11; Je. 8. 18; 20. 18; 31. 13; 45. 3; Ez. 23. 33.

SHEOL.] See note on 37. 35.

XLIII. 1. SEVERE,] lit. 'heavy, weighty,' as in 12. 10; 41. 31; 43. 1; 47. 4, 13; 50. 9, 10, 11; Ex. 4. 10; 7. 14, &c.

2. FINISHED EATING] the corn, which, not being like the widow's cruise of oil, was soon ended, and Jacob compelled, however reluctantly, to say,

BUY US A LITTLE FOOD,] fearing they might not find sufficient in Egypt on their return, and hoping that the famine might speedily pass away from Canaan.

3. THE MAN,] i.e. Joseph, the lord of the land.

6. WHY HAVE YE DONE EVIL TO ME?] This question only shows that Jacob could not answer the reasoning of Judah, and recalling what could not be helped.

7. ASKED DILIGENTLY,] lit. 'asking asked;' Joseph knowing the true state of things, put his questions so pointedly that they could not decline or evade speaking truth.

8. JUDAH SAITH.] Though only the fourth in order of the sons of Jacob, it is evident that Judah was already the real leader of the band; it was he who carried the proposal to sell Joseph; to burn Tamar; and now, when Reuben has failed, to overcome the feelings of Jacob. 'Judah! thy brethren praise thee!'

9. I AM SURETY FOR HIM,] as in 44. 32; (38. 17, 18, 20;) Job 17. 3; Ps. 104. 34; 119. 122; Pr. 3. 24; 6. 1; 11. 15; 13. 19; 14. 10; 17. 18, 20; 16. 19; 22. 26; 24. 21; 27. 13, &c.

THOU DOST REQUIRE HIM,] agreeably to Ge. 9. 5, 6.

I HAVE SINNED.] The word properly means 'to err, miss the mark,' as in Ju. 20. 16; Job 5. 24; Pr. 19. 2.

ALL THE DAYS,] of my life.

10. LINGERED,] as in 19. 16; 43. 10; Ex. 12. 39; Ju. 3. 26; 19. 8; Ps. 119. 60; 2 Sa. 15. 28; Is. 29. 9; Hab. 2. 3.

11. PRAISED THING.] See the use of the original word in Ps. 81. 2; 98. 5; Is. 51. 3; Am. 5. 23; and Ex. 15. 2.

A PRESENT,] as in Ge. 4. 3, 4, 5; 32. 13, 18. 20, 21, &c.; it is the custom in the East almost invariably to give a present to the master of the house, however small, (compare 1 Sa. 9. 7,) to show respect and good-will; in other cases, to pacify anger; see Pr. 21. 14.

BALM,] or rosin, mentioned again in Ge. 37. 25; 43. 11; Je. 8. 22; 46. 11; 51. 8; Ez. 27. 17.

HONEY,] either of bees or grapes; see Ex. 3. 8, 17; 13. 5; 16. 31; 33. 3; Le. 2. 11; 20. 24; Nu. 13. 27; 14. 8; 16. 13, 14; De. 6. 3; 8. 8; 11. 9; 26. 9, 15; 27. 3; 31. 20; 32. 13; Jo. 5. 6; some translate it 'dates.'

SPICES....MYRRH,] only mentioned elsewhere in Ge. 37. 25; rendered by some 'storax, wax...stacte, lotus, chesnuts.'

NUTS,] the original word is found nowhere else in SS.; pistachio nuts, said to grow on the terebinth tree.

ALMONDS,] mentioned also again in Nu. 17. 18; Ec. 12. 5; Je. 1. 11; Ex. 25. 33; 37. 19, 20.

12. DOUBLE,] lit. 'second' money for additional food, the 'first' referred to that which was brought back.

OVERSIGHT.] The original word is found nowhere else, but in its verbal form occurs in Le. 4. 13; Nu. 15. 22, &c.

14. ALMIGHTY,] rather, 'He who is sufficient;' committing them into His hands who had ever been with him, and who had promised to be so.

OTHER BROTHER,] i.e. Simeon.

BEREAVED.] See note on 42. 36; he seems to have lost all hope, and nigh to despair;

if anything could have touched his sons' hearts, this language might, and probably did, at least in the case of Judah, 44. 18—34.

15. STAND BEFORE JOSEPH,] according to his command.

16. SEETH BENJAMIN,] whom he had not seen for 22 years, and probably recognized from his likeness to Rachel, or his comparative youth, or from observing a new face.

INTO THE HOUSE,] i.e. Joseph's, as seen in next verse.

SLAUGHTER AN ANIMAL,] lit. 'a slaughter;' the Hebrews often use a noun and verb of the same root, as is done in English, 'to fight a fight.' Again in Pr. 9. 2, Ez. 21. 10.

18. AFRAID.] Business in the East is all transacted in the public bazaars or thoroughfares, and visitors or customers are rarely admitted into the houses, but only into the open space in the centre of the building; the affair was so unusual, that the brethren at once suspected treachery and danger.

TO ROLL HIMSELF UPON US.] Compare a similar phrase in 2 Sa. 20. 12; Je. 51. 25; Job 30. 14.

TO THROW HIMSELF ON US.] Compare the same phrase in De. 9. 18, 25; Ezra 10. 1.

20. WE REALLY CAME DOWN,] lit. 'coming down we came down.'

23. GOD OF YOUR FATHER,] which expression would seem to imply that he had received from Joseph some information regarding their true character and position.

HIDDEN TREASURE,] as in Job 3. 21; Pr. 2. 4; Is. 45. 3; Jo. 41. 8.

YOUR MONEY CAME UNTO ME.] Probably Joseph had repaid it into Pharaoh's treasury.

BRINGETH OUT SIMEON,] to quiet their fears still farther.

24. FEET,] which were weary and soiled with their journey.

ASSES.] A merciful man regards the life of his beast, and in the East the safety of the cattle is often more cared for than that of man. In India, at the present day, where numberless hospitals are erected by natives for the irrational creation, there is scarcely one erected for human beings, which has not been originated by Europeans or Christians.

25. PREPARE THE PRESENT,] i.e. arrange it in the most captivating form, as did Jacob, (32. 13—21.)

26. BOW THEMSELVES,] again unsuspectingly fulfilling his dreams, (37. 5—10.)

27. IS YOUR FATHER WELL?] His first questions very naturally were about his father who had loved him too fondly, and whose injudicious exhibition of it had been permitted to cause them all much sin and sorrow.

29. GOD FAVOUR THEE.] Same word as in Ge. 33. 5, 11; 43. 29; Ex. 33. 19; Nu. 6. 25; De. 7. 2; 28. 50; Job 19. 17, 21; 33. 34; Ju. 21. 22, &c.

MY SON.] A tender expression of regard; Joseph was only about 7 years older than he.

30. MOVED FOR,] or, 'unto his brother;' compare the use of the same word in 1 K. 3. 26· Ho. 11. 8; La. 5. 10.

INNER CHAMBER,] as in Ex. 8. 3; De. 32. 25; Ju. 3. 24; 15. 1; 16. 9, 12; 2 Sa. 4. 7; 13. 10, &c.

31. REFRAINETH HIMSELF,] as again in 45. 1; 1 Sa. 13. 12; Is. 42. 14; 63. 15; 64. 12, being all the passages where the original word occurs.

PLACE BREAD,] as in 2 Sa. 12. 20; 2 K. 6. 22; 'bread' in SS. often means 'food' in general.

32. NOT ABLE TO EAT.] Eating with anyone is always regarded in SS. as a token of intimate friendship; hence persons of different religions avoid all such manifestation of affection; e.g. a Jew will not eat with a Mohammedan, a Hindu, or a Bhuddist, and these have the same insuperable unwillingness to eat with him; the great majority of these would sooner die with hunger or thirst than touch either the bread or the water of a Christian: their consistency, however, does not go the length of refusing his money !

33. SIT BEFORE HIM] at the dinner; an arrangement evidently designed to surprise them, and it had the desired effect, for it is added,

THE MEN WONDER ONE AT ANOTHER,] *lit.* a man at his friend; the Hebrew word rendered 'wonder' does not occur in a verbal form elsewhere in the Pentateuch, (but is found in Job 26. 11; Ps. 48. 5; Ec. 5. 8; Is. 13. 8; 29. 9; Je. 4 9; Hab. 1. 5;) as a noun it is found in De. 28. 28; Zec. 12. 4; and in Da. 4. 2, 3; 6. 27.

34. GIFTS,] *lit.* 'a lift' of fruit, &c.; a special mark of respect; see the use of the word in 2 Sa. 11. 8; 2 Ch. 24. 6. 9; Est. 2. 18; Ps. 141. 2; Je. 40. 5; La. 2. 14; Ez. 20. 40; Am. 5. 11; Zep. 3. 18; and Ju. 20. 38, 40; Je. 6. 1.

FIVE HANDS,] i.e. times, parts, handfuls; as in 47. 24; Ne. 11. 1; Da. 1. 20; 2 Sa. 19. 43.

DRINK ABUNDANTLY.] This Hebrew word SHAKAR, only occurs in one other place in the Pentateuch as a verb, viz. Ge. 9. 21, where it is applied to Noah; it is doubtless the origin of the word 'sugar,' found transplanted into so many different languages, and denoting 'a sweet *or* satiating thing;' hence the verb signifies 'to be full *or* satiated' with any thing. In this passage, as well as in Song 5. 1, there seems to be no ground for supposing drunkenness to be implied, and it is worth considering whether even in Ge. 9. 21, any thing more is meant than in the verse before us—'satiety.'

XLIV. 2. BOWL,] a large cup *or* goblet, as in Je. 35. 5 : the same term is employed to denote a 'calix' of flowers, in the ornaments of the holy candlestick, Ex. 25. 31; 33. 34; 37, 17, 19, 20.

5. HE OBSERVETH DILIGENTLY WITH IT.] Same word as in Ge. 30. 27, on which see note.

7. FAR BE IT,] *lit.* profane ! as in Ge. 18 25; 44. 7, 17; Jo. 22. 29; 24. 16; 1 Sa. 2. 30; 12. 23; 14. 45; 20. 2, 9; 22. 15; 24. 6; 26. 11; 2 Sa. 20. 20; 23. 17; 1 K. 21. 3; 1 Ch. 11. 19; Job 27. 5; 34. 10. These are all the instances of its occurrence, and in

eleven of them it is in the Common Version irreverently rendered 'God forbid.'

8. HOW DO WE STEAL ?] Having already given such manifest proofs of their honesty, it was very painful to have such a charge laid against them; their positions of heads of an influential clan, their characters as members of a chosen race, induce them to denounce the offending party among them with death, and themselves with servitude, in which rash judgment they were like their father Jacob when charged with a somewhat similar offence; see Ge. 31. 32.

10. HE...BECOMETH MY SERVANT.] The messenger having been previously instructed, takes advantage of their concessions, and propounds the wished-for result.

ACQUITTED,] *lit.* 'innocent;' see the use of the word in Ge. 24. 41; 44. 10; Ex. 21. 28; 23. 7; Nu. 32. 22; De. 19. 10, 13; 21. 8, 9; 24. 5; 27. 25; Jo. 2. 17, 19, 20.

13. REND THEIR GARMENTS.] See note on Ge. 37. 39.

15. DILIGENTLY OBSERVE.] See note on Ge. 30. 27.

16. WHAT..WHAT..WHAT.] These abrupt interrogations show how great was the perplexity into which they had fallen.

GOD HATH FOUND OUT,] as in the case of Achan, (Jo. 7. 16—18,) of David, (2 Sa. 12. 10, 11,) of Jonah, (1. 7,) of Israel, (Nu. 32. 23,) of Adoni-Bezek, (Ju. 1. 7,) &c.

17. FAR BE IT] that the innocent should suffer for the guilty, see 18. 25; Ez. 18. 4, 20.

18. JUDAH COMETH NIGH.] Having pledged himself to his father to bring back Benjamin, he now felt it his duty to run all personal risk rather than falsify his word, and the simple yet graphic and eloquent address he now made is quite unparalleled in sacred or profane history : how far the adherence of the tribe of Benjamin in after days to that of Judah was affected by the generous sentiments of Judah, as here expressed, merits inquiry.

FOR THOU ART AS PHARAOH.] See 41. 40, 44.

30. HIS SOUL IS BOUND UP IN HIS SOUL.] Compare the love of Jonathan and David, 1 Sa. 18. 1.

34. DOTH FIND.] Compare Ex, 18. 8; 22. 6; Nu. 20. 14; 31. 50; De. 4. 30; 19. 5; 21. 17; 31. 17, 21.

XLV. 1. REFRAIN HIMSELF,] at the touching description of the fate of his aged father, and the evidence he had of their love to their father and to their younger brother, which he reckoned as to himself, being sons of the same mother—Rachel.

PUT OUT EVERY MAN,] not willing to expose their previous behaviour and bitter self-reproaches, which he felt convinced they would experience on knowing him.

2. THE EGYPTIANS HEAR,] those probably in the next room, or at the entrance, who quickly report it to the house of Pharaoh.

3. TROUBLED.] See the use of the same word in Ex. 15. 15; Job 4. 5; 21. 6; 22. 10; 23. 15, 16.

4. COME NIGH,] they appeared to have drawn off from him in dismay.

C

34   XLV. 5.—GENESIS.—XLVI. 3.

YOUR BROTHER.] This was to convince them that he had still a brotherly feeling towards them, not—their victim, or their accuser, or their judge, but their brother.
WHOM YE SOLD.] This is added to convince them that he was really Joseph, and to pave the way for expressing his matured views of the dealings of Providence with him.
5. BE NOT GRIEVED,] same word as in 1 Sa. 20. 3, 34; 2 Sa. 19. 2; Ec. 10. 9; Ne. 8. 10, 11; his meaning evidently is, not that they were blameless, but that the evil intended and executed was overruled for good by God.
6. HARVEST,] i.e. reaping.
8. YE HAVE NOT..BUT GOD,] who maketh even the wrath of man to praise him.
FATHER,] a title of respect, given in SS. to the founder of a nation, Ge. 10. 21; 17. 4, 5; 19. 37; 36. 9, 43; to the chief or first of a profession, Ge. 4. 21; to the author of anything, Job 38. 28; Is. 63. 16; to a protector, Ps. 68. 6; Is. 22. 21; to priests, prophets, teachers, superiors, 1 Sa. 10. 12; 2 K. 6. 21; 13. 14; Ju. 17. 10; 18. 19; to express intimate relationship, Job 17. 14; Ps. 88. 19.
LORD..RULER.] Compare 41. 40, 41, 43, 44.
9. JOSEPH THY SON,] lost but now found, recalling the memories of past days,
10. GOSHEN,] that part of Mitsraim next to Arabia, about 60 miles from Canaan, 'the best of the land' for pasturage—not for tillage : Joseph had evidently planned out this before-hand, which, as it was probably a thinly-peopled district, he could accomplish without difficulty.
11. NOURISHED.] Same word as in 47. 12; 50. 21; Ru. 4. 15; 2 Sa. 19. 32, 33; 20. 3; 1 K. 4. 7, 27; 8. 27; 17. 4, 9; 18. 4, 13, &c.
12. YOUR EYES ARE SEEING,] i.e. you know my face and voice.
MY MOUTH,] not merely that of an interpreter.
13. HONOUR,] lit. 'heaviness,' always used figuratively, as in Ge. 31. 1; 45. 13; 49. 6; Ex. 16. 6, 10; 24. 16, 17; 28. 2; 29. 43; 33. 18, 22; 40. 34, 35; Le. 9. 6, 23; Nu. 14. 10, 21, 22; 16. 19, 42; 20. 6; 24. 11.
17. LADE YOUR BEASTS] with corn and other provisions for the famine.
18. GOOD OF THE LAND.] See note on v. 10.
EAT THE FAT,] i.e. enjoy the fertility of the land of Egypt.
19. COMMANDED,] not merely permitted, but enjoined.
WAGGONS,] as in v. 21, 27; 46. 5; Nu. 7. 3, 6, 7, 8; 1 Sa. 6. 7, 8, 10, 11, 14; 2 Sa. 6. 3; 1 Ch. 13. 7; Ps. 46. 9; Is. 5. 18; 28. 27, 28; Am. 2. 13.
INFANTS,] as in Ge. 34. 29; 43. 8; 45. 19; 46. 5; 47. 12, 24; 50. 8, 21; Ex. 10. 10, 24; 12. 37; Nu. 14. 3, 31, &c.; opposed to young men and virgins, Ez. 9. 6; to men above 20 years of age, Ex. 12. 37; to the head of the house, 2 Ch. 20. 13; from a root signifying to move with short steps; see Is. 3. 16, the only instance of its occurrence.

20. YOUR EYE HATH NO PITY,] i.e. you do not grudge to leave it behind; compare same phrase in De. 7. 16; 13. 8; 19. 13, 21; 25. 12; 1 Sa. 24. 10; Ps. 72. 13; Is. 13. 18; Je. 13. 14; 21. 7; Ez. 5. 11; 7. 4, 9; 8. 18; 9. 5, 10; 16. 5; 20. 17; 24. 14; Jon. 4. 10, 11; Joel 2. 17; Ne. 13. 22.
VESSELS,] i e. goods, instruments, furniture, &c.; as in 24. 53; 27. 3; 31. 37; 42. 25; 43. 11; 45. 20; 49. 5.
21. PROVISION.] See note on 27. 3; several days' journey.
22. CHANGES OF GARMENTS.] The light white Eastern dress being easily soiled by the dust and heat, presents of such large outer garments as the word denotes—which serve alike for a covering by day and by night, (De. 22. 17,)—are common between friends; compare the use of the word in Ge. 9. 23; 35. 2; 37. 34; 41. 14; 44. 13; 45. 22; Ex. 3. 22; 12. 34, 35; 19. 10, 14; 22. 27; De. 8. 4; 10. 18; 21. 13; 22. 3, 5, 17; Jo. 7. 7; Ju. 8. 25; Ruth 3. 3; 1 Sa. 21. 9; 2 Sa. 12. 20; Pr. 30. 4; Is. 3. 6, 7; 41. 9. 5.
SILVERLINGS,] lit. 'silver,' the exact value of which is unknown, but reckoned by some as low as sixpence, and by others as high as two shillings; compare 20. 16; 37. 28; 44. 22; De. 22. 19; Ju. 9. 4; 16. 5; 17. 2, 3, 4, 10, &c.
23. FOOD.] This word only occurs elsewhere in 2 Ch. 11. 23; and Da. 4. 12, 21.
24. BE NOT ANGRY.]Same word as in Ex. 15. 14; De. 2. 25; 1 Sa. 14. 15; 2 Sa. 7. 10; 18. 33; 22. 8; 1 Ch. 17. 9; Ps. 4. 4; 18. 7; 77. 16, 18; 99. 1; Pr. 29. 9; 30. 21, &c. The exhortation was no doubt needed; they were very liable to fall into the error and sin of accusing each other in reference to their respective degrees of guilt in the sale of Joseph.
26. CEASETH] to beat, with astonishment, &c. for a time; the word is only found elsewhere in Ps. 38. 8; 77. 2; Hab. 1. 4; see also La. 2. 18.
GIVEN CREDENCE,] lit. 'remained steadfast ;' i.e. had no confidence in them.
27. LIVE,] as in Ge. 5. 3—30; 9. 28; 11. 11—26; 12. 13; 17. 18; 19. 20; 20. 7; 31. 32; 42. 2, 18; 43. 8; 45. 27; 47. 19, 28; 50. 22.
28. ENOUGH,] lit. 'abundant,' as in Ge. 6. 5; 7. 11; 13. 6; 18. 20; 21. 34; 24. 25; 25. 23; 26. 14; 30. 43; 33. 9; 36. 7; 37. 34; 45. 28; 50. 20.

XLVI. 1. BEER-SHEBA,] 16 miles from Hebron, where Abraham and Isaac had sojourned, and an altar had been built, Ge. 26. 25; where sacrifices were offered, which he now renews before going into a strange country, and which were accepted, for the next verses reveal the Divine answer.
GOD OF HIS FATHER ISAAC.] See Ge. 28. 13; 31. 53; 32. 9.
2. IN VISIONS OF THE NIGHT,] as he did afterwards to Samuel, Ezekiel, and Daniel, Nu. 12. 6; 1 Sa. 3. 15; Ez. 1. 1; 8. 3; 40. 2; 43. 3; Da. 10. 7, 8, 16. In the only remaining instance of its occurrence in Ex. 38. 8, it is translated 'looking-glasses.'
3. BE NOT AFRAID OF GOING DOWN TO EGYPT.] He may have felt hesitation about

the propriety of the step, as Isaac had been forbidden to do so during a season of famine, (Ge. 26. 1, 2,) and perhaps the prophecy in 15. 13 may have troubled him.

GREAT NATION,] as had been previously promised to Abraham, to Isaac, and to Jacob himself.

4. I GO DOWN WITH THEE,] agreeably to the promise in 28. 15.

I ALSO CERTAINLY BRING THEE UP,] as is recorded in 50. 13. Jacob could not have understood this of a return alive to the land of Canaan, for the next clause, JOSEPH DOTH PUT HIS HAND ON THINE EYES,] points to the last offices of affection on this side the grave; the phrase, however, does not occur elsewhere in SS.

5. THEIR WIVES,] i.e. his son's wives; no mention is made of his own wives; Rachel had died, (35. 9,) Leah also, as she is said by Jacob to have been buried by himself in the cave of Machpelah, (49. 31); Bilhah and Zilpah were probably dead likewise.

6. CATTLE] being their principal substance, wherein their wealth chiefly consisted.

8. FIRST-BORN OF JACOB—REUBEN,] as in 29. 32.

9. SONS OF REUBEN.] See Nu. 26. 5, 6, for an account of their respective families.

10. JEMUEL,] called also Nemuel in Nu. 26. 12; 1 Ch. 4. 24; evidently a scribe's error.

OHAD,] omitted in the above places, probably dying childless.

JACHIN,] called also Jarib, in 1 Ch. 4. 24.

ZOHAR,] called Zerah in 1 Ch. 4. 24, by a transposition of letters.

11. SONS OF LEVI.] Comp. Nu. 3. 1; 4. 1, &c.

12. DIE,] as recorded in 38. 7—10.

HEZRON...HAMUL,] whose father could not have been above 14 years of age; but instances of such early paternity are not uncommon in the East, where both sexes come much more rapidly to maturity than in colder regions.

13. TOLA,] whose descendants, in the days of David, numbered not less than 22,600; see 1 Ch. 7. 2.

PHUVAH..JOB..SHIMRON,] called in 1 Ch. 7. 1, 'Puah, Jashib, Shimrom,' and all heads of families.

14. SONS OF ZEBULUN.] Compare Nu. 26. 21.

15. PERSONS,] *lit.* 'souls;' see note on Ge. 12. 5.

16. SONS OF GAD.] Compare Nu. 26. 15-17.

17. SERAH,] in Nu. 26. 46, called Sarah.

SONS OF BERIAH,] who was the youngest son of Asher, and must have had sons very soon, like Pharez, noted in v. 12.

19. JACOB'S WIFE.] This title is not given to Leah in v. 15 above; it evidently points out Jacob's special affections being settled on her.

21. SONS OF BENJAMIN,] who was now about 32 years of age, and had no less than ten sons born up to this time.

24. SHILLEM,] called in 1 Ch. 7. 10, Shallum

26. SIXTY AND SIX,] viz. 32 of Leah's, (leaving out Er and Onan,) 16 of Zilpah's, 14 of Rachel's, and 7 of Bilhah's, in all 69; deduct Joseph and his two sons, and the exact number is sixty-six.

27. SEVENTY.] To the preceding 66 add Joseph, his two sons, and Jacob himself, and the number of 'the persons of the house of Jacob are seventy.' See also note on Acts 7. 14.

28. JUDAH,] being more honourable than his brethren, from his generous conduct throughout.

GOSHEN.] The Septuagint reads, 'to meet him at Heroopolis, or the city of the heroes, in the land of Rameses.'

29. HIS CHARIOT,] i.e. the one second to Pharaoh's; see 41. 43.

30. LET ME DIE,] aged and satisfied; yet he lived 17 years longer. Compare 45. 28; Nu. 23. 10; Ju. 16. 30; Ru. 1. 17.

31—34. These verses show very fully Joseph's anxiety to get his father settled, and his desire that it should be in the land of Goshen which he had previously fixed on, and that it should be with the consent of Pharaoh.

31. UNTO ME,] as the king himself had requested.

32. ALL THAT THEY HAVE;] in 45. 20, Pharaoh had told them not to regard their stuff, but Joseph and his father's household had no wish unnecessarily to test too much the generosity of Pharaoh.

MEN OF CATTLE,] i.e. a pastoral tribe, not agricultural like the Egyptians; but see note on Ge. 26. 12.

34. ABOMINATION.] It is difficult to say whence this hatred of shepherds actually arose : it has been supposed to have been a religious prejudice, arising from the use of the flesh of the cow, in sacrifices, (compare Ex. 8. 26); it may also have been a political and national feeling, from the predatory habits of the Beduwin Arabs, whose raids on their unprotected, unsuspecting neighbours, rendered the Egyptians suspicious of all pastoral visitors. In 47. 6, mention is made of Pharaoh himself having cattle.

XLVII. 1. GOSHEN,] according to his own command, and waiting for a further expression of his pleasure.

2. OUT OF HIS,] *lit.* 'from the extremity of his brethren,' i.e. the oldest, and the youngest, and the middle, to show their various ages and appearances.

4. TO SOJOURN,] because of the famine, not to abide permanently, having an eye to the better country; this was said also to allay any fears that may have been entertained of their ulterior designs.

6. THE LAND...IS BEFORE THEE.] This truly generous language shows the deep hold that Joseph's conduct had taken on Pharaoh and his courtiers, without whose consent he could scarcely have spoken so openly and frankly.

SET THEM OVER,] to attach them doubtless still more to his authority.

7. JACOB BLESSETH PHARAOH.] Age has always been regarded in the East quite as much as wealth or station ; yet the patriarch Jacob was no inconsiderable person in outward circumstances, seeing it has been calculated that he had four times the

number of the followers that his grandfather Abraham had, (Ge. 14. 14,) which would give 1272 fighting men, or a total of about five thousand persons, and that this number might increase in 215 (or rather 430) years to 600,000 armed men, is easily seen.

9. FEW,] i.e. comparatively so; Abraham living 175 years, (25. 7,) Isaac 180 years, (35. 28.)

EVIL,] or unfortunate, yet it was all the result of his own conduct—deceiving his father and brother; nothing could he bring against God, but undeserved mercy, (see 48. 15, 16.)

SOJOURNINGS,] in the land of promise as strangers and pilgrims.

11. RAMESES,] i.e. 'son of the sun,' supposed to be called after several Egyptian kings of that name, evidently another name for Goshen, lying on the eastern branch of the Nile; the capital city bore the same name, and was rebuilt by the Israelites, (Ex. 1. 11,) though the names are differently pronounced by the Masoretic scribes, 'Rameses—Raamses.'

12. ACCORDING TO THE MOUTH OF THE INFANTS,] i.e. their number and need.

13. FEEBLE.] The original word occurs nowhere else, but a cognate one is very common, denoting 'to be weary.'

15. CONSUMED,] at the end of the fifth, or the beginning of the sixth year of famine.

THOUGH,] or because.

16. FOR,] i.e. in exchange for, so in v. 17.

IF,] i.e. since.

17. TENDETH,] lit. 'leadeth,' as in Ge. 33. 14; Ex. 15. 13; Ps. 23. 2; 31. 3; Is. 40. 11; 49. 10; 51. 18; 2 Ch. 28. 15; 32. 22.

HORSES,] for which Egypt was proverbially famous; see De. 17. 6; 1 K. 10. 28; Is. 31. 1, 3.

18. SECOND YEAR,] being the seventh or last year of the famine, as it appears from v. 23, they received seed to sow the land.

BODIES...GROUND,] the one starving, the other desolate.

19. WE AND OUR GROUND ARE SERVANTS TO PHARAOH.] This offer Joseph does not appear to have accepted further than to claim a fifth of the increase of the land for Pharaoh, see v. 24; their personal service was not required, except it be implied in v. 21; and for this the people thank him in v. 25.

22. PRIESTS,] or 'ministers;' the word is used both of civil and sacred authorities; see 2 Sa. 8. 18; 1 Ch. 18. 17; Ge. 14. 18, &c. Junius, Tremellius, Piscator, and others take it in the former sense here, but the latter is preferable.

HAVE A PORTION,] as is testified by Herodotus, and as the Levites had afterwards among the Hebrews.

25. REVIVED,] or caused us to live, i.e. given us life.

26. UNTO THIS DAY,] when the historian was writing.

27. MULTIPLY EXCEEDINGLY,] agreeably to the promises, Ge. 28. 14; 46. 3.

28. SEVENTEEN YEARS] with Joseph his

son, just the same period he had lived with him before he was sold; see 37. 2.

29. ARE NEAR,] or, draw near—to die; there is no escaping the general doom, 'dust thou art :' very striking is the expression so often repeated in Ge. 5. 5—27, 'and he dieth,' used even of those whose age extended to more than ten times 'fourscore and ten.'

UNDER MY THIGH.] See note on 24. 2.

BURY ME NOT IN EGYPT.] It is, of course, of little importance to any one where the body may lie after the spirit has left it, still all who believe in its rising again have been careful to preserve the clay tabernacle as long as possible, and to find it a resting-place among the remains of its ancestors; Jacob, like Joseph, (50. 25,) moreover, remembering the unchangeable grant of Canaan to him, could not but desire to testify his belief in its realization by his body being deposited there, thus, even in death, as it were, taking possession of the land.

31. SWEAR TO ME,] not doubtless from any distrust of Joseph's word, but showing his own eagerness, and possibly with a view to prevent Pharaoh's hindering him from complying with this request; see 50. 5.

HEAD OF THE BED.] This is supposed by many to be referred to in Heb. 11. 21, where it is said Jacob bowed 'upon the top of his staff.' The Hebrew word may be rendered 'bed' or 'staff,' according to the vowels with which it is pronounced; the vowel signs are of modern invention, they are of no authority, and only valuable as showing the traditional interpretation of the Jews after the seventh century. Others consider the apostle as referring to some other circumstance connected with (but not mentioned in) the next chapter, regarding the blessings bestowed on the sons of Joseph.

XLVIII. 1. SICK,] i.e. ailing; believers are not exempt from any of the ordinary 'ills that flesh is heir to,'—'he whom thou lovest is sick,'—but the promise is sure : 'as thy day so is thy strength.'

TOOK WITH HIM HIS TWO SONS,] that they might receive his blessing, and see that the righteous hath peace in his death.

2. STRENGTHEN HIMSELF,] gathered up his energies, his heart growing lighter, and his hopes brighter, at the prospect of again seeing Joseph.

3. LUZ,] or Beth-El, at Jacob's departure for Padan-Aram, (28. 11—17,) and again at his return from thence, (35. 6—12.)

5. THY TWO SONS...ARE MINE,] i.e. by adoption, a very ancient and prevalent custom in the East.

AS REUBEN AND SIMEON,] they are not to be regarded as his grandsons, but as his own sons, and preferred to them, even to the eldest. The reason of Reuben's being deprived of the birthright is stated in 1 Ch. 5. 1, 2, Joseph coming in his place, and receiving a double portion, through Ephraim and Manasseh becoming two of the twelve tribes.

6. THEIR BRETHREN,] i.e. Ephraim and Manasseh.

7. PADAN.] In every other instance of its occurrence it is 'Padan-Aram.'

KIBRATH.] See note on Ge. 35. 16.

9. GOD HATH GIVEN.] Compare Ps. 127. 3; Ge. 16. 2; 30. 1; this sentiment has often been expressed in the very names of children, as Nathaniel, Mattaniah, Theodorus, Deodatus, Apollodorus, Artemidorus, &c., as noted by Gill.

10. UNABLE TO SEE,] i.e. distinctly, like his father Isaac, in 27. 1.

11. THOUGHT,] *lit.* 'judged,' as in 1 Sa. 2. 25; Ez. 16. 52; Ps. 106. 30.

14. UPON THE HEAD OF EPHRAIM.] This is the first mention of what is afterwards frequently noted as being done when blessing or appointing any one to an office; Nu. 27. 18, 23; De. 34. 9; (Mat. 19. 13, 15.)

15. FROM MY BEING,] since I came into being.

16. REDEEMING,] i.e. claiming and bringing back from evil. This is the first instance of the occurrence of this word, which is afterwards very frequently to be met with in the SS.

16. INCREASE.] The original word occurs nowhere else in SS. as a verb; as a noun it means 'a fish,' and as fish are proverbially prolific, the word has been thought to have been formed to express the idea of unbounded increase as fish; so Onkelos, Jarchi, Pagninus, Montanus, Junius, Tremellius, Piscator, Ainsworth, &c. From Nu. 25. 34—37 it appears that even in the wilderness the two tribes of Ephraim and Manasseh out-numbered by about *nine* thousand even the tribe of Judah.

17. WRONG.] Very naturally Joseph would have preferred that the blessing should come on the first-born, as did Isaac his grandfather with regard to Esau, &c.

18. THE FIRST-BORN,] whose rights were not to be set aside by mere caprice; see De. 21. 17.

19. GREATER THAN HE] in number, see Nu. 1. 33, 35: Ephraim's standard was placed before Manasseh's, Nu. 2. 18. 20; it was chief of the ten tribes, and sometimes gives its name to the whole of the others.

20. BY THEE,] i.e. by Joseph, in his sons.

EPHRAIM BEFORE MANASSEH.] Among the Tartars and other northern nations, and in old Saxon tenures, the second son was often preferred to the elder, who when grown up, was sent off with a portion of the father's goods, while the younger remained at home, and became heir to his father.

22. ONE PORTION,] *lit.* 'one shoulder,' i.e. a weight borne on the shoulder.

BOW.] This circumstance is not mentioned elsewhere, but apparently one in which the 'plain' Jacob, like the 'faithful' Abraham, had to fight the world with its own weapons.

XLIX 1. THE LATTER END OF THE DAYS,] meaning, generally, the latter end of the Jewish economy, and by the Jewish writers invariably interpreted of the days of Messiah, who was to inaugurate a new era.

2. This second verse is essentially a repetition of the first, expressing earnestness on the part of the speaker, and calling for the same from the hearers.

3. STRENGTH,] *or* 'iniquity,' *or* 'mourning; Sept. 'children.'

ABUNDANCE.] Same word in Ex. 10. 5; 23. 11; Le. 14. 17; Nu. 31. 32; De. 3. 11, 13; 28. 54.

EXALTATION.] Same word in Ge. 4. 7; Le. 13. 2, 10, 19, 28, 43; 14. 56; Job 13. 11; 31. 23; 41. 25; Ps. 62. 4; Hab. 1. 7.

STRENGTH,] as in. v. 7, ('fierce,') Ex. 14. 21; Nu. 13. 28; 21. 24; De. 28. 50.

4. UNSTABLE.] See Ju. 9. 4; Je. 23. 32; Zep. 3. 4.

ABUNDANT,] as in Ex. 10. 15; 12. 10; 16. 19, 20; 36. 7; Le. 22. 30; Nu. 33. 55; De. 28. 11, 54; 30. 9.

HE WENT UP.] Compare Ge. 35. 22, which 40 years had not obliterated from Jacob's memory.

5. BRETHREN] of the same disposition, temper, &c.

ESPOUSALS,] *lit.* 'sales,' referring to the espousal or sale of Dinah on a certain condition; so Aben Ezra.

6. SECRET,] i.e. hidden thing, (see 34. 25.)

ERADICATED A PRINCE,] i.e. Shechem. The verb is used in Jo. 11. 6, 9; 2 Sa. 8. 4; 1 Ch. 18. 4; Ec. 3. 2; Zep. 2. 4, in the same sense, viz. 'to root out;' so also in Da. 7. 4. The word rendered 'prince,' the Masorets have very stupidly rendered 'ox,' because the name of his father Hamor denotes '*an ass!*' The Chaldee, Arabic, and Syriac translate 'a wall.'

7. I DIVIDE THEM,] as Jeremiah (1. 10) is said to root out and pull down kingdoms, because he prophesied of such things. Simeon had only a portion of the tribe of Judah, (Jo. 19. 1—9, and compare 1 Ch. 4. 39, 42,) and Levi had 48 cities assigned them in the several tribes here and there.

8. JUDAH,] i.e. 'praise;' a play upon words.

NECK,] implying full triumph over them, verified in David, who was of this tribe; Ps. 18. 40.

BOW,] in token of superiority; everywhere in the Israelitish history, Judah is substantially leader.

9. LION'S WHELP,] full of courage, strength, and generosity, as in De. 33. 22; Na. 2. 11.

FOR PREY,] i.e. because of; some prefer 'from prey,' having been satisfied it goes up to the mountains, where its den is, where

HE HAS BENT] his knees, and

HE HAS CROUCHED] for rest; see note on Ge. 4. 7.

AS A LION.] Compare De. 23. 24; 24. 9, &c.

A LIONESS.] Compare Nu. 23. 24; 24. 9; De. 33. 20; Job 4. 11; 38. 39, &c.

10. SCEPTRE.] The original word occurs here for the first time, and again in v. 10, 26 of this chapter; in Ex. 21. 20 it denotes a rod with which a man might smite his servant; in Le. 27. 32 a rod of an inspector (or shepherd;) in Nu. 24. 17, a sceptre, or rod of power; in Ju. 5. 14, a reed of a writer; in every other instance in the Pentateuch it means 'a tribe.' Its parallelism with 'law-giver' in the next clause, favours the idea of regal authority.

LAWGIVER,] as the original word means in every other instance of its occurrence,

viz. Nu. 21. 18; De. 33. 21; Ju. 5-14; Ps. 60. 7; 108. 8; Is. 33. 22; from a root signifying 'to engrave.'
FROM BETWEEN HIS FEET.] Compare De. 28. 57; the only passage where the phrase occurs: it evidently means, 'from his seed.'
TILL.] Some render this particle 'for ever,' as it often signifies, (Ge. 13. 5,) which gives not a bad sense: 'the sceptre turneth not aside—for ever, for his seed cometh; and his is the obedience of peoples;' the sceptre and 'government is now upon his shoulder,' (see Is. 9. 6,) never to be removed till the work of redemption is complete.
HIS SEED,] so Calvin, Junius, Tremellius, Kimchi, Galatinus in Fagius, &c; SHILO being cognate with SHILYATHO, in De. 28. 57; in every other instance of its occurrence Shiloh is the name of a place in the tribe of Ephraim, north of Bethel; Jo. 18. 1, 8, 9, 10, &c., it is not mentioned at all in the Pentateuch, and only fancy could connect the two. All the Targums apply it to Messiah; the other versions vary.
OBEDIENCE,] as the word means in Pr. 30. 17, the only other instances of its occurrence.
11. VINE.] The idea is that the fertility of Judah's portion would be such that one might bind the animals to the vines from their size and abundance. The vineyards of En-Gedi (Song 1. 14,) and Eshcol, (Nu. 13. 23, 24,) are celebrated among those belonging to that tribe.
ASS,] as in Ge. 32. 15; Ju. 10. 4; 12. 14; Job 11. 12; Is. 30. 6, 24; Zec. 9. 9.
CHOICE VINE,] the Hebrew SOREK, occurs only elsewhere in Is. 5. 2; Je. 2. 21.
COLT,] lit. 'son.'
ASS,] a different word in Hebrew from the word rendered 'ass,' in the former clause, see also Ge. 12. 16; 32. 15; 45. 23; 49. 11; Nu. 22. 21—33; Ju. 5. 10. &c.
WASHED,] as in Ex. 19. 10, 14; Le. 6. 27; 11. 25, 28, 40.
WINE,] as in Ge. 9. 21, 24; 14. 18; 19. 32, 33, 34, 35; 27. 25; 49. 11, 12; Ex. 29. 40, &c., equivalent to 'the blood of grapes,' in the next clause, a phrase only occurring in De. 32. 14; Ez. 19. 10.
CLOTHING,] as in 2 Sa. 1. 24; 20. 4; 2 K. 10. 22; Job 24. 7, 10; 30. 18; 31, 19; 38. 9, 14; 41. 13; Es. 6. 8—11; Ps. 22. 8.
COVERING.] The Hebrew word SUTH is found nowhere else; it is probably a scribe's error for KESUTH, as in Ge. 20. 16; Ex. 21. 10; 22. 27; De. 22. 12; Job 24. 7; 26. 6; 31. 19; Is. 50. 3.
12. RED,] as in Pr. 23. 29, the only other passage where it occurs, denoting fire and brilliancy of expression.
WITH WINE,] lit. 'from, or because of, or than wine; same word as in v. 11.
WHITE,] as in Ge. 30. 35, 37; Ex. 16. 31; Le. 13. 3—43; Ec. 9. 8; Zec. 1. 8; 6. 3, 6.
WITH MILK,] lit. 'from, or because of, or than milk,' same word in Ge. 18. 8; Ex. 3. 8, 17; De. 32. 14; Job 21. 24; Song 5. 1, 12; Is. 55. 1; Joel 3. 18; La. 4. 7.
13. HAVEN,] as in De. 1. 7; Jo. 9. 1; Ju. 5. 17; Je. 47. 7; Ez. 25. 16; when the land

was divided by Lot, (Jo. 19. 10, 11,) Zebulun's portion fell towards the shore of the sea of Galilee, and the Great Sea, unto Sidon—not the city but the territory—thus remarkably fulfilling this prophecy to its very letter.
14. A STRONG ASS,] lit. 'an ass of bone;' this tribe numbered 54,400 when they came out of Egypt, and increased to 64,300 in the wilderness; they had their lot in lower Galilee between Zebulun and Manasseh; their leading men were Tola the judge, and Baasha the king; it does not appear to have been warlike, or to have taken a deep interest in public matters; they failed also to drive out the Canaanites.
TWO FOLDS,] The original word only occurs elsewhere in Ju. 5. 16, and is variously rendered; e.g. Jerome, Rosenmuller, Geddes, Boothroyd, &c. prefer 'boundaries,' Horsley, Patrick, Lee, &c. 'burdens or panniers;' Pool, 'burdens or folds,' Gesenius, 'folds for cattle.'
15. REST,] i.e. a place of rest, as in Nu. 19. 33; De. 12. 9; Onkelos has 'a portion,' probably reading MINCHAH, 'an offering or present,' instead of MENUCHAH; Syriac has 'his dwelling.'
PLEASANT,] including the vale of Jezreel, and the mountains of Gilboa; compare Ho. 1. 5; 2 Sa. 1. 21.
TO BEAR,] i.e. the burden willingly.
TRIBUTE.] Same word in Ex. 1. 11; De. 20. 11; Jo. 16. 10; 17. 13; Ju. 1. 28, 30, 33, 35; 2 Sa. 20. 24, &c.
16. JUDGE,] a play upon the meaning of his name, which means a 'judge or arbiter.'
AS ONE,] i.e. in the same way that the other tribes do—independently; Samson was of this tribe.
17. SERPENT.] See note on Ge. 3. 1.
ADDER.] The Hebrew word occurs nowhere else; rendered by some 'arrowsnake.'
WAY...PATH,] words having the same general meaning.
BITING...FALLETH BACKWARD.] Almost all references to this tribe indicate its subtile character and actions; see De. 33. 22; Jo. 19. 47; 21. 5; Ju. 18. 29, 30; 5. 17; 13. 25.
18. THY SALVATION.] The Targums paraphrastically explain: 'not for the salvation of Gideon...nor for Joash...nor for the salvation of Samson son of Manoah...but for the salvation of Messiah, son of David,' &c. The word 'salvation' occurs in Ex. 14. 13; 15. 2; De. 32. 15; 1 Sa. 2. 1; 14. 45; it is applied alike to temporal or spiritual deliverances.
19. GAD,] i.e. 'a troop,' as explained in 30. 5; there is here a two-fold paranomasia, lit. 'Troop! a troop doth troop him;' i.e. come upon him as a troop, fiercely, irresistibly, as recorded in Ju. 10. 8; Je. 49. 1.
LAST,] lit. 'heel;' see the use of the word in Ge. 3. 15; 25. 26; 49. 17, 19; Jo. 8. 13; Ju. 5. 22; Job 18. 9; Ps. 41. 9; 49. 5; 56. 6; 77. 19; 89. 51; Song 1. 8; Je. 13. 22.
20. ASHER,] i.e. 'happy;' his 'bread' is a general name for food; 'fat,' as in Nu. 13

20; Ju. 3. 29; 1 Ch. 4. 40; Ne. 9. 25, 35; Is. 30. 23; Ez. 34. 14, 16; Hab. 1. 6.

DAINTIES,] as in 1 Sa. 15. 32; Pr. 29. 17; La. 4. 5; and Job 38. 31; in Asher there was one of Solomon's puveyors, 1 K. 4. 16; its territory was about 20 miles long by 9 in breadth, and contained the valley of Asher, called the fat valley, De. 33. 24.

21. HIND,] as in 2 Sa. 22. 34; Job 39. 1; Ps. 18. 33; 29. 9; Song 2. 7; 3. 5; Hab. 3. 19.

SENT AWAY,] as in Ge. 32. 18; 49. 21; 1 K. 14. 6; Je. 49. 14; Ez. 2. 9; 3. 5; 23. 40.

GIVING,] i.e. yielding, bringing forth.

BEAUTEOUS YOUNG ONES,] *lit.* 'young ones of beauty.' The word EMER rendered 'words' in the Common Version is here evidently used in its Chaldee sense of 'a lamb,' or young hind, Ezra 6. 9, 17; 7. 17.

22. SON...DAUGHTERS,] are commonly understood as figurative appellations of the 'boughs or branches' of a tree, but are not found so applied in any other part of Scripture.

STEPPING BY A WALL.] For the word 'stepping,' see Ju. 5. 4; 2 K. 6. 13; Ps. 68. 7; Pr. 7. 8; Je. 10. 5; Hab. 3. 12; Job 18. 14.

23. EMBITTER,] see Ex. 1. 14; 23. 21.

STRIVEN,] as in Ge. 26. 22; Ex. 17. 2; Nu. 20. 13.

HATE,] same word in Ge. 27. 41; 49. 23; 50. 15; Job 16. 9; 30. 21; Ps. 55. 3.

ARCHERS,] *lit.* 'possessors of arrows,' a phrase which occurs nowhere else in SS., but referring doubtless to his brethren, his mistress, his rivals, &c.

24. BOW,] his weapon of defence and offence.

ABIDETH,] i.e. continueth, is not broken or injured by use.

MIGHTY ONE,] as in Ju. 5. 22; 1 Sa. 21. 7; Job 24. 22; 34. 20; Ps. 22. 12; 50. 13; 68. 30; 76. 5; 78. 25; 132. 2, 5; Is. 1. 24; 10. 13; 34. 7; 46. 12; 49. 26; 60. 16; Je. 6. 18; 46. 15; 47. 3; 50. 11; La. 1. 5.

WHENCE IS,] i.e. from the Mighty One of Israel came Joseph, son of Israel.

A SON.] The Hebrew word ABEN generally means 'a stone,' but is occasionally used (as in Arabic) in the sense of 'a son,' as here; it is found also in Ex. 1. 16, where, without the slightest appearance of sense or propriety, it is translated 'stool;' it also means 'son' in the following passages, viz., Job. 5. 23; Is. 14. 19.

25. BY THE GOD OF THY FATHER,] another appellation of 'the Mighty One of Jacob' in v. 24.

ALMIGHTY,] *lit.* ' He who is sufficient.'

BLESSINGS...FROM ABOVE,] copious dews and seasonable rains.

THE DEEP,] in its fountains, brooks, and rivers.

BREASTS AND WOMB,] an abundant and healthy household, and family, and stock.

26. THY FATHER'S BLESSINGS,] i.e. those Jacob gave to Joseph.

PROGENITORS.] The word is strictly applicable only to the female parent—*lit.* 'conceivers.'

UNTO THE LIMIT,] as far as the eye can reach.

THEY ARE,] i.e. his father's benedictions.

SEPARATE,] Hebrew NAZIR, a Nazarite, a person or thing separated (generally) by a vow; see Le. 25. 5, 11; Nu. 6. 2, 13, 18, 19, 20, 21; De. 33. 16; Ju. 13. 5, 7; 16. 17; La. 4. 7; Amos 2. 11, 12; compare also Le. 15. 31; 22. 2; Nu. 6. 2, 3, 5, 6, 12; Ho. 9. 10; Ez. 14. 7; Zec. 7. 3.

27. A WOLF.] Benjamin is here said to be a wolf, an animal remarkable for its ferocity and rapaciousness. The tribe is specially distinguished in Scripture by having (Ju. 20. 16,) no less than seven hundred men left-handed, who could sling stones at a hair-breadth and not miss; for its obstinate resistance to the whole of the remaining tribes, when it was almost wholly cut off, (Ju. 21. 3;) for its giving the first king to Israel, in the person of Saul, (1 Sa. 10. 20—24;) and for its adherence to the house of David when the ten tribes chose Jeroboam, 1 K. 12. 16—21.

MORNING...EVENING,] i.e. the beginning and end of the Israelitish state, (which is the subject of the whole prophecy), implying the existence of the tribe to the last, which was fully realized. Compare the similar expression in De. 33. 12; 'of Benjamin he said, The beloved of Jehovah doth tabernacle confidently by him, covering him over *all the day*.'

29. I AM BEING GATHERED;] in the course of being so, the process has begun, and cannot be delayed.

30—33. 'Had natural affection dictated this request, which was so important in his eyes as to be given to Joseph, (47. 29—31,) and repeated here to all the sons, he would have rather desired to be in Rachel's grave. But circumstances placed her body at a distance from the only spot which the patriarchs had procured as an earnest of the inheritance; and hence he fixed on this spot as his burial place, to show that, like his father, he died in the faith of the covenant of promise.'—*D. Davidson.*

33. EXPIRETH,] in the 147th year of his age, in the year of the world 2356, and before Christ 1689, according to Usher's Chronology.

L. 1. JOSEPH..WEEPETH.] Joseph is here mentioned as being the chief personage on whom the duties connected with the death and burial of Jacob depended. It is said he wept, which was no discredit to him either as a man, a ruler, a son, or a believer. A greater than Joseph wept at the grave of his friend Lazarus, (John 11. 35.)

2. PHYSICIANS,] *lit.* 'healers;' the word is again mentioned in Ex. 15. 26; 2 K. 20. 5; 2 Ch. 16. 12; Job 13. 4; Ps. 103. 3; 147. 3; Je. 8. 22.

TO EMBALM.] The original word occurs only elsewhere in Song 2. 13, and translated 'ripen,' being used of figs; the practice of embalming is not alluded to in any other place of SS.; it is a very ancient and widespread custom in Egypt, more than in any other nation. During the first thirty days the body lay in nitre, and the remaining forty days were spent in anointing it with gums and spices to preserve it; this explains the allusion to the 'forty' and the 'seventy' days in v. 3. This embalming of Jacob's body was not only in conformity to Egyptian usage, but necessary for the transport of it to Canaan.

3. SEVENTY DAYS.] For kings, Diodorus Siculus tells us, they mourned seventy-two days. 'Jarchi accounts for the number thus, 40 for embalming, 30 for mourning, which latter was the usual time for mourning with the Jews for principal men, and which the Egyptians added to their 40 of embalming, see Nu. 20. 29; De. 34. 8.'—*Gill.*

4. HOUSE,] i.e. household, not to Pharaoh himself, being hindered from doing so by his mourning, which required a degree of neglect of appearances distasteful to royalty, as in the case of Ahasuerus and Esther, (4. 2.)

5. CAUSED ME TO SWEAR,] as narrated in 47. 31.

PREPARED,] not necessarily or naturally 'digged,' as in the Common Version; see 2 K. 6. 23; Job 41. 6; Ps. 22. 16; 40. 6. Compare all the remaining passages where the word occurs, Ge. 26. 25; Ex. 21. 33; Nu. 18; De. 2. 6; Job 6. 27; Ps. 7. 15; 57. 6; 94. 13; 119. 85; Pr. 16. 27; 26. 27; 2 Ch. 16. 14; Je. 18. 20, 22; Ho. 3. 2.

6. AS HE CAUSED THEE TO SWEAR.] This, the only remark made by Pharaoh in giving the requisite permission, shows that the foresight of the aged patriarch, when he brought Joseph under a solemn oath, was not unnecessary or unmeaning.

7. ELDERS OF HIS HOUSE,] i.e. his court officers.

ELDERS OF THE LAND,] i.e. his state officials.

9. CAMP,] *or* encampment; 'company' is a very feeble word to express the force of the original; see also Ge. 32. 2, 7, 8, 10, 21; 33. 8; 50. 9; Ex. 14. 19, 20, 24; 16. 13; 19. 16, 17; 29. 14; 32. 17, 19, 26, 27; 33. 7, 11; 36. 6.

10. THRESHING-FLOOR,] as in Nu. 15. 20; 18. 27, 30; De. 15. 14; 16. 13; Ju. 6. 37, &c.

ATAD,] i.e. 'a thorn,' either the name of a man, or of a place 40 miles from Hebron, 16 from Jerusalem, and 250 from On, where Joseph is believed to have resided.

SEVEN DAYS,] which, according to 1 Sa. 31. 13, was the time of mourning afterwards among the Jews.

12. HIS SONS DO.] The plural is used, doubtless, to show that while Joseph was the chief mourner, yet Jacob's whole family united in carrying out his dying request, as in 49. 29.

14. TURNETH BACK,] according to his promise to Pharaoh, in v. 5.

15. PERADVENTURE.] Joseph had given them, for 17 years, unbounded proof of his forgiveness and affection; but a guilty conscience who can bear? They were no doubt sorry for their ill-treatment of him, but it is not said that they had ever frankly confessed their sin to God, or to Jacob, or to Joseph, and obtained in this manner a relief to their burdened spirits; their message shows that Jacob knew of it, but by what means we know not.

DOTH CERTAINLY RETURN,] as perhaps they felt they would have been inclined to do, had they been used as he had been; but 'to err is human—to forgive divine.'

17. WE PRAY THEE.] The Hebrew particle is precisely the same as in the preceding clause, 'I pray thee,' and may therefore be regarded as still the language of Jacob; but it is more likely to be their own language, repeating the supplication.

SERVANTS OF THE GOD OF THY FATHER,] thus calling Joseph's religious feelings into combination with his filial love, as the apostle reasons, (1 John 5.1,) 'Every one who is loving Him who begat, loveth also him who is begotten of Him.'

THEIR SPEAKING,] i.e. his brethren's messengers.

18. FOR SERVANTS,] as in 37. 7, 9; 42. 10—13; 43. 18; 44. 9—33.

19. IN THE PLACE OF GOD?] Compare 30. 2; 2 K. 5. 7; to Him vengeance belongs; De. 32. 35; Rom. 12. 19.

20. GOD DEVISED IT.] See the use of the same word in Ex. 31. 4; 35. 32, &c.

FOR GOOD,] as in 45. 5, 8; Ps. 76. 10; 105. 16, 17; 119. 71; Is. 10. 7.

22. 110 YEARS.] He was 17 years of age when sold into Egypt, (37. 2); 13 years in Potiphar's house, and in prison, for he was 30 years of age (41. 46) when he stood before Pharaoh, after which he lived 80 years, which united make 110 years.

23. BORN.] Compare the use of this word in 2 Sa. 21. 8.

24. INSPECT,] *or* look after.

HATH CAUSED YOU TO GO UP.] The use of the past tense here, as often elsewhere, is a very common and universally recognized way of expressing the certainty of an event taking place.

25. CAUSETH...TO SWEAR,] as his father had made him, (47. 31.)

MY BONES,] desiring to rest with his father in the land of Canaan, thus testifying his belief in the promises of God.

26. EMBALM,] as they had done his father, more especially with the view of fulfilling his last request, and as he had not requested them to bury him immediately.

A COFFIN,] the first instance of the occurrence of the word; it is the word so frequently used in the expression, 'ark' of the covenant;' and used twice of a money chest; 2 K. 12. 10, 11.

EGYPT,] where his body was preserved till the departure of the Israelites out of that land, when Moses took it with him, (Ex. 13. 19,) and it was eventually deposited in Shechem; Jo. 24. 32.

EXODUS

EXODUS is a Greek word, signifying 'outgoing,' and is applied to the second book of the Old Testament by the Septuagint translators, (B.C. 270,) from the earlier part of it being occupied with the deliverance and out-going of the Israelites from Egypt; it contains their history from the death of Joseph till the rearing up of the tabernacle in the wilderness, and is evidently a continuation of Genesis, without a previous knowledge of which Exodus would be very imperfectly, if at all understood. There are numerous references in the New Testament to this book, in which it is coupled with the name of Moses, implying its divine authority and his authorship, e.g. Mar. 12. 26; John 6. 31, 32, 49; Ac. 7. 24, 30; 1 Cor. 10. 2, 3, 4, 7; Heb. 9. 2, 19, 22; 11. 23, 24, 29; 12. 18, 20, 24; 1 Pet. 2. 9.

It has been divided into two parts, viz. : 1.) the historical part, chap. 1—11; 12. 21—42, 51; 13. 17—19. 25; 20. 15—18; 24. 1—18; 32—40; and, 2.) the legislative part, chap.12. 1—20, 43—50; 13. 1—16; 20. 1—14; 20. 19 to 23. 33; 25—31.

I. 1. NAMES,] as in Ge. 46. 8—27.

THEY HAVE COME,] none was left behind, each brought his household (generally his domestics, but here including his family) with him.

2—4. These verses enumerate first, the six sons of Leah, secondly, the younger son of Rachel, and thirdly, the four sons of the concubines.

5. COMING OUT OF THE THIGH,] as in Ge. 46. 26; Ju. 8. 30; being all the passages where the same phrase occurs.

SEVENTY,] as in Ge. 46. 27; see note thereon.

6. DIETH.] Gill gives the following dates of the death of the 12 patriarchs, from Rabbi Bechai in Shalshalesh Hakabala, fol. 3. 2, and 4. 1, but it is not to be trusted : viz. Joseph died first, at the age of 110 years, 'Reuben lived 124 years, and died two years after Joseph; Simeon 120 years, and died the year after Joseph; Levi 137 years, and died 24 years after Joseph; Judah 119 years; Issachar 122 years; Zebulun 124 years, and died two years after Joseph; Dan 127 years; Asher 123 years; Benjamin 111 years, and died 26 years before Levi; Gad 125 years, and Naphtali 133 years.'

BRETHREN.] According to Stephen's statement in Acts 7. 16, it would appear that their bodies were not buried in Egypt but in Sychar or Shechem ; whether they were carried thither immediately on their decease, or along with the bones of Joseph, it is impossible, to say, owing to the conciseness of the narrative.

THAT GENERATION,] whether Egyptians or Hebrews, who had seen and known the doings of Joseph.

7. Very striking is the multiplication of terms indicative of the increase of Israel, as had been promised in Ge. 12. 2; 13. 16; 15. 5; 17. 2, 4, 5, 6, 16; 18. 17; 22. 17; 26. 4, 24; 28. 14; 32. 12; 35. 11 : 46. 3; fruitful, (as in Ex. 23. 30;) teem, (as in Ex. 8. 3; Le. 11. 29—46; Ps. 105. 30; Ez. 47. 9;) multiply, (as in v. 10, 12, 20; 11. 9;) mighty, (as in v. 20; Ge. 26. 16.)

THE LAND,] not merely of Goshen, but of Egypt; compare 3. 22 : 5. 12, &c.

8. A NEW KING,] not merely another king, but one of another dynasty, a foreigner, under whose successor, whom Josephus calls king Ramses V., Amenophis, the last king of the 18th dynasty, the exodus took place.

NOT KNOWN,] i.e. appreciated the benefits conferred by Joseph on Egypt.

9. HIS PEOPLE,] who had assisted him to conquer Egypt, being Arabs.

MORE NUMEROUS AND MIGHTY THAN WE.] It is impossible the Israelites could be more numerous than the Egyptians, but it was likely enough they were more numerous than the band of foreigners who now domineered over the land.

10. GIVE HELP,] as in Ge. 11, 3, 4, 7; 29. 21; 30. 1; 38. 16; 47. 15, 16; De. 1. 13; 32. 3.

THOSE HATING US,] i.e. the native but oppressed Egyptians.

11. IT BUILDETH,] either by contributions, taxes, &c., or by manual labour—probably by both.

PITHOM,] a city in lower Egypt, east of the Nile, probably the same as that called Patamos by Herodotus.

RAAMSES,] a town generally distinguished from the land of Rameses, mentioned in Ge. 47. 11, and Ex. 12. 37, which is evidently identical with Goshen.

12. BREAKETH FORTH,] as in Ge. 28. 14; 30. 30, 43; 38. 29; Ex. 1. 12; 19. 22, 24.

VEXED,] as in Ge. 27. 46; Ex. 1. 12; Le. 20. 23; Nu. 21. 5; 22. 3; 1 K. 11. 25; Pr. 3. 11; Is. 7. 6, 16.

13. WITH RIGOUR,] as in v. 14; Le. 25. 43, 46, 53; Ez. 34. 4, being all the instances of the occurrence of the word.

14. MAKE BITTER,] as in Ge. 49. 23; Is. 42. 4; compare Ruth 1. 13; 1 Sa. 30. 6; 2 K. 4. 27; Is. 24. 9; 38. 17; La. 1. 4.

HARD BONDAGE.] See same phrase in 6. 9; De. 26. 6; 1 K. 12. 4; 2 Ch. 10. 4; Is. 14. 3.

IN BITUMEN.] Same word as in Ge. 11. 3; BRICK] as in 5. 7, 8, 16, 18, 19; Is. 9. 10; 65. 3; Ez. 4. 1; Ge. 11. 3.

THEY HAVE SERVED,] not, 'they made them serve,' as in the Common Version.

15. MIDWIVES, THE HEBREWESSES.] The supposition of Josephus and others that the midwives were Egyptian women, is inadmissible, as their names are not Egyptian

but Hebrew, and it is quite incredible that for this office strangers should be employed if others could be got ; the expression also in v. 17, 21, 'the midwives have feared God,' though not decisive, is favourable to the common interpretation. The circumstance that two only are mentioned has caused much conjecture : some have supposed them to have been chiefs of the profession, under whose directions the rest were to act, but it is much more probable that the sanguinary order concerned only a few of the principal Hebrew families, and not the whole nation. It is simply impossible to believe that a nation numbering two and a half millions, could be so reduced as to submit for a single day to allow all their male children to be destroyed ; if it concerned only a few of the principal families, it is easy to see how two midwives would suffice : the nation thus gradually deprived of its natural leaders might be kept in servitude for an indefinite time. It is remarkable also that there is not a single instance on record of the decree having been carried out, and very probably not even one perished ; see note on Mat. 2. 16.

SHIPHRAH,] i.e. 'beauty,' see Ge. 49. 21 ; Ps. 16. 6 ; Job 26. 13 ; Da. 4. 2, 27 ; 6. 1.

PUAH,] i.e. 'crying ;' see Is. 42. 14. Gesenius refers it to an Arabic root signifying 'a mouth.'

16. CHILDREN.] There is no passage in the book of Exodus which has caused greater perplexity to interpreters than this ; suffice it to say, the only way apparently to make sense at all of the passage is to consider the original word as an Arabism, i.e. ABEN for BEN, a son or child, see note on Ge. 49. 24 ; 'stones,stools,basins,' &c. are all unmeaning or unexampled.

17. FEAR GOD.] Same phrase as in Ge. 22. 12 ; 42. 18 ; Ex. 1. 17, 21 ; 9. 30 ; 18. 21 ; Le. 19. 14, 32 ; 25. 17, 36, 43 ; De. 6. 13 ; 10. 12, 20 ; 14. 23 ; 17. 19 ; 25. 18 ; 31. 12, &c.

19. LIVELY,] or 'living,' i.e. full of life, vigorous ; the Talmud (Sotahs, fol. 11. 1,) supposes it spoken contemptuously : 'they are beasts' which require no midwives.

BEFORE...COMETH IN.] It is well-known that child-birth is much easier in savage than in civilized life ; in warm than in colder regions.

21. MAKETH FOR THEM HOUSEHOLDS,] i.e. increased their own families ; the pronoun 'them' is masculine in the original, and has been supposed to refer to 'the people' in v. 20 ; but these interchanges of gender are not unfrequent, see Ge. 31. 9 ; Ex. 2. 17 ; 11. 6 ; Ruth 1. 8, 9, 11, 22 ; Ju. 19. 24 ; 21. 22 ; 2 K. 18. 16 ; Is. 3. 16 ; Da. 8. 9 ; 2 Ch. 29. 3 ; 1 K. 22. 17 ; 2 Ch. 18. 3 ; 1 Sa. 31. 7 ; 1 Ch. 10. 7, and it more naturally refers to the midwives.

22. EVERY SON...CAST.] See note on v. 15.

THE RIVER,] i.e. the Nile, which nevertheless was worshipped, and its water drank as the greatest delicacy.

II, 1. A MAN,] named in 6. 18, 20, Amram, i.e. 'a high people.'

THE DAUGHTER OF LEVI.] The original is not 'a daughter,' but 'the daughter.' Several Jewish commentators maintain that she was 130 years of age when she bore Moses, which is incredible ; it is better to consider this Levi not as the patriarch of that name, but as his grandson, the intermediate subordinate links being often omitted in Scripture genealogies, as is universally admitted to have been the case with those in Matthew 1. 1—17, &c.

2. BEARETH A SON.] She had before this born Aaron and Miriam, but the narrative is so entirely taken up with this particular child, which was born probably a few days after the issue of the king's charge, that the others are unnoticed ; most if not all of the real difficulties of Scripture arise from the conciseness of the narrative ; this remark is applicable alike to the Old and the New Testaments.

FAIR,] lit. 'good,' but of course referring to physical, not moral beauty : compare same word in Ge. 6. 2 ; 24. 16 ; &c. applied alike to human beings, the irrational beasts, and to the inanimate creation. See also Luke 7. 20.

3. ARK.] Same word as that applied to Noah's vessel.

RUSHES,] as in Job 8. 11 ; Is. 18. 2 ; 35. 7, the only other instances of its occurrence ; its Hebrew name GOMA is derived from a root signifying 'to suck up, swallow,' found in Job 39. 24 ; Ge. 24. 27.

PITCH,] mentioned only elsewhere in Is. 34. 9 ; the bitumen within would protect the child from the water, the pitch without would prevent the water getting in.

WEEDS,] the Hebrew word SUPH is thought to be the Egyptian SARI, 'alga nilotica.'

4. SISTER.] Miriam, who was then about 10 years of age.

STATIONETH HERSELF,] as in Ex. 8. 20 ; 9. 13 ; 14. 13 ; 19. 17 ; 34. 5 ; Nu. 11. 16 ; 22. 22 ; 23. 3, 15 ; De. 7. 24 ; 9. 2 ; 11. 25 ; 31. 14.

AFAR OFF,] i.e. at a distance, being, doubtless, directed by the parents to do so.

5. A DAUGHTER,] not necessarily the only daughter ; Josephus, after tradition, calls her name Thermuthis.

COMETH DOWN] from the palace to the river's side.

TO BATHE,] as in Ex. 29. 4, 17 ; 30. 18, 19, 20, 21 ; 40. 12, 20, 30, 31, 32, &c.; the word never means 'to wash' clothes, as some suppose.

6. HATH PITY.] Same word as in De. 13. 8 ; 1 Sa. 15. 3, 9, 15, &c.

HEBREWS' CHILDREN,] distinguishing it from its dress, &c.; being also, probably, acquainted with the recently issued royal order.

7. HIS SISTER SAITH.] There was doubtless a great commotion among the female attendants, and Miriam took the opportunity of drawing near and accomplishing her ingenious stratagem for obtaining maternal care for the babe.

8. VIRGIN,] lit. 'concealed or hidden one ;' the word only occurs elsewhere in Ge. 24. 43 ; Ex. 2. 8 ; Ps. 68. 25 ; Song 1. 3 ; 6. 8.

Is. 7. 14; to which some add Pr. 30. 19, but see note thereon, where it is translated 'youth.'

9. HIRE,] as in 22. 15; Nu. 18. 31; De. 15. 18; 24. 15; Ge. 15. 1; 30. 18, 28, 32, 33; 31. 8, &c.

10. GROWETH,] *lit.* 'becometh great,' see v. 11; Nu. 14. 17; Ge. 19. 13; 21. 8, 20; 24. 35; 25. 27; 26. 13; 38. 11, 14; 41. 40; 48. 19, &c.

BRINGETH HIM.] when he was weaned, which is generally at the age of two years in the East.

SON,] i.e. an adopted one.

MOSES,] from a root signifying 'to draw out,' as explained in this verse, and found in 2 Sa. 22. 17, and in Ps. 18. 16; the verb occurs nowhere else. By some it is supposed to be an Egyptian word, '*mo*, water, and *uses*, one rescued.'

11. IN THOSE DAYS,] when Moses was 40 years of age, see Acts 7. 23.

HIS BRETHREN,] the Israelites; knowing them to be such from common report, or from his adopted or his real mother.

LOOKETH ON,] as in Ex. 1. 16; Le. 13. 3; Ge. 21. 16; 34. 1; 44. 34, &c.

BURDENS,] as in Ex. 1. 11; 2. 11; 5. 4, 5; 6. 6, 7.

SMITING,] probably the Egyptian was one of the exactors who in 5. 16, are represented as acting thus to the Israelites; the smiting was probably though not necessarily fatal; compare the use of the word in Ge. 36. 35; Ex. 7. 17; 21. 12, 15, 19; Le. 24. 18, 21; Nu. 35. 11, 15, 21, 24, 30; De. 25. 11; 27. 24, &c.

12. TURNETH] his face, as the word literally means.

HITHER...THITHER,] see same phrase in Nu. 11. 31.

SMITETH,] same word as in v. 11, but here evidently fatal, as the next clause shows, as well as v. 14.

SAND] of the sea, on the border of which he may have been, or of some desert spot.

13. STRIVING,] as in 21. 22; Le. 24. 10; Nu. 26. 9; De. 25. 11; 2 Sa. 14. 6; Ps. 60.

WRONG-DOER,] *lit.* 'wicked one;' the word does not necessarily imply *moral* guilt, but simply that the party so called was 'wrong' in his plea or cause; in a court of law the party who lost his case was *legally* 'wicked,' and 'declared wicked' or condemned by the judge, see Ex. 22. 8; De. 25. 1, 2, &c., Ex. 2. 13; 9. 27; 23. 1, 7; Nu. 16. 26; 35. 31, &c.

NEIGHBOUR,] i.e. friend, companion, fellow.

14. SET,] as in 3. 22; 4. 11, 15, 21; 5. 14; 8. 12, 23; 9. 21, &c.

SAYING.] The original word never signifies to intend,' as the Common Version renders it.

FEAR...] In Hebrews 11, 27 it is said he was 'not afraid of the wrath of the king,' but the reference there is not to the present transaction, but to the final departure out of Israel.

15. TO SLAY MOSES] as a murderer, and as likely to set up an example of insurrection.

DWELLETH...DWELLETH.] The two words being the same in the original, ought not to be varied in the translation as the C. V. has done, viz. 'dwelt..sat down;' how long he dwelt in Midian before he dwelt in the vicinity of the well, is not stated; his marriage was probably late in life, as his children on his return to Egypt (4. 25) appear to have been quite young.

16. A PRIEST,] not necessarily or naturally 'the priest;' it is impossible to ascertain whether the word is to be taken in its common or in its more restricted application, i.e. priest *or* prince; it is probable he was an idolator.

SEVEN DAUGHTERS.] Romanism is, perhaps, the only religious society that has prohibited the marriage of priests.

TO WATER.] Compare the parallel example of Rebekah and Rachel.

17. THE SHEPHERDS.] Though Orientals are generally very polite to each other, they are not so much so to females, who are generally looked down upon by the male part of the population; only in Christian countries do the sex stand on a higher level.

DRIVE THEM AWAY.] The pronoun 'them' in Hebrew is masculine, and does not perhaps so much apply to the shepherdesses as to the flock.

SAVETH.] This is the first instance of the occurrence of this verb; it is only found elsewhere in the Pentateuch in 14. 30; Nu. 10. 9; De. 20. 4; 22. 27; 28. 29, 31; 33. 29, in all of which it is confined to temporal deliverances; compare note on Ge. 49. 18.

WATERETH THEIR FLOCK,] as Jacob did Rachel's.

18. REUEL,] i.e. 'friend of God;' he is called in 3. 1; 4. 18, 'Jethro,' and in Nu. 10. 29, 'Hobab son of Reuel;' the easiest way to explain the seeming difficulty is to suppose he had more than one name, like Abram, Sarai, Jacob, Esau, Solomon, &c.

COME IN] hastily, as their father's question indicates; compare the conduct of Rebekah and Rachel, glad to tell the news, and to introduce the stranger who had befriended them.

19. AN EGYPTIAN,] judging from Moses' dress, language, &c.

THE SHEPHERDS.] The language here is such as would lead to the belief that this was not the first time they had been ill-treated by the shepherds.

20. EAT BREAD,] i.e. take food.

21. IS WILLING,] i.e. desirous; the original word expresses much more than the 'content' of the Common Version; compare its use in Ge. 18. 27, 31; De. 1. 5; Jo. 7. 7; 17. 12, &c.

ZIPPORAH,] i.e. 'a bird.'

22. GERSHOM,] i.e. 'a sojourner there.'

23. DIETH...SIGH.] The death of the king produced no relief to the suffering Israelites; but man's extremity is God's opportunity.

CRY GOETH UP,] as in Ge. 18. 20, 21; 19. 13; 5. 12; 2 Sa. 22. 7; Ps. 18. 6; 34. 15; 39. 12; 40. 1; 102. 1; 145. 19; Je. 8. 19; La. 3. 56.

24. COVENANT.] Se. Ge. 12. 7; 13. 15; 15. 18; 17. 8; 24. 7; 26. 3, 4.

25. GOD KNOWETH.] See note on 6. 2.

III. 1. FEEDING THE FLOCK,] as did Abel, Joseph, David, &c.

THE WILDERNESS,] in the neighbourhood of Sinai; it has been already remarked (Ge. 14. 6) that the word does not denote a positive desert, but simply a comparatively uninhabited place.

MOUNT OF GOD,] i.e. 'Horeb;' so called by anticipation, because the glory and law of God were there displayed; only ignorance of Hebrew idiom could translate or explain it as 'a very high mountain.'

2. MESSENGER OF JEHOVAH,] who in v. 4 is called 'Jehovah,' and 'God;' in v. 6, 'God of Abraham, God of Isaac, and God of Jacob;' compare Ge. 16. 7, 9, 10, 11; 22. 11, 15, &c.

FLAME,] lit. a 'heart,' i.e. in the centre of the fire; so Rashi, Eben Ezra, &c.; it is more probably a scribe's error; see true form in Nu. 21. 28.

FIRE,] which from the earliest ages was a symbol of the Divine presence.

BUSH,] thorn-bush which grows abundantly about Sinai; the Septuagint renders it 'bramble,' which Pococke says is not found in the neighbourhood of Horeb.

CONSUMED,] referred to again in De. 33. 16; Mark 12. 26; Acts 7. 30, 35.

3. I PRAY THEE.] The particle NA, though often translated 'now' in the Common Version, is always a particle of respectful request; he spake, doubtless, to his attendant friends who were assisting him.

WHEREFORE?] The Hebrew particle is always interrogative; he had probably been viewing it for some time.

4. JEHOVAH...GOD.] These words are here so clearly interchangeable that the notion of some writers that they are always used strictly according to their meaning, as pointing out special qualities in the Divine Being, is only equalled in absurdity by those who consider their use as characteristic of Jehovistic and Elohistic writers.

MOSES.] In Ex. 33. 12, 17, God says that He knew him 'by name;' Abraham, Hagar, and Jacob were also thus addressed, see Ge. 16. 8; 21. 17; 22. 11; 31. 11, &c.

HERE AM I,] an expression of readiness, Ge. 22. 1, 7, 11; 27. 1, 18; 31. 11; 37. 13; 46. 2; Ex. 3. 4; 1 Sa. 3. 4, 5, 6, 8, 16; 2 Sa. 1. 7; 15. 26; Is. 6. 8, &c.

5. CAST THY SHOES FROM OFF THY FEET.] Compare Jo. 5. 15. an Eastern mode of expressing respect to God or man, precisely equivalent to our uncovering the head: in entering a temple, synagogue, or dwelling, it would be as disrespectful for an Oriental to remove his head-dress as a European would deem it to keep it on; in praying they invariably keep their heads covered, which Gill thinks 'a superstition!'

6. THY FATHER,] viz. Amram; Kalisch unnecessarily translates it, 'thy fathers,' in the plural.

GOD OF ABRAHAM, ETC.] This passage is quoted in Mark 12. 26, 27, to prove an after-life.

HIDETH HIS FACE,] as did Elijah (1 K. 19 13,) by covering it up with his mantle, because of the Divine brightness, and from the general belief that no one could see God and live.

7. CERTAINLY SEEN,] lit. 'seeing—I have seen;' implying both its certainty and its thoroughness.

EXACTORS,] who were Egyptians, see 5. 6, &c.

PAINS,] as the word always means, see Ge. 34. 25; Job 2. 13; 14. 22; 5. 18; 16. 6; 33. 19; &c., 'because of this I go down.'

8. GO DOWN,] as in Ge. 11. 5, 7; 18. 21; 46. 4; Ex. 3. 8; 19. 11; 18. 20; 34. 5; Nu. 11. 17, 25; 12. 5, &c.

THAT LAND,] i.e. of Goshen or of Egypt.

GOOD AND BROAD,] i.e. Canaan: its fertility has always been known and acknowledged; its length is 160 miles, its breadth 46 (in some places 60 miles) from the Jordan to the Great Sea. See Ne. 9. 35.

FLOWING WITH MILK AND HONEY,] a phrase expressive of abundance of those things which are dainties for pastoral tribes.

CANAANITE, ETC.] Compare Ge. 15. 18—21, where other four nations are enumerated.

9. CRY...HATH COME IN,] as in Ge. 18. 21; 1 Sa. 11. 16; Ex. 2. 23.

OPPRESSION,] as in De. 26. 7; Ex. 22. 21; 23. 9; Nu. 22. 25.

10. PHARAOH,] king of Egypt, for, as remarked already, it was a common name for the rulers of Egypt.

SONS OF ISRAEL,] the word 'sons' is not only the exact literal translation of the original, but is characteristic of the truly Eastern origin of Scripture, as the Orientals in speaking of a nation never think of its females at all.

11. WHO AM I?] a profound feeling of modesty is the best preparative for future actions; compare the language and conduct of Gideon, (Ju. 6. 15,) Samuel, (1 Sa. 16. 2,) Jonah, (1. 2,) Jeremiah, (1. 6,) &c.

12. BECAUSE I AM WITH THEE.] God does not answer the questions of Moses at all, but states why he should go, viz. that He was with him, and seeks to re-assure him by giving him a sign, which was, that they would serve God on this mount. This was a sign which required faith to be appreciated, just as did the sign of the birth of Immanuel to Ahaz and the house of David, (Is. 7. 14—16,) seven hundred and fifty years before the fulfilment.

13. NAME.] A name is that by which any person or thing is known and distinguished from anything else; the gods of the nations had all their specific names, and 'an unknown God' is treated very like a nonentity.

14. I AM THAT WHICH I AM,] i.e. incomprehensible; He declines giving his name to Moses, as He had before declined doing to Jacob, (Ge. 32. 29,) and afterwards to Manoah, (Ju. 13. 18.) In the next clause, however, He modifies the refusal so far as to select one of his characteristics, viz. existence, (by implication self-existence,) 'I AM.' The obvious lesson was: that He who was the

living and existing One was, and would always be, with them, to overcome all enemies, even the gods of Egypt, on which He afterwards promised to execute judgment (12. 12); but lest this might not suffice, he identifies himself with the God of their fathers—Jehovah ; a name known to Eve, (4. 1,) Noah, (9. 26,) Abraham, (14. 22,) Isaac, (26. 22,) Jacob, (32. 9,) Leah, (29. 32, 35,) Rachel, (30. 24,) and Laban, (30. 27.) See its appropriation by Jesus, John 8. 58.

15. NAME...MEMORIAL,] that by which I am known...that by which I cause myself to be remembered.

TO THE AGE...TO GENERATION—GENERATION,] which two clauses are evidently interchangeable.

16. ELDERS.] The word is literally descriptive of age, but it is evidently used in Scripture as an official title; state and court officials of Pharaoh are (in Ge. 50. 7) thus denominated ; and there can be no doubt but that the Israelites when in Egypt were under the leadership of an organized body of officials, whose existence and power were preserved in the national council—the Sanhedrim ; Ex. 6. 14, 25 ; 12. 21, &c.

18. THEY HAVE HEARKENED,] as we find they did in 4. 31 ; the past tense is here employed, according to the common idiom, to express the certainty of the thing; Kalisch unnecessarily resolves it into the 'omniscience of God.'

HEBREWS,] as in Ge. 14. 13 ; 39. 14 ; 40. 15 ; 41. 12 ; 43. 32 ; Ex. 2. 6, 11, 13 ; 3. 18 ; 5. 3 ; 7. 16 ; 9. 1, 13 ; 10. 3.

HATH MET,] as in Ge. 42. 29 ; 44. 19 ; De. 25. 18 ; Nu. 23. 3, 4, 15, 16 ; 2 Sa. 1. 6.

A JOURNEY OF THREE DAYS,] into the wilderness of Sinai, but they did not reach it till the third month of their going out of Egypt ; see 19. 1.

19. KNOWN.] Most unwarrantably does the Common Version translate 'sure,' which the original word never means.

21. EMPTY,] according to the promise in Ge. 15. 14.

22. ASKED.] The original word never signifies 'to borrow ;' and a knowledge or recollection of this might have saved many infidel objections, and antichristian evasions, and much dangerous morality ; sound grammatical and lexicographical principles are the best safeguards of Scripture and truth ; yet such is the power of tradition, that there is, perhaps, no Hebrew lexicon which does not give 'borrow' and 'lend' as the meaning of the word in some cases, e.g. Gesenius (among others) refers to Ex. 3. 22 ; 11. 2 ; 12. 35 ; 1 Sa. 1. 28 ; 2 K. 6. 5, as all signifying 'to borrow ;' and to 1 Sa. 2. 20, 'to lend.' The very slightest consideration bestowed on each of these passages as they are presented to the reader in the New Translation, shows the utter groundlessness of the supposition ; 'to ask, cause to ask, beg,' suit every passage.

SPOILED,] as in Ex. 12. 36 ; 2 Ch. 20. 25 ; in the only other instance of its occurrence in this (Peil) conjugation it means 'to deliver,' Ez. 14. 14 ; in the (Hiphil or)

causative conjugation it occurs in Ge. 31. 16, where it is used by Jacob's wives regarding God's 'taking' away Laban's substance, and giving it to Jacob.

IV. 1. AND IF] the supposition which Moses here makes requires 'What then ?' to be understood as an ellipsis at its close; the Septuagint has eán mē, 'if not ;' the Vulgate omits the particle entirely.

2. A ROD,] a shepherd's crook, or staff to lean on, as in Ge. 38. 18, 25 ; Ex. 4. 2, 4, 17, 20 ; 7. 9, 10, 12, 15, 17, 19, 20 ; 8. 5, 16, 17 ; 9. 23 ; 10. 13 ; 14. 16 ; in 17. 5, 9 ; 31. 2, 6 ; 35. 30, 34 ; 38. 22, 23, &c. it means 'a tribe.'

3. A SERPENT.] See note on Ge. 3. 1.

6. LEPROUS AS SNOW,] as in the case of Miriam, (Nu. 12. 10,) and Gehazi, (2 K. 5. 27) ; the excessive whiteness pointed out a very violent kind ; see Le. 13. 3. 4.

9. WATERS OF THE RIVER,] which were regarded as divine, being the first example of the way in which God would fulfil his promise of executing judgment on the gods of Egypt.

10. OH,] lit. perhaps, 'I pray thee ;' compare Ge. 43. 20 ; 44. 18 ; Ex. 4. 10, 13 ; Nu. 12. 11 ; Jo. 7. 8 ; Ju. 6. 13, 15 ; 13. 8 ; 1 Sa. 1. 26 ; 1 K. 3. 17, 26, being all the instances of its occurrence.

A MAN OF WORDS,] i.e. one accustomed or inclined to speak much.

SLOW...SLOW,] lit. 'heavy...heavy ;' applied, in Ge. 48. 10, to the eyes ; in Is. 59. 1, to the ears ; in Ex. 9. 7, to the mind ; in Ez. 3. 5, to a language.

11. APPOINTED,] lit. 'set,' as in Ex. 2. 24 ; 3. 22 ; 4. 11, 15, 21 ; 5. 14 ; 8. 12, 23 ; 9. 21 ; 10. 2 ; 15. 25, 26 ; 18. 21, &c.

OPEN,] as in Ge. 3. 5, 7 ; 21. 19 ; Job 14. 3 ; 27. 19 ; Ps. 146. 8 ; Pr. 20. 13 ; Is. 35. 5 ; 37. 17 ; 42. 7, 20 ; Je. 32. 19 ; 2 K. 6. 17, 20 ; 19. 16 ; 4. 35 ; 6. 17, 20 ; Da. 9. 18 ; Zec. 12. 4.

12. I AM WITH THY MOUTH,] 'and have directed thee that which thou speakest,' as in v. 15.

13. This obscure expression appears to point to a kind of belief that after all God would choose another messenger.

14. IS NOT AARON THY BROTHER—THE LEVITE ?] This, the strictly literal rendering, is preferable to that of the Common Version, or to that of Kalisch, viz. 'Do I not know Aaron the Levite thy brother, that he can speak well.'

AARON,] i.e. 'the shining one.'

THE LEVITE,] one of that tribe ; perhaps he had already become distinguished among his brethren.

HE SPEAKETH WELL.] The present (or so-called future) tense in Hebrew never should be rendered by 'can,' though it is done so in numerous instances in the Common Version, and (perhaps) in all translations, ancient and modern, save that executed by the present writer.

16. HE HATH SPOKEN.] The literal translation is infinitely preferable to that in the Common Version, 'he shall be thy spokesman.'

FOR GOD,] i.e. he will implicitly receive and obey thy directions in all things; Onkelos and Rashi weaken the sense unnecessarily by rendering it 'for a prince,' or civil magistrate; the word 'God' is never applied in the Old Testament to any but to the true God, and to those regarded as divine by the nations.

17. THE SIGNS] which God may enjoin on him.

18. JETHRO,] or 'Jether;' compare 'Geshem' and 'Geshmu,' in Je. 6. 1, 2, 6.

BRETHREN,] his father's family, not merely the nation of Israel, which he could scarcely doubt was yet 'alive.'

19. This verse seems out of its proper place, as do v. 21—23.

ALL...HAVE DIED.] Compare Mat. 2. 20, where a similar intimation is recorded.

20. THE ASS,] which along with the camel, was the principal beast for riding on; not a single ass, but the species is here meant.

21. I STRENGTHEN.] See note on Ge. 41.

13. Seven times (viz. 4. 21; 7. 3; 9. 12; 10. 1, 20, 27; 11. 10.) it is attributed to God, and seven times (viz. 7. 13. 22; 8. 11, 15, 28; 9. 7. 34,) to Pharaoh himself.

22. MY FIRST BORN,] as in Je. 31. 9; Ps. 89. 27.

23. THY FIRST BORN,] the fulfilment of which is found in 12. 29; 13. 15; Nu. 3. 13; 8. 17; 33. 4; Ps. 78. 51; 105. 36; 135. 8; 136. 10.

24. A LODGING PLACE.] See note on Ge. 42.

27; from v. 27 it appears to have been at the very beginning of his journey.

MEETETH.] Same word as in Ge. 32. 17; 33. 8; Ex. 4. 24, 27; Job 5. 14.

TO PUT HIM TO DEATH,] probably because of his having neglected circumcising his (infant) son to please his wife; he was now about to call Egypt and Israel to obey the command of God, and it behoved him to set them an example.

25. A FLINT,] as in Ez. 3. 9, the only other instance of its occurrence. Compare Jo. 5. 2, 3.

CAUSETH TO TOUCH,] as in Ge. 28. 12; Ex. 4. 25; 12. 12; Le. 5. 7; Job 20. 6; Ps. 32. 6; 88. 3; 107. 18, &c.

HIS FEET,] i.e. the feet of Moses, not of his son, as some suppose.

A BRIDEGROOM OF BLOOD,] as in the phrase 'a man of blood,' Ps. 7. 5; 26. 9; 55. 24. For the word rendered 'bridegroom,' see Ge. 19. 12, 14; Ex. 3. 1; 4. 18, 25, 28; 18. 1—27; Nu. 10. 29; De. 27. 23; Ps. 19. 5; Is. 61. 10; 62. 5; Je. 7. 34; 16. 9; 25. 10; 33. 11; Joel 2. 16; unsupported and unnatural is the supposition that this phrase was applied to the child rather than to the father.

26. HE DESISTETH] from attempting to put him to death; for the use of the verb see Ex. 5. 8, 17; De. 4. 31; 9. 14; 31. 6, 8.

THE CIRCUMCISION.] As suggested above, the motherly tenderness of Zipporah appears to have exceeded her love to her husband or to his God, and Moses felt it his duty to send her back to her father, lest she should prove a stumbling-block to him.

27. MOUNT OF GOD,] i.e. Horeb, as in 3. 1.

28. WITH WHICH...WITH WHICH,] as in 2 Sa. 11. 22. not 'who...which.'

29. GOETH] to Goshen where Israel dwelt.

30. THE SIGNS] mentioned in v. 2—9, viz. turning the rod into a serpent, and the water into blood, and perhaps making Moses' hand leprous.

31. THEY HEAR.] Sept. 'they rejoice.'

BOW,] as in 12. 27; 34. 8; Nu. 22. 31, &c. in eleven passages the Common Version translates it, 'bow the head,' in two 'bow' simply, and in two 'stoop;' it is used both in reference to God and to man; in the present passage it is evidently to God.

V. 1. ENTERED] with the elders of Israel, according to the command of God, 3. 18; see also 5. 4.

PHARAOH,] whom some name 'Cenchres,' others 'Amenophis,' the last king of the Diospolitican dynasty.

THUS SAID.] This formula is unaccountably rendered in the Common Version uniformly 'saith,' in the present tense, though it is always in the past tense in the original.

JEHOVAH, GOD OF ISRAEL.] This is the first mention of Him as the national God of themselves and their fathers, especially of the patriarch Jacob.

SEND AWAY,] as the verb always signifies, requiring not merely passive acquiescence but active obedience.

A FEAST] or festival, this is the first instance of the occurrence of the word; it comes from a root signifying 'to go round, to move or dance in a circle;' it always denotes a religious festival, except (perhaps) in 1 Sa. 30. 16; in Ps. 107. 27, it is used in the sense of 'reeling to and fro.'

IN THE WILDERNESS.] It is worthy of notice, no mention is made of how long time they would require (as in v. 3) nor of any return to Egypt.

2. WHO IS JEHOVAH.] This shows that the Hebrews could not have got the name 'Jehovah' from the Egyptians, as some have maintained; Pharaoh was entirely ignorant of a deity of this name, and like the ancient heathens generally, he believed that each nation had its own god, whose power was confined to its own followers; compare the language of the kings of Syria, (1 K. 20. 23,) of Sennacherib, (2 K. 18. 33—35,) &c.

I DO NOT SEND AWAY.] This refusal was foretold in 3. 19.

3. GOD OF THE HEBREWS,] dropping the name 'Jehovah,' and the appellation 'Israel,' they use another name by which the nation has been known from the beginning (see note on Ge. 14. 3,) indicating also their trans-jordanic origin.

LEST HE MEET, ETC.] This is their own language, not God's.

4. FREE.] This is the first instance of the occurrence of this word in SS.; see again Ex. 32. 25 (twice,) Le. 10. 6; 13. 45; 21. 10 Nu. 5. 18: 6. 5; De. 32. 42; Ju. 5. 2; Pr. 1. 25; 4. 5; 8. 33; 13. 18; 15. 32; 29. 18; 2 Ch. 28. 19; Ex. 24. 14; 44. 20.

GO,] this is addressed not to Moses and Aaron, but to the elders who accompanied them into the presence of Pharaoh.

5. THE PEOPLE OF THE LAND,] i.e. of Goshen ; but there is perhaps something contemptuous in the phrase.

BURDENS,] as in 1. 11, and in the following verse.

6. EXACTORS.] See note on 3. 7 ; these were Egyptians, while the 'authorities' were Hebrews.

AUTHORITIES.] This word is in the Common Version rendered 20 times 'officer,' once 'ruler,' and once ' overseer ;' it occurs in v. 10, 14 ; Nu. 11. 16 ; De. 1. 15 ; 16. 18 ; 20. 5, 8, 9 ; 29. 10 ; 31. 28 ; Jo. 1. 10 ; 3. 2 ; 8. 33 ; 23. 3 ; 24. 1 ; 1 Ch. 23. 4 ; 26. 29 ; 27. 1 ; 2 Ch. 19. 11 ; 26. 11 ; 34. 13 ; Pr. 6. 7 ; it occurs in the Chaldee part of Daniel (7. 5) as an abstract noun 'authority,' which the Common Version renders 'side.'

7. STRAW FOR THE MAKING OF BRICKS] to render them firmer and stronger by being mixed with the clay.

8. PROPER QUANTITY.] The original word only occurs elsewhere in Ez. 45. 11 ; as a verb it means 'to weigh, measure,' and occurs in Job 28. 25 ; Ps. 75. 3 ; Is. 40. 12, 13 ; Pr. 16. 2 ; 21. 2 ; 24. 12 ; 1 Sa. 2. 3 ; 2 K. 12. 11 ; another derivative occurs in Ez. 23. 12 ; 43. 10. Compare also its use in Ez. 18. 25, 29 ; 33. 17, 20.

REMISS,] as in v. 17, the only other instance of the occurrence of this word, from a root signifying 'to be weak, feeble, to relax, let down.'

9. LET THE SERVICE BE HEAVY,] i.e. burdensome, as Rehoboam threatened his should be, compared with his father's.

LET THEM WORK AT IT,] as if they were mere beasts of burdens, designed like the Sudras of India for being servants to others.

DAZZLED,] by 'looking' intensely to the signs and words of Moses, as in Is. 32. 3.

WORDS OF FALSEHOOD,] as in 23. 7 ; Pr. 3. 5 ; Is. 32. 7 ; 59. 13 ; Je. 7. 4, 8 ; 29. 23.

11. FOR] not 'yet,' as in the Common Version ; it gives a reason for their going and seeking straw; so Sept. Rosenmuller, Mendelssohn, Cahen, &c.

12. THE PEOPLE] of Israel, who dwelt in Goshen, at least that portion of them who were impressed and compelled to serve a certain time (in rotation) in the public service, without receiving any or very little remuneration for it ; this forced labour is common even yet in Egypt,

STUBBLE.] In Eastern countries the reapers sometimes only cut off the heads of the ears of corn, and leave most of the stalk in the ground for a considerable time.

14. ARE BEATING.] Corporal punishment prevails in the East generally, to an extraordinary extent ; instead of fining or imprisoning an offender, he is bastinadoed on the spot, and all classes of the community are liable to this summary punishment. The monumental remains of Egypt exhibit the overseers with a rod, which they were not slow in using.

YOUR PORTION,] i.e. of work set apart and allotted to you, as in Pr. 3. 15 ; Le. 10. 13, 14, &c.

16. THY PEOPLE HATH SINNED.] The exactors are the cause of all this suffering, and this diminution of bricks by refusing to give us straw ; ignorant (or at least appearing to be so) that these were only carrying out Pharaoh's express orders.

17. REMISS...REMISS,] as in v. 8.

19. SEE THEM,] the people of Israel and themselves.

20. STANDING TO MEET THEM,] to know the result of their appeal to Pharaoh.

21. JEHOVAH LOOK...JUDGE.] It is perhaps better to adhere to the literal rendering of the words, ' Jehovah doth look upon you and doth judge,' taking the language not as a prayer or imprecation, but as a solemn warning to Moses and Aaron, who had been the means of bringing on them this distress by their promises, predictions, and signs.

CAUSED...TO STINK IN THE EYES.] This mingling of imagery is not uncommon in Hebrew, the use of the five senses are sometimes interchanged, e.g. Ec. 7. 1, 'sweet is the light,' Ex. 20. 15, 'seeing the voices,' &c.

A SWORD INTO THEIR HAND,] i.e. an occasion of exerting their power more tyrannically.

22. TURNETH BACK] to him who had sent him, to give an account of his mission.

WHY HAST THOU DONE EVIL.] As remarked before, what one permits to be done when he has power to prevent it, in Scripture language he is said to do ; in the very next clause Moses declares Pharaoh to have been the doer of the evil.

23. NOT AT ALL,] lit. 'delivering Thou hast not delivered.'

VI. 1. SEND THEM AWAY...CAST THEM OUT.] See the fulfilment in 12. 33.

3. AS GOD ALMIGHTY.] The Hebrew particle BETH, signifying 'in,' gives no sense whatever without some supplement such as 'the name of,' or 'the character of,' which ellipsis is unparalleled in SS. ; it is better to consider it a scribe's error for CAPH 'as,' the difference in shape of the two letters in Hebrew being often undistinguishable in MSS. and sometimes even in print. Gesenius maintains that BETH is often equivalent to CAPH in meaning, but none of the passages he quotes (Job 34. 36 ; 37. 10 ; Is. 44. 10 ; 48. 10 ; Ps. 37. 20 ; 39. 7 ; 102. 4 ; Zec. 10. 5 ; Ho. 10. 15,) are unchallengeable.

AS TO MY NAME JEHOVAH,] i.e. 'He (who) is ; the Existing One ; it is only by inference that it can be held to express eternity, either past or future ; present existence is the fundamental idea.

I HAVE NOT BEEN KNOWN.] The word 'known' is in SS. often used in the sense of 'appreciating, caring for, approving, experiencing,' as in Is. 53. 3, 'acquainted with sickness ;' Ps. 1. 6, 'Jehovah knoweth (i.e. approveth) the way of the righteous ;'

Ps. 9. 11, 'those who know (i.e. appreciate) Thy name;' Ge. 39. 6, 'he hath not known (cared for) anything.' Amos 3. 2, 'you only have I known (cared for) of all the nations of the earth.'

4. TO GIVE TO THEM.] See Ge. 17. 7, 8; 26. 3 ; 35. 12.

6. BROUGHT OUT...DELIVERED...REDEEMED.] It is not easy to give the exact force of each of these words whose general meaning is the same ; the first, is the mere general notion of deliverance, the second, rescuing from danger, and the third, of avenging and reclaiming.

STRETCHED OUT ARM,] pointing to vigorous exertions, and personal interference.

GREAT JUDGMENTS,] such as the ten plagues.

7. FOR A PEOPLE,] for his own people— his peculiar treasure, (19. 5.)

FOR GOD,] i.e. for your God, not in a general way only, but as a covenant God.

8. LIFTED UP MY HAND,] as men do in swearing ; see Ge. 22. 16—18 ; Nu. 14. 30 ; De. 32. 40.

A POSSESSION,] not 'heritage,' as Gesenius justly remarks on the verb.

9. ANGUISH,] lit. 'shortness of spirit.'

11. AND HE DOTH SEND,] renewing the promise formerly given him in Ex. 3. 20.

12. HOW DOTH PHARAOH,] reasoning from the greater to the less : if thine own people have not obeyed my voice, how can I expect Pharaoh, a heathen, to do it, knowing as I do my own inability and unsuitableness?

AND I OF UNCIRCUMCISED LIPS,] i.e. unsanctified, unhallowed, undedicated, unprepared lips ; that which is growing wild, untrained, is in Scripture language uncircumcised, e.g. applied to a vineyard, tree, ear, lip, heart, &c.

13—30.] These verses are somewhat abruptly introduced here for the evident purpose of bringing out the genealogy of Moses and Aaron, through Levi the third son of Jacob ; the historian thought it necessary to preface the genealogy by giving the heads of the families of Reuben and Simeon, Levi's elder brothers ; why the families of the remaining tribes are not given it is not easy to say.

14—16. On these names, see Ge. 46. 9, 10, 11, and notes thereon.

17. LIBNI...SHIMI.] See Nu. 3. 21.

18. Compare Nu. 26. 58, and 1 Ch. 6. 18.

KOHATH] is said by the Jewish chronologists to have died just 100 years before the departure out of Egypt.

19. Compare Nu. 3. 33.

20. HIS AUNT,] i.e. his father's sister, for according to Nu. 26. 59, she was daughter of Levi, and sister of Kohath ; but the Septuagint and Syriac read 'the daughter of the brother of his father,' i.e. his cousin. After 'Moses,' some Hebrew MSS. and the Samaritan, Septuagint, and Syriac Versions add, 'and Miriam.'

21. KORAH,] who afterwards rebelled against Moses, (Nu. 16. 1, &c.) and whose posterity is often mentioned in the titles of the Psalms.

22. MISHAEL, AND ELZAPHAN,] who bore away the dead bodies of Aaron's sons, Nadab and Abihu, (Le. 10. 4, 5.)

23. NAASHON,] prince of Judah, Nu. 11. 12.

FOR A WIFE.] Intermarriage among the tribes was not allowed, lest their inheritances should be confounded, but perhaps this law or custom was not then observed.

NADAB AND ABIHU,] whose transgression and punishment, for offering strange fire before the Lord, are mentioned in Le. 10. 4, 5.

ELEAZAR,] who succeeded his father Aaron in the priesthood, Nu. 20. 26.

25. PHINEHAS,] whose zeal for the Lord is noted in Nu. 25. 11.

26. This verse resumes the narrative broken off at v. 13.

VII. 1. A GOD TO PHARAOH,] i.e. one whom he will fear, and seek to propitiate.

THY PROPHET,] i.e. thy mouth-piece ; as already remarked, the Hebrew idea of a prophet is not that of one who foretells future events, but one who receives a revelation of God's will, and proclaims it to others. Aaron is to be in this position, to receive the directions of Moses, and to declare them to Pharaoh, as the following clause shows.

3. HARDEN.] Compare note on Ge. 41. 13 ; Ex. 3. 19 ; 4. 21, &c.

4. AND I HAVE PUT,] not 'that I may put,' as the Common Version has rendered it.

6. SO THEY HAVE DONE.) This sentence is emphatic ; they never appear henceforth to have murmured at the Divine command.

7. EIGHTY YEARS.] He was forty years of age when he fled from Pharaoh ; he had now been the same period in Midian ; compare Acts 7. 23, 30.

9. A WONDER,] to show by what power or authority you ask the dismissal of Israel.

THY ROD,] which is here, and elsewhere, called Aaron's rod ; yet was originally Moses', having it with him in the wilderness, where it had been turned into a serpent, and which he brought into Egypt, where, apparently, he had transferred it to Aaron as his assistant.

MONSTER,] so also in v. 10, 12 ; an entirely different word from that used in v. 15 ; see also note on Ge. 1. 21.

11. WISE MEN,] as in Ge. 41. 8.

SORCERERS,] as in 22. 18 ; De. 18. 10 ; Da. 2. 2 ; Mal. 3. 5 ; Je. 27. 9 ; 2 K. 9. 22 ; Is. 47. 9, 12 ; Mic. 5. 12 ; Na. 3. 4 ; 2 Ch. 33. 6. Derived by Gesenius from a root signifying 'to pray, mutter.'

SCRIBES.] See note on Ge. 41. 8. The Septuagint renders the word 'quacks,' the Vulgate 'sooth-sayers,' or 'evil-doers.' The names of two of them are preserved by tradition, viz. 'Jamnes and Jambres,' 2 Ti. 3. 18.

FLASHINGS.] From a root signifying 'to burn, flame,' e.g. Ge. 3. 24 ; De. 32. 22 ; Job 41. 21 ; Ps. 57. 4 ; 83. 14 ; 97. 3 ; 106. 18 ; 104. 4 ; Is. 42. 25 ; Joel 1. 19 ; 2. 3 ; Mal. 4. 1. Gesenius gratuitously renders it 'incantations.'

12. AND THEY BECOME MONSTERS] in appearance, in the eyes of the beholders; by their flashings they so dazzled the eyes of the spectators that the deception was not discovered till the rod of Aaron
SWALLOWETH THEIR RODS,] which significantly showed how weak their power and skill was in the presence of the ambassadors of the God of Israel; there can be little doubt but that the pretended rods were charmed serpents, trained to appear motionless, as is done in Egypt at the present day.
13. IS STRONG,] as in Ge. 41. 56; Ex. 7. 13, 22 8. 19; 9. 35; 12. 33; quite unwarranted is ;he rendering 'he hardened.'
AS THE LORD HATH SPOKEN,] in 3. 19.
14. HARD,] *lit.* 'heavy.'
SEND...AWAY.] See note on 3. 20.
15. TO THE WATER,] i.e. the Nile, on which God was about to put forth his hand in judgment on Egypt and on its gods; it being regarded by the Egyptians as divine, the Lord resolved to show that He was above them all, that the water which they loved so much could be made an object of aversion.
16. THOU HAST NOT HEARKENED,] not 'thou wouldst not hear,' as in the C. V.
17. BY THIS,] i.e. by means of this judgment which I now announce.
TURNED TO BLOOD,] as the water was afterwards made wine in John 2. 9. The poetical language of Joel 2. 31, (Heb. 3. 4,) where a similar phrase is used, cannot justly fix the meaning of plain prose; it is not said 'red as blood,' but 'to *or* into blood.' Pococke, Maillet, Thevenot, and others inform us that yearly in the month of July, owing to the prevalence of certain winds, (according to Maundrell,) the Nile assumes a reddish hue; but any mere natural or regular occurrence could never have had an influence on the mind of the Egyptians, or proved to them that Jehovah was superior to their own deities; neither do the fish die during the occurrence of this natural phenomenon, but they did during the existence of this plague, which must have added very much to the distress of the country generally, fish being extensively exported.
18. WEARIED,] as the original word signifies in every instance of its occurrence, viz. Ge. 19. 11; Job 4. 2, 5; Je. 6. 7; Ps. 68. 9; Pr. 26. 15; Is. 1. 14; 7. 13; 16. 12; 47. 13; Je. 6. 11; 9. 5; 12. 5; 16. 7; 20. 9; Ez. 24. 12; Mic. 6. 3. Mascrier says 'the Turks find it [the Nile water] so exquisitely charming, that they excite themselves to drink of it by eating salt.'
19. STREAMS...RIVERS...PONDS...COLLECTIONS OF WATERS,] the various arms and mouths of the Nile, canals, trenches, lakes, pools, reservoirs, and cisterns, all became blood, throughout all the land of Egypt, except Goshen.
22. SCRIBES...DO SO,] they imitate the actions of Aaron to produce blood; in all cases they could only increase the evil, not mitigate it; the true test of their power would have been to remove it

23. TURNETH..GOETH IN..SET HIS HEART,] a striking description of stubborn, brutal obstinacy.
25. This last verse is obviously the beginning of a new paragraph, not the conclusion of the preceding, as the Masorets have marked it.

VIII. 1. SAITH.] After the plague of blood had continued seven days to try their obstinacy; the annual discolouration of the Nile above referred to, lasts about twenty days.
SEND MY PEOPLE AWAY.] This is the third demand of the same kind, see 5. 1; 8. 1.
2. IF THOU ART REFUSING,] then: 'I am smiting,'the parallelism is very remarkable, compare Ps. 18. 26; 1 Sa. 22. 27.
THY BORDER,] thy territory.
FROGS.] Most unaccountably have some Jewish writers rendered 'crocodiles,' which could scarcely have got into a kneading-trough, as they are said to do so in v. 3. The word occurs only v. 3, 4, 5, 6, 7, 8, 9, 10, 12, 13; Ps. 78. 45; 105. 30, which two latter passages are only references to the present chapter, and cast no additional light on the subject. The Egyptian god Ptha is represented with a frog's head.
3. THINE OVENS.] Layard says of the Arabs, they make rude ovens by digging a hole about three feet deep, like a reversed funnel, plastered with mud, heated with brushwood within, stick the dough to the sides, and the bread is ready in two or three minutes.
THE RIVER,] i.e. the Nile; in v. 5, the plague is extended to streams, rivers, &c.
KNEADING TROUGHS,] as in 12. 34; De. 28. 5, 17.
6. THE FROG.] The word is here in the singular, being used collectively; they are numerous at all times in Egypt, but the miracle consisted in their prodigious number, coming up even on the bodies of the Egyptians, so that Pharaoh was softened by it for a time, while the scribes could only add to the evil, not remove it.
8. MAKE SUPPLICATION,] as in Ex. 25. 21 (twice,) Ex. 8. 8, 9, 28, 29, 30; 9. 28; 10. 17, 10; Job 22. 27; 33. 26, &c.
TURN ASIDE,] as in v. 31; 10. 17; 14. 25.
I SEND,] as had been often requested, 5. 1, 3; 7. 16; 8. 1.
9. BEAUTIFY THYSELF,] as in Ju. 7. 2; Is. 10. 15; 44. 23; 49. 3; 60. 21; 61. 3; the meaning evidently is, 'Take advantage of my leniency, and make thyself comely in the sight of God and Israel.'
WHEN,] *lit.* 'for when,' i.e. for what time; Moses asked this question that Pharaoh might see that the departure of the plague was no chance event, but one executed at a given appointed time.
REMAIN] as they had been accustomed to do, see also v. 11.
10. TO-MORROW,] *lit.* 'for to-morrow,' as in v, 9.
12. MOSES CRIETH.] The original word is expressive of distress and anguish, see Ex. 5. 8, 15; 8. 12; 14. 10, 15; 15. 25; 17. 4, &c.

D

13. COURTS,] as in 27. 9, 12, 13, 16, 17, 18, 19; 35. 7, 18; 38. 9, 15, 16, 17, 18, 20, 31; 39. 40; 40. 8, 33, &c., the courts in the interior of Eastern houses is meant; the Septuagint, Vulgate, &c. have 'villages,' as in the Common Version.

14. TOGETHER,] *lit.* 'heaps, heaps,' i.e. numerous heaps.

15. BREATHING,] as in the only other instance of its occurrence, La. 3. 56.

HARDENED HIS HEART,] as in 7. 14.

16. GNATS.] Pharaoh having broken his word receives no warning regarding this third plague, that of mosquito gnats, as the word is rendered by the Septuagint; the word occurs only in v. 17, 18; Ps. 105. 31, which is merely a reference to this chapter, and in Is. 51. 6, where the Common Version reads 'manner,' i.e. thus, so. In v. 17, 'the gnats are,' and in v. 18, the same expression is very strangely pointed by the Masorets 'their gnats are,' i.e. those of Moses and Aaron; the Samaritan gives the true form and meaning: Jonathan, Onkelos, &c. agree with the Common Version in rendering the word 'lice.' Syriac has 'creeping locusts.'

19. FINGER OF GOD,] i.e. a direct interference of the Most High; they do not however acknowledge 'Jehovah, the God of the Hebrews,' but simply Deity; in opposition to their own doings—doings of men. See the same phrase in 31. 18; De. 9. 10, where the writing of the Ten Matters is noted.

STRONG,] as in 7. 13.

20. GOING OUT TO THE WATERS,] as in 7. 15.

21. IF THOU ART NOT SENDING,] mark the consequence : 'lo, I am sending.'

THE BEETLE.] The Septuagint renders this 'dog-fly,' so Rosenmuller, De Wette, Gesenius, &c. ; Onkelos, Jonathan, Vulgate, and the Rabbies generally: 'a mixture of wild animals;' Kirby, 'the cockroach ;' Kalisch, 'the beetle,' as these attack man, fill and waste the land, and are said to be rapacious in Ps. 78. 45 ; see Ps. 105. 31, the only other place where the word occurs out of this chapter.

22. SEPARATED,] as in 9. 4 ; 11. 7 ; 33. 16; Ps. 4. 3 ; 17. 7 ; 139. 14 ; the Septuagint, Vulgate, and Jonathan : 'make wonderful.'

24. DOTH SO,] apparently without the intervention of Aaron and his rod.

CORRUPTED,] i.e. spoiled, as in Ex. 21. 26; 32. 7 ; 12. 23 ; Le. 19. 27 ; De. 4. 16, 25. 31 ; 9. 12, 26 ; 10. 10 ; 20. 19, 20 ; 31. 29 ; 32. 5 ; Ge. 6. 11, 12, 13, 17, &c.

25. IN THE LAND,] i.e. of Egypt.

26. THE ABOMINATION,] i.e. that which the Egyptians think unlawful to be offered in sacrifice, such as the cow, &c.

STONE US.] Diodorus Siculus reports that for killing a cat accidentally, a Roman ambassador was put to death in Egypt.

27. SAITH,] not 'command' as in the C. V.

28. GO NOT VERY FAR OFF,] knowing probably their attachment to Palestine, he fears they may take the opportunity.

MAKE SUPPLICATION,] as in v. 8 above, unabashed by his former broken promise.

29. I AM GOING OUT.] Though Moses was doubtful of the king's sincerity, he does not hesitate to comply with his request, knowing Jehovah's kindness, and pitying the sufferings of the miserable people for the obstinacy of their ruler, see Pr. 28. 15.

32. HARDENETH.] Illustrating the truth of the saying, Is. 26. 10, 'the wicked findeth favour—he hath not learned righteousness !'

IX. 1. HORSES...ASSES...CAMELS,] all of which are found sculptured on the Egyptian monuments, and their horses are noted in Ge. 48. 17 ; De. 48. 17.

3. PESTILENCE.] as in 9. 3, 15 ; Le. 26. 25 ; Nu. 14. 12 ; De. 28. 31, &c. This kind of plague is also very common in Egypt, but the miraculous character of the present one consisted in its aggravated character, its instantaneous operation, its sudden departure, and the exemption of the Israelites.

6. ALL THE CATTLE,] perhaps 'all *kinds of* cattle,' as in Ex. 35. 35, ' all *kinds of* work.'

7. HARD,] *lit.* 'heavy.'

8. SOOT.] This word only occurs elsewhere in v. 10 ; it comes from a root signifying 'to blow, breathe,' hence anything that may be blown about.

FURNACE,] as in v. 10 ; 19. 18 ; Ge. 19. 28, being all the instances of its occurrence.

SPRINKLED,] as in v. 10 ; 24. 6, 8 ; 29. 16, 20, &c.

9. SMALL DUST,] as in De. 28. 24 ; Is. 5. 24 ; 29. 5 ; Ez. 26. 10 ; Na. 1. 3 ; Song 3. 6.

BOIL.] See v. 10, 11 ; in De. 28. 27, called the 'boil of Egypt,' and in v. 35 it is said to be incurable ; the word occurs also in Le. 13. 18, 19, 20, 23 ; Hezekiah was afflicted with one, (2 K. 20. 7 ; Is. 38. 21 ;) and Job, (2. 7.)

BREAKING FORTH,] as in v. 10 ; Le. 13. 12, 20, 25, 39, 42, 57 ; 14. 43 ; Nu. 17. 5, 8, &c.

BLAINS.] The word occurs nowhere else in SS. except in next verse.

12. DOTH STRENGTHEN,] as in 4. 21 ; 9. 12 ; 14. 4.

13. RISE EARLY,] as in 8. 20 ; 9. 13 ; 19. 2 ; 24. 4 ; 32 ; 6 ; 34. 4, &c.

STATION THYSELF,] as in 2. 4 ; 8. 20 ; 9. 13 ; 14. 13 ; 19. 17 ; 34. 5, &c.

GOD OF THE HEBREWS,] as in 5. 3 ; 7. 16 ; 9. 1, 13 ; 10. 3, &c.

14. UNTO THY HEART,] not 'upon thy heart,' as in the Common Version.

ALL MY PLAGUES,] those past as well as those still coming : they were all touching what was dearest to Pharaoh, his gods, his land, his substance, his character, his person, and his family.

15. PESTILENCE,] as in 5. 3.

HIDDEN,] as in Job 4. 7 ; 15. 28 ; 22. 20 ; Ps. 69. 5 ; 139, 15 ; Ho. 5. 3 ; 2 Sa. 18. 13 ; Zec. 11. 9, 16. The obvious meaning is, that being smitten he would pass away, and be seen no more in the land of the living.

I HAVE PUT FORTH.] Most unnecessarily and unwarrantably is this translated by some, 'I *might have* stretched out;' surely ATTAH, 'now,' is not supposed to be a 'conversive' particle like the famous WAW; the very evident explanation is by the well-known and universally admitted Hebrew idiom, which uses the preterite to express a future action on the ground of its *certainty in the mind of the speaker*; on any other principle, the Hebrew text is what is vulgarly called a mere nose of wax, a man of straw, which may be turned any way the critics please, proving black to be white, and white to be black. Hebrew syntax requires to be wholly rewritten for the Hebrew grammars.

16. I HAVE CAUSED THEE TO STAND,] a phrase occurring nowhere else in Exodus; in Ge. 47. 7; Le. 14. 11; 16. 7, 10; 27. 8, 11; Nu. 3. 6; 5. 16, 18, 30; 8. 13; 11. 24; 27. 19, 22, which are all the other instances of its occurrence in the Pentateuch, it denotes 'to present' any thing or person before another; it evidently means here 'to set up,' as in Ne. 6. 1; 1 K. 15. 4; Pr. 29. 4.

TO SHOW THEE.] The Septuagint, Vulgate, &c. read 'to show *in* thee;' which is, to say the least, not a natural translation.

OF DECLARING,] actively, not of 'being declared' or 'being acknowledged,' as some have rendered it; compare Ps. 26. 7; 40. 5; 50. 16; 73. 28; 102. 21, &c.

NAME,] *or* 'renown.'

EARTH,] *or* 'land, i.e. of Egypt; yet, in effect, wherever the Gospel is preached there it is declared.

18. HAIL,] as in v. 19—34; 10. 5, 12, 15; Jo. 10. 11, &c. Hail is not uncommon in Egypt, but this plague was to be unprecedented for its severity—killing man and beast.

TO-MORROW,] the fifth day of the month of Abib.

BEING FOUNDED,] as a nation, compare v. 24.

19. STRENGTHEN.] The original word here (and in Is. 10. 31; Je. 4. 6; 6. 1,) is unnecessarily derived by some from a fictitious root, supposed to mean 'gather, or set in safety;' the ordinary use of the word is as in Pr. 7. 13; 21. 29; Ju. 3. 10: 6. 2; Ps. 9. 19; 52. 7; 89. 13; Pr. 8. 28; Ec. 7. 19; Is. 30. 2; Da. 11. 12.

HAVE DIED,] as in Jo. 10. 11.

20. FEARING,] from sore experience, the truth of Jehovah's threatenings.

HOUSES] prepared for them where they were feeding.

21. SET THE HEART,] i.e. disregarded, was careless or indifferent or unbelieving.

22. IN ALL THE LAND,] whereas generally even the most terrific natural showers are confined to a portion of a country.

23. VOICES,] which is the simplest Hebrew form of expressing 'thunders.'

GOETH] from the Lord towards the earth; in Nu. 22. 37; De. 2. 14; 2 Sa. 10. 11; 1 K. 13. 9, 17; Is. 60. 3, 14, &c. the word is translated 'come' in the Common Version.

24. CATCHING ITSELF,] as in Ez. 1. 4, the only other place where the same form of the original word occurs.

25. EVERY TREE,] with the vines, and the fig-trees, according to Ps. 78. 47; 105. 33.

26. NO HAIL,] and none of the other plagues of Egypt; one is taken and another left.

27. THIS TIME.] Unwilling even in his distress, to acknowledge his sins fully.

28. MAKE YE SUPPLICATION,] as formerly, in Ex. 8. 8, 28.

AND PLEAD,] *or* 'and multiply' your supplications; the conjunction *and*, cannot here possibly be rendered 'for,' as is done in the Common Version; the Masoretic punctuation RAB for RIB has confused the meaning.

VOICES OF GOD,] i.e. thunders.

29. THE CITY,] supposed to have been Zoan; see Ps. 78, 12, 43.

I SPREAD MY PALMS,] as in v. 33; compare 1 K. 8. 38, 54; 2 Ch. 6. 12, 13, 29; Ezra 9. 5; Job 11. 13; Ps. 44. 20; 88. 9; Pr. 31. 20; Is. 1. 15; Je. 4. 31; La. 2. 19; 3. 41.

30. NOT YET AFRAID.] They were indeed afraid, in a certain sense, but their fear was only a temporary one.

31. FLAX,] a staple commodity of ancient Egypt; the stalk is about three feet in height, and as thick as a cane.

BARLEY.] Pliny observes that Egypt yields two crops of barley, one in spring and one in autumn; it was used as food for man and beast, especially horses; many Arabs live almost exclusively on unleavened barley bread, so that the plague must have affected the very lowest class in the country.

32. RYE,] *or* 'spelt,' (which is mentioned elsewhere in SS. only in Is. 28. 25; Ez. 4. 9,) grows as high as the barley, and is extensively cultivated in various species.

LATE,] *lit.* 'dark,' they are about a month later than the barley.

33. POURED OUT,] as in 2 Sa. 21. 10; 2 Ch. 34. 21; Je. 7. 20; 42. 18; Ez. 22. 21; 24. 11; Na. 1. 6. Rain is so very uncommon in Egypt that Herodotus asserts 'it never rains in that country;' but this is a mistake; still it is so rare that the outpouring of the text must have alarmed them excessively. We see here the efficacy of prayer, as in the case of Elijah noticed in Jas. 5. 17, 18.

34. CONTINUETH,] *or* 'addeth' to sin, as in Ps. 78. 17; Ho. 13. 2.

35. BY THE HAND OF MOSES,] see 4. 21; 7. 3.

X. 1. DECLARED HARD.] See 3. 19; the causative (*or* Hiphil) form of the Hebrew verb is often simply permissive or declarative, as has been already repeatedly noticed, and as is universally admitted by all Biblical critics; see Ex. 23. 7; 22. 9; De. 25. 1; 2 Sa. 15. 4; Is. 29. 21; 1 K. 8. 32; Job 9. 20, &c.

2. THOU.] Moses being addressed as the representative man of his people : He who has given man a memory would have them to treasure up in it the dealings of His providence, whether in mercy, (De. 5. 15,) or in anger, (De. 8. 2, 3.)

3. SEND AWAY,] as in 9. 1, 13.

4. THE LOCUST.] which is about five inches in length, and has four wings, green or

yellow: see Joel 1. 1—2, 10, for a very graphic account of their ravages.

TO-MORROW,] which Usher reckons as the seventh of the month of Abib.

5. EYE OF THE LAND,] as in v. 15; Nu. 22. 5, 11; the evident meaning is, its 'aspect, appearance.'

AND NONE IS ABLE TO SEE IT.] Volney writes : 'Everybody, except an eye-witness, must deem the enormous quantity of these insects incredible ; the ground is covered with them for several leagues...everything green vanishes momentarily from the fields, as if a curtain were rolled up.'

7. SNARE,] as in Ex. 23. 33; 34. 12; De. 7. 16; Jo. 23. 13; Ju. 2. 3; 8. 27; 1 Sa. 18. 21, &c.

NOT YET,] as in Ge. 2. 5.

PERISHED,] as in Le. 26. 38; Nu. 16. 33 ; 17. 12; 21. 29, 30; De. 4. 26; 7. 20; 8. 19, 20; 11. 17; 22. 3; 26. 5; 30. 18; 32. 28; the seven plagues had spread devastation everywhere among high and low.

8. WHO AND WHO ?] The repeated interrogative points out the earnest anxiety of Pharaoh to know how far he could risk the escape of such a numerous band of bondsmen.

9. WITH OUR YOUNG...AGED...WE GO.] As Pharaoh's courage fails him, so that of Moses increases ; he fears not the wrath of the king, nor seeks to compromise with him, or to propitiate him by leaving some of his people or their substance behind. to secure the deliverance of the rest.

A FESTIVAL.] The original word, though generally rendered 'feast,' is an entirely different word from that which occurs in Ge. 19. 3, (on which see note), &c.; the latter is properly a 'drinking,' and is used of ordinary entertainments ; the former is used only of religious rejoicings, accompanied with eating and 'dancing,' the literal meaning of the word being 'to move in a circle,' (compare Ps. 107. 27,) so in v. 12, 14; 13. 6; 23. 15, 16, 18; 32. 5; 34. 18, 22, 25, &c.; according to De. 16. 10, 11, all the people, without exception, were required to observe their 'festivals.'

10. FOR EVIL IS BEFORE YOU,] i.e. you are running to destruction by going into the wilderness, as it is said in Ex. 14. 3. Very unnaturally do some interpret : 'see, that you have evil plans before you.'

11. MEN.] Same word in 12. 37; Nu. 24. 3, 15; De. 22. 5, &c. Pharaoh seemed to think that the females were not required to take any part in the service of God ; yet the demand was, 'Send My people away ;' Rabbanism has a somewhat similar notion, that no conceivable number of women can constitute a synagogue without the presence of at least 'ten men.'

12. LEFT.]See the threatening in v. 5 above.

13. THE EAST WIND,] i.e. from Arabia ; very unnecessarily does the Septuagint, De Dieu, Bochart, &c., suppose a south wind meant, from Ethiopia.

LIFTED UP,] as the word always signifies ; see Ex. 6. 8; 18. 22; 28. 12, 29, 30, 38; 35. 21, 26; 36. 2.

14. VERY GRIEVOUS,] from their numbers, as noted in Ps. 105. 34 ; locusts are not uncommon in Egypt, but this visitation was unparalleled in severity.

16. SINNED AGAINST JEHOVAH YOUR GOD AND AGAINST YOU.] This humble confession is in words not unlike that of the repentant prodigal, Luke 15. 18, 21 ; but the expression 'your God,' points out the distance between Moses and Pharaoh.

17. BEAR WITH,] or 'lift up,' as in Ge. 13. 14 ; 21. 18; 27. 3; 31. 12; 50. 17; Le. 10. 4, &c.

THIS DEATH,] i.e. deadly pestilence of the locusts.

19. WEST WIND,] lit. 'sea-wind ;' the Mediterranean forming the western boundary of Palestine, the locusts were carried back again to whence they came, towards Arabia, and most of them perished in the Red Sea ; it is probable, however, that the 'sea wind' here mentioned may have been from an Egyptian point of view—north-west.

BLOWETH,] as in Nu. 10. 3, 4, 5, 6, 7, 8, 10, &c. ; very absurdly rendered by some, 'fixed' them in the sea.

RED SEA,] lit. 'Sea of Suph ;' so called after the name of some Egyptian king : there is really no foundation whatever for the idea that the name was derived from the abundance of 'weeds' (see Ex. 2, 3, 5) which grew in it ; it has no more weeds than any other inland sea. 'Red' is, of course, a translation of 'Edom,' whose descendants were the leading tribe or nation on its Arabian side, from whom it derived the appellation, 'Sea of Edom.'

NOT ONE LOCUST,] so that the removal was as miraculous as their bringing in.

20. JEHOVAH STRENGTHENETH.] See note on 3. 19; 4. 21.

21. DARKNESS.] This plague, like most, if not all of the preceding ones, was not uncommon in Egypt, only far more intense and sudden in its occurrence, while the land of Goshen was entirely exempt from the visitation. 'Where the Chamsin [or Samum] blows, the sun has a pale yellow colour ; his light is veiled, and darkness reaches sometimes such a degree, that it appears to be the most gloomy night, as we experienced it, about the middle of the day, at Kene, a city of the Said.'—Du Bois Ayme. Cicero (de Nat. Deor. ii. 96) says, that after an eruption of Etna, there was such darkness, that for 'two days no man could recognize any other person.'

DARKNESS IS FELT,] being so intense : see the use of the word in Ge. 27. 12, 21, 22 ; 31. 34, 37; Ex. 10. 21; De. 28. 29; Ju. 16. 26 ; Job 5. 14; 12. 25 ; Ps. 115. 7.

22. THICK,] lit. 'darkness,' as in De. 28. 29. The two synonymous nouns point out the 'dense' darkness.

24. STAYED,] lit. 'set, or set up,' as in Ge. 30. 38; 33. 15; 43. 9; 47. 2 ; De. 28. 56, &c.; this proposal was doubtless intended to prevent the Israelites from departing wholly from Egypt; the cattle were a kind of pledge for their return, as without these such a multitude would be distressed for want of food.

26. THERE IS NOT LEFT A HOOF,] i.e. even the most worthless of the herd and flock is taken with us.

27. JEHOVAH STRENGTHENETH.] See note on Ex. 3. 17; 4. 21, &c.

NOT WILLING.] Same word in De. 1. 26; 2. 30; 10. 10; 23. 5; 25. 7, &c. Except in Is. 1. 19, and Job 39. 9, this verb is always accompanied by a negative, as here.

29. RIGHTLY.] See note on Ge. 1. 7; Moses takes him at his word, but before leaving Pharaoh, proclaims the last and greatest plague of all, which was to come, being assured of its complete success; and he departs to see him no more, for there is no proof that Moses obeyed the summons recorded in 12. 31.

XI. 2. ASK.] See note on 3. 22; by 'asking or demanding' what things were necessary, they were prepared to start immediately.

VESSELS.] The original word means 'goods, instruments, implements' of any kind, rings, bracelets, necklaces, jars, cups, &c.

3. VERY GREAT,] from the signs and wonders he had performed.

5. MILL-STONES.] The original word is always in the old plural form, e.g. Nu. 11. 8; De. 24. 6; Is. 47. 2; Je. 25. 10; this occupation was principally followed by females, (Mat. 24. 21,) and those of the lowest order.

6. A GREAT CRY.] The Easterns think it necessary to make such lamentation at a death, that they hire persons to take a share in the crying and howling; the death of a firstborn is, of course, peculiarly distressing; compare Zec. 12. 10.

7. A DOG.] The word here is evidently used contemptuously, as in 1 Sa. 17. 43; 24. 14; 2 Sa. 2. 3; 9. 8; 16. 9; 2 K. 8. 13; Ps. 22. 16, 20; Is. 56. 10, 11; also Mat. 7. 6; Phil. 3. 2; Rev. 22. 15.

SHARPENETH NOT.] See the use of the original word in 2 Sa. 5. 24; Jo. 10. 21; 1 K. 20. 40.

8. COME DOWN] from the palace of Pharaoh, built, it may be, on an eminence.

AT THY FEET.] Compare De. 11. 6; Ju. 8. 5; 1 Sa. 25. 27, 42; 2 Sa. 15. 16, 17, 18; 1 K. 20. 10; 2 K. 3. 9.

HEAT OF ANGER,] as Jonathan did with Saul, 1 Sa. 20. 34; as the Israelites did with Amaziah, 2 Ch. 25. 10; see also De. 29. 24; Is. 7. 4; La. 2. 3. It must be acknowledged that while Moses was undoubtedly 'meek,' he was not less distinguished for warm zeal; see his slaying the Egyptian; his anger at Pharaoh; his impatience at the rock, &c.

XII 2. THIS MONTH,) i.e. Abib (13. 4; 23. 15) or Nisan, (Nah. 2. 1; Est. 3. 7.)

THE CHIEF OF MONTHS,] i.e. the head or principal one, not 'the beginning,' Oth.... the next clause would be superfluous.

3. COMPANY.) The first instance of the occurrence of this word, which literally means 'an appointed meeting;' it is rendered in the Common Version 121 times congregation, 13 times company, 9 times assembly, once multitude, once swarm, once people. It is applied to all Israel, to the followers of Korah, to a band of wicked men, (Ps. 22. 17,) and to a swarm of bees, (Ju. 14. 8.)

EACH MAN,) who was an householder.

A LAMB.) The Hebrew word denotes equally the young of a sheep or of a goat; see v. 5; and De. 14. 4. The animal chosen must be 1) perfect, 2) a male, 3) not exceeding a year old.

6. WHOLE ASSEMBLY OF THE COMPANY OF ISRAEL.] Every member was allowed to kill the passover for himself and his household, independently of priests and Levites, each one being a 'priest' in the sight of God; compare Rev. 20. 6.

BETWEEN THE EVENINGS.] The Jews are said to have reckoned two evenings, the first from the beginning of sunset, i.e. from four till six p.m. the second from six till about eight o'clock; the only other opinion worthy of notice is, that as the day was reckoned from sunset to sunset, the passage means that they were to slaughter the paschal-sacrifice any time between the sunset when the 14th day commenced, and the sunset with which it ended—a period of 24 hours.

7. SIDE POSTS,] as in v. 22, 23; 21. 6; to which the ear of the willing servant was to be bored, (21. 6,) on which they were to write the words of God, (De. 6. 9; 11. 20.)

LINTEL,] which is mentioned only in v. 22, 23 of this chapter.

8. ROAST WITH FIRE,] because thus prepared sooner than if boiled; other sanctified things were allowed to be boiled, 2 Ch. 35. 13.

UNLEAVENED THINGS.] The plural form points to the various forms into which the dough was moulded, thin, round cakes, &c.; these were to be eaten for seven days, leaven being considered a sign of corruption.

BITTERS,] as in Nu. 9. 11; La. 3. 15, the only other instances of its occurrence; there is nothing to limit it to 'herbs,' as in the Common Version.

9. RAW,] as the word is rendered in most versions; it occurs nowhere else in SS.

HEAD...LEGS...INWARDS,] i.e. all of it was to be sanctified, it was to be a whole sacrifice.

INWARDS,] as in Ex. 29. 13, 17, 22, &c.

10. NOT LEAVE OF IT,] lest it should become corrupted, being a holy thing.

BURN,] that it might not be retained as a superstitious relic.

11. LOINS GIRDED,] as in readiness for a journey or for action; the long flowing dress of an Oriental is quite unsuitable for active exertion; it must be tucked up and fastened round the waist with a girdle before he is fit for service; 2 K. 4. 29; 9. 1; Je. 1. 17; and Eph. 6. 14.

SANDALS,] which were seldom worn in the house, being reserved for the roads and streets, Jo. 9. 5, 13.

IN HASTE,] as in De. 16. 3; Is. 52. 12, the only other instances of its occurrence.

PASSOVER,] i.e. a 'passing over,' as explained in v. 13; see the use of the verb in v. 23, 27; 1 K. 18. 21, 26; (2 Sa. 4. 4;) Is. 31. 5.

12. EVERY FIRST-BORN,] as had been previously declared to Pharaoh, (11. 5.)

ALL THE GODS OF EGYPT,] by destroying their votaries and their reputation.

13. FOR YOU,] i.e. in your behalf, not ' to you,' as in the Common Version.

FOR DESTRUCTION.] as in 2 K. 23. 13; 2 Ch. 20. 23; 22. 4; Je. 5. 26; 51. 25; Ez. 5. 16; 9. 6; 21. 31; 25. 15; Da. 10. 8, being all the instances of its occurrence.

14. A MEMORIAL,] as in 13. 9; 17. 14; 28. 12, 29; 30. 16; 39. 7, &c.

AGE-DURING,] see note on Ge. 3. 22; 17. 7, &c.

15. CUT OFF.] See note on Ge. 17. 14.

16. CONVOCATION,] as in Le. 23. 2, 3, 4, 7, 8, 21, 24, 27, 35, 36, 37; Nu. 10. 2; 28. 18, 25, 26; 29. 1, 7, 12; Ne. 8. 8; Is. 1. 13; 4. 5; *lit.* ' a calling together.'

17. HOSTS.] See note on Ge. 2. 1.

19. NATIVES,] as in v. 48, 49; Le. 16. 29; 17. 15; 18. 26; 19. 34; 23. 42; 24. 16, 22; Nu. 9. 14; 15. 13, 29, 30; Jo. 8. 33; Ps. 37. 35; Ez. 47. 22, being all the instances of its occurrence, from a root signifying ' to rise,' see Ge. 32. 31; Ex. 22. 3; it means of course, Israelites born in Palestine, as distinguished from those born in other countries, and only sojourning for a time in that land.

21. DRAW OUT,] as in Ge. 37. 28; Ex. 12. 21; 19. 13; De. 21. 3, &c.

FLOCK,] not ' a lamb,' as in the Common Version, which the word never means; compare Ge. 4. 2; Ex. 2. 16, 17, 19; 3. 1; 9. 3; 10. 9, 24; 12. 21, 32, 38, &c.

PASSOVER-SACRIFICE,] as in De. 16. 2, 5, 6; 2 Ch. 30. 15, 17, 18; 35. 1, 6, 7, 8, 9, 11, 13; Ezra 6. 20.

22. A BUNCH,] as in 2 Sa. 2. 25; Is. 58. 6; Amos 9. 6, all the instances of its occurrence.

HYSSOP,] as in Le. 14. 4, 6, 49,. 51, 52; Nu. 19. 6, 18; 1 K. 4. 33; Ps. 51. 7; what particular herb is here meant is uncertain, whether mint, origanum, majoram, rosemary, &c. Boyle says ' the caper-plant;' Hazelquist ' a small red moss;' Kalisch, ' a species of origanum.'

BASIN,] as the word is rendered in 2 Sa. 17. 28; 1 K. 7. 50; 2 K. 12. 14; Je. 52. 19; Zec. 12. 2; in every other instance of its occurrence it is rendered ' threshold, door, gate, post,' (Ju. 19. 27, &c.) and it is so rendered in the present verse by the Septuagint, but improperly.

23. DESTRUCTION,] as in v. 13; Sept. Onk. and Vulg., have ' destroyer;' Jer. Targ. the destroying angel.

27. A SACRIFICE,] being not merely a commemorative ordinance, but an expiatory offering, the only one, indeed, which an Israelite was able to offer without the intervention of a priest.

BOW AND DO OBEISANCE,] indicating their concurrence and submission to the injunction.

29. AT MIDNIGHT] of the 15th day of Abib or Nisan, when they were asleep,

unsuspecting danger; compare Job 34. 20; Mat. 25. 5, 6; 1 Th. 5. 2, 3.

CAPTIVE.] The original word always denotes one taken captive in war, as in Nu. 21. 1; 31. 12, &c.; in 11. 5, the threatening reached to the ' maid-servant who is behind the millstones ;' from Ju. 16. 21, it appears to have been the custom to employ prisoners in the work of grinding.

BEASTS,] which, being reckoned by the Egyptians as divine, were cut off to fulfil the promise given, ' On all the gods of Egypt I do judgment,' in 11. 12.

30. NOT A HOUSE,] which contained a first-born, but the word ' first-born' in Ps. 89. 27, &c. is used figuratively for the ' most eminent.'

31. CALLETH FOR MOSES,] sending messengers to him with a message, for there is no reason to suppose that Moses came to him after what he said in 10. 29; compare also 11. 8.

RISE, GO OUT,] as in Ge. 19. 14; 31. 13, &c., fulfilling to the letter the language of Moses to Pharaoh in 11. 8.

32. AND GO] as in the wilderness; all without limitation are permitted, also all that they have.

BLESSED ALSO ME.] Most translators and interpreters understand this, ' pray for me ;' but the word is never used in this sense; the meaning appears to be that by their departure they were conferring a blessing on him as well as on the Egyptians.

33. THE EGYPTIANS ARE URGENT,] *lit.* ' Egypt is strong *or* hard ' upon the Israelites, by arguments, entreaties, gifts, &c.

34. DOUGH,] as in v. 39; 2 Sa. 13. 8; Je. 7. 18; Ho. 7. 4; from a root signifying to swell, found in De. 8. 4; Ne. 9. 21.

BOUND UP,] as in 1 Sa. 25. 29; 2 Sa. 20. 3; Ho. 13. 12.

35. WORD OF MOSES,] in 3. 22, and 11. 2, 3. ASK.] See note on 3. 22, &c.

36. CAUSE THEM TO ASK.] This is the literal and only true translation of the phrase; totally gratuitous and unfounded is the rendering of some, ' they gave them gladly,' which the verb cannot possibly mean. The simple form of the verb is ' to ask *or* to demand,' the causative (*or* Hiphil form) here used can only mean ' cause to ask :' the meaning is, the Egyptians cause the Israelites to ask whatever things they want for their journey, that they may be quit of their presence. Compare 1 Sa. 1. 28, the only other place where this Hiphil conjugation occurs, ' I have caused him to be asked.'

SPOILED,] as in Ex. 3. 22, (on which see note,) Ge. 15. 14.

37. RAMESES.] See note on Ge. 47. 11; Ex. 1. 11; Nu. 33. 3, 5.

SUCCOTH.] See Ex. 13. 20; Nu. 33. 5, 6, &c., not to be confounded with the place on this east of the Jordan, and south of the Sea of Galilee, where Jacob pitched his tent, (Ge. 33. 17,) afterwards in the territory of the tribe of Gad, (Jo. 13. 27; Ju. 8. 5—7, 14—16.) The Succoth mentioned in the text was, of course, in Egypt, supposed to be about eight miles from Rameses (or Raamses); the name is probably used by anticipation.

37. SIX HUNDRED THOUSAND MEN,] see Ex. 38. 16; Nu. 1. 46; 11. 21, where the same number is given. Very unreasonable have been the doubts cast on this number by Colenso and others, and equally so are some attempted solutions of the supposed difficulty; e.g. it has been said that the Hebrews used their letters as numerals, thus, *a* 1, *b* 2, &c.; many of the Hebrew letters being alike, there might be simply a scribe's error. But, ingenious as this is, there is not the slightest historical proof that the Hebrews before the Christian era, ever expressed their numbers in any other way than in *words*, as we find in all Hebrew MSS. There is not a single instance of the kind in the whole of the Old Testament; there are a few in the New Testament, viz. in Rev. 7. 4—8, and 13. 18.

A second unwarrantable mode of explaining the increase is to assert that, 'among the Hebrews, like the other Eastern nations, polygamy was the rule;' this is directly contrary to fact; so far from polygamy being the rule anywhere, it is and always has been the exception; the Koran allows four wives, but at least nineteen out of every twenty Musselmans have only one; so also among the Hindoos. It is clear from the number of male and female births being everywhere essentially equal, that universal and general polygamy is simply impossible.

The company of 70 persons who went down to Egypt (Ge. 46. 27) were undoubtedly accompanied by a numerous band of followers to watch their flocks and herds—all *circumcised*, (according to the law, Ge. 17. 12,) bearing the same *name* of 'Hebrews,' and *incorporated* thereby into the commonwealth of Israel; these, considering the superior blessings bestowed on Jacob above Esau (who had at least 400 male attendants, Ge. 33. 1,) have been reckoned at 1000 or 1200, but making a very moderate calculation of 500 or 600 males, and bearing in mind the fruitfulness promised and, according to Ex. 1. 7) realized, there can remain no possible difficulty for that number in 430 years (or 14 generations,) or even in 215 (seven generations,) to amount to 600,000 males; see note on Ge. 47. 7.

38. RABBLE,] see Nu. 11. 4, a mixture of native Egyptians, &c. who had become connected in some respect with Israel, and who were glad to escape from the tyranny of the usurping rulers of the land.

39. CAST OUT,] as in Job 30. 5; Ge. 3. 24; Ex. 2. 17; 6. 1; 10. 11; 11. 1; 23. 29, 30, &c.

DELAY,] as in Ge. 19. 16; 43. 10; Ju. 3. 26; 19. 8; Ps. 119. 60; Is. 29. 9; Hab. 2. 3; 2 Sa. 15. 28.

40. 𝔴𝔥𝔦𝔠𝔥 𝔰𝔥𝔢𝔶 𝔥𝔞𝔳𝔢 𝔡𝔴𝔢𝔩𝔱,] not, 'who have dwelt,' as in the Common Version, which is a compromise between two different chronologies, and sanctioned by (some copies of) the Sept., Jonathan, Talmud, and the ancient Jews generally; but see note on Ge. 15. 13; Ex. 2. 1. Jost, Ewald,

Kalisch, &c. justly contend for the 430 years being all spent in Egypt.

42. A NIGHT, ETC.] The meaning of this somewhat obscure verse appears to be, that as Jehovah had, as it were, to watch throughout that night to deliver Israel, so they were all to watch throughout their generations for, or with reference to, the Lord.

43. SON OF A STRANGER,] as in Ge. 12. 7; this is the general law, the next clause points out the limitation.

44. ANY MAN'S SERVANT,] who thus became one of the household, being 'purchased with money,' for his services for a longer or shorter period; having been circumcised, he was allowed to eat of the passover-sacrifice, Ge. 17. 13, 27.

45. A SETTLER,] i.e. one who has come from another country to fix his dwelling among them.

HIRED SERVANT,] *lit.* 'hireling,' i.e. one engaged from day to day.

46. IN ONE HOUSE IT IS EATEN.] If the household was too small, they were permitted to invite their neighbours.

NOT CARRY OUT,] as the remnant was to be wholly burnt, see v. 10.

BONE YE DO NOT BREAK,] to extract its marrow, as if the flesh were not sufficient; also to save time.

47. COMPANY,] or 'appointed assembly;' see note on v. 3.

48. A SOJOURNER,] i.e. a foreigner who has come for a short time into the land, intending to return to his own land again, thus differing from the 'settler,' who has no such intention, v. 45.

CIRCUMCISED,] as in Ge. 17. 10, 13.

49. ONE LAW.] The just and equitable arrangements of the Mosaic laws are in striking contrast to the narrow-minded, selfish policy that is found to prevail so much in mere worldly societies.

50. ALL...DO.] Being now convinced by the plagues inflicted on the Egyptians, and their own marvellous exemption from them, that it was at once their duty and their interest to do as they were commanded.

51. SELF-SAME DAY] in which they had observed the passover.

XIII. 2. SANCTIFY,] *lit.* 'separate, *or* set apart;' see note on Ge. 2. 3; 38. 21.

EVERY FIRST-BORN] if a male, (see v. 12); these might all have perished with the first-born of Egypt, but God spared them, and now claims them as his own; afterwards (in Nu. 3. 12, 13,) he exchanged them for the whole tribe of Levi, who were henceforth entirely separated to his service; the first-born, indeed, were from the beginning, the hereditary priests of their households.

OPENING ANY WOMB,] as in v. 12, 13, 15; 34. 19, 20; Nu. 3. 12; 18. 15; Ez. 20. 26.

5. 𝔴𝔥𝔦𝔠𝔥 𝔯𝔢𝔪𝔢𝔪𝔟𝔢𝔯,] as in 20, 8; De. 24. 9; 25. 17; Jo. 1. 13.

BEAST.] The firstling of beasts having also been spared, they are likewise claimed by the Lord as his own; if *unblemished* they were to be offered to the Lord; He accepted the fat and the blood ; the breast and the right shoulder were to the officiating priest, the remainder was allowed to be eaten by the offerer ; if *blemished*, they were to be killed and eaten at home, (De. 15. 21, 22.) The firstlings of unclean beasts were to be redeemed by a clean one, with the addition of a fifth of its value, or killed, (Le. 27. 26, 27.) The first-fruits of every field and garden were also claimed as His.

4. TO-DAY,] being the fifteenth of Nisan or Abib, answering to the latter half of March, and the former half of April ; a very suitable time for journeying, when there was neither heat, nor cold, nor rain.

5. SWORN.] See Ge. 15. 19 ; Ex. 3. 8, 17 ; De. 7. 1.

6. FEAST,] *or* 'festival;' see note on 10. 9 ; 12. 16.

7. NOT SEEN.] Compare the corresponding phrase, 'not found,' in 12. 19.

8. DECLARED,] *lit.* 'set before;' see note on Ge. 3. 11 ; Ex. 4. 28, &c.

THAT DAY,] when thou art in the promised land.

9. AND IT HATH BEEN.] This, as Gill remarks, is a continuation of the language of the parent ; for similar figures of speech, see Pr. 1. 9 ; 3. 3.

FOR A SIGN...FOR A MEMORIAL,] i.e. as a sign, and as a memorial ; the observance of the passover would be a perpetual sign and memorial of their deliverance, and the consequence would be, that they would be continually speaking of the 'law' of the Lord, who had saved them, and instituted this ordinance ; nothing but the grossest inattention could suppose that phylacteries are alluded to in this passage.

LAW OF JEHOVAH,] as in Ge. 26. 5 ; Ex. 16. 4 ; Ps. 1. 2 ; 2 K. 10. 31, &c.

IN THY MOUTH,] as in Ex. 4. 15.

10. FROM DAYS TO DAYS,] i.e. as Onkelos renders, 'from to time;' compare similar phrases in Ju. 11. 40; 21. 19; 1 Sa. 1. 3 ; 2. 19.

11. CANAANITE.] As noticed before, this tribe, though originally foreigners to the land of Palestine, succeeded in giving their own name to the land.

12. CAUSED TO PASS OVER,] as in Ge. 8. 1 ; Ex. 13. 12 : 33. 19; 36. 6, &c.

INCREASE,] as in De. 7. 13 ; 28. 4, 18, 21, all the passages where it occurs.

13. ASS,] as well as every other unclean animal, was to be ransomed with a lamb ; see Nu. 18. 15.

RANSOM.] This word, PADAH, differs from the word GAAL in this, that it always implies the paying of a price, whereas the latter may or may not do so, according to the context.

BEHEADED,] as in 34. 20 ; De. 21. 4, 6 ; Is. 66. 3 ; Ho. 10. 2 ; compare also De. 32. 2 ; 33. 28.

RANSOM,] within 30 days after birth, with five shekels of the sanctuary, Nu. 18. 16.

14. HEREAFTER,] *lit.* 'to-morrow;' see Ge. 30. 33 ; Ex. 8. 10, 23, 29 ; 9. 5, 18 ; 10. 4, &c.

15. WAS PAINED,] *or* 'pained himself;' see the use of the original word in Ge. 35. 17 ; Ex. 7. 3 ; 13. 15 ; De. 2. 30 ; 10. 16 ; 1 K.

12. 4, &c. Kalisch gratuitously inserts *not*, e.g. 'hardened himself not to let us go.'

16. FOR A TOKEN...FOR FRONTLETS.] See note on v. 9 above.

17. PHILISTINES,] whose five cities—Gaza, Askelon, Ashdod, Ekron, and Gath—lay between Egypt and Canaan, a journey of a few days, (Ge. 50. 7—13,) and the inhabitants of which were at once warlike and inimical to the Hebrews, (1 Ch. 7. 21, 22.)

FOR IT IS NEAR,] not 'although,' as in the Common Version ; but because it was near, and the consequence would be, that the people might be alarmed by being called upon to fight the warlike tribes who inhabited the land of promise, God led them round the way of the wilderness of the Red Sea ; so Septuagint, Targums, Aben Ezra, Rashi, Rosenmuller, &c.

18. TURNETH ROUND,] as in 1 K. 8. 14; 21. 4; 1 Sa. 5. 8, &c.

BY FIFTIES.] So Michaelis, Rosenmuller, Pococke, &c. This division is recognized everywhere by the Jews ; see Ex. 18. 21, 25 ; Nu. 31. 30, 47 ; De. 1. 15 ; 1 Sa. 8. 12; 2 Sa. 15. 1 ; 1 K. 1. 5 ; 18. 4, 13 ; 2 K. 1. 9, 10, 11, 12, 13, 14 ; 2. 7, 16, 17 ; 13. 7 ; 15. 25 ; Is. 3. 3. Puerile in all cases is the common notion of 'harnessed, girded ;' compare the passages, Jo. 1. 14 ; 4. 12 ; Ju. 7. 11.

19. SWEAR.] See Ge. 50. 25, 26 ; perhaps the remains of the other patriarchs were also taken with them, (Acts 7. 16.)

20. FROM SUCCOTH.] See note on 12. 37 ; this was on the 16th of Abib or Nisan.

ETHAM,] supposed to be the modern Ajrud, twelve miles north-east from Suez, being their third day's journey.

21. JEHOVAH IS GOING,] as noted in Ex. 33. 15 ; Nu. 14. 14; De. 1. 30, 33 ; 20. 4 ; 31. 6, 8 ; Is. 52. 12. In Ex. 14. 19, He is called a 'messenger of God ;' in 23. 20, simply a 'messenger.' Compare the practice of a shepherd preceding and leading, not following or driving, the flock, alluded to in John 10. 4.

CLOUD,] to shield them from the heat of the sun.

FIRE,] having a bright and a dark side, the one to the Israelites, the other to the pursuers.

TO GO BY DAY, ETC.] i.e. incessantly, if necessary.

22. HE REMOVETH NOT,] as in Mic. 2. 3 ; or, 'it removed not,' as in Ex. 33. 11 ; Job 23. 11, &c.

FROM BEFORE.] In Hebrew, verbs of motion often omit the preposition 'from,' as in 9. 33 ; but another construction of the original is perhaps preferable : ' He removeth not the pillar...(*which is*) before the people.'

XIV. 1. SPEAKETH] out of the pillar of the cloud.

2. PI-HAHIROTH,] i.e. 'mouth of the caverns,' *or* 'a grassy place,' situated east of Baal-Zephon, on the northern end of the Heroopolitan gulf ; only mentioned elsewhere in v. 9, and in Nu. 33. 7.

MIGDOL,] i.e. 'a tower,' *or* 'abundance of

hills,' mentioned in e. 44. 1; 46. 14: Ez.
29. 10; 30. 6.
BAAL-ZEPHON,] i.e. 'owner of Zephon,' or
Typhon,an evil demon among the Egyptians,
the enemy of fertility.
OVER AGAINST IT,] at Colzum, according
to Kalisch and others.
3. ENTANGLED,] as in Joel 1. 18; Est. 3. 15.
SHUT,] as in Nu. 12. 14, 15; Ge. 7. 16, &c.
4. STRENGTHENED,] as in Ex. 4. 21; 9. 12;
10. 20, 27; 11. 10; 14. 4, 8, 17.
PURSUE,] as the word always signifies;
see v. 9, 23; 15. 9; Ge. 14. 14, 15; Le. 26.
7, 8; De. 1. 44, &c.
FORCE,] as in v. 9, 17, 28; 15. 4; compare
the use of the word in 18. 21, 25, &c.
5. FLED.] This was not correct, they had
gone out openly and calmly, as in v. 8, but
the language was doubtless used to excite
Pharaoh to pursue them as a band of
fugitives, who could easily be overcome.
6. HARNESSETH,] as in Ge. 49. 29; 1 K.
6. 10; 18. 44; 2 K. 7. 10; 9. 21; Je. 46. 4;
1 Sa. 6. 7, &c.
HIS CHARIOT,] i.e. his own, anxious to be
present at the expected re-capture of the
fugitives, whether Israelites or Egyptians
who had joined them; there is no reason
for taking it as a collective noun.
HIS PEOPLE.] See note on Ex. 1. 9.
7. CHOSEN CHARIOTS,] for which the level
plains of Egypt were so suitable. They are
often found represented in the Egyptian
monuments as having two wheels, drawn
by two horses, with room for a warrior and
a driver. These were sought after by Israel, (2 K. 18. 24; Is. 31. 1; Ez. 17. 15, &c.)
EVEN ALL,] not 'and all;' the particle is
explicative rather than conjunctive.
CAPTAINS.] This word which occurs in 15.
4; 2 Sa. 23. 8; 1 K. 9. 22; 2 K. 7. 2, 17, 19;
9. 25; 10. 25; 15. 25; 1 Ch. 11. 11; 12. 18;
2 Ch. 8. 9; Ez. 23. 15, 23, is of very uncertain
meaning; 'captain over three, of the third
rank, a third person, mighty man, chariot
warrior,' &c., are the principal significations
attached to it. See also 1 Sa. 18. 6. (three-
stringed instrument); Ps. 80. 5, (a third
time); Pr. 22. 20, (three times); Is. 40. 12,
(tierce.)
8. HIGH HAND,] i.e. 'triumphantly.' See
the use of the same phrase in Nu. 33. 3; 15.
30, 'presumptuously;' compare Job 38. 15,
('high arm;') Ps. 18. 27, ('high looks.')
10. DRAWN NEAR,] *lit.* 'caused to draw
near,' i.e. his host; but compare Ge. 12. 11,
for the intransitive sense.
FEAR EXCEEDINGLY,] being unaccustomed
to arms, and broken-spirited by oppression.
CRY] of distress, as in Ge. 27. 34; 41. 55;
Ex. 5. 15; 8. 12; 14. 10, 15; 15. 25; 17. 4;
22. 23, 27, &c.
11. BECAUSE THERE ARE NO GRAVES,] an
emphatic assertion that there were abundance of them.
12. SPAKE...IN EGYPT.] See their grum-
bling noticed in 5. 21, and 6. 9.
13. SALVATION.] See note on Ge. 49. 18.
FOR AS YE HAVE SEEN,] not 'for...whom
ye have seen,' as in the Common Version;
so Sept., Onk. Rosenmuller, Kalisch, &c.

14. DOTH FIGHT,] as in v. 25; De. 1. 30;
3. 22; Jo. 10. 14, 42; 23. 3, 10; 2 Ch. 20. 29;
Ne. 4. 20.
KEEP SILENT,] as in Nu. 30. 4, 7, 14; Ge. 24.
21; 34. 5, &c.
15. THOU CRIEST.] Not only did the
Israelites generally cry unto the Lord, as
noted in v. 10, but Moses also; and the
answer was given to him as their leader.
16. LIFT UP THY ROD,] as he had done in
the case of the former wonders.
CLEAVE IT,] as in Ju. 15. 29; 2 Sa. 23. 16;
1 Ch. 11. 18; 2 Ch. 21. 17; 32. 1; Ps. 74. 15;
78. 13; 141. 7; Ec. 10. 9; Is. 34. 15; 48. 21;
63. 12; Ez. 29. 7; Ne. 9. 11; Amos 1. 13.
DRY LAND,] as in Ge. 1. 9, 10; Ex. 4. 9;
14. 16, 22, 29; 15. 19; Jo. 4. 22; Ne. 9. 11;
Ps. 66. 6; Is. 44. 3; Jon. 1. 9, 13; 2. 10.
17. STRENGTHENING,] as in Ex. 4. 21, &c.
18. I AM HONOURED,] as in v. 4.
19. MESSENGER OF GOD.] See note on 13. 21.
20. CLOUD AND THE DARKNESS ARE,] i.e.
continue to be where they have come in.
HE ENLIGHTENETH,] i.e. the messenger
of God does so.
21. EAST-WIND,] which the Sept. (as in
10. 13) renders a 'south-wind,' and the
Vulgate a 'burning wind;' Kalisch and
others referring to Ps. 48. 8; Ez. 27. 26;
Job 27. 21; Je. 18. 17; Is. 27. 8, consider
it only as a 'vehement wind;' but as the
Hebrews never express any points of the
wind otherwise than the four—north, south,
east, west—there is no reason to doubt but
that a north-east wind would be suitable,
and included under the designation 'east.'
DRY GROUND,] as in Ge. 7. 22; Jo. 3. 17;
4. 18; 2 K. 2. 8; Ez. 30. 12; Hag. 2. 6.
22. A WALL,] as in Le. 25. 29, 30, 31; De.
3. 5; 28. 52.
23. GO IN,] either ignorantly, owing to
the darkness, or blindly, from the desire of
vengeance.
24. MORNING WATCH,] i.e. from two to
six; there being three watches among the
Hebrews. the 1st from 6—10 p.m.; the 2nd
from 10—2 a.m.; the 3rd from 2—6 a.m.;
compare Ju. 7. 19; 1 Sa. 11. 11; Ps. 63. 6;
90. 4; 119. 148; La. 2. 19.
LOOKETH,] as in Ge. 18. 16; 19. 28; 26.
8; De. 26. 15; Ps. 14. 2; 53. 2; 102. 19.
TROUBLETH,] as in 23. 27; De. 2. 15; Jo.
10. 10; Ju. 4. 15; 1 Sa. 7. 10; 2 Sa. 22. 15;
Ps. 18. 14; 144. 6; Is. 28. 28; Je. 51. 34; 2
Ch. 15. 6; Est. 9. 24.
25. TURNETH ASIDE,] as in 8. 8, 31; 10.
17; 34. 34, &c. Totally unsupported is the
translation 'made glide.'
WHEELS,] as in 1 K. 7. 30; 32. 33; Pr. 20.
26; 25. 11; Is. 28. 27; Ez. 1. 15, 16, 19, 20,
21; 3. 13; 10. 6, 9, 10, 12, 13, 16, 19; 11. 22;
Na. 3. 2.
WITH DIFFICULTY,] i.e. 'heavily,' as a
more literal translation would be; without
the wheels they could only be dragged
through the sand.
IS FIGHTING,] as in v. 14, on which
see note.
27. TURNING OF THE MORNING.] See same
phrase in Ps. 46. 5; compare also Ge. 24
63; De. 23. 11; Ju. 19. 26.

PERENNIAL FLOW,] i.e. its usual one, as in De. 21. 4 ; 1 K. 8. 2 ; Amos 5. 24 ; the other instances of its occurrence are, Ge. 49. 24 ; Ex. 14. 27 ; Nu. 24. 21 ; Job 12. 19 ; 33. 19 ; Ps. 74. 15 ; Pr. 13. 15 ; Je. 5. 15 ; 49. 19 ; 50. 44 ; Mic. 6. 2.

AT ITS COMING,] or 'at meeting it;' see Ge. 14. 17 ; Ex. 4. 14, 27 ; 5. 20 ; 7. 15, &c.

SHAKETH OFF,] as in Ps. 136. 15 ; Neh. 5. 13, &c.

28. EVEN ALL,] or 'unto all.'
EVEN ONE,] i.e. of those who entered in.

30. THAT DAY,] reckoned to have been the seventh day from the passover, and the 21st of the month, which was to be a holy convocation to the Lord, see 12. 16.

31. GREAT HAND,] i.e. 'might, not 'work ;' compare 32. 11 ; Nu. 20. 20 ; De. 3. 24, &c.

REMAIN STEADFAST.] The root of the original word is 'to stay up, be stayed up, be steady, steadfast,' the causative (or Hiphel) conjugation of this verb is always intransitive, 'to remain steadfast, steady, in adherence to an object; it does not so much describe an act as a state. See note on Ge. 15. 6.

XV. 1. THEN SINGETH,] not 'sang,' as in the Common Version.

THIS SONG.] It still forms a part of the service of the synagogue on the seventh day of the passover.

I SING,] i.e. now, not 'I will sing,' as it is rendered in the Common Version.

TRIUMPHED,] i.e. risen high above his enemies ; see the use of the word in Job 8. 11 ; 10. 16 ; Ez. 47. 5 ; compare also v. 7 ; De. 33. 26, 29.

THROWN.] The original word is used of the 'throwing or shooting' of arrows, Ps. 78. 9 ; Je. 4. 29 ; 'of beguiling, deceiving, betraying,' in Ge. 29. 25 ; Jo. 9. 22 ; 1 Ch. 12. 17.

2. STRENGTH,] as in v. 13 ; Le. 26. 19 ; Ju. 5. 21 ; 9. 51 ; unnecessary is the supposed notion of 'praise.'

SONG,] as in Ps. 118. 14 ; Is. 12. 2.

JAH,] a contraction of 'Jehovah,' found also in 17. 16 ; Is. 12. 2 ; 26. 4 ; 38. 11 ; Ps. 68. 4, 18, &c.

SALVATION,] as in Ge. 49. 18 ; Ex. 14. 13 ; De. 32. 15, &c.

GOD,] lit. 'mighty one,' as in 6. 3 ; 15. 11.

GLORIFY,, lit. 'declare comely,' as in Sept., Vulg., Rashi, Luther, &c.

EXALT,] as in 2 Sa. 22. 49 ; Job 17. 4 ; Ps. 18. 48, &c.

3. MAN OF BATTLE,] i.e. warlike ; see same phrase in Nu. 31. 21, 28, 49 ; De. 2. 14, 16 ; compare Ex. 17. 16 ; 21. 14, &c.

NAME,] i.e. descriptive of his character, as in 6. 3 ; 3. 15, &c.

4. CAST,] as in Ge. 31. 15 ; Ex. 19. 13 ; Nu. 21. 30 ; Jo. 18. 6.

CHOICE,] as in Ge. 23. 6 ; De. 12. 11, &c.

CAPTAINS.] See note on Ex. 14. 7.

SUNK,] as in Ps. 9. 15 ; 69. 2, 14, &c.

5. DEPTHS,] as in v. 8 ; see note on Ge. 1. 2.

6. RIGHT HAND,] as in v. 12 ; De. 33. 2 ; 2 Ch. 18. 18 ; Ps. 16. 11 ; 17. 7 ; 18. 35, &c.

HONOURABLE,] as in v. 11 ; Is. 42. 21.

CRUSH,] as in Ju. 10. 8, the only other passage where it occurs.

AN ENEMY,] as in v. 9 ; not 'the enemy;' it is a general statement of Jehovah's power.

7. ABUNDANCE,] not 'greatness ;' compare the use of the word in Ge. 16. 10 ; Le. 25 16 ; De. 1. 10, &c.

EXCELLENCY,] as in Le. 26. 19 ; Job 35. 12 ; 37. 4 ; 38. 11 ; 40. 10 ; Ps. 47. 4 ; 59, 12, &c.

THROWEST DOWN,] as in 19. 21, 24 ; 23. 24 ; Ju. 6. 25, &c.

WITHSTANDERS,] lit. 'risers up ;' see 32. 35 ; De. 28. 7 ; 33. 11, &c.

WRATH,] as in 32. 12 ; Job 20. 23 ; Ps. 78. 49. &c.

8. SPIRIT OF THINE ANGER.] Compare 2 Sa. 22. 16 ; Job 4. 9 ; Ps. 18. 15.

HEAPED.] Compare the meaning of the noun in Ruth 3. 7 ; 2 Ch. 31. 6, 7, 8, 9 ; Ne. 4. 2, (3. 34) ; 13. 15 ; Song 7. 2 ; Je. 50. 26 ; Hag. 2. 16.

HEAP,] as the word denotes in Jo. 3. 13, 16 ; Ps. 33. 7 ; 78. 13 ; Is. 17. 11.

FLOWINGS,] as in Ps. 78. 16, 44 ; Pr. 5, 15 ; Song 4. 15 ; Is. 44. 3 ; Je. 18. 14.

CONGEALED,] as in Zep. 1. 12 ; Job 10. 10 ; (Zec. 14. 6.)

9. ENEMY,] i.e. Pharaoh ; his language is strikingly graphic and laconic, quite equal to Cæsar's : 'veni, vidi, vici.'

PURSUE...OVERTAKE...APPORTION SPOIL.] See 1.) Ex. 14. 8, 9, 23 ; 2.) Ex. 14. 9 ; 3.) Jo. 22. 8 ; Pr. 16. 19 ; Ps. 68. 12.

FILLED IS MY SOUL,] as in Ps. 107. 9 ; 123. 4 ; Pr. 6. 30 ; Ec. 6. 7.

DRAW OUT,] as in Ge. 14. 14 ; Le. 26. 33 ; &c., lit. 'empty.'

DESTROY,] lit. 'dispossess ;' see Ex. 34. 24, Nu. 14. 12, 24, &c.

10. THOU HAST BLOWN,] as in Is. 40. 24.

COVERED,] as in Ex. 10. 5, 6, 15 ; 14. 28 ; 15. 5, &c.

LEAD,] as found in Nu. 31, 22 ; Job 19. 24 ; Je. 6. 29 ; Ez. 22. 18, 20 ; 27. 12 ; Zec. 5. 7, 8.

MIGHTY,] as in Ju. 5. 13, 25 ; 1 Sa. 4. 8 ; Ps. 93. 4 ; Is. 33. 21, applied to God, gods, men, things, &c.

11. THE GODS,] lit. 'mighty ones,' as in 34. 14 ; Ps. 29. 1 ; 82. 1 ; 89. 6 ; Is. 57. 5 ; Ez. 31. 11 ; Da. 11. 36, &c.

HONOURABLE,] as in v. 6.

HOLINESS,] i.e. his state of separation from all creatures. The Septuagint reads, 'in the sanctuary ;' but the C. V. is preferable.

FEARFUL,] as in Ge. 28. 17 ; Ex. 34. 10 ; De. 1. 19 ; 7. 21, &c.

PRAISES,] as in Ge. 10. 21 ; 26, 19, &c.

WONDERS,] as in Ps. 77. 11, 14 ; Is. 9. 6, &c.

12. STRETCHED OUT,] as in Ex. 7. 5, 19 ; 8. 5, 16 ; 9. 22 ; 10. 12, &c.

SWALLOWETH,] as in Nu. 16. 30, 32, 34; reference to the fate of Korah, &c. is here made prophetically ; so must all the rest of the chapter be understood.

13. LED FORTH,] as in 13. 17, 21 ; 32. 34, &c. Very unjustifiable is the translation of some : 'Thou leadest forth,' in the present tense.

LED ON,] as in Ge. 47. 17 ; Ps. 23. 2 ; 31.

3; Is. 40. 11; 49. 10; 51. 18; 2 Ch. 28. 15; 32. 22.

KINDNESS.] The original word never means 'mercy,' though so rendered in the Common Version 144 times.

REDEEMED,] as in Ex. 6. 6; Le. 25. 25; Ge. 48. 16; Nu. 35. 12; Job 19. 25; Ps. 19. 14, &c.

HABITATION,] lit. 'a comely place;' see Job 5. 3, 24; 18. 15, &c.

14. PEOPLES,] i.e. of Canaan, Arabia, Aram, &c., 'have heard,' according to the prophetic style, not 'will hear.'

TROUBLED,] as in Is. 32. 11; Ps. 77. 16, &c.

PAIN,] as in Ps. 48. 6; Je. 6. 24; 22. 23; 50. 43; Mic. 4. 9; Job 6. 10.

SEIZED,] or 'laid hold on,' as in Ex. 4. 4; 15. 15; Ge. 25. 26, &c.

PHILISTIA,] as in Ps. 60. 8; 83. 7; 87. 4; 108. 9; Is. 14. 29, 31; Joel 3. 4; the narrow strip of land along the Mediteranean.

15. CHIEFS.] See the word used in Ge. 36. 15—43; 1 Ch. 1. 51—54, &c.

TROUBLED,] as in Ge. 45. 3; Ju. 20. 41, &c.

MIGHTY ONES,] as in 2 K. 24. 15; Job 24. 25; Is. 1. 29; 61. 3; Ez. 17. 13; 31. 14.

TREMBLING,] as in Ps. 55. 5; Job 4. 14; Ps. 2. 11; 48. 6; Is. 33. 14; Ps. 104. 32; Ezra 10. 9; Da. 10. 11.

MELTED,] like wax; compare Jo. 2. 9, 24, &c.

16. TERROR,] as in Ge. 15. 12; Ex. 23. 27, &c.

DREAD,] as in De. 2. 25; 11. 25; 28. 67, &c.

ARM,] as in Ex. 6. 6; De. 4. 34, &c.

STILL,] lit. 'dumb,' as in Le. 10. 3; Jo. 10. 12, 13; Job 29. 21, &c.

PASS OVER] the Jordan.

PURCHASED,] or 'acquired,' as in De. 32. 6; Ps. 74. 2; 78. 54, &c.

17. PLANT,] as in Nu. 24. 6; 2 Sa. 7. 10; 1 Ch. 17. 9; Ps. 80. 15, &c.

MOUNTAIN] of Moriah.

INHERITANCE,] which Israel is everywhere declared to be.

FIXED PLACE,] as in 1 K. 8. 13, 39, 43. 49, &c.

DWELLING.] The original is a verb in the infinitive, as in 16. 3.

SANCTUARY,] as in 25. 8; Le. 12. 4, &c.

ESTABLISHED,] as in De. 32. 6; 2 Sa. 7. 13, &c.

18. TO THE AGE—AND ONWARDS.] This phrase is found only in the Psalms, Isaiah, Micah, and Daniel, viz. in Ps. 9. 5; 10. 16; 21. 4; 45. 6, 17; 48. 14; 52. 8; 104. 5; 111. 8; 119. 44; 145. 1, 2, 21; Is. 30. 8; 45. 17; Mic. 4. 5; Da. 12. 3. The last word AD, is derived from a root signifying 'to pass on, away, by,' implying 'continuance' from and after any given point.

19. THE HORSE,] i.e. 'cavalry.'

20. INSPIRED ONE.] See note on Ge. 20. 7; Ex. 7. 1; Miriam, (compare also Nu. 12. 2) Deborah, (Ju. 4. 4,) Huldah, (2 K. 22. 14; 2 Ch. 34. 22,) Noadiah, (Ne. 6. 14,) are the only females thus denominated in SS.; Isaiah's wife is called by the same name (in Is. 8. 3,) but whether it was simply because she was the wife of the prophet, or because she really received Divine revelations, it is impossible to say positively.

TIMBREL,] as in Ge. 31. 27; Ju. 11. 34, &c., a kind of hand-drum, very common in the East, used principally by females, accompanied by dancing, or slow movements of the feet; in all Eastern festivals and entertainments, civil and sacred, the sexes are kept separate from each other: in every instance of singing recorded in Scripture, where the posture is mentioned, it is always standing; it was reserved for some modern churches to sanction the unnatural and unseemly—not to say un-Scriptural—practice of sitting during praise in the worship of God.

CHORUSES,] as in 32. 19; Ju. 11. 34; 21. 21; 1 Sa. 18. 6; 21. 11; 29. 5; Song 6. 13, (7. 1.)

21. ANSWERETH TO THEM,] i.e. respondeth to the male singers, as the masculine pronoun shows.

22. SHUR,] the western part of Arabia-Petræa, of which the desert of Etham was a part, lying next to Palestine.

23. MARAH,] supposed to be what is now called Howarah, about thirty miles from the shore of the Red Sea. It is impossible to say with certainty whether it was the Israelites who gave it this name or some of its former visitors—more probably the latter.

24. MURMUR,] lit. 'lodge, stay,' hence 'persist, be obstinate, murmur.'

25. CRIETH] from distress, as the word denotes; see note on Ge. 27. 34.

SHOWETH HIM,] by 'throwing' out the hand and finger, as the etymology of the word indicates, Pr. 6. 13; Ge. 46. 28; 2 Ch. 15. 3; 1 Sa. 20. 36. It is difficult to decide whether this was a direct miracle, or simply a supernatural direction, to make use of some medicinal herb or tree whose qualities were unknown to Moses and to the inhabitants of the place. Various plants, such as tea, the tree Nellimarum, the plant Yerva, the tree Sassafras, the Nelli (Phylanthus emblica,) are reputed to have this effect. In either case, without the Divine intervention, the agreeable change would not have been effected. Compare John 9. 6.

STATUTE...ORDINANCE.] See note on Ge. 47. 22, and on 18. 19.

TRIED] their faith, &c. as he had done Abraham, (Ge. 22. 1,) as the Queen of Sheba did Solomon, (2 Ch. 9. 1;) see also the use of the word in Ex. 16. 4; 17. 2, 7; 20. 20; Nu. 14. 22; De. 4. 34; 6. 16; 8. 2, 16; 13. 3; 28. 56; 33. 8.

26. HEARKEN..DO..GIVE EAR..KEEP.] The variety of language corresponds to the variety of ways in which man is required to serve God.

SICKNESS,] as in 23. 25; 1 K. 8. 27; 2 Ch. 6. 28; 21. 15; Pr. 18. 4.

HEALING THEE,] as He said to Hezekiah, (2 K. 20. 5;) compare also Ps. 103. 3; 147. 3; see also Ge. 20. 7; Nu. 12. 13; De. 32. 39; Job 5. 18; Ps. 30. 2; 107. 20; Is. 30. 26; 57. 18; Je. 3. 22; 30. 17; Ho. 6. 1; 14. 4.

27. ELIM,] on the 25th of Abib; supposed to be about four or eight miles from Marah

and two miles from Tor; Shaw found there nine fountains and about 2000 palms, which grew from 30 to 80 feet high.

XVi, 1. SIN.] According to Nu. 33. 10, 11, they went from Elim to the Red Sea, and thence to Sin; why they went back again to the Sea it is not easy to say, but nothing particular appearing to have happened to them there, the visit is here left unnoticed. This is a different wilderness from that of 'Zin,' mentioned in Nu. 20. 1, which was on the other side of Sinai, while this was on the way to it.

2. MURMUR,] for want of bread, as they had done in 15. 24, for water; see also 16. 2, 7, 8; 17. 3; Nu. 14. 2, 27, 29, 36; 16. 11, 41; 17. 5.

3. BY THE HAND OF THE LORD,] either a natural death, or as some understand it, a violent death, such as that inflicted on the first-born of the Egyptians, bringing their sufferings rapidly to a close.

FLESH-POT.] From this word and several other passages it is clear that, apart from the harsh involuntary service laid upon them in Egypt, their outward temporal comforts were not few; if indeed, mere food and raiment were all a man should desire, they might have been satisfied, but they were designed for another service than being 'beasts of burden' to the Egyptians; they were far, however, from aiming at this greater good, their better sympathies being blunted by a long course of servitude; yet this language which they use here, is doubtless exaggerated—present trials always appearing the worst.

4. I AM RAINING.] The use of the present participle here in the Original points to the immediate fulfilment of the promise—it is as good as done.

BREAD,] i.e. food; see note on Ge. 3. 19.

HEAVENS,] i.e. skies, as the word generally means; see note on Ge. 1. 8.

TRY,] i.e. prove them; see note on Ge. 22. 1.

5. THE SIXTH DAY] of the falling of the new food, viz. the 21st of the month.

PREPARED,] or made ready, as in Ge. 43. 16, 25; Ex. 23. 21.

DOUBLE,] lit. a 'second' quantity.

6. JEHOVAH HATH BROUGHT YOU OUT,] in opposition to what they had said in v. 3, 'ye have brought us out.'

7. SEEN THE HONOUR OF JEHOVAH,] in the cloud, as recorded in v. 10.

8. AGAINST JEHOVAH,] Moses and Aaron being merely His servants, doing as He directed them.

10. THE CLOUD,] which was going before them; see 13. 22.

11. UNTO MOSES,] out of the cloud.

12. I HAVE HEARD,] and will satisfy their murmurings.

BETWEEN THE EVENINGS.]See note on 12.6.

FLESH,] i.e. of the fowl—the quail, to be sent.

BREAD,] i.e. the manna.

13. THE QUAIL,] noticed again only in Nu. 11. 31, 32; Ps. 105. 40. Ludolph, Patrick, &c., translate it 'locust;' Josephus, &c.,

'quail;' in Ps. 78. 27, it is said to be 'winged fowl.' All critics agree that the quail is very numerous in these parts.

COVERETH,] by their abundance; according to Nu. 11. 31, the quails, like the locusts, (in 10. 13,) were brought from the sea by a wind; the miracle consisted in their numbers, and in the opportuneness of their arrival, and at the promised time.

DEW,] as in Nu. 11. 9; compare the blessings of Jacob and Esau, (Ge. 27. 28, 39.)

14. THING,] as in Ge. 41. 3, 4, 6, 7, 23, 24; Le. 13. 20; 16. 12; 21. 20; 1 K. 19. 12; Is. 29. 5; 40. 15.

BARE] or 'peeled' thing, the original word occurs nowhere else.

HOAR FROST,] as in Job 38. 29: Ps. 147. 16; in every other passage it signifies a 'basin,' e.g. 1 Ch. 18. 17; Ezra 1. 10; 8. 27.

15. WHAT IS IT ?] The original word MAN, which the English Translators (after Munster, Pagninus, Osiander,) supposed to be a name of the substance, is evidently a Chaldee (or Arabic) particle, found in Ezra 5. 3, 4, 9: Da. 3. 6, 11, 15; 4. 17, 25, 32; 5. 21, signifying, what? and so the Sept., Targums, Sam., Syr., Vulg., Ar., Piscator, Montanus, Josephus. Others render it a 'portion, gift, preparation,' &c.

16. OMER,] a measure containing 'three quarts in English,' or the tenth of an ephah; not a 'homer,' which contained ten baths; occurs in v. 18, 22, 32, 33, 36; Le. 23. 10, 11, 12, 15.

POLL,] properly 'scull,' from the idea of roundness; see again 38. 36; Nu. 1. 2, 18, 20, 22; 3. 47; Ju. 9. 53; 2 K. 9. 35; 1 Ch. 10. 10; 23, 3, 24.

11. GATHERING MUCH,] lit. 'multiplying,' as in v. 18; and in 36. 5; Le. 11. 42; 1 Ch. 8. 40; Ne. 6. 17; 9. 37; Pr. 23. 8; Ec. 6 11; Hab. 2. 6.

GATHERING LITTLE,] lit. 'lessening,' as in v. 18, and in Nu. 11. 32.

20. BRINGETH UP WORMS,] lit. 'it is high with worms.'

STINKETH,] as in 7. 18, 21; 8. 14; 16. 20.

21. MELTED,] as in De. 20. 8; Jo. 2. 11, &c.

22. PRINCES,] lit. 'lifted up ones,' as in Ge. 17. 20; Ex. 22. 28; 34. 31; 35. 27, &c., the same as those noticed in Ex. 12. 21; 17. 5, &c., under the title of 'elders.'

23. A REST.] This is the first instance of the occurrence of the word 'sabbath,' which is itself a Hebrew word signifying 'rest;' in Ge. 2. 2, 3, we read of God's 'resting' on the seventh day, and blessing it, and 'sanctifying' it, i.e. 'separating' it from the other days, so as to distinguish it from them. The division of time by weeks was thus marked from the beginning, and there cannot really be the slightest reasonable doubt but that those who feared God from Adam to Moses, were careful to distinguish the day set apart by Him. The allusions to sacrifices, (Ge. 4. 3, 4,) and to public preaching, (Ge. 4. 26,) would lead to the very natural belief, that as He had appointed, or at least sanctioned, such institutions and ordinances, there was a stated period for their observance.

There is a difficulty connected with these verses, viz. that the 'princes of the company' do not appear to have appreciated or understood the motives of the people in gathering an extra quantity (which they clearly did according to the express command in v. 5,) of manna on the sixth day, whereas, if the Sabbath had been a regularly authorized day of cessation from usual avocations, the rulers would have understood the cause immediately. It has been suggested, as a solution of this seeming difficulty, that the day of the Sabbath was now changed, being put forward one day, in which case, the first day of the week, now observed by Christians, will be identical with the day of the creation-Sabbath, as maintained by several critics. The order of the original words (disregarded by the Common Version) appears to support the hypothesis : 'A rest—a holy rest to Jehovah *is* to-morrow,' not '*the* rest,' or '*the* holy sabbath,' as might otherwise have been expected.

29. BECAUSE...THEREFORE.] God having given a command, will not allow those observing it to suffer any real evil, having inseparably connected duty with happiness; compare Ex. 34. 24.

PLACE...PLACE.] These are two different words in the original, but the difference is perhaps inexpressible in a translation ; the first, TAHATH, occurs in Zec. 6. 12; Ex. 16. 23, 29; Ju. 7. 21; 1 Sa. 14. 9; 2 Sa. 2. 23; 7. 10; 1 Ch. 17. 9; Job 36. 16, &c.; the second, MAKOM, in Ge. 1. 9; Ex. 3. 5, 8, &c.

31. MANNA,] rather, as in Hebrew, MAN, 'what;' see note on v. 15 for its origin.

CORIANDER,] i.e. in shape and abundance, not in colour. This seed is extensively used in the East as a spice for meats among bakers and confectioners. It is only mentioned elsewhere in Nu. 11. 7.

WHITE,] *or* whitish, inclining to yellow.

CAKE.] The original word occurs nowhere else ; its etymology is supposed to point to a broad, expanded cake of bread ; another word from the same root is generally rendered 'cruise,' i.e. of oil, water, &c. ; see 1 Sa. 28. 11, 12, 16; 1 K. 17. 12, 14, 16; 19. 6.

HONEY.] See note on Ge. 43. 11 ; Ex. 3. 8, 17 ; 13. 5, &c.

33. POT,] *or* basket, supposed to have been of wicker work ; the original word is found nowhere else. If the manna had been a mere natural production, it would have been unnecessary to preserve a specimen of it.

34. THE TESTIMONY,] i.e. the ark of the testimony, (25. 21, 22,) so called because it contained God's testimony to Israel, on the two tables of stone, with the Ten Matters, commonly called 'the ten commandments.'

35. LAND TO BE INHABITED,] not 'to a land inhabited;' they passed by various inhabited lands, such as Edom, Ammon, Amalek, Bashan, &c. As Moses led the people 'to the extremity of the land of Canaan,' it is not impossible nor improbable that he wrote this and the following verse, though not a few of the first critics consider it an addition of some later sacred writer, such as he who wrote the last chapter of Deuteronomy.

XVII. 1. REPHIDIM.] According to Nu. 33. 12, 13, after leaving the wilderness of Sin, they went to Dophkah, eight miles off, then to Alush, other twelve, and then to Rephidim, about eight miles further on the way to Sinai. Harmer writes : 'In the space of 315 miles, Mr Irwin found only four springs of water ; in another space of 115 miles, he found only four springs,' one of which was brackish, and another unwholesome.

2. STRIVE,] as in Nu. 20. 13 ; as the Philistines did with Isaac, (Ge. 26. 22 ;) as Jacob did with Laban, (Ge. 31. 36 ;) as the Ephraimites did with Gideon, (Ju. 8. 1 ;) as Nehemiah did with the nobles, (5. 7,) &c. TRY,] *or* prove : it is generally used in a good sense, (e.g. Ge. 22. 1 ; Ex. 15. 25 ; 16. 4 ; 20. 20, &c.,) but here evidently in a bad one, as in v. 7 ; Nu. 14. 22 ; De. 6. 6 ; 33. 8, &c.

3. MURMUR.] See note on 14. 2, &c.

4. STONED,] as in Ex. 8. 16 ; 19. 13 ; 21. 28, 29, 32 ; De. 13. 10 ; 17. 5 ; 22. 21, 24, &c.

5. THE ROCK.] The presence of the definite article points to some particular rock that was familiarly known and prominent. Monkish tradition points to a small piece of rock (having six openings like a lion's mouth on each side,) standing separate by itself. See an allusion to this miracle in 1 Cor. 10. 4, where it is spiritualized and applied to the Messiah.

6. HOREB.] See note on Ex. 3. 1.

7. MASSAH..MERIBAH,] i.e. 'trial..strife;' this naming of places and persons from particular events in their history is found throughout all the Holy Writings.

8. AMALEK,] generally supposed to be the posterity of Amalek, son of Eliphaz, (son of Esau,) by Timnah his concubine, (Ge. 36. 12, 16,) whose dwelling was the desert south of Judea, in Arabia-Petræa, in the neighbourhood of the Philistines, and of Mount Seir ; but, according to others, they were a different aboriginal tribe, said in Nu. 24. 20, to be 'the first of the Goyim,' or of the nations in that locality. Compare Ge. 14. 7.

COMETH,] out of their own territory to attack Israel, without having had received any cause of offence; compare De. 25. 17, 18.

9. JEHOSHUA,] elsewhere called 'Jeshua,' originally Hoshea, i.e. 'Jehovah saves,' was son of Nun, of the tribe of Ephraim, minister to Moses, and eventually his successor, privileged not only himself to enter the promised land as the reward of his faithful report of the state of the land, but to lead Israel into it ; his attachment to Moses manifested itself strikingly in his proposal to silence the two prophets in the camp ; see Ex. 24. 13 ; 32. 17 ; Nu. 11. 28 ; 13. 16 ; 14. 6 ; &c.

10. HUR,] according to Josephus, he was husband of Miriam : according to the Tal-

mud, son of Miriam and Caleb; see 1 Ch. 2. 5, 9, 19. 20.

11. LIFTETH UP HIS HAND,] in prayer to God, displaying also the staff as a kind of signal or banner, reminding those who beheld it of the wonders it had already accomplished.

13. WEAKENETH,] as in Job 14. 10; Is. 14. 12; Joel 3. 10.

14. WRITE...A BOOK.] This is the first mention of writing in the Bible; it clearly implies, however, that the art was already known and practised: it is straining the text too far to translate '*the* book,' as the Masorets have pointed it; there is no proof of its existence before this, though it is evident it was continued; see Ex. 24. 4, 7; 34. 27; Nu. 33. 1; 36. 13; De. 28. 61; Jo. 1. 7, 8.

WIPE AWAY,] as in Ge. 6. 7; 7. 4, 23; Ex. 32. 32, 33; Nu. 5. 23; De. 9. 14; 25. 6, 19; 29. 20, &c.

MEMORIAL,] as in 12. 14.

REMEMBRANCE,] as in 3. 15; De. 25. 19; 32. 26, &c.

15. ALTAR,] as Noah, Abraham, Isaac, and Jacob had done before him; see Ge. 8. 20; 12. 7; 26. 25; 35. 7.

NISSI,] i.e. 'my banner,' as the word is translated in Ps. 60. 4; see also its use in Nu. 21, 8, 9; 26. 10; Is. 5. 26; 11. 10, 12; 13. 2; 18. 3; 30. 17; 31. 9; 33. 23; 49. 22; 62. 10; Je. 4. 6, 21; 50. 2; 51. 12, 27; Ez. 27. 7.

16. A HAND IS AGAINST THE THRONE OF JAH.] This obscure expression has been rendered various ways, but that of the Common Version is most unlikely. 'Hand' has been taken to mean 'power,' i.e. 'because power is with Jehovah:' the word KES, 'throne,' is supposed to be a scribe's error for NES 'a banner,' i.e. because a hand (that of Moses) is on the banner of Jehovah;' the word 'on' may be justly rendered 'against,' i.e. because a hand (of Amalek) is against the throne of Jehovah.

XVIII. 1. JETHRO.] See Ex. 2. 1, &c.

2. BESIDES HER PRESENTS.] The original word only occurs elsewhere in 1 K. 9. 16; Mic. 1. 14, in both of which it signifies a (marriage)present: very weak is the idea of Gesenius and others, that it signifies 'a divorce, a bill of divorce.'

4. ELEAZAR,] i.e. my God is a help, as explained in the next clause.

6. SAITH UNTO MOSES,] by means of messengers sent beforehand.

7. WELFARE,] *lit.* 'peace.'

8. TRAVAIL,] as in Nu. 20. 14; Ne. 9. 32; La. 3. 5.

FOUND THEM,] as in Ge. 44. 34.

9. REJOICED,] as in Job 3. 6; Ps. 21. 6; 1 Ch. 16. 27; Ne. 8. 10; Ezra 6. 16.

11. IN THE THING THEY ACTED PROUDLY,] i.e. in oppressing the Israelites.

12. FOR GOD.] The change of name of the Divine Being might, at first sight, seem to imply that Jethro's acknowledgment of Jehovah was only that of one among many, though superior to every other, while his offerings were not to Jehovah but to God,

i.e. Deity in the abstract; but the next clause, where Aaron and the elders come in and feast with him 'before God,' shows that 'God' and 'Jehovah' are interchangeable, as already observed, as it is utterly unreasonable to suppose that they would recognize any God but Him whose name is 'Jehovah.'

TO EAT BREAD,] i.e. as a token of friendship sanctioned and sanctified by religion; see note on Ge. 43. 32, &c.; compare also Ge. 21, 28—30; 31. 46—49.

13. TO JUDGE,] as he was not only a prophet to reveal or declare the will of God to man, but a ruler, yea, a 'king in Jeshurun,' as it is said in De. 33. 5.

14. WHAT IS THIS?] The question does not imply ignorance of what was going on, but is simply a graceful way of opening up a conversation, in which he might find an opportunity of giving utterance to his sentiments.

15. TO SEEK GOD,] as in Ge. 25. 22; De. 4. 29; 2 K. 8. 8; 1 Ch. 10. 14; 2 Ch. 14. 7; 17. 4; 22. 9; Ps. 34. 5; 77. 2; 78. 34, &c.; the word 'God' is never applied to 'judges,' as some allege; see note on 21. 6.

17. NOT GOOD,] in the circumstances.

18. WEAR AWAY,] in body and in mind, as in Job 14. 18; Ps. 1. 3; 18. 45; 37. 2, &c., used of plants, trees, &c.

TOO HEAVY,] as he himself was sensible of afterwards, De. 1. 9.

19. I COUNSEL THEE,] as the word is used in Nu. 24. 14; 2 Ch. 26. 3, &c.

AND GOD IS WITH THEE,] from Him thou mayest enquire regarding the propriety of my advice.

OVER AGAINST,] as in 26. 9; 28. 25, 27 37; 34. 3; 39. 18, 20, &c.; it never means 'instead of,' as some have rendered it, but simply 'in the front of,'—before.

20. WARNED,] as in 2 K. 6. 10; 2 Ch. 19. 10; Ez. 3. 17, 18, 19, 20, 21; 33. 3, 7, 8, 9.

21. PROVIDE,] *lit.* 'see,' i.e. look out for; compare 24. 11; Ps. 11. 4; Pr. 24. 32; Is. 30. 10.

ABILITY,] *lit.* 'strength, might,' and, like the Latin '*virtus*,' applied often to the mind, Ge. 47. 6; De. 3. 18; Jo. 1. 14; 6. 2; 8. 3; 10. 7; Ruth 3. 11; Pr. 12. 4, &c.

FEARING GOD,] as in Ge. 22. 12; 42. 18; Ex. 9. 20; 1 K. 18. 3; Job 1. 1, 8; 2. 3, &c.

MEN OF TRUTH,] the phrase occurs no where else, but the meaning is plain.

DISHONEST GAIN,] as in Pr. 28. 16; Ps. 119. 36; Is. 33. 15, &c.

HEADS...OF TENS.] This advice, though excellent as a whole, was carrying the divisions too far; for 600,000 men there must have been, according to this plan, 60,000 heads of tens, 6000 heads of hundreds, 600 heads of thousands, in all 78,600 judges! It was apparently found unworkable, for at a later period seventy elders were chosen, and fitted to assist him.

23. AND GOD HATH COMMANDED THEE.] This language shows Jethro to have been a man of a truly godly spirit, proposing that his plans should only be adopted after receiving the Divine sanction.

STAND,] i.e. 'endure,' as in 21. 21.

ITS PLACE,] i.e. the promised land, or to their tents, returning from the tribunals.

27. HIS OWN LAND,] i.e. Midian; from Ju. 1. 16; 1 Ch. 2. 55; Je. 35. 2, it appears that the Kenites and the Rechabites, his descendants, afterwards lived among the Jews, and became proselytes.

XIX. 1. THIRD MONTH,] i.e. Sivan, part of May and June; see Est. 8. 9.

SINAI] is believed to be the name of a mountain forming part of a great range named Horeb; here the Israelites remained about eleven months and a half; compare Nu. 10. 11.

2. REPHIDIM...SINAI,] about eight miles distant from each other, the latter forming the 12th station of the Israelites after leaving Egypt.

3. UNTO GOD,] on the top of the mount.

4. EAGLE'S WINGS.] Compare De. 32. 11; the eagle is remarkable for its strength of wing, its long life, its love to its young, &c. He bore them out of the reach of danger, and set them in a place of safety—by Himself.

5. PECULIAR TREASURE,] as in De. 7. 6; 14. 2; 26. 18; Ps. 135. 4; Mal. 3. 17; compare its use in Ec. 2. 8; 1 Ch. 29. 3.

6. KINGDOM OF PRIESTS,] a title found nowhere else in the Old Testament; but compare 1 Peter 2. 9; Rev. 1. 6; they were so in respect of their being 'separated' or set apart to Him and his service in a special, peculiar way, to proclaim His truth and love in opposition to the gods of the nations.

HOLY NATION,] as repeated in De. 7. 6; 14. 2, 21; 26. 19; 28. 9; in respect of their being 'separated' from all the other peoples of the earth.

9. THE THICKNESS OF THE CLOUD,] as in v. 16; similar appearances of the Divine Being are noticed in Ex. 40. 34; 1 K. 8. 10, 11; Mat. 17. 5; Rev. 10. 1.

10. WASHED THEIR GARMENTS,] as in v. 14; Le. 11. 25, &c.; compare Ge. 35. 2, where ceremonial cleansing appears to have existed before the giving of the law of Moses.

11. PREPARED,] as in v. 15; 34. 2; Jo. 8. 4.

12. MADE A BORDER,] as in v. 23; De. 19. 14; Jo. 18. 20; Zec. 9. 2.

13. A HAND COMETH NOT AGAINST HIM,] i.e. the transgressor; so Aben Ezra: he was to be stoned or shot through.

DRAWING OUT,] i.e. prolongation of the sound, as in Jo. 6. 5; compare the use of the same original word in Ps. 10. 9; Ec. 2. 3.

JUBILEE-CORNET.] See the same word in Jo. 6. 4, 5, 6, 8, 13; Nu. 36. 4; De. 25. 10—54; 27. 17—24.

THEY GO UP,] i.e. the people go up a certain way, beyond the boundary line; compare 24. 9—15. Unnecessary is the refinement of certain critics in translating 'they go forward,' the word is always 'go up;' the distinction being one of degree, not of kind.

15. COME NOT NIGH.] This restraint is said to have been observed during religious festivals by the Babylonians, Arabians,

Egyptians, Greeks, and Romans, and is still among Mohammedans; compare 1 Sa. 21. 5.

16. VOICES,] i.e. thunders, as in 9. 23, on which see note.

LIGHTNINGS,] as in 2 Sa. 22. 15; Job 38. 35, &c.

A TRUMPET,] as in v. 19; 20. 18; Le. 25. 9; Jo. 6. 4—20; Ju. 3. 27, &c.

17. MEET GOD] in his promised manifestation as their Lawgiver, with which no other nation was ever so favoured.

18. SMOKE,] as in 20. 18, &c., arising from the dense clouds enveloping the mount.

IN FIRE,] i.e. flashes of lightning, as in v. 16.

SMOKE OF THE FURNACE.] Compare same phrase in Ge. 15. 17.

TREMBLETH,] same word as in v. 16.

19. SOUND,] lit. 'voice.'

MOSES SPEAKETH.] Though his words are not recorded, Gill and Macknight suggest they may have been the sentiment quoted in Heb. 12. 21, 'I am fearful exceedingly—and trembling,' which are not found recorded anywhere in the Old Testament.

20. GOETH UP,] into the mount still further.

21. PROTEST,] as in v. 23; Je. 32. 25; Amos 3. 13; Ge. 43. 3; Ex. 21. 29; De. 4. 26; 8. 19; 30. 19; 31. 28; 32. 46.

BREAK THROUGH,] or down; as in v. 24; compare Ex. 15. 7; Ju. 6. 25, &c.

FALLEN,] i.e. dead; as in Ge. 28. 15, &c.

22. PRIESTS.] Only in 28. 1, do we find Aaron and his sons set apart to the priests' office; who, then, were these priests? the easiest solution appears to be, that every head of a family or first-born was naturally the priest of his household. In 24. 5, mention is made of certain young men who offered sacrifices.

24. BREAK FORTH,] as in Ge. 38. 39; 2 Sa. 5. 20; 6. 8; Job 16. 16; 1 Ch. 13. 11, &c.

XX. 2. I, JEHOVAH, AM THY GOD,] and therefore claim thy willing ear and cheerful obedience; I am He who hath taken you to be my people, and have been taken by you to be your God; compare 19. 8.

WHO HAVE BROUGHT, ETC.] i.e. thy deliverer from a strange land, from a degrading, distressing state of servitude.

3. NO OTHER GODS,] i.e. no other being regarded as divine, to whom service is due.

BEFORE ME,] or 'against my face, or presence;' in v. 20, 'with me.'

4. A GRAVEN IMAGE,] as in Le. 26. 1; De. 4. 16, 23, 25; 5. 8; 27. 15; Ju. 17. 3, &c., compared with the use of the verb 'to grave,' in Ex. 34. 1, 4; De. 10. 1, 3; 1 K. 5. 18; Hab. 2. 18.

LIKENESS,] as in Nu. 12. 8; De. 4. 12, 15, 16, 23; 5. 8; Job 4. 16; Ps. 17. 15. In certain catechisms of the Romish Church this fourth verse is omitted. The prohibition is not against making statues or pictures of any object for ornament, (witness the cherub work in the tabernacle, 25. 18—20; compare 25. 34; 26. 32; Nu. 41. 8. 9; the twelve oxen 1 K. 7. 25: the *fourteen lions*, 1 K. 10. 20; the brazen *serpent*, Nu. 21. 9, &c.); but for *religious adoration*, as the next verse explicitly shows.

5. NOT BOW THYSELF TO THEM,] because they are senseless, useless, capable of doing neither good nor evil. The verb is often used of the respect due to any one, whether God or man, e.g. Ge. 18. 2; 19. 1; 22. 5; 23. 7, 12; 24. 26, 48, 52; 27. 29; 33. 3, 6, 7; 37. 7, 9, 10; 42. 6; 43. 26, 28; 47. 31; 48. 12; 49. 8; Ex. 4. 31; 11. 8; 12. 27; 18. 7, &c.

SERVE THEM,] i.e. keep their rites, ceremonies, &c.

ZEALOUS,] as repeated in 34. 14; De. 4. 24; 5. 9; 6. 15; compare Nu. 25. 11; 2 K. 10. 16; 19. 31; Ps. 69. 9.

CHARGING,] Common Version 'visiting.. upon,' is an unintelligible, and un-English phrase; the original word *never* means 'to visit,' i.e. come to see, though it is so translated several hundreds of times in the C. V.; it always has the idea of 'looking over, looking after, inspecting, examining;' and is sometimes used causatively, 'to set, appoint, lay a charge' upon anyone. 'Those hating me,' refer to the *children*, not to the *parents*. The vulgar interpretation is directly opposed to De. 24. 16; 2 K. 14. 5, 6; (Ex. 32. 33;) compare Ge. 18. 25; Le. 26. 39, 40; Je. 31, 29, 30; Ez. 18. 20—24. As the particle AL signifies not only '*on*,' but *with*,' (e.g. Ex. 35. 22, the men WITH the women,') the real translation probably is, 'looking after the iniquity of fathers WITH (the iniquity of) sons, WITH (the iniquity of) a third (generation,) and WITH (the iniquity of) a fourth—of those hating me.'

DOING KINDNESS,] the original verb *never* signifies 'showing,' but always 'doing;' and the noun *never* signifies 'mercy,' but always 'kindness.'

THOUSANDS] '*of generations*,' must here be supplied from the former clause.

7. TAKE UP,] on the lips, in conversation; it has no reference whatever to judicial proceedings.

VAIN THING,] i.e. a worthless, empty thing; it prohibits the unguarded use of the name of God on trivial occasions.

ACQUITTETH,] *or* 'declareth innocent,' as in Ex. 34. 7; Nu. 14. 18; De. 5. 11; 1 K. 2. 9; Job 9. 28; 10. 14; Je. 30. 11; 46. 28; Na. 1. 3; (Je. 49. 12.)

8. REMEMBER,] obviously implying the previous existence of the thing to be remembered.

THE SABBATH DAY,] *lit.* 'the day of the rest.'

TO SANCTIFY IT,] i.e. 'separate' *or* 'set it apart,' from all other days, (as in Ge. 2. 2, 3,) by a cessation from 'work *or* servile labour.'

9. THOU DOST LABOUR,] as in Ge. 2. 5, 15; De. 5. 13.

10. THE SEVENTH DAY,] as in Ge. 2. 2, 3. A SABBATH,] not '*the* sabbath.'

TO JEHOVAH,] i.e. 'the seventh day is a rest—with a view to Jehovah,' to keeping

his commandments, &c.; not 'of Jehovah, i.e. belonging to Him.

ANY WORK,] i.e. servile labour.

GATES,] i.e. 'cities,' as in De. 17. 2; 12. 12; 14. 27; 1 K. 8. 37; 2 Ch. 6. 28; but De. 6. 9, shows it may be also simply the gate of any private dwelling. The observance of *circumcision* by a sojourner was optional, his observance of the *passover* depended on his compliance with the former; but his observance of the sabbath rest was obligatory; the first being *personal*, the second *national*, the third *natural*. From 2 K. 4. 23, we infer that on the sabbath, prophets, teachers, and men of God, were accustomed to have meetings with the people, and on certain sabbaths at least, there were 'holy convocations' of all the people, though, doubtless, the actual laws on the subject are simply negative in their character—forbidding all servile labour, gathering of manna, wood, &c., kindling of fires, (by implication, cooking of dishes,) carrying of burdens, selling and buying, agricultural labour, &c. : a breach of these enactments involved the offender in a capital crime.

As all Christians admit the binding authority of the other nine commandments, there is reason, *prima facie*, to believe the fourth to be binding likewise, but if so, it must be taken *as a whole*, (not in part,) except in so far as it may have been repealed, expressly or by a irresistible inference. It must be admitted that the *whole tone* of the New Testament, without a single exception, is adverse to the rigid observance of the Jewish ritual, and that, probably, not a single individual in this land would insist on carrying out all the law as laid down in the Pentateuch on this subject. The truth of the matter appears to be, that we cannot place 'the Christian Sabbath' on the basis of the Mosaic legislation at all, the *time*, the *manner*, the *reason*, and the *penalty*, being all different.

Intelligent Christian men are now generally agreed, 1.) That during every age of the visible church of God, there has been a seventh portion of time set apart for cessation from worldly toils, and for the public service of God.

2.) That the Mosaic Sabbath law cannot be retained as a whole.

3.) That while there is no express law in the New Testament on the subject, it is evident that the first Christians and inspired followers of the Saviour, were accustomed to meet together for the service of God and mutual exhortation, and that on what is uniformly called 'the first day of the week.'

4.) That this *practice* appears to be once enjoined—'not forsaking the assembling of ourselves together as the manner of some is.'—And,

5.) That beyond this general duty of assembling together for the purpose of worship and mutual edification—there is not, and there ought not to be, anything required by the Church to bind any man's conscience.

11. SIX DAYS...MADE,] as recorded in the opening chapter of Genesis.

12. HONOUR,] *lit.* 'make heavy,' but always used figuratively; see De. 5. 16; 1 Sa. 15. 30; Ps. 22. 23; Pr. 3. 9; Is. 24. 15, comprehending, 1) reverence, 2) love, 3) obedience, 4) support; compare Mat. 15. 4—6; 1 Tim. 5. 17.

THY FATHER AND THY MOTHER,] as in Le. 19. 3; Mal. 1. 6; Eph. 6. 2; Heb. 12. 9. This command is carried to a very unnecessary degree of refinement in that really valuable compendium of faith and practice, where it is said, 'The fifth commandment requireth the preserving the honour, and performing the duties, belonging to every one in their several places and relations, as superiors, *inferiors*, and *equals*.' These duties are all enforced in SS., but not in the text; it is a well-meant specimen of rearing a mountain of meaning on a word or clause, for which certain Jewish writers are well known.

PROLONGED,] as in Nu. 9. 9; De. 4. 26, 40; 5. 16, 33; 6. 2; 11. 9; 17. 20; 22. 7; 25. 15; 30. 18; 32. 47, &c.

THE LAND,] i.e. of Canaan, but not necessarily restricted to it; in Ps. 115. 16, we read, 'The earth He hath given to the sons of men,' so that every place where a man is he may consider as the land which Jehovah his God is giving to him to live on and inherit; the promise, therefore, need not be considered as a special favour to Israel of old, but one which accompanies obedience to the law of God as much now as then, and always with the well-known Scriptural and common-sense limitation: 'as far as it shall serve for God's glory and their own good.'

13. MURDER,] not 'kill,' which is in certain cases 'lawful,' if not 'expedient.' Compare, however, the use of the word in Nu. 35. 6—31, where it is applied alike to a deliberate 'murderer,' and to an unintentional 'manslayer;' also De. 4. 42; 5. 17; 19. 3, 4, 6; 22. 26, &c.

14. COMMIT ADULTERY,] as in Le. 20. 10; De. 5. 18; Job 24. 15, &c. Compare Mat. 5. 28, 30.

15. STEAL,] as in Le. 19. 11; De. 5. 19. The primary idea of the original word is, 'to do a thing secretly,' as in Ge. 31. 27; 40. 15; 2 Sa. 15. 6; 19. 3, 41; Job 4. 12; 21. 18; 27. 20.

16. ANSWER,] as in Ex. 4. 1; 15. 21; 19. 8, 19; 23. 2; 24. 23, &c.

FALSE TESTIMONY,] *lit.* 'a testimony of falsehood,' as in De. 19. 18; Ps. 27. 12; Pr. 6. 19; 12. 17; 14. 5; 19. 5, 9; 25. 18, &c.

17. DESIRE,] as in 34. 24, De. 5. 21; 7. 25; Jo. 7. 21; Job 20. 20; Ps. 39. 11; 68. 16; Pr. 1. 22; 6. 25; 12. 12; Is. 1. 29; 53. 2; Mic. 2. 2, &c.

WIFE.] This clause has been made, in several Popish catechisms, a new commandment, to supply the lack of *the second*, which they had omitted, as noticed above. Strange to say, the Masorets had done the same before them, some time from the seventh to the tenth century. Were there Romanists among them? it is not improbable, as the punctuation system of the Masorets is much more in accordance with the Vulgate Translation, in use in the Romish Church, than with the older Septuagint one, the use of which was confined chiefly to the Greeks, their hated rivals.

18. SEEING THE VOICES,] i.e. the thunders; for the mixed imagery here used, see note on 5. 21.

19. LEST WE DIE,] it being a general belief of the ancients—Jews and Gentiles alike—that the presence of God is a consuming fire; compare the language of Manoah, Isaiah, &c. Compare Heb. 12. 19, 20, &c.

20. TO TRY YOU.] See note on Ge. 22. 1; Ex. 15. 15; 16. 4; 17. 2, 7, &c.

HIS FEAR,] i.e. the sense of reverence due to Him may be always before the eyes of their mind.

THAT YE SIN NOT,] i.e. that in your seeking to obey his commands, ye may not go aside from, nor fail of coming up to, the point to be aimed at, as the original word always implies.

21. THICK DARKNESS.] See 19. 9, 16, &c; compare also 1 K. 8. 12.

22. FROM THE HEAVENS.] Compare Ge. 21. 17; 22. 11, 15; De. 4. 36; 1 Sa. 2. 10; 2 Sa. 22. 14; 1 Ch. 21. 26; Ps. 18. 13; 20. 6; Ecc. 5. 2, &c.

23. GODS...TO YOURSELVES.] Idolatry was the great evil into which Israel all throughout their history were most liable to fall, hence we have 'line upon line, precept upon precept,' prohibiting it; the Babylonian captivity, however, appears to have nearly cured them, for since then, as a nation, they have abhorred idols—at least all outward visible symbols of such. The Masoretic accentuation of this verse is justly declared by Kalisch to be 'scarcely intelligible, much less logical.'

24. ALTAR OF EARTH,] probably in opposition to the gorgeous pagan ones, thus described (in Smith's Antiq., p. 116, *b*,) 'They were adorned with sculpture, and some were covered with the works of the most celebrated artists;' afterwards the altar for burnt-offerings was made of shittim-wood covered with brass, Ex. 27. 1, 2; and that in the temple was wholly of brass, 1 Ch. 4. 1.

PEACE-OFFERINGS.] This is the first occurrence of this word, which properly denotes 'a making complete' or perfect, a kind of repaying, recompensing, for benefits received, hence generally a thank-offering, but not always, (see Ju. 20. 26; 21. 4,) compare 24. 5; 29. 28; 32. 6; Le. 3. 1, 3, 6, 9, &c.

CAUSETH MY NAME TO BE REMEMBERED,] or 'to be made mention of,' see 23. 13; Jo. 23. 7; Ps. 20. 7; 45. 17; Is. 12. 4; 48. 1; 49. 1; 62. 6, &c.

I COME IN] not bodily, but spiritually; compare John 14. 21—23.

25. HEWN STONE,] which is prohibited doubtless for the general reason mentioned in the notes on the preceding verse.

TOOL,] *lit.* a 'wasting destroying' instrument of any kind, applied to a sword, knife, razor, axe, graving tool, &c.

E

WAVED,] as the word is used in 29. 24, 26; 35. 22; 2 K. 5. 11; Is. 11. 15.

POLLUTE,] as in 31. 14; Le. 18. 21; 19. 29, &c.

26. STEPS,] as in 1 K. 10. 19, 20; 2 K. 9. 13; 20. 9, 10, 11, &c. The altars were generally three feet high, but Solomon's was ten cubits high; they were gone up by a gentle ascent.

REVEALED,] or 'uncovered.'

XXI. 1. JUDGMENTS,] i.e. the sentences of a judge (even of God himself,) which the children of Israel were to obey; sometimes the word also denotes, 1) the act of judging, 2) the place of judgment, 3) a plea in law, 4) the offence, 5) a law, right, custom, habit.

2. BUYEST.] The primary idea of the original word is 'to acquire, get possession,' of anything, irrespective of the means, e.g. Pr. 4. 7; 15, 32; 16. 16; 19. 8; Ruth 4. 9, 10; Ge. 4. 1; also to buy, Ge. 25. 10; 47. 22; Is. 11. 11; Ne. 5. 8. A Hebrew *might sell himself* (for a number of years) on account of his poverty, or he might *be sold*, because of theft, debt, &c.

FREEMAN,] as in v. 5, 26, 27; De. 15. 12, 13, 18; 1 Sa. 17. 15; Job 3. 19; 39. 5; Ps. 88. 5; Is. 58. 6; Je. 34. 9, 10, 11, 14, 16.

FOR NOUGHT,] as in Ge. 29. 15; Ex. 21, 2, 11; Nu. 11. 5; 1 Sa. 19. 5; 25. 31, &c.

3. BY HIMSELF,] *lit.* 'in (*or* with) his body;' as in v. 4; Sept. 'alone;' the word is properly 'the back,' hence applied to an eminence, (Pr. 9. 3,) and to a wing, (Da. 7. 4, 6.

OWNER,] i.e. 'possessor, master.'

4. THE WIFE AND HER CHILDREN ARE HER LORD'S.] This is omitted in the parallel passage, De. 15. 12—18; by giving one of his female attendants to one of his male servants, the master was held to be still her's till she was redeemed : the servant must have known the law, and consented to it before he married her, he therefore could make no legal claim, and could only obtain his wife and family by paying their price, or by continuing in the service of her and his employer. Some regulations in the Mosaic code appear harsh, but this may be only in appearance, if we knew all the particulars of the cases; at the same time, the general spirit of the Mosaic legislation is truly admirable in its care for the poor and the stranger, its equitable claims for rich and poor, high and low, king, priest, and peasant.

5. UNTO GOD,] as the word always means in the Old Testament; it was probably to the priest as his representative, who would solemnly ratify the deed.

AWL,] as in De. 15. 17.

TO THE AGE.] i.e. all the days of his life, as in 1 Sa. 1. 11, 22, 28; not as Aben Ezra asserts, 'till the year of jubilee.' Very weak is the supposed reference to this act in Ps. 40. 7, rendered in the Common Version, 'my ears thou hast bored;' the argument rests only on the gratuitous uniformity of the Common Version; the *verbs* are entirely different in the two passages,

expressing different acts; the servant in Exodus also had only *one* ear bored, the servant in the Psalm speaks of *both* his ears; see note thereon.

7. HAND-MAID,] as in Ge. 20. 17; 21. 10, 12, 13; 30. 3; 31. 33; Ex. 2. 5; 20. 10, 17, &c.; it is not *necessary* to suppose with some that she was sold to be a concubine; the original word AMAH is familiar still in the East, denoting a lady's female attendant, generally a married woman who suckles her mistress's children.

NOT GO OUT] in the seventh year.

8. HE HATH NOT BETROTHED HER.] This is the rendering of the present Hebrew text; the Common Version follows the marginal reading, which has, 'to himself' instead of 'not,' a change of one Hebrew letter; Onkelos, Vulgate, De Wette, Winer, &c. support the marginal reading, while the Samaritan, Syriac, Symnachus, Theodotian, &c. agree with the text.

TO STRANGE PEOPLE,] whether Israelites or not; compare the use of the word in Pr. 2. 16; 5. 10, 20, &c.

RIGHT,] *lit.* 'judgment,' as in v. 1, 31; 23. 6; 24. 3; 26. 30.

9. DEALING TREACHEROUSLY;] have led her to expect marriage, and afterwards changed his purpose.

10. HABITATION.] The original word is only found elsewhere in Ho. 10. 10, where it is rendered 'iniquity,' which cannot be the meaning here; the probable root is AUN, to 'dwell.'

WITHDRAW,] as the word always means; see Job 36. 7; Ec. 5. 8, 19; De. 4. 2; 12. 32, &c.

13. LAID WAIT,] *or* 'hunted;' compare the use of the word in 1 Sa. 24. 11; Zep. 3. 6.

HATH BROUGHT] *or* 'caused to come;' compare Ps. 91. 10; Pr. 12. 21; 2 K. 5. 7.

14. PRESUME,] i.e. act proudly; compare De. 1. 43; 17. 13; 18. 20; Neh. 9. 10, 16, 29; in Ge. 25. 29, it is used in its primitive meaning of 'boiling, boiling over.'

ALTAR,] which was a sacred sanctified place, to which a murderer would naturally flee for safety, as was common among the Greeks and Romans; in 1 K. 1. 50, we read of Adonijah, and in 1 K. 2. 28, of Joab doing this, but in accordance with the law in the text, the latter was put to death even there.

15. SMITETH HIS FATHER,] not necessarily fatally, otherwise we would have expected the same clause to be added which is found in v. 12, 'so that he hath died;' in the East parental authority is scarcely, if at all, inferior to that of God himself—the parents being regarded as in his place; see also v. 17, which the Sept. places before v. 16, and with evident propriety.

16. STEALETH A MAN,] i.e. any one, not merely a 'Hebrew,' as Onkelos, Jonathan, and Sept. have rendered it, by confounding the present passage with De. 24. 7.

IN HIS HAND,] i.e. to have been in his possession.

17. REVILING,] as in Ge. 8. 21; 12. 3; Ex. 22. 28; Le. 19. 14; 20. 9; 24 11, 14. 15, 23, &c.

18. FALLEN ON THE BED.] The phrase occurs nowhere else, but the meaning is obvious.

19. HIS CESSATION,] i.e. the time of his being unable for his ordinary duties.

20. ROD,] i.e. staff, stick, crook, as in Ge. 38. 18, 25; Ex. 4. 2, 4, 17, 20, &c.

AVENGED,] as in Ju. 15. 7; 16. 28; 1 Sa. 14. 24; 18. 25; Is. 1. 24; Est. 8. 13 : Ez. 25. 12, 15; Je. 15. 15; 46. 10; 50. 15; the master must die the death of a murderer.

21. HIS MONEY,] i.e. the loss of the money which the master had paid for the services of the servant, being reckoned as a sufficient punishment for his unintentional homicide; this is doubtless one of the laws given to Israel for their 'hardness of heart,' just as the law of retaliation and the rights of the redeemer of blood were only partly modified, not entirely done away with.

22. SMITTEN,] as in 8. 2; 12. 23, 27; 21. 35; 32. 35.

MISCHIEF,] as in v. 23; Ge. 42. 4, 38; 44. 29; no mischief to her or her children—causing simply premature labour.

FINED,] as in De. 22. 19; 2 K. 23. 33; 2 Ch. 36.·3; Am. 2. 8; in Pr. 17. 26; 19. 19; 21. 11; 22. 3; 27. 12, the original word is used in the more general sense of 'punish.'

23. THROUGH THE JUDGES,] that there be no mistake nor second claim for damages.

24. EYE FOR EYE, ETC.] It has always been a question whether this is to be taken literally; the Jewish writers generally say it is figurative language, and so the Targum of Jonathan has 'the price of an eye for an eye,' &c. This is indeed the only reasonable interpretation, as it would be quite impossible to inflict upon an offender *exactly* the same amount of injury he had done to another, to exact the 'pound of flesh,' neither more nor less. It is perfectly evident, moreover, that these laws were not left to be executed by private individuals, but by the judge or civil magistrate.

25. BURNING.] This word is not found elsewhere in SS., but in a verbal form it occurs in Pr. 6. 28; Is. 43. 2.

26. DESTROYED,] *or* 'corrupted' it, as the original word is often translated; see its use in 8. 24; 32. 7, &c.

27. KNOCK OUT,] *lit.* 'cause to fall.'

28. THE OX IS STONED.] Compare the law as given to Noah and his posterity, in Ge.9. 5.

ITS FLESH IS NOT EATEN,] it being considered, in consequence of the act, unclean, and therefore polluting those who might eat it.

ACQUITTED,] *or* 'freed,' from blame and punishment.

29. OWNER IS ALSO PUT TO DEATH] by the hands of the civil magistrate, not 'by the hand of God,' as certain Jewish writers maintain; the next clause, however, shows that it was at the option of deceased's family to grant a remission of the capital punishment on payment of a sum of money, the deed being only one of culpable homicide, not of deliberate or intentional murder, for which latter offence no atonement whatever could be allowed.

30. ATONEMENT,] from a verb signifying 'to cover;' hence anything which one gives to cover over his fault; see 30. 12; Nu. 35. 31, 32; 1 Sa. 12. 3; Job 33. 24; 36. 18; Ps. 49. 7; Pr. 6. 35; 13. 8; 21. 18; Song 4. 13; Is. 43. 3; Am. 5. 12, translated in the Common Version, 'a sum of money, a ransom, satisfaction, bribe;' for the use of the verb, see Ge. 32. 20.

RANSOM,] *or* 'redemption,' as the original word is rendered in the only other instance of its occurrence, viz. Ps. 49. 8. Kindred words from the same root occur in Ex. 8. 23; Nu. 3. 46, 49, &c.

31. JUDGMENT,] *or* 'sentence,' here prescribed by God himself.

32. THIRTY SILVER SHEKELS,] being the recognized price of a slave; in the case of a son or daughter, mentioned in the preceding verse, no particular sum is specified, but from Le. 27. 3, we learn that fifty shekels (by the shekel of the sanctuary) was the estimated value for a freeman between the age of 20 and 60 years.

33. OPEN A PIT] which had been shut.

DIG A PIT,] i.e. a new one, in any public thoroughfare.

34. REPAY,] *or* 'recompence.'

35. DEAD ONE THEY HALVE,] i.e. its price or value, not its body.

36. THE DEAD IS HIS,] i.e. he who has to repay; but some say the first owner is here meant, and that the owner of the ox which gored its neighbour had not only to repair the loss, but was deprived of the dead carcase, as a punishment for his negligence.

XXII. 1. OX OR SHEEP.] These being the most common, are selected as specimens of cattle generally.

FIVE OF THE HERD..FOUR OF THE FLOCK.] The herd being generally more serviceable than the flock, theft out of it was more severely punished, and required greater compensation.

2. BREAKING THROUGH,] in order to steal, Eastern houses being generally of very fragile materials; compare the use of the word in Je. 2. 34, the only other instance of its occurrence; see also the verb in Job 24. 16; Amos 9. 2; Jon. 1. 13; Ez. 8. 8; 12, 5, 7, 12.

NO BLOOD FOR HIM,] i.e. the redeemer of blood has no right to avenge the death, the blow having been struck in the dark.

3. IF THE SUN HATH RISEN,] those in the house ought to have apprehended the thief, and the judge would have compelled him to pay the legal penalties, while, if he were unable to do this, he would be sold as a servant for a period of time to pay the legal damages; if those in the house smote him fatally instead of apprehending him, they were liable to death from the blood-avenger.

4. IF FOUND ALIVE...DOUBLE HE REPAYETH.] If slaughtered or sold (according to v. 1) he was to repay four or five-fold, here if found alive in his possession, he only restores double; this distinction was made probably to induce the guilty party to restore the stolen property of his own

accord, before he had put it out of his power by slaughtering or selling it.

5. DEPASTURETH,] *lit.* 'burneth *or* consumeth;' compare its use in 22. 6; Ju. 15. 5; 1 K. 16. 3; 2 Ch. 28. 3; Nah. 2. 13; Ez. 5. 2.

BEAST,] generally a beast of burden; see all the instances of its occurrence, viz. Ge. 45. 17; Nu. 20. 4, 8, 11; Ps. 78. 48.

PASTURED,] *lit.* 'burned or consumed;' see Le. 6. 12; Nu. 24. 22; De. 13. 5; 26. 13, &c.

6. FOUND.] Compare the expressions in Ge. 44. 34; Ex. 18. 18; Nu. 20. 14; 32. 23; Jo. 2. 23; Ju. 6. 13; Ps. 116. 3; 119; 143.

7. REPAYETH DOUBLE,] as in v. 4; but some are of opinion this was only if the stolen property was recovered in his possession—if the thief had sold it, they say he had to restore it fourfold; but this is doubtful.

8. NEAR UNTO GOD,] who by his regularly commissioned servants—the judge or the priest—would decide the matter in dispute. So in v. 10. twice.

WORK.] See the same word in v. 11; Ge. 33. 14; 1 Sa. 15. 9.

9. TRANSGRESSION,] not 'trespass,' which the original word never means; see 23. 21; 34. 7, &c.

CONDEMN,] *lit.* 'declare wicked,' as in De. 25. 1; 1 Sa. 14. 47 · 1 K. 8. 32; 2 Ch. 20. 35; 22. 3; Job 9. 20.

12. REPAY,] having been hired to keep it, as the Targum of Jonathan explains it.

14. ASK] the use of anything for which he pays.

16. ENTICE,] as in Ju. 14. 15; 16. 5; Pr. 1. 10; &c.

VIRGIN,] as in v. 17; Le. 21. 3, 14; De. 22. 19, 23, 28; 32. 25; Ge. 24. 16, on which see note.

BETROTHED.] Throughout the East children are betrothed to each other when very young, and there is no other ceremony when they come to live together; very rarely do either of the parties repudiate the engagement however unsuitable.

ENDOW.] The money or other equivalent given by the man for his wife properly belongs to her, not to her parents, and remains her own special property, over which the husband himself has no control whatever afterwards.

17. REFUSE] as being an improper or unequal match; she herself is never consulted.

MONEY...WEIGH OUT.] There being no *paper* currency in the East, and scarcely any *gold* money, silver and copper are the principal metals, which are weighed, not counted, when in any considerable quantity to save time. How much he had to pay is not stated, but probably it might be 50 shekels of silver, as in De. 22. 29.

18. A WITCH.] See note on Ex. 7. 11; also De. 18. 10; Da. 2. 2; Mal. 3. 5; 2 Ch. 33. 6; Je. 27. 9.

KEEP ALIVE,] as in Ge. 12. 12; 19. 32, 34; Ex. 1. 17, 18, 22; De. 20. 16; 32. 39.

19. A BEAST,] which also was to be stoned,

according to Le. 20. 15, 16. This was one of the abominations of the Egyptians, as well as of the Canaanites.

20. SACRIFICING.] This being the highest form of religious service, including all others, the early Christians were very frequently offered life if they would sacrifice to the gods.

DEVOTED] to the Lord (either for destruction or preservation), as the word always signifies, see Le. 27. 28, 29; Nu. 21. 2, 3: De. 3. 6; 7. 2; 20. 17, &c.

21. SOJOURNER,] not a 'stranger,' see Le. 25. 47.

OPPRESS,] not 'vex;' see Le. 19. 33; 25. 14, 17; De. 23. 16; Je. 22. 3; Is. 49. 26; Ez. 18. 7, 12, 16; 22. 7, 29; 45. 8.

25. USURER,] *lit.* a 'lifter up,' one who exacts something from another; compare De. 15. 2; 24. 10, 11; 2 K. 4. 1; Ne. 5. 7, 10, 11; Ps. 109. 11; Is. 24. 2; 50. 1; Je. 15. 10.

USURY,] *lit.* 'biting,' (Ge. 49. 17;) see Le. 25. 36, 37; De. 23. 19. 20; Ps. 15. 5; Pr. 28. 8; Ez. 18, 8, 13, 17 : 22. 12.

26. GARMENT.] The same long flowing garment which serves an Oriental for a day-dress is wrapped around him by night, and forms generally his only covering; they are commonly white, and easily washed and dried by the sun in a few minutes.

28. GOD,] not 'the gods;' the word 'revile' is literally 'disesteem,' and it could scarcely be expected that they would be required to 'esteem' the idols of the nations; but God himself is here referred to, and his appointed servant in the next clause—'a prince' among thy people; this latter clause is quoted by Paul in Acts 23. 5.

29. THY FULNESS,] i.e. the abundance of thy corn (De. 22. 9; Nu. 18. 27,) which was to be offered to the Lord as first-fruits, as well as the fulness of

THY LIQUIDS,] *lit.* 'thy tear,' used here metaphorically of olives and grapes, but nowhere else.

DELAY,] *or* 'defer,' as in Ge. 34. 19; 24. 56; De. 7. 10; 23. 21, &c.

FIRST BORN.] See note on 13. 2.

30. TO THINE OX, ETC.] i.e. their firstlings were the Lord's.

EIGHTH DAY.] From Nu. 18. 16, it appears they were obliged to ransom it at the end of a month by five silver shekels.

31. HOLY MEN TO ME,] i.e. persons separated, set apart to Him; compare 1 Pet. 2. 9.

XXIII. 1. LIFT UP,] i.e. propagate or fabricate in the sight of God or man.

A VAIN REPORT,] *lit.* 'a hearing of a vain thing,' i.e. anything unsubstantial, without foundation, worthless; see the use of the word in Ex. 20. 7; De. 5. 11, 20; Job 7. 3; 11. 11; 15. 31; 31. 5; 35. 13.

PUT THY HAND,] i.e. join in aiding or abetting their wicked plans.

VIOLENT WITNESS,] i.e. one doing violence to truth, justice, and his own conscience.

2. NOT AFTER MANY,] i.e. the majority, but some render it, 'not after great ones,' which seems supported by the next clause, where

'the poor' is introduced. We are not to follow for evil, either the many, or the great, or the poor; neither are we to cause others to turn aside from the path of rectitude.

3. A POOR MAN,] *lit.* 'weak, lean;' compare 30. 15; Le. 14. 21; 19. 15; Ju. 6. 15; Ruth 3. 10, &c.

HONOUR,] as in Le. 19. 15, 32.

STRIFE,] as in Ge. 13. 7; Ex. 17. 7; 23. 2, 3, 6; De. 1. 12; 17. 8; 19. 17; 21. 5; 25. 1, &c.

4. GOING ASTRAY,] as in Ge. 37. 15; Ps. 95. 10; Pr. 21. 16; Is. 29. 24, &c.

5. This verse, which has been rendered in a dozen different ways (of which that of the Common Version is least defensible) needs only a literal translation to become simple and intelligible: ' When thou seest the ass of him who is hating thee crouching under its burden, then thou hast ceased from leaving *it* [the burden] to it [the ass] —thou dost certainly leave *it* [the burden *or* the ass] with him [the owner.'] By this translation every word has its regular legitimate recognized sense.

6. TURN ASIDE,] as the original word always signifies.

THE JUDGMENT,] i.e. sentence, right.

NEEDY ONE.] This is the first instance of the occurrence of this word, which occurs again in v. 12; De. 15. 4, 7, 9, 11; 24. 14, &c.

STRIFE.] Same word as in v. 3 above; while they are not to be 'honoured' in their strife, they are not to be injured, or their right denied them.

7. DECLARE RIGHTEOUS,] as in De. 25. 1; Job 27. 5; 2 Sa. 15. 4; 1 K. 8. 32; 2 Ch. 6. 23; Ps. 82. 3; Pr. 17. 15; Is. 5. 23; 53. 11; 50. 8; Da. 12. 3.

8. A BRIBE,] not 'a gift;' compare De. 10. 17; 16. 19; 27. 25, &c.

OPEN-EYED,] as in Ex. 4. 11; Is. 61. 1; Ge. 21, 19, &c.

9. A SOJOURNER,] not a 'stranger;' see note on 22. 21.

SOUL,] not 'heart.'

11. RELEASE IT,] as in De. 15. 2, &c. Every one acquainted with agriculture knows the uselessness of endeavouring to secure abundant crops from the land for a long series of years without intermission; the Israelites were commanded to give the land a rest every seventh year, in proportion, as it were, to the rest enjoined on themselves, their servants, and their cattle, in the next verse. All experience, science, nature, and revelation agree in requiring this rest both for mind and matter.

12. THOU DOST REST,] *or* 'cease, *or* keep Sabbath,' being an entirely different word from that occurring in the next clause, ' doth rest.'

REFRESHED,] as in Ex. 31. 17; 2 Sa. 16. 12, being the only other passages where the same original word occurs.

13. NOT MENTION.] Than this nothing could be a better preservative against that tendency to fall into idolatry, which all along characterized the people of Israel, till the captivity of Babylon.

14. THREE TIMES,] *lit.* 'three feet' a

Hebrew idiom, found also in Nu. 22. 28; 32. 33.

15. FEAST OF UNLEAVENED THINGS,] beginning on the 14th of Abib (or Nisan,) lasting seven days, during which they refrained from leaven, in commemoration of their departure out of Egypt.

EMPTY,] i.e. without a gift, however small; in the East gifts are always presented to a superior on visiting him, but their intrinsic value may be very small—a flower, a bunch of grapes, &c. This token of respect paid to earthly superiors, is claimed by Him to whom belongs the earth and its fulness.

16. FEAST OF HARVEST,] sometimes called the ' feast of weeks,' there being seven weeks (or fifty days) between the wheat and the barley harvest, during which the first-fruits of the ground were brought near to the Lord.

FEAST OF THE IN-GATHERING,] sometimes called the ' feast of tabernacles,' at the end of the year, in the month Tisri.

17. THREE TIMES,] *lit.* 'three steps,' a Hebrew idiom, found also in Ge. 33. 3; 43. 10; Ex. 8. 32; 34. 23, 24; Le. 4. 6; De. 16. 16; Ju. 16. 15; 1. Sa. 20. 41; 1 K. 7. 4, &c. similar to that noticed in v. 14 above.

ALL THY MALES.] Females also often went up with them, as we find from various passages, but they were not expressly required to do so. This injunction, of course, could only be strictly applicable to those dwelling in the promised land, and is one of those things which show the unsuitableness of the 'old covenant' to the times prophesied of, when all ends of the earth turn unto the Lord.

18. NOT SACRIFICE, ETC.] i.e. in the feast of the passover; see 12. 27.

19. HOUSE OF JEHOVAH,] i.e. the tabernacle in the wilderness, or in Shiloh, and afterwards the temple at Jerusalem.

BOIL A KID,] as the heathen sometimes did for magical purposes, sprinkling their trees and fields to make them fruitful. This prohibition is repeated again in 34. 26; De. 14. 21; compare a somewhat similar injunction in Le. 22. 28, not to kill a beast and its mother on the same day.

20. A MESSENGER,] elsewhere it is, 'My messenger;' see v. 23. Compare note on Ge. 16. 7—11; Ex. 3. 2; 14. 19; 32. 34; 33. 2; Nu. 20. 16; 22. 22—35; Ju. 2. 1, 4, &c.

21. BE WATCHFUL.] See same phrase in Ex. 10. 28; 19. 12; 34. 12, &c.

HEARKEN.] See same phrase in Ex. 18. 19, &c.

REBEL NOT.] See same phrase in Nu. 20. 10, 24; 27. 14, &c.

BEARETH NOT WITH YOUR TRANSGRESSION.] See same phrase in Ge. 50. 17.

MY NAME IS IN HIS HEART,] *or* 'in his midst,' as in 1 K. 3. 28; Is. 63. 11; Je. 31. 33. The literal translation does away entirely with the inference which some theologians have drawn from the Common Version— ' My name is in him,' that this implies a divine nature in the being thus spoken of; but of any real saint it may be said, ' God's name is in his heart.' The divinity of the Messiah rests on much higher and more sure ground than this; see note on Ge. 16. 7.

22. THE JEBUSITE.] The Sept. adds 'the Girgashite,' bringing the number up to the usual seven; see note on 3. 8; 13. 5, &c. .

CUT THEM OFF,] *lit.* 'hide them,' as in 9. 13, on which see note.

24. STANDING-PILLARS,] as in Ge. 28. 18; Ex. 24, 4, &c.

26. MISCARRYING ONE.] Compare the use of the verb in Ge. 31. 38; Job 21. 10; 2 K. 2. 19, 21; Ez. 36. 13; Mal. 3. 11.

BARREN ONE,] as in De. 7. 14, &c.

NUMBER OF THY DAYS,] i.e. those allotted to each one by the Most High; compare Job 14. 5; 15. 20; 21. 21; 36. 26; Ec. 2. 3; 5. 18.

27. MY TERROR I SEND BEFORE THEE.] See the fulfilment of the promise in Jo. 2. 9—11; 5. 1, &c.

GIVEN THE NECK,] i.e. caused them to turn the back and flee before thee, as in Jo. 7. 8, 12; 2 Sa. 22. 41; 2 Ch. 29. 6; Ps. 18. 40, &c.

28. HORNET,] as promised again in De. 7. 20; Jo. 24. 12. A cognate word with the original for 'hornet,' signifies 'leprosy,' hence the Arabic Version and Aben Ezra understand it of a disease, not of an insect.

29. I CAST THEM NOT OUT.] The pronoun 'them' must refer not merely to the three or the six clans mentioned in v. 23, but to 'all the people among whom thou comest,' found within their 'border,' as described in v. 31, which they did not fully occupy till the times of David and Solomon, and even then only for a short time, 1 K. 5. 1—5.

THE BEASTS OF THE FIELD,] among which were found lions, bears, wolves, foxes, &c.

31. SEA OF THE PHILISTINES,] i.e. the great sea, the Mediterranean, on the west.

THE WILDERNESS] of Shur in Arabia (Ex. 15. 22,) to the River Euphrates, on the north; see Jo. 1. 4.

XXIV. 1. NADAB AND ABIHU.] The two elder sons of Aaron; see 6. 23. The Samaritan adds here the names of his other two sons.

3. ALL THE WORDS OF JEHOVAH] recorded in the three preceding chapters.

4. WRITETH,] as noted in Heb. 9. 19.

5. IN THE MORNING] of the 5th of Sivan, according to Rashi, or of the 8th of the same month, according to Gill.

THE YOUTHS.] According to most Jewish writers these were all first-born, to whom belonged the right of sacrificing, as a separate order of priests was not yet established.

CALVES.] The Vulgate adds 'twelve' calves, according to the number of the tribes, and probably of the youths.

6. HALF OF THE BLOOD] of these sacrifices, putting it into basins, with the view of afterwards sprinkling it on the people, i.e. on those representing them, probably on the youths who sacrificed; the other half he sprinkled on the altar, after which he declared anew the words of the Covenant, which they again confirm and ratify.

BOOK OF THE COVENANT,] i.e. the account of the promises and threatenings of God on the one hand, and the pledges of the people on the other.

8. ON THE PEOPLE,] as already noticed, on the youths who offered up sacrifices in the name of the whole twelve tribes, being probably one out of each tribe.

10. THEY SEE,] *or* perceive some appearance which was designed to impress them with reverence and fear, some spiritual manifestation, it may be, of Him whom no eye hath seen or can see; there is no form described, only the place of his feet is delineated.

WHITE WORK,] not 'paved work,' as the Common Version has it; see note on 16. 31.

SUBSTANCE,] *lit.* 'bone; see 12. 17, 41, 46, 51; 13. 19, &c.

PURITY,] as in Le. 12. 4, 6.

11. THOSE. . WHO ARE NEAR,] not 'nobles,' as in the Common Version; compare Is. 41. 9; De. 16. 21.

PUT NOT FORTH HIS HAND] either in anger or in favour, more probably the latter.

EAT AND DRINK.] It is not said of what they ate and drank; perhaps of the sacrifices they had offered, perhaps of the spiritual food only by which 'man liveth.'

12. THE TABLES OF STONE,] two in number, on which the Ten Matters were written. 'The law and the command' are perhaps in apposition to the expression 'the tables of stone.'

WHICH I HAVE WRITTEN,] with His own finger, as declared in 31. 18; De. 9. 10.

TO DIRECT THEM,] as in Ge. 46. 28; Ex. 35. 34; Le. 10. 11; 14. 57.

13. MOUNT OF GOD,] i.e. Mount Sinai, as in Ex. 3. 1; 4. 27; 18. 5.

14. THE ELDERS,] the seventy who had gone up with him: he thus endeavoured to provide for his continued absence.

16. COVERETH IT SIX DAYS.] What were Moses' feelings during this period is not said, nor can we give any satisfactory reason why that period of time was allowed to elapse before God's revealing himself, save that His servant might be more prepared by fasting, meditation, and prayer, for receiving additional divine communications; to the lowly He giveth grace.

18. FORTY DAYS AND FORTY NIGHTS,] as again narrated in De. 9. 9. Compare also note on Ge. 7. 4, 12.

XXV. 1. UNTO MOSES,] when in the mount with Him, as narrated in the close of the preceding chapter.

2. THEY TAKE FOR ME,] not 'bring me,' which the original verb never signifies.

HEAVE-OFFERING,] as in the margin of the Common Version, to distinguish it from KORBAN, an offering, TENUPHE, a wave-offering, MINCHAH, a present.

IMPELLETH,] as in 35. 21, 29; from this language it would appear that God would have His house built only by contributions willingly offered : this confidence in the voluntary liberality of the people was fully realized, for from 36. 7, we find the people had to be restrained from giving. The materials here mentioned may have been got from the presents of the Egyptians on the night of their departure out of Egypt, from the prey of those who were drowned, from the conquered Amalekites, the travelling merchants who passed by them during their sojourn in the wilderness, and from their own previous possessions.

3. GOLD, AND SILVER, AND BRASS.] Certain vessels were made of each of these metals, and certain others were only covered. The quantity used of each is stated in Ex. 38. 24—29, on which see note.

4. BLUE,] obtained from the juice of a shell-fish, a kind of mussel, found in rocks and clefts in the Mediterranean sea, with which woollen, linen, and cotton clothes were dyed by the Phenicians, Tyrians, &c.

PURPLE,] or 'red,' obtained also from a shell-fish, caught in the sea by bait.

SCARLET,] or 'crimson, or vermilion,' obtained from the carcases and eggs of an insect, the female of the coccus ilicis of Linnæus.

LINEN.] There are five Hebrew words all rendered 'linen,' and which it is almost impossible to distinguish in a translation, viz. SHESH, BAD, BUTS, PISHTEH, and KARPAS; the first is probably an Egyptian word, the second and third the same term, the fourth flax, the fifth, a Persian word.

GOATS' HAIR.] The finest and softest kind of which was manufactured into a solid and enduring substance.

5. RAMS' SKINS MADE RED.] Sept. translates, hyacinth or blue skins, with which Josephus agrees.

BADGER.] The original word thus translated occurs out of the Pentateuch only in Ez. 16. 10, so that the context throws no light on the subject. Many ancient interpreters understand it to denote a colour, though they differ in determining it: jackal, weasel, seal, boar, pardale, fitchet, dolphin, mermaid, dudong, hyæna, walrus, antelope, &c., have all been suggested in addition to badger, which has been objected to as an unclean animal, whose skin would have been unlawful for the tabernacle.

SHITTIM WOOD,] or 'acacia-wood,' which is the largest and most common tree in Arabia, especially near Sinai; whence the name of a place, Nu. 25. 1; 33. 49; Joel 3. 18.

6. OIL,] elsewhere called 'oil olive, pure, beaten,' of a white colour; the tree grows abundantly in Palestine, and rises to 20 or 30 feet, and lives many hundred years; it ripens in September. See 7. 20.

LIGHT,] or light-giver, as in Ge. 1. 14, 15, 16; Ex. 27. 20; 35. 8, 14, 28; 39. 37; Le. 24. 1; Nu. 4. 9, 16; Ps. 74. 16; 90. 8; Pr. 15. 30; Ez. 32. 8.

SPICES,] as in 30. 23; 35. 8; 1 K. 10. 2, &c.

ANOINTING OIL,] i.e. to anoint the priests, the tabernacle, and its vessels.

PERFUME,] as in 30. 1, 7, 8, 9, 27, 35, 37, &c.

SPICES,] as in 30. 7, 34; 31. 11, &c.

7. SHOHAM STONES.] as in Ge. 2. 12; Ex. 28. 9. 20. &c.

SETTING,] lit. 'fillings,', as in margin of Common Version; see again v. 20; 39. 13.

EPHOD,] a garment of the high priest worn over the tunic and robe, without sleeves, reaching to the middle of the thigh; worn by others besides the high priest, e.g. Samuel, (1 Sa. 2. 18, 28,) David, (2 Sa. 6. 14); these latter were of linen.

BREASTPLATE.] See 28. 4, 15, 22, 23, 24, 26, 28, 29, 30.

8. THEY HAVE MADE.] A common Hebrew way of expressing a command or desire that a thing should be done, by assuming or taking for granted that it is already done.

SANCTUARY,] i.e 'a holy or separate place,' as in 15. 13.

9. PATTERN,] as in v. 40; De. 4. 16, 17, 18, &c; 1 Ch. 28. 11, 12, 19; Heb. 8. 5.

10. ARK,] or 'chest,' as in Ge. 50. 26; 2 K. 12. 9, 10; 2 Ch. 24. 8, 10, 11.

CUBIT,] lit. 'fore-arm;' most of the Hebrew names of measures are taken from parts of the human body, e.g. 'hand-breadth, or palm, finger-breadth, span,' Ex. 28. 16. The cubit is generally six palms (De. 3. 11,) but in 2 Ch. 3. 3, and Ez. 40. 5, varieties of it are mentioned.

11. OVERLAID,] either by gilding, or by thin plates expanded.

RING,] or border; see 24. 25; 30. 3, 4; 37. 2, 11, 12, 26, 27.

12. RINGS,] properly 'seal-rings,' from a root, 'to sink.'

FEET,] not 'corners,' which the word never means; see 37. 3; 2 K. 19. 24; Ps. 17. 5, &c.

13. STAVES,] lit. 'parts, separated things;' compare Job 18. 13; 41. 4; Ez. 17. 6; 19. 14; Nu. 4. 6; Ho. 11. 6, &c.

14. BROUGHT,] lit. 'caused to go in.'

15. TURNED ASIDE,] at any time, that they might be always ready for use.

16. TESTIMONY,] as in 16. 34; 25. 16, 21, 22, &c.

17. MERCY-SEAT,] lit. 'a covering,' as in v. 18, 19, 20, 21, 22, &c.

18. CHERUBS.] See note on Ge. 3. 24.

BEATEN WORK,] as in v. 31, 36; 37. 7, 17, 22; Nu. 8. 4; 10. 2; Je. 10. 5.

22. I HAVE MET.] Compare 29. 42, 43; 30. 6, 36; Nu. 10. 3, 4; 17. 4; Jo. 17. 4; Ne. 6. 2, 10; Job 2. 11; Ps. 48. 4; Amos 3. 3; 1 K. 8. 5; 2 Ch. 5. 6, &c.

23. TABLE,] as in v. 27, 28, 30, &c.

25. BORDER,] or margin, from a verb 'to shut in;' see again v. 27; 37. 12, 14; 2 Sa. 22. 46; 1 K. 7. 28, 29, 31, 32, 35, 36, &c.

HAND-BREADTH.] Compare 37. 12; Ez. 40. 5, 43; 43. 13.

29. DISHES,] as in 37. 16; Nu. 4. 7; 7. 13, 19, 25, 31, 37, 43, 49, 55, 61, 67, 73, 79, 84, 85, being all the instances of its occurrence.

BOWLS,] as in 37. 16; Nu. 4. 7; 7. 14, 20, &c.; 1 K. 7. 50; 2 K. 25. 14; 2 Ch. 4. 22; 24. 14; Je. 52. 18, 19, &c.

COVERS,] as in 37. 16; Nu. 4. 7; 1 Ch. 28. 17.

CUPS,] as in 37. 16; Nu. 4. 7; Je. 52. 19.

30. BREAD OF THE PRESENCE,] elsewhere called 'bread of the arrangement,' twelve small loaves set before Jehovah weekly.

31. CANDLESTICK,] as in v. 32, 33, 34, 35, &c

BASE,] *lit.* 'thigh,' as in Ex. 1. 5; 28. 42, &c.
BRANCH,] *or* 'stalk,' as in Ge. 41. 5, 22, &c.
CALYXES,] *or* 'cups,' as in Ge. 44. 2, 12, 16, 17; Je. 35. 5; Ex. 25. 33, 34; 37. 17, 19, 20.
KNOPS,] as in Amos 9. 1; Zep. 2. 14; only found elsewhere in Exodus.
FLOWERS,] as in Nu. 17. 8; Is. 5. 24; 18. 5; Na. 1. 4, &c.
33. MADE LIKE ALMONDS,] as in v. 34; 37. 19, 20; compare Ge. 43. 11; Nu. 17. 8; Ec. 12. 5; Je. 1. 11.
37. LAMPS,] as in 1 Sa. 3. 3; 1 Ch. 28. 15, &c.
38. SNUFFERS,] as in 37. 23; Nu. 4. 9; 1 K. 7. 49: 2 Ch. 4. 21; Is. 6. 6.
SNUFF-DISHES,] as in 27. 3; 37. 23; 38. 3, &c.
39. TALENT,] equal to 3000 shekels of the sanctuary, Zec. 5. 7.

XXVI. 1. TABERNACLE,] i.e. habitation or dwelling-place, covered by a tent.
CURTAINS,] from a root signifying 'to move, shake.'
DESIGNER,] *or* 'deviser,' as in v. 31; 28. 6 15; 35. 35, &c.
4. LOOPS,] as in v. 5, 10, 11; 36. 11, 12, 17; not found elsewhere.
6. HOOKS,] as in v. 11, 33: 35. 11; 36. 13, 18; 39. 33.
7. CURTAINS.] There were four kinds of curtains, viz. of fine linen, goats' hair, rams' skins make red, and badgers' skin, which last was the outer covering, impervious to the rain.
12. THE SUPERFLUITY,] from a root signifying 'to spread out,' in the last clause of the verse, also in v. 13, Amos 6. 4; Ez. 17. 6; 23. 15; Je. 49. 7.
15. BOARDS,] as in v. 16—29; 35. 11; 36. 20—34; 39. 33; 40. 18; Nu. 3. 36; 4. 31; Ez. 27. 6.
STANDING UP,] as in 36. 20.
17. HANDLES,] *or* tenons, see v. 19; 36. 22, 24, &c.
19. SOCKETS,] as in v. 21, 25, 32, 37, &c. Job 38. 6; Song 5. 15.
22. SIDES,] *lit.* 'thighs,' as in Ex. 1. 5; 28. 42; 37. 17; 40. 22, 24, &c.
23. CORNERS,] as in 36. 29; 2 Ch. 26. 9; Ne. 3. 19, 20, 24, 25; Ez. 41. 22; 46. 21, 22, being all the instances of its occurrence.
24. PAIRS,] as in 36. 29; compare also Song 4. 2; 6. 6.
26. BARS,] as in 27, 28, 29, &c. also De. 3. 5; Ju. 16. 3, &c.
28. REACHING,] *lit.* fleeing; compare Job 41. 28; Pr. 19. 26; 1 Ch. 12. 15; Ne. 13. 28.
29. PLACES,] *lit.* 'houses,' as in 23. 19; 25. 27; 36. 34; 37. 14, 27; 38. 5.
30. RAISED UP,] as in Nu. 12. 21; De. 27. 2.
FASHION,] *lit.* 'judgment,' as in 28. 15, 29, 30.
SHEWN,] *lit.* 'was caused to see,' as in Le. 13. 49; De. 4. 35; Ex. 25. 40.
31. VAIL,] as in v. 33, 35, &c · 2 Ch. 3. 14.
32. PILLARS,] as in 13. 21; 26. 37; 27. 10 —17; Ju. 16. 25, 26, 29, &c.
PEGS,] as in v. 37; 27. 10, 11, 17; 36. 36, 38; 38. 10, 11, 12, 17, 19, 28, all the instances of its occurrence.
35. SIDE,] *lit.* 'rib,' as in Ge. 2. 21, 22; Ex. 25. 12, 14; 26. 20, 26, 27, 35, &c.

36. COVERING.] Compare Ez. 28. 13; Ju. 3. 24, &c.
OPENING.] i.e. the 'open' space of the door, as distinguished from the 'leaf' of the door itself.
EMBROIDERER,] as in 27. 16; 28. 39; 35. 35: 36. 37; 38. 18, 23; 39. 29; compare Ju. 5. 30, &c.
37. CAST,] *lit.* 'pour out,' as in Ge. 28. 18; 35. 14; Ex. 25. 12, &c.

XXVII. 1. ALTAR.] It is also called (in 38. 30) the 'altar of brass,' because it was overlaid with that metal, as in v. 2.
2. HORNS,] on which the blood of the sin-offering was sprinkled, and which was seized by those fleeing from death.
3. POTS,] as in 16. 3; 28. 3; 1 K. 7. 45, &c.
TO REMOVE ITS ASHES,] as in Nu. 4. 13; compare also Ps. 20. 3.
SHOVELS,] as in 38. 3; Nu. 4. 14; 1 K. 7. 40, 45; 2 K. 25. 14; 2 Ch. 4. 11, 16, Je. 52. 18.
BOWLS,] as in 38. 3; Nu. 4. 14; 7. 13, &c. Amos 6. 6; Zec. 9. 15; 14. 20.
FORKS,] as in 38. 3; Nu. 4. 14; 1 Ch. 28. 17; 2 Ch. 4. 16.
FIRE-PANS,] as in 27. 3: 37. 23; 38. 3; Le. 10. 1; 16. 12; Nu. 4. 9, 14; 16. 6, 7, 18, 37, 38, 39, 46; 1 K. 7. 50; 2 K. 25. 15; 2 Ch. 4. 22; Je. 52. 19.
4. GRATE,] as in 35. 16; 38. 4, 5, 30; 39. 39.
NET,] so in v. 5; 38. 4; Job 18. 8; Ps. 9. 15, &c.
EXTREMITIES,] as in 25. 18, 19; 26. 4, &c.
5. COMPASS,] as in 38. 4, the only other instance of its occurrence.
6. STAVES,] as in 25. 13, on which see note.
8. HOLLOW,] as in 38. 7; Job 11. 12; Je. 52. 21.
9. COURT,] as in Ex. 8. 13, which see.
HANGINGS,] as in v. 11, 12, 14, 15; 35. 17; 38. 9, 12, 14, 15, 16, 18; 39. 40; Nu. 3. 26; 4. 26; 1 K. 6. 34.
10. FILLETS,] *or* 'rods;' compare v. 11; 36. 38; 38. 10, 11, 12, 17, 19.
16. GATE.] This word which generally expresses the large outer gate of a court, city, &c., here denotes the 'open' space, not the gate itself.
19. PINS,] as in 35. 18; 38. 20, 21; 39. 40; Nu. 3. 37; 4. 32; De. 23. 13; Ju. 4. 21, &c.

XXVIII. 1. BEING PRIEST,] as in v. 3, 4. 41; 29. 1, 44; 30. 30; 31. 10; 35. 19; 39. 41; 40. 13, 15, &c.; compare Is. 61. 10.
2. HONOUR,] as in v. 40; 29. 43, &c.
BEAUTY,] as in v. 40; De. 26. 19; Ju. 4. 9; Ps. 71. 8, &c.
MITRE,] as in v. 37, 39; 29. 6; 39. 28, 31; Le. 8. 9; 16. 4; Ez. 21. 26, from a root signifying 'to wrap up.'
GIRDLE,] as in v. 39, 40; 29. 9; 30. 29; Le. 8. 7, 13; 16. 4; Is. 22. 21.
9. OPENED,] as in v. 11, 36; Job 12. 18; 39. 10, &c.
11. ENGRAVER,] as in 35. 35; 38. 23; De. 27 15; 1 Sa. 13. 19; 2 Sa. 5. 11; 2 K. 12. 11; 22. 6; 24. 14, 16, &c.
SIGNET,] as in Ge. 38. 18; Ex. 28. 11, 21, 36; 39. 6, 14, 30; 1 K. 21. 8; Job 38. 14. 41. 15; Song 8. 6; Je. 22. 24; Hag. 2. 23.

TURNED ROUND,] as in 39. 6, 13 ; Nu. 32. 38 ; Ez. 41. 24.

13. EMBROIDERED THINGS,] or 'settings ;' see v. 13, 14, 25 ; 39. 6. 13, 16, 18 ; Ps. 45. 13, being all the instances of its occurrence.

14. CHAINS,] as in 39. 15 ; 1 K. 7. 17 ; 2 Ch. 3. 5, 16.

WREATHED WORK.] This word occurs nowhere else ; but compare v. 22 ; 39. 15.

THICK BANDS,] as in 22, 24, 25 ; 39. 15, 17, 18 ; Ju. 15. 13, 14 ; 16. 11, 12, &c.

16. SQUARE,] as in 27. 1 ; 28. 16 ; 30. 2 ; 37. 25 ; 38. 1 ; 39. 9 ; 1 K. 7. 5, 31 ; Ez. 40. 47 ; 41. 21 ; 43. 16 ; 45. 2.

DOUBLED,] as in 39. 9 ; compare Ex. 26. 9 ; Ez. 21. 14, also Job 11. 6 ; 41. 13 ; Is. 40. 2.

SPAN,] as in 39. 9 ; 1 Sa. 17. 4 ; Is. 40. 12 ; Ez. 43. 13.

17. SETTINGS,] lit. 'fillings,' as in v. 20 ; 39. 13.

ROWS,] as in 18, 19, 20 ; 39. 10, 11, 12, 13 ; 1 K. 6. 36, &c.

SARDIUS,] or 'carnelian,' lit. 'red ;' see again 39. 10 : Ez. 28. 13.

TOPAZ,] or 'chrysolite ;' see Job 28. 19 ; Ez. 28. 13.

CARBUNCLE,] or 'smaragd,' lit. 'glittering ;' see Ez. 28. 13.

18. EMERALD.] or 'carbuncle ;' see 39. 11 ; Ez. 27. 16 ; 28. 13.

SAPPHIRE,] as in 24. 10 ; 28. 18 ; 39. 11 ; Job 28. 6, 16 ; Song 5. 14 ; Is. 54. 11 ; La. 4. 5 ; Ez. 1. 26 ; 10. 1 ; 28. 13.

DIAMOND,] or 'emerald ;' see Ez. 28. 13.

19. OPAL,] or 'ligure,' not found elsewhere in the Old Testament.

AGATE,] not found elsewhere in O. T.

AMETHYST,] not found elsewhere in the Old Testament.

20. BERYL,] or 'chrysolite,' lit. 'Tarshish ;' see 39. 13 ; Song 5. 14 ; Ez. 1. 16 ; 10. 9 ; 28. 13 ; Da. 10. 6.

ONYX,] or 'sardonix,' lit. 'shoham ;' see Ge. 2. 12 ; Ex. 25. 7 ; 28. 9, 20 ; 35. 9, 27 ; 39. 6, 13 ; 1 Ch. 29. 2 ; Job 28. 16 ; Ez. 28. 13.

JASPER,] as in 39. 13 ; Ez. 28. 13. All the preceding twelve stones are noticed again in 39. 10—13 ; Rev. 21. 19, 20.

28. RIBBON,] as in Ge. 38. 18, 25 ; Ex. 28. 28, 37 ; 39. 3, 21, 31 ; Nu. 15. 38 ; 19. 15 ; Ju. 16. 9 ; Ez. 40. 3.

LOOSED,] as in 39. 21, the only other place where the original verb occurs.

30. LIGHTS,] or 'fires ;' (see Is. 24. 15 ; 31. 9 ; 44. 16 ; 47. 14 ; 50. 11 ; Ez. 5. 2,) as in Le. 8. 8 ; Nu. 27. 21 ; De. 33. 8 ; 1 Sa. 28. 6 ; Ezra 2. 63 ; Ne. 7. 65.

PERFECTIONS,] as in Ge. 20. 5. 6 ; 2 Sa. 15. 11 ; 1 K. 9. 5 ; 22. 34 ; 2 Ch. 18. 33 ; Job 4. 6 ; 21. 23 ; Ps. 7. 8 ; 25. 21 ; 26. 1, &c.

THE URIM AND THUMMIM] are probably a general name for the twelve precious stones.

31. UPPER ROBE,] as in 28. 4, which see.

32. BORDER,] as in Ex. 2. 3 ; 7. 15 ; 26. 4, &c.

WEAVER,] as in 35. 35 ; 39. 22, 27, &c.

HABERGEON,] as in 39. 23, the only other passage where the word occurs.

33. HEM,] as in v. 34 ; 39. 24, 25, 26 ; Is. 6. 1 ; Je. 13. 22, 26 ; La. 1. 9 ; Na. 3. 5.

POMEGRANATES,] as in v. 34 ; 39. 24, 25, 26 ; Nu. 13. 23 ; 20. 5, &c.

BELLS,] as in v. 34 ; 39. 25, 26, being all the instances of its occurrence.

36. FLOWER,] as in 39. 30 ; Le. 8. 9 ; Nu. 17. 8 ; 1 K. 6. 18, 29, 32, 35 ; Job 14. 2 ; Ps. 103. 15 ; Is. 28. 1 ; 40. 6, 7, 8 ; Je. 48. 9.

38. PLEASING THING,] as in Le. 22. 20, 21 ; Ps. 19. 14 ; Pr. 10. 32 ; Is. 56. 7, &c.

39. COAT.] See note on Ge. 3. 21.

40. BONNETS,] as in 29. 9 ; 39. 29 ; Le. 8. 13, being all the instances of its occurrence.

41. CONSECRATED,] lit. 'filled,' as in Ex. 2. 16 ; 23. 26 ; 28. 3, 17, &c.

42. TROUSERS,] as in 39. 28 ; Le. 6. 10 ; 16. 4 ; Ez. 44. 18 ; the word is found nowhere else.

XXIX. 1. HALLOW,] i.e. sanctify or separate them to the service of God.

BULLOCK,] as in Ge. 32. 15 ; Ex. 24. 5 ; 29. 1, 3, 10, 11, 12, 14, 36, &c.

RAMS,] as in Ge. 15. 9 ; Ex. 25. 5, &c.

PERFECT ONES,] as in Ge. 6. 9 ; 17. 1 ; Ex. 12, 5 ; Le. 1. 3, &c.

2. ANOINTED,] as in Le. 2. 4 ; 7. 12 ; Nu. 3. 3 ; 6. 15 ; 2 Sa. 3. 39.

FLOUR,] as in Ge. 18. 6 ; Ex. 29. 2, 40 ; Le. 2. 1, &c.

3. BASKET,] as in Ge. 40. 16, 17, 18 ; Ex. 29. 3, 23, 32 ; Le. 8. 2, 26, 31 ; Nu. 6. 15, 17, 19 ; Ju. 6. 19.

4. BATHED,] as in Ex. 2. 5 ; 29. 4, 17 ; 30. 18, 19, 20, 21 ; 40. 12, 30, 31, 32.

6. CROWN,] as in 39. 30 ; Le. 8. 9 ; 21. 12 ; Nu. 6. 4, 5, 7, 8, 9, 12, 13, 18, 19, 21 ; 2 Sa. 1 10 ; 2 K. 11. 12 ; 2 Ch. 23. 11 ; Ps. 89. 39 132. 18 ; Pr. 27. 24 ; Je. 7. 29 ; Zec. 9. 16.

9. PRIESTHOOD,] as in 40. 15 ; Nu. 3. 10 , 16. 10 ; 18. 1, 7 ; 25. 13 ; Jo. 18. 7 ; 1 Sa. 2. 36 ; Ezra 2. 62 ; Ne. 7. 64 ; 13. 19.

12. FOUNDATION,] as in Le. 4. 7, 18, 25, 30, 34 ; 5. 9 ; 8. 15 ; 9. 9.

13. INWARDS,] as in v. 22 ; Le. 3. 3, 9, 14 4. 8 ; 7. 3 ; 8. 16, 25, &c.

REDUNDANCE,] or 'midriff, or caul, or lobe ;' see v. 22 ; Le. 3. 4, 10, 15 ; 4. 9 ; 7. 4 : 8. 16, 25 ; 9. 10, 19.

LIVER,] as in v. 22 ; Le. 3. 4, 10, 15 ; 4. 9 ; 7. 4 ; 8. 16, 25 ; 9. 10, 19 ; Pr. 7. 23 ; La. 2. 11 ; Ez. 2. 21.

KIDNEYS,] as in v. 22 ; Le. 3. 4, 10, 15 ; 4. 9 ; 7. 4 ; 8. 16, 25 ; 9. 10, 19 ; De. 32. 14 ; Job 16. 13 ; 19. 27, &c.

MADE PERFUME,] as in v. 18, 25 ; 30. 7, 8, 20 ; 40. 27, &c.

14. DUNG,] as in Le. 4. 11 ; 8. 17 ; 16. 27 ; Nu. 19. 5 ; Mal. 2. 3, being all the instances of its occurrence.

SIN-OFFERING,] lit. 'sin,' but often denoting the offering by which it is confessed, see Ge. 4. 7 ; Ex. 29. 14, 36 ; 30. 10, &c.

17. ITS PIECES,] as in Le. 1. 6, 8, 12 ; 8. 20 ; 9. 13 ; Ju. 19. 29 ; Ez. 24. 4, 6.

LEGS.] See note on Ex. 12. 9 ; also Le. 1. 9, 13 ; 4. 11 ; 8. 21 ; 9. 14 ; 11. 21 ; Amos 3. 12.

18. BURNT-OFFERING.] See Ge. 8. 20.

SWEET FRAGRANCE,] lit. 'fragrance of rest ;' see note on Ge. 8. 21.

FIRE-OFFERING,] as in v. 25, 21 ; 30. 20 ; Le. 1. 9, 13, 17, &c.

20. TIP,] as in Le. 8. 23, 24 ; 14. 14, 17, 25, 28.

GREAT TOE.] The original word, BOHEN, signifies the thumb, or the great toe, according as it is followed by YAD, a hand, or REGEL, a foot ; see Le. 8. 23, 24 ; 14. 14, 17, 25, 28; Ju. 1. 6, 7, being all the passages where it occurs.

22. FAT TAIL,] as in Le. 3. 9 ; 7. 3 ; 8. 25 ; 9. 19, and not found elsewhere.

CONSECRATION,] *lit.* 'fillings,' as in Ex. 25. 7 ; 29. 22, 26, 27, 31, 34 ; 35. 9, 27 ; Le. 7. 37 ; 8. 22, 28, 29, 31, 33 ; 1 Ch. 29. 2.

23. ROUND CAKE,] as in Ju. 8. 5 ; 1 Sa. 2. 36 ; 10. 3 ; 1 Ch. 16. 3 ; Pr. 6. 26 ; Je. 37. 21 ; everywhere else the word is translated 'circuit, talent.'

THIN CAKE,] as in v. 2. above ; Le. 2. 4 ; 7. 12 ; 8. 26 ; Nu. 6. 15, 19 ; 1 Ch. 23. 29.

24. WAVED,] as in Ex. 20. 25 ; 29. 24, 26 ; 35. 22 ; Le. 9. 21, &c.

26. BREAST,] as in v. 27 ; Le. 7. 30, 31, 34 ; 8. 29 ; 9. 20, 21 ; 10. 14, 15 ; Nu. 6. 20 ; 18. 18.

PORTION,] as in Le. 7. 33 ; 8. 29 ; 1 Sa. 1. 4, 5 ; 9. 23 ; 2 Ch. 31. 19 ; Ne. 8. 10, 12 ; Est. 2. 9 ; 9. 19, 22 ; Ps. 16. 5 ; Je. 13. 25.

28. HEAVE-OFFERING,] as in 25. 2, &c.

31. BOILED,] as in 12. 9 ; 16. 23.

36. FOR THE ATONEMENTS,] as in 30. 10, 16 ; Le. 23. 27, 28 ; 25. 9 ; Nu. 5. 8 ; 29. 11.

ATONED,] as in Le. 6. 26 ; 8. 15 ; 9. 15 ; 14. 49, 52 ; Nu. 19. 19 ; 2 Ch. 29. 24 ; Ps. 51. 7 ; Ez. 43. 20, 22, 23 ; 45. 18 ; Ge. 31. 19.

40. HIN,] a liquid measure containing the seventh part of a *bath*, or twelve *log ;* see 30. 24 ; Le. 19. 36 ; 23. 13, &c.

LIBATION,] as in Ge. 35. 14, &c.

41. PRESENT,] as in Ge. 4. 3, &c.

XXX. 1. PERFUME,] as in 25. 6, &c.

3. CROWN,] as in 25. 11, &c.

4. RIBS,] as in Ge. 2. 21, 22 ; Ex. 25. 12, &c.

6. TESTIMONY,] as in Ex. 16. 34, &c.

7. SPICES,] as in Ex. 25. 26, &c.

12. TAKEST UP,] *or* liftest up.

SUM,] *lit.* 'head.'

PLAGUE,] as in Ex. 12. 13, &c.

13. PASSING OVER,] as in v. 14 ; 38. 26, &c.

SHEKEL,] as in Ge. 23. 15, 16 ; Ex. 21. 32, &c.

SANCTUARY,] *lit.* 'holy *or* separate place,' as in Ex. 3. 5, &c.

GERAHS,] as in Le. 27. 25 ; Nu. 3. 47 ; 18. 16 ; Ez. 45. 12 ; the smallest Hebrew weight or coin.

15. RICH,] as in Ruth 3. 10 ; 2 Sa 12. 1, 2, 4 ; Job 27. 19 ; Ps. 45. 12 ; 49. 2 ; Pr. 10. 15, &c.

MULTIPLY,] as in 32. 13.

POOR,] as in 23. 3.

DIMINISH,] as in Le. 25. 16 ; 26. 22 ; Nu. 26. 54 ; 33. 54 ; 35. 8 ; 2 K. 4. 3 ; Ps. 107. 38 ; Je. 10. 24 ; Ez. 29. 15.

18. LAVER,] as in v. 28 ; 31. 9 ; 35. 16 ; 38. 8 ; 39. 39 ; 40. 7, 11, 30 ; Le. 8. 11 ; 1 Sa. 2. 14 ; 1 K. 7. 30. 38, 40, 43, &c.

BASE,] as in Ge. 30. 14 ; 41. 13 ; Ex. 30. 18, 28 ; 31. 9 ; 35. 16 ; 38. 8 ; 39. 39, &c.

WASHING,] as in Ge. 24. 32 ; Ex. 2. 5, &c.

19. AT IT,] *lit.* 'out of it.' Orientals never put their hands or feet *in* water to cleanse them, but *pour* water upon them.

23. SPICES,] as in 25. 6.

WILD,] *lit.* 'free,' as in Le. 25. 10 ; Is. 61. 1 ; Je. 34. 8, 15, 17 ; Ez. 46. 17.

CINNAMON,] as in Pr. 7. 17 ; Song 4. 14, not found elsewhere.

CANE,] as in Ge. 41. 5 ; Song 4. 14 ; Is. 43 24 ; Je. 6. 20 ; Ez. 27. 19.

24. CASSIA,] only found in Ez. 27. 19.

OLIVE OIL,] as in 27. 20, &c.

25. COMPOUND MIXTURE,] as in 1 Ch. 9. 30 ; 2 Ch. 16. 14.

32. PROPER PROPORTION,] as in Ex. 5. 8 ; 30. 32, 37 ; 2 Ch. 24. 13 ; Ez. 45. 11.

33. CUT OFF,] as in Ge. 17. 14, &c.

34. STACTE.]The original word only occurs elsewhere in Job 36. 27, translated 'drops.'

ONYCHA,] not found elsewhere in SS.

GALBANUM,] not found elsewhere in SS.

FRANKINCENSE,] as in Le. 2. 1, 2, 15, 16 ; 5. 11 : 6. 15 ; 24. 7 ; Nu. 5. 15 ; 1 Ch. 9. 29, &c.

PART.] In all other places where the original word is singular, it is used with prefixes as an adverb ; see Ex. 12. 27. &c.

35. SALTED,] compare Le. 2. 13 ; Ez. 16. 4.

36. BEATEN,] as in 2 Sa. 22. 43 ; Ps. 18. 42 ; Job 14. 19.

38. REFRESHED,] *or* 'smell,' as in Ge. 8. 21 ; 1 Sa. 16. 23, &c.

XXXI. 3. SPIRIT OF GOD.] See Gen. 1. 2.

WISDOM.] Compare 28. 3.

UNDERSTANDING,] as in 35. 31 ; 36. 1 ; De. 32. 28, &c.

KNOWLEDGE,] as in Ge. 2. 9, 17 ; Ex. 31. 3 ; 35. 31 ; Nu. 24. 16 ; De. 4. 42 ; 19. 4, &c.

4. DEVISE,] as in 26. 1, 31 ; 35. 22.

DEVICES,] as in Ge. 6. 4 ; Ex. 31. 4 ; 35. 32, 33, 35 ; 2 Sa. 14. 14, &c.

TO WORK,] as in v. 5 ; 35. 32, 35 ; 36. 1, &c.

5. GRAVING.] This word is found again only in 35. 33.

SETTINGS,] as in 35. 33.

10. COLOURED GARMENTS,] as in Ex. 35. 19 ; 39. 1, 41.

14. POLLUTING,] as in Le. 21. 9 ; 1 K. 1. 40 ; Ne. 13. 17 ; Ez. 24. 21 ; 28. 9 ; Mal. 1. 12.

17. CEASED,] as in Ge. 2. 3, &c.

REFRESHED.] See note on Ex. 23. 12.

18. TWO TABLES,] as in 32. 15 ; 34. 1, 4 ; De. 4. 13 ; 5. 22 ; 9. 10, 11, 15, 17 ; 10. 1, 3, &c.

STONE.] Compare Job 19. 24.

WRITTEN,] as in Ex. 8. 19 ; 29. 12, &c.

FINGER,] as in Ex. 8. 19 ; 29. 12, &c.

XXXII. 1. DELAYING,] as in Ju. 5. 28.

2. BREAK OFF,] as in Ge. 27. 40 ; 1 K. 19. 11 ; Ps. 7. 2 ; 136. 24 ; La. 5. 8 ; Zec. 11. 16 ; Da. 4. 27.

3. THEMSELVES BREAK OFF,] as in v. 34 ; Ez. 19. 12.

4. FASHION.] See note on Ge. 2. 7, 8, 19. The Masoretes have stupidly enough pointed the original word as if it meant 'distress,' he distressed it !

GRAVEN TOOL,] only found elsewhere in Is. 8. 1.

MOLTEN,] as in v. 8 ; 34. 17 ; Le. 19. 4 ; Nu. 33. 52 ; De. 9. 12, 16 ; 27. 15, &c.

5. FESTIVAL,] as in 10. 9, on which see note.

TO JEHOVAH,] not to the idol, as some have inadvertently supposed.

6. PLAY.] See note on Ge. 18. 13, 15 ; 17. 17 ; 18. 12 ; 19. 4 ; 21. 6, 9 ; 26. 8 ; 39. 14, 17 ; Ju. 16. 25.

7. DONE CORRUPTLY,] *or* 'is corrupted,

compare 21. 26; Nu. 32. 15; De. 9. 12; 32. 5, &c.

9. STIFF-NECKED,] as in 33. 3, 5; 34. 9; De. 9. 6, 13; 10. 16; 31. 27, &c.

10. LET ME ALONE,] as in 16. 24, 32, 33, 34. CONSUME,] as in 15. 7.

11. APPEASETH,] as in 1 Sa. 13. 12; 1 K. 13. 6; 2 K. 13. 4; 2 Ch. 33. 12; Job 11. 19; Ps. 45. 12; 77. 10; 119. 59; Pr. 19. 6; Je. 26. 19; Da. 9. 13; Zec. 7. 2; 8. 21, 22; Mal. 1. 9.

12. HEAT.] See note on 12. 7, also Nu. 25. 4; 32. 14; De. 13. 17, &c.

REPENT,] as in Ge. 6. 6, 7, on which see note.

13. BE MINDFUL OF,] as in De. 9. 27; Ps. 25. 27; 136. 23, &c.

SWORN,] as in Ge. 22. 16.

16. GRAVEN.] The original word does not occur elsewhere.

17. SHOUTING,] as in Job 36. 33; Mic. 4. 9.

18. MIGHT,] as in De. 3. 24; Jud. 5. 31; 8. 21, &c.

WEAKNESS,] not found elsewhere; but compare the root in Ex. 17. 13; Job 14. 10; Is. 14. 12, &c., Joel 3. 10.

19. DANCING,] or 'choruses,' as in 15. 20, &c.

20. GRINDETH,] as in Nu. 11. 8; De. 9. 21; Ju. 16. 21; Job 31. 10; Ec. 12. 3, 4; Is. 3. 15; 47. 2; La. 5. 13.

SCATTERETH,] as in Nu. 16. 34; Ruth 3. 2, &c.

22. IN EVIL.] Compare Ex. 5. 19; 2 Sa. 16. 8; Ps. 10. 6; 52. 1; 141. 5; Pr. 13. 17; 14. 32; 17. 20, &c.

23. MAKE,] as in v. 1.

25. UNBRIDLED,] lit. 'set free;' see note on Ex. 5. 4.

CONTEMPT.] The original word is found nowhere else.

WITHSTANDERS,] as in 15. 7, &c.

27. RELATION,] lit. 'one near,' as in Ge. 19. 20; 45. 10; Ex. 12. 4; 13. 7, &c.

29. CONSECRATE,] lit. 'fill, complete, perfect,' as in 28. 3; 29. 9, &c.

32. IF THOU TAKEST AWAY.] This form of expression is always according to Hebrew idiom left unfinished; the word 'well, good,' &c. being understood.

BLOT ME…OUT,] so v. 33; Ps. 69. 28; Ge. 6. 7; Ex. 17. 14; Is. 4. 3, &c.

34. LEAD,] as in Ge. 24. 27; Ex. 13. 17; 15. 13.

MY MESSENGER.] See note on Ge. 16. 7; Ex. 23. 23, &c.

CHARGING.] See note on Ge. 21. 1; Ex. 20. 5, &c.

35. PLAGUETH,] as in Ex. 8. 2; 12. 23, 27.

XXXIII. 2. A MESSENGER,] as in Ex. 23. 20.

3. CONSUME,] as in 15. 7.

4. SAD THING,] lit. 'evil thing.'

ORNAMENTS,] as in v. 5, 6; 2 Sa. 1. 24; Ps. 32. 9; 103. 5; Is. 49. 18; Je. 2. 32; 4. 30; Ez. 7. 20; 16. 7, 11; 23. 40; Is. 64. 6.

6. TAKE OFF.] Compare the use of the word in Ex. 3. 22; 12. 36; 2 Ch. 20. 25; Ez. 14. 14, &c.

7. STRETCHED,] as in Ge. 12. 8; Ex. 12. 15, &c.

MEETING,] i.e. the place where God meets with His people, as in 18. 7.

8. LOOKED EXPECTINGLY.] See note on Ge. 15. 5, &c.

9. PILLAR OF THE CLOUD,] in which Jehovah was.

10. STANDING,] i.e. abiding, remaining.

11. MINISTER,] or 'ministrant,' as in 24. 13; the same word is used of Samuel, Abishag, &c.

12. WHOM THOU DOST SEND,] i.e. his name, qualifications, &c.

BY NAME,] i.e. personally, intimately.

13. THY WAY] of dealing with me and with Israel.

14. MY PRESENCE,] lit. 'my faces,' i.e. manifestations of myself, in my several attributes.

16. DISTINGUISHED,] as in Ps. 139. 14; compare Ex. 8. 22; 9. 4; 11. 7; Ps. 4. 3; 17. 7; 139. 14.

18. THINE HONOUR,] as in 16. 7, 10; 24. 16, 17.

19. MY GOODNESS.] Compare same phrase in Neh. 9. 25, 35; Ps. 25. 7; 27. 13; 31. 19; 65. 4; 145. 7; Je. 31. 12, 14; Ho. 3. 5; Zec. 9. 17.

CALLED CONCERNING,] or 'in,' as the preposition often signifies.

NAME,] i.e. that by which one is distinguished from another.

FAVOURED,] as in Ge. 33. 5, 11; 43. 49; Nu. 6. 25; De. 7. 2; 28. 50.

20. MY FACE.] This evidently means the direct manifestation of his personal glory.

22. CLEFT,] as in Is. 2. 21.

SPREAD OUT.] The original word is not found elsewhere.

23. BACK-PARTS,] as in 26. 12; 1 K. 7. 25. Ez. 8. 16.

XXXIV. 1. HEW,] as in v. 4; De. 10. 1, 3; 1 K. 5. 18; Hab. 2. 18.

2. PREPARED,] as in Ge. 41. 32; Ex. 8. 16; 19. 11, 15; 34. 2.

5. CLOUD,] as heretofore.

CALLETH IN.] Compare 33. 19.

6. SLOW TO ANGER,] lit. 'long of nostrils,' i.e. patient.

ABUNDANT,] as the original word generally means, not 'great,' as in Ge. 6. 5, &c.

KINDNESS,] as the word always means; see note on Ge. 19. 19; Ex. 20. 5, &c.

TRUTH,] as in Ge. 24. 27.

7. KEEPING.] See 2 K. 17. 9; 18. 18; Job 7. 20; 27. 18; Ps. 25. 10; 31. 23; 119. 2, &c.

THOUSANDS.] The Targums and Rashi interpret: 'of generations,' and justly, perhaps, as in Ex. 20. 5.

TAKING AWAY,] or 'bearing away, or lifting up,' as the word often signifies.

INIQUITY.] See note on Ge. 15. 16; Ex. 20. 5, &c.

TRANSGRESSION.] See note on Ge. 31. 36; Ex. 23. 21, &c.

SIN,] as in Is. 5. 18; Amos 9. 8.

NOT ENTIRELY ACQUITTING.] See note on Ex. 20. 7; the word never means 'to cut off,' as some suppose.

CHARGING,] or 'looking after;' see note on Ex. 20. 5.

ON CHILDREN,] *or* 'with children;' see note on Ex. 20. 5.

THIRD,] i.e. generation, viz. grandchildren, as in Ge. 50. 23; Ex. 20. 5; 34. 7; Nu. 14. 18; De. 5. 9.

FOURTH,] i.e. generation, viz. great-grandchildren.

9. INHERITED,] as in 23. 30; 32. 13, &c.

10. WONDERS,] as in 3. 20.

FEARFUL,] as in Ge. 28. 17; Ex. 15. 11, &c.

11. OBSERVE,] as in De. 4. 9; 12. 28, &c.

12. TAKE HEED,] as in Ge. 24. 6; 31. 24, 29; Ex. 10. 28; 19. 12; 23. 21, &c.

SNARE,] as in 10. 7; 23. 33, &c.

13. BREAK DOWN,] as in Le. 14. 45; De. 7. 5.

SHIVER,] as in 9. 25; 23. 24; 32. 19, &c.

CUT DOWN,] as in Ex. 4. 25; Nu. 13. 23, &c.

14. ZEALOUS,] as in 20. 5; De. 4. 24; 5. 9; 6. 15; compare Jo. 24. 19; Nah. 1. 2.

15. GONE A-WHORING,] as in Ge. 38. 24; Ex. 34. 15, 16; Le. 19. 29; 20. 5; 21. 9.

17. MOLTEN.] See note on 32. 4.

18. FEAST OF UNLEAVENED THINGS,] as already noted in 12. 15—19; 13. 6, 7; 23. 15, &c.

19. OPENING.] See note on Ex. 13. 2, &c.

20. RANSOM,] as in 13. 13.

EMPTY.] See note on 23. 15.

21. WORK,] as in 20. 10; 23. 12; 31. 15, &c.

REST.] This latter clause is not found in the above quoted parallel passages.

22. FEAST OF WEEKS.] Comp. Le. 23. 15, 16.

IN-GATHERING.] See note on 23. 16.

REVOLUTION,] as in 1 Sa. 1. 20; 2 Ch. 24. 23; Ps. 19. 6.

23. TIMES,] *lit.* 'steps.' See note on Ge. 2. 23, &c.

24. DESIRE,] as in 20. 17; De. 5. 21; 7. 25.

25. FERMENTED,] as in 12. 15, &c.

26. BOIL,] as in 12. 9; 16. 23, &c.

27. TENOR,] *lit.* 'mouth.'

28. FORTY.] See note on Ge. 5. 13, &c.

29. SHONE.] The original word occurs only in v. 30. and 35; *lit.* 'emitted rays *or* beams.'

33. VAIL,] found only again in v. 34, 35.

XXXV. 2. DONE,] as noted in 31. 15.

3. BURN.] This command is nowhere repeated, nor is it said to be 'age-during;' it was, probably only kept in the wilderness.

4. COMMANDED,] *or* 'charged.'

6. HEAVE-OFFERING,] as in 25. 2, &c.

21. LIFTED,] as in 2 K. 10. 14; 2 Ch. 25. 19, &c.

MADE WILLING,] as in 25. 2; 35. 21, 29.

22. NOSE-RING,] as in 2 K. 19. 28; Is. 37. 29; Ez. 19. 4, 9; 29. 4; 38. 4.

EAR-RING,] as in Ge. 24. 22, &c.

SEAL-RING,] as in Ge. 41. 42; Ex. 25. 12, &c.

NECKLACE,] only elsewhere in Nu. 31. 50.

WAVED,] as in 20. 25; 29. 24, 26, &c.

25. SPUN,] only found elsewhere in v. 26; properly signifying 'to twist.'

YARN,] not found elsewhere, derived from the preceding root.

30. BY NAME,] as in 31. 2.

XXXVI. 1. BEZALEEL,] i.e. 'in the shadow of God.'

5. MORE THAN SUFFICIENT,] as in v. 7; 2 Ch. 30. 3; Es. 1. 18, &c.

6. CAUSE A VOICE TO PASS OVER,] as in 2 Ch. 30. 5; 36. 22; Ez. 1. 1; 10. 7; Ne. 8. 17.

RESTRAINED,] as in Ge. 8. 2; Ez. 31. 15.

7. LEAVE,] as in 2 K. 4. 43; 2 Ch. 31. 10, &c.

8—38.] See notes on chapter 26.

XXXVII. 1—28.] See notes on chapters 25 and 30.

XXXVIII. 1—7.] See note on 17. 1—8.

8. LOOKING-GLASSES] were commonly of brass, according to Pliny, Aristotle, &c.

9—20.] See notes on chap. 27. 9—19.

21. TABERNACLE OF TESTIMONY,] so called because the tent contained the Two Tables.

23. AHOLIAB,] i.e. 'tent of a father.'

AHISAMACH,] i.e. 'brother of support.'

24. GOLD OF THE WAVE-OFFERING,] noticed in 35. 22, and reckoned as equal to £148,719 pounds sterling.

25. SILVER,] as noted in 30. 12, 15, and reckoned at £37,721, 17s. 6d. sterling.

26. NUMBERED,] as ordered in 30. 12—15. 603,550.] Compare the census in 12. 37.

27. SOCKET,] each costing £353, 11s.

30. SOCKETS,] viz. five, as in 26. 37.

31. See 27. 19.

XXXIX. 1. COLOURED GARMENTS.] See note on 31. 10.

3—31.] See note on 28. 6—40.

32. COMPLETED,] according to the directions given by God through Moses.

33—41.] The several articles are here enumerated in the order in which they were directed to be made, and were brought before Moses, that he might examine each separately.

42. An emphatic repetition of v. 32.

46. BLESS THEM,] for their ready and cheerful and unreserved compliance.

XL 1. MONTH,] i.e. Nisan.

7. PUT,] as directed before in 30. 18, on which see notes.

8.] See note on 27. 9—16.

9—11.] See note on 30. 26—29.

12—15,] to separate them to the priesthood, as in 28. 41 : 29. 4—8.

16. DONE,] as a servant—stedfast and faithful.

17. SECOND YEAR,] from the time of the Exodus from Egypt.

19—32.] In these verses there are no less than seven repetitions of the phrase; 'as Jehovah hath commanded Moses,' all showing the desire of the Sacred Writer to proclaim that nothing that Moses ordered was of his own desiring, but according to the pattern shown him in the mount. Compare 26. 7, 14, 33, 34; 25. 30; Le. 24. 5. 8; Ex. 25. 37; 28. 38—42; 29. 1, 2, 18, 23.

33. THE COURT,] as in 27. 9, 16; Nu. 7. 1.

34. FILLED.] Compare 1 K. 8. 11.

35. TO ENTER,] till he was called, Le. 1. 1

36—38.] As God's people were at first chosen by Himself, delivered from the house of servitude by Himself, so they were conducted in all their journeyings by Himself, till their safe arrival in the promised land.

LEVITICUS

LEVITICUS, the third in order of the Sacred Writings, as its name denotes, treats of the duties to be performed by the tribe of LEVI, which was given to Aaron and his sons to serve and to help with them in the observance of the various ritual commands given by God to Moses at Mount Sinai. The best commentary on the spirit and intent of its manifold directions regarding sacrifices as a means of purifying and cleansing the guilty is to be found in the 'Epistle to the Hebrews,' where the only possible solution of the problem of how man can be just with God is given at length. Without the least desire unnecessarily to strain words and phrases beyond their logical and grammatical meaning, it is perfectly evident to the intelligent reader that a greater than Solomon is here, and that under the symbols of ancient times we have a view of the true state of man as guilty, and the possibility of his deliverance from it by accepting, *simpliciter*, the Divine directions for his cleansing. Apart, indeed, from Divine injunction, the doctrine of animal sacrifice is abhorrent to every rational mind, as rather increasing than diminishing guilt by taking the life of an unoffending creature, but as soon as it is known to be appointed by the Sovereign Lord of all, its propriety and beautiful adaptation to the condition of man is at once apparent.

The position of Leviticus is strikingly appropriate, Exodus having brought up the narrative to the erection and completion of the Tabernacle, the sacred writer proceeds to detail the work of the *priests* arising from it, but not confined to it, as the laws given to Moses were designed not only for Israel in the wilderness but for all ages, even till they should be abrogated by Him who at first gave them.

I. 1. AND JEHOVAH CALLETH.] This name, as already noticed, expresses simply 'existence;' it is the national appellation of the God of Israel, and it is here used to point out that He had a claim as such to obedience.

TO MOSES,] not to Aaron; Moses is everywhere the medium by which Israel learned God's will.

TENT OF MEETING,] which He had now chosen for His resting-place, from between the cherubs.

2. ANY MAN OF YOU,] none is exempted, all must comply with the same regulations, whether rich or poor, bond or free, high or low.

WHEN,] not 'if,' as in the Common Version.

BRING NEAR,] as the original word teaches.

AN OFFERING,] *lit.* a 'korban,' i.e. a thing brought near, an offering in general,

whether bloody or unbloody, compare Lev. 1. 2, 3, 10, 14; 2. 1, 4, 5, 7, 12, 13; 3. 1, 2, 6, 7, 8, 12, 14; 4. 23, 28, 32; 5. 11; 6. 20; 7. 13, 14, 15, 16, 29, 38; 9. 7, 15; 17. 4; 22. 18, 27; 23. 14; 27. 9, 11; Nu. 5. 15; 6. 14, 21; 7. 3. 10, 11, 12, 13, 17, 19; 23. 25, (31, 37, 43, 49, 55, 61, 67, 73, 79,) 29, 35, 41, 47, 53, 59, 65, 71, 77, 83; 9. 7, 13; 15. 4, 25; 18. 9; 28. 2; 31. 50. Its only other occurrences are Eze. 20. 28; 40. 43; Neh. 10. 34; 13. 31.

3. A BURNT-OFFERING,] *lit.* 'that which has gone up' on the altar, and is wholly burnt, and not eaten either by priest or offerer.

A MALE, A PERFECT ONE,] 'Male' as being reckoned more honourable, and 'perfect' as pointing to the best substitute.

TO THE OPENING OF THE TENT OF MEETING,] i.e. openly before God and man—not in secret, as if ashamed.

AT HIS PLEASURE,] *or* good-will, not by constraint.

BEFORE JEHOVAH,] not before gods of his own devising.

4. LAID HIS HAND,] testifing thereby the transmission of his guilt to his substitute.

ACCEPTED,] by the priest, and by the Lord.

TO MAKE ATONEMENT,] *lit.* 'to cover' him over.

5. SLAUGHTERED,] not 'killed;' the original word is appropriate to the slaughtering of animals for food or sacrifices, the offerer was to do this—himself to put his substitute to death. The Sept. apparently refers it to the priests.

THE PRIESTS,] who were to direct him, and help him to complete his work as those appointed by the Lord.

SPRINKLED THE BLOOD,] with their fingers.

ON THE ALTAR] of burnt-offering.

6. HE HATH STRIPPED,] that is, the offerer of the sacrifice, but probable it eventually came to be done by the priests and the Levites, in his stead. Sept. reads in the plural number.

TO PIECES,] pointing out its utter destruction.

9. WASH WITH WATER,] not *in* water; there is no proof whatever that the Hebrews ever put an object into water to cleanse it, the common mode being to pour water upon it.

MADE PERFUME,] *or* incense, with the whole of the offering, hence called a whole burnt-offering.

A FIRE-OFFERING,] see on Ex. 29. 18, 25, 41; 30. 20.

SWEET FRAGRANCE,] see on Ge. 8. 21, &c.

10. OUT OF THE FLOCK,] whether an ox, a sheep, or a goat—all must be males, and perfect ones, and precisely the same form must be gone through, only it is added here (in v. 11) that it must be slaughtered 'by the side of the altar northward.'

14. THE FOWL,] These being more easily obtained by the poor than a bullock, or sheep, or goat, (compare Lev. 5. 7; 12. 8,) besides being more suitable for sacrifice than birds of prey. No mention is made of their being male or female, perfect or blemished.

15. WRUNG OFF;] the original word is only found elsewhere in 5. 8.

16. FEATHERS.] There is not the slightest authority or necessity for translating the original word by 'filth,' as is done in the margin of the Common Bible, and by Gesenius and the Jerusalem Targum.

17. SEPARATE IT,] i.e. entirely.

II. **1. A PERSON,**] *lit.* a soul.

A PRESENT,] see note on Ge. 4. 3. There are five kinds—simple flour, oven cakes, cakes of the girdel, cakes of the frying-pan, and green ears of corn, see v. 4, 5, 7, 14.

2. HIS SONS,] agreeable to the law, that those serving at the altar should live of the altar, referred to in 1 Cor. 9. 13, 14.

4. OVEN,] These are sometimes in the East merely circular holes dug in the earth, from one to five feet in depth, the sides of which are covered with hardened plaster.

5. A GIRDEL,] a thin iron or copper plate.

6. PARTS,] for the priests, and for the Lord.

7. FRYING-PAN,] differs from the 'girdel' in being deeper, and having a cover, which the other has not.

10. REMNANT,] as in v. 3, above.

11. FERMENTED,] that it might be free from all hypocrisy and corruption; anything leavened soon spoiling in the East.

12. SWEET FRAGRANCE,] because they yielded none, if burned.

13. SALT,] to preserve it from putrefaction, salt being regarded as a symbol of perpetuity, hence the phrase 'a covenant of salt,' in Nu. 18. 19.

14. GREEN EARS, ROASTED WITH FIRE,] still an article of food among the very poorest people of Egypt and of Palestine, hence it was within the reach of all.

15. OIL,] as in v. 1, 4, 5, 7.

III. **1. PEACE-OFFERINGS,**] for favours received, see note on Ex. 20. 24.

2. LAID HIS HAND,] acknowledging it as his own offering.

3. THE FAT…THE FAT,] this being reckoned the best part of the animal.

6. THE FLOCK,] either a sheep, as in v. 7, or a goat, as in v. 12.

7. A SHEEP,] probably one of the first year, though not specified.

8. TENT OF MEETING,] as in v. 2 ; sacrifice being allowed no where else; see Jos. 22. 19, &c.

9. FAT TAIL,] which in some Eastern sheep, weighs fully fifty pounds weight.

11. BREAD,] i.e. food, so also in v. 16.

16. STATUTE,] *lit.* anything 'engraved or fixed.'

AGE-DURING,] i.e. till the end of the age or dispensation then in existence.

IV. **2. IGNORANCE,**] as in v. 22, 27 ; 5.

15, 18; 22. 14; Nu. 15. 24, 25, 26, 27, 28, 29; 35. 11, 15; Jos. 20. 3, 9; Ecc. 5. 6; 10. 5. The two kinds of commands here are called by the Jews 'Affirmative and Prohibitive;' of the first there are 248 (according to the number of the bones in a man's body!) and of the latter there are 365 (according to the number of days in the year,) in all 613 ; these were arranged in order by Maimonides, and have been published by the present writer in Hebrew and English, under the title of 'Book of the Precepts.'

3. ANOINTED,] i.e. the high priest, for the common priests were not anointed.

ACCORDING TO THE GUILT,] not 'sin,' as in Common Version, as in Ge. 26. 10, &c.

A BULLOCK,] of two years old.

4—12. Even the high priest had to do the very same thing as the common people; there is no exemption for them when they transgress the law of their God ; Judaism had this distinguishing feature when compared with other religions : it had no class legislation.

5. THE PRIEST] himself had to dip his finger in the blood, and to sprinkle it seven times, there being none superior to him of his brethren.

6. SEVEN TIMES,] which according to common Hebrew usage is a complete number.

7. HORNS] of the golden altar, see Ex. 30. 1—6.

POUR OUT] of the basin in which it had been received.

8—10. Compare the procedure in 3. 3—5.

11. THE SKIN,] which was generally the portion of the priest after being taken off the animal, appears here to have been burned with the other parts.

12. BROUGHT OUT,] *lit.* 'caused to go out,' either personally or by the aid of others ; very unreasonable and worthless is the notion that he *must* have done it himself; the SS. is full of the ordinary language of men, in which the actions of others are attributed to him who gives the order to do them.

13. THE WHOLE COMPANY,] by their rulers or heads, implying national responsibility and national guilt; and as a nation cannot be judged or punished in another world, national punishment and rewards must be in this one. Here we learn—*The Church may err.*

HIDDEN,] i.e. for a time.

14—15. Compare v. 3, 4, above.

15. ELDERS,] i.e. office-bearers, see Ex. 3. 16.

16. WHO IS ANOINTED,] that is, as explained above, the high-priest. The ritual ceremonies in the following verses form an exact counterpart to v. 5—12.

22. A PRINCE,] *lit.* one 'lifted up,' i.e. honoured. Having in the previous verses detailed the manner in which the high priest and the whole assembly were to make atonement, the law proceeds to the authorities of the land, and requires of them a sin-offering likewise ; the king was to be subject to the laws of God not less than the priest, and his means of atonement were the same, v. 22—26.

27. PEOPLE OF THE LAND,] i.e. of Israel; formerly it was the whole company, now it is a single individual, and his sin-offering is a female kid of the goats a sheep, whereas that of the prince was a male goat, while those of the 'anointed priest' was a bullock, as was likewise that of the 'whole company.'

28—35. Same as in v. 25. 26.

V. 1. AN OATH.] See the use of the same word in Ex. 24. 41; 26. 28; Nu. 5. 21, implying a 'curse' attending its falsity.

INIQUITY,] i.e. its guilt and punishment.

2. ANY THING UNCLEAN] ceremonially; they were to avoid even the appearance of evil.

UNCLEAN BEAST,] i.e. one declared so in the law, but nothing is unclean of itself, Lev. 11. 2—8.

TEEMING CREATURES,] see note on Ge. 1. 20. Compare Lev. 11. 29—31.

3. COMETH AGAINST,] undesignedly and unwittingly.

4. SWEARETH,] by appealing to God for the truth of his statement.

SPEAKING WRONGFULLY,] as did Moses, Ps. 106. 33; Pro. 12. 18; the word is found nowhere else in SS.

5. CONFESSED.] This is always the first and most important element in obtaining forgiveness from God or man; compare 1 John 1. 9.

6. GUILT-OFFERING,] a female lamb or kid, or two turtle-doves, or two young pigeons, or if poor, an offering of flour, that none might plead poverty for non-compliance with the divine requirements.

8. A SIN-OFFERING,] i.e. to atone for his sin, whereas the second pigeon was to be a burnt-offering, to denote the divine acceptance of the former.

10. THE ORDINANCE] of the burnt-offering, in 1. 15—17.

14. A TRESPASS,] from a root signifying 'to go up' above the law, over-ride it, as it were.

15. HOLY THINGS,] either by eating or desecrating or withholding them.

16. THE PRIEST] who is, as it were, in the place of God, whose holy things had been injured.

18. AT THY VALUATION,] i.e. the priest's.

VI. 2. AGAINST JEHOVAH,] in lying to his fellow; hence we see that an injury done to any one is treated as an injury done to God; compare Acts 9. 5; Mat. 25. 40, 45.

FELLOWSHIP,] lit. 'setting of hand.'

OPPRESSED,] so in v. 4; 19. 13; De. 24. 14; 28. 29, 33, &c.

FELLOW,] as in Zec. 13. 7; Lev. 18. 20; 19. 11, 19, 20, 21; 24. 19; 25. 14, 15, 17, one of the same people.

5. ITS FIFTH,] as in 5. 16.

6. GUILT-OFFERING,] not trespass-offering, as in Common Version.

8. COMMAND,] or charge; even Aaron had to receive his knowledge of the law of God

through the intervention of Moses.

LAW,] lit. 'direction.'

10. LONG ROBE,] as in Jud. 3. 16; 5. 10; 1 Sa. 4. 12; 17. 38, 39; 18. 4; 2 Sa. 20. 8; 21. 20; Job 11. 9; Ps. 109. 18; Jer. 13. 25.

11. OF THE CAMP,] i.e. of the priests, not of Israel.

12. MADE PERFUME,] i.e. by burning.

13. QUENCHED,] so in v. 13; 1 Sa. 3. 3; 2 K. 22. 17; 2 Ch. 34. 25; Pr. 26. 20; 31. 18; Isa. 34. 10; 66. 24; Jer. 7. 20; 17. 27; Ez. 20. 47, 48. The Zoroastrians, Brahmans, Greeks, and Romans, had each their sacred fire, which was constantly kept burning, doubtless in imitation of the Jews.

14. PRESENT.] Compare the directions in the first and second chapters of this book.

15. Compare 2. 2.

16. WITH UNLEAVENED THINGS,] or simply 'unleavened—it is eaten.'

17. MOST HOLY,] i.e. set apart to the exclusive use of the priests.

18. ALL THAT COMETH,] or 'all who cometh.'

20. OFFERING OF AARON.] The priests being sinful like other men, were also required to acknowledge and make atonement for it.

HIS BEING ANOINTED] to his office.

A TENTH OF THE EPHAH,] i.e. an omer.

21. BRING IT IN] before Jehovah, morning and evening.

23. IS NOT EATEN] by the priests, though they were permitted to eat of the people's offering, see Lev. 10. 11.

25. IN THE PLACE,] i.e. north of the altar, (see 1. 11,) where according to Aben Ezra and Ben Gershom, every sin-offering was slaughtered, and according to Gill, some expositors 'have observed that Mount Calvary, where our Lord was crucified, lay pretty much to the north of Jerusalem, see Ps. 48. 2.'

26. THE PRIEST...DOTH EAT IT,] thus denoting that he bore the sin of the offerer; his whole family, of course, partook of it with him.

28. EARTHEN VESSEL...BROKEN.] Such vessels are very common in the East, and are very cheap, sometimes even as low as a farthing, hence they are commanded, to be broken.

BRASS VESSELS,] which is a very common material of which cooking-pots and washing vessels are made, in the East, even to the present day, and the accuracy of the Scriptures in such little and incidental details is a most satisfactory proof of their authenticity.

VII. 1. THE GUILT-OFFERING] was presented for offences—unintentional or otherwise—against man; the sin-offering, with which it is often comfounded, for offences against God; compare Lev. 5. 1—6; 4. 2, 13, 22, 23. The details in this chapter may be considered as an enlargement of Lev. 3.

2. IN THE PLACE,] see 1. 11.

3. FAT TAIL,] see note in Ex. 29. 22; Lev. 3. 9.

6. IN THE HOLY PLACE,] not at the priest's

own dwelling, as was permitted with other sacrifices.

7. ONE LAW.] *or* 'direction;' see Lev. 6. 27, 28.

8. SKIN OF THE BURNT-OFFERING,] but not of the peace-offering, see 4. 11, 12.

9. IT IS HIS,] except the handful that was burned.

10. ONE AS ANOTHER,] not to the priest only who offered it.

11. PEACE-OFFERINGS.] See a full account of them in ch. 3.

12. SACRIFICE OF THANK-OFFERING,] a bullock, sheep or goat.

14. OUT OF IT ONE,] i.e. cake. HEAVE-OFFERING;] see note on Ex. 25. 2.

15. EATEN,] by the offerer and his family, the poor, and the priests, and Levites; see De. 12. 11, 12, 17, 18.

16. A VOW,] which he had uttered in distress; a *free-will* offering, to which his spirit inclined him.

17. BURNT,] that it might not become corrupt; compare Acts 13. 34, 35.

18. AN ABOMINABLE THING,] because kept in defiance of the divine directions.

20. CUT OFF] from Israel, as defiled, but not necessarily put to death; comp. Gal. 5. 12.

23. ANY FAT ...DO NOT EAT,] as already prohibited in 3. 17, because the fat was the Lord's, even of animals killed for common use; yet v. 25. would seem to restrict the prohibition to animals offered in sacrifice.

26. ANY BLOOD YE DO NOT EAT,] Compare Ge. 9. 4; Lev. 17. 10; Eze. 33. 25, &c.

VIII. 1. TAKE AARON.] Moses did not appoint his brother priest from any worldly motives, nor did Aaron assume the office of himself, but both were under the guidance of the great Lawgiver; compare Heb. 5. 4.

THE GARMENTS.] See an account of them in Ex. 30. 23; 37. 29.

THE ANOINTING OIL.] See Ex. 30. 23, and 37. 29, for the manner in which it is made.

BULLOCK...TWO RAMS,] as in Ex. 29. 1, 2.

5. JEHOVAH HATH COMMANDED.] Not from his own heart, but their own covenant God; Moses was faithful as a 'servant.'

6. BATHE THEM WITH WATER,] i.e. according to the language of common life and common sense, he directed that they should be bathed, not that he did it with his own hands.

7. THE COAT,] i.e. the embroidered one of fine linen, Ex. 28. 39.

THE GIRDLE] of needlework, Ex. 28. 39.

THE ROBE] of the ephod, Ex. 28. 31-35.

THE EPHOD] of gold, blue, &c. Ex. 28. 6—13.

8. URIM AND THUMMIM,] *lit.* 'lights and perfections,' i.e. the twelve precious stones set in the breast-plate, Ex. 28. 17—20; 29. 8—14.

9. THE MITRE] of fine linen, Ex. 38. 39.

11. SEVEN TIMES,] in token of perfection and completion.

ALTAR] of burnt-offering.

12. TO SANCTIFY THEM,] i.e. to separate *or* set them apart for God's service, as the original word properly means.

13. AARON'S SONS,] viz. Nadab and Abihu, Eleazar and Ithamar.

GIRDLES...BONNETS,] those made of fine linen; see Ex. 39. 27, 28.

17. SANCTIFIETH,] i.e. set apart as a sacred object, that atonement might be made upon it in time to come.

22. CONSECRATIONS,] *lit,* 'fillings,' viz. those things which filled up and completed the anointing of the priests for their office.

23—25. Compare Ex. 29. 19—22.

29. COMMANDED MOSES,] in Ex. 29. 26.

31. DO EAT IT.] Compare Ex. 29. 32.

32. THE REMNANT...YE BURN,] that it might not become putrid, nor be used for magical purposes.

33. CONSECRATE,] *lit.* 'fill your hand.' These consecrations or fillings were to be performed daily for seven days, to intimate their complete preparation for their work, which they were at the same time charged to do under the penalty of death.

IX. 1. EIGHTH DAY] of the consecration of Aaron and his sons, but others say it was the 8th day of Nisan or March, Ex. 40. 2.

ELDERS,] i.e. office-bearers and rulers who represented the whole assembly of Israel, the whole community being interested in the appointment of a priesthood.

2. A CALF,] probably as usual, of a year old; the Jewish writers think this selection was intended to remind Aaron and Israel of their sinful worship of the calf, which was now made a sin-offering.

3. THOU DOST SPEAK,] i.e. Aaron, in virtue of his appointment as God's high-priest in Israel.

5. STAND,] denoting their respect and reverence for the Lord, also their readiness to do His will. They also serve who only stand and wait.

7. SIN-OFFERING,] i.e. the calf.

BURNT-OFFERING,] i.e. the ram.

12. PRESENTED,] *lit.* 'caused to find;' so also in v. 13. 18, i.e. brought to him.

13. BY ITS PIECES,] i.e. piece by piece, not, with its pieces, as in the Common Version.

14. FOR THE BURNT-OFFERING,]not 'upon' them.

16. ORDINANCE,] as laid down in Lev. 1.

22. LIFTETH UP HIS HAND,] a token of earnestness and reverence; see the words of his blessing in Nu. 6. 24, 25.

COMETH DOWN] from off the altar, which was about three cubits high.

23. WENT IN,] to pray *or* to offer incense.

AND BLESS,] i.e. both of them, Moses and Aaron, the prophet and the priest.

APPEARETH,] how is not said; probably a brightness in the cloud which overshadowed the tabernacle.

24. CRY ALOUD.] The original word occurs in the Pentateuch only in De. 32. 43; compare its use in Job 29. 13; 38. 7, &c.

X. 1. NADAB AND ABIHU.] the two elder of his sons.

CENSER,] or fire-pan made of brass.

STRANGE FIRE,] i.e. not taken from the

fire which was on the altar of the burnt-offering.

NOT COMMANDED THEM.] They had not been commanded to offer perfume at all, much less to do it with strange fire.

2. CONSUMETH] their life, not their bodies.

3. HATH SPOKEN.] Perhaps Ex. 19. 22; 29. 43, may be referred to.

THOSE DRAWING NEAR TO ME.] This is one of the Hebrew forms expressive of the worshippers of God; they 'draw near' to Him, they 'know' Him; they do not worship an unknown God ; neither does Scripture reckon ignorance to be the mother of devotion.

I AM SANCTIFIED,] *lit.* 'set apart' as one above them, though near to them.

I AM HONOURED,] i.e. reverenced, respected, feared.

IS SILENT,] *lit.* 'is dumb,' i.e. remaineth as if dumb, not opening his lips.

4. COME NEAR.] These persons being Kohathites, and not priests, were not permitted to enter the holy place where the dead bodies lay, without a special call to do so by competent authority.

5. IN THEIR COATS,] i.e. just as they were when struck dead, in their priests' garments.

6. UNCOVER,] *lit.* 'make naked ;' see note on Ex. 32. 25.

REND.] The usual signs of mourning in the East, but the original word here occurring is only found elsewhere in this book of Lev. 13. 45; 21. 10.

7. GO OUT] to weep or lament in private, till (probably) their work was finished.

9. WINE AND STRONG DRINK.] From the mention and prohibition of these, it is natural to infer that Aaron's two sons had been guilty of over-indulgence in their use when they offered the 'strange fire.' The prohibition is limited to the period when the priests were about to engage in the worship of God; their use at other seasons was not disapproved of. The word rendered 'strong drink' occurs here for the first time; it properly means 'satiating,' or 'sweet,' rather than 'strong.' It is found elsewhere in Nu. 6. 3; 28. 7; De. 14. 26; 29. 6; Jud. 13. 4, 7, 14; 1 Sa. 1. 15; Ps. 69. 12 ; Pr. 20. 1 ; 31. 4, 6; Isa. 5. 11, 22; 24. 9; 28. 7; 29. 9; 56. 12; Mic. 2. 11. See the 'Wines of Scripture,' in the writer's Edinburgh 'Biblical Tracts.'

13. YE HAVE EATEN IT,] After the 'handful' had been taken away, the remnant was the priests.

PORTION,] not 'due ;' the word points to God's having appointed it to the priests, not to any right that the priests might have to claim it from the people, (so in v. 14.)

15. THEY DO BRING,] i.e. the offerers, not the priests; see 7. 29, 30.

COMMANDED,] see 7. 33, 34.

16. GOAT OF THE SIN OFFERING,] i.e. belonging to the people; see 9. 15.

WROTH,] being fearful that God might again manifest His displeasure at this neglect of the ordinance, which required that the remnant of the sin-offering should be eaten by the priests.

19. This verse is somewhat obscure in the original, and *utterly illogical* in the Common Version. The true meaning seems to be, that, in answer to Moses' rebuke to the two sons of Aaron, (who alone are blamed, not Aaron,) their father remarked that he, at least, had eaten of the sin-offering, and thus the law had not really been broken ; his question implies an affirmative answer.

XI. 2. THIS IS THE BEAST,] i.e. kind of beast. The distinction between clean and unclean beasts existed at least as early as the time of Noah, though whether in regard to general use or simply in sacrifices is not certain. The laws in the present chapter were very evidently designed to keep the people of Israel from connecting themselves with other nations. Eating with one, has, in all ages and countries, been regarded as denoting intimate friendship, and to prohibit this, or to throw any considerable barrier in the way of their so doing, was well calculated to secure the perpetual separation of the parties. The true Hindoo, Mussalman, Parsi, Jew, &c., would rather die from hunger or thirst than eat of the food prepared for each other. Christianity alone has risen above it.

3. DIVIDING.] The verb in the original is found in v. 4, 5, 6, 7, 26; De. 14. 6, 7, 8 ; Ps. 69. 31 ; and elsewhere only in Isa. 58. 7 ; Jer 16. 7, where it-is applied to the dividing *or* breaking *or* parting of bread to the hungry and the mourning.

HOOF.] See note on Ex. 10. 26, *lit.* a 'division *or* dividing.'

CLEAVING.] Compare Lev. 1. 17 ; 11. 3, 7 26 ; De. 14, 6, 7 ; Jud. 14. 6; 1 Sa. 24. 7.

CLEFT,] as in v. 7, 26 ; De. 14. 6.

BRINGING UP,] unnecessarily varied in the Common Version, 'chewed.'

CUD,] as in v. 4, 5, 6, 7, 26; De. 14. 6, 7, 8, and not found elsewhere.

4. CAMEL.] See note on Ge. 12. 6; so called from a root signifying 'to do, repay,' characterizing it as a 'working, useful' animal, a character it richly deserves in Eastern lands.

5. RABBIT,] *or* coney, *or* jerboa; its Hebrew name is from a root signifying (probably) 'to hide, conceal,' mentioned only in De. 14. 7; Ps. 104. 18 ; Pr. 30. 26.

6. HARE,] only noticed elsewhere in De. 14. 7 ; the etymology of its Hebrew name denotes a 'cropper of produce.'

7. SOW,] noticed again in De. 14. 8 ; Ps. 80. 13 ; Pr. 11. 22 ; Isa. 65. 4 ; 66. 3, 17 : the Mohammedans have the same distaste to this animal that the Jews have. The etymology of the Hebrew name is uncertain, probably 'to roll about.'

9. FINS,] as in v. 10, 12 ; De. 14. 9, 10; the etymology is unknown.

SCALES,] as in v. 10, 12 ; De. 14. 9, 10 ; 1 Sa. 17. 5; Ez. 29. 4; the etymology is unknown. Except in this chapter unclean *fish* are nowhere alluded to in SS.; probably the lack of fins and scales may render them difficult of digestion.

10. NOT FINS,] e.g. worms, horse-leeches, &c.

13. EAGLE.] According to some critics the original word includes the different kinds of vultures, and is derived from a root signifying 'to lacerate.' It occurs in Ex. 19. 4, &c. on which see note.

OSSIFRAGE,] a species of eagle, mentioned only elsewhere in De. 14. 12, from a root signifying ' to tear, divide.'

OSPRAY,] another species of eagle, noticed only in De. 14. 12; Sept. 'sea eagle.' Etymology unknown.

14. VULTURE.] The original word is not found elsewhere, (De. 14. 12). Sept. *gups,* Lat. *milvus.*

KITE,] only noticed elsewhere in De. 14. 13, (where its sharpness of sight is alluded to) ; and in Job 28. 7. Bochart suggests a kind of 'falcon ;' others, a vulture.

15. RAVEN.] See note on Ge. 8. 7, &c.

16. OWL,] *lit.* ' daughter of the owl,' i.e. a female owl, but Gesenius (with Sept. Vul. Targ. Onkelos, and Jonathan) prefers ' the daughter of the ostrich.' Compare its use in De. 14. 15 ; Job 30. 29; Isa. 13. 21 ; 34. 13 ; 43. 20 ; Jer. 50. 39. Mic. 1. 8.

NIGHT-HAWK,] only found elsewhere in De. 14. 15. Gesenius prefers 'the male ostrich.'

CUCKOO,] also in De. 14. 15; Gesenius prefers ' a gull,' from its leanness. So Ainsworth, Bochart, and Septuagint.

HAWK,] as in De. 14. 15 ; Job 39. 26 ; there are 16 kinds of these according to Pliny.

17. LITTLE OWL,] as in De. 14. 16; Ps. 107. 2; Bochart and Gesenius prefer ' pelican,' from its pouch.

CORMORANT,] as in De. 14. 17, a species of pelican ; Ainsworth has ' the little owl.'

GREAT OWL,] as in De. 14. 16; Isa. 34. 11; Sept. and Vulg. 'ibis,' i.e. Egyptian heron; Gesenius prefers 'heron or crane.'

18. SWAN,] not found elsewhere; Bochart prefers 'the chameleon,' Sept. and Vulg. *talpa,* Saad. Gaon, 'lizard.'

PELICAN,] as in De. 14. 17 ; Isa. 34. 11; Zeph. 2. 14; Ps. 102. 7.

GIER-EAGLE,] *lit.* ' the merciful one,' as in De. 14. 17 ; Bochart and Gesenius prefer a small kind of vulture.

19. STORK.] Its Hebrew name denotes ' kind,' being so-called from its love to its parents and its young ones ; see De. 14. 18; Ps. 104. 17 ; Jer. 8. 7; Zec. 5. 9 ; Job 29. 13. Gesenius unnecessarily objects to the last quoted passage.

HERON,] as in De. 14. 18 ; Bochart ' an angry bird ;' Gesenius 'perhaps *sand-piper;*' others, 'the parrot.'

LAPWING,] as in De. 14. 18; Sept. Vulg. and Saad. Gaon, the 'hoopoe,' Targ. 'mountain-cock.'

BAT,] as in Isa. 2. 10.

22. LOCUST.] The Hebrew name is from a root signifying 'to be many ;' see note on Ex. 10. 4, &c.

BALD LOCUST,] not referred to elsewhere, but apparently common food in the East.

BEETLE,] not referred to elsewhere; the Hebrew name is derived from its powers of ' leaping.'

GRASSHOPPER,] as in Nu. 13. 33 ; 2 Ch. 7.

13 ; Ecc. 12. 5 ; Isa. 40. 22 ; the name is derived from their abundance, covering or 'hiding' the ground.

29. WEASEL,] not mentioned elsewhere; others ' mole.'

MOUSE,] only found elsewhere in 1 Sa. 6. 4, 5, 11, 18; Isa. 66. 17.

TORTOISE,] not found elsewhere, Bochart and Gesenius suppose 'a lizard.'

30. FERRET,] not found elsewhere ; Sept. and Vulg. 'a shrew mouse.'

CHAMELEON,] not found elsewhere ; etymologically 'strength, power.'

LIZARD,] not mentioned elsewhere, Sept. *chalabotes,* Vulg. *stellio.*

SNAIL,] not found elsewhere, Sept. *saura,* Vulg. *lacerta.*

MOLE,] see on v. 18. above.

33. EARTHEN VESSEL...YE DO BREAK,] being, as before noted, of little value, but those of more valuable materials were rinsed and scoured.

36. A COLLECTION OF WATER,] see the use of the word in Ge. 1. 10 ; and Ex. 7. 19.

IS CLEAN,] because of the value of a well of water in the East. Mercy is here preferred to sacrifice.

THAT WHICH,] i.e. that water which may come or be put upon them.

37. SOWN SEED...IT IS CLEAN,] probably on the same ground as in the case of a well of water.

39. DIETH,] by a natural death.

CARCASE,] accidentally.

40. EATING,] unwittingly.

LIFTING UP,] to remove it out of the way.

44. YOUR PERSONS,] *lit* 'your souls.

45. WHO ARE BRINGING YOU UP,] the present participle in the original is more expressive than the present tense of the Common Version.

46. TEEMING,] not 'creeping' as in C.V.

XII. 2. GIVETH SEED,] see the use of the same word in Ge. 1. 11, 12.

SICKNESS,] i.e. menstrual.

3. EIGHTH DAY,] agreeably to Ge. 17. 12, Rom. 4. 14.

5. TWO WEEKS,] i.e. double the time appointed for a male.

SIXTY AND SIX DAYS,] i.e. double the number of days for a male.

6. A BURNT-OFFERING,] to express thankfulness for the life given, and the life spared.

YOUNG PIGEON OR A TURTLE DOVE ;] compare Luke 2. 22—24.

SIN-OFFERING ;] compare Ps. 51. 5.

FOUNDATION,] not 'issue' as in Common Version ; see the use of the word in 20. 13 ; Ps. 36. 9 ; 68. 26 ; Prov. 5. 18 ; 10. 11 ; 13. 14 ; 14. 27 ; 16. 22 ; 18. 4 ; 25. 26 ; Jer. 2. 13 ; 9. 1 ; 17. 13 ; 51. 36 ; Hos. 13. 15 ; Zec. 13. 1.

8. See notes on v. 6 above.

XIII. 2. SKIN OF THE FLESH,] i.e. his body.

A RISING,] as in v. 10, 19, 28, 43 ; compare its other occurrences in Ge. 4. 7 ; 49. 3 ; Job 13. 11 ; 31. 23 ; 41. 25 ; Ps. 62. 4 ; Hab. 1. 7.

SCAB,] as in 14. 56.

A BRIGHT SPOT,] as in v. 4, 19, 23, 24, 25, 26, 28, 38, 39; 14. 56.

IT HATH BECOME,] not 'it be...like,' as in the Common Version.

LEPROSY,] as in v. 3, 8, 9, 11, 13, 15, 20, 25, 30, 42, 43, 47, 49, 51, 52, 59; 14. 3, 7, 32, 34, 44, 54, 55, 57; De. 24. 8; 2 K. 5. 3, 6, 7, 27; 2 Ch. 26. 19. Leprosy was, and still is, common in Eastern countries, but perhaps all the cases of leprosy alluded to in Leviticus are rather marks of ceremonial uncleanness than of disease, requiring a priest, not a physician, to deal with it; the leper is rarely if ever said to be 'healed,' but generally to be 'cleansed.'

PLAGUE,] as in Ge. 12. 7; the original word is from a root signifying 'to come against, smite.'

3. HAIR] of the body in the plague spot.

PRONOUNCED HIM UNCLEAN,] *lit.* 'made him unclean.' This illustrates an important principle in Bible interpretation which is applicable to all such phrases as 'he hardened Pharoah's heart,'—'whosoever sins ye remit, they are remitted,' &c.

5. SEVEN DAYS,] for further examination.

A SECOND SEVEN DAYS,] the symptoms being yet undecided.

6. IS BECOME WEAK,] as in v. 21, 26, 28, 39, 56; 1 Sa. 3. 2; Isa. 42. 3; 61. 3; compare Nah. 3, 19, &c.

8. LEPROSY,] and believed to be incurable without the direct intervention of God.

13. SEEN,] as in v. 3, 5, 6, 8, 10.

18. FLESH,] i.e. any person, as in v. 24.

ULCER,] as in Ex. 9. 9, on which see note.

25. AND THE PRIEST,] not 'wherefore,' as in the Common Version.

30. SHINING,] *lit.* 'golden,' so in v. 32, 36.

SCALL,] as in v. 31, 32, 33, 34, 35, 36, 37; 14. 54, from a root signifying 'to draw out or away.'

33. SHAVETH HIMSELF,] i.e. causeth himself to be shaved.

35. AFTER HIS CLEANSING,] i.e. after his being declared clean.

39. FRECKLED SPOT,] the original word is found nowhere else.

BROKEN OUT,] as in v. 20, 25.

40. POLISHED,] as in v. 41; compare the use of the word in 1 K. 7. 45; Isa. 18. 2, 7; 50. 6; Eze. 21. 9, 10, 11, 28; 29. 18; Ezra 9. 3; Neh. 13. 25; also Dan. 7. 4.

42. PLAGUE,] not 'sore,' as in Common Version, and again in v. 43.

BALD BACK OF THE HEAD,] not 'bald head,' as in the C. V.; correct twice, and also in v. 43.

45. THE UPPER LIP,] not 'his' upper lip, there being no pronoun in the original text.

46. UNCOVERED,] *lit.* 'free,' as in Ex. 32. 25, &c.

CALLETH,] not 'cry;' the notion is not of expressing grief, but of warning others.

46. HE IS UNCLEAN,] as in the very next clause, and most unnecessarily and unwarrantably rendered 'defiled.'

ALONE,] as Uzziah the king did, 2 Ch. 26. 21.

OUTSIDE,] like Miriam, Nu. 12. 14, 15.

47. A GARMENT,] touched, it may be, by a leper.

50. SEVEN DAYS,] as in v. 5 above.

51. FRETTING,] as in v. 52; 14. 44; Eze. 28. 24.

55. ON THAT WHICH HATH THE PLAGUE,] compare parallel expression in v. 12, 13, 17, 31, 33, 50.

ITS ASPECT,] not its 'colour.'

BACK-PART...FRONT PART,] as in v. 42, 43.

57. BREAKING FORTH,] as in v. 20, 25.

XIV. 2. THAT HE HATH.] The Common Version omits the particle entirely.

IN THE DAY,] i.e. when he is cleansed; Jarchi absurdly enough says 'not in the night.'

OUTSIDE,] lepers not being allowed to enter a city.

3. CEASED FROM,] not 'healed in.' The verbs *rapha* to heal, and *raphah* 'to cease, desist,' are cognate.

4. BIRDS,] or 'sparrows,' see the use of the word in Ge. 7. 14; 15. 10; Ps. 84. 3; 102. 7, &c.

5. UPON,] or, 'at,' not *in* an earthen vessel.

DIPPED.] The Hebrew *tabal*, like the Greek *bapto* and *baptizo*, is here evidently used simply to express the notion of staining, dyeing, or covering an object with any thing, as it was clearly impossible to immerse a living bird in the blood of a single dead one.

7. SEND OUT,] actively, not merely 'let loose.'

WITH WATER,] not 'in water;' it is always done in the East by pouring or applying water to the body.

10. DAUGHTER OF A YEAR,] as in Ge. 17. 17.

12. GUILT-OFFERING,] not 'tresspass offering,' as in C. V.; compare Lev. 5. 6, &c.

13. SLAUGHTER,] the proper word for putting an irrational animal to death, either for food or sacrifice, as above noticed.

14. FOOT,] as was done at the consecration of the high priest, Ex. 29. 20; Lev. 8. 24.

15. LEFT PALM OF THE PRIEST,] not 'his own,' but that of another priest.

17. ON HIS PALM,] as in v. 15, not 'in his hand,' as in C. V.

18. PUTTETH,] not 'shall pour;' compare v. 17, same word in Hebrew.

19. MADE,] not 'offer.'

21. ONE TENTH DEAL,] instead of three-tenth deals.

24—30. From these verses it appears that precisely the same rites are enjoined on the poor as on the rich, leper; compare v. 12—20.

32. CLEANSING,] i.e. to the full demand of the law, in v. 10—20.

34. CANAAN,] whither they were going.

POSSESSION,] according to His promise to Abraham, Isaac, and Jacob.

I HAVE PUT,] *lit.* 'given.' Some have supposed this to indicate that the leprosy in this case was a direct divine infliction; but in Scripture language what God permits he is said to do.

36. THEY HAVE PREPARED.] The original verb never means 'to empty,' compare Ge. 24. 31; Ps. 80. 9; Zeph. 3. 15; Mal. 3. 1; Isa. 40. 3; 57. 14; 62. 10.

40. DRAWN OUT,] as in v. 43; Ps. 116. 8; Ps. 6. 4; 119. 153; 140. 1; 2 Sa. 22. 20; Job 36. 15; Ps. 7. 4; 18. 19; 34. 7; 50. 15; 31. 7; 91. 15.

42. CLAY,] *lit.* 'dust,' as in Ge. 2. 7; 3. 14, &c.

DAUBED,] as in v. 43, 48; Isa. 44. 18; Eze. 13. 10—15; 22. 28; 1 Ch. 29. 4.

46. HE HATH SHUT IT UP,] not ' that it is shut up ;' the verb is active.

48. CERTAINLY COME IN,] *lit.* 'coming, cometh in,' the C. V. omits the first word entirely.

49—53. Compare the same rites in v. 4—7, in the case of a leperous person.

57. TO DIRECT,] as in Ge. 46. 28, &c.

XV 2. ISSUE,] as in v. 3, 13, 15, 19, 25, 26, 28, 30, 33; compare the use of the verb in Ex. 3. 8, 17; 13. 5; 33. 3; Ps. 78. 20; Lam. 4. 9; Jer. 49. 4.

3. HATH RUN.] The original verb occurs nowhere else.

4. BED,] *lit.* 'lying place,' as in Ge. 29. 4; Ex. 8. 3; 21. 18, &c.

ALL] *or* every 'vessel,' or utensil, as the word properly denotes.

8. SPITTETH,] accidentally; compare the use of the word in Nu. 12. 14; De. 25. 9.

9. SADDLE,] *lit.* 'a place or object to ride on,' as in 1 K. 4. 26; Song 3. 10.

10. BEARING THEM] from one place to another.

11. RINSED,] *lit.* 'overflowed,' by pouring water upon them; compare the use of the word in Lev. 6. 28; 15. 12; 1 K. 22. 38.

12. WITH WATER,] not 'in water,' as in the Common Version.

15. HATH MADE,] not 'shall offer,' as in the Common Version.

16. Compare De. 23. 10, 11.

18. Compare Ex. 19. 15; 1 Sa. 21. 4.

19. IN HER SEPARATION,] as in 12. 2, 5, &c.

24. WITH HER] ignorantly, for if knowingly he was to be cut off, Lev. 20. 18.

25. WITHIN.] The phrase is somewhat doubtful, and translated variously : out of, beyond, before, not for, not with, without, not through, &c., *lit.* ' in not.'

30. HATH MADE,] not 'shall offer,' as in the Common Version.

32. SEED OF COPULATION;] as in v. 16, 17, 18 above.

33. SEPARATION,] as in v. 24.

XVI. 1. THEIR DRAWING NEAR,] with a view to offer perfume, as recorded in 10. 1, 2.

2. I AM SEEN,] not ' I will appear ;' the verb is in the Niphil or passive conjugation.

MERCY-SEAT,] *lit.* ' the covering,' i.e. the place where atonement was made.

4. AND] not ' therefore,' as in the C. V.

6. WHICH IS HIS OWN,] not as in the C. V. ' for himself ;' it is quite a different phrase from that in the next clause.

7. TWO GOATS,] belonging to the company.

8. GIVEN,] *or* given out, not 'cast,' which requires a different Hebrew word.

A GOAT OF DEPARTURE,] the original word 'Azazel" is only found elsewhere in v. 10, 26; and its meaning has been very unnecessarily controverted. It is evidently a compound word, made up of *az*, a goat, (v. 5,) and *azel*, to go away, (De. 32. 36, comp. 2. 10,)

10. BEFORE JEHOVAH.] Both goats were made sin-offerings to Jehovah, the one by being offered on the altar, the other by being sent away from man into the wilderness, where it probably was devoured by beasts.

12. SPICE-PERFUMES,] as in Ex. 25. 6; also Ex. 30. 34—37.

14. BLOOD,] which was caught in a vessel.

15. THE PEOPLE'S] not 'for the people,' as in the C. V.; compare the parallel phrases in v. 6, 11.

16.] WITH THEM,] not 'among them.'

18. THE ALTAR,] i.e. the golden altar of perfume, but others think the altar of burnt-offering is meant.

20. MAKING ATONEMENT,] *lit.* 'covering.'

21. FIT.] The original word is not found elsewhere ; it literally signifies ' timely, opportune, reasonable ;' others render it ' ready, prepared, appointed.'

22. SEPARATION,] so in the margin of the C. V., from a root signifying to cut off, divide ;' others render it ' decree,' i.e. a decreed place, comparing the use of the word in Dan. 4. 17, 24. But compare Ge. 41. 12, 13, 14, 15; 42. 1, 10, 13. Herodotus relates that the ancient Egyptians used to imprecate many things on the head of a sacrifice, and then sell it to a foreigner, or cast it into the river, hence he adds, the Egyptians do not eat the head of any animal. A similar custom existed among the Greeks.

23. PLACED,] see the use of the word in Nu. 17. 14; 19. 9; De. 14. 28; 26. 4, 10, &c.

25. ALTAR,] the brazen altar of burnt offering.

27. THE BULLOCK] belonging to Aaron, and the goat belonging to the people.

29. THE SEVENTH MONTH,] i.e. Tirsi.

YOURSELVES.] The word *nephesh* sometimes denotes the soul, but as often the *person*, sometimes even a carcase is so called. See Ge. 1. 20, 21, 24, 30, &c.

32. CONSECRATE.] *lit.* ' fill.'

34. ONCE IN A YEAR,] i.e. on the 10th day of the 7th month, viz. Tisri.

XVII. 3. SLAUGHTERETH] i.e. in sacrifice.

4. TENT OF MEETING,] where the altar of burnt-offering was.

CUT OFF,] i.e. excommunicate; comp. v. 10.

5. WITH THEM ;] i.e. along with them ; there is no necessity for the supplementary word '*for*,' as in the C. V.

7. TO GOATS,] as the word always means, not 'to devils;' compare the use of the word in Lev. 4. 23, 24; 9. 3, 15; 10. 16 : 16. 5, 7, 8, 9. 10, 15, 18, 20, 21, 26, 27 : 23. 19, &c.; idols in the form of goats are meant : comp. also 2 Ch. 11. 15.

10. SET MY FACE.] Compare this idiom again in Ge. 31. 21; Lev. 20. 3, 5, 6; 26. 17; Nu. 24. 1; 2. K. 12. 17.

12. I SAID.] See 3. 17; 7. 26, 27.

13. WHO HUNTETH VENISON,] lit. 'hunteth a hunting.'

15. A CARCASE,] lit. 'a faded, withered thing;' see Lev. 5. 2; 7. 24, &c.

TORN THING.] Compare Ge. 31. 39; Ex. 22. 13, &c.

NATIVES,] see on Ex. 12. 19, &c.

XVIII. 2. WORK,] as in Ge. 5. 29; not 'doings,' as in Ps. 9. 11.

STATUTES,] as in Ge. 26. 5; not 'ordinance,' as in Ex. 15. 25.

4. MY JUDGMENTS,] recorded in Ex. 21. 22, 23, and in this chapter.

5. IN THEM,] or by them.

6. NONE OF YOU,] lit. 'a man, a man,' i.e. any man, and with the succeeding negative —'no man.' Generally speaking, it may be laid down as a principle of interpretation that what a man is forbidden to do is unlawful to a woman also.

RELATION,] lit. 'flesh or food;' see Ex. 21. 10; a blood relative, Lev. 18. 6, 12, 13; 20. 19; 21. 2; 25. 49; Nu. 27. 11, &c.

TO UNCOVER,] or reveal, as in Job 20. 27, &c.

NAKEDNESS,] as in Ge. 9. 22, &c. The general opinion has always been that this phrase, 'to uncover nakedness,' is a prohibition of marriage between the parties mentioned in this chapter, but the common Hebrew expression for marriage is 'to take to wife,' 'to marry (lit. to be lord over) a wife,' 'to join in affinity with any one.' It seems, then, rather a prohibition of fornication or whoredom than of marriage, yet as these were unlawful at all times and with all persons, it is difficult to account for such minute details, if legal marriage be not meant here.

7. FATHER, EVEN.] The conjunction waw, which is here translated in the Common Version 'or,' is literally 'and,' but better 'even,' as explanatory of the first clause of the verse. History has recorded several violations of this prohibition, but none in Jewish History, except the case of Lot.

8. WIFE OF THY FATHER,] i.e. a stepmother; this was disregarded by Absalom, in 2 Sam. 16. 22.

9. SISTER, DAUGHTER OF THY FATHER.] Violated by Abraham in Ge. 20. 12.

WITHOUT,] i.e. a bastard.

10. SON'S DAUGHTER,] i.e. granddaughter. No reference is made to one's own daughter, but the more distant relationship being forbidden, the nearer must naturally be so also.

11. DAUGHTER OF THY FATHER'S WIFE,] i.e. step-sister.

12. SISTER OF THY FATHER,] i.e. aunt, as in v. 13, 14.

AUNT,] as in 20. 20. Violated by Amram, Ex. 6. 20.

15. DAUGHTER-IN-LAW,] as in Ge. 11. 31, &c. Violated by Judah, in Ge. 38. 11, 16, 24.

16. BROTHER'S WIFE.] Violated by Herod, in Mat 14. 3, &c.

17. HER DAUGHTER,] i.e. daughter-in-law, compare v. 14.

WICKEDNESS,] as in 29. 29; 20. 14; Jud. 20. 6; Job 31. 11; Ps. 26. 10; 119. 150; Pr. 10. 23; 21. 27; Isa. 32. 7; Jer. 13. 27; Eze. 16. 27, 43, 58; 22. 9, 11; 23. 21, 27, 29, 35, 44, 48, 49; 24. 13; Hos. 6. 9. In Job. 17. 11, and Pr. 24. 9, it means 'a device.'

18. A WOMAN UNTO ANOTHER,] lit. 'a woman unto her sister;' this is a common idiomatic Hebrew phrase, denoting 'one thing (added) to another;' compare all the passages where it occcurs, viz. Ex. 26. 3, 'five of the curtains joining one unto another,' lit. 'a woman to her sister.' So in v. 5, 6, 17; Eze. 1. 9, 23; 3. 13. These are all the passages where the phrase occurs, and it is quite evident that polygamy is what is here condemned. A parallel phrase is 'a man to his brother;' see Ge. 13. 11; 26. 31; 37. 19; Ex. 10. 23; 16. 15; 25. 20; 37. 9; Lev. 7. 10; 25. 14; 26. 37; Nu. 14. 4; De. 25. 11; 2 K. 7. 6; 1 Ch. 26. 12; Job 41. 17; Jer. 13. 14; 25. 26; Eze. 4. 17; 18. 10; 24. 23; 47. 14; Joel 2. 8; and there are also several passages where it is translated literally, and not idiomatically. The marriage of a man and his deceased wife's sister is not condemned here, and only by inference elsewhere. It was not only lawful but imperative for a man to marry the wife of his brother who died without issue.

TO BE AN ADVERSARY,] as in Ex. 23. 22; Isa. 11, 13, &c.

IN HER LIFE,] i.e during his life-time.

19. SEPARATION,] which lasted seven days; see 15. 19; the penalty was excision; see 20. 18.

20. FELLOW.] See note on this word in Lev. 6. 2, and compare the prohibition with Pr. 6. 32, 33.

21. THY SEED,] i.e. posterity.

TO PASS OVER] into his service, generally by passing through fire.

MOLECH,] lit. 'a king,' the name of an Ammonitish idol, called 'Milcom' in 1 K. 11. 5, and by some supposed to be the same as Baal, lit. 'a lord, master, superior;' Jer. 5. 31; mentioned elsewhere in Lev. 20. 2, 3, 4, 5; 1 K. 11. 7; 2 K. 23. 10; Jer. 32, 35. In 1 K. 21. 10, it is spelled 'Melech.'

POLLUTE,] as in Ge. 49. 8.

22. WOMAN.] Compare 1 Cor. 6. 9; Rom. 1. 24, &c.

23. CONFUSION,] as in 20. 12; compare also Isa. 10. 25.

24. I AM SENDING AWAY,] i.e. engaged in doing so even now.

25. I CHARGE.] The original word never means 'to visit;' see note on Ge. 21. 1; 'to visit upon' is not a phrase intelligible in English.

VOMITETH,] as in v. 28; 20. 22; Job 20. 15; Pr. 23. 8; 25. 13; Jon. 2. 10. Compare Rev. 3. 10.

27. BEFORE YOU.] The Hebrew particle generally refers to place, rarely to time.

28. IT HATH VOMITED OUT.] The past tense is here, as often elsewhere, used to denote the certainty of the event, as Matthew Henry remarks on the passage.

30. CHARGE,] as in Ge. 26. 5, &c.
STATUTES,] as in Ge. 26. 5. &c., not merely 'customs,' but statute laws.

XIX 2. ALL THE COMPANY,] either to their representatives, or by delegation.
HOLY...HOLY.] As observed already, the primitive idea of the original word is 'separation;' and it is by no means appropriately rendered by 'holy,' which expresses a moral quality, whereas the Hebrew word is used of God, men, cattle, places, things; even sodomites are described as such, because, of course, separated and dedicated to the temple services of idolatry.
3. FEAR,] as in Ex. 20. 12. In several ancient nations, and in China, at the present day, obedience to parents is the primary duty of every one, even before the worship of the deity.
SABBATHS,] i.e. the seventh day sabbath, the seventh year sabbath, the sabbath year of jubilee, and other appointed seasons of festival.
IDOLS,] lit. 'nothings,' see 26. 1; 1 Ch. 16. 26; Job 13. 4; Ps. 96. 5; 97. 7; Isa. 2. 8, 18, 20; 10. 10, 11; 19. 1. 3; 31. 7; Jer. 14. 14; Ez. 30. 13; Heb. 2. 18; Zec. 2. 17. Compare 1 Cor. 8. 4.
TURN NOT,] or 'look not,' lit. 'turn not the face.'
GOD.] Though this word is always in the plural number, the word rendered 'molten' is in the singular.
PEACE-OFFERINGS,] either as a thanksgiving, or for a vow, or for a freewill offering; see 7. 11, 12, 16.
6. BURNT,] as in 7. 16.
7. REALLY EATEN,] lit. 'eating it be eaten.'
PLEASING] to God, as in Lev. 7. 18, &c.
8. CUT OFF,] as in 7. 20.
9. YOUR LAND,] i.e. Canaan, which was theirs by promise, and the legislation of the Pentateuch generally was for the time when they were to dwell in it.
10. OMITTED PART.] The original word peret occurs no where else, but compare the use of the participial noun in Amos 6. 5.
11. STEAL,] as in Ex. 20. 15.
FEIGN,] as in Jos. 7. 11; Job 8. 18, &c.
FELLOW.] See note on Lev. 6. 2, &c.
13. OPPRESS,] as in Lev. 6. 2, &c. Vulg. reads improperly 'calumniate.'
HIRELING,] i.e. one hired only for a-day; wages in the East are generally paid monthly, to regular servants.
14. REVILE.] See note on Ex. 22. 28.
STUMBLING-BLOCK,] as in 1 Sa. 25. 31; Ps. 119. 165; Isa. 8. 14; 57. 14; Jer. 6. 21; Eze. 3. 20; 7. 19; 14. 3, 4, 7; 18. 30; 21. 15; 44. 12. Compare also Zeph. 1. 3; Isa. 3. 6.
15. LIFT UP THE FACE,] a common Hebrew idiom, as in Ge. 19. 21; 32. 20; De. 10. 17, &c.
FELLOW.] See note on Lev. 6. 2, &c. Compare Prov. 18. 5.
16. GO.] There is no necessity for the phrase 'up and down' of the Common Version; the original is simply 'go,' the next word, 'slanderer or tale-bearer,' is pro-

perly one who traffics, a merchant or pedlar, whose occupation affords, especially in the East, abundant opportunities for slander and gossip.
STAND AGAINST,] by bearing a false testimony.
17. THY BROTHER,] i.e. any one, according to Scripture idiom.
REPROVE,] as in Ge. 21. 25.
SUFFER,] or more lit. 'lift up' sin upon him.
18. WATCH,] as in Ps. 103. 9; Song 1. 6; 8. 11, 12; Jer. 3. 5, 12; Na. 1. 2; Dan. 7. 28.
19. CAUSE TO GENDER,] lit. 'cause to lie down;' compare Lev. 18. 23; 20. 6; Ps. 139. 3.
DIVERSE KINDS.] The original word occurs three times in this verse, and once again in De. 22. 9.
SHAATNEZ,] or mixed cloth; only found elsewhere in De. 22. 11, where it is added 'woollen and linen together;' the etymology is unknown; priests only were allowed to wear such a garment, according to Josephus, but Scripture is silent about such a permission.
20. MAID-SERVANT,] as in Ge. 12. 16; 16. 1, 2, 3, 5, 6, 8.
BETROTHED.] The original word occurs nowhere else, and has been variously rendered, e.g. gathered, plucked, reproached, by, to, or for a man.
REALLY RANSOMED,] lit. 'ransomed not ransomed.'
FREEDOM.] The original word is not found elsewhere, but compare Ex. 21. 2, &c.
AN INVESTIGATION THERE IS.] There is not the slightest ground for the monstrously unjust rendering of the Common Version; the noun occurring here is not found elsewhere, but the verbal form of the root occurs after. It never signifies 'to scourge,' nor 'to animadvert or punish any one,' as Gesenius pretends. The simple meaning is 'to search, seek, open up by examination;' compare all the passages where the verb occurs, viz., Lev. 13. 36; 27. 33; 2 K. 16. 15; Ps. 27. 4; Prov. 20. 25; Eze. 34. 11, 12; compare also Ezra 4. 15, 19; 5. 17; 6. 1; 7. 14.
24. PRAISES,] more lit. 'causing praises' to Jehovah. Compare its use in Jud. 9. 27.
26. WITH,] lit. 'on' the blood; Sept. on 'the mountains,' (as in Eze. 18. 6,) apparently having a different word in their Hebrew MSS.
ENCHANT,] lit. 'to observe diligently,' as may be seen in Ge. 20. 27; 44. 5, 16; De. 18. 10; 1 K. 20. 33; 2 K. 17. 17; 21. 6; 2 Ch. 33. 6, all the instances of its occurrence. Gesenius prefers the idea of 'hissing, whispering,' hence the Hebrew word for serpent.
OBSERVE CLOUDS,] as in Ge. 9. 14; compare also De. 18. 10, 14; Jud. 9. 37; 2 K. 21. 6; 2 Ch. 33. 6; Isa. 2. 6; 57. 3; Jer. 27. 9; Mic. 5. 12.
27. ROUND,] i.e. make the head round, by compressing it with boards and bandages, or by cutting the hair all round uniformly.

DESTROY,] *lit.* 'corrupt,' as in Ge. 6. 12; De. 4. 16, &c.

28. A CUTTING,] as in 21. 5; Zec. 12. 3.

SOUL.] There is not the slightest authority for abandoning the usual meaning of the word *nephesh*, or to suppose it denotes here a corpse or dead person.

A CROSS MARK.] This word *kaaka*, occurs nowhere else; supposed to mean to 'brand, a burn.'

29. GO NOT A WHORING.] This literal translation seems preferable to the C. V. 'fall.' The practice condemned is that of dedicating them to heathen temples, but the form of the original is sometimes only permissive, not causative.

31. TURN] or 'look,' i.e. turn the face to look.

FAMILIAR SPIRITS,] or necromancers, *lit.* 'auboth,' as in 20. 6, 27; De. 18. 11; 1 Sa. 28. 3, 7, 8, 9; 2 K. 21. 6; 23. 24; 1 Ch. 10. 13; 2 Ch. 33. 6: Isa. 8. 19; 19. 3; 29. 4. In Job 32. 19, the word signifies a 'bottle,' which favours the Sept. translation 'ventriloquists.'

WIZARDS,] *lit.* 'knowing ones,' as in 20. 6, 27; De. 18. 11; 1 Sa. 28. 3, 9; 2 K. 21, 6; 23. 24; 2 Ch. 33. 6; Isa. 8. 19; 19. 3.

32. GREY HAIRS,] *or* 'old age;' see Ge. 15. 5, &c.

33. OPPRESS,] not merely 'vex;' see note on Ex. 22. 21.

35. LIQUID MEASURE,] as in 1 Ch. 23. 29; Ez. 4. 11, 16.

36. WEIGHTS,] *lit.* 'stones,' these being anciently used for that purpose; so also De. 25. 13, 15; 2 Sa. 14. 26; Pr. 11. 1; 16. 11; 20. 10, 23; Mic. 6. 11; Zec. 5. 8.

XX. 2. MOLECH.] See note on 18. 21.

4. REALLY HIDE,] *lit.* 'hiding do hide.' To hide the eyes is a Hebrew phrase for conniving at a thing; see 1 Sa. 12. 3; or for disregarding it, as in Eze. 22. 26; Isa. 1. 15; La. 3. 5, 6; Pr. 28. 27.

5. THAT MAN,] i.e. of the people who conceals the guilt.

HIS FAMILY,] if they follow his example, of course.

6. TURNETH UNTO,] not 'after,' as in the Common Version.

TO GO A WHORING] spiritually, i.e. forsake Jehovah.

8. SANCTIFYING YOU,] as in Ex. 31. 13; on which see note.

9. REVILETH,] as in Ex. 22. 58, &c.

10. DEATH,] generally by stoning.

12. CONFUSION.] See on 18. 23.

14. THEY BURN,] not as in the C. V. 'they shall be burnt.'

WICKEDNESS,] as in Lev. 18. 17, &c.

15. GIVETH HIS LYING,] as in Lev. 18. 20, 23.

17. SHAME.] The original word occurs very often in the Old Testament, and with only two other exceptions is uniformly rendered 'kindness, loving kindness,' &c. In Job 6. 14, and in Pr. 13. 34, besides the present passage, it is rendered (by way of antiphrasis) '*shame*.'

SONS OF THEIR PEOPLE,] as in 2 Ch. 35.

5, 7, 12, but this form of expression is not found elsewhere.

19. SISTER,] are prohibited in 18. 13.

20. CHILDLESS,] as in Ge. 15, 2; Lev. 20 20, 21; Jer. 22. 30.

21. IMPURITY,] or, separated thing,' as in Lev. 12. 2, 5, &c.

23. STATUTES,] as in v. 22, not 'customs' merely.

SENDING AWAY,] as in Ge. 43. 4, not 'cast out.'

WEARIED,] as in Ge. 27. 46.

24. POSSESS,] as in next clause, not 'inherit;' compare Ge. 22. 17.

GROUND,] not 'land;' compare Ge. 2. 5.

25. YOURSELVES.] The original word is applied either to the soul or to the body.

ANYTHING,] There is no authority for, or propriety in, the addition of the Common Version, 'manner of living.'

26. SEPARATE YOU,] as in v. 25, not 'sever.'

27. THERE IS IN THEM,] compare 19, 31; Acts 16. 16; the spirit is said to be *in* them, not *with* them merely.

XXI. 1. PERSON.] That the person was dead is implied, but not *expressed* in the original.

RELATION.] See note on 18. 6.

3. THE VIRGIN.] The definite article is found in the original.

TO A MAN,] as in Nu. 30. 6; De. 25. 5; Ruth 1. 12, 13, &c. The Hebrews never thought of saying that a woman married a man, but that the man married the woman; he was not her property, but she was *his*.

5. BALDNESS.] See Lev. 19. 27, 28; De. 14. 1.

BEARD.] See Lev. 19. 27.

CUTTING.] See Lev. 19. 28.

6. BREAD.] This clause is explanatory of the preceding, there is no propriety therefore in the conjunction *and*, inserted in C.V.

9. BURNT,] whereas the daughter of any other but a priest was to be stoned; see De. 22. 23, 24.

10. HIGH PRIEST.] *lit.* 'great priest,' as in Nu. 35. 25, 28; Jos. 20. 6; 2 K. 12. 10; 22. 4, 8; 23. 4; 2 Ch. 34. 9; Neh. 3 1, 20: 13. 28; Hag. 1. 1, 12, 14: 2. 2, 4; Zec. 3. 1, 8; 6. 11. In 2 K. 25. 18; 1 Ch. 27. 5; 2. Ch. 19. 11; 24. 11; 26. 20; 36. 14; Ezra 7. 5; 8. 24, 29; 10. 5; Neh. 12. 7; Jer. 52. 24, he is called 'chief *or* head priest.'

POURED.] See Ex. 59. 7; Lev. 8. 12.

GARMENTS.] See Lev. 8. 7—9.

11. COME.] The priest of Jupiter among the Romans was under the same restraint.

DEFILE HIMSELF,] by rending his garments, shaving his hair, &c.

12. GO OUT,] i.e. during the time of divine service.

SANCTUARY,] by forsaking his duties unlawfully, and resuming them without atonement.

SEPARATION.] as in Nu. 6. 6.

15. SANCTIFYING HIM,] i.e. separating him or divine service.

17. BLEMISH,] such as those indicated in v. 18, 19, 20; such things being calculated to afford subjects of ridicule, and prevent them from possessing the authority and

reverence their office required. Hence we may with safety infer that the notion entertained by some that the Man of Sorrows was disfigured in countenance or appearance is highly improbable.

ENLARGED,] or 'stretched out,' (as in 22. 23; Isa. 28. 20,) e.g. the ear, &c.

18. DWARFED,] *lit.* 'stopped, shut up,' not found elsewhere, but in the causative conjugation it is common, and denotes 'to devote' to destruction or to God ; Ex. 22. 20.

20. MIXTURE.] The original word occurs only in this place; it is from a root signifying, 'to mix, anoint;' see Ge. 11. 7, 9; Ex. 29. 2, 40; Ps. 92. 11, &c.

22. EAT,] his blemish being his misfortune, not his fault, he is still permitted to share the priestly portion, and probably to engage in some of the menial services of the priesthood.

XXII. 2. THEY ARE SEPARATED.] The verb is in the *passive* not the *reflexive* form; compare Eze. 14. 7 ; Hos. 9. 10 ; Zec. 7. 3.

3. DRAWETH NEAR,] i.e. to eat, not merely 'goeth,' as in the C. V.; compare Ge. 20. 4.

4. ISSUE.] There is no necessity for the addition of the word 'running;' compare I5. 2, 25.

A PERSON,] not necessarily of a 'dead' person, as in the C. V.

FROM HIM,] probably by night in a dream; compare Nu. 15. 16.

5. TEEMING.] See note on Ge. 1. 20, 21.

6. TILL THE EVENING,] as already noticed in 11. 31 ; 15. 5, 7, 16.

7. GONE IN,] as in Ge. 7. 9, the Hebrews always regarding the sun as entering into his chambers, not merely as coming down or setting.

8. CARCASE.] There is no necessity or propriety in the rendering of the C. V. here, (or in 7. 24 ; 17. 15 ; De. 14. 21 ; Eze. 4. 14; 44. 31,) see Lev. 5. 2, &c.

9. CHARGE,] as in Ge. 26. 5.

10. A SETTLER,] as in Ge. 23. 4; not merely a 'sojourner,' but one who has deliberately taken up his habitation with them; compare 1 K. 17. 1, &c.

BUYETH A PERSON,] i.e. his services, for a period of years—more or less.

11. HE THAT IS BORN] among his domestics, belonging to his household, but not of his family.

18. A BURNT-OFFERING,] which was always to consist of either a bullock, sheep, or goat, (or fowls,) being males, perfect, (see 1. 3, 10,) but sin-offerings and peace-offerings might consist of females; (see 3. 1 ; 4. 32.)

20. PLEASING THING.] Compare Mal. 1. 8, 13, 14.

21. PEACE-OFFERINGS,] i.e. expressions of thanksgivings for mercies; see 7. 12.

22. BROKEN,] as in Ps. 147. 3.

MAIMED,] *lit.* 'cut or wounded;' only found elsewhere in Job 14. 5 ; Isa. 10. 22, where it is rendered 'determined, decreed.'

22. HAVING A WEN.] The word is not found elsewhere ; *lit.* a flowing out, i.e. with matter.

23. ENLARGED.] See on 21. 18 alone.

24. BRUISED.] Compare the use of the word in 1 Sa. 26. 7 ; Ez. 23. 3.

BEATEN,] as in De. 9. 21 ; Ps. 89. 23 ; Isa 30. 14 ; Joel 3. 10.

CUT,] as in De. 23. 1 ; 1 Sa. 5. 4.

25. SON OF A STRANGER,] as in Ge. 12. 17. &c.

CORRUPTION.] This word is not found elsewhere ; it is from a common root signifying 'to corrupt.'

27. DAM,] *lit.* ' its mother.'

28. ONE DAY,] to discourage cruelty, doubtless.

30. TILL MORNING,] as the word always means.

XXIII. 2. APPOINTED SEASONS,] as in Ge. 1. 14 : these were generally 'feasts' or festivals,' but the word does not mean so. and ought not to be so translated.

CONVOCATIONS,] as in Ex. 12. 16; *lit.* 1) a calling together, 2) those called together, 3) the place where they are called together.

MY APPOINTED SEASONS,] and therefore not of human origin.

3. A SABBATH OF REST.] This is the first of the 'appointed seasons of Jehovah.' It is here said to be a 'holy convocation', which shows or implies that it was the design of God that they should have stated meetings on that day ; and it need not be doubted but that these were for the reading of the Law, and the worship of God, by the priests, and especially the Levites, who are everywhere regarded as the instructors of Israel ; compare 1 K. 4. 23, &c.

5. BETWEEN THE EVENINGS,] See Ex. 12. 6, for further details of this festival.

6. FEAST OF UNLEAVENED THINGS.] See Ex. 12. 15, 18—20.

8. SEVEN DAYS,] i.e. daily for that period.

FIRE-OFFERING.] See Nu. 28. 19—24.

SEVENTH DAY,] in which the Egyptians were drowned, Ex. 12. 16.

10. HARVEST,] i.e. of barley ; see Ex. 9. 31 ; the wheat harvest was seven weeks later.

SHEAF,] as in v. 11. 12, 15; De. 24. 19 ; Ruth 2. 7, 15 ; Job 24. 10 ; it is elsewhere (Ex. 16. 16, 18, 22, 32, 33, 36,) considered as a measure called an " omer," hence it is a question whether the barley was to be waved before Jehovah before or after it was thrashed out.

13. TWO-TENTH DEALS.] From Ex. 29. 40, it appears that only one-tenth deal was commonly required for a present, here it is doubled, probably to express thankfulness.

A FOURTH OF THE HIN,] as in Ex. 29. 40.

14. FULL EARS,] not 'green ears;' see Lev. 2. 14, &c.

FIFTY DAYS,] from the 16th of Nisan, according to Josephus; hence called the feast of ' Pentecost.'

17. LEAVEN,] or yeast; none of these loaves were burnt; they became the priest's property.

FIRST FRUITS,] as in Ex. 23. 16, &c., hence in Ex. 34. 22, it is called the feast of the first fruits,' of wheat harvest.

22. LEAVE THEM,] as in 19. 9. 10.

24. A SABBATH,] *or* rest.

SHOUTING,] as in 25. 9; Nu. 10. 5, 6; 23. 21; 29. 1; 31. 6; Jos. 6. 5, 20; 1 Sa. 4. 5, 8; 2 Sa. 6. 15; 1 Ch. 25. 28; 2 Ch. 13. 12; 15. 14; Ezra 3. 11, 12, 13; Job 8. 21; 33. 26; 39. 25; Ps. 27. 6; 33. 3; 47. 5; 89. 15; 150. 5; Jer. 4. 19; 20. 16; 49. 2; Eze. 21. 22; Amos 1. 14; 2. 2; Zep. 1. 16.

25. FIRE-OFFERING.] See Nu. 29. 1—6.

27. ATONEMENTS.] The word is plural, as in Ex. 29. 36, on which see note.

FIRE-OFFERING.] See Nu. 29. 8—11.

34. SEVENTH MONTH] i.e. Tisri, part of September.

FESTIVAL.] See on Ex. 10. 9.

BOOTHS.] See on Ge. 33. 17; Lev. 23. 34, &c.

36. A RESTRAINT,] i.e. on their usual avocations, as in Nu. 29. 35; De. 16. 8; 2 Ch. 7. 9; Neh. 8. 18; Jer. 9. 2; Amos 5. 21; compare also 2 K. 10. 20; Isa. 1. 3; Joel 1. 14; 2. 15.

39. FIFTEENTH DAY,] i.e. as in v. .34 above, where the festival of booths is appointed (probably) to commemorate the dwelling of Israel in booths in the wilderness 40 years; in this 39th verse, the same festival is apparently to give thanks for the ingathering of the fruits of the land in autumn, hence in Ex. 23. 16, and 34. 22, it is called the feast of ingathering.

40. THE FRUIT,] as in Ge. 1. 11, &c.; the original word is entirely different from that translated 'boughs,' in the third clause of this verse, and should be distinguished in translation.

BEAUTIFUL.] Compare the use of the word in De. 33. 17; 1 Ch. 16. 27; Job 40. 10; Ps. 8. 5; 21. 5; 29. 4; 45. 3, 4; 90. 16; 96. 6; 104. 1; 110. 3; 111. 3; 145. 5, 12; 149. 9; Prov. 20. 29; 31. 25; Isa. 2. 10, 19, 21; 5. 14; 35. 2; 53. 2; La. 1. 6; Ez. 16. 14; 27. 10; Mic. 2. 9. Compare also Dan. 11. 20, and Dan. 4. 37, 36; 5. 18.

BRANCHES,] *lit.* 'bendings, or hands,' the word being used of the *sole* of the foot, the *palm* of the hands; compare also Job 18. 32; Isa. 9. 14; 19. 15.

PALMS,] as in Ex. 15. 27, &c.

BOUGHS,] as in Ps. 80. 10; Ez. 17. 8, 23; 31. 3; 36. 8; Mal. 4. 1; Da. 4. 12, 14, 21; Eze. 19. 19.

THICK,] as in Neh. 8. 15; Eze. 6. 13; 20. 18.

WILLOWS,] as in Job 40. 22; Ps. 137. 3; Isa. 15. 7; 44. 4.

BROOK,] as in Ge. 32. 23, &c.

42. NATIVES,] as in Ex. 12. 19, but not strangers, sojourners, or settlers.

XXIV 2. **COMMAND,]** or charge.

PURE OLIVE OIL,] at the public expense, for the charge is general—the sons of Israel.

LAMP,] as in Ge. 1. 14, 15, 16; Ex. 25. 6, &c.

LIGHT,] as in Ex. 25. 37, &c. These were seven in number, but the word is in the singular number here.

3. TENT.] See Heb. 9. 2

4. PURE,] being of gold.

5. FLOUR,] of wheat.

TWELVE CAKES,] one for each of the tribes of Israel.

DEALS] of an ephah, i.e. two omers.

6. RANKS,] as in Ex. 39. 37, &c.

RANK,] as in v. 7; 1 Ch. 9. 32; 23. 29; 28. 16; 2 Ch. 2. 4; 13. 11; 29. 18; Neh. 10. 33. The *second* rank or row was placed above the *first*.

PURE TABLE,] being overlaid with gold. Ex. 25. 24.

7. FRANKINCENSE,] two cups, each containing a handful.

TO THE BREAD,] not ' on the bread.'

10. GOETH OUT] in the midst of the sons of Israel; the original is ambiguous; some consider the going out to refer to the departure out of Egypt, others, that it refers to his going out of his tent into the public assembly, which latter aggravates his offence, as being publicly committed.

SON OF AN EGYPTIAN MAN.] Incidentally this shows that all who came out of Egypt were not exclusively of Israelitish origin.

STRIVE,] as in Ex. 2. 13, &c.

11. EXECRATE,] as in v. 16; Nu. 23. 8, 25, &c. from a root signifying ' to pierce;' 2 K. 18. 21, &c.

THE NAME,] i.e. of God; as in De. 28. 58.

MOSES,] as being one of the hard cases they were unable to settle of themselves.

SHELOMITH,] the feminine form of Solomon, like ' Shulammith.'

12. HE CAUSED,] not ' they caused,' as the Masorets have marked; thus a nominative is given to the next clause ' to explain,' unreasonably translated in the C. V. 'might be showed.'

EXPLAIN,] *lit.* 'spread out,' as in Nu. 15. 34; Ex. 4. 18; Neh. 8. 8; Ez. 34. 12.

MOUTH.] There is no necessity for, or propriety in, translating the original word by ' mind.'

14. REVILER,] as in Ge. 12. 3, &c.

17. SMITE A SOUL,] i.e. a person, so that he dieth.

18. BODY FOR BODY,] i.e. value for value.

19. FELLOW.] See note on Lev. 6. 2.

20. SO IT IS DONE IN HIM,] often, perhaps generally, a pecuniary recompense was accepted by the injured party instead of this; see on Ex. 21. 24, 25.

21. REPAYETH IT,] as in v. 18 above.

22. ONE JUDGMENT,] this shows the great superiority of the Mosaic laws and customs to those of other nations, even of some in the nineteenth century.

XXV 2. **KEPT A SABBATH,]** every seven years, as explained in v. 3—5, following: as is already noted, this was an important agricultural as well as ceremonial law.

3. SIX YEARS.] See Ex. 23. 10.

5. SPONTANEOUS GROWTH,] as in v. 11; 2 K. 19. 29; Job 14. 19; Isa. 37. 38.

SEPARATED THING] which hath been set apart to the Lord.

7. INCREASE,] as in Ge. 47. 24, &c.

9. SHOUTING,] as in 23. 24.

CAUSE TO PASS OVER] the land.

10. HALLOWED,] i.e. set apart.
LIBERTY,] as in Isa. 61. 1; Jer. 34. 8, 15,
17; Eze. 46. 17; liberty from bondage of all
kinds.
JUBILEE,] as in v. 14, 12, 13, 15, 28, 30, 31,
33, 40, 50, 52, 54; 27. 17, 18, 23, 24; Nu.
36. 4; Jos. 6. 4, 5, 6, 8, 13; comp. Ex. 19. 10.
TURN BACK] from servitude.
14. OPPRESS,] as in Ex. 22. 21, &c.
16. A NUMBER OF INCREASES.] There is no
necessity for the awkward supplement of
the C. V.
18. CONFIDENTLY,] as in v. 19; 26. 5;
Jud. 18. 7; De. 33. 12; the meaning is not
that they were to *be* safe, but to *feel* safe.
21. SIXTH YEAR,] as he had done on the
sixth day of the week with regard to the
manna, Ex. 16. 22.
23. TO EXTINCTION,] as in v. 30; it is not
to be sold so as absolutely to '*cut it off*'
permanently from its owners; property in
a walled city might be thus sold (see v. 30),
but not in the country. By this means
the possessions of any one tribe were prevented from being taken from them either
by sale or by marriage, as in the daughters
of Zelophehad, Nu. 36. 7.
24. A REDEMPTION,] as in v. 26, 29, 31, 32,
48, 51, 52; Ruth 4. 6, 7, 8; Eze. 11. 15.
25. REDEEMER,] as in v. 26; applied alike
to God and to man; see Ge. 48. 16; Nu. 5.
8; 35. 12, 19, 21, 24, 25, 27; De. 19. 6, 12;
Job 19. 25, &c.
29. DAYS.] For this peculiar mode of
expression see note on Ge. 1. 5, &c.
31. IN THE JUBILEE IT GOETH OUT.]
These stipulations being known to both
seller and buyer, there could be no complaint on the part of either, for the one in
asking a given price, and the other in paying it, would naturally reckon accordingly.
32. CITIES OF THE LEVITES,] i.e. those to
be given to them afterwards up and down
all the country, where they were settled as
teachers and instructors of the people.
REDEMPTION AGE-DURING] of property,
whether in a walled city or in the country,
was a peculiar privilege reserved for the
Levites, as these had neither fields nor
vineyards apart from the suburbs of their
cities.
34. A SUBURB,] which according to Nu.
35. 5, was to be two thousand cubits on
each side of the city, and the general
property of the tribe.
35. KEPT HOLD ON HIM,] as in De. 22. 25;
Job 27. 6, &c.
36. INCREASE,] as forbidden in Ex. 22.
25. This, of course, was only when the
recipient was poor; if borrowed to trade
with more largely, a share of the profits
was only reasonable.
39. HATH BEEN SOLD] by his debtor, or
his father, or himself, for a stated time.
Ex. 23. 3, &c.
40. AS AN HIRELING,] who receives his
allotted wages, and works a stipulated
time.
AS A SOJOURNER,] and therefore to be
treated in a friendly manner.
43. RIGOUR.] See note on Ex. 1. 13, 14, &c.

44. ROUND ABOUT YOU,] i.e. Amon, Aram,
Edom, Moab, Philistines, &c.
NATIONS.] There is no propriety in the
word 'heathen.'
46. TO OCCUPY,] not 'to inherit' as in the
C. V., being quite a different word from
that in the preceding clause; see same
word in 20. 24.
49. HE HATH BEEN REDEEMED,] not 'he
may redeem himself;' the word is in the
(Niphal or) passive conjugation, as in v
30, 54; 27. 20, 27, 28, 33; Isa. 52. 3.
55. MY SERVANTS,] and therefore they
cannot engage with any other master without my consent.
YOUR GOD,] and entitled to unlimited
obedience, both from families and from the
nation at large.

XXVI. 1. IDOLS,] lit. 'nothings;' com-
pare the same sentiment in 1 Cor. 8. 4.
GRAVEN IMAGE,] as in Ex. 20. 4.
STANDING IMAGE] or pillar, as in Ge. 28.
18, 22.
IMAGERY,] as in Nu. 33. 52; Ps. 73. 7;
Pr. 8. 11; 25. 11; Ez. 8. 12.
4. YOUR RAINS] or showers, those you re-
quire and expect for your land; distinguished as the former and the latter, or the
'gathered' and the 'sprinkling.'
THE TREE,] i.e. each one of them.
5. THE THRESHING, THE GATHERING,] i.e.
from March to July; compare Nu. 13. 20.
THE SOWING TIME,] i.e. October; see
Amos 9. 13.
6. CAUSING TREMBLING,] as in Ge. 27. 33.
CAUSED TO CEASE,] as in Ex. 5. 5, &c.
THE EVIL BEAST,] as in Ge. 37. 20, &c.
8. A MYRIAD,] as in Ge. 24. 60, &c.;
the Hebrews generally use the phrase 'ten
thousand,' when they desire to be particular,
as in Jud. 1. 4, &c. For the general sentiment see Jud. 7. 21, 22; 1 Sa. 14. 13, 14; 2
Sa. 23. 8—16, &c.
9. TURNED,] i.e. the face; to 'turn the
back' on one is to reject him.
MY COVENANT] with Abraham, and also
that made at Sinai.
10. BRING OUT] to make room for the new.
12. WALKING HABITUALLY,] as Ge. 6. 9;
2 Sa. 7. 6, &c.
13. BARS,] as in 1 Cor. 15. 15; Isa. 58. 6,
9; Jer. 27. 2; 28. 10, 12, 13; Eze. 30. 18;
34. 27.
ERECT.] This Hebrew word is not found
elsewhere; but it is derived from a very
common root, signifying 'to rise up.'
16. TROUBLE,] as in Ps. 78. 33; Isa. 65.
23; Jer. 15. 8.
THE CONSUMPTION.] The article is in the
Hebrew, as in the next clause.
CAUSING PAIN,] not found elsewhere; but
compare De. 28. 65; Job 41. 22.
SOUL,] as in v. 1, 15, &c.
17. SMITTEN,] as in Ex. 8. 2.
21. ARE NOT WILLING.] The verb is not
expressive of the simple future, but of a
positive resolution not to hearken.
22. THE FIELD.] There is no necessity
for translating the word by 'wild,' rather
than by the simple literal meaning.

BEREAVE YOU,] not merely of your children,' but also of your 'friends,' &c.

CUT OFF,] not necessarily by destroying them, but by giving them to the enemy.

FEW,] the supplement 'in number' is unnecessary.

WAYS,] not merely the 'high,' but 'the low,' and 'the bye-ways.'

23. INSTRUCTED,] as in Pr. 29. 19; Ps. 2. 10. Jer, 6. 8; 31. 18.

24. SMITTEN,] as in Ge. 8. 21, &c.

25. VENGEANCE,] as in De. 32. 35, 41, 43: Jud. 16. 28; Ps. 58. 10; Pr. 6. 34; Isa. 34. 8; 35. 5; 47. 3; 59. 17; 61. 2; 63. 4; Eze. 24. 8; 25. 12, 15; Mic. 5. 15; it never means 'quarrel.'

26. STAFF,] as in Ps. 105. 16; Eze. 4. 16; 5. 16; 14. 13.

TEN,] i.e. an indefinite number, as in Ge. 31. 7, &c.

29. EAT,] as in 2 K. 6. 29; La. 4 10; Eze.5.7.

30. HIGH PLACES,] as in Nu. 21. 28; 22. 41; 33. 52; De. 32. 13; 33. 29, &c.

IMAGES,] as in 2 Ch. 14. 5; 34. 4, 7; Isa. 17. 8; 27. 9; Eze. 6. 4, 6. The etymology of this word, which only occurs in the plural number, is altogether uncertain.

IDOLS,] as in De. 29. 17, J K. 15. 12; 21. 26; 2 K. 17. 12; 21. 11, 21; 23. 24; Jer. 50. 2; Eze. 6. 4, 5, 6, 9, 3; 8. 10; 14. 3, 4, 5, 6, 7; 16. 36; 18. 6, 12 15; 20. 7, 8, 16, 18, 24, 31, 39; 22. 34; 23.', 30, 37, 39, 49; 30. 13; 33. 25; 36. 18, 25, 37 23; 44. 10, 12. The word is only found, ike the preceding, in the plural form, *lit.* 'things rolled,' being unable to move of themselves.

31. A WASTE.] The original is a noun, not an adjective, as in the C. V.; so in v. 33.

33. A DESOLATION.] The orginal is a noun, not a verb or adjective.

35. THAT WHICH,] not 'because,' as in Common Version.

36. BROUGHT,] as in Je. 4. 4.

DRIVEN AWAY,] as in Job 13. 25; Pr. 21. 6; Isa. 41. 3; Ps. 68. 2; Isa. 19. 7.

37. STUMBLED,] as in Ps. 27. 2; Isa. 5. 27.

STANDING.] This original word does not occur elsewhere.

38. CONSUMED YOU,] by your being buried there.

39. CONSUME AWAY,] as in Eze. 4. 17; Zech. 12. 4; Ps. 38. 5; Isa. 34. 4; Eze. 24. 23; 33. 10.

45. FOR THEM,] not by any means 'for their sake,' as in the C. V.

46. GIVEN,] not 'made.'

XXVII. 2. WONDERFUL,] as in De. 28. 59; Jud. 13. 19; 2 Ch. 2. 9; 26. 15; Ps. 31. 21; Isa. 20. 29; 29. 14; Joel 2. 26; but compare the use of the word in Nu. 6. 2.

JEHOVAH'S.] Sometimes a person in his zeal for the Lord might wish to devote himself, or some of his family to His service, but as this would have unduly increased the number of those employed in divine service, while they were allowed thus to devote themselves, they were required also to redeem themselves by paying an equivalent for the services in money. The generous spirit of self-dedication was thus cherished and yet restrained at the same time.

VALUATION,] as in v. 18, *lit.* 'arrangement, ordering;' this was according to the probable value of the person's services and position, and was expressly defined to prevent an exorbitant overcharge on the one hand, or a rash vow on the other.

3. SHEKEL OF SILVER,] i.e. about two shillings.

SHEKEL OF THE SANCTUARY,] *or* 'holy shekel,' having always the same value.

8. HIM WHO IS VOWING.] A rich person might make a vow of some poorer person over whom he had authority, and this poor person might be unable to redeem himself by his poverty, and might claim a reduction thereupon, but the law here declares that the valuation is to be reckoned not by the ability of him who is vowed, but of him who is vowing.

9. ALL...IS HOLY,] i.e. separated and devoted; it cannot be redeemed like a human being, a house, c~ a field.

10. CHANGE,] as in Ge. 31. 45; an o~ for a sheep, or a sheep for an ox.

EXCHANGE,] as in Ps. 15. 4; 106. 20, an old for a young one, or a young one for an old one.

11. UNCLEAN BEAST,] for sacrifice or food; it might be sold, but if its owner wished to redeem it, he had to pay a fifth more than its valuation. These regulations would tend to prevent rash vows, and this shows how very far the spirit of the Mosaic legislation was from being allied to what is commonly called 'priest-craft.'

17. FIFTY SHEKELS,] the same as that of a full grown male, see v. 3.

16. POSSESSION,] i.e. derived from his parents, or by marriage, in opposition to 'the field of his purchase,' noticed in v. 22.

21. DEVOTED.] The original word denotes an object irrevocably devoted to God, either for preservation or destruction, more generally the latter. Compare v. 28, 29; Nu. 18. 14; De. 7. 26; 13. 17; Jos. 6. 17, 18; 7. 1, 11, 12, 13, 15; 22. 20; 1 Sa. 15. 21; 1 K. 20. 42; 1 Ch. 2, 7; Isa. 34. 5; 43. 28; Eze. 44. 29; Zec. 14. 11; Mal. 4. 6. See note on Ex. 22. 20.

26. JEHOVAH'S,] according to the law in Ex. 13. 2.

27. UNCLEAN BEASTS,] which are vowed, but not a firstling, for it would then be redeemed with a lamb.

28. DEVOTED THING.] See on v. 21 above.

29. WHICH IS DEVOTED OF MAN,] i.e. 'out of men;' the reference is to such cases as that of the Amalekites, and the Canaanites, who were thus devoted not by men, but by God 'out of men,' and not at all to the case of a person vowed to the Lord, as in v. 2—8, who were to be all redeemed, being not 'devoted,' but simply 'vowed.' The original words are quite different. This applies to the case of Jephthah's daughter.

32. ROD.] The allusion is to the practice of shepherds, who in counting their flocks caused them to pass by a narrow opening, where with their crooks they could easily number them in succession.

NUMBERS

THE BOOK OF NUMBERS, the fourth in order of the Books of the Old Covenant, as its name indicates, is chiefly occupied with the two numberings of the children of Israel, taken when they were in the wilderness. It embraces a period of about thirty-eight years in all, but its principal events took place in the second year of the exodus, and in the last year of the sojourn of the people in the desert. It is quoted *eighteen* times in the New Testament, e.g. Mat. 12. 5; Luke 2. 23; John 3. 14, 1 Cor. 10. 4; Heb. 9. 13, 14, &c. Its position is appropriate as presenting a return, in the narrative, to the political and general characteristics of the people, which was partly interrupted by the institutions of the Levites.

1. 1. IN THE TENT OF MEETING.] The commencement of the Book of Leviticus is almost in the same words with the present, naturally implying the same writer; on which see note.

2. SUM,] *lit.* 'the head,' the highest point, as in 5. 24.

ALL THE COMPANY,] except the Levites, see v. 47; the object was doubtless to enable them to see how God had fulfilled His word in multiplying them as He had promised. It is a question whether the mixed multitude that followed them out of Egypt were included in these numbers; probably they were.

FAMILIES,] securing regularity and precision.

FATHERS,] the mother's lineage not being reckoned, but the father's.

POLLS,] *lit.* 'sculls,' as in Jud. 9. 53; see note on Ex. 16. 16.

3. TO THE HOST,] for battle; the word is a noun not a verb as in C. V.

BY THEIR HOSTS,] belonging to their several tribes.

5. ELIZUR,] i.e. my God is a rock.
SHIDEUR,] i.e. my or the Mighty One is light.

6. SHELUMIEL.] i.e. my friend is God.
ZURISHADDAI,] i.e. my rock is the Mighty One.

7. NAHSHON,] i.e. a serpent *or* a diligent observer.
AMMINADAB,] i.e. my people is willing *or* noble.

8. NATHANEEL,] i.e. given by God.
ZUAR,] i.e. smallness.

9. ELIAB,] i.e. my God is father.
HELON,] i.e. strong.

10. ELISHAMA,] i.e. my God hath heard.
AMMIHUD,] i.e. my people is honourable.
GAMALIEL,] i.e. my rewarder is God.
PEDAHZUR,] i.e. the ransomed of the Rock.

11. ABIDAN,] i.e. my father is judge.

GIDEONI,] i.e. the cutter down.

12. AHIEZER,] i.e. my brother is a help.
AMMISHADDAI,] i.e. my people is mighty.

13. PAGIEL,] i.e. he who meeteth me is God.
OCRAN,] i.e. the troubled *or* the troubler.

14. ELIASAPH,] i.e. my God gathers.
DEUEL,] i.e. known of God: in 2. 14, Reuel, i.e a friend of God.

15. AHIRA,] i.e. my brother is evil.
ENAN,] i.e. having eyes.

16. CALLED,] as in 16. 2; called and chosen by God for the work.

17. DEFINED,] as in 1 Ch. 12. 31; 16. 41; 2 Ch. 28. 15; 31. 19; Ezra 8. 20. Compare the use of the verb in Ge. 30. 28; Lev. 24. 11. 16; Nu. 23. 8, 25.

18. THEY DECLARE THEIR BIRTHS.] The original word (from a root signifying 'to bear, beget,') does not occur elsewhere.

POLLS,] *lit.* 'sculls.' see note on Ex. 16. 16, &c.

20. FIRST BORN,] as in Ge. 10. 15; 35. 23; 46. 8; 49. 3, &c.

THEIR BIRTHS,] as in Ge. 2. 4; 5. 1; there is no necessity or propriety in the insertion of the particle *by*

BY THEIR FAMILIES,] not 'after.'

IN THE NUMBER OF NAMES,] not 'according to,' as in C. V.

A SON OF TWENTY YEARS.] See note on Ge. 5. 31, a common Hebrew idiom.

31. Reuben numbers 46,500 males; six of the tribes were more numerous, viz. Simeon, Judah, Issachar, Zebulon, Dan, and Naphtali, thus manifesting the fulfilment of his father's prophecy, in Ge. 49. 3, 4.

23. Simeon numbers 59,300, having only Judah and Dan more numerous.

25. Gad numbers 45,000, having seven tribes above it, and being next to Reuben.

27. Judah numbers 74,600, the highest of all the tribes.

29. Issachar numbers 54,400, having four above it.

31. Zebulon numbers 57,400, having three above it.

33. Ephraim numbers 40,500, having nine above it.

35. Manasseh numbers 32,200, the smallest of the tribes, and 8,300 below Ephraim his younger brother, agreeably to Ge. 48. 19, 20.

37. Benjamin numbers 35,400, having only Manasseh inferior to it.

39. Dan numbers 62,700, being next to Judah.

41. Asher numbers 41,500, having only Manasseh and Benjamin below it.

43. Naphtali numbers 53,400, being sixth in respect of number.

45. ALL...SONS OF ISRAEL,] except the Levites: see. v. 47

46. It is rather remarkable that the total number here given is precisely the same as that already recorded in Ex. 38. 26, as the result of a census apparently taken about seven months before this, at the setting up of the tabernacle, and a very little beyond the number who left Egypt, see Ex. 12. 37.

47. HAVE NOT BEEN NUMBERED,] *lit.* 'have not themselves been numbered,' so in 2. 33 ; 26. 62 ; 1 K. 20. 27.

49. NOT NUMBER,] because they were not to go out to the host, having been given by God to Aaron and to his sons, to serve, help, and minister to him and them in their work of serving the Lord and instructing Israel.

51. PUT TO DEATH,] by the hands of men, probably the Levites themselves ; whether this law was ever executed we know not, but in 2 Sam. 5. 6, 7, we have an instance of God himself punishing an offender (viz. Uzzah), for touching it.

52. HIS CAMP,] of which there were twelve, according to the number of the tribes.

STANDARD,] as in 2. 2, 3, 10, 17, 18, 25, 31, 34 ; 10. 14, 18, 22, 25 ; Song 2. 4. Compare 5. 10 ; 6. 4, 10 ; Ps. 20. 5.

53. THE CHARGE,] as in 3. 8.

II. 2. ENSIGNS,] as in Ps. 74. 4 ; or simply 'signs,' as in Ge. 1. 14, &c.

OVER AGAINST,] about 2000 cubits, judging from Jos. 3. 4, and supposed to be a sabbath day's journey.

3—8. Judah, Issachar, and Zebulon, being all children of the same mother, (Leah), are naturally and appropriately joined together, forming the largest of the four great camps.

9 THEY JOURNEY FIRST,] in all their journeyings in the wilderness, and also at war. Jud. 1. 1, 2.

10—16. Reuben, Simeon, and Gad, form the second great camp, but with 34,500 fewer men. Reuben and Simeon were the two elder of the sons of Jacob by Leah ; and Gad, being eldest son of Leah's handmaid Zilpah, occupies the place which properly fell to Levi, whose descendants had now the charge of

17. THE TENT OF MEETING,] surrounding and guarding it, in the midst of the four camps.

JOURNEY,] i.e. systematically, in order.

18—24. Ephraim, Manasseh, and Benjamin, form the third camp, 80,000 less than that of Judah's ; the two former tribes were descended from Joseph, to whom was added Benjamin, and thus the sons of Rachel were kept together.

25—31. Dan, Asher, and Naphtali, constitute the fourth camp, which is next in size to Judah's ; these were all children of the handmaids, the first and the last being from Bilhah, and Asher from Zilpah, Leah's handmaid.

32. The numbering here agrees precisely with that in 1. 46, which see.

33. HAVE NOT BEEN NUMBERED,] at the present time, but they are shortly afterwards, as recorded in 3. 15.

III. 1. MOSES.] There is no special notice of the children of Moses in this chapter, but some have supposed they are included under the Amramites, and were called by that name to show the magnanimity of Moses in declining to found for himself a name in Israel, which others so eagerly coveted. His highest honour, indeed, is in the characteristic quality ascribed to him by God himself in Joshua 1. 2, 'Moses My servant.'

2. ITHAMAR.] Compare Ex. 6. 23.

4. SONS,] not 'children,' as in C. V.

6. BRING NEAR,] i.e. before the Lord. PRIEST,] as His representative.

7. THE SERVICE.] Compare 1 Ch. 9. 14, 26—29 ; and 23. 3—5, 28—30.

8. VESSELS,] as particularized in v. 25, 26, 31, 36, 37.

10. KEPT,] i.e. watch, observed, not 'wait,' as in C. V.

STRANGER,] i.e. not of the seed of Aaron, who presumes to act as priest.

11—13. These verses give the reason for the injunction and gift recorded in v. 6—9 ; God, in sparing the first-born of man and beast among the Israelites when He destroyed those of the Egyptians, claimed them as his own ; He afterwards chose the tribe of Levi instead of these first-born, and now He transfers them as a gift to His servant Aaron and to his sons, for assistants in His service. See Ex. 13. 12, and compare 22. 26, 29 ; De. 33. 9.

16. MOSES,] also Aaron, as noticed in v. 39.

17. MERARI.] See Ge. 46. 11.

18. SHIMEI.] See Ex. 6. 17, and v. 21, below.

19. UZZIEL.] See Ex. 6. 18, and v. 27. below.

20. MUSHI.] See Ex. 6. 19; in all eight families.

25. THE TABERNACLE,] i.e. its linen curtains, Ex. 26. 1 ; the sons of Merari had charge of its boards, &c., see v. 36.

THE TENT,] i.e. the eleven curtains of goat's hair made for an outer cover for the tabernacle, Ex. 26. 7.

COVERING] of ram's and badger's skin, over the tent ; Ex. 26. 14.

OPENING,] i.e. the outer one.

26. COURT.] See Ex. 27. 9—13.

VAIL.] See Ex. 27. 16.

CORDS] of the tabernacle, see Ex. 38. 18; the sons of Merari had charge of the cords of the 'court ;' see v. 37.

TO ALL ITS SERVICE,] every part of the service of the 'tabernacle' was under the charge of the Gershonites.

27. KOHATH,] the second son of Levi.

AMRAMITE,] including of course all the descendants of Aaron and Moses.

IZEHARITES,] from whom came Korah, see 16. 1.

28. The Kohathites thus exceeded the Gershonites by 1100 males.

THE SANCTUARY,] or the holy place within the tent of meeting.

29. SOUTHWARD,] towards the camp of Reuben, among whom some of them had associates ; see 16. 1.

31. THE ARK.] See Ex. 25. 10.

TABLE.] See Ex. 25. 23.

CANDLESTICK.] See Ex. 25. 31.

ALTARS.] See Ex. 27. 1 ; 30. 1.

VAIL,] dividing the holy from the most holy place ; Ex. 29. 32 ; see on v. 25, 26, above.

32. OVERSIGHT,] as in v. 36 ; 4. 16 ; 16. 29, &c.

THE KEEPERS,] i.e. the Kohathites.

34. The sons of Merari are thus the fewest in number of the three sons of Levi.

35. NORTHWARD,] towards the camp of Dan.

36. BOARDS...BARS...PILLARS, &c.] Compare Ex. 26. 26, 32. 37 ; for which cause they had more waggons allowed to them than the sons of Gershon, while those of Kohath had none at all, see 7. 6—9.

37. SOCKETS...PINS...CORDS,] as in Ex. 27. 9—19.

39. AND AARON.] These words are omitted in the Samaritan and Syriac Versions, and are marked as peculiar by the Jewish scribes ; see note on v. 1 above.

22,000.] In adding up the previous numbers in v. 22, 28, and 34, we find 22,300 ; hence some suppose an omission in the present verse ; but others explain it as arising from there having been 300 first-born among the Levites, who, of course, were not redeemed, like the first-born of the other tribes. So the Talmud, Bab. Becoroth, fol. 5. 1, as noted by Gill.

43. 22,273.] Compare note on v. 39.

47. FIVE SHEKELS,] about eleven or twelve shillings of sterling money, which in 18. 16, is henceforth to be the fixed redemption price.

GERAHS.] See note on Lev. 27. 25.

IV. 2. TAKE UP THE SUM.] This second enumeration was confined to those between the ages of 30 and 50, with the view of setting such men directly apart to special services, (at the first of these ages began both John the Baptist and Jesus to fulfil their ministry) ; the Kohathites are probably mentioned first, as being most numerous, and as having charge of the ark, and other most holy things.

THIRTY.] Sept. here, as well as in v. 23, 30, reads 'twenty-five,' see 8. 24.

5. TAKEN DOWN] from off the pins on which it was suspended, Ex. 26. 31.

ARK OF TESTIMONY,] in Ex. 25. 10, 16.

6. COVERING] of the ark, not of the tabernacle ; see v. 25.

STAVES,] which had been removed while the ark was being covered, as they were otherwise to remain continually in their rings, see Ex. 25. 13—15.

7. TABLE OF THE PRESENCE.] See Ex. 25. 23, 29, 30 ; Lev. 24. 6, 8.

BREAD OF CONTINUITY,] so called because it was never lacking, but regularly replaced every week, see 2 Ch. 2. 4 ; the word is also applied to burnt-offerings, incense, presents, &c.

9. CANDLESTICK,] in Ex. 25. 31.

10. BAR,] as in v. 12 ; 13. 23 ; Nah. 1. 13.

11. GOLDEN ALTAR,] i.e. of incense, Ex. 20. 1—3.

14. CENSERS, &c.] See Ex. 27. 3.

BADGER SKIN.] The Sam. and Sept. Versions add here, 'and they take a purple cloth, and cover the laver, and its base, and put it into a covering of skin of a blue colour, and put it upon bearers.'

15. THE SANCTUARY.] Sept. reads 'the holy things.'

SONS OF KOHATH,] as in 7. 9 ; 10. 21 ; De. 31. 9 ; 2 Sa. 6. 13 ; 1 Ch. 15. 2, 15.

DIED.] See 2 Sa. 6. 6, 7 ; 1 Ch. 13. 9, 10.

THESE THINGS.] See 3. 31.

16. OIL.] Ex. 25. 6 ; 27. 20 ; Lev. 24. 2.

SWEET INCENSE,] as in Ex. 30. 40, 44.

PRESENT,] as directed in Ex. 30. 34—38.

ANOINTING OIL,] with which Aaron, his sons, the tabernacle, and its vessels, were all anointed. Ex. 30. 23—33.

18. YE DO NOT CUT OFF,] i.e. give occasion that it should be so, by negligence, &c.

20. HOLY THING,] not 'things,' as in the C. V.; any holy thing offered to God is meant.

HE HATH SWALLOWED.] This is one of the most difficult passages in the Book of Numbers ; the verb occurs very frequently, and its uniform meaning is 'to swallow up,' see Ge. 41. 7, 24 ; Ex. 7. 12 ; 15. 12, &c. The nearest parallel expression is in Pr. 20. 25 where a closely related cognate verb is employed ; it is 'a snare for a man to swallow a holy thing, and after vows to make inquiry.'

21. MOSES] and 'Aaron,' according to v. 41 below.

22. SONS OF GERSHON,] the second son of Levi, for a second numbering and selecting as in the case of the Kohathites, in v. 4—20.

23. THIRTY...FIFTY,] as in v. 3 above.

25. BORNE,] as in 3. 25, 26.

CURTAINS, &c.,] as in Ex. 26. 1, 7, 14, 36.

26. HANGINGS,] as in Ex. 27. 9, 16 ; 23. 26.

29. SONS OF MERARI,] the third and youngest son of Levi.

30. THIRTY...FIFTY.] See v. 3, 23 above.

31. BOARDS, &c.] See Ex. 26. 15—37.

32. PILLARS, &c.] See Ex. 27. 9—19.

33. ITHAMAR,] who had also charge of the Gershonites, while his brother Eleazar was over the Kohathites.

34. PRINCES] of the company, selected in 1. 5—16.

36. 2,750] males, between 30 and 50 years of age, leaving 5,850 beneath and above those limits.

40. 2,630] males, between 30 and 50 years of age, leaving 4,870 beneath and above those limits.

44. 3,200] males, between 30 and 50 years of age, leaving 3,000 beneath and above those limits.

48. 8,580] males, between 30 and 50 years of age, leaving 13,750 beneath and above those limits.

V. 2. LEPER.] See Lev. 13. 3, 46 ; 12. 14.

AN ISSUE.] See Lev. 15. 2, 19.

BY A BODY,] not necessarily a dead one,

as in C. V.; see Lev. 21. 1, 4; 9. 6, 10; 19. 11, 13; 22. 4; 31. 19, &c.

3. FEMALE,] as was done in the case of Miriam, 12. 14, 15.

TABERNACLE.] Compare Lev. 26. 11, 12; 2 Cor. 6. 16.

6. TRESPASS.] See the original law in Lev. 6. 1—7.

8. NO REDEEMER,] i.e. no one who had a right to claim from him the recompense due to the injured (and probably deceased) party, then it must be given to the Lord, to the priest as His representative.

RAM.] See Lev. 6. 6, 7; 7. 7.

9. HEAVE-OFFERING.] See Lev. 25. 2; 29. 28, &c.

10. BECOMETH HIS.] See Lev. 10. 13.

12. TURNETH ASIDE,] as in v. 19, 20, 29; Pr. 4. 15; 7. 25; all the places where the original word occurs.

TRESPASS,] i.e. a going over or beyond duty, as the etymology shows.

13. COPULATION,] as in Lev. 18. 20, 23; 20. 15.

CAUGHT,] as in Ps. 10. 2; Jer. 34. 3; 38. 23; 48. 41; 50. 24, 46; 51. 32, 41; Eze. 12. 13; 17. 20; 19. 4, 8; 21. 23, 24.

14. SPIRIT OF JEALOUSY.] This phrase is only found elsewhere in v. 30.

SHE HATH BEEN DEFILED.] If clear proof could be had of this, she was put to death, Lev. 10. 20; but if it was only suspicion, the following test was allowed; there is, however, no proof whatever that it ever was actually put into execution; perhaps a knowledge of its certainty as resulting from a direct injunction from God, may have sufficed to extort a confession from the guilty party.

15. TENTH OF AN EPHAH,] i.e. an omer, the quantity of manna allowed to each person daily (Ex. 16. 18), and for the daily present (Ex. 16. 36; 29. 40).

BARLEY-MEAL,] coarse and common food.

OIL...FRANKINCENSE,] which might render it more acceptable and pleasant, and not allowed in sin-offerings, Lev. 5. 11.

16. HER...HER,] or 'it...it,' referring to the present instead of the woman, (so Vulgate Version,) as the presentation of the woman is mentioned in v. 18.

17. HOLY WATER,] out of the laver of brass.

DUST,] which is said to be ever the serpent's food, and calculated to remind the spectators of the sense of the vileness of sin.

18. UNCOVERED,] generally reckoned a great disgrace and insult to Eastern females, and exposing her, as it were, to public gaze.

INTO HER HANDS,] that it might appear to be her own offering, and thus directly appealing to God.

19. UNDER,] i.e. being under thy husband, 'instead of' requires a violent and unnatural supplement to make it intelligible; so in v. 20.

21. EXECRATION,] as in Lev. 5. 1.

TO FALL,] i.e. become emaciated.

TO SWELL,] as in v. 22. 27, not found elsewhere.

22. AMEN, AMEN,] as in De. 27. 15—26; 1 K. 1. 36; 1 Ch. 6. 13; Neh. 5. 13; 8. 6; Ps. 41. 13; 72. 19; 89. 52; 106. 48; Isa. 65. 16 Jer. 11. 5; 28. 6. The literal meaning is 'stedfast;' it is used sometimes as an assent, 'It is stedfast;' at other times as a prayer, 'May it be stedfast.'

25. WAVE,] as directed in Lev. 8. 27.

26. MADE PERFUME,] as in Lev. 2. 2.

27. PEOPLE,] Similar tests were in use among the Greeks and Romans; the river Rhine, according to the Emperor Julian, tested the legitimacy of children, the Stygian lake perjury, one near Ephesus impurity, &c.

28. SEED,] i.e. may be, lawfully: by her husband, and he acquitted from iniquity.

VI. 2. SINGULARLY,] or wonderfully, as in Lev. 27. 2; De. 28. 59; Jud. 13. 19; 2 Ch. 2. 9; 26. 15; Ps. 31. 21; Isa. 28. 29; 29. 14.

NAZARITE.] lit. 'Nazir,' i.e. one separated, set apart; this might be for life, or for a definite time.

3. WINE AND STRONG DRINK.] See note on Lev. 10. 9, and especially the author's Biblical Tract on 'The Wines of Scripture.'

VINEGAR,] as in Ruth 2. 14; Ps. 69. 22; Prov. 10. 26.

JUICE.] The original word is not found elsewhere; it is supposed to be connected with a root signifying 'to loose, dissolve.'

MOIST.] Compare the use of the word in Ge. 30. 37; also De. 34. 7.

DRY,] as in 11. 6; Job 3. 25; Isa. 56. 3; Ez. 17. 24; 20. 47; 37. 2, 4; Nah. 1. 10.

4. WINE-VINE.] Compare Jud. 13. 14.

KERNELS.] The original word is not found elsewhere.

HUSK.] The original word is not found elsewhere.

5. UPPER PART.] Compare Eze. 44. 20, from a root signifying 'to be above, go before.'

7. THEIR DEATH,] as even the priests were allowed to be.

SEPARATION,] not 'consecration,' as in C. V. So again in v. 9.

9. SEVENTH DAY.] Compare 19. 11, 12.

10. YOUNG PIGEONS,] the poorest kind of offering; Lev. 12. 8; 15. 14, 29.

11. BODY.] The word 'dead' is not expressed, though implied.

HALLOWED,] beginning his vow afresh.

12. SEPARATED,] not 'consecrated,' as in v. 7.

GUILT-OFFERING,] not 'trespass-offering,' as in C. V.

14. BURNT-OFFERING,] as in Lev. 1. 31—10. SIN-OFFERING,] according to Lev. 4. 32. PEACE-OFFERINGS,] as in Lev. 3. 6.

15. UNLEAVENED THING,] as at the consecration of Aaron and his sons, Ex. 29. 2 compare Lev. 7. 13.

CAKES...THIN CAKES.] Compare Ex. 29. 2; Lev. 7. 12.

LIBATION,] which accompany all sacrifices.

17. LIBATION,] receiving his share, as usual.

18. AT THE OPENING,] that all might know he was now free from his vow.

19. PALMS,] as in Lev. 14. 15, 16, 27.

SEPARATION,] i.e. the sign of it.

21. BY THE LAW,] not 'after the law,' as in C. V.

22. SONS.] Compare De. 10. 8; 21. 5; 1 Ch. 23. 12.

25. CAUSE TO SHINE,] as in Ps. 31. 16; 67. 1; 80. 3, 19; 119. 135; Da. 9. 17.

FAVOUR,] as in Ge. 33. 5, 11; 43. 29, &c.

26. LIFT UP,] as in Ge. 19. 21; 32. 20; Lev. 19. 15; De. 10. 17; 28. 50.

APPOINT,] lit. 'set.'

PEACE,] as in Ge. 15. 15, where it ought to have been noticed that the original word shalom, denotes properly 'perfection, completion,' and not merely the idea of tranquillity or rest.

27. PUT MY NAME] upon them, that they should be called by his name.

VII. 1. DAY,] i.e. at the time, for the tabernacle was set up (Ex. 40. 17) on the first day of the first month of the second year of the Exodus, and the following offerings about a month later, (Nu. 1. 1.)

ANOINTETH,] as in Ex. 30. 23—28; Lev. 8. 10.

SANCTIFIETH,] i.e. separated them for divine service, Ex. 29. 35.

2. PRINCES,] 12 in number, as in 1. 5—15.

3. COVERED.] This word is only found elsewhere in Isa. 66. 20; in Lev. 11. 29 it is translated 'tortoise.'

WAGGONS,] as narrated in 4. 24—28.

7. SERVICE,] as in 4.

8. SERVICE,] as in 4. 29—33; both divisions of the Levites were under the charge of Ithamar, son of Aaron the priest; a double share was allotted to the sons of Merari, their service being the care of objects heavier than those committed to the sons of Gershon, while those of Kohath had none given, their duty being to bear on the

9. SHOULDER,] as charged in 4. 1—20; but compare Josh. 3. 17; 4. 10; 2 Sa. 6. 3, 13.

10. THE DEDICATION,] i.e. the things dedicated for the service of the altar.

ANOINTED] with the holy oil, and thus set apart for divine service.

11. ONE PRINCE A-DAY,] for the sake of order and solemnity.

12. NAHSHON.] See 2. 3.

13. DISH.] See Ex. 25. 29, &c.

130 SHEKELS] of silver, or £16, 5s. of English money.

BOWL.] See Ex. 27. 3.

70 SHEKELS] of silver, or £8, 15s. of English money.

SANCTUARY.] Compare Ex. 30. 13.

PRESENT,] part of which was burnt, and part fell to the priests.

14. SPOON.] See Ex. 25. 29.

TEN SHEKELS] of gold, or £7, 10s. of English money.

PERFUME,] to be offered with the sacrifices.

15. ONE BULLOCK,] of which the age is not specified, as is done with the ram and the lamb, &c.

17. PEACE-OFFERINGS] in addition to the present, the burnt-offering, and the sin-offering.

18—83. These verses contain an account of the offerings presented by the rest of the other princes, exactly the same as those of the first who offered; further annotations therefore are unnecessary.

84—88. A summary of the whole offerings; of which the silver is estimated at about £300; the gold at about £75; the value of the animals cannot to be ascertained.

89. AND IN THE GOING IN.] It is, perhaps, impossible to say whether this verse refers to the habitual manner in which Moses received divine directions, or whether it was on the occasion of the offering of the princes; most probably, however, the laws contained in the next chapter were delivered on the present occasion.

VIII. 2. AARON,] that he and his sons might direct the operation, if not do it themselves. Ex. 27. 21.

CAUSING TO GO UP,] as the original verb always denotes, see Ex. 3. 8; 27. 20, &c.; this was done in the evening, that they might burn all night, there being no window in the holy place. Ex. 25. 37.

4. WORK,] i.e. workmanship.

BEATEN GOLD.] Compare Ex. 25. 31, 36.

HE HATH MADE,] i.e. Bezaleel, under the direction of Moses, Ex. 25. 40.

6. CLEANSED THEM,] as in v. 7, 15; this is one of the many ceremonial cleansings which were significant of the inward purity required in those who serve the altar of God.

7. ATONEMENT,] lit. a sin-offering, as in v. 8, 12; Ge. 4. 7; Ex. 29. 14, &c.; the water was mixed with the ashes of a red heifer, ch. 19. 9, 17, 18.

SPRINKLE,] as in Ex. 29. 21.

CAUSED TO PASS OVER,] as in 6. 5, &c. like the leper in Lev. 14. 8, 9. The Egyptian priests are said to have done so every third day.

GARMENTS,] that every thing upon them might be clean.

8. BULLOCK] for a burnt-offering, as noted in v. 12 below.

OIL.] Compare 28. 12, 14.

9. WHOLE COMPANY] by its representatives, heads, chiefs, elders, &c.; see Lev. 8. 3.

10. LAID THEIR HANDS,] in token of their being set apart in behalf of the assembly; compare 1 Tim. 4. 14.

11. WAVED,] i.e. moved the hands up and down, as if presenting a wave-offering to the Lord.

JEHOVAH] instead of, and in behalf of, the whole nation of Israel.

12. HEAD] of each of the bullocks, thus testifying their assent to the substitution of the animal in their stead.

MAKE THOU,] not necessarily by his own hands, but by a priest's, probably Aaron.

LEVITES,] who required to offer atonement, as well as other Israelites.

14. SEPARATED,] as in Ge. 1. 4, 7, 14, &c.

MINE,] instead of every first-born of Israel, as recorded in v. 16, 18, and 3. 12, 13; Ex. 13. 2.

15. WAVED THEM—A WAVE-OFFERING,] as in Ex. 29. 24, 26, &c.

CLEANSED THEM,] or 'pronounced them clean,' as in Lev. 13. 6, &c.

16. FIRST-BORN.] These, having been spared to the children of Israel while those of the Egyptians were slain, were Jehovah's by right of redemption; afterwards He thought fit to take the whole of the males of the tribe of Levi for His ministering servants in their stead, as noted in 3. 12, 13.

17. AND AMONG BEASTS.] The firstlings of these were in the same position as the first-born of men, viz., set apart to the service of God, for the reason given in the close of the verse, compare Ex. 13. 2.

18. I TAKE.] Compare 3. 12.

19. I GIVE THE LEVITES GIFTS.] Being thus now His peculiar property He bestows them upon the chief priest, Aaron, and on his sons after him in the priesthood, that they may help him and them in the tent of meeting 'to do service' for the people, and to 'make atonement' for them, lest the divine regulations being infringed, the people might be smitten by plagues.

21. CLEANSE THEMSELVES,] as in 19. 12, 13, 20; 31. 19, 20, 23; Job 41. 25, being in the reflexive form.

WAVETH THEM—A WAVE OFFERING,] as in v. 11, 15, above.

24. FIVE AND TWENTY.] In 4. 3, 'thirty' is mentioned as the period of entrance into their work; perhaps the age was lowered for some reason not given in the text, or 4, 3, may refer to the age at which they were to be 'numbered;' a kind of five years' preparation-work being required.

IX. 2. APPOINTED SEASON.] It was now a twelvemonth since Israel had kept the feast of the passover, recorded in Ex. 12. 1—27; they probably thought it was not to be observed again till they got to the place where the Lord chose to put His name, and to prevent this misconception the precept is renewed, and its observance enjoined as before, as regards the month, day, time, manner, &c., see notes on Ex. 12. 1—27.

5. BETWEEN THE EVENINGS,] as in Ex. 12. 6, on which see note.

6. BY THE BODY,] not necessary a dead body; it may have been leprous, or covered with some defilement which was legally communicated to those coming in contact with it. So in v. 7, 10.

7. THE OFFERING,] that was appointed for the passover, not merely 'an offering,' as in the C. V.

8. AND I DO HEAR,] from Him who had appointed the ordinance, at the meeting-place, Ex. 25. 22.

10. GENERATIONS,] as in Ge. 6. 9. There is no propriety in rendering it 'posterity,' as is done in the C. V.

A PASSOVER,] not 'the passover,' there is no article in the original, and it was to be a month later, as narrated in the succeeding verse

12. ALL THE STATUTE.] The only difference permitted was in the time.

13. THAT PERSON,] or individual, high or low, rich or poor, young or old.

CUT OFF,] that is, excommunicated.

BEAR HIS SIN,] or suffer the consequences of his deliberate refusal to obey the Lord's command.

14. A SOJOURNER,] not 'a stranger,' one of another nation, but an Israelite from another tribe.

A NATIVE,] as in Ex. 12. 19, &c.

HE HATH PREPARED,] i. e. though he be now absent from his own tribe and home, he is not exempt from the obligation to keep the passover, but is bound to observe it with his neighbours among whom he is now sojourning.

15. THE DAY.] Which from Ex. 40. 1, 2, 17, appears to have been the first day of the first month of the second year of the departure out of Egypt.

APPEARANCE OF FIRE.] An emblem of the purifying and protecting presence of Jehovah, see Isa. 4. 5; Zech. 2. 5. Compare same phrase in v. 16; Ezek. 1. 27 (twice); 8. 2.

15—23. These verses very emphatically point out the ever-present watchful care of Jehovah over Israel, and their ready and complete obedience to His will in their travelling movements.

16. CONTINUALLY,] as long as they were in the wilderness.

17. TABERNACLE.] This literal rendering is far more expressive than that of 'abide,' given in the C. V.; the cloud formed, as it were, a covering over the 'tent of the testimony.'

18. COMMAND,] lit. 'mouth' of Jehovah.

19. PROLONGING ITSELF,] as in Ex. 20. 12, &c. so in v. 22, below.

THE CHARGE,] regarding their removal or non-removal.

22. OR DAYS.] This term is not necessarily to be understood of 'a year,' as is done in the C. V.; it probably is equal to: 'any number of days,' beyond a month.

X. 2. TRUMPETS.] There are two Hebrew words generally translated trumpets, and it is perhaps impossible to find suitable English terms to express the difference between them; the one in the text is supposed to have been straight in form, and the other crooked, like a horn. This one was made of silver, and appears to have been used exclusively in the service of God. See v. 8, 9, 10; 31. 6; 2 K. 11. 14; 12. 13; 1 Ch. 13. 8; 15. 24, 28; 16. 6, 42; 2 Ch. 5. 12, 13; 13. 14; 15. 14; 20. 28; 23. 13 29. 26, 27, 28; Ezra 3. 10; Neh. 12. 35, 41; Ps. 98. 6; Hos. 5. 8.

BEATEN WORK,] as in Ex. 25. 18, 31, 36, &c.

3. MET TOGETHER,] as in Ex. 25. 22; Josh. 11. 5, &c.

TENT OF MEETING,] that they might be where God had promised to meet with them.

5. BLOWN—A SHOUT,] or 'with a shout:

G

the word is generally used of a joyful shout, as in Lev. 23. 24, &c.

EASTWARD,] i. e. Judah, Issachar, and Zebulon, see 2. 3, 5, 7.

6. SOUTHWARD,] i.e. Reuben, Simeon, and Gad, see 2. 10, 12, 14. No intimation being given for those at the north and the west, there appears to be an omission here, which accordingly is supplied in the Septuagint Version.

7. ASSEMBLING OF THE ASSEMBLY,] referred to in the 3d verse above.

9. ADVERSARY,] as in Ex. 23. 22.

YE HAVE SHOUTED,] as in Josh. 6. 10.

10. GLADNESS,] any happy season of prosperity.

APPOINTED SEASONS,] or ordinances, appointed by God, Lev. 23. 2.

BEGINNINGS,] i.e. the new moons, especially of the seventh month, Lev. 23. 24.

AND THEY HAVE BEEN,] not 'that they may be,' as in the C. V.

11. GONE UP,] after they had been there a year; it was the recognised signal of their departure to another encampment, which they found in the wilderness of

12. PARAN,] see note on Ge. 21. 21.

13. AT FIRST,] or 'in the first place,' as in v. 14.

14—16.] For these names see 1. 7—9; 2. 3—7.

17. TAKEN DOWN,] and the Levites who had the charge of it, (see 1. 51), even the sons of Gershon and Merari.

18—20.] For these names see 1. 5, 6, 14; 2. 10—14.

21. SANCTUARY,] i. e. the ark, and all the holy things, which were to be borne on the shoulder by the Kohathites, while the Gershonites and Merari-ites had preceded them bearing the tabernacle itself on waggons, which they were required to have ready for the arrival of the holy things.

22—24.] For these names see 1. 10, 11; 2. 18—22.

25—27.] For these names see 1. 12, 13, 15; 2. 25—29.

28. THEY JOURNEY,] not knowing where they may next rest, like their great ancestor.

29. HOBAB,] lit. 'loving,' (compare De. 33. 3.) See note on Ex. 2. 18.

THE PLACE,] of rest and comfort, even Canaan.

I GIVE IT TO YOU,] see Ge. 12. 7, &c.

WE HAVE DONE GOOD,] compare its realization in Jud. 1. 16; 4. 11, 17; 1 Sa. 15. 6.

HATH SPOKEN GOOD,] see Ge. 32. 12; Ex. 3. 8, &c.

30. I DO NOT GO.] Very decisive language, yet it would seem he changed his mind afterwards.

LAND..KINDRED.] It might be a selfish love of home, or a desire for the welfare of his kindred that thus prompted him.

31. FORSAKE US NOT,] as in De. 12. 19, &c.

FOR EYES,] Hobab being acquainted with the wells, springs, fertile parts of the desert, could point these out.

32. WE HAVE DONE.] Being a partaker of

their trials, it was meet he should be a sharer of their joy.

TO THEE.] The text does not indicate here what was the result of this appeal, but from other passages quoted above it would appear that either he or some of his sons remained with Israel, and shared the blessings of the land.

33. MOUNT OF JEHOVAH,] i. e. Sinai, after being about a year at it.

TO SPY OUT,] as in 13. 2, 16, 17, 21, 25, 32; 14. 6, 7, 34, 36, 38; 15. 39; De. 1. 33, &c.

RESTING-PLACE,] as in Ge. 49. 15, &c.

35. ARE SCATTERED, ETC.] The simple present tense here used is much more appropriately and emphatically to be considered as expressing the result of the previous verb 'Rise,' than an additional entreaty; and this is the true usage of the Hebrew throughout.

36. THE MYRIADS,] as in Ge. 24. 60; Lev. 26. 8, &c.

XI. 1. SIGHING HABITUALLY.] The original word is only found elsewhere, in Lam. 3. 39.

EARS OF JEHOVAH,] as in v. 18; 14. 28, &c.

BURNETH,] as in Ex. 22. 24, &c.

A FIRE OF JEHOVAH,] i. e. one proceeding from Him, as in v. 3; 1 K. 18. 38; 2 K. 1. 12; Job 1. 16; see also Ge. 19. 24; Lev. 10. 2.

2. CRY.] The word is expressive of anguish, as in Ge. 4. 10, &c.

PRAYETH,] as in Ge. 20. 7, 17, &c.

QUENCHED,] or sunk, see Jer. 51. 64; Amos 9. 5; 8. 8; the causative form of the verb occurs in Job 41. 1; Ezek. 32. 14.

3. TABERAH,] i. e. 'a burning.' De. 9. 22.

4. RABBLE.] The original word does not occur elsewhere, but compare Ex. 12. 38; Lev. 24. 10, 11, &c.

LUSTED,] as in 11. 34; De. 5. 21; 2 Sa. 23. 15; 1 Ch. 11. 17; Ps. 45. 11; 106. 14; Prov. 13. 4; 21. 26; 23. 3, 6; 24. 1; Ecc. 6. 2; Jer. 17. 16; Amos 5. 8.

5. FOR NOUGHT,] as in Ge. 29. 15, &c.

CUCUMBERS.] This original word is not found elsewhere.

MELONS,] not mentioned elsewhere.

LEEK,] lit. grass, as in 1 K. 18. 5; 2 K. 19. 26; Job 8. 12; 40. 15; Ps. 37. 2; 90. 5; 103. 15; 104. 14; 129. 6; 147. 8; Prov. 27. 35; Isa. 15. 6; 35.7; 37. 27; 40. 6, 7, 8; 44. 4; 51. 12, being all the other passages where it occurs.

GARLICK,] not found elsewhere.

ONIONS,] not found elsewhere.

6. DRY,] as the word is used in 6. 3, &c.

7. MANNA.] See Ex. 16. 14, 31.

ASPECT,] lit. 'eye,' as in Ge. 3. 5, &c.

BDOLACH.] See note on Ge. 12. 2.

8. GONE TO AND FRO,] as in Job 1. 7; 2, 2; 2 Sa. 24. 28; Eze. 27. 8, 26; or 'turned aside,' as in Nu. 5. 12, 19, 20, 29; Prov. 4. 15; Hos. 5. 2, discarding the Masoretic distinction of points.

MILL-STONES,] as in Ex. 11. 5, &c.

TASTE,] as in Ex. 16. 31, &c.

MOISTURE,] as in Ps. 32. 4; not found elsewhere.

BOILED,] as in Ex. 16. 23.
10. EVIL,] i.e. the trial the Lord was sending on the people.
11. DONE EVIL,] as in Ge. 19. 7, 9.
12. NURSING FATHER,] as in 2 K. 10. 1, 5; Est. 2. 7; Isa. 49. 23; also Ruth 4. 16; 2 Sa. 4. 4.
SAYEST,] as in Ex. 32. 34.
SWEAREST,] as in Ge. 26. 3; 50. 24; Ex. 13. 5.
14. NOT ABLE.] Compare Ex. 18. 18.
15. SLAY.] The repetition marks emphasis; there is no propriety in translating it as in the C. V., 'out of hand.'
MY AFFLICTION.] Some Heb. MSS. read 'their affliction.'
16. ELDERS.] Compare Ex. 3. 16; 5. 6; 24. 9; 18. 21, 24; Lev. 4. 15, &c.
AUTHORITIES.] See Ex. 5. 6, &c.
STATIONED THEMSELVES,] as in Ex. 2. 4, &c.
17. KEPT BACK,] as in Ge. 27. 36, &c.
18. SANCTIFY YOURSELVES,] as in Ex. 19. 22.
20. ABOMINATION.] The original word found here does not occur elsewhere.
LOATHED,] as in Lev. 26. 43, &c.; Job 7. 6; Isa. 54. 6.
21. 600,000.] See Ex. 12. 37; 38. 26; Nu. 1. 46.
22. FOUND,] as in Ge. 2. 20, &c.
23. MEETETH,] as in Ge. 42. 29.
25. KEEPETH BACK,] as he had said in v. 17 above.
PROPHESY,] as in v. 27 below, see also note on Ge. 20. 7.
26. THE MEN,] i.e. the seventy elders.
ARE LEFT,] as in Ge. 7. 23.
WRITTEN,] as in Ex. 31. 18, &c.
27. THE YOUNG MAN,] probably he who had been appointed to summon them to appear before the Lord and the assembly.
28. RESTRAIN,] as in Ge. 23. 6, &c.
29. ZEALOUS,] as in Nu. 25. 13.
30 GATHERED,] as in v. 22 above. He had been at the opening of the Tent of Meeting.
31. JOURNEYED.] The original verb is never used of the wind except in Ps. 78. 26.
HE CUTTETH OFF,] as in Ps. 90. 10; Ge. 31. 19, &c., implying a forcible separation by the Lord.
QUAILS,] as in Ex. 16. 13, &c.,
SEA,] i.e. the sea of Suph.
TWO CUBITS,] from off the ground; the insertion of the word 'high' in the C. V. is unnatural and unnecessary.
32. HOMERS,] which contained ten ephahs each, or a cor.
33. CUT OFF,] as in Ge. 9. 11, &c.
SMITING,] as in Lev. 26. 21, &c.
34. KIBROTH-HATTAVAH,] i.e. 'graves of the desire.'
HAZEROTH,] i.e. 'courts, enclosures,' as in 12. 16; 33. 17; De. 1. 1; said to have been about eight miles distant from the previous station.

XII. 1. MIRIAM,] who was older than either Aaron or Moses.
CONCERNING.] This phrase occurs in Ge. 21. 11, which see.
CUSHITE WOMAN,] i.e. Zephorah, see Ex. 2. 21; Cush being a general title of Arabia, embracing Midian, &c.

TAKEN.] This is the usual phrase for marriage in SS.
2. BY US.] Compare Ex. 4. 14, 27; 15. 20; Mic. 6. 4.
3. HUMBLE,] as in Job. 24. 4; Ps. 9. 12, 18; 10. 12, 17; 22. 26.
6. I PRAY YOU.] There is no necessity for abandoning the proper and usual meaning of the original particle, in translating it 'now,' as in the C. V. So in v. 13.
YOUR PROPHET,] i.e. those you refer to, even you yourselves.
WITH HIM,] which he had probably never done to Aaron or Miriam.
8. RIDDLES,] as in Jud. 14. 12, 13, 14, 15, 16, 17, 18, 19; 1 K. 10. 1; 2 Ch. 9. 1; Ps. 49. 4; 78. 2; Prov. 1. 16; Eze. 17. 2; Dan. 8. 13; Hab. 2. 6.
FORM,] as in Ex. 20. 4, &c.
ATTENTIVELY,] as in Ge. 15. 5, &c.
10. TURNED ASIDE,] as in Ge. 19. 2, 3.
LEPROUS,] as in Ex. 4. 6; Lev. 14. 2, &c.
AS SNOW,] as in Ex. 4. 6; 2 K. 5. 27.
12. I PRAY THEE,] as in Ge. 12. 11, 13, &c.
14. SPAT,] as in De. 25. 9. Compare also Job 30. 10; Isa. 50. 6, where it is alluded to as the greatest disgrace.
GATHERED,] as in Ge. 25. 8, &c.
15. SEVEN DAYS.] Compare Lev. 13. 5, 6; 14. 8.
JOURNEYED,] as in Ge. 11. 2, &c.
16. PARAN,] about eight miles off; the particular place is called Rithmah in 33. 18.

XIII. 2. SPY,] as in 10. 33, &c.
PRINCE,] lit. 'an exalted, lifted up, honoured one,' as in Ge. 17. 20, &c.
4. SHAMMUA,] i.e. a rumour.
ZACCUR,] i.e. mindful.
5. SHAPHAT,] i.e. he judged.
HORI,] i.e. a worker in linen, or freeman of Jah, or my freeman.
6. CALEB,] i.e. a dog.
JEPHUNNEH,] i.e. for whom a way is prepared (according to Gesenius).
7. IGEL,] i.e. he redeems.
JOSEPH,] i.e. he adds.
8. OSHEA,] i.e. safety.
NUN,] i.e. a fish.
9. PALTI,] i.e. escape of Jah, or my escape.
RAPHU,] i.e. healed.
10. GADDIEL,] i.e. troop of God.
SODI,] i.e. counsel of God, or my counsel.
11. GADDI,] i.e. troop of Jah, or my troop.
SUSI,] i.e. horse of Jah, or my horse.
12. AMMIEL,] i.e. people of God.
GEMALLI,] i.e. deed of Jah or my deed.
13. SETHAR,] i.e. hidden.
MICHAEL,] i.e. who is like God?
14. NAHBI,] i.e. hidden.
VOPSHI,] i.e. my addition, or addition of Jah.
15. GEUEL,] i.e. excellency of God.
MACHI,] i.e. my lowness.
16. JEHOSHUA,] i.e. Jah is safety.
17. SENDETH THEM] from Kadesh-Barnea, Josh. 14. 7.
MOUNTAIN,] of the Amorites, De. 1. 44; afterwards of Judea, Luke. 1. 39, 65.
18. FEEBLE,] as in 2 Sa. 17. 3; Job 4. 3; Isa. 35. 3.

19. CAMPS,] as in Ge. 32. 2, 7, 8, 10, 21, &c.
FORTRESSES,] as in 32. 17, 36; Jos. 10.
20; 19. 29, 35; 1 Sa. 6. 18; 2 Sa. 24. 7; 2 K.
3. 19; 8. 12; 10. 2; 17. 9; 18. 8; 2 Ch. 17.
19, &c.
20. FAT,] as in Ge. 49. 20.
LEAN,] as in Eze. 34. 20.
STRENGTHENED,] as in Ge. 48. 2.
TAKEN,] as in Ge. 2. 15; 'bringing' is implied, not expressed.
DAYS,] not 'time,' as in C. V.
FIRST-FRUITS,] as in Ex. 23. 16, &c.
21. ZIN,] lit. 'a thorn,' west of Idumea,
see 20. 1; 27. 14; Zinah, in Nu. 34. 4; Jos.
15. 3; to be distinguished from 'Sin.'
REHOB,] lit. 'a broad place;' Jos. 19. 28,
30; 21. 31; Jud. 1. 13; 2 Sa. 8. 3, 12; 10. 8;
1 Ch. 6. 75.
HAMATH,] lit. 'a walled place;' 34. 8;
Jos. 13. 5; Jud. 3. 3; 2 Sa. 8. 9; 1 K. 8. 65. &c.
22. HEBRON,] lit. 'conjunction;' Ge. 13.
18. &c.
AHIMAN,] lit. 'brother of gift,' according
to Gesenius; Jos. 15. 14; Jud. 1. 10.
SHASHAI,] lit. 'whitish,' so Gesenius;
Josh. 15. 14; Jud. 1. 10.
TALMAI,] lit. 'my furrows;' Josh. 15. 14;
Jud. 1. 10.
ANAK,] lit. 'a chain;' so in v. 28, 33;
De. 9. 2; Jos. 15. 13; 14. 14; Jud. 1. 20, &c.
ZOAN,] lit. 'a low region;' Isa. 19. 11, 13;
30. 4; Eze. 30. 14.
23. ESHCOL,] lit. 'a cluster;' so in v. 24;
32. 9; De. 1. 24.
BROOK,] as in Ge. 32. 23, &c.
STAFF,] as in 4. 10, 12, &c.
POMEGRANATES,] as in Ex. 28. 33, &c.
FIGS,] as in Ge. 3. 7, &c.
26. KADESH,] as in Ge. 14. 7, &c.
27. RECOUNT,] as in Ge. 24. 66, &c.
28. FENCED,] as in De. 1. 28; 3. 5; 9. 1;
28. 52; Jos. 14. 12; 2 Sa. 20. 6; 2 K. 18. 13;
19. 25; 2 Ch. 17. 2; 19. 5; 32. 1; 33. 14;
Neh. 9. 25; Isa. 2. 15; 25. 2; 27. 10; 36. 1;
37. 26; Jer. 15. 20; 33. 3; Eze. 21. 20; 36.
35; Hos. 8. 14; Zep. 1. 16; Zec. 12. 2.
29. AMALEK,] see Ge. 36. 12. 16, &c.
HITTITE,] see Ge. 15. 20, &c.
JEBUSITE,] see Ge. 10. 16, &c.
AMORITE,] see Ge. 10. 16, &c.
CANAANITE,] see Ge. 10. 18, &c.
SIDE.] lit. 'hand,' as in Ex. 2. 5; Nu. 34. 3;
Jud. 11. 26; 1 Sa. 4. 13; 2 Sa. 8. 3; 15.2, &c.
30. STILLETH,] as in Jud. 3. 19, &c.
CONCERNING,] not 'before,' which the
original particle never means.
CERTAINLY,] lit. 'going up we go up.'
THOROUGHLY,] lit. 'able we are able.'
32. STATURE,] lit. 'measure,' as in Ex. 26.
2, &c.; 1 Ch. 11. 23; 20. 6; Isa. 45. 14.
33. NEPHILIM,] as in Ge. 6. 4.
GRASSHOPPERS,] as in Lev. 11. 22, &c.

XIV. 1. GIVE FORTH.] There is no necessity for paraphrasing instead of translating
the original word.
3. IS BRINGING.] The word is a present
participle in the original.
ARE BECOME,] or more literally still, 'are
for a prey.'
GOOD.] There is, properly speaking, no

comparative form in the original to justify
the C.V. 'better.'
4. APPOINT,] lit. 'give.'
HEAD,] as in Ex. 6. 14, &c.
8. HONEY.] Compare Ex. 3. 8, 17; 13. 5, &c.
9. BREAD,] i.e. food, as in Ge. 3. 19, &c.
DEFENCE,] lit. 'shadow,' as in Ge. 19. 8, &c.
10. UNTO,] not 'before,' as in C. V.
11. UNTIL WHEN,] as in Ex. 16. 28; Jer.
47. 6; Hab. 1. 2; Jos. 18. 3; Job 8. 2; 18. 2;
19. 2; Ps. 13. 2, 3; 62. 4.
DESPISE,] not 'provoke,' as in C. V.,
compare v. 23; 16. 30; De. 31. 30; 1 Sa. 2.
17; 2 Sa. 12. 14, &c.
DONE,] as in v. 22 below.
12. DISPOSSESS,] not 'disinherit;' compare
Ex. 15. 9, &c.
MAKE THEE,] not 'make of thee,' as in
C.V.
14. SAID,] as in v. 13.
INHABITANT.] The word is singular not
plural in the original.
EYE TO EYE,] as in Isa. 52. 8, but not
found elsewhere.
16. SLAUGHTER,] as in Ge. 22. 10; 37. 31;
Ex. 12. 6, 21, &c.
18. SLOW TO ANGER,] as in Ex. 34. 6, &c.
KINDNESS,] not 'mercy,' as in C. V., which
the word never means.
BEARING AWAY,] as in Ge. 37. 25; 45. 23, &c.
NOT ENTIRELY ACQUITTING.] See note on
Ex. 34. 6, 7.
CHARGING.] See note on Ex. 34. 6, 7.
19. BORNE WITH,] as in Ge. 4. 13; 13. 6, &c.
22. WHO ARE SEEING,] not 'which have
seen,' as in C.V.
MY SIGNS,] as in Ge. 1. 14; 4. 15; 9. 12,
13, 17, &c.
TRY ME,] as in Ge. 22. 1, &c.
TEN TIMES,] as in Ge. 31. 7, on which see
note.
23. DESPISING,] as in v. 11 above.
24. AND.] There is no necessity for translating 'but.'
HE IS FULLY AFTER ME,] as in 32. 11, 12;
De. 1. 36; Jos. 14. 8, 9, 14; 1 K. 11. 6, but
not occuring elsewhere.
25. AND THE AMALEKITE.] There does
not appear to be any sufficient reason for
supposing this to be a parenthetical addition of the writer, rather than the language of God himself.
CANAANITES,] at least that branch of
them called Amorites; compare De. 1. 19, 20.
DWELLING,] or perhaps simply 'abiding,'
as in 13. 29 they are said to dwell in the
hill-country. The reference here may be
to their 'abiding' in ambush in the
VALLEY,] as in Ge. 14. 3, 8, 10, 17, &c.,
on the other side of the Idumaean mountains where they were now encamped.
26. TO-MORROW,] as in Ge. 30. 33; Ex.
10, 23, 29, &c.
JOURNEY,] as in De. 1. 7, 40; 2. 24.
27. The literal translation shows how
unnecessary is the supplement adopted in
the C. V.
28. SPOKEN,] in v. 3 above.
30. HAVE LIFTED UP MY HAND,] as in Ex.
6. 8, &c.
TABERNACLE,] as in De 12. 11; 14. 23

₁6. 2, 6, 11; 26. 2; Neh. 1. 9; Ps. 78. 60; Jer. 7. 3, 7, 12.

31. INFANTS,] as in Ge. 34. 29, &c.

KICKED AGAINST,] as in Lev. 26. 15, &c.

33. ARE EVIL,] *or*, 'are feeding,' but the next clause shews that 'evil' is the true meaning.

CONSUMED,] as in v. 35 below.

34. BY THE NUMBER.] The Hebrew particle never means 'after.'

SPIED,] as in v. 6 above.

BREAKING OFF.] The original word only occurs elsewhere in Job 33. 10, from a root found in 30. 5, 8, 11; 32. 7, 9; Ps. 33. 10; 141. 5.

35. WHO ARE MEETING,] as in 16. 11; 27. 3; 1 K. 8. 5; 2 Ch. 5. 6; Ex. 25. 22, &c.

36. COMPANY,] not 'congregation.'

EVIL ACCOUNT,] as in Ge. 37. 2, &c.

39. SPEAKETH THESE WORDS.] There is no necessity for the free rendering of the C.V. : 'told these sayings.'

40. SPOKEN OF.] Not necessarily 'promised.'

43. TURNED BACK,] as in Ge. 3. 19, not 'turned aside.'

AND,] not 'therefore.'

44. PRESUME.] The original word is not found elsewhere, but compare Hab. 2. 4.

45. BEAT THEM DOWN,] as in De. 1. 44; compare Job 4. 20; Isa. 24. 12; Jer. 46. 5; Mic. 1. 7; also De. 9. 21.

XV. 2. I AM GIVING.] The present participle in the original is more expressive than the present tense.

3. AT SEPARATING,] as in Lev. 22. 21, on which see note.

YOUR APPOINTED THINGS,] as in Ge. 1. 14; 17. 21; 18. 14; 21. 2, &c.; but especially the passover, pentecost, &c. See Lev. 23. 4—37; Nu. 28 and 29.

4. Compare Ex. 24. 4—8; 29. 7, 10, 14, 27; 12. 15, &c.

5. FOR THE ONE LAMB] there was to be offered a present of flour, and a libation of wine, in certain proportions, which could neither be exceeded nor diminished; this was in order to prevent disputes, and also to secure a portion for the officiating priest.

6. FOR A RAM,] being double the quantity of flour required for a lamb, and also an increase of oil.

8. MAKEST,] not 'preparest,' as in C.V.

SEPARATING.] Compare note on v. 3 above.

9. BROUGHT NEAR,] as in v. 4 above, and in v. 10 below.

FOR,] not 'with,' as in C. V.

THREE TENTH-DEALS,] a bullock requiring as much as a lamb and a ram together.

13. NATIVE,] as in Ex. 12. 19, &c.

14. SOJOURNER,] as in Ge. 15. 13; and again in v. 15, 16 below.

TO YOUR GENERATIONS,] as in Ge. 9. 12; and again in v. 15, 21, below.

15. STATUTE,] as in Ge. 47. 26.

16. ORDINANCE,] as in Ex. 15. 25.

18. I AM BRINGING YOU IN.] The participial form of the original is more expressive than the simple present tense.

19. YE HEAVE UP,] as in v. 20.

22. AND WHEN,] not 'and if,' as in C. V.

ERR,] as in Lev. 4. 13, &c.

23. CHARGED UPON YOU,] as in Ge. 50. 16, &c

24. FROM THE EYES,] as in Ge. 31. 40, &c

PREPARED,] as in v. 8 above.

ORDINANCE,] as in v. 16 above.

27. DAUGHTER OF A YEAR,] as in Ge. 17. 17, &c.

28. ERRING,] as in Job 12. 16; Ps. 119. 67.

29. NATIVE,] as in Ex. 12. 19.

DOING ANYTHING,] as in 11. 15.

30. WITH A HIGH HAND,] as in Ex. 14. 8.

REVILING,] as in 2 K. 19. 6; Isa. 37. 6, 23; Eze. 20. 27; Ps. 44. 15; this peculiar word is not found elsewhere.

32. GATHERING,] not 'that gathered;' he was found in the act.

WILDERNESS] of Paran or Sinai.

34. EXPLAINED,] as in Lev. 24. 12; Neh 8. 8.

35. PUT TO DEATH,] for no fire was allowed (Ex. 35. 2, 3), it being unnecessary in these warm regions.

STONE HIM,] which was the most common mode of Hebrew punishments.

38. THOU HAST SAID UNTO THEM,] not 'bid,' as in C. V.

SKIRTS,] *lit.* 'wings,' as in Ge. 1. 21; and again in De. 22. 12; 1 Sa. 15. 27, &c.

RIBBONS,] as in Ge. 38. 18, 25; Ex. 28. 28, 37, &c.

39. FRINGE,] as in v. 38; compare its use in Eze. 8. 3.

SEARCH,] *or* spy, as in 10. 33, &c.

YE ARE GOING A-WHORING,] as in Lev. 17. 7.

XVI. 1. KORAH,] i.e. bald; he was cousin to Moses and Aaron, being great-grandson of Levi, Ex. 6. 16—21.

IZHAR,] i.e. oil; he was younger brother of Amram.

KOHATH,] i.e. obedience, father of Amram and Izhar.

DATHAN,] i.e. law.

ABIRAM,] i.e. my father is high.

ELIAB,] i.e. my God is father; he was son of Pallu, the second son of Reuben, 26. 5, 8

ON,] i.e. strength; he is not mentioned again elsewhere, probably he repented and left them.

PELETH,] i.e. escape. He, with Dathan and Abiram were sons of Reuben, and therefore, it may be, dissatisfied with the presidency of Judah, while Korah was dissatisfied with the superior authority of his cousins.

TAKETH.] The literal rendering makes it evident that Korah was the chief ringleader in this rebellion, compare v. 7 below.

2. PRINCES,] *lit.* 'honoured ones,' as in Ge. 17. 20.

CALLED OF THE CONVENTION,] *or* of the 'meeting,' as in Nu. 1. 16.

NAME,] as in Ge. 6. 4.

3. ARE ASSEMBLED,] as in Ex. 32. 1.

ENOUGH,] as in Ge. 33. 9; they would dispense with the services of Moses as 'king, and of Aaron as 'priest.'

5. MORNING !] as in Ge. 1. 5. The abruptness of the language is very impressive

MAKE KNOWN,] as in Jud. 8. 16; Ps. 103.
7; Isa. 40. 13, 14, &c.
6. CENSERS,] as in Ex. 25. 38.
7. PERFUME,] as in Ex. 25. 6.
HOLY,] i.e. separated, and 'set apart' for
God's service.
ENOUGH,] returning to them their own
words in v. 3 above.
SONS OF LEVI,] who were the instigators
of the whole affair, while the Reubenites
played a subordinate part.
9. IS IT LITTLE?] as in Ge. 30. 15; Nu. 16.
13; Jos. 22. 17; Job 15. 11; Isa. 7. 13; 29.
17; Eze. 16. 20; 34. 18; a strong way of implying a negative answer.
10. YE HAVE SOUGHT.] There is no necessity or propriety in reading this clause interrogatively, it is rather a kind of inter-
jection.
11. ARE MET,] as in Ex. 25. 22; 29. 42, 43;
30. 6, 36.
AGAINST JEHOVAH,] who had appointed
Aaron and his sons to the priesthood, which
they must have known, though in their
envy they shut their eyes to the fact.
Aaron, therefore, was doing nothing but
occupying the place God had given to him,
and in rejecting the servant they rejected
also the Master. Compare John 12. 48.
12. SENDETH TO CALL.] Moses, having re-
monstrated in vain with Korah and his
company, now turns to Dathan and Abiram,
hoping to turn them back to duty. The
phrase 'come up' does not necessarily imply that Moses was on a hill or a higher
ground than they were, but it is the natural
language of those who have been summoned
to meet a superior. They not only bluntly
refuse to come, but proceed to add insult
to their refusal. Compare Matt. 21. 29;
Luke 19. 14; John 5. 40, &c.
13. IS IT LITTLE?] repeating, as it were, in
derision, the language of Moses in v. 9
above.
A LAND FLOWING, ETC.] i.e. Egypt, but
fertile as that land undoubtedly was, it
was not distinguished either for milk or
honey; there appears to be a covert attack
upon Moses for having thus described the
promised land.
MAKEST THYSELF PRINCE.] This reflexive
form of the verb does not occur elsewhere;
in its simple form it occurs in Prov. 8. 16;
Isa. 32. 1; Est. 1. 22.
14. PICK OUT,] a horrible custom of abus-
ing prisoners or suspected persons in ancient
times; compare the use of the word in 1 Sa.
11. 2; Prov. 30. 17; Jud. 16. 21; Isa. 51. 1.
The expression 'these men,' refers to Korah
and his company, who were still remaining
in the presence of Moses, see v. 16.
15. DISPLEASING,] as in Ge. 4. 5, 6, &c.
TURN NOT THOU,] as in Ge. 18. 22, &c.,
Nu. 14. 25, &c.
PRESENT,] as in Ge. 4. 3, &c.
NOT ONE ASS.] Though this animal is
generally respectfully spoken of in the S.S.,
yet here it appears to be considered of
little or no value, as Sampson evidently
considered it in Jud. 15. 16.
16. BEFORE JEHOVAH,] i.e. at the opening

of the tent of meeting, agreeably to Ex. 25.
22, &c.
17. EACH HIS CENSER.] The object was to
afford an opportunity for Jehovah himself
to settle the dispute by declaring which of
the two parties he was inclined to accept
as his ministering servants.
18. THEY STAND,] openly accepting the
trial that Moses proposed.
21. BE YE SEPARATE,] as in Ezr. 6. 21;
9. 1; 10. 8, 11, 16; Neh. 9. 2; 10. 28; 1 Ch.
12. 8; 23. 13.
22. GOD OF THE SPIRITS.] Compare Heb.
12. 9.
WROTH.] There is nothing to mark this
clause as an interrogation in the original,
any more than in v. 10 above. These
groundless interrogatives are found dozens
of times in the C. V.
THE ONE MAN,] i.e. Korah, who was the
ringleader, as noted in v. 1. Compare a
similar plea in Ge. 18. 23; 20. 4. Yet by
one man's sin death entered into the world.
24. GO YE UP FROM, ETC.] God hearkens
to the prayer of Moses, and points out a
way of escape, of fleeing from the coming
wrath, after the announcement of which
to those concerned around the tent of
meeting,
25. MOSES RISETH AND GOETH] to Korah's
partners in guilt, and warns them likewise,
imitating him who willeth all men to be
saved. 1 Tim. 2. 4.
GO AFTER THEM,] that they also might
bear testimony to the truth. Compare 1
Tim. 5. 20; Nu. 35. 30; Matt. 18. 16, &c.
26. TURN ASIDE,] as in Ge. 19. 2, 3, &c.
27. STANDING,] still and upright, as if
daring Moses to do his utmost.
INFANTS,] same word as in Ge. 34. 29, &c.
28. MY OWN HEART,] as in 24. 13; 1 K. 12.
23; Neh. 6. 8; Job 8. 10.
THESE WORKS,] of guiding, directing, and
restraining Israel; like his brother Aaron,
he was 'called of God' for these very
things.
29. THE CHARGE OF ALL,] i.e. to return
to the dust, as found in Ge. 3. 19.
30. A STRANGE THING.] The original
word is not found elsewhere, but it is from
a very common root, see note on Ge. 1. 1.
The idea involved is rather that of being
out of the ordinary currents of events,
than of a merely new event.
DO,] i.e. prepare or perform.
ALIVE,] as in v. 33; Ps. 55. 15; Prov.
1. 12.
SHEOL,] i.e. the world of spirits, see note
on Ge. 37. 35, &c.
KNOWN,] not merely 'understood,' as in
C.V.
DESPISED,] as the word is used in Nu. 14.
11, 23; De. 31. 30; 32. 19, &c.
31—33. The terrible judgment here recorded would seem to have included the
'households' as well as the leaders, yet from
26. 11, it appears that the 'children' (more
lit. 'sons') of Korah did not die. The
orientals appear generally to have used
much more indeterminate language than
the westerns, so that what happened to the

greater part, or any large number, is said to have happened to ALL. A similar remark appears necessary in the case of Achan, recorded in Joshua 7. 24—26. The 'sons of Korah' were authors of many of the Psalms, in later ages.

34. FLED] at their voice, and because of the earthquake, as happened afterwards in the days of Uzziah, referred to in Zech. 14. 5; Amos 1. 1.

35. COME FORTH.] Compare a similar phrase in Ex. 22. 6; Lev. 9. 24; 10. 2; 21. 23, &c.

37. THE CENSERS,] belonging to Korah and the 250 men.

HAVE BEEN SANCTIFIED,] i.e. set apart as the Lord's property; the fire in them was to be scattered, to intimate its rejection as a thing displeasing to Jehovah.

38. SPREAD OUT.] The original word is not found elsewhere, except in a verbal form, as in Ex. 39. 3; Nu. 16. 39; Isa. 40. 19; Jer. 10. 9, &c.

PLATES,] as in Ex. 39. 3, &c.

A COVERING,] as in v. 39; Ex. 38. 17, 19; Isa. 30. 22; the altar referred to is the altar of burnt-offering.

A SIGN,] or memorial of the punishment of those who assumed the priest's office, which had been restricted to the family of Aaron; compare v. 40, and 2 Ch. 26. 18—23, where we find the king Uzziah disregarding it and punished accordingly.

40. A STRANGER,] as in Ex. 29. 33, &c. Here it simply means one not of the family of Aaron.

TO HIM,] i.e. Eleasar, as in v. 37.

41. YE—YE HAVE.] The reduplication of the pronoun shows the bitterness of the people; they thought that Moses and Aaron might have interceded with the Lord, and He would have spared even the guilty; they, not doing so, were held as having 'put them to death.' So, also, because Jeremiah (1. 10,) was commissioned to foretell the desolation of nations, he is said to do it himself; and God, because he foretold (Ex. 3. 19,) the obstinacy of Pharaoh, is said (in 4. 21,) to have produced it. The Hiphil (or causative) form of the Hebrew verb found here is often only permissive.

42. THEY TURN,] as in Ex. 18. 22, &c. It is not easy to decide whether it was the people or the accused that turned thus, probably it was the latter, to seek counsel and help from Him who had promised to meet there with those seeking Him.

THE CLOUD,] which was the symbol of the divine presence, while 'the glory' was probably a flame of fire.

43. COMETH.] Knowing that He was about to reveal His will, they draw near to the place of meeting to hear.

45. GET YOU UP,] or 'be lifted up,' as in Isa. 33. 10; Eze. 10. 15, 17, 19; (Isa. 33. 3; Job 24. 24; Ps. 118. 16).

CONSUME THEM,] as in v. 21, 24 above.

THEY FALL] before God in prayer, as in v. 22 above, and in 20. 6, &c.

46. THE CENSER,] i.e. Aaron's own, not 'a censer,' as in C.V.

THE WRATH] of God's judgment.

47. RUNNETH,] though now about 84 years of age; the case was urgent.

48. IS RESTRAINED.] See the use of the same Hebrew word in v. 50; 25. 8; 1 Sa 21. 7; 2 Sa. 24. 21, 25; 1 K. 8. 35; 1 Ch. 21 22; 2 Ch. 6. 26; Ps. 106. 30.

XVII. 2. A ROD,] as in Ge. 38. 18, 25; Ex. 4. 2, &c.

3. AARON'S NAME.] The parties who had opposed the authority of Aaron and Moses in the preceding chapter were of two classes; the first were members of their own tribe, that is, of Levi; the second were of the tribe of Reuben. The selection of Aaron's name for the rod of Levi, was a distinct rejection of the pretensions of the first, while those of the second, embracing a larger and more influential circle, were to be determined by a divine signal.

4. WHERE I MEET,] as promised in Ex. 25. 22, which see.

5. FLOURISH,] as in v. 8; Ge. 40. 10; Song 6. 11; 7. 12.

FROM OFF ME..AGAINST YOU.] It is a doctrine of Scripture, as well as of common sense, that an injury done to an ambassador, messenger, or steward, is held as done to him who sends him, as in the case of David and Hanan (2 Sa. 10. 1—8); Jesus and Saul (Acts 9. 5); John 12. 48, &c.

8. HATH FLOURISHED,] as in v. 8 above.

BLOSSOM BLOSSOMS,] as in Ps. 72. 16; 90. 6; 92. 7; 103. 15; 132. 18; Isa. 27. 6; Song 2. 9; Eze. 7. 10.

PRODUCE,] lit. 'do or recompense,' as in Ge. 50. 15, 17; De. 32. 6, &c.

ALMONDS.] See on Ge. 43. 11; Ecc. 12. 5; Jer. 1. 11.

10. FOR A CHARGE,] as in Ge. 26. 5; Ex. 12. 6; 16. 23; 32. 33, 34, &c. Compare the reference in Heb. 9. 4.

SONS OF REBELLION,] i.e. rebellious sons, those implicated in the rebellion of Korah and his company. See the tract on Hebrew Idioms, 'Son,' in my 'Biblical Tracts for every day in the Year.'

12. WE HAVE EXPIRED.] The perfect tenses of the original point out in a lively manner the anxiety of the speakers; they considered themselves as good as dead. See Ge. 6. 7, for a list of the occurrences of this verb.

WE HAVE PERISHED,] Ex. 10. 7, &c.

13. CONSUMED.] See the use of the original word in 14. 33, 35; 32. 13.

XVIII. 1. BEAR THE INIQUITY,] as in Ex. 28. 38; Lev. 10. 17, &c.

SANCTUARY,] i.e. all the evil committed there, whether by sins of omission or of commission.

YOUR PRIESTHOOD,] i.e. whatever evil may be done in the course of their services in behalf of the people.

2. BRING NEAR,] as in 3. 6; Lev. 6. 14; 9. 2; Mal. 1. 8, &c.

JOINED,] as in v. 4; Ge. 29. 34; Ps. 83. 8; Isa. 14. 1; 56. 3, 6; Jer. 50. 5; Dan. 11. 34; Zech. 2. 11; Est. 9. 27.

SERVE THEE,] as ministrants, in preparing the sacrifices, &c. see 3. 2.

THE TESTIMONY,] as in Ex. 38. 2; Nu. 1. 50, 53; 9. 15; 10. 11; 17. 7, 8.

3. THY CHARGE,] i.e. all that which thou dost command them.

THEY OR YOU,] because of their forwardness or your negligence.

4. A STRANGER,] who is not of the tribe of Levi; this precept was violated by king Uzziah.

5. NO MORE WRATH,] than had been experienced in the case of Korah and his company.

6. BY JEHOVAH,] not 'for the Lord,' as in the C. V.

7. VAIL.] See Ex. 26. 31; Heb. 9. 7, &c.

A SERVICE OF GIFT,] being freely and graciously given to them by God.

8. HALLOWED THINGS,] i.e. dedicated by vow, as distinguished from 'gifts,' in v. 11 below.

FOR THE ANOINTING,] as in Ex. 29. 29; not 'because of the anointing,' as in the C.V.

I HAVE GIVEN.] Compare Lev. 7. 34—36.

9. FROM THE FIRE,] i.e. of burnt-offerings.

OFFERING.] This general term includes 'presents' of flour and oil (Lev. 6. 14—18), 'sin-offerings' (Lev. 6. 25—30), 'guilt offerings' (Lev. 7. 5, 6, 15; 6. 6), the parts of these which were not consumed by the fire, were set apart for the maintenance of the priests.

10. HOLY OF HOLIES,] even the court of the tent of meeting; compare Lev. 6. 16, 26; 7. 6.

EVERY MALE,] as in Lev. 6. 18, 29, but not their wives or daughters.

HOLY TO THEE,] or for thee.

11. THEIR GIFT,] i.e. that which they offer of their own will, see Lev. 7. 14, 32; Nu. 6. 19, 20.

WAVE-OFFERINGS,] as in Lev. 7. 30, 34.

THY DAUGHTERS,] who were excluded from eating of the hallowed things, see v. 8.

EVERY CLEAN ONE,] i.e. ceremonially so; but from Lev. 22. 10—13, it appears that no stranger, settler, or hireling, nor any daughter married to a stranger, was permitted to eat of it.

12. NEW WINE,] as in Ge. 27. 28, &c.

13. THE BEST,] *lit.* 'fat,' as in Ge. 4. 4, &c.

ARE THINE.] See De. 26. 2—4.

14. DEVOTED,] as in Lev. 27. 21, &c; it might be a field, house, cattle, money, garments, vessels, or persons, Lev. 27. 1—34.

15. OPENING A WOMB.] See Ex. 13. 2, 12, 13, 15; 34. 19, 20; Nu. 3. 12; 18. 15; Eze. 20. 26.

RANSOM,] as in Ex. 13. 13, 15; 34. 20, &c. viz. by receiving five shekels as redemption-money, see v. 16, below.

TO JEHOVAH,] as His peculiar property, Ex. 13. 2, &c.

FIRSTLING,] with a lamb, Ex. 13. 13, when eight days old.

16. VALUATION,] as in Lev. 27. 5, 6.

FIVE SHEKELS,] or about ten shillings sterling. Compare 3. 47.

17. THOU DOST NOT RANSOM,] because capable of being offered in sacrifice, which the firstlings of an ass, or any other unclean

beast, was not, much less the first-born of man. Had Jephthah's vow been as some suppose, it would have been in violation of Jehovah's statute law imposed on Israel.

MAKEST PERFUME,] as in the case of all other animal sacrifices.

18. BREAST .. RIGHT LEG.] See Lev. 7. 35.

19. LIFT UP,] as in Ge. 14. 22, &c.

20. DOST NOT INHERIT,] as one of the twelve tribes; they were to have certain cities and suburbs, but not in one place, like the other tribes. Josh. 14. 4, &c.

I AM THY PORTION.] Compare De. 32. 9; Ps. 16. 5; 73. 26; 119. 57; 142. 5; Jer. 10. 16; 51. 19; Lam. 3. 24; Zech. 2. 12.

21. ALL THE TENTH.] As a tribe they were entitled to a twelfth, the additional *two* per cent. (besides the share of the sacrifices and offerings, cities and suburbs,) was given them for their religious services. Those who in modern times receive tithes, receive *five times* as much as did the Levites of old.

22. COME NO MORE NEAR] to offer their own sacrifices, which duty now devolved on the priests.

24. OF THEM,] not 'to them,' as in the C.V.

25. JEHOVAH SPEAKETH,] unto Moses, as was natural, rather than unto Aaron, for having already provided for the support of the Levites, as recorded in v. 21—24, he now proceeds to assign to Aaron his inheritance.

26. THE HEAVE OFFERING,] of Jehovah, even a tenth of the tithe which the children of Israel were to give to the Levites. Thus even the Levites who were engaged as ministrants in the divine service were not exempt from the duty of contributing to and sustaining it themselves.

27. RECKONED,] by God, as if it came from their own fields and vineyards.

28. YE ALSO,] that is, the Levites as well as Israel generally.

AARON THE PRIEST,] and to his successors after him in the priesthood.

29. YOUR GIFTS,] i.e. the things freely given to them by the people, and not merely out of the tithes.

THE WHOLE,] not a portion merely, but the full tenth.

ITS FAT,] or best part.

ITS HALLOWED PART,] or that portion which was especially set apart for God.

30. RECKONED,] as in v. 27 above.

31. HIRE,] as in Ge. 15. 1; 30. 18, 28, 32, 33, &c.

IN EXCHANGE FOR,] as in v. 21.

IN EVERY PLACE,] of the land of Israel.

32. FOR IT,] though otherwise a thing dedicated to God.

ITS FAT,] as in v. 29 above.

POLLUTE.] or 'render common,' as in De. 20. 6.

XIX. 2. A STATUTE,] as in Ge. 47. 26.

THEY BRING,] i.e. the whole assembly, because the benefit and use of the law was for the community at large.

A RED COW,] or perhaps merely a 'ruddy' fresh looking one, as the word is translated in Song 5. 10; a red heifer is said by Plutarch and Diodorus Siculus to have been offered to Typhon. From Lev. 3. 1, we see that females were allowed as sacrifices equally with males. This sacrifice was not strictly speaking a sin-offering, but it was appointed to procure the 'water of separation,' which was to be sprinkled over the penitent offender.

PERFECT..BLEMISH,] as in all other sacrifices.

YOKE,] as in De. 21. 3; 1 Sa. 6. 7. This regulation was designed to prevent them offering up in sacrifice any worn-out animal; what is given to God must be the best of the kind.

3. ELEAZAR,] son of Aaron, the priest, that he might be confirmed in his office.

AND ONE HATH BROUGHT IT.] There is no propriety in the Common rendering 'that he may bring it;' the literal rendering is preferable, and it is not likely that Eleazar would lead the animal out without the city, any more than that he would slay it himself; the language is indefinite, as in the next clause.

WITHOUT THE CAMP,] being legally reckoned as impure and unclean. Compare Heb. 13. 11—13.

BEFORE HIM,] that is, 'before' Eleazar, that he might be sure that all the conditions were complied with.

4. SEVEN TIMES,] denoting completeness. HE DOTH BURN,] so that it was a whole burnt-offering.

9. A CLEAN MAN,] one ceremonially so, a priest doubtless.

ASHES.] Compare Heb. 9. 13.

IT HATH BEEN FOR A CHARGE,] to be watched over and preserved for future use, day by day.

SEPARATION,] as in v. 13, 20, 21; 31. 23; Zec. 13. 1, &c.

A CLEANSING THING,] for the sinner from sin, as in v. 17.

10. WASHED..IS UNCLEAN,] like all the other persons who were engaged in the transaction.

11. COMING,] knowingly or unknowingly; he was unclean seven days, while if he had touched merely the carcase of a beast he would have been unclean only till the evening, see Lev. 11. 24.

12. FOR IT,] i.e. because of his transgression, or 'with it,' i.e. the water of separation, but the former is the preferable interpretation.

THE THIRD DAY,] which number Aben Erza here thinks a secret or mystery.

13. DOTH NOT CLEANSE HIMSELF,] i.e. will not, is heedless or indifferent to it, thereby shews his contempt for the divine law, and the 'tabernacle of Jehovah,' i.e. the people of Israel among whom He dwells; such a person

HATH DEFILED,] or, treated as defiled; see the use of the word in Lev. 13. 3, 8, 11, 15, 20, 22, 25, 27, 30.

CUT OFF,] as in Ge. 17. 16; Ex. 12. 15, &c. that is, excommunicated.

14. THE LAW,] or 'direction,' as the word properly means, see Ge. 26. 5, &c.

A TENT,] or 'house,' as the word is evidently used in 2 Sa. 20. 1, &c.

SEVEN DAYS,] as in v. 11.

COVERING,] lit. any thing 'joining or fastening' another, hence in every other instance of its occurrence, it is translated 'bracelet,' see Ge. 24. 22, 30, 47; Nu. 31. 50; Eze. 16. 11; 23. 42.

THREAD,] as in Jud. 16. 9, compare also Ge. 38. 18. 25; Ex. 28. 28, 37; 39. 3, 21, 31; Nu. 15. 38; Eze. 40. 3. Domestic vessels in the east are generally kept covered, to exclude the dust.

16. PIERCED OF A SWORD,] as in Jer. 14. 18; Lam. 4. 9; Eze. 31. 17, 18, &c.

THE DEAD,] who died naturally, in the field.

SEVEN DAYS,] as in v. 11, 14.

17. HE HATH PUT,] or, 'one hath put,' either the unclean person himself, or a priest; most probably the former.

RUNNING,] lit. 'living water.'

18. A CLEAN PERSON,] who might or might not be a priest.

19. THIRD..SEVENTH,] as in v. 12 above.

HATH CLEANSED HIM,] or 'pronounced him clean,' as in v. 13 above; not as in the C.V. 'he shall purify himself.'

20. See notes on v. 13 above, of which this verse is a repetition.

22. AND ALL] persons or things, see Hag. 2. 13.

XX. 1. ZIN,] south of Palestine, and west of Idumea, according to some; noticed also in 13. 21; 27. 14; 34. 4; Jos. 15. 3, distinct from that of Sin, which was on the shore of the Hero-opolitan gulf, Ex. 16. 1; 17. 1; Nu. 33. 12.

FIRST MONTH] of the thirty-ninth or fortieth year of their departure out of Egypt.

KADESH,] lit. the 'separated' place, elsewhere called Kadesh-Barnea, Nu. 34. 4; De. 1. 2, 19; 2. 14; compare Ps. 29. 8. Here the Israelites abode about four months, see 33. 38.

MIRIAM DIETH.] As she was the eldest of the family, she was also the first to die; owing probably to the distress of the people for want of water, as recorded in the next verse, there is no specific mention of any public mourning at her death, as is recorded took place at the death of Aaron (v. 29,) and Moses (De. 34. 8); the oriental mind, however, never seems to have been able thoroughly to entertain a belief of the equality of the sexes.

2. NO WATER,] as had happened to their fathers, and as recorded in Ex. 17. 1.

ARE ASSEMBLED,] as in Ex. 32. 1; Lev. 8. 4; Nu. 16. 3, 42; 20. 2.

3. STRIVE,] as in v. 16; Ge. 26. 20, 21, 22, &c.

AND OH THAT.] This simple literal rendering is infinitely superior to the profane and irreverent use of the name of God unhappily far too frequent in the C. V. See my letter to Dean Close on the 'Defects of King James' Bible '

OUR BRETHREN,] as recorded in 11. 33, and in 16. 33, 49.

EXPIRED,] as in Ge. 6. 17, &c.

4. BEASTS,] as in Ge. 45. 17, &c. For the language of complaint, compare Ex. 17. 3.

6. GO IN] to seek Jehovah where he had promised to meet with them, Ex. 25. 22; 29. 42.

FACES.] The Latin Vulgate Version adds here these words: 'and they cried to the Lord, and said, Lord God, hear the cry of this people, and open to them thy treasure, the fountain of living water, that, they being satiated, their murmuring may cease.' This addition is not found in any other version.

8. THE ROD] with which he had already done so many wonderful things.

THE ROCK] which was in the vicinity of the place where they now were. See the use of the original word in v. 10, 11; 24. 21; De. 32. 13; Jud. 1. 36; 6. 20; 15. 8, 11, 13; 20. 45, 47; 21. 13, &c.

9. FROM BEFORE JEHOVAH,] it being, like the rod of Aaron (17. 7, 10) preserved in the tabernacle.

10. I PRAY YOU.] There is no necessity nor authority for altering the well-known use of the Hebrew word, as is done by the C. V., which reads 'now.'

REBELS,] as in De. 21. 18, 20; Ps. 78. 8; Jer. 5. 23.   Compare Ps. 106. 32, 33.

11. TWICE.] The Chaldee Targum of the Pseudo-Jonathan has a curious remark here, that at the first stroke it dropped *blood*, at the second *water*.   Could this be an interpolation to suit John 19. 34?

WATER.] Compare Ps. 78. 15; 114. 8; De. 8. 15; Ex. 17. 6.

12. BELIEVED NOT,] which in 27. 14 is changed into 'ye rebelled.'   Unbelief is the source of all other evils.

13. MERIBAH,] i.e. 'strife,' this place is sometimes called Meribah Kadesh (De. 32. 51) to distinguish it from the place of the first strife, which was at Rephidim.

AMONG THEM,] i.e. Moses and Aaron, or more probably, the people of Israel.

14. KING OF EDOM.] In Ex. 15. 15, the rulers of Edom are spoken of as 'dukes' or 'chiefs,' some one of these by this time may have acquired a supremacy above his fellows.   Usher supposes him to be the same as Hadar, the last of those enumerated in Ge. 36. 39.

THY BROTHER.] Jacob or Israel being younger brother of Esau or Edom, see Ge. 25. 25—27.

TRAVAIL,] as in Ex. 18. 8; Neh. 9. 32; Lam. 3. 5.

FOUND US.] The travail being personified as seeking out its prey.

15. DO EVIL,] as in De. 26. 6; Ex. 5. 23, &c., compare Ex. 1. 8—22.

MANY DAYS,] even four hundred and thirty years, Ex. 12. 40, 41; Ge. 15. 13.

16. IS BRINGING US OUT.] The present participle is expressive of the feeling that they were not yet really out of Egypt—nor could be, till they had come to the promised land of rest.

17. THY LAND,] it being the nearest way.

FIELD..VINEYARD,] lest they should be injured by the passage of about three millions of people, besides cattle.

A WELL,] Water being perhaps the most valuable commodity in the East, and often sold for money, as noted in Lam. 5. 4, and in v. 19 below.

18. TO MEET THEE,] as in v. 20; 21. 23, 33; 22. 34; De. 1. 44; 2. 32; 3. 1; 29. 7, &c. The phrase 'with the sword,' shews the hostile purpose.

19. IT IS NOTHING] worth speaking of, of no importance.

20. NOT GO THROUGH.] Yet it appears they supplied Israel with food and drink for money, De. 2. 28, 29.

22. MOUNT HOR,] which is a day and a half's journey southward of the Dead Sea, at the foot of which was Petra (see Isa. 16. 1; Nu. 33. 32); another mount of the same name, noticed in Nu. 34. 7, 8, is part of Lebanon, at the north.

24. GATHERED TO HIS PEOPLE.] See same phrase in Ge. 25. 8, 17, &c. ; it is used both of good and bad.

YE PROVOKED,] i.e. made bitter, as in 27. 14 ; De. 1. 26, 43 ; Jos. 1. 18, &c.

26. GARMENTS,] priestly and official ones.

CLOTHED ELEAZAR,] to intimate his complete investiture with the priesthood in the room of his father.

28. DIETH,] on the first day of the fifth month, according to 33. 38; there is no mention made here of his being buried, but there is in De. 10. 6.

29. EXPIRED,] as in Ge. 6. 17.

THIRTY DAYS,] a whole month, as they did afterwards for Moses, De. 34. 8. Though Aaron was the elder brother of Moses, the whole narrative shews the propriety of the Divine choice of the latter as the natural leader of Israel.

XXI. 1. KING OF ARAD.] Arad appears to be the name of a place rather than that of a man, according to Jos. 12. 14; Jud. 1. 16, with which agree the Targums of Onkelos, Jonathan, and Jerusalem.

CANAANITE,] which may here be a general name for the Amorite, Amalekite, &c.

ATHARIM.] The Septuagint, Samaritan, and Arabic Versions understand this as a proper name.

2. DEVOTED.] See note on Ex. 22. 20, &c.

3. DEVOTETH] them and their cities, but as Arad is again referred to in Jos. 12. 14, some remnant probably was left unsubdued.

HORMAH] *or* destruction, and formerly called Zephath; here Israel had been defeated by Amalek (14. 45), and afterwards at this place Judah and Simeon were victorious (Jud. 1. 17.)

4. SOUL..IS SHORT,] as in Ex. 6. 9; Jud. 10. 16; 16. 16; Job 21. 4; Prov. 14. 29.

IN,] the way, not 'because of' it.

5. AGAINST GOD,] which the Targum of Jonathan renders 'against the Word of the Lord.'

WEARY,] as in Ge. 27. 46; Ex. 1. 12; Lev. 20. 23, &c.

VERY LIGHT BREAD,] i.e. the manna.

6. THE SERPENTS,] as in Ge. 3. 1, &c.

THE BURNING,] *Heb.* 'the seraphim;' compare v. 8; De. 8. 15; Isa. 6. 2, 6; 14. 29;

30. 6; as Isaiah speaks of the creatures whom he thus denominates as having wings, probably those referred to in our text were flying, as well as burning animals.

THEY BITE,] as in Ge. 49. 17, &c.

7. IN BEHALF OF,] as in Ge. 20. 7, &c.

8. ENSIGN,] as in Ex. 17. 15, &c.

9. BRASS,] hence the contemptuous language of Hezekiah, in 2 K. 18. 4.

LOOKED EXPECTINGLY,] or earnestly, as in Ge. 15. 5, &c.

10. JOURNEY,] from Zalmonah, where they now were, according to Nu. 33. 41, 42, 43, and encamp first at Punon, and afterwards at Oboth.

11. WILDERNESS.. OF MOAB,] as in De. 2. 8.

12. VALLEY,] or brook of Zared; in 33. 45 it is called Dibon-Gad, whence they removed to Almon-diblathaim, according to 33. 46, 47.

14. WAHEB.] This word is not found elsewhere; most probably it is the name of a place in 'Suphah,' which cannot mean the Red Sea, for in every instance where *it* is referred to, it has the word 'sea' annexed.

15. SPRING.] Compare the plural form in De. 3. 17; 4. 49; Jos. 10. 40; 12. 3, 8; 13. 20.

AR,] which in Isa. 15. 1, is called Ar of Moab.

TURNED ASIDE,] as in Ge. 38. 1, &c.

LEANED,] as in Ge. 18. 4; Jud. 16. 26, &c.

16. BEER,] so called from its well.

17. CONCERNING,] as in Ps. 32. 5; there seems no necessity or propriety in regarding the original word as an address to the well itself, while the next verb never really means to 'sing,' but simply to 'answer or respond,' which is a characteristic of Semitic poetry.

18. DIGGED,] as in Ge. 21. 30, &c.

PREPARED,] as in Ge. 26. 25; 2 K. 6. 23, &c.

PRINCES,] as in Ge. 12. 15; *lit.* 'heads.'

NOBLES,] as in Ps. 47. 9; 113. 8.

LAW-GIVER,] as in Ge. 49. 10; De. 33. 20; Jud. 5. 14; Ps. 60. 7; 108. 8; Isa. 33. 22.

STAVES,] as in Ex. 21. 19, &c.

WILDERNESS,] near Arnon, according to v. 13 above.

19. MATTANAH,] *lit.* a gift.

NAHALIEL,] *lit.* a valley or stream of God.

BAMOTH,] *lit.* high places; these places are not mentioned in Ch. 33, not being properly stations or encampments.

20. FIELD,] as in Ge. 2. 5; 32. 3; 36. 35; Jud. 5. 4; Ruth 1. 1, 2, 6, 22; 2. 6; 4. 3, &c.

PISGAH,] *lit.* a 'sight, or view.' Compare Ps. 48. 14.

THE WILDERNESS] of Kedemoth, De. 2. 26.

21. SIHON,] *lit.* 'a sweeping away,' referred to in v. 23, 28; Ps. 135. 11.

AMORITE.] See Ge. 10. 16, &c.

22. The proposals in this message to the king of the Amorites is almost verbally the same as those sent to the king of Moab, in 20. 17, which see.

23. HATH NOT SUFFERED] Israel to enter into his territory, because he did not 'trust' them, see Jud. 11. 20, while in De. 2. 30, it is attributed to God's providence.

THE WILDERNESS,] noticed in v. 20 above.

JAHAZ,] *lit.* a 'trodden down' place; in

latter times it was in the possession of the Reubenites, and given to the Levites, see De. 2. 32; Josh. 13. 8; Isa. 15. 4; Jer. 48. 21, 34.

24. ARNON.. JABBOK,] two rivers, the one at the north, forming the boundary of the Moabites, the other at the south, the boundary of the Ammonites.

STRONG,] and therefore Israel could not overcome it, being also prohibited by God from doing so, see De. 2. 19.

25. ALL THESE CITIES.] See their names in 32. 3, 34—38; they lay between Arnon and Jabbok.

ISRAEL,] even Reuben and Gad, see 32. 2, 33; De. 3. 12. 16.

VILLAGES,] *lit.* 'daughters,' the villages being reckoned as offshoots from the larger cities.

HESHBON,] *lit.* 'reason, or device,' referred to again in Isa. 15. 4.

27. SIMILES,] i.e. 'those comparing' one thing with another, as in Job 30. 19; Ps. 28. 1; 49. 12, 20; 143. 7; Isa. 14. 10; 46. 5, Eze. 12. 23; 16. 44; 17. 2; 18. 2, 3; 20. 49; 24. 3.

28. A FLAME,] as in Ps. 29. 7; 83. 14; 105. 32; 106. 18; Isa. 4. 5; 5. 24; 10. 17; 43. 2; 47. 14; Jer. 48. 45; La. 2. 3; Eze. 20. 47; Da. 11. 33; Hos. 7. 6; Joel 1. 19; 2. 3; Obad. 18.

AR OF MOAB,] as in Isa. 15. 1.

OWNERS,] *lit.* 'baalim,' as in Ge. 14. 3; Ex. 21. 28, &c.

29. PERISHED,] as in Ex. 10. 7, &c. This seems to be the language of the Amorites.

CHEMOSH,] *lit.* 'subduer,' the national deity of Moab and Ammon, Jud. 11. 24; 1 K. 11. 7, 33; 2 K. 23. 13; Jer. 48. 7, 13, 46.

HE HATH GIVEN,] i.e. Chemosh, who had proved unable to defend his sons and daughters, that is, his worshippers.

30. WE SHOOT THEM,] with arrows and darts, from a root signifying to 'throw, cast,' as in Ge. 31. 51; Ex. 15. 4; 19. 13, &c.

DIBON,] *lit.* 'pain, grief;' called Dibon-Gad, in 33. 45, because rebuilt by the Gadites; given to the Reubenites in Jos. 13. 9, 17, and afterwards occupied by the Moabites, Isa. 15. 2; Jer. 48. 18, 22. Doubtless it is the same place that is called *Dimon* in Isa. 15. 19; another town of the same name belonging to Judah is noticed in Neh. 11. 25, which in Josh. 15. 22 is called *Dimonah.*

NOPHAH,] *lit.* 'a blast;' not mentioned elsewhere except it be the same as Nebo, in Isa. 15. 2.

MEDEBA,] *lit.* 'water of strength,' a city in a plain of the same name, afterwards belonging to the Reubenites, Jos. 13. 9, 16; 1 Ch. 19. 7; Isa. 15. 2.

31. DWELLETH,] and thus the promise to Abraham was beginning to receive its accomplishment.

32. JAAZER,] given to the Gadites in 32. 1, 3, 35; Isa. 13. 25; 39; noticed in 2 Sa. 24. 5; Isa. 16. 8, 9; Jer. 48. 32; 1 Ch. 6. 81; and in 26. 31, where it is coupled with Gilead as in Nu. 32. 1.

VILLAGES,] *lit.* 'daughters,' as in v. 25 above.

POSSESS,] as in Ge. 15. 4, 7, 8, &c.

33. BASHAN,] *lit.* 'soft, sandy;' the northern part of the region beyond Jordan, and afterwards occupied by the half-tribe of Manasseh; it is celebrated for its oaks (Isa. 2. 13; Eze. 27. 6; Zec. 11. 2); its fertility and cattle (De. 32. 14; Ps. 22. 13; Amos 4. 1; Eze. 39. 18.)

OG,] *lit.* 'one who goes in a circle,' or rolls about, from fatness it may be; noticed again in 32. 32; De. 1. 4; 3. 1, 3, 4, 10, 11, 13; 4. 47; 29. 7; 31. 4; Jos. 2. 10; 9. 10; 12. 4; 13. 12, 30, 31; 1 K. 4. 19; Neh. 9. 22; Ps. 135. 11; 136. 20.

EDREI,] *lit.* 'strong;' afterwards occupied by Manasseh; noticed again in De. 1. 4; 3. 1, 10; Jos. 12. 4; 13. 12, 31. Another place of the same name belonging to Naphtali is mentioned in Jos. 19. 37.

35. A REMNANT,] as in 24. 19; De. 2. 34; 3. 3; Jos. 8. 22; 10. 20, 28, 30, 33, 37, 39, 40; 11. 8; Jud. 5. 13; 2 K. 10. 11; Job 18. 19; 20. 21, 26; 27. 15; Isa. 1. 9; Jer. 31. 2; 42. 17; 44. 14; 47. 4; La. 2. 22; Joel 2. 32; Obad. 14, 18; from a root which only occurs in Jos. 10. 20.

HIS LAND,] which was afterwards given to the half-tribe of Manasseh, De. 3. 4, 5, 13—15.

XXII. 1. JOURNEY] from the mountains of Abarim, according to 33. 48, 49, after the preceding events.

BEYOND] the Jordan, on the east side of it.

2. BALAK,] *lit.* 'waste, empty, void;' v. 4—41; 23. 1—30; 24. 10—25; Jos. 24. 9, Jud. 11. 25; Mic. 6. 5.

ZIPPOR,] *lit.* a 'bird, sparrow, *or* early;' v. 4, 10, 16; 23. 18; Jos. 24. 9; Jud. 11. 25.

AMORITE,] i.e. their two kings.

3. VEXED,] as in the parallel case of the Egyptians, Ex. 1. 12; and of Rezon, king of Syria, 1 K. 11. 25, compare Isa. 7. 16.

MIDIAN,] who were probably (Ge. 36. 35) tributary to Moab at this time; 31. 8; Jos. 13. 21.

4. LICK UP,] as in 1 K. 18. 38; Ps. 72. 9; Isa. 49. 23; Mic. 7. 17, which are all the occurrences of the original word.

GREEN THING,] as in Ge. 1. 30; 9. 3; Ex. 10. 15; Ps. 37. 2; Isa. 15. 6; compare De. 11. 10; 1 K. 21. 2; 2 K. 19. 26; Prov. 15. 17; Isa. 37. 27.

5. BALAAM,] i.e. 'not of the people,' that is 'a foreigner.'

BEOR,] i.e. a 'burning;' in Ge. 36. 32, and 1 Ch. 1. 43, it occurs as the name of the father of Bela, king of Edom.

PETHOR,] i.e. an 'interpretation,' a place on the Euphrates, in Aram, (23. 7,) which probably derived its name from being the abode of such men as Balaam, who in Jos. 13. 22, is called a diviner, against which class of men Israel is warned in De. 18. 10—14.

THE EYE,] as in Ex. 10. 5, 15; Nu. 22. 5, 11; not 'face,' as in C. V.

6. CURSE,] as in Ge. 3. 14; Nu. 23. 7, &c.

CURSED,] in opposition to which we are assured in Prov. 26. 2, that 'a reviling without cause doth not come.'

7. DIVINATIONS,] as in 23. 23; De. 18. 10; 1 Sa. 15. 23; 2 K. 17. 17; Prov. 16. 10; Jer. 14. 14; Eze. 13. 6, 23; 21. 21, 22. It never means the 'reward of divination;' it may mean the implements by which the art was to be practised. Aben Ezra suggests that it means that 'diviners were along with them,' but this is not so natural.

8. JEHOVAH.] It is rather singular to find this name used by Balaam (also in v. 13, 18, 19; 23. 3, 12, 21, 26; 24. 6, 13); it would imply that he had a knowledge of at least the incommunicable name of the God of Israel, and by thus using it would teach Balak whose was the people whom he sought to have cursed, and his own subjection to Jehovah's authority; yet, as Balaam's native tongue was Aramaean, probably the author of Numbers translated into Hebrew, Balaam's language, in which there may have been some peculiar intimation regarding the God of Israel, which warranted the translator's use of the peculiar name 'Jehovah.'

9. GOD COMETH IN] unto Balaam, in a dream or vision of the night, as he did in the case of Abimelech (Ge. 20. 3), and Laban (Ge. 31. 24); 'God,' is here used by the historian rather than 'Jehovah,' probably from the conception that the peculiar name was restricted to those who were His chosen people, and so in both of the above quoted passages He who reveals himself is spoken of as 'God,' not as Jehovah, i.e. the general instead of the specific.

WHO ARE THESE.] Compare the question in 2 K. 20. 14.

11. PIERCE IT,] as in v. 17; 23. 8, 11, 13, 25, 27; 24. 10, which are all the instances of its occurrence.

TO FIGHT,] as in Ex. 1. 10, &c.; to 'overcome,' only by inference.

CAST IT OUT] of the land of Moab.

12. NOT GO,] in opposition to the request in v. 6, 'come, I pray thee.'

NOT CURSE,] as required to do by Balak.

BLESSED,] as promised in Ge. 12. 3; 23. 20.

13. IS REFUSING,] as repeated in v. 14.

15. ADDETH TO SEND,] i.e. sends a second time, agreeably to a very common idiom, e.g. Ge. 4. 2, 12, &c.

16. BE NOT WITHHELD,] as in Job 38. 15; Jer. 3. 3; Joel 1. 13.

17. DO I HONOUR THEE,] i.e. hold thee in honour, not 'promote thee to honour,' as in C. V.

PIERCE,] as in v. 11 above.

18. COMMAND,] *lit.* 'mouth.'

20. GOD COMETH IN,] as in v. 9 above.

22. HE IS GOING,] without the condition being fulfilled on which the permission was granted, viz., the men coming to call for him, compare v. 20.

A MESSENGER OF JEHOVAH,] see note on Ge. 16. 7, &c.

STATIONETH HIMSELF,] as in Ex. 2. 5, &c.

AN ADVERSARY,] *lit.* a Satan, as in v. 32; 1 Sa. 29. 4; 2 Sa. 19. 22; 1 K. 5. 4; 11. 14, 23, 25; 1 Ch. 21. 1; Job 1. 6, 7, 8, 9, 12; 2. 1, 2, 4, 6, 7; Ps. 38. 20; 71. 13; 109. 4, 6, 20, 29; Zech. 3. 1, 2, being all the passages where the word occurs.

TWO OF HIS SERVANTS.] No mention is made of the princes of Moab, they had probably gone on before him, while the eyes of the servants were, like those of Elisha's young man in 2 K. 6. 17, unable to discern the appearance.

DRAWN SWORD,] as in Josh. 5. 13 ; 1 Ch. 21. 16.

TO TURN IT ASIDE,] as the word is rendered in the preceding clause.

24. NARROW PATH.] The original word is not found elsewhere.

A WALL,] as in Ezra 9. 9 ; Ps. 62. 30 ; 80. 12 ; Ecc. 10. 10 ; Isa. 5. 5 ; Eze. 13. 5 ; 22. 30 ; 42. 7 ; Hos. 2. 6 ; Mic. 7. 11.

25. IS PRESSED,] as in Ex. 3. 9, except that the verb here is passive not active, as in next clause.

26. TO TURN ASIDE,] as in v. 23 above.

27. CROUCHETH,] as in Ge. 4. 7, &c.

28. OPENETH.] Compare 2 Pet. 2. 16.

29. ROLLED THYSELF,] as in 1 Sa. 6. 6 ; 31. 4 ; 1 Ch. 10. 4 ; Jer. 38. 19 ; Jud. 19. 25.

OH THAT,] as in Ge. 17. 18, &c.

I HAD SLAIN,] not 'I would slay,' as in C.V.

31. UNCOVERETH,] as in Lev. 18. 7 ; Ps. 119. 18 ; Nu. 24. 4, 16, &c.

32. ADVERSARY,] as in v. 23 above.

PERVERSE.] Job 16. 11 is the only other place where the original word occurs.

BEFORE ME,] more *lit.* ' over against me.'

34. TO MEET ME,] as in Ge. 14. 17, &c.

EVIL IN THINE EYES,] as in Ge. 28. 8, &c.

39. KIRJATH-HUZOTH,] *lit.* ' city of streets *or* out-places,' not mentioned elsewhere.

40. SACRIFICETH,] as in Ge. 31. 54 ; the religious sentiment was probably stronger in ancient than in modern times, as no great event was ever attempted without a sacrifice being first offered to the God whom the actors served.

SENDETH] portions of the sacrifice, that by eating they might be joined in alliance with him.

41. HIGH-PLACES,] which might be either a tower or a hill dedicated to the worship of Baal-Peor, Chemosh, &c., see 25. 3.

THE EXTREMITY,] that portion of it only which lay nearest Kirjath-Huzoth ; not ' the whole' of Israel as some have imagined, compare 23. 13.

XXIII. 1. SEVEN ALTARS.] This number was probably chosen as a perfect number, that the sacrifice might be acceptable. Israel was not allowed to build any but one altar, and the patriarchs are never mentioned as having exceeded that number at one time.

RAMS.] Compare Job 42. 8 for a similar offering. It was an offering to Jehovah, see v. 4.

3. STATION THYSELF,] as in Ex. 2. 4, &c., that he might thus shew that they were his own.

HIGH PLACE,] even higher and more exposed than that on which he now was ; the original word occurs in Job 33. 21 ; Isa. 14. 18 ; 49. 9 ; Jer. 3. 2, 21 ; 4. 11 ; 7. 29 ; 12. 12 ; 14. 6. Compare Isa. 13. 2.

4. THE SEVEN ALTARS,] as in v. 1.

ARRANGED,] *or* 'set in order,' as in Ge. 14. 8, &c.

6. BURNT-OFFERING,] as in v. 3 above.

7. SIMILE,] see note on 21. 27.

LEAD ME,] as in Ge. 24. 48, &c

ARAM,] see Ge. 10. 22, &c.

THE EAST,] of Moab.

BE INDIGNANT,] as in v. 8 ; Ps. 7. 11 ; Prov. 22 14 ; 24. 24 ; 25. 23 ; Isa. 11. 30 ; 66. 14 ; Mic. 6. 10 ; Zec. 1. 12 ; Mal. 1. 4.

8. GOD..JEHOVAH.] The Targums of Jonathan and Jerusalem read, ' the Word of Jah,' twice.

8. PIERCE..PIERCED.] See note on 22. 11.

INDIGNANT,] as in v. 7.

9. TABERNACLE,] as in Ge. 9. 27, &c.

RECKON ITSELF.] This reflexive form of the verb is not found elsewhere.

10. WHO HATH COUNTED.] There is no necessity for the Common rendering, ' who *can* count ?' there is nothing in the original text to indicate non-potentiality, and this is only one of many scores of passages where the Common Version unnecessarily inserts the word '*can*,' which the simple past or present form of the verb never expresses.

UPRIGHT ONES,] as in Ex. 15. 26 ; De. 32. 4 ; 2 Ch. 29. 34, &c.

MY LAST END,] as in Ge. 49. 1 ; Nu. 24. 14, 20 ; De. 4. 30 ; 8. 16 ; 11. 12 ; 31. 29 ; 32. 20, 29, &c. Some render it 'my after-state ;' others, 'my posterity,' so Sept.

11. PIERCE,] as in 22. 11, above.

14. ZOPHIM,] *or* 'watchers;' not mentioned elsewhere.

PISGAH,] see note on 21. 20.

15. STATION THYSELF,] as in v. 3 above.

MEET,] as in v. 3 above ; Ge. 14. 17, &c.

18. SON OF ZIPPOR.] In v. 7, Balaam had spoken of him as ' King of Moab ;' he now speaks to him more personally, as a man.

19. GOD,] *lit.* AL, the 'mighty' one.

MAN..LIE.] Compare Ps. 62. 9 ; 89. 35 ; 116. 11.

SON OF MAN..REPENT.] Compare 1 Sa. 15. 29 ; Ps. 89. 34.

DO..CONFIRM,] Isa. 14. 24, 27.

21. BEHELD..SEEN.] Perhaps the nominative to these verbs is not 'God,' but 'no one' understood, as is common in S.S.

WITH HIM,] i.e. Jacob or Israel.

SHOUT,] as in Lev. 23. 24, &c.

KING,] either Jehovah (Ex. 15. 18,) or Moses (Deut. 33. 5), or Messiah (so the Targum of Jonathan).

22. GOD,] even EL, a mighty one.

IS BRINGING THEM.] The participial form denotes a present action.

SWIFTNESS,] as in 24. 8 ; compare Job 22. 25 ; Ps. 95. 4, the only other passages where the original word occurs.

REEM,] as in 24. 8 ; De. 33. 17 ; Job 39. 9, 10 ; Ps 22. 21 ; 29 6 ; 92. 10 ; Isa. 34. 7. The exact animal meant is not certain. The Sept. and Vulg. have 'unicorn ;' Gesenius, ' buffalo '

23. ENCHANTMENT,] as in 24. 1 ; compare Ge. 30. 27 ; 44 5, 15 ; Lev. 19. 26, &c.

DIVINATION,] as in 22. 7.

24. LIONESS,] as in Ge. 49. 9, &c.

LION,] see Ge. 49. 9, &c.

PREY,] see Ge. 49. 9, &c.

PIERCED ONES,] as in Ge. 34. 27, &c.

25. PIERCE.] See note on 22. 11, &c.

26. 1 DO.] not merely 'must do,' but 'do.'

27. EYES OF GOD,] as in Ge. 6. 8; 38. 7; Ex. 15. 26; Lev. 10. 19; Nu. 24. 1; De. 4. 25: 9. 18; 11. 12; 12. 28; 13. 18; 17. 2; 31. 29, &c.

28. PEOR,] *lit.* an 'opening or gape,' noticed again in 25. 18; 31. 16; Jos. 22. 17.

THE WILDERNESS,] *or* Jeshimon, the same as Beth-Jeshimoth, 33. 49, on which see note. The word literally means a 'waste desert place.'

XXIV. 1. GOOD,] as in De. 6. 18, &c.

TIME BY TIME,] *lit.* 'step by step,' as in Jud. 16. 20; 20. 30, 31; 1 Sa. 3. 10; 20. 25.

TO MEET,] as in Ge. 14. 47, not 'to seek for,' as in C.V.

SETTETH..HIS FACE,] as in Lev. 20. 5, &c.

2. TABERNACLING,] as in Ge. 9. 27, &c.

IS UPON HIM.] The verb in the original, though often translated 'come,' really and properly is simply 'to be.' See note on Ge. 1. 2.

SPIRIT OF GOD.] Compare Ge. 1. 2; 41. 38; Ex. 31. 3; 35. 31; Nu. 11. 29; Jud. 3. 10, &c. Compare also John 11. 51; Matt. 7. 22, 23, for his coming upon ungodly men.

3. AFFIRMATION.] See note on Ge. 22. 16.

BAALAM..BEOR.] Utterly ignoring Balak in the whole matter.

THE MAN,] *lit.* the 'mighty' one, as in Ex. 10. 11; 12. 37, &c.

SHUT.] Unaccountably and absurdly has the original word here been rendered 'open.' It occurs no where else, but compare cognate words in La. 3. 8; La. 12. 9, &c.

4. IS HEARING,] i.e. in the habit of doing so, and even now.

SAYINGS OF GOD,] as in Ps. 107. 11; Job 6. 10; Isa. 24. 27. See Nu. 22. 9, 20; 23. 4, 5, 16. VISION,] as in Ge. 15. 1; Eze. 13. 7; 1 K. 7. 4, 5.

ALMIGHTY,] *Heb.* 'shaddai,' as in Ge. 17. 1.

FALLING.] There is not the slightest authority for the addition: 'into a trance.'

UNCOVERED.] See the use of the original word in Esth. 3. 14; 8. 13; Jer. 32. 11, 14. Compare Ps. 119. 18.

5. STRETCHED OUT.] The people of Israel when in the wilderness were not crowded together, as some have supposed, but extending far and wide on every side, which they were compelled to do for pasturage, for though they themselves were supported to a large extent by the daily miraculous supply of manna, there is no reason for believing that their cattle were supported upon any thing beyond the pastures of the wilderness.

6. VALLEYS,] as in Ge. 26. 17, 19; sometimes the word signifies a 'brook or stream,' as in Ge. 32. 23, &c. In this latter sense it is understood here by the Targum of Jonathan, which yields not a bad sense.

RIVER,] which are consequently fruitful. Compare Ps. 1. 3; Song 4. 12—15.

ALOES,] as in Ps. 45. 8; Prov. 7. 17; Song 4. 14. Some read 'tents,' instead of aloes.

PLANTED,] as in Ge. 2. 8; Ex. 15. 17; 2 Sa. 7. 10; 1 Ch. 17. 9; Ps. 44. 2; 80. 8, 15; 104. 16; Isa. 5. 2; 51. 16; Jer. 2. 21; 11. 17; 12. 2; 24. 6; 31. 28; 32. 1; 42. 10; 45. 4; Am. 9. 15.

CEDARS,] to which the righteous are compared in Ps. 92. 12.

7. MAKETH FLOW,] compare the use of the original word in De. 32. 2; Jud. 5. 5; Job 36. 26; Ps. 147. 18; Song 4. 16; Isa. 45. 8; 48. 21; Jer. 9. 18; also Isa. 64. 1, 2.

BUCKETS,] as in Isa. 40. 15, from a root signifying 'to draw up' water.

SEED,] i.e. posterity.

MANY WATERS.] Compare the phrase in Jer. 51. 13; Prov. 17. 1, 15.

AGAG,] *lit.* 'burning, fiery,' apparently the general names of the kings of Amalek (1 Sa. 15. 8—32), like Pharaoh, Caesar, &c.

HIS KINGDOM.] According to the Targum of Jonathan, 'the kingdom of the Messiah.'

8. IS BRINGING,] as in 23. 22, on which see note.

SWIFTNESS..REEM,] as above.

EATETH UP,] so as to leave no remnant of them.

BONES,] as in Ge. 2. 23, &c.

BREAKETH.] See the use of the original verb in Eze. 23. 34; Zeph. 3. 3; Da. 6. 24.

ARROWS.] These being the chief weapons of attack in ancient times.

SMITETH,] as in v. 17; De. 32. 39; 33. 11, Jud. 5. 26; 2 Sa. 22. 39; Job 5. 18; 26. 12 Ps. 18. 38, &c.

9. BENT,] as in Ge. 49. 9, &c.

LAIN DOWN,] as in Ge. 19. 4; Job 40 21.

LION,] as in 23. 24 above.

LIONESS,] as in 23. 24.

RAISE UP,] as in Ge. 49. 9.

BLESSED..CURSED.] Compare Ge. 12. 3; 27. 29, &c.

10. BURNETH,] as in Ge. 30. 2; 39. 19; 44 18, &c.

STRIKETH HIS HANDS,] an eastern custom noticed in La. 2. 15; Job 34. 37.

PIERCE,] as in 22. 11, on which see note.

CERTAINLY BLESSED,] *lit.* 'blessing thou hast blessed.'

11. FLEE,] as in 27. 43.

PLACE,] i.e. Mesopotamia, see 22. 5; 23. 7, and notes thereon.

SAID,] not 'thought,' as in the C.V.

I DO GREATLY HONOUR,] as in 22. 17, 37.

KEPT BACK,] as in Ge. 30. 2; 1 Sa. 25. 26, 34; Ps. 84. 11, &c.

13. THE FULNESS OF HIS HOUSE,] as in 22. 18 above.

COMMAND,] *lit.* 'mouth,' as in Lev. 24. 12; Nu. 3. 16, 39, 51, &c.

OWN HEART,] as in 16. 28.

14. I COUNSEL THEE,] as in Ex. 18. 19; 1 K. 1. 12; Ps. 32. 8; Jer. 38. 15.

LATTER END OF THE DAYS.] See same phrase in Ge. 49. 1, on which see note.

15. SAITH,] in language almost literally word for word with his previous statement in v. 3, 4 above. In v. 16 however, he inserts a new clause, viz. 'and knowing knowledge of the Most High.'

16. KNOWLEDGE,] Compare Prov. 2. 5; 30. 3; Hos. 4. 1; 6 6

MOST HIGH,] as in Ge. 14. 18, 19, 20, 22.

17. SEE IT,] i.e. the circumstance he is going to narrate, viz. the appearance of a star.

NOT NOW,] already it had vanished from his sight—so transient was the glimpse he was permitted to obtain of the future, through his mental eye.

NOT NEAR,] in point of time or space.

STAR,] as in Ge. 1. 16; Amos 5. 26, &c. The Rabbis generally understood this of the Messiah, hence one impostor took the name of Son of the Star.

PROCEEDED,] lit. 'treaded,' see De. 1. 36; 11. 24, 25; 33. 29.

SCEPTRE,] as in Ge. 49. 10, &c.

SMITTEN,] as in v. 8 above.

CORNERS,] as in Ex. 25. 26; Jer. 48. 45. Compare 2 Sam. 8. 2; Ps. 60. 9, 12; 108. 9.

DESTROYED.] The original word is only found elsewhere in Isa. 22. 5.

SONS OF SHETH.] In Jer. 48. 45 it is 'sons of Shaon,' or 'wasting.'

18. POSSESSION,] as in De. 2. 5, 9, 12, 19; 3. 20. Compare 2 Sam. 8. 14, &c.

VALIANTLY,] or 'worthily,' as in Ge. 47. 6; Ex. 18. 21, 25; Ruth 3. 11, &c.

19. RULE,] as in Ge. 1. 26, 28; Lev. 25. 43, 46, 53, &c.

REMNANT,] as in 21. 35, &c.

AR,] a city of Moab, see 21. 15, 28, &c. The ordinary reading 'the city,' yields no intelligible sense.

20. AMALEK,] see Ge. 36. 12, 16; Ex. 17. 8, &c.

BEGINNING OF,] as in Ge. 10. 10, &c.

GOYIM,] as in Ge. 14. 1. In no sense was Amalek the first of 'the nations.'

LATTER END,] his posterity, or the latter state of his reign.

FOR EVER,] as in v. 24.

21. KENITE,] see note on Ge. 15. 19, where their land is promised to Israel.

ENDURING,] as in Ge. 49. 24.

DWELLING,] or 'seat,' Ge. 10. 30; 1 Sa. 20. 18, 25, &c.

A ROCK,] as in Nu. 20. 8; Jud. 15. 8; 20. 47; 2 K. 14. 7; Isa. 16. 1, &c.

NEST,] Heb. KEN, as in Ge. 6. 14; De. 22. 6, &c.

22. BURNING,] as in Ex. 35. 3; Isa. 5. 5, &c.

ASSHUR,] see note on Ge. 2. 14.

KEEP CAPTIVE,] as in Ge. 31. 26; 34. 29.

24. SHIPS,] as in Isa. 33. 21; Eze. 30. 9; Da. 11. 30.

SIDE,] lit. 'hand.'

CHITTIM,] see on Ge. 10. 4; where they are descendants of Japhet; compare also 1 Ch. 1. 7; Isa. 23. 1, 12; Jer. 2. 10; Ex. 27. 6; Da. 11. 30.

HUMBLED,] as in Ps. 35. 13; De. 8. 2, 3, 16, &c.

EBER,] i.e. the Hebrews, Ge. 10. 21, 24, 25, &c.

IS PERISHING,] as in v. 20 above.

25. HIS PLACE,] as in v. 11 above, but see note on 31. 8.

HIS WAY,] as in Ge. 19. 2, &c., i.e. to his own city and palace.

XXV. 1. DWELLETH,] till the death of Moses, see Josh. 2. 1; Nu. 33. 49, where it is called Abel-Shittim.

SHITTIM,] a valley of Moab near Palestine, so called from its wood. Compare Josh. 2. 1; 3. 1; Mic. 6. 5; Joel 4. 18.

GO A-WHORING.] From 31. 16 it appears this was the result of a deliberate plan on the part of Balaam.

MOAB,] and of Midian also, as appears from v. 6; 31. 9, 16.

2. EAT,] which is everywhere regarded as a token of intimate communion and fellowship.

3. IS JOINED] or coupled, as in v. 5; 2 Sa. 20. 8; Ps. 50. 19; 106. 28. Compare 1 Cor. 10. 14—21.

BAAL-PEOR.] See note on 23. 28; 25. 5; De. 4. 3; Ps. 106. 28; Hos. 9. 10, lit. 'lord of the opening.'

BURNETH,] as in 24. 10, &c.

4. HANG,] as in 2 Sa. 21. 6, 9, 13; the most ignominious punishment of those days.

5. JUDGES,] as in Ge. 18. 25; Ex. 2. 14; 18. 22; De. 1. 16, &c.

6. THE MIDIANITESS,] i.e. so distinguished because of high rank among her own people (v. 15), and of her conspicuous punishment.

A MAN,] even Zimri, son of Sallu, v. 14.

WEEPING,] because of the Lord's anger, and command to Moses.

MEETING,] where they had assembled to hear the word of the Lord, according to custom and appointment.

7. PHINEAS,] see Ex. 6. 25, &c.

JAVELIN,] as in Jud. 5. 8; 1 K. 18. 28; 1 Ch. 12. 8, 24; 2 Ch. 11. 12; 14. 8; 25. 5; 26. 14; Neh. 4. 13, 16, 21; Jer. 46. 4; Eze. 39. 9; Joel 3. 10; from a root probably signifying 'to throw.'

8. HOLLOW PLACE.] The noun does not occur elsewhere, but it is derived from a verb root signifying 'to pierce,' or 'make hollow.'

PIERCETH,] as in 1 Sa. 31. 4; Jud. 9. 54; 1 Ch. 10. 4; Zech. 12. 10; 13. 3, &c.

BELLY.] This original word does not occur elsewhere, and it is etymologically connected with the word which in the first clause is rendered 'hollow place.'

RESTRAINED,] as in Ge. 16. 2, &c.

9. FOUR AND TWENTY.] Paul in 1 Cor. 10. 8, speaks only of 23,000; perhaps the remainder were hanged.

11. WITH MY ZEAL,] not 'for my sake,' as in C.V.

MY ZEAL,] not 'my jealousy,' as in C.V.; same word as in previous clause, see note on Ex. 20. 25.

12. COVENANT OF PEACE.] Compare Isa. 54. 10; Eze. 34. 25; 37. 26; Mal. 2. 5; i.e. My covenant conferring peace.

MAKE ATONEMENT.] lit. 'make a covering' for their sins, i.e. do that by which their sins are hidden as it were, from God's sight. See note on Ge. 6. 14; 32. 20; Ex. 21. 30, &c.

14. ZIMRI,] lit. 'praised.'

SALU,] lit. 'valued.'

15. COZBI,] lit. 'lying.'

ZUR,] lit. 'a rock.'

17. DISTRESS,] as in Ex. 18. 18; Nu. 33. 55, &c.

18. ARE ADVERSARIES,] as in Ex. 23. 22, &c., or 'are distressing you.'

FRAUDS.] Not found elsewhere as a noun, but compare the verbal form in next clause, and in Mal. 1. 14; Ps. 105. 25; Ge. 37. 18.

ACTED FRAUDULENTLY.] See preceding remark.

PRINCE,] lit. 'lifted up' one, as in Ge. 17. 20.

FOR THE MATTER,] not 'for the sake' of Peor, as in C.V.

XXVI. 1. PLAGUE,] mentioned in the preceding chapter.

ELEAZAR.] Aaron being now dead, and his son officiating in his stead.

2. TAKE UP THE SUM,] as in Nu. 1. 2, &c., that it might be seen at the end of their journey how God had fulfilled his promise.

ALL THE COMPANY,] except the Levites, as appears from v. 62.

3. WITH THEM,] that is, 'the heads of the people,' as on the former occasion.

4. COMMANDED,] as He had done before; David's sin was in numbering the people without a command, and to gratify his vanity.

5. REUBEN.] At the previous numbering recorded in 1. 20, 21, this tribe consisted of 46,500, now only of 43,730, being a diminution of 2,770, which was partly caused by their having engaged in the conspiracy of Korah, and being punished for it.

HANOCH,] lit. 'trained, dedicated,' Ex. 6. 14.

PALLU,] lit. 'wonderful, separated.'

6. HEZRON,] lit. 'enclosure.'

CARMI,] lit. 'a vine-dresser.'

8. ELIAB,] lit. 'my God is Father,' Nu. 1. 9, &c.

9. NEMUEL,] lit. 'day of God,' so Gesenius.

DATHAN,] lit. 'a law.'

ABIRAM,] lit. 'my father is high.'

10. SIGN,] as in Ex. 17. 15; Nu. 21. 8, 9, &c.

11. DIED NOT.] See note on 16. 32, 33.

12. SIMEON.] This tribe previously numbered 59,300 and now only 22,200, a decrease of 37,100; it has been supposed that most of the 24,000 who were slain as recorded in the preceding chapter were of this tribe, as the most conspicuous offender, Cozbi, undoubtedly was (see 25. 14).

NEMUEL,] see on v. 9 above.

JAMIN,] lit. the 'right' hand.

JACHIN,] lit. 'he prepares, establishes.'

13. ZERAH,] lit. 'a rising, bursting forth.'

SHAUL,] lit. 'asked for.'

15. GAD.] This tribe previously numbered 45,650, and now only 40,500, a decrease of 5,150.

ZEPHON,] lit. 'a watching, looking out.'

HAGGI,] lit. 'festive.'

SHUNI,] lit. 'quiet.'

16. OZNI,] lit. 'hearing.'

ERI,] lit. 'watching.'

17. ARODI,] lit. 'a wild ass,' so Gesenius.

ARELI,] lit. 'son of a hero,' so Gesenius.

19. JUDAH.] This tribe previously numbered 74,600, and now 76,500, an increase of 1,900.

ER,] lit. 'a watcher.'

ONAN,] lit. 'strong.'

20. SHELAH,] lit. 'request.'

PHAREZ,] lit. 'a breaking forth.'

ZERAH,] as in v. 13 above.

21. HEZRON,] as in v. 6 above.

HAMUL,] lit. 'a pitied or spared one.'

23. ISSACHAR.] This tribe formerly numbered 54,400, and now 64,300, an increase of 9,900.

TOLA,] lit. 'a worm or scarlet.'

PUA,] lit. 'mouth.'

24. JASHUB,] lit. 'inhabited.'

SHIMRON,] lit. 'watch, guard.'

26. ZEBULON.] This tribe formerly numbered 57,400, and now 60,500, an increase of 3,100.

SERED,] lit. 'fear, humbling.'

ELON,] lit. 'an oak.'

JAHLEEL,] lit. 'waiting for God.'

29. MANASSEH.] This tribe formerly numbered 32,200, and now 52,700, an increase of 20,500.

MACHIR,] lit. 'sold.'

GILEAD,] lit. 'heap of testimony.'

30. JEEZER,] lit. 'where is help?' or 'there is no help.'

HELEK,] lit. 'a portion, share.'

31. ASRIEL,] lit. 'a binding of God.'

SHECHEM,] lit. 'a shoulder.'

32. SHEMIDA,] lit. 'fame of knowledge.'

HEPHER,] lit. 'a digging

33. ZELOPHEHAD,] lit. 'first-breach.'

MAHLAH,] lit. 'disease, sickness.'

NOAH,] lit. 'wandering.'

HOGLAH,] lit. 'a partridge?'

MILCAH,] lit. 'queen or counsel.'

TIRZAH,] lit. 'pleasure.'

35. EPHRAIM.] This tribe formerly numbered 40,500, and now only 32,500, a decrease of 8,000.

SHUTHELAH,] lit. 'crushing of rending,' so Gesenius.

BECHER,] lit. 'a young camel.'

TAHAN,] lit. 'a camp.

36. ERAN,] lit. 'watcher.'

38. BENJAMIN.] This tribe formerly numbered 35,400, and now 45,600, an increase of 10,200.

BELA,] lit. 'devouring, swallowing.'

ASHBEL,] lit. 'opinion of God,' so Gesenius.

AHIRAM,] lit. 'my brother is high.'

39. SHUPHAM,] lit. 'serpent?'

HUPHAM,] lit. 'inhabitant of a haven.'

40. ARD,] lit. 'a fugitive?'

NAAMAN,] lit. 'pleasant.'

42. DAN.] This tribe formerly numbered 62,700, and now 64,400, an increase of 1,700.

SHUHAM,] lit. 'a pit-digger.'

44. ASHER.] This tribe formerly numbered 41,500, and now 53,400, an increase of 11,900.

JIMNA,] lit. 'prosperity?'

JESUI,] lit. 'equal, level.'

BERIAH,] lit. 'in evil.'

45. HEBER,] lit. 'company.'

MALCHIEL,] lit. 'my king is God.'

46. SARAH,] lit. 'spread out.'

48. NAPHTALI.] This tribe formerly numbered 53,400, and now only 45,400, a decrease of 8,000.

JAHZEEL,] lit. 'God divides or halves.'

GUNI,] lit. 'coloured.'

49. JEZER,] lit. 'frame, formation '

SHILLEM,] lit. 'recompense.'

51. 601,730,] while formerly they numbered 603,550, showing a decrease of 1,820 on the whole; four tribes decreasing, and the others increasing.

52. TO THESE,] excluding the tribe of Levi.

55. ONLY,] not 'nevertheless,' as in C.V. Every thing was to be done by a direct appeal to God, which the use of the lot implies. How impious then for men—members of Christian Churches—to ask God to decide who of them shall get any paltry prize of a *chair*, or *book*, or *walking-stick!* See note on Lev. 16. 8; Prov. 16. 33, &c.

56. INHERITANCE,] not 'possession,' as in C.V.

57. FAMILIES,] even the three great divisions of the three sons of Levi.

58. LIBNITE,] son of Gershon, Ex. 6. 17.

HEBRONITE,] son of Kohath, Ex 6. 18.

MAHLITE,] son of Merari, Ex. 6. 19.

MUSHITE,] son of Merari, Ex. 6. 19.

KORATHITE,] son of Izhar, son of Kohath.

AMRAM,] Ex. 16. 18.

59. JOCHEBED,] his aunt, or father's sister.

SISTER,] the eldest of the family, though mentioned last.

60. ITHAMAR,] Ex. 6. 23.

61. STRANGE FIRE.] Lev. 10. 1, 2.

62. 23,000,] while in the previous numbering they were 22,000, being an increase of 1,000.

63. WHO NUMBERED,] by the hand of the heads of the people; what a person commands to be done is reckoned as being done by him.

64. SINAI,] thirty-eight years before.

65. SAID,] in 14. 32.

XXVII. 1. DAUGHTERS.] He had no sons, according to 26. 33; 27. 3.

TIRZAH.] See these names and their significations in notes on 26. 33.

3. KORAH,] as narrated in 16. 1, 2.

FOR HIS OWN SIN] against God, not for any special transgression among men.

4. WITHDRAWN,] as in Lev. 27. 18.

5. BEFORE JEHOVAH,] as in Ex. 18. 15, 19, being a case for which there was no precedent. Compare Lev. 24. 11; Nu. 9. 8; 15. 34.

7. GIVE,] see Josh. 17. 3, 4.

11. IT HATH BEEN,] not, 'it shall be,' as in the C.V.; it is evidently the language of the writer, not of God.

STATUTE OF JUDGMENT,] as in 35. 29.

12. ABARIM,] *lit.* 'the places beyond,' on the east of the Jordan; a mountain range, of which Nebo is one part (whose top is Pisgah); compare 33. 47, 48; De. 32. 49; Jer. 22. 20; also De. 34. 1.

13. GATHERED,] as in Ge. 25. 8, 17, &c. Compare Nu. 20. 26—28.

14. MY MOUTH,] as in 20. 24.

ZIN,] see note on 20. 12.

KADESH.] This is added to distinguish it from the previous strife at Rephidim, recorded in Ex. 17. 7. See De. 32. 51.

16. GOD..FLESH.] Compare the same expression in 16. 22.

APPOINT,] as in 3. 10, &c.

17. GO OUT..COME IN,] as in De. 31. 2; 1 Sa. 8. 20; 18. 13; 2 Ch. 1. 10

NO SHEPHERD,] as in 1 K. 22. 17; 2 Ch. 18. 16; Zech. 10. 2.

18. SPIRIT,] having his graces, even 'faith' in believing God's promise, as one of the spies, 'faithfulness' to Moses and his cause, 'courage' to fight, and 'skill' to lead on the hosts of the Lord, Ex. 17. 9—13; 24. 13; 33. 11.

LAID,] in token of a transference of authority from Moses to Joshua, indicating the concurrence of Moses.

19. PRIEST,] that he might receive the anointing oil, indicating the approval of God.

COMPANY,] that they might see him thus honoured, and testify their consent.

CHARGED HIM,] regarding his duty to God and to Israel.

20. HONOUR,] as in 1 Ch. 16. 27; 29. 11, 25; Job 37. 22; 39. 20; 40. 10; Ps. 8. 1; 21. 5; 45. 3; 96. 6; 104. 1; 111. 3; 145. 5; 148. 13; Prov. 21; Hos. 14. 6; Hab. 3. 3; Zech. 6. 13; 10. 3.

21. ASKED,] when necessary for public business, for only by God's words were they to do any thing nationally, as in next clause.

THE LIGHTS,] *lit.* 'the Urim,' as in Ex. 28. 30. &c., on which see note.

22. MOSES.] Here we have an example of his faithfulness and patriotism; no murmurings, or envyings, in his own sons being passed by unnoticed.

XXVIII. 2. OFFERING,] *lit.* any thing 'brought near,' as in Lev. 1. 2, &c., a general term.

BREAD,] i.e. food, see note on Ge. 3. 19, &c.

FIRE-OFFERINGS,] Ex. 29. 18, &c.

SWEET FRAGRANCE,] Ge. 8. 21, &c.

TAKE HEED,] as in 23. 12, &c.

BRING NEAR,] as in 5. 16, &c.

SEASON,] whether morning or evening, daily, weekly, monthly, or yearly.

3. FIRE-OFFERING.] Compare Ex. 29. 38, &c., for a similar account of the daily whole burnt-offering.

PERFECT ONES.] This phrase is lacking in the laws recorded in Ex. 29. 38.

4. PREPAREST,] *lit.* 'makest.'

MORNING..EVENINGS.] See note on Ex. 29. 39.

5. EPHAH.] See Ex. 16. 36, &c.

FLOUR,] as in Ge. 18. 6, &c.

PRESENT,] as in Ex. 4. 3, &c.

MIXED,] as in Ex. 29. 2, &c.

BEATEN OIL,] as in Ex. 27. 20, &c.

PIN,] as in Ex. 29. 40, &c.

6. CONTINUAL,] as in Ex. 25. 30, &c.

BURNT-OFFERING,] as in Ge. 8. 20, &c.

MADE,] not 'ordained,' as in the C.V.

SINAI.] See Ex. 29. 42, &c.

7. LIBATION,] as in Ge. 35. 14, &c.

SANCTUARY,] Ex. 30. 13, &c.

STRONG DRINK.] See on Lev. 10. 9, &c.

9. SABBATH-DAY,] twice as much as on other days.

11. BEGINNINGS,] on the first day of each month, at the new moon, Nu. 10. 10; 1 Sa. 20. 5; 2 K. 4. 23; 1 Ch. 23. 31; 2 Ch. 2. 4 Ezra 3. 5; Neh. 10. 33; Isa. 1. 13, 14; Eze 45. 17; 46. 6; Hos. 2. 11; Amos 8. 5.

H

BURNT-OFFERING,] very large, as only oc-
currrng once a month.
12—14.] as in 15. 4—10, only the quantity
of oil is not mentioned here.
15. KID,] as in 15. 24; 28. 22.
LIBATION,] which was not to be neglected,
though the special burnt-offering was so
great.
16. FIRST MONTH,] Nisan or Abib, Ex. 12.
2; 13. 4.
PASSOVER,] Ex. 12. 6—27.
17. A FESTIVAL,] as in Ex. 10. 9; Lev. 23.
6, of unleavened food.
EATEN.] See Ex. 12. 15, 18.
18. FIRST DAY] of unleavened food.
CONVOCATION,] as in Ex. 12. 16; or 'reading,' as in Neh. 8. 8.
SERVILE,] as in Lev. 23. 7, &c.
19. BURNT-OFFERING,] of the same kind
and number of animals as in v. 11 above.
20—21.] as in v. 12, 13 above.
23. THESE,] on the 15th day of the 1st
month till the 21st inclusive, even seven days.
25. CONVOCATION.] See on v. 18 above.
26. FIRST-FRUITS,] of the wheat-harvest,
called Pentecost, being fifty days from the
sheaf of the wave-offering being presented
to the Lord.
NEW PRESENT,] described in Lev. 23.15—17.
WEEKS,] i.e. seven complete ones.
CONVOCATION, ETC.] See Ex. 23. 21.
27—30.] Compare v. 11—24.
31. The necessity of keeping up the daily
sacrifice is again enjoined, which shews that
great special sacrifices and services rendered to God, do not supersede the necessity
of daily habitual obedience.

XXIX. 1. SEVENTH MONTH,] i.e. Tisri,
part of our September and October.
FIRST] of the month. Compare Lev. 23. 24.
SHOUTING,] indicating triumph.
2. PERFECT ONES.] Compare the numbers
with 28. 11, 19, 27.
3—5.] Compare the quantities with 28. 12,
13, 20, 21, 28, 29.
6. APART] from the usual burnt-offering
which is offered every month, and from the
daily sacrifice, so that on the first day of
the seventh month there were three distinct
sacrifices.
7. TENTH.] See Lev. 16. 29; 23. 27.
HUMBLED.] Compare Acts 27. 9.
8. BURNT-OFFERING,] as in v. 2 above.
9—11.] Compare v. 3—6 above.
12. FIFTEENTH.] Compare Lev. 23. 33; De.
16. 13; Eze. 45. 25.
FESTIVAL,] that of Tabernacles or Booths.
13. BROUGHT NEAR,] on the first day of
the festivals 13 bullocks, &c.
17. SECOND] day, 12 bullocks, &c.
20. THIRD] day, 11 bullocks, &c.
23. FOURTH] day, 10 bullocks, &c.
26. FIFTH] day, 9 bullocks, &c.
29. SIXTH] day, 8 bullocks, &c.
32. SEVENTH] day, 7 bullocks, &c.
35. EIGHTH] day, a restraint, as in Lev.
23. 36, &c.
36—38.] Compare v. 2, 8 above.
39. PEACE-OFFERINGS,] which were voluntary offerings. Lev. 7. 11—16; 22. 21, 23.

XXX. 1. HEADS] of the tribes, as in De.
1. 15; 5. 23.
2. WHEN,] a man, not 'if,' as in the C.V.;
so also in v. 3.
TO BIND] a bond upon his soul, not as in
the C.V. 'to bind his soul with a bond.'
POLLUTE,] as in Eze. 39. 7. Compare De.
23. 21—23; Ecc. 5. 4, 5.
HE DOTH,] if the thing in itself be lawful;
a thing in itself positively unlawful can
never become lawful by an oath.
3. A BOND] on her soul, as in v. 4.
HER FATHER,] being unmarried and under
his protection.
HER YOUTH,] i.e. in her virginity.
KEPT SILENT,] as in Ge. 24. 21, &c.
ESTABLISHED,] by his tacit consent; this
injunction was calculated to make parents
more watchful over their children and de-
pendants.
5. DISALLOWED,] as in v. 8, 11; Ps. 33. 10;
141. 5. Compare the use of the same original word in Nu. 32. 7, 9.
PROPITIOUS,] as in Ex. 34. 9, &c.; she
was guilty in speaking unadvisedly with her
lips.
DISALLOWED HER,] whether with or without reasons; parental authority was supreme.
6. BE AT ALL TO A] husband, not 'if she
had at all a husband,' the female in Scripture is always spoken of as belonging to the
man, not the man to the woman; she is
here supposed to be betrothed, but not yet
removed to her husband's house; her husband even now is her lord, and not her
father.
WRONGFUL UTTERANCE,] as in v. 8, and
compare Lev. 5. 4; Prov. 12. 18; Ps. 106. 33.
7. KEPT SILENT,] as in v. 3 above.
8. BROKEN,] as in Ge. 17. 14.
PROPITIOUS,] as in v. 5.
9. WIDOW,] lit. a dumb (i.e. silent) or forsaken one. Ge. 38. 11, &c.
CAST OUT ONE,] from her husband's house,
and no longer under law to him. Lev. 21.
7, 14, &c.
ESTABLISHED,] having no one to control
her actions.
10. HOUSE] of her husband, having been
removed there from (v. 6) her father's
dwelling.
11. KEPT SILENT,] as in v. 3, 7 above.
12. OUT-GOING,] as in Nu. 30. 12, &c.
13. HUMBLE,] as in Lev. 16. 31, &c.
15. INIQUITY,] or punishment, as in Ge. 4.
13. &c.
16. STATUTES,] as in Ge. 47. 26.

XXXI. 1. EXECUTE,] lit. 'avenge the vengeance,' as in Lev. 26. 25; Jud. 16. 28.
2. AGAINST,] lit. 'from the Midianites.
See 25. 17.
GATHERED.] See 27. 13.
3. BE YE ARMED,] or 'be ye delivered,' as
the word is used in Ps. 60. 5. 108. 6; Prov.
11. 8, 9; compare Nu. 32. 17, 20, also v. 5
below, where they are said to be 'given out.
HOST,] not 'war,' as in the C.V., which
the original word never means, see Ge. 2. 1,
&c. So in v. 4. 6.

THEY ARE,] not 'go.'
TO PUT,] *lit.* 'to give' the vengeance, as in 2 Sa. 4. 8; 22. 48; Ps. 18. 47.
5. GIVEN OUT,] compare v. 3, 'be ye delivered.'
6. ELEAZAR,] who was the Lord's representative, it being His war, and not merely the people's.
HOLY VESSELS,] probably the ark, &c., which were sometimes taken out to battle, (Jos. 6. 4; 1 Sam. 4. 3, 4,) but some think the next word 'and,' should be rendered 'even.' For 'holy vessels,' see 1 K. 8. 4; 2 Ch. 5. 5; Ezra 8. 28.
TRUMPETS] of the shouting, compare Lev. 23. 24; Nu. 10. 2, 8, 9, 10, &c.
7. EVERY MALE,] who fell into their hands, preserving the females, as in v. 9, 15, &c.
8. KINGS,] even Evi, Rekem, Zur, Hur, Reba, who in Josh. 13. 21, are styled 'princes,' or 'honoured ones.'
PIERCED ONES,] as in Ge. 34. 27, &c.
SWORD,] Josh. 13. 22.
9. THE WOMEN,] not 'all' the women, as the C.V. has it. See Jud. 6. 1, 2.
SUBSTANCE,] or 'gettings.'
WEALTH,] as in Ge. 34. 29, &c.
PLUNDERED,] as in Ge. 34. 27, &c.
10. WITH,] or 'among.'
HABITATIONS,] *lit.* 'seats,' Ge. 10. 30, &c.
TOWERS,] as in Ge. 25. 16.
12. JERICHO.] See 22. 1.
14. INSPECTORS] of the force, as in 2 K. 11. 15, &c.
THE HOST] of the battle, 132 in number, 13 belonging to each tribe.
15. FEMALE,] not 'woman,' as in Ge. 1. 27, &c.
16. WORD,] not 'counsel.'
PEOR.] See 23. 28, &c.
PLAGUE,] see 25. 9.
17. KNOWN,] compare Jud. 21. 11.
18. YOURSELVES,] for handmaids or wives.
19. ENCAMP YE,] as in Ge. 26. 17, &c.; the camp being legally reckoned pure, and they impure.
PIERCED ONE,] as in v. 8 above.
THIRD..SEVENTH.] Compare 19. 11.
20. GARMENT.] See Lev. 11. 25, 28, 40, &c.
SKIN-VESSEL.] See 11. 32, &c.
WORK] of goats' hair. See Ex. 25. 4, &c.
WOODEN VESSEL.] See Lev. 11. 32, &c.
YE YOURSELVES CLEANSE] by washing, Nu. 8. 21, &c.
21. STATUTE,] as in Ge. 26. 5, &c.
23. MAY GO INTO,] as in 27. 27, &c.
WATER] of separation, Compare 19. 9.
24. SEVENTH] day, like the leper, Lev. 14. 9.
26. TAKE THE SUM,] as in Ex. 30. 12.
HEADS] of the fathers, as in Ex. 6. 14.
27. HALVED,] as in Ge. 32. 7.
THOSE HANDLING] the battle, compare Ge. 4. 21; Jer. 2. 8; 46. 9, &c.
COMPANY.] Compare 1 Sa. 30. 24, 25; Ps. 68. 12.
28. RAISED,] as in 18. 26; 31. 52.
A BODY,] *lit.* 'breathing creature,' whether woman, or ox, or ass, or sheep.
HERD,] as in Ge. 12. 16.
FLOCK,] as in v. 30.

29. THE HEAVE-OFFERING,] not 'a heave-offering.'
30. ONE POSSESSION,] as in v. 47.
OF MAN,] i.e human beings, for only females were saved.
HERD,] as in v. 28.
ALL THE CATTLE,] as in Ge. 2. 20.
JEHOVAH,] that these also might have reason to rejoice over the victory.
32. PREY,] *lit.* 'captured thing.' Compare v. 11, 12, 26, 27.
SPOIL,] as in Nu. 14. 3, 31.
SPOILED,] as in Ge. 34. 27.
OF THE FLOCK,] i.e. sheep and goats.
33. OF THE HERD,] as in v. 28, 30.
35. HUMAN BEINGS,] as in Ge. 9. 5; Lev. 24. 17; Nu. 19. 11, 13, 40.
36. OF THE FLOCK,] as in v. 32.
38. THE HERD,] as in v. 28, 30.
40. HUMAN BEINGS,] as in v. 35 above.
MOSES,] in v. 29 above.
42. HALVED,] as in Ge. 32. 7.
43. OF THE FLOCK,] as in v. 32. 36.
44. OF THE HERD,] as in v. 28. 30.
46. HUMAN BEINGS,] as in Ge. 9. 5, &c.
47. THE ONE POSSESSION,] from the fifty as in v. 30 above.
MOSES,] in v. 30 above.
48. INSPECTORS,] as in v. 14.
HEADS,] as in v. 14 above.
49. WITH US,] *lit.* 'in our hand,' as in Ge 44. 16, &c.
MISSED,] as in Jud. 21. 3; 1 Sa. 20. 18, &c.
50. OFFERING,] as in Lev. 1. 2.
FOUND,] not 'gotten,' as in C.V. see Ge. 2,20
VESSELS,] *lit.* 'instruments,' as in v. 6. 20.
SEAL-RING,] as in Ge. 41. 21.
LEAD,] as in Ex. 35. 22; not found elsewhere.
51. MADE VESSEL,] *lit.* 'vessel of work.'
52. HEAVE OFFERING,] as in Ex. 25. 2.
LIFTED UP,] as in Ge. 14. 22.
HEADS,] as in v. 14 above.
54. JEHOVAH,] of His wonderful providential interference on their behalf, that not one of them had perished.

XXXII. 1. JAZER,] see Nu. 21. 32; previously part of the kingdom of Sihon.
GILEAD,] formerly part of the kingdom of Og, king of Bashan.
FOR CATTLE.] Compare the allusions in Jer. 48. 32; De. 32. 14; Ps. 22. 12; Song 4. 1; Mic. 7. 14.
3. ATAROTH,] see v. 34; Jos. 16. 2, 7; belonging to the Amorites, along with Dibon and Jazer.
DIBON,] see 21. 30; Isa. 15. 2.
JAZER,] see v. 1 above; 21. 32, fifteen miles from Heshbon.
NIMRAH,] not mentioned elsewhere, but compare Beth-Nimrah (v. 36), and Nimrim, Isa. 15. 6.
HESHBON,] see 21. 25, 26; Isa. 15. 4.
ELEALEH,] see v. 37; Isa. 15. 4; 16. 9; Jer. 48. 34, one mile from Heshbon.
SEBAM,] not mentioned elsewhere, but compare Shibmah, v. 38; Isa. 16. 18; Jer.48. 32.
NEBO,] see v. 38; 33. 47; De. 32. 49; 34. 1; 1 Ch. 5. 8; Ezra 2. 29; 10. 43; Neh. 7. 33; Isa. 15. 2; Jer. 48. 1, 22.

BEON,] not mentioned elsewhere, but compare Baal-Meon, v. 38, and Beth-Baal-Meon, Jos. 13. 17; nine miles from Heshbon.
6. THE CATTLE,] as in Ge. 14. 2, 8.
7. PASSING OVER] the Jordan into Canaan.
GIVEN] by oath to Abraham, Ge. 12. 7, &c.
8. KADESH-BARNEA,] see v. 13. 26; 34. 4; De. 1. 2, 19; 2. 14; 9. 23; Jos. 10. 41; 14. 6, 7; 15. 3.
9. ESHCOL,] see 13. 17, 23, 24.
10. BURNETH,] as in Ge. 30. 2, &c.
DAY,] not 'time,' as in C.V.
11. NOT SEE,] lit. 'if they see.'
BEEN FULLY AFTER ME,] as in v. 12; Jos. 14. 8, 9, 14; 1 K. 11. 6. Compare De. 1. 21.
SWORN,] as in 14. 28. 29.
12. CALEB,] see 13. 6; 14. 30.
JEPHUNNEH,] see 13. 6.
KENEZITE,] see Gen. 15. 19.
JOSHUA,] see Ex. 17. 9, &c.
NUN,] see Ex. 33. 11, &c.
BEEN FULLY AFTER] Jehovah, as in v. 11 above.
13. BURNETH,] as in v. 10 above.
FORTY,] strictly only 38 years, but compare the language in 14. 33.
15. HIM,] or 'it,' i.e. Israel.
DONE CORRUPTLY,] as in Ge. 38. 9, &c.
16. THEY,] i.e. sons of Reuben and Gad.
BUILT,] or rebuilded, as in v. 24.
17. ARE ARMED,] or 'are delivered,' see 31. 3; 34. 20, 21.
HASTING,] as in De. 32. 35; 1 Sa. 20. 38; Job 20. 2; 31. 5; Ps. 22. 19; 38. 22; 40. 13; 70. 1, 5; 71. 12; 119. 60; 141. 1; Ecc. 2. 25; Isa. 8. 1; Hab. 1. 8.
THEIR PLACE] of rest in Canaan, which God had given to them.
DEFENCE,] as in 13. 9, and v. 36 below.
18. INHERITANCE,] See Josh. 22. 1—6.
19. BEYOND] the Jordan, and yonder, on the west of the Jordan.
BEYOND] the Jordan, at the sun-rising, on the east side of it.
20. ARE ARMED,] or 'are delivered,' as 31. 3, &c.
JEHOVAH,] not merely before the sons of Israel, as they had said in v. 17.
21. DISPOSSESSING,] as in Ex. 15. 9; 34. 24, &c.
22. SUBDUED,] as in v. 29; Josh. 18. 1.
HAVE BEEN ACQUITTED,] or innocent, free, as in Gen. 24. 41.
BY JEHOVAH,] and by Israel, not 'before,' them as in C.V.
23. KNOW YE,] as in Ge. 20. 7.
FIND YOU OUT,] as in Ge. 44. 16.
25. IS COMMANDING,] and in v. 27, 'is saying,' more expressive than the simple present tense.
26. CATTLE,] or 'gettings.'
BEASTS,] as in Ge. 6. 7.
GILEAD,] see v. 1.
27. BEFORE JEHOVAH,] as in v. 20.
28. HEADS OF THE FATHERS,] as in Ex. 6. 14.
29. GILEAD,] see v. 1 above.
31. THAT WHICH,] not 'as, as in the C.V.
32. AND WITH US IS,] not 'that' it may be.
33. SIHON,] see 1. 21; 21. 24—35.
OG,] see 21. 33.
BORDERS,] not 'coasts.'

34. BUILT, or rebuilt.
AROER,] see De. 2. 36; 3. 12; 4. 48; Jos. 12. 2; 13. 9, 16, 25; Jud. 11. 33; 1 Sa. 30. 28; 2 Sa. 24. 5; 2 K. 10. 33; 1 Ch. 5. 8; Isa. 17. 2; Jer. 48. 19.
35. ATROTH, SHOPHAN,] not mentioned elsewhere.
JAAZER,] see 21. 32, and v. 3 above.
JOGBEAH,] as in Jud. 8. 11.
36. BETH-NIMRAH,] as in Jos. 13. 27, and in v. 3 above.
BETH-HARAN,] perhaps the same with Beth-Aram in Josh. 13. 27.
37. BUILT,] or rebuilt.
HESHBON,] see 21. 25.
ELEALEH,] as in v. 3 above.
KIRJATHAIM,] as in Jos. 13. 19; 1 Ch. 6. 76; Jer. 48. 1, 23; Eze. 25. 9.
38. NEBO,] see v. 3 above.
BAAL-MEON,] see 1 Ch. 5. 8; Eze. 25. 9.
SIBMAH,] see Josh. 13. 18; Isa. 16. 8, 9, Jer. 48. 32, and v. 3 below.
39. GILEAD,] see v. 1 above.
DISPOSSESS,] see v. 21 above.
40. MACHIR,] see Ge. 50. 23.
41. JAIR,] see De. 3. 14; Jos. 13. 30; Jud. 10. 3, 4, 5; 1 K. 4. 13; 1 Ch. 2. 22, 23; Esth. 2. 5.
TOWNS,] see De. 3. 14; Jos. 13. 30; Jud. 10. 4; 1 K. 4. 13; 1 Ch. 2. 23.
42. NOBAH,] see Jud. 8. 11.
KENATH,] see 1 Ch. 2. 23.
VILLAGES,] lit. ' daughters,' as in 21. 25.

XXXIII. 1. JOURNEYS,] as in Ge. 13. 3, Ex. 17. 1, &c. They are forty-two in number.
HOSTS,] as in Ex. 6. 26; 7. 4; 12. 17, 41, 51, &c.
2. OUT-GOINGS,] as in Ps. 65, 8.
MOUTH,] of Jehovah; his writings then were designed by God to be useful in after days.
3. RAMESES,] see Ex. 12. 37, and v. 5 below.
FIRST MONTH,] viz. Nisan or Abib, i.e. part of March and April.
MORROW] of the passover, which was held on the 14th of the month.
HIGH HAND,] as in Ex. 14. 8.
4. ARE BURYING,] in the very act of doing so, when Israel are going out; burial in the east is very rapid.
JUDGMENTS,] as in Ex. 12. 12; 18. 11; compare Isa. 19. 1; Rev. 12. 8.
5. ENCAMP,] as in v. 6, 15, 18, &c. below.
SUCCOTH,] see Ex. 12. 37.
6. ETHAM,] see Ex. 13. 20.
WILDERNESS] of Etham, Ex. 13. 20.
7. TURN BACK,] as in Ex. 14. 2.
PI-HAHIROTH,] Ex. 14. 2, 9.
BAAL-ZEPHON,] Ex. 14. 2, 9.
MIGDOL,] Ex. 14. 2.
8. SEA,] as in Ex. 14. 2.
MARAH,] Ex. 15. 23.
9. ELIM,] Ex. 15. 27.
TWELVE,] as in Ex. 15. 27.
SEVENTY,] as in Ex. 15. 27.
10. RED SEA,] lit. ' sea of Suph,' see note on Ex. 10. 19; this encampment is not mentioned in Ex. 16. 1.
11. SIN,] Ex. 16. 1.

12. DOPHKAH,] not mentioned elsewhere; *lit.* 'a beating *or* knocking.'

13. ALUSH,] not mentioned elsewhere.

14. REPHIDIM,] Ex. 17. 1, 8.

15. SINAI,] Ex. 16. 1.

16. KIBROTH-HATTAAVAH,] Nu. 11. 34. 35.

17. HAZEROTH,] Nu. 11. 35. Here Miriam was smitten with leprosy.

18. RITHMAH,] not mentioned elsewhere, but some suppose it the same as Kadesh-Barnea, compare 2. 16; 13. 1, 26; 32. 8; De. 2. 19; Josh. 14. 7.

19. RIMMON-PAREZ,] *lit.* 'pomegranate of the breach,' not mentioned elsewhere.

20. LIBNAH,] *lit.* 'whiteness,' not mentioned elsewhere.

21. RISSAH,] *lit.* 'a drop,' not mentioned elsewhere.

22. KEHELATHAH,] *lit.* 'an assembly,' not mentioned elsewhere.

23. SHAPHER,] *lit.* 'beauty,' not mentioned elsewhere.

24. HARADAH,] *lit.* 'fear, trembling,' not mentioned elsewhere.

25. MAKHELOTH,] *lit.* 'assemblies,' not mentioned elsewhere.

26. TAHATH,] *lit.* 'place,' not mentioned elsewhere.

27. TARAH,] *lit.* 'delay,' not mentioned elsewhere.

28. MITHCAH,] *lit.* 'sweetness,' not mentioned elsewhere.

29. HASHMONAH,] *lit.* 'fatness,' not mentioned elsewhere.

30. MOSEROTH,] *lit.* 'bonds;' in De. 10. 6 'Mosera.'

31. BENRE-JAAKAN,] *lit.* 'sons of Jaakan,' in De. 10. 6 more fully 'Beeroth (i.e. wells) of the sons of Jaakan.'

32. HOR HAGIDGAD] *or* Gudgodah, in De. 10. 7.

33. JOTBATHAH.] See De. 10. 7.

34. EBRONAH,] *lit.* 'a passage,' not mentioned elsewhere.

35. EZION-GEBER.] See De. 2. 8; 1 K. 9. 26; 22. 48; 2 Ch. 8. 17; 20. 36.

36. ZIN,] Nu. 13. 21.

KADESH,] Nu. 13. 26.

37. HOR,] Nu. 20. 22.

EDOM,] see 20. 16—23.

38. COMMAND,] *lit.* 'mouth,' as in v. 2.

OF THE GOING OUT,] not 'after,' as in C.V.

FIFTH] month, i.e. Ab, four months after Miriam, 20. 1, 25—29.

39. 123 YEARS.] He was 83 when he stood before Pharaoh (Ex. 7. 7), forty years before.

40. KING OF ARAD.] See note on 21. 1—3.

41. ZALMONAH,] *lit.* 'a shadow,' not mentioned elsewhere.

42. PUNON,] *lit.* 'distraction, pining away.'

43. OBOTH,] *lit.* 'bottles,' see 21. 10, 11.

44. IJE-ABARIM,] *lit.* 'heaps of Abarim,' Nu. 21. 11.

45. IIM,] *lit.* 'heaps,' Jos. 15. 29.

DIBON-GAD,] *lit.* 'pain *or* grief of Gad,' Nu. 21. 30.

46. ALMON-DIBLATHAIM,] *lit.* 'a concealment of branches of figs,' not mentioned elsewhere.

47. ABARIM,] *lit.* 'places beyond' *or* 'passages,' Nu. 27. 12.

NEBO,] *lit.* 'prophecy,' see v. 3 above.

48. PLAINS] of Moab, where they now were.

49. BETH-JESHIMOTH,] *lit.* 'house of the deserts,' Jos. 12. 3; 13. 20; Eze. 25. 9.

ABEL-SHITTIM,] *lit.* 'meadow *or* mount of shittim wood;' compare Nu. 25. 1; Mic. 6. 5.

52. DISPOSSESSED,] as in Ex. 34. 24, &c.

IMAGERY,] as in Lev. 26. 1.

MOLTEN] images, see on Ex. 32. 4, 8.

LAY WASTE,] as in Lev. 26. 30.

53. POSSESSED,] as in Ex. 15. 19.

54. INHERITED,] as in Lev. 25. 46.

INCREASE,] *or* 'multiply,' as in Ge. 3. 16

DIMINISH,] as in Ex. 30. 15.

GOETH OUT,] as in Ge. 2. 10; Jos. 19. 1, 7, 24, 32, 40; 21. 4; 1 Ch. 24. 7; 25. 9; 26. 14.

55. DISPOSSESS,] as in v. 52 above.

PRICKS.] This original word is not found elsewhere, but see the fulfilment in Jos. 23. 13; Jud. 2. 2; Ps. 106. 34, 36; Ex. 23. 33.

THORNS,] as in Jos. 23. 33.

DISTRESSED,] see on 25. 17.

56. THOUGHT,] as in Jud. 20. 5; Esth. 4. 13; Ps. 48. 9; 50. 21; Isa. 10. 7; 14. 24.

XXXIV. 2. COMMAND,] as in Lev. 24. 2; Nu. 5. 2; 28. 2; 34. 2; De. 2. 4.

BY,] *or* 'in' inheritance, not 'for.'

BY,] *or* 'to' its borders.

3. QUARTER,] as in Ex. 25. 26; 26. 18, 20.

ZIN.] See Nu. 13. 21. Miriam died there, see 20. 1; it is called Kadesh in 33. 36.

BY THE SIDES OF] Edom; compare Ex. 2. 5; De. 2. 37.

SALT SEA,] see Ge. 14. 3.

4. TURNED ROUND,] as in Ge. 19. 4; and v. 5 below.

ASCENT,] as in Ex. 20. 26; Jos. 10. 10; 15. 3, 7; 18. 17; Jud. 1. 36; 8. 13; 1 Sa. 9. 11; 2 Sa. 15. 30, &c.

AKRABBIM,] *lit.* 'scorpions.' Jos. 15. 3; Jud. 1. 36.

ZIN,] as in v. 3 above.

OUT-GOINGS,] as in v. 5. 8, 9, 12; Jos. 15. 4, 7, 11; 16. 3, 8; 17. 9, 18; 18. 12, 14, 19; 19. 14, 22, 29, 33; 1 Ch. 5. 16; Ps. 68. 20; Prov. 4. 23; Eze. 48. 30.

KADESH-BARNEA,] see Nu. 32. 8; 13. 17; 32. 8.

HAZAR-ADDAR,] called 'Adar,' in Jos. 15. 3.

AZMON,] *lit.* 'strong,' v. 5; Jos. 15. 4.

5. TURNED ROUND,] as in v. 4.

BROOK] of Egypt, now called Al-Arish. See Jos. 15. 4, 47; 1 K. 8. 65; 2 K. 24. 7; 2 Ch. 7. 8.

THE SEA,] i.e. the Mediterranean.

6. GREAT SEA,] as above.

7. MARK OUT,] for yourselves; the original verb is only found elsewhere in v. 8.

HOR,] not the mount where Aaron died, but a part of Lebanon, compare Jos. 13. 5.

8. MARK OUT,] as in v. 7.

HAMATH.] See Nu. 13. 21; called 'the great,' in Amos 6. 2.

ZEDAD,] only found elsewhere in Eze. 47. 15, which see.

GONE OUT,] not 'gone on.'

ZIPHRON,] *lit.* a 'sweet smell?' not mentioned elsewhere.

HAZAR-ENAN,] *lit.* 'court of fountains,' only mentioned elsewhere in Eze. 48. 1.

10. MARKED OUT.] The original word does not elsewhere occur with this signification.

SHEPHAM,] *lit.* 'high, sticking out,' not mentioned elsewhere.

11. RIBLAH,] *lit.* 'fertility,' 2 K. 23. 33; 25. 6, 20, 21; Jer. 39. 5, 6; 52. 9, 10, 26, 27; in the land of Hemath.

AIN,] *lit.* 'eye *or* fountain.' Jos. 15. 32; 19. 7; 21. 16; 1 Ch. 4. 32; a city in the tribe of Judah.

SMITTEN AGAINST.] The original word generally means 'to wipe *or* blot out,' as in Ge. 6. 7; 7. 4, 23, &c.

SHOULDER,] as in Ex. 26. 14, 15; 28. 7, 12, &c.

CHINNERETH,] *lit.* 'harps.' De. 3. 17; Jos. 13. 27; 19. 35; called in Eze. 47. 18 'the east sea,' in the New Testament 'sea of Tiberias,' and sea of Gennesaret.'

12. BY] *or* 'to' its borders.

13. TRIBE] of Manasseh.

14. HAVE RECEIVED,] see 32. 33.

17. GIVE THE INHERITANCE,] as in v. 29.

18. TO GIVE] the land, as in v. 17 above.

19. THE MEN,] i.e. the twelve princes or heads of the tribes of Israel.

20. SHEMUEL,] *lit.* 'heard of God,' see 1 Sa. 1. 20.

AMMIHUD,] as in Nu. 1. 10.

21. ELIDAD,] *lit.* 'my God is beloved,' not mentioned elsewhere.

CHISLON,] *lit.* 'folly, confidence,' not mentioned elsewhere.

22. BUKKI,] *lit.* 'my emptiness,' 1 Ch. 6. 5, 51; Ezr. 7. 4.

JOGLI,] *lit.* 'exiled,' not mentioned elsewhere.

23. HANNIEL,] *lit.* 'grace of God,' 1 Ch. 7. 39.

EPHOD,] *lit.* a 'girdle,' not mentioned elsewhere.

24. KEMUEL,] *lit.* 'gathered of God,'₁Ge. 22. 21; 1 Ch. 27. 17.

SHIPHTAN,] *lit.* 'judicial,' not mentioned elsewhere.

25. ELIZAPHAN,] *lit.* 'my God hath hidden,' Ex. 6. 22; Lev. 10. 4; Nu. 3. 30; 1 Ch. 15. 8; 2 Ch. 29. 13.

PARNACH,] *lit.* 'delicate,' not mentioned elsewhere.

26. PALTIEL,] *lit.* an 'escape of God,' 2 Sa. 3. 15.

AZZAN,] *lit.* 'strength,' not mentioned elsewhere.

27. AHIHUD,] *lit.* 'my brother is honour,' not mentioned elsewhere.

SHELOMI,] *lit.* 'my peaceful one,' not mentioned elsewhere.

28. PEDAHEL,] *lit.* 'ransom of God,' not mentioned elsewhere.

AMMIHUD,] see v. 20 above.

29. TO GIVE INHERITANCE,] as in v. 17.

XXXV. 2. COMMAND,] as in 34. 2.

BEASTS,] *lit.* 'living creatures,' as in Ge. 1. 20, 21, 24, 25, 28, 30.

4. 1000 CUBITS,] i.e. nearly half a mile, or half a sabbath day's journey, according to Gill.

2000] by the cubit. It is not easy to re-concile this verse with the preceding; it looks like an interpolation; some think the first thousand included in the 2000, others consider the whole suburb to have consisted of 3000 cubits.

6. REFUGE,] *lit.* a 'contracted place,' see v. 11—15, 25—28, 32; Jos. 20. 2, 3; 21. 13, 21, 27, 32, 38; 1 Ch. 6. 57, 67.

GIVE,] not 'appoint,' as in C.V.

YE GIVE,] not 'add,' as in C.V.

7. 48 CITIES,] whose names, &c. are recorded at length in Jos. 21. 10—37.

8. MULTIPLY,] as in 26. 54.

DIMINISH,] as in Ex. 30. 15.

11. PREPARED,] *lit.* 'caused to meet,' as in Ge. 24. 12; 27. 20, the only other passages where the word occurs.

UNAWARES,] as in Lev. 4. 2, 22, 27.

12. REDEEMER,] as in Ge. 48. 16; Lev. 25. 25, &c.

13. SIX,] out of the whole 48.

THREE,] Bezer, Ramoth, Golan, Jos. 20. 8.

THREE,] Kadesh, Shechem, and Kirjath-Arba, *or* Hebron, Jos. 20. 7. In De. 19. 8 it is enjoined that if God should enlarge their border, they were to add three more.

15. SOJOURNER,] as in Ge. 15. 13.

SETTLER,] as in Ge. 23. 4.

16. IRON,] as in Ge. 4. 22; e.g. hammer, hatchet, &c.

17. A STONE] in the hand, not by 'throwing a stone;' as the C.V., but striking him with it in his hand.

18. WOODEN INSTRUMENT,] as in Lev. 11. 32; 15. 12; Nu. 31. 20; e.g. a club, staff, or stick.

19. REDEEMER,] as in v. 12 above.

20. HATRED,] as in Ge. 24. 60.

THRUST THROUGH,] as in v. 22; De. 6. 19; 9. 4; Jos. 23. 5; 2 K. 4. 27; Job 18. 18; Prov. 10. 3; Isa. 22. 19; Jer. 46. 15; Eze 34. 21.

CAST,] as in Ge. 37. 20, &c.

LYING IN WAIT,] as in v. 22; Ex. 21. 13.

21. ENMITY,] as in Ge. 3. 15.

22. INSTANT,] as in 6. 9.

23. CAUSETH TO FALL,] as in Ge. 2. 21.

EVIL,] as in Ge. 2. 9; Nu. 11. 15, &c.

CAUSED TO TURN BACK,] as in Ge. 14. 16, &c.

HOLY OIL,] as in Ex. 30. 25; 37. 29.

29. STATUTE OF JUDGMENT,] as in 27. 11.

30. SMITETH,] i.e. mortally.

31. NO ATONEMENT,] i.e. 'covering' of the sin, by money, &c.

CONDEMNED—TO DIE,] by the law.

33. PROFANE,] as in Ps. 106. 38; Isa. 24. 5; Jer. 3. 1, 2, 9; 23. 11; Da. 11. 32; Mic. 4. 11.

34. TABERNACLE,] as in Ge. 9. 27; Ex. 25. 8, &c.

XXXVI. 1. HEADS] of the fathers, as in Ex. 6. 14.

MOSES.] The Sept. adds, 'and before Eleazar the priest,' as in 27. 2; 32. 2.

DAUGHTERS,] as in 27. 1—11.

3. BEEN..WIVES,] as in v. 6, 12; Jud. 3. 6.

WITHDRAWN,] as in Ex. 5. 11; Lev. 27. 18

4. JUBILEE.] See Lev. 25. 10—54.

5. RIGHTLY,] see note on Ge. 1. 7.

7. TURN ROUND,] as in Ge. 42. 24.

12. IS,] not 'remained,' as in C.V.

DEUTERONOMY

DEUTERONOMY, the fifth and last of the Books of Moses, derives its name from the Greek title given to it by the Septuagint translators, which denotes a 'second or repeated law,' because of its consisting of the last addresses of the great leader of Israel before his death. The Jews call it 'Alleh had-debarim,' from its initial phrase, 'These are the words,' but they sometimes call it also 'Mishneh Torah,' in imitation of the Septuagint, also occasionally 'The Book of Reproofs,' from the numerous and earnest ones it contains for Israel.

Nearly forty years had elapsed since God had delivered the people out of Egypt and given to them the laws at Sinai, almost all that generation were dead, and it was appropriate that the succeeding one should be reminded of their obligations to the God of Israel, and their duty toward him. Moses —his eye not dim, nor his natural force abated—repeats to them in the simplest and most majestic language these things. Cold indeed, must have been the heart that did not warm beneath his earnest appeals and warm pleadings on behalf of Jehovah God of Israel.

This glowing rhetorical style of the Book has induced some to suppose it to be the work of another author than Moses, but there is not the slightest real foundation for the allegation. Moses, learned in all the wisdom of the Egyptians, could no doubt adapt his style to his circumstances. Some phrases occurring in the former books are changed in this into others of a similar nature, but as language is always more or less changing, there is no reason why a writer should be compelled to use perpetually the same words and phrases when others of precisely the same force and value are at hand. The whole book bears the impress of a busy actor in the events described.

It is quoted about fifty times in the New Testament, viz., Matt. 4. 4, 7, 10; 5. 21, 27, 31, 38; 15. 4; 18. 16; 19. 18, 19; 22. 24, 37; Mark 7. 10; 10. 19; 12. 19, 29, 30; Luke 4. 4, 8, 12; 10. 27; 18. 20; 20. 28; John 8. 17; Acts 3. 22, 23; 7. 37; Rom. 7. 10. 6, 7, 8, 19; 12. 19; 15. 10; 13. 9; 1 Cor. 9. 9; 10. 20; 13. 1; Gal. 3. 10, 13; Eph. 6. 2, 3; 1 Tim. 5. 18; Heb. 10. 30; 12. 29; 13. 5; James 2. 11, &c. So strong is the evidence for its canonical authority.

I. 1. BEYOND] the Jordan eastward, where Israel now was, in the immediate prospect of entering the promised land, the forty years' wanderings which had been foretold now drawing to a close.
WILDERNESS] of Arabia, or properly of Moab.
PLAIN,] as in Nu. 22. 1; 'it is that low region into which the valley of the Jordan runs near Jericho, and which extends as far as the Ælanitic Gulf, in which are the Dead Sea (De. 4. 49, &c.,) and the brook Cedron, (Amos 6. 14); also the plains of Jericho, (Jos. 5. 10), and the plains of Moab. So Gesenius.
SUPH,] probably the same as 'Suphah' in Nu. 21. 14; very unreasonably has the C.V. confounded it with the Sea of Suph, i.e. Red Sea.
PARAN.] See on Ge. 21. 21; Nu. 10. 12, &c.
TOPHEL,] not mentioned elsewhere; Gill suggests it may be Zalmonah or Punon.
LABAN,] not mentioned elsewhere, but Jarchi identifies it with Libnah, Nu. 33. 20.
HAZEROTH.] See on Nu. 11. 35, &c.
DI-ZAHAB,] not mentioned elsewhere; the Sept. and Vul. versions render it 'golden mines,' and 'where there is much gold.'
2. ELEVEN DAYS'] journey; the orientals count distances by so many hours' or days' journey, not by miles or other measurements in length as in Europe.
HOREB.] See note on Ex. 3. 1, &c.
SEIR,] Ge. 14. 6, &c.
KADESH..BARNEA,] Nu. 32 8, &c.
3. FORTIETH YEAR.] Compare Nu. 33. 38.
ELEVENTH MONTH,] named Shebet, i.e. part of January and February.
4. SMITING,] as in Ge. 4. 15; 8. 21; 14. 17, &c.
HESHBON,] as in Nu. 21. 24—26.
EDREI.] See Nu. 21. 33.
5. BEGUN,] as in Ge. 18. 27, 31, on which see note; the original verb in the C.V. is rendered generally, 'to be pleased,' &c.
EXPLAIN,] as in De. 27. 8; Hab. 2. 2, the only other passages where the original verb occurs.
THIS LAW,] as follows, through the whole book of Deuteronomy.
6. ENOUGH,] as in Nu. 16. 3, 7, even a whole year save ten days, according to Ex. 19. 1; Nu. 10. 11.
7. JOURNEY] from Horeb to the mountainous country of the
AMORITE,] south of Canaan, the way of the spies; compare Nu. 13. 17, 29; 14. 40, 43. It was the greatest tribe in the land.
NEIGHBOURING PLACES,] viz. Moab, Ammon, and Seir; or 'its inhabited places,' see De.12. 5, or simply his 'neighbours.'
PLAIN,] as in v. 1 above.
HILL-COUNTRY] of Judea especially.
LOW-COUNTRY] toward the great sea.
SOUTH] of the promised land.
HAVEN] of the sea, i.e. the Mediterranean or great sea, even the land of the Philistines.
CANAANITE,] and the land of Lebanon on the north, unto the great river, the river PHRATH.] See Ge. 2. 14, &c.
8. SET,] lit. 'given.'
SWORN,] in Ge. 12. 7; 15. 18; 17. 7, 8; 26. 4; 28. 13.
9. SAYING,] in Ex. 18. 18; Nu. 11. 14.

10. MULTIPLIED YOU,] from seventy persons, see Ge. 46. 27.

STARS.] This is an example of the bold figures of speech so common in the Scriptures, and other oriental writings.

11. IS ADDING.] The declaration of a fact and promise, not a prayer, as in the C.V.

TIMES,] *lit.* 'steps,' as in Ge. 2. 23, on which see note.

12. PRESSURE,] as in Isa. 1. 14, the only other place where the original word occurs.

BURDEN,] as in Ex. 23. 5, &c.

STRIFE,] as in Ge. 13. 7, &c.

13. GIVE,] not 'take,' as in C.V.

INTELLIGENT,] as in Ge. 41. 33, 39.

KNOWN TO,] not 'among,' as in C.V.

SET,] as in Ge. 2. 8; 45. 8, &c.

FOR,] *or* 'with, among' them.

HEADS,] as in Ex. 6. 14, &c.

14. SAY.] This answer is not recorded elsewhere.

15. HEADS,] as in Nu. 30. 1, &c.

APPOINT,] *lit.* 'give.'

PRINCES,] in Hebrew 'sar,' from which is derived perhaps the English word 'sir.'

AUTHORITIES.] See note on Ex. 5. 6, &c.

16. HEARKENING,] i.e. at the time when ye do so.

RIGHTEOUSNESS] *or* rightness, as in Lev. 19. 15, &c.

BROTHER,] i.e. fellow Israelite.

17. DISCERN FACES,] as in 16. 19; Prov. 24. 23; 28. 21.

LITTLE] in outward appearance or rank.

FACE OF ANY.] Compare Job 31. 34.

GOD'S,] as in 2 Ch. 19. 6.

HARD,] *or* 'sharp,' i.e. severe and difficult.

HEARD IT,] as in Ex. 18. 22, 26.

18. TIME,] viz. when they were appointed.

YE DO] now, in reference to all matters, civil and sacred.

19. SEEN.] Compare 8. 15; Jer. 2. 6.

KADESH-BARNEA.] See Nu. 13. 26, &c.

20. MOUNT] or hill-country of the Amorite, the greatest of the seven nations who inhabited Canaan, as noted in v. 4 above.

TO US,] for an inheritance.

21. GIVEN UP] before thee the land, so that none can withstand thee.

AFFRIGHTED.] Compare the exhortation in Jos. 1. 9, &c.

22. SEARCH,] as in Jos. 2. 2, 3; Job 39. 29; everywhere else it is translated 'dig,' in the C.V., see Ge. 21. 30; 26. 15, 18, 19, 21, 22, 32, &c.

CITIES.] See Nu. 13. 19, 20.

23. EYES.] See note on Ge. 16. 6, &c.

TWELVE,] whose names are given in Nu. 13. 4—15.

24. HILL-COUNTRY,] as they had been directed to do by Moses, Nu. 13. 27.

ESHCOL,] *lit.* a 'cluster.'

SPY,] as in Nu. 21. 32. See note on the word as found in Ge. 42. 9, &c.

25. SAY,] as recorded in Nu. 13. 27.

26. MOUTH.] See note on Nu. 14. 41, &c.

27. MURMUR.] This original word is only found elsewhere in Ps. 106. 25; Isa. 29. 24.

TENTS,] first privately, and then openly. Nu. 14. 1, 2; De. 4. 37.

28. MELTED.] Compare Jos. 14. 8.

FENCED,] as again in 9. 1.

ANAKIM,] whose names are given in Nu. 3. 22—33, see also Jos. 14. 15; 15. 13, 14.

29. AFRAID,] as in v. 21 above; this address is not recorded in Nu. 14. 5.

30. IS GOING] habitually before you.

FIGHT,] by inspiring awe into the heart of their enemies, and by sending his armies—hail, fire, &c.

EYES,] which was thus palpable and manifest to them openly.

31. WILDERNESS,] against Amalek, Moab, Ammon, Sihon, Og, &c.

SON,] young, tender, feeble, i.e. gently and carefully.

PLACE,] even the plains of Moab, see v. 1 above.

32. NOT STEDFAST.] See note on Ge 15. 6, &c., Ps. 106. 24; Jude 5; Heb. 3. 19.

33. SEARCH OUT,] as in Nu. 10. 33, a different word from that found in v. 22 above.

34. SAYING,] in Nu. 14. 22, 28.

35. NOT ONE] more *lit.* 'if one,' the sentence being thus left imperfect, to be supplied mentally.

GOOD LAND] of Canaan, so called because of its fertility.

FATHERS,] Abraham, Isaac, and Jacob, see v. 8 above.

36. CALEB,] to whom must be added Joshua, see v. 38.

SONS.] See the fulfilment in Jos. 14. 13—15; 15. 13, 14.

FULLY AFTER.] See note on Nu. 14. 24.

37. SAKE.] This happened afterwards, and is only mentioned parenthetically, Nu. 20. 10—12; Ps. 106. 32, 33.

THITHER,] i.e. to Canaan; see 3. 25—27.

38. STANDING.] The position of a servant, ready for action.

STRENGTHEN,] more *lit.* 'harden,' for his work; see 31. 7, 8.

INHERIT] the promised land, as came to pass afterwards.

39. INFANTS,] as in Ge. 34. 29.

SAID,] in Nu. 24. 3.

40. RED SEA,] whence they had come.

41. SAY,] in Nu. 14. 40.

FOUGHT,] which, however, they had not been asked to do.

READY.] The original word does not occur elsewhere.

42. I AM NOT.] Compare Nu. 14. 44, where it is said that the ark, which usually went before them as a symbol of the Divine Presence, remained in the camp.

43. ACT PROUDLY,] see Ex. 18. 11; 21. 14.

44. TO MEET YOU.] See note on Ge. 14.17, &c.

PURSUE,] as in Ge. 14. 14, &c.

BEES,] as in Jud. 14. 8; Ps. 118. 12; Isa. 7. 18. They have been known to rout whole armies.

SMITE,] and beat down.

SEIR.] See note on Ge. 14. 6; 32. 3; 33. 14, 16; 36. 8, 9, 20, 21, 30, &c.

HORMAH.] See Nu. 14. 45; 21. 3, &c.

45. TURN BACK,] not merely to the camp, but to Jehovah their God.

46. DWELT,] i.e. before this took place.

II. 1. TURN] the face from Kadesh, where they had been residing, as in 1. 46.

WILDERNESS,] as commanded in 1. 40, which they had at first refused to obey.
SEIR,] see on 1. 44 above.
2. ENOUGH] to you, as in 1. 6 above.
3. NORTHWARD,] toward the land of Canaan. Compare Nu. 20. 14; 33. 36.
4. BORDER,] not 'coast,' as in C.V.
WATCHFUL,] as in 4. 15.
5. STRIVE,] as in v. 9, 19, 24; 2 K. 14. 10; 2 Ch. 25. 19; Prov. 28. 4; Da. 10. 11, 25.
TREADING,] of the sole of a foot; this phrase does not occur elsewhere. Nu. 24. 18, and Obad. 19, refer to the days of the Messiah, 2 Sa. 8. 14, to David.
POSSESSION,] as in Ge. 36. 8; Jos. 24. 4.
6. FOOD,] lit. 'eating.'
BUY,]or 'break,' as in Isa. 55. 1; Ge. 19. 9 &c.
MONEY,] lit. 'silver,' as always.
BUY,] or ' dig,' as in Ge. 26. 25.
7. BLESSED] thee, in cattle, &c.
KNOWN,] and cared for it.
8. PLAIN] of the wilderness of Zin, where Kadesh was.
ELATH,] compare 1 K. 9. 26.
EZION-GEBER,] near the Red Sea.
MOAB.] See Nu. 21. 11.
9. STIR THYSELF UP,] as in v. 5 above.
POSSESSION,] i.e. at this time, for compare 2 Sa. 8. 2.
AR,] Sept. 'Aroer,' but see Isa. 15. 1; Nu. 21. 28.
LOT.] Ge. 19. 37.
10. EMIM,] see Ge. 14. 5.
FORMERLY,] compare the same phrase in v. 12.
ANAKIM.] Nu. 13. 22, 23.
11. REPHAIM.] See Ge. 14. 5.
12. HORIM,] lit. 'mountaineers.'
FORMERLY,] as in v. 10 above.
DISPOSSESS,] as in Ex. 15. 9; 34. 24.
POSSESSION,] even the lands of Sihon and Og, already possessed by the two tribes and a half.
13. ZERED,] as in Nu. 21. 12.
14. DAYS,] not 'time,' as in C.V.
KADESH-BARNEA,] whence they sent the spies.
SWORN,] in Nu. 14. 21, 23, 30.
15. CAMP,] as in Ge. 32. 2, &c.
CONSUMED,] as in Ge. 47. 15, &c.
16. MEN OF BATTLE,] as in v. 14 above.
18. BORDER,] not ' coast,' as in C.V.
19. AMMON,] for they were neighbours to Moab, and brethren, Ge. 19. 37, 38.
POSSESSION,] save what Israel had already taken out of the hand of Sihon, Jos. 13. 25; Jud. 11. 13—23.
20. REPHAIM,] as in v. 11 above.
ZAMZUMMIN,] i.e. 'wicked devisers;' probably the same as the Zuzim in Ge. 15. 5.
21. DISPOSSESS,] as in v. 12 above.
22. DONE FOR,] not 'to,' as in the C.V.
23. AVIM,] lit. 'overturners,' mentioned again in Jos. 13. 3; 18. 23; 2 K. 17. 31, inhabitants of
HAZERIM,] lit. 'courts, villages;' not mentioned elsewhere.
AZZAH,] or Gaza, lit. 'a strong place.' See note on Ge. 10. 19, &c.
CAPHTORIM.] Most ancient authorities consider these Cappadocians, some few moderns

Cyprians or Cretans; but compare Ge. 10. 14, &c.
24. ARNON,] which divided the Moabites and the Amorites, Nu. 21. 13.
I HAVE GIVEN.] Here, as usual, the past tense is used for the future.
STIR UP THYSELF,] as in v. 5 above.
25. FAME,] as in 1 K. 10. 1; 2 Ch. 9. 1; Job 28. 22, &c., because of what the Lord had done to them.
PAINED,] as in Isa. 26. 18, &c., compare also Jos. 2. 9—11.
26. KEDEMOTH,] lit. 'eastern parts.' See Jos. 13. 18; 1 Ch. 6. 79. Probably the same as Jeshimon, Nu. 21. 20, 21.
SAYING,] as in Nu. 20. 10.
WORDS OF PEACE,] as in Est. 9. 30.
27. IN THE SEVERAL WAYS,] lit. 'in way and way.' They would not march through in one united body so as to injure the fruits of the ground by trespassing upon them, but by the several marked-out roads already made.
28. ON MY FEET.] They were all footmen (Nu. 11. 21), and do not appear to have had horses at all.
29. AS..HAVE DONE,] i.e. sold provisions to them.
30. HARDENED,] or sharpened; compare Ex. 7. 3, ; 13. 15, &c.
WAS NOT WILLING.] Compare Ex. 10. 27; De. 1. 26.
STRENGTHENED,] as in 3. 28; 15. 7, &c., Ge. 25. 23.
THIS DAY,] they now having received possession of it, see Nu. 21. 24, 25.
31. POSSESS..POSSESS.] The same verb is used twice, so there is no propriety in translating the second one by 'inherit,' as is done in the C.V.
32. TO MEET US,] to 'fight' with us, as expressed in next clause.
JAHAZ.] See note on Nu. 21. 23.
33. HIS SONS,] or 'his son.' The C.V. adheres to the Hebrew Marginal Reading.
34. DEVOTE,] as in Lev. 27. 28, they having been thus devoted by God for their wickedness.
THE WHOLE CITY,] even any and all that they captured, Nu. 21. 25, 30, 32; 32. 3, 34—38.
MEN,] as in Ge. 34. 30; De. 3. 6; 4. 27, &c.
INFANT.] See note on Ge. 34. 29, &c.
35. CAPTURED.] Which they were allowed to do.
36. BROOK,] as in Ge. 32. &c.
TOO HIGH,] not 'too strong,' as in C.V.; compare the use of the word in Job 5. 11, &c.
BEFORE US,] as in v. 33 above, not 'unto us,' as in the C.V.
37. DRAWN NEAR.] Compare note on v. 9 above.
JABBOK,] which was the boundary line of Ammon, see 3. 16; Ge. 32. 22.

III. 1. TURN] the face, as the word literally signifies.
BASHAN,] famous for its pastures and its oaks. See on Nu. 21. 23, &c.
OG.] See on Nu. 21. 33.
TO MEET US] with the sword in battle

EDREI,] said to have been six miles from Ashteroth, his capital city, see 1. 4; Nu. 21. 33.
2. SAITH,] as is recorded in Nu. 21. 34.
3. REMNANT,] compare Nu. 21. 35.
4. SIXTY CITIES.] Of course these cities were generally what we would call small towns or villages.
REGION,] *lit.* a 'portion,' compare v. 14; 32. 9; Jos. 2. 15; 17. 5, 14; 19. 9, 29; 1 Sa. 10. 5, 10; 2 Sa. 8. 2; 17. 13; 22. 6, &c.
ARGOB,] see v. 13, 14, also 1 K. 4. 13; the etymology of the name is unknown, propably the same as Trachonitis.
5. FENCED,] as in Nu. 13. 28.
TWO-LEAVED DOORS,] as in Jos. 2. 19; 6. 26; Jud. 3. 23, 24, 25, &c.
BARS,] as in Ex. 26. 26.
VILLAGES.] Compare 1 Sa. 6. 18; Est. 9. 19; also Ez. 38. 11; Zec. 2. 4.
6. DEVOTE,] as in 2. 34.
AS WE DID,] in 2. 34.
INFANTS,] as in 2. 35.
8. BEYOND] the Jordan eastward.
HERMON,] as in v. 8. 9; 4. 48; Jos. 11. 3, 17; 21. 1, 5; 13. 5, 11; 1 Ch. 5. 23; Ps. 89. 12; 133. 3; Song 4. 6. It is a mountain of Gilead, which ended where Lebanon began.
9. SIDONIANS,] i.e. inhabitants of Sidon, at the north.
SIRION,] *lit.* a 'coat of mail,' Ps. 29. 6.
AMORITE,] who last possessed it.
SHENIR,] *lit.* 'an apron,' according to some. Song 4. 8 is the only other place where the name occurs. Jarchi says it means 'snow,' with which agree the Targums of Onkelos and Jonathan. In De. 4. 48 it is also called 'Sion,' (*lit.* lifted up), which may be an error of the Scribes for 'Sirion.'
10. PLAIN] on the east side of Jordan, as in 4. 49.
GILEAD.] See note on Ge. 31. 21.
BASHAN,] on which see Nu. 21. 33, &c.
SALCHAH,] *lit.* 'a walk,' mentioned again in Jos. 12. 5; 13. 11; 1 Ch. 5. 11.
EDREI,] See Nu. 21. 33. Compare also De. 1. 4; 3. 1.
11. REPHAIM,] Ge. 14. 5, &c.
BEDSTEAD,] as in Job 7. 13; Ps. 6. 6; 41. 3; 132. 3; Prov. 7. 16; Song 1. 16; Amos 3. 12; 6. 4.
IRON.] Probably this was to shew his contempt for luxuries.
RABBATH,] *lit.* a 'great or populous place,' being the chief city of Ammon, 2 Sam. 12. 26.
NINE] cubits, or thirteen and a half feet long, and six feet broad; himself however was doubtless much less in magnitude.
12. GIVEN,] as recorded in Nu. 32. 33, &c.
13. GIVEN.] Compare Jos. 13. 29.
REPHAIM,] Ge. 14. 5, &c.
14. GESHURI,] or the Geshurite. See Jos. 12. 5; 13. 11, 13.
MAACHATHI,] or the Maachathite. See Jos. 12. 5; 13. 11, 13, &c.
15. GIVEN,] Nu. 32. 40.
16. BORDER,] as in Nu. 21. 24; Jos. 12. 2.
17. PLAIN,] east of the Jordan.
CHINNERETH.] See Nu. 34. 11.
SEA] of the plain, i.e. the salt or dead sea.
SPRINGS,] as in 4. 49.
18. ARMED.] See note on Nu. 31. 5.

PASS OVER] the river Jordan to meet the enemy.
SONS OF MIGHT.] See same phrase in Jud. 21. 10; 1 Sa. 18. 17; 2 Sa. 2. 7; 13. 28; 17. 10; 2 K. 2. 16; 1 Ch. 5. 18; 2 Ch. 28. 6, &c.
19. TO YOU,] beyond the Jordan.
GIVE REST,] from their wanderings and fears, as He had promised.
20. IS GIVING,] i.e. in the course of doing so.
21. COMMANDED.] See Nu. 27. 18.
ALL] the kingdoms of Canaan, of whom there were at least thirty-one; compare also Jud. 1. 7.
22. FOR YOU.] Compare Ex. 14. 14; De. 1. 30; 20. 4.
23. ENTREAT FOR GRACE.] Compare Ge. 42. 21, &c.
24. SHEW,] by the cases of Sihon and Og.
25. THIS GOOD HILL-COUNTRY,] i.e. the land of Israel, so called because of its general mountainous character; 'that goodly mountain,' conveys no intelligible sense.
26. SHEWETH HIMSELF WROTH,] as in Ps. 78. 21, 59, 62; 89. 38; Prov. 14. 6; 20. 2; 26. 17, being all the passages where this form of the verb occurs.
FOR YOUR SAKES,] i.e. on account of what you have been and done.
HEAR,] i.e. hearken, listen, consent to me.
ENOUGH FOR THEE,] as in Nu. 16. 3, 7, &c.
ADD NOT] to speak, as in Ge. 18. 29; Nu. 22. 19; De. 20. 8; Jud. 9. 37; Isa. 8. 5.
27. PISGAH,] or the Pisgah. See on Nu. 21. 20.
NOT PASS OVER,] as He had declared before, because of his not honouring God aright.
28. HARDEN] him against troubles, &c.
29. BETH-PEOR,] *lit.* a 'house of Peor,' mentioned again in 4. 46; 34. 6; Jos. 13. 20.

IV. 1. AND NOW] that he had narrated the way by which God had led them, he calls upon them to
HEARKEN] to and obey the laws and precepts which their covenant God had given to them, which are described as
STATUTES] that were 'engraved' as it were by the finger of God that they might never pass out of their memories, and as
JUDGMENTS] which He has judged and decided that they should follow after, and which Moses now proceeds to lay before them again, which he says
I AM TEACHING] you to do, and observe, and practise, the consequence of which obedience is that they
DO LIVE,] and not die, like their unbelieving fathers; and not only so, but they would go in and possess the land which their God is even now beginning to give the possession of to them.
2. YE DO NOT ADD] without divine directions to the words of the Lord which he was now
COMMANDING] in the name of the Lord.
NOR DIMINISH] from it, by leaving any part of it unobserved.
COMMANDS] of Jehovah their national Covenant God.

3. ARE SEEING,] day by day, so that they had no excuse for unbelief.

BAAL-PEOR,] recorded in Nu. 25. 4.

DESTROYED,] by the plague, even 24,000 persons.

4. CLEARING.] Compare the use of the original word in 2 Ch. 3. 12; Prov. 18. 24; also Da. 2. 43.

TO-DAY,] though there had been a war since then with Midian, Nu. 31. 49.

5. I HAVE TAUGHT.] The past tense is here used, as often, for the future.

COMMANDED ME,] not from my own heart, as he says in Nu. 16. 28.

6. AND] ye have kept, i.e. supposing ye have done so, then the people have said,

ONLY,] not 'surely,' as in C.V., see Ge. 6. 5, &c.

WISDOM]to do so, i.e. to observe God's laws.

7. UNTO HIM] to do in our behalf, to deliver us out of the hand of the king of Egypt, from the Egyptians, Amalekites, &c., from hunger, thirst, and fiery serpent, &c.

8. SETTING,] *lit.* 'giving.' This appeal of Moses to Israel still holds good up to the present day. The laws which God gave to them by his instrumentality are unsurpassed even yet, especially in regard to the poor and the unfortunate, and justice between man and man. It would be easy to show (as has often been done) that in many such points modern civil legislators might learn much from them still.

9. EXCEEDINGLY,] as in Ge. 7. 18, 19.

TURN ASIDE,] as in 17. 17, &c.

MADE..KNOWN.] Compare Ex. 18. 16; De. 6. 7.

10. THE DAY,] Ex. 19. 9, 16; 20. 18, &c.

GROUND,] as the word properly means, not 'earth.'

SONS.] The masculine gender being used as the more honourable.

11. UNDER,] i.e. at the foot of it, compare Ex. 19. 17.

HEART] of the heavens; this phrase is not found elsewhere, but parallel ones are found in Ex. 15. 8; 2 Sa. 18. 4, &c.

DARKNESS.] This word expresses the natural darkness of night, caused by the withdrawal of the sun, see Ge. 1. 2, &c.

CLOUD,] as in Ge. 9. 13.

THICK DARKNESS.] Compare Ex. 20. 21.

12. A VOICE,] as in v. 33, 36; Ex. 19. 19; 1 K. 19. 12, 13; Job 4. 16, &c.

SIMILITUDE.] Compare Ex. 20. 4; Nu. 12. 8.

13. TEN MATTERS,] *or* 'words,' i.e. ten different subjects they were to attend to, Ex. 20. 1—17; De. 5. 6—21.

STONE,] as in Ex. 31. 18.

15. SOULS.] A different phrase from that in v. 9 above.

16. DO CORRUPTLY,] as in Ge. 6. 12; De. 4. 25; 31. 29, &c.

GRAVEN IMAGE.] See Ex. 20. 4.

FIGURE.] Compare ? Da. 23. 7, 15; Ez. 8. 3, 5, the only other passages where the original word occurs.

FORM,] *or* 'structure,' see on Ex. 25. 9, 40, &c.

17. WINGED BIRD,] as in Ge. 7. 14.

18. CREEPING THING,] as in Ge. 1. 21.

19. HEAVENS.] Compare Ps. 8. 3, &c.; Ge. 15. 5; Job 35. 5; Isa. 51. 6; La. 3. 41.

SUN,] which was and is worshipped by the fire-worshippers of Persia and India. Job 31. 26.

MOON,] walking in brightness, as Job says; called also the queen of the heavens, Jer. 7. 18.

STARS,] which were supposed to exercise an influence on human destinies.

HOST,] as in Ge. 2. 1.

FORCED,] as in 13. 5, 10, 13; 19. 5; 20. 19; 22. 1; 30. 1, 4, 17, &c.

BOWED THYSELF,] as in Ge. 18. 2, &c.

APPORTIONED,] as in 29. 26, &c.

PEOPLES,] not 'nations,' as in C.V.; the one is a natural, the other a political, assembly. See note on Ge. 11. 6, compared with that on 10. 5.

20. IS BRINGING,] even now.

IRON FURNACE,] as in 1 K. 8. 51, also Prov 17. 3; 27. 21; Isa. 48. 10; Jer. 11. 4; Eze. 22. 18, 20, 22.

INHERITANCE,] not 'of inheritance;' the words are in apposition one to the other.

21. SHEWED HIMSELF ANGRY,] as in v. 4, 21; 9. 8, 20; 1 K. 11. 9; 2 K. 17. 18.

YOUR WORDS,] in murmuring and rebelling, Nu. 20. 12; De. 1. 37; 3. 26, &c.

22. I AM DYING,] even now, i.e. on the brink of it.

PASSING OVER,] *or* a 'passer-over.'

THIS LAND] of Moab, eastward of the Jordan.

23. FORGET,] Ge. 27. 45; 40. 23; De. 4. 23, 31; 6. 12, &c.

COVENANT,] *lit.* 'eating,' because it ratified the agreement. See Ge. 6. 18, &c.

WITH YOU,] as recorded in Ex. 19. 5.

GRAVEN IMAGE,] see v. 16 above.

SIMILITUDE,] as in v. 16 above.

CHARGED THEE,] as recorded in Ex. 20. 4.

24. CONSUMING FIRE.] Compare Ex. 24. 17; De. 9. 3; Isa. 29. 6; 30. 27; Joel 2. 5; also Heb. 12. 29.

ZEALOUS,] for his own glory, Ex. 20. 5, &c.

GOD,] *or* mighty one, as in Ge. 14. 18.

25. BECOME OLD.] Compare Lev. 13. 11; 25. 22; 26. 10; Neh. 3. 6; 12. 39; Song 7. 13; Isa. 22. 11.

DONE CORRUPTLY.] Compare v. 16 above.

GRAVEN IMAGE,] as in v. 16 above.

SIMILITUDE,] as in v. 16 above.

THE EVIL THING.] This phrase generally refers to idolatry.

TO MAKE HIM ANGRY,] as in 9. 18; 31. 29; 32. 16, 21.

26. I HAVE CAUSED TO TESTIFY,] as in 30. 19; 31. 28.

PERISH UTTERLY,] *lit.* 'perishing ye perish.'

HASTILY,] as in Ex. 32. 8.

27. SCATTERED,] as in 28. 64; 30. 3.

PEOPLE,] as in v. 19 above.

FEW,] *lit.* 'men of number,' as in Ge. 34. 30.

LEADETH,] as in Ge. 31. 18, 26; Ex. 3. 1; 10. 13; 14. 25; De. 28. 37, &c.

28. SERVED.] It has been remarked that though in former captivities the Jews have worshipped idols, they have not done so in their present dispersion, at least to any extent.

SMELL.] Compare Ps. 115. 4—7 ; 135. 15, 16.
29. SOUGHT] earnestly, as the word almost always implies, see Ge. 31. 39, &c.
FOUND,] as in 1 Ch. 28. 9 ; 2 Ch. 15. 2 ; Ps. 9. 10 ; Prov. 8. 17 ; Isa. 45. 19 ; Jer. 29. 13 ; Amos 5. 4 ; 8. 12.
HEART . . SOUL,] with thy whole being.
30. DISTRESS,] as in 2 Sa. 22. 7.
FOUND,] as in Ge. 44. 34.
LATTER END] of the days, compare Ge. 49. 1.
TURNED BACK,] which implies a previous departure, which the C. V. does not.
HEARKENED,] implying obedience, though not expressing it
31. MERCIFUL,] as in Ex. 34. 6 ; compare 33. 19.
FAIL,] as in 31. 6, 8.
DESTROY,] as in Ge. 6. 13.
FORGET,] see on v. 9 above.
COVENANT,] see v. 23 above.
FATHERS,] Abraham, Isaac, Jacob, &c.
32. ASK,] or demand ; compare Job 8. 8.
I PRAY THEE,] not 'now,' as in C.V.
FORMER DAYS,] as in Nu. 6. 12 ; De. 10. 10.
PREPARED.] See note on Ge. 1. 1.
33. A PEOPLE,] not 'people,' i.e. persons or individuals, but 'a (whole) people.'
FIRE,] as noted in v. 12. 15 above.
DOTH LIVE,] as thou still dost.
34. TRIED,] as the word is used in Ge. 22. 1 ; Ex. 15. 25 ; 16. 4 ; 17. 2, 7 ; 20. 20 ; Nu. 14. 22 ; De. 6. 16, &c.
NATION,] even that of Egypt.
TRIALS,] as in 7. 19 ; 29. 3 ; Ex. 17. 7 ; De. 6. 16 ; 9. 22 ; 33. 8 ; Job 9. 23 ; Ps. 95. 8.
SIGNS,] as in Ge. 1. 14.
WONDERS,] as in Ex. 4. 21.
WAR,] lit. 'battle,' as in 14. 2, 8.
STRONG HAND,] as noticed in Ex. 3. 19 ; 6. 1 ; 13. 9 ; 32. 11.
STRETCHED-OUT ARM,] as noticed in Ex. 6. 6, &c.
TERRORS,] or 'fears,' as in Ge. 9. 2.
35. GOD,] lit. 'the God,' i.e. the true and only one ; compare 1 K. 18. 21, 37 ; De. 7. 9 ; Ge. 5. 22 ; 6. 9, 11 ; 17. 18 ; 20. 6, 7, &c.
BESIDES HIM.] The precise Hebrew form of the phrase does not occur elsewhere, but compare 32. 39 ; 1 Sa. 2. 2 ; Isa. 45. 5, 18, 22 ; Mark 12. 29, 32.
36. HEAVENS,] as in Ex. 19. 9, 19 ; 20. 18, 22 ; 24. 16 ; Heb. 12. 18.   Compare also Job 26. 14 ; 40. 9 ; 29. 3.
EARTH,] i.e. at Sinai.
FIRE,] as noted in v. 12, 15, 33.
37. FATHERS,] especially Abraham, Isaac, and Jacob ; see 10. 15.
AFTER THEM,] to be to him a people for his glory.
EGYPT,] Ex. 13. 3, 9, 14.
38. NATIONS,] especially the seven in the land of Canaan ; see 7. 1 ; 9. 1, 4, 5.
THIS DAY.] Referring to the land of Og and Sihon which they already enjoyed as a first-fruit of the inheritance.
39. TURNED IT BACK,] as in 1 K. 8. 47 ; 2 Ch. 6. 37.
GOD.] See on v. 35 above, and Jos. 2. 11.
40. WELL.] See 5. 16 ; 6. 3, 18 ; 12. 25 28 ; 22. 7 ; Eph. 6. 3.

GROUND] of Israel.
ALL THE DAYS,] i.e. continually ; compare Ge. 6. 5 ; 43. 9 ; 44. 32 ; De. 5. 29 ; 6. 24 ; 11. 1 ; 14. 23 ; 18. 5 ; 19. 9 ; 28. 29, 32, 33 ; 31. 13 ; Jos. 4. 24 ; Jud. 16. 16 ; 1 Sa. 2. 32.
41. SEPARATETH.] See note on Ge. 1. 6.
THREE CITIES,] as commanded in Nu. 35.14.
SUN-RISING,] Josh. 20. 8.
42. UNKNOWINGLY,] lit. 'in want of knowledge,' as in 19. 4 ; Jos. 20. 5 ; Job 35. 16, &c.
HERETOFORE,] lit. 'yesterday third day.' as in Ge. 31. 2, &c.
43. BEZER,] as in Jos. 20. 8 ; 1 Ch. 6. 78 ; 7. 37.
WILDERNESS] of Moab, now occupied by the Reubenite.
PLAIN,] or level country, given to the Levites, 1 Ch. 6. 78.
RAMOTH.] See Jos. 20. 6 ; 1 Ch. 6. 73, 80 ; called Ramoth-Gilead, in
GILEAD,] now occupied by the Gadite, and given to the Levites, 1 Ch. 6. 80.
GOLAN,] as in Jos. 20. 8 ; 21. 27 ; 1 Ch. 6. 71.
BASHAN,] now occupied by the Manassehite, and given to the Levite.
44. THIS IS.] Many expositors are of opinion that this verse is the conclusion of the preceding address, but others think it the commencement of the succeeding one. The first supposition is to be preferred, while v. 45 seems an appropriate introduction to what remains.
LAW,] or 'direction,' see note on Ge. 26. 5.
45. TESTIMONIES,] or 'witnessings,' which the Lord bore against Israel.
STATUTES,] or engraved enactments.
JUDGMENTS,] or decisions, which they were to obey and carry out.
46. BETH-PEOR.] See 3. 29.
SMITTEN.] See Nu. 21. 21 ; De. 1. 4.
47. POSSESS,] i.e. the two tribes and a half.
48. AROER.] See on De. 32. 34.
ARNON,] as noted in 2. 36 ; 3. 2.
SION.] See note on 3. 8, 9.
49. PLAIN] of Moab, as in v. 43 above.
SEA,] i.e. the salt sea, on the border of which had stood Sodom and Gomorrah.
SPRINGS.] See on 3. 17.

V. 1. OBSERVED TO DO,] i.e. been careful to do them, not 'keep and do them,' as in C.V.
2. IN HOREB,] or Sinai, see Ex. 24. 7, 8.
3. OUR FATHERS] only, which word we must supply, agreeably to the oriental modes of expression, as the Saviour did in Mat. 4. 10, quoting De. 6. 13 ; 10. 20.
WITH US.] The covenant being not only with Abraham, but with his seed after him.
4. FACE TO FACE.] Compare the phrase in Ge. 32. 31 ; Ex. 33. 11 ; De. 34. 10 Jud. 6. 22 ; Prov. 27. 19.
FIRE,] as in Ex. 19. 9, 19, &c.
5. I AM STANDING.] See Ex. 20. 21.
DECLARE,] or 'set before,' see note on Ge. 3. 11.
AFRAID,] as in Ex. 19. 16 ; 20. 18 ; 24. 2, &c.
6. SERVANTS.] Compare Ex. 20. 2, and notes thereon.
7. BEFORE,] or 'over-against' my face.
8. GRAVEN IMAGE,] as in Ex. 20. 4, on which see note.

SIMILITUDE,] see note on Ex. 20. 4.

9. BOW THYSELF,] rendering them even outward acts of respect, as in Ge. 18. 2.

SERVE] them, by acknowledging their power.

ZEALOUS] for His own glory, and for the welfare of his people.

CHARGING,] or 'inspecting,' looking after.

ON SONS,] see note on Ex. 20. 5.

10. KINDNESS,] not 'mercy.'

THOUSANDS] of generations, as is to be understood in the 5th verse above.

11. TAKE UP,] upon thy lips, in a solemn affirmation.

VAIN THING,] i.e. 'empty worthless thing,' which might be settled without an appeal to the great Creator.

ACQUIT,] see note on Ex. 20. 7.

12. OBSERVE,] or 'watch,' its regular recurrence.

SABBATH,] i.e. 'cessation,' from usual avocations.

SANCTIFY,] i.e. 'separate or set it apart' from the midst of other days, to what God has destined it.

COMMANDED.] This clause is not in Ex. 20. 8, and seems a reference to it.

13. LABOUR,] for daily support, as in Ge. 2. 5, 15.

14. SEVENTH,] as in Ge. 2. 2, 3.

SABBATH TO,] not 'sabbath of;' it was to be kept as a day of cessation from usual labours, with a view to his example and command.

ANY WORK,] lit. 'all work,' i.e. all kinds of work.

GATES,] whether of private dwellings or of cities.

THYSELF.] Agreeably to Lev. 19. 18, 34, &c.

15. IS BRINGING] thee out, even now.

STRONG HAND,] as in Ex. 3. 19.

STRETCHED-OUT ARM,] as in Ex. 6. 6.

16. HONOUR,] as in Ex. 20. 12; Jud. 9. 9, &c.

COMMANDED,] in Ex. 20. 12.

17. MURDER.] Compare note on Ex. 20. 13.

18. COMMIT ADULTERY.] See note on Ex. 20. 14.

19. STEAL,] as in Ex. 20. 15; see note on Ge. 30. 33.

20. ANSWER,] in reply to the questions of a judge.

FALSE,] or 'empty, worthless,' testimony.

21. DESIRE,] as in Ex. 20. 17; also 34. 24; De. 7. 35, &c.

COVET.] See note on Nu. 11. 4.

22. WORDS,] or 'things.'

THICK DARKNESS,] see 4. 11.

ADDED] to say any more, at that time.

TO ME,] as in Ex 24. 12; 31. 18; De. 4. 13.

23. AND OF THE] not 'for the' mountain. Compare Ex. 19. 16—18.

ELDERS] who exercised authority among the people.

24. SHEWED,] lit. 'caused us to see.'

HONOUR,] i.e. a manifestation of his majesty.

GREATNESS] above all men, nations, and gods.

HEARD] with our own ears.

LIVED] notwithstanding all this; the common impression being that death would

ensue; compare the feelings of Hagar (Ge. 16. 13), Moses (Ex. 3. 6), Manoah (Jud. 13. 22), Elijah (1 K. 19. 13), Daniel (10. 9), John (Rev. 1. 17), Jacob (Ge. 32. 30).

25. DIED,] as did Korah's companions, Nu. 11. 1; 16. 35.

26. WHO OF ALL FLESH.] Such a thing had not occurred before, save to Moses (Ex. 3. 2—6).

27. DONE IT,] as they had often promised before.

28. UNTO ME] to encourage him to draw near to God, in accordance with the desire of the people, his natural backwardness preventing him at first.

29. THUS] sincerely afraid of offending me by their guilty and polluted presence.

HEART,] which in Hebrew often includes all the powers and faculties of man.

FEAR,] i.e. 'reverence,' as a child does a parent.

30. TURN BACK] from the presence of Moses, who probably stood in the Tent of Meeting.

31. WITH ME,] not 'by me,' as in the C.V.

COMMAND] or 'charge,' as in 6. 1.

32. LEFT.] Compare Ge. 13. 9; 24. 49; Nu. 20. 17; 22. 26; De. 2. 27; 17. 11, 20; 28. 14, &c.

33. THE WAY,] not 'ways,' as in C.V. Compare 10. 12; Ps. 119. 6; Jer. 7. 23; Luke 1. 6.

VI. 1. COMMAND] or 'charge,' as in 5. 31.

FEAR,] i.e. reverence.

PROLONGED,] as noted in 4. 26, 40; 5. 16, 33, &c.

3. MULTIPLY EXCEEDINGLY,] even as the 'stars of the heavens,' and as the 'sand which is upon the sea-shore,' in the oriental language of Scripture. Ge. 15. 5; 22. 17; 26. 4; 28. 14.

SPOKEN,] not necessarily 'promised,' though he really had done so to Abraham, &c.

HONEY,] even Canaan, Ex. 3. 8.

4. OUR GOD,] or perhaps 'Jehovah (is) our God, Jehovah (is) one.' So Vitringa. This seems the simplest and most appropriate sense, for the phrase 'one Jehovah,' is almost unintelligible. Two things are here asserted of Jehovah—the Being whose laws they were to keep—first, that he was their Covenant God, and entitled to their homage, and secondly, that he was One God, ever the same in his character, demands, &c.

5. AND THOU HAST LOVED.] The past tense is put for the imperative, as is common in Hebrew, as indicating rather what was naturally to be expected from them as a consequence of their having previously avouched Jehovah to be their God, than what they were to do positively.

6. HEART,] i.e. heartily, warmly.

SOUL,] i.e. intelligently.

MIGHT,] i.e. power or ability of body and spirit.

7. ON,] not 'in' thy heart, as in O.V.

REPEATED.] The original verb generally signifies 'to whet or sharpen;' I prefer deriving it from a root signifying to repeat, do a thing a second time.

SITTING..WALKING] i.e. however engaged.
LYING DOWN..RISING UP,] late and early.
8. SIGN,] or token.
HAND,] that it might ever be before his own eyes.
FRONTLETS,] as in Ex. 13. 16.
EYES,] that others may know it, and observe it, that they might thus be 'living epistles.' See Ex. 13. 16; De. 11. 18.
9. DOOR-POSTS,] as in 11. 20; and compare Zec. 14. 20, 21.
GATES,] i.e. even of thy cities; the profession and confession are to be national as well as personal.
10. SWORN,] many times to the patriarchs.
GOOD,] even well situated, well watered, with great walls and fortifications.
BUILT.] Compare Jos. 24. 13; Ps. 105. 44.
11. WELLS,] which are of primary and essential importance in Eastern lands for man and beast.
DIGGED,] ready to their hand, and for their use, thus saving them great labour and expense.
VINEYARDS,] producing the most luxuriant grapes and fruits.
OLIVEYARDS,] by which they were supplied with oil, so much used among orientals generally.
PLANTED,] thus saving them the anxiety of mind arising from the young plants.
SATISFIED] with their portion in the good land.
12. TAKE HEED,] or 'be watchful.'
FORGET,] or neglect Him who gave them these gifts.
SERVANTS,] when they were oppressed unmercifully.
13. FEAR,] i.e. reverence, as the Creator generally, and as 'thy God' especially.
SERVE,] according to his revealed will and law.
SWEAR,] in courts of justice, &c.
14. GODS,] to reverence, and serve them, because they had done, and could do nothing for any one.
PEOPLES,] Ammonites, Edomites, Egyptians, Moabites, Philistines, &c.
15. ZEALOUS] for His own glory, and the real welfare of His people.
MIDST,] having taken thee to be His people He resides and tabernacles within thee, and sees thy every action.
BURN,] and consume thee from off the GROUND] of Israel, as it did against the nations of Canaan.
16. TRY] his patience and forbearance, as in MASSEH,] in Ex. 17. 2, 7.
17. KEEP,] or 'observe.'
TESTIMONIES,] regarding Himself, and His STATUTES,] or positive enactments which he had laid upon them.
19. DRIVE AWAY,] that they might not be a snare to Israel.
SPOKEN,] in Nu. 33. 52, 53.
20. HEREAFTER,] lit. 'to-morrow,' as in Ex. 8. 10, &c.
21. SERVANTS,] against our will and consent.
HIGH HAND,] as noted often because of its importance.

22. GIVETH,] out of his treasury.
SIGNS,] and tokens of his love to Israel.
WONDERS,] which the land of Egypt, and the world, had never seen before.
SAD,] because of the obstinacy which caused them.
23. FATHERS,] Abraham, Isaac, and Jacob.
24. COMMANDETH,] as he was entitled to do by being the covenant-God of Israel.
STATUTES,] which he had prepared for them.
ALL THE DAYS,] i.e. continually.
25. RIGHTEOUSNESS,] or rightness, i.e. right state.
THIS COMMAND,] regarding the manner in which they were to reverence Him.

VII. 1. LAND] of Canaan, which he had promised to give to them.
POSSESS IT,] as the inheritance of the Lord.
CAST OUT,] with force and violence, because of their iniquities, and also as being themselves invaders and intruders.
HITTITE,] see on Ge. 15. 20, &c.
GIRGASHITE,] see on Ge. 10. 16, &c.
AMORITE,] see on Ge. 10. 16, &c.
CANAANITE,] see on Ge. 10. 18, &c.
PERIZZITE,] see on Ge. 13. 7, &c.
HIVITE,] see on Ge. 10. 17, &c.
JEBUSITE,] see on Ge. 10. 16, &c.
THOU,] not singly, but conjointly, considered.
2. GIVEN] them up into thy hand, that thou mayest do all his pleasure.
SMITTEN] them in battle, as God had commanded them.
DEVOTE,] to the good pleasure of God.
COVENANT] of peace and friendship.
FAVOUR THEM,] in any way, so as to prolong their stay in the promised land.
3. JOIN IN MARRIAGE,] as Esau had done with the daughters of Canaan.
4. TURN ASIDE,] into idolatry.
THEY HAVE SERVED,] and obeyed the (supposed) will and commands of false deities.
BURNED,] as in 6. 15, &c.
HASTILY,] as in Ex. 32. 8, &c.
5. ALTARS,] which they have erected for idolatrous worship.
BREAK DOWN,] as in Ex. 34. 13.
STANDING PILLARS,] which they set up in honour of their idols.
SHIVER,] as in 12. 3, &c.
SHRINES,] which they rear up to cover the idol.
CUT DOWN,] as in 12. 3, &c.
GRAVEN IMAGES,] which they bow before and serve.
WITH FIRE,] as polluting the land.
6. HOLY,] i.e. separated, set apart.
FIXED,] out of his own good pleasure.
PECULIAR,] as in Ex. 19. 5, &c.
GROUND,] which God made to be inhabited.
7. DELIGHTED,] as in Ge. 34. 8, &c.
LEAST,] as in Ex. 12. 4, &c.
OATH,] as in Ge. 26. 3, &c.
STRONG HAND,] and out-stretched arm.
RANSOM,] as in 9. 26.
8. GOD] or 'the God,' i.e. the only true God.

FAITHFUL,] i.e. stedfast.
THE COVENANT,] which Himself had made with them.
THE KINDNESS,] which he had promised to them.
9. GENERATIONS.] See note on Ex. 20. 5.
10. REPAYING,] or 'recompensing.'
FACE,] i.e. openly.
DESTROY THEM] from off the face of the earth.
DELAYETH NOT,] though men sometimes think he hath forgotten it all.
HATING HIM,] as it is said in Ps. 55. 23.
11. THE COMMAND] of God.
12. BECAUSE,] not 'if,' as in the C.V.
JUDGMENTS,] or decisions of what they were to do.
KINDNESS,] not 'mercy,' as in the C.V.
FATHERS,] to do to them.
13. LOVED THEE,] more than ever, because of this obedience.
BLESSED THEE,] in all things.
MULTIPLIED THEE,] as he had promised to thy fathers.
WOMB,] i.e. children.
GROUND,] in the land of Israel.
CORN,] as in Ge. 27. 28.
NEW WINE,] as in Ge. 27. 28.
OIL,] as in Nu. 18. 12.
INCREASE,] as in Ex. 13. 12; De. 28. 4, 18, 51.
OXEN,] as in De. 28. 4, 18, 51; Ps. 8. 8; Prov. 14. 4.
WEALTH,] as in De. 28. 4, 18, 51.
FLOCK] of sheep and goats.
14. PEOPLES] of the earth.
BARREN MAN.] This masculine form is not found elsewhere.
BARREN WOMEN,] as in Ge. 11. 30, &c.
CATTLE,] as in Ge. 1. 24.
15. TURNED ASIDE] so that it might not touch them.
SICKNESS,] as in 28. 59, 61; 1 K. 17. 17; 2 K. 1. 2; 8. 8, 9; 13, 14; 2 Ch. 16. 12; 21. 15, 18, 19; Ps. 41. 3; Ecc. 5. 17; 6. 2; Isa. 1. 5; 38. 9; 53. 34; Jer. 6. 7; 10. 19; Hos. 5. 13.
DISEASES,] as in 28. 60, but not elsewhere.
KNOWN] experimentally, being in Egypt, especially ophthalmia.
PUT,] or 'given.'
16. CONSUMED,] lit. 'devoured.'
TO THEE] for a prey, and a possession.
EYE,] which often affects the heart, as is well known.
PITY,] because they were wicked and abominable.
GODS,] of gold and silver, or wood, or stone.
SNARE,] bringing ruin and destruction.
17. HEART,] i.e. when the first symptoms of unbelief begin to arise, before being expressed in words or actions.
DISPOSSESS THEM,] as the Lord hath commanded.
18. OF THEM,] because of their number and strength.
REMEMBER,] i.e. call to mind, and take encouragement for the future from the personal dealings of God in the past.
19. TRIALS,] of strength between Jehovah and the gods of Egypt, &c.
SIGNS,] or tokens which God had given to manifest his power.

WONDERS] which had never been exhibited before.
STRONG HAND] and stretched-out arm.
20. LOCUST,] as in Ex. 23. 28; Jos. 24. 12.
LEFT] untouched by thy sword.
HIDDEN,] as in 28. 29; Ps. 19. 6, 12.
21. PRESENCE,] or 'face.'
FEARFUL,] as in Ge. 28. 17; Ex. 15. 11; 34. 10; De. 1. 19, &c.
22. LITTLE,] as in Ex. 23. 30.
HASTILY,] as in Ex. 32. 8, &c.
MULTIPLY,] so as to injure, harrass, and destroy thee.
23. BEFORE THEE] in battle.
HAND,] such as Og, Sihon, Adoni-Bezek, Agag, &c.
NAME,] or renown.
STATION HIMSELF] hostilely.
25. GRAVEN IMAGES,] which they worship as representatives of the deity.
DESIRE,] or be 'pleased' with it.
SILVER..GOLD] ornaments, which were often of great value, being gifts of their blind devotees.
SNARED,] or brought into danger by familiarity with things dedicated to idols.
26. HOUSE,] as Achan afterwards did.
DEVOTED] to destruction as it was.
DETEST . . . ABOMINATE.] The strongest terms are used to prevent any attaching themselves to it.
DEVOTED] to destruction, not for use in any way.

VIII. 1. COMMAND,] as in 6. 1.
FATHERS,] and repeated so often that it might not be forgotten.
2. REMEMBERED,] i.e. call to remembrance.
WAY,] from Egypt to Canaan.
FORTY YEARS,] as he had threatened them.
HUMBLE] them for their pride and unbelief.
TRY,] prove and test their obedience and professions.
HEART,] and not merely what they promised with the mouth.
3. HUMBLE] thee, as he had said he would do.
HUNGER,] that they might know their dependence upon him.
MANNA,] which was miraculously supplied to them each morning from the heavens.
KNOWN] before hand, it was not an ordinary substance of food.
BREAD,] i. e. food prepared by man. Mat. 4. 4.
PRODUCE,] i.e. by every thing which the Lord pleases to appoint for man's food, ordinary or extraordinary.
4. RAIMENT,] which they had brought out of Egypt with them, and taken from the Amalekites, &c.
WORN OUT,] as in 29. 5; Neh. 9. 21; compare Jos. 9. 13; Isa. 50. 9; 51. 6, &c.
SWELL,] as in Neh. 9. 21; the original word is used of the swelling of 'dough,' as in Ex. 12. 34, &c. Syr. and Arab. Versions read 'naked,' Sept. 'callous.'
5. KNOWN,] or experienced, not 'considered,' as in C. V.
WITH THY HEART,] or inmost soul, which

agrees in the testimony of thy outward experience.

SON,] i.e. tenderly, and with a true and sincere view to his profit.

THEE,] by keeping thee forty years in the wilderness, trying thee with hunger, thirst, and enemies.

7. BROOKS,] such as Jordan, Jabbok, Kishon, Cedron, Cherith, see 11. 10—12.

FOUNTAINS,] such as Siloam, Gihon, Etam, Tiberias, &c.

DEPTHS.] See on Ge. 1. 2 ; Ex. 15. 5, &c.

VALLEY..MOUNTAIN,] both of which abound in Canaan.

8. WHEAT,] the harvest beginning at Pentecost; see 1 K. 4. 22, 28 ; 5. 11 ; 2 Ch. 2. 10 ; Ezek. 27. 17 ; Acts 12. 20.

BARLEY,] which was begun to be gathered in at the season of the Passover.

VINE,] especially in Lebanon, Eshcol, Engedi, Ashcalon, Gaza, Sarepta, &c.

FIG.] Compare Nu. 13. 23.

POMEGRANATE.] See Nu. 13. 23 ; 20. 5, &c.

OLIVE OIL,] noticed in Ex. 30. 24 ; Lev. 24. 2.

HONEY.] See note on Ge. 43. 11 ; Ex. 3. 8, 17 ; 13. 5, &c.

9. SCARCITY.] This original word does not occur elsewhere, but cognate ones are common.

BREAD,] i.e. food generally.

LACK,] as in Ps. 23. 1, &c.

IRON,] i.e. like iron for hardness.

BRASS,] or 'copper.' Compare 33. 25 ; Job 28. 2.

10. EATEN..SATISFIED..BLESSED.] Compare 6. 11, 12.

12. INHABITED,] in the land of Canaan.

13. MULTIPLIED,] through the goodness and forbearance of God, as he had promised.

14. HIGH] in pride. Compare 1 Tim. 6. 17.

SERVANTS.] Repeated to remind them of their originally low condition.

15. TERRIBLE,] i.e. inspiring fear.

BURNING SERPENT.] See on Nu. 21. 6, 8.

SCORPION.] Compare the only other passages where the word occurs, 1 K. 12. 11, 14 ; 2 Ch. 10. 11, 14 ; Eze. 2. 6.

THIRST,] as in Ps. 107. 33 ; Isa. 35. 7, the only other places where the original word occurs.

FLINTY ROCK,] or 'rock of flint.' See 32. 13 ; Job 28. 9 ; Ps. 114. 8 ; Isa. 50. 7.

16. KNOWN,] as an article of food, Ex. 16. 15, &c.

HUMBLE] thee, and keep thee lowly in God's sight.

TRY,] or prove thy faith and endurance.

LATTER END,] i.e. hereafter. Jer. 24. 5, 6 ; Heb. 12. 11.

17. HEART,] if not with the lips, for the one precedes the other, see 9. 4.

WEALTH,] or 'strength, might, force,' so often. See Hos. 12. 8.

18. POWER,] or 'ability,' Ps. 127. 2 ; Prov. 10. 22 ; Ecc. 9. 11 ; 1 Ch. 29. 12.

ESTABLISH,] lit. ' cause to stand.'

19. PERISH,] because of your sin.

20. NATIONS] of Canaan.

NOT HEARKEN,] so as to be obedient to his voice.

IX. 1. TO-DAY.] The time was so short. (less than 2 months,) that it is regarded as if 'to-day,' see 1. 3, with Jos. 4. 19. Compare John 8. 56 ; 1 Cor. 4. 5 ; Rev. 16. 14.

THYSELF,] as noted in 7. 1.

2. TALL,] as in Nu. 13. 33.

KNOWN,] by the report of the spies.

STATION HIMSELF,] in hostility.

3. KNOWN] experimentally that thy God is greater than they.

CONSUMING,] as in 4. 24, &c.

HUMBLE,] as in Jud. 3. 30 ; 4. 23 ; 11. 33, &c.

DISPOSSESSED,] as in 7. 17.

HASTILY,] as in 7. 22.

4. HEART,] or even entertain the conception in the mind.

IN,] not 'after,' as in C.V.

RIGHTEOUSNESS,] i.e. because of my being in a right state before God, for, by the grace of God I am what I am.

WICKEDNESS.] This was the true cause of their being sentenced to expulsion and death ; each dieth for his own sin. See on this Lev. 18. 3—28, &c.

5. UPRIGHTNESS OF HEART,] as in 1 Ch. 29. 17 ; Job 33. 3 ; Ps. 119. 7 ; 1 K. 3. 6.

ESTABLISH,] as in 8. 18 above.

6. KNOWN,] and been conscious of its truth.

STIFF OF NECK,] as in Ex. 32. 9 ; 33. 3, 5 ; 34. 9 ; De. 9. 6, 13 ; 10. 16 ; 31. 27.

7. THAT WITH WHICH,] even their impatience, unbelief, &c.

WILDERNESS,] at Marah, Sin, Rephidim.

REBELS,] as in v. 24 ; 31. 27.

8. HOREB,] where they received the law.

DESTROY YOU,] because of idolatry. Ex. 32. 10.

9. MOUNT] Sinai, at the Lord's bidding.

STONE,] prepared by Jehovah himself.

COVENANT] of life and peace, which they had promised to keep.

YOU,] and your posterity.

NIGHTS,] see on Ex. 24. 18 ; 32. 1.

DRUNK,] during that period, showing that 'man doth not live on bread alone.'

10. WRITTEN] for perpetuity, not spoken merely.

ASSEMBLY,] Ex. 19. 17 ; De. 4. 10—12.

12. HATH DONE CORRUPTLY,] as in Ex. 32. 7.

WAY] of duty, in reference to idolatry, see Ex. 20. 1—3.

MOLTEN THING.] See note on Ex. 32. 4 ; a calf of gold.

13. SEEN,] and observed, and considered its doings.

STIFF OF NECK,] as in v. 6 above.

14. DESIST FROM ME,] as in Jud. 11. 37 ; 1 Sa. 11. 3 ; 15. 16 ; 2 Sa. 24. 16 ; 2 K. 4. 27 ; 1 Ch. 21. 15 ; Ps. 37. 8 ; 46. 10.

BLOT OUT,] as in Ge. 6. 7 ; 7. 4, &c.

TAKE IT.] See Ex. 32. 10.

15. ON,] not 'in,' as in C.V.

16. HALF] of your ear-rings, &c.

HASTILY,] within six weeks after his leaving them.

17. EYES,] implying a dissolution of the covenant which they were signs of.

18. THROW MYSELF,] in prayer and supplication.

THE EVIL THING,] i.e. idolatry.

19. AFRAID,] and trembled exceedingly, lest the Lord should execute his vengeance.

HEARKEN,] so as to grant his request, and spare the people.

ALSO,] as at other times, when he interceded for them.

20. AARON,] for complying with the sinful demands of the people; this special circumstance is not noticed elsewhere.

21. YOUR SIN,] i.e. your sinful formation—the calf.

DUST,] Ex. 32. 20.

BROOK,] and made them drink of it, as narrated in Exodus.

22. TABERAH,] Nu. 11. 1; 3. 5.

MASSAH,] Ex. 17. 7.

KIBROTH-HATTAAVAH,] Nu. 11. 4, 34.

23. KADESH-BARNEA,] Nu. 13. 3; 14. 1.

VOICE,] as noticed in Ps. 106. 24, 25.

24. REBELS,] as in v. 7 above.

KNOWING YOU,] Ex. 2. 11—14; Acts 7. 25; Ex. 5. 20, 21.

25. THROW MYSELF,] in prayer, as in v. 18 above.

26. DESTROY NOT,] in deprecation of what was said in v. 14 above.

PEOPLE,] as in Ex. 32. 11, &c.

INHERITANCE.] This clause is wanting in Ex. 32. 11.

RANSOMED,] as in 7. 8; 15. 15; 21. 8; 24. 18; 13. 5, &c.

HAND,] as noticed in Ex. 3. 19.

27. BE MINDFUL,] as in Ex. 32. 13.

STIFFNESS.] Compare Ex. 32. 9, &c.

WICKEDNESS,] generally in going astray from the path set before them.

SIN,] in this particular act of disobedience.

28. LAND,] i.e. its inhabitants.

BROUGHT US OUT,] i.e. Egypt.

WANT OF ABILITY,] as in Nu. 14. 16.

PUT..TO DEATH,] by various means, and not merely by 'slaying' them, as in the C.V.

29. PEOPLE,] by covenant engagement, and thy

INHERITANCE,] which he had voluntarily taken to himself.

X. 1. AT THAT TIME,] after Moses had appeased the Lord.

GRAVE,] as in Ex. 34. 1, 4, &c.

ARK,] see Ex. 25. 10.

2. ON THE FIRST,] not 'in,' as in C.V.

IN THE ARK,] for preservation, Ex. 25. 16, 21.

3. I MAKE,] by the hands of Bezeleel.

SHITTIM WOOD,] because of its durability, see Ex. 25. 5.

4. TEN MATTERS,] as in Ex. 34. 28.

ASSEMBLY,] as in 9. 10 above.

5. THERE,] when Moses was speaking, 38 years after they were made. Until the destruction of the temple by Nebuchadnezzar they doubtless remained in the ark, along with the other holy memorials, but what became of them afterwards is unknown. They may then have been destroyed by the fire, but as they were held in special reverence, it is perfectly possible that they may have been concealed by those who had the charge of them in the lower chambers of the temple, in the hope of their escaping

the hands of the invaders, and if so, they may yet be found entombed in the immense mass of ruined buildings which lie at the base of the Mosque of Omar. The possibility of recovering such treasure would warrant vigorous efforts being made for excavations in that locality.

6. BEEROTH,] lit. 'wells.' Aben Ezra supposes it to be Kadesh.

MOSERA,] not mentioned elsewhere except it be the same as Moseroth (Nu. 33. 31), the 27th station of the Israelites. The Samaritan reads the 6th and 7th verses thus: 'And the sons of Israel have journeyed from Moseroth, and they encamp in Bene-Yaakan; whence they have journeyed, and encamp in Gudgodah; whence they have journeyed, and encamp in Jotbathah, a land of brooks of water; whence they have journeyed, and encamp in Ebronah; whence they have journeyed, and encamp in Ezion-Geber; whence they have journeyed, and encamp in the wilderness of Zin, which is Kadesh; whence they have journeyed, and encamp in mount Hor, and there Aaron dieth, and he is buried there, and Eleazar his son doth act as priest in his stead,' which is more in accordance with Nu. 33. 31. Wall and Boothroyd omit v. 6—9 entirely as out of their proper place.

THERE,] i.e. Mosera, which may be another name for mount Hor.

8. AT THAT TIME.] Compare Nu. 3. 6; 4. 4; 8. 14; 16. 9.

TO BEAR] on the shoulder, which was the special duty of the Kohathites, Nu. 3. 31; 10. 21; 1 Ch. 5. 1.

TO STAND,] as a ministering servant.

TO SERVE HIM] in holy things, by bringing near to Him the offerings of the people, and by carrying out His will and directions to them.

TO BLESS] the people in His name, under the sanction of His authority.

UNTO THIS DAY] and for ever, i.e. until the close of that dispensation.

9. BRETHREN,] in the division of the land of Canaan, his share being given to Ephraim, the younger son of Joseph.

INHERITANCE,] i.e. all that the people were to give to the Lord, was given by him to the Levites.

10. STOOD] before God, in the mount, to hear and obey His commands.

HEARKENETH,] and complieth with the intercessory prayer of Moses for the people.

TIME,] lit. 'step,' see note on Ge. 2. 23.

NOT WILLED,] or 'not been willing,' as in Ex. 10. 27; De. 1. 26; 23. 5; 25. 7, &c.

11. GO TO THE JOURNEY,] which they yet had before they could come to the land of rest.

BEFORE THE PEOPLE,] as their leader and guide; as the shepherd goes before the flock, not after them. John 10. 4.

12. ASKING FROM THEE,] in return for all his kindnesses.

TO FEAR,] i.e. reverence him whom they had avouched to be their covenant-God.

WAYS,] which he had spoken of to them, all being holy, just, and good.

I

TO LOVE HIM] who first loved them; not as servants merely, but as friends.

TO SERVE HIM] as he himself had directed, without consulting their ownperverseminds.

HEART,] i.e. sincerely.

SOUL,] i.e. fully.

13. TO KEEP,] watch, and observe, all his laws.

GOOD.] Happiness being always associated with duty.

14. TO JEHOVAH..IN IT.] All things are God's, and he has numberless objects in which he might delight himself, but

15. ONLY,] or solely, in Israel did He please to manifest his special grace, not because they were more numerous or better than others, but agreeably to his good pleasure.

16. CIRCUMCISED,] i.e. removed or cut off that which prevents your hearts from being duly impressed by a sense of his love.

HARDEN,] or 'stiffen,' in pride and obstinacy.

17. YOUR GOD,] by your own solemn avowal.

GOD OF THE GODS,] i.e. supreme above all that is called God or worshipped.

LORD OF THE LORDS.] However great any may be in power and authority, there is one —the Lord Jehovah—who is greater still.

THE GOD,] lit. 'the Mighty One,' described as 'the great, the mighty (or hero), the fearful,' i.e. the one who inspires with awe and reverence his foes and his friends.

PERSONS,] or 'faces,' i.e. is not to be propitiated by outward appearances.

BRIBE,] as if he needed anything. Job 36. 18, 19.

18. HE IS DOING,] even now, habitually.

WIDOW,] or those who have no help in man.

SOJOURNER,] who has come from another land or tribe to be near Him.

RAIMENT,] which are all that are promised to God's own peculiar people. Isa. 33. 16.

19. YE WERE,] as in Lev. 19. 33, 34, &c.

20. FEAR,] i.e. reverence, and Him only.

SERVE,] in all the ways that God hath directed in his Word.

CLEAVE] continually, without intermission.

NAME,] when so required to do to promote the cause of justice.

21. THY PRAISE,] i.e. the object of thy praise, as in Ps. 22. 25; 40. 3; 15. 1; 71. 6; 109. 1; 148. 14; Jer. 17. 14.

THY GOD,] by thine entering into the covenant with him to be thy people.

FEARFUL,] i.e. inspiring awe and reverence.

SEEN] in Egypt, the wilderness, &c.

22. SEVENTY,] as in Ge. 46. 27, &c.

MULTITUDE,] i.e. very numerous, so much so that as one trying to count the stars would soon give it up from their number, so would it be with any one attempting to number Israel.

XI. 1. LOVED.] Without love all service or obedience rendered to God would be worthless.

KEPT] all these things—sacred and civil —which he has laid on Israel.

ALL THE DAYS,] of thy life on earth.

2. YOUR SONS,] of tender years and childish understanding.

CHASTISEMENT,] for sin which he has bestowed alike on his friends and his foes, especially however on the latter, as noted in the next verse.

3. SIGNS,] not 'miracles,' as in C.V.

4. FORCE,] i.e. power, vigour of its inhabitants, as collected in its army.

SEA OF SUPH,] see note on Ex. 10. 19, &c.

CAUSED TO FLOW.] This original verb is only found elsewhere in 2 K. 6. 6; Lam. 3. 54.

AGAINST THEIR FACES,] or 'over their faces.'

DESTROYED THEM,] their land and army, so that they had not as yet recovered their strength to pursue or harass them as they did afterwards in the days of Rehoboam, &c.

5. TO YOU,] in the way of mercy and of judgment.

6. DATHAN, ETC.] See Nu. 16. 1—33.

ALL THAT LIVETH,] as in Ge. 7. 4, 23, the only other passages where the original word occurs.

AT THEIR FEET.] Compare similar phrases in Ge. 30. 30; 33. 14; 49. 10; Ex. 11. 8; De. 28. 57; 33. 3.

7. YOUR EYES,] not those of your sons.

8. STRONG.] Compare Isa. 40. 1, &c.

9. PROLONG,] as in 4. 40, &c.

SWORN,] as in 9. 5, &c.

HONEY,] as in Ex. 3. 8, &c.

10. THY SEED,] after the overflowing of the Nile.

FOOT.] The foot is much more used by Orientals than by Westerns; having generally no stockings or shoes they can and do use it for various purposes where a European would use his hand, and in Egypt especially, various contrivances for watering the thirsty land are put in operation by the toes and feet, especially in gardens with artificial canals in them, conveying water from the rivers or wells in the neighbourhood.

11. HILLS AND VALLEYS,] hence called 'that goodly hill-country,' in 3. 25.

WATER,] whereas rain is very uncommon in Egypt.

12. SEARCHING,] that nothing evil may be in it; not merely 'caring for,' as in C.V.

YEAR,] that is, continually, in summer and winter, spring and autumn.

13. SOUL,] as in 10. 12 above.

14. SPRINKLING,] i.e. that gentle fertilizing rain which falls in drops; it is only mentioned elsewhere in Jer. 5. 24; it fell in October, after sowing.

GATHERED,] i.e. that which fell in heavy showers about March; noticed in Job 29. 23; Prov. 16. 15; Jer. 3. 3; 5. 24; Hos. 6. 3; Joel 2. 23; Zec. 10. 1.

GATHERED] into storehouses; without these rains there had been no crops whatever.

OIL.] All these were for themselves, while the

15. HERBS] in the field were abundant

for their cattle, so that both man and beast were
SATISFIED] with God's provision.
16. ENTICED,] as in Ex. 22. 16, &c.
BOWED THEMSELVES,] as in Ge. 18. 2, &c.
17. BURNED,] as in 7. 4, &c.
RESTRAINED,] as in 1 K. 8. 35; 2 Ch. 6. 26; 7. 13.
INCREASE,] as in Lev. 26. 4, 20, &c.
18. ON,] not 'in' the heart and soul; this, of course, could only be done figuratively, and hence there is no propriety in supposing that the
SIGN] on the hand, and the
FRONTLETS] between the eyes, are intended to be taken literally, as the Jews imagine.
19. SONS,] as they also were under the bond of the same covenant as their fathers.
SITTING] at ease in thy dwelling.
GOING] on to business in the ways and paths of the city.
LYING DOWN] to rest at night.
RISING UP] in the morning. All this was to indicate the care with which they were to train up their families in the ways of the Lord.
20. WRITTEN.] This implies, at least, that writing was a common acquirement among the Israelites even in the days of Moses. See note on Ex. 17. 14, &c.
GATES.] See notes on 6. 7—9.
21. ON THE GROUND,] not 'in the land,' as in the C.V. Ps. 91. 16, &c.
DAYS OF THE HEAVENS.] Ps. 89. 29, is the only other passage where this peculiar phrase occurs; it evidently means, 'as long as the heavens endure.'
EARTH,] or 'land,' i.e. of Canaan.
22. THIS COMMAND,] not 'these commandments,' as in the C.V.
CLEAVE.] See 10. 12, 20.
23. NATIONS.] See 7. 1, for the names of seven of these nations; also 9. 1.
24. WILDERNESS,] where they now were, at the south of Judea, on
LEBANON,] at the north of Palestine.
EUPHRATES,] on which see Ge. 2. 14; it was to form the eastern boundary of the land of promise, and was afterwards realized in the history of David, and Solomon, 1 K. 4. 21.
FARTHER SEA,] i.e. the Mediterranean; see 34. 2; Joel 2. 20; Zech. 14. 8.
25. STATION HIMSELF,]in a hostile manner.
PUT,] or 'give.'
SPOKEN.] See De. 2. 25; Ex. 15. 14—16; compare Jos. 2. 9—11.
26. SETTING,] or 'giving.' So in v. 32 below.
REVILING,] as in Ge. 27. 12, &c.
27. THE BLESSING,] of long life and prosperity, 28. 1—6.
28. THE REVILING] of God and men, 28. 15—20; 29. 20.
KNOWN] to be such, by receiving blessings from them, as they had received from Him.
29. GERIZIM,] noticed again in 27. 12; Jos. 8. 33; Jud. 9. 7.
EBAL,] opposite to Gerizim, 27. 4, 13; Jos. 8. 30, 33.
30. BEYOND] the Jordan, in the hill-

country of Samaria, sixty miles from where Israel now was.
GOING IN] of the sun, i.e. westward.
THE CANAANITE,] i.e. that special tribe which gave its name to the land, see on Ge. 13. 7; Nu. 13. 29, &c.
GILGAL,] which Lightfoot thinks means 'Galilee' here.
OAKS OF MOREH.]See on Ge. 12. 6; Jud. 7. 1. Jonathan reads 'Mamre,' as in Ge. 13. 18.

XII. 1. HATH GIVEN] by oath; not 'doth give,' as in C.V.
GROUND,] not 'earth.'
2. UTTERLY,]*lit.* 'destroying ye do destroy.'
PLACES] or spots whese they had set up their idols, &c.
MOUNTAINS..HEIGHTS.] Compare 2 K. 16. 4; 17. 10. 11; Jer. 2. 20; 3. 6; such places were frequented for the like purposes by the ancient Greeks, Romans, &c.
GREEN TREE.] The *oak* anciently was reckoned sacred to Jupiter, the *laurel* to Apollo, the *ivy* to Bacchus, the *olive* to Minerva, the *myrtle* to Venus, &c.
3. BROKEN DOWN,] as in Lev. 11. 35; Jud. 6. 28; 2 Ch. 31. 1; 33. 3; 34. 4, 7; 36. 19; Eze. 16. 39.
SHIVERED,] as in 7. 5; 9. 17, &c.
STANDING PILLARS,] as in Ex. 23. 24; 34. 13; De. 7. 5, &c.
SHRINES,] as in Ex. 34. 13; De. 7. 5; 16. 21, &c.
GRAVEN IMAGES,] as in 7. 5, 25
CUT DOWN,] as in 7. 5, &c.
NAME] *or* 'renown.'
4. DO SO,] i.e. sacrifice to him on hills or under trees, but only where he has appointed.
5. TABERNACLE,] which he himself had appointed.
SEEK,] or 'enquire.'
6. BURNT-OFFERINGS,] as in Ex. 20. 24; Lev. 17. 8, 9, &c.
SACRIFICES,] for sin, trespass, thanksgivings, &c.
TITHES,] of all their produce, for the Levites.
HEAVE-OFFERING,] as in Ex. 25. 2, &c.
VOWS,] as in v. 11, 17, 26, &c.
FREE-WILL OFFERINGS,]as in Ex. 35. 29,&c.
FIRSTLINGS] which were the Lord's, see Ex. 13. 2.
7. EATEN] of your sacrifices and offerings.
HAND,] i.e. every thing you do is a cause of rejoicing.
BLESSED THEE.] Compare Ps. 127. 5, for the psalmist's opinion to the same effect.
8. RIGHT..EYES,]being yet in an unsettled state, as it were; they had forgotten, for example, the rite of circumcision entirely, see Jos. 5. 2—9; and also for the reason assigned in the next verse.
9. REST,] as in Nu. 10. 33.
INHERITANCE,] as in Ex. 15. 17.
11. CHOICE OF YOUR VOWS.] Compare similar phrases in Ge. 23. 6; Ex. 15. 4; Isa. 22. 7; 37. 24; Jer. 22. 7, &c.
12. BEFORE JEHOVAH,] i.e. as in his presence, with his countenance and protection. Burdensome as the ceremonial rites undoubtedly were, they were commanded

to 'rejoice' in their celebration no less than believers are under the new covenant.   Phil. 3. 1; 4. 4, &c.

GATES,] whether those of a private dwelling or of a city; the Levites were the instructors of Israel along with the priests and prophets.

NO PART.] See 10. 9; 14. 29. &c.

13. BURNT OFFERINGS,] or animal sacrifices of any kind.

CAUSE TO ASCEND] on the altar of God.

THOU SEEST,] as suitable for building an altar; the *place*, as well as the *kind* of sacrifice was prescribed to them.

14. COMMANDING THEE] regarding sacrifices.

15. SACRIFICE,] as the word is used in Ge. 31. 54, &c.

UNCLEAN..CLEAN.] Those ceremonially so, which was forbidden with regard to the great festivals.

ROE,] as in v. 22; 14. 5; 15. 22; 2 Sa. 1. 19; 2. 18; 1 K. 4. 23; 1 Ch. 12. 8; Prov. 6. 5; Song 2. 7, &c.

HART,] as in v. 22; 14. 5; 15. 22; 1 K. 4. 23; Ps. 42. 1; Song 2. 9, 17; 8. 14; Isa. 35. 6; Lam. 1. 6.

16. BLOOD.] Compare Ge. 9. 4; Lev. 7. 26; 17. 10, &c,

EAT,] or 'consume,' as in v. 23 below.

POUR IT OUT,] as in Ex. 29. 12, &c.

17. TITHE.] Compare 14. 22—29.

FIRSTLINGS,] see v. 6 above.

HEAVE-OFFERING,] see 26. 1—11, &c.

18. FIX ON,] out of all their tribes, for a meeting with his people.

GATES,] either public or private.

REJOICED,] as in v. 12 above.

PUTTING FORTH,] i.e. exercise of thy hand, arm, or power.

19. FORSAKE,] by leaving him uncared for and unprovided.

THY GROUND,] not 'the earth,' as in C.V.

20. ENLARGE,] or 'make wide,' as in Ex. 34. 24; De. 19. 8.

BORDER,] or territory.

SPOKEN,] as in Ge. 15. 18; 28. 14; Ex. 34. 24, &c.

LONGETH,] as in 14. 26.

DESIRE,] as in v. 15 above.

21. SACRIFICED,] as in Ge. 21. 54, &c.

22. ROE..HART,] as in v. 15 above.

23. BE SURE,] *lit.* 'be strong,' as in 31. 6, 7, 23.

LIFE,] *lit.* 'soul,' or 'breathing' principle.

24. WATER,] see v. 16 above.

25. JEHOVAH,] the covenant-God of Israel.

26. HOLY THINGS,] i.e. things consecrated to God, viz. offerings, &c.

VOWS,] i.e. things vowed to him.

27. MADE,] or performed.

THY GOD,] to whom alone they were to offer them.

POURED OUT,] as commanded in Ex. 29. 12, &c.

29. CUT OFF] by a judicial decision, which Israel was to carry out.

30. SNARED,] and drawn into evil practices.

ENQUIRE,] or 'seek,' as in v. 5 above.

EVEN I.] Compare 2 K. 16. 10—16.

31. ABOMINATION,] or 'abominable thing.'

BURN,] thereby testifying their devotion to these gods; this God directly prohibited.

32. WHOLE THING,] not a part of it merely.

ADD,] anything out of your own imaginations, with the view of magnifying God.

DIMINISH,] so as to lessen His authority.

XIII. 1. PROPHET,] i.e. one who professes to declare, expound, or reveal, the will of God.

DREAM,] by which medium God often declared his will; see Ge. 20. 3, 6; 31. 10, 11, 12; 37. 5, &c.

SIGN,] or 'token,' as in Ge. 1. 14; 4. 15; 9. 12, 13, 17; 17. 11, &c.

WONDER,] as in Ex. 4. 21; 7. 3, 9; 11. 9, 10; De. 4. 34; 6. 22; 7. 19, &c.

2. HATH COME,] in the providence of God, that they might be 'tried,' and 'proved.'

OTHER GODS,] or objects of worship.

KNOWN,] as possessing power or ability to help any.

SERVE,] by extolling their name, or giving of substance to their honour.

3. TRYING,] or 'proving' your stedfastness to him.

4. WALK,] in your daily life and behaviour.

FEAR,] or reverence, as the 'trier of the heart and reins.'

KEEP,] watch, and observe.

HEARKEN,] as to the only authority over the soul.

SERVE] continually, and in the way he has appointed.

CLEAVE,] in love and devotedness, with the whole heart.

5. PUT TO DEATH,] by a legal sentence; Jehovah being supreme king in Israel.

IS RANSOMING] even now; they were still depending on him for complete deliverance.

DRIVE YOU AWAY,] by the force of his arguments and persuasion.

WALK,] habitually, and with the whole heart.

EVIL THING,] i.e. idolatry.

6. BROTHER..SON..DAUGHTER,] i.e. any of thy nearest relatives.

THINE OWN SOUL.] Compare the love of Jonathan and David, 1 Sa. 18. 1.

MOVE THEE,] as in Jos. 13. 18; Jud. 1. 14; 1 Sa. 26. 19; 2 Sa. 24. 1; 1 K. 21. 25; 2 K. 18. 32; 1 Ch. 21. 1, &c.

IN SECRET,] as in 27. 15, 24; 28. 57; Jud. 3. 19; 1 Sa. 19. 2; 25. 20; 2 Sa. 12. 12; Job 13. 10; 22. 14, &c.

7. THE PEOPLES,] i.e. Ammonites, Edomites, Moabites, Philistines, &c.

8. CONSENT,] as in 1 K. 20. 8; Prov. 1. 10, &c.

HAVE PITY,] as in 7. 16, &c.

SPARE,] as in 1 Sa. 15. 3, &c.

COVER HIM OVER,] as in Ge. 37. 26, &c.

9. SLAY] him, as an enemy of God, the supreme ruler in Israel; of course, this was to be done legally.

THY HAND,] as the accuser and witness, and that of

ALL THE PEOPLE,] as concurring in condemning his crime.

10. STONED.] This was a very old, and very natural way of putting criminals to

death, where a great number of persons were concerned.

DRIVE THEE.] See v. 5 above.

SERVANTS,] and who is therefore thine owner and thy Lord.

11. FEAR,] departing from the living God.

EVIL THING,] i.e. seducing to idolatry.

12. WHEN,] not 'if,' as in the C.V., which the original word never means.

13. WORTHLESSNESS,] i.e. worthless or useless sons, as the word Belial literally signifies.

FORCE AWAY,] by enticing arguments and persuasions.

14. ENQUIRED,] as in 17. 4, 9; 19. 18, &c.

SEARCHED,] as in Jud. 18. 2; 1 Sa. 20. 12; 2 Sa. 10. 3, &c.

ASKED DILIGENTLY,] that there might be no deception.

TRUTH.] It is really so, as reported.

ESTABLISHED,] as true, by competent witnesses.

ABOMINATION] of idolatry, which God hates.

15. SWORD,] because they had yielded to the temptation.

DEVOTING IT] to the will of God, which in such cases was utter destruction.

CATTLE,] that no living thing might escape.

16. SPOIL,] of silver, gold, merchandize, utensils, &c.

BROAD PLACE,] of public concourse.

BEFORE JEHOVAH,] i.e. as a religious act, and not a mere personal piece of revenge.

17. DEVOTED THING] of the city, even as a relict—it was all to be consumed by fire, as an emblem of the wrath of God against sin, and especially idolatry. Compare Joshua's treatment of Jericho, 6. 26.

MERCIES,] for soul and body.

FATHERS,] to be a God to them and to their seed after them.

XIV. 1. SONS YE ARE,] and therefore subject to God's authority. Mal. 1. 6; Eph. 5. 1; Rom. 8. 16; 9. 8, 26; Gal. 3 26.

CUT YOURSELVES] for the dead, as the nations did and still do, Lev. 19. 28, &c.

BALDNESS,] by shaving the eye-brows; this perhaps was in opposition to the Egyptian custom of serving Isis.

2. HOLY PEOPLE,] i.e. one separated or set apart for his service alone.

PEOPLE,] to show forth his praises, and a PECULIAR TREASURE,] as in Ex. 19. 5, on which see notes. De. 7. 6.

3. ABOMINABLE THING,] either in its own nature, or in consequence of its being directly prohibited by God.

4. OX..SHEEP..GOAT,] which were all used in sacrifice.

5. HART,] as in 12. 15.

ROE,] as in 12. 15.

FALLOW-DEER,] only noticed elsewhere in 1 K. 4. 23.

WILD GOAT,] not mentioned elsewhere.

PYGARG,] not mentioned elsewhere; in Heb. dishon.

WILD OX,] not mentioned elsewhere.

CHAMOIS,] not mentioned elsewhere.

6. HOOF,] as in Lev. 11 3, 4, 6, 7.

CLEFT,] as in Lev. 11. 3, 7, 26.

BRINGING UP] the cud, as in Lev. 11. 3, 4, 7, 26; and in v. 7. 8 below.

7. CAMEL,] as in Ge. 12. 16; Lev. 11. 4.

HARE,] as in Lev. 11. 16; not mentioned elsewhere.

RABBIT,] as in Lev. 11. 5; Ps. 104. 18; Prov. 30. 26.

UNCLEAN,] ceremonially for food or sacrifice

8. SOW,] as in Lev. 11. 7, &c.

CARCASE,] lit. 'fallen thing.' See Lev. 5. 2, &c.

9. FINS..SCALES,] as in Lev. 11. 9, 10, 12.

11. CLEAN BIRD,] i.e. fit for sacrifice.

12. EAGLE,] as in Ex. 19. 4; Lev. 11. 13, &c.

OSSIFRAGE,] as in Lev. 11. 13; not mentioned elsewhere.

OSPRAY,] as in Lev. 11. 13; not mentioned elsewhere.

13. GLEDE,] not mentioned elsewhere.

KITE,] as in Lev. 11. 14; Job 28. 7.

VULTURE,] only mentioned elsewhere in Isa. 34. 15.

14. RAVEN,] as in Ge. 8. 7, &c.

15. OWL,] lit. 'daughter of the ostrich, as in Lev. 11. 16.

NIGHT-HAWK,] as in Lev. 11. 16; not mentioned elsewhere.

CUCKOO,] as in Lev. 11. 16; not mentioned elsewhere.

HAWK,] as in Lev. 11. 16; Job 39. 26; not mentioned elsewhere.

16. LITTLE OWL,] as in Lev. 11. 17; Ps. 102. 6; not mentioned elsewhere.

GREAT OWL,] as in Lev. 11. 17; Isa. 34. 11; not mentioned elsewhere.

SWAN,] as in Lev. 11. 18, 30; not mentioned elsewhere.

17. PELICAN,] as in Lev. 11. 18, &c.

GIER EAGLE,] not mentioned elsewhere.

CORMORANT,] as in Lev. 11. 17; not mentioned elsewhere.

18. STORK,] as in Lev. 11. 19, &c.

HERON,] as in Lev. 11. 19; not mentioned elsewhere.

LAPWING,] as in Lev. 11. 19; not mentioned elsewhere.

BAT,] as in Lev. 11. 19; Isa. 2. 20; not mentioned elsewhere.

19. TEEMING THING.] See note on Ge. 1. 20.

20. CLEAN FOWL,] as in v. 11 above.

21. CARCASE,] as in v. 8 above.

GIVE,] in a present.

SELL,] for money.

BOIL A KID,] as in Ex. 16. 23; 23. 19; 34. 26, being a heathen practice for incantations.

22. INCREASE,] as in Ge. 47. 24, &c.

23. BEFORE JEHOVAH,] as in a religious festival.

FEAR,] i.e. reverence God, by obeying his commands.

ALL THE DAYS] of thy life.

24. TO BEAR] the increase of thy seed.

25. MONEY,] for money.

BOUND UP] into bags, as is common in the east, where money is not so much counted as weighed. See Ge. 23. 16, &c.

IN THY HAND,] i.e. along with thee.

26. STRONG DRINK.] See notes on Ge 9. 21; 43. 34; Lev. 10. 9, &c.

27 LEVITE,] see 12. 12, 18, 19.
INHERITANCE,] Nu. 18. 20; De. 18. 1, 2, &c.

XV. 1. SEVEN.] This number being a sign of perfection.
RELEASE,] i.e. of debts, as in v. 2, 3, 9; 31. 10; in Ex. 23. 11 a release of the land is spoken of.
2. MATTER] not 'manners,' as in C.V.
OWNER,] *lit.* 'lord of a loan;' this phrase is not found elsewhere.
LIFT UP,] as in 24. 10.
EXACT,] as in Ex. 3. 7; 5. 6, 10, 13, 14, &c.
PROCLAIMED,] *lit.* 'called,' i.e. publicly, that all who wished, might avail themselves of it.
TO,] *or* with a view to Jehovah's glory, honour, and will.
3. STRANGER,] as in Ge. 31. 15, &c.
4. ONLY,] as in Nu. 18. 28; 22. 35; 23. 13, &c.
WITH THEE,] *or* 'in thee.'
NEEDY ONE,] as in Ex. 23. 6, 11, &c.
5. ONLY,] as in Ge. 6. 5; 20. 11; 26. 29; 47. 26; Ex. 8. 29, &c.
6. HATH BLESSED,] not 'blesseth,' as in C.V.
SPOKEN,] not 'promised.'
LENT..BORROWED,] as in v. 8 below.
7. WHEN,] not 'if,' as in the C.V.
GATES,] *or* cities, because these generally had gates.
HARDEN,] as in 2. 30; 2 Ch. 36. 13, &c.
SHUT,] as the word is used in Job 5. 16; Ps. 77. 9; 107. 42; Isa. 52. 15.
8. CERTAINLY OPEN.] The *necessity* rather than the *extent* of the liberality is enjoined.
LEND,] as in v. 6 above.
SUFFICIENT,] as in Ex. 36. 5, 7.
LACK,] as in Jud. 18. 10; 19. 19, 20; Ps. 34. 9; Prov. 6. 11; 11. 24; 14. 23; 21. 5, 17; 22. 16; 24. 34; 28. 27.
9. WORD,] not 'thought,' as in C.V.
WORTHLESS,] as in 13. 13, which see.
EYE IS EVIL,] as in 28. 54, 56; Prov. 23. 6; 28. 22; Mat. 20. 15.
CALLED,] not necessarily 'cried.'
IN THEE,] not 'unto thee.'
10. SAD,] as in 1 Sa. 1. 8, &c.
FOR BECAUSE OF THIS,] not 'because that for this,' as in C.V.
PUTTING FORTH,] i.e. exercise.
11. CERTAINLY OPEN,] as in v. 8 above.
12. WHEN,] not 'if.'
SOLD,] for debt, for a limited period, a far more reasonable plan of dealing with a debtor, than that pursued in some countries, viz., imprisoning him perhaps for life!
SEND HIM AWAY,] as in Ge. 3. 23, not merely 'let him go.'
FREE,] as in Ex. 21. 2, &c., without ransom or payment of any kind.
13. EMPTY,] as in Ge. 31. 42, &c., lest he be 'poor and steal.'
14. ENCIRCLE,] as in Ps. 73. 6, &c., surround him with blessings.
WINE-VAT,] as in Nu. 18. 27, 30, &c.
15. REMEMBER.] Gratitude for past mercies is the best way of obtaining future ones.
17. AWL,] as in Ex. 21. 6, on which see note.
HAND-MAID,] or female servant, who had no desire to leave his service.

18. HARD,] *or* 'sharp,' as in 1. 17, &c.
DOUBLE,] as in Ge. 41. 43; 43. 12, 15, &c., *free*-labour is well known to be much more renumerative than *slave*-labour.
19. FIRSTLING..MALE,] as in Ex. 13. 2, &c.
SANCTIFY,] i.e. separate *or* set apart.
WORK,] do any servile labour, so as to injure or wear it out.
SHEAR,] to obtain profit from it, in any way.
21. BLEMISH,] as in Lev. 22. 20, &c., the *best* must be given to Him who gave it all.
22. ROE..HART,] as in 12. 15, 22.
23. BLOOD,] as in 12. 23, &c., because it contains the vital principle.
POUR IT,] as in 12. 16, &c.

XVI. 1. ABIB,] *or* Nisan, part of March and April, the corn beginning to ripen; the first of the sacred months.
A PASSOVER,] as in Ex. 12. 2; 13. 4.
BY NIGHT,] when the Egyptians were bury ing their dead.
2. A PASSOVER,] as in v. 1 above.
CHOOSE,] at any time hereafter.
3. ANY FERMENTED THING,] as in Ex. 12. 8.
UNLEAVENED THINGS,] i.e. food of any kind.
BREAD,] i.e. food of affliction, suitable for it.
IN HASTE,] being anxious to depart, and the Egyptians urgent in pressing them out.
4. LEAVEN,] not merely 'leavened bread,' but anything else with leaven.
BORDER,] not 'coast,' as in C.V.
REMAIN,] *lit.* 'lodge.'
5. GATES,] i.e. cities, as often.
6. TABERNACLE,] i. e. wherever the ark was.
EVENING,] *lit.* 'mixture,' see on Ge. 1. 5.
7. COOKED,] *lit.* 'boiled,' as in Ex. 16. 23; but Ex. 12. 8, 9, shows that the passover was not to be boiled; the original word here therefore must be understood in a wider sense.
MORNING,] after the last day of the feast was over, 1 K. 3. 66; 2 Ch. 7. 10.
TENTS,] i.e. dwellings, as the word often denotes.
8. RESTRAINT,] as in Lev. 23. 36, &c.
NO WORK,] as on other days.
9. SEVEN WEEKS,] i.e. forty-nine days after the festival of the passover, when the next festival, called Pentecost (meaning *fifty*) was observed.
SICKLE,] which was on the day following the conclusion of the passover, in the barley harvest. Lev. 23. 15.
10. MADE,] i.e. done, performed, observed FEAST OF WEEKS,] i.e. Pentecost.
TRIBUTE,] of honour and respect.
FREE-WILL OFFERING,] for God loveth a cheerful giver; while some things were enjoined as a law, others were left to *grace.*
11. REJOICED,] as in all the other festivals.
12. REMEMBERED,] with humility and gratitude their former servitude and distress.
STATUTES,] regarding the festivals.
13. BOOTHS.] See Lev. 23. 34, &c., so called because of their remaining during its con-

tinuance under these. It is called the 'feast of in-gathering,' in Ex. 23. 16.

IN-GATHERING,] on the 15th day of Tisri or September.

14. REJOICED,] as in v. 11 above.

15. SEVEN DAYS,] which also was the duration of the passover, and of the feast of weeks.

ONLY REJOICING.] No sorrow being allowed to interrupt their happiness.

16. THREE TIMES,] *lit.* ' steps;' see note on Ge. 2. 23.

MALES,] females being exempt; the rabbis in more modern times have perverted this by maintaining that females are exempt from the public worship of God even in the synagogues.

APPEAR,] *lit.* ' be seen;' it is much more naturally read actively: ' see,' discarding the Masoretic points, which in such phrases as the present, are evidently designed to suit such passages as Ex. 33. 20. A miserable human device to meet a fancied difficulty, as in Ex. 23. 16, &c.

UNLEAVENED THINGS,] before the barley-harvest.

WEEKS,] before the wheat-harvest.

BOOTHS,] after the in-gathering of the vintage and summer-fruits.

EMPTY,] seeing they had either the prospect, or the possession, of plenty. Compare Ex. 23. 16, &c.

17. GIFT OF HIS HAND,] i.e. whatever he had at the time, whether more or less.

18. JUDGES,] as in Ex. 2. 14; Nu. 25. 5; De. 1. 16, &c.

AUTHORITIES,] as in Ex. 5. 6, 10, 14, 15, 19; Nu. 11. 16; De. 1. 15, &c.

GATES,] *or* ' cities.'

TRIBES,] each having their own rulers selected out of themselves.

JUDGMENT,] they being, as it were, in the place of God.

19. TURN ASIDE,] as in Ex. 23. 2, 6; Prov. 17. 23; 18. 5; Isa. 10. 2; La. 3. 35.

DISCERN,] as in 1. 17; Prov. 24. 23; 28. 21, &c.

BRIBE,] as in Ex. 23. 8; De. 10. 17; 27. 25, &c.

BLINDETH,] as in Ex. 23. 8.

PERVERTETH,] as in Ex. 23. 8; Job 12. 19; Prov. 13. 6; 19. 3; 21. 12; 22. 12.

20. RIGHTEOUSNESS.] The repetition denotes the intensity of the command.

PURSUE,] as in Ps. 23. 6; 34. 14; 38. 20; Jud. 8. 4; Prov. 21. 21; Isa. 51. 1; Hos. 6. 3, &c.

21. PLANT,] as in Ge. 2. 8; 9. 20; 21. 33, &c.

SHRINE,] as in Ex. 34. 13; De. 7. 5, &c., on which see note.

22. STANDING IMAGE,] as in Ge. 28. 18, 22; 31. 13, &c.

HATH HATED,] as depriving him of his glory, as all sin does, see 12. 21; Ps. 5. 5; 11. 5; Prov. 6. 16, &c.

XVII. 1. BLEMISH.] See Lev. 22. 20.

EVIL THING,] which would lower it in the estimation of men.

2. WHEN,] not ' if,' as in C. V.

GATES,] *or* cities, as often elsewhere.

THE EVIL THING,] i.e. idolatry.

COVENANT,] which he had made with them as a nation.

3. OTHER GODS,] than the God of Israel.

BOW HIMSELF,] paying outward reverence to them, in addition to 'serving' them.

SUN,] which was perhaps the very earliest object of idolatrous worship, and still worshipped by the Parsees.

MOON,] called elsewhere the 'queen of heaven,' and worshipped by many, De. 4. 19; 2 K. 23. 5; Job 25. 5; 31. 26.

HOST,] as in Ge. 2. 1; De. 4. 19; 1 K. 22. 19; 2 K. 17. 16; 21. 3, 5; 23. 4, 5; 2 Ch. 33. 3, 5, &c.

4. DECLARED,] *lit.* 'put before,' (see Ge. 3. 11; 9. 22, &c.) i.e. designedly.

HEARD] of it accidentally, from whatever cause it may have come to their knowledge, then they

SEARCHED] 'well,' into the matter, as the original word implies.

TRUTH,] the accusation is correct, and the charge is

ESTABLISHED] beyond reasonable doubt.

5. GATES,] being the public places c judgment in the east, compare Ge. 19. 1; 23. 10, 18, &c.

STONES,] as in Lev. 20. 2, &c.

6. BY THE MOUTH] of 'testimony.'

HE WHO IS DEAD,] i.e. he is legally so already.

ONE WITNESS,] who might be deceived or a deceiver.

7. HAND..FIRST,] compelling them to carry out the just result of their own evidence and testimony.

HAND..LAST,] as manifesting their concurrence in the condemnation.

PUT AWAY,] *lit.* 'burned,' as in Ex. 35. 3.

8. TOO HARD,] *or* 'wonderful,' as in Ge. 18. 14; Ex. 3. 20, &c.

BLOOD,]i.e. regarding murder, manslaughter, &c.

PLEA,] i.e. civil controversies or disputes between man and man.

STROKE,] i.e. criminal assaults not issuing in death.

STRIFE,] *or* 'contention.'

GATES] whether public or private.

GONE UP.] The seat of justice being as it were on high.

9. PRIESTS, LEVITES,] who were to declare the laws of the Lord regarding such matters.

JUDGE] of Israel in civil matters.

INQUIRED,] at their mouth.

DECLARED,] *or* 'set before,' the parties litigating, the

WORD,] i.e. sentence of judgment which the law enforced.

10. TENOR,] *lit.* 'mouth,' as in v. 11 below.

DIRECT] thee to do, being God's appointed ministrants.

11. TENOR,] *lit.* 'mouth,' as in v. 10 above.

LAW] of the Lord, which was revealed on any subject.

JUDGMENT,] *or* decision.

TURN ASIDE,] avoiding, or declining, or refusing to comply with it.

12. PRESUMPTION,] as in 18. 22; 1 Sa. 17.

28; Prov. 11. 2; 13. 10; 21. 24; Jer. 49. 16;
50. 31, 32; Eze. 7. 10; Obad. 3.

PRIEST,] the appointed expositor of the divine law.

JUDGE,] who had been set up to execute the law of the Great King.

THE EVIL THING,] i.e. idolatry.

13. PRESUME,] in defiance of the divine injunctions.

14. KING,] or 'ruler;' this had been prophesied of in Ge. 17. 6, 16; 35. 11; 36. 31; Nu. 23. 21; 24. 7, &c.

15. FIX,] He reserving to Himself this right, as it was His throne the ruler would occupy, Jehovah being the Supreme King of Israel.

BRETHREN,] out of any of the twelve tribes, hence Saul was of Benjamin, and David of Judah.

STRANGER,] one of another nation, such as an Edomite, &c., which was violated in the case of Herod.

16. HORSES,] these being principally for warlike purposes in ancient times.

TURN BACK,] i.e. send back any of his servants or people, as Solomon did.

ADD.] See 28. 68, where it is repeated, and compare Jer. 42. 15; Hos. 11. 5.

17. WIVES,] as easterns were, and are fond of doing.

TURN ASIDE,] as in the case of Solomon, 1 K. 11. 3, 4, &c.

EXCEEDINGLY,] so as to set his heart upon them.

18. SITTETH,] i.e. is settled in his authority, he is to remember his position as God's vicegerent.

WRITTEN FOR HIMSELF,] by his own hand that he might be sure of his duty

THE COPY] or duplicate of

THIS LAW] regarding his kingly duties, and also of the 'statutes' alluded to in the next verse, which may include all the Mosaic legislation.

LEVITES,] even the original autograph, evidently preserved to prevent mistakes.

19. WITH HIM,] perpetually in his possession, not as a curiosity, but as a directory or guide.

READ,] lit. 'called,' reading in the east being almost invariably aloud, even when the reader is alone.

20. BRETHREN,] as if he had any superiority of his own to them; he was above them only through divine choice.

TURN ASIDE,] in any way, right or left, by acts of omission or of commission.

XVIII. 1. LEVI,] third son of Jacob.

PORTION] of the land; Ephraim coming in his place.

FIRE-OFFERINGS,] made by the people to the Lord, Lev. 2. 2, 3; 6. 17, 18.

INHERITANCE,] being all he required of them.

THEY EAT] habitually, as their appointed portion of food.

2. SPOKEN,] in Nu. 18. 8, 9.

3. RIGHT,] lit. 'judgment,' or 'judged thing,' being decided for him by the Lord Himself.

LEG,] lit. 'arm,' as in Ge. 49. 24; Ex. 6. 6; 15. 6; Nu. 6. 19, &c.

TWO CHEEKS,] as in Jud. 18. 15, 16, 17; 1 K. 22. 24; 2 Ch. 18. 23; Job 16. 10; 41. 2; Ps. 3. 7; Song 1. 10; 5. 13; Isa. 30. 28; 50. 6; La. 1. 2; 3. 20; Eze. 29. 4; 38. 4; Hos. 11. 4; Mic. 5. 1.

STOMACH,] compare Nu. 25. 8; not mentioned elsewhere.

4. FIRST,] or 'beginning.'

CORN,] whether wheat or barley.

NEW WINE,] with which the land of Canaan abounded.

OIL,] used so extensively by orientals.

FLEECE,] for his clothing; money being comparatively scarce, they gave goods instead of it.

5. FIXED,] from his own sovereign pleasure, instead of the first-born of each tribe.

ALL THE DAYS,] i.e. continually, while that covenant lasted.

6. WHEN,] not 'if.'

THE LEVITE,] not 'a Levite,' as in the C.V.

GATES,] or cities.

SOJOURNED,] for a time.

DESIRE,] as in 12. 15, 20, 21, which see.

7. MINISTERED,] in holy things, in the service of God, teaching, &c.

EAT,] i.e. they and he.

8. WITH,] i.e. along with the fathers or aged chief priests.

9. ART COMING,] or 'hast come.'

ABOMINATIONS,] recorded in the next two verses.

10. FIRE,] thus dedicating them to the false gods, like Ahaz, 2 K. 16. 3.

DIVINATIONS,] such as Balaam, Jos. 13. 22.

OBSERVER OF CLOUDS,] like Manasseh, 2 K. 21. 6.

ENCHANTER,] like Israel, 2 K. 17. 17.

SORCERER,] like the magicians of Egypt, and Pharaoh, Ex. 7. 11.

11. CHARMER,] as in Ps. 58. 5; Prov. 21. 9; 25. 24; Isa. 47. 9, 12; Hos. 6. 9.

FAMILIAR SPIRIT,] like Saul, 1 Sa. 28. 8, Manasseh, 2 K. 21. 6, &c.

WIZARD,] like Manasseh, 2 K. 21. 6, &c.

DEAD.] This phrase is not found elsewhere.

12. THEM,] i.e. the tribes of Canaan.

13. PERFECT,] like Noah (Ge. 6. 9); Abraham (17. 1); the passover lamb (Ex. 12. 5); God (De. 32. 4), &c.

14. HEARKEN,] as noticed in Isa. 2. 6.

SUFFERED,] lit. 'given to thee' to do.

15. PROPHET,] i.e. revealer and proclaimer of God's will. Acts 3. 22; 7. 37 (compare John 1. 45; 6. 14) apply this to the Messiah.

LIKE TO ME,] in nearness to God, and obedience to His will; Jonathan adds, 'in the Holy Spirit.'

HEARKEN] and obey; it is not a command, but a prophecy. Compare Ge. 49. 10, &c.

16. ACCORDING TO] their own desire, God would deal with them.

HOREB,] see 9. 10; Ex. 20. 19, &c.

17. DONE WELL,] in seeking a mediator between God and them.

18. RAISE UP,] in the latter end of the days, even 1450 years afterwards.

BRETHREN,] out of the tribe of Judah, of which our Lord was (Heb. 7. 14).

GIVEN] my words, so that they were God's, compare John 7. 16; 8. 28; 17. 6, 8.

SPOKEN,] and not kept silent, John 12. 49, 50; 15. 15; Heb. 2. 12.

19. I REQUIRE IT,] as in Ge. 9. 5; De. 23. 21; Job 3. 4; 10. 6; Ps. 10. 13; Eze. 20. 40; 33. 6, &c. Compare Luke 19. 27, 44.

20. PROPHET,] or 'proclaimer' of God's will.

PRESUMETH,] out of his own heart to say, 'The affirmation of Jehovah.'

NAME,] and as if by authority.

GODS,] as Baal, &c.

HATH DIED,] by the visitation of God, or the hands of men.

21. HEART,] pondering over the matter.

22. NOT SPOKEN.] The credentials of a true prophet are the fulfilment of his words, as in Jer. 18. 7—10; 28. 3.

AFRAID,] because he has no authority from God.

XIX. 1. CUT OFF,] judicially, for sin, the NATIONS,] seven in number, Ex. 23. 23; De. 12. 29.

CITIES..HOUSES,] which Israel did not build, but which the Lord gave to them.

2. THREE CITIES,] in the land of Israel, westward of the Jordan (Jos. 30. 7, 8), to which three others were (to be) added afterwards, eastward of the Jordan (De. 4. 41—43).

SEPARATE.] See note on Ge. 1. 4.

3. PREPARE,] or 'establish.'

THE WAY,] to each of the three cities.

DIVIDED INTO THREE PARTS,] lit. 'thirded,' see its use in 1 Sa. 20. 19; 1 K. 18. 34.

BORDER,] i.e. territory.

MAN-SLAYER,] as in Nu. 35. 6, &c.

4. UNKNOWINGLY,] as in De. 4. 42, &c.

HERETOFORE,] lit. 'yesterday, third day,' as in Ge. 31. 2, &c.

5. FOREST.] These are abundant in Canaan, see Jos. 17. 15, 18; 1 Sa. 14. 25, 26; 22. 5; 2 Sa. 18. 6, 8, 17; 1 K. 7. 2; 10. 17, 21, &c.

DRIVEN,] as the word is used in De. 4. 19; 22. 1; 30. 4, 17.

AXE,] as in 20. 19; 1 K. 6. 7; Isa. 10. 15; the original word is not found elsewhere.

IRON,] of which the 'head' was made.

WOOD,] which formed the 'handle.'

MET,] lit. 'found.'

6. REDEEMER,] as in Nu. 35. 19, 21, 24, 25, 27.

IS HOT,] with anger and revenge, for the death of his kinsman.

SMITTEN HIM—THE LIFE,] i.e. mortally.

SENTENCE OF DEATH,] not being yet legally tried for his offence.

HERETOFORE,] as in v. 4 above.

8. BORDER,] or territory.

SWORN.] See 12. 20.

ALL THE LAND,] from the sea of Egypt to the Euphrates, 1 K. 4. 21, 24.

9. TO LOVE] with the whole heart and soul, and to manifest that love by endeavouring

TO WALK] in the way which God has revealed for them.

ADDED] to these other three cities.

10. INNOCENT BLOOD,] even that of the man-slayer.

BLOOD] guiltiness, by the unlawful death of the unintentional man-slayer.

11. LAIN IN WAIT,] implying a settled purpose and determination.

SMITTEN HIM] as in v. 6 above.

12. ELDERS,] who had supreme authority in every city.

GIVEN] him up after trial and condemnation.

13. PITY,] because of his deliberate bloody cruelty in laying wait for his neighbour.

PUT AWAY,] lit. ' burned' away.

WELL,] because of having obeyed the law of God, with the performance of which happiness is inseparably connected.

14. REMOVE,] as in 27. 17; Prov. 22. 28; 23. 10; Hos. 5. 10, &c.

BORDER,] marks which indicate the separation of two properties.

15. ONE WITNESS,] 'only,' as in De. 6. 13; 10. 20, &c.

INIQUITY,] as in Ge. 15. 16, &c.

ESTABLISHED,] before one is punished.

16. VIOLENT WITNESS,] i.e. one who does violence to truth, as in Ex. 23. 1, &c.

APOSTACY,] lit. a 'turning aside,' as in 13. 5, &c.

17. STRIFE,] or 'controversy.'

PRIESTS AND JUDGES,] the representative. of Jehovah.

18. DILIGENTLY,] lit. 'well.'

FALSE WITNESS,] as in Ps. 27. 12; Prov. 6. 19, &c.

FALSEHOOD,] as in Ex. 5. 9.

HIS BROTHER] man, of the same great progenitor.

19. DEVISED,] as in Ge. 11. 6; Ps. 17. 3; 31. 13; 37. 12, &c.

PUT AWAY,] as in v. 13 above.

HEAR AND FEAR.] Compare the effect of the decision of Solomon, in 1 K. 3. 28.

THIS EVIL THING,] i.e. perjury, and apostacy from God.

21. PITY,] as in v. 13 above.

LIFE FOR LIFE.] See notes on Ex. 21. 23, 24; Lev. 24. 19, 20.

XX. 1. ENEMY,] in thine own land, for they were not allowed to extend their territory by conquest, being confined to the promised land.

HORSE AND CHARIOT,] as in Ex. 14. 9; Jos. 11. 4: 17. 6, &c.

NUMEROUS,] as in 2 Ch. 14. 9—12, &c.

WITH THEE.] Compare Nu. 23. 21; De. 31. 6, 8, &c.

2. PRIEST,] as representing the divine authority.

PEOPLE] in the camp, who are marching to the battle.

3. TENDER,] like that of a woman, or of a little child; 2 K. 22. 19; 2 Ch. 34. 27; Ps. 55. 21; Job 23. 16; Isa. 1. 6; 7. 4; Jer. 51. 46.

MAKE HASTE,] as in 1 Sa. 23. 26; 2 Sa. 4. 4; 2 K. 7. 15; Ps. 48. 5; 104. 7, &c.

PRESENCE,] or 'face,' because of their number, valour, &c.

WITH YOU,] as in v. 1 above.

TO FIGHT,] as in Ex. 14. 4; De. 1. 30, &c.

5. AUTHORITIES,] as representing the civil authority.
DEDICATED] it, as in 1 K. 8. 63; 2 Ch. 7.5,&c.
6. VINEYARD.] These are very common in the east.
MADE IT COMMON,] according to the law in Lev. 19. 23—25.
7. BETROTHED,] as in 22. 23, 25, 27, 28; 28. 30; Ex. 22. 16.
TAKEN HER] to his own house.
8. TENDER OF HEART,] as in v. 3 above.
MELT,] as in Jos. 2. 11; 5. 1; 7. 5; 2 Sa. 17. 10; Ps. 22. 14; Isa. 13. 7; 19. 1; Eze. 21. 7; De. 1. 28.
9. APPOINTED,] or 'charged.'
PEOPLE,] to go forth against the enemy, in the name of the Lord.
10. PEACE,] that the effusion of blood might be spared.
11. TRIBUTARIES.] This was only when the city was without the land of Canaan, 2 K. 3. 4.
12. LAID SEIGE,] as in v. 19, 2 Sa. 11. 1; 20. 15, &c.
13. MALE,] as in Nu. 31. 7, &c.
14. INFANTS,] as in Nu. 31. 9, &c.
SPOIL,] as in Ge. 49. 27, &c.
SEIZE,] as in Ge. 34. 27, &c.
EATEN,] i.e. used it for thyself.
15. THESE NATIONS,] of Canaan.
16. ANY BREATHING,] as in Jos. 10. 40; 11. 11, 14, &c.
17. DEVOTE] to destruction.
HITTITE.] See note on Ge. 15. 20.
AMORITE,] Ge. 10. 16.
CANAANITE,] Ge. 10. 6.
PERIZZITE,] Ge. 13. 7.
HIVITE,] Ge. 10. 17.
JEBUSITE] Ge. 10. 16; to whom should be added the Girgashites, Ge. 10. 16; 15, 21, &c.
COMMANDED,] in De. 7. 1—5, &c.
18. GODS.] See Lev. 18. 3, 24, 25, 27; 20. 2—23; De. 18. 9—12.
GOD,] by imitating their evil deeds.
19. CAPTURE] it, as in Jos. 8. 8, &c.
TREES,] i.e. fruit-trees.
FORCE,] as in 19. 5, &c.
EAT] fruit, i.e. it is a means of support and sustenance.
CUT DOWN,] or 'cut off,' i.e. any of their branches.
FOR MAN'S,] i.e. it belongs to him, being designed for his support.
GO IN] to the city.
SEIGE,] or 'bulwark,' as in next verse.
20. FRUIT TREE,] as in Ge. 2. 9; 3. 6; Lev. 19. 23; De. 28. 26; Neh. 9. 25; Ezek. 47. 12.
BULWARK,] as in v. 19; 28. 53, 55, 57; 2 K. 19. 24; 24. 10; 25. 2.
SUBDUED] it, and it has become tributary.

XXI. 1. WHEN,] not 'if,' as in the C.V.
SLAIN,] lit. 'pierced,' as in Ge. 34. 27.
GROUND,] not 'land.'
FALLEN,] not 'lying.'
SMITTEN] him so as to kill him.
2. ELDERS..JUDGES,] who exercised his authority in the place, and who by eastern customs, were responsible for the deed.
MEASURED,] if there was any doubt as to which was nearest the spot of the murder.

3. HEIFER OF THE HERD,] probably of a year old, as the Targum of Jonathan suggests.
WROUGHT WITH,] at any work whatever.
DRAWN IN THE YOKE.] Oxen are employed instead of horses for this work in various countries of Europe and Asia.
4. HARD VALLEY,] or 'perennial stream,' as in Amos 5. 24. the only other instance of the occurrence of this phrase, but the first translation is preferable.
TILLED NOT SOWN,] being wholly unculti- vated.
BEHEADED,] as in Ex. 13. 13, &c.
5. NIGH] to the slain heifer.
FIXED,] as in 10. 8.
BLESS,] as in Nu. 6. 23—27.
MOUTH,] i.e. decision.
STRIFE..STROKE] settled and decided.
6. WASH,] in token of their innocence of the crime, Ps. 26. 6; Mat. 27. 24.
7. BLOOD,] which the Lord was now re- quiring, as in Ge. 9. 5.
NOT SEEN] it shed; they were neither art nor part in the matter.
8. RECEIVE ATONEMENT FOR,] as in Eze 16. 63, &c.
RANSOMED,] from a house of servants, and from the power of Pharaoh.
SUFFER,] lit. 'give.'
PARDONED,] though they had not dis- covered him who shed it.
9. PUT AWAY,] lit. 'burned.'
10. ENEMIES,] who invade thee unjustly in thy land.
HAND,] as he would certainly do if they remained stedfast to him.
TAKEN CAPTIVE,] for bondsmen and bonds- women.
11. FAIR FORM,] as in Ge. 29. 17; 39. 6; Est. 2. 7.
DELIGHTED,] as in Ge. 34. 8, &c.
TAKEN,] or 'accepted.'
12. HOUSEHOLD,] that she might become one of them.
SHAVED,] as a sign and token of affliction, see 14. 1; Job 1. 20.
PREPARED,] lit. 'made.'
NAILS,] i.e. let them grow.
13. TURNED ASIDE,] from off her person.
RAIMENT,] in which she was dressed when taken captive, that nothing might remain to remind her of her former state.
BEWAILED,] as if they were dead; she should see them no more.
MONTH OF DAYS,] as in 2 K. 15. 13; com- pare also Nu. 20. 29; De. 34. 8.
GO IN,] as in Ge. 6. 4, &c.
MARRIED,] as in 24. 1, &c.
WIFE,] and help-meet, as in Ge. 2. 18, 24.
14. DELIGHTED,] as in v. 11 above.
SENT HER AWAY,] to her own people.
DESIRE,] lit. 'soul.'
SELL] her, either to an Israelite, or one of another nation.
TYRANNIZE,] as in 24. 7; from a root signifying 'to bind.'
HUMBLED,] or 'afflicted' her.
15. WHEN,] not 'if,' as in the C.V.
TWO WIVES,] one after the other, not necessarily at the same time. Compare the prohibition of polygamy in Lev. 18. 18.

LOVED..HATED,] i.e. the one loved more than the other, as in the case of Rachel and Leah. In scripture language that which is loved less is said to be 'hated.' Compare Ge. 29. 31, 33; Luke 14. 26, &c.

HATED ONE,] as in the case of Leah.

16. IN THE FACE,] or 'presence,' of the elder son, i.e. while he is alive. Ge. 49. 3, 4; 1 Ch. 5. 2, 3.

17. ACKNOWLEDGE,] as the rightful possessor of the birth-right.

DOUBLE PORTION,] as in 2 K. 2. 9.

FOUND WITH ME,] i.e. in his possession.

BEGINNING] of his strength, as Jacob says, in Ge. 49. 3.

RIGHT,] according to law.

18. WHEN,] not 'if.'

APOSTATIZING,] lit. 'turning aside,' as in v. 20; Neh. 9. 29; Ps. 66. 7; 68. 6, 18; 78. 8; Prov. 7. 11; Isa. 1. 23; 30. 1; 65. 2; Jer. 5. 23; 6. 28; Hos. 4. 16; 9. 15; Zec. 7. 11.

REBELLIOUS,] as in Nu. 20. 10, &c.

FATHER..MOTHER,] as in Prov. 30. 17.

CHASTISED,] as in 8. 5; Prov. 19. 18; 29. 17, &c.

HEARKEN,] so as to obey them.

19. LAID HOLD,] as in Ge. 4. 21; 39. 12; De. 22. 28, &c.

GATE,] which is the public place of judgment in the east, as in Ge. 19. 1; 23. 10, 18, &c.

20. OUR SON.] Parental authority in the east is held in the highest estimation.

GLUTTON,] as in Prov. 23. 20, 21; 28. 7; Jer. 15. 19; La. 1. 11.

DRUNKARD,] as in Prov. 23. 20. 21; Eze. 23. 42, &c.

21. STONES,] agreeably to the law.

PUT AWAY,] lit. 'burned.'

FEAR,] the sin and the punishment.

22. WHEN,] not 'if.'

JUDGMENT OF DEATH,] as in 19. 6.

HANGED,] as in Ge. 40. 19, &c.

23. CORPSE,] as in Lev. 5. 2; 7. 24; 11. 8, 11, 24, 25, 27, 28, 35, 36, 39, 40; 17. 15; 22. 8; De. 14. 8, 21, &c.

REMAIN,] as in Ge. 19. 2, &c.

BURY,] as in Ge. 23. 4.

LIGHTLY ESTEEMED,] as in Ge. 27. 12, 13; De. 11. 26, 28, 29, &c. Compare the use of the verb in Ge. 8. 8, &c.

DEFILE,] as in Ge. 34. 5; Nu. 35. 34, &c.

XXII. 1. DRIVEN AWAY,] as in 4. 19; 19. 5; 30. 4, 17, &c.

HIDDEN THYSELF,] as in v. 3, 4; Job 6. 16; Ps. 55. 1; Isa. 58. 7.

2. REMOVED IT,] lit. 'gathered it,' as in Ge. 6. 21, &c.

3. ASS..GARMENT,] as in Ex. 23. 4.

LOST THING,] as in Ex. 22. 9; Lev. 6. 3, 4.

HIDE THYSELF,] as in v. 1 above.

4. FALLING,] by weariness.

5. HABILIMENTS,] lit. 'vessels,' as in Ge. 24. 53; 42. 25; Lev. 13. 49; Isa. 61. 10; 2 Sa. 24. 22.

GARMENT,] as in v. 3 above.

6. WHEN,] not 'if,' as in v. 8.

COMETH,] lit. 'meeteth,' or 'happeneth, as in Ex. 5. 3; 2 Sa. 1. 6; 18. 9; 20. 1.

BROOD,] as in Job 39. 30; Ps. 84. 3.

EGGS,] as in Job 39. 14; Isa. 10. 14; 59. 5

WITH,] i.e. in addition to the young ones.

7. SEND AWAY,] the mother, free to join its mate.

PROLONG DAYS,] by obedience to the divine command.

8. PARAPET.] The original word does not occur elsewhere.

ROOF,] which is generally flat, and on which they often walk, and sit, and sleep.

PUT BLOOD,] i.e. blood-guiltiness.

9. DIVERS THINGS,] as in Ge. 19. 19; the original word is not found elsewhere.

FULNESS,] as in Ex. 22. 29; Nu. 18. 27.

INCREASE,] as in Ge. 47, 24, &c.

SEPARATE,] or 'set apart,' as in Ex. 29. 21, 37; 30. 29; Lev. 6. 18, 27; Nu. 16. 37, 38, &c.

10. OX..ASS,]their strength being unequal.

PUT ON,] i.e. 'clothe thyself.'

MIXED CLOTH,] as in Lev. 19. 19, which see.

WOOL..LINEN,] as in Lev. 13. 48, 52, 59, &c.

12. FRINGES.] The original word is only found elsewhere in 1 K. 7. 17.

SKIRTS,] or 'wings.'

COVERING,] as in Ge. 20. 16; Ex. 21. 10; 22. 27, &c.

13. WHEN,] as in v. 8; not 'if.'

GONE IN,] as in Ge. 6. 4, &c.

HATED,] from any cause.

14. LAID,] i.e. ascribed.

ACTIONS,] as in v. 17; 1 Sa. 2. 3; 1 Ch. 16. 8; Ps. 9. 11, &c.

EVIL NAME,] as in v. 19; Neh. 6. 13; Luke 6. 22.

TOKENS OF VIRGINITY,] as in v. 16,17, 20; compare Lev. 21. 13; Jud. 11. 37, 38; Eze. 23. 3, 8.

15. FATHER..MOTHER,] who were most interested in her case.

GATE,] where justice was dispensed in the east.

ELDERS,] who were the rulers of the city.

HATE HER,] i.e. without a cause.

17. ACTIONS OF WORDS,] as in v. 14 above.

SPREAD OUT,] as in Nu. 4. 7, 11.

THE GARMENT.] That worn by day often serves for night in the east.

18. CHASTISE] him, with stripes, according to the Jewish interpreters.

19. FINE,] as in Ex. 21. 22; 2 Ch. 36. 3; Prov. 17. 26; 21. 11; 22. 3; 27. 12; Amos 2. 8.

SILVERLINGS,] or about £12 sterling, being double the dowry of a divorced wife.

SEND HER AWAY,] from his house to that of her parents.

ALL HIS DAYS,] as a punishment for his wicked design.

20. THIS THING,] i.e. accusation of unchastity.

21. OPENING,] at the very door.

STONES,] which was the recognised punishment for whoredom.

DONE FULLY,] like Dinah in Ge. 34. 7.

FATHER'S HOUSE,] and while under his protection.

PUT AWAY,] lit. 'burned away.'

THE EVIL THING,] i.e. unchastity.

22. WHEN,] as in v. 8; not 'if.

DIED,] as a consequence and punishment of their sin.

THE WOMAN,] who might and ought to

have resisted, being in a city, within call. This is understood, though not expressed, as in v. 17.

PUT AWAY,] as in v. 21 above.

23. WHEN,] as in v. 8; not 'if.'
BETROTHED] to a man, and legally reckoned as a wife.

24. GATE,] or public place of judgment.
STONES,] as in v. 21 above.
CRIED OUT,] for help in her distress.
CITY,] and not in a field, where assistance could not be had.
HUMBLED,] or 'afflicted.'
PUT AWAY,] *lit.* 'burned.'
THE EVIL THING,] as in v. 21 above.

25. FIELD,] away from a city.
BETROTHED,] as in v. 23 above.
ALONE,] for he only was guilty.

26. DEADLY SIN,] i.e. worthy of death.
MURDERED HIM,] in spite of his resistance.

27. CRIED OUT,] for help in her distress.
SAVIOUR,] from the hand and power of the oppressor.

28. CAUGHT HER,] by force.

29. FIFTY SILVERLINGS,] the usual dowry paid to a divorced wife.
WIFE,] all his days, as in v 19 above.
HUMBLED,] or 'afflicted,' as in v. 24 above.
SEND HER AWAY,] i.e. divorce her, as in 19.
ALL HIS DAYS,] as in v. 18 above.

30. TAKE] to wife, whether she be his own mother, or merely his step-mother.
UNCOVER,] as in Lev. 18. 9, &c.
SKIRT,] *lit.* 'wing.'

XXIII. 1. WOUNDED,] as in 1 K. 20. 37; Song 5. 7; the only passages where the original word occurs.
BRUISED,] as in Ps. 10. 10; 38. 8; 44. 19; 51. 8, 17.
CUT,] as in Lev. 22. 24; 1 Sa. 5. 4.
MEMBER,] not mentioned elsewhere, from a root signifying 'to pour out.'
ASSEMBLY,] congregation or church on earth.

2. BASTARD,] as in Zech. 9. 6, not mentioned elsewhere.
TENTH GENERATION.] This round number implies that they can never obtain this privilege. Ge. 31. 7, 41.

3. AMMONITE.] See Ge. 19. 37.
MOABITE.] See Ge. 19. 38.
TO THE AGE,] i.e. *never*, but some say, 'till the age of Messiah.'

4. COME BEFORE YOU,] in a friendly manner, with
BREAD..WATER,] to support them in the wilderness.
HIRED,] with a promise of great honour and riches. Nu. 22. 7, &c.
REVILE,] i.e. speak lightly of them, and if possible, render them contemptible.

5. NOT BEEN WILLING,] though Balaam tried to please him by his burnt-offerings.
BLESSING,] by causing Balaam to pronounce upon them the blessings that should come to them.
LOVED] thee above all other nations, and chosen thee to be his people.

6. SEEK,] as if it were an object pleasing to God.

PEACE,] i.e. quietness.

7. EDOMITE,] being a descendant of Esau.
BROTHER,] born of the same parents with Jacob.
EGYPTIAN.] These being reserved for blessings, see Isa. 19. 25.
SOJOURNER,] for 430 years, or as some say 215 only, and others 400 years.

8. THIRD GENERATION.] There is little doubt but that it was the *king*, and not the *people*, of Egypt who oppressed Israel.

9. CAMP,] or 'encampment.'
EVIL THING,] forbidden in the law; especial care was needed, for they themselves required special care.

10. WHEN,] as in v. 9; not 'if.'
ACCIDENT] of any kind happening to him. Lev. 15. 16, &c.
OUTSIDE,] like a leprous person.

11. TURNING,] as in Ge. 24. 63.
BATHE,] as in Ge. 18. 4; 19. 2, &c.
GOING IN,] as in Ge. 15. 12, 17, &c.

12. STATION,] *lit.* 'hand,' as in Ez. 21. 19.

13. NAIL,] as in Ex. 27. 19, &c.
DIGGED,] as in Ge. 21. 30, &c.
FILTH,] as in Eze. 4. 12.

14. UP AND DOWN,] i.e. habitually.
DELIVER THEE,] as in Ex. 3. 8, &c.
HOLY,] i.e. separate, set apart.
NAKEDNESS,] as in 24. 1, &c.

15. SHUT UP,] as the men of Keilah wished to do with David, 1 Sa. 23. 11, 12.
DELIVERED,] as in Ge. 32. 30; 2 K. 19. 11.

16. OPPRESS] him, as in Ex. 22. 21; Lev 19. 33; 25. 14, 17, &c.

17. WHORE,] *lit.* a 'separated' one, as in Ge. 38. 21, 22; Hos. 4. 14.
WHOREMONGER,] *lit.* a 'separated one,' as in 1 K. 14. 24; 15. 12; 22. 46; 2 K. 23. 7; Job 36. 14.

18. GIFT,] as in Isa. 23. 17, 18; Eze. 16. 31, 34, 41; Hos. 9. 1; Mic. 1. 7.
DOG,] being an unclean animal, compare also Rev. 22. 15.
ANY VOW,] of any kind whatsoever.
LEND IN USURY,] *lit.* 'bite,' as in Ge. 49. 17, &c.
USURY,] as in Ex. 22. 25, &c.

20. STRANGER,] as in Ge. 31. 15; Ex. 2. 22, &c.
PUTTING FORTH,] i.e. exercise.

21. A VOW] to devote or give anything to God.
DELAY,] or 'be behind,' as in Ex. 22. 29; Ecc. 5. 4; Ge. 32. 4; 34. 19, &c.
COMPLETE] it, i.e. carry it into execution.
SIN] against God.

22. FORBEAREST,] or 'ceasest,' as in Ge. 11. 8; 18. 11; 41. 49, &c.

23. PRODUCE,] *lit.* 'outgoing,' as in Nu. 30. 12, &c.
KEEP,] i.e. watch, observe, preserve.
FREE-WILL OFFERING,] as in Ex. 35. 29, &c.

24. GRAPES,] as in Ge. 40. 10, &c.
DESIRE,] or 'soul,' as in Ps. 105. 22; Jer. 2. 24, &c.
SUFFICIENCY,] as in Ex. 16. 3; Lev. 25. 19; 26. 5, &c.
VESSEL,] bag, or anything with which travellers in the east are generally provided.

25. STANDING CORN,] as in Ex. 22. 6, &c.

PLUCKED,] as in Job 8. 12; 30. 4; Eze. 17. 4, 22.
SICKLE,] as in 16. 19.
WAVE,] as in Ex. 20. 25; De. 27. 5; Jos. 8. 31, &c.

XXIV. 1. FIND GRACE,] as in Ge. 6. 8, &c.
NAKEDNESS OF ANYTHING,] as in 23. 14 above.
SCROLL,] lit. 'book.'
DIVORCE,] lit. 'cutting off.'
HAND,] before witnesses doubtless.
SENT HER OUT,] of his house.
2. GONE OUT,] agreeable to his will and command.
ANOTHER MAN'S] wife, as she was at liberty to become.
3. HATED HER] like the first.
DIETH,] and she free to marry again.
4. DEFILED,] by another man.
CAUSE THE LAND TO SIN,] by suffering these abominations.
5. NEW WIFE,] i.e. another after the death of the former.
HOST,] for warlike purposes.
ANYTHING] of a public nature.
FREE] from civil and military burdens.
REJOICED,] by his presence.
6. TAKE IN PLEDGE,] for debt incurred by him.
MILL-STONES,] as Ex. 11. 5; Nu. 11. 8, &c.
RIDER,] as in 2 Sa. 11. 21; Jud. 9. 53.
LIFE,] i.e. means of sustaining life.
7. WHEN,] as in v. 5; not 'if.'
STEALING,] as in Ge. 40. 15.
PERSON,] lit. 'soul.'
TYRANNIZED,] as in 21. 14.
SOLD] him to another for money, or any other consideration.
DIED,] by the sentence of a judge.
PUT AWAY,] lit. 'burned.'
8. LEPROSY.] See Lev. 13. 2, &c.
TEACH YOU,] as they themselves had been directed by God.
9. MIRIAM,] in smiting her with leprosy, and in shutting her out of the camp seven days. See Nu. 12. 14—16.
10. LIFTEST UP,] as in 15. 2.
DEBT,] or 'burden,' as in Prov. 22. 26.
PLEDGE,] as in v. 11, 12, 13.
11. OUTSIDE] of his house.
LIFTING IT UP,] as in v. 10 above.
12. POOR MAN,] or 'afflicted,' as in Ex. 22. 24, &c.
LIE DOWN] to rest at night.
PLEDGE,] if it be his garment.
GOING IN] of the sun, i.e. daily.
RAIMENT,] which being poor, he uses by day and by night.
BLESSED THEE,] for being so considerate and kind.
RIGHTEOUSNESS,] i.e. a right state.
14. OPPRESS,] as in Lev. 6. 2, 4; 19. 13; De. 28. 29, 33, &c.
HIRELING,] as in Ex. 12. 45; 22. 15; Lev. 19. 13; 22. 10; 25. 6, 40, 50, 53, &c.
GATES,] public or private.
15. DAY,] i.e. daily.
HIRE] which he agreed for.
LIFTING UP,] anxiously his desire.
CALL,] or invoke punishment upon thee.

SIN] against God, as against man.
16. FOR SONS,] or perhaps it should be read, 'along with' or 'in addition to' sons. A man's crime ought not to be charged upon his relations, Ex. 20. 5.
FOR FATHERS,] or as in the above clause.
OWN SIN,] which he may commit. Eze. 18. 4.
17. TURN ASIDE,] or 'cause to incline,' from rectitude.
JUDGMENT,] or 'cause,' i.e. plea.
WIDOW.] Compare Job 24. 3, &c.
18. SERVANT,] and in hard drudgery.
RANSOM] thee to be his servant for ever.
THIS THING,] even to deal justly and mercifully.
19. REAPEST,] as in Lev. 19. 9, &c.
HARVEST,] whether of wheat or barley.
SHEAF,] lit. 'bundle,' tied together.
20. BEATEST,] as in Jud. 6. 11; Ruth 2. 17; Isa. 27. 12; 28. 27.
OLIVE,] with sticks and staves.
EXAMINE THE BRANCH.] The original word properly means 'to beautify,' and never occurs elsewhere with the present meaning.
21. CUTTEST,] as in Ge. 11. 6; Lev. 25. 5, &c.
GLEAN,] as in Lev. 19. 10, &c.
22. THIS THING,] of leaving the forgotten sheaf, olive and vineyard.

XXV. 1. STRIFE,] as in Ge. 13. 7; Ex. 17. 7, &c.
JUDGMENT,] or decision of the constituted judge.
THEY,] i.e. the judges have decided the matter in debate.
DECLARED RIGHTEOUS,] as in Ex. 23. 7, &c.
THE RIGHTEOUS,] i.e. he who has the right side of the strife.
DECLARED WRONG,] as in Ex. 22. 9, &c.
THE WRONG DOER,] i.e. he who is wrong in his plea.
2. SMITTEN] with a rod, as a punishment.
FALL DOWN] on the spot, and at the time; eastern justice is proverbially sharp.
HIS PRESENCE,] i.e. of the judge himself, that he may see it carried out.
SUFFICIENCY,] as in Ex. 36. 5, 7, &c.
3. FORTY.] Compare 2 Cor. 11. 24, &c.
LIGHTLY ESTEEMED,] as in 27. 16; 1 Sa. 18. 13; Prov. 12. 9; Isa. 3. 5; 16. 14.
4. MUZZLE,] or 'stop,' as in Eze. 39. 11, 1 Cor. 9. 9, 10; 1 Tim. 5. 17, 18.
OX,] which was generally used in agricultural labours.
THRESHING,] i.e. as it is engaged in this work.
5. WHEN,] not 'if,' as in the C.V.
DWELL TOGETHER] in the same house, as is often the case in the east, especially if only one of them be married.
DIED,] leaving a widow, but no
SON] The Hebrew word does indeed often include 'daughters,' but as these could not keep up the name of their father in their tribe and place, the probability is that the word is here used in its proper significance
STRANGE MAN] as a wife.
HUSBAND'S BROTHER,] as in Ge. 38. 8; De. 25. 5, 7.

PERFORM THE DUTY,] of a husband's brother, in raising up seed to bear the name of the deceased.

6. WIPED AWAY,] i.e. blotted out of the list of genealogies.

7. DELIGHT,] lest he should mar his own inheritance, as in the case of Ruth.

GATE] of the place, where justice was dispensed.

NAME.] i.e. one who would continue his name over his inheritance.

8. CALLED FOR HIM,] it being a violation of a divine injunction and statute law.

STOOD] up, and stood firm to his resolution not to take her.

9. DRAWN HIS SHOE,] or sandal, from off his feet, thus causing him to stand bare-foot in her presence, as a servant.

SPAT,] as a mark of ignominy; perhaps this latter part of the ceremony was not always carried out.

DRAWN OFF,] i.e. of one who has subjected himself to this reproach.

11. STRIVE TOGETHER,] in anger and fury, in their disputes or contentions.

SECRETS,] *lit.* 'shameful things;' not found elsewhere.

12. CUT OFF] by a judicial decision.

SPARE] because of her sex.

13. BAG,] as in Prov. 1. 14; 16. 11 ; 23. 31; Isa. 46. 6; Mic. 6. 11.

STONE,] i.e. divers stones or weights of different value for cheating customers, as in next clause.

14. EPHAH,] as in Ex. 16. 36, &c.

15. STONE,] i.e. weight.

COMPLETE,] perfect in size and weight.

JUST,] or 'right,' i.e. according to law. Lev. 19. 36.

THEY PROLONG,] i.e. doing justice to every one is productive of blessings to one's self, Ps. 55. 23.

16. INIQUITY,] or 'perverseness.'

17. AMALEK.] See Ge. 36. 12, 16.

EGYPT,] as in Ex. 17. 8, &c.

18. MET,] as in Ge. 42. 29; 44. 29; Ex. 3. 18, &c.

SMITETH THE TAIL,] as in Jos. 10. 19.

FEEBLE.] The original word here is not found elsewhere; it is probably the same word as that in Lev. 26. 27.

BEHIND THEE,] in the rear, unprotected stragglers.

WEARIED,] as in Ge. 25. 29, 30, &c.

FATIGUED,] as in 2 Sa. 17. 2; Ecc. 1. 8.

NOT FEARING GOD,] who was going before Israel, and had manifested His favour towards them so evidently.

19. BLOT OUT,] or 'wipe away.'

REMEMBRANCE,] i.e. anything that might mark its former existence.

HEAVENS,] i.e. from off the earth.

FORGET] this injunction, 1 Sa. 15. 2, &c.

XXVI. 2. FRUIT OF THE GROUND,] but not the same as in Lev. 23. 10, 17; Nu. 15. 20, 21.

BRING IN] to thy stores out of the land that He had given to them.

BASKET,] as in v. 4; 28. 5, 17.

DOTH CHOOSE] hereafter.

3. COME IN] unto the appointed place of sacrifice.

I HAVE DECLARED] by my presence here, openly, before God and men.

COME IN] and enjoy the good of the promised land.

TO US] on many occasions.

4. THY HAND,] accepting the offering and declaration of God's faithfulness.

PLACED,] *lit.* 'caused it to rest.'

BEFORE] the altar, not *upon* it.

5. ANSWERED AND SAID.] A very common Hebrew idiom, in continuing an address.

PERISHING] from hunger, as in Ge. 42. 2, &c.

ARAMEAN,] Jacob's mother—Rebecca—was a daughter of Aram, and Abraham himself came from Ur of the Chaldees.

EGYPT] for food.

SOJOURNETH] for 400 years.

FEW MEN,] compared with what there were now.

NATION,] or body politic, great in renown, mighty in power, and numerous, as in Ex. 1. 10.

6. DO US EVIL,] in reducing them to servitude.

AFFLICT] us in our families.

HARD SERVICE,] in making bricks without straw.

7. CRY OUT] in distress, as the word implies.

VOICE,] as He always does the voice of those who call upon Him.

AFFLICTION,] or 'humiliation,' or 'poverty.'

LABOUR,] or 'toil.'

OPPRESSION] by the king of Egypt.

8. STRONG HAND,] because it is almighty.

STRETCHED OUT ARM,] manifesting the greatness of the effort put forth.

GREAT FEAR] impressed upon the Egyptians, and on Israel.

SIGNS,] or 'tokens,' of His special presence.

WONDERS,] which astonished friends and foes alike.

9. THIS PLACE,] even where He chose to cause His name to tabernacle.

THIS LAND] of Canaan.

HONEY,] as it is everywhere represented in Scripture.

10. BROUGHT IN] to this place.

PLACED,] as in v. 9 above.

BOWED THYSELF,] in token of reverence.

11. MIDST.] None can be exempted from participating in the joy the Lord had given.

12. COMPLETE,] i.e. end, finish.

TO TITHE,] according to law.

INCREASE] of every kind, of cattle, fruits, &c.

THIRD YEAR,] of every seven.

GIVEN] the tithe of the increase.

SATISFIED] with God's care of them, and man's bounty.

13. PUT AWAY,] *lit.* 'burned.'

SEPARATED THING,] i.e. the tithe of the increase.

COMMANDED ME] in the law.

PASSED OVER,] knowingly.

FORGOTTEN,] as if they were of little importance.

14. OF IT,] that it might be diminished, on the ground of necessity.

UNCLEANNESS,] or any evil purpose.

FOR THE DEAD,] *or* 'to the dead,' i.e. idols.
15. LOOK,] Ex. 14. 24; Ps. 14. 2; 53. 2;85.
-1; 102. 19; Lam. 3. 50.
HABITATION,] as in 2 Ch. 30. 27; Ps. 68. 5;
Jer. 25. 30; Zec. 2. 13, &c.
THY PEOPLE,] as well as thy servant, and
the ground they cultivate which thou hast
given to them.
HONEY,] sufficient for the wants of all, as
in v. 9.
16. THIS DAY,] while Moses is speaking
to them.
HEART,] or mind.
SOUL,] or affections.
17. THOU HAST CAUSED TO PROMISE,] by
declaring their willingness to obey him.
WAYS,] which he had revealed for their
guidance.
STATUTES,] which he had enacted for them.
COMMANDS,] which he had pleased to lay
upon them.
JUDGMENTS] or decisions, which he had
declared to them.
VOICE] through his servants the prophets.
18. CAUSED THEE TO PROMISE] by offering
thee good laws and endless happiness.
PECULIAR TREASURE,] as in Ex. 19. 5, &c.
COMMANDS,] acknowledging in a practical
manner his sovereignty.
19. UPPERMOST,] *or* 'most high.'
MADE] of one blood.
PRAISE] to himself.
NAME,] *or* 'renown.'
BEAUTY,] as in Ps. 71. 8, &c.
HOLY PEOPLE,] i.e. a separated one.
SPOKEN] in 7. 6, 7.

XXVII. 1. ELDERS,] the recognized civil
authorities in Israel among the tribes.
2. GREAT STONES] on mount Ebal, as in v. 4.
PLAISTERED,] as in v. 4; this original
word is not found elsewhere.
PLAISTER,] as in v. 4; Isa. 33. 12; Amos 2. 1.
3. THIS LAW,] that Moses had been declaring; the whole Koran is said to be written
on the pillars of a mosque in Cairo.
4. MOUNT EBAL.] See on De. 11. 29; the
Samaritan Text and Version here reads
'Gerizzim.'
5. ALTAR] for sacrifices, see Josh. 8. 30.
STONES,] for durability.
IRON,] in hewing or fashioning them. See
Ex. 20. 25.
6. COMPLETE,] *or* 'perfect,' the most
suitable they could get without carving or
cutting.
BURNT-OFFERINGS] for sin.
7. PEACE-OFFERINGS,] as tokens of gratitude and thankfulness.
EATEN] the allotted portion of the sacrifices set apart for the offerer.
REJOICED,] because of God's acceptance
of the sacrifice.
8. THIS LAW,] as in v. 3 above.
WELL ENGRAVED,] for legibility. De. 1. 5;
Hab. 2. 2.
9. PRIESTS..LEVITES.] The ecclesiastical
authorities adding their sanction.
KEEP SILENT.] The original word does not
occur elsewhere.
BECOME,] *lit.* 'been for.'

12. MOUNT GERIZZIM.] See on 11 29, &c.
TO BLESS,] i.e. pronounce the blessings.
This idiom serves to explain Ge. 41. 13; Ex.
4. 21; Lev. 13. 6; Jer. 1. 10, &c.
SIMEON..BENJAMIN.] All these were children of Leah and Rachel.
13. EBAL,] as in v. 4 above.
REUBEN..NAPHTALI.] These were the
oldest and the youngest of the sons of Leah,
the other four were sons of the maid servant.
REVILING,] i.e. to pronounce it.
14. THE LEVITES,] i.e. the priests among
them, for the body of the tribe were on Gerizzim, as in v. 12.
15. CURSED,] as in Ge. 3. 14; it is not a
prayer but a declarative prophecy.
GRAVEN,] as in Ex. 20. 4, &c.
MOLTEN,] as in Ex. 32. 4, &c.
ABOMINATION,] as in 7. 25, &c.
ARTIFICER,] as in Ex. 28. 11, &c.
SECRET,] as in 13. 6, &c.
AMEN,] i.e. it is stedfast! it surely cometh.
16. MAKETH LIGHT,] in thought, word, or
act, Prov. 30. 17.
FATHER..MOTHER,] his parents, whom he
is bound to honour, as in Ex. 20. 12; De. 5.
16, &c.
17. REMOVING] secretly and unjustly.
BORDER,] i.e. the marks which pointed
it out.
18. CAUSING TO ERR,] as in Job 12. 16;
Prov. 28. 10.
BLIND,] as in Lev. 19. 14, &c.
19. TURNING ASIDE] in any way the
JUDGMENT] or plea of the
FATHERLESS, SOJOURNER, AND WIDOW,]
and of such as have no help in man.
20. WIFE,] as in Lev. 18. 8; Ge. 35. 22,
&c.
SKIRT,] *lit.* 'wing,' as in 22. 30.
21. BEAST,] as forbidden in Lev. 18. 23.
22. SISTER,] as in Lev. 18. 9.
23. MOTHER IN-LAW,] as in Lev. 18. 7, 8.
24. SMITING,] i.e. mortally.
SECRET,] as in v. 15 above.
25. BRIBE,] as in Ex. 23. 8, &c.
PERSON,] *lit.* 'soul.'
26. ESTABLISH,] *lit.* 'raise up.'

XXVIII. 1. UPPERMOST,] *or* 'most high,'
as in Ge. 14. 16.
2. COME UPON THEE] from on high, from
God himself.
OVERTAKEN THEE,] as in Ge. 31. 25; 44.
4, &c.
3. BLESSED,] as in Ge. 9. 26; it is not a
prayer, but a declarative prophecy, as in 27.
15 above.
A CITY,] i.e. when among men, or when in
A FIELD] alone, away from others.
4. FRUIT OF THY BODY] *or* 'belly,' as the
male is perhaps here referred to. Compare
Luke 1. 42.
GROUND,] which it gives for the use of
man, and of beast.
CATTLE,] as in v. 11; 30. 9.
INCREASE..WEALTH,] as in Ex. 13. 12.
5. BASKET,] as in 26. 2. 4.
KNEADING-TROUGH,] as in Ex. 8. 3; 12. 34.
6. COMING IN] to thine own house and
family.

GOING OUT] to transact business of any kind.

7. ONE WAY,] i.e. unitedly, in one band. SEVEN WAYS,] i.e. in any and every possible way.

8. STROE-HOUSES,] as in Prov. 3. 10, not found elsewhere.

PUTTING FORTH,] or exercise.

9. SWORN,] confirming it with an oath. De. 7. 12, 13.

10. THE LAND] of Canaan.

AFRAID,] because that God is on their side, 11. 25.

11. ABUNDANT] or ' to excel,' as in 30. 9, &c.

12. OPEN] freely without restraint. TREASURE,] i.e. of rain; see 32. 34; Job 38. 22; Ps. 33. 7; 135. 7, &c.

SEASON,] suitable for the land. Ge. 8. 22.

LENT,] or 'cause to borrow,' see v. 44 below.

BORROW] from them or any one.

13. FOR HEAD] of the nations, in privileges, honours, &c.

FOR TAIL,] i.e. to be among the last or lowest of the nations.

14. RIGHT OR LEFT,] one way or another.

SERVE THEM] instead of, or along with, the true and only Lord God.

15. REVILINGS] as in 27. 30, &c.

OVERTAKEN,] as in v. 2 above.

16. CURSED,] as in 27. 15, &c.

A CITY,] as in v. 3 above.

A FIELD,] as in v. 3 above.

17. BASKET,] as in v. 5 above.

KNEADING-TROUGH,] as in v. 5 above.

18. BODY,] as in v. 4 above.

LAND,] wherein thou dwellest.

INCREASE..WEALTH,] as in v. 4 above.

COMING IN,] as in v. 6 above.

GOING OUT,] as in v. 6 above.

20. THE CURSE,] as in Prov. 3. 33; 28. 27; Mal. 2. 2; 3. 9.

THE TROUBLE,] as in 7. 23, &c.

THE REBUKE.] The original form of the word is not found elsewhere, but compare 2 Sa. 22. 16, &c.

DESTROYED,] as in 4. 26; 7. 23; 12. 30; 28. 20, 34, 45, 51, 61; Ps. 92. 7, &c.

HASTILY,] as in Ex. 32. 8, &c.

21. CAUSE TO CLEAVE,] as in Jer. 13. 11; Eze. 3. 26; 29. 4.

PESTILENCE,] as in Ex. 5. 3; 9. 3, 15; Lev. 26. 25; Nu. 14. 12, &c.

22. CONSUMPTION,] as in Lev. 26. 16.

FEVER,] as in Lev. 26. 16.

INFLAMMATION.] The original word is not found elsewhere.

EXTREME BURNING.] Not mentioned elsewhere.

SWORD,] or perhaps 'drought,' according to Gill, Boothroyd, and Aben Ezra.

BLASTING,] as in 1 K. 8. 37; 2 Ch. 6. 28; Amos 4. 9; Hag. 2. 17; compare 2 K. 19. 26.

MILDEW,] as in 1 K. 8. 37; 2 Ch. 6. 28; Jer. 30. 6; Am. 4. 9; Hag. 2. 17.

23. THY HEAVENS,] as in Lev. 26. 19.

BRASS,] for hardness, through which no rain can pass.

24. IRON,] which can yield of itself no produce.

DUST AND ASHES,] as in Ex. 9. 9; De. 9 21, &c.

25. IN ONE WAY,] i.e. as a compact host—unitedly.

IN SEVEN WAYS,] i.e. in all directions, fleeing before the enemy.

A TREMBLING,] as in 2 Ch. 29. 8; Jer. 15. 4; 24. 9; 29. 18; 34. 17; Eze. 23. 46.

26. CARCASE,] as in 21. 23, &c.

CAUSING TREMBLING,] as in Lev. 26. 6, &c.

27. ULCER,] as in Ex. 9. 9, 10, 11, &c.

EMERODS,] as in 1 Sa. 5. 6, 9, 12; 6. 4, 5.

SCURVY,] as in Lev. 21. 20; 22. 22.

ITCH.] Everywhere else the original word means 'the sun,' as in Jud. 8. 13; 14. 18; Job 9. 7.

28. MADNESS,] as in 2 K. 9. 20; Zech. 12. 4.

BLINDNESS,] as in Zech. 12. 4.

ASTONISHMENT,] as in Zech. 12. 4.

29. GROPING,] as in Job 5. 14; 12. 25, &c.

DARKNESS,] as in Ex. 10. 22, &c.

CAUSE TO PROSPER,] as in 2 Ch. 13. 12; Prov. 28. 13; Jer. 2. 37; 32. 5, &c.

OPPRESSED,] as in v. 33; Ps. 103. 6; 146. 7; Prov. 28. 17; Ecc. 4. 1; Jer. 50. 33; Hos. 5. 11.

PLUNDERED,] as in v. 31; Jer. 21. 12; 22. 3; Mal. 1. 3.

SAVIOUR,] as in 22. 27, &c.

30. BETROTH] to thyself as a wife; after the betrothal an interval of time elapsed before she was taken home, but there was no other ceremony.

VINEYARD.] This is a common source of pleasure and profit in the east, as well as in France, Italy, &c.

MAKE IT COMMON,] as in 20. 6.

31. OX,] which was used for ploughing, &c.

ASS,] used for riding.

SHEEP,] affording milk, and clothing, and food to the family.

32. SONS..DAUGHTERS.] Regarded as such blessings in the east.

LOOKING] for their return to comfort thee.

CONSUMING] away for grief at their exile or death.

IS NOT TO GOD,] i.e. thou hast no power even to pray for them to God, Ge. 31. 29; Neh. 5. 5; Prov. 3. 27; Mic. 2. 1.

33. FRUIT OF THY GROUND,] which it bringeth forth spontaneously.

LABOUR,] which thou hast laboured at.

A PEOPLE,] i.e. Chaldeans, Romans, &c.

BRUISED,] as in 2 K. 18. 21; Isa. 36. 6; 42. 3; 58. 6; Hos. 5. 11.

34. MAD,] as in 1 Sa. 21. 15; 2 K. 9. 11; Jer. 29. 26; Hos. 9. 7.

35. EVIL ULCER,] as in Job 2. 7, &c.

SOLE..CROWN,] as in 2 Sa. 14. 25; Job 2. 7.

36. A NATION.] See v. 33 above.

SERVED,] i.e. worshipped and obeyed them.

STONE,] which can neither do good nor evil.

37. ASTONISHMENT,] as in 2 K. 22. 19; 2 Ch. 29. 8; 30. 7, &c.

SIMILE,] as in Nu. 23. 7, 18; 24. 3, 15, 20, 21, 23; 1 Sa. 10. 12; 24. 13; 1 K. 4. 32; 9. 7; 2 Ch. 7. 20, &c.

BYEWORD,] as in 1 K. 9. 7; 2 Ch. 7. 20; Jer. 24. 9.

LEAD,] i.e. captive

38. TAKE FORTH] out of thy store-house to sow in the field.
GATHER IN,] out of the harvest.
LOCUST,] which is well known to come in countless millions.
39. LABOURED] in tending it.
40. OLIVES,] either trees or leaves.
BORDER,] or territory.
OIL,] which is so much used in the east.
POUR OUT,] to anoint thyself or friend.
FALL OFF,] as in 19. 5, &c.
41. CAPTIVITY,] in other lands.
42. POSSESS,] or 'take possession of.'
43. VERY HIGH..VERY LOW,] lit. 'high high..low low.'
44. LEND,] money, food, clothes, &c.
HEAD..TAIL,] i.e. at the opposite extremes of honour and dishonour.
45. CURSES,] which are now revealed beforehand.
PURSUED,] as if they were wild beasts and furious enemies.
OVERTAKEN] thee, not one of them can fall to the ground.
46. SIGN,] or token of God's displeasure and justice.
WONDER] or marvellous thing, such as was never before heard of.
47. NOT SERVED] nor obeyed the Lord.
48. SERVED,] and obeyed thine enemies, and those who hate thee.
YOKE OF IRON,] i.e. heavy, burdensome, and degrading.
49. LIFT UP,] not merely 'bring,' as in the C.V.
END,] i.e. a far off place.
EAGLE,] i.e. swiftly and powerfully. Jer. 4. 19; Hab. 1. 8.
NOT HEARD,] as in Jer. 5. 15.
50. FIERCE OF COUNTENANCE,] lit. 'strong of face,' as in Da. 8. 23.
ACCEPTETH NOT,] lit. 'lifteth not up.'
AGED,] who is everywhere regarded with respect in the east.
FAVOUR,] as in 7. 2, &c.
51. EATEN,] or consumed.
LEAVETH NOT,] as in 2. 34; 3. 3, &c.
CORN,] as in Ge. 27. 28, 37, &c.
NEW WINE,] as in Ge. 27. 28, 37, &c.
OIL,] as in Nu. 18. 12, &c.
INCREASE,] as in v. 4, 18 above.
WEALTH,] as in v. 4, 18 above.
52. GATES,] or cities, which in ancient times generally had gates, and
WALLS,]which were often of great height, breadth, and strength.
FENCED,] by ditches, ramparts, &c.
53. FRUIT OF THY BODY,]as in Lev. 26, 28; 2 K. 6. 28, 29; Jer. 19. 9; Lam. 2. 20; 4.10, &c.
SIEGE,] as in 20. 19, 20; 28. 53, 55, 57, &c.
STRAITNESS,] as in v. 55, 57; 1 Sa. 22. 2; Ps. 119. 143; Jer. 19. 9.
STRAITEN THEE,] because of thy sins.
54. TENDER,] as in 1 Ch. 22. 5; 29. 1; 2 Ch. 13. 7; Prov. 4. 3, &c.
DELICATE,] as in v. 56; Isa. 47. 1.
IS EVIL,] as in 15. 9, which see.
LEAVETH] alone, not impelled by hunger to destroy him.
55. HE DOTH EAT,] lest he have not enough for himself.

56. TENDER WOMAN,] as in v. 54 above.
DELICATE,] as in v. 54 above.
TRIED,] as in 4. 34, &c.
DELICATENESS,] or 'delighting herself.'
TENDERNESS,] or 'being tender.'
IS EVIL,] as in 15. 9.
57. HER SEED,] as in Ge. 49. 10, on which see note.
IN SECRET,] as in 13. 7; 27. 15. 24, &c.
GATES,] as in v. 52 above.
58. THIS BOOK] of Moses.
FEAR,] i.e. reverence.
HONOURED,] as in Ge. 34. 19; Nu. 22. 15, &c.
FEARFUL,] as in Ge. 28. 17; Ex. 15. 11, &c.
59. MADE WONDERFUL,] as in Lev. 27. 2; Nu. 6. 2; Jud. 13. 19, &c.
STROKES,] lit. 'smitings,' as in Lev. 26. 21. &c.
STEDFAST,] as in Nu. 12. 7; De. 7. 9, &c.
SICKNESSES,] as in 7. 15, &c.
60. DISEASES,] as in 7. 15.
CLEAVED TO THEE,] without the possibility of being removed by human power.
61. SICKNESS,] as in 7. 15, &c.
STROKE,] as in v. 59 above.
62. FEW MEN,] as in 26. 5, which see.
STARS.] See the promise in Ge. 15. 5, &c.
NOT HEARKENED,] i.e. not obeyed.
63. REJOICED.] He not merely was pleased to do them good, but had pleasure in it.
LAY YOU WASTE,] as in v. 48 above.
PULLED AWAY,] as in Ps. 52. 5; Prov. 2. 22; 15. 25.
64. SCATTERED,] as in 4. 27; 28. 64, &c.
PEOPLES] of the earth.
SERVED,] either with or against their will.
65. NOT REST,] for any length of time; they were to be wandering exiles.
TREMBLING,] or 'raging,' as in Ge. 45. 24; De. 2. 25, &c.
FAILING,]or 'consumption,' as in Isa. 10.22.
GRIEF,] as in Job 41. 22.
66. HANGING IN SUSPENSE,] as in Hos. 11. 7; 2 Sa. 21. 12.
NOT BELIEVE,] that it is possible to escape from all these evils.
67. EVENING.] Compare Job 7. 4.
MORNING.] Compare Ps. 130. 6, 8.
68. TO EGYPT,] the dreaded place of servitude and oppression.
SHIPS,] as in Ge. 49. 13, &c.
SEE IT.] See 17. 16.
SOLD YOURSELVES,] or 'yourselves been sold;' 1 K. 21. 20, 25; 2 K. 17. 17.
NO BUYER,] because of their number and wretchedness.

XXIX. 1. THESE] words that follow, according to Gill, but Boothroyd and Clarke think they are those of the preceding chapter.
IN HOREB,] where: see 4. 23; 5. 2; Ex. 19. 5.
TO MAKE,] lit. 'to cut.'
2. SEEN,] and are therefore better prepared for what follows.
3. TRIALS..WONDERS,]as in 4. 34; 7. 19,&c.
4. A HEART,] to know or appreciate: wisdom and intelligence in the Hebrew are supposed to reside in the heart.

K

SEE] clearly the designs of the Lord.
HEAR,] and obey his will. Isa. 6. 9, 10, &c.
5. FORTY YEARS,] as in 1. 3; 8. 2, &c.
CONSUMED,] as in 8. 4; Neh. 9. 21.
WORN AWAY,] or 'consumed,' as in preceding clause.
6. EATEN,] i.e. as a general article of food.
DRUNK] habitually, as in Egypt.
7. THIS PLACE,] i.e. the wilderness of Moab, 2. 26; Nu. 21. 13, 20.
SIHON..OG.] See Nu. 21. 23—35.
8. THEIR LAND,] in Jazer, Gilead, and Bashan.
GIVE IT,] as in Nu. 32. 33; De. 3. 12, 13.
10. STANDING,] as in Ge. 24. 13, 43; Nu. 16. 27, &c.
11. INFANTS,] they also being in the covenant, as they had previously been in the Adamic and Abrahamic ones.
WIVES,] or 'women,' whom modern Rabbinism so despises.
SOJOURNER,] of whatever nation he might be.
HEWER] of wood for the fire, and
DRAWER] of water for man or beast; these were reckoned the most menial offices. Jos. 9. 21, 23, 27.
12. THY PASSING OVER.] Compare Ge. 15. 17; Jer. 34. 18.
13. ESTABLISH,] or 'cause to rise or stand.'
PEOPLE,] wholly his own, to be to him for glory and beauty.
GOD,] by covenant pledged to bless them.
SPOKEN] so often, and with his own voice.
SWORN,] which is to all a confirmation sure and stedfast.
14. YOU ALONE,] who are here present, but also with the absent, and those unborn.
16. DWELT,] for four generations.
NATIONS,] i. e. Ammonites, Edomites, Moabites, Midianites, Amalekites, &c.
17. ABOMINATIONS,] which they practice in honour of their
IDOLS,] which are incapable of doing either good or evil.
18. TURNING,] or 'looking,' lit. 'facing,' as in Jos. 15. 2, 7; Hos. 3. 1.
THE GODS] of these nations, such as Baal, Moloch, Malcom, &c.
FRUITFUL,] as in Ge. 49. 22.
GALL,] as in 32. 33; Job 20. 16; Ps. 69. 21; Jer. 8. 14; 9. 15; 23. 15; Lam. 3. 5, 15; Hos. 10. 4; Am. 6. 12.
WORMWOOD,] as in Prov. 5. 4; Jer. 9. 15; 23. 15; La. 3. 15, 19; Am. 5. 7; 6. 12.
19. OATH,] as in v. 14 above.
BLESSED HIMSELF,] as in Ge. 22. 18; 26. 4; Ps. 72. 17; Isa. 65. 16; Jer. 4. 2.
PEACE,] or completion, i.e. perfection of every thing.
STUBBORNNESS,] as in Ps. 81. 12; Jer. 3. 17; 7. 24; 9. 14; 11. 8; 13. 10; 16. 12; 18. 12; 23. 17.
END,] or 'add,' as in the C.V.
FULNESS.] This word is generally used of liquids, as in Ps. 36. 8; 65. 10; Prov. 5. 19; 7. 18; 11. 25, &c.
THIRST,] as in 2 Sa. 17. 29; Ps. 107. 5; Prov. 25. 21; Isa. 21. 14; 29. 8; 32. 6; 44. 3; 55. 1; Jer. 2. 25.
20. PROPITIOUS,] as in 2 K. 24. 4.
SMOKE,] as in Ps. 74. 1; 80. 4.

ZEAL,] for his own glory.
LAIN,] or 'crouched,' as in Ge. 4. 7, &c.
BLOTTED OUT,] or 'wiped away,' as in 9. 14, &c.
21. SEPARATED] him from the righteous.
22. STROKES,] lit. 'smitings.'
SICKNESSES,] as in 2 Ch. 21. 19; Ps. 103. 3
Jer. 14. 18; 16. 4.
23. BRIMSTONE,] as in Ge. 19. 24, &c.
SALT,] as in Jud. 9. 45.
BURNT,] i.e. a burnt thing, as in Isa. 9. 5; 64. 11, &c.
SOWN,] for the salt had rendered it barren.
SHOOT UP,] of itself, as even the wilderness does.
OVERTHROW,] recorded in Ge. 19. 24.
OVERTURNED,] because of sin.
24. JEHOVAH,] whom even they regarded as the God of the land.
25. THEY HAVE SAID,] i.e. some out of their number.
FORSAKEN,] which even the heathen were guiltless of, Jer. 2. 11.
HE MADE,] or 'cut.
26. NOT KNOWN,] as having done them any good.
APPORTIONED,] as in 4. 19; the ancients had the notion that each nation was bound to worship its own deity, and not that of another country.
27. BURNETH,] as in 6. 15; 7. 4; 11. 17; 29. 7.
REVILING,] as in 28. 15, &c.
THIS BOOK] of Deuteronomy.
28. PLUCK,] as in 1 K. 14. 15; 2 Ch. 7. 20, &c.
CAST,] as in Jer. 7. 15, &c.
29. HIDDEN,] as in 7. 20; Ps. 19. 6, 12, &c.
REVEALED] by God to men.

XXX. 1. REVILING,] as in 28. 15, &c.
SET BEFORE THEE,] by the command of God, so plainly and fully.
HEART,] which is here and elsewhere often regarded as the seat of thought.
DRIVEN] thee away by force because of sin.
2. TURNED BACK] from idolatry and sin.
HEARKENED,] and obeyed his voice, which is better than mere sacrifice.
HEART..SOUL,] even thy whole being.
3. TURNED BACK TO,] the captive ones who turn back to him.
PITIED] thee in thy misery.
GATHERED.] His pity is not inactive, but manifests itself in good.
4. OUTCAST,] as in 2 Sa. 14. 13, 14; Neh. 1. 9; Isa. 16. 3, 4; 27. 13; Jer. 30. 17; 49. 36; Eze. 34. 4, 16; Mic. 4. 6; Zeph. 3. 19.
GATHER THEE,] as in v. 3 above.
TAKE THEE,] in spite of all obstacles. Jonathan adds, 'by the hands of the king Messiah.'
5. THE LAND,] even of Canaan.
INHERITED IT,] as a gift of the heavenly Father.
GOOD,] both temporally and spiritually. Eze. 34. 24—31.
FATHERS.] See Hos. 1. 10, 11.
6. CIRCUMCISE] the heart, not the flesh which profiteth nothing.
7. THESE OATHS,] or 'execrations.'

PURSUED,] as if they were ravenous beasts of prey.

8. TURN BACK,] as in v. 2 above.

9. ABUNDANT,] as in 28. 11.

TURNETH BACK TO REJOICE,] i.e. for that purpose, not 'again rejoice,' as in the C. V.

FATHERS] in Egypt, the wilderness, Canaan, &c.

10. FOR,] not 'if,' as in the C. V.

THIS BOOK OF THE LAW.] This would seem to imply that there were several books of the law already in existence.

11. TOO WONDERFUL,] as in Job 42. 3; Ps. 131. 1.

FAR OFF,] requiring great exertion and expense to reach it. Compare Rom. 10. 6, &c.

12. CAUSE US TO HEAR,] as in De. 4. 10, &c. So again in v. 13.

13. WORD,] i.e. command, as in v. 11.

15. SET BEFORE THEE,] that thou mayest choose either of them.

16. LOVE..WALK..KEEP,] by doing which they would live, be multiplied, and blessed.

17. TURN,] lit. 'face,' as in 9. 15, 27; 10. 5, &c.

DRIVEN AWAY,] by force of sin, &c.

18. DECLARED.] There is not the slightest necessity nor propriety in the strong language of the C. V., 'I denounce,' which the original verb never means.

PROLONG.] This could only be done by obedience to the revealed will of God.

19. CAUSED TO TESTIFY,] that they had been duly warned and exhorted.

SET,] as in v. 1.

20. LOVE..HEARKEN..CLEAVE.] These are the necessary and natural results of each other.

TO THEM,] for an age-during inheritance.

XXXI. 1. ALL ISRAEL,] i.e. as represented by their heads and leaders.

2. 120 YEARS,] of which 40 were spent in Egypt, 40 in the service of Jethro, and 40 with Israel in the wilderness.

GO OUT AND COME IN,] as a public leader of the people.

JORDAN,] near which they now were; this was because of his sin, as noticed in 3. 27; Nu. 20. 12; 27. 13.

3. JEHOVAH,] the covenant-God of Israel.

POSSESSED THEM,] as he had promised.

JOSHUA,] son of Nun, is to be their leader henceforth.

SPOKEN,] as in 3. 28; Nu. 27. 21.

4. TO THEM,] i.e. to the nations of Canaan.

DESTROYED,] as in Nu. 21. 24, 33.

5. COMMANDED,] in 7. 1—5, &c.

6. THY GOD,] who is almighty.

FAIL..FORSAKE,] as in Jos. 1. 5; Heb. 13. 5.

7. DOST GO IN,] not 'must go in.'

INHERIT IT,] as came to pass afterwards.

8. FAIL..FORSAKE,] as in v. 6 above.

9. THIS LAW,] regarding the festivals of the Lord in v. 10.

PRIESTS..ELDERS,] who were respectively heads of the church and state.

10. SEVEN YEARS,] as in 15. 1, 2.

BOOTHS,] as in Lev. 23. 34.

11. TO SEE,] as in Ex. 23. 14—17.

CHOOSE.] first Shiloh, then Jerusalem.

PROCLAIM,] lit. 'call.'

12. ASSEMBLE,] as in Lev. 8. 3; 20. 8; De. 4. 10; 31. 12, 28.

WOMEN..INFANTS,] whose presence was not generally required at the three great festivals in the other six years.

HEAR..LEARN,] since faith comes by hearing, and hearing by the word of God.

FEARED..OBSERVED TO DO.] Reverence to God is the basis of obedience.

THIS LAW.] Evidently the Scriptures do not regard ignorance as the mother of devotion.

13. KNOWN,] by personal observation the doings of the Lord.

14. TO DIE,] this being the lot of all men. Ge. 3. 19.

STATION YOURSELVES,] as in Ex. 8. 20; 9. 13; 14. 13, &c.

TENT OF MEETING,] as in Ex. 27. 21, &c., for that was the Lord's meeting-place.

15. IS SEEN,] by those surrounding the tent.

CLOUD,] the usual symbol of his presence, Ex. 33. 9, &c.

AT,] not necessarily over, but 'beside' it.

16. LYING DOWN,] not necessarily to 'sleep,' but to 'rest.'

THE STRANGER,] of the land of Canaan, even the Canaanite, who was an intruder there.

GONE A-WHORING.] Compare Ps. 106. 35—39, &c.

17. FOUND IT,] as in 4. 30, &c.

18. HATH DONE,] not 'shall have done,' as in C. V.; the standing-point is after the commission of the evil.

19. WRITE,] that it may be preserved entire, and

TEACH,] that it may be fully understood.

20. BEEN SATISFIED] with God's goodness.

DESPISED,] as in Nu. 14. 11, 23; 16. 30.

21. DISTRESSES,] as in v. 17 above.

FIND IT,] as in v. 17 above.

IT IS DOING,] or 'making.'

TO-DAY.] There is no reason for the indefinite rendering ' even now.'

23. COURAGEOUS,] as in v. 7; Jos. 1. 6.

I—I AM WITH THEE.] This is apparently the language of Moses, quoting that of God.

24. THIS LAW,] recorded in v. 10—13, &c. These numerous references to writing down the laws and directions that God gave clearly indicate his design that they should be preserved for the guidance of future ages.

25. THE LEVITES,] who were the instructors of Israel, and had charge of all holy things.

26. THIS BOOK,] on which so many laws had been written from time to time.

ON THE SIDE,] lit. 'from the side,' not 'in the side.'

BEEN THERE,] with the other sacred relics and memorials of God's love and anger.

27. REBELLION,] against the just authority of God.

STIFF NECK,] the indication of pride and obstinacy.

REBELLIOUS,] see 9. 7, 24.

28. ELDERS, ETC.] The principle of repre-

sentation pervails everywhere throughout the 88.

29. I HAVE KNOWN,] by the Spirit of prophecy.

CORRUPTLY] against God, and law, and their own promises.

MET,] as in Ge. 42. 38, &c.

DAYS] of their natural existence.

THE EVIL THING,] especially idolatry.

30. SPEAKETH,] after having written it, and probably before copies of it were circulated among the people; the living voice thus authenticated the writing.

ALL THE ASSEMBLY,] by their representatives.

XXXII. 1. GIVE EAR.] Compare Isa. 1. 2.

2. DROP,] as in 33. 28.

RAIN,] as in De. 11. 11, 14, 17, &c.

DOCTRINE,] as in Job 11. 4; Prov. 1. 5; 4. 2; 7. 21; 9. 9; 16. 21, 23; Isa. 29. 24.

FLOW,] as in Nu. 24. 7; Jud. 5. 5; Job 36. 28; Ps. 147. 18; Song 4. 16; Isa. 45. 8; Jer. 9. 18, &c.

DEW,] as in Ge. 27. 28, 39, &c.

STORMS.] The original word is not found elsewhere in this sense; it means 'heavy, rough, tempestuous.'

TENDER GRASS,] as in Ge. 1. 11, 12, &c.

SHOWERS,] as in Ps. 65. 10 ; 72. 6; Jer. 3. 3; 14. 22; Mic. 5. 7.

HERB,] as in Ge. 1. 11, 12, 29, 30, &c.

3. NAME,] i.e. renown, fame.

ASCRIBE,] lit. 'give ye.'

4. THE ROCK.] This is a common appellation of God, see v. 15, 18, 31; 1 Sa. 2. 2; 22. 32, 47; 23. 3; Ps. 18. 2, 31, 46, &c.

STEDFASTNESS,] as in Ex. 17. 12; 1 Sa. 26. 23 ; 2 K. 12. 15; 22. 7, &c.

RIGHTEOUS,] or right.

UPRIGHT,] as in Ps. 25. 8; 92. 15, &c.

5. IT HATH DONE CORRUPTLY,] as in 9. 12, &c.

TO HIM,] i.e. to God.

PERVERSE,] as in 2 Sa. 22. 27; Ps. 18. 26; 101. 4; Prov. 2. 15; 8. 8; 11. 20; 17. 20; 19. 1; 22. 5; 28. 6.

CROOKED.] This word is not found elsewhere, but compare Job 5. 13 ; Prov. 8. 8.

6. DO YE ACT,] as in Ge. 50. 15, 17.

PURCHASED,] as in Ex. 15. 16; Ps. 74. 2; 78. 54.

7. DAYS OF OLD,] as in Isa. 63. 9; Amos 9. 11; Mic. 5. 2; 7. 14; Mal. 3. 4.

8. CAUSING TO INHERIT,] as in 21. 16, &c.

9. LINE,] as in 3. 4, 13 ; 32. 9; Jos. 2. 15; 17. 5, 14; 19. 9, 29.

10. VOID,] as in Ge. 1. 2, &c.

HOWLING,] as in Isa. 15. 8, &c.

APPLE,] lit. 'little man,' as in Ps. 17 8; Prov. 7. 2, 9; 20. 20.

11. WAKETH,] as in 1 Ch. 5. 26, &c.

NEST,] i.e. her brood.

FLUTTERETH,] as in Ge. 1. 2, &c.

PINIONS,] as in Job 39. 13 ; Ps. 68. 13; 91. 4.

12. LEAD HIM,] as in Ex. 13. 17; 15. 13, &c.

13. MAKETH HIM RIDE,] as in Isa. 58. 14; Hos. 10. 11, &c.

FLINT,] as in 8. 15; Job 28. 9; Ps. 114. 8; Isa. 50. 7.

14. HERD,] as in Ge. 12. 6.

FLOCK,] as in Ge. 4. 2.

SONS OF BASHAN.] Compare Ps. 22. 13. Amos 4. 1; Eze. 39. 18, &c.

HE-GOATS,] as in Ge. 31. 10, 11, &c.

KIDNEYS,] as in Ps. 81. 16; 147. 14.

WINE,] as in Isa. 27. 2.

15. JESHURUN,] as in 33. 5, 26; Isa. 44. 2, lit. 'the little upright one.'

FAT,] as in Jer. 5. 28.

KICK,] as in 1 Sa. 2. 29.

THICK,] as in 1 K. 12. 10 ; 2 Ch. 10. 10.

COVERED.] This original word is not found elsewhere.

DISHONOURETH,] as in Jer. 14. 21; Mic. 7. 6; Nah. 3. 6.

16. ZEALOUS,] of his own glory.

STRANGERS,] i.e. foreign gods.

ABOMINATIONS,] false gods and their customs.

17. DEMONS,] as in Ps. 106. 37.

VICINITY,] or 'near' place.

18. BEGAT,] or gave thee being.

FORMETH] thee to be a people.

19. DESPISETH,] as in La. 2. 6; Ps. 10. 3.

PROVOCATION] that they offered to him.

20. FORWARD,] as in Prov. 2. 12, 14; 6. 14; 8. 13; 10. 31, 32; 16. 28, 30; 23. 33.

STEDFASTNESS,] as in Prov. 13. 17; 14. 5; 20. 6; Isa. 26. 2.

21. ZEALOUS,] as in v. 16 above.

VANITIES,] as in 1 K. 16. 13; 2 K. 17. 15; Ps. 31. 6; Jer. 8. 19; 14. 22; 51. 18; Jon. 2. 8, &c.

22. KINDLED,] as in Jer. 15. 14; 17. 4.

LOWER,] as in Ps. 63. 9; 86. 13; 88. 6, &c.

23. GATHER] from all quarters.

CONSUME,] i.e. use them all up, reserving none.

24. EXHAUSTED.] This original word is not found elsewhere.

CONSUMED,] lit. 'eaten up.'

HEAT,] as in Job 5. 7; Ps. 76. 3; 78. 48; Song 8. 6; Hab. 3. 5.

DESTRUCTION,] as in Ps. 91. 6; Isa. 28. 2; Hos. 13. 14.

POISON,] as in v. 33; Job 6. 4; Ps. 58. 4; 140. 3; lit. 'heat, fury.'

FEARFUL THINGS,] as in Mic. 7. 17; compare Job 32. 6.

25. BEREAVE,] as in Ge. 42. 36.

INNER-CHAMBERS,] as in Ge. 43. 30.

26. I BLOW THEM AWAY.] This original word is not found elsewhere.

27. I FEAR,] as in 1. 17; 18. 22; this is spoken of course after the manner of men.

HIGH,] and more powerful than their's or than God's.

28. LOST TO COUNSELS,] refusing all advice; this is spoken of the enemy, not of Israel.

29. IF,] not 'oh that,' as in C.V.

DEAL WISELY,] as in 29. 9; Ps. 101. 2, &c.

LATTER END,] i.e. their future condition as a nation.

30. A THOUSAND] in battle.

MYRIAD,] i.e. ten thousand.

ROCK,] i.e. god.

SOLD] them, as no longer of any use to him.

SHUT THEM UP,] to the sword of the enemy.

32. VINE OF SODOM,] proverbially worthless, as in Isa. 1. 10, &c.

FIELDS OF GOMORRAH,] which were barren and useless.
GALL.] This original word is not found elsewhere.
33. POISON,] as in v. 24 above.
DRAGONS,] as in Ge. 1. 21; Ex. 7. 9, 10, 12; Ps. 74. 13, &c.
VENOM,] as in 29. 18, &c.
ASPS,] as in Job 20. 16.
35. VENGEANCE,] as in v. 41, 43, &c.
RECOMPENCE.] This original word is not found elsewhere.
SLIDE,] as in Ps. 38. 16; Ps. 94. 18, &c.
CALAMITY,] as in 2 Sa. 22. 19; Job 18. 12; 21. 17, &c.
HASTE,] as in Nu. 32. 17; Job 20. 2.
PREPARED,] as in Isa. 10. 13, &c.
36. JUDGE,] and not leave their wrongs unredeemed.
REPENT HIMSELF,] as in Ge. 37. 35; 27. 42; Nu. 23. 19; Ps. 119. 52; 135. 14; Eze. 5. 13.
THE GOING AWAY] of power, lit. of the 'hand,' as being the seat of power.
LEFT,] as in 1 K. 14. 10; 21. 21; 2 K. 9. 8; 14. 26.
37. ROCK,] i.e. God.
38. FAT,] as in Ge. 4. 4; Ex. 23. 18, &c.
LIBATION,] as in Ge. 35. 14; Ex. 29. 40.
HIDING-PLACE,] lit. 'secret place,' but the original word is not found elsewhere.
39. PUT TO DEATH,] i.e. I am the cause of death to every one.
KEEP ALIVE,] i.e. I give, preserve, or restore life.
SMITTEN,] according to my zeal against sin.
HEAL,] according to my good pleasure.
DELIVERER,] or 'rescuer.'
40. HAND,] the usual form of an oath.
41. SHARPENED,] as in Ps. 45. 5; 64. 3; 120. 4; 140. 3; Prov. 25. 18; Isa. 5. 28; De. 6. 7.
BRIGHTNESS,] or 'lightning,' as in Ex. 19. 16; 2 Sa. 22. 15, &c.
REPAY] their misdeeds.
42. MAKE DRUNK,] or 'merry,' as in Ge. 43. 34; i.e. it is satiated with blood.
DEVOURETH,] as in 2 Sa. 2. 26; 11. 25; 18. 8; Isa. 1. 20; Jer. 2. 30; Eze. 46. 10, 14; Nah. 2. 13, &c.
PIERCED,] as in Ge. 34. 27, &c.
FREEMAN,] as in Jud. 5. 2.
43. WITH HIS PEOPLE,] as in Rom. 15. 10, and in Septuagint Version here.
PARDONED,] lit. 'covered,' as in 2 Ch. 30. 18; Prov. 16. 14, &c.
44. SPEAKETH,] as in 31. 30 above.
46. SET YOUR HEART,] i.e. think seriously upon it.
47. VAIN,] or worthless, empty thing.
LIFE,] i.e. it secures it.
49. ABARIM,] see Nu. 21. 11; 27. 12; 33. 47.
NEBO.] See Nu. 32. 33.
MOAB,] now possessed by the two tribes and a half.
JERICHO,] on the west of the Jordan.
50. BE GATHERED,] as in Ge. 25. 8, 17, &c.
AARON,] recorded in Nu. 26. 25—29.
51. TRESPASSED,] i.e. went over or beyond the word of God.
MERIBATH-KADESH,] not the 'Meribah' referred to in Ex. 17. 7, but in Nu. 20. 1, 13.

ZIN,] see Nu. 13. 21, &c.

XXXIII. 1. BLESSING,] pronounced prophetically by Moses, who is the first person in the Bible described as a 'man of God.'
2. SINAI.] Compare Ex. 3. 1; 19. 18, 20, Jud. 5. 5.
SEIR,] see Jud. 5. 4.
PARAN,] see Heb. 3. 3.
MYRIADS,] i.e. tens of thousands.
SPRINGS,] as in De. 3. 17; 4. 49; Jos. 10. 40; 12. 3, 8; 13. 20. The Masorets have divided the word into two, lit. 'a fire of law,' which has no sense.
3. LOVING.] This original word is not found elsewhere.
PEOPLES,] i.e. of Israel, the twelve tribes
HAND,] or power.
FOOT,] to receive instruction.
4. LAW,] lit. 'a director,' guide.
POSSESSION,] not 'inheritance,' as in C.V.
5. JESHURUN,] as in 32. 15, &c.
6. A NUMBER,] as in Ge. 34. 30, &c. The Sept. applies this last clause to Simeon.
7. STRIVEN] for him, i.e. he is able to maintain his cause.
HELP,] as in Ex. 8. 4; De. 32. 26, 29; Ps. 20. 2, &c.
8. THUMMIM..URIM.] See on Ex. 28. 30.
PIOUS ONE,] i.e. Aaron, Ps. 106. 16.
TRIED,] by the sinfulness of the people.
MASSAH,] as in Ex. 17. 7, &c.
MERIBAH,] as in Nu. 20. 1, 13.
9. SEEN,] though they were his own parents, Lev. 21. 11.
DISCERNED,] yet they were out of the same loins, Ex. 32. 26, 27.
KNOWN,] though of his own flesh and blood. Compare Mat. 12. 49, 50.
COVENANT,] as in Mal. 2. 5, &c.
10. TEACH,] lit. 'shoot, throw.'
PERFUME,] as directed in the law, being part of their duty.
NOSE] for a sweet fragrance.
WHOLE-BURNT-OFFERING,] as in Lev. 1. 9, 13, 17, &c.
11. STRENGTH,] or 'force.'
ACCEPT,] favourably.
LOINS,] that they may become feeble.
WITHSTANDERS,] as in 28. 7, &c.
HATING HIM,] as in 32. 41, &c.
12. BELOVED,] as in Ps. 45. 1; 60. 5; 84. 1; 108. 6; 127. 2; Isa. 5. 1; Jer. 11. 15.
CONFIDENTLY,] i.e. not merely in safety, but with an assurance of safety.
COVERING.] This original word is not found elsewhere.
SHOULDERS.] Compare 1 Sa. 17. 6; the temple was on Moriah, part of Benjamin's inheritance.
13. LAND,] comprising Gilead, Bashan, and Samaria.
PRECIOUS THINGS,] as in v. 14, 15, 16: Song 4. 13, 16; 7. 13.
DEW,] so pleasant and fertilizing, Hos. 14. 5, &c.
DEEP,] as in Ge. 1. 2, &c.
CROUCHING,] as in Ge. 4. 7, &c.
14. FRUITS OF THE SUN,] i.e. produced by its heat.
MOONS,] or 'months.'

CAST FORTH.] Compare Eze. 45. 9; Isa. 57. 20.
15. CHIEF THINGS,] or 'best thing.'
ANCIENT,] as in v. 27 below.
AGE-DURING HEIGHTS,] as in Hab. 3. 6.
16. GOOD PLEASURE,] as in v. 23.
THE BUSH,] as in Ex. 32. 4.
CROWN] of the head, as in Ge. 49. 26; De.
28. 35, &c.
SEPARATE,] as in Ge. 49. 26, &c.
17. HONOUR,] as in 1 Ch. 16. 27, &c.
FIRSTLING,] which was dedicated to God.
REEM,] as in Nu. 23. 22; 24. 8, &c.
PUSH,] as in 1. K. 22. 11; 2 Ch. 18. 10; Ps.
44. 5; Eze. 34. 21; Dan. 8. 4.
MYRIADS,] i.e. ten thousands; the 'horns'
are Ephraim and Manasseh.
18. GOING OUT,] whether for peace or
war, Ge. 49. 19.
TENTS,] peaceably remaining at home, 1
Ch. 12. 32.
19. MOUNTAIN] of the Lord's house, Isa.
2. 2, 3.
SUCK,] Zebulun being a maritime tribe,
Ge. 49. 19.
HIDDEN THINGS.] This original word is
not found elsewhere.
HIDDEN,] as in Jos. 7. 21, 22.
20. ENLARGER,] i.e. God, as in Ge. 26. 22;
Ex. 34. 24; De. 12. 20; 19. 8, &c.
LIONESS,] as in Ge. 49. 9; Nu. 23. 24; 24.
9; compare 1 Ch. 12. 8.
ARM,] the seat of power.
CROWN,] the seat of honour and pride.
21. PROVIDETH,] as in Nu. 32. 1, 2.
PORTION,] as in Ge. 33. 19, &c.
LAW-GIVER,] as in Ge. 49. 10; Nu. 21. 18;
Jud. 5. 14; Ps. 60. 7; 108. 8; Isa. 33. 22.
COVERED,] as in 1 K. 7. 3, 7; Jer. 22. 14;
Hag. 1. 4.
22. WHELP,] as in Ge. 49. 9; compare Jud.
14. 5, 6.
LEAPS.] This original word is not found
elsewhere. See Jos. 19. 47; Jud. 18. 27.
BASHAN,] all the beasts of which are
strong and powerful.
23. PLEASURE,] as in v. 16 above.
SEA] of Tiberias.
24. SONS.] Compare Nu. 26, 47; Ps. 128.
3, 4; Luke 2. 36, 38.
DIPPING,] from its abundance, as in Job
29. 6.
FOOT,] when walking in the way.
25. IRON..BRASS,] which were common in
Canaan, see 8. 9.
SHOES,] or bolts or defence; the original
word is not found elsewhere.
STRENGTH.] Vulg. 'age,' Gesenius, 'rest,'
Chaldee, 'youth,' Sept. &c. 'strength.'
26. JESHURUN,] as in 32. 15, &c.
HELP,] see v. 3, 29, &c.
27. HABITATION.] Compare Ps. 71. 3; 90. 1;
91. 9, &c.
ETERNAL,] or 'of antiquity,' as in v. 15:
Ps. 74. 12, &c.

ARMS,] as in 4. 34, &c.
DESTROY,] as in 7. 24, &c.
28. CONFIDENCE,] not merely 'in safety.'
EYE,] as in Ge. 13. 10, &c.
CORN..WINE,] as in 8. 7, 8.
29. HAPPINESS,] as in Ps. 33. 12; 89. 15;
144. 15, &c.
SAVED,] from bondage and death.
SHIELD,] a common title given to God, as
in Ge. 15. 1, &c; a weapon of defence.
SWORD,] i.e. a weapon of offence.
ARE SUBDUED,] or 'feign obedience;' com-
pare Ge. 15. 18; Lev. 6. 2, 3; 19. 11; Jos. 7.
11; 24. 27.
TREAD,] as in 1. 36; 11. 24, 25, &c.

XXXIV. 1. MOAB,] on the east of the
Jordan, where Israel now was.
NEBO,] a part of the range of the moun-
tains of Abarim.
PISGAH,] the highest point of Nebo.
JERICHO,] on the west of the Jordan.
GILEAD,] where he now was, belonging to
the two tribes and a half.
DAN,] i.e. the city afterwards called by
that name.
2. NAPHTALI,] on the north,
EPHRAIM,] in the middle of the land, with
Manasseh.
JUDAH,] at the south of Canaan.
FURTHER SEA,] i.e. the great sea, or Medi-
terranean; see 11. 24.
3. SOUTH] of Judah, Heb. Nageb.
CIRCUIT,] as in Ge. 13. 10, 11, 12, &c.
VALLEY,] as in Jos. 5. 10.
PALMS,] so called because of the abundance
that grew there.
ZOAR,] as in Ge. 19. 22.
4. SWORN] in Ge. 15. 18; 26. 3; 28. 13.
NOT PASS OVER.] See Nu. 20. 12; De. 3.
25—27.
5. SERVANT,] as in Ex. 14. 31; Nu. 12. 7, &c.
6. BETH-PEOR.] See 3. 29.
7. 120 YEARS,] as in 31. 2.
DIM,] as were those of Isaac (Ge. 27. 1)
and Job (17. 7).
MOISTURE,] or 'freshness, greenness.'
FLED,] as in Song 2. 17; 4. 6; Isa. 35. 10;
51. 11; Ps. 104. 7; 114. 3, 5; Jud. 6. 11.
8. THIRTY DAYS,] as they had done for
his brother Aaron, Nu. 20. 29.
9. WISDOM,] like Moses himself, for peace
or for war.
HANDS,] at the command of God. Nu.
27. 23.
10. PROPHET,] or declarator of God's will.
FACE TO FACE,] as in Ex. 33. 11; Nu. 12.
6—8.
11. SIGNS AND WONDERS,] as in Ex. 7. 3;
De. 4. 34; 6. 22; 29. 3; 34. 11; Neh. 9. 10;
Ps. 135. 9; Isa. 8. 18; 20. 3; Jer. 32. 20.
12. STRONG HAND,] as in Ex. 3. 9; 6. 1; 13.
3, 9, 14, 16, 31, &c.
GREAT FEAR,] as in 4. 34; Jer. 32. 21.

JOSHUA

THIS BOOK is an evident continuation of the history of Israel as contained in the preceding Five Books, and from ch. 24. 26, it may be reasonably inferred that it is the writing of the great man whose name it bears; at all events, it is a record of the events which happened to Israel from the death of Moses till the conquest of the land of Canaan under Joshua. It is written in the same simple unaffected style in which the preceding books are written, as a whole, and embraces a period of from twenty-seven to thirty-one years. Its genuineness and authenticity have never been questioned in the Jewish Synagogue or Christian Church, and it is referred to in Acts 7. 45; 13. 19; Heb. 13. 5; 11. 30, 31; James 2. 25. Its great object is to show the fulfilment of the Divine promises in reference to the land of Canaan, in, *first*, its subjugation by, and, *second*, its assignment to, the twelve tribes of Israel.

I. 1. SERVANT OF JEHOVAH,] as in De. 34. 5.

JOSHUA,] *lit.* 'a saviour, preserver,' one who gives ease.

NUN,] as in Ex. 33. 11, &c.

MINISTER OF MOSES,] as so denominated in Ex. 24. 13; 33. 11; Nu. 11. 28, &c.

2. MY SERVANT,] as in v. 1 above; used of Abraham, Ge. 26. 24, and others.

JORDAN,] which separated them from the land of Canaan.

3. EVERY PLACE] of that land of Canaan.

HAVE GIVEN IT] by oath to the fathers, and renewed to Joshua's predecessor, in De. 11. 24, &c.

4. THIS WILDERNESS] of Kadesh and Sin, near Edom, Nu. 34. 3.

LEBANON,] the range of hills on the north, seen in the distance.

GREAT RIVER,] i.e. the river Phrath, on which see Ge. 2. 14.

HITTITES.] Compare Nu. 13. 33; 14. 1; 2 K. 7. 6.

GREAT SEA,] i.e. the Mediterranean.

THE SUN,] i.e. on the west.

BORDER,] *or* territory.

5. STATION HIMSELF,] with hostile purpose and success.

I AM WITH THEE,] to guide and bless, as in v. 9 below.

FAIL. . FORSAKE.] His power and his grace are unchangeable.

6. COURAGEOUS] in leading on the people.

SWORN] so often.

7. LAW,] *or* 'direction.'

COMMANDED THEE] in my name; thus God testified to the truth of Moses.

RIGHT OR LEFT,] either by omission or commission.

ACT WISELY] in every thing attempted.

8. THIS BOOK OF THE LAW,] can only be supposed to refer to that of Moses.

MOUTH,] i.e. thou art never to cease teaching it.

MEDITATED,] seriously and studiously and prayerfully; compare Ps. 1. 2.

DAY . . NIGHT,] i.e. always.

OBSERVE TO DO,] practice following study.

THY WAY] of living and acting among men upon earth.

ACT WISELY,] as in v. 7 above.

9. I COMMANDED,] and who can forbid, or resist?

AFFRIGHTED] because of the foes and the difficulties.

WITH THEE,] as in v. 5 above.

10. AUTHORITIES,] as in Ex. 5. 6, 10, 14, 15, 19, &c.

11. CAMP] of Israel.

PROVISION,] as in Ge. 27. 3; 42. 25; 45. 21; Ex. 12. 39, &c.

12. MANASSEH,] who had received their inheritance already, on the east of the Jordan where they now were.

13. COMMANDED,] in Nu. 32. 29, 30.

THIS LAND] of the two kings, Og and Sihon.

14. SUBSTANCE,] all of which might have hindered their journey.

BY FIFTIES,] as in Ex. 13. 18; Jos. 4. 12; Jud. 7. 11, &c.

HELPED THEM] to subdue the enemy.

POSSESSION] in Gilead, &c.

15. GIVING] by promise and oath.

SUN-RISING] eastward of Canaan.

16. WE DO] fully and cheerfully.

WE GO] to help our brethren.

THEE,] speaking by the command of God.

MOSES,] i.e. perpetually.

18. PROVOKE THY MOUTH,] to pass sentence upon him, as in De. 1. 26, 43; 9. 23, &c.

HEAR] so as to obey them.

COURAGEOUS,] as in v. 7, 9, &c.

II. 1. SHITTIM,] in Nu. 33. 49, called Abel Shittim, in the plains of Moab, where they now were.

SPIES,] *lit.* 'footmen,' as in Ge. 42. 9. 11, 14, 16, 30, 31, 34, &c.

SILENTLY,] as in Ex. 14. 14, &c.

LAND] of Canaan, beyond the river, and (not 'even') the city of Jericho.

HARLOT.] Some critics from the etymology of the original word think she was only an inn-keeper, from a root signifying 'to feed,' in Jer. 5. 8; Da. 4. 12.

RAHAB,] i.e. *lit.* 'broad, wide.'

LIE DOWN] to rest, (not 'to lodge,' as in the C. V.) after the fatigue of their wanderings.

2. KING OF JERICHO.] Every city almost in those days had its own king, there were 31 in Canaan alone who were conquered by Israel (see 12. 9—24), and in Jud. 1. 7, Adoni-Bezer speaks of having subdued seventy. The 'rajahs' of India are the nearest representatives of the 'melechs' of the Bible.

TO SEARCH.] The fame and purposes of Israel were well known to all.

3. BRING OUT.] The eastern respect for females probably prevented the king from taking more stringent measures to apprehend the men.

4. HIDETH,] as in v. 6 below.

NOT KNOWN.] No one need attempt to excuse this falsehood; in Heb. 11. 31, she is commended for her faith in God's promise that the land should be given to Israel, not for her falsehood.

5. TO BE SHUT.] The gates of eastern cities are always closed at night.

6. ROOF] of the house, which is generally flat in Palestine, India, &c.

FLAX-WOOD,] lit. 'flax of the tree,' i.e. cotton.

ARRANGED] that it might dry the better on the flat roof, exposed to the sun and air.

7. FORDS] where it was supposed that they would pass over.

AFTERWARDS,] to prevent the escape of the men, if they yet remained in the city, as well as because the night was advancing.

8. LIE DOWN] for a little rest, before resuming their way homeward.

9. JEHOVAH,] the recognized national God of Israel.

GIVEN] for an inheritance.

MELTED] like snow before the sun.

10. HEARD,] as in Ex. 15. 15, 16, &c.

DEVOTED] to destruction, as in Nu. 21. 21—35.

11. MELT,] as in v. 9 above.

ANY MORE SPIRIT,] as in 5. 1; 1 K. 10. 5; 2 Ch. 9. 4.

HE IS GOD.] This noble confession justifies Heb. 11. 31, and James 2. 25.

12. JEHOVAH] your God, and mine.

KINDNESS] in preserving your lives.

HOUSE,] i.e. household.

TRUE TOKEN,] lit. 'token of truth.'

13. KEPT ALIVE.] She appears to have known the Lord's resolution to devote the people to destruction.

THEY HAVE,] of servants, cattle, &c.

OUR SOULS,] i.e. ourselves.

14. SOUL,] i.e. selves, as in v. 13.

DECLARE NOT] to the king or citizens of Jericho, as in v. 20.

15. ROPE,] as in 2 Sa. 17. 13, &c.

IN THE SIDE OF THE WALL,] not 'upon the town-wall,' as in the C.V.

IN THE WALL,] not 'upon' it; their walls were very thick.

16. TO THE MOUNTAIN,] which Josephus says was a very barren one.

COME,] lit. 'kick or meet.'

HAVE BEEN HIDDEN,] as in 1 K. 22. 25; 2 K. 7. 12; Jer. 49. 10.

17. AQUITTED,] or 'innocent,' on the following condition.

SWEAR,] in v. 12 above.

18. LINE,] as in v. 21; every where else the original word is rendered 'hope.'

SCARLET,] as in Ge. 38. 28, 30.

THREAD,] as in Ge. 14. 23; Jud. 16. 12; 1 K. 7. 15; Ecc. 4. 12; Song 4. 3; Jer. 52. 21.

HOUSE,] or household, as in v. 13 above.

GATHER,] as in 24. 1, &c.

19. GOETH OUT,] and thus leaves the little sanctuary.

INNOCENT,] or 'acquitted,' as in v. 17 above

HIS HEAD,] i.e. he himself is to blame.

OUR HEAD,] i.e. we are guilty of it.

HAND,] of any Israelite is against him.

20. DECLARE,] as in v. 14 above.

21. SO IT IS,] agreeing to the terms of the stipulations as reasonable and just.

BINDETH,] immediately, as directed; her prudence and activity is here manifest; probably no one of her fellow citizens would notice—much less recognize the object of—the scarlet thread which fluttered with the wind.

22. MOUNTAIN,] as directed by Rahab in v. 16.

NOT FOUND,] God protecting his servants.

23. MOUNTAIN,] after hiding three days.

COME IN] to Shittim, where Israel now was, and whence they were sent, as in v. 1.

RECOUNT,] or 'rehearse.'

COME UPON THEM,] or lit. 'found them.'

24. HATH GIVEN,] even already; it is as good as done.

MELTED,] as Rahab said in v. 9 above.

III. 1. MORNING,] which is the best season for travelling in Canaan, before the sun is up.

THE JORDAN,] i.e. to its very banks.

LODGE,] lit. 'pass the night.'

2. THREE DAYS,] during which they rested by the river, while the opposite side was probably covered with spectators from Jericho.

AUTHORITIES,] as in 1. 10, &c.

CAMP,] as in 1. 11.

3. BEARING IT,] as directed in De. 31 9, 25.

JOURNEY,] as in v. 1, 14; 9. 17, &c. Compare the previous signal in Nu. 9. 17, &c.

4. A DISTANCE,] as in Ps. 10. 1, &c.

TWO THOUSAND CUBITS,] or three-quarters of a mile.

5. SANCTIFY YOURSELVES,] i.e. separate and set yourselves apart for the Lord.

WONDERS,] as in Ex. 3. 20, &c.

6. TAKE UP] on their shoulders, according to the law.

7. MAKE THEE GREAT,] by dividing the waters of the Jordan.

8. STAND,] till all Israel pass over.

9. WORDS,] which he himself had just heard.

10. LIVING GOD,] in opposition to the dead gods of Canaan.

DISPOSSESS,] as he had often promised.

CANAANITE..JEBUSITE,] as in Ge. 15. 19; Ex. 33. 2; De. 7. 1.

11. LORD OF ALL THE EARTH,] as in v. 13; Mic. 4. 13; Zech. 4. 14; 6. 5.

12. TRIBES,] that of Levi being exempted, as usual, as in Nu. 13. 4; 34. 19.

13. ONE HEAP,] not 'upon an heap,' as in the C.V.; so in v. 16.

14. JOURNEYING,] as in v. 1, 3 above.

15. EXTREMITY,] as in v. 8.

HARVEST,] i.e. of the barley-harvest; compare 1 Ch. 12. 15; in this the Jordan resembled the Nile.

16. ABOVE ADAM,] or 'in Adam;' this city is not mentioned elsewhere.

ZARETAN,] as in 1 K. 4. 12; 7. 46, a city on the west of the Jordan, in the tribe of Manasseh afterwards.

SEA OF THE PLAIN,] or 'of the Arabah,' i.e. the salt sea, noticed in Ge. 14. 3.

17. DRY GROUND,] as in Ge. 7. 22; Ex. 14. 21; Jos. 3. 17; 4. 18; 2 K. 2. 8; Eze. 30. 12; Hag. 2. 6.

ESTABLISHED,] as in 4. 3; 2 Ch. 12. 1; Jer. 33. 2.

THE NATION.] This word, though generally applied to the heathen, is occasionally given to Israel, as in Ge 12. 2; Ex. 19. 6, &c.

IV. 1. COMPLETED TO PASS,] as in 3. 17.

3. ESTABLISHED STANDING-PLACE,] as in 3. 17.

TWELVE STONES,] one for each tribe.

LODGING-PLACE,] see v. 19, 20.

4. HE PREPARED,] not 'had prepared.'

5. THE ARK,] which still remained on the shoulders of the priests in Jordan.

6. SIGN,] or 'token,' as in 2. 12; 24. 17.

HEREAFTER,] lit. 'to-morrow;' as in 3.5,&c.

7. MEMORIAL,] as in Ex. 12. 14, &c.

8. REMOVE,] lit. 'cause them to pass over.'

9. TWELVE STONES.] It is a question whether these were the same or different stones from those mentioned in the preceding verse; most probably they were the same, and were set up in Gilgal, as in v. 20. It is highly improbable that any twelve stones which any twelve men each could raise out of the Jordan could stand the current of the waters on their return, and especially at the annual over-flowing. The preposition beth 'in,' must be used for min, 'out of.'

10. MOSES,] as in De. 27. 2; 31. 7, but the Septuagint omits this whole clause.

HASTE,] as in 8. 14, 19.

11. PEOPLE,] they beholding the wondrous sight; the Sept. adds, 'and the stones before them.'

12. BY FIFTIES,] as in 1. 14; Jud. 7. 11; Ex. 13. 18.

SPOKEN,] in Nu. 32. 17—32.

13. FORTY THOUSAND,] of the tribes, these being sufficient.

ARMED,] as in Nu. 31. 5, &c.

THE PLAINS.] The Sept. reads 'the city' of Jericho.

14. MADE GREAT,] as he had promised in 3. 7.

MOSES,] see Ex. 14. 31, &c.

16. ARK OF THE TESTIMONY,] as in Ex. 25. 22, &c.; sometimes called 'the ark of the covenant.'

18. DRAWN UP,] as in 8. 16, &c.

HERETOFORE,] lit. 'yesterday, third day,' as in Ge. 31. 2, &c.

19. TENTH OF THE FIRST MONTH,] even Nisan or Abib, see Ex. 12. 2.

GILGAL,] so called because of the reason given in 5. 9.

20. RAISED UP,] not 'pitched,' as in C.V.

21. SONS,] as in v. 6 above.

22. DRY LAND,] as in Ge. 1. 9, 10; Ex. 4. 9; 14. 16, 22, 29; 15. 19; Neh. 9. 11; Ps. 66. 6; Isa. 44. 3; Jon. 1. 9, 13; 2. 10.

23. DRIED UP,] as in 4. 23.

24. PEOPLES OF THE EARTH,] as in 1 K. 8.

43, 53; 1 Ch. 5. 25; 2 Ch. 6. 33; 13. 9; 32. 19 Ezra 3. 3; 9. 1, 2, 11; 10. 11, &c.

V. 1. AMORITE,] see Ge. 10. 16; 14. 7, &c.

THE SEA,] i.e. Mediterranean, or great sea.

CANAANITE.] Sept. reads 'of Phenicia. See Nu. 13. 29.

THEIR PASSING OVER.] So in the margin of the Hebrew Bible.

MELTED,] as in De. 20. 8, &c.

ANY MORE SPIRIT,] as in 1 K. 10. 5, &c.

2. KNIVES OF FLINT.] Compare Ex. 4. 25.

A SECOND TIME,] i.e. their fathers who came out of Egypt had been circumcised, but not the new generation.

3. AT,] or 'unto.'

HEIGHT,] as in Ge. 49. 26; Ex. 17. 6.

4. ALL..MALES,] above twenty years of age, who were men of war, except Joshua and Caleb.

5. CIRCUMCISED,] agreeably to the law in Ge. 17. 10, &c.

NOT CIRCUMCISED.] Why, it is impossible to tell.

6. FORTY YEARS,] as threatened in Nu. 14. 34.

WHO,] or 'in that.'

HEARKENED NOT,] nor obeyed.

SWORN,] in Nu. 14. 23, &c.

SWARE.] in Ge. 22. 16, &c.

FLOWING,] as in Ex. 3. 8.

7. STEAD,] as he had promised in Nu. 14. 31.

8. NATION,] as in v. 6 above.

RECOVERING,] as in 2 K. 8. 10, 14, &c.

9. ROLLED,] as in 10. 18; Ps. 119. 22.

REPROACH,] as in Ge. 30. 23; 34. 14; 1 Sa. 11. 2, &c.

GILGAL,] i.e. 'a rolling' off.

10. MAKE,] or 'do,' as in Ex. 12. 48, &c.

FOURTEENTH DAY,] as in Ex. 12. 6.

AT EVENING,] the appointed time.

11. OLD CORN.] This original word is not found elsewhere.

ROASTED,] as in Lev. 2. 14.

12. MANNA,] which had been supplied to them for forty years.

INCREASE,] as in Ge. 47. 24, &c.

13. DRAWN SWORD,] as in Nu. 22. 23, 31; 1 Ch. 21. 16.

14. PRINCE,] as in Ge. 12. 15; 21. 22, 25; Dan. 10. 13, 20; 12, 1, &c.

JEHOVAH'S HOST,] as in Ex. 12. 41.

NOW I HAVE COME,] to ensure them the possession of the land.

15. CAST OFF THY SHOE,] the usual mark of respect in the east, Ex. 3. 5.

HOLY,] i.e. 'set apart' by my presence.

VI. 1. SHUTTETH ITSELF UP,] for fear of Israel.

IS SHUT UP,] by Israel in seige.

COMING IN,] to flee or to fight.

2. JEHOVAH,] evidently the same as the 'prince' mentioned in 5. 15.

3. COMPASSED,] or gone round the walls of the city.

ONCE,] daily, for six days in succession.

4. SEVEN PRIESTS,] as a round number denoting perfection.

OF THE JUBILEE,] as in Ex. 19. 13; Lev 25. 10, &c.

ARK,] which also was to go round the city in the midst of the host.
TRUMPETS,] every time they compassed it
5. PROLONGATION,] *lit.* 'drawing out,' as in Ex. 19. 13; Ps. 10. 9; Ecc. 2. 3.
OF THE JUBILEE,] as in v. 4.
UNDER IT,] i.e. the voice of the shout.
6. ARK OF THE COVENANT,] as in 3. 3, &c.
OF THE JUBILEE,] as in v. 4, 5.
7. ARMED,] as in 4. 13, &c.
9. IS GATHERING UP,] as in v. 13; Nu. 10. 25, &c.
10. CAUSE TO BE HEARD,] as if to terrify the enemy.
11. ONCE,] as directed in v. 3 above.
12. BEAR,] as beforehand they were accustomed to do.
13. TRUMPETS,] exactly as they had done the day before.
14. SIX DAYS,] as directed in v. 3 above.
15. ASCENDING OF THE DAWN,] as in Ge. 32. 24.
SEVEN TIMES,] as enjoined in v. 4 above.
16. SHOUT,] as in v. 10 above.
17. DEVOTED,] as in Lev. 27. 21, 28, 29; Nu. 18. 14; De. 7. 26; 13. 17, &c.
HID,] as in 2. 6, &c.
18. DEVOTED THING,] i.e. the wealth of Jericho.
TROUBLED IT,] as in Ge. 34. 30; Jos. 7. 25; Jud. 11. 35; 1 Sa. 14. 29; 1 K. 18. 17, 18; 1 Ch. 2. 7, &c.
19. TREASURY,] as in Nu. 31. 54, after the battle with Midian.
20. UNDER IT,] as in 6. 5.
21. DEVOTE,] according to the law in De. 7. 2, &c.
22. SWORN,] as recorded in 2. 12—20.
23. FAMILIES,] as in 7. 14, 17, &c.
24. TREASURY,] as directed in v. 19 above.
25. KEPT ALIVE,] as in 14. 10, &c.
UNTO THIS DAY,] when the writer lived.
26. ADJURETH,] *lit.* 'cause to swear,' as in Ge. 24. 3, 37, &c.
DOORS,] as in Ge. 19. 6, 9, 10; Ex. 21. 6; De. 3. 5; 15. 17; Jos. 2. 19, &c.
27. JOSHUA,] as he had been with Moses, causing him to prosper.
FAME,] as in 9. 9; Est. 9. 4; Jer. 6. 24.

VII. 1. COMMIT,] *lit.* 'trespass a trespass,' as in Lev. 5. 15; 6. 2, &c.
DEVOTED THING,] forbidden to them in 6. 18.
ACHAN,] i.e. 'a troubler,' as in 22. 20; in 1 Ch. 2. 7, it is written 'Achar.'
CARMI,] i.e. 'a vine-dresser;' the name also of a son of Reuben, Ge. 46. 9; Ex. 6. 14.
ZABDI,] i.e. 'my dowry;' in 1 Ch. 2. 7 it is written 'Zimri;' three other persons bear the same name in 1 Ch. 8. 19; 27. 27; Neh. 11. 17.
ZERAH,] i.e. *lit.* 'a rising,' son of Judah, Ge. 38. 30.
2. AI,] i.e. 'the heap,' as in Ge. 12. 8; 13. 3; Jos. 7. 2; 8. 1, &c.
BETH-AVEN,] i.e. 'house of iniquity, vanity, sorrow,' 1 Sa. 13. 5; Jos. 18. 12.
BETH-EL,] i.e. 'house of God,' where Abraham (Ge. 12. 8), and Jacob (Ge. 28. 19) built altars ; once called Luz.

SPY,] as in 2. 1, &c.
3. CAUSE TO LABOUR,] *or* 'weary,' as in Ecc. 10. 15, &c.
FEW,] i.e. the inhabitants of Ai, as in 8. 25.
5. THE GATE] of Ai.
SHEBARIM,] i. e. 'broken places;' not found elsewhere.
MORAD,] *lit.* 'descent *or* going down,' as in 10. 11.
MELTED,] as in 2. 11, &c.
BECOMETH,] *lit.* 'it is for water.'
6. RENDETH,] the usual sign of grief, as in Ge. 37. 29, &c.
FALLETH] in prayer and supplication.
DUST,] as in Job 16. 15; Ps. 7. 5; La. 2. 10; 3. 29; Eze. 24. 7; 27. 30, &c.
7. OH THAT,] as in Ge. 17. 18, &c. There is no reason for the profane exclamation of the C.V.
WILLING,] as in 1 Sa. 17. 39, &c.
8. NECK,] as in Ge. 49. 8; Ex. 23. 27, &c.
9. CANAANITE,] especially those dwelling in their immediate vicinity, see 11. 3.
COME ROUND,] as in Ge. 19. 4, &c.
CUT OFF OUR NAME,] as in Zech. 13. 2, &c.
GREAT NAME,] which would be left without a people to exalt it.
10. FALLING,] as in 1 Sa. 5. 3, 4, &c.
11. ISRAEL,] through one of its members.
COVENANT,] which required perfect obedience, see v. 15.
DEVOTED THING,] even Jericho and all that is in it.
STOLEN,] i.e. taken secretly.
DECEIVED,] *lit.* 'lied,' as in Ge. 18. 15; Lev. 6. 2, 3. &c.
VESSELS,] as in 6. 19, 24, &c.
12. TURN,] as in v. 8 above.
DEVOTED THING,] like Jericho itself, exposed to God's anger.
WITH YOU] as God and Saviour.
13. SANCTIFY,] *lit.* 'separate *or* set apart.'
14. BROUGHT NEAR,] before Jehovah, the supreme and infallible judge.
CAPTURE] by lot.
FAMILIES,] the minor subdivisions of each tribe.
MEN,] each one individually.
15. FIRE.] This being the destined punishment of Jericho, in v. 24.
ALL,] as in v. 24.
FOLLY,] as in Ge. 34. 7; De. 22. 21; 1 Sa. 25. 25; Job 42. 8, &c.
16. JUDAH,] the largest of the tribes.
17. FAMILY,] i.e. the several families of the tribe, one by one.
ZARHITE,] i.e. of Zerah, as in v. 1.
MEN,] as in v. 14, 18.
ZABDI,] see on v. 1.
18. HOUSEHOLD,] children and servants.
ACHAN,] see v. 1 above.
19. PUT..HONOUR,] as in Isa. 42. 12.
THANKS,] as in Lev. 7. 12, 13, 15; 22. 29.
DECLARE,] *lit.* 'bring before.'
HIDE NOT,] as in 1 Sa. 3. 17; 2 Sa. 14. 18, &c.
20. SINNED,] as in v. 11 above.
21. SPOIL] of Jericho.
ROBE,] as in Ge. 25. 25; Jos. 7. 24, &c.
SHINAR,] see Ge. 10. 10; 11. 2; 14. 1, 9, &c.
SHEKELS,] equal to about £25 sterling.
WEDGE,] *lit.* 'tongue.'

FIFTY,] equal to about £75 sterling.

DESIRE,] as in Ge. 2. 9; 3. 6, &c.

HID,] as in v. 22; De. 33. 19; Job 3. 16; 18. 10, &c.

UNDER IT,] even the garment.

22. RUN] to certify the facts stated to them.

23. POUR THEM OUT,] as in Ps. 45. 2, &c.

24. WITH HIM] as witnesses of the punishment to be inflicted.   .

ACHOR,] i.e. 'trouble,' it only now received this name, as stated in v. 26.

25. TROUBLED,] and brought Israel into danger.

AT HIM,] alone by himself.

BURN THEM,] i. e. the silver, gold, cattle, &c; if his family was included, it was doubtless because they were sharers of his guilt.

26. HEAP OF STONES,] as in 8. 29; 2 Sa. 18. 17.

UNTO THIS DAY,] when the author was writing.

TURNETH BACK,] as in Ex. 32. 12; Nu. 25. 4; De. 13. 17, &c.

VIII. 1. AFFRIGHTED,] as in 1. 9; 10. 25, &c.

ALL THE PEOPLE OF WAR,] that they might all share in the spoil.

2. KING,] i.e. destroy them utterly.

YOURSELVES,] which they had not been allowed to do in the case of Jericho, it being wholly devoted.

AMBUSH,] as in v. 4, 7, 12, 14, 19, 21; Jud. 16. 9, 12; 20. 29, 33, 36, 37, 38; 1 Sa. 22. 8, 13; Eze. 8. 31; Jer. 51. 12; La. 3. 10.

REAR,] as in v. 4, 14; Eze. 14. 19, &c.

4. LIERS IN WAIT,] i.e. an ambush.

PREPARED,] as in Ge. 41. 32 ; Hos. 6. 3, &c.

5. CITY,] openly and in the front.

THE FIRST,] recorded in 7. 4.

FLED] before them as if afraid of them.

6. CITY] entirely, leaving it defenceless.

7. AMBUSH] at the rear of the city, as in v. 4.

OCCUPIED,] or 'taken possession.'

8. FIRE,] but preserving the spoil for the men of war.

9. THEM,] i.e. the 30,000 men, mentioned in v. 3.

WEST,] see 7. 2.

PEOPLE] to encourage and direct them, as well as to share their hardships and dangers.

10. INSPECTETH,] to see they are all there, and in readiness for action.

BEFORE THE PEOPLE,] leading them on to the city.

12. 5,000 MEN] out of his remaining army.

WEST] where the first ambush was already.

13. SET,] i.e. in array for battle.

REAR,] lit. 'heel.'

VALLEY] nearer still to Ai.

14. SEETH] the arrangement of the Israelites for battle.

HASTEN,] remembering their former easy victory.

PLAIN] before the city, leading to the valley, in v. 11, 13.

AMBUSH,] as in v. 4.

15. STRICKEN,] as in Isa. 33. 4; Jud. 20.34, 41.

WILDERNESS] or pasture land; see 17. 12.

17. A MAN,] of those able to join in the pursuit of Israel.

OPEN] and unguarded.

18. JAVELIN,] as in v. 26; 1 Sa. 17. 6, 45 · Job 39. 23; 41. 29; Jer. 6. 23; 50. 42.

19. PLACE,] at the west of the city, as in v. 9.

HAND.] He was probably on some conspicuous place, where he could be seen, or it may have been so directed by God that the ambush should move forward at the very time of his stretching forth his hand, without their having observed it.

FIRE,] as directed in v. 8.

20. SMOKE,] as in Ge. 15. 17; Ex. 19. 18, &c.

HITHER AND THITHER,] as in 1 K. 2. 8; 20. 40.

PURSUER,] so that the men of Ai were hemmed in on both sides.

22. AND THESE,] who had captured the city.

REMNANT,] as in Nu. 21. 35; 24. 19; De. 2. 34; 3. 3, &c.

ESCAPED ONE,] as in Ge. 14. 13; Jud. 12. 4, 5, &c.

24. FIELD,] i.e. outside of the city, and in the

WILDERNESS] or pasture land noticed in v. 15 above.

CONSUMPTION,] as in 5. 6, &c.

25. MEN,] i.e. inhabitants.

27. COMMANDED,] in v. 2 above.

28. HEAP] of ruins, as a memorial of judgment.

THIS DAY,] when the author was writing.

29. HANGED ON THE TREE,] the most disgraceful mode of punishment in ancient times.

EVENTIME,] according to the law in De. 21. 23.

OPENING,] or open-place, that it might be observed and trodden down by every visitor or passer by.

HEAP OF STONES,] as in v. 7, 26, &c.

30. EBAL,] see De. 11. 29, &c.

31. WRITTEN,] in Ex. 20. 25; De. 27. 5, 6.

WHOLE,] lit. 'perfect,' as in De. 27. 6; 1 K. 6. 7.

WAVED IRON,] as in Ex. 20. 25; De. 27. 5.

BURNT-OFFERINGS,] for sin, and

PEACE-OFFERINGS,] for thanksgivings.

32. COPY,] or 'duplicate,' as in De. 17.18,&c

33. ALL ISRAEL,] i.e. the representatives of its several tribes.

ELDERS,] as in Ex. 3. 16, 18, &c.

AUTHORITIES,] as in Ex. 5. 6, 10, 14, 15, 19, &c.

JUDGES,] as in Nu. 25. 5, &c.

PRIESTS,] who were all of the tribe of Levi.

SOJOURNER,] from another country or nation.

NATIVE,] born in the land.

GERIZZIM,] as in De. 11. 29; 27. 12.

EBAL,] as in v. 30 above.

FIRST,] in De. 27. 12.

34. PROCLAIMED,] as in v. 35 below.

BLESSING] on the obedient, and the

REVILING,] on the disobedient.

WRITTEN,] in De. 27. 14—26; 28. 1—6.

35. ASSEMBLY,] as in Lev. 16. 17.

WOMEN,] as in Ex. 15. 20; 35. 22; De. 31. 12.
INFANTS,] as in 1. 14.
SOJOURNER,] as in v. 33 above.

IX. 1. JORDAN,] i.e. westward.
HILL-COUNTRY,] as in 10. 6, 40.
LOW-COUNTRY,] as in De. 1. 7; Jos. 10. 40;
11. 2, 16; 12. 8; 15. 33, &c.
HAVEN,] as in Ge. 49. 13; De. 1 7; Jud. 5.
17; Jer. 47. 7; Eze. 25. 16.
GREAT SEA,] i.e. the Mediterranean
LEBANON,] on the north.
HITTITE,] as in Ge. 15. 20, &c.
AMORITE,] as in Ge. 10. 16, &c.
CANAANITE,] as in Ge. 10. 15, &c.
PERIZZITE,] as in Ge. 15. 20, &c
HIVITE,] as in Ge. 10. 17, &c.
JEBUSITE,] as in Ge. 10. 16, &c.
2. ONE MONTH,] as in 2 Ch. 18. 12.
3. GIBEON,] lit. a 'little height,' see v. 17;
10. 1, 2, 4, 5, 6, 10, 12, 41; 11. 19; 18. 25; 21.
17; 2 Sa. 2. 12, 13, 16, 24, &c.
4. SUBTILTY,] as in Ex. 21. 14; Prov. 1. 4;
8. 5, 12.
FEIGN TO BE AMBASSADORS,] as in Prov.
13. 17; 25. 13, &c.
OLD SACKS,] containing food for them-
selves and their
ASSES,] which were much used for travelling in those days, see Ge. 22. 3; 42. 26;
Ex. 4. 20, &c.
BOTTLES] of skin; as in v. 13; Jud. 4. 19;
1 Sa. 6. 20; Ps. 56. 8; 119. 83.
RENT,] with much use.
BOUND UP,] with new skin. Ex. 12. 34;
1 Sa. 25. 29; 2 Sa. 20. 3; Hos. 13. 12.
5. SANDALS,] as in Ge. 14. 23; Ex. 3. 5;
12. 11, &c.
PATCHED,] lit. 'spotted,' as in Ge. 30. 32.
PROVISION,] lit. 'hunting,' as in Ge. 25.
28, &c.
CRUMBS,] as in v. 12; 1 K. 14. 3. Compare
Song 1. 11.
6. GILGAL,] as in 5. 10.
COVENANT] of peace and friendship.
7. HIVITE,] as in v. 1 above.
WITH THEE,] being one of the nations of
Canaan, which they were commanded to
expel.
8. SERVANTS,] professing submission at
once.
WHO..WHENCE.] Compare the anxiety of
Isaac before conferring the blessing of the
birth-right, in Ge. 27. 18, 26.
9. FAR OFF,] as in v. 6.
NAME,] or 'renown' of Jehovah, as in 1 K.
8. 41, &c.
FAME,] as in 6. 27; Esth. 9. 4; Jer. 6. 24;
Ex. 15. 14; Josh. 2. 10.
AMORITE,] as in v. 1 above.
HESHBON,] as narrated in Nu. 21. 21—30.
BASHAN,] in Nu. 21. 33—35.
ASHTAROTH,] see De. 1. 4, &c.
11. ELDERS,] as in Ge. 50. 7, &c.
IN YOUR HAND,] as in Ge. 9. 2, &c.
PROVISION,] as in v. 5.
MEET THEM,] at their entrance into the
land.
SERVANTS,] as in v. 8.
COVENANT,] as in v. 6.
12. WE PROVIDED OURSELVES.] This ori-

ginal word is not found elsewhere as a
verb.
DRY,] as in Ge. 8. 14; Jos 9. 5, &c.
CRUMBS,] as in v. 5.
13. WINE-BOTTLES,] not 'bottles of wine,'
as in C.V.
RENT,] as in v. 4.
14. THE MEN] of Israel, the elders, &c.
ASKED,] as in Ge. 24. 57; Isa. 30. 2.
15. SWEAR,] by way of confirming it, in
addition to the eating with them.
16. NEAR,] as in Ge. 45. 10, &c.
17. SONS OF ISRAEL,] i.e. a portion of them.
THIRD DAY,] after the covenant was
settled.
GIBEON,] as in v. 3.
CHEPHIRAH,] lit. 'a village,' as in 18. 16;
Ezra 2. 25; Neh. 7. 29.
BEEROTH,] lit. 'wells,' as in 18. 25; 2 Sa.
4. 2; Ezra 2. 25; Neh. 7. 29.
KIRJATH-JEARIM,] lit. 'city of forests,'
as in 15. 9, 60; 18. 14, 15; Jud. 18. 12; 1 Sa.
6. 21; 7. 1, 2; 1 Ch. 2. 50, 52, 53; 13. 5, 6; 2
Ch. 1. 4; Neh. 7. 29; Jer. 26. 20.
18. SWORN,] as in v. 15 above.
MURMUR,] as in Ex. 15. 24, &c.
19. PRINCES,] lit. 'lifted up, honoured
ones.'
AGAINST THEM,] hostilely.
WRATH,] i.e. of God.
20. OATH,] as in 2. 17, 20.
HEWERS OF WOOD,] as in De. 29. 11; and
DRAWERS OF WATER,] as in De. 29. 11; Ge.
24. 19, instead of the company, in the service of the sanctuary.
22. DECEIVED,] as in Ge. 29. 25, &c.
23. CURSED,] as in Ge. 3. 14, 17, &c.
HOUSE,] i.e. the place in which the ark of
the covenant may be.
24. COMMANDED,] as in Ex. 23. 22; De. 7.
1, 2.
FEAR GREATLY,] as in Ex. 15. 4; Jos. 2.
9, 24.
25. GOOD..RIGHT,] as in 2 Ch. 14. 2; 31.
20, &c.
26. DELIVERETH,] as in 24. 10.
27. CHOOSE,] whether at Gilgal, Shiloh, or
Jerusalem.

X. 1. ADONI-ZEDEK,] lit. 'lord of righte-
ousness.'
JERUSALEM,] lit. a 'possession or founda-
tion of peace;' supposed to be the same as
Salem, in Ge. 14. 18.
AI,] as narrated in 8. 1—28.
DEVOTE IT] to destruction, according to
the command of the Lord.
JERICHO,] in 6. 1—27.
PEACE,] as in 9. 15.
MIDST,] i.e. one with them, having friend-
ly intercourse.
2. ROYAL CITIES,] lit. 'cities of the king-
dom.'
HEROES,] or 'mighty men.'
3. HOHAM,] i.e. 'he impels;' not men-
tioned elsewhere.
HEBRON,] see Ge. 13. 18; Nu. 13. 22, &c.
PIRAM,] i.e. 'a wild ass.'
JARMUTH,] i.e. 'high,' as in 12. 11; 15 35;
Neh. 11. 29.
JAPHIA,] i.e. 'beautiful.'

LACHISH,] i.e. 'captured,' as in 12. 11; 15. 39; 2 K. 14. 19, &c.

DEBIR,] i.e. 'oracle.'

EGLON,] i.e. a 'little calf,' as in 12. 12; 15. 39. Sept. reads 'Adullam.'

5. AMORITE,] the most powerful tribe of the land.

6. GILGAL,] as in 9. 6.

CEASE,] as in 2 Sa. 24. 16.

GIVE SAFETY,] to us from our enemies on every hand.

HILL-COUNTRY,] of Judea especially.

8. STAND,] i.e. successfully.

9. SUDDENLY,] as in 11. 7, &c.

10. CRUSH,] as in Ex. 14. 24; 23. 27, &c.

BETH-HORON,] *lit.* 'house of the little cave;' there are two places of the same name, the 'upper,' and the 'lower;' see Jos. 16. 5; 21. 22; and Jos. 16. 3; 18. 13; also 2 Ch. 25. 13.

AZEKAH,] i.e. 'a fenced place,' 15. 35; 1 Sa. 17. 1; 2 Ch. 11. 9; Neh. 11. 30; Jer. 34. 7.

MAKKEDAH,] as in 12. 16; 15. 41; it fell to the tribe of Judah.

11. GREAT STONES.] Sept. reads 'hail-stones,' as in next clause.

HAIL-STONES,] as in Isa. 30. 30; Rev. 16. 21.

12. SUN,] as in Ge. 15. 12, 17; 29. 23; 28. 11; 32. 31; 37. 9; Ex. 16. 21; 17. 12; 22. 3, 26; Lev. 22. 7; Nu. 21. 11; 25. 4, &c., *lit.* 'ministrant, servant.'

STAND STILL,] *lit.* 'be dumb,' as in v. 13; Ex. 15. 16; Lev. 10. 3, &c.

MOON,] i.e. 'the yellow one,' as in Ge. 37. 9; De. 4. 19; 17. 3, &c.

VALLEY,] as in 7. 24, 26; 8. 13, &c.

AJALON,] i.e. a 'little hind,' as in 19. 42; 21. 24; Jud. 1. 35, afterwards a town of the Danites, given to the Levites.

13. STANDETH STILL,] see on v. 12.

STOOD,] as in Ex. 33. 9; Hab. 3. 11; Jos. 10. 8, 13, 19, &c.

A NATION,] in its natural character and capacity.

TAKETH VENGEANCE,] as in Nu. 31. 2; De. 32. 43, &c.

ON THE BOOK,] not 'in,' as in De. 17. 18; 31. 24, &c.

THE UPRIGHT,] not 'of Jasher,' as proper names do not admit of the article in Hebrew.

STANDETH,] as in Hab. 3. 11, &c.

MIDST,] *lit.* 'half,' as in Ex. 12. 29; 24. 6; Jos. 12. 2; 2 Sa. 10. 4; Ps. 102. 24; Isa. 44. 16; Da. 9. 27, &c.

HASTED,] as in Ex. 5. 13, &c.

AS A PERFECT DAY,] at its fullest limits, i.e. the longest day in the year.

14. A MAN,] for a lengthening of day-light.

IS FIGHTING,] as in v. 42; Ex. 14. 25, &c.

15. GILGAL.] Sept. omits this 15th verse.

16. MAKKEDAH,] see v. 10 above.

17. CAVE,] as in 1 Sa. 3 16; 22. 1; 24. 3, 7, 8, 10; 2 Sa. 23. 13; 1 K. 18. 4, 13; 19. 9, 13, &c.

18. ROLL,] as in Ge. 29. 3, 8; 1 Sa. 14. 33, &c.

APPOINT,] as in Nu. 1. 50, &c.

19. HINDMOST,] *lit.* 'tail,' as in De. 25. 18.

HAND,] as promised in v. 8.

20. CONSUMED,] as in 5. 6; 8. 24.

FENCED CITIES,] as in 19. 29, 35.

21. MOVED SHARPLY,] as in Ex. 11. 7; 2 Sa. 5. 24, &c.

22. UNTO ME,] for public judgment.

24. CAPTAINS,] as in Jud. 11. 6, 11; Prov. 6. 7; 25. 15; Isa. 1. 10; 3. 6, 7; 22. 3; Da. 11. 18; Mic. 3. 1, 9.

SET YOUR FEET,] as in Ps. 8. 6; 18. 38; 47. 3; 110. 1; La. 3. 34.

NECKS,] as in Ge. 27. 16, 40.

25. AFFRIGHTED,] as in 1. 9, &c.

26. HANGETH,] as in 8. 29.

EVENING,] agreeably to De. 21. 23.

27. CAVE,] as in v. 22 above.

THIS DAY,] when the author wrote.

28. THEM,] i. e. city and king; reserving the cattle for a prey.

REMNANT,] as in 8. 22, &c.

JERICHO,] recorded in 6. 21.

29. LIBNAH,] i.e. 'whiteness,' as in 12. 15; 15. 42; 21. 13; 22; 19. 8; 23. 31; it fell to the tribe of Judah.

30. REMNANT,] as in v. 28.

31. LACHISH,] as in v. 3, 5, &c.

32. SECOND DAY.] This implies that it was a place of considerable strength.

33. HORAM,] i.e. 'height.'

GEZER,] as in v. 3.

REMNANT,] as in v. 28.

34. EGLON,] as in v. 3.

35. DEVOTED,] as in Ex. 22. 20, &c.

36. HEBRON,] as in v. 3.

37. REMNANT,] as in v. 28; compare however Jud. 1. 10.

DEVOTE,] as in v. 35.

38. DEBIR,] as in v. 3.

DEVOTE.] as in v. 35.

REMNANT,] as in v. 28; compare however Jos. 1. 11, 12, 13.

40. HILL COUNTRY,] as in v. 6.

SOUTH] of Judah.

LOW COUNTRY,] as in De. 1. 7; 9. 1, &c.

SPRINGS,] as in De. 3. 17; 4. 49; compare 8. 7.

BREATHE,] as in De. 20—16, &c.

COMMANDED] Moses, in De. 20. 16, 17.

41. KADESH-BARNEA,] as in Nu. 32. 8; 34. 4, &c., in the south of Canaan.

GAZA,] as in Ge. 10. 19, &c., on the south west, a Philistine city, Amos 1. 7; Acts 8. 26.

GOSHEN,] as in 11, 16; 51. 51.

42. IS FIGHTING,] as in v. 14 above.

43. GILGAL,] as in v. 15.

XI. 1. JABIN,] i.e. 'he understands.'

HAZER,] i.e. 'court, village,' as in 12. 19; 19. 36; Jud. 4. 2; 1 K. 9. 15; 2 K. 15. 29; it fell to the tribe of Naphtali.

JOBAB,] i.e. 'an outcry.'

MADON,] i.e. 'contention,' as in 12. 19.

SHIMRON,] i.e. a 'little watch-tower,' as in 19. 12; it fell to the tribe of Zebulun, called Shimron Meron in 12. 20.

ACHSHAPH,] i.e. 'enchantment,' as in 19. 25; it fell to the tribe of Asher.

2. NORTH] of Canaan.

PLAIN,] not 'plains,' as in C.V.

CHINEROTH,] as in 12. 3; 1 K. 15. 20. See Nu. 34. 11.

LOW COUNTRY] of Jezreel, so in Hos. 1. 5, &c.

ELEVATIONS,] as in 12. 23; 1 K. 4. 11.

DOR,] *lit.* a 'habitation,' as in 17. 11; Jud. 1. 27; 1 K. 12. 2; it fell to Manasseh, near Carmel.

3. EAST..WEST] of the Jordan.

AMORITE,] as in Ge. 15. 21, &c.

HITTITE,] as in Ge. 15. 20, &c.

PERIZZITE,] as in Ge. 15. 20, &c.

JEBUSITE,] as in Ge. 15. 21, &c.

HILL-COUNTRY] of Judea, in which these four tribes dwelt.

HIVITE,] as in Ge. 10. 17, &c.

HERMON,] as in De. 3. 8, 9, &c.

MIZPEH,] as in Ge. 31. 49, &c.

4. MULTITUDE,] as in Ge. 22. 7; 32. 12; 41. 49, &c.

HORSE,] which they probably obtained from Egypt, and of which the Israelites were destitute.

CHARIOTEER,] as in Isa. 21. 7, &c.

5. MET TOGETHER,] by appointment, as the word implies.

WATERS OF MEROM,] lit. of a 'high place,' at the foot of Lebanon.

6. WOUNDED,] lit. 'pierced.'

HOUGH,] so as to disable them for warlike purposes.

FIRE,] that Israel might not be led to use and trust in them.

7. FALL] at once upon them, without allowing time for preparation.

8. GREAT ZIDON,] so called because of its great size and importance in those days.

MISREPHOTH MAIM,] lit. 'burnings of waters,' i.e. boilings ; Calmet identified it with the Sarepta in Luke 4. 26.

MIZPEH,] as in v. 3.

REMNANT,] as in all former victories.

FIRE,] as he had been expressly commanded.

10. HAZOR,] as in v. 1 above.

11. DEVOTED] to destruction without remedy.

FIRE,] though from Jud. 4. 2, it appears to have been rebuilt.

12. CITIES,] perhaps 'capital cities' are here meant.

COMMANDED,] in De. 7. 1, 2.

13. BY,] or 'on their hill,' as in De. 13. 16; Jos. 8. 28; Jer. 30. 18; 49. 2; the original word is not found elsewhere.

NOT BURNT,] but reserved for Israel.

14. SPOIL,] which was not set apart to the Lord.

ANY BREATHING,] lest they should be a snare to them, and because of their vile practices.

15. AS..SO..SO.] Compare Ex. 34. 11—13; Nu. 27. 19; 33. 52; De. 7. 1—7; 31. 7.

16. THIS LAND] as hereafter described.

HILL-COUNTRY] of Judea.

SOUTH] of Judea, as in 10. 40, &c.

GOSHEN,] see 10. 41.

17. HALAK,] lit. 'smooth,' as in 12. 7.

SEIR,] the mount of Esau and of the Edomites.

BAAL-GAD,] lit. 'lord of a troop or fortune.'

LEBANON,] on the north.

HERMON,] as in De. 3. 8, 9, near the source of the Jordan.

18. MANY DAYS,] between five and seven years.

19. GIBEON,] see 9. 15, &c.

BATTLE,] in spite of their walls and fortresses and cavalry.

20. STRENTHEN,] as in the case of Pharaoh.

GRACE,] as in Ezra 9. 8; or 'supplication,' as in 1 K. 8. 28, &c.

21. ANAKIM,] see De. 1. 28; 2. 10, &c.

HEBRON,] see Ge. 13. 18; 23. 2, &c., yet from Jud. 1. 10, we learn that they again possessed it.

DEBIR,] see 10. 3, 38, 39, &c.

ANAB,] i.e. 'a grape,' as in 15. 50.

22. GAZA,] as in Ge. 10. 19; De. 2. 23, &c.

GATH,] i.e. a 'wine-trough,' as in 19. 13; 1 Sa. 5. 8; 6. 17; 7. 14; 17. 4, 23, 52; 21. 10. 12; 27. 2, 3, 4, 11, &c.

ASHDOD,] i.e. 'fortified,' as in 15. 46, 47; 1 Sa. 5. 1, 5, 6, 7; 6. 17; 2 Ch. 26. 6; Isa. 20. 1; Jer. 25. 20; Amos 1. 8; Zeph. 2. 4; Zec. 9. 6. Azotus, in Acts 8. 40.

23. TAKETH,] or 'receiveth,' i.e. from the hand of God.

DIVISIONS,] as in 12. 7; 18. 10; 1 Ch. 23. 6; 24. 1; 36. 1, 12, 19; 27. 1, 15; 28. 1, 13, 21; 2 Ch. 5. 11; 8, 14; 23. 8; 31. 2, 15—17; 35. 4, 10; Neh. 11. 36; Eze. 48. 29.

TRIBES] as hereafter to be related.

REST,] as in 14. 15, &c.

XII. 1. SMITTEN] during the life-time of Moses.

JORDAN,] which runs through the centre of the land.

ARNON,] the boundary of the Moabites and Amonites.

HERMON] near Lebanon.

PLAIN] eastward of Jordan.

2. SIHON,] as in Nu. 21. 21, &c.

HESHBON,] previously occupied by the Moabites, Nu. 21. 26.

AROER,] a city of Moab.

OF GILEAD,] not 'and from half Gilead,' as in C.V.; Og ruled over the other half v. 5.

JABOK,] see Ge. 32. 22, &c.

BENE-AMMON,] sons of Lot, Ge. 19. 38.

3. PLAIN,] not 'and from the plain,' as in C.V.; it refers to the plain of Moab.

CHINNEROTH,] afterwards 'Genesaret,' and 'Galilee.'

SALT SEA,] into which the Jordan runs.

BETH-JESHIMOTH,] as in Nu. 33. 49.

PISGAH,] as in De. 3. 17, 49.

4. BORDER] or territory.

OG,] see Nu. 21. 33, &c.

BASHAN,] lit. 'the Bashan,' famous for pasturage.

REPHAIM,] as in De. 3. 11, &c.

EDREI,] as in De. 1. 4.

5. HERMON,] see De. 3. 8, 9.

SALCAH,] see De. 3. 10.

MAACHATHITE,] see De. 3. 14; Jos. 13. 13

GILEAD,] which belonged to Og.

BORDER,] as in v. 4 above.

6. SMITTEN,] as in Nu. 21. 21—35.

GIVETH,] as Nu. 32. 1—42.

7. WESTWARD,] to the great sea.

BAAL-GAD,] as in 11. 17.

LEBANON] on the north of Canaan.

HALAK,] as in 11. 17.

SEIR,] the possession of the Edomites.

DIVISIONS,] as in 11. 23.

8. HILL COUNTRY..SOUTH.] A striking description of the land of Canaan.

HITTITE..JEBUSITE,] all of whom were intruders and to be cast out.

9. JERICHO,] as in 6. 21; whose name is not mentioned.

AI,] as in 7. 2; 8. 27, 28: whose name is not mentioned.

BETH-EL,] as in 7. 2; 12. 16.

10. JERUSALEM,] as in 10. 1; called Adoni-Zedek.

HEBRON,] as in 10. 3; called Hoham.

11. JARMUTH,] as in 10. 3; called Piram.

LACHISH,] as in 10. 3; called Japhia.

12. EGLON,] as in 19. 3; called Debir.

GEZER,] as in 10. 33; called Horam.

13. DEBIR,] as in 10. 38; same as Kirjath-Sepher.

GEDER,] perhaps the same as Gedarah and Gedor, in 15. 36, 38.

14. HORMAH,] as in Jud. 1. 17; 15. 3, formerly called Zephath.

ARAD,] as in Nu. 21. 1; Jud. 1. 16.

15. LIBNAH,] as in 10. 29, 30.

ADULLUM,] as in 15. 35, where David hid himself, 1 Sa. 22. 1; Mic. 1. 15.

16. MAKKEDAH,] as in 10. 16; 15. 41.

BETH-EL,] as in 7. 2; 8. 17; 18. 22; it fell to Benjamin.

17. TAPPUAH,] as in 15. 34, 53; 17. 8.

HEPHER,] as in 19. 13; 2 K. 14. 25; 1 K. 4. 10.

18. APHEK,] as in 13. 14, 15, 53; 19. 30; 1 Sa. 4. 1; 29. 1; 1 K. 20. 26, 30; 2 K. 13. 17.

LASHARON,] or perhaps 'Sharon.'

19. MADON,] as in 11. 1; called Jobab.

HAZOR,] as in 11. 1; called Jabin.

20. SHIMRON-MERON,] as in 11. 1; it fell to Zebulun, 19. 15.

ACHSHAPH,] as in 11. 1; it fell to Asher, 19. 25.

21. TAANACH,] as in 17. 11; it fell to Manasseh, 19. 25.

MEGIDDO,] as in 17. 11; it also fell to Manasseh, Jud. 1. 17; 5. 19; 1 K. 4. 12; 9. 15; 2 K. 9. 27; 23. 29, 30; 1 Ch. 7. 29; 2 Ch. 35. 22.

22. KEDESH,] as in 19. 37; 20. 7; it fell to Naphtali, and became one of the cities of refuge.

JOKNEAM,] as in 19. 11; it fell to Zebulun, and was given to the Levites, 21. 34.

CARMEL,] i.e. 'a fruitful place,' as in 15. 55; 19. 26; 1 Sa. 15. 12; 25. 2, 2, 5, 7, 40; 1 K. 18. 19, 20, 42; 2 K. 2. 25; 4. 25, &c.

23. DOR,] as in 11. 2; it fell to Manasseh.

GOYIM,] as in Ge. 14. 1; Nu. 24. 20, &c, so Septuagint Version reads here.

GILGAL,] on the west coast of Palestine, according to Gesenius. Lightfoot and Sept. 'Galilee.'

24. TIRZAH,] i.e. 'pleasantness,' as in 1 K. 14. 17; 15. 21; 2 K. 15. 14; Song 6. 4.

XIII. 1. ENTERING INTO DAYS,] as in Ge. 18. 11; 24. 1; Jos. 23. 1, 2; 1 K. 1. 1.

POSSESS] as an inheritance.

2. CIRCUIT,] as in 22. 10, 11; Eze. 47. 8; Joel 3. 4.

PHILISTINES,] in the south-west of Canaan, on the shores of the great sea.

GESHURI,] see De. 3. 4; Jos. 12. 5, &c.

3. SIHOR,] i.e. black, supposed to be the Nile, Jer. 2. 18.

EKRON,] one of the five principalities of the Philistines.

RECKONED,] as belonging to them.

PRINCES,] *lit.* 'axles,' as in 1 K. 7. 30; this original word is only applied to the Philistine rulers, as in Jud. 3. 5, 8, 18, 23, 27, 30; 1 Sa. 5. 8, 11; 6. 4, 12, 16, 18; 7. 7; 29. 2, 6, 7; 1 Ch. 12. 19.

GAZATHITE,] as in Jud. 16. 2.

ASHDODITE,] as in 1 Sa. 5. 3, 6; Neh. 4. 7; 13. 23.

ESHKALONITE,] as in Jud. 1. 8.

GITTITE,] as in 2 Sa. 6. 10, &c.

EKRONITE,] as in 1 Sa. 5. 10.

AVIM,] as in De. 2. 23, &c.

4. MEAREH,] i.e. a 'forest, meadow,' belonging to the Sidonians, not merely 'beside' them, as in the C.V.

SIDONIANS,] or inhabitants of Sidon.

APHEK,] see on 12. 18.

5. GIBLITE,] i.e. 'stone-squarer,' see 1 K. 5. 18; Ps. 83. 7; Eze. 27. 9.

LEBANON] eastward.

BAAL-GAD,] as in 11. 17.

HERMON,] i.e. at the base of it.

HAMATH,] the northern border of the land, Nu. 34. 8.

6. MISREPHOTH-MAIM,] see 11. 8.

CAUSE IT TO FALL] by lot.

7. APPORTION,] as in 22. 8.

8. GIVEN,] as in Nu. 32. 1—42.

9. AROER,] a city of the Moabites, Nu. 21. 13.

ARNON,] which divided Moab from Ammon.

MEDEBA,] see Nu. 21. 30.

DIBON,] as in v. 17.

10. SIHON,] see Nu. 21. 21.

BORDER,] i.e. the river Jabbok.

11. GILEAD,] part of which belonged to Gilead, and part to

12. OG,] see 12. 4.

DISPOSSESS] them, and occupy their land.

13. GESHURITE,] see 2 Sa. 3. 3.

MAACHATHITE,] see 2 Sa. 10. 6.

DAY,] when the account was written.

14. NOT GIVEN,] because forbidden by God. Nu. 18. 20—24; Jos. 13. 3, 4.

SPOKEN,] in De. 18. 1, &c., Jos. 13. 33.

15. FOR,] not 'according to,' as in the C.V.; so in v. 23. 29.

16. AROER,] a city of Moab, on the northern side of the river, 12. 2.

ARNON,] which divided Moab from Ammon.

MEDEBA,] reaching unto Dibon, v. 9; Nu. 21. 30.

17. HESHBON.] See on Nu. 21. 25, &c.

DIBON,] which was rebuilt by Gad, whose territory bordered on that of Reuben.

RAMOTH-BAAL,] *lit.* 'high-places of Baal,' Nu. 22. 41.

BETH-BAAL-MEON,] the same as Baal-Meon in Nu. 32. 38.

18. JAHAZAH,] *or* 'Jahaz,' as in Nu. 21. 23; given to the Levites.

KEDEMOTH,] from the wilderness of which Moses sent messengers to Sihon, De. 2. 26; given to the Levites.

MEPHAATH,] given to the Levites, as in 21. 36, 37.

19. KIRJATHAIM,] as in Nu. 32. 3, 37. 38

SIBMAH,] as in Nu. 32. 38.
ZAROTH-SHAHAR,] i.e. 'brightness of the dawn.'
20. BETH-PEOR,]i.e. 'house of Peor,'De.3.29.
PISGAH,] as in De. 3. 17; Jos. 12. 3.
BETH-JESHIMOTH,] as in Nu. 33. 49.
21. THE PLAIN,] as in De. 3. 10.
SIHON,] see on Nu. 21. 21.
HESHBON,] as in v. 17 above.
MIDIAN,] see Nu. 31. 8; where they are called 'kings.'
22. BALAAM,] as in Nu. 22. 5; 31. 8.
DIVINER,] as in De. 18. 10, 14, &c.
WOUNDED] or 'pierced ones,' Nu. 31. 7, 8.
23. AND,] i.e. along with the villages a-round them, as in v. 28.
25. JAZER,] see Nu. 21. 32; 32. 35; Isa. 16. 8; Jer. 48. 32.
GILEAD.] Compare v. 31 above.
HALF,] which had previously been taken from Ammon by the Amorite; see Nu. 21. 26—29; De. 2. 19; Jud. 11. 13. 24.
RABBAH,] see 2 Sa. 11. 1; 12. 26.
26. HESHBON,] as in v. 17 above.
RAMATH-MIZPEH,] i.e. 'Ramoth-Gilead.'
BETONIM,] i.e. 'nuts;' not mentioned elsewhere.
MAHANAIM,] see Ge. 32. 2, near the river Jabbok.
DEBIR.] Sept. here reads 'Daibon.'
27. BETH-ARAM,] i.e Beth-Haran, in Nu. 32. 36.
BETH-NIMRAH,] see Nu. 32. 3, 36; compare Isa. 15. 6.
SUCCOTH,] as in Ge. 33. 17; 1 K. 7. 46.
ZAPHON,] i.e. 'north;' not mentioned else-where.
CHINNEROTH,] i.e. Geneserat or Galilee.
29. MAHANAIM,] see v. 26 above.
BASHAN,] see De. 3. 13, &c.
SMALL TOWNS] as in Nu. 32. 41; De. 3. 14, &c.
JAIR,] as in N.u. 33. 41; De. 3. 4, 14; 1 Ch. 2. 23.
31. GILEAD,] part being given to Gad and Manasseh, De. 3. 12, 13.
ASHTAROTH,] as in 22. 4; De. 1. 4, &c.
EDREI,] as in Nu. 21. 33, &c.
MACHIR,] only son of Manasseh, Ge. 50. 23; but compare 1 Ch. 7. 14.
32. EASTWARD] of Jordan.
33. GAVE NOT,] as in v. 14; 18. 7.
SPOKEN,] in Nu. 18. 20; De. 18. 1.

XIV. 1. CANAAN,] west of the Jordan.
ELEASER,] son of Aaron, the chief priest.
NUN,] along with ten heads, one of each tribe, appointed by name in Nu. 34. 17—29.
2. BY LOT,] to prevent all disputes and cavilings.
COMMANDED,]in Nu. 26. 55, 56; 33. 54 ;34.13.
3. GIVEN..NOT GIVEN,] as in 13. 8, 32, 33 above.
4. TWO TRIBES,] see Ge. 48. 5; 1 Ch. 5. 1, 2.
CITIES,] which could not be alienated by or from them.
SUBURBS,] as in Lev. 25. 34, &c.
5 APPORTION,] to the nine tribes and a nalf, as follows. Nu. 35. 2; Jos. 21. 2.
6. JUDAH,] the fourth son of Jacob, but now reckoned the 'first-born,' as in 1 Ch. 5. 2.

GILGAL,] where the ark was, as in 4. 19.
CALEB,] i.e. 'a dog.'
KENEZZITE,] Ge. 15. 19; Nu. 32. 12; Jos. 14. 6, 14.
SPOKEN,] recorded in Nu. 14. 24, 30; De. 1. 36, 38.
KADESH-BARNEA,] as in Nu. 13. 26.
7. FORTY YEARS,] when in the prime of his manhood.
SERVANT,] as in 1. 1.
SPY,] as in Nu. 13. 6; 14. 6.
WITH MY HEART,] i. e. honestly and heartily.
8. TO MELT,] with fear, because of the number and strength of the enemy.
FULLY AFTER,] as in Nu. 14. 24, &c.
9. SWEARETH,] in the name of Jehovah. Compare De. 1. 34—36; Nu. 14. 23, 24; Jos.1.3.
FULLY AFTER,] as in v. 8; Nu. 14. 24 : De. 1. 36.
10. FIVE AND FORTY YEARS,] of which 38 were spent in the wilderness, and 7 in Canaan.
FIVE AND EIGHTY YEARS,] being 40 years of age when he was sent as a spy.
11. STRONG,] as in 4. 24; 17. 18.
POWERS,] as in 17. 17.
GO OUT..COME IN,] as in De. 31. 2, &c.
12. THIS HILL-COUNTRY,] of Judea.
ANAKIM,] as in Nu. 13. 28; De. 1. 28, &c.
FENCED,] as in Nu. 13. 28; De. 1. 28, &c.
SPOKEN,] of Israel's doing, if they were obedient to His voice.
13. HEBRON,] not the city, for that was given to the Levites, but the country.
14. THIS DAY,] when the writer was writ-ing.
FULLY AFTER,] as in v. 8, 9 above.
15. KIRJATH-ARBA,] i.e. 'city of Arba,' as in Ge. 23. 2; 35. 27, &c.
REST,] as in 11. 25.

XV. 1. FOR,] not 'by' their families; so in v. 12, 20.
BORDER OF EDOM,] which lay at the south of Canaan, Nu. 34. 3.
ZIN,] i.e. Kadesh, as in Nu. 33. 36
SOUTH,] of the land of Canaan.
2. SALT SEA,] as in Ge. 14. 3, &c.; about 100 miles in length.
BAY,] lit. 'tongue,' as in v. 5; 18. 19; 7. 21, 24; 10. 21, &c.
3. MAALE-AKRABBIM,] as in Nu. 34. 4; i.e. 'ascent of scorpions.'
ZIN,] i.e. a 'low palm tree,' as in Nu. 13. 21; 20. 1, &c.
KADESH-BARNEA,] as noted in Nu. 34. 4.
HEZRON,] as in v. 25; it was near to, and is joined with the following place
ADAR,] in Nu. 34. 4.
KARKAA,] i.e. 'floor, bottom;' not men-tioned elsewhere.
4. AZMON,] as in Nu. 34. 4, 5; not men-tioned elsewhere.
BROOK OF EGYPT,] See Nu. 34. 5, &c.
OUT-GOINGS,] as in Nu. 34. 4, 5, 8, 9, 12, &c.
SEA,] i.e. 'the Mediterranean.
5. SALT SEA,] as in v. 2 above.
BAY,] as in v. 2 above.
6. BETH-HOGLAH,] i.e 'house of a par-tridge,' as in 18. 19, 21.

BETH-ARABAH,] i.e. 'house of the desert,' as in 18. 22; in 18. 18 it is simply 'Arabah.'
BOHAN,] i.e. 'thumb,' as in 18. 17.
7. DEBIR,] not far from Jericho; not the same as in v. 15, which was near Hebron, nor as in 13. 26, which was beyond Jordan.
ACHOR,] where Achan was put to death, as in 7. 26.
GILGAL,] i.e. Geliloth, in 18. 17.
ADUMMIM,] i.e. 'ruddy.'
THE BROOK,] or 'valley,' i.e. of Achan.
EN-SHEMESH,] i.e. 'fountain of the sun.'
EN-ROGEL,] i.e. 'fountain of the spy,' as in 18. 16; 2 Sa. 17. 17; 1 K. 1. 9.
8. SON OF HINNOM,] as in 18. 16; 2 Ch. 28. 3; 33. 6; 2 K. 23. 10; Neh. 11. 30; Jer. 7. 31, 32; 19. 26; 32. 35.
JEBUSITE,] as in Ge. 10. 16; 15. 21, &c.
JERUSALEM,] according to later usage.
WESTWARD,] even mount Moriah.
REPHAIM,] as in 2 Sa. 5. 18.
9. MARKED OUT,] as in v. 11; 18. 14, 17; Isa. 44. 13.
NEPHTOAH,] i.e. 'waters of the opening,' as in 18. 15.
EPHRON,] i.e. 'a little calf.'
BAALAH,] i.e. 'mistress,' 1 Ch. 13. 6.
KIRJATH-JEARIM,] i.e. Kirjath-Baal, as in v. 60; Jud. 18. 12.
10. SEIR,] supposed to be on the borders of Azotus and Ashcalon.
JEARIM,] i.e. 'forests.'
CHESALON,] i.e. 'confidence, hope.'
BETH-SHEMESH,] i.e. 'house of the sun,' compare 21. 16; and 1 Sa. 6. 12.
TIMNAH,] as in Ge. 38. 12; Jud. 14. 1.
11. EKRON,] one of the five Philistine principalities; 19. 43.
SHICRON,] i.e. 'merriment;' not mentioned elsewhere.
BAALAH,] i.e. 'mistress,' as in v. 9.
JABNEEL,] i.e. 'built of God;' not found elsewhere.
12. GREAT SEA,] i.e. the Mediterranean, as in v. 47; Nu. 34. 6, 7; part of the territory was afterwards given to Simeon, Dan, and Benjamin.
13. CALEB,] as in Nu. 13. 6, &c.
COMMANDED,] in De. 1. 36; Jos. 14. 12.
ARBA.] See on 14. 15.
14. THREE SONS,] as in Nu. 13. 22; Jud. 1. 10, 20.
15. DEBIR,] as in 10. 38; Jud. 1. 11.
KIRJATH-SEPHER,] i.e. 'city of books,' compare v. 49.
16. ACHSAH,] i.e. a 'tinkling ornament,' born to him by a concubine, 1 Ch. 2. 48. 49; see Jud. 1. 12.
17. OTHNIEL,] i.e. 'lion of God,' Jud. 1. 13; 3. 9.
KENAZ,] i.e. 'hunting,' Nu. 32. 12; Jos. 14. 6.
18. COMING IN] to her husband's house; see Jud. 1. 14.
PERSUADETH,] as in De. 13. 6, &c.
LIGHTETH,] as in Jud. 1. 14; 4. 21; Sept. 'crieth,' Vul. 'sighed.'
19. BLESSING,] or 'pool,' as in 2 Sa. 2. 13. &c.
LAND OF THE SOUTH,] a dry hill country.
SPRINGS OF WATERS,] so necessary in eastern lands.

LOWER SPRINGS,] as in Jud. 1. 15.
21. KABZEEL,] i.e. 'gathering of God,' called Jekabzeel in Neh. 11. 25; birth-place of Benaiah, 2 Sa. 23. 20.
EDER,] i.e. 'drove, arrangement;' not mentioned elsewhere.
JAGUR,] i.e. 'a lodging;' not mentioned elsewhere.
22. KINAH,] i.e. 'lamentation;' not mentioned elsewhere.
DIMONAH,] i.e. Dibon, Neh. 11. 25.
ADADAH,] i.e. 'a great company.'
23. KEDESH,] i.e. Kedesh-Barnea.
HAZOR,] not that in 11. 1.
ITHNAN,] i.e. 'a gift;' not mentioned elsewhere.
24. ZIPH,] i.e. 'a flowing;' not mentioned elsewhere.
TELEM,] i.e. Telaim, 1 Sa. 15. 4.
BEALOTH,] i.e. 'mistresses;' not mentioned elsewhere.
25. HAZOR, HADATTAH.] The Targum reads these two names as one; i.e. 'the new Hazor.'
KERIOTH, HEZRON.] The Targum reads these two names as one; Kerioth is supposed to be the birth place of Judas Iscariot, i.e. the man of Kerioth.
HAZOR,] i.e. Hezron.
26. AMAM.] The etymology is uncertain, and the place is not mentioned elsewhere.
SHEMA,] i.e. 'rumour.'
MOLADAH,] i.e. 'birth,' as in 19. 2; 1 Ch. 4. 28; Neh. 11. 26.
27. HAZAR-GADDAH,] i.e. 'village of the troop;' not mentioned elsewhere.
HESHMON,] i.e. 'little fertile place;' not mentioned elsewhere.
BETH-PELET,] i.e. 'house of escape,' as in Neh. 11. 26.
28. HAZAR-SHUAL,] i.e. 'village of a fox,' as in 19. 3; 1 Ch. 4. 28; Neh. 11. 27.
BEER-SHEBA,] the extreme south border of the land of Canaan; see Ge. 21. 14. &c.
BIZJOTHJAH,] i.e. 'contempt of Jah,' not mentioned elsewhere.
29. BAALAH,] i.e. 'mistress,' given to Simeon, 19. 3; 1 Ch. 4. 29.
JIM,] i.e. 'heaps,' not mentioned elsewhere.
AZEM,] i.e. 'strength,' 19. 3; 1 Ch. 4. 29.
30. ELTOLAD,] i.e. 'the generation;' in 1 Ch. 4. 29; called Tolad.
CHESIL,] i.e. 'confidence,' Sept. reads 'Baithel,' see 19. 4; 1 Ch. 4. 30.
HORMAH,] i.e. 'destruction,' the same as Zephath in Jud. 1. 17; these three cities were given to Simeon, 19. 4.
31. ZIKLAG,] i.e. 'outpouring of a spring,' as in 19. 5, &c. ; 1 Sa. 27. 6.
MADMANNAH,] i.e. 'dung-hill.'
SANSANNAH,] i.e. 'bushes or boughs;' not mentioned elsewhere.
32. LEBAOTH,] i.e. 'lionesses,' perhaps the same as Beth-Lebaoth in 19. 6.
SHILHIM,] i.e. 'presents;' not mentioned elsewhere.
AIN,] i.e. 'fountain,' compare Nu. 34. 11.
RIMMON,] i.e. 'pomegranate;' compare En-Rimmon in Neh. 11. 29.
33. LOW COUNTRY] of Judah.

L

ESHTAOL,] i.e. 'request,' Nu. 13. 23; Jos. 19. 21.

ZOREAH,]i.e. 'hornet;' not mentioned elsewhere, save in v. 43.

ASHNAH,] i.e. 'strong, mighty;' not mentioned elsewhere.

34. ZANOAH,] i. e. 'a rejected place;' not mentioned elsewhere.

EN-GANNIM,] i.e. 'fountain of gardens.'

TAPPUAH,] i.e. 'an apple,' as in 12. 17.

ENAM,] i.e. 'fountains;' not mentioned elsewhere.

35. JARMUTH,] i. e. 'a high place,' as in 10. 3.

ADULLAM.] The etymology is uncertain; see 12. 15.

SOCOH,] i.e. 'bough.'

AZEKAH,] i.e. 'fence, signet,' as in 10. 10.

36. SHARAIM,] i.e. 'two gates,' as in 1 Sa. 17. 52.

ADITHAIM,] i.e. 'two ornaments;' not mentioned elsewhere.

GEDERAH,] i.e. 'the fence;' perhaps the same as the next mentioned place.

GEDEROTHAIM,] i.e. 'two fences;' not mentioned elsewhere.

37. ZENAN,] i.e. 'a thorn;' perhaps the same as 'Zaanan,' in Mic. 1. 11.

HADASHAH,]i.e. 'the new one;' not mentioned elsewhere.

MIGDAL-GAD,] i.e. 'tower of Gad,' not mentioned elsewhere.

38. DILEAN.] The etymology is uncertain; not mentioned elsewhere.

MIZPEH,] i.e. 'the watch tower.'

JOKTHEEL,] i.e. 'obedient to God,' 2 K. 14. 7; not mentioned elsewhere.

39. LACHISH,] i.e. 'obstinate,' as in 10. 3.

BOZKATH,] i.e. 'a swelling,' 2 K. 21. 1.

EGLON,] i.e. 'a little calf,' as in 10. 3.

40. CABBON.] The etymology is uncertain; not mentioned elsewhere.

LAHMAS,] or as some Heb. MSS. 'Lachmam;' not mentioned elsewhere.

KITHLISH.] The etymology is uncertain; not mentioned elsewhere.

41. GEDEROTH,] i.e. 'fences,' 2 Ch. 28. 18.

BETH-DAGON,] i.e. 'house of Dagon;' see 1 Sa. 5. 2.

NAAMEH,] i.e. 'pleasantness;' not mentioned elsewhere.

MAKKEDAH,] as in 10. 10; 12. 16.

42. LIBNAH,] i.e. 'whiteness,' as in 10. 29; 12. 15.

ETHER,] i.e. 'abundance, supplicant;' 19. 7.

ASHAN,] i.e. 'smoke,' 19. 7.

43. JIPHTAH,] i.e. 'he opens;' not mentioned elsewhere.

ASHNAH,] see on v. 33.

NEZIB,] i.e. a 'pillar;' not mentioned elsewhere.

44. KEILAH,] i.e. a 'fortress,' as in 1 Sa. 23. 1.

ACHZIB,] i.e. 'a lie,' 19. 29; compare Ge. 38. 5; Mic. 1. 14.

MARESHAH,] i.e. 'the chief place,' as in 2 Ch. 11. 8; 14. 8, 9; Mic. 1. 15.

45. EKRON,] i.e. 'a little root,' see 13. 3.

46. ASHDOD.] The same as 'Azotus' in the New Testament; Amos 1. 8; Zeph. 2. 4.

47. GAZA,]i.e. 'strength,' Amos 1. 7; Zeph. 2. 4; Acts 8. 26.

BROOK OF EGYPT.] It is absurd to suppose that it refers to the Nile, see v. 4.

GREAT SEA,] i.e. the Mediterranean.

48. HILL COUNTRY] of Judea.

SHAMIR,] i.e. 'a brier, diamond.' Sept. reads 'Sophir.'

JATTIR,] i.e. 'excellent, abundant,' as in 21. 14; 1 Sa. 30. 27; 1 Ch. 6. 42.

SOCOH,] i.e. 'hedge, fence,' different from that in v. 35.

49. DANNAH,] i.e. 'a low place, or judgment;' not mentioned elsewhere.

KIRJATH-SANNAH,] i.e. 'city of the bush, or study,' with which agrees its other name

DEBIR,] i.e. 'an oracle,' as in 11. 21.

50. ANAB,] i.e. 'a grape,' as in 11. 21.

ESHTEMOH,] i.e. 'obedience,' as in 21. 14; 1 Sa. 30. 28.

ANIM,] i.e. 'fountains;' not mentioned elsewhere.

51. GOSHEN,] see 10. 41; 11. 6.

HOLON,] i.e. 'sandy,' as in 21. 15; not mentioned elsewhere, but perhaps the same as Hilen in 1 Ch. 6. 43.

GILOH,] i.e. 'exile,' the city of Ahitophel, 2 Sa. 15. 12.

52. ARAB,] i.e. 'ambush;' not mentioned elsewhere.

DUMAH,] i.e. 'silence,' in Ge. 25. 14; Isa. 21. 11: it is the name of a person and of a place in Arabia.

ESHEAN,] i.e. 'a prop, support;' not mentioned elsewhere.

53. JANUM,] i.e. 'sleep,' or Janus, 'slight;' not found elsewhere.

BETH-TAPHUAH,]i.e. 'house of the apple;' not mentioned elsewhere.

APHEKAH,] see 12. 18; 13. 4 for places of the same name.

54. HUMTAH,] i.e. 'place of lizards;' not mentioned elsewhere.

KIRJATH-ARBA,]i.e. 'city of Arba;' see 14. 15; 15. 13.

ZIOR,] i. e. 'a little one;' not mentioned elsewhere.

55. MAON,] i. e. 'habitation,' as in 1 Sa. 25. 2.

CARMEL,] i.e. 'fruitful field.'

ZIPH,] i.e.-'flowing,' 2 Ch. 11. 8; see 1 Sa. 23. 14.

JUTTAH,] i.e. 'stretched out;' not mentioned elsewhere.

56. JEZREEL,]i.e. 'God sows,' as in 1 Sa. 20. 1.

JOKDEAM.] The etymology is uncertain; not mentioned elsewhere.

ZANOAH,] i.e. 'a rejected place,' different from that in v. 34.

57. CAIN,] i.e. 'the acquisition,' as in 1 Sa. 23. 19.

GIBEAH,] i.e. 'height.'

TIMNAH.] The etymology is uncertain; see Ge. 38. 12, &c.

58. HALHUL,] i.e. 'very sandy,' or 'very painful;' not found elsewhere.

BETH-ZUR,] i.e. 'house of a rock.'

GEDOR,] i.e. 'hedge, fence,' see 12. 13.

59. MAARATH,]i.e. 'a cave or naked place;' not mentioned elsewhere.

BETH-ANOTH,] i.e. 'house of answers;' not mentioned elsewhere.

ELTEKON,] i.e. 'the straight or right place;' not mentioned elsewhere; compare Elteken, in 19. 44.

60. KIRJATH-BAAL,] i.e. 'city of Baal;' as in v. 9 above.

KIRJATH-JEARIM,] i.e. 'city of forests.'

RABBAH,] i.e. 'the great place;' not mentioned elsewhere.

61. WILDERNESS,] or pasture land of Judea.

BETH-ARABAH,] i.e. 'house of the desert;' see v. 6; 18. 22.

MIDDIN,] i.e. 'measures;' not mentioned elsewhere.

SECACAH,] i.e. 'enclosure;' not mentioned elsewhere.

62. NIBSHAN,] i.e. 'soft or sandy soil.'

SALT,] perhaps 'Zoar,' is meant, Ge. 19. 22.

ENGEDI,] i.e. 'fountain of the kid;' see 1 Sa. 24. 1, &c.

63. JEBUSITES,] as in Ge. 10. 16, &c.

NOT BEEN ABLE] entirely to dispossess them, till the time of David, 2 Sa. 5. 7; Jud. 1. 8, 21.

XVI. 1. SONS OF JOSEPH,] viz. Ephraim and Manasseh, as in Ge. 41. 50—52.

JERICHO,] as the southern border.

WILDERNESS,] or pasture land of Beth-aven, in 18. 12.

BETH-EL,] as in Ge. 12. 8.

2. LUZ,] as in Ge. 28. 11, 19; Jos. 18. 13; Jud. 1. 26.

ARCHI, ATAROTH.] Sept. reads these two words as one.

3. JAPHLETI,] i.e. 'it frees;' as in 1 Ch. 7. 32, 33; not mentioned elsewhere.

BETH-HORON,] i.e. 'house of the hollow;' as in 18. 13; 2 Ch. 8. 5; different from that in v. 5.

GEZER,] i.e. 'piece or part,' as in 10. 33; the same as 'Gadara,' 1 Ch. 7. 28; 1 K. 9. 15.

4. INHERIT] the land, as above apportioned to them; see 17. 14.

5. BY,] or 'for' their families.

ATROTH-ADDAR,] i.e. 'crowns of Addar,' as in 18. 13.

BETH-HORON,] as in v. 3; 2 Ch. 8. 5.

6. MICKMETHAH,] i.e. 'hiding place,' as in 17. 17.

TAANATH, SHILOH,] i.e. 'meeting of Shiloh;' not mentioned elsewhere.

JANOHAH,] i.e. 'rest,' as in v. 7.

7. ATAROTH,] i.e. 'crowns;' as in v. 5; 18. 13.

NAAROTH,] i.e. 'damsel;' called in 1 Ch. 7. 8 'Naaran.'

8. TAPPUAH,] i.e. 'apple;' as in 17. 8.

KANAH,] i.e. 'a reed;' see 17. 9; not mentioned elsewhere.

9. SEPARATE CITIES,] not alluded to elsewhere.

10. NOT DISPOSSESSED,] i.e. entirely as they ought to have done.

GEZER,] as in v. 3 above.

DAY,] and even till the days of Solomon, see 1 K. 9. 15—17; Jud. 1. 29.

TRIBUTE,] as in Ge. 49. 15; De. 20. 11; Jos. 17. 13; Jud. 1. 28; 30. 33, 35, &c

XVII. 1. FIRST BORN,] as in Ge. 41. 51, &c.

MACHIR,] so in Ge. 50. 23.

GILEAD,] i.e. 'the heap of witness.'

MAN OF WAR,] or 'of battle,' as in Ex. 15. 3; Nu. 31. 21, 28, 49, &c.

BASHAN,] see De. 3. 13, 15.

2. ABIEZER,] i.e. 'father of help,' called in Nu. 26. 30 'Jeizer.'

HELEK,] i.e. 'a portion.'

ASRIEL,] i.e. 'vow of God,' as in Nu. 26. 31; 1 Ch. 7. 14.

SHECHEM,] i.e. 'a shoulder.'

HEPHER,] i.e. 'a pit,' as in Nu. 26. 32; 27. 1.

SHEMIDA,] i.e. 'fame of knowledge,' as in Nu. 26. 32; 1 Ch. 7. 19.

3. ZELOPHEHAD,] i. e. 'fracture,' as in Nu. 26. 33, &c.

MAHLAH,] i.e. 'disease.'

NOAH,] i.e. 'motion.'

HOGLAH,] i.e. 'a partridge.'

MILCAH,] i.e. 'a queen or counsel.'

TIRZAH,] i.e. 'pleasantness.'

4. ELEAZAR,] the representative of the priesthood, and before

JOSHUA,] the representative of the civil authority.

PRINCES] of the congregation, who aided Joshua.

COMMANDED,] as in Nu. 27. 1—7.

HE GIVETH,] i.e. Joshua does so.

5. TEN PORTIONS,] for the six families in v. 2; the portion of Hepher being divided to the five daughters of Zelophehad.

6. DAUGHTERS,] as an exception to the general rule.

SONS,] i.e. the Machirites and the Gileadites, as in Nu. 26. 29.

7. ASHER,] i. e. 'happy;' a city not mentioned elsewhere.

MICHMETHAH,] as in 16. 6.

SHECHEM,] as in v. 2 above.

EN-TAPPUAH,] i.e. 'fountain of the apple.'

8. TAPPUAH,] i.e. 'an apple;' as in 16. 8.

9. BROOK OF KANAH,] as in 16. 8.

MIDST,] as in 16. 9.

10. NORTH,] as at mount Carmel.

EAST] towards Jordan.

11. BETH-SHEAN,] i.e. 'house of rest,' as in v. 16; 1 Sa. 31. 10; 1 K. 4. 12.

IBLEAM,] i.e. 'swallowing up a people,' as in Jud. 1. 27; 2 K. 9. 27; compare 1 Ch. 6. 25, 'Bileam.'

DOR,] as in 11. 2; 12. 23, &c.

EN-DOR,] i.e. 'fountain of Dor,' as in 1 Sa. 28. 7.

TAANACH,] as in 12. 22, &c.

MEGIDDO,] as in 12. 21, &c.

COUNTIES.] This original word in not found elsewhere; lit. 'elevated place.'

12. NOT ABLE,] from some cause left unexplained.

DESIROUS,] as in Jud. 1. 27, 35.

13. STRONG,] they assisted the tribe of Manasseh to subdue the Canaanites, and put them to

TRIBUTE,] as a mark of submission.

14. ONE PORTION,] which nevertheless was allotted to them by God.

BLESSED ME,] as in Ge. 48. 19; Nu. 26. 34. 37.

15. IF,] i.e. seeing, since.
FOREST] of Gilboa, &c.
PREPARED,] as in Ge. 1. 1, &c.
PERIZZITE,] as in 11. 3, &c.
REPHAIM,] as in Ge. 14. 5; 15. 20.
MOUNT EPHRAIM,] already allotted to them.
NARROW,] *lit.* 'hastened,' as in 10. 13; *or* 'because mount Ephraim hath hastened to thee.'
16. NOT FOUND,] as in Jos. 10. 17; i.e. we have not gained possession of it.
CHARIOT OF IRON,] of which Israel were entirely destitute.
LAND OF THE VALLEY,] at the bottom of the mountain.
BETH-SHEAN,] as in v. 11 above.
VALLEY OF JEZREEL,] as in 19. 18; 1 K. 4. 12.
17. POWER] in war.
18. FOREST,] as in v. 15.
PREPARED] it for a habitation, as in v. 15 above.
CHARIOTS OF IRON,] and therefore well able to defend themselves.
STRONG,] see De. 20. 1.

XVIII. 1. SHILOH,] a city allotted to Ephraim, about 15 miles from Jerusalem.
TENT OF MEETING,] which had been at Gilgal, as in 4. 19.
TO TABERNACLE] there, which it did for 328 years according to Usher, others say 369 years.
SUBDUED,] as had been promised by the Lord.
2. SHARED,] i.e. received any portion allotted to them.
SEVEN TRIBES,] viz. Benjamin, Simeon, Zebulun, Issacher, Asher, Naphtali, Dan.
3. REMISS,] *lit.* 'shew yourselves feeble,' as in Prov. 18. 9; 24. 10.
4. GO UP AND DOWN,] thoroughly examining the land.
DESCRIBE] it by its dimensions, localities, &c.
5. SEVEN PORTIONS,] for the seven tribes, in v. 2.
STAY,] content with their respective lots.
6. DESCRIBE,] as in v. 4.
CAST A LOT,] that there might be no ground for partiality.
7. NO PORTION] of the land of Canaan to them as one of the tribes of Israel.
INHERITANCE,] as he had repeatedly declared, see 13. 12.
GAVE] in answer to their own request.
8. SAYING,] as in v. 4, 6.
IN SHILOH,] where the ark of God now was.
9. BY CITIES,] one by one, in succession.
ON A BOOK,] not 'in a book.'
10. CASTETH A LOT,] as he had promised to do in v. 6 above.
JEHOVAH,] as the supreme Arbitrer.
DIVISIONS,] as in 11. 23, &c.
11. LOT GOETH UP,] as in Lev. 16. 9, &c.
12. BETH-AVEN,] near Beth-el and Ai, see 7. 2; 8. 20.
13. LUZ,] as in 16. 2.
BETH-EL,] where Jacob had the dream.

ATROTH-ADDAR,] see 16. 2, 5.
LOWER BETH-HORON,] as distinct from the 'upper Beth-Horon,' 16. 5; it was rebuilt by Solomon, 1 K. 4. 17.
14. MARKED OUT,] as in 15. 9.
WEST CORNER,] not 'corner of the sea,' for Benjamin had no sea coast; so in last clause of this verse.
KIRJATH-BAAL,] i.e. 'city of Baal.'
KIRJATH-JEARIM,] i.e. 'city of forests,' as in 15. 9, 60.
15. NEPHTOAH.] See 15. 9.
16. SON OF HINNOM.] See 15. 9.
REPHAIM,] as in 15. 8.
VALLEY OF HINNOM,] i.e. valley of the son of Hinnom.
JEBUSI,] as in 15. 8, i.e. Jerusalem.
EN-ROGEL.] See 15. 7.
17. MARKED OUT,] as in v. 14.
EN-SHEMESH,] as in 15. 7.
GELILOTH,] or as in 15. 7 'Gilgal.'
ADUMMIM,] between Jerusalem and Jericho, see 15. 7.
BOHAN,] as in 15. 6.
18. ARABAH,] i.e. 'Beth-Arabah,' as in 15. 6, and so Sept. reads here.
19. BETH-HOGLAH,] as in 15. 6.
NORTH BAY,] *lit.* 'tongue,' as in 15. 2.
SALT SEA,] on the banks of which had stood Sodom and Gomorrah.
20. EAST QUARTER,] having Dan on the west, Judah on the south, Ephraim on the north.
21. JERICHO,] See 2. 1.
BETH-HOGLAH,] as in 15. 6.
VALLEY OF KEZIZ,] *or* 'Emek-Keziz,' as in Sept.
22. BETH ARABAH,] as in 15. 6.
ZEMARAIM.] Compare 2 Ch. 13. 4; Ge. 10. 18.
BETH-EL,] as in 15. 6.
23. AVIM,] i.e. 'perverse places;' not mentioned elsewhere.
PAREH,] i.e. 'the cow;' not mentioned elsewhere.
OPHRAH,] i.e. 'a fawn,' as in 1 Sa. 13. 17; in Micah 1. 10, called Beth-Ophrah.
24. CHEPHER-HAAMMONAI,] i.e. 'village of the Ammonites;' not mentioned elsewhere.
OPHNI.] The etymology is uncertain; it is not mentioned elsewhere.
GABA,] the same as 'Gibeah;' Jud. 19. 12; Hos. 5. 8.
25. GIBEON,] See 10. 2.
RAMAH,] i.e. 'the lofty place,' as in Jud. 4. 5.
BEEROTH,] as in 9. 17.
26. MIZPEH,] as in Jud. 21. 1.
CHEPHIRAH,] as in 9. 17.
MOZAH,] i.e. 'an outlet;' not mentioned elsewhere.
27. REKEM,] 'variegated;' not mentioned elsewhere.
IRPEEL,] i.e. 'God heals;' not mentioned elsewhere.
TARALAH,] i.e. 'a reeling;' not mentioned elsewhere.
28. ZELAH,] i.e. 'a rib;' as in 2 Sa. 21. 14.
ELEPH,] i.e. 'the thousand *or* chief; not mentioned elsewhere.
JEBUSI,] as in v. 15, 18.

JERUSALEM,] as in 15. 63; it belonged partly to Benjamin, and partly to Judah; Moriah to the former, and Zion to the latter.
GIBEATH,] i.e. a 'high place;' see 15. 59.
KIRJATH,] i.e. 'a city;' not mentioned elsewhere.

XIX. 1. SECOND LOT,] the first being Benjamin's in this last division of the land.
MIDST,] as prophesied of in Ge. 49. 7; see Jud. 1. 3, and v. 9 below.
2. BEER-SHEBA,] i.e. 'well of an oath;' as in Ge. 21. 31, &c.
SHEBA,] i.e. 'oath;' this word is omitted in the enumeration in 1 Ch. 4. 28.
MOLADAH,] as in 15. 26.
3. HAZOR-SHUAL,] as in 15. 28.
BALAH,] as in 15. 29, i.e. Baalah.
AZEM,] as in 15. 29, i.e. Ezem.
4. ELTOLAD,] as in 15. 30, i.e. Tolad.
BETHUL,] as in 15. 30, i.e. Bethuel, in 1 Ch. 4. 29, 30, or Chesil, in 15. 30.
HORMAH,] as in 15. 30.
5. ZIKLAG,] as in 15. 31.
BETH-MARCABOTH,] i.e. 'a house of chariots.'
HAZAR-SUSAH,] i.e. a 'house of horses;' or as in 1 Ch. 4. 31 'Susim;' compare 2 K. 23. 11.
6. BETH-LEBAOTH,] perhaps the same as 'Lebaoth,' in 15. 32, i.e. 'house of lions.'
SHARUHEN,] i.e. 'a beginning of grace;' not mentioned elsewhere
7. AIN,] as in 15. 32.
REMMON,] as in 15. 32.
ETHER,] as in 15. 42.
ASHAN,] as in 15. 42.
8. BAALATH-BEER,] i.e. 'mistress of a well;' same as Baal in 1 Ch. 4. 33.
RAMOTH OF THE SOUTH,] as in 1 Sa. 30. 27.
9. TOO MUCH,] even 114 cities with their villages.
10. SARID,] i.e. 'a remnant;' as in v. 12.
11. THE SEA,] as prophesied of in Ge. 49. 13.
MARALAH,] i.e. 'trembling, shaking;' not found elsewhere.
DABBASHETH,] i. e. a 'humph,' or eminence, like a bee-hive; not mentioned elsewhere.
JOKNEAM,] as in 12. 22; near Carmel.
12. CHISLOTH-TABOR,] i.e. 'confidence of Tabor;' not mentioned elsewhere.
DABERATH,] see 21. 28.
JAPHIA,] as in 10. 3.
13. GITTAH-HEPHER,] i.e 'wine press of the well;' as in 2 K. 14. 25.
ITTAH KAZIN,] i.e. 'time of the captain;' not mentioned elsewhere.
RIMMON-METHOAR,] i.e. 'Rimmon that is marked out.'
NEAH,] i.e. 'moving, shaking;' not mentioned elsewhere.
14. HANNATHON,] i.e. 'gracious;' not mentioned elsewhere.
JIPHTHAH-EL,] i.e. 'God opens;' not mentioned elsewhere.
15. KITTATH,] i.e. 'Kitron,' a bond, as in Jud. 1. 30.
NAHALLEL,] i.e. 'pasture land,' as in 21. 35; Jud. 1. 30.
SHIMRON,] as in 11. 1; 12. 20.

IDALAH.] The etymology is uncertain; not mentioned elsewhere.
BETH-LEHEM,] i.e. 'house of bread;' different from that in Judah.
18. JEZREEL,] or royal residence of Ahab, 1 K. 21. 1; Jos. 1. 5.
CHESILOTH,] i.e. 'the confident places;' not mentioned elsewhere.
SHUNEM,] i.e. 'resting places;' as in 1 Sa. 28. 4; 2 K. 4. 8.
19. HAPHRAIM,] i.e. 'two pits;' not mentioned elsewhere.
SHIHON,] i.e. 'a waste;' not mentioned elsewhere.
ANAHARATH.] The etymology is uncertain; not mentioned elsewhere.
20. RABBITH,] i.e. 'multitude;' not mentioned elsewhere.
KISHION,] i.e. 'sharpness or hardness;' not mentioned elsewhere.
ABEZ,] i.e. 'tin;' not mentioned elsewhere.
21. REMETH,] i.e. 'a high place;' see 21. 29; 1 Ch. 6. 73.
EN-GANNIM,] i. e. 'fountain of gardens;' as in 21. 29; different from that in 15. 34.
EN-HADDAH,] i.e. 'fountain of sharpness;' not mentioned elsewhere.
BETH-PAZZEZ,] i.e. 'house of dispersion;' not mentioned elsewhere.
22. BETH-SHEMESH,] i.e. 'house of the sun;' other places of the same name occur in v. 38, and in 21. 16.
SHAHAZIMAH,] i.e. 'proud places;' not mentioned elsewhere.
22. TABOR.] The etymology is uncertain; as in Jud. 4. 6; 8. 18; Ps. 89. 13; Jer. 46. 18; Hos. 5. 1.
25. HELKATH,] i.e. 'a portion, field,' as in 21. 31.
HALI,] i.e. 'ornament;' not mentioned elsewhere.
BETEN,] i.e. 'belly or valley;' not mentioned elsewhere.
ACHSHAPH,] as in 11. 1.
26. ALAMMELECH,] i.e. 'the king;' not mentioned elsewhere.
AMAD,] i.e. 'people of old ' not mentioned elsewhere.
MISHEAL,] i.e. 'a request,' as in 21. 30; also 1 Ch. 6. 59.
CARMEL,] i.e. 'a fruitful place,' different from that in 15. 55.
SHIHOR-LIBNATH,] not mentioned elsewhere; the Sept. and Vulg. make two places of the word.
27. BETH-DAGON,] i. e. 'house of Dagon,' as in 15. 41.
ZEBULUN,] a city in Galilee, not mentioned elsewhere.
JIPHTHAH-EL,] as in v. 14.
BETH-EMEK,] i.e. 'house of the valley;' not mentioned elsewhere.
NEIEL,] i.e. 'motion of God;' not mentioned elsewhere.
CABUL,] i.e. 'a border;' a city not mentioned elsewhere.
28. HEBRON,] supposed to be the same as Abdon, in 21. 30; 1 Ch. 6. 74; different from that in 15. 54.
REHOB,] i.e. 'broad;' not mentioned elsewhere

HAMMON,] i.e. 'warm;' not mentioned elsewhere, and different from that in 1 Ch. 6. 6.

KANAH,] a city not mentioned elsewhere; supposed to be the *Cana* of John 2. 1, 11. GREAT ZIDON,] as in 11. 8; Jud. 1. 31.

29. RAMAH,] as in v. 36. FENCED CITY,] as in Nu. 13. 19; 2 Sa. 24. 7, &c.

TYRE,] i.e. 'a rock,' as in 2 Ch. 5. 11; 24. 7.; 1 K. 5. 1; 7. 13; 9. 11, 12; 1 Ch. 14. 1; 2 Ch. 2. 3, 11, &c. Some think it another place of the same name.

HOSAH,] i.e. 'a refuge;' not mentioned elsewhere.

ACHZIB,] i.e. 'a lie,' as in Jud. 1. 30; different from that in 15. 44; Mic. 1. 14.

30. UMMAH,] i.e. 'over-against, near;' not mentioned elsewhere.

APHEK,] i.e. 'strength,' as in 12. 18; 13. 4; Jud. 1. 31.

REHOB,] i. e. 'broad,' as in Nu. 13. 21; Jos. 19. 28, 30; 21. 13; Jud. 1. 31; compare 2 Sa. 10. 6, 8.

33. HELEPH,] i.e. 'an exchange;' not mentioned elsewhere.

ALLON,] i.e. 'an oak;' not mentioned elsewhere; or perhaps 'a plain.'

ZAANANNIM,] i.e. 'removings,' as in Jud. 4. 11.

ADAMI,] i.e. 'human;' not mentioned elsewhere; different from Adam in 3. 16.

NEKEB,] i. e. 'a cavern;' not mentioned elsewhere.

JABNEEL,] i.e. 'God builds;' not mentioned elsewhere, and different from that in 15. 11.

LAKKUM.] Etymology unknown; not found elsewhere.

34. AZNOTH-TABOR,] i.e. ' ears (summits) of Tabor;' not mentioned elsewhere.

HUKKOK,] i.e. 'things decreed,' as in 1 Ch. 6. 60, 75; v. 25 below.

35. ZIDDIM,] i.e. 'the sides;' not mentioned elsewhere.

ZER,] i.e. 'strait, flint;' not mentioned elsewhere.

HAMMATH,] i.e. 'warm baths;' not mentioned elsewhere, but compare Jos. 19. 35; Nu. 34. 8.

RAKKATH,] i.e. 'a shore;' not mentioned elsewhere.

CHINNEROTH,] as in De. 3. 17.

36. ADAMAH,] i.e. 'earth;' not mentioned elsewhere; different from Adami in v. 33.

RAMAH,] i.e. 'the high place;' not mentioned elsewhere; different from that in v. 13 above.

HAZOR,] i.e. 'village, hamlet;' as in 11. 1; 12. 19; Jud. 4. 2; 1 K. 9. 15; 2 K. 15. 29.

37. KADESH,] i.e. a place 'set apart,' as in 12. 22; Nu. 7; 21. 32; Jud. 4. 6; 1 Ch. 6. 61; Jud. 4. 9, 10.

EDREI,] i.e. 'strong;' not mentioned elsewhere, different from that in Nu. 21. 23.

EN-HAZOR,] i.e. 'fountain of the village;' not mentioned elsewhere.

38. IRON,] i.e. 'the little fearful one;' not mentioned elsewhere.

MIGDAL-EL,] i.e. 'tower of God;' not mentioned elsewhere, probably the Magdala of Matt. 15. 39.

HOREM,] i.e. 'devoted;' not mentioned elsewhere.

BETH-ANATH,] i.e. 'house of answers,' as in Jud. 1. 33; different from that in 15. 59.

BETH-SHEMESH,] i.e. 'house of the sun,' as in Jud. 1. 33; different from that in v. 22; 21. 16, &c.

41. ZORAH,] as in 15. 33, &c.

ESHTAOL,] as in 15. 33, &c.

IR-SHEMESH,] i. e. 'city of the sun;' not mentioned elsewhere.

42. SHALABIN,] i.e. 'place of foxes,' as in Jud. 1. 35; 1 K. 4. 19.

AIJALON,] as in 10. 12, &c.

JETHLAH,] i.e. 'lofty place;' not mentioned elsewhere.

43. ELON,] i.e. 'an oak;' not mentioned elsewhere.

TIMNATHAH,] as in Ge. 38. 12.

EKRON,] i.e. 'eradication;' as in 15. 45, &c.

44. ELTEKAH,] i.e. 'the object of fear,' as in 21. 23; compare 15. 59.

GIBBETHON,] i.e. 'a lofty place,' as in 21. 23; 1 K. 15. 27; 16. 15.

BAALATH,] i.e. 'mistress,' as in 1 K. 9. 18; different from that in 15. 29.

45. JEHUD,] i.e. 'praised;' not mentioned elsewhere.

BENE-BERAK,] i.e. 'sons of lightning;' not mentioned elsewhere.

GATH-RIMMON,] i.e. 'wine press of the pomegranate;' given to the Levites in 21. 24.

46. ME-JARKON,] i.e. 'waters of paleness;' not mentioned elsewhere.

RAKKON,] i.e. 'thinness;' not mentioned elsewhere.

JAPHO,] i.e. 'beauty,' as in 2 Ch. 2. 15; Ezra 3. 7; Jon. 1. 3; the 'Joppa' of Acts 9. 36. 38, and the 'Jaffa' of modern times.

47. LESHEM.] Etymology unknown; called also 'Laish' and 'Dan,' in Jud. 18. 29.

49. GIVE.] Joshua, though leader, did not 'take' anything to himself, and only 'received' a share after others were supplied.

50. TIMNATH-SERAH,] i.e. 'outspread portion;' as in 24. 30; compare Jud. 2. 9.

51. BY LOT,] that there might be no opportunity for partiality.

SHILOH,] where the ark was now resting.

MEETING,] as in 18. 1, 10.

XX. 1. JOSHUA,] renewing the command given in Ex. 21. 13; Nu. 35. 6, 11, 14; De. 19. 2, 9.

2. REFUGE,] or 'the contracted place,' as in Nu. 35. 6—32.

3. MAN SLAYER,] as in Nu. 35. 6—31, &c. INADVERTENTLY,] as in Lev. 4. 2, 22, 27; 5. 15, 18; 22. 14, &c.

REDEEMER OF BLOOD,] as in Nu. 35. 19. &c.

4. CITIES,] from any place or tribe in Israel, even to Kadesh, Shechem, Kirjath-Arba, Bezer, Ramoth, and Golan.

STOOD] seeking admission unto the city.

ELDERS,] the principal authorities in the place.

MATTER,] i.e. why he asks admission.

GATHERED,] as in 2. 18; 24. 1, &c.

PLACE] of habitation, during his residence therein.

5. PURSUE,] with the view of avenging the death of his kinsman.
SHUT UP] by seizing and binding.
SMITTEN,] i.e. mortally.
HERETOFORE,] lit. 'from yesterday third day,' as in Ge. 31. 2, &c.
6. JUDGMENT,] regarding his case.
TURN BACK,] in safety from the city of refuge to his former dwelling.
7. SANCTIFY,] or 'set apart.'
KEDESH,] i.e. 'a thing set apart,' see 19. 37.
GALILEE,] i.e. 'a circuit,' as in 21. 32; 1 K. 9. 11; 15. 29; 1 Ch. 6. 76; Isa. 9. 1.
NAPHTALI,] whose lot is described in 19. 32—39.
SHECHEM,] called Sichem in Ge. 12. 6; it belonged to Ephraim; in John 4. 5 it is called 'Sychar.'
EPHRAIM,] as in 16. 1—10.
KIRJATH-ARBA,] the city, not the country, which was given to Caleb, as in 14. 13.
JUDAH,] as in Luke 1. 39, 65.
8. BEZER,] as in De. 4. 43.
WILDERNESS,] or pasture land.
REUBEN,] as in 21. 36.
RAMOTH,] as in De. 4. 13.
GAD,] as in 21. 38.
GOLAN,] as in De. 4. 43.
9. CITIES OF THE MEETING,] i.e. places where those guilty of unintentional homicide were to meet their judge.
10. COMPANY,] and being condemned by impartial judges.

XXI. 1. HEADS OF THE FATHERS,] as in Ex. 6. 14.
LEVITES,] who were set apart to be servants of the Lord, and teachers of all Israel.
PRIEST,] as chief in religious matters.
JOSHUA,] as chief civil governor under God.
TRIBES,] the whole twelve; a certain number out of each tribe being appointed to assist in the administration of the affairs of the nation.
2. SHILOH,] where the ark now rested.
CANAAN,] of which the tribes now had possession.
COMMANDED,] as in Nu. 35. 2.
CATTLE,] in which the wealth of orientals principally consists.
3. THEIR INHERITANCE,] described in the preceding chapters.
COMMAND,] lit. 'mouth.'
CITIES..SUBURBS,] as about to be described in v. 4—48.
4. KOHATHITE,] as in Nu. 3. 27.
AARON,] grandson of Kohath, as in Ex. 6. 20.
TRIBE,] i.e. inheritance of the tribe.
THIRTEEN CITIES,] mentioned by name in v. 11—18.
5. LEFT,] even Izhar, Hebron, Uzziel.
TEN CITIES,] mentioned in v. 21—25.
6. GERSHON,] as in Nu. 3. 21.
THIRTEEN CITIES,] mentioned in v. 27—33.
7. MERARI,] as in Nu. 3. 20.
TWELVE CITIES,] mentioned in v. 34—39.
8. BY LOT,] that there might be no partiality in the matter.
.9 AARON,] as in v. 4.
11. ARBA,] as in 14. 15; 15. 13.

12. FIELD,] i.e. cultivated portion of land around the city.
POSSESSION,] as in 14. 6, 13; 15. 13.
13. HEBRON,] as in 10. 3, 5, &c.
LIBNAH,] on which see 10. 29, 30.
14. JATTIR,] see 15. 32.
ESHTEMOA,] see 15. 48.
15. HOLON,] see 15. 49.
DEBIR,] see 15. 50.
16. AIN,] see 15. 51.
JUTTAH,] see 15. 55.
BETH-SHEMESH,] see 15. 10; 1 Sa. 6. 9, 12.
17. GIBEON,] as in 18. 24.
GEBA,] as in 18. 25.
18. ANATHOTH,] i.e. 'answers,' as in Isa 10. 30; Jer. 1. 1; also 2 Sa. 23. 27.
ALMON,] i.e. 'hidden;' in 1 Ch. 6. 60 it is 'Alemeth.'
20. KOHATH,] as in v. 5 above.
21. SHECHEM,] see 20. 7.
GEZER,] see 16. 10.
22. KIBZAIM,] i.e. 'two gatherings;' perhaps the same as Jokdeam, 1 Ch. 6. 68.
BETH-HORON] the upper, see 16. 3. 5.
ELTEKEH,] as in 19. 44.
GIBBETHON,] as in 19. 44.
24. AIJALON,] as in 19. 42.
GATH-RIMMON,] as in 19. 45.
25. TANAACH,] as in 17. 10.
GATH-RIMMON,] the name was also given to a city in Dan, as in v. 24 above.
27. GERSHON,] the second son of Levi.
GOLAN,] as in 20. 8.
BEESHTARAH,] called in 1 Ch. 6. 71; and De. 1. 4 'Ashtaroth.'
28. KISHON,] or 'Kishion,' as in 19. 20, and called Kedesh in 1 Ch. 6. 72.
DABARATH,] as in 19. 12.
29. JARMUTH,] or Remeth in 19. 21; Ramoth in 1 Ch. 6. 73.
EN-GANNIM,] in 1 Ch. 6. 73 called 'Anen.
30. MISHAL,] or Mishael, as in 19. 26, Mashal, in 1 Ch. 6. 74.
ABDON,] perhaps the same as Hebron, in 19. 28.
HELKATH,] or Hukok in 1 Ch. 6. 75; see 19. 25.
REHOB,] as in 19. 28.
32. KEDESH,] as in 10. 7.
HAMMOTH-DOR,] the same as Hammon, 1 Ch. 6. 76, and Hammath in 19. 35.
KARTAN,] in 1 Ch. 6. 76 called Kirjathaim, but different from that in Nu. 32. 37.
34. JOKNEAM,] as in 12. 22
KARTAH,] perhaps the same as Kattah, 19. 15.
35. DIMNAH,] perhaps the same as Rimmon, in 1 Ch. 6. 77.
NAHALAL,] as in 19. 15.
36. BEZER,] as in 20. 8.
JAHAZAH] or Jahaz, as in Nu. 21. 33. This verse as well as the succeeding one, is wanting in most Hebrew MSS. but found in the Sept., Targ., Syr., and Arabic Versions, and in 1 Ch. 6. 78, 79, and both are necessary to suit v. 37.
37. KEDEMOTH,] as in De. 2. 26; Jos. 13. 18; 1 Ch. 6. 79.
MEPHAATH,] as in 13. 18.
38. RAMOTH,] as in 20. 8.
MAHANAIM,] as in Ge. 32. 1, 2; Jos. 13. 26; 2 Sa. 2. 8; 1 K. 2. 8.

39. HESHBON,] as in Nu. 21. 26, &c.
JAZER,] or Jaazer, as in Nu. 21. 32.
40. TWELVE CITIES,] four of Zebulun, four out of Reuben, and four out of Gad.
41. FORTY AND EIGHT,] as in Nu. 35. 7.
42. SUBURBS,] extending two thousand cubits on each side.
43. THE WHOLE] of the land, not merely a portion, as some pretend.
SWORN,] in Ge. 13. 15; 15. 18, &c
44. REST,] as in 11. 23; 22. 4.
NOT STOOD] successfully.
45. HATH COME] in unto them.

XXII. 1. MANASSEH,] after the division of the land, as already described in the preceding chapters.
2. COMMANDED,] in Nu. 32. 20; De. 3. 18.
MY VOICE,] as his successor and God's servant.
3. MANY DAYS,] even seven years, as already remarked.
4. SPAKE,] as in 21. 44; De. 12. 9, 10.
GIVEN] in Nu. 32. 33.
5. COMMAND..LAW,] i.e. charge and direction.
LOVE..WALK .. KEEP..CLEAVE..SERVE.] The various words here used shew the manifold ways of pleasing the Lord.
HEART..SOUL,] as in De. 10. 12, &c.
7. GIVEN,] as in De. 3. 13.
WESTWARD,] as in 17. 5.
BLESS,] as in v. 6 above.
8. RICHES,] as in 2 Ch. 1. 11, 12; Ecc. 5. 19; 6. 2; Ezra 6. 8; 7. 26.
DIVIDE,] i.e. share, apportion according to law, as in Nu. 31. 27; 1 Sa. 30. 24, 25; Ps. 68. 12.
BRETHREN] who had remained at home.
9. SHILOH,] see 18. 1, &c.
MOSES,] as in Nu. 32. 31.
10. DISTRICTS,] as in 13. 2, &c
ALTAR,] for the purposes afterwards explained in v. 26, 27.
FOR APPEARANCE,] as in Ge. 2. 9, &c.
11. PASSAGE,] or place where they passed over, in the front of Jericho.
12. SHILOH,] see 18. 1, &c.
WAR,] agreeably to De. 13. 12—16.
PHINEHAS,] whose zeal for God is manifest from Nu. 25. 7—13.
16. COMPANY,] as in Nu. 27. 17, &c.
TRESPASS,] as in Lev. 5. 15.
ALTAR,] which ought not to be done but by divine direction, see Ex. 20. 24; Lev. 17. 3, 4; De. 12. 5, 6.
17. PEOR,] on which see Nu. 25. 2, 3.
CLEANSED,] or 'have not cleansed ourselves,' as in Nu. 8. 7; 2 Ch. 30. 18; Ezra 6. 20; Neh. 12. 30.
PLAGUE,] as in Nu. 25. 9.
18. TO DAY..TO MORROW,] God will lose no time in punishing such apostacy.
WROTH,] and who can abide that day.
19. UNCLEAN,] by reason of the sins of its inhabitants.
LAND] westward of Jordan.
TABERNACLED] even in Shiloh.
BESIDES,] as in Nu. 5. 20; 2 Sa. 22. 32, &c.
20. ACHAN,] as in 7. 18, &c.
DEVOTED THING,] of the spoils of Jericho.

WRATH,] so that Israel was defeated and put to shame.
EXPIRED NOT,] thirty-six men being slain at Ai, as in 7. 5.
21. THOUSANDS,] even the ten princes and Phinehas.
22. GOD OF GODS,] lit. 'the mighty one of the gods.'
JEHOVAH,] the Existing One, the I am, the covenant God of Israel.
HE IS KNOWING,] because he sees and knows all things.
NOT SAVE] us from the punishment of sin.
23. BURNT-OFFERING,] lit. 'that which goes up upon the altar.'
PRESENT,] lit. 'a thing given or apportioned,' to God or man.
PEACE-OFFERINGS,] as in Ex. 20. 24, &c.
REQUIRE,] or 'seek,' as in 2. 22, &c.
24. TO YOU,] in common with the God of Israel.
25. NO PORTION,] in his promises and rewards.
FEAR,] i.e. reverence.
26. THE ALTAR,] which they had been speaking of building.
SACRIFICE,] which could only be done in some place which God himself should choose.
27. SERVICE,] as appointed in the law.
28. HEREAFTER,] as in 4. 6, 21.
PATTERN,] as in Ex. 25. 9, 40, &c.
29. TABERNACLE] in Shiloh.
30. PRINCES,] who were ten in number.
EYES.] A common Hebrew idiom.
31. KNOWN,] i.e. perceived experimentally.
TRESPASS,] of building an altar without his permission.
DELIVERED,] by their regard to God's law.
32. BLESS GOD,] i.e. declare him blessed.
34. PROCLAIM,] lit. 'call or cry.'
IS GOD,] lit. 'is the God;' i.e. the only one.

XXIII. 1. MANY DAYS,] supposed to be about 14 years.
ENTERING INTO DAYS,] as in 13. 1, &c.
3. IS FIGHTING,] as in 5. 14, 15.
4. CAUSED TO FALL] by lot, as in 13 2, 6; 18. 10.
CUT OFF] already.
5. THRUST] them violently from your presence.
DISPOSSESSED] them of their possessions.
POSSESSED,] or occupied their land.
SPOKEN,] in Nu. 33. 53.
6. VERY STRONG,] firmness and valour being required in God's service.
BOOK OF THE LAW,] here evidently recognized as an authority.
RIGHT OR LEFT,] as in 1. 7, &c.
7. GO IN,] so as to be reckoned with them.
LEFT,] unconquered in various parts of the land.
MAKE MENTION,] being forbidden in Ex. 23. 13, &c.
SWEAR,] as if they could hear you.
SERVE,] by offering sacrifice and gifts.
BOW,] as if they were your lords and superiors.
8. CLEAVE] unceasingly.
9. IS DISPOSSESSING] even now.

MIGHTY] in power and military force and strongholds.

STOOD] successfully.

10. PURSUE,] as in Lev. 26. 8.

11. VERY WATCHFUL,] as in De. 2. 4, &c.

12. AT ALL,] *lit.* 'turning back ye turn back.'

CLEAVED] in love, sympathy, or affection.

INTERMARRIED,] as in Ge. 34. 9; De. 7. 3, &c.

13, GIN,] as in Job 18. 9; 22. 10; Ps. 11. 6, &c.

SNARE,] as in Ex. 10. 7; 23. 33; 34. 12, &c.

SCOURGE,] as in 1 K. 12. 11, 14; 2 Ch. 10. 11, 14; Job 5. 21; 9. 23; Prov. 26. 3; Isa. 10. 26; 28. 15, 18; Nah. 3. 2.

SIDES,] as in Nu. 33. 55.

THORNS,] as in Nu. 33. 55.

EYES,] preventing them from seeing their duty or the way of escape.

14. TO DAY,] i.e. even now, very shortly.

WAY] of all men, to death, as in Ge. 3. 19.

KNOWN] experimentally.

HEART..SOUL,] as in De. 10. 12, &c.

NOT FALLEN] to the ground unfulfilled.

15. GOOD THING,] promised for obedience. De. 28. 1—14.

EVIL THING,] threatened to the disobedient.

GOOD GROUND,] as in Lev. 26. 14—39; De. 28. 15—68.

16. TRANSGRESSING,] or going beyond the command of the Lord.

COVENANT,] see Ex. 24. 7, 8.

SERVED,] as if they had any claim upon your obedience.

BOWED,] shewing outward homage and respect.

BURNED,] as in Nu. 11. 33, &c.

HASTILY,] as in De. 11. 17, &c.

GIVEN,] freely and unreservedly.

XXIV. 1. SHECHEM,] see Ge. 12. 6, &c.

STATION THEMSELVES,] as in Ex. 2. 4; 8. 20, &c.

2. THUS SAID] the Lord to Joshua himself, who now repeats it to all Israel.

GOD OF ISRAEL,] their national covenant God.

THE RIVER,] even the Euphrates, in Aram-Naharaim.

TERAH,] as in Ge. 11. 26, 28.

OTHER GODS,] being idolators like their neighbours.

3. ABRAHAM,] as in Ge. 12. 1.

TO GO THROUGH,] as in Ge. 12. 6, that he might see it.

SEED,] or posterity, as in Ge. 25. 1—4.

ISAAC,] the child of promise, as in Ge. 21. 3.

4. JACOB..ESAU,] as in Ge. 25. 25, 26.

MOUNT SEIR,] as in Ge. 32. 3; 33. 14, 16; 36. 8, 9, &c.

GONE DOWN,] as in Ge. 46. 3, 4.

5. SEND,] as in Ex. 3. 10.

MOSES..AARON,] as in Ex. 3. 10, 27, &c.

PLAGUE,] by ten plagues in succession.

BROUGHT YOU OUT,] with a high hand, and out-stretched arm.

6. GO INTO] the sea of Suph, as in Ex. 14. 2.

PURSUE,] as in Ex. 14. 9.

CHARIOT..HORSEMAN,] as in Ex. 14. 7—9.

7. CRY] for help, as in Ex. 14. 10.

THICK DARKNESS,] as in Ex. 14. 20.

THE SEA,] as in Ex. 14. 28.

YOUR EYES,] as in Ex. 14. 31.

A WILDERNESS,] not 'the wilderness;' there were many wildernesses.

8. AMORITE,] even the kingdoms of Og and Bashan.

JORDAN,] eastward of that river.

FIGHT,] as in Nu. 21. 21, 33; De. 2. 32; 3. 1.

HAND,] so that they could not escape destruction.

POSSESS,] or occupy their land as your own, it being given to the two and a half tribes.

DESTROY] them, so that they had neither name nor place.

9. BALAK,] as in Nu. 22. 2, &c.

MOAB,] descendants of Lot, as in Ge. 19. 37.

BALAAM,] the diviner, as in Nu. 22. 5.

REVILE,] as in De. 23. 4.

10. NOT BEEN WILLING,] as in De. 23. 5.

BLESS YOU,] against his will.

11. PASS OVER,] in a miraculous way towards

JERICHO,] about seven miles from the Jordan.

POSSESSORS,] or 'lords;' *lit.* 'Baalim,' see 6. 1.

HAND,] so that they could not escape.

12. THE HORNET,] see Ex. 23. 28; De. 7. 20.

CASTETH,] as in Ge. 3. 24, &c.

TWO KINGS,] Sihon and Og.

SWORD..BOW,] but by the help of the Lord himself, Ps. 44. 3, 6.

13. LABOURED,] in digging, ploughing, and sowing.

BUILT,] at great expense of time and money. De. 6. 10, 11.

PLANTED,] with care and skill.

14. FEAR,] i.e. reverence, De. 10. 12; 1 Sa. 12. 24.

SERVE,] by obeying his commands.

PERFECTION,] nothing lacking, Ge. 17. 1; 20. 5; De. 18. 13; Ps. 119. 1.

TRUTH,] i.e. sincerity and stedfastness.

TURN ASIDE,] i.e. remove entirely away, as in v. 2, 23 above; Lev. 17. 7.

IN EGYPT,] where almost every kind of creatures were adored. Eze. 20. 7, 8; 23. 3.

15. WRONG IN YOUR EYES.] A common Hebrew idiom.

CHOOSE,] as free men, for the Lord does not desire to be served ignorantly or unwillingly.

FATHERS,] when in Chaldea and in Egypt.

AMORITE,] the chief tribe of Canaan.

HOUSE,] or household.

WE SERVE,] i.e. we do even now serve him and will continue to do so.

16. THE PEOPLE] assembled, even their elders, &c., as in v. 1.

FAR BE IT FROM US.] A common Hebrew expression of abhorrence.

FORSAKE,] or abandon him whom we have promised to serve.

17. IS BRINGING US UP,] even now the deliverance is not entirely finished.

HOUSE OF SERVANTS,] as in Ex. 13. 3, &c.

GREAT SIGNS,] of power and kindness, as in Ps. 78. 11, 12, 43.

GONE,] from Egypt to Canaan.
PASSED,] in our journey to this land.
18. CASTETH OUT,] as in v. 12 above.
WE ALSO,] as well as thou and thy house.
OUR GOD,] by a covenant solemnly made.
19. NOT ABLE] of themselves, without God's aid.
MOST HOLY,] i.e. separate from all other beings.
ZEALOUS,] for his own glory. Ex. 20. 6.
BEAR WITH,] without punishing. Ex.23.21.
20. GODS OF A STRANGER,] as in v. 23; Ge. 35. 2, &c.
DONE EVIL,] according to your sins.
CONSUMED] you by sword and fire.
21. WE DO SERVE,] echoing Joshua's words in v. 15 above.
22. WITNESSES,] and therefore self-convicted.
CHOSEN,] voluntarily and without constraint, Ps. 119. 173.
WITNESSES,] adopting his words a second time.
23. TURN ASIDE,] as in v. 14 above.
INCLINE,] as in Ps. 119. 36, &c.
24. HEARKEN,] without murmurings or disputings.
25. COVENANT,] or agreement in behalf of the Lord. Ex. 15. 25; 2 K. 11. 17.
LAYETH ON IT,] i.e. the people.
STATUTE,] or thing decreed or engaged.
ORDINANCE,] or judgment, i.e. a thing decided according to law.
SCHECHEM,] where they were now assembled.
26. WRITETH,] to secure their permanence in Israel. De. 31. 26.
STONE,] as Jacob did, for a standing memorial.

OAK,] reckoned a sacred tree.
SANCTUARY,] in Shiloh.
27. THIS STONE,] as in Ge. 31. 45—47.
SPOKEN,] even now, by the mouth of Joshua.
LIE,] as in 7. 11.
28. INHERITANCE,] among the various tribes.
29. JOSHUA..DIETH,] the common lot of all men. Jud. 2. 8.
110 YEARS,] just the age of Joseph; before Christ, 1426.
30. TIMNATH-SERAH,] see 19. 50; Jud. 2. 9.
EPHRAIM,] where he lived, and where his inheritance had fallen.
HILL OF GAASH,] compare 2 Sa. 23. 30.
31. ALL THE DAYS] that Joshua lived, which would be a great comfort to him. Jud. 2. 7.
PROLONGED DAYS,] i.e. out-lived Joshua, being younger than he.
KNEW,] experimentally and who appreciated. De. 11. 2; 31. 13.
32. BONES OF JOSEPH,] who died in Egypt, as in Ge. 50. 26; Ex. 13. 19.
BROUGHT UP,] according to his last command, in Ge. 50. 25.
SHECHEM,] the portion allotted to Joseph.
HAMOR,] as in Ge. 33. 19.
KESITAH,] as in Ge. 33. 19.
THEY ARE,] i.e. the bones of Joseph as a sacred deposit.
33. ELEAZAR..DIETH,] sometime doubtless after Joshua, but not directly mentioned.
HILL OF PHINEHAS,] near Shechem. Ex. 6. 25; Jud. 20. 28.
GIVEN,] by the sons of Israel in the division of the land.

JUDGES

THE BOOK OF JUDGES contains a succinct history of Israel after the death of Joshua; its author however is unknown, but the Jewish writers generally ascribe it to Samuel, the last of the judges. From 2 Sa. 11. 21 it seems probable that it was written before the time of David; con.,are also the use of the ancient name of Jerusalem, in 19. 10, 11. Samuel himself (in 1 Sa. 12. 9—11) appears to refer to it, and Ps. 68. 8, 9; 97. 5, apparently allude to the language in 5. 4, 5. It is quoted in Acts 13. 20; Heb. 11. 32, 40. It contains a history of from 299 to 339 years, chronologically arranged, with the exception of the last five chapters, which are added to shew the rise of idolatry, and the almost complete destruction of the tribe of Benjamin.

I. 1. DEATH OF JOSHUA,] as recorded in Jos. 24. 29, at the age of 110 years, about B.C. 1426.

ASK,] by means of the Urim and Thummim, or by the priest, as in Nu. 27. 21; Jud. 20. 18.

CANAANITE,] who still inhabited various portions of the land. Joshua was dead, and no successor had been appointed.

2. JUDAH,] that is, the tribe of Judah, which was now regarded as the leading tribe in God's word and providence, Ge. 49.8.

I HAVE GIVEN,] that is, it is as good as done.

3. HIS BROTHER,] by the same father and mother, their lots also being together.

MY LOT,] as described in Jos. 15. 1—12, 20—62.

THY LOT,] as described in Jos. 19. 1—9. See v. 17 below.

4. PERIZZITE,] as in Ge. 13. 7, &c.

BEZEK,] i.e. 'a flash of lightning,' as in 1 Sa. 11. 8.

5. ADONI-BEZEK,] i.e. 'lord of Bezek.'

PERIZZITE,] as in v. 4 above.

6. CUT OFF,] as in De. 25. 12; 2 Sa. 4. 12, and v. 7 below.

THUMBS, ETC,] lit. 'thumbs of his hands and of his feet,' as in Ex. 29. 20; Lev. 8. 23, 24; 14. 14, 17, 25, 28, and in v. 7 below. The one loss prevented his fighting, the other his running.

7. SEVENTY KINGS,] or petty rulers in Canaan.

GATHERING] their food under the table, as a mark of degradation.

REPAID.] His awakened conscience was his own tormentor.

JERUSALEM,] part of which had been conquered, as in Jos. 15. 8, 63.

8. FIGHT.] There is no authority for the C. V. 'had fought,' so with the other verbs.

CAPTURE IT,] all except the part afterwards captured by Joab, in 2 Sa. 5. 6—9.

SENT INTO FIRE.] A common Hebrew idiom, as in 20. 48, &c.

9. GONE DOWN] from Jerusalem, which stands high.

INHABITING,] to some extent still.

10. HEBRON,] which was captured by Joshua, in 10. 36, 37.

KIRJATH-ARBA,] i.e. 'city of Arba.'

SHESHAI, AHIMAN, TALMAI.] See Nu. 13. 22; Jos. 15. 14, &c.

11. DEBIR,] as in Jos. 10. 3, 38, 39, &c.

KIRJATH-SEPHER,] i.e. 'city of the book,' as in Jos. 15. 15, 16.

12. CALEB,] son of Jephuneh, as in Jos. 15. 15, 16.

ACHSAH,] see on Jos. 15. 16.

13. OTHNIEL,] i.e. 'lion of God.'

KENAZ,] i.e. 'hunting.'

14. COMING IN] to her husband's home.

PERSUADETH,] as in De. 13. 6, &c.

THE FIELD,] round Kirjath-Sepher.

LIGHTETH,] as in Jos. 15. 18; Jud. 4. 21.

ASS,] on which she was riding; compare Jos. 15. 18; Ex. 4. 20; Jud. 19. 28.

15. BLESSING,] or 'pool;' as in Ps. 84. 6· Ecc. 2. 6, &c.

SOUTH-LAND,] one dry, arid, and mountainous.

SPRINGS OF WATER,] as in Jos. 15. 19.

UPPER..LOWER,] of the hill-country around.

16. KENITE,] as in 4. 11, 17; 1 Sa. 15. 6; 1 Ch. 2. 55; Jer. 35. 2.

CITY OF PALMS,] i.e. Jericho, as in De. 34. 3.

WILDERNESS,] or pasture land of Judah.

ARAD,] see Nu. 21. 1.

THE PEOPLE] of Judah, Jos. 15. 63.

17. BROTHER,] as promised in v. 3 above.

ZEPHATH,] i.e. 'a watch-tower;' perhaps the same as 'Zephathah,' in 2 Ch. 14. 9, 10.

HORMAH,] i.e. 'devotion or destruction, as in Nu. 14. 45; 21. 3; De. 1. 41; Jos. 12. 14; 19. 4.

18. GAZA,] as in Ge. 10. 17; De. 2. 23; Jos. 10. 41, &c.

ASHKELON,] i.e. 'migration or a weighing out,' as in 14. 19; 1 Sa. 6. 7; 2 Sa. 1. 20; Jos. 13. 3.

EKRON,] as in Jos. 13. 3, &c

JUDAH,] as in v. 2, &c.

IRON,] as in Jos. 17. 16, 18.

20. THEY GIVE,] as in Jos. 14. 9, 13; 15. 13, 14; 21. 11, 12.

SPOKEN,] in Nu. 14. 24; De. 1. 26.

ANAK,] named in v. 10 above.

21. JEBUSITE,] as in Ge. 10. 16; 15. 21.

JERUSALEM,] at least a portion of it, see 2 Sa. 5. 6—9.

TILL THIS DAY.] This phrase shews that the book was composed before the time of David, who entirely dispossessed them.

22. HOUSE OF JOSEPH,] Ephraim and Manasseh combinedly.

BETH-EL,] as in Jos. 8. 17; 16. 1, 2.

23. LUZ,] i.e. 'a nut;' as in Ge. 28. 19.

24. WATCHERS,] who were spying the city.

DONE,] not 'shewn,' as in C. V.

KINDNESS,] not merely 'mercy.'
25. SENT AWAY,] without injury.
26. HITTITES,] supposed to be in Edom or Arabia.
LUZ,] after the name of his former city.
27. OCCUPIED,] by dispossessing their inhabitants.
BETH-SHEAN,] as in Jos. 17. 11, 16.
TAANACH,] as in Jos. 12. 21, &c.
DOR,] as in Jos. 11. 2, &c.
IBLAIM,] as in Jos. 17. 11, &c.
MEGIDDO,] as in Jos. 12. 21, &c.
DESIROUS,] as in Jos. 17. 12, &c.
28. STRONG,] becoming more numerous, and their enemies less so, they put them to
TRIBUTE,] which may have arisen from their avarice and indolence.
29. GEZER,] as in Jos. 10. 33, &c.
30. KITRON,] not mentioned elsewhere, but supposed to be the same as Kattah in Jos. 19. 15, or Kartah, Jos. 21. 34.
NAHALOL,] as in Jos. 19. 15; 21. 34, 35.
TRIBUTARY,] as in v. 28 above.
31. ACCHO,] called Ptolemais, Acts 21. 7; now St Jean d'Acre.
ZIDON,] as in Jos. 19. 21.
AHLAB,] i.e. 'fatness, fat;' not mentioned elsewhere.
ACHZIB,] as in Jos. 19. 29.
HELBAH,]i.e. 'fat, fatness;' not mentioned elsewhere.
APHIK,] as in Jos. 19. 30 'Aphek.'
REHOB,] as in Jos. 19. 30.
33. BETH-SHEMESH,] as in Jos. 19. 38.
BETH-ANATH,] as in Jos. 19. 38.
TRIBUTARY,] as in v. 28 above.
34. THE MOUNTAIN,] Seir or Baalah; see Jos. 15. 10, 11.
SUFFERED,] lit. 'given.'
THE VALLEY] or plain of Sharon, which they afterwards possessed.
35. DESIROUS,] as in Jos. 17. 12, &c.
HERES,] i.e. 'heat or the sun;' not mentioned elsewhere.
AIJALON,] as in Jos. 19. 42.
SHAALBIM,] or Shaalabin, as in Jos. 19. 42.
HOUSE OF JOSEPH,] especially of the younger but more numerous section—Ephraim.
HEAVY] or 'weighty' upon the Amorites.
TRIBUTARY,] as in v. 28 above.
36. ASCENT OF AKRABBIM,] as in Nu. 34. 4; Jos. 15. 3.
THE ROCK,] perhaps the city Petra in Edumea is meant by this phrase.

II. 1. A MESSENGER,] a prophet, as the Targum remarks. Compare Ecc. 5. 6; Isa. 42. 19; Hag. 1. 13; Mal. 2.7; 3. 1.
FROM GILGAL,] where the ark was resting.
TO BOCHIM,] the exact site of which is unknown, and so called from the weeping mentioned in v. 5.
2. AND SAITH] in the name of the Lord.
EGYPT,] the place of hardest servitude.
FATHERS,] to Abraham, Isaac, and Jacob.
NO COVENANT] of alliance and friendship with the Canaanites, De. 7. 2.
BREAK DOWN,] as idolatrous and abominable, De. 7. 5; 12. 3.
VOICE,] in regard to this covenant.

3. CAST OUT,] as I promised to do, for the promise was conditional, being coupled with the due performance of their duties.
ADVERSARIES,] as in Da. 7. 24; or 'hunters,' as in Ge. 27. 33.
SNARE,] as in Ex. 23. 33.
4. ALL] who were there assembled.
WEEP] aloud, according to the eastern custom.
BOCHIM,] i.e. 'the weepers,' as in v. 1.
5. JEHOVAH,] not to the 'messenger,' which they would doubtless have done if they had understood him to have been a divine being, as some suppose, speaking in his own name.
6. INHERITANCE,] as in Jos. 24. 28.
7. ISRAEL,] as in Jos. 24. 31.
8. 110 YEARS,] as in Jos. 24. 29
9. GAASH,] as in Jos. 24. 30.
TIMNATH-HERES,] or as in Jos. 24. 30, 'Timnath-Serah.'
10. GATHERED,] as in Ge. 25. 8, where however the phrase is more general, 'to thy people.'
NOT KNOWN,] that is, fully appreciated.
11. THE EVIL THING,] which generally means idolatry.
THE BAALIM,] i.e. 'the lords,' as in 3. 7; 8. 33; 10. 6, 10; 1 Sa. 7. 4; 1 K. 8. 18; 2 Ch. 17. 3; 24. 7; 28. 2; 33. 3; 34. 4; Jer. 2. 23; 9. 14; Hos. 2. 13, 17.
12. GODS,] or objects of reverence and worship.
PEOPLES,] the Canaanites, Philistines, Phenicians, Amorites, Moabites, Edomites, Arabians, &c.
13. BAAL,] a Phenician idol supposed to denote the sun.
ASHTAROTH,]a Phenician female goddess, supposed to be Venus, see 10. 6; 1 Sa. 7. 3, 4; 12. 10; 31. 10; 1 K. 11. 5, 3; 2 K. 23. 13.
14. BURNETH,] as in Ex. 4. 14, &c.
SPOILERS,] as in 1 Sa. 17. 53; Ps. 89. 41; Isa. 13. 16; Jer. 30. 16; Zec. 14. 2.
SELLETH,] as in De. 32. 20; Jud. 3. 8, &c.
TO STAND] successfully in battle.
15. GONE OUT,] to conquer and subdue it.
SPOKEN . . . SWORN,] in De. 29. 12—20.
DISTRESSED GREATLY,] as i nGe. 32. 7; Jud. 10. 9, &c.
16. RAISETH UP,] or establisheth men who vindicated their rights, and did justice between man and man, as
JUDGES,] in the place of God executing vengeance.
SPOILERS,] as in v. 14.
17. HEARKENED] at all times, but only occasionally.
GONE A-WHORING,] seeking the society and fellowship of idols and idolators.
WITH HASTE,] as if it were a path of danger.
DONE SO,] as their fathers did, i.e. obeyed the Lord.
18. WITH THE JUDGE,] in making peace or war.
SAVED,] or 'gave them ease' from the cruel grasp of the oppressor.
REPENTETH,] as in Ge. 6. 6, 7; 24. 67; 38 12, &c.
GROANING,] as in Ex. 2. 24; 6. 5; Eze. 30. 24

OPPRESSORS,] as in Ex. 3. 9; Jud. 6. 9; 1
Sa. 10. 18; Isa. 19. 20; Jer. 30. 20.
THRUSTING THEM AWAY,] as in Joel 2. 8.
19. DONE CORRUPTLY,] as in De. 4. 25.
NOT FALLEN,] *lit.* 'caused *or* let 'themselves) fall,' as in 1 Sa. 3. 19.
STIFF,] as in Ex. 32. 9.
20. BURN,] as in v. 14 above.
TRANSGRESSED,] by turning aside to
idolatry.
NOT HEARKENED,] so as to obey his voice.
21. HATH LEFT,] unsubdued.
22. TO TRY,] prove, or test the stedfastness
of Israel.
KEEPING,] habitually, without turning to
the right hand or to the left.
23. LEAVETH] them yet a little longer unsubdued.
HASTILY,] nor indeed till the reign of
David.
JOSHUA,] when he was causing Israel to
inherit the land.

III. 1. LEFT] in the land unsubdued by
Joshua and Israel.
TO TRY] the faith and stedfastness of the
people.
NOT KNOWN] by personal aquaintance.
3. FIVE PRINCES,] of Ashdod, Ashkelon,
Ekron, Gath, and Gaza, as in Jos. 1. 18; and
13. 3.
CANAANITE,] the particular tribe so called,
Nu. 13. 29.
SIDONIAN,] or inhabitant of Sidon, as in
Ge. 10. 15, &c.
LEBANON,] at the north of Canaan.
BAAL-HERMON,] the eastern part of Leba-
non, i.e. Baal-Gad.
HAMATH,] the most northern part of the
land, Nu. 34. 8; Jos. 11. 3; 18. 5.
4. PROVE,] *or* 'try,' as in v. 1.
OBEY] fully and at all times.
COMMANDED,] in De. 7. 1—5, &c.
5. CANAANITE, &c.] instead of dispossess-
ing them utterly.
6. WIVES..SONS,] though directly forbidden in De. 7. 3, &c.
GODS,] as they had been warned would
be the case if they intermarried with the
natives.
7. THE EVIL THING,] even idolatry.
GOD,] by solemn covenant, and public
treaty.
THE BAALIM,] as in v. 11 above.
THE SHRINES,] as in Ex. 34. 13.
8. BURNETH,] as in Jud. 2. 14. &c.
SELLETH,] as in De. 32. 20; Jud. 2. 14, &c.
CHUSHAN-RISHATHAIM,] i.e. 'a Cushite
most wicked.'
ARAM-NAHARAIM,] i.e. 'Aram of the two
rivers,' e.g. Mesopotamia.
9. CRY,] in distress and anguish, as the
word indicates.
SAVIOUR,] as in De. 22. 27 ; 28. 29, &c.
SAVETH,] as in Ex. 2. 17, &c.
OTHNIEL,] as in 1. 12, 13.
10. SPIRIT OF JEHOVAH,] as in 6. 34; 11.
29 ; 13. 25; 14. 6, 19; 15. 14; 1 Sa. 10. 6; 16.
13, 16, &c.
BATTLE,] in the name of the Lord against
the oppressor.

STRONG,] as in 6. 2.
11. RESTETH] from war and foreign
oppression.
DIETH,] such being the lot even of the
greatest saints of God.
12. THE EVIL THING,] as in v. 7 above.
STRENGTHENETH,] as in Ex. 4. 21, &c.
EGLON,] i.e. 'a little calf,' as in v. 14,
15, 17.
13. BENE-AMMON,] who were akin to the
Moabites, and
AMALEK,] who still bore Israel an unex-
tinguishable enmity.
CITY OF PALMS,] even Jericho ; see De.
34. 3 ; Jud. 1. 16.
15. CRY,] as in v. 9 above.
A SAVIOUR,] as in v. 9 above
EHUD,] i.e. 'united.'
GERA,] i.e. 'a grain.'
SHUT,] restrained, as in 20. 16 ; Ps. 69. 15.
PRESENT,] as in Ge. 4. 5; 32. 13, 18,
20, 21.
16. TWO MONTHS,] compare Ps. 149. 6; Isa.
41. 15.
A CUBIT] or about 18 inches.
LONG ROBE,] as in Lev. 6. 10, &c.
17. BRINGETH NEAR,] for the purpose of
presenting it to the king.
FAT,] as in Ge. 41. 2, 4, 5, 7, 18, 20; K.
4. 23; Ps. 73. 4; Eze. 34. 3 Da. 1. 15; Hab. 1.
16; Zec. 11. 16.
19. GRAVEN IMAGES,] as in De. 7. 5, 25; 12.
3; Jud. 3. 26, &c.
GILGAL,] where the ark of God had rested ;
the profane sight seems to have nerved his
arm.
A SECRET WORD,] which could only be
confided to the king's own ear,
HUSH,] as in Ne. 8. 11; Amos 6. 10; 8. 3,
Hab. 2. 20; Zeph. 1. 7; Zec. 2. 13.
20. UPPER CHAMBER,] as in v. 23, 24, 25:
2 Sa. 18. 33; 1 K. 17. 19, 23; 2 K. 1. 2 ; 4. 10,
11 ; 23. 12; 1 Ch. 28. 11; 2 Ch. 3. 9; 9. 4 ; Neh.
3. 31, 32, Ps. 104. 3, 13; Jer. 22. 13, 14.
A WORD OF GOD,] *or* 'a matter of God.'
THRONE,] not merely 'the seat,' as in Ge.
41. 40; Ex. 11. 5; 12. 29; De. 17. 18; 1 Sa. 1.
9; 2. 8; 4. 13, 18, &c.
21. STRIKETH,] as in 4. 21, &c.
22. HALF.] This original word does not
occur elsewhere.
BLADE,] *lit.* 'flame,' as in 13. 20; Job 39.
23 ; 41. 21; Isa. 13. 8; 29. 6; 30. 30; 66. 15 ;
Joel 2. 5; Neh. 3. 3.
SHUTTETH,] as in Ex. 14. 3, &c.
FUNDAMENT.] This original word does not
occur elsewhere ; Targ., Vulg., Luther and
others read 'dung;' Syr., and Arabic Versions, 'he went out in haste.'
23. PORCH.] This original word is not
found elsewhere.
UPPER CHAMBER,] as in v. 20 above.
BOLTED IT,] as in 2 Sa. 13. 17, 18; Song
4. 12.
24. COVERING HIS FEET,] as in 1 Sa. 24. 3.
INNER CHAMBER,] as in v. 20 above
25. CONFOUNDED,] *or* 'ashamed,' as in 2
K. 2. 17; 8. 11; Jer. 6. 15; 8. 12.
KEY,] *lit.* 'opener,' as in 1 Ch. 9. 27; Isa.
22. 22 ; Prov. 8. 6.
26. ESCAPED,] as in 1 Sa. 23. 13, &c.

TARRYING,] as in Ge. 19. 16; 43. 10; Ex. 12. 39; Jud. 19. 18; 2 Sa. 15. 28; Ps. 119. 60; Isa. 29. 9; Hab. 2. 3.

IMAGES,] as in v. 9 above.

SEIRATH,] *lit.* 'a hairy *or* rough place;' not mentioned elsewhere.

27. COMING IN,] to the city of Seirath.

EPHRAIM,] to gather the inhabitants together.

28. HATH GIVEN.] The language of confidence.

GO DOWN,] from the hill-country to the Jordan, that they might obtain possession of the PASSAGES,] where the river was generally crossed and fordable,

29. ROBUST,] *lit.* 'oily, fat, shining,' as in Ge. 49. 20; Nu. 30. 20; 1 Ch. 4. 10; Neh. 9. 25, 35; Isa. 30. 23; Eze. 34. 14, 16; Hab. 1. 16.

VALOUR,] as in Ge. 47. 6; Ex. 18. 21, 25; Jos. 1. 14; 6. 2: 8. 3; 10. 7, &c.

ESCAPED,] over the Jordan.

30. HUMBLED,] as in 8. 28; 11. 23, &c.

RESTETH,] as in v. 11 above.

31. SHAMGAR.] Etymology unknown; as in 5. 6.

ANATH,] i.e. 'an answer,' not mentioned elsewhere, save in 5. 6.

PHILISTINES,] who dwelt on the shores of the great sea.

SIX HUNDRED,] a band who had invaded the place where he dwelt; he smote and defeated them, and drove them back.

OX-GOAD.] This phrase is not found elsewhere.

SAVETH,] i.e. giveth ease for a time, during his life.

IV. 1. THE EVIL THING,] as in 3. 7, 12, &c.

DEAD,] as in 2. 9, 10, 19; 3. 11, 12, &c.

2. SELLETH,] as in 3. 8 above.

JABIN,] i.e. 'he understands,' as in Jos. 11. 1; he was *a* king, not *the* king of Canaan.

HAZOR,] as in Jos. 11. 1, 10, 11, 13, &c.

SISERA.] Etymology unknown; see Ps. 83. 10; also Ezra 2. 53; Neh. 7. 55.

GOYIM,] as in v. 13, 16.

3. CRY,] as in 3. 9, 15, &c.

IRON,] as in 1. 19.

OPPRESSED,] as in 10. 12, &c.

4. DEBORAH,] i.e. 'a bee;' as in Ge. 35. 1.

INSPIRED,] as in Ex. 15. 20; 2 K. 22. 14; 2 Ch. 34. 22; Neh. 6. 14; Isa. 8. 3.

LAPIDOTH,] i.e. 'lamps;' not mentioned elsewhere; perhaps she was 'a maker of lamps.'

JUDGING.] Though not perhaps actually ordained to the office, she was regarded as 'a mother in Israel,' as in 5. 7.

5. PALM-TREE.] Her house was probably in a grove of these, and some one was specially prominent.

RAMAH,] as in Jos. 18. 25, &c.

BETH-EL,] as in Ge. 12. 8, &c.

EPHRAIM,] see Jos 16. 2; 18 22, 25.

JUDGMENT,] as they did to Moses, &c. Ex. 18. 13, &c.

6. BARAK,] i.e. 'lightning.'

ABINOAM,] i.e. 'my father is pleasant,' *or* 'father of pleasantness.'

KADESH-NAPHTALI,] a city of refuge, as in Jos. 20. 7.

HAST DRAWN] thyself out to meet the enemy.

MOUNT TABOR,] as in Jos. 19. 22.

7. HAVE DRAWN,] as in v. 6.

KISHON,] i.e. 'bending,' as in v. 13; 5. 21; 1 K. 18. 40; Ps. 83. 9; it flows into the gulf of Ptolemais.

HAVE GIVEN] up vanquished into thy control.

8. IF THOU,] who hast thyself received the assurance from the Lord. See Heb. 11. 32

9. THY GLORY,] *or* 'honour.'

SELL,] as in 3. 8, &c.

KEDESH,] in Naphtali, as in v. 6.

10. AT HIS FEET,] i. e. along with him, as in Ge. 30. 30; Ex. 11. 8; De. 11. 6; Jud. 8. 5, &c.

11. HEBER,] i.e. 'a companion, *or* charm,' as in v. 17.

KENITE,] as in Nu. 24. 22.

HOBAB,] as in Nu. 10. 29.

OAK OF ZAANAIM,] as in Jos. 19. 33

12. MOUNT TABOR,] as in v. 6.

13. CALLETH,] *or* 'cryeth,' as in v. 10; 2 Sa. 20. 4, 5; Job 35. 9; Jer. 3. 7; Zec. 6. 8.

IRON,] as in v. 3 above.

GOYIM,] as in v. 2 above.

KISHON,] as in v. 7 above.

14. GONE OUT,] to the battle against the foe.

MOUNT TABOR,] to attack Sisera and the Moabites.

15. DESTROYETH.] The honour is given to the Lord, and not to the warriors.

THE CHARIOT,] that he might be less observed.

16. LEFT EVEN ONE,] who attempted to resist.

17. ON HIS FEET,] as in v. 15 above.

JAEL,] i.e. 'a roe.'

HEBER,] as in v. 11.

18. GOETH OUT] of her tent, seeing him approaching it.

TURN ASIDE,] to lodge and rest.

MY LORD,] the courteous salutation of the east.

FEAR NOT,] as none would dare to enter it without her permission.

COVERLET.] This original word is not found elsewhere.

THE BOTTLE,] not 'a bottle;' they were made of skins, as in Jos. 9. 4, 13; 1 Sa. 16. 20; Ps. 56. 8; 119. 83.

COVERETH HIM] again, as in v. 18.

20. OPENING,] to be ready to prevent any one entering or observing him.

THERE IS NOT,] as in Ge. 2. 5, &c.

21. THE PIN,] some special one, made of wood or iron, as in 16. 14, &c.

THE HAMMER,] as in 1 K. 6. 7; Isa. 44. 12; Jer. 10. 4.

GENTLY,] as in 2 Sa. 18. 5; 1 K. 21. 27; Job 15. 11; Isa. 8. 6.

TEMPLES,] as in v. 22; 5. 26; Song 4. 3; 6. 7.

FASTENETH,] *or* 'lighteth,' as in Jos. 15. 18; Jud. 1. 14.

FAST ASLEEP,] as in Ps. 76. 6; Prov. 10. 5; Da. 8. 18; 10. 9; Jon. 1. 5.

WEARY,] as in 1 Sa. 14. 28, &c.

DIETH,] a death of violence, to which he himself had subjected many.

22. PURSUING,] as in 8. 4, 5, &c.
SEEKING] to capture.
23. HUMBLETH,] as in 3. 30, &c.
24. BECOMING HARD,] as in 1 Sa. 5. 7.
CUT OFF,] as in Jos. 11. 21, &c.

V. 1. SINGETH,] as in Ex. 15. 1; Nu. 21.
17, &c.
2. FREEING,] as in Ex. 32. 25; Nu. 5. 18.
FREEMEN,] as in De. 32. 42.
FOR THE PEOPLE,] not 'when,' as in C.V.
BLESS YE,] i.e. declare ye blessed.
JEHOVAH,] the God of Israel, as explained
in v. 3.
3. YE KINGS] of all lands.
YE PRINCES,] as in Ps. 2. 2; Prov. 8. 15;
31. 4; Isa. 40. 23; Hab. 1. 10.
I—I DO SING.] The repetition of the pro-
noun denotes the special emphasis.
I SING PRAISE,] as in 2 Sa. 22. 50; Ps. 7.
17, &c.
4. GOING FORTH,] as in De. 33. 2, &c.
FROM SEIR,] the inheritance of Edom, as
in Ge. 36. 8.
STEPPING OUT,] as in Ps. 68. 7; Hab. 3. 12.
FIELD OF EDOM,] as in Ge. 32. 3.
TREMBLED,] as in Ps. 68. 9; 2 Sa. 22. 8, &c.
DROPPED,] as in Ps. 68. 8; Song 5. 5, &c.
THICK CLOUDS,] as in Ex. 19. 9; 2 Sa. 22.
12, &c.
5. FLOWED,] as in De. 32. 2; Ps. 147. 18;
Song 4. 16.
SINAI,] i.e. trembled, as in v. 4; compare
Ex. 19. 18.
6. SHAMGAR,] as in 4. 31.
JAEL,] as in 4. 17, but Gesenius is pro-
bably correct in supposing this to have been
a different person.
CEASED] to be trodden, or used as such.
PATHS,] as in Job 19. 8, &c.
CROOKED WAYS,] as in Ps. 125. 5.
7. VILLAGES,] as in v. 11 below.
CEASED,] as in v. 6 above.
A MOTHER IN ISRAEL,] as in 2 Sa. 20. 19.
8. HE CHOOSETH,] that is, Israel doth so,
according to his own pleasure.
NEW GODS,] as in De. 32. 17, &c.
GATES,] of the cities of Israel.
SHIELD,] as a weapon of defence, and a
SPEAR,] as one of offence is almost un-
known.
9. LAW-GIVERS,] as in Isa. 10. 1; 22. 16;
and v. 14 below.
BLESS,] as in v. 2 above.
10. RIDERS,] as in 10. 4; 12. 14.
WHITE ASSES.] This colour of asses is not
mentioned elsewhere.
SITTERS,] as those at ease on
LONG ROBES,] as in Lev. 6. 3; Ps. 109. 18.
WALKERS,] being too poor to ride.
MEDITATE,] as in 1 Ch. 16. 9; Job 12. 8;
Ps. 105. 2.
11. SHOUTERS,] as in Prov. 30. 27.
PLACES OF DRAWING WATER,] as in Ge. 24.
11, 13, 19, 20, 43, 44, 45, &c.
GIVE OUT,] i.e. recount, rehearse.
VILLAGES,] as in v. 7 above.
RULED,] as in Nu. 24. 19, &c.
12. AWAKE,] as in Isa. 52. 1, &c.
UTTER,] lit. 'speak.'
THY CAPTIVITY,] as in Ps. 68 18, &c.

13. HIM WHO IS LEFT,] even Barak.
HONOURABLE ONES] in Israel.
HE CAUSED TO RULE,] i.e. God did so
among the mighty of the land.
CAUSED ME,] i.e. Deborah,'
14. EPHRAIM,] the tribe among whom she
was dwelling.
AMALEK,] the inveterate foe of Israel.
Ex. 17. 18.
BENJAMIN,] the youngest of the tribes,
and most fiery.
MACHIR,] the only son of Manasseh, half
of whose descendants dwelt beyond the
Jordan.
LAW-GIVERS,] as in v. 9 above.
ZEBULUN,] whose territories were close to
Phenicia, whence they early acquired the
art of
DRAWING,] with the wooden pen or
REED,] with which in the east letters are
written by the professional
WRITER,] or scribe, which is there a highly
honourable employment.
15. PRINCES,] or 'my princes.'
RIGHT,] as in Ge. 1. 7; 42. 11, &c.
THE VALLEY,] at the foot of mount Tabor.
ON HIS FEET,] without the chariots and
cavalry which the enemy had; or 'with his
footmen,' i.e. infantry.
DIVISIONS,] as in 2 Ch. 35. 5, &c.
DECREES,] as in Isa. 10. 1.
16. THE BOUNDARIES,] as in Ge. 49. 14.
LOWINGS.] See the use of the word in Jer.
18. 16.
DIVISIONS,] as in preceding verse.
SEARCHINGS,] as in Job 5. 9; 8. 8; 9. 10,
11. 7; 34. 24; 36. 26; 38. 16; Ps. 145. 3; Prov.
25. 3, 27; Isa. 40. 28.
17. TABERNACLE] at ease, indifferent to
the national struggle.
SOJOURN,] or 'fear,' among his ships at
Joppa, and on the great sea.
HAVEN OF THE SEAS,] where he was in
safety.
CREEKS,] i.e. breaches or broken places
of the land.
TABERNACLE] at ease quietly.
18. ZEBULUN,] as in v. 10 above.
EXPOSED,] lit. 'reproached,' as in 8. 15, &c.
NAPHTALI,] which was honourably allied
with Zebulun in its actings.
HIGH PLACES,] as in Prov. 9. 3.
19. KINGS] of Canaan, as in the next clause
FOUGHT] with Israel, in behalf of Jabin.
TAANACH,] as in Jos. 12. 21; 17. 11; Jud.
1. 27; 1 K. 4. 12.
MEGIDDO,] i.e. the river Kishon, which
ran near the city.
GAIN OF MONEY,] i.e. pecuniary profit.
THEY TOOK NOT] for fighting, it was no
mere mercenary warfare.
20. THEY FOUGHT,] against the enemies
of Israel—against Sisera.
HIGH WAYS,] as in Nu. 20. 19, &c.
21. KISHON,] as in v. 7 above.
SWEPT THEM AWAY.] This original word
does not occur elsewhere.
MOST ANCIENT,] in Heb. 'Kedumim,' which
some have supposed to be another name of
the river.
TREAD DOWN,] as in De. 33. 29; Ps. 91. 13.

22. BROKEN,] *or* 'hammered,' as in v. 26;
1 Sa. 14. 16; Prov. 23. 35; Ps. 74. 6; 141. 5;
Isa. 16. 8; 28. 1; 41. 7.
HORSE-HEELS,] as in Ge. 49. 17.
PRANCINGS,] as in Nah. 3. 2.
MIGHTY ONES,] as in 1 Sa. 21. 7; Job 24.
22; 34. 20; Ps. 22. 12; 50. 13; 68. 30; 76. 5;
78. 25; Isa. 10. 13; 34. 7; 46. 12; Jer. 8. 16;
46. 15; 47. 3; 50. 11; La. 1. 15.
23. CURSE,] as in Jer. 48. 10, &c.
MEROZ.] A place not mentioned elsewhere;
the etymology is uncertain; prob. 'a secret
place.'
MESSENGER,] perhaps Deborah himself;
others say Barak, and others a heavenly messenger.
AMONG,] not 'against,' as in the C.V.
24. BLESSED,] in opposition to the inhabitants of Meroz.
ABOVE WOMEN,] generally, and even above
those who live at ease at home.
KENITE,] as in 4. 17.
25. WATER,] as the most common beverage, he asked to quench his thirst, but
MILK,] she presented for his acceptance,
at once refreshing and strengthening.
DISH,] *or* 'bowl,' as in 6. 38; used by such
as those called 'honourable,' in v. 13.
BUTTER,] as in Ge. 18. 8; De. 32. 14; 2 Sa.
17. 29; Job 20. 17; Prov. 30. 33; Isa. 7. 15, 22.
26. THE PIN,] as in 4. 21.
LABOURER'S,] as in Job 3. 20; 20. 22; Prov.
16. 26; Ecc. 2. 18, 22; 3. 9; 4. 8; 9. 9.
HAMMERED,] as in Isa. 41. 7.
SMOTE.] This original word is not found
elsewhere.
SMOTE,] as in Ps. 68. 21; 110. 6; Hab. 3
13, &c.
TEMPLE,] as in 4. 21.
27. HE BOWED] the knee, as in 7. 5, 6, &c.
HE FELL,] exhausted by his flight.
HE LAY DOWN,] to rest and sleep.
DESTROYED,] as in Ps. 137. 8; Isa. 33. 1;
Jer. 4. 30.
28. THE WINDOW,] not 'a window,' as in
C.V.
LOOKED OUT,] as in 2 Sa. 6. 16; 1 Ch. 15.
29; Prov. 7. 6; 2 K. 9. 30, &c.
CRIETH OUT.] This original word is not
found elsewhere.
THE LATTICE,] as in Prov. 7. 6.
DELAYING,] as in Ex. 32. 1.
STEPS,] as in Ge. 2. 32; Ps. 17. 5, &c.
29. PRINCESSES,] as in 1 K. 11. 3; Est. 1.
18; Isa. 49. 23; La. 1. 1.
HER SAYINGS,] as in Prov. 7. 5, &c.
30. NOT FIND] the enemy, and conquered
him? yea, they
APPORTION] to each other respective
shares of
SPOIL,] which usually fell to the lot of the
victor.
FEMALE,] *lit.* 'a womb,' as in Ge. 49. 25;
Prov. 30. 16; Isa. 46. 3; Eze. 20. 26.
HEAD] or chief engaged in the battle.
FINGER-WORK.] This original word is not
found elsewhere.
EMBROIDERED,] as in 1 Ch. 29. 2; Ps. 45.
14; Eze. 16. 10, 13, 18; 17. 3; 26. 16; 27. 7,
16, 24.
THE SPOIL,] i e. made for those whose

bodies were now an object of spoilation.
31. PERISH,] i.e. shamefully and utterly.
LOVING,] as in Ex. 20. 6; De. 5. 10; Ps.
122. 6, &c.
SUN,] as in 2 Sa. 23. 4, &c.
MIGHT,] as in Ps. 19. 5, &c.
RESTETH,] as in 3. 11, 30.

VI. 1. THE EVIL THING,] even idolatry.
MIDIAN,] see Nu. 31. 1—12.
2. FLOWINGS] of water in trenches; this
original word is not found elsewhere.
CAVES,] as in 1 Sa. 13. 6, &c.
STRONGHOLDS,] as in 1 Sa. 23. 14, 19, 29;
1 Ch. 11. 7; 12. 8, 16; Isa. 33. 16; Jer. 48.
41; 51. 30; Eze. 33. 37.
3. SOWETH] the seed of their land.
AMALEK,] who seem to have embraced
every opportunity of harassing Israel.
SONS OF THE EAST,] as in v. 33; 7. 12;
8. 10; 1 K. 4. 30; Job 1. 3; Jer. 49. 28; Eze.
25. 4, 10.
4. DESTROY] maliciously, as the original
word implies.
GAZA,] a city of the Philistines, as in Ge.
10. 19.
SUSTENANCE,] as in 17. 10, &c.
5. TENTS,] that they might abide a long
time in the land wasting and destroying.
FULNESS OF THE LOCUST,] as in 7. 12, &c.
DESTROY,] *or* 'corrupt,' *or* 'mar' it, as in
v. 4 above.
6. WEAK,] as in Isa. 17. 4; Ps. 79. 8, &c.
CRY] for help, as the original word implies.
8. PROPHET,] to remind them of their
blessings, their pledges, and their sins.
EGYPT,] when they cried to him for help,
and had no power left in them.
SERVANTS,] toiling in the making of
bricks, &c.
9. DELIVER,] by a strong hand and out-
stretched arm.
OPPRESSORS,] such as Amalek, Midian, &c.
CAST..OUT] the tribes of Canaan.
LAND] as promised to the fathers.
10. GOD] by right of redemption, having
purchased them himself.
FEAR,] i.e. reverence,
NOT HEARKENED,] as they had solemnly
pledged themselves to do.
11. MESSENGER,] probably the same as in
v. 8 above.
OAK,] as in 1 K. 13. 14; and v. 19 below.
OPHRAH,] see 8. 27; 9. 5; different from
that in Jos. 18. 23, which belonged to Ben-
jamin.
JOASH,] not mentioned elsewhere.
ABI-EZRITE,] compare Jos. 17. 2.
GIDEON,] i.e. a 'cutter down.'
BEATING OUT,] as in De. 24. 20; Ruth 2.
17; Isa. 27. 12; 28. 27.
WHEAT,] as in 1 Ch. 21. 20.
WINE-PRESS,] as in Neh. 13. 15; Isa. 63. 2;
La. 1. 15; Joel 3. 13.
REMOVE,] *lit.* 'cause it to flee,' as in Ex.
9. 20; De. 32. 30; Jud. 7. 21.
MIDIANITES,] who were roving about for
plunder.
12. WITH THEE,] as in Ex. 3. 12; Jos. 1.
5, &c

VALOUR,] as in Jos. 1. 14; 6. 2; 8. 3; 10. 7, &c.

13. MY LORD,] a common title of respect.

WITH US,] an exclamation shewing a kind of incredulity.

ALL THIS] misery and oppression found us out?

RECOUNTED,] according to the divine command in the law.

LEFT] us, for had he been still with them, he would have remembered and delivered them, but now he

DOTH GIVE] them up helpless and apparently for ever.

14. JEHOVAH.] One of Kennicott's MSS. for 'Jehovah' reads 'the messenger;' the Sept. and Arabic Versions have it fully, i.e. 'the messenger of Jehovah,' the whole perhaps may be understood thus: 'and Jehovah turneth the face unto [the messenger, or unto] Gideon, and [the messenger] saith to Gideon.'

GO] on with the work of delivering Israel.

I SENT THEE] in the name of Jehovah of Hosts.

15. MY LORD,] as in v. 13 above; the Masorets have pointed it as if Gideon designedly used the phrase applicable only to God, but he seems still to have regarded the messenger only as a servant.

MY CHIEF,] or 'leader,' in the thousands of Manasseh, as in Mic. 5. 2.

WEAK,] as in 2 Sa. 3. 1.

THE LITTLE ONE,] as in 1 Sa. 9. 21; Ps. 68. 27. &c.

HOUSE,] or household.

16. JEHOVAH.] Sept. reads 'the messenger of the Lord,' as in v. 14 above.

BECAUSE,] not 'surely,' as in the C.V.

AS ONE MAN,] as if they were only one.

17. I PRAY THEE,] not 'now,' as in the C.V.; so in v. 18.

EYES,] as in Ge. 18. 3, &c.

SIGN,] or 'token.'

18. MOVE NOT,] as in Nu. 14 44.

PRESENT,] as in Ge. 4. 3, 4, 5.

19. GONE IN] unto his father's house.

A KID OF THE GOATS,] as in 13. 15, 19; 15. 1, &c.

EPHAH OF FLOUR,] as in 1 Sa. 1. 24.

UNLEAVENED THINGS,] i.e. cakes, &c.

FLESH] of the kid he hath placed in a BASKET,] as in Ge. 40. 16, 17, 18; Ex. 29. 3, 23, 32; Lev. 8. 2, 26, 31; Nu. 6. 15, 17, 19; it is not found elsewhere.

BROTH,] as in v. 20; Isa. 65. 4; not found elsewhere.

POT,] as in Nu. 11. 8; 1 Sa. 2. 14.

20. MESSENGER OF GOD,] i.e. of Jehovah, as in v. 11, 12 above.

THIS ROCK,] as in Eze. 24. 7, 8, &c.

POUR OUT,] as in Ex. 4. 9; Lev. 14. 41, &c.

21. MESSENGER OF JEHOVAH,] as in v. 11, 12, &c.

STAFF] for a support, and on which he leant.

THE FIRE,] miraculously brought out of the rock on which the flesh was lying.

CONSUMETH,] i.e. eateth the offering of Gideon

GONE] suddenly and entirely out of his sight.

22. MESSENGER OF JEHOVAH,] one sent direct by God to him with a divine message, he saith

ALAS!] as in 11. 35; Jos. 7. 7; 2 K. 3. 10: 6. 5, 15; Jer. 1. 6; 4. 10; 14. 13; 32. 17; Eze. 4. 14; 9. 8; 11. 13; 20. 49; Joel 1. 15.

MY LORD JEHOVAH,] as in Ge. 15. 2, 8; De. 3. 24; 9. 26; Jos. 7. 7; Jud. 16. 28; 2 Sa. 7. 18, &c.

MESSENGER OF JEHOVAH,] as in v. 11, 12.

FACE TO FACE,] as in Ge. 32. 30; Ex. 33 11; De. 34. 10, &c.

24. JEHOVAH,] not unto the 'messenger.'

SHALOM,] i.e. 'Jehovah (is) peace.'

ABI-EZRITES,] as in v. 11 above.

25. SAITH] in a dream or vision.

THE YOUNG OX.] The original phrase here is not found elsewhere.

THE SECOND BULLOCK] which was older, even

SEVEN YEARS,] when it is almost at its prime.

THROWN DOWN,] as in 1 K. 18. 30; 19. 10, 14, &c.

ALTAR OF BAAL,] the existence of which shews the laxity that prevailed.

SHRINE,] covering and enclosing the altar.

CUT DOWN,] as commanded in the law.

26. STRONGHOLD,] as in Nah. 1. 7, &c.

ARRANGEMENT,] as in Ex. 39. 37; Lev. 24. 6; 1 Ch. 12. 38; 1 Sa. 4. 2, &c.

THE SECOND BULLOCK] referred to in v. 25.

27. HOUSE,] or household.

NIGHT,] that it might not be known who did it.

28. BROKEN DOWN,] as in v. 30, 31, 32, &c

ALTAR OF BAAL,] at which they had so often worshipped.

SHRINE,] which had covered it was CUT DOWN,] violently by sharp weapons.

THE SECOND BULLOCK,] which perhaps had been remarkable for its appearance.

BUILT] rapidly by Gideon and his ten ser vants, in a single night.

29. THEY SAY,] i.e. some of the people in the place who may have noticed the operations.

30. BRING OUT] of the house where he was abiding.

DIETH,] the death of a criminal offender against Baal.

31. DO YE PLEAD,] or 'contend,' in his behalf?

YE SAVE HIM,] from destruction and contempt?

DURING THE MORNING,] i.e. immediately. A GOD] really, and not so merely nominally.

32. JERUBBAEL,] i.e. 'Baal doth plead or contend.'

33. MIDIAM, ETC,] as in v. 3 above.

GATHERED TOGETHER,] for another invasion of the land.

PASS OVER] the Jordan.

JEZREEL,] as in 17. 16, &c

34. CLOTHED] Gideon with zeal as with a garment, as in 1 Ch. 12. 18; 2 Ch. 24. 20.

M

TRUMPET,] the usual signal for summoning the people to war.
ABI-EZER,] one of the families of the ;ribe of
35. MANASSEH,] to which Gideon himself belonged.
NAPHTALI.] These three tribes lay nearest to him on the north.
COME UP] to where Gideon was, to Ophrah.
36. SAVIOUR,] as in 1 Sa. 14. 39; 2 K. 13. 5; [sa. 43. 3; 45. 15, &c.
BY MY HAND,] as by the hand of Moses and Aaron.
SPOKEN,] in v. 14 above.
37. FLEECE OF WOOL,] as in v. 38, 39, 40.
THRESHING FLOOR,] as in Ge. 50. 10, &c.
DEW,] as in Ge. 27. 28, 39, &c.
DROUGHT,] as in Ge. 31. 40, &c.
KNOWN,] assuredly by this sign or token being granted to strengthen his faith.
38. PRESSETH,] as in Job 39. 15; Isa. 1. 6.
WRINGETH,] as in Ps. 57. 8; Isa. 51. 17; Ezek. 23. 34.
BOWL,] as in 5. 25.
39. LET NOT BURN,] as in Ex. 32. 22, &c.
ONLY THIS TIME,] as in Ge. 18. 32, &c.
TRY,] as in Ge. 22. 1; Ecc. 2. 1, &c.
DEW,] reversing the former experiment.
40. DOTH SO,] to satisfy the soul of his servant who trusted in him.

VII. 1. JERUBBAAL,] i.e. ' Baal doth plead or contend.'
GIDEON,] as in 5. 11, 32.
FOUNTAIN OF HAROD,] compare 1 Sa. 29. 1; 2 Sa. 23. 25; lit. 'trembling,' as in v. 3 below.
HEIGHT OF MOREH,] i.e. of 'the teacher.'
VALLEY] of Jezreel, as in 5. 33.
2. TOO MANY] being 32,000.
BEAUTIFY ITSELF,] as in Ex. 8. 9; Isa. 10. 15; 44. 23; 49. 3; 60. 21; 61. 3.
3. AFRAID..TREMBLING,] compare the law in De. 20. 8,
MOUNT GILEAD,] which was westward of Jordan ; some read (without authority) ' to mount Gilead.'
4. TOO MANY] for the reason given in v. 2 above.
WATER] of the fountain of Harod.
REFINE,] as in 17. 4; Isa. 1. 25; 48. 10; Da. 11. 35; 12. 10; Ps. 105. 19; Zec. 13. 9.
5. LAPPETH,] as in v. 6, 7; 1 K. 21. 19; 22. 38.
SET HIM APART,] as in 6. 37; 8. 27; Ge. 30. 38, &c.
BOWETH ON HIS KNEES,] as in 1 K. 8. 54; 19. 18; 2 K. 1. 13; Ezra 9. 5.
6. THREE HUNDRED MEN,] not the one hundredth part of the original amount of his army.
7. I DO SAVE,] from the overpowering force of the enemy.
8. THE PROVISION,] as in 20. 10, &c.
TRUMPETS,] with which they appear to have been provided, to encourage themselves and frighten their enemies.
TENTS,] that is his own proper place of residence.
KEPT HOLD] for carrying on the war, as the Lord directed.

VALLEY,] as in v. 1 above.
9. CAMP] of Midian, in the valley, as in 6. 33.
10. PHURAH,] i.e. 'a branch or bough '
11. SPEAK,] to one another regarding themselves and thee.
STRENGTHENED] by the words he would hear.
THE FIFTIES,] as in Ex. 13. 8 ; Jos. 1. 14; 4. 12.
12. MIDIAN, &c.] as in 6. 33.
VALLEY] of Jezreel.
LOCUST,] as in 6. 5.
CAMELS,] generally used for bearing burdens.
SAND,] as in Ge. 22. 17, &c.
13. COMETH IN] unto the camp of Midian in the valley of Jezreel.
DREAM,] which was anciently a means of divine communications.
CAKE.] This original word is not found elsewhere.
BARLEY-BREAD,] compare Eze. 4. 12.
TURNING ITSELF,] as in Ge. 3. 24; Job 37. 12; 38. 14.
THE TENT,] perhaps that of the king is here alluded to, as the most conspicuous.
14. COMPANION,] or 'friend,' as in v. 13.
SWORD,] as in v. 20 below.
CAMP,] such as Amalek, and the sons of the east.
15. NARRATION,] as in 2 Sa. 24. 9; 1 Ch. 21. 5; 1 Ch. 27. 24.
INTERPRETATION,] lit. 'shivering or breaking,' as in Lev. 51. 19 ; 24. 20.
BOWETH HIMSELF] before Jehovah, in thankfulness for the encouragement afforded to him.
ISRAEL,] consisting of the 300 men, who were left.
HATH GIVEN.] The language of confident assurance.
16. DIVIDETH,] as in 9. 43, &c.
DETACHMENTS,] lit. 'heads,' as in v. 20; 9. 34, 37, 43 ; 1 Sa. 11. 11.
TRUMPETS] to blow with, so as to confound the enemy, and
PITCHERS,] as in Ge. 24. 14—46 ; 1 K. 17. 12—16; 18. 33; Ecc. 12. 6.
LAMPS,] as in Ge. 15. 17 ; Ex. 20. 18 ; Jud. 15. 4, 5; Job 12. 5, &c.
17. CAMP] of Midian, and their associates.
18. FOR JEHOVAH, &c.] i.e. we fight for them.
19. THE HUNDRED MEN,] who formed the first detachment.
MIDDLE-WATCH,] a little after midnight.
CONFIRMED,] or 'established.'
WATCHMEN,] who guarded the camp.
TRUMPETS] which they each had in their hands.
DASHING IN PIECES,] they being made of earthenware, as is common in the east.
20. BREAK,] lit. 'shiver.'
THE SWORD,] or ' a sword for the Lord and for Gideon.'
21. CAMP] in different directions.
RUNNETH] hastily hither and thither, and
SHOUT] to encourage themselves and their neighbours.

FLEE,] for escape from the sword of each other.

22. TRUMPETS,] as had been directed in order to heighten the confusion.

COMPANION,] mistaking them for enemies.

BETH-SHITTAH,] or Beth Hash-shittah, i.e. 'house (or place) of shittim wood ;' not mentioned elsewhere.

ZERARATH,] or as some MSS. read, Zereda, i.e. 'cooling,' as in 1 K. 11. 26; 2 Ch. 4. 17; it is called Zartan in Jos. 3. 16; 1 K. 4. 12; 7. 46.

ABEL-MEHOLAH,] i.e. 'a meadow of dancing,' as in 1 K. 4. 12; 19. 16.

TABBATH.] Etymology unknown ; not mentioned elsewhere.

23. NAPHTALI..ASHER..MANASSEH,] as in 6. 25; those especially who had returned home.

24. EPHRAIM,] on the south.

WATERS,] whose names are not mentioned.

BETH-BAREH,] i.e. 'house or place of passage,' as in John 1. 28.

25. HEADS,] i.e. chiefs.

OREB,] i.e. 'a raven,' as in 8. 3; Ps. 83. 11; Isa. 10. 26.

ZEEB,] i.e. 'a wolf,' as in 8. 3; Ps. 83. 11.

ROCK,] as in 6. 21.

WINE-FAT,] as in Nu. 18. 27, 30.

VIII. 1. EPHRAIM,] jealous at the appearance of being overlooked, while they were a most powerful tribe.

FOR US,] when those of Manasseh, Asher, Naphtali, and Zebulun, had been called.

STRIVE,] or 'contend.'

SEVERELY,] lit. 'with hardness.'

2. GLEANINGS,] as in Isa. 17. 6; 24. 13; Jer. 49. 9; Obad. 5. Mic. 7. 1.

HARVEST,] as in Lev. 26. 5; Isa. 24. 13; 32. 10; Jer. 48. 32; Mic. 7. 1; Zech. 11. 2.

3. HEADS,] as in 7. 25.

LIKE YOU,] in capturing the two chief leaders of the enemy.

TEMPER,] lit. 'spirit.'

DESISTED,] as in Ex. 4. 26, &c.

4. WEARIED,] as in Ge. 25. 29, 30; De. 25. 18.

PURSUING,] as in Jos. 2. 7.

5. SUCCOTH,] as in Ge. 33. 17.

OAKES,] as in Ex. 29. 23; 1 Sa. 2. 36; 10. 3; 1 Ch. 16. 3; Prov. 6. 26; Jer. 37. 21.

MY FEET,] as in 4. 10, &c.

WEARIED,] as in v. 4.

ZEBAH,] i.e. 'a sacrifice.'

ZALMUNNA,] i.e. 'a shadow withheld.'

6. HEADS,] as in 4. 2, 7; 5. 15; 7. 25; 8. 3; v. 14 below, &c.

HAND,] or power.

BREAD,] to support them, and expose ourselves to the enemy's wrath.

7. THRESHOLD,] as in Job 39. 15; 2 K. 13. 7, &c.

THORNS,] as in Ge. 3. 18; Ex. 22. 6, &c.

THRESHING INSTRUMENTS,] as in v. 16; not found elsewhere.

8. PENUEL,] i.e. 'face of God,' as in Ge. 32. 30; Jud. 8. 8, 9, 17; 1 K. 12. 25.

9. TOWER,] in which they were trusting confidently.

10. KARKOR,] Etymology unknown ; not mentioned elsewhere.

FALLING] away by death or desertion from the ranks.

DRAWING SWORD,] as in 20. 2, 15, 17, 25, 35, 46; 2 Sa. 24. 9; 2 K. 3. 27; 1 Ch. 21. 5.

11. TENTS,] generally supposed to be Arabians or Kederenes.

NOBAH,] i.e. 'a barking,' as in Nu. 32. 42.

JOGBEHAH,] i.e. 'lofty,' as in Nu. 32. 35.

CONFIDENT,] as in 18. 7.

12. CAUSED TO TREMBLE,] as in 2 Sa. 17. 2.

14. DESCRIBETH,] lit. 'writeth.'

15. REPROACHED,] as in 1 Sa. 17. 10, 26, 36, 45, &c.

BREAD,] as in v. 6 above.

16. THORNS,] as in v. 7 above.

THRESHING INSTRUMENTS,] as in v. 7 above.

TEACHETH,] as in 1 Sa. 14. 12; 16. 3.

17. BROKEN DOWN,] as in 6. 30, 31, 32.

18. TABOR,] as in Jos. 19. 22; Jud. 4. 6, 12, 14; 8. 18; 1 Sa. 10. 3; 1 Ch. 6. 77; Ps. 89. 12; Jer. 46. 18; Hos. 5. 1.

FORM,] as in 1 Sa. 16. 18, &c.

19. SONS OF MY MOTHER,] as in Ge. 27. 29; Ps. 69. 8; Song 1. 6, &c.

I HAD NOT SLAIN YOU,] which he had resolved upon.

20. JETHER,] i.e. 'superabundance, remnant.'

21. FALL UPON US,] and put us to death thyself.

MIGHT] as a general principle.

ROUND ORNAMENTS,] as in v. 26; Isa. 3. 18.

22. RULE,] as in 9. 2, &c.; they had a longing to be like the nations.

SAVED,] as in 2. 18, &c.

JEHOVAH,] as your only king and lawgiver.

23. PETITION,] lit. 'an asking.'

RING,] as in Ge. 24. 22, 30, 47; 35. 4; Ex. 32. 2, 3; Jud. 8. 24, 25, 26; Job 42. 11; Prov. 11. 22; 25. 12; Isa. 3. 21; Eze. 16. 12; Hos. 2. 13.

ISHMAELITES,] as in Ge. 37. 25, 27, 28; 39. 1; 1 Ch. 2. 17; 27. 30; Ps. 83. 6.

24. THE GARMENT,] as in 1 Sa. 21. 9.

25. OAST,] as in 9. 53, &c.

26. 1700] shekels, or about £2385 sterling, according to Gill.

ROUND ORNAMENTS,] as in v. 21; Isa. 3. 18.

DROPS,] as in Isa. 3. 19.

PURPLE,] as in Ex. 25. 4; 26. 1, 31, 36, &c.

CHAINS,] as in Prov. 1. 9; Song 4. 29.

27. EPHOD,] as in Ex. 25. 7; 28. 4, 6, 12, 15, 26, 27, 28, 31, &c.

OPHRAH,] as in Jos. 18. 23, &c.

GO A-WHORING,] i. e. forsake Jehovah, and worship before the ephod.

SNARE] inasmuch as it led them and others into sin.

28. HUMBLED,] as in Jud. 3. 30; by reason of Gideon's victory.

LIFT UP THEIR HEAD,] i.e. to exalt themselves at the expence of Israel.

RESTETH] from war, as in Jos. 11. 23; 14. 15.

29. JERUBBAAL,] as in 6. 32; 7. 1.
30. SEVENTY SONS,] as in 9. 2, 5.
LOIN,] as in Ge. 46. 26; Ex. 1. 5.
MANY WIVES,] contrary to Ge. 2. 24; Lev.
18. 18; in these troublous times every one
did very much what was right in his own
eyes; at the same time he may have had
them only in succession.
31. CONCUBINE,] as in Ge. 22. 24, &c.
SHECHEM,] a city in Ephraim, now called
Nablous.
APPOINTETH,] as in Da. 1. 7.
ABIMELECH,] i. e. 'my father is king, or
father of a king,' as in Ge. 20. 2.
32. DIETH,] according to the lot of all
men, Ge. 3. 19; Zech. 1. 5.
OLD AGE,] as in Ge. 15. 15; 25. 8; 1 Ch.
29. 28.
BURYING-PLACE,] as in 16. 31.
33. DEAD,] as in 2. 19.
BAALIM,] or 'lords,' as in 2. 11, 13.
BAAL-BERITH,] i.e. 'lord of a covenant,'
as in 9. 5.
34. REMEMBERED] his love or his hatred
against idolatry.
IS DELIVERING] from time to time.
35. DONE KINDNESS,] as in 1. 24, &c.
ISRAEL,] delivering them from the fear
and tyranny of their oppressors, and giving
them peace for forty years.

IX. 1. ABIMELECH,] as in 8. 31.
SHECHEM,] his mother's city, as in 8. 31
above.
2. MASTERS,] as in Nu. 21. 28; Jos. 24. 11;
Jud. 9. 2, 6, 7, 18, 20, 23, 24, 25, 26, 39, 46,
47, 51, &c.
RULING] which their and his father had
distinctly refused to do, as in 8. 23.
BONE..FLESH,] as in Ge. 2. 23; 29. 14; 2
Sa. 5. 1; 19. 12, 13; 1 Ch. 11. 1, &c.
3. MASTERS,] as in v. 2.
INCLINETH AFTER,] as in Ps. 119. 112; 1
K. 2. 28: 1 Sa. 8. 2.
BROTHER,] his mother being an inhabitant
of their city.
4. BAAL-BERITH,] as in 8. 33, the name of
their special deity.
HIRETH,] as in Neh. 13. 2.
VAIN,] as in 11. 3; 2 Sa. 6. 20; 2 Ch. 13.
7; Prov. 12. 11; 28. 19.
UNSTABLE,] as in Zeph. 4. 3; Ge. 49. 4; Jer.
23. 32.
5. SEVENTY MEN,] as in 8. 29.
ONE STONE,] which seems to imply that
they were treated as a sacrifice to Baal-
Berith, with whose money the bloody deed
was done.
JOTHAM,] i.e. 'Jah is perfect.'
LEFT,] as in 8. 10; 21. 7, 16.
WAS HIDDEN,] as in 1 Sa. 10. 22, &c.
6. MASTERS,] as in v. 3. 7.
MILLO,] i.e. 'fulness,' as in v. 20; different
from that in 2 Sa. 5. 9; 1 K. 9. 15, 24; 11.
27; 1 Ch. 11. 8; 2 Ch. 32. 5.
KING,] without apparently asking counsel
from God or Israel.
OAK,] as in Ge. 12 6; 13. 18; 14. 13; 18. 1;
De. 11. 30; Jud. 4. 11; 9, 6, 37; 1 Sa. 10. 3.
CAMP,] as in Isa. 29. 3; 1 Sa. 13. 23, &c.
7. GERIZIM,] whence the blessings had

been pronounced on Israel, as in De. 11.
29, &c.
8. TREES.] This is perhaps the oldest
specimen on record of parabolic instruction,
700 years before Æsop.
OLIVE,] with which the land abounded,
and greatly prized, as in De. 8. 8; Ps. 52. 8;
128. 3; Jer. 11. 16; Hos. 14. 6, &c.
REIGN] thou as a king over us.
9. CEASED,] as in 5. 6, 7; 9. 11, 13, &c.
FATNESS,] as in Job. 36. 16; Ps. 36. 8; 63.
5; 65. 11; Isa. 55. 2; Jer. 31. 14.
HONOUR,] by offering it in sacrifice, and
by consuming it.
GODS,] those who are regarded as deities,
and upon whose altars olive oil was poured
out.
STAGGER,] as in Isa. 29. 9; Ps. 107. 27.
10. FIGS,] as in Ge. 3. 7; Nu. 13. 23; 20. 5;
De. 8. 8; 1 K. 4. 25; 2 K. 18. 32; 20. 7; Neh.
13. 15, &c.
11. SWEETNESS,] as in Prov. 16. 21; 27. 9.
INCREASE,] as in De. 32. 13, &c.
STAGGER,] as in v. 9 above.
12. VINE,] as in Ge. 40. 9, 10; 49. 11.
13. NEW WINE,] as in Ge. 27. 28, 37, &c.
REJOICING,] as in Ps. 19. 8.
GODS,] as in v. 9 above.
STAGGER,] as in v. 9, 11 above.
14. BRAMBLE,] as in Ps. 58. 9, where it is
spoken of as being used for fuel only, while
olive, fig, and vine-trees were fruit-bearing.
15. TAKE REFUGE,] as in Isa. 30. 2.
SHADOW,] or 'shade.'
LEBANON,] which were great and power-
ful.
16. SINCERITY,] as in Jos. 24. 14; v. 19
below.
KING,] without consulting the tribes of
Israel, or their Divine King.
JERUBBAAL,] his father and their deliverer
from Midian, &c.
HOUSE] or household, especially his
seventy sons and Jotham.
DEED,] as in Prov. 12. 14; Isa. 3. 11.
17. FOUGHT] and conquered for you.
CAST AWAY,] as if it were a worthless
thing.
DELIVER,] by the help of God, as in 6. 12,
34, 36; 7. 7, 14, 15.
18. ONE STONE,] as in v. 5 above.
HANDMAID,] as in Ge. 21. 21, &c.
MASTERS OF SHECHEM,] but not recognized by the rest of Israel.
BROTHER,] as they had said in v. 3
above.
19. REJOICE,] as in De. 12. 7, &c.
20. FIRE COMETH OUT,] to consume each
other.
21. HASTETH,] as in Isa. 30. 16; lit. 'fleeth,'
as in v. 40 below.
FLEETH,] as in 11. 3, &c.
BEER,] supposed to be the same as
'Baalath-Beer,' in the tribe of Simeon, in
Jos. 19. 8; different from that in Nu. 21. 16
—18; Isa. 15. 8.
22. IS PRINCE,] as in Hos. 12. 4.
23. EVIL SPIRIT,] as in 1 Sa. 16. 14, 15, 16,
23; 18. 10; 19. 9.
DEAL TREACHEROUSLY,] as in Ex. 21.
8, &c.

24. VIOLENCE,] as in Ge. 6. 11, 13; 16. 5; 49. 5, &c.

PLACE IT ON,] as in Nu. 11. 11, &c.

SLEW THEM,] as in v. 5, without cause.

STRENGTHENED HIS HANDS,] by giving him the 70 shekels to hire murderers.

25. AMBUSHES,] as in 2 Ch. 20. 22.

HILLS,] which were Ebal and Gerizzim.

ROB,] shewing their disregard to his government and authority.

26. GAAL,] i.e. 'a loathing,' as in 28. 30.

EBED,] i.e. 'a servant,' as in v. 28.

PASS OVER,] probably the Jordan.

TRUST] in him as their deliverer from the power of Abimelech.

27. FIELD] around their city.

VINEYARDS,] at the proper time, as usual.

TREAD] the grapes in the wine-press.

MAKE PRAISES,] as in Lev. 19. 24.

GOD,] Baal-Berith, as in v. 4.

REVILE,] or 'disesteem,' as in Ge. 8. 21; 12. 3, &c.

28. SHECHEM,] i.e. a 'shoulder,' probably a youthful prince under the influence of Abimelech.

ZEBUL,] i.e. a 'habitation.'

COMMANDER,] overseer, or bishop, as in Ge. 41. 34, &c.

HAMOR,] i.e. 'an ass.'

29. OH THAT,] not 'would to God,' as in the C.V.

HAND,] or power.

TURN ASIDE,] or depose him from his rule over Israel.

INCREASE,] lit. 'make great.'

30. PRINCES,] or 'head,' as in Ge. 12. 15, &c.

BURNETH] at the audacity of the conspirators.

31. DECEITFULLY,] as in Ps. 119. 118, &c., or 'in Tormah,' according to Kinchi and Gershom; supposed to be the same as Arumah in v. 41.

FORTIFYING,] lit. 'straitening,' as in 1 K. 15. 27; Est. 8. 11, &c.

32. FIELD] round the city.

33. PUSHED,] as in v. 44; 20. 37; 1 Sa. 23. 27; 27. 8, 10; 30. 1, 14; 2 Ch. 28. 18, &c.

GOING OUT,] to meet thee in battle.

FIND] convenient, and expedient.

34. DETACHMENTS,] as in 7. 16, &c.

35. AMBUSH,] suggested in v. 32 by Zebul.

36. HILLS,] as in v. 25.

SHADOW,] as in Ge. 19. 8; Nu. 14. 9; 9. 15, &c.

37. HIGH PART,] as in Eze. 38, 12; this original word is not found elsewhere.

DETACHMENT,] that is, the third.

OAK,] as in Ge. 35. 8, &c.

MEONENIM,] i.e. 'observers of clouds;' not mentioned elsewhese.

38. MOUTH] speaking great things.

KICKED,] as in Lev. 26. 15, &c.

39. BEFORE,] i.e. at the head of them.

40. WOUNDED,] as in 16. 24, &c.

41. ARUMAH,] i.e. 'a high place,' perhaps the same as Rumah in 2 K. 23. 36; see also on v. 31 above.

42. FIELD] to perform their usual labours

DETACHMENTS,] as in v. 34.

44. PUSHED ON,] as in v. 33.

45. SLAIN] with the sword, sparing none.

BREAKETH DOWN] the walls and houses.

SALT,] to render it barren and unprofitable, and as a terror to others.

46. TOWER,] as in Ge. 11. 4, 5, &c.

HIGH PLACE,] as in v. 49; 1 Sa. 13. 6; lit. a 'place for crying out' war, compare Zeph. 1. 14; Isa. 42. 13.

BERITH,] as in 8. 33; and v. 4 above.

48. ZALMON,] i.e. a 'great shade,' thought to be the same as Salmon, in Ps. 68. 14.

THE GREAT AXE,] as in 1 Sa. 13. 20, 21; Ps. 74. 5; Jer. 46. 22.

BOUGH,] as in v. 49.

49. FIRE,] compare v. 20 above.

50. THEBEZ.] Etymology unknown; 2 Sa. 11. 21.

51. ROOF,] which was flat, as in most eastern towers and buildings.

52. OPENING,] that is, the open space before the gates.

A PIECE,] as in 1 Sa. 30. 12; 2 Sa. 11. 21; Job 41. 24; Song 4. 3; 6. 7.

A RIDER,] as in Ge. 11. 6; 2 Sa. 11. 21.

SKULL,] as in 2 K. 9. 35, &c.

54. BEARING HIS WEAPONS,] as in 1 Sa. 14. 1, 6, 7, 12, 13, 14, 17, &c.

A WOMAN,] as in 2 Sa. 11. 21.

PIERCED HIM THROUGH,] as in Nu. 25. 8; 1 Sa. 31. 4, &c.

55. HIS PLACE] of residence.

56. TURNETH BACK,] on himself.

CURSING,] or 'reviling,' as in Ge. 27. 12, 13, &c. ; see v. 20 above.

X. 1. SAVE ISRAEL,] from the hand of their enemies.

TOLA,] i.e. 'a worm.'

PUAH,] i.e. 'a mouth.'

DODO,] i.e. 'his beloved or his uncle.'

SHAMIR,] i.e. 'a thorn;' different from that in Jos. 15. 48, which was in Judah.

3. JAIR,] i.e. 'he enlightens.'

GILEADITE,] from beyond the Jordan.

4. ASS-COLTS,] as in Ge. 32. 15; 49. 11; Jud. 10. 4; 12. 14; Job 11. 12; Isa. 30. 6, 24; Zec. 9. 9.

HAVOTH,] i.e. 'villages,' as in Nu. 32. 41,&c.

5. KAMON,] i.e. 'abounding in stalks;' not mentioned elsewhere.

6. THE EVIL THING,] even idolatry.

BAALIM,] as in 2. 11, &c.

ASHTAROTH,] as in 2. 13, &c.

ARAM,] such as Belus, Saturn, Astarte, Dea Syria; see 2. 12.

ZIDON,] Ashtaroth, &c. ; 1 K. 11. 5, 33; Ps. 106. 36.

MOAB,] Baal-Peor, and Chemosh, Nu. 25. 2; 1 K. 11. 7.

BENE-AMMON,] Molech or Milcom, 1 K. 11. 5, 7.

PHILISTINES,] Dagon, Beelzebub, &c.

7. BURNETH,] as in 2. 14.

SELLETH,] as in 2. 14; 1 Sa. 12. 9, &c.

8. CRUSH,] as in Ex. 15. 6; this original word is not found elsewhere.

OPPRESS,] as in De. 28. 33, &c.

9. GREAT DISTRESS,] as in 2. 15, &c.

10. CRY,] because of their distress, for help, as the original word implies.

BAALIM,] as in v. 6 above.
11. EGYPTIANS,] see Ex. 14. 30.
AMORITE,] see Nu. 21. 21, 24, 25.
BENE-AMMON,] see 3. 12, 13.
PHILISTINES,] see 3. 31.
12. ZIDONIANS,] no mention occurs of it
elsewhere.
AMALEK,] see Ex. 17. 13 ; 3. 13; 6. 3.
MAON.] Sept. reads 'Midian.'
14. FIXED,] at your own good will and
pleasure.
15. SINNED,] in worshipping the creature
rather than the Creator.
EYES.] A very common Hebrew phrase.
16. TURN ASIDE,] from their houses and
households.
GODS OF THE STRANGER,] as in Ge. 35. 2.
GRIEVED,] *lit.* 'shortened,' as in 16. 16 ;
Nu. 21. 4 ; Job 21. 4, &c.
17. GILEAD,] beyond the Jordan.
MIZPEH,] as in 11. 11, 29; Ge. 31. 49.

XI. 1. JEPHTHAH,] i.e. 'he opens;' see
Heb. 11. 32.
HARLOT,] as in Ge. 34. 31; Jos. 2. 1; Jud.
16. 1, &c.
2. SONS,] after the birth of Jephthah.
ANOTHER,] not necessarily a 'strange'
woman, as in the C.V.
3. TOB,] i.e. 'good,' see 2 Sa. 10. 6.
VAIN MEN,] *lit.* 'empty,' as in 7. 16; 9.
4, &c.
4. BENE-AMMON.] as in 10. 17.
5. ELDERS,] or principal men of his native
district.
6. CAPTAIN,] as in Jos. 10. 24, &c.
7. HATED] me, without just cause, perverting justice.
CAST ME OUT,] as in v. 2 above.
DISTRESS,] *lit.* 'straitness, anguish,' because of the enemy.
8. TURNED BACK,] confessing their fault.
9. GIVEN THEM,] smitten before me in
battle.
FOR HEAD] of the nation of Israel, or at
least of his own city.
11. WORDS] or matters.
13. MY LAND] speaking as the chief ruler
and judge.
ARNON,] the river of that name unto
JABBOK] the brook, as in Nu. 21. 13, 24.
15. MOAB,] as in De. 2. 19.
BENE-AMMON,] being expressly forbidden
to do so by God.
16. RED SEA,] as in Nu. 33. 35.
KADESH,] as in Nu. 13. 26; 20. 1; De.
1. 46.
17. PASS OVER] into Canaan.
HEARKENED NOT,] being afraid of Israel.
MOAB,] compare De. 2. 29.
WILLING] to let them pass over through
his land to Canaan.
KADESH,] as noted in Nu. 20. 1.
18. WILDERNESS] of Paran.
EDOM..MOAB,] as in Nu. 21. 4—11; De.
1. 8.
ARNON] the river of that name. Nu. 21. 13.
BORDER] or territory of Moab.
19. SIHON,] as in Nu. 21. 2 ; De. 2. 26.
HESHBON.] which was part of the territory
in dispute]

MY PLACE] even Canaan.
20. TRUSTED,] fearing that it was only a
pretext for occupying his land.
JAHAZ,] as in Nu. 21. 13.
HAND,] that is, power.
SMITE] them so as to destroy them.
21. POSSESSETH] by right of conquest.
22. BORDER,] i.e. territory.
ARNON] on the south, to the river
JABBOK] on the north.
WILDERNESS] of Arabia to the river
JORDAN,] the western border of the
kingdom of Sihon.
23. DISPOSSESSED,] ascribing the praise not
to Israel but to Israel's God.
POSSESS IT] being covetous of it
24. CHEMOSH,] as in Nu. 21. 29.
CAUSETH.] It cannot be supposed that
Jephthah really believed this, but only that
he did not think it necessary to contro-
vert it.
WE DO POSSESS,] and nothing more.
25. BETTER] that is, more powerful and
able to subdue us.
BALAK,] Nu. 22. 2; Jos. 24. 9.
STRIVE,] in war with Israel in behalf of
Ammon; he strove with guile only for his
own ends.
26. THREE HUNDRED YEARS,] under eight
rulers and judges, from Joshua to Jephthah.
DELIVERED THEM] out of the (now pretended usurped) power of Israel; no claim
being made for restitution during that long
period showed that Ammon had no just
claim at all.
27. SINNED,] done any wrong against thee;
the war was thus unprovoked.
EVIL] in ravaging the land of Israel, and
proclaiming war.
THE JUDGE] of all the earth, as in Ge.
18. 25.
28. NOT HEARKENED,] trusting it may be
to his own superior force, for he does not
appear to have attempted a reply to the
arguments of Jephthah.
29. SPIRIT OF JEHOVAH,] as in 3. 10; 6.
34, &c.
MIZPEH] east of Jordan; different from
that in Jos. 15. 38.
AMMON] in their own land, as a judicious
warrior.
30. VOWETH A VOW,] as was often done
before undertaking any great matter.
31. THAT WHICH,] *or* 'he who,' as the
Hebrew language has no neuter gender.
IT HATH BEEN,] *or* 'he hath been.'
OR] *or* 'and.'
I HAVE OFFERED UP FOR IT,] as in Eze. 29.
3, 'I have made it (for) myself.
BURNT-OFFERING,] as in Ge. 8. 20, &c.
32. PASSETH OVER,] as in v. 29.
HAND,] as he had prayed in preceeding
verse.
33. AROER,] a city near the river Arnon,
De. 3. 12.
MINNETH,] a place famous for wheat, see
Eze. 27. 17.
MEADOW,] in *Heb.* Abel-Ceramin, whicl.
Eusebius says had even in his day good
vineyards.

HUMBLED,] as in 3. 30; 8. 28, &c.

34. MIZPEH,] as in v. 11.

TIMBRELS,] to welcome him back as a conqueror.

CHORUSES,] as in Ex. 15. 20; 32. 19, &c.

35. RENDETH,] as a common token of grief, Ge. 37. 34; Job 1. 20.

CAUSED TO BEND,] as in 2 Sa. 22. 40; Ps. 17. 13; 18. 39; 78. 31.

TROUBLING] me, by adding, however unwittingly, to his affliction.

OPENED,] as in v. 31 above.

TURN BACK] from my vow.

36. OPENED.] She had probably known of his vow, and here acknowledges it.

MOUTH,] without change of any kind.

VENGEANCE,] as in Nu. 31. 2, 3.

37. THIS THING,] thou hast vowed, or perhaps, the request which she was now about to make.

DESIST,] as in De. 9. 14; 1 Sa. 11. 3.

HILLS,] around Mizpeh.

VIRGINITY,] she being yet unmarried, the married life being in the east esteemed as the most honourable.

FRIENDS] or female companions, as in Song 1. 9, 15; 2. 2, 10, 13; 4. 1, 7; 5. 2; 6. 4.

39. VOWED,] as in v. 31 above.

KNEW NOT,] as in Ge. 19. 8, &c.

STATUTE,] as in Ge. 47. 26.

40. TIME TO TIME,] or more lit. 'from days to days.'

TO TALK TO] her, as in the margin of the C.V.; so Kimchi, Ben Melech, &c. The very common supposition that he made her a burnt-offering is without the slightest probability; human sacrifices are everywhere spoken of as an abomination in the Law; when in later times, the king of Moab, in utter despair, offered one, so great was the indignation against Israel, that they broke up the camp. The two months' interval allowed time for the Lord, the priests, the people, and Jephthah, to consider the matter dispassionately, and not one voice appears to have been raised against it. There can be no reasonable doubt but that she was set apart among the women who served the tabernacle. Had an unclean animal, such as a *dog*, come out to meet him, every one will see that to offer it would have been an *insult* to God, not an honour, and a vow more honoured in the breach than in the observance.

XII. 1. EPHRAIM,] as in 8. 1.

CALLED,] or 'cried,' as in 7. 23, 24; 10. 17.

NORTHWARD] to Mizpeh, where Jephthah was.

NOT CALLED.] See the exactly similar complaint made to Gideon in 8. 1.

FIRE,] their passion causing them to forget his great victory.

2. GREAT STRIFE,] well known to all men.

MY PEOPLE] that is, those of Gilead especially.

I CALL YOU,] so that their complaint was positively untrue.

NOT SAVED,] they were either unable or unwilling.

3. SAVIOUR,] paying no regard to the danger of the invasion.

PUT MY LIFE] in my hand, i.e. expose myself personally to danger.

PASS OVER,] as in 11. 29.

AGAINST ME,] with any just cause of offence.

4. GILEAD,] the Ephraimites having refused to hearken to his remonstrances.

FUGITIVES] from justice, escaping from their just punishment.

5. PASSAGES] or ferries across the river.

6. SHIBBOLETH,] i.e. ears (of corn.)

SIBBOLETH,] i.e. burdens.

NOT PREPARED,] or 'ready.'

RIGHT,] as in Ge. 1. 7; 42. 11, &c.

SLAUGHTER.] The word is appropriate to the putting to death of animals for food, as in Ex. 12. 21, &c.

CHIEFS,] not 'thousands,' as in the C.V.; compare Mic. 5. 2, &c.

7. DIETH] like all his predecessors.

GILEAD,] over which he has been head.

8. IBZAN,] i.e. 'tin.'

BETH-LEHEM,] his native city.

9. WITHOUT] to other tribes and perhaps to other nations.

11. ELON,] i.e. 'an oak.'

12. AIJALON,] a city different from that in 1. 35.

13. ABDON,] i.e. 'servile.'

HILLEL,] i.e. 'praising.'

PIRATHONITE,] being born in Pirathon, where he was also buried, as in v. 15.

14. GRANDSONS,] lit. 'sons of sons.

ASS-COLTS,] as in 10. 4, &c.

15. AMALEKITE,] so called probably because of some remarkable event happening to that nation there.

XIII. 1. THE EVIL THING,] even idolatry.

PHILISTINES,] dwelling on the coast of the great sea.

2. ZORAH,] as in Jos. 15. 33; 19. 41.

MANOAH,] i.e. 'rest.'

NOT BORNE] any children, either sons or daughters.

3. BARREN,] as in v. 2.

4. WINE,] as in 9. 21, 24, &c.

STRONG DRINK,] as in Lev. 10. 9, &c.

UNCLEAN THING,] as in Lev. 5. 2, &c.

5. RAZOR,] as in 16. 7; 1 Sa. 1. 11.

NAZARITE,] i.e. 'one separated,' as in Ge. 49. 26; Lev. 25. 5, 11; Nu. 6. 2, &c.

WOMB,] lit. 'belly.'

BEGIN TO SAVE,] but not complete their deliverance.

6. A MAN OF GOD,] i.e. a prophet.

MESSENGER OF GOD,] very solemn, impressive, and

VERY FEARFUL,] as in Joel 2. 11; Ge. 28. 17, &c.

7. PREGNANT,] as in Ge. 16. 11, &c.

WINE,] as in v. 4 above.

STRONG DRINK,] or sweet drink.

UNCLEAN THING,] forbidden by the law.

NAZARITE,] one separated to God, and his service.

WOMB] or 'belly.'

8. MAKETH ENTREATY,] as in Ge. 25. 21. &c

MY LORD,] as in Ge. 15. 2, 8, &c.

MAN OF GOD,] as in v. 6.
DIRECT,] as in Ge. 46. 28, &c.
9. HEARKENETH,] as in Ge. 30. 17, &c.
10. DECLARETH,] *lit.* 'setteth before.'
DURING THE DAY,] probably this second appearance was in the evening of the same day.
12. LET COME TO PASS,] rejoicing in the hope of a son and heir, who should also 'save' Israel.
CUSTOM,] as in Ge. 40. 13; there is no authority whatever for the strange rendering of the C.V.
WORK,] as in Ge. 5. 29, &c.
13. MESSENGER OF JEHOVAH,] as in v. 3.
TAKE HEED,] of disregarding in any way.
14. WINE-VINE,] as in Nu. 6. 4.
WINE,] as in v. 4, 7.
STRONG-DRINK,] as in v. 4, 7.
UNCLEAN THING,] as in v. 4, 7.
15. MESSENGER OF JEHOVAH,] as in v. 3, 13.
DETAIN,] as in 1 K. 18. 44.
BEFORE THEE,] not 'for thee,' as in C.V.
KID OF THE GOATS,] as in Ge. 27. 9, 16.
16. NOT EAT,] as in 1 Sa. 28. 23, &c.
TO JEHOVAH,] not to his messenger, turning his mind from the messenger to him who sent him.
18. THY NAME,] as in Ge. 32. 27; Ex. 3. 13.
HONOURED,] by gifts and respect.
MY NAME,] as in Ge. 32. 29.
WONDERFUL,] as in Ps. 139. 6; Isa. 9. 6.
19. THE KID OF THE GOATS,] as in v. 15.
THE PRESENT,] as in Nu. 15. 3, 4.
HE IS DOING WONDERFULLY,] i.e. Jehovah.
LOOKING ON,] *or* 'are seeing or beholding,' what is taking place.
20. FLAME,] which consumed the flesh.
GOETH UP,] out of their sight.
22. SEEN GOD,] as in Ge. 32. 30; Jud. 6. 22, 23; Ex. 33. 20.
23. DESIROUS,] as in 1 Sa. 2. 25; 2 Sa.15. 26.
RECEIVED,] acceptably, and sent fire to consume it.
THIS,] regarding the child and his work.
24. SAMSON,] i.e. 'a little sun *or* servant.'
BLESS HIM,] with bodily strength.
25. SPIRIT OF JEHOVAH,] as in 11. 29, &c.
MOVE,] as in Ge. 41. 8; Ps. 77. 4.
ZORAH,] as in v. 2 above.
ESHTAOL,] as in Jos. 15. 33; 19. 41.

XIV. 1. TIMNATH,] as in Jos. 15. 57; 19. 43.
2. TAKE,] *or* 'receive;' parents in the east are almost always those who contract marriages for the children.
3. MY PEOPLE,] the Danites, or the Israelites.
UNCIRCUMCISED,] as in Ge. 17. 14, &c.
RIGHT,] *or* 'upright.'
4. FROM JEHOVAH IT IS,] as in Jos. 11. 20; 1 K. 12. 15; 2 K. 6. 33; 2 Ch. 10. 15; 22. 7; 25. 30.
MEETING,] as in Jer. 2. 24.
RULING,] as the Ammonites had done before, in 10. 8.
5. VINEYARDS,] near the city and around it.
LION'S WHELP.] This original phrase does not occur elsewhere but it denotes a full-grown young lion.

ROARING,] as in Ps. 22. 13; 104. 21; Eze. 22. 25; Zeph. 3. 3.
6. SPIRIT OF JEHOVAH,] as a spirit of might and valour.
PROSPERETH,] as in v. 9; 15. 14; 1 Sa. 10. 10; 11. 6; 16. 3; 18. 10; Nu. 14. 41, &c.
RENDETH,] as in Lev. 1. 17; 1 Sa. 24. 7.
NOT DECLARED,] thinking it of no importance.
7. IS RIGHT,] as in Nu. 23. 27, &c.
8. DAYS,] as in Ge. 24. 55, &c.
BODY,] as in Ge. 47. 18, &c.
9. TAKETH DOWN,] *lit.* 'causeth to descend.'
BODY,] as in v. 8.
10. BANQUET,] *lit.* a 'drinking,' as in Ge. 19. 3; 21. 8, &c.
11. TAKE,] not 'bring' as in the C.V.
12. I PRAY YOU,] not 'now,' as in the C.V.
RIDDLE,] as in Nu. 12. 8, &c.
SEVEN DAYS,] as in Ge. 29. 27, 28, &c.
LINEN SHIRTS,] as in v. 13; Prov. 31. 24; Isa. 3. 23.
13. LINEN SHIRTS,] as in v. 12.
CHANGES OF GARMENTS,] as in Ge. 45. 22, &c.
14 EATER,] i.e. he who consumes and destroys, especially the young lion, as explained in v. 18 below.
FOOD,] that others may be fed.
STRONG,] as in v. 18, &c.
SWEETNESS,] as in Ps. 19. 10; Prov. 16. 24; 24. 13; 27. 7; Ecc. 5. 12; 11. 7; Song 2 3; Isa. 5. 20; Eze. 3. 3.
DECLARE,] *lit.* 'set before.'
15. ENTICE,] as in 16. 5, &c.
HUSBAND,] being betrothed.
TO POSSESS US,] i.e. all that we have.
16. FOR IT,] not ' before him,' as in the C.V.; so in v. 17.
THE RIDDLE,] as in v. 12 above.
SONS OF MY PEOPLE,] as in Ge. 23. 11, &c.
17. DISTRESSED,] as in 16. 16, &c.
18. GOETH IN,] which closes the day, according to Hebrew calculations.
HONEY,] as in Ps. 19. 10; 119. 103; Prov. 16. 24; Eze. 3. 3, &c.
LION,] as in 2 Sa. 1. 23; 17. 10; 1 Ch. 12. 8; Prov. 30. 30, &c.
PLOUGHED,] i.e. turned up the ground under which the prize was concealed.
HEIFER,] *or* 'young calf,' meaning with the aid of his betrothed wife.
19. SPIRIT OF JEHOVAH,] as in v. 6 above.
PROSPERETH,] as in v. 6 above.
ASHKELON,] a city of the Philistines.
SMITETH,] not necessarily 'killing' them.
ARMOUR,] as in 2 Sa. 2. 21.
CHANGES,] as in v. 13 above.
BURNETH,] against his betrothed wife and his companions, for their trick.
FATHER,] in Zorah, as in 13. 2.
20. WIFE,] who had been betrothed to him.
COMPANION'S,] some special one of the 30, whose name is not mentioned.
FRIEND,] during the seven days' feast.

XV. 1. DAYS,] as in 14. 8.
WHEAT-HARVEST,] which began at Pentecost.
LOOKETH AFTER,] as the word always

mplies; his anger had abated, and he wished to fulfil his engagement.

KID OF THE GOATS,] as a present to her.

INNER CHAMBER,] where she was abiding, and where only the members of the family were allowed to enter.

PERMITTED,] *lit.* 'given.'

2. HATE,] or at least, think of her lightly.

COMPANION,] as in 15. 20.

BETTER,] not necessarily 'fairer,' as in the C.V.

LET HER BE,] not 'take her,' as in the C.V.

3. INNOCENT,] and acquitted from blame.

THIS TIME,] than when he slew the 30 men at Ashkelon, noticed in 14. 19.

EVIL,] to their corn fields.

4. FOXES,] as in Neh. 4. 3; Ps. 63. 10; Song 2. 15; La. 5. 18; Eze. 13. 4.

TORCHES,] as in 7. 16, 20.

5. SENDETH FORTH,] bound two by two, that in their eager attempts to escape, their struggling might lead them to different parts of the field.

STANDING CORN,] as in Ex. 22. 6, &c.

HEAP,] *or* stack, as in Ex. 22. 6; Job 5. 26.

6. THEY SAY,] that is, some who had observed the action of Samson.

TIMNITE,] as in 14. 2, 5.

GO UP,] to Timnath.

FIRE,] so that, after all, she suffered the fate she had tried to avoid in 14. 15.

7. I CEASE,] for a little, till another suitable opportunity occurs.

8. HIP AND THIGH.] This phrase does not occur elsewhere.

SMITING,] not 'slaughter.'

CLIFT,] as in v. 11 ; Isa. 2. 21; 57. 5, &c.

ETAM,] i.e. 'ravenous birds,' near a city of the same name in 1 Ch. 4. 3, 32 ; 2 Ch. 11. 8.

9. GO UP,] from the borders of the great sea to the hill-country of Judah, and they

ARE SPREAD OUT,] watching and occupying the land, in the place afterwards called LEHI,] i.e. a 'jaw-bone,' from the circumstance to be mentioned.

10. BIND,] as a prisoner and criminal.

11. GO DOWN,] to the lower part of the country, where the rock Etam was.

CLIFT,] as in v. 8.

RULERS,] as in 14. 4, &c.

TO US,] bringing up a host of invaders on the land.

12. LEST] they should be tempted to put him to death themselves, with the view of avenging the Philistines.

13. THICK CORDS,] as in v. 14 ; 16. 11, 12, &c.

14. LEHI,] where the Philistines were, as in v. 9 above.

AT MEETING HIM.] 'Against him,' as in the C.V., is an old phrase, now conveying quite a different idea.

SPIRIT OF JEHOVAH,] as in 14. 19, &c.

THICK BANDS,] as in v. 13.

BANDS,] as in Ecc. 7. 26; Jer. 37. 15.

WASTED,] *or* 'melted,' as in Ex. 16. 21, &c.

15. FRESH.] This original word is only found elsewhere in Isa. 1. 6.

JAW-BONE,] as in De. 18. 3 ; 1 K. 22. 24, &c

SMITETH,] not necessarily 'slew' as in C.V.; so in v. 16.

1,000 MEN.] Compare 3. 31; 1 Ch. 11. 11, for similar deeds of valour.

16. ASS..ASSES.] An evident play on the word 'ass,' which was now beginning to be despised.

17. RAMOTH-LEHI,] i.e. 'the high place of the jaw-bone.'

18. SALVATION] to the land of Judah, which had been overrun by the

UNCIRCUMCISED] Philistines, who were not within the covenant of circumcision.

19. CLEAVETH,] as in Isa. 48. 21 ; Ecc. 10. 9, &c.

HOLLOW PLACE.] This original word is only found elsewhere in Prov. 27. 22.

LEHI,] not in the 'jaw-bone,' as in the C.V.

CALLING,] upon God in prayer, because of distress.

XVI. 1. GAZA,] one of the cities of the Philistines.

HARLOT.] The Targum reads an 'innkeeper,' as in Jos. 2. 1.

UNTO HER,] to lodge or abide.

2. GAZATHITES,] or inhabitants of Gaza.

GO ROUND] the walls of the house and city.

KEEP THEMSELVES SILENT,] *lit.* 'deaf.'

TILL] then, keep ye silent and watch for him.

3. LAYETH HOLD ON,] with all his might.

SIDE POSTS,] as in Ex. 12. 7, 22, 23, &c.

REMOVETH,] *lit.* 'causeth to journey.'

BAR] of iron, with which the leaves of the gate were fastened.

HEBRON,] but not necessarily near it.

4. SOREK,] i.e. 'a hisser;' not mentioned elsewhere.

DELILAH,] i.e. 'lean, poor, weak.'

5. PRINCES,] as in v. 8, 18, 23, of whom there were five, as in 3. 3.

ENTICE HIM,] as in 14. 15.

IN WHAT,] not 'by what means,' as in the C.V.

1,100 SILVERLINGS,] about £700 sterling.

7. GREEN WITHS,] *or* 'fresh cords,' as in v. 8, 9; Job 30. 11; Ps. 11. 2, but the former is preferable.

ONE OF THE HUMAN RACE,] as in v. 11, 17.

8. AMBUSH,] as in v. 12.

PHILISTINES,] not 'the Philistines;' so in v. 12, 14.

SMELLING,] as in Ge. 8. 21; 27. 27; Ex. 30. 38, &c.

10. PLAYED UPON ME,] as in v. 13, 15.

11. THICK BANDS,] as in v. 12.

13. WEAVEST,] as in Isa. 59. 5.

LOCKS,] *or* 'plaitings' of hair.

WEB,] *or* 'molten image,' as Gesenius suggests ; so in v. 14.

14. A PIN,] as in 4. 21, 22, &c.

WEAVING MACHINE,] as in Job 7. 6.

16. DISTRESSED,] as in 14. 17.

GRIEVED,] *lit.* 'shortened.'

17. RAZOR,] as in 13. 5, &c.

NAZARITE,] as in Nu. 6. 2, &c.

TURNED ASIDE,] as in v. 19.

18. ALL HIS HEART,] as in v. 17

THIS TIME,] as in v. 28.

THE MONEY,] *lit.* 'silver,' promised in v. 5

20. TIME BY TIME,] as in Nu. 24. 1; Jud 20. 30, 31 ; 1 Sa. 20. 25.

TURNED ASIDE,] because of his broken vows.
21. PICK OUT,] as in Nu. 16. 14; 1 Sa. 11. 2; Job 30. 17; Prov. 30. 17; Isa. 51. 1.
GAZA,] as in v. 1 above.
22. SHOOT UP,] as in Lev. 13. 37; 2 Sa. 10. 5; 1 Ch. 19. 5; Eze. 16. 7.
23. PRINCES,] as in v. 5 above.
DAGON,] i.e. 'a little fish,' the lower part of the image being that of a fish, and the upper part that of a man, see 1 Sa. 5. 2, 3, 4, 5, 7; 1 Ch. 10. 10.
24. LAYING WASTE,] as in Isa. 49. 17; 51. 10.
WOUNDED,] as in 9. 40, &c.
25. PLAY,] as in 2 Sa. 2. 14, &c., exhibiting his strength.
PILLARS,] as in v. 26.
26. ESTABLISHED,] as in v. 29.
27. PRINCES,] as in v. 5, 18,
29. TURNETH ASIDE,] as in Ruth 3. 8; Job 6. 18.
INCLINETH HIMSELF,] backward.
31. LIFT HIM UP,] out of the ruins of the place, no one venturing to interfere.

XVII. 1. MICAH,] i.e. who is like Jah?'
2. 1,100 SILVERLINGS,] which seem to have made 'a bag,' as in 16. 5.
TAKEN OF THINE,] not 'from thee,' as in C.V.
SWORN,] as in Hos. 4. 2; 10. 4.
BLESSED IS,] not 'blessed be,' as in C.V.
3. SET APART,] as in Ge. 2. 3, &c.
GRAVEN..MOLTEN,] both of which had been expressly forbidden in the law.
4. A REFINER,] as in Isa. 40. 19; 41. 7; 46. 6, &c.
5. HOUSE OF GODS,] or perhaps simply 'a house of God;' a place for worship.
EPHOD,] in imitation of Aaron's.
TERAPHIM,] as in Ge. 31. 19, 30; Hos. 3. 4, &c.
FILLETH THE HAND,] as in Ex. 28. 41, &c.
6. NO KING,] or general civil magistrate, whose authority was recognised; otherwise this idolatry might have been prevented.
OWN EYES,] without fear of punishment.
7. BETH-LEHEM,] in Judah, different from that in Jos. 19. 15, which was in Zebulun.
8. TO WORK HIS WAY,] or 'perform his calling,' i.e. act as teacher, &c.
10. FATHER..PRIEST,] that is, councillor and intercessor
TEN SILVERLINGS,] almost twenty-five shillings.
SUIT,] lit. 'arrangement or array.'
SUSTENANCE,] as in 6. 4, &c.
11. IS WILLING,] as in 1. 27, 35, &c.
12. CONSECRATETH,] lit. 'filleth.'
13. THE LEVITE,] as one of the sacred tribe.

XVIII. 1. NO KING,] as in 17. 6.
DANITE,] at least certain families of the tribe.
THAT DAY,] when the following circumstances took place.
2. OF THEM,] lit. 'from their extremity,' as in Ge. 47. 2.
SONS OF VALOUR,] or 'sons of worth.'
ZORAH..ESHTAOL,] as in 13. 25.

TRAVERSE,] or 'spy,' as in v. 14, 17.
3. WITH THE HOUSEHOLD,] not 'by the house' merely as in the C.V.; compare preceding clause.
DISCERNED,] as in 1 Sa. 26. 17, &c.
TURN ASIDE,] to where he was engaged probably in reading or teaching.
4. HIRETH,] as in 17. 10.
5. ASK,] or enquire, in our behalf.
6. OVER-AGAINST,] as in Prov. 5. 21; La. 2. 19.
7. LAISH,] called 'Leshem,' in Jos. 19. 47; afterwards 'Caesarea Philippi.'
CONFIDENTLY,] without distrust of any kind.
ZIDONIANS,] of whom they were probably a colony.
CONFIDENT,] in their remote position.
POSSESSING RESTRAINT,] over the populace.
WORD,] or matter, or communication.
8. WHAT—YE!] surprised at their return so speedily.
YE ARE KEEPING SILENT,] as in 1 K. 22. 3; 2 K. 7. 9; Neh. 8. 11; Isa. 57. 11.
10. CONFIDENT,] as in v. 7.
ON BOTH HANDS,] as in 1 Ch. 4. 40.
11. GUIDED,] as in Ex. 12. 11, &c.
12. KIRJATH-JEARIM,] see Jos. 15. 9, 60.
14. TRAVERSE,] as in v. 2, 17.
EPHOD,] as in 17. 5.
TERAPHIM,] as in 17. 5.
GRAVEN IMAGE,] as in 17. 4.
MOLTEN IMAGE,] as in 17. 4.
15. TURN ASIDE,] as in v. 3 above.
ASK HIM OF WELFARE,] their own and his
16. GIRDED,] as in v. 11.
18. GRAVEN IMAGE,] as in v. 14, not 'carved,' as in the C.V.
19. KEEP SILENT,] or 'be deaf.
FATHER..PRIEST,] as in 17. 10.
20. INTO THE MIDST,] not 'in the midst; he sought concealment and safety.
21. INFANTS,] whom they had brought with them.
BAGGAGE,] not 'carriage,' which has now changed its meaning, lit. 'the heavy or weighty thing.'
22. CALLED,] lit. 'cried' or summoned.
23. HAST BEEN CALLED TOGETHER,] as in v. 22.
25. BITTER IN SOUL,] as in 1 Sa. 1. 10; 22. 2; 2 Sa. 17. 8; Job 3. 30; Prov. 31. 6, &c.
GATHERED,] as in 1 Sa. 15. 6, &c.
27. LAISH,] which they had spied before hand.
CONFIDENT] in their own strength.
28. DELIVER,] to rescue it from the Danites.
ZIDON,] which city probably had the nominal sovereignty of it.
WORD]matter or business, or even communication, as in v. 7.
BETH-REHOB] on the north, see Nu. 13. 21.
29. BORN,] as narrated in Ge. 30. 6.
30. GRAVEN IMAGE,] which they had carried off from Micah.
JONATHAN,] i.e. 'Jehovah hath given;' probably this was the name of the Levite.
GERSHOM,] i.e. 'a sojourner there,' as in Ex. 2. 22.

MANASSEH,] or, as some MSS. and Versions read, 'Moses.'
LAND,] or, as some MSS. read, 'of the ark,' as in 1 Sa. 4. 5.
31. APPOINT,] not 'set up,' as in the C.V.
SHILOH,] even till it was removed to Nob.

XIX. 1. NO KING,] as in 17. 16; 18. 1.
CONCUBINE,] or secondary wife, as in Ge. 25. 1—6, &c.
BETH-LEHEM,] called of 'Judah,' to distinguish it from the place of the same name in Zebulun.
2. COMMIT WHOREDOM,] as in 8. 27, 33.
DAYS,] that is, a certain number, even four months.
3. UNTO HER HEART,] as in Ge. 34. 3, &c.
YOUNG MAN,] as in v. 19.
COUPLE OF ASSES,] one for himself and one for her.
REJOICETH,] in the hope of the reconciliation of his daughter with her husband.
5. SUPPORT,] as in Ge. 18. 5, &c.
MORSEL,] as in Ge. 18. 5; 1 Sa. 2. 36; 28. 22; 1 K. 17. 11; Prov. 28. 21.
6. BE WILLING,] as in 2 Sa. 7. 29; 2 K. 5. 23; 6. 3; Job 6. 28.
8. SUPPORT,] as in v. 5.
TURNING OF THE DAY,] as in 2 K. 20. 10; Ps. 109. 23.
9. HATH FALLEN,] as in 8. 3.
THE ENCAMPING,] as in Nu. 1. 51; 10. 31; De. 1. 33.
GONE TO THY TENT,] as in 7. 8; 20. 8.
10. NOT BEEN WILLING,] as in v. 25.
JEBUS,] as in 1 Ch. 11. 4, 5.
SADDLED,] as in 2 Sa. 16. 1.
11. GONE GREATLY DOWN,] or 'been greatly subdued,' as in Ps. 144. 2; Isa. 45. 1.
12. TURN ASIDE,] lest they should be defiled by contact with its inhabitants.
GIBEAH,] a Levitical city, as in Jos. 21. 17, &c.
13. RAMAH,] as in Jos. 18. 25.
14. BENJAMIN,] and therefore different from that in Jos. 15. 57, which belonged to Judah.
15. BROAD PLACE,] as in Ge. 19. 2.
GATHERING,] as in Nu. 10. 25; Jos. 6. 9, 13, &c.
17. TRAVELLER,] as in 2 Sa. 12. 4; Jer. 14. 8, &c.
BROAD PLACE,] as in v. 15, where travellers often encamped.
18. HOUSE OF JEHOVAH,] in Shiloh, where the ark now was abiding.
GATHERING ME,] as in v. 15, i.e. inviting me to the shelter of his roof.
19. STRAW..PROVENDER,] as in Ge. 24. 25, 32, &c.
BREAD..WINE,] as in Ge. 14. 8, &c.
HANDMAID,] his concubine, who was with him.
YOUNG MAN,] who was acting as servant.
20. PEACE,] the usual eastern salutation.
LODGE NOT,] because of the cold, and of the people.
21. MIXETH,] as in Ge. 11. 7, 9, &c.
FEET,] which being protected only by sandals, were exposed to the dust in travelling.

22. MAKING GLAD,] lit. 'good.'
SONS OF WORTHLESSNESS,] i.e. worthless persons.
KNOW,] as in Ge. 19. 5, &c.
23. DO NOT EVIL,] to these guests.
MY HOUSE,] and was therefore under his special protection.
FOLLY,] as in Ge. 34. 7; De. 22. 21; Jos. 7. 15, &c.
24. THE VIRGIN,] as in Ge. 24. 16, &c.
HUMBLE,] as in Ge. 34. 2, &c.
FOOLISH THING,] as in v. 23.
25. THE MAN,] apparently the Levite himself, not the master of the house.
KNOW,] as in v. 22.
ROLL THEMSELVES,] as in Nu. 22. 29, &c.
ASCENDING OF THE DAWN,] as in Ge. 32. 24, &c.
SEND HER AWAY,] from some house whither they had taken her, back to her husband.
26. TURNING OF THE MORNING,] as in Ex. 14. 27, &c.
27. TO GO ON] to his own dwelling, glad to escape with his life, intending to leave her behind.
THRESHOLD,] as in 1 K. 14. 17; 2 K. 12. 9; 22. 4; 23. 4; 25. 18; 1 Ch. 9. 19, 22, &c.
28. NONE ANSWERING,] as in 1 K. 18. 26, 29; Isa. 50. 2; 66. 4, &c.
HIS PLACE,] even Shechem.
29. THE KNIFE,] as in Ge. 22. 6, 10; Prov. 30. 14.
OUTTETH IN PIECES,] as in 20. 6; 1 Sa. 11. 7.
BORDER,] or 'territory.'
30. NOT BEEN..NOT BEEN SEEN,] in Israel at least.
SET,] as in Ex. 9. 21, &c.
TAKE COUNSEL,] as in Isa. 8. 10.
SPEAK] out boldly your opinion of it.

XX. 1. GO OUT,] of their own dwellings.
THE COMPANY] of the sons of Israel.
DAN..BEER-SHEBA,] the two extremities of the land, north and south.
GILEAD] beyond the Jordan, eastward.
MIZPEH,] a place near Shiloh.
2. CHIEFS,] lit. 'corners,' as in 1 Sa. 14. 38; Isa. 19. 13; Zech. 10. 4.
STATION THEMSELVES,] as in Ex. 2. 4, &c.
DRAWING SWORD,] as in 8. 10, &c.
3. BENJAMIN,] who were implicated in the murder of the woman by neglecting to punish the murderers.
4. MURDERED,] as in 19. 28.
GIBEAH] on his way home to Shechem.
BENJAMIN,] as in 19. 14.
5. MASTERS,] as in Jos. 24. 11; Jud. 9. 2, 6, 7, 18, 20, 23, 24, 25, 26, 39, &c.
HUMBLED,] as in 19. 25.
6. CUT IN PIECES,] as in 19. 29.
INHERITANCE,] given by God to Israel.
WICKEDNESS,] as in Lev. 18. 17, &c.
FOLLY,] as in 19. 23, 24.
7. GIVE,] as in Ge. 29. 21, &c.
COUNSEL,] as in De. 32. 28, &c.
8. TENT..HOUSE,] or dwellings of any kind in the city or in the field.
9. BY LOT,] allowing the place of honour to whomsoever God might give it.
10. MYRIAD,] as in Ge. 24. 60.

RECEIVE PROVISION] from those remaining at home for those engaged in the war.
11. COMPANIONS,] as in Ps. 45. 7; 119. 63; Prov. 28. 24; Ecc. 4. 10; Song 1. 7; 8. 13; Isa. 1. 23; 44. 11; Eze. 37. 16, 19.
12. TRIBES,] or families; compare Jos. 7. 17.
EVIL,] as in v. 3.
13. SONS OF WORTHLESSNESS,] as in 19. 22.
PUT TO DEATH,] according to law and justice.
PUT AWAY,] lit. 'burn away.'
15. NUMBER THEMSELVES,] as in v. 17; 21. 9, &c.
DAY,] when they feared an attack.
DRAWING SWORD,] as in v. 2.
CHOICE,] not 'chosen;' as in Ex. 14. 7, &c.
16. BOUND,] lit. 'shut,' as in 3. 15.
SLINGING,] as in Jer. 10. 18, &c.
HAIR,] as in 1 Sa. 14. 45, &c.
ERR,] lit. 'sin,' by missing the mark.
17. NUMBERED THEMSELVES,] as in v. 15.
DRAWING SWORD,] as in v. 2, 15.
MAN OF WAR,] as in Jos. 17. 1, &c.
18. GO UP] from Mizpeh to Beth-El.
ASK OF GOD,] by means of the priest, or by Urim and Thummim, as in Nu. 27. 21.
FOR US,] not 'of us,' as in the C.V.
JUDAH,] as in 1. 2, &c.
19. ENCAMP] with a force of 360,000 men, see v. 10.
21. DESTROY,] as in v. 25, 35; this defeat happened probably to shew their entire dependence on God; their own hands also were not clean.
22. STRENGTHEN THEMSELVES,] as in Ge. 48. 2; 1 Sa. 30. 6, &c
23. WEEP BEFORE JEHOVAH] in Shiloh, as again in v. 26.
ASK OF JEHOVAH] counsel as to continuing the war.
DRAW NIGH,] not 'go up,' as in the C.V.
MY BROTHER,] as in v. 28; they were beginning to relent somewhat.
25. TO MEET THEM,] in battle hostilely.
DESTROY,] as in v. 21 above, and for the same reason.
DRAWING SWORD,] as in v. 17.
26. BETH-EL,] where the ark of God was.
SIT] in prayer, as David did in 1 Ch. 17. 16; here we have a congregation, there an individual, worshipping God in a sitting posture; the mode is nothing, if the spirit be right.
FAST,] restraining the body to exercise the soul.
27. ASK OF JEHOVAH,] as in v. 23.
ARK,] which Moses had made by the command of God, by the hands of Bezaleel.
28. PHINEHAS.] As he died some time after Joshua, the events now recorded must have happened about the time of Othniel, 3. 9.
MY BROTHER,] as in v. 23.
CEASE, as in 1 K. 22. 6, 15.
29. LIERS IN WAIT,] or ambushes.
30. TIME BY TIME,] as in v. 31.
31. TO MEET,] as in v. 25.
WOUNDED,] lit. 'pierced.'
BETH-EL,] as in v. 26.
32. BEGINNING,] noticed in v. 21

33. BAAL-TAMAR,] i.e. 'possessing palms; not mentioned elsewhere.
AMBUSH,] mentioned in v. 29.
MEADOW,] lit. 'a naked place,' or perhaps 'cave,' as in 1 Sa. 13. 6.
34. GRIEVOUS,] lit. 'heavy.'
THE EVIL,] as in v. 41.
STRIKING,] as in v. 41.
35. IN BENJAMIN,] i.e. among them.
DRAWING SWORD,] as in v. 17.
36. AMBUSH,] as in v. 37.
AGAINST,] not 'beside,' as in the C.V.
37. PUSH,] as in 9. 33, 44, &c.
DRAWETH ITSELF OUT,] from the place of concealment.
38. THE APPOINTED SIGN,] the burning of the city.
VOLUME,] lit. 'burden.'
39. TURN] from their retreat before Benjamin.
THE WOUNDED,] or 'pierced.'
THIRTY MEN,] as in v. 31.
40. VOLUME,] noticed in v. 38.
PERFECTION,] i.e. the best part, not the 'whole' of it, nor the 'flame,' as in the C.V.
41. TROUBLED,] as in Ge. 45. 3, &c.
42. WILDERNESS] of Judah.
44. MEN OF VALOUR,] or strength or worth.
WILDERNESS,] as in v. 42.
RIMMON,] i.e. 'pomegranate,' as in 1 Sa. 14. 2.
GLEAN,] i.e. gather up here and there a few.
FOLLOW AFTER] the fugitives of Benjamin.
GIDOM,] i.e. a 'cutting down.'
46. DRAWING SWORD,] as in v. 17.
MEN OF VALOUR,] strength or worth, as in v. 44.
47. CATTLE,] both one and the other, as the Hebrew phrase implies.
FOUND,] by the pursuers.
INTO FIRE,] as devoted things.

XXI. 1. SWORN] before the battle, in the heat of their anger.
2. BETH-EL,] as in 20. 18, &c.
SIT] in prayer, as in 20. 26.
A GREAT WEEPING,] as in 2 Sa. 13. 36; 2 K. 20. 3; Isa. 38. 3.
3. FROM ISRAEL,] which had consisted of twelve tribes.
ALTAR,] in addition to the one already there, and probably because of the number of sacrifices, as in 1 K. 8. 64.
5. THE GREAT OATH,] as in v. 18.
6. REPENT,] as in v. 15.
7. WIVES,] that the tribe might not perish.
8. JABESH-GILEAD,] beyond the Jordan, eastward.
9. NUMBER THEMSELVES,] as in 20. 15, 17.
10. SONS OF VALOUR,] strength or worth.
INFANTS,] the whole being devoted.
11. LYING OF A MALE,] as in Nu. 31. 18.
DEVOTE] to destruction.
12. VIRGINS,] as in Ge. 24. 16.
CANAAN] west of Jordan.
13. PROCLAIM] publicly that all might know.

14. THE WOMEN,] who were virgins.
NOT FOUND] women as wives for the whole 600.
15. BREACH] by destroying one of the tribes.
16. REMNANT,] the two hundred.
17. POSSESSION,] as in Jos. 12. 6, 7.
ESCAPED PARTY,] as in Ex. 10. 5.
BLOTTED OUT,] as in Ge. 6. 7.
18. SWORN,] as in v. 1.
19. FESTIVAL,] as in Ex. 10. 9.
FROM TIME TO TIME,] *lit.* from days to days.'
LEBONAH,] i.e. 'frankincense;' not mentioned elsewhere.
20. VINEYARDS,] around the city.
21. DANCES,] during the festival.
BENJAMIN,] where they had been originally.

22. PLEAD] for restitution of their daughters.
FAVOUR US,] as in Ps. 123. 3; Isa. 33. 2.
WE HAVE NOT TAKEN] in battle with Benjamin or with Jabesh Gilead.
NOT GIVEN] willingly in violation of the oath.
GUILTY] before God and the people.
23. TAKEN VIOLENTLY AWAY,] as recommended in v. 21.
BUILD,] or rebuild the cities which had been burned, as in 20 48.
24. GO UP AND DOWN,] to every part of the country.
INHERITANCE,] in the land of Canaan and beyond the Jordan.
25. NO KING,] as in 17. 6; 18. 1; 19. 1.
EYES,] as in De. 12. 8; Jud. 17. 6.

RUTH

THE BOOK OF RUTH, according to Eusebius, was originally appended to the book of Judges, in the Hebrew Sacred Writings, though it is now put after the Song of Songs in the printed Hebrew Bibles. Its author is unknown, but the common tradition that it was written by Samuel is probably not unfounded. It professedly narrates an episode that occurred in the 'days of the judging of the Judges,' but critics are divided as to the particular judge who then lived. Eli, Ibzan, Ehud, and Shamger, Deborah and Barak, Gideon, &c., have been suggested. It is of importance in shewing the genealogy of David to be derived from a heathen woman whose affection for her mother-in-law brought her into Israel, and prepared her for being an ancestor of the Messiah. It must have given the ancient Jewish Church an opportunity of observing how the Gentiles might gradually be brought into the field of the Shepherd of Israel. Its facts are referred to in Mat. 1. 5; Luke 3. 31. 33.

I. 1. THE JUDGING,] not 'ruling' as in the C. V.; the two offices are quite distinct; compare Jud. 2. 16.

FAMINE,] perhaps that referred to in Jud. 6. 3, 4, caused by the ravages of Midian.

LAND] of Canaan, which was generally a very fruitful country.

BETH-LEHEM JUDAH,] so named to distinguish it from a Beth-Lehem in Zebulun, Jos. 19. 15; Jud. 17. 8.

SOJOURN,] for a time only, and then to return.

FIELDS,] i. e. level cultivated ground of the Moabites.

2. ELIMELECH,] i.e. 'my God is king.'

NAOMI,] i.e. 'my pleasant one,' as in v. 20.

MAHLON,] i.e. 'sickness.'

CHILION,] i.e. 'consumption.'

EPHRATHITES,] inhabitants of Ephratah (Ge. 35. 19; Mic. 5. 2;) so called from its fertility.

ARE THERE,] for some time not specified, but till Elimelech dieth.

3. LEFT,] as in v. 4; Ge. 7. 23, &c.

4. MOABITESSES,] contrary to the laws in De. 7. 3; 22. 3.

ORPAH,] i.e. 'a neck or hind.'

RUTH,] i.e. 'appearance or friend.

5. LEFT,] as in v. 3 above.

6. LOOKED AFTER,] as the original word always means, see Ex. 4. 31, &c.

BREAD,] the staff of life, but *food* in general is here evidently meant ; compare Ps. 132. 15.

7. HATH BEEN,] in the fields of Moab.

8. MOTHER,] to their nearest and dearest kindred.

THE DEAD,] even her two sons, and her husband, see 2. 20.

9. GRANT,] or 'give.'

FIND YE REST,] from sorrow and anxiety, see 3. 1.

KISSETH THEM,] in token of farewell.

WEEP] aloud, as the phrase implies.

10. THY PEOPLE,] even Israel, in the land of Canaan.

11. BOWELS,] as in Ps. 71. 6, &c.

12. TO BE TO A HUSBAND,] not 'to have an husband;' the wife in the old Testament is always represented as belonging to the husband, but never *vice versa*.

HOPE] of conceiving seed at all, in my old age.

SONS] rather than daughters, who would marry them, according to De. 25. 5.

13. SHUT YOURSELVES UP.] This original word is not found elsewhere.

AGAINST ME] in anger, cutting off husband, and sons, and all hope of others in their stead; compare Jud. 2. 15; Job 19. 21; Ps. 32. 4; 38. 2; 39. 9, 10.

14. CLEAVED] to her in love and affection, refusing to return.

15. PEOPLE,] the Moabites, and to her GOD,] whom she had been taught to reverence from her youth, perhaps Baal-Peor, Chemosh, &c., as in Nu. 21. 29; 25. 3.

16. URGE ME NOT,] lit. 'come not upon me,' as in 2. 22, &c.

MY GOD,] or object of worship, see 2. 11, 12.

17. ADD,] as in 1 Sa. 14. 44; 20. 13; 25. 22; 2 Sa. 3. 9, 35; 19. 13, &c.

PART,] as in 2 K. 2. 11; Prov. 18. 18.

18. IS STRENGTHENING HERSELF,] as in 1 K. 12. 8; 2 Ch. 10. 18; 13. 7.

TO SPEAK] about the subject of separation.

19. BETH-LEHEM,] whence Naomi had come originally, as in v. 1.

MOVED,] or 'sounded,' as in 1 Sa. 4. 5; 1 K. 1. 45; Syr. and Arab. read 'rejoiced.'

20. NAOMI,] i.e. 'my pleasant one ;' as in v. 2 above.

MARA,] i.e. 'bitter,' Ex. 15. 23.

DEALT BITTERLY,] as in Job. 27. 2; compare La. 3. 15, 19.

21. FULL] of husband, sons, and hopes of happiness.

EMPTY,] of all my former blessings, Job 1. 21.

TESTIFIED AGAINST ME,] that I have sinned.

DONE EVIL,] in taking away my hopes, Job 10. 17; 16. 8.

22. BARLEY-HARVEST,] on the 16th of Nisan, or 1st of April; see Lev. 23. 10, 14; Ruth 2. 23.

II. 1. ACQUAINTANCE,] as in 3. 2,12; Prov. 7. 4.

WEALTH,] or 'strength, or worth.'

BOAZ,] i.e. 'fleetness,' as in 4. 21; see Mat. 1. 5.

2. GATHER,] as in Lev. 19. 9, 10, &c. ; a privilege of the poor, the widow, and the fatherless, as in De. 24. 19.

EARS OF CORN,] as in Isa. 17. 5, &c.
FIND GRACE,] as in Ge. 6. 8, &c.
3. REAPERS,] as in v. 4, 5, 6, 7, 14 ; 1 Sa.
6. 13; 2 K. 4. 18; Ps. 129. 7; Jer. 9. 22; Am.
9. 13.
CHANCE,] as in 1 Sa. 6. 9; 20. 26; Ecc. 2.
14, 15; 3. 19; 9. 2, 3.
HAPPENETH,] as in Ecc. 2. 14, 15, &c.
PORTION,] as in 4. 3, &c.
4. WITH YOU,] as in Ps. 129. 7, 8.
BLESS THEE,] with a good harvest, &c.
5. YOUNG PERSON,] i.e. whose daughter is
she?
6. YOUNG MAN,] as in v. 5.
7. GLEAN,] as permitted by the law in De.
24. 19, &c.
SHEAVES,] as in v. 15 ; Job 24. 10 ; De. 24. 19.
8. PASS NOT OVER,] to any other field than
mine.
YOUNG WOMEN,] who are reaping the
harvest.
9. ATHIRST,] by the heat of the sun and
the toil of labour.
VESSELS,] in which water was kept.
DRAW] out of the wells for the use of the
reapers.
10. EARTH,] according to eastern custom
as in 1 Sa. 25. 23.
FOUND GRACE,] as in v. 2.
DISCERN,] recognize or distinguish from
the other gleaners around.
STRANGER,] or foreigner, from another
country, and race.
11. MOTHER-IN-LAW,] Naomi, a relative
of his own.
HUSBAND,] Mahlon.
BIRTH,] even Moab; in this she resembled
the father of the faithful.
HERETOFORE,] lit. 'yesterday, third day.'
12. WORK,] or 'doing, or deed.'
REWARD,] or 'hire.'
WINGS,] as in Ex. 25. 20, alluding to those
of the cherubim.
TAKE REFUGE,] as in Ps. 118. 9, 10; Isa.
30. 2; compare Ruth 1. 16.
13. COMFORTED] me, in loneliness and
widowhood.
HEART,] i.e. affectionately and kindly, as
in Ge. 34. 3; Jud. 19. 3, &c.
MAID-SERVANT,] being a foreigner and a
heathen, 1 Sa. 25. 41.
14. MEAL-TIME,] lit. 'time of eating.'
DIPPED,] as in 1 Sa. 14. 27, &c.
MORSEL,] as in Prov. 17. 1, &c.
VINEGAR,] as in Nu. 6. 3 ; Ps. 69. 21, &c. ;
a cooling refreshing beverage.
REACHETH.] This original word is not
found elsewhere.
ROASTED CORN,] as in Lev. 23. 14; 1 Sa. 17.
17; 25. 18; 2 Sa. 17. 28.
LEAVETH,] as in v. 18.
15. GLEAN,] that she may have sufficient
for her mother-in-law likewise.
CAUSE TO BLUSH,] as in Jud. 18. 7 ; 1 Sa.
20. 34, &c.
16. HANDFULS.] This original word is not
found elsewhere.
LEFT,] or 'forsaken,' designedly.
PUSH,] as in Ge. 37. 10, &c.
17. BEATETH OUT,] as in Jud. 6. 11 ; De
24. 20; Isa. 27. 12; 28 27.

EPHAH,] as in Ex. 16. 36, &c. ; about
bushel perhaps.
18. SATIETY,] as in Ex. 16. 3, &c.
19. DISCERNING,] recognizing or distin
guishing her from others, see v. 10; Ps. 41. 1.
20. FORSAKEN,] or 'left, or abandoned.'
RELATION,] as in 3. 12, &c.
REDEEMERS,] as in Ruth 3. 9; 4. 6; Lev.
25. 25, &c.
22. COME NOT AGAINST THEE,] as in 1. 16,&c.
23. WHEAT-HARVEST,] as in Ge. 30. 14,&c.,
which latter began at Pentecost.

III. 1. REST,] as in 1. 9, &c.
2. ACQUAINTANCE,] as in 2. 1, &c.
WINNOWING,] or 'fanning,' for the purpose
of cleansing.
THRESHING-FLOOR,] as in Ge. 50. 10, &c.
3. BATHED] thyself with water, and
ANOINTED THYSELF] with oil, according
to eastern customs, 2 Sa. 14. 2 ; Ps. 104. 15;
Mat. 6. 17.
4. LIETH DOWN,] to rest or sleep.
UNCOVERED,] or removed the covering
that is over him, thus claiming his protection
as a wife.
5. I DO,] giving the usual unreserved obedience of eastern daughters to their mother.
7. GLAD,] because of his harvest being
secured to him ; compare Jud. 19. 6, 9, 22
2 Sa. 13. 28 ; Est. 1. 10.
THE HEAP,] of corn or straw which had
been beaten out.
GENTLY,] as in 1 Sa. 18. 22 ; 24. 4, and
UNCOVERETH,] as she had been directed.
8. TREMBLETH,] as in Ge. 27. 33, &c., and
TURNETH HIMSELF,] as in Jud. 16. 29;
Job 6. 18.
9. HAND-MAID,] not now merely a 'maid-
servant,' as she had called herself in 2. 13.
SKIRT,] lit. 'wing,' as the emblem of protection, see Eze. 16. 8.
REDEEMER,] as in 2. 20 above.
10. DEALT MORE KINDLY,] lit. 'done thy
kindness well.'
POOR,] lit. 'lean, thin.'
RICH,] as in Prov. 14. 20, &c.
11. GATE,] i.e. city, or public men in it.
VIRTUOUS WOMAN,] lit. 'woman of strength
or worth;' see Prov. 12. 4.
12. REDEEMER,] as in v. 9; 4. 1.
13. LODGE,] as in Ge. 19. 2, &c.
REDEEM THEE,] by making thee his wife,
as in De. 25. 7, &c.
DELIGHT NOT,] as in 4. 5 it proved to be.
14. FLOOR,] i.e. threshing-floor, as in v. 2.
15. GIVE,] as in De. 1. 13, &c.
COVERING,] as in Isa. 3. 22; not a veil for
the face, but a covering for the head.
KEEP HOLD,] as in Ex. 4. 4, &c.
SIX MEASURES,] perhaps omers or pints.
HE GOETH,] not ' she goeth.'
16. WHO ART THOU,] being probably nearly
blind she could not see well.
18. SIT STILL,] as in Ps. 37. 3, 5.
FALLETH] out, in regard to the proceedings of Boaz.

IV. 1. GATE,] of his city, where the elders
assembled for the transaction of business,
as in Ge. 23. 10, 18 ; Prov. 31. 23.

SITTETH THERE,] among the people who were congregating.

SPOKEN] to Ruth, in 3. 11, 12.

SUCH A ONE, SUCH A ONE,] as in 1 Sa. 21. 2; 2 K. 6. 8.

2. TEN MEN,] this being probably the legal number of witnesses in such cases as the present.

3. A PORTION,] or 'share.'

BROTHER,] belonging to the same tribe.

SOLD,] in intention, but not yet in fact.

4. I UNCOVER THINE EAR,] as in 1 Sa. 9. 15; 20. 2, 12, 13; 22. 8, 17; 2 Sa. 7. 27; 1 Ch. 17. 25.

BUY,] as in Jer. 32. 7, 8, &c.

REDEEM,] as in Lev. 25. 25.

5. THE DEAD,] that he might not be forgotten, see Ge. 38. 8.

RAISE UP,] according to the law of Moses in De. 25. 5, 6.

6. DESTROY,] by bringing in additional heirs and claimants to his property.

MY RIGHT OF REDEMPTION,] as the nearest of kin.

7. FORMERLY.] This shews that the composition of this narrative was considerably after the occurrence of the events.

REDEMPTION] of property, as in De. 25. 7, 9.

CHANGING] one property for another.

DRAWN OFF,] as in v. 8, an indication of inferiority, De. 25. 9.

SANDAL,] as in Ex. 3. 5, &c.

TESTIMONY,] as in Isa. 8. 16, 20.

9. WITNESSES,] as in v. 10, 11.

MAHLON,] his two sons.

10. BROUGHT,] or 'acquired.'

INHERITANCE,] as in v. 5 above.

CUT OFF,] from being remembered, as in De. 25. 6.

GATE,] or public place of the city of his habitation.

11. GATE,] where the elders were assembled, as in v. 1.

BUILT,] by their twelve sons.

VIRTUOUSLY,] lit. 'mightily or worthily.'

PROCLAIM THE NAME] of God, as in Lev. 24. 11, 16; De. 28. 58.

EPHRATAH,] i.e. 'the fruitful place,' which is the same as

BETH-LEHEM,] i.e. 'the house of bread, as in Ge. 35. 19; Mic. 5. 2.

12. PHAREZ,] in Ge. 38. 29.

13. CONCEPTION,] as in Hos. 9. 11; compare Ge. 29. 31; 33. 5.

14. A REDEEMER,] in the person of her newly born grandson.

15. RESTORER OF LIFE,] as in La. 1. 16.

TO NOURISH,] as in 1 K. 17. 4, 9, &c.

SEVEN SONS,] the number of perfection, compare 1 Sa. 1. 8.

16. LAD,] as in Ex. 2. 9, &c.

BOSOM,] as in 1 K. 3. 20, &c.

NURSE,] lit. 'supporter,' as in Nu. 11. 12; 2 Sa. 4. 4; 2 K. 10. 1, 5; Est. 2. 7; Isa. 49. 23.

17. OBED,] i.e. 'servant.'

JESSE,] i.e. 'my substance, or wealthy.'

DAVID,] i.e. 'beloved.'

18. PHAREZ,] see Ge. 38. 29.

HEZRON,] see 46. 12, called Esrom in Mat. 1. 3; Luke 3. 33.

19. RAM,] or Aram, Mat. 1. 3; Luke 3. 33.

AMMINIDAB,] see Ex. 6. 27, &c.

NAHSHON,] see Nu. 7. 12, &c.

SALMON,] or Salmoh, 1 Ch. 2. 11.

BOAZ,] of Rahab, Mat. 1. 5.

FIRST BOOK OF SAMUEL

THIS BOOK contains an account of the government of the two last Judges, and of the first King, of Israel, embracing a period of about eighty years. Its author is unknown, but it has always formed part of the Sacred Canon of the Jews, and is referred to in Mat. 12. 3; Mark 2. 25; Luke 6. 4; Acts 7. 46; 13. 21, 23. It has sometimes been called the 'First Book of Kings,' because it contains the annals of the first Monarch who reigned over Israel.

I. 1. RAMATHAIM-ZOPHIM,] i.e. 'the two high places of the watchers;' not mentioned elsewhere.

EPHRAIM,] between Manasseh and Benjamin, having the one on the north, and the other on the south.

ELKANAH,] i.e. 'God has brought;' he had an ancestor of the same name, as in 1 Ch. 6. 23.

JEROHAM,] i.e. 'he is loved.'

ELIHU,] i.e. 'my God is he;' in 1 Ch. 6. 26 it is Eliab.

TOHU.] Etymology unknown, called Toah in 1 Ch. 6. 19; and Nahath in v. 11.

ZUPH,] i.e. 'dropping' of honey, in 1 Ch. 6. 20 it is Ziph, and in 1 Ch. 6. 11 Zaphai.

2. TWO WIVES,] a very uncommon circumstance in S.S.; and even in countries where polygamy is permitted.

HANNAH,] i.e. 'grace,' who being childless, he married also

PENINNAH,] i.e. 'pearl or coral.'

3. TIME TO TIME,] lit. 'days to days;' probably referring to the three great festivals. Ex. 23. 14; De. 16. 16.

SHILOH,] where the ark and altar of God were abiding. Jos. 18. 1.

ELI,] i.e. 'going up or pestle;' he succeeded Samson as judge.

HOPHNI,] i.e. 'a boxer.'

PHINEHAS,] i.e. 'mouth of brass.'

4. THE DAY] of his appearing before the Lord, according to appointment, and he

SACRIFICETH,] the appointed animal.

PORTIONS,] or gifts from his sacrifice, (De. 12. 5, 6, 7; 16. 10—15).

5. DOUBLE,] lit. 'of two faces.'

SHUT HER WOMB,] as in Ge. 20. 18; 30. 2.

6. ADVERSITY,] as in Ge. 35. 3; not 'adversary,' as in the C.V.

PROVOKED,] as in De. 32. 21, &c.

TREMBLE,] as in Eze. 27. 35; or 'thunder,' as in 2. 10; 7. 10; 2 Sa. 22. 14, &c.

7. YEAR BY YEAR,] according to the law.

NOT EAT,] as in Ps. 42. 3.

8. AFFLICTED,] lit. 'evil,' as in De. 15. 10; 28. 54, 56, &c.

TEN SONS,] that is, any number of sons.

9. DRINKING] water, not wine or strong drink, as in v. 15.

THRONE,] of the high priest, as in Ge. 41. 40; Ex. 11. 5; 12. 29; De. 17. 18; Jud. 3. 30; 1 Sa. 1. 9, 28; 4. 13. 18; Zec. 6. 13, &c.

SIDE-POST,] as in Prov. 8. 34; Ge. 12. 7, 22, 23.

TEMPLE,] as in 3. 3; 2 Sa. 22. 7; 1 K. 6. 3, 5, 17, 33; 7. 21, 50; 21. 1; 2 K. 18. 6; 20. 18; 23. 4; 24. 13, &c.

10. BITTER IN SOUL,] as in Jud. 18. 25; 1 Sa. 22. 2; 2 Sa. 17. 8; Job 3. 20; 7. 11; 10. 1; 21. 25; Prov. 31. 6; Isa. 38. 15.

11. VOWETH A VOW,] as in Ge. 28. 20; 31. 13; Nu. 6. 2, &c.

LOOK ON,] as in Ex. 3. 7.

REMEMBERED,] as in Ge. 8. 1; 30. 22, &c.

FORGET,] as in Ps. 9. 12.

SEED OF MEN.] A phrase not found elsewhere.

RAZOR,] for shaving the hair away; he was to be a Nazarite.

12. MULTIPLIED PRAYING,] as in 2 K. 21. 6; 2 Ch. 33. 6; 36. 14; Ps. 78. 38.

13. TO HER HEART,] that is, mentally.

MOVING,] as in Ge. 4. 12, 14; Ex. 20. 18.

RECKONETH,] as in Ge. 15. 6; 38. 15, &c.

DRUNKEN,] as in 25. 36; 1 K. 16. 9; 20. 16; Job 12. 25; Ps. 107. 27; Prov. 26. 9; Isa. 19. 14; 24. 20; 28. 1, 3; Jer. 23. 9; Joel 1. 5.

14. TURN ASIDE,] as in Ge. 35. 2; Jos. 24. 14, 23; 1 Sa. 7. 3; 1 K. 20. 24; Ps. 39. 10; 119. 29; Prov. 4. 24, 27; Ecc. 11. 10, &c.

15. SHARPLY PAINED,] because of her affliction.

POUR OUT] in prayer, as in Ps. 62. 8; 102. 1.

16. PUT NOT,] lit. 'give not.'

WORTHLESSNESS,] that is, a worthless woman, as in De. 13. 13, &c.

MEDITATION,] as in 1 K. 18. 27; 2 K. 9. 7; Job 7. 13; 7. 27; 10. 1; 21. 4; 23. 2; Ps. 55. 2; 64. 1; 102. 1; 104. 34; 142. 2; Prov. 23. 29.

PROVOCATION,] as in Ge. 32. 19, 27, &c.

18. FIND GRACE,] as in Ge. 6. 8; 18. 3, &c.

FOR IT,] or towards it, i.e. she no more regarded her adversary.

19. EARLY,] as most people do in the east.

RAMAH,] see v. 1.

KNEW,] as in Ge. 4. 1, &c.

REMEMBERETH,] as in Ge. 30. 22, &c.

20. REVOLUTION,] as in Ex. 34. 22; 2 Ch. 24. 23; Ps. 19. 6.

SAMUEL,] i.e. 'God hath heard.'

ASKED HIM,] in prayer, as in v. 11 above.

21. THE DAYS,] perhaps the feast of tabernacles.

VOW,] regarding his child, it may be.

22. YOUTH,] that is, her son Samuel.

WEANED,] which in the east is not for a considerable time, Ge. 21. 8.

23. HIS WORD,] or matter, viz., his becoming the Lord's, all the days of his life, as she had vowed, in v. 11.

SUCKLETH,] as in Ex. 2. 7, &c.

24. GO UP,] to Shiloh from Ramah, as in v. 7, 21, 22.

BULLOCKS,] as only one appears to have been sacrificed, perhaps the other two were for means of conveyance.

EPHAH,] compare Nu. 15. 9.

N

BOTTLE,] as in 10. 3; 25. 18; 2 Sa. 16. 1, &c.
25. SLAUGHTER,] for a sacrifice to the
Lord, and food for themselves.
THE BULLOCK,] which they had specially
brought with them for this end.
ELI,] the high priest, that the youth
might be formally presented to Jehovah's
service.
26. TO PRAY,] as in v. 10 above.
28. CAUSED HIM TO BE ASKED,] by husband and friends, as in Ex. 12. 36.
ASKED,] for the service of Jehovah, as in
2 K. 6. 5.
HE BOWETH HIMSELF,] either Eli or
Samuel, most probably the latter.

II. 1. PRAYETH,] as in 1. 10, 12, 26, 27;
2. 25; 7. 5; 8. 6; 12. 23, &c.
EXULTED,] as in 1 Ch. 16. 32; Ps. 5. 11;
9. 2; 25. 2; 68. 3; Prov. 11. 10; 28. 12.
HORN,] as in v. 10; Ps. 89. 17, &c.; the
emblem of power.
LARGE,] as in Ps. 81. 10.
SALVATION,] i.e. the safety and ease given
by Jehovah.
2. HOLY,] i.e. 'separate,' from evil, &c.
NONE,] no other God.
ROCK,] i.e. place of safety and strength.
3. MULTIPLY NOT,] any longer your proud
sayings.
HAUGHTILY,] ye are accustomed to do so,
but now the
OLD SAYING,] with which ye taunted me,
is for ever gone from you, and can return
no more.
KNOWLEDGE,] in reference even to the
thoughts of men.
WEIGHED,] in the balances of equity.
4. BOWS,] the chief weapons of offence
in ancient times.
ARE BROKEN,] and therefore worthless,
while, on the contrary
THE STUMBLING,] feeble ones have been
encompassed and clothed with might.
5. THE SATIATED] with much are reduced,
so that for a morsel of food they have
HIRED THEMSELVES OUT,] as servants to
others, but those formerly starved and
hungry have
CEASED,] out of the land, they are filled
now.
THE BARREN] wife has borne as many as
her soul desires, and she who once was
ABOUNDING] with the blessing of a numerous family
HATH LANGUISHED] for want of any to
comfort her, in latter years.
6. PUTTETH TO DEATH,] as in Isa. 14. 30;
65. 15, &c.
KEEPETH ALIVE,] as in Neh. 9. 6. &c.
SHEOL,] as in Ge. 37. 35; De. 32. 22; Ps.
9. 17, &c.
BRINGETH UP] from the gates of death and
of the other world.
7. DISPOSSESSETH] of health, wealth,
property, and power.
MAKETH RICH] in spiritual and temporal
matters.
MAKETH LOW] in the world's opinion.
MAKETH HIGH,] those who are low.
8. POOR.] as in Ps. 113. 7, 8; Da. 4. 17, &c.

DUNGHILL,] as in Ps. 113. 7, &c.
NEEDY,] as in Ex. 23. 6, 11.
NOBLES,] as in Nu. 21. 18; Ps. 113. 8.
THRONE OF HONOUR,] as in Jer. 17. 12, &c.
INHERIT,] as his own free gift for ever.
FIXTURES,] as in 14. 5.
HABITABLE WORLD,] as in 2 K. 22. 16; 1
Ch. 16. 30; Job 18. 18; 34. 13; 37. 12; Ps. 9.
8; 18. 15; 19. 4; 24. 1; 33. 8.
9. KEEPETH] from falling, as in De. 8. 4;
2 Ch. 33. 8; Ps. 25. 15; 56. 13; 91. 12; 121.
3, &c.
SILENT,] or 'cut off;' so Kimchi and Ben
Melech.   Ps. 31. 17.
POWER] of his own, but of God alone.
10. BROKEN DOWN,] as in Isa. 8. 9.
THUNDERETH,] as in 7. 10; 2 Sa. 22. 14;
Job 37. 4, 5; 40. 9; Ps. 18. 13; 29. 3.
ENDS OF EARTH,] as in De. 33. 17; Ps. 2.
8; 22. 27; 59. 13; 67. 7; 72. 8; 98. 3; Prov.
30. 4; Isa. 45. 22; 52. 10; Jer. 16. 19; Mic.
5. 4; Zec. 9. 10.
KING] that is, to any one whom the Lord
may set up.
HORN,] as in v. 1 above.
ANOINTED,] in Heb. Messiah, as in Lev. 4.
3, 5, 16; 6 22; 1 Sa. 2. 35; 12. 3, 5; 16. 6;
24. 6, 10; 26. 9, 11, 16, 23, &c.
11. RAMATH,] his place of residence, as
in 1. 1, 19; 2. 20.
SERVING] as a ministrant, compare Ex.
24. 13; 33. 11; Nu. 11. 28; Jos. 1. 1; 1 Sa. 2
11. 18; 2 Sa. 13. 17, &c.
12. WORTHLESSNESS,] i.e. worthless persons.
NOT KNOWN,] not appreciated his true
character as the heart-searching God.
13. CUSTOM,] lit. 'judgment.'
SACRIFICE] to Jehovah, especially peace-
offerings.
HOOK,] as in Ex. 27. 3; 38. 3; Nu. 4. 14;
1 Ch. 28. 17; 2 Ch. 4. 16, and v. 14 above.
14. PAN,] as in Ex. 30. 18, 28; 31. 9; 35.
16; 38. 8; 39. 39; 40. 7, 11, 30; Lev. 8. 11;
1 K. 7. 30, 38, 40, 43; 2 K. 16. 17; 2 Ch. 4.
6, 14; 6. 13; Zec. 12. 6.
KETTLE,] as in 2 K. 10. 7; 2 Ch. 35. 13;
Job 41. 20; Ps. 81. 6; Jer. 24. 2.
CALDRON,] as in Mic. 3. 3.
POT,] as in Nu. 11. 8; Jud. 6. 19.
FOR HIMSELF,] whereas the breast and
shoulder had been expressly allotted to
them, in Ex. 29. 27, 28; Lev. 7. 31.
SHILOH,] where the ark of God was abiding.
15. FAT,] commanded in Lev. 3. 3, 49;
7. 31.
TO ROAST,] as being more agreeable to the
appetite.   Isa. 44. 16, 19.
BOILED,] as in Ex. 12. 9, but rather
RAW,] lit. 'living.'
16. MAKE A PERFUME] of a sweet savour
to the Lord, according to law and custom.
DESIRETH,] as in De.. 12. 20; 14. 26.
STRENGTH,] as in Jud. 4. 3; 8. 1; 2 K. 12.
12; Eze. 34. 4; Jon. 3. 8.
17. THE MEN,] the young men, the sons of
Eli.
DESPISED,] as in Nu. 14. 11, 23; 16. 30;
De. 31. 20, &c.
18. MINISTERING,] as in v. 11 above

JEHOVAH,] or **as** in v. 11, of Eli.
EPHOD OF LINEN,] as in 22. 18; 2 Sa. 6.
14; 1 Ch. 15. 27; Eze. 9. 2, 3, 11, &c.
19. UPPER COAT,] as in Ex. 28. 4, 31, 34, &c.
TIME TO TIME,] *lit.* 'days to days,' as in
1. 3, &c.
THE TIME,] whether it was the feast of
the passover, tabernacle, &c.
20. APPOINT FOR THEE,] as in Ge. 4. 25, &c.
PETITION,] *lit.* 'asking.'
SHE ASKED,] as in 1. 11.
PLACE,] of abode, even Ramah, as in 1. 1,
19; 2. 11.
21. LOOKED AFTER,] as in Ge. 21. 1, &c.
WITH,] not 'before,' as in the C.V.
22. DO,] as in v. 15, 16 above.
ASSEMBLING,] as in Ex. 38. 8, &c.
24. TO TRANSGRESS,] or 'pass over' the
command of the Lord.
25. GOD,] not 'the judge,' as in the C.V.
JUDGED,] as in Ge. 48. 11; Ps. 106. 30;
Eze. 16. 52.
PRAY,] as in 1. 12, 26, 27; 12. 19, 23.
THOUGH,] or 'so that.'
DELIGHTED,] as in Nu. 14. 8; Jud. 13. 23;
Isa. 53. 10, &c.
26. GOOD,] compare v. 21 above.
MEN,] as in Prov. 3. 4; Luke 2. 52; Acts
2. 47; Rom. 14. 18.
27. REVEALED,] as in Ex. 4. 14, 27, &c.
FATHER,] Levi.
BEFORE,] not 'in,' as in the C.V.
28. PRIEST,] as in Ex. 28. 1, 4; Nu. 16. 5;
18. 1, 7, &c.
TO GO UP,] not 'to offer,' upon my al-
tar, as in the C.V.
PERFUME] morning and evening, in the
holy place.
EPHOD,] as in Ex. 25. 7; 28. 4, 6, 12, 15,
25, 26, 27, 28, 31; 29. 5; 35. 9, 27; 39. 2, 7,
8, 18, 19, 20, 21, 22, &c.
FIRE-OFFERINGS,] as in Lev. 2. 3, 10; 6.
16; 7. 8, 34, 35; 10. 14, 15; Nu. 5. 9, 10; 18.
8—10.
29. KICK,] as in De. 32. 15.
HABITATION,] as in v. 32; De. 26. 15, &c.
ABOVE ME,] respecting their pleasures
more than the express law of God.
FAT,] or 'let yourselves eat' of the first
or best part of the offerings, 2 Sa. 3. 35; 13. 5.
FIRST PART,] as in 15. 21, &c.
30. AFFIRMATION,] as in Ge. 22. 16, &c.
WALK UP AND DOWN,] as in Ge. 5. 22,
24, &c.
FAR BE IT FROM ME,] *lit.* a 'profane,
polluted thing it is to me.'
HONOUR,] as in Ps. 18. 20; 91. 14.
LIGHTLY ESTEEMED,] as in Mal. 2. 9.
31. CUT OFF,] as in Isa. 10. 33; 15. 2; La.
2. 3; Zec. 11. 10, 14.
ARM,] being the emblem and source of
power.
OLD MAN,] to be reverenced for his grey
hairs.
32. ADVERSARY,] as in 4. 4, 11.
HABITATION,] as in v. 29 above.
ALL THE DAYS] that it exists.
33. CONSUME] with tears, and to
GRIEVE] his soul with his wickedness and
calamities.
MEN] in the prime of their days.

34. SIGN,] or 'token.'
THEY DIE] a violent death, as in 4. 11.
35. STEDFAST,] as in Nu. 12. 7, &c.
STEDFAST HOUSE,] that cannot be moved.
WALKED UP AND DOWN] habitually, as in
v. 30 above.
ANOINTED,] or in Heb. 'Messiah,' as in v.10.
36. WAGE.] This original word is not
found elsewhere.
CAKE,] as in Ex. 29. 23, &c.
ADMIT ME.] Compare the use of the ori-
ginal word in 26. 19; Job 30. 7; Isa. 14. 1;
Hab. 2. 15.
OFFICES,] as in Ex. 29. 9, &c.
MORSEL,] as in Ge. 18. 5, &c.

III. 1. IS SERVING,] or 'ministering,' as
in v. 11, 18.
PRECIOUS,] as in 2 Sa. 12. 30; 1 K. 5.
17, &c.
VISION,] as in 1 Ch. 17. 15; 2 Ch. 32. 32;
Ps. 89. 19; Prov. 29. 18; Isa. 1. 1; 29. 7;
Jer. 14. 14; 23. 16; La. 2. 9; Eze. 7. 13, 26;
12. 22, 23, 24, 27; 13. 16; Da. 1. 17; 8. 1, 2,
13, 15, 17, 26; 9. 21, 24; 10. 14; 11. 14; Hos.
12. 10; Obad. 1; Mic. 3. 6; Na. 1. 1; Hab.
2. 2, 3.
BROKEN FORTH,] as in 1 Ch. 13. 2, &c.
2. LYING DOWN,] to rest and sleep.
DIM,] as in Ge. 27. 1, &c.
3. LAMP,] as in Ex. 25. 37; 27. 20, &c.
EXTINGUISHED,] as in Lev. 6. 12, 13.
TEMPLE,] as in 1. 9, &c.
ARK,] containing the manna, Aaron's
rod, &c.
4. CALLETH,] with an audible voice, probably naming him.
5. RUNNETH,] as was natural for a youth
anxious to shew his affection.
6. ADDETH TO CALL] a second time; compare Job 33. 14, &c.
7. NOT KNOWN] experimentally by receiving divine communications.
REVEALED,] by a direct personal grant.
8. ADDETH TO CALL,] as in v. 6.
UNDERSTANDETH,] as in Ps. 19. 12, &c.
9. IS HEARING,] or 'hearkening' to whatever may be said.
10. STATIONETH HIMSELF,] as in Ex. 34.
5; Nu. 22. 22.
TIME BY TIME,] *lit.* 'step by step,' as in
Nu. 24. 1; Jud. 16. 20; 20. 30, 31; 1 Sa. 20. 25.
11. TINGLE,] as in 2 K. 21. 12; Jer. 19. 3;
Hab. 3. 16.
12. ESTABLISH,] *lit.* 'raise up.'
BEGINNING AND COMPLETING,] taking the
whole into his own hands.
13. HAVE DECLARED,] as in 2. 27—36.
KNOWN,] hearing of it from the people,
and being warned by the man of God.
MAKING THEMSELVES VILE,] or 'lightly
esteemed' by God and man.
RESTRAINED,] *lit.* 'make dim.'
14. SWORN,] as in 2. 30.
NOT ATONED FOR,] as in De. 21. 8.
15. DOORS,] that the people might enter.
VISION,] which he had been shewn by
the Lord.
17. HIDE,] as in Ge. 47. 18, &c.
ADD,] as in Ruth 1. 17; 1 Sa. 14. 44; 20
13; 25. 22; 2 Sa. 3. 9, &c.

18. NOT HID,] not having been forbidden to tell it, but evidently the contrary.
JEHOVAH] who hath spoken, the greatest, and wisest, and best of beings.
DOTH,] and none can hinder.
19. WITH HIM,] filling him with His Spirit.
NOT LET FALL,] fruitless and unfulfilled.
20. DAN,] the most northern part of the land of Canaan, to
BEER-SHEBA,] the most southern.
21. SHILOH,] where the temple and the ark were.
REVEALED,] as in v. 7 above.
WORD OF JEHOVAH,] as in v. 1, 7.

IV. 1. SAMUEL,] universally regarded as a prophet of the Lord and judge of Israel, even before the death of Eli
PHILISTINES,] who dwelt on the coast of the great sea.
EBEN-EZER,] i.e. 'a stone of help,' as in 7. 12.
APHEK,] see Jos. 12. 18 ; 15. 53.
2. SPREADETH ITSELF,] or 'is left,' as in 10. 2 ; 12. 22 ; 17. 20, 22, 28 ; 30. 16, &c.
THE RANKS,] as in v. 12, 16, &c.
3. CAMP] in Eben-Ezer, as in v. 1.
ELDERS] who ruled the nation.
ARK,] the symbol of the presence of God.
4. SHILOH,] doubtless to Eli the chief priest.
CHERUBS,] as in 1 Ch. 13. 6 ; Ps. 80. 1 ; 99. 1 ; Isa. 37. 16.
5. CAMP] at Eben-Ezer.
SHOUT] of triumph, as the word implies.
MOVED,] as in Ruth 1. 19 ; 1 K. 1. 45.
6. HEBREWS,] see on Ge. 40. 15, &c.
PERCEIVE,] lit. 'know.'
7. GOD,] or 'a god.'
HERETOFORE,] lit. 'yesterday, third day.'
8. WO TO US,] as in v. 7 ; Jer. 4. 13 ; La. 5. 15, &c.
HONOURABLE,] as in Ex. 15. 10 ; Jud. 5. 13, 25 ; 2 Ch. 23. 20 ; Neh. 3. 5 ; 10. 29 ; Ps. 8. 1 ; 16. 3 ; 76. 4 ; 93. 4 ; 136. 18, &c.
PLAGUE,] lit. 'smiting,' as in Lev. 26. 21, Nu. 11. 33 ; De. 25. 3 ; 28. 59, 61 ; 29. 22 ; Jos. 10. 10, 20 ; Jud. 11. 33 ; 15. 8, &c.
WILDERNESS,] or 'pasture-land,' as in Ex. 13. 18, 20 ; 14. 3, 11, 12, &c.
9. STRENGTHEN YOURSELVES,] as in 1 K. 20. 22, &c.
BECOME MEN,] fighting for life, honour, and victory.
TO YOU,] as in Jud. 13. 1.
10. TENTS,] i.e. dwellings throughout the land.
BLOW,] lit. 'smiting,' as in v. 8 above.
FOOTMEN,] having no horsemen apparently.
11. TAKEN] by the Philistines from those Levites who guarded it.
DIED] by the wounds received in defending the ark.
12. RANKS] of the army of Israel, to SHILOH] where Eli was abiding, being unable to go out to battle, with his sons.
LONG ROBES,] with which the orientals delight to array themselves.
RENT,] as the usual token of grief.

EARTH,] as in 2 Sa. 15. 32, &c.
13. THE THRONE,] as in 1. 9 ; 2. 8 ; 4. 18, &c.
WAY,] waiting for the news of the battle, and watching or looking out for a messenger.
TREMBLING,] as in Jud. 7. 3 ; Ezra 9. 4 ; 10. 3 ; Isa. 66. 2, 5.
DECLARE] the tidings of the defeat, the capture of the ark, and the death of the two sons of Eli.
CRIETH OUT] in anguish, as the word implies.
14. TUMULT,] as in 14. 19 ; 2 Sa. 18. 29, &c.
15. A SON,] according to a common Hebrew idiom.
STOOD,] as in 1 K. 14. 4.
16. RANKS,] as in v. 12.
17. BEARING TIDINGS,] as in 2 Sa. 4. 10 ; 18. 26 ; Ps. 68. 11 ; Isa. 40. 9 ; 41. 27 ; 52. 7 ; Neh. 1. 15.
SLAUGHTER,] or 'plague,' as in 6. 4 ; Ex. 9. 14, &c.
DIED] in battle with the enemy.
TAKEN] by the Philistines.
18. THE THRONE,] as in v. 13.
NECK.] This original word is not found elsewhere.
BROKEN] in the falling from off his seat.
HEAVY,] as in 5. 6, 11, &c.
19. PREGNANT,] as in 16. 11 ; 38. 24 ; Ex. 21. 22 ; Jud. 13. 5, 7, &c.
BOWETH,] as in Ge. 49. 9, &c.
PAINS,] as in Isa. 21. 3, &c.
20. A SON] who would continue his father's name and race.
SET HER HEART,] as in Ex. 7. 23 ; 2 Sa. 13. 20 ; Ps. 48. 13 ; 62. 10 ; Prov. 22. 17 ; 24. 32 ; 27. 23.
21. I-CHABOD,] i.e. 'where is honour?' or 'there is no honour.'
REMOVED,] as in Isa. 24. 11, &c.
22. HONOUR,] especially the honour of being the custodiers of the visible symbol of the presence of God.
TAKEN,] as in v. 17 above.

V. 1. ASHDOD,] one of their five chief cities, afterwards called Azotus.
2. DAGON,] one of their principal gods, see Jud. 16. 23, &c.
3. MORROW,] to pay their devotions to their deity.
FACE,] prostrate as a worthless idol before the symbol of the presence of the God of Israel.
PLACE] from which it had fallen before the ark.
4. PALMS,] as in Lev. 14. 15, 16, &c.
THRESHOLD,] of the temple of Dagon in Ashdod.
FISHY PART,] lit. 'Dagon,' the 'little fish ;' see Jud. 16. 23.
5. TREAD NOT,] but 'leap over it,' as in Zeph. 1. 9, either reverencing or detesting it.
6. HEAVY,] as in v. 7, 11.
DESOLATE,] as in Nu. 21. 30, &c.
EMERODS,] as in De. 28. 27, &c.
BORDERS,] or 'territory.'
7. HARD,] as in Ge. 49. 7 ; De. 1. 17 ; 15. 18 ; 2 Sa. 19. 43.
GOD,] yet they did not seem to feel the

absurdity of continuing to serve one who could not help himself.

8. PRINCES,] who were five in number.

GATH,] another of their chief cities, not far from Ashdod (Jer. 25. 20); they were unwilling to restore it to Israel.

9. DESTRUCTION,] as in De. 7. 23; 28. 20, &c.

BREAK FORTH.] This original word is not found elsewhere.

EMERODS,] as in v. 6 above.

10. EKRON,] another chief city of the Philistines, when Beelzebub was worshipped.

PUT TO DEATH,] as in v. 11.

11. PRINCES,] as in v. 8.

DEADLY,] lit. a 'destruction of death.'

VERY HEAVY,] as in v. 6 above.

12. EMERODS,] as in v. 6, 9.

CRY,] as in Ex. 2. 23, &c.

VI. 1. FIELD,] i.e. cultivated country, as in 27. 11.

2. DIVINERS,] as in De. 18. 10, 14; Jos. 13. 22, &c.

3. EMPTY,] as in Ge. 31. 42; Ex. 3. 21; 23. 15; 34. 20, &c.

GUILT OFFERING,] as an acknowledgment and atonement for guilt.

HEALED,] having appeased the anger of the offended party by the offering and confession.

TURN ASIDE,] that is, cease from falling upon them.

4. GUILT-OFFERING,] as in v. 3.

MICE,] which had begun to overrun their fields and houses, as in v. 5.

5. IMAGES,] as in Eze. 7. 20, &c.

CORRUPTING,] as in 13. 17; 14. 15, &c.

HONOUR,] as to him who was punishing them for their sins.

LIGHTEN,] as in 1 K. 12. 4, 9, 10, &c.

6. HARDEN,] by trying to bear up against the heavy hand of God.

ROLLED HIMSELF,] in anger and fury.

GO] on their way to Canaan.

7. CART,] as in Ge. 45. 19, &c.

SUCKLING,] as in Ge. 33. 13; 1 Sa. 6. 7, 10; Ps. 78. 71; Isa. 40. 11.

YOKE,] as in Nu. 19. 2; De. 21. 3, &c.

8. COFFER,] as in v. 11, 15. This original word is not found elsewhere.

9. ITS OWN,] i.e. the ark's, even to Shiloh.

BETH-SHEMESH,] i.e. 'house of the sun,' see Jud. 15. 10.

EVIL] of plagues and sickness.

COME AGAINST US] intentionally, with a view to punish us.

ACCIDENT,] as in Ruth 2. 3; 1 Sa. 20. 26; Ecc. 2. 14, 15; 3. 9; 9. 2, 3.

11. SHUT UP] to prevent them following their dams.

12. GO STRAIGHT,] as in Prov. 9. 15; Job 37. 3, &c.

LOWING,] as in Job 6. 5. This original word is not found elsewhere.

13. WHEAT-HARVEST,] which began at Pentecost.

REJOICE,] deeming its return a token of God's presence again.

14 JOSHUA,] a chief man in that city.

STONE,] in the midst of the field or meadow, suitable for a sacrifice.

WOOD] for fuel to burn the sacrifice.

ASCEND,] on the stone as on an altar.

A BURNT-OFFERING,] from the Philistines to Jehovah, whom they feared, while they served their own gods.

15. TAKEN DOWN] from off the cart, as was their duty, according to the law.

VESSELS,] consisting of the images of the emerods and mice which had plagued the Philistines.

STONE,] as in v. 14 above.

BURNT-OFFERINGS,] to testify their pleasure in the return of the ark.

16. FIVE PRINCES,] as in v. 4.

EKRON,] whence they had brought the ark direct.

17. EMERODS,] as in v. 4, 5 above.

SENT BACK,] along with the ark of God, as in v. 5, 11.

GUILT OFFERING,] as in v. 3 above.

ASHDOD,] where the ark had been taken first.

GATH,] which had received the ark from Ashdod.

GAZA..ASHKELON,] which had escaped the plague.

EKRON,] which had refused to receive it.

18. MICE,] representatives of those destroying the land.

CITIES,] leading ones, at least.

FENCED CITY,] with walls and bulwarks, to the

HAMLET OF THE VILLAGES,] a small collection of tents or huts.

MEADOW,] as in v. 15 'stone;' others read 'Great Abel,' as a proper name.

UNTO THIS DAY,] i.e. the emerods and mice appear to have been preserved where they had been left by the Philistines, when this account was written.

19. LOOKED INTO] the ark, which was forbidden the Levites, in Nu. 4. 20.

SEVENTY MEN,] so Abarbanel, Josephus, and others.

FIFTY CHIEF MEN,] as the original word 'eleph' means in Mic. 5. 2, compared with Mat. 2. 6; it was only a small village.

MOURN,] as in Ge. 37. 34, &c.

SMITING,] as in Lev. 26. 21, &c.

20. STAND] accepted in his presence.

HOLY,] i.e. 'separate.'

21. KIRJATH-JEARIM,] or Kirjath-Baal, see Jos. 15. 9.

UNTO YOU,] being afraid of its presence among them, lest they should again be punished.

VII. 1. ABINADAB,] i.e. 'my father is noble,' 2 Sa. 6. 4.

HEIGHT,] above Beth-Shemesh.

ELEAZAR,] i.e. 'God is help.'

SANCTIFIED,] or 'set apart,' as a special attendant or

KEEP,] watch, and preserve it from curiosity and injury.

2. WAIL,] because of his long continued absence from them.

3. GODS OF THE STRANGER,] with which they were tempted.

ASHTAROTH,] see on Jud. 2. 13; 3. 7, &c.

PREPARE,] as in 1 Ch. 29. 16; 2 Ch. 12. 14; 19. 3; 30. 19; Ezra 7. 10; Job 11. 13; Ps. 10. 17; 78. 8.

ONLY,] as in De. 6. 13; 10. 20; 13. 4; Mat. 4. 10; Luke 4. 8.

DELIVER] you as his own people.

4. BAALIM,] *lit.* 'lords, masters, possessors,' as in Jud. 2. 13; 3. 7, &c.

ASHTAROTH,] as in v. 3.

5. MIZPEH,] of Benjamin, westward of Jordan, as in Jud. 20. 1.

6. DRAW WATER] out of some well or wells there.

POUR IT OUT,] as a drink-offering or libation.

FAST,] afflicting their bodies, as a token of the distress of their souls.

SINNED,] by going away from the path of duty, as well as in going beyond it.

JUDGETH,] as God's prophet and servant.

7. PRINCES,] five in number.

AFRAID,] being conscious of their own weakness.

8. KEEP NOT SILENT,] as in Ps. 28. 1; 35. 22; 39. 12; 50. 2; 83. 1; 109. 1.

SAVE,] being at once a hearer and an answerer of prayer.

9. LAMB.] The original word is only found in Isa. 65. 25.

WHOLE,] as in De. 33. 10, &c.

CRIETH] in distress, as the original word implies, for help.

10. THUNDER,] as in 2. 10, &c.

TROUBLETH,] as in Ex. 14. 24, &c.

11. BETH-CAR,] i.e. 'house of Car *or* a lamb.'

12. SHEN,] i.e. a 'tooth.'

EBEN-EZER,] i.e. 'stone of help,' as in 4. 1.

HELPED] against all enemies and oppressors.

13. HUMBLED,] by this defeat at the hand of God.

ANY MORE,] for some considerable time afterwards.

14. TAKEN] by force in their former victories.

EKRON.. GATH,] not these cities themselves, but the intervening and neighbouring ones.

BORDER,] i.e. territory.

AMORITE,] which appellation probably means the Canaanites generally.

15. OF HIS LIFE,] even after Saul had been appointed king, or civil ruler in Israel.

16. YEAR TO YEAR,] as in 1. 7; 1 K. 5. 11; 10. 25, &c.

BETH-EL,] near to Ai, not far from Shiloh, in the tribe of Benjamin.

GILGAL,] where Israel first encamped after passing the Jordan.

MIZPEH,] as in v. 5, 6, &c.

17. RAMATH,] as in 1. 1, 19.

AN ALTAR,] as in Jud. 21. 4; 2 Sa. 24. 25, &c.

VIII. 1. HIS SONS,] whose names are mentioned in the succeeding verse.

2. JOEL,] called in 1 Ch. 6. 28 Vashni.

ABIAH,] not mentioned elsewhere.

BEER-SHEBA,] in the southern extremity of Canaan.

3. WAYS,] of integrity and truth.

DISHONEST GAIN,] as in Ge. 37. 26; Ex. 18. 21; Jud. 5. 19, &c.

BRIBE,] as in Ex. 23. 8; De. 10. 17; 16. 19; 27. 25, &c.

JUDGMENT,] as in Ex. 23. 2, 6; De. 16. 19; 24. 17; 27. 19, &c.

4. ELDERS,] or leading men in the various tribes of Israel.

5. APPOINT,] *lit.* 'set, place,' leaving the selection of the person to Samuel himself.

KING,] as Moses had before spoken of, in De. 17. 4.

NATIONS,] most of whom were under the authority of one ruler.

6. IS EVIL,] because it shewed discontent with God's arrangements for his people.

PRAYETH,] for himself and the people, that His will might be manifested to Israel.

7. REJECTED.] Samuel appears to have still ruled in Israel till his death.

8. TO THEE,] disregarding the good government he had shewn to them as God's vicegerent. Mat. 10. 24, 25.

9. VOICE,] in reference to their request for a king.

PROTEST,] that they must bear the consequences of their request. Hos. 13. 11.

DECLARED,] *or* 'set before' them the royal prerogatives usually exercised.

CUSTOM,] *lit.* 'judgment,' as in 2. 13.

11. TAKE,] without asking permission or consent.

CHARIOTS,] whether for war or for pleasure.

HORSEMEN,] for glory or for war, according to his good will.

RUN,] on foot, shewing and doing him service, see 2 Sa. 15. 1; 1 K. 1. 9.

12. HEADS,] which, though honourable posts, were full of peril.

FIFTIES,] a constituted number among the Israelites.

PLOUGHING,] that he may be aggrandized and fed.

REAPING,] when his harvest is ripe, irrespective of their own will, and without proper remuneration.

WAR,] such as swords, spears, bows and arrows.

CHARIOTEER,] iron scythes, &c.

13. PERFUMERS,] to gratify his senses with delicious odours.

COOKS,] to satisfy his appetites by sumptuous dishes.

BAKERS,] to bake all manner of cakes and food.

14. SERVANTS,] as a reward for their services to him, but regardless of the loss of others.

15. SEED,] prepared for your own use.

TITHE,] exacting a tenth of all as a royal right.

EUNUCHS,] as in Ge. 37. 36; 39. 1; 40. 2, 7; 1 K. 22. 9; 2 K. 8. 6; 9. 32; 18. 17; 20. 18; 23. 11; 24. 12, 15; 25. 19, &c.

16. TAKE,] to himself, as if they were his own.

PREPARED,] made or used for his own labours.

OWN WORK,] whether public or private.

17. FLOCK,] of sheep and goats.

SERVANTS,] subject to his will and caprice.

18. CRIED OUT,] in distress and anguish, as the word implies.

NOT ANSWER,] but leave them to the consequences of their own choice.

19. REFUSED TO HEARKEN,] as in Jer. 11. 10; Zec. 7. 11.

20. NATIONS,] as in v. 5.

JUDGED] us in our disputes and contendings.

BEFORE US,] as our leader and head.

BATTLES,] with the nations around them.

21. SPEAKETH,] repeating, perhaps, the very words they used.

22. VOICE,] as he had said before in v. 9 above.

A KING,] as they desired, but without giving any indications of him whom he would appoint.

CITY,] till further revelations of God might be given him.

IX. 1. KISH,] i.e. 'laying a snare or bending.'

ABIEL,] i.e. 'my father is strong or is God.'

ZEROR,] i.e. a 'bundle or bag.'

BECHORATH,] i.e. a 'first-born.'

APHIAH,] i.e. 'blown or enflamed.'

VALOUR,] or ' might, or worth.'

2. SAUL,] i.e. 'asked.'

CHOICE,] as in Ex. 14. 7; Jud. 20. 15, 16, 34, &c.

GOODLY,] as to his stature and general appearance.

SHOULDER,] as in 10. 23.

3. SHE-ASSES,] as in Ex. 12. 16; 32. 15; 45. 23; 49. 11; Nu. 22. 21—33; Jud. 5. 10, &c.

YOUNG MEN,] the servants whom he had.

4. SHALISHA,] in 2 K. 4. 42, 'Baal-Shalisha.'

SHAALIM,] which is not mentioned elsewhere.

BENJAMIN,] or 'Imini.'

5. ZUPH,] compare 1. 1.

LEAVE OFF,] or ' cease,' as in Ge. 11. 8; 18. 11, &c.

SORROWFUL,] as in 10. 2; Ps. 38. 18; Isa. 57. 11; Jer. 17. 8; 38. 19; 42. 16.

6. A MAN OF GOD,] as in De. 33. 1; Jos. 14. 6; Jud. 13. 68; 1 Sa. 2. 27; 2 Sa. 9. 6, 7, 8, 10; 1 K. 12. 22; 13. 1—31, &c.

THIS CITY,] even Ramah, in the immediate neighbourhood.

HONOURED,] by God and men.

HAVE GONE,] in seeking the asses.

7. VESSELS,] which they carried along with them.

PRESENT,] compare Isa. 57. 9.

8. SILVER,] that is, about a sixpence in English money.

OUR WAY,] for finding the asses.

9. FORMERLY,] that is, when Samuel was alive; the narrative may have been written a century later.

SEEK GOD,] for guidance and help.

SEER,] lit. ' one who sees' visions from God.

PROPHET,] i.e. 'inspired one.'

10. GOOD,] and suitable to the circumstances.

ASCENT,] which led up to the city of Ramah.

DRAW WATER,] from the public wells for domestic use.

12. STATED SACRIFICE,] lit. 'the sacrifice of the day.'

A HIGH PLACE,] as in v. 13, 14, 19, 25; 10. 5, 13, &c.

13. TO EAT,] of the sacrifices.

BLESS,] as in Ex. 23. 25; Ps. 132. 15, &c.

CALLED,] or invited to the festival.

14. TO MEET THEM,] being divinely warned of their arrival beforehand.

15. UNCOVERED.] A common Hebrew phrase, as in Ruth 4. 4, &c.

16. ANOINTED,] pouring oil on his head, as in 10. 1, &c.

LEADER,] i.e. 'one in the fore-ground,' as in 10. 1; 13. 14; 25. 30; 2 Sa. 5. 2; 6. 21; 7. 8; 1 K. 1. 85; 14. 7; 16. 2; 2 K. 20. 5; 1 Ch. 5. 2; 9. 11, 20; 11. 2; 12. 27; 13. 1; 17. 7; 26. 24; 27. 4, 16; 28. 4; 29. 22; 2 Ch. 6. 5; 11. 11, 22; 19. 11; 28. 7; 31. 12, 13; 32. 21; 35. 8; Neh. 11. 11; Job 29. 10; 31. 37; Ps. 76. 12; Prov. 8. 6; 28. 16; Isa. 55. 4; Jer. 20. 1; Eze. 28. 2; Da. 9. 25, 26; 11. 22.

SAVED,] as in 14. 23; 18. 7, &c.

SEEN,] as in Ex. 3. 7, &c.

CRY,] as in Ex. 3. 7, &c.

17. RESTRAIN,] as in Job 29. 9, &c.

18. GATE,] or rather ' city,' as in v. 14 above.

19. EATEN,] as a token of friendship.

HEART,] regarding his future condition.

20. LOST,] as in v. 3 above.

THE DESIRE,] in the matter of a king.

21. SMALLEST,] owing especially to the fatal war narrated in the close of the Book of Judges.

FAMILY,] that is, the household of his father.

22. THE CHAMBER,] lit. perhaps, a place for 'reclining' at food, as in 2 K. 23. 11; 1 Ch. 9. 26, 33; 23. 28; 28. 12; 2 Ch. 31. 11; Ezra 8. 29; 10. 6; Neh. 10. 37, 38, 39; 13. 4, 5, 8, 9; Jer. 35. 2, 4; 36. 10, 12, 20, 21; Eze. 40. 17, 38, 44, 45, 46; 41. 10; 42. 1, 4, 5, 7, 8, 9, 10, 11, 12, 13; 44. 19; 45. 5; 46. 19.

CALLED,] or invited, as in v. 13.

23. COOK,] lit. 'slaughter-man,' as in Ge. 37. 36.

PORTION,] as in Ex. 29. 26, &c.

24. THE LEG,] as in Ex. 29. 22, &c.

LEFT,] or ' remains,' as in Ge. 14. 10, &c.

APPOINTED SEASON] of the festival, as in Ex. 13. 10, &c.

25. ROOF] of the house, which was flat, as most eastern houses are.

26. DAWN,] on the morrow.

27. EXTREMITY,] beyond the observation of spectators.

WORD OF GOD,] regarding the kingdom of Israel and himself, which had been revealed to Samuel.

X. 1. VIAL,] as in 2 K. 9. 1, 3.

OIL,] with which priests and others were anointed.

POURETH,] as in Ge. 28. 18, &c.

KISSETH] him, in token of affection and submission.

JEHOVAH,] the great king of Israel.
INHERITANCE,] that is, the twelve tribes of Israel, De. 32. 9.
LEADER,] as in 9. 16, &c.
2. GRAVE OF RACHEL,] as in Ge. 35. 19, 20; it was on the way to Bethlehem.
ZELZAH,] *lit.* 'shade from heat;' not mentioned elsewhere.
SEEK,] as in 9. 3, 4.
SORROWED,] as Saul had judged already, in 9. 5.
SON,] as in Ge. 42. 36; 2 Sa. 18. 33, &c.
3. OAK,] as in Ge. 12. 6, &c.
TABOR,] some distinguished man in those days, not the 'mountain,' which was in Zebulun.
BETH-EL,] which is Luz, as in Ge. 35. 6, 7.
KIDS,] for sacrifice to God.
CAKES] of bread, for a 'present,' or bread-offering.
BOTTLE] of skin, containing wine for an oblation.
4. WELFARE,] which is the common eastern salutation.
TWO LOAVES,] one for himself, and another for his servant.
5. HILL OF GOD,] as in v. 10.
GARRISON,] as in 13. 3.
CITY] of Geba, or near it.
BAND,] as in v. 10; Ps. 119. 61.
PROPHETS,] i.e. men who announced to others the will of God, whether it related to things past, present, or future.
HIGH-PLACE,] as in 9. 13, &c.
PSALTERY,] as in 2 Sa. 6. 5; 1 K. 10. 12; 1 Ch. 13. 8; 15. 16, 20, 28; 16. 5; 25. 16; 2 Ch. 5. 12; 9. 11; 20. 28; 29. 25, &c.
TABRET,] as in Ge. 31. 27, &c.
PIPE,] as in 1 K. 1. 40; Isa. 5. 12; 30. 29; Jer. 48. 36.
HARP,] as in Ge. 4. 21, &c.
PROPHESYING,] that is, singing the praises of God.
6. PROSPER,] subduing the natural backwardness of the man, and filling him with new zeal.
SPIRIT OF JEHOVAH,] the author of all spiritual influence.
PROPHESIED,] that is, sung and recounted the praises of God.
TURNED,] from his former character and habits to a new man.
7. SIGNS,] *or* 'tokens' just mentioned.
WITH THEE,] in the way of duty and trial to which he was called.
8. GILGAL,] where the Israelites first pitched after passing over the Jordan; compare 13. 1, 8, 13.
PEACE-OFFERINGS,] as in 11. 15; 13. 9—13.
WAIT,] see 12. 9—13.
9. SHOULDER,] as in 9. 2.
ANOTHER HEART,] as in Nu. 14. 24; v. 6 above.
SIGNS,] mentioned in v. 2—7.
10. HEIGHT,] as in v. 5.
MEET HIM,] and welcome him as the anointed of the Lord.
SPIRIT OF GOD,] as in v. 6.
MIDST,] as one of their number.
11. ACQUAINTANCE,] as in Job 13. 19; 42. 11.

HERETOFORE,] *lit.* 'from yesterday, third day.'
SON OF KISH.] In the east it is a very common thing to describe a man as the son of his father.
PROPHETS?] his previous character being contrary to all such things. Compare Acts 9. 21.
12. FATHER,] i.e. instructor.
SIMILE] in Israel, or at least among the inhabitants of his native place.
13. CEASETH,] other duties requiring his attention.
HIGH PLACE,] where the worship of God was performed.
14. UNCLE,] whose name was Ner, father of Abner, as in 14. 50, 51.
SAMUEL,] to seek God by him, as in 9. 6—10.
15. SAID,] regarding the asses, &c.
16. FOUND,] as in 9. 20.
NOT DECLARED,] probably from modesty or distrust.
17. MIZPEH,] of Benjamin, as in 7. 5.
18. BROUGHT UP,] as in Ge. 50. 24; Ex. 17. 3, &c.
DELIVER,] as in Ex. 18. 8; Jos. 19. 26; 24. 10, &c.
OPPRESSING] you on every side, from time to time.
19. REJECTED] from being king over you God himself, your
SAVIOUR,] and deliverer, as in Jud. 3. 9, 15; 6. 36.
EVILS,] or calamities, and from
DISTRESSES,] as in De. 31. 17, 21; Jud. 10. 14.
A KING,] such as the nations have over them.
STATION YOURSELVES,] as in 12. 7. 16.
20. CAPTURED,] by the lot, as the tribe out of which the new king must come.
21. FAMILIES,] or smaller divisions.
MATRI,] i.e. 'rainy.'
SAUL..KISH,] as in 9. 1.
22. VESSELS] that is, the waggons, &c., belonging to the assembly.
23. STATIONED HIMSELF,] as in v. 19.
UPWARD,] as in 9. 2.
24. FIXED] for king, according to their desire.
NONE LIKE HIM,] in regard to stature and outward appearance.
SHOUT] with joy, as the word implies.
LIVE,] not 'God save the king,' as it is profanely rendered in the C.V.
25. RIGHT,] *lit.* 'judgment.'
A BOOK,] for future guidance.
BEFORE JEHOVAH,] as a sacred deposit.
HOUSE,] without retaining any to serve the new king.
26. GIBEAH,] i.e. 'height *or* hill.'
FORCE,] as in Ex. 14. 4, 9, 28, &c.
TOUCHED,] *lit.* 'stricken,' as in Ge. 32. 32; Jer. 4. 18, &c.
27. WORTHLESSNESS,] i.e. worthless persons.
SAVE US] from the hand of the enemy.
DESPISE] him, probably from his youth inexperience, and common birth.
PRESENT,] as a mark of respect.

DEAF] to those who may have tried to stir him up against them.

XI. 1. NAHASH,] i.e. 'a serpent,' as in Ge. 3. 1, &c.

AMMONITE,] a descendant of Lot, as in Ge. 19. 38; king of Ammon, as in 1 Sa. 12. 12.

JABESH-GILEAD,] beyond the Jordan, in the tribe of Manasseh, Jud. 20. 8.

COVENANT,] of place and safety, and we SERVE] thee, by payment of tribute, &c.

2. PICKING OUT,] as in Nu. 16. 14; Jud. 16. 21; Job 30. 17; Prov. 30. 17; Isa. 51. 1.

RIGHT EYE,] so that they would be unfit for shooting in battle, and as a token of REPROACH] on their brethren that they could not help them in their extremity.

3. ELDERS,] who ruled in every city.

BORDER,] i.e. territory.

GIBEAH OF SAUL,] where he was born, brought up, and dwelt, since he had been appointed king, as in 10. 26.

WEEP,] because of their degradation and helplessness.

HERD,] with which he had been ploughing, which was an honourable occupation in those days even for chieftains.

6. SPIRIT OF GOD,] as in 9. 6, 10.

PROSPER,] as in 9. 10.

BURNETH] at the insult and injury intended for the people of God.

7. COUPLE OF OXEN,] probably those with which he had been labouring.

PIECES,] as in Jud. 19. 29; 20. 6.

SAMUEL,] who was still regarded as a leader in Israel.

FEAR OF JEHOVAH,] that is, of his wrath and judgment, as in Jud. 5. 23.

AS ONE MAN,] every one able to bear weapons.

8. INSPECTETH,] lest any of the tribes and families might be missing.

BEZEK,] as in Jud. 1. 4.

9. SAFETY,] confidently trusting in the justice of their cause, their great number, and the prayer of Samuel.

HEAT,] early morning being the best time for journeying in these countries.

REJOICE,] at the courage of Saul, and the hope of escape from injury and disgrace.

10. GOOD IN YOUR EYES,] as far as they had opportunity and power.

11. DETACHMENTS,] as in Jud. 7. 16.

CAMP] of the Ammonites, as in v. 1 above.

SCATTERED] abroad everywhere on the face of the field.

12. REIGN] as king, as in 10. 27.

GIVE YE UP] into our power, and to our will.

PUT TO DEATH,] for their disregard of the Lord's anointed.

WROUGHT SALVATION,] even for those disregarding his divine law and authority.

14. GILGAL,] as in 10. 8.

RENEW] before God and the world the oath of allegiance.

15. BEFORE JEHOVAH,] as in his sight, by his authority, and under his sanction.

REJOICETH,] because of the deliverance

from the enemy, and of the harmony prevailing among themselves.

XII. 1. VOICE,] as the Lord directed me, as in 8. 5, 19, 20.

A KING,] such as rules over the other nations of the earth.

2. WALKING HABITUALLY,] as in Ge. 3. 8; 5. 22, 24; 6. 9; 13. 7, &c.

GRAY-HEADED,] as in Job 15. 10.

WITH YOU] for judges, as in 8. 1.

YOUTH,] as in 1. 28; 2. 11, 18.

3. TESTIFY] before God and the assembly publicly.

ANOINTED] even Saul, as in 10. 1.

OX..ASS,] the chief beasts of burden in Canaan.

OPPRESSED,] as in Lev. 6. 2, 4.

BRUISED,] as in De. 28. 23; 2 K. 18. 21.

RANSOM,] lit. a 'covering,' as in Ge. 6. 14; Ex. 21. 20, &c.

HIDE MINE EYES,] as in Lev. 20. 4; Isa. 1. 15; Prov. 28. 27; Eze. 22. 26, &c.

4. OPPRESSED,] by unlawful exactions, nor CRUSHED,] by undue pressure.

TAKEN,] by any false pretence.

5. WITNESS,] who cannot lie nor be deceived.

FOUND,] being publicly called upon to search and exhibit it.

A WITNESS,] as in Jos. 24. 22.

6. MADE,] or perhaps 'prepared,' fitted them for their work.

BROUGHT UP] with a high hand, and an outstretched arm.

7. STATION YOURSELVES,] as in 10. 19.

JUDGE,] and by implication 'condemn' them for their sin.

RIGHTEOUS ACTS,] in leading and bringing them to Canaan.

8. EGYPT,] to see his son Joseph, and escape the famine in the land.

CRY,] because of their bondage and oppression.

CAUSE TO DWELL,] by casting lots for their inheritance.

9. FORGET] his benefits, his laws, and his threatenings.

SELLETH,] as in Jud. 2. 14.

HAZOR,] as in Jud. 4. 2.

PHILISTINES,] in the days of Samson, in Jud. 13. 1.

MOAB,] as in the times of Ehud, in Jud. 3. 14, 15.

10. CRY,] because of their distress, for help.

SINNED,] as in De. 1. 41.

BAALIM,] i.e. 'lords.'

ASHTAROTH,] as in Jud. 2. 11, 12.

DELIVER] us once more.

SERVE] as it is our duty to do.

11. JERUBBAAL,] that is Gideon, in Jud. 6. 23.

BEDAN,] not mentioned elsewhere, save in Heb. 11. 32; perhaps a contraction for the word 'Ben-Dan,' i.e. 'son of Dan,' viz. Samson.

JEPHTHAH,] as in Jud. 11. 1.

SAMUEL,] or as Syr. and Ar. Versions read 'Samson;' compare Heb. 11. 32.

CONFIDENTLY,] without fear of evil.

12. NAHASH,] as in 11. 1.

COME AGAINST YOU,] to subdue and oppress you.

A KING,] who shall go out and come in before them in war and in peace.

YOUR KING,] by right of purchase, inheritance, and solemn vows.

13. CHOSEN,] confirming God's choice by their own free will.

ASKED,] as in 8. 5.

PLACED,] *lit.* 'given.'

14. FEAR,] that is, 'reverence.'

SERVED,] him alone as your God and King.

VOICE,] in the mouth of his servants the prophets.

PROVOKE THE MOUTH,] as in Nu. 20. 24.

15. AGAINST YOU,] for evil and not for good.

16. STATION YOURSELVES,] as in v. 7 above.

GREAT THING,] sending thunder and rain in an unusual time.

17. WHEAT-HARVEST,] as in 7. 13, when rain is unknown.

VOICES,] that is, thunders, as in Ex. 9. 23.

RAIN,] as in Ex. 9. 33, 34, &c.

KNOW. SEE,] by this outward sign.

A KING,] instead of trusting to Jehovah their sole king.

18. VOICES... RAIN,] according to the prayer of Samuel.

19. PRAY FOR,] as in 2 Ch. 30. 18.

THY GOD,] afraid or unable to say ' our God.'

SINS,] this other sin with which Samuel had charged them.

20. EVIL.] He does not attempt to excuse or palliate it, but adopts their own words.

TURN NOT ASIDE] any more as in days past.

21. VAIN THINGS] that is, the idols, which are nothing in themselves.

PROFIT] those who serve them, as in Isa. 44. 10; Hab. 2. 18.

DELIVER] their worshippers, when they are in danger, as in De. 32. 30.

VAIN,] empty, worthless, as in 1 Cor. 8. 4.

22. LEAVE] them utterly, but remembers kindness for the sake of his own

NAME] or character, which he magnifies above all his works of creation.

PLEASED,] as in 1 Ch. 17. 27; 2 Sa. 7. 29; Job 6. 9.

PEOPLE,] to serve and glorify him, as in Ex. 6. 7, &c.

23. FAR BE IT FROM ME,] as in Ge. 18. 25, &c.

TO SIN] like you, in being regardless of the glory of God as exhibited by his people.

BY CEASING,] as in Jer. 44. 18.

DIRECTED,] as in Ex. 4. 12, 15.

UPRIGHT WAY,] being of the Lord's own choosing.

24. FEAR,] as a great God and King.

HEART,] as in De. 4. 29.

SEE] ye with your own eyes his working this day.

25. EVIL] as heretofore, notwithstanding these warnings and their profession of penitence.

CONSUMED] out of the land utterly.

XIII. 1. REIGNING] over Israel, by God's appointment.

2. CHOOSETH,] as foretold in 8. 11, 12.

MICHMASH,] i.e. 'treasure,' as in v. 5, 11, 16, 23; 14. 5, 31; Neh. 11. 31; Isa. 10. 28.

BETH-EL.] as in Ge. 12. 8, &c.

JONATHAN,] i.e. 'Jah hath given.'

GIBEAH OF BENJAMIN,] elsewhere called ' of Saul.'

TENTS,] or places of residence up and down the country.

3. GARRISON,] *lit.* 'set up thing,' as in Ge. 19. 26; 1 Sa. 13. 3, 4; 2 Sa. 8. 6, 14; 1 K. 4. 19; 1 Ch. 11. 16; 18. 13; 2 Ch. 8. 10; 17. 2.

GEBA,] i.e. 'a height,' as in Jos. 18. 24.

HEAR,] of this action of Jonathan.

TRUMPET,] proclaiming the victory, and summoning the people to the war.

HEAR,] the sound of the alarm.

4. SAUL,] rather Jonathan, but it was probably done under the direction of Saul.

ABHORRED,] because of this unexpected attack and victory.

GILGAL,] as in 11. 14, 15, &c.

5. CHARIOTS,] or 'charioteers,' as in 2 Sa. 10. 18; 1 K. 20. 21; 1 Ch. 19. 18; or 'thirty chief chariots;' Syr. and Ar. read '3000 chariots,' but even Pharaoh had only 600, (Ex. 14. 7); Jabin 900, (Jud. 4. 3); Zerah, 300, (2 Ch. 14. 9.)

SAND,] as in Ge. 22. 17, &c.

MICHMASH,] as in v. 2 above.

BETH-AVEN,] as in Jos. 7. 2.

6. DISTRESSED,] as in Jud. 11. 7.

OPPRESSED] by the multitude of the Philistines.

CAVES,] such as those of Adullam, Engedi, &c., with which the land abounded.

THICKETS,] as in 2 Ch. 33. 11.

ROCKS,] as in Nu. 24. 21; Jud. 15. 8; 20 45, 47.

HIGH-PLACES,] as in Jud. 9. 46. 49.

PITS,] as in Ge. 37. 20, &c.

7. HEBREWS,] as in Ge. 40. 15, &c.

GILEAD,] that they might escape the enemy.

TREMBLED,] as in 14. 15; 16. 4; 21. 1; 28 5, &c.

8. APPOINTMENT,] as in v. 11.

SCATTERED,] for fear of the Philistines.

ASCEND,] without waiting for the high priest.

10. BLESS,] i. e. salute or declare him blessed.

11. DONE?] seeing probably the offering burning on the altar.

SCATTERED,] as in v. 8.

THE DAYS,] as in v. 8.

MICHMASH,] as in v. 2, 5, 16.

12. UNTO ME,] to attack me in battle.

APPEASED,] *lit.* ' smoothed,' as in Ex. 32. 11, &c.

FORCE MYSELF,] against my own will and judgment.

ASCEND,] as in v. 9.

13. FOOLISH,] as in Ge. 31. 28; 1 Sa. 26. 21; 2 Sa. 15. 31; 24. 10; 1 Ch. 21. 8; 2 Ch. 16. 9; Isa. 44. 25.

COMMAND,] to hearken to the words of the Lord's prophets.

14. STAND,] established in thy family for ever.

SOUGHT] as a rare thing in the land.

HEART,] who would do all his pleasure.
LEADER,] as in 9. 16, &c.
15. GILGAL,] where Saul had been waiting for him.
GIBEAH OF BENJAMIN,] the dwelling-place of Saul.
INSPECTETH,] that he might know their condition and number.
16. MICHMASH,] as in v. 2, 5, 11.
17. DESTROYER,] as in 14. 15, &c.
DETACHMENTS,] as in Jud. 7. 16, &c.
OPHRAH,] as in Jos. 18. 23, a city of Benjamin.
SHUAL,] i.e. 'a fox.'
18. BETH-HORON,] as in Jos. 16. 3, 5, a city of Ephraim.
ZEBOIM,] in which was a city of that name, (Neh. 11. 34,) in the land of Benjamin.
WILDERNESS] of Jericho.
19. ARTIFICER,] as in Ex. 28. 11, and compare 2 K. 24. 14; Jer. 24. 1.
SWORD..SPEAR,] for warlike purposes, as in v. 22.
20. SHARPEN,] as in Ge. 4. 22; Job 16. 19; Ps. 7. 12; 52. 2.
PLOUGHSHARE,] as in v. 21.
COULTER,] as in v. 21; Isa. 2. 4; Joel 3. 10; Mic. 4. 3.
AXE,] as in Jud. 9. 48; v. 21 below; Ps. 74. 5; Jer. 46. 22.
MATTOCK,] as in v. 21.
21. FILE.] This original word is not found elsewhere.
THREE PRONGED RAKES.] This original word is not found elsewhere.
GOADS,] as in Ecc. 12. 11.
22. SWORD..SPEAR,] as in v. 19.
23. STATION,] as in Jos. 4. 3, 9; 1 Sa. 14. 1, 4, 6, 11, 15; 2 Sa. 23. 14; Isa. 22. 19.
PASSAGE,] as in Ge. 32. 22; Isa. 30. 32.

XIV. 1. THE DAY COMETH,] as in Job 1. 3, 13; 2. 1, &c.
BEARING HIS WEAPONS,] as in Jud. 9. 54, &c.
STATION,] as in 13. 23.
2. GIBEAH,] as in 13. 15, 16.
POMEGRANATE,] or 'Rimmon,' as in Jud. 20. 47.
MIGRON,] as in Isa. 10. 28.
SIX HUNDRED,] as in 13. 15.
3. AHIAH,] i.e. 'brother of Jah,' as in 22. 9, 11, 20, called 'Ahimelech,' i.e. 'brother of a king.'
AHITUB,] i.e. 'brother of goodness.'
I-CHABOD,] as in 4. 21.
EPHOD,] as every priest did, while ministering before the Lord.
4. PASSAGES,] as in 13. 23.
EDGE,] lit. 'tooth.'
BOZEZ,] i.e. 'shining.'
SENEH,] i.e. a 'bush or tooth.'
5. FIXED,] as in 2. 8.
6. UNCIRCUMCISED,] as in Jud. 14. 3, &c.
FOR US,] or 'by us.'
RESTRAINT,] as in Prov. 25. 28.
FEW,] as in Jud. 7. 4, 7; 2 Ch. 14. 11.
8. REVEALED,] as in 3. 21, &c.
10. SIGN,] or 'token.'
11. REVEALED,] as in v. 8.

HEBREWS,] as in 13. 7.
HOLES,] as in 2 K. 12. 8; Job 30. 6; Song 5. 4; Eze. 8. 7; Neh. 2. 12; Zec. 14. 12; compare 13. 6.
13. FALL,] wounded and slain.
14. SMITING] of the Philistines.
FURROW,] as in Ps. 129. 3.
YOKE,] as in 11. 7.
15. TREMBLING,] as in Da. 10. 7, &c.
DESTROYERS,] as in 13. 17.
SHAKETH,] as in Ps. 77. 18; Prov. 30. 21 ; Joel 2. 10; Amos 8. 8, &c.
OF GOD,] that is, a very great trembling, or rather one caused by God.
16. GIBEAH,, as in v. 2 above.
MELTED AWAY,] as in Ex. 15. 15; Jos. 2. 9, 24, &c.
BEATEN DOWN,] as in Ps. 5. 22, 26; Ps. 74. 6; 141. 5; Prov. 23. 35; Isa. 16. 8; 28. 1; 41. 7.
17. INSPECT] the six hundred who were with him, as in v. 2.
18. AHIAH,] as in v. 3.
ARK OF GOD,] to enquire of God by it, which he is not said to have done before.
19. GREAT,] so as to be heard at that distance.
REMOVE,] lit. 'gather,' as in Nu. 11. 16; 21. 16, &c.
20. CALLED,] or 'summoned,' as in Jos. 8. 6; Jud. 6. 34, 35; 18. 23.
DESTRUCTION,] as in De. 7. 23; 28. 20; 1 Sa. 5. 9, 11, &c.
21. FOR THE PHILISTINES,] that is, on their side, in the contest.
HERETOFORE,] lit. 'yesterday, third day.
22. HIDING THEMSELVES,] as in 13. 6.
23. SAVETH,] by the hand of Jonathan and his armour-bearer.
BETH-AVEN,] as in 13. 5.
24. DISTRESSED,] as in 13. 6; Isa. 3. 5; 53. 7
ADJURETH,] as in 1 K. 8. 31 ! 2 Ch. 6. 22.
CURSED,] as in v. 28; 26. 19; Ge. 3. 14, 17, &c.
FOOD,] in accordance with the king's oath.
25. FOREST,] between Beth-Aven and Aijalon, as in v. 31.
FIELD,] as they passed along; Canaan is frequently spoken of as a 'land of honey.'
26. DROPPED,] from the combs in the trees and shrubs.
MOUTH,] to taste a little of it, for they all feared the curse of the
OATH] that Saul had used in v. 24.
27. ROD,] as in v. 43; Ps. 110. 2, &c.
HONEY-COMB,] lit. 'forest of the honey,' not found elsewhere.
SEE,] whereas they had been dim with fatigue and exhaustion.
28. ADJURED,] as in v. 24 above.
WEARY,] as in v. 31.
29. TROUBLED,] as in Ge. 34. 30; Jos. 6. 18; 7. 25; Jud. 11. 35; 1 K. 18. 17, 18, &c.
BRIGHT,] as in v. 27; 29. 10; Ge. 44. 3; Prov. 4. 18, &c.
30. FOUND,] in the enemy's camp.
GREAT,] because of the weariness of the people.
31. AIJALON,] a city of Judah, as in 2 Ch. 11. 10.
VERY WEARY,] as in v. 28, by the heat of the day, and the pursuit of the enemy.

32. MAKE] their way, unto the spoil; the Marginal Reading 'flew,' is unnecessary.

BLOOD,] contrary to the express law of God in Ex. 33. 23; Lev. 19. 26.

33. SINNING,] in breaking his law.

DEALT TREACHEROUSLY,] as in Ex. 21. 8; Jud. 9. 23, &c.

ROLL,] as in Jos. 10. 18, &c.

GREAT STONE,] that it might serve as a table on which they could slaughter the animals properly.

34. SAITH,] to his officers and attendants.

35. ALTAR,] as Samuel had done in 7. 17.

JEHOVAH,] i.e. it was the first altar he built, but not the last.

36. PREY,] as in Ge. 34. 27, 29, &c.

UNTO GOD,] to ask his counsel and direction.

37. NOT ANSWERED,] as a punishment perhaps for his haste in v. 19.

38. CHIEFS,] lit. 'corners,' as in Jud. 20. 2, &c.

THIS SIN,] the existence of which he conjectured from the want of a divine response.

39. SAVING,] or 'the saviour of Israel.'

PEOPLE,] thus expressing their dissent from his judgment.

40. DO,] as in v. 36.

41. GIVE HELP,] as in Ge. 11. 3, 4, 7, &c.

O PERFECT ONE,] as in Job 36. 4; 37. 16; De. 32. 4; 2 Sa. 22. 31; Ps. 18. 30, &c.

CAPTURED,] by the lot.

43. DONE?] sinning against God.

TASTED,] as in v. 29.

ROD,] or staff, as in v. 27.

HONEY,] by which his eyes were refreshed, when weary.

44. ADD,] as in Ruth 1. 17, &c.

DIE,] to appease the anger of God, which had manifested itself by silence.

45. SALVATION,] from the power of the Philistines.

PROFANATION,] as in Ge. 18. 25, &c.

HAIR,] as in 2 Sa. 14. 11; 1 K. 1. 52.

WITH GOD,] along with him, in conjunction with him.

RESCUE,] as in Ex. 13. 13, &c.

46. PLACE,] on the coast of the great sea.

47. CAPTURED,] from all his enemies around.

MOAB,] on the east, along with the BENE-AMMON,] as in 11. 11, and EDOM,] on the south of Canaan.

ZOBAH,] near Damascus, 2 Sa. 8. 3, 5.

PHILISTINES,] in their five principalities.

VEX,] lit. 'make or declare wicked or wrong,' as in Ex. 22. 9; De. 25. 1, &c.

48. FORCE,] or 'doth mightily.'

AMALEK,] as in 15. 3, 7; compare Ex. 17. 8, 14, &c.

SPOILER,] as in Jud. 2. 14, 16.

49. JONATHAN,] as in 13. 2, &c.; he appears to have been the first-born.

ISHUI,] i.e. 'he is equal,' the same as Abinadab in 1 Ch. 8. 33; 9. 39.

MELCHI-SHUA,] i.e. 'my king is rich.' Ishbosheth (or Eshbaal) in 2 Sa. 2. 18; 1 Ch. 8. 33, was probably not then born, see also 2 Sa. 21. 8.

MERAB,] i.e. 'multiplication' as in 18. 17, 19.

MICHAL,] i.e. a 'brook,' who afterwards became the wife of David, as in 18. 27.

50. AHINOAM,] i.e. 'my brother is pleasant.'

AHIMAAZ,] i.e. 'my brother is angry.'

ABNER,] i.e. 'my father is light.'

NER,] i.e. 'light.'

51. KISH,] as in 9. 1.

ABIEL,] i.e. 'my father is strong or God,' as in 9. 1.

52. SEVERE,] as in 2 Sa. 11. 15.

MIGHTY MAN,] as in 9. 1, &c.

SON OF VALOUR,] or 'strength or worth,' as in De. 3. 18; Jud. 21. 10.

GATHER,] as foretold in 8. 11.

XV. 1. ME,] the prophet of the Lord, who now speaks to you.

ANOINT,] as in 9. 16.

2. LOOKED AFTER,] as in Ge. 21. 1; Ex. 3. 16, &c.

AMALEK,] the first of the Goyim, as in Nu. 24. 20.

LAID,] or 'set.'

3. SMITTEN,] with the sword in battle.

DEVOTED,] to the Lord, and to utter destruction.

PITY,] as it had no pity on the feeble rear of Israel, in Ex. 17. 8; De. 25. 17, 18, 19.

WOMAN,] as in Jos. 8. 25; 6. 21; 1 Sa. 22. 19.

SUCKLING,] as in 22. 19.

SHEEP,] as in Jos. 6. 21.

ASS,] that every living creature might be destroyed. De. 25. 19.

4. SUMMONETH,] lit. 'causeth to hear,' as in 23. 8.

INSPECTETH,] their condition and numbers.

TELAIM,] i.e. 'young lambs;' perhaps the same as Telem, in Jos. 15. 24.

5. STRIVETH,] as in Ge. 26. 20, 21, 22.

6. KENITE,] see Nu. 24. 21; Jud. 1. 16; 4. 11.

GO DOWN,] from their inaccessible heights, alluded to in Nu. 24. 21.

CONSUME] thee with the sword.

DIDST KINDNESS,] by the hands of Jethro and Hobab, Ex. 18. 10, 19; Nu. 10. 29, 32.

TURNETH ASIDE,] according to the advice of Saul.

7. HAVILAH,] as in Ge. 2. 11; 25. 18, on the north-east, to

SHUR,] as in Ge. 16. 7; on the south-west.

8. CATCHETH,] as in 2 K. 7. 12, &c.

AGAG,] a common name of the kings of Amalek, see Nu. 24. 2.

SWORD,] yet many escaped, see 27. 8; 30. 1.

9. PITY,] which had been expressly forbidden in v. 3 above.

BEST,] as in Ge. 47. 6, 11; Ex. 22. 5; 1 Sa. 15. 15.

NOT BEEN WILLING,] as in Ex. 10. 27, &c.

WORK,] as in Ge. 33. 14, &c.

DESPISED,] as in Mal. 1. 7, 12.

WASTED,] as in Ex. 16. 21.

10. ENGAGED,] as in Ge. 6. 6, 7, &c.

KING,] as in 8. 22.

TURNED BACK,] from following the law of Jehovah.

PERFORMED] fully, but according to his own pleasure only.

DISPLEASING,] that Saul had thus acted.

CRIETH,] because of his distress, as the word implies.

12. CARMEL,] a city of Judah, as in Jos. 15. 55.

MONUMENT,] *lit.* a 'hand,' as in 2 Sa. 18. 18; Isa. 56. 5.

GILGAL,] expecting perhaps to meet Samuel there as before, in 13. 8.

13. BLESSED,] as in Ge. 6. 26, &c.

WORD] of Jehovah regarding Amalek.

14. NOISE,] *lit.* 'voice.'

15. PITY,] as in Ex. 2. 6, &c.

BEST,] as in v. 9 above.

THY GOD,] he does not say 'my God.'

REMNANT,] being despised and wasted, as in v. 9.

16. DESIST,] as in De. 9. 14, &c.

SPEAK,] as in 3. 9, 10.

17. EYES,] as in 9. 1.

ANOINT] by the hands of his inspired servant.

18. SINNERS,] as in Ge. 13. 13, &c.

CONSUMED,] as in v. 3.

19. FLY,] as in 14. 32; 25. 14.

20. WAY,] as in v. 18.

21. FIRST PART,] as in 2. 29.

THY GOD,] as in v. 15 above.

22. SACRIFICES,] especially such as he hath not commanded.

HEARKENING,] and obeying the express law of God.

BETTER,] and more agreeable to the lawgiver.

FAT OF RAMS,] which was required by the ceremonial laws.

23. DIVINATION,] as in Nu. 22. 7; 23. 23, &c.

REBELLION,] against the will of God.

TERAPHIM,] as in Ge. 31. 19, 34, 35, &c.

STUBBORNNESS.] The original word is not found elsewhere.

KING] over Israel his own peculiar people.

24. SINNED,] against God and thee.

FEARED,] to oppose the wishes of the people, Ex. 23. 2; Prov. 29. 25; Isa. 51. 12, 13.

25. BEAR,] as in Ge. 50. 17, &c.

WITH ME,] to Gilgal.

JEHOVAH,] acknowledging his supreme authority as the God of Israel.

26. REJECTED,] by declining to carry out fully his wishes.

27. UPPER ROBE,] as in Ex. 28. 4, 31, 34, &c.

RENT,] as in 4. 12, &c.

28. NEIGHBOUR,] *or* 'friend,' as in 30. 26, &c.

PRE-EMINENCE,] as in 1 Ch. 29. 11; La. 3. 18; Isa. 63. 3, 5.

LIE,] regarding his promises or threats, nor

REPENT,] concerning his plans and purposes.

PENITENT,] but the all-seeing and all-knowing God.

30. SINNED,] as in v. 24.

HONOUR ME,] as in Ex. 20. 12; De. 5. 16; Ps. 22. 23; Prov. 3. 9; Isa. 24. 15.

WITH ME,] as in v. 25.

THY GOD,] as in v. 15.

31. TURNETH BACK,] at this second confession.

32. AGAG,] who had been captured, as in v. 8.

DAINTILY,] as in Ge. 49. 20; Prov. 29. 17; La. 4. 5.

BITTERNESS,] as in 2 Sa. 2. 26, &c.

33. BEREAVED,] as in La. 1. 20, &c.

HEWETH IN PIECES.] The original word is not found elsewhere; what one orders to be done is often said to be done by himself.

34. RAMATH,] his birth-place and usual residence.

OF SAUL,] as in 11. 4.

35. NOT ADDED TO SEE] him intentionally, once he saw him, as in 19. 24.

MOURNED,] as in v. 11; 16. 1.

REPENTED,] as in v. 11 above.

XVI. 1. MOURNING,] as in 15. 11, 35.

REJECTED,] for his disobedience, as in 15. 26.

HORN,] as in 1 K. 1. 39, &c.

JESSE,] see Ruth 4. 17, &c.

SONS,] even David, the youngest.

2. SLAIN] me, on the pretence of treason.

HEIFER,] as a peace-offering to the Lord.

SAID] to the elders and all those enquiring his purpose.

3. CALLED FOR JESSE] among those invited.

DO,] at the proper time; compare the promise in Mat. 10. 19.

ANOINTED,] for king, as in v. 1.

4. BETH-LEHEM,] where Jesse lived with his family, as in v. 1.

TREMBLE,] fearing that some visitation from God might be impending over the city.

PEACE,] that is, a token of peace.

6. COMING IN,] to the sacrifice, according to the invitation.

ELIAB,] i.e. 'my God is father;' he was the eldest and first-born; called Elihu in 1 Ch. 27. 18.

7. STATURE,] for in both these respects Saul himself was conspicuous.

THE EYES,] not 'the outward appearance,' as in the C.V.

THE HEART,] observing the thoughts and dispositions.

8. ABINADAB,] i.e. 'my father is noble ;' the second son, 17. 13.

FIXED,] for king over Israel instead of Saul.

9. SHAMMAH,] i.e. 'desolation *or* hearkening,' as in 1 Ch. 2. 13; 2 Sa. 13. 3; the third son.

10. SEVEN] in all, including Nathanael, Raddai, and Ozem (1 Ch. 2. 14, 15); the seventh is not mentioned by name.

11. YOUNGEST,] even David.

DELIGHTETH HIMSELF,] as in Ge. 37. 2, &c.

TURN ROUND,] not 'sit down,' as in C.V.

12. RUDDY,] as in 17. 42; Ge. 25. 25.

BEAUTY OF EYES.] This expression is not found elsewhere.

APPEARANCE,] *lit.* 'sight *or* vision.'

13. HORN,] which he had provided, as in v. 1.

BRETHREN,] doubtless, however, without mentioning for what purpose he did it.

PROSPER,] as in 10. 6, 10, &c.

RAMATH,] as in 15. 34.

14. TURNED ASIDE] because of disobedience, see 10. 11; 11. 6.

SPIRIT OF SADNESS,] *or* 'of evil.'

TERRIFIED,] as in 2 Sa. 22. 5, &c.

16. SKILFUL,] *lit.* 'knowing.'

PLAYING,] as in 18. 10; 19. 19; 2 Sa. 3. 15.
HARP,] as in v. 23.
HAND,] upon the harp.
17. PROVIDE,] *lit.* 'see ye.'
18. BETH-LEHEMITE,] as in 16. 1.
PLAYING] on the harp, as in v. 16.
VIRTUOUS,] *or* 'worthy.'
BATTLE,] known perhaps by some exploits not recorded.
INTELLIGENT,] as in Ge. 41. 33, 39.
FORM,] as in Ge. 29. 17; 39. 6; 41. 18. 19; compare Da. 1. 4.
WITH HIM,] as his helper in all things.
19. FLOCK,] as in 16. 11.
20. ASS,] for his son riding on, as was customary.
BREAD..WINE..GOATS,] as a present to SAUL,] the king of Israel; compare 9. 7.
21. LOVETH] him, before the passion of jealousy began to burn within him.
WEAPONS,] in Saul's going forth or coming in from war.
22. JESSE,] the father of David.
STAND BEFORE ME,] as my armour-bearer.
EYES.] This language, though courteous, could not but be regarded as a command.
23. ON SAUL,] rendering him unhappy.
HARP,] as in v. 16.
HAND,] using doubtless his best skill in producing harmony.
REFRESHMENT,] as in Job 32. 20,
TURNED ASIDE,] for a season, at least.

XVII. 1. CAMPS,] under their five different princes, encouraged perhaps by the dispondency of Saul.
SHOCHOH,] a city in Judah, as in Jos. 15. 35; 2 Ch. 28. 18.
AZEKAH,] see Jos. 10. 10.
EPHES-DAMMIM,] see 1 Ch. 11. 13, Pas-Dammim, i.e. 'extremity of Dammim.'
2. ELAH,] *lit.* a 'terebinth.'
4. DUELLISTS,] as in v. 23; *lit.* 'two who are between' other parties.
GOLIATH,] i.e. 'an exile,' as in v. 23; 21. 10: 22. 10.
GATH,] one of the five principalities of the Philistines, Jos. 11. 22.
A SPAN,] as in Ex. 28. 16; 39. 9; Isa. 40. 12; Eze. 43. 13.   He was 9½ feet high, which has been equalled in later times.
5. HELMET,] as in 2 K. 26. 14; Isa. 59. 17; Jer. 46. 4; Eze. 27. 10; 38. 5.
SCALED,] as in Lev. 11. 9, 10, 12; De. 14. 9, 10; Eze. 29. 4.
COAT OF MAIL,] as in v. 38; 2 Ch. 26. 14; Neh. 4. 16.
SHEKELS,] or about 156 lbs weight.
6. FRONTLET.] This original word is not found elsewhere,] but compare the word rendered 'forehead' in v. 49.
JAVELIN,] as in Jos. 8. 18, 26; v. 45 below; Job 39. 33; 41. 29; Jer. 6. 23; 50. 42.
7. SPEAR,] as in 13. 19, 22, &c.
BEAM,] as in 2 Sa. 21. 19; 1 Ch. 11. 23; 20. 5.
FLAME,] as in Nu. 21. 28, &c.
BUCKLER,] as in v. 41; 1 K. 10. 16; 1 Ch. 12. 8, 24, 34; 2 Ch. 9. 15; 11. 12; 14. 8; 25. 5,&c.
8. RANKS,] as in 4. 2, 12, 16, &c.

THE PHILISTINE,] the one pre-eminent,. so-—for stature and bravado.
COME DOWN] into the valley, in the midst of which he was standing.
9. SMITTEN ME] mortally in single combat.
10. REPROACHED,] as in Jud. 5. 18; 8. 15, &c.
11. BROKEN DOWN] in spirit, even Saul, Abner, Jonathan, and the rest of Israel.
AFRAID,] of meeting him in single combat.
12. From the 12th to the 31st verse is omitted in Septuagint.
13. TO BATTLE,] being summoned to meet the enemy, or perhaps from their own enthusiasm.
SHAMMAH,] as in 16. 6—9.
14. YOUNGEST] of the eight sons, as in 16. 11.
15. SAUL,] as in 16. 23, when the spirit of' sadness came upon him.
16. THE PHILISTINE,] that is Goliath of Gath, as in v. 8.
MORNING AND EVENING,] twice a day renewing his challenge.
STATIONETH HIMSELF,] in the front of Israel.
FORTY DAYS,] or nearly six weeks.
17. BRETHREN,] the three elder, as in v. 13, who were in the camp with Saul, at Elah.
EPHAH,] consisting of ten omers, Ex. 16. 16, 36.
ROASTED,] as in Lev. 23. 14; Ruth 2. 14. 1 Sa. 25. 18; 2 Sa. 17. 28.
LOAVES,] *lit.* 'ten bread.'
CAMP] at Elah, as in v. 2 above.
18. CUTTINGS.] Only found elsewhere in 2 Sa. 12. 31; 1 Ch. 20. 3.
CHEESE,] *lit.* 'milk,' as in Ge. 18. 8; 49. 12, &c.
THE THOUSAND,] among whom they were enrolled.
INSPECT,] *or* 'look after.'
PLEDGE] of safety and good behaviour.
19. ELAH,] as in v. 2 above.
20. LIFTETH UP] the goods for his brethren, as in v. 17, 18.
PATH,] as in Prov. 17. 5. 18; 5. 6, 21; Isa. 59. 8.
FORCE] of men of war going forth to battle.
RANK] in the front of the enemy.
SHOUTED,] according to the usual custom, inspiring themselves with courage, and dispiriting the enemy.
21. LETTETH DOWN] from off the beast of burden which bore the goods, or from off his own shoulder.
RANK,] unto his brethren.
23. DUELLISTS,] as in v. 4 above.
THOSE WORDS,] as in v. 8—10.
24. AFRAID] of engaging him in single combat, De. 32. 30.
25. COMING UP] from the valley, on the side where the Israelites were stationed.
DAUGHTER,] as in Jos. 15. 16.
REPROACH,] as he himself boasted in v. 10 above.
RICHES,] as a reward of his valour and skill.
MAKE FREE] from tribute, and servitude

26. WHAT IS DONE,] anxious to know the precise reward offered.
UNCIRCUMCISED,] as in Jud. 14. 3, &c.
27. THUS,] as in v. 25.
28. MEN,] standing round him in the ranks.
COME DOWN] from Beth-Lehem to the valley of Elah, where the enemy was met.
FEW SHEEP,] which he was accustomed to look after.
29. A WORD,] a matter of the lips, not worth speaking about. So the Targum reads it.
30. HEARD] by some of Saul's officers, from one to another.
31. RECEIVETH] him into his presence, knowing him of old.
32. FALL,] and become low and feeble.
FOUGHT] in single combat.
33. A YOUTH,] unaccustomed to contend with full grown men; he was about 18 or 20 years of age.
MAN OF WAR,] that is, one accustomed to it.
34. SHEPHERD,] entrusted with the care of a flock, and knowing the perils of such a life.
THE LION,] reckoned popularly the strongest of beasts, and
THE BEAR,] one of the most obstinate and powerful of the wild animals in Canaan.
DROVE,] which David had care of.
35. AFTER HIM] to the wilderness, whither he was retreating with his prey.
SMITTEN HIM,] with the staff perhaps which shepherds use.
DELIVERED] the trembling helpless prey.
BEARD,] as in 2 Sa. 20. 9, &c.
PUT HIM TO DEATH] for his rapacity.
36. HATH BEEN.] The language of confidence, not 'shall be,' as in the C.V.
LIVING GOD,] whose honour and name were reproached.
37. JEHOVAH,] the covenant-God of Israel.
PAW,] lit. 'hand.'
WITH THEE,] for help against the Philistines.
38. LONG ROBE,] as in Lev. 6. 10, &c.
HELMET,] as in Eze. 23. 24; this original word is not found elsewhere.
COAT OF MAIL,] as in v. 5 above.
39. GIRDED,] as in 25. 23, &c.
BEGINNETH,] or 'willeth,' as in Ex. 2. 21, &c.
TRIED] to use them beforehand, as in De. 28. 56.
40. STAFF,] or shepherd's crook for guiding the flock.
SMOOTH STONES,] fittest for the sling, which he intended to use.
BROOK,] which probably ran through the valley of Elah.
HABILIMENTS,] lit. 'vessel,' as in v. 49.
SCRIP.] This original word is not found elsewhere.
SLING,] a common instrument of defence and offence in ancient times.
41. BUCKLER,] as in v. 7.
42. LOOKETH ATTENTIVELY,] as in Ge. 15. 5. &c.
DESPISETH] him as an opponent unworthy of his prowess.
A YOUTH,] about 18 or 20 years of age.

RUDDY] with the freshness of youth, as in 16. 12.
FAIR APPEARANCE,] as in Ge. 39. 6.
43. A DOG,] one of the most despised of animals in the east.
STAVES,] fit only to drive away dogs and beggars.
44. HEAVENS,] as in De. 28. 26, &c.
FIELD,] as in Ex. 22. 31, &c.
45. SWORD..SPEAR..BUCKLER,] all implements of war.
REPROACHED,] as in v. 10 above.
46. SHUT THEE UP] helpless, without the possibility of escape from my hand.
TURNED ASIDE,] by cutting off and exposing to public view.
CARCASE,] as in Ge. 15. 12, &c.
EARTH,] as in v. 44 above.
EARTH,] or 'land,' i.e. of Canaan.
47. ASSEMBLY] of Israel and the Philistines.
SAVE,] or 'give ease' from oppression and danger.
JEHOVAH'S,] it belongs to him, and concerns his name and his people.
48. HASTETH,] as in 25. 18, 23, 42, &c.
49. VESSEL,] as in v. 40.
FOREHEAD,] which was probably uncovered for the purpose of seeing David properly, and of speaking with him.
50. STRONGER.] This verse is omitted by the Septuagint.
51. STANDETH OVER,] as he lay prostrate and wounded.
SHEATH,] as in 2 Sa. 20. 8; Jer. 47. 6; Eze. 21. 3, 4, 5, 30.
HEAD,] as a trophy of victory.
HERO,] as in Ge. 6. 4; 10. 8, 9; De. 10. 17, &c.
52. SHOUT] because of the victory.
THE VALLEY] of Elah.
EKRON,] another Philistine principality.
SHAARAIM,] or 'Sharaim,' as in Jos. 15. 36; 1 Ch. 4. 21.
GATH,] the birth-place of Goliath, about 24 miles off.
53. BURNING AFTER,] as in Ge. 31. 36, &c.
CAMPS,] as in v. 1.
54. HEAD,] as was customary in ancient warfare.
WEAPONS,] that is, those of Goliath.
TENT,] or dwelling, at Beth-Lehem, but see 21. 9.
55. GOING OUT,] as in v. 40 above. The Sept. omits v. 55—58; also 18. 1—5.
ABNER,] his uncle's son, see 14. 50.
WHOSE SON?] he had forgotten Jesse's name, which is not wonderful.
THY SOUL LIVETH,] as in 1. 26, &c.
NOT KNOWN] what was the name of David's father.
57. SMITING,] as in v. 49, 50, 51.
YOUTH.] He did not ask David's own name, knowing him well.
BETH-LEHEMITE,] as in 16. 1.

XVIII. 1. BOUND] by respect and affection and gratitude.
OWN SOUL,] as in De. 13. 6.
2. TAKETH HIM] into his own service entirely, and not partially as before.

PERMITTED,] *lit.* 'given.'
3. COVENANT] of friendship and peace.
4. STRIPPETH HIMSELF,] to make a present to David.
UPPER ROBE,] as in Lev. 8. 7, &c.
LONG ROBE,] as in Lev. 6. 10, &c.
SWORD..BOW..GIRDLE,] his chief weapons of warfare.
5. ACTETH WISELY,] as in Jos. 1. 7, 8, &c.
MEN OF WAR,] as their captain and leader.
GOOD,] that is, proper and suitable for his services.
6. COMING IN,] to the city from the valley of Elah.
WOMEN,] who had remained at home came forth
TO SING,] songs of triumph, as in Ex. 15. 20, &c.
DANCERS,] as in Ex. 15. 20 ; 32. 19, &c.
TABRETS,] as in Ge. 31. 27.
JOY,] and gladness, because of the return of peace.
7. ANSWER,] that is, respond to each other in the singing.
PLAYING] on the tabrets, &c.
SMITTEN AMONG,] not 'smitten,' as in the C.V.
8. DISPLEASING,] as in 15. 11.
GIVEN,] that is, 'ascribed.'
9. IS EYEING,] jealously and enviously. The Vatican MS. omits v. 9, 10, 11.
10. SPIRIT OF SADNESS,] as in 16. 14, &c.
PROPHESIETH,] *or* 'singeth praises,' as in 10. 5, &c.
IS PLAYING] on the harp, at the return of the king's distemper.
THE JAVELIN,] as in 19. 9, 10, &c.
11. CASTETH,] as in 20. 33, &c.
WALL,] as in 19. 10 ; 20. 25, &c.
TURNETH ROUND,] as in Ge. 42. 24, &c.
12. AFRAID,] as in v. 15, 29.
WITH HIM,] as he had formerly been with Saul, in 10. 7, &c.
TURNED ASIDE,] as in 16. 14 ; 28. 15.
13. FROM HIM,] that is, from his own immediate presence.
THOUSAND,] men in the army.
PEOPLE,] as a public servant of the state.
14. ACTING WISELY,] as in v. 5 above.
15. AFRAID,] as in v. 12, 29.
16. GOING OUT AND COMING IN,] as in v. 13.
17. MERAB,] as in 14. 49; the Vatican MS. omits v. 17—19.
WIFE,] according to the promise in 17. 25.
SON OF VALOUR,] as in Jud. 21. 10, &c.
JEHOVAH,] the king of Israel; he does not say 'my battles.'
UPON HIM,] hostilely, to put him to death.
18. MY LIFE,] worth, that exposing it to peril in battle should gain such a prize.
SON-IN-LAW,] as in Ge. 19. 12, 14, &c.
19. ADRIEL,] *lit.* 'drove of God ;' he was son of Barzillai, 2 Sa. 21. 8.
20. MICHAL,] as in 14. 49, &c.
21. SNARE,] by leading him to expose himself to danger.
SECOND] daughter, even Michal.
22. GENTLY,] without awakening his suspicions of any scheme to entrap him.

DELIGHTED,] because of thy character and works.
LOVED,] without being jealous of him.
SON-IN-LAW,] as in v. 18, by marrying his second daughter, as yet unmarried.
23. A LIGHT THING,] involving no responsibility and no hardship.
POOR MAN,] unable to give a dowry, such as might secure a princess.
LIGHTLY ESTEEMED] by many, as of poor extraction.
24. SPOKEN,] to excuse himself from the marriage proposed.
25. DOWRY,] which in the east the father generally asks and receives for giving a daughter in marriage.
FORESKINS,] as in Ge. 17. 11, &c.
AVENGED,] by the death of so many Philistines.
THOUGHT,] as in 1. 13.
26. RIGHT,] as shewing his valour in punishing the enemy.
FULL,] for his marriage being completed.
27. TWO HUNDRED.] Sept. reads only 100, and so in 2 Sa. 3. 14.
SET THEM,] *lit.* 'fill them.'
WIFE,] having no further pretence for delaying.
28. JEHOVAH,] as in v. 14.
LOVED,] as in v. 20.
29. ADDETH,] because of these two circumstances.
ALL THE DAYS,] of his life.
30. COME OUT] to battle with Israel from time to time.
NAME,] *or* 'renown.'
PRECIOUS,] among the Israelites generally, as a wise and successful leader.

XIX. 1. PUT TO DEATH,] as one dangerous to the community.
2. DELIGHTED,] *or* 'had pleasure.'
IS SEEKING] subtilely and by craft.
SECRET PLACE,] as in 25. 20, &c.
BEEN HIDDEN,] from the eyes of all passers by.
3. DECLARED,] as one bound by 'covenant' to help David in the time of danger.
4. SIN,] by seeking to bring evil upon an innocent servant.
GOOD,] fitted to strengthen his kingdom and authority among his enemies and his friends.
5. HAND,] risking it in battle many times against the enemies of Saul.
THE PHILISTINE,] Goliath of Gath, as in 17. 49, 50.
SALVATION,] from terror and oppression.
SEEN] with thine own eyes, as in 17. 55.
REJOICE] at his valour and success.
NOUGHT,] without any adequate cause.
6. JEHOVAH LIVETH !] the most solemn oath that can be imagined.
7. HERETOFORE,] *lit.* 'yesterday, third day.'
8 WAR,] with the Philistines.
SMITING,] so that they retreated in disorder and confusion.
FACE,] he apparently being the leader in the engagement.
9. SPIRIT OF SADNESS,] as in 16. 14 ; 18. 10, 11

JAVELIN,] as in 18. 10, 11.

HAND] on the harp, to drive away the despondency from Saul.

10. WALL,] as in 18. 11.

FREETH HIMSELF.] This original word only occurs elsewhere in 1 K. 6. 18, 29, 32, 35; 1 Ch. 9. 33; 2 Ch. 23. 8; Prov. 17. 14; Ps. 22. 7.

11. PUT TO DEATH] violently and in his own house.

WIFE,] as in 18. 27.

DELIVERING,] as in 2 Sa. 19. 5.

12. CAUSETH TO GO DOWN,] as in 30. 15, &c.

THE WINDOW,] as in Jos. 2. 15, &c.

13. TERAPHIM,] as in Ge. 31. 19, 34, 35; Jud. 17. 5; 18. 14, 17, 18, 20; 1 Sa. 15. 23; 19. 13, 16; 2 K. 23. 24; Eze. 21. 21; Hos. 3. 4; Zec. 10. 2.

MATTRESS,] as in v. 16.

PILLOWS,] as in Ge. 28. 11, 18; 1 Sa. 19. 13, 16; 26. 7, 11, 16; 1 K. 19. 6.

GARMENT,] as in Nu. 4. 7, 11, &c.

14. SICK,] as in Ge. 48. 1, &c.

15. BED,] as in v. 13.

16. TERAPHIM,] as in v. 13, &c.

MATTRESS..PILLOWS,] as in v. 13.

17. DECEIVED,] as in 28. 12, &c.

MINE ENEMY,] who yet was her husband.

18. FLED] from the court of Saul and his own dwelling, for his life.

ESCAPED,] from the messengers of Saul.

RAMATH,] where Samuel dwelt, as in 16. 13.

NAIOTH,] i.e. 'habitations,' as in v. 19. 22, 23; 20. 1.

20. ASSEMBLY.] This original word is not found elsewhere.

PROPHETS,] as in 10. 5, 6.

PROPHESYING,] i.e. 'praising,' and so the Targum explains it; compare 1 Cor. 14. 3, 24, 25.

SET OVER THEM,] as their leader and guide.

SPIRIT OF GOD,] as in 10. 10.

PROPHESY,] like the others who were there assembled, 1 Ch. 25. 1, &c.

21. OTHER MESSENGERS,] as in 2 K. 1. 11, 13.

22. RAMATH,] as in v. 18, 19.

SECHU,] perhaps the same as Sochoh in 17.1.

23. SPIRIT OF GOD,] as in v. 20.

PROPHESYETH,] as his former messengers had done.

24. STRIPPETH OFF,] as in Lev. 6. 11, &c.

NAKED,] that is without his outer garment, as in 2 Sa. 6. 20; Isa. 20. 2; Mic. 1. 8.

PROPHETS?] as before in 10. 11.

XX. 1. FLEETH,] while Saul was prophesying.

INIQUITY?] as in 3. 13, 14, &c.

LIFE?] lit. 'soul.'

2. FAR BE IT,] lit. 'profanation.'

UNCOVER,] as in Ruth 4. 4, &c.

3. SWEARETH,] to testify to Jonathan his own full conviction of the intensity of Saul's hatred.

GRACE] and acceptance before the son.

GRIEVED,] as in Ge. 45. 5, &c.

A STEP.] This original word is only found elsewhere in Isa. 27. 4.

4. SOUL] say should be done in the circumstances.

5. NEW MOON,] that is, the festival, enjoined in Nu. 10. 10; 28. 11, &c.

TO EAT,] according to the custom, as his son-in-law, armour-bearer, and chief officer.

HIDDEN,] or 'concealed' from the eyes of the servants of Saul.

6. LOOK AFTER ME,] lit. 'inspect me.'

TO RUN,] i. e. hasten from Gibeah of Saul to

BETH-LEHEM,] the birth-place and family residence of David.

A SACRIFICE OF THE DAYS,] as in 1. 21, &c.

FAMILY] of Jesse, of which David was the youngest son.

7. PEACE] on the part of Saul.

DISPLEASING,] and not received by Saul as a satisfactory excuse.

THE EVIL,] feared by David.

8. COVENANT,] as in 18. 3.

INIQUITY,] as in v. 1.

9. FAR BE IT,] lit. a 'profanation.'

DETERMINED,] or 'concluded.'

10. SHARPLY,] as in Ge. 42. 7, 30, &c.

11. THE FIELD,] away from the observation of men.

12. SEARCH,] as in Job 13. 9, &c.

UNCOVERED,] as in v. 2 above.

13. ADD,] as in Ruth 1. 17, &c.

IN PEACE,] fearing nothing from me.

FATHER,] in 11. 6, &c.

14. THE KINDNESS OF JEHOVAH,] inspired by him, and imitating the divine goodness.

15. CUT OFF,] that is, cease or abandon the brotherly covenant.

16. COVENANTETH,] not only for himself but for his posterity also, as in Ge. 21. 23.

SOUGHT,] the fulfilment of the covenant from Saul and all David's persecutors in his family.

17. OWN SOUL,] see 18. 1.

18. NEW MOON,] as in v. 5.

LOOKED AFTER] by my father, as in v. 6 above.

SEAT] at the king's table.

19. COME DOWN] to Gibeah from Beth-Lehem.

THE WORK,] perhaps that referred to in 19. 2.

EZEL,] i.e. 'going away;' or as in v. 41 'Etzel,' i.e. 'near.'

20. SHOOT] with a bow, as in v. 36, 37.

SIDE] of the stone, Jonathan standing by it.

MARK,] as in Job 16. 2; La. 3. 12.

21. THE YOUTH] who bare his weapons.

NOTHING] for thee to fear from my father Saul.

23. THE THING] that is, the matter of the covenant between them.

24. NEW MOON,] as in v. 5.

BY THE FOOD,] or 'unto the bread.'

25. WALL,] surveying the guests, or apart from them.

RISETH] from the side of his father, probably to escape all questioning.

LOOKED AFTER] and appointed to him by those who had charge of the guests.

26. ACCIDENT,] as in 6. 9.

NOT CLEAN,] according to the ceremonial law and therefore forbidden to appear at festivals.

o

27. LOOKED,] a second time, as in v. 25.
SON OF JESSE,] not mentioning David by
name, but the name of his father; this is
common in the east.
FOOD,] as customary for the king's son-in-
law and chief officer.
28. HATH BEEN ASKED.] The verb is
passive in the original, as in Neh. 13. 6.
BETH-LEHEM] his native city.
29. FAMILY SACRIFICE,] in v. 6 above.
MY BROTHER] the eldest, who in the east,
often exercises great power in the family,
as in the case of Laban.
30. BURNETH,] as in 11. 6, &c.
PERVERSE,] as in Prov. 12. 8.
REBELLIOUS WOMAN.] Nothing pains an
oriental more than reproach of his mother.
FIXING] thy love and affection.
SON OF JESSE,] as in v. 27.
SHAME,] as lacking spirit to take up his
father's quarrels.
31. ESTABLISHED,] free from dispute and
contention.
A SON OF DEATH,] i.e. doomed to die, as
in 26. 16; 2 Sa. 12. 5.
32. DONE?] worthy of such a punishment.
33. CASTETH,] as in 18. 11.
JAVELIN,] as in 19. 10.
DETERMINED,] or 'concluded.'
34. HEAT OF ANGER,] at this treatment
from his father.
GRIEVED,] as suggested by David in v. 3
above.
PUT HIM TO SHAME,] that is David, in
treating him as a traitor and criminal.
35. MORNING] of the third day.
APPOINTMENT,] as in v. 18—28.
36. RUNNING,] according to the instruction
of his master.
37. BEYOND THEE?] the words of the signal
in v. 27.
39. THE WORD] that had been determined
as a sign, viz. 'beyond' and 'on this side'
of thee.
40. WEAPONS,] his bow and arrows.
CITY] of Gibeah, to Jonathan's dwelling.
41. ETZEL,] i.e. 'near;' compare v. 19.
THREE TIMES,] in token of respect and
gratitude to his master's son.
KISS..WEEP,] expressing and manifesting
mutual love and sympathy.
EXERTED HIMSELF,] to control his feelings.
42. GO IN PEACE,] lit. 'go to peace.'
SWORN,] as in v. 16, 17.

XXI. 1. NOB,] i.e. 'fruit,' as in 1 Sa. 22.
9, 11, 19; Neh. 11. 32; Isa. 10. 32.
AHIMELECH,] i.e. 'brother of the king,'
he was brother of Ahijah, son of Ahitub.
TREMBLETH,] as in 16. 4.
2. COMMANDED,] being my rightful superior.
YOUNG MEN,] who were to attend him
were to meet him elsewhere.
3. HAND,] that is, under thy care, in thy
possession.
FOUND] readiest for immediate use.
4. COMMON BREAD,] such as the people
generally eat, but there is
HOLY,] or 'separate' bread, being that set
apart for the priests.

WOMEN,] ceremonial purity being required
in those partaking of it.
5. RESTRAINED,] or 'kept in.
HERETOFORE,] lit. 'yesterday third day.'
GOING OUT] on the king's business; this
speaks much for David's care for the morals
of his men.
VESSELS,] that is, their bodies.
IN THE VESSEL,] or 'for the vessel,' or
body.
6. HOLY THING,] set apart for God and
his ministering servants.
BREAD OF THE PRESENCE,] as in Ex. 25. 30.
TURNED ASIDE,] every seventh day, as in
Lev. 24. 8. 9.
JEHOVAH,] in the sanctuary.
HOT,] as in 11. 9, &c.
7. DETAINED,] or 'restrained,' from some
cause not mentioned.
DOEG,] i.e. 'sorrowful, fearful,' as in 22.
9, 18, 22; Ps. 52. 2.
EDOMITE,] one of a nation whose hatred
of Israel was unbending.
CHIEF,] lit. 'mighty one,' as in Jud. 5
22, &c.
SHEPHERDS,] kings in ancient times appear to have had their flocks as well as
private persons.
8. SPEAR OR SWORD,] as a weapon of de-
fence or offence.
VESSELS,] perhaps his bow and arrows
are meant.
URGENT.] This original word is not found
elsewhere.
9. ELAH,] as in 17. 2, 41.
WRAPT,] as in Isa. 25. 7; 1 K. 19. 13.
GARMENT,] as in Ge. 9. 23, &c.
EPHOD,] as in Ex. 25. 7; 28. 4, &c.
LIKE IT,] for size and temper.
10. ACHISH.] Etymology unknown; see
27. 2; 1 K. 2. 39.
GATH,] one of the five chief Philistine
cities.
11. A KING,] that is, a ruler of the land of
Canaan.
DANCES,] as in 18. 6; 29. 5.
MYRIADS,] repeating the chorus of the
singers.
12. HEART,] as an evident token of his
being discovered, and in danger.
13. CHANGETH,] as in Job 14. 20; Jer. 2. 39.
BEHAVIOUR,] lit. 'taste,' as in Ex. 16. 31;
Nu. 11. 8; 1 Sa. 25. 33; Job 6. 6; 12. 20; Ps.
34. 1; 119. 66; Prov. 11. 22; 26. 16; Jer. 48.
11; Jon. 3. 7.
FEIGNETH HIMSELF MAD,] as in Jer. 25.
16; 46. 9; 50. 38; 51. 7; Neh. 2. 4.
SCRIBBLETH,] or 'maketh marks,' as in
Eze. 9. 4.
LETTETH DOWN,] as in La. 2. 18; Ps. 78. 16.
SPITTLE.] This original word is only found
elsewhere in Job 6. 6.
BEARD,] which was reckoned an unfailible
sign of madness.
14. ACTING AS A MADMAN,] disfiguring his
beard, &c.
15. LACK,] as in 2 Sa. 3. 29; 1 K. 11. 22;
17. 16; Prov. 6. 32; 7. 7; 9. 4, 16; 10. 13, 21;
11. 12; 12. 9, 11; 15. 21; 17. 18; 24. 30; 28.
16; Ecc 6. 2; 10. 3.
BY ME,] lit. 'upon me.'

XXII. 1. CAVE OF ADULLAM,] a city in Judah, Jos. 15. 35.

GO DOWN,] to escape the fury of Saul.

2. GATHER THEMSELVES,] as a leader in Israel.

DISTRESS,] or 'straitness,' as in De. 28. 53, 55, 57; Ps. 119. 143; Jer. 19. 9.

EXACTOR,] as in Neh. 5. 7; Isa. 24. 2.

BITTER IN SOUL,] as in Jud. 18. 25.

3. MIZPEH,] i.e. a 'watch-tower,' in the land of

MOAB,] to distinguish it from the city of the same name in Israel.

FOR ME,] in the way of restoring him back to Israel.

4. LEADETH,] as in Ge. 24. 48.

FORTRESS,] as in v. 5; 24. 22, &c.

5. GAD,] i.e. 'a troop,' as in 2 Sa. 24. 14, &c.

PROPHET,] who declared the will of God to David.

JUDAH,] where he was born.

HARETH,] not mentioned elsewhere.

6. BECOME KNOWN,] or recognized by the inhabitants of the place.

GIBEAH,] his native place.

GROVE,] as in Ge. 21. 33; 1 Sa. 31. 13.

RAMAH,] or 'in the high place,' not the Ramah where Samuel dwelt.

7. BENJAMITES,] being of his own tribe, and personal retainers.

VINEYARDS.] The language is evidently that of derision.

HUNDREDS,] exalting them to places of trust, as perhaps Saul himself may have done. Bribery is irresistible in the east.

8. CONSPIRED,] as in v. 13; 1 K. 16. 16, 20, &c.

UNCOVERING,] as in 20. 12, &c.

COVENANTING,] as in 18. 3; 20. 30.

GRIEVING,] or 'sick for me,' as in Ge. 48. 1; 1 Sa. 19. 14, &c.

LIE IN WAIT,] as in 15. 5, &c.

9. SERVANTS,] that is, the herdsmen, as in 21. 7.

NOB,] a city of the Levites, the residence of Ahimelech son of

AHITUB,] as in 14. 3.

10. ASKED] counsel by the Urim and Thummim; this circumstance is not stated in the preceding chapter, but it is admitted in v. 15 below.

PROVISION,] even five loaves, as in 21. 3.

SWORD,] which properly was David's own property.

11. ALL THE HOUSE,] that none might escape the premeditated vengeance.

13. CONSPIRED,] as in v. 8 above.

LIE IN WAIT,] as in v. 8 above.

14. FAITHFUL,] that is, steady and loyal to the trust committed to him.

SON-IN-LAW,] as in 18. 27.

COUNCIL,] as in 2 Sa. 23. 23; 1 Ch. 11. 25; Isa. 11. 14.

HONOURED,] by all Israel and thine own household.

15. BEGUN.] He had done it often before for him apparently.

FAR BE IT,] lit. a 'profanation.'

LAY ANYTHING,] implying conspiracy or evil against the king and his kingdom.

ALL THIS] disagreement between Saul and David.

16. DIE,] refusing all excuse, without at tempting to reason.

FATHER,] which was contrary to the law

17. RUNNERS,] as in 20. 36; 2 Sa. 15. 1; 18 22, 24, 26; 1 K. 1. 5; 14. 27, 28, &c.

PRIESTS OF JEHOVAH,] acknowledging their official character, as the servants of the God of Israel.

HAND,] power and influence is used for David.

FLEEING,] from the sword of Saul.

UNCOVERED,] as in 20. 12, &c.

NOT BEEN WILLING,] because of their convictions of the priests' innocence, and also of the hasty disregard of legal forms.

18. TURN ROUND,] as in v. 17; 2 Sa. 18. 30, &c.

HIMSELF.] The pronoun is emphatic.

LINEN EPHOD,] their usual official robe.

19. A CITY,] as in v. 9, 11 above.

SWORD,] that no city hereafter might ven ture to harbour David, lest the same de struction should come upon them.

20. ABIATHAR,] i.e. 'father of abundance.

DAVID,] to Hareth, as in v. 5.

22. IS THERE,] as in 21. 7, detained before Jehovah.

BROUGHT IT ROUND,] that is, the death of the priests.

23. A CHARGE,] to be specially cared for, as the only recompense that could be made him.

XXIII. 1. KEILAH,] as in Jos. 15. 44, &c.

SPOILING,] as in Jud. 2. 14, 16, &c.

THRESHING-FLOORS,] as in Ge. 50. 10, 11.

2. ASKETH,] by Abiathar perhaps.

SAVED,] from the hand of the Philistines.

3. AFRAID,] though among friends.

RANKS,] of the armies of the warlike enemy.

4. ASK,] counsel and direction.

GO DOWN,] from Hareth, as in 22. 5.

5. LEADETH AWAY,] as spoil for the oppressed Israelites in Keilah.

6. EPHOD,] indispensable to an officiating priest.

7. MADE HIM KNOWN,] that is, revealed his hiding-place; Sept. 'sold him.'

BAR,] Keilah being a fortified city.

8. SUMMONETH,] lit. 'causeth to hear.'

9. DEVISING,] secretly and deliberately.

10. DESTROY,] lit. 'corrupt or mar,' as he had done Nob, in 22. 19.

11. POSSESSORS,] i.e. 'lords, masters, owners.'

COME DOWN,] as in v. 8.

THEY SHUT THEE UP,] though thou didst deliver them, as in v. 5.

13. SIX HUNDRED,] whereas he had only 400 in Adullam, in 22. 2.

GO UP AND DOWN,] every part of the wilderness or pasture land of Israel.

GO FORTH,] to seek him, for a time.

14. WILDERNESS,] or pasture land.

FORTRESSES,] as in 22. 4.

HILL-COUNTRY,] where the population is scanty.

ZIPH,] wherein was a city of the same name, as in Jos. 15. 55.

ALL THE DAYS,] that is, perpetually.

NOT GIVEN,] as Saul expected in v. 7 above.

15. SEEK] to put him to death, as a dangerous enemy.

FOREST,] residing with his men.

16. IN GOD,] as his only and effectual saviour.

17. SECOND] in the kingdom, after David.

KNOWETH.] Samuel's having anointed David had now probably become publicly known.

COVENANT,] as in 18. 3; 20. 6, 42.

18. BEFORE JEHOVAH,] as the witness, rewarder, and avenger.

FOREST,] near Ziph, as in v. 15.

HOUSE] in Gibeah, probably with his father.

19. HIDING HIMSELF,] as in 26. 1; Ps. 54. 1; Isa. 45. 15.

FORTRESSES,] as in v. 14.

HACHILAH,] i.e. 'red,' as in 26. 1—3.

DESOLATE PLACE,] lit. 'Jeshimon.'

20. DESIRE OF THY SOUL,] which burned intensely after David, as in 24. 14.

21. PITY,] as in Ex. 2. 6.

22. PREPARE,] or 'make ready.'

FOOT,] where he can last be traced.

SUBTILE,] in eluding his pursuers.

23. HIDING-PLACES,] whether caves or fortresses.

PREPARED] in this special manner.

LAND] of Israel, where Saul reigned, then he

SEARCHED HIM OUT,] and captured him, if in the land at all.

24. THEY RISE,] that is, the Ziphites.

MAON,] as in Jos. 15. 55.

PLAIN,] lit. 'Arabah,' as in De. 1. 1, &c.

DESOLATE PLACE,] lit. 'Jeshimon,' as in Nu. 21. 20, &c.

25. SEEK] for David and his company, to capture them.

THE ROCK,] afterwards called in v. 28, 'the rock of division.'

26. HASTENED TO GO,] by fear of being caught.

COMPASSING,] by dividing themselves into detachments.

TO CATCH THEM,] to put them to death.

27. HASTE,] for no time could be lost in repelling the invasion of the Philistines, who had unexpectedly

PUSHED] their forces into Israel, for plunder.

28. DIVISIONS,] because of the breaking up of the king's resolution to pursue David.

29. EN-GEDI,] on which see Jos. 15. 12.

XXIV. 1. PHILISTINES] who had invaded the land, as in 23. 27.

WILDERNESS,] that is, as in 23. 29, in the 'fortresses' in it.

2. WILD GOATS,] inaccessible to man, generally speaking.

3. FOLDS] where the flocks were gathered in the wilderness.

CAVE,] one of the many with which Canaan abounded.

ABIDING] for safety from the pursuit of man.

4. HAND,] as in 26. 8.

EYES,] wounding or killing him outright.

SKIRT,] lit. 'wing,' as in v. 11.

UPPER ROBE,] which covered him entirely.

GENTLY,] without awakening him.

5. SMITETH,] his reverence for the constituted king of Israel being so intense.

FAR BE IT,] lit. a 'profanation.'

ANOINTED] servant of Jehovah.

7. SUBDUETH,] or 'rendeth, divideth.'

WORDS,] reasoning calmly against their furious proposal.

PERMITTED,] lit. 'given.'

WAY] to seek David as before.

8. LOOKETH ATTENTIVELY,] because of the darkness.

OBEISANCE,] as was becoming a subject.

9. MAN,] who may lie or be deceived.

EVIL,] trying to supplant thy authority.

10. PITY,] as in Ge. 45. 20.

HE IS,] as in v. 6 above.

11. SKIRT,] lit. 'wing.'

UPPER ROBE,] as in v. 4.

TRANSGRESSION] against thee or thy kingdom.

HUNTING,] as in Ex. 21. 13; Eze. 13. 20.

12. JUDGE] impartially between man and man.

AVENGED] in his own way, time, and pleasure.

SIMILE,] as in Nu. 23. 7, &c.

ANCIENTS,] or 'eastern,' as in Job 18. 20, Isa. 43. 18; Eze. 10. 19; 11. 1; 38. 17; 47. 18; Joel 2. 20; Zec. 14. 8; Mal. 3. 4.

WICKED,] and 'good from the good,' by the same necessary law.

14. COME FORTH,] from his royal city to the wilderness.

PURSUING,] with so much persevering enmity.

A DEAD DOG,] which even when alive was despised.

A FLEA,] as in 26. 20.

PLEADETH,] or 'judgeth.'

HAND,] as he had already done on former occasions.

16. SON DAVID,] being overpowered by a sense of David's kindness in sparing his life, so that he

WEEPETH] in tears of gratitude, perhaps, rather than of sorrow.

17. MORE RIGHTEOUS] in the sight of God and men.

GOOD..EVIL,] all along from the beginning of their intercourse.

SHUT ME UP,] exposed and helpless.

19. ENEMY,] one seeking his hurt in every possible way.

GOOD MANNER,] without retaliating on him his wrongs.

REPAY,] both in this life and in the life that is to come.

20. REIGN,] in the room of Saul over the twelve tribes of Israel, according to God's promise and Samuel's anointing.

STOOD,] firm and stedfast.

21. JEHOVAH,] who is doing such things for thee.

SEED,] that is, posterity.

NAME,] *or* 'renown.'

23. SWEARETH,] as adjured by Saul, which satisfied him, and he went to his own HOUSE] in Gibeah, his capital city. FORTRESS] in En-Gedi, as in 23. 29; 24. 1.

XXV. 1. DIETH,] like all the prophets and judges who were before him; but the exact date is unknown.

RAMAH,] where he was born and had died.

PARAN,] as in Ge. 21. 21; it was to the south of Judah, near Edumea.

2. MAON,] a city near the wilderness of that name, see Jos. 15. 55.

WORK] of sheep-farming.

CARMEL] in the land of Judah, as in Jos. 15. 55.

GREAT] in worldly substance and general estimation.

SHEEP..GOATS,] in which the wealth of the east chiefly consists.

SHEARING] at the proper and ordinary time, about June or July.

3. NABAL,] i.e. 'folly,' as alluded to in v. 25.

ABIGAIL,] i.e. 'father of joy.'

UNDERSTANDING,] as in 1 Ch. 22. 12; 26. 14; 2 Ch. 2. 11; 30. 22; Ezra 8. 18; Neh. 8. 8; Job 17. 4; Ps. 111. 10; Prov. 3. 4; 12. 8; 13. 15; 16. 22; 19. 11; 23. 9; Da. 8. 25.

FAIR FORM,] as in Ge. 29. 17, &c.

HARD,] *or* 'sharp.'

DOINGS,] that is, his habitual actions, as the word implies.

CALEBITE,] of the family of Caleb, son of Jephunneh, but some understand it: 'as a dog.'

4. FLOCK,] as in v. 2 above.

5. WELFARE,] that is, given him the usual salutation.

6. TO LIFE,] may it be to life!

7. SHEARERS,] the present time being that of shearing, as in v. 2.

WITH US,] in the past season, in the wild pasture-land.

PUT THEM TO SHAME,] affronting or injuring anything under their care, as in v. 15.

LOOKED AFTER,] in the way of care and supervision, David's men having been a safeguard.

8. YOUNG MEN] who tend thy flocks, who can testify to our conduct.

YOUNG MEN] whom I have sent to salute thee.

GOOD,] that is, one of gladness and joy.

FINDETH] convenient, and at hand, more or less.

9. COME IN] to Carmel, where Nabal was.

THEY REST,] *or* 'are at rest *or* quiet,' as in Ge. 8. 4; 2 K. 2. 15; 2 Ch. 14. 7, &c.

10. WHO..WHO,] as if they were names quite unknown to him, though those of the king's son-in-law, and Israel's saviour.

BREAKING AWAY] violently and lawlessly from their masters, as in 22. 2.

11. BREAD WATER FLESH,] provided for his own shearers, who were doing him service, forgetting that David and his men had also done him service, and preserving from injury the flock he was shearing. For 'water,' the Sept. reads 'wine.'

12. COME IN] to Paran, as in v. 1.

GIRD YE ON,] for action in the field.

13. VESSELS,] of all kinds, which they carried systematically about with them for themselves and families.

14. WIFE,] as in v. 3.

BLESS,] that is, declare blessed, or to pray for a blessing on him.

FLIETH,] furiously and recklessly upon them as vagrants and impostors, as in v. 10, 11.

15. GOOD,] kind and obliging, in every thing.

SHAME,] as in v. 7, asserted by David.

NOT LOOKED AFTER,] *or* 'inspected,' as in v. 7 above.

GONE UP AND DOWN] the whole country side, seeking pasturage from place to place.

FIELD,] exposed to the attack of robbers and wild beasts.

16. A WALL] for defence against danger.

17. DETERMINED] by David, to punish this insult; some expressions of David's servants may have been overheard.

SON OF WORTHLESSNESS,] that is, a worthless person, as in De. 13. 14, &c.

18. HASTETH,] for the danger was pressing.

TWO HUNDRED LOAVES] of bread, which had doubtless been prepared for the shearers.

WINE,] which seems to have been scarce at this season, but the bottles being of leather, may have been able to hold several gallons each.

PREPARED,] that is, already dressed for food.

MEASURES,] as in Ge. 18. 6. &c.

ROASTED CORN,] as in Lev. 23. 14, &c.

RAISINS,] as in 30. 12; 2 Sa. 16. 1; 1 Ch. 12. 40.

FIGS,] as in 30. 12; 2 K. 20. 7; 1 Ch. 12. 40; Isa. 38. 21.

ASSES,] the most common beast of burden mentioned in the Scriptures.

19. PASS OVER] the hilly country, to David.

20. SECRET PART,] as in 19. 2, &c.

MEETETH,] as in 2 Sa. 2. 13; the idea of 'rushing' upon, is involved in the original word.

21. IN VAIN,] that is, for a 'false lying thing,' hope of a kindly recompence.

KEPT] from injury and destruction.

LOOKED AFTER,] as in v. 7, 15.

22. SITTING ON THE WALL.] There is some difficulty connected with this phrase, but one thing at least is certain, that the meaning cannot be as expressed in the C.V.; the practice there referred to, though common in this country, is totally unknown in the east. It is most probably derived from a root signifying 'to set, put, place,' and the plural feminine termination is used to denote those indolent effeminate persons who lolled at their ease on the roofs of their houses, which were generally flat. See also v. 34; 1 K. 14. 10; 16. 11; 21. 21; 2 K. 9. 8.

23. EARTH,] expressive of her desire to propitiate him if possible.

24. INIQUITY,] done to David's servants; she makes no attempt to excuse it—save ignorance.

25. MAN OF WORTHLESSNESS,] that is, worthless person, even Nabal.
FOLLY,] in Heb. 'nebalah,' being a play upon words.
SEND,] seeking an acknowledgment from Nabal, as in v. 5 above.
26. WITHHELD,] at least up to this present time.
BLOOD,] as he had proposed to himself in v. 22.
SAVE,] that is, 'give ease,' as in v. 33.
AS NABAL,] that is, as folly and foolishness.
27. BLESSING,] described in v. 18 above.
AT THE FEET,] that is, accompanying David, as in Ge. 30. 30, &c.
28. HAND-MAID,] taking again the blame upon herself, as in v. 24.
STEDFAST HOUSE,] that cannot be shaken or destroyed, like those of David's enemies.
FOUGHT] against the uncircumcised Philistines, &c.
29. MAN] but not God.
BUNDLE,] as in Ge. 42. 35, &c.
SLING THEM OUT] as worthless.
30. SPOKEN] by the prophet Samuel.
LEADER,] as in 9. 16; 10. 1; 13. 14; 25. 30; 2 Sa. 5. 2, &c.
31. STUMBLING-BLOCK,] as in Isa. 28. 7.
OFFENCE,] as in Lev. 19. 14; Ps. 119. 165, &c.
FOR NOUGHT,] without a just cause.
RESTRAINING HIMSELF] from executing his own feelings of private vengeance.
REMEMBERED] for good, and with gratitude, as he did afterwards in v. 39.
32. JEHOVAH,] whom he gratefully acknowledges as the great source of this relief.
33. DISCRETION,] lit. 'taste.'
RESTRAIN,] as in 6. 10 ; Ge. 8. 2, &c.
34. HASTED,] as in v. 18.
WALL.] See note on v. 22.
35. HOUSE,] to Carmel, as in v. 2.
FACE,] as in Ge. 19. 21, &c.
36. BANQUET,] lit. a 'drinking.'
GLAD,] lit. 'good.'
UNTO EXCESS,] lit. 'unto might,' as in 2 Ch. 16. 14; Ps. 119. 107; La. 5. 22; Da. 8. 8.
37. THESE THINGS,] recorded in v. 14—35.
HATH BEEN AS A STONE,] lit. 'hath become a stone;' compare the language in Ge. 19. 26; Ex. 4. 3; 7. 9—12, &c.
39. PLEADED,] as in 24. 15, &c.
EVIL] in shedding innocent blood.
HEAD,] as in 1 K. 2. 44, &c.
WIFE,] in addition to, or in the place of Michal.
41. WASH THE FEET,] or discharge the humblest duties.
42. THE ASS,] as in v. 20.
AT HER FEET,] as in v. 27.
43. AHINOAM,] i.e. 'brother of pleasantness;' compare 2 Sa. 3. 2, 3, where she seems to have been married before Abigail.
JEZREEL,] see Jos. 15. 56.
44. PHALTI,] i.e. 'escape of God,' as in 2 Sa. 3. 15.
LAISH,] i.e. 'a lion.'
GALLIM,] a city of Benjamin, as in Isa. 10. 29, 30.

XXVI. 1. ZIPHITES,] the inhabitants of Ziph, as in 23. 19; Ps. 54. 1; this was their second attempt to please Saul.
ON THE FRONT,] that is, as in 23. 19, 'at the south of the wilderness.'
2. ZIPH,] see Jos. 15. 24, 55.
CHOICE,] not ' chosen ;' as in Ex. 14. 7; Jud. 20. 15, 16, 34; 1 Sa. 24. 2; 2 Sa. 6. 1; 10. 9; 1 K. 12. 21; 1 Ch. 19. 10, &c.
3. SEETH,] or rather perhaps 'feareth,' and hence he sendeth forth
4. SPIES,] lit. 'footmen,' as in Ge. 42. 9, 11, 14, 16, 30, 31, 34, &c.
NACHON,] as in 23. 23; 2 Sa. 6. 6; in 1 Ch. 13. 9, 'Chidion.'
5. ENCAMPED] in Ziph, as in v. 3 above.
LAIN DOWN] to rest or sleep.
HOST,] as in 14. 50; 17. 55.
HATH,] as in 17. 20.
6. AHIMELECH,] i. e. 'brother of the king.'
HITTITE,] a proselyte of that people, attached to David.
ABISHAI,] i.e. 'father of presents,' as in v. 7, 8, 9; 2 Sa. 2. 18, 24; 3. 30; 10. 10, 14; 16. 9, 11; 18. 2, 5, 12, &c.
ZERUIAH,] i. e. perhaps a 'cleft,' as in 2 Sa. 2. 13. 18; 3. 39; 8. 16; 14. 1; 16. 9, 10; 17. 25; 18. 2 ; 19. 21, &c.
JOAB,] as in 2 Sa. 2. 13, 14, 18, 22, 24, 26, 27, 28, 30, 32; 3. 22, 23, 24, 26, 27, 29, 30, 31, &c.
7. PATH,] as in v. 5.
PILLOW,] as in Ge. 28. 11, 18; 1 Sa. 19. 13, 16; 26. 7, 11, 16; 1 K. 19. 6.
8. SHUT UP,] as in 24. 18, &c.
AT ONCE,] lit. 'one step or movement.'
NOT REPEAT,] as in 2 Sa. 20. 10, &c.
9. DESTROY NOT,] as in Ps. 57. 1; 58. 1 59. 1; 75. 1, &c.
ANOINTED,] lit. 'Messiah,' as in Lev. 4. 3, 5, 6, &c.
ACQUITTED,] as in Ge. 24. 8, 41; Ex. 21. 19, &c.
SMITE HIM,] by an outputting of direct power.
DIED] according to the lot of all men, as in Ge. 3. 19, &c.
CONSUMED] by the sword of the enemy, as afterwards came to pass, in 31. 3, 4.
11. FAR BE IT,] lit. a 'profanation.'
PUTTING FORTH] hostilely, as in 24. 6, 10.
PILLOW,] as in v. 7 above.
CRUISE,] as in v. 12, 16; 1 K. 17. 12, 14, 16; 19. 6.
12. DEEP SLEEP,] as in Ge. 2. 21; 15. 12; Job 4. 13; 33. 15; Prov. 19. 15; Isa. 29. 10.
13. OTHER SIDE] of the hill, that he might be out of danger.
14. UNTO THE KING,] or perhaps 'near the king,' disturbing him.
15. A MAN?] not a woman or a child.
LIKE THEE,] for courage, trustworthiness, &c.
THE KING,] while he was asleep.
ONE OF THE PEOPLE,] even Abishai, but without naming him.
16. SONS OF DEATH,] i.e. doomed to die for this negligence.
PILLOW,] as in v. 7.
17. DISCERNETH,] as in Jud. 18. 3, &c.

MY SON DAVID,] as in 24. 16.
18. EVIL,] compare the expostulations in
24. 9—15.
19. HEAR,] and consider calmly.
MOVED,] as in De. 13. 6; Jos. 15. 18; Jud.
1. 14; 2 Sa. 24. 1; 1 K. 21. 25, &c.
PRESENT,] for my sin, as in Ge. 4. 3, 4,
5, &c.
SONS OF MEN,] as in Ge. 11. 5, &c.
CURSED,] as in Ge. 3. 14, 17, &c.
BEFORE JEHOVAH,] as in Jos. 6. 26, &c.
CAST ME FORTH,] as in Ge. 3. 24; 4. 14;
21. 10, &c.
ADMITTED.] The special form of the
original word is not found elsewhere, but
compare 2. 36; Isa. 14. 1.
INHERITANCE,] as in 2 Sa. 14. 16; 20. 19.
20. FALL,] from violence and injustice.
ONE FLEA,] as in 24. 14, &c.
THE PARTRIDGE,] as in Jer. 17. 11; *lit.*
'the caller;' Sept. 'the owl;' Jarchi, 'the
cuckoo;' Bochart, 'the woodcock.'
21. SINNED,] as in 15. 24; 24. 17.
PRECIOUS,] as in 18. 30; 2 K. 1. 13, 14; Ps.
49. 8; 72. 14; 139. 17, &c.
ACTED FOOLISHLY,] as in Ge. 31. 28.
ERR,] as in Lev. 4. 13, &c.
22. PASS OVER] to the other side of the
hill, as in v. 13.
23. RIGHTEOUSNESS,] as in Ge. 15. 6; 18.
19; 30. 33, &c.
STEDFASTNESS,] as in De. 32. 4; 2 K. 12.
15; 22. 7, &c.
NOT BEEN WILLING,] as in Jos. 24. 10; Ex.
10. 27, &c.
24. GREAT] in value, as the anointed of
the Lord.
DISTRESS,] as in 2 Sa. 4. 9; 1 K. 1. 29, &c.
25. MY SON DAVID,] as in v. 17 above.
WORKING,] as in 25. 28; 2 Sa. 9. 7; Prov.
23. 5; Jer. 7. 5; 22. 4; 44. 17, 25.
PREVAIL,] as in Ge. 30. 8, &c.
PLACE,] in Gibeah, as in v. 1 above.

XXVII. 1. HEART,] as in Ge. 8. 21, &c.
CONSUMED,] as in 12. 25; 26. 10, &c.
PHILISTINES,] forgetting that he had formerly to leave it, as in 21. 10—15.
DESPAIRING,] as in Job 6. 26; Isa. 57. 10;
'er. 2. 25; 18, 12; Ecc. 2. 20.
2. SIX HUNDRED,] as in 23. 13.
ACHISH,] see 21. 10.
MAOCH,] i. e. 'bruising,' *or* Maacha, as in
1 K. 2. 39.
3. JEZREELITESS,] as in 25. 43.
CARMELITESS,] as in 25. 42.
4. TO SEEK HIM,] David being now beyond
his reach, in a foreign country.
5. FOUND GRACE,] as an inoffensive guest,
and true well-wisher.
CITIES OF THE FIELD,] smaller and less
conspicuous than the
ROYAL CITY] of Gath, which gave its name
to the whole principality.
6. ZIKLAG,] which was originally given to
Judah, and afterwards to Simeon, Jos. 15.
31; 19. 5.
THIS DAY,] when the narrative was
written.
7. FIELD,] as in 6. 1; 27. 11.
DAYS,] see note on Ge. 1. 5.

8. GOETH UP] from Ziklag, as in v. 6,
to the
GESHURITE,] as in De. 3. 14; Jos. 2. 5; 13.
2, 11, 13.
GERIZZITE,] inhabitants of Gezer, Jos. 10.
33; 12. 12; 16. 3, 10; 21. 21; Jud. 1. 29;
2 Sa. 5. 25; 1 K. 9. 15, 16, 17; 1 Ch. 6. 67; 7.
28; 14. 16; 20. 4.
AMALEKITE,] see Ex. 17. 16, &c.
OF OLD,] as in Ge. 6. 4; De. 32. 7, &c.
SHUR,] see 15. 7.
9. LAND] of these three tribes.
MAN..WOMAN,] as commanded in De. 7.
2; 25. 9.
TAKEN] from the vanquished tribes.
10. PUSHED,] as in 23. 27; 27. 8, 10; 30. 1, 14.
JERAHMEELITE,] descendants of the son
of Hezron, grandson of Judah, living at the
south of Judah, in 1 Ch. 2. 9, 25, 26.
KENITE,] as in Jud. 1. 16.
11. TO BRING IN,] not 'tidings,' as in the
C.V., but 'captives.'
CUSTOM,] and therefore he ought to be
expelled from the land of the Philistines.
12. BELIEVETH,] *or* 'remaineth stedfast,'
as in Ge. 15. 6, &c.
ABHORRED,] because of these pretended
excursions against Israel.
AGE-DURING,] that is, during his life-time,
as in De. 15. 17, &c.

XXVIII. 1. DAYS,] when David is residing in Ziklag.
CAMPS,] those of the five principalities.
KNOW,] as a matter of course, considering
the kindness he had received for Achish.
MEN] who were at least six hundred in
number.
2. THEREFORE,] because of this supposition.
KEEPER OF MY HEAD,] that is, captain of
his body-guard.
3. DIED,] as in 25. 1. This verse is introduced to shew why Saul went to a woman
at En-Dor.
MOURN,] because of the loss of his influence
with the king, and his prayers with God.
RAMAH] where he had been born, and
brought up.
FAMILIAR SPIRITS,] as in Lev. 19. 31; 20.
6, 27, &c.
WIZARDS,] as in Lev. 19. 31; 20. 6, 27, &c.
4. SHUNEM,] a city of Issachar, as in Jos.
19. 18; 2 K. 4. 8.
GILBOA,] a range of mountains near
Jezreel, as in 31. 1, 8; 2 Sa. 1. 6, 21; 21. 12;
1 Ch. 10. 1, 8.
5. TREMBLETH,] as in Ge. 27. 33; Job 37.
1; 1 Sa. 4. 13; 14. 15, &c.
6. ASKETH] counsel and direction.
DREAMS,] as in Nu. 12. 6, &c.
URIM,] as in Ex. 28. 30; Nu. 27. 21; De.
33. 8.
PROPHETS,] Samuel being dead, and Gad
being with David.
7. SEEK,] contrary to the law in Lev.
19. 31.
POSSESSING,] *or* 'mistress,' as in 1 K. 17.
17; Neh. 3. 4.
EN-DOR,] a city of Manasseh, as in Jos.
17. 11.

8. DISGUISETH HIMSELF,] as in 1 K. 20. 38;
22. 30; 2 Ch. 18. 29; Job 30. 18.
NIGHT,] as in 14. 36; 26. 7; 31. 12, &c., to
save time, and that he might not be known.
DIVINE,] as in De. 18. 10, 14; Eze. 21. 21,
23, 29, &c.
9. DONE,] in reference to such as she, that
he hath
CUT OFF] by a violent death.
LAYING A SNARE,] as in Ps. 38. 12; 109.
11; De. 12. 30; Ps. 9. 16.
10. SWEARETH,] an oath being to all men
an end of controversy.
PUNISHMENT,] lit. 'iniquity,' as in Ge. 4.
13; 15. 15; 19. 15; 44. 16, &c.
11. BRING UP] out of Sheol, the state of
the dead, supposed to be beneath the
ground.
SAMUEL] the prophet, who had died, as
in v. 3.
12. SEETH,] before she had time to commence her incantations.
LOUD VOICE,] from terror, as the word
implies, and for help.
DECEIVED ME,] as in Ge. 29. 25; Jos. 9.
22; 1 Sa. 19. 17; 2 Sa. 19. 26; 1 Ch. 12. 17;
Prov. 26. 19; La. 1. 19.
SAUL,] the arbitrary king of Israel.
13. GODS.] The noun as well as the verb
'coming up,' are plural.
14. HIS FORM,] as in Jud. 8. 18; Isa. 52.
14; 53. 2; La. 4. 8, &c.
UPPER ROBE,] as in 24. 4, 11.
OBEISANCE,] from fear, and a desire to
propitiate him.
15. TROUBLED,] as in Job 9. 6; 12. 6; Isa.
13. 13; 14. 16; 23. 11; Jer. 50. 34.
DISTRESS,] as in 2 Sa. 24. 14, &c.
FIGHTING,] as in v. 1.
TURNED ASIDE,] as in 18. 12.
PROPHETS,] as in v. 6.
DREAMS,] as in v. 6.
16. ASK ME,] the servant and prophet of
the Lord who had left him thus.
ENEMY,] as in Ps. 139. 20; Mic. 5. 14.
17. SPOKEN,] as in 13. 14.
RENDETH,] as in 15. 28.
DAVID,] as in 16. 1, 13.
18. NOT HEARKENED,] as in 13. 13, 14.
AMALEK,] as in 15. 9, 28.
19. GIVETH] up as spoil.
WITH ME,] in the world of spirits; this
was true at least of three sons, see 31. 2.
CAMP,] now at Gilboa.
20. FULNESS,] as in Ge. 48. 19; 2 Sa. 8.
2, &c.
POWER,] as in Lev. 26. 20; 1 Sa. 30. 4; 2
K. 19. 3; 2 Ch. 14. 11; 20. 12, &c.
BREAD,] that is, food.
21. COMETH IN,] into the apartment where
Saul was.
TROUBLED,] as in Ge. 45. 3, &c.
MAID-SERVANT,] as in 25. 27, 41, &c.
VOICE,] to bring up Saul.
HAND,] as in Jud. 12. 3; 1 Sa. 19. 5; Job
13. 14, &c.
22. MORSEL OF BREAD,] as in Ge. 18. 15;
Jud. 19. 5; 1 Sa. 2. 36; 2 Sa. 12. 3; 1 K. 17.
11; Prov. 28. 21, &c.
WAY,] back to the camp of Israel—to
Gilboa, as in v. 4.

23. URGE,] as in 2 Sa. 13. 25, 27; 2 K. 5.
23, &c.
BED,] as in 19. 13, 15, 16, &c.
24. STALL,] as in Jer. 46. 21; Amos 6. 4;
Mal. 4. 2.
FLOUR,] as in Ge. 18. 6; Nu. 5. 15; Jud.
6. 19; 1 Sa. 1. 24; 2 Sa. 17. 28; 1 K. 4. 22;
17. 12, 14, 16; 2 K. 4. 41; 1 Ch. 12. 40; Isa.
47. 2; Hos. 8. 7.
KNEADETH,] as in Ge. 18. 6; 2 Sa. 13. 8;
Jer. 7. 18; Hos. 7. 4.
25. GO ON,] their way back to Gilboa.

XXIX. 1. APHEK,] a city in Asher, as in
Jos. 19. 30.
JEZREEL,] the valley of that name, see
Jos. 19. 18.
2. PASSING ON,] in array, for inspection.
REAR,] as in Ge. 33. 2; De. 13. 9; 17. 7;
2 Sa. 2. 26; Da. 8. 3.
3. HEADS,] that is, the five princes.
WHAT?] distinguishing them by their
national dress perhaps.
ACHISH,] king of Gath, as in 27. 2.
SERVANT,] musician, armour-bearer, and
officer.
DAYS..YEARS,] not caring for stating the
exact time.
FALLING AWAY,] from the service of Saul
to that of Achish.
4. AGAINST HIM,] that is, against Achish,
being afraid of treachery on the part of
David.
HIS PLACE,] even Ziklag, as in 27. 5, 6.
GO DOWN,] from Aphek to the valley of
Jezreel, where Israel was encamped.
ADVERSARY,] turning against us at a
critical moment.
THOSE MEN,] in the ranks of the Philistines.
5. CHORUSES,] as in 18. 6, 7; 21. 11.
MYRIADS,] every where victorious and
dangerous.
6. UPRIGHT,] as in Nu. 23. 10, &c.
7. TURN BACK,] to Ziklag.
8. WHAT..WHAT?] as if displeased and
anxious to join in the battle.
9. MESSENGER OF GOD,] for his wisdom,
and inoffensive behaviour.
PRINCES,] that is, the heads, as in v. 3, 4.
10. THY LORD,] even Saul.
11. PHILISTINES,] from Aphek to Ziklag.
JEZREEL,] where Israel is encamping, as
in v. 1.

XXX. 1. THIRD DAY,] after their departure with Achish.
AMALEKITES,] in revenge for David's conduct in 27. 8.
SOUTH] of Judah.
FIRE,] destroying wantonly what they
could not remove.
2. LEAD AWAY,] towards their own land,
to keep them as slaves.
3. COMETH IN,] from the camp of the
Philistines, being sent back from it.
4. NO POWER,] from exhaustion of body
and spirit.
5. TWO WIVES,] whom he had left behind
when he went with Achish
6. STONE HIM,] as the cause of this
calamity coming upon them.

BITTER,] as in 2 K. 4. 27, &c.
STRENGTHEN HIMSELF,] as in Ge. 48. 2, &c.
7. ABIATHAR,] see 22. 20.
EPHOD,] as in 23. 6.
8. ASKETH] counsel and direction.
TROOP] of Amalekites, who had plundered Ziklag.
DELIVER,] the persons and the goods that have been carried away.
9. LEFT,] as in 2. 36.
10. STAND STILL,] at Besor, from fatigue.
FAINT,] as in v. 21.
BESOR,] supposed to be the 'river of the wilderness,' in Amos 6. 14.
11. FIELD,] lying sick and starving.
12. PIECE,] as in Jud. 9. 53; 2 Sa. 11. 21; Job 41. 24; Song 4. 3; 6. 7.
BUNCH OF DRIED FIGS,] as in 25. 18, &c.
BUNCHES OF RAISINS,] as in 25. 18; 2 Sa. 16. 1; 1 Ch. 12. 40.
THREE NIGHTS,] being sick, and also retreating in haste with the Amalekites.
13. FORSAKETH,] leaving him to die by hunger or an enemy.
14. PUSHED,] as in 27. 10, &c.
CHERETHITE,] a tribe of the Philistines, see Zeph. 2. 5.
CALEB,] the possessions of the son of Jephunneh, as in Jos. 15. 19.
FIRE,] as in v. 1.
15. TROOP] of Amalekites, as in v. 8.
GOD,] as in Ge. 21. 23; Jos. 2. 12.
SHUT ME UP,] as in 23. 11, 12.
16. SPREAD OUT,] in disorder and confusion.
FEASTING,] or 'holding a festival,' as in Ps. 42. 4.
SPOIL,] as in v. 1, 2.
17. TWILIGHT,] as in 2 K. 7. 5, 7; Job 3. 9; 7. 4; 24. 15; Ps. 119. 147; Isa. 5. 11; 21. 4; 59. 10; Jer. 13. 16.
CAMELS,] as in 15. 3; 27. 9, &c.
18. TAKEN,] from Ziklag, as in v. 2.
19. LACKED,] as in 2 Sa. 17. 22; 1 K. 4. 27; Isa. 34. 16; 40. 26; 59. 15; Zeph. 3. 5.
20. LED ON,] as in Ge. 31. 18, &c.
SPOIL,] as in Ge. 49. 27, &c.
21. WELFARE,] lit. 'peace, completion.'
22. WORTHLESS,] Heb. 'Belial,' as in De. 15. 9; 2 Sa. 22. 5; 23. 6; Job 34. 18; Ps. 18. 4; 41. 8; 101. 3; Nah. 1. 15, &c.
DELIVERED,] from the hand of the Amalekites, as in v. 18.
23. PRESERVE] us from the Philistines, the Amalekites, &c.
24. VESSELS,] keeping watch, while the rest were fighting.
SHARE,] in the spoils of the enemy, as in Nu. 31. 25; Ps. 68. 12.
25. FORWARD,] lit. 'upward,' as in Ge. 6.16.
26. FRIENDS,] those who in his own tribe sympathized with him in his trials.
JUDAH,] his own tribe, to the leading men of it, probably that they might be convinced of his love to them still.
BLESSING,] that is, the proof of one.
27. BETH-EL,] in Kirjath-Jearim, where the ark was, as in 7. 1; 9. 3; also called Baalah. Jos. 15. 9.
SOUTH RAMOTH,] a city of Simeon, Jos. 19.8.
JATTIR,] a city in Judah, as in Jos. 15. 48.

28. AROER,] in Judah, not mentioned elsewhere.
SIPHMOTH,] i.e. 'coverings,' not mentioned elsewhere.
ESHTEMOA,] a Levitical city, as in Jos. 21.14.
29. RACHAL,] i.e. 'traffic;' not mentioned elsewhere.
JERAHMEELITES,] as in 27. 10.
KENITES,] as in Jud. 1. 15.
30. HORMAH,] as in Jos. 15. 30.
CHOR-ASHAN,] i.e. 'a furnace of smoke;' elsewhere simply Ashan, in Jos. 15. 42; 19. 7; 1 Ch. 4. 32; 6. 44.
ATHACH,] i.e. perhaps 'a lodging place;' not mentioned elsewhere.
31. HEBRON,] as in Ge. 13. 18, &c.

XXXI. 1. GILBOA,] as in 28. 4.
2. FOLLOW] in pursuit, that they might capture them alive.
SONS OF SAUL,] as in 14. 49, only Abinadab is there called Ishua. Compare 1 Ch. 8. 33.
3. HARD,] lit. 'heavy,' as in Jud. 20. 34, &c.
ARCHERS,] lit. 'shooters,' as in 20. 36, &c.
PAINED,] as in 1 Ch. 10. 3, &c.
4. WEAPONS,] who now filled the place of David, as in 16. 21.
PIERCE,] as in Nu. 25. 8, &c. Compare the language of Abimelech, in Jud. 9. 54.
UNCIRCUMCISED] Philistines, as in Jud. 14. 3, &c.
ROLLED THEMSELVES,] as in Nu. 22. 29; Jud. 19. 25, &c.
NOT BEEN WILLING] to do anything against his lawful sovereign and the Lord's anointed.
AFRAID] of punishment from the hands of the elders of Israel. 2 Sa. 1. 14.
FALLETH] designedly with the view of destroying his own life. 2 Sa. 1. 10.
5. WITH HIM,] reckoning all things as lost.
ALL HIS MEN,] his body-guard, at least.
7. VALLEY] of Jezreel, where the battle took place.
JORDAN] on the east, among the two tribes and a half.
FLED] from before the victorious Philistines.
DIED] in battle as above narrated.
DWELL] at least for a time, till they were dispossessed by David.
8. STRIP,] as in 2 Sa. 23. 10; 1 Ch. 10. 8, &c.
9. HEAD,] to certify the fact of his death.
WEAPONS,] his coat of mail, sword, &c.
IDOLS,] such as Dagon, &c. Compare 21. 9.
10. ASHTAROTH,] as in Jud. 2. 13.
BETH-SHAN,] as in Jos. 17. 11; Jud. 1. 27.
11. JABESH-GILEAD,] whom Saul had delivered from Ammon, in 11. 1—11; 2 Sa. 2. 4—7.
12. VALOUR,] as in Jos 1. 14, &c.
BURN] them, that the enemy might not again possess them. See 2 Ch. 16. 14; Jer. 34. 5; Amos 6. 10.
13. BONES,] that is, the ashes of them after being burnt.
TAMARISK,] as in Ge. 21. 33; 1 Sa. 22. 6. Compare 1 Ch. 10. 12; Ge. 35 8.
SEVEN DAYS,] in token of their sense of the great calamity that had come upon their king, as in Ge. 50. 10.

SECOND BOOK OF SAMUEL

THE Title of this Book is evidently a misnomer, as it contains a narrative of transactions all of which happened after the death of Samuel; it was probably written by Nathan or Gad, (see 1 Ch. 29. 29), and extends over a period of forty years, the duration of David's reign. The author of the Epistle to the Hebrews (1. 5), refers to at least one statement in it, viz., in 7. 14. Compare also Mat. 1. 6, &c.

I. 1. SAUL] in battle with the Philistines, in mount Gilboa, as in 1 Sa. 31. 4—6.

AMALEKITE,] as narrated in 1 Sa. 30. 17—26.

TWO DAYS] after his return, resting from his fatigue, and making arrangements for his family and retainers.

2. CAMP] at Gilboa, where Israel was fighting with the Philistines.

RENT..HEAD,] displaying the usual signs of grief, as in 1 Sa. 4. 12.

OBEISANCE] to David, as his superior and lord.

3. ESCAPED,] from the sword of the enemy.

4. FLED,] being overpowered by the enemy, and disheartened by the loss of their leaders.

DIED,] from their wounds in the battle.

6. HAPPENED,] lit. 'meeting I met,' compare Ex. 5. 3; De. 22. 6; 2 Sa. 18. 9; 20. 1; Jer. 32. 23.

CHARIOTS] of war, belonging to the Philistines.

HORSES,] among the enemy, for the Israelites appear to have had no cavalry at this time.

8. AMALEKITE,] one of that nation whose enmity to Israel was proverbial.

9. SEIZED,] as in Ex. 15. 14, 15, &c.

ARROW,] lit. a thing 'embroidered;' not found elsewhere.

SOUL,] so that he was afraid he would be captured living.

10. FALLING,] being mortally wounded by the archers.

CROWN,] as in 2 K. 11. 10; 2 Ch. 23. 11; Ps. 89. 39; 132. 18; Prov. 27. 24; Jer. 7. 29; Zec. 9. 6.

BRACELET,] as in Nu. 31. 50; this original word is not found elsewhere.

11. RENDETH,] as in 3. 31; 13. 31.

12. EVENING,] as in Jud. 20. 26.

13. SOJOURNER,] lit. 'son of a man, a sojourner;' this phrase is not found elsewhere.

14. DESTROY,] as in 14. 11; 24. 16, &c.

ANOINTED,] in Heb. 'Messiah,' as in v. 16, 21, &c.

15. FALL UPON HIM,] as a murderer, smiting him with the sword, as in 4. 10, 12.

16. HEAD,] as in Jos. 2. 19, &c.

TESTIFIED,] as in v. 10 above.

17. LAMENTETH,] as in 3. 33; 2 Ch. 35. 25; Jer. 9. 17; Eze. 27. 32; 32. 16.

18. THE BOW,] that is, the following lines, whose title is taken from v. 22.

JUDAH,] rather than Israel, for the latter did not recognize him for several years afterwards.

THE UPRIGHT,] not of 'Jasher,' as in the C. V. ; the definite article shews it an appellative, not a proper name. See Jos. 10. 13.

19. THE ROEBUCK,] as in 2. 18, &c. ; the definite article shews that 'Israel' must be in the vocative case in Hebrew.

HIGH-PLACES,] even the mountains of Gilboa.

WOUNDED,] lit. 'pierced.'

FALLEN,] that is, Saul and Jonathan.

20. GATH,] the principality of the Philistines, where David himself had been residing.

ASHKELON,] as in Jud. 1. 18; 14. 19; 1 Sa. 6. 17; Jer. 25. 20, &c.

REJOICE,] as in Ex. 15. 20; Jud. 11. 34; 1 Sa. 18. 6, 7, &c.

EXULT,] as in Ps. 28. 7; 60. 6; 68. 4; 94. 3; 96. 12; 108. 7; 149. 5; Prov. 23. 6; Isa. 23. 12; Jer. 11. 15; 15. 17; 50. 11; 51. 39; Hab. 3. 18; Zeph. 3. 14.

UNCIRCUMCISED,] as in Jud. 14. 3, &c.

21. GILBOA,] in the tribe of Issachar, as in 1 Sa. 28. 4; 31. 1.

DEW NOR RAIN,] without which they would be barren and unfruitful, unable to yield the

HEAVE-OFFERINGS,] as in Ex. 25. 2, 3; 29. 27, 28, &c., which were presented to the Lord.

LOATHSOME,] as in Lev. 26. 11, 15, 30, 43, 44, &c.

MIGHTY,] as in v. 19, that is, of Saul and Jonathan.

WITHOUT,] that is, lacking him who bore it so bravely.

22. WOUNDED,] or 'pierced,' as in v. 19.

FAT,] as in Jud. 3. 22.

BOW,] as in 1 Sa. 18. 4.

TURNED BACKWARD.] This original verb is not found elsewhere.

EMPTY,] without accomplishing destruction on the enemy.

23. LOVED,] by their subjects and friends.

PLEASANT,] as in 23. 1; Job 36. 11; Ps. 16. 6, 11; 81. 2; 133. 1; 135. 3; 147. 1; Prov. 22. 18; 23. 8; 24. 4; Song 1. 16.

PARTED,] as in Ge. 2. 10; 10. 5, 32; 13. 9, 11, 14; 25. 23; Jud. 4. 11; Neh. 4. 19; Prov. 18. 1; 19. 4.

LIGHTER,] as in Jer. 4. 18; La. 4. 19, &c.

MIGHTIER,] as in Jud. 14. 18; 1 Sa. 17. 36, 37; 2 K. 23. 20; 1 Ch. 11. 22.

24. WEEP YE,] as in Jer. 22. 10, &c.

SCARLET,] as in Prov. 31. 21; Jer. 4. 30.

DELIGHTS,] as in Ps. 36. 8; Jer. 51. 34.

LIFTING UP,] lit. 'causing to go up,' as in 6. 15.

ORNAMENTS,] as in Ex. 33. 4, 5, 6, &c.

CLOTHING,] as in Ge. 49. 11, &c.

25. FALLEN,] wounded and slain.
HIGH-PLACES,] those of Israel in Gilboa.
WOUNDED,] or 'pierced,' as in v. 19.
26. IN DISTRESS,] *lit.* 'distress is to me.'
PLEASANT,] as in v. 23; compare 1 Sa. 18.
1, 3, 4; 19. 2, 4; 20. 30, 33.
WONDERFUL,] as in Ps. 118. 23; Prov. 30.
18; Zec. 8. 6, &c.
WOMEN,] as in Prov. 5. 19, &c.
27. FALLEN,] as in v. 19 above.
PERISH,] or 'are lost,' being taken and
destroyed by the enemy.

II. 1. AFTERWARDS,] perhaps next day,
compare 1. 12.
ASKETH,] as he had been accustomed to
do in serious cases.
JUDAH,] his own tribe, which was likely
to be most favourable.
HEBRON,] a city of refuge, belonging to
the Levites, about twenty miles from Jerusalem.
2. TWO WIVES,] as in 1 Sa. 30. 5.
3. HIS MEN,] six hundred in number, as
in 1 Sa. 27. 2, 3; 30. 1; 1 Ch. 12. 1.
4. ANOINT,] formally, according to the
usual custom.
BURIED,] as narrated in 1 Sa. 31. 11—13.
5. BLESSED,] as in Jud. 17. 2; Ruth 2. 20;
3. 10; 1 Sa. 15. 13; 23. 21, &c.
6. KINDNESS AND TRUTH,] as in Ex. 34.
6, &c.
7. SONS OF VALOUR,] that is, valiant
children and subjects; as in De. 3. 18; Jud.
21. 10, &c.
KING,] as in v. 4 above.
8. HEAD,] as in 1 Sa. 14. 50, &c.
ISH-BOSHETH,] i.e. a 'man of shame;'
named Ish-Baal, in 1 Ch. 8. 33; 9. 39.
MAHANAIM,] beyond the Jordan, in the
tribe of Gad, Jos. 13. 26—30; Ge. 32. 2.
9. GILEAD,] beyond the Jordan.
ASHUR,] perhaps another form of 'Asher;'
the Vul. reads 'Geshur,' erroneously; see 3.
3; Jos. 13. 13.
JEZREEL,] which bordered on and included Zebulun, Naphtali, and Issachar.
EPHRAIM,] next to Judah, the most
powerful tribe.
BENJAMIN,] the tribe to which Saul belonged.
10. SON OF FORTY YEARS,] born at the
beginning of his father's reign, see 1 Sa. 31. 6.
DAVID,] as the king of their own choice,
and God's selection.
12. GOETH FORTH,] probably with a view
to attack Judah.
MAHANAIM,] as in v. 8, which he had
apparently made his head-quarters.
GIBEON,] a city of Benjamin, as in Jos.
18. 25.
13. JOAB,] as in 1 Sa. 26. 6; he appears
now to be David's chief general.
ZERUIAH,] the sister of David, as in 1 Ch.
2. 16.
POOL,] which is called in Jer. 41. 12 'the
great waters.'
14. PLAY,] as in Jud. 16. 25, &c.
BENJAMIN,] to which tribe Abner himself belonged.
16. LAY HOLD,] as in Ge. 19. 16, &c.

HELKATH-HAZZURIM,] i. e. 'portion or
place of the sharp weapons.'
17. HARD,] or 'sharp.'
18. ABISHAI,] as in 1 Sa. 26. 6—9.
ASAHEL,] i.e. 'God made,' as in v. 19, 20
21, 22, 23, 30, 32; 3. 27, 30; 23. 24; 1 Ch. 2. 16.
LIGHT,] as in Ecc. 9. 11; Jer. 2. 23; 46. 6;
Amos 2. 14, 15, &c.; 1 Ch. 11. 26.
ROES,] as in 1. 19; 1 Ch. 12. 8; Song 2
7, &c.
21. LEFT,] as in v. 19, &c.
SEIZE] as a prisoner.
ARMOUR,] as in Jud. 14. 19.
22. LIFT UP] with confidence and hope
of friendship.
23. HINDER PART,] which appears to
have had a sharp point on it.
FIFTH RIB,] as in 3. 27; 4. 6; 20. 10.
STAND STILL] in grief and amazement.
24. GONE IN,] according to the usual
Hebrew phrase, as in Ge. 15. 12, 17, &c.
AMMAH,] i.e. 'cubit or pedestal;' not
mentioned elsewhere.
GIAH,] i.e. 'breaking forth' of a fountain;
not mentioned elsewhere.
GIBEON,] near the city of that name,
in v. 12.
25. ONE TROOP,] to make a final stand
against the enemy.
26. CONSUME,] as in De. 32. 42, &c.
BITTERNESS] to both parties, in the continuance of this unnatural contention.
BRETHREN] of the house of Israel, children of the same first parent.
27. SPOKEN,] as in v. 14 above.
28. A TRUMPET,] as in 6. 15; 15. 10; 18.
16; 20. 1, 22, &c.
29. PLAIN] towards the Jordan, *lit.* 'the
Arabah.'
BITHRON,] perhaps the same as 'Bether,'
in Song 2. 17; *lit.* a 'separation.'
MAHANAIM,] whence they had come out,
as in v. 12.
30. NINETEEN,] so that only seven appear
to have been killed in the general conflict,
see v. 16.
31. SMITTEN] mortally, not to speak of
the wounded.
32. FATHER,] whose name is nowhere
mentioned, only that of his mother.
IT IS LIGHT,] or 'there is light,' by the
rising of the sun.
HEBRON,] where David had fixed his
residence, as in v. 3, 11.

III. 1. THE WAR,] or 'battle,' as in 2.
17; it extended over five years, till the
death of Ish-Bosheth.
STRONG,] receiving accessions daily from
the other tribes.
WEAK,] by every successive contest.
2. AMNON,] i.e. 'stedfast,' as in 13. 1—39;
once called 'Aminon,' in 13. 20.
3. CHILEAB,] i.e. 'the father hath completed;' not mentioned elsewhere; called
Daniel in 1 Ch. 3. 1.
ABSALOM,] i.e. 'father of peace,' as in
13. 1, &c.
MAACAH,] i.e. 'oppression.'
TALMAI,] i.e. 'full of furrows,' as in 13. 37
GESHUR,] as in 13. 37.

4. ADONIJAH,] i.e. 'the Lord is Jah,' as in 1 K. 1. 5; 2. 25, &c.

HAGGITH,] i.e. 'festive,' as in 1 K. 1. 5, 11; 2. 13; 1 Ch. 3. 2.

SHEPHATIAH,] i.e. 'Jah hath judged,' as in 1 Ch. 3. 3, &c.

ABITAL,]i.e. 'father of dew,' as in 1 Ch. 3. 3.

5. ITHREAM,] i.e. 'abandance or remnant of a people,' as in 1 Ch. 3. 3.

EGLAH,] i.e. 'a calf,' as in 1 Ch. 3. 3.

6. STRENGTHENING HIMSELF,] as in 1 Ch. 11. 10; Da. 10. 21.

IN,] not 'for' the house of Saul, as in the C.V.

7. CONCUBINE,] as in 21. 11; Ge. 22. 24, &c.; by her he had two sons, as in 21. 8.

RiZPAH,] i.e. 'a burning coal.'

AIAH,] i.e. a 'kite or vulture,' as in 21. 8. GONE IN,] as in Ge. 6. 4, &c.

8. DISPLEASING,] that his conduct should be questioned by one who owed so much to him.

HEAD OF A DOG,] commonly reckoned in the east as a vile unclean animal, 1 Sa. 4. 24; 2 Sa. 9. 8.

DO KINDNESS] in risking his life while fighting their battles.

DELIVERED] thee as a prisoner, as he might have done, considering his power.

INIQUITY,] or 'punishment,' as in Ge. 4. 13.

9. ADD,] as in Ruth 1. 17, &c.

SWORN] in 1 Sa. 15. 28; 16. 1, 12; 28. 17; 1 Ch. 12. 23, &c.

10. BEER-SHEBA,] the two extremities of the land of Israel.

11. WORD,] as in 1 K. 12. 6; 2 Ch. 10. 6; Est. 4. 15; Job 33. 5.

12. FOR HIMSELF,] that is, in his own name and for his own behoof.

LAND,] that is, of Israel, about which there had been so much disputing and fighting.

WITH ME,] as the chief man in Israel hitherto opposed to David.

BRING ROUND,] so as to be on his side in future.

13. GOOD] is the proposal to unite the whole under one ruler.

MICHAL,] who had been unjustly taken from her husband.

COMING IN] to Hebron, where David was residing as his head quarters.

14. BETROTHED,] as in 1 Sa. 18. 25, 27.

15. SENDETH,] afraid to deny the request, which, nevertheless, was a just and reasonable one.

PHALTIEL,] i.e 'escape of God;' in 1 Sa. 25. 44 called 'Phalti.'

LAISH,] in Heb. 'Lavish.'

16. BAHURIM,] a city of Benjamin, as in 19. 16. Targum reads 'Almuth,' perhaps the same as Almon, in Jos. 21. 18, and Alemeth in 1 Ch. 6. 68.

TURNETH BACK] to his own house, justly punished for his taking David's wife.

17. ELDERS,] who ruled in every city.

HERETOFORE,] lit. 'yesterday, third day;' probably immediately after the death of Saul.

SEEKING,] agreeable to previous expectations of Saul and all Israel.

18. DO IT,] because it was sanctioned by the Divine word.

SAYING,] substantially, on various occasions.

ENEMIES,] around them on the north, east, and west.

19. BENJAMIN,] in which naturally he had most influence, and which was doubtless most attached to Saul's family.

ISRAEL,] especially the ten tribes.

BENJAMIN,] whom he appears to have won round to his plans.

20. TWENTY MEN,] probably chiefs of the tribes as delegates.

BANQUET,] lit. 'drinking.'

21. GATHER,] as in 2. 30.

COVENANT,] regarding the rights and duties of the kingly authority; it was not to be an absolute monarchy.

DESIRETH,] as in 1 K. 11. 37.

PEACE,] with David, having concluded the bargain.

22. JOAB,] their general, at their head.

TROOP,] which had been out on an excursion.

SPOIL,] belonging to the enemy.

23. THEY DECLARE,] that is, some of the friends of Joab, and enemies of Abner.

PEACE,] as in v. 21.

24. DONE?] boldly presuming on his value and relationship to the king.

GONE] in peace—after all the evil he had tried to do to David.

25. KNOWN,] in former days. Sept. Vulg. Syr. and Ar. Versions read this interrogatively.

DECEIVE,] and put thee off thy guard.

COMING IN,] thy plans and purposes.

26. ABNER,] as if by the command of David.

SIRAH,] i.e. 'the turning aside,' so called from this circumstance; or 'a pot, hook.'

27. TURNETH BACK,] at the request of Joab's messengers.

GATE,] probably 'city' is here meant.

QUIETLY,] or 'with ease or safety.'

FIFTH RIB,] as in 2. 23.

BLOOD,] which Abner had shed, though unwillingly.

28. ACQUITTED,] of all complicity, as in 14. 9, &c.

29. STAY,] unforgiven and unpropitiated. Compare 1 K. 2. 32, 33.

ISSUE] of blood, &c., and therefore unclean, as in Lev. 15. 2.

LEPROUS,] and generally incurable, as in Lev. 13. 44, 45, &c.

STAFF,] unable to walk actively; or distaff, as in Prov. 31. 9.

SWORD] in battle.

BREAD] for his daily food, and obliged to beg for it.

30. ABISHAI,] who probably had tempted Joab to this treacherous act.

BATTLE,] as in 2. 23.

31. REND,] as a public token of grief.

GIRD ON,] as in Ge. 37. 34, &c.

BEFORE] the body of Abner, as it was carried to the grave

BIER,] on which the body was lying.

32. HEBRON,] instead of taking him to Gibeah of Saul.

WEEP] in unison with the king, at the untimely death of a valiant warrior.
33. LAMENTETH,] as in 1. 17, &c.
FOOL,] in *Heb.* 'nabal;' Sept. reads 'Nabal.'
34. NOT BOUND,] so as to be unable to defend himself.
FETTERS,] as in Jud. 16. 21, &c.
SONS OF EVIL,] as in 7. 10; 1 Ch. 17. 8; Ps. 89. 22.
35. DAY,] he apparently intending to fast till sunset, fearing lest he may become exhausted.
SWEARETH,] to stop their importunity.
ADD,] as in Ruth 1. 7, &c.
TASTE,] as in 1 Sa. 14. 24, 29, 43.
36. DISCERNED] the object and intent of the oath and the fasting.
38. PRINCE,] *or* 'head.'
FALLEN,] destroyed and worthless.
39. TENDER] in point of feeling and authority.
ANOINTED KING,] with supreme power.
ZERUIAH,] his own sister.
HARD,] *or* 'sharp.'
EVIL,] as in 19. 13; 1 K. 2. 5, 6, 33, 34; Ps. 28. 4; 62. 12.

IV. 1. SON OF SAUL,] that is, Ish-Bosheth, as in 2. 8.
HEBRON,] and buried by David, as in 3. 22.
FEEBLE,] as in 2 Ch. 15. 7, &c.
TROUBLED] because of Abner's loss.
2. HEADS OF TROOPS,] chief officers in his army.
BAANAH,] i.e. 'son of affliction.'
RECHAB,] i.e. 'a rider.'
RIMMON,] i.e. 'a pomegranate.'
BEEROTH,] a city of Benjamin, as in Jos. 9. 17; 18. 25.
3. GITTAIM,] i.e. 'two wine-fats,' as in Neh. 11. 33; a city of Benjamin, perhaps.
SOJOURNERS,] without returning to Beeroth.
4. JONATHAN,] the eldest son of Saul, and heir to the throne.
LAME,] *lit.* 'smitten of the feet,' as in 9. 3.
JEZREEL,] where the battle was fought, as in 1 Sa. 29. 1, 11.
NURSE,] as in Ruth 4. 14, &c.
FLEE] with her charge, lest he should be taken by the Philistines.
MEPHIBOSHETH.] Etymology unknown; elsewhere called 'Merib-baal,' i.e. a 'contender against Baal,' as in 1 Ch. 8. 34; 9. 40.
5. HEAT OF THE DAY,] as in Ge. 18. 1; 1 Sa. 11. 11.
NOON,] as in Song 1. 7.
6. TAKING] away wheat for the troops as usual.
WHEAT,] as in 17. 28, &c.
FIFTH RIB,] as in 2. 23, &c.
ESCAPED] from the house and their pursuers.
7. BED,] as in Ge. 47. 31; 48. 2; 49. 33.
BED-CHAMBER,] *lit.* 'place of lying down,' as in Ex. 8. 3; 2 K. 6. 12; Ecc. 10. 20.
TURN ASIDE,] as in 2 K. 6. 32.
PLAIN] of the Jordan, from Mahanaim to 8. HEBRON,] where David was residing.

ENEMY,] this probably refers to Saul, not to Ish-Bosheth.
VENGEANCE,] *lit.* 'vengeances,' as in 22. 48.
SEED,] most of whom were now destroyed.
9. JEHOVAH LIVETH !] a solemn asseveration, as in Jud. 8. 19, &c.
REDEEMED,] as in Ex. 13. 13, &c.
ADVERSITY,] as in 1 K. 1. 29, &c.
10. ONE,] that is, the Amalekite, in 1. 4.
DEAD,] so that David should fear no longer.
TIDINGS,] not 'good tidings,' as in C.V.
TAKE HOLD,] lest he should attempt to escape.
ZIKLAG,] whither he had come with Saul's crown.
TIDINGS,] as he expected, and was customary.
11. THE RIGHTEOUS MAN,] that is, Ish-Bosheth, who had done them no wrong.
BED,] as in v. 7 above.
REQUIRE,] according to law and justice, as a ruler, as in Ge. 9. 5, 6, &c.
TAKEN YOU AWAY,] *lit.* 'burned you,' as in Lev. 6. 12, &c
12. THE YOUNG MEN] of his body-guard, as in 1. 15.
HANG,] as in Ge. 40. 19, 22; 41. 13, &c.
POOL,] a public place of resort, for a terror to others.
ABNER,] where he was buried by David, as in 3. 32.

V. 1. HEBRON,] after the death of Ish-Bosheth their king.
BONE..FLESH,] which was required of any one who was to be king among them, De. 17. 15.
2. HERETOFORE,] *lit.* 'yesterday, the third day.'
BRINGING OUT AND IN,] as a chief and leader.
FEED,] that is, take care of, and superintend, as in Ge. 29. 7; 30. 31; Ge. 4. 2, &c.
LEADER,] as in 1 Sa. 9. 16; 10. 1; 13. 14; 25. 30, &c.
3. ELDERS,] as representing the tribes in v. 1.
COVENANT,] securing the rights of both parties.
JEHOVAH,] the avenger of every transgression.
ANOINT,] as they had formerly done Saul.
4. KING] over Judah, as in 2. 4.
REIGNED] till his death, as in 1 K. 2. 11.
6. JERUSALEM,] which he conquered from the Jebusite, as in v. 6—9.
JEBUSITE,] as in Ge. 10. 16, &c.
BLIND..LAME,] as in v. 8; Lev. 21. 18; De. 15. 21; Jer. 31. 8; they proudly thought their city impregnable.
7. CAPTURETH,] by the aid of Joab, as in 1 Ch. 11. 6—9.
FORTRESS,] as in 1 Sa. 22. 4, 5, &c.
ZION,] i.e. 'the dry or sunny part' of Jerusalem, at the south.
CITY OF DAVID,] as in v. 9.
8. WATER-COURSE,] as in Ps. 42. 7.

HATED,] because of their boastful language.

HOUSE] of Millo, as in 2 K. 12. 21.

9. FORTRESS,] as in v. 6.

MILLO,] *lit.* 'a filling up,' i.e. a rampart, mound, see 1 K. 9. 15, 24; 11. 27; 1 Ch. 11. 8; 2 Ch. 32. 5.

10. BECOMING GREAT] in power and honour at home and abroad.

WITH HIM,] guiding and protecting and blessing him.

11. HIRAM,] i.e. 'freeman,' as in 1 K. 5. 15; *or* 'Huram,' as in 2 Ch. 2. 2.

TYRE,] as in Jos. 19. 29, &c.; a city of the Phenicians.

CEDAR-TREES,] as in Lev. 14. 4, 6, 49, 51, 52, &c.

ARTIFICERS,] as in 2 K. 12. 11; 1 Ch. 14. 1; 22. 15; Isa. 44. 13.

WALLS,] as in Ex. 30. 3; 37. 26; Lev. 1. 15; 5. 9; 14. 37, 39, &c.

HOUSE,] that is, a palace.

12. KNOWETH,] by the success of his undertakings.

LIFTED UP] above those around him.

PEOPLE,] whom he had chosen and redeemed.

13. CONCUBINES AND WIVES,] contrary to Lev. 18. 18; De. 17. 17.

14. SHAMMUAH,] i.e. 'heard,' as in 1 Ch. 14. 4; called 'Shimea,' in 1 Ch. 3. 5.

SHOBAB,] i.e. 'a bringer back,' as in 1 Ch. 3. 5; 14. 4.

NATHAN,] i.e. 'he gave.'

SOLOMON,] i.e. 'peace.'

15. IBHAR,] i.e. 'he chooses,' as in 1 Ch. 14. 5.

ELISHUA,] i.e. 'my God saves,' as in 1 Ch. 14. 5; called Elishama in 1 Ch. 3. 6.

NEPHEG,] i.e. 'a going forth,' as in 1 Ch. 3. 7; 14. 6.

JAPHIA,] i.e. 'he breathes.'

16. ELISHAMA,] i.e. 'God hears.'

ELIADA,] i.e. 'God knows;' in 1 Ch. 14. 7 called Bealiada.

ELIPHALET,] i.e. 'God escapes,' as in 1 Ch. 3. 6; 14. 5. 7.

17. ANOINTED,] as in v. 3.

SEEK DAVID,] to fight, and if possible, conquer him.

FORTRESS,] not for safety, but to gather his men; as in 23. 14.

18. SPREAD OUT] for plunder and devastation.

REPHAIM,] as in Jos. 15. 8, at the west of Jerusalem.

19. ASKETH] counsel and direction, as in 2. 1.

GO UP] from the valley to mount Perazim, as in Isa. 28. 21.

20. BAAL-PERAZIM,] i.e. 'lord of breaches,' as in 1 Ch. 14. 11.

BROKEN UP,] as in 2 Ch. 20. 37; 24. 7. &c.

21. IDOLS,] *lit.* 'grievous things,' as in 1 Sa. 31. 9; compare Isa. 58. 3, &c.

LIFT THEM UP,] not 'burn them,' as in the C.V. So Sept., Vulg., &c.

22. COME UP] from the shores of the great sea to the valley of Rephaim, as before.

SPREAD OUT,] as in v. 18.

23. ASKETH,] as in v. 19.

NOT GO UP] to meet them direct.

REAR,] to cut off their retreat, and attack the feeblest part of the camp.

MULBERRIES,] as in v. 24; 1 Ch. 14. 14, 15; Ps. 84. 6.

MOVE SHARPLY,] as in Ex. 11. 7, &c.

25. GEBA,] or Gibeon, as in 1 Ch. 14. 16, in the tribe of Judah.

GAZER,] as in Jos. 16. 10.

VI. 1. GATHERETH] by the advice of his officers, as in 1 Ch. 13. 1.

CHOICE ONE,] as in Ex. 14. 7, or 'young man,' as in De. 32. 25.

2. BAALE-JUDAH,] i.e. 'possessors of Judah,' called Baalah in Jos. 15. 9, and Kirjath-Jearim in 1 Ch. 13. 6; and Kirjath-Baal in Jos. 15. 60.

ARK,] see 1 Sa. 14. 18.

HOSTS,] as in 1 Sa. 1. 3, 11; 15. 2; 17. 45; 2 Sa. 5. 10, &c.

INHABITING THE CHERUBS,] as in 1 Sa. 4. 4, &c.

3. CAUSE TO RIDE,] as in 2 K. 9. 28; 13. 16; 1 Ch. 13. 7, &c.

CART,] as in 1 Sa. 6. 7, 8, 11, 14; 1 Ch. 13. 7, &c; it should have been carried on the shoulder, as in Nu. 7. 9.

4. ABINADAB,] as in 1 Sa. 7. 1.

HEIGHT,] in Kirjath-Jearim.

UZZAH,] i.e. 'strength.'

AHIO,] i.e. 'his brother.'

5. PLAYING,] as in 1 Sa. 18. 7; 1 Ch. 13. 8; 15. 29, &c.

FIR-WOOD,] as in 1 K. 5. 8, 10; 6. 15, 34; 9. 11; 2 K. 19. 23; 2 Ch. 2. 8; 3. 5; Ps. 104. 17; Isa. 14. 8; 37. 24; 41. 19; 55. 13; 60. 13; Eze. 27. 6; 31. 8; Hos. 14. 8; Na. 2. 3; Zec. 11. 2.

HARPS,] as in Ge. 4. 21; 31. 27; 1 Sa. 10. 5, &c

PSALTERIES,] as in 1 Sa. 10. 5, &c.

TIMBRELS,] as in Ge. 31. 27, &c.

CORNETS.] This original word is not found elsewhere.

CYMBALS,] as in Ps. 150. 5; this original word is not found elsewhere.

6. NACHON,] in 1 Ch. 13. 9 he is called 'Chidion.'

RELEASED] from the cart, as in 1 Ch. 13. 9; compare Ex. 23. 11; De. 15. 2, 3; 2 K. 9. 33; Ps. 141. 6; Jer. 17. 4.

OXEN,] which drew it along.

7. ERROR] in touching the ark, not being a Kohathite.

8. PERIZ-UZZAH,] i.e. 'breach of Uzzah.'

9. FEARETH] the purity and power of Jehovah, Ps. 119. 120.

UNTO ME] in my city—the city of David.

10. NOT BEEN WILLING,] because of this breach and fear.

CITY OF DAVID,] which he had conquered and beautified.

OBED-EDOM,] i.e. 'servant of Edom.'

GITTITE,] as in 1 Ch. 15. 18, 21, 24; 16. 5, 6; perhaps he was of Gath-Rimmon, a Levitical city, as in Jos. 21. 24.

11. INHABIT,] that is, dwell in.

BLESSETH] those who receive him gladly as this man appears to have done.

12. JOY,] freed from his fears by seeing the prosperity the ark had brought to Obed-Edom.

13. THOSE BEARING,] on the shoulders, that is, the Levites.

STEPPED,] as in Ge. 49. 22; Jud. 5. 4; Ps. 68. 7; Job 18. 14; Prov. 7. 8; Jer. 10. 5; Hab. 3. 12.

STEPS,] as in 22. 37; Job 14. 16; 18. 7; 31. 4, 37; 34. 21; Ps. 18. 36; Prov. 4. 12; 5. 5; 16. 19; 30. 29; Jer. 10. 23; La. 4. 18.

OX..FATLING.] Compare 1 Ch. 15. 26.

14. DANCING] with joy, as a religious service, as in v. 16.

LINEN EPHOD,] as in 1 Sa. 2. 18; 22. 18; 1 Ch. 15. 27.

15. SHOUTING,] as in 1 Sa. 4. 5, 6; 1 Ch. 15. 28, &c.

TRUMPET,] as in 1 Ch. 15. 28, &c.

16. CITY OF DAVID,] as in 5. 9; 6. 10, 12.

MICHAL] his first wife, now restored to him.

WINDOW] of her palace, too proud, it may be, to join the assembly.

MOVING,] as in Ge. 49. 24; compare 1 Ch. 15. 29.

DANCING,] as in v. 14.

DESPISETH,] or 'trampleth on him,' so in 1 Ch. 15. 29.

17. BRING IN] unto the city of David, as in v. 16.

SPREAD OUT,] as in Ge. 12. 8, &c.

BURNT-OFFERINGS,] for sin and transgression.

PEACE-OFFERINGS,] for mercies received.

18. BLESSETH,] as a prince and common father; compare 1 K. 8. 55; 1 Ch. 16. 2.

19. MULTITUDE] who were present.

CAKE,] as in Ex. 29. 2, 23; Lev. 2. 4; 7. 12, 13; 8. 26; 24. 5; Nu. 6. 15, 19; 15. 20.

ESHPAR,] as in 1 Ch. 16. 3; this word is not found elsewhere; Gesenius reads 'a measure.'

ASHISHA,] as in 1 Ch. 16. 3; compare Song 2. 4; Hos. 3. 1.

20. TURNETH BACK] from the tent where the ark was put.

HONOURABLE,] as in Ge. 34. 19, &c.

UNCOVERED,] removing perhaps his royal robes and upper garment.

HANDMAIDS,] who were accompanying the procession.

VAIN ONES,] or 'empty ones.'

21. BEFORE JEHOVAH,] in whose presence all pretensions must be put aside.

FIXED] of his own good will.

LEADER] and governor, under God.

PLAYED,] as in v. 5 above.

22. VILE,] or 'lightly esteemed.'

LOW] and humble before God.

HONOURED] as the servant of the Lord.

23. AS TO,] lit. 'and,' not 'therefore,' as in the C.V.

VII. 1. KING,] that is, David. Compare 1 Ch. 17. 1-16.

HOUSE,] which had been built of cedars, as in 5. 11.

GIVEN REST] as he had promised.

ENEMIES] at home and abroad.

2. NATHAN,] as in 1 Ch. 17. 1.

PROPHET,] who appears to have been attached to David.

CEDARS,] as in 5. 11.

CURTAIN,] as in Ex. 26. 1—13; 36. 8—17; Nu. 4. 25; 1 Ch. 17. 1; Ps. 104. 2; Song 1. 5; Isa. 54. 2; Jer. 4. 20; 10. 20; 49. 29; Hab.3.7.

3. HEART,] as in 1 K. 8. 17, 18; 1 Ch. 22. 7; 28. 2.

WITH THEE,] in the thought, and will be also in the execution, of it.

4. WORD OF JEHOVAH,] in reference to the proposal.

5. MY SERVANT,] though anointed king of Israel.

JEHOVAH] the covenant God and king of Israel.

HOUSE,] stable materials instead of a temporary tent.

6. BRINGING UP] with a high hand and an outstretched arm.

THIS DAY,] a period of about 450 years.

WALKING UP AND DOWN] habitually, as in a settled dwelling.

TENT,] of which the tabernacle was a small compartment, see Ex. 26. 1, 6, 11, 12, 13.

7. TRIBES,] or sceptres, perhaps 'sceptre-bearer' is meant; in 1 Ch. 17. 6 it is 'judges.'

FEED,] that is, take care of and overlook them.

8. MY SERVANT,] as in v. 5.

COMELY PLACE,] as in Hos. 9. 13; Ex. 15. 13, &c.

FLOCK] of which he was shepherd, as in 1 Sa. 16. 11—13.

LEADER,] in the place of Saul.

9. GONE] in peace and in war.

CUT OFF,] by giving success to David's arms everywhere.

NAME,] or 'renown.'

10. APPOINTED,] lit. 'set, placed.'

PLANTED] it deep in the land, that it may take root.

TROUBLED,] as in Ex. 15. 14; De. 2. 25.

SONS OF PERVERSENESS,] as in 3. 34, &c.

AFFLICT,] as in Ex. 1. 11; 22. 23, &c.

BEGINNING] of its history in Canaan, Egypt, the wilderness, &c.

11. JUDGES,] to execute justice between man and man.

GIVEN REST,] as in v. 1.

HOUSE,] that is, a family.

12. FULL,] as determined by God in his wisdom and foreknowledge, Ps. 90. 10.

FATHERS,] as in De. 31. 16, &c.

BOWELS,] as in Ge. 15. 4, &c.

KINGDOM,] as in 5. 12, &c.

13. MY NAME,] as in 1 K. 5. 5; 6. 12; 8. 19; 1 Ch. 22. 10; 8. 6; Zec. 6. 12, 13.

14. FATHER,] as in Ps. 89. 26, 27; Heb. 1. 5.

SON,] dutiful and obedient in all things.

DEALING PERVERSELY,] as in Jer. 9. 5.

REPROVED,] as in Ge. 21. 25, &c.

ROD,] with which men chastise their disobedient children.

STROKES,] as in De. 17. 8; 21. 5, &c.

SONS OF ADAM,] as in Nu. 23. 19, &c.

15. SAUL,] as in 1 Sa. 15. 23, 28; 16. 14 1 K. 11. 13, 34.

16. STEDFAST,] as in 1 Sa. 2. 35, &c.

ESTABLISHED,] as in v. 26.

17. WORDS..VISION,] neither adding to nor taking from it.

18. SITTETH,] in the attitude of prayer, as in Jud. 20. 26; 21. 2, &c.

COMETH IN] unto the tent where the ark was placed.

HITHERTO,] as in 1 Ch. 17. 16, &c.

19. LITTLE IN THINE EYES,] as in 1 Ch. 17. 17; 1 Sa. 15. 17, &c.

AFAR OFF,] as in Ge. 22. 4, &c.

LAW OF THE MAN.] The word 'law' never means 'custom' as in C.V., and there is no mark of interrogation; with Pye Smith we refer it to Messiah; so also Luther and Osiander.

MY LORD JEHOVAH,] as in Ge. 15. 2, 8, &c.

20. KNOWN] fully, and appreciated him.

21. WORD,] which cannot be allowed to fail.

HEART,] which had prompted this kindness.

GREATNESS] in making him king, and exalting his kingdom.

22. NONE,] in wonderful works of mercy; De. 3. 24; 4. 35; 32. 39; 1 Sa. 2. 2, &c.

SAVE THEE,] as in 1 Ch. 17. 20; Isa. 45. 5, 21; o4. 4; Hos. 13. 4.

EARS,] of God's doings.

23. AS ISRAEL,] over which David reigned as king.

ONE NATION,] small in number, and in influence in the

EARTH] or land of Canaan, in which it was dwelling.

REDEEM,] as in 1 Ch. 17. 21; De. 9. 26; 21. 8; 2 Sa. 4. 9; 7. 23, &c.

NAME,] as in v. 9, 13.

FOR YOU,] or as some read, 'for them.'

FEARFUL THINGS,] as in De. 10. 21, &c.

24. PEOPLE,] as in De. 26. 17, 18, &c.

GOD] rescuing and blessing them; Ps. 48. 14.

25. SPOKEN] by the mouth of Nathan, as in v. 12—16.

26. IS GREAT,] among thy people Israel.

27. UNCOVERED,] as in Ruth 4. 4; 1 Sa. 9. 15, &c.

HOUSE,] as in v. 11, 18, &c.

FOUND HIS HEART,] as in 1 Ch. 17. 25; Neh. 9. 8, &c.

28. GOD HIMSELF,] the fountain of all power.

TRUTH,] and therefore unchangeable; John 17. 17.

GOODNESS] regarding his house and family.

29. BEGIN,] as in De. 1. 5. So the Targum.

SPOKEN,] and will not draw back.

THY BLESSING,] which alone maketh rich, and addeth no sorrow with it.

VIII. 1. PHILISTINES,] as in 1 Ch. 18. 1.

HUMBLETH,] as in Lev. 26. 41; De. 9. 3, &c.

BRIDLE,] as in 2 K. 19. 28; Ps. 32. 9; Prov. 26. 3; Isa. 37. 29.

METROPOLIS,] lit. 'mother,' compare 20. 19.

2. MOAB,] fulfilling the prediction in Nu. 24. 17.

MEASURETH,] as in Ps. 60. 6; 108. 7.

LINE,] as in Jos. 2. 15; 2 Sa. 17. 13, &c.

KEEP ALIVE,] preserving a third of the prisoners.

PRESENT,] as in 2 K. 3. 4, 5; 2 Ch. 17. 11.

3. HADADEZER,] i.e. 'Hadad is help;' in 10. 16, 19; 1 Ch. 19. 16, 19 he is called 'Hadarezer'.

REHOB,] i.e. 'broad,' as in v. 12; 10. 8.

ZOBAH,] i.e. perhaps 'a station,' as in 10. 6; 1 Sa. 14. 47, &c.; called also 'Aram-Zobah.'

HIS POWER,] that is, of David; see Ge. 15. 18; 1 K. 4. 21—24.

RIVER.] The marginal reading of the Hebrew text supplies the proper name 'Euphrates.'

4. HORSEMEN,] as in Ge. 50. 6, &c, Compare 1 Ch. 18. 4 for an important variation.

FOOTMEN,] as in Ex. 12. 37, &c.

CHARIOTEERS,] as in Isa. 21. 7, &c.

LEAVETH,] for purposes of show and grandeur.

5. ARAM,] as in 1 K. 11. 23—25.

DAMASCUS,] in Heb. 'Dammesek.'

6. GARRISONS,] as in v. 14; 1 Sa. 10. 5, &c.

PRESENT,] as in v. 2 above.

SAVETH,] or 'easeth.'

7. SHIELDS,] as in 2 K. 11. 10; 1 Ch. 18. 7; 2 Ch. 23. 9; Song 4. 4; Jer. 51. 11; Eze. 27. 11.

ON,] or 'unto.'

8. BETAH,] i.e. 'confidence;' in 1 Ch. 18. 8 it is called Tibhath, i.e. 'slaughter.'

BEROTHIA,] i.e. 'my wells;' in 1 Ch. 18. called 'Chun.

BRASS.] Sept. adds, as in 1 Ch. 18. 8, ' wherewith Solomon made the brazen sea,' &c.

9. TOI,] i.e. 'erring;' in 1 Ch. 18. 9, 10 called 'Tou.'

HAMATH,] on which see Nu. 34. 8.

10. JORAM,] in 1 Ch. 18. 19 called 'Hadoram.'

MAN OF WARS,] as in Isa. 42. 13; 1 Ch. 18. 10.

SILVER..GOLD..BRASS,] as a present to king David.

11. SANCTIFY,] i.e. set apart for the house of the Lord which he had purposed to build.

12. ARAM] of Damascus, as in v. 5 above.

MOAB,] as in v. 2 above.

BENE-AMMON,] who probably joined themselves to Moab, as often elsewhere.

PHILISTINES,] as in v. 1.

AMALEK,] as in Ps. 83. 7.

SPOIL,] as in v. 3—6.

13. ARAM,] in 1 Ch. 18. 12 it is called 'Edom.'

18,000,] as in 1 Ch. 18. 12, but in Ps. 60. 1, only 12,000.

14. GARRISONS,] as in v. 6.

SERVANTS,] as in v. 2. Compare the prophecies in Ge. 25. 23; 27. 29, 40.

15. ALL ISRAEL,] the whole twelve tribes.

JUDGMENT AND RIGHTEOUSNESS,] as in Ge. 18. 19, &c.

16. HOST] of battle, as in 1 Ch. 11. 6, &c.

JEHOSHAPHAT,] as in 20. 24.

AHILUD,] as in 20. 24; 1 K. 4. 3.

REMEMBRANCER,] as in Ge. 41. 9; Nu. 5. 15; 2 Sa. 20. 24; 1 K. 4. 3; 2 K. 18. 18, 37; 1 Ch. 18. 15; 2 Ch. 34. 8; Isa. 36. 3, 22; 62. 6; 66. 3; Eze. 21. 23; 29. 16.

17. ZADOK,] i.e. 'just,' as in 15. 24

AHITUB,] i.e. 'brother of good.'

ABIATHAR,] or rather perhaps 'Abiathar, son of Ahimelech,' see 1 Sa. 21. 2; 22. 9; Ps. 52. 2; but compare 1 Ch. 24. 3, 6, 31.

PRIESTS,] officiating perhaps by turns; this one was of the family of Ithamar, the other of Eleazar.

SERAIAH,] i.e. 'Jah's prince;' in 20. 25 called Sheva; in 1 Ch. 18. 16 'Shausha;' in 1 K. 4. 2 'Shisha.'

SCRIBE,] that is, 'writer,' as in Jud. 5. 14. 18. BENAIAH,] as in 23. 20, 22.

JEHOIADA,] as in 1 Ch. 18. 17.

CHERETHITE,] i.e. 'cutters off,' that is, executioners. It is a gentile name in 1 Sa. 30. 14; Eze. 25. 16; Zeph. 2. 5.

PELETHITE,] i.e. 'runners,' as in 15. 18; 20. 7, 23.

SONS OF DAVID,] as in 3. 2—5; 5. 13—16.

MINISTERS,] *lit.* 'priests,' as in v. 17; in 1 Ch. 18. 17 they are said to be 'first.'

IX. 1. LEFT,] that is, alive after the disastrous battle of Gilboa, as in 1 Sa. 31. 6.

JONATHAN,] who had loved David so well in prosperity and in adversity.

2. ZIBA,]i.e. a 'thing planted,' as in 16. 1.

3. A MAN,] left alive, as in v. 1.

KINDNESS OF GOD,] such as he hath done with me. 1 Sa. 20. 14.

LAME,] *lit.* 'smitten of the feet,' as in v. 13; 4. 4, &c.

4. MACHIR,] i.e. 'sold,' as in 17. 27. Compare Ge. 50. 23; Jud. 5. 14.

AMMIEL,] i.e. 'people of God,' as in v. 5; 17. 27; compare Nu. 13. 12, &c.

LO-DEBAR,] *lit.* 'without anything or without pasture,' as in 17. 27; compare perhaps 'Lidbar' in Jos. 13. 26.

6. OBEISANCE,] as to his king and master.

MEPHIBOSHETH,] as in 4. 4; called Merib-Baal in 1 Ch. 8. 34.

SERVANT,] as in v. 2.

7. I CERTAINLY DO,] *lit.* 'doing I do.'

FIELD,] as in 1 Sa. 11. 5; 2 Sa. 19. 29.

BREAD,] that is, food.

CONTINUALLY,] all his lifetime—daily.

8. THE DEAD DOG,] as in 16. 9; 1 Sa. 24. 14. &c.

9. HOUSE,] that is, family.

SON OF THY LORD,] that is, to Mephibosheth.

10. SERVED,] as in Ge. 2. 15, &c.

BROUGHT IN]its produce from time to time.

EATEN] or consumed it, according to his pleasure.

TABLE,] as David had formerly done at Saul's table, in 1 Sa. 18. 2; 20. 5.

11. SONS OF THE KING,] because of Jonathan his father.

12. MICAH,] whose descendants are noted in 1 Ch. 8. 34—40.

SERVANTS,] according to the king's command.

13. EATING,] as in v. 10, 11.

LAME,] *lit.* 'smitten,' as in v. 9.

X. 1. BENE-AMMON,] named Nahash; perhaps the same as in 1 Sa. 11. 1, or his son.

HANAN,] i.e. 'gracious,' as in 1 Ch. 19. 2.

2. NAHASH,] i.e. a 'serpent.'

KINDNESS,] by sympathizing with him in the loss of his father.

TO COMFORT,] as in Ge. 37. 35; 1 Ch. 7. 22. 19. 2; Job 2. 11; Ps. 119. 76; Isa. 22. 4; 61. 2; Jer. 16. 7; Eze. 16. 54.

3. LORD,] that is, king, as in v. 1.

HONOURING,] as in 1 Sa. 2. 30; 1 Ch. 19. 3; Prov. 14. 31; La. 1. 8.

COMFORTERS,] as in 1 Ch. 19. 3; Job 15. 2; Ps. 69. 20; Ecc. 4. 1; Isa. 51. 12; La. 1. 2, 9, 16, 17, 21; Nah. 3. 7.

TO SEARCH,] as in Jud. 18. 2; 1 Ch. 19. 3; Prov. 23. 30; 25. 2.

THE CITY,] the capital, even Rabbah, as in 11. 1.

TO SPY,] as in Nu. 21. 32; Jos. 6. 25; 14. 7; Jud. 18. 2, 14, 17; 1 Ch. 19. 3.

TO OVERTHROW,] as in Ge. 19. 21, 29; 1 Ch. 19. 3; Prov. 12. 7; Isa. 29. 16.

4. SHAVETH OFF,] which in the east is never done save for a vow, a punishment, a disease or for mourning.

BEARD] of which they are specially careful.

LONG ROBES,] as in 1 Ch. 19. 2, in which the orientals pride themselves.

BUTTOCKS,] as in Isa. 20. 4.

5. THEY DECLARE,] by the hand of messengers.

ASHAMED,] as in 19. 3; 1 Ch. 19. 5; Ps. 74. 21; Eze. 16. 27.

JERICHO,] see Jos. 2. 1—3.

SPRING UP,] as in 1 Ch. 19. 5; Jud. 16. 22; Lev. 13. 37, &c.

RETURNED] to Jerusalem, to the court of the king.

6. ABHORRED,] because of this insult to his ambassadors. 1 Ch. 19. 6.

HIRE] for money, as was common (and still is) in time of war.

BETH-REHOB,] as in Jud. 18. 28; simply Rehob in v. 8 and elsewhere.

ZOBA,] as in 8. 3—5.

20,000,] out of both the preceding localities.

MAACAH,] as in Jos. 13. 11, 13; 1 Ch. 19. 6.

ISH-TOB,] i.e. the men of Tob, as in Jud. 11. 3, 5, whither Jephthah fled.

12,000,] in all 33,000, but 1 Ch. 19. 6, 7 has 32,000.

7. THE MIGHTY ONES] of war; perhaps those in 23. 8 may be referred to.

8. COME FORTH]from their city Rabbah, at the sight of Israel coming to their very gates.

GATE,] of the city, afraid to go out too far.

FIELD] around the city, not being permitted to enter.

9. FRONT,] *lit.* 'faces.'

CHOICE,] *or* 'young men.'

ARAM,]the auxiliaries of the Bene-Ammon, as in v. 6.

10. BROTHER] who was of a similar disposition with himself.

11. IF ARAM,] whom Joab himself undertook to fight.

SALVATION,] or 'ease, safety,' as in Ge. 49. 18, &c.

12. STRENGTHEN OURSELVES,] as 1 Ch. 19. 13; Ge. 48. 2, &c.

P

PEOPLE..CITIES,] which had been insulted, and might still be ravaged.
DOTH] according to his own good pleasure.
13. FLEE,] unable to resist his impetuous
attack, being merely hirelings, as in v. 6.
14. CITY,] that is, Rabbah, within shelter
of its walls and bars.
JERUSALEM,] not seeing at present any
opportunity of capturing the city.
15. ARAM] of Beth-Rehob and Zoba, as
in v. 6.
GATHERED TOGETHER] to try another
battle with Israel.
HADAREZER,] as in 8. 3.
RIVER] the Euphrates.
HELAM,] as in v. 17; not mentioned elsewhere.
SHOBACH,] as in v. 18; in 1 Ch. 19. 6 he is
called 'Shophach,' i.e. 'pouring out.'
17. ALL ISRAEL,] that is, all its soldiers.
HELAM,] as in v. 15; where the enemy
was assembled.
18. FLEETH,] as in v. 13.
CHARIOTEERS,] as in 1 Ch. 19. 18, where
there is mention of 7000.
HORSEMEN,] but in 1 Ch. 19. 18 it is 'footmen.'
SMITTEN] mortally in battle.
19. THE KINGS] of the surrounding localities.
SERVE,] by paying a tribute, so that Ge.
15. 18 was now fulfilled.
TO HELP,] lit. 'to save.'

XI. 1. REVOLUTION,] as in 1 K. 20. 22, 26;
1 Ch. 20. 1; 2 Ch. 36. 10.
MESSENGERS,] as in 10. 2; not 'kings,'
as in the C. V.
DESTROY,] or 'corrupt or mar.'
RABBAH,] their capital city, as in De. 3. 11.
2. DWELLING,] in his own new house of
cedars as in 5. 11.
EVENING-TIME,] when the breeze begins
to blow, as in Ge. 3. 8.
COUCH,] on which he had been resting
during the heat of the day.
ROOF,] which is generally flat in Palestine,
&c. De. 22. 8.
BATHING,] which is a daily operation in
eastern lands.
APPEARANCE,] as in Ge. 24. 16, &c.
3. BATH-SHEBA,] i.e. 'daughter of an oath,'
as in 1 K. 1. 15, &c. In 1 Ch. 3. 5, called
'Bath-Shua.'
ELIAM,] or, as in 1 Ch. 3. 5 'Ammiel.'
URIAH,] i.e. 'light of Jah;' as in 23. 39.
HITTITE,] perhaps a proselyte of that tribe.
4. LIETH,] see Ps. 51. 1, &c.
PURIFYING,] or 'separating herself,' as in
Isa. 66. 17.
UNCLEANNESS,] her monthly courses, as
in Lev. 15. 19, &c.
5. CONCEIVETH,] as in Ge. 4. 1, &c.
CONCEIVING,] as in Ge. 16. 11; 38. 24, 25,&c.
6. JOAB,] who was besieging Rabbah, as
in v. 1.
URIAH,] who was with Joab, being one of
David's mighty men, as in 23. 39.
8. HOUSE,] in the city, to Bath-Sheba.
FEET,] which being covered only with
sandals, were dusty.

GIFT,] as a token of respect, as in Ge. 43.
34; 2 Ch. 24. 6, 9; Est. 2. 18, &c.
9. LIETH DOWN,] to rest himself and to
sleep.
HOUSE,] as the king had wished, commanded, and expected.
10. THEY DECLARE,] that is, some of
David's spies.
JOURNEY,] from Rabbah to Jerusalem.
11. ARK,] as in 7. 2; compare 1 Sa. 4. 4;
14. 18, &c.
BOOTHS,] as in 22. 12, &c.
ENCAMPING] against Rabbah, as in v. 1.
EAT..DRINK..LIE,] that is, enjoy domestic
pleasures.
LIFE OF THY SOUL,] as in 1 Sa. 1. 26, &c.
12. ABIDE,] that he might give him another
trial.
SEND] back to Joab, to Rabbah.
13. DRINK,] lit. 'maketh him merry,' as
in Ge. 9. 21: 43. 34; Song 5. 1.
GOETH FORTH,] from the king's house.
COUCH,] probably in the open air, as is
customary in the east.
GONE DOWN,] as in v. 9.
14. LETTER,] as in 2 K. 10. 1, &c.
URIAH,] making him the unconscious
bearer of his own fate.
15. SEVEREST,] lit. 'strongest.'
TURNED BACK,] in retreat from before the
enemy, leaving him exposed.
SMITTEN,] by the enemy.
DIED,] ignorant of his wife's unfaithful-
ness, and freeing David from exposure.
16. CITY,] Rabbah, to capture it.
VALIANT MEN,] whose courage exposed
them to additional dangers.
17. GO FORTH,] seeing some part of the
army of Israel left exposed.
20. FURY,] because of this loss of men.
FIGHT,] instead of drawing the defenders
out to the open field.
SHOOT] with the bow, which was the
common weapon of offence in those days.
21. ABIMELECH,] i.e. 'my father is king.'
JERUBBESHETH,] i.e. 'let shame plead;'
in Jud. 6. 32 it is Jerubbaal, i.e. 'let Baal
plead.'
RIDER,] as in Jud. 8. 53.
THEBEZ,] as in Jud. 8. 50.
SAID,] as additional news, but really as
an apology.
DEAD,] as in v. 17.
23. THE MEN] of the city, that is, the
Bene-Ammon.
FIELD,] instead of confining themselves
to the city as heretofore.
UPON THEM,] in pursuit.
24. SHOOTING,] with bow and arrows, and
stones.
25. EVIL,] discouraging to thee in the pro-
secution of the war.
DEVOUR,] the good and the bad alike.
THROW IT DOWN,] as in 1 Ch. 20. 1.
26. WIFE,] that is, Bath-Sheba, as in v. 3.
LORD,] whose brave character could not
but endear him to her.
MOURNING,] probably only of a week or so.
WIFE,] in addition to those he already had,
see 3. 2—5; 5. 13.
SON,] whose name is not given.

JEHOVAH,] who seeth all things, though man continue ignorant.

XII. 1. NATHAN] the prophet, as in 7. 2, &c.
TWO MEN,] David and Uriah, they were also of the same race.
ONE CITY,] even Jerusalem.
ONE POOR,] relatively so, compared with the other.
2. FLOCKS AND HERDS,] the general sign of wealth in the east.
3. EWE-LAMB,] as in Ge. 21. 28, 29, 30, &c.
BOUGHT,] according to the usual practice, as in Ruth 4. 10.
GROWETH UP,] or 'becometh great.'
SONS,] perhaps she was his second and youngest wife.
MORSEL,] as in Ge. 18. 5, &c.
CUP,] as in Ge. 40. 11, &c.
LIETH,] for heat and safety.
DAUGHTER,] rather than as a wife.
4. TRAVELLER,] lit. 'goer.'
SPARETH,] as in 21. 7; Ex. 2. 6, &c
PREPARE,] lit. 'make.'
EWE-LAMB,] as in v. 3.
5. BURNETH,] with indignation, as the cruelty and selfishness described.
JEHOVAH LIVETH,] as in Jud. 8. 19, &c.
SON OF DEATH,] as in 1 Sa. 20. 31, &c.
6. FOURFOLD,] according to the law in Ex. 17. 1. The Jews remark that four of David's children, viz. Amnon, Tamar (or Adonijah), Absalom, and the son born to Bath-Sheba, were lost to him.
NO PITY,] on the affliction and poverty of his poor neighbour.
7. MAN!] who hath acted thus, and whose conduct thyself hast condemned.
OF ISRAEL,] and thy God and sovereign ruler.
KING,] by the hand of Samuel, as in 1 Sa. 16. 1—13.
DELIVERED,] as in Ps. 18. 1, &c.
8. HOUSE,] that is his family, &c.
WIVES,] who became, as it were, the property of the successor on the throne.
ISRAEL..JUDAH,] to serve and obey him.
SUCH AND SUCH,] lit. 'as these and as these,' as in Ge. 41. 19; Job 23. 14.
9. WORD,] concerning murder and adultery.
THE EVIL THING,] that is, rebellion and apostacy from God.
SWORD,] not personally, but yet really by the sword of the Bene-Ammon.
WIFE,] Bath-Sheba.
10. TURN ASIDE,] from smiting his household and family.
DESPISED,] as in v. 9 above.
11. EVIL,] as a recompense for the evil he had committed.
HOUSE,] or 'household,' by the hands of Absalom, Joab, Ahithophel, &c.
WIVES,] and concubines, who were secondary wives.
NEIGHBOUR,] lit. 'friend.'
SUN,] that is, in broad day light, and publicly.
12. SECRET,] at night, and none knowing of it.
BEFORE,] as in 16. 22.

13. SINNED.] Compare Ps. 51. 4; 32. 5.
CAUSED TO PASS AWAY,] as in 24. 10; 1 Ch. 21. 8; Job 7. 21; Ecc. 11. 10; Zec. 3. 4.
DIE,] as the law required.
14. DESPISE] the Lord, and his law, and his people, by this conduct.
SON,] as in v. 18.
15. INCURABLE,] as in Job 34. 6; Isa. 17. 11; Jer. 15. 18; 17. 9, 16; 30. 12, 15; Mic. 1. 9.
16. SEEKETH,] the favour and compassion of God.
FAST,] humbling himself for his sins.
GONE IN] unto the tent of meeting.
LODGED,] as in Joel 1. 13.
17. ELDERS,] who ruled over his affairs.
WILLING,] lest the child should die.
BREAD,] having resolved to fast and humble himself.
18. SEVENTH] day, probably from its birth.
DONE EVIL,] to himself or others.
19. WHISPERING,] as in Ps. 41. 7; 58. 5.
UNDERSTANDETH,] as in 1 Sa. 3. 8, &c.
20. BATHE,] which he had not done during his fast.
ANOINT,] as in De. 28. 40; Ruth 3. 3; 2 Sa. 14. 2, &c.
RAIMENT,] as in Ge. 35. 2; 41. 14.
HOUSE,] where the ark was, and where he had been seeking God.
BOWETH,]before the Lord who had smitten him.
EATETH,] to satisfy his hunger and strengthen his body.
21. DONE?] eating and refreshing himself, as if no calamity had befallen him.
WEEP,] in dread of his loss.
EAT BREAD,] as if it was a matter of no importance.
22. ALIVE,] and there was a chance of his recovery.
WHO KNOWETH] the loving kindness of the Lord.
PITY] my affliction and sorrow.
23. FAST,] when the last hope of his recovery is gone.
BRING BACK,] from the unseen world of spirits.
GOING,] slowly but surely to the same place.
NOT TURN BACK,] to comfort me any more.
24. COMFORTETH,] by these and similar considerations.
SOLOMON,] in Heb. 'Shelomoh,' as in 5. 14.
LOVED,] as in 7. 14, &c.
25. NATHAN,] as in 12. 1, &c.
JEDIDIAH,] i.e. 'dearly beloved of Jah.'
26. RABBAH,] as in 11. 1, &c.
ROYAL CITY,] that is, Rabbah itself, or at least, one portion of it.
27. CITY OF THE WATERS,] where the palace was.
28. NAME,] according to a common custom in ancient times.
29. CAPTURETH IT,] thus putting an end to the war.
30. CROWN,] of king Hanun, or 'of Malcom,' the idol of that name.
WEIGHT,] or perhaps value is here meant.
TALENT,] that is, of 3,000 shekels, as in Ex. 38. 25, 26.
STONES,] lit. 'stone,' simply.

SPOIL,] as in Ge. 49. 27, &c.
31. SETTETH TO,] not 'put under,' as in C. V. ; so Danzius, &c.
SAW,] as in 1 K. 7. 9 ; 1 Ch. 20. 3, &c.
CUTTING INSTRUMENTS,] as in 1 Ch. 20. 3 ; 1 Sa. 17. 18.
AXES.] This original word is not found elsewhere.
BRICK-KILN,] as in Jer. 43. 9 ; Nah. 3. 14.
ALL THE CITIES] that he captured.
JERUSALEM,] his capital city.

XIII. 1. AFTERWARDS,] but how long is not mentioned.
ABSALOM,] David's third son, of Maachah, daughter of Talmai, as in 3. 2.
FAIR,] as in Ge. 12. 11 14, &c.
TAMAR,] i. e. a 'palm-tree.'
AMNON,] David's eldest son by Ahinoam, as in 3. 2.
LOVETH HER,] because of her beauty ; being of different mothers they were doubtless brought up separate.
2. DISTRESS,] of body and of mind.
BECOME SICK,] and unable to discharge his usual duties.
VIRGIN,] unmarried as yet, pure in mind and body.
HARD,] as in Ge. 18. 14 ; De. 17. 18, &c.
3. FRIEND,]or 'neighbour,' as in 12. 11, &c.
JONADAB,] i.e. 'Jah made willing.'
SHIMEAH,]or 'Shammah,' as in 1 Sa. 16. 9.
WISE MAN,] as in Ge. 41. 8, 33, 39, &c.
4. LEAN,] or 'weak,' as in 3. 1, &c.
MORNING BY MORNING,] as in Ex. 16. 21 ; 30. 7 ; 36. 3 ; Lev. 6. 12 ; 1 Ch. 9. 27 ; 23. 30 ; 2 Ch. 13. 11 ; Isa. 28. 19 ; 50. 4 ; Eze. 46. 13, 14, 15 ; Zeph. 3. 5.
LOVING,] as in v. 1.
5. COUCH,] as in Ge. 49. 4, &c.
FEIGN SICK,] as in v. 2.
GIVE ME TO EAT,] as in 3. 35.
FOOD,] as in v. 7, 10.
6. CAKES] in the shape of 'hearts,' as the original word implies ; so in v. 8.
7. HOUSE OF AMNON;] who, being heir to the throne, lived in a house of his own.
THE FOOD] that he described.
8. DOUGH,] as in Ex. 12. 34, 39 ; Jer. 7. 18 ; Hos. 7. 4.
KNEADETH,] as in Ge. 18. 6 ; 1 Sa. 28. 24, &c.
MAKETH CAKES] in the shape of hearts, as desired in v. 6.
COOKETH,] lit. 'boileth,' as in Ex. 12. 9, &c.
9. FRYING-PAN.] This original word is not found elsewhere.
POURETH OUT,] as in 2 K. 4. 40.
TAKE OUT,] lit. 'cause ye to go out from off me.'
10. INNER CHAMBER,] as in Ge. 43. 30, &c.
11. LIE WITH ME,] as in Ge. 39. 12, &c.
12. HUMBLE,] as in Ge. 34. 2, &c.
DONE SO] in the case of brother and sister.
FOLLY,] as in Ge. 34. 7 ; De. 22. 21, &c.
13. REPROACH,] as in Ge. 30. 23, &c.
FOOLS,] as in De. 32. 6, 21, &c.
WITHHOLD,] remembering his love to his children.
14. HEARKEN] to her expostulations.

15. HATETH,] having gratified first his wishes.
16. BECAUSE OF THE CIRCUMSTANCES,] as in Ge. 21. 11, 25, &c.
GREATER] in repudiating her, because of the publicity.
17. THIS ONE,] that is, Tamar.
BOLT,] as in Jud. 3. 23, &c.
18. LONG COAT,] as in Ge. 37. 3, 23, 32.
UPPER ROBES,] as in Ex. 28. 4, 31, 34, &c.
VIRGINS,] and unmarried.
19. ASHES,] according to the usual custom.
BREAD,] as in Jer. 2. 37.
20. SET NOT,] as in Ex. 7. 23, &c.
DESOLATE] without society ; as in Isa. 49. 8, 19 ; 54. 1 ; 61. 4 ; La. 1. 4, 13, 16 ; 3. 11 ; Eze. 36. 4 ; Da. 8. 13 ; 9. 18, 26, 27 ; 12. 11.
21. HEARD] as Jacob did, in Ge. 35. 22.
DISPLEASING,] as in Ge. 4. 5, &c.
22. EVIL OR GOOD,] avoiding his society ; as in Ge. 24. 50 ; 31. 24, 29, &c.
HATING,] as might have been expected.
HUMBLED,] as in v. 14.
23. SHEARERS,] as in Ge. 38. 12 ; 1 Sa. 25. 4, 7, 11 ; v. 24 ; Isa. 53. 7.
BAAL-HAZOR,] i.e. 'possessor of Hazor,' see Jos. 15. 25.
EPHRAIM,] a city in the tribe of Judah, see John 11. 54.
CALLETH] them to the feast he proposed to have on the occasion.
24. SHEARERS] at present, as in v. 23.
GO] to enjoy the season of festivity.
25. HEAVY] and burdensome for him ; the orientals often ruin themselves by their extravagant banquets, &c.
PRESSETH,] or 'urgeth on him,' as in 1 Sa. 28. 23 ; 2 K. 5. 23.
BLESSETH HIM] because of his apparent kindness.
26. AMNON] his elder brother.
27. URGETH,] as in v. 25.
28. GLAD,] lit. 'good,' as in 1 Sa. 25. 36, &c
DEATH.] It is not said that he gave them any reason for his violent act, but such things in royal families have always been too common in the east.
FEAR NOT] the consequences, because I, the heir to the crown, will protect you.
SONS OF VALOUR,] as in De. 3. 18 ; Jud. 21. 10, &c.
29. COMMANDED] in v. 28.
MULE,] as in 18. 19 ; 1 K. 10. 25 ; 18. 5 ; 2 K. 5. 17 ; 1 Ch. 12. 40 ; 2 Ch. 9. 24 ; Ezra 2. 66 ; Neh. 7. 68 ; Ps. 32. 9 ; Isa. 66. 20 Eze. 27. 14 ; Zec. 14. 15.
30. WAY] to the king's house.
REPORT,] of the violence of Absalom.
ONE,] as Abimelech did to his seventy brethren, in Jud. 9. 5.
31. RENDETH,] as a usual token of grief, as in Ge. 37. 34.
EARTH,] as in 12. 16.
RENT GARMENTS,] expressive of their sympathy with him.
32. JONADAB,] as in v. 3 above.
APPOINTED,] lit. 'set.'
HUMBLING,] as in v. 14.
33. LAY UNTO HIS HEART.] as in v. 20.
ALONE,] because he alone was guilty.

34. FLEETH] from the face of David, as in v. 37.

WATCHING,] probably from the roof of the house.

HILL,] whose name is not mentioned.

35. HATH BEEN,] that there was none slain but Absalom.

36. WEEP] for joy at their escape, as well as sorrow for the dead.

37. FLED,] as in v. 34.

TALMAI,] her mother's father, as in 3. 3.

SON,] Absalom, or rather Ammon.

38. THREE YEARS] till his recall, as in 14. 23.

39.DETERMINETH,] or 'endeth,' to go out against Absalom, as in 8. 16, &c.

DEAD,] and could not be brought back again.

XIV. 1. JOAB,] who seems to have kept a strict watch on David's actions and feelings.

ABSALOM,] to bring him back from exile if possible.

2. TEKOAH,] a city of Judah, as in 1 Ch. 2. 24; 4. 5; 2 Ch. 11. 6; 20. 20; Jer. 6. 1; Amos 1. 1.

WISE WOMAN,] as in Ex. 35. 25; Jud. 5. 29; 2 Sa. 2. 16.

MOURNER,] as in Ge. 37. 34, &c.

GARMENTS] of sackcloth, such as those generally worn by mourners.

OIL,] as was customary daily, see De. 28. 40; Ruth 3. 3; 2 Sa. 12. 10; 2 Ch. 28. 15; Ezek. 16. 9; Mic. 6. 15; Da. 10. 3.

3. PUTTETH THE WORDS,] as in Ex. 4. 15; v. 19, &c.

4. SAVE,] as in Jos. 10. 6; 2 K. 6. 26; 16. 7; 19. 19, &c.

5. WIDOW-WOMAN,] as in 1 K. 17. 9, 10.

6. STRIVE] in some casual dispute.

DELIVERER,] as in De. 32. 39; Jud. 8. 34; 18. 28; Job 5. 4; 10. 7; Ps. 7. 2; 35. 10; 50. 22; 71. 11; Prov. 14. 25; Isa. 5. 29; 42. 22; 43. 13; Da. 8. 4, 7; Hos. 5. 14; Mic. 5. 8.

7. FAMILY] of the woman.

PUT TO DEATH,] on the principle of retaliation, as in Ex. 21. 23, &c.

HEIR] and inheritor of the family in Israel.

QUENCHED, as in 21. 17, &c.

MY COAL,] that is, my only remaining hope of continuing my husband's

NAME AND REMNANT,] which all prize so much in the world.

8. GIVE CHARGE] to the public officers under whose care such a matter lay.

9. INIQUITY,] if there should be any such, in preserving the man-slayer.

INNOCENT] of any blame.

10. AGAINST THEE,] because he would reprove and punish him.

11. THY GOD,] who had raised up David so prominently.

REDEEMER OF BLOOD,] whose duty it was to avenge the blood of the innocent.

JEHOVAH LIVETH,] adding the solemnity of an oath to satisfy her.

IF THERE.] A very common eliptical mode of expression in Hebrew.

12. A WORD,] once more, as in Ge. 18. 32.

13. THOUGHT THUS,] that they would seek the life of Absalom.

GUILTY ONE,] as in Ge. 42. 21, &c.

OUT-CAST,] that is, Absalom his son.

14. DIE,] at some time or other, this being the common lot of all men.

RUNNING DOWN,] as in Job 20. 28; Ps. 77. 2; La. 3. 49, &c.

GATHERED,] nor can be.

ACCEPT A PERSON,] as in Lev. 19. 15, &c.

DEVICES,] as in Ge. 6. 5; Ex. 31. 4; 35. 32, 33, 35.

HIM] for ever, but accept an atonement.

15. AFRAID,] asserting that the king would not hear her.

16. PAW,] as in Ge. 20. 5, &c.

INHERITANCE,] as in 1 Sa. 26. 19, &c.

17. EASE] to my soul regarding my trouble.

UNDERSTAND,] lit. 'hear.'

GOOD..EVIL,] of the course to be pursued.

WITH THEE,] as in 1 Sa. 16. 18, &c.

18. HIDE,] or 'cut off.'

19. MOUTH,] as in v. 3 above.

20. BRING ROUND,] that is, to accomplish it.

APPEARANCE,] lit. 'face.'

WISE,] to discern the intent of her story.

MESSENGER,] as in v. 17.

LAND] under his authority.

21. THOU] and thou only, thus casting the odium, if any, on him.

BRING BACK] from Geshur to Jerusalem.

22. OBEISANCE,] as to his king and superior.

SERVANT,] as suggested through the woman.

23. GESHUR,] whether Absalom had fled as in 13. 37.

24. TURN ROUND,] as in 1 Ch. 16. 43.

SEE,] as a punishment for his offence.

25. FAIR,] or 'beautiful.'

SOLE..CROWN,] as in De. 28. 35; Job 2. 7.

BLEMISH,] as in Lev. 22. 21; Nu. 19. 2; Job 11. 15; Song 4. 7; Da. 1. 4, &c.

26. POLLING,] lit. 'shaving,' as in Ge. 41. 14, &c.

HEAVY,] because of its abundance.

WEIGHED OUT,] as in Ge. 23. 16, &c.

SHEKELS,] as in Ge. 23. 15, 16; in value doubtless, not weight,

27. SONS,] whose names are not mentioned, and who appear to have died young, see 18.18

DAUGHTER,] whom Rehoboam afterwards married, see 1 K. 15. 22; 2 Ch. 11. 20.

TAMAR] after his sister, in 13. 1.

FAIR APPEARANCE,] as in Ge. 29. 17, &c.

28. TWO YEARS OF DAYS,] as in Ge. 41. 1, &c.

SEEN,] as in in v. 24 the king had said.

29. JOAB,] who had brought him back, and had influence with the king.

WILLING,] knowing the king's unwillingness, and Absalom's intriguing nature.

30. PORTION,] as in 23. 12, &c.

BARLEY,] as in 17. 18, &c.

FIRE,] as in Jos. 8. 18, 19; Jud. 9. 49; Jer. 11. 16; 17. 27; 21. 14; 32. 29; 43. 12; 49. 27; 50. 32; 51. 30; La. 4. 11; Eze. 20. 47; Amos 1. 14.

32. SENT,] as in v 29

GESHUR,] as in v. 23.

TEERE,] with my mother's father and other friends.

FACE,] and enjoy his favour again.

INIQUITY] against the king and his kingdom.

DEATH,] as a transgressor.

33. GIVETH A KISS,] in token of reconciliation and forgiveness.

XV. 1. AFTERWARDS,] but how long is not specified.

CHARIOT] for riding in.

HORSES,] instead of the mules on which the king's sons rode, as in 13. 29.

RUNNING,] as his guards and attendants.

2. RISEN EARLY,] as is customary in the east with public men and others.

GATE] of the city, that is, Jerusalem.

PLEADING,] or 'strife.'

JUDGMENT] or decision according to law.

3. STRAIGHTFORWARD,] as in Prov. 8. 9; 24. 26; Isa. 26. 10; 30. 10; 57. 2; 59. 14; Amos 3. 10.

KING,] insinuating the king's weakness.

4. JUDGE,] that is, a supreme decider of controversy.

PLEA,] or 'strife,' as in v. 2.

RIGHTEOUS,] or 'right' in the point in dispute.

5. BOW HIMSELF,] paying the usual respect to the king's son.

KISS] as if he were a dear familiar friend.

STEALETH,] as in Jer. 23. 30, &c.

7. FORTY YEARS,] from some date not mentioned; two Heb. MSS. read 'forty days;' Syr., Ar., and Vulg. 'four years.'

VOW,] as was customary in cases of distress.

HEBRON,] about 20 miles from Jerusalem, where David himself had been anointed king, as in 2. 1—4.

8. GESHUR,] with his mother's father.

ARAM,] at the south of Canaan.

SERVED,] by presenting gifts on the altar of God.

9. HEBRON,] as he had purposed.

10. SPIES,] lit. 'footmen,' as in Ge. 42. 9—34; Jos. 2. 1; 6. 22, 23; 1 Sa. 26. 4.

TRUMPET,] the signal agreed upon, to be observed throughout the various tribes.

REIGNED,] instead of David his father.

11. INVITED] to accompany him in the fulfilment of his vow.

SIMPLICITY,] as in Ge. 20. 5, 6; Ex. 28. 30; Lev. 8. 8; De. 33. 8; 1 K. 9. 4; 22. 23; 2 Ch. 18. 33; Ezra 2. 63, &c.

12. AHITHOPHEL,] i.e. 'brother of insipidity,' as in v. 31, 34; 16. 15, 20, 21, 23; 17. 1, 6, 7, 14, 15, 21, 23; 23. 34; 1 Ch. 27. 33, 34.

GILONITE,] that is, an inhabitant of Gilo, near Hebron, see Jos. 15. 48—54.

COUNCILLOR,] as in 1 Ch. 27. 33.

SACRIFICES] to obtain success, and feast his followers.

CONSPIRACY] against the royal authority of David.

INCREASING,] owing partly to the king's age, Absalom's courtesy and splendour, and a desire of change.

13. DECLARING,] as in Ge. 41. 24; Jud. 14. 19; 2 Sa. 1. 5, 6, 13; 4. 10, 18; Est. 2. 20; Ps 19. 1, &c.

AFTER ABSALOM] for king over Israel.

14. FLEE] out of Jerusalem, beyond the Jordan, eastward.

ESCAPE,] as in Ge. 32. 8; 45. 7; Ex. 10. 5; Jud. 21. 17; 2 K. 19. 30, 31; 1 Ch. 4. 43; 2 Ch. 12. 7, &c.

FORCE,] as in 2 Ch. 13. 9; De. 13. 5, 10. 13; 30. 1; 2 K. 17. 21; 2 Ch. 13. 9; 21. 11, &c.

CITY] of Jerusalem where David was residing.

15. CHOOSETH,] not 'appointeth,' as in the C.V.

16. AT HIS FEET,] as in Ge. 30. 30; Ex. 11. 8, &c.

CONCUBINES.] or secondary wives, as in Ge. 22. 24, &c.

17. FARTHEST OFF,] as in Ps. 138. 6; Prov. 25. 25; 31. 14; Isa. 8. 9; 10. 3; 13. 5; 17. 13; 30. 27; 33. 17, &c.

18. CHERETHITE,] his body-guard, as in 8. 18.

PELETHITE,] who are always associated with the Cherethite.

GITTITES,] as in Jos. 13. 3; 2 Sa. 6. 10, 11; 15. 18, 19, 22; 18. 2; 21. 19; 1 Ch. 13. 13; 20. 5.

GATH,] as in 1 Sa. 27. 2, 3.

19. ITTAI,] leader of the 600 men; as in v. 21; 18. 2.

GITTITE,] who had been attracted to the standard of king David.

THE KING,] with Absalom, whom the people had set up as king.

STRANGER,] that is, an alien, one of another nation than Israel.

EXILE,] whether voluntary or involuntary is not said.

20. MOVE,] as in Ge. 4. 12, 14; Ex. 20. 18; Jud. 9. 9, 11, 13; 1 Sa. 1. 13, &c.

GOING,] that is, I do not know where I may have to go.

BRETHREN,] the six hundred men of v. 18.

KINDNESS AND TRUTH] be with you and them, as the ellipsis required.

21. THE KING,] David, not Absalom.

DEATH..LIFE,] as in De. 30. 19, &c.

22. PASS-OVER] the Kidron, first in order.

INFANTS,] belonging to his and their respective families.

23. LAND,] that is, the people of the land, of Judah especially.

KIDRON,] which runs through the valley of Jehoshaphat; as in 1 K. 2. 37; 15. 13; 2 K. 23. 4, 6, 12; 2 Ch. 15. 16; 29. 16; 30. 14; Jer. 31. 40.

WILDERNESS] towards Jericho.

24. ZADOK] the priest, as in v. 27; as in 8. 17, &c.

BEARING,] as directed in Nu. 3. 31; 4, 15; 7. 9, &c.

FIRM] on the ground, as in Job 11. 15; 38. 38, &c.

ABIATHAR,] see 1 Sa. 22. 20, 21, 22; 23. 6, 9; 30. 7; 2 Sa. 8. 17, &c.

CITY OF JERUSALEM,] as in v. 14.

25. FIND GRACE,] as in Ge. 6. 8, &c.

HABITATION,] that is, the tent in which he had dwelt, in Jerusalem.

26. DELIGHTED,] as in Ge. 34. 19; Nu. 14. 8, &c.

EYES,] as in 1 Ch. 19. 13, &c.

27. SEER?] of visions of God, as in 1 Sa. 9. 9, 11, 18, 19; 1 Ch. 9. 22; 26. 28; 29. 29; 2 Ch. 16. 7, 10; Isa. 30. 10.

AHIMAAZ,] as in 1 Sa. 14. 50.

JONATHAN,] as in v. 36; 1 K. 1. 42, 43.

28. TARRYING,] as in Ge. 19. 16; 43. 10; Ex. 12. 39; Jud. 3. 26; 19. 8; Ps. 119. 60; Isa. 29. 9; Hab. 2. 3.

PLAINS,] as in 17. 16.

WILDERNESS] towards Jericho.

29. ABIDE] till the return of David and afterwards.

30. OLIVES,] as in Zec. 14. 4, and often in the New Testament narrative.

COVERED,] as in Est. 6. 12; 7. 8; Jer. 14. 3, 4.

BAREFOOTED,] as in Isa. 20. 2, 3, 4; Jer. 2. 25.

31. AHITHOPHEL,] as in v. 12 above.

CONSPIRATORS,] as in v. 12.

MAKE FOOLISH,] as in Isa. 44. 25.

COUNSEL,] which he may give to Absalom.

32. TOP] of the mount of the olives.

BOWETH HIMSELF] in token of thankfulness for his escape.

HUSHAI,] i.e. 'hasting,' as in v. 37; 16. 16, 17, 18; 17. 5, 6, 7, 8, 14, 15; 1 K. 4. 16; 1 Ch. 27. 33.

ARCHITE,] from Archi, of Ephraim, as in Jos. 16. 2.

RENT,] as in 13. 19, &c.

HEAD,] as in 1. 2, &c.

33. BURDEN,] being perhaps old and infirm.

34. MADE VOID,] as in Ge. 17. 14; Lev. 26. 15, 44, &c.

35. PRIESTS,] as in v. 29.

36. SONS,] as in v. 27.

HAND,] means or instrumentality.

37. DAVID'S FRIEND,] as in 16. 16; 1 Ch. 27. 33.

CITY] of Jerusalem, which David had left.

JERUSALEM,] to take full possession of the throne.

XVI. 1. TOP] of the mount of the olives, where Hushai met him.

ZIBA,] as in 9. 2.

SADDLED,] and ready for use.

LOAVES] of bread, and

BUNCHES OF RAISINS,] as in 1 Sa. 25. 18; 30. 12; 1 Ch. 12. 40.

SUMMER-FRUIT,] as in v. 2; Isa. 16. 9; 28. 4; Jer. 40. 10, 12; 48. 32; Am. 8. 12; Mic. 7. 1.

BOTTLE] made of leather, or earthenware.

WINE,] as in 1 Sa. 1. 24; 10. 3; 25. 18.

2. WEARIED] in the flight from Jerusalem.

WILDERNESS,] where such things were scarce and uncommon.

3. SON OF THY LORD,] as in 9. 9.

JERUSALEM] where he resided, eating daily at the king's table.

GIVE BACK] from David to him.

4. HATH,] that is, all his property, confiscating it for treason.

5. BAHURIM,] see 3. 16; Targum reads 'Alemath,' as in 1 Ch. 6. 60.

FAMILY,] a Benjamite, who appears to have entertained a grudge against David for supplanting the family of Saul.

SHEMEI,] i.e. 'famous,' as in 19. 16; 1 K. 2. 8, 44.

GERA,] i.e. perhaps a 'grain.'

REVILING,] as in Ge. 12. 3; Ex. 21. 17, &c.

6. STONETH,] as in 1 Sa. 30. 6, &c.

7. MAN OF BLOOD,] as in Ps. 5. 6; 26. 9; 55. 23, &c.

MAN OF WORTHLESSNESS,] as in 1 Sa. 25. 25, &c.

8. BLOOD,] none of which, however, had been shed by David.

REIGNED,] which, moreover, was of the Lord's good pleasure.

SON,] whom he expected to succeed in his treason.

THINE EVIL,] as the just reward of thy deeds.

MAN OF BLOOD,] as in v. 7.

9. ABISHAI,] brother of Joab, and as violent and unscrupulous.

DEAD DOG,] as in 1 Sa. 24. 14.

REVILE] in this unworthy manner.

.TURN ASIDE,] as in 1 Sa. 17. 46, &c.

10. SONS OF ZERUIAH] his own sister.

SAID,] not in words, but in the workings of providence.

WHEREFORE,] as in Da. 4. 35.

11. BOWELS,] and is bone of my bone, and flesh of my flesh.

THE BENJAMITE,] of the family of Saul, who persecuted me.

SAID,] as in v. 10.

12. LOOK] and consider it tenderly.

AFFLICTION] in this expulsion by his son.

13. WAY] to the wilderness of Jericho.

DUST,] expressing his animosity in every possible way.

14. WEARIED] with the heat and the dust.

REFRESHED] by rest and provisions.

15. JERUSALEM,] as in 15. 37.

AHITHOPHEL,] as in 15. 12, 21.

16. DAVID'S FRIEND,] as in 15. 37.

LET THE KING LIVE,] as in 1 Sa. 10. 24, &c.

17. FRIEND,] that is, David; their friendship was apparently well known everywhere.

18. CHOSEN.] This language is decidedly ambiguous; it really refers to David, not to Absalom.

ABIDE] as a friend and counsellor.

19. SECONDLY,] in addition to the former reason.

LABOUR,] or 'serve.'

SON,] his beloved one, and his legitimate successor.

GIVE,] as in Jud. 20. 7.

21. CONCUBINES,] as in 15. 16.

ABHORRED,] as in 10. 16; 1 Sa. 13. 4.

STRONG,] in fighting with the followers of David.

22. SPREAD OUT,] as in Ge. 12. 8, &c.

THE TENT] which was appropriate to the roof of the house.

THE ROOF] which was flat, as is common in Palestine.

BEFORE THE EYES,] that is, publicly.

23. WORD OF GOD,] by Urim and Thummim, &c.

DAVID,] while he was king heretofore.

XVII. 1. I PRAY THEE,] not 'now,' as in C.V.

TO-NIGHT,] that no time might be lost.

2. WEARY,] as in 16. 14.

FEEBLE-HANDED,] as in Job 4. 3; Isa. 35. 3.

TO TREMBLE,] as in Jud. 8. 12, &c.

FLED,] in terror, to places of safety, by the unexpected attack.

3. THE MAN,] even David himself.

PEACE,] that is, inclined for it, and peaceable.

4. RIGHT,] suitable for the times and circumstances.

ELDERS] who were aiding Absalom in his usurpation.

5. MOUTH,] what he is prepared to advise.

6. SPEAK THOU] as a friend and counsellor.

8. HEROES,] as in Ge. 6. 4; 10. 8, 9; De. 10. 17; Jos. 1. 14, &c.

BITTER IN SOUL,] as in Jud. 18. 25; 1 Sa. 1. 10; 22. 2, &c.

BEAR,] as in Prov. 17. 12; Hos. 13. 8.

MAN OF WAR,] as in Ex. 15. 3.

9. PITS,] as in 18. 17; Isa. 24. 17, 18; Jer. 48. 28, 43, 44; La. 3. 47.

10. SON OF VALOUR,] or 'of worth, might,' as in De. 3. 18, &c.

THE LION,] Compare 1 Ch. 12. 8.

MELT,] as in De. 20. 8; Jos 2. 11; 5. 1; 7. 5; Jud. 15. 14, &c.

HERO,] as in v. 8 above.

11. DAN..BEER-SHEBA,] the northern and southern extremities of the land.

SAND,] as in Ge. 22. 17, &c.

MIDST,] to encourage them, or perhaps with the view of his falling in battle.

12. DEW,] as in De. 32. 2; Ps. 133. 3; Prov. 19. 12; Isa. 18. 4; Hos. 14. 5; Mic. 5. 7, &c.

ONE] who would not be destroyed.

13. GATHERED] by the inhabitants, that is, received by them into their city as a place of refuge.

ROPES,] as in Jos. 2. 15; 2 Sa. 8. 2; 1 K. 20. 31, 32; Est. 1. 8; Job 41. 1, &c.

DRAWN,] or 'torn,' as in Jer. 15. 3; 22. 19; 49. 20; 50. 45.

BROOK,] or 'valley,' as in Ge. 26. 17. 19, &c.

A STONE,] as in Amos 9. 9.

14. BETTER,] in their estimation, as promising more glorious success, though slower.

WILLED,] or 'commanded,' as in 7. 11, &c.

MAKE VOID,] as prayed for by David in 15. 31, 34.

GOOD COUNSEL,] that is, really suitable for Absalom's interests.

THE EVIL] which he sought to bring upon his father.

15. PRIESTS,] as in 15. 35, &c.

16. WILDERNESS,] or pasture land.

PASS OVER] the river Jordan.

A SWALLOWING UP,] as in Job 37. 20, &c.

17. JONATHAN .. AHIMAAZ] as in 15. 36, &c.

EN-ROGEL,] see Jos. 15. 7, &c.

THE MAID SERVANT,] of the household, most probably.

CITY] of Jerusalem, lest their object should be suspected.

18. BAHURIM,] see 16. 14.

WELL,] or 'pit,' as in Ge. 14. 10, &c.

COURT,] as in Ge. 25. 16; 1 Sa. 6. 26, &c.

19. SPREADETH OUT,] as in Nu. 4. 6, 7, 8, 11, 13, 14.

THE COVERING,] as in Ps. 105. 39; Isa. 22. 8, &c.

SPREADETH,] as in Nu. 11. 32; Job 12. 23; Ps. 88. 9; Jer. 8. 9.

GROUND CORN,] as in Prov. 27. 22, &c.

20. THE BROOK.] This original word does not occur elsewhere, save as a proper name, 'Michal.'

21. THE WATERS] of the Jordan, as in v. 22.

22. THE JORDAN,] going eastward.

LACKING,] of the company following him.

23. DONE] by Absalom, but Hushai's preferred, as in v. 4.

THE ASS,] a common animal for riding, as in Ge. 22. 3; Ex. 4. 20; Jos. 15. 18; Jud. 1. 14, &c.

CITY] of Jerusalem, where Absalom was, as in 15. 37; 16. 15, &c.

STRANGLETH,] as in Nah. 2. 12; not 'hanged himself,' as in C.V.

BURIED,] as in Jud. 8. 32; 2 Sa. 2. 32, &c.

24. MAHANAIM,] a city of Gad, beyond Jordan, as in Ge. 32. 42; Jos. 13. 26, 30; 2 Sa. 2. 8, &c.

JORDAN,] in pursuit after David.

25. AMASA,] i.e. a 'load, burden;' as in 19. 14; 1 Ch. 2. 17.

JOAB,] who had adhered to David.

ITHRA,] i.e. 'super-abundance;' called 'Jether,' in 1 Ch. 2. 17; 1 K. 2. 5.

ISRAELITE,] but in 1 Ch. 2. 17 he is called an 'Ishmaelite,' probably because of some connection with the Ishmaelites.

ABIGAIL,] i.e. 'father of joy.'

NAHASH,] i.e. a 'serpent.'

ZERUIAH,] David's only sister, apparently.

26. GILEAD,] beyond the Jordan, in pursuit after David.

27. SHOBI,] i.e. 'one leading away captive.'

NAHASH,] i.e. a 'serpent.'

RABBAH,] the capital city of Ammon, as in 11. 1.

MACHIR,] i.e. 'sold.'

AMMIEL,] i.e. 'my people is strong.'

LO-DEBAR,] as in 9. 5; this person brought up Mephibosheth.

BARZILLAI,] i.e. 'iron;' as in 19. 32—39; 1 K. 2. 7.

ROGELIM,] as in 19. 32.

28. COUCH,] as in Ge. 49. 4, &c

BASIN,] as in Ex. 12. 22, &c.

EARTHEN VESSEL,] lit. 'vessel of a potter,' as in Ps. 2. 9; Isa. 29. 16; 30. 14; Jer. 19. 1, 11.

WHEAT,] as in Ge. 30. 14, &c.

BARLEY,] as in Ex. 9. 31, &c.

FLOUR,] as in Ge. 18. 6, &c.

ROASTED,] as in Lev. 23. 14, &c.

BEANS,] as in Eze. 4. 9; not found elsewhere.

LENTILES,] as in Ge. 25. 34, &c.

29. HONEY,] as in Ge. 43. 11, &c.

BUTTER,] as in Ge. 18. 8, &c.

SHEEP,] as in Ge. 4. 2, 4.

CHEESE OF KINE.] This original word is not found elsewhere.

WILDERNESS,] or pasture-land for cattle where they now were.

XVIII. 1. INSPECTETH,] as in Ge. 21. 1, &c.
HEADS,] as in Ex. 18. 21, 25, &c.
2. THIRD.] This threefold division was common in ancient times, as in Jud. 7. 16; 1 Sa. 11. 11; 2 K. 11. 5, 6; 2 Ch. 23. 4, 5; Eze. 5. 2, 12.
JOAB,] his steady but impetuous general.
ABISHAI,] whose disposition was akin to that of his brother Joab.
ITTAI,] who so firmly adhered to him, as in 15. 19.
3. TEN THOUSAND,] among the tribes of Israel—good as they.
HELPER,] in case of need.
4. GATE,] as they are going forth to the battle with Absalom and Israel.
5. CHARGETH] publicly, that there might be no excuse for disobedience.
GENTLY,] as in 1 K. 21. 27; Job 15. 11; Isa. 8. 6; Jud. 4. 21.
HEADS,] as in v. 1.
6. ISRAEL] in battle, under the command of Absalom and Amasa.
FOREST,] as in De. 19. 5; Ephraim here is not the name of the tribe but of a city.
7. TWENTY THOUSAND,] who were 'smitten,' not slain, as in C. V.
8. LAND,] Gilead, around Mahanaim and Ephraim.
DEVOUR,] *lit.* 'eat,' as in Ge. 31. 15; Nu. 26. 10; 2 Ch. 7. 13, &c.
9. MEETETH BEFORE,] as in De. 22. 6.
THE MULE,] as in 13. 29, &c.
ENTANGLED BOUGH.] Compare the use of a cognate Hebrew word in 1 K. 7. 17, 18, 20, 41; 2 K. 1. 2; Job 18. 8; also Ge. 22. 13; Ps. 74. 5; Isa. 9. 17; 10. 34; Jer. 4. 7.
OAK,] as in v. 10, 14.
PLACED,] *lit.* 'given.'
10. HANGED,] as in De. 21. 23; Jos. 10. 26; Song 4. 4.
11. TEN SILVERLINGS,] that is, about twenty shillings of English money.
ONE GIRDLE,] as a token of honour, 1 Sa. 18. 4.
12. WEIGHING,] as in Ge. 23. 16; Ex. 22. 17, &c.
CHARGED,] as in v. 5.
OBSERVE YE] that he may be punished.
13. A VAIN,] *or* 'lying, false' thing.
HID,] *lit.* 'cut off.'
OVER-AGAINST,] as an accuser and adversary.
14. NOT RIGHT,] as in 2 K. 7. 9, &c.
DARTS,] *lit.* 'rods,' as in Ex. 21. 20; probably with iron points.
15. SMITE] him again, to make his death certain.
16. TRUMPET,] as in 2. 28, &c.
KEPT BACK,] as in Ge. 20. 6; 22. 12, 16; 39. 9, &c.
17. PIT,] as in 17. 9, &c.
HEAP,] properly a 'round heap,' as in Ge. 31. 46—52; Jos. 7. 26; 8. 29, &c.
TENT,] as in 1 Sa. 4. 10; 2 Sa. 19. 8, &c.
18. STANDING PILLAR,] as in Ge. 35. 14, 20, &c.
KING'S VALLEY,] that is, the valley of Jehoshaphat.
NO SON] living, for he had had three, as in 14. 27.

MONUMENT,] *lit.* 'hand,' as in 1 Sa. 15.12, &c.
19. AHIMAAZ,] as in 15. 27.
DELIVERED,] *lit.* 'judged,' as in v. 31, &c.
20. MAN OF TIDINGS,] as in 4. 10; 18. 22, 25, 27; 2 K. 7. 9.
DEAD,] as in v. 15 above.
21. CUSHI,] i.e. a 'Cushite,' as in v. 22, 23, 31, 32.
SEEN,] regarding the end of the battle.
RUNNETH,] in haste to deliver his message to the king.
22. THE CUSHITE,] as in v. 21.
FOUND,] additional to what the first messenger would deliver.
23. CIRCUIT,] as in Ge. 13. 10, 11, 12, &c.
24. TWO GATES,] of the city on one side.
ROOF OF THE GATE,] to watch, doubtless by David's special directions.
25. MOUTH,] for had he been followed by others, it might have been the first of a retreating party.
26. ANOTHER MAN,] even the Cushite, as in v. 21, 23.
27. AHIMAAZ,] as in v. 19.
GOOD MAN,] well affected towards David.
28. PEACE,] the usual eastern salutation.
BLESSED,] as in Ge. 9. 26; 14. 19, 20; 24. 27, 31, &c.
SHUT UP,] as in 1 Sa. 17. 46; 24. 18; 26. 8.
29. TO ABSALOM,] for whom his affection extended so as to exclude every other consideration.
THE GREAT MULTITUDE,] of the army and the captives.
30. STATION THYSELF,] till the next messenger should arrive.
31. LET TIDINGS BE PROCLAIMED.] This original word or phrase does not occur elsewhere.
DELIVERED,] *lit.* 'judged,' as in v. 19.
32. TO ABSALOM,] as in v. 29.
33. TREMBLETH,] *or* 'is troubled, *or* is angry,' as in 7. 10; 22. 8; Ge. 45. 24, &c.
UPPER CHAMBER,] as in Jud. 3. 20, 23, 24, 25; 1 K. 17. 19, 23; 2 K. 1. 2; 4. 10, 11; 23. 12; 1 Ch. 28. 11, &c.
MY SON,] as again in 19. 4.
OH THAT,] *lit.* 'who doth give,' as in Ex. 16. 3; Nu. 11. 29; De. 5. 29; 28. 67; Jud. 9. 29, &c.

XIX. 1. JOAB,] on his return to the city from the battle, probably a few days after.
MOURNING,] *lit.* 'shewing himself a mourner,' as in Ge. 37. 34; Ex. 33. 4; Nu. 14. 39; 1 Sa. 16. 19; 15. 35; 16. 1; 2 Sa. 13. 37; 14. 2, &c.
2. SALVATION,] as in Jud. 15. 18, &c.
GRIEVED,] as in Ge. 45. 5; 1 Sa. 20. 3, 34, &c.
3. STEALETH AWAY,] *lit.* 'stealeth itself away;' a phrase not found elsewhere.
ASHAMED,] as in 10. 5; 1 Ch. 19. 5; Ps 74. 21; Eze. 16. 27.
4. COVERED.] Compare Job 15. 11.
MY SON,] as in 18. 33.
5. HOUSE] of the king, or, at least, where he was residing.
PUT TO SHAME,] by this inordinate manifestation of affection.
DELIVERING,] *lit.* 'causing to escape,' as in 1 Sa. 19. 11.

6. NO PRINCES,] who deserve respect or consideration.

7. HEART,] by thanking and encouraging them for their toils.
BY JEHOVAH,] as in Jud. 21. 7 ; 1 K. 1. 17, &c.
LODGE,] as in Ge. 19. 2, &c.
YOUTH,] by the persecution of his brothers, by Saul, Ish-Bosheth, &c.

8. GATE,] the public place of concourse in the east.
KING,] to congratulate him on his safety.

9. CONTENDING,] or 'judging' one another.
PHILISTINES,] often times in the days of Saul and afterwards.
ABSALOM,] as in 15. 14, &c.

10. ANOINTED.] This circumstance is not mentioned elsewhere.

11. PRIESTS,] as in 15. 35, &c.
ELDERS,] who ruled over each city.
WORD,] as in v. 9, 10.
MY BRETHREN,] of the same tribe.

13. AMASA,] as in 17. 25.
ADD,] as in Ruth 1. 17, &c.
JOAB,] who had acted so imperiously in the case of Abner, Absalom, and to David himself.

14. INCLINETH,] toward himself by these words.

15. GILGAL,] as in Jos. 2. 1 ; 4. 19, &c.

16. SHIMEI,] as in 16. 5, &c.

17. BENJAMIN,] of which tribe Shimei himself was.
ZIBA,] as in 9. 10; to whom David had given Mephibosheth's land, &c.
GONE PROSPEROUSLY,] lit. 'prospered,' as in Nu. 14. 14; Jud. 14. 6, 19; 15. 14; 1 Sa. 10. 10, &c.

18. FERRY-BOAT.] The original word is not found elsewhere with this meaning.

19. IMPUTE,] or 'reckon.'
INIQUITY,] as in 3. 8; 14. 9, 32, &c.
DID PERVERSELY,] as in 7. 14; 24. 17, &c.
HEART,] as in Ex. 9. 21, &c.

20. SINNED,] in reviling the Lord's anointed.
JOSEPH,] which perhaps here is equivalent to Israel, as distinguished from Judah.

21. ABISHAI,] as in 15. 9, &c.
REVILED,] or 'lightly esteemed.'
ANOINTED,] even David himself.

22. ADVERSARY,] Heb. 'Satan,' as in Nu. 22. 22, &c.
KING,] once more, by the assent of Israel and Judah.

23. SWEARETH,] that the word might be irreversible.

24. SON,] or rather grandson, being son of Jonathan.
PREPARED,] lit. 'made.'
UPPER LIP,] as in Lev. 13. 45; Eze. 24. 17, 22; Mic. 3. 7, &c.
WASHED NOT,] as a token of mourning.

25. JERUSALEM,] after the king's return.
GO WITH ME] into exile, instead of remaining quietly at home.

26. DECEIVED,] as in Ge. 29. 25, &c.
ASS,] which was, in those days, a common means of conveyance.
LAME,] as in 9. 13.

27. SLANDER,] as in Ps. 15. 3, &c.
MESSENGER OF GOD,] as in 14. 17, &c.

28. MEN OF DEATH,] as in 1 K. 2. 26.

TABLE,] as one of the king's sons; see 9. 7, 10, 13.
CRY] for help in distress, as the original word implies.

29. MATTERS,] or 'words.'
FIELD,] or property of Saul, as in 9. 7, &c.
HOUSE,] in Jerusalem, after the rebellion of Absalom.

30. BARZILLAI,] as in 17. 27.
SUSTAINED,] as in Ge. 45. 11, &c.
MAHANAIM,] as in 17. 24.
GREAT] in substance and honour.

33. SUSTAINED THEE,] as he had sustained the king.

34. HOW MANY,] as in Ge. 47. 8, &c.
JERUSALEM] the capital city where the king's court is.

35. KNOW] how to distinguish between good and evil, to be a counsellor of the king.
TASTE,] as in 1 Sa. 14. 24, 29, 43; 2 Sa. 3. 35, &c.
SONGSTRESSES,] as in 2 Ch. 35. 25; Ecc. 2. 3.
BURDEN,] as in 15. 33.

36. A LITTLE THING,] not worth mentioning, as in Ge. 26. 10, &c.
RECOMPENSE,] as in Prov. 12. 14, &c.

37. CITY,] that is, Rogelim, probably.
FATHER..MOTHER.] Compare Ge. 47. 30 ; 49. 29, 31.
CHIMHAM,] i.e. 'a longing,' as in v. 38; it is spelled Chimhan in v. 40.

38. FIX,] or 'choose.'

39. KISS,] in token of affection.
PLACE] of residence, even Rogelim.

40. GILGAL,] as in v. 15.

41. STOLEN,] that is, taken thee away privately; Ephraim was beginning to envy Judah.

42. NEAR,] being of the same tribe with themselves.
DISPLEASED,] as if an injury had been done them.
EATEN,] or 'consumed.'
GIFT,] or present from the royal funds.

43. TEN PARTS,] lit. 'ten hands,' as in Ge. 47. 24, &c.
DAVID,] as a man, seeing Absalom's followers were (not improbably) chiefly from the tribe of Judah.
LIGHTLY ESTEEMED,] as in Isa. 9. 1; 23. 9; Eze. 22. 7.
SHARPER,] or 'harder,' as in Ge. 49. 7; De. 1. 17; 15. 18; 1 Sa. 5. 7, &c.

XX. 1. MAN OF WORTHLESSNESS,] as in 1 Sa. 25. 25.
CALLED,] that is, invited, as in Est. 4.11, &c.
SHEBA,] i.e. 'seven.'
BICHRI,] i.e. 'my first born.'
BENJAMITE,] of the same tribe as Saul, whose family he probably thought unjustly supplanted.
TRUMPET,] to call the people after him to battle.
PORTION,] or 'share.'
INHERITANCE,] or special interest in maintaining the present royal family.
TENTS,] as in 1 K. 12. 16; 2 Ch. 10. 16.

2. EVERY MAN,] of those present in Jerusalem, where the dispute in 19. 41—43 took place.

CLEAVED,] *or* 'adhered.'
3. CONCUBINES,] as in 15. 16.
WARD,] for safe keeping.
SUSTAINETH,] as he was bound to do by law.
NOT GONE IN,] as formerly he had done.
SHUT UP,] *lit.* 'bound up,' as in Ex. 12. 34; 1 Sa. 25. 29; Hos. 13. 12.
WIDOWHOOD,] as in Ge. 38. 14, 19; Isa. 54. 4.
4. AMASA,] the new general of his army in the place of Joab.
CALL,] that is summon, *lit.* 'make a cry.'
STAND] at the appointed time.
5. ABISHAI,] brother of Joab.
FOUND FOR HIMSELF,] admission into fortresses.
EYE,] by keeping within fortified walls.
7. MEN OF JOAB,] the band specially attached to him, but who followed his brother.
CHERETHITE,] as in 2 Sa. 8. 18; 15. 18; 20. 7, 23; 1 K. 1. 38, 44; 1 Ch. 18. 17; Eze. 25. 76; Zeph 2. 5.
PELETHITE,] as in 2 Sa. 8. 18; 15. 18; 20. 7, 23; 1 K. 1. 38, 44; 1 Ch. 18. 17.
8. GIBEON,] on which see Jos. 9. 3, 17, &c.
BEFORE THEM,] as their head, in accordance with the king's order.
GIRDED,] ready for conflict or pursuit.
LONG ROBE,] as in Lev. 6. 10; Jud. 3, 16; 5. 10; 1 Sa. 4. 12. &c.
GIRDLE,] to bind it together, according to eastern usage.
SHEATH,] as in 1 Sa. 17. 51; Jer. 47. 6; Eze. 21. 3, 4, 5, 30.
FALLETH] to the ground.
9. MY BROTHER,] they were sister's children.
BEARD,] a not uncommon custom even among the Greeks, when one asked a special favour.
10. FIFTH RIB,] as in 2. 23; 3. 27; 4. 6; not found elsewhere.
DHEDDETH,] as in Ge. 9. 6, &c.
BOWELS,] as in Nu. 5. 22; 2 Ch. 21. 15, 18, 19, &c.
REPEATED IT,] because the first stroke was fatal; compare 1 Sa. 26. 8, &c.
11. DELIGHT,] in Joab as a victorious general.
12. ROLLING HIMSELF] in agony, as in Job 30. 14.
STOOD STILL,] in amazement and horror, at the death of their leader.
GARMENT,] to cover the dead body.
13. PURSUE,] before be got into a fenced city.
15. ABEL,] a city near.
BETH-MAACHAH,] a city of Manasseh, east of Jordan, near mount Lebanon, 1 K. 15. 20; 2 K. 15. 29; compare 2 Ch. 16. 4; 1 K. 15. 20; 2 Sa. 20. 18.
MOUNT,] as in 2 K. 19. 32; Isa. 37. 34; Jer. 6. 6; 32. 24; 33. 4; Eze. 4. 2; 17. 17; 21. 21; 26. 8; Da. 11. 15.
TRENCH,] as in Isa. 26. 1; Nah. 3. 8; La. 2. 8.
DNOTNOVING,] with instruments.
WALL,] of the city Abel.
16. WISE WOMAN,] as in Jud. 5. 29; 2 Sa. 14. 2, &c.
17. JOAB,] making certain that she was addressing the king's general.
18. FORMER TIMES,] *lit* 'at first.'

ASK] counsel from the wise ones of ABEL,] as in v. 14.
FINISHED] the controversy or dispute in hand.
19. STEDFAST] in adherence to the law of God and the king.
MOTHER.] This expression may refer to herself, or perhaps to the city Adel.
SWALLOW UP,] and put out of existence as a city in Israel, by destroying it.
INHERITANCE,] as in 21. 3, &c.
20. FAR BE IT FROM ME,] *lit.* 'a profanation it is to me.'
DESTROY] without sufficient cause.
21. EPHRAIM,] a Benjamite, according to v. 1.
LIFTED UP] in rebellion.
BY HIMSELF,] he being the ringleader.
WALL,] to satisfy him regarding the death of the disturber.
22. PEOPLE,] of her city, even Abel, as in v. 14.
TRUMPET,] as a signal for cessation of hostilities.
TENTS,] *or* habitations, the great body of the army being simply volunteers for the time being.
KING,] having by this exploit fully established his position as general of the host.
23. JOAB,] son of Zeruiah, sister of David, as in 8. 16. 18.
HOST] of the men of war in Israel.
CHERETHITE..PELETHITE,] as in 8. 18, &c.
24. TRIBUTE] exacted from all Israel, for civil and sacred purposes, as in 1 K. 4. 6.
REMEMBRANCER,] as in 8. 16; 1 K. 4. 3.
25. SHEVA,] *or* Seraiah, as in 8. 17; or Shausha, as in 1 Ch. 18. 16.
ZADOK..ABIATHAR..PRIESTS,] as in 8. 17; 1 K. 4. 4.
26. IRA,] i.e. 'stirring.'
JAIRITE,] a descendant of Jair the Gileadite. Jud. 10. 3.
MINISTER,] *or* 'priest.'

XXI. 1. FAMINE,] as in Ge. 12. 10; 29. 1, 41. 27, 30; Ruth 1. 1, &c.
SEEKETH,] as in Ps. 27. 8; 105. 4; 2 Ch. 7. 14; Hos. 5. 15.
BLOODY HOUSE,] the members of which appear to have incited or assisted him in his evil.
GIBEONITES,] or inhabitants of Gibeon; on which see Jos. 9. 3, 15, 16, 17.
2. AMORITE,] *or* 'Hivite,' as in Jos. 9. 7; 11. 19.
SMITE THEM,] by the mouth of the sword, so as to extirpate them in his
ZEAL,] while he spared the Amalekites, who were doomed to destruction for their cruelty.
3. MAKE ATONEMENT] to God, for the vow of Israel, broken by Saul.
INHERITANCE,] that is, the people of Israel, as in Ex. 15. 17.
4. BY SAUL,] that is by his interference with their peaceable pursuits.
NO MAN] of those who injured us.
5. CONSUMED US] with fire and sword.
DEVISED,] as in Nu. 33. 56; Jud. 20. 5, &c
DESTROYED,] as in Ge. 34. 30, &c.

STATIONING OURSELVES,] as in Ex. 2. 4; 8. 20, &c.
6. SEVEN,] as a perfect number.
HANGED] them publicly before Jehovah, to appease his anger.
HEIGHT,] or Gibeah, or hill, as in 1 Sa. 10. 26; 11. 4, &c.
CHOSEN,] as in 1 Sa. 10. 24, &c.
7. MEPHIBOSHETH,] as in 4. 4, &c.
OATH,] as in 1 Sa. 18. 3; 20. 8, 15, 42; 23. 18.
8. AIAH,] as in 3. 7.
ARMONI,] i.e. 'palatial.'
MEPHIBOSHETH,] a brother (not the son) of Jonathan.
MICHAL,] an evident mistake for Merab; see 1 Sa. 18. 9.
MEHOLATHITE,] to distinguish him from the Gileadite, in 17. 27, &c.
9. HILL,] or height of Gibeah.
FALL,] that is, suffer death together.
HARVEST,] which begun on the 16th of Nisan, or the beginning of April; see Lev. 23. 10, 11.
10. SACKCLOTH,] the usual sign of mourning.
ROCK] on the side of the hill where they were hanged.
POURED OUT,] as in Ex. 9. 33, &c.
SUFFERED,] lit. 'given.'
11. CONCUBINE,] as in 3. 7.
12. JABESH-GILEAD,] who had buried them, as in 1 Sa. 31. 13.
BETH-SHAN,] a city of the Philistines.
13. HANGED,] that is, of the seven mentioned in v. 9.
BENJAMIN,] they being of that tribe.
ZELAH,] as in Jos. 18. 26.
KISH,] as in 1 Sa. 9. 1, 2, &c.
ENTREATED,] as in Ge. 25. 21, &c.
15. AGAIN,] after that 8. 1.
GOETH DOWN] to the land of the Philistines on the sea-shore.
WEARY,] as in Jud. 4. 21; 1 Sa. 14. 28, 31; everywhere else the original word signifies 'to fly,' as in 22. 7, &c.
16. ISHBI-BENOB,] i.e. 'whose seat is in Nob.'
GIANT,] in Hebrew 'Raphah,' as in v. 18, 20, 22.
BRASS,] just half the weight of Goliath's, as in 1 Sa. 17. 7.
SPEAKETH,] lit. 'saith,' to his companions boastingly.
17. ABISHAI,] brother of Joab, as in 1 Sa. 26. 6, &c.
SWARE] to make it more solemn.
QUENCH,] as in 14. 7, &c.
LAMP,] as in Ex. 25. 37, &c.
18. GOB,] i.e. 'a pit;' in 1 Ch. 20. 4 it is Gezer.
SIBBECHAI,] i.e. 'my thicket,' as in 1 Ch. 11. 29; 20. 4; 27. 11; in 2 Sa. 23. 27 it is 'Mebunnai.'
HUSHATHITE.] See 1 Ch. 4. 4; 11. 29; 20. 4.
SAPH,] i.e. 'bason;' in 1 Ch. 20. 4 it is 'Sippai.'
19. ELHANAN,] as in 23. 24; 1 Ch. 11. 16; 20. 5.
JAARE-OREGIM,] in 1 Ch. 20. 5 it is simply 'Jair.'
A BROTHER OF,] as in 1 Ch. 20. 5; the Hebrew particle ath is doubtless a mistake for ach, 'brother.'

GITTITE,] whom David slew, as in 1 Sa. 17. 4.
BEAM OF WEAVERS,] as in 1 Sa. 17. 7; 1 Ch. 11. 23; 20. 5.
20. GATH,] one of the five Philistine principalities.
MAN OF STATURE,] or 'of contention,' as in Prov. 26. 21; Jer. 15. 10.
TOES,] lit. 'fingers,' as in 1 Ch. 20. 6; Ex. 8. 19, &c.
21. REPROACHETH,] as in Jud. 8. 15; 1 Sa. 17. 10, 25, 26, 36, 45, &c.
JONATHAN,] brother of Jonedab, in 13. 3.
SHIMEAH,] in 1 Sa. 16. 9 it is 'Shammah,' and in 1 Ch. 2. 13 it is 'Shimma.'
22. THE GIANT,] as in v. 16, 18, 20.

XXII. 1. SONG,] which is found again in Ps. XVIII. with upwards of seventy-four corrections or alterations, on which see notes.
THE DAY,] that is, the time.
2. JEHOVAH,] the covenant-God of Israel is MY ROCK,] or elevated place, as in Nu. 20. 8, 10, 11; 24. 21; De. 32. 13; Jud. 1. 36; 6. 20; 15. 8, &c.
MY BULWARK,] as in 1 Sa. 22. 4, 5; 24. 22 2 Sa. 5. 7, 9, 17, &c.
DELIVERER,] lit. 'he who is giving escape to me,' as in Ps. 18. 2, 48; 40. 17; 144. 2.
3. MY GOD,] that is, Jehovah is my rock, as in De. 32. 37, &c.
TAKE REFUGE,] as in De. 32. 37; Jud. 9. 15; Ruth 2. 12, &c.
MY SHIELD,] as in Ge. 15. 1; De. 33. 29, &c.
HORN,] as in 1 Sa. 2. 1; Ps. 132. 17; Luke 1. 69, &c.
HIGH TOWER,] as in Ps. 9. 9; 18. 2; 46. 7; 48. 3; 59. 9, 16; 62. 2; 94. 22; 144. 2; Isa 25. 12; 33. 16; Jer. 48. 1.
REFUGE,] as in Job 11. 20; Ps. 59. 16, 142. 4; Jer. 16. 19; 25. 35; 46. 5; Am. 2. 14.
SAVIOUR,] as in De. 22. 27; 28. 29, 31; Jud. 3. 9, 15; 6. 36; 12. 3; 1 Sa. 10. 19; 11. 3; 14. 39, &c.
VIOLENCE,] as in Ge. 6. 11, 13; 16. 5; 49. 5; Ex. 23. 1; De. 19. 16; Jud. 9. 24.
4. PRAISED ONE,] as in 1 Ch. 16. 25; Ps. 18. 3; 48. 1; 96. 4; 113. 3; 145. 3; Eze. 26. 17.
5. BREAKERS,] as in Ps. 42. 7; 88. 7, 93. 4; Jon. 2. 3.
STREAMS,] as in Ge. 32. 23; Job 6. 15; Ps. 18. 4; Isa. 30. 28; 66. 12; Amos 5. 24, &c.
CORDS,] as in Jos. 2. 15; 2 Sa. 8. 2; 17. 13; 1 K. 20. 31, 32; Est. 1 6; Job 18. 10; 36. 6; Ps. 18. 4, 5; 116. 3; 119. 61, &c.
SNARES,] as in Ex. 10. 7; Ps. 18. 5; Prov 13. 14; 14. 27, &c.
7. JEHOVAH.. MY GOD,] the existing one —whom I serve and own.
TEMPLE] in heaven, where his seat is.
CRY,] of help, for ease, as in Ex. 2. 23; 1 Sa. 5. 12; Ps. 18. 6; 34. 15; 39. 12; 40. 1, 102. 1; 145. 19, &c.
SHAKE,] as in Ps. 18. 7; Job 34. 20.
TREMBLE,] as in Jud. 5. 4; Ps. 18. 7; 46. 3; 68. 8; 72. 16; 77. 18, &c.
8. FOUNDATIONS,] as in De. 32. 22; 2 Sa. 22. 16; Ps. 18. 7, 15; 82. 5; Prov. 8. 29, &c.
TROUBLED,] as in Ge. 45. 24; Ex. 15. 14; De. 2. 25; 1 Sa. 14. 15; 2 Sa. 7. 10; 18. 33, &c.
SHAKEN,] lit. 'shake themselves,' as in Ps. 18. 7; Jer. 5. 22; 25. 16; 46. 7, 8.

WRATH,] as in Ps. 18. 7; Ge. 18. 30, 32, &c.
9. SMOKE,] as in Ps. 18. 8; compare Job 41. 20.
NOSTRILS,] *lit.* 'nose.'
DEVOURETH] all that oppose it.
BRANDS,] as in Lev. 16. 12; 2 Sa. 14. 7; 22. 9,13; Job 41. 21; Ps. 18. 8, 12; 120. 4;140.10,&c.
KINDLED,] *or* 'burnt,' as in Ex. 3. 2, 3, &c.
10. INCLINETH,] as in Ps. 18. 9, &c.
THICK DARKNESS,] as in Ex. 20. 21; De. 4. 11; 5. 22, &c.
11. CHERUB,] as in Ge. 3. 24; Ps. 18. 10, &c.
FLY,] as in Ps. 18. 10; De. 4. 11, &c.
SEEN,] in Ps. 18. 10, it is 'he flieth,' by the change of a Hebrew letter.
WINGS OF THE WIND,] as in Ps. 18. 10; 104. 3.
12. SETTETH,] as in Ps. 18. 11; 104. 20; Jer. 13. 16, &c.
TABERNACLES,] as in Ps. 18. 11; Ge. 33. 17; Lev. 23. 34, &c.
DARKNESS,] *or* 'collection;' but in Ps. 18. 12, it is 'darkness.'
THICK CLOUDS,] as in Ps. 18. 11; Ex. 19. 9; Jud. 5. 4, &c.
SKIES,] as in De. 33. 26, &c.
13. BRIGHTNESS,] as in 23. 4; Ps. 18. 12; Prov. 4. 18; Isa. 4. 5; 50. 10; 60. 3, 19; 62. 1; Eze. 1. 4, 13, 27, 28; 10. 4; Joel 2. 10; 3. 15; Amos 5. 20; Hab. 3. 4, 11.
BRANDS OF FIRE,] as in Lev. 16. 5; Ps. 18. 12, 13; Eze. 1. 13; 10. 2.
KINDLED,] *or* 'burnt,' as in v. 9.
14. THUNDER,] as in 1 Sa. 2. 10; 7. 10; Ps. 18. 3; 29. 3; Job 37. 4, 5; 40. 9, &c.
MOST HIGH,] as in Ge. 14. 18, 19, 20, 22, &c.
VOICE,] in these thunders.
15. ARROWS,] as in Ge. 49. 23; Nu. 24. 8; De. 32. 23, 42; 1 Sa. 17. 7; 20. 20, 21, 22, 36, 38, &c.
SCATTERETH,] as in Ps. 18. 14; Ge. 11. 8, 9, &c.
LIGHTNING,] as in Ex. 19. 16; De. 32.41,&c.
TROUBLETH,] as in Ex. 14. 24, &c.
16. STREAMS,] as in Job 6. 15; 12. 21; 40. 18; 41. 15; Ps. 18. 15; 42. 1; 126. 4; Song 5. 12; Isa. 8. 7; Eze. 6. 3; 31. 12; 32. 6; 34. 13; 35. 8; 36. 4; Joel 1. 20; 3. 18.
FOUNDATIONS,] as in v. 8; De. 32. 22; Ps. 18. 7, 15; 82. 5; Prov. 8. 29, &c.
WORLD,] as in 1 Sa. 2. 8; 1 Ch. 16. 30; Job 18. 18; 34. 13; 37. 12; Ps. 9. 8; 18. 15; 19. 4; 24. 1; 33. 8; 50. 12; 77. 18, &c.
REBUKE,] as in Job 26. 11; Ps. 18. 15; 76. 6; 80. 16; 104. 7; Prov. 13. 1, 8; 17. 10; Ecc. 7. 5; Isa. 30. 17; 50. 2; 51. 20; 66. 15.
BREATH,] as in Ps. 18. 15; Ge. 2. 7, &c.
17. DRAWETH,] as in Ex. 2. 10; Ps. 18. 16.
MANY WATERS] of affliction.
18. STRONG ENEMY,] such as Saul, &c.
19. BEFORE ME,] as opposing enemies.
SUPPORT,] *or* 'stay,' as in Ps. 18. 18; Isa.3.1.
20. LARGE PLACE,] as in Ps. 18. 10; 31. 8; 118, 5; Hos. 4. 16; Hab. 1. 6.
DRAWETH OUT,] as in Ps. 18. 19; Lev. 14. 40, 43; Job 36. 15; Ps. 6. 4; 7. 4; 54. 7; 60. 15; 81. 7; 91. 15; 116. 8; 119. 153; 140. 1.
DELIGHTED,] as in Ps. 18. 19; Ge.34. 19, &c.
21. RECOMPENSETH,] *or* 'doth,' as in Ps. 18. 20; Ge. 50. 15, &c.
RIGHTEOUSNESS,] in my controversy with my enemies.

CLEANNESS,] as in v. 25; Job 9. 30; 22. 30; Ps. 18. 20; Isa. 1. 25.
22. KEPT,] as in Ps. 18. 21; Ge. 18. 19, &c.
DONE WICKEDLY,] as in 1 K. 8. 47; 2 Ch. 6. 37; Job 9. 29; 10. 7, 15; Ps. 18. 21; Ecc. 7. 17; Da. 9. 15.
23. JUDGMENTS..STATUTES,] as in Ps. 18. 22; De. 8. 11, &c.
24. PERFECT,] as in Ge. 6. 9; 17. 1, &c.
MINE INIQUITY,] that to which I am prone, or am accused of.
25. RIGHTEOUSNESS,] as in v. 21.
CLEANNESS,] as in v. 21.
26. KIND,] that is, benevolent, well disposed, as in De. 33. 8; 1 Sa. 2. 9, &c.
PERFECT,] as in v. 24.
27. PURE,] as in Ps. 18. 26; Isa. 52. 11, &c.
PERVERSE,] as in De. 32. 5; Ps. 18. 26; 101. 4; Prov. 2. 15; 8. 8; 11. 20; 17. 20; 19. 1; 22. 5; 28. 6.
WRESTLER,] as in Ps. 18. 26.
28. POOR PEOPLE,] as in Ex. 22. 25; Ps. 18. 27; 72. 4; Isa. 14. 32; Zeph. 3. 12, &c.
FALL] in indignation and fury.
29. LAMP,] as in 1 K. 11. 36; 15. 4; 2 K. 8 19; 2 Ch. 21. 7, &c.
LIGHTEN,] as in Ps. 18. 10; Isa. 13. 10.
30. A TROOP,] in number, not alone; as in Ge. 49. 19; 1 Sa. 30. 8,15, 23; 2 Sa. 3. 23; 4. 2,&c.
LEAP,] as in Ps. 18. 29; Isa. 35. 6; Song 2. 8; Zeph. 1. 9.
31. WAY,] of dealing with his creatures.
TRIED,] *or* 'refined,' as in Ps. 12. 6; 18. 30; 119. 140; Prov. 30. 5.
SHIELD,] as in Ge. 15. 1; De. 33. 29.
TRUSTING,] as in Ps. 2. 12; 5. 11; 17. 7; 18. 30; 31. 19; 34. 22; Prov. 14. 32; 30. 5; Isa. 57. 13; Nah. 1. 7.
32. GOD,] that is, a 'mighty one,' save Jehovah, the revealed God of Israel.
ROCK,] as in v. 3.
33. BULWARK,] as in Jud. 6. 26; Neh. 8. 10; Ps. 27. 1; 28. 8; 31. 2, 4; 37. 39; 43. 2; 52. 7; 60. 7; 108. 8, &c.
STRENGTH,] as in v. 40.
MY WAY,] *or* 'his way,' as in Hebrew *chetib.*
34. HINDS,] as in Ge. 49. 21; Job 39. 1; Ps. 18. 33; 29. 9; Song 2. 7; 3. 5; Hab. 3. 19.
HIGH PLACES,] as in Lev. 26. 30; Nu. 21. 28; 22. 41; 33. 52, &c.
35. TEACHING,] as in De. 4. 1; Ps. 18. 34; 94. 10; 119. 99; 144. 1; Prov. 5. 13; Isa. 48. 17.
BOW OF BRASS,] as in Job 20. 24; Ps. 18. 34.
BROUGHT DOWN,] i.e. bent, as in Ps. 18. 34; 65. 10.
36. SHIELD OF SALVATION,] as in Ps. 18. 35.
LOWLINESS,] as in Ps. 18. 35; 45. 4; Prov. 15. 33; 18. 12; 22. 4; Zeph. 2. 3.
GREAT,] *or* 'multiplied me,' as in Ps. 18. 35; Ge. 3. 16; 16. 10, &c.
37. SLIPPED,] as in Ps. 18. 36; 2 Sa. 6. 13; Job 14. 16; 18. 7; 31. 4, 37; 34. 21; Prov. 4. 12; 5. 5; 16. 9; 30. 29; Jer. 10. 28; La. 4. 18.
ANCLES,] as in Ps. 18. 36; this original word is not found elsewhere.
38. DESTROY,] as in 14. 7, 11.
39. FEET,] as in Jos. 10. 24, &c.
40. CAUSEST TO BOW,] as in Jud. 11. 35; Ps. 17. 13; 18. 39; 78. 31.
WITHSTANDERS,] as in v. 49; Ex. 15. 7. 32. 25, &c.

41. THE NECK,] as in Ge. 49. 8; Ex. 23. 27, &c.
CUT THEM OFF,] as in Ps. 18. 40; 54. 7; 69. 4; 73. 27; 94. 23; 101. 5, 8; 143. 12.
42. LOOK,] as in Ge. 4. 4, 5; Ex. 5. 9; Job 7. 19; 14. 6, &c.
SAVIOUR,] give ease and safety.
43. BEAT,] as in Ps. 18. 42; Ex. 30. 36; Job 14. 19.
MIRE,] as in Job 41. 30; Ps. 18. 42; 40. 2; 69. 14; Isa. 41. 25; 57. 20; Jer. 38. 6; Mic. 7. 10; Nah. 3. 14; Zec. 9. 3; 10. 5.
BEAT SMALL,] as in Ex. 30. 36, &c.
SPREAD OUT,] as in Ps. 136. 6; Isa. 42. 5; 44. 24, &c.
44. STRIVINGS,] or 'contendings,' as in Ge. 13, 7, &c.
NATIONS,] others than that of Israel.
45. SONS OF A STRANGER,] as in Ge. 17. 12, 27; 35. 2, 4, &c.
FEIGN OBEDIENCE,] or 'make themselves liars;' the original form of this verb is not found elsewhere.
46. FADE AWAY,] as in Ps. 18. 45; Ex. 18. 18, &c.
GIRD THEMSELVES,] as in Ex.12.11;29.9,&c.
CLOSE PLACES,] as in Ps. 18. 45; Mic. 7. 7; everywhere else the original word is translated 'border,' as in Ex. 25. 25.
47. ROCK,] as in v. 3 above.
48. VENGEANCE,] lit. 'vengeances.'
49. WITHSTANDERS,] as in v. 40 above.
VIOLENCE,] lit. 'violences.'
50. CONFESS,] as in Ge. 29. 35; 49. 8; Job 40. 14; Ps. 6. 5, &c.
NATIONS] of the earth wherever I go.
SING PRAISE,] as in Jud. 5. 3; 1 Ch. 16. 9; Ps. 7. 17, &c.
51. MAGNIFYING,] or 'making great.'
SALVATIONS,] or acts of safety shewn to him whom he had chosen as
HIS KING] over Israel.
ANOINTED,] to David himself.

XXIII. 1. LAST WORDS,] as in 1 Ch. 23. 27.
AFFIRMATION,] as in Ge. 22. 16; Nu. 14. 28; 24. 3, 15; 4. 16; 1 Sa. 2. 30, &c.
SON OF JESSE,] as in 1 Sa. 16. 1, 18, &c.
MAN,] lit. 'hero or mighty man.'
ANOINTED,] in Heb. 'Messiah.'
GOD OF JACOB,] as in Ge. 49. 24; Ex. 3. 6, 15, 16; 4. 5; Ps. 20. 1; 46. 7, 11; 75. 9; 76. 6; 81. 1, 4; 84. 8; 94. 7; 114. 7; 132. 2, 5; 146. 5; Isa. 2. 3, &c.
SWEETNESS,] as in 1. 23; Job 36. 11; Ps. 16. 6, 11; 81. 2; 133. 1; 135. 3; 147. 1; Prov. 22. 18; 23. 8; 24. 4; Song 1. 16.
2. SPIRIT OF JEHOVAH,] as in Jud. 3. 10,&c.
SPOKEN] in prophetic psalms, &c.
HIS WORD] even now is on my tongue, ready for utterance.
3. HE SAID,] where is not mentioned; most likely in prophetic vision.
ROCK OF ISRAEL,] as in Isa. 30. 29; compare De. 32. 4, &c.
RULING OVER MAN,] in the heavens, directing all according to his will—the Messiah, in v. 1, and so the Targum.
RIGHTEOUS,] or 'just.' in his dealings.
FEAR OF GOD,] as in Ge. 20. 11; 2 Ch. 19. 9; Neh. 5. 9, 15.

4. LIGHT OF MORNING,] as in Jud. 16. 2; 1 Sa. 14. 36; 25. 22, 34, 36; 2 Sa. 17. 22; 2 K. 7. 9; Mic. 2. 1.
HE RISETH,] as in De. 33. 2; Isa. 60. 1, 2, 3; 2 Ch. 26. 19, &c.
A MORNING SUN.] One of Kennicott's Heb. MSS. reads 'Jehovah the sun.'
CLOUDS,] as in Jud. 5. 4; 2 Sa. 22. 12; 1 K. 18. 44, &c.
SHINING,] as in 22. 13; Ps. 18. 12; Prov. 4. 18; Isa. 4. 5; 50. 10; 60. 3, 19; Eze. 1. 4, 13, 27, 28; 10. 4; Joel 2. 10; 3. 15; Amos 5. 20; Hab. 3. 4, 11.
RAIN,] as in Ex. 9. 33, 34; De. 11. 11, 14, 17; 28. 12, 24; 32. 2; 1 Sa. 12. 17, 18; 2 Sa. 1. 21, &c.
TENDER GRASS] springs up, as in Ge. 1. 1, 12; De. 32. 2; Joel 2. 22, &c.
5. FOR,] or 'because' of the following things, God has revealed himself thus.
NOT SO,] as I could wish, is the conduct of my household and family, and I am liable to be discouraged.
A COVENANT,] as in 7. 15, 16; Ps. 89. 22; Isa. 55. 3, &c.; and he reveals his secrets to his servants.
ARRANGED,] as in Jos. 2. 6; Isa. 30. 33. Jer. 6. 23; 50. 42; Eze. 23. 41; Joel 2. 5.
KEPT] by him who made it.
SALVATION..DESIRE] is in it and in him.
SPRING UP,] as yet, but will do so in his own time.
6. WORTHLESS,] as in 1 Sa. 30. 22; 2 Sa. 22. 5; Job 34. 18; Ps. 18. 4; Nah. 1. 15.
DRIVEN AWAY,] as in Job 20. 8; Ps. 64. 8.
7. IS FILLED,] that is, furnished, supplied CESSATION,] when they are gathered together into one heap.
8. MIGHTY ONES,] or 'heroes.'
SITTING IN THE SEAT,] as the head and chief of them all, or perhaps the phrase is a proper noun 'Josheb-Bashebeth;' in 1 Ch. 11. 11 it is 'Jashobeam son of Hachmonite.'
TACHMONITE,] probably a mistake for 'Hachmonite.'
ADINO,] i.e. 'his delight;' see 1 Ch. 11. 11 for an important difference.
HARDENED HIMSELF.] This original word is not found elsewhere; in 1 Ch. 11. 11 it is only 300.
WOUNDED,] lit. 'pierced;' Sept. omits the word entirely, and it seems out of place.
9. ELEAZAR,] as in 1 Ch. 11. 12.
DODO,] as in 1 Ch. 11. 12; 27. 4.
AHOHI,] perhaps the same as Ahoah, a descendant of Benjamin, 1 Ch. 8. 4; 11.12; 27.4.
EXPOSING,] lit. 'reproaching.'
GO UP] to Pasdammim, as in 1 Ch. 11. 13.
10. CLEAVETH,] by the sweat and blood.
SALVATION,] as in v. 12.
STRIP OFF,] the spoils of their slain enemies.
11. SHAMMAH,] as in 1 Ch. 11. 27; there was one of this name among the thirty, as in v. 33.
AGEE,] i.e. a 'fugitive.'
HARARITE,] i.e. 'mountaineer.'
COMPANY,] as in v. 13; the Targum reads the word as the name of a place, viz. Chayah.
LENTILES,] as in Ge. 25. 34; 2 Sa. 17. 28; Eze. 4. 9.

12. STATIONETH HIMSELF,]as in Ex. 2. 4,&c.
13. THREE,] probably Adino, Eleazar, and Shammah.
ADULLAM,] as in 1 Sa. 22. 1, &c.
COMPANY,] as in v. 11.
VALLEY OF REPHAIM.] See Jos. 15. 8.
14. FORTRESS.]See 1 Ch. 11. 15; 1 Sa. 22. 4, 5.
STATION,] as in Jos. 4. 3, 9; 1 Sa. 13. 23; 14. 1, 4, 6, 11, 15; Isa. 22. 19.
BETH-LEHEM,] David's native place.
15. LONGETH,] as in 1 Ch. 11. 17; Nu. 11. 4; 34. 10; De. 5. 21; 1 Sa. 2. 16; 2 Sa. 3. 21, &c.
BY THE GATE] of the village, or, perhaps, 'within the gate.'
16. CLEAVE,] as in 1 Ch. 11. 18; Ex. 14. 16; Jud. 15. 19, &c.
POURETH OUT,] as in 1 Ch. 11. 18; Ge. 35. 14; Nu. 28. 7, &c.
17. FAR BE IT,] lit. 'a profanation.'
18. ABISHAI,] as in 1 Sa. 26. 6, 7, 8, 9, &c.
LIFT UP,] as in 1 Ch. 11. 11, 20, &c.
WOUNDED,] lit. 'pierced.'
20. BENAIAH,] as in 2 Sa. 8. 18, &c.
KABZEEL.] See Jos. 15. 21; 1 Ch. 11. 22.
LION-LIKE,] as in 1 Ch. 11. 22; Isa. 29. 1, 2, 7; Eze. 43. 15, 16.
THE LION] itself, which had fallen into a PIT,] or 'well,' as in v. 15, 16 above.
SNOW,] as in 1 Ch. 11. 22; Ex. 4. 6; Nu. 12. 10; 2 K. 5. 27; Job 6. 16; 9. 30; 24. 19; 37. 6; 38. 22; Ps. 51. 7, &c.
21. APPEARANCE,] as in Ge. 2. 9; 12. 11; 24. 16; 26. 7; 29. 17; 39. 6; 41, 2, 3, 4, 21, &c.
SPEAR,] as in 1 Sa. 13. 19, 22; 17. 7, 45, 47; 18. 10, 11; 19. 9, 10, &c.
ROD,] as in 7. 14; 18. 14, &c.
TAKETH VIOLENTLY AWAY,] as in Ge. 21. 25, &c.
OWN SPEAR,] as David did Goliath with his own sword.
23. GUARD,] or 'council,' as in 1 Sa. 22. 14; 1 Ch. 11. 25; Isa. 11. 14.
24. ASAHEL,] as in 2. 18, &c.; he was slain by Abner.
ELHANAN,] as in 21. 19.
DODO,] lit. 'his love or his uncle.'
25. SHAMMAH,]in 1 Ch. 11. 27 it is 'Shammoth,' in 1 Ch. 27. 8 it is 'Shamhuth.'
HARODITE,]in 1 Ch. 11. 27 it is 'Harorite;' see Jud. 7. 1.
ELIKA.] Etymology unknown.
26. HELEZ,] as in 1 Ch. 11. 27; 27. 10.
PALTITE,]in 1 Ch. 11. 27, it is 'Pelonite.'
IRA,] i.e. 'watchful,' as in v. 38.
IKKESH,] i.e. 'perverse.'
TEKOITE,] as in 14. 4, 9, &c.
27. ABIEZER,] i.e. 'father of help,' as in 1 Ch. 11. 28; 27. 12.
ANNETHOTHITE,] as in 1 Ch. 11. 28; 12. 3; 27. 12; Jer. 29. 27.
MEBUNNAI,]in 21. 18 it is Sibbecai, so also in 1 Ch. 11. 29; 27. 11.
. HUSHATHITE,] a descendant of Judah, as in 1 Ch. 4. 4.
28. TALMON,] in 1 Ch. 11. 29 it is Ilai.
AHOHITE,] a descendant of Benjamin, as in 1 Ch. 8. 4.
MAHARAI,] i.e. 'hasting,' as in 1 Ch. 11. 30; 27. 12.
NETOPHATHITE,] a city of Judah, as in Neh. 7. 26.

29. HELEB,] in 1 Ch. 11. 30; 27. 15 it is Heled.
BAANAH,] i.e. 'son of affliction,' as in 1 Ch. 11. 30.
ITTAI,] not the Gittite in 15. 19.
RIBAI,]i.e. 'my striving,'as in 1 Ch. 11. 31.
GIBEAH] of Saul, or of Benjamin.
30. BENAIAH,] as in 1 Ch. 11. 31; 27. 14.
PIRATHONITE,] of the tribe of Ephraim, Jud. 12. 15.
HIDDAI,] in 1 Ch. 11. 32 it is Hurai.
GAASH,] in the tribe of Ephraim, as in Jos. 24. 30.
31. ABI-ALBON,] in 1 Ch. 11. 32 it is 'Abiel.'
ARBATHITE,] of the tribe of Judah, (Jos. 15. 6, 7) or of Benjamin (Jos. 18. 22).
AZMAVETH,] i.e. 'strong to death;' see 1 Ch. 27. 25.
BARHUMITE,] perhaps an error for 'Bahuramite;' see 16. 5; 19. 16.
32. ELIAHBA,] i.e. 'God hides.'
SHAALBONITE,] in the tribe of Dan, Jos. 19. 42.
JASHEN,] in 1 Ch. 11. 34 it is Hashem the Gizonite.
33. SHAMMAH,] i.e. 'desolation, astonishment.'
HARARITE,] i.e. 'mountaineer,'
AHIAM,] i.e. 'brother of a mother.'
SHARAR,] in 1 Ch. 11. 35 it is 'Sacar.'
34. ELIPHELET,] in 1 Ch. 11. 35 it is Eliphal son of Ur.
AHASBAI.] Etymology unknown
MAACHATHITE,] as in De. 3. 14; Jos. 12. 5, &c.
ELIAM,] perhaps the same as Ahijah the Pelonite, in 1 Ch. 11. 36.
AHITHOPHEL,] as in 15. 12, &c.
35. HEZRAI,] i.e. 'my court or village.'
CARMELITE.] See 1 Sa. 25. 2; in 1 Ch. 11. 37 it is Hezro.
PAARAI,] perhaps the same as Naarai, son of Ezbai.
ARBITE,] of the tribe of Judah, Jos. 15. 52.
36. IGAL,] perhaps the same as Joel, in 1 Ch. 11. 38.
NATHAN,] i.e. 'he gave.'
ZOBAH] of Aram, as in 8. 3, &c.
BANI,] in 1 Ch. 11. 38 it is Mibhar, son of Haggeri.
37. ZELAK,] i.e. 'a cleft,' as in 1 Ch. 11. 39.
AMMONITE,] a convert of that nation.
NAHARAI,] i.e. 'my snorting,' as in 1 Ch. 11. 39.
BEEROTHITE,] in the tribe of Benjamin, as in Jos. 18. 25.
38. IRA,] as in v. 26 above.
ITHRITE,] of the the tribe of Judah, 1 Ch. 2. 50, 53; 4. 15. 17.
GAREB,] i.e. 'scrabby,' as in 1 Ch. 11. 8.
39. URIAH,] husband of Bath-Sheba, as in 11. 3.

XXXIV. 1. ADDETH TO BURN,] because of the following circumstance.
ADVERSARY,] This supplement is in accordance with 1 Ch. 21. 1.
MOVETH,]as in De. 13. 6; Jos. 15. 18; Jud. 1. 14; 1 Sa. 26. 19, &c.
NUMBER,] as in Ge. 13. 16; Nu. 23. 10, &c.
2. GO TO AND FRO,] as in Nu. 11. 8, &c.

DAN..BEER-SHEBA,] the two extremities of the land of Israel.
INSPECT,] as in Ge. 21. 1, &c.
3. DESIROUS,] as in Ge. 34. 19, &c.
4. SEVERE,] or 'hard, strong.'
5. AROER,] a city of Gad, as in Nu. 32. 34.
BROOK OF GAD,] that is, the brook of Arnon, as in Jos. 13. 9.
JAZER,] another city of Gad, as in Nu. 32. 3, 35.
6. GILEAD,] the land of that name, as in De. 3. 12, 13.
TATTIM-HODSHI,] i.e. 'my new places.'
DAN-JAAN,] formerly called Leshem, Jos. 19. 47; elsewhere simply Dan.
ZIDON.] See Jos. 11. 8.
7. TYRE.] See Isa. 23. 1.
HIVITE,] about mount Hermon and Anti-Lebanon.
CANAANITE,] westward of the Jordan.
BEER-SHEBA,] the extreme southren border of the land.
8. GO TO AND FRO,] as in v. 2.
9. ACCOUNT,] lit. 'enumeration,' as in Ge. 34. 30; 41. 49, &c.
INSPECTION,] as in 1 Ch. 21. 5; 2 Ch. 31. 13; Neh. 3. 33; Eze. 43. 21.
800,000,] in 1 Ch. 21. 5 it is 1,100,000, being 300,000 more; perhaps the larger number included those referred to in 1 Ch. 27. 1—15.
DRAWING SWORD,] probably above 20 years of age.
500,000,] in 1 Ch. 21. 5 it is 470,000.
10. SMITETH,] as in 1 Sa. 24. 5, &c.
I HAVE SINNED,] as in 1 Ch. 21. 8, &c.
CAUSE TO PASS AWAY,] as in 1 Ch. 21. 8, &c.
INIQUITY,] or 'punishment.'
ACTED FOOLISHLY,] as in Ge. 31. 28; 1 Sa. 13. 13; 26. 21; 2 Sa. 15. 31; 24. 10; 1 Ch. 21. 8; 2 Ch. 16. 9; Isa. 44. 25.
GAD,] i.e. a 'troop.'
PROPHET,] as in 1 Sa. 22. 5, &c.
SEER OF DAVID,] as in 1 Ch. 21. 9; 2 Ch. 29. 25.
12. LIFTING UP,] as in Isa. 40. 15; La. 3. 28; Isa. 63. 9.
CHOOSE,] or 'fix,' as in 1 Ch. 21. 10; Ex. 17. 9; Jos. 24. 15; 1 K. 18. 25.
13. SEVEN YEARS,] in 1 Ch. 21. 12, it is 'three years,' and so the Sept. reads here.
PESTILENCE,] as in Ex. 5. 3; 9. 3, 15.
KNOW] which is best for thee.
14. GREAT DISTRESS,] as in 1 Ch. 21. 13, &c.
MERCIES,] as in Ge. 43. 14, 30; De. 13. 17, &c.
NOT FALL,] as in 1 Ch. 21. 13.
15. GIVETH as in 1 Ch. 21. 14.

PESTILENCE,] in the hand of a messenger of wrath.
MORNING,] as ' v. 11.
TIME APPOINTED] of the third day.
DAN..BEER-SHEBA,] the whole extent of Canaan.
16. THE MESSENGER] who held the pestilence.
REPENTETH,] as in 1 Ch. 21. 15; Ge. 6. 6, &c.
CEASE,] as in 1 Ch. 21. 15; Jos. 10. 6.
MESSENGER OF JEHOVAH,] as in Ge. 16. 7, &c.
THRESHING-FLOOR,] as in Ge. 50. 10, 11, &c.; it was on mount Moriah.
ARAUNAH,] in v. 20 it is 'Aurenah;' in v. 18 'Araniah;' in 1 Ch. 21. 18 'Ornan.'
JEBUSITE,] a convert of that tribe perhaps.
17. I HAVE SINNED,] as in v. 10 above.
DONE PERVERSELY,] as in 19. 19, &c.
THE FLOCK] committed to his care, as the king of Israel.
ME..FATHER,] rather than on the people generally.
18. GO UP] from his palace to mount Moriah.
ALTAR] for sacrifices, which was only allowed by a divine command.
20. LOOKETH] out of his hiding-place, as in 1 Ch. 21. 20.
KING,] recognizing him as such.
21. BUY,] lit. 'acquire,' as in Ge. 4. 1, &c.
PLAGUE] of the pestilence in the hand of the messenger of Jehovah.
RESTRAINED,] as in Nu. 16. 48, 50 ; 25. 8. 1 Ch. 21. 22 ; Ps. 106. 30.
22. OXEN,] employed in treading the corn, as in De. 25. 4.
BURNT-OFFERING] to Jehovah for sin.
THRESHING-INSTRUMENTS,] as in 1 Ch 21. 23; Isa. 41. 15.
WOOD,] to burn the sacrifice.
23. AS A KING.] The Sept. Syr. Ar. &c. omit 'as a king.'
ACCEPT,] as in De. 33. 11, 34; Ecc. 9. 7; Ps. 119. 108, &c.
24. BUY,] or 'acquire,' as in v. 21.
PRICE.] as in De. 23. 18, &c.
FOR NOUGHT,] as in Ge. 29. 15, &c.
FIFTY SHEKELS OF SILVER,] in 1 Ch. 21 25 it is '600 shekels of gold,' perhaps it was afterwards made up to the larger sum.
25. ALTAR,] as commanded in v. 18.
BURNT-OFFERINGS] for sin, and
PEACE-OFFERINGS] for benefits received
ENTREATED,] as in 21. 14, &c.
PLAGUE] of the pestilence.
RESTRAINED] as in v. 21.

FIRST BOOK OF KINGS

THIS and the following Book are most evidently a direct continuation of the two preceding Books of Samuel, which, after narrating the birth, actions, and death of Samuel, continue the narrative of the history of Israel under its first two kings, Saul and David, and are therefore as well entitled to the name of the 'Book of the Kings' as the two succeeding, and hence in the Latin Version they are so denominated, while the others are called the Third and the Fourth Book of Kings.

This first book contains a history of about 120 years, from the accession of Solomon to the throne until the death of Jehoshaphat, grandson of Abijam, grandson of Solomon. Its facts are referred to in Mat 12. 42; Luke 4. 25—28; 11. 31; Acts 2. 29; Rom. 11. 2—4; James 5. 17, 18.

I. 1. ENTERING INTO DAYS,] as in Ge. 24. 1, &c.; he was about eighty years of age; compare Ps. 90. 10.

GARMENTS,] as in Ge. 24. 53; 27. 15, 27, &c.

HEAT,] as in De. 19. 6; Ecc. 4. 11; Eze. 24. 11.

2. LET THEM SEEK,] not 'let there be sought,' as in C.V.

STOOD] to serve and minister to him habitually.

COMPANION,] as in v. 4; Isa. 22. 15; Job 15. 3; 22. 2; 34. 9; 35. 3; Nu. 22. 30; Job 22. 21; Ps. 139. 3.

BOSOM,] as a wife and friend, as in Mic. 7. 5, &c.

3. BORDER,] as in Jud. 19. 29; 1 Sa. 11. 7; 29. 1; 2 Sa. 21. 5, &c.

ABISHAG,] i.e. 'father of error,' as in 2. 17.

SHUNAMMITE,] of the tribe of Isachar, as in Jos. 19. 18.

VERY VERY,] lit. 'unto might,' as in 1 Sa. 25. 36, &c.

COMPANION,] as in v. 2.

NOT KNOWN,] being eighty years of age, and exhausted by labours and trials.

5. ADONIJAH,] the third and eldest surviving son of David, Amnon and Absalom being dead.

LIFTING HIMSELF UP,] as in 1 Ch. 29. 11; Nu. 16. 3, &c.

PREPARETH,] like his brother Absalom, in 2 Sa. 15. 1.

CHARIOT .. HORSEMEN .. MEN RUNNING,] the usual attendants of rank in the east.

6. GRIEVED,] as in 1 Ch. 4. 10; Isa. 54. 9, &c.

GOOD FORM,] which generally goes far with the multitude, as in 1 Sa. 9. 2.

7. HIS WORDS,] i.e. matters.

JOAB,] the general of the army, as in v. 19.

ABIATHAR,] of the family of Eli.

HELP AFTER.] This phrase occurs nowhere else.

8. ZADOK,] a son of Ahitub, as in 2 Sa. 8. 17; 15. 24.

BENAIAH,] chief of the guard or council, as in 2 Sa. 8. 18; 23. 20, 22.

NATHAN,] as in 2 Sa. 7. 2; 12. 1.

SHIMEI,] as in 4. 18.

REI,] i.e. my friend; not mentioned elsewhere.

MIGHTY ONES,] thirty in number, as in 2 Sa. 23. 8.

9. SACRIFICETH,] that he may obtain the favour of God; as in v. 19, 25, &c.

FATLINGS,] as in 2 Sa. 6. 13, &c.

ZOHELETH,] i.e. a fearful, creeping thing.

EN-ROGEL,] a fountain near the royal gardens, without the walls of the city.

SONS,] those mentioned in 2 Sa. 3. 2—5.

SERVANTS,] that is, that of his own tribe, in official positions.

10. SOLOMON,] whom David had sworn to make his heir, as appears from v. 13, 17, &c.

NOT CALLED] to the feast, lest they should spoil his plans.

11. NATHAN,] anxious to secure the succession to the throne to Solomon, the favourite son of

BATH-SHEBA,] the favourite wife of David.

HATH REIGNED,] as in v. 13, 18; not 'doth reign,' as in C.V.

OUR LORD] and sovereign, whose will was law.

12. DELIVER,] or 'cause to escape;' compare Jud. 9. 5.

13. SWORN.] This is not expressly recorded elsewhere.

HANDMAID,] the language of humility.

14. COMPLETED,] as in v. 22—27.

15. INNER CHAMBER,] as in Ge. 43. 30, &c.

AGED,] as in v. 1.

MINISTERED,] as in v. 4.

OBEISANCE,] probably to attract his attention.

WHAT TO THEE,] i.e. what hast thou? not 'what wouldst thou,' as in the C.V.

17. SWORN,] as in v. 13.

JEHOVAH THY GOD,] as in Ge. 9. 26; 27. 20; 28. 21, &c.

19. SACRIFICETH,] as in v. 9, 25.

SONS,] as in v. 9.

THY SERVANT.] She does not say 'my son, lest it should appear too much a personal matter.

20. DECLARE.] Authority in the east is not necessarily hereditary.

21. LIETH,] as in Ge. 47. 30, &c.

SINNERS,] lit. 'those missing the mark;' as in Ge. 13. 13, &c.

22. COME,] according to the arrangement in v. 14.

24. THOU HAST SAID,] an affirmation, not a question, as in C.V.

25. GONE DOWN] to En-Rogel, as in v. 9.

LET..LIVE,] as in De. 33. 6; 1 Sa. 10. 24, &c.

NOT CALLED,] as in v. 10, 19.

28. BATH-SHEBA,] who it, appears, had

Q

gone out that the intercourse of the king and the prophet might be more unrestrained.

29. SWEARETH] to certify her the more. JEHOVAH LIVETH,] as in Jud. 8. 19, &c. ADVERSITY,] as in 2 Sa. 4. 9, &c. JEHOVAH, GOD OF ISRAEL,] as in Ge. 33. 20, &c.

32. ZADOK..NATHAN..BENAIAH,]as in v.8. 33. YOUR LORD,] that is, David himself. MULE,] as in 38. 44; 2 Sa. 13. 29; 18. 9, &c. GIHON,] a fountain west of Jerusalem; see 2 Ch. 32. 30. 34. ZADOK..NATHAN,] the religious representatives of the kingdom. TRUMPET,] to make it appear a public transaction, not a secret one. LET..LIVE,] as in v. 25.

35. HATH SAT] down on the throne, as taking actual possession of it. LEADER,] as in 1 Sa. 9. 16; 10. 1, &c. 36. AMEN!] that is, 'it is stedfast;' as in Nu. 5. 22, &c. 37. WITH MY LORD,] as in 1 Sa. 20. 13. GREATER,] as in v. 47. 38. GOETH DOWN] to Gihon, as in v. 33. CHERETHITE..PELETHITE,] the king's usual body-guard. MULE,] which was appropriated to the king's special use. 39. THE HORN OF OIL,] as in 1 Sa. 16. 1, 13, &c. THE TENT] which David had spread out for the ark, as in 2 Sa. 6. 17. TRUMPET,] according to the king's direction in v. 34. LET..LIVE,] as in v. 25, 34, &c. 40. PIPING WITH PIPES,] as in 1 Sa. 10. 5; [sa. 5. 12; 30. 29; Jer. 48. 36. GREAT JOY,] as in 1 Ch. 29. 9, 22; 2 Ch. 30. 21, 26; Neh. 8. 12, 17; 12. 43. IS RENT,] as we sometimes say, 'the air is rent with their voice.' 41. THOSE CALLED,] or invited, as in v. 9. ROARING,] as in Prov. 1. 21; 7. 11; 9. 13; 20. 1; Isa. 22. 2; Jer. 4. 19; Eze. 7. 16. 42. JONATHAN,] as in 2 Sa. 15. 36, &c. VALOUR,] or worth, or might, as in 2 Sa. 18. 27, &c. TIDINGS,] as in 1 Sa. 31. 9; 2 Sa. 1. 20; 18. 19, 20; 1 Ch. 10. 9; 16. 23, &c. 43. OUR LORD] and master, whom we are all bound to obey. 44. ZADOK..MULE,] as in v. 32, 33, 38. 45. GIHON,] as in v. 33, 38. MOVED,] as in Ruth 1. 17. 46. HATH SAT] down, and already taken possession of the throne and its authority. 47. COME IN] to the royal palace, to David. BETTER..GREATER,] as in v. 37. BED,] before Jehovah, as Jacob did in Ge. 47. 31. 48. SEEING,] as in Ge. 45. 12; De. 3. 21; 4. 3; 11. 7; 28. 32; 2 Sa. 24. 3; 2 K. 7. 2, 19, &c. 49. TREMBLE] for fear of being implicated in Adonijah's attempts. THOSE CALLED,] as in v. 9, 41. 50. ALTAR,] as criminals often did, to escape the punishment of their enemies. 51. HIS SERVANT,] confessing Solomon's right to rule. 52. VIRTUOUS,] or 'worthy, or mighty.'

HAIR,] as in 1 Sa. 14. 45; 2 Sa. 14. 11. EVIL] towards the king or his kingdom. 53. FROM OFF] the altar, on the top of which he appears to have gone up. BOWETH HIMSELF,] as an humble servant and subject. HOUSE,] in peace and safety; it was wise in not beginning his reign in blood.

II. 1. DRAW NEAR,] as in Ge. 47. 29, &c., compare Job 14. 5. 2. THE WAY,] as in Jos. 23. 14. BECOME A MAN,] lit. 'been for a man.' 3. CHARGE,] as in Ge. 26. 5, &c. WALK,] or 'go on.' KEEP,] i.e. 'watch, guard.' STATUTES..TESTIMONIES,]the varied forms in which he revealed his will to man. LAW OF MOSES,] which each king was enjoined to copy, preserve, read, and obey. DOST WISELY] and suitably for the time and the circumstances. 4. ESTABLISH,] not 'continue,' as in the C.V. UNTO,] not 'concerning' me, as in C.V. HEART..SOUL,] as in De. 4. 29, &c. CUT OFF,] as in 8. 25; 9. 5; 2 Ch. 6. 16; 7. 18, &c. 5. TO ME,] in the matter of Absalom, as in 2 Sa. 18. 14; 19. 5—7. TWO HEADS,] or 'princes,' as in 2 Sa. 3. 27; 20. 10. MAKETH,] lit. 'setteth, or placeth.' GIRDLE,] as in 2 Sa. 18. 11, &c. SANDAL,] as in Ex. 3. 5; 12. 11, &c. 6. WISDOM,] which had already manifested itself. OLD AGE,] as in Ge. 15. 15, &c. SHEOL,] the place of departed spirits. 7. BARZILLAI.] See 2 Sa. 12. 31, 38. TABLE,] like the king's sons, as in 2 Sa. 9. 7, 10; 19. 28. DREW NEAR,] to provide the king and his followers with provision. 8. SHIMEI,] as in 2 Sa. 16. 5. THE BENJAMITE,] a chief man of that tribe. REVILING,] disesteeming or making light of him. MAHANAIM,] beyond the Jordan. COME DOWN] from the hill-country to the banks of the river. SWEAR] to satisfy his doubts and fears. 9. ACQUIT HIM NOT,] as in Ex. 20. 7; 34. 7, &c. WISE MEN,] even from childhood perhaps, being the 'beloved of Jehovah.' OLD AGE..SHEOL,] as in v. 6. 10. LYETH DOWN,] as in 1. 21; Ge. 47. 30. CITY OF DAVID,] as in 2 Sa. 7. 5; compare Acts 2. 29; 13. 36. 11. FORTY YEARS,] as in 2 Sa. 5. 4; 1 Ch. 29. 26, 27. SEVEN YEARS,] over the tribe of Judah only. THIRTY AND THREE YEARS,] over the twelve tribes of Israel. 12. ESTABLISHED,] as in v. 46; Prov. 16. 12; 25. 5; 29. 14, &c. 13. ADONIJAH,] David's eldest surviving son.

BATH-SHEBA,] who, as the king's mother, was supposed to have great influence with him.

PEACE?] that is, a sign or token of it.

14. A WORD,] or 'matter.'

SPEAK,] as in v. 16; Ge. 24. 33, &c.

15. MINE,] as the eldest surviving son of the king, according to law, entitled to rule.

SET THEIR FACES,] as in 2 K. 12. 7.

TURNED ROUND ABOUT] from me to my brother.

JEHOVAH,] the supreme king of Israel.

16. PETITION,] or 'request.'

TURN NOT BACK MY FACE] in sadness, by a refusal.

SPEAK,] as in v. 14.

17. TURN BACK THY FACE,] as in v. 16.

ABISHAG,] king David's last wife, as in 1. 3, 4.

18. GOOD,] thinking probably it might strengthen his gratitude to Solomon.

19. RISETH,] expressive of the parental respect received in the east generally.

BOWETH HIMSELF] in salutation and filial greeting; see Ex. 20. 12, &c.

A THRONE,] not a 'seat' merely, as in C.V.

MOTHER OF THE KING,] who is, in the east, generally supreme in the king's household.

RIGHT HAND,] as the seat of honour; see Ps. 45. 9.

20. I ASK,] not 'I desire,' as in C.V.; neither is there any necessity for the supplement, 'I pray thee.'

TURN NOT BACK MY FACE,] as in v. 16.

21. WIFE,] according to his request.

22. KINGDOM,] because the pretender to a throne in the east generally endeavoured to get the king's wives to himself.

ELDER BROTHER,] and expects therefore the kingdom.

ABIATHAR..JOAB,] who were his friends and favourites.

23. SWEARETH,] to render his word more unchangeable.

ADD.] The usual form of an oath or imprecation.

SOUL,] that is, against himself.

24. JEHOVAH LIVETH,] as the hearer and avenger of vows.

MADE AN HOUSE,] or household, as in Ex. 1. 21, &c.

SPAKE] to David, in 2 Sa. 7. 11, 13; 1 Ch. 22. 10.

25. BENAIAH,] now the head of the host.

26. ABIATHAR,] who had joined with Adonijah, as in 1. 7, &c.

ANATHOTH,] a city of Benjamin, given to the priests, as in Jos. 21. 18, &c.

A MAN OF DEATH,] as in 2 Sa. 19. 28, &c.

THIS DAY,] not 'this time,' as in C.V.

BORNE THE ARK,] as in 2 Sa. 15. 24, &c.

AFFLICTED IN,] by Saul, Absalom, &c.

27. CASTETH OUT,] as in Ge. 3. 24; 4. 14,&c.

SPAKE,] in 1 Sa. 2. 31—36; 3 12—14.

SHILOH,] through the mouth of Samuel.

28. REPORT,] or rumour, of what had been done to Adonijah and Abiathar.

TURNED ASIDE,] from David and Solomon.

TENT,] which was at Gibeon; see 2 Ch. 1. 3, &c.

ALTAR,] as in 1. 50.

29. BENAIAH,] as in v. 25.

FALL UPON HIM,] and apprehend him as a prisoner of state.

30. TENT,] as in v. 28.

COME FORTH,] not being willing to seize him violently in that holy place.

HERE,] if die I must.

31. BURIED HIM,] that is, caused him to be buried.

CAUSELESS,] as in Ge. 29. 15; Ex. 21. 2, 11; Nu. 11. 5; 1 Sa. 19. 5; 25. 31; 2 Sa. 24. 24, &c.

32. HIS OWN HEAD,] as in Jud. 9. 57; 1 Sa. 25. 39; 2 Sa. 1. 16, &c.

TWO MEN,] heads of the host of Israel.

SWORD,] privately and unjustly.

KNEW NOT,] nor consented to the cruel and treacherous action.

33. SEED,] as in 2 Sa. 3. 29.

HOUSE,] or household.

34. GOETH UP] to Gibeon, the great high place, as in 3. 4, &c.

WILDERNESS,] or pasture-land.

35. HOST] of Israel and Judah.

ZADOK,] son of Ahitub, as in 2 Sa. 8. 17, &c., of the family of Eleazar.

36. SHIMEI,] who dwelt at Bahurim, in the tribe of Benjamin, as in 2 Sa. 16. 5.

JERUSALEM,] the capital city, where the king himself dwelt.

37. KIDRON,] as in 2 Sa. 15. 23, &c.; half a mile from the city.

HEAD,] as in v. 32.

38. GOOD,] being conscious that he deserved harsher treatment.

DO,] which promise, it would appear from v. 42, 43, the king made him swear to.

39. FLEE,] probably because of Shimei's bad usage.

GATH,] a principality of the Philistines, about 34 miles from Jerusalem.

40. ASS,] a common beast used for riding in those days.

BRINGETH] in to Jerusalem.

42. SWEAR] that thou wouldest keep thy word and my command in v. 38.

TESTIFY] publicly, before witnesses doubtless.

GOOD,] as in v. 38.

43. OATH,] taken in the presence of Jehovah, and under his sanction.

CHARGE] of not leaving Jerusalem.

44. EVIL] in thought, word, and action.

HATH KNOWN,] and are fully conscious of.

HEAD,] as in v. 32. 37.

45. BLESSED] by Jehovah the covenant-keeping God of Israel.

ESTABLISHED,] as in 2 Sa. 7. 16, 26, &c.

46. BENAIAH,] as in v. 25, 29.

FALLETH ON HIM] with the sword, and putteth him to death, as in v. 25, 34.

III. 1. JOINETH IN MARRIAGE,] as in Ge. 34. 9; De. 7. 3; Jos. 23. 12; 1 Sa. 18. 21, 22, 23, 26, 27; 2 Ch. 18. 1; Eze. 9. 14.

PHARAOH,] which was a common name of the kings of Egypt.

CITY OF DAVID,] which he had conquered from the Jebusites, and rebuilt and enlarged.

OWN HOUSE,] which was 13 years in building, as in 7. 1.

HOUSE OF JEHOVAH,] which was 7 years in building, and begun in the 4th year of his reign; see 6. 37, 38.

WALL,] for protecting the city round about, as in 9. 15, 19.

2. HIGH PLACES,] as in Lev. 26. 30; Nu. 21. 28; 22. 21; 35. 52, &c.

NAME,] or 'renown.'

3. LOVETH,] as in Ps. 116. 1, &c.

STATUTES,] which David had made for the service of God and man.

MAKING PERFUME,] as in Ex. 29. 13, &c.

4. GIBEON.] See on 2. 28: 1 Ch. 16. 39; 2 Ch. 1. 3.

GREAT HIGH PLACE.] where the tent and the ark were. 1 Ch. 16. 39.

A THOUSAND,] as in 2 Ch. 1. 6.

5. DREAM OF THE NIGHT,] as in Ge. 20. 3, &c.

ASK,] as in 2 Ch. 1. 7; Ps. 2. 8, &c.

6. DONE..KINDNESS,] as in 2 Sa. 22. 21, &c.

TRUTH..RIGHTEOUSNESS,] that is stedfastly and rightly.

UPRIGHTNESS,] as in De. 9. 5, &c.

7. JEHOVAH MY GOD] as well as the God of my father David.

A LITTLE CHILD,] in understanding compared with the work before me.

TO GO OUT AND TO COME IN,] that is, conduct himself as the supreme leader in Israel.

8. CHOSEN,] to be to thyself for a peculiar people, that thou mayest be my God.

NUMEROUS,] already counting several millions.

9. UNDERSTANDING,] *lit.* 'hearing *or* hearkening.'

TO JUDGE] correctly and justly.

TO DISCERN,] as in v. 11; Ps. 32. 9; Prov. 1. 2, 6; 14. 8; Isa. 28. 19; 56. 11; Da. 10. 12, 14.

10. IS GOOD,] as in Lev. 10. 19, &c.

11. MANY DAYS,] to enjoy the glory bestowed on him.

RICHES,] as if they could add to his happiness.

DISCERNMENT,] *lit.* 'to discern,' as in v. 9

12. WORDS,] as in v. 9 above.

THEE] for wisdom and discernment.

13. RICHES..HONOUR,] which men covet most earnestly.

14. MY WAYS,] that are revealed in the law.

WALKED,] generally speaking with his whole heart.

PROLONGED.] But his idolatrous compliances prevented this.

15. DREAM,] in which God anciently spoke often to men.

JERUSALEM,] from Gibeon, as in v. 5.

ARK,] as in 2 Sa. 6. 17.

BANQUET,] *lit.* 'drinking.'

16. HARLOTS.] The Targum reads 'innkeepers,' but without much authority.

STAND] for judgment in their controversy.

17. BRING FORTH] a child, a son, as appears from v. 20.

18. STRANGER,] as in Ex. 29. 33 &c.

19. SON,] not 'child,' as in C. V.

LAIN UPON IT,] and accidently smothered it.

21. SUCKLE,] as in Ge. 21. 7; Ex. 2. 7, 9, &c.

MY SON,] knowing it from some particular mark upon it.

24. TAKE FOR ME,] not 'bring me,' as in C. V.

25. CUT,] as in v. 26; 2 K. 6. 4; Isa. 9. 20; Hab. 3. 17; Ps. 136. 13, &c.

26. SON,] not 'child,' as in C. V.

YEARNED,] as in Ge. 43. 30, &c.

CUT,] this horrible language plainly showed it was not her own child.

28. JUDGED,] in the case just narrated.

WISDOM OF GOD,] derived from him and of him.

IN HIS HEART,] or 'in his midst.'

IV. 1. ALL ISRAEL,] like his father David.

2. HEADS,] or chief men around him in public departments.

AZARIAH,] son of Ahimaaz, son of

ZADOK,] the head of the family of Eleazar, son of Aaron.

3. ELIHOREPH,] i.e. 'God of my maturity.'

AHIAH,] i.e. 'brother of Jah.'

SHISHA,] or 'Sheva,' as in 2 Sa. 20. 25: 'Shausha' in 1 Ch. 18. 16; 'Seraiah' in 2 Sa. 8. 17.

SCRIBES,] as in 2 Sa. 20. 25.

JEHOSHAPHAT,] as in 2 Sa. 8. 16; 20. 24.

AHILUD,] as in 2 Sa. 8. 16; 20. 24.

REMEMBRANCER,] as in 2 Sa. 8. 16; 20. 24.

4. BENAIAH,] as in 2 Sa. 8. 18, &c.

HOST] of the men of war, instead of Joab, see 2. 35.

ZADOK,] as in v. 2.

ABIATHAR,] as in 2. 27.

PRIESTS,] that is, of course, head priests.

5 NATHAN,] the prophet, most likely.

OFFICERS,] as in v. 7, &c.

ZABUD,] i.e. 'endowed.'

MINISTER,] or 'priest,' as in 2 Sa. 8. 18; 20. 26.

FRIEND OF THE KING,] as in 2 Sa. 15 37; 16. 16; 1 Ch. 27. 33.

6. ABISHAR,] i.e. 'brother of a singer,' or of 'the upright.'

HOUSEHOLD,] as in 2 Sa. 20. 24.

ADONIRAM,] as in 5. 14; in 2 Sa. 20. 24; 1 K. 12. 18 it is Adoram; in 2 Ch. 10. 8 Hadoram.

ABDA,] i.e. a 'servant.'

TRIBUTE,] as in 5. 13, 14; 9. 15, 21.

7. OFFICERS,] as in v. 5, 27; 5. 16; 9. 23; 2 Ch. 8. 10, &c.

SUSTAINED,] as in v. 27; compare Ge. 45. 11; 47. 12; 50. 21, &c.

SUSTENANCE,] *lit.* 'to sustain,' as in Ruth 4. 15; 1 K. 17. 4, 9; Jer. 20. 9.

8. BEN-HUR,] i.e. 'son of whiteness.'

9. BEN-DEKAR,] i.e. 'son of piercing through.'

MAKAZ.] Not mentioned elsewhere, but apparently in Dan.

SHAALBIM,] as in Jos. 19. 41.

BETH-SHEMESH,] as in Jos. 19. 42

ELON-BETH-HANAN,] as Jos. 19. 43.

10. BEN HESED,] i.e. 'son of kindness.'

ARUBOTH.] Not mentioned elsewhere.

SHOCHOH.] There were two places of this

name in the tribe of Judah; see Jos. 15. 35, 48.

HEPHER.] Compare Jos. 12. 17; 17. 3; 1 Ch. 4, 6.

11. BEN-ABINADAB,] i.e. 'son of Abinadab.' ELEVATION OF DOR,] as in Jos. 17. 11, in the half-tribe of Manasseh.

TAPHATH,] i.e. 'a drop or dropping.'

12. BAANA,] i.e. 'son of affliction.' TAANACH,] as in Jos. 17. 11; in Manasseh. MEGIDDO,] as in Jos. 17. 11. BETH-SHEAN,] as in Jos. 17. 11. ZARTANAH,] not that referred to in Jos. 3. 16. JEZREEL,] either the city (Jos. 19. 18) or the valley (Jos. 17. 16) of that name. ABEL-MEHOLAH,] as in Jud. 7. 22; 1 K. 19. 16. JOKNEAM,] as in Jos. 19. 11, in the tribe of Manasseh.

13. BEN-GEBER,] i.e. 'son of a mighty one.' RAMOTH-GILEAD,] a city of refuge, in Gad, as in Jos. 20. 8. SMALL TOWNS OF JAIR,] as in Nu. 32. 41; De. 3. 14; Jos. 13. 30; Jud. 10. 4; 1 Ch. 2. 23. GILEAD,] beyond the Jordan. ARGOB.] See De. 3. 4, &c. BASHAN,] i.e. 'the soft, sandy soil,' as in Nu. 21. 23; 32. 33, &c. BAR,] as in De. 3. 5; 1 Sa. 23. 7; 2 Ch. 8. 5; 14. 7, &c.

14. MAHANAIM,] as in Ge. 32. 3; Jos. 13. 26, 30; 21. 38; 2 Sa. 2. 8; 12. 29; 17. 24, 27; 1 K. 2. 8.

15. AHIMAAZ,] son of Zadok, as in 2 Sa. 15. 27, 36; 17. 17, 20; 18. 19, &c. NAPHTALI,] whose bounds are described in Jos. 19. 32—39. BASEMATH,] i.e. 'spicy.'

16. HUSHAI,] as in 2 Sa. 15. 32, &c. ASHER.] See its bounds in Jos. 19. 24—31. ALOTH,] i.e. 'ascents;' not mentioned elsewhere.

17. PARUAH,] i. e. 'flourishing.' ISSACHAR,] as in Jos. 19. 17—23.

18. ELAH,] i. e. a 'terebinth.' BENJAMIN,] as in Jos. 18. 21, &c.

19. URI,] i. e. 'my light,' probably father of the officer in v.13. GILEAD,] beyond the Jordan eastward. SIHON..OG,] as in De. 3. 8, &c. LAND] of Gilead already, whose name is not mentioned.

20. SAND,] according to the promise in Ge. 22. 17. REJOICING,] this 20th verse is omitted in the Septuagent.

21. THE KINGDOMS] of the surrounding tribes. RIVER,] the Euphrates, according to the Targum. PHILISTINES,] on the coast of the great sea, the Mediterranean. BORDER OF EGYPT,] on the south of Canaan. PRESENT,] as a token of subjection

22. PROVISION,] lit. 'bread.' CORS,] as in 5. 11; 2 Ch. 2. 10; 27. 5; Eze. 45. 14; a dry and liquid measure, containing ten ephahs or baths. FAT OXEN,] as in Ge. 41. 2, 4, 5, 7, 18, 20;

Jud. 3. 17; Ps. 73. 4; Eze. 34. 3; Da. 1. 15; Hab. 1. 16; Zec. 11. 16. FEEDING OXEN,] grazing in the fields perhaps. FLOCK,] both sheep and goats. ROE..HART,] as in De. 12 15, 22; 14. 5; 15. 22, &c. FALLOW-DEER,] as in De. 14. 5. FATTED BEASTS.] This original word is not found elsewhere. STALLS,] as in Prov. 15. 17; 14. 4; Job 39. 9; Isa. 1. 3.

24. RIVER] Euphrates. TIPHSAH,] i.e. a 'passage over,' as in 2 K. 15.16, on the westren bank of the Euphrates, mentioned by Xenophen, Arrian, Strabo. GAZA,] a principality of the Philistines. PEACE] until the latter years of his reign.

25. CONFIDENCE,] as in Ge. 34. 25; Lev. 25. 18, 19; 26. 5. VINE..FIG-TREE,] as in Mic. 4. 4; Zec. 3. 10. DAN..BEER-SHEBA,] the two extremities of Canaan.

26. FORTY THOUSAND,] in 2 Ch. 9. 25 it is four thousand. STALLS,] as in 2 Ch. 9. 25; 32. 28. CHARIOTS,] of which he had 1,400, as in 10. 26. TWELVE THOUSAND,] probably one thousand for each tribe. HORSEMEN,] spread up and down the various cities, as well as in Jerusalem, as in 2 Ch. 9. 25.

27. THESE OFFICERS,] mentioned in v 8—19 above. LACKING,] of what was required by the king for the support of his household.

28. BARLEY,] as in Ex. 9. 31; Lev. 27. 16; Nu. 5. 15; De. 8. 8; Jud. 7. 13; Ruth 1. 22; 2. 17, 23; 3. 2, 15, 17, &c. STRAW,] as in Ge. 24. 25, 32; Ex. 5. 7, 10—18; Jud. 19. 19; Job 21. 14; 41. 27; Isa. 11. 7; 65. 25; Jer. 23. 28. HORSES,] which Solomon was the first to multiply in Israel. DROMEDARIES,] as in Est. 8. 10, 14; Mic. 1. 3. ORDINANCE,] given him by the king.

29. WISDOM,] as in 3. 12. BREADTH OF HEART.] This phrase is not found elsewhere. SAND,] a common mode of expressing immensity.

30. SONS OF THE EAST,] lit. 'sons of Kedem;' as in Jud. 6. 3, 33; 7. 12; 8. 10, 11, &c.; the Arabians, Persians, &c. EGYPT,] which was famous for its wise men. Acts 7. 22.

31. EZRAHITE,] to whom Ps. 89 is ascribed in its title. HEMAN,] of the tribe of Judah, 1 Ch. 2. 6. CHALCOL,] as in 1 Ch. 2. 6. DARDA,] in 1 Ch. 2. 6 it is Dara. MAHOL,] in 1 Ch. 2. 6 it is Zerah.

32. SIMILES,] as in Prov. 1. 1, 6; 10. 1; 25. 1; Ecc. 12. 9, &c. SONGS ARE FIVE.] The Sept. reads five thousand; Ps. 72 and 127 are two of them. CHIEF ONE,] that is, the Song of Songs.

33. TREES,] including shrubs and plants, as the original word shews.

CEDAR,] the tallest and statliest of them all, to the
HYSSOP,] used in purification, as in Ex. 12. 12, &c.
WALL] of houses and gardens.
CATTLE,] quadrupeds of all kinds.
FOWL,] every bird possessing wings.
CREEPING THINGS,] or reptiles of every sort.
FISHES] of the sea, especially the Mediterranean.
34. THE PEOPLES] round about Israel.

V. 1. HIRAM,] as in v. 10, 18; 2 Sa. 5. 11, but in 2 Ch 2. 2 it is Huram.
TYRE,] the celebrated city of the Phenicians, for traffic and wealth.
ANOINTED,] as in 1. 34, 39, 45.
LOVER,] as in 2 Sa. 5. 11; 1 Ch. 14. 1; Amos 1. 9.
EVERY SIDE] with the Edomites, Moabites, Amonites, Aramaeans, Philistines, &c.
HIS FEET,] or 'my feet,' as in the margin of the Hebrew text. Compare Ge. 8. 9; De. 2. 5; 11. 24, &c.
4. REST,] from wars of all kinds.
ADVERSARY,] Heb. 'Satan,' as in Nu. 22. 22, 23 &c.
OCCURRENCE,] as in Ecc. 9. 11.
5. SAYING] to my people and servants.
HE DOTH BUILD,] as in 2 Sa. 7. 13; 1 Ch. 17. 12; 22. 10.
6. CUT DOWN,] as in Nu. 13. 23, 24, &c.
LEBANON,] part of which belonged to Tyre, and part to Israel.
THOU SAYEST,] having abundance of means within his power.
ACQUAINTED,] lit. 'knowing.'
SIDONIANS,] or inhabitants of Zidon, which was under the same authority as Tyre.
7. REJOICETH,] because of the prospect of peace with Israel, and of mutual commercial intercourse.
JEHOVAH] the God of Israel, whom Hiram probably knew of from David and others.
NUMEROUS,] rather than 'great,' as in C.V.
8. HEARD,] not 'considered,' as in the C.V.
9. SEA,] that is, the Mediterranean or great sea.
FLOATS.] This original word does not occur elsewhere.
SPREAD OUT,] as in Ge. 9, 19; 1 Sa. 13. 11; Isa. 11. 12; 33. 3; Da. 12. 7, &c.
EXECUTE,] lit. 'do.'
11. CORS,] as in 4. 22, &c.
WHEAT,] which abounded in Canaan.
TWENTY.] In 2 Ch. 2. 10, it is 'twenty-thousand baths;' Sept. here reads 'twenty thousand.
BEATEN OIL,] as in Ex. 27. 20; 29. 40; Lev. 24. 2; Nu. 28. 5, &c.
12. SPAKE,] in 3. 12.
COVENANT,] of friendship and amity, the Tyrians not being of the nations of Canaan.
13. TRIBUTE,] as in Ge. 49. 15; Ex. 1. 11; De. 20. 11; Jos. 16. 10; 17. 13; Jud. 1. 28, 30, 33, 35; 2 Sa. 20. 24, &c.
14. CHANGES,] as in Ge. 45. 22; Jud. 14. 12, 13, 19; 2 K. 5. 5, 22, 23; Job 10. 17; 14. 14; Ps. 55. 19.
ADONIRAM,] as in 4. 6, &c.

15. BURDENS,] as in 2 Ch. 2. 2, 18; 34. 13 Neh. 4. 10.
HEWING,] as in 2 K. 12. 12; 1 Ch. 22. 2, 15; 2 Ch. 2. 2, 18; 24. 12; Eze. 2. 7; Ps. 29. 7; Isa. 10. 15; 22. 16, &c.
16. 3,300,] in 2 Ch. 2. 18, it is 3,600.
17. PRECIOUS STONES,] as in 2 Sa. 12. 30; 1 K. 7. 9, 10, 11; 10. 2, 10, 11; 1 Ch. 20. 2; 29. 2; 2 Ch. 3. 6, &c.
HOUSE] of the Lord, as in v. 3.
HEWN STONES,] as in Ex. 20. 25, &c.
18. GIBLITES,] as in Eze. 27. 9; men of Gebal.

VI. 1. 480TH YEAR,] 57 under Moses and Joshua, 299 under judges, 80 under Eli, Samuel, and Saul, 40 under David, and 3 under Solomon.
FOURTH YEAR,] as in 2 Ch. 3. 2.
ZIF,] as in v. 37, part of May and June.
BUILDETH,] that is, proceeds to build.
2. SIXTY CUBITS,] from east to west; the holy place was 40, the most holy 20 cubits.
3. PORCH] on the east side.
TEMPLE,] as in 1 Sa. 1. 9; 2. 3, &c.
4. NARROW,] as in Eze. 40. 16, 26.
LIGHTS,] as in 7. 4, 5.
5. A COUCH,] as in Ge. 49. 6; 1 K. 6. 5, 6 10; 1 Ch. 5. 1; Job 17. 13; Ps. 63. 6; 132. 3.
ORACLE,] as in v. 16, 19, 20, 21, 22, 23, 31, 7. 49; 8. 6, 8; 2 Ch. 3. 16; 4. 20; 5. 7, 9, Ps. 28. 2.
SIDES,] lit. 'ribs.'
6. COUCH,] as in v. 5.
WITHDRAWINGS.] This original word is not found elsewhere.
LAY HOLD,] as in 1 Ch. 13. 9; Job 38. 13 Ps. 56. 1; Ecc. 2. 3.
7. PERFECT STONE,] as in De. 25. 15; 27. 6; Jos. 8. 31; Prov. 11. 1.
HAMMER,] as in Isa. 44. 12; Jer. 10. 4.
AXE,] as in De. 19. 5; 20. 19; Isa. 10. 15.
8. MIDDLE-SIDE,] or 'rib,' as in v. 5, &c.
SHOULDER,] as in 7. 30, 34, 39; 2 K. 11. 11, &c.
WINDINGS.] This original word is not found elsewhere.
9. COVERETH,] as in 7. 3, 7; Jer. 22. 14; Hag. 1. 4; De. 33. 21.
VOWS,] as in 2 K. 11. 8, 15; 2 Ch. 23. 14.
10. THE COUCH,] as in v. 5, 6.
TAKETH HOLD,] as in v. 6.
11. WORD OF JEHOVAH,] as in Ge. 15. 1, 4, &c.
12. WALK..DO,] as in 2. 4; 9. 4, &c.
STATUTES..JUDGMENTS..COMMANDS,] the various appointments of Jehovah.
SPAKE,] in 2 Sa. 7. 31; 1 Ch. 22. 10.
13. TABERNACLED,] as in Ge. 9. 27; 14. 13; 16. 12, &c.
FORSAKE,] as in Ge. 28. 15, &c.
15. BEAMS,] lit. 'ribs.'
FLOOR,] as in Nu. 5. 17; 1 K. 6. 15, 16, 30; 7. 7; Amos 9. 3.
OVERLAID,] as in v. 20, 22, 30, 32, 35, &c.
RIBS,] as in v. 5.
16. HOLY OF HOLIES,] as in Ex. 26. 33, 34; 29. 37; 30. 10, 29, 36; 40. 10; Lev. 2. 3, 10, &c.
17. FORTY CUBITS,] as noted on v. 2.
18. CARVINGS,] as in v. 29, 32; 7. 31

KNOBS,] as in 7. 24. This original word is not found elsewhere.

FLOWERS,] as in Ex. 28. 36; 39. 30; Lev. 8. 9; Nu. 17. 8; 1 K. 6. 18, 29, 32, 35; Job 14. 2; Ps. 103. 15, &c.

19. ARK,] which had been made in the wilderness.

20. REFINED,] as in v. 21; 7. 49, 50; 10. 21; 2 Ch. 4. 20, 22; 9. 20, &c.

OVERLAYETH,] as in v. 15.

21. CHAINS,] as in Eze. 7. 23.

23. CHERUBS,] as in Ge. 3. 24; Ex. 25. 18, 19, &c.

OIL-TREE,] as in v. 31, 32, 33; Ne. 8. 15; Isa. 41. 19.

24. TEN CUBITS,] or half the breadth of the house.

25. FORM,] as in 7. 37; Jon. 2. 6; lit. 'cuttings.'

29. COMING,] as in Ge. 3. 3; 26. 11, &c.

OPENINGS OF CARVINGS,] as in v. 18.

PALM-TREES,] as in v. 32, 35; 7. 36; 2 Ch. 3. 5; Eze. 40. 16, 22, 26, 31, 34, 37; 41. 18, 19, 20, 25, 26.

31. OPENING,] that is, the open space before it.

OIL-TREE,] as in v. 23.

LINTEL,] as in Eze. 40. 9—49; 41. 1, 3.

SIDE-POSTS,] as in Ex. 12. 7, 22, 23; 21. 6, &c.

32. CAUSETH TO GO DOWN,] as in Jud. 19. 11; Isa. 45. 1; Ps. 144. 2.

33. OPENING,] as in v. 31.

34. SIDES,] lit. 'ribs.'

REVOLVING,] lit. 'rolling.'

HANGINGS,] as in Ex. 27. 9, 11, 12, 14, 15; 35. 17; 38. 9, 12, 14, 15, 16, 18; 39. 40; Nu. 3. 26; 4. 26.

35. STRAIGHTENED,] that is, made straight, stretched out.

36. INNER COURT] for the priests, as in 2 Ch. 4. 9.

37. FOUNDED,] as in Ezra 3. 6; Hag. 2. 18; Zec. 8. 9.

ZIF,] as in v. 1.

38. ELEVENTH YEAR] of the reign of Solomon.

BUL,] part of October and November.

MATTERS,] lit. 'words.'

ORDINANCES,] lit. 'judgments.'

SEVEN YEARS] and six months, see v. 1.

VII. 1. THIRTEEN YEARS,] commencing to it after finishing the house of the Lord, as appears from 2 Ch. 8. 1.

2. FOREST OF LEBANON,] so called, either because it was on the sides of Lebanon, or because it was a court of judicatory (v. 7), and an armoury (10. 17), for those of his subjects who may have resided there.

3. SIDES,] lit. 'ribs.'

4. SIGHT..SIGHT,] as in v. 5.

5. SQUARE,] as in Ex. 27. 1; Eze. 41. 21; 43. 16, &c.

6. A THICK PLACE,] as in Eze. 41. 25; 2 Ch. 4. 17, &c.

8 THIS WORK] of the house of the forest of Lebanon.

PHARAOH.] See 3. 1.

9. PRECIOUS STONES,] as in 5. 17, &c.

HEWN WORK,] as in v. 11, 12.

SAW,] as in 2 Sa. 12. 31; 1 Ch. 20. 3.

COPING,] lit. 'hand-breadth,' as in v. 26; 2 Ch. 4. 5; Ps. 39. 5.

10. GREAT STONES,] twelve and fifteen feet in length, and of proportionable height and thickness.

11. ABOVE] the foundation, mentioned in v. 10.

12. THE HOUSE] probably of Solomon.

13. HIRAM,] who, probably, being a favourite of the king of Tyre, had received or adopted his name.

14. NAPHTALI,] in the vicinity of Tyre and Zidon ; in 1 Ch. 2. 14, she is said to be of the daughters of Dan.

MAN OF TYRE,] an inhabitant, not necessarily a native, of it.

WORKER,] or 'plower, graver,' as in 19. 19; Job 1. 14, &c.

WISDOM..UNDERSTANDING..KNOWLEDGE,] such as Bezaleel and Aholiab possessed in the making of the tent of the tabernacle.

15. FORMETH,] by cutting and carving, not 'cast,' as in C.V. Compare Ex. 32. 4.

CORD,] as in Ge. 14. 23; Jos. 2. 18; Jud. 16. 12; Ecc. 4. 12; Song 4. 3; Jer. 52. 21.

16. CHAPITERS,] or 'crowns,' as in v. 17, 18, 19, 20, 31, 41, 42; 2 K. 25. 17; 2 Ch. 4. 12; Jer. 52. 22.

CAST,] as in v. 23, 33; 2 K. 4. 5; 2 Ch. 4. 2, Job 11. 15; 37. 18.

17. NET WORK,] as in v. 18, 20, 41, 42; 2 K. 1. 2; 25. 17; 2 Ch. 4. 12, 13; Job 18. 8; Jer. 52. 22, 23.

WREATHS,] as in De. 22. 12.

CHAINWORK,] as in Ex. 28. 14; 39. 15; 2 Ch. 3. 5, 16.

19. LILY-WORK,] as in v. 26; Ps. 45. 1; 69. 1; 80. 1; Song 2. 16; 4. 5; 5. 13; 6. 2, 3; 7. 2.

20. PROTUBERANCE,] lit. 'belly.'

21. FOR,] not 'in,' as in C.V.

JACHIN,] i.e. 'he prepares or establishes.'

BOAZ,] i.e. 'fleetness,' as in 1 Ch. 3. 17.

22. LILY-WORK,] as in v. 19.

23. MOLTEN,] lit. 'cast,' as in v. 16.

24. KNOBS,] as in 6. 18.

25. TWELVE OXEN,] as in 2 Ch. 4. 4, 5; Jer. 52. 20.

26. HAND BREADTH.] See on v. 9 above.

CUP,] as in 2 Ch. 4. 5; Ge. 40. 11, &c.

2,000] regularly; it could contain 3,000 if necessary, see 2 Ch. 4. 5.

BATHS,] as in v. 38, &c.

27. BASES,] for the ten lavers in v. 38.

28. BORDERS,] as in Ex. 25. 25, 27; 37. 12, 14; 2 Sa. 22. 46; 1 K. 7. 29, 31, 32, 35, 36; 2 K. 16. 17; Ps. 18. 4, 5; Mic. 7. 17.

JOININGS,] as in v. 29.

29. ADDITIONS,] as in v. 30, 31.

SLOPING WORK,] that is, pensile work, festoons.

30. WHEELS,] as in Ex. 14. 25; 1 K. 7. 32, 33; Prov. 20. 26; 25. 11; Isa. 28. 27; Eze. 1. 15, 16, 19, 20; 3. 13; 10. 6, 9, 10, 12, 13, 16 19; 11. 22; Nah. 3. 2.

AXLES.] This original word is only applied elsewhere to the princes of the Philistines Jos. 13. 0, &c.

CORNERS,] lit. 'steps.'

SHOULDERS,] as in 6. 8, &c.

MOLTEN,] as in v. 16, 23, &c.

31. CARVINGS,] as in 6. 18, 29, 32.

32. SPOKES,] *lit.* 'hands,' as in v. 33.
33. AXLES,] as in Eze. 1. 16, &c.
FELLOES,] by which the nave and the rim were joined.
NAVES.] The original word is not found elsewhere.
34. SHOULDERS,] as in v. 30, &c.
35. SPOKES,] as in v. 32.
36. TABLETS,] as in Ex. 24. 12, &c.
VOID SPACE,] *lit.* 'nakedness,' as in Nah. 2. 5.
37. CASTING,] as in v. 16, 23, &c.
MEASURE,] as in Ex. 26. 2, &c.
FORM,] as in 6. 25.
38. LAVERS,] as in Ex. 30. 18, 28, &c.
BATHS,] as in v. 26; 2 Ch. 2. 10; 4. 5; Isa. 5. 10; Eze. 45. 10, 11, 14.
39. SIDE,] *lit.* 'shoulder,' as in 6. 8, &c.
40. HIRAM,] as in v. 13.
BASONS,] as in Ex. 27. 3, &c.
41. BOWLS,] as in v. 42; 2 Ch. 4. 12, 13; Ecc. 12. 6; Zec. 4. 3.
42. POMEGRANATES,] as in v. 18, 20.
43. BASES..LAVERS,] as in v. 27, 38.
44. SEA..OXEN,] as in v. 23. 25.
45. POLISHED,] as in Isa. 18. 2, 7; Eze. 21. 10. 11.
46. CIRCUIT,] as in Ge. 13. 10, 11, &c.
THICK SOIL.] This original word is not found elsewhere.
SUCCOTH,] in the tribe of Gad, beyond Jordan.
ZARTHAN,] on the west of Jordan, in Manasseh, called Zartanah in 4. 12; Zaretan in Jos. 3. 16; Zaredathah in 2 Ch. 4. 7.
47. PLACETH,] as in 13. 29, 30; 19. 3, &c.
SEARCHED OUT,] as in 2 Ch. 4. 18; Jer. 31. 37; 46. 23.
48. ALTAR OF GOLD,] that is, covered with it, as in 6. 20; compare Rev. 8. 3.
TABLE,] which consisted of ten parts, as in 2 Ch. 4. 8.
BREAD OF THE PRESENCE,] as in Ex. 25. 30, &c.
49. REFINED,] as in 6. 20, 21, &c.
TONGS,] as in 2 Ch. 4. 21; Isa. 6. 6.
50. BASONS,] as in Ex. 12. 12; 2 Sa. 17. 28, &c.
SNUFFERS,] as in 2 K. 12. 13; 25. 14; 2 Ch. 4. 22; Jer. 52. 18.
BOWLS,] as in v. 40, 45; Ex. 27. 3.
CENSERS,] as in Ex. 25. 38, &c.
HINGES.] This original word is not found elsewhere, with this meaning.
51. SANCTIFIED THINGS,] those 'set apart' for divine service,
TREASURIES,] as in De. 28. 12; 32. 34, &c.

VIII. 1. ELDERS,] who exercised authority in the various tribes.
HEADS,] by birth and succession—the chief men.
PRINCES,] as in 2 Ch. 5. 2, &c.
CITY OF DAVID,] as in 2 Sa. 6. 12.
ZION,] *lit.* 'the sunny place,' as in 2 Sa. 5. 7; 2 K. 19, 21, 31; 1 Ch. 11. 5; 2 Ch. 5. 2; Ps. 2. 6, &c.
2. ARE ASSEMBLED,] not 'assemble themselves,' as in C.V.
ETHANIM,] i.e. 'perenial streams,' the same as Tisri, part of September and October.

3. COME IN] to Jerusalem, to the tent that David spread out for the ark, as in 2 Sa. 6. 17.
LIFT UP] upon their shoulders, according to the law; compare 2 Ch. 5. 4.
4. BRING UP] to mount Moriah, to the temple.
TENT OF MEETING,] constructed by Moses in the wilderness.
HOLY VESSELS,] as in Nu. 31. 6, &c.
5. MET] by agreement, as the original word indicates, as in Nu. 14. 35; 16. 11; 27. 3; 2 Ch. 5. 6.
NOT COUNTED,] as in Ge. 16. 10; 32. 12; 1 K. 3. 8; 2 Ch. 5. 6; Jer. 33. 22; Hos. 1. 10; 1 Ch. 23. 3.
6. ORACLE,] as in 6. 5, 16, 19, 20, 21, 22, 23, 31; 7. 49; 8. 6, 8; 2 Ch. 3. 16; 4. 20; 5. 7, 9; Ps. 28. 2.
WINGS,] as in Ex. 25. 20; 37. 9; Ruth 2. 12; 1 K. 6. 24, 27; 8. 6, 7; 2 Ch. 3. 11, 12, 13; 5. 7, 8, &c.
COVER,] so that the ends of the staves were not seen.
8. LENGTHEN,] as in 2 Ch. 5 9.
9. THERE IS NOTHING.] Perhaps the other articles were lost when the Philistines carried the ark away.
10. THE CLOUD,] the usual symbol of the Divine Presence, as in Ex. 40. 34, 35; 2 Ch. 5. 13, 14; 7. 2.
11. HONOUR,] *lit.* 'weight, heaviness.'
12. SAID,] perhaps in Lev. 16. 2; so 2 Ch. 6. 1.
THICK DARKNESS] of clouds, as the original word appears to signify; see Ex. 20. 21; De. 4. 11; 5. 22; 2 Sa. 22. 10; 2 Ch. 6. 1; Job 22. 13; 38. 9; Ps. 18. 9; 97. 2; Isa. 60. 2; Jer. 13. 16; Eze. 34. 12; Joel 2. 2; Zeph. 1. 15.
13. HOUSE OF HABITATION,] as in 2 Ch. 6. 2; Ps. 49. 14; Isa. 63. 15; Hab. 3. 11.
FIXED PLACE,] as in Ex. 15. 17, &c.
14. TURNETH ROUND] from before the altar, as in v. 22.
STANDING] as a mark of respect for the king.
15. SPAKE,] in 2 Sa. 7. 5, 25.
16. FROM THE DAY,] four hundred and eighty-eight years before, as in 6. 1, 38; 8. 2.
FIXED,] though he had indicated his intention of doing so, in De. 12. 5, 11, &c.
BEING THERE,] as in v. 29.
MY PEOPLE,] as their leader and king, under God.
17. WITH THE HEART,] that is, in accordance with it, not 'in,' it, as in the C.V.
18. SAID,] in 2 Ch. 6. 8, 9.
19. THOU DOST NOT,] being a man of war and blood.
20. ESTABLISH,] *or* 'raise up.'
SPOKE,] in 1 Ch. 28. 5, 6.
21. COVENANT,] as in v. 9; De. 31. 26.
22. ALTAR,] as in 2 Ch. 6. 12.
23. LIKE THEE] in respect to the following particulars.
THE COVENANT] specially entered into by himself with his people
THE KINDNESS] which he promised to shew to them.
HEART,] as in 3. 6, &c.
24. FOR,] not 'with,' as in C.V.
SPAKEST,] as in 2. 4; 2 Sa. 7. 12. 16.
MOUTH..HAND,] as in v. 15.

25. NOT CUT OFF] finally and for ever.

26. STEDFAST,] as in 2 Ch. 1. 9, &c.

27. IS IT TRUE?] as in Ge. 18. 13; Nu. 22. 32; 2 Ch. 6. 18; Ps. 58. 1.

HEAVENS OF THE HEAVENS,] as in De. 10. 14.

CONTAIN,] as in 2 Ch. 2. 6; 6. 18, &c.

28. TURNED] thy face, as the original word indicates, as in Ge. 18. 22, &c.

PRAYER,] as in 2 Sa. 7. 27; 1 K. 8. 28, 29, 38, 45, 49, 54; 9. 3; 2 K. 19. 4; 20 .5; 2 Ch. 6. 19, 20, 29, 35, 39, 40, &c.

SUPPLICATION,] as in Jos. 11. 20.

CRY,] as in 22. 26; 2 Ch. 6. 19; 20. 22; Ps. 17. 1; 30. 5; 42. 4; 47. 1; 61. 1; 88. 2; 105. 43; 106. 44; 107. 22; 118. 15; 119. 169; 126. 2, 5, 6; 142. 6; Prov. 11. 10; Isa. 14. 7; 35. 10; 43. 14; 44. 23; 48. 20; 49. 13; 51. 11; 54. 1; 55. 12; Jer. 7. 16; 11. 14; 14. 12; Zep. 3. 17.

29. SAIDST,] in De. 12. 11.

30. PRAY TOWARD,] as in Da. 6. 10; Jon. 2. 4.

31. SINNETH,] being unfaithful to his trust.

LIFTED UP,] as in 2 Ch. 6. 22.

OATH,] as in Ge. 24. 41, &c.

32. TO DECLARE WICKED,] as in Ex. 22. 9, &c, PUT HIS WAY,] as in 2 Ch. 6. 23.

TO DECLARE RIGHTEOUS,] as in Ex. 23. 7; De. 25. 1.

RIGHTEOUSNESS,] as in 2 Sa. 21. 21, 25; 2 Ch. 6. 23.

33. SMITTEN,] as in Jud. 20. 39; Lev. 26. 17, &c.

TURNED BACK,] as in De. 1. 45; 4. 30.

CONFESSED,] as in v. 35; 2 Ch. 6. 24, 26; 1 Ch. 16. 35; Ps. 44. 8; 54. 6; 99. 3; 106. 47; 122. 4; 138. 2; 140. 13; 142. 7; Isa. 25. 1.

34. GROUND,] as in Nu. 11. 12, &c.

FATHERS,] in promises many and clear.

35. RESTRAINED,] as in 2 Ch. 6. 26; 7. 13; De. 11. 17; Job 12. 15.

AFFLICT,] as in 2 Ch. 6. 26.

36. DIRECTEST,] as in Ex. 15. 25, &c.

THE GOOD WAY,] as in 1 Sa. 12. 23; 2 Ch. 6. 27, &c.

INHERITANCE,] as in Nu. 18. 20, &c.

37. FAMINE,] lit. 'hunger,' as in Ge. 12. 9; 26. 1; 41. 27—57, &c,

PESTILENCE,] as in Ex. 5. 3; 9. 3, 15, &c.

BLASTING,] as in De. 28. 22; 2 Ch. 6. 28; Amos 4. 9; Hag. 2. 17.

MILDEW,] as in De. 28. 22; 2 Ch. 6. 26; Jer. 30. 6; Amos 4. 9; Hag. 2. 17.

LOCUST,] as in Ex. 10. 4, 12, 13, 14, 19; Lev. 11. 22; De. 28. 38; Jud. 6. 5; 7. 12; 2 Ch. 6. 28; Job 39. 20; Ps. 78. 46, &c.

CATERPILLAR,] as in 2 Ch. 9. 28; Ps. 78. 46; Isa. 33. 4; Joel 1. 4; 2. 25.

GATES,] as in Ge. 19. 1; De. 28. 52, 55, 57; 2 Ch. 6. 28, &c.

PLAGUE,] or 'stroke.'

SICKNESS,] as in Ex. 15. 26; 23. 25; 2 Ch. 6. 28.

38. OWN HEART,] in 2 Ch. 6. 29 it is 'his own plague and his own pain.'

39. THYSELF ALONE,] as in Jer. 17. 10, &c.

40. FACE OF THE GROUND,] as in Ge. 2. 6, &c.

41. STRANGER,] as in Ge. 31. 15, &c.

42. NAME..HAND..ARM,] that is, of his character and actings to his friends and his enemies.

43. SETTLED PLACE,] as in Ex. 15. 17, &c.

ALL PEOPLES,] as in 1 Sa. 17. 46; 2 K. 19. 19; Ps. 67. 2.

CALLED,] as in 2 Ch. 6. 33; Jer. 7. 10, 11, 14, 30; 32. 34; 34. 15.

44. SEND,] for they could only go at his command.

45. CAUSE,] lit. 'done their judgment,' as in v. 49, 59; 2 Ch. 6. 35, 39, &c.

46. SINNETH NOT,] as in 2 Ch. 6. 36; Ecc. 7. 20.

ANGRY,] as in 2 Ch. 6. 36; Ezra 9. 14; Ps. 2. 12; 60. 1; 79. 5; 85. 5; Isa. 12. 1.

TAKEN CAPTIVE,] as in Ge. 34. 29.

THEIR CAPTIVITY,] as in De. 21. 10; 2 Ch. 6. 36; 28. 11; Ps. 68. 18.

47. TURNED IT BACK,] as in Lev. 26. 40, &c.

TURNED BACK] to God in penitence.

DONE PERVERSELY,] according to our own wishes, and against many promises.

DONE WICKEDLY] or wrongly against ourselves and our God.

48. HEART..SOUL,] as in De. 4. 29, &c.

PRAYED,] as in Da. 6. 10.

LAND..CITY..HOUSE,] all of which were meeting-places of God with his people.

49. SETTLED PLACE,] as in v. 43.

50. MERCIES,] lit. 'for or to mercies.'

51. PEOPLE,] prepared and adapted for himself.

INHERITANCE,] as in Ex. 15. 17, &c.

FURNACE,] as in De. 4. 20; Prov. 17. 3; 27. 21; Isa. 48. 10; Jer. 11. 4; Ecc. 22. 18, 20, 22.

52. IN ALL] that is consistent with God's glory.

SEPARATED,] as in Lev. 20. 24, &c.

SPEAK,] as in Ex. 19. 5, 6.

54. ALTAR] of burnt-offering.

KNEES,] on the brazen scaffold, as in 2 Ch. 6. 13.

SPREAD OUT,] as in v. 38.

55. BLESSETH,] as David did in 2 Sa. 6. 18.

56. GIVEN REST,] from internal strife and outward foes.

SPOKEN,] as in De. 12. 9, 10.

ONE WORD,] as in Jos. 23. 14.

57. FORSAKE..LEAVE,] as in Jos. 1. 5.

58. INCLINE,] as in Jos. 24. 23; 2 Sa. 19. 14; Ps. 119. 36; 141. 4; Prov. 2. 2; 21. 1.

WAYS .. COMMANDS .. STATUTES .. JUDGMENTS,] his various directions to men.

59. CAUSE,] as in v. 45, 49.

THE MATTER,] as in Ex. 5. 11; 16. 4; 2 Ch. 8. 13; Ezra 3. 4.

60. PEOPLES,] not 'people,' as in C.V.

GOD,] lit. 'the God,' that is, the only true one, as in Ge. 5. 22; 6. 9, 11; 17. 18; 20. 6, 7; De. 4. 35; 1 K. 18. 21; Da. 9. 11, &c.

NONE ELSE,] as in De. 4. 35.

61. PERFECT,] as in 11. 4: 15. 3, 14; 2 K. 20. 3; 1 Ch. 12. 38; 28. 9; 29. 9, 19; 2 Ch. 15. 17; 16. 9; 19. 9; 25. 2; Isa. 38. 3.

62. ARE SACRIFICING,] as in 2 Ch. 7. 1—3.

63. PEACE-OFFERINGS,] part of which were consumed by those offering. 22,000..120,000,] during the fourteen days of the feast.

DEDICATE,] lit. 'to make narrow,' hence to 'set apart,' as in De. 20. 5; 2 Ch. 7. 5; Prov. 22. 6; Nu. 7. 10, 11, 84, 88.

64. MIDDLE,] as in 2 Ch. 7. 7.

ALTAR OF BRASS,] as in 2 Ch. 4. 1.

CONTAIN,] because of its abundance, as in v. 63.
65. THE FESTIVAL,] as in v. 2.
HAMATH,] as in Nu. 13. 21; 34. 8, &c.
BROOK OF EGYPT,] as in Nu. 34. 5.
FOURTEEN DAYS,] seven for the dedication of the house, and seven for the feast of tabernacles; see 2 Ch. 7. 8, 8. The Vatican M.S. omits the second 'seven days.'
66. EIGHTH DAY] of the second festival.
TENTS,] or dwellings throughout the whole land.
GLAD OF HEART,] as in 1 Sa. 25. 36; 2 Sa. 13. 28; 2 Ch. 7. 10, &c.

IX. 1. DESIRE,] as in v. 19; 2 Ch. 8. 6; Isa. 21. 4.
DELIGHTED,] as in Ge. 34. 19, &c. See 2 Ch. 7. 11; Ecc. 2. 4—6.
2. APPEARETH,] lit. 'is seen.'
GIBEON,] as in 3. 5; 2 Ch. 7. 12.
3. PRAYER..SUPPLICATION,] recorded in 8. 23—53.
NAME,] as in 8. 29.
EYES..HEART,] as in De. 11. 12.
4. SIMPLICITY OF HEART,] as in Ge. 20. 56; Ps. 78. 72; 101. 2.
UPRIGHTNESS,] as in De. 9. 5; 1 Ch. 29. 17, &c.
5. SPAKE,] in 2 Sa. 7. 12, 13, &c.
6. FROM AFTER ME,] as in Nu. 14. 43, &c.
7. NAME,] being there, as in De. 12. 11, &c.
SIMILE,] as in De. 28. 37, &c.
BYE-WORD,] as in De. 28. 37; 2 Ch. 7. 20; Jer. 24. 9.
8. ASTONISHED,] at its degradation and abasement.
HISS,] as in Job 27. 23; Isa. 5. 26; 7. 18; Jer. 19. 8; 49. 17; 50. 13; La. 2. 15, 16; Eze. 27. 36; Zep. 2. 15; Zec. 10. 8.
9. SAID,] not 'answer,' as in C.V.
LAY HOLD,] firmly with their own free will and determination.
10. TWENTY YEARS,] seven and thirteen, as in 6. 83; 7. 1.
11. CEDAR..FIR,] for both his houses, as in 5. 8, 10.
GOLD,] which Hiram also got from Ophir, as in 9. 27.
GALILEE,] nearest Tyre and Zidon.
12. NOT RIGHT,] as in Jud. 14. 3, &c; perhaps they were lying waste.
13. CABUL.] Etymology unknown; perhaps an errata for Gebul, a 'boundary.'
14. GOLD,] as in v. 11.
15. MATTER,] or cause.
TRIBUTE,] as in 4. 6; 5. 13, 14; 9. 15, 21; 12. 18 &c.
MILLO,] which he repaired; see 2 Sa. 5. 9.
HAZOR,] in the tribe of Naphtali; see Jos. 11. 1; 19. 36.
MEGIDDO,] in Manasseh; see Jos. 17. 11.
GEZER,] in Ephraim; see Jos. 10. 33; 16. 3.
16. PRESENTS,] as in Ex. 18. 2; Mic. 1. 14.
WIFE OF SOLOMON,] as in 3. 1, &c.
17. BUILDETH] anew Gezer, it having been burnt with fire, as in v. 16.
BETH-HORON THE LOWER,] and also the Upper, as in 2 Ch. 8. 5, between Ephraim and Benjamin, Jos. 16. 3, 5; 18. 13. 14.
18. BAALATH,] in Dan, Jos. 19. 44.

TADMOR,] or 'Tamor,' a 'palm-tree,' in Greek 'Palmyra,' 2 Ch. 8. 3, 4; Eze. 47. 19.
WILDERNESS,] or pasture-land, between Damascus and the Euphrates.
LAND] of Hamath-Zobah, as in 2 Ch. 8. 3, 4.
19. CITIES OF STORES,] as in Ex. 1. 11; 2 Ch. 8. 4, 6; 16. 4; 17. 12; 32. 28.
CHARIOTS,] as in 10. 26; 2 Ch. 1. 14; 8. 6; 9. 25.
HORSEMEN,] as in 2 Ch. 8. 6.
JERUSALEM,] the capital city, as in Ecc. 2. 4.
LEBANON,] especially 'the house of the forest of Lebanon,' as in 7. 2; 2 Ch. 8. 3, 6.
20. AMORITE..JEBUSITE,] left by Joshua and David unsubdued; see Jud. 1. 19, 21, 27, 29, 30, &c.
21. LEFT] unexterminated.
DEVOTE] to God by utter destruction.
22. APPOINTED,] lit. 'given.'
24. WENT UP,] from the 'city of David' below; see 3. 1; 2 Ch. 8. 11.
25. THREE TIMES,] at the Passover, Pentecost, and Tabernacle festivals.
26. NAVY,] as in v. 27; 10. 11, 22; Isa. 33. 21.
EZION-GEBER,] as in Nu. 33. 35, 36; De. 2. 8; 1 K. 9. 26; 22. 48; 2 Ch. 8. 17; 20. 36.
ELOTH,] as in 2 K. 16. 6; 2 Ch. 8. 17; 26. 2.
SEA OF SUPH,] the southern border of Arabia.
27. SERVANTS,] and according to 2 Ch. 8. 18, a navy also of his own.
28. OPHIR,] the locality of which is un known; some say, in Arabia, near Aden, others India, and others Mozambique, in Africa; see 10. 11; 22. 48; 1 Ch. 1. 23; 29. 4; 2 Ch. 8. 18; 9. 10; Job 22. 24; 28. 16; Ps. 45. 9; Isa. 13. 12.
420 TALENTS,] in 2 Ch. 8. 18, it is 450.

X. 1. SHEBA,] in Arabia Felix, as in v. 4, 10, 13; Job 1. 15; 6. 19; Ps. 72. 10, 15; Isa. 60. 6; Jer. 6. 20; Eze. 27. 22, 23; 38. 13.
TO TRY,] as in Ge. 22. 1; Ex. 15. 25, &c.
ENIGMAS,] as in Nu. 12. 8; Jud. 14. 12—19; 2 Ch. 9. 1; Ps. 49. 4; 78. 2; Prov. 1. 6; Eze. 17. 2; Da. 8. 23; Hab. 2. 6.
2. GREAT COMPANY,] or 'heavy force,' as in 2 K. 7. 6; 2 Ch. 9. 1; 24. 24, &c.
SPICES,] as in Ex. 25. 6; 30. 23; 35. 8, &c.
PRECIOUS STONE,] as in 2 Sa. 12. 30, &c.
WITH HER HEART,] or 'near' it; as in 2 Ch. 9. 1, &c.
3. MATTERS,] not 'questions,' as in C.V.
4. HOUSE] for the Lord, or for himself, or that of the forest of Lebanon.
5. FOOD,] as in 2 Ch. 9. 4; Ge. 2. 9, &c.
SITTING,] or 'seat,' as in Ge. 10. 30; 27. 39; 36. 43, &c.
STANDING] as in 1 Ch. 23. 28; 2 Ch. 9. 4; 35. 15; Isa. 22. 19.
BUTLERS,] as in Ge. 40. 21; Lev. 11. 34; 2 Ch. 9. 20; Isa. 32. 6; Eze. 45. 15, &c.
BURNT-OFFERINGS.] So Sept. Lat. Syr. and Arabic Versions; as in 9. 25, &c.
SPIRIT,] as in 2 Ch. 9. 4; Jos. 2. 11; 5. 1
6. MATTERS,] lit. 'words.'
7. HALF,] as in 2 Ch. 9. 6; Ps. 102. 24; Eze. 16. 51.
8. HAPPINESS,] as in De. 33. 39; 2 Ch. 9. 7; Job 5. 17; Ps. 1. 1, &c.

9. SET,] as in De. 1. 13; 17. 14, 15, &c.
10. 120 TALENTS.] See 9. 14.
11. NAVY,] as in 9. 26, &c.
OPHIR,] as in 9. 28.
ALMUG TREES,] as in v. 12; in 2 Ch. 2. 8; 9. 10, 11, it is 'algum-trees;' supposed to be red sandal wood, or Brazil wood.
12. SUPPORT.] This original word is not found elsewhere.
13.MEMORIAL,] lit. 'a hand;' see Est. 1. 7; 2. 18.
14. 666 TALENTS,] variously reckoned from two to five million pounds sterling.
15. TOURISTS,] as in 2 Ch. 9. 14; in Nu. 14. 6, the word is used of the spies.
TRAFFIC,] as in Prov. 3. 14; 31. 18; Isa. 23. 3, 18; 45. 14.
MERCHANTS,] not 'spice-merchants,' as in C.V.; see Neh. 3. 31, 32; 13. 20; Song 3. 6; Eze. 17. 4; 27. 3, 13, 15, 17, 20, 22, 23, 24; Nah. 3. 16.
ARABIA,] who were subject to him, or who made presents, as in 4. 21, 24.
GOVERNORS,] as in 20. 24; 2 K. 18. 24; 2 Ch. 9. 14; Ezra 8. 36; Neh. 2. 7, 9; 3. 7; 5. 14, 15, 18; 12. 26; Est. 3. 12; 8. 9; 9. 3; Isa. 36. 9; Jer. 51. 23, 28, 57; Eze. 23. 6, 12, 23; Hag. 1. 1, 14; 2. 2, 21; Mal. 1. 8.
16. TARGETS,] as in 1 Sa. 17. 7, 41, &c.
ALLOYED,] lit. 'slaughtered,' as in Lev. 14. 6, 51; 1 K. 10. 16, 17; 2 Ch. 9. 15, 16; Jer. 9. 8.
17. SHIELDS,] as in Ge. 15. 1, &c.
HOUSE,] as in 7. 2; see Song 4. 4.
18. IVORY,] brought from Tarshish, as in v. 22; see 22. 39; 2 Ch. 9. 17; Ps. 45. 8; Song 5. 14; Eze. 27. 6, 15; Amos 3. 15; 6. 4.
OVERLAYETH,]as in Ex. 25. 11, 13, 24, 28,&c.
REFINED,] or as in 2 Ch. 9. 17 'pure,' using however, a different Hebrew word.
19. STEPS,] lit. 'ascents.'
ROUND,] as in 7. 23, 31, 35; 2 Ch. 4. 2.
HANDS,] as in 7. 35, 36.
20. TWELVE LIONS,] two on each step.
21. DRINKING VESSELS,] as in 2 Ch. 9. 20.
REFINED,] as in 6. 20, 21; 7. 49, 50; 2 Ch. 4. 20, 22; 9. 20; Job 41. 15; Eze. 44. 1, 2; 46. 1.
22. TARSHISH.] See on Ge. 10. 4; generally believed to have been Tartessus in Spain; as in v. 22; 22. 48; 1 Ch. 1. 7, &c.
APES,] as in 2 Ch. 9. 21.
PEACOCKS,] as in 2 Ch. 9. 21.
24. SEEKING THE PRESENCE,] or 'face,' as in 2 Ch. 9. 23, &c.
25. PRESENT,] as in Ge. 4. 3—5; 32. 13, 18, 20, 21, &c.
ARMOUR,] as in 2 K. 10. 2; 2 Ch. 9. 24; Neh. 3. 19; Job 20. 24; 39. 21; Ps. 140. 7; Isa. 22. 8; Eze. 39. 9, 10.
SPICES,] as in v. 2, 10 above.
MULES,] as in 2 Sa. 13. 29; 18. 9; 1 K. 18. 5; 2 K. 5. 17; 1 Ch. 12. 40; 2 Ch. 9. 24; Eze. 2. 66; Neh. 7. 68; Ps. 32. 9; Isa. 66. 20. Eze. 27. 14; Zec. 14. 15.
26. CHARIOTS . . HORSEMEN,] contrary to De. 17. 16.
12,000,] as in 4. 90; 2 Ch. 1. 14; 9. 25.
PLACETH,] as in 2 Ch. 9. 25.
27. SYCAMORES,] as in 1 Ch. 27. 28; 2 Ch. 1. 15; 9. 27; Ps. 78. 47; Isa. 9. 10; Amos 7. 14.
LOW COUNTRY,] as in De. 1. 7; Jos. 9. 1, &c.
28. OUT-GOING,] as in 2 Ch. 1. 16

KEVAH,] the name of a place in Egypt, so Geddes and Boothroyd; very unnatural is Gesenius' conjecture.
PRICE,] as in De. 23. 18; 2 Sa. 24. 24; 1 K. 21. 2; 2 Ch. 1. 16; Job 28. 15; Ps. 44. 12; Prov. 17. 16, &c.
29. 600 SILVERLINGS,] or about sixty pounds sterling.
150,] or about fifteen pounds sterling.
HITTITES,] as in 2 K. 7. 6.
ARAM,] those of Damascus, Zobah, &c.

XI. 1. STRANGE WOMEN,] i.e. foreigners, as in v. 8; Ezra 10. 2, 10. 11, 14, 17, 18, 44; Neh. 13. 26, 27, &c.
DAUGHTER,] whom he had married, as in 3. 1, whom he married after the death of his first wife, as in 14. 21, 31.
2. SAID,] as in De. 7. 1—3.
CLEAVED,] as in Ge. 2. 24, &c.
3. WOMEN,] not 'wives,' as in the C.V.; they were probably the captive wives and daughters of the princes conquered by David, and brought as pledges to Jerusalem. It is not said that he 'married' them, or 'took them to wife,' or had any intercourse with them but that of friendship, and he had only one son, viz., Rehoboam.
PRINCESSES,] as in Jud. 5. 29; Est. 1. 18; Isa. 49. 23; La. 1. 1.
CONCUBINES,] as in Ge. 22. 24; companions in misfortune of the preceding.
4. OLD AGE,] as in Ge. 24. 36; 1 K. 15. 23; Ps. 71. 9, 18; Isa. 46. 4.
PERFECT,] as in 8. 61, &c.
5. ASHTORETH,] as in v. 33; 2 K. 23. 13; see De. 1. 4: Jos. 9. 10; 12. 4: 13. 12, 31, &c.
GODDESS,] lit. 'god.' The Hebrew has no feminine form for the word.
MILCOM,] as in v. 33; 2 K. 23. 13.
6. THE EVIL THING,] that is, idolatry or apostacy.
7. HIGH PLACE,] as in Lev. 26. 30, &c.
CHEMOSH,] as in Nu. 21. 29, &c.
ABOMINATION,] as in De. 29. 17, &c.
HILL,] that is, the mount of the olives.
MOLECH,] as in Lev. 18. 21, &c.
8. STRANGE WOMEN,] as in v. 1.
9. SHEWETH HIMSELF ANGRY,] as in De. 1. 37; 4. 21; 9. 8, 20; 2 K. 17. 18.
TWICE,] as in 3. 5; 9. 2.
10. CHARGE,] as in 9. 5, 6, 7.
11. SAITH,] perhaps by Ahijah, as in v. 29.
WITH THEE,] not 'done of thee,' as in C.V.
REND,] as in 1 Sa. 15. 28; 28. 17.
12. SAKE,] as in 8. 7. 12, 13.
13. CHOSEN] for a habitation.
14. RAISETH UP,] during the king's lifetime; see 2 Sa. 7. 14.
ADVERSARY,] lit. 'a satan.'
HADAD,] the name of a former king of Edom, as in Ge. 35. 36; 1 Ch. 1. 46, &c.
15. WITH EDOM,] not 'in Edom,' as in C.V.
EVERY MALE] whom he could find, but many escaped; see 2 K. 8. 20—22.
16.CUT OFF] judicially, as the word implies as in De. 12. 29, &c.
17. YOUTH,] as in 1 Sa. 20. 35; 1 K. 3. 7 2 K. 2. 23; 5. 14; Isa. 11. 6.
18. PARAN,] as in Ge. 21. 21, &c.
COMMANDED,] lit. 'said.'

19. TAHPENES,] i.e. 'head of the age,' according to Gesenius.
MISTRESS,] as in 15. 13; 2 K. 10. 13; 2 Ch. 15. 16; Jer. 13. 18; 29. 2.
20. GENUBATH,] i.e. 'theft.'
WEANETH,] implying that from his birth till then he had been brought up in the palace.
SONS,] as one of their number.
21. LAIN,] as in 2. 10.
DEAD,] as in 2. 34.
LAND,] that of Edom, as in v. 14.
22. LACKING,] seeing he had been treated as one of the royal family.
23. RAISETH,] as in v. 14.
ADVERSARY,] lit. 'satan,' as in v. 14.
REZON,] i.e. a 'prince.'
ELIADAH,] i.e. 'God has known.'
HADADEZER,] as in 2 Sa. 8. 3.
ZOBAH,] as in 1 Sa. 14. 47, &c.
24. DAMASCUS,] the largest city of Aram.
25. CUTTETH OFF,] lit. 'maketh an end,' or 'is disgusted with' Israel.
ARAM] of Damascus, as in v. 24.
26. JEROBOAM,] i.e. 'he multiplies the people,' as in v. 28, 29, 31, 40; 12. 2, 3, 12, 15, 20, 25, 26, 32; 13. 1, &c.
NEBAT,] i.e. 'aspect.'
ZEREDA,] as in 2 Ch. 4. 17; perhaps the same as Zererah in Jud. 7. 22, and Zarathan in Jos. 3. 16; 1 K. 4. 14; 7. 46.
ZERUAH,] i.e. 'leprous.'
WIDOW WOMAN,] as in 2 Sa. 14. 5, &c.
27. MILLO,] as noted in 9. 24.
SHUT UP,] as in Ge. 2. 21; 7. 16; 19. 6, 10, &c.
BREACH,] as in Ge. 39. 29, &c.
28. MIGHTY IN VALOUR,] as in Jos. 1. 14, &c.
DOING BUSINESS,] or a 'doer of business,' as in 2 K. 12. 11, 14, 15; 22. 5, 9; 1 Ch. 22. 15, &c.
BURDEN,] as in Neh. 4. 17; Ps. 81. 6.
JOSEPH,] that is, of Ephraim and Manasseh; perhaps even the ten tribes are thus designated, which would partly account for his influence over them afterwards.
29. AHIJAH,] i.e. 'brother of Jah,' as in 12, 15; 14. 6, 18; 2 Ch. 10. 15.
SHILONITE,] an inhabitant of Shiloh, as in 14. 2, &c.
PROPHET,] as in 14. 2, 18.
COVERING HIMSELF,] as in Ge. 24. 65; 2 K. 19. 1, 2; Prov. 26. 26; Isa. 37. 42; 59. 6; Jon. 3. 8.
30. RENDETH,] as in 1 Sa. 15. 27, &c.
PIECES,] as in v. 31; 2 K. 2. 12; Prov. 23. 21.
31. TEN TRIBES,] that he might rule over them as God's servant.
32. ONE TRIBE,] besides the tribe of Judah, from which he had sprung.
33. ASHTEROTH..CHEMOSH..MILCOM,] as in v. 5—7.
34. PRINCE,] lit. a 'lifted up or honoured one.'
35. SON,] Rehoboam.
36. A LAMP,] as in 15. 4; 2 K. 8. 19; 2 Ch. 21. 7; 2 Sa. 22. 29.
ALL THE DAYS,] as in Ge. 43. 9, &c.
37. SOUL DESIRETH,] as in 2 Sa. 3. 21; De. 12. 20; 14. 26; 1 Sa. 2. 16; Job 23. 13; Prov. 21. 10; Isa. 26. 9; Mic. 7. 1.
38. SERVANT,] as in 2 Sa. 3. 18; 7. 5, 8, &c.
39. HUMBLE.] or 'afflict.'
40. SHISHAK,] as in 14. 25; 2 Ch. 12. 5;

Gesenius says, 'this seems to be Sesocchis, the first of the 22nd dynasty of Manetho.'
41. MATTERS,] lit. 'words.'
ON THE BOOK,] not 'in' it, as in C.V.; the eference is to the rolls of ancient times.
42. FORTY YEARS,] like David and Saul.
43. LIETH,] as in 2. 10, &c.
CITY OF DAVID,] that is, Zion, as in 2. 10.

XII. 1. SHECHEM,] a city of Ephraim, as in Ge. 33. 18, 19; 34. 2, 26; 35. 4; 37. 12, 14; Nu. 26. 31; Jos. 17. 2, &c.
2. FLED] for fear of Solomon.
3. CALL FOR HIM] to come and be their head and leader in their appeal to the king.
4. MADE HARD,] or 'sharp,' by his magnificence and splendour.
MAKE LIGHT,] by reducing the expenditure and taxes of labour and money.
HARD,] or 'sharp.'
HEAVY,] or 'weighty.'
6. CONSULTETH,] remembering perhaps Prov. 11. 14; 24. 6, &c.
ELDERS,] or official counsellors and rulers, as in Ge. 50. 7; 2 Sa. 12. 17, &c.
STANDING,] as ministering servants.
7. SERVANT,] in yielding to their request, and gratifying their wishes.
8. LADS,] lit. 'children,' as in Ge. 33. 13, 14, &c.
GROWN UP,] lit. 'become great.'
STANDING BEFORE HIM] as his attendants.
9. WE ANSWER,] courteously associating them with himself.
10. MY LITTLE,] as in 2 Ch. 10. 10.
THICKER,] as in 2 Ch. 10. 10; De. 32. 15.
LOINS,] as in 2 Ch. 10. 10; Ge. 37. 34; Ex. 12. 11; 28. 42.
11. CHASTISED,] as in Lev. 26. 18, 28; De. 8. 5, &c.
WHIPS,] as in v. 14; 2 Ch. 10. 11, 14; Job 5. 21; 9. 23; Prov. 26. 3; Isa. 10. 26; 28. 15, 18; Nah. 3. 2.
SCORPIONS,] as in De. 8. 15; 2 Ch. 10. 11, 14; Eze. 2. 6.
12. SPOKEN,] as in v. 5.
13. SHARPLY,] as in 2 Ch. 10. 13; Ge. 42. 7, 30, &c.
COUNSELLED HIM,] to speak kindly to the people.
15. REVOLUTION,] as in 2 Ch. 10. 15; lit 'the bringing round about.'
SPAKE,] in 11. 29—39.
16. SEND BACK WORD,] probably after return ing and mutual consultation.
PORTION..INHERITANCE,] as in Ge. 31. 14, &c.
TENTS,] as in 2 Sa. 20. 1; 2 Ch. 10. 16, &c.
SEE,] that is, behold thy house, what it has come; to, not 'see to it,' as in the C.V.
17. SONS OF ISRAEL,] that is, those belonging to the ten tribes.
18. ADORAM,] as in 4. 6; 5. 14.
TRIBUTE] of money and labour exacted from the people by government.
STRENGTHENED HIMSELF,] as in 2 Ch. 10. 18; 13. 7; Ruth 1. 18.
JERUSALEM,] his capital city, on the fidelity of whose inhabitants he trusted.
19. TRANSGRESSETH,] as in 8. 50, &c.
20. RETURNED,] from Egypt, as in v. 3.

HOUSE OF DAVID,] as the rightful possessor of regal powers.

21. 180,000 CHOICE,] as in 2 Ch. 11. 1.

22. OF GOD,] *lit.* 'of the (true) God,' hence in 2 Ch. 12. 15, he is called a 'prophet.'

SHEMAIAH,] i.e. 'heard of Jah.'

A MAN OF GOD,] as in De. 33. 1.

23. KING OF JUDAH,] thus recognizing and yet limiting his title and power.

REST OF THE PEOPLE] of Israel, who adhered to the old dynasty.

24. GO UP] to the mountains of Israel.

FROM ME,] as in v. 15 above.

25. SHECHEM,] probably strengthening and enlarging it. See Jud. 9. 45.

PENUEL,] destroyed by Gideon, as in Jud. 8. 17.

26. TURN BACK,] if not prevented.

27. GO UP,] to Mount Zion and Moriah.

JERUSALEM,] three times a year, as the law directed.

SLAIN ME,] to ingratiate themselves with their late master, as in 1 Sa. 29. 4.

28. TAKETH COUNSEL,] as Rehoboam had done in v. 6 above.

TWO CALVES OF GOLD,] in imitation of Aaron, and having seen such worship in Egypt during his sojourn there.

ENOUGH TO YOU,] not 'too much for you,' as in C.V.

THY GODS,] as in Ex. 32. 4, 8.

29. BETH-EL,] in the southern part of the land, on the borders of Ephraim and Benjamin; see Ge. 28. 19, &c.

DAN,] in the northern part of the land of Israel; see Jud. 18. 29, &c.

30. SIN,] *or* a 'thing causing sin.'

GO BEFORE,] to do service to it.

UNTO DAN,] at the extreme north.

31. THE HOUSE OF HIGH PLACES,] as in 13. 32, for the residence of the priests.

EXTREMITIES,] of the various classes of society, whether high or low.

LEVI,] to whom God, in the law, had committed the charge of all divine ordinances.

32. FESTIVAL,] as in Ex. 10. 9, &c.

EIGHTH MONTH,] called Marchesvan or Bul, part of October and November.

JUDAH,] that of 'tabernacles *or* booths.'

HE OFFERETH,] by his own hands, as in 13. 4.

APPOINTED,] *lit.* 'caused to stand.'

33. HEART,] to prevent Israel from going up to Jerusalem.

MAKETH,] not 'ordaineth,' as in C.V.

TO MAKE PERFUME,] when the following incident took place.

XIII. 1. A MAN OF GOD,] as in 12. 22, &c.

WORD OF JEHOVAH,] directing him.

BETH-EL,] where Jeroboam had placed a golden calf, and was now present.

2. A SON,] not 'a child,' as in C.V.

JOSIAH,] as in 2 Ch. 23. 15, 16, &c.

SACRIFICED,] that is, put on the altar and burnt them as if they were a sacrifice.

BONES OF MAN,] abominable in the sight of God and men.

3. SIGN,] *or* 'wonder,' as in Ex. 4. 21; 7. 3, 9; 11. 9, 10, &c.

RENT,] as in v. 5; Ex. 28. 32; 39. 23; 1 Sa. 15. 27.

POURED FORTH,] as in Lev. 14. 41, &c.

4. CATCH HIM,] as in 18. 40; 20. 18; 2 K. 10. 14; Ps. 71. 11, &c.

DRIED UP,] as in 17. 7; Ps. 22. 15; Eze. 37. 11; Zec. 11. 17, &c.

5. RENT,] as in v. 3 above.

6. APPEASE,] as in Mal. 1. 9, &c.

I PRAY THEE,] not 'now,' as in C.V.

PRAY FOR ME,] as in Nu. 21. 7; 1 Sa. 12. 19; Jer. 29. 7; 37. 3; 42. 2, 20, &c.

7. REFRESH THYSELF,] *lit.* 'support thyself,' as in Ge. 18. 5; Jud. 19. 5, 8; Ps. 119. 117, &c.

GIFT,] as in Prov. 25. 14; Ecc. 3. 13; 5. 19; Eze. 46. 5, 11.

8. HALF OF THINE HOUSE,] as in Est. 5. 3, 6; 7. 2, &c.

9. HE COMMANDED,] not 'it was charged,' as in C.V.

10. NOT TURNED BACK,] according to the command in v. 9.

11. PROPHET,] that is, preacher or declarer of the will of God.

12. WHERE IS THIS,] as in 1 Sa. 9. 18, &c.

13. SADDLE,] as in v. 27; Ge. 22. 3, &c.

14. THE OAK,] as in Ge. 35. 4; Jud. 6. 11, 19; 1 Sa. 17. 2, 19; 21. 9; 2 Sa. 18. 9, 10, 14; 1 Ch. 10. 12; Isa. 1. 30; 6. 13; Eze. 6. 13; Hos. 4. 13.

15. EAT BREAD,] as in 21. 7, &c.

16. NOT ABLE,] being prohibited by God, as in v. 8, 9.

17. A WORD IS,] not 'it was said,' as in C.V.

18. PROPHET,] as in v. 11.

LIED,] as in Ge. 18. 15; Lev. 6. 2, 3; 19. 11, &c.

20. PROPHET,] as in v. 11, 18.

21. CALLETH,] not 'cried,' as in C.V.

PROVOKED,] as in Nu. 20. 24, &c.

22. CARCASE,] as in Lev. 5. 2; 7. 24; 11. 8, 11, 24, 25, 27, 28, 35, 36, 37, 38, 39, 40, &c.

BURYING-PLACE,] as in Jud. 8. 32; 16. 31; 2 Sa. 2. 32; 17. 23; 19. 37; 21. 14, &c.

23. THE ASS,] of the lying prophet, for the other does not appear to have had any.

24. FINDETH,] not 'met,' as in C.V.

25. CITY,] even Beth-El, as in v. 11.

26. PROVOKED,] as in v. 21.

DESTROYETH,] *lit.* 'breaketh.'

27. THE ASS,] another that he appears to have had.

28. CAST,] as in 2 Sa. 20. 21; 1 K. 13. 24, 25, 28; Jer. 14. 16; 36. 30.

DESTROYED,] *lit.* 'broken,' as in v. 26.

29. MOURN,] according to the usual custom.

30. MY BROTHER,] as in Jer. 22. 18, &c.

31. MY BONES,] that they might not be disturbed when the prediction came to pass.

32. HOUSES OF THE HIGH PLACES,] as in 12. 13.

CITIES OF SAMARIA,] round about on every side.

33. EXTREMITIES,] as in 12. 31.

CONSECRATETH,] *lit.* 'filleth.'

34. IN THIS THING IS THE SIN,] that is, the special cause of offence to God.

CUT IT OFF,] *lit.* 'hide it,' as in Ex. 28. 23; 2 Ch. 32. 21; Job 20. 12; Ps. 83. 4; Zec. 11. 8.

XIV. 1. ABIJAH,] i.e. 'my father is Jah.'
SICK,] as in Ge. 48. 1, &c.
2. CHANGE,] as in 1 Sa. 21. 13.
SHILOH,] about 24 miles from Tirzah,
where Jeroboam now lived, as in v. 17; see
11. 29.
SPAKE,] as in 11. 31.
3. IN THY HAND,] as in Ge. 24. 10, &c.; it
was customary (and still is) for visitors to
take a small present with them.
LOAVES,] lit. 'bread.'
CRUMBS,] as in Jos. 9. 5, 12.
BOTTLE,] as in Jer. 19. 1, 10.
YOUTH,] as in Ge. 14. 24; 18. 7, &c.
4. STOOD,] as in 1 Sa. 4. 15.
5. SAITH.] Compare 1 Sa. 9. 15, 16.
SEEK A WORD,] not 'ask a thing.'
SICK,] as in v. 1.
THUS AND THUS,] as in Jud. 18. 4; 2 Sa. 11. 25.
MAKING HERSELF STRANGE,] as in v. 6;
Ge. 42. 7; Prov. 20. 11.
6. SOUND OF HER FEET,] as in 2 K. 6. 32.
OPENING] of the house of the prophet.
A SHARP THING,] as in 12. 4, 13, &c.
7. MADE THEE HIGH,] when he had been
only a poor widow's son, as in 16.2; compare
2 Sa. 12. 7, 8.
APPOINT,] lit. 'give.'
LEADER,] as in 1 Sa. 9. 16; 10. 1; 13. 14;
25. 30; 2 Sa. 5. 2, &c.
8. REND,] at least ten parts of the kingdom;
see 11. 31.
MY SERVANT,] God has pleasure in acknowledging those who fear him.
ALL HIS HEART,] as in 11. 33. 38; 15. 5.
9. BEFORE THEE,] among the judges and
leaders in Israel.
MOLTEN IMAGES,] as in 12. 28; 2 Ch. 11. 15.
PROVOKE ME TO ANGER,] as in De. 4. 25;
9. 18; 31. 29; 1 K. 14. 9, &c.
CAST ME,] as in Ex. 23. 35; Neh. 9. 26; Ps.
50. 17.
10. EVIL,] that is, misfortune and calamity;
see 15. 29.
CUT OFF,] violently and because of sin.
SITTING ON THE WALL,] as in 1 Sa. 25. 22,
34; 1 K. 16. 11; 21. 21; 2 K. 9. 8.
SHUT UP..LEFT,] as in De. 32. 36, &c.
PUT AWAY,] lit. 'burned,' as in De. 13.
6, &c.
POSTERITY, as in 16. 3; 21. 21, &c.
DUNG,] as in Job 20. 7; Eze. 4. 12, 15;
Zeph. 1. 17.
11. DOGS EAT,] as in Ex. 22. 31; 1 K. 16. 4;
21. 24; 2 K. 9. 10; Jer. 15. 3.
FOWLS EAT,] as in Ge. 40. 19; De. 28. 26;
1 Sa. 17. 44, 46; 2 Sa. 21. 10; 1 K. 16. 4; 21.
24; Ps. 79. 2; Jer. 7. 33; 16. 4; 19. 7; 34. 20;
Eze. 29. 5.
12. HOUSE] in Tirzah, as in v. 17.
LAD,] not child,' as in C. V.
13. MOURNED,] shewing their affection
and respect.
A GRAVE,] the rest being devoured or
left unburied.
FOUND,] by the searching eye of God; see
2 Ch. 12. 12; 19. 3.
14. OUTTETH OFF,] by violence for their
sin in judicial vengeance; see 15. 27—29.
EVEN NOW,] that is, very shortly, it must
begin.

15. SMITTEN,] by the sword of their enemies on every side.
REED,] which grows by the river side.
MOVED] to and fro by the force of the tide.
PLUCKED UP,] as a corrupt and degenerate
plant, worthless and noxious; see 2 K. 15. 29;
17. 6; Ps. 52. 5.
GOOD GROUND,] flowing with milk and
honey; see Jos. 23. 15, 16.
SCATTERED] them, as chaff is scattered by
the wind.
RIVER,] the Euphrates, or Gozan, as in
2 K. 17. 6; 15. 29.
SHRINES,] for covering their idols on
every high hill and under every green-tree;
Ex. 34. 13; De. 12. 3, 4.
16. GIVETH UP,] as apostate and rebellious.
SINNED..TO SIN,] ruining himself and
others; see 12. 30; 13. 34; 15. 30, 34; 16. 2.
17. TIRZAH,] a city of Manasseh, as in
Jos. 12. 24; 1 K. 16. 6, 8, 15, 23; Song 6. 4.
THRESHOLD,] as in Jud. 19. 27; 2 K. 12. 9;
24. 4, &c.
18. PROPHET,] as in v. 13.
MATTERS,] not 'acts,' as in C.V.
FOUGHT,] with Rehoboam in v. 30, and
with Abijam in 2 Ch. 13. 1—20·
REIGNED,] whether he moderated the
heavy burdens of Solomon, because of
which the people revolted is not said.
ON,] not 'in,' the book of the
CHRONICLES,] lit. 'words or matters of
the days.'
20. 22 YEARS,] over the ten tribes.
LIETH,] as in 21. 43, &c.
NADAB,] i.e. 'liberal, impulsive.'
21. IN JUDAH,] over the two tribes which
adhered to him.
41 YEARS,] being born one year before
Solomon ascended the throne; 2 Ch. 22. 13.
CHOSE,] as in 11. 36.
MOTHER,] who appears to have been
Solomon's first wife, the second being
Pharaoh's daughter.
NAAMAH,] i.e. 'pleasantness;' see v. 31.
AMMONITESS,] perhaps a captive in war of
that race.
22. THE EVIL THING,] that is, idolatry,
2 Ch. 12. 1.
ZEALOUS] for his own glory, and their
own good.
23. HIGH PLACES,] which implied their
rejection of the temple as God's appointed
place of sacrifice.
STANDING-PILLARS,] for paying adoration
to, as figures of God.
SHRINES,] for covering their idols.
HIGH HEIGHT..GREEN TREE,] the usual
places for idolatrous worship.
24. WHOREMONGER,] as in De. 23. 17; 1 K.
14. 24; 15. 12; 22. 46; 2 K. 23. 7; Job 36. 14.
ABOMINATIONS,] offensive to God and man,
for doing which God had already
DISPOSSESSED,] by violence and blood
25. FIFTH YEAR,] that is, B.C. 971.
COME UP,] from Egypt to Canaan.
SHISHAK,] as in 11. 40; 2 Ch. 12. 2.
26. TAKETH] to himself for spoil.
TREASURES,] as in 7. 51.
MADE,] as in 10. 16, 17.
27. BRASS,] as in 2 Ch. 12. 10.

RUNNERS,] as in 1 Sa. 22. 17; 2 Sa. 15. 1,&c.
29. JUDAH,] as distinct from Israel, in v. 19.
30. WAR,] *lit.* 'battle.'
31. LIETH,] as in v. 20.
CITY OF DAVID,] that is, Zion, as in 2. 10; 11. 43.
ABIJAM,] as in 15. 1; 7. 8; in 2 Ch. 13. 1, &c., it is Abijah.

XV. 1. 18TH YEAR,] that is, B.C. 958.
JUDAH] and Benjamin, which adhered to the house of David.
2. MAACHAH,] i.e. 'oppression,' as in 10. 13; (in 13. 2, Michaiah); 2 Ch. 11. 20.
ABISHALOM,] i.e. 'father of peace;' in 2 Ch. 11. 20, 21, it is Absalom.
3. SINS] of idolatry, in the matter of the two calves of gold, &c.
PERFECT,] as in 11. 4.
FATHER,] strictly, his father's grandfather.
4. SAKE,] who followed the Lord with his whole heart.
LAMP,] as in 11. 36.
ESTABLISH] it as a settled place of abode for the Most High.
5. RIGHT,] as in 14. 8.
TURNED NOT ASIDE,] willingly nor habitually.
MATTER,] as in 2 Sa. 11. 4, 15; 12. 9.
6. WAR,] *lit.* 'battle,' as in 14. 30.
8. CITY OF DAVID,] that is, Zion.
ASA,] i.e. 'healer.'
9. 20TH YEAR,] that is, B.C. 955.
10. MAACHAH,] as in v. 2, 13.
11. FATHER,] as in v. 3.
12. REMOVETH,] *lit.* 'causeth to pass over or away.'
WHOREMONGERS,] as in 14. 24.
IDOLS,] as in Lev. 26. 30, &c.
FATHERS,] Abijah, Rehoboam, and Solomon.
13. MISTRESS,] as in 11. 19; 2 K. 10. 13; 2 Ch. 15. 16; Jer. 13. 18; 29. 2.
HORRIBLE THING,] as in 2 Ch. 15. 16.
SHRINE,] as in Ex. 24. 13, &c.
CUTTETH DOWN,] *or* 'cutteth off.'
BURNETH,] as in Ge. 11. 3, &c.
KIDRON,] as in 1 K. 2. 37, &c.
14. HIGH PLACES,] as in 22. 43; 2 Ch. 15. 17, 18.
PERFECT,] as in v. 3.
15. VESSELS,] out of the spoils of war, taken from the Cushites, as in 2 Ch. 14. 13, 14.
16. WAR,] *lit.* 'battle.'
BAASHA,] i.e. 'evil,' as in 2 Ch. 16. 1; Jer. 41. 9, &c.
17. RAMAH,] a city of Benjamin, as in Jos. 18. 25.
PERMIT,] *lit.* 'give.'
18. LEFT] by Shishak, as in 14. 26.
BEN-HADAD,] i.e. 'son of shouting,' as in 2 Ch. 16. 2.
TABRIMON,] i.e. 'good is the pomegranate,' *or* 'good is Rimmon,' the Syrian deity.
HEZION,] i.e 'vision;' perhaps the same as Rezon in 11. 25.
DAMASCUS,] as in 11. 24.
19. REWARD,] as in Ex. 23. 8; De. 10. 17, &c.
BREAK,] as in 2 Ch. 16. 3, &c.
20. IJON,] i.e. 'ruin,' as in 2 Ch. 16. 4.

DAN,] as in Jos. 19. 47; Jud. 18. 29, &c.
ABEL-BETH-MAACHAH,] as in 2 Sa. 20. 14, 15; 2 K. 15. 29; compare 2 Ch. 16. 4; 2 Sa. 20. 18.
CHINNEROTH,] as in Nu. 34. 11; De. 3. 17; Jos. 11. 2.
NAPHTALI,] of which the places above noted were parts.
21. TIRZAH.] See 14. 17; his capital city.
22. SUMMONED,] *lit.* 'caused to hear.'
EXEMPT,] *lit.* 'innocent, free.'
BUILT,] but not finished, because of the invasion of the Syrians.
GEBA,] as in Jos. 18. 24; 21. 17.
MIZPAH,] as in Jos. 18. 26.
23. MIGHT,] as in 16. 5, 27; 22. 45, &c.
CITIES,] such as Geba, Mizpah, &c.
FEET,] two years before his death; see 2 Ch. 16. 12, 13.
24. JEHOSHAPHAT,] i.e. 'Jehovah has judged,' as in 2 Ch. 17. 1.
25. NADAB,] i.e. 'liberal.'
TWO YEARS,] or nearly so; see v. 28.
26. THE EVIL THING,] that is, idolatry.
FATHER] Jeroboam, who first set up idols in Israel.
27. CONSPIRE,] as in 1 Sa. 22. 8, 13; 1 K. 16. 9, 16, 20.
BAASHA,] as in v. 16 above.
AHIJAH,] i.e. 'brother of Jah.'
GIBBETHON,] a city of Dan, as in Jos. 19. 44; 21. 23, &c.
29. THE WHOLE HOUSE,] that he might have no rival.
ANY BREATHING,] as in De. 20. 16; Jos. 10. 40; 11. 11, &c.
SHILONITE,] as in 14. 10, 14.
30. SINNED..SIN,] as in 14. 9, 16.
31. MATTERS,] as in v. 7. 23, &c.
32. WAR,] *or* 'battle,' as in v. 6. 16, &c.
33. 3D YEAR,] as in v. 28.
TIRZAH,] his capital city, as in 14. 17.
34. THE EVIL THING,] that is, idolatry.

XVI. 1. A WORD OF JEHOVAH,] as in 13. 1, 20, &c.
JEHU,] i.e. 'he is;' he reproved Asa in 2 Ch. 16. 7; and Jehoshaphat in 2 Ch. 19. 2; and wrote a history, as in 2 Ch. 20. 34.
2. DUST,] as in 1 Sa. 2. 8; Job 4. 19; 8. 19, &c.
APPOINT,] *lit.* 'give.'
LEADER,] as in 1 Sa. 6. 19, &c.
WAY,] as in 15. 34.
3. PUTTING AWAY,] *lit.* 'burning away,' as in 14. 10, &c.
4. DOGS..FOWLS,] as in 14. 11, &c.
5. MATTERS,] as in 15. 31, &c.
6. LIETH,] being one of the few kings of Israel who died a natural death.
TIRZAH,] as in 14. 17; 15. 21.
ELAH,] i.e. 'a terebinth tree.'
7. THE PROPHET,] as in v. 12, &c.
8. 26TH YEAR,] B.C. 930.
9. CONSPIRE,] as in 15. 27, &c.
ZIMRI,] i.e. 'my song.'
DRUNKARD,] *or* 'merry,' as in Ge. 9. 21; 43. 34, &c.
ARZA,] i.e. 'earth.'
10. STEAD,] but only for seven days; see v. 15.
11. SITTING,] as in 1 Sa. 25. 22, &c.

REDEEMERS,] as in Ge. 48. 16; Ex. 6. 6; 15. 3; Lev. 25. 25, &c.
12. DESTROYETH,] as in Ge. 34. 30, &c.
PROPHET,] as in v. 1, 7.
13. VANITITES,] as in De. 32. 21, &c.
14. MATTERS,] as in v. 5.
15. 27TH YEAR,] that is, B.C. 929.
TIRZAH,] as in v. 6 above.
GIBBETHON,] as in 15. 27.
16. ENCAMPING,] in the field round the city, that is, the soldiers.
CONSPIRED..SMITTEN,] as in v. 9, 10.
OMRI,] i.e. 'my sheaf.'
17. TIRZAH,] as in v. 6 above.
18. HIGH-PLACE,] as in 2 K. 15. 25; 2 Ch. 36. 19; Ps. 48. 3, 13; 122. 7; Prov. 18. 19; Isa. 23. 13; 25. 2; 32. 14; 34. 13; Jer. 6. 5; 9. 21; 17. 27; 30. 18; 49. 27; La. 2. 5, 7; Hos. 8. 14; Amos 1. 4, 7, 10, 12, 14; 2. 2, 5; 3. 9, 10, 11; 6. 5; Mic. 5. 5.
19 TO SIN,] as in 12. 28.
20. MATTERS,] as in v. 5 above.
21. TIBNI,] i.e. 'my structure.'
GINATH,] i.e. 'a garden,' perhaps.
22. DIETH,] whether by violence or by natural causes is not said.
23. 31ST YEAR,] B.C. 925.
TIRZAH,] the first capital of the ten tribes, and the remaining six years in Samaria.
24. SAMARIA,] *Heb.* 'Shomeron,' from SHEMER,] i.e. 'dregs.'
TWO TALENTS,] about £750 sterling.
25. THE EVIL THING,] as in 13. 32, &c.
VANITIES,] as in v. 13 above.
27. GOT,] *lit.* 'made.'
28. LIETH,] as in v. 6.
AHAB,] i.e. 'father's brother.'
29. 38TH YEAR] B.C. 918.
22 YEARS,] like Jeroboam, in 14. 20.
30. ABOVE ALL,] as in v. 25.
31. HATH IT BEEN,] an interrogation, not an affirmation, as in C.V.
JEZEBEL,] i.e. 'without habitation.'
ETHBAAL,] i.e. 'with Baal.'
ZIDONIANS,] under which name the Tyrians were included, whose god BAAL,] he publicly worshipped in Samaria.
32. THE BAAL,] as in 2 K. 10. 21, 26, 27.
33. THE SHRINE,] as in Ex. 34. 13, &c.
ADDETH TO DO,] as in De. 13. 11; 19. 20; Jud. 3. 12, &c.
ABOVE ALL,] as in v. 25, 30.
34. HIEL,] i.e. 'God liveth.'
BETH-ELITE.] The original form of the word is not found elsewhere.
JERICHO,] which had been destroyed by Joshua, as in Jos. 6. 26.
ABIRAM,] i.e. 'my father is high.'
SEGUB,] i.e. 'set on high.'
SPAKE,] as in Jos. 6. 26.

XVII. 1. ELIJAH,] i.e. 'my God is He.'
TISHBITE,] as in 21. 17; from Tishbe a city of Naphtali in Galilee.
GILEAD,] whether he had gone to sojourn.
LIVETH,] as in 2 K. 3. 14, &c.
STOOD,] as a ministering servant.
DEW..RAIN.] See James 5. 17.
3. HIDDEN] from Ahab and Jezebel, as in 18. 10, &c.
CHERITH,] i.e. 'a cutting off,' as in v. 5

4. RAVENS,] *or* 'Arabs,' *or* 'mixed people,' *or* 'traders,' *or* 'Orbim,' the inhabitants of Oreb, Jud. 7. 25.
6. ARE BRINGING,] day by day systematically.
7. DAYS,] as in Ge. 4. 3; probably of a week.
9. ZAREPHATH,] i.e. 'a refining place;' not as in Obad, 20.
ZIDON,] whence Jezebel herself had come, as in 16. 31.
WIDOW WOMAN,] as in 2 Sa. 14. 5, &c.
SUSTAIN,] as in Ge. 45. 11, &c.
10. STICKS,] as in Nu. 15. 32. 33, &c.
11. MORSEL,] as in Ge. 18. 5, &c.
12. LIVETH,] as in Jud. 8. 19, &c.
CAKE.] The original word is only found elsewhere in Ps. 35. 16.
FULNESS OF THE HAND,] as in Ex. 9. 8; Lev. 2. 2, &c.
MEAL,] as in Ge. 18. 6, &c.
PITCHER,] as in v. 14, 16; 18. 33; Ge. 24. 14, 15, 16, 17, 18, 20, 43, 45, 46; Jud. 7. 16, 19, 20; Ecc. 12. 6.
OIL,] as in Ge. 28. 18, &c.
DISH,] as in v. 14, 16; 19. 6; 1 Sa. 26. 11, 12, 16.
TWO STICKS,] that is, a few.
PREPARED,] *lit.* 'made.'
13. FEAR NOT] to do according to my request.
THY WORD,] that is, make food for thyself and son.
BROUGHT FORTH,] out of the house to where he was then.
14. CONSUMED,] *or* 'ended.'
LACKING,] as in Ge. 8. 3; 18. 28, &c.
SHOWER,] as in Ge. 7. 12; 8. 2, &c.
15. HOUSEHOLD,] now, perhaps, having servants.
17. MISTRESS,] *lit.* 'lady,' as in 1 Sa. 28. 7; Nah. 3. 4.
SEVERE,] *or* 'strong.'
BREATH,] as in Ge. 2. 7, &c.
18. TO ME, AND TO THEE] in common, that thou hast brought this evil upon me.
MAN OF GOD,] as in 12. 22, &c.
INIQUITY,] as in Nu. 5. 15; Eze. 21. 24; 29. 16.
19. THE UPPER CHAMBER,] as in Jud. 3. 20, &c.
20. CALLETH,] not 'crieth,' as in the C. V.
21. STRETCHETH HIMSELF,] *lit.* 'measureth himself;' compare 2 K. 4. 34, 35.
22. MIDST,] as in Ge. 18. 12, 24, &c.
LIVETH] as before, but for how long a time is not noted.
23. HIS MOTHER.] See Heb. 11. 35.
24. NOW THIS,] not 'now by this,' as in C.V.
MAN OF GOD,] as in v. 18.
TRUTH,] regarding the famine and her household.

XVIII. 1. THIRD YEAR] of the drought.
APPEAR,] *lit.* 'be seen.'
GIVE,] not 'send,' as in C.V.
GROUND,] not 'earth,' as in C.V.
2. APPEAR,] *lit.* 'be seen.'
FAMINE,] by reason of the drought so long continued.
SEVERE,] *or* 'hard.'

3. OBADIAH,] i.e. 'servant of Jah.'
FEARING,] that is, reverencing Jehovah,
in the midst of an idolatrous court.

4. JEZEBEL,] the wife of Ahab, as in 16.
31, &c.

CUTTING OFF,] by a violent death.

PROPHETS] who proclaimed the revealed
will of God to the people.

HIDDETH,] as in Jos. 6. 17, &c.

CARE,] as in 1 Sa. 22. 1; 24. 3, &c.

BREAD AND WATER,] the simplest food
possible, yet sufficient to preserve life.

5. BROOKS,] to find water and pasturage.

HAY,] as in Nu. 11. 5; 2 K. 19. 26; Job 8.
12; 40. 15, &c.

MULE,] as in 2 Sa. 13. 29; 18. 9; 1 K. 10. 25;
2 K. 5. 17; 1 Ch. 12. 40; 2 Ch. 9. 24; Ezra 2.
66; Neh. 7. 68; Ps. 32. 9; Isa. 66. 20; Eze. 17.
14; Zec. 14. 15.

OUT NOT OFF,] by failing to provide pasturage for them.

6. APPORTION,] as in Ge. 49. 27, &c.

7. TO MEET HIM,] is standing, waiting for
him.

DISCERNETH,] as in 20. 41, &c.

9. SINNED] against God or man.

10. LIVETH !] the most solemn oath of an
Israelite.

IF THERE IS.] A common Hebrew form of
expressing a negative more strongly.

CAUSED TO SWEAR,] as in 2. 42.

FIND] by a diligent searching.

12. SPIRIT OF JEHOVAH,] as in 2 K. 2. 16;
Eze. 3. 12, 14; Mat. 4. 1; Acts 8. 34.

FEARING,] as in v. 3 above.

13. BREAD AND WATER,] as in v. 4 above.

14. SLAIN ME,] because I did not at once
apprehend thee.

15. JEHOVAH OF HOSTS,] as in 2 K. 3.
14, &c.

STOOD,] as in 17. 1, &c.

17. TROUBLER,] as in Jud. 11. 35, &c.

18. BAALIM,] as in 16. 31, 32, &c.

19. CARMEL] in Issachar, Jos. 19. 26, &c.
450..400,] who were doubtless scattered
over all Israel.

TABLE,] or supported at her expense.

20. GATHERETH] the one class of prophets,
but not the other.

21. COMETH NIGH,] as in Ge. 18. 23, &c.

LEAPING,] or 'passing over,' as in v. 26;
Ex. 12. 13, 23, 27, Isa. 31. 5.

THE TWO BRANCHES,] as in Eze. 31. 6, 8;
like birds unable to settle anywhere.

GOD,] lit. 'the God.'

FOLLOW HIM] unreservedly as the only
being worthy of adoration.

IF BAAL] be God, he only is entitled to
worship.

NOT A WORD,] unable to decide, fearing the
wrath of Jezebel, and the continued indignation of God.

22. BY MYSELF,] without co-operation from
others.

450 MEN,] as in v. 19.

23. TWO BULLOCKS,] to offer sacrifice to
their respective objects of worship.

CUT IT IN PIECES,] as was commonly done
before placing on the altar.

WOOD,] which was first of all laid on the
altar.

NO FIRE,] that the sacrifice might be manifestly seen to be consumed by divine inter-
position.

24. CALLED IN,] not ' on,' as in C.V.

FIRE,] consuming the sacrifice offered to
him.

THE GOD,] that is, the only true one.

25. FIRST,] the sacrifice to your god—even
Baal.

THE MULTITUDE,] being 450 in number.

26. PREPARE,] lit. 'make, do.'

NOON,] as in v. 27, 29.

ANSWER,] not 'hear,' as in C.V.

LEAP,] as in v. 21.

27. PLAYETH ON THEM,] as in Ge. 31. 7;
Jud. 16. 10, 13, 15; Job 13. 9; Jer. 9. 4.

A GOD,] at least in your estimation.

MEDITATING,] as in 1 Sa. 1. 16; 2 K. 9 11,
Job 7. 13; 9. 27; 10. 1; 21. 4; 23. 2; Ps. 55. 2;
64. 1; 102. 1; 104. 34; 142. 3; Ps. 23. 29.

PURSUING.] This original word is not
found elsewhere.

JOURNEY,] to some other place or worshipper.

ASLEEP] from fatigue, as the heathen
believed their gods often to be.

28. CUT THEMSELVES,] as in De. 14. 1; Jer.
5. 7; 16. 6; 47. 5; Mic. 5. 1; Jer. 41. 5.

ORDINANCE,] lit. 'judgment.'

SWORDS,] as in 19. 1, 10, 14, 17.

SPEARS,] as in Nu. 25. 7; Jud. 5. 8, &c.

FLOWING OF BLOOD,] as in 1 Sa. 25. 31;
Prov. 1. 16; Isa. 59. 7; Jer. 6. 11; 22. 17; Eze
9. 8; 17. 17; 20. 8, 13, 21, &c.

29. NOON,] as in v. 26.

FEIGN THEMSELVES PROPHETS,] as in 22.10.

PRESENT] in the temple of the Lord day
by day.

NONE ATTENDING,] or any indication of
an answer to their prayers.

30. REPAIRETH,] lit. 'healeth.'

BROKEN DOWN] the ruins of some one that
had been injured in some way.

31. WAS,] as in Ge. 32. 28; 35. 10, &c.

32. AN ALTAR,] along side of the previous
one, probably so as to form one altar.

TRENCH,] as in v. 35, 38; 2 K. 18. 17; 20.
20; Job 38. 25; Isa. 7. 3; 36. 2, &c.

AS THE SPACE,] lit. 'as the house.'

MEASURES,] as in Ge. 16. 3; 1 Sa. 25. 18;
2 K. 7. 1, 16, 18.

CUTTETH IN PIECES,] as in v. 23.

PITCHERS,] as in 17. 12, 14, 16.

34. A SECOND TIME,] lit. 'repeat it.'

A THIRD TIME.] lit. 'third it.'

35. WATER,] so that the possibility of the
sacrifice being consumed from natural fire
was almost impossible.

36. PRESENT,] as in v. 29.

ISRAEL,] as in Ex. 3. 6, &c.

SERVANT,] that henceforth the people
might listen to him.

THOSE THINGS,] restraining the rain, &c.

37. ANSWER ME,] not 'hear me,' as in C.V.

BACKWARD,] from their idols unto the
true God.

38. FALLETH,] as in Job 1. 16; compare
Lev. 9. 24, &c.

LICKED UP,] as in Nu. 22. 4; Ps. 72. 9; Isa.
49. 23; Mic. 7. 17.

39. FALL,] confounded and terrified.

R

THE GOD,] that is, the only true and living
one.
40. CATCH,] as in 13. 4, &c.
ESCAPE] the punishment of the law
against idolatry.
KISHON,] as in Jud. 4. 7; 5. 21, &c.
SLAUGHTER,] as in Ge. 22. 10; 37. 31; Ex.
12. 6, 21, &c.
41. GO UP,] from the brook of Kishon to
the sides of Carmel.
SHOWER] of rain that was about to come.
42. CARMEL,] near the altar perhaps,
that he had built.
STRETCHETH HIMSELF,] as in 2 K. 4. 34, 35.
43. I PRAY THEE,] not 'now,' as in C.V.
LOOK ATTENTIVELY,] as in Ge. 15. 5.
SEA,] the Mediterranean.
SEVEN TIMES.] This is rather the language
of the historian than of the prophet.
44. A LITTLE THICKNESS,] as in Ex. 19. 9, &c.
BIND,] as in 2 K. 9. 21; Ps. 118. 27; Jer. 46. 4.
GO DOWN,] from the sides of Carmel to
Jezreel.
SHOWER,] as in v. 41.
RESTRAIN,] by reason of its abundance.
45. BLACK.] See Jer. 4. 28.
THICK CLOUDS,] as in Jud. 5. 4, &c.
JEZREEL,] reckoned as 16 miles from
Carmel.
46. HAND,] as in Ex. 9. 3; 16. 3; Nu. 11.
23; De. 2. 15; Jos. 4. 24; 22. 31; Jud. 2. 15;
Ruth 1. 13; 5. 6, 9; 7. 13; 12. 15; 2 Sa. 24. 14;
2 K. 3. 15; 2 Ch. 29. 25, &c.
LOINS,] as in 2 K. 4. 29; 9. 1, &c.
RUNNETH,] as a servant of the king, an-
nouncing his approach.

XIX. 1. THE PROPHETS] of Baal, 450 in
number.
2. THE GODS,] Baal, Ashtaroth, &c.
3. FEARETH.] So the Sept. Vulg. and
Syriac Versions read the original.
FOR HIS LIFE.] Sept. reads, 'according to
his soul or desire.'
BEER-SHEBA,] 84 miles from Jezreel, beyond the rule of Ahab.
4. WILDERNESS] of Paran.
RETEM-TREE,] as in v. 5; Job 30. 4; Ps.
120. 4.
DESIRETH HIS SOUL,] as in Jon. 4. 3; compare Nu. 11. 15.
TAKE MY SOUL,] as in Jon. 4. 3.
5. RISE, EAT,] as in v. 7; 21. 7, &c.
6. BOLSTER,] as in Ge. 28. 11, 18; 1 Sa. 19.
13, 16; 26. 7, 11, 16.
CAKE,] as in Ge. 18. 6; Ex. 12. 39; Nu. 11.
8; 1 K. 17. 13; 19. 6; Eze. 4. 12; Hos. 7. 8.
BURNING STONES,] as in Isa. 6. 6.
DISH,] as in 1 Sa. 26. 11, 12; 1 K. 17. 12,
14, 16.
7. WAY] to Horeb, as in v. 8.
8. FORTY DAYS AND FORTY NIGHTS,] as in
Ex. 34. 28; De. 9. 9, 18; Mat. 4. 2.
HOREB.] See Ex. 3. 1, &c.
9. THE CAVE,] as in Ge. 19. 30, &c.
LODGETH,] how long is not said, perhaps
only a single night.
WHAT TO THEE,] not 'what dost thou?'
but 'what hast thou.'
10. ZEALOUS,] as in v. 14; Nu. 25. 11, 13·
2 Sa. 21. 2.

THROWN DOWN,] as in 18. 30.
SLAIN,] as in 18. 4.
BY MYSELF,] as in 18. 22.
11. PASSING BY,] before the mouth of the
cave.
SHIVERING,] as in Ex. 9. 25, &c.
SHAKING,] as in v. 12; Job 39. 34; 41. 29;
Isa. 9. 5; 29. 6; Jer. 10. 22; 47. 3; Eze. 3. 12,
13; 12. 18; 37. 7; 38. 19; Amos 1. 1; Neh. 3.
2; Zec. 14. 5.
12. FIRE,] as in Ex. 3. 2; 13. 21, 22; 14. 24;
19. 18, &c.
STILL,] as in Job 4. 16; Ps. 107. 29.
13. WRAPPETH,] as in 1 Sa. 21. 9; Isa. 25. 1.
ROBE,] as in Ge. 25. 25; Jos. 7. 1, 24; 1 K.
19. 19; 2 K. 2. 8, 13, 14; Eze. 17. 6; Jon. 3. 6;
Zec. 11. 3; 13. 4.
WHAT—TO THEE,] as in v. 9.
14. ZEALOUS,] as in v. 10.
15. DAMASCUS,] the chief city of Aram.
HAZAEL,] i.e. 'God has seen.'
16. JEHU,] i.e. 'he is.'
NIMSHI,] i.e. 'drawn out.'
ELISHA,] i.e. 'God of safety.'
SHAPHAT,] i.e. 'he judged.'
ABEL-MEHOLAH.] See Jud. 7. 22.
PROPHET,] or proclaimer of the will of God.
17. ESCAPED.] Compare 2 K. 10. 23, 33; 9.
24, 33; 10. 1—7, 23, 33.
18. LEFT,] that is, suffered to remain as a
remnant.
7000,] as in Rom. 11. 4.
BAAL,] the god of the Zidonians, as a
mark of homage and respect.
KISSED HIM,] according to an ancient rite
of worship, as in Ge. 41. 40; Job 31. 27; Ps.
2. 12; Hos. 13. 2.
19. PLOWING,] in his native place, Abel-
Meholah.
TWELVE YOKE,] so that he was a man of
property.
20. FORSAKETH,] as a thing of no value
compared to the call he had now received.
KISS.] Compare Mat. 8. 21, 22; Luke 9. 61, 62.
DONE,] to prevent him settling his own
affairs first.
21. SACRIFICETH,] as a token of his joy at
the call given him.
PEOPLE] of the village or place where he
dwelt.
SERVETH HIM,] as a ministering attendant,
receiving doubtless those instructions which
Elijah alone could impart.

XX. 1. BEN-HADAD.] See on 15. 18.
ARAM,] of Damascus, the greatest of all
the rulers on the north of Canaan.
32 KINGS,] or petty princes, of whom he
was chief.
HORSE AND CHARIOT,] of which Israel
generally had few.
3. MINE,] claiming to be sovereign lord
of all.
4. KING,] timidly admitting the arrogant
presumption.
6. DESIRABLE THING,] as in 2 Ch. 36. 19;
Song 5. 16; Isa. 64. 11; La. 1. 10, 11; 2. 4;
Eze. 24. 16, 21, 25; Hos. 9. 6, 16; Joel 3. 5.
7. ELDERS,] who ruled in every city.
WITHHELD,] acknowledging him as superior.

8. PEOPLE,] indignant at the insulting language.

9. NOT ABLE,] without the consent of the elders and people of Israel.

10. ADD,] as in 19. 2, &c.

DUST] of the houses which he would destroy.

HANDFULS,] as in Isa. 40. 12; Eze. 13. 19.

AT MY FEET,] as in Ge. 30. 30; Eze. 11. 8, &c.

11. GIRDING ON,] that is, only preparing himself for the contest.

BOAST HIMSELF,] as in 1 Ch. 16. 10; Ps. 34. 2; 49. 6; 52. 1; 63. 11; 64. 10; 97. 7; 105. 3; 106. 5; Prov. 20. 14, &c.

LOOSING,] lit. 'opening.'

12. DRINKING,] as in 1 Sa. 30. 16; 1 K. 1. 25; 4. 20; 16. 9; 20. 16; 1 Ch. 12. 39; Job 1. 13, 18; 6. 4; 15. 16; Ps. 69. 12; Prov. 26. 6, &c.

BOOTHS,] in the fields round the city, in which they were abiding.

13. MULTITUDE,] of Aram, and its 32 kings, with horse and chariot.

14. PROVINCES,] as in v. 15, 17, 19; Ezra 2. 1; Neh. 1. 3; 7. 6; 11. 3; Est. 1. 1, 3, 16, 22; 2. 3, 18; 3. 8, 12, 13, 14; 4. 3, 11; 8. 5, 9, 11, 12, 13, 17; 9. 2, 3, 4, 12, 16, 20, 28, 30; Ecc. 2. 8; 5. 8; La. 1. 1; Eze. 19. 8; Da. 3. 2; 11. 24.

DIRECT,] lit. 'gird.'

15. INSPECTETH,] as in Ge. 21. 1, &c.

232,] less even than Gideon's three hundred.

PEOPLE,] who are ready to go forth to the field.

16. NOON,] when the sun was most powerful, thinking to find the enemy unprepared.

DRUNK,] or 'merry.'

17. COME FORTH,] but for what object they could not say.

18. CATCH,] as in Ge. 39. 12, &c.

19. FORCE] of 7000 men, as in v. 15.

21. SMITING,] as in Jos. 10. 10, 20; Jud. 11. 33; 15. 8; 1 Sa. 4. 10; 6. 19; 14. 30; 19. 8; 23. 5.

22. COMETH NIGH,] a second time; see v. 13.

STRENGTHEN THYSELF,] as in 1 Sa. 4. 9.

TURN OF THE YEAR,] as in v. 26; 2 Sa. 11. 1; 1 Ch. 20. 1; 2 Ch. 36. 10.

23. HILLS.] Canaan being a remarkably hilly country compared with Aram.

PLAIN,] where the Syrian cavalry could be of use.

24. STEAD,] as more fitted for active service.

25. FALLEN,] either wounded, or dead, or captive, or deserted.

26. TURN OF THE YEAR,] as in v. 22.

INSPECTETH] the condition of the army newly raised.

APHEK,] east of the sea of Galilee; distinct from that in Jos. 13. 4; 19. 30, which was in Asher, and from that in 1 Sa. 4. 1; 29. 1, which was in Issachar, and from that in Jos. 15. 53, which was in Judah.

27. SUPPORTED,] or 'sustained,' not 'present,' as in C.V.

GOATS,] helpless and insignificant.

28. COMETH NIGH,] as in v. 13, 22.

SAID,] as in v. 23, 24.

VALLEYS,] as in Ge. 14. 3, 8, 10, 17; 37. 14; Nu. 14. 25; Jos. 7. 24, &c.

29. DRAWETH NEAR,] as in De. 20. 2, 3.

SMITE,] not 'slew,' as in C.V.

30. APHEK,] as in v. 26.

CHIEF MEN,] not 'thousand men,' as in C.V.

INNERMOST PART,] as in 22. 25; 2 K. 9. 2; 2 Ch. 18. 24.

31. WE PRAY THEE,] not 'now,' as in C.V.

KIND,] not merely 'merciful,' as in C.V.

LOINS,] as a token of mourning.

ROPES,] as indicating we deserve death.

KEEP THEE ALIVE,] though he might put the others to death.

32. SERVANT,] his pride being now thoroughly humbled.

LET ME LIVE,] afraid of being captured and punished.

MY BROTHER,] a monarch like himself, hoping yet to gain him as an ally.

33. OBSERVE DILIGENTLY,] as in Ge. 30. 27; 44. 5, 15; Lev. 19. 26; De. 18. 10; 2 K. 17. 7; 21. 6; 2 Ch. 33. 6.

BROTHER,] adopting his words.

34. CITIES] of Israel on the north.

STREETS,] for the traffic of Israelitish merchants.

35. SONS OF THE PROPHETS,] one of those instructed by them.

36. THE LION,] as in 13, 24, &c.

37. SMITING AND WOUNDING,] so as to leave scars.

38. DISGUISETH HIMSELF,] as in 1 Sa. 28. 8, &c.

EYES,] that is, of course, on his eye-lids.

39. MISSING,] lit. 'inspected,' and not found, as in Nu. 16. 29; 31. 49; Jud. 21. 3, &c.

TALENT OF SILVER,] i.e. about £375.

WEIGH OUT,] money in the east being generally weighed not counted.

40. IS WORKING,] lit. 'doing.'

HE IS NOT] to be found, having escaped unobserved.

RIGHT,] agreeably to law and equity, according to the bargain.

JUDGMENT] of condemnation.

DETERMINED,] as in Job 14. 5; Isa. 10. 22.

41. EYES,] as in v. 38; not 'face,' as in C.V.

DISCERNETH,] having probably seen him before.

42. SENT AWAY] in peace and amity, as in v. 34.

DEVOTED] to death and destruction.

43. SULKY,] as in 21. 4, 5.

WROTH,] as in 21. 4; 2 Ch. 16. 10; 28. 9, &c.

XXI. 1. NABOTH,] i.e. 'increase, produce.'

JEZREEL,] in Issachar (Jos. 19. 18), where was a great valley of the same name, (Jos. 17. 16.)

PALACE,] or 'temple,' as in 1 Sa. 1. 9; 3. 3, &c.

2. GREEN HERBS,] as in De. 11. 10; 2 K. 19. 26; Prov. 15. 17; Isa. 37. 27.

SILVER,] or 'money.'

3. FAR BE IT FROM ME,] lit. 'a profanation it is to me.'

FATHERS,] which they had left to him, and was endeared by many associations.

4. SULKY AND WROTH,] as in 20. 43.

BED,] or couch 'stretched out' for him, as the original indicates.

NOT EATEN BREAD,] nor taken his usual food.

5. JEZEBEL,] as in 16. 31, &c.

6. NOT GIVE,] forgetting however to give the cause of the refusal.

7. EXECUTE RULE,] *lit.* 'do the kingdom.'

8. SEAL,] thus stamping them with royal authority.

FREE MEN,] as in v. 11; Neh. 2. 16; 4. 14; 5. 7; 6. 17; 7. 5; 13. 7; Ecc. 10. 17; Isa. 34. 12; Jer. 27. 20; 39. 6.

9. FAST,] as in 2 Sa. 12. 16; 2 Ch. 20. 3; Ezra 8. 21; Neh. 9. 1; Est. 4. 3; 9. 31, &c.

AT THE HEAD,] as in 1 Sa. 9. 22, &c.

10. SONS OF WORTHLESSNESS,] as in Jud. 19. 22, &c.

BLESSED,] as in v. 13; Job 1. 11; 2. 5. 9; the word never has anything but the one meaning 'to bless.'

MELECH,] *or* 'Molech.' So Syr. Sept. Vulg.

STONED] him for an idolater, according to the law, Ex. 22. 28; Lev. 24. 15. 16.

11. HIS CITY,] that is, Jezreel, as in v. 1.

13. OVER-AGAINST HIM,] as in v. 10.

BLESSED,, MELECH,] as in v. 10.

OUTSIDE,] as an unclean place, without the camp, according to the law.

14. DEAD,] as she had desired.

15. POSSESS] without fear or hindrance.

DEAD,] and his property as a criminal, falling to the crown.

16. GO DOWN,] probably from Samaria to Jezreel.

POSSESS IT,] as his own and enjoy its fruit.

18. GO DOWN,] from some place not mentioned.

19. MURDERED,] as in Ex. 20. 13, &c.

LICKED,] as in Jud. 7. 5—7; 1 K. 22. 38.

THINE,] that of his son, as in 2 K. 9. 26.

20. FOUND ME,] his conscience, doubtless, prompting him to put the question.

ENEMY,] for such he reckoned him because he spoke the truth.

SELLING THYSELF,] as in v. 25; De. 28. 68; 2 K. 17. 17.

THE EVIL THING,] that is, idolatry.

21. I AM BRINGING IN,] even now it is beginning.

POSTERITY,] as in 16. 3, &c.

SITTING,] as in 1 Sa. 25. 22, 34; 1 K. 14. 10; 16. 11; 2 K. 9. 8.

RESTRAINED . . LEFT,] as in 14. 10, &c.

22. JEROBOAM,] the first king of the ten tribes, as in 15. 29.

BAASHA,] as in 16. 3, 11.

23. JEZEBEL,] the active agent in all this.

BULWARK,] as in 2 Sa. 20. 15; Ps. 122. 7; Isa. 26. 1; La. 2. 8; Nah. 3. 8.

24. FOWLS OF THE HEAVENS,] as in 14. 11; 16. 4.

25. NONE,] as in 16. 30.

SELL HIMSELF,] as in v. 20 above.

MOVED,] as in De. 13. 6, &c.

26. ABOMINABLY,] as in Ps. 14. 1; 53. 1; Eze. 16. 52.

IDOLS,] as in Lev. 26. 30, &c.

AMORITE,] as in Ge. 15. 16, &c.

DISPOSSESSED,] as in 14. 24, &c.

27. GARMENTS,] as a token of his grief at the threatened calamity.

GENTLY,] as in 2 Sa. 18. 5; Job 15. 11; Isa. 8. 6, &c.

29. HATH BEEN HUMBLED,] as in Lev. 26. 21, &c..

EVIL,] which had been denounced, as in v. 24.

SON.] See 2 K. 9. 25.

XXII. 1. IS STILL,] that is, the Aramaeans and Israel refrain from mutual hostilities.

2. JEHOSHAPHAT,] whose son had married Ahab's daughter, as in 2 K. 8. 18; 2 Ch.18. 1.

COMETH DOWN,] from Jerusalem to Samaria, a distance of 32 miles.

3. SERVANTS,] that is, his officers and chief men, encouraged by the expected aid of his guest.

RAMOTH-GILEAD,] a city of Gad, beyond Jordan, as in Jos. 20. 8, &c.

OURS,] belonging properly to Israel.

KEEPING SILENT,] only meditating on its possibility and propriety.

ARAM,] who had (in 20. 34) agreed to give up all his father's conquests.

4. AS I AM, SO THOU, &c.] The C.V. unnecessarily transposes the language, which is elliptical.

5. SEEK,] as in Ge. 25. 22, &c.

JEHOVAH,] regarding the propriety of the enterprize.

6. PROPHETS] of Baal, not of Jehovah, those left by Elijah and the people.

FOUR HUNDRED,] as in 18. 19.

FORBEAR,] *lit.* 'cease,' from pursuing the plan adopted.

THE LORD,] *Heb.* 'Adonai,' not 'Jehovah.'

7. PROPHET OF JEHOVAH,] whom he himself served.

SEEK BY HIM,] *lit.* 'from with him.'

8. MICAIAH,] i.e. 'who is like him,' as in 2 Ch. 18. 7; in v. 24 below it is 'Micah.'

IMLAH,] i.e. 'he fills.'

HATED] him all along for his words, which were generally of

EVIL,] towards the king Ahab and his kingdom.

SAY SO,] regarding a servant of Jehovah.

9. EUNUCH,] as in Ge. 37. 36, &c.

10. THRONE,] in the midst of the royal counsellors, &c.

GARMENTS,] suitable for their rank.

THRESHING FLOOR,] as in Ge. 50. 10, 11, &c.

11. ZEDEKIAH,] i.e. 'righteousness of Jah.'

CHENAANAH,] i.e. a 'Canaanites,' as in 2 Ch. 18. 10.

HORNS OF IRON,] emblems of mighty power.

JEHOVAH,] using this name doubtless to please Jehoshaphat.

PUSH,] as in De. 33. 17; 2 Ch. 18. 10; Ps. 44. 5; Eze. 34. 21; Dan. 8. 4.

12. PROSPER,] as in v. 15; 2 Ch. 18. 11, 14; 20. 20; Neh. 1. 11; Ps. 118. 25.

13. I PRAY THEE,] not 'now,' as in C.V.

ONE MOUTH,] as in 2 Ch. 18. 12.

14. I SPEAK.] Compare Nu. 22. 38.

15. WE GO,] including Jehoshaphat with himself; compare v. 6.

FORBEAR,] *lit.* 'cease,' as in v. 6.

16. ADJURING,] *lit.* 'causing to swear'

17. SCATTERED,] as in 2 Ch. 18. 16.

NO SHEPHERD,] and thus exposed to every enemy.
MASTER,] *or* 'lord,' as in Ge. 18. 12; 19. 2, 18, &c.
18. EVIL,] as in v. 8 above.
19. SITTING,] as in 2 Ch. 18. 18; Ps. 9. 4; 47. 8; Isa. 6. 1.
HOST OF THE HEAVENS,] as in Ge. 2. 1; De. 4. 19; 17. 3; 2 K. 17. 6; 21. 3, 5; 23. 4, 5; 2 Ch. 18. 18; 33. 3, 5; Neh. 9. 6, &c.
STANDING,] as ministering servants.
20. ENTICE,] as in Ex. 22. 16, &c.
21. THE SPIRIT] of falsehood, not 'a spirit,' as in C.V.
22. SPIRIT OF FALSEHOOD,] as in 2 Ch. 18. 21, 22.
ABLE] to entice him to his ruin.
23. PUT,] *lit.* 'given.'
24. CHEEK,] as in 2 Ch. 18. 23; Job. 16. 10; Ps. 3. 7; La. 3. 30; Mic. 5. 1.
25. BE HIDDEN,] for fear of punishment as a false prophet.
26. AMON,] i.e. 'workman, artificer.'
JOASH,] who is not mentioned elsewhere.
27. THIS ONE,] not 'this fellow,' as in C.V.
HOUSE OF RESTRAINT,] as in 2 K. 17. 4; 25. 27, 29; 2 Ch. 18. 26; Isa. 42. 7, 22; Jer. 37. 15, 18; 52. 33.
OPPRESSION,] as in Ex. 3. 9, &c.
28. NOT SPOKEN,] as in Nu. 16. 29; De. 18. 20, 21, 22.
PEOPLES,] of Israel and Judah.
30. DISGUISE HIMSELF,] as in 2 Ch. 18. 29; 1 Sa. 28. 8; 1 K. 20. 38; 22. 30; Job 30. 18.
GARMENTS,] of royal state, that he might appear as the leader.
31. SMALL..GREAT,] as far as that could be avoided.
BY HIMSELF,] as the real originator of the war.
32. ONLY,] judging by his royal apparel.
CRIETH OUT,] for help, as the original word implies.
34. IN HIS SIMPLICITY,] as in 9. 4; 2 Ch. 19. 33.
JOININGS,] as in 2 Ch. 18. 33; Isa. 41. 7.
COAT OF MAIL,] as in 2 Ch. 18. 33; Isa. 59. 17; 1 Sa. 17. 5; 2 Ch. 26. 14; Neh. 4. 16.
BECOME SICK,] for want of blood.
35. INCREASETH,] *lit.* 'goeth up.'
CAUSED TO STAND,] *or* 'remain,' in the battle-field.
MIDST,] *lit.* 'bosom.'
36. CRY,] as in 8. 22; 2 Ch. 6. 19; 20. 22; Ps. 17. 1; 30. 5; 42. 4; 47. 1; 61. 1; 88. 2; 105. 43; 106. 44; 107. 22, &c.
LAND,] dispersing the armies and closing the war.

37. COMETH,] as a corpse.
SAMARIA,] beside his father Omri, as in 16. 28.
38. RINSETH,] as in Lev. 15. 11, 12; 6. 28.
POOL,] as in 2 Sa. 2. 13; 4. 12, &c.
ARMOUR.] This original word does not occur elsewhere.
SPAKE,] as in 21. 19.
39. MATTERS,] not 'acts,' as in C.V.
IVORY,] as in Amos 3. 15.
40. LIETH,] as in 16. 28.
AHAZIAH,] i.e. 'laid hold off by Jah.'
41. FOURTH YEAR.] See 2 Ch. 20. 31.
42. 25 YEARS,] so that he was sixty when he died.
AZUBAH,] i.e. a 'forsaken woman.'
SHILHI,] i.e. 'my shoot or dart.'
43. WALKETH,] as in 2 Ch. 17. 3.
RIGHT,] *or* 'upright.'
44. HIGH PLACES,] as in 14. 23; 15. 14; 2 K. 12. 3.
MAKING PERFUME,] as in 2 K. 12. 3; 14. 4; 15. 4, 35; 18. 4; 23. 5; Isa. 65. 3; Jer. 11. 12; 44. 15, 19.
45. MAKETH PEACE] by intermarriage, as in 2 Ch. 18. 1; 19. 2, &c.
MATTERS,] not 'acts,' as in C.V.
GOT,] *lit.* 'made.'
FOUGHT,] against Moab, Ammon, &c., in 2 Ch. 20. 1.
46. WHOREMONGERS,] as in 14. 24; 15. 12.
LAND] of Judah and Benjamin.
47. EDOM.] See 2 Sa. 8. 14; 2 K. 8. 20.
HE SET UP,] *or* 'an officer,' as in 1 K. 4. 5,. 7, &c.
48. MADE.] The Keri is 'ten,' not 'made SHIPS OF TARSHISH,] as in 10. 22.
OPHIR,] as in 9. 28.
BROKEN,] *lit.* 'shivered.'
EZION-GEBER,] a port of Edom, in the Red Sea.
49. AHAZIAH,] as in v. 40.
WILLING,] being warned by the prophet and the destruction of his navy; 2 Ch. 20 35—37.
50. LIETH,] as in v. 40.
CITY OF DAVID,] that is, Zion.
JEHORAM,] i.e. 'Jah is high.'
51. TWO YEARS,] not complete; see 2 K. 3. 1.
52. THE EVIL THING,] i.e. idolatry.
MOTHER,] that is, Jezebel.
SIN,] as in 15. 26.
53. THE BAAL,] the chief god of the Zidonians.
BOWETH HIMSELF,] in token of reverence.
DONE,] who had exceeded in this all who were before him.

SECOND BOOK OF KINGS

THIS BOOK is most evidently a continuation of the preceding one, and carries down the history of Israel and Judah from the death of Ahab and Jehoshaphat, A.M. 3115, to the destruction of Jerusalem, A.M. 3416, a period of 301 years. It is referred to in Luke 4. 27; 10. 4, &c.

I. 1. MOAB,] a country on the east of the Dead Sea unto Arnon.

TRANSGRESSETH,] as in 1 K. 8. 50; 12. 19,&c.

2. LATTICE,] as in 1 K. 7. 17, 18, 20, 41, 42, &c.

BAAL-ZEBUB,] i.e. 'lord of a fly,' as in v. 3, 6, 16.

EKRON,] one of the five Philistine principalities.

SICKNESS,] as in De. 7. 15; 28. 59, 61; 1 K. 17. 17; 2 K. 8. 8, 9; 2 Ch. 16. 12; 21. 15, 18, 19; Ps. 41. 3, &c.

3. TISHBITE,] as in 1 K. 17. 1.

NOT A GOD,] able to save, and to destroy, and to reveal the future.

4. BED,] as in Ge. 47. 31, &c.

GOETH ON,] his journey to meet the messengers.

6. COME UP] towards Samaria.

· 7. FASHION,] lit. 'judgment.'

8. HAIRY,] lit. 'a lord, master, or possessor of hair;' a phrase not found elsewhere.

GIRDLE OF SKIN.] This phrase is not found elsewhere; but compare Mat. 3. 4; Zec. 13. 4.

9. FIFTY,] as in Ex. 18. 21, 25, &c.

THE HILL,] perhaps Carmel, as in 2. 25.

MAN OF GOD,] recognising him as a devout man.

SPOKEN,] with regal authority that cannot be resisted.

. 10. COME DOWN,] from God, as in Luke 9.54.

CONSUMETH,] lit. 'eateth.'

11. HASTE,] language more imperious than even the first.

13. BOWETH,] as in Ge. 49. 9; Nu. 24. 9; Jud. 5. 27; 7. 5, 6; 1 Sa. 4. 19; 1 K. 8. 54; 19. 18; 2 K. 9. 24; 20. 29; Ezra 9. 5; Est. 3. 2, 5; Job 4. 4, &c.

MAKETH SUPPLICATION,] as in Ge. 42. 21, &c.

PRECIOUS,] as in 1 Sa. 18. 30; 26. 21; Ps. 49. 8; 72. 14; Isa. 43. 4; Zec. 11. 13, &c.

15. BE NOT AFRAID,] as in Ge. 15. 1, &c.

16. JEHOVAH,] the God of truth, in opposition to the lying vanities of the Philistines.

HIS WORD,] regarding any matter of life and death.

17. JEHORAM,] as in 3. 1.

SON,] and thus the threatened cutting off of Ahab's family was beginning.

18. MATTERS,] not 'acts,' as in C.V.

II. 1. AT TAKING UP,] not 'would take up,' as in C.V.

WHIRLWIND,] as in v. 11; Job 38. 1; 40. 6; Ps. 107. 25, 29; 148. 8; Isa. 29. 6; 40. 24; 41.

16; Jer. 23. 19; 30. 23; Eze. 1. 4; 13. 11, 13; Zec. 9. 14.

GILGAL,] where Israel first encamped after passing the Jordan, Jos. 4. 19; 5. 9.

2. ABIDE,] probably to try his faith and affection to himself.

BETH-EL,] where there was a school of the prophets.

GO DOWN,] from Gilgal.

3. SONS OF THE PROPHETS,] as in 1 K. 20. 35, &c.

KEEP SILENT,] as in v. 5; not to aggravate his grief.

4. ELISHA,] naming him tenderly, as he had not done before.

JERICHO,] about four miles from Beth-El.

5. HEAD,] as in v. 3.

6. THE JORDAN,] about six miles from Jericho.

7. OVER-AGAINST,] not 'to view,' as in C.V.

8. ROBE,] as in Ge. 25. 25; Jos. 7. 21, 24; 1 K. 19. 13, 19; 2 K. 2. 13, 14; Eze. 17. 8; Jon. 3. 6; Zec. 11. 3; 13. 4.

WRAPPETH.] This original word is not found elsewhere.

WATERS,] as in v. 14.

HALVED,] as in v. 14; Eze. 37. 22; Dan.11.4.

DRY LAND,] as in Ge. 7. 22; Ex. 14. 21; Jos. 3. 17; 4. 18; 2 K. 2. 8; Eze. 30. 12; Hag. 2. 6.

9. BEFORE,] not 'after;' the intercession of saints is only on earth.

A DOUBLE PORTION,] lit. 'two mouths,' as in De. 21. 17; Zec. 13. 8.

10. ASKED A HARD THING,] lit. 'made hard to ask.'

11. HORSES OF FIRE,] as in 6. 17; compare Ps. 104. 4.

SEPARATE,] as in Ge. 30. 40; De. 32. 8; Ruth 1. 17; Prov. 16. 23; 17. 9; 18. 18.

WHIRLWIND,] as in v. 1.

12. MY FATHER,] as in 13. 14.

CHARIOT OF ISRAEL, ETC.,] an acknowledgment that the friends of God are the true defence of a land.

TWO PIECES,] as a token of bereavement.

13. ROBE,] as in v. 8.

EDGE,] lit. 'lip.'

14. WATERS,] as Elijah had done; some copies of Sept. and Vulg. add, 'but the waters were not divided, then he said.'

EVEN HE.] These two words are unaccountably left out in the C. V., and the Sept.

HALVED,] as in v. 8.

15. OVER-AGAINST,] as in v.'7; not 'to view,' as in C.V.

RESTED,] as in Nu. 11. 25, 26; Isa. 11. 2, &c.

SPIRIT OF ELIJAH,] judging from his miraculously dividing the water.

BOW THEMSELVES,] as to their inspired teacher and guide.

16. WE PRAY THEE,] not 'now,' as in C.V.

SONS OF VALOUR,] or 'of worth or virtue.'

SPIRIT OF JEHOVAH,] as in 1 K 18. 12, &c.

HILLS . . VALLEYS,] with which the land of Israel abounded.

NOT SEND,] knowing that he was really taken up into heaven.
17. PRESS,] as in Ge. 19. 3, 9; 33. 11; Jud. 19. 7; 2 K. 5. 16.
ASHAMED,] as in 8. 11.
FIFTY MEN,] in different directions.
18. DO NOT GO,] knowing it was useless.
19. THE CITY] of Jericho.
SITE,] *lit.* 'seat.'
STERILE,] *lit.* 'causing to miscarry.'
20. DISH,] as in 21. 13; 2 Ch. 35. 13; Prov. 19. 24; 26. 15.
21. SOURCE,] as in 2 Ch. 32. 20; Ps. 107. 33, 35; Isa. 41. 18; 58. 11.
STERILITY,] *lit.* 'causing to miscarry,' as in v. 19.
23. BETH-EL,] as in v. 3.
YOUTHS,] not 'children,' as in C.V.
SCOFF,] as in Eze. 22. 5; Hab. 1. 10.
BALDHEAD,] as in Lev. 13. 40; 21. 5; De. 14. 1, &c.
24. DECLARETH THEM VILE,] as in Ge. 8. 21; 12. 3; Ex. 21. 17; 22. 28, &c.
BEARS,] as in 1 Sa. 17. 34, 36, 37; 2 Sa. 17. 8; Prov. 17. 12; 28. 15; Isa. 11. 7; 59. 11; La. 3. 10; Hos. 13. 18; Am. 5. 19.
REND,] as in Ge. 22. 3; 1 Sa. 6. 14; 2 K. 8 12; 15. 16; Ps. 78. 15; Job 28. 10; Isa. 59. 5; Eze. 13. 11, 13; Hos. 13. 8; Hab. 3. 9.
LADS,] as in Ge. 4. 23, &c.
25. CARMEL,] about fifty-six miles from Beth-El.
SAMARIA,] about thirty-two miles from Carmel.

III. 1. JEHORAM,] as in 1. 17.
2. THE EVIL THING,] that is, idolatry.
FATHER..MOTHER,] Ahab and Jezebel.
STANDING PILLAR,] as in Ge. 28. 18, 22, &c.
3. SINS,] as in 1 K. 12. 28, 31, 32.
4. MESHA,] i.e. 'safety.'
SHEEPMASTER,] as in Amos 1. 1.
RENDERED,] as tribute year by year.
WOOL,] as in Lev. 13. 47, 48, 52, 59; De. 22. 11; Jud. 6. 37, &c.
5. TRANSGRESSETH,] as in 1. 1.
6. INSPECTETH] all the army of Israel.
7. JEHOSHAPHAT,] his relative, as in 8. 18; 2 Ch. 18. 1.
UNTO MOAB,] not 'against it,' as in C.V.
8. GO UP,] towards the mountains of Moab.
AS I, SO THOU.] The C.V. transposes the thought of the original.
WILDERNESS,] or pasture-land.
9. EDOM,] whom they had got to join them against Moab.
SEVEN DAYS] round the Dead Sea, and through the wilderness of Edom.
NO WATER,] by reason of the drought and the large force with them.
AT THEIR FEET,] as in Ge. 30. 30; Ex. 11. 8.
10. JEHOVAH,] whom perhaps he regarded as his enemy.
11. HERE] in this pasture land of Edom.
BY HIM,] *lit.* 'from with him.'
POURED WATER,] according to a well-known eastern custom.
12. WITH HIM,] recognizing him as a true prophet of Jehovah.
GO DOWN] to his dwelling in the valley.

13. TO THEE,] in common, that he should expect assistance.
PROPHETS] of Baal, whom he and his parents patronized.
JEHOVAH,] as in v. 10.
14. JEHOVAH OF HOSTS,] as in 1 Sa. 1. 3, &c.
STOOD] as a ministering servant.
FACE..LIFTING UP,] a common phrase denoting respect.
15. MINSTREL,] as in 1 Sa. 16. 16; 18. 10; 19. 9
HAND,] as in 1 K. 18. 46.
16. DITCHES,] as in Isa. 10. 31; Jer. 14. 3.
17. WIND,] driving the clouds towards them, that
RAIN] from the heavens might satisfy them.
WATER,] by the direct intervention of God.
BEASTS,] and been refreshed and strengthened.
18. LIGHT,] being the fountain of all goodness.
19. FENCED CITY,] as in Nu. 13. 19; 32. 17, 36; Jos. 10. 20; 19. 29, 35; 1 Sa. 6. 18; 2 Sa. 24. 7, &c.
CHOICE,] as in 19. 23.
FALL,] as in 6. 5.
FOUNTAINS,] as in Ge. 7. 11; 8. 2; Lev. 11. 36; Jos. 15. 9; 18. 15; 1 K. 18. 5, &c.
STOP,] with dust and stones, as in v. 25; 2 Ch. 32. 3, 4, 30.
GOOD PORTION] of cultivated ground.
MAR,] *lit.* 'pain,' as in Job 5. 18; Eze. 13. 22; 28. 24.
20. PRESENT,] on the altar of God in Jerusalem, as in Ex. 29. 41, &c.
21. THE KINGS] of Israel, Judah, and Edom.
CALLED TOGETHER,] as in Jos. 8. 16, &c.
GIRDLE,] as in Ex. 12. 11; 1 K. 20. 11, &c.
BORDER] of their land, awaiting the approach of the invaders.
22. SHONE,] *lit.* 'arisen,' as in Ge. 32. 31.
RED,] as in Ge. 25. 30; Nu. 19. 2; Song 5. 10; Isa. 63. 2; Zec. 1. 8; 6. 2.
23. DESTROYED,] *lit.* 'dried up,' as in Ge. 8. 13; Eze. 26. 19; 30. 7, &c.
SPOIL,] as in Ge. 49. 27, &c.
24. MOAB,] as Elisha had foretold.
25. BREAK DOWN,] to render uninhabitable.
GOOD PORTION,] as in v. 19.
KIR-HARASETH,] i.e. 'wall of clay;' see Isa. 16. 7, 11; Jer. 48. 31, 36.
SLINGERS,] as in 1 Sa. 17. 40, 50; 25. 29; 2 Ch. 26. 14; Job. 41. 28; Zec. 9. 15.
26. TOO STRONG,] there being three kings united against one.
DRAWING SWORD,] as in Jud. 8. 10, &c.
TO CLEAVE THROUGH,] as in Isa. 7. 6; Jer. 39. 2, &c.
EDOM,] thinking him most probably the weakest or the most friendly of his assailants.
27. FIRST BORN,] as in De. 21. 15—17.
WALL] of the capital city, in the sight of friend and foe.
GREAT WRATH,] against or over Israel.
LAND] of Israel, Judah, and Edom.

IV. 1. SONS OF THE PROPHETS,] as in 1 K. 20. 35.

CRIED,] because of her distress, as the original word implies.
FEARING,] that is, reverencing the true God.
LENDER,] as in Ex. 22. 25; De. 24. 11; Neh.
5. 7, 10, 11; Ps. 109. 11; Isa. 24. 2; 50. 1.
CHILDREN,] not 'sons,' as in C.V.
SERVANTS,] not 'bondmen,' as in C.V. Compare Ex. 21. 2; Lev. 25. 39, &c.
2. MAID-SERVANT,] as in Ge. 12. 16, &c.
POT.] The original word is not found elsewhere.
3. VESSELS] for holding oil.
FEW,] as the supply of oil would not be scanty.
4. POURED OUT,] from the one pot of oil.
REMOVE] into a safe place.
5. SHUTTETH,] as directed in v. 4.
POURING FORTH] with her own hands.
6. STAYETH] from flowing.
7. SELL,] having more than would supply her own present lack.
REPAY,] lit. 'make complete.'
LOAN,] as was only just and proper.
8. SHUNEM,] in Issachar, as in Jos. 19. 18.
GREAT WOMAN] in station, wealth, goodness, &c.
EAT BREAD,] that is, partake of food.
9. I PRAY THEE,] not 'now,' as in C.V.
HOLY,] i.e. 'separate, set apart.'
10. WALL,] as in Jud. 3. 20, &c.
BED,] lit. 'a thing stretched out,' as in Ge. 47. 31, &c.
TABLE,] as in Ge. 25. 23, &c.
HIGH SEAT,] lit. 'a throne,' as in Ge. 41. 40; Ex. 11. 5; 12. 29; De. 17. 18; Jud. 3. 20; 1 Sa. 1. 9; 2. 8; 4. 13, 18, &c.
CANDLESTICK,] as in Ex. 25. 31, &c.
11. THE DAY COMETH,] as in Job 1. 6, 13.
12. GEHAZI,] i.e. 'valley of vision.'
SHUNAMMITE,] or inhabitant of Shunem, as in v. 8.
13. I PRAY THEE,] not 'now,' as in C.V.
TROUBLED THYSELF,] lit. 'trembled,' as in Ge. 27. 33; 42. 28, &c.
HEAD OF THE HOST,] that her husband or friends might be promoted.
DWELLING] without a desire of change.
14. NO SON,] which in the east is reckoned a great lack.
AGED,] so that there was no likelihood of the lack being supplied.
15. OPENING] of his chamber.
16. SEASON,] next year.
TIME OF LIFE,] as in Ge. 18. 10, 14.
EMBRACING] with a mother's affection.
NOT LIE,] as in Nu. 23. 19; Job 6. 28; 24. 25; 34. 6; 41. 9; Ps. 78. 36; 116. 11; Prov. 14. 5; 30. 6; Isa. 57. 11; 58. 11; Eze. 13. 19; Hab. 2. 3; Mic. 2. 11.
18. GROWETH,] lit. 'becometh great.'
19. MY HEAD,] caused probably by sunstroke.
HIS MOTHER,] who was best qualified to take care of him.
20. DIETH,] notwithstanding all a mother's care.
21. BED] in the upper chamber.
SHUTTETH,] or 'maketh secure.'
22. ASSES,] the most common means of conveyance mentioned in the Scriptures.

23. NEW MOON,] when the monthly festival was held.
SABBATH,] when the prophets and Levites instructed the people.
PEACE,] be not afraid, all is well.
24. LEAD] on the way before her.
RESTRAIN,] the full speed of the asses.
25. CARMEL,] sixteen miles from Shunem.
SHUNAMMITE,] as in v. 8, 12.
26. THEE..HUSBAND..LAD,] herself, and nearest relatives.
PEACE,] as she had said to her husband, in v. 23.
27. FEET,] in humility and earnestness.
THRUST,] as an impertinent intruder.
ALONE,] suffer her to explain her conduct.
BITTER,] because of some great sorrow.
HIDDEN,] or left it unrevealed.
28. DID I ASK,] or importune thee for any gift or blessing.
DO NOT DECEIVE,] with illusive hopes.
29. GIRD UP,] the long flowing oriental dress and go.
MY STAFF,] as an emblem of authority.
SALUTE,] lit. 'bless.'
ANSWER,] to prevent loss of time.
30. LIVETH,] as in 2. 2, &c.
HE RISETH,] that is, Elisha himself.
31. NO VOICE..NO ATTENTION,] as in 1 K. 18. 29; Isa. 21. 7.
NOT AWAKED,] as in 1 Sa. 26. 12; Job 14. 12; Ps. 3. 5; 17. 15; 35. 23; 44. 23; 59. 5; 73. 20; 139. 18; Prov. 6. 22; 23. 35; Isa. 29. 8; 26. 19; Jer. 31. 26; 51. 39, 57; Eze. 7. 6; Da. 12. 2; Joel 1. 5; Hab. 2. 19.
32. HIS BED,] as in v. 21.
33. SHUTTETH..PRAYETH,] in secret; compare Matt. 6. 6.
34. GOETH UP,] on to the bed, and
STRETCHETH HIMSELF,] as in v. 35; 1 K. 18. 42.
BECOMETH WARM,] as in Ex. 16. 21; 1 K. 1. 2; Ps. 39. 3; Ecc. 4. 11; Isa. 44. 15, 16; 47. 14.
35. STRETCHETH HIMSELF,] as in v. 34.
SNEEZETH.] The original word is not found elsewhere.
EYES,] as in Ge. 21. 19, &c.
36. SHUNAMMITE,] as in v. 12.
LIFT UP] from off the bed.
38. GILGAL,] as in 2. 1, &c.
FAMINE,] as in 8. 1, &c.
SITTING,] receiving instruction; compare Acts 22. 3.
POT,] as in Ex. 16. 3, &c.
POTTAGE,] as in Ge. 25, 34; Hag. 2. 12.
39. HERBS,] as in Isa. 26. 19.
VINE OF THE FIELD,] supposed by Gill to be 'coloquintida.'
GOURDS,] or wild cucumbers; not mentioned elsewhere.
SPLITTETH,] as in Ps. 141. 7; Job 16. 13; 39. 3; Prov. 7. 23.
40. DEATH,] as the consequence of partaking of the pottage.
41. MEAL,] as in Ge. 18. 6, &c.
NO EVIL THING,] that could cause injury.
42. BAAL-SHALISHAH,] as in 1 Sa. 9. 4.
FIRST-FRUITS] of barley harvest, as in Lev. 23. 10.
FULL EARS,] as in Lev. 2. 14, &c.

HUSK.] The original word is not found elsewhere.

43. MINISTER,] as in 6. 15; Ex. 24. 13, &c. LEAVE,] as in Ex. 36. 7; 2 Ch. 31. 10; Jer. 44. 7.

V. 1. NAAMAN,] i.e. 'pleasantness,' as in Ge. 46. 21; Nu. 26. 40.
ACCEPTED OF FACE,] as in Job 22. 8; Isa. 3. 3; 9. 15.
SAFETY,] as in Jud. 15. 18; 1 Sa. 11. 9, 13; 19. 5, &c.
LEPROUS,] as in v. 11, 27; 7. 3, 8; 15. 5; Ex. 4. 6, &c.
2. TROOPS,] as in Ge. 49. 19; 1 Sa. 30. 8, &c.
WIFE OF NAAMAN,] as an attendant.
3. MISTRESS,] as in Ge. 16. 4, 8, 9, &c.
THE PROPHET] Elisha.
RECOVER,] lit. 'gather.'
LEPROSY,] as he had raised even the dead, as in v. 36.
5. ENTER] into the plan, and into Israel.
IN HIS HAND,] that is, along with him.
TEN TALENTS,] about £3750.
6000] of gold, about £4500.
TEN CHANGES,] for presents to the king and prophet.
6. LEPROSY,] as suggested by the damsel in v. 3.
7. RENDETH,] the usual token of grief.
GOD,] or 'a god,' in whose hands only it is to take life or to keep ALIVE,] as in Ge. 30. 2; De. 32. 39; 1 Sa. 2. 6.
PRESENTING HIMSELF.] The original word is not found elsewhere, but it is from a root found in Ex. 21. 13; Ps. 91. 10; Prov. 12. 21.
8. MAN OF GOD,] as in De. 33. 1, &c.
I PRAY THEE,] not 'now,' as in C.V.
PROPHET,] or revealer and announcer of the will of God to men.
9. HORSES..CHARIOT,] suitable to his rank, and in accordance with eastern fashions.
OPENING,] expecting the prophet to come forth to meet him, as in v. 11.
10. SEVEN TIMES,] according to the law of cleansing the leper, in Lev. 14. 7, 9.
BE THOU CLEAN,] as in Lev. 13. 3.
11. WROTH,] as in Ge. 40. 2, &c.
CALLED IN,] not 'on,' as in Ge.
WAVED,] as in Ex. 20. 25; 29. 24, 26; 35. 22, &c.
RECOVERED,] lit. 'gathered.'
12. ABANA,] or Amana, as in Song 4. 8.
PHARPAR,] i.e. 'swift.'
FURY,] as in Ge. 27. 44, &c.
13. MY FATHER,] Naaman was doubtless a kind master, or they would not have used such language.
A GREAT THING,] requiring much labour and expense.
14. DIPPETH,] as in Ge. 37. 31; Ex. 12. 22; Lev. 4. 6, 17; 9. 9; 14. 6, 16, 51; Nu. 19. 18; De. 33. 34, &c.
CLEAN,] as the prophet had foretold.
15. CAMP,] of horses and chariots, as in v. 9.
I PRAY THEE,] not 'now,' as in C.V.
NOT A GOD,] able to remove disease.
BLESSING,] that is, a present, expressive of his gratitude.
16. PRESSETH,] as in Ge. 19. 3, 9, 11; Jud. 19. 7; 2 K. 2. 17; 5. 16.

REFUSETH,] as in Ge. 37. 35; 39. 8; 48.19,&c.
17. COUPLE,] as in Jud. 19. 3, 10; 1 Sa. 11. 7; 14. 14; 2 Sa. 16. 1; 1 K. 19. 19, 21, 2 K. 9. 25; Job 1. 3; 42. 12; Isa. 5. 10; 21. 7, 9; Jer. 51. 23.
JEHOVAH,] the God of Israel.
18. RIMMON,] i.e. 'pomegranate,' a Syrian idol.
WAS SUPPORTED,] as in 7. 2, 17.
I BOWED MYSELF,} in token of respect to the idol.
BE PROPITIOUS,] as in Ex. 34. 9, &c.
19. KIBRATH OF LAND,] as in Ge. 35. 16; 48. 7.
20. GEHAZI,] as in 4. 12.
SPARED,] lit. 'withheld.'
21. SLIGHTETH,] lit. 'falleth.'
22. MY LORD,] that is, Elisha his master.
HILL-COUNTRY,] to receive instructions from the prophet.
A TALENT OF SILVER,] about £375.
TWO CHANGES,] one for each of the young men.
23. BE PLEASED,] as in 6. 3; Jud. 19. 6; 2 Sa. 7. 29; Job 6. 28.
TWO TALENTS,] about £750.
URGETH,] as in 1 Sa. 28. 23; 2 Sa. 13. 25, 27, &c.
PURSES,] as in Isa. 3. 22.
24. HIGH PLACE,] Heb. 'Ophel,' as in 2 Ch. 27. 3; 33. 14; Neh. 3. 26, 27; 11. 21; Isa. 32. 14; Mic. 4. 8; compare Hab. 2. 4; Nu. 14. 14.
25. STAND BY] Elisha, ready to serve him, according to his custom.
WHENCE?] a searching question which does not require the supplement of the C.V. 'camest thou?'
26. WENT NOT,] an affirmation, not a question, as in C.V.
A TIME,] when the Lord is manifesting his mighty power and grace.
27. CLEAVE,] as in Ge. 2. 24, &c.
SNOW,] as in Ex. 4. 6; Nu. 12. 10; 2 Sa. 23. 20; 1 Ch. 11. 22; Job 6. 16; 9. 30; 24. 19; 37. 6; 38. 22; Ps. 51. 7; 147. 16; 148. 8; Prov. 25. 13; 26. 1; 31; Isa. 1. 18; 55. 10; Jer. 18. 14; La. 4. 7.

VI. 1. SONS OF THE PROPHETS,] as in 4. 38.
STRAIT,] as in Isa. 49. 20; Nu. 22. 26.
2. JORDAN,] on its banks, about six miles from Gilgal.
BEAM,] as in v. 5; Ge. 19. 8; 2 Ch. 3. 7; Song 1. 17.
3. BE PLEASED,] as in 5. 23.
5. FELLING,] with repeated strokes.
THE IRON,] with which he was hewing.
IT IS ASKED,] or 'begged.'
6. STICK,] from off the boughs of the tree.
CAUSETH TO SWIM,] contrary to the nature of things.
8. FIGHTING,] but from what cause is not said.
TAKETH COUNSEL,] like a prudent warrior.
ENCAMPING,] to surprize the king of Israel and his army.
9. MAN OF GOD,] that is, Elisha.
PASSING BY] with his troops, exposing himself to the assaults of the enemy.
COMING DOWN,] not 'come down,' as in C.V

10. HE IS PRESERVED,] not 'he saved himself,' as in C.V.

11. IS TOSSED ABOUT,] as by a tempest; compare Isa. 54. 11; Hos. .13. 3; Hab. 3. 14; Jon. 1. 11; Zec. 7. 14.

WHO OF US,] as in 1 Sa. 22. 7, 8.

12. INNER PART,] as in Ge. 43. 30; Ex. 8. 3, &c.

13. SEE,] not 'spy,' as in C.V.

DOTHAN,] in Manasseh, near Shechem, as in Ge. 37. 17; twelve miles from Samaria.

14. HORSES..CHARIOT,] as in 1 K. 20. 1.

HEAVY FORCE,] as in 18. 17; 2 Ch. 9. 1.

15. SERVANT,] whose name is not mentioned.

FORCE,] as in v. 14.

YOUNG MAN,] as in Ge. 14. 24, &c.

16. FEAR NOT,] as in Ge. 15. 1, &c.

MORE,] as in 2 Ch. 32. 7; Ps. 55. 18; Rom. 8 31.

17. OPEN HIS EYES,] to behold spiritual objects concealed from the natural eye.

THE HILL,] around Gilgal.

CHARIOTS OF FIRE,] as in 2. 11.

18. IT,] that is, the camp.

THIS NATION] of Aram, those warriors of it who were present.

BLINDNESS,] lit. 'blindnesses,' as in Ge. 19. 11.

19. SAMARIA] the capital city of Israel.

21. KING,] even Jehoram, as in 1. 17.

DO I SMITE,] when the Lord had thus brought them into his hand, as in 1 K. 20. 42.

MY FATHER,] a title of honour, as in Ge. 45. 8, &c.

22. NOT SMITE,] they being simply captives of war.

SWORD..BOW,] the usual weapons of war.

BREAD AND WATER,] the usual food of simple orientals.

23. PREPARETH,] as in Ps. 40. 6; Job 41. 6; Hos. 3. 2.

PROVISION,] or 'preparation.'

TROOPS,] as in Ge. 49. 19; 1 Sa. 30. 8, 15, 23; 2 Sa. 3. 22; 4. 2; 22. 30; 1 K. 11. 24; 2 K. 5. 2; 13. 20, 21; 24. 2, &c.

ANY MORE,] in marauding excursions, though, as appears immediately, they came in open warfare.

24. SAMARIA,] with the hope of overturning the throne of Israel.

25. FAMINE,] through the long continuance of the unexpected seige.

HEAD OF AN ASS,] not mentioned elsewhere as an article of food.

SILVERLINGS,] about £8.

CAB,] a Hebrew measure not noticed elsewhere.

DOVES' DUNG,] probably some kind of pulse or pease so called.

26. ON THE WALL] of the city, which was usually of great breadth.

SAVE] from hunger and misery.

27. NOT SAVE,] by giving victory over the foe, and a return of plenty.

WINE-VAT,] that is, food or drink.

28. WHAT TO THEE,] not 'what aileth thee,' as in C.V., but 'what have you to say.'

EAT] to sustain life, as in De. 28. 53.

29. BOIL,] as in Ex. 12. 9; 16. 23, &c.

HIDETH,] as in Jos. 6. 17, 25; 1 K. 18. 4, 13; Isa. 49. 2.

30. RENDETH,] testifying his grief at the distress.

ON THE WALL,] as in v. 26.

SACKCLOTH,] indicative of his humiliation and sorrow.

31. ADD,] as in Ruth 1. 17, &c.

32. HOUSE,] instructing the elders and the people, as in Eze. 8. 1; 20. 1.

SON OF THE MURDERER,] i.e. a murderous person.

33. THE EVIL,] not 'this evil,' as in C.V.

WAIT,] or 'tarry,' as in 1 Sa. 10. 8; 13. 8; 2 Sa. 18. 14, &c.

VII. 1. MEASURE,] in Heb. 'seah,' as in v. 16, 18; Ge. 18. 6; 1 Sa. 25. 18; 1 K. 18. 32.

FINE FLOUR,] as in Ge. 18. 6, &c.

SHEKEL,] as in Ge. 23. 15, 16, &c.

BARLEY,] as in Ex. 9. 31, &c.

GATE,] where the public markets were held.

2. CAPTAIN,] lit. 'third,' as in Ex. 14. 7; 15. 4 &c.

SUPPORTED,] as in 5. 18, &c.

WINDOWS,] as in v. 19; Ge. 7. 11; 8. 2; Ecc. 12. 3; Isa. 24. 18; 60. 8; Hos. 13. 3; Mal. 3. 10.

NOT EAT,] a prophecy of his sudden death.

3. LEPROUS,] and therefore cast out from society by themselves.

GATE] of Samaria, on the outside most probably.

4. FAMINE,] as in v. 25.

ARAM,] where there was abundance.

DIED,] judging they might as well die by violence as by famine.

5. TWILIGHT,] as in 1 Sa. 30. 17, &c.

EXTREMITY,] on the side next Samaria.

6. HEAR,] as in De. 4. 10, 36, &c.

HIRED,] as in Ge. 30. 16; De. 23. 4; Jud. 9. 4; 18. 4; 2 Sa. 10. 6; 1 Ch. 19. 6, 7; 2 Ch. 24. 12; 25. 6; Neh. 6. 12, 13; 13. 2; Isa. 46. 6; Prov. 26. 10; Isa. 46. 6.

HITTITES,] as in 1 K. 10. 29.

EGYPT,] whose resources were great.

7. FLEE] in the direction of Damascus.

8. HIDE,] for future use.

9. RIGHT,] as in Ge. 1. 7; Ex. 10. 29; Nu. 27. 7, &c.

TIDINGS,] as in 2 Sa. 4. 10; 18. 20, 22, 25, 27.

KEEPING SILENT,] as in Jud. 18. 9; 1 K. 22. 3; Neh. 8. 11; Isa. 57. 11.

LIGHT OF THE MORNING,] as in Jud. 16. 2; 1 Sa. 14. 36; 25. 22, 34, 36; 2 Sa. 17. 22; 23. 4, &c.

PUNISHMENT,] as in Ge. 4. 13, &c.

FOUND] as a just reward for their selfishness.

10. GATE-KEEPER,] the chief one of the whole number.

BOUND] to prevent them straying by night.

12. DECLARE,] not 'shew,' as in C.V.

I PRAY YOU,] not 'now,' as in C.V.

FAMISHED,] by reason of the seige.

TO BE HIDDEN] in the caves and valleys around the city.

CATCH] and make prisoners for the sake of ransom.

ENTER] and spoil the city.

13. This verse is much obscured by its apparent tautologies.

14. CHARIOT-HORSES,] having probably none others to ride on.

15. HASTE,] as in v. 7.

16. SPOIL,] as in Ge. 34. 27, 29, &c.

WORD,] as in v. 1 above.

17. CAPTAIN,] *lit.* 'third,' as in v. 2.

18. GATE,] or perhaps 'city.'

20. TREAD HIM DOWN] in their anxiety to secure food for themselves.

VIII. 1. REVIVED,] as in 4. 35, &c.

SOJOURN,] that is, wherein she could.

FAMINE,] noticed in the preceding chapter.

SEVEN YEARS,] double the length of that for which Elijah prayed.

2. PHILISTINES,] on the coast of the Mediterranean Sea.

3. TO CRY] in her distress, for help.

FIELD,] which, during her absence, had been appropriated by some one, thinking her dead.

4. GEHAZI,] as in 5. 27, &c.

DONE,] some of which he knew only by report.

5. REVIVED,] as in 4. 35.

6. EUNUCH,] as in Ge. 37. 36; 39. 1; 40. 2, 7, &c.

INCREASE,] as in Ge. 47. 24, &c.

7. DAMASCUS,] to confirm Naaman, or appoint Hazael to be king; see 1 K. 19. 15.

SICK,] as in 1. 2, &c.

THE MAN OF GOD,] that is, Elisha, who had cured his former general.

8. HAZAEL,] i.e. 'God has seen.'

PRESENT,] as is customary in the east.

JEHOVAH,] the covenant-God of Israel.

SICKNESS,] as in 1. 2, &c.

9. GOOD THING,] suitable for a king to offer.

FORTY CAMELS,] each of them, however, probably carrying only a very small burden, the whole being for shew.

10. NOT REVILE.] The C.V. follows the Rabbies, who represent the prophet as uttering a falsehood.

11. SETTETH,] *lit.* 'causeth to stand.'

WEEPETH,] affected by the passing thought.

12. EVIL,] delineated in the following particulars.

FENCED PLACES,] as in Nu. 13. 39, &c.

SEND INTO FIRE,] as in Jos. 8. 8, &c.

SUCKLINGS,] as in 1 Sa. 15. 3; 22. 19; Job 3. 16; Ps. 8. 2; 17. 14; 137. 9, &c.

DASH TO PIECES,] as in Isa. 13. 16, 18; Hos. 10. 14; 13. 16; Neh. 3. 10.

PREGNANT,] as in Ge. 16. 11; 38. 24, 25, &c.

RIP UP,] as in 15. 16; Hos. 13. 16; Amos 1. 13.

13. THE DOG,] one of the most unclean and least regarded animals in the east.

GREAT THING,] its magnitude rather than its vileness appears to have affected him.

SHEWED,] *lit.* 'caused me to see.'

14. RECOVER,] which was not true; see v.10.

15. COARSE CLOTH.] This original word is not found elsewhere.

STEAD,] as had been foretold.

16. FIFTH YEAR,] B.C. 892; compare 3. 1.

JEHORAM,] as in 1 K. 22. 50

17. 32 YEARS,] as in 2 Ch. 21. 5.

8 YEARS,] till B.C. 884.

18. WAY] of idolatry and wickedness.

WIFE,] as in v. 26.

19. NOT WILLING,] as in De. 10. 10; 23. 5, &c.

LAMP,] as in 1 K. 11. 36; 15. 4; 2 Ch. 21. 7.

20. EDOM,] subdued by David.

REVOLTED,] *lit.* 'transgressed,' as in 1 K. 8. 50; Ge. 31. 36; 50. 17, &c.

21. ZAIR,] i.e. 'little, small.'

HIMSELF,] the original is very emphatic.

TENTS,] according to the usual custom of oriental armies.

22. EDOM,] according to Ge. 27. 40.

LIBNAH,] as in Jos. 10. 29; 21. 13, &c.

23. MATTERS,] not 'acts,' as in C.V.

24. CITY OF DAVID,] that is, Zion.

AHAZIAH,] i.e. 'laid hold of by Jah;' in 2 Ch. 21. 17 he is called 'Jehoahaz,' and in 2 Ch. 22. 6 'Azariah.'

26. 22 YEARS,] in 2 Ch. 22. 2 it is 42 years.

ATHALIAH,] i.e. 'afflicted of Jah,' as in 11. 1, 2.

OMRI,] father of Ahab, as in v. 18

27. SON-IN-LAW,] or rather, his father was so.

28. HAZAEL,] as in v. 15.

RAMOTH-GILEAD,] which still remained in the possession of Aram, after the death of Ahab.

29. WOUNDS,] *lit.* 'smitings.'

RAMAH] of Gilead, as in v. 28.

GONE DOWN] to Samaria from Jerusalem.

JEZREEL,] where he had a palace.

SICK,] by reason of his wounds.

IX. 1. SONS OF THE PROPHETS,] or young men whom they instructed.

GIRD UP] the long flowing oriental robes.

VIAL OF OIL,] as in v. 3; 1 Sa. 10. 1.

RAMOTH-GILEAD,] where Joram had left his army besieging the city.

2. JEHU,] i.e. 'he is,' as in 1 K. 19. 16; 21. 29.

JEHOSHAPHAT,] i.e. 'Jah has judged.'

NIMSHI,] as in 1 K. 19. 16.

INNER CHAMBER,] as in 1 K. 20. 30, &c.

3. POURED] the oil out of the vessel, anointing him.

FOR KING,] instead of Joram.

WAIT,] to answer any enquiries or receive any reward.

4. THE PROPHET,] or announcer of the will of God.

5. O CHIEF,] as in Ge. 12. 15; 21. 22, 32, &c.

6. ANOINTED] by the hand of his servant.

7. SMITTEN] with utter destruction.

REQUIRED,] as in Ge. 4. 15, 24; Ex. 21. 20, 21, &c.

JEZEBEL,] wife of Ahab, who put the Lord's servants to death.

8. PERISHED] because of their iniquity.

CUT OFF,] judicially, by a violent death.

SITTING,] as in 1 K. 14. 10; 21. 21, &c.

9. JEROBOAM,] as in 1 K. 15. 29.

BAASHA,] as in 1 K. 16. 3, 11.

10. PORTION OF JEZREEL,] as in 1 K. 21. 23, &c.

NONE BURYING,] her body being devoured, as in v. 35, 36 below.

FLEETH,] as directed in v. 3.
11. SERVANTS,] his fellow chiefs, as in v. 4.
MADMAN,] as in De. 28. 34; 1 Sa. 21. 15;
Jer. 29. 26; Hos. 9. 7, &c.
TALK,] as in 1 Sa. 1. 16; 1 K. 18. 27; Job 7.
13; 9. 27; 10. 1; 21. 4; 23. 2; Ps. 55. 2; 64. 1;
102. 1; 104. 34; 142. 2; Prov. 23. 29.
12. FALSE,] as in Ex. 5. 9; 20. 16, &c.
KING,] instead of Joram.
13. GARMENT,] his upper robe, for a seat
to the new king.
TOP,] lit. 'bone,' as in Ge. 49. 14; Job 40.
18; Prov. 17. 22; 25. 15; Da. 6. 24.
TRUMPET,] that all the camp might hear.
14. CONSPIRETH,] lit. 'bindeth himself,'
as in 2 Ch. 24. 25, 26.
KEEPING IN,] or 'watching over.'
15. JEZREEL,] as in 8. 29.
WOUNDS,] lit. 'smitings.'
MIND,] lit. 'soul, or desire.'
CITY] of Ramoth-Gilead.
16. LYING,] sick and wounded.
GONE DOWN,] from Jerusalem to Jezreel,
as in 8. 29.
17. WATCHMAN,] as in Nu. 23. 14; 1 Sa. 1.
1; 14. 16; 2 Sa. 13. 34; 18. 24, 25, 26, 27, &c.
TOWER,] as in Ge. 11. 4, 5, &c.
COMPANY,] as in Job 22. 11; 38. 34; Isa. 60.
6; Eze. 26. 10.
PEACE?] fearing some hostile attack in his
enfeebled state.
18. THE KING,] Joram, whose officer Jehu
was.
TURN ROUND,] lest he should warn Joram
of the coming danger.
20. DRIVING,] or 'leading.'
MADNESS,] as in De. 28. 28; Zec. 12. 4.
21. HARNESS,] lit. 'bind,' as in 1 K. 18. 44;
Jer. 46. 4.
NABOTH,] who had been unjustly stoned
to death, as in 1 K. 21. 13.
22. WHOREDOMS,] in following Baal and
not Jehovah.
WITCHCRAFTS,] as in Isa. 47. 9, 12; Mic.
5. 12; Nah. 3. 4.
23. TURNETH HIS HANDS,] as in 1 K. 22.
34; 2 Ch. 18. 33.
DECEIT,] as in Ge. 27. 35, &c.
24. FILLED HIS HAND,] so as to be ready
for action.
ARMS,] on the shoulder at the back.
BOWETH DOWN,] as in Ge. 49. 9, &c.
25. BIDKAR,]i.e. 'son of piercing through.'
CAPTAIN,] lit. 'third,' as in 7. 2, &c.
PORTION,] as in v. 21.
BURDEN,] as in Ex. 23. 5, &c.
26. NABOTH . . SONS,] who might have
sprung from him.
AFFIRMATION,] as in Ge. 22. 16, &c.
RECOMPENSED,] as in Ge. 44. 4; De. 7. 10;
32. 41, &c.
WORD,] as in 1 K. 21. 19.
27. GARDEN HOUSE.] See 1 K. 21. 2.
GUR,] i.e. a 'whelp or sojourner.'
IBLEAM,] in Manasseh, as in Jos. 17. 11.
MEGIDDO,] as in Jos. 17. 11; also in Man-
asseh.
28. JERUSALEM,] his capital city.
CITY OF DAVID,] that is, Zion, 1 K. 22. 50.
29. ELEVENTH YEAR,] in 8 25 it is said to
have been the 12th year.

30. JEZREEL,] after having slain the two
kings.
JEZEBEL,] the wife of Ahab.
PUTTETH HER EYES IN PAINT.] See Jer.
4. 30.
MAKETH RIGHT,] lit. 'good.'
WINDOW,] of the palace or tower.
31. GATE,] of the palace.
SLAYER OF HIS LORD,] as in 1 K. 16.
9, 10.
32. WITH ME,] that is, on my side.
EUNUCHS,] who had charge of the royal
harem.
33. LET HER GO,] as in Ex. 23. 11; De. 15.
2, 3; 2 Sa. 6. 6; 2 K. 9. 33; 1 Ch. 13. 9; Jer.
17. 4; Ps. 141. 6.
SPRINKLED,] as in Lev. 6. 27; Isa. 63. 6.
WALL,] of the palace.
TREADETH HER DOWN,] with the hoofs of
his horses.
34. DRINKETH,] as if it were a matter of
no importance.
LOOK AFTER,] or 'inspect.'
I PRAY YOU,] not 'now,' as in C.V.
CURSED ONE,] as in Ge. 3. 14, 17, &c.
KING'S DAUGHTER,] even Ethbaal, king of
the Sidonians, as in 1 K. 16. 31.
35. SKULL,] as in Ex. 16. 16; 38. 26; Nu. 1.
2, 18, 20, 22; 3. 47; Jud. 9. 53; 1 Ch. 10. 10;
23. 3, 24.
PALMS OF THE HANDS,] as in Lev. 14. 15,
26; 1 Sa. 5. 4, &c.
36. SPAKE,] in 1 K. 21. 23.
37. CARCASE,] lit. 'fallen thing.'
DUNG,] as in Ps. 83. 10; Jer. 8. 2; 9. 22; 16.
4; 25. 33.

X. 1. SEVENTY SONS,] including grandsons
doubtless.
SAMARIA,] the capital of the kingdom of
Israel.
JEZREEL,] who had probably fled thither;
Sept. has 'Samaria;' Vulg. 'the city.'
ELDERS] of Samaria, and the
SUPPORTERS,] of the family and house of
Ahab.
2. LORD,] even Ahab.
CHARIOTS .. HORSES,] belonging to the
whole kingdom.
FENCED CITY..ARMOUR,] so that they had
no excuse for declining.
3. BEST..UPRIGHTEST,] for ruling in the
stead of his father.
FIGHT,] as loyal servants.
4. GREATLY,] knowing how helpless they
were in reality.
THE TWO KINGS,] of Israel and Judah.
5. HOUSE,] of the king.
CITY,] of Samaria.
ELDERS..SUPPORTERS,] of the house of
Ahab.
DO,] thus acknowledging his supreme
authority.
6. HEADS OF THE MEN,] by putting them
to death.
GREAT ONES,] in rank, station, and influence, most worthy of confidence.
BRINGING THEM UP,] lit. 'making them
great.'
7. SLAUGHTER,] as in Ge. 22. 10; 37. 31;
Ex. 12. 6, &c.

BASKETS,] as in 2 Sa. 2. 14; 2 Ch. 35. 13; Job 41. 20; Ps. 81. 6; Jer. 24. 2.

8. TWO HEAPS,] one on each side of the way.

MORNING,] when he would take public notice of them.

9. RIGHTEOUS,] having taken no part in these troubles.

CONSPIRED,] as in 9. 14.

SLAY HIM,] as in 9. 24.

ALL THESE] seventy innocent men.

10. SPAKE,] as in 1 K. 21. 21, 29.

11. GREAT MEN,] as in v. 6.

ACQUAINTANCES,] as in Ruth 2. 1; Job 19. 14; Ps. 31. 11; 55. 13; 88. 9, 18; Isa. 12. 5.

PRIESTS,] who supported him in idolatry.

REMNANT,] in Jezreel, at least.

12. SAMARIA,] from Jezreel, to take possession of the throne.

SHEARING,] lit. 'binding' for shearing.

13. SALUTE,] lit. 'peace.'

MISTRESS,] as in 1 K. 11. 19; 15. 13; 2 Ch. 15. 16; Jer. 13. 18; 29. 2.

14. CATCH,] as in Ge. 39. 12, &c.

SLAUGHTER,] as in v. 7.

PIT,] as in Ge. 37. 20, 22, 24, 28, 29, &c.

42 MEN,] of the company.

15. JEHONADAB,] a Kenite, as in 1 Ch. 2. 55; Jer. 35. 6—10.

RECHAB,] i.e. 'a rider, charioteer.'

RIGHT,] lit. 'upright.'

HAND,] as a token of friendship.

16. ZEAL,] as in Nu. 25. 11, &c.

17. LEFT,] beyond the 70 in v. 7.

18. BAAL,] the god of the Sidonians.

19. PROPHETS,] who proclaimed his praises.

PRIESTS,] who offered sacrifices to him.

LACKING,] lit. 'inspected,' and found absent.

SUBTILTY,] as Jacob did to Isaac and Esau.

20. SANCTIFY,] separate or set apart.

RESTRAINT,] as in Isa. 1. 13; Joel 1. 14; 2. 15.

21. MOUTH TO MOUTH,] as in 21. 16; Ezr. 9. 11.

22. WARDROBE.] This original word is not found elsewhere.

CLOTHING,] suitable for a festival of Baal, to mark them conspicuously.

23. SEARCH,] as in Ge. 31. 35; 44. 12; 1 Sa. 23. 23; 1 K. 20. 6, &c.

24. SOUL,] as in 1 K. 20. 39, &c.

25. BURNT-OFFERING,] to Baal, as in v. 19.

RUNNERS,] as in 1 Sa. 22. 17, &c.

CAPTAINS,] as in Ex. 14. 7, &c.

HOUSE OF BAAL,] as in 1 K. 16. 32, &c.

26. STANDING-PILLARS,] as in Ge. 28. 18, 22; 31. 13, 45, 51, 52; 35. 14, 20; Ex. 23. 24; 24. 4; 34. 13; Lev. 26. 1, &c.

BURN,] as directed in the law.

27. BREAK DOWN,] as in Ex. 34. 13, &c.

APPOINT,] lit. 'set.'

DRAUGHT-HOUSE.] The original word is not found elsewhere.

28. ISRAEL,] at least for a time.

29. CALVES,] as in 1 K. 12. 28, 29.

30. DONE WELL,] so far as he executed justice on the house of Ahab.

IN MY HEART,] as in 1 Sa. 2. 35, &c.

FOURTH,] as in 15. 12; Ge. 15. 16

31. LAW,] as revealed to Moses and the prophets.

ALL HIS HEART,] as he was required to do.

32. CUT OFF,] as in Prov. 26. 6; Hab. 2. 10.

HAZAEL,] as foretold in 8. 12.

33. GILEAD AND BASHAN,] the first conquered and the first lost.

34. MATTERS,] not 'acts,' as in C.V.

35. SAMARIA,] where the former kings were buried.

JEHOAHAZ,] i.e. 'Jah has taken hold,' who reigned 17 years, as in 13. 1.

36. 28 YEARS,] being longer than any other king of Israel.

XI. 1. ATHALIAH,] daughter of Ahab, and grand-daughter of Omri, as in 8. 18, 26.

AHAZIAH,] the last king of Judah.

DEAD,] slain by Jehu, as in 9. 27.

SEED OF THE KINGDOM,] as in 1 K. 11. 14; 2 K. 25. 25; 2 Ch. 22. 10; Eze. 17. 13; Da. 1. 3.

2. JEHOSHEBA,] i.e. 'sworn of Jehovah;' in 2 Ch. 22. 11, it is 'Jehoshabeath.'

JORAM,] i.e. 'Jehovah is high.'

JOASH,] i.e. 'Jehovah is foundation.'

STEALETH,] as in 2 Ch. 22. 11.

NURSE,] as in Ge. 24. 59; 32. 15; 35. 8; Ex. 2. 7; 2 Ch. 22. 11; Isa. 49. 23.

INNER PART,] as in Ex. 3. 8; 2 Sa. 4. 7; 2 K. 6. 12; 2 Ch. 22. 11; Ecc. 10. 20.

3. HOUSE OF JEHOVAH,] which phrase often includes the priests' dwellings around the temple proper.

HIDING HIMSELF,] as in 1 Sa. 14. 22; 1 Ch. 21. 20; 2 Ch. 22. 9, 12.

REIGNING,] without interruption or opposition.

4. JEHOIADA,] i.e. 'Jehovah hath known,' husband of Jehosheba, and high priest, as in 2 Ch. 22. 11.

THE HUNDREDS,] as in Ex. 18. 21, 25, &c.

EXECUTIONERS..RUNNERS,] as in 2 Sa. 20. 23; v. 19 below.

CAUSETH TO SWEAR,] as in Ge. 24. 3, 37,&c.

SON OF THE KING,] even Joash, as in v. 2.

5. GOING IN,] to perform the services of the temple.

6. SUR,] i.e. 'turning aside;' in 2 Ch. 33. 5, it is 'the foundation,' by changing a Hebrew letter.

RUNNERS,] in 2 Ch. 35. 4, called 'of the thresholds.'

PULLED DOWN,] not 'from being pulled down,' as some suppose—a very unlikely supposition.

7. TWO PARTS,] lit. 'two of the hands,' as in Ge. 47. 24; Neh. 11. 1; Da. 1. 20.

GOING OUT,] from the service of the temple.

8. COMPASSED,] as in Jos. 6. 3, 11; 2 K. 6. 14, &c.

WEAPONS,] shields and spears, as in v. 10.

RANGES,] as in v. 15; 2 Ch. 23. 14; 1 K. 6. 9.

9. COMMANDED,] as in 2 Ch. 23. 8.

10. THE PRIEST,] that is, Jehoiada.

SPEARS..SHIELDS,] probably laid up as trophies in the temple.

11. SHOULDER,] as in Ex. 20. 14, 15; 28. 7, 12, 25, 27, &c.

HOUSE,] not 'temple,' as in C.V.

12. TESTIMONY,] as in Ex. 16. 34, &c.

ANOINT,] with the holy oil.

SMITE THE HAND,] as in Nu. 24. 10; Job 27. 23; Ps. 47. 1; 98. 8, &c,
LIVE,] as in 1 Sa. 10. 24, &c.
13. HOUSE,] not 'temple,' as in C.V.
14. THE PILLAR,] called 'his pillar,' in 2 Ch. 23. 13; compare 2 Ch. 34. 1; 2 K. 23. 3.
ORDINANCE,] *lit.* 'judgment.'
TRUMPETS,] not 'trumpeters,' as in C.V.; see Nu. 10. 2, 8, 9, 10; 31. 6; 2 K. 12. 13; 1 Ch. 13. 8; 15. 24, 28; 16. 6, 42, &c.
TRUMPETS,] to testify congratulations.
CONSPIRACY,] as in 2 Ch. 15. 12; 1 K. 16. 20; 2 K. 12. 20; 14. 19; 15. 15, 30; 17. 4; 2 Ch. 23. 13; 25. 27; Isa. 8. 12; Jer. 11. 9; Ez. 22. 25.
15. INSPECTORS,] as in Nu. 31. 14, 48, &c.
RANGES,] as in v. 8.
HOUSE OF JEHOVAH,] lest it should be defiled with blood.
16. SIDES,] *lit.* 'hands.'
PUT TO DEATH,] as a usurper and tyrant.
17. JEHOVAH..KING..PEOPLE,] as in 2 Ch. 23. 16.
KING..PEOPLE,] as in 2 Sa. 5. 3.
18. HOUSE OF BAAL,] perhaps on the mount of the olives, called the mount of corruption, in 23. 13.
BREAK IT DOWN,] as in Ex. 34. 13, &c.
IMAGES,] as in Nu. 33. 52; 1 Sa. 6. 5, 11; 2 Ch. 23. 17, &c.
THOROUGHLY,] *lit.* 'well.'
MATTAN,] i.e. 'a gift,' as in 2 Ch. 23. 17.
ALTARS,] which were many.
THE PRIEST,] Jehoiada, as in v. 9.
INSPECTORS,] as in v. 15.
19. EXECUTIONERS ... RUNNERS,] as in v. 4.
BRING DOWN,] from Mount Moriah to the king's house.
THRONE,] which had been occupied by David, &c.
20. LAND,] of Judah and Benjamin.
CITY,] Jerusalem.
21. SEVEN YEARS,] as in v. 4; 22. 1; 2 Ch. 24. 1.
JEHOASH,] *or* Joash, as in v. 2.

XII. 1. JEHU,] king of Israel.
JEHOASH,] son of Ahaziah, as in 11. 2.
FORTY YEARS,] like David and Solomon.
JERUSALEM,] over Judah and Benjamin.
ZIBIAH,] i.e. 'a roe.'
BEER-SHEBA,] in the tribe of Simeon, on the extreme south.
2. RIGHT,] *or* 'upright.'
DIRECTED,] as in Ge. 46. 28; Ex. 4. 12, 15, &c.
3. HIGH PLACES] on the mountains, &c.
MAKING PERFUME] with the sacrifices.
4. PRIESTS,] who had charge of the temple.
SANCTIFIED THINGS,] offerings of every kind.
PASSING OVER,] in the numbering of the people, as in Ex. 30. 13, 14.
VALUATION,] as in Lev. 5. 15, 18, &c.
GOETH UP] spontaneously.
5. ACQUAINTANCE,] as in v. 7.
THE BREACH,] *or* broken down place.
NOT STRENGTHENED,] either from want of means or of willingness.
7. JEHOIADA,] who had instructed him, as in v. 2.

GIVE IT,] as he had formerly commanded in v. 5.
8. CONSENT,] as in Ge. 34. 15, 22, 23.
9. CHEST,] as in Ge. 50. 26; Ex. 25. 10; 2 Ch 24. 8, 10, 11.
PIERCETH,] as in 18. 21, &c.
HOLE,] as in 1 Sa. 14. 11, &c.
LID,] *lit.* 'door.'
ALTAR] of burnt-offering.
THRESHOLD,] as in 23. 4; 25. 18; 1 Ch. 9. 19; 2 Ch. 34. 9; Est. 2. 21; 6. 2; Jer. 35. 4; 52. 24.
10. ABUNDANT,] from the free-will offerings.
OF THE HIGH PRIEST,] not 'the high priest' himself as in the C.V.
BIND IT UP] in bags, according to the custom.
COUNT,] as in Ge. 13. 16, &c.
11. WEIGHED,] as in Job 28. 25; Ps. 75. 3; Isa. 40. 12, 13, &c.
INSPECTING,] *or* 'overseeing.'
WORKING IN THE WOOD,] as in 2 Sa. 5. 11, &c.
12. WALL] of the temple.
BREACH,] as in v. 5.
13. BASINS,] as in Ex. 12. 22, &c.
SNUFFERS,] as in 1 K. 7. 50, &c.
BOWLS,] as in Ex. 27. 3, &c.
15. FAITHFULNESS,] as in Ex. 17. 12; De 32. 4; 1 Sa. 26. 23, &c.
16. GUILT-OFFERING,] as in Ge. 26. 10; Ex. 5. 6, 7, 15, 16, 19, &c.
SIN-OFFERING,] as in Ge. 4. 7, &c.
IT IS,] according to the law in Lev. 7. 7; Nu. 18. 9.
17. GO UP] from Damascus to
GATH,] one of the five Philistine cities, and
SETTETH HIS FACE,] as in Ge. 31. 21, &c.
18. SANCTIFIED THINGS,] as in v. 4; 18. 15, 16; 1 K. 15. 18.
SENDETH] as a present, tribute, or bribe.
19. MATTERS,] not 'acts,' as in C.V.
20. CONSPIRACY,] probably to avenge the death of Zechariah, as in 2 Ch. 24. 21.
MILLO,] as in 2 Sa. 5. 9, &c.
SILLA,] i.e. 'a basket;' not mentioned elsewhere.
21. JOZACHAR,] i.e. 'Jehovah has remembered.'
SHIMEATH,] i.e. 'hearing.'
JEHOZABAD,] i.e. 'Jehovah has endowed.'
SHEMER,] i.e. 'a keeper.'
CITY OF DAVID,] that is, Zion.
AMAZIAH,] i.e. 'strengthened by Jah.'

XIII. 1. TWENTY AND THIRD.] See 12. 6.
JEHOAHAZ,] i.e. 'Jehovah has laid hold.'
SEVENTEEN YEARS,] the two last with his son; see v. 10; 14. 1.
2. THE EVIL THING,] that is, idolatry.
THE SINS,] as in 1 K. 13. 33, &c.
3. BURNETH,] as in Ex. 4. 14; 22. 24, &c.
HAZAEL,] as in 12. 17.
BEN-HADAD,] i.e. 'son of shouting.'
4. APPEASETH,] as in Ex. 32. 11, &c.
OPPRESSED,] as in Ex. 3. 9, &c.
5. SAVIOUR,] perhaps Joash, as in v. 25.
6. TO SIN,] by making the two calves of gold.

SHRINE,] which Ahab made, 1 K. 16. 33, and Jehu had spared.

7. 10,000 FOOTMEN,] whereas Jeroboam had once 800,000, as in 2 Ch. 12. 3.

THRESHING,] as in Hos. 10. 11; Amos 1.3,&c.

8. MATTERS,] not 'acts,' as in C.V.

9. SAMARIA,] his capital city, where Omri and the other kings of Israel were buried.

JOASH,] in v. 10 it is Jehoash.

10. 37TH YEAR,] B.C. 841.

JEHOASH,] or 'Joash.'

11. THE EVIL THING,] that is, idolatry.

12. MATTERS,] not 'acts,' as in C.V.

AMAZIAH,] as in 12. 21.

13. JEROBOAM,] as in 1 K. 11. 26.

ISRAEL,] as in v. 9.

14. SICKNESS,] as in De. 7. 15, &c.

COME DOWN] from his palace to the prophet's house.

CHARIOT..HORSEMEN,] as in 2. 12.

15. BOW AND ARROWS,] the usual weapons of war.

16. PLACE,] lit. 'cause to ride.'

17. EASTWARD,] as in Ge. 13. 14, &c.

SALVATION,] or 'safety,' as in Jud. 15. 18, &c.

APHEK,] see 1 K. 20. 26, 29, 30.

19. WROTH,] as in Ge. 40. 2, &c.

CONSUMING,] as in Ex. 32. 12, &c.

20. TROOPS,] as in Ge. 49. 19; 1 Sa. 30. 8, 15, 23, &c.

MOAB,] on the east of the Dead Sea unto Arnon.

21. SEEN,] not 'spied,' as in C.V.

GOETH AND COMETH,] by the force of the fall.

FEET,] God thus honouring even the mortal remains of his servant.

22. OPPRESSED,] as in 13. 4, &c.

23. FAVOUR,] as in Ge. 33. 5, 11; 43. 29; Ex. 33. 19, &c.

PITY,] as in Ex. 33. 19; De. 13. 17, &c.

TURN,] as in Ex. 18. 22, &c.

COVENANT,] as in Ex. 32. 13.

NOT BEEN WILLING,] as in Ex. 10. 27; De. 1. 16; 2. 30; 10. 10, &c.

AS YET,] lit. 'until now.'

24. STEAD,] being the third king of that name over Aram.

25. CITIES,] in Gilead and Bashan, as in 10. 33.

THREE TIMES,] as in v. 18, 19.

BRINGETH BACK] under his own authority.

XIV. 1. SECOND YEAR,] of his reigning alone, after the death of his father, B.C.839.

AMAZIAH,] as in 2 Ch. 25. 1.

2. 29 YEARS,] 14 of which were contemporary with Joash, and 15 after him, see 13. 10; v. 17 below.

JEHOADDAN,] as in 2 Ch. 25. 1.

3. RIGHT,] or 'upright.'

NOT LIKE DAVID,] so thoroughly and sincerely; see 2 Ch. 25. 2.

DID] first good and then evil.

4. HIGH PLACES,] as in 12. 3.

5. STRONG,] by his good government.

SMITING,] as in 12. 20.

6. SONS] or descendants.

WRITTEN] in De. 24. 16.

7. EDOM] lying between the Dead Sea and the Ælanitic Gulf of the Sea of Suph.

VALLEY OF SALT,] on which see 2 Sa. 8. 13.

10,000,] besides other 10,000 taken alive, as in 2 Ch. 25. 5—12.

SELAH,] lit. 'the rock,' same as Petra, the capital city of Edom.

JOKTHEEL,] i.e. 'obedience of God;' see 2 Ch. 25. 8, 9.

8. LOOK ONE ANOTHER,] as in Ge. 42. 1; 2 Ch. 25. 17, 21; v. 11 below.

9. THORN,] as in 1 Sa. 13. 6; 2 Ch. 25. 18; 33. 11; Job 31. 40; 41. 2; Prov. 26. 9; Song 2. 2; Isa. 34. 13; Hos. 9. 6.

CEDAR,] one of the largest trees in the country.

PASS BY,] accidentally as a matter of course.

BEAST,] lit. 'living creature.'

TREADETH DOWN] with ease, without opposition.

10. SMITTEN,] as in v. 7.

LIFTED THEE UP] with pride and conceit.

BE HONOURED,] in thine own circle and kingdom.

STIR THYSELF UP,] as in De. 2. 5, 9, 19, 24, &c.

11. HEARKENED,] trusting to the gods of Edom, as in 2 Ch. 25. 14, 20.

LOOK ONE ANOTHER,] as in v. 8.

BETH-SHEMESH,] i.e. 'house of the sun,' as in Jos. 19. 38, &c.

12. TENT,] as in Jud. 7. 8; 1 Sa. 4. 10, &c.

13. CAUGHT] alive, a prisoner of war.

THEY COME IN,] both of the kings.

BURSTETH,] as in Ge. 28. 14; 30. 30, 43; 38. 39.

GATE,] leading in the direction of Ephraim.

GATE OF THE CORNER,] as in 2 Ch. 26. 9; Jer. 31. 38, &c.

14. GOLD..SILVER..VESSELS,] with Obed-Edom their keeper, as in 2 Ch. 25. 24.

PLEDGES,] or 'sureties,' as in 2 Ch. 25. 24.

15. MATTERS,] not 'acts,' as in C.V.

16. IN SAMARIA,] his capital city.

JEROBOAM] the second of that name.

17. FIFTEEN YEARS.] See on v. 2; Vulg. has '25 years.'

18. MATTERS,] not 'acts,' as in C.V.

19. CONSPIRACY,] because of the troubles he had brought upon the state by his pride and idolatry.

LACHISH,] as in Jos. 15. 39.

20. CITY OF DAVID,] that is, Zion.

21. AZARIAH,] i.e. 'help of Jah;' called 'Uzziah' in 15. 13; 2 Ch. 26. 1; 'strength of Jah.'

16 YEARS,] as in 15. 2.

22. ELATH,] a port of the Sea of Suph, belonging to Edom, as in De. 2. 8; 1 K. 9. 26.

BACK] from the power of Edom.

THE KING,] his father.

23. 15TH YEAR,] B.C. 825.

41 YEARS.] Josephus has 40.

24. THE EVIL THING,] that is, idolatry.

TO SIN,] by setting up the calves of gold.

25. BORDER,] that is, territory.

HAMATH.] See Nu. 34. 8.

SEA OF THE DESERT] of Jordan, the salt or Dead Sea.

JONAH,] i.e. 'a dove.'

AMITTAI,] i.e. 'true, stedfast.'

GATH-HEPHER,] in Zebulun, in Galilee see Jos. 19. 13, and John 7. 52.
26. BITTER,] *lit.* 'rebellious,' as in Nu. 20. 10; De. 21. 18, 20; Ps. 78. 8; Jer. 5. 23.
RESTRAINED..LEFT,] as in De. 32. 36, &c.
HELPER,] as in Job 29. 12; 30. 13; Ps. 22. 11; 72. 12; Isa. 63. 5; La. 1. 7; Da. 11. 45.
27. BLOT OUT,] as in Ge. 6. 7; 7. 4, 23, &c.
28. MATTERS,] not 'acts,' as in C.V.
DAMASCUS,] the chief city of Aram, on the north of Israel.
HAMATH.] See v. 25.
29. WITH THE KINGS,] in Samaria.
ZECHARIAH,] i.e. 'remembered by Jah.'

XV. 1. 27TH YEAR,] B.C. 810.
AZARIAH,] as in 14. 21.
2. 52 YEARS,] longer than any other of the kings of Judah.
JECHOLIAH,] i.e. 'ability of Jah,' as in 2 Ch. 26. 3.
3. RIGHT,] *or* 'upright.'
DID,] as in 14. 3.
4. HIGH PLACES,] as in 14. 4.
5. SMITETH,] with leprosy, as in 2 Ch. 24. 19, 20.
SEPARATE,] *lit.* 'free.'
JOTHAM,] i.e. 'Jah is perfect.'
THE HOUSE] of the king.
6. MATTERS,] not 'acts,' as in C.V.
7. CITY OF DAVID,] that is, Zion.
8. ZECHARIAH,] as in 14. 29.
9. THE EVIL THING,] that is, idolatry.
TO SIN,] as in 14. 24.
10. SHALLUM,] i.e. 'recompense.'
JABESH,] i.e. 'dry.'
BEFORE,] in an open public manner.
11. MATTERS,] not 'acts,' as in C.V.
12. SAYING,] in 10. 30.
13. 39TH YEAR,] B.C. 772.
UZZIAH,] or Azariah, as in 13. 21.
MONTH OF DAYS,] as in De. 21. 13.
14. MENAHEM,] i.e. 'a comforter.'
GADI,] i.e. 'a Gadite.'
TIRZAH,] as in Jos. 12. 24.
15. CONSPIRACY,] against Zechariah, as in v. 10.
16. TIPHSAH,] as in 1 K. 4. 24.
RIPPED UP,] as in 8. 12; Amos 1. 13.
17. 39TH YEAR,] B.C. 772.
18. THE EVIL THING,] that is, idolatry.
19. PUL,] i.e. 'a lord, elephant, *or* bean.'
ASSHUR,] east of the Euphrates.
1000 TALENTS,] about £375,000.
HAND,] against all competitors.
20. WEALTH,] as in Ge. 34. 29, &c.
50 SHEKELS,] about £6.
21. MATTERS,] not 'acts,' as in C.V.
22. PEKAHIAH,] i.e. 'opened by Jah.'
23. 50TH YEAR,] B.C. 761.
24. THE EVIL THING,] that is, idolatry.
25. PEKAH,] i.e. 'opening,' see Isa. 7. 1.
REMALIAH.] Etymology uncertain.
CAPTAIN,] *lit.* 'third.'
HIGH PLACE,] as in 1 K. 16. 18, &c.
ARGOB.] Etymology uncertain, probably so called from his birth-place.
ARIEH,] i.e. 'the lion.'
GILEADITES,] beyond the Jordan, near Argob, see De. 3. 13.
26. MATTERS,] not 'acts,' as in C.V.

27. 52ND YEAR,] B.C. 759.
28. THE EVIL THING,] that is, idolatry
29. TIGLATH-PILESER,] i.e. 'lord of the Tigris.'
ASSHUR,] as in v. 19.
IJON-..ABEL-BETH-MAACHAH,] as in 1 K. 15. 20.
JANOAH,] in Ephraim, as in Jos. 16. 6.
KEDESH..HAZOR,] in Naphtali, see Jos 19. 36, 37.
GILEAD,] beyond the Jordan.
GALILEE,] north of Canaan.
NAPHTALI,] or upper Galilee.
ASSHUR,] thus beginning the threatened captivity of the ten tribes.
30. HOSHEA,] i.e. 'ease, safety.'
ELAH,] i.e. 'an oak.'
JOTHAM,] as in v. 7.
31. MATTERS,] not 'acts,' as in C.V.
32. UZZIAH,] *or* Azariah, as in 14. 21.
33. 25 YEARS,] B.C. 758.
JERUSHA,] i.e. a 'possession.'
ZADOK,] i.e. 'righteous.'
34. RIGHT,] *or* 'upright.'
DONE,] except interfering with the priests' duties.
35. HIGH PLACES,] as in v. 4.
HIGH GATE,] as in 2 Ch. 27. 3.
36. MATTERS,] not 'acts,' as in C.V.
37. REZIN,] i.e. 'a prince.'
38. CITY OF DAVID,] that is, Zion.
AHAZ,] i.e. 'he laid hold.'

XVI. 1. 17TH YEAR,] B.C. 742.
2. 20 YEARS.] See 18. 2.
16 YEARS,] like his father.
3. THE WAY] of idolatry, as in 8. 18.
PASSOVER,] as in Lev. 18. 21.
ABOMINATIONS,] as in Ge. 43. 32; 46. 34; Ex. 8. 16, &c.
DISPOSSESSED,] as in Ex. 34. 24, &c.
4. HIGH PLACES,] as in 1 K. 3. 2, &c.
HEIGHTS,] as in 1 K. 14. 23, &c.
GREEN TREE,] as in De. 12. 2, &c.
5. GO UP,] from Samaria and Damascus.
AHAZ,] the king himself, in Jerusalem.
FIGHT,] as in Nu. 22. 11, &c.
6. ELATH.] See 14. 22, &c.
CASTETH OUT,] as in Ex. 3. 5; De. 7. 1, 22; 19. 5; 28. 40; Jos. 5. 15.
7. SERVANT..SON,] needing protection and assistance.
8. BRIBE,] as in Ex. 23. 8, &c.
9. DAMASCUS,] the capital of Rezin.
KIR,] beyond the Euxine, on the river Cyrus ; see Isa. 22. 6; Amos 1. 5: 9. 7.
10. ALTAR,] on which perhaps the king of Aram used to offer.
URIJAH,] i.e. 'light of Jah,' as in Isa. 8. 2
PATTERN,] as in Ex. 25. 9, &c.
11. BUILDETH,] contrary to the law of God, and apparently without hesitation.
12. OFFERETH,] which was the duty of the priests only.
13. PERFUMETH,] with sweet fragrance.
PRESENT,] as in Ge. 4. 3, 4, 5, &c.
LIBATION,] as in Ex. 35. 14, &c.
SPRINKLETH,] as in Ex. 9. 8, 10; 24. 6, 8; 29. 16, 20, &c.
14. ALTAR OF BRASS,] as in 2 Ch. 4. 1.
NORTHWARD,] out of view.

15. GREAT ALTAR,] the new one he had built.
INQUIRE BY,] or seek the Lord.
16. DOTH,] according to the proverb, 'like king, like priest.'
17. CUTTETH OFF,] as in 18. 16; 24. 13; 2 Ch. 28. 24.
BASES,] as in 1 K. 7. 27, 28.
LAVER,] for the use of the priests.
SEA,] which Solomon had made.
BRAZEN OXEN,] twelve in number.
18. COVERED PLACE,] probably to shield the people from the rain.
ASSHUR,] to please him, or for fear of him.
19. MATTERS,] not 'acts,' as in C.V.
20. CITY OF DAVID,] that is, Zion.
HEZEKIAH,] i.e. 'strength of Jah.'

XVII. 1. 12TH YEAR,] B.C. 730.
HOSHEA,] as in 15. 30, &c.
2. THE EVIL THING,] that is, idolatry.
3. SHALMANESER,] in Hos. 10. 14, it is 'Shalman.'
PRESENT,] as a token of respect and submission.
4. CONSPIRACY,] against his rule over him.
SO,] the Sevechus of Manetho.
RESTRAINT,] as in 1 K. 22. 27, &c.
5. THREE YEARS.] See 18. 9, 10.
6. 9TH YEAR,] B.C. 721.
HALAH,] probably Calachene, north of Asshur, next Armenia.
HABOR,] i.e. 'a joining together,' a river in Aram Naharaim, falling into the Euphrates at Circesium, as in 18. 11; 1 Ch. 5. 26.
GOZAN,] as in 18. 11; 19. 12; 1 Ch. 5. 26; Isa. 37. 12.
MEDES,] such as Hara, in 1 Ch. 5. 26.
7. SINNED,] especially by idolatry.
OTHER GODS,] of the nations around them.
8. STATUTES,] against which they had been warned, as in Lev. 18. 3.
MADE,] to themselves.
9. DO COVERTLY,] or perhaps, simply 'they cover' from themselves the iniquity of their doings.
TOWER OF THE WATCHERS,] in a lonely field or garden to the
FENCED CITY,] with bars and gates; see 18. 8.
10. STANDING-PILLARS,] as in 1 K. 14. 23, &c.
SHRINES,] as in Jud. 3. 7, &c.
HIGH HEIGHT,] as in 1 K. 14. 23; 2 Ch. 28. 4, &c.
GREEN TREE,] as in De. 12. 2, &c.
11. MAKE PERFUME,] to their idols over their sacrifices.
REMOVED,] as in 15. 29; 16. 9; 17. 6, &c.
PROVOKE,] as in De. 4. 25, &c.
12. SAID,] in Ex. 20. 3, 4, 5, 23.
13. TESTIFIETH,] as in 1 Sa. 9. 9, &c.
PROPHET..SEER,] never leaving himself without a witness.
TURN BACK,] as in 2 Ch. 30. 6, &c.
KEEP,] as in Ex. 34. 11, &c.
LAW,] or 'direction.'
14. HARDEN,] as in De. 10. 16, &c.
REMAIN STEDFAST,] as in De. 20. 12, &c.
15. REJECT,] as in Lev. 26. 15, &c.
VAIN THING,] as in De. 32. 21.

BECOME VAIN,] like the objects of their veneration.
NOT TO DO,] as in De. 6. 13, 14, &c.
16. MOLTEN IMAGE,] as in Ex. 32. 4, 8, &c.
TWO CALVES,] as in 1 K. 12. 28, &c.
SHRINE,] as in v. 10 above.
HOST,] as in Ge. 2. 1; De. 4. 19; 17. 3, &c.
BAAL,] lit. 'the Baal.'
17. FIRE,] as in 16. 3; to Baal or Moloch.
DIVINE DIVINATIONS,] as in De. 18. 10, 14, &c.
USE ENCHANTMENTS,] as in Lev. 19. 26,&c.
SELL THEMSELVES,] as in 1 K. 21. 20, 25.
PROVOKE,] as in v. 11 above.
18. SHEWETH HIMSELF ANGRY,] as in De. 1. 37; 4. 21; 9. 8, 20; 1 K. 11. 9.
LEFT,] in the promised land.
19. NOT KEPT,] fully and sincerely.
20. KICKETH,] as in Lev. 26. 15, &c.
SPOILERS,] as in Jud. 2. 14, 16; 1 Sa. 14. 48; 23. 1; Isa. 17. 14; Jer. 30. 16; 50. 11.
PRESENCE,] as in v. 18 above.
21. RENT,] as in 1 K. 11. 11, 31.
KING,] as in 1 K. 12. 20, 28.
DRIVETH,] by persuasions, and commands, and example.
SIN,] in committing idolatry.
23. SPAKE,] in 1 K. 13. 32; 14. 15, 16, &c.
REMOVED,] as in v. 6.
24. BABYLON,] at this time under Asshur.
CUTHA.] See Ge. 10. 6.
AVA,] same as Ivah, in Isa. 33. 13; compare De. 2. 23.
HAMATH,] north of Canaan, as in Nu. 34. 8
SEPHARVAIM,] probably Sipphara on the Euphrates, as in 18. 34; 19. 13; Isa. 36. 19; 37. 13.
25. NOT FEARED,] or paid any regard to Him.
LIONS,] as in Jud. 14. 5; 1 Sa. 17. 34; 2 Sa. 23. 20; 1 K. 13. 24; 20. 36, &c.
26. REMOVED,] as in v. 24.
CUSTOM,] lit. 'judgment.'
27. PRIESTS,] of the land.
28. BETH-EL,] as in Ge. 12. 8, &c.
FEAR,] that is, worship Him.
29. GODS,] as when in their own land.
HIGH PLACES,] as in 1 K. 12. 31, &c.
30. MEN OF BABYLON,] as in v. 24.
SUCCOTH-BENOTH,] i.e. 'booths of daughters.'
CUTH,] as in v. 24.
NERGAL.] Etymology uncertain.
HAMATH,] as in v. 24.
ASHIMA.] Etymology uncertain.
31. AVITES,] from Ava, as in v. 24.
NIBHAZ.] Etymology uncertain.
TARTAK.] Etymology uncertain.
SEPHARVITES,]fromSepharvim, as in v. 24.
ADRAMMELECH,] i.e. 'honour of the king.'
ANNAMELECH.] Etymology uncertain.
SEPHARVAIM,] as in v. 24.
32. FEARING,] the power and anger of Jehovah.
EXTREMITIES,] as in Ge. 47. 2; Jud. 18. 2; 1 K. 12. 31; 13. 33.
ACTING FOR THEM,] as priests.
33. SERVING,] with good will.
34. FORMER CUSTOMS,] of their own land
ISRAEL,] as in Ge. 32. 28; 35. 10.
35. SAYING,] in Jud. 5. 10, &c.

36. ARM,] as in Ex. 6. 6, &c.
37. WROTE,] with his own finger and by his servants.
38. COVENANT,] to be their God.
39. ENEMIES,] in virtue of their obedience.
40. FORMER CUSTOM,] as in v. 34.
41. GRAVEN IMAGES,] as in De. 7. 5, 25; 12. 3, &c.
DAY,] when the Book of the Kings was written.

XVIII. 1. THIRD YEAR,] B.C. 726.
HOSHEA,] as in 15. 30, &c.
HEZEKIAH,] as in 16. 20.
2. ABI,] i.e. 'my father;' in 2 Ch. 29. 1, it is Abijah.
ZECHARIAH,] perhaps the same mentioned in Isa. 8. 3.
3. DID,] an expression used of no other king before him.
4. HIGH PLACES,] which none of them had ever done ; 2 Ch. 31. 1.
BRAZEN SERPENT,] in Nu. 21. 9.
MAKING PERFUME,] as if it were a god.
PIECE OF BRASS,] having no value in itself.
5. TRUSTED,] for guidance and protection; as in 19. 10.
LIKE HIM,] in his fear of God and love of justice, as in 23. 25.
6. CLEAVETH,] in love and obedience, as in De. 10. 20.
COMMANDED,] by the hand of Moses in the wilderness.
7. WITH HIM,] in all his actings; 2 Ch.15.2.
ACTETH WISELY,] so as to gain success.
REBELLETH,] his father Ahaz having acknowledged subjection to Asshur.
SERVED HIM,] with tribute and present.
8. GAZA,] one of their five principal cities.
FROM..UNTO,] as in 17. 9.
9. HOSHEA,] as in v. 1.
SHALMANESER,] as in 17. 5.
10. THREE YEARS,] as in 17. 5.
11. REMOVETH,] as in 17. 6.
13. SENNACCERIB.] Etymology uncertain; see Isa. 36. 1.
FENCED CITY,] as in 2 Sa. 20. 6, &c.
14. LACHISH,] twenty miles south-west of Jerusalem.
SINNED,] lit. 'erred.'
BEAR,] or 'lift up,' from my people.
LAYETH,] lit. 'setteth,' as a burden.
300..20,] about £247,500.
TREASURES,] as in 12. 18; 16. 8.
16. CUT OFF,] as in 16. 17; 24. 13.
PILLARS,] or 'supports,' not mentioned elsewhere.
17. TARTAN.] Etymology uncertain; see Isa. 20. 1.
CHIEF OF THE EUNUCHS,] in Heb. Rab-Saris.
CHIEF OF THE BUTLERS,] in Heb. Rab-Shakeh.
HEAVY FORCE,] as in 6. 14.
CONDUIT,] as in 1 K. 18. 32, 35, 38; 2 K. 20. 20; Job 38. 25; Isa. 7. 3; 36. 2; Jer. 30. 13; 46. 11; Eze. 31. 4.
FULLER'S FIELD,] as in Isa. 7. 3; 36. 2.
18. ELIAKIM,] i.e. 'God raises up.'
HILKIAH,] i.e. 'portion of Jah.'
SHEBNA.] Etymology uncertain.

JOAH,] i.e. 'Jah is brother.'
ASAPH,] i.e. 'gatherer.'
REMEMBRANCER,] as in 2 Sa. 8. 16, &c.
19. CHIEF OF THE BUTLERS,] as in v. 17.
THE GREAT KING,] really the greatest of his day.
CONFIDED,] as a shield against an enemy.
20. THOU HAST SAID,] in thy confidence.
LIPS,] is the threat of the king of Asshur, for
COUNSEL..MIGHT,] are required, and these are with the king of Egypt.
21. STAFF,] as in Ex. 21. 19, &c.
BROKEN REED,] as in Isa. 36. 6; 42. 3.
LEANETH ON,] as in Isa. 36. 6; Jud. 16. 29, &c.
PIERCED,] as in Isa. 36. 6; Hab. 3. 14, &c.
22. OUR GOD,] by express covenant engagements.
HIGH PLACES..ALTARS,] places of worship.
23. GIVE A PLEDGE,] as in Isa. 36. 8.
2000 HORSES,] of which Canaan was generally deficient.
24. TURN BACK,] in battle.
CHARIOT..HORSEMEN,] of which they had abundance.
25. WITHOUT,] the countenance and aid of Judah's God himself.
SAID,] perhaps by false prophets.
26. JOAH,] as in v. 18.
ARAMAEAN,] the language of Aram, a sister dialect of the Hebrew.
UNDERSTANDING,] the language of Aram.
JEWISH,] that is, Hebrew.
WALL,] watching and hearing the interview.
27. UNTO THEE] only, must be supplied.
SITTING ON THE WALL] guarding it.
DUNG,] as in 6. 25.
WATER,] as in Isa. 36. 12.
28. JEWISH,] that all the people might understand.
THE GREAT KING,] as in v. 19.
29. LIFT YOU UP] with pride.
HIS HAND,] viz., that of the king of Asshur.
30. JEHOVAH] the national God of Israel.
31. BLESSING,] expressive of friendship.
VINE..FIG-TREE,] as in Isa. 36. 16.
OWN WELL,] as is customary in the east.
32. CORN..HONEY,] as in De. 8. 7, 8.
33. GODS,] as in 19. 12.
34. HAMATH.] as in 17. 24.
ASHPAD,] as in 19. 13.
SEPHARVAIM,] as in 17. 24; 19. 13.
HENA,] as in 19. 13.
IVVAH,] or Ava, as in 17. 24; 19. 13.
35. GODS,] as in v. 33.
36. KEPT SILENT,] as in Ge. 34. 5, &c.
37. JOAH,] as in v. 18.
RENT GARMENTS,] in token of their grief.

XIX. 1. SACKCLOTH,] as a mark of humiliation.
HOUSE] to seek guidance.
2. ELDERS OF THE PRIESTS,] as in Isa. 37. 2; Jer. 19. 1, &c.
ISAIAH,] i.e. 'safety of Jah.'
AMOZ,] i.e. 'a strong one.'
3. DISTRESS,] as in Ge. 35. 3, &c.
REBUKE,] as in Ps. 149. 7; Isa. 37. 3; Hos. 5. 9.

DESPISING,] as in Isa. 37. 3; Neh. 9. 18, 20; Eze. 35. 12.
BIRTH,] as in Isa. 37. 3; Hos. 13. 13.
4. REPROACH,] as in 1 Sa. 17. 25; 2 Sa. 23. 9; 2 Ch. 32. 17; Isa. 37. 4, 17.
LIVING GOD,] as in De. 5. 26, &c.
DECIDED,] as in Isa. 37. 4, &c.
LIFTED UP] to God in the heavens.
FOUND] present in Jerusalem.
6. WORDS,] for they were only words.
REVILED,] as in Nu. 15. 30, &c.
7. GIVING,] not 'send,' as in C.V.
A SPIRIT,] or simply 'spirit.'
REPORT,] as in 1 Sa. 2. 24; 4. 19, &c.
HIS LAND,] even Asshur.
SWORD] of his own sons, as in v. 37.
8. TURNETH BACK] from Jerusalem to his master.
LIBNAH.] See 8. 22.
LACHISH,] as in 18. 14.
9. TIRHAKAH,] as in Isa. 37. 9.
10. LIFT THEE UP,] as in 18. 29.
11. TO DEVOTE,] as in De. 3. 6, &c.
DELIVERED,] as if Hezekiah were stronger than all of them.
12. DESTROYED,] from being independent powers.
GOZAN,] as in 17. 6, &c.
HARAN,] as in Ge. 11. 31, &c.
REZEPH,] as in Isa. 37. 12.
EDEN,] as in Ge. 2. 8, &c.
THELASSAR,] as in Isa. 37. 12.
13. HAMATH..IVVAH,] as in 18. 34, &c.
14. SPREADETH IT] out, as if to let it be seen.
15. PRAYETH,] as in Ge. 20. 7, 17, &c.
JEHOVAH,] the Existing One.
GOD OF ISRAEL,] and therefore its guardian.
CHERUBS,] as in 1 Sa. 4. 4, &c.
ALONE,] without any equal or partner.
MADE,] as in Ge. 2. 4, &c.
16. INCLINE,] as in Ps. 17. 6, &c.
OPEN,] as in Prov. 20. 13, &c.
REPROACH,] as in v. 4.
17. LAID WASTE,] as in Isa. 37. 18, &c.
18. PUT,] lit. 'given.'
HANDS,] as in Ps. 115. 4, &c.
WOOD..STONE,] as in De. 4. 28, &c.
DESTROY THEM] from under the heavens, as in Jer. 10. 3.
19. SAVE,] lit. 'give ease.'
ALONE,] as in v. 15.
20. HEARD,] and now answer.
21. TRAMPLED,] as in Isa. 37. 22, &c.
LAUGHED,] as in Job 22. 19, &c.
VIRGIN DAUGHTER,] as in Isa. 37. 22; 47. 1; Jer. 14. 17; 46. 11; La. 1. 15; 2. 10, 13.
ZION,] i.e. 'a sunny place.'
SHAKEN THE HEAD,] as in Isa 37. 22.
DAUGHTER OF JERUSALEM,] as in Song 1. 5, &c.
22. REPROACHED,] as in v. 4, 16.
REVILED,] as in v. 6 above.
ON HIGH,] as in Isa. 40. 26, &c.
HOLY ONE,] i.e. he who is separate from all others.
23. HIGH PLACE,] as in Isa. 37. 24; Jer. 49. 16; Eze. 34. 14.
SIDES,] lit. 'thighs.'
HEIGHT,] or 'stature,' as in Ge. 6. 14, &c.
CHOICE,] as in Ge. 23. 6, &c.
LODGING,] as in Ge. 42. 27, &c.

EXTREMITY,] or 'end.'
CARMEL,] as in Lev. 2. 14; 23. 14; 2 K. 4. 42, &c.
24. DIGGED,] as in Isa. 37. 25.
STRANGE WATERS,] as in Jer. 18. 14.
SOLES OF MY FEET,] as in Isa. 37. 25.
FLOODS,] as in Ge. 41. 1, 2, 3, 17, 18, &c.
BULWARK,] as in De. 20. 19, 20, &c., or Matzor may be a proper name for Egypt; so Gesenius.
25. AFAR,] in point of place or time.
DAYS OF OLD,] as in Neh. 12. 46; Ps. 77. 5; 143. 5; Isa. 19. 11; 23. 7; 37. 26; 45. 23; 51. 9; Jer. 46. 26; La. 1. 7; 2. 17; Mic. 7. 20.
FORMED,] as in Ge. 2. 7, 8, 19, &c.
DESOLATION,] as in Isa. 37. 26.
RUINOUS,] as in Jer. 4. 7.
26. FEEBLE HANDED,] lit. 'short of hand.'
BROKEN DOWN,] as in Job 32. 15; Isa. 20. 5; 31. 9; 37. 27; Jer. 8. 9; 14. 4; 48. 1, 20, 39; 50. 2, 36; Obad. 9.
DRIED UP,] or 'confounded.'
HERB,] as in Ge. 2. 5; 3. 18, &c.
GREENNESS,] as in De. 11. 10; 1 K. 21. 2; Prov. 15. 17; Isa. 37. 27.
TENDER GRASS,] as in Ge. 1. 11, 12, &c.
GRASS OF THE ROOF,] as in Ps. 129. 6; Isa. 37. 27.
BLASTED CORN,] as in Ge. 41. 6; 23. 27.
RISEN UP,] as in Isa. 37. 27; Ex. 22. 6; De. 16, 9; 23. 25; Jud. 15. 5; Isa. 17. 5; Hos. 8. 7.
27. SITTING DOWN,] as in Ex. 15. 17, &c.
ANGER,] as in v. 28; Isa. 37. 28, 29.
NOISE,] as in Job 12. 5; Ps. 123. 4; Isa. 32. 9, 11, 18; 33. 20; 37. 29; Amos 6. 1; Zec. 1. 15.
EARS,] as in 2 Sa. 22. 7, &c.
HOOK,] as in Isa. 35. 22; Isa. 37. 29; Eze. 19 4, 9: 29. 4; 38. 4.
NOSE,] as in Ge. 24. 47, &c.
LIPS,] as in Isa. 37. 29, &c.
29. TO THEE,] that is, to Hezekiah.
SIGN,] or 'token.'
SPONTANEOUS GROWTH,] as in Lev. 25. 5, 11; Job 14. 19; Isa. 37. 30.
SELF-PRODUCED.] This original word is not found elsewhere.
30. CONTINUED,] or 'added.'
ESCAPED,] as in Ge. 32. 8; 45. 7, &c.
ROOT,] as in Ge. 29. 18, &c.
MADE FRUIT,] as in Ge. 1. 11, 12, &c.
31. REMNANT,] as in Ge. 45. 7, &c.
ESCAPE,] as in v. 30 above.
ZEAL,] as in Ex. 20. 5; 34. 14; De. 4. 24; 5. 9; 6. 15.
32. THIS CITY] of Jerusalem.
ARROW,] against its defenders.
SHIELD,] protecting the soldiers from the projected missiles.
POUR OUT] stones and rubbish to form a MOUNT,] by which he might capture the city.
33. AFFIRMATION,] as in Ge. 22. 16, &c.
34. COVERED,] as in 20. 6; Isa. 37. 35; 38 6; 31. 5; Zec. 9. 15; 12. 8.
SERVANT] which he delighted to honour.
35. A MESSENGER OF JEHOVAH,] as in Ge. 16. 7, 9, 10, 11, &c.
SMITETH.] There is some ambiguity about the exact number in the Hebrew text: it may be 100×80×5000=5,180, or better perhaps

100×85,000=85,100; (compare the order in Eze. 48. 30—35 for the same principle of computation.)
THEY RISE,] that is, men rise as usual.
CORPSES,] as in Ge. 14. 11; Lev. 26. 30, &c.
36. NISROCH,] i.e. 'great eagle,' as in Isa. 37. 38.
ADRAMMELECH,] as in Isa. 37. 38; compare 2 K. 17. 31.
SHAREZER,] i.e. 'prince of fire,' as in Isa. 37. 38; compare Zec. 7. 2.
SWORD,] as foretold in v. 7.
ARARAT,] as in Ge. 8. 4, &c.
ESARHADDON,] as in Isa. 37. 38; Ezra 4. 2.

XX. 1. SICK UNTO DEATH,] as in 2 Ch. 32. 24; Isa. 38. 1.
ISAIAH,] as in 19. 2.
GIVE A CHARGE,] as in 2 Sa. 17. 23, &c.
2. PRAYETH,] as in Ge. 20. 7, 17, &c.
3. I PRAY THEE,] as in Ge. 50. 17; Ex. 32. 31; Neh. 1. 5, 11; Ps. 116. 4, 16; 118. 25; Isa. 38. 3; Da. 9. 4; Jon. 1. 14; 4. 2.
WALKED HABITUALLY,] as in Ge. 5. 22, 24, &c.
PERFECT HEART,] as in 1 K. 8. 61; 11. 4; 15. 3, 14; 1 Ch. 12. 38; 15. 17; 16. 9; 19. 9; 25. 2; Isa. 38. 3.
GREAT WEEPING,] as in Jud. 21. 2, &c.
4. COURT] of the king's palace; most MSS. read 'city' for 'court;' compare 1 K. 7. 8.
5. LEADER,] as in 1 Sa. 9. 16, &c.
TEAR,] not 'tears,' as in C.V.
HOUSE,] that is, the temple.
6. FIFTEEN YEARS,] as in Isa. 38. 5.
SERVANT,] as in 19. 34.
7. CAKE,] as in 1 Sa. 25. 18; 30. 12; 1 Ch. 12. 40; Isa. 38. 21.
BOIL,] as in Ex. 9. 9, 10, 11, &c.
8. SIGN,] or 'token.'
9. SHADOW] of the sun, as in Job 7. 2; Isa. 38. 8.
DEGREES,] lit. 'goings up or steps,' as in Ex. 20. 26; 1 K. 10. 19, 20, &c.
10. LIGHT,] comparatively speaking it might be deemed an accident or overlooked entirely.
INCLINE,] as in Ex. 7. 5; 23. 2, &c.
BACKWARD,] as in Ge. 9. 23, &c.
11. CALLETH] in prayer.
AHAZ] his father, which he had made.
12. BERODACH-BALADAN,] in Isa. 39. 1 called 'Merodach-Baladan.'
PRESENT,] according to eastern customs.
SICK,] as in v. 1.
13. HEARKENETH] to their request, whatever it might be; but compare Isa. 39. 2.
HOUSE OF HIS TREASURY.] So Syr. Targ. Saad.; but Aq. Sym. Vulg. 'spices.'
HOUSE OF HIS VESSELS,] as in Isa. 39. 2.
DOMINION,] as in 2 K. 20. 13; 2 Ch. 8. 6, &c.
14. PROPHET,] as in v. 1.
BABYLON,] the capital of Asshur.
15. TREASURIES,] as noted in v. 13 above.
17. TREASURED UP,] as most rare and valuable.
18. EUNUCHS,] as in Ge. 37. 36, &c.
19. GOOD,] for God's glory, and especially because of the promised delay.
MY DAYS,] a matter of grateful acknowledgement.

20. MATTERS,] not 'acts,' as in C.V.
POOL,] as in Neh. 3. 16.
CONDUIT,] as in 1 K. 18. 32, 35, 38; 2 K. 18. 17; Job 38. 25; Isa. 7. 3; 36. 2; Eze. 31. 4.
WATERS,] as in 2 Ch. 32. 3, 4, 30.
CITY] of Jerusalem, to provide against a siege.
21. MANASSEH,] i.e. 'causing to forget,' as in Ge. 41. 51.

XXI. 1. 12 YEARS,] being born in 710 B.C.
55 YEARS,] as in 2 Ch. 33. 1; it was longer than any other of the kings of Israel or Judea.
HEPHZI-BAH,] i.e. 'my delight is in her;' as in Isa. 62. 4.
2. EVIL THING,] that is, idolatry.
DISPOSSESSED,] as in 16. 3, &c.
3. DESTROYED,] as in 18. 4.
BAAL,] the god of the Sidonians.
AHAB,] in 1 K. 18. 32, 33.
4. ALTARS,] to Baal, and other deities.
NAME,] as in 2 Sa. 7. 13, &c.
TWO COURTS,] outer and inner.
6. FIRE,] as in Lev. 18. 21, &c.
OBSERVED CLOUDS,] as in Lev. 19. 26; De. 18. 10, 14; Jud. 9. 37; 2 Ch. 33. 6; Isa. 2. 6 57. 3; Jer. 27. 9; Mic. 5. 12.
USED ENCHANTMENT,] as in Ge. 30. 27; 44. 5, 15; Lev. 19. 26; De. 18. 10; 1 K. 20. 33; 2 K. 17. 17; 2 Ch. 33. 6.
FAMILIAR SPIRIT,] as in Lev. 19. 31; 20. 6, 27; De. 18. 11; 1 Sa. 28. 3, 7, 8, 9; 2 K. 23. 24, &c.
WIZARDS,] as in Lev. 19. 31; 20. 6, 27; De. 18. 11; 1 Sa. 28. 3, 9; 2 K. 23. 24; 2 Ch. 33. 6. Isa. 8. 19; 19. 3.
MULTIPLIED TO DO,] as in 2 Ch. 33. 6, &c.
7. GRAVEN IMAGE,] as in Ex. 20. 4; Lev. 26. 1, &c.
SAID,] in 2 Sa. 7. 13, &c.
8. MOVE,] as in 2 Sa. 7. 10, &c.
9. ERR,] as in Ge. 20. 13; 2 Ch. 33. 9; Job 12. 24, 25, &c.
10. PROPHETS,] Isaiah, Joel, Nahum, Habakkuk.
11. ABOMINATIONS,] described in v. 3—7
AMORITES,] as in 1 K. 21. 26, &c.
IDOLS,] as in v. 9.
12. TINGLE,] as in 1 Sa. 3. 11; Jer. 19. 3; Hab. 3. 16.
13. LINE,] with which He had measured the iniquity and the punishment of Samaria.
PLUMMET,] with which he had guaged the house of Ahab.
WIPED,] as in Ge. 6. 7; 7. 4, 23, &c.
DISH,] as in Prov. 19. 24; 26. 15, &c.
14. LEFT,] as in Jud. 6. 13; 1 Sa. 12. 22, &c.
ENEMIES,] the Chaldeans, Edomites, &c.
15. THIS DAY,] as in De. 9. 24, &c.
16. INNOCENT BLOOD,] as in De. 19. 10, 13, &c.
MOUTH TO MOUTH,] as in 10. 21, &c.
17. MATTERS,] not 'acts,' as in C.V.
SIN] of idolatry.
18. GARDEN,] a not unfrequent place of burial; compare John 19. 41.
UZZA,] i.e. 'strength.'
AMON,] i.e. 'an artificer.'
19. 22 YEARS,] as in 2 Ch. 33. 21.
MESHULLEMETH,] i.e. 'one recompensed.'

HARUZ,] i.e. 'sharp-pointed, diligent.'
JOTBAH,] i.e. 'goodness;' as in Nu. 33. 33;
De. 10. 7, &c.
20. FATHER,] in 2 Ch. 33. 23.
21. SERVED,] as in 2 Ch. 33. 22.
22. WAY,] revealed by Moses and the
prophets.
23. CONSPIRE.] as in 1 Sa. 22. 8, &c.
24. PEOPLE OF THE LAND,] as in Ge. 23.
7, &c.
JOSIAH,] prophesied of in 1 K. 13. 2.
25. MATTERS,] not 'acts,' as in C.V.
26. GARDEN,] as in v. 18 above.

XXII. 1. 8 YEARS,] as in 2 Ch. 34. 1.
31 YEARS,] B.C. 641—610.
JEDIDAH,] i.e. 'beloved.'
ADAIAH,] i.e. 'adorned of Jah.'
BOSKATH,] as in Jos. 15. 39, &c.
2. RIGHT OR LEFT,] as in De. 5. 32.
3. 18TH YEAR,] of his reign, as in 2 Ch.
34. 3—7.
SHAPHAN,] i.e. 'a coney;' as in v. 12; Jer.
36. 10; Eze. 8. 11.
AZALIAH,] i.e. 'kept back by Jah.'
MESHULLAM,] i.e. 'recompensed.'
4. HILKIAH,] i.e. 'portion of Jah;' as in
Jer. 1. 1, 2.
COMPLETE,] lit. 'make perfect;' 2 Sa. 20.
18; Job 22. 3; Isa. 33. 1; Eze. 22. 15; 24. 10;
Da. 8. 23; 9. 24.
THRESHOLD,] as in 12. 9, 13, &c.
5. OVERSEERS,] as in 12. 11, &c.; see 2 Ch.
34. 9.
BREACH,] as in 12. 8, 12, &c.
6. ARTIFICERS,] as in Ex. 28. 11; 35. 35;
38. 23, &c.
BUILDERS,] as in Ge. 4. 17; 1 K. 5. 18; 6.
12; 2 K. 12. 11, &c.
WALL,] as in 2 K. 12. 12; Isa. 58. 12; Eze.
22. 30.
7. FAITHFULNESS,] as in Ex. 17. 12; De.
32. 4; 1 Sa. 26. 23; 2 K. 12. 15, &c.
8. A BOOK,] not 'the book,' as in C.V.; in
2 Ch. 34. 14 it is added, 'by the hand of
Moses,' which may mean, but not necessarily, his autograph.
9. THY SERVANTS,] Hilkiah and Shaphan.
POURED OUT,] as in 2 Ch. 34. 17; Job 10.
10, &c.
INSPECTORS,] as in v. 5.
10. DECLARETH,] not 'sheweth,' as in C.V.
11. RENDETH,] in token of grief.
12. AHIKAM,] i.e. 'brother of a withstander.'
ACHBOR,] i.e. 'a mouse;' in 2 Ch. 34. 20,
it is 'Abdon, son of Micah.'
MICAIAH,] i.e. 'who is like Jah.'
ASAHIAH,] i.e. 'doing of Jah.'
13. SEEK JEHOVAH,] his counsel and favour, by the intervention of the prophets.
KINDLED,] as in Jos. 8. 8, 19; Jud. 9. 49;
2 Sa. 14. 30, 31, &c.
14. HULDAH,] i.e. 'a mole or weasel;' as
in 2 Ch. 34. 22.
PROPHETESS,] as in Ex. 15. 20; Jud. 4. 4;
2 Ch. 34. 22; Neh. 6. 14; Isa. 8. 3.
SHALLUM,] i.e. 'recompense.'
TIKVAH,] i.e. 'hope.'
HARHAS,] or Hasrah, as in 2 Ch. 34. 22.
GARMENTS,] of the priests, most probably.

SECOND] part of the city, as in Zeph. 1.
19; Neh. 11. 9.
15. THE MAN,] that is, Josiah the king; it
is the language of God, not of the prophetess.
16. I AM BRINGING IN,] even now, not 'I
will bring,' as in C.V.
17. FORSAKEN,] as in De. 20. 25, 26, 27.
HATH BEEN KINDLED,] not 'shall be,' as
in C.V.
QUENCHED,] by repentance and reformation.
18. KING OF JUDAH,] this is the language
of Huldah.
19. TENDER,] afraid of incurring the wrath
of God.
HUMBLED,] in mind and body.
DESOLATION,] as in De. 28. 37, &c.
REVILING,] as in Ge. 27. 12, 13; De. 11. 26,
28, 29, &c.
AFFIRMATION,] as in Ge. 22. 16, &c.
20. PEACE,] for his encounter with the
king of Egypt was more a personal than a
national act, see 2 Ch. 35. 24.
NOT LOOK,] he dying beforehand.

XXIII. 1. ELDERS,] who ruled in each
city, 2 Ch. 34. 29, 30.
2. FROM SMALL UNTO GREAT,] as in Ge.
19. 11, &c.
READETH,] or 'proclaimeth.'
BOOK OF THE COVENANT,] made by Moses
as in 22. 8, 9.
3. THE PILLAR,] in the temple, as in 11.
14; 2 Ch. 6. 13; 34. 31.
STAND,] or 'remain in' the covenant.
4. SECOND ORDER,] as in 25. 18; 1 Ch. 15. 18.
THRESHOLD,] as in 22. 4, &c.
BAAL,] by former kings of Judah
SHRINE,] as in 21. 3, 7.
BURNETH,] as in De. 7. 5, 25, &c.
KIDRON,] as in v. 4.
BETH-EL,] which had been captured, as in
2 Ch. 13. 19; Jer. 52. 24.
5. CAUSED TO CEASE,] as in Ex. 5. 5; 12.
15, &c.
IDOLATROUS PRIESTS,] as in Hos. 10. 5;
Zeph. 1. 4.
APPOINTED,] not 'ordained,' as in the C.V.
SUBURBS,] as in 1 K. 6. 29; Job 37. 12; Ps.
140. 9; Song 1. 12.
MAKING PERFUME] over sacrifices.
BAAL] the god of the Sidonians.
SUN,] as in De. 4. 19; 17. 3; Eze. 8. 16.
MOON,] as in De. 4. 19; 17. 3; Job 31. 26.
PLANETS,] or perhaps the 12 signs of the
Zodiac; the original word is not found else-
where.
6. SHRINE,] as in 21. 7, &c.
KIDRON,] as in v. 4.
BEATETH SMALL,] as in Ex. 30. 36, &c.
SONS OF THE PEOPLE,] in 2 Ch. 34. 4 it is
'of those sacrificing to them.'
7. WHOREMONGERS,] as in De. 23 17; 1 K.
14. 24; 15. 12; 22. 46; Job 36. 14.
HOUSES,] not 'hangings,' as in C.V.
8. DEFILETH] by casting filth upon them.
GEBA,] as in 1 K. 15. 22, the northern
boundary of Judah.
BEER-SHEBA,] the southern boundary of
Judah.

JOSHUA,] i.e. a 'saviour.'
9. UNLEAVENED BREAD,] according to the law in Lev. 2. 4, 5; Eze. 44. 10—15.
10. DEFILED,] as in v. 8.
TOPHETH,] i.e. 'the wonder,' as in Jer. 7. 31. 32; 19. 6, 13, 14.
HINNOM,] as in Jos. 15. 8, &c.
MOLOCH,] the god of the Ammonites, called also Milcom and Malcom; see v. 13.
11. CAUSETH TO CEASE,] as in v. 5.
HORSES,] which were sometimes dedicated and consecrated.
SUN,] as in v. 5.
NATHAN-MELECH,] i. e. 'given by the king.
EUNUCH,] not 'chamberlain,' as in C.V.
SUBURBS,] as in 1 Ch. 26. 18.
CHARIOTS,] consecrated to the sun.
12. TOP,] which was flat, as in most eastern dwellings.
TWO COURTS,] as in 21. 5.
BROKEN DOWN,] as commanded in Ex. 34. 13.
KIDRON,] which ran into the Dead Sea.
13. CORRUPTION,] that is, the mount of the olives, as in 1 K. 11. 7.
ASHTAROTH,] as in 1 K. 11. 5, 33.
CHEMOSH,] as in Nu. 21. 29; Jud. 11. 24; 1 K. 11. 7, 33; Jer. 48. 7, 13, 46.
MILCOM] or Moloch, as in v. 10.
DEFILED,] as in v. 10.
14. STANDING-PILLARS,] as commanded in Ex. 23. 24, &c.
SHRINES,] as in De. 7. 5, &c.
BONES,] which by the law were unclean, as in Nu. 19. 16.
15. BETH-EL,] for the worship of the calf.
MADE,] as in 1 K. 12. 28, 33.
BEAT IT SMALL,] as in v. 6.
16. MOUNT,] where people often were buried, as in Jos. 24. 30, 33.
WORD,] three hundred years before.
17. SIGN,] not 'title,' as in C.V.
18. LET HIM ALONE,] he being a man of God, though deceived.
ESCAPE] burning on the defiled altars, as in v. 16.
19. HOUSES OF THE HIGH-PLACES,] in which their priests resided.
20. SLAYETH,] lit. 'sacrificeth.'
BONES,] as in v. 16.
21. PASSOVER,] as in Ex. 12. 3, &c.
22. JUDGES,] who succeeded Joshua, and preceded Saul.
23. 18TH YEAR,] B.C. 623.
24. FAMILIAR SPIRITS,] as in Lev. 19. 31; 20. 6, 27, &c.
WIZARDS,] as in Lev. 19. 31; 20. 6, 27, &c.
TERAPHIM,] as in Ge. 31. 19, 34, 35; Jud. 7. 5, &c.
IDOLS,] as in Lev. 26. 30; De. 29. 17, &c.
ABOMINATIONS,] as in De. 29. 17, &c.
FOUND,] as in 22. 8, 10.
25. TURNED BACK,] from the idolatrous ways of his fathers.
HEART..SOUL..MIGHT,] as in De. 6. 5, &c.
26. NOT TURNED BACK,] because of the sins of the people yet unrepented of.
27. TURN ASIDE,] as in 17. 18, 20, &c.
REJECTED,] because of its wickedness.
THERE,] as in 1 K. 8. 29, &c.

28. MATTERS,] not 'acts,' as in C.V.
29. PHARAOH-NECHOH.] Targum reads 'Pharaoh the lame.'
PHRAT,] at Carchemish, as in 2 Ch. 35. 26 : Isa. 46. 2.
MEGIDDO] in Manasseh, as in Jos. 17. 11, &c.
30. JEHOAHAZ,] see 1 K. 13. 3, &c.; in Jer. 22. 11 called 'Shallum;' so in 1 Ch. 3. 15.
ANOINT,] as in 1 Sa. 9. 14, &c.
31. THREE MONTHS,] till deposed as in v. 33.
HAMUTAL,] as in 24. 18; Jer. 52. 1.
LIBNAH,] in Judah, as in Jos. 10. 29; 15. 42.
32. FATHERS,] Amon and Manasseh.
33. RIBLAH,] as in Nu. 34. 11, &c.
HAMATH] in Aram, as in Nu. 13. 21, &c.
FINE,] as in Prov. 19. 19; Ex. 21. 22, &c.
100 TALENTS,] about £37,500.
A TALENT,] about £4,500 or £5067.
34. ELIAKIM,] as in Jos. 18. 18, &c.
JEHOIAKIM,] i.e. 'Jah raises up.'
35. SILVER..GOLD,] as in v. 33.
VALUED,] as in Lev. 27. 8, 12, 14.
EXACTED,] as in Ex. 3. 7, &c.
36. 25 YEARS,] two years older than his brother Jehoahaz, as in v. 31; B.C. 610.
11 YEARS,] till B.C. 599.
ZEBUDAH,] i.e. 'endowed.'
PEDAIAH,] i.e. 'ransomed.'
RUMAH,] i.e. 'height.'
37. DID,] as in v. 32.

XXIV. 1. NEBUCHADNEZZAR,] i.e. 'Nebo is prince of gods, or god of fire, or prince of the god Mercury; sometimes spelled 'Nebuchadrezzer,' as in Jer. 39. 1, 11; 43. 10; Eze. 29. 18.
THREE YEARS,] the 5th, 6th, 7th of his reign.
REBELLETH,] but for what cause is not mentioned.
2. TROOPS,] as in Ge. 49. 19, &c.
CHALDEANS,] as in Ge. 11. 31; 15. 7; 2 K. 25. 4, &c.
ARAM,] from the north, beyond Lebanon.
MOAB,] from the east, beyond the Jordan.
SONS OF AMMON,] north of Moab.
SPAKE,] in 20. 17, &c.
3. MANASSEH,] recorded in 21. 2, 11, &c.
4. FORGIVE,] without publicly shewing his displeasure.
5. MATTERS,] not 'acts,' as in C.V.
6. JEHOIACHIN,] i.e. 'Jah establishes.'
7. EGYPT,] who had established 'Jehoiakim,' as in 23. 34.
BROOK OF EGYPT,] as in Nu. 34. 5, &c.
PHRAT,] as in Ge. 2. 14, &c.
8. 18 YEARS,] in 2 Ch. 36. 9 it is only eight years.
NEHUSHTA,] i.e. 'brass;' see v. 15.
ELNATHAN,] i.e. 'God hath given.'
9. THE EVIL THING,] that is, idolatry
10. SEIGE,] as in De. 20. 19, 20, &c.
11. NEBUCHADNEZZAR,] the king himself.
12. GOETH FORTH,] seeing no other chance of escape.
CHIEFS,] as in Ge. 12. 15, &c.
EUNUCHS,] as in Ge. 37. 36, &c.
13. BRINGETH OUT,] as spoil for himself and his army.
CUTTETH IN PIECES,] as in 16. 17, &c.
SPOKEN,] in 20. 17, &c.

14. REMOVED] to Babylon, to prevent future revolts.
10,000,] as explained in v. 15, 16.
ARTIFICER,] as in Ex. 28. 11, &c.
SMITH,] as in v. 16; Jer. 24. 1; 29. 2.
15. BABYLON,] where he lived 37 years, as in 25. 27.
16. WARRIORS,] as in De. 20. 20; 1 K. 12. 21, &c.
17. MATTANIAH,] i.e. 'gift of Jah,' third son of Josiah.
FATHER'S BROTHER,] as in Lev. 10. 4, &c.
ZEDEKIAH,] i.e. 'righteousness of Jah.'
18. 21 YEARS,] as in 2 Ch. 36. 11.
LIBNAH,] as in 23. 31.
19. THE EVIL THING,] as in v. 9.
20. REBELLETH,] as in v. 1.

XXV. 1. NINTH YEAR,] B.C. 597.
FORTIFICATION,] as in Jer. 52. 4; Eze. 4. 2; 17. 17; 21. 22; 26. 8.
2. SEIGE,] as in 24. 10, &c.
ELEVENTH YEAR,] the fourth month, as in Jer. 39. 2; 52. 6.
3. SEVERE,] lit. 'strong.'
4. BROKEN UP,] as in Jer. 52. 7.
TWO WALLS,] as in Jer. 39. 4.
PLAIN] of Jericho, as in Jer. 39. 4—7; 52. 7; Eze. 12. 12.
5. OVERTAKE,] as in Ge. 31. 25, &c.
SCATTERED,] as in Ge. 10. 18, &c.
6. RIBLAH,] as in 23. 33; Jer. 52. 9.
JUDGMENT,] because of his perjury and rebellion.
7. SLAUGHTERED,] as in Ge. 22. 10, &c.
BLINDED,] as in Jer. 39. 7; Eze. 12. 13.
BRAZEN FETTERS,] as in Jud. 16. 21, &c.
BABYLON,] as in 23. 15; fulfilling Jer. 32. 5; 34. 3, and Eze. 12. 13.
8. SEVENTH,] in Jer. 52. 12 it is the 'tenth.'
19TH YEAR,] as in 24. 12; v. 27.
NEBUZARADDAN,] as in v. 11, 20; Jer. 39. 9—13; 40. 1; 41. 10; 43. 6; 52. 12—30.
EXECUTIONERS,] as in Ge. 37. 36, &c.
9. BURNETH,] as in 2 Ch. 36. 19, after lasting according to Usher 424 years, 3 months, and 8 days.
GREAT HOUSE,] as in Jer. 39. 8; Amos 2. 5.
BROKEN DOWN,] as in Neh. 1. 3; Jer. 52. 14.
11. LEFT] by Nebuchadnezzar, as in Jer. 39. 9; 52. 15.
12. HUSBANDMEN,] as in 2 Ch. 26. 10.
13. PILLARS OF BRASS,] called Jachin and Boaz.
BASES,] as in 1 K. 7. 27.
SEA OF BRASS,] as in 1 K. 7. 23.
14. POTS..SHOVELS,] as in Ex. 27. 3, &c.
SNUFFERS..SPOONS,] as in 1 K. 7. 50, &c.
15. FIRE-PANS..BOWLS,] as in Ex. 27. 3.

TAKEN,] from the temple to Babylon.
16. WEIGHING,] as in 1 K. 7. 47.
17. EIGHTEEN CUBITS,] as in 1 K. 7. 15; Jer. 52. 21.
CHAPITER,] as in 1 K. 7. 16, &c.
NET..POMEGRANATE,] as in 1 K. 7. 17, 18, 20, 42.
18. SERAIAH,] as in 1 Ch. 6. 14; Ezra 7. 1.
ZEPHANIAH,] i.e. 'hidden of Jah.' as in Jer. 21. 1; 29. 25.
SECOND PRIEST,] as in Jer. 52. 24.
THRESHOLD] of the temple.
19. EUNUCH,] as in Jer. 52. 25.
SEEING THE KING'S FACE,] as in Est. 1. 14.
MINISTERETH,] as in Jer. 52. 25.
20. RIBLAH,] as in Nu. 34. 11, &c.
21. HAMATH,] as in Nu. 13. 21, &c.
REMOVETH,] 468 years after the death of Saul, 388 after the death of Solomon, and 134 after the captivity of the ten tribes.
22. GEDALIAH,] i.e. 'greatness of Jah.'
AHIKAM,] i.e. 'my brother has risen.'
SHAPHAN,] i.e. a 'coney.'
23. HEADS OF THE FORCE,] as in Jer. 40. 7, 8, 9, &c.
MIZPEH,] as in Ge. 31. 49, &c.
ISHMAEL,] i.e. 'God hears.'
NETHANIAH,] i.e. 'given of Jah.'
JOHANAN,] i.e. 'Jah is gracious.'
KAREAH,] i.e. 'bald.'
SERAIAH,] as in v. 18.
TANHUMETH,] i.e. 'consolation.'
NETOPHATHITE,] as in 2 Sa. 23. 28, 29.
JAAZANIAH,] i.e. 'Jah gives ear.'
MAACHATHITE,] as in De. 3. 14, &c.
24. SWEARETH,] as in Jer. 40. 9.
25. ISHMAEL,] as in v. 23.
ELISHAMA,] i.e. 'my God has heard.'
SEED OF THE KINGDOM,] as in Jer. 41. 1; Ezek. 17. 13; Da. 1. 3.
SMITE,] as in Jer. 41. 1, 2.
MIZPEH,] as in v. 23.
26. EGYPT,] contrary to the command of God, as in Jer. 43. 4—7, leaving Judah a desolation.
27. 37TH YEAR,] being 55 years of age.
27TH DAY,] in Jer. 52. 31 it is the 25th day.
EVIL-MERODACH,] i.e. 'the fool of Merodach,' as in Jer. 52. 31.
RESTRAINT,] as in 1 K. 22. 27; 2 K. 17. 4; 25. 29; 2 Ch. 18. 26; Isa. 42. 7, 22; Jer. 37. 15, 18; 52. 33.
28. GOOD THINGS,] as in Nu. 10. 29; 1 K. 12. 7, &c.
THRONE] or royal state.
29. CHANGED,] as a mark of regard.
EATEN BREAD,] as in 2 Sa. 9. 7.
30. ALLOWANCE,] as in Prov. 15. 17; Jer. 40. 5; 52. 34.
IN ITS DAY,] as in Ex. 5. 13, &c.

FIRST BOOK OF CHRONICLES

THE two succeeding Books, generally known as the 'Books of Chronicles,' are evidently from the same compiler, who lived after the return from Babylon, see 1 Ch. 3. 19—24; 9. 1, &c. The author is unknown, and it is a matter of no importance, as the whole has always formed a part of the sacred Writings of the Jews, which have been universally received as such in the Jewish and Christian Churches.

Like most other portions of the Scriptures, the title is of human authority; the Masorets entitle it 'Matters of the days;' the Septuagint translators 'Things left,' as if it were a supplement to the preceding books of Samuel and Kings; Jerome is said to have first given it its present name.

The *first* Book or division reaches from Adam till the death of David, the *second* from the ascension of Solomon to the return from Babylon; the former embraces a period of nearly 3,000 years, the latter of about 450 years.

I. 1. ADAM,] i.e. a 'ruddy' man, as in Ge. 1. 26, &c.

SHETH, ENOSH,] son and grandson of Adam, see Ge. 5. 1—8.

2. See Ge. 5. 9—20.

3. See Ge. 5. 18—31.

4. See Ge. 5. 32; 6. 8—10; 7. 1; 9. 18, 29; 10. 1.

5. See Ge. 10. 1—5, &c.

6. RIPHATH,] or Diphath; see Ge. 10. 3; Eze. 38. 6.

7. DODANIM,] or Rodanim; see Ge. 10. 4.

8. See Ge. 10. 6, 7, 29.

9. See Ge. 10. 7.

10. See Ge. 10. 8—13; Mic. 5. 6.

11. See Ge. 10. 13, 14.

12. See Ge. 10. 14; De. 2. 23; Jer. 47. 4; Amos 9. 7.

13. See Ge. 9. 22, 25, 26; 10. 15, 19, &c.

14. See Ge. 15. 21; 48. 22, &c.

15. See Ge. 13. 5; Ex. 3. 8, 17; 13. 5; Jos. 9. 17; 1 K. 9. 20.

16. See Nu. 34. 8; 1 K. 8. 65; Ezek. 27. 8.

17. MESHECH,] or Mash; see Ge. 10. 22, 32; 11. 10; 14. 1.

18. See Ge. 10. 24; 11. 12, 15.

19. PELEG,] i.e. 'division;' see Ge. 10. 21, 25; 11. 7, 16, 17; Nu. 24. 24.

20. See Ge. 10. 26, 27.

22. See Ge. 10. 28.

23. See Ge. 2. 11; 10. 29; 25. 18.

24. See Ge. 11. 10, 26.

25. See Ge. 11. 15, 18.

26. See Ge. 11. 25; 24. 47.

27. See Ge. 11. 26, 27, 32; 17. 5.

28. See Ge. 16. 11, 16; 17. 19, 21; 21. 2, 5, 9, 10, 12.

29. See Ge. 25. 12, 16; 28. 9.

30. HADAD,] or Hadar; see Ge. 25. 15; Isa. 21. 11.

32. See Ge. 18. 12; 25. 1, 4; 35. 22; 37. 28.

33. See Ge 25. 4; Isa. 60. 6.

34. See Ge. 21. 2, 3; 25. 19, 21, 24, 28; 32. 28

35. See Ge. 36. 4, 5, 9, 10.

36. ZEPHI,] or Zepho; see Ge. 36. 10, 15; v. 53; Timna; see Ge. 36. 12.

37. See Ge. 36. 13.

38. See Ge. 32. 3; 36. 20, 21, 24, 29, 30; De. 2. 20.

39. HOMAM,] or Heman; see Ge. 36. 22; De. 2. 12, 22.

40. ALIAN,] or Alvan; Shephi or Shepho; see Ge. 36. 23, 24.

AMRAM,] or Hemdan; see Ge. 36. 25, 26.

42. JAKAN,] or Achan; see Ge. 36. 27, 28.

43. See Ge. 14. 1; 36. 31, 39; 49. 10.

44. See Ge. 36. 33; Isa. 34. 6; 63. 1; Jer. 49. 13; Amos 1. 12; Mic. 2. 12.

45. See Ge. 36. 34; Jer. 4. 9; Amos 1. 12.

46. See Nu. 22. 4; 1 K. 11. 14.

48. See Ge. 36. 37; Ge. 2. 10, 14.

50. HADAD,] or Hadar; Pai or Pau; see Ge. 36. 29, 39.

51. ALIAH,] or Alvah; see Ge. 36. 40.

54. See Ge. 36. 41—43.

II. 1. ISRAEL,] or Jacob; see Ge. 29. 32, 35.

3. See Ge. 38. 2, 10; 46. 12.

4. See Ge. 4. 1; 9. 4, 6; 38. 13. 30.

5. See Ge. 46. 12; Nu. 26. 21.

6. ZIMRI,] or Zabdi; see Jos. 7. 1. 17, 18; 1 K. 4. 31.

7. ACHAR,] or Achan; see 4. 1.

8. See v. 31; Ge. 46. 23.

9. RAM,] or Aram; Chelubai or Caleb; see v. 2, 33, 42.

10. See Nu. 1. 7; 2. 3; 7. 12, 17; 10. 14.

11. SALMA,] or Salmon; see Ruth 4. 1, 21.

12. See 10. 14; Ruth 4. 22.

13. SHIMMA,] or Shammah; see 20. 7; 27. 18.

15. See 1 Sa. 16. 10, 11; 17. 12—14.

16. See 1 Sa. 26. 6; 2 Sa. 2. 18—23.

17. JETHER AN ISHMAELITE,] or Ithra an Israelite; see 2 Sa. 17. 25.

18. See v. 9. 42.

19. See v. 24, 50; 4. 4; Mic. 5. 2.

20. See Ex. 17. 10, 14; 24. 14; 31. 1, 2; 36. 1, 2; 37. 1; 38. 22; 2 Ch. 1. 5.

21. See Ge. 4. 1; 6. 4; 50. 23.

22. See Nu. 32. 40; De. 3. 14; Jos. 13. 30.

23. See Nu. 32. 41; De. 3. 14; Jos. 13. 30.

24. See v. 4, 5, 9, 18, 19; 4. 5.

25. See v. 9.

27. See v. 25.

28. See v. 26.

30. See v. 34, 35.

31. See v. 34, 35

33. JERAHMEEL,] see 1 Sa. 27. 10.

35. See v. 31; Ge. 21. 21.

36. See 11. 41; 1 Ch. 13. 41.

42. See v. 9, 18, 23, 24, 45, 49, 60, 62; 8. 9; Ge. 49. 3.

45. See Jos. 15. 58.

46. See v. 18, 19, 48; 1. 32; Ge. 22. 24; 25. 1. 5.

48. See v. 49; Ge. 25. 5, 6; 1 K. 11. 3.

49. See v. 42; Jos. 15. 17, 31, 35, 57

50. EPHRATHA,] or Ephrath; see v. 19, 20, 42, 53; 13. 5, 6; Jos. 15. 9, 60.
51. See 4. 4; Ge. 35. 19.
52. HAROE,] or Reaiah; half of the Manahethites or Menuchites; see 4. 2; 9. 16; 2 Sa. 23. 23.
.53. See 11. 40; Jos. 15. 33.
54. ATAROTH,] or Asarites, or crowns of the house of Joab; see v. 51; 11. 30.
55. See v. 2; 4. 9, 10; Nu. 24. 21.

III. 1. DANIEL,] or Chileab; see 2 Sa. 3. 3.
2. See 2. 23; Jos. 13. 13.
3. See 2 Sa. 3. 5.
4. See 2 Sa. 2. 11; 3. 5; 5. 4, 5; 1 K. 2. 11.
5. SHIMEA,] or Shammuah; Bathshua or Bath-Sheba; Ammiel or Eliam; see 14. 4; 23. 5, 6.
6. ELISHAMA,] or Elishua; Eliphelet or Elpalet; see 14. 5; 2 Sa. 5. 15.
7. See 2 Sa. 5. 15, 16.
8. ELIADA,] or Beeliada; see 14. 7; 2 Sa. 5. 14, 16.
9. See 2 Sa. 5. 13; 13. 1, 20; 1 K. 11. 3.
10. ABIA,] or Abijam; see 1 K. 11. 43.
11. AHAZIAH,]or Azariah or Jehoahaz; see 1 K. 5. 50.
12. AZARIAH,] or Uzziah; see 2 K. 12. 21.
13. AHAZ,]or Achaz; Hezekiah or Ezekias; Manasseh or Menasses; see 2 K. 15. 38.
14. JOSIAH,]or Josias; see 2 K. 21. 18,19, 26.
15. JOHANAN,] or Jehoahaz; Jehoiakim or Eliakim; Zedekiah or Mattaniah; see 2 K. 23. 30, 34.
16. JECHONIAH,] or Jehoiakim, or Coniah; see v. 15; 2 K. 24. 6, 8, 17.
17. SALATHIEL,]or Shealtiel; see 2 K. 24. 15.
19. ZERUBBABEL,] or Zorobabel; see Ez. 2. 2; 3. 2.
21. See Ne. 10. 22.
22. See Ezra 8. 2.
23. HEZEKIAH,] or Hiskijahu.

IV. 1. CARMI,] or Chelubai, or Caleb; see 2. 4, 5, 9, 18; Ge. 38. 3, 39; 46. 12.
2. REAIAH,] or Haroch; see 2. 52, 54.
3. See Jud. 15. 11; 2 Ch. 11. 6.
4. See v. 11, 18, 39; 2. 19, 50, 51.
5. See v. 6, 7; 2. 24.
9. JABEZ,] i.e. 'sorrowful;' see v. 10.
10. See v. 9; 16. 8.
12. IR-NAHASH,] i.e. 'city of Nahash.'
13. See Nu. 32. 12; Jos. 15. 17, &c.
14. See 2. 11; 1 Sa. 26. 6.
15. KENAZ,] or Uknaz; see Nu. 13. 6, 30.
16. See 2. 42.
17. ESHTEMOA,] or Eshtemoh; see v. 19.
18. JEHUDIJAH,] or the Jewess; Socho, or Socoh; see v. 4, 39.
19. HODIAH,] or Jehudijah; see v. 18.
20. See Ge. 38. 1, 5.
21. SHELA,] or Shiloni; see 2. 3; 9. 5.
22. CHOZEBA,] i.e. 'a lie.'
23. See v. 14; Jer. 45. 5.
24. NEMUEL,] or Jemuel; Jarib or Jachin; Zerah or Zohar; see Ge. 46. 10, &c.
27. See Nu. 2. 4, 13; 26. 14, 22.
28. See Ge. 21. 25; 26. 33.
29. BILHA,] or Balah; Tolad, or El-Tolad; see Nu. 14. 45.
30. See Jos. 15. 31; 19. 5, 6.

31. HAZAR-SUSIM,] or Hazar-Susah.
32. ETAM,] or Ether; see Jos. 19. 7.
33. BAAL,] or Baalath-Beer; see Jos. 19. 8.
38. See v. 24; Ge. 6. 4.
39. GEDOR,] or Geder; see v. 4, 18.
40. See Ge. 9. 22; 10. 6.
41. See v. 33, 38; Nu. 32. 1—4.
42. See Ge. 36. 8; Ex. 17. 8.
43. See Ex. 17. 14, 16; De. 25. 17—19

V. 1. See 2. 1; Ge. 25. 23, 31, &c.
2. See Ge. 48. 5; 49. 8—10, &c.
3. PALLU,] or Phallu; see Ge. 46. 9.
6. TILGATH-PILNESER,] or Tiglath-Pileser; see v. 26.
7. See v. 17.
8. SHEMA,] or Shemaiah; see v. 4.
9. See v. 7; Jos. 22. 8, 9; 1 Ch. 2. 21.
10. See v. 19, 20; Ge. 21. 9; 25. 12.
11. See Nu. 32. 1, 34—36; De. 3. 10, 17.
12. See 2 Ch. 27. 29.
16. See 27. 29; Jos. 17. 8; Isa. 35. 2.
17. See v. 7; 2 K. 14. 16, 23, 28.
18. See Jos. 4. 12, 13; 2 Ch. 13. 3.
19. NEPHISH,] or Naphish; see v. 10.
20. See v. 22; Ex. 17. 11; Jos. 10. 14, 42.
21. See Nu. 31. 35; Jud. 5. 10; 10. 14.
22. See v. 26; Jos. 23. 12; 2 K. 15. 29.
23. See De. 3. 8, 11; 4. 48; 23. 9.
24. See 4. 28; Ge. 6. 4; Nu. 31. 35.
25. See Jud. 2. 12, 17; 8. 33.
26. See v. 6; 2 Sa. 24. 1; 2 K. 12. 13.

VI. 1. GERSHON,] or Gershom; see v. 16 17, 20; Ge. 46. 11; Ex. 6. 16.
2. See v. 22; 23. 12; Ex. 2. 7, 8, &c.
3. See 23. 13; 24. 1—6; Ex. 2. 4, 7, &c.
4. See v. 10; 9. 20; Ex. 6. 25.
7. See 2 Sa. 15. 27; 17. 17; 18. 19.
8. See 2 Sa. 8. 7, 17; 15. 27, 35, 36.
10. HOUSE,] as in v. 31.
11. See 2 K. 22. 4; Ezra 7. 3.
12. SHALLUM,] or Meshullam; see 9. 11.
13. See 2 K. 22. 12, 14.
14. See 2 K. 25. 16, 18.
15. JEHOZADAK,]or Jozadak, or Josedech
16. GERSHOM,]see v. 1; Ge. 6. 16, 17.
17. See 27. 3; Ex. 6. 17; Nu. 3. 18, 21
18. See v. 2, 3; 23. 12.
19. See 23. 21; 24. 26; Ex. 6. 19.
20. See v. 17, 42.
21. JOAH,] or Ethan; Iddo, or Adaiah; Jeaterai, or Ethni.
22. AMMINADAB,] or Izhar, v. 2, 18.
23. See 1 Sa. 1. 1.
24. URIEL,] or Zephaniah; Uzziah, or Azariah; Shaul, or Joel.
25. See v. 35, 36; Ex. 6. 24
26. ZOPHAI,] or Zuph; Nahath, or Toah.
27. ELIAB,] or Eliel, v. 34.
28. VASHNI,] or Joel, v. 33; 1 Sa. 8. 2.
29. See v. 19; Nu. 3. 33.
31. See 15. 16, 22, 27; 16. 1; 25. 1—31.
32. See v. 10; 9. 33; 16. 4—6, 37—42.
34. TOAH,] or Nahath, v. 26, 27.
35. ZUPH,] or Zophai, v. 26.
36. JOEL,] or Shaul; Uzziah or Uriel.
37. EBIASAPH,] or Abiasaph, Ex. 6. 21.
38. See Nu. 3. 19; 16. 1.
39. See v. 33, 44; 15. 17—19; 16. 7.
41. See v. 21.

42. See **v.** 21.
43. See **v.** 1, 16, 17, 20; 23. 6.
44. ETHAN,] *or* Jeduthan ; Kishi *or* Kushaiah.
47. See 23. 21, 23; Ex. 6. 19.
48. See **v.** 41; 23. 2, &c.
49. See Ex. 28. 6; 29. 33, 36, 37.
50. See **v.** 3, 9; 9. 20; 24. 1.
53. See 12. 23; 18. 16; 24. 3, 31.
54. See Ge. 25. 16; Nu. 35. 1—9.
55. See Ge. 23. 2; Jos. 14. 13; 15. 13; 21. 11—13.
56. See Jos. 14. 13; 15. 13; 21. 12.
57. See 4. 17; Nu. 35. 13—15.
58. HILEN,] *or* Holon ; Jos. 12. 13.
59. ASHAN,] *or* Ain ; Jos. 15. 10.
60. ALEMETH,] *or* Almon ; 8. 6.
61. See **v.** 1, 2, 18, 33, 66; Jos. 20; 21. 1, 4, 5, 8, 20—26.
62. See **v.** 71, 76; Jos. 21. 27—33.
63. See **v.** 77, 81; Jos. 21. 7, 34—40.
64. See Nu. 35. 2, 5; Jos. 21. 41, 42.
65. See **v.** 57, 60.
66. See **v.** 61; Jos. 21. 21.
67. See Ge. 35. 4; Nu. 18. 20, &c.
68. JOKNEAM,] see Jos. 10. 11; 16. 5.
69. See Jos. 10. 12; 21. 23, 24.
70. See Jos. 17. 11; 21. 25.
71. See De. 1. 4; 4. 43; Jos. 9. 10.
72. See Jos. 19. 37; 21. 28, 29, 32; Jud. 4. 9.
73. See Jos. 19. 21.
74. See Jos. 21. 30.
75. See Jos. 21. 31.
76. See Jos. 12. 22; 19. 37; 20. 7; 21. 32.
77. See Jos. 21. 34, 35.
78. See De. 4. 32; Jos. 20. 8; 31. 36, 37.
80. See Ge. 32. 2; Jos. 21. 38, 39.
81. See Nu. 21. 25, 34; 23. 7; 32. 1, 3, 4, 37.

VII. 1. PUAH,] *or* Phuvah; Jashub, *or* Job.
2. See **v.** 5; 21. 1—5; 27. 1, 23, 24.
3. See 3. 22.
4. See **v.** 5; 12. 32; Ge. 49. 25.
6. See **v.** 10, 11; 8. 1; Ge. 35. 18; 42. 13.
7. See 21. 1, 5; 2 Ch. 17. 17.
10. See Jud. 3. 15, &c.
12. SHUPPIM,] *or* Shupham; Huppim, *or* Hupham; Ir, *or* Iri; Aher, *or* Ahiram.
13. SHALLUM,] *or* Shillem; Ge. 30. 3—8.
14. See 2. 21, 23; Ge. 50. 23; Nu. 26. 29.
15. See **v.** 12; Nu. 26. 33.
17. See 2. 31, 34; 1 Sa. 12. 11.
18. ABIEZER,] *or* Jezer; Nu. 26. 30, 32.
19. See Nu. 26. 30—32.
20. See Ge. 47. 52; 48. 19, 20; Nu. 26. 35, 36.
21. See Jos. 21. 11; 1 Sa. 5. 8.
22. See Ge. 37. 34; Job 2. 11.
23. BERIAH,] i.e. 'in evil;' 4. 9.
24. See Jos. 16. 3, 5; 1 K. 9. 17; 2 Ch. 8. 5.
26. See Nu. 1. 10.
27. NON,] *or* Nun; Ex. 17. 9—13.
28. NAARAN,] *or* Naarath; Gaza, *or* Adasa.
29. BETH-SHEAN,] *or* Beth-Shan; Jos. 11. 2.
30. IMNAH,] *or* Jimnah; Ishuai, *or* Isui.
31. See 2. 42; Ge. 46. 17.
32. SHOMER,] *or* Shamer ; **v.** 34.
34. SHAMER,] *or* Shomer ; **v.** 32.
37. ITHRAN,] *or* Jether ; **v.** 38.
38. See **v.** 37.
40. See 21. 1, 5; 2 Sa. 24. 1—9.

VIII. 1. AHARA,] *or* Ahiram.
2. RAPHA,] *or* Rosh; Ge. 46. 21.
3. ADDAR,] *or* Ard; 7. 6, 12.
4. AHOAH,] *or* Echi; Ge. 46. 21.
5. SHEPHUPHAN,] *or* Shupham; 7. 12.
6. See 2. 52; 5. 22; 6. 60; 7. 10.
8. See **v.** 7; 7. 12; Ge. 24. 6; 25. 6.
12. See **v.** 21; Ezra 2. 33; Neh. 6. 2.
13. SHEMA,] *or* Shimhi; Aijalon *or* Ajalon; **v.** 21.
16. See **v.** 13.
21. SHIMHI,] *or* Shema; **v.** 13.
25. SHASHAK,] son of Elpaal, as in **v.** 14.
27. JEROHAM,] *or* Jerimoth, another son of Elpaal.
28. See **v.** 14; Ge. 14. 18.
29. FATHER,] called Jehiel, 9. 35.
30. See 9. 36, 37.
31. ZACHER,] *or* Zechariah, 9. 37, 38.
32. SHIMEAH,] *or* Shimeam, 9. 38.
33. ABINADAB,] *or* Ishui; Ish-Baal *or* Ish-Bosheth, 9. 39; 1 Sa. 9. 1, &c.
34. MERIB-BAAL,] *or* Mephibosheth, 2 Sa. 4. 4.
35. TAREA,] *or* Tahrea, 9. 41.
36. JEHOADAH,] *or* Jarah, 9. 42.
37. RAPHA,] *or* Rephaiah, 9. 43.
40. See 12. 2; 2 Ch. 14. 8; 26. 14.

IX. 1. See 2 Ch. 33. 11; 36. 9, 10, 14, 18, 20.
2. See Jos. 9. 21, 27; 2 Ch. 11. 16; 30. 11, 18.
3. See 2 Ch. 11. 36; 30. 11, 18; 34. 6.
4. See 2. 5; 4. 1; Ge. 46. 12; Nu. 26. 20.
5. See Ge. 38. 5; Nu. 26. 20; Neh. 11. 5.
6. See **v.** 9; 2. 4, 6; 6. 39, 44; 7. 5.
7. See Neh. 8. 4; 10. 20; 11. 7.
9. See Neh. 11. 8.
10. See Neh. 11. 10; 12. 19.
11. AZARIAH,] *or* Seraiah; 6. 8—15.
12. See 24. 14; Neh. 10. 11; 11. 12, 13.
13. VALOUR,] as in 26. 6; 30. 32; Neh. 11. 14.
14. See 6. 19, 29, 63; Nu. 26. 57; Neh. 10. 11.
15. See 6. 17; 25. 2; Neh. 10. 12; 11. 17, 22.
16. See 2. 54; 12. 25; 25. 1, 3, 6.
17. See. **v.** 19; 23. 5; 26. 1; Neh. 11. 19.
18. See 26. 12—19; 1 K. 10. 5; 2 K. 11. 19.
19. THRESHOLDS,] as in 2 K. 12. 9, &c.
20. See Nu. 3. 32; 4. 16, 28, 33; 25. 11—13.
21. See 26. 1, 14.
22. APPOINTED,] *lit.* 'founded.'
23. See 23. 32; 2 Ch. 1. 3, 5; 23. 19.
24. See 26. 1, 14, 18; 1 K. 6. 5.
25. See 2 K. 11. 5, 7; 2 Ch. 23. 8; Eze. 4. 10. 11.
26. OFFICE,] *lit.* 'stedfastness.'
27. See 23. 32; 1 Sa. 3. 15; Mal. 1. 10.
28. NUMBER,] as in Ge. 34. 30, &c.
29. VESSELS,] as in Ex. 27. 20; 30. 23—28.
30. See Ex. 30. 7, 23, 25, 33, 35—38; 37. 29.
31. OFFICE,] as in **v.** 26.
32. ARRANGEMENT,] as in Ex. 25. 30, &c.
33. SING,] as in 6. 31; 25. 1.
34. See **v.** 13; Neh. 11. 1—15.
35. See 2. 23, 24, 45, 50—52; 8. 29—40.
36. See **v.** 39, 5; 8. 33; 1 Sa. 14. 50, 51.
37. GEDOR,] *or* Geder; Zechariah *or* Zacher; 8. 31.
38. SHIMEAM,] *or* Shimeah; 8. 32.
39. See 8. 33, 38; 10. 2; 1 Sa. 13. 22; 14. 1.
40. See 8. 34—36; 2 Sa. 4. 4.
41. See 8. 35.

42. JARAH,] or Jehoadah; 8. 36.
43. See 8. 37.

X. 1. FOUGHT,] as recorded in 1 K. 31. 1—13, on which see notes.
GILBOA,] as in 1 Sa. 28. 4; 31. 1, 8; 2 Sa. 1. 6, 21; 21. 12; v. 8 below.
2. PURSUE,] lit. 'cleave.'
ABINADAB,] as in 8. 33; 1 K. 31. 2; called Ishui in 1 Sa. 14. 49.
3. HEAVY,] as in Jud. 20. 34, &c.
SHOOTING,] as in 2 Ch. 35. 23; Prov. 26. 18, &c.
4. BEARER,] as in 16. 21.
PIERCE,] as in Nu. 25. 8; comp. Jud. 9. 54.
UNCIRCUMCISED,] as in Jud. 14. 3.
ROLL THEMSELVES,] as in Nu. 22. 29, &c.
NOT WILLING,] to do any evil to the anointed of Jehovah.
FEARETH] punishment, as in 2 Sa. 1. 14.
FALLETH] designedly,] as in 2 Sa. 1. 10.
6. HOUSE,] or household, that is, his bodyguard.
7. VALLEY] of Jezreel.
DWELL,] till dispossessed by David.
8. STRIP,] as in 2 Sa. 23. 10; 1 Sa. 31. 8.
9. HEAD,] to certify his death.
WEAPONS,] his coat of mail, sword, &c.
IDOLS,] such as Dagon; comp. 1 Sa. 21. 9.
10. GODS,] as trophies of victory.
DAGON,] their chief idol.
11. JABESH-GILEAD,] as in 1 Sa. 11. 1—11; ! Sa. 2. 4—7.
12. VALOUR,] as in Jos. 1. 14, &c.
BURY,] after burning, as in 1 Sa. 31, 12, 13.
FAST,] in token of sorrow, as in Ge. 50. 10.
13. BECAUSE OF,] or 'in.'
KEPT NOT,] as in 1 Sa. 13. 13, 14; 15. 3, 9.
FAMILIAR SPIRIT,] as in 1 Sa. 28. 8, 15.
14. INQUIRED NOT,] in a right spirit, evidently.
TURNETH ROUND,] as in 1 Sa. 15. 23; 2 Sa. 3, 9, 10; 5. 3.

XI. 1. HEBRON, as in 2 Sa. 5. 1, &c.
BONE..FLESH,] not a foreigner, forbidden in the law, see De. 17. 15.
2. TIME PAST,] lit. 'yesterday, third day.'
TAKING OUT..BRINGING IN,] as chief ruler.
SAITH,] as in Ps. 78. 71.
FEED,] as a shepherd does his flock.
LEADER,] as in 1 Sa. 9. 16, &c.
3. ELDERS] who ruled in every city.
COVENANT] of mutual rights.
ANOINT,] as in 2 Sa. 5. 3.
SAMUEL,] as in 16. 1, 12, 13.
4. JERUSALEM,] as in 2 Sa. 5. 6, &c.
JEBUS,] as in Jud. 1. 21; 19. 10.
5. CAPTURETH,] as in Nu. 31. 22, &c.
FORTRESS,] as in 1 Sa. 22. 4, &c.
CITY OF DAVID,] as in v. 9; 6. 10, &c.
6. HEAD AND PRINCE] of the army.
JOAB,] nephew of David.
8. MILLO,] as in 2 Sa. 5. 9; 1 K. 9. 15, 24; 11. 27; 2 Ch. 32. 5; in 2 Ch. 12. 21 it is called 'house of Millo.'
RESTORETH,] lit. 'reviveth.'
9. GREAT,] as in 2 Sa. 5. 10, &c.
WITH HIM,] as in Ps. 46. 7, 11; Am. 5. 14; Hag. 2. 4.
10. HEADS,] as in 2 Sa. 23. 8

STRENGTHENING THEMSELVES,] as in Ge. 48. 2; 2 Sa. 3. 6; Da. 10. 21.
WORD,] as in 1 Sa. 16. 1, 12.
11. ACCOUNT,] not merely 'number,' as ir C.V.
HACHMONITE,] in 2 Sa. 23. 8 it is 'Tachmonite.'
300.] In the parallel passage it is 800.
WOUNDED,] lit. 'pierced.'
12. ELEAZAR,] i.e. 'God is help.'
DODO,] i.e. 'his uncle or beloved.'
AHOHITE,] a descendant of Benjamin.
13. PAS-DAMMIM,] or Ephes-Dammim, 1 Sa. 17. 1.
14. STATION THEMSELVES,] as in Ex. 2. 4, &c.
SMITE,] not 'slay,' as in C.V.
SALVATION,] or 'safety.'
15. THE ROCK,] as in 2 Sa. 23. 13.
ADULLAM,] as in 1 Sa. 22. 1.
REPHAIM,] as in 14. 9.
16. FORTRESS,] as in 1 Sa. 22. 4, 5.
BETH-LEHEM,] his native city.
17. LONGETH,] as in Nu. 11. 4, &c.
GATE] of the city, beyond the wall doubtless.
18. NOT BEEN WILLING,] as in Ex. 10. 27, &c.
POURETH,] as a drink-offering or libation.
19. FAR BE IT,] as in Ge. 18. 25, &c.
WITH THEIR LIVES,] or souls.
20. ABISHAI,] as in 2 Sa. 23. 18.
LIFTING UP,] as in v. 11.
WOUNDED,] lit. 'pierced,' as in v. 11.
21. HONOURED,] as in 2 Sa. 23. 19.
22. BENAIAH,] i.e. 'built or son of Jah.'
JEHOIADA,] i.e. 'Jah hath known.'
KABZEEL] in the south of Judah.
LION-LIKE,] as in 2 Sa. 23. 30.
PIT,] into which it had fallen.
23. MEASURE,] as in Nu. 13. 32, &c.
FIVE BY THE CUBIT,] that is, about seven and a half feet.
BEAM OF WEAVERS,] as in 1 Sa. 17. 7, 2 Sa. 21. 19; 1 Ch. 20. 5.
ROD,] as in Ex. 21. 20, &c.
25. GUARD,] around himself.
26. MIGHTY ONES,] not 'valiant men,' as in C.V.
ASAHEL,] as in 2 Sa. 23. 24.
ELHANAN,] i.e. 'God hath grace.'
27. SHAMMOTH,] or Shammah.
HELEZ,] in 2 Sa. 23. 26 he is called a 'Paltite.'
28. IRA,] i.e. a 'watcher.'
ABI-EZER,] i.e. 'father of help.'
29. SIBBECAI,] or Meburnai.
ILAI,] or Zalmon.
30. MAHARAI,] i.e. 'hasting.'
HELED,] or Heleb.
31. ITHAI,] i.e. 'there is.'
BENAIAH,] i.e. 'built or son of Jah.'
32. HURAI,] or Hiddai.
ABIEL,] or Abi-Albon.
33. ARMAVETH,] i.e. 'strength of death.'
ELIAHBA,] i.e. 'God hides.'
34. HASHEM,] or Jashen, 2 Sa. 23. 32, 35.
JONATHAN,] i.e. 'Jah hath given.'
35. AHIAM,] i.e. 'brother of a mother.'
SACAR,] or Sharer.
ELIPHAL,] or Eliphelet.

UR,] or Ahasbai.
36. HEPHER,] i.e. 'a pit.'
AHIJAH,] i.e. 'brother of Jah.'
37. HEZRO,] or Hezrai.
NAARAI,] or Paarai the Arbite.
38. JOEL,] i.e. 'Jah is God.'
MIBHAR] the Haggeret.
39. ZELEK,] i.e. a 'cleft.'
NAHARAI,] i.e. 'my snorting.'
40. IRA,] i.e. a 'watcher,' as in v. 28.
GAREB,] i.e. 'scurvy.'
41. URIAH,] i.e. 'light of Jah.'
ZABAD,] i.e. 'dowry;' this name, and those
following in v. 42—47 are additional to the
list in 2 Sa. 23. 8—39.
42. ADINA,] i.e. 'luxuriant.'
BY HIM,] by his side, under his command.
43. HANAN,] i.e. 'gracious.'
JOSHAPHET,] i.e. 'Jah has judged.'
44. UZZIA,] i.e. 'strength of Jah.'
SHAMA,] i.e. 'heaving.'
JEHIEL,] i.e. 'removed of God.'
45. JEDAIEL] the Shimrite.
JOHA.] Etymology uncertain.
46. ELIEL,] i.e. 'my God is God.'
JERIBAI,] i.e. 'my contender.'
JOSHAVIAH.] Etymology uncertain.
ITHMAH,] i.e. 'orphanage.'
47. ELIEL,] as in v. 46.
OBED,] i.e. 'serving.'
JAASIEL,] i.e. 'made by God.'

XII. 1. ZIKLAG,] given to him by Achish,
as in 1 Sa. 27. 2, 6.
SHUT UP,] not 'kept himself close,' as in
C.V.
HELPING,] as in v. 18, against Amalek, &c.
2. BOW,] as in 2 Ch. 17. 17; Ps. 78. 9.
RIGHT AND LEFTHANDED,] as in Jud.
20. 16.
BENJAMIN,] the youngest son of Jacob.
3. AHIEZER,] i.e. 'brother of help.'
JOASH.] Etymology uncertain.
SHEMAAH,] or Hasmaah.
GIBEATHITE,] of Gibeah in Benjamin, as
in 1 Sa. 11. 4.
JEZIEL.] Etymology uncertain.
PELET,] i.e. 'escape.'
AZMAVETH,] i.e. 'strength of death.'
BERACHAH,] i.e. 'blessing.'
JEHU,] i.e. 'he is.'
ANTOTHITE,] or Anathothite, as in Vul-
gate.
4. ISHMAIAH,] i.e. 'Jah hears.'
GIBEONITE] of Gibeon, as in Jos. 18. 25.
JEREMIAH.] Etymology uncertain.
JAHAZIEL,] i.e. 'God sees.'
JOHANAN,] i.e. 'God has grace.'
JOSABAD,] i.e. 'God has endowed.'
GEDERATHITE,] of Gedera, on the borders
of Judah and Benjamin.
5. ELUZAI,] i.e. 'God is my refuge or
strength.'
JERIMOTH,] i.e. 'high places' perhaps.
BEALIAH,] i.e. 'possessed of Jah.'
SHEMAIAH,] i.e. 'kept by Jah.'
SHEPHATIAH,] i.e. 'judged by Jah.'
HARUPHITE,] of Haruph, or Hariph, as in
Neh. 7. 24.
6. ELKANAH,] i.e. 'God has acquired.'
JESIAH.] Etymology uncertain.

AZAREEL,] i.e. 'helped by God.'
JOEZER,] i.e. 'Jah is help.'
JASHOBEAM,] i.e. 'the people hath dwelt.'
KORHITES,] not 'Korahites.'
7. JOELAH.] Etymology uncertain.
ZEBADIAH,] i.e. 'endowed by Jah.'
JEROHAM,] i.e. 'he has pity.'
GEDOR,] in Judah, as in Jos. 15. 58.
8. GADITE,] descendants of the fifth son of
Leah by Zilpah.
HAVE BEEN SEPARATED,] by causes not
mentioned.
WILDERNESS,] of Ziph or Maon or Judah.
SETTING IN ARRAY,] as in v. 33, 35; Isa.
65. 11.
FACE OF THE LION,] as in Eze. 1. 10; 10. 14.
ROES,] as in De. 12. 15, 22, &c.
SPEED,] as in 2 Sa. 2. 18.
9. EZER,] i.e. 'help.'
OBADIAH,] i.e. 'servant of Jah.'
ELIAB,] i.e. 'my God is father.'
10. MISHMANNAH,] i.e. 'fatness.'
JEREMIAH,] as in v. 4.
11. ATTAI,] i.e. 'my time.'
ELIEL,] i.e. 'my God is God.'
12. JOHANAN,] i.e. 'God has grace.'
ELZABAD,] i.e. 'God has endowed.'
JEREMIAH,] as in v. 4.
MACHBANNAI,] i.e. 'a bond.'
14. GAD,] as in v. 8.
15. FIRST MONTH,] that is, Nisan or Ab;
compare Jos. 3. 15.
THE VALLEY] of the Jordan, east and
west.
16. BENJAMIN,] as in v. 2.
JUDAH,] his own proper tribe.
STRONGHOLD,] or 'fortress,' as in v. 8.
17. I HAVE A HEART,] ready and willing to
UNITE] as brethren in a common cause.
BETRAY,] or 'deceive,' as in Ge. 29. 25;
Jos. 9. 22; 1 Sa. 19. 17; 28. 12; 2 Sa. 19. 26;
Prov. 26. 19; La. 1. 19.
VIOLENCE,] as in Job 16. 17; Isa. 53. 9, &c.
REPROVE,] as in Ge. 31. 42, &c.
18. SPIRIT] of God.
CLOTHED,] as in Jud. 6. 34, &c.
AMASAI,] as in 2 Sa. 17. 25, son of Zeruiah
David's sister, afterwards slain by Joab.
HELPER,] even God, as in next clause.
TROOP] which followed him, as their
leader.
19. MANASSEH,] the elder son of Joseph.
BATTLE,] as narrated in 1 Sa. 29. 2.
OUR HEADS,] as in 1 Sa. 29. 4.
20. ZIKLAG,] as in v. 1 above.
ADNAH,] i.e. 'time or pleasure.'
JOZABAD,] i.e. 'Jah has endowed.
JEDIAEL,] i.e. 'God knows.'
MICHAEL,] i.e. 'who is like God?'
ELIHU,] i.e. 'my God is He.'
ZILLTHAI,] i.e. 'my shadow.'
21. HELPED,] that is, gave help along
with him over the unruly spirits in his own
band.
22. CAMP OF GOD,] as in Ge. 32. 3.
23. HEADS,] not 'bands,' as in C.V.
HEBRON,] as in 2 Sa. 2. 3, 4; 5. 1; 1 Ch.
11. 1.
TURN ROUND,] as in 10. 14.
MOUTH,] as in 1 Sa. 16. 1, 3.
24. JUDAH,] as in v 16.

TARGET AND SPEAR,] as in v. 8; 2 Ch. 25. 5; Jer. 46. 3; Eze. 39. 9.

6,800,] David being already recognized as king over Judah, fewer of that tribe apparently took part in this transaction.

25. SIMEON,] second son of Jacob.

26. LEVI,] third son of Jacob.

27. JEHOIADA,] i.e. 'Jah hath known.'

28. ZADOK,] as in 2 Sa. 8. 17.

HEADS] of the courses, as in 24. 4.

29. BENJAMIN,] the youngest son of Jacob. 3,000,] the bulk of the tribe remaining neutral.

CHARGE,] as in 2 Sa. 2. 8, 9.

30. EPHRAIM,] the younger son of Joseph. NAME,] renowned among their tribe.

31. HALF-TRIBE,] west of Jordan. DEFINED,] that is, pointed out as fit persons.

32. ISSACHAR,] Leah's fifth son. TIMES,] as in Est. 1. 13, &c. SHOULD DO,] in circumstances of perplexity. COMMAND,] willing to follow their guidance.

33. ZEBULON,] Leah's sixth son. HOST] of battle, when necessary. ARRANGING,] as in v. 8 above. KEEPING RANK,] as in v. 38. DOUBLE HEART,] lit. 'heart and heart.'

34. NAPHTALI,] the second son of Bilhah, Rachel's maid.

35. DANITE,] descendants of the first son of Bilhah, Rachel's maid. ARRANGING,] as in v. 33.

36. ASHER,] second son of Zilpah, Leah's maid.

37. JORDAN,] eastward.

38. KEEPING RANK,] as in v. 33. ONE HEART,] as in 2 Ch. 30. 12.

39. BRETHREN] in Hebron.

40. NEAR,] reaching unto the three tribes mentioned afterwards. BREAD,] Sept reads 'to or for them,' by the change of one Hebrew letter. ASSES..OXEN,] all kinds of cattle. FINE FLOUR,] as in Ge. 18. 6; Nu. 5. 15; Jud. 6. 19; 1 Sa. 1. 24; 28. 24; 2 Sa. 17. 28; 1 K. 4. 22; 17. 12, 14, 16, &c. FIG-CAKES,] as in 1 Sa. 25. 18; 30. 12; 2 K. 20. 7; Isa. 38. 21. GRAPE-CAKES,] as in 1 Sa. 25. 18; 30. 12; 2 Sa. 16. 1. WINE,] as in Ge. 9. 21, &c. OIL,] as in 9. 29, &c. OXEN AND SHEEP,] as in Ge. 12. 16, &c.

XIII. 1. CONSULTETH,] as in 1 K. 12. 6, &c. LEADER,] as in 1 Sa. 9. 16, &c.

2. BROKEN FORTH,] not 'let us send abroad,' as in C.V. LEFT,] not having come up to the coronation. SUBURBS,] as in 6. 54—81. GATHERED,] as in 11. 1; 2 Sa. 6. 1.

3. BRING ROUND,] not 'bring again,' as in C.V. ARK,] being the symbol of the divine presence. SOUGHT NOT] rightly nor diligently.

4. TO DO SO,] not 'that they would do so.' as in C.V.

5. SHIHOR,] as in Jos. 13. 3, on the south of Canaan; i.e. 'the brook of Egypt.' HAMATH,] on the north of Canaan. KIRJATH-JEARIM,] where it had remained since the days of Samuel, as in 1 Sa. 7. 1.

6. GOETH UP] from Hebron, as in v. 12, 38. BAALAH,] as in Jos. 15. 9; called Kirjath-Baal in Jos. 15. 60; and Baale-Judah in 2 Sa. 6. 2. INHABITING,] as in 1 Sa. 4. 4, &c. CALLED ON,] in prayer and supplication. So Targum.

7. PLACE,] lit. 'cause to ride,' as in 2 K. 9. 28; 13. 16; 2 Sa. 6. 3. CART,] as in 1 Sa. 6. 7, 8, 11, 14, &c.; it should have been carried on the shoulders, as in Nu. 7. 9. ABINADAB,] as in 1 Sa. 7. 1. UZZA,] i.e. 'strength.' AHIO,] i.e. 'his brother.' LEADING,] not 'driving,' as in C.V.

8. PLAYING,] as in 1 Sa. 18. 7; 1 Ch. 13. 8, &c. STRENGTH,] as in 2 Sa. 6. 14; 2 Ch. 30. 21, &c. SONGS,] as in Ge. 31. 27; Jud. 5. 12; 1 K. 4. 32, &c. HARPS,] as in Ge. 4. 21; 31. 27, &c. PSALTERIES,] as in 1 Sa. 10. 5, &c. TIMBRELS,] as in Ge. 31. 27, &c. CYMBALS,] as in 15. 16, 19, 28: 16. 5, 42; 25. 1, 6; 2 Ch. 5. 12, 13; 29. 25; Ezra 3. 10; Neh. 12. 27. TRUMPETS,] as in Nu. 10. 2, 8, 9, 10.

9. THRESHING-FLOOR,] as in Ge. 50. 10, 11, &c. CHIDION,] in 2 Sa. 6. 6 it is Nachon. RELEASED] from the cart, as in 2 Sa. 6. 6; compare Ex. 23. 11; De. 15. 2, 3; 2 K. 9. 33; Ps. 141. 6; Jer. 17. 4.

10. KINDLED,] as in Ge. 30. 2, &c. DIETH,] as in Lev. 10. 2.

11. DISPLEASING,] as in Ge. 4. 5, &c. BREACH,] as in Ge. 38. 29; Jud. 21. 15; 2 Sa. 5. 20; 6. 8; 1 K. 11. 27; 1 Ch. 14. 11; Neh. 6. 1; Job 16. 14; 30. 14, &c.

12. UNTO ME,] in my city—the city of David.

13. CITY OF DAVID,] that is, Zion, which he had conquered and beautified. OBED-EDOM,] i.e. 'servant of Edom.' GITTITE,] as in 1 Ch. 15. 18, 21, 24; 26. 5, 6; perhaps he was of Gath-Rimmon, a Levitical city, as in Jos. 21. 24.

XIV. 1. HURAM,] or Hiram; as in 2 Sa. 5. 11; 1 K. 5. 15; 2 Ch. 2. 2. TYRE,] a city of Phenicia; as in Jos. 19. 29, &c. CEDAR,] from Lebanon, as in Lev. 14. 4, 6, &c. ARTIFICERS,] as in Ex. 28. 11, &c. ARTIFICERS OF WOOD,] as in 2 Sa. 5. 11, &c. HOUSE,] that is, a palace.

2. KNOWETH,] by the success he had. LIFTING UP ON HIGH,] above all around him. PEOPLE,] whom he had redeemed.

3. JERUSALEM,] as in 2 Sa. 5. 13, &c.

4. SHAMMUA,] i.e. 'heard;' *or* Shimea, as in 1 Ch. 3. 5, &c.
SHOBAB,] i.e. a 'bringer back,' as in 2 Sa. 5. 14.
NATHAN,] i.e. 'he gave.'
SOLOMON,] i.e. 'peace.'
5. IBHAR,] i.e. 'he chooses,' as in 2 Sa. 5. 15.
ELISHUA,] i.e. 'my God saves,' as in 2 Sa. 5. 15.
ELPALET,] i.e. 'God has escaped.'
6. NOGAH,] i.e. 'shining, brightness.'
NEPHEG,] i.e. 'a going forth.'
JAPHIA,] i.e. 'he breathes.'
7. ELISHAMA,] i.e. 'God hears.'
BEELIADA,] in 2 Sa. 5. 16 it is Eliada.
ELIPHALET,] i.e. 'God escapes,' as in 2 Sa. 5. 16.
8. ANOINTED] in the place of Saul, whom they had slain in Gilboa.
GO UP,] from the sea-coast to the valley of Rephaim; as in v. 9.
9. RUSH,] as in Jud. 9. 33, &c.
REPHAIM,] as in Jos. 15. 8, west of Jerusalem.
ASKETH,] as in 2 Sa. 5. 19, 23.
11. BAAL-PERAZIM,] i.e. 'lord of breaches,' as in 2 Sa. 5. 20.
BROKEN UP,] as in 2 Ch. 20. 37.
12. GODS,] such as Dagon, &c.
FIRE,] as directed in De. 7. 5, 25, &c.
13. VALLEY] of Rephaim, as in v. 9.
14. MULBERRIES,] as in 2 Sa. 5. 23. 24; Ps. 84. 6.
15. STEPPING,] as in 2 Sa. 5. 24.
16. GIBEON,] *or* Geba, as in 2 Sa. 5. 25.
GAZER,] as in Jos. 16. 10.
17. NAME] or renown of David as a successful warrior.
FEAR,] as in Ex. 15. 16; De. 2. 25, &c.

XV. 1. HOUSES,] for his wives, his household, and his captives.
ARK,] which had been left with Obed-Edom, as in 14. 13.
TENT,] under which it might remain, as in 2 Sa. 6. 1, 17.
2. CARRY] from one place to another.
LEVITES,] who were given as assistants to Aaron and the priests.
FIXED] he preferred them to the first born. Nu. 1. 50; 4. 15; 7. 9.
3. BRING UP] from the house of Obed-Edom.
4. SONS OF AARON,] the priests, and their assistants the Levites.
5. KOHATH,] the second son of Aaron, as in Ex. 6. 16.
URIEL,] i.e. 'light of God.'
6. MERARI,] the youngest son of Aaron.
ASAIAH,] i.e. 'made by Jah.'
7. GERSHOM,] the eldest son of Aaron.
JOEL,] i.e. 'Jah is God.'
8. ELIZPHAN,] i.e. 'my God has hidden.'
SHEMAIAH,] i.e. 'heard by Jah.'
9. HEBRON,] i.e. 'companionship.'
ELIEL,] i.e. 'my God is God.'
10. UZZIEL,] i.e. 'my strength is God.'
AMMINADAB,] i.e. 'my people is willing.'
11. ZADOK..ABIATHAR,] as in 2 Sa. 8. 17; 15. 27, 29; 1 K. 4. 4.

12. SANCTIFY YOURSELVES,] from all uncleanness or legal defilement.
13. AT THE FIRST] attempt to bring up the ark, as in 13. 7.
BREACH,] by smiting Uzzah.
ORDINANCE,] *or* 'judgment' that the Lord set upon Israel.
14. PRIESTS,] as in Jos. 3. 13, 14; 6. 6.
15. COMMANDED,] in Ex. 25. 14; Nu. 4. 15; 7. 9, &c.
STAVES,] as in Nu. 4. 10, 12; 13. 23; Nah. 1. 13, &c.
16. APPOINT,] not assuming the nomination to himself as some do now-a-days.
SINGERS,] in the public service of the sanctuary.
JOY,] because of the presence of the ark.
17. HEMAN,] i.e. 'stedfast.'
JOEL,] i.e. 'Jah is God;' he was son of Samuel, as in 6. 33.
ASAPH,] i.e. 'he gathers,' as in 6. 39.
BERACHIAH,] i.e. 'blessed of Jah.'
MERARI,] as in v. 6.
ETHAN,] i.e. 'perennial.'
KUSHAIAH,] i.e. 'bow *or* snare of Jah;' *or* Kishi, as in 6. 44.
18. ZECHARIAH,] i.e. 'remembered by Jah.'
BEN,] i.e. a 'son.'
JAAZIEL,] *or* Aziel, as in v. 20.
SHEMIRAMOTH,] i.e. 'renown of high places,' as in v. 20; 16. 5; 2 Ch. 17. 8.
JEHIEL,] i.e. 'God lives.'
UNNI,] i.e. 'afflicted.'
ELIAB,] i.e. 'my God is father.'
BENAIAH,] i.e. 'son of Jah.'
MAASEIAH,] i.e. 'work of Jah.'
MATTITHIAH,] i.e. 'gift of Jah.'
ELIPHELEH,] i.e. 'God makes him wonderful.'
MIKNEIAH,] i.e. 'possession of Jah.'
OBED-EDOM,] i.e. 'servant of Edom.'
JEIEL.] See on 5. 7.
GATE-KEEPERS,] as in 2 Sa. 18. 26, &c.
19. HEMAN..ASAPH..ETHAN,] as in v. 17.
CYMBALS,] as in 13. 8, &c.
20. PSALTERIES,] as in 1 Sa. 10. 5, &c.
VIRGINS,] who joined in the triumphal processions, as in Ex. 15. 20, &c.
21. HARPS,] as in v. 26.
OCTAVE,] as in Ps. 6. 1; 12. 1.
TO OVERSEE,] as in 23. 4; 2 Ch. 34. 12; Ezr. 3. 8, 9.
22. CHENANIAH,] i.e. 'covered by Jah,' as in v. 27.
BURDEN] of the song.
INTELLIGENT,] as in 25. 7, 8; 27. 32; 28. 9; 2 Ch. 26. 5; 34. 12; 35. 3; Eze. 8. 16; Neh. 8. 2, 3, 7, 9; 10. 28, &c.
23. BERECHIAH,] as in v. 17.
ELKANAH,] i.e. 'God has got.'
24. SHEBANIAH,] Etymology uncertain.
JOSHAPHAT,] i.e. 'Jah has judged.'
NETHANEEL,] i.e. 'gift of God.'
AMASAI,] i.e. 'borne by Jah.'
ZECHARIAH,] as in v. 18.
BENAIAH,] as in v. 18.
ELIEZER,] i.e. 'my God is help.'
BLOWING WITH TRUMPETS] of silver, as in Nu. 10. 5, 6.
JEHIAH,] *or* 'Jeiel,' as in v. 18.

25. DAVID] himself, the King of Israel, as in 2 Sa. 6. 12, 13; 1 K. 8. 1.
OBED-EDOM,] as in 13. 14.
26. HELPING,] so that no evil befell them or the ark.
SACRIFICE] to him, as in 2 Sa. 6. 13.
27. WRAPPED.] The original word is not found elsewhere.
FINE LINEN,] as in 4. 21, &c.
EPHOD,] as in 1 Sa. 2. 18; 22. 18.
28. SHOUTING,] as in 1 Sa. 4. 5, 6; 2 Sa. 6. 15.
CORNET,] as in Ex. 19. 16, &c.
29. ARK OF THE COVENANT,] as in Nu. 10. 33, &c.
MICHAL] his first wife, daughter of Saul.
WINDOW] of the palace, as in 2 Sa. 6. 16, &c.
DANCING,] or 'skipping,' as in Job 21. 11; Ps. 29. 6; 114. 4, 6; Ecc. 3. 4; Isa. 13. 21; Joel 2. 5; Nah. 3. 2.
PLAYING,] as in 1 Sa. 18. 7; 2 Sa. 6. 5, &c.
DESPISETH,] as in 2 Sa. 6. 16.

XVI. 1. BRING IN] unto the city of David.
TENT,] as in 15. 1.
2. BLESSETH,] as a prince and common father; compare 1 K. 8. 55; 2 Sa. 6. 18.
3. PORTION,] or 'share,' of good provided.
CAKE,] as in Ex. 29. 23, &c.
MEASURE,]in Heb. 'esphar,' as in 2 Sa. 6. 19.
GRAPE-CAKE,] in Heb. 'ashisha,' as in 2 Sa. 6. 19; compare Song 2. 4; Hos. 3. 1.
4. MINISTERS,] as in Ex. 24. 13; 33. 11, &c.
MAKE MENTION OF,] as in 1 Sa. 4. 18, &c.
THANKS,] as in v. 7, 35, 41; 23. 30; 25. 3; 2 Ch. 5. 13; 7. 3, 6; 31. 2; Ezr. 3. 11; Neh. 12. 24, 46; Ps. 92. 1, &c.
GIVE PRAISE,] as in 2 Sa. 14. 25, &c.
5. SECOND,] or substitute.
6. COVENANT,] as in 15. 29.
7. GIVEN,] that is, 'appointed.'
BEGINNING] of the service. V. 8—22 are as in Ps. 105. 1—15; v. 23—33 as in Ps. 96.
8. GIVE THANKS,] as in v. 34; 2 Ch. 20. 21; Ps. 30. 4; 33. 2; 97. 12; 100. 4; 105. 1; 106. 1; 107. 1; 118. 1, 29; 136. 1, 2, 3, 26; Isa. 12. 4; Jer. 33. 11.
CALL,] or 'preach' in his name.
PEOPLES] of Israel, or of the lands.
9. SING,] as in Ex. 15. 21, &c.
SING PSALMS,] as in Ps. 9. 5; 30. 4; 33. 2; 47. 6, 7; 66. 2; 68. 4, 5; 105. 2; 135. 3; 147. 7; Isa. 12. 5.
MEDITATE,] as in Jud. 5. 10; Job 12. 8; Ps. 105. 2.
10. BOAST YOURSELVES,] as in Ps. 105. 3; 1 K. 20. 11, &c.
SEEKING,] by prayer, as in Ps. 24. 6; 40. 16; 69. 6; 70. 4; 105. 3; Prov. 28. 5; Isa. 51. 1; Mal. 3. 1, &c.
11. STRENGTH,] as in Ex. 15. 2, 13, &c.
FACE,] or countenance, that is, his favour.
12. DID,] in times past.
SIGNS,] as in Ex. 4. 21; 7. 3, 9; 11. 9, 10.
JUDGMENTS,] that he pronounced.
13. SEED,] as in 2 Sa. 17. 20, &c.
SERVANT,] which they have vowed to be.
14. CHOSEN,] or choice ones, as in 2 Sa. 21. 6, &c.

OUR GOD,] by covenant voluntarily entered into.
EARTH,] or land, that is, of Israel.
JUDGMENTS,] of mercy and of wrath.
15. COVENANT,] as described in v. 18.
WORD,] or thing.
16. ABRAHAM,] as in Ge. 17. 2.
ISAAC,] as in Ge. 26. 3.
17. JACOB,] as in Ge. 28. 13; 35. 11.
STATUTE,] or 'portion,' as in Ge. 47. 22, 26; Ex. 5. 14, &c.
COVENANT AGE-DURING,] as in Ge. 9. 6; 17. 7, &c.
18. CANAAN,] a land of hills and valleys.
INHERITANCE,] as in De. 3. 4, 13, 14; 32. 9, &c,
19. FEW OF NUMBER,] as in Ge. 34. 30, &c.
SOJOURNERS,] as in Ge. 15. 13; 23. 4, &c.
20. GO UP AND DOWN,] as in Ge. 13. 17, &c.
PEOPLE,] viz., the Egyptians.
21. SUFFERED,] lit. 'left.'
OPPRESS,] as in Ps. 105. 14; Hos. 12. 7; Lev. 6. 2, &c.
KINGS,] such as Abimelech, Pharaoh, &c.
22. COME NOT] hostilely, 'to plague,' as the word often means.
ANOINTED ONES,] as in Ps. 105. 15.
PROPHETS,] those who communicated his will to men.
23. SING,] as in v. 9 above.
SALVATION,] or 'safety,' which he bestows on his people.
24. REHEARSE,] or 'recount,' as in Ge. 40. 8, &c.
GLORY,] lit. 'weightiness.'
WONDERS,] as in v. 12.
25. PRAISED GREATLY,] by all who knew him.
FEARFUL,] i.e. 'causing fear.'
26. NOUGHT,] as in Lev. 19. 4; 26. 1; Job 13. 4, &c.
MADE,] as in Ge. 2. 1, &c.
27. BEFORE HIM,] lit. 'at his face.'
HIS PLACE] of standing, wherever he is.
28. ASCRIBE,] lit. 'give.'
FAMILIES OF PEOPLES,] as in Ps. 22. 27; 96. 7.
29. NAME,] or character.
PRESENT,] as in Ge. 4. 3, 4, &c.
BEFORE HIM,] in his appointed meeting-place.
BOW YOURSELVES,] as in Ps. 29. 2; 45. 11; 96. 9; 97. 7; 99. 5, 6.
HOLINESS,] as in 2 Ch. 20. 21; Ps. 29. 2; 96. 9.
30. PAINED,] as in Ps. 96. 9; 114. 7; Mic. 4. 10.
31. WORLD,] as in 1 Sa. 2. 8, &c.
NOT MOVED,] as in Ps. 93. 1; 96. 10; 104. 5, &c.
REJOICE..GLAD,] as in Ps. 96. 11; 97. 1, Isa. 49. 13; Joel 2. 21.
REIGNED,] as supreme king and ruler.
32. ROAR,] as in Ps. 96. 11; 98. 7.
EXULT,] as in 1 Sa. 2. 1, &c.
33. FOREST,] as in De. 19. 5; Jos. 17. 15, 18, &c.
EARTH] or land, as in v. 14.
34. GIVE THANKS,] as in v. 8 above.
KINDNESS,] not 'mercy,' as in C.V.
35. SALVATION,] or 'safety,' as in 2 Sa. 22. 3, 36, &c.
GATHER,] as in Ps. 106. 47.
NATIONS,] who were harassing them.

GIVE THANKS,] as in v. 8.
TRIUMPH,] as in Ps. 106. 47.
36. BLESSED,] as in 1 K. 8. 15, &c
AGE..AGE,] as in 29. 10; Neh. 9. 5; Ps. 41. 14, &c.
AMEN,] i.e. 'so it is,' as in Nu. 5. 22; De. 27. 15—26; 1 K. 1. 36; Neh. 5. 13; 8. 6; Ps. 41. 13; 72. 19, &c.
37. LEAVETH] Obed-Edom, &c.; as in v. 38, 39.
DAY,] as in Ex. 5. 13, &c.
38. OBED-EDOM,] as in v. 18, 21.
JEDUTHUN,] i.e. 'confessing.'
HOSAH,] i.e. 'trusting, taking refuge.'
39. ZADOK,] i.e. 'righteous.'
40. GIBEON,] as in 21. 28; 1 K. 3. 4; 8. 4.
CHARGED,] as in Ex. 29. 38—42.
41. CHOSEN,] or 'choice,' as in 7. 40; 9. 22; Neh. 5. 18; Job 33. 3; Isa. 49. 2; Zeph. 3. 9.
DEFINED,] as in Nu. 1. 17, &c.
GIVE THANKS,] as in v. 4, 7, 35.
KINDNESS,] not 'mercy,' as in C.V.
42. SOUNDING,] lit. 'causing to hear.'
GATE] of the tent of the testimony.
43. HOUSE,] as in 2 Sa. 6. 19.

XVII. 1. SAT] at rest, after the preceding transactions.
NATHAN,] as in 2 Sa. 7. 2.
PROPHET,] who was specially attached to David.
CEDARS,] as in 2 Sa. 5. 11.
CURTAINS,] as in Ex. 26. 1—13; 36. 8—17; Nu. 4. 25; 2 Sa. 7. 1; Ps. 104. 2; Song 1. 5; Isa. 54. 2; Jer. 4. 20; 10. 20; 49. 29; Hab. 3. 7.
2. HEART,] as in 1 K. 8. 17, 18; 2 Sa. 7. 3; 1 Ch. 22. 7; 28. 2.
WITH THEE,] in all that he did.
3. A WORD,] in reference to the proposal.
4. SERVANT,] though anointed king.
THE HOUSE,] not 'an house,' as in C.V.
THIS DAY,] a period of 450 years.
TENT,] without a settled dwelling.
TABERNACLE,] one compartment of the tent.
WALKED UP AND DOWN] habitually.
JUDGES,] in 2 Sa. 7. 7 it is 'tribes.'
FEED,] that is, take care of.
CEDARS,] instead of a simple tent.
6. SERVANT,] as in v. 4.
OF HOSTS.] This phrase is added to the expression in v. 4.
HABITATION,] or 'comely place,' as in Hos. 9. 13; Ex. 15. 13, &c.
7. FLOCK,] as in 1 Sa. 16. 11—13.
LEADER] in the place of Saul, who was disobedient.
8. WALKED,] or 'gone' in peace or in war.
CUT OFF,] by causing David always to prosper.
NAME,] for glory and honour.
9. PREPARED,] lit. 'set, appointed.'
PLANTED,] that it might take root perpetually.
DWELT,] lit. 'tabernacled,' as in Ge. 9. 27.
TROUBLED,] as in Ex. 15. 14; De. 2. 25.
SONS OF PERVERSENESS,] as in 2 Sa. 3. 34; 7. 10, &c.
WEAR IT OUT,] as in Ps. 49. 14, &c.
10. APPOINTED,] or 'commanded.'
HUMBLED,] as in De. 9. 3, &c.

HOUSE,] that is, a family.
11. FATHERS,] as in De. 31. 16, &c.
RAISED UP,] as in Jos. 5. 7, &c.
ESTABLISHED,] as in 2 Sa. 7. 12, &c.
12. HOUSE] of sacrifice and prayer.
13. FATHER,] guiding, protecting, and helping him.
SON,] obedient and submissive, as in 2 Sa. 7. 14, 15.
KINDNESS,] not 'mercy,' as in C.V.
TURNED ASIDE,] as in 1 Sa. 15. 23, 28; 16. 14; 1 K. 11. 13, 34; 2 Sa. 7. 15, &c.
14. MY HOUSE,] or 'household.'
MY KINGDOM,] over Israel.
15. WORDS..VISION,] without adding or diminishing.
16. COMETH IN] to the tabernacle, where the ark was.
SITTETH] in prayer, as in Jud. 20. 26; 21. 2; 2 Sa. 7. 18.
17. SMALL,] as in 2 Sa. 7. 19; 1 Sa. 15. 17, &c.
AFAR OFF,] as in Ge. 22. 4, &c.
SEEN,] not 'regarded,' as in C.V.
TYPE,] lit. 'turn, row,' as in Est. 2. 12, 15; Song 1. 10, 11; in 2 Sa. 7. 19 it is 'law.'
THE MAN,] not 'a man,' as in C.V.
WHO IS ON HIGH,] as in De. 28. 43, &c.
18. ADD MORE] to say; as in Nu. 11. 25; De. 5. 22, &c.
KNOWN,] fully and appreciated.
19. THY SERVANT] David; in 2 Sa. 7. 21 it is 'thy word.'
OWN HEART,] as in 1 K. 9. 3; 2 Ch. 7. 16; 1 Sa. 2. 35.
20. NONE LIKE THEE,] in truth and kindness, as in De. 3. 24; 4. 35; 32. 39; 1 Sa. 2. 2, &c.
SAVE THEE,] as in 2 Sa. 7. 22; Isa. 45. 5, 21; 64. 4; Hos. 13. 4.
EARS,] of God's dealings with men.
21. WHO,] among the nations of the earth.
RANSOM,] as in 2 Sa. 7. 23, &c.
NAME,] or 'renown.'
CAST OUT] of their inheritances, as in Ex. 23. 28, 29, &c.
22. APPOINT,] lit. 'give.'
GOD,] rescuing and blessing, Ps. 48. 14.
23. STEDFAST] and unchangeable.
24. GREAT,] among thy people Israel.
GOD,] acknowledged and served.
HOUSE,] or household.
25. UNCOVERED THE EAR,] as in Ruth 4. 4, &c.
HOUSE,] or household, as in v. 24.
FOUND] in his heart, as in 2 Sa. 7. 27.
26. GOD HIMSELF,] able to do all things, the fountain of all power.
GOODNESS,] regarding his house and family.
27. PLEASED,] of his own good will and grace.
BLESSED,] and none can revoke it.

XVIII. 1. PHILISTINES,] as in 2 Sa. 8. 1.
HUMBLETH,] as in Lev. 26. 41; De. 9. 3, &c.
GATH,] one of the Philistine principalities.
SMALL TOWNS] round about it.
2. MOAB,] as prophesied of in Nu. 24. 17.
PRESENT,] at set times, as a token of submission. 2 K. 3. 4, 5; 2 Sa. 8. 2.

3. HADAREZER,] or Hadadezer, as in 2 Sa.
8. 3; 10. 16, 19; 1 Ch. 19. 16, 19.
ZOBAH,] as in 2 Sa. 8. 3; 10. 6; 1 Sa. 14. 47.
HAMATH.] See Nu. 34. 8; 2 Sa. 8. 9.
POWER,] not 'dominion,' as in C.V.
PHRAT,] as in Ge. 2. 14.
4. FOOTMEN,] as in Ex. 12, 37, &c.
DESTROYETH UTTERLY,] *lit.* 'eradicateth.'
100 CHARIOTS,] as in 2 Sa. 8. 4.
5. DAMASCUS,] *in Heb.* 'Demmesek.'
22,000,] as in 2 Sa. 8. 5.
6. PRESENT,] as in v. 2 above.
SALVATION,] or 'safety.'
7. SHIELDS,] as in 2 Sa. 8. 7, &c.
JERUSALEM] his own capital.
8. TIBHATH,] in 2 Sa. 8. 8 it is 'Betah.
CHUN,] in 2 Sa. 8. 8 it is 'Berothia.'
9. TOU,] in 2 Sa. 8. 9 it is 'Toi.'
10. HADORAM,] in 2 Sa. 8. 9 it is 'Joram.'
PEACE] and friendship.
BLESS HIM,] wishing him all happiness
and success.
MAN OF WARS,] as in 2 Sa. 8. 10; Isa. 42. 13.
11. SANCTIFIED,] for the house of the Lord
which he purposed to build.
EDOM,] in 2 Sa. 8. 12 it is 'Aram.'
MOAB,] east of the Dead Sea, unto Arnon.
AMMON,] between the rivers Jabbok and
Arnon.
PHILISTINES,] on the coast of the great Sea.
AMALEK,] south of Canaan between Edom
and Egypt.
12. ABISHAI,] who commanded, as in
2 Sa. 8. 13.
ZERUIAH,] sister of David.
VALLEY OF SALT,] as in 2 Sa. 8. 13, &c.;
Ps. 60. 1.
18,000,] as in 2 Sa. 8. 13; but in Ps. 60. 1
it is 12,000.
13. GARRISONS,] as in 2 Sa. 8. 6, 14, &c.
14. ALL] the twelve tribes of Israel.
DOING] habitually.
15. JOAB] his nephew, son of his sister.
HOST,] as in 11. 6, &c.
JEHOSHAPHAT,] as in 2 Sa. 8. 16; 20. 24.
AHILUD,] as in 2 Sa. 8. 16; 20. 24; 1 K. 4. 3.
REMEMBRANCER,] as in Ge. 41. 9; Nu. 5.
15; 2 Sa. 8. 16; 20. 24; 1 K. 4. 3, &c.
16. ZADOK,] i.e. 'just,' as in 2 Sa. 8. 17;
15. 25.
AHITUB,] i.e. 'brother of good.'
ABIMELECH,] in 2 Sa. 8. 17 it is 'Ahimelech.'
ABIATHAR,] i.e. 'father of abundance.'
PRIESTS,] the one of the family of Ithamar,
the other of Eleazar.
SHAVSHA,] in 2 Sa. 8. 17 it is 'Seraiah;' in
1 K. 4. 3 it is 'Shisha.'
SCRIBE,] that is, writer, as in Jud. 5. 14.
17. BENAIAH,] as in 2 Sa. 23. 20, 22.
JEHOIADA,] as in 2 Sa. 8. 18.
CHERETHITE..PELETHITE,] as in 2 Sa. 8.
18; 15. 18; 20. 7, 23.
HAND OF THE KING,] in 2 Sa. 8. 18 it is
'priests.'

XIX. 1. NAHASH,] i.o. 'serpent,' as in Ge.
3. 1; 1 Sa. 11. 1; 2 Sa. 10. 1.
AMMON] son of Lot, nephew of Abraham.
2. HANAN,] i.e. 'gracious,' as in 2 Sa. 10. 1.
KINDNESS] in the days of Saul.
COMFORT,] as in Ge. 37. 35; 2 Sa. 10. 2, &c.

3. HONOURING,] as in 1 Sa. 2. 30; 2 Sa 10.
2, &c.
SEARCH,] as in Jud. 18. 2; 2 Sa. 10. 3;
Prov. 23. 30; 25. 2.
OVERTHROW,] as in Ge. 19. 21, 29; 2 Sa.
10. 3; Prov. 12. 7; Isa. 29. 16.
SPY OUT,] as in Nu. 21. 32; Jos. 6. 25; 14.
7; Jud. 18. 2, 14, 17; 2 Sa. 10. 3.
4. SHAVETH,] which in the east is never
done save for a vow, a punishment, a disease, or for mourning.
LONG ROBES,] in which orientals pride
themselves.
BUTTOCKS,] as in Isa. 20. 4, &c.
5. ASHAMED,] as in 2 Sa. 10. 5; 19. 3; Ps.
74. 21; Eze. 16. 27.
JERICHO.] See Jos. 2. 1—3.
GROWN,] or 'spring up,' as in 2 Sa. 10. 5;
Jud. 16. 22; Lev. 13. 37.
6. ABHORRED,] because of this insult to
his ambassadors.
1,000 TALENTS,] in 2 Sa. 10. 6 the amount
is not specified.
NAHARAIM,] i.e. 'between the two rivers.'
MAACHAH,] as in Jos. 13. 11—13; 2 Sa.
10. 6.
ZOBAH,] as in 2 Sa. 8. 3—5; 1 Ch. 18. 5, 9.
7. 32,000,] in 2 Sa. 8. 6 it is 33,000.
PEOPLE,] they hired also, to the amount
of 1000 men, as in 2 Sa. 10. 6.
MEDEBA,] as in Nu. 21. 30.
BATTLE] against Israel, hoping for plunder.
8. JOAB,] his chief general and tried
warrior.
9. CITY] of Medeba, as in v. 7.
FIELD] ready for action.
10. FRONT,] *lit.* 'faces.'
CHOICE,] that is, most select young men.
SETTETH IN ARRAY,] for an immediate
contest.
ARAM,] the auxiliaries of Ammon, as in v.
6, 7.
11. AMMON,] who were within the city
walls, or on the front of them.
12. SALVATION,] or 'safety,' as in Ge. 49.
18, &c.
SAVED THEE] from their hand.
13. STRENGTHEN OURSELVES,] as in 2 Sa.
10. 12; Ge. 48. 2, &c.
GOOD] and proper in the circumstances.
14. FLEE,] without waiting for a contest,
like true mercenaries.
AMMON,] who were before the walls of
the city.
ABISHAI,] as in v. 11.
CITY] of Medeba, as in v. 7.
JERUSALEM,] to receive further instructions.
16. ARAM,] beyond the Euphrates.
SHOPHACH,] in 2 Sa. 10. 16, 18 it is 'Shobach.'
HADAREZER,] as in 2 Sa. 8. 3; 10. 15.
17. HE GATHERETH,] he himself, along
with Joab.
JORDAN,] eastwards towards Ammon, between Jabbok and Arnon.
SETTETH IN ARRAY,] as in v. 10.
18. 7,000,] in 2 Sa. 10. 18 it is 700.
FOOTMEN,] in 2 Sa. 10. 18 it is 'horsemen.'
SHOPHACH,] as in v 16.

T

19. HADAREZER,] as in v. 16.
SERVE HIM,] bringing tribute at stated times; see Ge. 15. 18.
HELP,] *lit.* 'save,' as in 2 Sa. 10. 19.

XX. 1. TURN OF THE YEAR,] as in 2 Sa. 11. 1; 1 K. 20. 22, 26; 2 Ch. 36. 10.
MESSENGERS] of David to Hanun, as in 19. 1, 2; 2 Sa. 10. 2.
DESTROYETH,] that is, 'marreth.'
RABBAH,] their chief city, as in De. 3. 11.
JERUSALEM,] where he saw Beth-Sheba.
BREAKETH IT DOWN.] This is not mentioned in 2 Sa. 12. 29.
2. THEIR KING,] *or* of 'Malcom,' their idol.
TALENT,] or 3000 shekels, as in Ex. 38. 25, 26.
A PRECIOUS STONE,] as in 2 Sa. 12. 30.
SPOIL,] as in Ge. 49. 27, &c.
3. SETTETH TO,] not 'under,' as in *C.V.*
CUTTING INSTRUMENTS,] as in 2 Sa. 12. 31; 1 Sa. 17. 18.
AXES,] as in 1 K. 7. 9.
4. GEZER,] in 2 Sa. 21. 18 it is 'Gob.'
SIBBECHAI,] in 2 Sa. 23. 27 it is 'Mebunnai.'
HUSHATHITE.] See 2 Sa. 21. 18; 1 Ch. 4. 4; 11. 29.
SIPPAI,] in 2 Sa. 21. 18 it is 'Saph.'
GIANT,] *in Heb.* 'the Rapha.'
HUMBLED] before Israel.
5. ELHANAN,] as in 2 Sa. 21. 19; 23. 24; 1 Ch. 11. 16.
JAIR,] in 2 Sa. 21. 19 it is 'Jaare-Oregim.'
LAHMI,] i.e. 'my bread;' but compare 2 Sa. 21. 19.
GOLIATH,] whom David slew, as in 1 Sa. 17. 4.
GITTITE,] a native of Gath.
BEAM OF WEAVERS,] as in 1 Sa. 17. 7; 1 Ch. 11. 23.
6. GATH,] one of the five Philistine principalities.
MAN OF MEASURE,] as in Nu. 13. 32, &c.
TOES,] *lit.* 'fingers.'
GIANT,] *in Heb.* 'the Rapha.'
7. REPROACHETH,] as in Jud. 3. 15, &c.
JONATHAN,] brother of Jonedab, as in 2 Sa. 13. 3.
SHIMMA,] in 1 Sa. 16. 9 it is 'Shammah,' in 2 Sa. 21. 21 it is Shimeah.
8. GIANT,] as in v. 4, 6.

XXI. 1. ADVERSARY,] *in Heb.* a 'satan,' as in Nu. 22. 22, 32, &c.
PERSUADETH,] as in De. 13. 6; Jos. 15. 18; Jud. 1. 14; 1 Sa. 26. 19; 2 Sa. 24. 1.
NUMBER,] as in Ge. 13. 16; Nu. 23. 10, &c.
2. BEER-SHEBA..DAN,] the two extremities of the land of Israel.
3. ADD,] as he had promised.
SERVANTS] acknowledging his authority.
CAUSE OF GUILT,] and bringing punishment.
4. SEVERE,] *lit.* 'hard, strong.'
GOETH UP AND DOWN,] as in Ge. 3. 8; 13. 17, &c.
5. ACCOUNT,] or narrative.
1,100,000,] in 2 Sa. 24. 9 it is 800,000.
DRAWING SWORD,] above 20 years of age.

470,000,] in 2 Sa. 24. 9 it is 500,000.
6. NOT NUMBERED,] as in 27. 24.
ABOMINABLE,] as in Job 15. 16; Isa. 14. 19, &c.
7. EVIL,] as in Ge. 38. 10, &c.
SMITETH,] as in 1 Sa. 24. 5, &c.
8. CAUSED TO PASS AWAY,] as in 2 Sa. 24. 10.
INIQUITY,] *or* 'punishment.'
ACTED VERY FOOLISHLY,] as in Ge. 31. 28; 1 Sa. 13. 13; 2 Sa. 24. 10; 2 Ch. 16. 9.
9. GAD,] i.e. 'a troop.'
SEER OF DAVID,] as in 2 Sa. 24. 10; 2 Ch. 29 25; 1 Sa. 9. 9.
10. I AM STRETCHING OUT,] as in Job 9. 8; 26. 7; Ps. 104. 2; Isa. 40. 22; 42. 5; 44. 24; 51. 13; 66. 12; Jer. 10. 20; Eze. 25. 16; Zec. 12. 1.
CHOOSE,] *or* 'fix,' as in 2 Sa. 24. 12, &c.
11. TAKE,] *or* 'receive,' as in Prov. 19. 20, &c.
12. THREE YEARS,] in 2 Sa. 24. 13 it is 'seven years.'
PESTILENCE,] as in Ex. 5. 3; 9. 3, 15, &c.
A MESSENGER,] as in v. 15, &c.
13. GREATLY DISTRESSED,] as in 2 Sa. 24. 14.
MERCIES,] as in Ge. 43. 14, 30; De. 13. 17.
NOT FALL,] as in 2 Sa. 24. 15.
14. PESTILENCE,] as in v. 12 above.
70,000,] as in 2 Sa. 24. 15.
15. MESSENGER,] as in v. 12; 2 Sa. 24. 16.
DESTROY,] *or* 'mar' it.
COMFORTED,] as in 2 Sa. 24. 16; Ge. 6. 6, &c.
CEASE,] as in 2 Sa. 34. 16; Jos. 10. 6, &c.
THRESHING FLOOR,] on mount Moriah.
ORNAN,] in 2 Sa. 24. 16 it 'Araunah;' in v. 18 it is 'Araniah;' in v. 20 it is 'Aurenah.'
JEBUSITE,] perhaps a convert of that tribe.
16. DRAWN,] as in Nu. 22. 23, 31; Jos. 5. 13.
ELDERS] of Israel, whom he had probably summoned.
SACKCLOTH,] in token of grief and humiliation.
17. I] alone against advice and warning.
THE FLOCK] committed to his care, over whom he ruled.
PLAGUED,] and punished for sin.
18. MESSENGER..SPAKE.] This circumstance is not expressly mentioned in 2 Sa. 24. 18, though it is implied.
SURELY,] *or* 'because.'
ALTAR,] for sacrifice to Jehovah, to appease his wrath against Israel.
19. JEHOVAH,] as in 2 Sa. 24. 19.
20. MESSENGER.] Sept. reads 'king;' see 2 Sa. 24. 19.
HIDING THEMSELVES] for fear of the destroyer.
THRESHING WHEAT,] their usual occupation.
21. LOOKETH ATTENTIVELY,] as in Ge. 15. 5, &c.
EARTH,] as to his king and lord.
22. ALTAR] for sacrifice, as commanded by God.
FULL SILVER,] that is, its full value, without reduction.
PLAGUE] of the pestilence sent against them.
RESTRAINED,] as in Nu. 16. 48, 50, &c.
23. I HAVE GIVEN,] without being asked, and without reward.

BURNT OFFERINGS,] that no time might be lost.

WOOD,] for a fire to burn the sacrifices. PRESENT,] as in Ge. 4. 3—5.

24. FULL SILVER,] as in v. 22 he had already offered.

LIFT UP] on the altar, as an offering to God.

WITHOUT COST,] as in Ge. 29. 15, &c.

25. SIX HUNDRED,] in 2 Sa. 24. 24 it is 'fifty shekels of silver.'

26. ALTAR,] as commanded in v. 18 by Gad.

CALLETH] in prayer for mercy.

FIRE,] as in Lev. 9. 24, &c.; a token of acceptance.

27. SHEATH,] justice being fully satisfied.

28. ANSWERED] his prayer, as in v. 26 above.

29. TABERNACLE,] containing the ark, and other sacred vessels.

MADE,] by the hands of Bezaleel.

GIBEON,] as in 16. 39; 1 K. 3. 4, &c.; four or five miles from Jerusalem.

30. NOT ABLE,] for want of time, perhaps.

SWORD,] as in v. 16, threatening destruction.

XXII. 1. A HOUSE,] a place of dwelling for Jehovah the true God.

AN ALTAR,] or place of sacrifice.

2. SOJOURNERS,] as in Ge. 15. 13; 23. 4; Ex. 2. 22, &c.; compare 1 K. 9. 21.

APPOINTETH,] lit. 'causeth to stand.'

HEWERS,] as in 1 K. 5. 15; 2 K. 12. 12.

HEWN STONES,] as in Ex. 20. 25; 1 K. 5. 17; 6. 36; 7. 9, 11, 12, &c.

3. IRON,] as in Ge. 4. 22; Lev. 26. 19, &c.

NAILS,] as in 2 Ch. 3. 9; Isa. 41. 7; Jer. 10. 4.

GATES] of the proposed temple.

COUPLINGS,] as in 2 Ch. 34. 11.

NO WEIGHING,] as in v. 14; 1 K. 7. 47; 2 K. 25. 16; 2 Ch. 4. 18; Jer. 52. 20.

4. CEDAR TREES,] as in Lev. 14. 4, 6, 49, 51, 52, &c.

ZIDONIANS AND TYRIANS,] by command of their king Hiram or Huram, 1 K. 5. 6.

5. TENDER] in disposition and constitution, perhaps; see 29. 1.

NAME,] or 'renown.'

BEAUTY,] as in Ex. 28. 2, 40; De. 26. 19, &c.

PREPARE,],] as in Ge. 43. 16, 25, &c.

6. CHARGETH,] or 'commandeth.'

7. WITH MY HEART,] as in Jos. 14. 7, &c.; compare 2 Sa. 7. 2, 3; 1 K. 8. 17; 1 Ch. 17. 1; 28. 2.

8. SAYING,] as in 28. 3; 1 K. 5. 3.

BLOOD . . WARS,] being a man of strife from his youth.

9. SON,] as in 2 Sa. 7. 12; 12. 24; compare 28. 5.

MAN OF REST,] as in Jer. 51. 59.

SOLOMON,] i.e. 'peace;' like Ishmael, Josiah, Cyrus, &c. he was named before his birth. QUIETNESS,] see 1 K. 4. 24, 25; 5. 3, 4.

10. NAME.] See 2 Sa. 7. 13; 1 K. 5. 5; see 17. 12, 13; 28. 6.

SON . . FATHER,] as in 2 Sa. 7. 13, 14; Heb. 1. 5.

11. WITH THEE,] as in v. 16 below.

PROSPERED] in every undertaking.

12. WISDOM,] as in 1 K. 3. 9, 12; Ps. 72. 1.

CHARGE,] or 'command,' as in v. 6.

13. MOSES,] as in 1 K. 2. 2, 3.

COURAGEOUS,] in seeking to glorify God.

CAST DOWN,] by reason of any difficulty.

14. AFFLICTION,] or 'poverty.'

PREPARED,] as in v. 3, 4 above.

1,000,000 TALENTS,] supposed to amount to about fifty millions sterling.

WEIGHING,] as in v. 3 above.

PREPARED,] as in v. 3, 4 above.

15. WORKMEN,] of the various kinds enumerated.

HEWERS,] as in v. 2.

ARTIFICERS OF STONE,] as in 2 Sa. 5. 11; 2 K. 12. 11; 1 Ch. 14. 1.

SKILFUL MAN,] lit. 'wise man.'

16. NUMBER,] or 'numbering.'

17. HEADS] of the tribes of Israel.

18. WITH YOU,] in giving peace and prosperity.

GIVEN REST,] as in 23. 25; 2 Sa. 7. 1

MY HAND] and authority.

SUBDUED,] as in Ge. 1. 28; Nu. 32. 22, 29; Jos. 18. 1, &c.

19. SEEK,] or 'enquire,' as in Ge. 25. 22; Ex. 18. 15, &c.

SANCTUARY,] that is, the place that should be set apart for his service.

ARK,] which was made in the wilderness.

HOLY VESSELS] used in the tabernacle.

XXIII. 1. OLD,] about 70 years of age; see 2 Sa. 5. 4.

SATISFIED] like Abraham, in Ge. 25. 28; 35. 29, &c.

CAUSETH TO REIGN] while yet alive, as in 28. 5; 1 K. 1. 43.

3. NUMBERED, as in Nu. 4. 3, 47.

POLLS,] as in Ex. 16. 16; 38. 26; Nu. 1. 2, 18, 20, 22; 3. 47; Jud. 9. 53; 2 K. 9. 35; 1 Ch. 10. 10; 23. 3, 24.

38,000,] while they were only 8,580 when in the wilderness; see Nu. 4. 47, 48.

4. PRESIDE,] or 'oversee,' as in 15. 21, &c.

WORK] of slaughtering, stripping, and washing the sacrifices, &c.

24,000,] of whom 1000 served weekly in rotation; see 9. 25.

6,000,] who decided all ceremonial questions that might arise.

5. 4,000 GATE KEEPERS,] to prevent the unclean from entering.

4,000] players on musical instruments.

6. DISTRIBUTETH,] or 'apportioneth.'

COURSES,] in three great divisions, according to the following names.

LEVI] the third son of Jacob, see Ge. 29. 34

GERSHON, &c.] as in Ex. 6. 16, &c.

7. LAADAN,] or 'Libni,' as in 6. 17; 15. 7 26. 21.

SHIMEI,] or 'Shimi,' as in Ex. 6. 17.

8. JEHIEL,] i.e. 'God lives,' as in 15. 18.

ZETHAM,] as in 26. 22.

JOEL,] i.e. 'Jah is God,' as in 6. 33; 15. 7

9. SHELOMITH,] i.e. 'peaceful.'

HAZIEL,] i.e. 'seen of God.'

HARAN,] i.e. a 'mountaineer.'

10. JAHATH,] as in 4. 2; 6. 5, 28.

ZINAH,] or Zizah, as in v. 11.

JEUSH.] See Ge. 36. 18; 2 Ch. 11. 18, &c.
BERIAH,] i.e. 'a gift,' perhaps.
11. ZIZAH,] or Zinah, as in v. 10.
12. KOHATH] the second son of Levi, see Ex. 6. 18.
AMRAM.] See Ex. 6. 20.
IZHAR,] i.e. 'he shines or is bright.'
HEBRON,] i.e. 'companionship.'
UZZIEL,] i.e. 'strength of God.'
13. AARON,] i.e. a 'mountaineer,' perhaps.
MOSES,] i.e. 'a drawer out.'
SEPARATED,] as in Ex. 28. 1; Heb. 5. 4.
HOLY OF HOLIES,] as in Ex. 26. 33.
MAKE PERFUME,] as in Ex. 30. 7; Nu. 16. 40.
BLESS,] as in Nu. 6. 23—27, &c.
14. MAN OF GOD,] as in De. 33. 1.
ARE CALLED] and designated by the common name of Levites, see 26. 23—25.
15. GERSHOM,] i.e. 'a sojourner there,' as in Ex. 2. 22.
ELIEZAR,] i.e. 'my God is help,' as in Ex. 18. 3, 4.
16. SHEBUL,] i.e. 'captive of God;' see 24. 20, where it is 'Shubael.'
17. REHABIAH,] i.e. 'breadth of Jah;' 26. 25.
18. SHELOMITH,] i.e. 'peaceful;' in 24. 22 it is 'Shelomoth.'
19. JERIAH,] i.e. 'cast by God.'
AMARIAH,] i.e. 'saying of Jah.'
JAHAZIEL,] i.e. 'Jah sees.'
JEKAMEAM,] i.e. 'a people rises.'
20. MICAH,] i.e. 'who is thus?'
ISHSHIAH,] i.e. 'forgotten of Jah,' perhaps.
21. MAHLI,] i.e. 'sickly.'
MUSHI,] i.e. 'touched of Jah.'
ELEAZAR,] i.e. 'God has help.'
KISH,] i.e. 'a snaring;' 24. 29.
22. TAKE THEM] in marriage, to prevent their inheritance being alienated, Nu. 36. 6—8.
23. MAHLI,] as in v. 21.
EDER,] i.e. 'drove, order.'
24. APPOINTMENT] to their various offices.
POLLS,] as in v. 3.
TWENTY YEARS,] as in v. 27; Nu. 1. 3; 4. 3; 8. 24; Ezra 3. 8.
25. GIVEN REST,] from outward warfare and internal contention, see 22. 18.
TABERNACLE,] in the tent which David stretched out for the ark.
26. TO BEAR] on the shoulder hereafter, as in Nu. 4. 5.
28. STATION,] as in 1 K. 10. 5; 2 Ch. 9. 4; 35. 15; Isa. 22. 19.
SIDE,] lit. 'hand.'
COURTS,] outer and inner.
CHAMBERS,] as in 1 Sa. 9. 22; 2 K. 23. 11; 1 Ch. 9. 26. 33; 28. 12; 2 Ch. 31. 11; Ezra 8. 29; 10. 6; Neh. 10. 37, 38, 39, &c.
29. ARRANGEMENT,] on the pure table, as in 9. 32; Ex. 25. 30.
FINE FLOUR,] as in 9. 29; Lev. 6. 20, &c.
PRESENT] with every sacrifice.
THIN UNLEAVENED CAKES,] as in Lev. 2. 4, &c.
PAN,] as in Lev. 2. 5; 6. 21; 7. 9; Eze. 4. 3.
FRIED,] as in Lev. 6. 21; 7. 12.
MEASURE,] as in Lev. 19. 35; Eze. 4. 11, 16.
MEASURE,] as in Ex. 26. 2, 8; 36. 9, 15, &c.

30. GIVE THANKS,] or confessions.
GIVE PRAISE,] as in 16. 4, 7, 35, 41; 25. 3; 2 Ch. 5. 13; 7. 3, 6; 31. 2; Ezra 3. 11; Neh. 12. 24, 46, &c.
31. SABBATHS,] as in Nu. 28. 10, &c.
NEW MOONS,] as in Nu. 28. 14, &c.
APPOINTED SEASONS,] as in Lev. 23. 2, &c.
ORDINANCE,] lit. 'judgment;' in Nu. 28. 1—31; 29. 1—40.
32. SANCTUARY,] where the ark, and the cherubs were.
SONS OF AARON] the priests, to whose ser·vice God had appointed them in the wilderness.

XXIV. 1. AARON] the high-priest, who had four sons, as in 6. 3; Ex. 6. 23, &c.
COURSES,] that all things might be done decently and in order.
NADAB,] i.e. 'a willing one.'
ABIHU,] i.e. 'my father is he.'
ELEAZAR,] i.e. 'God is help.'
ITHAMAR,] i.e. 'land of palms,' or 'where is the palm?'
2. DIETH,] as in Nu. 3. 4; 26. 61; Lev. 10. 1, 2.
ACT AS PRIESTS,] as in Ex. 28. 1, 3, 4, &c.
3. DISTRIBUTETH,] or 'apportioneth.'
ZADOK,] i.e. 'just.'
ABIMELECH,] i.e. 'my brother is king;' same as (Abiathar or) Abiah, as in 14. 3; Mark 2. 26.
OFFICE,] as in Nu. 3. 32, 36; 4. 16; 16. 29; 2 K. 11. 18; 1 Ch. 23. 11; 24. 19; 26. 30, &c.
5. LOTS,] that there might be no partialities or prejudices.
SANCTUARY] to direct all things in it.
GOD,] in religious matters.
6. SHEMAIAH,] i.e. 'heard of Jah.'
NETHANEEL,] i.e. 'gift of Jah.'
7. JEHOIARIB,] i.e. 'Jah strives.'
JEDAIAH,] i.e. 'known of Jah.'
8. HARIM,] i.e. 'flat-nosed, compressed.'
SEORIM,] i.e. 'barley.'
9. MALCHIJAH,] i.e. 'king of Jah.'
MIJAMIM,] i.e. 'from the right hand.'
10. HAKKOZ,] i.e. 'the thorn,' as in Ezra 2. 61; Neh. 3. 4, 21; 7. 63; it is Koz in 1 Ch. 4. 8
ABIJAH,] i.e. 'my father is Jah;' see Neh. 12. 4, 17; Luke 1. 5.
11. JESHUAH,] i.e. 'a saviour.'
SHECANIAH,] i.e. 'tabernacle of Jah.'
12. ELIASHIB,] i.e. 'God brings back.'
JAKIM,] i.e. 'He raises up.'
13. HUPPAH,] i.e. a 'covering.'
JESHEBEAB,] i.e. 'seat of a father.'
14. BILGAH,] i.e. 'brightness.'
IMMER,] i.e. 'a sayer.'
15. HEZIR,] i.e. 'a sow.'
APHSES,] i.e. 'the scatterer, breaker.'
16. PETHAHIAH,] i.e. 'opening of Jah.'
JEHEZEKIEL,] i.e. 'God is strong.'
17. JACHIN,] i.e. 'He prepares.'
GAMUL,] i.e. 'deed, recompense.'
18. DELAIAH,] i.e. 'drawn up of Jah.'
MAAZIAH,] i.e. 'strength of Jah.'
19. APPOINTMENTS,] or 'offices,' as in v. 3 above.
ORDINANCE,] lit. 'judgment.'
20. SHUBAEL,] i.e. 'returning of God;' in 23. 16 it is 'Shebuel.'

JEHDEIAH,] i.e. 'unity of Jah.'
REHABIAH,]i. e. 'breadth of Jah;' see 23.17.
ISHSHIAH,] i.e. 'forgotten of Jah.'
22. IZHARITE,] brother of Amram.
SHELOMOTH,] i.e. 'peaceful;' in 23. 18 it
is 'Shelomith.'
JAHATH,] i.e. 'he affrights.'
23. JERIAH, &c.] See 23. 19; 26. 31.
24. UZZIEL,] i.e. 'strength of God.'
MICHAH,] i.e. 'who is thus?' in 23. 20, it is
'Micah.'
SHAMIR,] i.e. 'a briar, diamond.'
25. ISHSHIAH,] i.e. 'forgotten of Jah;' in
33. 20 it is Jesiah.
ZECHARIAH,] i.e. 'remembered by Jah.'
26. BENO,] i.e. 'his son.'
27. SHOHAM,] i.e. 'an onyx stone.'
ZACCUR,] i.e. 'mindful.'
IBRI,] i.e. 'a passer over.'
29. JERAHMEEL,] i.e. 'God is merciful.'
30. JERIMOTH,] i.e. 'high places.'
31. CAST LOTS,] as in v. 5 above.

XXV. 1. SERVICE,] in the worship of God
in public.
ASAPH, &c.,] as in 6. 33, 39, 44.
PROPHESYING,] that is, proclaiming the
praises and doings of God, as the word ordi-
narily means.
HARPS,] as in Ge. 4. 21; 31. 27; 1 Sa. 10. 5;
16. 16, 23; 2 Sa. 6. 5; 1 K. 10. 12; 1 Ch. 13. 8;
15. 16, 21, 28; 16. 5, &c.
PSALTERIES,] as in 1 Sa. 10. 5; 2 Sa. 6. 5;
1 K. 10. 12; 1 Ch. 13. 8; 15. 16, 20, 28; 16.
15, &c.
CYMBALS,] as in 13. 8; 15. 16, 19, 28; 16. 5,
42; 25. 1, 6; 2 Ch. 5. 12, 13; 29. 25; Ezra 3.
10; Neh. 12. 27.
2. ZACCUR,] i.e. 'mindful.'
JOSEPH,] i.e. 'he is adding.'
NETHANIAH,] i.e. 'gift of Jah.'
ASARELAH,] i.e. 'uprightness of an oak;'
in v. 14 it is 'Jesharelah.'
SIDE,] lit. 'hand.'
3. GEDALIAH,] i.e. greatness of Jah.'
ZERI,] i.e. 'balm, or formation;' in v. 11 it
is 'Izri.'
JESHAIAH,] i.e. 'safety of Jah.'
HASHABIAH,] i.e. 'reckoning of Jah.'
MATTITHIAH,] i.e. 'gift of Jah.'
SHISHAH,] i.e. 'six;' perhaps the same
as 'Shimea' in v. 17.
GIVING OF THANKS,] or confession, as in
23. 30, &c.
4. BUKKIAH,] i.e. 'emptiness of Jah.'
MATTANIAH,] i.e. 'gift of Jah.'
UZZIEL,] i.e. 'strength of God;' in v. 18 it
is 'Azareel.'
HANANIAH,] i.e. 'grace of Jah.'
HANANI,] i.e. 'my grace.'
ELIATHAH,] i.e. 'my God hath come.'
GIDDALTI,] i.e. 'I have made great.'
ROMAMTI-EZER,] i.e. 'I have heightened
help.'
JOSHBEKASHAH,] i.e. 'a sharp seat.'
MALLOTHI,] i.e. 'my fulness.'
HOTHIR,] i.e. 'he made abundant.'
MAHAZIOTH,] i.e. 'vision of a sign.'
5. SEER,] as in 2 Sa. 24. 11; 2 K. 17. 13;
1 Ch. 21. 9; 29. 29; 2 Ch. 9. 29; 12. 15; 19. 2;
29. 25, 30, &c.

HORN,] that is, exult in God's goodness.
6. SIDE,] lit. 'hand.'
CYMBALS, &c.,] as in v. 1 above.
7. TAUGHT,] as in Song 3. 8; Isa. 29. 13;
Hos. 10. 11.
INTELLIGENT] in music, &c.; as in 15 22;
25. 7, 8; 27. 32; 28. 9; 2 Ch. 26. 5; 34. 12; 35.
3; Ezra 8. 16, &c.
8. LOTS,] as in 24. 5, &c.
SMALL..GREAT,] making no distinction of
ranks and the
INTELLIGENT..LEARNER,] having different degrees of ability.
9. JOSEPH,] i.e. 'he is adding;' as in v. 2.
GEDALIAH,] i.e. 'greatness of Jah.'
10. ZACCUR,] i.e. 'mindful,' as in v. 2.
11. IZRI,] i.e. 'my formation ;' in v. 3 it
is 'Zeri.'
12. NETHANIAH,] i.e. 'gift of Jah,' as in
v. 2.
13. BUKKIAH,] i.e. 'emptied by Jah.'
14. JESHARELAH,] i.e. 'uprightness of
an oak;' in v. 2 it is 'Asareleh.'
15. JESHAIAH,] i.e. 'safety of Jah.'
16. MATTANIAH,] i.e. 'gift of Jah.'
17. SHIMEI,] i.e. 'hearing.'
18. AZAREEL,] i.e. 'help of God,' as in v. 4.
19. HASHABIAH,] i.e. 'reckoning of Jah,
as in v. 3.
20. SHUBAEL,] i.e. 'return of God;' in v.
4, it is 'Shebuel.'
21. MATTITHIAH,] i.e. 'gift of Jah.'
22. JERIMOTH,] i.e. 'high places.'
23. HANANIAH,] i.e. 'grace of Jah.'
24. JOSHBEKAHAH,] i.e. 'sharp seat.'
25. HANANI,] i.e. 'my grace.'
26. MALLOTHI,] i.e. 'my fulness.'
27. ELIATHAH,] i.e. 'my God hath come.'
28. HOTHIR,] i.e. 'he has made abundant.'
29. GIDDALTI,] i.e. 'I have made great.'
30. MAHAZIOTH,] i.e. 'vision of a sign,' as
in v. 4.
31. ROMAMTI-EZER,] i.e. 'I have exalted
help.'

XXVI. 1. COURSES,] as in 23. 6, &c.
GATE KEEPERS] of the sanctuary.
KORHITES,] as in Ex. 6. 24; Nu. 26. 58;
1 Ch. 9. 19, 31; 12. 6; 26. 19; 2 Ch. 20. 19.
MESHELEMIAH,] or 'Shelemiah,' as in
v. 14.
KORE,] i.e. 'a partridge,' as in 9. 19.
ASAPH,] or Abiasaph, as in 6. 37; 9. 19.
2. ZECHARIAH,] i.e. 'remembered by Jah.'
JEDIAEL,] i.e. 'known of God.'
ZEBADIAH,] i.e. 'endowed of Jah.'
JATHNIEL,] i.e. 'given of God.'
3. ELAM,] i.e. 'hidden.'
JEHOHANAN,] i.e. 'Jah has grace.'
ELIOENAI,] i.e. 'unto Jah are mine eyes.'
4. OBED-EDOM,] i.e. 'servant of Edom,' as
in 13. 14, &c.
SHEMAIAH,] i.e. 'heard of Jah.'
JEHOZABAD,] i.e. 'Jah has endowed.'
JOAH,] i.e. 'Jah is brother.'
SACAR,] i.e. 'sweetness, hire, reward.'
NETHANEEL,] i.e. 'given by God.'
5. AMMIEL,] i.e. 'people of God.'
ISSACHAR,] 'there is a hire or reward.'
PEULTHAI,] i.e. 'my work or wage.'

BLESSED HIM] with many sons; that is, Obed-Edom, as in v. 4; 13. 14; 15. 24; 16. 38.
6. RULING,] or 'having dominion.'
VALOUR,] or 'worth or might.'
7. OTHNI,] i.e. 'my lion.'
REPHAEL,] i.e. 'feebleness of God.'
OBED,] i.e. 'a servant.'
ELZABAD,] i.e. 'God has endowed.'
ELIHU,] i.e. 'my God is he.'
SEMACHIAH,] i.e. 'supported by Jah.'
9. MESHELEMIAH,] as in v. 1 above.
10. HOSAH,] i.e. 'taking refuge;' see 16. 38.
SHIMRI,] i.e. 'watchful.'
11. HILKIAH,] i.e. 'portion of Jah.'
TEBALIAH,] i.e. 'dipped of Jah.'
ZECHARIAH,] i.e. 'remembered of Jah.'
13. Compare 24. 31; 25. 8.
14. SHELEMIAH,] or Meshelemiah, as in v. 1, 2, 9.
ZECHARIAH,] i.e 'remembered of Jah.'
COUNSELLOR,] as in 2 Sa. 15. 12, &c.
UNDERSTANDING,] as in 1 Sa. 25. 3; 1 Ch. 22. 12, &c.
15. GATHERINGS,] of gold, silver, vessels, perhaps, as in 2 Ch. 25. 24.
16. SHUPPHIM,] i.e. 'adders, serpents.'
SHALLECHETH,] i.e. 'a casting forth.'
HIGHWAY,] as in Nu. 20. 19; Jud. 5. 20, &c.
ASCENT,] as in 1 K. 10. 5; 2 Ch. 9. 4.
17. Compare 9. 24.
18. PARBAR,] or Parvar, as in 2 K. 23. 11.
19. KORHITE.] See Nu. 23. 11.
20. AHIJAH,] i.e. 'brother of Jah.'
HOLY THINGS,] as in 28. 12.
21. LAADAN,] or Libni, as in 6. 17.
JEHIELI,] i.e. 'my God lives;' or Jehiel, as in 23. 8; 29. 8.
22. ZETHAM,] as in 23. 8.
JOEL,] i.e. 'Jah is God.'
AMRAMITE, &c.] See Ex. 6. 18.
24. SHEBUEL,] i.e. 'captive of God,' 23. 16.
GERSHOM,] i.e. 'a sojourner there.'
MOSES,] i.e. 'a drawer out.'
PRESIDENT,] or 'leader.'
25. ELEAZAR,] i.e. 'my God is help,'
REHABIAH,] i.e. 'breadth of Jah.'
JESHAIAH,] i.e. 'safety of Jah.'
JORAM,] i.e. 'Jah is exalted.'
ZICHRI,] i.e. 'mindful,'
SHELOMITH,] i.e. 'peaceful;' see 23. 18.
26. SANCTIFIED,] as in 2 Sa. 8. 11; compare Nu. 31. 48, 50.
27. SPOIL] of the enemy.
STRENGTHEN,] by giving it a deep foundation, strong walls, &c,
28. SEER,] as in 1 Sa. 9. 9.
KISH,] i.e. 'a snare.'
NER,] i.e. 'a light, lamp.'
ZERUIAH,] i.e. 'cleft of Jah,' as in 1 Sa. 26. 6; 2 Sa. 2. 13.
SIDE,] lit. 'hand.'
29. IZHARITE,] about 1,600 in number; compare v. 30, 32; 23. 4.   See Ex. 6. 18.
CHENANIAH,] i.e. 'prepared by Jah.'
OUTWARD WORK,] as in Neh. 11. 16.
OFFICERS..JUDGES,] as in 23. 4.
30. HEBRONITE,] grandson of Kohath, as in Ex. 6. 18.
HASHABIAH,] i.e. 'reckoning of Jah.'
1700.] Compare v. 29, 32, &c.

INSPECTION,] as in Nu. 3. 32, 36, &c.
WESTWARD,] that is, the two tribes and a half.
JEHOVAH..KING,] that is, both civil and religious, as in v. 32 below.
31. JERIJAH,] i.e. 'shot by Jah;' see 23. 19.
SOUGHT OUT,] as in Ge. 42. 22; Isa. 65. 1; Eze. 14. 3; 20. 3, 31; 36. 37.
JAZER] beyond Jordan, a city of Gad; see Nu. 21. 32; 32. 1, 3, 35; Jos. 21. 39.
32. 2,700,] in all 6,000, as in 23. 4.
REUBENITE, &c.] who were beyond Jordan westward, as in v. 30.
GOD..KING,] as in v. 30; 2 Ch. 19. 11.

XXVII. 1. HEADS OF THE FATHERS,] as in Ex. 6. 25, &c.
AUTHORITES,] as in Ex. 5. 6, 10, 14, 15, 19, &c.
COURSES,] as in 23. 6, &c.
MONTH,] as in 1 K. 4. 7, 27.
24,000,] which, in the year would require 288,000 men's service, for a month each.
2. FIRST MONTH,] called Nisan or Abib.
JASHOBEAM,] i.e. 'sitting of the people;' chief of David's worthies, as in 11. 11; 2 Sa. 23. 8.
ZABDIEL,] i.e. 'endowed of God.'
3. PEREZ,] i.e. a 'breach,' as in Ge. 38. 20.
4. SECOND MONTH,] called Ziv or Ijar.
DODAI,] i.e. 'my beloved;' or Dodo, as in 11. 12; 2 Sa. 23. 9, 28.
MIKLOTH,] i.e. 'rods, staves.'
PRESIDENT,] or 'leader,' as in 26. 24.
5. THIRD MONTH,] called Sivan.
BENAIAH,] i.e. 'built up by Jah;' see 11. 22, 24; 1 Sa. 4. 5; 2 Sa. 23. 20, 22, 23.
JEHOIADA,] i.e. 'Jah has known.'
6. THIRTY] mighty warriors whom David had gathered around him.
AMMIZABAD,] i.e. 'my people is endowed.'
7. FOURTH MONTH,] called Tammuz.
ASAHEL,] i.e. 'made by God;' see 11. 26; 2 Sa. 23. 24.
ZEBADIAH,] i.e. 'endowed by Jah.'
8. FIFTH MONTH,] called Ab.
SHAMHUTH,] i.e. 'desolation, astonishment,' or Shammah, as in 2 Sa. 23. 11; Shammoth in 11. 27.
IZRAHITE,] or Ezrahite, or Zerahite.
9. SIXTH MONTH,] called Elul, see 11. 28.
IRA,] i.e. 'watchful;' see 11. 28.
IKKESH,] i.e. 'perverse.'
TEKOITE,] as in 2 Sa. 14. 14, &c.
10. SEVENTH MONTH,] called Tizri; see 11. 27.
HELEZ,]i.e. 'armed, drawn out;' see 11. 27.
PELONITE,] as in v. 36.
11. EIGHTH MONTH,] called Marchesvan or Bul.
SIBBECAI,] i.e. 'my thicket;' see 11. 29; 2 Sa. 21. 18.
HUSHATHITE,] as in 2 Sa. 21. 18.
ZARHITE,] as in Nu. 26. 13, 20, &c.
12. NINTH MONTH,] called Cisleu; see 11. 29.
ABIEZER,] i.e. 'my father is help;' see 11. 28.
ANTOTHITE,] as in 2 Sa. 23. 27.
13. TENTH MONTH,] called Tebet; see 11. 30.

MAHARAI,] i.e. 'hasting;' see 11. 30; 2 Sa. 23. 23.

NETOPHATHITE,] as in 2 Sa. 23. 28, 29, &c.

ZARHITE,] as in v. 11 above.

14. ELEVENTH MONTH,] called Shebet; see 11. 31.

BENAIAH,] i.e. 'built up by Jah;' see 11. 31.

PIRATHONITE,] as in Jud. 12. 13, 15, &c.

15. TWELFTH MONTH,] called Adar; see 11. 30.

HELDAI,] i.e. 'worldly;' or Heled, as in 11. 30.

OTHNIEL,] i.e. 'lion of God;' see Jud. 1. 13; 3. 9.

16. ELIEZAR,] i.e. 'my God is help.'

SHEPHATIAH,] i.e. 'judged of Jah.'

17. HASHABIAH,] i.e. 'reckoning of Jah;' see 26. 30.

ZADOK,] i.e. 'just.'

18. ELIHU,] i.e. 'my God is he;' or Eliab, 1 Sa. 16. 6.

OMRI,] i.e. 'my sheaf.'

19. ISHMAIAH,] i.e. 'Jah hears.'

JERIMOTH,] i.e. 'high places.'

20. HOSHEA,] i.e. 'safety.'

JOEL,] i.e. 'Jah is God.'

21. IDDO,] i.e. 'throwing, casting.'

JAASIEL,] i.e. 'God makes, does.'

AZAREEL,] i.e. 'help of God.'

23. 20 YEARS.] See Nu. 1. 3, 18, &c.

STARS,] as in Ge. 15. 5; 22. 17.

24. NOT FINISHED,] Levi and Benjamin being omitted; see 21. 6, 7; 2 Sa. 24. 15.

GONE UP,] on the roll of the account prepared for the king.

ACCOUNT,] as in Ge. 34. 30, &c.

CHRONICLES,] lit. 'words or matters of the days,' as in 1 K. 14. 19, &c.

25. TREASURES] of the king, in Jerusalem, apparently.

AZMAVETH,] i.e. 'strength of death.'

FIELD,] that is, the cultivated land, as in Ge. 27. 27, &c.

CITIES,] with or without walls, as in Ge. 41. 35, 48, &c.

VILLAGES,] lit. 'coverings,' as in Song 7. 11; Jos. 18. 24; Neh. 6. 2; 1 Sa. 6. 18.

TOWERS,] lit. 'great places.'

JEHONATHAN,] i.e. 'Jah has given.

26. EZRI,] i.e. 'helpful.'

27. SHIMEI,] i.e. 'hearing.'

RAMATHITE,] from Ramah, in Benjamin.

ZABDI,] i.e. 'endowed.'

SHIPHMITE,] from Shepham; see Nu. 34. 10, 11.

28. OLIVES,] as in De. 6. 11; 8. 8, &c.

SYCAMORES,] as in 1 K. 10. 27, &c.

BAAL-HANAN,] i.e. 'master of grace or favour.'

GEDERITE] in the tribe of Judah; see Jos. 15. 36, 58.

JOASH;] see 1 Ch. 7. 8.

29. SHARON,] as in 1 Ch. 5. 16 in Bashan, or as in Jos. 12. 18 between Caesarea and Joppa.

SHITRAI,] or Shirtai.

SHAPHET,] i.e. 'he judged.'

30. OBIL.] Etymology uncertain.

ISHMEELITE,] as in 2. 17.

JEHDEIAH,] i.e. 'unity of Jah.'

MERONOTHITE,] as in Neh. 3. 7.

31. JAZIZ.] Etymology unknown.

HAGERITE,] as in 11. 38.

32. COUNSELLOR;] see 2 Sa. 21. 21.

UNDERSTANDING,] as in Prov. 28. 2.

SCRIBE,] as in Jud. 5. 14, &c.

JEHIEL,] i.e. 'God lives.'

HACHMONI,] as in 11. 11.

33. AHITHOPHAL,] i.e. 'brother of folly or my brother is foolish;' see 2 Sa. 15. 12.

HUSHAI,] i.e. 'hasty, hasting;' see 2 Sa. 15. 37; 16. 16.

ARCHITE,] from Ephraim, as in Jos. 16. 2.

FRIEND,] as in 2 Sa. 15. 37; 16. 16.

34. JEHOIADA,] i.e. 'Jah has known.'

BENAIAH,] i.e. 'built up by Jah.'

ABIATHAR,] i.e. 'father of abundance;' see 1 K. 1. 7.

JOAB,] i.e. 'Jah is father,' as in 11. 6.

XXVIII. 1. ISRAEL., TRIBES,] enumerated in 27. 16—22.

COURSES,] mentioned in 27. 2—15.

SUBSTANCE,] noticed in 27. 25—31.

2. FEET] from off his throne.

MY BRETHREN . . . PEOPLE,] identifying himself with them.

WITH MY HEART,] as in 2 Sa. 7. 2; Ps. 132. 4, 5.

REST,] as in Ge. 49. 15, &c.

ARK OF THE COVENANT,] as in Nu. 10. 33, &c.

FOOTSTOOL,] as the ark is called in Ps. 99. 5; 132. 7, 8.

PREPARED,] as narrated in 22. 3, 4, 14, 15, 16; 29. 2—5.

3. SAID,] by the mouth of Nathan, as in 17. 4; 22. 8; 2 Sa. 7. 5, 13; 1 K. 5. 3.

MAN OF WARS,] that is, accustomed to them, as in 22. 8, &c.

4. FIX,] of his own free will and pleasure, as in 1 Sa. 16. 7—13.

LEADER,] to lead out and to lead in Israel in peace or war; compare 5. 2; Ge. 49. 10; Ps. 60. 7; 78. 68.

PLEASED,] as in 1 Sa. 16. 10, 12.

5. MANY SONS,] whose names are mentioned in 3. 1—9; 23. 1.

SOLOMON,] as in 22. 9.

6. MY COURTS,] around the temple; see 2 Sa. 7. 13, 14; 22. 9, 10.

SON..FATHER,] as in 2 Sa. 7. 14.

7. STRONG,] in mind and in deed.

8. ALL ISRAEL,] now assembled before him.

SEEK,] the true nature and extent of the law of God.

POSSESS,] in peace and prosperity without hindrance.

INHERIT,] the good land promised to them.

9. KNOW,] by a practical acquaintance with his law.

SERVE,] as a son does his father.

SEEKING,] to worship him, as their creator and preserver, and judge.

FOUND,] without fail, being a God at hand, and not one afar off.

CASTETH OFF,] as a worthless, rotten thing.

10. FIXED,] of his own good pleasure.

SANCTUARY,] where he may rest with and bless his people.

11. PATTERN,] as in Ex. 25. 9, &c.

PORCH,] before the temple.

HOUSES,] the holy and the most holy, as in 2 Ch. 3. 5.

UPPER CHAMBERS,] as in Jer. 35. 2; Acts 1. 13.

INNERMOST ONES,] as in 1 K. 6. 5; built against the wall of the temple round about.

ATONEMENT,] *lit.* 'covering,' as in Ex. 25. 17, &c.

12. SPIRIT] of God, which guided him.

COURTS,] the outer and the inner.

CHAMBERS,] as in 1 K. 6. 5.

TREASURES,] as in 26. 20.

13. COURSES,] as described in 1 Ch. 24. 25, 26.

14. See Ex. 36. 30; 1 K. 7. 48, 49.

15. CANDLESTICKS,] ten in number, each having seven

LAMPS,] as in 1 K. 7. 49.

16. TABLES,] of which there were ten, as in 2 Ch. 4. 8.

ARRANGEMENTS,] on which the bread of the presence was placed.

17. FORKS,] by which they took the flesh out of the pots in which it was boiled.

BOWLS..CUPS..BASINS,] for receiving and sprinkling the blood of the sacrifices.

18. ALTAR OF PERFUME,] which was to be overlayed with gold.

REFINED,] as in 29. 4; Ps. 12. 6; Isa. 25. 6; compare Job 28. 1; 36. 27; Mal. 3. 3.

CHARIOT,] as in 1 K. 7. 33; 2 K. 23. 11.

CHERUBS,] as in Ge. 3. 24; Ex. 25. 18, 19, 20, 22, &c.

SPREADING,] as in 1 K. 6. 27, &c.

COVERING,] as in 1 K. 8. 7, &c.

ARK,] as in 2 Ch. 5. 8, &c.

19. WRITING,] as in 2 Ch. 2. 11; 35. 4, &c.

HAND OF JEHOVAH,] the Spirit, as in v. 12 above.

UNDERSTAND,] so as to prevent mistakes.

20. COURAGEOUS,] as in De. 31. 6, 7, 23; Jos. 1. 6, 7, 9, 18; 10. 25, &c.

AFFRIGHTED,] as in 22. 13, &c.

WITH THEE,] as he had been with David.

FAIL..FORSAKE,] as in Jos. 1. 5, &c.

21. COURSES,] as described in 1 Ch. 24. 25, 26.

WILLING ONE,] as in Ex. 35. 5, &c.

WORDS,] that is, at thy command.

XXIX. 1. FIXED,] as in 28. 5, 10; 1 K. 3. 7, &c.

TENDER,] as in 22. 5; he was now married; see 2 Ch. 9. 30; 12. 13.

PALACE,] as in v. 19; Neh. 1. 1; 2. 8; 7. 2; Est. 1. 2, 5; 2. 3, 5, 8; 3. 15; 8. 14; 9. 6, 11, 12; Da. 8. 2; Ezra 6. 2; compare 2 Ch. 7. 12; 27. 4.

2. PREPARED,] *or* 'made ready,' as in Ge. 43. 16, 45, &c.

SHOHAM STONES,] as in Ge. 2. 12; Ex. 25. 7; 28. 9, 20; 35. 9, 27; 39. 6, 13; Job 28. 16; Eze. 28. 13.

SETTINGS,] as in Ex. 25. 7; 35. 9, 27, &c.

PAINTING,] as in 2 K. 9. 30; Isa. 54. 11; Jer. 4. 30.

DIVERS COLOURS,] as in Jud. 5. 30; Ps.

45. 14; Eze. 16. 10, 13, 18; 17. 3; 26. 16; 27. 7, 16, 24.

PRECIOUS STONE,] as in 2 Ch. 3. 6; 2 Sa. 12. 30, &c.

WHITE MARBLE,] as in Est. 1. 16; Song 5. 16.

3. DELIGHTING,] as in Job 34. 9; Ps. 77. 7; Prov. 16. 7.

SUBSTANCE,] as in Prov. 8. 21.

PECULIAR TREASURE,] as in Ex. 19. 5; De. 7. 6; 14. 2; 26. 18; Ps. 135. 4; Ec. 2. 8; Mal. 3. 17.

4. 3000 TALENTS] of gold, about 13½ millions sterling.

7000 TALENTS] of silver, about 2,625,000 pounds sterling.

REFINED,] as in 28. 18.

OVERLAY,] *lit.* 'plaister, daub,' as in Lev. 14. 42, 43, &c.

5. ARTIFICERS,] as in Ex. 28. 11, &c.

OFFERING WILLINGLY,] as in Jud. 5. 9; 2 Ch. 17. 16; Ezra 3. 5; Neh. 11. 2.

CONSECRATE,] *lit.* 'fill,' as in Ex. 29. 29, &c.

6. HEADS,] as in 27. 1; 28. 1.

7. 5000 TALENTS] of gold, about 22½ millions sterling.

10,000 DRAMS,] about 22,507,500 pounds sterling.

10,000 TALENTS] of silver, about 3,750,000.

18,000 TALENTS] of brass, the value of which is unknown.

100,000 TALENTS] of iron, also of unknown value.

8. STONES,] not necessarily 'precious stones,' as in C.V.

JEHIEL,] *or* Jehieli, who with his sons, were over the treasury, as in 26. 21, 22.

9. PERFECT HEART,] as in 1 K. 8. 61; 11. 4; 15. 3, 14; 1 Ch. 12. 38; 28. 9; 29. 19; 2 Ch. 15. 17; 16. 9; 19. 9; 25. 2; Isa. 38. 3.

10. BLESSETH,] that is, declareth Him worthy of all praise.

OUR FATHER.] This expression may refer either to God or to Israel, more probably the latter.

11. GREATNESS,] as in 17. 19, 21; Ps. 145. 3, 6, &c.

MIGHT,] as in v. 12; De. 3. 24; Job 12. 13; 26. 14; 41. 12; Ps. 21. 13; 54. 1; 65. 6, &c.

BEAUTY,] as in Ex. 28. 2, 40; De. 26. 19, &c.

VICTORY,] as in Isa. 25. 8.

HONOUR,] as in 16. 27; 29. 25, &c.

KINGDOM,] as in 2 Ch. 13. 8, &c.

LIFTING HIMSELF UP,] as in 1 K. 1. 5; Nu. 16. 3; 23. 24; 24. 7; Prov. 30. 32; Eze. 17. 14; 29. 15; Da. 11. 14.

12. RICHES,] as in Ge. 31. 16; 1 Sa. 17. 25, &c.

RULING,] as in Ge. 45. 8, 26; 2 Sa. 23. 3; 2 Ch. 20. 6; Ps. 22. 28, &c.

POWER .. MIGHT,] over all things and beings.

13. GIVING THANKS,] *or* 'making confession,' as in Prov. 28. 13.

GIVING PRAISE,] as in 23. 5; 2 Ch. 20. 21; 23. 12; 30. 21.

BEAUTEOUS NAME,] *lit.* 'name of thy beauty,' as in Ex. 28. 2, 40, &c.

14. RETAIN POWER,] as in 2 Ch. 2. 6, &c.

WHOLE] of what we have, the means and the grace.

15. SOJOURNERS,] as in Ge. 23. 4, &c.

SETTLERS,] as in Ge. 23. 4; Ex. 12. 45, &c.

SHADOW,] as in Job 8. 9; 14. 2; Ps. 102. 11; 109. 23; 144. 4; Ecc. 6. 12; 8. 13.

NONE ABIDING,] or 'no hope' of continuance here; as in Ezra 10. 2; Jer. 14. 8; 17. 13; 50. 7.

16. STORE] of materials and wealth; as in Ps. 37. 16; Ecc. 5. 9; Isa. 60. 5.

WHOLE,] as in v. 14 above.

17. TRYING,] that is, proving and sifting.

UPRIGHTNESS,] or 'upright ones.'

WILLINGLY OFFERED,]for the glory of God.

FOUND] present in Jerusalem, on being summoned.

18. IMAGINATION,] as in Ge. 6. 5; 8. 21; De. 31. 21, &c.

PREPARE,] or 'establish.'

19. PERFECT HEART,] as in v. 9 above.

COMMANDS..STATUTES,] all the revealed will of God.

PALACE,] as in v. 1 above.

20. I PRAY YOU,] not 'now,' as in C.V.

KING,] as his representative, see 21. 21.

21. SACRIFICES] of thanksgiving and praise.

CAUSE TO ASCEND,] on the altar of burnt-offerings.

OBLATIONS,] as commanded in the law, see Lev. 23. 13, &c.

22. BEFORE JEHOVAH,] as in a religious festival.

SECOND TIME,] for the first occasion see 1 K. 1. 35, 39.

LEADER,] as in 1 Sa. 9. 16, &c.

PRIEST,] after expelling Abiathar, as in 1 K. 2. 35.

23. PROSPERETH,]as God had said of him in 28. 7.

24. GIVEN A HAND UNDER,] as a token of allegiance and submission, see 2 K. 10. 15; Ezra 10. 19; 2 Ch. 30. 8, &c.

25. EXCEEDINGLY GREAT,] as in 2 Ch. 1. 1, &c.

HONOUR,] as in Nu. 27. 20, &c.

26. ALL ISRAEL,] the whole twelve tribes.

27. FORTY YEARS,] as in 1 K. 2. 11; 2 Sa. 5. 4.

HEBRON,] over the tribe of Judah only.

SEVEN YEARS,] as in.2 Sa. 5. 5.

JERUSALEM,] over the twelve tribes.

33 YEARS,] as in 3. 4; 2 Sa. 5. 3—5; 1 K. 2. 11, 14.

28. OLD AGE,] even seventy years of age; see Ge. 15. 15; 25. 8; Jud. 8. 32; Ruth 4. 15.

SATISFIED WITH DAYS,] as in Ge. 25. 8; 35. 39; Job 42. 17.

RICHES AND HONOUR,]as in v. 12 above.

29. MATTERS,] not 'acts,' as in C.V.

SEER,] as in 1 Sa. 9. 9, 11, 18, 19; 2 Sa. 15. 27; 1 Ch. 9. 22; 26. 28, &c.

SEER,] as in 2 Sa. 24. 11; 2 K. 17. 13; 1 Ch. 21. 9; 2 Ch. 9. 29; 12. 15; 19. 2; 29. 25, &c.

PROPHET,] as in 2 Sa. 7. 2; 12. 25, &c.

30. LANDS,]such as Ammon, Aram, Moab Philistia, &c.

SECOND BOOK OF CHRONICLES

I. 1. STRENGTHEN HIMSELF,] by doing justice and judgment, as in 1 K. 3. 28.

WITH HIM,] to counsel and aid him, as in Ge. 21. 20, &c.

GREAT,] in honour, wisdom, and position, as in 1 Ch. 29. 25, &c.

2. HONOURABLE ONE,] as in Ge. 17. 20, &c.

3. HIGH PLACE,] where they offered sacrifices, as in 1 Sa. 9. 12, &c.

GIBEON,] a city of the Hivites (Jos. 10. 2; 11. 19) given to Benjamin, Jos. 18. 25; 21. 17.

TENT OF MEETING,] with his people, as in Ex. 25. 22, &c.

WILDERNESS] of Sinai, as in Ex. 19. 1, &c.

4. ARK OF GOD,] containing the rod of Aaron, the pot of manna, &c.

KIRJATH-JEARIM,] a city of Judah or Benjamin, as in Jos. 9. 17; 18. 15, &c.

PREPARED,] or 'established,' or 'made ready.'

STRETCHED OUT,] as in Ge. 12. 8; 2 Sa. 6. 17, &c.

JERUSALEM,] which he had captured from the Jebusites, as in 2 Sa. 5. 7, &c.

5. ALTAR OF BRASS,] for burnt-offerings.

MADE,] as recorded in Ex. 38. 1, &c.

TABERNACLE,] in the tent of meeting at Gibeah.

SEEK HIM,] that is Jehovah, not the altar.

6. BURNT-OFFERINGS,] as in 1 K. 3. 4, &c.

7. NIGHT,] in a dream, according to 1 K. 3. 5.

8. KINDNESS,] as in 2 Sa. 22. 21, &c.

9. STEDFAST,] as in Ge. 42. 20, &c.

DUST,] as in Ge. 13. 16; 28. 14, &c.

10. WISDOM..KNOWLEDGE,] as in v. 11, 12; Da. 1. 17.

GO OUT..COME IN,] that is, conduct himself as the supreme leader in Israel.

JUDGE,] correctly and justly.

11. WITH,] not 'in,' as in C.V.

RICHES . . . WEALTH . . . HONOUR,] things which most men desire.

LIFE,] *lit.* 'soul.'

MANY DAYS,] to enjoy the glory bestowed on him.

WISDOM..KNOWLEDGE,] as in v. 10.

MY PEOPLE,] compare v. 10.

12. GIVEN,] without upbraiding.

13. HIGH PLACE,] as in v. 3.

14. CHARIOTS AND HORSEMEN,] contrary to De. 17. 16.

1400 CHARIOTS,] as in 1 K. 10. 26.

12,000 HORSEMEN,] as in 9. 25; 1 K. 4. 26; 10. 26.

15. STONES,] for abundance.

CEDARS..SYCAMORES,] as in 9. 27; 1 K. 10. 27; 1 Ch. 27. 28; Ps. 78. 47; Isa. 9. 10; Am. 7. 14.

16. SOURCE,] as in 1 K. 10. 28.

KEVA,] the name of a place in Egypt, see 1 K. 10. 28.

PRICE,] as in De. 23. 18; 2 Sa. 24. 24, &c.

17. 600 SILVERLINGS,] about £60 sterling. 150,] about £15 sterling.

II. 1. NAME,] that is, the renown and character of the God of Israel.

KINGDOM,] in which he himself might dwell.

2. BEARING BURDEN,] as in v. 18; 34. 13; Neh. 4. 10; 1 K. 5. 15.

HEWING] stones, as in 1 K. 5. 15; 2 K. 12. 12; 1 Ch. 22. 2, 15; 2 Ch. 2. 18; 24. 12; Ezra 2. 7; Ps. 29. 7; Isa. 10. 15; 22. 16, &c.

OVERSEERS,] as in v. 18; 34. 13; Ps. 4. 5. 6. 8. 9. 11. 12. 13. 14. 18. 19. 20. 21. 22. 31. 36. 39. 40. 41. 42. 44. 45. 46. 47. 49. &c.

3,600,] in 1 K. 5. 16 it is 3,300 only.

3. HURAM,] in 1 K. 5. 1 it is Hiram.

HOUSE,] as noticed in 1 Ch. 14. 2.

4. NAME,] as in v. 1.

SANCTIFY,] that is, separate or set it apart for him.

MAKE PERFUME,] as commanded in the law.

SPICES,] as in Ex. 25. 6; 30. 7, &c.

CONTINUAL ARRANGEMENT,] of bread upon the table before God.

SABBATHS,] the weekly ones.

NEW MOONS,] or beginning of each month.

APPOINTED SEASONS,] such as that of the passover, tabernacles, pentecost, &c.

5. GREAT,] in extent and magnificence.

GODS] of the nations, which were only wood, stone, &c.

6. RETAIN STRENGTH,] as in 1 Ch. 29. 14, &c.

HEAVENS OF THE HEAVENS,] as in 1 K. 8. 27: De. 10. 14, &c.

CONTAIN,] as in 6. 18; 1 K. 8. 27.

MAKE PERFUME,] as in v. 4.

7. WISE MAN,] that is, skilful in the things mentioned.

GRAVE GRAVINGS,] *lit.* 'open openings,' as in Zec. 3. 9, &c.

PREPARED,] established or made ready.

8. CEDAR-TREES,] which were most suitable and lasting.

FIRS,] as in 2 Sa. 6. 5; 1 K. 5. 8, 10; 6. 15, 34; 9. 11; 2 K. 19. 23; 2 Ch. 3. 5, &c.

ALGUMS,] or 'almugs,' as in 9. 10, 11; 1 K. 10. 11, 12.

LEBANON,] part of which was under Hiram.

SERVANTS,] to help them in accomplishing the work.

9. AND WONDERFUL,] *lit.* 'and to make wonderful,' as in Isa. 29. 14; Joel 2. 26.

10. BEATEN,] *lit.* 'smitten.'

CORS,] a dry and liquid measure, containing ten ephahs or

BATHS,] ten of which make a homer, (Eze. 45. 11, 14), while the tenth of a bath is an omer.

11. WRITING,] as in 1 Ch. 28. 19, &c.

12. BLESSED,] *lit.* 'kneeled to,' as in Ge. 14. 20, &c.

MADE,] as in Ge. 2. 4, &c.

WISE SON,] meaning Solomon.

KINGDOM,] as in v. 1.

14. DAN,] whose territories lay northward, near the city of

TYRE,] the capital of the Zidonians.

DEVICE,] as in Ge. 6. 5; Ex. 31. 4; 35. 32, 33, 35, &c.

15. WHEAT..WINE,] as in v. 10 above.

16. NEED.] This original word is not found elsewhere.

FLOATS.] This original word is not found elsewhere.

JOPPA,] a sea-port, as in Jos. 19. 46, &c.

JERUSALEM,] where the temple and palace were to be built, about 40 miles from Joppa.

17. SOJOURNERS] from among the Canaanites,·&c.

FATHER,] as in 1 Ch. 22. 2, 8, 14.

18. 70,000×80,000×3,600,] which together amount to 153,600 as in v. 17.

III. 1. MORIAH,] as in Ge. 22. 2, 8, 14.

ORNAN,] or 'Araunah,' as in 2 Sa. 24. 18; see 1 Ch. 21. 18; 22. 1.

2. SECOND MONTH,] that is, Zif, as in 1 K. 6. 1.

FOURTH YEAR,] as in 1 K. 6. 1; B.C. 1012.

3. INSTRUCTED,] lit. 'founded' by his father David, who was guided by inspiration to do so, as in 1 Ch. 28. 11.

CUBITS,] from east to west; the holy place was 40, the most holy 20 cubits.

FORMER MEASURE,] used in former times by Moses, perhaps.

4. PORCH] on the east side, as in 1 K. 6. 3.

FRONT] of the temple.

20. CUBITS,] as noted in v. 3.

OVERLAYETH,] as in Ex. 25. 11, 13, 24, 28, &c.

PURE GOLD,] as in Ex. 25. 11, 17, 24, 29, 31, 36, 38, 39, &c.

5. LARGE HOUSE,] the holy place, in opposition to the most holy, as in v. 8.

COVERED,] both inside and outside, as in v. 7, 8, 9.

FIR TREES,] as in 2. 8, &c.

GOOD GOLD,] as in v. 8; Ge. 2. 12.

PALMS,] as in 1 K. 6. 29, 32, 35; 7. 36; Eze. 40. 16, 22, 26, 31, 34, 37; 41. 18, 19, 20, 25, 26.

CHAINS,] as in Ex. 28. 14; 39. 15; 1 K. 7. 17; v. 16 below.

6. PRECIOUS STONE,] as in 1 K. 5. 17; 7. 9, 10, 11, &c.

BEAUTY,] as in Ex. 28. 2, 40, &c.

PARVAIM,] perhaps 'the east;' or 'Ophir.'

7. HOUSE,] that is, the larger one, as in v. 5.

BEAMS,] as in Ge. 19. 8; 2 K. 6. 2, 5; Song 1. 7.

THRESHOLDS] of its various doors and entrances.

WALLS] round about, from the floor to the ceiling.

DOORS,] made of olive and firs, as in 1 K. 6. 31, 34.

GRAVED,] as in 1 K. 7. 36.

CHERUBS,] as in Ge. 3. 24; Ex. 25. 18, 19, 20, 22, &c.

8. MOST HOLY HOUSE,] the smaller one of the two; see v. 5.

600 TALENTS,] about three millions sterling.

9. NAILS,] as in 1 Ch. 22. 3; Isa. 41. 7; Jer. 10. 4.

50 SHEKELS,] about £75 sterling.

UPPER CHAMBERS,] as in 1 Ch. 28. 11.

10. TWO CHERUBS,] as in 1 K. 6. 23.

IMAGE-WORK.] This original word is not found elsewhere.

11. WINGS,] as in Ex. 25. 20; 37. 9, &c.

TOUCHING,] as in v. 12; 1 K. 6. 27.

12. ADHERING,] as in De. 4. 4; Prov. 18. 24.

13. 20 CUBITS,] the whole breadth of the holy of holies, as in v. 8.

FEET,] which were probably 'straight,' as in Eze. 1. 7, &c.

INWARD,] lit. 'to the house.'

14. VAIL,] as in Ex. 26. 31, 33, 35, &c.

BLUE,] as in Ex. 26. 31; 36. 35.

PURPLE, &c.] similar to that made by Moses, as in Ex. 26. 31; 36. 35, &c.

15. TWO PILLARS,] as in 1 K. 7. 15—21; Jer. 52. 21; they were chiefly ornamental.

LENGTH,] that is, of course, when raised up, height.

ORNAMENT.] This original word is not found elsewhere.

16. CHAINS,] as in v. 5; Ex. 28. 14; 39. 15; 1 K. 7. 17.

ORACLE,] as in 4. 20; 5. 7, 9; Ps. 28. 2; 1 K. 6. 5, 16, 19, 20, 21, 22, 23, 31; 7. 49; 8. 6, 8.

POMEGRANATES,] as in 1 K. 7. 20.

17. JACHIN..BOAZ,] as in 1 K. 7. 21.

IV. 1. ALTAR,] as in Ex. 27. 1, 2; this brazen one was four times as long and broad, and three times as high.

2. MOLTEN SEA,] as in 1 K. 7. 23, for holding an abundance of pure water.

EDGE,] lit. 'lip,' that is, its diameter was ten cubits.

COMPASS,] as in 1 K. 7. 23, 31, 35; 10. 19.

LINE,] as in 1 K. 7. 23; 2 K. 21. 13; Job 38. 5; Ps. 19. 4; Isa. 18. 2, 7; 28. 10, 13, 17; 34. 11, 17; 44. 13; Jer. 31. 39; La. 2. 8; Eze. 47. 3; Zec. 1. 16.

3. LIKENESS,] as in Ge. 1. 26; 5. 1, 3; 2 K. 16. 10, &c.

OXEN,] as in 1 K. 7. 25, 29, 44, &c.

ROWS,] as in v. 13; Ex. 28. 17, 18, 19, 20; 39. 10, 11, 12, 13; 1 K. 6. 36; 7. 2, 3, 4, 12, 18, 20, 24, 42; Ez. 46. 23.

CAST,] as in v. 17 below.

4. TWELVE OXEN,] probably according to the number of the tribes.

HINDER PARTS,] as in Ex. 33. 23; 1 K. 7. 25; Ps. 78. 66; Eze. 8. 16.

5. THICKNESS,] as in 1 K. 7. 26; Jer. 52. 21.

HAND-BREADTH,] as in 1 K. 7. 26; Ps. 39. 5; Ex. 25. 25; 37. 12; Eze. 40. 5, 43; 43. 13.

LIP,] as in v. 2 above.

CUP,] as in 1 K. 7. 26; Ge. 40. 11, 13, 21, &c.

FLOWER,] as in v. 21; Ex. 25. 31, 33, 34; 37. 17, 19, 20; Nu. 8. 4; 17. 8; 1 K. 7. 26, 49; Isa. 5. 24; 18. 5; Nah. 1. 4.

LILY,] as in Song 2. 1, 2; Hos. 14. 5.

TAKING HOLD,] that is, having once received 3000 baths of water it was able to contain that quantity, but generally it had only about 2000 in it.

6. LAVERS,] as in v. 14; Ex. 30. 18, 28; 31. 9; 35. 16; 38. 8; 39. 39; 40. 7, 11, 30; Lev. 8. 11; 1 Sa. 2. 14; 1 K. 7. 30, 38, 40, 43; 2 K. 16. 17; 2 Ch. 6. 13; Zec. 12. 6.

WITH THEM,] not 'in them,' as in C. V

PURGE,] as in Isa. 4. 4; Eze. 40. 38; Jer. 51. 34.

7. CANDLESTICKS,] as in 1 K. 7. 49; Ex. 25. 31, &c.
ORDINANCE,] *lit.* 'judgment.'

8. TABLES,] as in 1 K. 7. 48; Ex. 25. 23, &c.
BOWLS,] as in v. 11; 1 K. 7. 40, 45, 50; Ex. 27. 3, &c.

9. COURT OF THE PRIESTS,&c.] as in 1 K. 6. 36; 7. 12.
GREAT COURT,] as in 6. 13; Eze. 43. 14, 17, 20; 45. 19.

10. SHOULDER,] of the house, as in 1 K. 7. 39, &c.

11. HURAM,] as in 1 K. 7. 40, &c.
POTS,] as in v. 16; Ex. 16. 3; 27. 3; 1 K. 7. 45; 2 K. 4. 38—41; 25. 14; 2 Ch. 35. 13, &c.
SHOVELS,] as in v. 16; Ex. 27. 3; 38. 3; Nu. 4. 14; 1 K. 7. 40, 45; 2 K. 25. 14; Jer. 52. 18.
BOWLS,] as in v. 8 above.

12. CROWNS,] as in v. 13; 1 K. 7. 16, 17, 18, 19, 20, 31, 41, 42; 2 K. 25. 17; Jer. 52. 22.
WREATHS,] as in v. 13; 1 K. 7. 17, 18, 20, 41, 42; 2 K. 1. 2; 25. 17; Job 18. 8; Jer. 5. 22. 23.

14. BASES,] which according to 1 K. 7. 27 were ten in number and of brass.
LAVERS,] as in v. 6.

15. SEA..TWELVE OXEN,] as in v. 2, 4.

16. FORKS,] as in Ex. 27. 3; 38. 3; Nu. 4. 14; 1 Ch. 28. 17.
HIS FATHER,] in Heb. 'Abiv.'
PURIFIED,] as in Lev. 26. 28; Jer. 46. 4.

17. CIRCUIT,] as in Ge. 13. 10, 11, 12; 19. 17, 25, 28, 29, &c.
CAST,] as in v. 3 above.
THICK PARTS,] as in Ex. 19. 9; Jud. 5. 4, &c.
SUCCOTH,] in the tribe of Gad, as in Ge. 33. 17; Jos. 13. 27; Jud. 8. 5; 1 K. 7. 46.
ZERADATHAH,] in Manasseh, as in 4. 12; 7 46; 11. 26; compare Jos. 3. 16; Jud. 7. 22.

18. SEARCHED OUT,] as in 1 K. 7. 47; Jer. 31. 37; 46. 23.

19. ALTAR OF GOLD,] as in 1 K. 7. 48.
BREAD OF THE PRESENCE,] as in Ex. 25. 30, &c.

20. ORACLE,] as in 3. 16, &c.

21. TONGS,] as in 1 K. 7. 49; Isa. 6. 6.
PERFECTION,] *lit.* 'perfections.'

22. SNUFFERS,] as in 1 K. 7. 50; 2 K. 12. 13; 25. 14; Jer. 52. 18.
CENSERS,] as in Ex. 25. 38; 27. 3; 37. 23; 38. 3; Lev. 10. 1; 16. 12; Nu. 4. 9, 14; 16. 6, 7, 18, 37, 38, 39, 46; 1 K. 7. 50; 2 K. 25. 15; Jer. 52. 19.
HOLY OF HOLIES,] as in Ex. 26. 33, 34, &c.

V. 1. FINISHED,] *or* 'completed,' as in 1 K. 7. 51.
SANCTIFIED THINGS,] which were dedicated to the temple service.

2. ELDERS,] or official rulers.
BRING UP] to mount Moriah, where the temple had just been built.

3. FEAST] of the dedication.
SEVENTH MONTH,] that is, Tisri.

4. LIFT UP,] as commanded in the law, on their shoulders.

5. ARK, &c.] to the newly built temple.

6. CONVENED,] as in Nu. 14. 35; 16. 11; 27. 3; 1 K. 8. 5.
MULTITUDE,] as in Ge. 16. 10; 32. 12; 1 K. 3. 8; 8. 5; Jer. 33. 22; Hos. 1. 10.

7. ORACLE,] as in 3. 16; 4. 20, &c.
HOLY OF HOLIES,] as in 4. 22, &c.

8. SPREADING OUT,] as in 3. 3; Ex. 25. 20; 37. 9; 1 K. 8. 7; 1 Ch. 28. 18.
STAVES,] by which it was borne.

9. WITHOUT,] as in 1 K. 8. 8.
DAY] when the writer lived, before the captivity.

10. HOREB,] as in De. 10. 2, &c.

11. SANCTUARY,] after having set down the ark.
COURSES,] as in 1 Ch. 23. 6; 24. 1; 26. 1, 12, 19; 27. 1, 2, 4—15; 28. 1, 13, 21; 2 Ch. 8. 14; 23. 8; 31. 2, 15, 16, 17; 35. 4, 10; Neh. 11. 26; Eze. 48. 29.

12. SINGERS,] as in v. 13; 1 K. 6. 33; 9. 33; 15. 16, 19, 27, &c.
WHITE LINEN,] as in 2. 14; 3. 14; 1 Ch. 4. 21; 15. 27; Est. 1. 6; 8. 15; Eze. 27. 16.
CYMBALS,] as in 1 Ch. 13. 8; 15. 16, 19, 28, &c.
PSALTERIES,] as in 1 Sa. 10. 5; 2 Sa. 6. 5, &c.
HARPS,] as in Ge. 4. 21; 37. 27, &c.
PRIESTS,] sons of Aaron.
TRUMPETS,] as in Nu. 10. 2; 1 Ch. 15. 24; 16. 6; 2 Ch. 13. 12, 14; 29. 26; Ezra 3. 10; Neh. 12. 35, 41.

13. TO SOUND,] *lit.* 'cause to hear,' as in 1 Ch. 15. 19; Ps. 26. 7; Isa. 58. 4.
TO PRAISE,] as in 2 Sa. 14. 25; 1 Ch. 16. 4, 36; 23. 5, 30; 25. 3, &c.
TO GIVE THANKS,] *or* 'confessions,' as in 1 Ch. 16. 4, 7, 35, 41; 23. 30; 25. 3, &c.
KINDNESS,] not 'mercy,' as in C.V.
CLOUD,] the usual symbol of the Divine presence, as in Ex. 13. 21, 22; 14. 19, 20, 24; 16. 10; 19. 9, 16; 24. 15, 16, 18, &c.

14. HONOUR,] *lit.* 'weightiness,' as in Ge. 31. 1; 45. 13; 49. 6, &c.
FILLED,] as in v. 14; 7. 1, 2; Ex. 40. 34, 35; 1 K. 8. 10, 11.

VI. 1. SOLOMON,] who, though only a king, and not a priest, appears a chief performer.
SAID,] as in 1 K. 8. 12.
THICK DARKNESS,] as in Ex. 20. 20, 21; De. 4. 11; 5. 22; 2 Sa. 22. 10; 1 K. 8. 12; Job 22. 13; 38. 9; Ps. 18. 9; 97. 2; Isa. 60. 2; Jer. 13. 16; Ezek. 34. 12; Joel 2. 2; Zep. 1. 15.

2. HOUSE OF HABITATION,] as in 1 K. 8. 13; Ps. 49. 14; Isa. 63. 15. Hab. 3. 11.
FIXED PLACE,] as in Ex. 15. 17, &c.

3. TURNETH ROUND] from facing the altar, as in v. 12.
STANDING,] a mark of respect for the king.

4. BLESSED,] as in Ge. 14. 20; 24. 27, &c.
SPOKEN,] as in 2 Sa. 7. 5, 25.

5. DAY,] 488 years before, as in 1 K. 6. 1, 38; 8. 2.
FIXED,] though he had indicated an intention to do so in De. 12. 5, 11, &c.
LEADER,] as in 1 Sa. 6. 9, &c.

6. NAME,] or renown, that is, his character
MY PEOPLE] as their leader and king.

WITH THE HEART,] that is, in accordance with it, not 'in it,' as in the C.V.
8. SAITH,] as in 1 K. 8. 18.
9. NOT BUILD,] being a man of wars and blood, as in 1 K. 8. 19, &c.
SON,] even Solomon.
10. ESTABLISH,] not 'perform,' as in C.V.
11.'MADE,]by the hands of Moses at Horeb.
12. STANDETH,] as in 1 K. 8. 22.
SPREADETH OUT,] as in v. 13, 29; Ex. 9. 29, 33; 1 K. 8. 22, 38, 54; Ezra 9. 5, &c.
13. SCAFFOLD.] This original word is not found elsewhere in this sense.
COURT,] as in 4. 9; Eze. 43. 14, 17, 20; 45. 19.
KNEELETH,] as in Jud. 7. 5, 6; 1 K. 8. 54; Da. 6. 10.
14. NOT LIKE THEE] in the following particulars.
KEEPING THE COVENANT] between himself and his people.
AND THE KINDNESS] he promised to do to them.
ALL THEIR HEART,] as in 1 K. 3. 6, &c.
15. KEPT,] laid up, as it were, in store.
16. GOD OF ISRAEL,] as in v. 1.
NOT CUT OFF] finally and for ever.
WALK,] habitually and fully.
17. STEDFAST,] as in 1 K. 8. 26, &c.
18. TRUE,] as in Ge. 18. 13; Nu. 22. 32; 1 K. 8. 27; Ps. 58. 1.
DWELLETH,] lit. 'sitteth.'
HEAVENS OF THE HEAVENS,] as in De. 10. 14.
CONTAIN,] as in 2. 6; 1 K. 8. 27.
19. TURNED] thy face, as the original word indicates; see Ge. 18. 22, &c.
PRAYER,] as in 2 Sa. 7. 27; 1 K. 8. 28, 29, &c.
SUPPLICATION,] as in Jos. 11. 20; 1 K. 8. 28, &c.
MY GOD,] by covenant engagements.
CRY,] as in 1 K. 8. 28; 22. 26, &c.
20. OPEN,] as in v. 40; 1 K. 8. 29, 52; Neh. 1. 6.
NIGHT,] as in Ex. 13. 21; Lev. 8. 35, &c.
NAME,] as in v. 6 above.
TOWARDS,] as in 1 K. 8. 30; Da. 6. 10, &c.
21. HEARKENED,] and by inference received favourably.
PLACE OF THY DWELLING,] as in 6. 2, &c.
FORGIVEN,] as in Ex. 34. 9; Lev. 4. 20, 26, &c.
22. SIN,] that is, miss the performance of any duty laid upon him in reference to his neighbour.
LIFTED UP,] as in 1 K. 8. 31, &c.
OATH,] as in Ge. 24. 41, &c.
ALTAR,] in the presence of the priest or messenger of Jehovah.
23. DONE] judgment and justice.
JUDGED] in truth and uprightness.
HEAD,] as in 1 K. 8. 32, &c.
RIGHTEOUS,] as in Ex. 23. 7; De. 25. 1.
24. SMITTEN,] as in Jud. 20. 39; Lev. 26. 17.
SIN,] whether wilfully or ignorantly.
CONFESSED,] as in 1 K. 8. 33, 35; 1 Ch. 16. 35, &c.
25. TURN BACK] out of captivity and oppression.
FATHERS,] in promises many and clear.
26. RESTRAINED,] as in 7. 13; 1 K. 8. 35; De. 11. 17; Job 12. 15.

RAIN,] to water the earth, and support man and beast.
TURN BACK,] as in De. 1. 45; 4. 30, &c.
AFFLICT THEM,] as in 1 K. 8. 35.
27. DIRECTEST THEM,] as in Ex. 15. 25, &c.
GOOD WAY,] as in 1 Sa. 12. 23; 1 K. 8. 36, &c.
INHERITANCE,] as in Nu. 18. 20, &c.
28. FAMINE,] lit. 'hunger,' as in Ge. 12. 9; 26. 1; 41. 27—57, &c.
PESTILENCE,] as in Ex. 5. 3; 9. 3, 15, &c.
BLASTING,] as in De. 28. 22; 1 K. 8. 37; Amos 4. 9; Hag. 2. 17.
MILDEW,] as in De. 28. 22; 1 K. 8. 37; Jer. 30. 6; Amos 4. 9; Hag. 2. 17.
LOCUST,] as in Ex. 10. 4, 12, 13, 14, 19, &c.
CATERPILLAR,] as in 1 K. 8. 37; Ps. 78. 46, Isa. 33. 4; Joel 1. 4; 2. 25.
DISTRESSED IT] by oppression and war.
PLAGUE,] or 'stroke.'
SICKNESS,] as in Ex. 15. 26; 23. 25, &c.
29. SUPPLICATION,] for mercy and help.
PAIN,] in 1 K. 8. 38 it is 'his own heart.'
30. DWELLING,] as in v. 2, 21, &c.
ALL HIS WAYS,] whether right or wrong.
HEART,] as in Jer. 17. 10; 1 K. 8. 39.
31. FEAR,] that is, reverence, as a just God.
THY WAYS,] so far as they are revealed for men's guidance.
FATHERS,] Abraham, Isaac, Jacob, &c.
32. STRANGER,] as in Ge. 31. 15; Ex. 2. 22, &c.
AFAR OFF,] as in Ge. 22. 4; 37. 18, &c.
NAME..HAND..ARM,] that is, of his actings to his friends and his enemies.
33. SETTLED PLACE,] as in Ex. 15. 17, &c.
ALL THE PEOPLES,] as in 1 Sa. 17. 46; 2 K. 19. 19; Ps. 67. 2.
FEAR,] that is, reverence.
CALLED ON,] as in 1 K. 8. 43; Jer. 7. 10, 11, 14, 30; 32. 34; 34. 15.
34. SEND,] for they could only go at his command.
FIXED ON,] even Jerusalem, as in v. 6.
35. PRAYER..SUPPLICATION,] as in v. 19, 24, 29, &c.
CAUSE,] lit. 'done their judgment,' as in v. 39; 1 K. 8. 45, 49, 59, &c.
36. WHO SINNETH NOT,] as in 1 K. 8. 46; Ecc. 7. 20.
ANGRY,] as in 1 K. 8. 46; Ezra 9. 14; Ps. 2. 12; 60. 1; 79. 5; 85. 5; Isa. 12. 1.
GIVEN THEM] up helpless as prey.
CAPTIVE,] as in Ge. 34. 29, &c.
37. TURNED IT BACK,] as in Lev. 26. 40, &c.
TURNED BACK,] to God in penitence.
SINNED,] as in De. 1. 41; Jud. 10. 10, &c.
DONE PERVERSELY,] according to our own wishes, and against many promises.
DONE WICKEDLY,] or 'wrongly,' as in 1 K. 8. 47.
38. HEART..SOUL,] as in De. 4. 29, &c.
39. SETTLED PLACE,] as in v. 30, 33.
MAINTAINED THEIR CAUSE,] as in v. 35.
40. OPEN,] as in v. 20.
ATTENTIVE,] as in 7. 15; Ps. 10. 17; 130. 2; Neh. 1. 6, 11; Isa. 32. 3.
41 REST,] as in Est. 9. 16, 17, 18; compare Nu. 10. 33; Ps. 95. 11; 132. 8, 14; Isa. 66. 1.
ARK OF THY STRENGTH,] as in Ps. 132. 8.
SALVATION,] or 'safety,' as in Jud. 15. 18, &c.

GOODNESS,] as in Ex. 18. 9; De. 26. 11; Ecc. 2. 1, 24; 3. 13; 5. 18; 7. 14.
42. TURN NOT BACK,] in shame and confusion, by rejecting his prayer.
KIND ACTS,] promised to David by God.

VII. 1. FIRE,] as in 2 K. 1. 10, 12.
CONSUMETH,] the usual token of divine acceptance.
FILLED,] as in 1 K. 8. 10, 11.
2. TO GO IN,] much less to 'minister,' as in 5. 14.
3. BOW] the knee, as the word implies; see Ge. 49. 9; Nu. 24. 9; Jud. 5. 27, &c.
FACES TO THE EARTH,] as in Ge. 19. 1; 42. 6; 48. 12; Nu. 22. 31; 1 Sa. 20. 41; 24. 8, &c.
PAVEMENT,] as in Est. 1. 6; Eze. 40. 17, 18; 42. 3.
DO OBEISANCE,] as in Ge. 18. 2; 19. 1; 22. 5, &c.
KINDNESS,] as in Ge. 19. 19; 1 Ch. 16. 34, 41, &c.
5. 22,000..120,000,] during the fourteen days of the feast.
DEDICATE,] lit. 'make narrow,' hence 'to set apart,' as in De. 20. 5; 1 K. 8. 63; Prov. 22. 6; Nu. 7. 10, 11, 84, 88.
6. CHARGES] as in 1 Ch. 9. 23, 27; 23. 32, &c.
SONG OF JEHOVAH,] as in 1 Ch. 15. 7; 2 Ch. 29. 27; Ps. 137. 4.
MADE,] as in 1 Ch. 23. 5, &c.
BLESSING,] as in 5. 12 above.
STANDING,] to join in the song of praise.
7. MIDDLE OF THE COURT,] as in 1 K. 8. 64.
FAT,] as in Ge. 4. 4; Ex. 23. 18; 29. 13, &c.
ALTAR OF BRASS,] as in 4. 1.
8. FEAST,] as in Ex. 10. 9; 12. 14; 13. 6, &c.
SEVEN DAYS,] the usual period of religious festivals in Israel.
HAMATH,] as in Nu. 13. 21; 34. 8, &c.
BROOK OF EGYPT,] as in Nu. 34. 5, &c.
9. A RESTRAINT,] as in Lev. 23. 36; Nu. 29. 35; De. 16. 8; Neh. 8. 18; Jer. 9. 2; Am. 5. 21.
DEDICATION,] as in Nu. 7. 10, 11, 84, 88; Neh. 12. 27; Ps. 30. 1.
10. SEVENTH MONTH,] that is, Tisri.
TENTS,] that is, dwellings.
GLAD IN HEART,] as in 1 Sa. 25. 36, &c.
11. FINISHETH,] as in 5. 1, &c.
PROSPER,] being guided by divine wisdom.
12. BY NIGHT,] as in Ge. 20. 3; 31. 24, &c.
PRAYER,] as recorded in the preceding chapter.
FIXED,] as in 6. 6, &c.
13. RESTRAIN,] as in 6. 25, &c.
LOCUST,] as in 6. 28, &c.
PESTILENCE,] as in 6. 28, &c.
14. IS CALLED,] as in De. 28. 10, &c.
HUMBLED,] because of their sin.
SEEK,] with all their heart and soul.
TURN BACK,] as Solomon prayed in v. 6.
FORGIVE,] as in 6. 39, &c.
HEAL,] from its drought and barrenness.
15. OPEN,] as prayed for by Solomon.
ATTENTIVE,] as in v. 6.
16. CHOSEN,] or 'fixed on,' as in v. 12.
EYES..HEART,] as in 1 K. 9. 3, &c.
17. WALKED,] in sincerity and stedfastuess.
KEEP,] watch, and observe to do.
18. ESTABLISHED,] lit. 'caused to rise up.'

COVENANTED,] as in 2 Sa. 23. 5, &c.
NOT CUT OFF] for ever.
RULER,] as in 2 Sa. 23. 3, &c.
19. PLACED,] lit. 'given.'
SERVED,] and obeyed their laws.
BOWED YOURSELVES,] in token of obeisance.
PLUCKED,] as in De. 29. 28, &c.
MY GROUND,] which he still claims as his own.
20. CAST,] as a polluted thing.
PROVERB,] as in De. 28. 27; 1 Sa. 10. 12, &c.
BYEWORD,] as in De. 28. 27, &c.
21. HIGH,] in honour and glory among men.
ASTONISHMENT,] as in De. 29. 24; Jer. 22. 8, 9.
22. FORSAKEN,] the covenant God of their fathers.
EGYPT,] where they were in grievous bondage.
LAY HOLD,] of their own free will and determination.
EVIL,] of ruin, and desolation, and misery.

VIII. 1. TWENTY YEARS,] as in 1 K. 9. 10, &c.
2. CITIES,] in the land of Galilee, which, probably because of their inland position, were rejected by the king of Tyre, and returned to Solomon.
BUILT,] or rebuilt, and extended.
DWELL,] settling colonies there, to take possession of the land.
3. HAMATH-ZOBAH] in Aram, called 'Zobah the great,' in Amos 6. 2.
LAYETH HOLD,] by force of arms; this is the only military expedition mentioned in connection with Solomon.
4. TADMOR,] in 1 K. 9. 18 it is 'Tamar;' otherwise called Palmyra.
WILDERNESS,] or pasture land of Aram, between Damascus and the Euphrates.
CITIES OF STORE,] as in Ex. 1. 11; 1 K. 9. 18, &c.
5. BETH-HORON,] the upper, of which there is no mention in 1 K. 9. 17.
CITIES OF DEFENCE,] all in the tribe of Ephraim.
WALLS..BAR,] as in De. 3. 5; 1 Sa. 23. 7, &c.
6. BAALATH,] in the tribe of Dan, Jos. 19. 44.
CHARIOT,] of which he had 1400; see 1. 14; 9. 25; 1 K. 9. 19; 10. 26.
HORSEMEN,] of whom he had 12,000; see 1 K. 9. 19.
DESIRE,] as in 1 K. 9. 1, 19; Isa. 21. 4.
JERUSALEM,] his capital city; as in Ecc. 2. 4.
LEBANON,] part of which was under his authority; see 1 K. 7. 2; 9. 19.
DOMINION,] extending from the river of Egypt to the Euphrates.
7. LEFT] alive in different parts of the land of Israel; see 1 K. 9. 20, &c.
HITTITE..JEBUSITE,] left unsubdued; see Jud. 1. 19, 21, 27, 29, 30, &c.
8. CONSUMED NOT,] in battle.
TRIBUTE,] of money and service, as in 1 K. 4. 6; 5. 13, 14; 9. 15. 21; 12. 18, &c.
9. SERVANTS,] engaged in menial employments.
MEN OF WAR,] as in Nu. 31. 28, 49, &c.
10. OFFICERS,] or 'garrisons,' as in 17. 2;

1 Sa. 10. 5; 13. 3, 4; 2 Sa. 8. 6, 14; 1 K. 4. 19;
1 Ch. 11. 16; 18. 13.
RULERS,] as in 1 K. 9. 23, &c.
11. DAUGHTER OF PHARAOH,] whom he
had married, as in 1 K. 3. 1, &c.
CITY OF DAVID,]that is, Zion, as in 2 Sa. 5. 7.
HOLY,] or 'separate.'
ARK,] the symbol of the divine presence.
12. PORCH,] as in 4. 1.
13. ITS DAY,] morning and evening, as in
Ex. 29. 38, 39.
SABBATHS,] which were weekly, as in Nu.
28. 9, &c.
NEW MOONS,] which were monthly.
APPOINTED SEASONS,] which were three
times in a year, as in Ex. 23. 14; De. 16.
16, &c.
UNLEAVENED THINGS,] as in Ex. 12. 17, &c.
WEEKS,] as in De. 16. 10, &c.
BOOTHS,] as in De. 16. 13, &c.
14. ORDINANCE,] lit. 'judgment.'
COURSES,] as in 1 Ch. 24. 1; twenty-four in
number.
CHARGES,] as in 1 Ch. 25. 1.
ITS DAY,] as in v. 13.
COMMAND,] as in 1 Ch. 9. 17; 26. 1.
15. KING] Solomon or David, most probably the former.
TREASURES,] as in 1 Ch. 26. 20, &c.
16. PREPARED] beforehand, to prevent
loss of time, &c.
COMPLETION,] a period of seven years, as
in 1 K. 6. 38.
PERFECT,] in all its proportions.
17. EZION-GEBER,] as in 1 K. 9. 2; Nu. 33.
35, &c.
ELOTH,] or 'Elath,' as in De. 2. 8; 2 K.
14. 22.
SEA] of Suph, as in 1 K. 9. 26; the southern
border of Arabia.
EDOM,] whence the sea received its name,
'the Red Sea.'
18. HURAM,] king of Tyre, as in 9. 10, 13;
1 K. 9. 27.
OPHIR,] as in 1 K. 9. 28, &c.
450 TALENTS,] in 1 K. 9. 28 it is 420
talents.
SOLOMON,] as in 9. 10.

IX. 1. SHEBA,] in Arabia Felix, as in 1 K.
10. 1, 4, 10, 13, &c.
FAME,] for riches and wisdom, which all
kings desired to see and to hear.
TRY,] as in Ge. 22. 1; Ex. 15. 15, &c.
ACUTE SAYINGS,] as in Nu. 12. 8; Jud. 14.
12—19; 1 K. 10. 1, &c.
GREAT,] lit. 'heavy,' as in 2 K. 7. 6, &c.
SPICES,] as in Ex. 25. 6; 30. 23; 35. 8.
PRECIOUS STONE,] as in 2 Sa. 12. 30, &c.
WITH HER HEART,] not 'in' it, as in C.V.
2. MATTERS,] not 'questions,' as in C.V.
HID,] or 'concealed,' as in Lev. 4. 13; 5. 2,
3, 4, &c.
3. WISDOM,] the exhibition of it in his
rule and government.
HOUSE,] that is, his palace; but see 1 K.
10. 4, &c.
4. TABLE,] so much variety and abund-
ance.
SITTING,] as in Ge. 30; 27. 39; 36. 43, &c.
STANDING,] as in 1 K. 10. 5; 1 Ch. 23. 28, &c.

MINISTERS,] as in Ex. 24. 13; 1 Ch. 27.
1, &c.
CLOTHING,] as in 1 K. 10. 5; 2 K. 10. 22, &c
BUTLERS,] as in Ge. 40. 1—23; 1 K. 10.
5, &c.
BURNT-OFFERING,] or 'ascent.'
OFFERETH UP,] or 'goeth up.'
SPIRIT,] as in 1 K. 10. 5; Jos. 2. 11; 5. 1.
5. WORD,] or 'thing.'
WISDOM,] which extended to the surround-
ing lands.
6. NO CREDENCE,] lit. 'did not remain
stedfast.'
HALF,] as in 1 K. 10. 7; Ps. 102. 24, &c.
REPORT,] or 'rumour.'
7. HAPPINESS,] lit. 'happinesses.'
STANDING,] as his immediate attendants
8. BLESSED,] that is, 'kneeled to.'
DELIGHTED,] as in 1 K. 10. 9; Nu. 14. 8, &c.
FOR JEHOVAH,] as His vicegerent.
RIGHTEOUSNESS,] as in 1 K. 10. 9, &c.
9. 120 TALENTS.] See 1 K. 9. 14, &c.
SPICES..PRECIOUS STONE,] as in 1 K. 10.
10, &c.
10. HURAM,] king of Tyre, his ally.
OPHIR,] as in 1 K. 9. 28, &c.
ALGUM-TREES,] or 'almug-trees,' as in 2. 8;
1 K. 10. 11, 12.
11. STAIRCASES,] or 'highways,' as in Nu.
20. 19; Jud. 5. 20, &c.
HARPS AND PSALTERIES,] as in 2 Sa. 6. 5;
1 K. 10. 12; 1 Ch. 13. 8; 15. 16, 28; 16. 5; 25.
6, &c.
JUDAH,] this last clause is omitted in 1
K. 10. 12.
12. DESIRE,] as in 1 Sa. 15. 22; 18. 25, &c.
BROUGHT,] as in v. 1. 9 above.
LAND,] even Sheba, in Arabia.
13. 666 TALENTS,] variously reckoned from
two to five millions pounds sterling.
14. TOURISTS,] as in 1 K. 10. 15; in Nu. 14.
6, it is the word used of the spies.
MERCHANTS,] as in Ge. 23. 16; 37. 28, &c.
ARABIA,] who were subject to him, or
who made presents, as in 1 K. 4. 21, 24.
GOVERNORS,] as in 1 K. 10. 15, &c.
15. TARGETS,] as in 1 Sa. 17. 7, 41, &c.
ALLOYED,] lit. 'slaughtered,' as in Lev. 14.
6, 51; 1 K. 10. 16, 17; Jer. 9. 8.
16. SHIELDS,] as in Ge. 15. 1; 1 K. 10.
17, &c.
HOUSE OF THE FOREST,] as in 1 K. 7. 2;
10. 17, 21.
17. IVORY,] brought from Tarshish, as in
1 K. 10. 18, 22; 22. 39, &c.
OVERLAYETH,] as in Ex. 25. 11, 13, 24,
28, &c.
18. STEPS,] lit. 'ascents.'
FOOTSTOOL.] This original word is not
found elsewhere.
HANDS,] as in 1 K. 7. 35, 36, &c.
19. FOR,] not 'in' any kingdom, as in C.V.
20. DRINKING VESSELS,] as in 1 K. 10.
21, &c.
REFINED,] as in 1 K. 6. 20, 21; 7. 49, 50.
2 Ch. 4. 10, 22; Job 41. 15; Eze. 44. 1, 2; 46. 1.
RECKONED,] or 'thought of.'
21. TARSHISH,] as in Ge. 10. 4; 1 K. 10
22; 22. 48; 1 Ch. 1. 7, &c.
HURAM,] as in v. 10.
THREE YEARS,] as in 1 K. 10. 22, &c.

IVORY,] as in v. 17 above.
APES,] as in 1 K. 10. 22, &c.
PEACOCKS,] as in 1 K. 10. 22, &c.
22. EARTH,] or 'land.'
23. PRESENCE,] lit. 'face.'
IN HIS HEART,] as in 1. 12, &c.
24. PRESENT,] as in Ge. 4. 3—5; 32. 13, &c.
GARMENTS,] as in Ex. 22. 9, 26; De. 24. 13;
29. 5; Jos. 9. 5, 13; 22. 8; 1 K. 10. 25; 11. 29,
30; Neh. 9. 21; Job 9. 31; Ps. 104. 2; Song 4.
11; Mic. 2. 8.
HARNESS,] or 'armour;' as in 1 K. 10. 25;
2 K. 10. 2, &c.
SPICES,] as in 2 Sa. 13. 29; 18. 9, &c.
HORSES,] which were not very suitable for
the hilly character of Palestine,
MULES,] as in 2 Sa. 13. 29; 18. 9; 1 K. 10.
25; 18. 5; 2 K. 5. 17; 1 Ch. 12. 40; Ezra 2.
66; Neh. 7. 68; Ps. 32. 9; Isa. 66. 20; Eze. 27.
14; Zec. 14. 15.
A RATE,] lit. a 'matter,' as in De. 15. 20;
1 Sa. 7. 16.
25. 4,000 STALLS,] as in 32. 28; in 1 K. 4.
26 it is 40,000.
12,000 HORSEMEN,] as in 1. 14; 1 K. 4. 26;
10. 2, 6.
26. RULING,] as in Ge. 24. 2; 45. 8, 26; Jos.
12. 2, 5, &c.
THE RIVER,] the Euphrates, on the east.
PHILISTINES,] on the border of the great
sea, on the west.
EGYPT,] on the south of Canaan.
27. MAKETH,] lit. 'giveth.'
CEDARS,] which he brought from Lebanon
at great expense.
SYCAMORES,] as in 1. 15; 1 K. 10. 27; 1 Ch.
27. 28; Ps. 78. 47; Isa. 9. 10; Amos 7. 14.
LOW COUNTRY,] as in De. 1. 7; Jos. 9. 1, &c.
28. HORSES,] for warfare and for show.
EGYPT,] where they were found in abundance.
29. MATTERS,] not 'acts,' as in C.V.
NATHAN,] the companion of David his
father.
PROPHECY,] that is, declaration of God's
truth.
AHIJAH,] i. e. 'brother of Jah.'
SHILONITE,] from Shiloh, as in 1 K. 11.
29, &c.
VISIONS,] or spiritual 'sights,' as in 1 Sa.
3. 1; 1 Ch. 17. 15; 2 Ch. 32. 32; Ps. 89. 19, &c.
IDDO,] or Iddai, i.e. 'timely,' as in 12. 15;
13. 22.
SEER,] as in 2 Sa. 24. 11, &c.
JEROBOAM,] i.e. 'he multiplies the people.'
30. 40 YEARS,] like Saul and David.
31. LIETH,] as in 1 K. 2. 10, &c.
CITY OF DAVID,] Zion, as in 1 K. 2. 10.
REHOBOAM,] i.e. 'breadth or enlargement
of a people.'

X. 1. SHECHEM] in Ephraim, as in Ge. 33.
18, 19; 34. 2, 26; 35. 4; 37. 12, 14; Nu. 26. 31;
Jos. 17. 2, &c.
REIGN] over Israel, in the place of his
father.
2. JEROBOAM,] as in 9. 29, &c.
FLED,] for fear of Solomon, as in 1 K. 11. 40.
3. SEND,] for him to be their leader, knowing his ability, as in 1 K. 11. 28.
SAYING,] as in 1 K. 12. 3.

4. SHARP,] or 'hard;' by his magnificent
works and plans.
MAKE LIGHT,] by reducing the expenditure of money and labour.
6. CONSULTETH,] remembering perhaps
Prov. 11. 14; 24. 6, &c.
AGED MEN,] official counsellors and rulers,
as in Ge. 50. 7; 2 Sa. 12. 17, &c.
STANDING] as ministering servants.
YE COUNSELLING,] as in v. 9 below.
7. BECOME GOOD,] not 'be kind,' as in C.V.
PLEASED WITH THEM,] not 'pleased them,'
as in C.V.
GOOD WORDS,] suitable for them in their
circumstances.
8. LADS,] lit. 'children,' as in Ge. 13.13, &c.
GROWN UP,] lit. 'become great.'
9. YE COUNSELLING,] as in v. 6 above.
WE ANSWER,] associating them with himself.
11. HEAVY YOKE,] as in v. 4 above.
ADD,] by additional burdens.
CHASTISED,] as in Lev. 26. 18, 28, &c.
WHIPS,] as in v. 14; 1 K. 12. 11, 14.
SCORPIONS,] as in v. 14; De. 8. 15; Eze. 2. 6.
12. SPAKE,] not 'bade,' as in C.V.
13. SHARPLY,] as in 1 K. 12. 13; Ge. 42. 7, &c.
14. SPEAKETH,] not 'answereth,' as in C.V.
15. REVOLUTION,] lit. 'the bringing round
about,' as in 1 K. 12. 15.
FROM GOD,] determined by his foreknowledge and will.
SPAKE,] as in 1 K. 11. 29—39.
16. SEND BACK WORD,] probably after re-
tiring and mutual consultation.
PORTION..INHERITANCE,] as in Ge. 31. 14.
SEE,] that is, 'behold it,' not 'see to it,'
as in C.V.
TENTS,] or dwellings, as in 1 K. 12. 16.
17. SONS OF ISRAEL,] belonging to the ten
tribes.
JUDAH] and Benjamin, as in 11. 1.
18. HADORAM,] in 1 K. 4. 6; 5. 14; 12. 18 it
is 'Adoram.'
TRIBUTE,] of labour and money exacted
from the people by the government.
STRENGTHENED HIMSELF,] as in 1 K. 12.
18; Ruth 1. 18; 2 Ch. 13. 7.
CHARIOT,] as in 1 K. 12. 18.
JERUSALEM,] his capital city, on the
fidelity of whose inhabitants he trusted.
19. TRANSGRESS,] as in 1 K. 8. 50; 12. 19.

XI. 1. 180,000 CHOICE,] as in 1 K. 12. 21, &c.
BENJAMIN,] which also adhered to him.
2. SHEMAIAH,] i.e. 'heard of Jah,' as in
1 K. 12. 22.
3. JUDAH,] thus at once confirming and
limiting his authority.
4. BRETHREN] of the ten tribes.
FROM ME,] as in 10. 15.
5. BULWARK,] against Jeroboam and the
ten tribes.
6. BETH-LEHEM,] about six miles from
Jerusalem.
ETAM,] where was a rock of the same
name, as in Jud. 15. 8.
TEKOA,] about twelve miles from Jerusalem, and birth-place of Amos the prophet.
7. BETH-ZUR.] as in Jos. 15. 35.

SHOCHO,] as in Jos. 15. 35, 48.
ADULLAM,] as in Jos. 15. 35.
8. GATH,] or Moresheth-Gath, birth-place of Micah the prophet, as in Mic. 1. 14.
MARESHAH,] in the plain country, as in 14. 8, 9; Mic. 1. 15.
ZIPH,] which is the name of two distinct places; see Jos. 15. 24, 55.
9. ADORAIM.] Not mentioned elsewhere.
LACHISH,] as in Jos. 12. 11; 15. 39.
AZEKAH,] as in Jos. 10. 10; 15. 35.
10. ZORAH,] or 'Zoreah,' as in Jos. 15. 33.
AIJALON,] not that in Dan, Jos. 10. 10; 19. 42, but one in Judah.
HEBRON,] about twenty miles from Jerusalem, as in Jos. 15. 54; 20. 7.
BULWARKS,] as in v. 5, against Israel.
11. STRENGTHENETH] those already in existence.
LEADERS,] as in 1 Sa. 6. 9, &c.
TREASURES,] for defence in time of seige or war.
12. TARGETS,] as in 9. 15; 11. 12; 14. 8; 25. 5; 1 Sa. 17. 7, 41; 1 K. 10. 16; 1 Ch. 12. 8, 24, 34; Ps. 5. 12; 35. 2; 91. 4; Jer. 46. 3; Eze. 23. 24; 26. 8; 38. 4; 39. 9.
SPEARS,] as in 14. 8; 25. 5; 26. 14; Nu. 25. 7; Jud. 5. 8; 1 K. 18. 28; 1 Ch. 12. 8, 24; Neh. 4. 13, 16, 21; Jer. 46. 4; Eze. 39. 9; Joel 3. 10.
HATH,] for his subjects who cleaved to him.
13. ISRAEL,] belonging to the ten tribes, who had revolted from him.
STATIONED THEMSELVES] of their own free will and determination.
14. LEFT,] throughout the territory of the ten tribes; compare Jos. 21. 1—41.
CAST THEM OFF,] probably because of their unwillingness to comply with his idolatrous movements.
15. PRIESTS,] not of the sons of Aaron, as directed in the law, but of every class in the community who offered themselves.
HIGH PLACES,] where the people might offer sacrifices, as in 1 K. 12. 31.
GOATS,] as in 29. 23; Isa. 13. 21; 34. 14, &c.
CALVES,] one at Dan, and the other at Beth-El; see 1 K. 12. 28, 29.
16. SEEK] the knowledge and favour of the covenant-king and God of Israel.
SACRIFICE,] at the appointed seasons, and in solemn vows.
17. STRENGHEN,] by encouraging his heart and hands in good.
THREE YEARS,] after which they began to become careless and indifferent; see 12. 1.
18. MAHALATH,] i. e. a 'flute,' as in Ps. 53. 1; 88. 1; compare Ge. 28. 9.
CHILD.] The Hebrew text has 'son,' the margin has 'daughter,' the Hebrew BEN sometimes includes both genders.
JERIMOTH,] i. e. 'high places.'
ABIHAIL,] i. e. 'father of might.'
ELIAB,] i.e. 'my God is father,' as in 1 Sa. 17. 13, 28.
19. JEUSH,] i.e. 'he hastens.'
SHAMARIAH,] i.e. 'preserved of Jah.'
ZAHUM,] i e. 'nausea, abhorrence.'
20. MAACHAH,] i.e. a 'bruise' called Michaiah in 13. 2.

ABSALOM,] called Abishalom in 1 K. 15. 2, and Uriel in 13. 2, of Gibeah, a Benjamite, not the rebellious son of David.
ABIJAH,] i.e. 'my father is Jah;' in 1 K. 14. 31 it is Abijam.
ATTAI,] i.e. 'timely.'
ZIZA,] i.e. 'abundance, brightness.'
SHELOMITH,] i.e. 'peaceful, complete.'
21. CONCUBINES,] contrary to the express law of God, in De. 17. 17, &c.
60 DAUGHTERS,] which was doubtless reckoned a great blessing and honour.
22. APPOINTETH,] lit. 'causeth to stand.'
ABIJAH,] as in v. 20.
LEADER,] as in 1 Sa. 9. 16, &c.
23. UNDERSTANDING,] of the times and seasons.
SPREADETH OUT,] as a matter of policy, to establish his kingdom.
BULWARKS,] as in v. 10 above.
PROVISION] of food, wine, oil, as in v. 11.
ASKETH] from their parents, not 'desired,' as in C.V.

XII. 1. STRENGTHENING HIMSELF,] as in 11. 5—12; 22. 23.
THE LAW,] as given by Moses and the prophets, as in 1 K. 14. 22—24.
2. FIFTH YEAR,] the second of his apostacy; see 11. 17; B.C. 971.
SHISHAK,] as in 1 K. 11. 40; 14. 25.
3. 1,200 CHARIOTS,] as in Ex. 14. 7; Jud. 4. 3, 13; 1 Sa. 13. 5; 2 Sa. 10. 18; 1 K. 10. 26, &c.
60,000 HORSEMEN,] of which the Jews were always deficient.
LUBIM,] that is, Lybians; see Ge. 10. 13, &c.
SUKKUM.] Sept. and Vulg. 'Troglodytae;' not mentioned elsewhere.
CUSHIM.] See Ge. 2. 13; 10. 6, 7, 8; Nu. 12. 1; 2 Sa. 18. 21, &c.
4. BULWARKS,] as in 11. 5, 10, 23.
5. SHEMAIAH,] i.e. 'heard of Jah,' as in 11.2.
FORSAKEN.. LEFT,] as in v. 1.
6. HUMBLED,] not 'humbled themselves,' as in C.V.
RIGHTEOUS] in inflicting their punishment; compare Ex. 9. 27, &c.
7. DESTROY,] lit. 'mar,' as in Ge. 6. 7, &c.
AS A LITTLE THING,] as in Ge. 26. 10, &c.
ESCAPE] from the hand of Shishak; compare Ge. 32. 8, &c.
POUR OUT] wholly and at once.
8. BECOME SERVANTS,] yielding him tribute; see 1 K. 14. 26—28.
MY SERVICE,] which is light, easy, and safe, as in Matt. 11. 30.
9. TREASURES,] as in 1 K. 7. 51, &c.
SHIELDS,] as in 9. 6; 1 K. 10. 17; 14. 26, &c.
10. BRASS,] as in 1 K. 14. 27.
RUNNERS,] as in 1 Sa. 22. 17; 14. 26, &c.
11. CHAMBER,] as in 1 K. 14. 28; Eze. 40. 7, 10, 12, 13, 16, 21, 29, 33, 36.
12. WRATH,] as in Ge. 27. 45; Eze. 32. 12; De. 13. 17; Jos. 7. 26, &c.
COMPLETION,] as in Eze. 13. 13.
THINGS,] or 'matters.'
13. STRENGTHENETH HIMSELF,] as in Ge. 48. 2; Nu. 13. 20; Jud. 20. 22, &c.
41 YEARS,] being born one year before his father Solomon mounted the throne.

U

17 YEARS,] twelve years after his defeat.
CHOSEN,] as in 6. 6, &c.
NAAMAH,] i.e. 'pleasantness.'
14. EVIL THING,] that is, idolatry, as in v. 1, 5.
PREPARED,] or 'established, made ready,' as in 19. 3; 20. 33; 29. 18; 30. 19; 1 Sa. 7. 3; Ezra 7. 10; Job 11. 13; Ps. 78. 8, &c.
SEEK] the favour and guidance of Jehovah, as in Ge. 25. 22, &c.
15. MATTERS,] not 'acts,' as in C. V.
SHEMAIAH,] as in 11. 2; 12. 5.
IDDO,] as in 13. 22.
GENEALOGY,] as in 1 Ch. 4. 33; 5. 1, 7, 17; 7. 5, 7, 9, 40; 9. 1, 22; 2 Ch. 31. 16—19; Ezra 2. 62; 8. 1, 3; Neh. 7. 5, 64.
WAR,] lit. 'battles,' as in Ge. 14. 2, 8.
16. LIETH,] as in Ge. 47, 30, &c.
CITY OF DAVID,] that is, Zion.
ABIJAH,] or Abijam, as in 1 K. 14. 31.

XIII. 1. JEROBOAM,] who reigned over the ten tribes; 1 K. 15. 1.
JUDAH] and Benjamin, as in 11. 1.
2. JERUSALEM,] the capital city of Judah.
MICHAIAH,] as in 11. 20; 1 K. 13. 2, &c.
URIEL,] i.e. 'my light is God.'
GIBEAH] in Benjamin, as in 1 Sa. 13. 5, &c.
3. DIRECTETH,] lit. 'bindeth.'
400,000..800,000.] Some of Kennicott's MSS. read 40,000 and 80,000.
4. ZEMARAIM,] as in Jos. 18. 22; Ge. 10. 18.
EPHRAIM,] on the border of Benjamin.
GIVEN,] as in 2 Sa. 7. 12, 13, 16.
COVENANT OF SALT,] as in Nu. 18. 19.
SERVANT,] as in 1 K. 11. 28.
REBELLETH,] as in Ge. 14. 4; Nu. 14. 9, &c.
7. VAIN MEN,] or 'empty ones,' as in Ge. 37. 24; 41. 27; De. 32. 47; Jud. 7. 16; 9. 4; 11. 3; 2 Sa. 6. 20; 2 K. 4. 3, &c.
SONS OF WORTHLESSNESS,] as in Jud. 19. 22, &c.
YOUTH,] comparatively speaking, for he was 41 years of age, as in 12. 13.
STRENGTHENED HIMSELF] beforehand, by ascertaining their real designs.
8. BEFORE,] that is, in the face or presence of.
MULTITUDE,] double the whole force of Judah, as in v. 3.
CALVES,] as in 11. 15, &c.
9. CAST OUT,] refusing their services because of their attachment to the law.
LIKE THE PEOPLES,] the Canaanites, &c.
FILL HIS HAND,] as in Ex. 28. 41, &c.
SEVEN RAMS,] a perfect sacrifice, as in Nu. 23. 1, &c., but five more than required in Ex. 29. 1.
NO-GODS,] being only gold and silver, wood and stone; see 1 K. 13. 31.
10. JEHOVAH,] the ever living God of Israel.
NOT FORSAKEN,] as the ten tribes had done.
MINISTERING,] performing their appointed duties in the law.
11. MAKING PERFUME,] as in 1 Ch. 6. 49.
PERFUMES OF SPICES,] as in Ex. 25. 6, &c.
ARRANGEMENT OF BREAD,] changed weekly, as in Lev. 24. 6, 7, &c.
PURE TABLE,] as in Lev. 24. 6.
CANDLESTICKS..LAMPS,] as in Ex. 25. 31, &c.

CHARGE,] as in Ge. 26. 5; Ex. 12. 6; 16. 23, 32, 33, 34; Lev. 8. 30, &c.
12. GOD,] as our king and leader; compare Nu. 23. 21, &c.
SHOUT,] an alarm of battle, as in Nu. 10. 7, 9, &c.
NOT PROSPER,] fighting against Omnipotence.
13. AMBUSH,] as in Jos. 8. 9; Jud. 9. 35; Ps. 10. 8.
14. CRY,] in distress for help, as the original word implies; see Ge. 4. 10; 27. 34; 41. 55, &c.
TRUMPETS,] to encourage them in the battle.
15. SHOUT,] encouraged by the blowing of the trumpets; see 1 Sa. 17. 20.
SMITTEN,] with fear and confusion.
16. FLEE,] to their tents for safety.
17. SMITING,] as in Nu. 11. 33; De. 25. 3; 28. 59; Jos. 10. 10, 20; Jud. 11. 33; 15. 8; 1 Sa. 4. 10; 6. 19, &c.
WOUNDED,] lit. 'pierced.'
500,000.] Jerome makes it 50,000.
18. HUMBLED,] by this unexpected and disastrous defeat.
LEANT,] or 'been supported by,' as in Ge. 18. 4; Nu. 21. 15; Jud. 16. 26, &c.
19. BETH-EL,] where one of the calves was set up.
SMALL TOWNS,] lit. 'daughters,' as in Jos. 15. 45, &c.
JESHANAH,] i.e. 'old;' not mentioned elsewhere.
EPHRAIM,] a city of that name.
20. NOT RETAINED POWER,] as in 2. 6; 20. 37; 22. 9; Da. 10. 8, 16; 11. 6; 1 Ch. 29. 14.
DIETH,] being one of the very few kings who died peaceably on his bed; it was two years after Abijah; see 1 K. 14. 20; 15. 9.
21. STRENGTHENETH HIMSELF,] as in v. 7.
FOURTEEN WIVES,] his father had 18, as in 11. 21.
22 SONS.—16 DAUGHTERS,] his father had 28 sons, and 60 daughters.
23. MATTERS,] not 'acts,' as in C. V.
INQUIRY,] as in 24. 27.
IDDO,] as in 12. 15.

XIV. 1. LIETH,] as in 12. 6, &c. ; see 1 K. 15. 8.
CITY OF DAVID,] that is, Zion, as in 2 Sa. 5. 7, &c.
ASA,] i.e. 'a healer.'
QUIET,] from war, as in Jos. 11. 23; 14. 15, &c.
2. GOOD..RIGHT,] as in 31. 20, &c. ; see 1 K. 15. 11.
3. STRANGER,] such as the Edomite, Moabite, Aramaean, Philistine, Ammonite, &c. ; see 1 K. 11. 7. 8.
HIGH PLACES,] where the people worshipped God at Jerusalem, or rather idolatrous ones; see 1 K. 15. 14.
BREAKETH,] as commanded in the law of Moses.
STANDING PILLARS,] which they set up to their idols.
CUTTETH DOWN,] with sharp weapons.
SHRINES,] dedicated to the false gods of the nations.

4. SEEK,] as directed in the law, for his favour and countenance.

DO,] or perform all required in the directions and commands that God had given them.

5. IMAGES,] probably those of the sun; compare Lev. 26. 30; 2 Ch. 34. 4, 7; Isa. 17. 8; 27. 9; Eze. 6. 4, 6.

QUIET,] as in v. 1 above.

6. BULWARKS,] as in 11. 5, &c.; compare 12. 4.

GIVEN REST,] as a reward for his obedience.

7. BUILD,] that is, 'build up,' out of their comparatively ruined condition.

WALL..BARS,] for defence against foes.

SOUGHT,] as himself had directed in v. 4.

PROSPER,] bringing their purposes to completion.

8. TARGET..SPEAR,] as in 1 Ch. 12. 8, &c. 300,000..280,000,] nearly a half more than his father Abijah could raise; see 13. 3.

9. ZERAH,] i.e. a 'rising.'

CUSHITE,] from southern Arabia. 1,000,000,] of whom Josephus says 100,000 were horsemen, and compare 16. 8.

CHARIOTS 300,] a comparatively small number.

MARESHAH,] on the southern border of Judah, as in 11. 8; Jos. 15. 44. &c.

10. ZEPHATHAH,] i.e. an 'ornament;' not mentioned elsewhere.

11. HIS GOD,] whom he had avouched to be so.

HELP,] in time of trouble and distress.

NO POWER,] as in 1 Sa. 14. 6, &c.

LEANT,] or 'been supported,' as in 13. 18, &c.

OUR GOD,] his own and his people's God.

PREVAIL,] lit. 'retain (power) or restrain,' as in Ge. 16. 2; 20. 18, &c.

MORTAL MAN,] as in Ge. 13. 8, &c.

12. CUSHIM,] as in v. 9 above.

13. GERAR,] a city of the Philistines; see Ge. 10. 19; 20. 1.

NO PRESERVING,] as in Ge. 45. 5; Ezra 9. 8, 9; Jud. 6. 4.

BROKEN,] lit. 'shivered,' as in 20. 37; Ex. 22. 10, 14; Lev. 6. 28; 15. 12, &c.

HIS CAMP,] that is, Israel, as in Ge. 32. 2, 7, 8, 10, 21; 33. 8; 50. 9; Ex. 14. 19, 20, &c.

BEAR AWAY,] lit. 'lift up,' as in Ge. 4. 13; 7. 17, &c.

SPOIL,] from the camp of the enemy; see Ge. 49. 27; Ex. 15. 9, &c.

14. FEAR OF JEHOVAH,] as in 17. 10; 19. 7; 1 Sa. 11. 7, &c.

15. TENTS OF CATTLE,] probably belonging to the inhabitants of Gerer, who sided with the Cushim.

SHEEP..CAMELS,] which the Cushim had brought with them.

XV. 1. AZARIAH,] i.e. 'help of Jah.'

ODED,] i.e. 'causing to stand,' as in v. 8.

2. WITH YOU,] to give quiet, and safety, and victory.

SEEK,] his favour and protection in obeying his commands.

FORSAKE,] his directions and laws.

3. MANY DAYS,] probably during the times of the judges; see Jud. 5. 6.

TRUE GOD,] lit. 'God of truth,' as in Ps. 31. 5; Jer. 10. 10.

TEACHING,] lit. 'directing,' as in 2 K. 17. 28; Job 36. 22; Prov. 5. 13; 6. 13; Isa. 9. 15; 30. 20; Hab. 2. 18.

WITHOUT LAW,] lit. 'direction,' as in Ge. 26. 5, &c.

4. DISTRESS,] as in De. 4. 30; 2 Sa. 22. 7, &c.

FOUND,] as in v. 2, 15; 1 Ch. 28. 9.

5. GOING OUT..COMING IN,] as in Jos. 6. 1; 1 Sa. 18. 16; 1 Ch. 27. 1; 2 Ch. 16. 1; Jer. 37. 4; Zec. 8. 10.

TROUBLES,] as in De. 7. 23; 28. 20; 1 Sa. 5. 9, 11; 14. 20; Prov. 15. 16; Isa. 22. 5; Eze. 7. 7; 22. 5; Amos 3. 9; Zec. 14. 13.

6. BEATEN DOWN,] not 'destroyed,' as in C.V.

ADVERSITY,] or 'distress,' as in Ge. 35. 3, &c.

7. FEEBLE,] or 'fall down,' as in 2 Sa. 4. 1, &c.

REWARD,] or 'hire,' as in Ge. 15. 1, &c.

8. ODED.] Alex. MS. Sept., Vulg., Syr., read as in v. 1, 'Azariah son of Oded.'

PROPHECY,] or proclamation of God's truth.

ABOMINATIONS,] as in De. 29. 17; 1 K. 11. 5, &c.

CAPTURED,] as in 13. 19 perhaps.

RENEWETH,] as in 24. 4, 12; 1 Sa. 11. 14; Job 10. 17; Ps. 51. 10; 104. 30; Isa. 61. 4; La. 5. 21.

PORCH,] as in 1 K. 6. 3; 7. 6, 7, 8, 12, &c.

9. SOJOURNERS,] as in Ge. 15. 13; 23. 4, &c.

SIMEON,] three of the revolting tribes.

WITH HIM,] especially in his contest with the Cushim.

10. THIRD MONTH,] that is, Sivan, about the time of pentecost, or feast of weeks; so Targum.

11. SACRIFICE,] not 'offer,' as in C.V.

12. COVENANT,] with each other and with God.

HEART..SOUL,] as in De. 4. 29, &c.

13. NOT SEEK,] after having entered into the covenant.

PUT TO DEATH,] as in De. 17. 2—6.

14. SWEAR,] lit. 'are sworn,' as in Ge. 21. 23, 24, 31, &c.

SHOUTING,] as in Lev. 23. 24; 25. 9, &c.

TRUMPETS,] as in Nu. 10. 2, 8, 9, 10, &c.

CORNETS,] as in Ex. 19. 16, 19; 20. 18, &c.

15. OATH,] as in Ge. 24. 8; 26. 3, &c.

GOOD WILL,] as in Ge. 49. 6; Ex. 28. 38, &c.

GIVETH REST,] as in 14. 6, &c.

16. MAACHAH,] properly his grand-mother, as in 1 K. 15. 10.

MISTRESS,] as in 1 K. 11. 19; 15. 13; 2 K. 10. 13; Jer. 13. 8; 29. 4, queen-dowager, perhaps; Sept. has 'that she should not minister to Astaste.'

SHRINE,] as in Ex. 34. 13; De. 7. 5, &c.

HORRIBLE THING,] as in 1 K. 15. 13.

CUTTETH DOWN,] as in Ex. 34. 13; Nu. 13. 23, 24, &c.

BEATETH SMALL,] as in Ex. 30. 36, &c.

KIDRON,] which flows between Jerusalem and the mount of the Olives, and falls into the Salt Sea.

17. HIGH PLACES,] where Jehovah himself was worshipped.

PERFECT,] comparatively speaking, as in 1 K. 8. 61; 11. 4; 15. 3, 14; 2 K. 20. 3; 1 Ch. 12. 38; 28. 9; 29. 9, 19, &c. 19. 35TH YEAR,] B.C. 940.

XVI. 1. BAASHA,] i.e. 'evil;' see 1 K. 15. 17; Jer. 41. 9, &c.
RAMAH,] in Benjamin; see Jos. 18. 25, &c.
COMING IN,] as in 15. 9 they are said to do.
2. TREASURES,] which were increased from time to time by gifts and spoils.
BEN-HADAD,] i.e. 'son of shouting.'
DAMASCUS,] as in 1 K. 11. 24; 14. 18, &c.
3. COVENANT,] of friendship and amity.
BREAK,] as in 1 K. 15. 19, &c.
4. IJON,] i.e. 'ruin,' as in 1 K. 15. 20.
DAN,] as in Jos. 19. 47; Jud. 18. 29, &c.
ABEL-MAIM.] See 2 Sa. 20. 14, 15, &c.
STORES,] as in Ex. 1. 11; 1 K. 9. 19; 2 Ch. 8. 4, 6; 17. 12; 32. 28.
NAPHTALI,] of which the above mentioned places were parts.
5. REST,] lit. 'keep sabbath.'
6. STONES ... WOOD,] which had been gathered together.
GEBA,] as in Jos. 18. 24; 21. 17.
MIZPAH,] as in Jos. 18. 26.
7. HANANI,] i.e. 'my grace;' compare 19. 2; 20. 34; 1 K. 16. 1.
SEER,] as in 1 Sa. 9. 9, 11, 18, 19, &c.
LEANING,] or 'being supported by,' as in 13. 18; 14. 11; 16. 7, 8.
ESCAPED,] capture and destruction.
8. CUSHIM..LUBIM,] under Zerah, as in 14. 9; 12. 3.
9. GO TO AND FRO,] as in Da. 12. 4; Amos 8. 12; Zec. 4. 10; see Nu. 11. 8, &c.
SHEW HIMSELF STRONG,] as in Nu. 13. 20, &c.
PERFECT,] as in 15. 17, &c.
FOOLISH,] as in 1 Sa. 13. 13, &c.
WARS,] or 'battles,' as in Ge. 14. 2, 8, &c.
10. ANGRY,] as in Neh. 4. 1; Ps. 112. 10; Ecc. 5. 17; 7. 9; Eze. 16. 42.
TORTURE,] lit. 'overturning,' as in Jer. 20. 2, 3; 29. 26; see De. 29. 23, &c.
RAGE,] as in 28. 9; Prov. 19. 12; Isa. 30. 30; Jon. 1. 15; Mic. 7. 9.
OPPRESSETH,] as in De. 28. 33; Jud.10.8,&c.
11. MATTERS,] not 'acts,' as in C.V.
12. DISEASED,] as in 1 K. 15. 23; Ge. 48. 1, &c.
EXCESSIVE,] or 'at the highest' point.
PHYSICIANS,] as in Ge. 50. 2; Ex. 15. 26; 2 K. 20. 5; Job 13. 4; Ps. 103. 3; 147. 3; Jer. 8. 22.
13. LIETH,] as in Ge. 47. 30, &c.
41ST YEAR,] two years after his disease began.
14. GRAVES,] as in Ge. 23. 4, 6, 9, 20, &c.
CITY OF DAVID,] that is, Zion, as in 2 Sa. 5. 7, the usual burial-place of the kings of Judah.
BED,] as in Ge. 49. 4; Ex. 8. 3; 21. 18, &c.
SPICES,] as in Ex. 25. 6; 30. 23; 35. 8, &c.
PERFUMED WORK,] as in Ex. 30. 25; 1 Ch. 9. 30.
BURNING,] as in 21. 19; see Ge. 11. 3, &c.

XVII. 1. JEHOSHAPHAT,] i.e. 'Jah has judged,' as in 1 K. 15. 24.

STRENGTHENETH HIMSELF,] as in Ge. 48. 2, &c.
2. FENCED CITIES,] as in Nu. 13. 28; De. 1. 28, &c.
GARRISONS,] as in 1 Sa. 10. 5; 13. 3, 4, &c.
CAPTURED,] as in 15. 8.
3. FIRST WAYS,] as the best, wherein he served God most faithfully; Sept. omits 'David.'
BAALIM,] as in 1 K. 15. 24; 16. 32.
4. ISRAEL,] which was almost wholly given to idolatry, as in 1 K. 12. 28.
5. ESTABLISH,] lit. 'make right or ready, as in Ge. 43. 16; 43. 25; Ex. 16. 5, &c.
PRESENT,] in token of allegiance and respect; see 1 Sa. 10. 27; 1 K. 10. 25.
6. HIGH,] as in 26. 16; 32. 25; 1 Sa. 10. 23.
TURNED ASIDE,] by destroying and prohibiting them; but see 20. 33.
7. BEN-HAIL,] i.e. 'son of might or valour or worth.'
OBADIAH,] i.e. 'servant of Jah.'
ZECHARIAH,] i.e. 'remembered of Jah.'
NETHANEEL,] i.e. 'given of God.'
MICHAIAH,] i.e. 'who is like Jah?'
TEACH,] both the civil laws of the kingdom, and the sacred.
8. SHEMAIAH,] i.e. 'heard of Jah.'
NETHANIAH,] i.e. 'given of Jah.'
ZEBADIAH,] i.e. 'endowed of Jah.'
AZAHEL,] i.e. 'made of God.'
SHEMIRAMOTH,] as in 1 Ch. 15. 18, 20; 16. 5
JEHONATHAN,] i.e. 'Jah has given.'
ADONIJAH,] i.e. 'my lord is Jah.'
TOBIJAH,] i.e. 'goodness of Jah.'
TOB ADONIJAH,] i.e. 'goodness of the lord Jah.'
ELISHAMA,] i.e. 'my God has heard.'
JEHORAM,] i.e. 'Jah is high.'
9. TEACH,] as in v. 7 above.
BOOK OF THE LAW,] as in De. 28. 61; 30. 10; 31. 26; Jos. 1. 8; 8. 31, 34.
10. FEAR OF JEHOVAH,] as in 1 Sa. 11. 7; 2 Ch. 14. 14, &c.
11. PHILISTINES,] perhaps those about Gerar; see 14. 14, 15.
PRESENT,] as in v. 5 above.
TRIBUTE,] lit. 'burden,' as in Ex. 23. 5, &c.
ARABIANS,] on the east and south of Palestine to the Red Sea.
FLOCK,] consisting of sheep and goats.
RAMS,] as in Ge. 15. 9; 22. 13, &c.
HE-GOATS,] as in Ge. 30. 35; 32. 14; Prov. 30. 31.
12. PALACES,] as in 27. 4; 1 Ch. 29. 1, 19; Ezra 6. 2, &c.
CITIES OF STORE,] as in Ex. 1. 11; 1 K. 9. 19; 2 Ch. 8. 4, 6; 16. 4; 32. 28.
13. WORK,] as in Ge. 2. 2, 3; 33. 14, &c.
14. ADNAH,] i.e. 'pleasure.'
300 CHIEFS,] not 'thousands,' as in the C.V.; see 1 Sa. 6. 19; 1 K. 20. 30; Job 33. 23; Song 4. 4; Isa. 60. 22; Mic. 5. 2.
15. HAND,] as in Jos. 15. 46, &c.
JEHOHANAN,] i.e. 'Jah has grace.'
280 CHIEFS,] as in v. 14 above.
16. AMASIAH,] i.e. 'lord of Jah.'
ZICHRI,] i.e. 'mindful.'
WILLINGLY OFFERING HIMSELF] as a soldier.
200 CHIEFS,] as in v. 14 above.

17. BENJAMIN,] which adhered to Judah, when the ten tribes broke off.
ELIADA,] i.e. 'God has known.'
200 CHIEFS,] as in v. 14 above.
18. JEHOZABAD,] i.e. 'Jah has endowed.'
180 CHIEFS,] as in v. 14 above.
19. FORTRESS,] as in Nu. 13. 19; 32. 17, 36; Jos. 10. 20, &c.

XVIII. 1. RICHES..HONOUR,] as stated in 17. 5.
JOINETH AFFINITY,] by marrying his son Joram to Athaliah, a daughter of Ahab and Jezebel.
2. GOETH DOWN] from Jerusalem his capital city; see 1 K. 22. 2.
SACRIFICETH.] All important events were anciently marked by special sacrifices to God.
PERSUADETH,] by some reasons not mentioned.
RAMOTH-GILEAD,] a city of Gad, beyond Jordan, as in Jos. 20. 8, &c.
3. AS I—SO THOU, &c.] The C.V. unnecessarily transposes the language, which is elliptical.
4. SEEK..JEHOVAH,] regarding the propriety of the enterprize.
5. THE PROPHETS] of Baal, not of Jehovah, those left alive by Elijah and the people.
400 MEN,] as in 1 K. 18. 19; 22. 6.
WE GO..I FORBEAR,] lit. 'cease,' from pursuing the plan adopted.
THE KING,] but which king is not indicated, whether the king of Israel or of Aram.
6. JEHOVAH,] whom he himself served.
7. HATED] without a just cause.
PROPHESYING,] or proclaiming the truth of God.
MICAIAH,] i.e. 'who is like Jah?' or 'like him;' see 1 K. 22. 8, 24.
IMLAH,] i.e. 'he fills.'
THE KING,] that is, Ahab.
8. EUNUCH,] as in Ge. 37. 36, &c.
HASTEN,] as in Ge. 18. 6; 19. 22; 45. 9; Jud. 9. 48; 1 Sa. 9. 12; 23. 27; 2 Sa. 15. 14; 1 K. 22. 9; Est. 5. 5; 6. 10.
9. THRONE,] in the midst of the council.
GARMENTS,] suitable for their rank.
THRESHING-FLOOR,] as in Ge. 50. 10, 11, &c.
THE GATE,] where in the east justice is administrated.
10. ZEDEKIAH,] i.e. 'rightness of Jah.'
CHENAANAH,] i.e. 'a Canaanitess.'
IRON,] indicative of great strength.
11. PUSH,] as in De. 33. 7; 1 K. 22. 11; Ps. 44. 5; Eze. 34. 21; Da. 8. 4.
CONSUMED,] or 'ended' them.
PROSPER,] as in v. 14; 20. 20; 1 K. 22. 12, 15; Neh. 1. 11; Ps. 118. 25.
KING,] as in v. 5 above.
12. ONE MONTH,] as in 1 K. 22. 13.
GOOD,] that is, agreeable to his wishes.
13. LIVETH,] as in Nu. 14. 21, 28; Jos. 3. 10; Jud. 8. 19, &c.
MY GOD,] he whom I worship as such.
SPEAK,] as in Nu. 22. 38, &c.
14. WE GO..I FORBEAR,] as in v. 5 above.
THEY] are given, that is, the Aramaeans.
15. ADJURING,] lit. 'causing to swear,' as in 1 K. 22. 16.

16. SEEN] in spiritual vision, as in Ge. 32. 30, &c.
MOUNTAINS] of Israel, where flocks were accustomed to graze.
NO SHEPHERD,] exposed to every enemy that might assail them.
MASTERS,] or 'lords.'
17. GOOD..EVIL,] as in v. 7 above.
18. SITTING,] as in 1 K. 22. 19; Ps. 9. 4; 47. 8; Isa. 6. 1.
HOST,] as in Ge. 2. 1; De. 4. 19; 17. 3, &c.
RIGHT AND LEFT,] as in Ex. 14. 22, 29; 2 Sa. 16. 16, &c.
19. ENTICE,] as in Ex. 22. 16, &c.
20. THE SPIRIT,] not 'a spirit,' as in C.V.
21. SPIRIT OF FALSEHOOD,] as in 1 K. 22. 22.
ABLE] to entice him to his ruin.
DO SO,] a permission, not a command.
22. EVIL,] that is, misfortune and calamity.
23. CHEEK,] as in 1 K. 22. 24; Job 16. 10; Ps. 3. 7; La. 3. 30; Mic. 5. 1.
PASSED OVER,] as in 1 K. 22. 24.
24. INNERMOST CHAMBERS,] as in 1 K. 20. 30, &c.
HIDDEN] for fear of punishment, as a false prophet.
25. AMON,] i.e. 'workman, artificer.'
JOASH,] as in 1 K. 22. 26.
26. HOUSE OF RESTRAINT,] as in 1 K. 22. 27; 2 K. 17. 4; 25. 27, 29; Isa. 42. 7, 22; Jer. 37. 15, 18; 52. 33.
OPPRESSION,] as in Ex. 3. 9, &c.
27. SPOKEN,] as in Nu. 16. 29; De. 18. 20, &c.
PEOPLES] of Israel and Judah.
28. GOETH UP] from Samaria his capital city.
29. DISGUISE HIMSELF,] as in 1 Sa. 28. 8; 1 K. 20. 38; 22. 30; Job 30. 18.
GARMENTS] of royalty, as the leader of the host in battle.
30. CHARIOTEERS,] not 'chariots,' as in C.V.
SMALL..GREAT,] as far as possible.
ISRAEL,] whom he looked upon as the chief opponent.
31. JEHOSHAPHAT,] dressed in his royal robes.
CRIETH OUT] for help, as the original word implies.
HELPED,] agreeably to the prayer offered.
ENTICETH,] as in De. 13. 6; Jos. 15. 18, &c.
32. TURN BACK] from their pursuit of him.
33. BOW,] apparently in the camp of Aram.
SIMPLICITY,] as in 1 K. 22. 34; Isa. 41. 7.
JOININGS,] as in 1 K. 22. 34; Isa. 41. 7.
COAT OF MAIL,] as in 26. 14; 1 K. 22. 34; 1 Sa. 17. 5; Neh. 4. 16; Isa. 59. 17.
TURN THY HAND,] as in 1 K. 22. 34.
CAMP,] into the background of the battle.
BECOME SICK] for loss of blood.
34. INCREASED,] lit. 'goeth up.'
STAYED UP,] as in 1 K. 22. 35.
GOING IN,] as in Ge. 15. 12, 17, &c.

XIX. 1. TURNETH BACK] from Ramoth-Gilead, as in 18. 28, after the death of Ahab.
2. JEHU,] i.e. 'he is,' as in 20. 34; 1 K. 16. 1.
HANANI,] i.e. 'my grace,' as in 16. 7, 10.
SEER,] as in 1 Sa. 9. 9, &c.
WICKED..HATING JEHOVAH,] that is, Ahab and Israel; see Ps. 139. 21.

WRATH,] which was manifested in his danger from the Moabites, &c., in the violent death of his sons and grandsons, as in 20. 1; 21. 4; 22. 8; 32. 25.

3. FOUND,] by the all searching God, who looks for the good as well as for the evil.

SHRINES,] where idols were worshipped.

PREPARED,] *or* 'made ready *or* established;' see 30. 19; Eze. 7. 10.

4. JERUSALEM,] the capital city of Judah.

BEER-SHEBA,] i.e. 'the well of the oath,' on the south of Judah.

EPHRAIM,] on the north, towards Samaria.

GOETH OUT] to visit and inspect them personally.

BRINGETH BACK,] by persuasive teachings, as in 17. 7—9.

5. ESTABLISHETH,] *lit.* 'causeth to stand.'

FENCED CITIES,] as in 17. 2; compare 1 Ch. 26. 29, 32.

6. DOING,] that it be right and just, according to law and equity.

JEHOVAH,] who was the real and sole judge of Israel; see De. 1. 17.

JUDGMENT] between right and wrong; see Ps. 82. 1.

7. FEAR OF JEHOVAH,] as in 1 Sa. 11. 7; 2 Ch. 14. 14; 17. 10, &c.

PERVERSENESS,] as in 2 Sa. 3. 34; Ps. 92. 15; Zeph. 3. 5; Mal. 2. 6, &c.

ACCEPTANCE,] *lit.* 'lifting up.'

BRIBE,] as in Ex. 23. 8; De. 10. 17, &c.

8. JUDGMENT OF JEHOVAH,] as in Ps. 19. 9; Isa. 58. 2; Jer. 5. 4, 5; 8. 7.

STRIFE,] *or* 'controversy, contention.'

AND THEY TURN BACK TO.] Sept. and Vulg. read 'inhabitants of;' so Kennicott.

9. CHARGE,] *or* 'precept.'

FAITHFULNESS,] *or* 'stedfastness,' as in Ex. 17. 12; De. 32. 4, &c.

PERFECT HEART,] as in 1 K. 8. 61. 11. 4; 15. 3, 14, &c.

10. STRIFE,] as in v. 8 above.

BLOOD AND BLOOD,] as in De. 17. 8.

LAW AND COMMAND,] as in Ex. 24. 12, &c.

STATUTES AND JUDGMENTS,] as in Ex. 15. 25, &c.

WARNED,] *lit.* 'made clear *or* shining.'

GUILTY,] as in Lev. 4. 13, 22, 27; 5. 2, 3, 4, 5, &c.

WRATH,] as in v. 2 above.

11. AMARIAH,] i.e. 'said by Jah.'

ZEBADIAH,] i.e. 'endowed by Jah.'

ISHMAEL,] i.e. 'God hears.'

LEADER,] as in 1 Sa. 9. 16, &c.

OFFICERS,] as in Ex. 5. 6, 10, 14, 15, 19; Nu. 11. 16; De. 1. 15; 16. 18; 20. 5, 8, 9; 29. 10; 31. 28; Jos. 1. 10; 3. 2; 8. 33, &c.

DO,] all that is commanded you.

GOOD,] in heart and life; as in Ecc. 2. 26.

XX. 1. SONS OF MOAB,] beyond the Salt Sea, eastward.

SONS OF AMMON,] beyond the Jordan, north of Moab; compare Ps. 83. 8.

THE PEOPLES,] round about them, enemies of Israel, especially Edom; see 10, 22, 23; Sept. 'Mineans,' as in Jud. 10. 12.

2. THE SEA,] that is, the Salt Sea.

ARAM,] on the north of Canaan.

HAZEZON-TAMAR,] as in Ge. 14. 7, afterwards called

EN-GEDI,] i.e. 'fountain of a kid.'

3. FEARETH,] the wrath of the Lord, as in 19. 2.

SETTETH,] *lit.* 'giveth.'

FAST,] as in 2 Sa. 12. 16; 1 K. 21. 9, 12, &c.

4. ENQUIRE,] *or* 'seek,' as in 11. 16.

5. STANDETH,] in prayer and confession.

NEW COURT,] of the priests; compare 15. 8; 2 K. 21. 5; 23. 12.

6. FATHERS,] Abraham, Isaac, and Jacob.

HEAVENS,] high above all things.

RULING,] as in 1 Ch. 29. 12; Ps. 22. 26; 59. 13; 66. 7; 89. 9; Isa. 40. 10; Mic. 5. 2.

POWER AND MIGHT,] as in 1 Ch. 29. 12; Est. 10. 2.

STATION HIMSELF,] in opposition or contrariety.

7. OUR GOD,] the direct object of our worship.

DISPOSSESSED,] by the hands of Moses, Joshua, and others.

GIVE] it in actual possession, as promised in Ge. 12. 7.

8. DWELL,] up to the time of the present invasion.

BUILD,] by the hands of David and Solomon, as in 1 Ch. 28. 1—6.

9. EVIL,] that is, misfortune of any kind, especially the

SWORD,] of the enemy from without, or

JUDGMENT,] of any kind from the direct hand of God, such as

PESTILENCE,] because of unforgiven sin, or

FAMINE,] by reason of continued drought.

NAME,] that is, renown, character, as the God of Israel.

CRY,] for help, as the original word implies.

DISTRESS,] as in Ge. 35. 3; 42. 21, &c.

SAVE,] as promised in 1 K. 8. 33, 37; 9. 3.

10. AMMON . . MOAB,] as in v. 1 above.

MOUNT SEIR,] as in v. 22, 23.

NOT GRANT.] See De. 2. 5, 9, 19.

11. RECOMPENSING,] *or* 'doing against us,' as in Ge. 50. 15, 17, &c.

THY POSSESSION,] where he dwells, and which he had given to his people.

12. UPON,] *or* 'among them.'

NO POWER,] as in 14. 11; 22. 9; 1 Sa. 28. 20; 30. 4; 2 K. 19. 3; Ezra 10. 13; Job 26. 2; Isa. 37. 3; 50. 2; Da. 8. 7, 22; 10. 8, 16, 17, &c.

WE DO,] whether it be for the best or not.

EYES,] for help, and for guidance, as thy servants.

13. STANDING,] along with the king, in v. 5.

INFANTS,] as in Ge. 34. 29; 43. 8, &c.

14. JAHAZIEL,] i.e. 'God sees.'

ZECHARIAH,] i.e. 'remembered of Jah.'

BENAIAH,] i.e. 'built up by Jah.'

JEIEL,] i.e. 'heaps of Jah.'

MATTANIAH,] i.e. 'gift of Jah.'

ASAPH,] i.e. 'he gathered.'

BEEN,] as in Nu. 24. 2; Jud. 3. 10, &c.

15. ATTEND,] as in Job 13. 6; 33. 31; Ps. 5. 2; 17. 1; 55. 2; 61. 2; 86. 6; 142. 6; Prov. 4. 1, 20; 5. 1, 7, 24; Isa. 28. 23; 34. 1; 49. 1; 51. 4; Jer. 6. 17; 18. 19; Da. 9. 19; Hos. 5. 1 Mic. 1. 2.

NOT FOR YOU,] being beyond their power

16. ZIZ,] i.e. a 'blossom, fringe;' a place not mentioned elsewhere in S.S.
VALLEY,] as in Ge. 26. 17, 19; 32. 23, &c.
JERUEL,] i.e. 'foundation of God;' not mentioned elsewhere.
17. NOT FOR YOU,] as in v. 15.
STATION YOURSELVES,] as in Ex. 8. 20; 19. 13; 14. 13; Nu. 23. 3, 15; De. 31. 14; 1 Sa. 10. 19; 12. 7, 16; 2 Sa. 18. 30; Job 33. 5; Jer. 46. 4, 14.
SALVATION,] or 'safety,' as in Ge. 49. 18; Ex. 14. 13; 15. 2, &c.
WITH YOU,] to bless, and guide, and protect.
18. BOWETH,] the head, as in 29. 30; Ge. 24. 26, 48; 43. 28; Ex. 4. 31; 12. 27; 34. 8; Nu. 22. 31; 1 Sa. 24. 8; 28. 14; 1 K. 1. 16, 31; 1 Ch. 29. 20; Neh. 8. 6.
EARTH,] in token of reverence.
FALLEN,] down on their knees.
BOW THEMSELVES,] as in Ge. 37. 10; Lev. 26. 1; Jud. 2. 19; 1 Sa. 1. 3; 2. 36; 2 Sa. 15. 5; 2 K. 5. 18; Isa. 2. 20, &c.
19. KOHATHITES,] sons of Kohath, as in Nu. 3. 27, 30; 4. 18, 34, 37; 10. 21; 26. 57, &c.
KORHITES,] sons of Korah, as in Ex. 6. 24; Nu. 26. 58, &c.
GIVE PRAISE,] as in 1 Ch. 16. 4, 36, &c.
20. TEKOA,] part of the pasture-land of Judah, as in 2 Sa. 14. 2; 1 Ch. 2. 24; Jer. 6. 1; Amos 1. 1.
REMAIN STEDFAST,] as in Ge. 15. 6; 45. 26, &c.
YE BECOME STEDFAST,] as in 1. 9; 6. 17; Ge. 42. 20; 2 Sa. 7. 16; 1 K. 8. 26; 1 Ch. 17. 23, 24, &c.
PROSPER,] as in 18. 11, 14; 1 K. 22. 12, 15; Neh. 1. 11; Ps. 118. 25.
21. TAKETH COUNSEL,] as in 1 K. 12. 6, 8, 28, &c.
APPOINTETH,] lit. 'causeth to stand.'
SINGERS,] as in 1 Ch. 6. 33; 9. 33; 15. 16, 19, 27; 2 Ch. 5. 12, 13: 23. 13; 29. 28; 35. 15; Ezra 2. 42, &c.
GIVING PRAISE,] as in v. 19 above.
HONOUR OF HOLINESS,] as in 1 Ch. 16. 29; Ps. 29. 2; 96. 9.
ARMED MEN,] as in Nu. 31. 5; 32. 21, &c.
GIVE THANKS,] or 'confession,' as in 1 Ch. 16. 8, 34, &c.
KINDNESS,] not 'mercy,' as in C.V.
22. SINGING,] as in 1 K. 8. 28; 22. 36; 2 Ch. 6. 19; Ps. 17. 1; 30. 5; 42. 4; 47. 1; 61. 1; 88. 2; 105. 43, &c.
AMBUSHMENTS,] as in Jud. 9. 25.
23. DEVOTE,] as in De. 3. 6; 7. 2; 20. 17, &c.
DESTROY,] each other to the uttermost, as in De. 1. 27; 7. 24; 9. 8, 18, 20, 25; 28. 48, 63, &c.
24. WATCHTOWER,] as in Isa. 21. 8.
WILDERNESS] of Jeruel, as in v. 16.
CARCASES,] as in Ge. 15. 11; Lev. 26. 30, &c.
NONE ESCAPED,] as in 2 Sa. 15. 14; Ezra 9. 14; Jer. 50. 29; Da. 11. 42; Joel 2. 3.
25. SPOIL,] as in Ge. 49. 27; Ex. 15. 9, &c.
GOODS,] as in Ge. 12. 5; 13. 6; 14. 11, 12, 16, 21, &c.
CARCASES.] Eight MSS. read 'garments.'
DESIRABLE VESSELS,] as in 32. 27; 36. 10; Jer. 25. 34; Da. 11. 8; Hos. 13. 15; Neh. 2. 9.

PROHIBITION,] or 'burden,' as in Ex. 23. 5, &c.
26. BLESSING,] in Heb. 'Berachah.'
27. REJOICE,] as in De. 24. 5; Jud. 9. 13 Ezra 6. 22; Neh. 12. 43; Ps. 19. 8; 30. 1; 45. 8; 46. 4; 86. 4; 90. 15; 92. 4; 104. 15, &c.
28. PSALTERIES,] as in 1 Sa. 10. 5; 2 Sa. 6. 5, &c.
HARPS,] as in Ge. 4. 21; 31. 27; 1 Sa. 10. 5, &c.
TRUMPETS,] as in Nu. 10. 2, 8, 9, 10; 31. 6, &c.
29. FEAR OF GOD,] as in Ps. 36. 1; compare 1 Sa. 11. 7, &c.
30. QUIET,] as in 14. 5.
GIVETH REST,] as in 15. 15.
31. 35 YEARS.] See 1 K. 22. 42.
25 YEARS,] being sixty years old at his death.
AZUBAH,] i.e. a 'forsaken one.'
SHILHI,] i.e. 'my shoot or dart,' as in 1 K. 22. 42.
32. ASA,] i.e. 'a healer.'
RIGHT,] or 'upright.'
33. HIGH PLACES,] as in 17. 6; 1 K. 14. 23, &c.
NOT PREPARED,] or 'made ready.'
34. MATTERS,] not 'acts,' as in C.V.
JEHU,] i.e. 'he is.'
BEEN MENTIONED,] as in 1 K. 16. 1, 7.
35. AHAZIAH,] i.e. 'laid hold of by Jah.'
DID WICKEDLY,] against God, his people, and himself.
36. JOINETH HIM,] though at first unwilling; see 1 K. 22. 49.
TARSHISH,] as in 1 K. 22. 48.
EZION-GEBER,] a port of the Red Sea; see 1 K. 9. 26.
37. PROPHESY,] or 'shew himself a prophet.'
ELEAZAR,] i.e. 'my God is help.'
DODAVAH,] i.e. 'love of Jah.'
MARESHAH,] of Judah, as in Jos. 15. 44.
BROKEN UP,] not 'broken' merely, as in C.V.
BROKEN,] lit. 'shivered,' as in 1 K. 22. 48.

XXI. 1. LIETH,] as in 1 K. 22. 50.
CITY OF DAVID,] that is, Zion, the usual burying-place of the kings.
JEHORAM,] i.e. 'Jah is high.'
2. AZARIAH,] i.e. 'help of Jah.'
JEHIEL,] i.e. 'God lives.'
ZECHARIAH,] i.e. 'remembered of Jah.'
AZARIAH,] a second son probably of the same name, the first having died.
MICHAEL,] i.e. 'who is like God?'
SHEPHATIAH,] i.e. 'judge of Jah.'
ISRAEL,] Sept., Vulg., Syr., and Arabic Versions read 'Judah;' so also 40 Heb. MSS.
3. GIFTS,] to make them happy and contented.
PRECIOUS THINGS,] as in 32. 23; Ge. 24. 53; Ezra 1. 6.
FENCED CITIES,] for them to rule in, under their brother Jehoram.
FIRST-BORN,] according to the law in De. 21. 16, 17.
4. STRENGTHENETH HIMSELF,] on the throne against all competitors.
SWORD,] as Abimelech did, in Jud. 9. 5.

HEADS,] who probably opposed his cruelties.

5. 32 YEARS,] as in 2 K. 8. 17.

8 YEARS,] till B.C. 884.

ISRAEL,] that is, the ten tribes.

WIFE,] as in 2 K. 8. 17, 26.

EVIL THING,] even idolatry.

7. NOT BEEN WILLING,] as in De. 10. 10, &c.

LAMP,] as in 1 K. 11. 36; 15. 1; 2 K. 8. 19.

8. EDOM,] according to Ge. 27. 40.

REVOLTED,] *lit.* 'transgressed,' as in 1 K. 8. 50; Ge. 31. 36; 50. 17, &c.

HAND,] that is, power and authority.

9. PASSETH OVER,] the desert of Zin, and the ascent of Maale-Akrabbim.

COMING ROUND,] as in 2 K. 8. 21, &c.

10. LIBNAH,] as in Jos. 10. 29; 21. 13, &c.

FORSAKEN,] as in v. 6 above.

11. MOUNTAINS,] a common custom in the east.

WHOREDOM,] against God by following idols.

COMPELLETH,] as in De. 13. 5, 10, 13; 30. 1; 2 Sa. 15. 4; 2 K. 17. 21; 2 Ch. 13. 9; Ps. 5. 10, &c.

12. WRITING,] as in Ex. 32. 16; 39. 30; De. 10. 4; 2 Ch. 35. 4; 36. 22; Ezra 1. 1; Isa. 38. 9.

ELIJAH,] written before his translation to heaven.

FATHER,] who prospered in all his ways.

ASA,] his grandfather, as in 14. 2—6.

13. ISRAEL,] especially Ahab, as in 1 K. 16. 30—33.

WHOREDOM,] as in v. 11 above.

SLAIN,] with the sword, as in v. 4.

14. SMITING,] as in Ex. 9. 14; Nu. 14. 37; 16. 48, 49, 50; 25. 8, 9, 18; 26. 1; 31. 16; 1 Sa. 4. 17; 6. 1; 2 Sa. 17. 9, &c.

15. SICKNESSES,] as in De. 7. 15; 28. 59, 61; 1 K. 17. 17; 2 K. 1. 2; 8. 8, 9; 13. 14; 2 Ch. 16. 12; 21. 18, 19; Ps. 41. 3, &c.

DISEASE,] as in Prov. 18. 14, &c.

DAY BY DAY,] for two years, as in v. 19.

16. WAKETH UP,] as in 36. 22; De. 32. 11; 1 Ch. 5. 26; Ezra 1. 1, &c.; Job 8. 6; 41. 10; Ps. 35. 23; 57. 8; 108. 2, &c.

PHILISTINES,] who brought tribute to Jehoshaphat, as in 17. 11.

ARABIANS,] on the south-east of Palestine.

CUSHIM,] as in Nu. 12. 1; 2 Sa. 18. 21, &c.

17. REND,] several cities from under its authority.

TAKE CAPTIVE,] to their own lands, afar off.

JEHOAHAZ,] also called Ahaziah and Azariah, as in 22. 1, 6; see v. 14.

18. PLAGUED,] as in v. 15 above.

HEALING,] as in 36. 16; Prov. 4. 22; 6. 15; 12. 18; 13. 17; 16. 24; 29. 1; Jer. 8. 15; 14. 19; 33. 6; Mal. 4. 2.

19. WITH,] along with his sickness, not 'by reason of' it, as in C.V.

DISEASES,] as in De. 29. 22; Ps. 103. 3; Jer. 14. 18; 16. 4.

BURNING,] as they did for his grandfather Asa, in 16. 14.

20. 32 YEARS,] as in 2 K. 8. 17.

8 YEARS,] as in v. 5 above.

WITHOUT DESIRE,] of remaining any longer, on the part of himself or of his subjects.

CITY OF DAVID,] that is, Zion, as in v. 1.

XXII. 1. AHAZIAH,] *or* Jehoahaz, as in 21. 17.

THE TROOP] of Philistines, as in 21. 16.

2. 42,] in 1 K. 8. 26 it is 22; so (Sept.) Syr., Arab., Versions.

ATHALIAH,] i.e. 'afflicted of Jah.'

OMRI,] father of Ahab, as in 2 K. 8. 18, 26.

3. AHAB,] as his father Jehoram had done, in 21. 6; 2 K. 8. 27.

COUNSELLOR,] as in v. 4: 25. 16, &c.

TO DO WICKEDLY,] *or* 'wrongly,' as in 20. 35, &c.

4. EVIL THING,] as in 2 K. 8. 27.

DESTRUCTION,] as in Ex. 12. 13; 2 K. 23. 23; 2 Ch. 20. 23; Jer. 5. 26; 51. 25; Eze. 5. 16; 9. 6; 21. 31; 25. 15; Da. 10. 8.

5. WALKED.] Compare Ps. 1. 1, &c.

JEHORAM,] i.e. 'Jah is high.'

HAZAEL,] as in 2 K. 8. 15, 28.

RAMOTH-GILEAD,] which remained in the hands of Aram, after Ahab's death.

RAMAH,] of Gilead, as in 2 K. 8. 28, 29.

6. AZARIAH,] *or* Ahaziah, as in v. 1; *or* Jehoahaz, as in 21. 17.

JEZREEL,] as in 2 K. 9. 15.

SICK,] by reason of his wounds.

7. FROM GOD,] as in 10. 15; Jud. 14. 4, 1 K. 12. 15.

GONE FORTH] unsuspecting danger from JEHU,] as in 2 K. 9. 21.

ANOINTED,] as in 2 K. 9. 1, 2.

8. EXECUTING JUDGMENT,] pronounced beforehand by the Lord's prophets.

SLAYETH] forty-two of them, as in 2 K. 10. 12—14.

9. AHAZIAH,] who fled when Joram was wounded.

HIDING HIMSELF,] in Megiddo, (as in 2 K. 8. 28,) a city of Samaria.

JEHU,] who was in Jezreel; see 2 K. 9. 27.

BURY HIM,] in the sepulchre of his fathers, in Jerusalem, as in 2 K. 9. 28.

ALL HIS HEART,] as in 17. 4.

NONE,] left alive of sufficient age and ability.

10. ATHALIAH,] daughter of Ahab, and grand-daughter of Omri, as in 2 K. 8. 18, 26; 11. 1, &c.

DESTROYETH,] as in 2 K. 11. 1; *lit.* 'speaketh,' with them.

11. JEHOSHABEATH,] in 1 K. 11. 2 it is 'Jehosheba.'

JOASH,] i.e. 'Jah is foundation.'

STEALETH,] as in 2 K. 11. 2.

BED-CHAMBERS,] *lit.* 'beds,' as in Ge. 47. 31; 48. 2; 49. 33, &c.

JEHORAM,] as in 21. 1, &c.

JEHOIADA,] i.e. 'Jah hath known.'

AHAZIAH,] as in 21. 1, &c.

12. HOUSE OF GOD,] in the priests' dwellings in the temple.

HIDING HIMSELF,] as in 1 Sa. 14. 22, &c.

REIGNING,] without interruption or fear.

XXIII. 1. SEVENTH YEAR,] after the death of Ahaziah.

STRENGTHENED HIMSELF,] for restoring the kingdom to Joash.

HUNDREDS,] as in Ex. 18. 21, 25, &c.

AZARIAH,] i.e. 'help of Jah.'
JEROHAM,] i.e. 'he is loved.'
ISHMAEL,] i.e. 'God hears.'
JEHOHANAN,] i.e. 'Jah has grace.'
OBED,] i.e. a 'servant.'
MAASEIAH,] i.e. 'work of Jah.'
ADAIAH,] i.e. 'adorned by Jah.'
ELISHAPHAT,] i.e. 'my God has judged.'
ZICHRI,] i.e. 'mindful.'
COVENANT,] to restore the crown to its rightful heir.
2. LEVITES,] of which tribe Jehoiada himself was.
HEADS,] as in Ex. 6. 14, &c.
3. WITH THE KING,] securing mutual rights, as in 2 Sa. 5. 3.
SPAKE,] as in 6. 16; 7. 18; 21. 7; 2 Sa. 7. 12; 1 K. 2. 4; 9. 5.
4. GOING IN] to perform temple-service.
THRESHOLDS] of the temple, as in Jud. 19. 27; 1 K. 14. 17; 2 K. 12. 9, 13; 22. 4; 23. 4; 25. 18, &c.
5. FOUNDATION,] in 2 K. 11. 6 it is 'Sur.'
COURTS] around the temple.
6. MINISTERING] at the altar of the Lord.
HOLY,] that is, set apart for that purpose.
WATCH OF JEHOVAH,] as in Lev. 8. 35; Nu. 9. 23; 1 K. 2. 3; 2 Ch. 13. 11, &c.
7. LEVITES,] in whom Jehoiada had confidence.
WEAPON,] as in Ge. 27. 3; 49. 5, &c.
PUT TO DEATH,] as an intruder and rebel.
8. COMMANDED,] his sacred character giving him authority.
SABBATH,] as in v. 4 above.
COURSES] of the Levites, who had finished their period of service.
9. HEADS,] as in v. 1 above.
SPEARS,] as in 1 Sa. 13. 9, 22; 17. 7, 45, 47, &c.
SHIELDS,] as in Ge. 15. 1; De. 33. 29, &c.
BUCKLERS,] as in 2 Sa. 8. 7; 2 K. 11. 10; 1 Ch. 18. 7; Song 4. 4; Jer. 51. 11; Eze. 27. 11.
HOUSE OF GOD,] laid up as trophies of victory, most probably; see 1 K. 11. 10.
10. STATIONETH,] lit. 'causeth to stand.'
DART,] as in 32. 5; Neh. 4. 17, 23; Job 33. 18; 36. 12; Song 4. 13; Joel 2. 8.
SHOULDER,] as in Ex. 26. 14, 15; 28. 7, 12, 15, 27, &c.
ALTAR,] of burnt-offering.
HOUSE,] the most holy of holies.
11. CROWN,] as in Ex. 29. 6; 39. 30; Lev. 8. 9; 21. 12; Nu. 6. 4, 5, 7, 8, 9, 12, 13,18, 19, 21; 2 Sa. 1. 10; 2 K. 11. 10; Ps. 89. 39; 132. 18; Prov. 27. 24; Jer. 7. 29; Zec. 9. 16.
TESTIMONY,] as in Ex. 16. 34; 25. 16, 21, 22, &c.
ANOINT,] as in 1 Ch. 11. 3; 29. 22, &c.
LIVE,] as in 1 Sa. 10. 24, &c.
12. ATHALIAH,] the young king's grandmother.
RUNNING] backward and forwards to the temple.
PRAISING,] as in 1 Ch. 23. 5; 29. 13; 2 Ch. 20. 21; 30. 21.
13. STANDING,] as in 2 K. 11. 14, &c.
HIS PILLAR,] as in 2 K. 11. 14; compare 2 Ch. 34. 1; 2 K. 23. 3.
TRUMPETS,] as in 2 K. 11. 14, &c.

SHOUTING,] as in Jos. 6. 9; 2 K. 11. 14; Neh. 4. 18; Prov. 11. 14; 17. 18; 22. 26.
SONG,] as in 5. 13; 7. 6; 34. 12; 1 Ch. 15. 16; 16. 42; Neh. 12. 36; Amos 6. 5.
TEACHERS,] as in Isa. 47. 13; Jer. 16. 21; Da. 3. 19.
PRAISE] God and the king.
CONSPIRACY,] as in 15. 12; 25. 27; 1 K. 16. 20; 2 K. 11. 14; 12. 20; 14. 19; 15. 15, 30; 17. 4; Isa. 8. 12; Jer. 11. 9; Eze. 22. 25.
14. HEADS,] as in v. 1, 9.
INSPECTORS,] as in Nu. 31. 14, 48, &c.
ROWS,] as in 2 K. 11. 8 15; 6. 9, &c.
HOUSE,] lest it should be defiled.
15. SIDES,] lit. 'hands.'
HORSES,] as in 2 K. 11. 16.
16. PEOPLE] of Judah and Benjamin, as in v. 2.
17. BAAL,] perhaps on the mount of the olives, called the mount of corruption, as in 1 K. 11. 15; 23. 13.
IMAGES,] as in Nu. 33. 52; 1 Sa. 6. 5, 11, &c.
MATTAN,] i.e. 'a gift,' as in 2 K. 11. 18.
18. OFFICES,] as in Nu. 3. 32, 36; 4. 16; 16. 29, &c.
APPORTIONED,] as in 1 Ch. 23. 6, 30, 31; 24. 1, &c.
WRITTEN] in Nu. 28. 2.
HANDS,] as in 1 Ch. 25. 2, 6.
19. UNCLEAN,] those ceremonially defiled, as in Lev. 5. 2; 7. 19, 21, &c.
20. HONOURABLE ONES,] as in Ex. 15. 10; Jud. 5. 13, 25; 1 Sa. 4. 8; Neh. 3. 5, &c.
RULERS,] as in Ge. 24. 2; 45. 8, 26; Jos. 12 2, 5; Jud. 14. 4; 15. 11; 2 Sa. 23. 3; 1 K. 4. 21; 1 Ch. 29. 12; 2 Ch. 7. 18; 9. 26; 20. 6.
HIGH GATE,] as in 27. 3; 2 K. 15. 35.
TO SIT] as king, thus formally taking possession of it.
21. REJOICE] at the peaceful settlement of the rightful heir to the throne.
QUIET,] as in 2 K. 11. 20.
SWORD,] as in v. 15 above.

XXIV. 1. SEVEN YEARS,] as in 2 K. 11. 4, 21; 22. 1, &c.
40 YEARS,] the same length of period as David, Solomon, &c.
ZIBIAH,] i.e. 'a roe.'
BEER-SHEBA,] in the tribe of Simeon, on the extreme south of Canaan.
2. RIGHT,] or 'upright,' as in Ex. 15. 26, &c.
3. TWO WIVES,] not necessarily at the same time.
4. WITH THE HEART,] not 'in,' as in C.V.
RENEW,] as in v. 12; 15. 8; 1 Sa. 11. 14; Job 10. 17; Ps. 51. 10; 103. 5; 104. 30; Isa. 61. 4; La. 5. 21.
MONEY,] lit. 'silver,' as in Ge. 13. 2, &c.
NOT HASTED] from some cause not mentioned.
6. HEAD] of the priests.
LEVITES,] who were given to the priests to minister to them.
TRIBUTE,] as in v. 9; Ge. 43. 34; Jud. 20. 38, 40; 2 Sa. 11. 8; Est. 2. 18, &c.
TENT OF THE TESTIMONY,] as in Ex. 38. 21; Nu. 1. 50, &c.
7. ATHALIAH,] as in 22. 10.
WICKED ONE.] This original word is not found elsewhere.

BROKEN UP] by violence, the treasures laid up there.
PREPARED,] *lit.* 'made,' that is, used.
8. CHEST,] as in Ge. 50. 26; Ex. 25. 10; 1 K. 12. 9, &c.
9. INTIMATION,] *lit.* 'voice.'
10. REJOICE] at the opportunity of offering gifts for the temple.
COMPLETION,] that is, till it was full.
11. INSPECTION,] as in Nu. 3. 32, 36, &c.
MONEY,] *lit.* 'silver,' as in v. 4 above.
SCRIBE OF THE KING,] as in 2 K. 12. 10, &c.
OFFICER OF THE HIGH PRIEST,] as in 31. 13, Ge. 41. 34; Jud. 9. 28; 2 K. 25. 19.
EMPTY,] as in Ge. 24. 20, &c.
12. SERVICE,] as in 8. 14; 29. 35, &c.
HEWERS,] as in 1 K. 5. 15; 2 K. 12. 12; 1 Ch. 22. 2, 15.
ARTIFICERS,] as in Ex. 28. 11; 35. 35; 38. 23, &c.
RENEW,] as in v. 4 above.
STRENGTHEN,] as in v. 5 above.
13. WORK,] heartily and continuously.
LENGTHENING,] as in Neh. 4. 7; Isa. 58. 8; Jer. 8. 22; 30. 17; 33. 6, &c.
PROPER MEASURE,] as in Ex. 5. 8; 30. 32, 37; Eze. 45. 11.
14. MONEY,] *lit.* 'silver,' as in v. 4, 11.
SPOONS,] as in Ex. 25. 29; 37. 16, &c.
15. SATISFIED WITH DAYS,] like Abraham in Ge. 25. 8, &c.
130 YEARS,] the age of Jacob when he stood before Pharaoh ; see Ge. 47. 9.
16. CITY OF DAVID,] that is, Zion, the usual burial-place of the KINGS] of Judah.
HOUSE,] *or* 'household,' either his own or God's.
17. BOW THEMSELVES] in token of their continued allegiance and of their desire to please the king.
HEARKENED] to their wishes, which were evidently idolatrous.
18. FORSAKE,] as in Ex. 34. 13; De. 7. 5, &c.
SHRINES,] as in Ex. 34. 13; De. 7. 5, &c.
IDOLS] of the nations around them.
GUILT,] in violating their covenant with the Most High; see v. 23.
19. PROPHETS,] those proclaiming his will whether it refers to past, present, or future events.
TESTIFY] to the guilt and danger of their conduct.
GIVEN EAR] to their warnings and exhortations.
20. CLOTHED,] as in Jud. 6. 34; 1 Ch. 12. 8.
ZECHARIAH,] i.e. 'remembered of Jah.
OVER-AGAINST,] not 'above,' as in C.V.
JEHOVAH,] the covenant-God of Israel.
PROSPER NOT,] in national affairs.
FORSAKE,] as Himself had said in De. 31. 17.
21. CONSPIRE,] that is, the princes, most probably.
STONES,] as one speaking evil of the king.
COURT,] the outer one, where the people used to assemble; compare Matt. 23. 35.
22. KINDNESS,] in securing him the throne, as in 23. 1—21.

REQUIRE.] A prophecy not a prayer, as in C.V.
23. TURN,] as in Ex. 34. 22; 1 Sa. 1. 20; Ps. 19. 6.
ARAM,] from the north of Canaan.
DESTROY,] *or* 'mar,' that is, injure and impoverish.
DAMASCUS,] the chief power in Aram; see 2 K. 12. 17.
24. FEW MEN,] comparatively speaking.
MIGHTY FORCE,] belonging to Judah.
FORSAKEN,] as in v. 21 above.
EXECUTED JUDGMENTS,] as in Ex. 12. 12, &c.
25. DISEASES,] as in 6. 28; 21. 15; Ex. 15. 26; 23. 25; 1 K. 8. 37; Prov. 18. 14.
CONSPIRED,] as in v. 21 above.
SONS,] only one is mentioned in v. 21 above, but probably there were others.
BED,] in the house of Millo; see 2 K. 12. 20.
CITY OF DAVID,] that is, Zion.
GRAVES,] because of his cruelty, oppression, and idolatry.
26. CONSPIRING,] as in v. 25.
ZABAD,] i.e. 'dowry;' in 2 K. 12. 21 it is Jozachar, son of 'Shimeah.'
SHIMEATH,] i.e. 'hearing, hearkening.'
JEHOZABAD,] i.e. 'Jah has endowed.'
SHIMRITH,] in 2 K. 12. 21 it is 'Shomer.'
27. SONS,] whose names are not mentioned in 8.8.
BURDEN] of wrath, as in v. 18 above.
FOUNDATION,] as in v. 4—14.
INQUIRY,] as in 13. 22.
AMAZIAH,] i.e. 'strength of Jah,' as in 2 K. 12. 21.

XXV. 1. 25 YEARS,] as in 2 K. 14. 2.
29 YEARS,]14 of which were contemporary with Joash, and 15 after him; see 2 K. 13. 10; 14. 2, 17.
JEHOADDAN,] as in 2 K. 14. 2.
2. RIGHT,] *or* 'upright.'
PERFECT HEART,] like David his father.
3. STRONG,] by his good government, &c.
SMITING,] as in 24. 25; 2 K. 12. 20; 14 5.
4. SONS,] or descendants.
LAW,] of God, the supreme king in Israel.
MOSES,] in De. 24. 16.
5. APPOINTETH,] *lit.* 'causeth to stand.'
INSPECTETH,] to see that none are lacking.
20 YEARS,] as in Ex. 30. 14, 38. 26, &c.
300,000.] Some copies of the Vulgate have 30,000.
SPEAR AND TARGET,] as in 1 Ch. 12. 8, &c.
6. HIRETH,] not thinking himself strong enough.
100,000,] equal to a third of his own army.
100 TALENTS,] about £35,300 sterling.
7. A MAN OF GOD,] whose name is not mentioned.
WITH ISRAEL,] because it had wholly gone astray after idols.
EPHRAIM,] which is often put for the ten tribes.
8. STUMBLE,] as in La. 1. 14, &c.
HELP,] against all enemies, whether with few or with many.
9. TROOP,] of 100,000 as in v. 6 above.
MORE] in his storehouse that can be exhausted.

10. SEPARATETH,] as the man of God recommended, trusting to Jehovah's help.
ANGER,] being deprived of their hopes of spoil from the enemy.

11. STRENGTHENED HIMSELF,] by relying on God's promise.
LEADETH,] as their king and general, confident of victory.
VALLEY OF SALT,] on which see 2 Sa. 8. 13.
SEIR,] that is, of Edom, thus surnamed. 10,000,] as in 2 K. 14. 7.

12. ROCK,] *Heb.* 'Selah,' as in 2 K. 14. 7; the same with Petra.
CAST THEM,] according to the cruel customs of eastern warfare.
BROKEN,] *or* 'broken up,' as in Ge. 7. 11, &c.

13. SONS OF THE TROOP,] that is, those belonging to it, probably the younger and more fiery portion of it.
RUSH,] *or* 'push,' as in Jud. 9. 33, 44, &c.
SAMARIA,] the capital city of Israel.
BETH-HORON,] on the border of Benjamin.
PREY,] from the defenceless inhabitants, whose armed men had gone with their king against Edom.

14. EDOMITES,] in mount Seir, as in v. 11, 12.
GODS,] whose names are nowhere mentioned in S.S.
BOW HIMSELF,] offering the usual outward token of respect.
MAKETH PERFUME,] as if they were capable of being pleased with it.

15. BURNETH,] *or* 'is hot,' as in Ge. 4. 5, 3, &c.
PROPHET,] whose name is not mentioned, probably the 'man of God,' in v. 9.
PEOPLE,] that is, the Edomites.

16. COUNSELLOR,] who might be expected to offer his advice.
APPOINTED,] *lit.* 'given.'
CEASE,] as in 35. 21; Ex. 14. 12, &c.
THEY SMITE] thee on the cheek, as an impertinent adviser.
COUNSELLED,] that is, given counsel, agreeably to the well known scripture idiom whereby what God allows he is said to do.

17. TAKETH COUNSEL,] with his generals and his advisers.
JOASH,] i.e. 'Jah is foundation.'
JEHOAHAZ,] i.e. 'Jah has laid hold.'
JEHU,] i.e. 'he is.'

18. LOOK ONE ANOTHER,] as in v. 21; Ge. 42. 1; 2 K. 14. 8, 11.
THORN,] as in 33. 11; 1 Sa. 13. 6; 2 K. 14. 9; Job 31. 40; 41. 2; Prov. 26. 9; Song 2. 2; Isa. 34. 13; Hos. 9. 6.
LEBANON,] the mountain range of that name.
CEDAR,] the largest tree in the whole land.
WIFE,] as if it were equal to the other in importance.
BEAST OF THE FIELD,] any one, however insignificant, and otherwise harmless.
TREADETH DOWN,] without thinking of it, or regarding it.

19. EDOM,] as in v. 11, 12 above.
BOAST,] as if by his own power he had done it, and was able to do the same to Israel.
STIR THYSELF UP,] as in De. 2. 5, 9, 19, &c.

20. FROM GOD,] as the being in whose hands are all events, prosperous or adverse.
SOUGHT,] and worshipped, as in v. 14.

21. LOOK ONE ANOTHER,] as in v. 18 above.
BETH-SHEMESH,] i.e. 'house of the sun,' as in Jos. 19. 38, &c.

22. TENTS,] as in Jud. 7. 8; 1 Sa. 4. 10, &c.
23. CAUGHT] alive, as a prisoner of war.
BREAKETH DOWN,] so as to render it open to every assailant.
GATE,] leading towards Ephraim.
CORNER,] as in 2 K. 14. 13, &c.
400 CUBITS,] that is, 600 feet.

24. OBED-EDOM,] i.e. 'servant of Edom.'
SONS OF THE PLEDGE,] as in 2 K. 14. 14.
25. 15 YEARS.] Vulg. has '25 years.'
26. MATTERS,] not 'acts,' as in C.V.
27. CONSPIRACY,] because of the troubles he brought upon them by pride and idolatry.
LACHISH,] as in Jos. 15. 39, &c.
28. THE CITY OF JUDAH,] that is, Jerusalem; see 2 K. 14. 20.

XXVI. 1. UZZIAH,] i.e. 'strength of Jah,' as in 2 K. 15. 13; in 2 K. 21 it is 'Azariah.'
16 YEARS,] as in 2 K. 14. 21; 15. 2.
2. ELOTH,] a port of the Sea of Suph, belonging to Edom, as in De. 2. 8; 1 K. 9. 26; *or* 'Elath,' as in 2 K. 14. 22.
3. 52 YEARS,] being a longer period than any other of the kings of Judah or Israel reigned.
JECHOLIAH,] i.e. 'ability of Jah,' as in 2 K. 15. 2.
4. RIGHT,] *or* 'upright.'
DID,] as in 2 K. 14. 3; 15. 3.
5. SEEKING GOD,] as in Ps. 9. 10; 14. 2; 22. 26; 24. 6; 34. 10; 53. 2; 69. 32, &c.
ZECHARIAH,] i.e. 'remembered of Jah,' as in 2 K. 14. 29; 15. 8; Isa. 8. 2.
GIVING UNDERSTANDING.] So Syr., Sept., Targ., Arabic.
VISIONS,] *lit.* 'sights;' Sept., Syr., Arab., and Targum read 'fear.'
PROSPER,] in every putting forth of his hand.
6. PHILISTINES,] on the shores of the great sea, who had distressed them in the days of Jehoram, as in 21. 16.
GATH,] one of their five principalities.
JABNEH,] not mentioned elsewhere.
ASHDOD,] the Azotus of the New Testament; Amos 1. 8.
7. GOD HELPETH,] and thus caused him to prosper, as in v. 5.
ARABIANS,] or mixed races.
GUR-BAAL,] i.e. 'sojourning of Baal,' the same as 'Gerar,' according to the Targum, or 'Ashkelon.'
MEHUMIM.] Sept. has 'Minaeans;' see 20. 1.
8. AMMONITES,] north of the Moabites, beyond the Jordan.
PRESENT,] as a token of respect, if not of submission.
ENTERING IN,] as in Ge. 12. 11, &c.
9. TOWERS,] *lit.* 'great places.'
CORNER,] it had been broken down; see 25. 23.
VALLEY,] as in Neh. 2. 13; 3. 13, through which Kidron ran; see Jer. 31. 40.
ANGLE,] of the wall of the city.

10. WILDERNESS] of Judah, that is, its pasture-land.

WELLS,] which are of great value in the east.

MUCH CATTLE,] as kings often had and have in these lands, e. g. Pharaoh, Saul, Mesha, &c.

MOUNTAINS.] Compare Ps. 72. 16.

CARMEL,] where Nabal dwelt; see 1 Sa. 25. 2.

LOVER OF THE GROUND,] that is, given to agricultural pursuits.

11. JEHIEL,] i. e. a 'heap of God.'

MAASAIAH,] i. e. 'work of Jah.'

OFFICER,] as in Ex. 5. 6, 10, 14, 15, 19, &c.

HANANIAH,] i. e. 'grace of Jah.'

12. 2,600,] captains of hundreds and of thousands.

13. HAND,] under their authority.

307,500,] being 7,500 more than his father had; see 25. 5.

14. PREPARETH,] or 'maketh ready,' as in Ge. 43. 16, 25, &c.

SHIELDS,] as in Ge. 15. 1; De. 33. 27, &c.

SPEARS,] as in Nu. 25. 7; Jud. 5. 8, &c.

HELMETS,] as in 1 Sa. 17. 5; Isa. 59. 17; Jer. 46. 4; Eze. 27. 10; 38. 5.

COATS OF MAIL.] as in 1 Sa. 17. 5; Neh. 4. 16; 1 K. 22. 34; Isa. 59. 17.

BOWS,] as in Ge. 9. 13—16; 21. 16, &c.

SLINGS,] as in 1 Sa. 17. 40, 50; 25. 29; Job 41. 28; Zec. 9. 15; 2 K. 3. 25.

15. INVENTIONS,] as in Ec. 7. 29.

DEVICE,] as in Ge. 6. 5; Ex. 31. 4, &c.

INVENTOR,] as in Ex. 26. 1, 31; 28. 6, &c.

TOWERS..CORNERS,] as in v. 9 above.

SHOOT,] against an enemy approaching.

WONDERFULLY,] as in De. 28. 59; Ps. 31. 21; Isa. 28. 29.

16. HIGH,] with pride, as in 17. 6; 32. 25, &c.

TRESPASSETH,] as in Lev. 5. 6, 15; 6. 2, &c.

PERFUME,] as in Ex. 25. 6; 30. 1, &c.

17. AZARIAH,] i. e. 'help of Jah;' chief priest, see v. 20; 1 Ch. 6. 10.

VALOUR,] or 'worth,' as in De. 3. 18, &c.

18. SONS OF AARON,] the first high priest, as in Nu. 16. 35.

TRESPASSED,] as in v. 16.

19. WROTH,] as in Ge. 40. 6; Prov. 19. 3, &c.

CENSER,] as in Eze. 8. 11.

LEPROSY,] as in Lev. 13. 2, 3, 8, 9, 11, &c.

FOREHEAD,] where it could not be concealed.

PLAGUED,] leprosy being regarded as a direct visitation of God, as in the case of Miriam.

21. LEPER,] as in 2 K. 15. 5.

SEPARATE,] lit. 'free,' as in 2 K. 15. 5.

CUT OFF,] not allowed to enter it, being unclean and defiled.

HOUSE,] or 'household.'

JUDGING,] according to the law of the kingdom.

22. MATTERS,] not 'acts,' as in C.V.

ISAIAH,] i. e. 'safety of Jah.'

AMOZ,] i. e. 'the strong one.'

23. LIETH,] as in 2 K. 15. 6; see Isa. 6. 1.

LEPER,] and therefore ceremonially unclean.

JOTHAM,] i. e. 'Jah is perfect.'

XXVII. 1. 25 YEARS,] B.C. 758; see 2 K. 15. 34.

16 YEARS,] like his son; see 28. 1.

JERUSHAH,] i. e. a 'possession.'

ZADOK,] i. e. 'just.'

2. RIGHT,] or 'upright.'

DID,] except assuming the priest's office.

COME IN,] to worship and burn incense, but for what reason is not stated.

DOING CORRUPTLY,] against God and their own good, in attending the high places; see 2 K. 15. 35.

3. UPPER GATE,] as in 2 K. 15. 35.

OPHEL,] i. e. a 'height,' on the east of Zion; see 33. 14; 2 K. 5. 24; Neh. 3. 27; 11. 21.

4. FORESTS,] as in 1 Sa. 23. 15, 16, 18, 19; Isa. 17. 9; Eze. 31. 3.

PALACES,] as in 17. 12; Ezra 6. 2; 1 Ch. 29 1, 19, &c.

TOWERS,] lit. 'great places,' as in Ge. 11. 4, 5; 35. 21, &c.

5. AMMON,] beyond the Jordan, northward of Moab; see Amos 1. 13.

100 TALENTS,] about £35,300 sterling.

CORS,] the same as the 'homer.'

SECOND..THIRD,] after which it stopped.

6. PREPARED,] or 'established or made ready.'

7. MATTERS,] not 'acts,' as in C.V.

8. 25..16,] as in v. 1, 2.

9. LIETH,] as in Ge. 47. 30, &c.

CITY OF DAVID,] that is, Zion.

AHAZ,] i. e. 'he laid hold.'

XXVIII. 1. 20 YEARS.] See 2 K. 16. 2; 18. 2.

16 YEARS,] like his father; see 27. 1.

RIGHT,] or 'upright.'

2. WAYS,] idolatrous ones.

MOLTEN IMAGES,] as in Ex. 32. 4, 8, &c.

BAALIM,] as in Jud. 2. 11, 13; 3. 7; 6. 25, 28, 30, 31, 32; 8. 33; 10. 6, 10, &c.

3. MADE PERFUME,] to Moloch who was worshipped in the valley of the son of HINNOM,] as in Jos. 15. 8; 18. 16, &c.

BURNETH,] as in Ex. 22. 5, 6; Jud. 15. 5; 1 K. 16. 3; Eze. 5. 2; Nah. 2. 3.

ABOMINATIONS,] as in Ge. 43. 32; 46. 34, &c.

DISPOSSESSED] because of their wickedness.

4. HIGH PLACES,] to the gods of the nations.

HEIGHTS..GREEN TREES,] the usual places of resort for idolaters.

5. ARAM,] on the north of Canaan, whose name was Rezin, 2 K. 16. 5.

DAMASCUS,] on the river Pharpar and Amana.

KING OF ISRAEL,] whose name was Pekah, as in v. 6.

SMITING,] as in Lev. 26. 21; Nu. 11. 33, &c.

6. PEKAH,] i. e. 'opening.'

REMALIAH.] Etymology uncertain.

120,000.] Compare 13. 17.

7. ZICHRI,] i. e. 'mindful.'

EPHRAIM,] that is, of the ten tribes, often so denominated.

MAASEIAH,] i. e. 'work of Jah.'

AZRIKAM,] i. e. 'my help is risen.'

LEADER,] as in 1 Sa. 9. 16; 10. 1, &c.

ELKANAH,] i. e. 'God has brought.'

SECOND,] as in Ge. 41. 43; 43. 12, 15, &c.

8. SPOIL,] as in Ge. 49. 27; Ex. 15. 9, &c.
SAMARIA,] the capital city of Israel.
9. ODED,] i.e. 'causing to stand.'
FURY,] *lit.* 'heat,' as in Ge. 27. 44, &c.
RAGE,] as in 16. 10; Prov. 19. 12; Isa. 30.
30; Jon. 1. 15; Mic. 7. 9.
COME,] *or* 'touched,' as in Ge. 28. 12, &c.
10. SUBDUE,] as in Ge. 1. 28; Neh. 5. 5;
Est. 7. 8; Jer. 34. 11, 16; Mic. 7. 19; Zec.
9. 15.
CAUSES OF GUILT,] as in Lev. 4. 3; 6. 5, 7;
22. 16; 1 Ch. 21. 3; 2 Ch. 24. 18; 28. 13; 33. 23;
Ezra 9. 6, &c.
11. HEAT OF THE ANGER,] as in Ex. 32. 12;
Nu. 25. 4; 32. 14; De. 13. 17, &c.
12. EPHRAIM,] as in v. 7 above.
AZARIAH,] i.e. 'help of Jah.'
JOHANAN,] i.e. 'Jah has grace.'
BERECHIAH,] i.e. 'blessed of Jah.'
MESHILLEMOTH,] i.e. 'recompenses.'
JEHIZKIAH,] i.e. 'strengthened by Jah.'
SHALLUM,] i.e. 'recompensed.'
AMASA,] i.e. 'a load.'
HADLAI,] i.e. 'ceasing, worldly.'
13. TO GUILT,] already contracted by idol-
atry, &c.
FIERCENESS,] *or* 'heat,' as in v. 11.
14. ARMED MEN,] as in Nu. 31. 5; 32. 21,
27, 29, 30, 32; De. 3. 18; 25. 10; Jos. 4. 13; 6. 7,
9, 13; 1 Ch. 12. 23, 24; 2 Ch. 17. 18; 20. 21;
Isa. 15. 4.
PREY,] as in 14. 14; 25. 13; Ezra 9. 7; Est.
9. 10, 15, 16; Dan. 11. 24, 33.
15. EXPRESSED BY NAME,] as in v. 12
above; compare Nu. 1. 17, &c.
SHOE,] as in Eze. 16. 10.
ANOINT,] as in De. 28. 40; Ruth 3. 3, &c.
FEEBLE ONE,] as in Job 4. 4; Ps. 105. 37;
Isa. 5. 27; 35. 3; Jer. 46. 16.
JERICHO,] in Benjamin, a fertile spot.
CITY OF PALMS,] as in De. 34. 3; Jud. 1. 16;
3. 13.
16. ASSHUR,] that is, Tiglath-Pileser and
his son, 2 K. 16. 7.
17. EDOMITES,] as in 20. 10.
CAPTIVITY,] as in Ex. 12. 29; Nu. 1; 31.
12, 19, 26, &c.
18. PHILISTINES,] on the shores of the
great Sea.
BETH-SHEMESH,] a Levitical city, between
Judah and Dan, as in Jos. 15. 10, &c.
AIJALON,] a Levitical city in Dan, as in
Jos. 10. 12; 19. 42; 21. 24; Jud. 1. 35.
GEDEROTH,] in the tribe of Judah.
SHOCHO,] in the plain (Jos. 15. 35), or in
the mountains (Jos. 15. 48) of Judah.
TIMNAH,] first in Judah (Jos. 15. 10, 57),
and then in Dan (Jos. 19. 43).
GIMZO.] Not mentioned elsewhere.
19. HUMBLED,] under all its enemies.
MADE FREE,] as in Ex. 5. 6.
20. TILGATH-PILNESER,] *or* Tiglath-Pileser,
as in 2 K. 15. 29; 16. 10; see 1 Ch. 5. 6, 26.
DISTRESS,] by exactions of money, &c.
21. PORTION,] *or* share of the treasures
gathered up there.
NO HELP] in his extremity.
22. TRESPASS,] as in v. 19.
23. DAMASCUS,] that is, of the people of
Damascus, who were smiting him all the
time.

CAUSE TO STUMBLE,] into greater calamities than before.
24. CUTTETH IN PIECES,] with the view of
disposing of them.
SHUTTETH THE DOORS,] to prevent the
public worship of God.
CORNER] of the public streets and thoroughfares.
25. HIGH PLACES,] forbidden in the law of
Moses, and repeatedly removed by pious
kings.
PROVOKETH,] by this daring attempt to
put down the service of God.
26. MATTERS,] not 'acts,' as in the C.V.
27. LIETH,] as in 27. 9.
GRAVES,] as in 16. 14; 21. 20; 24. 25; 32. 33;
34. 4, 28; 35. 24.
HEZEKIAH,] i.e. 'strength of Jah.'

XXIX. 1. **25 YEARS,]** in the third year of
Hoshea, son of Elah, king of Israel.
29 YEARS,] till B.C. 698.
ABIJAH,] in 2 K. 18. 2 it is 'Abi.'
ZECHARIAH,] perhaps the same as in
Jos. 8. 3.
2. RIGHT,] *or* 'upright.'
DID,] language used of no other king.
3. FIRST MONTH,] on the first day of it, as
in v. 17; the month of Ab *or* Nisan.
OPENED,] they having been shut by Ahaz,
as in 28. 24.
4. BROAD PLACE,] as in Ge. 19. 2; De. 13.
5. IMPURITY,] as in Lev. 12. 2, 5; 15. 19, 20,
24, 25, 26, 33; 18. 19; 20. 21; Nu. 19. 9, 13, 20,
21; Ezra 9. 11; La. 1. 17; Eze. 7. 19, 20; 18. 6;
22. 10; 36. 17; Zec. 13. 1.
6. TRESPASSED,] as in Lev. 5. 15; 6. 2; 26.
40, &c.
FACES,] as in 6. 3; 35. 22; Jud. 18. 23; 1 K.
8. 14; 21. 4, &c.
NECK,] not 'back,' as in C.V.
7. SHUT,] as in Ge. 2. 21; 7. 16; 19. 6,
10, &c.
PORCH,] so that none could enter the
temple; see 28. 24.
QUENCH,] as in Lev. 6. 12, 13; 1 Sa. 3. 3;
2 Sa. 14. 7; 21. 17, &c.
LAMPS,] as in Ex. 25. 37; 27. 20; 30. 7, 8;
35. 14; 37. 23; 39. 37; 40. 4, 25; Lev. 24. 2, 4;
Nu. 4. 9; 8. 2.
PERFUME,] as in Ex. 25. 6; 10. 1, 7, 8, 9,
27, 35, 37; 31. 8. 11; 35. 8, &c.
8. WRATH,] as in Nu. 1. 53; 16. 46; 18.
5, &c.
TREMBLING,] as in Isa. 28. 19; Jer. 15. 4;
24. 9; 29. 19; 34. 17.
ASTONISHMENT,] as in De. 28. 37; 2 K. 22.
19, &c.
HISSING,] as in Jer. 19. 8; 25. 9, 18; 29. 18;
51. 37; Mic. 6. 16.
9. CAPTIVITY,] as in 28. 8, 15, 17.
10. WITH MY HEART,] as in Jos. 14. 7, &c.
COVENANT] of peace and reconciliation,
as in Ge. 6. 18; 9. 9—16; 14. 3, &c.
FIERCENESS,] as in Ex. 32. 12; Nu. 25.
4, &c.
11. AT REST,] *or* 'deceived.'
FIXED,] of his own good pleasure in the
wilderness, instead of the first born of every
house.

PERFUME,] when sacrifices are being offered to him.
12. MAHATH,] i.e. 'taking hold.'
AMASAI,] i.e. 'my load.'
JOEL,] i.e. 'Jah is God.'
AZARIAH,] i.e. 'strength of Jah.'
KOHATHITE,] as in Nu. 3. 27, 30; 4. 18, 34, 37; 10. 21; 26. 57, &c.
MERARI,] as in Ge. 46. 11; Ex. 6. 16, 19; Nu. 3. 17, 20, 33, 35, 36, &c.
KISH,] i.e. 'snaring.'
ABDI,] i.e. 'my servant.'
JEHALELEL,] i.e. 'he praises God.'
GERSHONITE,] as in Nu. 3. 21, 23, 24; 4. 24, 27, 28; 26. 57, &c.
JOAH,] i.e. 'Jah is brother.'
ZIMMAH,] i.e. 'device.'
EDEN,] i.e. 'delight.'
13. ELIZAPHAN,] i.e. 'my God has hidden.'
SHIMRI,] i.e. 'watchful.'
JEIEL,] i.e. 'God lives.'
ASAPH,] i.e. 'he gathered.'
ZECHARIAH,] i.e. 'remembered of Jah.'
MATTANIAH,] i.e. 'gift of Jah.'
14. HEMAN,] i.e. 'stedfast.'
JEHIEL,] i.e. 'God lives.'
SHIMEI,] i.e. 'hearkening.'
JEDUTHUN,] i.e. 'beloved.'
SHEMAIAH,] i.e. 'heard of Jah.'
UZZIEL,] i.e. 'my strength is God.'
15. CLEANSE] from the impurity in v. 5.
16. UNCLEANNESS,] as in Lev. 5. 3; 7. 20, 21, &c.
COURT,] the outer one, open to all.
KIDRON,] running through the valley of the son of Hinnom, that it might be carried off to the Dead Sea.
17. PORCH,] as in v. 7.
18. ARRANGEMENT,] on which the bread of the presence was placed weekly.
19. CAST AWAY] as worthless, as in 11. 14; 28. 9; Isa. 19. 6.
TRESPASS,] as in 28. 24.
PREPARED,] or 'made ready or established.'
20. RISETH EARLY,] as in Ge. 19. 2, 27; 20. 8; 21. 14, &c.
21. SEVEN BULLOCKS, &c.] as in Nu. 23. 1, 14, 29, &c.
SIN-OFFERING,] as in Lev. 4. 3, 14, &c.
22. SLAUGHTER,] as in Ge. 22. 10; 37. 31, &c.
SPRINKLE,] as in Ex. 9. 8, 10; 24. 6. 8, &c.
23. HE-GOATS,] as in v. 21.
LAY HANDS,] as in Lev. 4. 15, 24, &c.
24. MAKE ATONEMENT,] as in Ge. 32. 20; Ex. 29. 36, &c.
SIN-OFFERING,] and not for those only who were present; see 30. 1.
25. APPOINTETH,] lit. 'causeth to stand.'
CYMBALS,] as in 1 Ch. 13, 8; 15. 16, 19, 28; 16. 5, 42; 25. 1, 6; 2 Ch. 5. 12, 13; 29. 25; Ezra 3. 10; Neh. 12. 27.
PSALTERIES,] as in 1 Sa. 10. 5; 2 Sa. 6. 5, &c.
HARPS,] as in Ge. 4. 21; 31. 27; 1 Sa. 10. 5; 16. 16, 23; 2 Sa. 6. 5; 1 K. 10. 12, &c.
SEER,] as in 2 Sa. 24. 11; 2 K. 17. 15; 1 Ch. 21. 9; 25. 5; 29. 9; 2 Ch. 9. 29; 12. 15; 19. 2; 29. 25, 30, &c.
PROPHET,] as in 2 Sa. 7. 2; 12. 25, &c.

26. INSTRUMENTS,] as in 1 Ch. 23. 5, &c.
TRUMPETS,] as in Nu. 10. 2, &c.
27. SONG OF JEHOVAH,] as in 1 Ch. 25. 7, 2 Ch. 7. 6; Ps. 137. 4.
28. DOING OBEISANCE,] as in Ge. 37. 9; 2 K. 19. 37; Neh. 9. 3, 6; Est. 3. 2, 5; Isa. 37. 38; Eze. 8. 16; Zeph. 1. 5.
29. BOWED] before Jehovah, as in 7. 3, &c.
30. GIVE PRAISE,] as in 2 Sa. 14. 25; 1 Ch. 16. 4, &c.
WORDS OF DAVID,] in the psalms written by him.
SEER,] in such psalms as the fiftieth, &c.
31. FILLED YOUR HAND,] as in Ex. 27. 41, &c.
WILLING-HEARTED ONE,] as in Ex. 35. 5, 22, &c.
32. BURNT-OFFERINGS,] which were wholly consumed on the altar.
33. SANCTIFIED THINGS,] part of which was partaken of by the worshipper.
34. FEW,] through the closing of the temple by Ahaz.
STRIP,] the skin off the burnt-offering.
STRENGTHEN THEM,] as in 35. 11.
SANCTIFY THEMSELVES,] as directed in v. 5.
UPRIGHT OF HEART,] as in De. 9. 5; 2 K. 10. 15; 1 Ch. 29. 17; Job 33. 3; Ps. 7. 10; 11. 2; 32. 11; 64. 10; 94. 15; 97. 11; 119. 7.
35. FAT,] as in Lev. 3. 16.
OBLATIONS,] as in Nu. 15. 5, 7, 10.
ESTABLISHED,] anew, after it had been stopped by Ahaz.
36. PREPARATION,] or 'establishment.'
SUDDENLY,] as in Nu. 6. 9; 12. 4; Jos. 10. 9; 11. 7; Job 5. 3; 9. 23; 22. 10; Ps. 64. 4, 7; Prov. 3. 25, &c.

XXX. 1. ISRAEL,] belonging to the ten tribes.
EPHRAIM AND MANASSEH,] the two nearest tribes on the north.
PASSOVER,] as commanded in Ex. 12. 14; De. 16. 1—6.
2. TAKETH COUNSEL,] as a thing touching the glory of God, and the welfare of the state.
SECOND MONTH,] that is, Ijar, (so the Targum), instead of the first as in the law.
3. AT THAT TIME,] in the month Nisan; see 29. 17.
SUFFICIENTLY,] in such numbers as were necessary for such an assembly.
4. RIGHT,] or 'upright.'
5. ESTABLISH,] lit. 'cause to stand.'
INTIMATION,] lit. a 'voice.'
BEER-SHEBA,] the southern extremity of Canaan.
DAN,] its most northern province.
WRITTEN,] in the law of Moses.
6. RUNNERS,] as in 1 Sa. 22. 17, &c.; see v. 10; Est. 3. 13, 15; 8. 10, 14; Job 9. 25; Jer. 51. 31, &c.
LETTERS,] as in v. 6; Neh. 2. 7, 8, 9; 6. 5, 17, 19; Est. 9. 26, 29.
ESCAPED PART,] as in Ge. 32. 8; 45. 7; Ex. 10. 5; Jud. 21. 17, &c.
ASSHUR,] who had carried them off captive, as in 2 K. 15. 19, 29.
7. TRESPASSED,] against the laws of God, by idolatry

DESOLATION,] as in De. 28. 37; 2 K. 22. 19, &c.
8. HARDEN NOT YOUR NECK,] as in Ex. 32. 9; 33. 3, 5; 34. 9; De. 9. 6, 13; 10. 16; 31. 37, &c.
GIVE A HAND,] according to an eastern mode of indicating submission
9. MERCIES,] or 'are objects of mercy,' as in 1 K. 8. 50.
THE FACE,] that is, refuse to hear and accept you.
10. ZEBULUN,] north of Issachar, not being interfered with by Hoshea, king of Israel.
LAUGHING,] as in Job 5. 22; 29. 24, &c.
MOCKING,] as in Neh. 2. 19; 4. 1; Job 21. 3; Ps. 22. 7.
11. ASHER,] near Tyre and Zidon, in the north of Canaan.
MANASSEH,] east of the Jordan, in Bashan.
HUMBLED,] because of their sin and desolation.
12. ONE HEART,] so that there were none opposing or keeping aloof.
13. FEAST,] or 'festival.'
SECOND MONTH,] as decided in v. 2.
14. ALTARS,] of the idols, that had been worshipped; see 28. 24.
KIDRON,] that they might be carried into the Salt Sea; see 29. 16.
15. FOURTEENTH,] the day appointed in the law.
ASHAMED,] of their long delay and distrust of the willingness of the people.
16. STATION,] as in 34. 31; 35. 10; Neh. 8. 7; 9. 3; 13. 11; Da. 8. 17, 18; 10. 11; 11. 1.
ORDINANCE,] lit. 'judgment.'
SPRINKLING,] according to the custom; see Lev. 1. 5.
17. NOT SANCTIFIED THEMSELVES,] fully and thoroughly, as required in the law.
NOT CLEAN,] that is, ceremonially so.
18. ISSACHAR,] north of Manasseh, west of Jordan.
WRITTEN,] in Ex. 12. 1—28.
PRAYETH,] as in Ge. 20. 7, 17; Nu. 11. 2, &c.
GOOD,] as in Ge. 50. 20; Ex. 18. 9, &c.
RECEIVE ATONEMENT,] as in De. 21. 8; 32.43.
19. PREPARED HIS HEART,] as in 12. 14; 19. 3, &c.
20. HEALETH,] from their sins and sufferings.
21. SEVEN DAYS,] according to the law in Ex. 12. 18, 19.
GIVING PRAISE,] as in 1 Ch. 23. 5; 29. 13; 2 Ch. 20. 21; 23. 12.
PRAISE,] or 'strength,' as in Ex. 15. 2, 13, &c.
22. UNTO THE HEART,] as in Ge. 34. 3, &c.
GIVING GOOD UNDERSTANDING,] in reference to law and duty.
APPOINTED THING,] set apart for them.
MAKING CONFESSION,] as in Neh. 1. 6; 9. 3; Da. 9. 20.
23. OTHER SEVEN DAYS,] as a religious festival, offering thanksgivings.
24. PRESENTED,] from his own flocks and herds.
25. REJOICE,] as in Lev. 23. 40; De. 12. 7, &c.
ISRAEL,] that is, the ten tribes.
SOJOURNERS,] as in Ex. 3. 22; 12. 49, &c.

26. SOLOMON,] a period of nearly 300 years.
BLESS,] as directed in Nu. 6. 24, 25.
HEARD,] by the hearer of prayer.
HABITATION,] as in De. 26. 15; 1 Sa. 2. 29, 32, &c.

XXXI. 1. STANDING-PILLARS,] as in Ge. 28. 18, 22; 31. 13, 45, 51, 52; 35. 14, 20; Ex. 23. 24, &c.
SHRINES,] as in Ex. 34. 13; De. 7. 5; 12. 3; 16. 21; Jud. 3. 7, &c.
HIGH PLACES..ALTARS,] erected by Ahaz, in 28. 25; see also 2 K. 18. 4 for the destruction of the brazen serpent.
POSSESSION,] as in Ge. 17. 8; 23. 4; 23. 9, 20; 36. 43; 47. 11; 48. 4; 49. 30; 50. 13; Lev. 4. 34, &c.
2. COURSES,] established by David and Solomon, in 1 Ch. 23. 6; 24. 1.
TO MINISTER,] as in Ge. 39. 4; 40. 4; Ex. 24. 13; 28. 35, 43; 29. 30, &c.
TO GIVE THANKS,] as in Ge. 29. 35; 49. 8; 2 Sa. 22. 50, &c.
CAMPS,] not 'tents,' as in C.V.
3. PORTION,] as in v. 4; Neh. 12. 44, 47; 13. 10; Ps. 11. 6; 63. 10.
SUBSTANCE,] as in Ge. 12. 5; 13. 6; 14. 11, &c.
MORNING..EVENING,] that is, the daily sacrifices.
SABBATHS,] or days of rest appointed in the law.
NEW MOONS,] as in 1 Sa. 20. 5, 18, 24, &c.
APPOINTED SEASONS,] as in Ge. 1. 14; 17. 21; 18. 14; 21. 2; Ex. 9. 5; 13. 10; 23. 15, &c.
WRITTEN,] in Nu. 28. 9—31; 29. 1—40.
4. PORTION,] as in v. 3.
5. SPREADING-FORTH,] as in Ge. 28. 14; 30. 30, 43; 38. 29; Ex. 1. 12, &c.
FIRST-FRUIT,] as in Ge. 1. 1; 10. 10; 49. 3; Ex. 23. 19; 34. 26; Lev. 2. 2; 23. 10; Nu. 15. 20, &c.
INCREASE,] as in Ge. 47. 24; Ex. 23. 10, &c.
TITHE,] as in Ge. 14. 20; 27. 30, 31, 32, &c.
6. HERD AND FLOCK,] as commanded in Lev. 27. 32.
HEAP..HEAPS,] as in v. 7, 8, 9; Ruth 3. 7; Neh. 4. 2; 13. 15; Song 7. 2; Jer. 50. 26; Hag. 2. 16.
7. THIRD MONTH,] that is, Sivan.
LAY THE FOUNDATION,] as in Ezra 3. 12; Job 38. 4, &c.
SEVENTH MONTH,] that is, Tisri.
FINISHED,] or 'ended,' as in Ge. 2. 2, &c.
8. BLESS,] because of the abundance of the offerings.
9. HEAPS,] how they became so great and valuable.
10. AZARIAH,] i.e. 'help of Jah;' see 26. 17.
ZADOK,] i.e. 'just;' made high priest by Solomon after the expulsion of Abiathar for his connection with Adonijah.
HEAVE OFFERING,] as in Ex. 25. 2, 3; 29. 27, 28, &c.
EAT..SATISFIED,] as in De. 6. 11; Joel 2. 26, &c.
LEAVE ABUNDANTLY,] as in Ex. 36. 7; 2 K. 4. 43, &c.
STORE,] as in 1 Ch. 29. 16, &c.
11. CHAMBERS,] as in 1 Sa. 9. 22; 2 K. 23. 11; 1 Ch. 9. 26, 33; 23. 28; 28. 12; Ezra 8. 29; 10. 6; Neh. 10. 37, 38, 39, &c.

12. HEAVE-OFFERING,] as in v. 10.
FAITHFULLY,] that is, stedfastly, as in Ex.
17. 12; De. 32. 4; 1 Sa. 26. 23; 2 K. 12. 15; 22.
7, &c.
LEADER,] as in 1 Sa. 9. 16, &c.
CONANIAH,] i.e. 'prepared of Jah.'
SHIMEI,] i.e. 'hearkening.'
SECOND,] as in 28. 7, &c.
13. JEHIEL,] i.e. 'God lives.'
AZAZIAH,] i.e. 'strength of Jah.'
NABATH,] i.e. 'quiescence, descent.'
AZAHEL,] i.e. 'made of God.'
JERIMOTH,] i.e. 'heights.'
JOZABAD,] i.e. 'Jah has endowed.'
ELIEL,] i.e. 'my God is God.'
ISHMACHIAH,] i.e. 'supported of Jah.'
MAHATH,] i.e. 'laying hold of.'
BENAIAH,] i.e. 'built up of Jah.'
INSPECTORS,] of the other priests and
Levites.
APPOINTMENT,] as in Neh. 3. 31.
14. KORE,] i.e. a 'caller, partridge.'
IMNAH,] i.e. 'southward.'
WILLING-OFFERINGS,] as in Ex. 35. 29; 36.
3, &c.
15. EDEN,] i.e. 'delight.'
MINIAMIN,] i.e. 'from or at the right hand
or south.'
JESHUA,] i.e. 'he gives safety.'
SHEMAIAH,] i.e. 'heard of Jah.'
AMARIAH,] i.e. 'saying of Jah.'
SHECANIAH,] i.e. 'tabernacle of Jah.'
FAITHFULLY,] as in v. 12.
COURSES,] as in 1 Ch. 23. 6; 24. 1, &c.
16. THREE YEARS,] which seems a very
early age.
IN ITS DAY,] as in Ex. 5. 13; 16. 4, &c.
CHARGES,] as in 7. 6, &c.
17. 20 YEARS,] as in 1 Ch. 23. 24.
18. INFANTS,] as in Ge. 34. 29; 43. 8, &c.
FAITHFULNESS,] or 'stedfastness.'
19. SUBURB,] as in Lev. 25. 34; 35. 2, 3, 4,
5, 7, &c.
DEFINED,] as in Nu. 1. 17; 1 Ch. 12. 31; 16.
41; 2 Ch. 28. 15; Ezra 8. 20.
GENEALOGY,] as in 1 Ch. 4. 33; 5. 1, 7, &c.
20. TRUE,] lit. 'truth, stedfastness,' as in
Ge. 24. 27, 48, 49; 32. 10; 42. 16; 47. 29, &c.
21. PROSPERED,] lit. 'made to prosper.'

XXXII. 1. THIS TRUTH,] as in 31. 20, &c.
SENNACHERIB,] as in 2 K. 18. 13; 19. 16—
36; Isa. 36. 1.
ASSHUR,] the most powerful state in the
east at that time.
THE DEFENCED,] as in Nu. 13. 28; De. 1.
28, &c.
REND] it from the power of Hezekiah.
3. TAKETH COUNSEL,] as in 1 K. 12. 6, 8, 9,
28, &c.
STOP] the mouths, that they might not be
discovered.
HELP,] as in Ge. 49. 25; De. 32. 38, &c.
4. FOUNTAINS,] as in Ge. 7. 11; 8. 2; Lev.
11. 36; Jos. 15. 9; 18. 15; 1 K. 18. 5; 2 K. 3.
19, 25; Ps. 74. 15, &c.
BROOK,] that is, Gihon, most probably.
5. STRENGTHENETH HIMSELF,] as in Ge.
48. 2, &c.
WALL,] broken down, as in 25. 23; 26. 9;
28. 6, 7.

TOWERS,] lit. 'great places.'
MILLO,] as in 2 Sa. 5. 9; 1 K. 9. 15, 24; 11.
27; 2 K. 12. 20; 1 Ch. 11. 8.
CITY OF DAVID,] that is, Zion.
DARTS,] as in 23. 10; Neh. 4. 17, 23; Job
33. 18; 36. 12; Song 4. 13; Joel 2. 8.
SHIELDS,] as in Ge. 15. 1; De. 33. 29; Jud.
5. 8; 2 Sa. 1. 21, &c.
6. BROAD PLACE,] as in Ge. 19. 2; De. 13.
16; Jud. 19. 15, &c.
HEART,] as in Ge. 34. 3, &c.
7. COURAGEOUS,] as in Jer. 31. 6, 7, 23;
Jos. 1. 6, 7, 9, 18; 10. 25; 1 Ch. 22. 13; 28. 20.
CAST DOWN,] as in De. 1. 21; 31. 8; Jos. 1.
9; 8. 1; 10. 25, &c.
MORE] helpers—myriads of heavenly messengers.
8. ARM OF FLESH,] finite in power.
HELP] against all enemies whatever.
FIGHT,] as in Ex. 17. 10; Nu. 22. 11; De.
20. 4, 10, 19; Jos. 9. 2; 11. 5; Jud. 1. 1, 9; 8.
1; 10. 9, 18; 11. 9, &c.
SUPPORTED,] as in Jud. 16. 29; 2 K. 18. 21;
Isa. 36. 6.
9. LACHISH,] twenty miles south-west of
Jerusalem; see Isa. 36. 2.
SERVANTS,] mentioned in 2 K. 18. 14—17.
10. BULWARK,] as in De. 20. 19, 20; 28. 53,
55, 57; 2 K. 19. 24; 24. 10; 25. 2; 2 Ch. 8. 5,
11. 5; Ps. 31. 21, &c.
11. PERSUADING,] as in Jer. 43. 3.
FAMINE..THIRST,] within the walls of
Jerusalem.
OUR GOD,] the national covenant-God of
Israel.
12. TURNED ASIDE] and destroyed, as in
31. 1.
BOW YOURSELVES,] as in Ge. 18. 2; 19. 1;
22. 5, &c.
MAKE PERFUME,] as in Ex. 29. 13, 18, 25;
30. 7, 8, 20, &c.
13. LANDS,] round about Asshur and
Canaan.
AT ALL ABLE,] lit. 'to be able, were they
able.'
14. DEVOTED TO DESTRUCTION,] as in Ex.
22. 20; Lev. 27. 28, 29; Nu. 21. 2, 3, &c.
15. LIFT YOU UP] with pride and conceit.
PERSUADE,] as in De. 13. 6; Jos. 15. 18, &c.
17. GIVE REPROACH,] as in 2 K. 19. 9—14;
Isa. 37. 9—14.
18. JEWISH,] that is, Hebrew, as in 2 K.
18. 26.
WALL,] defending it and observing what
was said and transacted.
FRIGHTEN,] as in Neh. 6. 19.
TROUBLE,] or 'hasten,' as in 35. 21.
19. HANDS,] and therefore utterly helpless.
20. PRAYETH,] as in Isa. 37. 15—20; 38. 4, 21.
21. MESSENGER.] The Targum has 'Gabriel.'
CUTTETH OFF,] lit. 'hiddeth,' as in Ex. 23.
23; 1 K. 13. 34; Job 20. 12; Ps. 83. 4; Zec.
11. 8.
SHAME OF FACE,] as in Ezra 9. 7; Ps. 44.
15; Jer. 7. 19; Da. 9. 7, 8.
GOD] Nisroch, as in 2 K. 19. 37; Isa.
37. 38.
BOWELS,] that is, his sons Adrammelech
and Sharezer, Isa. 37. 38.

22. SAVETH,] as in Ex. 2. 17; 14. 30, &c.
LEADETH,] as in 23. 15; Ge. 47. 17; Ex. 15. 13, &c.
23. OFFERING,] as in Ge. 4. 3, 4, 5; 32. 13, &c.
PRECIOUS THINGS,] as in 21. 3; Ex. 24. 53.
LIFTED UP,] as in 1 Ch. 15. 2, &c.
24. SICK UNTO DEATH,] as in 2 K. 20. 1; Isa. 38. 1.
PRAYETH,] as in Ge. 20. 7, 17; Nu. 11. 2, &c.
WONDER,] as in Ex. 4. 21; 7. 3, 9; 11. 9, 10, &c.
25. NOT RETURNED,] thanks and gratitude to God.
DEED] of kindness and mercy.
LOFTY,] as if his greatness were his own.
WRATH,] from God his sovereign and protector.
26. HUMBLED,] at the denouncement of Isaiah the prophet.
DAYS OF HEZEKIAH,] but in those of his son's son; see Isa. 39. 7, 8.
27. RICHES..HONOUR,] as in v. 23 above.
PRECIOUS STONE,] as in 2 Sa. 12. 30; 1 K. 5. 17, &c.
SPICES,] as in Ex. 25. 6; 30. 23; 35. 8; 1 K. 10. 2, 10, 25, &c.
SHIELDS,] as in Ge. 15. 1, &c.
28. STOREHOUSES,] as in Ex. 1. 11; 1 K. 9. 19; 2 Ch. 8. 4, 6; 16. 4; 17. 12.
STALLS,] as in 1 K. 4. 26; 2 Ch. 9. 25.
29. MADE,] that is, built or acquired.
POSSESSIONS,] as in Ge. 26. 14, &c.
SUBSTANCE,] as in Ge. 12. 5; 13. 6, &c.
30. STOPPED,] as in v. 3, 4 above.
SOURCE,] or 'outlet,' as in 2 K. 2. 21, &c.
GIHON,] as in 33. 14; 1 K. 1. 33, 38.
DIRECTETH,] as in Job 37. 3; Ps. 119. 128; Prov. 3. 6; 9. 15; 11. 5; 15. 21; Isa. 40. 3.
PROSPERETH,] as in 31. 21.
31. AMBASSADORS,] or 'interpreters,' as in Ge. 42. 23; Job 16. 20; 33. 23; Isa. 43. 27.
WONDER,] as in v. 24.
TRY,] as in Ge. 22. 1; Ex. 15. 25, &c.
HEART,] whether good or evil.
32. MATTERS,] not 'acts,' as in the C.V.
KIND ACTS,] as in 6. 42; 35. 26, &c.
VISION.] See Isa. 1. 1; 36. 37—39.
33. LIETH,] as in Ge. 47. 30.
UPPERMOST,] or 'ascent.'
DONE HONOUR,] probably by a national mourning.
MANASSEH,] i.e. 'causing to forget.'

XXXIII. 1. 12 YEARS,] being born in 710 B.C.; see 2 K. 21. 1.
55 YEARS,] a longer period than any of the other kings of Israel and Judah.
2. EVIL THING,] that is, idolatry.
ABOMINATIONS,] as in Ge. 43. 32; 46. 34; Ex. 8. 26; Lev. 18. 22, 26, 27, 29, 30; 20. 13; De. 7. 25, 26, &c.
DISPOSSESSED,] as in 2 K. 16. 3; 21. 2, &c.
3. BROKEN DOWN,] as related in 30. 14; 31. 1; 32. 12.
BAALIM,] as in 1 K. 16. 32, &c.
SHRINES,] as in 1 K. 14. 15; 15. 13; 2 K. 17. 16; 21. 3, &c.
SERVETH,] as if they were gods.
4. IN THE HOUSE,] or temple of Jehovah himself.

SAID,] in 6. 6; 7. 16, &c.
5. TWO COURTS,] the outer and inner.
6. FIRE,] as in Lev. 18. 21, &c.
HINNOM,] as in 2 K. 23. 10, &c.
OBSERVED CLOUDS,] as in Lev. 19. 26; De. 18. 10, 14; Jud. 9. 37; 2 K. 21. 6; Isa. 2. 6; 57. 3; Jer. 27. 9; Mic. 5. 12.
USED ENCHANTMENTS,] as in Ge. 30. 27; 44. 5, 15; Lev. 19. 26; De. 18. 10; 1 K. 20. 33; 2 K. 17. 17; 21. 6.
WITCHCRAFT,] as in 2 K. 9. 22; Isa. 47. 9, 12; Mic. 5. 12; Nah. 3. 4, &c.
FAMILIAR SPIRIT,] as in Lev. 19. 31; 20. 6, 27; De. 18. 11; 1 Sa. 28. 3, 7, 8, 9; 2 K. 21. 6; 23. 24, &c.
WIZARD,] as in Lev. 19. 31; 20. 6, 27; De. 18. 11; 1 Sa. 28. 3, 9; 2 K. 21. 6; 23. 24; Isa. 8. 19; 19. 3.
ANGER,] as in De. 4. 25; 9. 18; 31. 29; 32. 16, 21, &c.
7. GRAVEN IMAGE,] as in Ex. 20. 4; Lev. 26. 1, &c.
IDOL,] as in v. 15; De. 4. 16; Eze. 8. 3, 5.
SAID,] in 2 Sa. 17. 13, &c.
8. FOOT,] as in 2 Sa. 7. 10, &c.
9. ERR,] as in Ge. 20. 13; 2 K. 21. 9; Job 12. 24, 25, &c.
NATIONS] of the Canaanites, &c.
10. ATTENDED,] as in 20. 15; 1 Sa. 15. 22; Neh. 9. 34, &c.
11. ASSHUR,] Ezarhaddon, son and successor of Sennacherib; see 2 K. 19. 37.
THICKETS] whether he had fled for safety; not 'thorns,' as in the C.V.
BRAZEN FETTERS.] as in 36. 6; Jud. 16. 21; 2 Sa. 3. 34; 2 K. 25. 7; Jer. 39. 7; 52. 11.
BABYLON,] now apparently become the capital of Asshur.
12. APPEASED,] as in Ex. 32. 11, &c.
HUMBLED,] as in Lev. 26. 41; De. 9. 3, &c.
13. PRAYETH,] as in Ge. 20. 7, 17; Nu. 11. 2, &c.
ENTREATED,] as in Ge. 25. 21; 2 Sa. 21. 14, &c.
SUPPLICATION,] as in Jos. 11. 20; 1 K. 8. 28, 30, 38, 45, 49, 52, 54; 9. 3; 2 Ch. 6. 19, 29, 35, 39, &c.
KNOWETH,] by experience of good and evil.
GOD,] ruling over all men and things.
14. CITY OF DAVID,] that is, Zion.
GIHON,] the brook of that name, stopped by Hezekiah, as in 32. 10.
FISH-GATE,] as in Neh. 3. 3; 12. 39; Zeph. 1. 10.
TOWER,] in Heb. 'Ophel,' as in 27. 3; 2 K. 5. 24; Neh. 3. 26, 27; 11. 21; Mic. 4. 8; Isa. 32. 14.
DEFENCED,] as in Nu. 13. 28; De, 1. 28; 3. 5; 9. 1; 28. 52; Jos. 14. 12; 2 Sa. 20. 6; 2 K. 18. 13, &c.
15. STRANGER,] as in Ge. 35. 24; De. 31. 16; 32. 12; Jos. 24. 20, 23; Jud. 10. 16; 1 Sa. 7, 3; 2 Ch. 14. 3, &c.
IDOL.] See v. 7 above.
16. THE ALTAR,] which had fallen into ruin, or been destroyed.
THANK-OFFERING,] as in Lev. 7. 12, 13, 15; 22. 29; Jos. 7. 19; 2 Ch. 29. 31; Ezra 10. 11; Neh. 12. 27, &c.
17. HIGH PLACES,] as in 1 Sa. 9. 12, 13, 14, 19, 25, &c.
18. MATTERS,] not 'acts,' as in C.V.

PRAYER,] said to be preserved in the Apocrypha.
SEERS,] perhaps Joel, Nahum, Habakkuk.
19. ENTREATY,] as in v. 13.
GRAVEN IMAGES,] as in v. 22; 34. 3, 4, 7.
HOZAI.] So Targum and Vulgate.
20. LIETH,] as in Ge. 47. 30, &c.
OWN HOUSE,] in his garden, as in 2 K. 21. 18; compare John 19. 41.
AMON,] i.e. an 'artificer.'
21. 22 YEARS,] as in 2 K. 21. 19.
22. EVIL THING,] as in v. 2 above.
GRAVEN IMAGES,] as in De. 7. 5, 25; 12. 3; Jud. 3. 19, 26; 2 K. 17. 41; 2 Ch. 33. 19, 22; 34. 3, 4, 7, &c.
23. HUMBLING,] as in v. 12 above.
GUILT,] as in Lev. 4. 3; 6. 5.
24. CONSPIRE,] as in 1 Sa. 22. 8, &c.
OWN HOUSE,] as in 2 Sa. 4. 5—12; 2 K. 20. 1; 21. 23, 26; 2 Ch. 24. 25; 26. 25—28.
25. SMITE,] as in 2 Sa. 1. 15; 2 K. 21. 24, &c.
JOSIAH,] prophesied in 1 K. 13. 2.

XXXIV. 1. 8 YEARS,] as in 2 K. 22. 1.
31 YEARS,] B.C. 641—610.
RIGHT,] or 'upright.'
RIGHT OR LEFT,] as in De. 5. 32, &c.
3. 8TH YEAR,] B.C. 634.
YOUTH,] being 16 years of age.
SEEK,] the knowledge and favour of Jehovah.
12TH YEAR] of his reign, having received confidence and encouragement.
CLEANSE,] as in 29. 15, 16; and v. 8 below.
MOLTEN IMAGES,] left by Manasseh, or set up since his death.
4. BAALIM,] as in 33. 3, &c.
BEATEN SMALL,] as in Ex. 30. 36, &c.
SPRINKLETH,] as in 2 K. 23. 6, &c.
5. BURNT,] as foretold 350 years before, in 1 K. 13. 2.
6. MANASSEH..NAPHTALI,] which were left nearly desolate by the captivity of the ten tribes, 2 K. 18. 11, 12.
TOOLS,] as in Ex. 20. 25; Jos. 5. 2, 3, &c.
7. BREAKETH DOWN,] as in Ex. 34. 13, &c.
CUT DOWN,] as in De. 7. 5; 12. 3; Jud. 21. 6, &c.
8. 18TH YEAR,] when he was 26 years of age; see 2 K. 22. 3.
CLEANSE,] as in v. 3.
SHAPHAN,] i.e. a 'rabbit, or coney.'
AZALIAH,] i.e. 'kept back by Jah.'
MAASEIAH,] i.e. 'work of Jah.'
JOAH,] i.e. 'Jah is brother.'
JOHAZ,] i.e. 'Jah has laid hold.'
REMEMBRANCER,] as in Ge. 41. 9; Nu. 5. 15; 2 Sa. 8. 16; 20. 24; 1 K. 4. 3; 2 K. 18. 18, 37; 1 Ch. 18. 15; Isa. 36. 3, 22; 62. 6; 66. 3; Eze. 21. 23; 29. 16.
9. HILKIAH,] i.e. 'portion of Jah.'
THRESHOLD,] of the temple, as in 2 K. 12. 9, &c.
MANASSEH, &c.,] those remaining of the ten tribes, after their captivity.
10. WORKMEN,] lit. 'doers of the work,' as in Ex. 31. 14, 15; 35. 2, 35, &c.
TO REPAIR.] This original verb is not found elsewhere.
11. ARTIFICERS,] as in Ex. 28. 11; 35. 35; 38. 23, &c.

BUILDERS,] as in Ge. 4. 17; 1 K. 5. 18; 6. 2; 2 K. 12. 11, &c.
HEWN STONES,] as in 2 K. 12. 12; 22. 6.
COUPLINGS,] as in 1 Ch. 22. 3.
BEAMS,] as in Neh. 2. 8
DESTROYED,] lit. 'marred,' as in Ge. 6. 7.
12. JAHATH,] i.e. 'union,' perhaps.
OBADIAH,] i.e. 'servant of Jah.'
MERARI,] as in Ex. 6. 16, the third son of Levi.
ZECHARIAH,] i.e. 'remembered of Jah.'
MESHULLAM,] i.e. 'recompensed.'
KOHATHITE,] the second son of Levi, as in Ex. 6. 16, &c.
OVERLOOK,] as in 1 Ch. 15. 21; 23. 4, &c.
13. BURDEN-BEARERS,] as in 1 K. 5. 15; 2 Ch. 2. 2, 18; Neh. 4. 10.
SCRIBES,] as in Jud. 5. 14; 2 Sa. 8. 17, &c.
OFFICERS,] as in Ex. 5. 6, 10, 14, 15, 19; Nu. 11. 16, &c.
GATE-KEEPERS,] as in 2 Sa. 18. 26; 2 K. 7. 10, 11; 1 Ch. 9. 17, 18, 21, 22, 24, 26, &c.
14. THE BOOK,] not 'a book,' as in C.V.; but see 2 K. 22. 8.
BY THE HAND,] this is not in 2 K. 22. 8.
16. THY SERVANTS,] Hilkiah and Shaphan.
17. POUR OUT,] as in 2 K. 22. 9; Job 10. 10, &c.
18. READETH] aloud, as orientals generally do, even when alone.
19. LAW] of God, as written by Moses.
RENDETH,] in token of grief at the denunciations it contains.
20. AHIKAM,] i.e. 'brother of a withstander.'
ABDON,] i.e. 'servile.'
MICAH,] i.e. 'who is like Jah?'
ASAIAH,] i.e. 'doing of Jah.'
21. SEEK,] the favour and good will of the God of Israel.
LEFT,] by the Assyrians who had carried the ten tribes captive.
FURY,] lit. 'heat.'
POURED OUT,] as in 12. 7; Job 3. 24, &c.
22. HULDAH,] i.e. a 'mole or weasel.'
PROPHETESS,] as in Ex. 15. 20; Jud. 4. 4; 2 K. 22. 14; Neh. 6. 14; Isa. 8. 3.
SHALLUM,] i.e. 'recompense.'
TIKVATH,] i.e. 'hope.'
HASRAH,] or Harhas, as in 2 K. 22. 14.
GARMENTS,] of the priests most probably.
SECOND] part of the city of Jerusalem, as in Zeph. 1. 19; Neh. 11. 9.
23. THE MAN,] Josiah the king; this is the language of God, not of the prophetess.
24. EXECRATIONS,] as in Ge. 24. 41.
25. PROVOKE,] as in De. 4. 25; 9. 18; 31. 29; 32. 16, 21, &c.
POURED FORTH,] as in v. 21.
QUENCHED,] by repentance and reformation.
26. KING OF JUDAH,] this is the language of Huldah.
HEARD] read out of the book that was found in the temple.
27. TENDER,] afraid of incurring the wrath of God.
HUMBLED,] in body and in mind.
REND,] as in v. 19 above.
AFFIRMATION,] as in Ge. 22. 16, &c.
28. GATHERED,] as in 2 K. 22. 20, &c.

29. ELDERS,] who ruled in each city; see 2 K. 23. 1.

30. GREAT..SMALL,] as in Ge. 19. 11, &c. READETH,] or 'proclaimeth.'

31. STATION,] as in 30. 16; 35. 10; Neh. 8. 7; 9. 3; 13. 11; Da. 8. 17, 18; 10. 11; 11. 1. HEART..SOUL,] as in De. 4. 29; 6. 5; 10. 12; 11. 13, 18; 13. 3; 26. 26; 30. 2, 6, 10, &c. COVENANT,] as in Ex. 24. 7; 34. 27, 28; De. 4. 13; 29. 19, &c.

32. PRESENTETH,] *lit.* 'causeth to stand,' as in Ge. 47. 7; Ex. 9. 16; Lev. 14. 11, &c. FOUND,] as in Ge. 19. 15; 47. 14; De. 20. 11; Jud. 20. 48; 1 Sa. 13. 15, 16; 21. 3; 2 K. 12. 10, 18; 14. 14, &c.

33. ABOMINATIONS,] as in Ge. 43. 32; 46. 34; Ex. 8. 26, &c. THEIR GOD,] by this renewed profession, as well as the God of their fathers.

XXXV. 1. PASSOVER,] as in Ex. 12. 3, &c. MONTH,] that is, Nisan, the time appointed for its celebration; see Ex. 12. 6.

2. CHARGES,] that all things might be done decently and in order. STRENGTHENETH,] by encouraging words and promises.

3. TEACHING,] as in 1 Ch. 15. 22; 25. 7, 8; 27. 32; 28. 9; 2 Ch. 26. 5; 34. 12; Ezra 8. 16, &c. ARK,] which probably had been removed during the cleansing and repairing of the temple. SHOULDER,] having now a fixed abode.

4. PREPARE,] or 'make ready,' for their several duties. WRITING,] as in 1 Ch. 28. 19; 2 Ch. 2. 11; Ezra 2. 62; 4. 7; Neh. 7. 64; Est. 1. 22; 3. 12, 14; 4. 8; 8. 8, 9, 13; 9. 27; Eze. 13. 9; Da. 10. 21.

5. STAND,] or 'continue, abide.' DIVISIONS,] as in Ezra 6. 18. SONS OF THE PEOPLE,] that is, common people, as in v. 7, 12. PORTION,] of duty and privilege.

6. MOSES,] as in Ex. 12. 1—28, 43—49.

7. LIFTETH UP,] as presents for the use of the general public. SUBSTANCE,] as in Ge. 12. 5; 13. 6; 14. 11, 12, 16, 21; 15. 14, &c.

8. WILLING-OFFERING,] as in Ex. 35. 29; 36. 3, &c JEHIEL,] i.e. 'God lives.' LEADERS,] as in 1 Sa. 9. 16; 10. 1; 13. 14; 25. 30; 2 Sa. 5. 2; 6. 21; 7. 8; 1 K. 1. 35; 14. 7; 16. 2; 2 K. 20. 5, &c. 9. CONANIAH,] i.e. 'prepared of Jah;' see 31. 12 SHEMAIAH,] i.e. 'heard of Jah.' NETHANEEL,] i.e. 'gift of Jah.' HASHABIAH,] i.e. 'reckoning of Jah.' JEIEL.] Etymology uncertain. JOZABAD,] i.e. 'Jah has endowed.'

10. PREPARED,] or 'made ready,' or 'established.' STATION,] according to their rank and office, each in his place.

11. SLAUGHTER,] in behalf of the whole multitude, according to the law. SPRINKLE,] the blood, as in 30. 16, &c. STRIPPING] off the skins of the animals for sacrifice.

12. DIVISIONS,] as in v. 5. WRITTEN,] as in Lev. 3. 3, &c.

13. COOK,] as in Ex. 12. 9; 16. 23; 23. 19; 29. 31; 34. 26; Lev. 6. 28; 8. 31, &c. ORDINANCE,] *lit.* 'judgment;' as in Ex. 12. 8, 9. POTS,] as in Ex. 16. 3; 27. 3; 38. 3; 1 K. 7. 45, &c. KETTLES,] as in 1 Sa. 2. 14; 2 K. 10. 7; Job 41. 20; Ps. 81. 6; Jer. 24. 2. PANS,] as in 2 K. 2. 20; 21. 13; Prov. 19. 24; 26. 15.

14. PREPARED,] as in v. 10. NIGHT,] the number of sacrifices being so great.

15. SINGERS,] as in 1 Ch. 6. 33; 9. 33; 15. 16, 19, 27; 2 Ch. 5. 12, 13; 20. 21; 23. 13; 29. 28; Ezra 2. 41, &c. STATION,] as in v. 10. SEER,] as in 2 Sa. 24. 11; 2 K. 17. 13; 1 Ch. 21. 9; 25. 5; 29. 29; 2 Ch. 9. 29; 12. 15; 19. 2; 29. 25, 30; 33. 18, &c. GATE-KEEPERS,] as in 2 Sa. 18. 26; 2 K. 7. 10, 11; 1 Ch. 9. 17, 18, 21, 22, 24, 26; 15. 18, &c. PREPARED,] as in v. 4, 10, 14.

16. TO KEEP,] *lit.* 'do,' as in Ex. 12. 47.

17. FOUND,] present in Jerusalem at that time. SEVEN DAYS,] as in 30. 21.

18. PROPHET,] the last of the judges, before Saul, B.C. 1060. NONE.] Compare 2 K. 23. 22, 23.

19. 18TH YEAR,] B.C. 623.

20. HOUSE] of Jehovah, as in 34. 8. NECHO,] i.e. the 'smitten,' that is 'lame,' so Targum; see 2 K. 23. 29; Jer. 46. 2. CARCHEMISH,] a city on the Euphrates, as in Isa. 10. 9; Jer. 46. 2. PHRAT,] the river of that name, as in Ge. 2. 14.

21. TO ME AND TO THEE,] in common, as often elsewhere. WAR,] viz., the king of Asshur. GOD,] in *Heb.* Elohim, as in Ge. 1. 1, &c. HASTE,] and not to prevent him from executing vengeance. CEASE,] as in Ex. 14. 12; 2 Ch. 25. 16, &c. WITH ME,] in the expedition against Asshur. DESTROY,] or 'mar,' as in Ge. 6. 12, 13, &c.

22. TURNED ROUND,] as in Jud. 18. 23; 1 K. 8. 14, &c. DISGUISED HIMSELF,] as in 1 Sa. 28. 8, &c. GOD,] not believing that it was the word of God. MEGIDDO,] in Manasseh, as in Jos. 17. 11, &c.

23. ARCHERS,] as in 1 Sa. 31. 3; 2 K. 17. 28, &c. REMOVE,] *lit.* 'cause to pass over or away.' SICK,] as in 18. 33; 1 K. 22. 34.

24. SECOND CHARIOT,] as in Ge. 41. 43, &c. MOURNING,] as in Ge. 37. 34; Ex. 33. 4, &c.

25. JEREMIAH,] the prophet. LAMENTETH,] as in 2 Sa. 1. 17; 3. 33; Jer. 9. 17; Eze. 27. 32; 32. 16. SONGSTRESSES,] as in 2 Sa. 19. 35; Ecc. 2. 8; Ezra 2. 65; Neh. 7. 67. LAMENTATIONS,] as in 2 Sa. 1. 17; Jer. 7. 29; 9. 10, 20; Eze. 2. 10; 19. 1, 14; 26. 17; 27. 2, 32 28. 12; 32. 2, 16; Amos 5. 1; 8. 10.

STATUTE,] as in Jud. 11. 39, &c.
26. MATTERS,] not 'acts,' as in C.V.
KIND ACTS,] as in 32. 32; Ge. 32. 10.
27. WRITTEN,] as in 36. 8, &c.

XXXVI. 1. JEHOAHAZ.] See 1 K. 13. 3,
&c., in Jer. 22. 11 called 'Shallum;' so in
1 Ch. 3. 15.
2. 23 YEARS,] being two years younger
than his brother Jehoiakim; as in v. 5.
3. TURN HIM ASIDE,] as a usurper and not
sufficiently pliable.
FINETH,] as in Prov. 19. 19; Ex. 21. 22, &c.
100 TALENTS,] about £37,500.
A TALENT,] about £4,500, or £5,067.
4. ELIAKIM,] as in Jos. 18. 18, &c.
JEHOIAKIM,] i.e. 'Jah raises up.'
5. 25 YEARS,] two years older than his
brother Jehoahaz; see 2 K. 23. 31; B.C. 610.
11 YEARS,] till B.C. 599.
EVIL THING,] that is, idolatry.
6. NEBUCHADNEZZAR,] i.e. 'Nebo is prince
of gods, or god of fire, or prince of Mercury;'
sometimes spelled 'Nebuchadrezzar,' as in
Jer. 39. 1, 11; 43. 11; Eze. 29. 18.
BRAZEN FETTERS,] as in Jud. 16. 21; 2 Sa.
3. 34, &c.
7. TEMPLE,] of idols, which he worshipped.
8. MATTERS,] not 'acts,' as in C.V.
ABOMINATIONS,] of idolatry, &c.
JEHOIACHIN,] i.e. 'Jah makes ready;' in
1 Ch. 3. 16 it is 'Jeconiah;' in Jer. 22. 24 it
is 'Coniah.'
9. 8 YEARS,] in 2 K. 24. 8 it is 18 years.
EVIL THING,] that is, idolatry, as in v. 5.
10. TURN OF THE YEAR,] B.C. 599.
DESIRABLE VESSELS,] as in 32. 27; Jer. 25.
34; Da. 11. 8; Hos. 13. 15; Nah. 2. 9.
ZEDEKIAH,] i.e. 'rightness of Jah;' in 2
K. 24. 17 it is 'Mattaniah,' his father's
brother.
11. 21 YEARS,] as in 2 K. 24. 18.
11 YEARS,] till B.C. 588.
12. EVIL THING,] as in v. 5, 9.
HUMBLED,] as in Lev. 26. 41; De. 9. 3, &c.
13. REBELLED,] as in Ge. 14. 4; Nu. 14. 9,
&c.
SWEAR,] as in Ge. 24. 3, 37; 50. 5, 6, 25, &c.
NECK,] as in 29. 6; 30. 8, &c.
HEART,] as in De. 2. 30; 15. 7, &c.
14. ABOMINATIONS,] connected with idolatry especially.

DEFILE,] as in Ge. 34. 5; 12. 27; Lev. 11.
44, &c.
15. SENDING,] as in Jer. 7. 25.
PITY,] as in Ex. 2. 6; De. 13. 8, &c.
HABITATION,] as in De. 26. 15; 1 Sa. 2. 29,
32; 1 Ch. 4. 41; 2 Ch. 30. 27; Ps. 26. 8, &c.
16. MOCKING.] This original word is not
found elsewhere.
DESPISING,] as in Ge. 25. 34; Nu. 15. 31, &c.
ACTING DECEITFULLY,] as in Ge. 27. 12;
Prov. 4. 22; 6. 15; 12. 18; 13. 17; 16. 24; 29.
1; Jer. 8. 15; 14. 19; 33. 6; Mal. 4. 2.
HEALING,] as in 21. 18.
17. CHALDEANS,] that is, Nebuchadnezzar,
as in v. 6.
CHOICE ONES,] as in De. 32. 25, &c.
PITY,] as in v. 15.
VIRGIN,] as in Ge. 24. 16; Ex. 22. 16, 17, &c.
VERY AGED.] This original word is not
found elsewhere.
18. GREAT..SMALL,] of all sizes and kinds.
19. BURN,] as in 2 K. 25. 9, &c.
WALL,] to prevent it being a fortified
place, as in 2 K. 25. 10.
PALACES,] as in 1 K. 16. 18; 2 K. 15. 25;
Ps. 48. 3, 13; 122. 7; Prov. 18. 19; Isa. 23. 13;
25. 2, &c.
TO DESTRUCTION,] or 'marring,' as in Ge.
6. 12, 13, &c.
20. REMOVETH,] as in 2 K. 15. 29; 17. 11, &c.
SONS,] Evil Merodach and Belshazzar;
see Jer. 27. 7.
PERSIA,] over Babylon and the Chaldeans,
B.C. 536.
21. WORD,] as in Jer. 25. 12; 27. 7; 29. 10.
SABBATHS,] as in Lev. 26. 34, 35.
DESOLATION,] caused by removing the
inhabitants to Babylon.
70 YEARS,] as prophesied of by Jeremiah
the prophet; see Jer. 25. 9—12; 26. 6, 7; 29.
10, Da. 9. 2.
22. CYRUS,] i.e. 'a son or lord.'
JEREMIAH,] as in v. 21.
WAKED UP,] as in Ezra 1. 1, 5; Jer. 51. 11;
Hag. 1. 14.
INTIMATION,] lit. 'voice.'
WRITING,] to make it more certain and
irreversible.
23. EARTH,] so far as known in his day.
CHARGE,] as in Ezra 1. 2; Job 34. 13; Jer.
44. 13; Zeph. 3. 7; Ex. 32. 34; Isa. 13. 11, &c.
GO UP,] to Jerusalem, as in Ezra 1. 3.

EZRA

THE BOOK OF EZRA is so evidently a continuation of the 'Book of Chronicles,' that the first two verses of it are found in almost all Hebrew MSS. attached to the conclusion of the latter, and they are so naturally and necessarily connected with 2 Ch. 36. 21, that it is most probable they were written by the same author. Ezra, the reputed writer, according to ch. 7. 1, was son of Seraiah, the high-priest, who was slain by Nebuchadnezzar, as noted in Jer. 52. 24, 27; he was brother of Josedech and uncle of Joshua, who were both high-priests in succession, and he is described as a ready scribe in the law of Moses.

It embraces a period of about eighty years, from B.C. 536 to B.C. 458, from the decree of Cyrus, for the rebuilding of the temple, till the reconstruction of the Mosaic laws regarding marriage, &c., and its contents may be arranged under five divisions, viz. Ch. I., the decree of Cyrus; II., III., the proceedings of the people in consequence of that decree; IV—VI., the hindrances they met with, and their ultimate success; VII—VIII.; the mission of Ezra; and IX—X., his trials and final success. With the Book of Ezra may be studied the prophecies of Haggai and Zechariah.

I. 1. FIRST YEAR] of his reign over Babylon, B.C. 536.

CYRUS,] i.e. a 'sun *or* lord.'

PERSIA,] as in 2 Ch. 36. 20, 22.

COMPLETION] of the seventy years, foretold by Jeremiah, 25. 1, 11, 12; 29. 10.

JEREMIAH,] as in 2 Ch. 36. 21.

WAKED UP,] as in 2 Ch. 36. 21; Jer. 51. 11; Hag. 1. 14.

INTIMATION,] *lit.* 'voice.'

WRITING,] to make it more certain and irreversible.

2. EARTH,] so far as known in his day.

HEAVENS,] who rules over all.

GIVEN] in accordance with his promise, as in Isa. 44. 28.

LAID A CHARGE,] as in Ezra 1. 2; Job 34. 13; Zeph. 3. 7; Ex. 32. 34; Isa. 13. 11, &c.

HOUSE] where he might be publicly worshipped.

JERUSALEM,] which he had before chosen as his habitation.

JUDAH,] which was now a province of the Persian empire.

3. PEOPLE,] the Jews, whom he had selected.

WITH HIM] to help and guide him in duty.

GO UP] from Babylon and Persia.

GOD OF ISRAEL,] by especial covenant.

THE GOD,] the only true one, as in Ge. 6. 2, &c.

4. LEFT] alive of the captives of Israel, too poor to return of himself.

SOJOURNER,] for the time being, as in Ge. 12. 10. &c.

ASSIST,] *lit.* 'lift him up,' as in 2 Sa. 5. 12; 19. 42, &c.

BEASTS,] or 'cattle,' as in Ge. 1. 24—26; 2. 20; 3. 14, &c.

FREE-WILL OFFERING,] of their own, in addition to the preceding items which were under the nature of a command.

5. HEADS OF THE FATHERS,] as in Nu. 31. 26; 32. 28; 36. 1, &c.

PRIESTS..LEVITES,] the leaders and teachers in all matters.

WAKED UP,] as in v. 1.

6. STRENGTHENED,] as in Ex. 4. 21; 9. 12, 10. 20, 27; 11. 10; 14. 4, 8, 17; De. 1. 38, &c.

GOODS,] as in Ge. 12. 5; 13. 6; 14. 11, 12, 16, 21; 15. 14; 31. 18, &c.

PRECIOUS THINGS,] as in Ge. 24. 53; 2 Ch. 21. 3; 32. 23.

OFFERED WILLINGLY,] as in v. 4 above.

7. BROUGHT OUT] from the place where they had been laid up by Nebuchadnezzar, even the

HOUSE OF HIS GODS.] See 2 Ch. 36. 7; Da. 1. 2; 5. 2. 3.

8. MITHREDATH,] i.e. 'given by Mithras,' as in 4. 7.

TREASURER,] as in 7. 21.

SHESHBAZZAR,] i.e. 'worshipper of fire,' perhaps; another name of Zerubbabel, as in v. 11; 5. 14.

PRINCE,] *lit.* 'lifted up one.'

9. DISHES.] This original word is not found elsewhere.

KNIVES.] The original word is not found elsewhere.

10. BASINS,] as in 8. 27; 1 Ch. 28. 17.

SECONDS,] as in Ge. 41. 43; 43. 12, 15; Ex 16. 5, 22, &c.

OTHER VESSELS,] belonging to the temple service.

11. 5,400.] This number probably included those given in presents, as in v. 6 above.

REMOVAL] of the captive Jews.

BABYLON,] the city or the province of that name.

II. 1. SONS OF THE PROVINCE,] of Babylon, or of Judea, as in 5. 8.

CAPTIVES,] as in Ex. 12. 29; Nu. 21. 1; 31. 12, 19, 26, &c.

THE REMOVAL] from Jerusalem and Judah.

REMOVED,] as in 2 Ch. 36. 20.

CITY] in which he or his family previously resided; see Neh. 11. 1, &c.

2. ZERUBBABEL,] i.e. 'scattered *or* born at Babylon.'

JESHUA,] i.e. a 'saviour;' in Haggai 1. 1 it is Joshua, son of Josedech.

NEHEMIAH,] i.e. 'comforted of Jah;' see Neh. 1. 1.

SERAIAH,] i.e. 'head of Jah,' supposed to be Azariah in Neh. 7. 7, and the same with Ezra the scribe.

REELAIAH,] i.e. 'a reeling of Jah.'

MORDECAI,] i.e. 'a little man *or* worshipper of Mars.'
BILSHAN,] i.e. 'son of tongue,' that is, loquacious or eloquent, as in Neh. 7. 7.
MISPAR,] i.e. 'number.'
BIGVAI,] i.e. 'a gardener' perhaps, as in v. 14; 8. 14; Neh. 7. 19.
REHUM,] i.e. 'merciful.'
BAANAH,] i.e. 'son of affliction.'
PEOPLE OF ISRAEL] in general, as distinguished from those of particular classes and localities.
3. PAROSH,] i.e. 'a flea,' as in 10. 25; Neh. 3. 25.
4. SHEPHATIAH,] i.e. 'judged of Jah.'
5. ARAH,] i.e. 'a path.'
6. PAHATH-MOAB,] i.e. 'pit, snare, *or* governor of Moab.'
JESHUA,] i.e. 'a saviour.'
JOAB,] i.e. 'Jah is father.'
7. ELAM,] i.e. 'concealed.'
8. ZATTU.] Etymology uncertain; see 10. 27; Neh. 7. 13; 10. 5.
9. ZACCAI,] i.e. 'pure.'
10. BANI,] i.e. 'built up.'
11. BEBAI.] Etymology uncertain; see 8. 11; Neh. 7. 16.
12. AZGAD,] i.e. 'strength of a troop;' see 8. 12; Neh. 7. 17; 10. 16.
13. ADONIKAM,] i.e. 'my lord has risen.'
14. BIGVAI.] See v. 2 above.
15. ADIN,] i.e. 'luxuriant,' as in Neh. 7. 20.
16. ATER,] i.e. 'shut, stopped,' as in Neh. 7. 21.
17. BEZAI,] i.e. 'miry,' as in Neh. 7. 23; 10. 19.
18. JORAH,] i.e. 'casting, shooting, sprinkling.'
19. HASHUM,] i.e. 'rich, wealthy,' as in 10. 33; Neh. 7. 22; 8. 4; 10. 19.
20. GIBBAR,] i.e. 'mighty,' perhaps for Gibeon, as in Neh. 7. 25.
21. BETH-LEHEM,] about six miles from Jerusalem.
22. NETOPHAH,] i.e. a 'dropping,' as in Neh. 7. 26; see 2 Sa. 23. 28, 29; 2 K. 25. 23.
23. ANATHOTH,] i.e. 'responses,' as in Jos. 21. 18, &c.
24. AZMAVETH,] i.e. 'strength of death.'
25. KIRJATH-ARIM,] i.e. 'city of forests.'
CHEPHIRAH,] i.e. 'a village,' as in Jos. 9. 17; 18. 26; Neh. 7. 29.
BEEROTH,] i.e. 'wells.'
26. RAMAH,] i.e. 'high place.'
GABA,] i.e. 'a height, hill.'
27. MICHMAS,] i.e. 'laid up, a treasure.'
28. BETHEL,] i.e. 'house of God.'
AI,] i.e. 'heap.'
29. NEBO,] i.e. a 'prophet.'
30. MAGBISH,] i.e. 'congregating.'
31. ELAM,] i.e. 'hidden, concealed.'
32. HARIM.] i.e. 'flat nosed,' as in 10. 31; Neh. 3. 11.
33. LOD,] i.e. 'contention, strife.'
HADID,] i.e. 'sharp,' as in Neh. 7. 37; 11. 34.
ONO,] i.e. 'strong,' as in Neh. 7. 37; 11. 35; 1 Ch. 8. 12.
34. JERICHO,] as in Nu. 22. 1; Jos. 2. 1, &c.
35. SENAAH,] i.e. 'thorny, bushy.'
36. PRIESTS,] sons of Aaron, as distinguished from the common people in v. 2.

JEDAIAH,] i.e. 'known of Jah.'
JESHUA,] i.e. 'a saviour.'
37. IMMER,] i.e. 'lamb, talkative.'
38. PASHHUR,] i. e. 'prosperity everywhere.'
39. HARIM,] i.e. 'flat-nosed.'
40. LEVITES,] who had been given by God as assistants to the priests.
JESHUA,] i.e. 'a saviour.'
KADMIEL,] i.e. 'before God.'
HODAVIAH,] i.e. 'praise Jah.'
41. SINGERS,] who conducted the temple psalmody, as in 2 Ch. 35. 15.
ASAPH,] i.e. 'he gathers.'
42. GATE-KEEPERS,] of the temple, as in 1 Ch. 9. 7.
SHALLUM,] i.e. 'recompensed.'
ATER,] i.e. 'bound, shut.'
TALMON,] i.e. 'oppressed.'
AKKUB,] i.e. 'taken by the heel.'
HATITA,] i.e. 'digging, exploring.'
SHOBAI,] i.e. 'a captor.'
43. NETHINIM,] i.e. 'given' to the service of the Levites (see Nu. 8. 19), as in 7. 24; 8. 17, 20; Neh. 3. 31; 7. 46, 60, 70; 11. 3, 21, &c.
ZIHA,] i.e. 'dryness.'
HASUPHA,] i.e. 'made naked,' as in Neh. 7. 46.
TABBAOTH,] i.e. 'signets.'
44. KEROS,] i.e. 'a weaver's comb,' as in Neh. 7. 47.
SIAHA,] i.e. 'counsel, congregation,' as in Neh. 7. 47.
PADON,] i.e. 'liberation, redemption,' as in Neh. 7. 47.
45. LEBANAH,] i.e. 'white, the moon,' as in Neh. 7. 48.
HAGABAH,] i.e. 'a locust,' as in Neh. 7. 48.
AKKUB,] i.e. 'taken by the heel.'
46. HAGAB,] i.e. 'a locust.'
SHALMAI,] i.e. 'peaceable;' *or* Shamlai.
HANAN,] i.e. 'he has grace.'
47. GIDDEL,] i.e. 'too great.'
GAHAR,] i.e. 'hiding-place,' as in Neh. 7.49.
REAIAH,] i.e. 'seen of Jah.'
48. REZIN,] i.e. 'firm, stable, prince.'
NEKODA,] i.e. 'speckled, spotted.'
GAZZAM,] i.e. 'palmer-worm.'
49. UZZA,] i.e. 'strength.'
PASEAH,] i.e. 'lame.'
BESAI,] i.e. 'a sword,' perhaps.
50. ASNAH,] i.e. 'storehouse, bramble.'
MEHUNIM,] i.e. 'dwellings, habitation.'
NEPHUSIM,] i.e. 'expansions.'
51. BAKKUK,] i.e. 'a bottle.'
HAKUPHA,] i.e. 'bent.'
HARHUR,] i.e. 'inflammation, burning fever.'
52. BAZLUTH,] i.e. 'a making naked.'
MEHIDA,] i.e. 'a joining together.'
HARSHA,] i.e. 'enchanter, magician.'
53. BARKOS,] i.e. 'a painter.'
SISERA,] i.e. 'a field of battle.'
THAMAH,] i.e. 'laughter.'
54. NEZIAH,] i.e. 'pure, sincere.'
HATIPHA,] i.e. 'seized, caught.'
55. SERVANTS OF SOLOMON,] who probably had some peculiar privilege conferred by that monarch.
SOTAI,] i.e. 'drawing back.'
SOPHERETH,] i.e. 'scribe.'

PERUDA,] i.e. 'grain, kernel,' as in Neh. 7. 57.
56. JAALAH,] i.e. 'female ibex, chamois.'
DARKON,] i.e. 'a scatterer,' perhaps.
GIDDEL,] i.e. 'too great, giant.'
57. SHEPHATIAH,] i.e. 'judged of Jah.'
HATTIL,] i.e. 'waving,' perhaps.
POCHERETH,] i.e. 'a snaring.'
ZEBAIM,] i.e. 'gazelles.'
AMI,] in Neh. 7. 59 it is Amon, 'a workman.'
58. NETHINIM,] as in v. 43 above.
SERVANTS OF SOLOMON,] as in v. 55.
59. TEL-MELAH,] i.e. 'hill or heap of salt.'
TEL-HARSA,] i.e. 'hill of a wood.'
CHERUB.] See Ge. 3. 24, &c.
ADDAN,] i.e. 'lord, judge;' in Neh. 7. 61 it is Addon.
IMMER,] i.e. 'talkative, loquacious.'
DECLARE,] as in Ge. 32. 5; 46. 3; De. 5. 5; Jud. 14. 12, 13, 14, &c.
ISRAEL,] or of the nations round them.
60. DELAIAH,] i.e. 'drawn up by Jah.'
TOBIAH,] i.e. 'goodness of Jah.'
NEKODA,] i.e. 'speckled, spotted.'
61. SONS OF THE PRIESTS,] as in v. 36.
HABAIAH,] i.e. 'hidden of Jah.'
KOZ,] i.e. 'the thorn.'
BARZILLAI,] i.e. 'of iron.'
GILEADITE,] as in 2 Sa. 17. 27, &c.
NAME,] as in Ge. 4. 17; 48. 6, 16, &c.
62. REGISTER,] lit. 'writing,' as in 4. 7; 1 Ch. 28. 19; 2 Ch. 2. 11; 35. 4; Neh. 7. 64; Est. 1. 22; 3. 12, 14; 4. 8; 8. 8, 9, 13; 9. 27; Eze. 13. 19; Da. 10. 21.
GENEALOGY,] as in v. 3; 1 Ch. 4. 33; 5. 1, 7; 7. 5, 7, 9, 40; 9. 22; 2 Ch. 12. 15; 31. 16—19; Neh. 7. 5, 64.
REDEEMED,] not 'polluted;' see Nu. 3. 46—51.
63. TIRSHATHA,] i.e. 'severity;' as in Neh. 7. 65, 70; 8. 9; 10. 2; compare Neh. 12. 26.
MOST HOLY THINGS,] which were offered in sacrifices.
URIM..THUMMIM,] as in Ex. 32. 30, &c.
64. ASSEMBLY,] gathered together at this time in Jerusalem.
42,360,] which includes those who had been in Jerusalem before the arrival of Zerubbabel.
65. SERVANTS..HANDMAIDS,] who were many of them probably not of Israel.
SINGERS . . . SONGSTRESSES,] who could minister in the temple in the praise of God.
66. MULES,] as in 2 Sa. 13. 29; 18. 9; 1 K. 10. 25; 18. 5; 2 K. 5. 17; 1 Ch. 12. 40; 2 Ch. 9. 24; Neh. 7. 68, &c.
67. ASSES,] as in Ge. 12. 16; 22. 3, 5; 24. 35; 30. 43; 32. 5; 34. 28; 36. 24; 42. 26, 27; 43. 18, 24; 44. 3, 13; 45. 23; 47. 17; 49. 14; Ex. 4. 20, &c.
68. HOUSE,] which was then lying in ruins, as burnt by Nebuchadnezzar.
OFFERED WILLINGLY,] as in Jud. 5. 2, 9, &c.
BASE,] as in 3. 2; 1 K. 7. 27—43; 2 K. 16. 17; 25. 13, 16; 2 Ch. 4. 14; Jer. 27. 29; 52. 17, 20.
69. POWER,] as in Ge. 4. 12; 31. 6; 49. 3; Ex. 9. 16, &c.
TREASURE,] as in De. 28. 12; 32. 34; Jos. 6. 19, 24; 1 K. 7. 51; 14. 26; 15. 18; 2 K. 12. 18, &c.

DRAMS,] as in Neh. 7. 70—72; compare 1 Ch. 29. 7; Ezra 8. 27; worth about 13s. 6d. sterling.
POUNDS,] as in 1 K. 10. 17; Neh. 7. 71, 72; Eze. 45. 12.
PRIESTS' COAT,] as in Neh. 7. 70, 72; Ex. 28. 4, &c.
70. PRIESTS..LEVITES,] as the spiritual guides and instructors of the people.
PEOPLE,] that is, the common people.
SINGERS,] as in v. 65 above.
GATE-KEEPERS,] as in v. 42 above.
NETHINIM,] as in v. 43 above.
CITIES,] scattered up and down through out the land.

III. 1. SEVENTH MONTH,] that is, Tisri.
CITIES,] as in 2. 70.
AS ONE MAN,] as in Nu. 14. 15, &c.
JERUSALEM,] where the temple had formerly been, and was to be again.
2. JESHUA,] i.e. 'a saviour.'
JOZADAK,] i.e. 'Jah is just.'
ZERUBBABEL,] i.e. 'scattered to Babel.'
SHEALTIEL,] i.e. 'I have asked of God.'
THE ALTAR,] which had been in ruins before.
BURNT-OFFERINGS,] for sin, as in Ge. 8. 20; 22. 2, &c.
WRITTEN,] in Lev. 1. 1—17.
MAN OF GOD,] as in De. 33. 1, &c.
3. BASES,] as in 1 K. 7. 27—43, &c.
FEAR,] as in Neh. 5. 12; Ex. 15. 16; 23. 27; De. 32. 25, &c.
PEOPLES OF THE LAND,] as in Ge. 23. 7, &c
MORNING..EVENING,] as directed in Ex. 29. 38, 39.
4. FEAST,] or 'festival,' as in Ex. 10. 9, &c.
THE BOOTHS,] as in Ge. 33. 17; Lev. 23. 24, &c.
WRITTEN,] in Lev. 23. 34—42.
THE DAY,] during the eight days of the festival.
ORDINANCE,] lit. 'judgment,' as in Nu. 29. 12—38.
IN ITS DAY,] as in Ex. 5. 13, 19; 16. 4, &c.
5. CONTINUAL,] as in Ex. 29. 42; Nu. 28. 3, &c.
NEW MOONS,] as in 1 Sa. 20. 5, 18, 24, &c.
APPOINTED SEASONS,] as in Ge. 1. 14; Lev. 23. 2, 4, 37, 44, &c.
SANCTIFIED,] that is, set apart to him and his service.
WILLING-OFFERING,] as in Ex. 35. 29; 36. 3, &c.
6. SEVENTH MONTH,] that is, Tisri, as in v. 1, on the first day of which was the blowing of trumpets, as in Lev. 23. 24, 25.
CAUSE TO ASCEND,] on the altar; the tenth of this month was the day of atonement; see Lev. 23. 27—32.
JEHOVAH,] as the covenant God of Israel.
TEMPLE OF JEHOVAH,] as in 1 Sa. 1. 9; 3 3, &c.
FOUNDED,] as yet by Zerubbabel, after the return from Babylon.
7. MONEY,] lit. 'silver.'
HEWERS,] as in 1 K. 5. 15; 2 K. 12. 12, &c.
ARTIFICERS,] as in Ex. 28. 11; 35. 35, &c.
FOOD,] as in Ge. 2. 9; 3. 6; 6. 21, &c.
DRINK,] as in Ge. 19. 3; 21. 8; 26. 30, &c.

OIL,] as in Ge. 28. 18; 35. 14; Ex. 25. 6; 27. 20; 29. 2, &c.

ZIDONIANS,] the inhabitants of Zidon, and TYRIANS,] the inhabitants of Tyre, in Phenicia, or the coast of the great sea.

CEDAR-TREES,] as in Lev. 14. 4, 6, 49, 51, 52, &c.

LEBANON,] which partly belonged to the Phenicians, and partly to the land of Israel, at one time.

JOPPA,] a sea-port, about forty miles from Jerusalem ; see 2 Ch. 2. 16.

PERMISSION,] not 'grant,' as in C.V.

8. SECOND YEAR,] B.C. 535.

SECOND MONTH,] that is, Ijar.

CAPTIVITY,] as in 2. 1, 2.

LEVITES,] who were naturally regarded as the leaders of the work.

TWENTY YEARS,] as in Ex. 30. 14; 38. 26; Lev. 27. 3, 5; Nu. 1. 3, &c.; see 1 Ch. 23. 24.

OVERLOOK,] as in 1 Ch. 15. 21; 23. 4; 2 Ch. 34. 12; v. 9 below.

9. JESHUA,] the Levite, as in 2. 40, not the high priest of that name.

KADMIEL,] i.e. 'before God ;' or Hodaviah, as in 2. 40.

OVERLOOK,] as in v. 8.

HENADAD,] i.e. 'grace of Hadad;' compare Neh. 3. 18, 24; 10. 9.

10. FOUNDED,] as in 1 K. 5. 17; 6. 37; 16. 34, &c.

CLOTHED,] with the proper priests' dresses, as in 2. 69.

TRUMPETS,] as in Nu. 10. 2—10; 31. 6, &c.

ASAPH,] i.e. 'he gathered.'

CYMBALS,] as in 1 Ch. 13. 8; 15. 16, 19, 28; 16. 5, 42; 25. 1, 6; 2 Ch. 5. 12, 13; 29. 25; Ezra 3. 10; Neh. 12. 27.

PRAISE,] as in 2 Sa. 14. 25; 1 Ch. 16. 4, &c.

BY MEANS OF,] lit. 'by the hands of ;' see 1 Ch. 15. 16.

11. RESPOND,] as in Ge. 18. 27; 23. 5, 10, 14; 24. 50; 27. 37, 39; 30. 33, &c.

PRAISING,] as in 2 Sa. 14. 25, &c.

GIVING THANKS,] as in 1 Ch. 16. 4, 7, 35, 41, &c.

KINDNESS,] as in Ge. 19. 19; 20. 13; 21, 23, &c.

12. SHOUTED,] as in Nu. 10. 7; Isa. 6. 5, 10, 16, 20, &c.

GIVING PRAISE,] as in v. 10, 11.

FOUNDED,] as in 2 Ch. 31. 7; Job 38. 4; Isa. 51. 16.

13. AGED MEN,] who must have been above eighty years of age.

FIRST HOUSE] which Solomon built.

WEEPING] with mingled feelings of joy and sorrow.

SHOUT,] as in Lev. 23. 24; 25. 9, &c.

VOICE,] as in Ge. 39. 18; Nu. 18. 30, 32; 1 Ch. 15. 16; 25. 5; 2 Ch. 5. 13, &c.

14. DISCERNING,] as in Ruth 2. 19; Neh. 13. 24; Ps. 142. 4, &c.

DISTANCE,] as in 2 Sa. 7. 19, &c.

IV. 1. ADVERSARIES,] the Samaritans, as appears from v. 2, 10.

SONS OF THE CAPTIVITY,] as in 6. 19, 20; 8. 35; 10. 7, 16.

TEMPLE,] for offering up sacrifices and vows.

2. ZERUBABBEL,] the chief civil ruler of the Jews, as in 2. 2.

WE SEEK,] the face and favour of Jehovah, the God of Israel.

NOT SACRIFICING,] to Him, for want of a suitable place.

ESAR-HADDON,] as in 2 K. 19. 37; Isa. 37. 38.

BROUGHT UP HITHER] from Babylon, &c.; as in 2 K. 17. 24.

3. JESHUA,] the high priest, as in 2. 2; 3. 2, &c.

OUR GOD,] for his worship and praise.

ISRAEL,] by covenant engagements often repeated.

COMMANDED,] or 'wished,' as in Ezra 1. 1—3.

4. PEOPLE OF THE LAND,] the Samaritans, &c.

FEEBLE,] as in Jer. 38. 4, &c.

TROUBLING,] as in 2 Ch. 32. 18, &c.

5. HIRING,] as in Neh. 6. 12, 13, &c.

MAKE VOID,] as in Lev. 26. 15, 44; Nu. 30. 12, 15; 2 Sa. 17. 14, &c.

DARIUS] Hystaspis, all the reign of Cambyses and of Smerdis the impostor, which lasted 15 years.

6. AHASUERUS,] that is, of Cambyses or Artaxerxes.

COMMENCEMENT,] B.C. 529.

ACCUSATION.] This original word is not found elsewhere.

7. BISHLAM,] i.e. 'son of peace.'

MITHREDATH,] as in 1. 8.

TABEEL,] i.e. 'goodness of God.'

COMPANIONS,] or associates; see v. 9, 17, 23; 5. 3, 6; 6. 6, 13.

LETTER,] as in v. 18, 23; 5. 5; 7. 11.

ARAMAEAN,] as in 2 K. 18. 26; Isa. 36. 11; Da. 2. 4.

INTERPRETED.] This original word is not found elsewhere.

8. REHUM,] i.e. 'merciful.'

COUNSELLOR,] lit. 'master of taste,' that is, discretion, counsel.

SHIMSHAI,] i.e. 'sunny,' as in v. 17.

SCRIBE,] as in v. 9, 17, 23; 7. 12, 21.

9. DINAITES,] from some part of Asshur, unknown.

APHARSATHCHITES,] perhaps the Paroetaceni, between Persia and Media; see Herod. 1., 101.

TARPELITES.] Not mentioned elsewhere.

APHARSITES,] perhaps the Parrhasii or the Persians.

ARCHEVITES,] the Arecenses.

BABYLONIANS] from Babylon.

SUSANCHITES,] from Susa, in Persia.

ELAMITES,] that is, natives of Elam.

10. HONOURABLE,] lit. 'rare,' as in Da. 2. 11.

ASNAPPER.] Not mentioned elsewhere.

REMOVED] from the Assyrian dominions to SAMARIA,] the ancient capital of the two tribes.

RIVER,] the Euphrates, westward.

11. COPY,] as in v. 23; 5. 6; 7. 11.

AT SUCH A TIME,] or 'so on,' as in v. 10, 17. 7. 12.

12. REBELLIOUS,] as in v. 15.

BASE,] or 'ill-flavoured.'

WALLS,] which had previously been in ruins.

FOUNDATIONS,] as in 5. 16; 6. 3.

JOIN,] *lit.* 'sew.'

13. THIS CITY] Jerusalem, as the metropolis of the country.

FINISHED,] as proposed by the Jews.

TOLL,] as in 7. 24.

TRIBUTE,] as in v. 20; 7. 24.

CUSTOM,] as in v. 20; 7. 24.

AT LENGTH.] This original phrase is not found elsewhere; Aben Ezra reads 'treasury, revenue.'

LOSS,] as in v. 15, 22; Da. 6. 2; Est. 7. 4.

14. SALT,] that is, sustenance.

PALACE,] as in Da. 4. 1, 26; 5. 2, 3, 5.

OUR SALT,] being, as it were, public property.

NAKEDNESS,] as in Ge. 9. 22, 23; 42. 9, 12, &c.

NO PATIENCE,] *lit.* 'no length.'

15. RECORDS,] as in 6. 2.

REBELLIOUS CITY,] as in v. 12 above.

CAUSING LOSS,] as in v. 13.

PROVINCES,] as in 5. 8; 6. 2; 7. 16; Da. 2. 48, 49; 3. 1, 2, 3, 12, 30.

SEDITION,] as in v. 9.

DAYS OF OLD,] as in v. 19.

WASTED,] as in Jer. 26. 9; Eze. 6. 6, &c.

16. A PORTION,] as in Da. 4. 15, 23.

17. AN ANSWER,] as in 5. 7, 11; 6. 11; Da. 3. 16; 4. 17.

PEACE,] the usual oriental salutation.

AT SUCH A TIME,] *or* 'so on,' as in v. 11.

18. EXPLAINED,] as in Lev. 24. 12; Nu. 15. 34; Neh. 8. 8.

19. DECREE,] as in v. 8, 9, 17, 21; 5. 3, 9, 13, 17, &c.

LIFTING ITSELF UP,] as in Nu. 16. 3, &c.

20. MIGHTY KINGS,] such as David, Solomon, &c.

RULERS,] as in 7. 24; Da. 2. 10, 15; 4. 17, 25, 26, 32; 5. 21, 29.

TOLL, TRIBUTE AND CUSTOM,] as in v. 13.

21. DECREE,] as in v. 19.

IS MADE,] as in Da. 2. 5; Ezra 5. 8.

22. NEGLIGENCE,] as in 6. 9; Da. 3. 29; 6. 4.

THE HEART,] as in Da. 6. 23.

LOSS,] as in v. 13.

23. COPY,] as in v. 11.

FORCE,] *lit.* 'arm.'

24. SERVICE,] as in 5. 8; 6. 7, 18; Da. 2. 49; 3. 12.

SECOND YEAR.] B.C. 520.

V. 1. PROPHESIED,] that is, proclaimed the will of God that they should resume the building of the temple, in the second year of Darius, as in Hag. 1. 1; Zec. 1. 1.

HAGGAI,] i.e. 'festive.'

ZECHARIAH,] i.e. 'remembered by Jah.'

SON OF IDDO,] or rather grandson, for his father's name was Barachiah, as in Zec. 1. 1.

2. ZERUBBABEL..JESHUA,] the leading civil and ecclesiastical rulers.

BUILD,] that part which had been left unfinished, as in 4. 23, 24.

PROPHETS,] especially the two above mentioned, Haggai and Zechariah.

SUPPORTING,] by word and deed.

3. TATNAI,] i.e. 'a gift,' *or* 'liberal.'

GOVERNOR,] as in v. 6, 14; 6. 6, 7, 13; Da 3. 2, 3, 27; 6. 7.

THE RIVER] Euphrates, westward.

SHETHAR-BOZNAI,] i.e. 'bright star,' as in 6. 6.

COMPANIONS,] as in 6. 2; Da. 2. 24, 25; 4. 14; 6. 6; 7. 5, 23.

DECREE,] as in 4. 8, 9, 17, 19, 21, &c.

FINISH,] as in v. 9, 11; 4. 12, 13, 16; 6. 14.

4. ARE BUILDING,] as in v. 11; 4. 12; 6. 14.

5. EYE,] as in Nu. 14. 14; De. 11. 12; Job 7. 8.

ELDERS,] that is, official men.

DARIUS,] Hystaspis, as in 4. 24.

6. COPY,] as in 4. 11, 23.

APHARSACHITES.] See 4. 9.

8. PEACE,] the usual eastern salutation.

PROVINCE,] as in 4. 15; 6. 2; 7. 16; Da. 2. 48, 49; 3. 1, 2, 3, 12, 30.

GREAT HOUSE,] not 'great God,' as in C.V.

ROLLED STONES,] as in 6. 4.

WOOD,] for greater strength.

SPEEDILY] within a few months.

PROSPERING,] through the blessing of him whose house it was.

9. ELDERS,] as in v. 5 above.

FINISH,] as in v. 3, 11; 4. 12, 13, 16; 6. 14.

10. NAMES,] as in v. 4 above.

HEAD,] that they might be called to account for it.

11. SERVANTS,] doing the will of their lord.

GREAT KING,] even Solomon, 500 years before.

12. ANGRY,] by their continued idolatries.

DESTROYED,] *lit.* 'hid.'

REMOVED,] as in 2 Ch. 36. 19, 20.

13. FIRST YEAR] of his reign over Babylon.

DECREE,] recited in 1. 1—4.

14. VESSELS,] with which the priests and Levites performed the service of God.

TEMPLE] of his own gods, Nisroch, &c.

GIVEN,] as in 1. 8, 11.

GOVERNOR] of Jerusalem, subject to the king of Persia.

15. PUT THEM DOWN,] as in 6. 1, 5; Da. 5. 20.

PLACE] where it had been before.

16. LAID,] *lit.* 'given.'

NOT FINISHED,] through the interruption of the Samaritans, &c.

17. GOOD] for the public safety, and his own royal authority.

TREASURE-HOUSE,] as in 6. 1; 7. 20.

WILL,] as in 7. 15.

VI. 1. TREASURIES,] as in 5. 17; 7. 20.

2. ACHMETHA,] the capital of ancient Media, and summer residence of the kings of Persia, called Hamedan, Ecbatana, Ispahan.

PALACE,] as in 1 Ch. 29. 1, 19; Neh. 1. 1; 2. 8; 7. 2, &c.

PROVINCE,] as in 4. 15; 5. 8; 7. 16; Da. 2 48, 49; 3. 1, 2, 3, 12, 30.

MEDIA,] as in Da. 5. 28; 6. 13.

ROLL,] as in Ps. 40. 7; Jer. 36. 2, 4. &c.

RECORD,] as in 4. 15.

3. FIRST YEAR,] B.C. 536; see 1. 1—4; Isa 44. 28.

SACRIFICES,] to the God of heaven.

STRONGLY LAID,] *or* 'borne up.'
SIXTY CUBITS,] double that of Solomon's temple (1 K. 6. 2), though only half the height of the porch, 2 Ch. 3. 4.
SIXTY CUBITS,] three times the breadth of Solomon's; 1 K. 6. 2.
4. ROWS,] *lit.* a 'cleaving together.'
ROLLED STONES,] as in 5. 8.
NEW WOOD,] for greater stability.
OUTLAY,] as in v. 8.
5. VESSELS,] with which the priests and Levites ministered.
GIVEN BACK] to the Jews, especially Sheshbazzar.
PUT THEM DOWN,] as in 5. 15.
6. BE YE FAR FROM HENCE,] as impertinent intruders.
7. LET ALONE,] as in Da. 2. 44; 4. 15, 23, 26.
GOVERNOR,] even Zerubbabel *or* Sheshbazzar.
PLACE,] where it had been before.
8. DECREE,] in addition to that made by Cyrus, as in 1. 1—4.
RICHES OF THE KING,] his own personal property.
TRIBUTE,] paid by the subject princes and people.
SPEEDILY,] as in v. 12.
OUTLAY,] as in v. 4 above.
9. NEEDING,] for the due performance of their services in the temple.
BULLOCKS..RAMS..LAMBS,] all of which were used in burnt-offerings.
WHEAT..OIL,] as required in Lev. 2. 1—16.
PRIESTS,] the sons of Aaron, who minister at the altar; see Ex. 29. 38—41.
WITHOUT FAIL,] as in 4. 22; Da. 3. 29; 6. 4.
10. SWEET SAVOURS,] as in Da. 2. 46.
LIFE] and prosperity, as in Jer. 29. 7; 1 Tim. 2. 1, 2.
11. CHANGETH,] or attempted to do so.
PULLED DOWN,] as in Prov. 15. 25.
RAISED UP] as a scaffold on high.
SMITTEN ON IT,] that is, pierced through or hanged.
DUNGHILL,] as in Da. 2. 5; 3. 29.
12. TO DWELL,] as his own immediate habitation.
CAST DOWN,] to the earth and dust from their former glory.
SPEEDILY,] as in v. 8.
13. DONE,] knowing the despotic power of eastern kings.
14. PROPHECY,] or preaching of the will of God that they should continue and complete their work.
FINISHED,] in spite of the opposition of the Samaritans, &c.
15. HOUSE,] that is, the second temple of the Lord.
GONE OUT,] extending and becoming more complete.
ADAR,] or part of Febuary and March.
SIXTH YEAR,] four years from the issuing of his decree, as above.
16. SONS OF THE CAPTIVITY,] the returned captives.
DEDICATION,] or solemn setting apart of it to the public service of God.
17. BROUGHT NEAR] to the altar of God, to the priests.

BULLOCKS..RAMS..LAMBS,] as in v. 9.
YOUNG HE-GOATS,] as in 8. 35: 2 Ch. 29. 21; Da. 8. 5, 21.
SIN-OFFERING,] as in Lev. 4. 13—21.
18. DIVISIONS,] as in 2 Ch. 35. 5.
COURSES,] as in 1 Ch. 23. 6.
SERVICE,] publicly in the temple day by day.
WRITTEN,] in Nu. 3. 6; 8. 11, 14, 15.
19. SONS OF THE CAPTIVITY,] as in v. 16.
PASSOVER,] the great national festival of Israel.
FOURTEENTH OF THE FIRST MONTH,] Nisan *or* Abib, as in Ex. 12. 2, 6.
20. PURIFIED THEMSELVES,] as in Ge. 35. 2; Nu. 8. 7; Jos. 22. 17; 2 Ch. 30. 18; Lev. 14. 4—31; Neh. 13. 22; Isa. 66. 17.
PURE.] Compare 2 Ch. 29. 34.
THEMSELVES,] after the others were served.
21. SEPARATED,] as in Neh. 10. 28.
UNCLEANNESS,] as in Lev. 5. 2; 7. 20. 21, &c.
TO SEEK] the favour of Jehovah.
EAT,] of the paschal sacrifice, as commanded in the law.
22. FEAST OF UNLEAVENED THINGS,] which followed the passover, as in Ex. 12. 18, 19.
REJOICE] in the midst of their sorrow.
TURNED ROUND,] from emnity or indifference into favour and friendship.
STRENGTHEN,] by his gifts and his decrees in their favour.

VII. 1. ARTAXERXES,] or Darius, as in preceding chapter; in the seventh year of his reign, as in v. 7, 8.
EZRA,] i.e. 'help,' B.C. 458.
SERAIAH] the high priest, slain by Nebuchadnezzar, Jer. 52. 24, 27.
AZARIAH,] i.e. 'help of Jah.'
HILKIAH,] i.e. 'portion of Jah.'
2. SHALLUM,] i.e. 'recompence.'
ZADOK,] i.e. 'right, just.'
AHITUB,] i.e. 'brother of goodness.'
3. AMARIAH,] i.e. 'saying of Jah.'
AZARIAH,] i.e. 'help of Jah;' six generations are omitted between him and Meraioth, see 1 Ch. 6. 7—10.
MERAIOTH,] i.e. 'high places.'
4. ZERAHIAH,] i.e. 'rising of Jah.'
UZZI,] i.e. 'my strength.'
BUKKI,] i.e. 'cast off by Jah.
5. ABISHUA,] i.e. 'father of riches.'
PHINEHAS,] i.e. 'mouth of brass.'
ELEAZAR,] i.e. 'God is help.'
AARON,] i.e. 'a mountaineer,' perhaps.
6. HIMSELF,] a second time; see 5. 4; Neh. 12. 1.
SCRIBE,] as in v. 11; Neh. 8. 1, 4, 9, 13; 12. 26, 36.
READY,] as in Ps. 45. 1; Prov. 22. 29; Isa. 16. 5.
GAVE] in the wilderness, at Sinai.
THE KING,] Ahasuerus *or* Artaxerxes.
REQUEST,] regarding the Jews and the temple.
7. GO UP,] from the remnant of the Jews left still in Babylon.
ISRAEL..NETHINIM,] as in 2. 70.
SEVENTH YEAR,] B.C. 457.

8. FIFTH MONTH,] that is called Ab.
FIRST MONTH,] that is called Nisan.
FOUNDED THE ASCENT,] that is, began it.
HAND..UPON HIM,] as in v. 6.
10. PREPARED,] as in 1 Sa. 7. 3, &c.
SEEK..DO..TEACH,] the law of God more
perfectly.
STATUTE AND JUDGMENT,] set forth in
the written word.
11. COPY,] as in 4. 11, 23; 5. 6.
PRIEST..SCRIBE,] as in v. 5, 6.
COMMANDS..STATUTES,] as contained in
the law.
12. KING OF KINGS,] having many other
kings under him, as in 1. 1.
PERFECT,] as in Ps. 57. 2; 138. 8.
GOD OF HEAVEN,] because its maker.
AT SUCH A TIME,] or 'so on;' see 4. 10.
13. DECREE,] in addition to that of Cyrus
in 1. 1—4.
WILLING,] of his own free consent.
14. SEVEN COUNSELLORS,] as in Est. 1. 14.
INQUIRE,] by personal inspection and examination.
LAW OF GOD,] as written by Moses and
the prophets.
15. WILLINGLY OFFERED,] that the wrath
of God might be averted, and his favour
supplicated.
TABERNACLE,] dwelling-place or temple.
16. FINDEST,] offered by the friends of
the Jews anywhere in the
PROVINCE] of the Persian empire, called
Babylon.
FREEWILL OFFERING,] as in v. 13, 15.
17. PRESENTS,] offered with every sacrifice,
as in Lev. 23. 18, &c.
LIBATIONS,] as in Ge. 35. 14; Ex. 29. 40, &c.
ALTAR,] as in 3. 3.
18. WILL,] as in 5. 17.
19. VESSELS,] as in 5. 14, 15; 6. 5; Da. 5.
2, 3, 23.
MAKE PERFECT,] as in 5. 16; Da. 5. 26.
20. NEEDFUL THINGS,] as in 6. 9; Da. 3. 16.
TREASURE HOUSE,] as in 5. 17; 6. 1.
21. TREASURERS,] as in 1. 8.
SPEEDILY,] as in 5. 8; 6. 8, 12, 13; 7.
17, 26.
22. 100 TALENTS,] about £35,300.
100 CORS] or homers, each holding ten
ephahs.
100 BATHS,] or ten cors or homers.
SALT,] which was required for every sacrifice, and cheap.
RECKONING,] lit. 'writing.'
23. GOD OF HEAVEN,] as in v. 12.
WRATH,] from heaven.
24. PRIESTS..NETHINIM,] as in 2. 70.
TOLL, TRIBUTE, AND CUSTOM,] as in 4. 13.
AUTHORITY] from the laws of the kingdom.
25. WISDOM OF THY GOD,] as in Da. 2. 20,
21, 23, 30; 5. 11, 14.
IN THY HAND,] that is, with thee.
APPOINT,] as in Da. 2. 24, 49; 3. 12.
MAGISTRATES,] to carry out existing
laws, and
JUDGES,] to enact new ones.
THE RIVER] Euphrates, westward.
KNOWING,] that is, recognising and adher-
ing to the law revealed to Moses.

CAUSE TO KNOW,] whether Jews or of the
nations.
26. NOT DO,] having professed to adhere
to the law.
LAW OF THE KING,] in reference to this
matter of the Jews.
CONFISCATION,] as in 2 K. 23. 33; Prov.
19. 19.
BONDS,] as in Da. 4. 15, 23.
27. OUR FATHERS,] as in De. 26. 7, &c.
GIVEN,] of his own free grace and mercy.
BEAUTIFY,] as in Isa. 60. 7, 13.
28. STRETCHED OUT,] as in 9. 9.
KINDNESS,] as in Ge. 19. 19; 20. 13; 21. 23;
24. 12, 14, 27, 49, &c.
HAND..UPON ME,] as in v. 6, 9; 8. 22. 31;
Neh. 2. 8, 18, &c.

VIII. 1. HEADS,] as in Ex. 6. 14, 25, &c.
GENEALOGY,] as in v. 3; 2. 62; 1 Ch. 4. 33;
5. 1, 7; 7. 5, 7, 9, 40; 9. 22; 2 Ch. 12. 15; 31.
16—19; Neh. 7. 5, 64.
BABYLON,] on the Euphrates, in Lat. 32. deg.
32. min.
2. PHINEHAS,] son of Eleasar the third
son of Aaron, brother of Moses.
GERSHOM,] i.e. a 'stranger there.'
ITHAMAR,] the fourth son of Aaron.
DANIEL,] i.e. 'judge of God.'
DAVID,] the king, son of Jesse.
HATTUSH.] Etymology uncertain; see
1 Ch. 3. 22.
3. SHECHANIAH,] i.e. a 'neighbour with
Jah.'
PHAROSH,] i.e. 'a flea,' as in 2. 3; 10. 25;
Neh. 3. 25.
ZECHARIAH,] i.e. 'remembered of Jah.'
GENEALOGY,] as in v. 1.
4. PAHATH-MOAB,] i.e. 'pit, snare, or gov-
ernor of Moab.'
ELIHOENAI,] i.e. 'unto Jah are mine eyes.'
ZERAHIAH,] i.e. 'rising of Jah.'
5. SHECHANIAH,] as in v. 3.
JAHAZIEL,] i.e. 'seen of God.'
6. ADIN,] i.e. 'luxuriant.'
EBED,] i.e. a 'servant.'
JONATHAN,] i.e. 'Jah has given.'
7. ELAM,] a province of Persia.
JESHAIAH,] i.e. 'safety of Jah.'
ATHALIAH,] i.e. 'afflicted of Jah.'
8. SHEPHATIAH,] i.e. 'judged of Jah.'
ZEBADIAH,] i.e. 'endowed of Jah.'
MICHAEL,] i.e. 'who is like God?'
9. JOAB,] i.e. 'Jah is father.'
OBADIAH,] i.e. 'servant of Jah.'
JEHIEL,] i.e. 'God lives.'
10. SHELOMITH,] i.e. 'peaceful.'
JOSIPHIAH,] i.e. 'added to by Jah '
11. BEBAI.] Etymology unknown.
ZECHARIAH,] i.e. 'remembered of Jah.'
12. AZGAD,] i.e. 'strength of a troop.'
JOHANAN,] i.e. 'Jah has grace.'
BEN-HAKKATAN,] i.e. 'son of the little one.'
13. ADONIKAM,] i.e. 'my lord has risen.'
ELIPHELET,] i.e. 'God delivers.'
JEIEL,] i.e. 'removed of God.'
SHEMAIAH,] i.e. 'heard of Jah.'
14. BIGVAI.] Etymology uncertain.
UTHAI,] i.e. 'aided by God.'
ZABBUD,, i.e. 'endowed.'
15. RIVER,] perhaps the Euphrates.

AHAVA,] as in v. 21, 31.
CONSIDER,] *or* 'understand,' as in De. 32.
7. 29, &c.
16. ELIEZER,] i.e. 'my God is help.'
ARIEL,] i.e. 'lion of God.'
SHEMAIAH,] i.e. 'heard of Jah.'
ELNATHAN,] i.e. 'God hath given.'
JARIB,] i.e. 'he strives, contends.'
NATHAN,] i.e. 'he gave.'
ZECHARIAH,] i.e. 'remembered of Jah.'
MESHULLAM,] i.e. 'recompensed.'
JOIARIB,] i.e. 'Jah contends.'
MEN OF UNDERSTANDING,] *or* 'giving understanding.'
17. IDDO.] Etymology unknown.
CASIPHIA.] Etymology and situation unknown.
PUT IN THEIR MOUTH,] as in Ex. 4. 15;
Nu. 22. 38; 23. 5, 12, 16; De. 31. 19; 2 Sa. 14.
3, 19; Isa. 51. 16; 59. 21.
NETHINIM,] as in 2. 43, 70, &c.
MINISTRANTS,] as in Ex. 24. 13; 33. 11;
Nu. 11. 28; Jos. 1. 1; 1 Sa. 2. 11, 18; 3. 1; 2
Sa. 13. 17, 18; 1 K. 1. 5, &c.
18. HAND..UPON US,] as in v. 22, 31, &c.
UNDERSTANDING,] as in 1 Sa. 25. 3: 1 Ch.
22. 12, &c.
MAHLI,] i.e. 'sick.'
SHEREBIAH,] i.e. 'heat of Jah.'
19. HASHABIAH,] i.e. 'reckoning of Jah.
JESHAIAH,] i.e. 'safety of Jah.'
MERARI.] i.e. 'bitter.'
20. NETHINIM,] as in v. 17 above.
GAVE.] Not mentioned elsewhere.
DEFINED,] as in Nu. 1. 17; 1 Ch. 12. 31; 16.
41; 2 Ch. 28. 15; 31. 19.
21. PROCLAIM,] *lit.* 'call.'
FAST,] as in 2 Sa. 12. 16; 1 K. 21. 9, 12; 2
Ch. 20. 3; Neh. 9. 1; Est. 4. 3; 9. 31, &c.
RIVER AHAVA,] as in v. 15.
AFFLICT,] *or* 'humble ourselves,' as in
Ge. 16. 9; 1 K. 2. 26; Ps. 107. 17; Da. 10.
4; 105. 3; Prov. 28. 5, &c.
RIGHT WAY,] as in 1 Sa. 12. 23; Ps. 107. 7;
Prov. 14. 12; 15. 19; 16. 25, &c.
INFANTS,] as in Ge. 34. 29; 43. 8; 45. 19, &c.
SUBSTANCE,] as in Ge. 12. 5; 13. 6; 14.
11, &c.
22. ASHAMED,] as in 9. 6.
FORCE,] as in Ge. 34. 29; 47. 6; Ex. 14. 4,
9, 17, 28; 15. 4; 18. 21, 25, &c.
HORSEMEN,] as in Ge. 50. 9; Ex. 14. 9, 17,
18, 23, 26, 28, &c.
ENEMY,] the wandering marauders who
extorted prey from the unprotected travellers.
HAND..UPON US,] as in v. 8 above.
SEEKING HIM,] by prayer and supplication, as in 1 Ch. 16. 10; Ps. 40. 16; 69. 6; 70.
4; 105. 3; Prov. 28. 5, &c.
STRENGTH,] as in Ex. 15. 2, 14; Lev. 26.
19, &c.
WRATH,] as in Ex. 4. 14; 15. 8; 22. 24; 32.
10, 11, 12, &c.
FORSAKING,] as in Ps. 119. 53; Prov. 2. 13,
17; 17. 10; 28. 4, 13; Isa. 1. 28; 65. 11; Jer.
17. 3; Da. 11. 30; Zec. 11. 17.
23. FAST,] as in v. 21.
SEEK] a gracious answer.
ENTREATED,] as in Ge. 25. 21, &c.
24. SEPARATE,] as in Ge. 1. 6, 7, &c.
SHEREBIAH,] i.e. 'heat of Jah,' as in v. 18

HASHABIAH,] i.e. 'reckoning of Jah,' as
in v. 19.
TWELVE,] as representing the twelve
tribes.
25. WEIGH,] as is still customary in the
east.
HEAVE-OFFERING,] as in Ex. 25. 2. 3; 29.
27, &c.
PRESENT,] in the captivity.
LIFTED UP,] as an offering to God and his
temple, as in 7. 15, 16.
26. TALENTS 650,] or about £2,229,450.
100 TALENTS,] about £35,300.
27. BASINS,] as in 1 Ch. 28. 17; Ezra 1. 10.
DRAMS,] as in 1 Ch. 29. 7.
SHINING,] *lit.* 'gold *or* yellow.
DESIRABLE,] as in Ge. 27. 15; 2 Ch. 20. 25;
Da. 9. 23; 10. 3; 11. 19; 11. 38, 43.
28. HOLY,] that is, separate and set apart.
WILLING-OFFERING FROM THE PEOPLE,]
as in 7. 15, 16.
29. WATCH,] as in Job 21. 32; Ps. 102. 7;
127. 1; Prov. 8. 34; Isa. 29. 20; Jer. 1. 12; 5.
6; 31. 28; 44. 27.
KEEP,] *or* 'preserve, observe.'
WEIGH,] to certify their good conduct.
CHAMBERS,] where they were to be kept
30. WEIGHT,] as noted above in v. 26, 27.
31. RIVER AHAVA,] that is, v. 15, 21.
FIRST MONTH,] that is, Nisan.
HAND..UPON US,] as in v. 8, 22 above.
THE ENEMY,] as in v. 22.
THE LIER OF WAIT,] as in Jos. 8. 2, 4, 7,
12, 14, 19, 21; Jud. 16. 9, 12; 20. 29, 33, 36.
37, 38; 1 Sa. 22. 8, 13; Jer. 51. 12; La. 3. 10.
32. THREE DAYS,] for rest after their long
journey of four months, as in 7. 9.
33. WEIGHED,] as directed by Ezra in
v. 30.
MEREMOTH,] i.e. 'heights.'
URIAH,] i.e. 'light of Jah.'
ELEAZAR,] i.e. 'God is help.'
PHINEHAS,] i.e. 'mouth of brass.'
JOZABAD,] i.e. 'Jah has endowed.'
JESHUA,] i.e. 'a saviour.'
NOADIAH,] i.e. 'met by Jah.'
BINNUI,] i.e. 'built up.'
34. NUMBER..WEIGHT,] as in v. 26, 27.
WRITTEN,] that it might be permanently
preserved.
35. CAPTIVES,] from Babylon at this time
with Ezra.
SONS OF THE REMOVAL,] as in 4. 1; 6. 19,
20, &c.
BULLOCKS 12,] the number of the tribes.
RAMS 96,] eight for each bullock.
LAMBS 77,] which, with the rams and
bullocks, were for burnt-offerings.
HE-GOATS 12,] one for each tribe.
36. LAWS,] given in behalf of the Jews.
LIEUTENANTS,] as in Est. 3. 12; 8. 9; 9. 3.
GOVERNORS,] as in 1 K. 10. 15; 20. 24; 2
K. 18. 24; 2 Ch. 19. 14; Neh. 2. 7, &c.
THEY LIFTED UP,] that is, the lieutenants
and governors, or perhaps the returned
captives.

IX. 1. SEPARATED,] as required to be by
the law, in relation to marriage, &c.
CANAANITE..AMORITE,] with whom they

were forbidden to have social intercourse, as in De. 7. 1—3.

2. TAKEN] to wife, as the phrase generally means.

HOLY SEED,] of Abraham, which was set apart to Jehovah.

MINGLED THEMSELVES,] by intermarriage; compare Mal. 2. 13—15.

SECONDS,] in authority and rank among the Jews.

FIRST,] in point of time and degree.

TRESPASS,] against the positive revealed law of Moses.

3. THIS WORD,] of confession and sorrow.

GARMENT,] according to a common eastern practice; Job 1. 20, &c.

UPPER ROBE,] which covered the other garments.

BEARD,] as is often done in great distress; see Lev. 19. 27; Isa. 15. 2.

ASTONISHED,] as in v. 4; or 'desolate,' as in Da. 9. 27; 11. 31.

4. GATHERED,] to hear the result of this communication.

TREMBLING] with reverential awe; as in 10. 3; Jud. 7. 3; 1 Sa. 4. 13; Isa. 66. 2, 5.

REMOVAL,] in intermarrying with the nations.

5. PRESENT OF THE EVENING,] about three o'clock in the afternoon.

AFFLICTION,] because of the trespass of the people, as in v. 2 above.

BOW DOWN,] as in Ge. 49. 9; Nu. 24. 9; Jud. 5. 27; 7. 5, 6; 1 Sa. 4. 19; 1 K. 8. 54, &c.

SPREAD OUT] in prayer and supplication, as in Ex. 9. 29, 33, &c.

6. ASHAMED,] as in 8. 22, &c.

BLUSHED,] as in Nu. 12. 14; 2 Sa. 10. 5, &c.

INIQUITIES,] as in Ge. 4. 13; 15. 16; 19. 15, &c.

GUILT,] as in Lev. 4. 3; 6. 5, 7; 22. 16, &c.

7. GIVEN] by God, the offended king of Israel.

SPOILING] of goods, as foretold by Moses and the prophets.

SHAME OF FACE,] as in 2 Ch. 32. 21; Ps. 44. 15; Jer. 7. 19; Da. 9. 7, 8.

8. AS A SMALL MOMENT,] as in Isa. 26. 20; 54. 7.

GRACE,] that is, unmerited favour and kindness.

AN ESCAPE,] from the hands of the Babylonian oppressors.

A NAIL,] as in Isa. 22. 23, 25; 33. 20; 54. 2; Eze. 15. 3; Zec. 10. 4, &c.

ENLIGHTENING,] as in Ps. 13. 3; 19. 8; Prov. 29. 13; 1 Sa. 14. 27, 29, &c.

QUICKENING,] as in Ge. 45. 5; Lev. 13. 10, 24; Jud. 6. 4; 17. 10; 2 Ch. 14. 13.

SERVITUDE,] as in Ex. 1. 14; 2. 23; 5. 9, &c.

9. SERVANTS] to the kings of Persia.

STRETCHETH OUT,] as in 7. 28, &c.

KINDNESS,] not 'mercy,' as in C.V.

A QUICKENING,] as in v. 8.

TO LIFT UP,] out of its ruins, and rebuild for public service.

WASTES,] as in Lev. 26. 31, 33; Job 3. 14; Ps. 9. 6; 102. 6; 109. 10; Isa. 5. 17, &c.

A WELL,] as in Nu. 22. 24; Ps. 62. 3; 80. 12; Ecc. 10. 8; Isa. 5. 5; Eze. 13. 5; 22. 30; 42. 7; Hos. 2. 6; Mic. 7. 11.

10. COMMANDS,] in reference to intermarriage with the nations.

11. SAYING,] in De. 6. 3; Jos. 23. 12; Jud. 2. 2.

IMPURITY,] as in Lev. 12. 2, 5; 15. 19, 20, 24, 25, 26, 33; 18. 19; 20. 21; Nu. 19. 9, 13, 20, 21; 31. 23; 2 Ch. 29. 5, &c.

ABOMINATIONS,] as in Lev. 18. 22—30; 20. 13, &c.

MOUTH UNTO MOUTH,] as in 2 K. 10. 21, &c.

UNCLEANNESS,] as in 6. 12, &c.

12. NOT GIVE..NOT TAKE,] as in De. 7 3, &c.

NOT SEEK,] as in De. 23. 6, &c.

STRONG,] to do the revealed will of God.

EATEN,] as in Ge. 45. 18, &c.

GIVEN POSSESSION,] as in Jud. 11. 24; 1 Sa. 2. 7; Job 13. 26, &c.

13. COME UPON US,] of misery and suffering from the avenging hand of God.

GUILT,] as in v. 6, 7, 15; 10. 10, 19, &c.

KEPT BACK,] as in Ge. 20. 6; 22. 12, 16; 39. 9, &c.

ROD,] as in Ge. 38. 18, 25; Ex. 4. 2, 4, 17, 20, &c.

ESCAPE,] as in v. 8, 14, 15, &c.

14. JOIN,] as in Ge. 34. 9; De. 7. 3, &c.

ABOMINATIONS,] as in Ge. 43. 32; 46. 34 Ex. 8. 26; Lev. 18. 22, 26, 27, 29, 30, &c.

ANGRY,] as in 1 K. 8. 46; 2 Ch. 6. 36; Ps. 2. 12; 60. 1; 79. 5; 85. 6; Isa. 12. 1.

CONSUMPTION,] as in Ex. 31. 18; 32. 12; Lev. 26. 24, &c.

REMNANT,] as in Ge. 45. 7; 2 Sa. 14. 7, &c.

ESCAPED PART,] as in v. 8; 13. 15, &c.

15. RIGHTEOUS,] as in Ex. 9. 27; De. 32. 4, 2 Ch. 12. 6; Neh. 9. 8, 33; Job 34. 17, &c.

GUILT,] as in v. 6, 7, 13; 10. 10, 19, &c.

STAND] acquitted or blameless, in this matter.

X. 1. PRAYING,] as in 9. 6—15 above.

MAKING CONFESSION] of sin, as in Lev. 5. 5; 16. 21; 26. 40, &c.

WEEPING,] as in 3. 12, &c.

CASTING HIMSELF DOWN,] as in Ge. 43. 18; De. 9. 18, 25.

ASSEMBLY,] as in Ge. 28. 3; 35. 11; 48. 4; 49. 6; Ex. 12. 6; 16. 3, &c.

2. SHECHANIAH,] i.e. 'neighbour of Jah.'

JEHIEL,] i.e. 'God lives.'

SONS OF ELAM,] as in 2. 7, 31; 8. 7, &c.

TRESPASSED,] as in v. 10.

SETTLE,] as in v. 10, 14, 17, 18; Ge. 47. 6, 11, &c.

STRANGE WOMEN,] as in v. 10, 11, 14, 17, 18, 44; 1 K. 11. 18; Neh. 13. 26, 27, &c.

HOPE,] seeing they were convinced of their own sin, and had confessed it.

3. COVENANT,] as in De. 29. 12; 2 K. 23. 3, &c.

GO FORTH,] from their houses to their own.

COUNSEL,] as in De. 32. 28; Jud. 20. 5; 2 Sa. 15. 31, &c.

THE LORD,] or 'my lord;' that is, Ezra.

TREMBLING,] as in 9. 4 above.

LAW,] that no injustice might be done.

4. ON THEE,] as the chief ecclesiastical ruler, and expositor of the law of God.

WITH THEE,] to take part in the labour and odium.
BE STRONG,] as in De. 12. 23; 31. 6, 7, 23; Jos. 1. 6, 7, 9, 18, &c.
5. CAUSETH..TO SWEAR,] as in Ge. 24. 3, 37, &c.
6. FROM BEFORE] the porch of the temple.
CHAMBER,] as in 1 Sa. 9. 22; 2 K. 23. 11; 1 Ch. 9. 26, 33; 23. 28; 28. 12; 2 Ch. 31. 11; Ezra 8. 29; Neh. 10. 37, &c.
JEHOHANAN,] i.e. 'Jah has grace.'
ELIASHIB,] i.e. 'God turns back;' he was grandson of Joshua.
EATEN..DRUNK,] since he had been informed of the trespass in 9. 3.
MOURNING,] as in Ge. 37. 34, &c.
TRESPASS,] in the matter of strange marriages.
7. A VOICE,] as in Ex. 36. 6; 2 Ch. 24. 9; 30. 5, &c.
SONS OF THE REMOVAL,] who had come from Babylon, as in 4. 1.
8. COMETH NOT IN,] to be examined by Ezra and the Levites, as in v. 4, 5.
COUNSEL,] as in v. 3.
SUBSTANCE,] as in Ge. 12. 5; 13. 6; 14. 11, &c.
DEVOTED,] to the public service of God.
SEPARATED,] as one wilfully disobedient and rebellious, as in v. 16; Nu. 16. 21, &c.
9. NINTH MONTH,] that is, Chisleu, five months after Ezra came to Jerusalem.
SIT] on the ground, or simply 'abide.'
BROAD PLACE,] as in Ge. 19. 2; De. 13. 16; Jud. 19. 15, 17, 20; 2 Sa. 21. 12; 2 Ch. 29. 4; 32. 6; Neh. 8. 1, &c.
TREMBLING,] as in Ps. 104. 32; Da. 10. 11.
SHOWERS] of rain, as in v. 13 below.
10. TRESPASSED,] as in v. 2; 9. 2, &c.
SETTLE,] as in v. 2, 14, 17, 18, &c.
STRANGE WOMEN,] as in v. 2, 11, 14, 17, 18, 44, &c.
TO ADD,] as in Lev. 19. 25; 2 Ch. 28. 13; Ecc. 3. 14.
11. MAKE,] *lit.* 'give,' as in Jos. 7. 19.
GOOD PLEASURE,] as in Ge. 49. 6; Ex. 28. 38; Lev. 1. 3, &c.
BE SEPARATED,] as in Nu. 16. 21, &c.
12. RIGHT,] as in Ex. 10. 29; Nu. 27. 7, &c.
13. MANY,] who are involved in the same trespass.
TIME OF SHOWERS,] as in v. 9 above.
WITHOUT,] in the broad place in the front of the temple.
MULTIPLIED TO TRANSGRESS,] as in Amos 4. 4.
14. STAND,] as judge to decide in this matter.
SETTLED,] as in v. 2 above.
TIMES APPOINTED,] as in Neh. 10. 34; 13. 31.
ELDERS..JUDGES,] who had supreme authority.
FURY OF THE WRATH,] as in Ex. 32. 12: Nu. 25. 4; 32. 14, &c.
15. JONATHAN,] i.e. 'Jah hath given.'
ASAHEL,] i.e. 'made or done by God.'
JAHAZIAH,] i.e. 'seen of Jah.'
TIKVAH,] i.e. 'hope, expectation.'
AGAINST,] not 'employed about,' as in C.V.; so Jarchi and Lightfoot.

MESHULLAM,] i.e. 'recompensed.'
SHABBETHAI,] i.e. 'sabbatic,' as in Neh. 8. 7; 11. 16.
HELPED THEM,] to resist the proposal of Ezra and the elders.
16. SONS OF THE REMOVAL,] as in v. 7.
SEPARATED,] for the work of examination.
BY NAME,] being men specially chosen for this purpose.
TENTH MONTH,] that is, Tebeth.
EXAMINE,] or 'seek,' as in Ge. 25. 22; Ex. 18. 15; Lev. 10. 16, &c.
17. FIRST MONTH,] that is, Nisan, so that it occupied them three months.
18. SONS OF THE PRIESTS,] as in 2. 61, &c.
JESHUA,] i.e. 'saviour;' compare Zec. 3. 3.
JOZADAK,] i.e. 'Jah is just.'
MAASEIAH,] i.e. 'work of Jah.'
ELIEZER,] i.e. 'my God is help.'
JARIB,] i.e. 'he contends.'
GEDALIAH,] i.e. 'greatness of Jah.'
19. GIVE THEIR HAND,] as in 1 Ch. 29. 24, &c.
SEND FORTH,] as in v. 3 above.
BEING GUILTY,] as in Ge. 42. 21; 2 Sa. 14. 13.
RAM OF THE FLOCK,] as in Ge. 31. 38.
GUILT,] as in v. 10 above.
20. IMMER,] i.e. 'talkative, loquacious.'
HANANI,] i.e. 'my grace.'
ZEBADIAH,] i.e. 'endowed by Jah.'
21. HARIM,] i.e. 'flat-nosed, or devoted.
MAASEIAH,] i.e. 'work of Jah.'
ELIJAH,] i.e. 'God is Jah.'
SHEMAIAH,] i.e. 'heard of Jah.'
JEHIEL,] i.e. 'God lives.'
UZZIAH,] i.e. 'strength of Jah.'
22. PASHHUR,] i.e. 'prosperity everywhere.'
ELIOENAI,] i.e. 'unto Jah are my eyes.'
MAASEIAH,] i.e. 'work of Jah.'
ISHMAEL,] i.e. 'God hears.'
NETHANEEL,] i.e. 'gift of God.'
JOZABAD,] i.e. 'Jah has endowed.'
ELASAH,] i.e. 'God has made.'
23. THE LEVITES,] the instructors of Israel, along with the priests.
JOZABAD,] i.e. 'Jah has endowed.'
SHIMEI,] i.e. 'hearkening.'
KELAIAH,] i.e. 'light or swift one of Jah.'
KELITA,] i.e. 'contracted, lacking,'
PETHAHIAH,] i.e. 'opening of Jah.'
JUDAH,] i.e. 'confessed, praised.'
ELIEZER,] i.e. 'my God is help.'
24. SINGERS,] in the public worship of God in the temple service.
ELIASHIB,] i.e. 'God brings back.'
GATE-KEEPERS,] of the temple.
SHALLUM,] i.e. 'recompensed.'
TELEM,] i.e. 'oppression.'
URI,] i.e. 'my light.'
25. ISRAEL] in general, that is, the common people.
PAROSH,] i.e. a 'flea.'
RAMIAH,] i.e. 'exaltation of Jah.
JEZIAH,] i.e. 'sprinkled of Jah.'
MALCHIJAH,] i.e. 'my king is Jah.'
MIAMIN,] i.e. 'southward, on the right hand.'
ELEAZAR, i.e. 'God is help.'
BENAIAH,] i.e. 'built up of Jah.'
26. SONS OF ELAM,] as in 2. 7, 31; 8. 7, &c
MATTANIAH,] i.e. 'gift of Jah.'

ZECHARIAH,] i.e. 'remembered of Jah.'
JEHIEL,] i.e. 'God lives.'
ABDI,] i.e. 'my servant.'
JEREMOTH,] i.e. 'heights.'
ELIJAH,] i.e. 'God is Jah.'
27. ZATTU,] as in 2. 8; Neh. 7. 13; 10. 15.
ELIOENAI,] i.e. 'unto Jah are my eyes.'
ELIASHIB,] i.e. 'God brings back.'
MATTANIAH,] i.e. 'gift of Jah.'
JEREMOTH,] i.e. 'heights.'
ZABAD,] i.e. 'he endowed.'
AZIZA,] i.e. 'strong.'
28. BEBAI,] as in 2. 17; Neh. 7. 16.
JEHOHANAN,] i.e. 'Jah has grace.'
HANANIAH,] i.e. 'grace of Jah.'
ZABBAI,] as in Neh. 3. 20; in Ezra 2. 9;
and Neh. 7. 14 it is Zaccai.
ATHLI.] Etymology uncertain.
29. BANI,] i.e. 'built up.'
MESHULLAM,] i.e. 'recompensed.'
MALLUCH,] i.e. 'reigning or counsellor.'
ADAIAH,] i.e. 'adorned of Jah.'
JASHUB,] i.e. 'he turns back.'
SHEAL,] i.e. 'he asked.'
RAMOTH,] i.e. 'heights.'
30. TAHATH-MOAB,] i.e. 'fear or governor
of Moab.'
ADNA,] i.e. 'pleasure.'
CHELAL,] i.e. 'completion, perfection.'
BENAIAH,] i.e. 'built up of Jah.'
MAASEIAH,] i.e. 'work of Jah.'
MATTANIAH,] i.e. 'gift of Jah.'
BEZALEEL,] i.e. 'in the shadow of God.'
BINNUI,] i.e. 'built up.'
MANASSEH,] i.e. 'causing to forget.'
31. HARIM,] i.e. 'flat-nosed or devoted.'
ELIEZER,] i.e. 'my God is help.'
ISHIJAH,] as in 1 Ch. 7. 3, &c.
MALCHIAH,] i.e. 'my king is Jah.'
SHEMAIAH,] i.e. 'heard of Jah.'
SHIMEON,] i.e. 'hearkening.'
32. BENJAMIN,] i.e. 'son of the right hand.'
MALLUCH,] i.e. 'reigning, or counsellor.'
SHEMARIAH,] i.e. 'kept of Jah.
33. HASHUM,] i.e. 'rich, wealthy.'

MATTENAI,] i.e. 'gift of Jah.'
MATTATHAH,] i.e. 'gift of Jah.'
ZABAD,] i.e. 'he endowed.'
ELIPHELET,] i.e. 'God causes to escape.'
JEREMAI,] i.e. 'dweller on high.'
MANASSEH,] i.e. 'causing to forget.'
SHIMEI,] i.e. 'hearing.'
34. BANI,] i.e. 'built up.'
MAADAI,] i.e. 'ornament.'
AMRAM,] i.e. 'exalted people.'
UEL,] i.e. 'desire of God.'
35. BENAIAH,] i.e. 'built up of Jah.'
BEDEIAH.] Etymology uncertain.
CHELUHU,] i.e. 'completion of Jah.'
36. VANIAH,] i.e. 'torpid,' perhaps.
MEREMOTH,] i.e. 'heights.'
ELIASHIB,] i.e. 'God brings back.'
37. MATTANIAH,] i.e. 'gift of Jah.'
MATTENAI,] i.e. 'gift of Jah.'
JAASAU,] i.e. 'made by Jah.'
38. BANI,] i.e. 'built up.'
BINNUI,] i.e. 'building up.'
SHIMEI,] i.e. 'hearkening.'
39. SHELEMIAH,] i.e. 'peace of Jah.'
NATHAN,] i.e. 'he gave.'
ADAIAH,] i.e. 'made by Jah.'
40. MACHNADBAI,] i.e. 'a bond,' perhaps
SHASHAI,] i.e. 'whitish, or sixth.'
SHARAI,] i.e. 'beginning.'
41. AZAREEL,] i.e. 'help of God.
SHELEMIAH,] i.e. 'peace of Jah.
SHEMARIAH,] i.e. 'kept of Jah.'
42. SHALLUM,] i.e. 'recompensed.'
AMARIAH,] i.e. 'saying of Jah.'
JOSEPH,] i.e. 'he adds.'
43. NEBO,] i.e. 'a prophet.'
JEIEL,] i.e. 'heaps of God.'
MATTITHIAH,] i.e. 'gift of Jah.'
ZABAD,] i.e. 'he endowed.'
ZEBINA,] i.e. 'bought.'
JADAU] i.e. 'loving or judging.'
JOEL,] i.e. 'Jah is God.'
BENAIAH,] i.e. 'built up of Jah.'
WHO ADOPT,] lit. 'who set, place.

NEHEMIAH

THE BOOK OF NEHEMIAH carries on the history of the Jewish state for a period of twelve years from the reformation effected by Ezra, and is therefore called in the Septuagint and Vulgate Versions, the 'Second Book of Ezra.' It professes (ch. 1. 1) to be the work of Nehemiah himself, and throughout the narrative is in the first person. It is not certain whether he was of priestly origin,—most probably not,—but he appears to have had considerable means (see 5. 14—19); he came up from Babylon with Ezra (see 2. 2; 7. 7), and returned to Shushan, where he was cup-bearer to Artaxerxes the king, through whose favour he once more returned to Jerusalem with full authority to restore the walls and city of Jerusalem, with which he chiefly occupied himself, as Ezra had done with the temple and its services.

I. 1. WORDS,] or 'matters.'
NEHEMIAH,] i.e. 'comforted of Jah.'
HACHALIAH,] i.e. 'reddened or dimmed oy Jah.'
CHISLEU,] that is, the ninth month; see Ezra 10. 9.
20TH YEAR] of the reign of Artaxerxes; see 2. 1.
SHUSHAN,] i.e. 'lily.'
PALACE,] as in 2. 8; 7. 2; 1 Ch. 29. 1, 19; Est. 1. 2, 5; 2. 3, 5, 8; 3. 15; 8. 14; 9. 6, 11, 12; Da. 8. 2.
2. HANANI,] i.e. 'my grace.'
JEWS,] as in 2 K. 16. 6; 25. 25, &c.
ESCAPED PART] from the bondage of Babylon.
JERUSALEM,] whither the returned exiles had gone.
3. LEFT,] or 'remaining,' as in Ge. 14. 10; 32. 8; Ex. 10. 5, &c.
PROVINCE] of Judah, under the Persian empire.
EVIL,] or 'sadness.'
REPROACH,] of the nations around because of their small numbers and poverty.
BROKEN DOWN,] having been destroyed by the Chaldeans.
FIRE,] as in 2 Ch. 36. 19.
4. SAT DOWN] on the ground, as mourners do in the east.
WEEP.. MOURN,] for their misery and wretchedness.
FASTING.. PRAYING,] to appease the anger of the Lord, and obtain his mercy.
GOD OF THE HEAVENS,] as in Ge. 24. 3, &c.
5. I BESEECH THEE,] as in v. 11; Ge. 50. 17; Ex. 32. 31; 2 K. 20. 3; Ps. 116. 4, 16; 118. 25; Isa. 38. 3; Da. 9. 4; Jon. 1. 14; 4. 2.
THE GOD,] lit. 'the mighty one.'
THE FEARFUL,] as in Ge. 28. 17; Ex. 15. 11; 34. 10; De. 1. 19, &c.
COVENANT.. KINDNESS,] as in De. 7. 9; 1 K. 8. 23; 2 Ch. 6. 14; Neh. 9. 32; Da. 9. 4.

LOVING.. KEEPING,] as in Ex. 20. 6; De. 5. 10; 7. 9; Da. 9. 4.
6. ATTENTIVE,] as in v. 11; 2 Ch. 6. 40; 7. 15; Ps. 130. 2.
OPEN,] as in 1 K. 8. 29, 52; 2 Ch. 6. 20, 40; 7. 15, &c.
SERVANTS,] by profession and by covenant engagements.
CONFESSING,] as in 9. 2, 3; Lev. 5. 5; 16. 24; 26. 40; Nu. 5. 7; 2 Ch. 30. 22; Ezra 10. 1; Da. 9. 4, 20.
SINNED,] for there is no one who doeth good, and sinneth not.
7. CORRUPTLY,] or 'taken a pledge,' as in Ex. 22. 26, &c.
8. SAYING,] in Lev. 26. 33; De. 4. 25; 28. 64, &c.
TRESPASS,] as in Lev. 5. 15, &c.
SCATTER,] as in Ge. 11. 8, 9; 49. 7, &c.
9. OUTCAST,] as in De. 22. 1; 30. 4; 2 Sa. 14. 13, 14; Isa. 16. 3, 4; 27. 13; Jer. 30. 17; 49. 36; Eze. 34. 4, 16, &c.
GATHER,] as in De. 30. 3, 4, &c.
TABERNACLE,] as in De. 12. 11; 14. 23; 16. 2, 11; 26. 2, &c.
10. SERVANTS,] as in v. 6 above.
PEOPLE,] set apart to bear testimony to God.
RANSOMED,] as in Ex. 13. 13, 15; 34. 20, &c.
POWER.. HAND,] as in Ex. 32. 11, &c.
11. ATTENTIVE,] as in v. 6 above.
DELIGHTING,] as in 1 K. 13. 33; 21. 6; 1 Ch. 28. 9; Ps. 5. 4; 34. 12; 35. 27; 40. 14; 70. 2; Mal. 3. 1.
GIVE PROSPERITY,] as in Ps. 119. 25, &c.
FOR MERCIES,] as in 1 K. 8. 50, &c.
THIS MAN,] even king Artaxerxes.
BUTLER,] as in Ge. 40. 1—23; 41. 9; 1 K. 10. 5; 2 Ch. 9. 4; Ps. 104. 13; Hab. 2. 15.

II. 1. NISAN,] the first month of the Jewish calendar.
20TH YEAR,] as in 1. 1; B.C. 446.
WINE,] on his table, during one of his feasts.
SAD,] lit. 'evil,' as in Ge. 40. 7, &c.
2. SICK,] as in Ge. 48. 1; 1 Sa. 19. 14, &c.
SADNESS OF HEART,] as in 1 Sa. 17. 28, &c.
FEAR,] lest some one had been speaking to the king about him.
3. LIVE,] as in 1 K. 1. 31, &c.
THE CITY,] Jerusalem; see 1. 2.
PLACE OF THE GRAVES,] as in v. 5.
WASTE,] as in v. 17; Jer. 33. 10, 12; Eze. 36. 35, 38; Hag. 1. 4, 9.
FIRE,] as in 1. 3.
4. SEEKING,] as in Ge. 37. 16; Ex. 4. 19; 10. 11; 33. 7; Nu. 34. 23; Jud. 4. 22, &c.
PRAY,] as in Ge. 20. 7, 17; Nu. 11. 2, &c.
5. PLEASING,] lit. 'good.'
CITY OF THE GRAVES,] as in v. 3 above.
6. QUEEN,] as in Ps. 45. 9; Da. 5. 2, 3, 23.
JOURNEY,] as in Eze. 42. 4; Jon. 3. 3, 4.
SET,] lit. 'give.'
7. LETTERS] of safe conduct and protection.

GOVERNORS,] as in 1 K. 10. 15; 20. 24; 2 K. 18. 24; 2 Ch. 9. 14; Ezra 8. 36; Neh. 2. 9; 3. 7; 5. 14, 15, 18; 12. 26, &c.

8. ASAPH,] i.e. 'he gathers.'

PARADISE,] as in Ecc. 2. 5; Song 4. 13.

BEAMS,] as in 2 Ch. 34. 11.

PALACE,] as in 1 Ch. 29. 1, 19; Neh. 1. 1; 7. 2; Est. 1. 2, 5; 2. 3, &c.

WALL,] which had been broken down, as in 1. 3.

HAND..UPON ME,] as in v. 18.

9. FORCE,] as in 2 Sa. 24. 2, 4, &c.

10. SANBALLAT.] Etymology uncertain.

HORONITE.] See Isa. 15. 5; Jer. 48. 3, 5, 34.

TOBIAH,] i.e. 'goodness of Jah.'

SERVANT,] who had probably been a slave, though now a ruler.

AMMONITE,] which tribe bore a grudge against Israel.

EVIL,] as in v. 1 above.

SEEK GOOD,] as in Ps. 122. 9.

11. THREE DAYS,] resting himself and laying plans for the future.

12. BY NIGHT,] during moonlight, that he might not be noticed particularly.

GIVING,] every good resolution being the fruit of His grace.

BEAST,] lit. 'cattle,' as in Ge. 1. 24, 25, 26; 2. 20, &c.

13. VALLEY] of Jehoshaphat, or that referred to in 2 Ch. 26. 9; Jer. 31. 4.

DRAGON,] as in Ge. 1. 21; Ex. 7. 9, 10, 12; De. 32. 33; Job 7. 11; Ps. 74. 13; 91. 13; 148. 7; Isa. 27. 1; 51. 9; Jer. 51. 34; La. 4. 3.

DUNGHILL,] as in 3. 13, 14; 12. 31; 1 Sa. 1. 2; Ps. 113. 7; La. 4. 5.

MEASURING,] as in v. 15; Job 38. 10.

FIRE,] as in 1. 3, &c.

14. FOUNTAIN] of Siloah.

POOL,] as in 2 Sa. 2. 13; 4. 12; 1 K. 22. 38; 2 K. 18. 17; 20. 20; Neh. 3. 15, 16; Ecc. 2. 6; Song 7. 4; Isa. 7. 3; 22. 9, 11; 36. 2; Nah. 2. 8.

15. BROOK,] Kidron, as in 1 K. 2. 37, &c.

MEASURING,] as in v. 13.

VALLEY,] whence he had gone out, as in v. 13.

16. PREFECTS,] as in Ezra 9. 2; Neh. 4. 14, 19; 5. 7, 17; 7. 5; 12. 40; 13. 11; Isa. 41. 25; Jer. 51. 23, 28, 57; Eze. 23. 6, 12, 23.

FREEMEN,] as in 1 K. 21. 8, 11; Neh. 4. 14, 19; 5. 7; 6. 11; 7. 5; 13. 17; Ecc. 10. 17; Isa. 34. 12; Jer. 27. 20; 39. 6.

17. EVIL,] that is, misfortune and sadness.

WASTE,] as in v. 3 above.

FIRE,] as in v. 3; 1. 3, &c.

WALL,] which was broken down, as in 1. 3.

REPROACH,] as a helpless, feeble people.

18. HAND..UPON ME,] as in v. 8.

SAID,] as in v. 2—18.

GOOD,] for a good purpose, essential for their national prosperity.

19. SANBALLAT..TOBIAH,] as in v. 10.

GESHEM,] i.e. 'a shower.'

MOCK,] as in 4. 1; 2 K. 10. 21; 2 Ch. 30. 10, &c.

DESPISE,] lit. 'trample on us.'

REBELLING,] as in Job 24. 13; Eze. 2. 3; 20. 38.

20 WORD,] as in Ge. 37. 14, &c.

GOD OF THE HEAVENS,] as in Ge. 24. 3, &c.

GIVE PROSPERITY,] as in 1. 11, &c.

PORTION,] as in 14. 24; 31. 14, &c.

RIGHT,] as in Ge. 15. 6; 18. 19; 30. 33, &c.

MEMORIAL,] as in 12. 14; 13. 9, &c.

III. 1. ELIASHIB,] i.e. 'God brings back, as in 12. 10; son of Joiakim, son of Joshua.

SHEEP-GATE,] as in v. 32; 12. 39, &c.

SANCTIFIED,] that is, set apart.

SET UP,] lit. 'caused to stand.'

MEAH,] i.e. 'the hundred.'

HANANEEL,] i.e. 'grace of God.'

2. HAND,] as in Ex. 2. 5; Nu. 2. 17, &c.

JERICHO,] some who had come from that city to inhabit Jerusalem.

ZACCUR,] i.e. 'mindful.'

IMRI,] i.e. 'eloquent, talkative.'

3. FISH-GATE,] as in 12. 39.

HASSENAH,] i.e. a 'thorny place.'

WALLED IT,] as in v. 6; 2. 8; 2 Ch. 34. 11; Ps. 104. 3.

DOORS,] as in v. 6, 13, 14, 15; 6. 1, 10; 7. 1, 3; 13. 19, &c.

LOCKS,] as in v. 6, 13, 14, 15; Song 5. 5.

BARS,] as in v. 6, 13, 14, 15; Ex. 26. 26, &c.

4. MEREMOTH,] i.e. 'high places.'

URIJAH,] i.e. 'light of Jah.'

KOZ,] i.e. 'the thorn.'

MESHULLAM,] i.e. 'recompensed.'

BERECHIAH,] i.e. 'blessed of Jah.'

MESHEZABEEL,] i.e. 'delivered of God.'

ZADOK,] i.e. 'right, just.'

BAANA,] i.e. 'son of affliction.'

5. TEKOITES,] from Tekoa, south east of Beth-Lehem in Judah, as in 2 Sa. 14. 4; 1 Ch. 11. 28.

HONOURABLE ONES,] as in Ex. 15. 10; Jud. 5. 13, 25; 1 Sa. 4. 8; 2 Ch. 23. 20; Neh. 10. 29; Ps. 8. 1, &c.

NECK,] as in Jer. 27. 11, 12, &c.

6. OLD GATE,] as in 12. 39.

JEHOIADA,] i.e. 'Jah has known.'

PASEAH,] i.e. 'passing over, lame.'

MESHULLAM,] i.e. 'recompensed.'

BESODEIAH,] i.e. 'in the counsel of Jah.'

WALLED UP,] as in v. 3.

DOORS..LOCKS..BARS,] as in v. 3.

7. MELATIAH,] i.e. 'escaped of Jah.'

GIBEONITE,] from Gibeon, north west of Geba and Gibeah; see 2 Sa. 21. 1.

JADAN,] i.e. 'he judges.'

MERONOTHITE,] as in 1 Ch. 27. 30; not mentioned elsewhere.

MIZPAH,] in Benjamin, as in v. 19.

THRONE,] as in Ge. 41. 40; Ex. 11. 5; 12. 29; De.17. 18; Jud. 3.20; 1 Sa. 1. 9; 2. 8; 4. 13 18; 2 Sa. 3. 10, &c.

GOVERNOR,] as in 1 K. 10. 15; 20. 24, &c.

8. UZZIEL,] i.e 'strength of God.'

HARHAIAH,] i.e. 'dried up,' perhaps.

REFINERS,] as in Jud. 17. 4; Neh. 3. 32; Prov. 4; Isa. 40. 19.

HANANIAH,] i.e. 'grace of Jah.'

COMPOUNDERS,] as in Ex. 30. 25, 35; 37. 29, &c.

LEAVE,] or 'forsake,' as in Ge. 2. 24.

BROAD WALLS,] broken down by Joash, but repaired by Uzziah; see 2 Ch. 25. 23: 26. 9.

9. REPHAIAH,] i.e. 'healed of Jah.'

Y

HUR,] i.e. 'a hole, whiteness.'
HALF OF THE DISTRICT,] as in v. 12; probably that part of the city which belonged to Benjamin.
10. JEDAIAH,] i. e. 'he confesses Jah.'
HARUMAPH,] i.e. 'flattened in the nose.'
HATTUSH,] i.e. 'assembled,' perhaps.
HASHABNIAH,] i.e. 'reckoning of Jah.'
11. MALCHIJAH,] i.e. 'king of Jah.'
HARIM,] i.e. 'flat-nosed, devoted;' see Ezra 2. 6.
HASHUB,] i.e. 'imputed.'
PAHATH-MOAB,] i.e. 'fear *or* governor of Moab;' see Ezra 2. 32.
FURNACES,] as in 12. 38; Ge. 15. 17, &c.
12. SHALLUM,] i.e. 'recompensed.'
HALOHESH,] i. e. 'the whisperer, charmer.'
HALF OF THE DISTRICT,] as in v. 9; belonging to Judah.
DAUGHTERS,] having probably no sons.
13. VALLEY,] as in 2. 13.
HANUN,] i.e. 'gracious.'
ZANOAH,] a city of Judah, as in Jos. 15. 34, &c.
DOORS..LOCKS..BARS,] as in v. 3 above.
DUNG-GATE,] as in 2. 13.
14. MALCHIJAH,] i.e. 'king of Jah.'
RECHEB,] i.e. 'a rider, chariot.'
DISTRICT,] as in v. 9, 12, 15, 16, 17, 18.
BETH-HACCEREM,] i.e. 'house of the vineyard;' between Tekoa and Jerusalem; see Jer. 6. 1.
DOORS..LOCKS..BARS,] as in v. 3.
15. FOUNTAIN,] as in 2. 14.
SHALLUM,] i.e. 'recompensed.'
COL-HOZAH,] i.e. 'every seer.'
MIZPAH,] see v. 7 above.
DOORS..LOCKS..BARS,] as in v. 3 above.
SILOAH,] i.e. 'sent.'
GARDEN OF THE KING,] as in 2 K. 25. 4.
STEPS,] as in 12. 37; Ex. 20. 26, &c.
CITY OF DAVID,] that is, Zion.
16. NEHEMIAH,] i.e. 'comforted of Jah.'
AZBUK,] i.e. 'wholly forsaken.'
BETH-ZUR,] a strong place in Judah; see Jos. 15. 58.
GRAVES OF DAVID,] as in Acts 2. 29.
MADE,] that is, not a natural one.
MIGHTY ONES,] in wealth and station.
17. LEVITES,] who aided the priests in their services.
REHUM,] i.e. 'merciful.'
BANI,] i.e. 'built up.'
HASHABIAH,] i.e. 'reckoning of Jah.'
KEILAH] of Judah, as in Jos. 15. 4.
18. BAVAI.] Etymology uncertain.
HENADAD,] i.e. 'grace of Hadad.'
KEILAH,] as in v. 17.
19. EZER,] i.e. 'help.'
JESHUA,] i.e. 'a saviour.'
MIZPAH,] as in v. 15.
MEASURE,] as in Ex. 26. 2, 8; 36. 9, 15, &c.
ARMOURY,] where the weapons of war were laid up.
ANGLE,] as in Ex. 26. 24; 36. 29; 2 Ch. 26. 9; Neh. 3. 19, 20, 24, 25; Eze. 41. 21, 22.
20. BARUCH,] i.e. 'blessed.'
ZABBAI.] Compare Ezra 10. 28.
ELIASHIB.] See v. 1 above.

21. MEREMOTH.] See v. 4 above.
22. PRIESTS,] of the family of Aaron.
CIRCUIT,] of the Jordan, as in 12. 28.
23. BENJAMIN,] i.e. 'son of the right hand.'
HASHUB,] i.e. 'imputed.'
AZARIAH,] i.e. 'help of Jah.'
24. CORNER,] as in v. 31, 32; Ex. 27. 2; 38. 2; Jud. 20. 2; 1 Sa. 14. 38; 1 K. 7. 34; 2 K. 14. 13; 2 Ch. 26. 9, 15; 28. 24; Job 1. 19, &c.
25. PALAL,] i.e. 'he judged.'
UZAI,] i.e. 'strong.'
PRISON,] as in 12. 39; Job 16. 12; Jer. 32. 2, 8, 12; 33. 1; 37. 21; 38. 6, 13, 28; 39. 14, 15.
PEDAIAH,] i.e. 'ransomed of Jah.'
PAROSH,] i.e. a 'flea.'
26. NETHINIM,] i.e. 'given ones.'
OPHEL,] i.e. 'fort, secret *or* high place.'
WATER-GATE,] as in 8. 1, 3, 16; 12. 37.
GOETH FORTH] from the wall.
27. TEKOITES,] as in v. 5.
OPHEL,] as in v. 26.
28. HORSE-GATE,] as in 2 Ch. 23. 15.
29. ZADOK,] i.e. 'right, just.'
IMMER,] i.e. 'talkative, loquacious.'
SHEMAIAH,] i.e. 'heard of Jah.'
SHECHANIAH,] i.e. 'neighbour of Jah.'
30. HANANIAH,] i.e. 'grace of Jah.'
SHELEMIAH,] i.e. 'peace of Jah.'
HANUM,] i.e. 'gracious.'
ZALAPH,] i.e. 'fracture, wound.'
MESHULLAM,] i.e. 'recompensed,' as in v. 4.
BERECHIAH,] i.e. 'blessed of Jah.'
CHAMBER,] as in 12. 44; 13. 7.
31. MALCHIJAH,] i.e. 'king of Jah.'
REFINER.] Compare v. 8, 32, &c.
NETHINIM,] i.e. 'given ones.'
MERCHANTS,] as in v. 32; 13. 20; 1 K. 10. 15; Song 3. 6; Eze. 17. 4; 27. 3, 13, 15, 17, 20, 22, 23, 24; Nah. 3. 16.
MIPHKAD,] i.e. 'inspection.'
CORNER,] from east to west.
32. SHEEP-GATE,] as in v. 1; 12. 39, &c.

IV. 1. SANBALLAT,] as in 2. 10; 6. 1, 2, 12, 14; 13. 28.
WALL,] of Jerusalem, as detailed in 3. 1—32.
DISPLEASING,] *lit.* 'there is heat,' as in Ge. 4. 5, 6, &c.
VERY ANGRY,] *lit.* 'angry, multiplying.'
MOCKETH,] as in v. 2 K. 19. 21, &c.
2. FORCE,] as in 2. 9, &c.
WEAK,] as in Ps. 6. 2.
LEFT TO THEMSELVES,] not 'fortify themselves,' as in C.V.
SACRIFICE,] as in the days of old.
IN A DAY,] implying it was beyond their strength.
REVIVE,] that is, bring them into use again.
HEAPS,] as in Ruth 3. 7; 2 Ch. 31. 6, 7, 8, 9; Neh. 13. 15; Song 7. 2; Jer. 50. 26; Hag. 2. 16.
RUBBISH,] *lit.* 'dust.'
3. TOBIAH,] i.e. 'goodness of Jah.'
FOX,] as in Jud. 15. 4; Ps. 63. 10; Song 2. 15; La. 5. 18; Eze. 13. 4.
BROKEN DOWN] by its weight.

4. DESPISED,] as feeble and insane, by the enemy.

REPROACH,] which they had cast on the Jews.

SPOIL,] as a reward of their enmity to the Jews.

CAPTIVITY,] such as the Jews had lately been in.

5. INIQUITY,] in wishing evil to their neighbours who had done them no wrong.

BLOTTED OUT,] from the book of God's remembrance.

ANGER,] which might lead on to sin.

6. BUILD,] without heeding the opposition of Sanballat and Tobiah.

JOINED,] *lit.* 'bound.'

HEART,] so that the work came speedily to conclusion.

7. ARABIANS,] of whom Geshem was probably chief.

AMMONITES,] with Tobiah as their head, see v. 3.

ASHDODITES,] from Ashdod, once a city of the Philistines, afterwards called Azotus.

LENGTHENING,] or prolongation in height and length.

BREACHES,] in various parts of the walls.

STOPPED,] and filled up by new buildings.

DISPLEASING,] *lit.* 'there is heat.'

8. CONSPIRE,] that is, bind themselves together by a mutual engagement.

INJURY,] by setting it on fire, or casting down its wall, &c.

9. PRAY] habitually, as the word often indicates.

WATCH,] *or* 'guard.'

10. JUDAH,] the returned Jews as a body; it was a general impression.

BURDEN-BEARERS,] as in 1 K. 5. 15; 2 Ch. 2. 2, 18; 34. 13.

FEEBLE,] by continued exercise and exertion.

RUBBISH,] *lit.* 'dust,' as in v. 2.

11. ADVERSARIES,] mentioned in v. 7.

CEASE,] leaving Jerusalem in its ruins.

12. COME,] to Jerusalem from time to time.

TEN TIMES,] that is, many times, as in Ge. 31. 41, &c.

13. LOWEST] part of the wall, most easily scaled.

CLEAR PLACES,] freed from rubbish.

FAMILIES,] that they might be united together in action.

SWORDS .. SPEARS ... BOWS,] the usual weapons of war in those days.

14. FREEMEN .. PREFECTS,] as in v. 19.

FEARFUL,] as in Ge. 28. 17; Ex. 15. 11, &c.

BRETHREN .. HOUSES,] for life and everything dear to man.

15. FRUSTRATE,] *or* 'make void.'

WORK,] assigned to them by Nehemiah, or taken up by themselves.

16. BUSINESS,] of building the walls, clearing the rubbish, &c.

KEEPING HOLD,] ready for action.

SHIELDS..COATS OF MAIL,] and other weapons of offence and defence.

17. LADING,] the carts and other vehicles for conveying away the rubbish.

MISSILE,] *or* 'dart.'

18. LOINS,] that he might be prepared for an assault.

BLOWING,] when necessary to summon the people.

19. FREEMEN .. PREFECTS,] as in v. 14.

LARGE,] *or* 'broad.'

SEPARATED] from each other by distance.

20. GATHERED,] for consultation or war.

FIGHT] against all oppressors.

21. BUSINESS,] of building the walls, as in v. 17.

SPEARS,] as in v. 16.

DAWN,] as in Ge. 19. 15; 32. 24, 26, &c.

STARS,] as in Ge. 1. 16; 15. 5, &c.

22. LODGE] all night habitually, that they might be at hand.

GUARD,] *or* 'watch.'

PUTTING OFF,] as in Lev. 6. 11; 16. 23, &c.

VESSEL OF WATER,] for pouring on the hands, &c., when washing.

V. 1. CRY] of distress, as in Ge. 18. 21; 19. 13; 27. 34; Ex. 3. 7, 9; 11. 6, &c.

JEWS,] who were wealthy and powerful.

2. MANY,] increasing in numbers from all parts of the land.

CORN,] as in Ge. 27. 28, 37; Nu. 18. 12, 27; De. 7. 13, &c.

3. PLEDGING,] as in Prov. 17. 18; 22. 26; Eze. 27. 27, &c.

FAMINE,] *lit.* 'hunger;' compare Ezra 6. 8; 7. 24.

4. BORROWED,] as in De. 28. 12; Ecc. 8. 15; Ps. 37. 21; Prov. 22. 7; Isa. 24. 2, &c.

TRIBUTE,] *lit.* 'measure,' as in 3. 11, 19, 20, 21, 24, 27, 30, &c.

5. SUBDUING,] as in Ge. 1. 28; 2 Ch. 28. 10; Est. 7. 8; Jer. 34. 11, 16; Mic. 7. 19; Zec. 9. 15; compare Ex. 21. 7; 2 K. 4. 1.

HATH NO MIGHT,] *or* 'is not to God,' as in Ge. 31. 29, &c.

6. DISPLEASING,] *lit.* 'there is heat.'

CRY,] as in v. 1.

7. REIGNETH OVER ME,] not 'consulteth with myself,' as in C.V.

STRIVE,] as in 13. 11, 17, 25; Ge. 26. 20, 21, 22, &c.

FREEMEN .. PREFECTS,] as in 4. 19, &c.

USURY,] as in v. 10; *or* 'burden,' as in Ex. 23. 5.

EXACTING,] *lit.* 'lifting up,' as in 4. 7; Ge. 37. 25, &c.

SET,] *lit.* 'give.'

8. ACQUIRED,] as in Ge. 4. 1; 14. 19, 22; 25. 10; 33. 19; 39. 1; 47. 19, 20, 22, 23, &c.

SOLD,] as in Ex. 22. 3; Lev. 25. 23, 34, 39, 42, 47, 48, &c.

ABILITY,] *lit.* 'sufficiency.'

SILENT,] as in Ge. 24. 21; 34. 5.

NOT FOUND,] as in Job 32. 3; 2 Sa. 18. 22.

9. NOT GOOD,] as in Ge. 2. 18; Ex. 18. 17, &c.

FEAR,] as in v. 15; Ge. 20. 11; Ex. 20. 20, &c.

REPROACH,] as in Ge. 30. 23; 34. 14, &c.

10. EXACTING,] as in v. 7, 11; Ex. 22. 25; De. 15. 2; 24. 10, 11; 2 K. 4. 1, &c.

CORN,] as in v. 2, 3; Ge. 27. 28, 37, &c.

USURY,] as in v. 7 above.

11. HUNDREDTH PART,] probably for the

purpose of helping them to resume the cultivation of the land.

12. PRIESTS,] the natural instructors of the people.

SWEAR,] as in Ge. 24. 3, 37; 50. 5, 6, &c.

13. LAP,] as in Isa. 49. 22; Ps. 129. 7.

SHAKEN,] as in Ex. 14. 27; Jud. 16. 20, &c.

PERFORM,] *lit.* 'cause to rise.'

LABOUR,] as in Ge. 31. 42; De. 28. 33, &c.

EMPTY,] as in Ge. 37. 34; 41. 27; De. 32. 47; Jud. 7. 16; 9. 4; 11. 3; 2 K. 6. 20, &c.

AMEN,] as in Nu. 5. 22; De. 27. 15, &c.

PRAISE,] as in Ge. 12. 15; Jud. 16. 24, &c.

14. APPOINTED,] as in 1. 7, 8, &c.

GOVERNOR,] as in 1 K. 10. 15; 20. 24, &c.

TWELVE YEARS,] B.C. 446 to B.C. 434; see 13. 6.

BREAD,] provision and allowance made for the chief ruler.

15. HEAVY,] exacting tribute, presents, &c.

40 SHEKELS,] or four or five pounds sterling daily.

RULED,] without hindrance from the governor.

FEAR,] as in v. 9.

16. MIGHTILY,] and made strong efforts to complete it as far as possible.

BOUGHT] or acquired, with either public or private money.

17. 150 MEN,] chief in rank and character.

NATIONS,] such as the Syrians, Arabs, &c.

TABLE,] daily receiving support from him.

18. PREPARED,] *lit.* 'made, done.'

FAT SHEEP,] *or* 'choice ones.'

FOWLS,] *lit.* 'birds,' as in Ge. 7. 16; 15. 10; Lev. 14. 4, &c.

SOUGHT,] or required for the people.

HEAVY,] considering their poverty and numbers.

19. FOR GOOD,] as in Ge. 50. 20, &c.

VI. 1. HEARD,] being informed by his spies and friends.

TOBIAH,] i.e. 'goodness of Jah.'

GESHEM,] i.e. 'shower.'

WALL] of Jerusalem round about.

BREACH,] it being wholly finished.

DOORS,] or leaves of its large public

GATES,] at different sides of the city.

2. MEET TOGETHER,] by appointment, as the original word indicates, as in v. 10; Ex. 25. 22, &c.

VILLAGES,] where they would not be observed, *or* in Chephirim, which Jarchi thinks to be Chephirah, in Benjamin; see Jos. 18. 26.

ONO,] *lit.* 'strong,' as in 7. 37; 11. 3; 1 Ch. 8. 12; Ezra 2. 33.

EVIL,] and put Jerusalem in confusion.

3. GREAT WORK,] rebuilding the temple and city of the great king.

COME DOWN,] from Jerusalem to the valley of Ono.

CEASE,] there being none to fill his place.

4. FOUR TIMES,] hoping by this repetition to gain their object.

5. OPEN LETTER,] being a public insult.

NATIONS,] that is, those not Jews.

GASHMU,] another form of Geshem, in v. 1.

REBEL] against the king of Persia.

WALL,] so as to be able to endure an assault.

KING,] exercising supreme authority.

7. PROPHETS,] as if sent from God to authorise this authority.

APPOINTED] of his own will, as Jeroboam did his priests.

CALL,] or proclaim publicly, that all might acknowledge him.

TAKE COUNSEL,] how to stop these rumours.

8. OWN HEART,] which was meditating evil to Jerusalem and the Jews.

DEVISING,] as in 1 K. 12. 33.

9. MAKING US AFRAID,] trying to do so at least.

FEEBLE,] unaccustomed to such a thing and too few in number.

DONE,] the wish being father to the thought.

STRENGTHEN THOU,] turning to the omniscient hearer of prayer.

10. SHEMAIAH,] i.e. 'heard of Jah.'

DELAIAH,] i.e. 'drawn up of Jah.'

MEHETABEEL,] i.e. 'done good to by God.'

RESTRAINED,] as in De. 32. 36; 1 Sa. 21. 5; 1 K. 14. 10; 21. 21, &c.

MEET] by appointment, as in v. 2.

11. FLEE,] as in Ge. 16. 6, 8; 27. 43, &c.

TEMPLE,] as to a sanctuary or place of refuge.

12. DISCERN,] as in Ge. 27. 23; 31. 32, &c.

SENT HIM,] to warn him of impending danger.

PROPHECY,] or declaration of danger to Nehemiah.

HIRED HIM,] as an intimate friend.

13. HIRELING,] receiving a bribe to deceive Nehemiah.

FEAR,] being cut off by the emissaries of Sanballat and Tobiah.

SINNED,] in forsaking the work of God which he had begun and was carrying on.

REPROACH ME,] as a coward and apostate.

14. BE MINDFUL,] as in 5. 19, &c.

NOADIAH,] i.e. 'met by Jah.'

PROPHETESS,] who probably was a songstress in the temple.

MAKING ME AFRAID,] as in v. 9.

15. WALL,] of the city of Jerusalem.

ELUL,] the sixth month, part of August and September.

52d DAY,] from some date not specified.

16. ENEMIES,] the Samaritans, Ammonites, &c.

FALL,] so that they are ashamed.

BY OUR GOD,] the God of Israel.

17. FREEMEN,] who had been reproved, as in 5. 7, by Nehemiah.

18. SWORN,] *lit.* 'lords, possessors of an oath.'

SON-IN-LAW,] as in 13. 28, Ge. 19. 12, 14, &c.

SHECHANIAH,] i.e. 'neighbour of Jah.'

ARAH,] i.e. 'path,' as in Ezra 2. 5.

JEHOHANAN,] i.e. 'Jah has grace.'

MESHULLAM,] i.e. 'recompensed;' see 3. 4, 30.

BERECHIAH,] i.e. 'blessed of Jah.'

19. GOOD DEEDS,] whatever these were.

MY WORDS] *or* 'matters,' regarding public affairs.

LETTERS,] as in 2 Ch. 30. 1, 6; Neh. 2. 7, 8, 9; 6. 5, 17; Est. 9. 26, 29.

VII. 1. BUILT,] and finished, as above.
DOORS,] of the large gates of the city and temple.
GATE-KEEPERS,] to open and shut them by day and by night.
SINGERS,] to conduct the psalmody in the public service of God.
LEVITES,] to stand in their proper place and discharge their respective duties, see 3. 17.
2. HANANI,] i.e. 'my grace,' as in 1 2; Nehemiah was probably returning to Persia, as promised in 2. 6.
HANANIAH,] i.e. 'grace of Jah.'
PALACE,] as in 1 Ch. 29. 1, 19; Neh. 1. 1, &c.
MAN OF TRUTH,] as in Ex. 18. 21.
FEARING,] as in Ge. 22. 12; 42. 18, &c.
3. GATES,] which were now set up, as in v. 1.
HEAT OF THE SUN,] as in 1 Sa. 11. 9, 11.
FASTEN,] lit 'take or keep hold of,' as in Ex. 4. 4; 15. 14, 15, &c.
GUARDS,] as in 4. 9, 22, 23; 12. 24, 25; 13. 14, &c.
HOUSE,] that he might be always at hand.
4. BROAD,] as in Jud. 18. 10; 1 Ch. 4. 40; Ps. 104. 25; Isa. 22. 18; 33. 21.
FEW,] compared with its former population.
HOUSES,] most of them living in tents.
5. PUTTETH,] lit. 'giveth.'
FREEMEN .. PREFECTS,] as in 5. 7, &c.
GENEALOGY,] as in 1 Ch. 4. 33; 5. 1, 7, 17; 7. 5, 7, 9, 40; 9. 1, 22; 2 Ch. 12. 15, &c.
BEGINNING,] at the command of Cyrus, as in 1. 1—4, &c.
6. SONS OF THE PROVINCE,] as in 1 K. 20. 14, 15, 17, 19; Ezra 2. 1; Neh. 11. 3.
REMOVED,] as in 2 Ch. 36. 20.
CITY,] wherein they or their fathers had dwelt formerly; see Ezra 2. 1—70.
7. ZERUBBABEL,] i.e. 'scattered to Babel.'
8. PAROSH,] i.e. 'a flea.'
9. SHEPHATIAH,] i.e. 'judged of Jah.'
10. ARIAH,] i.e. 'path.'
11. PAHATH-MOAB,] i.e. 'fear or governor of Moab.'
12. ELAM,] i.e. 'hidden, concealed.'
13. ZATTU,] as in Ezra 2. 18; 10. 27; Neh. 10. 15.
14. ZACCAI,] i.e. 'pure.'
15. BINNUI,] i.e. 'building.'
16. BEBAI,] as in Ezra 2. 11; 8. 11.
17. AZGAD,] i.e. 'strength of a troop.'
18. ADONIKAM,] i.e. 'my lord hath risen.'
19. BIGVAI,] as in v. 7.
20. ADIN,] i.e. 'delicate,' as in Ezra 2. 15.
21. ATER,] i.e. 'bound.'
22. HASHUM,] i.e. 'rich, wealthy.'
23. BEZAI,] as in Ezra 2. 17; Neh. 10. 19.
24. HARIPH,] as in 10. 20; in Ezra 2. 18 it 's Jore.
25. GIBEON,] i.e. 'high place.'
26. BETH-LEHEM,] i.e. 'house of bread.'
27. ANATHOTH,] i.e. 'responses.'
28. BETH-AZMAVETH,] i.e. 'house of the strength of death;' see 12. 29; Ezra 2 24.

29. KIRJATH-JEARIM,] i.e. 'city of forests.
CHEPHIRAH,] i.e. 'a village,' as in Jos. 9. 17; 18. 26; Ezra 2. 25.
BEEROTH,] i.e. 'wells.'
30. RAMAH,] i.e. 'high place.'
GABA,] i.e. a 'height.'
31. MICHMAS,] i.e. 'laid up treasure,' west of Beth-Aven.
32. BETHEL,] i.e. 'house of God.'
AI,] i.e. 'heap.'
33. NEBO,] i.e. 'prophet, Mercury.'
34. ELAM,] i.e. 'hidden, concealed.'
35. HARIM,] i.e. 'flat-nosed, devoted.'
36. JERICHO,] near the Jordan and Dead Sea.
37. LOD,] i.e. ' contention, strife.'
HADID,] i.e. 'sharp.'
ONO,] i.e. 'strong.'
38. SENAAH,] i.e. 'thorn bush.'
39. PRIESTS,] being sons of Aaron.
JEDAIAH,] i.e. 'known of Jah.'
JESHUA,] i.e. a 'saviour.'
40. IMMER,] i.e. 'lamb, talkative.'
41. PASHUR,] i.e. 'prosperity everywhere.'
42. HARIM,] i.e. 'flat-nosed, devoted.'
43. LEVITES,] who were helpers of the priests.
JESHUA,] i.e. a 'saviour.'
KADMIEL,] i.e. 'before God.'
HODEVAH,] i.e. 'honour of Jah.'
44. SINGERS,] in the public service of God.
ASAPH,] i.e. 'he gathers.'
45. GATE-KEEPERS] of the temple.
SHALLUM,] i.e. 'recompensed.'
ATER,] i.e. 'shut, bound, dumb.'
TALMON,] i.e. 'oppressed.'
AKKUB,] i.e. 'supplanted.'
HATITA,] i.e. 'digging, exploring.'
SHOBAI,] i.e. 'leading captive.'
46. NETHIAIM,] i.e. 'given ones.'
ZIHA,] i.e. 'drought.'
HASUPHA,] i.e. 'made naked.'
TABBAOTH] i.e. 'signets.'
47. KEROS,] i.e. 'a weaver's comb.'
SIA,] i.e. 'counsel or congregation.'
PADON,] i.e. 'ransom.'
48. LEBANAH,] i.e. 'whiteness, brick.'
HAGABA,] i.e. a 'locust.'
SALMAI,] i.e. 'clothed;' in Ezra 2. 46 it is Shalmai.
49. HANAN,] i.e. 'he has grace.'
GIDDEL,] i.e. 'great, giant.'
GAHAR,] i.e. a 'hiding-place.'
50. REAIAH,] i.e. 'seen of Jah.'
REZIN,] i.e. 'prince, firm, stable.'
NEKODA,] i.e. 'spotted, speckled.'
51. GAZZAM,] i.e. 'a locust.'
UZZA,] i.e. 'strength.'
PHASEAH,] i.e. 'lame.'
52. BEZAI,] as in Ezra 2. 49.
MEUNIM,] as in Ezra 2. 50.
NEPHISHESIM,] i.e. 'expansions,' as in Ezra 2. 50.
53. BAKBUK,] i.e. a 'bottle,' as in Ezra 2. 51
HAKUPHA,] i.e. 'bent,' as in Ezra 2. 1.
HARHUR,] i. e. ' inflammation, burning fever.'
54. BAZLITH,] i.e. 'making naked.
MEHIDA,] i.e. a 'joining together.'
HARSHA,] i.e. 'enchanter, magician.
55. BARKOS,] i.e. a 'painter.'
SISERA,] i.e. 'a field of battle.'

TAMAH,] i.e. 'laughter.'
56. NEZIAH,] i.e. 'pure, sincere.'
HATIPHA,] i.e. 'seized, caught.'
57. SERVANTS OF SOLOMON,] who were probably a privileged class.
SOTAI,] as in Ezra 2. 55.
SOPHERETH,] i.e. 'a scribe.'
PERIDA,] i.e. 'grain, kernel.'
58. JAALA,] i.e. a 'female ibex, chamois.'
DARKON,] i.e. 'scattering,' perhaps.
GIDDEL,] i.e. 'great, giant.'
59. SHEPHATIAH,] i.e. 'judged of Jah.'
HATTIL,] i.e. 'warning.'
POCHERETH,] i.e. 'snaring' of ZEBAIM,] i.e. 'gazelles.'
AMON,] i.e. 'workman, artificer.'
60. NETHINIM,] i.e. 'given ones.'
SERVANTS OF SOLOMON,] as in v. 57 above.
61. TEL-MELAH,] i.e. 'height of salt.'
TEL-HARSHA,] i. e. 'height of an en-chanter.'
CHERUB,] as in Ezra 2. 59.
ADDON,] as in Ezra 2. 59.
IMMER,] i.e. 'lamb, talkative.'
DECLARE,] or 'set before' the priests and rulers.
ISRAEL,] or proselytes of the nations.
62. DELAIAH,] i.e. 'drawn up of Jah.'
TOBIAH,] i.e. 'goodness of Jah.'
NEKODA,] i.e. 'speckled, spotted.'
63. PRIESTS,] the sons of Aaron.
HABAIAH,] i.e. 'hidden of Jah.'
KOZ,] i.e. 'thorn.'
BARZILLAI,] i.e. 'of iron.'
GILEADITE,] as in 2 Sa. 17. 27; 19. 32—39; 1 K. 2. 7.
NAME,] to perpetuate their father's memory.
64. REGISTER,] *lit.* 'writing.'
GENEALOGY,] as in Ezra 2. 62.
REDEEMED,] by a payment of money, as in 2. 62, &c.
65. TIRSHATHA,] that is, Nehemiah the governor.
URIM AND THUMMIM,] as in Ex. 28. 30; Lev. 8. 8; Nu. 27. 21; De. 33. 8, &c.
66. 42,360,] as in Ezra 2. 64.
67. HANDMAIDS,] as in Ge. 20. 17; 21. 10, &c.
7,337,] as in Ezra 2. 64.
245,] in Ezra 2. 67 it is 200 only.
68. MULES,] as in 2 Sa. 13. 29; 18. 19, &c.
69. ASSES,] as in Ge. 12. 16; 22. 3, 5, &c.
70. EXTREMITY,] as in Ge. 19. 4; 47. 2, &c.
TIRSHATHA,] as in v. 65, &c.
DRAMS 1000,] about £1000 sterling.
BOWLS,] as in Ex. 27. 3; 38. 3, &c.
COATS,] as in Ge. 3. 21: 27. 3, &c.
71. POUNDS 2,200,] each worth 60 shekels, Eze. 14. 12.
72. POUNDS 2,000,] or 120,000 shekels.
73. CITIES,] where their fathers had dwelt.
SEVENTH MONTH,] that is, Tisri, in which was the feast of tabernacles.

VIII. 1. AS ONE MAN,] as in Nu. 14. 15, &c.
WATER-GATE,] as in 3. 26, &c.
SCRIBE,] as in 7. 6, 11, 12, who had been in Jerusalem 13 years before, and was come again.

MOSES,] containing the national covenant with God.
2. MEN AND WOMEN,] no sex being exempt from obedience to its requirements, &c.
SEVENTH MONTH,] that is, Tisri, on this day was the festival of blowing of trumpets, as in Lev. 23. 24; it was also the first day of their civil year, and that on which the altar had been set up, see Ezra 3. 6.
3. READETH,] *lit.* 'calleth,' that is, aloud.
4. TOWER,] *lit.* 'great place,' some kind of platform that he might be seen and heard.
MATTITHIAH,] i.e. 'gift of Jah.'
5. OPENETH,] as in Da. 7. 10.
STOOD UP,] in token of respect for the law, like a servant before his master.
6. BLESSETH,] that is, declareth him blessed.
AMEN,] that is, 'It is so!' not 'Let it be so.'
HANDS,] in prayer and thanksgiving; compare 1 Tim. 2. 8.
BOW] the head, as in Ge. 24. 26, 48; 43. 28; Ex. 4. 31, &c.
DO OBEISANCE,] as in Ge. 18. 2; 19. 1, &c.
7. JESHUA,] i.e. 'a saviour.'
UNDERSTANDING,] as in v. 2, 3, 9; 10. 28, &c.
STATION,] according to the direction of Ezra.
8. BOOK] of Moses as in v. 1.
EXPLAINING,] or 'explained;' *lit.* 'spread out,' as in Lev. 24. 12; Nu. 15. 34; Eze. 34. 12; Ezra 4. 18.
MEANING,] as in 1 Sa. 25. 3; 1 Ch. 22. 12, &c.
CONVOCATION,] not 'reading,' as in C. V.
9. NEHEMIAH,] i.e. 'comforted of Jah.'
TIRSHATHA,] or 'governor.'
INSTRUCTING,] as in v. 2, 3, 7, &c.
HOLY,] that is, separate, set apart.
MOURN..WEEP,] seeing it ought to be a day of gladness.
10. FAT THINGS,] as in Ge. 27. 28, 39; Ps. 78. 31; Isa. 10. 16; 17. 4; Da. 11. 24.
SWEET THINGS,] as in Song 5. 16.
PORTION,] of the things they themselves enjoyed.
11. SILENT] from weeping.
GRIEVED,] as in v. 10; Ge. 45. 5, &c.
12. CONCERNING] the true meaning and intent.
THEY MADE KNOWN,] not 'were declared,' as in C.V.
13. HEADS OF THE FATHERS,] as in 7. 70, 71, &c.
TO ACT WISELY,] as in 9. 20; Ge. 3. 6, &c.
14. WRITTEN,] in Lev. 23. 39—43; De. 16. 13.
SEVENTH MONTH,] that is, Tisri, as in v. 2.
15. PROCLAIM,] *lit.* 'cause to hear.'
MOUNT,] especially that of the Olives, near Jerusalem.
LEAVES,] as in Ge. 3. 7; 8. 11, &c.
OLIVE,] as in Ge. 8. 11; Ex. 23. 11, &c.
OIL-TREE,] as in De. 8. 8, &c.
MYRTLE,] as in Isa. 41. 19; 55. 13; Zec. 1. 8, 10, 11.
PALMS,] as in Ex. 15. 27; Lev. 23. 40.
THICK,] as in 1 K. 7. 6, &c.
WRITTEN,] in Lev. 23. 40, &c.

16. ROOF,] which was generally flat in the east.

COURTS,] as in Ge. 25. 16; Ex. 8. 13, &c.

WATER-GATE,] as in 3. 26; 8. 1, 3, 16, &c.

EPHRAIM,] leading toward Israel.

17. CAPTIVITY,] which had returned from Babylon.

SIT,] or 'dwell.'

NUN,] who conquered Canaan.

18. READETH] publicly, in the hearing of the people.

SEVEN DAYS,] the usual period of feasts.

RESTRAINT,] as in Lev. 23. 36.

ORDINANCE,] *lit.* 'judgment.'

IX. 1. FASTING, &c.,] the usual token of mourning, as in 1 Sa. 4. 12; Joel 1. 8, &c.

2. SEED OF ISRAEL] who were in Jerusalem.

SONS OF A STRANGER,] belonging to other nations.

CONFESS,] without which is no forgiveness.

3. STATION,] according to their families, &c.

. A FOURTH,] from six to nine a. m.

BOWING THEMSELVES,] in token of submission.

4. ASCENT,] as in 3. 15; Ex. 20. 26, &c.

JESHUA,] as in 8. 17, &c.

BANI,] i.e. 'built up.'

KADMIEL,] i.e. 'before God.'

SHEBANIAH.] Etymology uncertain.

BUNNI,] i.e. 'built up.'

SHEREBIAH,] i.e. 'heat of Jah.'

CHENANI,] i.e. a 'protector;' all Levites.

CRY] in distress, as the original implies.

5. JESHUA..PETHAHIAH,] as in v. 4.

HASHABNIAH,] i.e. 'reckoning of Jah.'

HODIJAH,] i.e. 'honour of Jah.'

PETHAHIAH,] i.e. 'opening of Jah.'

BLESS,] that is, declare him so.

HONOUR,] as in Ps. 29. 2, &c.

PRAISE,] as in Ex. 15. 11; De. 10. 21, &c.

6. THYSELF] alone and no other.

HEAVENS,] as in De. 10. 14, &c.

HOST,] whether animate or inanimate.

EARTH,] the habitable globe.

SEAS,] or collections of water, Acts 4. 24.

ALIVE,] by his word and providence; see Ps. 36. 6; Heb. 1. 3; Col. 1. 17.

BOWING THEMSELVES,] as servants; see Ps. 148. 2. 3; Heb. 1. 6.

7. FIX ON,] out of his good pleasure.

UR,] i.e. 'light,' Ge. 11. 28, 31; 12. 1.

ABRAHAM,] formerly Abram, Ge. 17. 5.

8. STEDFAST,] in adherence to duty, Ge. 17. 6; 22. 1, 2, 12.

COVENANT] of circumcision, Ge. 15. 18—21.

SEED,] after him.

ESTABLISH,] *lit.* 'raisest up.'

RIGHTEOUS,] that is, right, correct, just.

9. AFFLICTION,] from heavy bondage, Ex. 1. 23; 3. 7.

CRY] of distress, as the word implies.

SUPH,] the eastern extremity of Egypt, Ex. 14. 10, 13.

10. SIGNS,] as in Ge. 1. 14; 4. 15; 9. 12, 13, .7; 17. 11; Ex. 3. 12; 4. 8, 9, 17, 28, 30, &c.

WONDERS,] as in Ex. 4. 21; 7. 3, 9, &c.

ACTED PROUDLY,] as in v. 16, 29, &c. Ex. 18. 11.

NAME,] for power and justice, Ex. 9. 16.

11. CLEAVED,] as in Ex. 14. 21, &c.

DRY LAND,] as in Ge. 1. 9, 10; Ex. 4. 9, &c

PURSUERS,] as in Lev. 26. 17, 36, 37, &c

CAST,] as in Ge. 21. 15; 37. 20, &c.

DEPTHS,] as in Ex. 15. 5; Ps. 88. 6.

STRONG WATERS.] See Ex. 15. 4, 10.

12. PILLAR OF CLOUD,] as in Ex. 13. 21, 22.

LED,] as in Ge. 24. 48; Ex. 13. 21, &c.

PILLAR OF FIRE,] as in Ex. 13. 21, 22; 14. 24, &c.

13. SINAI,] as in Ex. 16. 1; 19. 1, &c.

COME DOWN,] as in Ex. 19. 18.

TO SPEAK,] as in Ex. 20. 1, &c.

RIGHT,] or 'upright, straightforward.'

TRUE,] stedfast and abiding.

GOOD,] suitable for the times and places.

COMMANDS,] expressions of God's will.

14. HOLY SABBATH,] day set apart for God.

MADE KNOWN,] a second time; see Ge. 2. 1—4.

STATUTES,] as in De. 14. 8, &c.

15. BREAD,] the manna, which fell daily.

HUNGER,] as in Ex. 16. 3, 4.

ROCK,] in the midst of a desert.

THIRST,] as in Ex. 17. 6; Nu. 20. 8, 11.

POSSESS,] for themselves and children.

LIFTED UP THY HAND,] as in Ge. 14. 22, &c.

16. ACTED PROUDLY,] as in v. 10, 29, &c.

NECK,] as an obstinate bullock.

NOT HEARKENED,] so as to obey.

17. REFUSE,] by acts, if not by words.

WONDERS,] of mercy and judgment.

APPOINT A HEAD,] as in Nu. 14. 4.

SERVICE,] in the land of Egypt.

REBELLION,] against God's dealings.

GOD OF PARDONS,] as in Ps. 130. 4; Da. 9. 9.

GRACIOUS..ABUNDANT IN KINDNESS,] as in Ex. 34. 6, 7.

NOT FORSAKEN,] utterly and for ever.

18. MOLTEN CALF,] in imitation of the Egyptians.

THY GOD,] as in Ex. 32. 4.

DESPISING,] as if God could not punish.

19. MERCIES,] as in Ge. 43. 14, 30; De. 13. 17, &c.

WILDERNESS,] or pasture land by miracles.

LEAD,] safely from enemies of all kinds.

20. GOOD SPIRIT,] as in Nu. 11. 17, 25.

ACT WISELY,] wherever they might go.

MANNA,] as in Ex. 16. 15.

WITHHELD,] for a single day.

THIRST,] as in Nu. 20. 11.

21. FORTY YEARS,] half of the ordinary life of man.

NOURISHED,] with manna, &c.

LACKED] any good thing; see Ps. 23. 1.

SWELLED,] as in De. 8. 4.

22. KINGDOMS] of Og and Sihon.

APPORTION,] as in 13. 13, &c.

CORNER,] so that no portion was unoccupied.

SIHON..HESHBON,] his capital city.

OG..BASHAN,] the fat fertile land.

23. STARS,] as in Ge. 15. 5; 22. 17; De. 1. 10.

24. SONS,] the first generation dying in the wilderness for sin, as in Nu. 14. 30—33.

HUMBLEST,] by successive defeats.

KINGS,] thirty one, as in Jos. 12. 9—24.

PLEASURE,] to kill or to keep alive.

25. CAPTURE,] all cities resisting.

FENCED CITIES,] walled up to heaven, as in De. 1. 28.
FAT GROUND,] as in De. 8. 7, 8.
ALL GOOD,] all kind of good things.
DIGGED WELLS,] which were expensive.
FRUIT-TREES,] *lit.* 'trees of food.'
SATISFIED,] as in Ex. 16. 8, 12, &c.
BECOME FAT,] in body and in mind; see De. 32. 15; Isa. 6. 10.
DELIGHT THEMSELVES,] compare Isa. 47. 8; Ge. 18. 12; 2 Sa. 1. 24; Ps. 36. 8; Jer. 51. 34.
26. DISOBEDIENT,] *or* 'bitter,' as in De. 1. 26, 43, &c.
REBEL,] as in Ge. 14. 14; Nu. 14. 9, &c.
BACK,] as in 1 K. 14. 9; Ezra 23. 35.
PROPHETS,] as in Matt. 23. 37; Acts 7. 52.
TESTIFIED,] as in Ge. 43. 3; Ex. 19. 21, &c.
DESPISINGS,] as in v. 26; Eze. 35. 12.
27. ADVERSARIES,] the kings of Aram, Moab, &c.
DISTRESS THEM,] as in De. 28. 52, &c.
CRY,] as in Jud. 3. 9, 15; 4. 3; 6. 6, 7.
MERCIES,] as in v. 19 above.
SAVIOURS,] such as Othniel, Ehud, &c.
28. REST,] from enemies within or around.
EVIL,] especially idolatry.
LEAVE,] forsake or abandon.
RULE,] as in Jud. 13. 1.
MANY TIMES,] as in the Book of Judges.
29. TESTIFY,] as in v. 26, &c.
ACTED PROUDLY,] as in v. 10, 16, &c.
SINNED,] by acts of omission and commission.
LIVED,] as in Lev. 18. 5, &c.
REFRACTORY SHOULDER,] as a bullock unaccustomed to the yoke.
HARDENED,] so as not to feel the pain of the many rebukes and checks of God.
30. DRAWEST,] causest many years to pass by.
TESTIFIEST,] as in v. 26, 29, &c.
SPIRIT,] the Holy Spirit of God.
PROPHETS,] such as Samuel, Jeremiah, &c.
GIVEN EAR] or been willing to listen.
31. MERCIES,] as in v. 19, 27, &c.
CONSUMPTION,] as in Isa. 10. 23; 28. 22, &c.
FORSAKEN,] as in v. 17 above.
GRACIOUS AND MERCIFUL,] as in v. 17.
32. GREAT..MIGHTY..FEARFUL,] as in 1. 5.
COVENANT..KINDNESS,] promised by himself.
TRAVAIL,] as in Ex. 18. 8; Nu. 20. 14; La. 3. 5.
FOUND US,] being sent, as it were, by God.
ASSHUR,] who harassed Hezekiah.
33. RIGHTEOUS,] right, just.
TRUTH,] stedfastness.
DONE WICKEDLY,] as in 2 Ch 20. 35; 22. 3. &c.
KING .. FATHERS,] the leaders in Israel.
LAW..TESTIMONIES,] every revealed direction.
TESTIFIED,] as in v. 26, 29, &c.
KINGDOM,] where they had their own rulers.
FAT,] as in Ge. 49. 20; Nu. 13. 20, &c.
36. SERVANTS] to the kings of Persia.
FRUIT..GOOD,] without tax or tribute.
37. KINGS] of Persia and Media.
RULING,] exercising dominion.

PLEASURE,] putting to death or keeping alive.
DISTRESS,] of body and mind.
38. STEDFAST,] permanent and abiding.
WRITING,] in token of our sincerity.
SEALED,] having subscribed his name.
PRIESTS,] all who were in authority.

X. 1. NEHEMIAH,] i.e. 'comforted of Jah.
TIRSHATHA,] the governor of the Jews.
2. SERAIAH,] i.e. 'head of Jah.'
3. PASHHUR,] i.e. 'prosperity everywhere.'
4. HATTUSH,] i.e. 'assembled.'
5. HARIM,] i.e. 'flat-nosed *or* devoted.'
6. DANIEL,] i.e. 'judge of God.'
7. MESHULLAM,] i.e. 'recompensed.'
8. MAAZIAH,] i.e. 'strength of Jah.'
9. LEVITES,] who assisted the priests.
10. SHEBANIAH.] Etymology uncertain.
11. MICHA,] i.e. 'who is thus?'
12. ZACCUR,] i.e. 'remembered.'
13. HODIJAH,] i.e. 'honour of Jah.'
14. HEADS,] belonging to the various tribes.
15. BUNNI,] i.e. 'built up.'
16. ADONIJAH,] i.e. 'the lord is Jah.'
17. ATER,] i.e. 'bound, shut.'
18. HODIJAH,] i.e. 'honour of Jah.'
19. HARIPH,] i.e. 'autumnal showers.'
20. MAGPIASH,] i.e. 'killer of moths.'
21. MESHEZABEEL,] i.e. 'freed by God.'
22. PELATIAH,] i.e. 'escaped of Jah.'
23. HOSHEA,] i.e. 'he gave safety.'
24. HALLOHESH,] i.e. 'the whisperer.'
25. REHUM,] i.e. 'merciful.'
26. AHIJAH,] i.e. 'brother of Jah.'
27. MALLUCH,] i.e. 'counselled.'
28. SEPARATED,] as in 9. 2.
INTELLIGENT ONE,] as in 8. 2, 3, 7, 9, &c.
29. LAYING HOLD,] as in 4. 16, 17. 21, &c.
HONOURABLE ONES,] as in Ex. 15. 12; Jud. 5. 13, &c.
EXECRATION,] as in Ge. 24. 41; 28. 26, &c.
OATH,] as in Ge. 24. 8; 26. 3, &c.
WALK..OBSERVE..DO,] according to law.
30. GIVE NOT..TAKE NOT,] so as to be wholly free.
31. WARES.] This original word is not found elsewhere.
CORN,] as in Ge. 42. 1, 2, 19, 26; 43. 2; 44. 2; 47. 14; Amos 8. 5.
SABBATH-DAY,] the seventh day of the week.
HOLY DAY,] set apart for God's service.
LEAVE] the land uncultivated.
USURY,] *lit.* 'a burden.'
32. COMMANDS,] as in Ge. 26. 5; Ex. 15. 26, &c.
THIRD OF A SHEKEL,] about ten pence.
33. ARRANGEMENT,] as in Lev. 24. 6, 7, &c.
CONTINUAL PRESENT,] as in Lev. 6. 20, &c.
SABBATHS,] as in Ex. 31. 13; Lev. 19. 3, &c.
NEW MOONS,] as in 1 Sa. 20. 5, 18, 24, &c.
APPOINTED SEASONS,] as in Ge. 1. 14; 17. 21.
HOLY THINGS,] as in Ex. 28. 28; Lev. 5. 15.
SIN-OFFERING,] as in Ge. 1. 7; Ex. 29. 14.
MAKE ATONEMENT,] as in Ex. 29. 26; 30. 15.
34. LOTS,] as in Lev. 16. 8, 9, 10; Nu. 26. 55.
OFFERING OF WOOD,] not mentioned elsewhere.
TIME APPOINTED,] as in 13. 31; Ezra 10. 14
BURN,] as in Nu. 24. 2; 2 Ch. 4. 20, &c.

WRITTEN,] as in Lev. 6. 12, 13.
FIRST-FRUITS,] as in Ex. 23. 19; Lev. 23. 10, 17; De. 8. 8.
36. FIRSTLINGS,] as in Ex. 13. 2, 13; Nu. 18. 15, 16, 17, 18.
MINISTERING,] as in Ex. 24. 13; 33. 11, &c.
37. BEGINNING,] as in Ge. 1. 1; 10. 10, &c.
DROUGH,] as in Nu. 15. 20, 21; Eze. 44. 30.
HEAVE-OFFERINGS,] as in Ex. 25. 2, 3, &c.
NEW WINE,] as in Ge. 27. 28, 37; Nu. 18. 12.
OIL,] as in Nu. 18. 12; De. 7. 13, &c.
CHAMBERS,] as in 1 Sa. 9. 22; 2 K. 23. 11, &c.
TITHE,] as in Ge. 14. 20; Lev. 27. 30, &c.
TILLAGE,] *lit.* 'service.'
38. PRIEST] who offered sacrifices.
TITHING,] which was required of them.
TREASURE-HOUSE,] as in Da. 1. 2, &c.
39. CHAMBERS,] as in v. 37.
HEAVE-OFFERING,] as in v. 37.
VESSELS OF THE SANCTUARY,] for receiving them.
NOT FORSAKE,] but frequent it.

XI. 1. HEADS,] as in 2 Ch. 24. 23, &c.
HOLY CITY,] as in v. 18; Isa. 48. 2; 52. 1; 64. 10; Da. 9. 24.
PARTS,] *lit.* 'hands.'
CITIES,] of Judea generally.
2. BLESSING,] that is, presents, as in Ge. 33. 11, &c.
OFFERING THEMSELVES WILLINGLY,] as in Jud. 5. 2, 9, &c.
3. PROVINCE,] as in 1. 3; 7. 6, &c.
POSSESSION,] in which their fathers dwelt.
SERVANTS OF SOLOMON,] as in 7. 57, 60, &c.
4. JUDAH,] the fourth son of Jacob; see Jos. 15. 63; 18. 28.
5. MASSEIAH,] i.e. 'work of Jah;' see 1 Ch. 9. 5.
6. PEREZ,] *lit.* a 'breaking forth.'
7. BENJAMIN,] the youngest son of Jacob.
8. GABBAI,] i.e. 'exactor of tribute.'
9. JOEL,] i.e. 'Jah is God.'
SECOND] in rank and authority.
10. PRIESTS,] the descendants of Aaron.
11. SERAIAH,] i.e. 'head of Jah;' see 1 Ch. 9. 10, 11.
LEADER,] as in 1 Sa. 9. 16, &c.
12. ADAIAH,] i.e. 'adorned of Jah;' see 1 Ch. 9. 12.
13. AMASHSAI,] i.e. 'burdensome;' see 1 Ch. 9. 12.
14. VALOUR,] *or* 'worth.'
INSPECTOR,] as in Ge. 41. 34; Jud. 9. 28, &c.
ZABDIEL,] i.e. 'endowed of God.'
15. LEVITES,] who assisted the priests.
16. SHABBETHAI,] i.e. 'sabbatic.'
JOZABAD,] i.e. 'Jah has endowed.'
17. OUTWARD WORK,] in caring for the temple buildings.
18. MATTANIAH,] i.e. 'gift of Jah.'
MICHA,] i.e. 'who is so?'
ZABDI,] i.e. 'endowed;' in 1 Ch. 9. 15 it is Zichri.
ASAPH,] i.e. 'he gathered.'
COMMENCEMENT,] as in Ge. 13. 3; 41. 21, &c.
GIVETH THANKS,] *or* 'confession.'
BAKBUKIAH,] i.e. 'emptying of Jah.'
SECOND] in rank and authority.
ABDA,] i.e. a 'servant.'
SHAMMUA,] i.e. 'heard.'

GALAL,] i.e. 'weighty, worthy.'
JEDUTHUN,] i.e. 'confessing.'
HOLY CITY,] as in v. 1.
19. GATE KEEPERS,] of the temple.
AKKUB,] i.e. 'supplanted.'
TALMON,] i.e. 'oppressed.'
20. INHERITANCE,] received from his fathers.
21. NETHINIM,] as in 3. 26, 31; 7. 46, &c.
OPHEL,] i.e. 'high *or* secret place.'
ZIHA,] i.e. 'drought,' as in 7. 46; Ezra 2. 43.
GISHPA,] i.e. 'soothing.'
22. OVERSEER,] as in v. 14 above.
23. KING] of Persia.
SUPPORT,] *lit.* a 'stedfast thing,' as in 9. 38.
IN ITS DAY,] as in Ex. 5. 13, 19, &c.
24. PETHAHIAH,] i.e. 'opening of Jah.'
MESHEZABEEL,] i.e. 'freed by God.'
ZERAH,] i.e. 'rising.'
JUDAH,] as in Ge. 38. 30.
HAND OF THE KING,] as in 1 Ch. 18. 17.
25. VILLAGES,] as in Ge. 25. 16; Ex. 8. 13, &c.
KIRJATH-ARBA,] as in Jos. 15. 54; called also Hebron.
SMALL TOWNS,] *lit.* 'daughters.'
DIBON,] as in Jos. 15. 22, called also Dimonah.
JEKABZEEL,] as in Jos. 15. 21, called also Kabzeel.
26. JESHUA.] Not mentioned elsewhere.
MOLADAH,] as in Jos. 15. 26; 1 Ch. 4. 28.
BETH-PHELET,] as in Jos. 15. 27.
27. HAZAR-SHAUL,] as in Jos. 15. 28; 19. 3; 1 Ch. 4. 28.
BEER-SHEBA,] as in Ge. 21. 14, 31, 32, &c.
28. ZIKLAG.] as in Jos. 15. 13; 19. 5, &c.
MEKONAH.] Not mentioned elsewhere.
29. EN-RIMMON.] Not mentioned elsewhere.
ZAREAH,] as in Jos. 15. 33; 19. 41, &c.
JARMUTH,] as in Jos. 10. 3, 5, 23; 12. 11; 15. 35; 21. 29.
30. ZANOAH,] as in 3. 13; Jos. 15. 34, 56; 1 Ch. 4. 18.
ADULLAM,] as in Jos. 12. 15; 15. 35, &c.
VILLAGES,] as in Ge. 25. 16; Ex. 8. 13, &c.
LACHISH,] as in Jos. 10. 3, 5, 23, &c.
AZEKAH,] as in Jos. 10. 10, 11, &c.
SMALL TOWNS,] *lit.* 'daughters.'
BEER-SHEBA,] as in Ge. 21. 14, &c.
HINNOM,] beside Jerusalem.
31. BENJAMIN,] the youngest son of Jacob.
GEBA,] as in Jos. 18. 24.
MICHMASH,] as in 1 Sa. 13. 2.
AIJA,] in Jos. 7. 2 called Ai.
BETH-EL,] as in Ge. 12. 8, &c.
SMALL TOWNS,] *lit.* 'daughters.'
32. ANATHOTH,] as in 1 Ch. 7. 8.
NOB,] as in 1 Sa. 21. 1; 22. 9, &c.
ANANIAH.] Not mentioned elsewhere.
33. HAZOR,] as in Jos. 19. 36.
RAMAH,] as in Jos. 18. 25.
GITTAIM,] as in 2 Sa. 4. 3.
34. HADID,] as in 7. 37; Ezra 2. 33.
ZEBOIM,] as in 1 Sa. 13. 18.
NEBALLAT.] Not mentioned elsewhere.
35. LOD,] as in 7. 37; 1 Ch. 8. 12; Ezra 2. 33.
ONO,] as in 6. 2; 7. 37; 1 Ch. 8. 12; Ezra 2. 33.
ARTIFICERS,] as in 1 Ch. 4. 14.
38. LEVITES,] who assisted the priests.
COURSES,] as in 1 Ch. 23. 6; 24. 1, &c.

XII. 1. ZERUBABBEL,] i. e.'scattered to Babel.'
2. AMARIAH,] i.e. 'saying of Jah,' as in 10. 3, 4.
3. SHECHANIAH,] i.e. 'neighbour of Jah;' in v. 14 and 10. 4 it is 'Shebaniah.'
4. IDDO,] i.e. 'timely.'
5. MIAMIN,] i.e. 'on the right hand;' in v. 17 it is 'Miniamin.'
6. SHEMAIAH,] i.e. 'heard of Jah.'
7. SALLU,] i.e. 'elevation;' in v. 20 it is Sallai,' i.e. 'lifted up or basket-weaver.'
8. JESHUA,] i.e. 'a saviour,' as in 8. 7; 10. 9, 10; 11. 15, 17.
THANKSGIVING,] or 'confession.'
9. BAKBUKIAH,] i.e. 'emptying of Jah,' as in 11. 17.
CHARGES,] of which there were 24; see 1 Ch. 23. 6; 26. 12.
10. JESHUA,] i.e. 'a saviour;' the high-priest.
11. JONATHAN,] i.e. 'Jah hath given.'
JADDUA,] who met Alexander the Great.
12. SERAIAH,] i.e. 'head of Jah.'
13. EZRA,] i.e. 'help.'
14. MELICU,] i.e. 'my reign or counsel.'
15. HARIM,] i.e. 'flat-nosed, devoted.'
16. IDDO,] i.e. 'timely.'
17. ABIJAH,] i.e. 'my father is Jah.'
18. BILGAH,] i.e. 'cheerfulness.'
19. JOIARIB,] i.e. 'Jah contends.'
20. SALLAI,] i.e. 'lifted up or basket-weaver.'
21. HILKIAH,] i.e. 'portion of Jah.'
22. ELIASHIB,] i.e. 'God brings back.'
WRITTEN,] as in 7. 5; Nu. 11. 26, &c.
PERSIAN,] surnamed Codomannus, the last king.
23. CHRONICLES,] as in 1 Ch. 9. 14, &c.
24. HASHABIAH,] i.e. 'reckoning of Jah.'
TO GIVE PRAISE,] as in 2 Sa. 14. 25, &c.
TO GIVE THANKS,] as in 1 Ch. 16. 4, 7, 35, &c.
MAN OF GOD,] as in v. 36; De. 33. 1, &c.
CHARGE,] as in 1 Ch. 23. 5, 36.
25. MATTANIAH,] i.e. 'gift of Jah.'
GATHERINGS,] as in 1 Ch. 26. 15, 17.
26. JOIAKIM,] i.e. 'Jah raises up.'
GOVERNOR,] as in 5. 14, 15, 18, &c.
SCRIBE,] as in v. 36; 8. 1, 4, 9, 13; 13. 13.
27. DEDICATION,] as in Nu. 7. 10, 11, 84. 88; 2 Ch. 7. 9; Ps. 30. 1.
PLACES] up and down the country.
THANKSGIVINGS,] as in v. 31, 33, 40; Lev. 7. 12, &c.
SINGING,] as in v. 36, 46; Ge. 31. 27, &c.
CYMBALS,] as in 1 Ch. 3. 8; 15. 16, &c.
PSALTERIES,] as in 1 Sa. 10. 5, &c.
HARPS,] as in Ge. 4. 21; 31. 27, &c.
28. SINGERS,] as in 1 Ch. 6. 33; 9. 33, &c.
CIRCUIT,] as in Ge. 13. 10, 11, 12; 19. 17, &c.
NETOPHATH,] as in 1 Ch. 9. 16.
29. GILGAL,] as in De. 11. 30; Jos. 5. 9, 10.
GEBA,] as in Jos. 21. 17.
AZMAVETH,] as in 7. 28; Ezra 2. 24.
VILLAGES,] as in Ge. 25. 16; Ex. 8. 13, &c.
30. CLEANSED,] or 'cleansed themselves,' as in Ge. 35. 2.
31. THANKSGIVING COMPANIES,] as in v. 27.
PROCESSIONS,] lit. 'goings.'
DUNG-GATE,] as in 2. 13.
32. HOSHAIAH,] i.e. 'saved by Jah.'
33. AZARIAH,] i.e. 'help of Jah.'

34. JUDAH,] i.e. 'he confesses;' not the patriarch.
35. SONS OF THE PRIESTS,] as in 1 Ch. 9. 30.
TRUMPETS,] as in v. 41; Nu. 10. 2, 8, &c.
36. SHEMAIAH,] i.e. 'heard of Jah.'
INSTRUMENTS OF SONG,] as in 1 Ch. 15. 16, &c.
MAN OF GOD,] as in v. 24; De. 33. 1, &c.
37. FOUNTAIN,] as in 2. 14.
STEPS,] or 'ascents.'
WATER-GATE,] as in 3. 26; 8. 16.
THANKSGIVING COMPANY,] as in v. 27, 31.
FURNACES,] as in 3. 11.
BROAD WALL,] as in 3. 8.
39. GATE OF EPHRAIM,] as in 8. 16.
OLD GATE,] as in 3. 6.
FISH-GATE,] as in 3. 1.
GATE OF HANANEEL,] as in 3. 1.
MEAH,] as in 3. 2.
SHEEP-GATE,] as in 3. 2.
PRISON-GATE,] as in 3. 25; Jer. 20. 1, 2; 32. 2.
40. THANKSGIVING COMPANIES,] as in v. 27, 31, 33, &c.
STAND] still in their posts.
PREFECTS,] as in 2. 16; 4. 14, 19; 5. 7, 17; 7. 5; 13. 11; Ezra 9. 2; Isa. 41. 25; Jer. 51. 23, 28, 57; Eze. 23. 9, 12, 23.
42. MAASEIAH,] i.e. 'work of Jah.'
INSPECTOR,] as in 11. 9, 14, 22; Ge. 41. 34, &c
43. DISTANCE,] as in Ezra 3. 13.
44. APPOINTED,] as in 7. 1.
CHAMBERS,] as in 3. 30; 13. 7.
TREASURIES,] as in 7. 70, 71; 10. 38; 13. 12.
HEAVE-OFFERINGS,] as in 10. 37, 39; 13. 5.
FIRST-FRUITS,] as in 10. 37, &c.
TITHES,] as in 10. 37, 38; 13. 5, 12.
FIELDS OF THE CITIES,] as in Jos. 21. 12; 1 Ch. 6. 56.
PORTIONS,] as in 10. 35—39.
STANDING UP,] to serve the Lord publicly
45. CHARGE,] laid on them especially.
CLEANSING,] as in Lev. 12. 4, 5; 13. 8, 35, &c.
COMMAND,] as in 1 Ch. 25. 1; 26.1; 2 Ch. 8. 14.
46. OF OLD;] see 1 Ch. 25, 2—8.
47. ISRAEL,] belonging to the twelve tribes.
ITS DAY,] as in Ge. 39. 10; Ex. 5. 13, &c.
SANCTIFYING,] that is, setting apart.

XIII. 1. READ,] by Ezra or the priests.
EARS OF THE PEOPLE,] assembled together.
WRITTEN,] in De. 23. 3.
AMMONITE,] descendant of Lot, Ge. 19. 38.
MOABITE,] descendant of Lot, Ge. 19. 37.
ASSEMBLY,] as in 5. 13; 7. 66; 8. 2, 17.
2. NOT COME,] as in De. 23. 4, 5.
BREAD..WATER,] the most necessary food
HIRE,] as in 6. 12, 13, &c.
BALAAM,] as in Nu. 22. 5, &c.
REVILE,] as in Jos. 24. 9, &c.
BLESSING,] as in 9. 5; Ge. 12. 2, &c.
3. LAW,] or 'direction,' as above.
SEPARATE,] as in 1. 4, 7, 14, 18, &c.
MIXED PEOPLE,] as in Ex. 12. 38; Lev. 13. 48, 49, 51, 52, 53, 56, 57, 58, 59.
4. ELIASHIB,] as in 3. 1, 20, 21; 12. 10, &c.
APPOINTED,] lit. 'given.'
CHAMBERS,] as in 10. 37, 38, 39, &c.
RELATION,] as in Ge. 19. 20; 45. 10, &c.
TOBIAH,] as in 2. 10, though he was an Ammonite.
5. CHAMBER,] though he was an Ammonite.
PRESENT,] as in Ge. 4. 3, 4, 5; 32. 13, &c.
FRANKINCENSE,] as in v. 9; Ex. 30. 34, &c.

VESSELS,] used by priests and Levites.
TITHE,] as in Ge. 14. 20; Lev. 27. 30, &c.
CORN,] as in Ge. 27. 28, 37; Nu. 18. 11, &c.
NEW WINE,] as in Ge. 27. 28, 37; Nu. 18. 12.
OIL,] as in Nu. 18. 12; De. 7. 13, &c.
COMMANDED THING,] for their support.
HEAVE-OFFERING,] as in Ex. 25. 2, 3, &c.
6. ARTAXERXES,] or Darius Hystaspis.
BABYLON,] as well as of Persia.
KING,] to Babylon again.
DAYS,] a week perhaps, as in Ge. 4. 3, &c.
7. JERUSALEM,] as permitted by the king.
EVIL,] in desecrating the temple.
CHAMBER,] as in v. 5.
8. DISPLEASING,] *lit.* 'evil, wrong.'
CAST FORTH,] as polluted and polluting.
VESSELS,] furniture of every kind.
9. CLEANSE] for the future use of the priests.
VESSELS,] which belonged to the temple.
FRANKINCENSE,] as in v. 5.
10. PORTIONS,] necessary for their support.
FLEE,] to work for food elsewhere.
11. STRIVE,] or 'contend.'
PREFECTS,] who were over the people.
FORSAKEN,] by the priests and Levites.
GATHER] the Levites who had fled.
STATION,] according to their abilities.
TITHE,] as commanded in the law.
TREASURIES,] of the temple, as formerly.
13. SHELEMIAH,] i.e. 'peace of Jah.'
ZADOK,] i.e. 'right, just.'
PEDAIAH,] i.e. 'ransomed of Jah.'
HANUN,] i.e. 'grace.'
ZACCUR,] i.e. 'mindful.'
MATTANIAH,] i.e. 'gift of Jah.'
STEDFAST] in adherence to their duty.
PORTION,] of food, at set times.
14. BE MINDFUL,] as in 1. 8; 4. 14; 5. 19, &c.
BLOT OUT,] as in Prov. 31. 3; Jer. 18. 23.
KIND ACTS,] in behalf of Israel.
CHARGES,] as in 4. 9, 22, 23; 7. 3, &c.
15. TREADING,] as in 1 Ch. 5. 18; 8. 40; 2
Ch. 14. 8; Job 9. 8; Isa. 16. 10, &c.
WINE-VATS,] as in Jud. 6. 11; Isa. 63. 2;
La. 1. 15; Joel 3. 13.
SABBATH,] the sixth day of the week.
SHEAVES,] as in v. 2; Ruth 3. 7; 2 Ch. 31.
6, 7, 8, 9; Song 7. 2; Jer. 50. 26; Hag. 2. 16.
LADING,] as in Zec. 12. 3.
ASSES,] as in 7. 69; Ge. 12. 16, &c.
WINE,] as in 2. 1; 5. 15, 18; Ge. 9. 21, &c.
GRAPES,] as in Ge. 40. 10, 11; 49. 11, &c.
FIGS,] as in Ge. 3. 7; Nu. 13. 23, &c.
BURDEN,] as in v. 19; 10. 31; Ex. 23. 5, &c.
TESTIFY,] as in v. 21; 9. 26, 29, 30, 34.
PROVISION,] as in Ge. 10. 9; 25. 27, &c.
16. TYRIANS,] inhabitants of Tyre.
FISH,] caught on their shores.
WARE,] as in Nu. 20. 19; Prov. 31. 10.
17. FREEMEN,] as in 2. 16; 4. 14; 5. 7; 6. 17.
POLLUTING,] as in Ex. 31. 14; Lev. 21. 9, &c.
18. DO,] as in Jer. 17. 21—23.
EVIL,] or 'misfortune.'

FIERCENESS,] of the wrath of God.
19. DARK,] or 'shadowed,' as in Eze. 31. 3.
DOORS,] or 'leaves' of the gates.
SHUT,] as is done nightly in the east.
STATIONED,] to see his orders executed.
BURDEN] of any kind of merchandise.
20. LODGE,] or 'pass the night.'
MERCHANTS,] as in 3. 31, 32; 1 K. 10. 15, &c.
SELLERS,] as in v. 16; Lev. 25. 16, &c.
WARE,] as in v. 16 above.
21. TESTIFY,] as in v. 15 above.
PUT FORTH,] to punish for obstinacy.
22. CLEANSED,] as in 12. 30; Ge. 35. 2, &c.
KEEPING THE GATES,] that they may not
be opened.
REMEMBER,] as in v. 14 above.
HAVE PITY,] as in Ge. 45. 20; De. 7. 16, &c.
KINDNESS,] not 'mercy,' as in the C. V.
23. SETTLED,] *lit.* 'caused to dwell.'
ASHDOD,] as in 4. 7; Jos. 13. 3; 1 Sa. 5. 3, 6.
AMMON..MOAB,] the children of Lot.
24. ASHDODITISH,] the peculiarities of
which are unknown.
JEWISH,] the language of the Jews on their
return from Babylon, a corrupted Hebrew.
PEOPLE AND PEOPLE,] with which their
mothers were connected.
25. STRIVE,] as in v. 17.
DECLARE VILE,] as in v. 2; Ge. 3. 21, &c.
SMITE,] as in Ge. 4. 15; 8. 21, &c.
PLUCK OFF,] as in Ezra 9. 3; Isa. 50. 6.
CAUSE TO SWEAR,] as in 5. 12; Ge. 24. 3, 37.
BY GOD,] as in Ge. 21. 23; 1 Sa. 30. 15;
2 Ch. 36. 13; Isa. 65. 16.
GIVE..TAKE,] as they had sworn in 10. 29,30.
26. SOLOMON,] as in 1 K. 11. 3, 4.
NO KING,] in point of wisdom and honour.
BELOVED,] as 'Jedidiah' indicates.
KING,] in preference to all David's sons.
STRANGE WOMEN,] Moabites, Ammonites,
Edomites, Zidonians, Hittites, &c.
CAUSE TO SIN,] by seducing him to idolatry.
27. HEARKEN,] so as to obey the word.
EVIL,] of intermarriage with heathens.
TRESPASS,] as in De. 7. 1, 8; 1 K. 11. 1, 2.
SETTLE,] as in v. 23.
28. JOIADA,] i.e. 'Jah hath known.'
ELIASHIB,] i.e. 'God brings back.'
SON-IN-LAW,] as in 6. 18.
SANBALLAT,] as in 2. 10, 19; 4. 1, 7, &c.
CAUSE TO FLEE,] as in Ex. 28. 26; 1 Ch. 8. 13.
29. BE MINDFUL,] as in v. 14, 22.
REDEEMED,] as in 7. 64; Ezra 2. 62.
COVENANT,] made in Nu. 24. 11—13; Mal.
2. 4—8.
30. CLEANSED,] as in v. 17; 12. 30, &c.
CHARGES,] as in 7. 3; 12. 9, 45.
31. WOOD-OFFERING,] as in 10. 39.
APPOINTED TIMES,] as in 10. 34; Ezr. 10. 14.
FIRST FRUITS,] as in 10. 35; Ex. 23. 16, &c.
BE MINDFUL,] as in v. 14, 22, 29.
GOOD,] rendering to him according to his
works.

ESTHER

THE Book of Esther contains the narrative of a wonderful deliverance of the Jews in the Persian empire by the intervention of a Jewess of that name, when they were in danger of being cut off by the malignant vengeance of Haman, an Agagite, a hereditary foe of Israel. The author's name is not mentioned, but the supposition that it was written by Mordecai—whose behaviour to Haman brought on the danger—is as likely as any other, see 9. 20, 32. The Book is not quoted in the New Testament, nor referred to by Philo, nor even by Melito, A.D. 170, when naming the books of the Old Testament, yet there is no good ground for doubting its genuineness as a portion of the Jewish Canon. Another peculiarity is that there is not a single allusion to God throughout the narrative, but though his name be unmentioned his finger is evident. It comprises a period of about ten years, (see 1. 3, and 3. 7,) and is, and has always been a favourite book with the Jews, as narrating the origin of the feast of Purim, &c.

I. 1. AHASUERUS,] i.e. 'lion-king,' in Greek Xerxes,' who invaded Greece.
HODU,] that is, India, so Syr. 'Hendu,' Arab. 'Hind,' Zend and Pehlvi 'Heando.'
CUSH,] i.e. southern Arabia and Abyssinia.
127 PROVINCES ;] in Da. 6. 1 it is 120.
2. SHUSHAN,] i.e. a 'lily,' as in Neh. 1. 1; Da. 8. 2. Now called Shuster, anciently Susa.
PALACE,] as in 1 Ch. 29. 1, 19; Neh. 1. 1, &c.
3. 3D YEAR,] B.C. 519.
BANQUET,] *lit.* a 'drinking,' as in Ge. 19. 3.
FORCE,] as in 8. 11; Ge. 34. 29; 47. 6, &c.
4. SHEWING,] to gratify his vanity.
WEALTH,] as in 5. 11; Ge. 31. 16, &c.
BEAUTY,] as in Ex. 28. 2, 40; De. 26. 19, &c.
180 DAYS,] almost six months, but this is not uncommon in eastern story.
5. FOUND] present, as in 4. 16; Ge. 19. 15.
SEVEN DAYS,] an additional week.
COURT,] as in 2. 11; 4. 11; 5. 1, 2; 6. 4, 5, &c.
6. WHITE LINEN,] as in 8. 15.
WHITE COTTON.] Not mentioned elsewhere; Ben-Melech has 'green.'
BLUE,] as in 8. 15; Ex. 25. 4, &c.
FASTENED,] as in 1 Ch. 24. 6; Ecc. 9. 12, &c.
CORDS,] as in Jos. 2. 15; 2 Sa. 8. 2, &c.
FINE LINEN,] as in 8. 15; 1 Ch. 4. 21, &c.
PURPLE,] as in 8. 15; Ex. 25. 4, &c.
RINGS,] as in Song 5. 14.
PILLARS,] as in Ex. 13. 21, 22; 14. 19, &c.
WHITE MARBLE,] as in Song 5. 15.
COUCHES,] as in 7. 8; Ge. 47. 31; 48. 2, &c.
PAVEMENT,] as in 2 Ch. 7. 3; Eze. 40. 17, 18; 42. 3.
SMARAGDUS.] Not mentioned elsewhere; Targum has 'crystal.'
MOTHER OF PEARL.] Not mentioned elsewhere; Bochart has 'pearl.'
BLACK MARBLE.] Not mentioned elsewhere ; Hartman has 'tortoise-shell.'

7. DRINK,] as in Ge. 2. 10; 24. 19; Ex. 2. 16
ROYAL WINE,] *lit.* 'wine of the kingdom.
MEMORIAL,] *lit.* 'hand.'
8. LAW,] as in v. 13, 15, 19; 2. 8, 12; 3. 8, &c.
PRESSING,] as in Da. 4. 9.
APPOINTED,] *lit.* 'founded,' as in Jos. 6. 26.
CHIEF ONE,] *or* 'great one.'
PLEASURE,] as in 9. 5; Ge. 49. 6, &c.
MAN AND MAN,] each individual.
9. VASHTI,] i.e. 'beautiful.'
QUEEN,] as in v. 11, 12, 15, 16, 17, 18.
BANQUET,] as in v. 3.
WOMEN,] who were not allowed to associate with men publicly, not even in festivity.
ROYAL HOUSE,] *lit.* 'house of the kingdom.'
10. SEVENTH DAY,] the day of the feast.
GLAD,] *lit.* 'good,' as in 5. 9, &c.
MEHUMAN,] i.e. 'stedfast.'
BIZTHA,] i.e. 'a eunuch.'
HARBONA,] i.e. an 'ass-driver.'
BIGTHA,] i.e. 'gardener.'
ABAGTHA,] i.e. 'gardener.'
ZETHER,] i.e. a 'star.'
CARCAS,] i.e. an 'eagle.'
EUNUCHS,] as in v. 12, 15; 2. 3, 4, &c.
MINISTERING,] as in 2. 2; 6. 3; Ex. 24. 13. &c.
11. ROYAL CROWN,] *lit.* 'crown of the kingdom.'
BEAUTY,] as in Ps. 45. 11; 50. 2; Prov. 6. 25.
GOOD APPEARANCE,] as in 2. 2, 3, 7; Ge.12.11.
12. REFUSETH,] as in Ge. 37. 35; 39. 8, &c.
BY THE HAND,] or instrumentality.
WROTH,] as in 2. 21; Ge. 40. 2, &c.
FURY,] as in 2. 1; 3. 5; 5. 9; 7. 7, 10, &c.
13. WISE MEN,] as in 6. 13; Ge. 41. 8, &c.; compare Ezra 7. 14.
KNOWING THE TIMES,] as in 1 Ch. 12. 32.
JUDGMENT,] as in De. 17. 6; Job 19. 29, &c.
14. CARSHENA,] i.e. 'spoiling of war, *or* black.'
SHETHAR,] i.e. a 'star.'
ADMATHA,] i.e. 'human,' perhaps.
TARSHISH,] i.e. 'breaking, subjection.'
MERES,] i.e. 'lofty, worthy.'
MARSENA,] i.e. 'lofty, worthy.'
MEMUCAN,] i.e. 'established, prepared.'
SEEING THE FACE,] a peculiar privilege.
SITTING FIRST.] Compare Ezra 7. 14.
15. LAW,] obligatory even on the king.
16. MEMUCAN,] as in v. 14.
DONE PERVERSELY,] as in Da. 9. 5, &c.
PROVINCES,] numbering 127, as in v. 1.
17. WORD] of refusal, as in v. 12.
CONTEMPTIBLE,] as in Mal. 2. 9.
18. PRINCESSES,] as in Jud. 5. 29; 1 K. 11. 3.
SUFFICIENCY,] as in Ex. 36. 5, 7; Lev. 5. 7.
WRATH,] as in Nu. 1. 53; 16. 46, &c.
19. GOOD,] as in De. 23. 16, &c.
WORD,] not 'commandment,' as in C.V.
WRITTEN,] as in 2. 23; 3. 9, 12; 8. 5, 9, &c.
NOT PASS AWAY,] as in 4. 17; 9. 27, 28, &c.
ROYALTY,] *lit.* 'kingdom,' as in 1. 2, 4, 7 9, 11, 14, 20.
COMPANION,] not 'another,' as in C.V. see Ex. 11. 2; Isa. 34. 15, 16; Jer. 9. 20; Zec. 11. 9.

20. SENTENCE,] not 'decree;' see Ecc. 8. 11.
GREAT,] consisting of 127 provinces.
HONOUR,] or 'glory,' as in v. 4; 6. 3, 6, 7, 9, 11.
21. GOOD IN THE EYES,] as in Nu. 24. 1, &c.
PRINCES,] the other six, as in v. 14.
22. LETTERS,] lit. 'books;' as in 2. 23; 3. 13.
WRITING,] as in 3. 12, 14; 4. 8; 8. 8, 9, 13, &c.
PEOPLE,] as in 3. 12; 8. 9.
TONGUE,] as in 3. 12; 8. 9; Ge. 10. 5, &c.
HEAD,] as in Prov. 8. 16; Isa 32. 1; Nu. 16. 13.

II. 1. CEASING,] not 'appeased,' as in C.V.
FURY,] as in 1. 12; 3. 5; 5. 9; 7. 7, 10, &c.
REMEMBERED,] as in Ge. 8. 1; 9. 15, 16, &c.
DECREED,] lit. 'cut off,' as in 2 Ch. 26. 21.
2. MINISTERS,] as in 1. 10; 6. 3; Ex. 24. 13.
VIRGINS,] as in v. 3, 17, 19; Ge. 24. 16, &c.
GOOD APPEARANCE,] as in v. 3, 7; 1. 11.
3. INSPECTORS,] as in Ge. 41. 34; Jud. 9. 28.
HEGE,] i.e. a 'eunuch,' as in v. 8, 15.
EUNUCH,] not 'chamberlain,' as in C.V.
PURIFICATIONS,] as in v. 9, 12; Prov. 20. 30.
4. GOOD IN THE EYES,] as in 1. 21, &c.
REIGN,] as in 2 K. 11. 3; 2 Ch. 22. 12, &c.
5. JEW,] by religion, not by birth only.
SHUSHAN,] as in 1. 2, &c.
MORDECAI,] i.e. a 'little man,' worshipper of Mars.'
JAIR,] i.e. 'he enlightens.'
SHIMEI,] i.e. 'hearing.'
KISH,] i.e. 'snaring with the bow.'
BENJAMITE,] of the same tribe with the father of Saul.
6. REMOVED,] eleven years before the destruction of the temple.
7. SUPPORTING,] as in Nu. 11. 12, &c.
HADASSAH,] i.e. a 'myrtle.'
ESTHER,] i.e. a 'star.'
UNCLE,] as in v. 15; Lev. 10. 4; 20. 20, &c.
FAIR FORM,] as in Ge. 29. 17; 39. 6, &c.
GOOD APPEARANCE,] as in v. 2, 3; 1. 11.
8. LAW,] regarding the virgins.
HEGAI,] in v. 8 it is 'Hege.'
TAKEN,] probably by force without consent.
9. GOOD,] as in 1. 21, &c.
RECEIVETH,] not 'obtaineth,' as in C.V.
HASTENETH,] as in 8. 14; 2 Ch. 35. 21, &c.
PURIFICATIONS,] as in v. 3 above.
PORTIONS,] as in 9. 19, 22; Ex. 29. 26, &c.
PROVIDED,] no 'meet,' as in C.V.
CHANGETH,] as in 1 Sa. 21. 13; Ps. 34. 1, &c.
10. DECLARED,] lit. 'set before.'
KINDRED,] as in v. 20; 8. 6; Ge. 11. 28, &c.
LAID A CHARGE,] for what reason is unknown, probably lest she should be despised.
11. WALKING UP AND DOWN,] as in Ge. 3. 8.
COURT,] as in 1. 5, &c.
WELFARE,] that is, peace and prosperity.
12. TURN,] as in v. 15; comp. Song 1. 10, 11.
PURIFICATIONS,] as in v. 3, 9.
MYRRH,] as in Ex. 30. 23; Ps. 45. 8, &c.
SPICES,] as in Ex. 25. 6; 30. 23, &c.
13. SAITH,] not 'desireth,' as in C.V.
14. SECOND HOUSE,] where the concubines were kept.
SHAASHGAZ,] i.e. 'servant of the beautiful.'
CONCUBINES,] or secondary wives; Darius, whom Alexander conquered, had 300.
DELIGHTED,] as in 6. 6, 7, 9, 11; Ge. 34. 19, &c.
NAME,] as in Ex. 31. 2, &c.
15. TURN,] as in v. 12.

ABIHAIL,] i.e. 'father of strength.'
DAUGHTER,] as in v. 7.
NOT SOUGHT,] not being anxious perhaps for the perilous dignity of a queen.
GRACE,] as in v. 17; 5. 2, 8; 7. 3; 8. 5, &c.
16. ROYAL HOUSE,] as in 1. 9.
10TH MONTH.] Sept. and Josephus read 'twelfth.'
TEBETH,] part of December and January.
7TH YEAR,] four years after the divorce of Vashti, see 1. 3.
17. KINDNESS,] as in v. 9.
VIRGINS,] who had come before her.
ROYAL CROWN,] as in 1. 11.
REIGN,] as in v. 4.
18. BANQUET,] lit. 'drinking.'
RELEASE.] The original word is not found elsewhere.
GIFTS,] as in Ge. 43. 34; Jud. 20. 38, 40, &c.
MEMORIAL,] lit. 'hands.'
19. SECOND TIME,] for what purpose is unknown.
SITTING IN THE GATE,] as in v. 21; 5. 13.
20. NOT DECLARING,] as in v. 10.
TRULY,] lit. 'in truth, stedfastness;' see Ge. 30. 12; Jos. 7. 20.
21. SITTING,] as in v. 19.
BIGTHAN,] i.e. 'a gift.'
TERESH,] i.e. 'severe, austere.'
THRESHOLD,] as in 6. 2, &c.
PUT FORTH A HAND,] as in 3. 6, &c.
22. IN THE NAME,] and by the authority of Mordecai.
23. SOUGHT OUT,] by legal investigations.
FOUND,] to be true and accurate.
HANGED,] as in La. 5. 12, &c.
CHRONICLES,] lit. 'words or matters of the days.'

III. 1. EXALTED,] lit. 'made great.'
HAMAN,] i.e. 'magnificent, Mercury.'
HAMMEDATHA.] Not mentioned elsewhere.
AGAGITE,] probably of the seed royal.
THRONE,] which subject princes occupied.
2. IN THE GATE,] waiting to attend the king.
ARE BOWING] the knee, as in v. 5; Ge. 49. 9.
DOING OBEISANCE,] as to their superior.
DOTH NOT,] either because it seemed too much like worship or from natural pride.
3. TRANSGRESSING,] by refusing to comply with the law.
4. DAY BY DAY,] to overcome his resolution.
NOT HEARKENED,] so as to obey the law.
DECLARE,] lit. 'set before.'
STAND] unchangeable, by becoming known.
JEW,] which he previously avoided doing.
5. FURY,] lit. 'heat.'
6. CONTEMPTIBLE,] or 'despicable.'
PUT FORTH A HAND,] as in 2. 21, &c.
DESTROY,] as in v. 13; 4. 8; 7. 4; 8. 11, &c.
7. NISAN,] part of February and March.
12TH YEAR,] see 1. 3; 2. 16.
PUR,] i.e. 'a part, portion,' a common practice in the east.
HAMAN,] that he might judge for himself.
DAY TO DAY,] to obtain a lucky day.
MONTH TO MONTH,] throughout a year.
ADAR,] part of January and February.
8. SCATTERED,] as in Jer. 50. 17; Joel 3. 2, &c., though many had returned to Judah.
SEPARATED,] lit. 'parted.'

PROVINCES,] the whole of the 127; compare Acts 2. 5.
DIVERSE,] as in 1. 7, &c.; they were so designedly.
NOT DOING,] an assertion without proof.
PROFITABLE,] as in 5. 13; 7. 14, &c.
SUFFER,] as in Nu. 32. 15, &c.
9. GOOD,] as in 1. 19, &c.
WRITTEN] among the king's enactments.
10,000 TALENTS,] two millions sterling.
WEIGH,] as in 4. 7; Ge. 22. 16, &c.
DOING THE WORK] of writing and sealing the law.
10. SIGNET,] as in v. 12; 8. 2, 8, 10; Ge. 41. 42.
ADVERSARY,] lit. 'distresser, strainer.'
11. GIVEN,] as a free gift and grant.
12. SCRIBES,] as in 8. 9; Jud. 5. 14, &c.
FIRST MONTH,] that is, Nisan.
COMMANDED,] as authorized by the king.
LIEUTENANTS,] as in 8. 9; 9. 3; Ezra 8. 36.
GOVERNORS,] as in 8. 9; 9. 3; 1 K. 10. 15, &c.
PROVINCE,] as in 1. 22, &c.
PEOPLE,] as in 1. 22, &c.
WRITING,] as in 1. 22, &c.
TONGUE,] as in 1. 22, &c.
SEALED,] as in 8. 8, 10; De. 32. 34, &c.
13. RUNNERS,] as in v. 15; 8. 10, 14, &c.
CUT OFF,] as in v. 6 above.
STAY,] as in 7. 4; 8. 11; 9. 16, &c.
DESTROY,] as in v. 9; 4. 7; 7. 4; 8. 5, 11, &c.
YOUNG..OLD,] as in Ge. 19. 4; Ex. 10. 9, &c.
INFANT..WOMEN,] as in 8. 11; Nu. 14. 3, &c.
ADAR,] as in v. 7 above.
SEIZE,] for their own behoof.
14. COPY,] as in 4. 8; 8. 13.
REVEALED,] as in 8. 13; Nu. 24. 4, 6; Jer. 32. 11, 14.
READY,] for assaulting the Jews.
RUNNERS,] as in v. 13.
HASTENED,] as in 6. 12; 8. 14; 2 Ch. 26. 20.
LAW,] for the destruction of the Jews.
DRINK,] as in Ex. 32. 6; 2 Sa. 11. 11, &c.
PERPLEXED,] as in Ex. 14. 3; Joel 1. 18.

IV. 1. DONE,] by the king and Haman.
RENDETH,] as in Ge. 37. 29, 34; 44. 13, &c.
SACKCLOTH AND ASHES,] as in v. 3; Isa. 58. 5; Da. 9. 3.
CRY] of distress, for help.
BITTER,] as in Ge. 27. 34; Ex. 15. 23, &c.
2. FRONT,] that Esther might see or hear.
GARMENT,] that the king be not disturbed.
3. LAW,] as in 3. 15, &c.
MOURNING,] as in 9. 22; Ge. 27. 41, &c.
FASTING,] as in 9. 31; 2 Sa. 12. 16, &c.
WEEPING,] as in Ge. 45. 2; De. 34. 8, &c.
LAMENTING,] as in Ge. 50. 10; Ps. 30. 11, &c.
SPREAD OUT,] as in Ps. 139. 8; Isa. 14. 11.
4. EUNUCHS,] as in 1. 10, 12, 15; 2. 3, 14.
PAINED,] at this unknown sorrow.
NOT RECEIVED,] being in such distress.
5. HATACH.] Etymology unknown.
6. BROAD PLACE,] as in 6. 9, 11; Ge. 19. 2, &c.
7. MET HIM,] as in 6. 13; Ge. 42. 29, &c.
EXPLANATION,] as in 10. 2.
WEIGH,] as in 3. 9 above.
DESTROY,] as in 3. 13, &c.
8. COPY,] as in 3. 14, &c.
SHEW,] that she might have the testimony of her own eyes.
LAY A CHARGE,] as in Ge. 49. 33; Lev 7. 38

MAKE SUPPLICATION,] as in 8. 3; Ge. 42. 21.
9. DECLARETH,] lit. 'setteth before.'
11. INNER COURT,] as in 5. 1; 1 K. 6. 36, &c.
CALLED] by name, and specially invited.
PUT TO DEATH,] as in Ge. 18. 25; 37. 18, &c.; first enacted by Dejoceo, king of Media, according to Herodotus.
GOLDEN SCEPTRE,] as in 5. 2; 8. 4.
THIRTY DAYS,] or a whole month.
13. SPEAKETH,] not 'commandeth,' as in C. V.
SEND BACK,] as in v. 15.
THINK,] as in Nu. 33. 56; Jud. 20. 5, &c.
DELIVERED,] from the threatened danger.
14. SILENT,] as in Nu. 30. 14; Job 13. 5, &c.
RESPITE,] as in Ge. 32. 16.
DELIVERANCE.] This original word is not found elsewhere.
ANOTHER PLACE,] even a heavenly throne.
DESTROYED,] as proposed by Haman.
KINGDOM,] as queen over Persia.
15. SEND BACK,] as in v. 13.
FOUND,] present at that time in the city.
FAST,] before God in humility.
THREE DAYS,] one whole day and part of two others.
NIGHT..DAY,] to shew their sincerity.
LAW,] as in v. 11 above.
PERISHED,] in the cause of humanity.
16. PASSETH ON,] to his house and people.
CHARGED,] as in v. 15.

V. 1. THIRD DAY,] after the agreement.
ROYALTY,] as in 1. 19.
INNER COURT,] as in 4. 11; 1 K. 6. 36, &c.
ROYAL THRONE,] lit. 'throne of his kingdom.
ROYAL HOUSE,] lit. 'house of the kingdom.'
OPENING,] as in Ge. 43. 19; Ex. 12. 22, &c.
2. STANDING,] as in 6. 5; 7. 9; Ge. 18. 8, &c.
GOLDEN SCEPTRE,] as in 4. 11; 8. 4.
TOUCHETH,] as in Ge. 3. 3; 20. 6, &c.
3. QUEEN,] recognizing her royal dignity.
REQUEST,] as in v. 7, 8; 7. 2, 3; 9. 12; Ezra 7. 6.
HALF OF THE KINGDOM,] as in v. 6; 7. 2; compare Mark 6. 23.
4. GOOD,] as in 1. 19, &c.
BANQUET,] lit. 'drinking.'
5. HASTE,] as in 6. 10; Ge. 18. 6, &c.
6. BANQUET OF WINE,] as in 7. 2, 7, 8.
PETITION,] as in v. 7, 8; 7. 2, 3; 9. 12, &c.
REQUEST,] as in v. 8, 7, 8; 7. 2, 3, 9, 12.
8. FOUND GRACE,] as in 2. 15, 17; 5. 2, 8.
GOOD,] as in v. 4 above.
9. GLAD,] lit. 'good.'
MOVED,] as in Ecc. 12. 3.
FURY,] lit. 'heat.'
10. FORCETH HIMSELF,] as in Ge. 43. 31, &c.
ZERESH,] i.e. 'golden,' perhaps.
11. RECOUNTETH,] as in 6. 13; Ge. 24. 66, &c.
WEALTH,] as in 3. 9—11.
ABUNDANCE,] or 'greatness.'
MADE HIM GREAT,] as in 3. 1, 2.
12. BANQUET,] as in v. 4.
13. PROFITABLE,] as in 3. 8, &c.
14. TREE,] not a 'gallows,' as in C. V.
50 CUBITS,] or 75 feet high.
HANG,] as in 2. 23, &c.
REJOICING,] in the thought of victory.

VI. 1. SLEEP,] as in Ge 28. 16; 31. 40:

Jud. 16. 14, &c.; Sept. 'the Lord moved the king that night by dreams.'
FLED AWAY,] as in Ge. 31. 40; Ps. 31. 11, &c.
MEMORIALS,] as in Ex. 17. 14; Mal. 3. 16, &c.
CHRONICLES,] as in 2. 23.
2. BIGTHANA,] in 2. 21 it is 'Bigthan.'
TERESH,] as in 2. 21.
3. HONOUR,] or 'glory,' as in v. 6, 7, 9, &c.
GREATNESS,] as in 1. 4; 10. 2; 2 Sa. 7. 21, &c.
MINISTER,] as in 2. 2, &c.
4. COURT,] waiting for an audience.
HANG,] as proposed in 5. 14.
5. STANDING,] or 'abiding.'
6. DELIGHTED,] as in 2. 14.
IN HIS HEART,] as in 7. 5; Ge. 8. 21, &c.
MYSELF,] as his chief favourite.
8. ROYAL CLOTHING,] lit. 'clothing of the kingdom.'
RIDDEN,] which was reserved for his own use, like the clothing.
ROYAL CROWN,] lit. 'crown of the kingdom.'
9. CHIEFS,] as in 1. 3; Da. 1. 3.
BROAD PLACE,] as in 4. 6, &c.
CALLED,] or 'proclaimed.'
10. HASTE,] as in 5. 5, &c.
DO SO,] in the manner described.
JEW,] as in 2. 5, &c.
FALL] unfulfilled any part of the honour.
11. TAKETH,] or 'receiveth.'
CALLETH,] as he himself had proposed.
12. TURNETH BACK,] as if nothing had happened.
BEEN HASTENED,] by his own fears.
MOURNING,] because of the unexpected events.
COVERED HEAD,] indicating his deep distress; see 2 Sa. 15. 30; 19. 4; Jer. 14. 3, 4.
13. RECOUNTETH,] as in 5. 11, &c.
WIFE,] his principal adviser, as in 5. 14.
MET,] as in 4. 17.
WISE MEN,] as in 1. 3; Ge. 41. 8, &c.
SEED,] that is, posterity, as in 9. 27, &c.
FALL,] in the king's favour.
NOT ABLE,] to overcome him.
14. YET SPEAKING,] as in Job 1. 16, 17, 18.
EUNUCHS,] as in 1. 10, &c.
HASTE,] as in 5. 5.

VII. 1. DRINK,] as in 3. 15; Ge. 24. 19, &c.
2. PETITION..REQUEST,] as in 5. 6, &c.
3. FOUND GRACE,] as in 2. 15, 17; 5. 2, 8; 8. 5.
4. SOLD,] as in Ex. 22. 3; Lev. 25. 39, &c.
TO CUT OFF,] as in 3. 13, &c.
MEN SERVANTS,] as in 1. 3; 2. 18; 3. 2, &c.
MAID-SERVANTS,] as in Ge. 12. 16; 16. 1, &c.
KEPT SILENT,] as in 4. 14, &c.
ADVERSITY,] or 'adversary,' as in v. 6; De. 4. 30, &c.
EQUAL,] as in 3. 8; 5. 13, &c.
LOSS,] as in Ezra 4. 13, 15, 22; Da. 6. 2; of subjects and property and peace.
5. WHO..WHERE,] that he may be caught.
FILLED,] with such a scheme of blood.
6. ADVERSARY,] lit. 'distresser, straitener.'
ENEMY,] as in 8. 13; 9. 1, 5, 16, 22.
WICKED,] or 'evil, wrong-doer.'
AFRAID,] as in 1 Ch. 21. 30; Da. 8. 17.
7. FURY,] lit. 'heat.'
GARDEN,] as in 1. 5, &c.
DETERMINED,] as in 1 Sa. 20. 7, 9; 25. 17, &c.
8. COUCH,] as in 1. 6; Ge. 47. 31, &c.

SUBDUE,] as in Ge. 1. 28; Nu. 32. 22, &c.
COVERED,] as himself had done in 6. 12.
9. HARBONAH,] as in 1. 10 perhaps.
TREE,] as in 5. 14.
SPAKE GOOD,] in revealing the king's danger.
HOUSE,] that he might feast his eyes.
50 CUBITS,] as in 5. 14.
HANG,] as a traitor and troubler; Sept. 'crucify.'
10. LAIN DOWN,] to rest, being appeased.

VIII. 1. GIVEN]up to be punished, as in 3. 11.
HOUSE,] or 'household.'
ADVERSARY,] as in 7. 6, &c.
COME IN,] called to narrate the whole scheme of Haman.
TO HER,] her uncle's brother.
2. SIGNET,] thus conferring authority; see Ge. 41. 42, &c.
CAUSED TO PASS AWAY,] as in 3. 10, &c.
SETTETH,] or 'placeth.'
3. ADDETH AND SPEAKETH,] as in Ge. 18. 19.
FEET,] in lowliest supplication.
MAKETH SUPPLICATION,] as in Ge. 42. 21.
DEVICE,] as in v. 5; 9. 25, &c.
DEVISED,] as in 9. 24, 25, &c.
4. GOLDEN SCEPTRE,] as in 4. 11; 5. 2.
5. GOOD,] as in 1. 19, &c.
FOUND GRACE,] as in 2. 15, 17; 5. 2, 8, &c.
RIGHT,] as in Ecc. 10. 10; 11. 6.
WRITTEN,] that there might be no mistake.
LETTERS,] lit. 'books.'
DEVICE,] as in v. 3.
DESTROY,] as in 3. 13, &c.
PROVINCES,] which were 127 in all.
6. ENDURE,] lit. 'am able.'
FIND,] as a wild beast doth its prey.
KINDRED,] as in v. 1.
7. GIVEN,] as in 7. 10.
HANGED,] as in 7. 10.
PUT FORTH,] as in 3. 6, &c.
8. NAME,] as in 3. 12, &c.
9. SCRIBES,] as in 3. 12, &c.
SIVAN,] part of May and June.
COMMANDED,] being now chief favourite.
LIEUTENANTS,] as in 3. 12; 9. 3; Ezra 8. 36.
GOVERNORS,] as in 3. 12; 9. 3; 1 K. 10. 15.
HODU..CUSH,] as described in 1. 2.
TONGUE,] as in 3. 12.
10. NAME..SIGNET,] as Haman had done.
LETTERS,] lit. 'books.'
RUNNERS,] who acted as postmen.
DROMEDARY,] as in v. 14; 1 K. 4. 28; Mic. 1. 13.
MULES,] as in v. 14.
YOUNG MARES.] Not mentioned elsewhere
11. GIVEN] permission and authority.
ASSEMBLED,] for mutual consultation.
STAND,] against all opposers.
CUT OFF..SLAY..DESTROY,] as in 3. 13.
FORCE,] whether armed or otherwise.
INFANTS,] as in 3. 13.
SEIZE,] should they thus attack them.
12. ADAR,] fixed on by Haman.
13. COPY,] as in 3. 14.
REVEALED,] and made known by heralds.
READY,] and prepared beforehand.
AVENGED,] for the meditated massacre.
14. RUNNERS, &c.,] as in v. 10.
HASTENED,] as in Prov. 20. 21.
PRESSED,] as in 3. 15.
PALACE,] the royal residence.

15. ROYAL CLOTHING,] *lit.* 'clothing of the kingdom.'
CROWN,] as now chief minister of state.
FINE LINEN,] as in 1. 6; 1 Ch. 4. 21; 15. 27; 2 Ch. 2. 14; 3. 14; 5. 12; Eze. 27. 16.
GLAD,] at the deliverance of the Jews.
16. LIGHT,] as in Ps. 139. 12.
GLADNESS,] as in v. 17; 9. 17, 18, 19, 22.
JOY,] as in v. 17; Ps. 45. 7; 51. 8, 12, &c.
HONOUR,] *or* 'glory.'
17. LAW,] authorizing the Jews to fight.
GOOD DAY,] as in 9. 19, 22.
BECOMING JEWS,] conforming to the law of Moses.
FEAR,] of their power and influence.

IX. 1. ADAR,] as in 8. 12 above.
HOPED,] as in Ps. 119. 166, &c.
TO RULE,] without restraint over their bodies and property.
TURNED,] by the discovery of Haman's plot.
HATING THEM,] and longing for their destruction.
2. ASSEMBLED,] as in 8. 11.
PUT FORTH,] in their own defence.
EVIL,] *or* 'misfortune.'
STOOD] up to assault them.
FEAR,] caused by the king's favour.
3. HEADS..GOVERNORS,] as in 8. 9, &c.
FEAR OF MORDECAI,] who stood so near the king.
4. FAME,] as a wise, powerful counsellor.
BECOMING GREAT,] in the estimation of the court.
5. SMITING,] authorized by the king in 8. 11.
PLEASURE,] no one interfering with their vengeance.
6. SLAIN AND DESTROYED,] of those assaulting them.
7. PARSHANDATHA,] i.e. 'given forth to light.'
DALPHON,] i.e. a 'dropping,' perhaps.
ASPATHA,] i.e. 'given by the horse.'
8. PORATHA,] i.e. 'ornament.'
ADALIA.] Etymology uncertain.
ARIDATHA,] i.e. 'strong.'
9. PARMASHTA,] i.e. 'strong-fisted.'
ARISAI,] i.e. 'lion-like.'
ARIDAI,] i.e. 'strong.'
VEJEZATHA,] i.e. 'pure, white.'
10. ADVERSARY,] *lit.* 'distresser, strainener.'
PREY,] or spoil of the dead enemies.
11. NUMBER,] even 510 in all.
12. DONE?] wishing further information.
PETITION..REQUEST,] as in 5. 6, &c.
13. GOOD,] as in 1. 19, &c.
TO-DAY,] that is, have permission to resist their assailants.
HANG] their dead bodies for a public terror.
15. 14TH,] on the morrow, as Esther requested.
300,] who assailed them violently.
PREY,] as in v. 10, 16.
16. HATING,] as in v. 1.
PREY,] as in v. 10, 15.
17. 13TH,] as in 3. 13, &c.
18. ASSEMBLED,] to defend themselves, as in 8. 11.
REST,] from fear and war.
19. VILLAGES,] as in Ex. 38. 11; Est. 9. 19.
CITIES,] as in Ge. 4. 17, &c.

GOOD DAY,] as in 8. 17, &c.
PORTIONS,] as in v. 22; 2. 9; Ex. 29. 26, &c.
20. WRITETH,] an account of the matter.
LETTERS,] *lit.* 'books.'
21. ESTABLISH,] *lit.* 'cause to stand.'
KEEPING,] *lit.* 'doing,' as in v. 27.
22. RESTED,] as in v. 17, 18.
TURNED,] by the providence of God.
GOOD DAY,] as in 8. 17, &c.
PORTIONS,] as in v. 19, &c.
GIFTS,] as in Ge. 25. 6; Ex. 28. 38, &c.
NEEDY,] as in Ex. 23. 6, 11; De. 15. 4, 7, 9, 11.
23. RECEIVED,] as in v. 27; 4. 4; 1 Ch. 12. 8.
BEGUN TO DO,] of their own free choice.
24. ADVERSARY,] as in 3. 10; 7. 6, &c.
DEVISED,] as in v. 25; 8. 3.
DESTROY,] as in 3. 13.
PUR,] as in 3. 7.
CRUSH,] as in Ex. 14. 24; 23. 27, &c.
25. IN HER COMING,] with tears and supplications.
LETTER,] *or* 'book,' as in v. 20.
DEVICE,] as in 8. 3, 5.
HEAD,] as in Jud. 9. 57; 1 Sa. 25. 39, &c.
HANGED,] as in 7. 10, &c.
26. PURIM,] as in v. 24; 3. 7.
LETTER,] as in v. 29; 2 Ch. 30. 1, 6, &c.
27. ESTABLISHED,] as in v. 21, 31.
RECEIVED,] as in v. 23.
JOINED,] by embracing Judaism.
NOT PASS AWAY,] from being observed.
KEEPING,] *lit.* 'doing,' as in v. 21.
TWO DAYS,] the 14th and 15th of Adar.
SEASON,] as in v. 31; Neh. 2. 6.
28. REMEMBERED,] as in Nu. 10. 9; Job 24. 20.
KEPT,] *lit.* 'done,' as in v. 21. 27.
GENERATION,] as in Ps. 45. 17; 145. 13, &c.
FAMILY,] as in Zec. 12. 12, 14.
PROVINCE,] as in 1. 22; 3. 12, 14; 4. 3; 8. 9, 13, 17.
CITY,] as in 8. 11, &c.
MEMORIAL,] as in Ex. 3. 15; 17. 14; De. 25. 19.
29. ABIHAIL,] as in 2. 15.
MIGHT,] as in 10. 2; Da. 11. 17.
30. 127 PROVINCES,] as in 1. 1, &c.
PEACE AND TRUTH,] as in Isa. 39. 8; Jer. 14. 13; 33. 6.
31. ESTABLISH,] as in v. 21, 27.
THEMSELVES,] of their own free will.
FASTINGS,] as in 4. 3; 2 Sa. 12. 16, &c.
CRY,] of distress, as the original indicates.
31. SAYING,] as in 1. 15; 2. 20.
THE BOOK,] *or* 'in a book.'

X. 1. AHASUERUS,] as in 1. 1, 16, 19, 21, &c.
SETTETH,] *or* 'placeth.'
TRIBUTE,] as in Ge. 49. 15; Ex. 1. 11, &c.
LAND,] the 127 provinces.
ISLES OF THE SEA,] as in Isa. 11. 11; 24. 1b 2. WORK,] not 'acts,' as in C.V.
STRENGTH,] as in 9. 29; Da. 11. 17.
MIGHT,] as in Ex. 32. 18; De. 3. 24, &c.
EXPLANATION,] as in 4. 7.
GREAT,] as in 8. 1, 7, &c.
CHRONICLES,] *lit.* 'words of the days.'
3. JEW,] as in 2. 5; 5. 13; 6. 10, &c.
SECOND,] in power and station, being prime minister or vizier.
ACCEPTED,] as in De. 33. 24.
SEEKING,] as in De. 11. 12, &c.
SPEAKING PEACE,] as in Ps. 28. 3, &c.

THE BOOK OF JOB

THIS Book is the oldest composition in the world, except the primeval records embodied in the earlier parts of Genesis. There seems no good ground for questioning the universal tradition of the Church in all ages and countries, that the book of Job was first introduced into the Hebrew Sacred Literature by Moses, who wrote the first two chapters as an introduction, and ch. 42. 7—17 as the finale of the whole. These portions are simple prose, while the body of the work is highly poetic, and easily distinguishable by its antique vocables and idioms. We cannot reasonably suppose that the speeches of Job and the other speakers are word for word as originally delivered, though it is undoubtedly true that orientals in their positions do occasionally manifest the highest eloquence and persuasive powers, while instances have been known of individuals whose memory seemed capable of retaining almost any amount of poetry. But as Job lived 140 years after his restoration to prosperity, it is not unnatural to suppose that he himself gave the final cast to the whole. This, falling into the hands of Moses, was, by divine direction, introduced to the Israelites, for their warning and encouragement. As it bears no marks whatever of being a translation, it was doubtless written in Hebrew, which was then very extensively spoken. As Job and his three friends are all rebuked, and confessed that they had spoken in many things unadvisedly with their lips, their reasonings, principles and facts, are to be judged of by the clearer and fuller revelations of the Divine Will in later times.

Two great questions are raised and treated of in this Book, both quite distinct from each other, and between different parties. The first is between GOD and the ADVERSARY regarding the question 'Does Job serve God for nought?' and is answered in the negative by the stedfast adherence of Job to truth and duty. The second is between Job and his THREE FRIENDS, on the point 'Do sufferings imply guilt?' The negative side is triumphantly upheld by Job to the utter discomfiture of his opponents, but as Job had appeared at least to impugn the justice of God, a fourth disputant stands forth to vindicate that justice, which he does by shewing that these sufferings are corrective, not punitive merely. Job tacitly acknowledging the justice of the remarks by his silence, God himself appears, and closes the discussion by referring the whole to his own omnipotence and omniscience. Job humbly confessed his folly, his three friends offer a sin-offering, and peace and prosperity return to Job, who survived his troubles a hundred and forty years, dying about the time of the birth of Isaac, B.C. 1900.

The Book is systematically arranged as follows : I.) An introduction, (i. ii); II.) Job's complaint, (iii); Eliphaz's address, (iv. v), with Job's reply, (vi. vii); Bildad's address, (viii), with Job's reply, (ix. x); Zophar's address, (xi), with Job's reply, (xii. xiii. xiv); Eliphaz's *second* address, (xv). with Job's reply, (xvi. xvii); Bildad's second address, (xviii), with Job's reply (xix); Zophar's second address, (xx), with Job's reply, (xxi); Eliphaz's *third* address, (xxii), with Job's reply, (xxiii. xxiv); Bildad's third address, (xxv), with Job's reply, (xxvi—xxxi); Elihu's address to Job, (xxxii—xxxvii) Jehovah's address to Job,(xxxviii—xli); Job's confession, (xlii. 1—6); III.) conclusion, (xlii. 7—17.)

I. 1. MAN,] an individual, a person of station.

UZ,] *lit.* 'counsel ;' as in Jer. 25, 20 ; La. 4. 21, between Palestine, Edumea and the Euphrates ; see Ge. 10. 23 ; 22. 21 ; 36. 28.

JOB,] i.e. 'hated, at enmity with.'

PERFECT,] as in v. 8 ; 23. 8, 20 ; 9. 20, 21, 22 ; Ge. 25. 27 ; Ps. 37. 37 ; 64. 4 ; Prov. 29. 10 ; Song 5. 2 ; 6. 9.

UPRIGHT,] as in v. 8 ; 2. 3 ; 4. 7 ; 8. 6 ; 17. 8 ; 23. 7 ; 33. 27 ; Ex. 15. 26, &c.

FEARING,] as in v. 8 ; 2. 3 ; Ge. 22. 12, &c.

GOD,] the creator, preserver, and judge.

TURNING ASIDE,] as in v. 8 ; 2. 3 ; Prov. 11. 22 ; 14. 16 ; Jer. 6. 28.

EVIL,] *or* the 'evil one.'

2. THREE DAUGHTERS.] Compare 42 13.

3. SUBSTANCE,] *lit.* 'acquisition,' as in v. 10 ; 36. 33 ; Ge. 4. 20, &c.

SHEEP,] *or* 'flock,' which included goats, as in v. 16 : 21. 11 ; 30. 1 ; 42. 12 ; Ge. 4. 2, &c.

CAMELS,] as in v. 17 ; 42. 12 ; Ge. 12. 16, &c.

PAIRS,] as in 42. 12 ; Jud. 19. 3, 10, &c.

OXEN,] as in v. 14 ; 40. 15 ; 42, 12 ; Ge. 12. 16.

SHE ASSES,] as in v. 14 ; 42. 12 ; Ge. 12. 16.

SERVICE,] as in Ge. 26. 14.

ABUNDANT,] as in 4. 3 ; 22. 5 ; 31. 25, &c.

THAT MAN,] not 'this man,' as in C. V.

4. MADE A BANQUET,] *lit.* 'drinking,' as in v. 5 ; Ge. 19. 3, &c.

5. HAVE GONE ROUND,] not 'were gone about,' as in C. V. ; see 19. 6 ; Lev. 19. 27, &c.

SANCTIFY,] *lit.* 'separate,' as in Ge. 2. 3 ;

CAUSE TO GO UP] on the altar, as in 42. 8 ; Ge. 8. 20, &c.

BURNT-OFFERINGS,] as in 42. 8 ; Ge. 8. 20.

YET BLESSED.] So Vulgate, Lee, Hengstenberg, and others. The original word occurs 320 times in the O. T., and in all passages with the exception of 1 K. 21. 10, 13 ; Job 1. 5, 11 ; 2. 5, 9, it is universally admitted as meaning 'to bless,' as in v. 10, 21 of this very chapter ; forsaken—renounced —cursed, are equally false and worthless ;

z

the simple meaning here is, 'they blessed God in their self-satisfaction, as if He had not seen or known or cared for sin.'
HEART,] as in 9. 4; 10. 13; 12. 3; 17. 11; 22. 22; 27. 6; 34. 10, 34; Ge. 20. 5, &c.
ALL THE DAYS,] as in 15. 20; Ge. 6. 5, &c.
6. THE DAY IS,] as in v. 13; 2. 1; probably the sabbath, as in Ge. 2. 2, &c.
SONS OF GOD,] as in 2. 1; 38. 7; Ge. 6. 2, 4.
STATION THEMSELVES,] as in 2. 1; Ex. 8. 20.
JEHOVAH,] as in v. 7, 8, 9, 12, 21; 2. 1, 2, 3, 4, 6, 7; 12. 9; 38. 1; 40. 1, 3, 6; 42. 1, 7, 9, 10, 11, 12, &c.; Ge. 2. 4, &c.
THE ADVERSARY,] as in v. 7, 8, 9, 12; 2. 1, 2, 3, 4, 6, 7; Nu. 22. 22, 32, &c.
7. GOING TO AND FRO,] as in 2. 2; Nu. 11. 8.
WALKING UP AND DOWN,] as in 2. 2; 18. 8; 22. 14; 38. 16; Ge. 3. 8, &c.
LAND] of Uz, not the 'earth,' as in C.V.
8. SET THY HEART,] as in 2. 3; Ex. 9. 21, &c.
PERFECT..UPRIGHT, &c.] as in v. 1 above.
9. FOR NOUGHT,] as in 2. 3; 9. 17; 22. 6, &c.
FEARING,] as in v. 1 above.
10. MADE A HEDGE,] as in 11. 10; Hos. 2. 6.
FOR HIM,] not 'about him,' as in C.V.
WORK OF HIS HANDS,] as in 14. 15; 34. 19; Ge. 5. 29, &c.
SPREAD ABROAD,] as in 16. 14; 28. 4, &c.
11. I PRAY THEE,] not 'now,' as in C.V.
STRIKE,] as in v. 19; 2. 5; 4. 5; 5. 19; 6. 7; 19. 21; Isa. 53. 4, &c.
IF NOT,] if you do not injure him.
BLESS,] or 'declare thee blessed.'
12. HAND,] not 'power,' as in C.V.
UNTO HIM,] not 'upon himself,' as in C.V.
13. THE DAY IS,] as in v. 18; 18. 13, &c.
THE FIRST-BORN,] as in v. 18; 18. 13, &c.
14. COME IN,] unto Job's house probably.
PLOWING,] as in 4. 8; 1 K. 19. 19, &c.
SIDES,] lit. 'hands.'
15. SHEBA,] the tribe of that name, (see Ge. 10. 7, 28; 25. 3), as in 1 K. 10. 1, 4, 10, 13; Job 6. 19; Ps. 72. 10, 15; Isa. 60. 6; Jer. 6. 20; Eze. 27. 22, 23; 38. 13.
TAKE,] not necessarily 'take away.'
YOUNG MEN,] as in v. 16, 19; 24. 5; 29. 5, 8; Ge. 14. 24, &c.
SMITTEN,] not 'slain,' as in C.V.
MOUTH OF THE SWORD,] as in Ge. 34. 26; Ex. 17. 13, &c.
ESCAPED,] as in v. 16, 17, 19· Ge. 19. 17, &c.
DECLARE,] as in v. 16, 17, 19; 11. 6; 12. 7; 15. 18; 17. 5; 21. 31; 26. 4; 31. 37; 33. 23; 36. 9, 33; 38. 4, 18; 42. 3; Ge. 3. 11, &c.
16. THIS ONE,] not 'he,' as in C.V.
FIRE OF GOD,] as in 2 K. 1. 12; Nu. 11. 1, 3; 1 K. 18. 38.
BURN AMONG,] not 'burned up,' as in C.V.
FLOCK,] including goats, as in v. 3.
CONSUME,] lit. 'eat, devour.'
17. CHALDEANS,] from Chaldea and Mesopotamia.
MADE,] not 'made out,' as in C.V.
HEADS,] or 'detachments,' as in Jud. 7. 16, 20; 9. 34, 37, 43; 1 Sa. 11. 11, &c.
RUSH,] not 'fell,' as in C.V.; see Jud. 9. 33, 44; 20. 37, &c.
18. FIRST-BORN,] as in v. 13 above.
19.FROM OVER,]not 'from'merely,as in C.V.
WILDERNESS,] or 'pasture-land,' as in 24. 5; 38. 26; Ge. 14. 6, &c.

STRIKETH,] as in v. 11 above.
CORNERS,] as in 38. 6; Ex. 27. 2; 38. 2, &c.
YOUNG MEN,] as in v. 16.
20. UPPER ROBE,] as in 2. 12; 29. 14; Ex. 28. 4.
SHAVETH,] as in Jer. 7. 29; Mic. 1. 16; compare Ge. 31. 19, &c.
EARTH,] before God, in humiliation.
OBEISANCE,] as in Ge. 18. 2; 19. 1, &c.
21. NAKED,] as in 22. 6; 24. 7, 10; 26. 6; Ge. 2. 25, &c.
WOMB,] lit. 'belly.'
BLESSED,] as in Ps. 113. 2.
22. SINNED,] lit. 'missed the mark.'
GIVEN FOLLY,] as in 24. 12; Jer. 23. 13.
GOD,] as in v. 1, 5.

II. 1. THE DAY IS,] as in 1. 6, 13.
BY] the side of, not 'before,' as in C.V.
2. WHENCE?] as in 1. 7.
3. SET THY HEART,] as in 1. 8.
UNTO,] or 'towards' him.
KEEPING HOLD,] as in v. 9; Ex. 9. 2, &c.
MOVE ME,] as in 36. 16, 18; De. 13. 6, &c.
SWALLOW,] as in 7. 19; 8. 18; 10. 8; 20. 15, 18; Ge. 41. 7, &c.
FOR NOUGHT,] as in v. 9.
4. A SKIN FOR A SKIN,] an eastern proverb, like the Scotch : 'giff-gaff makes good friends.'
AND,] not 'yea,' as in C.V.
LIFE,] lit. 'soul, person.'
5. I PRAY THEE,] not 'now,' as in C.V.
STRIKE,] as in 1. 11.
BONE..FLESH,] his own person, not his property or family merely.
IF NOT,] if you do not do so; as in 1. 11.
6. HAND,] as in 1. 12.
TAKE CARE OF,] or 'guard, watch.'
7. ULCER,] as in Ex. 9. 9, 10, 11; Lev. 13. 18, 19, 20, 23; De. 28. 27, 35; 2 K. 20.7; Isa.38.21.
CROWN,] as in Ge. 49. 26; De. 28. 35, &c.
8. POTSHERD,] as in 41. 30; Lev. 6.28, &c.
SCRAPE HIMSELF.] The original word is not found elsewhere.
IS SITTING,] habitually during his illness.
ASHES,] as in 13. 12; 30. 19; 42. 6; Ge. 18. 27; Nu. 19. 9, 10, &c.
9. WIFE,] whose name is not mentioned.
THOU ART,] an affirmation, not a question as in C.V.
BLESS] God for this comfort and grace ; so Targum, &c.
DIE,] give up hopes of recovery.
10. FOOLISH WOMEN,] as in 30. 8; De. 32. 6.
YEA,] not 'what ;' an affirmation, not a question as in C.V.
NOT RECEIVE.] He seems persuaded his troubles came from the Adversary, not from God, see 9. 24.
SIN WITH HIS LIPS,] though he did so afterwards.
11. THREE OF THE FRIENDS,] not 'his three friends.'
ELIPHAZ,] i.e. 'my God is strong.'
TEMANITE,] from Teman, in Edom, as in Jer. 49. 7, 20; Eze. 25. 13; Amos 1. 12; Obad. 9; Hab. 3. 3.
BILDAD,] i.e. 'son of contention.'
SHUHITE,] from Shuah, in Arabia Petraea.
ZOPHAR,] i.e. 'a chirper.'
NAAMATHITE,] from Naamah, in Edom.

ARE MET TOGETHER,] as in Ex. 25. 22; 29. 42, 43; 30. 6, 36, &c.
MOAN FOR HIM,] *lit.* 'nod to him,' as in 42. 11, &c.
12. LIFT UP THEIR EYES,] as in Ge. 13. 10, 14.
DISCERNED,] as in 4. 16; 7. 10; 24. 17; 34. 13, 25; Ge. 27. 23, &c.
LIFT UP THEIR VOICE,] as in 38. 34; Ge. 21. 16, &c.
ROBE,] as in 1. 20.
SPRINKLE,] as in Ex. 9. 8, 10; 24. 6, 8; 29. 16, 20, &c.
13. SIT,] not 'sit down,' as in C.V.
EARTH,] as in 1. 20.
SEVEN,] a round, sacred number.
WHEN,] not 'for,' as in C.V.; it is incredible that they sat so long without speaking.
THE PAIN,] not 'grief;' as in 16. 6; Ps. 39. 2; Isa. 17. 11; 65. 14; Jer. 15. 18; also Job 5. 18; 14. 22, &c.

III. 1. OPENED HIS MOUTH,] as in 29. 23; 33. 2; 35. 16; Nu. 22. 28, &c.
REVILETH,] *or* 'maketh light of,' as in Ge. 8. 21; 12. 3; Ex. 21. 17, &c.
HIS DAY,] his birth-day, and his whole life.
3. PERISH,] *or* 'be lost,' to memory.
I AM BORN,] not 'was born;' he goes back in poetic fancy to that day.
THAT HATH SAID,] night being personified here.
MAN-CHILD,] *or* 'man,' as in v. 23; 4. 17; 10. 5; 14. 10, 14; 16. 21; 22. 2; 33. 17, 29; 34. 7, 9, 34; 38. 3; 40. 7.
CONCEIVED.] Sept. 'behold a man-child.'
4. DARKNESS,] the darkness of 'night,' as in v. 5; 5. 14; 10. 21; 12. 22, 25; 15. 22, 23, 30.
REQUIRE,] as in 5. 8; 10. 6; 39. 8.
LIGHT.] This original word is not found elsewhere.
SHINE,] as in 10. 3, 22; 37. 15; De. 33. 2; Ps. 50. 2; 80. 1; 94. 1.
5. DEATH-SHADE,] or simply 'a deep shade,' as in 10. 21, 22; 12. 22; 16. 16; 24. 17; 28. 3; 34. 22; 38. 17; Ps. 23. 4, &c.
REDEEM,] not 'stain,' as in C.V.; as in 19. 25; Ge. 48. 16; Ex. 6. 6, &c.
CLOUD,] as in 7. 9; 26. 8, 9; 37. 11, 15, &c.
TABERNACLE,] as in Ex. 40. 35; Nu. 9. 17.
MOST BITTER,] as in De. 32. 24, 32; Job 13. 26; 20. 14, 25.
6. THICK DARKNESS,] as in 10. 22; 23. 27; 28. 3; 30. 26; Ps. 11. 2; 91. 6; Isa. 29. 18.
TAKE IT,] as in 1. 15.
BE UNITED,] as in Ge. 49. 6; Isa. 14. 20; Ps. 86. 11.
MONTHS,] as in 7. 3; 29. 2; 39. 2; Ex. 2. 2.
7. GLOOMY,] as in 15. 34; 30. 3; Isa. 49. 21.
SINGING,] as in 20. 5; Ps. 63. 5; 100. 2.
8. CURSERS,] as in Ge. 27. 29; Nu. 24. 9.
MARK,] as in Ge. 30. 28; 5. 3; Isa. 62. 2; Amos 6. 1; *or* 'pierce,' as in 40. 24; 41. 2.
READY,] as in 15. 24; De. 32. 35, &c.
WAKE UP,] as in 2 Sa. 23. 18; 1 Ch. 11. 11.
LEVIATHAN,] as in 41. 1; Ps. 74. 14, &c.
9. TWILIGHT,] as in 7. 4; 24. 15; 1 Sa. 30. 17.
WAIT,] as in 6. 19; 7. 2; 17. 3; 30. 26, &c.
LIGHT,] as in v. 16, 20; 12. 22, 25, &c.
EYE-LIDS OF THE DAWN,] as in 41. 18.
10. DOORS,] as in 31. 32; 38. 8, 10; 41. 14.
WOMB,] *lit.* 'belly;' to prevent conception.

MISERY,] as in 4. 8; 5. 6, 7; 7. 3; 11. 16; 15. 35; 16. 2, &c.
HIDE,] as in 13. 24; 14. 13; 34. 29, &c.
11. DIE,] not 'died,' as in C.V.
BELLY,] as in v. 10; 1. 21; 10. 19, &c.
I GASP,] as in 10. 18; 13. 19; 14. 10, &c.
12. KNEES,] as in 4. 4; Ge. 30. 3, &c.
BEEN BEFORE,] as in 30. 27; 41. 11, &c.
BREASTS,] as in Ge. 49. 25; Ps. 22. 9, &c.
SUCK,] as in 20. 16; Nu. 11. 12, &c.
13. LAIN DOWN,] as in 7. 4, 21; 11. 18; 14. 12.
AM QUIET,] as in v. 26.
REST,] as in v. 17, 26; Ge. 8. 4, &c.
14. COUNSELLORS,] as in 12. 17; 2 Sa. 15. 12.
WASTES,] as in Lev. 26. 31, 33; Ezra 9. 9, &c.
15. PRINCES,] as in 29. 9; 34. 19; 39. 25, &c.
16. ABORTION,] as in Ps. 58. 8; Ecc. 6. 3.
INFANTS,] as in 1 Sa. 15. 3; 22. 19, &c.
LIGHT,] as in v. 9.
17. WICKED,] those in a wrong state towards God or man, as in 8. 22; 9. 22, 24, &c., Ge. 18. 23, &c.
TROUBLING,] *or* 'trouble,' as in v. 26; 14. 1; 37. 2; 39. 24; Isa. 14. 3; Hab. 3. 2.
WEARIED,] as in De. 25.18; 2 Sa.17.2; Ecc.1.8.
18. AT EASE,] as in Prov. 1. 33; Jer. 30. 10; 46. 27; 48. 11.
EXACTOR,] as in 39. 7; Ex. 3. 7, &c.
19. SAME,] *or* 'there is he,' i.e. each of them.
LORD,] as in 28. 28; Ge. 18. 12, &c.
20. GIVETH HE,] not 'is given,' as in C.V.
BITTER IN SOUL,] as in Jud. 18. 25; 1 Sa. 1. 10; 22. 2; 2 Sa. 17. 8; Prov. 31. 6.
21. WAITING,] as in Isa. 64. 4; Da. 12. 12.
SEEK,] as in 11. 18; 39. 21, 29; Ge. 21. 30.
HID TREASURES,] as in Ge. 43. 23; Prov. 2. 4; Isa. 45. 3; Jer. 41. 8.
22. JOY,] as in 39. 4; 45. 15; 65. 12; Prov. 23. 24; Isa.16. 10; Jer. 48. 33; Da. 1.10; Joel 1.16.
GRAVE,] as in 5. 26; 10. 19; 17. 1; 21. 32; Ge. 23. 4, &c.
23. HIDDEN,] as in 13. 20; 28. 21; 34. 22; Ge. 4. 14, &c.
SHUT UP,] as in 38. 8; Ex. 40. 21, &c.
24. FOOD,] *lit.* 'bread,' as in 6. 7; 15. 23, &c.
SIGHING,] as in 23. 2; 6. 6; 31. 10; 38.9; Ps.102. 5; Isa. 21. 2; 35. 10; 51. 11; Jer. 45. 3; La. 1. 22.
POURED OUT,] as in 10. 10; 2 Ch. 12. 7, &c.
25. FEAR,] as in 4. 14; 13. 11; 15. 21; 21. 9; 22. 10; 25. 2; 31. 33; 39. 16, 22; Ge. 31. 42, &c.
MEETETH,] *or* 'cometh,' as in 16. 22; 30. 14; 37. 22.
26. SAFE,] as in 12. 6; Ps. 122. 6; Jer. 12. 1; La. 1. 5.
QUIET,] as in v. 13 above.
AT REST,] as in v. 13, 17.
TROUBLE,] as in v. 17.

IV. 1. ELIPHAZ,] from Teman, as in 2. 11.
2. HAS ONE TRIED,] as in Ge. 22. 1; Ex. 15. 25.
A WORD,] of reasoning and expostulation.
WEARY,] as in v. 5; Ge. 19. 11.
KEEP IN,] as in 12. 15; 29. 9; Ge. 16. 2, &c.
3. INSTRUCTED,] as in De. 4. 36; Ps. 16. 7.
FEEBLE HANDS,] as in Nu. 13. 18; 2 Sa. 17. 2; Isa. 35. 3.
4. STUMBLING,] as in 2 Ch. 28. 15; Ps. 105. 37; Isa. 5. 27; 35. 3; Jer. 46. 16.
BOWING,] as in 31. 10; 39. 3; Est. 3. 2, 5.
5. TO THEE,] in his own person and family.
WEARY,] as in v. 2.

STRIKETH,] as in 1. 11; 2. 5.
TROUBLED,] as in 21. 6; 22. 10; 23. 15, 16.
6. REVERENCE,] for God, the source of thy
CONFIDENCE,] in the divine protection
and blessing.
HOPE,] of prosperity based upon the
PERFECTION] of his ways toward God and
man.
7. INNOCENT,] as in 9. 23; 17. 8; 22. 19, 30;
27. 17; Ge. 24. 41, &c.
PERISHED,] as in v. 9, 11, 20; 3. 3; 6. 18, &c.
UPRIGHT,] as in 1. 1, 8; 2. 3, &c.
CUT OFF,] lit. 'hidden,' as in 15. 28; 22. 20.
8. PLOUGHERS OF INIQUITY,] as in Prov.
6. 14, 18; 12. 20; 14. 22; Ps. 129. 3, &c.
SOWERS OF MISERY,] as in Prov. 11. 18; 22. 8.
REAP,] as in 24. 26; Lev. 19. 9, &c.
9. BREATH,] as in 32. 8; 33. 4; 37. 10, &c.
SPIRIT OF HIS ANGER,] as in Ex. 15. 8; 2
Sa. 22. 16, &c.
CONSUMED,] as in 7. 6, 9; 11. 20; 17. 5; 19.
27; 33. 21, &c.
10. LION,] as in Ge. 49. 9; Nu. 23. 24, &c.
FIERCE LION,] as in 10. 16; 28. 8; Ps. 91.
13; Prov. 26. 13; Hos. 5. 14; 13. 7.
YOUNG LIONS,] as in 38. 39; Jud. 14. 5, &c.
BROKEN,] as in Ps. 58. 6.
11. OLD LION,] as in Prov. 30. 30; Isa. 30. 6.
PREY,] as in 24. 5; 29. 17; 38. 39, &c.
WHELPS,] lit. 'sons.'
LIONESS,] as in 38. 39; Ge. 49. 9, &c.
SEPARATE,] as in 41. 17; Ps. 22. 14; 92. 9.
12. SECRETLY BROUGHT,] lit. 'is stolen,'
as in Ge. 40. 15.
LITTLE,] as in 26. 14, or a 'report.'
13. THOUGHTS,] as in 20. 2.
DEEP SLEEP,] as in 33. 15; Ge. 2. 21; 15. 12.
14. MET,] as in 39. 21; Ge. 42. 38, &c.
TREMBLING,] as in Ps. 2. 11; 48. 6; Isa. 33. 14.
CAUSED TO FEAR,] as in 3. 25; 23. 15.
15. HAIR,] as in Jud. 20. 16; 1 Sa. 14. 45.
STAND UP,] as in Ps. 119. 120.
16. DISCERN,] as in 2. 12; 7. 10, &c.
ASPECT,] as in 41. 9; Ge. 2. 9, &c.
SIMILITUDE,] as in Ex. 20. 4; Nu. 12. 8; De.
4. 12, 15, 16, 23, 25; 5. 8; Job 4. 16; Ps. 17. 15.
SILENCE,] as in 1 K. 19. 12; Ps. 107. 29.
17. MORTAL MAN,] as in v. 17; 5. 17, &c.
JUST,] or 'right,' as in 9. 2, 15, 20; 10. 15; 11. 2.
CLEANER,] as in Lev. 11. 32; 12. 7, 8; 13. 6.
18. CREDENCE,] as in 9. 16; 15. 15, 22, 31;
24. 22, &c.
MESSENGERS,] as in 1. 14; 33. 23; Ge. 16. 7.
SETTETH,] as in 1. 8, 17; 2. 3; 4. 20; 5. 8,
11; 7. 20, &c.
PRAISE,] as in Ex. 15. 11; De. 10. 21; 26. 19.
19. CLAY,] as in 10. 9; 13. 12; 27. 16, &c.
FOUNDATION,] as in 22. 16; Ex. 29. 12.
THEY BRUISE THEM,] as in 6. 9; 19. 2; Ps.
72. 4; 94. 5, &c.
MOTH,] as in 13, 28; 27. 18; Ps. 39. 11, &c.
20. BEATEN DOWN,] as in Isa. 24. 12; Jer.
46. 5; Mic. 1. 7.
21. EXCELLENCY,] or 'remnant,' as in 22.
20; Ge. 49. 3; Ex. 10. 5, &c.
REMOVED,] lit. 'journey,' as in Isa. 38. 12.

V. 1. PRAY,] not 'now,' as in C.V.
HOLY ONES,] as in 15. 15; Ex. 19. 6, &c.
TURN] thy face, as in 6. 28; 21. 5; 24. 18; 36. 21.
2. PROVOCATION,] as in 6. 2; 10. 17; 17. 7.

PERVERSE,] as in v. 3; Ps. 107. 17; Prov.
1. 7; 7. 22; 10. 8, 10, 14, 21; 11. 29; 12. 15, 16
14. 3, 9; 15. 5, &c.
ENVY,] or 'zeal, jealousy,' as in Nu. 5. 14.
SIMPLE,] as in Prov. 20. 19; Hos. 7. 11.
3. PERVERSE,] as in v. 2.
TAKING ROOT,] as in Ps. 80. 9; Isa. 27. 6.
MARK,] as in 3. 8 above.
HABITATION,] as in v. 24; 18. 15; Ex. 15. 13.
STRAIGHTWAY,] as in 9. 23; 22. 10; Nu. 6. 5.
4. SAFETY,] as in v. 11; 2 Sa. 22. 3, 36, 47.
BRUISED] or 'bruise themselves,' as in 34. 25.
GATE,] when brought to judgment.
DELIVERER,] from their opponents.
5. HARVEST,] or 'crop;' as in 14. 9; 18.
16; 29. 19, &c.
THORNS,] as in Prov. 22. 5.
DESIGNING,] as in 18. 9; or 'thirsty.'
SWALLOWED UP,] as in 7. 2; Ps. 56. 1; 57. 3.
WEALTH,] as in 15. 29; 20. 15, 18; 21. 7, &c.
6. SORROW,] or 'iniquity,' as in 4. 8, &c.
SPRINGETH UP,] as in 8. 19; Ge. 2. 5, &c.
MISERY,] as in 3. 10; 4. 8, &c.
7. MAN,] the human race.
BORN,] as in Ge. 4. 26; 6. 1; 10. 21, &c.
SPARKS,] lit. 'sons of the flame.'
GO HIGH,] as in 3. 4; 10. 6; 39. 8, &c.
TO FLY,] as in Prov. 26. 2.
8. ENQUIRE,] as in 4: 10. 6; 39. 8, &c.
FOR GOD,] in behalf of Him.
GIVE,] lit. 'set, place.'
9. SEARCHING,] as in 8. 8; 9. 10; 11. 7; 34.
24; 36. 26; 38. 6; Jud. 5. 16; Ps. 145. 3; Prov.
25. 3, 27; Isa. 40. 28.
WONDERFUL,] as in 9. 10; 37. 5, 14; 42. 3, &c.
TILL,] as in Ge. 3. 19; 6. 7; 8. 5, &c.
10. LAND,] or 'earth.'
OUT-PLACES,] as in 18. 17; 31. 32, &c.
11. LOW,] or 'humbled,' as in Lev. 13. 20.
HIGH PLACE,] as in 16. 19; 25. 2; 31. 2, &c.
MOURNERS,] as in 30. 28; in 6. 16 it is
'blackish.'
HIGH,] as in De. 2. 36.
SAFETY,] as in v. 4 above.
12. MAKING VOID,] as in 15. 4; 40. 8, &c.
THOUGHTS,] as in 15. 5; Ge. 3. 1; Prov. 12. 16.
SUBTILE,] as in 15. 5; Ge. 3. 1; Prov. 12. 16.
WISDOM,] as in 6. 13; 11. 6; 12. 16; 26. 3;
30. 22; Prov. 2. 7; 3. 21; 8. 14; 18. 1; Isa
28. 29; Mic. 6. 9.
13. CAPTURING,] as in Prov. 16. 32, &c.
WRESTLING ONES,] as in Prov. 8. 8, &c.
HASTENED,] as in Isa. 32. 4; 35. 4; Hab. 1. 6.
14. MEET,] as in Ge. 32. 17; 33. 8; Ex. 4. 24.
GROPE,] as in 12. 25; Ge. 27. 12, 22; 31. 34,
37; De. 28. 29; Ex. 10. 21.
15. WASTED,] as in Eze. 29. 12; 26. 2, &c.
NEEDY,] as in 24. 4, 14; 29. 16; 30. 25; 31.
19; Ex. 23. 6, 11, &c.
16. POOR,] as in 20. 10, 19; 31. 16; 34. 19, 28.
HOPE,] as in 4. 6; 6. 8; 7. 6; 8. 13, &c.
PERVERSENESS,] as in Ps. 58. 2; 64. 6, &c.
SHUT,] as in 24. 24; De. 15. 7; Ps. 77. 9, &c.
17. MORTAL MAN,] as in 4. 3, 17; 5. 17, &c.
REPROVETH,] as in 6. 25, 20; 9. 33; 13. 3.
MIGHTY,] or 'sufficient' one.
18. PAIN,] as in 2 K. 3. 19; Eze. 13. 22, &c.
BINDETH UP,] as in 28. 11; 34. 17; Ge. 22. 3.
SMITETH,] as in 26. 12; Nu. 24. 17, &c.
HEAL,] as in 13. 4; Ge. 20. 17; 50. 2, &c.
19. DISTRESSES,] as in 27. 9; Ge. 35. 3, &c

SEVEN,] that is, any indefinite number.
STRIKETH,] as in 1. 19; 4. 5; 6. 7; 19. 21, &c.
20. FAMINE,] as in Ge. 12. 10; 26. 1; 41. 27.
REDEEMETH,] as in 6. 23; 33. 28; Ex. 13. 13.
BATTLE,] as in 38. 23; 39. 25; 41. 8, &c.
HANDS OF THE SWORD,] as in Ps. 63. 10.
21. SCOURGETH,] as in 9. 23, &c.
HID,] as in 29. 8, 10; 24. 4, &c.
DESTRUCTION,] as in v. 22; Ps. 12. 5; Prov. 21. 7; 24. 2; Isa. 13. 6; 16. 4, &c.
22. HUNGER,] as in 30. 3.
MOCKEST,] as in 29. 24; 30. 1; 39. 7, 18, 22; 41. 29; Ps. 2. 4, &c.
BEAST OF THE EARTH,] as in Ge. 1. 24, 25.
23. SONS,] as in Ge. 49. 24; Ex. 1. 16, &c.
BEAST OF THE FIELD,] as in 39. 15; 40. 20.
24. TENT,] as in 8. 22; 11. 14; 12. 6; 15. 34.
INSPECTED,] as in 7. 18; 31. 14, &c.
ERR,] in the examination.
25. NUMEROUS,] not 'great,' as in C.V.
OFFSPRING,] as in 21. 8; 27. 14; 31. 8; Isa. 22. 24; 34. 1; 42. 5; 44. 3; 48. 19; 61. 9; 65. 23.
HERB OF THE EARTH,] as in Ex. 10. 12, 15.
26. FULL AGE,] as in 30. 2.
GOING UP,] as in 36. 20; Ge. 32. 24, &c.
STALK,] as in 21. 32; Ex. 22. 6; Jud. 15. 5.
27. SEARCHED,] as in 13. 9; 28. 3, 27; 29. 16.
RIGHT,] as in Ge. 10. 29, &c.
FOR THYSELF,] not 'for thy good,' as in C.V.

VI. 2. PROVOCATION,] as in 5. 2; 10. 17; 17. 7.
WEIGHED,] as in 28. 15; 31. 6; Ge. 23. 16.
CALAMITY,] as in v. 30; 30. 13; Ps. 5. 9, &c.
BALANCES,] as in 31. 6; Lev. 19. 36, &c.
LIFT UP,] not 'were laid,' as in C.V.
3. SANDS OF THE SEA,] as in Ge. 32. 12, &c.
RASH.] So Gesenius; Sept. 'evil.'
4. ARROWS,] as in 34. 6; Ge. 49. 23, &c.
DRINKING UP,] as in 15. 16; comp. 1. 13, &c.
TERRORS OF GOD,] as in 88. 16.
ARRAY THEMSELVES,] as in 13. 18; 23. 4; 28. 17, 19; 32. 14; 33. 5; 36. 19; 37. 19, &c.
5. BRAYETH,] as in 30. 7.
WILD ASS,] as in 11. 12; 24. 5; 39. 5, &c.
TENDER GRASS,] as in 38. 27; Ge. 1. 11, &c.
LOWETH,] as in 1 Sa. 6. 12.
PROVENDER,] as in 24. 6; Isa. 30. 24.
6. INSIPID THING,] as in La. 2. 14; Eze. 13. 10, 11, 14, 15; 22. 28.
SENSE,] as in 12. 20; 1 Sa. 21. 13; 25. 33; Ps. 34. 1; 119. 66; Prov. 11. 22; 26. 16; Jon. 3. 7; also Ex. 16. 31; Nu. 11. 8; Jer. 48. 11.
DRIVEL,] as in 1 Sa. 21. 13; Vulg. 'food of death.'
DREAMS,] as in 7. 14; 20. 8; 33. 15. So Sept. 'vain words.'
7. TOUCH,] as in Ge. 20. 6; Ex. 19. 12, &c.
SICKENING,] as in Ps. 41. 3; Isa. 1. 5, &c.
8. MAY COME,] in answer to my prayer.
MY HOPE,] of being eased from pain.
9. PLEASE,] as in v. 28, &c.
BRUISE,] as in 4. 19; 19. 2, &c.
LOOSE,] as in Ps. 105. 20; 146. 7; Hab. 3. 6; Isa. 58. 6.
CUT OFF,] as in Isa. 10. 12; 38. 12; Eze. 22. 12.
10. COMFORT,] as in Ps. 119. 50.
EXULT.] This original word is not found elsewhere.
PAIN,] as in Ex. 15. 14; Ps. 48. 6, &c.
SPARE,] as in 16. 13; 20. 13; 27. 22.
HIDDEN,] as in 15. 18; 27. 11; Ge. 47. 18.

11. POWER,] as in v. 12, 22; 3. 7; 9. 4, 19.
HOPE,] as in 13. 15; 14. 14; 29. 21, 23, &c.
END,] as in 16. 3; 18. 2; 22. 5; 28. 3, &c.
PROLONG,] as in Ex. 20. 12; De. 4. 26, &c.
12. STONES,] as in 41. 24, &c.
BRAZEN,] as in 20. 24; 28. 2; 40. 18; 41. 27.
13. HELP,] as in 31. 21; Jud. 5. 23, &c.
SUBSTANCE,] as in 5. 12; 11. 6; 12. 16; 26. 3; 30. 22; Prov. 2. 7; 3. 21; 8. 14; 18. 1; Isa. 28. 29; Mic. 6. 9.
DRIVEN,] as in De. 4. 19; 13. 5, 10; 19. 5.
14. DESPISER.] So Good; comp. 5. 17, &c.
SHAME,] as in Lev. 20. 17; lit. 'kindness.'
15. DECEIVED,] as in Ex. 21. 8; Jud. 9. 23.
STREAM,] as in 2 Sa. 22. 16; lit. 'strong one.'
PASS AWAY,] as in 9. 11; 11. 16; 13. 13; 14. 5.
16. BLACK,] as in 5. 15; 30. 28; Ps. 35. 14.
ICE,] as in 37. 10; 38. 29; Ge. 31. 40; Jer. 36. 30; Eze. 1. 22; Ps. 147. 17.
HID ITSELF,] as in De. 22. 1, 3, 4; Ps. 55. 1; Isa. 58. 2.
17. WARM.] This original word is not found elsewhere.
CUT OFF,] as in 23. 17.
HOT,] as in 24. 19; Ge. 8. 22; 18. 1, &c.
EXTINGUISHED,] as in 18. 5, 6; 21. 17, &c.
18. TURN ASIDE,] as in Ruth 3. 8; Jud. 16. 20.
PATHS OF THEIR WAY,] in Isa. 3. 12 it is 'way of thy paths.'
ASCEND,] or 'go up,' not merely 'go,' as in C.V.
EMPTINESS,] as in 12. 24; 26. 7; Ge. 1. 2.
ARE LOST,] as in 3. 3; 4. 7, 9, 11, 20; 8. 13.
19. PASSENGERS,] as in 31. 32; lit. 'paths.
TEMA,] lit. 'untilled,' north of Arabia Deserta; as in Isa. 21. 14; Jer. 25. 23. Sept. 'Thaiman.'
LOOKED EXPECTINGLY,] as in 28. 24; 35. 5; 36. 25; 39. 29, &c.
TRAVELLERS,] lit. 'goings,' as in 29. 6; Ps. 68. 24; Prov. 31. 27; Nah. 2. 5; Hab. 3. 6.
SHEBA,] as in 1. 15, &c.
HOPED,] as in 3. 9; 7. 2; 17. 13; 30. 26, &c.
20. ASHAMED,] as in 19. 3, &c.
TRUSTED,] as in 11. 18; 39. 11; 40. 23, &c.
CONFOUNDED,] as in 34. 5; 35. 4, 26; 40. 14.
21. BECOME THE SAME,] as these deceitful brooks.
DOWNFALL,] in the case of Job.
22. GIVE] help, as in Ge. 11. 3, 4, 7; 29. 21.
POWER,] as in 3. 7; 6. 11, 12, 22; 9. 4, &c.
BRIBE,] as in 15. 34; Eze. 16. 33.
23. ADVERSARY,] as in 7. 11; 15. 24; 16. 9.
TERRIBLE ONES,] as in 15. 20; 27. 13, &c.
RANSOM,] as in 5. 20; 33. 28; Ex. 13. 13, &c.
24. SHOW,] as in 8. 10; 12. 7, 8; 27. 11 34. 32; 36. 22, &c.
KEEP SILENT,] as in 11. 3; 13. 5, 13, 19, &c.
ERRED,] as in 19. 4; Lev. 4. 13, &c.
25. POWERFUL,] as in 1 K. 2. 8; Mic. 2. 10.
UPRIGHT,] as in 33. 3, 23; De. 9. 5, &c.
REPROOF,] as in v. 26; 13. 3, 10; 15. 3, &c.
26. RECKON,] as in 13. 24; 19. 11, 15.
DESPERATE,] as in Isa. 57. 10; Jer. 2. 25 18. 12; 1 Sa. 27. 1; Ecc. 2. 20.
27. ANGER,] as in 4. 9; 9. 5, 13; 16. 9, &c. So Targum and Rashi.
ARE STRANGE,] as in 21. 29; 34. 19; so Cocceius and Poole.
28. PLEASE,] as in v. 9 above.

FACE,] openly, publicly.
LIE,] as in 34. 6; 41. 9; Nu. 23. 19, &c.
29. PERVERSENESS,] as in v. 30; 11. 14;
13 7; 15. 16, &c.
RIGHTEOUSNESS,] right state before God
and men.
30. PALATE,] as in 12. 11; 20. 13; 29. 10;
31. 30; 33. 2; 34. 3; Ps. 119. 103, &c.
DESIRABLE THINGS,] as in v. 2; 30. 13.

VII. 1. WARFARE,] as in 10. 17; 14. 14, &c.
HIRELING,] as in v. 2; 14. 6; Ex. 12. 45.
2. DESIRETH,] as in 5. 5; 36. 20; Ps. 56. 1.
SHADOW,] as in 8. 9; 14. 2; 17. 7; Ge. 19. 8.
EXPECTETH,] as in 3. 9; 6. 19; 17. 13; 30. 26.
WAGE,] lit. 'work;' as in 24. 5; 34. 11; 36.
9, 24; 37. 12; De. 32. 4, &c.
3. INHERIT,] as in De. 1. 38; 3. 28, &c.
VARIETY,] as in 11. 11; 15. 31; 31. 5; 35. 13.
MISERY,] as in 3. 10; 4. 8; 5. 6, 7; 7. 3, &c.
NUMBERED,] as in Ge. 13. 16.
4. EVENING,] as in 4. 12; Ge. 1. 5, 8, 13, 19.
MEASURED,] as in 28. 25; Hab. 3. 6, &c.
TOSSINGS,] or 'movings,' as in 15. 23, &c.
DAWN,] as in 3. 9; 24. 15; 1 Sa. 30, 17, &c.
5. CLOD.] Original word is not found else
where.
SHRIVELLED.] So Gesenius; Syr. 'con-
tracted.'
LOATHSOME,] as in Ps. 58. 7.
6. WEAVING MACHINE,] as in Jud. 16. 14.
CONSUMED,] as in v. 9; 4. 9; 11. 20; 17. 5.
7. BREATH,] or 'wind,' as in 1. 19; 4. 9, 15.
SEE GOOD,] as in Ps. 27. 13; 34. 12; 106. 5.
8. BEHOLDER,] as in Ge. 13. 16, &c.
I AM NOT,] being consumed by the sight.
9. CLOUD,] as in 26. 8, 9; 37. 11, 15; 38. 9.
SHEOL,] as in 11. 8; 14. 13; 17. 13, 16, &c.
10. DISCERN,] as in 2. 12; 4. 16; 24. 13, 17.
11. WITHHOLD,] as in 16. 5, 6; 21. 30; 30.
10; 33. 18; 38. 23, &c.
DISTRESS,] as in 15. 24; 38. 23, &c.
TALK,] as in 12. 8; Jud. 5. 10; 1 Ch. 16. 9.
BITTERNESS,] as in 10. 1; 21. 5; Isa. 38. 15.
12. SEA-MONSTER.] So Reiske, Good, &c.
DRAGON,] as in Ge. 1. 21; Ex. 7. 9, 10, 12.
GUARD,] as in Ge. 40. 3, 4, 7; 41. 10, &c.
13. BED,] as in De. 3. 11; Ps. 6. 6; 41. 3, &c.
TAKETH AWAY,] as in v. 21; not 'ease, as
in C. V.
TALKING,] as in 9. 27; 10. 1; 21. 4; 23. 2, &c.
MY COUCH,] as in 33. 15, 19; Ge. 49. 4, &c.
14. AFFRIGHTED,] as in 31. 34; 32. 15; 39.
22; De. 1. 21, &c.
DREAMS,] as in 6. 6; 20. 8; 33. 15; Ge. 20. 3.
VISIONS,] as in 4. 13; 20. 8; 33. 15; 2 Sa. 7. 17.
TERRIFIEST,] as in 3. 5; 9. 34; 13. 11, 21, &c.
15. STRANGLING,] as in 2 Sa. 17. 23;
Nah. 2. 12.
BONES,] in his body sticking out.
16. WASTED AWAY,] or 'been despised;'
as in 19. 18, &c.
CEASE,] as in 10. 20; Ex. 14. 12; 2 Ch. 25. 16.
17. HEART,] as in 2. 3, &c.
INSPECTEST,] as in 5. 24, &c.
EVENINGS,] as in Isa. 27. 3; lit. 'quiet times.'
19. LOOK,] as in 14. 6; Ge. 4. 4, 5, &c.
DESIST,] as in 27. 6; De. 4. 31.
SPITTLE,] as in 30. 10; Isa. 50. 5.
20. WATCHER,] as in 27. 18; Ex. 34. 7, &c.
MARK,] anything for striking against.

BURDEN,] as in Ex. 23. 5; Nu. 4. 15, &c.
21. TAKE AWAY,] as in v. 13.
CAUSE TO PASS AWAY,] as in 2 Sa. 12. 13;
31; 24. 10; 1 Ch. 21. 8; Zec. 3. 4.
FOR DUST,] not 'in dust,' as in C.V.
SOUGHT ME] diligently, as in 8. 5; 24. 5, &c.

VIII. 1. BILDAD THE SHUHITE,] as in 2. 11.
2. TILL WHEN,] as in 18. 2; Ex. 16. 28, &c.
3. PERVERT,] as in 19. 6; 34. 12; Ps. 119. 78.
4. BEFORE HIM,] or 'in regard to him.'
HAND,] medium or instrumentality.
5. EARLY,] or diligently, as in 7. 21, &c.
SUPPLICATION,] as in 9. 15; 19. 16; Ge. 42. 21.
6. PURE..UPRIGHT,] as in Prov. 21. 8.
WALKETH,] as in 41. 10; De. 32. 11, &c.
COMPLETED,] as in 21. 19, 31; 22. 27, &c.
7. GREAT,] as in v. 11; Ps. 92. 12.
8. GENERATION,] through the medium of
their records.
9. YESTERDAY,] as in Ge. 31. 2, 5; Ex. 4. 10.
KNOW NOT] the whole of the facts of the
case.
SHADOW,] as in 7. 2; 14. 2; 17. 7, &c.
10. SHEW,] as in 6. 24, &c.
BRING FORTH,] as in 10. 18; 12. 22; 15. 13;
28. 11; 38. 32, &c.
11. RUSH,] as in Ex. 2. 8; Isa. 18. 2; 35. 7
MIRE,] as in 40. 21; Eze. 47. 11.
REED,] as in Ge. 41. 2, 18.
INCREASE,] as in v. 7.
12. BUDDING,] as in Song 6. 11; Da. 4. 12, 14
UNCROPT,] as in 30. 4; De. 23. 25; Eze. 17. 4, 22.
HERB,] as in 40. 15; Nu. 11. 5, &c.
WITHERETH,] as in 12. 15; 14. 11; 18. 16.
13. PROFANE,] as in 13. 16; 15. 34; 17. 8;
20. 5; 27. 8; 34. 30; 36. 13; Ps. 35. 16; Prov.
11. 9; Isa. 9. 17; 10. 6; 33. 14.
14. CONFIDENCE,] as in 15. 27; 31. 24, &c
LOATHSOME,] as in Eze. 16. 47.
HOUSE OF A SPIDER,] as in Isa. 59. 5.
TRUST,] as in 18. 14; 31. 24; Ps. 40. 4, &c.
15. LEANETH,] as in 24. 23; Ge. 18. 4, &c.
TAKETH HOLD,] as in v. 20; 2. 3, 9; 18. 9; 27. 6.
16. GREEN,] as in 14. 8.
BRANCH,] as in 14. 7; 15. 30; Ps. 80. 11;
Eze. 17. 22; Hos. 14. 6.
17. HEAP,] as in 15. 28; 38. 11; Ge. 31. 46.
WRAPPED,] as in Nah. 1. 10.
HOUSE OF STONES]as a permanent dwelling.
18. FEIGNED,] as in 16. 8; 31. 28; Ge. 18. 15.
19. DUST,] of the plant, or of the ground
SPRING UP,] as in 5. 6; Ge. 2. 5, &c.
20. REJECT,] as in 5. 17, &c.
PERFECT,] as in 1. 1, 8; 2. 3; 9. 20, 21, 22.
TAKETH HOLD,] as in v. 15, &c.
21. WHILE,] or 'till.'
LAUGHTER,] as in 12. 4; Ps. 126. 2; Prov. 10. 23.
SHOUTING,] as in 33. 26; 39. 25; Lev. 23. 24.
22. PUT ON,] as in 7. 5; 10. 11; 29. 14; 27. 17.
TENT,] as in 5. 24; 11. 14; 12. 6; 15. 34, &c.

IX. 2. TRULY,] as in 12. 2; 19. 4, 5; 34. 12.
RIGHTEOUS,] as in v. 15, 20; 4. 17, &c.
3. DELIGHT,] as in 13. 3; 21. 14; 33. 32; 40. 17.
STRIVE,] as in 10. 2; 13. 8, 19; 23. 6; 33. 13.
THOUSAND,] as in 33. 23, &c.
4. WISE IN HEART,] as in 37. 24; Ex. 28. 3.
STRONG IN POWER,] as in v. 19; Isa. 40. 26.
HARDENED,] his heart and mind.
PEACE,] without internal or external fears

5. REMOVING,] as in 32. 15; Ge. 12. 8; 26.
22; Prov. 25. 1.
OVERTURNED,] as in 12. 5; 28. 9; 34. 25, &c.
6. SHAKING,] as in 12.6; 1 Sa. 28.15; Isa.13.13.
PILLARS,] as in 26. 11; Ex. 13. 21, &c.
MOVE THEMSELVES,] with trembling and
horror.
7. SPEAKING,] *lit.* 'saying.'
SEALETH UP,] as in 14.17; 24. 16; 33.16;37.7.
8. STRETCHING OUT,] as in 26. 7; 1 Ch. 21. 10.
TREADING,] as in 22. 15; 24. 11; 28. 8, &c.
HEIGHTS,] as in Lev. 26. 30; Nu. 21. 28, &c.
9. OSH,] *lit.* 'moth;' see 38. 32.
KESIL,] *lit.* 'fool;' as in 38. 31.
KIMAH,] as in 38. 31; Am. 5. 8.
INNER CHAMBERS OF THE SOUTH,] as in 37.9.
10. SEARCHING,] as in 5. 9; 8. 8; 34. 24, &c.
NUMBERING,] as in 1. 5; 3. 6; 5. 9; 14. 5, &c.
11. BY ME,] *or* 'above me.'
PASSETH ON,] as in v. 26; 4. 15; 11. 10, &c.
ATTEND,] as in 6. 30; 13. 1; 14. 21; 15. 9, &c.
12. SNATCHES AWAY,] as prey.
BRINGETH BACK,] *or* 'causeth to turn back.'
13. TURN BACK,] as in Nu. 25. 11; Prov. 24.18.
BOWED,] as in 38. 40; Ps. 10. 10, &c.
PROUD HELPERS,] *lit.* 'helpers of pride *or*
breadth.'
14. CHOOSE,] as in 7. 15; 15. 5; 29. 25, &c.
15. JUDGMENT,] whether favourable or
adverse.
SUPPLICATION,] as in 8. 5; 19. 16; Ge. 42. 21.
16. GIVETH EAR,] as in 32. 11; 33. 1; 34.
2, 16; 37. 14.
17. TEMPEST,] as in Nah. 1. 3.
BRUISETH,] as in Ge. 3. 15; Ps. 139. 11.
WOUNDS,] as in Ge.4.23; Ex.21.25;Pro. 20. 30.
18. REFRESH,] *lit.* 'bring back.'
19. STRONG ONE,] as in v. 4; 2 Sa. 15. 12, &c.
CONVENE,] as in Jer. 49. 19; 50. 44.
20. RIGHTEOUS,] as in v. 2, 15, &c.
DECLARE WICKED,] as in v. 29; 10. 2, 7, 15.
PERFECT,] as in v. 21, 22; 1. 1, 8; 2. 3; 8. 20.
DECLARETH PERVERSE,] as in Prov. 10. 9.
. 21. KNOW NOT,] fully and perfectly.
DESPISE,] as in 5. 17; 7. 16; 8. 21, &c.
22. THE SAME THING,] whether one be
good or bad.
CONSUMING,] as in Lev. 26. 16; Jer. 14. 12.
23. SCOURGE,] as in 5. 21; 1 K. 12. 11, 14. &c.
TRIAL,] as in Ex. 17. 7; De. 4. 34; 6. 16, &c.
24. WICKED ONE,] the Satan of 1. 6, &c.
COVERETH,] as in 15. 27; 16. 18; 21. 26, &c.
25. RUNNER,] as in 1 Sa. 20. 36; 22. 17, &c.
GOOD,] as in 2. 10; 7. 7; 21. 13, 25, &c.
26. REED,] *or* 'desire, *or* enmity.'
EAGLE,] as in 39. 27; Ex. 19. 4; De. 14. 12.
DARTETH.] Original word not found else-
where.
FOOD,] as in 12. 11; 20. 21; 36. 31; 38. 41, &c.
27. TALKING,] as in 7. 13; 10. 1; 21. 4; 23. 2.
FORSAKE,] as in 6. 14; 10. 1; 20. 13, &c.
CORNER,] as in Prov. 7. 8; Zec. 14. 10.
BRIGHTEN UP,] as in 10. 20; Ps. 39. 13;
Amos 5. 9.
28. SORROWS,] as in Ps. 16. 4; 147. 3; Prov.
10. 10; 15. 13.
ACQUIT,] as in 10. 14; Ex. 20. 7; 34. 7, &c.
29. VAIN,] as in 7. 16; 21. 34; 27. 12; 35. 16.
30. WASHED MYSELF.] Compare 29. 6.
PURIFIED.] Compare 15. 15; 25. 5.
SOAP,] as in Isa. 1. 25.

31. CORRUPTION,] as in 17. 14; 33. 18, 22, &c.
DIP,] as in Ge. 37. 31; Ex. 12. 22, &c.
ABOMINATED,] as in 19. 19; 30. 10; De. 7. 26.
32. BUT IF,] instead of being God—wise
and strong.
33. UMPIRE,] *lit.* a 'reasoner,' as in 32.
12; 40. 2.
34. ROD,] as in 21. 9; 37. 13.
35. NOT RIGHT,] as in margin of C.V.

X. 1. WEARY,] as in 8. 14; Ps. 95. 10, &c.
TALKING,] as in 7. 13; 9. 27, &c.
2. CONDEMN,] *lit.* 'declare wicked.'
LET ME KNOW,] as in 13. 23; 37. 19; 38. 3
3. OPPRESS,] as in 40. 23; Lev. 6. 2, &c.
DESPISEST,] as in 5, 17, &c.
LABOUR,] as in 39. 11, 16; Ge. 31. 42, &c.
4. EYES OF FLESH,] such as men have.
6. INQUIREST,] as in Ge. 31. 37, &c.
SEEKEST,] as in 3. 4; 5. 8; 39. 8, &c.
7. FOR THOU KNOWEST,] *lit.* 'because of
thy knowledge.'
8. TAKEN PAINS,] *or* 'grieved me;' as in
Ps. 56. 5; Isa. 63. 10.
ROUND ABOUT,] in every particular.
SWALLOWEST,] as in 2. 3; 8. 18; 20. 15, 18.
9. CLAY,] as in 4. 19; 13. 12; 27. 16, &c.
DUST,] as in 2. 12; 4. 19; 5. 6; 7. 5, 21, &c.
10. POUR ME OUT,] as in 3. 24; 2 K. 22. 9.
MILK,] as in 21. 24; Ge. 18. 8, &c.
CHEESE.] Original word not found else-
where.
CURDLE,] as in Ex. 15. 8; Zech. 14. 6;
Zeph. 1. 12.
11. PUT UPON ME,] as in 39. 19.
FENCE,] as in 1. 10; Hos. 2. 6.
12. DONE,] *or* 'performed.'
INSPECTION,] as in Nu. 3. 32, 36; 4. 16, &c.
13. LAID UP,] as in 17. 4; 20. 26; 21. 19, &c.
14. OBSERVED,] as in 2. 6; 13. 27; 14. 16, &c.
ACQUIT,] as in 9. 28, &c.
15. DONE WICKEDLY,] as in 9. 29; 10. 7, &c.
WO,] as in Mic. 7. 1.
RIGHTEOUSLY,] as in 4. 17; 9. 2, 15, 20, &c.
SHAME,] as in Ps. 83. 16; Prov. 3. 35, &c.
AFFLICTION,] as in 30. 16, 27; 36. 8, 15, 21.
16. RISETH,] as in 8. 11; Ex.15.1,21; Eze.47.5.
LION,] as in 4. 10; 28. 8; Ps. 91. 13.
HUNTEST,] as in 38. 39; Ge. 27. 3, 5, &c.
WONDERFUL,] as in Ex. 15. 11; Ps. 77. 11, 14.
17. RENEWEST,] as in 1 Sa. 11. 14; 2 Ch.15.8.
WITNESSES,] as in 16. 8, 9; Ge. 31. 44, &c.
MULTIPLY,] as in 9. 17, &c.
CHANGES,] as in 14. 14; Ge. 45. 22; Jud. 14. 12.
WARFARE,] as in 7. 1; 14. 14, &c.
18. WOMB,] as in 3. 11; 24. 20; 31. 15; 38. 8.
EXPIRE,] as in 3. 11; 13. 19; 14. 10, &c.
19. BELLY,] as in 1. 21; 3. 10, 11; 15. 2, 35
20. FEW,] as in 15. 11; 14. 24; 32. 22, &c.
CEASE,] as in 7. 16; Ex. 14. 12; 2 Ch. 25. 16
BRIGHTEN UP,] as in 9. 27; Ps. 39. 13.
21. DARKNESS,] as in 3. 4, 5. 5. 14; 12. 22
DEATH-SHADE,] as in v. 22; 3. 5; 12. 22, &c
22. OBSCURITY,] as in Amos 4. 13.
THICK DARKNESS,] as in 3. 6; 23. 17; 28. 3
ORDER,] *or* 'arrangement.'
THE SHINING,] *or* 'it shineth.'

XI. 1. ZOPHAR,] as in 2. 11.
2. MULTITUDE,] as in 4. 14, &c.
MAN OF LIPS.] Compare Prov. 10. 8, 10, &c

JUSTIFIED,] as in 4. 17; 9. 2, 15, 20; 10. 15.
3. DEVICES,] as in 41. 12; Isa. 16. 6; 44. 25.
KEEP SILENT,] as in 6. 24; 13. 5, 13, 19, &c.
SCORNEST,] as in 9. 23; 22. 19; 2 K. 19. 21.
CAUSING BLUSHING,] as in 19. 3; Jud. 18. 7.
4. PURE,] as in 8. 6; 16. 17; 33. 9, &c.
DISCOURSE,] as in De. 32. 2; Prov. 1. 5, &c.
CLEAN,] as in Ps. 19. 9; 24. 4; 73. 1, &c.
5. GOD,] instead of mere men.
OPEN HIS LIPS,] as in 32. 20; Ps. 51. 15, &c.
6. SECRETS,] as in 28. 11; Ps. 44. 21, &c.
COUNSEL,] as in 5. 12; 6. 13; 12. 16, &c.
FOLDINGS,] or 'doublings,' as in 41. 13;
Isa. 40. 2.
FORGETTETH,] as in 39. 17; Ge. 41. 51, &c.
7. SEARCHING,] as in 5. 9; 8. 8; 9. 10, &c.
PERFECTION,] as in 26. 10; 28. 3; Neh. 3.
21; Ps. 139. 22.
8. HEIGHTS,] as in 22. 12; 40. 10; 1 Sa. 17. 4.
DEEPER,] as in 12. 22; Lev. 13. 3, 4, &c.
SHEOL,] as in 7. 9; 14. 13; 17. 13, 16, &c.
9. LONGER,] as in 2 Sa. 3. 1; Jer. 29. 28, &c.
MEASURE,] as in Jer. 13. 25.
BROADER,] as in 30. 14; Ge. 34. 21, &c.
10. PASS ON,] as in 4. 15; 9. 11, 26; 20. 24.
SHUT UP,] as in 16. 11; Lev. 13. 4, 5, 11, &c.
ASSEMBLE,] as in Ex. 35. 1; Lev. 8. 3, &c.
REVERSE,] lit. 'cause to turn back.'
11. MEN OF VANITY,] as in Ps. 26. 4.
CONSIDER,] as in 23. 15; 26. 14; 30. 20; 31.
1; 32. 12; 37. 14; 38. 18, &c.
12. EMPTY MAN,] as in Ex. 27. 8; 38. 7;
Jer. 52. 31.
BOLD,] or 'takes heart;' as in Song 4. 9; 2
Sa. 13. 6, 8.
COLT,] as in Ge. 32. 15; 49. 11; Jud. 10. 4, &c.
WILD ASS,] as in 6. 5; 24. 5; 39. 5, &c.
13. PREPARED,] as in 17. 5; 27. 16, 17, &c.
SPREAD OUT,] as in 36. 30; 39. 26.
14. PUT IT FAR OFF,] as in 13. 21; 19. 13, &c.
PERVERSENESS,] as in 6. 29, 30; 13. 7, &c.
TENTS,] as in 5. 24; 8. 22, &c.
15. BLEMISH,] as in Lev. 21. 17, 18, 1, 23.
FIRM,] lit. 'molten;' as in 37. 18.
16. FORGET,] as in 9. 27; 19. 14; 24. 20, &c.
MISERY,] as in 3. 10; 4. 8; 5. 6, 7; 15. 35, &c.
17. NOON,] as in 5. 14; Ge. 6. 6; 43. 16, 25.
AGE,] as in Ps. 17. 14; 39. 5; 49. 1; 89. 47.
FLIEST,] as in 5. 7; 20. 8; De. 4. 17, &c.
18. HOPE,] as in v. 20; 4. 6; 5. 16; 6. 8, &c.
SEARCHED,] as in 3. 21; 39. 21, 29, &c.
IN CONFIDENCE,] as in 24. 23; Ge. 34. 25,&c.
19. RESTED,] lit. 'crouched,' as in Ge. 4. 7.
CAUSING TREMBLING,] as in Lev. 26. 6, &c.
ENTREATED,]lit. 'smoothed,'asin1Sa.13.12.
20. CONSUMED,] as in 4. 9; 7. 6, 9; 17. 5, &c.
REFUGE,] as in 2 Sa. 22. 3; Ps. 59. 16, &c.
BREATHING OUT,] or a 'puff.'

XII. 2. TRULY,] as in 9. 2; 19. 4, 5; 34. 12.
THE PEOPLE,] the many, the multitude.
3. HEART,] as in 1. 5; 9. 4; 10. 13; 17. 11, &c.
FALLEN,] as in 13. 2; 14. 18, &c.
4. LAUGHTER,] as in 8. 21; Ps. 126. 2, &c.
FRIEND,] as in 2. 11; 6. 14; 16. 20, 21; 17. 5.
PERFECT,] as in 36. 4; 37. 16; Ge. 6. 9, &c.
5. TORCH,] as in 41. 19; Ge. 15. 17; Ex.
20. 18, &c.
DESPISED,] as in v. 21; 31. 34; Ge. 38. 23.
SECURE,] as in 2 K. 19. 28; Ps. 123. 4, &c.
PREPARED,] as in 15. 23; 18. 12; 21. 12, &c.

SLIDING,] as in 2 Sa. 22. 37; Ps. 18. 36;
26. 1; 37. 31.
6. SPOILERS,] as in 15. 21; Isa. 16. 4; 21. 2.
PROVOKING,] as in 9. 6; Isa. 14. 16, &c.
CONFIDENCE,] lit. 'confidences;' not
'secure,' as in C.V.
BROUGHT,] the spoil they captured.
7. BEASTS,] as in 18. 3; 35. 11; 40. 15.
SHEW,] as in v. 8; 6. 24; 8. 10, &c.
FOWL OF THE HEAVENS,] as in 18. 21; 35. 11.
DECLARE,] or 'set before,' as in Ge. 3. 11.
8. TALK,] as in 7. 11; Jud. 5. 10; 1 Ch. 16. 9.
FISHES OF THE SEA,] as in Ge. 9. 2, &c.
RECOUNT,] as in 15. 17; 28. 27; 38. 37, &c.
9. JEHOVAH.] Some MSS. read 'God.'
10. BREATH,] or 'soul;' as in 2. 4, 6; 3. 20.
LIVING THING,] as in 3. 20; 5. 22, 23; 7. 7.
FLESH OF MAN,] or 'mankind.'
11. EAR,] as in 4. 12; 13. 1, 17; 15. 21, &c.
TRY,] as in 7. 18; 23. 10; 34. 3, 36, &c.
PALATE,] as in 6. 30; 20. 13; 29. 10; 31. 30.
TASTE,] as in 34. 3; 1 Sa. 14. 24, 29, 43, &c
12. VERY AGED,] as in 15. 10; 29. 8; 32. 6.
LENGTH OF DAYS,] as in De. 30. 20; Ps. 21. 4
UNDERSTANDING,]as in v. 13; 26. 12; 32. 11.
13. MIGHT,] as in 26. 14; 39. 19; 41. 12, &c
COUNSEL,] as in 5. 13; 10. 3; 18. 7; 21. 16.
14. BREAKETH DOWN,] as in Ex. 15. 7; 19
21, 24; Jud. 6. 25, &c.
SHUTTETH,] as in 3. 10; 41. 15; Ge. 2. 21,&c
15. KEEPETH IN,] as in 4. 2; 29. 9; Ge. 16. 2
DRIED UP,] as in 8. 12, &c.
OVERTURN,] as in 9. 5, &c.
16. STRENGTH,] as in 26. 2; 37. 6; 41. 22, &c.
WISDOM,] as in 5. 12; 6. 13; 11. 6; 26. 3, &c.
DECEIVED,] as in Nu. 15. 28; Ps. 119. 67.
DECEIVER,] as in De. 27. 18; Prov. 28. 10.
17. COUNSELLORS,] as in 3. 14; 2 Sa. 15. 12.
SPOIL,]as in Jer. 50. 10; Eze. 39. 10; Zec. 2. 8.
JUDGES,] who administer the law.
FOOLISH,] as in Ecc. 2. 2; 7. 7; Ps. 102. 8.
18. BAND,] as in 5. 17; 20. 3; 36. 10, &c.
GIRDLE,] as in 2 K. 1. 8; Isa. 5. 27; 11. 5.
19. MINISTERS,] or 'priests,' as in Ge. 14. 18.
STRONG ONES,] as in 33. 19; Ge. 49. 24, &c.
OVERTHROWETH,] as in Ex. 23. 8; De. 16. 19.
20. LIP,] that is, 'pronunciation, utter-
ance.'
STEDFAST,] as in Nu. 12. 7; De. 7. 9; 28. 59.
REASON,] as in 6. 6; Ex. 16. 31; Nu. 11. 8.
AGED,] as in 32. 4, 9; 42. 17; Ge. 18. 11, &c.
21. POURING,] as in Ge. 9. 6; Nu. 35. 33.
CONTEMPT,] as in v. 5; 31. 34; Ge. 38. 23.
PRINCES,] as in 21. 28; 34. 18; Ex. 35. 5, &c.
FEEBLE,] as in Ezra 4. 4; Jer. 38. 4, &c.
22. REMOVING,] or 'revealing;' as in
Prov. 11. 13.
DEEP THINGS,] as in 11. 8, &c.
DEATH-SHADE,] as in 3. 5; 10. 21, ' 16. 16.
23. MAGNIFYING,] as in 36. 24.
DESTROYETH,] as in Nu. 33. 52; De. 11. 4;
12. 2, 3, &c.
SPREADING OUT,]as in Nu. 11. 32; 2 Sa.17.19.
QUIETETH,] or 'causeth them to rest.'
24. TURNING ASIDE,] as in v. 20; Prov. 28.
9; Isa. 3. 1.
HEADS,] as in 29. 25.
WANDER,] as in v. 25; Ge. 20. 13; 2 K. 21. 9.
VACANCY,] as in 6. 18; 26. 7; Ge. 1. 2, &c.
25. FEEL,] as in 5. 14; Ge. 27. 12, 22; 31. 34.
DRUNKARD,] as in 1 Sa. 1. 13; 25. 36, &c.

XIII. 1. EYE..EAR,] of the things they had noted.
2. KNOWLEDGE,] as in 10. 7, &c.
FALLEN,] as in 12. 3; 14. 18.
3. ARGUE,] or 'reason,' as in v. 10; 15. 13.
DELIGHT,] as in 9. 3; 21. 14; 33. 32, &c.
4. FORGERS,] lit. 'sewers up,' as in 14. 17; Ps. 119. 69.
PHYSICIANS,] as in Ge. 50. 2; Ex. 15. 26, &c.
5. SILENT,] as in v. 19; Nu. 30. 14, &c.
6. ARGUMENT,] as in 23. 4; Ps. 38. 14; 39. 11.
PLEADINGS,] as in 29. 16; 31. 13, 35; 33. 19.
7. PERVERSENESS,] as in 6. 29, 30; 11. 14.
DECEIT,] as in 27. 4; Ps. 32. 2; 52. 2, &c.
8. ACCEPT,] lit. 'lift up.'
STRIVE,] as in v. 19; 9. 3; 10. 2; 23. 6, &c.
9. SEARCH,] as in 5. 27; 28. 3, 27; 29. 16, &c.
MOCK,] as in Ge. 31. 7; Ex. 8. 29; Jud. 16. 10.
10. REPROVE,] as in v. 3 above.
SECRET,] as in 22. 14; 24. 15; 31. 27; 40. 21.
11. EXCELLENCY,] as in 31. 23; 41. 25, &c.
TERRIFY,] as in v. 21; 3. 5; 7. 14; 9. 34, &c.
DREAD,] as in 3. 25; 4. 14; 15. 21; 21. 9, &c.
12. REMEMBRANCES,] as in Ex. 12. 14; 13. 9.
SIMILES,] as in 27. 1; 29. 1; Nu. 21. 7, 8, &c.
ASHES,] as in 2. 8; 30. 19; 42. 6, &c.
CLAY,] as in 4. 19; 10. 9; 27. 16, &c.
HEIGHTS,] as in 15. 26; Lev. 14. 9; 1 K. 7. 33.
13. KEEP SILENT,] as in 33. 31, 33; Isa. 41. 1.
14. TEETH,] as in 4. 10; 16. 9; 19. 20; 29. 17.
HAND,] as in v. 21; 2. 7; 9. 30; 10. 3; 11. 13.
15. SLAY,] as in 24. 14; Ps. 139. 19.
WAIT,] as in 6. 11; 14. 14; 29. 21, 23, &c.
ARGUE,] as in v. 3 above.
16. SALVATION,] as in 30. 15; Ge. 49. 18, &c.
PROFANE,] as in 8. 13; 15. 34; 17. 8; 20. 5.
17. DECLARATION,] lit. 'shewing.'
18. SET IN ARRAY,] as in 6. 4; 23. 4; 28. 17, 19.
CAUSE,] lit. 'judgment.'
RIGHTEOUS,] as in 4. 17; 9. 2, 15, 20; 10. 15.
19. STRIVE,] as in v. 8.
GASP,] as in 3. 11; 10. 18; 14. 10; 27. 5, &c.
20. GOD.] The C.V. is exactly the reverse of what Job desires in v. 21.
HIDDEN,] as in 3. 10, 23, &c.
21. PUT FAR OFF,] as in 11. 14, &c.
TERRIFY,] as in v. 11; 3. 5, &c.
22. CALL THOU,] as an accuser.
SPEAK,] in vindication of my innocence.
23. HOW MANY,] as in Ge. 47. 8, &c.
LET ME KNOW,] as in 10. 2; 37. 19, &c.
24. HIDE,] as in 34. 29; De. 31. 17, 18, &c.
RECKONEST,] as in 6. 26; 19. 11, 15; 33. 10.
25. LEAF,] as in Ge. 3. 7; 8. 11; Lev. 26. 36.
DRIVEN AWAY,] as in Lev. 26. 36; Prov. 21. 6; Isa. 41. 2.
TERRIFY,] as in 31. 34; De. 1. 29; 7. 21, &c.
STUBBLE,] as in 14. 28, 29; Ps. 83. 13, &c.
PURSUE,] as in 19. 22, 28.
26. WRITEST,] as in 31. 35; 19. 23.
BITTER THINGS,] as in 20. 14, 25.
POSSESS,] as in Ex. 15. 9; Nu. 14. 24, &c.
YOUTH,] as in 31. 18; Ge. 8. 31; 46. 34, &c.
27. STOCKS,] as in 33. 11.
OBSERVEST,] or 'watchest.'
ROOTS,] as in 8. 17; 14. 8; 18. 16; 19. 28, &c.
PRINT,] as in 1 K. 6. 35; Eze. 8. 10; 23. 14.
28. ROTTEN THING,] as in Prov. 12. 4; 14. 30; Hos. 5. 12, &c.
WEARETH AWAY,] as in 21. 13; Ge. 18. 12.
GARMENT,] as in 22. 6; 37. 17, &c.

MOTH,] as in 4. 19; 27. 18, Ps. 39. 11, &c.

XIV. 1. MAN,] earthly man, as in Ge. 1. 26
BORN OF WOMAN,] as in 15. 14; 25. 4, &c.
FEW DAYS,] lit. 'short of days.'
TROUBLE,] as in 3. 17, 26; 37. 2; 39. 24, &c
2. FLOWER,] as in Ex. 28. 36; 39. 30, &c.
CUT OFF,] as in 18. 16; 24. 24; Ge. 17. 11. Ps. 37. 2.
FLEETH,] as in 9. 25; 20. 24; 27. 22, &c.
SHADOW,] as in 7. 2; 8. 9; 17. 7, &c.
3. EYES.] Not an interrogation, as in C. V.
4. CLEAN,] as in 28. 19; Ge. 7. 2, 8; 8. 20, &c.
UNCLEAN,] as in Lev. 5. 2; 7. 19, 21; 10. 10.
5. DETERMINED,] as in Isa. 10. 22.
MONTHS,] as in 21. 21; Ge. 7. 11, &c.
LIMIT,] as in v. 13; 23. 12, 14; 26. 10, &c.
PASSETH NOT OVER,] as in 19. 8, &c.
6. LOOK AWAY,] as in 19. 8; Ps. 104. 9, &c.
CEASE,] as in v. 7; 3. 17; 7. 16; 10. 20; 16. 6.
ENJOY,] as in 33. 26; 34. 9, &c.
HIRELING,] as in 7. 1, 2; Ex. 12. 43; 22, 15.
7. HOPE,] as in 4. 6; 5. 16; 6. 8; 7. 6; 8. 13.
CHANGE,] as in 29. 20; Ge. 31. 7, 41; 35. 2.
TENDER BRANCH,] lit. 'suckling,' as in 8. 16.
8. OLD,] as in Prov. 22. 6.
STEM,] as in Isa. 11. 1; 40. 24.
9. FRAGRANCE,] as in Ge. 8. 21; 27. 27, &c.
FLOURISH,] as in Ps. 92. 13; Prov. 14. 11, Isa. 17. 11; Eze. 17. 24.
CROP,] or 'harvest;' as in 5. 5; 18. 16, &c.
PLANT,] as in 1 Ch. 4. 23; Isa. 5. 7; 17. 10, 11.
10. WEAK,] as in Ex. 17. 16; Isa. 14. 12; Joel 3. 10.
EXPIRETH,] as in 3. 11; 10. 18; 13. 19, &c.
11. GONE AWAY,] as in De. 32. 36; 1 Sa. 9. 7; Prov. 20. 14; Jer. 2. 36; Eze. 27. 19.
WASTE,] as in Ge. 8. 13; Ps. 106. 9, &c.
12. LAIN DOWN,] as in 3. 13; 7. 4, 21; 11. 18.
WEARING OUT,] as a garment, Isa. 50. 9, &c.
ROUSED,] as in 1 Sa. 26. 12; 2 K. 4. 31, &c.
13. SHEOL,] as in 7. 9; 11. 8; 17. 13, 16, &c.
CONCEAL,] as in Ex. 2. 3; Ps. 56. 6.
HIDE,] as in 3. 10; 13. 24; 39. 29, &c.
LIMIT,] as in v. 5; 23. 12, 14; 26. 10, &c.
14. REVIVE,] or 'live;' as in 7. 6; 21. 7, &c.
WARFARE,] as in 7. 1; 10. 17, &c.
CHANGE,] as in 10. 17; Ge. 45. 22; Jud. 14. 12.
15. DESIRE,] as in Ge. 31. 30; Ps. 17. 12, 84. 2; Zeph. 2. 1.
16. STEPS,] as in 18. 7; 31. 4, 37; 34. 21, &c.
NUMBEREST,] or 'recountest;' as in 12. 8.
WATCH.] Not an interrogation, as in C. V.
17. SEALED UP,] as in De. 32. 34; Neh. 9. 38.
BAG,] or 'bundle,' as in Ge. 42. 35, &c.
SEWEST UP,] as in 13. 4; Ps. 119. 69.
18. WASTETH AWAY,] as in v. 12; Ex. 18. 18.
REMOVED,] as in 18. 4; Ps. 6. 5, &c.
19. WORN AWAY,] as in Ex. 30. 36; 2 Sa. 22. 43; Ps. 18. 43.
OUT-POURINGS,] as in Lev. 25. 5, 11; 2 K. 19. 29; Isa. 37. 30.
WASH AWAY,] as in Lev. 15. 11; 1 K. 22. 38.
DESTROYED,] as in 23. 30; Nu. 24. 19.
20. PREVAILEST,] as in 15. 24; Ecc. 4. 12.
CHANGING,] as in 1 Sa. 21. 13; Est. 2. 9, &c.
21. HONOURED,] lit. 'become heavy,' as in 6. 3, &c.
LITTLE,] as in Jer. 30. 19; Zec. 13. 7.
22. PAINED,] as in 5. 18; Ge. 34. 25.
MOURN,] as in Isa. 3. 26; 19. 8; 24. 4, &c.

XV. 1. ELIPHAZ,] as in 2. 11; 4. 1.
2. VAIN KNOWLEDGE,] *lit.* 'knowledge of wind.'
EAST WIND,] as in 27. 21; 38. 24, &c.
3. REASON,] as in 13. 3, 10, &c.
NOT USEFUL,] as in 22. 2; 34. 9; 35. 3, &c.
SPEECHES,] as in 4. 2, 4; 6. 26; 8. 10; 12. 11.
PROFIT,] as in 21. 15; 30. 13; 35. 3, &c.
4. MAKE VOID,] as in 5. 12; 40. 8, &c.
REVERENCE,] as in 4. 6; 6. 14; 22. 4; 28. 28.
DIMINISH,] as in v. 8; 36. 7, 27.
MEDITATION,] as in Ps. 119. 97, 99.
5. TEACHETH,] as in 33. 33; 35. 11; Prov. 22. 25.
CHOOSEST,] as in 7. 15; 9. 14; 29. 25; 34. 4, 33; 36. 21.
SUBTILE,] as in 5. 12; Ge. 2. 25, &c.
6. DECLARETH THEE WICKED,] as in 9. 20.
TESTIFY,] *lit.* 'answer, respond.'
7. BORN,] as in 1. 2; 3. 3; 11. 12; 38. 21, &c.
HEIGHTS,] as in Ge. 49. 26; Ex. 17. 9, 10. &c.
FORMED,] as in 26. 5, 13; 35. 14, 19; 39. 1, &c.
8. SECRET COUNSEL,] as in 19. 19; 29. 4, &c.
WITHDRAWEST,] as in v. 4; 36. 7, 27, &c.
10. GRAY-HEADED,] as in 1 Sa. 12. 2.
VERY AGED,] as in 12. 12; 29. 8; 32. 6.
11. FEW,] *or* 'little;' as in 10. 20; 24. 24, &c.
COMFORTS,] as in 21. 2.
GENTLE,] as in 2 Sa. 18. 5; Isa. 8. 6.
12. TAKE THEE AWAY,] as in 1. 15, 17, 21, &c.
HIGH.] So Sept., Vulgate, &c.
14. MAN,] *or* 'mortal man,' as in 4. 13, 17.
PURE,] as in 25. 4; Ps. 51. 4; Mic. 6. 11, &c.
RIGHTEOUS,] as in 4. 7; 9. 2, 15, 20, &c.
BORN,] as in 14. 1; 25. 4, &c.
15. HOLY ONES,] as in 5. 1; 6. 10; Ex. 19. 6.
CREDENCE,] as in 4. 18; 9. 16, &c.
PURE,] as in 9. 30; 25. 5; La. 4. 7.
16. ABOMINABLE,] as in 1 Ch. 21. 6; Isa. 14. 19.
FILTHY,] as in Ps. 14. 3; 53. 3.
PERVERSENESS,] as in 6. 29, 30; 11. 14, &c.
18. DECLARE,] *lit.* 'set before.'
HID,] as in 6. 10; 27. 11, &c.
19. LAND,] in which they dwelt.
STRANGER,] as in 19. 15, 27, &c.
20. PAINING HIMSELF,] as in Est. 4. 4; Ps. 37. 7; Jer. 23. 19.
FEW,] *lit.* a 'number,' as in 1. 5; 3. 6, &c.
LAID UP,] as in 24. 1, &c.
TERRIBLE ONE,] as in 6. 23; 27. 13; Ps. 37. 35.
21. FEARFUL VOICE,] *lit.* 'voice of fears.'
DESTROYER,] as in 12. 6, &c.
22. BELIEVETH,] *lit.* 'is not stedfast.'
WATCHED,] as in Ge. 31. 49; Nu. 23. 14, &c.
23. WANDERING,] as in Prov. 27. 8; Isa. 10. 14.
READY,] *or* 'prepared,' as in 12. 5; 18. 12.
24. TERRIFY,] as in 3. 5; 7. 14; 9. 34, &c.
ADVERSITY,] as in 6. 23; 7. 11; 16. 9, &c.
DISTRESS,] as in Ps. 25. 17; 107. 6, 13, 19, 28; Zeph. 1. 15.
PREVAIL,] as in 14. 20; Ecc. 4. 12.
READY,] as in 3. 8; De. 32. 35; Est. 3. 14; 8. 13; Isa. 10. 13.
BOASTER,] as in Isa. 22. 18.
25. MIGHTY,] as in 36. 9; Isa. 42. 13.
26. NECK,] as in 39. 19; 41. 22; Ge. 27. 16, &c.
BOSSES,] as in 13. 12; Lev. 14. 9, &c.
27. FAT,] as in Ge. 4. 4; 45. 18, &c.
VIGOUR.] Original word not found again.
CONFIDENCE,] as in 8. 14; 31. 24, &c.
28. CUT OFF,] as in 4. 7; 22. 20, &c.
ARE READY,] as in v. 24; Prov. 24. 27.

HEAPS,] as in 8. 17; 38. 11; Ge. 31. 46, &c.
29. RICH,] as in 12. 8.
WEALTH,] *or* 'strength,' as in Ge. 34. 29, &c.
RISE,] as in 1. 20; 7. 4; 8. 15; 11. 17, &c.
STRETCH OUT,] as in v. 25, &c.
CONTINUANCE.] Original word is not found elsewhere.
30. TENDER BRANCH,] as in 8. 16; 14. 7; Ps. 80. 11; Eze. 17. 22; Hos. 14. 6.
DRY UP,] as in Prov. 17. 22; Nah. 1. 4.
BREATH,] *lit.* 'wind, spirit.'
31. VANITY,] as in 7. 3; 11. 11; 31. 5, &c.
DECEIVED,] as in 38. 41; Isa. 19. 14, &c.
RECOMPENCE,] as in 20. 18; 28. 17, &c.
32. COMPLETED,] *or* 'fulfilled,' as in Ge. 6. 11.
BENDING BRANCH,] as in Isa. 9. 14; 19. 15.
GREEN,] as in De. 12. 2; 1 K. 14. 23, &c.
33. SHAKETH,] as in 21. 27; Jer. 22. 3, &c.
UNRIPE FRUIT,] as in Isa. 18. 5; Jer. 31. 29.
CASTETH OFF,] as in 18. 7; 27. 22; 29. 17.
BLOSSOM,] as in Isa. 18. 5.
34. COMPANY,] as in 16. 7; Ex. 12. 3, &c.
PROFANE,] as in 8. 13; 13. 16; 17. 8, &c.
GLOOMY,] as in 3. 7; 30. 3; Isa. 49. 21, &c.
BRIBERY,] as in Ex. 23. 8; De. 10. 17, &c.
35. CONCEIVE,] as in Isa. 59. 4, &c.
MISCHIEF,] as in 3. 10; 4. 8; 5. 6, 7, &c.
BEAR,] as in 39. 1, 2, &c.
HEART,] *lit.* 'belly,' as in 1. 21; 3. 10, &c.
PREPARE,] as in 11. 13; 27. 16, 17; 28. 27, &c.
DECEIT,] as in 31. 5; Ge. 27. 35, &c.

XVI. 2. MISERABLE,] as in 3. 10; 4. 8, &c.
COMFORTERS,] as in 2 Sa. 10. 3; 1 Ch. 19. 3.
3. WORDS OF WIND,] unsubstantial as such.
EMBOLDEN,] as in 6. 25; 1 K. 2. 8; Mic. 2. 10.
4. STEAD,] overborne by sorrow.
JOIN,] in the cry of the multitude.
NOD,] as in Nu. 32. 13; 2 Sa. 15. 13, &c.
5. HARDEN,] as in 4. 4; De. 2. 30; 3. 28, &c.
SPARING,] as in 7. 11; 30. 10; 33. 18; 38. 23.
6. PAIN,] as in 2. 13; Ps. 39. 2; Isa. 17. 11.
CEASE,] as in 10. 20; 14. 6, 7, &c.
7. WEARIED,] as in Isa. 7. 13; Jer. 12. 5, &c.
DESOLATED,] as in Lev. 26. 31, 32; Nu. 21. 30.
COMPANY,] as in 15. 34; Ex. 12. 3, &c.
8. LOATHE,] as in 22. 16.
WITNESS,] as in v. 19; 10. 17; Ge. 31. 44, &c.
FAILURE,] as in Ps. 59. 12; Hos. 7. 3, &c.
TESTIFIETH,] *lit.* 'answereth,' as in 1. 7, 9.
9. TORN,] as in 18. 4; Ge. 37. 33, &c.
HATETH,] as in 30. 21; Ge. 27. 41; 49. 23.
GNASHED,] as Ps. 35. 16; 37. 12; 112. 10; La. 2. 16.
ADVERSARY,] as in 6. 23; 7. 11; 15. 24, &c.
SHARPENETH,] as in Ge. 4. 22; 1 Sa. 13. 20.
SET,] as in 29. 23; Ps. 119. 131; Isa. 5. 14.
REPROACH,] as in 19. 5; Ge. 30. 23, &c.
CHEEKS,] as in 41. 2; De. 18. 3, &c.
SET,] *lit.* 'filled.'
11. SHUTTETH ME UP,] as in 11. 10; Lev. 13. 4.
PERVERSE,] *lit.* 'evil.'
WICKED,] as in 3. 17; 8. 22; 9. 22, 24, &c.
TURNETH ME OVER,] as in Nu. 22. 32.
12. EASE,] as in 20. 20; 21. 13; 1 Ch. 4. 20.
BREAKETH,] as in 5. 12, &c.
NECK,] as in Ge. 49. 8; Ex. 23. 27, &c.
BREAKETH ME IN PIECES,] as in Jer. 23. 29
MARK,] as in 1 Sa. 20. 20; Neh. 3. 25, &c.
13. ARCHERS.] *or* 'great ones,' as in Jer. 50. 29

SPLITTETH,] as in 39. 3; 2 K. 4. 39, &c.
REINS,] as in 19. 27; Ex. 29. 13, 22, &c.
SPARETH NOT,] as in 6. 10; 20. 13; 27. 22.
POURETH OUT,] 12. 21; Ge. 9. 6, &c.
GALL.] Original word not found elsewhere.
14. BREAKETH,] as in 1. 10; 28. 4, &c.
BREACH,] as in 30. 14; Ge. 38. 29; Jud. 21. 15.
MIGHTY ONE,] as in Ge. 6. 4; 10. 8, 9, &c.
15. SEWED,] as in Ge. 3. 7; Ecc. 3. 7, &c.
ROLLED,] and thus 'defiled' it.
HORN,] as in De. 33. 17; 1 Sa. 2. 1, &c.
16. FOUL,] as in La. 1. 20; 2. 11.
EYE-LIDS,] as in 3. 19; 41. 18; Ps. 11. 4, &c.
DEATH-SHADE,] as in 3. 5; 10. 21, 22, &c.
17. VIOLENCE,] as in 19. 7; Ge. 6. 11, 13, &c.
PRAYER,] as in 2 Sa. 7. 27; 1 K. 8. 28, &c.
PURE,] as in 8. 6; 11. 4; 33. 9, &c.
18. O EARTH,] as in De. 32. 1; Isa. 1. 2; 49.
13; Jer. 6. 13; Mic. 1. 2.
COVER,] as in 9. 24; 15. 27, &c.
CRY,] as in Ge. 18. 20; Neh. 5. 6; 9. 9, &c.
19. WITNESS,] as in v. 8; 10. 17; Ge. 31. 44.
TESTIFIER.] Compare Ge. 31. 47.
HIGH PLACES,] as in 5. 11; 25. 2; 31. 2, &c.
20. INTERPRETER,] as in 33. 23; Ge. 42. 23;
2 Ch. 32. 31; Isa. 43. 27.
FRIEND,] as in v. 21; 2. 11; 6. 14; 12. 4, &c.
DROPPED,] as in Ps. 119. 28; Ecc. 10. 18.
21. REASONETH,] as in 5. 17; 6. 25; 13. 10, 15.
A SON OF MAN,] as in Nu. 23. 19, &c.
22. FEW YEARS,] *lit.* 'a number of years.'
PATH,] as in 6. 18, 19; 8. 13; 13. 27, &c.

XVII. 1. DESTROYED,] as in Isa. 10. 27.
EXTINGUISHED.] Original word not found
elsewhere.
GRAVES,] as in 3. 22; 5. 26; 10. 19; 21. 32.
2. MOCKERIES,] as in 13. 9.
PROVOKINGS,] as in Ps. 78. 17; Isa. 3. 8.
LODGE,] as in 19. 4; 29. 19; 31. 32, &c.
3. PLACE,] as in 21. 5; 22. 22; 41. 8, &c.
I PRAY THEE,] not 'now,' as in C.V.
PLEDGE,] as in 1 Sa. 17. 18; Prov. 17. 18.
STRIKETH HAND,] as in Prov. 6. 1; 11. 15;
17. 18; 22. 26.
4. HIDDEN,] as in 10. 13; 23. 12; 21. 19, &c.
EXALT,] as in Ex. 15. 2; 2 Sa. 22. 49, &c.
5. PORTION,] as in 20. 29; 27. 13; 31. 2, &c.
FRIENDSHIP,] *lit.* 'friends.'
CONSUMED,] as in 4. 9; 7. 6; 11. 20, &c.
6. SET ME UP,] as in Ge. 30. 38; 33. 15; 43. 9.
PROVERB,] as in 13. 12; 27. 1; 29. 1, &c.
PEOPLES,] as in 12. 2, 24; 18. 19; 34. 20, 30.
WONDER,] *lit.* 'a fair thing.'
7. DIM,] as in Ge. 27. 1; De. 34. 7, &c.
MEMBERS,] *lit.* 'formations.'
SHADOW,] as in 7. 2; 8. 9; 14. 2, &c.
8. ASTONISHED,] as in Lev. 26. 32; 1 K. 9. 8.
PROFANE,] as in 8. 13; 13. 16; 15. 34, &c.
STIRRETH HIMSELF UP,] as in 31. 29; Isa.
51. 17; 64. 7, &c.
9. LAYETH HOLD,] as in 16. 12; 18. 9, 20, &c.
CLEAN OF HANDS,] as in Prov. 22. 11.
DUMB,] as in Ex. 4. 11; Ps. 38. 13; Prov. 31. 8.
10. I PRAY YOU,] not 'now,' as in C.V.
11. PASSED BY,] as in 6. 15; 9. 11; 11. 16, &c.
DEVICES,] as in 31. 11; Lev. 18. 17, &c.
BROKEN OFF,] as in 18. 14; Jos. 4. 18, &c.
POSSESSIONS,] as in Isa. 14. 23; Obad. 17.
12. APPOINT,] *lit.* 'set *or* place.'
NEAR,] as in 19. 14; 20. 5.

13. WAIT,] as in 3. 9; 6. 19; 7. 2; 30. 26, &c.
SHEOL,] as in v. 16; 7. 9; 11. 8; 14. 13, &c.
SPREAD OUT,] as in 41. 10; Song 2. 5.
COUCH,] as in Ge. 49. 4; 1 K. 6. 5, 6, 10, &c.
14. CORRUPTION,] as in 9. 31; 33. 18, 22, 24.
FATHER,] the source of his being.
MOTHER..SISTER,] his nearest kindred.
WORM,] as in 7. 5; 21. 26; 24. 20; 25. 6, &c.
15. HOPE,] as in 4. 6; 5. 16; 6. 8; 7. 6; 8. 13.
16. PARTS,] as in 11. 3; 18. 13; 41. 12, &c.
REST,] *or* 'come down,' as in 21. 13; 36. 16.

XVIII. 1. BILDAD,] as in 2. 11, &c.
2. SET AN END,] as in 16. 3; 28. 3, &c.
CONSIDER,] as in 6. 30; 9. 11; 13. 1; 14. 21.
3. RECKONED,] as in 41. 29; Ge. 31. 15, &c.
CATTLE,] as in 12. 7; 35. 11; 40. 15, &c.
DEFILED,] as in Lev. 18. 24; Nu. 5. 13, &c.
4. TEARING,] as in 16. 9; Ps. 22. 13, &c.
SAKE,] as in Ge. 12. 13; 18. 24; 50. 20, &c.
FORSAKEN,] as in Lev. 26. 43; Neh. 13. 11.
REMOVED,] as in 14. 18; 21. 7; Ps. 6. 7, &c.
5. LIGHT,] as in 3. 9, 16, 20; 12. 22, 25, &c.
EXTINGUISHED,] as in v. 6; Prov.13.9; 20.20.
SHINE,] as in 22. 28; Isa. 9. 2, &c.
SPARK,] as in Da. 3. 22; 7. 9.
6. TENT,] as in 5. 24; 8. 22; 11. 14, &c.
LAMP,] as in 21. 17; 29. 3; Ex. 25. 37, &c.
7. STRAITENED,] as in 20. 22; Ge. 32. 7, &c.
STEPS,] as in 14. 16; 31. 4, 37; 34. 21, &c.
COUNSEL,] as in 5. 13; 10. 3; 12. 13; 21. 16.
8. SENT,] as in Ge. 44. 3; Jud. 5. 15, &c.
NET,] as in Ex. 27. 4, 5; Ps. 9. 5, &c.
SNARE,] *lit.* 'checker-work,' as in 1 K. 7. 17.
WALKETH HABITUALLY,] as in 1. 7; 2. 2;
22. 14; 38. 16.
9. SEIZE,] as in v. 20; 16 12; 17. 9; 21. 6.
HEEL,] as in Ge. 3. 15; 25. 26; 49. 17, 19.
GIN,] as in 22. 10; Ex. 39. 3; Nu. 16. 38.
DESIGNING,] as in 5. 5.
10. HIDDEN,] as in 3. 16; 20. 26; 40. 13, &c.
CORD,] as in 21. 17; 36. 8; 39. 3; 41. 1, &c.
TRAP.] Original word not found elsewhere.
11. TERRORS,] as in v. 14; 24. 17; 27. 20, &c.
SCATTERED,] as in 37. 11; 38. 24; Ge. 11. 8.
12. SORROW,] as in 5. 6; 15. 35; 21. 19, &c
CALAMITY,] as in 17,30; 30. 12; 31. 3, &c.
READY,] as in 12. 5; 15. 23; 21. 8; 42. 7, &c.
13. PARTS OF HIS SKIN,] as in 11. 3; 17. 16.
DEATH'S FIRST-BORN.] Comp. Isa. 14. 30.
14. DRAWN,] as in 17. 11; Jos. 4. 18; 8. 16.
CONFIDENCE,] as in 8. 14; 31. 24; Ps. 40. 4.
TO STEP,] as in Ge. 49. 22; Jud. 5. 4, &c.
KING OF TERRORS,] that is, death itself.
15. PROVENDER,] as in 6. 5; 24. 6; Isa. 30. 24.
SCATTERED,] *or* 'spread,' as in Prov. 1. 17.
SULPHUR,] as in Ge. 19. 24; De. 29. 23, &c.
16. ROOTS,] as in 8. 17; 13. 27; 14. 8; 19. 28.
DRIED UP,] as in 8. 12; 12. 15; 14. 11, &c.
CUT OFF,] as in 14. 2; 24. 24; Ps. 37. 2;
Ge. 17. 11.
CROP,] *or* 'harvest,' as in 5. 5; 14. 9, &c.
17. MEMORIAL,] as in Ex. 3. 15; 17. 14, &c.
NAME,] *or* 'renown.'
18. THRUST,] as in Nu. 35. 20; De. 6. 19
HABITABLE EARTH,] as in 34. 13; 37. 12.
CAST HIM OUT,] as in 20. 8, &c.
19.CONTINUATOR,] as in Ge. 21. 23; Isa.14.22
SUCCESSOR,] as in Ge. 21. 23; Isa. 14. 22.
20. WESTERN,] *lit.* 'those behind.'
ASTONISHED,] as in Jer. 4. 9; Eze. 4. 17, &c

EASTERN,] *lit.* 'those before.'
TAKEN,] as in Isa. 21. 3.
FRIGHT,] as in Isa. 28. 2; Eze. 27. 35; 32. 10.
21. PERVERSE,] as in 27. 7; 29. 17; 31. 3;
Zeph. 3. 5.
KNOWN,] nor regarded.

XIX. 2. AFFLICT,] as in Isa. 51. 23; La. 1.
5, 12; 3. 32, &c.
BRUISE,] as in 4. 19; 6. 9, &c.
3. TEN TIMES,] as in Nu. 14. 22; Neh. 4. 12.
SHAME,] as in 11. 3; Jud. 18. 7, &c.
BLUSH,] as in 6. 20; Jud. 3. 25, &c.
STRANGE,] *or* 'harden yourselves.'
4. TRULY,] as in v. 5; 9. 2; 12. 2; 34. 12, &c.
ERRED,] as in 6. 24; Lev. 4. 13, &c.
REMAIN,] *lit.* 'lodge.'
5. MAGNIFY YOURSELF,] as in Ge. 19. 19, &c.
DECIDE,] as in Ge. 24. 14, 44, &c.
REPROACH,] as in 16. 10; Ge. 30. 23, &c.
TURNED ME UPSIDE DOWN,] as in 8. 33, &c.
NET,] as in Prov. 12. 12; Ecc. 7. 26.
7. CRY OUT,] as in 35. 12; Ge. 4. 10, &c.
VIOLENCE,] as in 16. 17; Ge. 6. 11, 13, &c.
CRY ALOUD,] as in 19. 7; 24. 12; 29. 12, &c.
8. HEDGED UP,] as in La. 3. 7, 9; Eze. 13. 5.
PASS NOT OVER,] as in 14. 5, &c.
9. HONOUR,] *lit.* 'weightiness.'
STRIPPETH,] as in 22. 6; Ge. 37. 23, &c.
CROWN,] as in 31. 36; 2 Sa. 12. 30, &c.
10. BREAKETH ME DOWN,] as in Ex. 34. 13.
REMOVETH,] *lit.* 'causeth to journey.'
11. KINDLETH,] as in Neh. 3. 20.
RECKONETH,] as in v. 15; 6. 26; 13. 24, &c.
ADVERSARIES,] as in 6. 23; 7. 11; 15. 24, &c.
12. TROOPS,] as in 25. 3; 29. 25; Ge. 49. 19.
RAISE UP,] as in 30. 12; Ps. 68. 4; Prov.15. 19.
ENCAMP,] as in Ge. 26. 17; 33. 18; Ex. 13. 20.
13. PUT FAR OFF,] as in 11. 14; 13. 21, &c.
ACQUAINTANCES,] as in 24. 1; 34. 2; 42. 11.
ESTRANGED,] as in v. 17; Ps. 58. 3; 78. 30.
14. CEASED,] as in 3. 17; 7. 16; 10. 20; 14. 6.
NEIGHBOURS,] as in 17. 12; 20. 5; Ge. 19. 20.
FAMILIAR FRIENDS,] as in 2 K. 10. 11, &c.
FORGOTTEN,] as in 9. 27; 11. 16; 24. 20, &c.
15. SOJOURNERS,] as in 28. 4; Ex. 3. 22, &c.
MAIDS,] as in 31. 13; Ge. 20. 17, &c.
STRANGER,] as in v. 27; 15. 19; Ex. 29. 33.
RECKON,] as in v. 11.
ALIEN,] as in Ge. 31. 15; Ex. 2. 22, &c.
16. MAKE SUPPLICATION,] as in 8. 5; 9. 15.
17. SPIRIT,] as in 7. 11; 9. 18; 15. 6. 4, 26.
STRANGE,] as in v. 13; Ps. 58. 3; 78. 30.
FAVOURS,] *or* 'entreatings.'
MY WOMB,] that from which I came.
18. SUCKLINGS,] *or* 'perverse,' as in 16. 11.
DESPISED,] as in 5. 17; 7. 16; 8. 20; 9. 21.
19. ABOMINATE ME,] as in 9. 31; 30. 10, &c.
MEN OF MY COUNSEL,] those whom I consulted.
20. CLEAVED,] as in 29. 10; 31. 7; 41. 23, &c.
SOME,] as in 2. 5; 4. 14; 7. 15; 10. 11, &c.
DELIVER MYSELF,] as in 41. 19.
TEETH,] *or* 'a scarlet *or* second skin.'
21. PITY,] *or* 'favour.'
STRICKEN,] as in 1. 11, 19; 2. 5; 4. 5; 5. 19.
22. PURSUE,] as in v. 28; 13. 25; 30. 15, &c.
FLESH,] as in 2. 5; 4. 15; 6. 12; 7. 5, &c.
23. WHO DOTH GRANT,] *lit.* 'give,' as in
Ex. 16. 3, &c.
WRITTEN,] as in 13. 36; 31. 35; Ezra 8. 34.

A BOOK,] *or* 'in the book,' as in 31. 35.
GRAVEN,] as in Isa. 10. 1; 22. 16; 30. 8, &c
24. PEN,] as in Ps. 45. 1; Jer. 8. 8; 17. 1.
IRON,] as in Jer. 17. 1, &c.
LEAD,] as in Ex. 15. 10; Nu. 31. 22, &c.
ROCK,] as in 14. 18; 18. 4; 22. 24; 24. 8, &c
HEWN,] as in De. 6. 11; 8. 9, &c.
25. REDEEMER,] as in Ge. 48 16; Lev. 25. 25.
LIVING,] as in 27. 2; Ge. 16. 14; Nu. 4. 21
LAST,] as in Isa. 41. 4; 44. 6; 48. 12, &c
FOR,] because of, on account of.
DUST,] i.e. the dead, as in 34. 15, &c.
RISE,] not 'stand,' as in C.V.
26. SKIN,] in its various parts.
COMPASSED,] as in Isa. 10. 34; 29. 1; Job
1. 5; 19. 6; Lev. 19. 27; Jos. 6. 3, 11; 1 K. 7.
24; 2 K. 6. 14; 11. 8; 2 Ch. 4. 3; 23. 7; Ps. 17.
9; 22. 16; 48. 12; 88. 7; Isa. 15. 8; La. 3. 5.
It never means 'destroy,' as in C.V.
FROM MY FLESH,] not 'in' it, as in C.V.
27. ON MY SIDE,] *lit.* 'for me.'
STRANGER,] as in v. 13, 15, 17; 15. 19, &c.
CONSUMED,] as in 4. 9; 7. 6, 9; 11. 20, &c.
REINS,] as in 16. 13; Ex. 29. 13, &c.
BOSOM,] as in Ge. 16. 5; Ex. 4. 6, 7, &c.
28. PURSUE,] as in v. 22 above.
OF THE MATTER,] *or* 'of a word' of vindication.
29. FURIOUS,] *lit.* 'heat *or* hot.'
JUDGMENT,] as in 35. 14; 36. 17, &c.

XX. 1. ZOPHAR,] as in 2. 11; 11. 1, &c.
2. THEREFORE,] because of these things.
THOUGHTS,] as in 4. 13.
SENSATIONS,] of shame and anger.
3. CHASTISEMENT,] as in 5. 17; 12. 18, &c.
SHAME,] as in Ps. 4. 2; 35. 26; 44. 15, &c.
4. ANTIQUITY,] as in 19. 24; Ex. 15. 16, &c
PLACING,] as in 5. 11; 37. 15; 38. 9, &c.
5. SINGING,] as in 3. 7; Ps. 63. 5; 100. 2.
PROFANE,] as in 8. 13; 13. 16; 15. 34, &c.
MOMENT,] as in 7. 18; 21. 13; 34. 20, &c.
6. EXCELLENCY,] *or* 'lifting up.'
CLOUD,] as in 22. 14; 26. 8; 30. 15, &c.
7. DUNG,] as in Eze. 4. 12, 15; Zeph. 1. 17.
8. DREAM,] as in 7. 14; 33. 15, &c.
DRIVEN AWAY,] as in 18. 18, &c.
VISION OF THE NIGHT,] as in 4. 13; 7. 14, &c.
9. SEEN,] as in 28. 7; Song 1. 6.
10. OPPRESS,] as in v. 19; 2 Ch.16.10;Ps.74.14.
WEALTH,] as in 18. 7, 12; 40. 60; Ge. 49. 3.
11. BONES,] as in 2. 5; 4. 14; 7. 15; 10. 11, &c.
YOUTH,] as in 33. 25; Ps. 89. 45; Isa. 54. 4
12. SWEETEN,] as in Ps. 55. 14.
HIDE,] as in 6. 10; 15. 18; 27. 11, &c.
13. PITY,] as in 6. 10; 16. 13; 27. 22, &c.
KEEP IT BACK,] as in 7. 12; 31. 36, &c.
PALATE,] as in 6. 30; 12. 11; 29. 10, &c.
14. FOOD,] *lit.* 'bread.'
BITTERNESS,] as in v. 25; 13. 26; De. 32. 32.
ASPS,] as in v. 16; De. 32. 33; Ps. 58. 4, &c
HEART,] *or* 'midst,' as in Ge. 18. 12, &c.
15. WEALTH,] as in v. 18; 5. 5; 15. 29; 21. 7
SWALLOWED,] as in v. 18; 7. 19; Ge. 41. 7.
VOMIT,] as in Lev. 18. 25, 28; 20. 22, &c.
BELLY,] as in 3. 11; 21. 3. 10, &c.
DRIVETH IT OUT,] as in Ex. 34. 24, &c.
16. GALL,] as in Ge. 29. 18; 32. 33; Ps. 69. 21
SUCKETH,] as in 3. 12; De. 33. 19, &c.
VIPER,] as in Isa. 30. 6; 59. 5.
17. RIVULETS,] as in 29. 6; Ps. 1. 3; 46. 4

FLOWINGS,] as in 14. 11; 22. 16; 28. 11, &c.
BROOKS,] as in 6. 15; 21. 33; 22. 24, &c.
HONEY,] as in Ge. 43. 11; Ex. 3. 8, 17, &c.
BUTTER,] as in Ge. 18. 8; De. 32. 14, &c.
18. LABOURED FOR,] as in 9. 29, &c.
CONSUME,] *lit.* 'swallow.'
BULWARK,] as in 2 Sa. 20. 15; 1 K. 21. 23.
EXCHANGE,] as in 15. 31; 28. 17; Lev. 27. 10.
EXULTS,] as in 39. 13.
19. OPPRESSED,] as in v. 10 above.
POOR,] as in v. 10; 5. 16; 31. 16; 34. 19, &c.
TAKEN VIOLENTLY AWAY,] as in 24. 2, 9, 19.
20. EASE,] as in 16. 12; 21. 23; 1 Ch. 4. 40.
DESIRABLE THING,] as in Ps. 39. 11; 44. 9.
DELIVERETH,] as in 6. 23; 22. 30; 29. 12.
21. REMNANT,] as in v. 26; 18. 19; 27. 15, &c.
STAY,] as in Ge. 8. 10; Jud. 3. 25, &c.
22. SUFFICIENCY,] *or* 'smiting.'
STRAITENED,] *lit.* 'there is straitness to him.'
PERVERSE,] as in 3. .20, &c.
MEET,] as an enemy.
23. FIERCENESS OF HIS ANGER,] as in Ex. 15. 12, &c.
24. FLEETH,] as in 9. 25; 14. 2; 27. 22, &c.
WEAPON,] as in 39. 21; 1 K. 10. 25, &c.
BOW OF STEEL,] as in 2 Sa. 22. 35; Ps. 18. 34.
25. BODY,] *or* 'back,' as in 1 K. 14. 9, &c.
GLITTERING WEAPON,] *lit.* 'lightning,' as in 38. 35, &c.
GALL,] as in v. 14 above.
TERRORS,] as in 9. 34; 13. 21; 33. 7; 39. 20.
26. HID,] as in 3. 16; 18. 10; 40. 13, &c.
TREASURES,] as in Ps. 17. 14; 83. 3, &c.
NOT BLOWN,] as in Eze. 22. 20; 37. 9, &c.
BROKEN,] *or* 'evil, unfortunate.'
27. REVEAL,] as in 12. 22; 41. 13, &c.
RAISING ITSELF UP,] as in 27. 7; Ps. 17. 7.
28. REMOVE,] as in 1 Sa. 4. 21, 22; 9. 15, &c.
INCREASE,] as in Lev. 26. 4, 20; De. 11. 17.
POURED FORTH,] as in Ps. 77. 2; La. 3. 49; 2 Sa. 14. 14.
29. PORTION,] as in 17. 5; 27. 13; 31. 2, &c.
INHERITANCE,] as in Ps. 16. 6.
APPOINTED,] *lit.* 'said.'

XXI. 2. WORD,] as in 4. 2, 4; 6. 26; 8. 10, &c.
CONSOLATIONS,] as in 15. 11.
3. BEAR,] *lit.* 'lift me up.'
DERIDE,] as in Neh. 2. 19; 4. 1; Ps. 22. 7.
4. COMPLAINT,] as in 7. 13; 9. 27; 10. 1; 23. 2.
TEMPER,] *lit.* 'spirit.'
SHORT,] as in Nu. 21. 4; Jud. 10. 16; 16. 16; Mic. 2. 7.
5. TURN,] *lit.* 'face;' as in 6. 28, &c.
ASTONISHED,] as in 17. 3; 18. 20; Lev. 26. 32.
HAND TO MOUTH,] as in 29. 9; 39. 34; Mic. 7. 16.
6. TROUBLED,] as in 4. 5; 23. 15; Ge. 45. 3.
TAKEN FRIGHT,] *lit.* 'laid hold on trembling.'
7. LIVE,] and enjoy life without fear.
OLD,] as in Ps. 6. 7.
WEALTH,] *lit.* 'strength.'
8. SEED,] as in 5. 25; 39. 12; Ge. 1. 11, &c.
OFFSPRING,] as in 5. 25; 27. 14; 31. 8, &c.
9. FEAR,] as in 9. 25; 4. 14; 13. 11; 15. 21, &c.
ROD,] as in 9. 34; 37. 13; Ge. 49. 10, &c.
10. BULLOCK,] as in 6. 5; 24. 3; Ge. 32. 5, &c.
EATEN CORN,] old corn, as in Jos. 5. 11, 12.
LOATHE,] as in Lev. 26. 11, 15, 30, 43, 44, &c.
COW,] as in Ge. 32. 15; 41. 2, 3, 4, 18, 19, &c.

BRINGETH FORTH SAFELY,] *lit.* 'causeth to escape.'
MISCARRY,] as in Ge. 27. 45; 31. 38; 42. 36.
11. FLOCK,] as in 1. 3, 16; 30. 1; 42. 12, &c.
SUCKLINGS,] as in 19. 18, &c.
SKIP,] as in 1 Ch. 15. 29, &c.
12. LIFT THEMSELVES UP,] not 'they take' up, as in C.V.
TIMBREL,] as in Ge. 31. 27; Ex. 15. 20, &c.
HARP,] as in 30. 31; Ge. 4. 21; 31. 27, &c.
ORGAN,] as in 30. 31; Ge. 4. 21; Ps. 150. 4.
13. WEAR OUT,] as in 13. 28; Ge. 18. 12, &c.
MOMENT,] as in 7. 18; 20. 5; 34. 20, &c.
SHEOL,] as in 7. 9; 11. 8; 14. 13; 17. 13, &c.
14. AND,] not 'therefore,' as in C.V.
TURN ASIDE,] as in 22. 17; Ge. 19. 2; Nu. 16. 26.
WAYS,] of providence and grace.
DESIRED,] as in 9. 3, 13; 33. 22, &c.
15. SERVE HIM,] by obeying his commands.
PROFIT,] as in 15. 3; 30. 13; 35. 3, &c.
MEET,] as in 36. 32; Ge. 23. 8; 28. 11, &c.
16. COUNSEL OF THE WICKED,] as in 10. 3, &c.
17. HOW OFT,] as in Ps. 78. 40, &c.
LAMP,] as in 18. 6; 29. 3, &c.
EXTINGUISHED,] as in 18. 5, 6, &c.
CALAMITY,] as in v. 30; 18. 12; 30. 12, &c.
PANGS,] as in 18. 10; 36. 8; 39. 3; 41. 1, &c.
APPORTIONETH,] as in 27. 17; 38. 24; 39. 17.
18. STRAW,] as in 41. 27; Ge. 24. 25, 32, &c.
CHAFF,] as in Ps. 1. 4; 35. 5; Isa. 17. 13, &c.
HURRICANE,] as in 27. 30; 37. 9; Ps. 83. 15.
STOLEN AWAY,] as in 27. 20, &c.
19. LAYETH UP,] as in 13; 17. 4; 23. 12.
SORROW,] as in 4. 8; 5. 6; 11. 11, 14; 15. 35.
RECOMPENSE,] as in v. 31; 22. 27; 34. 11, 33.
20. DESTRUCTION.] Original word not found elsewhere.
DRINKETH,] as in 34. 7, &c.
21. DELIGHT,] as in 22. 3; 31. 16; 1 Sa. 15. 22.
NUMBER OF HIS MONTHS,] as in 14. 5, &c.
CUT OFF,] as in 41. 6, &c.
22. KNOWLEDGE,] as in 10. 7; 13. 2; 15. 2, &c.
HIGH,] as in 38. 15; Ex. 14. 8; Nu. 15. 30, &c.
23. PERFECT STRENGTH,] *lit.* 'bone of his perfection.'
EASE,] as in 3. 18; 12. 5; the original word is not found elsewhere.
QUIET,] as in 16. 12; 20. 20; 1 Ch. 4. 40, &c.
24. BREASTS.] Original word is not found elsewhere.
MILK,] as in 10. 10; Ge. 18. 8, &c.
MARROW,] *or* 'fat;' as in Ps. 66. 15; Isa. 5. 17.
MOISTEN,] *or* 'water;' as in Prov. 3. 8, &c.
25. BITTER SOUL,] as in 3. 20; 7. 11; 10. 1.
GLADNESS,] *lit.* 'goodness.'
26. TOGETHER,] not 'alike,' as in C.V.
WORM,] as in 7. 5; 17. 14; 24. 20; 25. 6, &c.
COVER,] as in 9. 24; 15. 27; 16. 18; 22. 11, &c.
27. THOUGHTS,] as in 5. 12; Ge. 6. 5; Ex. 31. 4.
DEVICES,] as in 42. 2; Ps. 10. 2, 4; 21. 11, &c.
DO WRONGFULLY,] *or* 'violently,' as in 15. 33.
28. NOBLE,] *or* 'willing, liberal one.'
29. SIGNS,] as in Ge. 1. 14; 4. 15; 9. 12, 13, 17.
30. CALAMITY,] as in v. 17; 18. 2; 30. 12, &c.
SPARED,] *lit.* 'restrained, kept back.'
BROUGHT,] as in v. 32; 10. 19; Ps. 45. 14, &c.
31. DECLARE,] *or* 'set before.'
RECOMPENSE,] as in v. 19 above.
32. GRAVES,] as in 5. 5; 26; 10. 19, &c.
HEAP,] as in 5. 26; Ex. 22. 5; Jud. 15. 5.
WATCH,] as in Ps. 102. 7; 127. 1; Prov. 8. 34

33. SWEET,] as in 20. 12; 24. 20; Ex. 15. 25.
CLODS,] as in 38. 38.
DRAWETH,] as in 24. 22; 41. 1, &c
NUMBERING,] as in 5. 9; 9. 10, &c.
34. COMFORT,]as in 2. 11; 7. 13; 16.2;29.25,&c.
VANITY,] as in 7. 16; 9. 29; 27. 12; 35. 16, &c.
LEFT,] as in 7. 23; 14. 10; 32. 8; 42. 38, &c.
TRESPASS,] as in Lev. 5. 15; 6. 2; 26. 40, &c.

XXII. 1. ELIPHAZ,] as in 2. 11; 4. 1; 15. 1.
2. PROFITABLE,] as in 15. 3; 34. 9; 35. 3, &c.
3. DELIGHT,]as in 21. 21; 31. 16; 1 Sa. 15. 22.
GAIN,] as in Ge. 37. 26; Ex. 18. 21; Jud. 5. 19.
MAKEST PERFECT,] as in 2 K. 22. 4.
4. REVERENCE,] as in 4. 6; 6. 14; 15. 4, &c.
REASON,] as in 5. 17; 6. 25, &c.
5. ABUNDANT,] as in 1. 3; 5. 25; 31. 25, &c.
NO END,] as in Ecc. 4. 8, 16; 12. 12; Isa. 9. 7.
6. TAKEST A PLEDGE,] as in 24. 3, 9; 34. 31.
NOUGHT,] as in 1. 9; 2. 3; 9. 17; Ge. 29. 15.
STRIP OFF,] as in 19. 9; Ge. 37. 23, &c.
7. WEARY,] as in Ge. 25. 29, 30; De. 25. 18.
DRINK,]as in Ge. 2. 6, 10; 19. 32—35; 21. 19.
WITHHOLDEST,]asin 20. 13; 31. 16; Ge. 30. 2.
8. MAN OF ARM,] that is, of power.
EARTH,] or 'land.'
ACCEPTED OF FACE,] as in 2 K. 5. 1; Isa.
3. 3; 9. 15.
9. WIDOWS,]as in 24. 3, 21; 27. 15; 29. 13, &c.
EMPTY,] as in Ge. 31. 42; Ex. 3. 21; 23. 15.
BRUISED,] as in Isa. 19. 10; 53. 5, &c.
10. SNARES,]as in 18. 9; Jos. 23. 13; Ps. 11. 6.
TROUBLE,] as in 2 Ch. 32. 18; Est. 2. 9, &c.
SUDDENLY,] as in 5. 3; 9. 23; Nu. 6. 9, &c.
11. DARKNESS,] as in 3. 4, 5; 5. 14; 10. 21.
ABUNDANCE,] as in 38. 34; Isa. 60. 6; Eze.
26. 10.
COVER,] as in 9. 24; 15. 17; 16. 18; 21. 26, &c.
12. HIGH,] as in 11. 8; 40. 10, &c.
SUMMIT,] lit. 'head.'
STARS,] as in 3. 9; 9. 7; 25. 5; 38. 7, &c.
HIGH,] as in 21. 22; 38. 15, &c.
13. THICKNESS,] as in 38. 9; Ex 20. 21, &c.
14. THICK CLOUDS,] as in 20. 6; 26. 8; 30. 15.
SECRET PLACE,] as in 13. 10; 24. 15; 31. 27.
CIRCLE,] as in Prov. 8. 14; Isa. 40. 22.
WALKETH HABITUALLY,]or 'up and down.'
15. AGE,] as in 7. 16; 41. 4; Ge. 3. 22, &c.
OBSERVE,] or 'watch.'
INIQUITY,] as in 4. 8; 5. 6; 11. 11, 14, &c.
TRODDEN,] as in 9. 8; 24. 11; Nu. 24. 17, &c.
16. CUT DOWN,] or 'firmly seized;' compare 16. 8.
UNEXPECTEDLY,] lit. 'and no time.'
FLOOD,] as in 14. 11; 20. 17; 28. 11; 40. 23.
POURED OUT,] as in Lev. 21. 10; Ps. 45. 2, &c.
FOUNDATION,] as in 4. 19; Ex. 29. 12, &c.
17. TURN ASIDE,] as in 21. 14; Ge. 19. 2, &c.
18. GOOD,] as in 2. 10; 7. 7; 9. 25; 21. 13, &c.
COUNSEL OF THE WICKED,] as in 10. 3, &c.
19. MOCKETH,] as in 9. 23; 11. 3, &c.
20. SURELY,] lit. 'if not,' as in Ge. 24. 38.
SUBSTANCE,] or 'uprising.'
CUT OFF,] as in 4. 7, &c.
EXCELLENCY,] as in 4. 21; Ge. 49. 3, &c.
21. ACQUAINT THYSELF,]as in Nu. 20. 30,&c.
I PRAY THEE,] not 'now,' as in C.V.
PEACE,] or 'be complete.'
INCREASE,] as in 31. 12; Ge. 47. 24; Ex.23.10.
22. SET,] as in 17. 3; 22. 22; 41. 8, &c.
23. BUILT UP,] as in 12. 14, &c.

24. DUST,] as in 2. 12; 4. 19; 5. 6; 7. 5, 21
DEFENCE,] as in v. 25; 36. 19; Mic. 2. 12.
VALLEYS,] as in 21. 33; 30. 6, &c.
COVERING,] Heb. 'ophir.'
25. DEFENCE,] as in v. 24.
STRENGTH,] as in Nu. 23. 22; 24. 8; Ps. 95. 4
26. DELIGHTEST THYSELF,] as in 27. 10, &c
LIFT UP,] as in 11. 15; 13. 8, 10; 32. 21, &c.
27. SUPPLICATION,] as in Ex. 8. 8, 9; 28. 29.
VOWS,] as in Ge. 28. 20; 31. 13; Lev. 7. 16.
COMPLETEST,] as in De. 23. 21; 2 Sa. 15. 7.
28. DECREEST,] as in Est. 2. 1; lit. 'cut.'
SHONE,] as in 18. 5; Isa. 9. 2.
29. LOW,] as in 40. 11; 1 Sa. 2. 7; 2 Sa. 22. 28.
LIFT UP,] lit. 'pride,' as in 33. 17, &c.
BOWED DOWN,] as in 9. 3; 38. 40, &c.
SAVETH,] as in 5. 15; 26. 3; 40. 14; Ex. 2. 17.
30. NOT INNOCENT.] So Targum ; Sept.
and Vulg. omit 'not.'
DELIVERED,] as in 1. 15, 16, 17, 19, &c.
CLEANNESS,] as in 9: 30; 2 Sa. 22. 21, 25, &c.

XXIII. 2. COMPLAINT,]as in 7. 13; 9. 27, &c.
BITTER,] as in Nu. 17. 11; De. 31. 27, &c.
HAND,] not 'stroke,' as in C.V.
HEAVY,] as in Ge. 13. 2; 18. 20; 48. 10, &c.
SIGHING,] as in 3. 24; Ps. 6. 6; 31. 10, &c.
3. SEAT.] Compare De. 33. 3.
4. A CAUSE,] lit. 'a judgment.'
6. ABUNDANCE,] not 'great,' as in C.V.
STRIVE,] as in 9. 3; 10. 2; 13. 8, 19; 40. 2.
PUTTETH,] placeth or setteth.
7. UPRIGHT,] as in 1. 1, 8; 2. 3; 4. 7; 8. 6, &c
REASON,] as in Ge. 20. 16; Isa. 1. 18.
ESCAPE,] as in 21. 10; 2 Sa. 22. 2, 44, &c.
8. FORWARD,] lit. 'eastward,' as in Ge. 2. 8.
BACKWARD,] as in Ge. 49. 17; Ex. 26. 12, &c
9. LEFT,] as in Ge. 13. 9; 14. 15; 24. 49, &c.
WORKING,] lit. 'doing.'
COVERED,] as in Ps. 61. 2; 65. 13; 73. 6, &c.
RIGHT,] as in 30. 12; 40. 14; Ge. 13. 9, &c.
10. WITH ME,]as in Ge. 21. 23; 29. 19, 27,&c
TRIED,] as in 7. 18; 12. 11; 34. 3, 36, &c
GO FORTH,] from the trial and test.
11. STEP,] as in 31. 7; Ps. 17. 5, 11; 37. 31.
FOOT,] as in 2. 7; 12. 5; 13. 27; 18. 8, 11, &c.
LAID HOLD,]as in 16. 12; 17. 9; 18. 9, 20, &c.
KEPT,] observed, watched, guarded.
TURN NOT ASIDE,] as in 24. 4; 36. 18, &c.
12. COMMAND,] as in Ge. 26. 5; Ex. 15. 26
DEPART NOT,] as in Ex. 13. 22; 33. 11, &c.
ALLOTTED PORTION,] as in v. 14; 14. 5, 13.
LAID UP,] as in 10. 13; 17. 4; 21. 19, &c.
13. DESIRED,] as in 13. 9; Ps. 40. 14. 26, &c.
14. COMPLETE,] as in De. 20. 12; Jos. 10. 1, 4.
PORTION,] as in v. 12.
15. TROUBLED,] as in 4. 5; 21. 6; Ge. 45. 3.
16. SOFT,] or 'tender.'
17. CUT OFF,] as in 6. 17; 2 Sa. 22. 41, &c
DARKNESS,]lit. 'from the face of darkness.'
COVERED,] as in 9. 24; 17. 16; 8; 21. 16.
THICK DARKNESS,] as in 3. 6; 10. 22; 28. 3.

XXIV. 1. WHEREFORE,] as in Ge. 26. 27.
HIDDEN,] as in 24. 1; Jer. 16. 17.
DAYS,] of vengeance and recompense.
2. BORDERS,] as in 38. 20, &c.
REACH,] as in 7. 20; 41. 26; Ge. 31. 25, &c
DROVE,] as in Ge. 29. 2, 3, 8; 30. 40; 32. 16
TAKEN VIOLENTLY AWAY,] as in v. 9, 19, &c
DO EVIL,] as in v. 9, 19; 20. 19; Ge. 21. 25

3. LEAD AWAY,] as in Ge. 31. 18, 26; Ex. 3. 1.
TAKE IN PLEDGE,] as in v. 9; 22. 6; 34. 31.
4. NEEDY,] as in v. 14; 5. 25; 29. 16; 30. 25.
HID,] as in 5. 21; 29. 8, 10, &c.
5. WILD ASSES,] as in 6. 5; 11. 12; 39. 5, &c.
WILDERNESS,] or pasture-land.
WORK,] as in 7. 2; 34. 11; 36. 9, 24; 37. 12.
SEEKING EARLY,] as in 7. 21; 8. 5; Prov.8.17.
PREY,] as in 4. 11; 29. 17; 38. 39; Ge. 49. 9.
MIXTURE.] Sept. 'sweetness.'
FOOD,] *lit.* 'bread,' as in 3. 24; 6. 7; 15. 23.
YOUNG ONES,] as in 1. 5, 16, 17, 19; 29. 5, 8.
6. PROVENDER,] as in 6. 5; Isa. 30. 24.
REAP,] as in 4. 8; 21. 4; Lev. 19. 9, &c.
GLEAN,] the latter growth; Amos 7. 1.
7. CAUSE TO LODGE,] as in Jer. 4. 14.
COLD,] as in 37. 9; Ps. 147. 17; Prov. 25.
20; Nah. 3. 11.
8. INUNDATION,] as in Isa. 4. 6; 25. 4; 28.
2; 30. 30; 32. 2; Hab. 3. 10.
WET,] as in 8. 16.
REFUGE,] as in Ps. 14. 6; 46. 1; 61. 3; 62. 7,
8; 71. 7; 73. 28; 91. 2, 9; 94. 22; 104. 18; 142. 5.
EMBRACED,] as in Ge. 29. 13; 33. 4; 48. 10.
9. ORPHAN,] as in v. 3.
LAY A PLEDGE,] as in v. 3 above.
10. SHEAF,] or 'omer,' as in Ex. 16. 16, &c.
11. WALLS,] as in Ge. 49. 22; 2 Sa. 23. 30;
Ps. 18. 29.
MAKE OIL,] *lit.* 'brightness.'
WINE-PRESSES,] as in Nu. 18. 27, 30, &c.
TRODDEN,] as in 9. 8; 22. 5; Nu. 24. 17, &c.
12. ENMITY,] as in Ps. 73. 20; Hos. 11. 9, &c.
GROAN,] as in Eze. 30. 24; Ex. 2. 24; 6. 5, &c.
PIERCED ONES,] as in 39. 30; Ge. 34. 27, &c.
GIVE,] *lit.* 'set, place.'
13. REBELLIOUS ONES,] as in Neh. 2. 19;
Eze. 2. 3; 20. 38.
DISCERNED,] as in v. 17; 2. 12; 4. 16; 7. 10.
14. LIGHT,] as in v. 13, 16; 3. 9, 16, 20, &c.
MURDERER,] as in Nu. 35. 6, 11, 12, 16, &c.
POOR,] as in v. 4, 9; 29. 12; 34. 28; 36. 6, &c.
THIEF,] as in 30. 5; Ex. 22. 2, 7, 8; De. 24. 7.
15. ADULTERER,] as in Lev. 20. 10.
OBSERVED,] or 'watched.'
TWILIGHT,] as in 3. 9; 7. 4; 1 Sa. 30. 17, &c.
SECRET,] as in 13. 10; 23. 14; 31. 27; 40. 21.
16. DUG,] as in Eze. 8. 8; 12. 5, 7, 12; Am.
9. 2; Jon. 1. 13.
SHUT THEMSELVES UP,] as in 9. 7; 14. 17.
17. DEATH SHADE,] as in 3. 5; 10. 21, 22, &c.
TERRORS,] as in 18. 11, 14; 27. 20; 30. 15.
18. LIGHT,] as in 2. Sa. 2. 18; Ecc. 9. 11, &c.
VILIFIED,] or 'made light of,' as in Ge. 8. 8.
PORTION,] as in Ge. 33. 19; De. 33. 21, &c.
VINEYARDS,] as in v. 6; Ge. 9. 20; Ex. 22. 5.
19. DROUGHT,] as in 30. 3; Ps. 63. 1; 78. 17.
HEAT,] as in 6. 17; Ge. 8. 22; 18. 1; 1 Sa. 11. 9.
SNOW-WATERS,] as in 9. 30.
SHEOL,] as in 7. 9; 11. 8; 14. 13; 17. 13, 16.
SINNED,] that is, 'missed the mark.'
20. WOMB,] as in 3. 11; 10. 18; 31. 15; 38. 8.
SWEETEN,] as in 21. 23, &c.
WORM,] as in 7. 5; 17. 14; 21. 26; 25. 6, &c.
BROKEN,] as in 31. 22; 38. 15; Ex. 22. 10, 14.
21. TREATING EVIL,] or 'feeding' on, as
in 1. 14.
BARREN, as in Ge. 11.30; 25.21; 29.31, &c.
22. DRAWN,] as in 21. 33; 41. 1; Ge. 37. 28.
BELIEVETH,] *lit.* 'remaineth stedfast.'
23. CONFIDENCE,] as in 11. 18; Ge. 34. 25.

SUPPORTED,] as in 8. 15; Ge. 18. 4; Nu. 21. 15.
24. BROUGHT LOW,] as in Ps. 106. 43
Ecc. 10. 18.
SHUT UP,] as in 5. 16; De. 15. 7, &c.
EAR OF CORN,] as in Ge. 41. 5, 6, 7, 22, 23, &c.
OUT OFF,] as in 14. 2; 18. 16; Ge. 17. 11;
Ps. 37. 2.
25. LIAR,] as in 6. 28; 34. 6; 41. 9; Nu. 23. 19.

XXV. 1. BILDAD,] as in 2. 11; 8. 1; 18. 1.
2. RULE,] the exercise of dominion.
FEAR,] as in 3. 25; 4. 14; 13. 11; 15. 21, &c.
MAKING,] *lit.* 'doing.'
HIGH-PLACES,] as in 5. 11; 16. 19; 31. 2, &c.
3. TROOPS,] as in 19. 12; 29. 25; Ge. 49. 19.
LIGHT,] as in 3. 9, 16, 20; 12. 22, 25; 7. 12.
4. RIGHTEOUS,] as in 9. 2, 15, 20; 10. 15, &c.
PURE,] as in 15. 14; Ps. 51. 4; 73. 13, &c.
BORN OF A WOMEN,] as in 14. 1; 15. 14, &c.
5. MOON,] as in 31. 26; Ge. 37. 9; De. 4. 19.
SHINETH.] This original word is not found
elsewhere in this sense.
STARS,] as in 3. 9; 9. 7; 22. 12; 38. 7, &c.
6. GRUB,] as in 7. 5; 17. 14; 21. 26; 24. 20.
WORM,] as in De. 28. 39; Ps. 22. 6; Isa. 14. 11.

XXVI. 2. HELPED,] as in 9. 13; 29. 12, &c.
POWERLESS,] as in La. 1. 6, &c.
SAVED,] or 'eased.'
3. GIVEN COUNSEL,] as in 3. 14; 12. 17, &c.
UNWISE,] *lit.* 'non-wisdom.'
WISE PLANS,] as in 5. 12; 6. 13; 11. 6, &c.
ABUNDANCE,] as in Ge. 30. 30; 48. 16, &c.
4. DECLARED,] *lit.* 'set before.'
BREATH,] as in 4. 9; 27. 3; 32. 8; 33. 4, &c.
5. REPHAIM,] as in Ps. 88. 10; Prov. 2. 18.
FORMED,] as in v. 13; 15. 7; 35. 14; 39. 1.
WATERS,] as in v. 8, 10; 3. 24; 5. 10; 8. 11.
INHABITANTS,] as in 4. 19; Ge. 14. 13, &c.
6. NAKED,] as in 1. 21; 22. 6; 24. 7, 10, &c.
SHEOL,] as in 7. 9; 11. 8; 14. 13; 17. 13, &c.
COVERING,] as in 24. 7; 31. 19; Ge. 20. 16.
DESTRUCTION,] as in 28. 22; 31. 12; Ps. 88. 1.
7. STRETCHING OUT,] as in 9. 8; 1 Ch. 21. 10.
NORTH,] as in 37. 22; Ge. 13. 14; 28. 14, &c.
DESOLATION,] as in 6. 18; 12. 24; Ge. 1. 2.
HANGING,] as in Ge. 40. 19, 22; 41. 13, &c.
NOTHING.] So Sept., Syr., Vulg., Targ., &c.
8. BINDING UP,] as in Prov. 26. 8; 30. 4, &c.
THICK CLOUDS,] as in 20. 6; 22. 14; 30. 15.
CLOUD,] as in v. 9; 7. 9; 37. 11, 15; 38. 9.
RENT,] as in 32. 19; Ge. 7. 11; De. 14. 21.
9. TAKING HOLD,] not 'hold back,' as in C. V.
THRONE,] as in 36. 7; 1 K. 10. 19; Ge. 41. 40.
SPREADING.] This original word is not
found elsewhere.
CLOUD,] as in v. 8.
10. LIMIT,] or 'statute,' as in 14. 5, 13, &c.
PLACED,] This original word is not found
elsewhere.
BOUNDARY,] or 'completion,' as in 11. 7, &c..
LIGHT,] as in 3. 9; 16. 20; 12. 22, 25, &c.
DARKNESS,] as in 3. 4, 5; 5. 14; 10. 21, &c.
11. PILLARS,] as in 9. 6; Ex. 13. 21, 22; 14. 19.
TREMBLE,] or 'are weak, feeble.'
WONDER,] as in 5. 9; Ps. 48. 5, &c.
REBUKE,] as in 2 Sa. 22. 16; Ps. 18. 15, &c.
12. QUIETED,] as in 5. 5; Isa. 51. 15, &c.
SMITTEN,] as in 5. 18; Nu. 24. 8, 17, &c.
PROUD,] as in 9. 13; Ps. 40. 4; 87. 6; 89. 10,
Isa. 30. 7; 51. 9.

SEA,] as in 6. 3; 7. 12; 9. 8; 11. 9, &c.
13. SPIRIT,] as in Ge. 1. 2; Ps. 33. 6; 104. 30.
BEAUTIFIED,] or 'made fair.'
FORMED,] as in v. 5.
FLEEING SERPENT,] as in Isa. 27. 1.
14. BORDERS,] lit. 'ends, extremities.'
LITTLE,] as in 4. 12.
THUNDER,]as in 39. 25; Ps. 77. 18; 81. 7, &c.

XXVII. 1. SIMILE,] as in 13. 12; 29. 1, &c.
2. LIVETH,] as in Jud. 8. 19; Ruth 3. 13, &c.
JUDGMENT,] as in 8. 3; 9. 19, 32; 13, 18, &c.
MIGHTY,] as in 5. 17; 6. 4, 14; 8. 3, 5; 11. 7.
BITTER,] as in 23. 21; Ruth 1. 20; Zec. 12. 10.
3. BREATH,] as in 4. 9; 26. 4; 32. 8; 33. 4.
SPIRIT OF GOD,] as in 33. 4; Ge. 1. 2; 41. 38.
NOSTRILS,] as in 4. 9; 40. 24; 41. 2; Ge. 2. 7.
4. PERVERSENESS,] as in 6. 29, 30; 11. 14.
DECEIT,] as in 13. 7; Ps. 32. 2; 52. 2, &c.
5. POLLUTION TO ME,] as in 34. 10, &c.
JUSTIFY,] as in Ex. 23. 7; De. 25. 1, &c.
EXPIRE,] as in 3. 11; 10. 18; 13. 19; 14. 10.
INTEGRITY,] as in 2. 3, 9; 31. 6; Prov. 11. 3.
6. LAID HOLD,] as in 2. 3, 9; 8. 15, 20; 18. 9.
REPROACH,] as in Ps. 69. 9; 119. 42, &c.
LIVE,] lit. 'from my days.'
7. WICKED,] as in 3. 7; 8. 22; 9. 22, 24; 10, 3.
IS,] not 'let be,' as in C.V.
WITHSTANDER,] as in 20. 27; Ps. 17. 7, &c.
PERVERSE,] as in 18. 21; 29. 17; 31. 3;
Zeph. 3. 5.
8. PROFANE,] as in 8. 13; 13. 16; 15. 34, &c.
CUT OFF,] as in 6. 9; Ps. 10. 3; Prov. 1. 19.
CAST OFF,] or 'draw out,' from the body.
9. CRY] of distress, as the word indicates.
DISTRESS,] as in 5. 19; Ge. 35. 3; 42. 21, &c.
10. DELIGHT HIMSELF,] as in 22. 26; De.
28. 56; Ps. 37. 4, &c.
AT ALL TIMES,] or 'in all time.'
11. SHEW,] as in 6. 24; 8. 10; 12. 7, 8; 30. 19.
HIDE NOT,] as in 6. 10; 15. 18, &c.
12. VAIN,] as in 2 K. 17. 15; Ps. 62. 10, &c.
13. PORTION,] as in 17. 5; 20. 29; 31. 2, &c.
INHERITANCE,] as in 20. 29; 31. 2; 42. 15.
TERRIBLE ONES,] as in 6. 23; 15. 20, &c.
14. SWORD,] as in 1. 15, 17; 5. 20; 15. 22, &c.
OFFSPRING,] as in 5. 25; 21. 8; 31. 8, &c.
SATISFIED,] as in 19. 22; 31. 31; Ex. 16. 8.
15. REMNANT,] as in 18. 19; 20. 21, 26, &c.
WIDOWS,] as in 22. 9; 24. 3, 21; 29. 13, &c.
WEEP,] as in 2. 12; 30. 25, 31; 31. 38, &c.
16. HEAP UP,] as in Ge. 41, 35, 49; Ex. 8. 14.
CLAY,] as in 4. 19; 10. 9; 13. 12; 30. 19, &c.
PREPARE,] as in 11. 13; 15. 35, &c.
CLOTHING,] as in 1 K. 10. 5; 2 K. 10. 22, &c.
17. PUTTETH IT ON,] as in 7. 5; 8. 22; 29. 14.
APPORTION,] as in 39. 17; De. 4. 19; 29. 26.
18. MOTH,] as in 4. 19; 13. 28; Ps. 39. 11, &c.
BOOTH,] as in 36. 29; 38. 40; Ge. 33. 17, &c.
WATCHMAN,]as in 7. 20; Ex. 34. 7; 2 K. 17. 9.
19. RICH,] as in Ex. 30. 15; Ruth 3. 10, &c.
GATHERED,] as in Ge. 25. 8, 17, &c.
OPENED,] as in 14. 3; Ge. 21. 19, &c.
20. OVERTAKE,]as in 24. 2; 41. 26; Ge. 31. 25.
TERRORS,] as in 18. 11, 14; 24. 17; 30. 15, &c.
STOLEN HIM AWAY,] as in 21. 18; 4. 12, &c.
WHIRLWIND,] as in 21. 18; 37. 9; Ps. 83. 15.
21. EAST WIND,] as in 2; 38. 24; Ge. 41. 6.
FRIGHTENETH,] as in Ps. 58. 9; 50. 3, &c.
22. CASTETH,] its force and violence.
SPARE,] as in 6. 10; 16. 13; 20. 13; Ex. 2. 6.

FLEETH,] as in 9. 25; 14. 2; 20. 24, &c.
23. CLAPPETH.] Compare Isa. 2. 6.
HISSETH,] as in 1 K. 9. 8; Isa. 5. 26; 7. 18

XXVIII. 1. SOURCE,] as in 38. 27; Nu. 30. 12
REFINE,] as in 36. 27; Mal. 3. 3; 1 Ch. 28. 18
2. IRON,] as in 19. 24; 20. 24; 40. 18; 41. 27
DUST,] as in 2. 12; 4. 19; 5. 6; 7. 5, 21, &c
FIRM,] as in 41. 23, 24, &c.
BRASS,] as in 20. 24; 40. 18; 41. 27, &c.
3. END,] as in 6. 11; 16. 3; 18. 2; 22. 5, &c.
PERFECTION,] as in 11. 7; 28. 3; Ps. 139
22; Neh. 3. 21.
SEARCHING,] as in 5. 27; 13. 9; 28. 27, &c.
DEATH-SHADE,] as in 3. 5; 10. 21, 22; 12. 22.
4. STREAM,] or 'valley,' that is, a mine.
BROKEN OUT,] or 'he hath broken out.'
SOJOURNER,] as in 19. 15; Ex. 3. 22; 12. 49
THOSE FORGOTTEN OF THE FOOT,] that is
unvisited.
LOW,] as in Ps. 79. 8; 116. 6; 142. 6, &c.
WANDERED,] or 'moved,' as in Ex. 20. 18.
5. BREAD,] as in 3. 24; 6. 7; 15. 23; 20. 14.
UNDER PARTS.] that is, below the surface.
TURNED,] as in 19. 19; 20. 14; 41. 28, &c.
6. SAPPHIRE,] as in v. 16; Ex. 24. 10; 28. 18.
DUST OF GOLD,] that is, golden ore.
7. RAVENOUS FOWL,] as in Ge. 15. 11, &c.
SCORCHED,] as in 20. 9; Song 1. 6.
KITE,] as in Lev. 11. 14; De. 14. 13.
8. TRODDEN,] as in Jud. 20. 43; Ps. 25. 5, 9.
SONS OF PRIDE,] as in 41. 34.
FIERCE LION,] as in 4. 10; 10. 16; Ps. 91. 13.
9. FLINT,] as in De. 8. 15; 32. 13; Ps. 114.
8; Isa. 50. 7.
OVERTURNED,] as in 9. 5; 12. 15; 34. 25, &c.
10. BROOKS,] as in Ge. 41. 1, 2, 3, 17, 18, &c.
CLEAVED,] as in 26. 8; Ge. 22. 3, &c.
PRECIOUS THING,] as in v. 16; 31. 26, &c.
11. OVERFLOWING,] lit. 'weeping.'
BOUND,] as in 5. 18; 34. 17; 40. 13, &c.
HIDDEN THING,] as in 11. 6; Ps. 44. 21, &c.
12. WISDOM,] as in v. 18, 20, 28, &c.
UNDERSTANDING,] as in v. 20, 28, &c.
13. ARRANGEMENT,] as in 41. 12; Ex. 40. 4.
LAND OF THE LIVING,] as in Ps. 27. 13; 52. 5.
14. DEEP,] as in 38. 16, 30; Ge. 1. 2; 7. 11.
SEA,] as in 6. 3; 7. 12; 9. 8; 11. 9; 12. 8, &c.
15. GOLD.] The original word is only
found elsewhere in Hos. 13. 8.
WEIGHED,] as in 6. 2; 31. 6; Ge. 23. 13, &c.
PRICE,] as in De. 23. 18; 2 Sa. 24 24, &c.
16. VALUED,] as in v. 19; lit. 'trodden
down.'
PURE GOLD,] as in v. 19; 31. 24; Ps. 45. 9.
OPHIR,] as in 22. 24; Ge. 10. 29, &c.
PRECIOUS,] as in v. 10.
ONYX,] as in Ge. 2. 12; Ex. 25. 7; 28. 9, 20.
SAPHIRE,] as in v. 6.
17. EQUAL,] as in v. 19; lit. 'set in array.'
CRYSTAL.] Not mentioned elsewhere.
EXCHANGE,] as in 15. 31; 20. 18; Lev. 27. 10.
FINE GOLD,]as Ps. 19. 10; 21. 3; 119. 127,&c.
18. CORAL,] as in Eze. 27. 16.
PEARL.] Not mentioned elsewhere.
ACQUISITION,] lit. 'drawing.'
RUBIES,] as in Prov. 3. 15; 8. 11; 20. 15; 31
10; La. 4. 7.
19. EQUAL,] as in v. 17.
TOPAZ,] as in Ex. 28. 17; 39. 10; Eze. 28. 13
CUSH,] as in Ge. 2. 13, &c.

PURE GOLD,] as in v. 16.
VALUED,] as in v. 16.
20. WISDOM..UNDERSTANDING,] as in v. 12.
21. HID,] as in Lev. 4. 13; 5. 2, 3, 4; Nu. 5. 13.
22. DESTRUCTION,] as in 26. 6; 31. 12, &c.
DEATH,] as in 3. 21; 5. 20; 7. 15; 18. 13, &c.
FAME,] *lit.* 'hearing;' as in 42. 5, &c.
24. ENDS OF THE EARTH,] as in Ex. 16. 35;
De. 13. 7; 28. 49, 64, &c.
25. WEIGHT,] as in Ge. 24. 22; 43. 21, &c.
METED OUT,] as in Ps. 75. 3; Isa. 40. 12, 13.
MEASURE,] as in Ex. 26. 2, 8; 36. 9, 15, &c.
26. LIMIT,] as in 14. 5, 13; 23. 12, 14; 26. 10.
BRIGHTNESS,] as in 38. 25; Zec. 10. 1.
27. DECLARETH,] rehearseth, recounteth.
PREPARED,] *or* 'made ready.'
SEARCHED IT OUT,] as in 5. 27; 13. 9; 29. 16.
28. FEAR OF JEHOVAH,] as in 2 Ch. 19. 9, &c.
TURN FROM EVIL,] as in 1. 1, 8; 2. 3, &c.

XXIX. 1. ADDETH,] as in 27. 1, &c.
2. WHO DOTH MAKE,] *lit.* 'give *or* grant.'
PRESERVING,] watching, guarding, keeping.
3. CAUSING TO SHINE,] as in 31. 26; 41. 18.
LAMP,] as in 18. 6; 21. 17; Ex. 25. 37, &c.
4. MATURITY,] *lit.* 'winter,' as in Ge. 8. 22.
COUNSEL OF GOD,] as in 15. 8; 19. 19, &c.
5. MIGHTY ONE,] who is 'sufficient.'
YOUNG ONES,] as in v. 8; 1. 15, 16, 17, &c.
6. WASHING,] as in 9. 30; Ge. 18. 4; 19. 2.
GOINGS,] as in 6. 19; Ps. 68. 24; Prov. 31.
27; Na. 2. 5; Hab. 3. 6.
BUTTER,] as in 20. 17; Ge. 18. 8; De. 32. 14.
FIRM,] as in 28. 2, &c.
RIVULETS,] as in Ps. 1. 3; 46. 4; 65. 9; 119. 136.
OIL,] as in Ge. 28. 18; 35. 14; Ex. 25. 6, &c.
7. CITY,] *or* 'wall;' as in Prov. 8. 3; 9. 3,
14; 11. 11.
BROAD PLACE,] as in Ge. 19. 2; De. 13. 16, &c.
PREPARE,] *or* 'make ready.'
SEAT,] as in Ge. 10. 30; 27. 39; 36. 43, &c.
8. YOUTHS,] as in v. 5.
HIDDEN,] as in v. 10; 5. 21; 24. 4; Ge. 3. 10.
AGED,] as in 12. 12; 15. 10; 32. 6.
STOOD UP,] as in 4. 16; 8. 15; 14. 2, &c.
9. PRINCES,] as in 3. 15; 34. 14; 39. 25, &c.
KEPT IN,] as in 4. 2; 12. 15; Ge. 16. 2, &c.
MOUTH,] as in 21. 5; 40. 4, &c.
10. LEADERS,] as in 31. 37; 1 Sa. 9. 16, &c.
PALATE,] as in 6. 30; 12. 11; 20. 13; 31. 30.
CLEAVED,] as in 19. 20; 31. 7, &c.
11. DECLARETH ME HAPPY,] as in Ge. 30. 13.
TESTIFIETH,] as in Ge. 43. 3, 13; Ex. 19. 21, 23.
12. DELIVER,] as in 6. 23; 20. 20; 22. 30, &c.
AFFLICTED,] as in 24. 4, 9, 14; 34. 28, &c.
CRYING,] as in 19. 7; 30. 20, 28; 35. 9, &c.
HELPER,] as in 9. 13; 30. 13, &c.
13. PERISHING,] as in 4. 11; 31. 19; De. 26. 5.
CAUSE TO SING,] as in Ps. 65. 8, &c.
14. PUT ON,] as in 7. 5; 8. 22; 27. 17; 40. 10.
ROBE,] as in 1. 20; 2. 12; Ex. 28. 4, &c.
DIADEM,] as in Isa 3. 23; 62. 3; Zec. 3. 5.
15. BLIND,] as in Ex. 4. 11; Lev. 19. 14, &c.
LAME,] *or* 'limping,' as in Lev. 21. 18, &c.
16. NEEDY,] as in 5. 15; 24. 4, 14, &c.
CAUSE,] as in 5. 15; 24. 4, 14; 30. 25; 31. 19.
SEARCH OUT,] as in 5. 27; 13. 9; 28. 3, 27, &c.
17. BREAK,] *lit.* 'shiver.'
JAW-TEETH,] as in Prov. 30. 14; Joel 1. 6.
PERVERSE,] as in 18. 21; 27. 7; 31. 3; Zep. 3. 5.
CAST AWAY,] as in 15. 33; 18. 7; 27. 22. &c.

PREY,] as in 4. 11; 24. 5; 38. 39, &c.
18. WITH MY NEST,] not 'in' it, as in C. V.
EXPIRE,] as in 3. 11; 10. 18; 13. 19; 14. 10.
SAND,] as in 6. 3; Ge. 22. 17; 32. 12; 41. 49.
19. ROOT,] as in 8. 17; 13. 27; 14. 8; 18. 16.
OPEN,] as in Nu. 19. 15; Jos. 8. 17; 1 K. 8. 29.
DEW,] as in 38. 28; Ge. 27. 28, 39, &c.
BRANCH,] *or* 'harvest, crop,' as in 5. 5, &c.
20. HONOUR,] as in 19. 9; Ge. 31. 1; 45. 13.
FRESH,] *lit.* 'new.'
RENEWED,] *lit.* 'changed ;' as in 14. 7, &c.
21. WAIT,] as in v. 23; 6. 11; 13. 15; 14. 14.
SILENT,] as in 30. 27; 31. 34; Jos. 10. 12, &c.
22. CHANGE,] as in 14. 20; 1 Sa. 21. 13, &c.
SPEECH,] as in 4. 2, 4; 6. 26; 8. 10; 12. 11, &c.
DROP,] as in Jud. 5. 4; Ps. 68. 8; Prov. 5. 3.
23. WAIT,] as in v. 21.
RAIN,] as in 5. 10; 28. 26; 36. 37; 37. 6, &c.
OPENED WIDE,] as in 16. 10; Ps. 119. 131;
Isa. 5. 14.
LATTER RAIN,] as in De. 11. 14; Prov. 16. 15.
24. LAUGH,] as in 5. 22; 30. 1; 39. 7, 18, &c.
CREDENCE,] as in 4. 18; 9. 16; 15. 15, 21, 31.
FALL,] as in 6. 27; Ge. 2. 21; Ex. 21. 27, &c.
25. CHOOSE,] as in 7. 15; 9. 14, 15. 5; 34. 4, &c.
HEAD,] as in 1. 17, 20; 2. 12; 10. 15; 12. 24.
TROOP,] as in 19. 12; 25. 3; Ge. 49. 19, &c.
COMFORT,] as in 2. 11; 16. 2; 17. 13; 42. 11.

XXX. 1. LAUGHED,] as in 5. 22; 29. 24, &c.
YOUNGER,] *lit.* 'lesser.'
LOATHED,] as in 5. 17; 7. 16; 8. 20; 9. 21, &c.
FLOCK,] as in 1. 3, 16; 21. 11; 42. 12, &c.
2. POWER OF THEIR HANDS,] as in Isa. 10. 13.
OLD AGE,] as in 5. 26.
3. WANT,] as in Prov. 28. 22.
FAMINE,] as in 5. 22.
GLOOMY,] as in 3. 7; 15. 34; Isa. 49. 21.
FLEEING,] as in v. 17.
DRY PLACE,] as in 24. 19; Ps. 63. 1; 78. 17
FORMERLY,] *lit.* 'yesternight.'
DESOLATION,] as in v. 14; 38. 27; Ps. 35. 8.
WASTE,] as in 38. 37; Zeph. 1. 5.
4. CROPPING,] as in 8. 12; De. 23. 25; Eze
17. 4, 22.
MALLOWS.] Not noticed elsewhere.
SHRUB,] as in v. 7; Ge. 2. 5; 21. 15.
BROOM,] as in 1 K. 19. 4, 5; Ps. 120. 4.
5. MIDST,] *or* 'body' politic.
CAST OUT,] as in Ge. 3. 24; 4. 14; Ex. 2. 17.
SHOUT,] as in 38. 7; Nu. 10. 7, 9, &c.
THIEF,] as in 24. 14; Ex. 22. 2, 7, 8, &c.
6. FRIGHTFUL PLACE,] as in 6. 23; 15. 20, &c.
VALLEYS,] as in 31. 34; 38. 22, 24; 28. 4, &c.
HOLES,] as in 1 Sa. 14. 11; 2 K. 12. 9, &c.
CLEFTS,] as in Jer. 4. 29.
7. SHRUBS,] as in v. 4.
GROAN,] *or* 'bray,' as in 6. 5.
NETTLES,] as in Jud. 9. 14; 2 K. 14. 9.
GATHERED,] as in 1 Sa. 2. 36; Isa. 14. 1;
Hab. 2. 15.
8. FOLLY,] as in 2. 10; De. 32. 6, 21, &c.
SONS WITHOUT NAME] orrenown, unknown.
SMITTEN,] as in Ps. 109. 16; Da. 11. 30;
Eze. 13. 22.
9. SONG,] as in Ps. 4. 1; 6. 1; 54. 1; 55. 1;
61. 1; 67. 1; 69. 12; 76. 1; 77. 6; Isa. 38. 30;
La. 3. 14; 5. 14; Hab. 3. 19.
BYEWORD,] *or* simply a 'word,' as in 4. 2.
10. ABOMINATED,] as in 9. 31; 15. 16; 19. 19.
KEPT FAR,] as in 5. 4; 21. 16; 22. 18, &c.

2 A

SPARED,] as in 7. 11; 16. 5; 33. 18; 38. 23, &c.
SPIT,] as in 7. 19; Lev. 15. 8; Isa. 50. 6.
11. CORD,] as in Jud. 16. 7, 8, 9; Ps. 11. 2.
LOOSED] or 'opened,' as in 11. 12; 39. 5, &c.
AFFLICTETH,] as in 37. 23; Ge. 15. 13, &c.
BRIDLE,] as in 41. 13; Ps. 32. 9; Isa. 30. 28.
CAST AWAY,] as in 8. 4; 12. 15; 14. 20, &c.
12. BROOD.] So Sept. Vulg. 'calamities.'
CAST AWAY,] as in v. 11.
CALAMITY,] as in 18. 12; 21. 17, 30; 31. 3, &c.
13. BROKEN DOWN,] or 'plucked up,' perhaps.
PROFIT,] as in 15. 3; 21. 15; 35. 3; 1 Sa. 12. 21.
HELPER,] as in 9. 13; 26. 2; 29. 12, &c.
14. WIDE BREACH,] as in 16. 14; 11. 9, &c.
DESOLATION,] as in v. 3; 38. 27; Ps. 35. 8.
ROLLED THEMSELVES,] as in Ge. 43. 18; 2 Sa. 20. 12.
15. TERRORS,] as in 18. 11, 14; 24. 17, &c.
PURSUETH,] as in 13. 25; 19. 22, 28; Ge. 14. 14.
ABUNDANCE,] or 'nobleness;' as in 12. 21.
THICK CLOUD,] as in 20. 6; 22. 14; 26. 8, &c.
SAFETY,] as in 13. 16; Ge. 49. 18, &c.
16. POURETH ITSELF OUT,] as in La. 2.12; 4.1.
SEIZE,] as in 16. 12; 17. 9; 18. 9, 20; 21. 6.
DAYS OF AFFLICTION,] as in v. 27; La. 1. 7.
17. BONE,] as in 2. 5; 4. 14; 7. 15; 10. 11, &c.
PIERCED,] as in Nu. 16. 14; Jud. 16. 21, &c.
EYE-LID,] as in v. 3.
18. ABUNDANCE OF POWER,] as in 23. 6, &c.
CLOTHING,] as in 24. 7, 10; 31. 19; 38. 9, &c.
CHANGED,] or 'change itself,' as in 1 Sa. 28. 8, &c.
COAT,] as in Ge. 3. 21; 27. 3, 23, 31, 32, &c.
GIRD,] as in 38. 3; 40. 7; 1 Sa. 2. 4, &c.
19. CASTING,] as in 38. 6, &c.
MIRE,] as in 4. 19; 10. 9; 13. 12; 27. 16, &c.
DUST AND ASHES,] as in 42. 6; Ge. 18. 27.
20. CRY,] as in v. 28; 19. 7; 24. 12; 35. 9, &c.
STOOD] up or still, as in 4. 16; 8. 15; 14. 2.
CONSIDER,] as in 11. 11; 23. 15; 26. 14, &c.
21. FIERCE,] as in 41. 10; De. 32. 33; La. 4. 3.
OPPOSEST,] as in 16. 9; Ge. 27. 41; 49. 23; 50. 15; Ps. 55. 3.
22. LIFT ME UP,] as in 2. 12; 6. 2; 7. 13, &c.
TO RIDE,] as in Ge. 41. 43; Ex. 4. 20, &c.
MELTEST,] as in Ps. 65. 10.
LEVELEST,] as in Isa. 28. 25.
23. BRING ME BACK,] as in 9. 12, 13; 10. 9.
APPOINTED,] as in 1 Sa. 13. 11, &c.
24. HEAP,] as in Ps. 79. 1; Jer. 26. 19; Mic. 1. 6; 3. 12.
RUIN,] as in 31. 29; Prov. 24. 22.
SAFETY,] or 'opulence,' as in 36. 19, &c.
25. WEEP,] as in v. 31; 2. 12; 27. 15; 31. 38.
HARD,] as in Ge. 42. 7, 30; Ex. 1. 14; 6. 9, &c.
GRIEVED.] The original word is not found elsewhere.
NEEDY,] as in 5. 15; 24. 4, 14; 29. 16, &c.
26. EXPECTED,] as in 3. 9; 6. 19; 7. 2, &c.
WAIT,] as in 6. 11; 13. 15; 14. 14; 29. 21, &c.
27. BOWELS,] as in 20. 14; Ge. 15. 4; 25. 23.
BOILED,] as in 41. 31; Eze. 24. 5.
CEASED,] lit. 'dumb, silent.'
DAYS OF AFFLICTION,] as in v. 16.
28. MOURNING,] or 'black,' as in 5. 11, &c.
SUN,] as in Ps. 19. 6; Song 6. 10; Isa. 24. 23; 30. 26.
ASSEMBLY,] as in Ge. 28. 3; 35. 11; 48. 4, &c.
CRY,] as in v. 20.
29. BROTHER,] as in Prov. 18. 9.
DRAGONS,] as in Ps. 44. 19; Isa. 33. 22, &c.

COMPANION,] lit. 'friend.'
DAUGHTERS OF THE OSTRICH,] as in Lev. 11. 16; De. 14. 15, &c.
30. SKIN,] as in 2. 4; 7. 5; 10. 11; 18. 13, &c.
BLACK,] as in Lev. 13. 31, 37; Song 1. 5, &c.
BONE,] as in v. 17.
BURNED,] or 'kindled,' as in 32. 2, 3; 42. 7.
HEAT,] as in Ge. 31. 40; Jud. 6. 37, 39, &c.
31. HARP,] as in 21. 12; Ge. 4. 21; 31. 27, &c.
MOURNING,] as in Ge. 27. 41; 50. 10, 11, &c.
ORGAN,] as in 21. 12; Ge. 4. 21; Ps. 150. 4.
SOUND OF WEEPING,] or 'weepers,' as in Ex. 2. 6, &c.

XXXI. 1. COVENANT,] as in 5. 23; 41. 4, &c.
ATTEND,] as in 11. 11; 23. 15.
VIRGIN,] as in Ge. 24. 16; Ex. 22. 16, 17, &c.
2. PORTION,] as in 20. 29; 27. 13; 32. 17.
INHERITANCE,] as in 20. 29; 27. 13; 42. 15, &c.
HEIGHTS,] as in 5. 11; 16. 19; 25. 2; 39. 18.
3. CALAMITY,] as in v. 23; 18. 12; 21. 17, &c.
PERVERSE,] as in 18. 21; 27. 7; 29. 17; Zep. 3.5.
STRANGENESS,] or a 'strange thing.'
WORKERS OF INIQUITY,] as in 34. 8, 22, &c.
4. STEPS,] as in v. 37; 14. 16; 18. 7; 34. 21.
NUMBER,] as in 14. 16; 39. 2, &c.
5. VANITY,] as in 7. 3; 11. 11; 15. 31; 35. 15.
HASTEN,] as in 20. 2; De. 32. 35, &c.
TO DECEIT,] lit. 'on or with deceit.'
6. WEIGH,] as in Ge. 23. 16; Ex. 22. 17, &c.
BALANCES,] as in 6. 2; Lev. 19. 36; Ps. 62. 9.
INTEGRITY,] as in 2. 3, 9; 27. 5; Prov. 11. 3.
7. STEP,] as in 23.16; Ps. 17. 5, 11; 37. 31, &c.
HEART,] as in v. 9, 27, &c.
CLEAVED,] as in 19. 20; 29. 10; 41. 23, &c.
BLEMISH,] as in Da. 1. 4.
8. SOW,] as in 4. 8; Ge. 26. 12; 47. 23, &c.
PRODUCTS,] as in 5. 25; 21. 8; 27. 14, &c.
ROOTED OUT,] as in v. 12.
9. ENTICED,] as in v. 27; 5. 2; Ex. 22. 16, &c.
OPENING,] as in v. 34; Ge. 4. 7; 6. 16, &c.
LAID WAIT,] as in De. 19. 11; Jud. 9. 31, &c.
10. GRIND,] as in Ex. 32. 20; Nu. 11. 8, &c.
BEND,] as in 4. 4; 39. 3; Ge. 49. 9, &c.
11. WICKED THING,] as in 17. 11; Lev. 18. 17.
JUDICIAL,] lit. 'iniquity (for) judges.'
12. FIRE,] as in 1. 16; 15. 34; 18. 5; 20. 26.
DESTRUCTION,] as in 26. 6; 28. 22; Ps. 88. 1.
INCREASE,] as in Ge. 47. 24; Ex. 23. 10, &c.
TAKE ROOT,] as in Ps. 52. 5; Isa. 40. 24, &c.
13. DESPISE,] as in 5. 17; 7. 16; 8. 20; 9. 21.
MAN-SERVANT,] as in 1. 8; 2. 3; 3. 19; 4. 18.
HAND-MAID,] as in 19. 15; Ge. 20. 17, &c.
CONTENDING,] as in v. 35; 13. 6; 19. 16, &c.
14. ARISETH,] as in Ps. 12. 5; 68. 1; 102. 13.
INSPECT,] as in 5. 24; 7. 18; 34. 13; 35. 15.
15. WOMB,] as in v. 18; 1. 21; 3. 10, 11, &c.
PREPARE,] or 'make ready,' as in 8. 8, &c.
ONE,] as in 13. 4; 23; Mal. 2. 10, 15, &c.
16. WITHHELD,] as in 20. 13; 22. 7; 38. 15.
PLEASURE,] as in 21. 21; 22. 3; 1 Sa. 15. 22.
POOR,] as in 5. 16; 20. 10, 19; 34. 19, 28, &c.
CONSUME,] as in 9. 22; 21. 13; 36. 11, &c.
17. MORSEL,] as in 42. 11; Ge. 18. 5; Lev. 2. 6, &c.
ORPHAN,] as in v. 21; 6. 27; 22. 9; 24. 3, &c.
18. YOUTH,] as in 13. 26; Ge. 8. 21, &c.
GREW UP] or 'he made me great as a father.'
LED,] as in 12. 23; 38. 32; Ge. 24. 48, &c.
19. PERISHING,] as in 4. 11; 29. 13; De. 26. 5.
COVERING,] as in 24. 7; 26. 6; Ge. 20. 16, &c.
20. LOINS,] as in 38. 3; 40. 7; Ge. 35. 11, &c.

FLEECE,] as in De 18. 4; Ps. 72. 6; Am. 7. 1.
WARM HIMSELF,] as in 39. 14, &c.
21. WAVED,] as in Ex. 20. 25; 29. 24, 26, &c.
COURT,] as in 2 Ch. 4. 9; 6. 13; Eze. 43. 14,
17, 20; 45. 19.
22. SHOULDER,] as in Ex. 26. 14, 15; 28. 7, &c.
BLADE,] as in v. 36; Ge. 9. 23; 21. 14, &c.
ARM,] as in Jer. 32. 21.
BROKEN,] *lit.* 'shivered.'
23. DREAD,] as in 3. 25; 4. 14; 13. 11; 15. 21.
CALAMITY,] as in v. 3; 18. 12; 21. 17, 30.
EXCELLENCY,] as in 13. 11; 41. 25; Ge. 4. 7.
24. CONFIDENCE,] as in 8. 14; 15. 27, &c.
PURE GOLD,] as in 28. 16, 19; Ps. 45. 9, &c.
TRUST,] as in 8. 14; 18. 14; Ps. 40. 4, &c.
25. WEALTH,] as in 5. 5; 15. 29; 20. 15, &c.
FOUND,] as in v. 29; 3. 33; 11. 7; 17. 10, &c.
26. LIGHT,] as in 3. 9, 16, 20; 12. 22, 25, &c.
PRECIOUS,] as in 28. 16; 1 Sa. 3. 1, &c.
27. ENTICED,] as in v. 9 above.
SECRET,] as in 13. 10; 22. 14; 24. 15, &c.
KISS,] as in Ge. 27. 26, 27; 29. 11; 33. 4, &c.
28. JUDICIAL.] Compare v. 11.
LIED,] as in 8. 18; Ge. 18. 15; Lev. 6. 2, &c.
29. RUIN,] as in 30. 24; Prov. 24. 22.
STIRRED UP MYSELF,] as in 17. 8; Isa. 51. 17.
FOUND,] as in v. 25.
30. SUFFERED,] *lit.* 'given.'
OATH,] as in Ge. 24. 41; 26. 28; Lev. 5. 1, &c.
31. MEN,] as in 11. 3, 11; 19. 19; 22. 15, &c.
TENT,] as in 5. 24; 8. 22; 11. 14; 12. 6, &c.
OH THAT,] *lit.* 'who doth give,' as in 6. 8.
SATISFIED,] as in 19. 22; 27. 14; Ex. 16. 12.
32. STREET,] *lit.* 'out-place,' as in 5. 10, &c.
STRANGER,] *or* 'sojourner,' as in Ge. 15. 13.
TRAVELLER,] *lit.* 'path,' as in 6. 18, 19, &c.
33. COVERED,] as in 9. 24; 15. 27; 16. 18, &c.
ADAM.] So Targ., Schultens, Rosenmuller,
&c., *or* 'as a man;' so Vulg., Luther, &c.
BOSOM.] Original word not found again.
34. FEAR,] as in 13. 25; De. 1. 29; 7. 21, &c.
MULTITUDE,] as in 39. 7; Ge. 17. 4, 5, &c.
CONTEMPT,] as in 12. 5, 21; Ge. 38. 23, &c.
FAMILIES,] as in 32. 2; Ge. 8. 19; 10. 5, &c.
AFFRIGHT,] *or* 'break down,' as in 32. 15, &c.
SILENT,] as in 29. 21; 30. 27; Ex. 15. 16, &c.
OPENING,] as in v. 9.
35. HEARING,] as in 34. 34; Ge. 18. 10, &c.
MARK,] as in Eze. 9. 4, 6.
MIGHTY ONE,] as in 5. 17; 6. 4, 14; 8. 3, &c.
BILL,] *lit.* a 'book.'
ADVERSARY,] *lit.* 'man of my strife.'
36. SHOULDER,] as in Ge. 9. 23; 21. 14, &c.
BIND,] as in Prov. 6. 21.
CROWN,] as in 19. 9; 2 Sa. 12. 30; 1 Ch. 20. 2.
37. STEPS,] as in v. 4.
LEADER,] as in 29. 10; 1 Sa. 9. 16; 10. 1, &c.
APPROACH,] as in 33. 22; Ge. 20. 4; 27. 41.
38. LAND,] *or* 'ground,' as in 5. 6; Ge. 1. 25.
CRY OUT,] as in Ex. 2. 23; Jud. 3. 9, 15, &c.
FURROWS,] as in 39. 10; Ps. 65. 10; Hos.
0. 4; 12. 11.
39. STRENGTH,] *or* 'power,' as in Ge. 4. 12.
MONEY,] *lit.* 'silver.'
POSSESSORS,] *or* 'lords, owners.'
BREATHE OUT,] as in Mal. 1. 13.
40. WHEAT,] as in Ge. 30. 14; Ex. 9. 32, &c.
THORN,] as in 41. 2; 1 Sa. 13. 6; 2 K. 14. 9.
BARLEY,] as in Ex. 9. 31; Lev. 27. 16, &c.
USELESS WEED,] *lit.* 'stinking.'
ARE FINISHED,] *lit.* 'have been finished.'

XXXII. 1. THREE MEN,] Eliphaz, Bildad,
and Zophar.
EYES,] as in 11. 4; 15. 15; 18. 3; 19. 15, &c.
2. BURN,] as in v. 3, 5; 42. 7; Ge. 30. 2, &c.
ELIHU,] i.e. 'my God (is) He;' as in v. 5,
6; 34. 1; 36. 1.
BARACHEL,] i.e. 'blessed of God,' as in v. 6.
BUZITE,] i.e. 'despised one;' see Jer. 25. 23.
FAMILY,] as in 31. 34; Ge. 8. 19; 10. 5, 18, &c.
RAM,] i.e. 'high one.'
MORE THAN,] was more anxious to do so.
3. NOT FOUND,] arguments sufficiently
strong.
CONDEMN,] *or* 'declare him in a wrong
state.'
4. WAITED EARNESTLY,] as in 3. 21, &c.
IN DAYS,] in respect of days.
5. NO ANSWER,] as in v. 1, 3.
6. ANSWERETH,] as in 3. 2; 4. 1; 6. 1; 8. 1.
YOUNG,] *lit.* 'little,' as in 30. 1, &c.
AGED,] as in 12. 12; 15. 10; 29. 8.
SHOWING,] as in v. 10, 17; 15. 17; 36. 2; Ps. 19. 2.
OPINION,] as in v. 10, 17; 36. 3; 37. 16, &c.
7. DAYS,] as in 12. 12, &c.
TEACH,] *lit.* 'make known,' as in 10. 2, &c.
8. SPIRIT,] as in 2 K. 19. 28, &c.
BREATH,] as in 4. 9; 33. 4; 37. 10, &c.
UNDERSTAND,] as in v. 9; 6. 24, &c.
9. MULTITUDE,] not 'great;' as in 35. 9, &c.
JUDGMENT,] as in 8. 3; 9. 19, 32; 13. 18, &c
10. OPINION,] as in v. 7.
11. WAITED,] as in v. 16; 1 Sa. 10. 8; 13. 8.
REASONS,] as in 12. 12, 13; 26. 12; Ex. 31. 3.
SEARCH OUT,] as in 5. 27; 13. 9; 28. 27, &c.
12. ATTENDED,] as in 11. 11; 23. 15; 26. 14, &c.
FOR JOB,] fit for him, not 'like' him, as in C. V
13. THRUST AWAY,] as in 13. 25; Ps. 1. 4; 68. 2.
14. SET IN ARRAY,] as in 6. 4; 13. 18; 23. 4.
SAYINGS,] as in v. 12; 6. 10, 25, 26; 8. 2, &c.
15. BROKEN DOWN,] as in 2 K. 19. 26, &c.
REMOVED,] as in 9. 5; Ge. 12. 8; 26. 22, &c.
16. WAITED,] as in v. 11.
STOOD STILL,] as in 4. 16; 8. 15; 14. 2, &c.
17. SHARE,] *or* 'portion,' as in 20. 29, &c.
OPINION,] as in v. 6, 10.
18. FULL OF WORDS,] as in 4. 2; 16. 4, &c.
DISTRESSED ME,] as in De. 28. 53, 55, 57, &c.
BREAST,] *lit.* 'belly, body.'
19. OPENED,] as in 12. 14; Ge. 7. 11, &c.
BOTTLES.] Everywhere else the original
word signifies a 'familiar spirit;' as in Lev.
19. 31, &c.
BROKEN UP,] as in 26. 8; Ge. 7. 11, &c.
20. REFRESHMENT,] as in 1 Sa. 16. 23.
21. ACCEPT,] *lit.* 'lift up,' as in 11. 15, &c.
GIVE FLATTERING TITLES,] as in v. 22; Isa.
44. 5; 45. 4.
22. NOT KNOWN,] as in 5. 24, 25; 9. 2, 5, &c.
IN A LITTLE,] *lit.* 'as a little thing.'
MAKER,] as in 4. 17; 31. 15; 35. 10; 40. 19.

XXXIII. 1. SPEECHES,] as in v. 8, 32, &c.
GIVE EAR,] as in 34. 2, 16; 37. 14, &c.
2. I PRAY THEE,] not 'now,' as in C. V.
PALATE,] as in 6. 30; 12. 11; 20. 13; 29. 13.
3. UPRIGHTNESS,] as in v. 23; 6. 25; De. 9. 5.
CLEARLY,] as in Zeph. 3. 9; Isa. 40. 2, &c
4. SPIRIT OF GOD,] as in 27. 3; 26. 13.
MADE,] as in 10. 9; 12. 9; 31. 15; 40. 15, &c
BREATH,] as in 32. 8, &c.
QUICKEN ME,] *or* 'give me life.'

5. SET IN ARRAY,] as in 6. 4; 13. 18; 23. 4.
STATION THYSELF,] as in Ex. 8. 20; 9. 13.
6. WORD,] *lit.* 'mouth.'
CLAY,] as in 4. 19; 10. 9; 13. 12; 27. 16, &c.
FORMED,] *lit.* 'nipped;' as in Ps. 35. 19, &c.
7. TERROR,] as in 9. 34; 13. 21; 20. 25, &c.
FRIGHTEN,] as in 3. 5; 7. 14; 9. 34; 13. 11, &c.
BURDEN.] The original word is not found elsewhere.
HEAVY,] as in 6. 3; 23. 2; Ex. 5. 9, &c.
8. EARS,] as in 4. 12; 12. 11; 13. 1, 17, &c.
9. PURE,] as in 8. 6; 11. 4; 16. 17; Ex. 27. 20.
TRANSGRESSION,] as in 7. 21; 8. 4; 13. 23, &c.
INNOCENT.] The original word is not found elsewhere.
10. OCCASIONS,] as in Nu. 14. 34.
RECKON,] as in 6. 26; 13. 24; 19. 11, 15, &c.
11. STOCKS,] as in 13. 27.
WATCH,] *or* 'observe.'
12. RIGHT,] *or* 'just.'
GREATER,] in wisdom, power and uprightness.
13. STRIVEN,] as in 9. 3; 10. 2; 13. 8, 19, &c.
ANSWERETH NOT,] nor giveth account.
14. ONCE..TWICE,] *lit.* 'in one..in two.'
15. DREAM,] as in 7. 14; 20. 8; Ge. 20. 3, &c.
VISION OF NIGHT,] as in 4. 13; 7. 14; 20. 8.
DEEP SLEEP,] as in 4. 13; Ge. 2. 21; 15. 12.
SLUMBERINGS,] as in Ps. 132. 4;Prov.6.4,10.
BED,] as in v. 19; 7. 13; Ge. 49. 4; Ex. 8. 3.
16. UNCOVERETH THE EAR,] as in 36. 10, 15.
INSTRUCTION,] as in 5. 17; 12. 18; 20. 3, &c.
SEALETH,] as in 9. 7; 14. 17; 24. 16; 37. 7.
17. DOING] unrighteousness ; so Sept.
PRIDE,] as in 22. 29; Jer. 13. 17; Da. 4. 37.
CONCEALETH,] as in 9. 24; 15. 27; 16. 18, &c.
18. CORRUPTION,] as in v. 22, 24, 28, 30, &c.
DART,] as in 36. 12; 2 Ch. 23. 10; 32. 5, &c.
19. REPROVED,] as in 5. 17; 6. 25, 26, &c.
PAIN,] as in Ex. 7. 3; 2 Ch. 6. 29; Ps. 32. 10.
BED,] as in v. 15.
STRIFE,] as in 13. 6; 29. 16; 31. 13, 35, &c.
ENDURING,] as in 12. 19; Ge. 49. 24, &c.
20. NAUSEATED.] Original word not found again.
DESIRABLE,] as in Ge. 3. 6; 49. 26; Nu. 11. 4.
21. CONSUMED,] as in 4. 9; 7. 6, 9; 11. 20, &c.
HIGH,] as in Isa. 13. 2.
NOT SEEN,] formerly, in his prosperity.
22. DRAW NEAR,] as in Ge. 27. 41; 47. 29; De. 31. 14, &c.
CAUSING DEATH,] as in 1 Sa. 2. 6; 2 K. 17. 26; Jer. 26. 15.
23. MESSENGER,] as in 1. 14; 4. 18; Ge. 16. 7.
INTERPRETER,] *lit.* 'sweetener,' as in 16. 20; Ps. 119. 103; 2 Ch. 32. 31; Isa. 43. 27.
ONE OF A THOUSAND,] as in 9. 3, &c.
UPRIGHTNESS,] as in v. 3.
24. FAVOUR,] as in Ge. 33. 5, 11; 43. 29,&c.
RANSOM,] as in v. 28; 5. 20; 6. 23; Ex. 13. 13.
PIT,] *or* 'corruption,' as in v. 18, 22, &c.
ATONEMENT,] *lit.* 'covering,' as in 36. 18.
25. FRESHER.] Original word not found again.
CHILD'S,] as in 36. 14; Ps. 88. 15; Prov. 20. 21.
YOUTH,] as in 20. 11; Ps. 89. 45; Isa. 54. 4.
26. SUPPLICATION,] as in 22. 27; Ge. 25. 21.
ACCEPTETH HIM,] as in 14. 6; 20. 10; 34. 9.
SHOUTING,] as in 8. 21; 39. 25; Lev. 23. 24.
RIGHTNESS,] as in 27. 6; 35. 8; 37. 23, &c.
27. SINNED,] as in 1. 5, 22, &c.

UPRIGHTNESS,] as in 1. 1, 8; 2. 3; 4. 7; 8. 6.
PERVERTED,] as in 2 Sa. 7. 14; 19. 19; 24. 17.
PROFITABLE,] as in Est. 3. 8; 5. 13; 7. 4, &c.
28. RANSOMED,] as in 5. 20; 6. 23, &c.
PIT,] *or* 'corruption,' as in v. 18, 22, 24, &c.
LIGHT,] as in v. 30; 3. 9, 16, 20; 12. 22, 25.
29. WORK,] as in 7. 20; 11. 8; 22. 17; 34. 32.
TWICE—THRICE,] that is, many times.
30. ENLIGHTENED,] as in 2 Sa. 2. 32; Ps. 76. 4.
LIGHT OF THE LIVING,] which living men enjoy.
31. ATTEND,] as in 13. 6; 2 Ch. 20. 15, &c.
KEEP SILENT,] as in v. 33; 13. 13; Jud. 18. 19
32. DESIRE,] as in 9. 3; 13. 3, 21. 14; 40. 17
JUSTIFY,] as in 32. 2; Eze. 16. 52, &c.
33. WISDOM,] as in 4. 21; 11. 6; 12. 2, &c.

XXXIV. 2. WISE MEN,] as in v. 34; 5. 13.
KNOWING ONES,] as in 19. 13; 24. 1; 42. 11
3. TRY,] as in 7. 18; 12. 11; 23. 10, &c.
PALATE,] as in 6. 30; 12. 11; 20. 13; 29. 10
TASTETH,] as in 12. 11; 1 Sa. 14. 24, 29, &c
4. CHOOSE,] as in 7. 15; 9. 14; 15. 5; 29. 25
5. RIGHT,] as in 4. 17; 9. 2, 15, 20; 10. 15, &c
RIGHT,] *lit.* 'judgment.'
6. LIE,] as in 6. 28; Nu. 23. 19; 2 K. 4. 16
MORTAL,] as in Isa. 17. 11; 15. 18; 17. 9, &c
ARROW,] as in 6. 4; Ge. 49. 23; Nu. 24. 8.
TRANSGRESSION,] as in v. 37; 7. 21; 8. 4, &c
7. SCOFFING,] as in Ps. 44. 13; 79. 4; 123. 4
9. TRAVELLED,] as in Ge. 37. 25, &c.
COMPANY,] as in 41. 6; Da. 7. 20; Mal. 2. 14
WORKERS OF INIQUITY,] as in v. 22; 31. 3
WICKEDNESS,] as in v. 10; De. 9. 27, &c.
10. MEN OF HEART,] as in v. 34.
PERVERSENESS,] as in v. 32; Lev. 19. 15, &c
11. REPAYETH,] as in 33; 21. 19, 31; 22. 27
PATH,] as in 6. 18, 19; 8. 13; 13. 27; 16. 22
12. DO WICKEDLY,] as in v. 17, 29; 9. 20, &c.
PERVERT,] as in 8. 3; 19. 6; Ps. 119. 78, &c.
13. INSPECTED,] as in 5. 24; 7. 8; 31. 14, &c.
PLACED,] as in 1. 8, 17; 2. 3; 4. 18; 5. 8, &c.
HABITABLE WORLD,] as in 18. 18; 37. 12, &c
14. SET,] as in v. 23.
SPIRIT,] as in Ps. 104. 29, &c.
BREATH,] as in 4. 9; 26. 4; 27. 3; 32. 8, &c.
GATHERETH,] as in 39. 12; Ps. 104. 29, &c
15. EXPIRE,] as in 3. 11; 10. 18; 13. 19; 14. 10
RETURNETH,] as in Ge. 3. 19; 10. 9; Ps. 104
29; Ecc. 3. 20; 12. 7.
16. UNDERSTANDING,] as in 20. 3; 28. 12, &c
17. GOVERN,] *lit.* 'bind up,' as in 5. 18, &c.
MOST,] as in v. 24; 8. 2; 15. 10; 31. 25; 36. 5.
CONDEMN,] *or* 'declare wicked *or* wrong.'
18. WORTHLESS,] as in De. 13. 13; 15. 9, &c.
PRINCES,] as in 12. 21; 21. 28; Ex. 35. 5, &c.
WICKED,] as in 3. 17; 8. 22; 9. 22, 24; 10. 2.
19. ACCEPTED,] *lit.* 'lifted up.'
NOT KNOWN,] as in 21. 29; Ge. 23. 27;
1 Sa. 3. 7; Jer. 19. 4.
RICH,] as in Isa. 22. 5; 32. 5; Eze. 23. 23.
POOR,] as in v. 28; 5. 16; 20. 10, 19; 31. 16
WORK OF HIS HANDS,] as in 1. 10; 14. 15, &c.
20. MOMENT,] as in 7. 18; 20. 5; 21. 13, &c.
MIDNIGHT,] as in Ex. 11. 4; Ps. 119. 62.
SHAKE,] as in 2 Sa. 22. 8; Ps. 18. 7, &c.
REMOVE,] as in 9. 34; 19. 9; 27. 2, 5, &c.
WITHOUT HAND,] *lit.* 'not by hand.'
21. WAYS,] as in v. 27; 3. 23; 4. 6, &c.
STEPS,] as in 14. 16; 18. 7; 31. 4, 37, &c.
22. DARKNESS,] as in 3. 4, 5; 5. 14; 10. 21

DEATH-SHADE,] as in 3. 5; 10. 21, 22; 12. 22.
WORKERS OF INIQUITY,] as in v. 8.
HIDDEN,] as in 3. 23; 13. 20; 28. 21, &c.
23. SUFFER,] *lit.* 'set, place.'
24. BREAKETH,] as in Ps. 2. 9; Jer. 15. 12.
SEARCHING,] as in 5. 9; 8. 8; 9. 10; 11. 7.
APPOINTETH,] *lit.* 'causeth to stand.'
25. OVERTURNED,] as in 9. 5; 12. 15; 28. 19.
BRUISED,] as in 5. 4.
26. STRICKEN,] as in v. 37; 20. 22; Nu. 24. 10.
27. RIGHT,] as in Ge. 42. 11, 19, 31, 33, 34, &c.
CONSIDERED WISELY,] as in v. 35; 22. 2, &c.
28. CRY,] as in 37. 9; Ge. 18. 21; 19. 13, &c.
AFFLICTED,] as in 24. 4, 9, 14; 29. 12, &c.
29. REST,] as in 37. 17; Ps. 94. 13; Prov. 15. 18.
MAKETH WRONG,] as in v. 12, 17.
HIDETH THE FACE,] as in 13. 24; Ex. 3. 6.
THE SAME,] *lit.* 'together,' as in 2. 11; 3. 18.
30. REIGNING,] as in Ge. 36. 31; 37. 8, &c.
PROFANE MAN,] as in 8. 13; 13. 16; 15. 34.
SNARES,] as in 40. 24; Ex. 10. 7; 23. 33, &c.
31. TAKEN AWAY,] *lit.* 'lifted up.'
DO CORRUPTLY,] as in 22. 6; 24. 3, 9, &c.
32. ADD,] as in v. 37.
33. BY THEE,] *lit.* 'from with thee.'
RECOMPENSE,] as in v. 11.
REFUSED,] as in 5. 17; 7. 16; 8. 20; 9. 21, &c.
CHOOSE,] as in v. 4.
34. MEN OF HEART,] as in v. 10.
WISE MAN,] as in Prov. 24. 5.
35. KNOWLEDGE,] as in 35. 16; 36. 12; 38. 2.
WISDOM,] as in Prov. 1. 3; 21. 16; Jer. 3. 15.
36. MY FATHER.] So Vulgate, &c.
TRIED,] as in v. 3; 7. 18; 12. 11; 23. 10;
Ge. 42. 15, 16, &c.
VICTORY,] as in 4. 20; 14. 20; 20. 7; 23. 7, &c.
MEN OF INIQUITY,] as in 22. 15; Prov. 6. 12.
37. ADD,] as in v. 32.
VOMITETH,] as in Jer. 48. 26.

XXXV. 2. RECKONED,] as in 6. 26; 13. 24.
MORE THAN,] *or* 'from' God.
3. USEFUL,] as 15. 3; 22. 2; 34. 9.
PROFIT,] as in 15. 3; 21. 15; 30. 13, &c.
5. BEHOLD ATTENTIVELY,] as in Ge. 15. 5.
CLOUDS,] as in 36. 28; 37. 18, 21; 38. 37, &c.
HIGHER,] as in 36. 7; 1 Sa. 10. 23, &c.
6. AGAINST HIM,] *or* 'with him.'
7. RIGHTEOUS,] as in 4. 17; 9. 2, 15, 20, &c.
RECEIVE,] *or* 'take.'
8. A MAN,] as in 1. 1, &c.
A SON OF MAN,] as in 16. 21, 25. 6, &c.
9. OPPRESSIONS,] as in Ecc. 4. 1; Am. 3. 9.
CRY OUT,] as in Zec. 6. 8, &c.
CRY,] as in 19. 7; 24. 12; 30. 20, 28, &c.
MIGHTY,] *or* 'many *or* great.'
10. MAKER,] as in 4. 17; 5. 9; 9. 9, 10, &c.
SONGS,] *or* 'psalms,' as in 2 Sa. 23. 1, &c.
11. TEACHING,] as in 15. 5; 33. 33.
BEASTS OF THE EARTH,] as in De. 28. 26.
FOWL OF THE HEAVENS,] as in 12. 7; 28. 21.
MAKETH US WISER,] as in Ps. 105. 22, &c.
12. CRY,] as in 19. 7; Ge. 27. 34; 41. 55, &c.
PRIDE,] as in 37. 4; 38. 11; 40. 10, &c.
EVIL-DOERS,] as in 21. 30; Ge. 13. 13, &c.
13. VANITY,] as in 7. 3; 11. 11; 15. 31; 31. 5.
14. STAY,] *or* 'be pained.'
15. APPOINTED,] as in 36. 23, &c.
EXTREMITY.] Sept., 'offence.' Vulg.,
transgression.'
16. VANITY,] as in 7. 16; 9. 29; 21. 34, &c.

WITHOUT KNOWLEDGE,] *lit.* 'in lack of knowledge.'
MULTIPLIETH,] as in 36 31.

XXXVI. 2. HONOUR,] *lit.* 'compass, as in Jud. 20. 43; Ps. 22. 12.
SHEW,] as in 15. 17, 32. 10, 17; Ps. 19. 2.
3. AFAR,] as in v. 25; 2. 12; 39. 25, 29.
MAKER,] *lit.* 'worker,' as in 31. 3; 34. 8, &c.
4. FALSE,] as in 13. 4; Ex. 5. 9; 20. 16, &c.
PERFECT IN KNOWLEDGE,] as in 37. 16.
5. DESPISETH,] as in 5. 17; 7. 16; 8. 20, &c.
MIGHTY,] as in 8. 2; 15. 10; 31. 25, &c.
6. REVIVETH,] as in 33. 4; Ge. 7. 3; 12. 12.
APPOINTETH,] *lit.* 'giveth.'
7. WITHDRAWETH,] as in 15. 4, 8; Ex. 5. 18.
THRONE,] sitting as his vicegerents.
CAUSETH TO SIT,] *or* 'abide.'
HIGH,] as in 35. 5; 1 Sa. 10. 23, &c.
8. PRISONERS,] *lit.* 'bound ones.'
FETTERS,] as in Ps. 49. 8; Prov. 26. 14, &c.
CAPTURED,] as in Jos. 7. 16, 17, 18, &c.
CORDS,] as in 18. 10; 21. 17; 39 3; 41. 1, &c.
9. WORK,] as in v. 24; 7. 2; 24. 5; 34. 11, &c.
MIGHTY,] as in 15. 25; Isa. 42. 13.
10. UNCOVERETH THEIR EAR,] as in v. 15.
INSTRUCTION,] as in 5. 17; 12. 18; 20. 3, &c.
INIQUITY,] as in v. 21; 4. 8; 5. 6; 11. 11, &c.
11. SERVE,] as in 21. 15; 39. 9, &c.
COMPLETE,] as in 21. 13; 31. 16, &c.
GOOD,] as in 21. 13; 22. 18, &c.
PLEASANTNESS,] as in 2 Sa. 1. 23; 23. 1, &c.
12. DART,] as in 33. 18; 2 Ch. 23. 10; 32. 5.
EXPIRE,] as in 3. 11; 10. 18; 13. 19; 14. 10.
13. PROFANE,] as in 8. 13; 13. 16; 15. 34, &c.
FACE,] *lit.* 'nose,' as in 4. 9; 9. 5, 13; 14. 13.
14. YOUTH,] as in 33. 25; Ps. 88. 15, &c.
DEFILED,] *lit* 'separated,' as in De. 23. 17.
15. DRAWETH,] as in Lev. 14. 40, 43, &c.
AFFLICTED,] as in v. 6.
UNCOVERETH,] as in v. 10.
OPPRESSION,] as in Ex. 3. 9; De. 26. 7, &c.
16. MOVED,] as in v. 18; 2. 3; De. 13. 6, &c.
STRAIT PLACE,] *lit.* 'mouth of straitness '
BROAD PLACE,] as in 38. 18.
STRAITNESS,] as in 37. 10; Isa. 9. 1, &c.
SITTING DOWN,] *lit.* 'rest, quietness.'
TABLE,] as in Ex. 25. 23, 27; 28. 30; 26. 35.
FATNESS,] as in Jud. 6. 6; Ps. 36. 8; 63. 5.
17. FULFILLED,] *or* 'filled up.'
UPHELD,] as in Ge. 48. 17; Ex. 17. 12, &c.
FURY,] *lit.* 'heat.'
18. MOVE,] as in v. 16.
STROKE,] as in 34. 26.
ABUNDANCE.] as in 4. 14; 11. 2; 23. 6; 26. 3.
ATONEMENT,] *lit.* 'covering,' as in 33. 24.
19. VALUE,] as in 28. 17, 19, &c.
RICHES,] as in 20. 34; 34. 19.
GOLD,] as in 22. 24, 25.
FORCES.] Original word not found again.
20. DESIRE,] as in 5. 5; 7. 2; Ps. 56. 1, &c.
GOING UP,] as in 5. 26; Ge. 32. 24, &c.
STEAD,] *lit.* 'under them.'
21. TAKE HEED,] as in Ge. 24. 6; 31. 24, &c.
FIXED,] as in 7. 15; 9. 14; 15. 5; 29. 25, &c.
AFFLICTION,] as in v. 8. 15.
RATHER THAN,] *or* 'because of, from.'
22. SET ON HIGH,] as in 5. 11; Ps. 20. 1, &c
TEACHER,] as in Ps. 9. 20; 84. 6; Joel 2. 23
2 K. 17. 28; 2 Ch. 15. 3; Prov. 5. 13; 6. 13
Isa. 9. 15; 30. 20; Hab. 2. 18.

23. APPOINTED,] as in 34. 13; 35. 15, &c.
INIQUITY,] as in 6. 29, 30; 11. 14; 13. 7, &c.
24. MAGNIFY,] as in 12. 23.
25. LOOKETH ATTENTIVELY,] as in 6. 19, &c.
26. HIGH,] as in 37. 23.
NUMBER OF HIS YEARS,] as in 15. 20; 16. 22.
SEARCHING,] as in 5. 9; 8. 8; 9. 10; 11. 7, &c.
27. DIMINISH,] as in v. 7.
DROPPINGS,] as in Ex. 30. 34.
REFINE,] as in 28. 1; Mal. 3. 3, &c.
VAPOUR,] as in Ge. 2. 6.
28. CLOUDS,] as in 35. 5; 36. 28; 37. 18, &c.
DROP,] as in Nu. 24.7; De. 32. 2; Jud. 5. 5.
DISTRESS,] as in Ps. 65. 11, 12; Prov. 3. 20.
29. SPREADINGS OUT,] as in Eze. 27. 7.
THICK CLOUD,] as in 20. 6; 22. 14; 26. 8, &c.
NOISES,] as in 39. 7; Isa. 22. 2; Zec. 4. 7.
TABERNACLE,] as in 27. 18; 38. 40, &c.
30. SPREAD,] as in 11. 13; 39. 26; Ex. 9. 29.
ROOTS,] as in 8. 17; 13. 27; 14. 8; 18. 16, &c.
COVERED,] as in 9. 24; 15. 27; 16. 18; 21. 26.
31. PEOPLES,] as in v. 20; 12. 2, 24; 17. 6.
FOOD,] as in 9. 26; 12. 11; 20. 21; 38. 41, &c.
32. TWO-PALMS,] or 'palms,' as in 2. 7, &c.
COVERED,] as in v. 30.
LAYETH A CHARGE,] as in 37. 12; 38. 12, &c.
MEETING,] lit. 'striking against.'
33. FRIEND,] as in 2. 11; 6. 14; 12. 4; 16. 20.
SUBSTANCE,] as in 1. 3, 10; Ge. 4. 20, &c.
ANGER,] as in v. 13.
PERVERSITY,] as in v. 23.

XXXVII. 1. TREMBLETH,] as in Ge. 27. 33.
MOVETH,] as in 6. 9, &c.
2. TREMBLING,] as in 3. 17, 26; 14. 1, &c.
SOUND,] as in Ps. 90. 9; Eze. 2. 10.
3. DIRECTETH IT,] as in 2 Ch. 32. 30, &c.
SKIRTS,] lit. 'wings,' as in 38. 13; 39. 13, &c.
4. ROAR,] as in Jud. 14. 5; Ps. 22. 13, &c.
THUNDERETH,] as in 5; 40. 9. 1 Sa. 2. 10.
EXCELLENCY,] as in 35. 12; 38. 11; 40. 10.
HOLD BACK,] as in Ge. 27. 36; Jer. 9. 4;
Hos. 12. 3.
5. WONDERFULLY,] as in v. 14; 5. 9; 9. 10.
GREAT THINGS,] as in 5. 9; 9. 10, &c.
6. SNOW,] as in 6. 16; 9. 30; 24. 19; 38. 22.
SMALL RAIN,] lit. 'shower of rain.'
GREAT RAIN,] lit. 'shower of rains.'
7. SEALETH,] as in 9. 7; 14. 17; 24. 16, &c.
MEN OF HIS WORK,] those whom he made.
8. BEAST,] lit. 'living creature.'
COVERT,] as in 38. 40.
HABITATIONS,] as in 38. 40; De. 26. 15, &c.
CONTINUE,] lit. 'tabernacle.'
9. INNER CHAMBER,] as in 9. 9; Ge. 43. 30.
HURRICANE,] as in 21. 18; 27. 20; Ps. 83. 15.
SCATTERING WINDS,] Heb. 'Mezarim,'
compare 38. 32.
COLD,] as in 24. 7; Ps. 147. 17; Prov. 25. 20;
Nah. 3. 17.
10. BREATH OF GOD,] as in 4. 9; 32. 8; 33. 4.
FROST,] as in 6. 16; 38. 29; Ge. 31. 40, &c.
BREADTH,] as in Ge. 6. 15; 13. 17; Ex. 25. 10.
STRAITENED,] lit. 'in straitness.'
11. FILLING.] Original word is not found
again.
PRESS OUT,] as in De. 1. 12; Isa. 1. 14.
SCATTER,] as in 18. 11; 38. 24; Ge. 11. 8, &c.
LIGHT,] as in v. 3, 15, 21.
12. TURNING ITSELF,] as in 38. 14; Ge. 3.
24; Jud. 7. 13.

COUNSELS,] as in Prov. 1. 5; 11. 14; 12. 5.
20. 18; 24. 6.
COMMANDETH,] as in 36. 32; 38. 12.
13. ROD,] as in 9. 34; 21. 9; Ge. 49. 10, &c.
KINDNESS,] as in 6. 14; 10. 12; Ge. 19. 19.
14. CONSIDER,] as in 11. 11; 23. 15; 26. 14.
WONDERS,] as in v. 5.
15. PLACE,] as in 5. 11; 20. 4; 38. 9, &c.
CAUSED TO SHINE,] as in 3. 4; 10. 3, 22;
De. 33. 2; Ps. 50. 2; 80. 1; 94. 1.
16. BALANCINGS.] Original word not found
again.
PERFECT IN KNOWLEDGE,] as in 32. 6,10; 36. 3.
17. WARM,] as in Jos. 9. 12.
QUIETING,] as in Ps. 94. 13; Isa. 30. 15, &c.
SOUTH,] as in De. 33. 23; Ecc. 1. 6; 11. 3, &c.
18. EXPANSE,] as in Ge. 1. 6, 7, 8, 14, 15, &c.
STRONG,] as in 5. 15; Ex. 3. 19; 6. 1, &c.
HARD,] as in v. 10; 36. 16; 38. 38; 41. 23, &c
MIRROR] for obtaining a 'sight, appearance.
19. SET IN ARRAY,] as in 6. 4; 13. 8; 23. 4.
20. DECLARED,] as in 12. 8; 15. 17; 28. 27.
SWALLOWED UP,] as in 2. 3; 7. 19; 8. 18, &c.
21. LIGHT,] as in v. 3, 11, 15, &c.
BRIGHT,] as in Lev. 13. 2, &c.
CLEANSETH,] as in Lev 11. 32, &c.
22. GOLDEN NORTH,] or 'north, brightness
cometh.'
FEARFUL HONOUR,] lit. 'fear, honour.'
23. FOUND OUT,] as in 11. 7; 23. 3, &c.
HIGH,] or 'great,' as in 36. 26.
ANSWER,] as in 9. 15; 19. 16; 30. 20; 33. 13.
ABUNDANT,] as in 4. 14; 11. 2; 23. 6; 26. 3.
24. FEAR,] or 'reverence.'
SEETH NOT,] nor regardeth them.
WISE OF HEART,] as in 9. 4; Ex. 35. 10, &c.

XXXVIII. 1. JEHOVAH,] as in 1. 6; 2. 1, &c.
WHIRLWIND,] as in 40. 6; 2 K. 2. 1, 11, &c
2. DARKENING,] as in Ps. 105. 28; 139. 12.
COUNSEL,] as in 5. 13; 10. 3; 12. 13; 18. 7.
KNOWLEDGE,] as in 34. 35; 35. 16; 36. 12.
3. GIRD,] as in 40. 7; 30. 18; 1 Sa. 2. 4, &c.
I PRAY THEE,] now! as in C.V.
MAN,] as in 3. 3, 23; 4. 17; 10. 5, &c.
LOINS,] as 31. 20; 40. 7; Ge. 35. 11, &c.
4. FOUNDED,] as in Isa. 51. 16; Ps. 24. 2, &c.
5. PLACED,] or 'set,' as in 1. 8, 17; 2. 3, &c.
MEASURES,] as in 28. 25.
STRETCHED OUT,] as in 9. 8; 15. 25, 29, &c.
LINE,] as in 1 K. 7. 23; 2 K. 21. 13, &c.
6. SOCKETS,] as in Ex. 26. 19, 21, 25, 32, &c.
SUNK,] as in Prov. 8. 25; Jer. 38. 32, &c.
CAST,] as in Ex. 31. 51; Ex. 19. 13, &c.
CORNER,] as in 1. 19; Ex. 27. 2; 38. 2, &c.
7. SINGING, as in Lev. 9. 24; Ezra. 3. 11, &c.
STARS,] as in 3. 9; 9. 7; 22. 12; 25. 5, &c.
SONS OF GOD,] as in 1. 6; 2. 1; Ge. 6. 4, &c.
SHOUT,] as in 30. 5.
8. SHUTTETH UP,] as in 3. 23; Ex. 40. 20.
DOORS,] as in v. 10; 3. 10; 31. 32; 41. 14, &c.
SEA,] as in v. 16; 6. 3; 7. 12; 9. 8; 11. 9, &c.
9. CLOTHING,] as in v. 14; 24. 7, 10; 30. 18.
THICK DARKNESS,] as in 22. 13; Ex. 20. 21.
SWADDLING BAND,] as in Eze. 16. 4.
10. MEASURE.] So Gesenius, &c.
STATUTE,] as in 14. 5, 13; 23. 12, 14; 26. 10.
PLACE,] or 'set,' as in v. 5.
BARS,] as in Ex. 26. 26, 27, 28, 29, &c.
DOORS,] as in v. 8.
11. ADD NOT,] as in 20. 9; 34. 32; 40 5, &c

COMMAND,] *lit.* 'mouth;' as in 33. 6, &c.
PRIDE,] as in 35. 12; 37. 4; 40. 10, &c.
BILLOWS,] as in Ps. 42. 7; 65. 7; 89. 9, &c.
12. MORNING,] as in v. 7.
SINCE THY DAYS,] as in 27. 6, &c.
DAWN,] as in 3. 9; 41. 18; Ge. 19. 15, &c.
13. TAKE HOLD,] as in 16. 12; 17. 9; 18. 20.
SKIRTS,] *lit.*'wings,' as in 37.3; 39.13, &c.
SHAKEN,] as in Jud. 16.20, Ps.109.23, &c.
14. TURNETH ITSELF,] as in 37. 12, &c.
CLAY,] as in 4. 19; 10. 9; 13. 12; 27.16, &c.
SEAL,] as in 41. 15; Ge. 38, 18; Ex. 28. 11.
STATION THEMSELVES,] as in 1. 6; 2. 1, &c.
15. WITHHELD,] as in 20.13; 22.7; Ge.30.2.
LIGHT,] as in v. 19, 24.
ARM,] as in 22. 8, 9; 26. 2; 35.9; 38. 15, &c.
BROKEN,] *or* 'shivered;' as in v. 10.
16.SPRINGS.]Originalwordnotfoundagain.
SEARCHING,] as in 5. 9; 8. 8; 9. 10; 11.7,&c.
DEEP,] as in v. 30; 28. 14; 41. 32, &c.
WALKED UP AND DOWN,] as in 1.7; 2.2, &c.
17. REVEALED,] as in Ge. 35.7; 1 Sa. 2. 27.
GATES OF DEATH,] as in Ps. 9. 13; 107. 18.
DEATH-SHADE,] as in 3. 5; 10. 21. 22, &c.
18. BROAD PLACES,] as in 36. 16.
19. LIGHT,] as in v. 15, 24.
20. BOUNDARY,] as in Ge.10.19; 23.17, &c.
21. BORN.] as in 1. 2; 3. 3; 11. 12; 15.7, &c.
22. TREASURES,] as in De. 28. 12; 32. 34.
SNOW,] as in 6. 16; 9. 30; 24. 19; 37. 6, &c.
HAIL,] as in Ex. 9.18, 19, 22, 23, 24, 25, &c.
23. KEPT BACK,] as in 7. 11; 16. 5, 6, &c.
DISTRESS,] as in 6. 23; 7. 11; 15. 24; 16. 9.
CONFLICT,] as in 2 Sa. 17.11; Ps. 55.18,&c.
BATTLE,] as in 5. 20; 39. 25; 41. 8, &c.
24. APPORTIONED,] as in Ge. 14. 15, &c.
SCATTERETH,] as in 18. 11; 37. 11; 40. 11.
EAST WIND,] as in 15. 2; 27. 21; Ge. 41. 6.
25. DIVIDED,] as in Ps. 55. 9.
FLOOD,] as in Ps. 32. 6; Prov. 27. 4, &c.
CONDUIT,] as in 1 K. 18, 32. 35, 38, &c.
LIGHTNING,] as in 28. 26; Zec. 10. 1, &c.
26. CAUSE..RAIN,] as in 20. 23; Ge. 2. 5.
WILDERNESS,] *or* pasture land.
27. SATISFY,] as in 9. 18; Ps. 81. 16, &c.
DESOLATE,] as in 30. 3, 14; Ps. 35. 8, &c.
WASTE PLACE,] as in 30. 3; Zeph. 1. 15.
CAUSE TO SHOOT UP,] as in Ge. 2. 9; 3. 18.
PRODUCE,] as in 28.1; Nu. 30.12; 32.2, &c.
TENDER GRASS,] as in 6. 5; Ge. 1. 11,12,&c.
28. FATHER,] that is, a creator, source ;
hence in Hebrew 'creator-hood' is the same
as 'father-hood,' while 'creature-hood' is
'son-ship.'
BEGOTTEN,] as in Ge. 5. 3—32; 6. 10, &c.
DROPS.] Original word not found again.
DEW,] as in 29.19; Ge. 27.28,39; Ex.16.13.
29. ICE,] as in 6.16; 37.10; 38.29; Ge.31.40.
HOAR-FROST,] as in Ex. 16.14; 1 Ch. 28.17.
30. HIDDEN,] *or* 'hid themselves.'
CAPTURED,] as in 41. 17.
31. BIND,] as in 39.10; 41.5; Ge. 38.28, &c.
SWEET INFLUENCES,] as in Ge. 49. 20, &c.
KIMAH,] as in 9. 9; Am. 5. 8.
ATTRACTIONS,] *lit.* 'drawings.'
KESIL,] *lit.* 'a fool;' as in 9. 9; Am. 5. 8.
OPEN,] as in 12.18; 30.11; 39. 5; 41. 14, &c.
32. MAZZAROTH,] as in 37. 9.
SEASON,] as in v. 23.
AYSH,] *lit.* a 'moth;' as in 9. 9.
SONS,] *or* 'children.'

COMFORT,] they being, as it were, lost to
view.
33. STATUTES,]asinGe.26.5; Ex.12.14,&c.
APPOINT,] *lit.* 'set, place.'
DOMINION,] *or* 'authority.'
34. THICK CLOUD,] as in 20. 6; 22. 14, &c.
ABUNDANCE,] as in 22. 11; 2 K. 9. 17; Isa.
60. 6; Eze. 26. 10.
COVER,] as in 9. 24; 16. 18; 21. 26; 22. 11.
35. LIGHTNINGS,] as in 20. 25; Ex. 19. 16.
36. INWARD PARTS,] as in Ps. 51. 6.
COVERED PART.] Original word not found
elsewhere.
37. NUMBER,] as in 12. 8; 14. 16; 15.17, &c.
BOTTLES,] as in 1 Sa. 1. 24; 10. 3; 25. 18.
LIE DOWN,] as in 2 Sa. 8. 2; 1 K. 3, 20, &c.
38.HARDENING,]*lit.*'pouring out, casting.'
HARDNESS,] as in 1 K. 7. 37.
CLODS,] as in 21. 33.
CLEAVE,] as in 41. 17.
39. HUNT,] as in 10. 16; Ge. 27. 3,5,33,&c.
LION,] as in 4. 11; Ge. 49.9; Nu. 23. 24,&c.
PREY,] as in 4.11; 24. 5; 29. 17, &c.
DESIRE,] *or* 'life,' as in 3. 20; 7. 7, &c.
YOUNG LIONS,] as in 4. 10; Jud. 14. 5, &c.
FULFIL,] *or* 'fill out, complete.]
40. BOW DOWN,] as in 9. 3; Ps. 10. 10, &c.
DENS,] as in 37. 8; De. 33. 27; Ps. 76.2,&c.
ABIDE,] *lit.* 'sit.'
THICKET,]asin27.18; 36.29; Ge.33.17,&c.
COVERT,] as in 37. 8.
41. PREPARE,]*or* 'make ready,' as in 11.13.
RAVEN,] as in Ge. 8. 7; Lev. 11. 15, &c.
PROVISION,] *lit.* 'hunting;' as in Ge. 10. 9.
YOUNG ONE,] as in 21. 11; 39. 3; Ge. 4. 23.
CRY,] as in 19. 7; 24. 12; 30. 20, 28, &c.
WANDER,] as in Ge. 21. 14; 37. 15; Ex.23.4.

XXXIX.1.BEARING,]asinv.2; 15.35,&c.
WILD GOATS,] as in 1 Sa. 24. 2; Ps. 104. 18.
BRINGING FORTH,] *lit.* 'paining.'
HINDS,] as in Ge. 49. 21; 2 Sa. 22. 34, &c.
MARK,] watch, observe.
2. FULFIL,] before bringing forth young.
3. BOW DOWN,] as in 31. 10; Ge. 49, 9, &c.
YOUNG ONES,] as in 21.11; 38,41; Ge.4.23.
BRING FORTH SAFELY,] *lit.* 'cleave,' as in
16. 13, &c.
PANGS,] as in 18. 10; 21. 17; 36.8; 41. 1, &c.
CAST FORTH,] as in 8. 4; 12.15; 14. 20, &c.
4. SAFE.] Original word not found again
in this sense.
GROW UP,] *or* ' become great.'
5. WILD ASS,] as in 6. 5; 11. 12; 24. 5, &c.
FREE,] as in 3. 19; Ex. 21. 2, 5, 26, 27, &c.
BANDS,] as in Ps. 2. 3; 107. 14; 116. 16, &c.
WILD ASS,] as in Da. 5. 21.
6. WILDERNESS,]asin24.5; Nu.22.1,&c.
BARREN LAND,]asin Ps. 107.34; Jer.17.6.
7. LAUGH,] as in v. 18, 22; 5.22; 29.24, &c.
MULTITUDE,] as in 31. 34; Ge. 17. 4, 5, &c.
CRIES,] as in 36. 29; Isa. 22; Zec. 4. 7.
EXACTOR,] as in 3. 18; Ex. 3. 7; 5. 6,10,&c.
8. RANGE.] Original word not found again.
PASTURE,] as in Ge. 47. 4; 1 Ch. 4. 39, &c.
GREEN THING,] as in Ge. 1. 30, &c.
9. REEM,] as in 10; Nu. 23. 22; 24. 8, &c.
WILLING,] as in Ge. 20. 5, 8; Ex. 10.27,&c.
CRIB,] as in Prov. 14. 4; Isa. 1. 3.
10. BIND,] as in 38.31; 41.5; Ge. 38.28, &c.
FURROW] as in 31.38; Ps. 65.10; Hos.10.4.

THICK BAND,] as in Ex. 28. 14, 22, 24, 25, &c.
HARROW,] as in Isa. 28. 24; Hos. 10. 11.
11. TRUST,] as in 6. 20; 11. 18; 40. 23, &c.
LABOUR,] as in v. 16; 10. 3; Ge. 31. 42, &c.
12. SEED,] as in 5. 25; 21. 8; Ge. 1. 11, &c.
THRESHING-FLOOR,] as in Ge. 50. 10, 11, &c.
GATHER,] as in 34. 14; Ge. 6. 21; 29. 22, &c.
13. WING,] as in v. 26; 37. 3; 38. 13.
RATTLING ONES,] as in v. 23; 3. 7; 20. 5, &c.
EXULTETH,] as in 20. 18.
PINION,] as in De. 32. 11; Ps. 68. 13; 91. 4.
OSTRICH,] as in Lev. 11. 19; De. 14. 18, &c.
HAWK,] as in Eze. 17. 3, 7.
14. EGGS,] as in De. 22. 6; Isa. 10. 14; 59. 5.
WARM,] by the rays of the sun.
15. PRESS,] as in Jud. 6. 38; Isa. 1. 6.
TREAD IT DOWN,] as in Da. 7. 23.
16. HARDENED,] as in Isa. 63. 17.
VAIN,] as in Lev. 26. 16, 20; Ps. 2. 1, &c.
LABOUR,] as in v. 11.
17. CAUSED HER TO FORGET,] as in 11. 6.
GIVEN A PORTION,] as in 27. 17; De. 4. 19.
18. LIFTETH HERSELF UP,] as in Zeph. 2. 1.
LAUGHETH,] as in v. 7, 22.
RIDER,] in their attempts to catch her.
19. MIGHT,] as in 12. 13; 26. 14; 41. 12, &c.
NECK,] as in 15. 26; 41. 22; Ge. 27. 16, &c.
MANE,] lit. a 'waving, raging' thing.
20. CAUSE HIM TO RUSH,] as in Ps. 60. 2.
LOCUST,] as in Ex. 10. 4, 12, 13, 14, 19, &c.
MAJESTY,] as in 33. 22; 40. 10; Nu. 27. 20.
SNORTING,] as in Jer. 8. 16.
TERRIBLE,] as in 9. 34; 13. 21; 20. 25, &c.
21. DIG,] as in v. 29; 3. 21; 11. 18, &c.
VALLEY,] as in v. 10.
ARMOUR,] as in 20. 24; 1 K. 10. 25, &c.
22. LAUGHETH,] as in v. 7, 18.
AFFRIGHTED,] as in 32. 15; De. 1. 21, &c.
FACE OF THE SWORD,] as in 19. 29, &c.
23. RATTLE,] as in v. 13.
QUIVER,] as in Ps. 127. 5; Isa. 22. 6; 49. 2;
Jer. 5. 16; La. 3. 13.
FLAME,] as in 41. 21; Jud. 3. 22; 13. 20, &c.
SPEAR,] as in 41. 26; 1 Sa. 13. 19, 22, &c.
HALBERT,] as in 41. 29; Jos. 8. 18, 26, &c.
24. TREMBLING,] as in 41. 29; 1 K. 19. 11.
RAGE,] as in 3. 17, 26; 14. 1; 37. 2; Isa. 14. 3.
SWALLOWETH,] as in Ge. 24. 17.
STEDFAST,] as in 4. 18; 9. 16; 15. 15, 22, &c.
TRUMPET,] as in v. 25; Ex. 19. 16, 19, &c.
25. AHA,] as in Ps. 35. 21, 25; 40. 15; 70. 3.
.sa. 44. 16; Eze. 25. 3; 26. 2; 36. 2.
SMELL,] as in Ge. 8. 21; 27. 27; Ex. 30. 38.
ROARING,] as in 16; Ps. 77. 18; 81. 7.
PRINCES,] lit. 'heads.'
SHOUTING,] as in 8. 21; 33. 26; Lev. 23. 24.
26. HAWK,] as in Lev. 11. 16; De. 14. 15.
SPREADETH,] as in 11. 13; 36. 30; De. 32. 11.
WINGS,] as in v. 13.
SOUTH,] as in 9. 9; Ex. 26. 18, 35; 27. 9, &c.
27. EAGLE,] as in 9. 26; Ex. 19. 4, &c.
HIGH,] as in 38. 34; Ge. 14. 32; 31. 45, &c.
NEST,] as in 29. 18; Ge. 6. 14; Nu. 24. 21, &c.
28. ROCK,] as in v. 1.
INHABIT,] as in 3. 5; 4. 19, &c.
TOOTH,] as in 4. 10; 13. 14; 16. 9; 19. 20, &c.
FORTRESS,] as in 1 Sa. 22. 4, 5; 24. 22, &c.
LOOK ATTENTIVELY,] as in 6. 19; 2. 24, &c.
30. BROOD,] as in De. 22. 6; Ps. 84. 3.
GULP UP.] Original word not found again.
PIERCED,] as in 24. 12; Ge. 34. 37; Lev. 21. 7.

XL. 1. JEHOVAH,] as in 38. 1.
2. STRIVER,] as in Isa. 45. 9; Jer. 51. 36.
INSTRUCTED,] as in Lev. 26. 23; Ps. 2. 10
REPROVER,] as in 9. 33; 32. 12; Prov. 9. 7
4. VILE,] as in Ge. 16. 4, 5; Nah. 1. 14, &c
RETURN,] as in 31. 14, &c.
MOUTH,] as in 21. 5; 29. 9; Prov. 30. 32, &c
5. ANSWER,] or 'respond.'
ADD,] as in 20. 5; 34. 32; 38. 11; 41. 8, &c.
6. WHIRLWIND,] as in 38. 1; 2 K. 2. 1, &c.
7. GIRD,] as in 38. 3, &c.
I PRAY THEE,] not 'now,' as in C.V.
MAN,] as in 3. 3, 23; 4. 17; 10. 5, &c.
LOINS,] as in 31. 30; 38. 3; Ge. 35. 11, &c.
8. MAKE VOID,] as in 5. 12; 15. 4; Ge. 17. 14.
CONDEMN,] or 'declare wrong.'
RIGHTEOUS,] as in 4. 17; 9. 2, 15, 20; 10. 15.
9. ARM,] as in 22. 8, 9; 26. 2; 35. 9; 38. 15.
THUNDER,] as in 37. 4, 5; 1 Sa. 2. 10, &c.
10. PUT ON,] as in Isa. 61. 10; Jer. 4. 30, &c.
I PRAY THEE,] not 'now,' as in C.V.
EXCELLENCY,] as in 35. 12; 37. 4; 38. 11.
LOFTINESS,] as in 11. 8; 22. 12; 1 Sa. 17. 4.
HONOUR,] as in 37. 22; 39. 20; Nu. 27. 30.
BEAUTY,] as in Lev. 23. 40; De. 33. 17, &c.
11. SCATTER ABROAD,] as in 18. 11; 37. 11.
WRATH,] as in 21. 30; Ge. 49. 7; Ps. 7. 6, &c.
PROUD ONE,] as in v. 12; Ps. 9. 4, 2; 13. 4.
LOW,] as in 22. 29; 1 Sa. 2. 7; 2 Sa. 22 28.
12. HUMBLE,] as in De. 9. 3; Jud. 4. 23, &c.
TREAD DOWN.] Original word not found
again.
13. HIDE,] as in 31. 33; Ge. 35. 4; Ex. 2. 12.
SECRET,] as in 3. 16; 18. 10; 20. 26, &c.
14. PRAISE,] as in Ex. 29. 35; 49. 8, &c.
SALVATION,] as in 5. 15; 22. 29; 26. 2, &c.
15. I PRAY THEE,] not 'now,' as in C.V.
BEHEMOTH,] lit. 'beasts, cattle,' or 'great
beast.'
GRASS,] as in 8. 12; Nu. 11. 5; 1 K. 18. 5.
OX,] as in 1. 3, 14; 42. 15; Ge. 12. 16, &c.
16. LOINS,] as in 12. 18; Ge. 37. 34; Ex. 12. 11.
MUSCLES,] as in Song 7. 2.
17. BEND,] lit. 'delighteth, desireth,' as
in 9. 3, &c.
TAIL,] as in Ex. 4. 4; De. 28. 13, 44, &c.
CEDAR,] as in Lev. 14. 4, 6, 49, 51, 52, &c.
SINEWS,] as in 10. 11; Ge. 32. 32; Isa. 48.
4; Eze. 37. 6, 8.
THIGHS,] lit. 'fearful things,' as in 3. 25.
WRAPPED TOGETHER,] as in La. 1. 14.
18. TRIBES,] as in 6. 15; 12. 21; 41. 15, &c.
BAR.] Original word not found again.
19. BEGINNING,] as in 8; 7; 42. 12; Ge. 1. 1.
MAKER,] as in 4. 17; 5. 9; 9. 9, 10; 25. 2, &c.
SWORD,] as in 1. 15, 17; 5. 15, 20; 15. 22, &c.
20. FOOD,] as in Isa. 44. 19.
BEAR,] lit. 'lift up.'
PLAY,] as in 41. 5; Jud. 16. 25; 1 Sa. 18. 17.
21. SHADES,] as in v. 22.
LIETH DOWN,] as in 7. 21; 11. 18; 20. 11, &c.
SECRET PLACE,] as in 13. 10; 22. 14, &c.
REED,] as in 31. 22; Ge. 41. 5, 18; Ex. 25. 31.
MIRE,] as in 8. 11; Eze. 47. 11; Jer. 38. 22.
22. COVER,] as in Ex. 25. 20; 37. 9; 40. 3.
SHADOW,] as in Song 2. 17; 4. 6; Jer. 6. 4.
WILLOWS OF THE BROOK,] as in Lev. 23. 40.
23. FLOOD,] or 'river.'
OPPRESSETH,] as in 10. 3; Lev. 6. 2, 4, &c.
HASTE,] as in De. 20. 3; 2 Sa. 4. 4; 2 K. 7. 15.
CONFIDENT,] as in 6. 20; 11. 18; 39. 11, &c

JORDAN,] as in Ge. **13.** 10. 11; 32. 10, &c.
24. TAKE] him captive against his will.
SNARES,] as in 34. 30; Ex. 10. 7; 23. 33, &c.
PIERCE,] as in 3. 8; 5. 3; 40. 24, &c.

XLI. 1. DRAW,] as in 21. 33; 24. 22; Ex. 12. 21.
LEVIATHAN,] as in 3. 8; Ps. 74. 14; 104. 26;
Isa. 27. 1.
ANGLE,] as in Isa. 19. 8; Hab. 1. 15.
ROPE,] as in 18. 10; 21. 17; 36. 8, &c.
2. REED,] as in v. 20; Isa. 9. 14; 19. 15; 58. 5.
THORN,] as in 31. 40; 1 Sa. 13. 6; 2 K. 14. 9.
JAW,] as in 16. 10; De. 18. 3; Jud. 15. 15.
3. SUPPLICATIONS,] as in 2 Ch. 6. 21; Ps. 28. 2.
TENDER,] as in Ge. 18. 7; 29. 17; 33. 13, &c.
4. COVENANT,] as in 5. 23; 31. 1; Ge. 6. 18.
AGE-DURING,] as in 7. 16; 22. 15; Ex. 21. 6.
5. PLAY,] as in 40. 20, &c.
BIRD,] as in Ge. 7. 14; 15. 10; Lev. 4. 4, 5, &c.
BIND,] as in 38. 31; 39. 10; Ge. 38. 28, &c.
DAMSELS,] as in Ge. 24. 14, 16, 28, 55, &c.
6. FEAST,] or 'make provision' on him.
COMPANIONS,] as in 34. 8; Jud. 20. 11, &c.
DIVIDE,] as in Ge. 32. 7; 33. 1; Ex. 21. 35.
MERCHANTS,] as in Prov. 31. 24; Zec. 14. 21.
7. BARBED IRONS.] Not mentioned else-
where.
SPEARS,] *lit.* 'a tinkling instrument.'
8. HAND,] as in 2. 7; 9. 30; 10. 3; 11. 13, &c.
BATTLE,] as in 5. 20; 38. 23; 39. 25; Ge. 14. 2.
ADD,] as in 40. 5, &c.
9. HOPE] of catching him.
LIAR,] as in 6. 28; 34. 6; Prov. 30. 6.
APPEARANCE,] as in 4. 16; Ge. 2. 9; 12. 11.
CAST DOWN,] as in Ps. 37. 24; Prov. 16. 33.
Jer. 22. 28.
10. FIERCE,] as in 30. 21; De. 32. 33; La. 4. 3.
AWAKE,] as in 8. 16; De. 32. 11; 1 Ch. 5. 26.
STATIONETH HIMSELF,] as in 1. 6; 2. 1, &c.
11. REPAY,] as in 8. 6, 21. 19, 31; 22. 27;
34. 11, 33.
12. KEEP SILENT,] as in 6. 24; 11. 3; 13. 5.
PARTS,] as in 11. 3; 18. 13, &c.
MIGHT,] as in 12. 13; 26. 14; 39. 19, &c.
GRACE,] as in Ge. 6. 8; 18. 3; 19. 19; 30. 27.
ARRANGEMENT,] as in 28. 13; Ex. 40. 4, &c.
13. UNCOVERED,] as in 12. 22; 20. 27, 28, &c.
CLOTHING,] as in 24. 7, 10; 30. 18; 31. 19.
DOUBLE,] as in 11. 6; Isa. 40. 2.
BRIDLE,] as in 30. 11; Ps. 32. 9; Isa. 30. 28.
14. OPENED,] as in 12. 18; 30. 11; 38. 31, &c.
TERRIBLE,] as in 9. 34; 13. 21; 20. 25; 33. 7.
15. PRIDE] they are to him; De. 33. 26, &c.
STRONG ONES,] as in 6. 15; 12. 21; 40. 18, &c.
SHIELDS,] as in 15. 26; Ge. 15. 1; De. 33. 29.
SHUT UP,] as in Eze. 44. 1, 2; 46. 1, &c.
SEAL,] as in 38. 14; Ge. 38. 18; Ex. 28. 11.
16. DRAW NIGH,] as in Ge. 18. 23; 19. 9, &c.
AIR,] or 'wind,' as in 1. 19; 4. 9, 15; 6. 4.
17. ADHERE,] as in 19. 20; 29. 10; 31. 7, &c.
STICK TOGETHER,] *lit.* 'capture them-
selves.'
SEPARATED,] *lit.* 'do not separate them-
selves.'
18. SNEEZINGS.] Original word not found
again.
CAUSE TO SHINE,] as in 29. 3; 31. 26.
EYE-LIDS OF THE DAWN,] as in 3. 9; 16. 16.
19. FLAMES,] as in 12. 5; Ge. 15. 17; Ex. 20. 8.
SPARKS.] Original word not found again.
ESCAPE.] *lit.* 'deliver themselves.'

20. NOSTRILS.] Original word not found
again.
SMOKE,] as in Ge. 15. 17; Ex. 19. 18, &c.
BLOWN,] as in 20. 26; Jer. 1. 13, &c.
POT,] as in 1 Sa. 2. 14; 2 K. 10. 7, &c.
REEDS,] as in v. 2 above.
21. BREATH,] *lit.* 'soul.'
COALS,] as in Lev. 16. 12; 2 Sa. 14. 7, &c.
SETTETH ON FIRE,] as in De. 32. 22; Ps.
57. 4.
FLAME,] as in 39. 23; Jud. 3. 22, &c.
22. NECK,] as in 15. 26; 39. 19; Ge. 27. 16.
STRENGTH,] as in 12. 16; 26. 2; 37. 6, &c.
QUIET,] as in De. 28. 58.
EXULT.] Original word not again found.
23. FLAKES,] or 'falling parts,' as in A-
mos 8. 6.
ADHERED,] as in 19. 20; 29. 10; 31. 7, &c.
FIRM,] as in v. 24; 28. 2, &c.
MOVED,] as in 1 Ch. 16. 30; Ps. 10. 6; 13. 4.
24. FIRM,] as in v. 23.
LOWER PIECE,] as in Ge. 6. 16; Ex. 19. 17.
25. BREAKINGS,] or 'because of destruc-
tions.'
KEEP THEMSELVES FREE,] *lit.* 'purify
themselves.'
26. OVERTAKER,] as in Lev. 14. 21; 1 Sa.
14. 26; 1 Ch. 21. 12.
SPEAR,] as in 39. 23; 1 Sa. 13. 19, 22; 17. 7
DART.] Original word not found again.
LANCE.] Original word not found again.
27. RECKONETH,] as in 6. 26; 13. 24; 19. 11.
IRON,] as in 19. 24; 20. 24; 28. 2; 40. 18, &c.
STRAW,] as in 21. 18; Ge. 24. 25, 32, &c.
BRASS,] as in 20. 24; 28. 2; 40. 18, &c.
ROTTEN WOOD,] as in 13. 28; Prov. 10. 7, &c.
28. SON OF THE BOW,] that is, an arrow.
STUBBLE,] as in v. 29; 13. 25; Ex. 5. 12, &c.
STONES OF A SLING,] as in 2 Ch. 26. 14;
Zec. 9. 15.
29. DARTS.] Original word not found again.
SHAKING,] as in 39. 24; 1 K. 19. 11, 12, &c.
JAVELIN,] as in 39. 23; Jos. 8. 18, 26, &c.
30. SHARP-POINTS.] Original word not
found again.
CLAY,] as in 2. 8; Lev. 6. 28; 11. 33, &c.
SPREADETH,] as in 17. 13.
GOLD,] as in Ps. 68. 13; Prov. 3. 14; 8. 10, &c.
MIRE,] as in 2 Sa. 22. 43; Ps. 18. 42, &c.
31. TO BOIL,] as in 30. 27; Eze. 34. 5, &c.
POT,] as in Ex. 16. 2; 27. 3; 38. 3; 1 K. 7. 45.
DEEP,] as in Ps. 68. 22; 69. 2, 15; 107. 24.
OINTMENT,] as in Eze. 24. 10.
32. CAUSETH TO SHINE,] as in Ge. 1. 15, &c.
THINKETH,] or 'reckoneth.'
DEEP,] as in 28. 14; 38. 16, 30; Ge. 1. 2, &c.
HEAVY,] as in Ex. 15. 15; 25. 8; 42. 38, &c.
33. TERROR,] as in Ge. 9. 2; 1 Sa. 2. 4;
Jer. 46. 5.
34. HIGH THING,] as in Ge. 7. 10; De. 3. 5.
SONS OF PRIDE,] as in 28. 8; Sept. and
Targ. read 'sons of teeming creatures.'

XLII. 1. ANSWERETH,] as in 40. 3.
2. THOU HAST KNOWN,] not 'I have known.
ABLE,] as in 40. 9, &c.
WITHHELD,] as in Ge. 11. 6, &c.
DEVICE,] as in 21. 27; Ps. 10. 2, 4, &c.
3. HIDING,] as in 28. 21, &c.
WONDERFUL,] as in 5. 9; 9. 10; 37. 5, 14, &c.
4. KNOW,] as in 38. 3, &c.

5. EAR,] as in 28. 22; Ps. 18. 44, &c.
EYE,] seeth the outward manifestations of his power.
6. LOATHE,] as in 5. 17; 7. 16; 8. 20; 9. 21, &c.
REPENTED,] as in Ge. 6. 6, 7; 24. 67; 38. 12, &c.
DUST AND ASHES,] as in 30. 19; Ge. 18. 27.
7. ELIPHAZ,]'as in v. 9; 2. 11; 4. 1; 15. 1; 22. 1.
BURNED,] as in 32. 2, 3, 5; Ge. 30. 2, &c.
RIGHTLY,] or 'preparedly,' as in 21. 8, &c.
MY SERVANT,] as in v. 8; 1. 3; 2. 3, &c.
8. SEVEN BULLOCKS,] as in Nu. 23. 1, 29, &c.
SEVEN RAMS,] as in Nu. 23. 1, 29, &c.
BURNT OFFERING,] as in 1. 5; Ge. 8. 20, &c.
PRAY,] as in v. 10; Ge. 20. 7, &c.
ACCEPT,] lit. 'lift up.'
FOLLY,] as in Ge. 34. 7; De. 22. 21, &c.
10. TURNED BACK,] having as it were left him for a time.
CAPTIVITY,] he being removed from his comforts.
DOUBLE,] as in Ge. 41. 43; 43. 12, 15, &c.
11. BRETHREN,] his male kindred and relations.
SISTERS,' his female kindred and relations.

ACQUAINTANCES,] as in 19. 3; 24. 1; 34. 2, &c.
EAT BREAD,] as in 19. 13; 24. 1; 34. 2, &c.
BEMOAN,] as in 2. 11, &c.
EVIL,] or 'misfortune.'
KESITAH,] as in Ge. 33. 19; Jos. 24. 32.
RING,] as in Ge. 24. 22, 30, 47; 35. 4, &c.
12. BLESSED,] as in 1. 5, 10; 31. 20, &c.
LATTER END,] as in 8. 7; Ge. 49. 1, &c.
BEGINNING,] as in 8. 7; 40. 19; Ge. 1. 1, &c.
14,000,] in 1. 3 it was 7,000.
6000,] in 1. 3 it was 3000.
1000,] in 1. 3 it was 500.
1000,] in 1. 3 it was 500.
13. SEVEN..THREE,] as in 1. 2.
14. JEMINA,] i.e. a 'dove,' perhaps.
KEZIA,] i.e. 'cassia,' as in Ps. 45. 9.
KEREN-HAPPUCH,] i.e. 'horn of painting.'
15. FAIR,] as in Ge. 12. 11, 14; 29. 17; 39. 6, &c.
LAND] of Uz, as in 1. 1.
INHERITANCE,] as in 20. 29; 27. 13; 31. 2, &c.
16. 140 YEARS,] nearly the whole age of Jacob.
FOUR GENERATIONS,] as in Ge. 15. 16.
AGED,] about 230 or 240 years.
DAYS,] as in Ge. 25. 8; 35. 39; 1 Ch. 29. 28.

BOOK OF PSALMS

THE BOOK OF PSALMS consists of 150 compositions, of which 75 (or exactly one-half) are ascribed in their titles to David, 12 to Asaph, 11 to sons of Korah, 2 to Solomon, 1 to Ethan, 1 to Heman, 1 to Moses, and the rest (47) are anonymous. The Jews call the book *Tehillim*, i.e. 'praises,' but the Septuagint title *Psalmos* (whence comes the English word *Psalm*) is preferable, as it exactly corresponds to the Hebrew *Mizmor* a 'plucking' of the harp or lyre, which is prefixed to 57; 30 are simply called '*Songs*,' 15 are '*Songs of Ascents*,' 13 are '*Causing to act wisely*,' 10 are called '*Prayers*,' only one '*Praise*,' and the rest have no particular title. Some of the titles are, however, of doubtful origin.

The whole collection consists of five books, each ending with 'Amen,' or 'Hallelujah'. The First Division I—XLI, is wholly ascribed to David, with the (apparent) exception of Ps. I. II.

The Second Division XLII—LXXII, contains 18 by David, 7 by sons of Korah, 1 by Asaph 1 by Solomon, and 4 anonymous.

The Third Division LXXIII—LXXXIX, contains 1 by David, 11 by Asaph, 4 by sons of Korah, 1 by Ethan, and 1 by Heman.

The Fourth Division XC—CVI, contains 2 by David, 1by Moses, and 14 anonymous.

The Fifth Division CVII—CL, contains 15 by David, 1 by Solomon, and 18 anonymous.

Most of the Psalms were doubtless designed for public worship in the tabernacle and in the temple, some for the great public festivals, others for family or personal use only. In the ancient synagogue, the whole collection was used rather as a 'Prayer-Book' than a 'Praise-Book,' at least on Sabbaths, when they had no service of praise distinct from that of prayer.

The New Testament references to the Book are too numerous to be specified here.

1's. I. This and the succeeding one are anonymous, but both were really written by David, for 2. 7 is quoted as his in Acts 13. 13, where instead of 'the second Psalm,' the best MSS. read 'the first Psalm.' This accords with the Talmudic tradition noticed by Gill, that the two psalms were originally one, and thus we have both Christian and Jewish authority for ascribing them to David. (See also Acts 4.25; Heb. 1. 5; 5. 1). They are both Messianic, the first describing the truly 'happy' one, as the undefiled Servant, and contrasts him with those who are in a 'wrong' state and 'missing' the mark he set before his eyes, and the second describing him as the 'anointed' King and Son, against whom they 'assemble tumultuously,' but in vain.

1. HAPPINESS,] as in De. 33.39; 1 K. 10.

8; 2 Ch.9. 7; Job.5.17; Ps.2. 12; 31. 1, 2; 33 12; 34. 8; 40. 4; 41. 1; 65. 1; 84. 4, &c.

THE MAN,] that is, the individual.

WALKED,] or 'gone,'at any time; which is true only of the Lord Jesus.

COUNSEL,] as in De. 32. 18; Jud. 20. 7; 2 Sa. 15. 31, 24; 16. 20, 23; 17. 7, 14, 23; 1 K. 1. 12; 12. 8, 13, 14; 2 K. 18. 20, &c.

WICKED,] *lit.* one in a 'wrong' state toward God or man, as in v. 4, 5, 6; Ge. 18, 23, 25; Ex. 2. 13; 9. 27; 2. 23, 1, &c.

WAY,] as in v. 6; 2. 12; Ge. 3. 24; 6. 12; 16. 7; 18. 19; 19. 2, 31, &c.

SINNERS,] *lit.* those 'missing' the mark; as in v. 5; Ge. 13. 13; Nu. 16. 38; 32. 14; 1 Sa. 15. 18; 1 K. 1. 21, &c.

STOOD,]that is, still: as in 10.1; 26.12, &c. SEAT,] as in 107. 4, 7, 32, 36; 132. 3; Ge. 10. 30; 27. 39; 36. 43, &c.

SCORNERS,] as in Prov. 1. 22; 3. 24; 9. 7, 8; 13. 1; 14. 6; 15. 12; 19. 25, &c.

SAT,]that is, sat down; as in 9. 4; 23. 6; 26. 4; 29. 10; 47. 8, &c.

2. BUT RATHER,] as in Ge. 32. 26; 39. 6; Ex. 22. 23; Lev. 22. 6; Nu. 24. 22, &c.

LAW,] *lit.* 'direction;' as in 19. 7 ; 37. 31; 40. 8; 78. 1, 5, 10; 89. 30, 30, &c.

JEHOVAH,] the 'existing one,' the revealed national God of Israel and of the earth.

DELIGHT,] as in 16. 3; 107. 30; 111. 2; 1 Sa. 15. 22; 18. 25; 2 Sa. 23. 5; 1 K. 5. 8, 9; 9. 11; 10. 13; 2 Ch. 9. 12; Job 21. 21, &c.

MEDITATE] as in 2. 1; 35. 28, 37. 30; 38. 12; 63. 6; 71.24; 77.12; 115.7; 143.5; Jos.1.8, &c.

DAILY,] as in 13. 2; 22. 2; 32. 4; 42. 3, 8; 55. 10; 78. 14; 91. 5; 121. 6; Ex. 13. 21, 22, &c.

NIGHTLY,] as in 22. 2; 32. 4; 42. 3, 8, &c. 3. TREE,] as in 74, 5; 96. 12; 104. 16, &c.

PLANTED,] as in 92. 13; 128. 3; Jer. 17. 8; Eze. 17. 8, 10, 22, 23; 19. 10, 13; Hos. 9. 13.

RIVULETS,]as in 46.4; 65.9; 119.136; Job 29. 6; Prov. 5. 16; 21. 1; Isa. 30. 25; 32. 2; La. 3. 48.

WATERS,] so necessary to vegetable life.

GIVETH,] as in 2. 8; 14. 7; 16. 10; 18. 13, &c. FRUIT,] as in 21. 10; 58. 11; 72. 16; 104. 13.

SEASON,] as in 4. 7; 9. 9; 10. 1, 5; 21. 9, &c. LEAF,] as in Ge. 3. 7; 8. 11; Lev. 26. 26, &c.

WITHER,] as in 18. 45; 37. 2; Ex.18.18,&c. CAUSETH TO PROSPER,] as in Ge. 24. 21, &c.

4. WICKED,] as in v. 1.

BUT RATHER,] as in v. 2.

CHAFF,] as in 35. 5; Job 21. 18; Isa. 17. 13. WIND,] as in 11. 6; 18. 10, 15, 42; 31. 5, &c.

DRIVETH AWAY,] as in 68. 2; Lev. 26. 36, &c. 5. RISE,] as in 12. 5; 20. 8; 24. 3; 27. 3, &c.

JUDGMENT,] as in 7. 6; 9. 4, 7 16; 10. 5, &c. SINNERs,] as in v. 1.

COMPANY,] as in 7. 7; 22. 16; 68. 30; 74. 2. RIGHTEOUS,] or 'just,' or 'right,' as in v. 6; 7. 9, 7. 9, 11; 11. 3, 5, 7; 14. 5, &c.

6. IS KNOWING,] as in 9. 11; 36. 10; 37. 18. WAY,] as in v. 1.

RIGHTEOUS,] or 'just,' or 'right,' as in v. 5. IS LOST.] as in 2. 12; 9. 3, 6, 18; 10. 16 &c.

II. 1. NATIONS,] as in v. 3; 9. 5, 15, 17, &c.
TUMULTUOUSLY ASSEMBLED,] as in 55. 14;
Da. 6. 6, 11.
PEOPLES,] as in 7. 7; 9. 8; 44. 2, 14; 47. 3.
MEDITATE,] as in 1. 2, &c.
VANITY,] as in 4. 2; 73. 13; Lev. 26. 16, &c.
2. STATION THEMSELVES,] as in 5. 5, &c.
KINGS OF EARTH,] as in 76. 12; 89. 27, &c.
PRINCES,] as in Jud. 5. 3; Prov. 8. 15; 31.
4; Isa. 40. 23; Hab. 1. 10.
UNITED,] *lit.* 'founded;' as in 31. 13; Ex.
9. 18; Isa. 44. 28, &c.
MESSIAH,] i.e. 'anointed;' as in 18. 50; 20.
3; 28. 8; 84. 9; 89. 38, 51, &c.
3. DRAW OFF,] as in 107. 14; Jud. 16. 9, 12.
CORDS,] as in 107. 14; 116. 16; Job 39. 5, &c.
CAST,] as in 50. 17; 51. 11; 60. 8; 71. 9, &c.
THICK BANDS,] as in 118. 27; 129. 4, &c.
4. IS SITTING,] as in 9. 11; 17. 12; 22. 3, &c.
HEAVENS,] as in 11. 4; 14. 2; 20. 6; 33. 13.
LAUGH,] as in 37. 13; 52. 6; 59. 8, &c.
LORD,] as in 16. 2; 22. 30; 35. 17, &c.
MOCK,] as in 59. 8; 80. 6, &c.
5. ANGER,] as in v. 12; 6. 1; 7. 6; 10. 4, &c.
WRATH,] as in 58. 9; 69. 24; 78. 49, &c.
TROUBLE,] as in 83. 15; Job 22. 10, &c.
6. ANOINTED,] *lit.* 'poured out,' as in Isa.
29. 10, &c.
KING,] the one whom I have chosen.
ZION,] i.e. 'the sunny place;' as in 9. 11, &c.
HILL,] as in 3. 4; 15. 1; 43. 3, &c.
HOLINESS,] as in 4; 5. 7; 11. 4; 15. 1, &c.
7. DECLARE,] *or* 'recount, rehearse,' as in
9. 1, 14, &c.
STATUTE,] as in 50. 16; 81. 4; 94. 20; 99. 7.
SON,] as in Ex. 4. 22, 23; De. 14. 1, &c.
TO-DAY,] the day of inauguration.
BROUGHT THEE FORTH,] into the world as
a servant and king.
8. ASK,] *or* 'demand,' as a matter of right.
GIVE,] not 'make,' as in C.V.
NATIONS,] as in v. 1.
INHERITANCE,] as in 28. 9; 33. 12; 37. 18, &c.
POSSESSION,] as in Ge. 17. 8; 23. 4, 9, 20, &c.
ENDS OF EARTH,] *or* 'land;' as in 59. 13;
72. 8; 98. 3; De. 33. 17; 1 Sa. 2. 10, &c.
9. RULE,] *or* 'feed, *or* break.'
SCEPTRE,] as in 23. 4; 46. 7; 74. 2; 78. 55, &c.
IRON,] as in 105. 18; 107. 10, 16; 149. 8, &c.
VESSEL,] as in 7. 13; 31. 12; 71. 22, &c.
POTTER,] as in 33. 15; 94. 9, 20; 2 Sa. 17. 28.
CRUSH,] as in 137. 9; 1 K. 5. 9; Jer. 13. 14.
10. KINGS,] as in v. 2.
ACT WISELY,] as in 14. 2; 32. 8; 36. 3, &c.
BE INSTRUCTED,] as in Jer. 6. 8; Lev. 26. 23.
JUDGES OF EARTH,] *or* 'land;' as in 148. 11.
11. SERVE,] as in 100. 2; Ex. 10. 8, 11, &c.
FEAR,] *or* 'reverence;' as in 7; 19. 9, &c.
REJOICE,] as in 32. 11; Isa. 49. 13; 65. 18, &c.
TREMBLING,] as in 48. 6; Job 4. 14; Isa. 33. 14.
12. KISS,] as in Ge. 27. 26; Ge. 41. 40, &c.
CHOSEN ONE,] the 'Messiah' of v. 2; as in
Song 6. 9.
LEST,] *lit.* 'facing, fronting.'
ANGRY,] as in 60. 1; 79. 5; 85. 5, &c.
LOSE,] as in 1. 6; 9. 3, 6, 18; 10. 16, &c.
WAY,] of life and peace to God.
ANGER,] as in v. 5.
BURNETH,] as in 18. 8; 39. 3; 79. 5; 83. 14, &c.
AS A LITTLE THING,] as in 73. 2; 81. 15, &c.
HAPPINESS,] as in 1. 1, &c.

TRUSTING,] *lit.* 'taking refuge;' as in 5.
11; 17. 7, &c.

III. PSALM.] This title is prefixed to 57 of
the 'Psalms,' it denotes a poem accompanied
by the 'plucking' or 'twanging' of a harp
or lyre.
DAVID,] whose name is prefixed to 75
psalms.
FLEEING,] as in 57. 1; 2 Sa. 15. 14, &c.
ABSALOM,] i.e. 'father of peace.'
1. JEHOVAH,] as in 1. 2, &c.
HOW,] *lit.* 'what.'
DISTRESSES,] as in 4. 1; 18. 6; 32. 7, &c.
MULTIPLIED,] as in 4. 7; 25. 19; 38. 19, &c.
RISING UP,] as in 18. 39, 48; 44. 5, &c.
2. SOUL,] *lit.* a 'breathing' creature, as
in 6. 3.
SAFETY,] as in v. 8; 9. 14; 13. 5; 14. 7, &c.
GOD,] *in Heb.* 'Alohim.'
SELAH,] *lit.* 'pause!' So Sept.
3. SHIELD,] as in 7. 10; 18. 2, 30, 35, &c.
FOR ME,] in my behalf.
HONOUR,] as in 4. 2; 7. 5; 8. 5; 16. 9, &c.
LIFTER UP,] as in Ex. 35. 24; Prov. 3. 35, &c.
HEAD,] as in 23. 5; 27. 6; 60. 7, &c.
4. VOICE,] as the outward manifestation
of his inward feelings.
CALL,] upon him in prayer for help.
ANSWERETH,] not 'heard,' as in C.V.
HILL,] even Mount Zion, as in 2. 6, &c.
5. LAIN DOWN,] as in 8; 41. 8; 57. 4, &c.
SLEEP,] as in 4. 8; 13. 3; 44. 23; 121. 4, &c.
WAKED,] as in 35. 23; 44. 23; 59. 5; 139. 18.
SUSTAIN,] as in 37. 17, 34; 51. 12; 54. 4, &c.
6. AFRAID,] as in 23. 4; 27. 1, 3; 33. 8, &c.
MYRIADS,] as in 91. 7; Ge. 24. 60; Lev. 26. 8.
A PEOPLE,] as in v. 8; 7. 8; 9. 11; 14. 4, &c.
ROUND ABOUT,] as in 12. 8; 18. 11; 27. 6, &c.
SET,] not 'set themselves,' as in C.V.
7. RISE,] as in 7. 6; 9. 19; 10. 12; 17. 13, &c.
JEHOVAH,] the God of Israel.
SAVE,] as in 6. 4; 7. 1; 12. 1; 20. 9, &c.
MY GOD,] by a personal covenant.
SMITTEN,] as in 69. 26; 73. 51, 66; 135. 8, &c.
ENEMIES,] as in 10; 7. 5; 8. 2; 9. 3, &c.
CHEEK,] as in De. 18. 3; Jud. 15. 15, 16, &c.
TEETH,] as in 35. 16; 37. 12; 45. 8; 57. 4, &c.
BROKEN,] as in 29. 5; 46. 9; 48. 7; 74. 13, &c.
8. OF JEHOVAH,] *or* 'by Jehovah.'
SAFETY,] as in v. 2.
PEOPLE,] as in v. 6.
BLESSING,] as in 21. 3, 6; 24. 5; 37. 26, &c.

IV. OVERSEER,] as in 2 Ch. 2. 2, 18; 34. 13;
this title is prefixed to 55 psalms.
STRINGED INSTRUMENTS,] as in Hab. 3. 19,
&c.; as in Ps. 4. 6. 54. 55. 61. 67. 76; also in
69. 12; 77. 6; Job 30. 1; Isa. 38. 20; La. 3.
14; 5. 14.
1. CALLING,] in prayer unto Jehovah.
ANSWER,] not 'hear,' as in C.V.
GOD,] that is, source and fountain of my
RIGHTEOUSNESS,] towards God or men.
ADVERSITY,] as in 18. 6; 32. 7; 59. 16, &c.
GAVEST ENLARGEMENT,] as in Ge. 26. 22, &c
FAVOUR,] not 'have mercy,' as in C.V.
HEAR,] as in 17. 1, 6; 27. 7; 28. 2; 30. 10, &c.
PRAYER,] as in 6. 9; 17. 1; 35. 13; 39. 12, &c
2. SONS OF MEN,] as in 49. 2; 62. 9, &c.
TILL WHEN,] as in 74. 9, &c.

GLORY,] that which I value most, reckoned for
SHAME,] *or* a 'shameful thing.'
LOVE,] as in 11. 5; 52. 3, 4; 109. 17, &c.
VAIN THING,] as in 2. 1, &c.
SEEK,] *or* 'enquire.'
LIE,] as in 5. 6; 40. 4; 58. 3; 62. 4, 9, &c.
3. KNOW,] as in 46. 10; 100. 3; 139. 23, &c.
SEPARATED,] as in 17. 7; 139. 14, &c.
KIND ONE,] not 'godly,' as in C.V.
4. TREMBLE,] not 'stand in awe,' as in C.V.
SIN,] that is, 'miss the mark.
HEART,] as in 13. 2; 15. 2; 20. 4; 22. 26, &c.
BED,] as in 36. 4; 41. 3; 149. 5; Ge. 49. 4, &c.
SILENT,] *lit.* 'dumb,' as in 37. 7; 62. 5, &c.
5. SACRIFICE,] as in 50. 14; Ex. 8. 25, &c.
SACRIFICES,] as in 27. 6; 40. 6; 50. 5, 8, &c.
TRUST,] *or* 'lean,' as in 37. 3, 5; 62. 8, &c.
6. DISPLAY AS A BANNER.] So Sept.,
Vulg., &c.
LIGHT OF THY FACE,] as in 44. 3; 89. 15, &c.
7. GIVEN,] not 'put,' as in C.V.
JOY,] as in 16. 11; 21. 6; 30. 11; 43. 4, &c.
FROM THE TIME,] not 'more than in the time.' So Sept., Vulg., &c.
CORN,] as in 65. 9; 78. 24; Ge. 27. 28, &c.
NEW WINE,] as in Ge. 27. 28, 37; Nu. 18. 12.
MULTIPLIED,] as in 3. 1, &c.
8. PEACE,] as in 28. 3; 29. 11; 34. 14; 35. 20.
LIE DOWN,] as in 3. 5, &c.
SLEEP,] as in 3. 5, &c.
ALONE,] as in Nu. 23. 9; Mic. 7. 14.
CONFIDENTLY,] not 'in safety,' as in C.V.
DWELL,] as in 68. 6; 107. 36; 113. 8; 143. 3.

V. INHERITANCES.] So Sept., Vulg., &c.
1. SAYINGS,] as in 19. 14; 54. 2; 78. 1; 107. 11.
HEAR,] as in 17. 1; 39. 12; 49. 1; 54. 2, &c.
CONSIDER,] as in 50. 22; 94. 8; De. 32. 7, &c.
MEDITATION,] as in 39. 3.
2. BE ATTENTIVE,] not 'hearken;' as in 17. 1; 55. 2; 61. 1; 86. 6, &c.
CRY,] as in 18. 6; 34. 5; 39. 12; 40. 1, &c.
KING..GOD,] as in 44. 4; 74. 12; 84. 3, &c.
3. MORNING,] as in 59. 16; 92. 2, &c.
SET IN ARRAY,] not 'direct;' as in 50. 21.
LOOK OUT,] not 'look up;' as in 37. 32, &c.
4. DESIRING,] as in 34. 12; 35. 27; 40. 14, &c.
INHABIT,] as in 15. 1; 33. 8; 56. 6, &c.
5. BOASTFUL,] not 'foolish,' as in 73. 3, &c.
STATION THEMSELVES,] as in 2. 36. 4, &c.
HATED,] as in 9. 13; 11. 5; 25. 19; 26. 5.
WORKERS OF INIQUITY,] as in 6. 8; 14. 4.
6. LIE,] as in 4. 2, &c.
MAN OF BLOOD,] as in 26. 9; 55. 23; 59. 2.
DECEIT,] as in 10. 7; 17. 1; 24. 4, &c.
ABOMINATE,] as in 106. 40; 107. 18; 119. 163.
7. ABUNDANCE,] as in 69. 13; 106. 7, 45, &c
KINDNESS,] not 'mercy;' as in 6. 4; 13. 5.
HOUSE,] as in 23. 6; 26. 8; 27. 4, &c.
BOW MYSELF,] as in 138. 2, &c.
TEMPLE,] as in 11. 4; 18. 6; 27. 4; 29. 9, &c.
FEAR,] as in 2. 11; 19. 9; 34. 11, &c.
8. LEAD,] as in 27. 11; 139. 24, &c.
OBSERVING,] as in 54. 5; 65. 2; 59. 10, &c.
STRAIGHT,] as in Prov. 4. 25; Isa. 45. 2.
WAY,] as in 18. 21, 30; 25. 4, 8, 9, 12, &c.
9. STABILITY,] *or* 'preparedness, readiness.'
INWARD PART,] as in 36. 1; 39. 3; 46. 5, &c.
MISCHIEFS,] as in 33. 12; 52. 2, 7; 55. 11.

OPEN GRAVE,] as in Jer. 5. 16.
THROAT,] as in 69. 3; 115. 7; 149. 6; Isa. 3. 6.
TONGUE,] as in 10. 7; 12. 3, 4; 15. 3; 22. 15.
SMOOTH,] as in 36. 2; Prov. 2. 16; 7. 5, &c.
10. DECLARE GUILTY,] not 'destroy,' as in C.V.; as in 34. 21, 22.
FROM,] away from, *or* 'by means of.'
TRANSGRESSIONS,] as in 19. 13; 25. 7; 32. 1.
DRIVE AWAY,] as in 62. 4; De. 13. 5, 10, 13.
REBELLED,] as in 78. 8; 105. 28; Nu. 20. 10.
11. REJOICE,] as in 9. 2; 14. 7; 21. 1; 31. 7
TRUSTING,] *lit.* 'taking refuge.'
AGE,] as in 30. 12; 44. 8, &c.
SING,] as in 20. 5; 51. 14; 59. 16; 63. 7, &c.
COVEREST,] as in 91. 4; Ex. 40. 21; Jud. 3. 24
EXULT,] as in 9. 2; 25. 2; 68. 3, &c.
12. BLESS,] as in 29. 11; 65. 10; 67. 1, &c.
BUCKLER,] as in 35. 2; 91. 4; 1 Sa. 17. 7, &c
FORMER,] as in 19. 14; 30. 5, 7; 40. 8, &c
COMPASS,] as in 8. 5; 65. 11; 103. 4, &c.

VI. OCTAVE,] as in 12. 1. So Sept., Vulg., &c.
1. REPROVE,] as in 38. 1; 50. 8, 21; 94. 10, &c.
ANGER,] as in 2. 5, 12, &c.
FURY,] as in 37. 8; 38. 1; 58. 4; 59. 13, &c
CHASTISE,] as in 16. 7; 38. 1: 39. 21; 94. 12
2. FAVOUR,] not 'have mercy, as in C.V.; so in 4. 1, &c.
WEAK,] as in Neh. 4. 2; 1 Sa. 2. 5, &c.
HEAL,] as in 41. 4; 60. 2; Nu. 12. 13, &c.
TROUBLED,] as in v. 3, 10; 48. 5; 83. 17, &c
BONES,] as in 22. 14, 17; 31. 10; 32. 3, &c.
3. TILL WHEN,] as in Ge. 30. 30; Ex. 10. 3.
4. DRAW OUT,] as in 119. 153; 140. 1, &c.
SAVE,] as in 3. 7; 7. 1; 12. 1; 20. 9, &c.
KINDNESS' SAKE,] as in 31. 16; 44. 26, &c.
5. MEMORIAL,] as in 9. 6; 30. 4· 34. 16, &c.
DEATH,] during its dominion.
SHEOL,] not 'grave,' as in C.V.; as in 9. 17.
GIVE THANKS,] as in Isa. 38. 18, &c.
6. WEARY,] as in 69. 3; Jos. 24. 13; 2 Sa. 23. 10.
SIGHING,] as in 31. 10; 38. 9; 102. 5, &c.
MEDITATE,] not 'make to swim,' as in C.V.; as in Ge. 24. 63.
NIGHT,] as in 78. 14; Ex. 10. 13; 14. 20, &c.
BED,] as in Ge. 47. 31; 48. 2; 49. 33, &c.
TEAR,] not 'tears,' as in C.V
COUCH,] as in 41. 3; 132. 3; De. 3. 11, &c.
WASTE,] not 'water,' as in C.V.; as in 39. 11.
7. OLD,] not 'consumed,' as in C.V.; as in 31. 9, 10.
PROVOCATION,] as in 10. 14; 31. 9; 85. 4, &c
EYE,] as in 31. 9; 38. 10; 54. 7; 69. 3, &c.
OLD,] as in Job 21. 7, &c.
ADVERSARIES,] as in 7. 4, 6; 8. 2; 10. 5, &c.
8. WORKERS OF INIQUITY,] as in 5. 5; 14. 4.
WEEPING,] as in 30. 5; 102. 9; Ge. 45. 2, &c.
9. SUPPLICATION,] as in 55. 1; 119. 170, &c.
PRAYER,] as in 4. 1; 17. 1; 35. 13; 39. 12.
RECEIVETH,] that is, accepteth and granteth it.
10. ASHAMED,] as in 22. 5; 25. 2, 3, 20, &c.
TROUBLED,] as in Isa. 38. 18, &c.
ENEMIES,] as in 3. 7; 7. 5; 8. 2; 9. 3, 6, &c.
MOMENT,] as in 30. 5; 73. 19; Ex. 33. 5, &c.

VII. ERRING ONE,] as in Hab. 3. 1; Sept., and Vulg. 'psalm.'
SUNG,] as in 13. 6; 21. 13; 27. 6, &c.

WORDS,] or 'matters.
CUSH.] Not mentioned elsewhere; probably some follower of Saul.
BENJAMITE,] of which tribe Saul was.
1. TRUSTED,] or 'taken refuge,' as in 2. 12.
SAVE,] as in 3. 7; 6. 4; 12. 1; 20. 9, &c.
PURSUERS,] not 'persecutors,' as in C.V; as in 31. 15; 35. 3, 6, &c.
DELIVER,] as in 22. 20; 25. 20; 31. 3, 15, &c.
2. TEAR,] as in 17. 12; 22. 13; 50. 22, &c.
LION,] as in 10. 9; 17. 12; 22. 13, 16, &c.
RENDING,] as in 1 K. 19. 11; La. 5. 8, &c.
DELIVER,] as in 35. 10; 50. 22; 71. 11, &c.
3. THIS] thing, imputed to him by others.
INIQUITY,] as in 53. 1; 82. 2; Lev. 19. 15.
HAND,] as in 9. 16; 18. 1; 24. 4: 26. 6, &c.
4. WELL-WISHER,] or 'peaceful one;' as in 2 Sa. 20. 19, &c.
EVIL,] as in v. 9; 5. 4, &c.
DRAW OUT,] as in 6. 4, &c.
ADVERSARY,] as in v. 6; 6. 7; 8. 2; 10. 5.
WITHOUT CAUSE,] as in 25. 3; Ge. 31. 42, &c.
5. ENEMY,] as in 3. 7; 6. 10; 8. 2; 9. 3, 6, &c.
PURSUE,] not 'persecute,' as in C.V.; as in 18. 37, &c.
SOUL,] as in v. 2; 3. 2; 6. 3, 4; 10. 3, &c.
OVERTAKETH,] not 'take;' as in 18. 37, &c.
TREADETH DOWN,] as in 91. 13; 2 K. 7. 17.
EARTH,] as in 2. 2, 8, 10, &c.
LIFE,] as in 16. 11; 17. 14; 18. 46; 21. 4, &c.
HONOUR,] as in 3. 3; 4. 2; 7. 5; 8. 5, &c.
PLACETH,] lit. 'causeth to tabernacle.'
DUST,] as in 18. 42; 22. 15, 29; 30. 9, &c.
6. RISE,] as in 3. 7; 9. 19; 10. 12; 17. 3, &c.
ANGER,] as in 2. 5, 12, &c.
BE LIFTED UP,] not 'lift thyself up,' as in C.V.; as in 24. 7; 94. 2, &c.
WRATH,] as in 78. 49; 85. 3; 90. 9, &c.
ADVERSARIES,] as in v. 4, &c.
AWAKE,] as in 44. 23; 57. 8; 59. 4; 108. 2, &c.
COMMANDED,] as in 33. 9; 42. 8; 68. 28, &c.
7. COMPANY,] not 'congregation,' as in C.V.; as in 1. 5; 22. 16, &c.
PEOPLES,] as in 2. 1; 9. 8; 44. 2, 14; 47. 3.
COMPASS,] as in 26. 6; 32. 7, 10; 55. 10, &c.
ON HIGH,] as in 10. 5; 18. 16; 56. 2; 68. 18.
8. JUDGE,] as a legislator, as in 9. 8; 54. 1.
JUDGE ME,] as a magistrate; as in 26. 1, &c.
RIGHTEOUSNESS,] as in v. 17; 18. 20, 24, &c.
INTEGRITY,] as in 25. 21; 26. 1, 11; 41. 12.
ON ME,] not 'in me,' as in C.V.
9. ENDED,] as in 12. 1; 57. 2; 77. 8; 138. 8.
EVIL,] as in v. 4, &c.
ESTABLISH,] or 'prepare,' as in v. 12, &c.
TRIER,] as in 11. 4, 5; 17. 3; 26. 2; 66. 10.
HEARTS,] as in 17. 3; 1 Ch. 29. 17; Prov. 17. 3.
REINS,] as in 16. 7; 26. 2; 73. 21; 139. 13, &c.
RIGHTEOUS GOD.] Sept. and Vulg. omit 'righteous.'
10. SHIELD,] not 'defence,' as in C.V.; as in 3. 3, &c.
ON GOD,] not 'of God,' as in C.V.
SAVIOUR,] as in 17. 7; 18. 46; 106. 21, &c.
UPRIGHT IN HEART,] as in 11. 2; 32. 11, &c.
11. JUDGE,] as in 2. 10; 9. 4; 50. 6; 58. 11.
NOT ANGRY,] not 'God is angry, as in C.V. So Sept. and Vulg.
AT ALL TIMES,] or 'during every day.'
12. TURN] not back from his ways.
SWORD,] as in 17. 13; 22. 20; 37. 14, 15, &c.
SHARPENETH,] as in Ge. 4. 22; 1 Sa. 13. 20.

BOW,] as in 11. 2; 18. 34; 37. 14, 15; 44. 6.
TRODDEN,] not 'bent,' as in C.V.; as in 11. 2, &c.
PREPARETH,] as in v. 9, &c.
13. INSTRUMENTS OF DEATH,] that is, deadly ones.
ARROWS,] as in 11. 2; 18. 14; 38. 2; 45. 5, &c.
BURNING PURSUERS,] as in Prov. 26. 23, &c.
MAKETH,] not 'ordaineth,' as in C.V.; as in v. 15.
14. TRAVAILETH,] or 'destroyeth,' or 'corrupteth.'
INIQUITY,] as in 5. 6; 6. 8; 10. 7, &c.
PERVERSENESS,] as in 16; 10. 7, 14, &c.
CONCEIVED,] as in Ge. 4. 1, 17; 16. 4, 5, &c.
BROUGHT FORTH,] as in 2. 7, &c.
FALSEHOOD,] as in 27. 12; 31. 18; 33. 17, &c.
15. PREPARED,] not 'made,' as in C.V.; as in 22. 16, &c.
PIT,] as in 28. 1; 30. 3; 40. 2, &c.
DIGGETH,] as in 35. 7; Ge. 21. 30, &c.
DITCH,] or 'marring;' as in 9. 15; 16. 10, &c.
MAKETH,] as in v. 13.
16. PERVERSENESS,] not 'mischief,' as in C.V.; as in v. 14.
HEAD,] as in Jos. 2. 19; Jud. 9. 57, &c.
CROWN,] as in 68. 21; Ge. 49. 26, &c.
VIOLENCE,] as in 11. 5: 18. 48; 25. 19, &c.
COMETH DOWN,] in the providence of God.
17. THANK,] not 'praise,' as in C.V.; as in 6. 5, &c.
PRAISE,] as in 6. 5; 9. 1; 18. 49, &c.
MOST HIGH,] as in 9. 2; 18. 13; 21. 7, &c.

VIII. GITTITH,] as in 81. 1; 84. 1; Sept and Vulg. 'wine-presses;' Targ. 'harp of Gath.'
1. LORD,] as in 12. 4; 45. 11; 97. 5; 105. 21.
HONOURABLE,] as in v. 9; 16. 3; 76. 4, &c.
NAME,] as in 5. 11; 7. 17: 9. 2, 5, 10, &c.
EARTH,] or 'land.'
SETTEST,] lit. 'givest.'
HONOUR,] as in 21. 5; 45. 3; 96. 6; 104. 1, &c.
ABOVE,] or 'upon the heavens.'
2. INFANTS,] as in 17. 4; 137. 9; 1 Sa. 15. 3.
SUCKLINGS,] as in Nu. 11. 12; De. 32. 25, &c.
FOUNDED,] not 'ordained,' as in C.V.; as in 24. 2; 78. 69; 89. 11; 102. 25, &c.
STRENGTH,] as in 21. 1, 13; 28. 7; 8; 29. 1, 11.
ADVERSARIES,] as in 6. 7; 7. 4, 6; 10. 5, &c.
TO STILL,] as in 46. 9; 89. 44; 119. 119, &c.
ENEMY,] as in 3. 7; 6. 10; 7. 5; 9. 3, 6, &c.
SELF-AVENGER,] as in 44. 16; Jer. 5. 9, 29, &c.
3. FOR,] not 'when,' as in C.V.
WORK,] as in v. 6; 19. 2; 28. 4, 5, &c.
FINGERS,] as in 144. 1; Ex. 18. 19; 29. 21, &c.
MOON,] as in 72. 5, 7; 89. 37; 104. 19, &c.
STARS,] as in 136. 9; 147. 4; 148. 3, &c.
ESTABLISH,] or 'prepare,' not 'ordain,' as in C.V.
4. MAN,] as in 9. 19, 20; 10. 18; 26. 9, &c.
INSPECTEST,] not 'visitest,' as in C.V.; as in 17. 3; 65. 9; 89. 32, &c.
SON OF MAN,] as in 11. 4; 12. 1; 14. 2, &c.
REMEMBEREST,] as in 9. 12; 20. 3; 22. 27, &c.
5. TO LACK,] not 'lower,' as in C.V.
A LITTLE,] as in 23. 1; 34. 10; Ge. 8. 3, 5, &c.
GODHEAD,] or 'God,' not 'angels,' as in C.V.; in Heb. 2. 7 the Sept. is quoted as an argumentum ad hominem, which is true so far as the greater includes the less.

HONOUR,] as in 3. 3; 4. 2; 7. 5; 16. 9, &c.
MAJESTY,] as in 21. 5; 29. 4; 45. 3, 4, &c.
COMPASSEST,] as in 5. 12; 65. 11; 103. 4, &c.
6. RULE,] as in Da. 11. 39.
WORKS OF THY HANDS,] as in v. 3; 19. 1, &c.
PLACED,] as in 3. 6; 9. 20; 12. 5, &c.
FEET,] as in 9. 15; 18. 9, 33. 38; 22. 16, &c.
7. SHEEP,] as in Nu. 32. 24.
OXEN,] as in 50. 10; De. 7. 13; 28. 4, 18, 51.
BEASTS OF THE FIELD,] as in 50. 11; 80. 13.
8. BIRD,] not 'fowl,' as in C.V.; as in 11. 1.
FISH,] as in Ge. 9. 2; Nu. 11. 22, &c.
PASSING THROUGH,] as in 80. 12; 84. 6, &c.
PATHS,] as in 16. 11; 17. 4; 19. 5; 25. 4, &c.
9. EARTH,] as in v. 1.

IX. DEATH OF LABBEN,] Targ. 'death of his son;' Sept. and Vulg. 'hidden things of the son;' others 'on death, to Ben;' see 1 Ch. 15. 18.
1. CONFESS,] not 'praise,' as in C.V.; as in 6. 5, &c.
WHOLE HEART,] as in 119. 2, 10, 34, 58, &c.
RECOUNT,] not 'shew forth,' as in C.V.; as in v. 14; 2. 7; 22. 17, &c.
WONDERS,] as in 26. 7; 40. 5; 71. 17, &c.
2. REJOICE,] as in 5. 11; 14. 7; 21. 1; 31. 7.
EXULT,] as in 5. 11; 25. 2; 68. 3, &c.
PRAISE,] as in v. 11; 7. 17; 18. 49; 21. 13, &c.
NAME,] as in v. 5, 10; 5. 11; 7. 17; 8. 1, &c.
MOST HIGH,] as in 7. 17; 18. 13; 21. 7, &c.
3. ENEMIES,] as in v. 6; 3. 7; 6. 10; 7. 5, &c.
BACKWARD,] as in 35. 4; 40. 14; 44. 10, 18.
STUMBLE,] not 'fall,' as in C.V.; as in 1 Sa. 2. 4.
PERISH,] as in v. 6, 18; 1. 6; 2. 12; 10. 16, &c.
FACE,] or 'presence.'
4. DONE,] that is, performed or executed.
JUDGMENT,] as in v. 7, 16; 1. 5; 7. 6; 10. 5.
RIGHT,] as in 76. 8; 140. 12; De. 17. 18, &c.
SAT,] or 'sat down.'
THRONE,] as in v. 7; 11. 4; 45. 6; 47. 8, &c.
JUDGE,] as in 2. 10; 7. 11; 50. 6; 58. 11, &c.
5. REBUKED,] as in 68. 30; 106. 9; 119. 21.
NATIONS,] not 'heathen,' as in C.V.; as in 2. 1, &c.
DESTROYED,] as in 5. 6; 21. 10, &c.
NAME,] as in v. 2, 10, &c.
BLOTTED OUT,] as in 51. 1, 9; 69. 28, &c.
FOR EVER,] as in v. 7; 5. 11; 10. 16; 12. 7, &c.
6. ENEMY,] as in v. 3.
FINISHED,] as in 64. 6; 73. 19, &c.
DESTRUCTIONS,] as in 102. 6; 109. 10, &c.
FOR EVER,] or 'to victory;' as in v. 18, &c.
CITIES,] as in 31. 21; 46. 4; 48. 1, 8, &c.
PLUCKED UP,] not 'destroyed,' as in C.V.; as in De. 29. 28, &c.
PERISHED,] as in 1. 6, &c.
MEMORIAL,] as in 6. 5; 30. 4; 34. 16, &c.
WITH THEM,] or 'they themselves,' as in C.V.
7. ABIDETH,] or 'sitteth.'
PREPARING,] as in 8. 3; 11. 2; 40 2; 68. 9.
THRONE,] as in v. 4.
8. JUDGETH,] as in 98. 9, &c.
WORLD,] as in 18. 15; 19. 4; 24. 1; 33. 8, &c.
JUDGETH,] as in 7. 8, &c.
PEOPLE,] as in 2. 1; 7. 7; 44. 2, &c.
UPRIGHTNESS,] as in 17. 2; 58. 1; 75. 2, &c.
9. TOWER,] not 'refuge,' as in C.V.; as in 18. 2, &c.

BRUISED,] not 'oppressed,' as in C.V.
TIMES,] as in 10. 18; 74. 21; Prov. 26. 28.
ADVERSITY,] as in 10. 1; 20. 1; 22. 11, &c.
10. TRUST,] as in 4. 5, &c.
KNOW,] as in 1. 6; 36. 10; 37. 18; 44. 21, &c.
NAME,] as in v. 2, 5; 5. 11; 7. 17; 8. 1, &c.
FORSAKEN,] as in 16. 10; 22. 1; 27. 9, 10, &c.
SEEKING,] as in v. 12; 14. 2; 22. 26; 24. 6, &c.
11. PRAISE,] or 'psalms,' as in v. 2; 7. 17, &c.
INHABITING,] lit. 'sitting.'
ZION,] as in 2. 6, &c.
DECLARE,] lit. 'set before,' as in Ge. 24. 23, 49, &c.
PEOPLES,] as in 3. 6, 8; 7. 8; 14. 4, 7, &c.
ACTS,] as in 14. 1; 66. 5; 77. 12; 78. 11, &c.
12. SEEKING,] as in v. 10.
BLOOD,] as in Ge. 4. 10, 11; 9. 4, 5, 6, &c.
REMEMBERED,] as in 8. 4; 25. 6, 7, &c.
FORGOTTEN,] as in v. 18; 10. 11, 12; 13. 1, &c.
CRY,] as in Ge. 18. 21; 19. 13; 27. 34, &c.
AFFLICTED,] or 'humble;' as in C.V.
13. FAVOUR,] not 'have mercy,' as in C.V.
AFFLICTION,] as in v. 18.
HATING,] as in 18. 17; 21. 8; 34. 21; 35. 19.
LIFTEST UP,] as in 18. 48; 1 Sa. 2. 7, &c.
GATES OF DEATH,] as in 107. 18; Job 38. 17.
14. SO THAT,] or 'in order that.'
RECOUNT,] not 'shew forth,' as in C.V.
PRAISE,] as in 22. 3, 25; 33. 1; 34. 1, &c.
GATES,] as in v. 13.
DAUGHTER OF ZION,] as in Isa. 1. 8, &c.
REJOICE,] as in 2. 11; 13. 4, 5; 14. 7, &c.
SALVATION,] as in 3. 2, 8; 13. 5; 14. 7, &c.
15. SUNK,] as in 69. 2, 14; Ex. 15. 4, &c.
PIT,] or 'marring;' as in 7. 15, &c.
NET,] as in 10. 9; 25. 15; 31. 4; 35. 7, &c.
HID,] as in 31. 4; 35. 7, 8; 140. 5, &c.
CAPTURED,] as in 59. 12; Jos. 7. 15, 16, &c.
16. KNOWN,] as in 48. 3; 74. 5; 77. 19, &c.
DONE,] as in v. 4; 99. 4, &c.
WORK OF HIS HAND,] as in De. 33. 11, &c.
SNARED,] as in De. 7. 25; 12. 30, &c.
MEDITATION,] as in 19. 14; 92. 3; La. 3. 62.
17. SHEOL,] not 'hell,' as in C.V.
FORGETTING,] as in v. 12.
18. FOR EVER,] as in v. 6.
NEEDY,] as in 12. 5; 35. 10; 37. 14, &c.
HOPE,] as in 62. 5; 71. 5, &c.
HUMBLE,] as in v. 12.
LOST,] as in 1. 6; 2. 12, &c.
19. RISE,] as in 3. 7; 7. 6; 10. 12; 17. 13, &c.
MAN,] as in 8. 4; 10. 18; 26. 9; 55. 13, &c.
BE STRONG,] as in 52. 7; 89. 13, &c.
20. APPOINT,] lit. 'set;' as in 48. 13, &c.
DIRECTOR,] that is, one who shews the way; as in 84. 6; Joel 2. 23.
MEN,] as in v. 19; 8. 6; 10. 18, &c.; or 'mortal men.'

X. 1. DISTANCE,] or 'in a far off place.' The Sept. and Vulg. justly consider this psalm as part of the preceding one.
HIDEST,] as in Lev. 20. 4; 1 Sa. 12. 3, &c.
TIMES,] as in v. 5; 1. 3; 4. 7; 9. 9, &c.
ADVERSITY,] as in 9. 9; 20. 1; 22. 11, &c.
2. PRIDE,] as in 31. 18, 23; 36. 11; 46. 3, &c.
POOR,] as in v. 9, 12; 9. 12, 18, &c.
ENFLAMED,] not 'persecuted,' as in C.V.; so Sept., Targ., Vulg., Cocceius, &c.
THEY ARE CAUGHT.] So Sept., Vulg., &c.
DEVICES,] as in v. 4; 21. 11; 37. 7; 139. 20.

DEVISED,] as in 21. 1; 32. 2; 35. 20, &c.
3. BOASTED,] as in 44. 8; 119. 164, &c.
DESIRE,] as in v. 17; 21. 3; 38. 9; 78. 29, &c.
DISHONEST GAINER,] not 'covetous;' as
in C.V.
BLESSED.] Gesenius and others strangely
enough read 'cursed.'
DESPISED,] not 'abhorred,' as in C.V.; so
Horsley, Hammond, &c.
4. HEIGHT,] as in 1 Sa. 17. 4; 2 Ch. 3. 4, &c.
INQUIRETH,] the path of duty and honour.
Targum supplies 'after God.'
DEVICES,] not 'thoughts;' as in v. 2. Sept.
Vulg. Arab. 'God is not before him.'
5. PAIN.] Sept. 'polluted or profaned;'
Targ. 'prosperous.'
WAYS,] towards God and man.
TIMES,] as in v. 1.
ON HIGH,] or 'a high place.'
ADVERSARIES,] lit. 'distressors.'
PUFFETH,] as in 12. 5; Prov. 6. 19; 12. 17.
6. HEART,] as in v. 11.
MOVED,] as in 13. 4; 15. 5; 16. 8, &c.
GENERATION,] as in 33. 11; 45. 17; 49. 11.
EVIL,] that is, misfortune.
7. OATHS,] not 'cursing,' as in C.V.
MOUTH,] as in 5. 9; 8. 2; 17. 3, 10, &c.
FULL,] as in 26. 10; 33. 5; 38. 7, &c.
DECEITS..FRAUD,] in Rom. 3. 6 it is simply
rendered 'bitternesses,' like Sept.
TONGUE,] as in 5. 9; 12. 3, 4, &c.
PERVERSENESS,] as in v. 14; 7. 14, 16, &c.
INIQUITY,] as in 5. 5; 6. 8; 7. 14, &c.
8. SITTING,] or 'abiding.'
AMBUSH,] as in Jos. 8. 9, &c.
VILLAGES,] or 'courts;' so Targ. and Syr.
But Arab. Ethiop. Sept. Vulg. &c., 'with
the rich.'
SECRET PLACES,] as in v. 9; 17. 12; 64. 4, &c.
SLAY,] as in 59. 11; 78. 31, &c.
INNOCENT,] as in 15. 5; 24. 4; 94. 21, &c.
AFFLICTED.] Sept. and Targ. read 'poor,'
as in C.V.
WATCH SECRETLY,] as in 27. 5; 31. 19, 20.
9. LIETH IN WAIT,] as in 59. 3, &c.
SECRET PLACE,] as in v. 8.
LION,] as in 7. 2, &c.
COVERT,] not 'den,' as in C.V.
CATCH,] as in Jud. 21. 21.
POOR,] as in v. 2.
DRAW,] as in 28. 3; 36. 10; 85. 5, &c.
NET,] as in 9. 15, &c.
10. BRUISED,] as in 38. 8, &c.
BOWETH DOWN,] as in 35. 4; 38. 6, &c.
MIGHTY ONES,] as in 35. 18; 135. 10, &c.
AFFLICTED,] not 'poor,' as in C.V.
FALLEN,] injured and dead.
11. HEART,] as in v. 6; if not in open words.
GOD,] lit. 'the mighty' one.
FORGOTTEN,] the actions of the sinner.
HID HIS FACE,] as unable or unwilling to
prevent evil.
SEEN,] and therefore is ignorant of the
crime.
12. ARISE,] as in 3. 7; 7. 6; 9. 19, &c.
LIFT UP] to execute vengeance.
HUMBLE,] as in v. 2, 9; or 'afflicted.'
13. DESPISED,] as in v. 3.
HEART,] as in v. 11.
REQUIRED,] not 'thou wilt not require,'
as in C.V.; So Vulg.

14. SEEN,] all the actions of the wicked in
his hiding place.
PERVERSENESS,] as in v. 7.
ANGER,] not 'spite,' as in C.V.
BEHOLDEST,] as in 13. 3, &c.
GIVING,] not 'requiting,' as in C.V.
AFFLICTED,] not 'poor,' as in C.V.
LEAVETH.] So Montanus, Michaelis, Coc-
ceius, &c.
FATHERLESS,] as in v. 18; 68. 5; 82. 3, &c.
HELPER,] as in 22. 11; 30. 10; 54. 4, &c.
15. BREAK,] as in Jer. 17. 18, &c.
ARM,] that is, the power.
SEEK OUT,] as in 4. 13.
FIND NOT,] as in 17. 3, &c.
16. KING,] supreme ruler over all.
PERISHED,] or 'lost.'
17. DESIRE,] as in v. 3.
HUMBLE,] as in 9. 12, 18, &c.
HEARD,] and accepted favourably.
PREPAREST,] makest ready or firm.
ATTEND,] as in 66. 19, &c.
18. JUDGE,] as in 51. 4; 96. 13; 98. 9, &c
FATHERLESS,] as in v. 14.
BRUISED,] as in 9. 9; 74. 21; Prov. 26. 28.
MORTAL MAN,] as in 8. 4; 9. 19, 20, &c.
EARTH,] or 'land,' perhaps.
OPPRESS,] or 'terrify.' So Ainsworth, Pis-
cator, Musculus, Vatablus, &c.

XI. OVERSEER,] as in Ps. 4. 5. 6. 8. 9. &c.
DAVID.] Sept. adds a 'psalm by David,' as
it often does elsewhere.
1. TRUSTED,] or 'taken refuge,' as in 2. 12.
SOUL,] that is, to myself, as often.
THEY MOVED,] not 'flee ye,' as in C.V.
THY MOUNTAIN,] a usual place of retreat.
Sept. Targ. 'to the mount, as a sparrow.'
BECAUSE OF,] by reason of, on account of
THE BIRD,] in order to catch it.
2. TREAD A BOW,] by putting their foot
upon it to bend it, in order to
SHOOT,] as in 64. 4; Ex. 19. 13, &c.
THICK DARKNESS,] as in 91. 6; Job. 3. 6.
UPRIGHT IN HEART,] as in v. 7; 7. 10, &c.
3. WHEN,] not 'if,' as in C.V.
FOUNDATIONS,] on which his hopes are
built; Sept. 'things thou hast perfected or
prepared.'
DESTROYED,] as in Prov. 11. 11; 24. 31, &c.
HATH HE DONE] in time past? he will do
so in time to come; but 'what can he do,' as
in C.V. So Sept. Vulg., &c.
4. HOLY TEMPLE,] as in 5. 7; 65. 4; 79. 1.
THRONE,] as in 9, 4, 7, &c.
SEE,] as in v. 7.
EYE-LIDS,] as in 132. 4; Job 3. 9, &c.
TRY,] as in 5; 7. 9; 17. 3, &c.
SONS OF MEN,] or 'of Adam,' as in 8. 4, &c
5. TRIETH,] as in v. 4; in order to prove
him.
VIOLENCE,] as in 7. 16; 18. 48; 25. 19, &c.
HATED,] as in 5. 5, &c.
6. POURETH,] lit. 'raineth,' as in 78. 24, 27.
SNARES,] as in 69. 22; 91. 3; 119. 110, &c.;
the original word never means 'lightning,'
as some suppose.
FIRE,] as in 18. 8, 12, 13; 21. 9, &c.
BRIMSTONE,] as in Ge. 19. 24; De. 29. 23.
HORRIBLE,] as in 119. 53; La. 5. 11
WIND,] not 'tempest,' as in C.V.

PORTION,] as in Ex. 29. 26; Lev. 7. 33, &c.
CUP,] as in 16. 5; 23. 5; 75. 8, &c. So
Sept. Syr. Vulg. &c.
7. RIGHTEOUS,] as in v. 5; 7. 9, 11; 116. 5.
LOVED,] as in 45. 7, &c.
UPRIGHT,] as in v. 2.
SEE.] Sept. 'his face seeth righteousness;'
as in v. 4; the Targ. and Arab. read, 'the
upright see His face

XII. OVERSEER,] as in Ps. 4. 5. 6. 8. 9. &c.
OCTAVE,] as in Ps. 6.
1. SAVE,] not 'help,' as in C.V.   So Sept.
and Vulg.
KIND,] not 'godly,' as in C.V.; so every-
where.
FAILED,] as in 7. 9; 57. 2; 77. 8; 138. 8, &c.
STEDFAST,] as in 31. 23; 2 Sa. 20. 19. Sept.
'the truths.'
CEASED,] Original word not found again.
SONS OF MEN,] or 'sons of Adam,' as in 8. 4.
2. VANITY,] as in 24. 4; 26. 4; 31. 6, &c.
EACH,] lit. a 'man.'
NEIGHBOUR,] lit. 'friend,' as in 15. 3; 28. 3.
LIP OF FLATTERY,] as in v. 3; 5. 9, &c.
HEART AND HEART,] as in 1 Ch. 12. 33, &c.
3. CUTTETH OFF,] as in 34. 16; 101. 8, &c.
GREAT THINGS]not 'proud things,'asinC.V.
4. DO MIGHTILY,] not 'prevail,' as in C.V.
OUR OWN,] lit. 'with us.'
LORD,] as in 8. 1, 9; 45. 11; 97. 5, &c.
5. SPOILING,] not 'oppression,' as in C.V.
POOR,] as in 9. 12, 18; 10. 2, 9, 12, &c.
GROANING,] not 'sighing,' as in C.V.
NEEDY,] as in 9. 18; 35. 10; 37. 14; 40. 17.
ARISE,] as in 68. 1; 76. 9; 102. 13, &c.
Targ. adds 'for judgment.'
SET,] as in 3. 6; 8. 6; 9. 20, &c.
HE BREATHES FOR IT,] as his due and por-
tion. Sept. and Vulg. 'I will act boldly with
him.'
6. SAYINGS,] as in 17. 6; 18. 30; 105. 19, &c.
PURE,] as in 19. 9; 51. 10, &c.
SILVER,] as in 15. 5; 66. 10; 68. 13, 30, &c.
TRIED,] as in 18. 30; 119. 140; 2 Sa. 22. 31.
FURNACE.] Original word not found again.
REFINED,] as in 1 Ch. 28. 18; 29. 4, &c.
SEVEN-FOLD,] as in 79. 12; Ge. 4. 15, 24, &c.
7. PRESERVE,] or watch. Sept. Vulg.
Arab. Ethiop. read 'us' for 'them,' as in
next clause.
KEEPEST,] as in 25. 21; 32. 7; 40. 11, &c.
GENERATION,] as in 10. 6; 14. 5, &c.
8. WALK CONTINUALLY,] as in 26. 3; 39. 6.
VILENESS,] not 'vilest men,' as in C.V.
EXALTED,] lit. 'to the exaltation of vile-
ness.'
SONS OF MEN,] as in v. 1, &c.

XIII. OVERSEER,] as in Ps. 4. 5. 6. 8. &c.
1. TILL WHEN,] as in Job 8. 2; 18. 2, &c.
FORGET,] as in 9. 12; 10. 11, 12; 13. 1, &c.
FOR EVER,] as in 9. 6; 13; 10. 11; 16. 11, &c.
HIDE THY FACE,] as in 10. 11; 22. 24, &c.
2. SET,] not 'take,' as in C.V.; so Sept.
Vulg. &c.
COUNSELS,] not 'counsel,' as in C.V.
SORROW,] as in 31. 10; 107. 39; 116. 3, &c.
DAILY.] Sept. reads 'day and night.'
ENEMY,] as in 3. 7; 6. 10; 7. 5; 8. 2; 9. 3, &c.
EXALTED,] as in 18. 46; 27. 6; 46. 10, &c.

3. LOOK ATTENTIVELY,] as in 74. 20, &c.
ANSWER,] not 'hear' merely, as in C.V.
ENLIGHTEN,] as in 31. 16; 80. 3, 19; 119. 135.
SLEEP,] as in 3. 5; 4. 8; 44. 23, &c.
IN DEATH,] lit. 'the death.'Sept. 'to death.'
4. OVERCAME,] or 'I am abler (than) he.'
ADVERSARIES,] lit. 'distressors.'
JOY,] or 'are glad,' as in v. 4.
MOVED,] as in 10. 6; 15. 5; 16. 8; the Targ.
adds 'from thy ways.'
5. KINDNESS,] not 'mercy,' as in C.V.
TRUSTED,] or 'leant.'
REJOICE,] or 'is glad,' as in v. 5.
HEART,] as in 4. 7; 16. 9; 19. 8; 28. 7, &c.
SALVATION,] or 'safety' afforded by thee.
6. SING,] as in 21. 13; 27. 6; 33. 3, &c.
CONFERRED BENEFITS,] as in 7. 4, &c.
Sept. and Vulg. add 'and I sing psalms to
the name of the Lord Most High.'

XIV. OVERSEER,] as in Ps. 4. 5. 6. 8. 9. &c.
1. FOOL,] as in 39. 8; 53. 1; 74. 18, 21, &c.
HEART,] as in 4. 7; 7. 10; 9. 1; 10. 6, &c.
NO GOD,] or 'there is not a God;' Targ.
'no rule or authority.'
DONE CORRUPTLY,] as in 53. 1; 78. 38, &c.
DONE ABOMINABLY,] as in 53. 1; 1 K. 21. 26
ACTIONS,] as in 9. 11; 66. 5; 77. 12; 78. 11
DOER OF GOOD,] as in v. 3; 53. 1, 3, &c.
2. LOOKED,] as in 53. 2; 102. 19; Ge. 18. 16
SONS OF MEN,] or 'of Adam,' as in 8. 4, &c.
WISE ONE,] as in 32. 1; 41. 1; 42. 1; 44. 1.
SEEKING GOD,] as in 9. 10; 22. 26; 24. 6, &c
3. WHOLE] of the 'sons of Adam,' as in v. 2,
TURNED ASIDE,] as in 44. 4; 119. 102, &c.
TOGETHER,] as in 2. 2; 4. 8; 19. 9; 31. 13.
FILTHY,] as in 53. 3; Job 15. 16.
DOER OF GOOD,] as in v. 1.
ONE,] as in 27. 4; 34. 20; 53. 3; 62. 11, &c.
The Vat. MSS. of Sept. adds here eight
verses, as in Rom. 3. 13—18.
4. WORKING INIQUITY,] as in 5. 6; 8. 9, &c.
CONSUMING,] lit. 'eating,' as in 53. 4, &c.
ATE BREAD,] that is, 'taken their food;' a
common Hebrew idiom.
CALLED,] or 'invited' to come and bless
them.
5. FEARED A FEAR,] as in 53. 5; Job 3. 25.
GENERATION,] as in 112. 2, &c.
6. COUNSEL,] as in 1; 13. 2; 20. 4; 33. 10.
POOR,] as in 9. 12, 18; 10. 2, 9, 12; 12. 5, &c.
STINK,] as in 44. 7; 53. 5; 119. 31, 116, &c.
REFUGE,] as in 46. 1; 61. 3; 62. 7, 8; 71. 7.
7. GIVETH,] as in 53. 6; 55. 6; Ex. 16. 3, &c.
ZION,] as in 2. 6; 9. 11, 14; 20. 2; 48. 2, &c.
SAFETY OF ISRAEL,] as in 53. 6; compare
44. 4, &c.
TURNETH BACK,] not 'bringeth back,' as
in C.V.
CAPTIVITY,] as in 53. 6; 85. 1; 126. 4, &c.
JACOB,] as in 20. 1; 22. 23; 44. 4, &c.
REJOICE,] as in 2. 1; 9. 14; 13. 4, 5, &c.
ISRAEL,] as in 22. 23; 25. 22; 68. 26, &c.
GLAD,] as in 5. 11; 9. 2; 16. 9, &c.

XV. 1. SOJOURN,] not 'abide,' as in C.V.;
as in 5. 4; 61. 4; 105. 12, 23, &c.
TENT,] not 'tabernacle,' as in C.V.; as in
19. 4; 27. 5, &c.
DWELL,] or 'tabernacle,' as in 16. 9, &c.
HOLY HILL,] as in 2. 6; 3. 4; 43. 3 &c.
2 B

2. WALKING UPRIGHTLY,] as in 84. 11; Prov 28. 18..

WORKING RIGHTEOUSNESS,] as in 119. 121; Isa. 64. 5.

SPEAKING TRUTH,] not 'the truth,' as in C.V.

IN HIS HEART,] or 'with his heart,' i.e. cheerfully.

3. SLANDERED,] lit. 'traversed,' as in 2 Sa. 19. 27.

BY,] by means of or on.

FRIEND,] as in 12. 2; 28. 3; 35. 14, &c.

REPROACH,] as in 22. 6; 31. 11; 39. 8, &c.

LIFTED UP,] not 'taketh up,' as in C.V.

NEIGHBOUR,] lit. 'near one,' as in 22. 11.

4. DESPISED,] as in 119. 141; Isa. 53. 3, &c.

REJECTED ONE,] rejected by Jehovah.

FEARING,] as in 22. 23, 25; 25. 12, 14, &c.

HONOURETH,] as in 50. 15, 23; 86. 9, 12, &c.

SWORN,] as in 24. 4; 89. 3, 35, 49; 95. 11, &c.

TO SUFFER EVIL,] lit. 'to do evil,' i.e. some action which may be injurious to his personal interests. Sept. Vulg. Syr. Arab. Ethiop. read 'to his friend.'

CHANGETH,] as in 46. 2; 106. 20, &c.

5. SILVER,] all 'money' then being of that metal.

USURY,] lit. 'biting;' as in Ex. 22. 25, &c.

BRIBE,] as in 26. 10; Ex. 23. 8; De. 10. 17.

INNOCENT,] as in 10. 8; 24. 4; 94. 21, &c.

IS DOING] habitually, as a matter of course.

MOVED,] as in 10. 6; 13. 4; 16. 8; 17. 5, &c.

XVI. SECRET TREASURE.] Sept. and Vulg. an 'inscription;' Targ. a 'right engraving;' Luther, a 'golden psalm.'

1. PRESERVE,] watch or guard.

TRUSTED,] lit. 'taken refuge,' as in 2. 12.

2. THOU HAST SAID.] Sept. Vulg. &c., 'I have said.' Targ. adds 'O my soul.'

LORD.] Vulg. reads 'God.'

GOOD] acts or deeds, as in 35. 12, &c.

FOR THINE OWN SAKE,] or 'because of thee.' Sept. 'thou hast no need of;' Syr. Targ. 'not from thee.'

3. FOR] the sake of, not 'to,' as in C.V.

HOLY ONES,] those separated to God.

LAND] of Israel, not 'earth,' as in C.V.

HONOURABLE,] as in 8. 1, 9; 76. 4; 93. 4, &c.

DELIGHT,] as in 1. 2; 107. 30; 111. 2, &c.

4. MULTIPLIED,] as in 49. 16; 107. 38, &c.

GRIEF.] Targum 'idols.'

BACKWARD,] not 'another,' as in C.V.

POUR,] not 'offer,' as in C.V.

LIBATIONS,] as in Ge. 35. 14; Ex. 29. 40, &c.

OF BLOOD,] or 'because of blood.' So Michaelis, Cocceius, Gejerus, &c.

TAKE UP,] as in 24. 5; 25. 1; 50. 16, &c.

NAMES,] as in Ex. 20. 7; 23. 13; De. 7. 24.

5. PORTION,] as in Ex. 29. 26; Lev. 7. 33, &c.

SHARE,] as in 17. 14; 50. 18; 73. 26, &c.

CUP,] as in 16. 6; 23. 5; 75. 8, &c.

UPHOLDEST,] as in Prov. 3. 18; Am. 1. 5, 8.

LOT,] as in 22. 18; 125. 3, &c.

6. LINES,] as in 18. 4, 6; 78. 55, &c.

PLEASANT PLACES,] as in v. 11; 81. 3, &c.

BEAUTEOUS,] as in 49. 21; Da. 4. 2, &c.

INHERITANCE,] as in 2. 8; 28. 9; 33. 12, &c.

7. COUNSELLED,] as in 32. 8; 62. 4, &c.

NIGHTS,] as in 42. 8; 92. 2; Job 4. 13, &c.

REINS,] as in 7. 9; 26. 2; 73. 21, &c.

INSTRUCT,] as in 39. 11; 118. 18, &c.

8. PLACED,] as in 18. 33; 21. 5; 89. 19, &c.

CONTINUALLY,] as in 25. 15; 34. 1; 35. 27.

RIGHT HAND,] as in 110. 1, 5; 121. 5; 142. 4.

MOVED,] as in 10. 6; 13. 4; 15. 5, &c.

9. GLAD,] as in 33. 21; 105. 3, &c.

HONOUR.] Sept. 'tongue.'

REJOICETH,] as in 9. 14; 13. 4, 5; 14. 7, &c.

FLESH,] as in 27. 2; 38. 3; 50. 13, &c.

DWELLETH,] not 'rest' merely, as in C.V.

CONFIDENTLY,] not 'in hope,' as in C.V.

10. LEAVE,] as in 10. 14; 27. 9; 37. 28, &c.

SOUL,] as in 3. 2; 6. 3, 4; 7. 2, 5; 10. 3, &c.

TO SHEOL,] not 'in hell,' but to (the power of) sheol, the unseen world.

GIVE,] as in 1. 3; 2. 8; 14. 7; 18. 13, &c.

KIND ONE,] lit. 'kind ones;' but all the ancient versions read in the singular, with 284 Heb. MSS.

SEE,] that is, experience.

CORRUPTION,] or 'marring,' as in 7. 15, &c.

11. TO KNOW,] not 'shew,' as in C.V.

PATH OF LIFE,] as in Prov. 2. 19; 5. 6, &c.

FULNESS,] as in 78. 25; Ex. 16. 3, &c.

WITH THY PRESENCE,] not 'in' it merely, as in C.V.

PLEASANT THINGS,] as in v. 6.

BY,] or 'in,' not 'at' thy right hand, as in C.V.

XVII. 1. HEAR,] as in v. 6; 4. 1; 27. 7, &c

RIGHTEOUSNESS.] Sept. Vul. Arab. Eth. 'my righteousness.' Syr. 'O righteou' Lord;' so Jerome, Aquila, &c.

ATTEND,] as in 5. 2; 55. 2; 61. 1, &c.

GIVE EAR,] as in 5. 1; 39. 12; 49. 1. &c.

DECEIT,] as in 5. 6; 10. 7; 24. 4, &c.

PRAYER,] as in 4. 1; 6. 9; 35. 13, &c.

2. JUDGMENT,] as in 5. 1; 7. 6; 9. 4, 7, &c.

UPRIGHTLY,] not 'things that are equal, as in C.V.

3. PROVED,] as in 7. 9; 11. 4, 5, &c.

INSPECTED,]not 'visited' merely, as in C.V.

TRIED,] as in 12. 6; 18. 30, &c.

NOTHING,] Sept. Vulg. Eth. 'in me un-righteousness.' Syr. Targ. Arab. 'unright-eousness.'

THOUGHTS,] or 'thinking.'

PASS OVER,] as in 37. 36; 42. 4; 57. 1, &c.

MOUTH,] as in v. 10; 5. 9; 8. 2; 10. 7, &c.

4. DOINGS,] as in 28. 5; 109. 20, &c.

WORD OF THY LIPS,] as in 59. 12; 2 K. 18. 20. .

OBSERVED,] or watched and avoided.

PATHS,] as in 8. 8; 16. 11; 19. 5, &c.

DESTROYER,]lit. 'breaker forth,' as in Eze. 7. 22; 18. 10, &c.

5. TO UPHOLD,] with the view of doing so.

GOINGS,] as in 37. 31; 40. 2; 44. 18, &c.

PATHS,] as in 1 Sa. 17. 20; Prov. 2. 15, &c.

STEPS,] as in 17. 57. 6; 58. 10; 74. 3, &c.

SLIDDEN,]lit. 'been moved,' as in 10. 6, &c.

6. CALLED,] as in 14. 4; 31. 17; 34. 6, &c.

ANSWEREST,]not 'hear' merely, as in C.V.

INCLINE,] as in 31. 2; 45. 10; 71. 2; 78. 2.

SPEECH,] lit. 'saying,' as in 12. 6; 18. 30.

7. SEPARATE WONDERFULLY,]as in 4. 3, &c.

KINDNESSES,] as in 5. 7; 6. 4; 13. 5, &c.

SAVIOUR,] as in 7. 10; 18. 41; 106. 21, &c.

CONFIDING,] lit. 'taking refuge,' as in 2. 12.

RIGHT,] as in 16. 11; 18. 35; 20. 6; 21. 8. &c.

WITHSTANDERS,] as in 59. 1; Job 20. 27; 27. 7.

8. KEEP,] watch, guard, as in v. 4.

APPLE,] *lit.* 'little man,' as in De. 32. 10; Prov. 7. 2, 9; 20. 20.

DAUGHTER OF THE EYE,] as in La. 2. 18.

SHADOW,] as in 36. 7; 57. 1; 63. 7; 80. 10.

WINGS,] as in 18. 10; 36. 7; 57. 1; 61. 4, &c.

HIDE,] *lit.* 'keep me secret.'

9. PRESENCE,] *lit.* 'face.'

SPOILED,] not 'oppressed' merely, as in C.V.

SOUL,] that is, spiritual foes.

GO ROUND,] as in 22. 16; 48. 12; 88. 17, &c.

10. FAT,] as in 63. 5; 73. 7; 81. 16, &c.

CLOSED UP,] not 'they are enclosed,' as in C.V.

MOUTHS,] as in v. 3.

PRIDE,] as in 89. 9; 93. 1; Isa. 9. 18, &c.

11. STEPS,] as in v. 5.

COMPASSED,] as in 18. 5; 22. 12, 16; 88. 17.

SET,] as in 12. 5; 13. 2; 18. 11; 21. 3, &c.

TURN ASIDE.] Syr. Arab. 'cast me down.'

LAND,] *or* 'earth.'

12. LIKENESS,] as in 58. 4, &c.

LION,] as in 7. 2; 10. 9; 22. 13, 16. 21, &c.

DESIROUS,] as in 84. 2; Job 14. 11, &c.

TEAR,] as in 7. 2; 22. 13; 50. 22, &c.

YOUNG LION,] as in 34. 10; 35. 17; 58. 6, &c.

DWELLING,] not 'lurking,' as in C.V.

SECRET PLACES,] as in 10. 8, 9; 64. 4, &c.

13. ARISE,] as in 3. 7; 7. 6; 9. 19; 10. 12, &c.

GO BEFORE,] not 'disappoint,' as in C.V.

TO BEND,] as in 18. 39; 78. 31; Jud. 11. 35.

DELIVER,] *lit.* 'cause to escape.'

SWORD.] Targ. 'by thy sword.'

14. MEN,] as in 26. 4; 105. 12; Ge. 34. 30, &c.

HAND.] Targ. ' by thy hand.'

MEN OF THE WORLD,] *or* 'age,' as in 39. 5; ... 1; 89. 47; Job 11. 17.

PORTION,] as in 16. 5; 50. 18; 73. 26, &c.

LIFE,] *or* 'among the living,' as in 27. 13.

HIDDEN THINGS,] as in 83. 3; Job 20. 26; Prov. 13. 22, &c.

BELLY,] as in 22. 9, 10; 31. 9; 44. 25, &c.

SATISFIED,] not 'full' merely, as in C.V.

SONS,] not 'children' merely, as in C.V.

LEFT,] *lit.* 'caused to rest,' as in Ge. 42. 33, &c.

ABUNDANCE,] or superfluity, as in 31. 23.

SUCKLINGS,] as in 8. 2; 137. 9; 1 Sa. 15. 3.

15. RIGHTEOUSNESS,] as in v. 1.

SEE,] as in v. 2.

SATISFIED,] as in v. 14.

AWAKING,] *or* 'in the awaking of' thy FORM.] Sept. Vulg. Eth. Arab. 'glory.'

XVIII. OVERSEER.] Another version of this Psalm is in 2 Sa. xxii., which see for many interesting variations.

SERVANT OF JEHOVAH,] as in 36. 1; 78. 70.

SONG,] as in 2 Sa. 22. 1; Ex. 15. 1, &c.

DELIVERED,] as in 34. 4, 17; 54. 7; 56. 13.

HAND,] *lit.* 'paw,' as in 7. 3; 9. 16, &c.

SAUL,] the king of Israel.

1. LOVE] with deepest intensity, as the original word generally means.

STRENGTH.] This verse is omitted in 2 Sa. xxii.

2. ROCK,] as in 31. 3; 40. 2; 42. 9, &c.

BULWARK,] as in 31. 2, 3; 66. 11; 71. 3, &c.

DELIVERER,] *lit.* 'causer to escape,' as in v. 48; 40. 17; 144. 2, &c.

TRUST,] *or* 'take refuge.'

SHIELD,] as in v. 30, 35; 3. 3; 7. 10, &c.

HORN,] as in 22. 21; 75. 4, 5, 10, &c.

HIGH TOWER.] See the addition in 2 Sa. 22, 3.

3. PRAISED ONE,] not 'worthy to be praised,' as in C.V.

CALL,] not 'call upon,' as in C.V.

SAVED,] as in 80. 3, 7, 19; 119. 117, &c.

4. COMPASSED,] as in 40. 12; 116. 3; Jon. 2. 5.

CORDS OF DEATH,] not 'sorrows;' in 2 Sa. 22. 5 it is 'breakers.'

STREAMS,] as in 36. 8; 74. 15; 78. 20; 83. 9.

WORTHLESS,] not 'ungodly;' Sept. 'iniquity.

AFRAID.] Sept. 'troubled me.'

5. CORDS OF SHEOL,] not 'sorrows,' as in C.V.

SNARES OF DEATH,] as in Prov. 13. 14, &c.

HAVE BEEN BEFORE ME,] not 'prevented me,' as in C.V.

6. ADVERSITY,] *lit.* 'straitness.'

CALL,] not 'call upon,' as in C.V.

CRY,] as in v. 41; 22. 24; 28. 2, &c.

CRY,] as in 34. 15; 39. 12; 40. 1, &c

EARS,] as in v. 44; 10. 17; 31. 2, &c.

7. SHAKE,] as in 2 Sa. 22. 8; Job 34. 20, &c.

TREMBLE,] as in 46. 3; 68. 8; 72. 16, &c.

EARTH,] *or* 'land.'

FOUNDATIONS,] as in v. 15; 82. 5; De. 32. 22.

HILLS.] In 2 Sa. 22. 8 it is 'heavens.'

TROUBLED,] not 'moved,' as in C.V.

SHAKE,] not 'were shaken,' as in C.V.

WRATH,] *or* 'heat,' as in Ge. 6. 4, &c.

8. SMOKE,] as in 37. 20; 68. 2; 102. 3, &c.

NOSTRILS,] *lit.* 'nose,' as in v. 15.

FIRE,] as in v. 12, 13; 11. 6; 21. 9, &c.

CONSUMETH,] *lit.* 'eateth.'

COALS,] as in v. 12; 120. 4; 140. 10, &c.

KINDLED,] *or* 'burned,' as in 2. 12; 39. 3.

9. INCLINETH,] as in 17. 11; 21. 11; 40. 1.

HEAVENS,] as in 104. 2; Job 9. 8; Isa. 40. 22.

COMETH DOWN,] as in 7. 16; 49. 17; 55. 15.

THICK DARKNESS,] as in 97. 2; Ex. 20. 21.

FEET,] as in v. 33, 38, &c.

RIDETH,] as in 45. 4; 68. 4, 33.

10. CHERUB.] Sept. Syr. Targ. Arab. 'cherubs.'

FLY,] as in 55. 6; 90. 10; 91. 5, &c.

FLEETH.] In 2 Sa. 22. 11 it is 'seen;' as in De. 28. 49; Jer. 48. 40; 49. 22.

WINGS OF WIND,] as in 104. 3; 2 Sa. 22. 11.

11. DARKNESS,] as in v. 28; 35. 6; 88. 12.

SECRET PLACE,] as in 27. 5; 31. 20; 32. 7.

TABERNACLE,] as in 31. 20; Ge. 33. 17, &c.

DARKNESS OF WATERS.] A phrase not found again.

THICK CLOUDS,] as in v. 12; 77. 17; 104. 3.

SKIES,] as in 36. 5; 57. 10; 68. 34, &c.

12. BRIGHTNESS,] as in v. 28; 22. 13; 23. 4.

OVER-AGAINST,] as in v. 24; 31. 22; 38. 11.

THICK CLOUDS,] as in v. 11.

PASSED ON,] *or* 'over *or* away *or* by.'

HAIL,] as in 78. 47, 48; 105. 32; 148. 8, &c

COALS OF FIRE.] See omission in 2 Sa. 22. 18.

13. THUNDER,] as in 29. 3; 1 Sa. 2. 10, &c.

MOST HIGH,] as in 7. 17; 9. 2; 21. 7, &c.

VOICE,] as in 29. 3, 4, 5, 7, 8, 9, &c.

14. ARROWS,] as in 7. 13; 11. 2; 38. 2, &c.

SCATTERETH,] as in 144. 6; Ge. 11. 8, 9, &c.
MUCH LIGHTNING,] not 'he shot out.' So
Targ., &c.
LIGHTNING,] as in 77. 18; 97. 4; 135. 7, &c.
CRUSHETH,] not merely 'discomfiteth,' as
in C.V.
15. STREAMS OF WATERS.] In 2 Sa. 22. 16 it
is 'sea.'
REVEALED,] as in Ge. 35. 7; Ex. 20. 26, &c.
FOUNDATIONS,] as in v. 7.
REBUKE,] as in 76. 6; 80. 16; 104. 7, &c.
BREATH,] not 'blast,' as in C.V.
SPIRIT,] not 'breath,' as in C.V.
ANGER,] not 'nostrils,' as in C.V.
16. DRAWETH,] as in 2 Sa. 22. 17; Ex. 2. 10.
MANY WATERS,] as in 29. 3; 32. 6; 77. 19.
17. DELIVERETH,] as in v. 48; 22. 8; 34. 19.
STRONG,] as in 59. 3; 2 Sa. 22. 18, &c.
HATING,] as in 9. 13; 21. 8; 34. 21, &c.
STRONGER,] as in 142. 6; 2 Sa. 22. 18, &c.
18. GO BEFORE,] not 'prevent,' as in C.V.
CALAMITY,] as in De. 32. 35; 2 Sa. 22. 19.
SUPPORT,] as in 23. 4; Isa. 3. 1, &c.
19. LARGE PLACE,] as in 31. 8; 118. 5, &c.
DRAWETH OUT,] as in 7. 4; 34. 7; 50. 15, &c.
DELIGHTED,] as in 22. 8; 40. 6, 8; 41. 11, &c.
20. RECOMPENSE,] as in 7. 4; 13. 6; 103. 10.
RIGHTEOUSNESS,] as in v. 24; 7. 8, &c.
CLEANNESS,] as in Job 9. 30; 22. 30, &c.
HANDS,] as in 2 Sa. 22. 21, 25, &c.
RETURN,] as in v. 24; 54. 5, &c.
21. KEPT,] watched or observed.
WAYS,] as in v. 30; 5. 8; 25. 4, 9, &c.
DONE WICKEDLY,] as in 2 Sa. 22. 22, &c.
22. JUDGMENTS,] as in 1. 5; 7. 6; 9. 4, 7, &c.
STATUTES,] as in 89. 31; 119. 16, &c.
FROM ME.] In 2 Sa. 22. 23 it is 'from
them.'
23. PERFECT,] not 'upright' merely, as
in C.V.
KEEP MYSELF,] as in 2 Sa. 22. 24; Mic. 6. 16.
INIQUITY,] as in 25. 11; 31. 10; 32. 2, 5, &c.
24. RETURN,] as in v. 20.
OVER-AGAINST,] as in v. 12, &c.
25. KIND,] not 'merciful' merely, as
in C.V.
PERFECT,] not 'upright' merely, as in C.V.
26. PURE,] or 'purified,' as in 2 Sa. 22. 27;
Isa. 52. 11.
PERVERSE,] as in 101. 4; De. 32. 5, &c.
WRESTLER,] not 'froward,' as in C.V.
27. POOR,] not 'afflicted,' as in C.V.
SAVEST,] as in 34. 18; 36. 6; 37. 40, &c.
HIGH,] as in 131. 1; Prov. 6. 17, &c.
TO FALL,] or 'makest low or humble.'
28. LIGHTEST,] as in 13. 3; 19. 8, &c.
LAMP,] not 'candle,' as in 2 Sa. 22. 9.
ENLIGHTENETH,] as in Isa. 13. 10, &c.
DARKNESS,] as in v. 11.
29. RUN,] as in 19. 5; 59. 4; 119. 32, &c.
TROOP,] in number, not 'through' one, as
in C.V.
LEAP,] as in Song 2. 8; Isa. 35. 6; Zeph. 1. 9.
WALL,] as in Ge. 49. 22; Job 24. 11.
30. PERFECT.] Sept. 'without spot.'
TRIED,] as in 12. 6; 119. 140, &c.
SHIELD,] as in v. 2, 30, &c.
TRUSTING,] lit. 'taking refuge.'
31. BESIDES,] as in Nu. 5. 20; Isa. 36. 10.
ROCK,] as in v. 2, 46, &c.
SAVE,] as in De. 1. 36; 4. 12; Jos. 11. 13.

32. GIRDING.] In 2 Sa. 22. 23 it is 'my bul-
wark—strength.'
STRENGTH,] might or wealth.
MAKETH PERFECT,] lit. 'giving perfect.'
WAY,] as in 39. 1; 119. 26, 30, 59, &c.
33. MAKING,] as in 2 Sa. 22. 34, &c.
HINDS,] not 'like hinds' feet,' as in C.V.
HIGH PLACES,] as in 78. 58; Lev. 26. 30, &c.
TO STAND,] not 'setteth' merely, as in C.V.
34. TEACHING,] as in 94. 10; 119. 99; 141. 1.
BATTLE,] as in v. 39; 24. 8; 27. 3; 46. 9, &c.
BOW OF BRASS,] not 'steel,' as in C.V.
BROUGHT DOWN,] not 'broken,' as in C.V.
35. SHIELD,] as in v. 2, 30, &c.
RIGHT HAND,] as in 16. 11; 17. 7; 20. 6, &c.
SUPPORT.] This clause is omitted in 2 Sa.
22. 36.
LOWLINESS,] not 'gentleness;' Sept. Vulg.
&c., 'discipline;' Targ. 'word.'
GREAT,] as in 71. 21; 2 Sa. 22. 36, &c.
36. ENLARGEST,] lit. 'makest broad.'
STEP,] as in 2 Sa. 6. 13; 22. 37; Job 14. 16.
ANCLES,] not 'feet,' as in C.V.
SLIDDEN,] or 'moved,' as in 26. 1; 37. 31.
37. PURSUE,] as in 23. 6; 34. 14; 38. 20, &c
OVERTAKE,] as in 7. 5; 40. 12; 69. 24, &c.
CONSUMED,] lit. 'their consumption.'
38. SMITE,] not 'wound,' as in C.V.
FULL,] as in 5. 10; 7. 15; 35. 8, &c.
39. GIRDEST,] as in v. 32; 30. 11, &c.
STRENGTH,] might or wealth.
BATTLE,] as in v. 34.
WITHSTANDERS,] as in v. 48; 3. 1; 44. 5, &c.
TO BOW,] not 'subdued,' as in C.V.
40. NECK,] as in Ge. 49. 8; Ex. 23. 27; 32. 9
HATING,] as in 44. 7, 10; 55. 12; 68. 1, &c.
CUT OFF,] as in 94. 23; 101. 5, 8; 143. 12, &c.
41. CRY,] as in v. 6.
SAVIOUR,] as in 7. 10; 17. 7; 106. 21, &c.
ANSWER,] as in 22. 2; 1 Sa. 8. 18, &c.
42. BEAT,] as in Ex. 30. 36; Job 14. 19.
DUST,] as in 7. 5; 22. 15, 29; 30. 9, &c.
BEFORE,] lit. 'on or by the face of wind.'
MIRE,] as in 40. 2; 69. 14, &c.
STREETS,] or 'out-places,' as in 31. 11, &c.
EMPTY OUT.] In 2 Sa. 22. 43 it is 'beat
them small.'
43. DELIVER,] lit. 'cause to escape.'
STRIVINGS,] as in 31. 20; 35. 23; 43. 1, &c.
THE PEOPLE.] In 2 Sa. 22. 44 it is 'my
people.'
PLACEST,] as in 39. 8; 44. 13, 14; 52. 7, &c.
SERVE,] as in 22. 30; 72. 11; 106. 36, &c.
44. HEARING,] or 'report,' as in 150. 5, &c.
HEARKEN,] not 'obey,' necessarily, as
in C.V.
SONS OF A STRANGER,] not 'strangers'
merely, as in C.V.
FEIGN OBEDIENCE,] not 'submit themselves,' as in C.V.
45. FADE AWAY,] as in 1. 3; 37. 2; Ex. 18. 18.
SLAIN,] not 'be afraid;' in 2 Sa. 22. 46 it is
'gird themselves.'
CLOSE PLACES,] as in Mic. 7. 17; 2 Sa. 22. 46.
46. LIVETH,] as in Jud. 8. 19; Ruth 3. 13.
ROCK,] as in v. 2, 31, &c.
GOD.] In 2 Sa. 22. 47 it is 'God of the
rock' of my
SALVATION,] as in v. 2, 35, &c.
47. GIVING VENGEANCE,] not 'avengeth,
as in C.V.

SUBDUETH,] *lit.* 'speaketh.'
48. DELIVERER,] as in v. 2.
WITHSTANDERS,] as in v. 39.
MAN OF VIOLENCE,] as in 140. 1, 4, 11, &c.
49. CONFESS,] not 'give thanks,' as in C.V.
SING PRAISE,] as in 7. 17; 9. 2; 21. 13, &c.
50. MAGNIFYING,] as in 35. 26; 2 Sa. 22. 51.
KING,] whom he had anointed.
DOING KINDNESS,] not 'sheweth mercy,' as in C.V.
ANOINTED,] *in Heb.* 'Messiah,' as in 2. 2.
DAVID,] the author of this Psalm.
SEED,] as in 2 Sa. 7. 12; 22. 51, &c.

XIX. OVERSEER,] as in Ps. 4. 5. 6. 8. 9. &c.
1. HEAVENS,] as in 2. 4; 8. 1, 3, 8; 11. 4, &c.
RECOUNTING,] not 'declare,' as in C.V.
GOD,] the 'mighty' one.
WORK OF HIS HAND,] as in 8. 6; 28. 4, 5, &c.
EXPANSE,] as in 150. 1; Ge. 1. 6, 7, 8, &c.
DECLARETH,] not 'sheweth,' as in 7.
2. UTTERETH,] as in 59. 7; 78. 2; 94. 4, &c.
SPEECH,] *lit.* 'saying,' as in v. 3; 68. 11, &c.
SHEWETH,] as in Job 15. 17; 32. 6, 10, &c.
KNOWLEDGE,] as in 94. 10; 119. 66; 139. 6.
3. NO SPEECH,] as in v. 2.
NO WORDS,] not 'language,' as in C.V.
VOICE,] *or* 'sound.'
HEARD,] at all by the outward ear.
4. EARTH,] *or* 'land.'
LINE.] In Rom. 10. 18 it is 'sound,' like Sept.
WORLD,] as in 9. 8; 18. 5; 24. 1, &c.
SAYINGS,] not 'words,' as in C.V.
SUN,] as in 50. 1; 58. 8; 72. 5, 17; 74. 16, &c.
PLACED,] *or* 'set,' as in 40. 4, &c.
TENT,] not 'tabernacle,' as in C.V.
5. BRIDEGROOM,] *or* 'son-in-law,' as in Ge. 19. 12, 14, &c.
COVERING,] as in Isa. 4. 5; Joel 2. 16.
MIGHTY ONE,] as in 24. 8; 33. 16; 45. 3, &c.
PATH,] not 'race,' as in C.V.
6. END OF THE HEAVENS,] as in De. 4. 32.
REVOLUTION,] as in Ex. 34. 22; 1 Sa. 1. 20; 2 Ch. 24. 23.
HID,] as in v. 12; De. 7. 20; 29. 29, &c.
HEAT,] as in Job 30. 28; Song 6. 10, &c.
7. LAW OF JEHOVAH,] as in 1. 2; 119. 1; Ex. 13. 9, &c.
PERFECT,] as in 18. 23, 25, 30, 32, &c.
REFRESHING,] *lit.* 'bringing back,' as in Ge. 20. 7, &c.
SOUL,] as in Ruth 4. 15; La. 1. 16.
TESTIMONY,] as in 60. 1; 78. 5; 80. 1, &c.
STEDFAST,] as in 89. 28, 37; 101. 6; 111. 7.
MAKING WISE,] as in 105. 22; 119. 98, &c.
SIMPLE.] Sept. Vulg. Syr. Arab. Ethiop. read 'babes.'
8. PRECEPTS,] not 'statutes,' as in C.V.
UPRIGHT,] not 'right,' as in C.V.
HEART,] as in 104. 15, &c.
COMMAND,] as in 78. 7; 89. 31; 112. 1, &c.
PURE,] as in 24. 4; 73. 1; Job 11. 4, &c.
ENLIGHTENING,] as in 13. 3; Prov. 29. 13.
9. FEAR,] *or* 'reverence' due to him.
CLEAN,] as in 12. 6; 51. 10, &c.
STANDING,] as in 111. 3, 10; 112. 3, 9, &c.
JUDGMENT,] as in 81. 4; 2 Ch. 19. 8, &c.
TRUE,] *lit.* 'truth;' as in 15. 2; 25. 5, &c.
TOGETHER,] not 'altogether,' as in C.V.
10. DESIRABLE,] as in Ge. 2. 9; 3. 6, &c.

GOLD,] as in 45. 13; 72. 15; 105. 37, &c.
FINE GOLD,] as in 21. 3; 119. 127; Job 28. 17.
SWEETER,] as in Jud. 14. 14, 18; Pr. 16. 24.
HONEY,] as in 81. 16; 119. 103; Ge. 43. 11.
LIQUID HONEY,] as in Prov. 5. 3; 24. 13; 27. 7; Song 4. 11.
COMB,] as in Prov. 16. 24.
11. WARNED,] *or* 'made bright.' So Pagninus, Montanus, Rivetus.
KEEPING,] *or* 'observing.'
REWARD,] *or* 'consequence;' *lit.* 'heel.'
12. ERRORS.] Original word is not found again.
UNDERSTAND,] as in 28. 5; 49. 20.
HIDDEN ONES,] as in v. 6.
INNOCENT,] not 'cleanse,' as in C.V.
13. PRESUMPTUOUS ONES.]Sept 'strangers.'
KEEP BACK,] as in 78. 50, &c.
RULE,] as in 103. 19; 106. 41, &c.
PERFECT,] not 'upright,' as in C.V.
MUCH,] not 'the great,' as in C.V.
TRANSGRESSION,] as in 5. 10; 25. 7; 32. 1.
14. SAYINGS,] not 'words,' as in C.V.
MOUTH,] as in 54. 2; 78. 1; 138. 4, &c.
MEDITATION,] as in 9. 16; 92. 3; La. 3. 62.
HEART,] as in 49. 3, &c.
PLEASING THING,] as in 5. 12; 30. 5, 7, &c.
ROCK,] not 'strength,' as in C.V.
REDEEMER,] as in 78. 35; 103. 4, &c.

XX. OVERSEER,] as in Ps. 4. 5. 6. 8. 9. &c.
1. ANSWER,] not 'hear,' as in C.V.; as in 3. 4, &c.
ADVERSITY,] as in 9. 9; 10. 1; 22. 11; 25. 17.
NAME,] as in v. 5, 7; Ps. 5. 11; 7. 17; 8. 1.
GOD OF JACOB,] as in 46. 7; 76. 6; 81. 4, &c.
SET ON HIGH,] not 'defend,' as in C.V.; as in 59. 1, &c.
2. HELP,] as in 33. 20; 70. 5; 89. 19; 115. 9.
SANCTUARY,] as in v. 6; 2. 6, 3, 4; 5. 7, &c.
ZION,] as in 2. 6; 9. 11, 14; 14. 7, &c.
SUPPORT,] as in 18. 35; 41. 3; 94. 18, &c.
3. REMEMBER,] as in 8. 4; 9. 12; 22. 27, &c.
PRESENTS,] as in 40. 6; 45. 12; 72. 10, &c.
BURNT-OFFERING,] as in 40. 6; 50. 8; 51. 16.
REDUCE TO ASHES,]not 'accept,' as in C.V.; as in Ex. 27. 3; Nu. 4. 13, &c. So Kimchi, Vat., Mont., Ains., &c. Sept. 'be made fat.'
4. HEART,] as in v. 3; 13. 2; 15. 2; 22. 26.
COUNSEL,] as in 1. 1; 13. 2; 14. 6; 33. 10, &c.
FULFIL,] as in v. 5; 17. 14; 80. 9, &c.
5. SING,] not 'rejoice,' as in C.V.; as in 5. 11, &c.
SALVATION,] as in 3. 2, 8; 9. 14; 13. 5, &c.
NAME,] as in v. 1, 7, &c.
BANNER,] as in Song 5. 10; 6. 4, 10, &c.
REQUESTS,] as in 37. 4.
6. KNOWN,] by past personal experience.
SAVED,] as in 3. 7; 6. 4; 7. 1, &c.
ANOINTED,] as in 2. 2; 18. 50; 28. 8, &c.
ANSWERETH,] not 'hear,' as in C.V.; as in v. 1 above.
HOLY HEAVENS.]Original phrase not found again.
SAVING,] as in 12. 5; 18. 2, 35, 46; 24. 5, &c.
MIGHT,] as in 21. 13; 54. 1; 65. 6; 66. 7, &c.
RIGHT HAND,] as in 10. 8, 11; 17. 7; 18. 35.
7. SOME,] *lit.* 'these.'
OF CHARIOTS,] not 'in chariots,' as in C.V.
OF HORSES,] not 'in horses,' as in C.V.
NAME,] as in v. 1, 5, &c.

MAKE MENTION,] not 'remember,' as in
C.V.; as in 45. 17; 71. 16; 77. 11, &c.
8. BOWED,] as in 22. 29; 72. 9; 95. 6, &c.
FALLEN,] as in 27. 2; 36. 12; 57. 6, &c.
RISEN,] as in 27. 12; 54. 3; 86. 14, &c.
STATION OURSELVES,] not 'stand,' as in
C.V.
9. SAVE,] as in 3. 7; 6. 4; 7. 1; 12. 1, &c.
SAVE THE KING.] So Sept. Eth. Arab.
Vulg.
ANSWER,] not 'hear,' as in C.V.; as in v.
1, 6, &c.
CALL,] as in 4. 1, 3; 69. 3; 141. 1, &c.

XXI. OVERSEER,] as in Ps. 4. 5. 6. 8. 9. &c.
1. STRENGTH,] as in v. 13; 8. 2; 28. 7. &c.
JOYFUL,] as in 5. 11; 9. 2; 14. 7; 16. 9, &c.
SALVATION,] as in v. 5; Ps. 3. 2, 8; 9. 14, &c.
REJOICETH,] as in 2. 11; 9. 14; 13. 4, 5, &c.
2. DESIRE,] as in 10. 3, 17; 38. 9; 78. 29, &c.
REQUEST.] Original word not found again.
LIPS,] as in 12. 2, 3, 4; 16. 4; 17. 1, 4, &c.
WITHHELD,] as in 84. 11; Ge. 30. 2, &c.
3. PUTTEST BEFORE HIM,] not 'preventest
him,' as in C.V.; as in 18. 5, 18; 59. 10, &c.
BLESSINGS,] as in v. 6; 3. 8; 24. 5, &c.
SETTEST,] as in v. 6; 3. 6; 8. 6; 12. 5, 6, &c.
HEAD,] as in 3. 3; 7. 16; 18. 43; 22. 7, &c.
CROWN,] as in 2 Sa. 12. 30; 1 Ch. 20. 2, &c.
FINE GOLD.] Sept. Vulg. 'precious stone.'
4. LIFE,] as in 7. 5; 16. 11; 17. 14; 18. 46.
ASKED,] as in 27. 4; 35. 11; 40. 6, &c.
LENGTH OF DAYS,] as in 23. 6; 91. 16; 93. 5.
AGE-DURING,] as in 5. 11; 9. 5, 7; 10. 16, &c.
FOR EVER,] as in v. 6; 9. 5, 18; 10. 16, &c.
5. HONOUR,] as in 3. 3; 4. 2; 7. 5; 8. 5, &c.
SALVATION,] as in v. 1 above.
MAJESTY,] as in 8. 5; 29. 4; 45. 3, 4, &c.
PLACEST,] as in 16. 8; 18. 33; 89. 19, &c.
6. SETTEST,] as in v. 3 above.
BLESSINGS,] not 'most blessed,' as in C.V.
JOY,] as in 4. 7; 16. 11; 30. 11; 43. 4, &c.
BY,] not 'with,' as in C.V.
7. TRUSTING,] as in 27. 3; 32. 10; 49. 6, &c.
KINDNESS,] not 'mercy,' as in C.V.
MOST HIGH,] as in 7. 17; 9. 2; 18. 13; 46. 4.
MOVED,] as in 10. 16; 13. 4; 15. 5, &c.
8. FIND,] as in 10. 15; 17. 3; 116. 3, &c.
9. FURNACE,] as in Ge. 15. 17; Ex. 8. 3, &c.
PRESENCE,] not 'anger,' as in C.V. So
Sept. Vulg, &c.
ANGER,] as in 2. 5, 12; 6. 1; 7. 6, &c.
SWALLOW,] as in 35. 25; 55. 9, &c.
DEVOUR,] as in 14. 4; 18. 8; 22. 26, &c.
10. FRUIT,] as in 1. 3; 58. 11; 72. 16, &c.
DESTROYEST,] as in 5. 6; 9. 5; 119. 95, &c.
SEED,] as in 18. 50; 22. 23, 30; 25. 13, &c.
SONS OF MEN,] or 'of Adam,' as in 8. 4, &c.
11. STRETCHED OUT,] not 'intended,' as
in C.V.
DEVISED,] as in 10. 2; 32. 2; 35. 4, 20, &c.
WICKED DEVICE,] as in 10. 2, 4; 37. 7, &c.
PREVAIL NOT,] lit. 'are not able.'
12. BUTT,] not 'turn their back,' as in C.V.;
so Gill, Ainsworth, Horsley, Boothroyd, &c.
STRINGS,] as in Ex. 35. 18; 39. 40; Nu. 3.
26, 27; 4. 26, 32; Isa. 54. 2; Jer. 10. 20.
PREPAREST,] as in 7. 9, 12; 8. 3; 9. 7, &c.
13. EXALTED,] as in 57. 5, 11; 108. 5, &c.
STRENGTH,] as in v. 1 above.
SING,] as in 13. 6; 27. 6; 33. 3, &c.

PRAISE,] as in 7. 17; 9. 2, 11; 18. 49, &c
MIGHT,] as in 20. 6; 54. 1; 65. 6, &c.

XXII. OVERSEER,] as in Ps. 4. 5. 6. 8. &c.
HIND,] as in Prov. 5. 19; Jer. 14. 5. Sept.
'help;' Targ. 'daily sacrifice;' Kimchi, 'star.'
MORNING,] as in 57. 8; 108. 2; 139. 9, &c.
1. MY GOD,] as in v. 10; 18. 2; 63. 1; 68.
24; 89. 26; 102. 24; 118. 28; 140. 6, &c. Sept.
Vulg. 'God, my God, haste to me.'
FORSAKEN,] as in 9. 10; 10. 14; 16. 10, &c.
FAR,] as in 10. 1; 38. 11; 56. 1; 65. 5, &c.
SALVATION,] as in 3. 2, 8; 9. 14; 13. 5, &c.
ROARING,] as in 32. 3; Job 3. 24; 4. 10; Isa.
5. 29; Eze. 19. 7; Zec. 11. 3.
2. CALL,] not 'cry,' as in C.V.
BY DAY,] as in 1. 2; 13. 2; 32. 4; 42. 3, &c.
ANSWER,] not 'hear,' as in C.V.; as in v. 21.
BY NIGHT,] as in 1. 2; 6. 9; 16. 7; 17. 3, &c.
SILENCE,] as in 39. 2; 62. 1; 65. 1.
3. HOLY,] as in 71. 22; 78. 41; 89. 18, &c.
Sept. Vulg. 'in the holy place hast dwelt.'
SITTING,] not 'inhabiting,' as in C.V.
PRAISE,] that is, the 'object of praise.'
4. TRUST,] as in v. 5; 4. 5; 9. 10; 13. 5, &c.
DELIVER,] or 'cause to escape,' as in v. 8.
5. CRIED] in distress for help, as the ori-
ginal word indicates.
ASHAMED,] not 'confounded,' as in C.V.
6. WORM,] as in De. 28. 29; Job 25. 6; Isa.
14. 11; 41. 14; 66. 24; Jon. 4. 7.
MAN,] having no strength left.
REPROACH,] as in 15. 3; 31. 11; 39. 8; 44. 13.
DESPISED,] as in Ecc. 9. 16; Jer. 49. 15;
Obad. 2; Isa. 53. 3, &c.
7. BEHOLDING,] as in 31. 14; 64. 8, &c.
MOCK,] as in Neh. 2. 19; 4. 1; Job 21. 3;
2 Ch. 30. 10, &c.
MAKE FREE,] not 'shoot out,' as in C.V.
Sept. Vulg. 'spake.'
LIPS,] as in 12. 2, 3, 4; 16. 4; 17. 1, &c.
SHAKE,] as in 109. 25; 2 K. 19. 21; Isa. 37.
22; Job 16. 4; La. 2. 15, &c.
8. ROLL,] not 'trusted,' as in C.V.; as in
37. 5, &c.
DELIVER,] as in v. 5 above.
DELIGHTED.] as in 18. 19; 37. 23; 40. 6, 8.
9. BRINGING FORTH,] as in Job 38. 8; 40. 23;
Eze. 32. 2; Mic. 4. 10.
WOMB,] as in v. 10; 17. 14; 31. 9; 44. 25, &c.
TRUST,] or 'lean,' as in 2 K. 18. 30; Isa. 36.
15; Jer. 38. 15; 29. 31. Sept. Vulg. 'my
hope.'
BREASTS,] as in Ge. 49. 25; Job 3. 12, &c.
10. CAST,] as in Isa. 14. 19; Jer. 22. 28, &c
BELLY,] as in 58. 3; 110. 3; Ge. 20. 18, &c
MY GOD,] as in v. 1 above.
11. FAR,] as in v. 19; 35. 22; 38. 21, &c.
ADVERSITY,] as in 9. 9; 10. 1; 22. 11, &c.
NEAR,] as in De. 32. 35; Jer. 48. 16, &c.
HELPER,] as in 10. 14; 30. 10; 54. 4; 72. 12.
12. BULLS,] as in 50. 9; 51. 19; 69. 31, &c.
SURROUNDED,] as in v. 16; 17. 11; 18. 5, &c.
MIGHTY ONES,] as in 76. 5; 78. 25, &c.
BASHAN,] as in 68. 15, 22; 135. 11, &c.
Sept. Vulg. 'fat ones.'
COMPASSED,] as in Jud. 20. 43.
13. OPENED,] as in 66. 14; 144. 7, 10, 11, &c.
LION,] as in v. 16, 21; 7. 2; 10. 9, &c. Sept.
Vulg. 'as a lion.'
TEARING,] not 'a ravening,' as in C.V.

ROARING,] as in 104. 21; Jud. 14. 5; Eze.
22. 25; Zeph. 3. 3.
14. POURED OUT,] as in De. 12. 27, &c.
SEPARATED THEMSELVES,] not 'are out of
joint,' as in C.V.; as in 92. 9; Job 4. 11; 41. 17.
BONES,] as in v. 17; 6. 2; 31. 10; 32. 3, &c.
WAX,] as in 68. 2; 97. 5; Mic. 1. 4.
MELTED,] as in 68. 2; 97. 5; 112. 10, &c.
BOWELS,] as in 40. 8; 71. 6; Ge. 15. 14, &c.
15. DRIED UP,] as in 90. 6; 102. 4, 11; 129. 6;
102. 4, 11, &c.
POWER,] as in 31. 10; 38. 10; 71. 9, &c.
EARTHEN VESSEL,] as in Lev. 6. 28; 11. 33.
CLEAVING,] as in Eze. 3. 16, &c.
JAWS.] Everywhere else the original word
denotes 'prey'—a thing captured.
DUST,] as in v. 29; 7. 5; 18. 42; 30. 9, &c.
APPOINTEST,] as in Isa. 26. 2; Eze. 24. 3;
2 K. 4. 38.
16. SURROUNDED,] as in v. 12; 17. 11, &c.
DOGS,] as in v. 20; 59. 6, 14; 68. 23, &c.
Sept. Vulg. 'many dogs.'
COMPANY,] not 'assembly,' as in C.V.
Sept. 'synagogue.'
EVIL-DOERS,] as in 26. 5; 27. 2; 37. 1, &c.
COMPASSED,] as in 17. 9; 48. 12; 88. 17, &c.
PIERCING.] So Sept. Vulg. Syr. Arab. Eth.;
the Targ. has 'biting as a lion.'
HANDS..FEET,] to disable from fighting
and running.
17. I COUNT,] not 'I tell;' the Sept. Vulg.
Arab. Eth. 'they have numbered.'
BONES,] as in v. 14.
LOOK EXPECTINGLY,] as in 10. 14; 91. 8, &c.
LOOK,] as in 8. 3; 35. 17; 36. 9; 37. 34, &c.
18. APPORTION,] not 'part' merely, as
in C.V.
GARMENTS,] as in 45. 8; 102. 26; 109. 19, &c.
CLOTHING,] as in 35. 13; 45. 13; 69. 11, &c.
FALL,] as in 1 Ch. 24. 31; 25. 8; 26. 13, &c.
19. FAR OFF,] as in v. 10 above.
STRENGTH.] Original word is not found
again.
HASTE,] as in 38. 22; 40. 13; 70. 1, 5, &c.
20. DELIVER,] as in 7. 1; 25. 20; 31. 2, &c.
SWORD,] as in 7. 12; 7. 13; 37. 14, 15, &c.
SOUL,] as in v. 29; 3. 2; 6. 3, 4; 7. 2, &c.
PAW,] or 'hand,' not 'power,' as in C.V.
DOG,] as in v. 16 above.
ONLY ONE,] Sept. 'only begotten;' not
'darling,' as in C.V.; as in 25. 16; 35. 17; 68.
6; Ge. 22. 2, 12, 16; Jud. 11. 34; Prov. 4. 3;
Jer. 6. 26; Amos 8. 10; Zec. 12. 10.
21. SAVE,] as in 3. 7; 6. 4; 7. 1; 12. 1; 20. 9.
LION,] as in v. 13, 16. Here ends abruptly
the cry of the sufferer, and the joy of the
deliverance begins.
HORNS,] as in 18. 2; 75. 4, 5, 10; 89. 17, &c.
A HIGH PLACE,] as in 78. 69; that is, the
altar of God, whose horns were seized by
the pursued and distressed. Sept. 'the one-
horned.'
THOU HAST ANSWERED,] not 'heard,' as in
C.V.; as in v. 2 above.
22. DECLARE,] lit. 'recount, rehearse.'
NAME,] or 'renown,' as in 5. 11; 7. 17, &c.
BRETHREN,] as in 69. 8; 122. 8; 133. 1, &c.
ASSEMBLY,] as in v. 23; 26. 5.
PRAISE,] as in v. 26; 35. 18; 56. 4, &c.
23. FEAR,] or 'reverence,' as in v. 25, &c.
PRAISE YE,] as in Ps. 104. 35; 105. 45, &c.

SEED OF JACOB,] as in Isa. 45. 19; 65. 9;
Jer. 33. 26; Eze. 20. 5.
HONOUR,] as in Ex. 20. 12; De. 5. 16; 1 Sa.
15. 30; Prov. 3. 9; Isa. 25. 14.
BE AFRAID,] as in Job 19. 29; Ps. 33. 8.
SEED OF ISRAEL,] as in 2 K. 17. 20; 1 Ch.
16. 13; Neh. 9. 2; Isa. 45. 25; Jer. 31. 36, 37.
24. DESPISED,] as in 69. 33; 102. 17.
ABOMINATED,] as in Lev. 11. 11, 13, 43; 20.
25; De. 7. 26.
AFFLICTION.] Sept. Vulg. 'supplication.'
AFFLICTED,] as in 9. 12, 18; 10. 2, 9, 12; 12.
5, &c. Sept. Vulg. 'poor.'
HIDDEN HIS FACE,] as in 10. 11; 13. 1, &c.
FROM HIM.] Sept. Vulg. 'from me.'
HIS CRYING,] as in 28. 2; 31. 22, &c. Sept.
Vulg. 'my crying.'
HEARETH,] as in 38. 14; 59. 7; 65. 2, &c.
25. OF THEE,] or 'from thee.' So Sept. &c.
PRAISE,] as in v. 3 above.
ASSEMBLY,] as in 23 above.
VOWS,] as in 50. 14; 56. 12; 61. 5, 8, &c.
COMPLETE,] not 'pay,' as in C.V.; as in
50. 14; 66. 13; 76. 11; 116. 14, 18, &c.
FEARERS,] as in v. 23; Sept. prefixes 'all.'
26. HUMBLE,] as in 9. 12, 18; 10. 12, 17, &c.
EAT,] their daily portion, and are
SATISFIED,] as in 17. 14, 15; 37. 19; 59. 15
PRAISE,] as in v. 22 above.
SEEKING HIM,] as in 9. 10, 12; 14. 2; 24. 6
27. REMEMBER,] as in 8. 4; 20. 3; 25. 7, &c
RETURN,] not 'turn,' as in C.V.; as in 6
10; 7. 12, &c.
ENDS OF THE EARTH,] as in 2. 8; 59. 13.
BEFORE THEE.] Sept. Vulg. 'before him.'
BOW THEMSELVES,] as in v. 29; 5. 7; 66. 4.
FAMILIES,] not 'kindreds,' as in C.V.; as
in 96. 7; 107. 41, &c.
28. KINGDOM,] as in 1 Sa. 10. 16, 25; 11. 14.
RULING,] as in 59. 13; 66. 7; 89. 9, &c.
29. FAT ONES,] as in 92. 14; Isa. 30. 23.
Sept. Vulg. prefix 'all.'
BOW THEMSELVES,] as in v. 27.
BOW,] as in 20. 8; 72. 9; 95. 6, &c.
GOING DOWN,] as in 28. 1; 30. 3; 88. 4, &c.
DUST,] as in v. 15.
REVIVED,] lit. 'caused to live.' Sept.
Vulg. 'and my soul shall live to him.'
30. A SEED.] Targ. 'the seed of Abraham;
Sept. 'his seed;' Vulg. 'my seed.'
REHEARSED,] or 'recounted;' as in C.V.
GENERATION,] as in 10. 6; 12. 7; 14. 5, &c.
31. COME IN,] to the temple and assembly
of God.
DECLARE,] as in 30. 9; 38. 8; 40. 5; 50. 6.
BORN,] as in Ge. 21. 3; 48. 5, &c.
MADE,] not 'done.' Sept. Vulg. 'whom
the Lord hath made.'

XXIII. 1. SHEPHERD,] as in 80. 1; Ge.
4. 2, &c.
LACK,] as in 34. 10; De. 2. 7; 8. 9, &c.
2. PASTURES,] as in 65. 12; 74. 20; 83. 12;
Jer. 9. 10; 23. 10; 25. 37; La. 2. 2; Joel 1. 19,
20; 2. 22; Amos 1. 2.
TENDER GRASS,] not 'green,' as in C.V.;
as in 37. 2; Ge. 1. 11, 12, &c.
LIE DOWN,] lit. 'crouch;' as in Song 1. 7;
Isa. 13. 20; 54. 11; Jer. 33. 12; Eze. 34. 15.
3. REFRESHETH,] lit. 'bringeth back.'
LEADETH,] as in 5. 8; 27. 11; 31. 3; 43. 3, &c.

PATHS,] as in 65. 11; 140. 5, &c.
NAME'S SAKE,] as in 25. 11; 31. 3; 79. 9;
106. 8; 109. 21; 143. 11, &c.
4. WALK,] *or* 'go.' Sept. Vulg. add 'in
the midst, instead of'
VALLEY,] as in 60. 2; Nu. 21. 20, &c.
DEATH-SHADE,] as in 44. 19; 107. 10, 14, &c.
FEAR,] as in 3. 6; 27. 1, 3; 33. 8; 40. 3, &c.
EVIL,] as in 5. 4; 7. 4, 9; 10. 6, 15; 15. 3, &c.
ROD,] as in 2. 9; 45. 6; 74. 2; 78. 55, &c.
STAFF,] as in Ex. 21. 19; Nu. 21. 18; Jud.
6. 21; 2 K. 4. 29, 31; 18. 21; Isa. 36. 6; Eze.
29. 6; Zec. 8. 4.
COMFORT,] as in 69. 20; 71. 21; 119. 76, 82.
5. ARRANGEST,] not 'preparest' merely, as
in C.V.; as in 5. 3; 40. 5, &c.
TABLE,] as in 69. 22; 78. 19; 128. 3, &c.
OVER-AGAINST,] not 'in the presence of,'
as in C.V.; as in 31. 22; 33. 11, &c.
ADVERSARIES,] *lit.* 'distressors;' as in 6.
7; 7. 4, &c.
ANOINTED,] *or* 'made fat;' as in Prov. 15.
30, &c.
OIL,] as in 45. 7; 55. 21; 89. 20, &c.
HEAD,] as in Ge. 28. 18; Lev. 21. 10; 2 K.
9. 6; Ecc. 9. 8; Isa. 28. 1, 4, &c.
CUP,] as in 11. 6; 16. 5; 75. 8; 116. 13, &c.
FULL,] not 'runneth over,' as in C.V.; as
in 66. 12.
6. ONLY,] not 'surely,' as in C.V.
GOODNESS,] as in 4. 6; 14. 1; 16. 2; 21. 3,
&c. Sept. Vulg. omit.
KINDNESS,] not 'mercy,' as in C.V.
PURSUE,] not 'follow' merely, as in C.V.
DAYS OF LIFE,] as in 27. 4; 128. 5; Ge. 3. 14.
MY DWELLING,] *or* 'I have dwelt.'
HOUSE OF JEHOVAH,] the temple or taber-
nacle where God's worship is performed.
A LENGTH OF DAYS,] not 'for ever,' as in
C.V.; as in 21. 4; 91. 16; 93. 5; Job 12. 12;
Prov. 3. 2, 16; Lam. 5. 20, &c.

XXIV. PSALM OF DAVID.] Sept. Vulg. add,
'for the first sabbath.'
1. EARTH,] both land and sea.
FULNESS,] as in 50. 12; 89. 11; 96. 11; 98. 7.
WORLD,] the habitable or fruit-bearing
earth; as in 9. 8, &c.
INHABITANTS.] Sept. Vulg. prefix 'all.'
2. SEAS,] as in 8. 8; 65. 7; 69. 34; 135. 6, &c.
FOUNDED,] as in 78. 69; 89. 11; 102. 25, &c.
FLOODS,] as in 46. 4; 66. 6; 72. 8, &c.
ESTABLISH,] as in 7. 9, 12; 21. 12; 48. 8, &c.
3. HILL,] as in 2. 6; 3. 4; 11. 1; 15. 1, &c.
RISETH,] not 'stand,' as in C.V.; as in 1. 5.
HOLY PLACE,] as in Ex. 29. 31; Lev. 6. 26.
4. CLEAN,] *lit.* 'innocent;' as in 10. 8, &c.
PURE OF HEART,] as in 73. 1.
LIFTED UP,] as in 15. 3; 32. 5; 69. 7, &c.
VANITY,] as in 12. 2; 26. 4; 31. 6, &c.
HIS SOUL.] Sept. 'my soul.'
SWORN,] as in 15. 4; 89. 3, 35, 49, &c.
DECEIT,] as in 5. 6; 10. 7; 17. 1, &c.
5. BEARETH AWAY,] *or* 'lifteth up;' as in
16. 4; 25. 1, &c.
BLESSING,] as in 3. 8; 21. 3, 6; 37. 26, &c.
RIGHTEOUSNESS.] Sept. Vulg. 'kindness
from God his saviour.'
SALVATION,] as in 18. 46; 25. 5; 27. 9, &c.
6. GENERATION,] as in 10. 16; 12. 7; 14. 5.
SEEKING,] as in 9. 10; 14. 2; 22. 26, &c.

FACE,] as in 27. 8; 105. 4; 2 Sa. 21. 1, &c.
JACOB.] Sept. Vulg. Syr. Ar. 'O God of
Jacob.'
SELAH,] as in v. 10; 2. 3, 4, 8; 4. 2, 4, &c.
7. LIFT UP,] as in v. 9; 4. 6; 10. 12; 25. 18.
GATES,] as in v. 9; 9. 13. 14; 69. 12, &c.
HEADS,] as in 3. 3; 7. 16; 18. 43; 21. 3, &c.
BE LIFTED UP,] as in 7. 6; 94. 2.
DOORS,] *lit.* 'openings;' as in v. 9; Ge. 4. 7.
KING OF GLORY,] *or* 'of the glory,' as in
v. 8, 10.
8. STRONG,] as in Isa. 43. 17.
MIGHTY,] as in 19. 5; 33. 16; 45. 3, &c.
BATTLE,] as in 18. 34, 39; 27. 3; 46. 9, &c.
9. LIFT UP,] as in v. 7.
10. HOSTS,] as in 46. 7, 11; 48. 8; 59. 5, &c.

XXV. BY DAVID.] Sept. and Vulg. pre
fix 'a psalm.'
1. LIFT UP.] In the original Hebrew text
each of the 22 verses of this Psalm commences with a different letter of the alphabet.
2. TRUSTED,] as in 13. 5; 22. 4, 5; 26. 1, &c.
ASHAMED,] as in v. 3, 20; 6. 10; 31. 1, &c.
EXULT,] as in 5. 11; 9. 2; 68. 3, &c.
3. WAITING,] as in 37. 9; 69. 6; Isa. 40. 31;
49. 23; La. 3. 25.
TREACHEROUS DEALERS,] not ' transgressors,' as in C.V.; as in 59. 5; 119. 158,
&c. Sept. Vulg. prefix 'all.'
WITHOUT CAUSE,] as in 7. 4; Ge. 31. 43; Ex
3. 21; 23. 15; 34. 20; De. 15. 13; 16. 16, &c.
4. THY WAYS,] as in v. 8, 9, 12; 5. 8, &c.
TO KNOW,] not 'show,' as in C.V.; as in
39. 4; 90. 12; 105. 1; 143. 8, &c.
THY PATHS,] as in v. 10; 44. 18; 119. 15, &c.
TEACH,] as in v. 5; 119. 12, 26, 64, 68, &c.
5. TO TREAD,] not 'lead,' as in C.V.; as in
v. 9; 119. 35, &c.
TRUTH,] as in v. 10; 15. 2; 19. 9, &c.
TEACH,] as in v. 4.
SALVATION,] as in 18. 46; 27. 9, &c. Sept.
Vulg. 'God my saviour.'
NEAR THEE,] not 'on thee,' as in C.V.
WAITED,] as in v. 3.
ALL THE DAY,] as in 32. 3; 35. 28; 38. 6, &c.
6. REMEMBER,] as in v. 7; 74. 2, 18, 22, &c.
MERCIES,] as in 40. 11; 51. 1; 69. 16, &c.
KINDNESSES,] as in v. 7; 5. 7; 6. 4, &c.
7. SINS,] as in v. 18; 32. 5; 38. 3, 18, &c.
YOUTH,] as in 71. 5, 17; 103. 5; 127. 4, &c.
TRANSGRESSIONS,] as in 5. 10; 19. 13; 32.
1, &c. Sept. Vulg. 'ignorance.'
REMEMBER,] as in v. 6.
BE MINDFUL,] *or* 'remember about' me.
GOODNESS,] as in 27. 13; 31. 19; 65. 4, &c.
8. GOOD,] as in 34. 8; 54. 6; 73. 1, &c.
UPRIGHT,] as in 92. 15; De. 32. 4; Isa. 26. 7.
DIRECTETH,] not 'teach,' as in C.V.; as in
v. 12; 32. 8, &c.
SINNERS,] as in 1. 5; 26. 9; 51. 13, &c.
WAY,] as in v. 4, 9, 12.
9. HUMBLE,] as in 9. 12, 18; 10. 12, 17, &c.
TO TREAD,] not 'guide,' as in C.V.; as in v. 5.
JUDGMENT,] as in 1. 5; 7. 6; 9. 4, 7, 16, &c.
TEACHETH,] as in v. 4.
10. PATHS,] as in v. 4.
KINDNESS,] not 'mercy,' as in C.V.; as in
v. 6, 7, &c.
TRUTH,] as in v. 5.
KEEPING,] as in 31. 23; 119. 2; Prov. 13. 3.

COVENANT,] as in v. 14; 44. 17; 50. 5, 16, &c.
TESTIMONIES,] as in 78. 56; 93. 5; 99. 7, &c.
11. NAME'S SAKE,] as in 31. 3; 79. 7; 106. 8.
THOU HAST PARDONED,] not 'pardon,' as in C.V.; Sept. Vulg. 'propitious.'
INIQUITY,] as in 18. 23; 31. 10; 32. 2, 5, &c.
GREAT,] or 'abundant.'
12. FEARING,] as in v. 14; 15. 4; 22. 23, 25.
DIRECTETH,] not 'teach,' as in C.V.; as in v. 8.
CHOOSE,] as in 33. 12; 47. 4; 65. 4, &c.
13. GOOD,] not 'ease,' as in C.V.; as in v. 8.
REMAIN,] lit. 'lodge;' as in 30. 5; 49. 12, &c.
SEED,] as in 18. 50; 21. 10; 22. 23, 30, &c.
POSSESS,] not 'inherit,' as in C.V.; as in 37. 9, 11, 22, 29, 34, &c.
LAND,] in which he dwells.
14. SECRET,] as in 55. 14; 64. 2; 8. 3; 89. 7; 111. 1; Ge. 49. 6, &c.
FEARING,] as in v. 12.
COVENANT,] as in v. 10.
TO KNOW,] not 'shew;' as in 78. 5; 106. 8; 145. 12, &c.
15. EYES,] as in 123. 2, &c.
NET,] as in 9. 15; 10. 9; 31. 4; 35. 7, 8; 57. 6; 140. 5, &c.
16. TURN,] the face, as the original word implies; as in 69. 16; 86. 16; 119. 132, &c.
FAVOUR,] not 'have mercy,' as in C.V.; as in 4. 1; 6. 2, &c.
LONELY,] as in 22. 20; 35. 17; 68. 6, &c. Sept. 'only begotten.'
AFFLICTED,] as in 9. 12, 18; 10. 2, 9, 12.
17. DISTRESSES,] as in v. 22; 9. 9; 10. 1, &c.
ENLARGED THEMSELVES,] not 'are enlarged,' as in C.V.; as in 4. 1; 18. 36; 35. 12; 81. 10; 119. 32, &c.
DISTRESSES,] as in 107. 6, 13, 19, 28; Job 15. 24; Zeph. 1. 15.
18. AFFLICTION,] as in 9. 13; 31. 7; 44. 24.
MISERY,] as in 7. 14, 16; 10. 7, 14; 55. 10, &c.
BEAR WITH,] as in Ge. 50. 17; 1 Sa. 25. 28, &c.
SIN,] as in v. 7.
19. SEE,] not ' consider,' as in C V. ; as in v. 18, &c.
MANY,] as in 3. 1; 4. 7; 38. 19; 69. 4, &c.
VIOLENT,] not ' cruel,' as in C.V. ; as in 7. 16, &c. Sept. and Vulg. 'unjust.'
HATED,] as in 109. 3, 5; 139. 22, &c.
20. KEEP,] or 'watch, guard.'
DELIVER,] as in 7. 1; 22. 20; 31. 2, 15, &c.
ASHAMED,] as in v. 2, 3.
TRUSTED,] lit. ' taken refuge;' as in v. 2, 3.
21. INTEGRITY,] as in 7. 8; 26. 1, 11; 41. 12; 78. 72, &c. Sept. 'harmlessness;' Vulg. 'innocence.'
UPRIGHTNESS,] as in 119. 7; De. 9. 5; 1 K. 9. 4, &c.
KEEP,] as in 12. 7; 32. 7; 40. 11; 61. 7, &c.
WAITED,] as in v. 5.
22. REDEEM,] as in 26. 11; 44. 26; 69. 18, &c.
ISRAEL,] God's peculiar people.
DISTRESS,] as in v. 17 above.

XXVI. BY DAVID.] Vulg. prefixes 'a psalm.'
1. JUDGE,] as in 7. 8; 35. 24; 43. 1; 82. 3, &c.
INTEGRITY.] Sept. 'harmlessness,' Vulg. 'innocence;' as in 7. 8, &c.
WALKED,] and gone on all my days.
TRUSTED,] or 'leant;' as in 13. 5; 22. 4, &c.

SLIDE,] or 'am not moved;' as in 18. 36, 37. 31; 2 Sa. 22. 37; Job 12. 5.
2. TRY,] as in 129. 23; Mal. 3. 10, &c.
PROVE,] as in Da. 1. 12, &c.
PURIFIED,] not 'try,' as in C.V.; as in 12. 6; 18. 30; 119. 140, &c.
REINS..HEART,] as in 7. 9; Jer. 11. 20, &c.
3. KINDNESS,] as in 5. 7; 6. 4; 13. 5; 17. 7.
WALKED HABITUALLY,] as in 12. 8; 35. 14.
TRUTH,] as in 12. 2; 19. 9; 25. 5, 10; 30. 9.
4. SAT,] as in 1. 1; 9. 4; 23. 6; 29. 10, &c.
VAIN MEN,] as in Job 11. 11, &c.
DISSEMBLERS,] lit. 'hidden,' as in 1 K. 10. 3; Ecc. 12. 14; Nah. 3. 11.
ENTER,] as in 5. 7; 18. 6; 22. 31; 24. 7, &c.
5. HATED,] as in 5. 5; 11. 5; 25. 19, &c.
ASSEMBLY,] as in 22. 22, 25; 35. 18, &c.
EVIL-DOERS,] as in 22. 16; 27. 2; 37. 1, &c.
WICKED,] as in 1. 1, 4, 5, 6; 3. 7; 7. 9, &c.
SIT,] as in v. 4.
6. WASH,] as in 58. 10; 73. 17; Ex. 30. 21, &c.
INNOCENCY,] as in 73. 17; Ge. 20. 5; Hos. 8. 5, Am. 4. 6.
HANDS,] as in 7. 3; 9. 16; 18. 1; 24. 4, &c.
COMPASS,] as in 7. 7; 32. 7, 10; 55. 10, &c.
ALTAR,] as in 43. 4; 51. 19; 84. 3; 118. 27, &c.
7. SOUND,] lit. ' cause to hear,' as in 1 Ch. 15. 19; 2 Ch. 15. 13; Isa. 58. 4.
CONFESSION,] as in 42. 4; 50. 14, 23, &c.
RECOUNT,] not 'tell,' merely, as in C.V.; as in 40. 5; 50. 16; 73. 28; 102. 21, &c.
WONDERS,] as in 9. 1; 40. 5; 71. 17; 72. 18.
8. LOVED,] as in 11. 7; 45. 7; 47. 4; 52. 3, &c.
HABITATION,] as in 65. 5; 71. 3; 90. 1, &c.
PLACE,] as in 24. 3; 37. 10; 44. 19; 103. 16.
HONOUR,] as in 3. 3; 4. 2; 7. 5; 8. 5; 16. 9.
9. GATHER.] Sept. Vulg. 'destroy not;' as in 27. 10; 39. 6; 50. 5; 85. 3; 104. 29, &c.
SINNERS,] as in 1. 1, 5; 26. 9; 51. 13, &c.
MEN OF BLOOD,] as in 5. 6; 55. 23; 59. 2, &c.
LIFE,] as in 75. 16, 11; 17. 14; 18. 46, &c.
10. WICKED DEVICE,] not 'mischief,' as in C.V.; Sept. 'lawlessnesses,' Vulg. 'iniquities.'
BRIBES,] as in 15. 5; Ex. 23. 8; De. 10. 17.
11. INTEGRITY.] Sept. Vulg. as in v. 1.
WALK,] as in v. 1.
REDEEM.] Sept. adds ' O Lord.'
FAVOUR,] not 'be merciful,' as in C.V.
12. FOOT,] as in 8. 6; 9. 15; 18. 9, 33, &c.
UPRIGHTNESS,] as in 27. 11; 45. 6; 67. 4, &c.
ASSEMBLIES,] as in 68. 26.
BLESS,] Sept. and Vulg. add 'thee.'

XXVII. BY DAVID.] Sept. and Vulg. add 'before the anointing.'
1. LIGHT,] as in 4. 6; 36. 9; 37. 6, &c.
SALVATION.] Sept. 'saviour;' as in v. 9, &c.
FEAR,] as in v. 3; 3. 6; 23. 4; 33. 8, &c.
STRENGTH.] Vulg. 'protector;' as in 28. 8.
AFRAID,] as in 14. 5; 53. 5; 78. 53, &c.
2. EVIL-DOERS,] not 'wicked,' as in C.V.; as in 22. 16, &c.
EAT MY FLESH,] as in 50. 13; 79. 2, &c.
ADVERSARIES,] as in v. 12; 3. 1; 4. 1, &c.
ENEMIES,] as in v. 6; 3. 7; 6. 10; 7. 5, &c.
STUMBLED,] as in 31. 10; 107. 12; 100. 24.
FALLEN,] as in 10. 10; 16. 16; 20. 8, &c.
3. HOST,] as in 78. 28; 106. 16, &c.
ENCAMP,] as in 34. 7; 53. 5; Ge. 26. 17, &c.
FEAR,] as in v. 1.

WAR,] *or* 'battle;' as in 18. 34, 39; 24. 8, &c.
CONFIDENT,] as in 21. 7; 32. 10; 49. 6, &c.
4. ASKED,] not 'desired' merely, as in C.V.;
as in 21. 4, &c.
SEEK,] as in v. 8; 4. 2; 37. 36; 63. 9, &c.
DWELLING,] as in 23. 6; 139. 2, &c.
LOOK ON,] as in Eze. 21. 29, &c.
PLEASANTNESS,] not 'beauty,' as in C.V.
ENQUIRE,] as in Lev. 13. 36; 27. 33; 2 K.
16. 15; Prov. 20. 25; Eze. 34. 11, 12.
TEMPLE.] Sept. 'holy temple.'
5. HIDETH,] as in 10. 8; 17. 14; 31. 19, &c.
TABERNACLE,] not 'pavilion.' Sept. Vulg.
his 'tabernacle.'
DAY OF EVIL.] Sept. 'day of my evil;' as in
5. 7; 11. 4, &c.
HIDETH,] *lit.* 'keepeth secret;' as in v. 9;
10. 11; 13. 1, &c.
SECRET PLACE,] as in 18. 11; 31. 20; 32. 7.
TENT,] not 'tabernacle;' as in v. 6; 15. 1, &c.
ROCK,] as in 18. 2, 31, 46; 19. 14; 28. 1, &c.
6. LIFTED UP.] Sept. 'lo, the Lord hath
lifted up.'
ENEMIES,] as in v. 2.
MY SURROUNDERS.] Sept. Vulg. 'I have
surrounded.'
SACRIFICE,] as in 54. 6; 116. 117, &c.
SHOUTING,] not 'joy,' as in C.V.; as in 33. 3.
SING,] as in 3. 6; 21. 13; 57. 7; 59. 16, &c.
SING PRAISE,] as in 7. 17; 9. 2; 18. 49, &c.
7. HEAR,] as in 4. 1; 17. 1, 6; 28. 2; 30. 10.
CALL,] not 'cry,' as in C.V.; Sept. Vulg.
add 'to thee.'
FAVOUR,] not 'have mercy;' as in 4. 1, &c.
ANSWER,] as in 4. 1; 13. 3; 55. 2; 60. 5, &c.
8. HEART,] as in v. 3, 14, &c.
THEY SOUGHT,] not 'seek ye,' as in C.V.;
Sept. 'I have sought thy face;' Vulg. 'my
face hath sought thee.'
I SEEK,] as in v. 4.
9. HIDE,] as in 69. 17; 102. 2; 119. 19, &c.
TURN ASIDE,] not 'put away,' as in C.V.;
as in 141. 4, &c.
ANGER,] as in 2. 5, 12; 6. 1; 7. 6; 10. 4, &c.
THY SERVANT.] Sept. Vulg. 'from thy ser-
vant.'
HELP,] as in 22. 19; 35. 2; 38. 22, &c.
LEAVE,] as in 78. 60; 94. 14, &c.
FORSAKE,] as in 10. 14; 16. 10; 37. 28, &c.
SALVATION,] as in v. 1 above. Sept. 'God
my saviour.'
10. HAVE FORSAKEN,] not 'do forsake.' So
Sept. Vulg. &c.
DOTH GATHER,] not 'will take up,' as in
C.V.; as in 26. 9, &c.
11. SHEW,] not 'teach,' as in C.V.; as in
86. 11, &c.
THY WAY,] as in 5. 8; 25. 4; 51. 13, &c.
LEAD,] as in 5. 8; 139. 24, &c.
PATH,] as in 8. 8; 16. 11; 17. 4; 19. 5, &c.
UPRIGHTNESS,] as in 26. 12; 45. 6; 67. 4, &c.
FOR THE SAKE OF,] not 'because of,'
merely, as in C.V.
BEHOLDERS,] not necessarily 'enemies,' as
in C.V. Sept. Vulg. &c.
12. WILL,] *lit.* 'soul,' as in 3. 2; 6. 3, 4, &c.
FALSE,] Sept. Vulg. 'unjust,' as in 7. 14, &c.
BREATHE OUT,] as in 10. 5; 12. 5, &c.
VIOLENCE,] not 'cruelty,' as in C.V.; Sept.
the injustice.'
13. NOT BELIEVED.] Sept. Vulg. 'I believe.'

LOOK ON,] not 'see, merely, as in C.V.
LIVING,] as in 52. 5; 116. 9; 142. 5, &c.
14. LOOK,] not 'wait,' as in C.V.; as in
37. 34, &c.
STRONG,] not 'of good courage,' as in C.V.;
as in 31. 24, &c.
HEART,] as in v. 3, 8 above.
LOOK,] not 'wait,' as in C.V.

XXVIII. 1. CALL,] not 'cry,' as in C.V.; as
in 3. 4, &c.
ROCK,] as in 18. 2, 31, 46; 19. 14; 27. 5, &c.
Sept. and Vulg. 'my God.'
NOT SILENT,] as in 35. 22; 39. 12; 50. 3, &c.
COMPARED,] not 'become like,' as in C.V.;
as in 49. 12, &c.
GOING DOWN,] as in 22. 29; 30. 3; 88. 4, &c.
PIT,] as in 7. 15; 30. 3; 40. 2; 88. 4, 6, &c.
2. SUPPLICATION,] as in v. 6; 31. 22; 116. 1,
&c. Vulg. adds 'O Lord.'
CRYING,] as in 22. 24; 31. 22, &c.; Vulg.
'praying.'
LIFTING UP,] as in 63. 4; 106. 26; 119. 48, &c.
ORACLE,] as in 1 K. 6. 5—31; 7. 49; 8. 6, 8, &c.
Sept. 'sanctuary;' Vulg. 'temple.'
3. DRAW,] as in 10. 9; 36. 10; 85. 5, &c.;
Sept. adds 'my soul.'
WICKED,] as in 1. 1, 4, 5, 6; 3. 7; 9. 5, &c.
WORKERS OF INIQUITY,] as in 5. 5; 6. 8; 7.
14, &c. Sept. Vulg. add 'destroy me not.'
SPEAKING PEACE,] as in 35.20; 85. 8, &c.
NEIGHBOURS,] *lit.* 'friends,' as in 12. 2, &c.
EVIL,] as in 5. 4; 7. 4, 9; 10. 6, 15; 15. 3, &c.
HEART,] as in 4. 4; 13. 2; 15. 2; 20. 4, &c.
4. ACTING,] *or* 'act,' as in 9. 16; 44. 1; 64.
9; 77. 12; 90. 16; 92. 4; 95. 9, &c. Sept.
'works.'
DOINGS,] not 'endeavours,' as in C.V.; as
in 77. 11, &c.
WORK OF THEIR HANDS,] as in v. 5; 8. 6, &c.
RETURN,] as in 79. 12; 94. 2, &c.
DEED,] not 'desert,' as in C.V.; as in 94. 2.
5. ATTEND,] as in 19. 12; 49. 20; 58. 9, &c.
DOINGS,] as in 27. 4; 109. 20; Lev. 19. 13, &c.
WORK OF HIS HANDS,] as in v. 5.
THROWETH DOWN,] as in Ex. 15. 7; 19. 21.
BUILD UP,] as in 51. 18; 69. 35; 78. 69, &c.
6. HEARD,] as in 6. 8, 9; 10. 17; 31. 13, &c.
SUPPLICATIONS,] as in v. 2 above.
7. STRENGTH,] as in v. 8; 8. 2; 21. 1, 13;
29. 1, 11, &c. Sept. Vulg. 'help.'
SHIELD,] as in 3. 3; 7. 10; 18. 2, 30, 35, &c.
TRUSTED,] as in 13. 5; 22. 4, 5; 25. 2; 26. 1.
HELPED,] as in 1 Ch. 5. 20; 2 Ch. 26. 15, &c.
HEART.] Sept. Vulg. 'flesh.'
EXULTETH,] as in 60. 6; 94. 3; 96. 12, &c.
SONG,] as in 30. 1; 33. 3; 40. 3; 42. 8, &c.
Sept. Vulg. 'good-will.'
THANK,] not 'praise,' merely, as in C.V.
as in 6. 5, &c.
8. STRENGTH,] as in v. 7 above.
TO HIM.] Sept. Vulg. 'to his people.'
STRENGTH,] as in 27. 1; 31. 2, 4; 37. 39, &c.
SALVATION,] as in 3. 2, 8; 9. 14; 13. 5, &c.
ANOINTED,] *in Heb.* 'Mashiach,' as in 2. 2.
9. SAVE,] as in 3. 7; 6. 4; 7. 1; 12. 1; 20. 9.
PEOPLE,] as in 3. 8, &c.; Vulg. adds 'O Lord.
BLESS,] as in 66. 8; 68. 26; 92. 12, &c.
INHERITANCE,] as in 2. 8; 33. 12; 37. 18, &c.
FEED,] as in 37. 3, &c. Vulg. 'rule.'
CARRY,] not 'lift up,' merely, as in C.V.

XXIX. DAVID.] Sept. Vulg. add 'at the completion of the tabernacle.'
1. ASCRIBE,] not 'give,' merely, as in C.V.; as in v. 2; 60. 11; 96. 7, 8; 108. 12, &c.
SONS OF THE MIGHTY,] not 'mighty,' merely, as in C.V.; as in 89. 6, &c.
HONOUR,] as in v. 2, 3, 9; 3. 3; 4. 2; 7. 5, &c.
STRENGTH,] as in v. 11; 8. 2; 21. 1, 13, &c.
2. NAME,] as in 66. 2; 96. 8.
BOW YOURSELVES,] not 'worship,' as in C.V.; as in 45. 11, &c.
BEAUTY OF HOLINESS.] Sept. Vulg. 'court of his sanctuary,' as in 1 Ch. 16. 29; Ps. 96. 9.
3. VOICE,] as in v. 4, 5, 7, 8, 9, &c.
WATERS,] as in 1. 3; 18. 11, 15, 16; 22. 14.
GOD OF GLORY.] Compare 24. 7—10.
THUNDERED,] as in 18. 13; 1 Sa. 2. 10, &c.
MANY WATERS,] as in 18. 16; 32. 6; 77. 19.
4. WITH POWER,] or 'in power.'
WITH MAJESTY,] or 'in majesty.'
5. SHIVERING,] not merely 'breaking,' as in C.V.
CEDARS,] as in 80. 10; 92. 12; 104. 16, &c.
LEBANON,] as in 92. 12; 104. 16, &c.
6. TO SKIP,] as in 114. 4, 6; 1 Ch. 15. 29, &c.
CALF,] as in 68. 30; 106. 19; Ex. 32. 4, &c. Sept. Vulg. 'of Lebanon.'
SIRION,] another name of Hermon; Sept. translates it 'the beloved.'
REEMS,] as in 22. 21; 92. 10; Nu. 23. 22, &c.
7. HEWING,] not 'divideth;' as in 1 K. 5. 15.
FLAMES OF FIRE,] as in 105. 32; Isa. 4. 5.
8. PAINETH,] not 'shaketh;' as in 10. 5, &c.
WILDERNESS,] as in 55. 7; 63. 1; 65. 12, &c.
KADESH,] called in Nu. 33. 36 'Zin.'
9. PAINETH,] or 'maketh to calve;' as in 90. 2, &c.
OAKS,] or 'hinds;' so Sept. Vulg.; but Horsley, Boothroyd, Lowth, Green, prefer 'oaks.'
MAKETH BARE,] not 'discovereth;' as in Isa. 20. 4; 30. 14; 47. 2; 52. 10, &c.
FORESTS,] as in 50. 10; 80. 13; 83. 14, &c.
TEMPLE,] as in 5. 7; 11. 4; 18. 6; 27. 4, &c. Sept. 'sanctuary.'
SAITH,] not 'speaketh of,' as in C.V.
10. DELUGE,] not 'flood;' as in 6. 17; 7. 6—17; 9. 16, 15, 28; 10. 1, 32; 11. 10.
HATH SAT,] as in 1. 1; 9. 4; 23. 6; 26. 4, &c. Vulg. 'made the deluge to sit.'
KING,] as in 5. 2; 10. 16; 24. 7, 8, 9, 10, &c.
11. STRUGGLE,] as in v. 1.
PEACE,] as in 4. 8; 28. 3; 34. 14; 35. 20, &c.

XXX. SONG,] as in 28. 7; 33. 3; 40. 3; 42. 8. Sept. 'ode.'
DEDICATION,] as in Nu. 7. 10, 11, 84, 88; 2 Ch. 7. 9; Neh. 12. 27.
HOUSE OF DAVID,] as in 2 Sa. 5. 11; 7. 1, &c.
1. EXALT,] as in 18. 48; 27. 5; 34. 3; 37. 34.
DRAWN UP,] not 'lifted up;' as in Prov. 20. 5; Ex. 2. 6, 19.
REJOICE,] as in 45. 8; 92. 4, &c.
2. MY GOD,] as in v. 12; 18. 28; 35. 24, &c.
CRIED,] as in 18. 6; 28. 2; 31. 22; 88. 13, &c.
HEAT,] as in 103. 3; 107. 20; 147. 3, &c.
3. SHEOL,] not the 'grave;' as in 6. 5; 9. 17. FROM GOING DOWN.] Sept. Vulg. 'from those going down.'
KEPT ALIVE,] as in 22. 29; 119 50, 93, &c. Sept. Vulg. 'saved.'

PIT,] as in 7. 15; 28. 1; 40. 2; 88. 4, 6, &c.
4. SING PRAISE,] not 'sing,' merely; as in 9. 11; 33. 2, &c.
SAINTS,] as in 4. 3; 12. 1; 16. 10; 18. 25, &c.
GIVE THANKS,] as in 33. 2; 97. 12; 100. 4.
REMEMBRANCE,] as in 6. 5; 9. 6; 34. 16, &c.
5. MOMENT,] as in 6. 10; 73. 17; Ex. 33. 5, &c. Sept. Vulg. 'ire.'
ANGER,] as in 2. 5, 12; 6. 1; 7. 6; 10. 4, &c.
LIFE,] as in 16. 11; 17. 14; 21. 4; 34. 12, &c.
GOOD WILL,] as in v. 7; 5. 19; 19. 14; 40. 8.
EVEN,] not 'night;' as in 55. 17; 59. 6, &c.
REMAINETH,] lit. 'lodgeth;' as in 25. 13, &c.
WEEPING,] as in 6. 8; 102. 9; Ge. 45. 2, &c.
MORN,] as in 5. 3; 46. 5; 49. 14; 55. 17, &c.
SINGING,] not 'joy,' merely; as in 17. 1, &c.
6. EASE,] as in 73. 12; 122. 7, &c.
MOVED,] as in 10. 6; 13. 4; 15. 5; 16. 8, &c.
7. GOOD PLEASURE,] not 'favour' merely; as in v. 5.
CAUSED TO REMAIN,] or 'to stand;' as in 31. 8, &c.
STRENGTH,] as in 8. 2; 21. 1, 13; 28. 7, &c.
MY MOUNTAIN,] as in 36. 6; 50. 10; 76. 4; 87. 1, &c. Sept. Vulg. 'my beauty.'
HIDDEN THY FACE,] as in 10. 11; 13. 1; 22. 24, &c. Vulg. adds 'from me.'
TROUBLED,] as in 6. 2, 3, 10; 104. 29, &c.
8. CALL,] not 'cried;' as in 3. 4; 18. 3, &c.
JEHOVAH,] Sept. Vulg. 'my God.'
MAKE SUPPLICATION,] as in 142. 1, &c.
9. GAIN,] as in 119. 36; Ge. 37. 26; Ex. 18. 21, &c.
BLOOD,] as in 5. 6; 9. 12; 16. 4; 26. 9, &c.
CORRUPTION,] not 'the pit;' as in 7. 15, &c.
DUST,] not 'the dust,' as in C.V.
THANK,] not 'praise;' as in v. 12; 6. 5, &c.
DECLARE,] as in 22. 31; 38. 18; 40. 5, &c.
TRUTH,] as in 15. 2; 19. 9; 25. 5, 10, &c.
10. FAVOUR,] not 'have mercy;' as in 4. 1
HELPER,] as in 10. 14; 22. 11; 54. 4; 72. 12.
11. TURNED,] as in 41. 3; 66. 6; 78, 9, &c.
MOURNING,] as in Ge. 50. 10; Est. 4. 3, &c.
DANCING,] as in 149. 3; 150. 4; Jer. 31. 4, 13; La. 5. 15. Vulg. 'joy.'
LOOSED,] lit. 'opened;' as in 116. 16, &c.
SACKCLOTH,] as in 35. 13; 69. 11; Ge. 37. 34
GIRDEST,] as in 18. 32, 39, &c.
JOY,] as in 4. 7; 16. 10; 21. 6; 43. 4, &c.
12. HONOUR,] as in 3. 3; 4. 2; 7. 5; 8. 5; 16. 9, &c. Sept. Vulg. 'my honour.'
PRAISE,] as in 7. 17; 9. 2; 18. 49; 21. 13, &c.
SILENT,] as in 4. 14; 31. 17; 37. 7; 62. 5, &c.
MY GOD,] as in v. 2 above.
THANK,] as in v. 9 above.

XXXI. OVERSEER,] as in Ps. 45. 6. 8, &c.
DAVID,] Sept. Vulg. add 'an extasy.'
1. TRUSTED,] lit. 'taken refuge;' as in 7. 1
ASHAMED,] as in v. 17; 6. 10; 25. 2, 3, &c.
RIGHTEOUSNESS,] as in 11. 7; 22. 31, &c.
DELIVER,] as in 17. 13; 71. 4; 82. 4, &c. Sept. 'free me and lift me up.'
2. INCLINE,] as in 17. 6; 45. 10; 71. 2; 78. 1, &c.
EAR,] as in 10. 17; 17. 6; 18. 6, 44, &c.
HASTILY,] as in 37. 2; 147. 16; Nu. 16. 46, &c. Sept. Vulg. connect this with the next clause.
DELIVERANCE,] as in v. 15; 7. 1; 22. 20, &c.
ROCK,] as in 18. 2, 31, 46; 19. 14; 27. 5; 28. 1, &c. Sept. Vulg. 'God.'

BULWARKS,] not 'defence;' as in v. 3, &c.
SAVE,] as in 71. 3; 76. 9; 109. 31, &c.
3. ROCK,] as in 18. 2; 40. 2; 42. 9; 71. 3, &c.
BULWARK,] as in v. 2.
NAME'S SAKE,] as in 23. 3; 25. 11; 79. 9, &c.
LEAD,] as in 23. 3; 43. 3; 61. 2; 67. 4, &c.
TEND,] not 'guide;' as in 23. 2; Ge. 47. 17.
4. BRING OUT,] not 'pull out;' as in 18. 19.
NET,] as in 9. 15; 10. 9; 25. 15, &c.
HID,] as in 9. 15; 35. 7, 8; 140. 5; 142. 3, &c.
STRENGTH,] as in v. 2. Sept. adds 'O Lord.'
5. HAND,] as in 8. 6; 10. 12, 14; 17. 14, &c.
COMMIT,] as in 1 K. 14. 27; 2 Ch. 12. 10, &c.
REDEEMED,] as in 55. 18; 71. 23; 78. 42, &c.
TRUTH,] as in 15. 2; 19. 9; 25. 5, 10; 26. 3, &c.
6. HATED,] as in 5. 5; 11. 5; 25. 19; 26. 6, &c.
OBSERVERS,] as in 34. 20; 71. 10; 97. 10, &c.
LYING VANITIES,] or 'vanities of emptiness;' as in Jon. 2. 8.
TOWARDS,] not 'in,' as in C. V.; Sept. 'upon.'
CONFIDENT,] lit. 'leant;' as in v. 14; 13. 5.
7. REJOICE,] as in 9. 13; 13. 4, 5; 14. 7, &c.
GLAD,] as in 5. 11; 9. 2; 14. 7; 21. 1, &c.
KINDNESS,] not 'mercy,' as in C. V.
SEEN,] not 'considered,' as in C.V.
AFFLICTION,] as in 9. 13; 25. 18; 44. 24, &c.
KNOWN,] as in 14. 4; 18. 43; 20. 6; 31. 7, &c. Sept. Vulg. 'saved.'
ADVERSITIES,] as in 9. 9; 10. 1; 20. 1, &c.
8. SHUT UP,] as in 78. 48, 50, 62; Lev. 13. 4, 5, 11, &c.
ENEMY,] as in v. 15; 18. 1; Lev. 26. 25, &c.
FEET] as in 8. 6; 9. 15; 18. 9, 33, 38, &c.
TO STAND,] not 'set,' as in C. V.; as in 18. 33.
BROAD PLACE,] not 'large room;' as in 18. 19; 118. 5; 2 Sa. 22. 20; Hos. 4. 16; Hab. 1. 6.
9. FAVOUR,] not ' have mercy;' as in 4. 1; 6. 2; 9. 13, &c.
DISTRESS,] as in 3. 1; 4. 1; 13. 4; 18. 6, &c.
EYE..SOUL..BELLY,] that is, my whole being.
OLD,] as in v. 10; Ps. 6. 7.
PROVOCATION,] not 'grief;' as in 6. 7; 10. 14; 85. 4, &c.
10. CONSUMED,] not 'spent;' as in 37. 20; 39. 10; 69. 3, &c.
SORROW,] as in 13. 2; 107. 39; 116. 3, &c.
SIGHING,] as in 6. 6; 38. 9; 102. 5, &c.
FEEBLE,] as in 27. 2; 107. 12; 109. 24, &c.
INIQUITY,] as in 18. 23; 25. 11; 32. 3, 5, &c. Sept. Vulg. 'poverty.'
STRENGTH,] as in 22. 15; 29. 4; 33. 16, &c.
BONES,] as in 6. 2; 22. 14, 17; 32. 3, &c.
OLD,] as in v. 10.
11. ADVERSARIES,] as in 6. 7; 7. 4, 6; 8. 2.
REPROACH,] as in 15. 3; 22. 6; 39. 8, &c.
NEIGHBOURS,] as in 44. 13; 79. 4, 12; 80. 6.
FEAR,] as in 14. 5; 36. 11; 53. 5; 64. 1, &c.
ACQUAINTANCES,] as in 55. 13; 88. 8, 18, &c.
WITHOUT,] as in 18. 42; 41. 6; 144. 13, &c.
FLED,] as in 55. 7; 68. 12; Ge. 31. 40, &c.
12. FORGOTTEN,] as in 9. 18; Ge. 41. 30, &c.
OUT OF MIND,] or 'from the heart.'
VESSEL,] as in 2. 9; 7. 13; 71. 22; Ge. 24. 53.
13. EVIL ACCOUNT,] not 'slander;' as in Ge. 37. 2, &c. Sept. 'disparagement;' Vul. 'vituperation.'
FEAR,] as in Isa. 31. 9; Jer. 6. 25; 87. 1, &c.
BEING UNITED,] not 'took counsel;' as in 2. 2; Ex. 9. 18; Isa. 44. 28.
DEVISED,] as in 17. 3; 37. 12; Ge. 11. 6, &c.

14. ON THEE,] not 'in thee,' as in C. V.
TRUSTED,] as in v. 6.
MY GOD,] as in 3. 7; 5. 2; 7. 1, 3; 13. 3, &c.
15. TIMES,] as in 1. 3; 4. 7; 9. 9; 10. 1, 5, &c. Sept. Vulg. 'lots.'
DELIVER,] as in v. 2.
ENEMY,] as in v. 8.
PURSUERS,] as in 7. 1; 35. 3, 6; 119. 84, &c.
16. CAUSE TO SHINE,] as in 13. 3; 80. 3, 19.
SAVE,] as in 3. 7; 6. 4; 7. 1; 12. 1; 20. 9, &c.
KINDNESS,] not 'mercies,' as in C.V.
17. ASHAMED,] as in v. 1 above.
CALLED,] as in 14. 4; 17. 6; 34. 6; 49. 11, &c.
WICKED,] as in 1. 1, 4, 5, 6; 3. 7; 7. 9, &c.
BECOME SILENT,] as in 4. 4; 30. 12; 35. 15.
SHEOL,] not 'the grave,' as in C.V.
18. LIPS OF FALSEHOOD,] as in 120. 2, &c.
DUMB,] as in 39. 2, 9; Isa. 53. 7; Eze. 3. 26.
RIGHTEOUS ONE,] as in 1. 5, 6; 5. 12, &c.
ANCIENT SAYINGS,] not 'grievous things; as in 75. 5; 94. 4; 1 Sa. 2. 3. Sept. 'lawlessness;' Vulg. 'iniquity.'
PRIDE,] as in v. 23; 10. 2; 36. 11; 46. 3, &c.
CONTEMPT,] as in 107. 40; 119. 22; 123. 3, 4.
19. ABUNDANT,] not 'great,' as in C.V.
GOODNESS,] as in 25. 7; 27. 13; 65. 4, &c.
LAID UP,] as in v. 20; 10. 8; 27. 5; 56. 6, &c.
FEARING,] as in 15. 4; 22. 23, 25; 25. 12, 14.
20. WROUGHT,] as in 11. 3; 44. 1; 68. 28, &c.
TRUSTING,] as in 2. 12; 5. 11; 17. 7; 18. 30.
SONS OF MEN,] as in 8. 4; 11. 4; 12. 1, 8, &c.
HIDEST,] as in 10. 11; 13. 1; 17. 8; 22. 24, &c
SECRET PLACE,] as in 18. 11; 27. 5; 32. 7.
ARTIFICES.] Sept. Vulg. ' troubles, turmoils;' Gesenius 'conspiracies.'
CONCEALEST,] as in v. 19 above.
A TABERNACLE,] not 'pavilion;' as in 18. 11, &c. Vulg. prefixes 'thy.'
STRIFE,] as in 18. 43; 35. 23; 43. 1, &c.
21. BLESSED,] as in 18. 46; 28. 6; 41. 13, &c.
MADE MARVELLOUS,] as in De. 28. 59; Lev 27. 2; Nu. 6. 2; Jud. 13. 19; 2 Ch. 2. 9; 26. 15; Isa. 29. 14; Joel 2. 22.
CITY OF BULWARKS,] as in 60. 6; 2 Ch. 8. 5; 11. 5.
22. HASTING,] as in 116. 11; 2 Sa. 4. 4; 2 K. 7. 14, &c. Sept. 'extasy;' Vulg. 'excess of my mind.'
CUT OFF.] Sept. 'gone;' Vulg. 'cast out.' Original word is not found again.
BUT.] Sept. Vulg. 'because of this, therefore.'
SUPPLICATIONS,] as in 28. 2, 6; 116. 1, &c.
CRYING,] as in 22. 24; 28. 2, &c.
23. LOVE,] as in Prov. 4. 6; Hos. 3. 1; Amos 5. 15; Zec. 8. 19.
SAINTS,] as in 4. 3; 12. 1; 16. 10; 18. 25, &c.
KEEPING,] as in 25. 10; 119. 2; De. 32. 20, &c. Sept. Vulg. 'requireth.'
FAITHFUL,] as in 12. 1; 2 Sa. 20. 19, &c. Sept. Vulg. 'truth.'
RECOMPENSING,] as in 38. 20; De. 7. 10; Isa. 66. 6; Jer. 32. 18; 57. 6; Joel 3. 4.
PROUD DOER,] as in v. 18.
24. BE STRONG,] not 'be of good courage,' as in C.V.; Sept. Vulg. 'be men.'
STRENGTHEN,] as in 27. 14.
WAITING,] not 'hope,' as in C.V.

XXXII. INSTRUCTION,] as in 14. 2; 41. 1; 42. 1; 44. 1, &c.

BY DAVID.] Sept. prefixes 'a psalm.'
1. HAPPINESS,] not 'blessed,' as in C.**V.** ;
as in 1. 1, &c. So Sept. Vulg.
TRANSGRESSION,] as in v. 5; 5. 10; 19. 13;
25. 7, &c. Sept. 'lawlessnesses ;' Vulg. 'iniquities.'
FORGIVEN,] as in 2 K. 5. 1; Job 22. 8; Isa.
3. 3; 9. 15; 33. 24; 46. 3.
SIN,] as in 40. 6; 109. 7; Ge. 20. 9, &c.
Sept. Vulg. 'sins.'
COVERED,] as in v. 5; 85. 2; Job 31. 33, &c.
2. HAPPINESS,] as in v. 1.
MAN,] the human being, as in 8. 4; 11. 4.
IMPUTETH,] as in 10. 2; 21. 11; 35. 20, &c.
INIQUITY,] as in v. 5; 18. 23; 25. 11; 31. 10.
SPIRIT,] as in 31. 5; 34. 18; 51. 10, 17, &c.
Sept. 'mouth.'
DECEIT,] as in 52. 2; 78. 57; 101. 7, &c.
3. KEPT SILENCE,] as in 50. 21; Ge. 24. 21.
BECOME OLD,] as in 49. 14;102. 26;Ge. 18. 12.
MY BONES,] as in 6. 2; 22. 14, 17; 31. 10, &c.
4. BY DAY AND BY NIGHT,] as in 1. 2; 42. 3.
IS HEAVY,] as in 38. 4; Jud. 1. 35; 1 Sa. 5. 11.
MOISTURE,] as in Nu. 11. 8; the original
word is not found again.
CHANGED,] as in 78. 58, &c.
DROUGHTS.] Original word is not found
again.
SUMMER,] as in 74. 17; Ge. 8. 22; 2 Sa. 16. 1.
5. TO KNOW,] as in 16. 11; 51. 6; 89. 1, &c.
COVERED,] not 'hid;' as in v. 1.
CONFESS,] as in 6. 5; 7. 17; 9. 1; 18. 49, &c.
TAKEN AWAY,] as in 24. 5; 25. 1; 50. 16, &c.
SIN.] Sept. 'heart.'
SELAH,] as in v. 4, 7; 3. 2, 4, 8; 4. 2, 4, &c.
6. SAINTLY ONE,] not 'godly;' as in 4. 3;
12. 1; 16. 10, &c.
PRAY,] as in 5. 2; 72. 15; Ge. 20. 7, &c.
TO FIND,] as in 36. 2; Ge. 19. 11; 27. 20, &c.
SURELY,] as in Ge. 6. 5; 20. 11; 26. 29, &c.
OVERFLOWING,] as in Job 38. 25; Prov.27.4.
MANY WATERS,]not 'great waters,'as in C.V.
7. HIDING-PLACE,] as in 18. 11; 27. 5, &c.
DISTRESS,] as in 3. 1; 4. 1; 13. 4; 18. 6, &c.
KEEP,] as in 12. 7; 25. 21; 40. 11, &c.
SONGS.] Sept. Vulg. 'my exaltation.'
DELIVERANCE,] as in 56. 7; Sept. Vulg.
'deliver me.'
COMPASS,] as in v. 10; 7. 7; 26. 6; 55. 10, &c.
Sept. Vulg. 'from those surrounding me.'
8. TO ACT WISELY,] not 'instruct,' as in
C.V.; as in 94. 8; 101. 2, &c.
DIRECT,] not 'teach,' as in C.V.; as in 25.
8, 12; 45. 4, &c.
EYE,] as in 11. 4; 17. 2; 18. 24; 31. 9, 22, &c.
TO TAKE COUNSEL,] not 'guide,' as in C.V.;
as in 7. 5; 14. 24, 27, &c.
9. HORSE,] as in 20. 7; 33. 17; 76. 6; 147. 10.
AS A MULE,] as in 2 Sa. 13. 29; 18. 9; 1 K.
10. 25, &c. Sept. Vulg.,read 'and' for 'as.'
UNDERSTANDING,] as in 1 K. 3. 9, 11; Prov.
1. 2, 6, &c.
BRIDLE,] as in 2 Sa. 8. 1; 2 K. 19. 27; Prov.
26. 3; Isa. 37. 29.
BIT,] as in Job 30. 11; 41. 43; Isa. 30. 28.
ORNAMENTS,] not 'mouth;' as in 103. 5; Ex.
33. 4, 5, 6; 2 Sa. 1. 24; Jer. 49. 18, &c. Sept.
Vulg. 'jaws.'
CURB.] Original word not found again.
10. PAINS,] not 'sorrows' merely, as in
C.V.; as in 38. 17 &c. Sept. Vulg. 'floggings.'

TRUSTING,] as in 21. 7; 27. 3; 49. 6; 84. 12
KINDNESS,] not 'mercy,' as in C.V.; as in
5. 7; 6. 4; 13. 5, &c.
COMPASS,] as in v. 7 above.
11. BE GLAD,] as in 97. 12; De. 33. 18, &c.
REJOICE,] as in 2. 11; Isa. 49. 13; 65. 18, &c.
SING,]not 'shout,' as in C.V.; as in 81. 1, &c.
UPRIGHT OF HEART,] as in 7. 10; 11. 2, &c.

XXXIII. 1. SING,]not 'rejoice,' as in C.V.
as in 98. 4, &c.
UPRIGHT ONES,] as in v. 4; 7. 10; 11. 2, 7.
PRAISE,] as in 9. 14; 22. 3, 25; 34. 1, &c.
COMELY,] as in 147. 1; Prov. 17. 7;19. 10, &c.
2. GIVE THANKS,] not 'praise,' as in C.V.;
as in 30. 4, &c.
HARP,] as in 43. 4; 49. 4; 57. 8, &c.
PSALTERY,] as in 57. 8; 71. 22; 81. 2; 92. 3.
TEN STRINGS,] as in 92. 3; 144. 9; Ge. 24. 55.
SING PRAISE,]not 'sing' merely, as in C.V.;
as in 9. 11, &c.
3. NEW SONG,] as in 40. 3; 96. 1; 98. 1, &c.
PLAY SKILFULLY,] *lit.* 'do well to play.'
SHOUTING,] not a 'loud voice,' as in C.V.;
as in 27. 6, &c.
4. UPRIGHT,] not 'right,' as in C.V.; as
in v. 1.
WORKS,] as in 8. 3, 6; 19. 1; 28. 5; 64. 9, &c.
FAITHFULNESS,] not 'truth,' as in C.V.; as
in 36. 5, &c.
5. RIGHTEOUSNESS,] as in 5. 8; 11. 7; 22. 31.
JUDGMENT,] as in 1. 5; 7. 6; 9. 4, 7, 16, &c.
KINDNESS,] as in v. 18, 22; 5. 7; 6. 4, &c.
FULL,] as in 10. 7; 26. 10; 33. 7, &c.
6. WORD OF JEHOVAH,] as in v. 4.
MADE,] as in 96. 5, &c. Sept. Vulg. 'established.'
SPIRIT OF HIS MOUTH,] as in 135. 17, &c.
HOST,] as in 24. 10; 44. 9; 46. 7, &c. Sept.
Vulg. 'powers.'
7. GATHERING, as in 147. 2; 1 Ch. 22. 2, &c.
HEAP,] as in 78. 13; Ps. 15. 8; Jos. 3. 13.
16; Isa. 17. 11.
WATERS OF THE SEA,] as in Ge. 1. 22, &c.
TREASURIES,] as in 135. 7; De. 28. 12, &c.
DEPTHS,] as in 36. 6; 42. 7; 71. 20, &c.
Sept. Vulg. 'abyss.'
8. AFRAID,] as in 67. 7; 72. 5; 102. 15, &c.
EARTH,] *or* 'land.'
WORLD,] as in 9. 8; 18. 15; 19. 4; 24. 1, &c.
AFRAID,] not 'stand in awe,' as in C.V.;
as in 22. 23, &c.
9. SAID,] not 'spake,' as in C.V.; as in
2. 7, &c.
IT IS,] not 'it was done,' as in C.V.
COMMANDED,] as in 7. 6; 68. 28; 71. 3, &c.
STANDETH,] as in v. 11; Vulg. 'they were
created.'
10. MAKE VOID,] not 'bring to nought;'
as in 89. 33; Ex. 17. 19.
COUNSEL,] as in v. 11; 1. 1; 13. 2; 14. 6, &c.
NATIONS,] as in 2. 1, 8; 9. 5, 15, 17, 19, &c.
DISALLOWED,] not 'maketh of none effect.'
THOUGHTS,] not 'devices,' as in C.V.; as
in v. 11; 40. 6; 56. 5; 92. 5; 94. 11, &c.
PEOPLES,] as in v. 12; 3. 6, 8; 7. 8; 9. 11, &c.
Sept. Vulg. adds, 'and he disallowed the
counsel of princes.'
11. STANDETH,] *or* 'remaineth.'
THOUGHTS,] as in v. 10.
GENERATIONS,] as in 10. 6; 45. 17; 49. 11,

12. HAPPINESS,] not 'blessed;' as in 1. 1;
2. 12; 32. 1, 2; 34. 8; 40. 4; 41. 1; 65. 4, &c.
NATION,] as in v. 10.
GOD,] as in 3. 2, 7; 4. 1; 5. 2, 10; 7. 1, &c.
JEHOVAH,] the Existing One, God of
Israel.
PEOPLE,] as in v. 10.
CHOOSE,] as in 78. 67; 84. 10; 105. 26, &c.
INHERITANCE,] as in 2. 8; 28. 9; 37. 18, &c.
13. LOOKED,] as in 34. 5; 102. 19, &c.
SEEN,] as in 10. 11, 14; 31. 7; 35. 21, &c.
SONS OF MEN,] as in 8. 4; 11. 4; 12. 1, &c.
14. FIXED PLACE,] not 'place,' as in C.V.;
Sept. Vulg. 'prepared place.'
DWELLING,] as in 89. 14; 97. 2. 104. 5, &c.
LOOKED,] as in Song 2. 9; Isa. 14. 16.
EARTH,] as in 49. 1; Ge. 34. 30, &c.
15. FORMING,] as in 2. 9; 94. 9, 20, &c.
TOGETHER,] not 'alike,' as in C.V.; as in
2. 2, &c.
ATTENDING,] as in 119. 130; 1 Ch. 15. 22, &c.
WORKS,] as in v. 4.
16. THE KING,] as in 2. 6, 10; 5. 2; 10. 16.
SAVED,] as in De. 33. 29; Zec. 9. 9, &c.
FORCE,] not 'host,' as in C.V.; as in v. 17;
18. 32, &c. Sept. Vulg. 'much power.'
MIGHTY MAN,] as in 19. 5; 24. 8; 45. 3, &c.
Sept. Vulg. 'giant.'
DELIVERED,] as in 69. 14; Ge. 32. 30, &c.
POWER,] as in 22. 15; 29. 4; 31. 10, &c.
Sept. Vulg. 'his strength.'
17. FALSE THING,] not 'vain thing,' as in
C.V.; as in 7. 14; 27. 12; 31. 18, &c.
THE HORSE,] not 'a horse,' as in C.V.
SAFETY,] as in 37. 39; 38. 22; 40. 10, &c.
STRENGTH,] as in v. 16.
DELIVER,] as in 41. 1; 89. 48; 107. 20, &c.
18. EYE,] as in 5. 5; 11. 4; 17. 2; 34. 15, &c.
Sept. Vulg. 'eyes.'
FEARING,] as in 15. 4; 22. 23, 25, &c.
WAITING,] not 'hope,' as in C.V.; as in
31. 24; 69. 3; 147. 11, &c.
KINDNESS,] not 'mercy;' as in v. 5.
19. DELIVER,] as in 40. 13; 70. 1; Ge. 37. 22.
DEATH,] as in 6. 5; 7. 13; 9. 13; 13. 3, &c.
SOUL,] as in 3. 2; 6. 3, 4; 7. 2, 5, &c.
KEEP ALIVE,] as in Ge. 7. 3; De. 6. 24, &c.
FAMINE,] as in 105. 16; Ge. 12. 10; 26. 1. &c.
20. WAITED,] as in 106. 13; 2 K. 7. 9, &c.
HELP,] as in 20. 2; 70. 5; 89. 19, &c.
SHIELD,] as in 3. 2; 7. 10; 18. 2, 30, &c.
21. REJOICE,] as in 5. 11; 9. 2; 14. 7; 21. 1.
NAME,] as in 5. 11; 7. 17; 8. 1; 9. 2, 5, &c.
TRUSTED,] as in 13. 5; 22. 4, 5; 25. 2, &c.
22. KINDNESS,] not 'mercy;' as in v. 2, 18.
WAITED,] not 'hope;' as in v. 18.

XXXIV. CHANGING,] as in Jer. 2. 36, &c.
BEHAVIOUR,] as in 119. 66; Ex. 16. 31, &c.
ABIMELECH,] i.e. 'my father is king.'
DRIVETH AWAY,] as in 78. 60. 9, &c.
1. I BLESS,] as in 5. 12; 16. 7; 26. 12, &c.
THROUGHOUT ALL TIME,] as in 10. 5, &c.
CONTINUALLY,] as in 16. 8; 25. 15; 34. 1, &c.
PRAISE,] as in 9. 14; 22. 3, 25; 33. 1, &c.
MOUTH,] as in 51. 15; 71. 6, 8; 145. 21, &c.
2. BOAST HERSELF,] as in 49. 6; 52. 1, &c.
HUMBLE,] as in 9. 12, 18; 10. 12, 17; 22. 26.
REJOICE,] as in 5. 11; 9. 2; 14. 7; 21. 1, &c.
3. GREATNESS,] as in 69. 30; Ge. 12. 2, &c.
EXALT,] as in 18. 48; 27. 5; 30. 1, &c.

4. I SOUGHT,] as in 77. 2; 78. 34; 109. 10, &c.
ANSWERED,] not 'heard' merely, as in C.V.
FEARS,] as in Isa. 66. 4; 31. 9; Prov. 10.
24; Sept. Vulg. 'tribulations.'
DELIVER,] as in v. 17; 18. 1; 54. 7; 56. 13.
5. LOOKED EXPECTINGLY,] as in 33. 13;
102. 19, &c. Sept. Vulg. 'look ye.'
BECAME BRIGHT.] Sept. Vulg. read as an
imperative.
ASHAMED,] as in 35. 4, 26; 40. 14; 83. 17, &c.
6. POOR ONE,] as in 9. 12, 18; 10. 2, 9, &c.
CALLED,] not 'cried,' as in C.V.
HEARD,] as in 6. 8, 9; 10. 17; 28. 6, &c.
DISTRESSES,] as in v. 17; 9. 9; 10. 1; 20. 1.
7. MESSENGER,] as in 35. 5, 6; 78. 49; 91. 11.
ENCAMPING,] as in 53. 5; Ex. 14. 9; 18. 15.
ARMETH,] not 'delivereth,' as in C.V.; as
in 7. 4, &c.
8. TASTE,] as in 1 Sa. 14. 24, 43; 2 Sa. 3. 35
SEE,] as in 9. 13; 25. 18, 19; 37. 37, &c.
HAPPINESS,] not 'blessed,' as in C.V.
TRUSTETH,] as in 18. 2; 36. 7; 57. 1; 61. 4, &c.
9. FEAR,] as in Jos. 24. 14; 1 Sa. 12. 24, &c.
HOLY ONES,] as in 16. 3; 22. 3; 46. 4; 65. 4.
LACK,] as in De. 15. 8; Jud 18. 10; 19. 19.
10. YOUNG LIONS,] as in 17. 12; 35. 17; 58.
6, &c. Sept. Vulg. 'rich men.'
LACKED,] or 'been poor;' as in Ps. 82. 3.
HUNGRY,] as in 50. 12; Ge. 41. 55; Prov. 6. 30.
SEEKING,] as in 9. 10, 12; 14. 2; 22. 26, &c.
GOOD.] Sept. adds 'diapsalma.'
11. SONS,] as in 4. 2; 11. 4; 12. 1, 8; 14, 2, &c.
TEACH,] as in 25. 9; 51. 13; 94. 12; 119. 171
12. MAN,] that is, the 'individual.'
DESIRING,] as in 5. 4; 35. 27; 40. 14; 70. 2.
DAYS,] that is, length of life.
SEE,] enjoy or experience good things.
13. HEARD,] as in 141. 3; Prov. 3. 21; 4. 13.
TONGUE,] as in 5. 21; 6. 30; 15. 5; 20. 12, &c.
LIPS,] as in 12. 2, 3, 4; 16. 4; 17. 1, 4, &c.
DECEIT,] as in 5. 6; 10. 7; 17. 1; 24 4, &c.
14. TURN ASIDE,] not 'depart,' as in C.V.;
as in 6. 8; 119. 115; 139. 19, &c.
DO GOOD,] as in 37. 3, 27, &c.
SEEK,] as in 27. 8; 105. 4; 119. 176, &c.
PURSUE,] as in 71. 11; Ge. 44. 4; Jos. 2. 5.
15. EYES,] as in 33. 18, &c.
EARS,] as in 10. 17; 17. 6; 18. 6, 44, &c.
CRY,] as in 18. 6; 39. 12; 40. 1; 102. 1, &c.
16. FACE,] as in 9. 3, 19; 68. 1, 2, &c.
DOERS OF EVIL,] as in 15. 3; 28. 3, &c.
CUT OFF,] as in 101. 8; 109. 13; Ex. 8. 9, &c.
MEMORIAL,] as in 6. 5; 9. 6; 30. 4; 97. 12.
17. CRIED,] as in 77. 1; 88. 1; 107. 6, 28;
Sept. Vulg. Syr. Targ. Arab. prefix 'the
just.'
HEARD,] as in v. 6.
DISTRESSES,] as in v. 6.
18. NEAR,] as in 75. 1; 85. 9; 145. 18, &c.
BROKEN OF HEART,] as in 51. 17; 147. 3, &c.
BRUISED OF SPIRIT,] as in Isa. 57. 15;
Sept. Vulg. 'humble.'
SAVETH,] as in 18. 27; 36. 6; 37. 40; 44. 6.
19. EVILS,] not 'afflictions,' as in C.V.
DELIVER,] as in 18. 17, 48; 22. 8; 71. 2, &c.
20. KEEPING,] as in 31. 6; 71. 10; 97. 10
&c. Sept. Vulg. prefix 'the Lord.'
BONES,] as in 6. 2; 22. 14, 17; 31. 10, &c.
BROKEN,] as in 37. 15, 17; 124. 7, &c.
21. EVIL,] as in v. 3, 14, 16, 19.
PUT TO DEATH,] not 'slay,' as in C.V.

HATING,] as in 9. 13; 18. 17; 21. 8; 35. 19.
DESOLATE,] or 'guilty;' as in v. 22, &c.
22. REDEEMETH,] as in De. 13. 5, &c.
SERVANTS,] as in 18. 1; 19. 11, 13; 27. 9, &c.
TRUSTING,] as in 2. 12; 5. 11; 17. 7; 18. 30.
DESOLATE,] as in v. 21.

XXXV. 1. STRIVE,] not 'plead,' as in C.V.;
as in 43. 1; 74. 22; 119. 154, &c. Sept. Vulg.
'judge.'
STRIVERS,] as in Isa. 49. 25; Jer. 18. 19.
FIGHT,] lit. 'eat, consume.'
FIGHTERS,] as in 56. 1, 2, &c.
2. TAKE HOLD,] as in Ge. 21. 18; 2 Sa. 11. 25.
SHIELD,] as in 3. 3; 7. 10; 18. 2, 30, &c.
BUCKLER,] as in 5. 12; 91. 4; 1 Sa. 17. 7, &c.
HELP,] as in 22. 19; 27. 9; 38. 22, &c.
3. DRAW OUT,] lit. 'make empty,' as in 18.
42; Ge. 14. 14, &c.
SPEAR,] as in 46. 9; 57. 4; 1 Sa. 13. 19, &c.
Sept. 'thy spear.'
LANCE.] So Drusius, Mich. Vitr. Walf. &c.
TO MEET,] as in 59. 4; Ge. 14. 17; 15. 10, &c.
PURSUERS,] as in v. 6; 7. 1; 31. 15, &c..
SALVATION,] as in v. 9; 3. 2, 8; 9. 14, &c.
4. ASHAMED,] not 'confounded,' as in C.V.
BLUSH,] as in 40. 14; 69. 6; 70. 2, &c.
SEEKING,] as in 24. 6; 37. 25, 32; 38. 12, &c.
TURNED BACKWARD,] as in 40. 14; 70. 2, &c.
CONFOUNDED,] as in v. 26; 34. 5; 40. 14, &c.
DEVISING,] as in Ex. 26. 1, 31; 28. 6, &c.
5. CHAFF,] as in 1. 4; Job 21. 18; Isa. 17.
13; 29. 5; 41. 15; Hos. 13. 3; Zeph. 2. 2.
Sept. Vulg. 'dust.'
WIND,] as in 1. 4; 11. 6; 18. 10, 15, 42, &c.
MESSENGER,] as in v. 6; 34. 7, &c.
DRIVING,] as in 62. 3; 118. 13; 140. 4, &c.
6. WAY,] as in 1. 1, 6; 2. 12; 5. 8; 10. 5, &c.
DARKNESS,] as in 18. 11, 28; 88. 12; 104. 20.
SLIPPERINESS,] as in Jer. 23. 12; Da. 11.
21. 34.
PURSUER,] as in v. 3.
7. WITHOUT CAUSE,] as in v. 19; 69. 4, &c.
DIGGED,] as in 7. 15; Ge. 21. 30; 26. 15, &c.
8. MEET,] not 'come upon,' as in C.V.
DESOLATION,] not 'destruction,' as in C.V.;
as in 63. 9, &c.
KNOWETH NOT,] as in 39. 6; 73. 22; 92. 6, &c.
NET,] as in v. 7; 9. 15; 10. 9; 25. 5, &c.
HID,] as in v. 7; 9. 15; 31. 4; 140. 5, &c.
CATCHETH,] as in Nu. 21. 32; 32. 39, &c.
9. JOYFUL,] as in 9. 14; 13. 4, 5; 14. 7, &c.
SALVATION,] as in v. 3.
10. BONES,] as in 6. 2; 22. 14, 17; 31. 10, &c.
JEHOVAH.] Sept. repeats the name.
LIKE THEE,] as in Isa. 46. 9, &c.
DELIVERING,] as in 7. 2; 50. 22; 71. 11, &c.
POOR,] as in 9. 12, 18; 10. 2, 9, 12; 12. 5, &c.
NEEDY,] as in 9. 18; 12. 5; 35. 10; 37. 14, &c.
PLUNDERER,] as in Prov. 28. 24; Mic. 3. 2.
11. VIOLENT WITNESSES,] not 'false wit-
nesses,' as in C.V.; Sept. Vulg. 'unjust wit-
nesses.'
RISE UP,] as in 1. 5; 12. 5; 24. 3; 27. 3, &c.
NOT KNOWN,] as in v. 15; 18. 43, &c.
ASK,] not 'lay to my charge,' as in C.V.
12. REPAY,] as in 37. 21; 41. 10; 137. 8, &c.
EVIL FOR GOOD,] as in 38. 20; 109. 5, &c.
BEREAVING,] as in Isa. 47. 8, 9, &c.
13. SICKNESS,] as in Isa. 38. 9, &c.
CLOTHING,] as in 22. 18; 45. 13; 69. 11, &c.

SACKCLOTH,] as in 30. 11; 69. 11; Ge. 37. 14.
HUMBLED,] as in 88. 7; 9. 15; 102. 23, &c.
FASTINGS,] as in 69. 10; 109. 24; 2 Sa. 12. 16.
PRAYER,] as in 4. 1; 6. 9; 17. 1, 2; 39. 12.
BOSOM,] as in 74. 11; 79. 12; 89. 50, &c.
14. FRIEND,] as in 12. 2; 15. 3; 28. 3; 38.
11, &c. Sept. Vulg. 'neighbour.'
BROTHER,] as in 22. 22; 49. 7; 50. 20, &c.
Sept. Vulg. 'our brother.'
WALKED HABITUALLY,] not 'behaved my-
self,' as in C.V.; as in 26. 3, &c.
MOURNER,] as in Ge. 37. 35; Est. 6. 12, &c.
MOTHER,] as in 22. 9, 10; 27. 10; 50. 20, &c.
MOURNING,] not 'heavily,' as in C.V.; as
in 38. 6; 42. 9; 43. 2; Job 5. 11; 6. 16; 30. 28.
BOWED DOWN,] as in 10. 10; 38. 6; 107. 39.
15. HALTING,] not 'adversity,' as in C.V.;
as in 38. 17; Jer. 20. 10. Sept. Vulg. 'against
me.'
REJOICED,] as in 16. 9; 105. 38; 122. 1, &c.
GATHERED TOGETHER,] as in 47. 9; 104. 22.
SMITERS,] not 'abjects,' as in C.V. So
Sept. Vulg. &c.
NOT KNOWN,] as in v. 11.
RENT,] as in 1 Sa. 15. 28; Hos. 13. 8, &c.
CEASED,] lit. 'been silent, dumb;' as in
30. 12; 31. 17, &c.
16. PROFANE,] not 'hypocritical,' as in
C.V.; as in Job 8. 13; 13. 16; 15. 34; 17. 8, &c.
Sept. Vulg. 'they tempted me.'
MOCKERS,] as in Isa. 28. 11.
A FEAST,] lit. a 'circle;' hence a 'cake,'
as in 1 K. 17. 12.
GNASHING,] as in 37. 12; 112. 10; Job 16. 9.
La. 2. 16.
TEETH,] as in 3. 7; 37. 12; 45. 8; 57. 4, &c.
17. LORD,] or 'my lord;' as in v. 22, 23, &c.
BEHOLD,] quietly as if there were no dan-
ger.
KEEP BACK,] not 'rescue,' as in C.V.; as
in 28. 4; 51. 12; 79. 12; 80. 3, 7, 9, &c.
DESOLATIONS,] not 'destructions,' as in
C.V. Sept. Vulg. 'evil, malignity.'
YOUNG LIONS,] as in 17. 12; 34. 10; 58. 6;
91. 13, &c.
ONLY ONE,] not 'darling,' as in C.V.; as in
22. 20; 25. 16; 68. 6, &c.
18. THANK,] as in 6. 5; 7. 17; 9. 1; 18. 49.
GREAT ASSEMBLY,] as in 22. 25; 40. 9, &c.
A MIGHTY PEOPLE,] not 'much people,'
as in C.V.; as in Nu. 22. 6; Da. 8. 24; Joel
2. 2, 5.
I PRAISE,] as in 22. 22, 26; 56. 4, 10; 63. 5.
19. FALSEHOOD,] not 'wrongfully,' as in
C.V.; as in 7. 14, &c.
WITHOUT CAUSE,] as in v. 7.
WINK,] as in Prov. 6. 13; 10. 10; 16. 30, &c.
20. SPEAK NOT,] Sept. Vulg. 'speak to me.'
PEACE,] as in 27; 28. 3; 85. 8; 120. 7, &c.
QUIET,] lit. 'shrivelled,' i.e. timid.
DECEITFUL,] as in 12; 109. 2, &c.
DEVISE,] as in 10. 2; 21. 11; 32. 2; 36. 4, &c.
21. ENLARGE,] as in 4. 1; 18. 36; 25. 17, &c.
MOUTH,] as in 81. 10; 1 Sa. 2. 1; Isa. 57. 4.
AHA,] as in v. 25; 40. 15; 70. 3; Job 39. 25.
SEEN] the accomplishment of their plans.
22. SEEN,] their plans and devices.
SILENT,] as in 28. 1; 39. 12; 50. 3; 83. 1, &c.
LORD,] as in v. 17. 23.
BE NOT FAR,] as in 22. 11, 19; 38. 21, &c.
23. STIR UP,] as in Joel 3. 9; Ps. 57 8, &c

WAKE,] as in 44. 23; 59. 5, &c.
JUDGMENT,] as in 1. 5; 7. 6; 9. 4, 7, 16, &c.
PLEA,] not 'cause,' as in C.V.; as in 18.
43; 31. 20; 43. 1; 55. 9; 74. 22; 119. 154, &c.
24. JUDGE,] as in 7. 8; 26. 1; 43. 1; 82. 3, &c.
RIGHTEOUSNESS,] as in v. 27; 4. 1, 5; 7. 8.
GOD,] as in v. 23; 3. 2, 7; 4. 1; 5. 2, 10, &c.
NOT REJOICE,] as in v. 19 above.
25. HEART,] as in 10. 6, 11, 13; 14. 1; 36. 1.
AHA,] as in v. 21 above.
DESIRE,] lit. 'soul;' as in v. 3, 4, 7, 9. &c.
SWALLOWED UP,] as in 21. 9; 55. 9; 69. 15.
26. ASHAMED,] as in v. 4.
CONFOUNDED,] as in v. 4.
EVIL,] not 'hurt,' as in C.V.; as in v. 4, &c.
PUT ON,] not 'be clothed with,' as in C.V.;
as in 109. 18, 29; 132. 9, &c.
SHAME,] as in 40. 15; 44. 15; 69. 19; 70. 3.
CONFUSION,] as in 4. 2; 44. 15; 69. 7, &c.
MAGNIFYING,] as in 38. 16; 41. 9; 55. 12, &c.
27. SING,] not 'shout,' as in C.V.; as in 5.
11; 20. 5, &c.
REJOICE,] as in v. 15 above.
DESIRING,] not 'favour,' as in C.V.; as in
5. 4; 34. 12; 40. 14; 70. 2, &c.
RIGHTEOUSNESS,] as in v. 24.
MAGNIFIED,] as in 40. 16; 70. 4; 92. 5, &c.
PEACE,] as in v. 20.
SERVANT,] as in 18. 1; 19. 11, 13; 27. 9, &c.
28. UTTERETH,] not 'speak,' as in C.V.; as
in 1. 2; 2. 1; 37. 30, &c.
PRAISE,] as in 9. 14; 22. 3, 25; 33. 1; 34. 1.

XXXVI. OVERSEER,] as in Ps. 4. 5. 6. &c.
SERVANT,] as in 18. 1; 19. 11, 13; 27. 9, &c.
DAVID.] Sept. adds 'a psalm.'
1. TRANSGRESSION,] as in 5. 10; 19. 13, &c.
AFFIRMING,] not 'saith,' as in C.V.; as in
110. 1; Ge. 22. 16, &c.
FEAR OF GOD,] as in 2 Ch. 20. 29, &c.
2. MADE SMOOTH,] not 'flattereth,' as in
C.V.; as in 5. 9, &c. Sept. Vulg. 'made
grievous.'
TO FIND,] as in 32. 6; Ge. 19. 11; 27. 20, &c.
INIQUITY,] as in 18. 23; 25. 11; 31. 10, &c.
TO BE HATED,] as in 105. 25; Ge. 37. 5, &c.
3. WORDS OF HIS MOUTH,] as in 19. 14, &c.
DECEIT,] as in 5. 6; 10. 7; 17. 1; 24. 4, &c.
CEASED,] as in 49. 8; Ge. 11. 8; 18. 11; 41.
49, &c. Sept. Vulg. 'would not.'
TO ACT PRUDENTLY,] not 'to be wise,' as
in C.V.; as in Ge. 3. 6; Neh. 8. 13; 9. 20, &c.
TO DO GOOD,] as in Lev. 5. 4; Isa. 1. 17, &c.
4. DEVISETH,] as in 10. 2; 21. 11; 35. 20, &c.
BED,] as in 4. 4; 41. 3; 149. 5, &c.
STATIONETH HIMSELF,] as in 2. 2; 5. 2, &c.
ON A WAY.] Sept. Vulg. 'all the way.'
EVIL,] as in 5. 4; 7. 4, 9; 10. 6, 15; 15. 3, &c.
REFUSE,] not 'abhorreth,' as in C.V.; as in
53. 5; 78. 59, 67, &c. Sept. 'offended at.'
Vulg. 'hate.'
5. KINDNESS,] not 'mercy,' as in C.V.; as
in v. 7, 10; 5. 7; 6. 4; 13. 5, &c.
FAITHFULNESS,] as in 33. 4; 37. 3; 40. 10.
CLOUDS,] as in 18. 11; 57. 10; 68. 34; 77. 17.
6. RIGHTEOUSNESS,] as in v. 10, &c.
MOUNTAINS OF GOD,] not 'great moun-
tains,' as in C.V.
JUDGMENTS] on men and nations.
GREAT DEEP,] as in Ge. 7. 11; Isa. 51. 10;
Amos 7. 4

BEAST,] as in 8. 7; 49. 12; 50. 10; 73. 22, &c
SAVEST,] as in 18. 27; 34. 18; 37. 40; 44. 6
7. PRECIOUS,] not 'excellent,' as in C.V.
as in 37. 20; 45. 9; 116. 15, &c. Sept. Vulg.
'hast thou multiplied.'
SONS OF MEN,] as in v. 6; 11. 4; 12. 1, &c.
WINGS,] as in 17. 8; 57. 1; 63. 7, &c.
TRUST,] as in 7. 1; 11. 1; 16. 1; 18. 2, &c.
8. FILLED,] not 'satisfied,' as in C.V.; as
in 65. 10; Prov. 7. 18, &c. Sept. Vulg. 'in-
toxicated.'
FATNESS,] as in 63. 5; 65. 11; Jud. 9. 9, &c.
STREAM,] not 'river,' as in C.V.; as in 18.
4; 74. 15; 78. 20, &c.
DELIGHTS,] as in 2 Sa. 1. 24; Jer. 51. 34.
TO DRINK,] as in 60. 3; 69. 21; 78. 15, &c.
9. FOUNTAIN,] as in 68. 26; Lev. 12. 7, &c.
LIGHT,] as in 4. 6; 27. 1; 37. 6; 38. 10, &c.
10. DRAW OUT,] not 'continue,' as in C.V.:
as in Ex. 12. 21; Song 1. 4; Eze. 32. 20.
KNOWING,] as in 9. 10; 87. 4; 89. 15, &c.
UPRIGHT OF HEART,] as in 7. 10; 11. 2, &c.
11. PRIDE,] as in 10. 2; 31. 18, 23; 36. 11, &c.
MEET,] as in 35. 8; 55. 5; 109. 17, &c.
MOVE,] not 'remove,' as in C.V.; as in 2
K. 21. 8; Jer. 18. 16.
12. WORKERS OF INIQUITY,] as in 5. 5, &c.
OVERTHROWN,] as in 35. 5; 62. 3; 118. 13,
&c. Sept. Vulg. 'expelled.'
ARISE,] as in 18. 38; 41. 8; 76. 9; 124. 2, &c.
Sept. Vulg. 'stand.'

XXXVII. BY DAVID.] Sept. Vulg. prefix
'a psalm.'
1. FRET,] as in v. 7, 8; Prov. 24. 19.   Sept.
Vulg. 'emulous.'
EVIL DOERS,] as in v. 9; 22. 16; 26. 5, &c.
ENVIOUS,] as in 73. 3; 106. 16; Ge. 26. 14.
INIQUITY,] as in 43. 1; 89. 22; 92. 15, &c.
2. GRASS,] as in 90. 5; 103. 15; 104. 14, &c.
SPEEDILY,] as in 37. 2; 147. 15, &c.
CUT OFF,] as in Ge. 17. 11; Job 14. 2; 18.
10; 24. 24.   Sept. Vulg. 'become dry.'
GREENNESS,] as in Ge. 1. 30; 9. 3; Ex. 10.
15; Nu. 22. 4; Isa. 15. 6.
TENDER HERB,] not 'green herb,' as in
C.V.; as in 23. 2.
FADE,] as in 1. 3; 18. 45; Ex. 18. 18, &c.
Sept. Vulg. add 'suddenly.'
3. TRUST,] as in v. 5; 4. 5; 62. 8; 115. 9,
10, 11; Prov. 3. 5; Isa. 26. 4, &c.
DO GOOD,] as in v. 27; 34. 14, &c.
DWELL,] as in v. 27; Ge. 26. 2; Jer. 48. 28.
ENJOY,] as in 28. 9; Ge. 29. 7; Song 1. 8;
Mic. 7. 14; Zech. 11. 4.
FAITHFULNESS,] or 'stedfastness,' as in
33. 4; 36. 5, &c. Sept. Vulg. 'its riches.'
4. DELIGHT THYSELF,] as in v. 11; De. 28.
56; Job 22. 26; 27. 10; Isa. 55. 2; 57. 4; 58.
14; 66. 11.
PETITIONS.] not 'desires,' as in C.V.; as
in 20. 5.
5. ROLL,] not 'commit,' as in C.V.; as in
119. 22; Jos. 10. 18; 1 Sa. 14. 33; Prov. 16. 3.
Sept. Vulg. 'reveal.'
WAY,] as in v. 7, 14, 23, 34; 1. 1, 6; 2. 12, &c.
TRUST,] as in v. 3.
WORKETH,] not 'shall bring it to pass,' as
in C.V.
6. BROUGHT OUT.] as in 18. 19; 25. 15, &c.
LIGHT,] as in 4. 6; 27. 1; 36. 9; 38. 10, &c.

RIGHTEOUSNESS,] as in 4. 1, 5; 7. 8, &c.
JUDGMENT,] as in v. 28, 30; 1. 5; 7. 6, &c.
NOON-DAY,] as in 55. 17; 91. 6, &c.
7. BE SILENT,] not 'rest,' as in C.V.; Sept. Vulg. 'be subject.'
STAY THYSELF,] not 'wait patiently,' as in C.V.; Sept. Vulg. 'entreat him.'
FRET,] as in v. 1, 8, &c.
MAKING PROSPEROUS,] not 'who prospereth,' as in C.V.; as in Ge. 24. 42; 39. 2, 3, 23.
WICKED DEVICES,] as in 10. 2, 4; 21. 11; 139. 20, &c. Sept. Vulg. 'injustice.'
8. DESIST,] as in 46. 10; De. 9. 14, &c.
ANGER,] as in 2. 5, 12; 6. 1; 7. 6; 10. 4, &c.
FORSAKE,] as in Prov. 9. 6; Jer. 48. 28; 49. 11; 51. 9.
FURY,] as in 6. 1; 38. 1; 58. 4; 59. 13, &c.
ONLY,] not 'in any wise,' as in C.V.; as in Ge. 7. 23, &c.
TO DO EVIL,] as in 15. 4; Ge. 31. 7; Lev. 5. 4.
9. EVIL DOERS,] as in v. 1.
CUT OFF,] as in v. 22, 28, 34, 38.
WAITING,] as in 25. 3; 69. 6, &c.
POSSESS,] not 'inherit,' as in C.V.
LAND,] not 'earth,' as in C.V.
10. A LITTLE,] as in v. 16; 2. 12; 8. 5, &c.
IS NOT,] as in 38. 10; 73. 2; Ge. 2, 5, &c.
CONSIDERED,] as in 107. 43; 119. 95, 100, 104, &c. Sept. Vulg. 'sought.'
PLACE,] as in 24. 3; 26. 8; 44. 19; 103. 16, &c.
IT IS NOT.] Sept. Vulg. add 'found.'
11. HUMBLE,] as in 9. 12, 18; 10. 12, 17, &c.
DELIGHTED THEMSELVES,] as in v. 4.
PEACE,] as in v. 37; 4. 8; 28. 3; 29. 11, &c.
12. DESIRING,] as in 31. 13: Ge. 11. 6; De. 19. 19, &c. Sept. Vulg. 'watching.'
GNASHING,] as in 35. 16; 112. 10; Job 16. 9; La. 2. 6.
13. LORD,] as in 2. 4; 16. 2; 22. 30; 35. 17.
LAUGH,] as in 2. 4; 5. 2, 6; 59. 8, &c.
DAY,] of punishment and retribution, as in 1 Sa. 26. 10, &c.
14. SWORD,] as in v. 15; 7. 12; 7. 13; 22. 10.
OPENED,] not 'drawn out,' as in C.V.; as in Eze. 21. 28, &c.
TRODDEN,] not 'bent,' as in C.V.; as in 7. 12, &c.
POOR,] as in 9. 12, 18; 10. 2, 9, 12; 12. 5, &c.
NEEDY,] as in 9. 18; 12. 5; 35. 10; 40. 17, &c.
TO SLAUGHTER,] as in Ge. 43. 16; Jer. 11. 16; 25. 34; 51. 40; Eze. 21. 10, &c.
OF THE WAY,] not 'of conversation,' as in C.V. Sept. Vulg. 'of heart.'
15. HEART,] as in v. 4, 31, &c.
BOWS,] as in v. 14; 7. 12; 11. 2; 18. 34, &c.
SHIVERED,] as in v. 17; 34. 20; 124. 7, &c.
16. LITTLE,] as in v. 10 above.
STORE,] not 'riches,' as in C.V.; as in 42. 4; 65. 7, &c.
17. ARMS,] as in 10. 15; 18. 34; 44. 3, &c.
SUSTAINING,] as in v. 24; 54. 4; 145. 14, &c.
18. KNOWETH,] as in 1. 6; 9. 10; 36. 10, &c.
PERFECT,] not 'upright,' as in C.V.; as in 15. 2; 18. 23, 25, 30, 32, &c.
INHERITANCE,] as in 2. 8; 28. 9; 33. 12, &c.
19. ASHAMED,] as in 6. 10; 22. 5; 25. 2, &c.
TIME OF EVIL,] as in Eccl. 9. 12; Jer. 15. 11; Amos 5. 13.
FAMINE,] as in Ge. 42. 19, 33.
SATISFIED,] as in 17. 14, 15; 22. 26; 59. 15.
20. PERISH,] or 'are lost,' as in 1. 6; 2. 12.

PRECIOUSNESS,] not 'fat,' as in C.V.; as in 36. 7, &c.
LAMBS,] as in 65. 13; Ge. 31. 34; De. 32. 14.
CONSUMED,] as in 31. 10; 39. 10; 69. 3, &c.
SMOKE,] as in 18. 8; 68. 2; 102. 3, &c.
21. BORROWING,] as in Prov. 22. 7; Isa. 24. 2.
REPAYETH,] as in 22. 25; 35. 12; 41. 10, &c.
GRACIOUS,] not 'sheweth mercy,' as in C.V.; as in v. 26; 109. 12; 112. 5, &c.
GIVING,] as in 18. 47; 33. 7; 68. 35, &c.
22. BLESSED ONES,] as in 113. 2; Nu. 22. 6.
POSSESS,] not 'inherit,' as in C.V.; as in v. 9, 11, 29, &c.
LAND,] not 'earth,' as in C.V.
REVILED ME,] not 'cursed,' as in C.V.; as in Job 24. 18; Isa. 65. 20.
CUT OFF,] as in v. 9, 28, 34, 38, &c.
23. FROM JEHOVAH,] not 'by,' as in C.V.
STEPS,] as in Prov. 20. 24; Da. 11. 43.
PREPARED,] not 'ordered,' as in C.V.; as in Eze. 23. 18, &c.
DESIRETH,] not 'delighteth,' as in C.V.: as in 51. 16, 19; 68. 30; 147. 10, &c.
24. CAST DOWN,] as in Job 41. 9; Prov. 16. 33.
SUSTAINING,] as in v. 17.
25. YOUNG,] as in 119. 9; 148. 12; Ge. 14. 24.
OLD,] as in Ge. 18. 12, 13; 19. 31; 24. 1, &c.
FORSAKEN,] as in Isa. 27. 10; 62. 12, &c.
SEED,] as in v. 26, 28; 18. 50; 21. 10, &c.
BEGGING,] as in v. 32; 24. 6; 35. 4, &c.
BREAD,] as in 14. 4; 41. 9; 42. 3; 53. 4, &c.
26. GRACIOUS,] not 'merciful,' as in C.V.; as in v. 21.
LENDING,] as in 112. 5; Prov. 19. 17; 22. 7; Isa. 24. 2.
BLESSING,] as in 3. 8; 21. 3, 6; 24. 5; 84. 6.
27. TURN ASIDE,] not 'depart,' as in C.V.; as in 6. 8; 34. 14; 119. 115; 139. 19, &c.
DO GOOD,] as in v. 3 above.
DWELL,] as in v. 3 above.
28. JUDGMENT,] as in v. 6, 30, &c.
FORSAKE,] as in v. 33; 10. 14; 16. 10; 27. 9.
SAINTLY ONES,] as in 4. 3; 12. 1; 16. 10, &c.
KEPT,] as in 2 K. 6. 10; Hos. 12. 13, &c.
CUT OFF,] as in v. 9, 22, 34, 38, &c.
29. POSSESS,] not 'inherit,' as in C.V.; as in v. 9, 11, 22, &c.
DWELL,] as in 15. 1; 16. 9; 55. 6; 65. 4, &c.
30. MOUTH,] as in 5. 9; 8. 2; 10. 7; 17. 3, &c.
UTTERETH,] not 'speaketh,' as in C.V.; as in 1. 2; 2. 1; 35. 28; 38. 12, &c.
WISDOM,] as in 51. 6; 90. 12; 104. 24, &c.
TONGUE,] as in 5. 9; 10. 7; 12. 3, 4; 15. 3.
JUDGMENT,] as in v. 6, 28, &c.
31. LAW,] as in 1. 2; 19. 7; 40. 8; 78. 1, &c.
HEART,] as in Isa. 81. 33; 51. 7, &c.
STEPS,] as in 17. 5; 40. 2; 44. 18; 73. 2; Job 23. 11; Prov. 14. 15; Eze. 27. 6.
SLIDE,] as in 18. 36; 26. 1; 2 Sa. 22. 37; Job 12. 5.
32. WATCHING,] as in Nu. 23. 14; 1 Sa. 1. 1.
SEEK,] as in v. 25.
PUT TO DEATH,] as in 59. 1; Ge. 18. 25, &c.
33. NOT LEAVE,] as in v. 28.
HAND.] Sept. Vulg. 'hands.'
CONDEMN,] or 'declare him wrong.'
JUDGED,] as in 109. 7; 2 Ch. 22. 8.
34. LOOK,] not 'wait;' as in 27. 14; Prov. 20. 22; Hos. 12. 6.
KEEP,] or 'watch, observe,' as in 16. 1, &c.
EXALT,] as in 18. 48; 27. 5: 30. 1; 34. 3, &c

POSSESS,] not 'inherit,' as in C.V.
LAND,] as in Ge. 15. 7; 28. 4; Lev. 20. 24.
CUT OFF,] as in v. 9, 22, 28, 38, &c.
THOU SEEST] and markest their fall.
35. TERRIBLE,] as in 54. 3; 86. 14; Job 6.
23, &c. Sept. Vulg. 'highly exalted.'
SPREADING,] *lit.* 'making himself naked;
as in La. 4. 21.
NATIVE PLANT,] as in Ex. 12. 19, 48, 49;
Lev. 16. 29; 17. 15; 18. 26; 19. 34, &c. Sept.
Vulg. 'cedars of Lebanon.'
36. PASSETH AWAY,] *or* 'by,' as in 17. 3;
42. 4; 57. 1, &c. Vulg. 'I passed by.'
HE IS NOT,] does not exist, is not seen.
SEEK,] as in 4. 2; 27. 4, 8; 37. 36; 63. 9, &c.
FOUND,] as in 46. 1; Ge. 44. 16, 17; 21. 16,
&c. Sept. Vulg. add 'his place.'
37. OBSERVE,] as in v. 34, &c.
PERFECT,] as in 64. 4; Ge. 25. 27; Job 1. 1,
&c. Sept. 'harmless;' Vulg. 'innocent.'
UPRIGHT,] as in v. 14, &c.
LATTER END,] as in v. 38; 73. 17; 109. 13.
PEACE,] as in v. 11.
38. TRANSGRESSORS,] as in 51. 13; Isa. 1.
28; 46. 8; 48. 8, &c.
DESTROYED,] as in 83. 10; 92. 7; Ge. 34. 30.
TOGETHER,] as in 2. 2; 4. 8; 14. 3; 19. 9, &c.
CUT OFF,] as in v. 9, 22, 28, 34, &c.
39. SALVATION,] as in 33. 17; 38. 22; 40. 10.
STRONG PLACE,] not 'strength,' as in C.V.;
as in 27. 1, &c. Vulg. 'protector.'
ADVERSITY,] as in 9. 9; 10. 1; 20. 1; 22. 11.
40. HELP,] as in 46. 5; 86. 17; 119. 175, &c.
DELIVER,] as in 18. 43; 22. 4, 8; 43. 1, &c.
SAVETH,] as in 18. 27; 34. 18; 86. 6; 44. 6.
TRUSTED,] as in 7. 1; 11. 1; 16. 1; 25. 20, &c.

XXXVIII. TO CAUSE TO REMEMBER,] as
in 70. 1; 1 Sa. 4. 18; 2 Sa. 18. 18; 1 K. 17. 18;
1 Ch. 16. 4; Eze. 21. 24; Am. 6. 10. Sept.
Vulg. 'in commemoration of the sabbath.'
1. WRATH,] as in 102. 10; Nu. 1. 53; 16. 46.
REPROVE,] not 'rebuke,' as in C.V.; as in
6. 1, &c. Sept. 'convict,' Vulg. 'argue.'
FURY,] as in 6. 1; 37. 8; 58. 4; 59. 13, &c.
CHASTISE,] *or* 'instruct,' as in 6. 1; 16. 7;
39. 11; 94. 12; 118. 18, &c.
2. ARROWS,] as in 7. 13; 11. 2; 18. 14, &c.
COME DOWN,] not 'stick fast,' as in Prov.
17. 10; Jer. 21. 13; Job 21. 13.
LETTEST DOWN,] not 'presseth sore,' as in
C.V.
3. SOUNDNESS,] as in v. 3; Isa. 1. 6.
FLESH,] as in 16. 9; 27. 2; 50. 13; 56. 4, &c.
INDIGNATION,] not 'anger,' as in C.V.; as
in 69. 24; 78. 48; 102. 10, &c.
BONES,] as in 6. 2; 22. 14, 17; 31. 10; 32. 3.
SIN,] as in v. 18; 25. 7, 18; 32. 5, &c. Sept.
Vulg. 'sins.'
4. INIQUITY,] as in v. 18; 18. 23; 25. 11, &c.
BURDEN,] as in Ex. 23. 5; Nu. 4. 15, 19, 24,
27, 31, 32, 47, 49; 11. 11, 17, &c.
5. STUNK,] as in Ge. 34. 30; Ex. 5. 21; 16.
24; 1 Sa. 27. 12.
CORRUPT,] as in Lev. 26. 39; Isa. 34. 4; Eze.
4. 17; 24. 23; 33. 10; Zec. 14. 12.
BRUISES,] as in Ge. 4. 23; Ex. 21. 25; Prov.
20. 30; Isa. 1. 6; 53. 5.
FOLLY,] as in 69. 5; Prov. 5. 23; 12. 23, &c.
6. BENT DOWN,] not 'troubled,' as in C.V;
as in Isa. 21. 3, &c.

BOWED DOWN,] as in 10. 10; 35. 4; 107. 39.
EXCESS,] as in 119. 107; 1 Sa. 25. 36; 2 Ch.
16. 14; La. 5. 22; Da. 8. 8.
MOURNING,] as in 35. 14; 42. 9; 43. 2, &c.
7. FLANKS,] as in Lev. 3. 4, 10, 15; 4. 9, &c.
DROUGHT,] not 'a loathsome disease,' as
in C.V. Sept. Vulg. 'jeering.'
SOUNDNESS,] as in v. 3.
8. FEEBLE.] Sept. Vulg. 'afflicted.'
SMITTEN,] not 'broken,' as in C.V.; as in
51. 17.
ROARED,] as in 22. 13; 74. 4; 104. 21, &c.
DISQUIETUDE,] as in Isa. 5. 30.
HEART.] Sept. Vulg. 'my heart.'
9. LORD,] as in v. 15, 22; 2. 4; 16. 2; 22. 30.
DESIRE,] as in 10. 3, 17; 21. 2; 78. 29, &c.
SIGHING,] not 'groaning,' as in 6. 6; 31. 10.
HID,] as in 16. 9, 12; 55. 12; 89. 46, &c.
10. PANTING,] *or* 'going up and down.'
POWER,] as in 22. 15; 31. 10; 33. 16, &c.
LIGHT OF MINE EYES,] a phrase not found
again in S.S.
11. LOVERS,] as in 88. 18; 2 Sa. 19. 6, &c.
FRIENDS,] as in 12. 2; 15. 3; 28. 3; 35. 14,
&c. Sept. Vulg. 'neighbours.'
PLAGUE,] not 'sore,' as in C.V.; as in 39.
10; 89. 32; 91. 10, &c.
NEIGHBOURS,] not 'kinsmen,' as in C.V.
12. SEEKING,] as in 15. 3; 22. 11; 34. 18, &c.
SNARE,] as in 109. 11; 9. 6; De. 12. 30; 1
Sa. 28. 9. Sept. Vulg. 'use violence.'
EVIL,] not 'hurt,' as in C.V.; as in v. 20;
5. 4, &c.
MISCHIEVOUS THINGS,] as in 5. 9; 52. 2, 7
55. 11, &c. Sept. Vulg. 'vanities.
DECEITS,] as in 5. 6; 10. 7; 17. 1; 24. 4, &c.
MEDITATE,] not 'imagine,' as in 1. 2; 2. 1
13. DEAF,] as in 58. 4; Ex. 4. 11; Lev. 19.
14; Isa. 29. 18; 35. 5; 42. 18, 19; 43. 8.
HEAR,] as in 58. 5; 66. 18; 94. 9, &c.
DUMB,] as in Ex. 4. 11; Prov. 31. 8; Isa.
35. 6; 56. 10; Hab. 2. 18.
MOUTH,] as in 39. 9; 78. 2; 109. 2, &c.
14. REPROOFS,] as in 39. 11; 73. 14, &c.
15. WAITED,] not 'hope,' as in C.V.; as in
42. 5, 11; 43. 5; 130. 5, &c.
ANSWER,] not 'hear,' as in C.V.; as in 3.
4; 17. 6, &c.
16. REJOICE,] as in 35. 19, 24, &c. Sept.
Vulg. add, 'my enemies.'
SLIPPING,] *lit.* 'moving,' as in 46. 2, &c.
MAGNIFIED THEMSELVES,] as in 41. 9; 55.
12; 126. 2, 3; 138. 2, &c.
17. READY,] as in 9. 9; 51. 10; 57. 7; 78. 37.
TO HALT,] as in 35. 15; Jer. 20. 20, &c.
Sept. Vulg. 'for floggings.'
PAIN,] not 'sorrow,' as in C.V.; as in 32.
10; 69. 26, &c.
18. DECLARE,] as in 22. 31; 30. 9; 40. 5, &c.
SORRY,] as in 1 Sa. 9. 5; 10. 2; Isa. 57. 11;
Jer. 17. 8; 88. 19; 42. 16. Sept. 'careful about.'
Vulg. 'think about.'
19. LIVELY,] *lit.* 'living;' So Sept. Vulg, &c.
STRONG,] as in 40. 5, 12; 69. 4; 139. 17; Ge.
26. 16, &c. Sept. Vulg. 'confirmed against
me.'
WITHOUT CAUSE,] *lit.* 'false, lying;' as in
7. 14; 27. 12; 31. 18; 33. 1?, &c.
MULTIPLIED,] as in 3. 1; 4. 7; 25. 19, &c.
20. PAYING,] as in 31. 23, De. 7. 10; Isa. 66.
6; Jer. 32. 18; 51. 6; Joel 3. 4. Sept. adds 'me.

ACCUSE,] not 'are my adversaries,' as in C.V.

PURSUING,] not 'follow,' as in C.V.; as in 7. 1; 31. 15; 33. 3, 6, &c.

21. FORSAKE,] as in 10. 14; 16. 10; 27. 9, &c.

NOT FAR,] as in 22. 11, 19; 35. 22; 71. 12, &c.

22. HASTE,] as in 22. 19; 40. 13; 70. 1, 5; 71. 12; 141. 1.

HELP,] as in 22. 19; 27. 9; 35. 2; 40. 13, &c.

LORD,] as in v. 9, 15 above.

SALVATION,] as in 33. 17; 37. 39; 40. 10, &c.

XXXIX. OVERSEER,] as in Ps. 4. 5. 6, &c.

JEDUTHUN,] as in Ps. 30. 39. 62; 1 Ch. 16. 38.

1. OBSERVE,] or 'keep;' as in 12. 7; 41. 2, &c.

WAYS,] as in 1. 1, 6; 2. 12; 5. 8; 10. 5, &c.

SINNING,] as in 78. 17; Ge. 20. 6; Ex. 9, 34.

TONGUE,] as in v. 3; 5. 9; 10. 7; 12. 3, 4, &c.

KEEP.] Sept. Vulg. 'placed.'

CURB,] not 'bridle,' as in C.V.; the original word is not found again.

2. DUMB,] as in v. 9; 31. 18; Isa. 53. 7; Ex. 2. 26; 24. 27; 33. 22; Da. 10. 15.

SILENCE,] as in 22. 2; 39. 2; 62. 1; 65. 1. Sept. Vulg. 'and was humbled.'

PAIN,] not 'sorrow,' as in C.V.; as in Job 2. 13; 16. 6; Isa. 17. 11; 65. 14; Jer. 15. 18.

EXCITED,] as in Prov. 15. 6. Sept. Vulg. 'renewed.'

3. HOT,] as in Ex. 16. 21; 1 K. 1. 2; 2 K. 4. 34; Ecc. 4. 11; Isa. 44. 15, 16; 47. 14.

MEDITATING,] not 'musing,' as in C.V.; as in 5. 1.

FIRE,] as in 11. 6; 18. 9, 12; 21. 9; 29. 7, &c.

BURN,] as in 2. 12; 79. 5; 83. 14; 89. 46, &c.

4. END,] as in 119. 96; Ge. 4. 3; 6. 13, &c.

MEASURE,] as in Ex. 26. 2, 8; 36. 9, 15; Lev. 19. 35, &c. Sept. Vulg. 'number.'

FRAIL,] as in Isa. 53. 3; Eze. 3. 27, &c. Sept. Vulg. 'what I lack.'

5. HAND-BREADTHS,] as in 1 K. 7. 26; 2 Ch. 2. 4. Vulg. 'measureable.'

AGE,] as in 17. 14; 49. 1; 89. 47; Job 11. 17. Sept. Vulg. 'substance.'

VANITY,] as in v. 6, 11; 31. 6; 62. 9, &c.

SET UP,] not 'at his best estate;' as in 82. 1; 119. 89, &c. Sept. Vulg. 'living.'

SELAH,] as in v. 11; 3. 2, 4, 8; 4. 2, 4, &c.

6. IMAGE,] not 'shew,' as in C.V.; as in 73. 20, &c.

WALK HABITUALLY,] as in 12. 8; 43. 2, &c.

VAIN,] or 'vanity;' as in v. 5.

DISQUIETED,] as in 42. 5, 11; 46. 3; 55. 17.

HEAPETH UP,] as in Ge. 41. 35, 49; Ex. 8. 14; Job 27. 16; Hab. 1. 10; Zec. 9. 3. Sept. Vulg. 'treasures up.'

GATHERETH,] as in Nu. 19. 10; 2 K. 22. 20; 2 Ch. 34. 28.

7. EXPECTED,] not 'wait,' as in C.V.; as in 25. 5, 21, &c.

O LORD,] or 'my lord;' as in 2. 4; 16. 2, &c. Sept. Vulg. 'is it not the Lord?'

HOPE,] as in Job 41. 9; Prov. 10. 28; 11. 7; 13. 12; La. 3. 18. Sept. Vulg. 'substance.'

8. TRANSGRESSIONS,] as in 5. 10; 19. 13, &c.

DELIVER,] as in 7. 1; 22. 20; 25. 20, &c.

REPROACH,] as in 15. 3; 22. 6; 31. 11, &c.

FOOL,] as in 14. 1; 53. 1; 74. 18, 22, &c.

9. DUMB,] as in v. 2.

OPEN NOT,] as in 38. 13; 49. 4; 51. 15, &c.

DONE IT.] Sept. 'made me.'

10. TURN ASIDE,] not 'remove,' as in 119. 29, &c.

STROKE,] or 'plague;' as in 38. 11; 89. 32.

STRIVING.] Original word not found again. Sept. Vulg. 'strength.'

CONSUMED,] as in 31. 10; 37. 20; 69. 3, &c.

11. WITH REPROOFS,] not 'rebukes;' as in 38. 14; 73. 14, &c. Vulg. joins this to the preceding verse.

CORRECTED,] as in 6. 1; 16. 9; 38. 1; 94. 12.

WASTE,] as in 6. 6; 147. 18.

MOTH,] as in 4. 19; 13. 28; 27. 18; Isa. 50. 9; 51. 8; Hos. 5. 12.

DESIRABLENESS,] not 'beauty;' as in Job 20. 20; Isa. 14. 9. Sept. Vulg. 'soul or life.'

VANITY,] as in v. 5, 6. Vulg. 'in vain is every man disquieted.'

12. HEAR,] as in 4. 1; 17. 1, 6; 27. 7; 28. 2.

PRAYER,] as in 4. 1; 6. 9; 17. 1; 35. 13, &c.

CRY,] as in 18. 6; 34. 15; 40. 1; 102. 1, &c.

GIVE EAR,] as in 5. 1; 17. 1; 39. 12; 49. 1.

TEAR,] as in 6. 2; 42. 3; 56. 8; 80. 5, &c.

SILENT,] as in 28. 1; 35. 22; 50. 3; 83. 1, &c.

SOJOURNER,] as in 94. 6; 119. 19; 146. 9, &c.

SETTLER,] as in Ge. 23. 4; Ex. 12. 45, &c.

13. LOOK FROM ME,] not 'spare me;' as in Job 14. 6; Isa. 22. 4.

BRIGHTEN UP,] not 'recover strength;' as in Job 9. 27; 10. 20; Am. 5. 9.

XL. OVERSEER,] as in Ps. 4. 5. 6. 8. 9. &c.

1. EXPECTED,] not 'waited;' as in Jer. 8 15; 14. 19, &c.

INCLINETH,] as in 18. 9; 21. 11; 44. 18, &c

CRY,] as in 18. 6; 34. 15; 39. 12; 102. 1, &c. Sept. Vulg. 'supplications.'

2. PIT,] as in 7. 15; 28. 1; 30. 3; 88. 4, &c.

DESOLATION,] not 'horrible;' as in 65. 7; 74. 23, &c. Sept. Vulg. 'misery.'

MIRE,] as in 18. 42; 69. 14; 2 Sa. 22. 41, &c.

MUD,] not 'clay,' as in 69. 2.

ROCK,] as in 18. 2; 31. 3; 42. 9; 71. 3, &c.

ESTABLISHING,] as in 8. 3; 9. 7; 11. 2; 68. 9, &c. Sept. Vulg. 'directeth.'

STEPS,] not 'goings;' as in 17. 5; 37. 31; 44. 18; 73. 2; Job 23. 11; Prov. 14. 15; Eze. 27. 6.

3. NEW SONG,] as in 144. 9; 149. 1; Isa. 42. 10.

PRAISE,] as in 9. 14; 22. 3, 25; 33. 1; 34. 1, &c. Sept. 'a hymn.'

FEAR,] as in 6; 23. 4; 27. 1, 3; 33. 8, &c.

TRUST,] as in 9. 10; 44. 6; 52. 7; 55. 23, &c.

4. HAPPINESS,] not 'blessed;' as in 1. 2, &c.

JEHOVAH.] Sept. Vulg. 'the name of the Lord.'

TRUST,] as in 65. 5; 71. 5; Job 8. 14, &c. Sept. Vulg. 'vain.'

PROUD,] Sept. Vulg. 'vain.'

TURNING ASIDE,] as in Nu. 5. 12, 19, 20, 29; Prov. 4. 15; 7. 25.

LIES,] as in 4. 2; 5. 6; 58. 3; 62. 4, 9, &c.

5. WONDERS,] as in 9. 1; 26. 7; 71. 17, &c.

THOUGHTS,] as in 33. 10, 11; 56. 5; 92. 5, &c.

ARRANGE,] as in 78. 19; Jud. 20. 22; 1 Sa.

7. 8, &c. Sept. Vulg. 'compare.'

DECLARE,] as in 22. 31; 30. 9; 38. 18, &c.

SPEAK,] as in 2. 5; 12. 2; 35. 20; 37. 30, &c

NUMBERED,] as in 26. 7; 50. 16; 73. 28, &c

6. SACRIFICE,] as in 4. 5; 27. 6; 50. 5, &c.

PRESENT,] not 'offering;' as in 20. 3, &c.

DESIRED,] as in v. 8; 18. 19; 22. 8; 41. 11

EARS,] as in 10. 17; 17. 6; 18. 6, 44; 31. 2, &c. Vulg. 'a body.'
PREPARED,] not 'opened;' as in 7. 15; 22. 16; 57. 6; 119. 85; 2 K. 6. 23; Job 41. 6, &c.
BURNT-OFFERING,] as in 20. 3; 50. 8, &c.
SIN-OFFERING,] as in Ge. 4. 7; Ex. 29. 14.
ASKED,] as in 21. 4; 27. 4; 105. 40; 137. 3.
7. COME,] as in 41. 6; 44. 17; 51. 1; 52. 1, &c.
ROLL,] as in Jer. 36. 2, 4, 6, 14, 20, 21, 23, &c. Vulg. 'chapter.'
BOOK,] as in 69. 28; 139. 16; Ge. 5. 1, &c.
WRITTEN,] as in 149. 9; Ex. 31. 18; 32. 15.
8. PLEASURE,] as in 5. 12; 19. 14; 30. 5, &c.
DELIGHTED,] as in v. 7. Sept. 'counselled.'
LAW,] as in 1. 2; 19. 17; 37. 31; 78. 1, 5, &c.
BOWELS.] Vulg. 'heart.'
9. PROCLAIMED TIDINGS,] as in 68. 11; 96. 2; 1 Sa. 4. 17; 31. 9; 2 Sa. 1. 20, &c.
RIGHTEOUSNESS,] as in 4. 1, 5; 7. 8, 17; 9. 4, 8, &c. Vulg. 'thy righteousness.'
GREAT ASSEMBLY,] as in v. 10; 22. 25, &c.
RESTRAIN,] as in v. 11; 119. 101, &c.
KNOWN,] as in 31. 7; 69. 5, 19; 103. 14, &c.
10. CONCEALED,] as in 32. 5; 44. 15; 69. 7.
FAITHFULNESS,] as in 33. 4; 36. 5; 37. 3; 88. 11, &c. Sept. 'truth.'
SALVATION,] as in 33. 17; 37. 39, &c.
TOLD,] lit. 'said.'
HIDDEN,] as in 69. 5; 78. 4; 139. 15, &c.
KINDNESS,] as in v. 11; 5. 7; 6. 4; 13. 5, &c.
TRUTH,] as in v. 11; 15. 2; 19. 9; 25. 5, &c.
GREAT ASSEMBLY,] as in v. 9.
11. RESTRAINEST,] as in v. 9.
MERCIES,] as in 25. 6; 51. 1; 77. 9; 79. 8, &c.
KEEP,] as in 12. 7; 25. 21; 32. 7, &c. Sept. Vulg. 'sustain.'
12. COMPASSED,] as in 18. 4; 116. 3; 2 Sa. 22. 2; Jon. 2. 5.
EVILS,] as in v. 14; 5. 4; 7. 4, 9; 10. 6, &c.
INNUMERABLE,] as in 104. 25; 105. 34, &c.
OVERTAKEN,] not 'taken hold;' as in 7. 5.
INIQUITIES,] as in 18. 23; 25. 11; 31. 10, &c.
HAIRS OF MY HEAD,] as in 69. 4; 1 Sa. 14. 45.
HEART,] as in v. 10.
FORSAKEN,] not 'falleth;' as in 9. 10; 22. 1.
13. BE PLEASED,] as in 119. 108; 44. 3, &c.
DELIVER,] as in 33. 19; 70. 1; Ge. 37. 22.
HELP,] as in v. 17; 22. 19; 27. 9; 35. 2.
MAKE HASTE,] as in 22. 19; 38. 22; 40. 13.
14. ASHAMED,] as in 6. 10; 25. 2, 3, 20, &c.
CONFOUNDED,] as in 34. 5; 35. 4, 26; 70. 2.
DESTROY,] lit. 'end;' as in Ge. 18. 23, &c.
TURNED,] as in 35. 4; 70. 2; 78. 57; 129. 5.
DESIRING,] as in 35. 4; 69. 6; 70. 2, &c.
EVIL,] as in v. 12.
15. DESOLATE,] as in Lev. 26. 32; 1 K. 9. 8.
SHAME,] as in 35. 26; 44. 15; 69. 19, &c.
AHA,] as in 35. 21, 25; 70. 3; Job 39. 25, &c.
16. SEEKING,] as in v. 14; 24. 6; 35. 4, &c.
REJOICE,] as in 19. 5; 35. 9; 68. 3; 70. 4, &c.
ARE GLAD,] as in 5. 11; 9. 2; 14. 7; 21. 1, &c.
SALVATION,] as in v. 10.
MAGNIFIED,] as in 35. 27; 70. 4; 92. 5, &c.
17. POOR,] as in 9. 12, 18; 10. 2, 9, 12, &c.
NEEDY,] as in 9. 18; 12. 5; 35. 10; 37. 14, &c.
DEVISE,] not 'thinketh;' as in 32. 2; 35. 20.
HELP,] as in v. 13.
DELIVERER,] as in 18. 2, 48; 70. 5; 144. 2.
TARRY NOT,] as in 70. 5; Ge. 24. 56, &c.

XLI. OVERSEER,] as in Ps. 4. 5. 6. 8. &c.
1. HAPPINESS,] not 'blessed;' as in 1. 1, &c.
ACTING WISELY,] not 'considereth;' as in 14. 2; 32. 1; 42. 1; 44. 1, &c.
POOR,] as in 72. 13; 82. 3, 4; 113. 7, &c. Sept. Vulg. 'poor and needy.'
DAY OF EVIL,] not 'time of trouble;' as in 49. 5, &c.
DELIVER,] as in 33. 17; 89. 48; 107. 20, &c.
2. PRESERVE,] as in 12. 7; 39. 1; 56. 6, &c.
REVIVE,] lit. 'causeth to live;' as in 71. 20; 80. 18; 85. 6; 138. 7; 143. 11, &c.
HAPPY,] not 'blessed;' as in 1. 1; 2. 12, &c. Sept. 'he makes him happy.'
LAND,] not 'earth,' as in C.V.
WILL,] lit. 'soul;' Sept. 'hand.'
3. SUPPORTETH,] not 'strengthen;' as in 18. 35; 20. 2; 94. 18; 104. 15; 119. 117, &c.
COUCH,] not 'bed;' as in 6. 6; 132. 3, &c.
SICKNESS,] not 'languishing;' as in Job 6. 7.
BED,] as in 4. 4; 36. 4; 149. 5, &c.
TURNED,] as in 30. 11; 66. 6; 78. 9, &c.
WEAKNESS,] as in De. 7. 15; 28. 59, 61, &c.
4. FAVOUR,] not 'be merciful;' as in v. 10; 4. 1; 6. 2, &c.
HEAL,] as in 6. 20; 60. 2; Nu. 12. 13, &c.
5. EVIL,] as in 5. 4; 7. 4. 9; 10. 6, 15; 15. 3.
NAME,] as in 5. 11; 7. 17; 8. 1; 9. 2, 5, &c.
PERISHED,] as in 9. 6; 10. 16; 119. 92; 142. 5, &c. Sept. Vulg. read interrogatively.
6. TO SEE,] as in 14. 2; 16. 10; 27. 13, &c.
VANITY,] as in 12. 2; 24. 4; 26. 4; 31. 6, &c.
GATHERETH,] as in Ge. 41. 35, 48; De. 13. 16
INIQUITY,] as in 5. 5; 6. 8; 7. 14; 10. 7, &c.
GOETH OUT,] as in 17. 2; 44. 9; 60. 10, &c.
STREET,] lit. 'outside;' as in 18. 42; 31. 11.
7. WHISPER,] as in 2 Sa. 12. 19.
TOGETHER,] as in 2. 2; 4. 8; 14. 3; 19. 9, &c.
DEVISE,] as in 2. 2; 35. 20; 36. 4; 40. 17.
8. THING,] or 'word.'
BELIAL,] or 'worthlessness;' Sept. Vulg. 'unlawful.'
POURED OUT,] not 'cleaveth fast;' as in 45. 2; Sept. Vulg. 'placed.'
LAY DOWN,] not 'lieth;' as in 3. 5, &c.
9. ALLY,] lit. 'man of my peace;' as in Jer. 20. 10; 38. 22.
TRUSTED,] as in 13. 5; 22. 4, 5; 25. 2; 26. 1.
BREAD,] as in Obad. 7.
MADE GREAT,] not 'lifted up;' as in 38. 16; 55. 12, &c.
HEEL,] as in 49. 5; 56. 6; 77. 19; 89. 51, &c.
10. FAVOUR,] not 'be merciful;' as in v. 4.
GIVE RECOMPENSE,] as in 22. 25; 35. 12, &c.
11. DELIGHTED,] not 'favourest;' as in 18. 19; 22. 8, &c.
SHOUTETH,] not 'triumph;' as in 95. 1, &c.
12. INTEGRITY,] as in 7. 8; 25. 21; 26. 1, 11, &c. Sept. 'harmlessness;' Vulg 'innocence.'
TAKEN HOLD,] not 'upholdest;' as in 63. 8; 16. 5.
13. BLESSED,] as in 18. 46; 28. 6; 31. 21, &c.
JEHOVAH,] the Existing One, the covenant keeping.
GOD OF ISRAEL,] as in 59. 5; 68. 9; 69. 6, &c.
AGE..AGE,] as in 90. 2; 103. 17; 106. 48, &c.
AMEN,] as in 72. 19; 89. 52; 106. 48, &c.
Here ends the first of the five great divisions of the Psalms.

XLII. OVERSEER,] as in Ps. 4. 5. 6. 8 &c.
INSTRUCTION,] as in 14. 2; 32. 1; 41. 1, &c.
SONS OF KORAH,] as in Ps. 44. 45. 46. 47.
48. 49. 84. 85. 87. 88. Sept. adds 'a Psalm
of David.'
1. HART,] as in De. 12. 15, 22; 14. 5; 15. 22.
PANT,] as in Joel 1. 20.
STREAMS,] as in 18. 15; 126. 4; 2 Sa. 22. 6.
2. THIRSTED,] as in 63. 1; Ex. 17. 3; Jud.
4. 19; 15. 18, &c.
LIVING GOD,] as in 84. 2; Isa. 37. 4, &c.
Sept. Vulg. 'living strong one.'
ENTER,] not 'come,' as in C.V.
SEE THE FACE,] not 'appear before God;'
as in C.V.
3. TEAR,] not 'tears;' as in 6. 6; 39. 12, &c.
BREAD,] not 'meat;' as in 14. 4; 37. 25, &c.
DAY AND NIGHT,] as in v. 9; 1. 2; 22. 3, &c.
4. REMEMBER,] as in v. 6; 77. 3, 6, 11, &c.
POUR OUT, as in 102. 1; 106. 38; 142. 2, &c.
PASS OVER,] as in 17. 3; 37. 36; 57. 1, &c.
BOOTH,] not 'multitude;' as in 10. 9; 27. 5;
76. 2; Jer. 25. 38.
GO SOFTLY,] not 'went,' merely; as in Isa.
38. 15.
HOUSE OF GOD,] as in 55. 14, &c.
SINGING,] not 'joy;' as in 17. 1; 30. 5; 47. 1.
CONFESSION,] not 'praise;' as in 26. 7, &c.
MULTITUDE,] as in 37. 16; 65. 7; Ge. 17. 4.
KEEPING FEAST,] not 'holyday;' as in 1 Sa.
30. 16, &c.
5. BOWEST THOU THYSELF,] not 'cast
down;' as in v. 6, 11; 43. 5.
TROUBLED,] as in v. 11; 39. 6; 43. 5; 46. 3.
WAIT,] not 'hope;' as in v. 11; 43. 5.
CONFESS,] not 'praise;' as in v. 11; 6. 5, &c.
SALVATION,] not 'help;' as in v. 11; 3. 2, &c.
HIS COUNTENANCE.] Sept. Vulg. 'my
countenance,' as in v. 11.
MY GOD.] Sept. Vulg. 'and my God.'
6. BOW ITSELF,] not 'cast down;' as in v.
5, 11. Sept. Vulg. 'troubled.'
REMEMBER,] as in v. 4.
JORDAN,] the river of that name.
HERMONS.] The pl. form is not found again;
eastward of Canaan.
MIZAR,] or 'little one.' So Sept. Vulg. &c.
7. DEEP,] as in 33. 7; 36. 6; 71. 20; 77. 16.
WATER SPOUTS,] as in 2 Sa. 5. 8. Sept.
Vulg. 'cataracts.'
BREAKERS,] not 'waves;' as in 88. 7; 93. 4;
2 Sa. 22. 5; Jon. 2. 3.
BILLOWS,] as in 65. 7; 89. 9; 107. 25, 29.
PASSED OVER,] as in 18. 12; 33. 4; 48. 4, &c.
8. BY DAY,] as in v. 9; 1. 2; 22. 3; 32. 4, &c.
COMMANDETH,] as in 78. 23; 91. 11, &c.
KINDNESS,] as in 5. 7; 6. 4; 13. 5; 17. 7, &c.
BY NIGHT,] as in v. 9.
HIS SONG,] as in 28. 7; 30. 1; 33. 3; 40. 3.
PRAYER,] as in 4. 1; 6. 9; 17. 1; 35. 13, &c.
GOD,] or 'mighty one,' as in v. 2.
9. ROCK,] as in 18. 2; 31. 3; 40. 2; 71. 3, &c.
Sept. Vulg. 'my supporters.'
FORGOTTEN,] as in 9. 12; 10. 11; 44. 17, &c.
MOURNING,] as in 35. 14; 38. 6; 43. 2.
OPPRESSION,] as in 44. 24; Ex. 3. 9, &c.
10. SWORD,] or 'murder,' as in Eze. 21. 22.
Sept. Vulg. 'bruising.'
BONES,] as in 6. 2; 22. 14, 17; 31. 10; 32. 3.
REPROACHED,] as in 57. 3; 74. 18; 79. 12, &c.
WHERE,] as in v. 3.

11. BOWEST THOU THYSELF,] not 'cast
down;' as in v. 5, 6; 43. 5.
TROUBLED,] as in v. 5; 39. 6; 43. 5; 46. 3.
WAIT,] not 'hope;' as in v. 5; 43. 5.
CONFESS,] not 'praise;' as in v. 5; 6. 5, &c.
SALVATION,] not 'health;' as in v. 5; 3. 2.
MY COUNTENANCE.] Compare v. 5.
AND MY GOD.] Compare v. 5.

XLIII. This Psalm in Hebrew has no title.
Sept. has same title as in Ps. 42; Vulg. 'a
Psalm of David.' Thirty Heb. MSS. join it
to the preceding psalm.
1. JUDGE,] as in 7. 8; 26. 1; 35. 24; 82. 3.
PLEAD,] as in 35. 1; 74. 22; 119. 154, &c.
CAUSE,] lit. 'pleading,' as in 18. 43; 31. 20;
35. 23; 55. 9; 74. 22; 119. 154, &c.
NOT PIOUS,] or 'kind,' not 'ungodly;' as
in 4. 3, &c.
DECEIT,] as in 5. 6; 10. 7; 17. 1; 24. 4, &c.
PERVERSENESS, as in 37. 1; 89. 22; 92. 15.
2. THE GOD OF,] Sept. Vulg. 'O God my
strength.'
STRENGTH,] as in 27. 1; 28. 8; 31. 2, &c.
CAST OFF,] as in 44. 9; 60. 1, 10; 74. 1, &c.
MOURNING,] as in 35. 14; 38. 6; 42. 9, &c.
GO UP AND DOWN,] as in 12. 8; 39. 6; 58. 7.
OPPRESSION,] as in 42. 9; 44. 24; Ex. 3. 9.
AN ENEMY,] Sept. 'my enemy.'
3. SEND FORTH,] as in 144. 6, 7; Ge. 42. 6.
LIGHT,] as in 4. 6; 27. 1; 36. 9; 37. 6, &c.
TRUTH,] as in 15. 2; 19. 9; 25. 5, 10; 26. 3.
LEAD,] as in 23. 3; 31. 3; 61. 2; 67. 4, &c.
BRING ME IN,] as in 78. 29, 54; 90. 12, &c.
HOLY HILL,] as in 2. 6; 3. 4; 15. 1; 99. 9.
TABERNACLES,] as in 26. 8; 46. 4; 49. 11, &c.
4. ALTAR,] as in 26. 6; 51. 19; 84. 3; 118. 27.
JOY,] as in 4. 7; 16. 11; 21. 6; 30. 11; 45. 15.
REJOICING,] as in 45. 15; 65. 12; Job 3. 22,
&c. Sept. Vulg. 'youth.'
THANK,] not 'praise,' as in v. 5; 6. 5, &c.
HARP,] as in 33. 2; 49. 4; 57. 8; 71. 22, &c.
5. BOWEST THOU THYSELF,] not 'cast
down;' as in 42. 5, 6, 11. Sept. Vulg.
'sorrowful.'
TROUBLED,] as in 42. 5, 11; 39. 6; 46. 3, &c.
WAIT,] not 'hope;' as in 42. 5, 11.
CONFESS,] not 'praise;' as in v. 4; 6. 5, &c.
SALVATION,] not 'health;' as in 3. 2, 8, &c.
MY COUNTENANCE,] as in 42. 5, 11, &c.
AND MY GOD,] as in 42. 5, 11, &c.

XLIV. OVERSEER,] as in Ps. 4. 5. 6. 8. 9. &c.
SONS OF KORAH,] as in Ps. 42. 45. 46. &c.
INSTRUCTION,] as in Ps. 32. 41. 42. 45. &c.
1. GOD,] as in v. 4, 8, 20, 21, &c.
HEARD,] as in 48. 8; 62. 11; 78. 3; 97. 8.
WORK,] as in 9. 16; 28. 4; 64. 9; 77. 12, &c.
DAYS OF OLD,] not 'times of old;' as in 77.
5; 143. 5, &c.
2. HAND,] as in 8. 6; 10. 12, 14; 17. 14, &c.
DISPOSSESSED,] as in Ex. 15. 9; 34. 24, &c.
PLANT,] as in 80. 8, 15; 107. 37; 104. 16, &c.
AFFLICTEST,] as in 105. 15, &c.
SENDEST AWAY,] not 'cast out;' as in 78.
45, 49; 80. 11; 81. 12; 104. 30; 106. 15, &c.
3. SWORD,] as in v. 6; 7. 12; 17. 13; 22. 20.
POSSESSED,] as in 25. 13; 37. 9, 11, 22, &c.
LAND] of Israel.
ARM,] as in 10. 15; 18. 34; 37. 17; 71. 18, &c.
SALVATION,] as in 20. 6; 34. 6; 44. 3, 7, &c

RIGHT HAND,] as in 16. 8, 11; 17. 7; 18. 35.
LIGHT OF THY COUNTENANCE,] as in 4. 6, &c.
ACCEPTED,] not 'hadst a favour;' as in 85.
1; 102. 4, &c.
4. HE.] The pronoun is emphatic.
MY KING,] as in 5. 2; 68. 24; 74. 12; 84. 3.
O GOD,] Sept. Vulg. 'my God.'
COMMAND,] as in Lev. 6. 9; 24. 2; Nu. 5. 2.
DELIVERANCES,] as in 3. 2, 8; 9. 14; 13. 5.
JACOB,] as in 14. 7; 20. 1; 22. 23; 24. 6, &c.
5. ADVERSARIES,] as in v. 7, 10; 3. 1, &c.
PUSH,] as in De. 33. 17; 1 K. 22. 11, &c.
NAME,] as in v. 8, 20; 5. 11; 7. 17; 18. 1, &c.
TREAD DOWN,] as in 60. 12; 108. 13; Prov.
27. 7, &c.   Sept. Vulg. 'contemn.'
WITHSTANDERS,] as in 3. 1; 18. 39, 48, &c.
6. BOW,] as in 7. 12; 11. 2; 18. 34; 37. 14, 15.
TRUST,] as in 9. 10; 40. 3; 44. 6; 52. 7, &c.
SWORD,] as in v. 3.
SAVE,] as in 18. 27; 34. 18; 36. 6; 37. 40, &c.
7. ADVERSARIES,] as in v. 5, 10.
PUT TO SHAME,] as in 14. 6; 53. 5; 119. 31.
8. BOASTED,] as in 10. 3; 119. 164, &c.
THANK,] not 'praise;' as in 6. 5; 7. 17, &c.
SELAH,] i.e. 'pause.'   Vulg. omits.
9. IN ANGER,] or 'also;' Sept. Vulg. 'but
now.'
CAST OFF,] as in 43. 2; 60. 1, 10; 74. 1, &c.
TO BLUSH,] not 'put to shame;' as in Ruth
2. 15, &c.
GOEST FORTH,] as in 17. 2; 41. 6; 60. 10; 88.
8, &c.   Sept. Vulg. add, 'O God.'
HOSTS,] as in 24. 10; 33. 6; 46. 7; 48. 8, &c.
10. TO TURN BACKWARD,] as in 18. 20, &c.
AN ADVERSARY,] Sept. 'our adversary.'
SPOILED,] as in Jud. 2. 14, 16; 1 Sa. 14. 48.
11. MAKEST,] lit. 'givest.'
FOOD,] not 'meat;' as in 74. 14; 79. 2, &c.
SHEEP,] as in v. 22; 49. 14; 65. 13; 74. 1, &c.
SCATTERED,] as in 106. 27; 139. 3, &c.
12. SELLEST,] as in Ge. 25. 33; 31. 15, &c.
WITHOUT WEALTH,] not 'for nought;' as
in 112. 2; 119, 14, &c.   Sept. Vulg. 'price.
PRICE,] as in De. 23. 18; 2 Sa. 24. 24, &c.
Sept. 'shouting;' Vulg. 'change.'
13. REPROACH,] as in 15. 3; 22. 6; 31. 11, &c.
NEIGHBOURS,] as in 31. 11; 79. 4, 12, &c.
SCORN,] as in 79. 4; 123. 4; Job 34. 37, &c.
REPROACH,] as in 79. 4; Jer. 20. 8.
SURROUNDERS,] as in 3. 6; 12. 8; 18. 11, &c.
14. SIMILE,] not 'a byword;' as in 49. 4;
69. 11; 78. 2, &c.
SHAKING OF THE HEAD,] as in 22. 7, &c.
15. CONFUSION,] as in 4. 2; 35. 26; 69. 7, &c.
SHAME,] as in 35. 26; 40. 15; 69. 19, &c.
COVERED,] as in 32. 5; 40. 10; 69. 7; 78. 53.
16. REPROACHER,] as in 69. 9; 119. 42;
Prov. 27. 11.
REVILER,] not 'blasphemeth;' as in Nu.
15. 30.
SELF-AVENGER,] not 'avenger' merely; as
in 8. 2.
17. MET,] or 'come to us.'
FORGET,] as in v. 20; 9. 12; 10. 11; 42. 9, &c.
DEALT FALSELY,] as in 89. 33; Ge. 21. 23.
COVENANT,] as in 25. 10, 14; 50. 5, 16, &c.
18. TURN BACKWARD,] as in 35. 4; 40. 14, &c.
HEART,] as in 4. 7; 7. 10; 9. 1; 10. 6, &c.
TURN ASIDE,] as in 18. 19; 21. 11; 40. 1, &c.
STEP,] as in 17. 5; 37. 31; 40. 2; 73. 2, &c.
PATH,] as in 8. 8; 16. 11; 17. 4; 19. 5, &c.

19. SMITTEN,] not 'sore broken;' as in 51.
18; 10. 10, &c.
DRAGONS,] as in Job 30. 29; Isa. 13. 22; 34.
13, &c.   Sept. Vulg. 'affliction.'
SEVER,] as in 55. 5; 116. 11, 17; 140. 9, &c.
DEATH-SHADE,] as in 23. 4; 107. 10, 14, &c.
20. FORGOTTEN,] as in v. 17.
NAME,] as in v. 5, 8.
SPREAD OUT,] as in 68. 14; 105. 39; 140. 5.
HANDS,] as in Ex. 9. 29, 33; 1 K. 8. 38, &c
STRANGE,] as in 54. 3; 81. 9; 109. 11, &c.
21. SEARCH OUT,] as in 139. 1, 23; De. 13. 14.
SECRETS,] as in Job 11. 6; 28. 11.
22. SURELY,] or 'because;' not 'yea,' as in
C.V.   So Sept. Vulg.
SAKE,] or 'because of thee.'   See Rom.
8. 36.
SLAIN,] as in Isa. 27. 7.
RECKONED,] as in 88. 4; 106. 31; Ge. 31. 15.
SLAUGHTER,] as in 1 Sa. 25. 11; Jer. 12. 3.
23. STIR UP,] as in 7. 6; 57. 8; 59. 4; 108. 2.
SLEEP,] as in 3. 5; 4. 8; 13. 3; 121. 4, &c.
AWAKE,] as in 35. 23; 59. 5; Isa. 26. 19,
&c.   Sept. 'stand up.'
CAST OFF,] as in 43. 2; 44. 9; 60. 1, 10, &c.
24. HIDEST,] lit. 'makest secret;' as in 13.
1; 17. 8, &c.   Sept. Vulg. 'turn aside.'
FORGETTEST,] as in 10. 12; 13. 1; 59. 11, &c
AFFLICTIONS,] as in 9. 13; 25. 8; 31. 17,
&c.   Sept. Vulg. 'poverty.'
OPPRESSION,] as in 42. 9; Ex. 3. 9; De. 26. 7
25. BOWED,] as in Prov. 2. 8; La. 3. 20.
DUST,] as in 7. 5; 18. 42; 22. 15, 29, &c.
CLEAVED,] as in 63. 8; 101. 3; 102. 5, &c.
BELLY,] as in 17. 14; 22. 9, 10; 31. 9, &c.
26. RISE,] as in 3. 7; 7. 6; 9. 19; 10. 12; 17.
13, &c;   Sept. Vulg. add, 'O Lord.'
HELP,] as in 22. 19; 27. 9; 35. 2; 38. 22, &c.
RANSOM,] not 'redeem;' as in 25. 22; 26.
11; 69. 18; 119. 134, &s.
KINDNESS,] not 'mercies;' as in 5. 7; 6. 4,
&c.   Sept. Vulg. 'name.'

XLV. OVERSEER,] as in Ps. 4. 5. 6. 8. &c.
LILIES,] as in Ps. 60. 80; 1 K. 7. 22, 26.
Song 2. 16; 4. 5; 5. 13; 6. 2, 3; 7. 2.   Sept.
Vulg. 'those who are changed.'
SONS OF KORAH,] as in Ps. 42. 44. 44. 46. &c.
INSTRUCTION,] as in Ps. 32. 41. 42. 44. &c.
SONG,] as in Ps. 30. 46. 48. 65. 66. &c
Sept. 'ode.'
LOVES,] as in 60. 5; 84. 1; 108. 6; 127. 2,
&c.   Sept. Vulg. 'for the beloved.'
1. HEART,] as in v. 5; 4. 7; 7. 10; 9. 1, &c.
INDITED.] Original word not found again.
Sept. Vulg. 'sent forth.'
GOOD THING,] or 'word.'
TELLING,] lit. 'saying;' as in 3. 2; 4. 6, &c.
WORKS,] as in 8. 6; 19. 1; 28. 4, 5; 33. 4.
KING,] as in v. 5, 9, 11, 13, 14, 15; 2. 2, &c.
TONGUE,] as in v. 9; 10. 7; 12. 3, 4; 15. 3.
PEN,] as in Job 19. 24; Jer. 8. 8; 17. 1.
SPEEDY,] as in Ezra 7. 6; Prov. 22. 29; Isa.
16. 5.
WRITER,] as in Jud. 5. 14; 2 Sa 8. 17, &c.
2. BEAUTIFIED,] not 'fairer;' as in Jer. 10.
4; Song 4. 10; 7. 1, 6; Eze. 16. 13; 31. 7, &c.
SONS OF MEN,] as in 11. 4; 12. 1; 14. 2, &c.
GRACE,] as in 84. 11; Ge. 6. 8; 18. 3; 19. 19.
POURED,] as in Lev. 21. 10; 2 K. 4. 5; Job
22. 16.

LIPS,] as in 12. 2, 3, 4; 16. 4; 17. 1, 4, &c.
THEREFORE,] as in Ge. 2. 24; 10. 9, &c.
BLESSED,] as in 10. 3; 118. 26; 129. 8, &c.
3. GIRD,] as in 1 Sa. 25. 13; 2 Sa. 3. 31, &c.
SWORD,] as in 7. 12; 17. 13; 22. 20; 37. 14.
THIGH,] as in Ge. 24. 2, 9; 32. 25, 31, 32,
&c. Sept. Vulg. 'thy thigh.'
MIGHTY,] as in 19. 6; 24. 8; 33. 16; 52. 1, &c.
GLORY,] as in 8. 1; 21. 5; 96. 6; 104. 1, &c.
MAJESTY,] as in 8. 5; 21. 5; 29. 4; 45. 3, &c.
4. PROSPER,] as in 118. 25; 1 K. 22. 12, 15,
&c. Sept. Vulg. 'and stretch out, and di-
rect, and reign, because of,' &c.
RIDE,] as in 18. 10; 68. 4, 33; Ge. 24. 61, &c.
TRUTH,] as in 15. 2; 19. 9; 25. 5, 10; 26. 3.
MEEKNESS,] as in 18. 35.
RIGHTEOUSNESS,] as in v. 7; 4. 1, 5; 7. 8.
RIGHT HAND,] as in v. 9; 16. 8, 11; 17. 7.
SHEWETH,] as in 28. 5, 12; 32. 8; 64. 4, &c.
FEARFUL THINGS,] as in 47. 2; 65. 4; 66. 3.
5. ARROWS,] as in 7. 13; 11. 2; 18. 14; 38. 2.
SHARP,] as in 120. 4; Prov. 25. 18; Isa. 5.
28. Sept. adds, 'O mighty one.'
PEOPLES,] as in v. 10, 12, 17; 3. 6, 8; 7. 8.
HEART,] as in v. 1.
6. THRONE,] as in 9. 4, 7; 11. 4; 47. 8; 89.
4, &c. Vulg. 'seat.'
O GOD,] as in v. 2, 7.
AGE-DURING,] as in v. 2, 17; 5. 11; 9. 5, &c.
FOR EVER,] as in v. 7; 9. 5, 18; 10. 16, &c.
SCEPTRE,] as in 2. 9; 23. 4; 74. 2; 78. 55, &c.
UPRIGHTNESS,] as in 26. 12; 27. 11; 67. 4;
143. 10, &c. Vulg. 'direction.'
7. LOVED,] as in 11. 7; 26. 8; 47. 4; 52. 3.
HATE,] as in 5. 5; 11. 5; 25. 19; 139. 21, &c.
THY GOD,] as in 42. 4, 11; 50. 7; 68. 28, &c.
ANOINTED,] as in 89. 20; Ge. 31. 13; Ex.
30. 30, &c. Targ. adds, 'Lord.'
OIL,] as in 23. 5; 45. 7; 55. 21; 89. 20, &c.
JOY,] as in 51. 8, 12; 105. 43; 119. 111, &c.
COMPANIONS,] as in 119. 63; Jud. 20. 11, &c.
8. MYRRH,] as in Ex. 30. 23; Est. 2. 12, &c.
ALOES,] as in Nu. 24. 6; Prov. 7. 17; Song
4. 14.
CASSIA.] Original word not found again.
GARMENTS,] as in 22. 18; 102. 26; 109. 19,
&c. Sept. Vulg. 'are from thy garments.'
PALACES,] as in v. 15; 5. 7; 11. 4; 18. 6, &c.
IVORY,] as in 1 K. 10. 18; 22. 39; 2 Ch. 9.
17; Song. 5. 14; 7. 4; Eze. 27. 6, 15. Amos 3.
15; 6. 4.
STRINGED INSTRUMENTS,] as in 150. 4.
Sept. Vulg. 'out of which.'
GLAD,] as in 30. 1; 46. 4; 92. 4; 104. 15, &c.
Sept. Vulg. make 'daughters of kings,' the
nominative to the verb.
9. DAUGHTERS,] as in v. 10, 12, 13; 9. 14, &c.
PRECIOUS,] as in 36. 7; 37. 20; 116. 15, &c.
Sept. Vulg. 'in thy honour.'
QUEEN,] as in Neh. 2. 6; Da. 5. 2, 3, 23.
PURE GOLD,] as in Job 28. 16, 19; 31. 24;
Prov. 25. 12, &c. Sept. Vulg. 'arrayed in
garments of gold, embroidered.'
OPHIR,] as in 1 K. 9. 28; 2 Ch. 8. 18; 9. 10.
10. HEARKEN,] as in 4. 1; 17. 1, 6; 27. 7, &c.
DAUGHTER,] as in v. 9, 12, 13.
SEE,] not 'consider;' as in 9. 13; 25. 18, &c.
INCLINE,] as in 17. 6; 31. 2; 45. 10; 71. 2.
FORGET,] as in Ge. 40. 23, &c.
HOUSE,] or 'household.'
11. THE KING,] as in v. 1, 5.

DESIRE,] as in 106. 14; Nu. 11. 4, 34, &c.
BEAUTY,] as in 50. 2; Est. 1. 11; Prov. 6. 25.
LORD,] lit. 'lords;' as in 123. 2; 136. 2, &c.
Vulg. 'the Lord thy God.'
BOW THYSELF,] not 'worship;' as in 29.
2; 96. 9, &c.
12. DAUGHTER OF TYRE,] that is, Zidon;
83. 7; 87. 4; Sept. makes this the nomina-
tive to the preceding verb.
PRESENT,] as in 20. 3; 40. 6; 72. 10; 96. 8;
141. 2, &c.
RICH,] as in 49. 2; Ex. 30. 15; Ruth 3. 10.
APPEASE,] lit, 'smooth;' as in 119. 58; Ex.
32. 11, &c. Targ. 'seek.'
13. ALL GLORY.] Vulg. 'all his glory.'
DAUGHTER OF THE KING,] as in v. 9, 10, &c.
WITHIN,] in the inside of the palace, not
'inwardly,' in her mind, as most critics
suppose, but which the original text cannot
possibly mean.
EMBROIDERED,] as in Ex. 28. 11, 13, 14, &c.
CLOTHING,] as in 22. 18; 35. 13; 69. 11, &c.
14. DIVERS COLOURS,] not 'raiment of
needle-work;' as in Jud. 5. 30; 1 Ch. 29. 2.
VIRGINS,] as in 78. 63; 148. 13; Ge. 24. 16.
COMPANIONS,] as in Jud. 11. 37, 38.
BROUGHT,] as in v. 15; 60. 9; 68. 29, &c.
15. JOY,] as in 4. 7; 16. 7; 21. 6; 30. 11, &c
GLADNESS,] as in 43. 4; 65. 12; Job 3. 22.
PALACE,] as in v. 8. Sept. 'sanctuary.'
16. SONS,] not 'children,' as in C.V.; Sept
Vulg. 'are born to thee.'
SET,] not 'make;' as in 5. 5; 13. 2, &c.
PRINCES,] or 'heads,' as in 68. 27; 82. 7, &c.
EARTH,] or 'land.'
17. MAKE MENTION,] not 'cause to be re-
membered,' as in C.V.
NAME,] as in 5. 11; 7. 17; 8. 1; 9. 2, 5, &c.
GENERATIONS,] as in 10. 6; 33. 11; 47. 15.
PEOPLES,] as in v. 5, 10, 12.
PRAISE,] as in 6. 5; 7. 17; 9. 1; 18. 49, &c.

XLVI.

OVERSEER,] as in Ps. 4. 5. 6. 8. &c.
SONS OF KORAH,] as in Ps. 42. 44. 45, &c.
VIRGINS,] as in 1 Ch. 15. 20. Sept. Vulg
'for or concerning the hidden ones.' Sept.
adds 'of David.'
1. GOD IS TO US,] as in v. 4, 5, 7, 10, 11;
3. 2, 7; 4. 1, &c. Sept. Vulg. 'our God.'
REFUGE,] as in 14. 6; 61. 3; 62. 7, 8; 71. 7.
STRENGTH,] as in 8. 2; 21. 1, 13; 28. 7, &c.
HELP,] as in 22. 19; 27. 9; 35. 2; 38. 22, &c.
ADVERSITIES,] as in 9. 9; 10. 1: 20. 1, &c.
FOUND,] as in 37. 36; Ge. 18. 29, 30, 31, &c.
MOST SURELY,] or 'with might.' Sept.
Vulg. 'to those finding us speedily.'
2. FEAR,] as in 3. 6; 23. 4; 27. 1, 3; 33. 8.
CHANGING,] not 'be removed;' as in 15. 4;
106. 20, &c. Vulg. 'troubled.' Sept. 'dis-
turbed.'
EARTH,] or 'land.'
SLIPPING,] not 'be carried;' as in 60. 2, &c.
HEART OF THE SEAS,] as in Ex. 15. 8, &c.
3. ROAR,] as in v. 6; 39. 6; 42. 5, 11; 55. 17.
TROUBLED,] as in 75. 8; Ex. 2. 3. Targ.
'polluted.'
SHAKE,] as in 18. 7; 72. 16; 77. 18, &c.
PRIDE,] not 'swelling;' as in 10. 2; 31. 18
&c. Sept. Vulg. 'strength.'
SELAH.] Vulg. omits.
4. RIVER,] as in 24. 2; 60. 1; 66. 6; 72. 8.

RIVULETS,] as in 1, 3; 65. 9; 119. 136, &c.
Sept. Vulg. 'the rushings of the river.'
REJOICE,] as in 30. 1; 45. 8; 92. 4; 104. 15.
CITY OF GOD,] as in 48. 1, 8; 87. 3; 101. 8.
HOLY PLACE,] as in 2. 6; 3. 4; 5. 7; 11. 4; 15. 1, &c. Sept. Vulg. 'the Most High sanctified his tabernacle.'
TABERNACLES,] as in 26. 8; 43. 3; 49. 11, &c.
MOST HIGH,] as in 7. 17; 9. 2; 18. 13; 21. 7.
5. MIDST,] as in 5. 9; 36. 1; 39. 3; 48. 9, &c.
MOVED,] as in v. 2, 6.
HELP,] as in 37. 40; 119. 175.
TURN OF THE MORN,] not 'right early;' as in Ex. 14. 27; Jud. 19. 26.
6. TROUBLED,] not 'raged;' as in v. 3.
MOVED,] as in v. 2, 5. Sept. Vulg. 'bent.'
GIVEN FORTH.] Sept. adds, 'the Most High.'
MELTETH,] as in Isa. 64. 7; Am. 9. 5; Eze. 21. 15. Sept. Vulg. 'tottereth.'
7. JEHOVAH OF HOSTS,] as in v. 11; 24. 10.
TOWER,] not 'refuge;' as in v. 11; 9. 9; 18. 2; 48. 3, &c. Sept. Vulg. 'supporter.'
GOD OF JACOB,] as in v. 11; 20. 1; 41. 13, &c.
SELAH.] Vulg. omits.
8. WORKS,] as in 66. 5.
JEHOVAH.] Sept. 'God.'
ASTONISHING THINGS,] not 'desolations;' as in 73. 19; De. 28. 37; 2 K. 22. 19, &c.
EARTH,] or 'land.'
9. WARS,] as in 18. 34, 39; 24. 8; 27. 3, &c.
TO CEASE,] as in 8. 2; 89. 44; 119. 119, &c. Sept. Vulg. 'removing wars to the ends of the earth.'
BOW,] as in 7. 12; 11. 2; 18. 34; 37. 14, &c.
SPEAR,] as in 35. 3; 57. 4; 1 Sa. 13. 19, &c. Sept. Vulg. 'armour.'
CUT ASUNDER,] as in 129. 4; Ex. 39. 3, &c.
CHARIOTS,] wagons, or carts, as in Ge. 45. 19, 21, 27, &c. Sept. Vulg. 'shields.'
BURN,] as in 21. 3; Ex. 12. 10; 29. 14, &c.
FIRE,] as in 11. 6; 18. 8, 12; 21. 9; 29.⁴, &c.
10. DESIST,] as in 37. 8; De. 9. 14, &c.
KNOW,] as in 4. 3; 100. 3, &c. Vulg. 'see.'
GOD,] as in v. 1, 4, 5.
EXALTED,] as in 13. 2; 18. 46; 27. 6; 61. 2.
EARTH,] or 'land;' as in v. 2, 6, 8.
11. JEHOVAH OF HOSTS,] as in v. 7.
TOWER,] not 'refuge;' as in v. 7.
GOD OF JACOB,] as in v. 7.
SELAH.] Sept. Vulg. omit.

XLVII. OVERSEER,] as in Ps. 4. 5. 6. &c.
BY SONS OF KORAH,] Sept. 'concerning' them.
PSALM,] Sept. adds 'of David.'
1. PEOPLES,] not 'people;' as in v. 3, 9; 7. 8, &c. Sept. Vulg. 'nations.'
CLAP,] as in Job 17. 3; Prov. 6. 1; 11. 15; 17. 18; 22. 26; Nah. 3. 19.
SHOUT,] as in 66. 1; 81. 1; 98. 4, 6; 100. 1.
SINGING,] not 'triumph;' as in 17. 1; 30. 5; 2. MOST HIGH,] as in 7. 17; 9. 2; 18. 13, &c.
FEARFUL,] not 'terrible;' as in 45. 4, &c.
GREAT KING,] as in 95. 3; 2 K. 18. 19, 28; Ecc. 9. 14; Isa. 36. 4, 13; Jer. 25. 14; 27. 7; Mal. 1. 14.
EARTH,] or 'land;' as in v. 7, 9.
3. LEADETH,] as in 18. 47; Sept. Vulg. 'subdueth.'
PEOPLES,] not 'people;' as in v. 1, 9.

NATIONS,] as in v. 8.
FEET,] as in 8. 16; 9. 15; 18. 9; 33. 38, &c.
4. CHOOSE,] as in 25. 12; 65. 4; 78. 68, &c.
OUR INHERITANCE,] as in 2. 8; 28. 9; 33. 12; 37. 18, &c. Sept. Vulg. 'inheritance.'
EXCELLENCY,] as in 59. 12; Ex. 15. 7, &c.
LOVED,] as in 78. 68; 87. 2; De. 4. 37, &c.
SELAH,] Vulg. omits.
5. GONE UP,] as in 68. 18; Ge. 17. 22, &c.
SHOUT,] as in 27. 6; 33. 3; 89. 15; 150. 5, &c
TRUMPET,] as in 81. 3; 98. 6; 150. 3, &c.
6. PRAISE,] as in v. 7; 9. 11; 30. 4; 33. 2, &c.
GOD.] Sept. Vulg. 'our God.'
7. KING,] as in v. 2.
EARTH,] or 'land;' as in v. 2, 9.
UNDERSTANDING ONE,] not 'with under standing;' as in 14. 2, &c.
8. REIGNED,] as in 93. 1; 96. 10; 97. 1, &c.
NATIONS.] Sept. 'all the nations.'
SAT,] as in 9. 4, 7; 29. 10; 102. 12; 132. 14, &c.
THRONE,] as in 9. 4, 7; 11. 4; 45. 6, &c.
9. NOBLES,] as in 51. 12; 83. 11; 107. 40, &c.
GATHERED,] as in 35. 15; 104. 22; Ge. 25. 8.
WITH THE PEOPLE,] as in v. 1, 3. Sept. Vulg. read simply 'with the God of Abraham.'
GOD OF ABRAHAM,] as in Ge. 24. 42; 31. 42.
SHIELDS,] as in 3. 3; 7. 10; 18. 2, 30, 35, &c.
BEEN EXALTED,] lit. 'gone up;' as in 97. 9, &c.

XLVIII. SONG.] Sept. 'ode.'
PSALM,] Sept. adds 'to David.'
BY SONS OF KORAH,] not 'for them;' as in C.V.; Vulg. adds, 'for the second sabbath.'
1. GREAT,] as in 47. 2; 76. 1; 77. 13; 86. 10.
PRAISED,] as in 18. 3; 96. 4; 113. 3; 145. 3.
CITY OF GOD,] as in v. 8; 46. 4; 87. 3, &c.
HOLY HILL,] as in 2. 6; 3. 4; 15. 1; 43. 3, &c.
2. BEAUTIFUL,] as in Ge. 12. 11; 39. 6; Ecc. 3. 11; 5. 18, &c. Vulg. 'founded with joy of all the land.'
ELEVATION,] not 'situation,' as in C.V.
JOY,] as in Job 8. 19; Isa. 8. 6; 24. 8, &c.
LAND,] not 'earth,' as in C.V.
MOUNT ZION,] as in v. 11; 2. 6; 74. 2, &c
SIDES,] lit. 'thighs;' as in 128. 3; Ge. 49. 13.
NORTH,] as in 89. 12; 107. 3; Ge. 13. 14, &c.
CITY,] as in Nu. 21. 28; De. 2. 36; 3. 4, &c.
A GREAT KING,] David or Solomon perhaps.
3. GOD,] as in v. 1, 8, 9, 14.
HIGH PLACES,] not 'palaces;' as in v. 13; 122. 7, &c. Sept. 'burdens;' Vulg. 'houses.
KNOWN,] as in 9. 16; 76. 1; 77. 19, &c.
TOWER,] not 'refuge;' as in 9. 9; 18. 2; 46.
7. 11, &c. Sept. Vulg. 'when he helps her.'
4. KINGS,] Sept. Vulg. 'kings of the earth.'
MET,] not 'assembled;' as in Ex. 25. 22, &c.
PASSED OVER,] as in 18. 12; 38. 4; 42. 7; 73. 7, &c. Vulg. 'convened.'
TOGETHER,] as in 2. 2; 4. 8; 14. 3; 19. 9, &c.
5. SEEN] the position of Jerusalem, and known the power of her God.'
MARVELLED,] as in Ge. 43. 33; Job 26. 11.
TROUBLED,] as in 6. 2, 3, 10; 83. 7; 90. 7; 104. 29, &c.
HASTENED AWAY,] as in 104. 7; 1 Sa. 23. 26. Targ. 'fled.'
6. TREMBLING,] not 'fear;' as in 2. 11; Job 4. 14; Isa. 33. 14.

SEIZED,] as in 73. 23; 77. 4; 119. 53, &c.
THERE.] Sept. Vulg. connect 'there' with next clause.
PAIN,] as in Ex. 15. 14; Jer. 6. 24; 22. 23; 50. 43; Mic. 4. 9.
TRAVAILING WOMAN,] as in Ge. 16. 11.
7. EAST WIND,] as in 78. 26; Ge. 41. 6, 23, 27, &c. Sept. Vulg. 'vehement wind.'
SHIVEREST,] as in 29. 5; 46. 9; 105. 33, &c.
SHIPS OF TARSHISH,] as in 1 K. 22. 18; 2 Ch. 9. 21; Isa. 2. 16; 23. 1, 14; 60. 9; Eze. 27. 25.
8. HEARD] reports of the glory of Zion, so we have
SEEN] their truthfulness and accuracy.
JEHOVAH OF HOSTS,] as in 24. 10; 33. 6, &c.
CITY OF OUR GOD,] as in v. 1.
ESTABLISH,] or 'prepare,' as in 7. 9, 10; 21. 12, &c. Sept. Vulg. 'found.'
SELAH.] Vulg. omits.
9. THOUGHT,] as in 50. 21; Nu. 33. 56; Jud. 20. 5, &c. Sept. Vulg. 'received, under-taken;' Targ. 'compared.'
KINDNESS,] as in 5. 7; 6. 4; 13. 5: 17. 7, &c.
TEMPLE,] as in 5. 7; 11. 4; 18. 6; 27. 4, &c.
10. NAME,] as in 5. 11; 7. 17; 8. 1; 9. 2, &c.
PRAISE,] as in 9. 14; 22. 3, 25; 33. 1; 34. 1.
ENDS OF THE EARTH,] or 'land;' as in 65. 5; Isa. 26. 15.
FILLED,] as in 10. 7; 26. 10; 33. 5; 38. 7, &c.
RIGHT HAND,] as in 16. 8, 11; 17. 7; 18. 35.
11. REJOICE,] as in 5. 11; 9. 2; 14. 7; 21. 1.
MOUNT ZION,] as in v. 2.
DAUGHTERS OF JUDAH,] as in 97. 8; La. 1. 15; 2. 1.
JOYFUL,] as in 9. 14; 13. 4, 5; 14. 7; 16. 9.
JUDGMENTS,] as in 10. 5; 36. 6; 72. 1; 97. 8, &c. Sept. Vulg. add, 'O Lord.'
12. COMPASS,] not 'walk about;' as in Jos. 6. 7; 1 Sa. 22. 17; 2 K. 9. 18, 19, &c.
ZION,] as in v. 2, 11.
GO ROUND,] as in 17. 9; 22. 16; 88. 17, &c.
COUNT,] not 'tell;' as in Ge. 15. 5; 1 Ch. 21. 2.
TOWERS,] as in 61. 3; Ge. 11. 4, 5; 35. 21, &c.
13. SET YOUR HEART,] not 'mark well;' as in 62. 10; Ex. 7. 23; 1 Sa. 4. 20; 2 Sa. 13. 20; Prov. 22. 17; 24. 32; 27. 23.
BULWARK,] as in 10. 10; 122. 7, &c.
CONSIDER.] Original word not found again. Sept. Vulg. 'distribute.'
HIGH PLACES,] not 'palaces;' as in v. 3.
RECOUNT,] not 'tell;' as in 9. 1, 14, &c.
LATER GENERATION,] as in 78. 4, 6; 102. 18; 109. 13.
14. GOD,] as in v. 3, 9, 10. Sept. omits.
OUR GOD,] as in v. 1, 8.
FOR EVER,] or 'age-during and onwards;' as in 9. 5; 10. 16; 21. 4; 45. 6, 17, &c.
LEAD,] as in 78. 26; 80. 1, &c. Sept. 'feed.'
OVER DEATH,] not 'unto death.' Sept. Vulg. 'to the ages.'

XLIX. OVERSEER,] as in Ps. 4. 5. 6. 8. 9. 11. &c.
BY SONS OF KORAH,] not 'for' them, as in C.V.
PSALM,] as in Ps. 3. 4. 5. 6. 8. 9. 12. 13. &c.
1. HEAR,] as in 4. 1; 17. 1, 6; 27. 7; 28. 2.
PEOPLES,] not 'people;' as in 7. 8; 9. 12, &c. Sept. Vulg. 'nations.'
GIVE EAR,] as in 5. 1; 17. 1; 39. 12; 49. 1, &c.

WORLD,] or 'age;' as in 17. 14; 39. 5; 89. 47; Job 11. 17.
2. LOW,] lit. 'sons of Adam;' as in 8. 4; 11. 4, &c. Sept. Vulg. 'earth-born.'
HIGH,] lit. 'sons of a man;' as in 4. 2, &c.
RICH,] as in 45. 12; Ex. 30. 15; Ruth 3. 10.
NEEDY,] not 'poor;' as in 9. 18; 12. 5, &c.
3. WISE THINGS,] or 'wisdoms;' as in Prov. 1. 20; 9. 1; 24. 7.
MEDITATION.] Sept. 'care.'
HEART,] as in 4. 7; 9. 1; 13. 5; 16. 9, &c.
UNDERSTANDING,] as in 78. 72; 136. 5; 147. 5, &c. Vulg. 'prudence.'
4. INCLINE,] as in 17. 6; 31. 2; 45. 10, &c.
SIMILE,] as in 44. 14; 69. 11; 78. 2; Nu. 23. 7.
OPEN,] as in 38. 13; 39. 9; 51. 15; 78. 2, &c.
HARP,] as in 33. 2; 43. 4; 49. 4; 57. 8, &c. Sept. Vulg. 'psaltery.'
RIDDLE,] not 'dark saying;' as in 78. 2, &c. Sept. 'problem;' Vulg. 'proposition.'
5. FEAR,] as in v. 16.
DAYS OF EVIL,] as in 27. 5; 37. 19; 41. 1, &c.
INIQUITY,] as in 18. 23; 25. 11; 31. 10, &c.
SUPPLANTERS,] or 'heels;' as in 41. 9; 56. 6; 77. 19; 89. 51, &c.
COMPASS,] as in 17. 11; 18. 6; 22. 12, 16, &c.
6. TRUSTING,] as in 21. 7; 27. 3; 32. 10, &c
WEALTH,] or 'strength;' as in v. 10; 18. 32 &c. Sept. Vulg. 'strength.'
ABUNDANCE,] as in 5. 7, 10; 33. 16, 17, &c
RICHES,] as in 57. 7; 112. 3; Ge. 31. 16, &c
FOOLISH,] or 'boast themselves;' as in 34. 2; 52. 1; 63. 11; 64. 10; 97. 7; 105. 3; 106. 5, &c.
7. BROTHER,] as in 22. 22; 35. 14; 50. 20, &c.
AT ALL.] Sept. Vulg. 'doth he ransom a man?'
RANSOM,] as in v. 15; 25. 22; 26. 11; 31. 5.
ATONEMENT,] not 'ransom;' as in Ex. 21. 30; 30. 12, &c.
8. PRECIOUS,] as in 72. 14; 139. 17; 1 Sa. 18. 30, &c. Sept. 'and the price of the re-demption of his soul.'
REDEMPTION,] as in Ex. 21. 30.
SOUL,] as in v. 15, 18.
CEASED,] as in 36. 3; Ge. 11. 8; 18. 11; 41. 49, &c. Sept. Vulg. 'and he labours for ever.'
9. FOR EVER,] for a hidden indefinite period.
PIT,] not 'corruption;' as in 7. 15; 9. 15, &c.
10. WISE MEN,] as in 107. 43; Ge. 41. 8, &q
FOOLISH,] as in 92. 6; 94. 8; Prov. 1. 22, &c.
BRUTISH,] as in 73. 22; 92. 6; Prov. 12. 1; 30. 2.
PERISH,] as in 1. 6; 2. 12; 9. 3, 18; 37. 20.
LEFT,] as in 9. 10; 22. 1; 27. 10; 38. 10, &c.
WEALTH,] as in v. 6.
11. HEART,] as in 5. 9; 36. 1; 39. 3; 46. 5, &c. Sept. Vulg. 'graves are their house.'
HOUSES,] as in v. 16.
TABERNACLES,] not 'dwelling places;' as in 26. 8; 43. 3, &c.
GENERATIONS,] as in 10. 6; 33. 11; 45. 17, &c.
NAMES,] as in Ge. 4. 17; Jos. 19. 47, &c.
LANDS,] as in 83. 10; 104. 30; 105. 35, &c.
12. MAN,] as in v. 20; 8. 4; 11. 4; 12. 1, &c.
HONOUR,] as in v. 20; 8. 5; 4. 2; 20; 6. 3, &c.
REMAIN,] lit. 'lodge;' as in 25. 13; 30. 5, &c. Sept. Vulg. 'understand;' with which compare v. 20.
BEEN LIKE,] as in v. 20; 28. 1; 143. 7; Isa 14. 10.

BEASTS,] as in v. 20; 8. 7; 36. 6; 50. 10, &c.
Sept. Vulg. adds 'the irrational.'
CUT OFF,] not 'perish;' as in v. 20; Isa. 6.
5, &c.   Sept. Vulg. 'made like.'
13. WAY,] as in 1. 1, 6; 2. 12; 5. 8; 10. 5, &c.
FOLLY,] as in Ecc. 7. 25.   Sept. Vulg.
'stumbling-block.'
POSTERITY,] *lit.* those 'after' them.   Sept.
'and with these in their mouth are pleased.'
SAYINGS,] *lit.* 'mouth.'
PLEASED,] as in 50. 18; 51. 16; 62. 4, &c.
SELAH.] Vulg. omits.
14. SHEEP,] *or* 'a flock;' as in 44. 11, 22, &c.
SHEOL,] not 'the grave;' as in v. 15; 6. 5.
SET THEMSELVES,] as in 73. 9.
DEATH,] as in v. 17; 6. 5; 7. 13; 9. 13, &c.
AFFLICT,] not 'feed upon;' as in Jer. 2.
16, &c.
UPRIGHT,] as in 7. 10; 11. 2, 7; 19. 8; 25. 8.
RULE,] as in 72. 8; 110. 2, &c.
MORNING,] as in 5. 3; 30. 5; 46. 5; 49. 14, &c.
FORM,] not 'beauty;' as in Isa. 45. 16. Sept.
Vulg. 'help grows old in Hades, from their
glory being expelled.'
CONSUMPTION,] as in 1 Ch. 17. 9.
DWELLING,] as in 1 K. 8. 13; 2 Ch. 6. 2; Isa.
63. 15; Hab. 3. 11.
15. ONLY,] not 'but;' as in 37. 8, &c.
RANSOM,] not 'redeem;' as in v. 7.
HAND OF SHEOL,] as in 89. 48.
RECEIVE,] as in 6. 9; 73. 24; 75. 2, &c.
16. FEAR,] as in v. 5.
MAKETH WEALTH,] not 'is made rich;' as
in 65. 9, &c.
HONOUR,] *lit.* 'weightiness.'
ABUNDANT,] as in 16. 4; 107. 38; 139. 18, &c.
17. DEATH,] as in v. 14; 6. 5; 7. 13; 9. 13, &c.
RECEIVETH,] not 'carryeth away;' as in
v. 15.
GOETH NOT DOWN,] as in 7. 16; 18. 9; 55. 15.
18. SOUL,] as in v. 8, 15.
LIFE,] as in 7. 5; 16. 11; 17. 14; 18. 46, &c.
BLESSETH,] as in 5. 12; 16. 7; 26. 12; 29. 11.
PRAISE,] as in 6. 5; 7. 17; 9. 1; 18. 49, &c.
DOST WELL,] as in 36. 3; Ge. 4. 7; 12. 16, &c.
19. COMETH,] as in 45. 15; 42. 2; 63. 9, &c.
GENERATION,] as in v. 11; 10. 6; 12. 7, &c.
LIGHT,] as in 4. 6; 27. 1; 36. 9; 37. 6, &c.
20. MAN IN HONOUR,] as in v. 12.
UNDERSTANDETH,] Compare v. 12 above.
BEASTS .. CUT OFF,] as in v. 12.

L. ASAPH,] *i* e. 'gatherer;' as in Ps. 73—
83; 2 K. 18. 18, &c.
PSALM.] Sept. adds 'to the chief.'
1. GOD,] *lit.* ' mighty one.'
OF GODS,] those regarded as such by man.
JEHOVAH,] the God of the Hebrews.
SPOKEN,] as in 60. 6; 62. 10; 89. 19; 108. 7.
CALLETH,] as in v. 4; 105. 16; 147. 4, &c.
EARTH,] *or* 'land.'
RISING OF THE SUN,] as in 113. 3; Nu. 2. 3.
GOING IN,] not 'going down;' as in 104.
19; 113. 3, &c.
2. ZION,] as in 2. 6; 9. 11, 14; 14. 7; 20. 2, &c.
PERFECTION,] as in Eze. 27. 24; 2 Ch. 4. 21.
BEAUTY.] Sept. Vulg. 'his beauty.'
SHONE,] as in De. 33. 2; Job 10. 3; 37. 15;
Ps. 80. 1; 94. 1; Job 3. 4; 10. 22.   Sept. Vulg.
God came manifestly, our God.'
3. SILENT,] as in 28. 1; 35. 22; 39. 12; 83. 1.

DEVOUR,] as in v. 13; 18. 8; 21. 9; 22. 26.
TEMPESTUOUS,] as in 58. 9.
4. HEAVENS,] as in v. 6; 2. 4; 8. 1 3, 8, &c.
EARTH,] as in v. 1.
JUDGE,] as in Ecc. 6. 13; Isa. 3. 13, &c.
Sept. 'judge thoroughly,' Vulg. 'discern.'
5. GATHER,] as in Nu. 11. 16; 21. 16; 1 Sa.
14. 19, &c.   Sept. Vulg. ' gather ye to him
his saints.'
SAINTS,] as in 4. 3; 12. 1; 16. 10; 18. 25, &c.
COVENANT,] as in Ex. 34. 10; De. 29. 12,
14, &c.   Sept. Vulg. 'his covenant.'
SACRIFICE,] as in v. 8; 4. 5; 27. 6; 40. 6, &c.
6. DECLARE,] as in 22. 31; 30. 9; 38. 18, &c.
JUDGE,] as in 2. 10; 7. 11; 9. 4; 58. 11, &c.
SELAH,] as in 3. 2, 4, 8; 4. 2, 4; 7. 5, &c.
7. HEAR,] as in 4. 1; 17. 1, 6; 27. 7; 28. 2, &c.
SPEAK,] as in 2. 5; 85. 8; 99. 7, &c.   Sept
adds 'to thee.'
MY PEOPLE,] as in 3. 8; 14. 7; 28. 9; 29. 11.
O ISRAEL,] as in 81. 8; 115. 9; De. 4. 1, &c.
TESTIFY,] as in 81. 8; Ge. 43. 3; Ex. 19. 21.
GOD,] the great object of worship, who
alone ought to be worshipped.
THY GOD,] whom they had vowed to serve.
8. SACRIFICE,] as in v. 5.
REPROVE,] as in v. 21; 6. 1; 38. 1; 94. 10, &c.
BURNT-OFFERINGS,] as in 20. 3; 40. 6, &c.
CONTINUALLY,] as in 16. 28; 24. 15; 34. 1, &c.
9. TAKE,] *or* 'receive;' as in 6. 9; 18. 16, &c.
BULLOCK,] as in 22. 12; 50. 9; 51. 19; 69. 31.
FOLD,] as in 78. 70; Hab. 3. 17. Sept. Vulg.
' flocks.'
HE-GOATS,] as in v. 13; 66. 15; Ge. 31. 10.
10. BEAST,] as in Ge. 1. 24, 25, &c.
FOREST,] as in 80. 13; 83. 14; 96. 12; 104. 20.
CATTLE,] as in 8. 7; 36. 6; 49. 12, 20, &c.
HILLS OF OXEN,] not a 'thousand hills,' as
in C. V.   Sept. Vulg. 'cattle on the hills, and
oxen.'
11. FOWL,] as in 78. 27; 79. 2; 104. 12, &c.
MOUNTAINS.] Sept. Vulg. 'heavens.'
WILD BEAST,] as in 80. 13; Isa. 66. 11.
FIELD,] as in 8. 7; 80. 13; 96. 12; 104. 11, &c.
12. HUNGRY,] as in 10; Ge. 41. 55, &c.
TELL,] *lit.* 'say' to thee.
WORLD,] as in 7. 9; 13. 4; 24. 1, &c.
FULNESS,] as in 24. 1; 89. 11; 96. 11; 98. 7.
13. EAT,] as in v. 3.   Vulg. 'masticate.'
FLESH,] as in 16. 9; 27. 2; 38. 3; 56. 4, &c.
BULLS,] *lit.* 'mighty ones;' as in 22. 12; 68.
30· 76. 5: 78. 25, &c.
DRINK,] as in 75. 8; 78. 44; 110. 7, &c.
BLOOD,] as in 9. 12; 16. 4; 26. 9, &c
HE-GOATS,] not 'goats;' as in v. 9.
14. SACRIFICE,] as in 4. 5; Ex. 8. 25.
CONFESSION,] as in v. 23; 26. 7, &c.   Sept.
Vulg. 'a sacrifice of praise.'
COMPLETE,] not 'pay;' as in 76. 11, &c.
Sept. Vulg. 'render.'
MOST HIGH,] as in 7. 17; 9. 2; 18. 13; 21. 7
VOWS,] as in 22. 25; 56. 12; 61. 5, 8; 65. 1.
15. CALL,] as in 105. 1; Ex. 2. 20; De. 31. 14.
DAY OF ADVERSITY,] as in 20. 1; 77. 2; 86.
7, &c.   Sept. 'day of thy tribulation.'
DELIVER,] as in 7. 14; 18. 19; 34. 7; 81. 7.
HONOUREST,] as in v. 23; 15. 4; 86. 9, 12;
91. 15, &c.   Sept. adds 'Selah.'
16. WICKED,] as in 1. 1, 4, 5, 6; 3. 7; 7. 9. &c.
RECOUNT,] not 'declare;' as in 26. 7; 40
5; 73. 38, &c.

STATUTES,] as in 2. 7; 81. 4; 94. 20; 99. 7, &c. Sept. Vulg. 'righteous acts.'
LIFTEST UP,] not 'take;' as in 16. 4; 24. 5.
COVENANT,] as in v. 5.
MOUTH,] as in v. 19; 5. 9; 8. 2; 10. 7, &c.
17. HATED,] as in 5. 5; 11. 5; 25. 9; 26. 5.
INSTRUCTION,] as in De. 11. 2; Isa. 5. 17; 12. 18; 20. 3, &c.
CAST,] as in 2. 3; 51. 11; 60. 8; 71. 9, &c.
18. THIEF,] as in Ex. 22. 1, 7, 8; De. 24. 7.
PLEASED,] not 'consentest;' as in 49. 13, &c. Sept. Vulg. 'runnest.'
ADULTERERS,] as in Prov. 30. 20, &c.
PORTION,] as in 16. 5; 17. 14; 73. 26; 119. 57, &c. Sept. Vulg. adds, 'thou hast placed.'
19. MOUTH,] as in v. 17.
SENT FORTH,] not 'givest;' as in 55. 20; 78. 25, &c. Sept. Vulg. 'has abounded.'
EVIL,] as in 5. 4; 7. 4, 9; 10. 6, 15; 15. 3, &c
JOINETH,] not 'frameth;' as in 106. 28; Nu. 25. 3, 5; 2 Sa. 20. 8.
DECEIT,] as in 5. 6; 10. 7; 17. 1; 24. 4, &c.
20. SITTEST,] as in 9. 7; 10. 8; 26. 5, &c.
BROTHER,] as in 22. 22; 35. 14; 49. 7, &c
SON OF THY MOTHER,] as in 69. 8, &c.
GIVEST SLANDER.] A phrase not found again. Sept. Vulg. 'a stumbling block.'
21. KEPT SILENT,] as in 32. 3; Ge. 24. 21, &c.
THOUGHT,] as in 48. 9; Nu. 33. 56, &c.
Sept. Vulg. add 'unjustly.'
REPROVE,] as in v. 8.
SET IN ARRAY,] as in 5. 3; 23. 5; 89. 6, &c.
22. UNDERSTAND,] as in 5. 1; 94. 8.
PRAY YOU,] as in Ge. 12. 11, 13; 18. 4, &c.
FORGETTING,] as in Job 8. 13, &c.
TEAR,] as in 7. 2; 17. 12; 22. 13, &c.
DELIVER,] as in 7. 2; 35. 10; 71. 11, &c.
23. SACRIFICING,] as in Ex. 13. 15; 22. 20; Lev. 17. 5, &c. Sept. Vulg. 'a sacrifice of praise.'
CONFESSION,] as in v. 14.
HONOURETH,] not 'glorifieth;' as in v. 15.
MAKETH A WAY,] not 'ordereth his conversation.' Sept. Vulg. 'and there a way.'
TO LOOK,] as in 4. 6; 59. 10; 60. 3; 91. 16.
SALVATION,] as in 12. 5; 18. 2, 35; 18. 46.

LI. OVERSEER,] as in Ps. 4. 5. 6. 8. 9. &c
NATHAN,] as in 2 Sa. 5. 14; 7. 2, 3, 4, &c.
BATH-SHEBA,] as in 2 Sa. 11. 3; 12. 24, &c
1. FAVOUR,] not 'have mercy;' as in 4. 1.
KINDNESS,] as in 5. 7; 6. 1; 13. 5; 17. 7, &c. Sept. Vulg. 'greatness of thy kindness.'
ABUNDANCE,] not 'multitude;' as in 5. 7, 10, &c.
MERCIES,] as in 25. 6; 40. 11; 69. 16, &c.
BLOT OUT,] as in v. 9; 9. 5; 69. 28, 109. 13.
TRANSGRESSIONS,] as in v. 3; 5. 10; 9. 13.
2. WASH,] as in v. 7; Ge. 49. 11; Ex. 19. 10.
INIQUITY,] as in v. 5, 9; 18. 23; 25. 11, &c.
SIN,] as in v. 3; 25. 7, 18; 32. 5; 38. 3, &c.
CLEANSE,] as in Lev. 13. 6, 13, 17, 23, &c.
3. TRANSGRESSIONS,] as in v. 1.
KNOW,] not 'acknowledge;' as in 9. 20, &c.
CONTINUALLY,] as in 16. 8; 25. 15; 34. 1.
4. ONLY,] lit. 'alone—thyself.'
SINNED,] as in 41. 14; 78. 32; 106. 6, &c.
THE EVIL THING,] not 'this evil;'as in Nu. 32. 13, &c.
RIGHTEOUS,] as in 143. 2; Ge. 38. 36, &c

SO THAT,] not 'in order that;' as in Ge. 18. 19, &c.
IN THY WORDS.] So Sept. Vulg. &c.
PURE,] not 'clear;' as in Job 15. 14; 25. 4; Mic. 6. 11. Sept. Vulg. 'conquer.'
JUDGING,] as in 10. 18; 51. 4; 96. 13, &c.
5. BROUGHT FORTH,] not 'shapen;' as in Job 15. 7; Prov. 8. 24, 25, &c.
SIN,] as in v. 9; 103. 10; Ge. 41. 9, &c.
CONCEIVE,] as in Ge. 30. 38, 39, 41; 31. 10.
6. TRUTH,] as in 15. 2; 19. 9; 25. 5, 10, &c.
DESIRED,] as in 18. 19; 22. 8; 40. 6, 8, &c.
INWARD PARTS,] as in Job 38. 36. Sept. Vulg. 'the uncertain and hidden things of thy wisdom.'
HIDDEN PART,] as Eze. 28. 3; Da. 12. 9.
WISDOM,] as in 37. 30; 90. 12; 104. 24, &c.
TO KNOW,] as in 16. 11; 32. 5; 89. 1, &c.
7. CLEANSEST,] as in Ge. 31. 39; Ex. 29. 36; Lev. 8. 15, &c. Sept. Vulg. 'sprinklest.'
HYSSOP,] as in Ex. 12. 22; Lev. 14. 4, &c.
CLEAN,] as in Lev. 11. 32; 12. 7, 8; 13. 6, &c.
SNOW,] as in 147. 16; 148. 6; Ex. 4. 6, &c.
WHITER,] as in Isa. 1. 18; Da. 11. 35 Joel 1. 7.
8. TO HEAR,] as in 26. 7; 66. 8; 76. 8, &c.
JOY,] as in v. 12; 45. 7; 105. 43; 119. 111.
GLADNESS,] as in 4. 7; 16. 11; 21. 6; 30. 11.
MAKEST JOYFUL,] as in 9. 14; 13. 4, 5, &c.
BONES,] as in 6. 2; 32. 14, 17; 31, 10, &c.
BRUISED,] not 'broken;' as in v. 17; 10. 10; 44. 19, &c. Sept. Vulg. 'humbled.'
9. HIDE,] as in 10. 11; 13. 1; 17. 8; 22. 24.
BLOT OUT,] as in v. 1.
10. CLEAN,] as in 12. 6; 19. 9; Ge. 7. 2, &c.
PREPARE,] not 'create;' as in Eze. 21. 19.
RIGHT,] as in v. 9; 33. 17; 57. 7; 78. 38, &c.
RENEW,] as in 104. 30; La. 5. 21, &c.
WITHIN ME.] Sept. Vulg. 'in my bowels.'
11. CAST NOT FORTH,] as in 2. 3; 50. 17, &c.
PRESENCE,] lit. 'face.'
HOLY SPIRIT,] as in Isa. 63. 11, 12, &c.
12. RESTORE,] as in 23. 4; 35. 17; 79. 12, &c.
JOY,] as in v. 8.
SALVATION,] as in 12. 5; 18. 2, 35, 46; 20. 6.
WILLING SPIRIT,] as in 47. 9; 83. 11; 107. 40. &c. Sept. Vulg. 'guiding spirit.'
SUSTAIN,] as in 3. 5; 37. 17, 24; 54. 4, &c.
13. TEACH,] as in 25. 9; 34. 11; 94. 12, &c.
TRANSGRESSORS,] as in 37. 38; Isa. 1. 28.
WAYS,] as in 5. 8; 18. 21, 30; 25. 4, 9, &c.
SINNERS,] as in 1. 1, 5; 25. 8; 26. 9, &c.
RETURN,] not 'be converted;' as in 6. 10.
14. DELIVER,] as in 7. 1; 22. 20; 25. 20, &c.
BLOOD,] as in 5. 6; 9. 12; 16. 4; 26. 9, &c.
SALVATION,] as in 33. 17; 37. 38; 88. 22, &c.
SINGETH,] as in 5. 11; 20. 5; 59. 16; 63. 7.
15. LORD,] or 'my lord.'
OPEN,] as in 38. 13; 39. 9; 49. 4; 78. 2, &c.
DECLARETH,] not 'shew forth;' as in 22. 31; 30. 9; 38. 18, &c.
PRAISE,] as in 9. 14; 22. 3, 25; 33. 1; 34. 1.
16. DESIREST,] as in v. 19; 37. 23; 68. 30.
NOT.] Sept. Vulg. 'if.'
SACRIFICE,] as in v. 17, 19; 4. 5; 27. 6, &c.
BURNT-OFFERING,] as in v. 19; 20. 3, &c.
ACCEPTEST,] not 'delightest;' as in 49 13; 50. 18, &c.
17. SACRIFICES,] as in v. 16, 19.
BROKEN,] as in 34. 18; Isa. 61 1, &c.
BRUISED,] not 'contrite;' as in v. 8.

DESPISE,] as in 22. 24; 69. 33; 73. 20, &c.
18. DO GOOD,] as in 33. 3; 36. 3; 49. 18, &c.
Sept. Vulg. add, 'O Lord.'
GOOD PLEASURE,] as in 5. 12; 19. 14, &c.
ZION,] as in 2. 6; 9. 11, 14; 14. 7; 20. 2, &c.
BUILD,] as in 28. 5; 69. 35; 78. 69; 127. 1.
WALLS,] as in 55. 10, &c.
JERUSALEM,] as in 68. 29; 79. 1, 3, &c.
19. DESIREST,] not 'be pleased;' as in v. 16.
SACRIFICES OF RIGHTEOUSNESS,] as in 4.
5; De. 33. 19.
BURNT-ONFERING,] as in v. 16.
WHOLE BURNT-OFFERING,] as in Lev. 6.
22. 23; De. 33. 10; 1 Sa. 7. 9.
BULLOCKS,] as in 22. 12; 50. 9; 69. 31, &c.
ALTAR,] as in 26. 6; 43. 4; 51. 19; 84. 3, &c.

LII. OVERSEER,] as in Ps. 4. 5. 6. 8. 9, &c.
INSTRUCTION,] as in 14. 2; 32. 1; 41. 1, &c.
DOEG,] as in 1 Sa. 21. 7; 22. 9, 18, 22.
DECLARETH,] as in 22. 32; 30. 9; 38. 18, &c.
SAUL,] the first king of Israel.
AHIMELECH,] as in 1 Sa. 21. 1, 2, 8; 22.
9—20; 23. 6; 26. 6; 30. 7, &c. Sept. 'Abime-leoh.'
1. WHAT?] not 'why?' as in C.V.
BOASTEST,] as in 34. 2; 49. 6; 63. 11, &c.
EVIL,] as in v. 3; 5. 4; 7. 4, 9; 10. 6, &c.
MIGHTY ONE,] as in 19. 5; 24. 8; 33. 16; 45.
3, &c. Sept. Vulg. 'who art powerful in
iniquity? All the day thy tongue deviseth
injustice.'
KINDNESS,] as in v. 8; 5. 7; 6. 4; 13. 5, &c.
2. MISCHIEFS,] as in v. 7; 5. 9; 38. 12, &c.
DEVISE,] as in 32. 2; 35. 20; 36. 4; 40. 17.
SHARP,] as in 7. 2; Ge. 4. 22; 1 Sa. 13.
20; Job 16. 9.
RAZOR,] as in Nu. 6. 5; 8. 7; 1 Sa. 17. 52.
DECEIT,] as in 32. 2; 78. 57; 101. 7, &c.
3. LOVED,] as in v. 4; 11. 7; 26. 8; 45. 7, &c.
LYING,] as in 7. 14; 27. 12; 31. 18; 33. 17,
&c. Sept. Vulg. 'injustice.'
SELAH.] Vulg. omits.
4. ALL-DEVOURING.] Sept. 'all words of
throwing into the sea.'
DECEITFUL,] as in 5. 6; 10. 7; 17. 1; 24. 4.
5. BREAK DOWN,] not 'destroy;' as in 58.
6; Ex. 34. 13, &c.
TAKETH,] as in Prov. 6. 27; 25. 22, &c.
PULLETH,] as in Prov. 2. 22; 15. 25.
TENT.] Vulg. 'thy tent.'
UPROOTED,] as in Job 31. 8, 12; Sept. Vulg.
'and thy root.'
LAND OF THE LIVING,] as in 27. 13; 116. 9.
6. SEE,] as in 37. 34; 40. 3; 91. 8, &c.
FEAR,] as in 3. 6; 23. 4; 27. 1, 3; 33. 8, &c.
LAUGH,] as in 2. 4; 37. 13; 59. 8; Job 5. 22,
&c. Sept. Vulg. add 'and say.'
7. STRONG PLACE,] not 'strength;' as in 27.
1; 28. 8; 31. 2, 4, &c. Sept. Vulg. 'help.'
TRUSTETH,] as in 9. 10; 40. 3; 44. 6, &c.
ABUNDANCE,] as in 5. 7, 10; 33. 16, 17, &c.
RICHES,] as in 49. 6; 112. 3; Ge. 31. 16, &c.
STRONG,] as in 19; 89. 13; Jud. 3. 10, &c.
MISCHIEFS,] not 'wickedness;' as in v. 5.
Sept. Vulg. 'vanities.'
8. GREEN,] as in 37. 35; 92. 10, 14; De. 12.
2, &c. Sept. Vulg. 'fruitful.'
HOUSE OF GOD,] as in 23. 6; 27. 4; 42. 5, &c.
TRUSTED,] as in v. 7.
KINDNESS,] not 'mercy;' as in v. 1

FOR EVER,] as in 9. 5; 10. 16; 21. 4; 45. 6.
9. THANK,] not 'praise;' as in 6. 5; 7. 17.
WAIT,] as in 25. 5, 20; 39. 7; 40. 1; 56. 6, &c.
NAME,] as in 5. 11; 7. 17; 8. 1; 9. 2, 5, &c.
SAINTS,] as in 4. 3; 12. 1; 16. 10; 18. 25, &c.

LIII. OVERSEER,] as in Ps. 4. 5. 6. 8. &c.
DISEASE,] as in 88. 1; Sept. Vulg. 'Mae-leth.'
INSTRUCTION,] as in 14. 2; 32. 1; 41. 1; 42.
1; 44. 1, &c.
1. FOOL,] as in 14. 1; 39. 8; 74. 18, 22, &c.
THERE IS NOT A GOD,] that is, he does not
exist.
DONE CORRUPTLY,] not 'are corrupt;' as
in 14. 1, &c.
DONE ABOMINABLY,] as in 14. 1; 1 K. 21.
26; Eze. 16. 52.
INIQUITY,] as in 7. 3; 82. 2; Lev. 19. 15, &c.
DOING GOOD,] as in 14. 1, 3, &c.
2. LOOKED FORTH,] not 'looked down;' as
in 14. 2; 102. 19, &c.
SONS OF MEN,] as in 11. 4; 12. 1; 14. 2, &c.
UNDERSTANDING ONE,] as in 14. 2, &c.
SEEKING GOD,] as in 14. 2; 69. 32, &c.
3. WENT BACK,] as in 80. 18; Prov. 14. 14,
&c. Sept. Vulg. 'gone aside.'
TOGETHER,] as in 2. 2; 4. 8; 14. 3; 19. 9, &c.
FILTHY,] as in 14. 3; Job 15. 16. Sept.
Vulg. 'useless.'
ONE,] as in 14. 3; 27. 4; 34. 20; 62. 11, &c.
4. WORKERS OF INIQUITY,] as in 5. 5; 6. 8;
14. 4, &c. Sept. Vulg. prefix 'all.'
EATING,] as in 14. 4; 41. 9; 106. 20; 127. 2.
PEOPLE,] as in 14. 4; 59. 11; 78. 1, &c.
EATEN BREAD,] that is, partaken of their
usual food.
CALLED,] or 'invited.'
5. THERE,] at that place and time.
FEARED,] as in 14. 5; 78. 53; 119. 161, &c.
FEAR,] as in 14. 5; 31. 11; 36. 1; 64. 1, &c.
NO FEAR,] that is, no just cause of fear.
SCATTERED,] as in 80. 10; 112. 9; 147. 16.
BONES,] as in 6. 2; 22. 14, 17; 31. 10, &c.
ENCAMPING,] as in 34. 7; Ex. 14. 9; 18. 5,
&c. Sept. Vulg. 'men-pleasers.'
PUT TO SHAME,] as in 14. 6; 44. 7; 119. 31,
116, &c. Sept. Vulg. 'they have been put
to shame.'
DESPISED,] as in 36. 4; 78. 59, 67; 89. 38.
6. WHO DOTH GIVE,] not 'oh that;' as in
14. 7, &c.
ZION,] the special dwelling of God.
SALVATION,] or 'safety,' temporal and
spiritual.
TURNETH BACK,] not 'bringeth back;' as
in 9. 3, &c.
CAPTIVITY,] as in 14. 7; 85. 1; 126. 4; &c.
JACOB,] the first name of the third pat-riarch.
REJOICE,] as in 9. 14; 13. 4, 5; 14. 7; 16. 9.
ISRAEL,] the new name of Jacob.
IS GLAD,] as in 5. 11; 9. 2; 14. 7; 21. 1, &c.

LIV. OVERSEER,] as in Ps. 4. 5. 6. 8. 9. &c.
STRINGED INSTRUMENTS,] as in Ps. 4. 6.
55. 61. 67. &c. Sept. Vulg. 'hymns of un-
derstanding by David.'
INSTRUCTION,] as in 14. 2; 32. 1; 41 1, &c.
ZIPHIM,] as in 1 Sa. 23. 19; 26. 1.
SAUL,] the enemy of David.

HIDING HIMSELF,] as in Isa. 29. 14; 45. 15; 1 Sa. 23. 19; 26. 1.

1. GOD,] as in v. 2, 3, 4.
NAME,] as in v. 6; 5. 11; 7. 17; 8. 1; 9. 2.
SAVE,] as in 3. 7; 6. 4; 7. 1; 12. 1; 20. 9, &c.
MIGHT,] as in 20. 6; 21. 13; 65. 6; 66. 7, &c.
JUDGE,] as in 7. 8; 9. 8; 72. 2; 96. 10, &c.
2. PRAYER,] as in 4. 1; 6. 9; 17. 1; 35. 13.
GIVE EAR,] as in 5. 1; 17. 1; 39. 12; 49. 1.
SAYINGS OF MY MOUTH,] as in 19. 14, &c.
3. STRANGERS,] as in 44. 20; 81. 9; 109. 11.
RISE UP,] as in 20. 8; 27. 12; 86. 14, &c.
TERRIBLE ONES,] not 'oppressors;' as in 37. 35; 86. 14, &c.
SOUGHT,] as in 35. 4; 40. 14; 63. 9; 70. 2, &c.
SET,] as in 19. 4; 40. 4; 46. 8; 50. 23, &c.
4. HELPER,] as in 10. 14; 22. 11; 30. 10, &c.
GOD,] as in v. 1.
THE LORD,] or 'my lord;' as in 2. 4; 16. 2.
WITH THOSE SUPPORTING.] Sept. Vulg. 'is the supporter of my soul.'
5. TURN BACK,] not 'reward;' as in 6. 10; 7. 12, 16; 9. 17, &c.
TRUTH,] as in 15. 2; 19. 9; 25. 5, 10, &c.
CUT THEM OFF,] as in 18. 40; 69. 4; 73. 27.
6. FREE-WILL OFFERING,] not 'freely;' as in 68. 9; 110. 3, &c.
SACRIFICE,] as in 27. 6; 106. 37; 107. 22, &c.
THANK,] not 'praise;' as in 6. 5; 7. 17, &c.
NAME,] as in v. 1.
GOOD,] to do so, or good in itself.
7. ADVERSITY,] as in 9. 9; 10. 1; 20. 1, &c.
DELIVERED,] as in 18. 1; 34. 4, 17; 56. 13.
LOOKED,] in calm disdain; as in 35. 21.

LV. OVERSEER,] as in Ps. 4. 5. 6. 8. 9. &c.
STRINGED INSTRUMENTS,] as in Ps. 4. 6. 55. 61. &c. Sept. Vulg. 'hymns.'
INSTRUCTION,] as in 14. 2; 32. 1; 41. 1, &c.
1. GIVE EAR,] as in 5. 1; 17. 1; 39. 12, &c.
GOD,] as in v. 14, 16, 18, 23, &c.
PRAYER,] as in 4. 1; 6. 9; 17. 1; 35. 13, &c.
HIDE THYSELF,] as in De. 22. 1, 3, 4; Job 6. 16; Isa. 58. 7.
SUPPLICATION,] as in 6. 9; 119. 170, &c.
2. ATTEND,] as in 5. 2; 17. 1; 61. 1; 86. 6.
ANSWER,] not 'hear;' as in 4. 1; 13. 3, &c.
MOURN.] Original word not found again.
MEDITATION,] not 'complaint;' as in 64. 1.
MAKE A NOISE,] as in Mic. 2. 12. Sept. Vulg. 'am troubled.'
3. VOICE,] or 'sound.'
OPPRESSION.] Original word not found again.
CAUSE TO MOVE,] not 'cast;' as in 140. 10.
SORROW,] not 'iniquity;' as in v. 10; 90. 10, &c. Sept. Vulg. 'lawlessness.'
ANGER,] as in 2. 5, 12; 6. 1; 7. 6; 10. 4, &c.
HATE,] as in Ge. 27. 41; 49. 23; 50. 15; Job 16. 9; 30. 21. Sept. Vulg. 'are troubling me.'
4. HEART,] as in v. 21; 4. 7; 7. 10; 9. 1, &c.
PAINED,] as in 10. 5; 29. 8; 77. 16; 97. 4, &c.
TERRORS OF DEATH,] as in 88. 15; Ge. 15. 12; Ex. 15. 12, &c.
5. FEAR,] as in 2. 11; 5. 7; 19. 9; 34. 11, &c.
TREMBLING,] as in Ex. 15. 15.
HORROR,] as in Job 21. 6; Isa. 21. 4; Eze. 7. 18. Sept. Vulg. 'darkness.'
6. WHO DOTH GIVE,] not 'oh that;' as in 14. 7, &c.

PINION,] not 'wings;' as in Isa. 40. 31; Eze. 17. 8.
DOVE,] as in 56. 1; 68. 13; Ge. 8. 8, 9, &c.
FLY AWAY,] as in 18. 10; 90. 10; 91. 5, &c.
REST,] as in 15. 1; 16. 9; 37. 29; 65. 4, &c.
7. MOVE,] not 'wander;' as in 31. 11; 68. 12, &c. Sept. Vulg. 'flee.'
LODGE,] as in 25. 13; 30. 5; 49. 12; 59. 15.
A WILDERNESS,] as in 29. 8; 63. 1; 65. 12; 75. 6, &c. Vulg. 'solitude.'
8. HASTEN,] as in Jud. 20. 37; Isa. 5. 19; 28. 16; 60. 22. Sept. Vulg. 'I expect him who is saving me from feebleness of soul, and tempest.'
RUSHING.] Original word not found again.
WHIRLWIND,] as in 83. 15; Jer. 23. 19, &c.
9. SWALLOW UP,] not 'destroy;' as in 21. 9.
DIVIDE,] as in Job 38. 25.
TONGUE,] as in 5. 9; 10. 7; 12. 3, 4; 15. 3.
VIOLENCE,] as in 7. 16; 11. 5; 18. 48, &c.
STRIFE,] as in 18. 43; 31. 20; 35. 23; 43. 1.
CITY,] as in 9. 6; 31. 21; 46. 4; 48. 1, 8, &c.
10. BY DAY,] as in 1. 2; 13. 2; 22. 2; 32. 4.
BY NIGHT,] as in 1. 2; 6. 6; 16. 7; 17. 3, &c.
GO ROUND,] as in 7. 7; 26. 6; 32. 7, 10, &c.
WALLS,] as in 51. 18; Ex. 14. 22, 29, &c.
INIQUITY,] as in v. 3.
PERVERSENESS,] not 'sorrow;' as in 7. 14 16; 10. 7, 14, &c.
11. MISCHIEFS,] not 'wickedness;' as in 5 9; 38. 12, &c.
MIDST,] as in v. 4, 11, 15.
FRAUD,] as in 10. 7; 72. 14. Sept. Vulg. 'usury.'
DECEIT,] as in 5. 6; 10. 7; 17. 1; 24. 4, &c.
STREET,] lit. 'broad place.'
12. REPROACHETH,] as in 42. 10, 57. 3, &c.
BEAR,] lit. 'lift up.'
HATING,] as in 9. 13; 18. 17; 21. 8; 34. 21.
MAGNIFIED HIMSELF,] as in 38. 16; 41. 9.
AM HIDDEN,] as in 19. 6, 12; 38. 9; 89. 46.
13. MAN,] as in 9; 23; 8. 4; 9. 19, 20; 10. 18.
EQUAL,] as in Ex. 40. 4, 23; Lev. 5. 15, 18; 6. 6, &c. Sept. Vulg. 'one-souled.'
FAMILIAR FRIEND,] as in Prov. 2. 17, &c.
ACQUAINTANCE,] as in 33. 11; 88. 8, 18, &c.
14. SWEETEN,] as in Job. 20. 12, &c.
HOUSE OF GOD,] as in 23. 6; 27. 4; 52. 1, &c.
COMPANY,] as in 2. 1; 64. 2, &c. Sept. Vulg. 'concord.'
15. DESOLATIONS,] not 'let death seize.'
GO DOWN,] as in 7. 16; 18. 9; 49. 17, &c.
SHEOL,] not 'hell;' as in 6. 5; 9. 17; 16. 10
ALIVE,] or 'living;' not 'quick.'
EVILS,] as in 5. 4; 7. 4, 9; 10. 6, 15; 15. 3, &c.
DWELLINGS,] lit. 'sojournings;' as in 119. 54.
MIDST,] as in v. 4, 11.
16. CALL,] as in 3. 4; 18. 3, 6; 22. 2; 27. 7.
SAVETH,] as in 18. 27; 34. 18; 36. 6; 37. 40.
17. EVENING,] as in 30. 5; 59. 6, 14; 65. 8.
MORNING,] as in 5. 3; 30. 5; 46. 5; 49. 14.
NOON,] as in 37. 6; 91. 6; Ge. 43. 16, &c.
MEDITATE,] not 'pray;' as in 69. 12; 77. 3, 6, &c. Sept. Vulg. 'declare.'
MAKE A NOISE,] not 'cry aloud.' Sept. Vulg. 'announce.'
VOICE,] as in 3. 4; 5. 2, 3; 6. 8; 18. 6, &c.
18. RANSOMED,] not 'delivered;' as in 31. 5; 71. 23, &c.
IN PEACE,] as in 4. 8; 28. 3; 29. 11; 34. 14

NEAR,] not 'battle.' So Sept. Vulg. &c.
THE MULTITUDE,] not 'many,' as in C.V.
19. AFFLICT,] as in 89. 22; 94. 5; 119. 67, &c.
OF OLD,] as in 44. 1; 68. 33; 74. 2, 12; 77. 5,
11, &c. Sept. Vulg. 'who is from the ages.'
CHANGES,] as in Job 10. 17; 14. 14, &c.
FEARED NOT,] as in 76. 8; 112. 1; 119. 63.
20. SENT FORTH,] as in 144. 7; 125. 3, &c.
WELL-WISHER,] or 'peaceful one;' as in
49. 1, &c. Sept. Vulg. 'in retribution.'
POLLUTED,] not 'broken;' as in 74. 7;
89. 39.
COVENANT,] as in 25. 10, 14; 44. 17; 50. 5.
21. SWEETER,] as in De. 4. 19; 29. 26, &c.
BUTTER,] as in Ge. 18. 8; De. 32. 14; Jud.
5. 25; 2 Sa. 17. 29; Job 20. 17; Prov. 30. 33;
Isa. 7. 15, 22. Sept. Vulg. 'divided from
fury hath been his face.'
HIS MOUTH,] as in 10. 7; 18. 8; 33. 6; 36. 3.
HEART,] as in v. 4.
WAR,] as in 68. 30; 78. 9; 144. 1; 2 Sa. 17.
11, &c. Sept. Vulg. 'has drawn near.'
SOFTER,] as in 2 K. 22. 19; 2 Ch. 34. 27, &c.
OIL,] as in 23. 5; 45. 7; 89. 20; 92. 10, &c.
DRAWN,] *lit.* 'open ones.' Sept. Vulg.
'missiles.'
22. CAST,] as in Ge. 37. 22; Ex. 4. 3; 7. 9, &c.
GIVEN,] not 'burden;' as in C.V. Sept.
Vulg. 'care.'
SUSTAIN,] as in 112. 5; Ge. 45. 11; 47. 12;
50. 21, &c. Sept. Vulg. 'nourish.'
SUFFER,] *lit.* 'give.'
THE MOVING,] as in 38. 16; 46. 2; Isa. 24. 19.
23. GOD,] as in v. 1, 14, 16, 19.
BRING THEM DOWN,] as in 56. 7; 59. 11, &c.
PIT,] as in 69. 15; Ge. 14. 10; 16. 14; 21. 10.
DESTRUCTION,] as in 7. 15; 9. 15; 16. 10, &c.
MEN OF BLOOD,] as in 5. 6; 26. 9; 59. 2, &c.
DECEIT,] as in 5. 6; 10. 7; 17. 1; 24. 4, &c.
REACH NOT TO HALF,] as in Isa. 30. 28, &c.
TRUST,] as in 9. 10; 40. 3; 44. 6; 52. 7, &c.

LVI. OVERSEER,] as in Ps. 4. 5. 6. 8. 9. &c.
DUMB DOVE,] *lit.* 'dove of dumbness.'
Sept. Vulg. 'people who are far from the
saints.'
SECRET TREASURE,] as in Ps. 16. 57. 58. 60.
PHILISTINES,] as in Ge. 10. 4; 21. 32, 34;
26. 1, &c. Sept. 'aliens.'
GATH,] as in Jos. 11. 22; 19. 13; 1 Sa. 5. 8.
1. FAVOUR,] not 'be merciful;' as in 4. 1.
GOD,] as in v. 4, 7, 10, 12, 13.
SWALLOWED ME UP,] as in v. 2; 57. 3; 119.
131, &c. Sept. Vulg. 'trample.'
FIGHTING,] as in v. 2; 35. 1.
OPPRESSETH,] as in 106. 42; Ex. 3. 9, &c.
2. SWALLOWED UP,] as in v. 1.
MOST HIGH,] as in 7. 7; 10. 5; 18. 16; 68. 18,
&c. Sept. 'from the height of the day.'
3. AFRAID,] as in v. 4, 11; 3. 6; 23. 4, &c.
CONFIDENT,] as in 9. 10; 40. 3; 44. 6, &c.
4. PRAISE,] as in v. 10; 22. 22, 26; 35. 18, &c.
HIS WORD.] Sept. Vulg. 'my words.'
TRUSTED,] as in v. 11; 13. 5; 22. 4, 5; 25. 2.
FEAR,] as in v. 3, 11.
FLESH,] as in 65. 2; 78. 39; 136. 25, &c.
DOTH,] not 'can do,' as in C.V. Sept.
reads interrogatively.
5. WREST,] or 'make grievous;' as in Isa.
63. 10.
THOUGHTS,] as in 33. 10, 11; 40. 5; 92. 5, &c.

EVIL,] as in 5. 4; 7. 4, 9; 10. 6, 15, &c.
6. ASSEMBLE,] as in 59. 3; 140. 2; Nu. 22.
3, &c. Sept. Vulg. 'sojourn.'
HIDE,] as in 10. 8; 27. 5; 31. 19, 20; 119. 11
WATCH,] as in 12. 7; 39. 1; 41. 2; 59. 1, &c
HEELS,] not 'steps;' as in 41. 9; 49. 5, &c.
EXPECTED,] as in 25. 5, 21; 39. 7; 40. 1, &c.
7. INIQUITY,] an affirmation, not a ques
tion, as in C.V. Sept. 'for nothing dost thou
save them?' Vulg. reads the same affirma
tively.
ESCAPE,] as in 32. 7.
ANGER,] as in 2. 5, 12; 6. 1; 7. 6; 10. 4, &c.
PUT DOWN,] not 'cast down;' as in 59. 11.
8. WANDERING,] as in Ge. 4. 16. Sept.
Vulg. 'my life I tell to thee.'
COUNTED,] as in 48. 12; 87. 6; 139. 18.
TEAR,] not 'tears;' as in 6. 6; 39. 12; 42. 3.
BOTTLE,] as in 119; 83; Jos. 9. 4, 13; Jud.
4. 19; 1 Sa. 16. 20, &c. Sept. Vulg. 'sight.
BOOK,] as in 40. 7; 69. 28; 139. 16. &c.
Sept. Vulg. 'promise.'
9. TURN BACK,] as in 6. 10; 7. 12, 16, &c.
I CALL, not 'cry;' as in 3. 4; 18. 3, 6; 22. 2,
&c. Sept. Vulg. add 'thee.
FOR ME.] Sept. Vulg. 'my God thou art.'
10. THE WORD,] or 'thing, not 'his word,
as in C.V.
IN JEHOVAH,] the covenant God of Israel.
I PRAISE,] as in v. 4.
11. IN GOD,] in his strength.
TRUSTED,] as in v. 4.
FEAR,] as in v. 3, 4.
MAN,] in v. 4 it is 'flesh.'
DOTH,] not 'can do,' as in C.V. Sept. reads
interrogatively.
12. VOWS,] as in 22. 25; 50. 14; 61. 5, 8, &c.
REPAY,] not 'render;' as in 22. 25; 35. 12.
THANK-OFFERINGS,] not 'praises;' as in
26. 7, &c.
13. DELIVERED,] as in 18. 1; 34. 4, 17, &c.
DEATH,] as in 6. 5; 7 13; 9. 13; 13. 3, &c.
MY FEET,] as in 18. 33, 38; 22. 16; 25. 15, &c.
FALLING,] as in 116. 8.
TO WALK HABITUALLY,] as in Job 1. 7; 2.
2; Prov. 6. 22; Zec. 1. 10; 6. 7.
LIGHT,] as in 4. 6; 27. 1; 36. 9; 37. 6, &c.
LIVING,] as in 27. 13; 52. 5; 69. 28, &c.

LVII. OVERSEER,] as in Ps. 4. 5. 6. 8. &c.
DESTROY NOT,] as in Ps. 58. 59. 75; 78. 88.
SECRET TREASURE,] as in Ps. 16. 56. 58. 60.
CAVE,] as in Ps. 141; Ge. 19. 30; 23. 9, &c.
1. FAVOUR,] not 'be merciful;' as in 4. 1.
TRUSTED,] as in 7. 1; 11. 1; 16. 1; 25. 20, &c.
SHADOW OF THY WINGS,] as in 17. 8; 36. 7.
TRUST,] as in 18. 2; 34. 8; 36. 7; 61. 4, &c.
CALAMITIES,] or 'mischiefs;' as in 5. 9;
38. 12; 52. 2, 7; 55. 11; 91. 3; 94. 20. So Sept.
Vulg. &c.
PASS OVER,] as in 17. 3; 37. 36; 42. 4, &c.
2. CALL,] not 'cry;' as in 3. 4; 18. 3, 6, &c.
MOST HIGH,] as in 7. 17; 9. 2; 18. 13; 21. 7.
GOD,] *lit.* the 'mighty' one.
PERFECTING,] as in 7. 9; 12. 1; 77. 8; 138.
8, &c. Sept. Vulg. 'does good.' Sept. adds
'Selah.'
3. SENDETH,] as in 18. 14, 16; 20. 2; 107. 20.
HEAVENS,] as in v. 5, 10, 11; 2. 4; 8. 1, &c.
SAVETH,] as in 18. 27; 34. 18; 36. 6; 87. 40.
REPROACHED,] as in 42. 10; 74. 18; 79. 12.

PANTING,] as in 56. 1, 2; 119. 131, &c. Sept.
Vulg. 'those who are trampling me.'
KINDNESS,] not 'mercy;' as in v. 10; 5. 7, &c.
TRUTH,] as in v. 10; 15. 2; 19. 9; 25. 5, 10.
4. LIONS,] as in Ge. 49. 9; Nu. 23. 24, &c.
Sept. Vulg. adds 'he delivereth.'
I LIE DOWN,] as in 3. 5; 4. 8; 41. 8; 68. 13.
FLAMES,] not 'them that are set on fire;'
as in 104. 4.
SONS OF MEN,] as in 11. 4; 12. 1; 14. 2, &c.
TEETH,] as in 3. 7; 35. 16; 37. 12; 45. 8, &c.
SPEAR,] as in 35. 3; 46. 9; 1 Sa. 13. 19, &c.
ARROWS,] as in 7. 13; 11. 2; 18. 14; 38. 2, &c.
SHARP,] as in Prov. 5. 4; Isa. 49. 2; Eze. 5. 1.
5. EXALTED,] as in v. 11; 21. 13; 108. 5, &c.
HONOUR,] as in v. 8, 11; 3. 3; 4. 2; 7. 5, &c.
6. NET,] as in 9. 15; 10. 9; 25. 15; 31. 4, &c.
PREPARED,] as in 7. 13; 74. 16; 78. 8, &c.
STEPS,] as in 17. 5; 58. 10; 74. 3; 85. 13, &c.
BOWED DOWN,] as in 145. 14; 146. 8; Isa. 58.
5. Sept. Vulg. 'they have bowed down.'
DIGGED,] or 'prepared;' as in 7. 15, &c.
PIT,] as in 119. 85; Jer. 18. 22.
FALLEN,] as in 10. 10; 16. 6; 20. 8; 27. 2, &c.
7. PREPARED,] not 'fixed;' as in 5. 9, &c.
HEART,] as in 4. 7; 7. 10; 9. 1; 10. 6, &c.
SING,] as in 13. 6; 21. 13; 27. 6; 57. 7, &c.
PRAISE,] as in v. 9; 7. 17; 9. 2; 18. 49, &c.
8. AWAKE,] as in 7. 6; 44. 23; 59. 4; 108. 2.
HONOUR,] as in v. 5, 11.
PSALTERY,] as in 33. 2; 71. 22; 81. 2, &c.
HARP,] as in 33. 2; 43. 4; 49. 4; 71. 22, &c.
MORNING DAWN,] not 'will awake early;'
as in 22. 1; 108. 2; 139. 9, &c.
9. THANK,] not 'praise;' as in 6. 5; 7. 17.
PEOPLES,] perhaps those of Israel.
PRAISE,] not 'sing;' as in v. 7.
NATIONS,] not belonging to Israel.
10. GREAT,] as in 86. 13; 108. 4; 145. 8, &c.
KINDNESS,] not 'mercy;' as in v. 3.
CLOUDS,] as in 18. 11; 36. 5; 68. 34; 77. 17.
TRUTH,] as in v. 3.
11. EXALTED,] as in v. 5.
HONOUR,] as in v. 5, 8.

LVIII. OVERSEER,] as in Ps. 4. 5. 6. 8. &c.
DESTROY NOT,] as in Ps. 57. 59. 75; 78. 38.
SECRET TREASURE,] as in Ps. 16. 56. 57. 60.
1. IS IT TRUE,] not 'indeed;' as in Ge. 18.
13; Nu. 22. 23; 1 K. 3. 27; 2 Ch. 6. 18.
DUMB,] not 'congregation;' as in 56. 1.
Sept. Vulg. omit.
RIGHTEOUSLY,] as in 4. 1, 5; 7. 8, 17, &c.
UPRIGHTLY,] as in 9. 8; 17. 2; 75. 2; 96. 10.
JUDGE,] as in 9. 8; 67. 4; 72. 4; 75. 2, &c.
2. IN HEART,] as in 4. 7; 7. 10; 9. 1; 10. 6.
VIOLENCE,] as in 7. 16; 11. 5; 18. 48; 25. 19.
PONDER,] not 'weigh;' as in 78. 50; Prov.
4. 26; 5. 6, 21; Isa. 26. 5.
3. ESTRANGED,] as in 78. 30; Job 19. 13, &c.
WOMB,] as in 22. 10; 110. 3; Ge. 20. 18, &c.
ERRED,] as in 95. 10; 107. 4; 119. 110, &c.
BELLY,] as in 17. 14; 22. 9, 10; 31. 9; 44. 25.
LIES,] as in 4. 2; 5. 6; 40. 4; 62. 4, 9, &c.
4. POISON,] lit. 'heat;' as in 6. 1; 37. 8, &c.
SERPENT,] as in 140. 3; Ge. 3. 1, 2, 4, &c.
DEAF,] as in 38. 13; Ex. 4. 11; Lev. 19. 14.
ASP,] as in 91. 13; De. 32. 33; Job 20. 14.
16; Isa. 11. 8.
SHUTTING,] as in Prov. 17. 28; 21. 13; Isa.
33 15.

5. HEARKENETH,] as in 4. 3; 5. 3; 18. 6, &c.
CHARMERS,] lit. 'whisperers.'
CHARMER OF CHARMS,] as in De. 18. 11,
Prov. 21. 9; 25. 24; Isa. 47. 9, 12; Hos. 6. 9.
MOST SKILFUL,] as in Prov. 30. 24.
6. GOD,] as in v. 11.
BEAK,] as in 2 Sa. 11. 25; Ps. 28. 5, &c.
TEETH,] as in 3. 7; 35. 16; 37. 12; 45. 8, &c.
JAW-TEETH.] Original word not found
again.
YOUNG LIONS,] as in 17. 12; 34. 10; 35. 17.
BREAK DOWN,] as in Jer. 1. 10; 18. 17, &c.
7. MELTED,] lit. 'refused;' as in 15. 4, &c
Compare Job 7. 5. Sept. 'set at nought.'
WATERS,] as in 1. 3; 18. 11, 15, 16; 22. 14, &c.
GO UP AND DOWN,] as in 12. 8; 39. 6; 43. 2.
ARROW,] as in 7. 13; 11. 2; 18. 14; 38. 2, &c.
PROCEEDETH,] as in Nu. 24. 17; Mic. 1. 3.
CUT THEMSELVES OFF,] not 'cut in pieces;'
as in C. V. Sept. Vulg. 'become weak.'
8. SNAIL.] Original word not found again.
UNTIMELY BIRTH,] as in Job 3. 16; Ecc. 6.
3, &c. Sept. Vulg. 'fire falls.'
SEEN,] as in v. 10; 27. 4; 46. 8; 63. 2, &c.
SUN,] as in 19. 4; 50. 1; 72. 5, 17, &c.
9. POTS,] as in 60. 8; Ex. 16. 3; 27. 3; 38. 3,
&c. Sept. Vulg. 'thorns.'
DISCERN,] not 'feel;' as in 19. 12; 28. 5, &c.
BRAMBLE,] not 'thorns;' as in Ge. 50. 10,
11; Jud. 9. 14, 15.
RAW,] lit. 'living.'
HEATED,] lit. 'heat;' as in 69. 24; 78. 49, &c.
WHIRLETH AWAY,] as in Job 27. 21, &c
Sept. Vulg. 'consumeth.'
10. REJOICETH,] as in 5. 11; 9. 2; 14. 7, &c.
VENGEANCE,] as in Lev. 26. 25; De. 32. 25.
STEPS,] not 'feet;' as in 17. 5; 57. 6; 74. 3,
&c. Sept. Vulg. 'hands.'
WASHETH,] as in 26. 6; 73. 13; Ge. 24. 32, &c.
BLOOD,] as in 5. 6; 9. 12; 16. 4; 26. 9, &c.
11. MAN,] as in 17. 4; 22. 6; 32. 2; 39. 5, &c.
SURELY,] or 'only;' as in 7. 23; 9. 4, &c.
FRUIT,] not 'reward;' as in 1. 3; 21. 10, &c.
JUDGING,] as in 2. 10; 7. 11; 9. 4; 50. 6, &c.
Sept. Vulg. add 'them.'
EARTH,] or 'land.'

LIX. OVERSEER,] as in Ps. 4. 5. 6. 8. &c.
DESTROY NOT,] as in Ps. 57. 58. 75; 78. 38.
SECRET TREASURE,] as in Ps. 16. 56. 57 58.
THE HOUSE.] Sept. Vulg. 'his house.'
PUT HIM TO DEATH,] as in 37. 32; Ge. 18. 25.
1. DELIVER,] as in v. 2; 7. 1; 22. 20; 25. 20.
MY GOD,] as in 3. 7; 5. 2; 7 1, 3; 13. 3, &c.
WITHSTANDERS,] as in 17. 7; Job 20. 27,
27. 7, &c.
SET ME ON HIGH,] as in 20. 1; 69. 29; 91. 14,
&c. Sept. Vulg. 'free me.'
2. WORKERS OF INIQUITY,] as in 5. 5; 6. 8.
MEN OF BLOOD,] as in 5. 6; 26. 9; 55. 23, &c.
SAVE,] as in 3. 7; 6. 4; 7. 1; 12. 1; 20. 9, &c.
3. LAID WAIT,] as in 10. 9; De. 19. 11, &c.
ASSEMBLED,] as in 56. 6; 140. 2, &c.
STRONG ONES,] as in 18. 17; Nu. 13. 28, &c
TRANSGRESSION,] as in 5. 10; 19. 13; 25. 7.
SIN,] as in v. 12; 25. 7, 18; 32. 5, &c.
4. PUNISHMENT,] not 'fault;' as in 69. 27.
RUN,] as in 18. 29; 119. 32; 147. 15, &c.
PREPARE THEMSELVES,] as in Nu. 21. 27,
Prov. 24. 3; Isa. 54. 14, &c.
STIR UP,] as in 7. 6; 44. 23; 57. 8; 108. 2, &c

MEET ME,] not 'help' me; as in 35. 3, &c.
Sept. 'stand with me.'
5. JEHOVAH,] as in v. 8.
GOD OF HOSTS,] as in 69. 6; 80. 4, 7, 14, &c.
GOD OF ISRAEL,] as in 41. 13; 68. 8; 69. 6.
AWAKE,] as in 35. 23; 44. 23, &c.
INSPECT,] not 'visit;' as in Ge. 50. 24, 25;
Ex. 3. 16, &c.
FAVOUR,] not 'merciful;' as in 67. 1; 123. 2.
TREACHEROUS DEALERS,] as in 25. 3; 119.
158; Prov. 2. 22, &c. Sept. Vulg. simply
'workers.'
INIQUITY,] as in v. 2.
SELAH,] as in 3. 2, 4, 8; 4. 2, 4; 7. 5, &c.
6. TURN BACK,] as in v. 14; 6. 10; 7. 12, &c.
EVENING,] as in v. 14; 30. 5; 55. 17; 65. 8.
MAKE A NOISE,] as in v. 14; 39. 6; 42. 5, 11,
&c. Sept. Vulg. 'suffer famine.'
DOG,] as in v. 14; 22. 16, 20; 68. 23, &c.
GO ROUND,] as in 7. 7; 26. 6; 32. 7, 10, &c.
CITY,] as in v. 14; 9. 6; 31. 21; 46. 4, &c.
7. BELCH OUT,] as in 19. 2; 78. 2; 94. 4;
119. 171, &c. Sept. 'speak out plainly.' Vulg.
'speak.'
SWORDS,] as in 7. 12; 17. 13; 22. 20; 37. 14.
HEARETH,] as in 38. 14; 65. 2; 69. 33; 81. 13.
8. LAUGH,] as in 2. 4; 37. 13; 52. 6, &c.
MOCK,] as in 2. 4; 80. 6; 2 K. 19. 21, &c.
Sept. Vulg. 'set or brought to nought.'
NATIONS,] as in v. 5.
9. MY STRENGTH.] So Sept. Vulg. &c.
I TAKE HEED,] or 'watch;' as in v. 1; 12. 7.
GOD.] Sept. Vulg. 'thou, O God.'
TOWER,] not 'defence;' as in v. 16; 9. 9;
18. 2; 46. 7, &c. Sept. Vulg. 'supporter.'
KINDNESS,] not 'mercy;' as in v. 16, 17; 5.
7, &c. Sept. Vulg. 'my God, his kindness
goes before me.'
10. GO BEFORE ME,] not 'prevent me;' as
in 17. 13, &c.
LOOK,] in calmness, not 'see my desire,'
as in C.V.
11. SLAY,] as in 10. 8; 78. 31, 47; 94. 6, &c.
PEOPLE.] Sept. 'thy law.'
FORGET,] as in 10. 12; 13. 1; 44. 24; 74. 19.
SHAKE,] not 'scatter;' as in 22. 7, &c.
STRENGTH,] as in 18. 32, 39; 33. 16, 17, &c.
BRING THEM DOWN,] as in 56. 7, &c.
SHIELD,] as in 3. 3; 7. 10; 18. 2, 30, 35, &c.
Sept Vulg. 'my protector.'
12. SIN,] as in v. 3.
WORD OF THEIR LIPS,] as in 17. 4, &c.
CAPTURED,] as in Jos. 7. 16, 17, 18; 1 Sa. 10. 20.
PRIDE,] as in 47. 4; Ex. 15. 7; Lev. 26. 19.
CURSE,] or 'execration;' as in 10. 7, &c.
LYING,] as in Hos. 7. 3; 10. 13; 11. 12; Nah.
3. 1; Job 16. 8.
RECOUNT,] not 'speak;' as in 2. 7; 9. 1, 14.
13. CONSUME,] as in 78. 33; 90. 9; 119. 87, &c.
FURY,] as in 6. 1; 37. 8; 38. 1; 58. 4, &c.
ARE NOT,] as in 7. 7; Eze. 28. 19, &c.
KNOW,] as in 9. 20; 35. 8; 39. 4, 6; 51. 3, &c.
RULING,] as in 22. 28; 66. 7; 89. 9; 105. 20.
IN JACOB,] as in 58. 5; 99. 4, &c. Sept.
'the God of Jacob doth rule.'
ENDS OF THE EARTH,] or 'land' of Israel.
SELAH,] as in v. 5.
14. TURN BACK,] as in v. 6.
EVENING,] as in v. 6.
MAKE A NOISE,] as in v. 6. Sept. Vulg. as
in v. 6.

A DOG,] as in v. 6.
GO ROUND ABOUT,] as in v. 6.
CITY,] as in v. 6; a very common custom
in the east.
15. WANDER,] as in 107. 27; 109. 10, &c.
FOOD,] or 'to eat;' as in 27. 2; 78. 24, &c.
SATISFIED,] as in 17. 4, 15; 22. 26; 37. 19.
MURMUR,] as in Ex. 16. 7; 17. 3; Nu. 14.
36, &c.; or 'lodge.'
16. SING,] as in 13. 6; 21. 13; 27. 6; 57. 7, &c.
STRENGTH,] as in v. 1, 17.
MORN,] as in 5. 3; 30. 5; 46. 5; 49. 14, &c.
KINDNESS,] not 'mercy;' as in v. 9, 17.
TOWER,] not 'defence;' as in v. 9. Sept.
Vulg. 'supporter.'
REFUGE,] as in 142. 4; 2 Sa. 22. 3, &c.
DAY OF ADVERSITY,] as in 102. 2; Prov. 24.
10, &c. Sept. Vulg. 'my adversity.'
17. MY STRENGTH,] as in v. 9, 16. Sept.
Vulg. 'my help.'
I SING PRAISE,] as in 7. 17; 9. 12; 18. 49,
&c. Sept. Vulg. 'exult.'
FOR GOD.] Sept. 'my God, thou art my
supporter.'
TOWER,] not 'defence;' as in 9. 9; 18. 2, &c.
KINDNESS,] not 'mercy;' as in v. 9, 16.
Sept. Vulg. 'my God, my kind one.'

LX. OVERSEER,] as in Ps. 4. 5. 6. 8. 9. &c.
LILY,] as in 45. 1; 80. 1; 1 K. 7. 22, 26.
Song 2. 6; 4. 5; 5. 13; 6, 2, 3; 7. 2. Sept
Vulg. 'those who are changed.'
TESTIMONY,] as in 19. 7; 78. 5; 81. 5, &c.
SECRET TREASURE,] as in Ps. 16. 56. 57. 58.
TO TEACH,] as in De. 4. 14; 6. 1; Jud. 3. 2.
STRIVING,] as in Nu. 26. 9; Ex. 21. 22, &c.
ARAM-NAHARAIM,] as in Ge. 24. 10; De. 23.
4; Jud. 3. 8; 1 Ch. 19. 6. Sept. Vulg. 'Me-
sopotamia.'
ARAM-ZOBAH,] as in 2 Sa. 10. 6. 8. Sept.
Vulg. 'Sobal.'
JOAB,] as in 1 Sa. 26. 6; 2 Sa. 2. 13, 14, &c.
EDOM.] Sept. omits.
VALLEY OF SALT,] as in 2 Sa. 8. 13; 2 K.
14. 7; 1 Ch. 18. 12; 2 Ch. 25. 11.
12,000,] in 2 Sa. 8. 13 it is 18,000.
1. GOD,] as in v. 6, 10, 12.
HADST CAST,] not 'hast cast;' as in 43. 2.
BROKEN,] not 'scattered;' as in 80. 12; 89.
40, &c. Sept. 'destroyed.'
ANGRY,] as in 2. 12; 79. 5; 85. 5.
DOST TURN BACK,] not 'turn thyself;' as
in 23. 3, &c.
2. LAND,] or 'earth.
TO TREMBLE,] as in Job 39. 20; Isa. 14. 16;
Eze. 31. 16; Hag. 2. 6, 7, 21.
BROKEN.] Original word not found again.
HEAL,] as in 6. 2; 41. 4; Nu. 12. 13, &c.
BREACHES,] as in Lev. 21. 19; 24. 20, &c.
MOVED,] as in 38. 16; 46. 4; 94. 18, &c.
3. SHEWN,] as in 4. 6; 50. 23; 59. 10, &c.
HARD THING,[as in Ge. 42. 7, 30; Ex. 1. 14
TO DRINK,] as in 36. 8; 69. 21; 78. 15; 80. 5.
TREMBLING,] not 'astonishment;' as in
Isa. 51. 17, 22.
4. FEARING THEE,] as in 15. 4; 22. 23, 25.
ENSIGN,] as in Ex. 17. 15; Nu. 21. 8, 9, &c
LIFTED UP,] as in Zec. 9. 16. Sept. Vulg.
'to flee from the face of the bow.'
TRUTH,] as in Prov. 22. 21; Da. 2. 47; 4. 37.
SELAH,] as in 3. 2, 4, 8; 4. 2, 4; 7. 5, &c.

5. BELOVED ONES,] as in 45. 1; 84. 1; 108.
6; 127. 2; De. 33. 12; Isa. 5. 1; Jer. 11. 15.
DRAWN OUT,] as in 108. 6; Prov. 11. 8, &c.
SAVE,] as in 3. 7; 6. 4; 7. 1; 12. 1, &c.
RIGHT HAND,] as in 16. 8, 11; 17. 7; 18. 35.
ANSWER US,] not 'hear;' as in 4. 1; 13. 3;
27. 7, &c. Sept. Vulg. 'me.'
6. HOLINESS,] as in 29. 2; 30. 4; 47. 8, &c.
EXULT,] as in 28. 7; 94. 3; 96. 12; 108. 7, &c.
APPORTION,] as in 22. 18; 68. 12; 108. 7, &c.
SHECHEM,] as in 108. 7; Ge. 12. 6; 33. 18.
VALLEY OF SUCCOTH,] as in 108. 7; Jos. 13.
27. Sept. Vulg. 'of tabernacles.'
MEASURE,] as in 108. 7; 2 Sa. 8. 2, &c.
7. GILEAD,] as in Nu. 32. 1, 40; De. 3. 15.
MANASSEH,] as in 80. 2; 108. 8; Ge. 41. 51.
EPHRAIM,] as in 78. 9; 80. 2; 108. 8, &c.
STRENGTH,] as in 27. 1; 28. 8; 31. 2, 4, &c.
HEAD,] as in 3. 3; 7. 16; 18. 43; 21. 3, &c.
JUDAH,] as in 76. 1; 108. 8; 114. 2, &c.
LAWGIVER,] as in 108. 8; Ge. 49. 10; Nu. 21.
18, &c. Sept. Vulg. 'king.'
8. MOAB,] as in 83. 6; 108. 9; Ge. 19. 37, &c.
POT,] as in 58. 9; 108. 9; Ex. 16. 3; 27. 3, &c.
WASHING] the hands, not 'wash;' as in
108. 9. Sept. Vulg. 'hope.'
EDOM,] as in v. 1, 9, &c.
CAST,] as in 2. 3; 50. 17; 51. 11; 71. 9, &c.
SHOE,] as in 108. 9; Ge. 14. 23; Ex. 3. 5, &c.
SHOUT,] not 'triumph;' as in 65. 13; 108. 9,
&c. Sept. Vulg. read, 'to me strangers are
subdued.'
PHILISTINES,] as in 83. 7; 87. 4; 108. 9, &c.
9. BRING ME,] as in 68. 29; 76. 11; 108. 10.
CITY OF BULWARKS,] not 'strong city;' as
in 31. 21, &c.
LED ME,] as in 77. 20; 108. 10; 139. 24, &c.
EDOM,] as in v. 1, 8.
10. CAST US OFF,] as in v. 1.
HOSTS,] as in 60. 10; 108. 11; Ex. 6. 26, &c.
11. HELP,] as in 22. 19; 27. 9; 35. 2; 38. 22.
ADVERSITY,] or 'an adversary;' as in v.
12; 3. 1, &c.
VAIN,] as in 12. 2; 24. 4; 26. 4; 31. 6, &c.
SAFETY,] as in 33. 17; 37. 39; 38. 22, &c.
12. IN GOD,] not 'through God,' as in C.V.
DO MIGHTILY,] not 'valiantly;' as in 18. 32.
TREADETH DOWN,] as in 44. 5; 108. 13;
Prov. 27. 7; Isa. 14. 26; 63. 6; Zec. 10. 5. Sept.
Vulg. 'makes nought.'
ADVERSARIES,] as in v. 11; 3. 1; 4. 1; 13. 4.

LXI. OVERSEER,] as in Ps. 4. 5. 6. 8. 9. &c.
STRINGED INSTRUMENTS,] as in Ps. 4. 6.
54. 55. 67; 69. 12; 76. 77. 6, &c. Sept. Vulg.
'hymns.'
1. HEAR,] as in 4. 1; 17. 1, 6; 27. 7; 28. 2.
LOUD CRY,] as in 17. 1; 30. 5; 42. 4; 47. 1.
ATTEND,] as in 5. 2; 17. 1; 55. 2; 86. 6, &c.
PRAYER,] as in 4. 1; 6. 9; 17. 1; 35. 13, &c.
2. END OF THE LAND,] or 'earth.'
CALL,] not 'cry;' as in 3. 4; 18. 3, 6; 22. 2.
FEEBLENESS,] as in Ge. 30. 42; La. 2. 19, &c.
ROCK,] as in 18. 2, 31, 46; 19. 14; 27. 5, &c.
HIGHER THAN I.] Sept. Vulg. 'thou hast
exalted me.'
LEAD ME,] as in 23. 3; 31. 3; 43. 3; 67. 4, &c.
3. REFUGE,] as in 14. 6; 46. 1; 62. 7, 8; 71.
7, &c. Sept. Vulg. 'my hope.'
TOWER,] as in 48. 12; Ge. 11. 4, 5; 35. 21, &c.
4. SOJOURN,] not 'abide;' as in 5. 4; 15. 1.

TENT,] not 'tabernacle;' as in 15. 1; 19. 4.
AGES,] as in v. 7; 5. 11; 9. 5, 7; 10. 6; 12. 7.
TAKE REFUGE,] as in 18. 2; 34. 8; 36. 7, &c.
SECRET PLACE,] as in 18. 11; 27. 5; 31. 20.
WINGS,] as in 17. 8; 36. 7; 57. 1; 63. 7, &c.
SELAH,] as in 3. 2, 4, 8; 4. 2, 4; 7. 5, &c.
5. GOD.] Vulg. 'my God.'
VOWS,] as in v. 8; 22. 25; 50. 14; 56. 12, &c.
Sept. Vulg. 'prayers.'
APPOINTED,] lit. 'given.'
INHERITANCE,] or 'possession;' as in De.
2. 5, 9, 12, 19; 3. 20, &c.
FEARING THY NAME,] that is, reverencing
thy character.
6. DAYS,] as in 21. 4; 23. 6; 34. 12; 37. 18.
THE KING] David, the anointed of the
Lord.
ADDEST,] as in 10. 18; 41. 8; 77. 7; 78. 17, &c.
YEARS,] as in 31. 10; 65. 11; 77. 5, 10; 78.
33, &c. Sept. Vulg. add 'unto the days of
generation,' &c.
GENERATIONS,] as in 10. 6; 12. 7; 14. 5, &c.
7. DWELLETH,] as in 2. 4; 9. 11; 17. 12, &c.
KINDNESS,] not 'mercy;' as in 5. 7; 6. 4
13. 5, &c. Sept. Vulg. 'his kindness and
truth, who doth seek them?'
TRUTH,] as in 15. 2; 19. 9; 25. 5, 10; 26. 3.
APPOINT,] not 'prepare;' as in Job 7. 3;
Da. 1. 5, 10, 11; Jon. 1. 7; 4. 6, 7, 8.
KEEP,] as in 12. 7; 21; 32. 7; 40. 11, &c.
8. PRAISE,] as in 7. 17; 9. 2; 18. 49; 21. 13.
NAME,] as in 5. 11; 7. 17; 8. 1; 9. 2, 5, &c.
FOR EVER.] Sept. Vulg. add 'and ever.'
PAY,] as in Ex. 21. 36; 22. 3, 6, 14; De. 23. 21.
VOWS,] as in v. 5; 22. 25; 50. 14; 56. 12, &c.
DAY BY DAY,] as in 68. 19, &c.

LXII. OVERSEER,] as in Ps. 4. 5. 6. 8. &c.
JEDUTHUN,] as in Ps. 39. 77; 1 Ch. 9. 16, &c.
1. ONLY,] not 'truly;' as in v. 2, 4, 5, 6, 9.
Sept. Vulg. 'shall not my soul be subject to
God?'
SILENT,] lit. 'silence;' as in 22. 2; 39. 2; 65. 1.
SALVATION,] as in v. 2; 3. 8; 9. 14; 13. 5.
2. ROCK,] as in v. 6. 7; 18. 2, 31, 46; 19. 14,
&c. Sept. Vulg. 'God.'
SALVATION,] as in v. 1. Sept. Vulg. 'sa-
viour.'
TOWER,] not 'defence;' as in v. 6; 9. 9; 18.
2, &c. Sept. Vulg. 'supporter.'
MOVED,] as in v. 6; 10. 6; 13. 4; 15. 5, &c.
3. TILL WHEN,] as in Job 8. 2; 18. 2, &c.
DEVISE MISCHIEF.] Original word not
found again. Sept. Vulg. 'rush upon.'
DESTROYED,] lit. 'murdered;' as in Prov.
22. 13, &c.
WALL,] as in Ex. 30. 3; 37. 26; Lev. 1. 15
INCLINED,] as in 73. 2; 102. 11; 136. 12, &c.
HEDGE,] as in 80. 12; Nu. 22. 24, &c.
CAST DOWN,] not 'tottering;' as in 36. 12.
4. EXCELLENCY,] as in Ge. 4. 7; 49. 3; Lev.
13. 2, &c. Sept. Vulg. 'my honour.'
COUNSELLED,] as in 16. 7; 32. 8; Ex. 18. 19.
DRIVE AWAY,] not 'cast down;' as in De.
13. 5, 10, &c.
ENJOY,] as in 49. 13; 50. 18; 51. 16; 147. 10,
&c. Sept. Vulg. 'ran.'
LIE,] as in v. 9; 4. 2; 5. 6; 40. 4; 58. 3, &c.
Sept. Vulg. 'thirst.'
BLESS,] as in 5. 12; 16. 7; 26. 12; 29. 11, &c.
REVILE,]not 'curse;' as in 109 28; Ge 8. 21
2 D

SELAH,] as in v. 8; 3. 2, 4, 8; 4. 2, 4, &c.
5. BE SILENT,] not 'wait;' as in 4. 4; 37.
7, &c. Sept. Vulg. 'subject.'
HOPE,] as in 9. 18; 71. 5; Ruth 1. 12, &c.
6. ROCK,] as in v. 2, 7. Sept. Vulg. 'God.'
SALVATION,] as in v. 1, 2. Sept. Vulg.
'saviour.'
TOWER,] not 'defence;' as in v. 2. Sept.
Vulg. 'supporter.'
MOVED,] as in v. 2.
7. ON GOD,] not 'in God.' So Sept.
SALVATION,] as in 12. 5; 18. 2, 35; 18. 46.
HONOUR,] as in 3. 3; 4. 2; 7. 5; 8. 5; 16. 9.
ROCK,] as in v. 6. Sept. Vulg. 'the God.'
STRENGTH,] as in v. 11; 8. 2; 21. 1, 13, &c.
REFUGE,] as in v. 8; 14. 6; 46. 1; 61. 3; 62.
7, &c. Sept. Vulg. 'hope.'
8. TRUST,] as in 4. 5; 37. 3, 5; 115. 9, &c.
AT ALL TIMES,] as in 10. 5; 34. 1; 106. 3;
119. 20, &c. Sept. Vulg. 'all ye assemblies
of people.'
PEOPLE,] as in 3. 6, 8; 7. 8; 9. 11; 14. 4, &c.
POUR FORTH,] as in 69. 24; 79. 6; Jud. 6. 20.
HEART,] as in 4. 4; 13. 2; 15. 2; 20. 4, &c.
REFUGE,] as in v. 7. Sept. Vulg. 'helper.'
Vulg. adds 'for ever.'
9 VANITY,] as in 31. 6; 39. 5, 6, 11; 78. 33.
LOW,] lit. 'sons of Adam;' as in 49. 2, &c.
LIE,] as in v. 4.
HIGH,] lit. 'sons of a man;' as in 49. 2, &c.
BALANCES,] as in Lev. 19. 36; Job 6. 2, &c.
LIGHTER,] lit. 'sharper.'
10. OPPRESSION,] as in 72. 8; 119. 134; Lev.
6. 4, &c. Sept. Vulg. 'injustice.'
VALLEY,] as in Lev. 6. 2; Isa. 61. 8; Eze.
22. 29.
VAIN,] as in 2 K. 17. 15; Job 27. 12; Jer.
2. 5. Sept. Vulg. 'do not desire.'
WEALTH,] or 'strength;' as in 18. 32, 39, &c.
INCREASETH,] as in 92. 14; Prov. 10. 31;
Zec. 9. 17.
SET NOT THE HEART,] as in 1 Sa. 4. 20; 2
Sa. 13. 20; Ps. 48. 13; Prov. 22. 17; 24. 32;
27. 23; Jer. 31. 21.
11. ONCE,] as in 89. 35; Job 33. 14; 40. 5.
TWICE,] as in Job 33. 14; 40. 5; Ge. 22. 15,
&c. Sept. Vulg. 'these two.'
STRENGTH,] as in v. 7, &c. Sept. Vulg.
'of God.'
12. KINDNESS,] not 'mercy;' as in 5. 7, &c.
RECOMPENSE,] as in 22. 25; 35. 12; 37. 31.
WORK,] as in 8. 3, 6; 19. 1; 28. 4, 5, &c.
Sept. Vulg. 'works.'

LXIII. WILDERNESS,] as in 29. 8; 55. 7, &c.

JUDEA.] Vulg. 'Idumea.'
1. GOD,] as in v. 11; 3. 2, 7; 4. 1; 5. 2, &c.
MY GOD,] as in 18. 2; 22. 1, 10; 68. 24, &c.
EARNESTLY,] as in 78. 34; Job 8. 5; 24. 5,
&c. Sept. Vulg. 'early.'
THIRSTED,] as in 42. 2; Ex. 17. 3; Jud. 4. 19;
15. 18, &c.
LONGED.] Original word not found else-
where. Sept. Vulg. 'how greatly.'
DRY,] as in 78. 17; 105. 41; 137. 35, &c.
Sept. Vulg. 'desert.'
WEARY,] not 'thirsty;' as in 143. 6; Ge. 25.
29, 30, &c. Sept. Vulg. 'untrodden, path-
less.'
WATERS,] as in 1. 3; 18. 11, 15, 16; 22. 14.
2. SANCTUARY,] as in 2. 6; 3. 4; 5. 7; 11. 4.

SEEN,] as in 11. 4, 7; 17. 2, 15; 58. 8, 10, &c.
Sept. Vulg. 'appeared.'
BEHOLD,] as in 14. 2; 16. 10; 27. 13; 34. 12
STRENGTH,] as in 8. 2; 21. 1, 13; 28. 7. 8, &c
HONOUR,] as in 3. 3; 4. 2; 7. 5; 8. 5; 16. 9.
3. KINDNESS,] as in 5. 7; 6. 4; 13. 5, &c.
LIFE,] as in v. 4; 7. 5; 16. 11; 17. 14; 18. 46.
LIPS,] as in 12. 2, 3, 4; 16. 4; 17. 1, 4, &c.
PRAISE,] as in 117. 1; 145. 4; 147. 12.
Ecc. 8. 13.
4. BLESS,] as in 5. 12; 16. 7; 26, 12; 29. 11.
NAME,] as in 5. 11; 7. 17; 8. 1; 9. 2, 5, &c.
LIFT UP,] as in 16. 4; 24. 5; 25. 1; 50. 16.
5. MILK,] not 'marrow;' as in 17. 10; 73. 7.
FATNESS,] as in 36. 8; 65. 11; Jud. 9. 9, &c.
SATISFIED,] as in 17. 14, 15; 22. 26; 37. 19.
SINGING,] not 'joyful;' as in 100. 2; Job 3.
7; 20. 5.
MY MOUTH.] Sept. 'thy name.'
PRAISE,] as in 22. 22, 26; 35. 18; 56. 4, 10.
6. REMEMBERED,] as in 9. 12; 78. 42; 88. 5.
COUCH,] as in 132. 3; Ge. 49. 4; 1 K. 6. 5, 6,
10; 1 Ch. 5. 1; Job 17. 13.
WATCHES,] as in 90. 4; 119. 148; Ex. 14. 24,
&c. Sept. Vulg. 'mornings.'
MEDITATE,] as in 1. 2; 2. 1; 35. 28; 37. 20,
&c. Sept. 'is careful.'
7. HELP,] as in 22. 19; 27. 9; 35. 2; 38. 22.
SHADOW OF THY WINGS,] as in 17. 8; 36. 7.
SING,] not 'rejoice;' as in 5. 11; 20. 5, &c.
8. CLEAVED,] as in 44. 25; 63. 8; 102. 5, &c.
RIGHT HAND,] as in 16. 8, 11; 17. 7; 18. 35.
TAKEN HOLD,] not 'upholdeth;' as in 16.
5; 17. 5; 41. 12, &c.
9. DESOLATION,] as in 35. 8; Job 30. 3, 14;
38. 27, &c. Sept. Vulg. 'a vain thing.'
LOWER PARTS,] as in 86. 13; 88. 6; 139. 15.
EARTH,] or 'land.'
10. TO RUN,] as in 75. 8; Eze. 35. 5, &c.
Sept. Vulg. 'they are delivered.'
EDGE,] lit. 'hands.'
PORTION,] as in 11. 6; 2 Ch. 31. 3, 4, &c.
FOXES,] as in Jud. 15. 4; Neh. 4. 3; Song
2. 15; La. 5. 18; Eze. 13. 4.
11. THE KING,] that is, David himself.
REJOICE,] as in 5. 11; 9. 2; 14. 7; 21. 1, &c.
BOAST HIMSELF,] as in 34. 2; 49. 6; 52. 1.
SWEARING,] as in Ecc. 9. 2; Isa. 19. 18, &c.
BUT.] Sept. Vulg. 'because.'
STOPPED,] as in Ge. 8. 2; Isa. 19. 4.
FALSEHOOD,] as in 7. 14; 27. 12; 31. 18;
33. 17, &c. Sept. Vulg. 'injustice.'

LXIV. OVERSEER,] as in Ps. 4. 5. 6. 8. &c.

1. HEAR,] as in 4. 1; 17. 1, 6; 27. 7; 28. 2, &c.
GOD,] as in v. 7, 9, &c.
VOICE,] as in 3. 4; 5. 2, 2; 6. 8; 18. 6, 13,
&c. Sept. Vulg. 'prayer.'
MEDITATION,] not 'prayer.' Sept. Vulg.
'supplication.' Sept. adds 'to thee.'
FEAR,] as in 55. 2; 102. 1; 104. 34; 142. 3.
LIFE,] as in 7. 5; 16. 11; 17. 14; 18. 46, &c
2. HIDEST,] as in 13. 1; 17. 8; 27. 5, 9, &c.
SECRET COUNSEL,] as in 25. 14; 55. 14; 64.
2, &c. Sept. Vulg. 'assembly.'
EVIL DOERS,] as in 22. 16; 26. 5; 27. 2, &c.
TUMULT,] not 'insurrection,' as in C.V.
Sept. Vulg. 'multitude.'
WORKERS OF INIQUITY,] as in 5. 5; 6. 8, &c
3. SHARPENED,] as in 45. 5; 120. 4; 140. 3
&c. Targ 'relate.'

SWORD,] as in 7. 12; 17. 13; 22. 20; 37. 14, &c.
DIRECTED,] not 'bent;' as in 7. 12; 58. 7, &c.
ARROW,] as in v. 7; 7. 13; 11. 2; 18. 14, &c.
Sept. Vulg. 'bow.'
BITTER,] as in Ge. 27. 34; Ex. 15. 23, &c.
SHOOT,] as in v. 7; 11. 2; Ex. 19. 13, &c.
SECRET PLACES,] as in 10. 8, 9; 17. 12; Isa.
45. 3; Jer. 13. 17; 23. 24; 49. 10; La. 3. 10;
Hab. 3. 14.
PERFECT,] as in 37. 37; Ge. 25. 27; Job 1.
1, 8; 2. 3, &c.   Sept. Vulg. 'blameless.'
SUDDENLY,] as in v. 7; Nu. 6. 9; 12. 4, &c.
5. STRENGTHEN,] as in 147. 13; Ex. 4. 21, &c.
RECOUNT,] not 'commune,' as in 2. 7; 9. 1.
HIDING,] as in Job 31. 33; Jer. 13. 6, &c.
SNARES,] as in 18. 5; 69. 22; 106. 36; 140. 5.
AT IT.] Sept. Vulg. 'them.'
6. SEARCH OUT,] as in 77. 6; Ge. 31. 35, &c.
PERVERSE THINGS,] as in 58. 2; 92. 15; Job
5. 16.   Sept. Vulg. 'lawlessness.'
PERFECTED,] as in 9. 6; 73. 19; Ge. 47. 15.
INWARD PART,] not 'thought;' as in 5. 9;
36. 1; 39. 3, &c.   Sept. Vulg. 'man has
drawn near.'
DEEP,] as in Lev. 13. 3, 4, 25, 30, 31, 32, &c.
7. SHOOT,] as in v. 4.   Sept. Vulg. 'shall
be exalted.'
ARROW,] as in v. 3.   Sept. Vulg. 'arrows
of babes become their plagues.'
SUDDEN,] as in v. 4.
WOUNDS,] lit. 'smitings;' as in Lev. 26. 21.
8. TO STUMBLE,] not 'to fall;' as in 2 Ch.
25. 8; 28. 23, &c.   Sept. 'their own tongue
set him at nought.'
MOVETH HIMSELF AWAY,] as in 31. 11; 55.
7; 68. 12, &c.   Sept. Vulg. 'confounded.'
9. FEAR,] as in v. 4.
DECLARE,] as in 22. 31; 30. 9; 38. 18; 40. 5.
WORK OF GOD,] as in 44. 1; 77. 12; 90. 16,
&c.   Sept. Vulg. 'works.'
DEED,] as in 8. 3, 6; 19. 1; 28. 4, 5; 33. 4,
&c.   Sept. Vulg. 'deeds.'
CONSIDERED WISELY,] as in 32. 8; 106. 7, &c.
10. REJOICE,] as in 5. 11; 9. 2; 14. 7; 21. 1.
TRUSTED,] as in 7. 1; 11. 1; 16. 1; 25. 20, &c.
BOAST THEMSELVES,] as in 34. 2; 49. 6, &c.
UPRIGHT OF HEART,] as in 7. 10; 11. 2, &c.

LXV. OVERSEER,] as in Ps. 4. 5. 6. 8. 9, &c.
SONG.] Sept. 'Ode.'
1. SILENCE,] as in 22. 3; 39. 2; 62. 1.   Sept.
Vulg. 'becoming is an hymn.'
PRAISE,] as in 9. 14; 22. 3, 24; 33. 1; 34. 1.
ZION,] as in 2. 6; 9. 11; 48. 12; 51. 18, &c.
VOW,] as in 22. 25; 50. 14; 56. 12; 61. 5, &c.
COMPLETED,] not 'performed;' Vulg. adds
in Jerusalem.'
2. HEARER,] as in 38. 14; 59. 7; 65. 2, &c.
PRAYER,] as in 4. 1; 6. 9; 17. 1, 2; 35. 13,
&c.   Sept. Vulg. 'hear my prayer.'
FLESH,] as in 56. 4; 78. 39; 136. 25, &c.
3. INIQUITIES,] as in 18. 23; 25. 11; 31. 10.
MIGHTIER,] as in 103. 11; 117. 2; Ge. 7. 19,
&c.   Sept. Vulg. 'than we.'
TRANSGRESSIONS,] as in 5. 10; 18. 13; 25. 7.
COVER,] not 'purge away;' as in 78. 38, &c.
4. HAPPINESS,] not 'blessed;' as in 1. 1, &c.
CHOOSEST,] as in 25. 12; 47. 4; 78. 68, &c.
DRAWEST NEAR,] as in Job. 31. 37, &c.
INHABITETH,] as in 15. 1; 16. 9; 37. 29, &c.
COURTS,] as in 10. 8; 84. 2, 10; 92. 13, &c.

SATISFIED,] as in 17. 14, 15; 22. 26; 37. 19.
TEMPLE,] as in 5. 7; 11. 4; 18. 6; 27. 4, &c.
Sept. Vulg. 'holy is thy temple.'
5. FEARFUL THINGS,] as in 45. 4; 47. 2; 65.
6; 66. 3, 5, &c.   Sept. Vulg. 'O fearful one in
righteousness.'
ANSWEREST,] as in 3. 4; 17. 6; 20. 1, 6, &c.
GOD OF OUR SALVATION,] as in 18. 46; 24.
5; 25. 5, &c.   Sept. Vulg. 'God is our saviour.'
CONFIDENCE,] as in 40. 4; 71. 5; Job 8. 14.
ENDS,] as in 48. 10; Isa. 26. 15.
6. ESTABLISHING,] not 'setting fast;' as in
147. 8; Jer. 10. 12; 51. 15.   Sept. Vulg. 'preparing.'
HIS POWER.] Sept. Vulg. 'thy power.'
GIRDED,] as in Ps. 18. 32, 39; 30. 11, &c.
7. RESTRAINING,] not 'stilleth;' as in 89.
9; Prov. 29. 11.   Sept. Vulg. 'troubling the
depths of the sea.'
SEAS,] as in 8. 8; 24. 2; 65. 7; 69. 34, &c.
BILLOWS,] as in 42. 7; 89. 8; 107. 25, &c.
MULTITUDE,] not 'tumult;' as in 37. 16; 42.
4, &c.   Sept. Vulg. 'troubled are the nations.'
8. UTTERMOST PARTS,] lit. 'ends, extremi-
ties.'
SIGNS,] as in 74. 4, 9; 78. 43; 86. 17; 105. 27.
AFRAID,] as in 3. 6; 23. 4; 27. 1, 3; 33. 8.
OUT-GOINGS,] as in 19. 6. 75. 6; 89. 34, &c.
MORNING AND EVENING,] as in Ge. 1. 5, &c.
TO SING,] not 'rejoice;' as in 32. 11; 81. 1.
9. INSPECTED,] not 'visitest;' as in 17. 3, &c.
WATEREST,] as in 36. 8; 69. 21; 78. 15, &c.
RICH,] as in 49. 16; Ge. 14. 24; 1 Sa. 2. 7,
&c.   Sept. Vulg. 'thou multipliest its
riches.'
RIVULET,] not 'river;' as in 1. 3; 46. 4, &c.
PREPAREST,] as in 10. 17; 68. 10; 78. 20, &c.
CORN,] as in 4. 7; 78. 24; Ge. 27. 28, 37, &c.
Sept. Vulg. 'food.'
10. RIDGES,] as in Job 31. 38; 39. 10; Hos.
10. 4; 12. 11.
FILLED,] not 'waterest;' as in 36. 8; Prov.
5. 10; 7. 18, &c.
TO GO DOWN,] as in 18. 34; 38. 2; 2 Sa. 18.
34. &c.   Sept. Vulg. 'multiply.'
FURROWS,] as in Jer. 48. 37.   Sept. Vulg.
'products.'
SHOWERS,] as in 72. 6; De. 32. 2; Jer. 3. 3;
14. 22; Mic. 5. 7.
SOFTEN,] as in 46. 6; 75. 3; Job. 30. 22, &c.
SPRINGING UP,] as in Ge. 19. 24; Isa. 4. 2.
BLESSEST,] Sept. Vulg. 'blessest the crown
of the year,' &c.
11. CROWNED,] as in 5. 12; 8. 5; 103. 4, &c.
YEAR OF THY GOODNESS,] not 'with' it, as
in C.V.
PATHS,] as in 23. 3; 140. 5; 1 Sa. 26. 5, 7;
Prov. 2. 9; 4. 11, 26; Isa. 26. 7.   Sept. Vulg.
'feet.'
DROP,] as in v. 12; Job. 36. 28; Prov. 3. 20.
FATNESS,] as in 36. 8; 63. 5; Jud. 9. 9; Job
36. 16; Isa 55. 2; Jer. 31. 14.
12. PASTURES,] as in 33. 2; 74. 20; 83. 12;
Jer. 9. 10, &c.   Sept. 'fat are the mountains.'
WILDERNESS,] as in 29. 6; 55. 7; 63. 1; 75. 6.
JOY,] as in 43. 4; 45. 15; Job 3. 22, &c.
HEIGHTS,] as in 72. 3; 114. 4, 6; 148. 9, &c.
GIRDEST ON,] as in 45. 3; 76. 10; 109. 19, &c.
Sept. Vulg. 'and with gladness the heights
are girded.'

CLOTHED,] as in 35. 26; 93. 1; 104. 1; 109. 18.
LAMBS,] not 'pastures;' as in 37. 20, &c.
FLOCK,] as in 44. 11, 22; 49. 14; 74. 1, &c.
VALLEYS,] as in 60. 6; 84. 6; 108. 7, &c.
COVERED,] as in 61. 2; 73. 6; 102. 1; Job
23. 9, &c. Sept. Vulg. 'full.'
CORN,] as in 72. 16; Ge. 41. 35, 49; 42. 3, &c.
SHOUT,] as in 60. 8; 108. 9.
SING,] as in 13. 6; 21. 13; 27. 6; 57. 7, &c.
Sept. Vulg. 'sing a hymn.'

LXVI. OVERSEER,] as in Ps. 4. 5. 6. 8. &c.
PSALM,] as in Ps. 3. 4. 5. 6. 8. 9. 12. &c.
SONG,] as in Ps. 30. 45. 46. 48. 65. &c. Sept.
Vulg. 'an ode of the resurrection.'
1. SHOUT,] not 'make a joyful noise;' as in
47. 1; 81. 1; 98. 4, 6; 100. 1, &c.
EARTH,] not 'lands,' as in C.V.
2. NAME,] as in v. 4. Sept. Vulg. 'sing
psalms to his name.'
HONOURABLE,] lit. 'honour.'
PRAISE,] as in v. 8; 9. 14; 22. 3, 25; 33. 1.
3. FEARFUL,] not 'terrible;' as in v. 5, &c.
WORKS,] as in 8. 3, 6; 19. 1; 28. 4, 5; 33. 4,
&c. Vulg. adds 'O Lord.'
ABUNDANCE,] not 'greatness;' as in 5. 7, &c.
STRENGTH,] as in 8. 2; 21. 1, 13; 28. 7, &c.
FEIGN OBEDIENCE,] lit. 'lie;' not 'submit
themselves;' as in 18. 1, 4; 81. 15, &c.
4. EARTH,] or 'land.'
BOW,] not 'worship;' as in 5. 7; 22. 27, &c.
SING PRAISE,] as in 7. 17; 9. 2; 18. 49, &c.
SELAH,] as in v. 7, 15; 3. 2, 4, 8; 4. 2, &c.
5. COME,] as in v. 16; 34. 11; 46. 8; 80. 2.
ACTS,] as in 9. 11; 14. 1; 77. 12; 78. 11, &c.
Sept. Vulg. 'counsel.'
SONS OF MEN,] as in 11. 4; 12. 1; 14. 2, &c.
6. TURNED,] as in 30. 11; 41. 3; 78. 9, &c.
SEA,] as in 8. 8; 24. 2; 33. 7; 46. 2, &c.
DRY LAND,] as in Ge. 1. 9, 10; Ex. 4. 9, &c.
RIVER,] not 'flood;' as in 24. 2; 46. 4, &c.
FOOT,] as in v. 9; 8. 6; 9. 15; 18. 9, 33, &c.
REJOICE,] as in 5. 11; 9. 2; 14. 7; 21. 1, &c.
7. RULING,] as in 22. 28; 59. 13; 89. 9, &c.
MIGHT,] as in 20. 6; 21. 13; 54. 1; 65. 6, &c.
WATCH,] not 'behold;' as in Ge. 31. 49; Isa.
21. 5.
REFRACTORY,] not 'rebellious;' as in 68.
6. 18; 78. 8, &c.
EXALT THEMSELVES,] as in 12. 2; 18. 46, &c.
8. PEOPLES,] as in 3. 6, 8; 7. 8; 9. 11, &c.
SOUND,] as in 143. 8; Song 2. 14; 8. 13, &c.
9. PLACED,] not 'holdeth;' as in 104. 3, &c.
OUR SOUL.] Sept. Vulg. 'my soul.'
LIFE,] as in 7. 5; 16. 11; 17. 14; 18. 46, &c.
SUFFERED,] lit. 'given.'
OUR FEET.] Sept. Vulg. 'my feet.'
MOVED,] as in 121. 3.
10. TRIED,] as in 26. 2; 17. 3; 66. 10; 95. 9.
REFINED,] not 'tried,' as in 26. 2; 17. 3; 105;
19, &c. Sept. Vulg. adds 'with fire.'
REFINING,] as in Da. 11. 35; Zec. 13. 9, &c.
11. NET,] as in Eze. 12. 13; 32. 3; 17. 20.
PRESSURE,] Original word not found again.
LOINS,] as in 69. 23; Ge. 37. 34; Ex. 12. 11.
Sept. Vulg. 'back.'
12. TO RIDE,] as in Ge. 41. 43; Ex. 4. 20, &c.
FIRE,] as in 11. 6; 18. 8, 12, 13; 21. 9, &c.
WATER,] as in 18. 16; 69. 12, 14, 15; 88. 17.
WATERED PLACE,] not 'wealthy;' as in 23.
5. Sept. Vulg. 'cooling, refreshing.'

13. HOUSE,] as in 5. 7; 23. 6; 26. 8; 27. 4.
BURNT-OFFERINGS,] as in v. 15: 20. 3, &c.
COMPLETE,] not 'pay;' as in 22. 25; 35. 12.
VOWS,] as in 22. 25; 50. 14; 56. 12; 61. 5.
14. OPENED,] not 'uttered;' as in 22. 13
144. 7, 10, 11, &c. Sept. Vulg. 'commanded.
DISTRESS,] as in 3. 1; 4. 1; 13. 4; 18. 6, &c.
15. FATLINGS,] as in Isa. 5. 17, &c.
OFFER,] lit. 'cause to go up.'
PERFUME,] as in 141. 2; Ex. 25. 6; 30. 1, &c.
RAMS,] as in 14. 4, 6; Ge. 15. 9; 22. 13, &c.
PREPARE,] lit. 'make;' as in 1. 3; 37. 5, &c.
BULLOCK,] as in Ge. 12. 16; 13. 5; 18. 7, &c.
HE GOATS,] not 'goats;' as in 50. 9, 13, &c.
SELAH,] as in v. 4, 7.
16. COME,] as in v. 16.
HEAR,] as in 4. 1; 17. 1, 6; 27. 7; 28. 2, &c.
FEAR,] as in 15. 4; 22. 23, 25; 25. 12, 14.
RECOUNT,] not 'declare;' as in 2. 7; 9. 1, &c.
17. CALLED,] not 'cried;' as in 14. 4; 17. 6.
EXALTATION,] not 'he was extolled;' as in
149. 6, &c.
18. INIQUITY,] as in 5. 5; 6. 8; 7. 14; 10. 7.
HEART,] as in 4. 7; 7. 10; 9. 1; 10. 6, 11, &c.
LORD,] as in 2. 4; 16. 2; 22. 30; 35. 17, &c.
HEAR,] as in 4. 3: 5. 3; 18. 6; 34. 2; 38. 13.
19. BUT.] Sept. Vulg. 'therefore.'
ATTENDED,] as in 5. 2; 10. 17; 17. 1, &c.
PRAYER,] as in v. 20; 4. 1; 6. 9; 17. 1, &c.
20. BLESSED,] as in 18. 46; 28. 6; 31. 21, &c.
TURNED ASIDE,] as in 18. 22; 39. 10; 119. 29.
LOVING-KINDNESS,] not 'mercy;' as in 5.
7; 6. 4; 13. 5; 17. 7, &c.

LXVII. OVERSEER,] as in Ps. 4. 5. 6. &c.
STRINGED INSTRUMENTS,] as in Ps. 4. 6.
54. 56. &c.
PSALM,] as in Ps. 3. 4. 5. 6. 8. 9. 12. 13. &c.
SONG,] as in 28. 7; 30. 1; 33. 3; 40. 3, &c.
1. FAVOUR,] not 'be merciful;' as in 59.
5; 123. 2, &c.
BLESS,] as in v. 6, 7; 5. 12; 16. 7; 26. 12.
TO SHINE,] as in 18. 28; 118. 27; 119. 30;
139. 12, &c. Vulg. adds 'and doth pity us.'
SELAH,] as in v. 4; 3. 2, 4, 8; 4. 2, 4, &c.
2. EARTH,] or 'land.'
WAY,] as in 1. 1, 6; 2. 12; 5. 8; 10. 5, &c.
NATIONS,] as in 2. 1, 8; 9. 5, 15, 17, 19, &c
SALVATION,] not 'saving health;' as in 3
2, 8; 9. 14; 13. 5; 14. 7, &c.
3. CONFESS,] as in v. 5; 6. 5; 17. 17; 9. 1.
PEOPLES,] as in v. 4; 3. 6, 8; 7. 8; 9. 11, &c
4. REJOICE,] as in 5. 11; 9. 2; 14. 7; 21. 1.
SING,] as in 5. 11: 20. 5; 51. 14; 59. 16, &c
JUDGEST,] as in 9. 8; 58. 11.
UPRIGHT,] as in 9. 8; 58. 1; 67. 4; 72. 4, &c
COMFORTEST,] not 'govern;' as in C.V
Sept. Vulg. 'directest.'
5. CONFESS,] not 'praise,' as in v. 5.
6. INCREASE,] as in 78. 46; 95. 12, &c.
Sept. Vulg. 'fruit.'
OUR GOD,] as in 18. 31; 20. 5, 7; 40. 3, &c.
7. ENDS OF EARTH,] or 'land.'
FEAR,] as in 33. 8; 40. 3; 52. 6; 64. 9, &c.

LXVIII. OVERSEER,] as in Ps. 4. 5. 6. 8. &c
PSALM..SONG,] as in Ps. 30. 48. 65. 67. 75
76. 83. 87. 88. 92. 108.
1. RISE,] as in 1. 5; 12. 5; 24. 3; 27. 3, &c.
GOD,] as in v. 2, 4, 5, 7, 10. 15, 21. 24, 26
28, 31, 32, 34, 35, &c.

SCATTERED,] as in Ge. 11. 4; Nu. 20. 35, &c.
HATING,] as in 18. 40; 44. 7, 10; 55. 12, &c.
FLEE,] as in 104. 7; 114 3, 5; Ge. 14. 10, &c.
2. DRIVING AWAY,] as in 1. 4; Lev. 26. 36;
Job 13. 25, &c. Sept. Vulg. 'disappear-
ance..they disappear.'
SMOKE,] as in 18. 8; 37. 20; 102. 3, &c.
MELTING,] as in 22. 14; 97. 5; 112. 10, &c.
WAX,] as in 72. 14; 97. 5; Mic. 1. 4.
PERISH,] as in 1. 6; 2. 12; 9. 3, 18; 37. 20.
PRESENCE,] lit. 'face.'
3. REJOICE,] as in 5. 11; 9. 2; 14. 7; 21. 1.
EXULT,] as in 5. 11; 9. 2; 25. 2; 68. 3, &c.
JOY,] as in 19. 5; 35. 9; 40. 16; 70. 4, &c.
GLADNESS,] as in 4. 7; 16. 11; 21. 6; 30. 11.
4. SING,] as in v. 32; 33. 3; 96. 1, 2; 98. 1.
PRAISE,] as in 9. 11; 30. 4; 33. 2; 47. 6, &c.
RAISE UP A HIGHWAY,] not 'extol;' as in
Isa. 57. 14; 62. 10; Jer. 50. 26, &c.
RIDING,] as in v. 33; Ge. 1. 9, 17; Ex. 15. 1,
&c. Sept. Vulg. 'goes up upon the sun-
sets.'
IN JAH,] as in v. 18; 77. 11; 89. 8; 94. 7, 12;
102. 18, &c. Sept. Vulg. omit 'in.'
EXULT,] as in 28. 7; 60. 6; 94. 3; 96. 12,
&c. Sept. Vulg. add 'they are confounded
from his presence.'
5. FATHER,] as in 22. 4; 27. 10; 39. 12, &c.
FATHERLESS,] as in Ps. 10. 14, 18; 82. 3, &c.
JUDGE,] as in 1 Sa. 24. 15.
WIDOWS,] as in 78. 64; 94. 6; 109. 9; 146. 9.
HABITATION,] as in 26. 8; 71. 3; 90. 1; 91.
9, &c. Sept. Vulg. 'place.'
6. GOD,] as in v. 1.
LONELY,] as in 22. 20; 25. 16; 35. 17, &c.
TO DWELL,] as in 113. 9.
AT HOME,] as in Ex. 28. 26; 39. 19, &c.
BOUND ONES,] as in Ps. 69. 33; 79. 11, &c.
PROSPERITY.] Original word not found
again.
ONLY,] as in 37. 8, &c.
REFRACTORY,] not 'rebellious;' as in v.
18; 66. 7; 78. 8, &c.
DRY PLACE,] as in Neh. 4. 13; Eze. 24. 7,
8; 26. 4, 14, &c. Sept. Vulg. 'sepulchres.'
7. GOING FORTH,] as in 81. 5; 105. 38, &c.
STEPPING,] as in Jud. 5. 4; Ge. 49. 22, &c.
WILDERNESS,] as in 78. 40; 106. 14; 107. 4.
8. EARTH,] or 'land.'
SHAKEN,] as in 18. 7; 46. 3; 72. 16; 77. 18.
DROPPED,] as in Jud. 5. 4; Job 29. 22, &c.
SINAI,] as in v. 17; De. 33. 2; Jud. 5. 5.
Sept. Vulg. 'from the face of the God of
Sinai.'
GOD OF ISRAEL,] as in 41. 13; 69. 6; 72. 18.
9. SHOWER,] not 'rain;' as in 105. 32, &c.
FREEWILL BLESSINGS,] not 'plentiful;' as
in 54. 6; 110. 3; 119. 108, &c.
SHAKEST,] not 'send;' as in Ex. 20. 25, &c.
INHERITANCE,] as in 2. 8; 28. 9; 33. 12, &c.
WEARY,] as in Ex. 7. 18; Prov. 26. 15, &c.
ESTABLISHED,] as in 8. 3; 9. 7; 11. 2; 40. 2.
10. COMPANY,] lit. 'living one.' So Sept.
Vulg. &c.
DWELT,] as in 1. 1; 9. 4; 23. 6; 26. 4; 29. 10.
PREPAREST,] as in 10. 17; 65. 9; 78. 20, &c.
POOR,] as in 9. 12, 18; 10. 2, 9, 12; 12. 5, &c.
11. LORD,] as in v. 17, 19, 20, 22, 26, 32, &c.
SAYING,] as in 19. 2, 3; 77. 8; Job 22. 28;
Hab. 3. 9.
FEMALE PROCLAIMERS,] as in 1 Sa. 4. 17;

Sa. 4. 10; 18. 26; Isa. 40. 9; 41. 27; 52. 7;
Neh. 1. 13. Sept. Vulg. 'evangelists.'
NUMEROUS,] as in 3. 1, 2; 4. 6; 18. 16, &c.
HOST,] as in 24. 10; 33. 6; 44. 9; 46. 7, &c.
12. KINGS,] as in v. 14, 29; 2. 2, 10; 48. 4.
FLEE,] as in 31. 11; 55. 7; Ge. 31. 40, &c.
Sept. Vulg. 'the king of the hosts, the most
beloved.'
FEMALE INHABITANT,] as in Jer. 6. 2.
Sept. Vulg. 'comeliness.'
APPORTIONETH,] not 'divided;' as in 22.
18; 60. 6; 108. 7, &c.
SPOIL,] as in 119. 162; Ge. 49. 27; Ex. 15. 9.
13. LIE,] as in 3. 5; 4. 8; 41. 8; 57. 4; 88. 5,
&c. Sept. Vulg. 'slept.'
TWO BOUNDARIES,] not 'pots,' as in C.V.
Sept. Vulg. 'lots.'
WINGS,] as in 17. 8; 18. 10; 36. 7; 57. 1, &c.
DOVE,] as in 55. 6; 56. 1; Ge. 8. 8, 9, 10, &c.
COVERED,] as in 2 Sa. 15. 30; 2 Ch. 3. 5, &c.
SILVER,] as in v. 30; 12. 6; 15. 5; 66. 10, &c.
PINIONS,] not 'feathers;' as in 91. 4; De.
32. 11; Job 39. 13. Sept. Vulg. 'back.'
YELLOW GOLD,] as in Job 41. 30; Prov. 3. 14.
14. MIGHTY,] as in 91. 1; Ge. 17. 1; 28. 3.
SPREADETH,] not 'scattered;' as in Isa.
1. 14, &c.
KINGS.] Sept. Vulg. 'heavenly kings.'
SNOW.] Original word not found again.
SALMON,] as in Jud. 9. 48.
15. HILL OF GOD,] that is one belonging to
him.
BASHAN,] thought to be Hermon. Sept.
Vulg. 'a fertile hill.'
HILL OF HEIGHTS,] a very high hill. Sept.
Vulg. 'a hill of milk.'
16. ENVY.] Original word not found
again. Sept. Vulg. 'distrust.'
HIGH HILLS,] as in v. 15.
DESIRED,] as in Ex. 20. 17; 34. 24; De. 5. 21.
SEAT,] as in 27. 4; 33. 14; 101. 6; 113. 5, &c.
TABERNACLE,] as in 15. 1; 16. 9; 37. 29, &c.
17. CHARIOTS,] as in 20. 17; 76. 6; Ge. 50. 9.
MYRIADS,] as in Neh. 7. 71.
CHANGES.] Original word not found again.
Sept. 'vigorous ones.' Vulg. 'rejoicing
ones.'
SINAI,] as in v. 8.
SANCTUARY,] as in v. 5, 24.
18. ON HIGH,] as in 7. 7; 10. 5; 18. 16, &c.
CAPTIVITY,] as in 78. 61; Ex. 12. 29; 81. 12.
TAKEN,] or 'received;' as in 15. 5; or
'given,' as in Hos. 14. 2.
GIFTS,] as in 96. 6; Ex. 28. 38, &c.
FOR MEN,] or 'among men.'
REFRACTORY,] not 'rebellious;' as in v. 6.
Sept. Vulg. 'unbelieving.'
REST,] lit. 'tabernacle;' as in 85. 9; Ge.
35. 22, &c.
O JAH, GOD] of Israel, as in v. 4.
19. LORD,] as in v. 4.
DAY BY DAY,] as in 61. 8.
LAYETH,] as in Ge. 44. 13; Neh. 13. 15, &c.
SALVATION,] as in 3. 2, 8; 9. 14; 13. 5, &c.
20. DELIVERANCES.] Original word not
found again.
JEHOVAH, LORD] of heaven and earth.
OUT-GOINGS,] as in Prov. 4. 23; Eze. 48. 30.
21. SMITE,] not 'wound;' as in v. 23; 18. 38.
HEAD,] as the most vital part.
CROWN,] as in 7. 16; Ge. 49. 26; De. 28. 35.

HABITUAL WALKER,] as in Ge. 3. 8; De.
23. 14; 1 Sa. 12. 2; 25. 27; 2 Sa. 7. 6; Est. 2.
11; Prov. 20. 7; 24. 34; Eze. 1. 13.
GUILT,] not 'trespasses;' as in Ge. 26. 10;
Lev. 5. 6, 7, 15, 18, &c.
22. LORD,] as in v. 11, 17, 19, 20, 26, 32.
BASHAN,] as in v. 15.
DEPTHS OF THE SEA,] as in 69. 2, 15, &c.
23. DASHEST,] or 'smitest;' as in v. 21.
BLOOD,] as in 5. 6; 9. 12; 16. 4; 26. 9, &c.
DOGS,] as in 22. 16, 20; 59. 6, 14; Ex. 11. 7.
24. GOINGS,] as in Job 6. 19; Prov. 31. 27;
Neh. 2. 5; Hab. 3. 6.
MY GOD,] as in 18. 2; 22. 1, 10; 63. 1; 89. 26.
MY KING,] as in 2. 6; 5. 2; 44. 4; 74. 12, &c.
Sept. Vulg. 'the king.'
SANCTUARY,] as in v. 5, 17.
25. SINGERS,] as in 87. 7; 2 Sa. 19. 35; 1 K.
10. 12, &c.   Sept. Vulg. 'princes.'
PLAYERS ON INSTRUMENTS,] as in 1 Sa. 16.
16; 18. 10; 19. 9; 2 K. 3. 15.
VIRGINS,] as in Ge. 24. 43; Ex. 2. 8; Prov.
30. 19; Song 1. 3; 6. 8; Isa. 7. 14.
TIMBRELS,] as in Na. 2. 7.
26. ASSEMBLIES,] as in 26. 12.
GOD,] as in v. 1, 2.
LORD,] as in v. 11, 17, 20, 22, 26, 32.
FOUNTAIN,] as in 36. 9; Lev. 12. 7; 20. 18.
27. LITTLE,] as in 119. 141; Ge. 19. 31, &c.
BENJAMIN,] as in 1 Sa. 9. 21.
RULER,] as in 1 K. 4. 24; 5. 16; 9. 23; 2 Ch.
8. 10; Isa. 14. 6.   Sept. Vulg. 'in ecstasy.'
HEADS,] as in 45. 16; 82. 7; 105. 22; 119. 23.
JUDAH] the fourth son of Leah.
DEFENCE.] Original word is not found
again.
ZEBULUN,] the tenth son of Jacob by
Leah.
NAPHTALI,] a son of Bilhah.
28. THY GOD,] as in 42. 3, 10; 45. 7; 50. 7,
&c.   Sept. Vulg. omit 'thy.'
COMMANDED,] as in 7. 6; 33. 9; 68. 28, &c.
STRENGTH,] as in v. 33, 34, 35.
BE STRONG,] as in 9. 9; 52. 7; 89. 13, &c.
WROUGHT,] as in 11. 3; 31. 19; 44. 1; 119. 3.
29. BECAUSE,] lit. 'from.'   So Sept. Vulg.
TEMPLE,] as in 5. 7; 11. 4; 18. 6; 27. 4, &c.
JERUSALEM,] where David had put the
ark.
PRESENT,] as in 76. 11; Isa. 18. 7.
30. REBUKE,] as in 9. 5; 119. 21; Ge. 37. 10.
BEAST.] So Sept. Vulg. &c.
REEDS,] not 'spearmen;' as in Ge. 41. 5,
22, 31, 32, 33, 35, 36, &c.
COMPANY,] not 'multitude;' as in 1. 5; 7. 7.
BULLS,] lit. 'mighty ones;' as in 22. 12, &c.
CALVES,] as in 29. 6; 106. 19; Ex. 32. 4, &c.
PEOPLES,] as in v. 7, 35.
HUMBLING,] not 'submit;' as in Prov. 6. 3.
Sept. Vulg. 'to exclude those tried with
silver.'
PIECES.] Original word is not found again.
SCATTER,] as in Da. 11. 24.
DELIGHTING,] as in 37. 23; 51. 16, 19, &c.
CONFLICTS,] as in 55. 18. 21; 78. 9; 144. 1.
31. FAT ONES.] Original word is not found
again.   Sept. 'honoured ones;' Vulg. 'le-
gates.'
EGYPT,] on the south-west of Canaan.
CUSH,] on the northern coast of the Red
Sea.

TO RUN,] as in Ge. 41. 14; 1 Sa. 17. 17, &c.
32. SING,] as in v. 4.
PRAISE,] as in v. 4.   Vulg. 'sing psalms to
God.'
33. RIDING,] as in v. 4.   Sept. Vulg. 'goes
up.'
HEAVENS OF THE HEAVENS,] as in De. 10.
14; 1 K. 8. 27.
OF OLD,] as in 44. 1; 55. 19; 74. 2, 12; 77. 5,
&c.   Sept. Vulg. 'from the east.'
GIVETH,] not 'send,' as in C.V.
STRONG,] as in v. 28, 34, 35.
34. ASCRIBE,] lit. 'give.'
STRENGTH,] as in v. 28.
EXCELLENCY,] as in 10. 2; 31. 18, 23; 36. 11.
CLOUDS,] as in 18. 11; 36. 5; 57. 10; 77. 17.
35. FEARFUL,] not 'terrible,' as in C.V.
OUT OF.] Sept. Vulg. 'in.'
SANCTUARIES,] as in 73. 17; 74. 7; 78. 69.
STRENGTH AND MIGHT,] as in v. 28.
PEOPLE,] as in v. 7, 30.   Sept. Vulg. 'his
people.'
GOD,] as in v. 19; 28. 6; 31. 21; 66. 20, &c.

LXIX. OVERSEER,] as in Ps. 4. 5. 6. 8. &c.
LILIES,] as in Ps. 45. 80; 1 K. 7. 22, 26;
Song 2. 16; 4. 5; 5. 13; 6. 2, 3; 7. 2.   Sept.
Vulg. 'those who are changed.'
1. SAVE,] as in 3. 7; 6. 4; 7. 1; 12. 1; 20. 9.
WATERS,] as in v. 2, 14, 15.
SOUL,] as in v. 10, 18.   Sept. Vulg. 'my
soul.'
2. SUNK,] as in v. 14; 9. 15; 1 Sa. 17. 49, &c.
DEEP,] as in v. 15; 68. 22; 107. 24, &c.
MIRE,] as in 40. 2.
STANDING,] as in 1 K. 10. 5; 1 Ch. 23. 28;
2 Ch. 9. 4; 35. 15; Isa. 22. 19.   Sept. Vulg.
'substance.'
DEPTHS,] as in v. 14; 130. 1; Isa. 51. 10;
Eze. 28. 34.   Vulg. 'heights.'
FLOOD,] as in v. 15; Isa. 27. 12.
OVER-FLOWN,] as in v. 15; 78. 20; 124. 4, &c.
3. WEARIED,] as in 6. 6; Jos. 24. 13, &c.
CALLING,] not 'crying;' as in 4. 1, 3; 26. 9.
BURNT,] not 'dried;' as in 102. 3; Song 1. 6.
THROAT,] as in 5. 9; 115. 7; 149. 6, &c.
CONSUMED,] not 'fail;' as in 31. 10; 37. 20.
EYES,] as in 119. 82, 123; Jer. 14. 6, &c.
4. HATING,] as in v. 14.
WITHOUT CAUSE,] as in 35. 7, 19; 109. 3, &c.
HAIRS OF MY HEAD,] as in 40. 12, &c.
MIGHTY,] as in 38. 19; 40. 5, 12; 139. 17, &c.
DESTROYERS,] lit. 'cutters off.'
LYING,] not 'wrongfully;' as in 7. 14, &c.
TOOK NOT AWAY,] as in Ge. 21. 25; 31. 31.
BRING BACK,] as in 18. 20, 24; 44. 10, &c.
5. GOD,] as in v. 1, 6, 13, 29, 32, 35.
OVERTURN,] not 'foolishness.'   Sept. Vulg.
'heedlessness.'
DESOLATIONS,] not 'sins.'   Sept. 'discord-
ance.'
HID,] lit. 'cut off;' as in 139. 15, &c.
6. JEHOVAH OF HOSTS,] as in 24. 10; 46. 7.
SEEKING,] as in 24. 6; 35. 5; 37. 27, &c.
BLUSH,] not 'be ashamed;' as in 6. 10, &c.
GOD OF ISRAEL,] as in 20. 1; 41. 13; 59, 5.
7. BORNE,] as in 15. 3; 24. 4; 32. 5; 83. 2, &c.
REPROACH,] as in v. 9, 10, 19, 20; 15. 3, &c.
SHAME,] as in v. 19; 4. 2; 35. 26; 44. 15, &c.
COVERED,] as in 32. 5; 40. 10; 44. 15, &c.

8. STRANGER.] Original word not found again.
BROTHER,] as in 22. 22; 35. 14; 49. 7, &c.
FOREIGNER,] as in Ge. 31. 15, Ex. 2. 22, &c.
SONS OF MY MOTHER,] as in 50. 20, &c.
9. ZEAL.] as in 79. 5; 119. 139; Nu. 5. 14, &c.
HOUSE,] as in 5. 7; 23. 6; 26. 8; 27. 4, &c.
CONSUMED,] as in 14. 4; 22. 29; 53. 4, &c.
REPROACHES,] as in v. 7, 10, 19, 20.
REPROACHERS,] as in 119. 42; Prov. 27. 11.
FALLEN,] as in 10. 10; 16. 6; 20. 8; 27. 2, &c.
10. WEEP,] as in 78. 64; 126. 6; 137. 1, &c.
FASTING,] as in 35. 13; 109. 24; 2 Sa. 12. 16.
REPROACH,] as in v. 7, 9, 19, 20.
11. CLOTHING,] as in 22. 18; 35. 13; 45. 13.
SACKCLOTH,] as in 30. 11; 35. 13; Ge. 37. 34.
SIMILE,] as in 44. 14; 49. 4; 78. 2; Nu. 23. 7.
12. SITTING,] as in v. 25; 2. 4; 9. 11; 17. 12.
GATE,] as in 9. 13, 14; 24. 7, 9; 87. 2, &c.
MEDITATE,] not 'speak;' as in 55. 17, &c.
DRINKING,] as in 1 Sa. 30. 16; 1 K. 1. 25, &c.
STRONG DRINK,] as in Lev. 10. 9; Nu. 6. 3;
28. 7, &c. Sept. Vulg. 'wine.'
PLAY ON INSTRUMENTS,] as in Ps. 4. 6. 54.
55. &c. Sept. Vulg. 'sing psalms.'
13. PRAYER,] as in 4. 1; 6. 9; 17. 1; 35. 13.
GOOD PLEASURE,] as in 5. 12; 19. 14; 30. 5.
ABUNDANCE,] as in v. 16; 5. 7, &c. Sept.
'fulness.'
KINDNESS,] not 'mercy;' as in v. 16; 5. 7.
ANSWER,] not 'hear;' as in v. 16, 17; 4. 1.
TRUTH,] as in 15. 2; 19. 9; 25. 5, 10; 26. 3.
SALVATION,] as in 12. 5; 18. 2, 35, 46, &c.
14. DELIVER,] as in 7. 1; 22. 20; 25. 20; 31.
2, 15, &c. Sept. 'save.'
MIRE,] as in 18. 42; 40. 2; 2 Sa. 22. 43, &c.
SINK,] as in v. 2.
HATING,] as in v. 4.
DEEP PLACES,] as in v. 14.
15. FLOOD,] as in v. 2.
OVERFLOW,] as in v. 2.
DEEP,] as in v. 2.
SWALLOW UP,] as in 21. 19; 35. 25; 55. 9;
106. 17.
PIT,] as in 55. 23; Ge. 14. 10; 16. 14, &c.
SHUT.] Original verb not found again.
16. ANSWER,] not 'hear;' as in v. 13, 17.
KINDNESS,] as in v. 13.
MERCIES,] as in 25. 6; 40. 11; 51. 1, &c.
17. HIDE,] as in 13. 1; 17. 8; 27. 5, 9; 31.
20, &c. Sept. Vulg. 'turn away.'
SERVANT,] as in v. 36; 18. 1; 19. 11, 13, &c.
DISTRESS,] as in 31. 9; 129. 1, &c.
HASTE,] as in 79. 8; 102. 2; 143. 7, &c.
ANSWER,] not 'hear;' as in v. 13, 16.
18. BE NEAR,] not 'draw nigh;' as in Ex.
16. 9; Lev. 9. 7, &c.
REDEEM,] as in 2. 14; 106. 10; 119. 154, &c.
RANSOM,] not 'deliver;' as in 25. 22; 26. 11.
19. REPROACH,] as in v. 7, 9, 10, 20.
SHAME,] as in v. 7.
BLUSHING,] not 'dishonour;' as in v. 7.
ADVERSARIES,] as in 6. 7; 7. 4, 6; 8. 2, &c.
20. BROKEN MY HEART,] as in 34. 18; 51.
17; Isa. 61. 1; Jer. 23. 9, &c. Sept. 'hath my
soul expected, and misery.'
SICK,] not 'full of heaviness;' as in 2 Sa.
12. 15.
LOOK,] or 'wait;' as in 27. 40; 37. 34; 40. 1.
BEMOANER,] not 'take pity;' as in Job 2.
11; Prov. 26. 2, &c. Sept. 'sympathizers.'

NONE,] as in 38. 10; 73. 3, &c.
COMFORTERS,] as in 2 Sa. 10. 3; 1 Ch. 19. 3.
FOUND,] as in 76. 5; 84. 3; 89. 20; 107. 4, &c.
21. FOOD.] Original word not found again.
Vulg. 'in my food.'
GALL,] as in De. 29. 18; 32. 33; Job 20. 16.
THIRST,] as in 104. 11; Ex. 17. 3; De. 28. 48.
TO DRINK,] as in 36. 10; 78. 15; 80. 5, &c.
VINEGAR,] as in Nu. 6. 3; Ruth 2. 14; Prov.
10. 26; 25. 20.
22. TABLE,] as in 23. 5; 78. 19; 128. 3, &c.
SNARE,] as in 11. 6; 91. 3; 119. 110; 124. 7.
RECOMPENSE,] not 'welfare;' as in Isa. 34.
8; Hos. 9. 7; Mic. 7. 3. So Sept. Vulg.
TRAP,] as in 18. 5; 64. 5; 106. 36; 140. 5, &c.
Sept. Vulg. 'stumbling-block.'
23. DARKENED,] as in Ex. 10. 15; Job 3. 9.
FROM SEEING,] as in 119. 37, &c.
LOINS,] as in 66. 11; Ge. 37. 34; Ex. 12. 11,
&c. Sept. Vulg. 'back.'
SHAKE,] or 'slip, slide;' as in 18. 36, &c.
Sept. Vulg. 'bend.'
24. POUR,] as in 62. 8; 79. 6; Jud. 6. 20, &c.
INDIGNATION,] as in 38. 3; 78. 49; 102. 10, &c.
FIERCENESS,] as in 2. 5; 58. 9; 78. 49. &c.
ANGER,] as in 2. 5, 12; 6. 1; 7. 6; 10. 4, &c
SEIZE,] or 'overtake;' as in 7. 5; 18. 37, &c.
25. TOWER,] not 'habitation;' as in Ge. 25.
16; Nu. 31. 10, &c.
DESOLATED,] as in 54. 3; Jer. 33. 10; Eze.
29. 12, &c. Sept. Vulg. 'deserted.'
TENTS,] as in 19. 4; 52. 5; 78. 51, 55, &c.
DWELLER,] as in v. 12.
26. PURSUED,] not 'persecute;' as in 119 86.
161; 143. 3, &c.
SMITTEN,] as in 3. 7; 78. 20; 135. 8, 10.
RECOUNT,] not 'talk;' as in 2. 7; 9. 1, &c.
PAIN,] not 'grief;' as in 32. 10; 38. 17, &c.
PIERCED ONES,] as in 88. 5; 89. 10; Ge. 34.
27, &c. Sept. Vulg. 'my wounds.'
27. PUNISHMENT,] as in Ge. 4. 13; 19. 15, &c.
FOR,] lit. 'upon, along with.'
INIQUITY,] or 'punishment,' as in preced-
ing word.
RIGHTEOUSNESS,] as in 5. 8; 11. 7; 22. 31.
28. BLOTTED,] as in 109. 13, 14; Ge. 7. 23.
BOOK,] as in 40. 7; 139. 16; Ex. 32. 32, &c.
RIGHTEOUS,] as in 1. 5, 6; 5. 12; 7. 9, &c.
WRITTEN,] as in 102. 18; 139. 16; Ezr. 8. 34.
29. AFFLICTED,] as in 9. 12, 18; 10. 2, 9, &c.
PAINED,] as in Ge. 34. 25, &c.
SALVATION,] as in 3. 2, 8; 9. 14; 13. 5, &c.
O GOD.] Sept. 'of thy countenance.'
SET ON HIGH,] as in 20. 1; 59. 1; 91. 14;
107. 41, &c. Sept. Vulg. 'sustain.'
30. PRAISE,] as in v. 34; 22. 22, 26; 35. 18.
NAME,] as in v. 36; 5. 11; 7. 17; 8. 1; 9. 2.
SONG,] as in 28. 7; 31. 1; 33. 3; 40. 3, &c.
Sept. 'ode.'
MAGNIFY,] as in 34. 3; Ge. 12. 2; Jos. 4. 14.
THANKSGIVING,] as in 26. 7; 42. 4; 50. 14,
23, &c. Sept. Vulg. 'praise.'
31. BETTER,] as in Ps. 4. 6; 19; De. 1. 23; &c.
OX,] as in 106. 20; Ge. 32. 5; 49. 6; Ex. 20.
17, &c. Sept. Vulg. 'young ox.'
BULLOCK,] as in 22. 12; 50. 9; 51. 19, &c.
HORNED.] Original word not found again.
HOOFED,] as in Lev. 11. 3, 4, 5, 6, 7, 26, &c.
32. HUMBLE,] as in 9. 12, 18; 10. 12, 17; 22
26, &c. Sept. Vulg. 'poor.'
SEEN,] as in 10. 11, 14; 31. 7; 33. 13; 35. 21

REJOICE,] as in 5. 11; 9. 2; 14. 7; 21. 1, &c.
SEEK,] as in 9. 10, 12; 14. 2; 22. 26; 24. 6,
&c.   Sept. Vulg. 'seek ye God, and live.'
LIVETH,] as in 22. 26; 49. 9; 72. 15; 89. 48.
33. HEARKENETH,] not 'heareth;' as in 38.
14; 59. 7, &c.
NEEDY,] not 'poor;' as in 9. 18; 12. 5, &c.
BOUND ONES,] as in 68. 6; 79. 11; 102. 20.
DESPISED,] as in 22. 24; 51. 11; 73. 20, &c.
34. HEAVENS,] as in 148. 14, &c.
EARTH,] or 'land.'
PRAISE,] as in v. 30.
SEAS,] as in 8. 8; 24. 2; 33. 7; 46. 2, &c.
MOVING THING,] as in Ge. 1. 21, 26, 28, &c.
35. SAVE,] as in 18. 27; 34. 18; 36. 6, &c.
ZION,] as in 2. 6; 9. 11; 48. 2, 11, 12; 51. 18.
BUILD,] as in 28. 5; 51. 18; 78. 69; 127. 1.
CITIES,] as in 9. 6; 31. 21; 46. 4; 48. 1, &c.
JUDAH,] as in 48. 11; 60. 7; 63. 1; 68. 27, &c.
DWELT,] as in 68. 10; 119. 23; 122. 5; 137. 1.
POSSESS,] as in 25. 13; 37. 9, 34; 44. 3, &c.
36. SEED,] as in 18. 50; 21. 10; 22. 23, &c.
SERVANTS,] as in v. 17.
INHERIT,] as in 82. 8; 119. 111; Ex. 23. 30.
LOVING,] as in 5. 11; 11. 5; 33. 5; 34. 12, &c.
NAME,] as in v. 30.
DWELL,] as in 15. 1; 16. 9; 37. 29; 55. 6, &c.

LXX. OVERSEER,] as in Ps. 4. 5. 6. 8. 9. &c.
DAVID.] Vulg. adds 'a psalm.'
TO CAUSE TO REMEMBER,] as in 38. 1.
Sept. Vulg. add, 'in the Lord's delivering
him.'
1. GOD,] as in v. 4, 5; the creator of all.
DELIVER,] as in 33. 19; 40. 13, &c.   Sept.
omits.
JEHOVAH,] as in v. 5; the covenant God.
Sept. omits.
HELP,] as in 22. 19; 27. 9; 35. 2; 38. 22, &c.
HASTE,] as in v. 5; 22. 19; 38. 22; 40. 13, &c.
2. ASHAMED,] as in 6. 10; 25. 2, 3, 20, &c.
CONFOUNDED,] as in 34. 5; 35. 4, 26; 40. 14.
SEEKING,] as in v. 4; 24. 6; 35. 4; 37. 25, &c.
TURNED,] as in 35. 4; 40. 14; 78. 57; 120. 5.
BACKWARD,] as in 9. 3; 35. 4; 40. 14, &c.
BLUSH,] not 'put to confusion;' as in 35.
4, &c.
EVIL,] as in 5. 4; 7. 4, 9; 10. 6, 15, &c.
3. TURN BACK,] as in 6. 10; 7. 12, 16; 9. 17;
18. 37, &c.   Sept. Vulg. 'instantly.'
SHAME,] as in 35. 26; 40. 15; 44. 15; 69. 19.
AHA,] as in 35. 21, 25; 40. 15; Job 39. 25,
&c.   Sept. Vulg. add 'to me.'
4. SEEKING,] as in v. 2.
JOY,] as in 19. 5; 35. 9; 40. 16; 68. 3, &c.
BE GLAD,] as in 5. 11; 9. 2; 14. 7; 21. 1, &c.
LOVING, as in 5. 11; 11. 5; 33. 5; 34. 12, &c.
SALVATION,] as in 3. 2, 8; 9. 14; 13. 5, &c.
CONTINUALLY,] as in 16. 8; 25. 15; 34. 1, &c.
MAGNIFIED,] as in 35. 27; 40. 16, &c.
5. POOR,] as in 9. 12, 18; 10. 2, 9, 12; 12. 5.
NEEDY,] as in 9. 18; 12. 5: 35. 10; 37. 14, &c.
HASTE,] as in v. 1.   Sept. Vulg. 'help.'
HELP,] as in 20. 3; 33. 20; 89. 19; 115. 9, &c.
DELIVERER,] as in 18. 2, 48; 40. 17; 144. 2.
TARRY,] as in 40. 17; 127. 2; Ge. 24. 56, &c.

LXXI. This Psalm is probably a continua-
tion of the preceding as in 27 MSS.   Sept.
Vulg. Ar. add 'By David, for the sons of
Jonadab, and the first of the captives.'

1. JEHOVAH,] as in v. 5, 16.
TRUSTED,] as in 7. 1; 11. 1; 16. 1; 25. 20, &c
ASHAMED,] as in v. 13, 24; 6. 10; 22. 5, &c
TO THE AGE,] as in 5. 11; 9. 5, 7; 10. 16, &c.
2. RIGHTEOUSNESS,] as in v. 15, 16, 19, &c
DELIVER,] as in 18. 17, 48; 22. 8; 34. 19, &c.
TO ESCAPE,] as in 18. 43; 22. 4, 8; 37. 40, &c.
INCLINE,] as in 17. 6; 31. 2; 45. 10; 78. 1, &c.
EAR,] as in 10. 17; 17. 6; 18. 6, 44; 31. 2, &c.
SAVE,] as in 3. 7; 6. 4; 7. 1; 12. 1; 20. 9, &c.
3. ROCK,] not 'strong;' as in 18. 2, 31, 46;
19. 14, &c.   Sept. Vulg. 'for God.'
HABITATION,] as in 26. 8; 68. 5; 90. 1, &c.
CONTINUALLY,] as in v. 6, 14; 16. 8; 25. 15,
&c.   Sept. Vulg. 'for a strong place to save
me.'
GIVEN COMMAND,] as in 7. 6; 33. 9; 68. 28.
ROCK,] as in 18. 2; 31. 3; 40. 2; 42. 9, &c
BULWARK,] as in 18. 2; 31. 2, 3; 66. 11; 91. 2,
&c.   Sept. Vulg. 'refuge.'
4. MY GOD,] as in v. 12, 22.
HAND OF THE WICKED,] as in 36. 11; 82.
4; 97. 10; 140. 4, &c.
PERVERSE,] not 'unrighteous,' as in C.V.
VIOLENT,] not 'cruel;' as in Isa. 26. 10, &c.
Sept. Vulg. 'unjust.'
5. HOPE,] as in 9. 18; 62. 5; Ruth 1. 12, &c.
LORD JEHOVAH,] as in v. 1, 16.
TRUST,] as in 40. 4; 65. 5; Job 8. 14; 18. 14.
YOUTH,] as in v. 17; 25. 7; 103. 5; 127. 4, &c.
6. SUPPORTED,] as in Jud. 16. 29; 2 K. 18.
21; 2 Ch. 32. 8; Isa. 36. 6; 48. 2.
BELLY,] as in 17. 14; 22. 9, 10; 31. 9; 44. 25.
BOWELS,] as in 22. 14; 40. 8; Ge. 15. 4, &c.
CUT ME OUT,] not 'took me out,' as in C.V.
Sept. Vulg. 'my shelter or protector.'
IN THEE,] not 'of thee,' as in C.V.
PRAISE,] as in v. 8, 14; 9. 14; 22. 3, 25, &c.
7. WONDER,] as in 78. 43; 105. 5, 27; 135. 8.
MANY,] or 'a multitude.'
STRONG,] as in 8. 2; 21. 1, 13; 28. 7, 8, &c.
REFUGE,] as in 14. 6; 46. 1; 61. 3; 62. 7, 8,
&c.   Sept. Vulg. 'help.'
8. FILLED,] as in 72. 19; 107. 9; 126. 2, &c.
MOUTH,] as in v. 15.
THY PRAISE,] as in v. 6, 14.   Sept. Vulg.
omit 'my,' but add 'and I praise thy glory.'
BEAUTY,] not 'honour;' as in 78. 61; 89. 17,
&c.   Sept. Vulg. 'greatness.'
9. ACCORDING TO,] Sept. Vulg. 'in.'
CAST AWAY,] as in 2. 3; 50. 17; 51. 11, &c.
OLD AGE,] as in v. 18; Ge. 24. 36; 1 K. 11
4; 15. 23; Isa. 46. 4.
CONSUMPTION,] as in Ruth 2. 23; 1 Ch. 28.
FORSAKE,] as in v. 18; 10. 14; 16. 10; 27. 9.
10. ENEMIES,] as in 3. 7; 6. 10; 7. 5; 8. 2.
WATCHING,] as in 31. 6; 34. 20; 97. 10, &c.
TAKEN COUNSEL,] as in 83. 5; 1 K. 12. 6, &c.
11. FORSAKEN, as in 9. 10; 22. 1; 27. 10, &c.
PURSUE,] not 'persecute;' as in 34. 14, &c.
CATCH,] as in 1 K. 13. 4; 18. 40; 20. 18, &c.
DELIVERER,] as in 7. 2; 35. 10; 50. 22, &c.
12. FAR,] as in 22. 1, 11, 19; 35. 22; 38. 21, &c.
HELP,] as in 22. 19; 27. 9; 35. 2; 38. 22, &c.
HASTE,] as in 22. 19; 38. 22; 40. 13; 70 1, &c.
13. ASHAMED,] not 'confounded;' as in
v. 1, 24.
CONSUMED,] as in 31. 10; 37. 20; 39. 10, &c
OPPOSING,] as in 109. 4, 6: 20. 29, &c.
COVERED,] as in 84. 6; 104. 2; 109. 19, &c
REPROACH,] as in 15. 3; 22. 6; 31. 11, &c.

BLUSHING,] not 'dishonour;' as in 4. 2, &c.
SEEKING,] as in v. 24; 24. 6; 35. 4; 37. 25.
EVIL,] as in v. 20, 24.
14. WAIT WITH HOPE,] as in 33. 22; 119. 43.
ADDED,] as in 10. 18; 41. 8; 61. 6; 77. 7, &c.
PRAISE,] as in v. 6, 8.
15. RECOUNTETH,] not 'shew forth;' as in 2. 7; 9. 1, 14, &c.
RIGHTEOUSNESS,] as in v. 2, 16, 19, 24.
SALVATION,] as in 33. 17; 37. 39; 38. 22, &c.
NUMBERS.] Sept. 'deeds;' Vulg. 'letters.'
16. COME,] not 'go,' as in C.V.
MIGHT,] as in v. 18; 20. 6; 21. 13; 54. 1, &c.
LORD,] as in v. 1, 5.
JEHOVAH.] Sept. and Vulg. make this word the beginning of the next sentence.
MENTION,] as in 20. 7; 45. 17; 77. 11; 87. 4.
ONLY,] *lit.* 'thyself alone.'
17. TAUGHT,] as in 25. 9; 34. 11; 51. 13, &c.
YOUTH,] as in v. 5. Sept. 'in my youth.'
HITHERTO,] as in Ge. 15. 16; 44. 28, &c.
DECLARE,] as in v. 18; 22. 31; 30. 9; 38. 18.
WONDERS,] as in 9. 1; 26. 7; 40. 5; 72. 18, &c.
18. OLD AGE,] as in v. 9.
GREY HAIRS,] as in 92. 14; Ge. 15. 15, &c.
FORSAKE,] as in v. 9.
DECLARE,] as in v. 17.
STRENGTH.] Sept. Vulg. 'arm.'
GENERATION,] as in 10. 6; 12. 7; 14. 5; 22. 30, &c. Sept. Vulg. 'all the generation.'
MIGHT,] as in v. 16.
19. HEIGHT,] not 'very high;' as in 7. 7, &c.
BECAUSE,] *or* 'in that.'
GREAT THINGS,] as in 12. 3; 106. 21; 111. 2.
LIKE THEE,] as in Ex. 3. 10; 9. 14, &c.
20. SHOWED,] *lit.* 'caused me to see;' as in 60. 3, &c.
DISTRESSES,] as in 9. 9; 10. 1; 20. 1; 22. 1.
TURNEST BACK,] as in 6. 10; 7. 12, 16, &c.
REVIVEST,] as in 41. 2; 80. 18; 85. 6, &c.
DEPTHS,] as in 33. 7; 36. 8; 42. 7; 77. 16, &c.
BRINGEST ME UP,] as in 40. 2; 51. 19; 66. 15, &c. Sept. repeats this after v. 21.
21. INCREASE,] as in 18. 35; 78. 38, &c.
GREATNESS,] as in 145. 3, 6; 1 Ch. 17. 20, 21, &c. Sept. 'thy righteousness;' Vulg. 'thy greatness.'
SURROUNDEST,] as in 119. 3, 4; Ge. 19. 4; 42. 24, &c. Sept. Vulg. 'turnest back.'
COMFORTEST,] as in 23. 4; 86. 17; 119. 82.
22. THANK,] not 'praise;' as in 6. 5; 7. 17; 9. 1, &c. Sept. Vulg. 'confess.'
VESSEL OF PSALTERY,] as in Isa. 22. 24, &c.
TRUTH,] as in 15. 2; 19. 9; 25. 5, 10, &c.
23. CRY ALOUD,] not 'greatly rejoice;' as in 5. 11; 20. 5; 51. 14, &c.
SING PRAISE,] not 'sing;' as in v. 22; 7. 17.
REDEEMED,] as in 31. 5; 55. 18; 78. 42, &c.
24. UTTERETH,] not 'talk,' as in 1. 2; 2. 1.
ASHAMED,] as in v. 1, 13.
CONFOUNDED,] not 'brought to shame;' as in 34. 5, &c.
EVIL,] as in v. 13, 20.

LXXII. BY,] not 'for' Solomon. Vulg. prefixes a 'psalm.'
1. GOD,] as in v. 18.
JUDGMENTS,] as in v. 2; 1. 5; 7. 6; 9. 4, 7, &c. Sept. Vulg. 'judgment.'
KING,] as in v. 10, 11; 2. 6; 18 50; 20. 9, &c.
RIGHTEOUSNESS,] as in 4. 1, 5; 7. 8, 17, &c.

KING'S SON,] as in 2 Sa. 9. 11; 13. 23, &c.
2. JUDGE,] as in 7. 8; 9. 8; 50. 4; 54. 1, &c.
Sept. Vulg. 'to judge.'
PEOPLE,] as in v. 3, 4.
POOR,] as in v. 4, 12.
3. MOUNTAINS,] as in v. 16; 2. 6; 3. 4, &c.
BEAR,] not 'bring;' as in 16. 4; 24. 5; 25. 1.
PEACE,] as in v. 7; 4. 8; 28. 3; 29. 11, &c.
HEIGHTS,] as in 65. 12; 114. 4, 6; 148. 9, &c.
THE PEOPLE.] Sept. 'thy people,..to the cattle.'
BY RIGHTEOUSNESS.] Sept. prefixes this to next verse.
POOR,] as in v. 2, 12.
4. JUDGETH,] as in 9. 8; 58. 1; 67. 4; 75. 2.
PEOPLE,] as in v. 2, 3.
DELIVERANCE,] as in v. 13; 18. 27; 34. 18.
NEEDY,] as in v. 12, 13; 9. 18; 12. 5; 35. 10.
BRUISETH,] not 'break in pieces;' as in 89. 10; 94. 5; 143. 3, &c. Sept. Vulg. 'humbleth.'
OPPRESSOR,] as in 119. 121; Prov. 14. 31; 22. 16, &c. Sept. Vulg. 'calumniator.'
5. FEAR.] Sept. Vulg. 'he endures with.'
SUN,] as in v. 17; 19. 4; 50. 1; 58. 8, &c.
MOON,] as in v. 7; 8. 3; 89. 37; 104. 19, &c.
GENERATIONS,] as in 10. 6; 33. 11; 45. 17.
6. RAIN,] as in 135. 7; 147. 8; Ex. 9. 33, &c.
MOWN GRASS,] as in Amos 7. 1.
SHOWERS,] as in 65. 10; De. 32. 2; Jer. 3. 3; 14. 22; Mic. 5. 7.
SPRINKLING.] Original word not found again.
7. FLOURISH,] as in 92. 7, 12; Ge. 40. 10, &c.
RIGHTEOUS,] as in 1. 5, 6; 5. 12; 7. 9, 11, &c. Sept. Vulg. 'righteousness.'
ABUNDANCE,] as in 5. 7, 10; 33. 16, 17, &c.
PEACE,] as in v. 3.
MOON,] as in v. 5.
8. RULETH,] as in 49. 14; 68. 27; Ge. 1. 26.
SEA,] as in 80. 11, &c.
RIVER,] as in 80. 11; the Euphrates.
ENDS OF EARTH,] as in 2. 8; 59. 13; 67. 7; 98. 3, &c. Sept. Vulg. 'habitable earth.'
9. BOW,] as in 20. 8; 22. 29; 95. 6; Ge. 49. 9.
DRY PLACES,] not 'wilderness;' as in 74. 14; Isa. 13. 21; 23. 13; 34. 14; Jer. 50. 39.
Sept. Vulg. 'Ethiopians.'
LICK,] as in Nu. 22. 4; 1 K. 18. 38; Isa. 49. 23; Mic. 7. 17.
DUST,] as in 7. 5; 18. 42; 22. 15, 29; 30. 9.
10. TARSHISH,] as in 48. 7; Ge. 10. 4, &c.
ISLES,] as in 97. 1; Ge. 10. 5; Est. 10. 1, &c.
SEND BACK,] not 'bring;' as in 18. 20, &c.
PRESENT,] as in 20. 3; 40. 6; 45. 12; 96. 8.
SHEBA,] as in v. 15; 1 K. 10. 1, 4, 10, 13; Job 1. 15; 6. 19, &c. Sept. Vulg. 'Arabia.'
SEBA,] as in Ge. 10. 7; 1 Ch. 1. 9; Isa. 43. 3.
REWARD,] not 'offer;' as in Eze. 27. 15.
BRING NEAR,] not 'offer;' as in Ge. 12. 11; Ex. 14. 10; 28. 1, &c.
11. BOW THEMSELVES,] not 'fall down;' as in 5. 7; 22. 27, &c. Vulg. prefixes 'of the land *or* earth.'
SERVE,] as in 18. 43; 22. 30; 106. 36, &c.
12. DELIVERETH,] as in 18. 17, 48; 22. 8, &c.
NEEDY,] as in v. 4, 13.
CRIETH,] as in Job 29. 12; Ps. 18. 6, 41; 22. 24; 28. 2, &c. Sept. Vulg. 'from the power ful.'
POOR,] as in v. 2, 4.

HELPER,] as in 10. 14; 22. 11; 30. 10; 54. 4.
13. PITY,] not 'spare;' as in Ge. 45. 20, &c.
POOR,] as in 41. 1; 82. 3, 4; 113. 7; Ex. 23. 3.
NEEDY,] as in v. 4, 12.
SOULS,] or 'persons;' as in v. 14; 3. 2, &c.
SAVETH,] as in v. 4.
14. FRAUD,] as in 10. 7; 55. 11. Sept. Vulg.
'usury.'
VIOLENCE,] as in 7. 16; 11. 5; 18. 48; 25.
19, &c. Sept. Vulg. 'injustice.'
REDEEMETH,] as in 74. 2; 77. 15; 106. 10.
SOUL,] as in v. 13.
PRECIOUS,] as in 49. 8; 139. 17; 1 Sa. 18. 30,
&c. Sept. 'honourable.'
BLOOD,] as in 9. 12; 30. 9, &c. Sept. Vulg.
'name.'
15. LIVETH,] that is, the poor and the
needy one who is delivered.
HE GIVETH,] not 'shall be given,' as in
C.V.; the king's son giveth a gift of his royal
bounty.
GOLD OF SHEBA,] as in 60. 6. Sept. Vulg.
'of Arabia.'
PRAYETH,] as in 5. 2; 32. 6; Ge. 20. 7, &c.
CONTINUALLY,] as in 16. 8; 25. 15; 34. 1, &c.
ALL THE DAY,] as in 37. 26; 42. 3, 10, &c.
BLESS,] not 'shall he be praised;' as in 5.
2, &c.
16. HANDFUL.] Original word not found
again. Sept. Vulg. 'support, stay.'
CORN,] as in 65. 13; Ge. 41. 35, 39; 42. 3, &c.
EARTH,] or 'land.'
MOUNTAINS,] as in v. 3.
SHAKE,] as in 18. 7; 46. 3; 68. 8; 77. 18, &c.
LEBANON,] as in 29. 5, 6; 92. 12; 104. 16, &c.
FRUIT,] as in 1. 3; 21. 10; 58. 11; 104. 13.
FLOURISH,] as in 90. 6; 92. 7; 103. 15.
CITY,] as in 9. 6; 31. 21; 46. 4; 48. 1, 8, &c.
HERB,] not 'grass,' as in 92. 7; 102. 4, &c.
17. NAME,] as in v. 19; 5. 11; 7. 17; 8. 6, &c.
Sept. Vulg. add, 'is blessed.'
AGE,] as in 5. 11; 9. 5, 7; 10. 16; 12. 7, &c.
SUN,] as in v. 5.
CONTINUED.] Original word not found
again.
BLESS THEMSELVES,] not 'be blessed.'
Sept. Vulg. add 'all the tribes of the land.'
PRONOUNCE HIM HAPPY,] not 'blessed;' as
in Ge. 22. 18; 26. 4; De. 29. 19; Isa. 65. 16;
Jer. 4. 2.
18. BLESSED,] as in v. 19; 18. 4, 6; 28. 6, &c.
JEHOVAH GOD,] as in 41. 13, &c. Sept.
Vulg. omit 'God.'
GOD OF ISRAEL,] as in 41. 13; 59. 5; 68. 8.
ALONE,] lit. 'apart by himself.'
WONDERS,] as in 9. 1; 26. 7; 40. 5; 71. 17.
19. BLESSED,] as in v. 18.
NAME,] as in v. 17.
HONOUR,] as in 3. 3; 4. 2; 7. 5; 8. 5, &c.
Vulg. 'majesty.'
AGE.]Sept. adds, 'and to the age of the age.'
EARTH,] or 'land.'
FIELD,] as in 71. 8; 126. 2; Ge. 6. 11, &c.
AMEN,] as in 41. 13; 89. 52; 106. 48, &c.
20. PRAYERS,] as in 4. 1; 6. 9; 17. 1; 35. 13,
&c. Sept. 'hymns;' Vulg. 'praises.'
DAVID,] as in 17. 1; 86. 1; 142. 1.
SON OF JESSE,] as in Ruth 4. 22, &c.
ENDED,] as in 31. 10; 37. 20; 39. 10; 69. 3,
&c. Here ends the Second Book or Collection of Psalms.

75. 76. 77. 79. 80. 82. 83.
1. ONLY,] not 'truly;' as in v. 13, 18; Ge. 7.
23, &c. Sept. Vulg. 'how.'
GOOD,] as in 4. 16; 14. 1; 16. 2; 21. 3, &c.
ISRAEL,] as in 14. 7; 22. 3, 23; 25. 22, &c.
GOD,] as in v. 26, 28.
CLEAN OF HEART,] as in 24. 4. Sept. Vulg.
'upright of heart.'
2. AS A LITTLE THING,] not 'almost;' as in
2. 12, &c.
FEET,] as in 8. 6; 9. 15; 18. 9, 33, 38; 22. 16.
TURNED ASIDE,] as in 62. 3; 102. 11, &c.
AS NOTHING,] as in 38. 10, &c.
STEPS,] as in 17. 5; 37. 31; 40. 2; 44. 18, &c.
SLIPPED,] lit. 'been poured forth;' as in
Nu. 35. 33; Zeph. 1. 17.
3. ENVIOUS,] as in 37. 1; 106. 16; Ge. 26. 14.
BOASTFUL,] not 'foolish;' as in 5. 5; 75. 4.
Sept. Vulg. 'lawless.'
PEACE,] not 'prosperity,' as in C.V.
WICKED,] as in v. 12; 1. 1, 4, 5, 6; 3. 7, &c.
SEE,] as in 35. 17; 36. 9; 37. 34; 40. 3, &c.
4. BANDS,] as in Isa. 58. 6.
MIGHT,] as in 2 K. 24. 15. Sept. Vulg.
'plagues.'
FIRM,] or 'fat;' as in 41. 2, 4, 5, 7, 18, 20.
5. MISERY,] not 'trouble;' as in v. 16; 7.
14, 16; 10. 7, 14, &c.
MORTALS,] as in 8. 4; 9. 19, 20; 10. 18, &c.
COMMON MEN,] as in 8. 4; 11. 4; 12. 1, 8, &c.
PLAGUED,] lit. 'touched or smitten.'
6. PRIDE,] as in 10. 2; 31. 18, 23; 36. 11, &c.
ENCIRCLED] as with a chain; compare De.
15. 14. Sept. Vulg. 'held them.'
VIOLENCE,] as in 7. 16; 11. 5; 18. 48; 25.
19, &c. Sept. Vulg. 'injustice.'
COVERETH,] as in 61. 2; 65. 13; 102. 1, &c.
DRESS,] as in Prov. 7. 20. Sept. Vulg.
'impiety.'
7. EYE,] as in v. 16; 5. 5; 6. 7; 10. 8, 11, &c.
Sept. Vulg. 'iniquity.'
COME OUT,] as in 17. 2; 19. 4; 41. 6; 44. 9.
FAT,] as in 17. 10; 63. 5; 81. 16; 119.
70, &c.
IMAGINATIONS,] as in Lev. 26. 1; Nu. 33.
52; Prov. 18. 11; 25. 11; Eze. 8. 12.
TRANSGRESSED,] as in 18. 12; 38. 4; 42. 7.
8. DO CORRUPTLY,] not 'are corrupt,' as
in C.V.
WICKEDNESS,] as in 5. 4; 7. 4, 9; 10. 6, &c.
OPPRESSION,] as in 62. 10; 119. 134, &c.
HIGH,] as in 7. 7; 10. 5; 18. 16; 56. 2, &c.
9. SET IN,] not 'against;' as in v. 18, 28, &c.
MOUTH,] as in 5. 9; 8. 2; 10. 7; 17. 3, &c.
WALKETH,] as in 1. 1; 26. 1; 58. 8; 91. 6, &c.
10. HIS PEOPLE.] Sept. Vulg. 'my people.'
HITHER,] as in Ge. 16. 13; Ex. 3. 5; Jud.
18. 3; 20. 7; Ruth 2. 14; 1 Sa. 10. 22; 14. 36,
38; 2 Sa. 7. 18; 1 Ch. 17. 16.
WATERS OF FULNESS,] as in 75. 8; 144. 13;
Ge. 23. 9, &c. Sept. Vulg. 'days of fulness
are found in them.'
WRUNG OUT,] as in 75. 8; Lev. 1. 15; 5. 9.
11. KNOWN,] as in 14. 4; 18. 43; 20. 6, &c.
KNOWLEDGE,] as in 1 Sa. 2. 3; Job 36. 4;
Isa. 11. 9; 28. 9; Jer. 3. 15.
MOST HIGH,] as in 7. 17; 9. 2; 18. 13; 21. 7.
12. WICKED,] as in v. 3.
EASY ONES,] not 'who prosper;' as in 1 Ch
4. 14, &c.

AGE,] not 'world,' as in C.V.
INCREASED,] as in 92. 12; Job 8. 7, 11.
Sept. 'obtained.' Targ. 'acquired.'
STRENGTH,] not 'riches;' as in 18. 32, 39;
33. 16, 17, &c. Sept. Vulg. add 'and I said.'
13. ONLY,] not 'verily;' as in v. 1, 18.
A VAIN THING,] as in 2. 1; 4. 2; Lev. 26. 16.
PURIFIED,] as in 119. 9; Prov. 20. 9, &c.
Sept. Vulg. 'justified.'
HEART,] as in v. 1, 7, 21, 26; 4. 4; 13. 2, &c.
WASH,] as in 26. 6; 58. 10; Ge. 18. 4, &c.
INNOCENCY,] as in 26. 6; Ge. 20. 5; Hos. 8.
5; Am. 4. 6.
HANDS,] as in 7. 3; 9. 16; 18. 1; 24. 4, &c.
14. PLAGUED,] as in Isa. 53. 4.
ALL THE DAY,] as in 25. 5; 32. 3; 35. 28, &c.
REPROOF,] not 'chastened;' as in 38. 14, &c.
EVERY MORNING,] lit. 'at the mornings.'
15. RECOUNT,] not 'speak;' as in 2. 7; 9. 1.
GENERATION,] as in 10. 6; 12. 7; 14. 5, &c.
DECEIVED,] not 'offered;' as in 25. 3; 59. 5.
16. THINK,] as in 77. 5; 119. 59; 144. 3, &c.
KNOW,] as in 67. 2, &c.
PERVERSENESS,] as in v. 5. Sept. Vulg.
'labour, weariness.'
17. SANCTUARIES,] as in 68. 35; 74. 7; 78. 69.
ATTEND,] as in 19. 12; 28. 5; 49. 20; 58. 9.
LATTER END,] as in 37. 37, 38; 109. 13; 139.
9, &c. Sept. 'the last things.'
18. ONLY,] not 'surely;' as in v. 1, 13.
SLIPPERY PLACES,] as in 12. 2, 3; Ge. 27.
16, &c. Sept. Vulg. 'because of grief.'
SET,] as in v. 9, 28.
TO FALL,] as in 22. 18; 37. 14; 78. 28, &c.
DESOLATIONS,] not 'destructions;' as in
74. 3. Sept. Vulg. 'in being elevated.'
19. DESOLATION,] as in 46. 8; De. 28. 37, &c.
MOMENT,] as in 6. 10; 30. 5; Ex. 33. 5, &c.
Sept. Vulg. 'suddenly they have been ended.'
ENDED,] as in Est. 9. 28; Isa. 66. 17; Amos
3. 15.
CONSUMED,] as in 9. 6; 64. 6; Ge. 47. 18, &c.
TERRORS,] as in Job 18. 11, 14; 24. 17; 27.
20, &c. Sept. Vulg. 'because of their iniquity.'
20. DREAM,] as in Ge. 20. 3, 6; 31. 10, &c.
AWAKENING,] as in 3. 5; 17. 15; 35. 23, &c.
LORD,] as in v. 28; 2. 4; 16. 2; 22. 30, &c.
AWAKING,] or 'in enmity.' Sept. Vulg.
'in thy city.'
IMAGE,] as in 39. 6; Ge. 1. 26, 27; 5. 3, &c.
DESPISEST,] as in 22. 24; 51. 17; 69. 33, &c.
Sept. Vulg. 'bringest to nought.'
21. VIOLENT,] not 'grieved;' as in 71. 4.
Sept. 'inflamed;' Targ. 'saddened.'
REINS,] as in 7. 9; 16. 7; 26. 2; 139. 13, &c.
PRICK THEMSELVES,] not 'was pricked,'
as in C.V. Sept. Vulg. 'are changed.'
22. BRUTISH,] not 'foolish;' as in 49. 10;
92. 6; Prov. 12. 1; 30. 2. Sept. Vulg. 'reduced to nothing.'
KNOW,] as in 35. 8; 39. 6; 92. 6; 101. 4, &c.
BEAST,] in Heb. 'behemoth,' i.e. a large
beast, Job 40. 15. Vulg. 'as a beast.'
23. CONTINUALLY,] as in 16. 8; 25. 15; 34. 1.
LAID HOLD,] as in 48. 6; 77. 4; 119. 53, &c.
RIGHT HAND,] as in 16. 8, 11; 17. 7; 18. 35.
24. COUNSEL,] as in 1. 1; 13. 2; 14. 6; 20. 4,
&c. Vulg. 'good pleasure.'
LEAD,] as in 23. 3; 31. 3; 43. 3; 61. 2, &c.

HONOUR,] as in 3. 3; 4. 2; 7. 5; 8. 5; 16. 9,
&c. Vulg. 'with honour.'
RECEIVE,] as in 6. 9; 18. 16; 49. 15, 17, &c.
25. HEAVENS,] as in v. 9.
DESIRED,] as in 18. 19; 22. 8; 40. 6, 8, &c.
EARTH,] as in v. 9.
26. CONSUMED,] as in 31. 10; 37. 20; 39. 10.
FLESH,] as in 78. 20, 27; Ex. 21. 10, &c.
HEART,] as in v. 1, 7, 13, 21.
ROCK,] not 'strength;' as in 18. 2, 31, 46;
19. 14, &c. Sept. Vulg. 'God.'
PORTION,] as in 16. 5; 17. 14; 50. 18, &c.
27. FAR OFF.] Sept. 'remove far off.'
PERISH,] as in 1. 6; 2. 12; 9. 3, 18; 37. 20.
CUT OFF,] not 'destroyed;' as in 18. 40; 54.
5; 94. 23, &c.
A WHORING,] as in Ge. 34. 31; 38. 15, &c.
28. NEARNESS,] not 'to draw near;' as in
Isa. 58. 2. Vulg. 'to adhere.'
GOOD,] as in v. 1.
PLACED,] as in 3. 6; 8. 6; 84. 3; 88. 6, &c.
LORD JEHOVAH,] as in v. 20. Sept. omits
'Jehovah.'
REFUGE,] not 'trust;' as in 14. 6; 46. 1; 61.
3; 62. 7, &c. Sept. Vulg. 'hope.'
RECOUNT,] not 'declare;' as in 26. 7; 40. 5.
WORKS,] as in 107. 23; Ge. 2. 2, 3; 33. 14,
&c. Sept. Vulg. 'praises in the gates of the
daughter of Zion.'

LXXIV. INSTRUCTION,] as in Ps. 32. 42.
44. 45. 52. 53. 54. 55. 78. 88. 89. 142.
ASAPH,] as in Ps. 50. 75. 76. 77. 79. 80.
82. 83.
1. CAST OFF,] as in 43. 2; 44. 9, 23; 60. 1, &c.
SMOKETH,] as in 80. 4; 104. 32; 144. 5; Ex.
19. 18; De. 29. 20. Sept. 'is incensed.'
FLOCK,] as in 44. 11, 22; 49. 14; 65. 13, &c.
2. REMEMBER,] as in v. 18, 22; 25. 6, 7, &c.
COMPANY,] not 'congregation;' as in 1. 5;
7. 7; 22. 16, &c.
PURCHASE,] as in 78. 54; 139. 13; Ge. 4. 1,
&c.; or 'acquire;' Sept. Vulg. 'possess.'
OF OLD,] as in v. 12; 44. 1; 55. 19; 68. 33,
&c. Sept. Vulg. 'from the beginning.'
REDEEM,] as in 72. 14; 77. 15; 107. 2, &c.
ROD,] as in 2. 9; 23. 4; 45. 6; 78. 55, &c.
INHERITANCE,] as in 2. 8; 28. 9; 33. 12, &c.
MOUNT ZION,] as in 2. 6; 48. 11; 78. 68, &c.
DWELL,] as in 15. 1; 16. 9; 37. 3, 27, 29, &c.
3. STEPS,] not 'feet;' as in 17. 5; 57. 6; 58.
10, &c. Sept. Vulg. 'hand upon their pride
for ever.'
PERPETUAL,] as in v. 1, 10, 19.
DESOLATIONS,] as in 73. 18.
DID WICKEDLY,] as in 15. 4; 37. 8; 44. 2, &c.
SANCTUARIES,] as in 2. 6; 3. 4; 5. 7; 11. 4,
&c. Sept. Vulg. 'thy sanctuaries.'
4. ROARED,] as in 38. 8; Job 37. 4; Isa. 5.
29, &c. Sept. Vulg. 'gloried.'
ADVERSARIES,] as in v. 23; 6. 7; 7. 4, 6; 8.
2, &c. Sept. Vulg. 'those hating thee.'
MEETING-PLACES,] not 'congregations;' as
in v. 8; 75. 2, &c. Sept. Vulg. 'festivals.'
SET,] as in 19. 4; 40. 4; 46. 8; 50. 23, &c.
ENSIGNS,] as in v. 9; 65. 8; 78. 43; 86. 17.
5. HE IS KNOWN,] not 'famous;' as in 79.
10; 88. 12, &c.
BRINGING IN,] not 'lifted up;' as in Ge. 6
17, &c. Sept. Vulg. 'and they have not
known.'

ON HIGH,] as in Ex. 25. 20; 37. 9; De. 28. 13.
THICKET,] as in Ge. 22. 13; Isa. 9. 18, &c.
WOOD,] as in 1. 3; 96. 12; 104. 16; 105. 33.
AXES,] as in Jud. 9. 48; 1 Sa. 13. 20, 21; Jer. 46. 22.
6. CARVINGS,] *lit.* 'openings;' as in Ex. 28. 11, &c. So Sept. Vulg.
AXE,] *lit.* 'one causing to stumble.'
HATCHET.] Original word not found again.
BREAK DOWN,] as in 141. 5; Jud. 5. 22, &c.
7. SENT INTO FIRE,] not 'cast fire into,' as in C.V.
SANCTUARY,] as in 68. 35; 74. 7; 78. 69, &c.
EARTH,] as in v. 8, 12, 17, 20.
POLLUTED,] as in 55. 20; 89. 31, 34, 39, &c.
TABERNACLE,] not 'dwelling-place;' as in 26. 8; 43. 3, &c.
8. HEART,] as in 10. 6, 11, 13; 14. 1; 35. 25.
OPPRESS,] not 'destroy;' as in 123. 4; Jer. 25. 38, &c. Sept. Vulg. 'in their relationship;' Targ. 'their sons.'
BURN,] as in 46. 9; 80. 16; Ge. 11. 3, &c. Sept. Vulg. 'cause to cease.'
MEETING PLACES,] not 'synagogues;' as in v. 4. Sept. Vulg. 'festivals.'
GOD.] Sept. 'the Lord.'
LAND,] as in v. 7, 12, 17, 20.
9. ENSIGNS,] as in v. 4.
SEEN,] as in 10. 11; 37. 25, &c.
PROPHET,] as in 51. 2; 105. 15; Ge. 20. 17.
HOW LONG,] as in 4. 2, &c.
10. TILL WHEN,] *lit.* 'till what.'
ADVERSARY,] as in 3. 1; 4. 1; 13. 4; 18. 6.
REPROACH,] as in 42. 10; 55. 12: 57. 3, &c.
DESPISE,] not 'blaspheme;' as in v. 18, &c.
FOR EVER,] as in v. 1, 3, 19.
11. TURN BACK,] as in 81. 14; Ex. 4. 7, &c.
RIGHT HAND,] as in 16. 8, 11; 17. 7; 18. 35.
BOSOM,] as in 35. 13; 79. 12; 89. 50, &c.
REMOVE,] not 'pluck;' as in 59. 13; Ex. 5. 13, &c.
12. KING,] as in 2. 6; 5. 2; 44. 4; 68. 24, &c. Sept. Vulg. 'our king.'
OF OLD,] as in v. 2.
SALVATIONS,] as in 3. 2, 8; 9. 14; 13. 5, &c.
EARTH,] as in v. 7, 8, 17, 20.
13. BROKEN,] not 'divide,' as in C.V.
STRENGTH,] as in 8. 2; 21. 1, 13; 28. 7, &c.
SEA MONSTER,] not 'sea,' as in C.V.
SHIVERED,] as in 3. 7; 76. 3; 105. 33; 107. 16.
DRAGONS,] as in 91. 13; 148. 7; Ge. 1. 21, &c.
14. BROKEN,] as in 2 Ch. 16. 10; Job 20. 19; 1 Sa. 12. 3, 4, &c. Sept. Vulg. 'strengthened.'
LEVIATHAN,] as in 104. 26; Job 3. 8; 41. 1; Isa. 27. 1.
FOOD,] not 'meat;' as in 44. 11; 79. 2, &c.
DRY PLACES,] not 'wilderness;' as in 72. 9; Isa. 13. 21; 23. 13; 34. 14; Jer. 50. 39. Sept. Vulg. 'Ethiopia.'
15. CLEAVED,] as in 78. 13; 141. 7, &c.
FOUNTAIN,] as in 84. 6; 87. 7; 107. 10, &c.
STREAM,] not 'flood;' as in 18. 4; 36. 8; 78. 20, &c. Sept. Vulg. 'torrents.'
DRIED UP,] as in Jos. 2. 10; 4. 23; 5. 1, &c.
PERENNIAL,] Sept. Vulg. 'of Etham.'
FLOWINGS,] as in 24. 2; 46. 4; 60. 1; 66. 8, &c.
16. DAY..NIGHT,] as in Ge. 1. 5, 8, 13, &c.
PREPARED,] as in 7. 13; 57 6; 78. 8; 103. 19.

LIGHT-GIVER,] as in 90. 8; Ge. 1, 14, 15, 16, &c. Sept. 'sun and moon.'
SUN,] as in 19. 4; 15. 1; 58. 8; 72. 5, &c.
17. SET UP,] as in 41. 12; 78. 13; Ge. 21. 28, &c. Sept. Vulg. 'made.'
BORDERS,] as in Nu. 32. 33; 34. 2, 12, &c.
SUMMER,] as in 32. 4; Ge. 8. 22; 2 Sa. 16. 1.
WINTER,] as in Ge. 8. 22; Job 29. 4, &c.
FORMED,] not 'made;' as in 95. 5; 104. 26.
18. REMEMBER.] as in v. 2, 22. Sept. adds 'of thy creation.'
REPROACHED,] as in 42. 10; 57. 3; 79. 12.
FOOLISH.] as in v. 22; 14. 1; 39. 8; 53. 1, &c.
DESPISED,] not 'blasphemed;' as in 10. 3, 13; 107. 11, &c.
19. COMPANY,] *lit.* 'living one.' Sept. Vulg. 'beasts.'
TURTLE-DOVE,] as in Ge. 15. 9; Lev. 1, 14; 5. 7, 11, &c. Sept. Vulg. 'those confessing thee.'
COMPANY.] Sept. Vulg. 'souls.'
POOR ONES,] as in v. 21; 9. 12, 18; 10. 2, &c.
FORGET,] as in v. 23; 10. 12; 13. 1; 44. 24.
FOR EVER,] as in v. 1, 3, 10.
20. LOOK ATTENTIVELY,] as in 13. 3; 80. 14.
COVENANT,] as in 25. 10, 14; 44. 17; 50. 5; &c. Sept. Vulg. 'thy covenant.'
DARK PLACES,] as in 88. 6, 18; 143. 3, &c.
EARTH,] as in v. 7, 8, 12, 17.
HABITATIONS,] as in 23. 2; 65. 12; 83. 12.
VIOLENCE,] not 'cruelty;' as in 9. 16; 11. 5, 18. 48, &c. Sept. Vulg. 'lawlessness.'
21. OPPRESSED,] as in 9. 9; 10. 18; Prov. 26. 28. Sept. Vulg. 'humble.'
TURN BACK,] as in 6. 10; 7. 12, 16; 9. 17, &c.
ASHAMED,] as in 2 Sa. 10. 5; 19. 3; 1 Ch. 19. 5, &c. Sept. 'and the ashamed.'
POOR,] as in v. 19.
NEEDY,] as in 9. 18; 12. 5; 35. 10; 37. 14, &c.
PRAISE,] as in 22. 22, 26; 35. 18; 56. 4, &c.
22. ARISE,] as in 3. 7; 7. 6; 9. 19; 10. 12, &c.
PLEAD,] as in 35. 1; 43. 1; 119. 154, &c.
PLEA,] not 'cause;' as in 18. 43; 31. 20, &c.
REMEMBER,] as in v. 2, 18.
REPROACH,] as in v. 18.
FOOT,] as in v. 18.
23. VOICE,] as in 3. 4; 5. 2, 3; 6. 8; 18. 6, &c.
NOISE,] not 'tumult;' as in 40. 2; 65. 7, &c. Sept. Vulg. 'pride.'
WITHSTANDERS,] as in 3. 1; 18. 39, 48; 44. 5, &c. Sept. Vulg. 'haters.'
GOING UP,] not 'increaseth;' as in Ge. 28. 12, &c. Sept. adds 'before thee.'

LXXV. OVERSEER,] as in Ps. 4. 5. 6. 8. 9. &c.
DO NOT DESTROY,] as in Ps. 57. 58. 59.
SONG,] as in Ps. 76. 83. Sept. 'ode.'
1. GIVEN THANKS,] as in 6. 5; 7. 17; 9. 1.
NEAR,] as in 34. 18; 85. 9; 119. 151; 148. 14, &c. Sept. Vulg. 'and we call on thy name.'
RECOUNTED,] as in 44. 1; 78. 3; 119. 113, 126. Sept. 'to recount;' Vulg. 'we recount.'
WONDERS,] as in 9. 1; 26. 7; 40. 5; 71. 17, &c. Sept. 'all thy wonders.'
2. RECEIVE,] as in 9. 18: 16; 49. 15, &c.
APPOINTMENT,] not 'congregation;' as in 74. 4, 8, &c. Sept. Vulg. 'set time *or* season.'
JUDGE,] as in 9. 8; 58. 1; 67. 4; 72. 4, &c.
UPRIGHTLY,] as in 9. 8; 17. 2; 58. 1; 96. 10

3. MELTED,] as in Ex. 15. 5; Jos. 2. 9, 24;
1 Sa. 14. 16, &c.
EARTH,] or 'land.'
INHABITANTS,] as in 2. 4; 9. 11; 17. 12, &c.
PONDERED,] not 'bear up;' as in Job 28.
25; Isa. 12. 13. Sept. Vulg. 'confirmed.'
PILLARS,] as in 99. 7; Ex. 13. 21, 22; 14. 19.
SELAH,] as in 3. 2, 8; 4. 2, 4; 7. 5; 9. 16, &c.
4. BOASTFUL,] not 'fools;' as in 5. 5; 73. 3.
Sept. Vulg. 'lawless.'
HORN,] as in v. 5, 10; 18. 2; 22. 21; 89. 17.
5. SPEAK,] as in 2. 5; 12. 2; 35. 20; 37. 30.
STIFF,] as in 31. 18; 94. 4; 1 Sa. 2. 3.
NECK,] as in Ge. 27. 16, 40; 33. 4; 41. 42,
&c. Sept. Vulg. 'against God iniquity.'
6. EAST,] lit. 'out-going;' as in 19. 6; 65. 8.
WEST,] as in 103. 12; 107. 3; 1 Ch. 7. 28, &c.
WILDERNESS,] not 'south;' as in 29. 8, &c.
ELEVATION,] as in Ge. 39. 18; Nu. 13. 30,
32; 1 Ch. 15. 16, &c. Sept. Vulg. 'of moun-
tains.'
7. JUDGE,] as in 2. 10; 7. 11; 9. 4; 50. 6, &c.
LOW,] as in 18. 27; 113. 6; 147. 6, &c.
LIFTETH UP,] as in 110. 7; 113. 7; 148. 14.
8. CUP,] as in 11. 6; 16. 5; 23. 5; 75. 8, &c.
HAND,] as in 8. 6; 10. 12, 14; 17. 14; 18. 1.
WINE,] as in 60. 3; 78. 65; 104. 15, &c.
FOAMED,] not 'is red;' as in 46. 3; Ex. 2. 3.
MIXTURE.] Original word not found
again.
POURETH OUT,] as in 63. 10; Jer. 18. 21;
Eze. 35. 5, &c. Sept. Vulg. add 'from this
to that.'
ONLY,] as in Ge. 7, 23; 9. 4; 18. 32; 20. 9.
DREGS,] as in Isa. 25. 6; Jer. 48. 11; Zeph.
1. 12.
WRING OUT,] as in Jud. 6. 38; Isa. 51. 17;
Eze. 23. 34. Sept. Vulg. prefixes 'not.'
DRINK,] as in 50. 13; 78. 44; 110. 7, &c.
EARTH,] or 'land.
9. DECLARE,] as in 22. 31; 30. 9; 38. 18; 40.
5, &c. Sept. 'I am glad.'
SING PRAISE,] as in 7. 17; 9. 2; 18. 49, &c.
GOD OF JACOB,] as in 20. 1; 41. 13; 46. 7, &c.
10. HORNS,] as in v. 4, 5.
CUT OFF,] as in 107. 16; De. 7. 5; 12. 3, &c.
EXALTED,] as in 66. 17; Neh. 9. 5.

LXXVI. OVERSEER,] as in Ps. 4. 5. 6. 8.
9. 11. &c.
STRINGED INSTRUMENTS,] as in Ps. 4. 6.
54. 55. 61. 67. Sept. 'hymns;' Vulg. 'praises.'
PSALM OF ASAPH,] as in Ps. 50. 73. 75. &c.
SONG,] as in Ps. 30. 45. 46. 48. 65. &c. Sept.
Vulg. add 'for the Assyrian.'
1. JUDAH,] as in 60. 7; 108. 8; 114. 2, &c.
KNOWN,] as in 9. 16; 48. 3; 77. 19, &c.
ISRAEL,] as in 78. 5; Ge. 34. 7, &c.
GREAT,] as in 21. 5; 47. 2; 48. 1; 57. 10, &c.
2. TABERNACLE,] as in 10. 9; 27. 5; Jer. 25.
38. Sept. Vulg. 'place.'
SALEM,] as in Ge. 14. 18; 33. 18. Sept.
Vulg. 'in peace.'
HABITATION,] as in 104. 22; De. 33. 27, &c.
ZION,] as in 2 K. 23. 17; Jer. 31. 21; Ezek.
39. 15.
3. SHIVERED,] as in 3. 7; 74. 13; 107. 16;
Isa. 21. 9.
ARROWS,] as in 78. 48; Song 8. 6; Hab. 3.
5: Job 5. 7. Sept. Vulg. 'power.'
BOW,] as in 78. 9, 57; Isa. 5. 23; 7. 24, &c.

SHIELD,] as in 84. 9; 89. 18; 115. 9; 119. 114.
SWORD,] as in 78. 62; 89. 43; 144. 10, &c.
BATTLE,] as in 89. 43; 120. 7; 140. 2; 144. 1.
SELAH,] as in v. 9; 77. 3; 81. 7; 82. 2, &c.
4. BRIGHT,] not 'glorious,' as in C.V.
HONOURABLE,] not 'excellent,' as in C.V.
Sept. Vulg. 'wonderfully.'
HILLS OF PREY,] as in 87. 1; 133. 3; Song
4. 8; Hab. 3. 6, &c. Sept. Vulg. 'from ever-
lasting mountains.'
5. SPOILED THEMSELVES,] not 'are spoiled;'
Sept. Vulg. 'troubled.'
MIGHTY OF HEART,] Sept. Vulg. 'sense-
less of heart.'
SLEPT,] as in Nah. 3. 18.
SLEEP,] as in 90. 5; Prov. 3. 24; 4. 16, &c.
MEN OF MIGHT,] as in 139. 19; Prov. 29. 10.
Isa. 5. 22; 45. 14, &c. Sept. Vulg. 'men of
riches.'
HANDS,] as in 77. 2; 78. 42; 80. 17; 81. 14.
6. REBUKE,] as in 80. 16; 104. 7; Prov. 13.
1; 17. 10, &c.
GOD OF JACOB,] as in 81. 4; 84. 4; 94. 7, &c.
RIDER,] not 'chariot;' as in 20. 7; 68. 17;
76. 6; Song 1. 9, &c. Sept. Vulg. 'riders
and horses.'
HORSE,] as in 32. 9; 33. 17; 147. 10, &c.
FAST ASLEEP,] as in Prov. 16. 5; Dan. 10. 9;
Jon. 1. 6.
7. FEARFUL,] as in v. 12; 89. 7; 96. 4; 99. 3
STAND,] as in 102. 26; 104. 6; 106. 36, &c.
ANGRY,] as in 77. 9; 78. 21; 85. 3; 86. 15, &c.
8. SOUNDED,] as in Isa. 30. 30; 43. 12; 44. 8.
JUDGMENT,] as in 140. 12; Prov. 20. 8, &c.
FEARED,] as in 112. 1; 119. 63, 120; Jer. 3. 8.
STILL,] as in Isa. 14. 7; Jer. 30. 10; 46. 27.
9. RISING,] as in 124. 2; 127. 2; 139. 2;
Prov. 23. 12.
JUDGMENT,] as in 81. 4; 89. 14; 94. 15, &c.
SAVE,] as in 109. 31; Isa. 37. 35; 38. 20, &c.
HUMBLE,] as in 147. 6; 149. 4; Prov. 3. 34.
EARTH.] Sept. 'heart.'
10. FIERCENESS,] as in 78. 38; 79. 6; 88. 7;
89. 46, &c. Sept. Vulg. 'inward thought.'
REMNANT,] as in Isa. 14. 30; 15. 9; 37. 4, &c.
GIRDEST ON,] not 'restrain;' as in 109. 19;
Eze. 44. 18; Ps. 65. 12; 1 K. 20. 32, &c.
Sept. Vulg. 'shall keep a feast to thee.'
11. COMPLETE,] not 'pay;' as in 50. 14; Ecc.
5. 4; Jer. 50. 29; Nah. 1. 15.
YOUR GOD,] Sept. 'our God.'
SURROUNDING,] as in 78. 28; 79. 3; 89. 7.
PRESENTS,] as in 68. 29; Isa. 18. 7.
FEARFUL ONE,] as in 9. 20; Isa. 8. 12; Jer.
32. 21; Mal. 1. 6, &c.
12. GATHER,] not 'cut off;' as in Lev. 25.
5, 11; De. 24. 21; Jud. 9. 27.
SPIRIT,] as in 77. 3, 6; 78. 8, 39; 83. 13, &c.
LEADERS,] not 'princes;' as in Prov. 8. 6;
28. 16; Isa. 55. 4; Jer. 20. 1, &c.
FEARFUL,] not 'terrible;' as in v. 7.
KINGS OF EARTH,] as in 89. 27; 102. 15;
138. 4; 148. 11, &c.

LXXVII. OVERSEER,] as in Ps. 4. 5. 6. 8.
9. 11. &c.
JEDUTHUN,] as in Ps. 39. 62. 75. 76. 79. 80
82. 83.
PSALM OF ASAPH.] as in 50. 73.
1. VOICE,] as in v. 17, 18; 81. 11; 86. 6, &c
GOD,] as in v. 3, 13, 16; 78. 7 10, &c.

CRY,] as in 107. 6, 28; Isa. 19. 20; 42. 2, &c.
GIVEN EAR,] as in Isa. 64. 4; Ex. 15. 26;
De. 1. 45; 2 Ch. 24. 19, &c.
2. DISTRESS,] as in 78. 49; 81. 7; 86. 7, &c.
LORD,] as in v. 7; 78. 65; 79. 12; 86. 3, &c.
SOUGHT,] as in 78. 34; 109. 10; 119. 10, &c.
HAND,] not 'sore;' as in v. 20; 78. 42, 61;
80. 17, &c. Sept. Vulg. 'with my hands by
night before him, and I was not deceived.'
SPREAD OUT,] not 'ran;' as in Lam. 3. 49.
CEASE,] as in Ge. 45. 26; Hab. 1. 4.
REFUSED,] as in 78. 10; Prov. 21. 7, 25, &c.
COMFORTED,] as in 1 Sa. 15. 20; Jer. 15. 6;
31. 15.
3. REMEMBER,] as in v. 6, 11; 78. 35, 39, &c.
MAKE A NOISE,] not 'was troubled;' as in
83. 2; 39. 6; 42. 5; 46. 3, &c. Sept. Vulg.
'was glad.'
MEDITATE,] not 'complained;' as in v. 6.
FEEBLE,] not 'overwhelmed;' as in 107. 5;
143. 4.
SELAH,] as in v. 9, 15; 81. 7; 82. 2, &c.
4. TAKEN HOLD,] as in 48. 6; 73. 23; 119.
53; Song 3. 4, &c.
WATCHES,] Sept. 'all my enemies set a
watch.'
5. RECKONED,] not 'considered;' as in 119.
59; Jon. 1. 4; Lev. 25. 27, 50, &c.
OF OLD,] as in v. 11; 78. 2; 119. 152; 139. 5.
OF THE AGES,] not 'of ancient times;' as
in v. 7; 78. 66, 69; 79. 13, &c. Sept. Vulg.
add 'I remembered.'
6. MUSIC,] not 'song;' as in 61. 1; Lam. 3.
14; 5. 14; Hab. 3. 19, &c.
NIGHT,] as in v. 2; 78. 14; 88. 1; 90. 4, &c.
HEART,] as in 78. 18; 84. 5; 86. 11, &c.
MEDITATE,] not 'commune;' as in v. 3.
SEARCH,] as in Ge. 31. 35; 44. 12; Am. 9. 3;
Zeph. 1. 12.
7. LORD,] as in v. 2.
CAST OFF,] as in 44. 23; 88. 14; Lam. 3.
17, 31.
ADD,] as in 78. 17; 115. 14; 120. 3; 10. 18.
PLEASED,] as in 1 Ch. 29. 3; Job 34. 9;
Prov. 16. 7.
8. KINDNESS,] not 'mercy;' as in 85. 7, &c.
CEASED,] as in Ge. 47. 15, 16; Isa. 16. 4; 29.
20. Sept. 'cut off.'
SAYING,] not 'promise;' as in 19. 2, 3; 68.
11; Hab. 3. 9; Job 22. 28.
FAILED,] as in 12. 1.
GENERATIONS,] as in 78. 4, 6, 8; 79. 13, &c.
9. FORGOTTEN,] as in 102. 4; 106. 13, &c.
FAVOURS,] as in 102. 13; Job 19. 17; Isa.
30. 18, 19.
SHUT UP,] as in 107. 42; Job 5. 16.
ANGER,] as in 78. 21, 31, 38, 49, &c.
MERCIES,] as in 78. 43; 4; 106. 46, &c.
10. WEAKNESS,] as in Zech. 7. 2; 8. 21, 22.
Sept. Vulg. 'now I have begun.'
CHANGES,] not 'years;' as in v. 5; 78. 33.
RIGHT HAND,] as in 78. 54; 80. 15, 17, &c.
MOST HIGH,] as in 78. 17, 35. 56; 82. 6, &c.
11. MENTION,] as in v. 3, 6. Sept. Vulg.
'remembered.'
DOINGS,] not 'works;' as in 28. 4; 78. 7, &c.
JAH,] as in 68. 4, 18; 89. 8; 94. 7, 12, &c.
REMEMBER,] as in v. 3, 6.
OF OLD,] as in v. 5; 78. 2; 119. 152; 139. 5,
&c. Sept. Vulg. 'from the beginning.'
WONDERS,] as in v. 14; 78. 12; 88. 10, &c.

12. MEDITATED,] as in 143. 5; Jos. 1. 8.
WORKING,] not 'work;' as in 90. 16; 92. 4
TALK,] as in v. 3, 6; 119. 15. 23, 27, &c.
DOINGS,] as in 78. 11; 99. 8; 103. 7; 105. 1.
13. HOLINESS,] as in 78. 54; 79. 1; 87. 1, &c.
WAY,] as in v. 19; 80. 12; 81. 13; 85. 13, &c.
GOD,] as in v. 1, 3, 16; 78. 7, 10, &c. Sept.
Vulg. 'like our God.'
14. THE GOD,] as in v. 9, 13; 78. 7; 80. 10.
WONDERS,] as in v. 11.
KNOWN,] not 'declared;' as in 98. 2; Pro.
22. 19; Jer. 11. 18; Eze. 20. 11, &c.
STRENGTH,] as in 78. 26, 61; 81. 1; 84. 5, &c.
15. REDEEMED,] as in 74. 2; 107. 2, &c.
STRENGTH,] Sept. Vulg. 'thine arm.'
PEOPLE,] as in v. 14; 78. 1; 79. 13, &c.
SONS OF JACOB AND JOSEPH,] that is, the
whole twelve tribes.
16. WATERS,] as in v. 17, 19.
SEEN,] as in 90. 15; 95. 9; 97. 4, 6, &c.
GOD,] as in v. 1, 3, 13.
AFRAID,] as in 10. 5; 29. 8; 55. 4; 77. 16, &c.
DEPTHS,] as in 78. 15; 104. 6; 106. 9; 107
26, &c. Sept. Vulg. 'abysses.'
TROUBLED,] as in 18. 7; 99. 1; Isa. 5. 25, &c.
17. POURED OUT,] as in 90. 5.
THICK CLOUDS,] as in 18. 11, 12; 104. 3, &c.
SKIES,] as in 78. 83; 89. 6, 37; 108. 4, &c.
NOISE,] as in v. 1, 18.
ARROWS,] as in Pro. 20. 17; Lam. 3. 16.
GO UP AND DOWN,] not 'went abroad;' as
in 82. 5; 101. 2; 105. 13; 116. 9, &c.
18. THUNDER,] as in 81. 17; 104. 7; Job 26.
14; 39. 35.
SPHERES,] not 'heavens;' as in 83. 13; Zec.
12. 6; Isa. 5. 28; 17. 13, &c.
LIGHTNINGS,] as in 18. 14; 97. 4; 135. 7;
144. 6, &c. Sept. Vulg. 'thy lightnings.'
LIGHTENED,] as in Ex. 25. 37; Ps. 97. 4;
Eze. 43. 2.
WORLD,] as in 9. 8; 18. 15; 19. 4; 24. 1, &c.
EARTH,] as in 78. 12, 69; 79. 2; 80. 9, &c.
TREMBLED,] as in Pro. 29. 9; 30. 21; Isa.
14. 9; Jer. 33. 9, &c.
SHAKETH,] as in 18. 7; 46. 3; 72. 16, &c.
19. SEA,] as in 78. 13; 27. 53; 80. 11, &c.
WAY,] as in v. 13.
PATHS,] as in Jer. 18. 15.
TRACKS,] not 'footsteps;' as in 41. 9; 49. 5.
KNOWN,] as in 9. 16; 48. 3; 77. 19; Isa. 19. 21.
20. LED,] as in 60. 9; 108. 10; Isa. 58. 11, &c.
FLOCK,] as in 78. 52, 70; 79. 13; 80. 1, &c.
PEOPLE,] as in v. 15.
HAND,] as in v. 15.
MOSES AND AARON,] the sons of Amram.

LXXVIII. INSTRUCTION,] as in Ps. 74.
ASAPH,] as in Ps. 74.
1. GIVE EAR,] as in 80. 1; 84. 8; 86. 6, &c.
PEOPLE,] as in v. 20, 52, 62, 71.
LAW,] as in v. 5, 10.
INCLINE YOUR EAR,] as in 86. 1; 88. 2, &c.
SAYINGS OF MY MOUTH,] as in 5. 1; 19. 14.
2. OPEN,] as in 38. 13; 39. 9; 49. 4; 51. 15.
SIMILE,] as in 44. 14; 49. 4; 69. 11, &c.
BRING FORTH,] not 'utter;' as in 19. 2, &c.
HIDDEN THINGS,] not 'dark things;' as in
49. 4; Nu. 12. 8; Jud. 14. 12, 13, &c.
OF OLD,] as in 44. 1; 55. 19; 68. 33; 74. 2.
3. HEARD,] as in v. 21, 59.
KNOW,] as in 9. 20; 35. 8; 39. 4; 5* &c.

RECOUNTED,] not 'told;' as in 44. 1; 75. 1.
4. HIDE,] as in Ge. 47. 18; Jos. 7. 19; 1 Sa.
3. 17; 2 Sa. 16. 18, &c. Sept. Vulg. 'they
were not hidden.'
LATER GENERATION,] not the one 'to
come:' as in v. 6.
RECOUNTING,] not 'shewing;' as in 19. 1;
Jud. 7. 13; 2 K. 8. 5.
PRAISES,] as in 9. 14; 22. 3, 25; 33. 1, &c.
STRENGTH,] as in 145. 6; Isa. 42. 25.
WONDERS,] as in v. 11, 32.
5. RAISETH UP,] not 'establisheth;' as in
40. 2; 107. 29; Ecc. 4. 10; Jer. 23. 6, &c.
TESTIMONY,] as in 19. 7; 81. 5; 119. 14, &c.
LAW,] as in v. 1, 10.
PLACED,] not 'appointed;' as in v. 43.
COMMANDED,] as in 7. 6; 33. 9; 68. 28, &c.
KNOWN,] as in 25. 14; 106. 8; 145. 12, &c.
6. LATER GENERATION,] as in v. 4.
BORN,] as in Ge. 4. 18; 10. 1; 17. 17; 46. 20.
RISE,] as in 1. 5; 12. 5; 24. 3; 27. 3, &c.
RECOUNT,] not 'declare;' as in 2. 7; 9. 1, &c.
7. PLACE,] as in 18. 43; 39. 8; 44. 13, &c.
CONFIDENCE,] not 'hope;' as in 33. 7; 49.
13; Prov. 3. 26; Ecc. 7. 25, &c.
FORGET,] as in 10. 12; 13. 1; 44. 24, &c
DOINGS,] not 'works;' as in 28. 4; 77. 11.
GOD,] as in v. 8, 18, 19, 34, &c.
KEEP.] Sept. Vulg. 'seek.'
COMMANDS,] as in 19. 8; 89. 31; 112. 1, &c.
8. GENERATION,] as in v. 4, 6.
APOSTATE,] not 'stubborn;' as in 66. 7, &c.
REBELLIOUS,] as in Nu. 20. 10; De. 21. 18,
20; 2 K. 14. 26, &c. Sept. Vulg. 'provok-
ing.'
PREPARED,] not 'set aright;' as in 7. 13, &c.
HEART,] as in 4. 7; 7. 10; 9. 1; 10. 6, &c.
STEDFAST,] as in v. 37.
9. ARMED BEARERS,] as in 1 Ch. 12. 2;
2 Ch. 17. 17.
BOW,] as in v. 57.
TURNED,] as in 30. 11; 41. 3; 66. 6; 105. 25.
CONFLICT,] not 'battle;' as in 55. 18, &c.
10. KEPT,] as in 17. 4; 18. 21; 99. 7, &c.
COVENANT,] as in v. 37.
LAW,] as in v. 1, 5.
REFUSED,] as in 77. 2; Ex. 7. 14; 10. 3, &c.
WALK,] as in 107. 7; Ge. 11. 31; 12. 5, &c.
11. FORGET,] as in v. 7.
DOINGS,] not 'works;' as in 9. 11; 14. 1, &c.
DOINGS.] Sept. Vulg. 'benefits.'
WONDERS,] as in v. 4, 32.
12. FIELD,] as in v. 43.
ZOAN,] as in v. 43. Sept. Vulg. 'Tanes.'
13. CLEFT,] not 'divided;' as in 74. 15, &c.
SEA,] as in v. 27, 53.
TO PASS OVER,] as in Ge. 8. 1; 32. 23, &c.
TO STAND,] as in 41. 12; Ge. 21. 28; 33. 20.
HEAP,] as in 33. 7; Ex. 15. 8; Jos. 3. 13;
Isa. 17. 11. Sept. Vulg. 'as in a bottle.'
14. LEADETH,] as in v. 53, 72.
CLOUD,] as in 97. 2; 99. 7; 105. 39, &c.
LIGHT,] as in 4. 6; 27. 1; 36. 9, &c.
15. CLEAVETH,] as in Ge. 22. 3; 1 Sa. 6. 14.
ROCKS,] as in v. 20, 35.
WILDERNESS,] as in v. 19, 40, 52.
GIVETH DRINK,] as in 36. 8; 69. 21; 80. 5.
DEEP,] as in 33. 7; 36. 6; 42. 7, &c.
16. BRINGETH OUT,] as in 18. 19; 25. 15, &c.
STREAMS,] as in v. 44.
ROCK,] as in 18. 2; 31. 3; 40. 2; 42. 9, &c.

TO COME DOWN,] not 'run down;' as in 55.
23; Ge. 24. 18; 44. 11; Nu. 1. 51, &c.
RIVERS,] as in 24. 2; 46. 4; 66. 6; 72. 8, &c.
17. ADD,] as in 10. 18; 41. 8; 61. 6; 77. 7, &c.
TO SIN,] as in 39. 1; Ge. 20. 6; Ex. 9. 34, &c.
PROVOKE,] as in Job 17. 2; Isa. 3. 8.
MOST HIGH,] as in 7. 17; 9. 2; 18. 13; 21. 7.
DRY PLACE,] not 'wilderness;' as in 63. 1.
18. TRY,] not 'tempt;' as in v. 41, 56.
HEART,] as in v. 72.
FOOD,] not 'meat;' as in v. 30.
LUST,] as in v. 50.
19. ABLE,] as in v. 20.
ARRAY,] not 'furnish;' as in 40. 5, &c.
TABLE,] as in 23. 5; 69. 22; 128. 3, &c.
WILDERNESS,] as in v. 15.
20. SMITTEN,] as in 3. 7; 69. 26; 135. 8, &c.
ROCK,] as in v. 15.
FLOW,] not 'gush out;' as in 105. 41; Lev.
15. 25; Isa. 48. 21; Lam. 4. 9.
STREAMS,] as in 18. 4; 36. 8; 74. 15; 83. 9.
OVERFLOW,] as in 69. 15; 1 K. 22. 38, &c.
BREAD,] as in v. 25.
PREPARE,] not 'provide; as in 10. 17, &c.
FLESH,] as in v. 27. Sept. Vulg. 'a table.'
21. HEARD,] as in v. 59.
WROTH,] as in v. 59; De. 3. 26.
GONE UP,] as in v. 31.
22. BELIEVED,] as in v. 32.
TRUSTED,] as in 13. 5; 22. 4, 5; 25. 2, &c.
SALVATION,] as in 3. 8; 9. 14; 13. 5; 14. 7.
23. CLOUDS,] as in 18. 11; 36. 5; 57. 10, &c.
DOORS,] as in 107. 16, &c.
OPENED,] as in 37. 14; 105. 41; 109. 2, &c.
24. RAINETH,] as in v. 27.
MANNA,] as in Ex. 16. 15, 31, 33, 35, &c.
CORN,] as in 6. 7; 65. 9; Isa 36. 17; 62. 8,
&c. Sept. Vulg. 'bread of heaven.'
25. FOOD,] as in v. 20.
MIGHTY,] not 'angels;' as in 22. 12;
50. 13.
VENISON,] not 'meat;' as in Ge. 27. 3, &c.
TO SATIETY,] as in 17. 14; 22. 26; 37. 19, &c.
26. TO JOURNEY,] not 'to blow;' as in v. 52.
EAST WIND,] as in 48. 7; Ge. 41. 6, 23, 27,
&c. Sept. Vulg. 'south-wind.'
LEADETH,] not 'brought;' as in v. 52;
48. 14.
SOUTH-WIND,] as in v. 52. Sept. Vulg.
'south-west wind.'
27. RAINETH,] as in v. 24.
FLESH,] as in v. 20.
DUST,] as in 7. 5; 18. 42; 22. 15; 30. 9, &c.
SAND,] as in 139. 18; Ex. 2. 12; De. 33. 19.
WINGED,] not 'feathered;' as in 17. 8, &c.
28. TO FALL,] as in v. 55. Sept. Vulg.
'they fell.'
CAMP,] as in 27. 3; 106. 16; Song 6. 13, &c.
TABERNACLES,] not 'habitations;' as in v.
60. Sept. Vulg. 'their tabernacle.'
29. SATISFIED,] not 'well-filled;' as in 17.
14; 22. 26; 37. 19; 59. 15, &c.
DESIRE,] as in v. 30.
BRINGETH,] not 'gave;' as in v. 54.
30. ESTRANGED,] Sept. Vulg. 'disappoint-
ed.'
DESIRE,] not 'lust;' as in v. 29.
FOOD,] not 'meat;' as in v. 18.
MOUTH,] as in v. 1, 2, 36.
31. GONE UP,] not 'came;' as in v. 21.
SLAYETH,] as in v. 47.

FAT ONES,] as in Ge. 27. 28; Isa. 10. 16; 17.
4; Dan. 11. 24.
YOUTHS,] as in v. 63.
TO BEND,] not 'smote down;' as in Jud.
11. 35.
32. SINNED,] as in 41. 4; 51. 4; 106. 6, &c.
BELIEVED,] as in v. 22.
WONDERS,] as in v. 4, 11.
33. CONSUMETH,] as in Ge. 2. 2; 6. 16, &c.
VANITY,] as in 31. 6; 39. 5, 6, 11, &c.
TROUBLE,] as in Lev. 26. 16; Isa. 65. 23;
Jer. 15. 18.
34. SLEW,] as in 135. 10; Ge. 4. 23; 12. 12.
SOUGHT,] as in 34. 4; 77. 2; 109. 10; 119. 10.
TURNED BACK,] as in 85. 1; Ge. 18. 33, &c.
EARNESTLY,] not 'early;' as in Job 7. 21.
35. REMEMBER,] as in v. 39.
ROCK,] as in v. 15, 20.   Sept. Vulg. 'help-
er.'
MOST HIGH,] as in v. 17, 56.
REDEEMER,] as in 19. 14; 103. 4; Job 19. 25.
36. DECEIVE,] not 'flatter;' as in Ex. 22.
16; 1 K. 22. 20, 21, 22, &c.   Sept. Vulg. 'lov-
ed.'
LIE,] as in 89. 35; Nu. 23. 19; 2 K. 4. 16.
37. RIGHT,] as in 5. 9; 38. 17; 51. 10; 57. 7.
STEDFAST,] as in v. 8.
COVENANT.] as in v. 10.
38. MERCIFUL ONE,] as in 86. 15; 103. 8, &c.
PARDONETH,] as in 65. 3; Ge. 32. 20, &c.
INIQUITY,] as in 18. 23; 25. 11; 31. 10, &c.
DESTROYETH,] as in v. 45.
TURNED BACK,] not 'away;' as in 106. 23.
WALKED,] as in 57. 9; 108. 2; Song 2. 7, &c.
FURY,] as in 6. 1; 37. 8; 38. 1; 58. 4, &c.
39. FLESH,] as in 16. 9; 27. 2; 38. 3; 50. 13.
WIND,] as in v. 8.
RETURNETH,] as in v. 41.
40. PROVOKE,] as in Job. 17. 2; Isa. 3. 8.
WILDERNESS,] as in v. 15, 19, 52.
GRIEVE,] Sept. Vulg. 'anger him.'
DESOLATE PLACE,] as in 63. 7; 106. 14, &c.
41. TRY,] not 'tempt;' as in v. 18, 56.
HOLY ONE OF ISRAEL,] as in 71. 22; 89. 18.
LIMITED,] as in Eze. 9. 4.   Sept. Vulg.
'provoked.'
42. HAND,] as in v. 61.
RANSOMED,] not 'delivered;' as in 31. 5, &c.
ADVERSARY,] as in v. 61, 66.
43. SET,] not 'wrought;' as in v. 5.
SIGNS,] as in 65. 8; 74. 4, 9; 86. 17, &c.
WONDERS,] as in 71. 7; 105. 5, 27; 135. 9.
FIELD OF ZOAN,] as in v. 12.   Sept. Vulg.
'Tanes.'
44. TURNETH,] as in Ge. 19. 25; Ex. 10. 19.
BLOOD,] as in 5. 6; 9. 12; 16. 4; 26. 9, &c.
STREAMS,] not 'rivers;' as in Ge. 41. 1, &c.
FLOODS,] as in v. 16.
DRINK,] as in 50. 13; 75. 8; 110. 7, &c.
45. SENDETH,] as in v. 49.
BEETLE,] not 'divers sort of flies;' as in
105. 31; Ex. 8. 21, 22, 24, &c.   Sept. 'dog-
-ly.'
CONSUMETH,] not 'demand;' as in v. 29.
FROG,] as in 105. 30.
DESTROYETH,] as in v. 38.
46. CATERPILLAR,] as in 1 K. 8. 37, &c.
INCREASE,] as in 67. 6; 85. 12; Lev. 26. 4.
LABOUR,] as in 109. 11; 128. 2; Isa. 45. 14.
LOCUST,] as in 105. 34; 109. 23; Prov. 30. 27.
47. DESTROYETH,] as in v. 31.

HAIL,] as in v. 48.
VINE,] as in 80. 8, 14; 105. 33; 128. 3, &c.
SYCAMORES,] as in 1 K. 10. 27; 1 Ch. 27. 28
FROST.] Original word not found again.
48. DELIVERETH UP,] as in v. 62.
HAIL,] as in v. 47.
BEASTS,] not 'cattle;' as in Ge. 45. 17, &c
CATTLE,] not 'flocks;' as in Ge. 4. 20, &c.
BURNING FLAMES,] as in 76. 3; De. 32. 24
49. SENDETH,] not 'cast;' as in v. 45.
FURY OF HIS ANGER,] as in 2. 5; 58. 9, &c.
WRATH,] as in 7. 6; 85. 3; 90. 9, 11, &c.
INDIGNATION,] as in 38. 3; 69. 24; 102. 10.
DISTRESS,] as in 9. 9; 10. 1; 20. 22, 11, &c.
DISCHARGE,] as in Zec. 8. 8.   Sept. 'mes-
sage.'
EVIL MESSENGERS,] not 'angels;' as in
Prov. 16. 14; Isa. 14. 32; 33. 7; 37. 9, &c.
50. PONDERETH,] not 'made;' as in 58. 2;
Prov. 5. 6; Isa. 26. 7.
PATH,] as in 119. 35; Job 18. 10; 28. 7;
41. 32.
ANGER,] as in v. 21, 38, 49.
KEPT BACK,] as in Ge. 22. 12, 16; 39. 9, &c
LIFE,] as in v. 18.   Sept. Vulg. 'cattle.'
PESTILENCE,] as in 91. 3, 6; Ex. 5. 3; 9. 3,
15, &c.   Sept. Vulg. 'death.'
DELIVERED UP,] as in 31. 8; Lev. 13. 4, &c.
51. SMITETH,] as in v. 66.
FIRST-BORN,] as in 89. 27; 105. 36; 135. 8.
EGYPT.] Sept. Vulg. 'land of Egypt.'
FIRST-FRUIT,] not 'chief;' as in 105. 36, &c.
STRONG,] as in 105. 35; Isa. 40. 26, 29; Hos.
12. 3, &c.   Sept. Vulg. 'all their labours.'
TENTS OF HAM,] not 'tabernacles;' as in v.
55, 60, 67.
52. TO JOURNEY,] not 'go forth;' as in v. 26.
FLOCK,] not 'sheep;' as in v. 70.
GUIDETH,] as in v. 26.
DROVE,] not 'flock;' as in Ge. 29. 2, 3, &c.
WILDERNESS,] as in v. 15, 19, 40.
52. LEADETH,] as in v. 14, 72.
CONFIDENTLY,] not 'safely;' as in 4. 8, &c.
AFRAID,] as in 14. 5; 53. 5; 119. 161, &c.
SEA,] as in v. 13, 27.
COVERED,] not 'overwhelmed;' as in 32.
5; 40. 10; 44. 15; 69. 7, &c.
54. BORDER,] as in 104. 9; 105. 31, 33; 147.
14, &c.   Sept. Vulg. 'mountain.'
SANCTUARY,] that is, the land of Canaan;
as in 2. 5; 3. 4; 5. 7; 11. 4, &c.
MOUNTAIN,] or hill-country, as in v. 68.
RIGHT HAND,] as in 16. 8, 11; 17. 7; 18. 35.
GOT] not 'purchased;' as in 74. 2; 139. 13;
Prov. 8. 22; Ecc. 2. 7.
55. CASTETH OUT,] as in 80. 8; Ge. 3. 24, &c.
NATIONS,] not 'heathen;' as in 2. 1, 8, &c.
TO FALL,] as in v. 28.   Sept. 'he made
them to inherit.'
LINE,] as in 16. 6; 18. 4; 105. 11; 116. 3, &c.
INHERITANCE,] as in v. 62, 71.
TO DWELL,] as in 7. 5; Ge. 3. 24; Jos. 18. 1;
Job 11. 14.
TRIBES,] as in v. 67, 68.
TENTS,] as in v. 51, 60, 67.
56. TEMPT,]or 'try;' as in v. 41; 106. 14, &c.
PROVOKE,] as in v. 40.
MOST HIGH,] as in v. 17, 35.
TESTIMONIES,] as in 119. 14, 31, 36, 38, &c
KEPT,] as in v. 10.
57. TURN BACK,] as in 35. 4; 40. 14; 70. 2.

DEAL TREACHEROUSLY,] as in Jud. 9. 23; Isa. 33. 1; 48. 8; Mal. 2. 10, &c. Sept. 'brake covenant.'
FATHERS,] as in v. 3, 5, 8, 12.
TURNED,] as in 32. 4; Ex. 7. 15, 17, &c.
DECEITFUL.] Sept. 'crooked.'
BOW,] as in v. 9.
58. ANGRY,] as in 106. 29; De. 32. 16, 21, &c.
HIGH PLACES,] as in 18. 33; Lev. 26. 30, &c.
GRAVEN IMAGES,] as in De. 7. 5, 25; 12. 3.
ZEALOUS,] as in De. 32. 16, 21.
59. HEARD,] as in v. 3, 21.
WROTH,] as in 89. 38. Sept. 'overlooked them.'
KICKETH,] not 'abhorred;' as in v. 67.
60. LEAVETH,] as in 27. 9; 94. 14; Prov. 1. 8; Jer. 7. 29, &c. Sept. Vulg. 'rejecteth.'
TABERNACLE,] as in v. 28.
TENT,] as in v. 51, 55, 66.
PLACED,] as in Jer. 7. 7, 12, &c. Sept. Vulg. 'where he dwelt.'
61. STRENGTH,] as in v. 26.
CAPTIVITY,] as in 68. 18; Ex. 12. 29, &c.
BEAUTY,] not 'glory;' as in 71. 8; 89. 17, &c.
ADVERSARY,] as in v. 42, 66.
62. SWORD,] as in v. 64.
PEOPLE,] as in v. 1, 20, 52, 71.
INHERITANCE,] as in v. 55, 71.
ANGRY,] as in 89. 38. Sept. Vulg. 'spurned.'
63. YOUNG MEN,] as in v. 31.
CONSUMED,] as in v. 25.
VIRGINS,] as in 45. 14; 148. 12; Ge. 24. 16.
PRAISED,] not 'given to marriage.' Sept. Vulg. 'did not mourn.'
64. PRIESTS,] as in 99. 6; 110. 4; 132. 9, &c.
SWORD,] as in v. 62.
FALLEN,] as in 10. 10; 16. 6; 20. 8; 27. 2.
WIDOWS, as in 68. 5; 94. 6; 109. 9; 146. 9.
WEEP,] as in 69. 10; Ge. 21. 16; 27. 38; 29. 11, &c. Sept. Vulg. 'not wept for.'
65. LORD,] as in 2. 4; 16. 2; 22. 30; 35. 17.
WAKETH,] as in Ge. 9. 24; 28. 16; 41. 4, &c.
SLEEPER,] as in 1 Sa. 26. 7, 12; 1 K. 3. 20.
MIGHTY ONE,] as in 19. 5; 24. 8; 33. 16, &c.
CRYING ALOUD.] Sept. Vulg. 'heated by wine.'
WINE,] as in 60. 3; 78. 8; 104. 15, &c.
66. SMITETH,] as in v. 51.
ADVERSARIES,] as in v. 42, 61.
BACKWARD,] as in 9. 3; 35. 4; 40. 14, &c.
REPROACH,] as in 15. 3; 22. 6; 31. 11, &c
AGE-DURING,] as in v. 69.
67. KICKETH,] not 'refused,' as in v. 59.
TENT,] not 'tabernacle;' as in v. 60.
TRIBE,] as in v. 68.
FIXED,] as in 33. 12; 84. 10; 105. 26, &c.
68. CHOOSETH,] as in v. 70.
MOUNT ZION,] as in 2. 6; 48. 2; 74. 2, &c.
LOVED,] as in 11. 7; 26. 8; 45. 7; 47. 4, &c.
69. BUILDETH,] as in 28. 5; 51. 18; 69. 35.
SANCTUARY,] as in 68. 35; 73. 17; 74. 7, &c.
HIGH PLACE,] as in 18. 27; 113. 4; 138. 6; Prov. 6. 17, &c. Sept. Vulg. 'as of unicorns.'
EARTH,] as in 2. 2; 7. 5; 8. 1; 10. 16, &c. Sept. 'on the earth.'
FOUNDED,] not 'established;' as in 89. 11.
70. FIXETH,] as in v. 68.
SERVANT,] as in 27. 9; 31. 16; 34. 22; 35. 27.
FOLDS,] as in 50. 9; Hab. 3. 17, &c.
FLOCK,] as in v. 52.

71. SUCKLING ONES,] not 'great with young,' as in C. V.
RULE,] as in Ge. 36. 24; 37. 12; 1 Sa. 17. 15.
PEOPLE,] as in v. 62. Sept. Vulg. 'servant'
INHERITANCE,] as in v. 62.
72. INTEGRITY,] as in 7. 8; 25. 21; 26. 1; 41. 12, &c. Sept. Vulg. 'innocency.'
SKILFULNESS,] as in 49. 3; 136. 5; 147. 5.
LEADETH,] not 'guideth;' as in v. 14, 53.

LXXIX. PSALM OF ASAPH,] as in Ps. 73.
1. GOD,] as in v. 9, 10.
NATIONS,] not 'heathen;' as in v. 6, 10.
INHERITANCE,] as in 2. 8; 28. 9; 33. 12, &c.
DEFILED,] as in Ge. 34. 5, 13, 27; Lev. 13. 3.
HOLY TEMPLE,] as in 5. 7; 11. 4; 18. 6, &c.
HEAPS,] as in Nu. 21. 11; 33. 44, 45; Jer 26. 18, &c. Sept. Vulg. 'a storehouse of fruits.'
2. DEAD BODIES,] as in Lev. 5. 2; 7. 24, &c.
SERVANTS,] as in v. 10.
FOOD,] not 'meat;' as in 44. 11; 74. 14, &c.
FOWLS OF THE HEAVENS,] as in 104. 12; Ge. 1. 26, 28, &c.
FLESH,] as in 16. 9; 27. 2; 38. 3; 50. 13, &c.
SAINTS,] as in 4. 3; 12. 1; 16. 10; 18. 25, &c.
WILD BEAST,] not 'beasts;' as in 7. 5, &c.
EARTH,] as in 2. 2, 8, 10; 7. 5, &c.
3. SHED,] as in Ex. 4. 9; Lev. 14. 41; 17. 4.
BLOOD,] as in v. 10.
BURYING,] as in 2 K. 9. 10; 13. 21.
4. REPROACH,] as in v. 12.
NEIGHBOURS,] as in v. 12.
SCORN,] as in 44. 13; 123. 4; Eze. 23. 32, &c.
DERISION,] as in 44. 13; Ge. 20. 8.
SURROUNDERS,] as in v. 12.
5. TILL WHEN,] as in 4. 2; 74. 9.
ANGRY,] as in 2. 12; 85. 5.
FOR EVER,] as in 9. 6, 18; 10. 11; 13. 1, &c.
JEALOUSY,] as in 69. 9; 119. 139; De. 29. 19.
BURN,] as in 2. 12; 39. 3; 83. 14; 89. 46, &c.
6. POUR,] as in 62. 8; 69. 24; Jer. 6. 6, &c.
FURY,] as in 6. 1; 37. 8; 38. 1; 58. 4, &c.
KNOWN,] as in 14. 4; 18. 43; 20. 6; 31. 7, &c.
KINGDOMS,] as in 46. 6; 68. 32; 102. 22, &c
CALLED IN,] not 'upon;' as in 14. 4; 17. 6.
7. DEVOURED,] as in 14. 4; 22. 29; 53. 4, &c.
JACOB,] as in C.V.
HABITATION,] as in Ex. 15. 13; 2 Sa. 7. 8; 15. 25; 1 Ch. 17. 7, &c. Sept. Vulg. 'place.'
DESOLATE,] as in Lev. 26. 31; Job 16. 7, &c.
8. REMEMBER,] as in 8. 4; 20. 3; 22. 27, &c.
INIQUITIES,] as in 18. 23; 25. 11; 31, 10, &c.
FORE-FATHERS.] Sept. Vulg. 'our old.'
HASTE,] as in 69. 17; 102. 2; 143. 7, &c.
MERCIES,] as in 25. 6; 40. 11; 51. 1; 77. 9.
GO BEFORE,] not 'prevent;' as in 18. 8, &c.
WEAK,] not 'low;' as in 106. 6; 142. 6; Job 28. 4; Prov. 26. 7, &c. Sept. Vulg. 'poor.'
9. HELP,] as in 109. 26; 119. 86; Jos. 10. 4; 2 Ch. 14. 11.
GOD OF OUR SALVATION,] as in 18. 46; 24. 5; 25. 5; 27. 9, &c. Sept. Vulg. 'God our saviour.'
HONOUR OF THY NAME,] as in 66. 2; 72. 19.
DELIVER,] as in 7. 1; 22. 20; 25. 20; 31. 2
COVER OVER,] not 'purge away;' as in Lev. 9. 7; Nu. 16. 46; De. 21. 8.
NAME'S SAKE,] as in 25. 11; 31. 3; 106. 8, &c
10. NATIONS,] not 'heathen;' as in v. 1.

GOD,] as in v. 1.
KNOWN,] as in 74. 5; 88. 12; Ge. 41. 21, &c.
VENGEANCE,] as in 18. 47; 94. 1; 149. 7, &c.
SHED,] as in Eze. 20. 33, 34.
11. GROANING,] not 'sighing;' as in 12. 5;
102. 20; Lev. 11. 30; Mal. 2. 13.
PRISONER,] as in 69. 6; 69. 33; 102. 20;
107. 10, &c. Sept. Vulg. 'prisoners.'
ARM,] not 'power;' as in 10. 15; 18. 34, &c.
LEAVE,] not 'presence,' as in C. V.
SONS OF DEATH,] not 'appointed to die;'
as in 102. 20, &c.
12. TURN BACK,] as in 23. 4; 35. 17; 51. 12.
NEIGHBOURS,] as in v. 4.
SEVENFOLD,] as in 12. 6; Ge. 4. 15, 24; 2 Sa.
21. 9.
BOSOM,] as in 35. 13; 74. 11; 89. 50; Prov.
5. 20.
REPROACH,] as in v. 4.
REPROACHED,] as in v. 4.
LORD,] as in 2. 4; 16. 2; 22. 30; 35. 16, &c.
13. PEOPLE,] as in 3. 6, 8; 7. 8; 9. 11, &c.
FLOCK,] not 'sheep;' as in 44. 11; 49. 14;
65. 13; 74. 1, &c.
PASTURE,] as in 74. 1; 95. 7; 100. 3, &c.
GIVE THANKS,] as in 6. 5; 7. 17, 9. 1, &c.
AGE,] as in 5. 11; 9. 5, 7; 10. 16, &c.
GENERATIONS,] as in 10. 6; 12. 7; 14. 5, &c.
RECOUNT,] not 'shew forth;' as in 2. 7, &c.
PRAISE,] as in 9. 14; 22. 3, 25; 33. 1, &c.

LXXX. OVERSEER,] as in Ps. 4. 5. 6. 8. 9.
LILIES,] as in Ps. 45. 69. 80. &c.
TESTIMONY,] as in Ps. 60. 80.
ASAPH,] as in Ps. 75. 76. 77. 79. &c.
PSALM,] as in Ps. 75. 76. 77. 79. &c. Sept.
adds 'concerning the Assyrian.'
1. SHEPHERD,] as in 23. 1; Prov. 13. 20, &c.
GIVE EAR,] as in 5. 1; 17. 1; 39. 12; 49. 1.
LEADING,] as in 2 Sa. 6. 3; 1 Ch. 13. 7; Zec.
2. 3; Isa. 11. 6.
FLOCK,] as in 44. 11, 22; 49. 14; 65. 13, &c.
INHABITING,] not 'dwelling between;' as
in 2. 4; 9. 11; 17. 12; 22. 3, &c.
SHINE FORTH,] as in 94. 1.
2. EPHRAIM,] the youngest but favourite
son of Joseph.
BENJAMIN,] the youngest son of Jacob.
MANASSEH,] the elder brother of Ephraim.
WAKE UP,] as in 7. 6; 44. 23; 57. 8; 59. 4, &c.
MIGHTY,] as in 20. 6; 21. 13; 54. 1; 64. 6, &c.
SALVATION,] as in 3. 2, 8, 9. 14; 13. 5, &c.
3. GOD,] as in v. 4, 7, 14, 19.
TO TURN BACK,] as in v. 7, 19.
CAUSE TO SHINE,] as in v. 19.
SAVED,] as in 18. 3; 119. 117; 2 Sa. 22. 4.
4. JEHOVAH,] as in v. 7, 14, 19.
GOD OF HOSTS,] as in v. 7, 14, 19.
BURNED,] as in Ex. 9. 18.
PRAYER,] as in 4. 1; 6. 9; 35. 13; 39. 12, &c.
5. TO EAT,] not 'feedest;' as in Ex. 16. 32;
Isa. 49. 26; 58. 14; Jer. 19. 9, &c.
TEARS,] as in 78. 24; 104. 14, &c.
TO DRINK,] as in 36. 8; 69. 21; 78. 15, &c.
TEARS,] as in 6. 6; 39. 12; 42. 3; 56. 8, &c.
THIRD TIME,] not 'in great measure;' as
in Ex. 14. 7; 15. 4; 1 Sa. 18. 6; 2 Sa. 23. 8, &c.
6. STRIFE,] as in Prov. 6. 14; 15. 18; 16. 28.
NEIGHBOURS,] as in 31. 11; 44. 13; 79. 4, &c.
MOCK,] as in 2. 4; 59. 8; Prov. 1. 26; 30. 17.
AT IT.] Sept. Vulg. 'at us.'

7. GOD OF HOSTS,] as in v. 4, 14, 19. Sept.
prefixes 'Lord.'
TURN US BACK,] as in v. 3, 19.
SAVED,] as in v. 3, 19.
8. VINE,] as in 78. 47; 105. 33; 128. 3, &c.
BRING.] Sept. Vulg. 'transplant.'
CAST OUT,] as in 78. 55; Hos. 9. 15; Mic. 2. 9.
NATIONS,] not 'heathen;' as in 2. 1, 8; 9. 5.
PLANTEST,] as in 44. 2; 107. 37; Isa. 5. 2, &c.
9. LOOKED,] not 'preparest;' as in Ge. 24.
31; Lev. 14. 36; Zeph. 3. 15; Mal. 3. 15. Sept.
'make a way.'
ROOT,] as in De. 29. 18; Jud. 5. 14; 2 K. 19. 30.
LAND,] as in 2. 2, 8, 10; 7. 5, &c.
10. COVERED,] as in Prov. 24. 31.
SHADOW,] as in 17. 8; 36. 7; 57. 1; 63. 7, &c.
BOUGHS,] as in Lev. 23. 40; Eze. 17. 8. &c.
CEDARS OF GOD,] not 'goodly cedars;' as
in C. V.
11. SENDETH FORTH,] as in 44. 2; 78. &c.
BRANCHES,] as in Ge. 8. 22; 30. 14; 45. 6.
SEA,] as in 8. 8; 24. 2; 33. 7. 46. 2. &c.
RIVER,] as in 24. 2; 46. 4; 66. 6; 72. 8, &c.
SUCKLINGS,] not 'branches;' as in Job 8.
16: 14. 7; 15. 30; Eze. 17. 22, &c.
12. BROKEN DOWN,] as in 60. 1; 89. 40, &c.
HEDGES,] as in 62. 3; Nu. 22. 24; Ezra 9. 9.
PASSING BY,] as in 84. 6; 89. 41; 129. 8, &c.
PLUCKED,] as in Song 5. 1.
13. BOAR,] as in Lev. 11. 7; De. 14. 8, &c.
FOREST,] as in 50. 10; 83. 14; 96. 12; 104. 20.
WASTE.] Original word not found again.
WILD BEAST,] as in 50. 11; Isa. 66. 11.
FIELDS,] as in 8. 7; 50. 11; 96. 12; 104. 11.
CONSUMETH,] not 'devour;' as in Ge. 30.
31; 41. 2; Ex. 34. 3; 2 Sa. 5. 2, &c.
14. GOD OF HOSTS,] as in v. 4, 7, 19.
TURN BACK,] as in 6. 4; 7. 7; 85. 3; 90. 3.
WE BESEECH THEE,] as in Ge. 12. 11, &c.
LOOK,] as in 13. 3; 74. 20; 84. 9; 142. 4, &c.
SEE,] as in 9. 13; 25. 18, 19; 34. 8, &c.
INSPECT,] not 'visit;' as in 106. 4, &c.
VINE,] as in v. 8.
15. ROOT,] not 'vineyard.' Sept. 'and pre-
pare that which.'
RIGHT HAND,] as in v. 17.
PLANTED,] as in 104. 16; Lev. 19. 23, &c.
BRANCH,] Sept. Vulg. 'son of man.'
MADEST STRONG,] as in v. 17.
16. BURNT,] as in Nu. 16. 39; 1 Sa. 30. 3.
CUT DOWN,] as in Isa. 23. 12. Sept. Vulg
'dug up.'
REBUKE,] as in 18. 15; 76. 6; 104. 7, &c.
PERISH,] as in 1. 6; 2. 12; 9. 3, 18, &c.
17. HAND,] as in 8. 6; 10. 12; 17. 14; 19. 1.
MAN,] as in 1. 1; 4. 2; 5. 6; 12. 2, &c.
SON OF MAN,] as in 8. 4; Zec. 1. 1; 10. 17.
STRENGTHENED,] as in v. 15.
18. GO BACK,] as in 53. 3, &c.
REVIVE,] as in 41. 2; 71. 20; 85. 6; 138. 7.
IN,] not 'upon;' as in 20. 5; 33. 21; 63. 4.
CALL,] as in 3. 4; 18. 3, 6; 22. 2; 27. 7, &c.
19. JEHOVAH,] as in v. 4.
GOD OF HOSTS,] as in v. 4.
TURN US BACK,] as in v. 3, 7.
TO SHINE,] as in v. 3.
SAVED,] as in v. 3.

LXXXI. OVERSEER,] as in Ps. 4. 5. 6. &c.
GITTITH.] Sept. Vulg. 'concerning the
wine-presses.'

BY ASAPH.] The Alex. MS. reads 'David.'
1. CRY ALOUD,] not 'sing aloud;' as in 32.
11; De. 32. 43.
STRENGTH,] as in 8. 2; 21. 1, 13; 28. 7, 8,
&c. Sept. Vulg. 'helper.'
SHOUT,] not 'make a joyful noise;' as in
47. 1; 66. 1; 98. 4; 100. 1, &c.
GOD OF JACOB,] as in 20. 1; 76. 6; 84. 8, &c.
2. LIFT UP,] not 'take;' as in 4. 6; 10. 12.
SONG,] not 'psalm;' as in 98. 5; Ge. 43. 11;
Isa. 51. 3; Am. 5. 23.
GIVE OUT,] not 'bring hither;' as in 8. 1;
28. 4; 68. 34; 69. 27, &c.
TIMBREL,] as in 149. 3; 150. 4; Ge. 31. 27.
HARP,] as in 33. 2; 43. 4; 49. 4, &c.
PSALTERY,] as in 33. 2; 57. 8; 71. 22; 92. 3
3. BLOW,] as in 47. 1; Jer. 4. 5; 6. 1; 51. 27.
MONTH,] not 'new moon;' as in Ge. 7. 11.
TRUMPET,] as in 47. 5; 98. 6; 150. 3, &c.
NEW MOON,] not 'time appointed,' as
in C.V.
FESTIVAL,] not 'solemn feast day;' as in
118. 27; Isa. 29. 1; 30. 29; Eze. 45. 17, &c.
4. STATUTE,] as in 2. 7; 50. 16; 94. 20, &c.
ORDINANCE,] not 'law;' as in 1. 5; 7. 6, &c.
GOD OF JACOB,] as in v. 1.
5. TESTIMONY,] as in 19. 7; 78. 5; 119. 14.
PLACED,] not 'ordained;' as in 19. 4; 40. 4.
GOING FORTH,] as in 68. 7; 105. 38; 114. 1.
LIPS,] not 'language;' as in 12. 2, 3, 4, &c.
KNOWN,] as in 14. 4; 18. 43; 20. 6; 31. 7,
&c. Sept. Vulg. 'he did not know, he
heard.'
HEAR,] as in 4. 3; 5. 3; 18. 6; 34. 2, &c.
6. BURDEN,] as in 1 K. 11. 28; 2 Ch. 2. 2;
34. 13; Neh. 4. 10.
SHOULDER,] as in 21. 12; Isa. 9. 4; 10. 27;
14. 25, &c. Sept. Vulg. 'back.'
TURN ASIDE,] as in 66. 20; Isa. 18. 5; 31. 2.
HANDS,] as in 7. 3; 9. 16; 24. 4; 26. 6, &c.
BASKET,] not 'pots;' as in 1 Sa. 2. 14; 2 K.
10. 7; 2 Ch. 35. 13; Job 41. 20, &c.
PASS OVER,] not 'were delivered;' as in
17. 3; 37. 36; 42. 4; 57. 1, &c. Sept. Vulg.
'among the baskets served.'
7. DISTRESS,] as in 9. 9; 10. 1; 20. 1; 22. 11.
CALLED,] as in 14. 4; 17. 6; 31. 17; 34. 6, &c.
Sept. Vulg. add 'upon me.'
DELIVER,] as in 7. 4; 18. 19; 34. 7; 50. 15.
ANSWER,] as in 3. 4; 17. 6; 20. 1, 6, &c.
SECRET PLACE,] as in 18. 11; 27. 5; 31. 20.
THUNDER,] as in 77. 18; 104. 7; Job 26. 14;
39. 25, &c. Sept. Vulg. 'tempest.'
TRY,] not 'prove;' as in 11. 4, 5; Job 7. 18;
12. 11; 34. 3.
MERIBAH,] i.e. 'strife;' as in 95. 8; 106. 32;
Ge. 13. 8; Ex. 17. 7, &c. Sept. Vulg. 'strife.'
SELAH,] as in 3. 2, 4, 8; 4. 2, &c.
8. HEAR,] as in 4. 1; 17. 1, 6; 27. 7, &c.
PEOPLE,] as in v. 11, 13.
TESTIFY,] as in 50. 7; Isa. 8. 2; Jer. 6. 10.
HEARKEN,] as in v. 5.
9. A STRANGE,] as in 44. 20; 54. 3; 109.
11; Prov. 2. 16, &c. Sept. Vulg. 'a new
God.'
BOWEST THYSELF,] not 'worship;' as in 5.
7; 22. 27, 29; 66. 4; 72. 11; 81. 9, &c.
STRANGE GOD,] as in De. 32. 12; Jos. 24. 20.
10. THY GOD,] as in Ex. 20. 2, 5, 7, 10, &c.
ENLARGE,] not 'open;' as in Isa. 54. 2;
Mic. 1. 16.

FILL,] as in 17. 14; 20. 4, 5; 80. 9, &c.
11. PEOPLE,] as in v. 8.
CONSENTED,] as in Ex. 10. 27; De. 1. 26; 2.
30; 10. 10, &c. Sept. Vulg. 'gave heed,
attend.'
12. SEND AWAY,] not 'gave up;' as in 44.
2; 78. 45, 49; 80. 11, &c.
ENMITY,] not 'lust;' as in De. 29. 19; Jer.
3. 17; 7. 24; 9. 14, &c. Sept. Vulg. 'according to the desire.'
WALK,] as in 23. 4; 26. 11; 32. 8; 39. 13, &c.
COUNSELS,] as in 5. 10; Prov. 1. 31; 22. 20.
13. O THAT,] as in Ge. 17. 18; 23. 13; 30. 34;
50. 15, &c. Sept. Vulg. 'if.'
WAYS,] as in 1. 1, 6; 2. 12; 5. 8, &c.
WALK,] as in 55. 14; 85. 13; 86. 11; 89. 15.
14. AS A LITTLE THING,] not 'soon;' as in
2. 12; 8. 5; 37. 10, 16, &c.
ENEMIES,] as in 3. 7; 6. 10; 7. 5; 8. 2, &c.
TO BOW,] not 'subdued;' as in De. 9. 3;
Jud. 4. 23; 2 Sa. 8. 1; 1 Ch. 18. 1, &c.
ADVERSARIES,] as in 3. 1; 4. 1; 13. 4; 18. 6.
HAND,] as in 8. 6; 10. 12; 17. 14; 19. 1, &c
15. HATING,] as in 18. 40; 44. 7; 55. 10, &c
FEIGN OBEDIENCE,] not 'submitted them-
selves;' as in 18. 44; 66. 3; Ge. 18. 15, &c.
TIME,] as in 1. 3; 4. 7; 9. 9; 10. 1, &c.
AGE,] as in 5. 11; 9. 5, 7; 10. 16, &c.
16. TO EAT,] not 'fed;' as in Nu. 11. 4; De.
8. 3; 2 Ch. 28. 15; Eze. 3. 2, &c.
FAT,] not 'finest;' as in 7. 10; 63. 5; 78. 7.
WHEAT,] as in 147. 14; Ge. 30. 14, &c.
HONEY,] as in 19. 10; 119. 103; Ge. 43. 11.
ROCK,] as in 18. 2, 31, 46; 19. 14, &c.
SATISFY,] as in Job 19. 28; 91. 16; 105. 40;
132. 15, &c. Sept. Vulg. 'he satisfieth
them.'

LXXXII. PSALM OF ASAPH,] as in Ps. 50.
73. 75. 76. 77. 79. 80. &c.
1. GOD,] as in 3. 2, 7; 4. 1; 5. 2, &c.
COMPANY,] as in 5. 4; 7. 7; 22. 16; 68. 30,
&c. Sept. Vulg. 'synagogue.'
GOD,] not 'mighty;' as in 5. 4; 7. 11; 10. 11,
12, &c. Sept. Vulg. 'he doth judge gods.'
JUDGE,] as in 9. 8; 58. 8; 67. 4; 72. 4, &c.
2. TILL WHEN,] as in Ge. 30. 30; Ex. 10. 3.
JUDGE,] as in v. 1.
PERVERSELY,] not 'unjustly;' as in 7. 3;
53. 1; Prov. 29. 27; Jer. 2. 5, &c.
LIFT UP,] not 'accept;' as in 16. 4; 24. 5.
SELAH,] as in 3. 2, 4, 8; 4. 2, &c.
3. JUDGE,] not 'defend;' as in v. 8.
WEAK,] not 'poor;' as in v. 4.
FATHERLESS,] as in 10. 14, 18; 68. 5; 94. 6.
AFFLICTED,] as in 9. 12, 18; 10. 2, 9, &c.
POOR,] as in 1 Sa. 18. 23; 2 Sa. 12. 1, 3, &c.
DECLARE RIGHTEOUS,] not 'do justice;' as
in Ex. 23. 7; De. 25. 1; 2 Sa. 15. 4, &c.
4. WEAK,] not 'poor;' as in v. 3.
NEEDY,] as in 18. 12. 5; 35. 10; 37. 14, &c.
ESCAPE,] not 'deliver;' as in 17. 13; 31. 1.
HAND,] as in 8. 6; 10. 12; 17. 14; 19. 1, &c.
DELIVER,] not 'rid;' as in 7. 1; 22. 20, &c.
5. KNEW,] as in 14. 4; 18. 43; 20. 6; 31. 7.
UNDERSTAND,] as in 19. 12; 28. 5; 49. 20.
DARKNESS,] as in 139. 12; Ge. 15. 12; Isa.
8. 22; 50. 10.
WALK HABITUALLY,] not 'walk on;' as in
12. 8; 39. 6; 43. 2; 58. 7, &c.
MOVED.] not 'out of course;' as in 10. 6, &c.

FOUNDATIONS,] as in 18. 7. 15; De. 32. 22.
6. GODS,] as in v. 1.
SONS OF THE MOST HIGH,] A phrase not
found elsewhere.
7. MAN,] as in 84. 5, 12; 80. 47; 90. 3; 94. 10.
HEADS,] as in 45. 16; 68. 27; 105. 22, &c.
8. RISE,] as in 3. 7; 7. 6; 9. 19; 10. 12, &c.
GOD,] as in v. 1, 6.
JUDGE,] as in v. 3.
EARTH,] as in v. 5.
INHERITANCE,] as in 69. 36; Prov. 3. 35.
AMONG ALL,] not 'all' merely, as in the
C. V.

LXXXIII. SONG,] as in Ps. 30. 45. 46, &c.
PSALM OF ASAPH,] as in Ps. 50. 73. 75, &c.
1. GOD,] as in v. 12, 13.
SILENCE,] as in Isa. 62. 6, 7.   Sept Vulg.
'who shall be compared to thee.'
SILENT,] not 'hold thy peace;' as in 28. 1;
35. 22; 39. 12; 80. 3, &c.
GUILT,] as in Jud. 3. 11, 13; 5. 31; 8. 28, &c.
2. ROAR,] not 'make a tumult;' as in 39. 6;
42. 5, 11; 46. 3, &c.
HATING,] as in 18. 40; 44. 7, 10; 55. 12, &c.
LIFTED UP,] as in 15. 3; 24. 4, &c.
3. PEOPLE,] as in 85. 2, 6, 8; 87. 6, &c.
TAKE COUNSEL,] as in 1 Sa. 23. 22; Prov.
15. 5; 19. 25.
HIDDEN ONES,] as in 17. 14; Job 20. 26;
Prov. 13. 22; Eze. 7. 22, &c.   Sept. Vulg.
'saints.'
4. COME,] as in 34. 11; 46. 8; 66. 5; 80. 2, &c.
CUT OFF,] as in 2 Ch. 32. 21; Job 20. 12, &c.
NATION,] as in 2. 1, 8; 9. 5, 15, 17, &c.
Sept. Vulg. 'out of the nations.'
NAME,] as in v. 16, 18.
5. CONSULTED,] as in 7. 10; Isa. 40. 14.
HEART,] not 'consent;' as in 4. 7; 7. 10, &c.
COVENANT,] as in 25. 10, 14; 44. 17; 50. 5.
MAKE,] as in Ge. 21. 27, 32; 26. 28; 31. 44.
6. TENTS,] that is, those dwelling in them;
as in 15. 1; 19. 4; 27. 5, 6, &c.
EDOM,] the elder son of Isaac.
ISHMAELITES,] children of the elder son
of Abraham.
MOAB,] the elder son of Lot.
HAGARENES,] or Hagarites, as in 1 Ch. 5.
10, 19, 20.
7. GEBAL.] Compare Jos. 13. 5; 1 K. 5. 18;
Eze. 27. 9.
AMMON,] the younger son of Lot.
AMALEK,] a grandson of Esau, Ge. 36. 12.
PHILISTIA.] Sept. Vulg. 'the strangers or
others.'
TYRE,] the chief city of Phoenicia.
8. ASSHUR,] as in Ge. 2. 14; 10. 11, 22, &c.
JOINED,] as in Nu. 18. 4; Isa. 14. 1; 56. 3.
ARM,] as in 10. 15; 18. 34; 37. 17; 44. 3, &c.
Sept. Vulg. 'help.'
SONS OF LOT,] nephew of Abraham.
SELAH,] as in 3. 2, 4, 8; 4. 2, &c.
9. MIDIAN,] as in Ge. 25. 2, 4; 36. 35; Eze.
2. 15, &c.   Sept. 'Mediam.'
SISERA,] as in Jud. 4. 2, 7, 9, 12, 13, 14, &c.
JABIN,] as in Jos. 11. 1; Jud. 4. 2, 7, 17,
23, 24.
KISHON,] as in Jud. 4. 7. 13; 5. 21, &c.
10. DESTROYED,] as in 37. 38; Ge. 34. 30;
Jud. 21. 16; 2 Sa. 21. 5, &c.
EN-DOR,] as in Jos. 17. 11; 1 Sa. 28. 7.

DUNG,] as in 2 K. 9. 37; Jer. 8. 2; 9. 22, &c.
GROUND,] not 'earth;' as in 49. 11; 104. 30.
11. NOBLES,] as in 47. 9; 51. 12; 107. 40, &c.
OREB,] as in Jud. 7. 25; 8. 3; Isa. 10. 26.
ZEEB,] i.e. 'a wolf.'
ZEBAH,] i.e. 'a sacrifice.'
ZALMUNNA,] i.e. 'a shadow withdrawn.'
PRINCES,] as in De. 32. 38; Jos. 13. 21, &c.
12. OCCUPY,] as in 25. 13; 37. 9, 11, 22, &c.
COMELY PLACES,] not 'houses;' as in 23. 2;
65. 12; 74. 20; Jer. 9. 10, &c.   Sept. Vulg.
'sanctuaries.'
13. ROLLING THING,] not 'wheel;' as in 77.
18; Ecc. 12. 6; Isa. 5. 28; 17. 13, &c.   Sept.
Vulg. 'wheel.'
STUBBLE,] as in Ex. 5, 12; 15. 7; Job 13. 25.
14. BURN,] as in Ex. 3. 3; Nu. 11. 1, &c.
FOREST,] as in 50. 10; 80. 13; 96. 12, &c.
FLAME,] as in 29. 7; 105. 32; 106. 18, &c.
SETTETH ON FIRE,] as in 97. 3; 106. 18;
Isa. 42. 25; Joel 2. 3.
15. PURSUE,] not 'persecute;' as in 18. 37;
23. 6; 109. 16; Isa. 5. 11, &c.
WHIRLWIND,] not 'tempest;' as in 55. 8;
Jer. 23. 19; 25. 32; 30. 23, &c.
HURRICANE,] not 'storm;' as in Job 21.
18; 27. 20; 37. 9; Prov. 1. 27, &c.
TROUBLEST,] not 'make afraid;' as in 2. 5;
Est. 2. 9; Job 22. 10; Ecc. 5. 2, &c.
16. SHAME,] as in Job 10. 15; Prov. 3. 35.
SEEK,] as in 4. 2; 27. 4, 8; 37. 36, &c.
NAME,] as in v. 4, 18.
17. ASHAMED,] not 'confounded;' as in 6.
10; 25. 2, 3, 20, &c.
TROUBLED,] as in 6. 10; Jud. 20. 41, &c.
CONFOUNDED,] not 'put to shame;' as in
34. 5; 35. 4, 26; 40. 14, &c.
LOST,] as in 1. 6; 2. 12; 9. 3, 18, &c.
18. JEHOVAH,] as in v. 16.
MOST HIGH,] as in 7. 17; 9. 2; 18. 13; 21. 7.
EARTH,] as in 2. 2, 8, 10; 7. 5, &c.

LXXXIV. OVERSEER,] as in Ps. 4. 5. 6. 8.
9. 11. &c.
GITTITH.] Sept. Vulg. 'concerning the
wine-presses.'
SONS OF KORAH,] as in Ps. 42. 44. 45. 46, &c.
PSALM,] as in Ps. 3. 4. 5. 6. &c.
1. BELOVED,] not 'amiable;' as in 60. 5;
108. 6; 127. 2; Isa. 5. 1, &c.
TABERNACLES,] as in 26. 8; 43. 3; 46. 4, &c.
JEHOVAH OF HOSTS,] as in v. 3, 8, 12.
2. DESIRED,] not 'longeth;' as in Ge. 31. 30.
CONSUMED,] not 'fainteth,' as in C.V.
COURTS,] as in v. 10.
HEART..FLESH,] his whole nature.
CRY ALOUD,] as in 5. 11; 20. 5; 51. 14; 59.
16, &c.   Sept. Vulg. 'were glad.'
LIVING GOD,] as in 42. 2; 84. 2, &c.
3. SPARROW,] as in 8. 8; 11. 1; 102. 7, &c.
HOUSE,] as in 5. 7; 23. 6; 26. 8; 27. 4, &c.
SWALLOW,] as in Prov. 26. 2.   Sept. Vulg.
'turtle-dove.'
NEST,] as in Ge. 6. 14; Nu. 24. 21, &c.
PLACED,] not 'lay;' as in 3. 6; 8. 6; 73. 28.
BROOD,] not 'young;' as in De. 22. 6; Job
39. 30.
ALTARS,] as in 26. 6; 43. 4; 51. 19; 118. 27.
KING..GOD,] as in 5. 2; 68. 24; 74. 12, &c.
4. HAPPINESS,] not 'blessed;' as in v. 5, 12.
HOUSE,] as in v. 3.

PRAISE,] as in 22. 22, 26; 35. 18; 56. 4, &c.
SELAH,] as in 3. 2, 4, 8; 4. 2, &c.
5. STRENGTH,] as in 8. 2; 21. 1, 13; 28. 7,
8, &c. Sept. Vulg. 'help is of thee.'
HIGHWAYS,] as in Nu. 20. 19; Jud. 5. 20;
20. 31; 21. 19, &c. Sept. Vulg. 'to go up he
hath purposed in his heart to the valley of
weeping, to the place which he purposed.'
6. PASSING THROUGH,] as in 8. 8; 80. 12, &c.
VALLEY,] as in 60. 6; 65. 13; 108. 7, &c.
WEEPING,] not 'Baca;' as in 2 Sa. 5, 23, 24;
1 Ch. 14. 14, 15.
FOUNTAIN,] as in 74. 15; 87. 7; 104. 10, &c.
BLESSINGS,] not 'pools;' as in 3. 8; 21. 3.
COVER,] not 'filleth;' as in 71. 13; 109. 19,
29; Isa. 59. 17, &c. Sept. 'for the law-giver
blessings.'
DIRECTOR,] not 'rain;' as in Joel 2. 23.
7. STRENGTH,] as in 18. 32, 39; 33. 16, &c.
APPEARETH,] as in 18. 15; 42. 2; 90. 16;
Isa. 47. 3, &c. Sept. Vulg. 'the god of gods
shall be seen in Zion.'
ZION,] as in 2. 6; 9. 11, 14; 14. 7, &c.
8. JEHOVAH,] as in v. 1, 2, 3, 11, 12.
GOD OF HOSTS,] as in 59. 5; 80. 4, 7, 19, &c.
PRAYER,] as in 4. 1; 6. 9; 35. 13; 39. 12, &c.
GIVE EAR,] as in 5. 1; 17. 1; 39. 12; 49. 1.
GOD OF JACOB,] as in 20. 1; 46. 7; 76. 6, &c.
SELAH,] as in 3. 2, 4, 8; 4. 2, &c.
9. SHIELD,] as in 3. 3; 7. 10; 18. 2; 28. 7.
SEE,] as in 9. 13; 25. 18; 34. 8; 37. 37, &c.
BEHOLD,] as in 13. 3; 74. 20; 80. 14; 142. 4.
ANOINTED,] as in 2. 2; 18. 50, 20. 6; 28. 8.
10. COURTS,] as in v. 2.
TEACHER,]not'than a thousand;' as in C.V.
CHOSEN,] not 'had;' as in 33. 12; 78. 67, &c.
OF THE THRESHOLD,] not 'a door-keeper.'
Sept. Vulg. 'be an abject.'
HOUSE,] as in 5. 7; 23. 6; 26. 8; 27. 4, &c.
DWELL,] as in Da. 4. 12, &c.
TENTS,] as in 78. 51, 67; 83. 6; 120. 5, &c.
Sept. Vulg. 'sinners.'
11. SUN,] as in 19. 4; 50. 1; 58. 8; 72. 5, &c.
Sept. Vulg. 'the Lord God loves mercy and
truth.'
SHIELD,] as in 3. 3; 7. 10; 18. 2, 30, &c.
JEHOVAH GOD,] as in 7. 1, 3; 13. 3; 18. 28.
GRACE,] as in 45. 2; Ge. 6. 8; 18. 3; 19. 19.
HONOUR,] as in 3. 3; 4. 2; 7. 5; 8. 5, &c.
WITHHOLDETH,] as in 1 Sa. 13. 13, &c.
WALKING,] as in 15. 2; 78. 39; 101. 6, &c.
IN UPRIGHTNESS,] as in 15. 2; 18. 23; 19. 7;
37. 18, &c. Sept. Vulg. 'in innocency.'
12. JEHOVAH OF HOSTS,] as in v. 1.
HAPPINESS,] not 'blessed;' as in v. 5.
TRUSTING,] as in 21. 7; 27. 3; 32. 10; 49. 6.

LXXXV. OVERSEER,] as in Ps. 4. 5. 6. 8.
9. 11. &c.
BY SONS OF KORAH.] as in Ps. 42. 44. 45. 46.
PSALM,] as in Ps. 3. 4. 5. 6. &c.
1. ACCEPTED,] not 'been favourable;' as in
44. 3; 102. 14; Ecc. 9. 7; Isa. 42. 1, &c.
JEHOVAH,] as in v. 7, 8, 12.
LAND,] as in 2. 2, 8, 10; 7. 5, &c.
TURNED TO,] not 'brought back;' as in 78.
54; Ge. 18. 33; 28. 21; 43. 10, &c.
CAPTIVITY,] as in 14. 7, &c.
2. BORNE AWAY,] as in 15. 3; 24. 4; 32. 5.
INIQUITY,] as in 18. 23; 25. 11; 31. 10, &c.
PEOPLE,] as in v. 6. 8.

COVERED,] as in 32. 5; 40. 10; 44. 15, &c.
SIN,] as in 25. 7; 32. 5; 38. 3; 51. 2, &c.
SELAH,] as in 2. 2, 4, 8; 4. 2, &c.
3. GATHERED UP,] not 'taken away;' as in
Ge. 6. 21; 30. 23; Ex. 3. 16; 23. 10, &c.
WRATH,] as in 7. 6; 78. 49; 90. 9, 11, &c.
ANGER,] as in v. 5.
4. TURN BACK TO US,] not 'turn us;' as in
6. 4; 7. 7; 80. 14; 90. 3, &c.
SALVATION,] as in v. 7, 9.
MAKE VOID,] not 'cause to cease;' as in 1
K. 15. 19; 2 Ch. 16. 3.
ANGER,] as in 6. 7; 10. 14; 31. 9; Prov.
12. 16.
5. AGE,] as in 5. 11; 9. 5; 10. 16; 12. 7, &c
ANGRY,] as in 2. 12; 79. 5; Ezra 9. 14.
DRAW OUT,] as in 28. 3; Job 21. 33; 41. 1.
GENERATION,] as in 10. 6; 12. 7; 14. 5, &c.
6. TURN BACK,] as in v. 8.
REVIVEST,] as in 41. 2; 71. 20; 80. 18, &c.
REJOICE,] as in 5. 11; 9. 2; 14. 7; 21. 1, &c.
7. SHOW,] as in Ex. 33. 18; Jud. 1. 24;
Song 2. 14.
JEHOVAH,] as in v. 1, 8, 12.
KINDNESS,] as in v. 10.
SALVATION,] as in v. 4, 9.
GIVE,] as in v. 12.
8. HEAR,] as in 4. 3; 5. 3; 18. 6; 34. 2, &c.
GOD JEHOVAH,] as in 31. 5; 50. 1; 94. 1;
95. 3, &c. Sept. Vulg. add 'concerning me.'
PEACE,] as in v. 10.
SAINTS,] as in 4. 3; 12. 1; 16. 10; 18. 25, &c.
FOLLY,] as in Job 4. 6. Sept. 'and to
those turning their heart towards him.'
9. ONLY,] not 'surely;' as in 37. 8; Ge. 7. 23.
NEAR,] as in 15. 3; 22. 11; 34. 18; 38. 11, &c.
FEARING,] as in 15. 4; 22. 23, 25; 25. 12, &c.
SALVATION,] as in v. 4, 7.
HONOUR,] as in 3. 3; 4. 2; 7. 5; 8. 5, &c.
LAND,] as in 10. 6; 16. 3; 21. 10; 24. 1, &c.
10. KINDNESS,] not 'mercy;' as in v. 7.
TRUTH,] as in v. 11.
MET,] as in Prov. 22. 2; 29. 13.
RIGHTEOUSNESS,] as in v. 11, 13.
PEACE,] as in v. 9.
KISSED,] as in 2 Sa. 15. 5; 1 K. 19. 18;
Prov. 7. 13.
11. TRUTH,] as in v. 10.
EARTH,] as in v. 9.
SPRINGETH UP,] as in Ge. 2. 5; Job 5. 6, &c.
LOOKETH DOWN,] as in Nu. 21. 20, &c.
12. GOOD,] as in 4. 6; 14. 1; 16. 2; 21. 3, &c.
INCREASE,] as in 67. 6; 78. 46; Eze. 34. 27.
YIELD,] as in v. 7.
13. GOETH,] as in 55. 14; 81. 13; 86. 11, &c.
MAKETH,] not 'set;' as in 18. 43; 39. 8, &c.
FOOTSTEPS,] as in 17. 5; 57. 6; 58. 10, &c.
FOR A WAY,] for 'in the way;' as in 10. 5;
18. 21; 25. 9; 27. 11, &c.

LXXXVI. PRAYER OF DAVID,] as in Ps. 17.
90. 102. 142.
1. INCLINE,] not 'bow down;' as in 17. 6;
31. 2; 45. 10; 71. 2, &c.
JEHOVAH,] as in v. 6, 11, 17.
EAR,] as in 17; 17. 6; 18. 6; 31. 2, &c.
ANSWER,] not 'hear;' as in 4. 1; 13. 3, &c.
POOR,] as in 9. 12, 18; 10. 2, 9, &c.
NEEDY,] as in 9. 18; 12. 5; 35. 10; 37. 14, &c.
2. KEEP,] as in 16. 1; 17. 8; 25. 20; 37. 34.
PIOUS,] or 'kind,' not 'holy;' as in 4. 3. &c

SAVE,] as in v. 16.
SERVANT,] as in v. 4, 16.
TRUSTING,] as in 21. 7; 27. 3; 32. 10; 49. 6.
MY GOD,] as in 22. 1; 63. 1; 68. 24; 89. 26.
3. FAVOUR,] not 'be merciful;' as in v. 16.
LORD,] as in v. 4, 5, 8, 9, 12, 15.
CALL,] not 'cry;' as in v. 7.
ALL THE DAY,] not 'daily;' as in 25. 5; 32.
3; 35. 28; 38. 6, &c.
4. REJOICE,] as in 90. 15; Prov. 27. 11.
LIFT UP,] as in 16. 4; 24. 5; 25. 1; 50. 16.
5. GOOD,] as in v. 17.
FORGIVING,] not 'ready to forgive,' as in
C.V.
KINDNESS,] not 'mercy;' as in v. 13.
CALLING THEE,] not 'upon thee;' as in 42.
7; 99. 6; 145. 18; Isa. 6. 4, &c.
6. HEAR,] as in 5. 1; 17. 1; 39. 12; 49. 1, &c.
SUPPLICATIONS,] as in 18. 2, 6, &c.
PRAYER,] as in 4. 1; 6. 9; 35. 13; 30. 12, &c.
ATTEND,] as in 5. 2; 17. 1; 55. 2; 61. 1, &c.
7. DAY OF MY DISTRESS,] as in 20. 1; 50. 15.
CALL THEE,] not 'upon thee;' as in v. 3.
ANSWER ME,] as in 3. 4; 17. 6; 20. 1, &c.
8. LIKE THEE,] as in Ex. 9. 18; Lev. 19. 18.
GODS,] as in 8. 5; 82. 1, 6; 97. 9, &c.
LORD,] as in v. 3, 4, 5, 9, 12.
WORKS,] as in 8. 3, 6; 19. 1; 28. 4, &c.
9. NATIONS,] as in 2. 1, 8; 9. 5, 15, &c.
MADE,] as in 7. 3; 9. 4; 15. 3; 22. 31, &c.
BOW THEMSELVES,] not 'worship,' as in
C.V.
GIVE HONOUR,] as in v. 12
NAME,] as in v. 11, 12.
10. GREAT,] as in v. 13.
DOING WONDERS,] as in 9. 1; 26. 7; 40. 5.
ALONE,] as in Ex. 12. 37; Est. 4. 11, &c.
11. SHEW,] not 'teach,' as in C.V. Sept.
Vulg. 'guide.'
WAY,] as in 1. 1, 6; 2. 12; 5. 8; 10. 5, &c.
WALK,] as in 55. 14; 81. 13; 85. 13; 89. 15.
TRUTH,] as in 15. 2; 19. 9; 25. 5, 10, &c.
REJOICE,] not 'unite,' as in C.V
TO FEAR,] as in De. 4. 10; 5. 29; 6. 24, &c.
12. CONFESS,] not 'praise,' as in C.V.
LORD MY GOD,] as in 38. 15, &c.
HEART,] as in 4. 4; 13. 2; 15. 2; 20. 4, &c.
AGE,] as in 5. 11; 9. 5, 7; 10. 16, &c.
13. KINDNESS,] not 'mercy;' as in v. 5, 15.
DELIVERED,] as in 34. 4; 54.7; 56. 13, &c.
SHEOL,] not 'hell;' as in 6. 5; 9. 17, &c.
14. PROUD,] as in 19. 13; 119. 21, 51, 69, &c.
Sept. Vulg. 'lawless.'
COMPANY,] as in 1. 5; 7. 7; 22. 16; 68. 30.
TERRIBLE,] not 'violent;' as in 37. 35; 54.
3; Prov. 11. 16; Isa. 13. 11, &c.
PLACED,] as in 19. 4; 40. 4; 46. 8; 50. 23.
15. LORD,] as in v. 3, 4, 5, 8, 9, 12.
MERCIFUL,] as in 78. 38; 103. 8; 111. 4, &c.
GRACIOUS,] as in 103. 8; 111. 4; 116. 5, &c.
SLOW TO ANGER,] as in 103. 8; 145. 8, &c.
KINDNESS,] not 'mercy;' as in v. 5, 13.
TRUTH,] as in v. 11.
16. LOOK,] not 'turn;' as in 25. 16; 69. 16.
FAVOUR,] not 'have mercy;' as in 4. 1; 25.
16; 26. 11; 27. 7, &c.
SERVANT,] as in v. 2, 4.
SALVATION,] as in v. 2.
HAND-MAID,] as in 116. 16; Ge. 20. 17, &c.
17. DO,] not 'show;' as in 34. 14; 37. 3, &c.
SON,] as in 65. 8; 74. 4, 9; 78. 43, &c.

GOOD,] as in v. 5.
HATING,] as in 9. 13; 18. 17; 21. 8; 34. 21.
ASHAMED,] as in 6. 10; 25. 2, 3, 20, &c.
HELPED,] as in 118. 13; Jos. 1. 14; 1. a. 7. 12.
COMFORTED,] as in Ruth 2. 13; Isa. 49. 13.

LXXXVII. BY 'SONS OF KORAH,] as in Ps.
42. 44. 45. 46. &c.
PSALM..SONG,] as in Ps. 30. 65. 76. 88. &c.
1. FOUNDATION,] as in Job 4. 19, &c.
HOLY MOUNTAINS,] as in 2. 6; 3. 4; 15. 1.
2. JEHOVAH,] as in v. 6.
LOVING,] as in 5. 11; 11. 5; 33. 5; 34. 12.
GATES,] as in 9. 13, 14; 24. 7, &c.
TABERNACLES,] not 'dwellings;' as in 26.
8; 43. 3; 46. 4; 49. 11, &c.
3. HONOURABLE THINGS,] as in 149. 8.
IN THEE,] not 'of thee;' as in v. 5.
CITY OF GOD,] as in 46. 4; 48. 1, 8; 101. 8.
SELAH,] as in 3. 2, 4, 8; 4. 2, &c.
4. MENTION,] as in 20. 7; 45. 17; 71. 16, &c.
RAHAB,] as in 89. 10.
BABEL,] as in 137. 1, 8.
KNOWING ME,] as in 1. 6; 9. 10; 36. 10, &c.
PHILISTIA,] as in 45. 12.
TYRE,] as in 45. 12.
CUSH.] Sept. Vulg. 'and the people of the
Ethiopians.'
BORN,] as in v. 5, 6.
5. ZION.] Sept. 'a mother is Zion, shall a
man say.'
EACH ONE,] lit. 'a man and a man.'
MOST HIGH,] as in 7. 17; 9. 2; 18. 13, &c.
ESTABLISH,] as in 7. 9, &c.
6. RECOUNT,] not 'count;' as in 139. 18;
Lev. 23. 16; De. 16. 9; 2 Ch. 2. 2, &c.
DESCRIBINGS,] as in De. 31. 34; Jos. 18. 8;
Jer. 32. 44; 45. 1.
PEOPLES,] not 'people;' as in 3. 6; 9. 11;
57. 9; 77. 14, &c. Sept. 'and of those per-
sons born in her.'
THERE,] as in Ge. 2. 8; Ex. 40. 3; De. 1. 37.
7. SINGERS,] as in 68. 25; 2 Sa. 19. 35, &c.
PLAYERS ON INSTRUMENTS.] Sept. Vulg.
'as of rejoicing ones is the dwelling of all in
thee.'
FOUNTAINS,] as in 74. 15; 84. 6; 104. 10, &c.

LXXXVIII. SONG..PSALM,] as in Ps. 30.
65. 76. 87. &c
BY,] not 'for sons of Korah;' as in Ps. 42.
44. 45. 46. &c.
OVERSEER,] as in Ps. 4. 5. 6. 8. 9. 11. &c.
SICKNESS,] as in Ps. 53. Sept. 'Maeleth.'
AFFLICTIONS,] as in Ps. 22. 24.
INSTRUCTION,] as in Ps. 32. 42. 44. 45. &c.
HEMAN,] as in 1 Ch. 6. 33, &c.
EZRAHITE.] Sept. 'Israelite.'
1. JEHOVAH,] as in v. 9, 13, 14.
SALVATION,] as in 3. 2; 9. 14; 13. 5; 14. 7.
DAILY,] not 'day;' as in 2. 7; 7. 11; 20. 1.
CRIED,] as in 34. 17; De. 22. 24, 27; 1 K.
20. 39.
NIGHTLY,] not 'night;' as in 90. 4; 92. 2, &c.
2. PRAYER,] as in v. 13.
INCLINE,] as in 17. 6; 31. 2; 45. 10; 71. 2.
LOUD CRY,] not 'cry;' as in 17. 1; 30. 5; 42.
4; 47. 1, &c. Sept. 'supplication, O Lord.'
3. EVILS,] not 'troubles;' as in 5. 4; 7. 4.
LIFE,] as in 7. 5; 16. 11; 17. 14; 18. 46, &c.
SHEOL,] not 'grave;' as in 6. 5; 9. 17, &c.

4. RECKONED,] as in 44. 22; Ge. 31. 15, &c.
GOING DOWN,] as in 22. 29; 28. 1; 30. 3, &c.
PIT,] as in 7. 15; 28. 1; 30. 3; 40. 2, &c.
STRENGTH.] Original word not found again.
Sept. Vulg. 'help.'
5. DEAD,] as in v. 10.
FREE,] as in Ex. 21. 2, 5, 26; De. 15. 12, &c.
PIERCED ONES,] not 'slain;' as in 69. 26; 89.
10; Prov. 7. 26; Isa. 22. 2, &c.
LYING,] as in Ge. 28. 13; Ex. 22. 19, &c.
GRAVE,] as in v. 11; 5. 9; Ge. 23. 4, 6, &c.
REMEMBERED,] as in 19. 13; 63. 6; 78. 42.
HAND,] as in 8. 6; 10. 12, 14; 17. 14, &c.
CUT OFF,] as in 2 Ch. 26. 21; Est. 2. 1; Isa.
53. 8; Lam. 3. 54, &c. Sept. Vulg. 'cast
away.'
6. PUT,] not 'laid;' as in 3. 6; 8. 6; 73. 28;
84. 3, &c. Sept. Vulg. 'they put.'
LOWEST PIT,] as in 7. 15; 28. 1; 30. 3, &c.
DARK PLACES,] not 'darkness;' as in v. 18;
74. 20; 143. 8; Isa. 29. 15, &c.
DEPTHS,] as in Ex. 15. 5; Neh. 9. 11. Sept.
Vulg. 'shadow of death.'
7. FURY,] as in 6. 1; 37. 8; 38. 1; 58. 4, &c.
LAIN,] not 'lieth hard;' as in Ge. 27. 37;
Ex. 29. 10; Lev. 1. 4; 3. 2, &c.
BREAKERS,] not 'waves;' as in 42. 7; 93.
4; 2 Sa. 22. 5; Jon. 2. 3, &c.
AFFLICTED,] as in 35. 13; 90. 15; 102. 23;
105. 18, &c. Sept. Vulg. 'brought.'
SELAH,] as in 3. 2, 4, 8; 4. 2, &c.
8. PUT,] as in v. 18.
THOU HAST MADE.] Sept. Vulg. 'they have
made.'
ABOMINATION,] as in Ge. 43. 32; 46. 34, &c.
SHUT UP.] as in Jer. 32. 2.
9. GRIEVED,] not 'mourned;' as in Jer. 31.
25. Sept. Vulg. 'languid.'
AFFLICTION,] as in 9. 13; 25. 18; 31. 7; 44.
24, &c. Sept. Vulg. 'poverty.'
CALLED THEE,] not 'upon thee;' as in 14.
4; 17. 6; 31. 17; 34. 6, &c.
ALL THE DAY,] not 'daily;' as in 25. 5, &c.
SPREAD OUT,] as in Nu. 11. 32; 2 Sa. 17. 19;
Job 12. 23; Jer. 8. 2.
10. DEAD,] as in v. 5.
WONDERS,] as in v. 12.
REPHAIM,] as in Job 26. 5; Prov. 2. 18; 9.
18, &c. Sept. Vulg. 'physicians.'
RISE,] as in 1. 5; 12. 5; 24. 3; 27. 3, &c.
THANK,] not 'praise;' as in 6. 5; 7. 17; 9.
1, &c. Sept. Vulg. 'confess.'
SELAH,] as in v. 7.
11. KINDNESS,] as in 5. 7; 6. 4; 13. 5, &c.
RECOUNTED,] not 'declared;' as in 22. 30;
Job 37. 20; Hab. 1. 5.
GRAVE,] as in v. 5.
FAITHFULNESS,] as in 33. 4; 36. 5; 37. 3.
DESTRUCTION,] as in Job 26. 2; 28. 22, &c.
12. WONDERS,] as in v. 10.
KNOWN,] as in 74. 5; 79. 10; Prov. 10. 9, &c.
DARKNESS,] as in 18. 11, 28; 35. 6; 104. 20.
FORGETFULNESS.] Original word not found
again. Sept. 'a forgotten land.'
13. CRIED,] as in 30. 2; Jon. 2. 2; Hab. 1. 2.
MORNING,] as in 5. 3; 30. 5; 46. 5; 49. 14.
PRAYER,] as in v. 2.
COME BEFORE,] not 'prevent;' as in 18. 18;
21. 3; 59. 10; 79. 8, &c.
14. CASTEST OFF,] as in 44. 23; 77. 7; Lam.
3. 17, 31.

HIDEST,] as in 13. 1; 17. 8; 27. 5, 9, &c.
Sept. Vulg. 'turnest away.'
15. AFFLICTED,] as in 9. 12, 18; 10. 2, 9, &c.
Sept. Vulg. 'poor.'
EXPIRING,] or 'being gathered;' as in Ge.
6. 17, &c. Sept. Vulg. 'in labours.'
YOUTH,] as in Job 33. 25; 36. 14; Ps. 29. 21.
BORNE,] not 'suffer;' as in 15. 3; 24. 4; 32.
5; 69. 7. Sept. Vulg. 'been exalted.'
TERRORS,] as in 55. 4; Ge. 15. 12; Ex. 15. 16.
PINE AWAY,] not 'am distracted.' Origi-
nal word not found again.
16. WRATH,] as in 2. 5; 58. 9; 69. 24, &c.
PASSED,] as in 18. 12; 38. 4; 42. 7; 48. 4, &c.
TERRORS,] as in Job 6. 4.
CUT OFF,] as in 18. 40; 54. 5; 73. 27; 119.
139, &c. Sept. Vulg. 'troubled.'
17. SURROUNDED,] as in 17. 11; 18. 5, &c.
ALL THE DAY,] not 'daily;' as in v. 9.
GONE ROUND,] as in 22. 16; 2 K. 11. 8, &c.
18. PUT FAR,] as in v. 8.
LOVER,] as in 5. 11; 11. 5; 33. 5; 34. 12. &c.
FRIEND,] as in 12. 2; 15. 3; 28. 3; 35. 14.
ACQUAINTANCE,] as in v. 8.
PLACE OF DARKNESS,] Sept. Vulg. 'because
of misery.'

LXXXIX. INSTRUCTION,] as in Ps. 32. 42.
44. 45. &c.
ETHAN,] as in 1 K. 4. 31; 1 Ch. 2. 6, &c.
EZRAHITE,] as in Ps. 88. Sept. 'Israel-
ite.'
1. KIND ACTS,] not 'mercies;' as in v. 2,
14, 24, 28, 33, 49. Sept. 'thy kindness, O
Lord.'
SING,] as in 13. 6; 21. 13; 27. 6; 57. 7, &c.
GENERATION,] as in v. 4.
FAITHFULNESS,] as in v. 2, 5, 8, 24, 33. 49.
MOUTH,] as in 5. 9; 8. 2; 10. 7; 17. 3, &c.
2. I SAID.] Sept. Vulg. 'thou hast said.'
KINDNESS,] not 'mercy;' as in v. 1.
BUILT,] as in Ge. 16. 2; 30. 3; Nu. 21 27.
HEAVENS,] as in v. 5, 11, 29.
ESTABLISH,] as in v. 4; 10. 17; 65. 9, &c.
FAITHFULNESS,] as in v. 1.
3. COVENANT,] as in v. 28, 34, 39.
CHOSEN,] as in 105. 6, 43; 106. 5, 23, &c.
SWORN,] as in v. 35, 49.
SERVANT,] as in v. 20, 39, 50.
4. ESTABLISH,] as in v. 2. Sept. Vulg.
'prepare.'
SEED,] as in v. 29, 36.
BUILT,] as in 102. 16; Ge. 11. 5; Nu. 32. 37.
GENERATION,] as in v. 1.
SELAH,] as in 3. 2, 4, 8; 4. 2, &c.
5. HEAVENS,] as in v. 2.
CONFESS,] as in 6. 5; 7. 17; 9. 1; 18. 49, &c.
WONDERS,] as in 77. 11, 14; 78. 12; 88. 10.
JEHOVAH,] as in v. 1, 6, 8, 46, 50.
FAITHFULNESS,] as in v. 2.
ASSEMBLY,] as in 22. 22; 26. 5; 35. 18, &c.
HOLY ONES,] as in v. 6.
6. SKY.] Sept. Vulg. 'clouds.'
COMPARED HIMSELF,] not 'can be com-
pared;' as in 5. 3; 23. 5; 50. 21; Isa. 40. 18, &c.
IS LIKE,] not 'can be likened,' as in C.V.
MIGHTY.] Sept. Vulg. 'God.'
7. VERY TERRIBLE.] Compare Isa. 8. 13; 2.
19, 21. Sept. Vulg. 'glorified.'
SECRET COUNSEL,] as in 25. 14; 55. 14; 64.
2; 83. 3, &c.

FEARFUL,] as in 45. 4; 47. 2; 65. 5; 66. 3, &c.
Sept. Vulg. 'great and fearful.'
8. GOD OF HOSTS,] as in 80. 4, 7, 19; 84. 8.
JAH,] as in 68. 4, 18; 77. 11; 89. 8, &c.
Sept. Vulg. 'strong art thou, O Lord.'
FAITHFULNESS,] as in v. 5.
9. PRIDE,] not 'raging;' as in 17. 10; 93. 1;
Isa. 9. 18; 12. 5, &c. Sept. Vulg. 'power.'
LIFTING UP,] as in v. 50; 28. 2, &c. Sept.
Vulg. 'tumult or motion.'
BILLOWS,] as in 42. 7; 64. 7; 107. 25, &c.
RESTRAIN,] as in 63. 3; 145. 4; Prov. 29. 11.
10. BRUISED,] as in 143. 3. Sept. Vulg.
'humbled.'
RACHAB,] as in 87. 4; Job 9. 13; 26. 12;
Isa. 30. 7, &c. Sept. Vulg. 'proud.'
WOUNDED,] as in 69. 26; 88. 5; Prov. 7. 26.
STRENGTH,] as in v. 17.
SCATTERED,] as in 53. 5; 112. 9; Joel 3. 2.
ENEMIES,] as in v. 22, 42, 51.
11. HEAVENS..EARTH,] as in 69. 34; 103. 11.
HABITABLE WORLD,] as in 9. 8; 18. 15, &c.
FULNESS,] as in 24. 1; 50. 12; 96. 11, &c.
FOUNDED,] as in 24. 2; 78. 69; 102. 25, &c.
12. NORTH,] as in 48. 2; 107. 3; Ge. 13. 14.
SOUTH,] as in v. 13, 25, 42. Sept. Vulg.
'sea,' i.e. the west.
APPOINTED,] as in v. 47.
TABOR,] as in Jos. 19. 22; Jud. 4. 6, 12, &c.
HERMON,] as in 133. 3; De. 3. 8, 9; 4. 48, &c.
NAME,] as in v. 16, 24.
SING,] as in 5. 11; 20. 5; 51. 14; 59. 16, &c.
13. ARM,] as in v. 10; 21.
MIGHT,] as in 20. 6; 21. 13; 54. 1; 65. 6, &c.
STRONG,] as in 9. 19; 52. 7, &c.
HIGH,] as in v. 16, 17, 24.
14. RIGHTEOUSNESS,] as in 4. 1, 5; 7. 8, &c.
JUDGMENT,] as in v. 30.
FIXED PLACE,] as in 33. 14; 97. 2; 104. 5;
Isa. 4. 5, &c. Sept. Vulg. 'preparation.'
THRONE,] as in v. 4, 29, 36, 44.
KINDNESS,] as in v. 1, 2, 24, 28, 33, 49.
TRUTH,] as in 15. 2; 19. 9; 25. 5, 10, &c.
15. HAPPINESS,] as in 1. 1; 2. 12; 32. 1, &c.
SHOUT,] as in 27. 6; 33. 3; 47. 5; 150. 5, &c.
LIGHT,] as in 4. 6; 27. 1; 36. 9; 37. 6, &c.
WALK HABITUALLY,] as in 55. 14; 81. 13.
16. REJOICE,] as in 9. 14; 13. 4, 5; 14. 7, &c.
EXALTED,] as in v. 13, 17, 24.
17. BEAUTY,] not 'glory;' as in 71. 8; 78.
61; 96. 6; Prov. 4. 9, &c. Sept. 'boast.'
GOOD PLEASURE,] as in 5. 12; 19. 14; 30. 5.
HORN,] as in v. 24.
18. OF JEHOVAH,] coming from him.
SHIELD,] as in 3. 3; 7. 10; 18. 2, 30, &c.
Sept. Vulg 'the help.'
HOLY ONE OF ISRAEL,] as in 71. 22; 78. 41.
KING,] as in v. 27.
19. VISION,] as in 1 Sa. 3. 1; 1 Ch. 17. 15.
SAINT,] as in 4. 3; 12. 1; 16. 10; 18. 25, &c.
Sept. 'sons.'
HELP,] as in 20. 2; 33. 20; 70. 5; 115. 9, &c.
MIGHTY ONE,] as in 19. 5; 24. 8; 33. 16, &c.
EXALTED,] as in v. 42.
CHOSEN ONE,] as in 78. 31; 148. 12, &c.
PEOPLE,] as in v. 15, 50. Sept. Vulg. 'my
people.'
20. FOUND,] as in 69. 20; 76. 5; 84. 3, &c.
SERVANT,] as in v. 3, 39, 50, &c.
HOLY OIL,] as in 23. 5; 45. 7; 55. 21, &c.
ANOINTED,] as in 45. 7; Ge. 31. 13; Ex. 28. 41.

21. ESTABLISHED,] as in v. 37. Sept. Vulg
'shall help.'
STRENGTHEN,] as in De. 15. 7; 2 Ch. 11. 7.
22. EXACTETH.] Sept. 'hath no advantage
over him.'
PERVERSENESS,] as in 37. 1; 43. 1; 92. 15;
107. 42, &c. Sept. 'lawlessness.'
AFFLICTETH,] as in 94. 5; Ge. 16. 6; 31. 50.
23. BEATEN DOWN,] as in Lev. 22. 24, &c.
ADVERSARIES,] as in v. 42.
PLAGUE,] as in 91. 12; Ex. 21. 35; 32. 35;
Jos. 24. 5, &c. Sept. Vulg. 'put to flight.'
24. KINDNESS,] as in v. 1, 2, &c.
NAME,] as in v. 12, 16.
HORN,] as in v. 17.
25. SEA,] as in v. 9.
RIVERS,] as in 24. 2; 46. 4; 66. 6; 72. 8, &c.
26. PROCLAIMETH ME,] as in 3. 4; 18. 3, &c
FATHER,] as in 27. 10; 45. 10; 68. 5; 103. 13
GOD,] as in v. 6, 7.
ROCK,] Sept. Vulg. 'helper.'
SALVATION,] as in 3. 2; 9. 14; 13. 5; 14. 7
27. FIRST-BORN,] as in 78. 51; 105. 36, &c
APPOINT,] as in 1. 3; 2. 8; 14. 7; 16. 10, &c
HIGHEST,] as in 7. 17; 9. 2; 18. 13; 21. 7
28. KINDNESS,] as in v. 24, &c.
COVENANT,] as in v. 3, &c.
STEDFAST,] as in v. 37.
29. SET,] not 'make to endure;' as in v.
25, 40.
THRONE,] as in v. 4, 14, 36, 44.
DAYS OF THE HEAVENS,] as in De. 11. 21.
30. FORSAKE,] as in 10. 14; 16. 10; 27. 9, &c.
LAW,] as in 1. 2; 19. 7; 37. 31; 40. 8, &c.
JUDGMENTS,] as in v. 14.
WALK,] as in 23. 4; 26. 11; 32. 8; 39. 13, &c.
31. STATUTES,] as in 18. 22; 119. 16, &c.
POLLUTE,] as in v. 34.
COMMANDS,] as in 19. 8; 78. 7; 112. 1, &c.
32. LOOKED AFTER,] not 'visited;' as in 17.
3; 65. 9; Isa. 13. 11; 26. 14, &c.
TRANSGRESSION,] as in 5. 10; 19. 13; 25. 7.
ROD,] as in 2. 9; 23. 4; 45. 6; 74. 2, &c.
STROKES,] as in 38. 11; 39. 10; 91. 10, &c.
INIQUITY,] as in 18. 23; 25. 11; 31. 10, &c.
33. BREAK,] as in 33. 10; Eze. 17. 19, &c.
DEAL FALSELY,] as in Lev. 19. 11, &c.
FAITHFULNESS,] as in v. 2, 5, 8, 24, 49.
34. PROFANE,] as in v. 31.
COVENANT,] as in v. 3, 28.
GOING FORTH,] as in 19. 6; 65. 8; 75. 6, &c.
LIPS,] as in 12. 2, 3, 6; 16. 4, &c.
CHANGE,] as in 1 Sa. 21. 13; Est. 2. 9; Prov.
31. 5. Sept. 'make not void.'
35. ONCE,] as in 14. 3; 27. 4; 34. 20; 53. 3.
SWORN,] as in v. 3, 49.
HOLINESS,] as in v. 20; 2. 6; 3. 4; 5. 7, &c
LIE,] as in 78. 36; Nu. 23. 19; 2 K. 4. 16, &c
36. SEED,] as in v. 4, 29.
THRONE,] as in v. 4, 14, 44.
SUN,] as in 19. 4; 50. 1; 58. 8; 72. 5. &c.
37. MOON,] as in 8. 3; 72. 5, 7; 104. 19, &c.
ESTABLISHED,] as in v. 21.
WITNESS,] as in 27. 12; 35. 11; Prov. 6. 19.
SKY,] as in v. 6. Sept. Vulg. 'heavens.'
STEDFAST,] as in v. 28.
38. CAST OFF,] as in 43. 2; 44. 9; 60. 1, &c.
REJECT,] as in 36. 4; 78. 59; 106. 24, &c.
WROTH,] as in 78. 62. Sept. Vulg 'reject-
ed.'
ANOINTED,] as in v. 20.

SERVANT,] as in v. 3, 20, 50.
POLLUTED,] as in 55. 20; 74. 7; Isa. 47. 6
CROWN,] as in 132. 18; Ex. 29. 6; 39. 30;
Lev. 8. 9, &c. Sept. Vulg. 'sanctuary.'
40. BROKEN DOWN,] as in 60. 1; 80. 12, &c.
HEDGES,] as in Nu. 32. 16, 24, 36, &c. ·
FENCED PLACES,] as in 108. 10; Isa. 17. 3.
RUIN,] as in Prov. 10. 14, 15, 29; 13. 3, &c.
Sept. 'terror.'
41. SPOILED,] as in 44. 10; Jud. 2. 14, &c.
PASSING BY,] as in 8. 8; 80. 12; 84. 6, &c.
REPROACH,] as in v. 50.
NEIGHBOURS,] as in 31. 11; 44. 13; 79. 4, &c.
42. EXALTED,] as in v. 13, 17, 24.
ADVERSARIES,] as in v. 23.
ENEMIES,] as in v. 10, 22, 51.
CAUSED TO REJOICE.] Compare 30. 1, &c.
43. SHARPNESS,] as in v. 26. Sept. Vulg.
'help.'
BATTLE,] as in 18. 34, 39; 24. 8; 27. 3, &c.
44. TO CEASE,] as in 46. 4; 119. 119, &c.
BRIGHTNESS.] or 'purity;' as in Ex. 24. 10.
THRONE,] as in v. 4, 14, 29, 36.
CAST DOWN,] as in Ezr. 6. 12.
45. SHORTENED,] lit. 'reaped.'
YOUTH,] as in Job 20. 11; 33. 25; Isa. 54. 4.
Sept. Vulg. 'time.'
COVERED.] Compare 71. 13, &c.
SHAME,] as in Eze. 7. 18; Obad. 10; Mic.7.10.
46. TILL WHEN,] as in 4. 2; 74. 9.
HIDDEN,] as in 55. 12; Ge. 4. 14; 31. 49;
1 Sa. 20. 24, &c. Sept. Vulg. 'turn away.'
FURY,] as in 6. 1; 37. 8; 38. 1; 58. 4, &c.
BURN,] as in 2. 12; 39. 3; 79. 5; 83. 14, &c.
FIRE,] as in 11. 6; 18. 8, 12; 21. 9, &c.
47. REMEMBER,] as in v. 50.
I PRAY THEE.] Sept. Vulg. omit.
LIFE-TIME,] as in 17. 14; 39. 5; 49. 1; Job
11. 17. Sept. Vulg. 'my substance.'
IN VAIN,] as in 12. 2; 24. 4; 26. 4; 31. 6, &c.
CREATED,] as in v. 12.
48. LIVETH,] as in 22. 26; 49. 9; 69. 32, &c.
SEE,] as in 8. 3; 22. 17; 35. 17; 36. 9, &c.
DELIVERETH,] as in 33. 17; 41. 1; 107. 20.
HAND OF SHEOL,] as in 49. 15, &c.
49. KINDNESSES,] as in v. 2, 14, 24, 28, 33.
LORD,] as in v. 50.
SWORN,] as in v. 3, 35.
FAITHFULNESS,] as in v. 2, 5, 8, 24, 33.
50. REPROACH,] as in v. 41.
BORNE,] as in v. 9.
BOSOM,] as in 35. 13; 74. 11; 79. 12, &c.
STRIVINGS,] as in 3. 1, 2; 4. 6; 18. 16, &c.
Sept. Vulg. 'of many nations.'
51. ENEMIES,] as in v. 10, 22, 42.
STEPS,] as in 41. 9; 49. 5; 56. 6; 77. 19, &c.
Sept. Vulg. 'recompense.'
ANOINTED,] as in v. 20, 38.
52. BLESSED,] as in 18. 46; 28. 6; 31. 21, &c.
AMEN,] as in 41. 13; 72. 19; 106. 48; Isa. 65.
16, &c. Here ends the Third Collection of
the Psalms.

XC. PRAYER,] as in Ps. 17. 86. 102. 142.
MOSES,] generally supposed to be the son
of Amram.
MAN OF GOD,] as in 1 K. 12. 12; 13. 1, &c.
1. LORD,] as in 2. 4; 16, 2; 22, 30; 35. 17
HABITATION,] as in 26. 8; 68. 5; 71. 3; 91.
9, &c. Sept. Vulg. 'refuge.'
GENERATION,] as in 10. 6; 12. 7; 14. 5, &c.

2. MOUNTAINS,] as in 46. 2, 3; 65. 6; 72. 3.
BROUGHT FORTH,] as in 87. 4, 5, 6, &c.
FORM,] as in 29. 9; Job 26. 15; 35. 14, &c.
EARTH,] as in 2. 2, 8, 10; 7. 5, &c.
WORLD,] as in 9. 8; 18. 15; 19. 4; 24. 1, &c.
AGE TO AGE,] as in 5. 11; 9. 5, 7; 10. 16, &c
GOD,] as in 5. 4; 7. 11; 10. 11, 12, &c. Sept.
omits 'God.'
3. TURNEST,] as in 18. 20, 24; 44. 10; 54. 5,
&c. Sept. Vulg. 'turn not back.'
BRUISED THING,] as in 34. 18; Isa. 57. 15
Sept. Vulg. 'low, humble place.'
TURN BACK,] as in v. 13.
SONS OF MEN,] as in v. 16.
4. THOUSAND,] as in 8. 7; 50. 10; 68. 17:
84. 10, &c. Sept. adds 'O Lord.'
YESTERDAY,] as in v. 9, 10, 12, 14, 15.
PASSETH ON,] as in 17. 3; 37. 36; 42. 4, &c.
WATCH,] as in 63. 6; 119. 148; Ex. 14. 24, &c.
5. INUNDATED,] as in 77. 17; Job 24. 8, &c.
Sept. 'the vanities of them shall be years.'
ASLEEP,] as in 76. 5; Ge. 28. 16; 31. 40;
Jud. 16. 14, &c. Sept. Vulg. 'years.'
MORNING,] as in v. 6, 14.
GRASS,] as in 37. 2; 103. 15; 104. 14; 129. 6
CHANGETH,] as in Jud. 5. 26; 1 Sa. 10. 3, &c.
6. FLOURISHETH,] as in 72. 16; 92. 7, &c.
CUT DOWN.] Compare 58. 7; 118. 10, 11, 12.
WITHERED,] as in 22. 15; 129. 6; Isa. 15. 6;
19. 5; 40. 7, &c. Sept. Vulg. add 'and dried
up.'
7. CONSUMED,] as in 31. 10; 37. 20; 39. 10.
ANGER,] as in v. 11.
FURY,] as in 6. 1; 37. 8; 38. 1; 58. 4, &c.
TROUBLED,] as in 6. 2, 3; 48. 5; Isa. 13. 8.
8. INIQUITIES,] as in 18. 23; 25. 11; 31. 10.
HIDDEN THINGS,] not merely sins. Sept.
Vulg. 'age.'
9. PINED AWAY,] as in 40. 4; 102. 17, &c.
WRATH,] as in v. 11.
MEDITATION,] as in Job 37. 2; Eze. 2. 10.
10. SEVENTY,] as in Ge. 4. 24; 5. 12, &c.
MIGHT,] as in 20. 6; 21. 13; 54. 1; 65. 6, &c.
EIGHTY,] as in Ge. 5. 25, 26, 28; 16. 16, &c.
ENLARGEMENT,] lit. 'breadth.' Sept. Vulg.
'greater part.'
LABOUR,] as in 7. 14, 16; 10. 7, 14; 25. 18, &c.
VANITY,] as in 5. 5; 6. 8; 7. 14; 10. 7, &c.
CUT OFF,] as in Nu. 11. 31.
HASTILY.] Compare 71. 12.
FLY AWAY,] as in 18. 10; 55. 6; 98. 5; Prov.
23. 5, &c. Sept. Vulg. 'are chastised.'
11. ANGER,] as in v. 7.
FEAR,] as in 2. 11; 5. 7; 19. 9; 34. 11, &c.
WRATH,] as in v. 9.
12. TO NUMBER,] as in Ge. 13. 16; 1 Ch. 21. 1.
OUR DAYS.] Sept. Vulg. 'thy right hand so
make known to me.'
ARIGHT,] or 'so,' as in C.V.
HEART,] as in 4. 4; 13. 2; 15. 2; 20. 4, &c.
WISDOM,] as in 37. 30; 51. 6; 104. 24, &c.
13. TILL WHEN,] as in Ge. 30. 30; Ex. 10. 3.
REPENT,] as in Ex. 32. 12.
SERVANTS,] as in v. 16.
14. SATISFY,] as in Prov. 20. 13; Eze. 7. 19.
KINDNESS,] as in 5. 7; 6. 4; 13. 5; 17. 7, &c.
SING,] as in 5. 11; 20. 5; 51. 14; 59. 16, &c.
REJOICE,] as in 5. 11; 9. 2; 14. 7; 21. 1, &c.
15. TO REJOICE,] as in 86. 4; Prov. 27. 11.
AFFLICTED,] as in 35. 13; 88. 7; 102. 23, &c.
EVIL,] as in 5. 4; 7. 4, 9; 10. 6, 15, &c.

16. WORK,] as in 9. 16; 28. 4; 44. 1; 64. 9
APPEAR,] as in 18. 5; 42. 2; 84. 7, &c.
HONOUR,] as in 8. 5; 21. 5; 29. 4; 45. 3, &c.
Sept. Vulg. 'and guide their sons.'
17. PLEASANTNESS,] as in 27. 4; Prov. 3. 17;
15. 26; 16. 24, &c. Sept. Vulg. 'brightness.'
ESTABLISH,] as in Job 8. 8.

XCI. Sept. Vulg. prefix 'Praise of an
Ode,—to David.'
1. DWELLING,] as in 2. 4; 9. 11; 17. 12, &c.
SECRET PLACE,] as in 18. 11; 27. 5; 31. 20;
32. 7, &c. Sept. Vulg. 'help.'
MOST HIGH,] as in v. 9.
SHADE,] as in 17. 8; 36. 7; 57. 1; 63. 7. &c.
MIGHTY,] as in 68. 14; Ge. 17. 1; 28. 3; 35.
11, &c. Sept. Vulg. 'God of heaven.'
LODGE HABITUALLY,] as in Job 39. 28.
2. REFUGE,] as in v. 9. Sept. Vulg. prefix
'thou art.'
BULWARK,] as in 18. 2; 31. 2, 3; 66. 11, &c.
GOD,] as in 3. 2, 7; 4. 1; 5. 2, &c.
TRUST,] as in 9. 10; 40. 3; 44. 6; 52. 7, &c.
3. DELIVERETH,] as in 18. 17; 22. 8; 34. 19.
THEE.] Sept. Vulg. 'me.'
SNARE,] as in 11. 6; 69. 22; 91. 3; 119. 110.
FOWLER,] as in Prov. 6. 5; Jer. 5. 26.
CALAMITIES,] as in 5. 9; 38. 12; 52. 2, &c.
PESTILENCE,] as in v. 6. Sept. Vulg.
'word or matter.'
4. PINION,] as in 68. 13; De. 32. 11; Job
39. 13. Sept. Vulg. 'shoulders.'
COVERETH,] as in 17. 8; 18. 10; 36. 7; 57. 1, &c.
WINGS,] as in 17. 8; 18. 10; 36. 7; 57. 1, &c.
SHIELD,] as in 5. 12; 35. 2; Jer. 46. 3, &c.
BUCKLER,] as in 5. 12; 35. 2; 1 Sa. 17. 7,
&c. Sept. 'cover thee with a shield doth
his truth.'
TRUTH,] as in 15. 2; 19. 9; 25. 5; 26. 3, &c.
5. AFRAID,] as in 3. 6; 23. 4; 27. 1, 3, &c.
FEAR,] as in 5; 31. 11; 36. 1; 53. 5, &c.
ARROW,] as in 7. 13; 11. 2; 18. 14; 38. 2, &c.
FLIETH,] as in 18. 10; 55. 6; 90. 10, &c.
6. PESTILENCE,] as in v. 3. Sept. Vulg.
'thing or matter.'
THICK DARKNESS,] as in 11. 2; Job 3. 6, &c.
WALKETH,] as in 58. 8; 73. 9; Ex. 9. 23, &c.
DESTRUCTION,] as in De. 32. 24;[Isa. 28. 2.
Sept. Vulg. 'demon.'
DESTROYETH,] as in Prov. 11. 3; Jer. 5. 6.
NOON,] as in 37. 6; 55. 17; Song 1. 7, &c.
7. SIDE,] as in Ge. 6. 16; 25. 32; 26. 13, &c.
THOUSAND,] as in 8. 7; 50. 10; 68. 17, &c.
MYRIAD,] as in 3. 6; Ge. 24. 60; Lev. 26. 8.
COMETH NIGH,] as in Ge. 18. 23; 19. 9, &c.
8. LOOKEST,] as in 10. 14; 22. 17; 92. 11, &c.
REWARD,] as lit. 'recompence.'
WICKED,] as in 1. 1, 4, 5, 6, &c.
9. REFUGE,] as in v. 2. Sept. Vulg. 'hope.
MOST HIGH,] as in v. 1.
HABITATION,] as in 26. 8; 68. 5; 71. 3; 90.
1, &c. Sept. Vulg. 'refuge.'
10. EVIL,] as in 5. 4; 7. 4, 9; 10. 6, &c.
HAPPENETH,] as in Prov. 12. 21.
PLAGUE,] as in 38. 11; 39. 10; 89. 32, &c.
TENT,] as in 15. 1; 19. 4; 27. 5, 6, &c.
11. MESSENGERS,] as in 34. 7; 35. 5, &c.
WAYS,] as in 1. 1, 6; 2. 12; 5. 8, &c.
12. HANDS,] as in 7. 3; 9. 16; 24. 4; 26. 6.
BEAR UP,] as in 16. 4; 24. 5; 25. 1; 50. 16.

SMITE,] as in 89. 23; Ex. 21. 35; 32. 35, &c.
STONE,] as in 102. 14; 113. 22; Prov. 11. 1.
FOOT,] as in 8. 6; 9. 15; 18. 9; 22. 16, &c.
13. LION,] as in 4. 10; 10. 16; 28. 8; Prov.
26. 13, &c. Sept. 'basilisk.'
ASP,] as in 58. 4; De. 32. 23; Job 20. 14, &c.
TREADEST,] as in 11. 2; 58. 7; De. 11. 24.
TRAMPLEST,] as in 7. 5; 2 K. 7. 17; 9. 33.
YOUNG LION,] as in 17. 12; 34. 10; 35. 17, &c.
DRAGON,] as in 74. 13; 148. 7; Ge. 1. 21, &c.
14. DELIGHTED,] as in Ge. 34. 8; De. 7. 7;
10. 15; 21. 11, &c. Sept. Vulg. 'hoped.'
DELIVER,] as in 18. 43; 22. 4; 37. 40; 43. 1.
SET ON HIGH,] as in 20. 1; 59. 1; 69. 29; 107.
41, &c. Sept. Vulg. 'protect.'
KNOWN,] as in 14. 4; 18. 43; 20. 6; 31. 7, &c.
15. CALL,] as in 3. 4; 18. 3, 6; 22. 2; 27. 7.
ANSWER,] as in 3. 4; 17. 6; 20. 1, 6, &c.
Sept. Vulg. 'hearken.'
DISTRESS,] as in 9. 9; 10. 1; 20. 1; 22. 11.
HONOUR,] as in 15. 4; 50. 15; 86. 9, 12, &c.
16. LENGTH OF DAYS,] as in 21. 4; 23. 6, &c.
SATISFY,] as in 81. 16; 105. 40; 132. 15, &c.
TO LOOK,] as in 4. 6; 50. 23; 59. 10, &c.
SALVATION,] as in 3. 2, 8; 9. 14; 13. 5, &c.

XCII. PSALM,] as in Ps. 3. 4. 5. 6. &c.
SONG,] as in Ps. 30. 45. 46. 48. &c.
SABBATH-DAY,] as in Ex. 20. 8; Lev. 24. 8.
1. GOOD,] as in 100. 5; 103. 5; 104. 28, &c.
GIVE THANKS,] as in 106. 47; 119. 62; 122.
4; 142. 7, &c. Sept. Vulg. 'confess.'
SING PRAISE,] as in 147. 1.
MOST HIGH,] as in 7. 17; 9. 2; 18. 13; 21. 7.
2. DECLARE,] as in 9. 6; Ge. 32. 5; 43. 6.
KINDNESS] as in 5. 7; 6. 4; 13. 5; 17. 7, &c.
FAITHFULNESS,] as in 33. 4; 36. 5; 37. 3, &c.
3. TEN STRINGS,] as in 33. 2; 149. 9, &c.
PSALTERY,] as in 33. 2; 57. 8; 71. 22; 81. 2.
HIGGAION,] as in 9. 16; 19. 14; La. 3. 62.
Sept. Vulg. 'with an ode.'
HARP,] as in 33. 2; 43. 4; 49. 4; 57. 8, &c.
4. TO REJOICE,] as in 30. 1; 45. 8; Isa. 56. 7.
WORK,] as in 9. 16; 28. 4; 44. 1; 64. 9, &c.
SING,] as in 5. 11; 20. 5; 51. 14; 59. 16, &c.
5. GREAT,] as in 104. 1; Ge. 19. 14; 26. 13.
DEEP,] or 'profound.'
THOUGHTS,] as in 33. 10, 11; 40. 5; 56. 5, &c.
6. BRUTISH,] as in 49. 10; 73. 22; Prov. 12.
1; 30. 2.
FOOL,] as in 49. 10; 94. 8; Prov. 1. 22, &c.
7. WICKED,] as in 1. 1, 4, 5, 6, &c.
FLOURISH,] as in Lev. 13. 12; Isa. 25. 2.
HERB,] as in 72. 16; 102. 4, 11; 104. 14, &c.
BLOSSOM,] as in 72. 16; 90. 6; 103. 15; 132.
18, &c. Sept. Vulg. 'appeared.'
WORKERS OF INIQUITY,] as in v. 9.
DESTROYED,] as in De. 4. 26; 7. 23; 12. 30.
8. HIGH,] as in 7. 7; 10. 5; 18. 16; 56. 2, &c.
9. ENEMIES,] as in 3. 7; 6. 10; 7. 5; 8. 2, &c.
PERISH,] as in 1. 6; 2. 12; 9. 3; 37. 20, &c.
SEPARATE THEMSELVES,] as in Job 4. 11.
10. EXALTEST,] as in 66. 7; 75. 4, 5, 7, &c.
REEM,] as in 22. 21; 29. 6; Job 39. 8; Isa.
34. 7.
HORN,] as in 18. 2; 22. 21; 75. 4, 5, &c.
ANOINTED,] as in Ge. 11. 9. Sept. 'and
mine old age.'
OIL,] as in 23. 5; 45. 7; 55. 21; 89. 20, &c.
11. LOOKETH,] as in 10. 14; 22. 17; 91. 8.
RISING UP,] as in 3. 1; 18. 39, 48; 44. 5, &c.

EVIL-DOERS,] as in 22. 16; 26. 5; 27. 2, &c.
HEAR,] as in 4. 3; 5. 3; 18. 6; 34. 2, &c.
12. RIGHTEOUS,] as in 1. 5, 6; 5. 12; 7. 9.
PALM-TREE,] as in Ex. 15. 27; 23. 40, &c.
FLOURISHETH,] as in 72. 7; Lev. 13. 12, &c.
CEDAR,] as in 29. 5; 80. 10; 104. 16; 148. 9.
GROWETH,] as in Job 8. 7, 11.
13. PLANTED,] as in 1. 3; Jer. 17. 8, &c.
HOUSE OF JEHOVAH,] as in 23. 6; 27. 4, &c.
COURTS,] as in 10. 8; 65. 4; 84. 2; 96. 8, &c.
14. BRING FORTH,] as in 62. 10; Prov. 10. 31.
OLD AGE,] as in 71. 18; Prov. 16. 31, &c.
FAT,] as in 22. 29; Isa. 30. 23.
FLOURISHING,] as in v. 10.
13. TO DECLARE,] as in v. 2.
UPRIGHT,] as in 7. 10; 11. 2, 7; 19. 8, &c.
ROCK,] as in 18. 2, 31, 46; 19. 14, &c. Sept.
Vulg. 'our God.'
PERVERSENESS,] as in 37. 1; 43. 1; 80. 22.

XCIII. Sept. Vulg. prefix, 'For the days of
the Sabbath, when the land was inhabited,
praise of an ode—to David.'
1. JEHOVAH,] as in v. 3, 4, 5.
REIGNED,] as in 47. 8; 97. 10; 99. 1, &c.
EXCELLENCY,] as in 17. 10; 89. 9; Isa. 9. 18.
PUT ON,] as in 65. 13; 104. 1; Eze. 42. 14.
STRENGTH,] as in 6. 2; 21. 1, 13; 28. 7, &c.
GIRDED HIMSELF,] as in Isa. 9. 9.
ESTABLISHED,] as in 89. 21, 37; 96. 10, &c.
WORLD,] as in 9. 8; 18. 15; 19. 4; 24. 1, &c.
UNMOVED,] as in 10. 6; 13. 4; 15. 5; 16. 8.
2. THRONE,] as in 9. 4, 7; 11. 4; 45. 6, &c.
AGE,] as in 5. 11; 9. 5, 7; 10. 16, &c.
3. FLOODS,] as in 24. 2; 46. 4; 66. 6; 72. 8.
LIFTED UP,] as in 15. 3; 24. 4; 32. 5; 69. 7.
VOICE,] as in 3. 4; 5. 2, 3; 6. 8, &c.
BREAKERS,] not 'waves,' as in C.V.
4. THAN.] Sept. Vulg. 'from.'
MIGHTY WATERS,] as in 18. 16; 29. 3, &c.
SEA,] as in 8. 8; 24. 2; 33. 7; 46. 2, &c.
Sept. Vulg. add, 'are wonderful.'
MIGHTY.] Sept. Vulg. 'wonderful.'
ON HIGH,] as in 7. 7; 10. 5; 18. 16; 56. 2.
5. TESTIMONIES,] as in 19. 7; 78. 5; 81. 5.
STEDFAST,] as in 78. 8, 37; 2 Sa. 7. 16, &c.
HOUSE,] or 'household;' as in 5. 7; 23. 6.
COMELY,] as in Song 1. 7; Isa. 52. 7.
HOLINESS,] as in 2. 6; 3. 4; 5. 7; 11. 4, &c.

XCIV. Sept. Vulg. prefix, 'a Psalm of an
ode—to David, the fourth of the sabbath,'
i.e. week.
1. GOD OF VENGEANCE,] as in 18. 47.
JEHOVAH,] as in v. 3. 5, 7, 14, 17, &c.
SHINE FORTH,] as in 80. 1.
2. BE LIFTED UP,] as in 7. 6; 24. 7.
JUDGE,] as in 2. 10; 7. 11; 9. 4; 50. 6, &c.
RECOMPENCE,] as in 28. 4; 35. 17; 51. 12.
PROUD,] as in 123. 4; 140. 5; Prov. 15. 25.
3. TILL WHEN,] as in Ge. 30. 30; Ex. 10. 3.
WICKED,] as in v. 13.
EXULT,] as in 23. 7; 60. 6; 96. 12; 108. 7, &c.
Sept. Vulg. 'boast.'
4. UTTER,] as in 19. 2; 59. 7; 78. 2; 119. 171.
OLD SAW,] as in 31. 18; 75. 5; 1 Sa. 2. 3, &c.
Sept. Vulg. 'injustice.'
WORKING INIQUITY,] as in v. 16.
BOAST THEMSELVES.] Original word not
found again. Sept. Vulg. simply 'speak.'
5. PEOPLE,] as in v. 8, 14.

BRUISE,] as in 72. 4; Job 4. 19; 6. 9; 19. 2,
&c. Sept. Vulg. 'humble.'
INHERITANCE,] as in v. 14.
AFFLICT,] as in 89. 22; Ge. 16. 6; 31. 50, &c.
6. WIDOW,] as in 68. 5; 78. 64; 109. 9, &c.
SOJOURNER,] as in 39. 12; 119. 19; 146. 9.
SLAY,] as in 10. 8; 59. 11; 78. 31, 47, &c.
FATHERLESS ONES,] as in 10. 14, 18; 68. 5.
MURDER,] as in Hos. 6. 9.
7. SEE,] as in 8. 3; 22. 17; 35. 17; 36. 9, &c.
GOD OF JACOB,] as in 4. 1; 20. 1; 41. 13, &c.
CONSIDER,] as in 19. 12; 28. 5; 49. 20, &c.
8. BRUTISH,] as in 49. 10; 92. 22; 92. 6, &c.
FOOLISH,] as in 49. 10; 92. 6; Job 9. 9, &c.
ACT WISELY,] as in 32. 8; 101. 2; De. 29. 9.
9. PLANTETH,] as in Jer. 11. 17; 31. 5.
EAR,] as in 10. 17; 17. 6; 18. 6, 44, &c.
FORMETH,] as in 2. 9; 33. 15; Isa. 22. 11.
EYE,] as in 5. 5; 6. 7; 10. 8; 11. 4, &c.
INSTRUCTING,] as in Prov. 9. 7.
REPROVE,] as in 6. 1; 38. 1; 50. 8, 21, &c.
TEACHING,] as in 18. 34; 119. 99; 144. 1, &c.
KNOWLEDGE,] as in 19. 2; 119. 66; 139. 6.
11. THOUGHTS,] as in 33. 10, 11; 40. 5, &c.
VANITY,] as in 31. 6; 39. 5; 62. 9; 78. 33.
12. HAPPINESS,] as in 1. 1; 2. 12; 32. 1, &c.
JAH,] as in v. 7; 68. 4, 18; 77. 11, &c.
LAW,] as in 1. 2; 19. 7; 37. 31; 40. 8, &c.
13. GIVE REST,] as in Job 37. 17; Isa. 30. 15.
EVIL,] as in v. 22.
PIT,] as in 7. 15; 9. 15; 16. 10; 30. 9, &c.
DIGGED,] as in 7. 15; 57. 6; 119. 85, &c.
WICKED,] as in v. 3.
14. LEAVETH,] as in 27. 9; 78. 7; Prov. 1. 8;
6. 12, &c. Sept. 'rejecteth.'
FORSAKETH,] as in 10. 14; 16. 10; 27. 14, &c.
15. RIGHTEOUSNESS,] as in 4. 1, 5; 7. 8, &c.
TURNETH BACK,] as in 6. 10; 7. 12, 16, &c.
UPRIGHT OF HEART,] as in 7. 10; 11. 2, &c.
16. RISETH UP,] as in 1. 5; 12. 5; 24. 3, &c.
EVIL-DOERS,] as in 22. 16; 26. 5; 27. 2; 37.
1, &c. Sept. Vulg. 'against evil-doers.'
STATIONETH HIMSELF,] as in 2. 2; 5. 5, &c.
WORKERS OF INIQUITY,] as in v. 4.
17. HELP,] as in 22. 19; 27. 9; 35. 2; 38. 22.
INHABITED,] as in 68. 6; 74. 2; 120. 5, &c.
SILENCE,] as in 115. 17. Sept. Vulg.
'Hades.'
18. FOOT,] as in 8. 6; 9. 15; 18. 9; 22. 16, &c.
SLIPPED,] as in 46. 6; 60. 2; Lev. 25. 35, &c.
KINDNESS,] as in 5. 7; 6. 4; 13. 5; 17. 7, &c.
SUPPORTETH,] as in 18. 35; 20. 2; 41. 3; 104.15.
19. ABUNDANCE,] as in 5. 7, 10; 33. 16, &c.
THOUGHTS,] as in 139. 23. Sept. Vulg.
'griefs.'
COMFORTS,] as in Isa. 66. 11; Jer. 16. 7, &c.
DELIGHT,] as in 119. 70; Isa. 11. 8, &c.
20. MISCHIEF,] as in 7. 14, 16; 10. 7, 14, &c.
Sept. Vulg. 'lawlessness.'
JOINED,] as in 122. 3; Ex. 28. 7; 39. 4, &c.
FRAMER,] as in v. 9.
PERVERSENESS,] as in 7. 14, 16; 10. 7, &c.
STATUTE,] as in 49. 10; 52. 16; 81. 4; 99. 7, &c.
21. DECREE.] Sep. Vulg. 'hunt for.'
RIGHTEOUS,] as in 1. 5, 6; 5. 12; 7. 9, &c.
BLOOD,] as in 5. 6; 9. 12; 16. 4; 26. 9, &c.
DECLARE WICKED,] as in 37. 33; Prov. 12. 2.
22. HIGH PLACES,] as in 9. 9; 18. 2; 46. 7;
48. 3, &c. Sept. Vulg. 'refuge.'
ROCK,] as in 18. 2, 31, 46; 19. 14, &c. Sept.
Vulg. 'helper.'

REFUGE,] as in 14. 6; 46. 1; 61. 3; 62. 7,
&c. Sept. Vulg. 'hope.'
23. INIQUITY,] as in v. 4, 16. Sept. prefixes
'according to.'
WICKEDNESS,] as in v. 13.
CUTTETH THEM OFF,] as in 18. 40; 101. 5,
8; 143. 12, &c. Sept. omits.

XCV. 1. COME,] as in 34. 11; 46. 8; 66. 5.
SING,] as in 5. 11; 20. 5; 51. 14; 59. 16, &c.
JEHOVAH,] as in v. 3.
SHOUT,] as in v. 2.
ROCK,] as in 18. 2, 31, 46; 19. 14, &c.
SALVATION,] as in 12. 5; 18. 2, 35, 46, &c.
sept. Vulg. 'God our saviour.'
2. COME BEFORE,] as in 18. 18; 21. 3, &c.
THANKSGIVING,] as in 16. 7; 42. 4; 50. 14;
'6. 12, &c. Sept. Vulg. 'confession.'
PSALMS,] as in 119. 54; 2 Sa. 23. 1, &c.
3. GREAT GOD,] as in 48. 1; 77. 13; 96. 4, &c.
GREAT KING,] as in 47. 2; 48. 2; Ecc. 9. 14.
4. DEEP PLACES.] Original word not found
again. Sept. Vulg. 'ends.'
STRONG PLACES,] as in Nu. 23. 22; Job 22.
25. Sept. Vulg. 'high places.'
HILLS,] as in 2. 6; 3. 4; 11. 1; 15. 1, &c.
5. SEA,] as in 8. 8; 24. 2; 33. 7; 46. 2, &c.
MADE,] as in 7. 3; 9. 4, 15, 16, &c.
FENCED,] as in 74. 17; 104. 26; Ge. 2. 8, &c.
DRY LAND,] as in Ex. 4. 9.
6. COME IN,] as in 96. 8; 100. 2, 4; Ge. 7. 1.
BOW OURSELVES,] as in 22. 29; 72. 9, &c.
BEND,] as in 22. 29; 72. 9, &c. Sept. adds
to him.'
KNEEL,] as in 2 Ch. 6. 13. Sept. Vulg.
.ament.'
MAKER,] as in 14. 1, 3; 15. 5; 18. 50; 31. 23.
7. GOD,] as in 3. 2, 7; 4. 1; 5. 2, 10, &c.
PEOPLE,] as in v. 10.
PASTURE,] as in 74. 1; 79. 13; 100. 3, &c.
FLOCK,] as in 44. 11; 49. 14; 65. 13; 74. 1.
TO-DAY,] as in 2. 7; 7. 11; 19. 2; 20. 1, &c.
VOICE,] as in 3. 4; 5. 2, 3; 6. 8, &c.
HEARKEN,] as in 4. 3; 5. 3; 18. 6; 34. 2, &c.
8. HARDEN,] as in Ex. 7. 3; De. 10. 16, &c.
HEARTS,] as in 4. 4; 13. 2; 15. 2; 20. 4, &c.
MERIBAH,] i.e. 'strife.'
MASSAH.] i.e. 'trial.'
WILDERNESS,] as in 29. 8; 55. 7; 65. 12, &c.
9. TRIED,] as in Ge. 22. 1; 15. 25; De. 4. 34.
PROVED,] as in 17. 3; 66. 10; Job 23. 10, &c.
SEEN,] as in 10. 11, 14; 31. 7; 33. 13, &c.
10. FORTY YEARS,] as in Ge. 26. 34, &c.
WEARY,] as in Eze. 16. 47. Sept. Vulg.
add 'always.'
GENERATION,] as in 10. 6; 12. 7; 14. 5, &c.
ERRING,] as in Ge. 37. 15; Ex. 23. 4; Prov.
21. 16; Isa. 29. 24.
HEART,] as in v. 8.
WAYS,] as in 39. 1; 51. 13; 81. 13; 91. 11.
11. SWARE,] as in 15. 4; 24. 4; 89. 3, 35, &c.
ANGER,] as in 2. 5, 12; 6. 1; 7. 6; 10. 4, &c.
IF,} as in Ge. 4. 7; 14. 23; 24. 21; 38. 4, &c.
REST,] as in 23. 2; 132. 8, 14; Ge. 49. 15, &c.

XCVI. Sept. Vulg. prefix, 'An ode of
David, when the house was built after the
captivity.'
1. SING,] as in v. 2.
SONG,] as in 28. 7; 33. 3; 40. 3; 42. 8, &c.
EARTH,] as in 2. 2, 8, 10; 7. 5, &c.

2. BLESS,] as in 28. 9; 66. 8; 68. 26; 104. 1.
NAME,] as in v. 8.
PROCLAIM,] as in 1 Ch. 16. 23.
SALVATION,] as in 3. 2, 8; 9. 14; 13. 5, &c
3. DECLARE,] as in Ge. 40. 8; 2 K. 8. 4, &c
HONOUR,] as in 3. 3; 4. 2; 7. 5; 8. 5, &c.
WONDERS,] as in 9. 1; 26. 7; 40. 5; 71. 17.
4. GREAT,] as in 48. 1; 77. 13; 86. 10; 95. 3.
PRAISED,] as in 18. 3; 48. 1; 113. 3; 145. 3.
FEARFUL,] as in 45. 4; 47. 2; 65. 5; 66. 3.
5. NOUGHT,] as in 97. 7; Lev. 19. 4; 26. 1;
1 Ch. 16. 26, &c. Sept. Vulg. 'demon.'
MADE,] as in 7. 3; 9. 4, 15, 16, &c.
6. HONOUR,] as in 8. 1; 21. 5; 45. 3; 104. 1,
&c. Sept. Vulg. 'thanksgiving.'
MAJESTY,] as in 8. 5; 21. 5; 29. 4; 45. 3, &c.
Sept. Vulg. 'beauty.'
STRENGTH,] as in v. 7. Sept. Vulg. 'sanc-
tity.'
BEAUTY,] as in 71. 8; 78. 61; 89. 17; Ex.
28. 2, &c. Sept. Vulg. 'magnificence.'
SANCTUARY,] as in 68. 35; 73. 17; 74. 7, &c.
7. ASCRIBE,] as in v. 8; 29. 1, 2; 60. 11, &c.
FAMILIES,] as in 22. 27; 107. 41; Ge. 8. 19
HONOUR,] as in v. 3. Sept. Vulg. 'glory.'
STRENGTH,] as in v. 6. Sept. Vulg. 'hon
our.'
8. PRESENT,] as in 20. 3; 40. 6; 45. 12; 72.
10, &c. Sept. Vulg. 'sacrifice.'
COURTS,] as in 10. 8; 65. 4; 84. 2; 92. 13, &c.
9. BOW YOURSELVES,] as in 29. 2; 45. 11, &c.
HONOUR OF HOLINESS,] as in 29. 2; 1 Ch.
16. 29; 2 Ch. 20. 21. Sept. Vulg. 'his holy
court.'
AFRAID,] as in 114. 7; 1 Ch. 16. 30, &c.
10. REIGNED,] as in 47. 1; 93. 1; 97. 1, &c.
ESTABLISHED,] as in 89. 21, 37; 93. 1, &c.
WORLD,] as in 9. 8; 18. 15; 19. 4; 24. 1, &c.
UNMOVED,] as in 10. 6; 13. 4; 15. 5; 16. 8.
UPRIGHTNESS,] as in 9. 8; 17. 2; 58. 1, &c.
11. JOY,] as in 5. 11; 9. 2; 14. 7; 21. 1, &c.
IS JOYFUL,] as in 9. 14; 13. 4, 5; 14. 7, &c.
ROAR,] as in 98. 7; 1 Ch. 16. 32, &c.
12. FIELDS,] as in 8. 7; 50. 11; 80. 13; 104. 11,
&c. Sept. Vulg. 'plains.'
EXULTETH,] as in 28. 7; 60. 6; 94. 3, &c.
SING,] as in 5. 11; 20. 5; 51. 14; 59. 16, &c
FOREST,] as in 50. 10; 80. 13; 83. 14; 104. 20
13. TO JUDGE,] as in 10. 18; 51. 4; 98. 9, &c
WORLD,] as in 2. 2, 8, 10; 7. 5, &c.
RIGHTEOUSNESS,] as in 4. 1, 5; 7. 8, 17, &c.
FAITHFULNESS,] as in 33. 4; 36. 5; 37. 3, &c.

XCVII. Sept. Vulg. prefix, 'By David,
when his land was established.'
1. REIGNED,] as in 47. 8; 93. 1; 96. 10, &c.
IS JOYFUL,] as in v. 8.
ISLES,] as in 72. 10; Ge. 10. 5; Est. 10. 1.
REJOICE,] as in v. 8.
2. CLOUD,] as in 78. 14; 99. 7; 105. 39, &c.
DARKNESS,] as in 18. 9; Ex. 20. 21; De. 4. 11.
RIGHTEOUSNESS,] as in v. 6.
JUDGMENT,] as in v. 8.
BASIS,] as in 33. 14; 89. 14; 104. 5; Ex. 15. 17.
THRONE,] as in 9. 4, 7; 11. 4; 45. 6, &c.
3. FIRE,] as in 11. 6; 18. 8, 12; 21. 9, &c.
BURNETH,] as in 83. 14; 106. 18; De. 32. 22.
ADVERSARIES,] as in 3. 1; 4. 1; 13. 4, &c.
4. LIGHTENED,] as in 77. 18; Ex. 15. 37;
Eze. 43. 2.
LIGHTNINGS,] as in 18. 14; 77. 18; 135. 7.

WORLD,] as in 9. 8; 18. 15; 19. 4; 24. 1, &c.
SEEN,] as in v. 6.
PAINED,] as in 10. 5; 29. 8; 55. 4; 77. 16, &c.
5. HILLS,] as in 18. 7; 46. 2; 68. 16; 72. 3.
WAX,] as in 22. 14; 68. 2; Mic. 1. 4.
MELTED,] as in 22. 14; 112. 10; Ex. 16. 21.
LORD,] as in 8. 1; 12. 4; 45. 11; 105. 21, &c.
6. DECLARED,] as in 22. 31; 30. 9; 38. 18, &c.
HONOUR,] as in 3. 3; 4. 2; 7. 5; 8. 5, &c.
7. ASHAMED,] as in 6. 10; 25. 2, 3, 20, &c.
SERVANTS,] as in Ge. 4. 2; 49. 15; Nu. 4. 37.
GRAVEN IMAGE,] as in Ex. 20. 4; Lev. 26. 1.
BOASTING THEMSELVES,] as in Prov. 25. 14;
Jer. 9. 24.
IDOLS,] as in 96. 5; Lev. 19. 4; 26. 1, &c.
BOW YOURSELVES,] as in 29. 2; 45. 11, &c.
GODS,] as in 3. 2, 7; 4. 1; 5. 2, &c. Sept.
Vulg. 'angels.'
8. HEARD,] as in 6. 8, 9; 10. 17; 28. 6, &c.
REJOICETH,] as in v. 1.
DAUGHTERS OF JUDAH,] as in La. 1. 15; 2. 2.
JOYFUL,] as in v. 1.
JUDGMENTS,] as in v. 2.
9. MOST HIGH,] as in 7. 17; 9. 2; 18. 13, &c.
EXALTED,] as in 47. 9; Nu. 9. 21; 10. 11, &c.
ALL GODS,] as in v. 7.
10. LOVE,] as in 5. 11; 11. 5; 33. 5; 34. 12.
HATE,] as in Am. 5. 15.
EVIL,] as in 5. 4; 7. 4, 9; 10. 6, &c.
KEEPING,] as in 31. 6; 34. 20; 71. 10, &c.
SAINTS,] as in 4. 3; 12. 1; 16. 10; 18. 25, &c.
WICKED,] as in 1. 1, 4, 5, 6, &c.
DELIVERETH,] as in 18. 17, 48; 22. 8, &c.
11. LIGHT,] as in 4. 6; 27. 1; 36. 9; 37. 6, &c.
SOWN,] as in Jer. 2. 2. Sept. Vulg. 'sprung
up.'
RIGHTEOUS,] as in v. 12.
UPRIGHT OF HEART,] as in 7. 10; 11. 2, &c.
JOY,] as in 4. 7; 16 11; 21. 6; 30. 11, &c.
12. GIVE THANKS,] as in 6. 5; 30. 4, &c.
REMEMBRANCE,] as in 6. 5; 9. 6; 30. 4, &c.
HOLINESS,] as in 2. 6; 3. 4; 5. 7; 11. 4, &c.

XCVIII. PSALM,] as in Ps. 3. 4. 5. 6. &c.
Sept. Vulg. add, 'of David.'
1. SING,] as in 33. 3; 68. 4; 96. 1, 2, &c.
NEW SONG,] as in 33. 3; 40. 3; 144. 9, &c.
WONDERS,] as in 9. 1; 26. 7; 40. 5; 71. 17.
DONE,] as in 7. 3; 9. 4, 15, 16, &c.
GIVEN SALVATION,] as in 20. 6; 34. 6, &c.
RIGHT HAND,] as in 16. 8, 11; 17. 7; 18. 35.
ARM,] as in 10. 15; 18. 34; 87. 17; 44. 3, &c.
2. MADE KNOWN,] as in 77. 14; Ex. 18. 16.
SALVATION,] as in v. 3.
REVEALED,] as in Lev. 20. 11, 17, 18, &c.
RIGHTEOUSNESS,] as in 5. 8; 11. 7; 22. 31.
3. REMEMBERED,] as in 9. 12; 63. 6; 78. 42.
KINDNESS,] as in 5. 7; 6. 4; 13. 5; 17. 7, &c.
Sept. adds 'to Jacob.'
FAITHFULNESS,] as in 33. 4; 36. 5; 37. 3, &c.
HOUSE OF ISRAEL,] as in 115. 12; 135. 19.
ENDS OF EARTH,] as in 2. 8; 22. 27; 59. 13.
SALVATION,] as in v. 2
4. SHOUT,] as in v. 6.
BREAK FORTH,] as in Isa. 44. 23; 49. 13;
52. 9; 54. 1.
CRY ALOUD,] as in 33. 1; Isa. 26. 19; 52. 9.
SING,] as in v. 5.
5. HARP,] as in 33. 2; 43. 4; 49. 4; 57. 8, &c.
PRAISE,] as in 81. 2; Ge. 43. 11; Isa. 51. 3;
Am. 5. 23.

6. TRUMPETS,] as in Nu. 10. 2, 8, 9, 10, &c.
Sept. Vulg. add, 'of metal.'
CORNET,] as in 47. 5; 81. 3; 150. 3; Ex. 19.
16, &c. Sept. Vulg. add, 'of horn.'
SHOUT,] as in v. 4.
KING,] as in 2. 6; 5. 2; 18. 16; 18. 50, &c.
7. ROAR,] as in 96. 11; 1 Ch. 16. 32.
FULNESS,] as in 24. 1; 50. 12; 89. 11, &c.
WORLD,] as in 9. 8; 18. 15; 19. 4; 24. 1, &c.
8. FLOODS,] as in 24. 2; 46. 4; 66. 6; 72. 8.
CLAP,] as in Isa. 55. 12.
CRY ALOUD,] as in 5. 11; 20. 5; 51. 14, &c.
9. TO JUDGE,] as in 10. 18; 51. 4; 96. 13, &c.
RIGHTEOUSNESS,] as in 4. 1, 5; 7. 8; 9. 4, &c.
UPRIGHTNESS,] as in 9. 8; 17. 2; 58. 1, &c.

XCIX. 1. REIGNED,] as in 47. 8; 93. 1, &c
TREMBLE,] as in 18. 7; 77. 16; Ge. 45. 24.
INHABITANT OF THE CHERUB,] as in 1 Sa.
4. 4; 2 Sa. 6. 2, &c.
SHAKETH.] Original word not found again
2. GREAT,] as in v. 3.
HIGH,] as in 131. 1; De. 8. 14; 32. 27, &c.
3. PRAISE,] as in 6. 5; 7. 17; 9. 1; 18. 49, &c.
FEARFUL,] as in 45. 4; 47. 2; 65. 5; 66. 3, &c.
STRENGTH,] as in 8. 2; 21. 1, 13; 28. 7, &c.
Sept. Vulg. 'honour.'
JUDGMENT,] as in 1. 5; 7. 6; 9. 4, 7, &c.
ESTABLISHED,] as in 8. 3; 9. 7; 11. 2, &c.
UPRIGHTNESS,] as in 9. 8; 17. 2; 58. 1, &c.
5. EXALT,] as in v. 9.
BOW YOURSELVES,] as in v. 9.
FOOT STOOL,] as in 110. 1; 132. 9; 1 Ch. 28. 2
HOLY,] as in v. 3, 9.
6. MOSES,] the great lawgiver of Israel.
AARON,] as in 77. 20; 105. 26; 106. 16, &c.
PRIESTS,] as in 78. 64; 110. 4; 132. 9. 16, &c.
SAMUEL,] as in 1 Sa. 1. 20; 2. 18, 21, 26;
PROCLAIMING,] as in 42. 7; 86. 5; 145. 18.
CALLING,] as in 3. 4; 17. 6; 20. 1; 22. 2, &c.
ANSWER,] as in 3. 4; 17. 6; 20. 1; 22. 2, &c.
7. PILLAR OF CLOUD,] as in Ex. 13. 21, &c.
SPEAKETH,] as in 2. 5; 12. 2; 35. 20; 37. 30.
KEPT,] as in 17. 4; 18. 21; 78. 10; 119. 67,
&c. Sept. prefixes 'because.'
TESTIMONIES,] as in 25. 10; 78. 56; 93. 5.
STATUTE,] as in 2. 7; 50. 16; 81. 4; 94. 20.
8. AFFLICTED.] Sept. Vulg. 'hearkened to
them.'
FORGIVING,] as in 126. 6; Ge. 37. 25; 45. 23;
Ex. 34. 7, &c. Sept. Vulg. 'propitious.'
TAKING VENGEANCE,] as in Lev. 26. 25;
Nah. 1. 2.
ACTIONS,] as in 9. 11; 14. 1; 66. 5; 77. 22,
&c. Sept. Vulg. prefix, 'all.'
9. EXALT,] as in v. 5.
HOLY HILL,] as in 2. 6; 3 4; 11. 1; 15. 1, &c.
HOLY,] as in v. 3, 5.
OUR GOD,] as in v. 5, 8.

C. PSALM,] as in Ps. 3. 4. 5. 6. &c.
THANKSGIVING,] as in 26. 7; 42. 4; 50. 14;
56. 12, &c. Sept. Vulg. 'confession;' as in v. 4.
1. SHOUT,] as in 47. 1; 66. 1; 81. 1; 98. 4.
2. SERVE,] as in 2. 11; Ex. 5. 18; 10. 8, &c.
JOY,] as in 4. 7; 16. 11; 21. 6; 30. 11, &c.
SINGING,] as in 63. 5; Job 3. 7; 20. 5
3. KNOW,] as in 4. 3; 46. 10; 139. 23, &c.
JEHOVAH,] as in v. 2, 5.
GOD,] as in 3. 2, 7; 4. 1; 5. 2, &c. Sept.
'our God.'

MADE,] as in 7. 3; 9. 4; 15. 3; 22. 31, &c.
ARE HIS,] not 'and not we ourselves;' as in.C.V. Sept. Vulg. &c.
PEOPLE,] as in 3. 6, 8; 7. 8; 9. 11, &c.
FLOCK,] as in 44. 11; 49. 14; 65. 13; 74. 1.
PASTURE,] as in 74. 1; 79. 13; 95. 7; 100. 3.
4. GATES,] as in 9. 13, 14; 24. 7; 69. 12, &c.
COURTS,] as in 10. 8; 65. 4; 84. 2, 10, &c.
PRAISE,] as in 9. 14; 22. 3; 33. 1; 34. 1, &c. Sept. Vulg. 'hymns.'
GIVE THANKS,] as in 30. 4; 33. 2; 97. 12, &c.
NAME,] as in 5. 11; 7. 17; 8. 1; 9. 2, &c.
5. GOOD,] as in 4. 6; 14. 1; 16. 2; 21. 3, &c.
KINDNESS,] as in 5. 7; 6. 4; 13. 5; 17. 7, &c.
GENERATION,] as in 10. 6; 12. 7; 14. 5, &c.
FAITHFULNESS,] as in 33. 4; 36. 5; 37. 3; 40 10, &c.

CI. PSALM,]as in Ps. 3. 4. 5. 6. 8. 9. 12. &c.
1. KINDNESS,] not 'mercy,' as in C.V.
JUDGMENT,] upon his enemies or upon himself.
SING,] a song of joy and praise.
SING PRAISE,] not 'sing' merely, as in C.V.; he would also play upon musical instruments, as the word implies.
2. ACT WISELY,] as in 32. 8; 94. 8, &c.
PERFECT WAY,] as in v. 6; 18. 30, 32, &c. Sept. Vulg. 'blameless.'
WALK HABITUALLY,] as the form of the original word implies, or 'up and down.'
INTEGRITY OF MY HEART,] not with 'a perfect heart,' as in C.V. Sept. ·harmlessness,' Vulg. 'innocency.'
3. SET,] as in 12. 5· 13. 2; 17. 11; 18. 11, &c.
WORTHLESS THING,] or a 'wicked thing,' as in C.V. Vulg. 'unjust.'
WORK,] or 'doing.' Sept. Vulg. 'those doing evil, I have hated.'
TURNING ASIDE] from duty and God.
HATED,] as in 5. 5; 11. 5; 25. 19; 26. 5, &c.
ADHERETH,] as in 44. 25; 63 8; 102. 5, &c.
4. PERVERSE,] as in 18. 26; De. 32. 5, &c.
EVIL,] as in 5. 4; 7. 4, 9; 10. 6, 15, &c.
5. SLANDERETH,] as in Prov. 30. 10.
SECRET,] as in 27. 5; 31. 20; 61. 4; 81. 7, &c.
CUT OFF,] as in v. 8; 18. 40; 94. 23, &c. Vulg. 'pursue.'
HIGH OF EYES,] as in Isa. 5. 15; 10. 33.
PROUD OF HEART,] as in Prov. 21. 4. Sept. Vulg. 'insatiable of heart.'
ENDURE,] as in Isa. 1. 13, &c. Sept. Vulg. with him I do not eat.'
6. FAITHFUL,] or 'stedfast,' in their allegiance to God.'
TO DWELL,] as in 27. 4; 33. 14; 68. 16, &c. Sept. Vulg. 'to seat them with me.'
WALKING,] as in 15. 2; 78. 39; 84. 1; 101. 6.
SERVETH,] not 'shall serve;' he doth so already.
7. DWELLETH,] or 'abideth.'
HOUSE,] or 'among my household.'
DECEIT,]as in 32. 2; 52. 2; 78. 57, &c. Sept. Vulg. 'pride.'
LIES,] or 'falsehoods;' as in 7. 14; 27. 12; 31. 18, &c. Sept. Vulg. 'injustice.'
ESTABLISHED,] as in 89. 21, 27; 93. 1, &c.
8.CUT OFF,]as in v.5. Sept.Vulg.'disperse.'
WICKED,] as in 1. 1, 4, 5, 6; 3. 7; 7. 9, &c.
CITY OF JEHOVAH,] as in 46. 4; 48. 1, &c.
WORKERS OF INIQUITY,] as in 5. 5; 6. 8, &c.

CII. PRAYER,] as in v. 1, 17; 4. 1; 6. 9, &c.
AFFLICTED,] as in 9. 12, 18; 10. 2, 9, 12, &c. Sept. Vulg. 'poor.'
FEEBLE,] as in 61, 2; 65. 13; 73. 6, &c. Sept. Vulg. 'anxious.'
POURETH OUT,] as in 42. 4; 106. 38; 142. 2.
PLAINT,] as in 55. 2; 64. 1; 104. 34; 142. 2, &c. Sept. Vulg. 'supplication.'
1. HEAR,] as in 4. 1; 17. 1, 6; 27. 7; 28. 2.
CRY,] as in 18. 6; 34. 15; 39. 12; 40. 1, &c.
2. HIDE,] as in 13. 1; 17. 8; 27. 5, 9; 31. 20, &c. Sept. Vulg. 'turn not away.'
ADVERSITY,] as in 3. 1; 4. 1; 13. 4; 18. 6.
INCLINE,] as in 17. 6; 31. 2; 45. 10; 71. 2.
CALL] upon thee in prayer for help.
ANSWER,] as in 4. 1; 13. 3; 27. 7; 55. 2, &c.
3. CONSUMED,] as in 31. 10; 37. 20; 39. 10.
SMOKE.] Sept. Vulg. 'as smoke.'
BONES,] as in v. 5; 6. 2; 22. 14, 17, &c.
FIRE-BRAND,] as in Isa. 33. 14.
BURNED,] as in 69. 3, &c.
4. SMITTEN.] Vulg. adds, 'I am.'
HERB,] as in v. 11; 72. 16; 9. 2; 104. 14, &c.
WITHERED,] as in v. 11; 22. 15; 90. 6, &c.
HEART,] as in 4. 7; 7. 10; 9. 1; 10. 6, 11, &c.
FORGOTTEN,] as in 9. 12; 10. 11; 42. 9, &c.
BREAD,] as in v. 9; 14. 4; 37. 25; 41. 9, &c.
5. SIGHING,] as in 6. 6; 31. 10; 38. 9, &c.
BONE,] as in v. 3.
CLEAVED,] as in 44. 25; 63. 8; 119. 25, &c.
6. PELICAN,] as in Lev. 11. 18; De. 14. 7, Isa. 34. 11; Zeph. 2. 14.
WILDERNESS,] as in 29. 8; 55. 7; 63. 1, &c.
OWL,] as in Lev. 11. 17; De. 14. 16.
DRY PLACES.] Sept. Vulg. 'house-sites.'
7. WATCHED,] as in 127. 1; Eze. 8. 29, &c.
BIRD,] as in 8. 8; 11. 1; 84. 3; 104. 17, &c.
ROOF,] as in 129. 6; Ex. 30. 3; 37. 26, &c.
8. REPROACHED,] as in 42. 10; 55. 12, &c.
MAD.] Sept. Vulg. 'praising one.' Ecc. 2. 2; 7. 7; Job 12. 17; Isa. 44. 25.
SWORN,] as in 15. 4; 24. 4; 35, 39, &c.
9. ASHES,] as in 147. 16; Ge. 18. 27, &c.
EATEN,] as in 14. 4; 22. 29; 53. 4; 69. 9, &c.
DRINK,] as in Prov. 3. 8; Hos. 2. 7.
WEEPING,] as in 6. 8; 30. 5; Ge. 45. 2, &c.
MINGLED,] as in Prov. 9. 2, 5; Isa. 5. 22; 19. 14.
10. INDIGNATION,] as in 38. 3; 69. 24, &c.
WRATH,] as in 38. 1; Nu. 1. 53; 16. 46, &c.
LIFTED UP,] as in 15. 3; 24. 4; 32. 5; 69. 7.
CAST DOWN,] as in 2. 3; 50. 17; 51. 11, &c.
11. SHADOW,] as in 17. 8; 36. 7; 57. 1, &c.
STRETCHED OUT,] as in 62. 3; 73. 2;136. 12.
12. ABIDEST,] as in 9. 7; 10. 8; 26. 5, &c.
MEMORIAL,] as in 6. 5; 9. 6; 30. 4; 34. 16.
GENERATIONS,] as in v. 18, 24; 10. 6; 12. 7.
13. RISETH,] as in 1. 5; 12. 5; 20. 8; 24. 3.
PITIEST,] as in 103. 13; Ex. 33. 16, &c.
TIME,] as in 1. 3; 4. 7; 9. 9; 10. 1, 5, &c.
TO FAVOUR,] as in 77. 9; 16. 38, 19, &c.
APPOINTED TIME,] as in 74. 4, 8; 75. 2, &c.
14. SERVANTS,] as in v. 28; 19. 11, 13, &c.
PLEASED,] as in 44. 3; 49. 13; 50. 18, &c.
STONES,] as in 91. 12; 118. 22; Ge. 2. 12, &c.
DUST,] as in 7. 5; 18. 42; 22. 15, 29; 30. 9, &c. Vulg. 'land,'
FAVOUR,] as in v. 13.
15. FEAR,] as in 3. 6; 23. 4; 27. 1, 3; 33. 8.
NAME.] Sept. Vulg. 'thy name, O Lord.'
HONOUR,] as in v. 16; 96. 8; 97. 6; 104. 31

16. BUILDED,] as in 28. 5; 51. 18; 69. **35, &c.**
SEEN,] as in 18. 15; 42. 2; 84. 7; 90. 16, **&c.**
17. TURNED,] as in 40. 4; 90. 9, &c.
DESTITUTE,] as in Jer. 17. 6.
DESPISED,] as in 22. 24; 69. 33; 73. 20, &c.
18. WRITTEN,] as in 69. 28; 139. 16, &c.
LATER GENERATION,] as in 48. 13; 78. 4.
CREATED,] as in 104. 13; 148. 5, &c.
PRAISE,] as in 22. 22, 23, 26; 35. 18, &c.
JAH,] as in 68. 4, 18; 77. 11; 89. 8; 94. 7, &c.
19. LOOKED,] as in 14. 2; 53. 2, &c.
HIGH PLACE,] as in 7. 7; 10. 5; 18. 16, &c.
SANCTUARY,] as in 2. 6; 3. 4; 5. 7; 11. 4, &c.
LOOKED ATTENTIVELY,} as in 33. 13; 34. 5.
20. GROAN,] as in 12. 5; 79. 11; Lev. 11. 30;
Mal. 2. 18.
PRISONER,] as in 68. 6; 69. 33; 79. 11, &c.
LOOSE,] *lit.* 'open.'
SONS OF DEATH,] as in 79. 11.   Sept. Vulg.
'sons of the slain.'
21. DECLARE,] as in 26. 7; 40. 5; 50. 16, &c.
NAME,] as in v. 15; 5. 11; 7. 17; 8. 1, &c.
PRAISE,] as in 9. 14; 22. 3, 25; 33. 1, &c.
22. GATHERED TOGETHER,] as in Ezra 10.
7; Est. 2. 8, 19, &c.
KINGDOM.] Sept. Vulg. 'kings.'
SERVE,] as in Ex. 10. 26; De. 10. 12, &c.
23. HUMBLED.] Sept. Vulg. 'responded.'
WAY,] as in 1. 1, 6; 2. 12; 5. 8; 10. 5, &c.
POWER,] as in 22. 15; 29. 4; 31. 10; 33. 16.
Sept. Vulg. 'his power.'
SHORTENED,] as in 126. 5; 129. 7, &c.
Sept. Vulg. 'the fewness of my days tell
me.'
DAYS,] as in v. 2, 8, 11, 24, &c.
24. MY GOD,] as in 5. 4; 18. 2; 22. 1, 10, &c.
Sept. Vulg. 'tell to me.'
GENERATIONS,] as in v. 12, 18, 24; 10. 6, &c.
25. BEFORE TIME,] as in De. 2. 10, 12, &c.
FOUND,] as in 8. 2; 24. 2; 78. 69; 89. 11, &c.
WORK OF THY HANDS,] as in 90. 17; 135. 15.
26. PERISH,] as in 1. 6; 2. 12; 9. 3, 18, &c.
REMAINEST,] as in 10. 1; 33. 9, 11; 38. 11.
GARMENT,] as in 22. 18; 45. 8; 109. 19, &c.
BECOME OLD,] as in 32. 3; 49. 14; Ge. 18. 12.
CLOTHING,] as in 22. 18; 35. 13; 45. 13, &c.
CHANGEST,] as in Ge. 31. 7, 41; 35. 2, &c.
27. FINISHED,] as in 104. 35; Nu. 14. 35, &c.
28. SERVANTS,] as in v. 14.
CONTINUE,] *lit.* 'tabernacle.'
SEED,] as in 18. 50; 21. 10; 22. 23, 30, &c.
ESTABLISHED,] as in 89. 21, 37; 93. 1; 96.
10, &c.   Sept. Vulg. 'directed.'

CIII. BY DAVID.] Luther adds, 'a Psalm.'
1. BLESS,] as in v. 2, 20, 21, 22; 28. 9, &c.
JEHOVAH,] the God of Israel.
INWARD PARTS,] as in 5. 9; 36. 1; 39. 3, &c.
NAME,] as in 5. 11; 7. 17; 8. 1; 9, 2, 5, 10.
2. FORGET,] as in 10. 12; 13. 1; 44. 24, &c.
BENEFITS,] as in 28. 4; 94. 2; 137. 8, &c.
3. FORGIVING,] as in 25. 11; Ex. 34. 9, &c.
INIQUITIES,] as in v. 10; 18. 23; 25. 11, &c.
HEALING,] as in 147. 3; Ex. 15. 26, &c.
DISEASES,] as in De. 29. 22; 2 Ch. 21. 19;
Jer. 14. 18; 16. 4.
4. REDEEMING,] as in 19. 4; 78. 35, &c.
DESTRUCTION,] as in 7. 15; 9. 15; 16. 10, &c.
LIFE,] as in 7. 5; 16. 11; 17. 14; 18. 46, &c.
CROWNING,] as in 8. 5; 5. 12; 65. 11, &c.
KINDNESS,] as in v. 8, 11, 17; 5. 7; 6. 4, &c.

MERCIES,] as in 25. 6; 40. 11; 51. 1; 77. 9.
5. SATISFYING,] as in 145. 16, &c.
DESIRE,] as in 32. 9; 33. 4, 5, 6, &c.
RENEW ITSELF.] Original word not found
again.
EAGLE,] as in Ex. 19. 4; Lev. 11. 13, &c.
YOUTH,] as in 25. 7; 71. 5, 17; 127. 4, &c.
6. RIGHTEOUSNESS,] as in v. 17; 5. 8, &c.
JUDGMENTS,] as in 1. 5; 7. 6; 9. 4, 7, &c.
OPPRESSED,] as in 146. 7; De. 28. 29, &c.
7. MAKETH KNOWN,] as in 16. 11; 32. 5, &c.
WAYS,] as in 1. 1, 6; 2. 12; 5. 8; 10. 5, &c.
MOSES,] as the appointed leader of his
people.
ACTS,] as in 9. 11; 14. 1; 66. 5; 77. 12, &c.
Sept. Vulg. 'volitions.'
8. MERCIFUL,] as in 78. 38; 86. 15; 111. 4.
GRACIOUS,] as in 86. 15; 111. 4; 112. 4, &c.
SLOW,] as in 86. 15; 145. 8; Ex. 34. 6, &c.
ANGER,] as in 2. 5, 12; 6. 1; 10. 4, &c.
ABUNDANT,] as in 3. 1, 2; 4. 6; 18. 16, &c.
9. STRIVE.] Sept. Vulg. 'angry.'
WATCH.] Sept. Vulg. 'wrathful.'
10. SINS,] as in 51. 5, 9; Ge. 41. 9; Lev. 19. 17.
DONE,] as in 7. 3; 9. 4; 15. 16; 15. 3; 22. 3.
CONFERRED BENEFITS,] as in 7. 4; 13. 6.
11. HEIGHT,] as in 113. 5; 131. 1; 2 Ch. 26. 16
MIGHTY,] as in 12. 4; 65. 3; 117. 2; Ge. 7. 19.
FEARING,] as in v. 13, 17; 15. 4; 22. 23, &c.
12. DISTANCE,] as in 22. 11, 19; 35. 22, &c.
EAST,] as in 50. 1; 107. 3; 113. 3; Ex. 27. 13.
WEST,] as in 75. 6; 107. 3; 1 Ch. 7. 28; 12. 15.
PUT FAR,] as in 88. 8, 18; 55. 7, &c.
TRANSGRESSIONS,] as in 5. 10; 19. 13, &c.
13. FATHER,] as in 27. 10; 39. 12; 44. 1, &c.
MERCY,] as in 18. 1; 102. 13; 116. 5, &c.
14. FRAME,] as in Ge. 6. 5; 8. 21; De. 31. 21.
REMEMBERING,] *or* 'reminded.'
DUST,] as in 7. 5; 18. 42; 22. 15, 29, &c.
15. MORTAL MAN,] as in 8. 4; 9. 19, 20, &c.
GRASS,] as in 37. 2; 90. 5; 104. 14; 129. 6.
FLOWER,] as in Ex. 28. 26; 39. 30; Lev. 8. 9.
FIELD,] as in 78. 12, 43; 107. 37; 132. 6, &c.
FLOURISHETH,] as in 72. 16; 90. 6; 92. 7.
16. WIND,] as in 1. 4; 11. 6; 18. 10, 15, &c.
PASSED,] as in 18. 12; 38. 4; 42. 7; 48. 4, &c.
PLEA,] as in 2. 3; 26. 3; 37. 10; 44. 19, &c.
DISCERN,] as in 142. 4; Ge. 27. 23, &c.
17. KINDNESS,] as in v. 4.
RIGHTEOUSNESS,] as in v. 6.
18. COVENANT,] as in 25. 10, 14; 44. 17, &c.
PRECEPTS,] as in 19. 8; 111. 7; 119. 4, &c.
19. ESTABLISHED,] as in 7. 13; 57. 6; 74. 16.
THRONE,] as in 9. 4, 7; 11. 4; 45. 6; 47. 8.
RULED,] as in 19. 13; 22. 28; 59. 13; 66. 7.
20. MESSENGERS,] as in 34. 7; 35. 5, 6, &c.
MIGHTY,] as in 19. 5; 24. 8; 33. 16; 45. 3.
POWER,] as in 19. 5; 29. 4; 31. 10; 33. 16.
DOING,] as in v. 6, 21; 14. 1, 3; 15. 5, &c.
TO HEARKEN,] as in 102. 20; 106. 4, &c.
WORD,] as in 17. 4; 19. 8; 22. 1; 33. 4, &c.
21. HOSTS,] as in 24. 18; 33. 6; 44. 9; 46. 7.
MINISTERS,] as in 72. 16; 101. 6; Nu. 3. 6.
PLEASURE,] as in 5. 12; 19. 14; 30. 5, &c.
22. WORKS,] as in 9. 16, &c.
DOMINION,] as in 114. 2; 136. 8, 9; 144. 13.

CIV. 1. BLESS,] as in v. 35; 28. 9; 66. 8, &c.
MY GOD,] as in v. 33; 3. 7; 5. 2; 7. 1, 3, &c.
GREAT,] as in 92. 5; 35. 27; 40. 16; 70. 4, &c.
HONOUR,] as in 8. 1; 21. 5; 45. 3; 96. 6, &c

MAJESTY,] as in 8. 5; 21. 5; 29. 4; 45. 3, &c.
PUT ON,] as in 65. 13; 93. 1; 109. 18, 20, &c.
2. COVERING HIMSELF,] as in 1 Sa. 28. 14;
Song 1. 5; Isa. 22. 17.
LIGHT,] as in 4. 6; 27. 1; 36. 9; 37. 6, &c.
GARMENT,] as in Ex. 22. 9, 26; De. 24. 13.
STRETCHING OUT,] as in 1 Ch. 21. 10, &c.
CURTAINS,] as in Ex. 25. 1; Lev. 2. 8; 9. 10.
3. LAYING THE BEAM,] as in Neh. 2. 8; 3.
3, 6; 2 Ch. 34. 11.
UPPER CHAMBER,] as in v. 13; Jud. 3. 20.
THICK CLOUDS,] as in 18. 11, 12; 77. 17, &c.
CHARIOT.] Original word not found again.
WALKING,] as in Prov. 6. 11; Ecc. 4. 15, &c.
WINGS,] as in 17. 8; 18. 10; 36. 7; 57. 1, &c.
WIND,] as in v. 4, 29, 30; 1. 4; 11. 6, &c.
4. MESSENGERS,] as in 34. 7; 35. 5, 6, &c.
MINISTERS,] as in 103. 21; 101. 6; Nu. 3. 6.
FLAMING FIRE,] as in 57. 4; 83. 14; 106. 18.
5. FOUNDED,] as in v. 8; 24. 2; 78. 69, &c.
BASES,] as in 33. 14; 89. 14; 97. 2; Ex. 15. 17.
MOVED,] as in 10. 6; 13. 4; 15. 5; 16. 8, &c.
6. ABYSS,] as in 33. 7; 36. 6; 42. 7; 71. 20.
CLOTHING,] as in 22. 18; 35. 13; 45. 13, &c.
COVERED,] as in 32. 5; 40. 10; 44. 15, &c.
HILLS,] as in v. 8, 10, 13, 18, 32, &c.
STANDS,] as in 10. 1; 33. 9, 11; 38. 11, &c.
7. REBUKE,] as in 18. 15; 76. 6; 80. 16, &c.
FLEE,] as in 68. 1; 114. 3, 5, &c.
THUNDER,] as in 77. 18; 81. 7; Job 26. 14;
39. 25; Isa. 29. 6.
HASTE AWAY,] as in 48. 5; 1 Sa. 23. 26.
8. GO UP,] as in 24. 3; 107. 26; 132. 3, &c.
GO DOWN,] as in 7. 16; 18. 9; 49. 17; 55. 15.
VALLEYS,] as in v. 10; Ge. 11. 2; De. 8. 7.
PLACE,] as in 24. 3; 26. 8; 37. 10; 44. 19.
9. BORDER,] as in 78. 54; 105. 31, 33, &c.
SET,] as in 19. 4; 40. 4; 46. 8; 50. 23, &c.
PASS OVER,] as in 17. 3; 37. 36; 42. 4, &c.
TURN BACK,] as in v. 29; 6. 10; 7. 12, &c.
TO COVER,] as in Ex. 26. 13; 28. 42, &c.
10. SENDING FORTH,] as Ge. 43. 45, &c.
FOUNTAINS,] as in 74. 15; 84. 6; 87. 7, &c.
GO ON.] Sept. Vulg. add 'waters.'
11. WATER,] as in 36. 8; 69. 21; 78. 15, &c.
BEAST,] as in v. 20, 25, 33; 7. 5, 16, 11, &c.
FIELD,] as in 8. 7; 50. 11; 80. 13; 96. 12, &c.
WILD ASSES,] as in Ge. 16. 12; Job 6. 5, &c.
QUENCH,] lit. 'break.'
THIRST,] as in 69. 21; Ex. 17. 3; De. 28. 48.
12. FOWL OF THE HEAVENS,] as in 50. 11;
78. 27; 79. 2; Ge. 1. 26, &c.
DWELL,] as in 15. 1; 16. 9; 37. 29; 55. 6, &c.
BRANCHES.] Sept. Vulg. 'rocks.'
13. WATERING,] as in Ge. 13. 10; Lev. 11. 34.
FRUIT,] as in 1. 3; 24. 10; 58. 11; 72. 16, &c.
SATISFIED,] as in v. 16; 17. 14, 15; 22. 26.
14. GRASS,] as in 37. 2; 90. 5; 103. 15;
129. 6.
TO SPRING UP,] as in 147. 8, &c.
CATTLE,] as in 8. 7; 36. 6; 49. 12; 50. 10, &c.
HERB,] as in 72. 16; 92. 7; 102. 4, 11, &c.
SERVICE,] as in v. 23; Ge. 29. 27; 30. 26, &c.
MAN,] as in v. 23; 8. 4; 1u. 4; 12. 1, 8, &c.
15. WINE,] as in 60. 3; 75. 8; 78. 65, &c.
REJOICETH,] as in Prov. 10. 1; 15. 20, &c.
HEART,] as in 4. 4; 13. 2; 15. 2; 20. 4, &c.
TO SHINE,] or 'be bright.'
OIL,] as in 23. 5; 45. 7; 55. 21; 89. 20, &c.
BREAD,] as in v. 14; 14. 4; 37. 25; 41. 9, &c.
SUPPORTETH,] as in 18. 35; 20. 2; 41. 3, &c.

16. SATISFIED,] as in v. 13.
TREES,] as in 1. 3; 74. 5; 96. 12; 105. 33, &c.
JEHOVAH.] Sept. Vulg. 'the plain.'
CEDARS,] as in 29. 5; 80. 10; 92. 12; 148. 9
PLANTED,] as in 80. 15; 44. 2; 80. 8, &c.
17. BIRD,] as in 8. 8; 11. 1; 84. 3; 104. 17.
NESTS,] as in Isa. 34, 15; Eze. 31. 6; Jer.
48. 28; 22. 23.
STORK,] as in Lev. 11. 19; De. 14. 18; Job
39. 13; Jer. 8. 7, &c.   Sept. Vulg. 'the house
of the heron leadeth them.'
FIRS,] as in 2 Sa. 6. 5; 1 K. 5. 8; 6. 15, &c.
18. HIGH HILLS,] as in v. 6.
WILD GOATS,] as in 1 Sa. 24. 2; Job 39. 1.
ROCKS,] as in 18. 2; 31. 3; 40. 2; 42. 9, &c.
REFUGE,] as in 14. 6; 46. 1; 61. 3; 62. 7, &c.
CONIES,] as in Lev. 11. 5; De. 14. 7; Prov.
30. 26.
19. MOON,] as in 8. 3; 72. 5, 7; 89. 37, &c.
SEASONS,] as in 74. 4, 8; 75. 2; 102. 13, &c.
SUN,] as in v. 22; 19. 4; 50. 1; 58. 8, &c.
PLACE OF ENTRANCE,] as in 50. 1; 113. 3.
20. SETTETH,] as in 21. 4, &c.
DARKNESS,] as in 18. 11; 35. 6; 88. 12, &c.
NIGHT.] as in 1. 2; 6. 6; 16. 7; 17. 3, &c.
CREEP,] as in 69. 34; Ge. 9. 2; Lev. 20. 25:
21. YOUNG LIONS,] as in 17. 12; 34. 10, &c.
ROARING,] as in 22. 13; 38. 8; 74. 4, &c.
PREY,] as in 76. 4; 111. 5; 124. 6; Ge. 49. 9.
FOOD,] as in v. 27; 78. 18; 80; 107. 18, &c.
22. RISETH,] as in 112. 4, &c.
GATHERED,] as in 35. 12, &c.
DENS,] as in 76. 2; De; 33. 27; Job 38. 40.
CROUCH,] as in Zeph. 2. 7, &c.
23. GOETH FORTH,] as in 17. 2. 41. 6; 44. 9.
WORK,] as in 9. 16; 28. 4; 44. 1; 64. 9, &c.
EVENING,] as in 30. 5; 55. 17; 59. 6, 14, &c.
24. HOW MANY,] as in 3. 1; 4. 7; 25. 19, &c.
WORKS,] as in v. 13, 31; 8. 3; 19. 1; 28. 4.
WISDOM,] as in 37. 30; 51. 6; 90. 12, &c.
MADE,] as in v. 19; 7. 3; 9. 4, 15, 16; 15. 3.
FULL,] as in 10. 7; 26. 10; 33. 5; 38. 7, &c.
POSSESSIONS,] as in 105. 21; Ge. 31. 18; 34.
23; 36. 6, &c.   Sept. 'creation.'
25. SEA,] as in 8. 8; 24. 2; 33. 7; 46. 2, &c.
BROAD OF SIDES,] lit. 'of hands.'
MOVING THINGS,] as in 148. 10; Ge. 1. 24.
INNUMERABLE,] as in 40. 12; 105. 12, 34, &c.
LIVING CREATURES,] as in 143. 3, &c.
26. SHIPS,] as in 48. 7; 107. 23; Ge. 49. 13.
LEVIATHAN,] as in 74. 14; Job 3. 8; 41. 1;
[Isa. 27. 1.   Sept. Vulg. 'this dragon.'
FORMED,] as in 74. 17; 94. 9, 20; 95. 5, &c.
TO PLAY,] as in 2. 4; 37. 13; 52. 6; 59. 8, &c.
27. LOOK,] as in 119. 166; 145. 15; Neh. 2. 13.
FOOD,] as in v. 21, &c.
SEASON,] as in 1. 3; 4. 7; 9. 9; 10. 1, &c.
28. GATHER,] as in Ex. 16. 4, 18, 22; Nu. 11. 8.
OPEN,] as in 38. 13; 39. 9; 49. 4; 51. 15, &c.
SATISFIED,] as in v. 13, &c.
29. HIDEST,] as in 31. 20; 44. 24; 64. 2; 69
17, &c.   Sept. Vulg. 'turnest aside.'
TROUBLED,] as in 6. 10; 5; 83. 17; 90. 7
GATHEREST,] as in 26. 9; 27. 10; 50. 5; 85
3, &c.   Vulg. 'bearest away.'
SPIRIT,] as in v. 3, &c.
EXPIRE,] as in Ge. 6. 17; 7. 21; 25. 8; 35. 29
DUST,] as in 7. 5; 18. 42; 22. 15; 30. 9, &c.
TURN BACK,] as in v. 9, &c.
30. SENDEST FORTH,] as in 44. 2; 78. 45, &c
SPIRIT,] as in v. 3, &c.

CREATED,] as in 51. 10; 80. 12, 47; 148. 5.
RENEWEST,] as in 51. 10; 103. 5; 1 Sa. 11. 14.
GROUND,] as in 49. 11; 83. 10; 105. 35, &c.
31. HONOUR,] as in 3. 3; 4. 2; 7. 5; 8. 5, &c.
REJOICETH,] as in v. 34; 5. 11; 9. 2; 14. 7.
WORKS,] as in v. 13, &c.
32. TREMBLETH,]as in Ezr. 10. 9; Da. 10. 11.
HILLS,] as in v. 6, &c.
SMOKE,] as in 74. 1; 80. 4; 144. 5; Ex. 19.
18; De. 29. 20.
33. SING,] as in 13. 6; 21. 13; 27. 6; 33. 3, &c.
LIFE,] as in v. 11, &c.
SING PRAISE,] as in 7. 17; 9. 2; 18. 49, &c.
EXIST,] as in 139. 18; Ge. 18. 22; 29. 9, &c.
34. SWEET,] as in 106. 35; 119. 22; Ge. 43. 9.
MEDITATION,]as in 55. 2; 64. 1; 142. 2, &c.
REJOICE,] as in v. 31, &c.
35. CONSUMED,] as in 9. 6; 19. 13; 102. 27.
SINNERS,] as in 1. 1; 25. 8; 26. 9; 51. 13, &c.
WICKED,] as in 1. 1; 3. 7: 7. 9; 9. 5, &c.
BLESS,] as in v. 1, &c.
PRAISE,] as in 105. 45; 106. 1; 111. 1; 112.
1. &c. This last clause in Sept. and Vulg.
is put at the beginning of the next Psalm.

CV. 1. GIVE THANKS,] as in 106. 1; 107. 1.
CALL,] as in 50. 15; 53. 4; 66. 17; 79. 6, &c.
MAKE KNOWN,]as in 25. 4; 39. 4; 90. 12, &c.
PEOPLES,] as in v. 13, 20, 24, 25, 43.
ACTS,] as in 9. 11; 14. 1; 66. 5; 77. 12, &c.
2. SING,] as in 33. 3; 68. 4; 96. 1; 137. 3, &c.
SING PRAISE,] as in 9. 11: 30. 4: 33. 2, &c.
MEDITATE,] as in 55. 17; 69. 12; 77. 3, 6,
12, &c. Sept. Vulg. 'declare or narrate,'
WONDERS,] as in v. 5, 9. 1; 26. 7; 40. 5, &c.
3. BOAST YOURSELVES,] as in 1 Ch. 16. 10.
HOLY NAME,] as in 33. 21; 103. 1; 106. 47.
SEEKING,] as in 24. 6; 35. 4; 37. 25, 32, &c.
REJOICETH,]as in 5. 11; 9. 2; 14. 7; 21. 1, &c.
4. SEEK,] as in 1 K. 22. 5; 2 K. 1. 2; 22. 13.
STRENGTH,] as in 8. 2; 21. 1; 28. 7: 29. 1,
&c. Sept. Vulg. 'be confirmed.'
FACE,] or 'presence,' as in v. 17; 5. 8, &c.
CONTINUALLY,] as in 16. 8; 25. 15; 34. 1, &c.
5. REMEMBER,] as in 25. 6; 74. 2; 89. 7, &c.
WONDERS,] as in v. 2, &c.
SIGNS,] as in v. 27; 71. 7; 78. 43; 135. 9, &c.
JUDGMENTS,] as in v. 7; 1. 5; 7. 6; 9. 4, 7.
6. SEED,] as in 18. 50; 21. 10; 22. 23; 25. 13
SERVANT,] as in v. 17, 25, 26, 42, &c.
SONS,] as in 4. 2; 11. 4; 12. 1, 8, &c.
CHOSEN ONES,] as in v. 43; 89. 3; 106. 5, &c.
7. OUR GOD,] as in 20. 5, 7; 40. 3; 44. 20, &c.
EARTH,] or 'land,' as in v. 11, 16, 23, 27, &c.
JUDGMENTS,] as in v. 5, &c.
8. REMEMBERED,] as in v. 42; 9. 12; 63. 6.
COVENANT,] as in v. 10; 25. 10: 44. 17, &c.
WORD,]or 'thing,' as in v. 19, 27, 28, 42, &c.
COMMANDED,] as in 7. 6; 33. 9; 68. 28, &c.
GENERATIONS,] as in 10. 6; 12. 7; 14. 5, &c.
9. OATH,] as in Ge. 24. 8; 26 3; Ex. 22. 11.
10. ESTABLISH,] as in 18. 33; 107. 25, &c.
STATUTE,] as in v. 45; 2. 7; 50. 16; 81. 4, &c.
COVENANT AGE-DURING,] as in Ge. 9. 16,&c.
11. GIVE,] as in v. 44: 1. 3; 2. 8: 14. 7, &c.
PORTION,] as in 16. 6; 18. 4. 5; 78. 55, &c.
INHERITANCE,] as in 2. 8; 28. 9; 33. 12. &c.
12. FEW,] as in 109. 8; Lev. 25. 52. &c.
SOJOURNERS,] as in 39. 12; 94. 6: 119. 19.
13. GO UP AND DOWN,] as in 12. 8; 39. 6, &c.
14. SUFFERED,] as in 17. 14; Lev. 16. 23, &c.

REPROVED,] as in 6. 1; 38. 1; 50. 8; 94. 10
KINGS,] such as Pharaoh, Og, &c.
15. STRIKE,] as in 104. 32; Ge. 3. 3; 32. 25.
ANOINTED,] as in 2. 2; 18. 50; 20. 6, &c.
PROPHETS,] as in 74. 9; Ge. 20. 7; Ex. 7. 1.
EVIL,]as in 44. 2; 74. 3; Ge. 19. 7; Nu. 20. 15.
16. CALLETH,] as in 3. 4; 18. 3, 6; 22. 2, &c.
FAMINE,] as in 33. 19; Ge. 12. 10; 26. 1, &c.
STAFF,] as in 110. 2; Gen. 38. 18; Ex. 4. 2.
BROKEN,] as in 69. 20; 104. 11; Lev. 26. 19.
17. SENT,] as in v. 19, 20, 26, 28, 50, &c.
SERVANT,] as in v. 6, &c.
SOLD,] as in Ex. 22. 3; Lev. 25. 39; 27. 27.
18. AFFLICTED,] as in 35. 13; 88. 7; 90. 15;
102. 23, &c. Sept. Vulg. 'humbled.'
FETTERS,] as in 149. 8.
FEET,] as in 8. 6; 9. 15; 18. 9, 33, 38, &c.
IRON,] as in 107. 10, 16; 149. 8; Ge. 4. 22, &c.
SOUL,] as in v. 22; 3. 2; 6. 3; 7. 2; 10. 3, &c
19. TIME,] as in 1. 3; 4. 7; 9. 9; 10. 1, 5, &c.
SAYING OF JEHOVAH,]as in 12. 6; 18. 30,&c.
TRIED,] as in 17. 3; 66. 10; Isa. 48. 10; Jer.
6 29, &c. Sept. Vulg. 'inflamed.'
20. LOOSETH,] as in 2 Sa. 22. 33; Job 6. 9.
RULER,] as in v. 21; 22. 28: 59. 30; 66. 7, &c
21. LORD,] as in 8. 1; 12. 4: 45. 11; 97. 5, &c.
HOUSE,] or 'household,' as in 5. 7; 23. 6, &c.
RULER,] as in v. 20, &c.
POSSESSIONS,] as in 104. 24; Ge. 31. 18, &c.
22. BIND,] as in Nu. 30. 2; Jud. 15. 10, 12,
13, &c. Sept. Vulg. 'to instruct.'
CHIEFS,] as in 45. 16; 68. 27; 82. 7; 119. 23.
PLEASURE,] as in v. 18, &c. Sept. Vulg
' as himself.'
ELDERS,] as in 107. 32; 119. 100; 148. 12, &c.
MAKETH WISE,] as in 119. 98; Job 35. 11.
23. SOJOURNED,] as in 120. 5; Ge. 21. 23, &c.
LAND OF HAM,] as in v. 23, &c.
24. PEOPLE,] as in v. 1, 13, 20, 24, 43, &c.
FRUITFUL,] as in Ge. 17. 6, 20; 28. 3, &c.
ADVERSARIES,] as in 3. 1; 4. 1; 13. 4, &c.
25. TURNED,] as in v. 20; 30. 11; 41. 3, &c.
HEART,] as in v. 3; 4. 7; 7. 10; 9. 1; 10. 6.
TO HATE,] as in 36. 2; Ge. 37. 5, 8; Jud. 15. 2.
CONSPIRE,] as in Ge. 37. 18.
SERVANTS,] as in v. 6, &c.
26. SENT,] as in v. 17, &c. Sept. 'sent
forth.'
FIXED ON,] as in 33. 12; 78. 67; 84. 10, &c.
27. SET,] as in 8. 1; 12. 4; 40. 4; 46. 8, &c.
SIGNS,] as in v. 5, &c.
WONDERS,] as in v. 2, &c.
LAND OF HAM,] as in v. 23, &c
28. DARKNESS,] as in 18. 11; 35. 6; 88. 12.
DARK,] as in 139. 12; Job 38. 2: Jer. 13. 16.
PROVOKED,] as in 5. 10; Nu. 20. 4; 27. 14
WORD,] as in v. 8, &c.
29. TURNED,] as in v. 25, &c.
WATERS,] as in v. 1, 3; 18. 11, 15, &c.
BLOOD,] as in 5. 6; 9. 12; 16. 4; 26. 9, &c
PUTTETH TO DEATH,] as in Ge. 38. 7; 42. 37.
FISH,] as in Ge. 1. 26, 28; Ex. 7. 18, 21, &c.
30. TEEMED,] as in Ge. 1. 21; 8. 17; Ex. 8. 3.
FROGS,] as in 78. 45; Ex. 8. 2, 3, 4, 5, 6, &c.
INNER-CHAMBERS,] as in Ge. 43. 30; Ex.8.3.
KINGS,] as in v. 14, &c.
31. SAID,] as in 42. 9, 10; 71. 11; 119. 82, &c
BEETLE,] as in 78. 45; Ex. 8. 2, 22, 24, &c.
LICE,] as in Ex 8. 16, 17, 18; Isa. 51. 6.
BORDER,] as in v. 33; 78. 54; 104. 9, &c.
32. SHOWERS,] as in 68. 9; Ge. 7. 12; 8. 2.

2 F

HAIL,] as in 18. 12; 78. 47, 48; 148. 8, &c.
FLAMING FIRE,] as in v. 39; 11. 6; 18. 8, &c.
33. SMITETH,] as in v. 36; 78. 51, 66; 121. 6.
VINE,] as in 78. 47; 80. 8, 14; 128. 3, &c.
FIG,] as in Ge. 3. 7; Nu. 13. 23; 20. 5, &c.
SHIVERETH,] as in 29. 5; 46. 9; 48. 7, &c.
TREES,] as in 1. 3; 74. 5; 96. 12; 104. 16, &c.
34. SAID,] as in v. 31, &c.
LOCUST,] as in 78. 46; 109. 23; Ex. 10. 4, &c.
CANKERWORM,] as in Jer. 51. 14, 27; Joel
1. 4; 2. 25; Nah. 3. 15, 16.
INNUMERABLE,] as in 40. 12; 104. 25, &c.
CONSUMETH,] as in 18. 8; 21. 9; 22. 26, &c.
HERB,] as in 72. 16; 92. 7; 102. 4, 11, &c.
FRUIT,] as in 1. 3; 21. 10; 58. 11; 72. 16, &c.
36. SMITETH,] as in v. 33.
FIRST-BORN,] as in 78. 51; 89. 27; 135. 8, &c.
FIRST-FRUIT,] as in 78. 51; 111. 10; Ex.23.19.
STRENGTH,] as in 78. 51; Ge. 43. 3; De. 21.
17; Job 18. 7, &c.   Sept. Vulg. 'labour.'
37. BRINGETH OUT,] as in v. 43; 18. 19, &c.
SILVER,] as in 12. 6; 15. 5; 66. 10; 68. 13, &c.
GOLD,] as in 19. 10; 45. 13; 72. 15; 115. 4, &c.
TRIBES,] as in 74. 2; 78. 55, 67, 68, &c.
FEEBLE ONE,] as in 2 Ch. 28. 15; Job 4. 4.
38. REJOICED,] as in 16. 9; 35. 15; 122. 1, &c.
FEAR,] as in 14. 5; 31. 11; 36. 1; 53. 5, &c.
FALLEN,] as in 10. 10; 16. 6; 20. 8; 27. 2, &c.
39. SPREAD,] as in 104. 5; Nu. 4. 6, 8, &c.
CLOUD,] as in 78. 14; 97. 2; 99. 7; Ge. 9. 13.
COVERING,] as in Ex. 26. 36, 37; 27. 16, &c.
FIRE,] as in v. 32, &c.
ENLIGHTEN,] as in Ge. 1. 15, 17; Ex. 13. 21.
NIGHT,] as in 1. 2; 6. 6; 16. 7; 17. 3, &c.
40. ASKED,] as in 21. 4; 27. 4; 40. 6, &c.
QUAILS,] as in Ex. 16. 13; Nu. 11. 31, 32.
SATISFIETH,] as in 81. 16; 91. 16; 132. 15.
41. OPENED,] as in 37. 14; 78. 23; 109. 2, &c.
ROCK,] as in 18. 2, 31, 46; 19. 14, &c.
ISSUE,] as in 78. 20; Lev. 15. 25; Isa. 48. 21.
GO ON,] as in 1. 1; 26. 1; 119. 3; Ge. 19. 2.
DRY LAND,] as in 63. 1; 78. 17; 107. 35, &c.
RIVER,] as in 24. 2; 46. 4; 66. 6; 72. 8, &c.
Sept. Vulg. 'rivers.'
42. REMEMBERED,] as in v. 8, &c.
SERVANT,] as in v. 6, &c.
43. BRINGETH FORTH,] as in v. 37, &c.
PEOPLE,] as in v. 1, &c.
JOY,] as in 45. 7; 51. 8, 12; 119. 111, &c.
SINGING,] as in 17. 1; 30. 5; 42. 4; 47. 1, &c.
CHOSEN ONES,] as in 106. 5, &c.
44. GIVETH,] as in v. 10, &c.
NATIONS,] as in 2. 1, 8, &c.
LABOUR,] as in 7. 14; 10. 7; 90. 10; 107. 12.
POSSESS,] as in 25. 13; 37. 9, 11, 22; 83. 12.
45. OBSERVE,] as in 12. 7; 39. 1; 41. 2, &c.
STATUTES,] as in v. 10, &c.
LAWS,] as in 1. 2; 19. 7; 37. 31; 40. 8, &c.
KEEP,] as in 12. 7; 25. 21; 32. 7; 40. 11, &c.
Sept. Vulg. 'seek out.'
PRAISE,] as in 104. 35; 106. 1, 48; 111. 1;
112. 1, &c.   Sept. Vulg. omit this last clause.

CVI. 1. PRAISE,] as in 104. 35; 105. 45, &c.
GIVE THANKS,] as in 105. 1; 107. 1; 118. 1.
GOOD,] as in v. 5; 4. 6; 14. 1, 3; 34. 8, &c.
KINDNESS,] as in v. 7, 45; 5. 7; 6. 4; 13. 5.
2. UTTER,] as in Ge. 21. 7; Job 8. 2; 33. 3;
Prov. 6. 13.
MIGHTY ACTS,] as in v. 8; 145. 4, 12, &c.
SOUNDETH,] as in 51. 8; 143. 8; De. 4. 10.

PRAISE,] as in v. 12, 47; 9. 14; 22. 3, &c.
3. HAPPINESS,] as in 1. 1; 2. 12; 32. 1, &c
KEEPING,] as in 31. 6; 34. 20; 71. 10; 97. 10.
JUDGMENT,] as in 1. 5; 7. 6; 9. 4; 10. 5, &c.
RIGHTEOUSNESS,] as in v. 31; 5. 8; 11. 7.
TIMES,] as in 1. 3; 4. 7; 9. 9; 10. 1, &c.
4. REMEMBER,] as in 25. 6; 74. 2; 89. 47;
105. 5, &c.   Sept. Vulg. 'us.'
FAVOUR,] as in 5. 12; 30. 5; 89. 17, &c.
LOOK AFTER,] as in 80. 14; 59. 5; 1 Sa. 14.
17: 2 Sa. 24. 2, &c.   Sept. Vulg. 'us.'
SALVATION,] as in 3. 2; 3. 8; 9. 14; 13. 5.
5. LOOK,] as in 14. 2; 16. 10; 27. 13; 34. 12.
GOOD,] as in v. 1, &c.
CHOSEN ONES,] as in v. 23; 105. 6, 43, &c.
REJOICE,] as in Ecc. 3. 12; 5. 19; 8. 15, &c
JOY,] as in 4. 7; 16. 11; 21. 6; 30. 11, &c.
NATION,] as in v. 27, 35, 41, 47, &c.
BOAST MYSELF,] as in 34. 2; 49. 6; 52. 1, &c
INHERITANCE,] as in v. 40; 2. 8; 28. 9, &c
6. SINNED,] as in 41. 4; 51. 4; 78. 32, &c.
FATHERS,] as in v. 7; 22. 4; 27. 10; 39. 12.
DONE PERVERSELY,] as in 2 Sa. 19. 19, &c.
DONE WICKEDLY,] as in 2 Ch. 20. 35, &c.
7. CONSIDERED WISELY,] as in 64. 9, &c.
WONDERS,] as in 9. 1; 26. 7; 40. 5; 71. 17.
ABUNDANCE,] as in 5. 7, 10; 33. 16; 37. 11.
KIND ACTS,] as in v. 1, &c.
PROVOKE,] as in v. 33, 43; 78. 17, 40, 53, &c.
Sept. Vulg. add, 'going up.'
8. SAVETH,] as in v. 10; 18. 27; 34. 18, &c
NAME'S SAKE,] as in 23. 3; 31. 3; 79. 9, &c
MAKE KNOWN,] as in 25. 14; 78. 5; 105. 1.
MIGHT,] as in v. 2, &c.
9. REBUKETH,] as in 9. 5; 68. 30; 119. 12.
DRIED UP,] as in Job 14. 11; Isa. 19. 5, &c.
TO GO,] as in 125. 5; Ex. 14. 12; Lev. 26. 13.
DEPTHS,] as in 33. 7; 36. 6; 42. 7; 71. 20, &c.
WILDERNESS,] as in v. 14, 26; 29. 8; 55. 7.
10. HATING,] as in v. 41; 9. 13; 18. 17, &c.
REDEEMETH,] as in 72. 14; 74. 2; 77. 15, &c.
ENEMY,] as in 8. 7; 6. 10; 7. 5; 8. 2; 9. 3.
11. COVER,] as in v. 17; 44. 19; 55. 5; 140. 9.
ADVERSARIES,] as in v. 44; 27. 2; 44. 7, &c.
12. BELIEVE,] as in v. 24; 27. 13; 78. 22, &c.
SING,] as in 13. 6; 21. 13; 27. 6; 57. 7, &c.
PRAISE,] as in v. 2, &c.
13. HASTED,] as in Ge. 27. 20; 45. 13, &c.
FORGOTTEN,] as in v. 21; 9. 12; 10. 11, &c.
WAITED,] as in 33. 20; 2 K. 7. 9; Job 32.
4; Isa. 8. 17, &c.   Sept. 'sustain.'
COUNSEL,] as in v. 1; 13. 2; 14. 6, &c.
14. LUST,] as in 10. 3; 31. 2; 78. 29, 30, &c.
WILDERNESS,] as in v. 9, &c.
TRY,] as in 78. 18, 41, 56; Ex. 16. 4; 17. 2.
DESERT,] as in 68. 7; 78. 40; 107. 4; De. 32.
10, &c.   Sept. Vulg. 'waterless place.'
15. REQUEST,] as in Jud. 8. 24; 1 Sa. 1. 17.
LEANNESS,] as in Isa. 10. 16; Mic. 6. 10.
16. ENVIOUS,] as in 37. 1; Ge. 26. 14; 30. 1;
37. 11, &c.   Sept. Vulg. 'irritate.'
CAMP,] as in 78. 28; Ge. 32. 2; Ex. 14. 19.
HOLY ONE,] as in 16. 3; 22. 3; 71. 22, &c.
17. OPENETH,] as in 38. 13; 39. 9; 49. 4, &c.
SWALLOWETH UP,] as in 69. 15; 124. 3, &c.
COVERETH,] as in v. 11, &c.
COMPANY,] as in v. 18; 1. 5; 7. 7; 22. 16, &c.
18. FIRE,] as in 6; 18. 8; 21. 9; 29. 7, &c.
BURNETH,] as in 2. 12; 39. 3; 79. 5; 83. 14.
FLAME,] as in 29. 7; 83. 14; 105. 32, &c.
SETTETH ON FIRE,] as in 83. 14; 97. 3, &c

WICKED,] as in 1. 1; 3. 7; 7. 9; 9. 5, &c.
19. CALF,] as in 29. 6; 68. 30; Ex. 32. 4, &c.
BOW THEMSELVES,] as in 5. 7; 22. 27, &c.
MOLTEN IMAGE,] as in Ex. 32. 4; 34. 17, &c.
20. HONOUR,] as in 3. 3; 8. 5; 10. 9; 26. 8.
FORM,] as in 144. 12; De. 4. 16; Jos. 22. 28.
OX,] as in 69. 31; Ge. 32. 5; 49. 6; Ex. 20. 17.
HERBS,] as in 72. 16; 92. 7; 102. 4, 11, &c.
21. FORGOTTEN,] as in v. 13, &c.
SAVIOUR,] as in 7. 10; 17. 7; 18. 41, &c.
GREAT THINGS,] as in 12. 3; 21. 5; 47. 2, &c.
22. WONDERFUL THINGS,] as in v. 7, &c.
FEARFUL THINGS,] as in 45. 4; 47. 2; 65. 5.
SEA OF SUPH,] as in v. 7, &c.
23. TO DESTROY,] as in v. 34; 145. 20, &c.
CHOSEN ONE,] as in v. 5, &c.
BREACH,] as in 144. 14; Ge. 38. 29, &c.
TO TURN BACK,] as in 78. 38; Ge. 24. 5, &c.
WRATH,] as in 6. 1; 37. 8; 38. 1; 58. 4, &c.
DESTROYING,] as in De. 10. 10; 31. 29, &c.
24. KICK,] as in 36. 4; 78. 59, 67; 89. 38, &c.
Vulg. 'reckon as nothing.'
DESIRABLE,] as in 1 Sa. 9. 20; 2 Ch. 21. 20.
GIVEN CREDENCE,] as in v. 12, &c.
MURMUR,] as in Isa. 29. 24; De. 1. 27.
TENTS,] as in 15. 1; 19. 4; 27. 5; 52. 5, &c.
HEARKENED,] as in 6. 8; 10. 17; 28. 6, &c.
26. LIFTETH UP,] as in 16. 4; 24. 5; 25. 1.
TO FALL,] as in v. 27; Nu. 5. 22; 1 Sa. 18. 25.
WILDERNESS,] as in v. 9, &c.
27. SEED,] as in 18. 50; 21. 10; 22. 23, &c.
SCATTER,] as in Lev. 26. 33; Prov. 15. 7, &c.
28. COUPLED,] as in Nu. 25. 3, 5. Sept.
Vulg. 'initiated to.'
EAT,] as in 18. 8; 21. 9; 22. 26; 50. 3, &c.
SACRIFICE,] as in 4. 5; 27. 6; 40. 6; 50. 5.
DEAD,] as in 31. 12; 88. 5, 10; 115. 7, &c.
29. PROVOKE TO ANGER,] as in 78. 58; De.
32. 16; Jud. 2. 12; 1 K. 22. 53.
ACTIONS,] as in v. 39; 28. 4; 77. 11; 78. 7.
PLAGUE,] as in v. 30; Ex. 9. 14; Nu. 14. 37.
BREAKETH FORTH,] as in Ge. 30. 30, &c.
30. RESTRAINED,] as in Nu. 16. 48; 25. 8, &c.
31. RECKONED,] as in 44. 22; 88. 4, &c.
RIGHTEOUSNESS,] as in v. 3, &c.
GENERATIONS,] as in 10. 6; 12. 7; 14. 5, &c.
32. CAUSE WRATH,] as in Zec. 8. 14, &c.
EVIL,] as in Ge. 21. 11; 38. 10; De. 15. 10.
33. PROVOKED,] as in v. 7.
LIPS,] as in 12. 2, 3, 4; 16. 4, &c.
34. DESTROY,] as in v. 23, &c.
35. MIX THEMSELVES,] as in Prov. 14. 10.
LEARN,] as in 119. 71, 73; De. 4. 10; 14. 22.
36. SERVE,] as in 18. 34; 22. 30; 72. 11, &c.
IDOLS,] as in v. 38; 115. 4; 135. 15; 1 Sa.
31. 9, &c. Sept. Vulg. 'graven images.'
SNARE,] as in 18. 5; 64. 5; 69. 22; 140. 5, &c.
Sept. Vulg. 'stumbling-block.'
37. SACRIFICE,] as in 27. 6; 54. 6; 107. 22.
DESTROYERS,] as in De. 32. 17; Sept. Vulg.
'demons.'
SHED,] as in 42. 4; 142. 2; Ge. 37. 22, &c.
INNOCENT BLOOD,] as in 94. 21; 1 Sa. 19. 5.
PROFANED,] as in Jer. 3. 1, 9; Nu. 35. 33.
39. DEFILED,] as in Lev. 5. 3; 11. 24, 26, &c.
WORKS,] as in v. 13, &c.
HABITUAL DOINGS,] as in v. 29, &c.
40. ANGER,] as in 2. 5; 6. 1; 7. 6; 10. 4, &c.
KINDLED,] as in Ge. 4. 5; 18. 30; 30. 2, &c.
ABOMINATE,] as in 5. 6; 107. 18; 119. 163.
INHERITANCE,] as in v. 5, &c.

41. HATING,] as in v. 10, &c.
RULE,] as in 19. 3; 103. 19; Ge. 3. 16, &c.
42. ENEMIES,] as in v. 10, &c.
OPPRESS,] as in Ex. 22. 21; 23. 9; Nu. 22. 25.
HUMBLED,] as in Lev. 26. 41; Jud. 3. 30, &c.
43. DELIVER,] as in 18. 17; 22. 8; 34. 19, &c.
REBEL,] as in v. 7, &c.
COUNSEL,] as in v. 13, &c.
INIQUITY,] as in 18. 23; 25. 11; 31. 10, &c.
44. LOOKETH,] as in 8. 3; 22. 17; 35. 17, &c.
DISTRESS,] as in v. 11, &c.
CRY,] as in 17. 1; 30. 5; 42. 4; 47. 1, &c.
45. REMEMBERETH,] as in 8. 4; 20. 3, &c.
COVENANT,] as in 25. 10; 44. 17; 50. 5, &c.
COMFORTED,] as in 110. 4; Ge. 24. 67, &c.
ABUNDANCE,] as in v. 7, &c.
KINDNESS,] as in v. 1, &c.
46. APPOINTETH,] as in v. 15, &c.
MERCIES,] as in 25. 6; 40. 11; 51. 1; 77. 9, &c.
CAPTORS,] as in 137. 3; 1 K. 8. 46; 2 Ch. 6. 36.
47. OUR GOD,] as in 44. 20; 48. 1; 67. 6, &c.
GATHER,] as in 107. 3; De. 30. 3; 1 Ch. 16. 35.
HOLY NAME,] as in 33. 21; 103. 1; 145. 21, &c.
TO GLORY,] as in 1 Ch. 16. 35.
PRAISE,] as in v. 2, &c.
48. BLESSED,] as in 18. 46; 28. 6; 31. 21, &c.
AGE..AGE,] as in v. 1, 31, &c.
AMEN,] as in 41. 13; 72. 19; 89. 52, &c.
Sept. Vulg. repeat twice.
PRAISE JAH,] as in v. 1, &c. Here ends
the Fourth Division of the Book of Psalms.

CVII. 1. GIVE THANKS,] as in 105. 1, &c.
GOOD,] as in v. 9; 4. 6; 14. 1, 3; 16. 2, &c.
KINDNESS,] as in 8, 43; 5. 7; 6. 4, &c.
2. REDEEMED,] as in 74. 2; 77. 15; Ex. 6. 6.
ADVERSARY,] as in 6. 19; 27. 12; 32. 7, &c.
3. GATHERED,] as in De. 30. 3; Isa. 34. 16.
EAST,] as in 50. 1; 103. 12; 113. 3; Ex. 27. 13.
WEST,] as in 75. 6; 103. 12; 1 Ch. 7. 28, &c.
NORTH,] as in 48. 2; 89. 12; Ge. 13. 14, &c.
SEA,] or 'west,' as in v. 23; 8. 8; 24. 2, &c.
4. WILDERNESS,] as in v. 33, 35; 29. 8; 55.
7; 65. 12, &c. Vulg. 'solitude.'
DESERT,] as in 68. 7; 78. 40; 106. 14; Nu.
21. 20; Sept. Vulg. 'waterless place.'
WAY,] as in v. 7, 17, 40; 1. 1; 2. 12, &c.
CITY,] as in v. 7, 36; 9. 6; 31. 21; 46. 4, &c.
HABITATION,] as in v. 7, 32, 36, &c.
FOUND,] as in 69. 20; 76. 5; 84. 3; 89. 20, &c.
5. HUNGRY,] as in v. 9, 36; 146. 7; 1 Sa. 2. 5.
THIRSTY,] as in De. 29. 19; 2 Sa. 17. 29, &c.
FEEBLE,] as in 77. 3; 142. 3; 143. 4, &c.
CRY,] as in v. 28; 77. 1; 88. 1; Ge. 27. 34, &c.
ADVERSITY,] as in v. 2, &c.
DISTRESS,] as in v. 13, 19, 28; 25. 17; Job
15. 24; Zep. 1. 15.
DELIVERETH,] as in 18. 17; 22. 8; 34. 10, &c.
6. TO TREAD,] as in 25. 9; Isa. 42. 16; Jer.
9. 3; Hab. 3. 19, &c. Sept. Vulg. 'leadeth.
8. CONFESS,] as in 15, 21, 31, &c.
KINDNESS,] as in v. 1, 43, &c.
WONDERS,] as in v. 15, 21, 31; 40. 5; 71. 17.
SONS OF MEN,] as in v. 15, 21, 31; 8. 4, &c.
SATISFIED,] as in 81. 16; 91. 16; 105. 40, &c.
LONGING,] as in Prov. 28. 15; Isa. 29. 8; 33. 4.
HUNGRY,] as in v. 5, 36, &c.
FILLED,] as in 127. 5; 129. 7; Ex. 28. 3, &c.
10. INHABITANTS,] as in v. 34; 33. 8; 49. 1.
DARK PLACES,] as in v. 14; 18. 11; 35. 6, &c
DEATH-SHADE,] as in v. 14; 23. 4; 44. 19, &c.

PRISONERS,] as in 68. 6; 69. 13; 79. 11, &c.
AFFLICTION,] as in v. 41; 9. 13; 25. 18, &c.
IRON,] as in v. 16; 2. 9; 105. 18; 149. 8, &c.
11. CHANGED,] as in 78. 17; 106. 7, 33, 43,
&c. Sept. Vulg. 'embittered.'
SAYING,] as in 5. 1; 19. 4; 54. 2; 78. 1, &c.
COUNSEL,] as in 1. 1; 13. 2; 14. 6; 20. 4, &c.
MOST HIGH,] as in 7. 17; 9. 2; 18. 13; 21. 7.
DESPISED,] as in Prov. 1. 30; 5. 12; 15. 5.
12. HUMBLE,] as in 81. 14; 106. 42; De. 9. 3.
LABOUR,] as in 73. 16; 90. 10; 105. 44, &c.
FEEBLE,] as in 27. 2; 31. 10; 109. 24, &c.
HELPER,] as in 10. 14; 22. 11; 30. 10, &c.
13. CRY,] as in v. 6, 28, &c.
ADVERSITY,] as in v. 26, 19, &c.
DISTRESSES,] as in v. 6, 19, 28, &c.
SAVETH,] as in v. 19; 18. 27; 34. 18; 36. 6,
&c. Vulg. 'freeth.'
14. BRINGETH OUT,] as in v. 28; 18. 19, &c.
DARK PLACE,] as in v. 10, &c.
DEATH-SHADE,] as in v. 10, &c.
BANDS,] as in 2. 3; 116. 6; Job 39. 5, &c.
DRAWETH AWAY,] as in 2. 3; Jud. 16. 9, 12;
Jos. 8. 16, &c. Sept. Vulg. 'breaketh up.'
15. CONFESS,] as in v. 8, 21, 31, &c.
KINDNESS,] as in v. 1, 8, 43, &c.
WONDERS,] as in v. 8, 21, 31, &c.
16. BROKEN,] as in 3. 7; 74. 13; 76. 3, &c.
BARS OF IRON,] as in 2. 9; Isa. 45. 2; Job
40. 18.
CUT,] as in 75. 10; De. 7. 5; 12. 13; 2 Ch.
34. 4, 7, &c. Sept. Vulg. 'broken together.'
17. FOOLS,] as in 5. 2; Prov. 1. 7; 7. 22; 10.
8, &c. Sept. Vulg. 'he receiveth them.'
TRANSGRESSION,] as in 5. 10; 19. 13; 25. 7.
INIQUITIES,] as in 18. 23; 25. 11; 31. 10, &c.
AFFLICT THEMSELVES,] as in 1 K. 2. 26;
Ezra 8. 21; Da. 10. 12.
18. FOOD,] as in 78. 18, 30; 104. 21, 27, &c.
ABOMINATE,] as in 5. 6; 106. 40; 119. 163.
COME NIGH,] as in 32. 6; 88. 3; Ex. 4. 25.
GATES OF DEATH,] as in 9. 13; 107. 18; Job
38. 17.
19. CRY,] as in v. 6, 13, 28, &c.
ADVERSITY,] as in v. 2, 6, 13, &c.
DISTRESSES,] as in v. 6, 13, 28, &c.
SAVETH,] as in v. 13, &c.
20. SENDETH,] as in 18. 14; 20. 2; 57. 3, &c.
HEALETH,] as in 30. 2; 41. 4; 60. 2, &c.
DELIVERETH,] as in 33. 17; 41. 1; 89. 48.
DESTRUCTIONS,] as in La. 4. 20.
21. CONFESS,] as in v. 8, 15, 31, &c.
22. SACRIFICE,] as in 27. 6; 54. 6; 106. 37.
THANKSGIVING,] as in 26. 7; 42. 4; 50. 14.
RECOUNT,] as in 2. 7; 9. 1, 14; 22. 17, &c.
WORKS,] as in v. 24; 8. 3; 19. 1; 28. 4, &c.
SINGING,] as in 17. 1; 30. 5; 42. 4; 47. 1, &c.
23. GOING DOWN,] as in 22. 29; 28. 1; 30. 3.
SEA,] as in v. 3, &c.
SHIPS,] as in 48. 7; 104. 26; Ge. 49. 13, &c.
BUSINESS,] as in 73. 28; 1 Ch. 26. 29, &c.
MANY WATERS,] as in 29. 3; 32. 6; 77. 19.
24. SEEN,] as in 10. 11, 14; 31. 7; 33. 13, &c.
WORKS OF JEHOVAH,] as in v. 22, &c.
WONDERS,] as in v. 8, 15, 21, 31.
DEEP,] as in 68. 22; 69. 2, 15; Job 41. 31.
25. APPOINTETH,] lit. 'causeth to stand.'
TEMPEST,] as in 1. 4; 11. 6; 18, 10, 15, &c.
LIFTETH UP,] as in v. 32; 18. 48; 27. 5, &c.
BILLOWS,] as in v. 29; 148. 8; 2 K. 2. 1, &c.
26. GO UP,] as in 24. 3; 104. 8; 132. 3, &c.

GO DOWN,] as in 7. 16; 18. 9; 49. 17; 55. 15.
DEPTHS,] as in 33. 7; 36. 6; 42. 7; 71. 20, &c.
EVIL,] as in v. 34, 39; 5. 4; 7. 4; 7. 9, &c.
MELTED,] as in Nah. 1. 5; Am. 9. 13.
27. REEL TO AND FRO.] Original word not
found again in this sense.
MOVE,] as in 59. 15; 109. 10; Ex. 20. 18, &c.
DRUNKARD,] as in 1 Sa. 1. 13; 25. 36, &c.
WISDOM,] as in 37. 13; 51. 6; 90. 12; 104. 24.
SWALLOWED UP.] This form of the original
word not found elsewhere.
28. CRY,] as in v. 6, &c.
DISTRESSES,] as in v. 6, 13, 19, &c.
BRINGETH OUT,] as in v. 14, &c.
29. ESTABLISHETH,] as in 40. 2; 78. 5; 89. 43.
WHIRLWIND,] as in v. 25, &c.
CALM,] as in 1 K. 19. 12; Job 4. 16.
HUSHED,] as in 28. 1; Isa. 62. 1, 6; 84. 12.
BILLOWS,] as in v. 25; 42. 7; 65. 7; 89. 9.
30. REJOICE,] as in v. 42; 5. 11; 9. 2, &c.
QUIET,] as in Prov. 26. 30; Jon. 1. 11, 12.
LEADETH,] as in 23. 3; 31. 3; 43. 3; 61. 2.
HAVEN.] Original word not found again.
DESIRE,] as in 1. 2; 16. 3; 111. 2; 1 Sa. 15. 22.
31. CONFESS,] as in v. 8, 15, 21, &c.
32. EXALT,] as in v. 25, &c.
ASSEMBLY,] as in 22. 22; 26. 5; 35. 18, &c.
SEAT,] as in v. 4, 7, 32, &c. not 'assemble,'
as in C.V.
ELDERS,] as in 105. 22; 119. 100; 148. 12, &c.
PRAISE,] as in 22. 22, 26; 35. 18; 56. 4, &c.
33. RIVERS,] as in 24. 2; 46. 4; 66. 6; 72. 8.
WILDERNESS,] as in v. 4, 35, &c.
FOUNTAINS,] as in v. 35; 19. 6; 65. 8, &c.
DRY LAND,] as in De. 8. 15; Isa. 35. 7.
34. FRUITFUL,] as in v. 37; 1. 3; 21. 10, &c.
BARREN PLACE,] as in Job 39. 6; Jer. 17. 6.
WICKEDNESS,] as in v. 26, 39.
INHABITANTS,] as in v. 10, &c.
35. WILDERNESS,] as in v. 4, 33, &c.
POOL OF WATER,] as in 114. 8; Ex. 7. 19,
8. 5, &c.; not 'standing waters,' as in C.V.
DRY LAND,] as in 63. 1; 105. 41; Isa. 41. 18.
FOUNTAINS OF WATERS,] as in v. 33, &c.
36. HUNGRY,] as in v. 5, 9, &c.
TO DWELL,] as in 4. 8; 143. 3; 1 Sa. 12. 8.
PREPARE,] as in 7. 9, 12; 21. 12; 24. 2, &c.
CITY OF HABITATION,] as in v. 4, 7, &c.
37. SOW,] as in 126. 5; Ex. 23. 10, &c.
FIELDS,] as in 78. 12; 103. 15; 132. 6, &c.
PLANT,] as in 44. 2; 80. 2; Ge. 2. 8; 9. 20.
VINEYARDS,] as in Ge. 9. 20; Ex. 22. 5, &c.
INCREASE,] as in Ge. 47. 24; Ex. 23. 10, &c.
38. BLESSETH,] as in 5. 12; 16. 7; 26. 12, &c.
MULTIPLY,] as in 16. 4; 49. 16; 139. 18, &c.
CATTLE,] as in 8. 7; 36. 6; 49. 12; 50. 10, &c.
DIMINISH,] as in Ex. 30. 15; Lev. 25. 16, &c.
39. BOW DOWN,] as in 10. 10; Isa. 60. 14;
Job 38. 40.
RESTRAINT,] as in Prov. 30. 16; Isa. 53. 8.
EVIL,] as in v. 26, 34, &c.
SORROW,] as in 13. 2; 31. 10; 116. 3, &c.
40. POURING,] as in Ge. 9. 6; Nu. 35. 33, &c.
CONTEMPT,] as in 31. 18; 119. 22; 123. 3, &c.
NOBLES,] as in 47. 9; 51. 12; 83. 11; 113. 8,
&c. Sept. prefixes 'their.'
TO WANDER,] as in 2 K. 21. 9; 2 Ch. 33. 9.
VACANCY,] as in 2. 1; De. 32. 10, &c.
WAY,] as in v. 4, 7, 17, &c.
41. SETTETH ON HIGH,] as in 20. 1; 59. 1.
NEEDY,] as in 9. 18; 12. 5; 35. 10; 37. 14.

AFFLICTION,] as in v. 10, &c.
PLACETH,] as in v. 33, 35, &c.
FAMILIES,] as in 22. 27; 96. 7; Ge. 8. 19.
FLOCK,] as in 44. 11; 49. 14; 65. 13; 74. 1.
42. UPRIGHT,] as in v. 7, &c.
REJOICE,] as in v. 30, &c.
PERVERSITY,] as in 37. 1; 43. 1; 80. 22, &c.
SHUT,] as in 77. 9; Job 5. 16.
43. WISE,] as in 49. 10; Ge. 41. 8, 33, &c.
OBSERVETH,] as in 12. 7; 39. 1; 41. 2, &c.
KIND ACTS,] as in v. 1, 8, &c.

CVIII. SONG,] as in 28. 7; 33. 3; 40. 3, &c.
PSALM,] as in Ps. 3. 4. 5. 6. 8. &c.
1. PREPARED,] as in 5. 9; 38. 17; 51. 10, &c.
HEART,] as in 4. 7; 7. 10; 9. 1; 10. 6, &c.
Sept. Vulg. repeat twice, 'prepared is my
heart.'
GOD,] as in v. 5, 7, 11; 3. 2, &c.
SING,] as in 13. 6; 21. 13; 27. 6; 57. 7, &c.
SING PRAISE,] as in v. 3; 7. 17; 9. 2; 18. 49.
ALSO,] Sept. Vulg. 'in.'
HONOUR,] as in v. 5; 3. 8; 4. 2; 7. 5; 8. 5.
2. AWAKE,] as in 7. 6; 44. 23; 57. 8; 59. 4,
&c. Vulg. adds 'my glory, awake.'
PSALTERY,] as in 33. 2; 57. 8; 71. 22; 81. 2.
HARP,] as in 33. 2; 43. 4; 49. 4; 57. 8, &c.
I AWAKE,] as in 57. 8; 78. 38; De. 32. 11.
DAWN,] as in 57. 8; 139. 9; Ge. 19. 15, &c.;
not 'early,' as in C.V.
3. I THANK,] as in 6. 5; 7. 17; 9. 1; 18. 49.
PRAISE,] as in v. 1, &c.
4. GREAT,] as in 12. 3; 21. 5; 47. 2; 48. 1.
KINDNESS,] as in 5. 7; 6. 4; 13. 5; 17. 7, &c.
CLOUDS,] as in 18. 11; 36. 5; 57. 10; 68. 34.
TRUTH,] as in 15. 2; 19. 9; 25. 5, 10, &c.
5. EXALTED,] as in 7. 5, 11, 21, 13.
HONOUR,] as in v. 1, &c.
6. BELOVED ONES,] as in 60. 5; 127. 2; Isa.
5. 1; Jer. 11. 15.
DELIVERED,] as in 60. 5; Nu. 32. 17, 20;
Prov. 11. 9.
RIGHT HAND,] as in 16. 8; 17. 7; 18. 35, &c.
ANSWER,] as in 4. 1; 13. 3; 27. 7; 55. 2, &c.
US.] Sept. Vulg. 'me.'
7. HOLINESS,] as in 2. 6; 3. 4; 5. 7; 11. 4, &c.
I EXULT,] as in 28. 7; 60. 6; 94. 3; 96. 12.
I APPORTION,] as in 22. 18; 60. 6; 68. 12, &c.
VALLEY,] as in 60. 6; 65. 13; 84. 6; Ge. 14. 3.
SUCCOTH.] Sept. Vulg. 'tabernacles.'
MEASURE,] as in 60. 6; 2 Sa. 8. 2.
8. STRENGTH,] as in 27. 1; 28. 8; 31. 2, &c.
HEAD,] as in 3. 3; 7. 16; 18. 43; 21. 3, &c.
LAW-GIVER,] as in 60. 7; Ge. 49. 10; Nu.
21. 18; De. 33. 21, &c. Sept. Vulg. 'king.'
9. POT,] as in 58. 9; 60. 8; Ex. 16. 3; 27. 3.
WASHING,] as in 60. 8, &c. Sept. Vulg.
'hope.'
I CAST,] as in 2. 3; 50. 17; 51. 11; 60. 8, &c.
SHOE,] as in 60. 8; Ge. 14. 23; Ex. 3. 5, &c.
PHILISTIA.] Sept. Vulg. 'others.'
SHOUT HABITUALLY,] as in 60. 8; 65. 13.
10. BRING IN,] as in 60. 8; 68. 29; 76. 11, &c.
FENCED CITY,] as in 89. 40; Nu. 32. 17.
LED,] as in 60. 9; 77. 20; Ge. 24. 27, &c.
11. CAST OFF,] as in 43. 2; 44. 9; 60. 1, &c.
GOEST FORTH,] as in 17. 2; 41. 6; 44. 9, &c.
HOSTS,] as in 24. 10; 33. 6; 44. 9; 46. 7, &c
12. HELP,] as in 22. 19; 27. 9; 35. 2; 38. 22.
ADVERSITY,] as in v. 13; 3. 1; 4. 1; 13. 4.
VAIN,] as in 12. 2; 24. 4; 26. 4; 31. 6, &c.

13. MIGHTILY,] as in 18. 32, 38; 33. 16, &c.
TREAD DOWN,] as in 44. 5; 60. 12.

CIX. OVERSEER,] as in Ps. 4. 5. 6. 8. &c.
PSALM OF DAVID,] as in Ps. 3. 4. 5. 6. 8, &c.
1. GOD,] as in v. 26; 3. 2; 4. 1; 5. 2; 7. 1, &c
Sept. Vulg. 'O God, my praise.'
PRAISE,] as in 9. 14; 22. 3; 33. 1; 35. 28, &c.
SILENT,] as in 22. 18; 28. 1; 35. 22; 39. 12.
2. WICKEDNESS,] as in v. 6, 7: 1. 1; 3. 7, &c.
DECEIT,] as in 5. 6; 10. 7; 17. 1; 24. 4, &c.
OPENED,] as in 37. 14; 78. 23; 105. 41, &c.
FALSEHOOD,] as in 7. 14; 27. 12; 31. 18, &c.
HATRED,] as in v. 5; 25. 19; 139. 22, &c.
3. COMPASSED,] as in 17. 11; 18. 5; 22. 12, &c
FIGHT,] as in Ex. 14. 14; 17. 8; Nu. 21. 1.
WITHOUT CAUSE,] as in 35. 7, 19; 69. 4, &c.
4. LOVE,] as in v. 5; Ge. 29. 20; De. 7. 8.
OPPOSE,] as in 38. 20; Zec. 3. 1.
PRAYER,] as in v. '· that is, full of it.
5. SET,] as in 18. 48; 39. 8; 44. 13; 52. 7, &c.
EVIL,] as in v. 20; 5. 4; 7. 4; 10. 6; 15. 3.
6. APPOINT,] as in Nu. 1. 50; Jos. 10. 18.
WICKED,] as in v. 2, 7, &c.
ADVERSARY,] as in Nu. 22. 22; 1 Sa. 29. 4.
STANDETH,] as in v. 31; 10. 1; 33. 9, 11, &c.
RIGHT HAND,] as in v. 31; 16. 8, 11; 17. 7.
7. BEING JUDGED,] as in 37. 33; 2 Ch. 22. 8.
GOETH FORTH,] from the presence of the
judge, declared and proved to be
WICKED,] as in v. 2, 6, &c.
PRAYER,] as in v. 4, &c.
SIN,] as in 32. 1; 40. 6; Ge. 20. 9; Ex. 32. 21.
8. FEW,] as in 2. 12; 8. 5; 37. 10; 73. 2, &c.
OVERSIGHT,] as in 8. 6; 4. 16; 16. 29.
TAKETH,] or 'receiveth;' as in 6. 9; 18. 16.
9. FATHERLESS,] as in v. 12; 10. 14, 18, &c.
WIDOW,] as in 68. 5; 78. 64; 94. 6; 146. 9.
10. WANDER,] as in 59. 15; 107. 27, &c.
CONTINUALLY,] as in Jud. 9. 9, 11, 13, &c.
SOUGHT,] as in 34. 4; 77. 2; 78. 34; 119. 10,
&c. Sept. Vulg. 'cast.'
DRY PLACES,] as in 9. 6; 102. 6; Isa. 5. 17.
11. EXACTOR,] as in Ex. 22. 25; De. 24. 11.
LAYETH A SNARE,] as in 38. 12.
STRANGERS,] as in 44. 20; 54. 3; 81. 9, &c.
SPOIL,] as in Ge. 34. 27, 29; De. 20. 14, &c.
LABOUR,] as in 78. 46; 128. 2; Ge. 31. 42.
12. TO EXTEND,] as in Jud. 5. 14; Isa. 5. 18;
66. 19; Am. 9. 13.
KINDNESS,] as in v. 16, 21, 26, &c.
SHOWING FAVOUR,] as in 37. 21, 26; 112. 5.
ORPHANS,] as in v. 9, &c.
13. POSTERITY,] as in 37. 37, 38; 73. 17;
139. 9, &c. Sept. Vulg. 'children.'
CUTTING OFF,] as in 34. 16; 101. 8, &c.
GENERATION,] as in 10. 6; 12. 7; 14. 5, &c.
BLOTTED OUT,] as in v. 14; 69. 28; Ge. 7. 23.
14. INIQUITY,] as in 18. 23; 25. 11; 31. 10.
REMEMBERED,] as in 83. 4; Ex. 34. 19, &c.
SIN,] as in 25. 7, 18; 32. 5; 38. 3; 51. 2, &c.
BLOTTED OUT,] as in v. 13, &c.
15. CONTINUALLY,] as in v. 19; 16. 8; 25. 15.
CUTTETH OFF,] as in 34. 16; 101. 8, &c.
MEMORIAL,] as in v. 6; 30. 4; 34. 16.
KINDNESS,] as in v. 12, 21, 26, &c.
PURSUETH,] as in 18. 37; 23. 6; 83. 15, &c.
POOR MAN,] as in v. 22; 9. 12; 10. 2; 12. 5.
NEEDY,] as in v. 22, 31, &c.
17. LOVETH,] as in 4. 2; 119. 167; Ge. 24. 57
REVILING,] as in v. 18; Ge. 27. 12; De. 11. 26.

MEETETH HIM,] as in v. 18; 5. 7; 18. 6, &c.
DELIGHTED,] as in 18. 19; 22. 8; 40. 6, &c.
BLESSING,] as in 3. 8; 21. 3, 6; 24. 5, &c.
FAR,] as in 22. 11, 19; 35. 22; 38. 21, &c.
18. PUTTETH ON,] as in v. 29; 35. 26; 132. 9.
ROBE,] as in Lev. 6. 10; Jud. 3. 16; 5. 10.
MIDST,] as in v. 22; 5. 9; 36. 1; 39. 3, &c.
OIL,] as in v. 24; 23. 5; 45. 7; 55. 21, &c.
BONES,] as in 6. 2; 22. 14; 31. 10; 32. 3, &c.
19. APPAREL,] as in 22. 18; 45. 8; 102. 26.
COVERETH HIMSELF,] as in v. 29; 71. 13, &c.
CONTINUAL,] as in v. 15, &c.
GIRDLE,] as in Job 12. 21; Isa. 23. 10.
GIRDETH,] as in 65. 12; 76. 10; Lev. 8. 7, &c.
20. WAGE,] as in 17. 4; 28. 5; Lev. 19. 13;
2 Ch. 15. 7, &c. Sept. Vulg. 'work.'
ACCUSERS,] as in v. 29; 71. 13, &c.
SPEAKING EVIL,] as in 5. 6; 31. 18; 58. 3.
21. DEAL.] Sept. adds 'mercifully.'
NAME'S SAKE,] as in 23. 3; 25. 11; 31. 3, &c.
KINDNESS,] as in v. 12, 16, 26, &c.
DELIVER,] as in 7. 1; 22. 20; 25. 20; 31. 2.
22. POOR,] as in v. 16, &c.
NEEDY,] as in v. 16, &c.
HEART,] as in 51. 10, 17; 53. 1; 55. 4, &c.
PIERCED.] Sept. Vulg. 'troubled.'
MIDST,] as in v. 18, &c.
23. SHADOW,] as in 17. 8; 36. 7; 57. 1, &c.
STRETCHED OUT,] as in 17. 11; Ex. 7. 5, &c.
DRIVEN AWAY,] as in Jud. 16. 20; Job
38. 13.
LOCUST,] as in 78. 46; 105. 34; Ex. 10. 4, &c.
24. KNEES,] as in Ge. 30. 3; 48. 12; 50. 23.
FEEBLE,] as in 27. 2; 31. 10; 107. 12, &c.
FASTING,] as in 35. 13; 69. 10; 2 Sa. 12. 16.
FLESH,] as in 16. 9; 27. 2; 38. 3; 50. 13, &c.
FAILED.] Sept. Vulg. 'changed.'
FATNESS,] as in v. 18, &c.
25. REPROACH,] as in 15. 3; 22. 6; 31. 11, &c.
SHAKE THE HEAD,] as in 22. 7; Job 16. 4.
26. HELP,] as in 79. 9; 119. 86; Jos. 10. 4.
MY GOD,] as in 3. 7; 5. 2; 7. 1; 13. 3; 18. 21.
SAVE,] as in 3. 7; 6. 4; 7. 1; 12. 1, &c.
KINDNESS,] as in v. 12, 16, 21, &c.
27. HAND,] which hath done it.
28. REVILE,] as in 62. 4; Ex. 22. 28, &c.
BLESS,] as in 5. 12; 16. 7; 26. 12; 29. 11, &c.
RISEN,] as in 20. 8; 27. 12; 54. 3; 86. 14, &c.
Sept. Vulg. add 'against me.'
ASHAMED,] as in 6. 10; 25. 2, 3; 31. 1, &c.
SERVANT,] as in 19. 11, 13; 27. 9; 31. 16, &c.
REJOICE,] as in 5. 11; 9. 2; 14. 7; 21. 1, &c.
29. ACCUSERS,] as in v. 20, &c.
PUT ON,] as in v. 18, &c.
BLUSHING,] as in 4. 2; 35. 26; 44. 15, &c.
COVERED,] as in v. 19, &c.
UPPER ROBE,] as in Ex. 28. 4; 29. 5; 39. 22;
Lev. 8. 7, &c.
SHAME,] as in 35. 26; 40. 15; 44. 15; 69. 19.
30. THANK,] as in 6. 5; 7. 17; 9. 1; 18. 49.
MOUTH,] as in v. 2; 5. 9; 8. 2; 10. 7, &c.
MANY,] as in 3. 1, 2; 4. 6; 18. 16, &c.
PRAISE,] as in 22. 22, 26; 35. 18; 56. 4, &c.
31. STANDETH,] as in v. 6, &c.
RIGHT HAND,] as in v. 6, &c.
NEEDY,] as in v. 16, 22, &c.
TO SAVE,] as in 31. 2; 71. 3; 76. 9; De. 20. 4.
HIS SOUL.] Sept. Vulg. 'my soul.'

CX. PSALM OF DAVID,] as in Ps. 3. 4. 5. &c.
1. AFFIRMATION,] as in 36. 2. &c.

MY LORD,] a title of honour, never given
by a superior to an inferior.
SIT,] as in Ge. 20. 15; 22. 5; 27. 19; 29. 19.
RIGHT HAND,] as in 5; 16. 8, 11; 17. 7.
ENEMIES,] as in v. 2; 3. 7; 6. 10; 7. 5, &c.
FOOTSTOOL,] as in 99. 5; 132. 7; 1 Ch. 28.
2; Isa. 66. 1; Lam. 2. 1.
2. ROD,] as in 105. 16; Ge. 38. 18; Ex. 4. 2.
STRENGTH,] as in 8. 2; 21. 1, 13; 28. 7, &c.
RULE,] as in Ge. 1. 28, &c.
3. PEOPLE,] as in 3. 6, 8; 7. 8; 9. 11; 14. 4,
&c. Sept. Vulg. 'with thee is principality.'
FREE-WILL GIFTS,] as in 54. 6; 68. 9, &c.
HONOURS, as in 8. 5; 21. 5; 29. 4; 45. 3, &c.
HOLINESS,] as in 2. 6; 20. 2; 30. 4; 47. 8,
&c. Sept. Vulg. 'holy ones.'
WOMB,] as in 22. 10; 58. 3; Ge. 20. 18, &c.
DEW,] as in 133. 3; Ge. 27. 28; Ex. 16. 13,
14, &c. Sept. Vulg. omit.
YOUTH,] as in Ecc. 11. 9, 11. Sept. Vulg.
'from the morning I have begotten thee.'
4. SWORN,] as in 15. 4; 24. 4; 89. 3, 35, &c.
REPENT,] as in 106. 45; Ge. 6. 6; 24. 67, &c
PRIEST,] as in 78. 64; 99. 6; 132. 9, 16, &c.
ORDER,] as in Job 5. 8; Ecc. 3. 18; 7. 14, &c.
5. THE LORD,] as in 2. 4; 35. 17, 22, &c.
RIGHT HAND,] as in v. 1, &c.
SMOTE,] as in v. 6; Nu. 24. 17; De. 32. 39.
KINGS] as in 2. 2, 6; 5. 2; 10. 16, &c.
ANGER,] as in 2. 5, 12; 6. 1; 7. 6; 10. 4, &c.
6. JUDGE,] as in 7. 8; 9. 8. 54. 1; 72. 2, &c.
COMPLETED,] as in 10. 7; 26. 10; 33. 5, &c.
CARCASES,] as in Ge. 47. 18; Jud. 14. 8, &c.
SMITTEN.] as in v. 5, &c.
HEAD,] as in v. 7; 3. 3; 7. 16; 18. 43; 21. 3.
MIGHTY,] as in 3. 1, 2; 4. 6; 18. 16; 19. 10,
&c. Sept. Vulg. 'heads of many on the
earth.'
7. BROOK,] as in 18. 4; 36. 8; 74. 15; 78. 20.
DRINKETH,] as in 50. 13; 75. 8; 78. 44, &c.
LIFT UP THE HEAD] with hope and joy.

CXI. 1. PRAISE JAH,] as in Ps. 112. 113.
I THANK,] as in 6. 5; 7. 17; 9. 1; 18. 49, &c
Sept. Vulg. add 'thee.'
WHOLE HEART,] as in De. 4. 29; 10. 12; 13
3; Isa. 1. 5, &c. Sept. Vulg. add 'my.'
SECRET MEETING,] as in 89. 7; Jer. 6. 11.
UPRIGHT,] as in v 8; 7. 10; 11. 2; 7; 19. 8.
COMPANY,] as in 1. 5; 7. 7; 22. 16; 68. 30, &c.
2. GREAT,] as in 12. 3; 21. 5; 47. 2; 48. 1, &c.
WORKS OF JEHOVAH,] as in 92. 5; 107. 24.
SOUGHT OUT,] as in Isa. 62. 12.
DESIRING,] as in 1. 2; 16. 3; 107. 30, &c.
3. HONOURABLE,] as in 8. 1; 21. 5; 45. 3, &c.
MAJESTIC,] as in 8. 5; 21. 5; 29. 4; 45. 3, &c.
RIGHTEOUSNESS,] as in 5. 8; 11. 7; 22. 31.
STANDING,] as in v. 10; 19. 9; 112. 3, &c.
4. MEMORIAL,] as in 6. 5; 9. 6; 30. 4, &c.
WONDERS,] as in 40. 5; 71. 17; 72. 18, &c.
GRACIOUS,] as in 25; 103. 8; 116. 5, &c.
MERCIFUL,] as in 78. 38; 86. 15; 103. 8, &c.
5. PREY,] as in 14. 4; 124. 6; Ge. 49. 9, &c.
FEARING,] as in 15 4; 22. 23; 25. 12; 31. 19.
REMEMBERETH,] as in v. 9; 25. 10, 14; 44. 17, &c.
COVENANT,] as in v. 9; 25. 10, 14; 44. 17, &c.
6. POWER,] as in 22. 15; 29. 4; 31. 10, &c.
DECLARED,] as in 97. 6; Ge. 3. 11; 12. 18.
PEOPLE,] as in v. 3. 6; 7. 8; 9. 11; 14. 4.
INHERITANCE,] as in 2. 8; 28. 9; 33. 12, &c.
7. WORKS OF HIS HANDS,] as in 8. 3, 6, &c.

TRUE,] as in v. 8; 15. 2; 19. 9; 25. 5; 26 3.
JUST,] as in 9. 4; 10. 5; 18. 22; 19. 9; 25. 9.
STEDFAST,] as in 19. 7; 89. 28, 37; 101. 6.
APPOINTMENTS,] as in 19. 8; 103. 18; 119. 4.
8. SUSTAINED,] as in 112. 8; Isa. 26. 3.
TRUTH,] as in v. 7, &c.
UPRIGHTNESS,] as in v. 1, &c.
9. REDEMPTION,] as in 130. 7; Ex. 8. 23;
Isa. 50. 2.
APPOINTED,] as in 50. 19; 55. 20; 78. 25, &c.
COVENANT,] as in v. 5, &c.
HOLY,] as in 16. 3; 22. 3; 34. 9; 46. 4, &c.
FEARFUL,] as in 45. 4; 47. 2; 65. 5; 66. 3.
10. BEGINNING OF WISDOM,] as in Prov. 9. 10.
FEAR OF JEHOVAH,] as in 19. 9; 34. 11, &c.
UNDERSTANDING,] as in 1 Sa. 25. 3, &c.
DOING,] as in 14. 1, 3; 15. 5; 18. 50; 31. 23.
PRAISE,] as in 9. 14; 22. 3; 33. 1; 34. 1, &c.
STANDING,] as in v. 3, &c.

CXII. 1. PRAISE YE JAH,] as in Ps. 111.
113, &c. Vulg. adds 'on the return of
Haggai and Zechariah.'
HAPPINESS,] as in 32. 1, 2; 33. 12; 34. 8, &c.
FEARING,] as in 55. 19; 76. 8; 119. 63, &c.
COMMANDS,] as in 19. 8; 78. 7; 89. 31, &c.
DELIGHTED,] as in 18. 19; 22. 8; 40. 6, &c.
2. MIGHTY,] as in 19. 5; 24. 8; 33. 16.
SEED,] as in 18. 50; 21. 10; 22. 23; 25. 13.
GENERATION,] as in 10. 6; 12. 7; 14. 5, &c.
UPRIGHT,] as in v. 4; 7. 10; 11. 2, 7; 19. 8.
BLESSED,] as in 128. 4; Jud. 5. 24, &c.
3. WEALTH,] as in 44. 12; 119. 14; Prov. 1.
13; 3. 9, &c. Sept. Vulg. 'glory.'
RICHES,] as in 49. 6; 52. 7; Ge. 31. 16, &c.
RIGHTEOUSNESS,] as in v. 9; 5. 8; 11. 7, &c.
STANDING,] as in v. 9; 19. 9; 111. 3; 122. 2.
4. LIGHT,] as in 4. 6; 27. 1; 36. 9; 37. 6, &c.
RISEN,] as in Ex. 22. 3; De. 33. 2; 2 K. 3. 22.
DARKNESS,] as in 18. 11; 35. 6; 88. 12, &c.
UPRIGHT,] as in v. 2, &c.
GRACIOUS,] as in 86. 15; 103. 8; 111. 4, &c.
MERCIFUL,] as in 78. 38; 86. 15; 103. 8, &c.
RIGHTEOUS,] as in v. 6; 1. 5; 5. 12; 7. 9, &c.
5. LENDING,] as in 37. 26; Prov. 19. 17; 22.
7; Isa. 24. 2.
JUDGMENT,] as in 1. 5; 7. 6; 9. 4; 10. 5, &c.
6. MOVED,] as in 10. 6; 13. 4; 15. 5; 16. 8.
MEMORIAL,] as in 6. 5; 9. 6; 30. 4; 34. 16.
7. EVIL REPORT,] as in Isa. 37. 7; Jer. 49. 14.
AFRAID,] as in v. 8; 3. 6; 23. 4; 27. 1, &c.
PREPARED,] as in 5. 9; 38. 17; 51. 10, &c.
HEART,] as in v. 8; 4. 7; 7. 10; 9. 1, &c.
CONFIDENT,] as in Isa. 26. 3.
8. SUSTAINED,] as in 111. 8; Isa. 26. 3.
FEARETH,] as in v. 7, &c. Vulg. 'he is
not moved.'
LOOK,] as in v. 10; 8. 3; 22. 17; 35. 17, &c.
ADVERSARIES,] as in 3. 1; 4. 1; 13. 4, &c.
9. SCATTERED,] as in 53. 5; 89. 10, &c.
NEEDY,] as in 9. 18; 12. 5; 35. 10; 37. 14.
RIGHTEOUSNESS,] as in 5. 8; 11. 7; 22. 31.
STANDING,] as in v. 3, &c.
HORN,] as in 18. 2; 22. 21; 75. 4; 89. 17, &c.
EXALTED,] as in 13. 2; 18. 46; 27. 6; 46. 10.
HONOUR,] as in 3. 3; 4. 2; 7. 5; 8. 5, &c.
10. WICKED,] as in 1. 1; 3. 7; 7. 9; 9. 5, &c.
ANGRY,] as in 2 Ch. 16. 10; Ecc. 5. 17, &c.
TEETH,] as in 3. 7; 35. 16; 37. 12; 45. 8, &c.
GNASHETH,] as in Job 16. 9; Lam. 2. 16.
MELTED,] as in 22. 14; 97. 5; Ex. 16. 21, &c.

DESIRE,] as in 10. 3; 21. 2; 38. 9; 78. 29, &c
PERISH,] as in 1. 6; 2. 12; 9. 3, 18; 37. 20.

CXIII. 1. PRAISE YE JAH,] as in Ps. 111. 112.
SERVANTS OF JEHOVAH,] as in 27. 9; 31. 6.
NAME,] as in v. 2, 3; 5. 11; 7. 17; 8. 1, &c.
2. BLESSED,] as in 37. 22; Nu. 22. 6, &c.
HENCEFORTH,] as in Ge. 22. 12; 26. 22, &c.
3. RISING OF THE SUN,] as in 50. 1; 103. 12
GOING IN,] as in 50. 1; 104. 19; De. 11. 30.
4. HIGH,] as in 18. 27; 78. 69; 138. 6, &c.
HONOUR,] as in 3. 3; 4. 2; 7. 5; 8. 5, &c.
5. OUR GOD,] as in 18. 31; 20. 5, 7; 40. 3, &c.
EXALTING,] as in Prov. 17. 19. Sept. Vulg.
'who is dwelling in the high places.'
TO SET,] as in 27. 4; 33. 14; 68. 16; 101. 6.
6. HUMBLING,] as in 147. 6; 1 Sa. 2. 7.
Sept. Vulg. 'low things he beholdeth.'
TO LOOK,] as in 14. 2; 16. 10; 27. 13; 34. 12.
7. RAISING UP,] as in Ge. 9. 9; 1 Sa. 2. 8, &c.
DUST,] as in 7. 5; 18. 42; 22. 15; 30. 9; 44.
25, &c. Sept. Vulg. 'earth.'
POOR,] as in 41. 1; 72. 13; 82. 3, 4, &c.
DUNGHILL,] as in 1 Sa. 2. 8; Neh. 2 13, &c.
EXALTETH,] as in 66. 7; 75. 4; 89. 17, &c.
NEEDY,] as in 9. 18; 12. 5; 35. 10; 37. 14, &c.
8. TO CAUSE TO SIT,] as in 1 Sa. 2. 8; Neh.
13. 27.
PRINCES,] as in 1 Sa. 2. 8; Job 12. 21, &c.
9. BARREN ONE,] as in Ge. 11. 30; 25. 21, &c.
JOYFUL,] as in 35. 26; 126. 3; De. 16. 15, &c.
MOTHER,] as in 22. 9, 10; 27. 10; 35. 14, &c.
PRAISE YE JAH,] as in v. 1; but this clause
should commence Ps. 114.

CXIV. 1. GOING OUT,] as in 81. 6.
HOUSE OF JACOB,] as in Ge. 46. 27; Ex. 19. 3.
STRANGE,] or 'barbarian.' So Sept. Vulg.
2. SANCTUARY,] as in 2. 6; 11. 4; 24. 3, &c.
DOMINION,] as in 103.,22; 136. 8, 9; 145. 13.
3. SEA,] as in v. 5; 8. 8: 24. 2; 33. 7; 46. 2.
FLEETH,] as in v. 5; 68. 1; 104. 7; Ge. 14. 10.
TURNETH,] as in v. 5; 71. 21; Ge. 42. 24, &c.
BACKWARD,] as in v. 5; 9. 3; 35. 4; 40. 14.
4. MOUNTAINS,] as in v. 6; 50. 11; 65. 6, &c.
SKIPPED,] as in v. 6, &c. Vulg. 'exulted.'
RAMS,] as in v. 6; 66. 15; Ex. 25. 5; 26. 14.
HEIGHTS,] as in v. 6; 65. 12; 72. 3; 148. 9.
SONS OF A FLOCK,] as in v. 6, &c.
7. LORD,] as in 8. 1; 12. 4; 45. 11; 97. 5, &c.
AFRAID,] as in 96. 9; 1 Ch. 16. 30; Mic. 4.
10. Sept. Vulg. 'moved.'
GOD OF JACOB,] as in 46. 7; 81. 4; 94. 7.
8. ROCK,] as in 18. 2; 19. 14; 27. 5; 28. 1, &c.
POOL OF WATERS,] as in 107. 35; Isa. 14. 23.
FLINT,] as in De. 8. 15; 32. 13; Job 28. 9;
Isa. 50. 10.
FOUNTAIN OF WATERS,] as in Job 15. 9;
1 K. 18. 5; 2 K. 3. 19, 25, &c.

CXV. 1. JEHOVAH,] God of Israel.
NAME,] as in 5. 11; 7. 17; 8. 1; 9. 2, 5, &c.
HONOUR,] as in 3. 3; 4. 2; 7. 5; 8. 5, &c.
2. THEIR GOD,] as in Ex. 29. 46; Lev. 21. 6.
OUR GOD,] as in 18. 31; 20. 5; 40. 3; 44. 20.
PLEASED,] as in 18. 19; 22. 8; 40. 6; 41. 11.
&c. Sept. adds, 'on the earth.'
4. IDOLS,] as in 106. 36, 38; 135. 15; 1 Sa.
31. 9; 2 Sa. 5. 21, &c. Sept. Vulg. add 'of
the nations.
SILVER,] as in 12. 6; 15. 5; 66. 10; 68. 13

GOLD,] as in 19. 10; 45. 13; 72. 15; 105. 37.
WORKS OF MEN'S HANDS,] as in 135. 15; De.
4. 28; 2 K. 19. 18, &c.
5. MOUTH,] as in 5. 9; 8. 2; 10. 7; 17. 3, &c.
EYES,] as in 5. 5; 6. 7; 10. 8; 11. 4; 13. 3.
6. EARS,] as in 10. 7; 17. 6; 18. 6; 31. 2, &c.
NOSE,] as in 18. 15; Ge. 2. 7; 7. 22; 24. 47.
SMELL,] as in Ge. 8. 21; 27. 27; Lev. 26. 31.
HANDS,] as in v. 4; 8. 6; 10. 12; 17. 14, &c.
FEET,] as in 8. 6; 18. 9; 22. 16; 25. 15, &c.
WALK,] as in 55. 14; 81. 13; 85. 13; 86. 11.
8. MUTTER,] as in 35. 28; 37. 30; 71. 24, &c.
THROAT,] as in 5. 9; 69. 3; 149. 6; Isa. 51. 1.
MAKERS,] as in v. 15; 14. 1; 15. 5; 34. 16.
TRUSTING,] as in 21. 7; 27. 3; 32. 18; 49. 6.
9. ISRAEL.] Sept. Vulg. 'house of Israel
hath trusted.'
HELP,] as in v. 10, 11; 20. 2; 33. 20; 70. 5.
SHIELD,] as in v. 10, 11; 3. 3; 7. 10; 18. 2.
10. HOUSE OF AARON,] as in v. 12; 118. 3.
11. FEARING,] as in v. 15; 15. 4; 22. 23, &c.
12. REMEMBERED,] as in 9. 12; 63. 6; 78. 42.
BLESSETH,] as in v. 13, 18: 5. 12; 49. 18, &c.
HOUSE OF ISRAEL,] as in 98. 3; 135. 19, &c.
SMALL..GREAT,] as in 104. 25; De. 25. 13.
14. ADDETH,] as in 10. 18; 41. 8; 65. 1, &c.
15. MAKER,] as in v. 8, &c.
HEAVENS,] as in v. 3, 16; 2. 4; 8. 1; 11. 4.
EARTH,] as in v. 16; 2. 2; 7. 5; 8. 1; 10. 16.
SONS OF MEN,] as in 11. 4; 12. 1; 14. 2, &c.
17. DEAD,] as in 31. 12; 88. 5, 10; 106. 28.
PRAISE,] as in 22. 22; 35. 18; 56. 4; 63. 5,
&c. Sept. Vulg. add 'thee.'
GOING DOWN,] as in 22. 29; 28. 1; 30. 3, &c.
SILENCE,] as in 94. 17. Sept. 'hades;' Vulg.
'infernum.'
18. WE.] Sept. Vulg. add 'the living.'
PRAISE YE JAH.] This should commence
Ps. 116.

CXVI. 1. LOVED,] as in 26. 8; 119. 47, &c.
HEARETH,] as in 4. 3; 5. 3; 18. 6; 34. 2, &c.
VOICE,] as in 3. 4; 5. 2; 6. 8; 18. 6, &c.
SUPPLICATION,] as in 28. 2; 31. 22; 130. 2.
2. INCLINED HIS EAR,] as in 45. 10; 49. 4.
CALL,] as in v. 4, 13, 17; 3. 4; 18. 3; 22. 2,
&c. Sept. adds 'upon him.'
3. CORDS OF DEATH,] as in 18. 4. Sept.
Vulg. 'pains or sorrows.'
STRAITS,] as in 118. 5; Lam. 1. 3.
DISTRESS,] as in 9. 9; 10. 1; 20. 1; 22. 11.
SORROW,] as in 13. 2; 31. 10; 107. 39, &c.
4. NAME,] as in v. 13, 17; 5. 11; 7. 17, &c.
PRAY THEE,] as in 118. 25; Ge. 50. 17; Ex.
32. 31, &c. Sept. Vulg. omit.
DELIVER,] as in 1 K. 1. 12: Job 6. 23; Jer.
48. 6; 51. 6, 45.
5. GRACIOUS,] as in 86. 15; 103, 8; 111. 4.
RIGHTEOUS,] as in 1. 5; 5. 12; 7. 9; 11. 3.
MERCIFUL,] as in Isa. 49. 10; 54. 10.
6. PRESERVER,] as in 31. 6; 34. 20; 71. 10.
SIMPLE,] as in 19. 7; 119. 130; Prov. 1. 4.
LOW,] as in 79. 8; 142. 6; Job 28. 4, &c.
GIVETH SALVATION,] as in 18. 27; 34. 18;
36. 6; 37. 49, &c. Vulg. 'freed.'
7. TURN BACK,] as in 6. 4; 7. 7; 80. 14, &c.
REST,] as in Ge. 8. 9; De. 28. 65; Ru. 3. 1.
CONFERRED BENEFITS,] as in 7. 4; 13. 6, &c.
8. DELIVERED,] as in 7. 4; 18. 19; 34. 7, &c.
DEATH,] as in v. 3, 15; 6. 5; 7. 13; 9. 13, &c.
EYES,] as in v. 15; 5. 5; 6. 7; 10. 8, &c.

TEARS,] as in 6. 6; 39. 12; 42. 3; 56. 8, &c.
FEET,] as in 8. 6; 9. 15; 18. 9; 22. 16, &c.
OVERTHROWING,] as in 56. 13.
9. WALK HABITUALLY,] as in 12. 8; 39. 6;
43. 2; 58. 7, &c. Sept. Vulg. 'I am well-
pleasing.'
LANDS OF THE LIVING,] as in 52. 5; 142. 5.
10. BELIEVED,] as in 27. 13; 78. 22; 106. 24;
119. 66, &c. Sept. Vulg. make this verse
begin a new Psalm, prefixing 'Praise ye Jah.'
SPEAK,] as in 2. 5; 12. 2; 35. 20; 37. 30, &c.
AFFLICTED,] as in 119. 67.
11. HASTE,] as in 2. 5; 12. 2; 20. 3; 2 Sa. 4.
4; 2 K. 7. 15, &c. Sept. 'extacy;' Vulg. 'excess.'
LIAR,] or 'deceiver.'
12. RETURN,] as in 18. 20; 44. 10; 54. 5, &c.
BENEFITS.]Original word not found again.
13. CUP,] as in 11. 6; 16. 5; 23. 5, &c.
LIFT UP,] as in 16. 4; 24. 5; 25. 1; 50. 16, &c.
CALL,] as in v. 2, 4, 17, &c.
14. VOWS,] as in v. 18; 22. 25; 50. 14; 56. 12.
COMPLETE,] as in v. 18; 22. 25; 35. 12, &c.
PEOPLE,] as in v. 18; 3. 6; 7. 8; 9. 11, &c.
15. PRECIOUS,] as in 36. 7; 37. 20; 45. 9, &c.
THE DEATH,] of the sacrifice for sin.
FOR HIS SAINTS,] as in 4. 3; 31. 23; 37. 28.
16. CAUSE TO COME,] as in Ex. 21. 13, &c.
Sept. Vulg. omit.
SERVANT,] as in 19. 11; 27. 9; 31. 16, &c.
HAND-MAID,] as in 86. 16; Ge. 20. 17, &c.
OPENED,] as in 38. 13; 39. 9; 49. 4; 51. 15,
&c. Sept. Vulg. 'broken up.'
BONDS,] as in 2. 3; 107. 14; Job 39. 5, &c.
17. I SACRIFICE,] as in 27. 6; 54. 6; 106. 37.
THANKS,] as in 26. 7; 42. 4; 50. 14; 56. 12.
CALL,] as in v. 2, 4, 13, &c.
18. VOWS,] as in v. 14, &c.
19. COURTS OF THE HOUSE,] as in 135. 2.
1 Ch. 29. 16; 33. 5; Neh. 8. 16, &c.
PRAISE YE JAH,] See note on Ps. 113.

CXVII. 1. PRAISE,] as in v. 2; 22. 23, &c.
NATIONS,] as in 2. 1; 9. 5; 10. 16; 18. 43, &c.
GLORIFY,] as in 147. 12; 63. 3; 89. 9, &c.
PEOPLES,] as in Ge. 25. 16; Nu. 25. 15.
2. MIGHTY,] as in 65. 3; 103. 11; Ge. 7. 19.
KINDNESS,] as in 5. 7; 6. 4; 13. 5; 17. 7, &c.
TRUTH,] as in 15. 2; 19. 9; 25. 5; 26. 3, &c.
PRAISE YE JAH,] See note on Ps. 113.

CXVIII. 1. GIVE THANKS,] as in 30. 4, &c.
GOOD,] as in v. 8, 20.
KINDNESS,] as in v. 2, 3, 4, 29, &c.
2 ISRAEL,] Sept. 'the house of Israel.'
3. HOUSE OF AARON.] as in 115. 10, 12, &c.
4. FEARING,] as in 15. 4; 22. 23; 25. 12, &c.
5. STRAITNESS,] as in 116. 3; Lam. 1. 3.
CALLED,] as in 14. 4; 17. 6; 31. 17; 34. 6, &c.
ANSWERED,] as in v. 21; 18. 41; 22. 21, &c.
BROAD PLACE,] as in 18. 19; 31. 8; 2 Sa. 22. 20.
6. FEAR,] as in 3. 6; 23. 4; 33. 8; 40. 3, &c.
7. HELPERS,] as in 10. 14; 22. 11; 30. 10.
LOOK,] as in 8. 3; 22. 17; 35. 17; 36. 9, &c.
HATING,] as in 9. 13; 18. 17; 21. 8; 34. 21.
8. TAKE REFUGE,] as in Ruth 2. 12; Isa
30. 2.
TRUST,] as in v. 9; Isa. 59. 4; Jer. 48. 7, &c
PRINCES,] as in 47. 9; 83. 11; 107. 40, &c.
10. COMPASSED ABOUT,] as in v. 11, 12, &c
CUT OFF,] as in v. 11, 12, &c.

12. BEES,] as in De. 1. 44; Jud. 14. 8, &c.
EXTINGUISHED,] Sept. 'they burst into flame.'
13. THRUST,] as in 140, 4, &c.
HELPED,] as in 86. 17; 119. 157; Jos. 1. 14.
14. STRENGTH,] as in 8. 2; 21. 1; 28. 7, &c.
SONG,] as in Ex. 15. 2; Isa. 12. 2.
SALVATION,] as in v. 15, 21; 3. 8; 9. 14, &c.
15. SINGING,] as in 17. 1; 30. 5; 42. 4; 47. 1; 61. 1, &c. Sept. 'gladness;' Vulg. 'exaltation.'
TENTS,] as in 15. 1; 19. 4; 27. 5; 52. 5, &c.
RIGHTEOUS,] as in v. 20; 1. 5; 5. 12; 7. 9.
RIGHT HAND,] as in v. 16; 16. 8; 17. 7, &c.
VALIANTLY,] as in v. 16; 18. 32; 33. 16, &c.
16. EXALTED.] Sept. 'exalted me.' So Vulg.
17. DIE,] as in 41, 5; 49. 10; 82. 7; Ge. 2. 17.
LIVE,] as in 22. 26; 49. 9; 69. 32. 72. 15, &c.
RECOUNT,] as in 2. 7; 9. 1; 22. 17; 48. 13, &c.
WORKS OF JAH,] as in 107. 24; 138. 8, &c.
18. CHASTENED,] as in 16. 7; 39. 11, &c.
DEATH,] as in 6. 5; 7. 13; 9. 13; 13. 3, &c.
19. OPEN,] as in Jos. 10. 22; 2 K. 13. 17, &c.
GATES OF RIGHTEOUSNESS,] as in Prov. 14. 19.
THANK,] as in v. 21, 28; 6. 5; 7. 17; 9. 1, &c.
20. GATE,] as in 9. 13; 24. 7; 69. 12; 87. 2.
RIGHTEOUS,] as in v. 15, &c.
21. ANSWERED,] as in v. 5, &c.
SALVATION,] as in v. 14, &c.
22. STONE,] as in 91. 12; 102. 14; Ge. 2. 12.
BUILDERS,] as in 127. 1; 147. 2; 1 K. 5. 18.
REFUSED,] as in 53. 5; Lev. 26. 43, 44; Nu. 11. 20, &c. Vulg. 'reprobated.'
HEAD,] as in 3. 3; 7. 16; 18. 43; 21. 3, &c.
CORNER,] as in Ex. 27. 2; 38. 2; Jud. 20. 2.
23. WONDERFUL,] as in 2 Sa. 1. 26, &c.
24. MADE,] as in 7. 3; 9. 4; 15. 3; 22. 31, &c.
REJOICE,] as in 9. 14; 13. 4; 14. 7; 16. 9, &c.
GLAD,] as in 5. 11; 9. 2; 14. 7; 21. 1, &c.
25. BESEECH,] as in 116. 4, 16; Ge. 50. 17.
SAVE,] as in 3. 7; 6. 4, 7. 1; 12. 1, &c. Vulg. adds 'me.'
PROSPER,] as in 1 K. 22. 12, 15; 2 Ch. 18. 11.
26. BLESSED,] as in 18. 46; 28. 6; 31. 21, &c.
COMING,] as in Ge. 7. 16; 18. 11; 23. 10.
NAME,] as in v. 10, 11, 12, &c.
HOUSE OF JEHOVAH,] as in 27. 4; 55. 14; 116. 19; 135. 2, &c.
27. GOD,] as in v. 28; 5. 4; 7. 11; 10. 11, &c.
LIGHT,] as in 18. 28; 67. 1; 119. 130; 139. 12.
DIRECT,] as in 1 K. 18. 44; 2 K. 9. 21; Jer. 46. 4, &c. Sept. Vulg. 'celebrate.'
FESTAL-SACRIFICE,] as in 81. 2; Ex. 10. 9; 12. 14; 13. 6, &c. Vulg. 'day of solemnity.'
CORDS,] as in 2. 3; 129. 4; Ex. 28. 14, &c.
HORNS OF THE ALTAR,] as in Ex. 29. 12, &c.
28. MY GOD,] as in 22. 1; 63. 1; 89. 26, &c.
EXALT,] as in 18. 48; 27. 5; 30. 1; 34. 3, &c.
Sept. Vulg. add, 'I confess thee, because thou hast heard me, and art become to me for salvation.'
29. GIVE THANKS,] as in v. 19, 21, &c.
GOOD,] as in v. 1, 8, &c.
KINDNESS,] as in v. 1, 2, 3, 4, &c.

CXIX. Each of the 22 parts of this Psalm commences with a separate letter of the Hebrew alphabet. Sept. Vulg. prefix 'Praise ye Jah.'

1. HAPPINESS,] as in v. 2; 1. 1; 2. 12; 32. 1.
PERFECT,] as in v. 80; 15. 2; 18. 23; 19. 7, &c. Sept. Vulg. 'blameless.'
WAY,] as in v. 3, 5, 14, 26, 27, 29, 30, &c.
WALKING,] as in 15. 2; 78. 39; 84. 11, &c.
LAW,] as in v. 18, 29, 34, 44, &c.
JEHOVAH,] the 'Existing' one, the national covenant God of Israel.
2. KEEPING,] as in 25. 10; 31. 23; Ex. 34. 7; 2 K. 17. 9, &c. Sept. Vulg. 'searching out.'
TESTIMONIES,] as in v. 22, 24, 46, 59, &c.
WHOLE HEART,] as in v. 10, 34, 58, 69, &c.
SEEK,] as in 10. 4, 13, 15; Ge. 9. 5; De. 4. 29.
3. INIQUITY,] as in 37, 1; 43. 1; 89. 22, &c.
WALKED,] as in 1. 1; 26. 1; 105. 41; Ge. 19. 9.
4. COMMANDED,] as in v. 138; 7. 6; 33. 9, &c.
PRECEPTS,] as in v. 15, 27, 40, 45, 56, &c.
DILIGENTLY,] as in v. 8, 43, 51, 96, 107, &c.
5. PREPARED,] as in 89. 21; 93. 1; 96. 10, &c.
STATUTES,] as in v. 8, 12, 23, 33, &c.
6. ASHAMED,] as in v. 46, 78, 80; 6. 10.
COMMANDS,] as in v. 10, 19, 21, 32, 35, &c.
7. UPRIGHTNESS OF HEART,] as in De. 9. 5; 1 K. 9. 4; 1 Ch. 29. 17, &c.
LEARNING,] as in Jer. 12. 16.
JUDGMENTS,] as in v. 13, 20, 30, 39, &c.
RIGHTEOUSNESS,] as in v. 62, 75, 106, &c.
8. STATUTES,] as in v. 5, 12, 23, 33, &c.
KEEP,] as in v. 17, 34, 44, 55, 88, 101, &c.
LEAVE,] as in 10. 4; 16. 10; 27. 9; 37. 28, &c.
UTTERLY,] as in v. 43, 51, 96, 107, 138, &c.
9. YOUNG MAN,] as in 37. 25; 148. 12, &c.
PURIFY,] as in 73. 13; Prov. 20. 9. Sept. 'direct;' Vulg. 'correct.'
PATH,] as in v. 15, 101, 104, 128, &c.
OBSERVE,] as in v. 4, 5, 57, 60, 106, &c. Sept. Vulg. 'in the keeping of thy words.'
WORD,] as in v. 16, 17, 25, 28, 42, 43, 49, &c.
10. ALL MY HEART,] as in v. 2, &c.
SOUGHT,] as in v. 45, 94, 155; 34. 4; 109. 10.
ERR,] as in De. 27. 18; Job 12. 16; Prov. 28. 10. Sept. Vulg. 'cast me not away from thy commands.'
COMMANDS,] as in v. 6, 19, 21, 32, 35, &c.
11. HID,] as in 31. 19; 56. 6; Job 10. 13, &c.
SAYING,] as in v. 38, 41, 50, 58, 67, &c.
SIN,] as in 4. 4; 41. 4; 51. 4; 78. 32, &c.
12. BLESSED,] as in 18. 46; 28. 6; 31. 21, &c.
TEACH,] as in v. 26, 64, 68, 124, &c.
STATUTES,] as in v. 5, 8, 26, 33, 48, 54, &c.
13. LIPS,] as in v. 171; 12. 2; 16. 4; 17. 1.
RECOUNTED,] as in v. 26; 44. 1; 75. 1; 78. 3.
MOUTH,] as in v. 43, 72, 88, 103, &c.
14. JOYFUL,] as in v. 162; 12. 94. 6; 146. 9.
WEALTH,] as in 44. 12; 112. 3; Prov. 1. 13.
15. PRECEPTS,] as in v. 4, &c.
MEDITATE,] as in v. 23, 27, 48, 78, &c.
BEHOLD ATTENTIVELY,] as in v. 18; 10. 14; 22. 17; 91. 8, &c.
16. DELIGHT MYSELF,] as in v. 47, &c. Sept. Vulg. 'meditate.'
FORGET,] as in v. 93; 10. 12; 13. 1; 44. 24.
17. SERVANT,] as in v. 23, 38, 49, 65, 76, &c.
I LIVE,] as in v. 77, 116, 144, 175, &c.
18. UNCOVER,] as in v. 37, 82, 123, 136, 148, &c.
EYES,] as in v. 37, 82, 123, 136, 148, &c.
WONDERS,] as in v. 27; 9. 1; 26. 7; 40. 5, &c.
19. SOJOURNER,] as in 39. 12; 94. 6; 146. 9.
EARTH,] as in v. 64, 87, 90; 2. 2; 7. 5, &c.
HIDE,] as in 13. 1; 17. 8; 27. 5; 31. 20, &c.
20. BROKEN.] Sept. Vulg. 'desired.'

AT ALL TIMES,] as in 34. 1; 62. 8; 106. 3, &c.
21. REBUKED,] as in 9. 5; Isa. 17. 13; Jer.
29. 27; Mal. 3. 11.
CURSED,] as in Ge. 3. 14; 4. 11; 9. 25; 27.
29, &c. Sept. Vulg. 'proud, cursed me.'
PROUD,] as in v. 51, 69, 78, 85, 122, &c.
22. REMOVE,] as in v. 18, &c.
REPROACH,] as in v. 39; 15. 3; 22. 6; 31. 11.
CONTEMPT,] as in 31. 18; 107. 40; 123. 3, &c.
KEPT.] Sept. Vulg. 'sought out.'
23. PRINCES,] as in v. 161; 45. 16; 68. 27, &c.
SAT,] as in 1. 1; 9. 4; 23. 6; 26. 4, &c.
SPAKE,] as in Mal. 3. 13, 16.
24. DELIGHT,] as in v. 77, 92, 143, 174, &c.
Sept. Vulg. 'meditation.'
MEN OF MY COUNSEL.] Sept. Vulg. 'and my
counsel are thy righteous acts.'
25. CLEAVED,] as in v. 31; 44. 25; 63. 8, &c.
DUST,] as in 7. 5; 18. 42; 22. 15; 30. 9, &c.
QUICKEN,] as in v. 37, 40, 88, 107, 149, &c.
26. RECOUNTED,] as in v. 13, &c.
ANSWEREST,] as in v. 42, 172; 3. 4; 17. 6.
27. CAUSE TO UNDERSTAND,] as in v. 34.
73, 125, 144, 169, &c.
28. DROPPED,] as in Job 16. 20; Ecc. 10. 18.
Sept. Vulg. 'slumbered.'
AFFLICTION,] as in Prov. 10. 1; 14. 13; 17. 21;
ACCORDING TO.] Sept. Vulg. 'with thy
words.'
29. FALSEHOOD,] as in v. 69, 78, 86, 104, &c.
Sept. Vulg. 'unrighteousness.'
TURN ASIDE,] as in 39. 10; Ge. 35. 2, &c.
FAVOUR,] as in v. 58, 132; 4. 1; 25, 16, &c.
30. FAITHFULNESS,] as in v. 75, 86, 90, &c.
CHOSEN,] as in v. 173; 33. 12; 78. 67; 84. 10.
COMPARED,] as in 16. 8; 89. 19; 131. 2; Isa.
28. 25, &c. Sept. Vulg. 'not forgotten.'
31. ADHERED,] as in v. 25, &c.
PUT TO SHAME,] as in v. 116; 14. 6; 44. 7.
32. RUN,] as in 18. 29; 59. 4; 147. 15, &c.
ENLARGE,] as in 18. 36; 35. 21; De. 12. 20.
33. SHOW,] as in 27. 11; 86. 11; Job 6. 24;
34. 32.
END,] as in v. 112; 19. 11; 40. 15; 70. 3, &c.
34. CAUSE TO UNDERSTAND,] as in v. 27, &c.
KEEP.] Sept. Vulg. 'search out.'
35. TO TREAD,] as in 25. 5, &c.
DELIGHTED,] as in 18. 19; 22. 8; 40. 6, &c.
36. INCLINE,] as in 17. 6; 31. 2; 45. 10, &c.
DISHONEST GAIN,] as in 30. 9; Ex. 18. 21.
37. REMOVE,] as in v. 39; 2 Sa. 14. 19, &c.
VANITY,] as in 12. 2; 24. 4; 26. 4; 31. 6, &c.
38. ESTABLISH,] as in 41. 10, &c.
SAYING,] as in v. 11; Ge. 38. 8; 2 Sa. 7. 25.
FEAR,] as in 2. 11; 5. 7; 19. 9; 34. 11; 55. 5.
39. REMOVE,] as in v. 37, &c.
FEARED,] as in De. 9. 19; 28. 60; Job 3. 25.
GOOD,] as in v. 65, 68, 71, 72, 122, &c.
40. LONGED,] as in v. 174, &c.
RIGHTEOUSNESS,] as in v. 142; 5. 8; 11. 7.
41. MEET,] as in v. 77, 170; 5. 7; 18. 6, &c.
KINDNESS,] as in v. 64, 76, 88, 124, 149, &c.
SALVATION,] as in v. 81; 33. 17; 37. 39, &c.
42. ANSWER,] as in v. 26, &c.
REPROACHING,] as in 69. 9; Prov. 27. 11.
TRUSTED,] as in 13. 5; 22. 4; 25. 2; 26. 1, &c.
WORD.] Sept. Vulg. 'words.'
43. TAKEST AWAY,] as in 18. 17; 22. 8, &c.
WORD OF TRUTH,] as in v. 160; 2 Sa. 7. 28.
HOPED,] as in v. 49, 74, 81, 147, &c.
44. CONTINUALLY,] as in v. 109, 117; 16. 8

EVER,] as in v. 52, 89, 93, 98, &c.
45. WALK HABITUALLY,] as in 12. 8; 39. 6.
BROAD PLACE,] as in v. 96; 101. 5; 104. 25.
SOUGHT,] as in v. 10, 94, 155.
46. KINGS,] as in 2. 2; 72. 10, 11; 102. 15.
ASHAMED,] as in v. 6, 78, 80, &c.
47. DELIGHT MYSELF,] as in v. 16, &c.
Sept. Vulg. 'meditate.'
LOVED,] as in v. 48, 97, 113, 119, 127, &c.
Sept. adds 'greatly.'
48. LIFT UP HANDS,] as in 106.26; Lev. 9. 22
49. REMEMBER,] as in 25. 6; 74. 2; 89. 47.
THE WORD.] Sept. Vulg. 'thy word.'
TO HOPE,] as in v. 43, &c.
50. COMFORT,] as in Job 6. 10.
AFFLICTION,] as in v. 92, 153; 9. 13; 25. 18.
51. PROUD,] as in v. 21, &c.
SCORNED,] as in Prov. 3. 34; 14. 9; 19. 28.
Sept. Vulg. 'transgressed greatly.'
TURNED ASIDE,] as in v. 112, 157; 21. 11, &c.
52. OF OLD,] as in v. 44, &c.
COMFORT MYSELF,] as in 135. 14; Nu. 23. 19.
53. HORROR,] as in 11. 6; Lam. 5. 10.
SEIZED,] as in 48. 6; 73. 23; 77. 4; Ex. 15. 14.
WICKED.] as in v. 61, 95, 110, 119, 155, &c.
FORSAKING,] as in Ezr. 8. 22; Prov. 2. 13;
10. 17; 15. 10, &c.
54. SONGS,] as in 95. 2; 2 Sa. 23. 1; Job 35.
10; Isa. 24. 16; 25. 5.
SOJOURNINGS,] as in 55. 15; Ge. 17. 8, &c.
55. NIGHT,] as in v. 62; 1. 2; 6. 6; 16. 7, &c.
NAME,] as in v. 132; 5. 11; 7. 17; 8. 1; 9. 2.
56. PRECEPTS,] as in v. 4, 15, 27, 35.
KEPT.] Sept. Vulg. 'sought out.'
57. PORTION,] as in 16. 5; 17. 14; 50. 18; 73.
26, &c. Sept. adds, 'thou art, O Lord.'
WORDS.] Sept. Vulg. 'law.'
58. APPEASED THY FACE,] as in 45. 12; De.
29. 22; 1 Sa. 13. 12, &c.
WHOLE HEART,] as in v. 2, &c.
59. RECKONED,] as in 73. 16; 77. 5; 144. 3.
MY WAYS.] Sept. 'thy ways.'
TURN BACK,] as in 18. 20, 24; 44. 10; 54. 5.
FEET,] as in v. 101, 105; 8. 6; 9. 15; 18. 9.
60. MADE HASTE.] Sept. Vulg. 'prepared
myself.'
DELAYED,] as in Ge. 19. 16; 43. 10; Jud. 19.
8, &c. Sept. Vulg. 'troubled.'
61. CORDS,] as in 16. 10; 18. 4, 5; 78. 55, &c.
62. MIDNIGHT,] as in v. 55, &c.
TO GIVE THANKS,] as in 92. 1; 106. 47, &c.
63. COMPANION,] as in 45. 7; Jud. 20. 11, &c.
FEAR,] as in v. 120; 55. 19; 76. 8; 112. 1, &c.
64. EARTH,] or 'land;' as in v. 19, &c.
FULL,] as in 10. 7; 26. 10; 33. 5; 38. 7, &c.
65. GOOD,] as in v. 68, &c.
GOODNESS,] as in 25. 7; 27. 13; 31. 19, &c.
REASON,] as in Ex. 16. 31; Nu. 11. 8, &c.
KNOWLEDGE,] as in 19. 2; 94. 10; 139. 6, &c.
BELIEVED,] as in 27. 13; 78. 22; 106. 24, &c.
67. AFFLICTED,] as in 116. 10; Isa. 31. 4;
Zec. 10. 2.
ERRING,] as in Nu. 15. 28; Job 12. 16.
68. DOING GOOD,] as in Prov. 30. 29; Eze.
33. 32. Sept. 'O Lord, in thy goodness.'
69. FORGED,] as in Job 14. 17; Sept. Vulg.
'multiplied.'
WHOLE HEART,] as in v. 2, &c.
70. INSENSIATE.] Sept. Vulg. 'curdled.'
FAT,] as in 17. 10; 63. 5; 73. 10; 81. 16; 147.
14, &c. Sept. Vulg. 'milk.'

DELIGHTED,] as in Isa. 11. 8.   Sept. Vulg. 'meditated.'
71. GOOD,] as in v. 39, &c.
AFFLICTED.] Sept. Vulg. 'thou hast afflicted me.'
LEARN,] as in v. 73; 106. 35; De. 4. 10, &c.
72. LAW OF THY MOUTH,] as in Mal. 2. 7.
THOUSANDS,] as in 8. 7; 50. 10; 68. 17, &c.
GOLD AND SILVER,] as in v. 127: 105. 37, &c.
73 MADE ME,] as in v. 65, 121, 166; 7. 3, &c.
ESTABLISH,] as in 7. 9; 21. 12; 24. 2; 48. 8, &c.   Sept. Vulg. 'fashioned.'
CAUSE ME TO UNDERSTAND,] as in v. 27, &c.
74. FEARING,] as in v. 79; 15. 4; 22. 23, &c.
REJOICE,] as in 5. 11; 9. 2; 14. 7; 21. 1, &c.
WORD.] Sept. Vulg. 'words.'
75. KNOWN,] as in v. 79, 152; 14. 4; 18. 43.
RIGHTEOUS,] as in v. 7, 62, 106, 121, 123, &c.
FAITHFULNESS,] as in v. 30, &c.
76. TO COMFORT,] as in Ge. 37. 35; 2 Sa. 10. 2.
77. MEET,] as in v. 41, &c.
MERCIES,] as in v. 156; 25. 6; 40. 11; 51. 1.
DELIGHT,] as in v. 24, &c.   Sept. Vulg. 'meditation.'
78. ASHAMED,] as in v. 6, 46, 80, &c.
FALSEHOOD,] as in v. 29, &c.
DEALT PERVERSELY,] as in 146. 9; Job 19. 3; Ecc. 7. 13, &c.
79. FEARING,] as in v. 74, &c.
TURN BACK,] as in 6. 10; 7. 12; 9. 17; 18. 37.
KNOWING,] as in 36. 10; 37. 18; 44. 21, &c.
80. PERFECT,] as in v. 1, &c.
ASHAMED,] as in v. 6, 46, 78, &c.
81. CONSUMED,] as in v. 82, 123; 31. 10, &c.
HOPED,] as in v. 43, &c.
82. EYES,] as in v. 18, &c.
COMFORT,] as in 23. 4; 71. 21; Ge. 5. 29, &c.
83. BOTTLE,] as in 55. 8; Jos. 9. 4, 13; Jud. 1. 19; 1 Sa. 16. 20.
SMOKE,] as in 148. 8; Ge. 19. 28.   Sept. Vulg. 'frost.'
FORGOTTEN,] as in v. 61, 109, 139, 141, &c.
84. EXECUTE,] as in 1. 3; 37. 5; 56. 4; 60. 12.
PURSUERS,] as in v. 150, 157; 7. 1; 31. 15.
85. PROUD,] as in v. 21, &c.   Sept. Vulg. 'iniquitous.'
DIGGED,] as in 7. 15; 22. 16; 40. 6; 57. 6, &c. Sept. Vulg. 'declared or narrated.'
PITS,] as in 57. 6; Jer. 18. 22.   Sept. Vulg. 'fables.'
86. FAITHFULNESS,] as in v. 30, &c.
PURSUED,] as in v. 161; 69. 26; 143. 3, &c.
HELP,] as in 79. 9; 109. 26; Jos. 10. 4, &c.
87. CONSUMED,] as in 90. 9; Ge. 18. 33, &c.
PRECEPTS,] as in v. 4, &c.
88. KINDNESS,] as in v. 41, &c.
TESTIMONY,] as in v. 14, 31, 36, 99, &c.
89. SET UP,] as in 39. 5; 82. 12; Ge. 18. 2, &c.
90. GENERATIONS,] as in 10. 6; 12. 7; 14. 5
ESTABLISH,] as in 8. 3; 9. 7; 11. 2; 40. 2, &c.   Sept. Vulg. 'founded.'
STANDETH,] as in 10. 1; 33. 9; 38. 11; 76. 7.
91. ORDINANCES,] as in v. 7, &c.
STOOD,] as in 1. 1; 26. 12; 38. 11; 106. 23.
THIS DAY.] Sept. Vulg. 'the day remaineth.'
92. UNLESS,] as in 94. 17; 106. 23; 124. 1, &c.
DELIGHTS.] Sept. Vulg. 'meditation.'
PERISHED,] as in 9. 6; 10. 16; 41. 5; 142. 4.
93. FORGET,] as in v. 16, &c.
QUICKENED,] as in v. 50; 22. 29; 30. 3, &c.
94 SAVE,] as in v. 146; 3. 7; 6. 4; 7. 1, &c.

SOUGHT,] as in v. 10, &c.
95. WICKED,] as in v. 53, &c.
WAITED,] as in 25. 5; 39. 7; 40. 1; 56. 6, &c.
DESTROY,] as in De. 12. 2; Est. 3. 9; 4. 7.
UNDERSTAND,] as in v. 100, 104; 107. 43, &c.
96. PERFECTION.] Original word not found again.
END,] as in 39. 4; Ge. 4. 3; 6. 13; 8. 6, &c.
EXCEEDINGLY,] as in v. 4, 51, &c.
97. LOVED,] as in v. 47, &c.
LAW.] Sept. Vulg. add 'O Lord.'
MEDITATION,] as in v. 99; Job 15. 4.
98. ENEMIES,] as in 3. 7; 6. 10; 7. 5; 8. 2, &c.
MAKETH WISER,] as in 105. 22; Job 35. 11.
99. TEACHERS,] as in 18. 34; 94. 10; 144. 1.
ACTED WISELY,] as in 64. 9; 106. 7, &c.
TESTIMONIES,] as in v. 88, &c.
100. ELDERS,] as in 105. 22; 107. 32; 148. 12.
UNDERSTAND,] as in v. 95, &c.
KEPT.] Sept. Vulg. 'sought out.'
101. EVIL PATH,] as in v. 104, 128, &c.
RESTRAINED,] as in 40. 9, 11; 1 Sa. 25. 33.
WORD.] Sept. Vulg. 'words.'
102. TURNED ASIDE,] as in 14. 3; Ex. 3. 4.
DIRECTED,] as in Ex. 4. 12; 1 Sa. 12. 23, &c.
Sept. Vulg. 'give me a law.'
103. SWEET.] Original word not found again.
PALATE,] as in 137. 6; Job 6. 30; 12. 11, &c.
HONEY,] as in 19. 10; 81. 16; Ge. 43. 11, &c.
104. PRECEPTS,] as in v. 4, &c.
UNDERSTANDING,] as in v. 95, &c.
HATED,] as in v. 113, 128, 163; 5. 5; 11. 5.
FALSE PATH,] as in v. 29, &c.
105. LAMP,] as in 18. 28; 132. 17; Ex. 25. 37.
WORD.] Sept. Vulg. 'law.'
LIGHT,] as in 4. 6; 27. 1; 36. 9; 37. 6, &c.
PATH,] as in 142. 3; Jud. 5. 6; Job 19. 8; 24. 13, &c.   Sept. Vulg. 'paths.'
106. SWORN,] as in 15. 4; 24. 4; 89. 3, &c.
CONFIRM,] as in Ru. 4. 7; Est. 9. 27, 31, &c.
RIGHTEOUSNESS,] as in v. 7, 62, 75, 121, &c.
107. AFFLICTED,] or 'humbled.'
QUICKEN,] as in v. 25, &c.
108. FREE-WILL OFFERINGS,] as in 54. 6, &c.
ACCEPT,] as in 40. 13, &c.
TEACH,] as in v. 12, &c.
109. CONTINUALLY,] as in v. 44, &c.
FORGOTTEN,] as in v. 83, &c.
110. WICKED,] as in v. 53, &c.
LAID A SNARE,] as in 140. 5; 142. 3, &c.
111. INHERITED,] as in Ex. 23. 30; 32. 13.
TESTIMONIES,] as in v. 14, 31, 36, 88, &c.
JOY OF MY HEART,] as in Jer. 15. 16.
112. INCLINED MY HEART,] as in v. 51, &c.
END,] as in v. 33, &c.
113. DOUBTING ONES.] Sept. Vulg. 'iniquitous ones'
LOVED,] as in v. 47, &c.
114. HIDING-PLACE,] as in 18. 11; 27. 5; 31. 20; 32. 7, &c.   Sept. Vulg. 'helper.'
SHIELD,] as in 3. 3; 7. 10; 18. 2; 28. 7, &c.
Sept. Vulg. 'supporter.'
WORD.] Sept. Vulg. 'words.'
115. TURN ASIDE,] as in 6. 8; 34. 14; 139. 19.
EVIL-DOERS,] as in 22. 16; 26. 5; 27. 2, &c.
KEEP] Sept. Vulg. 'search out.'
MY GOD,] as in 4. 1; 5. 2; 7. 1; 13. 3, &c.
116. SUSTAIN.] Sept. 'receive.'
LIVE,] as in v. 17, &c.   Sept. Vulg. 'quicken me.'

PUTTEST TO SHAME,] as in v. 31, &c.
117. SUPPORT,] as in Ge. 18. 5; Jud. 19. 5.
SAVED,] as in 18. 3; 80. 3; 2 Sa. 22. 4, &c.
LOOK,] as in Ge. 4. 4; Ex. 5. 9; 2 Sa. 22. 42,
&c. Sept. Vulg. 'meditate.'
118. TRODDEN DOWN.] Sept. 'brought to
nought.'
FALSEHOOD,] as in v. 29, &c. Sept. Vulg.
unrighteous.'
DECEIT,] as in Jer. 8. 5; 14. 14; 23. 26; Zep.
3. 13. Sept. Vulg. 'inmost thought.'
119. DROSS,] as in Prov. 25. 4; 26. 23; Isa.
1. 22; Eze. 22. 18, &c. Sept. Vulg. 'transgressors.'
CAUSED TO CEASE.] Sept. Vulg. 'I have
reckoned.'
WICKED.] as in v. 53, &c.
120. TREMBLED.] Sept. Vulg. 'penetrate
my heart with thy fear.'
FLESH,] as in 16. 9; 27. 2; 38. 3; 50. 13, &c.
121. DONE,] as in v. 73, &c.
RIGHTEOUSNESS,] as in v. 7, 62, 75, 106, &c.
LEAVE,] as in 17. 14; 1 K. 7. 47; 19. 3; Ecc.
2. 18, &c. Sept. Vulg. 'deliver up.'
OPPRESSORS,] as in 72. 4; Prov. 14. 31, &c.
122. MAKE SURE,] as in Job 17. 3; Isa. 38. 14.
PROUD,] as in v 21, &c.
OPPRESS,] as in Lev. 19. 13; De. 24. 14, &c.
123. CONSUMED,] as in v. 81, &c.
SALVATION,] as in v. 155, 166, 174; 3. 2, &c.
124. KINDNESS,] as in v. 41, &c.
TEACH,] as in v. 12, &c.
125. CAUSE TO UNDERSTAND,] as in v. 27,
34, 144, 169, &c.
KNOW,] as in 9. 20; 35. 8; 39. 4; 51. 3, &c.
126. TIME,] as in 1. 3; 4. 7; 9. 9; 10. 1. &c.
TO WORK,] as in v. 112; 40. 8; 101. 3, &c.
MADE VOID,] as in Ge. 17. 14; Nu. 15. 31, &c.
127. LOVED,] as in v. 47, &c.
GOLD,] as in 19. 10; 45. 13; 72. 15: 105. 37.
FINE GOLD,] as in 19. 10; 21. 3; Job 28. 17;
Prov. 8. 19, &c. Sept. Vulg. 'topaz.'
128. APPOINTMENTS,] as in v. 4, &c. Sept.
Vulg. 'thy commands.'
DECLARED RIGHT,] as in Prov. 3. 6; 11. 5;
15. 21; Isa. 45. 2, 13, &c. Sept. Vulg. 'direc-
ted myself.'
WHOLLY.] Sept. Vulg. omit
129. WONDERFUL,] as in 77. 11; 78. 12, &c.
KEPT,] as in v. 22, &c. Sept. Vulg. 'sought
out.'
130. OPENING.] Sept. Vulg. 'declaration.'
ENLIGHTENETH,] as in 33. 15; 1 Ch. 15. 22.
INSTRUCTING,] as in 33, 15; 1 Ch. 25. 8, &c.
SIMPLE,] as in 19. 7; 116. 6; Prov. 1. 4, &c.
131. OPENED,] as in Job 16. 10; 29. 23; Isa.
5. 14.
PANT,] as in Job 7. 2; 36. 20; Isa. 42. 14.
Sept. Vulg. 'draw breath.'
132. LOOK,] as in 25. 16; 69. 16; 86. 16, &c.
CUSTOMARY,] as in Ge. 40. 13; Ex. 21. 9, &c.
LOVING,] as in v. 165; 5. 11; 33. 5; 34. 12.
133. STEPS,] as in 17. 5; 57. 6; 58. 10; 74. 3.
ESTABLISH,] as in Ge. 43. 16; Nu. 23. 1, &c.
INIQUITY,] as in 5. 5; 6. 8; 7. 14; 10. 7, &c.
RULE,] as in Ecc. 5. 19; 6. 2.
134. RANSOM,] as in 25. 22; 26. 11; 44. 26.
OPPRESSION,] as in 62. 10; 73. 8; Ecc. 5. 8;
7. 7, &c. Sept. Vulg. 'calumny.'
135. CAUSE TO SHINE,] as in 13 3; 31. 16.
TEACH,] as in v. 12, &c.

136. RIVULETS,] as in 1. 3; 46. 4; 65. 9, &c.
COME DOWN,] as in Ge. 43. 20; Ex. 9. 19, &c.
THEY HAVE NOT KEPT.] Sept. 'I have not
kept.'
137. RIGHTEOUS,] as in 1. 3; 5. 12; 7. 9, &c.
UPRIGHT,] as in 7. 10; 11. 2; 19. 8; 25. 8, &c.
FAITHFUL,] as in v. 30; 75. 86, 90, &c.
139. CUT OFF.] Sept. Vulg. 'wasted.'
ZEAL,] as in 69. 9; 79. 5; Nu. 5. 14; 25. 11.
ADVERSARIES,] as in v. 143, 157; 3. 1; 4. 1.
140. TRIED,] as in 12. 6: 18. 30; 2 Sa. 22. 31;
Prov. 30. 5.
EXCEEDINGLY,] as in v. 4, &c.
141. SMALL,] as in 68. 27; Ge. 19. 31; 25. 23;
29. 26, &c. Sept. Vulg. 'young.'
DESPISED,] as in 15. 4; Isa. 53. 3; Jer. 22. 28.
142. RIGHTEOUSNESS,] as in v. 7, 62, 75, &c.
TRUTH,] as in v. 43, &c.
143. ADVERSITY,] as in v. 139, &c.
DISTRESS,] as in De. 28. 53, 55, 57; 1 Sa. 22.
2; Jer. 19. 9.
FOUND,] as in 69. 20; 76. 5; 84. 3; 89. 20, &c.
DELIGHTS,] as in v. 24, &c. Sept. Vulg.
'meditations.'
144. CAUSE TO UNDERSTAND,] as in v. 27.
LIVE,] as in v. 17, &c.
145. I HAVE CALLED,] as in v. 146; 14. 4, &c.
ANSWER,] as in 4. 1; 13. 3; 27. 7; 55. 2, &c.
KEEP.] Sept. Vulg. 'search out.'
146. SAVE,] as in v. 94, &c.
TESTIMONIES,] as in v. 2, 22, 24, 46, 59, &c.
147. GONE FORWARD,] as in v. 148; 18. 5, &c.
DAWN,] as in 1 Sa. 30. 17; 2 K. 7. 5; Job 3. 9.
CRY,] as in 18. 6, 41; Job 19. 7; 24. 12, &c.
148. WATCHES,] as in 63. 6; 90. 4; Ex. 14. 24.
149. HEAR,] as in 27. 7; 31. 22; 55. 17, &c.
150. NEAR,] as in Ge. 20. 4; Ex. 14. 20, &c.
WICKED,] as in 26. 10; Lev. 18. 7; 19. 29.
FAR OFF,] as in Job 21. 16; 22. 18; 30. 10.
151. TRUTH,] as in v. 43, &c.
152. OF OLD,] as in v. 44, &c.
FOUNDED,] as in 24. 2; 78. 69; 89. 11, &c.
153. AFFLICTION,] as in v. 50, &c.
DELIVER,] as in 6. 4; 140. 1.
154. PLEAD,] as in 35. 1; 43. 1; 74. 22, &c.
PLEA,] as in 18. 43; 31. 20; 35. 23; 43. 1, &c
REDEEM,] as in 69. 18; Ru. 4. 4, 6.
155. FAR,] as in 10. 1; 22. 1; 38. 11; 65. 5
SALVATION,] as in v. 123, &c.
SOUGHT,] as in v. 10, &c.
156. MERCIES,] as in v. 77, &c.
MANY,] as in v. 157, 162, 165; 3. 1, &c.
157. PURSUERS,] as in v. 84, &c.
TURNED ASIDE,] as in v. 51, &c.
158. TREACHEROUS ONES,] as in 25. 3; 59.
5; Prov. 2. 22; 11. 3, &c. Sept. Vulg. 'unin-
telligent.'
GRIEVE MYSELF,] as in 139. 21, &c. Sept.
Vulg. 'pined away.'
159. SEE,] as in v. 153; 9. 13; 25. 18; 34. 8.
160. SUM,] as in 139. 17; Nu. 26. 2 Sept
Vulg. 'beginning.'
RIGHTEOUSNESS,] as in v. 7, 62, 75, 106, &c
161. PRINCES,] as in v. 23, &c.
WITHOUT CAUSE,] as in 35. 7, 19; 69. 4, &c
AFRAID,] as in 14. 5; 53. 5; 78. 53, &c.
162. REJOICE,] as in Isa. 64. 5.
FINDING,] as in Ge. 4. 14; Nu. 15. 33, &c
SPOIL,] as in 68. 12; Ge. 49. 27; Ex. 15. 9
163. FALSEHOOD,] as in v. 29, &c.
ABOMINATE,] as in 5. 6; 106. 40; 107. 18, &c

164. SEVEN,] as in Ge. 4. 24; 5. 7; 7. 2, &c.
PRAISED,] as in 10. 3; 44. 8; Isa. 62. 9, &c.
165. PEACE,] as in 4. 8; 28 3; 29. 11, &c.
LOVING,] as in v. 132, &c.
STUMBLING-BLOCK,] as in Lev. 19. 14, &c.
166. WAITED,] as in 104. 27; 145. 15, &c.
SALVATION,] as in v. 123, &c.
DONE.] Sept. Vulg. 'lord.'
167. TESTIMONIES,] as in v. 146, &c.
EXCEEDINGLY,] as in v. 4, &c.
168. PRECEPTS,] as in v. 4, &c.
WAYS,] as in v. 1, &c. Sept. adds 'O Lord.'
169. LOUD CRY,] as in 17. 1; 30. 5; 42. 4; 47.
1, &c. Sept. Vulg. 'supplication.'
COMETH NEAR,] as in v. 150; 91. 10, &c.
CAUSE TO UNDERSTAND,] as in v. 34, &c.
170. SUPPLICATION,] as in 6. 9; 55. 1; 1 K.
8. 28; 9. 3, &c. Sept. adds 'O Lord.'
DELIVER,] as in 7. 1; 22. 20; 25. 30; 31. 2.
171. LIPS,] as in v. 13, &c.
UTTER,] as in 19. 2; 59. 7; 78. 2; 94. 4, &c.
PRAISE,] as in 9. 14; 22. 3; 33. 1; 34. 1; 35.
28, &c. Sept. Vulg. 'hymn.'
TEACH,] as in 25. 9; 34. 11; 51. 13; 94. 12.
STATUTES,] as in v. 5, 12, 26, 33, &c.
172. TONGUE,] as in 5. 9; 10. 7; 12. 3, &c.
RIGHTEOUS,] as in v. 7, 62, 75, 106, 121, &c.
173. HELP,] as in Jos. 10. 33; 2 Sa. 8. 5; 18.
3; 1 Ch. 12. 17, &c. Sept. Vulg. 'to save
me.'
CHOSEN,] as in v. 30, &c.
174. LONGED,] as in v. 40, &c.
DELIGHT,] as in v. 24, &c. Sept. Vulg.
'meditation.'
175. LIVETH,] as in v. 17, &c.
PRAISE,] as in 22. 22; 35. 18; 56. 4; 63. 5.
HELP.] as in 37. 40; 46. 5; 86. 17; 118. 13.
176. WANDERED,] as in 31. 12; 1 Sa. 9. 20.
LOST SHEEP,] as in Jer. 50. 6.
SEEK,] as in 27. 8; 34. 14; 105. 4; 1 Sa. 9. 3.
PRECEPTS,] as in v. 6, &c.

CXX. SONG.] as in 28. 7; 33. 3; 40. 3; 42. 8,
&c. Sept. 'ode of those going up.'
ASCENTS,] as in Ps. 121. 122. 123. 124. &c.
Most probably the goings up Mount Zion to
the temple are meant.
1. JEHOVAH,] the national God of Israel.
DISTRESS,] as in 9. 9; 10. 1; 20. 1; 22. 11.
CALLED,] as in 14. 4; 17. 6; 31. 17; 34. 6.
ANSWERETH,] as in 3. 4; 17. 6; 20. 1; 22.
2, &c. Sept. Vulg. 'giveth ear.'
2. DELIVER,] as in 7. 1; 22. 20; 25. 20, &c.
LYING,] as in 7. 14; 27. 12; 31. 18; 33. 17,
&c. Sept. Vulg. 'unrighteous.'
LIP,] as in 12. 2, 3, 4; 16. 4, &c. Sept.
Vulg. 'lips.'
DECEITFUL,] as in v. 3; 32. 2; 52. 2; 78. 57,
&c. Sept. Vulg. 'for the deceitful tongue.'
TONGUE,] as in v. 3; 5. 9; 10. 7; 12. 3, &c.
3. GIVE,] as in 1. 3; 2. 8; 14. 7; 16. 10, &c.
ADD,] as in 10. 18; 41. 8; 61. 6; 77. 7. &c.
4. SHARP,] as in 45. 5; Prov. 25. 18; Isa.
5. 28.
ARROWS,] as in 7. 13; 11. 2; 18. 14; 38 2.
MIGHTY ONE,] as in 19. 5; 24. 8; 33. 16, &c.
BROOM-COALS.] Sept. Vulg. 'coals of the
desert.'
5. INHABITED,] as in 10'. 23; Ge. 21. 23, &c.
MESECH.] Sept. Vulg. 'my sojourning has
been prolonged.'

TENTS,] as in 15. 1: 19. 4; 27. 5; 52. 5, &c.
6. TOO MUCH,] as in 3. 1; 4. 6; 18. 16, &c.
HATING,] as in 9. 13; 18. 17; 21. 8; 34.
21, &c. Sept. Vulg. 'those hating.'
7. PEACE,] as in v. 6; 4. 8; 28. 3; 29. 11, &c.
WAR,] as in 18. 34; 24. 8; 27. 3; 46. 9, &c.
Sept. Vulg. 'they were warring against me
for nought.'

CXXI. SONG OF THE ASCENTS,] as in Ps.
120. 123. 124. &c.
1. LIFT UP EYES,] as in Ge. 24. 64; 33. 1, &c.
HILLS.] as in 2. 6; 3. 4; 11. 1; 15 1; 18. 7.
WHENCE,] as in Ge. 29. 4: 42 7; Nu.
11. 13, &c.
HELP,] as in v. 2; 20. 2; 33. 20; 70. 5, &c.
2. JEHOVAH,] as in v. 3, 7, 8.
MAKER,] as in 14. 1; 15. 5; 18. 50; 31. 23.
3. SUFFERETH,] as in 16. 10; 55. 22, &c.
FOOT,] as in 8. 6; 9. 15; 18. 9; 22. 16, &c.
PRESERVER,] as in v. 4, 5; 31. 6; 34. 20, &c.
SLUMBERETH,] as in v. 4; 76. 5; Isa. 5. 27;
Nah. 3. 18.
4. SLUMBERETH,] as in v. 3, &c.
SLEEPETH,] as in 3. 5; 4. 8; 13. 3; 44. 23.
5. SHADE,] as in 17. 8; 36. 7: 57. 1; 63 7.
RIGHT HAND,] as in 16. 8; 17. 7; 18. 35, &c.
6. BY DAY,] as in 1. 2; 13. 2; 22. 2; 32. 4.
SUN,] as in 19. 4; 50. 1; 58. 8; 72. 5, &c.
SMITE,] as in 78. 51, 60; 105. 33, 36, &c.
Sept. Vulg. 'burn.'
MOON,] as in 8. 3; 72. 5; 89. 37; 104. 19, &c.
BY NIGHT,] as in 1. 2; 6. 6; 16. 7; 17. 3, &c.
7. EVIL,] as in 5. 4; 7. 4; 10. 6; 15. 3, &c.
8. GOING OUT.] Sept. Vulg. transpose the
parts of this clause.
COMING IN,] as in 71. 3; 105. 19; 126. 6, &c
HENCE FORTH,] as in 113. 2, &c.

CXXII. SONG OF THE ASCENTS,] as in Ps
120. 121. 123. 124. &c.
BY DAVID.] Sept. Vulg omit.
1. REJOICED,] as in 16. 9; 35. 15; 105. 38.
HOUSE OF JEHOVAH,] as in v. 9; 27. 4, &c.
2. FAST,] as in 8. 6; 9. 15; 18. 9; 22. 16, &c.
STANDING,] as in 19. 9; 111. 3; 112. 9, &c.
GATES,] as in 9. 13; 24. 7; 69. 12; 87. 2. &c.
Sept. Vulg. 'courts.'
JERUSALEM,] as in v. 3, 6.
3. BUILDED ONE,] as in Jud. 6. 28, &c.
CITY,] as in 9. 6; 31. 21; 46. 4; 48. 1; 55. 9.
JOINED,] as in Ex. 28. 7; 39. 4; Ecc. 9. 4.
4. TRIBES,] as in 9; 23. 4; 45. 6; 74. 2, &c.
GONE UP,] as in 18. 8; 47 5; 68. 18; 78. 21.
COMPANIES.] Sept. Vulg. 'a testimony to
Israel.'
TO GIVE THANKS,] as in 92 1; 106. 47, &c.
5. SAT,] as in 1. 1; 9. 4; 22. 6; 26. 4. &c.
THRONES,] as in 9. 4; 11. 4; 45. 6; 47. 8, &c.
JUDGMENT,] as in 9. 4; 72. 2, &c.
HOUSE OF DAVID,] as in 1 Ch. 17. 24, &c.
6. ARK,] as in 2; De. 4. 32; 32. 7, &c.
PEACE,] as in v. 7, 8; 4. 8; 28. 3; 29. 11, &c.
AT REST,] as in Job 3. 26; 12. 6; Jer. 12. 1;
Lam. 1. 5.
LOVING,] as in 5. 11; 11. 5; 33. 5; 34. 12, &c.
7. BULWARK,] as in 9; 23. 4; 48. 20. 15, &c.
REST,] as in Prov. 1. 32: 17. 1; Jer. 22. 21.
HIGH PLACES,] as in 48. 3. 13; 1 K. 16. 18
8. BRETHREN,] as in 22. 22; 35. 14; 49. 7

COMPANIONS,] as in 12. 2; 15. 3; 28. 3, &c.
9. HOUSE OF JEHOVAH,] as in v. 1, &c.
SEEK,] as in 4. 2; 27. 4; 37. 36; 63. 9, &c.

CXXIII. SONG OF THE ASCENTS,] as in Ps.
120. 121. 122. 124. &c.
1. LIFTED UP EYES,] as in Ge. 13. 10, &c.
DWELLER IN THE HEAVENS,] as in 2. 4, &c.
2. MEN-SERVANTS,] as in 19. 11; 27. 9, &c.
MASTERS,] as in 8. 1; 12. 4; 45. 11; 97. 5.
MAID-SERVANTS,] as in Ge. 12. 16; 16. 1.
MISTRESS,] as in Ge. 16. 4, 8, 9; 2 K. 5. 3.
JEHOVAH,] as in v. 3.
OUR GOD,] as in 18. 31; 20. 5; 40. 3; 44. 20.
FAVOUR,] as in 59. 5; 67. 1; 77. 9; 102. 13.
3. FILLED,] as in v. 4; 88. 3; 104. 13, &c.
CONTEMPT,] as in v. 4; 31. 18; 107. 40, &c.
4. SCORNING,] as in 44. 13; 97. 4; Job 34. 7.
EASY ONES,] as in Job 12. 5; Isa. 32. 9, &c.
CONTEMPT,] as in v. 3.
ARROGANT.] Sept. 'the scorning is to the
easy ones, and the contempt to the proud.'

CXXIV. SONG OF THE ASCENTS,] as in Ps.
120. 121. 122. 123. &c.
BY DAVID.] Sept. Vulg. omit.
1. SAVE,] as in v. 2; 94. 17; 106. 23; 119. 92.
JEHOVAH,] as in v. 2, 6, 8, &c.
2. RISING UP,] as in 18. 38; 36. 12; 41. 8, &c.
MAN,] as in 8. 4; 11. 4; 12. 1; 14. 2; 17. 4.
3. ALIVE,] as in 7. 5; 16. 11; 17. 14: 18. 46.
SWALLOWED UP,] as in 69. 15; 106. 17, &c.
BURNING,] as in 1 Sa. 20. 7; 2 Sa. 24. 1.
ANGER,] as in 2. 5; 6. 1; 7. 6; 10. 4, &c.
4. WATERS,] as in v. 5; 1. 3; 18. 11; 22. 14.
OVERWHELMED,] as in 69. 2, 15; 78. 20, &c.
STREAM,] as in 18. 4; 36. 8; 74. 15; 78. 20.
PASSED OVER,] as in v. 5; 18. 12; 38. 4, &c.
PROUD.] Original form of the word not
found again.
6. BLESSED,] as in 18. 46; 28. 6; 31. 21, &c.
PREY,] as in 76. 4; 104. 21; 111. 5; Ge. 49. 9.
TEETH,] as in 3. 7; 35. 16; 37. 12; 45. 8, &c.
7. BIRD,] as in 8. 8; 11. 1; 84. 3; 102. 7, &c.
ESCAPED,] as in 22. 5; Jud. 3. 26; 1 Sa. 23. 13.
SNARE,] as in 11. 6; 69. 22; 91. 3; 119. 110.
FOWLERS.] Original word not found again.
BROKEN,] as in 34. 20; 37. 15, 17; Ex. 22. 10.
ESCAPED,] as in 22. 5; Jud. 3. 26, 29, &c.
8. HELP,] as in 20. 2; 33. 20; 70. 5; 89. 19.
MAKER,] as in 14. 1; 15. 5; 18. 50; 31. 23.

CXXV. SONG OF THE ASCENTS,] as in Ps.
120. 121. 122. 123. &c.
1. TRUSTING,] as in 21. 7; 27. 3; 32. 10, &c.
JEHOVAH,] as in v. 2, 4, 5.
MOUNT ZION,] on which the temple was
built.
MOVED,] as in 10. 6; 13. 4; 15. 5; 16. 8, &c.
ABIDETH,] as in 9. 7; 10. 8; 26. 5; 29. 10.
2. JERUSALEM.] Sept. Vulg. 'he is not
moved to the age who is dwelling in Jer-
usalem.'
MOUNTAINS,] as in v. 1; 2. 6; 3. 4; 11. 1.
PEOPLE,] as in in 3. 6; 7. 8; 9. 11; 14. 4, &c.
3. ROD,] as in 2. 9; 23. 4; 45. 6; 74. 2, &c.
WICKEDNESS,] as in 5. 4; 10. 15; 45. 7, &c.
Sept. Vulg. 'the wicked.'
RESTETH.] as in Ge. 8. 4; Ex. 10. 14; 20. 11.
LOT,] as in 16. 5; 22. 18; Lev. 16. 8, &c.
RIGHTEOUS,] as in 1. 5; 5. 12; 7. 9; 11. 3.

PUT FORTH,] as in 18. 14, 16 20. 2; 57. 3.
INIQUITY,] as in 37. 1; 43. 1; 80. 22; 92. 15.
4. DO GOOD,] as in 51. 20.
UPRIGHT IN HEART,] as in 7. 10; 11. 2, &c.
5. TURNING,] as in Mal. 3. 5.
CROOKED WAYS,] as in Jud. 5. 6.
CAUSETH TO GO,] as in 106. 9; Ex. 14. 21.
WORKERS OF INIQUITY,] as in 5. 5; 6. 8, &c.
PEACE,] as in 4. 8; 28. 3; 29. 11; 34. 14, &c.
ISRAEL,] as in 128. 6.

CXXVI. SONG OF THE ASCENTS,] as in
Ps. 120. 121. 122. 123. &c.
1. JEHOVAH,] as in v. 3, 4, &c.
TURNING BACK,] as in 9. 3; 14. 7; 53. 6, &c.
CAPTIVITY,] as in 14. 7; 53. 7, &c.
DREAMERS,] as in Ge. 41. 1; De. 13. 1, 3, 5.
Sept. Vulg. 'comforted ones.'
2. FILLED,] as in 71. 8; 72. 19; Ge. 6. 11, &c.
LAUGHTER,] as in Job 8. 21; 12. 4, &c.
TONGUE,] as in 5. 9; 10. 7; 12. 3; 15. 3, &c.
SINGING,] as in v. 5, 6; 30. 5; 42. 4; 47, 1.
3. GREAT THINGS,] as in v. 2; 38. 16; 41. 9.
JOYFUL,] as in 35. 26; 113. 9; De. 16. 15, &c.
4. TURN AGAIN,] as in 6. 4; 7. 7; 80. 14, &c.
CAPTIVITY,] as in 14. 7; 53. 6; 85. 1, &c.
STREAMS,] as in 18. 15; 42. 1; Job 6. 15, &c.
SOUTH,] or 'in Negeb.'
5. SOWING,] as in Job 4. 8; Prov. 11. 18, &c.
TEARS,] as in 6. 6; 39. 12; 42. 3; 56. 8, &c.
SINGING,] as in v. 2, &c.
REAP,] as in Lev. 25. 5; Nu. 11. 23; 21. 4.
6. WEEPETH,] as in Ge. 23. 2; 43. 30, &c.
BEARING,] as in 99. 8; Ge. 37. 25; 45. 23.
BASKET,] as in Job 28. 18. Sept. Vulg
omit.
SEED,] as in 18. 50; 21. 10; 22. 23; 25. 13.
SHEAVES,] as in Ge. 37. 7.

CXXVII. SONG OF THE ASCENTS,] as in Ps.
120. 121. 122. 123. &c.
BY SOLOMON.] Sept. omits.
1. JEHOVAH,] as in v. 3, &c.
BUILD,] as in 28. 5; 51. 18; 69. 35; 78. 69
HOUSE,] as in 5. 7; 23. 6; 26. 8; 27. 4, &c.
IN VAIN,] as in v. 2; 12. 2; 24. 4; 26. 4, &c.
BUILDERS,] as in 118. 22; 147. 2; 1 K. 5. 18.
LABOURED,] as in Prov. 16. 26; Ecc. 2. 11.
WATCH,] as in 12. 7; 39. 1; 41. 2; 56. 6, &c.
CITY,] as in 9. 6; 31. 21; 46. 4; 48. 1, &c.
WAKED,] as in 102. 7; Job 21. 32, &c.
2. VAIN,] as in v. 1, &c.
RISING EARLY,] as in 18. 38; 36. 12; 41. 8.
DELAY SITTING, as in 27. 4; 33. 14; 68. 16;
101. 6, &c. Sept. Vulg. 'to rise up after
resting.'
BREAD OF GRIEFS,] that is, suitable for
mourners.
BELOVED ONE,] as in 60. 5; 84. 1; 108. 6;
De. 33. 12; Isa. 5. 1, &c. Sept. Vulg. 'be
loved ones.'
SLEEP.] Original word not found again.
3. INHERITANCE,] as in 2. 8; 28. 9; 33. 12
SONS,] as in v. 4; 4. 2; 11. 4; 12. 1, &c.
REWARD,] as in Ge. 15. 1; 30. 18; 31. 8, &c.
FRUIT OF THE WOMB,] as in De. 7. 13.
4. ARROWS,] as in 7. 13; 11. 2; 18. 14, &c.
MIGHTY ONE,] as in 15. 24. 8; 33. 16, &c.
YOUNG MEN,] as in 25. 7; 71. 5; 129. 1, 2, &c
Sept. Vulg. 'outcasts.'
5. HAPPINESS,] as in 1. 1; 2. 12; 32. 1, &c

SLUMBER,] as in Job 33. 15; Prov. 6. 4, 10:
24. 33. Sept. Vulg. add, 'and rest to my
temples.'
5. PLACE,] as in 24. 3; 26. 8; 37. 10; 44. 19.
TABERNACLES,] as in v. 7; 26. 8; 43. 3, &c.
MIGHTY ONE OF JACOB,] as in v. 2, &c.
Sept. Vulg. 'God of Jacob.'
6. HEARD,] as in 6. 8; 10. 17; 22. 24; 28. 6.
EPHRATHAH,] the birth-place of Benjamin.
FOUND,] as in v. 5; 69. 20; 76. 5; 84. 3, &c.
FIELDS OF THE FOREST,] as in Isa. 29. 17;
32. 15.
7. TABERNACLE,] as in v. 5.
BOW OURSELVES,] as in 95. 6, &c.
FOOTSTOOL,] as in 99. 5; 110. 1; 1 Ch. 28. 2;
Isa. 66. 1; Lam. 2. 1.
8. ARISE,] as in 3. 7; 7. 6; 9. 19; 10. 12, &c.
REST,] as in v. 14; 23. 2; 95. 11; Ge. 49. 15.
ARK OF THY STRENGTH,] as in 62. 7; 71. 7.
Sept. Vulg. 'of thy sanctification.'
9. PRIESTS,] as in v. 16; 78. 64; 99. 6, &c.
PUT ON,] as in 35. 26; 109. 18, 29; Ge. 38. 39.
RIGHTEOUSNESS,] as in 4. 1; 7. 8; 9. 4, &c.
PIOUS ONES,] as in v. 16; 4. 3; 12. 1; 16. 10.
CRY ALOUD,] as in 5. 11; 20. 5; 51. 14; 59.
16. &c. Sept. 'are glad with gladness.'
10. SAKE,] as in 1 Ch. 17. 19, &c.
SERVANT,] as in 19. 11; 27. 9; 31. 16, &c.
TURN BACK,] as in 6. 10; 7. 12; 9. 17, &c.
ANOINTED,] as in v. 17; 2. 2; 18. 50; 20. 6.
11. SWORN,] as in v. 2, &c.
TRUTH,] as in 15. 2; 19. 9; 25. 5; 26. 3, &c.
FRUIT OF THY BODY,] as in De. 28. 4, 11,
18; Mic. 6. 7.
SET,] as in 12. 5; 13. 2; 17. 11; 18. 11; 21. 3.
THRONE,] as in v. 12; 9. 4; 11. 4; 45. 6, &c.
12. COVENANT,] as in 25. 10; 44. 17; 50. 5.
TESTIMONIES,] as in 25. 10; 78. 56; 93. 5.
TEACH,] as in 25. 9; 34. 11; 51. 13; 94. 12.
13. FIXED ON,] as in 33. 12; 78. 67; 84. 10.
ZION,] as his holy hill.
DESIRED,] as in v. 14; Job 23. 13, &c.
SEAT,] as in 1. 1; 107. 4, 7, 32, 36, &c.
14. REST,] as in v. 8, &c.
SIT,] as in v. 12; 9. 7; 10. 8; 26. 5; 29. 10.
15. PROVISION,] as in Ge. 10. 28; 27. 3, &c.
BLESS,] as in 5. 12; 16. 7; 26. 12; 19. 11, &c.
NEEDY ONES,] as in 9. 18; 12. 5; 35. 10, &c.
SATISFY,] as in 16. 2; 14. 1, 3; 16. 2; 34. 8, &c.
BREAD,] as in 14. 4; 37. 25; 41. 9; 42. 3, &c.
16. PRIESTS,] as in v. 9, &c.
CLOTHE,] as in v. 18; Ge. 3. 21; 27. 15, &c.
SALVATION,] as in 12. 5; 18. 2; 20. 6; 24. 5.
PIOUS ONES,] as in v. 9, &c.
SING ALOUD,] as in v. 9, &c. So Sept.
Vulg.
17. CAUSE TO SPRING UP,] as in Ge. 2. 9, &c.
HORN,] as in 18. 2; 22. 21; 75. 4; 89. 17, &c.
ARRANGED,] as in Ex. 40. 4; Lev. 1. 7, &c.
LAMP,] as in 18. 28; 119. 105; Ex. 25. 37, &c.
ANOINTED,] as in v. 10.
18. ENEMIES,] as in 3. 7; 6. 10; 7. 5; 8. 2.
CLOTHE,] as in 35. 26; 40. 15; 44. 15; 69. 19.
CROWN,] as in 89. 39; Ex. 29. 6; 39. 30; Lev.
3. 9, &c. Sept. Vulg. 'sanctification.'
FLOURISH,] as in 72. 16; 90. 6; 92. 7, &c.

CXXXIII. SONG OF THE ASCENTS,] as in
Ps. 120. 121. 122. 123. &c.
BY DAVID,] as in Ps. 122. 124. 131.

1. GOOD,] as in v. 2; 4. 6; 14. 3; 16. 2, &c.
PLEASANT,] as in 16. 6, 11; 81. 2; 135. 3.
DWELLING,] as in 27. 4; 33. 14; 68. 16, &c.
BRETHREN,] as in 22. 22; 35. 14; 49. 7, &c
2. OIL,] as in 23. 5; 45. 7; 55. 21; 89. 20;
92. 10. &c. Sept. Vulg. omit 'good.'
HEAD,] as in 3. 3; 7. 16; 18. 43; 21. 3, &c.
BEARD,] as in Lev. 13. 29; 14. 9; 19. 27, &c.
AARON,] the first anointed priest.
SKIRT,] as in De. 33. 15; Jos. 28. 30, &c.
ROBES,] as in Ex. 36. 9; Neh. 3. 11.
3. DEW,] as in 110. 3; Ge. 27. 28; Ex. 16. 13.
HERMON,] which was copious and refresh-
ing.
HILLS OF ZION,] those around Jerusalem.
BLESSING,] as in 3. 8; 21. 3; 24. 5; 37. 26,
&c. Sept. 'his blessing.'
LIFE,] as in 7. 5; 16. 11; 17. 14; 18. 46, &c.

CXXXIV. SONG OF THE ASCENTS,] as in
Ps. 120. 121. 122. 123. &c,
1. BLESS,] as in 28. 9; 66. 8; 96. 2; 100. 4.
SERVANTS,] as in 19. 11; 27. 9; 31. 16, &c.
STANDING,] as in 19. 9; 111. 3, 10; 112. 3.
HOUSE OF JEHOVAH,] where he was wor-
shipped.
BY NIGHT,] as in 1. 2; 6. 6; 16. 7; 17. 3, &c.
Sept. Vulg. adds, 'in the courts of the house
of our God,' as in 135. 2.
2. LIFT UP HANDS,] as in 10. 12, &c.
SANCTUARY,] as in 2. 6; 3. 4; 5. 7; 11. 4,
&c. Sept. 'to the holy things.'
BLESS,] as in 5. 12; 16. 7; 26. 12; 29. 11, &c
3. ZION,] where His seat is.
MAKER,] as in 14. 1; 15. 5; 18. 50; 31. 23.

CXXXV. 1. PRAISE YE JAH,] as in v. 3, 21,
22. 23; 104. 35; 105. 45, &c.
NAME OF JEHOVAH,] as in v. 3, 13; 20. 7;
54. 1; 83. 18, &c. Sept. 'ye servants, Je-
hovah.'
SERVANTS OF JEHOVAH,] as in 86. 2; 113. 1.
2. STANDING,] as in 19. 9; 111. 3, 10; 112. 3.
HOUSE OF JEHOVAH,] as in 5. 7; 23. 6, &c.
COURTS OF THE HOUSE,] as in 116. 19; 2 K.
21. 5; 2 Ch. 33. 5, &c.
OUR GOD,] as in 18. 31; 20. 3; 44. 20; 48. 1.
3. PRAISE YE JAH,] as in v. 1, 21, &c.
GOOD,] as in 4. 6; 14. 1, 3; 16. 2; 34. 8, &c
SING PRAISE,] as in 9. 11; 30. 4; 33. 2, &c.
PLEASANT,] as in 16. 6, 11; 81. 2; 133. 3, &c.
4. CHOSEN,] as in 33. 12; 78. 67; 84. 10, &c.
PECULIAR TREASURE,] as in Ex. 19. 5, &c.
5. KNOWN,] as in 14. 4; 18. 43; 20. 6; 31. 7.
GREAT,] as in 12. 3; 21. 5; 47. 2; 48. 1, &c.
OUR LORD] and master, supporter of all
things.
ALL GODS,] of the heathen worshipped
elsewhere.
6. PLEASED,] as in 18. 19; 22. 8; 40. 6, &c.
DEEP PLACES,] as in 33. 7; 36. 6; 42. 7; 71.
20; 77. 16, &c. Sept. Vulg. 'abysses.'
7. CAUSING TO ASCEND,] as in 81. 10; Lev.
11. 3; Jos. 24. 17, &c.
VAPOURS,] lit. 'things lifted up.' Sept.
Vulg. 'clouds.'
END OF THE EARTH,] as in 46. 9; 61. 2, &c.
LIGHTNINGS,] as in 18. 14; 77. 18; 97. 4, &c.
RAIN,] as in 72. 6; 147. 8; Ex. 9. 33, &c.
BRINGING FORTH,] at his good pleasure.
WIND,] as in v. 17; 1. 4; 11. 6; 18. 10, &c

2 G

TRUTH,] as in 15. 2; 19. 9; 25. 5; 26. 3, &c.
MADE GREAT,] as in 38. 16; 41. 9; 55. 12.
SAYING,] as in 12. 6; 17. 6; 18. 30; 105. 19;
119. 11, &c.   Sept. Vulg. 'sanctuary.'
3. CALLED,] as in 14. 4; 17. 6; 31. 17; 34. 6.
ANSWER,] as in 3. 4; 17. 6; 20. 1; 22. 2, &c.
STRENGTHEN,] as in Song 6. 5. &c.
STRENGTH,] as in 8. 2; 21. 1; 28. 7; 29. 1.
4. KINGS,] as in 2. 2; 5. 2; 10. 16; 18. 50, &c.
CONFESS,] as in v. 1, 2, &c.
HEARD,] as in 6. 8, 10, 17; 22. 24; 28. 6, &c.
SAYINGS OF THY MOUTH,] as in 19. 14, &c.
5. SING,] as in 13. 6; 21. 13; 27. 6; 57. 7, &c.
WAYS OF JEHOVAH,] as in 18. 21; 77. 13, &c.
GREAT,] as in 12. 3; 21. 5; 47. 2; 48. 1, &c.
HONOUR OF JEHOVAH,] as in 19. 1; 29. 5.
6. HIGH,] as in 18. 27; 78. 69; 113. 4, &c.
LOWLY,] as in Lev. 13. 20; 14. 37; 2 Sa. 6.
22; Job 5. 11, &c.   Sept. 'lowly things.'
SEETH,] as in 8. 3; 22. 17; 35. 17; 36. 9, &c.
HAUGHTY,] as in 104. 18; 1 Sa. 2. 3; Job
41. 34; Ecc. 5. 8, &c.   Sept. 'haughty things.'
FROM AFAR,] as in Prov. 25. 25; 31. 14, &c.
KNOWETH,] as in 9. 20; 35. 8; 39. 4; 51. 3.
7. WALK,] as in 23. 4; 26.11; 32. 8; 39.13.
DISTRESS,] as in 9. 9; 10. 1; 10. 1; 22. 11, &c.
QUICKENEST,] as in 41.2; 71. 20; 80. 18; 85.
6; 143. 11, &c.   Sept. 'savest.'
ANGER,] as in 2. 5; 6. 1; 7. 6; 10. 4; 18. 8.
ENEMIES,] as in 3. 7; 6. 10; 7. 5; 8. 2, &c.
SENDEST FORTH,] as in 18. 14; 20. 2; 57. 3.
RIGHT HAND,] as in 16. 8; 17. 7; 18. 35, &c.
SAVE,] as in 18. 27; 34. 18; 36. 6; 37. 40, &c.
8. PERFECT,] as in 7. 9; 12. 1; 77. 8.
KINDNESS,] as in v. 2, &c.
WORKS OF THY HANDS,] as in 8. 3; 90. 17.
FALL,] as in De. 4. 31; 31. 6, 8; Jos. 1. 5.

CXXXIX. OVERSEER,] as in Ps. 4. 5. 6, &c.
PSALM,] as in Ps. 3. 4. 5. 6. 7. &c.
DAVID,] as in Ps. 138. &c.   Sept. adds, 'a
psalm of Zechariah in the dispersion.'
1. JEHOVAH,] as in v. 4. 21, &c.
SEARCHED,] as in 44. 21; De. 3. 14, &c.
KNOWEST,] as in 9. 20; 35. 8; 39. 4; 51. 3.
2. SITTING DOWN,] as in 27. 4; 33. 14, &c.
RISING UP,] as in 18. 38; 36. 12; 41. 8; 76. 9.
THOUGHTS,] as in v. 17, &c.
3. PATH,] as in 8. 8; 16. 11; 17. 4; 19. 5, &c.
FANNED,] as in 44. 11; 1 K. 14. 15, &c.
WAYS,] as in v. 24; 1. 1; 2. 12; 5. 8; 10. 5.
ACQUAINTED,] as in Nu. 22. 30.
4. A WORD.] Sept. 'unrighteous word.'
TONGUE,] as in 5. 9; 10. 7; 12. 3; 15. 3, &c.
5. BEFORE AND BEHIND.] Sept. Vulg. "the
last things and the first,' joining it to the
preceding clause.
BESEIGED,] as in 12. 5; 13, 2; 17. 11; 18. 11.
HAND,] as in 7. 3; 9. 16; 24. 4; 26. 6, &c.
6. KNOWLEDGE,] as in 19. 2; 94. 10: 119. 66.
WONDERFUL,] as in Jud. 13. 18, &c.
SET ON HIGH,] as in Prov. 18. 10; Isa. 2.
11, 17.
NOT ABLE,] as in 18. 38; 21. 11; 78. 19, &c.
7. THY SPIRIT,] as in 18. 15; 51. 11; 104. 30.
FLEE,] as in Ge. 16. 6; 31. 21; Ex. 2. 15, &c.
8. SPREAD OUT,] as in Isa. 58. 5, &c.
9. TAKE,] as in 16. 4; 24. 5; 25. 1; 50. 16.
WINGS,] as in 17. 8; 18. 10; 36. 7; 57. 1; 61.
4, &c.   Sept. Vulg. 'my wings early.'
MORNING,] as in 57. 8; 108. 2; Ge. 19. 15.

UTTERMOST PARTS,] as in 37. 37; 73. 17, &c.
10. LEAD,] as in 23. 3; 43. 3; 61. 2.
RIGHT HAND,] as in 16. 8; 17. 7; 18. 35, &c.
HOLD.] as in 48. 6; 73. 23; 77. 4; 137. 9, &c.
11. DARKNESS,] as in v. 12; 18. 11; 35. 6.
BRUISETH,] as in Ge. 3. 15; Job 9. 17.
NIGHT,] as in v. 12; 1. 2; 6. 6; 16. 7; 17. 3.
LIGHT,] as in 4. 6; 27. 1; 36. 9; 37. 6, &c.
12. HIDETH,] as in 105 28; Jer. 13. 16, &c.
SHINETH,] as in 18. 28; 67. 1; 118. 27, &c.
13. POSSESSED,] as in 74. 2; 78. 54; Ge. 4. 1.
REINS,] as in 7. 9; 16. 7; 26. 2; 73. 21, &c.
Sept. adds 'O God.'
COVER,] as in 140. 7; Ex. 40. 3; 1 K. 8. 7.
BELLY,] as in 17. 14; 22. 9; 31. 9; 44. 25, &c.
14. CONFESS,] as in 6. 5; 7. 17; 9. 1; 18. 49.
WONDERS,] as in 9. 1; 26. 7; 40. 5; 71. 17.
WONDERFUL,] as in Ex. 33. 16.
WORKS,] as in 8. 6; 33. 15; 66. 3; 86. 8, &c
WELL,] as in 6. 3; 21. 1; 31. 11; 38. 6, &c.
15. SUBSTANCE,] as in De. 8. 17; Job 30. 21.
HID,] as in 69. 5; Job 4. 7; 22. 20; Hos. 5. 3
SECRET,] as in 18. 11; 27. 5; 31. 20; 32. 7.
CURIOUSLY WROUGHT.] Sept. Vulg. 'my
'substance.'
LOWER PART,] as in 63. 9; 86. 13; 88. 6, &c
16. UNFORMED SUBSTANCE.] Original word
not found again.
THY BOOK,] as in 40. 7; 69. 28; Ex. 32. 32.
WRITTEN,] as in 69. 28; 102. 18; Ezr. 8. 34.
17. PRECIOUS,] as in 49. 8; 72. 14; 1 Sa. 26. 21.
THOUGHTS,] as in v. 2, &c.   Sept. Vulg.
'friends.'
GOD,] as in v. 23; 5. 4; 7. 11; 10. 11; 16. 1.
SUM,] as in 18. 43; Ex. 30. 12; Nu. 1. 49, &c.
18. RECOUNT,] as in 87. 6; Lev. 23. 16, &c.
SAND,] as in 78. 27; Ge. 22. 17; 32. 12, &c.
WAKED,] as in 3. 5; 2 K. 4. 31; Prov. 6. 22.
19. SLAY,] as in Job 13. 15; 24. 14, &c.
GOD,] as in 18. 31; 50. 22; 114. 7, &c.
WICKED,] as in 1. 1; 3. 7; 7. 9; 9. 5; 10. 2.
MEN OF BLOOD,] as in 5. 6; 26. 9; 55. 23;
59. 2.
TURN ASIDE,] as in 6. 8; 34. 14; 119. 115.
20. EXCHANGE.] Sept. Vulg. 'thou sayest,
concerning the thought, take for a vain
thing thy cities.'
WICKEDNESS,] as in 10. 2; 21. 11; 37. 7, &c.
LIFTED UP,] as in 15. 3; 24. 4; 32. 5, &c.
VANITY,] as in 12. 2; 24. 4; 26. 4; 31. 6, &c.
ENEMIES,] as in 9. 6; 1 Sa. 28. 16; Isa. 14.
21; Mic. 5. 11, 14.
21. HATING,] as in 18. 40; 44. 7; 55. 12, &c.
WITHSTANDERS.] Sept. Vulg. 'enemies.'
GRIEVE MYSELF,] as in 119. 158, &c.   Sept.
Vulg. 'waste away.'
22. HATED,] as in 25. 19; 109. 3, 5, &c.
23. SEARCH,] as in Jud. 18. 2, &c.
KNOW,] as in 4. 3; 46. 10; 100. 3; Ge. 20. 7.
TRY,] as in 26. 2; Mal. 3. 10, &c.
THOUGHTS,] as in 94. 19, &c.   Sept. Vulg.
'paths.'
24. GRIEVOUS,] as in 1 Ch. 4. 9; Isa. 14. 3;
48. 5.
LEAD,] as in 23. 3; 31. 3; 43. 3; 61. 2, &c.
WAY,] as in v. 3, &c.

CXL. OVERSEER,] as in Ps. 4. 5. 6. 8. 9. &c.
PSALM OF DAVID,] as in Ps. 3. 4. 5. 6. &c.
1. DELIVER,] as in 6. 4; 119. 153.
EVIL,] as in v. 2, 11: 5. 4; 7. 4; 10. 6, &c.

SOUL,] as in v. 7; 3, 2; 6, 3; 7. 2; 10, 3, &c.
5. CRIED,] as in 22. 5; Jud. 6. 7; 1 Sa. 8. 18.
REFUGE,] as in 14. 6; 46. 1; 61. 3; 62. 7;
71. 7, &c.   Sept. Vulg. 'hope.'
PORTION,] as in 16. 5; 17. 14; 50. 18; 73. 26.
LAND OF THE LIVING,] as in 27. 13; 52. 5.
6 ATTEND,] as in 5. 2; 17. 1; 55. 2; 61. 1.
LOUD CRY,] as in 17, 1; 30. 5; 42. 4; 47. 1.
LOW,] as in 79. 8; 116. 6; Job. 28. 4, &c.
DELIVER,] as in 7. 1; 22. 20; 25. 20; 31. 2.
PURSUERS,] as in 7. 1; 31. 15; 35. 3; 119. 84.
STRONGER,] as in 18. 17; Ge. 25. 23, &c.
7. BRING FORTH,] as in 25. 17; Gen. 8. 17.
PRISON,] as in Isa. 24. 22; 42. 7; Jer. 24. 1.
CONFESS,] as in 92. 1; 106. 47; 110. 62, &c.
COMPASS ABOUT,] as in Prov. 14. 18.
CONFERREST BENEFITS,] as in 18. 20; Nu.
17. 8; De. 32. 6; 2 Sa. 19. 36, &c.

CXLIII. PSALM OF DAVID.] Sept. adds,
'when the son pursued him.' So Vulg.
1. JEHOVAH,] as in v. 7, 8, 9, 11, &c.
HEAR,] as in 4. 1; 17. 1; 27. 7; 28. 2; 30. 10.
PRAYER,] as in 4. 1; 6. 9; 35. 13; 39. 12, &c.
GIVE EAR,] as in 5. 1; 17, 1; 39. 12; 49. 1..
SUPPLICATIONS,] as in 28. 2; 31. 22; 116. 1.
FAITHFULNESS,] as in 33. 4; 36. 5; 37. 3, &c.
ANSWER,] as in v. 7; 4. 1; 13. 3; 27. 7, &c.
2. JUDGMENT,] as in 1. 5; 7. 6; 9. 4; 10. 5.
SERVANT,] as in v. 12; 19. 11; 27. 9; 31. 16.
JUSTIFIED,] as in 51. 4; Job 4. 17; 9. 2, &c.
3. ENEMY,] as in v. 9, 12; 3. 7; 6. 10; 7. 5 .
PURSUED,] as in 18. 37; 23. 6; 69. 26, &c.
BRUISED,] as in 72. 4; 89. 10; 94. 5, &c.
LIFE,] as in v. 1; 7. 5; 16. 11; 17. 14; 10. 46.
CAUSED TO DWELL,] as in Lev. 23. 43, &c.
DARK PLACES,] as in 74. 20; 88. 6, 18, &c.
DEAD,] as in 31. 12; 88. 5, 10; 106. 28, &c.
OF OLD,] as in 5. 11; 9. 5; 10. 16; 12. 7, &c.
4. FEEBLE,] as in 77. 3; 107. 5; 142. 3; Lam.
2. 12, &c.   Sept. Vulg. 'grieved.'
DESOLATE,] as in Ecc. 7. 16; Isa. 79. 16;
3. 35; Dan. 8. 27.   Sept. Vulg. 'troubled.'
5. REMEMBERED,] as in 9. 12; 63. 6; 78. 42.
MEDITATED,] as in 1. 2; 2. 1; 35. 28; 37. 30.
ACTS,] as in 9. 16; 28. 4; 44. 1; 64. 9; 77. 12.
MUSE,] as in Isa. 53. 8, &c.
6. SPREAD FORTH,] as in Isa. 25. 11; 65. 2.
WEARY LAND,] as in 63. 1; Isa. 32. 2. Sept.
Vulg. 'waterless land.'
7. HASTE, as in 69. 17; 79. 8; 102. 2, &c.
ANSWER,] as in v. 1, &c.
CONSUMED,] as in 31. 10; 37. 20; 39. 10, &c.
HIDE,] as in 13. 1; 17. 8; 27. 5; 31. 20; 44.
14, &c.   Sept. Vulg. 'turn not away.'
COMPARED,] as in 28. 1; 49. 12, 20, &c.
GOING DOWN,] as in 22. 29; 28. 1; 30. 3, &c.
PIT,] as in 7. 15; 28. 1; 30. 3; 40. 2; 88. 4.
8. CAUSE TO HEAR,] as in 66. 8; Song 2. 14.
KINDNESS,] as in v. 12; 5. 7; 6. 4; 13. 5, &c.
TRUSTED,] as in 13. 5; 22. 4; 25. 2; 26. 1.
CAUSE TO KNOW,] as in 25. 4; 39. 4; 90. 12.
WAY,] as in 1. 1; 2. 12; 5. 8; 10. 5; 18. 21.
LIFTED UP,] as in 15. 3; 24. 4; 32. 5; 69. 7.
9. DELIVER,] as in 7. 1; 22. 20; 25. 20, &c.
ENEMY,] as in v. 3, 12, &c.
COVERED,] as in 32. 5; 40. 10; 44. 15; 69. 7;
78. 53, &c.   Sept. Vulg. 'taken refuge.'
10. TEACH,] as in 25. 4; 119. 12, 26, 68, 124.
GOOD PLEASURE,] as in 5. 12; 19. 14; 40. 8.
MY GOD,] as in 3. 7; 5. 2; 7. 1; 13. 3; 18. 21.

THY SPIRIT,] as in 51. 11; 104. 30; 139. 7.
&c.   Sept. Vulg. 'thy good spirit.'
LEAD,] as in 23. 3; 31. 3; 43. 3; 61. 2, &c.
UPRIGHTNESS,] as in 26. 12; 27. 11; 45. 6.
11. NAME'S SAKE,] as in 23. 3; 25. 11; 31. 3.
QUICKEN,] as in 41. 2; 71. 20; 80. 18; 85. 6.
RIGHTEOUSNESS,] as in v. 1; 5. 8; 11. 7, &c.
BRINGEST OUT,] as in 18. 19; 25. 15; 31. 4.
DISTRESS,] as in 9. 9; 10. 1; 20. 1; 22. 11.
12. KINDNESS,] as in v. 8, &c.
CUTTEST OFF,] as in 18. 40; 94. 23; 101. 5, 8.
ENEMIES,] as in v. 3. 9, &c.
DESTROYED,] as in Lev. 23. 30; Nu. 24. 19.
ADVERSARIES,] as in 6. 7; 7. 4; 8. 2; 10. 5.
SERVANT,] as in v. 2, &c.

CXLIV. BY DAVID.] Sept. Vulg. add 'con-
cerning Goliath.'
1. BLESSED,] as in 18. 46; 28. 6; 31. 21, &c.
JEHOVAH,] as in v. 3. 5, 15, &c.
ROCK,] as in 18. 2; 19. 14; 27. 5; 28. 1, &c.
TEACHING,] as in 18. 34; 94. 10; 119. 99, &c.
WAR,] as in 55. 18; 68. 30; 78. 9; 2 Sa. 17. 11.
FINGERS,] as in 8. 3; Ex. 8. 19; 29. 12, &c.
BATTLE,] as in 18. 34; 24. 8; 27. 3; 46. 9, &c.
2. KIND ONE,] as in 52. 1; 57. 3; 59. 10, &c.
BULWARK,] as in 18. 2; 31. 2, 3; 66. 11; 71.
3, &c.   Sept. Vulg. 'refuge.'
TOWER,] as in 9. 9; 18. 2; 46. 7, 11; 48. 3.
DELIVER,] as in 18. 2, 48; 40. 17; 2 Sa. 22. 2.
SHIELD,] as in 3. 3; 7. 10; 18. 2; 28. 7, &c.
TRUSTED,] as in 7. 1; 11. 1; 16. 1; 25. 20.
3. MAN,] as in v. 4; 8. 4; 11. 4; 12. 1; 14. 2.
KNOWEST,] as in 9. 20; 35. 8; 39. 4; 51. 3;
59. 13, &c.   Sept. 'art made known.'
SON OF MAN,] as in 8. 4; 11. 4; 12. 1; 14. 2.
ESTEEMEST,] as in 77. 5; 119. 59; 2 K. 12. 15.
4. VANITY,] as in 31. 6; 39. 5; 62. 9; 78. 3.
LIKE,] as in 102. 6; Song 7. 7; Isa. 1. 9, &c.
SHADOW,] as in 17. 8; 36. 7; 57. 1; 63. 7, &c.
PASSING BY,] as in 8. 8; 80. 12; 84. 6, &c.
5. INCLINE,] lit. 'stretch out.'
COME DOWN,] as in 7. 16; 18. 9; 49. 17, &c.
STRIKE,] as in Job 1. 11; 2. 5.
MOUNTAINS,] as in 2. 6; 3. 4; 11. 1; 15. 1.
SMOKE,] as in 74. 1; 80. 4; 104. 32, &c.
6. LIGHTNING,] as in 18. 14; 77. 18; 97. 4.
SCATTER,] as in 18. 14; Ge. 11. 8; 49. 7, &c.
ARROWS,] as in 7. 13; 11. 2; 18. 14; 38. 2.
7. ON HIGH,] as in 7. 7; 10. 5; 18. 16; 56. 2.
FREE,] as in v. 7; Eze. 2. 8.
DELIVER,] as in v. 11; 7. 1; 22. 20; 25. 20.
MANY WATERS,] as in 18. 16; 29. 3; 77. 19.
SONS OF A STRANGER,] as in v. 11; 18. 44.
8. VANITY,] as in v. 11; 12. 2; 24. 4; 31. 6.
RIGHT HAND,] as in v. 11; 16. 8; 17. 7, &c.
FALSEHOOD,] as in v. 11; 7. 14; 27. 12, &c.
9. GOD,] as in v. 15; 4. 1; 5. 10; 7. 11, &c.
NEW SONG,] as in 33. 3; 40. 3; 96. 1; 98. 1.
I SING,] as in 13. 6; 21. 13; 27. 6; 57. 7, &c.
PSALTERY,] as in 33. 2; 57. 8; 71. 22; 81. 2.
TEN STRINGS,] as in 33. 2; 92. 3.
I SING PRAISE,] as in 7. 17; 9. 2; 27. 6, &c.
10. GIVING DELIVERANCE,] as in Jud. 15. 18;
2 K. 5. 1.
FREEING,] as in Isa. 10. 14.
11. FREE,] as in v. 7, &c.
VANITY,] as in v. 8, &c.
12. PLANTS,] as in 1 Ch. 4. 23; Job 14. 9;
Isa. 5. 7; 17. 10, 11.
BECOMING GREAT.] Sept 'strengthened.'

YOUTH,] as in 25. 7; 71. 5; 103. 5; 127. 4, &c.
HEWN STONES,] as in Zec. 9. 15.
LIKENESS,] as in 106. 20; Ex. 25. 9. &c.
PALACE,] as in 5. 7; 11. 4; 18. 6; 27. 4; 29.
9, &c. Sept. Vulg. 'temple.'
13. FULL,] as in 73. 10; 75. 8; Ge. 23. 9, &c.
BRINGING OUT.] Sept. 'bursting.'
KIND,] as in 2 Ch. 16. 14.
FLOCKS,] as in 44. 11; 49. 14; 65. 13; 74. 1.
TEN THOUSANDS,] as in 3. 6; 91. 7, &c.
OUT-PLACES,] as in 18. 42; 31. 11; 41. 6, &c.
14. OXEN,] as in Jer. 11. 19.
CARRYING.] Sept. Vulg. 'fat.'
BREACH,] as in 106. 23; Ge. 38. 29; Jud. 21.
15; 2 Sa. 5. 20, &c. Sept. 'falling of a
hedge.'
OUT-GOING,] as in 19. 5; Ge. 2. 10; 9. 10, &c.
CRYING,] as in Isa. 24. 11; Jer. 14. 2; 46. 12.
BROAD PLACES,] as in 55. 11; Ge. 19. 2; De.
13. 16; Jud. 19. 15, &c. Sept. 'folds.'
15. HAPPINESS,] as in 1. 1; 2. 12; 32. 1, &c.
JEHOVAH,] as in v. 1, 3, 5, &c.

CXLV. PRAISE,] as in v. 21; 9. 14; 22. 3.
1. EXALT,] as in 18. 48; 27. 5; 30. 1; 34. 3.
MY GOD,] as in 3. 7; 5. 2; 7. 1; 13. 3; 18. 6.
O KING,] as in 2. 10; 1 Sa. 23. 20; 26. 17;
2 Sa. 14. 4, &c. Sept. 'my king.'
BLESS THY NAME,] as in v. 2, 10, 21; 16. 7.
2 EVERY DAY,] as in 32. 3; 35. 28; 38. 6.
PRAISE,] as in 22. 22; 35. 18; 56. 4; 63. 5.
3. GREAT,] as in v. 8; 12. 3; 21. 5; 47. 2, &c.
PRAISED,] as in 18. 3; 48. 1; 113. 3, &c.
SEARCHING,] as in Jud. 5. 16; Job 5. 9; 8.
8; 9. 10, &c. Sept. Vulg. 'end.'
4. GENERATION,] as in v. 13; 10. 6; 12. 7.
WORKS,] as in v. 9, 10, 17; 8. 3; 19. 1, &c.
MIGHTY ACTS,] as in v. 11, 12; 106. 2, &c.
DECLARE,] as in 22. 31; 30. 9; 38. 18; 40. 5.
5. HONOUR,] as in v. 12; 8. 5; 21. 5; 29. 4.
GLORY,] as in v. 11, 12; 3. 3; 7. 5; 8. 5, &c.
MAJESTY,] as in 8. 1; 21. 5; 45. 3; 96. 6, &c.
WONDERS,] as in 9. 1; 26. 7; 40 5; 71. 17.
DECLARE,] as in 55. 17; 69. 12; 77. 3, &c.
6. STRENGTH,] as in 78. 4; Isa. 42. 25.
FEARFUL ACTS,] as in 45. 4; 65. 5; 66. 3, &c.
TELL,] as in v. 11; 11. 1; 12. 5; 13. 4; 35. 10.
GREATNESS,] as in v. 3; 71. 21; 1 Sa. 7. 21.
RECOUNT,] as in 2. 7; 9. 1; 22. 17; 48. 13
7. MEMORIAL,] as in 6. 5; 9. 6; 30. 4; 34. 16.
ABUNDANCE,] as in 31. 19; 97. 1; 103. 8, &c.
GOODNESS,] as in 4. 6; 14. 1; 16. 2; 31. 3.
SEND FORTH,] as in 19. 2; 50. 7; 78. 2, &c.
RIGHTEOUSNESS,] as in 5. 8; 11. 7; 22. 31.
SING,] as in 5. 11; 20. 5; 51 14; 59. 16; 63.
&c Sept. Vulg. 'are glad.'
8. GRACIOUS,] as in 86. 15; 103. 8; 111. 4.
MERCIFUL,] as in 78. 38; 86. 15; 103. 8, &c.
SLOW TO ANGER,] as in 86. 15; 103. 8, &c.
GREAT IN KINDNESS,] as in 3. 7; 17. 7, &c.
9. MERCIES,] as in 25. 6; 40. 11; 51. 1, &c.
WORKS,] as in v. 4, 10, 17, &c.
10. CONFESS,] as in 6. 5; 7. 17; 9. 1; 18. 49.
WORKS,] as in v. 4, 9, 17, &c.
SAINTS.] as in v. 17; 4. 3; 12. 1; 16. 10, &c.
BLESS,] as in v. 1, 2, 21, &c.
11 HONOUR.] as in v. 5, 12, &c,
KINGDOM.] as in v. 12, 13; 45. 6; 103. 19.
TELL.] as in v 6. &c.
MIGHT,] as in v. 4. 12. &c.
12. MAKE KNOWN,] as in 25. 14; 78. 5, &c.

SONS OF MEN,] as in 8. 4; 11. 4; 12. 1, &c.
MIGHTY ACTS,] as in v. 4, 11, &c.
HONOUR,] as in v. 5, 11, &c.
MAJESTY,] as in v. 5, &c,
13. ALL AGES,] as in 93. 2; 100. 5; 103. 17.
DOMINION,] as in 103. 22; 114. 2; 136. 8, &c.
GENERATIONS,] as in v. 4, &c.
14. SUPPORTING,] as in 37. 17, 24; 54. 4, &c.
FALLING,] as in Ge. 15. 12; Nu. 5. 12, &c.
RAISING,] as in 146. 8, &c.
BOWED DOWN,] as in 146. 8, &c.
15. LOOK,] as in 104. 27; 119. 166; Ru. 1. 13.
FOOD,] as in 78. 18; 104. 21, 27; 107. 18, &c.
SEASON,] as in 1. 3; 4. 7; 9. 9; 10. 1; 21. 9.
16. OPENING,] as in Jud. 3. 25; Isa. 22. 22.
SATISFYING,] as in 103. 5, &c.
DESIRE,] as in v. 19; 5. 12; 19. 14; 30. 5, &c.
LIVING THING,] as in 27. 13; 50. 10; 69. 28.
17. RIGHTEOUS,] as in 1. 5; 5. 12; 7. 9, &c.
WAYS,] as in 1. 1; 2. 12; 5. 8; 10. 5, &c.
WORKS,] as in v. 4, 9, 10, &c. Sept. Vulg.
add here v. 17.
18. NEAR,] as in 15. 3; 22. 11; 34. 18; 38. 11.
CALLING,] as in 42. 7; 86. 5; 99. 6, &c.
TRUTH,] as in 15. 2; 19. 9; 25. 5; 26. 3, &c.
19. FEARING,] as in 15. 4; 22. 23; 25. 12, &c.
CRY,] as in 18. 6; 34. 15; 39. 12; 40. 1, &c.
SAVETH,] as in 18. 27; 34. 18; 36. 6; 37. 40
20. PRESERVETH,] as in 31. 6; 34. 20, &c.
LOVING,] as in 5. 11; 11. 5; 33. 5; 34. 12, &c.
WICKED,] as in 1. 1; 3. 7; 7. 7; 9. 5, &c.
DESTROYETH,] as in 106. 34; Nu. 33. 52, &c.
21. PRAISE,] as in v. 1, &c.
FLESH,] as in 16. 9; 27. 2; 38. 3; 50. 13, &c.
HOLY NAME,] as in 33. 21; 103. 1; 105. 3, &c.
FOR EVER,] as in 5. 11; 9. 5; 10. 16; 12. 7.

CXLVI. PRAISE YE JAH.] as in v. 10; 115.
18; 116. 19; 117. 1, &c. Sept. Vulg. add, 'of
Haggai and Zechariah.'
LIFE,] as in 7. 2; 16. 11; 17. 14; 18. 46, &c.
SING PRAISE,] as in 22. 22, 26; 35. 18; 56. 4.
MY GOD,] as in 3. 7; 5. 2; 7. 1; 13. 3; 18. 6.
3. TRUST,] as in 9. 10; 40. 3; 44. 6; 52. 7, &c.
PRINCES,] as in 47. 9; 83. 11; 107. 40; 113. 8.
SON OF MAN,] as in 8. 4; 11. 4; 12. 1; 14. 2,
&c. Sept. Vulg. 'sons of men.'
DELIVERANCE,] as in 33. 17; 37. 39; 40. 10.
GOETH FORTH,] as in 17. 2; 41. 6; 44. 9, &c.
RETURNETH,] as in 6. 10; 7. 12; 9. 17, &c.
PERISHED,] as in 9. 6; 10. 16; 41. 15; 119. 92.
5. HAPPINESS,] as in 1. 1; 2. 12; 32. 1, &c.
HELP,] as in 20. 2; 33. 20; 70. 5; 89. 19, &c.
HOPE,] as in 119. 116, &c.
6. MAKING,] as in v. 1; 14. 1; 15. 5; 18. 50.
SEA,] as in 8. 8; 24. 2; 33. 7; 46. 2, &c.
7. KEEPING,] as in v. 9; 31. 6; 34. 20; 71. 10.
TRUTH,] as in 15. 2; 19. 9; 25. 5; 26. 3, &c.
DOING JUDGMENT,] as in 99. 4; 119. 84, &c.
OPPRESSED,] as in 103. 6; De. 28. 29, 33, &c.
BREAD,] as in 14. 4; 37. 25; 41. 9; 42. 3, &c.
HUNGRY,] as in 107. 5, 9, 36; 1 Sa. 2. 5, &c.
8. PRISONERS,] as in Ge. 39. 20; 40. 3, &c.
OPENING.] Sept. Vulg. 'enlightens.'
BLIND,] as in Ex. 4 11; Lev. 19. 14; 21. 18.
RAISING,] as in 145. 14, &c.
BOWED DOWN,] as in 145. 14, &c.
LOVING,] as in 5. 11; 11. 5; 33. 5; 34. 12. &c.
RIGHTEOUS,] as in 1. 5; 5. 12; 7. 9; 11. 3.
9. PRESERVING.] as in v. 7, &c.
FATHERLESS,] as in 10. 14; 68. 5; 82. 3, &c.

WIDOW,] as in 68. 5; 78. 64; 94. 6; 109. 9.
CAUSETH TO STAND.]Sept. Vulg. 'helpeth.'
WICKED,] as in 1. 1; 3. 7; 7. 9; 9. 5; 10. 2.
TURNETH UPSIDE DOWN,]as in Job 8. 3, &c.
10. REIGN,] as in 47. 8; 93. 1; 96. 10; 97. 1.
GENERATION,] as in 10. 6; 12. 7; 14. 5, &c.
PRAISE YE JAH,] as in v. 1, &c. Sept.
Vulg. make this the title of the next psalm,
and add 'of Haggai and Zechariah.'

CXLVII. 1. PRAISE YE JAH,] as in v. 20;
115. 18; 116. 19; 117. 1, &c.
OUR GOD,] as in v. 7; 20. 7; 40. 3; 44. 20, &c.
PLEASANT,] as in 16. 6; 81. 2; 123. 1; 135. 3.
COMELY,] as in 33. 1; Prov. 17. 7; 19. 10, &c.
PRAISE,] as in 9. 14; 22. 3; 33. 1; 34. 1, &c.
2. BUILDING,] as in 118. 22; 127. 1, &c.
DRIVEN AWAY,] as in De. 22. 1; 30. 4, &c.
GATHERETH,] as in Eze. 22. 21; 39. 28.
3. GIVING HEALING,]as in 103. 3; Ex. 15. 26.
GRIEFS,] as in 16. 4; Job 9. 28; Prov. 10.
10; 15. 13.
4. APPOINTING,] as in Jer. 33. 13.
NUMBER,] as in v. 5; 40. 12; 104. 25; 105. 12.
STARS,] as in 8. 3; 136. 9; 148. 3; Ge. 1. 16.
NAMES,] as in 5. 11; 7. 17; 8. 1; 9. 2; 16. 4.
5. OUR LORD,] as in 135. 5; 1 Sa. 25. 14, &c.
POWER,] as in 22. 15; 29. 4; 31. 10; 33. 16.
UNDERSTANDING,] as in 49. 3; 78. 72, &c.
NARRATION,] as in v. 4. &c.
6. MEEK,] as in 9. 12; 10. 12; 22. 26; 25. 9.
MAKING LOW,] as in 113. 6; 1 Sa. 2. 7.
WICKED,] as in 1. 1; 3. 7; 9. 5; 10. 2; 11. 2.
7. ANSWER,] as in 4. 1; 13. 3; 27. 7; 55. 2.
THANKSGIVING,] as in 26. 7; 42. 4; 50. 14.
SING,] as in 9. 11; 30. 4; 33. 2; 47. 6; 66. 2.
OUR GOD,] as in v. 1, &c.
HARP,] as in 33. 2; 43. 4; 49. 4; 57. 8, &c.
8. COVERING,] as in Ge. 18. 17; Ex. 29. 13.
HEAVENS,] as in 2. 4; 8. 1; 11. 4; 14. 2, &c.
CLOUDS,] as in 18. 11, 12; 77. 17; 104. 3, &c.
PREPARING,] as in 65. 6; Jer. 10. 12; 51. 15.
RAIN,] as in 72. 6; 135. 7; Ex. 9. 33, &c.
CAUSING TO SPRING UP,] as in 104. 14, &c.
GRASS,] as in 37. 2; 90. 5; 103. 15; 104. 14.
MOUNTAINS,] as in 2. 6; 3. 4; 11. 1; 15. 1;
10. 7, &c. Sept. Vulg. add Ps. 104. 14 here.
9. BEAST,] as in 8. 7; 36. 6; 49. 12; 50. 10.
FOOD,]as in 14. 4; 37. 25; 41. 9; 42. 3, &c.
RAVENS,] as in Ge. 8. 7; Lev. 11. 15, &c.
10. MIGHT,] as in 20. 6; 21. 13; 54. 1; 65. 6.
HORSE,]as in 20. 7; 32. 9; 33. 17; 76. 6, &c
DELIGHT,]as in 37. 23; 51. 16; 68. 30; 73. 25.
LEGS,] as in De. 28. 35; Prov. 26. 7, &c.
PLEASED,] as in 49. 13; 50. 18; 51. 16; 62. 4.
11. FEARING,]as in 15. 4; 22. 23; 25. 12, &c.
WAITING,] as in 31. 24; 33. 18; 69. 3.
KINDNESS,] as in 5. 7; 6. 4; 13. 5; 17. 7, &c.
12. GLORIFY,] as in 117. 1, &c. Sept.
Vulg. prefix 'praise ye the Lord,' and be-
gin a new Psalm; Sept. also adding, 'of
Haggai and Zechariah.'
ZION,] lit. the 'sunny or dry place.'
13. STRENGTHEN,]as in Ex. 14. 4; Jud. 9. 24.
BARS,] as in 107. 16; Ex. 26. 26; 27. 2, &c.
GATES,] as in 9. 13; 24. 7; 69. 12; 87. 2, &c.
BLESSED,] as in 10. 3; 45. 2; 118. 26; 129. 8.
SONS,] as in v. 9; 2. 7; 11. 4; 12. 1, &c.
MIDST,] as in 5. 9; 36. 1; 39. 3; 46. 5; 48. 9.
14. BORDER,] as in 78. 56; 104. 9; 105. 31.
PEACE,] as in 4. 8; 28. 3; 29. 11; 34. 14, &c

FAT,] as in 17. 10; 63. 5; 73. 7; 81. 16, &c.
WHEAT,] as in 81. 16; Ge. 30. 14; Ex. 9. 32
SATISFIETH,] as in 81. 16; 91. 16; 105. 40.
15. SENDING FORTH,]as in Ex. 9 14; 23. 20.
SAYING,] as in 12. 6; 17. 6; 18. 30; 105. 19.
SPEEDILY,] as in 31. 2; 37. 2; Nu. 16. 46.
RUN,] as in 18. 29; 59. 4; 119. 32; Ge. 10. 2.
16. SNOW,] as in 51. 7; 148. 8; Nu. 4. 6, &c.
WOOD,] as in Lev. 13. 47; Jud. 6. 37, &c.
HOAR FROST,] as in Ex. 16. 14; Job 38. 29.
ASHES,] as in 102. 9; Ge. 18. 27; Nu. 19. 9.
SCATTERETH,]as in 53. 5; 89. 10; 112. 9, &c.
17. CASTING FORTH,] as in Isa. 19. 8, &c.
ICE,] as in Ge. 31. 40; Job 6. 16; 37. 10; 38.
29; Jer. 36. 30; Eze. 1. 22.
MORSELS,] as in Ge. 18. 5; Lev. 2. 6; 6. 12.
COLD,] as in Job 24. 7; 37. 9; Prov. 25. 20;
Nah. 3. 17.
18. SENDEST FORTH,] as in 18. 14; 20. 2, &c.
MELTETH,] as in De. 20. 8; Jos. 2. 11; 5. 1.
TO BLOW,] according to his pleasure.
FLOW,] as in Nu. 24. 7; De. 32. 2; Job 36. 28.
19. DECLARING,] as in 19. 1; Ge. 41. 24, &c.
WORDS,] or 'matters.'
STATUTES,] as in v. 20; 2. 7; 50. 16; 81. 4.
JUDGMENTS,] as in 1. 5; 7. 6; 9. 4, 7; 10. 5.
20. NATION,] as in 9. 17; 22. 27; 43. 1; 66. 7.
JUDGMENTS,] as in v. 19, &c. Sept. Vulg
'his judgments.'
KNOWN,] as in 15. 4; 18. 43; 20. 6; 31. 7, &c.
PRAISE YE JAH,] as in v. 1, &c. Sept.
omits.

CXLVIII. PRAISE YE JAH.]Sept. adds 'by
Haggai and Zechariah.'
1. HIGH PLACES,] as in 102. 19; Jud. 5. 18.
2. MESSENGERS,]as in 34. 7; 35. 5; 78. 49, &c.
HOSTS,] as in 24. 2; 33. 6; 44. 9; 46. 7; 48. 8.
3. SUN,] as in 19. 4; 50. 1; 58. 8; 72. 5, &c
MOON,] as in 8. 3; 72. 5; 89. 37; 104. 19, &c
STARS,] as in 8. 3; 136. 9; 147. 4; Ge. 1. 16,
&c. Sept. Vulg. 'stars and the light.'
4. HEAVENS OF HEAVENS,] as in 115. 6; 1
K. 8. 27.
WATERS,] as in 18. 11; 23. 2; 29. 3; 32. 6.
5. NAME OF JEHOVAH,] as in v. 13; 7. 17.
COMMANDED,] as in 7. 6; 33. 9; 68. 28; 71.
3; 78. 5, &c. Sept. Vulg. add, 'For he
spake and they were made.'
CREATED,] as in 104. 30; Ex. 34. 10, &c.
6. ESTABLISH,] as in 18. 33; 105. 10, &c.
STATUTE,] as in 2. 7; 50. 16; 81. 4; 94. 20.
PASS OVER,] as in 17. 3; 37. 36; 42. 4; 57. 1.
7. DRAGONS,] as in 74. 13; 91. 13; Ge. 1. 21.
DEEPS,] as in 33. 7; 36. 6; 42. 7; 71. 20, &c.
8. FIRE,] as in 11. 6; 18. 8; 21. 9; 29. 7, &c.
HAIL,] as in 18. 12; 78. 47, 48; 105. 32, &c.
SNOW,] as in 51. 7; 147. 16; Ex. 4. 6, &c.
VAPOUR,] as in 119. 83; Ge. 19. 28.
WHIRLWIND,] as in 107. 25; 2 K. 2. 1, &c.
9. MOUNTAINS,] as in 2. 6; 3. 4; 11. 1, &c.
HEIGHTS,] as in 65. 12; 72. 3; 114. 4, 6, &c.
FRUIT-TREE,] as in 1. 11; Neh. 9. 25.
CEDARS,] as in 29. 5; 80. 10; 92. 12; 104. 16.
10. WILD BEAST,] as in 17. 17. 7; 17. 14.
CATTLE,] as in 8. 7; 36. 6; 49. 12; 50. 10, &c.
CREEPING THING,] as in 104. 25; Ge. 1. 24.
WINGED BIRD,] as in 8; 11. 1; 84. 3, &c.
11. KINGS OF EARTH,] as in 76. 12; 89. 27.
PEOPLES,] as in 3. 6; 7. 8; 9. 11; 14. 4, &c
CHIEFS.] as in 45. 16; 68. 27; 82. 7, &c

JUDGES OF EARTH,] as in 2. 10; 58. 11, &c.
12. YOUNG MEN,] as in 78. 31, 63; De. 32. 35.
MAIDENS,] as in 45. 14; 78. 63; Ge. 24. 16.
AGED MEN,] as in 105. 22; 107. 32; 119. 100.
YOUTHS,] as in 37. 25; 119. 9; Ge. 14. 24.
13. NAME OF JEHOVAH,] as in v. 5, &c.
SET ON HIGH,] as in Prov. 18. 11; Isa. 12. 4.
HONOUR,] as in 8. 1; 21. 5; 45. 3; 96. 6, &c.
14. EXALTETH,] as in 66. 7; 75. 4; 89. 17.
SAINTS,] as in 4. 3; 30. 4; 31. 23; 37. 28, &c.
NEAR,] as in 15. 3; 22. 11; 34. 18; 88. 11, &c.
PRAISE YE JAH,] as in v. 1, &c. Sept.
omits.

CXLIX. 1. PRAISE YE JAH,] as in v. 9, &c.
SING,] as in 33. 3; 68. 4; 96. 1; 98. 1, &c.
NEW SONG,] as in 33. 3; 40. 3; 96. 1; 98. 1.
PRAISE,] as in 9. 14; 22. 3; 33. 1; 34. 1, &c.
ASSEMBLY,] as in 22. 22; 26. 5; 35. 18, &c.
SAINTS,] as in v. 5, 9; 4. 3; 12. 1; 30. 4, &c.
2. ISRAEL,] who is a 'prince with God.'
REJOICE,] as in 5. 11; 9. 2; 14. 7; 21. 1, &c.
MAKER,] as in 14. 1; 15. 5; 18. 50; 31. 23.
ZION,] the 'sunny place.'
JOY,] as in 9. 14; 13. 4; 14. 7; 16. 9; 21. 1.
KING,] as in v. 8; 2. 2; 5. 2; 10. 16; 18. 50.
3. PRAISE,] as in 22. 22; 35. 18; 56. 4; 63. 5.
DANCE,] as in 30. 11; 150. 4; Jer. 31. 4;
Lam. 5. 15. Sept. Vulg. 'chorus.'
TIMBREL,] as in 81. 2; 150. 4; Ex. 15. 20, &c.
HARP,] as in 33. 2; 43. 4; 49. 4; 57. 8, &c.
SING PRAISE,] as in 22. 22; 35. 18; 56. 4, &c.
4. PLEASED,] as in 147. 11; Jer. 14. 12.
BEAUTIFIETH,] as in De. 24. 20; Isa. 55. 5;
60. 9, 13, &c. Sept. Vulg. 'exalt.'
HUMBLE,] as in 9. 12; 10. 12; 22. 26; 25. 9.
SALVATION,] as in 3. 2; 9. 14; 13. 5; 14. 7.
5. EXULT,] as in 28. 7; 60. 6; 94. 3; 96. 12.
SAINTS,] as in v. 1, 9.
HONOUR,] as in 3. 3; 7. 5; 8. 5; 16. 9, &c.
SING ALOUD,] as in 5. 11; 20. 5; 51. 14, &c.
BEDS,] as in 4. 4; 36. 4; 41. 3; Ge. 49. 4, &c.

6. EXALTATION,] as in 66. 17.
THROAT,] as in 5. 9; 69. 3; 115. 7, &c.
TWO-EDGED,] as in Isa. 41. 15.
7 VENGEANCE,] as in 18. 47; 79. 10; 94. 1.
PUNISHMENTS,] as in 2 K. 19. 3; Isa. 37. 3;
Hos. 5. 9.
8. BIND,] as in 105. 22; Nu. 30. 2, &c.
CHAINS,] as in Job 36. 8; Prov. 26. 18;
Isa. 45. 14; Nah. 3. 10.
HONOURED ONES,] as in 87. 3; Ge. 24. 19.
FETTERS,] as in 105. 18.
IRON,] as in 2. 9; 105. 18; 107. 10, 16, &c.
9. WRITTEN,] as in 40. 7; Ex. 31. 18; 32. 15.
HONOUR,] as in 8. 5; 21. 5; 29. 4; 45. 3, &c.
SAINTS,] as in v. 1, 5, &c.
PRAISE YE JAH,] as in v. 1, &c. Sept.
omits.

CL. 1. PRAISE YE JAH,] as in v. 6; 115. 18.
HOLY PLACE,] as in 2. 7; 3. 4; 5. 7; 11. 4.
EXPANSE,] as in 19. 1; Ge. 1. 6, 7, 8, 14, 15,
17, 20, &c. Aben Ezra, 'the ark.'
STRENGTH,] as in 8. 2; 21. 1; 28. 7; 29. 1.
2. MIGHTY ACTS,] as in 106. 2; 145. 4, 11, 12.
ABUNDANCE OF HIS GREATNESS,] as in Ex.
15. 7.
3. BLOWING.] Sept. 'echo.'
TRUMPET,] as in 47. 5; 81. 3; 98. 6, &c.
PSALTERY,] as in 33. 2; 57. 8; 71. 22; 81. 2.
HARP,] as in 33. 2; 43. 4; 49. 4; 57. 8, &c.
4. TIMBREL,] as in 81. 2; 149. 3; Ex. 15. 20.
DANCE,] as in 30. 11; 149. 3; Jer. 31. 4, 13;
Lam. 5. 15, &c. Sept. 'chorus.'
STRINGED INSTRUMENTS,] as in 45. 8, &c.
5. CYMBALS,] as in 2 Sa. 6. 5; Job 41. 7; Isa
18. 1.
SOUNDING,] as in 18. 44; Ge. 29. 13, &c.
SHOUTING,] as in 27. 6; 33. 3; 47. 5; 89. 15.
BREATHE,] as in 18. 15; Ge. 2. 7; 7. 22, &c.
PRAISE YE JAH,] as in v. 1, &c. Sept.
omits this clause, but adds an additional
Psalm, not found in any Hebrew MSS.

THE BOOK OF PROVERBS

THE BOOK OF PROVERBS (*lit.* ruling things), is divided into seven parts, the *first* (Ch. i.—ix. inclusive) probably committed to writing, and issued by Solomon himself; the *second*, (Ch. x.—xxii. 16, inclusive) probably spoken, but not written by him; the *third,* (Ch. xxii. 17—to xxiv. inclusive) professedly those which the men of Hezekiah transcribed from documents left by Solomon; the *fourth,* (Ch. xxv.—xxix. inclusive) an additional collection which is simply said to be 'For the wise;' the *fifth,* (Ch. xxx.) professedly the words of one who styles himself *Agur,* a 'Gatherer,' with which may be compared *Koheleth* and *Asaph;* the *sixth,* (Ch. xxxi. 1—9) the words of King Lemuel; and the *seventh,* (Ch. xxxi. 10—31) a description of a 'woman of worth,' physically, mentally, and morally.

It is quoted repeatedly in the New Testament, e. g. Prov. 1. 16 in Rom. 3. 10, 15; 3. 7 in Rom. 12. 16; 3. 11, 12 in Heb. 12. 5, 6. and in Rev. 3. 19; 3. 34 in James 4. 6; 10. 12 in 1 Pet. 4. 8; 11. 31 in 2 Pet. 4. 18; 17. 13 in Rom. 12. 17; 1 Thes. 5. 15; 1 Peter 3. 9; 17. 27 in Jas. 1. 19; 20. 9 in 1 John 1. 8; 20. 20 in Mat. 15. 4; Mark 7. 10; 20. 22 in Rom. 12. 17; 25. 21 in Rom. 12. 20; 26. 11 in 2 Pet. 2. 22.

In 1 K. 4. 32 Solomon is said to have spoken 'three thousand' similes or proverbs, but they have not all been preserved, yet there are sufficient to excite our admiration of the wisdom conferred upon him.

I. 1. PROVERBS,] as in v. 6; 10. 1; 25. 1, &c.
SOLOMON,] i. e. the 'peaceful one.'
SON OF DAVID,] as in 1 Ch. 17. 17; 29. 22
KING OF ISRAEL,] as in 1 Sa. 24. 14; 26. 20.
2. KNOWING,] as in 4. 1; 27. 23; Ge. 3. 22.
WISDOM,] as in v. 7; 2. 2; 6. 10; 3. 13; 4. 5.
INSTRUCTION,] as in v. 3; 7. 8; 3. 11; 4. 1.
UNDERSTANDING,] as in v. 6; 14. 8, &c.
SAYINGS,] as in v. 21; 2. 1, 16; 4. 5, 10, 20.
INTELLIGENCE,] as in 2. 3; 3. 5; 4. 1; 7. 4.
3. RECEIVING,] as in Ge. 4. 11; 24. 48, &c.
INSTRUCTION.] Sept. 'turning of words to understand true justice.'
WISDOM,] as in 3. 4; 12. 8; 13. 15; 16. 22.
RIGHTEOUSNESS,] as in 2. 9; 8. 8, 15; 12. 17.
JUDGMENT,] as in 2. 8, 9; 8. 20; 12. 5, &c.
UPRIGHTNESS.] Sept. 'and to direct judgment.'
4. SIMPLE ONES,] as in v. 22, 32; 7. 7; 8. 5.
PRUDENCE,] as in 8. 5, 12; Ex. 21. 14; Jos. 9. 4.
YOUTH,] as in 7. 7; 20. 11; 22. 6, 15; 23. 13.
KNOWLEDGE,] as in v. 7, 22, 29; 2. 5, 6, &c.
DISCRETION,] as in 2. 11; 3. 21; 5. 2; 8. 12.
5. WISE,] as in v. 6; 3. 7, 35; 9. 8, 9; 10. 1.
HEAR,] as in 15. 29; 18. 13; 29. 24; Ge. 3. 8.
INCREASETH,] as in 3. 2; 9. 9, 11; 10. 22.
LEARNING,] as in 4. 2; 7. 21; 9. 9; 16. 21.
INTELLIGENT,] as in 10. 13; 14. 6, 33, &c.

OBTAIN,] as in 8. 22; 18. 15; Ge. 33. 19, &c.
COUNSELS,] as in 11. 14; 12. 5; 20. 18; 24 6; Job 37. 12.
6. UNDERSTANDING,] as in v. 2.
PROVERB,] as in v. 1, &c. Sept. Vulg 'parable.'
SWEETNESS,] as in Hab. 2. 6. Sept. a 'dark word;' Vulg. 'interpretation.'
WORDS OF THE WISE,] as Ecc. 10. 12; 12. 11.
ACUTE SAYINGS,] as in Nu. 12. 8; Jud. 14. 12.
7. FEAR OF JEHOVAH,] as in v. 29; 8. 13.
BEGINNING,] as in 3. 9; 4. 7; 8. 22; 17. 14, &c. Sept. adds, 'and good understanding have all doing it; reverence also to God is the beginning of understanding.'
FOOLS,] as in 7. 22; 10. 8, 14; 11. 29; 12. 15.
DESPISED,] as in 6. 30; 23. 9; 30. 17, &c.
8. HEAR,] as in 4. 1, 10; 5. 7; 7. 24; 8. 6, &c.
SON,] as in v. 10. 15; 2. 1; 3. 1; 4. 1, &c.
INSTRUCTION,] as in v. 3, 7. Sept. 'law.'
LEAVE,] as in 6. 20; Nu. 11. 31; De. 32. 15.
LAW,] as in 3. 1; 4. 2; 6. 20; 7. 2, &c.
9. GRACEFUL,] as in 3. 4, 22; 4. 9, 5. 19; 11. 16, &c. Sept. 'rules.'
WREATH,] as in 4. 9. Sept. 'crown.'
CHAINS,] as in Jud. 8. 26; Song 4. 9. Sept. adds, 'of gold.'
NECK,] as in 3. 3, 22; 26. 1.
10. SINNERS,] as in 13. 21; 33. 17; Ge. 13. 13.
ENTICE,] as in 16. 29; 24. 28; Ex. 22, 16, &c.
WILLING,] or consent.
11. COME,] as in 3. 28; 6. 3, 6; 7. 18; 9. 5.
LAY WAIT,] as in v. 18; 7. 12; 23. 28; 24. 15, &c. Sept. 'have fellowship.'
BLOOD,] as in v. 16, 18; 6. 17; 12. 6; 28. 17.
WATCH SECRETLY,] as in v. 18; 2. 1; 7. 1; 10. 14, &c. Sept. 'hide in the earth the just man unjustly.'
INNOCENT,] as in 6. 17; Ge. 24. 41; 44. 10.
WITHOUT CAUSE,] as in v. 17; 3. 30; 23. 29.
12. SWALLOW,] as in Ge. 41. 7; Ex. 7. 12,&c.
SHEOL,] the world of spirits.
ALIVE,] as in 2. 19; 3. 2, 18, 22; 4. 10; 5. 6.
WHOLE,] as in 2. 21; 11. 5, 20; 20, 10, 18, &c. Sept. 'and remove his memorial from the earth.'
GOING DOWN,] as in 5. 5; 7. 27; Ge. 28. 12.
PIT,] as in 5. 15; 28. 17; Ge. 37. 12, &c.
13. PRECIOUS,] as in 3. 15; 6. 26; 12. 27, &c.
SUBSTANCE,] as in 3. 9; 6. 31; 8. 18; 10. 15.
FIND,] as in v. 28; 2. 6; 3. 13; 7. 15; 8. 12.
SPOIL,] as in 16. 19; 31. 11; Ge. 49. 27, &c.
14. LOT,] as in 16. 33; 18. 18; Lev. 16. 8, 9.
CAST,] *lit* 'cause to fall.'
15. WAY,] as in v. 31; 2. 8, 12, 13, 20; 3. 6.
WITHHOLD,] as in Jer. 2. 25; 31. 16.
FOOT,] as in 3. 23; 4. 26; 5. 5, &c.
PATH,] as in 3. 17; 7. 25; 8. 2, 20; 12. 28.
16. EVIL,] as in v. 33; 2. 12; 3. 7; 4. 14, &c.
RUN,] as in 4. 12; 18. 10; Ge. 18. 2; 24. 17.
HASTE,] as in Ge. 18. 6, 7; 24. 18, 20, 46.
SHED BLOOD,] as in 6. 17; Ge. 9. 6; 37. 22.
17. IN VAIN,] as in v. 11, &c.

NET,] as in 29. 5; Ex. 27. 4, 5; 38. 4, &c.
BIRD,] as in 23. 5; Ge. 1. 21; 7. 14, &c.
18. LAY WAIT,] as in v. 11, &c.
WATCH SECRETLY,] as in v. 11, &c.
19. PATHS,] as in 2. 8, 13, 15, 19, 20; 3. 6.
GAINER,] as in 15. 27; Ps. 10. 3; Jer. 6. 13.
DISHONEST GAIN,] as in 15. 27; 28. 16, &c.
OWNERS,] as in 3. 27; 12. 4; 16. 22; 17. 8.
20. WISDOM,] as in 9. 1; 24. 7; Ps. 49. 3.
OUT-PLACE,] as in 5. 16; 7. 12; 8. 26; 22. 13.
CRIETH ALOUD,] as in 8. 3; 29. 6; Lev. 9. 24.
BROAD PLACE,] as in 5. 16; 7. 12; 22. 13, &c.
GIVETH FORTH HER VOICE,] as in 8. 1, &c.
21. MULTITUDES,] as in 7. 11; 9. 13; 20. 1.
CALLETH,] as in v. 28; 2. 3; 7. 4; 8. 1, &c.
OPENINGS OF THE GATES,] as in Jos. 8. 29.
CITY,] as in 16. 32; 21. 22; 25. 28; Ge. 4. 17.
SAYINGS,] as in v. 2, &c.
22. SIMPLE,] as in v. 4, 32. &c.
SIMPLICITY,] as in 7. 7; 8. 5; 9. 4, 16, &c.
SCORNING,] as in 29. 8; Isa. 28. 14.
DESIRED,] as in 12. 12; Ps. 68. 16; Isa. 1. 29.
FOOLS,] as in v. 32; 3. 35; 8. 5; 10. 1, &c.
HATE,] as in 9. 8; 13. 5; 26. 28; 29. 10, &c.
KNOWLEDGE,] as in v. 4, 7, 29, &c.
23. TURN BACK,] as in 2. 19; 12. 14; 25. 10.
REPROOF,] as in v. 25, 30; 3. 11; 5. 12, &c.
SPIRIT,] as in 11. 13; 14. 29; 15. 4; 16. 2, &c.
MAKE KNOWN,] as in Nu. 16. 5; Jud. 8. 16.
24. CALLED,] as in Ge. 1. 5, 10; 11. 9; 16. 11.
REFUGE,] as in Ge. 37. 25; 39. 8; 48. 19, &c.
STRETCHED OUT MY HAND,] as in Ex. 15. 12.
ATTENDING,] as in 17. 4; 29. 12; Song 8. 13.
25. SLIGHT,] as in 8. 33; Ex. 32. 25, &c.
COUNSEL,] as in v. 30; 8, 14; 12. 15; 19. 20.
REPROOF,] as in v. 23, 30.
DESIRED,] as in v. 30; Ex. 10. 27; De. 1. 26.
26. CALAMITY,] as in v. 27; 6. 15; 17. 5, &c.
LAUGH,] as in 31. 25; Job 5. 22; 29. 24, &c.
DERIDE,] as in 30. 17; Job 9. 23; 11. 3, &c.
FEAR,] as in v. 27, 33; 3. 25; Ge. 31. 42, &c.
27. HURRICANE,] as in 10. 25; Job 21. 18.
DISTRESS,] as in 11. 8; 12. 13; 17. 17, &c.
28. CALL,] as in v. 21, &c.
ANSWER,] as in 18. 23; 26. 4; Ge. 18. 27, &c.
FIND,] as in v. 13, &c.
29. HATED,] as in 5. 12; 6. 16; 8. 13; 19. 7.
KNOWLEDGE,] as in v. 4, 7, 22.
FEAR OF JEHOVAH,] as in v. 7, &c.
CHOSEN,] as in 3. 31; Ge. 6. 2; De. 7. 6, &c.
30. CONSENTED,] as in v. 25, &c.
DESPISED,] as in 5. 12; 15. 5; Ps. 107. 11.
REPROOF,] as in v. 23, 25, &c.
31. EAT,] as in 13. 2; 18. 21; 27. 18, &c.
FRUIT,] as in 8. 19; 11. 30; 12. 14; 13. 2, &c.
WAY,] as in v. 15, &c.
COUNSELS,] as in v. 25, &c.
FILLED,] as in 5. 10; 12. 11; 14. 14; 18. 20.
32. SIMPLE,] as in v. 4, 22, &c.
SLAYETH,] as in Ge. 4. 8; 20. 4; 26. 7, &c.
SECURITY,] as in 17. 1; Ps. 122. 7, &c.
FOOLISH,] as in v. 22, &c.
DESTROYETH,] as in 29. 3; Nu. 33. 52, &c.
33. HEARKENING,] as in 8. 34; 12. 15; 15. 31.
CONFIDENTLY,] as in 3. 23, 29; 10. 9, &c.
QUIET,] as in Job 3. 18; Jer. 30. 10; 46. 27.
FEAR,] as in v. 26, 27, &c.
EVIL,] as in v. 16, &c.

II. 1. MY SON,] as in 1. 1, 8, 10, 15; 3. 1, &c.
ACCEPT,] as in 1. 19; 6. 25; 10. 8; 17. 23, &c.

SAYING,] as in v. 16; 1. 2, 21; 4. 5; 5. 7, &c.
COMMAND,] as in 3. 1; 4. 4; 6. 20: 7. 1, 2.
LAY UP,] as in v. 7; 1. 11, 18; 7. 1; 27. 16.
2. CAUSE TO ATTEND,] as in 1 Sa. 15. 22;
Jer. 6. 10; Zec. 7. 11.
EAR,] as in 4. 20; 5. 1, 13; 15. 31; 18. 15.
WISDOM,] as in v. 6, 10; 2. 7; 3. 13, 18, &c.
UNDERSTANDING,] as in v. 3, 6, 11; 3. 13.
3. INTELLIGENCE,] as in 1. 2; 3. 5; 4. 1, &c.
CALLEST,] as in 1. 21; 7. 4; 8. 1; 9. 3, &c.
GIVEST FORTH THY VOICE,] as in 1. 20, &c.
4. SEEK,] as in 11. 27; 15. 14; 17. 11; 18. 1.
SILVER,] as in 3. 14; 7. 20; 8. 10; 10. 20, &c.
HID TREASURES,] as in Ge. 43. 23; Job 3.
21; Isa. 45. 3; Jer. 41. 8.
SEARCHEST,] as in Ps. 64. 6; Lam. 3. 40.
5. UNDERSTANDEST,] as in v. 9; 7. 7; 14. 15
FEAR OF JEHOVAH,] as in 1. 7, 29; 8. 13.
KNOWLEDGE OF GOD,] as in Hos. 4. 1; 6. 6
FINDEST,] as in 1. 13, 28; 6. 33; 7. 15; 8. 12
6. JEHOVAH,] as in 1. 7, 29, &c.
MOUTH,] as in 4. 5; 5. 4; 6. 2, 12; 7. 24, &c
7. UPRIGHT,] as in v. 21; 3. 32; 8. 9, &c.
SUBSTANCE,] as in 3. 21; 8. 14; 81. 1, &c.
SHIELD,] as in 6. 11; 24. 34; 30. 5; Ge. 15. 1
WALKING UPRIGHTLY,] as in 10. 9; 19. 1.
8. KEEP,] as in 3. 1; 4. 6; 5. 2; 13. 6; 20. 28
PATHS OF JUDGMENT,] as in 17. 23; Isa
26. 8.
SAINTS,] as in 1 Sa. 2. 9; 2 Ch. 6. 41, &c.
PRESERVETH,] as in v. 11, 20; 4. 6; 6. 22
9. RIGHTEOUSNESS,] as in 1. 3; 8. 8, 15, &c
JUDGMENT,] as in v. 8; 1. 3; 8. 20; 12. 5.
10. HEART,] as in v. 3; 2. 2, 10; 4. 4; 5. 12
PLEASANT,] as in 9. 17; 24. 5; Ge. 49. 15.
11. THOUGHTFULNESS,] as in 1. 4; 3. 21, &c
UNDERSTANDING,] as in v. 2, 3, 6, &c.
KEEP,] as in v. 8, 20, &c.
12. DELIVER,] as in v. 16; Ge. 37. 22, &c.
EVIL WAY,] as in 4. 14; 8. 13; 16. 17; 28. 10.
FROWARD THINGS,] as in 10. 32; 23. 33.
13. FORSAKING,] as in v. 17; 10. 17; 15. 10.
UPRIGHTNESS,] as in 4. 11; 11, 24; 14. 2, &c.
DARKNESS,] as in 20. 20; Ge. 1. 2, 4, 5, 18.
14. REJOICING,] as in 15. 13; 17. 5, 22, &c.
EVIL,] as in 1. 16, 33; 3. 7; 4. 14; 5. 14, &c.
DELIGHT,] as in 23. 24; 24. 17; 1 Ch. 16. 31.
FROWARDNESS,] as in v. 12; 6. 14; 8. 13, &c.
WICKED,] as in v. 12, &c.
15. CROOKED,] as in 8. 8; 11. 20; 17. 20, &c.
PERVERTED,] as in 3. 22; 14. 2: Isa. 30. 12.
16. DELIVER,] as in v. 12, &c.
STRANGE WOMAN,] as in 7. 5, &c.
STRANGER,] as in 5. 10; 6. 24; 7. 5; 20. 16.
MADE SMOOTH,] as in 7. 5; Ps. 5. 9; 36. 2.
17. FORSAKING,] as in v. 13, &c.
GUIDE,] as in 16. 28; 17. 9; Ps. 55, 13, &c.
YOUTH,] as in 5. 18; Ge. 8. 21; 46. 34, &c.
COVENANT,] as in Ge. 6. 18; 9. 9; 14. 13, &c.
FORGOTTEN,] as in 3. 1; 4. 5; 31. 5, 7, &c.
18. INCLINED,] as in Ps. 44. 25, &c.
DEATH,] as in 5. 5; 7. 27; 8. 36; 10. 2, &c.
REPHAIM,] Sept. 'giants.'
PATHS,] as in 4. 11, 26; 1 Sa. 20. 5; Ps. 23. 3.
19. TURN BACK,] as in 1. 23; 12. 14; 25. 10.
REACH,] as in Ge. 31. 25; 44. 6; Ex. 14. 9.
PATHS OF LIFE,] as in 5. 6; 6. 23; 10. 17, &c.
20. GO,] as in 15: 3. 23; 10. 9; 15. 12, &c.
KEEP,] as in v. 8, 11, &c.
21. INHABIT,] as in 1. 33; 7. 11; 10. 30, &c.
PERFECT,] as in 1. 12; 11. 5; 28. 10, 18, &c

INCLINED MINE EAR,] as in Jer. 7. 24, &c.
14. AS A LITTLE THING,] as in 6. 10; 10. 20.
ALL EVIL,] as in 20. 8; Jud. 9. 57, &c.
ASSEMBLY,] as in 21. 16; 26. 26; Ge. 28. 3.
COMPANY,] as in Ex. 12. 3; 16. 1; 17. 1, &c.
15. DRINK,] as in 9. 5; 23. 7; Ge. 24. 14, &c.
CISTERN,] as in 1. 12; 28. 17; Ge. 37. 20, &c.
FLOWING ONES,] as in Ex. 15. 8; Ps. 78. 16.
WELL,] as in 23. 27; Ge. 16. 14; 21. 19, &c.
16. FOUNTAINS,] as in 8. 24; 25. 26, &c.
SCATTERED ABROAD,] as in Ge. 11. 4. &c.
BROAD PLACES,] as in 1. 20; 7. 12; 22. 13.
RIVULETS,} as in 21. 1; Job 29. 6; Ps. 1. 3.
17. STRANGERS,] as in v. 3, 10, 20, &c.
18. FOUNTAIN,] as in 10. 11; 13. 14; 14. 27.
REJOICE,] as in De. 33. 18; Jud. 9. 19. &c.
WIFE OF THY YOUTH,] as in Isa. 54. 6; Mal.
2. 14, 15.
19. HIND,] as in Jer. 14. 5, &c.
LOVES,] as in 10. 12; 15. 17; 17. 9; 27. 5, &c.
GRACE,] as in 1. 9; 3. 4, 22; 4. 9; 11. 16, &c.
SATISFY,] as in Isa. 16. 9; 34. 5, 7, &c.
MAGNIFY,] as in v. 20, 23; Lev. 4. 13, &c.
CONTINUALLY,] as in 6. 21; 15. 15; 28. 14.
20. MAGNIFY THYSELF,] as in v. 19, 23. &c.
STRANGER,] as in v. 10, &c.
EMBRACE,] as in 4. 8; Ge. 29. 13; 33. 4, &c.
BOSOM,] as in 6. 27; 16. 33; 17. 23; 21. 14.
STRANGE WOMAN,] as in v. 3, 10, 17, &c.
21. OVER-AGAINST,] as in 4. 25; Ge. 30. 38.
22. INIQUITIES,] as in 16. 6; Ge. 4. 13, &c.
CAPTURE,] as in Nu. 31. 32; 32. 39, 41, &c.
WICKED,] as in 2. 22; 3. 25, 33; 4. 14; 9. 7.
ROPES,] as in De. 3. 4, 13; 32. 9; Jos. 2. 15.
23. INSTRUCTION,] as in v. 12 &c.
ABUNDANCE,] as in 7. 21; 10. 19; 11. 14, &c.
FOLLY,] as in 12. 23; 13. 16; 14. 1, 8, 17.
MAGNIFIETH HIMSELF,] as in v. 19, 20.

VI. 1. MY SON,] as in v. 3; 1. 8, 10, 15; 2. 1.
SURETY,] as in 3. 24; 11. 15; 20. 16; 27. 13.
FRIEND,] as in v. 3, 26; 3. 28, 29; 11. 9, 12.
STRICKEN,] as in Ge. 31. 25; Nu. 10. 3, &c.
STRANGER,] as in 2. 16; 5. 3, 10, 17, 20, &c.
2. SNARED,] as in Isa. 8. 15; 28. 13, &c.
SAYINGS OF THY MOUTH,] as in 4. 5; 7. 24.
CAPTURED,] as in 1 K. 16. 18; 2 K. 18. 10.
3. BE DELIVERED,] as in v. 5, &c.
4. SLEEP,] as in v. 9, 10; 3. 24; 4. 16; 20. 13.
SLUMBER,] as in v. 10; 24. 33; Job 33. 15.
EYE-LIDS,] as in v. 25; 4. 25; 30. 13, &c.
5. BE DELIVERED,] as in v. 3, &c.
ROE,] as in De. 12. 15, 22; 14. 5; 15. 22, &c.
BIRD,] as in 7. 23; 16. 2; 27. 8; Ge. 7. 14.
FOWLER,] as in Ps. 91. 3; Jer. 5. 26, &c.
6. ANT,] as in 30. 25, &c.
SLOTHFUL ONE,] as in v. 9; 10. 26; 13. 4.
BE WISE,] as in 8. 33; 23. 19; 27. 11.
7. CAPTAIN,] as in 25. 15; Jos. 10. 24, &c.
OVERSEER,] as in Ex. 5. 6; Nu. 11. 16, &c.
RULER,] as in 16. 32; 23. 1; 28. 15; 29. 12.
8. PREPARE,] as in 16. 9; 21. 29; 30. 25, &c.
SUMMER,] as in 10. 5; 26. 1; 30. 25; Ge. 8. 22.
BREAD,] as in v. 26; 4. 17; 9. 5, 17; 12. 9, 11.
GATHERED,] as in De. 28. 39.
HARVEST,] as in 10. 5; 20. 4; 25. 13; 26. 1.
FOOD,] as in Ge. 2. 9; 3. 6; 6. 21; 40. 17, &c.
9. SLOTHFUL ONE,] as in v. 6, &c.
LIE,] as in 3. 24; Ge. 19. 4; 28. 11; 30. 15.
SLEEP,] as in v. 4, 10, &c.
10. SLUMBER,] as in v. 4, &c.

CLASPING,] as in 24. 33, &c.
TO REST,] as in v. 22; 24. 33; Ge. 19. 33, &c.
11. POVERTY,] as in 30. 8, &c.
TRAVELLER,] as in Ps. 104. 3; Ecc. 4. 15.
WANT,] as in 11. 24; 14. 23; 21. 5, 17; 22. 16.
ARMED MAN,] as in 24. 34; 30. 5, &c.
12. WORTHLESSNESS,] as in 16. 27; 19. 28.
INIQUITY,] as in v. 18; 10. 29; 11. 7; 12. 21.
WALKING,] as in 2. 7; 4. 18; 7. 22; 10. 9, &c.
PERVERSENESS,] as in 4. 24, &c.
13. WINKING,] as in 10. 10; 16. 30, &c.
FEET,] as in v. 18, 28; 1. 15, 16; 3. 23, 26.
FINGERS,] as in 7. 3; Ex. 8. 19; 29. 12, &c.
14. FROWARDNESS,] as in 2. 12; 8. 13; 10. 31.
DEVISING,] as in v. 18; 12. 20; 14. 22, &c.
CONTENTIONS,] as in v. 19; 10. 12; 18. 18.
SENDETH FORTH,] as in 16. 28; 31. 19, 20, &c.
15. SUDDENLY,] as in 3. 25; 7. 22; 24. 22, &c.
CALAMITY,] as in 1. 26, 27; 17. 5; 24. 22, &c.
INSTANTLY,] as in 29. 1; Nu. 9. 6; 35. 22.
BROKEN,] as in 29. 1; Lev. 6. 28; 15. 12, &c.
HEALING,] as in 4. 22; 12. 18; 13. 17; 16. 24.
16. HATED,] as in 1. 29; 5. 12; 8. 13; 19. 7.
ABOMINATIONS,] as in 3. 22; 8. 7; 11. 1, 20.
17. HIGH,] as in 24. 7; Ex. 14. 8; Nu. 15. 30.
FALSE,] as in v. 19; 10. 18; 11. 18; 12. 17.
SHEDDING,] as in Ge. 9. 6; Nu. 35. 33, &c.
INNOCENT BLOOD,] as in De. 21. 8, &c.
18. DEVISING,] as in v. 14, &c.
THOUGHTS,] as in 12. 5; 15. 22; 16. 3, &c.
VANITY,] as in v. 12, &c.
HASTING,] as in Ge. 41. 32; Mal. 3. 5.
RUN,] as in 1 Sa. 20. 6; Ps. 19. 5.
EVIL,] as in v. 14, 24, &c.
19. FALSE,] as in v. 17, &c.
WITNESS,] as in 12. 17; 14. 5, 25; 19. 5, 9.
BREATHE OUT,] as in 12. 17; 14. 5, 25; 19. 5.
LIES,] as in 14. 5, 25; 19. 5, 9; 21. 28; 23. 3.
SENDING FORTH,] as in Ge. 43. 4; Ex. 8. 21.
CONTENTIONS,] as in v. 14, &c.
20. COMMAND,] as in v. 23; 2. 1; 3. 1; 4. 4.
FATHER,] as in 1. 8; 3. 12; 4. 1, 3; 10. 1; 13. 1.
LEAVE,] as in 1. 8; Nu. 11. 31; De. 32. 15.
LAW,] as in v. 23; 1. 8; 3. 1; 4. 2; 7. 2, &c.
21. BIND,] as in 3. 3; 7. 3, &c.
CONTINUALLY,] as in 5. 19; 15. 15; 28. 14.
TIE,] as in Job 31. 36, &c.
NECK,] as in 1. 9; 3. 3, 22; 26. 1.
22. GOING UP AND DOWN,] as in Job 1. 7, &c.
LEADETH,] as in 11. 3; 18. 16; De. 32. 12.
LYING DOWN,] as in v. 10, &c.
WATCHETH,] as in 2. 8, 11; 4. 6; 8, 32; 14. 3.
AWAKED,] as in 2 K. 4. 31; Ps. 3. 5; 139. 18.
TALKETH,] as in Job 11. 7; Ps. 55. 17; 69. 12.
23. LAMP,] as in v. 13; 9. 20, 27; 24. 20, &c.
LIGHT,] as in 5. 18; 13. 9; 16. 15; Ge. 1. 3.
WAY OF LIFE,] as in 10. 17; 15. 24, &c.
REPROOF,] as in 1. 23, 25, 30; 3. 11; 5. 12.
INSTRUCTION,] as in 1. 2, 3, 7, 8; 3. 11, &c.
24. FLATTERY,] as in Ps. 12. 2; 73. 18; Isa.
30. 10; Jer. 12. 10.
STRANGE WOMAN,] as in 2 17; 5. 10; 7. 5.
25. DESIRE,] as in 1. 22; 12. 12; Ex. 20. 17.
BEAUTY,] as in 31. 30; Est. 1. 11; Ps. 45. 11.
EYE-LIDS,] as in v. 4, &c.
26. HARLOT,] as in 7. 10; 23. 27; 29. 3, &c.
ADULTERESS,] as in 30. 20; Lev. 20. 10.
PRECIOUS,] as in 1. 13; 3. 15; 20. 15; 27. 27
HUNTETH,] as in Lev. 17. 13; Job 10. 16.
27. FIRE,] as in Ps. 52. 5; Isa. 30. 14.
BOSOM,] as in 5. 20; 16. 33; 17. 23; 21. 14.

GARMENTS,] as in 20. 16; 25. 20; 27. 13, &c.
BURNT,] as in Ge. 38. 24; Lev. 4. 12; 6. 30.
28. HOT COALS,] as in 25. 22; 26. 21, &c.
SCORCHED,] as in Isa. 43. 2, &c.
29. NEIGHBOUR,] as in v. 1, 3, &c.
TOUCH,] as in Ge. 26. 11; Ex. 19. 12; 29. 37.
INNOCENT,] as in 11. 21; 16. 5; 17. 5; 19. 5.
30. DESPISE,] as in 23. 9, 22; 30. 17, &c.
THIEF,] as in 29. 24; Ex. 22. 2, 7; De. 24. 7.
STEALETH,] as in Ge. 31. 19; 44. 8; Ex. 20. 15.
HUNGRY,] as in 19. 15; Ge. 41. 55, &c.
31. REPAYETH,] as in 13. 21; 19. 17; 20. 22.
SEVEN-FOLD,] as in Ge. 4. 15, 24; 2 Sa. 21. 9.
32. COMMITTETH ADULTERY,] as in Lev.
20. 10: Job 24. 15; Eze. 16. 38; 23. 45, &c.
LACKETH,] as in 7. 7; 9. 4, 16; 10. 13, 21.
DESTROYING,] as in 18. 9; 28. 24; Ge. 6. 13.
33. STROKE,] as in De. 17. 8; 21. 5; Ps. 38. 11.
SHAME,] as in 3. 35; 9. 7; 11. 2; 12. 16, &c.
REPROACH,] as in 18. 3; Ge. 30. 23; 34. 14.
WIPED AWAY,] as in Ge. 7. 23; De. 25. 6.
34. JEALOUSY,] as in 14. 30; 27. 4; Nu. 5. 14.
FURY,] as in 15. 1; 16. 14; 19. 19; 21. 14, &c.
SPARE,] as in Ex. 2. 6; De. 13. 8; 1 Sa. 15. 3.
VENGEANCE,] as in De. 32. 35; Jud. 16. 28.
35. APPEARANCE,] as in 4. 3; 7. 13; 8. 25.
ATONEMENT,] as in 13. 8; 21. 18; Ex. 30. 12.
CONSENT,] as in 1. 10; Ge. 24. 5; Lev. 26. 21.
MULTIPLY,] as in 13. 11; Ge. 3. 16; 16. 10.
BRIBES,] as in 17. 8, 23; 21. 14; Ex. 23. 8.

VII. 1. MY SON,] as in 1. 8, 10, 15; 2. 1; 3. 1.
SAYINGS,] as in v. 5, 24; 1. 2, 21; 2. 1, 16.
LAY UP,] as in 1. 11; 2. 1, 7; 10. 14, &c.
2. LIVE,] as in 4. 4; 9. 6; Ge. 20. 7; 42. 18.
LAW,] as in 1. 8; 3. 1; 4. 2; 6. 20, 23, &c.
PUPIL,] as in v. 9; 20. 20; De. 32. 10; Ps.
17. 8.
3. BIND,] as in 3. 3; 6. 21, &c.
FINGERS,] as in 6. 13; Ex. 8. 19; 29. 12, &c.
WRITE,] as in 3. 3; Ex. 17. 14; 34. 27, &c.
TABLET,] as in 3. 3; Ex. 24. 12; 27. 8, &c.
4. WISDOM,] as in 1. 2, 7; 2. 2, 6; 3. 13, 19.
SISTER,] as in Ge. 4. 22; 12. 13; 20. 2, 5, 12.
CRY,] as in 1. 21; 2. 3; 8. 1, 4; 9. 3, &c.
UNDERSTANDING,] as in 1. 2; 2. 3; 3. 5; 4.
1; 8. 14.
KINSWOMAN,] as in Ru. 4. 1, &c.
5. STRANGE WOMAN,] as in 2. 16; 5. 3, 20.
MADE SMOOTH,] as in 2. 16; Ps. 5. 9; 36. 2.
6. WINDOW,] as in Ge. 8. 6; 26. 8; Jos. 2. 15.
CASEMENT,] as in Jud. 5 28, &c.
LOOKED OUT,] as in Nu. 21. 10; Jud. 5. 28.
7. SIMPLE ONES,] as in 1. 4, 22, 32; 8. 5, &c.
DISCERN,] as in 2. 5, 9; 14. 15; 19. 25; 20. 24.
YOUNG MAN,] as in 1. 4, 10; 11; 22. 6, 15.
LACKING,] as in 6. 32; 9. 4, 16; 10. 13. 21.
8. PASSING ON,] as in 9. 15; 26. 10, 17, &c.
STREET,] as in Ecc. 12. 4, 5; Song 3. 2.
CORNER,] as in 21. 9; 25. 24; Ex. 27. 2, &c.
STEP,] as in Ge. 49. 22; 2 Sa. 6. 13; Jer. 10.
5; Hab. 3. 12.
9. TWILIGHT,] as in 1 Sa. 30. 17; 2 K. 7. 5.
DARKNESS,] as in 4. 19; Ex. 10. 22, &c.
BLACKNESS,] as in v. 2, &c.
10. MEET,] as in v. 15; Ge. 14. 17; 15. 10.
DRESS,] as in Ps. 73. 6.
11. NOISY,] as in 1. 21; 9 18; 20. 1, &c.
STUBBORN,] as in De. 21 18; Neh. 9. 29, &c.
REST,] as in 1. 33; 2. 21; 10. 30; Ge. 9. 27.
12. OUT-PLACE,] as in 1. 20; 5. 16; 9. 26, &c.

BROAD-PLACES,] as in 1. 20; 5. 16; 7. 12, &c.
LIETH IN WAIT,] as in 1. 11, 18; 23. 28, &c.
13. LAID HOLD,] as in Job 27. 6; Isa. 4. 1.
KISSED,] as in 2 Sa. 15. 5; 1 K. 10. 18, &c.
HARDENED,] as in 21. 29, &c.
14. SACRIFICES,] as in 15. 8; 17. 1; 21. 3, 27.
PEACE-OFFERINGS,] as in Ex. 20. 24; 24. 5.
COMPLETED,] as in 6. 31; 13. 21; 19. 17, &c.
VOWS,] as in 20. 25, 31. 2; Ge. 28. 20; 21. 13.
15. MEET,] as in v. 10, &c.
16. ORNAMENTAL COVERINGS,] as in 31. 22.
COUCH,] as in De. 3. 11; Job 7. 13; Ps. 6 6
17. BED,] as in 22. 27; Ge. 49. 4; Ex. 8. 3.
MYRRH,] as in Ex. 30. 23; Est. 2. 12, &c.
ALOES,] as in Nu. 24. 6; Ps. 45. 8, &c.
CINNAMON,] as in Ex. 30. 23; Song 4. 14, &c.
18. LOVES,] as in Song 1. 2; 2. 3; 4. 10, &c.
MORNING,] as in 27. 14; Ge. 1. 5; 19. 27, &c.
LOVES,] as in 5. 9; Hos. 8. 9.
19. THE MAN,] as in 2. 12; 3. 31; 5. 21, &c.
LONG,] as in 25. 25; 31. 14; 2 Sa. 15. 17, &c.
JOURNEY,] as in v. 8, 25, 27, &c.
20. BAG,] as in 26. 8; Ge. 42. 25; 1 Sa. 25. 29.
MONEY,] as in 2. 4; 3. 14; 8. 10, 19; 10. 20.
21. TURNETH ASIDE,] as in 5. 13; 1 K. 11. 4.
SPEECH,] as in 1. 5; 4. 2; 9. 9; 16. 21, 23.
FLATTERY,] as in Job 17. 5; 20. 29; 27. 13.
22. STRAIGHTWAY,] as in 25; 6. 15; 24. 22.
OX,] as in 14. 4; 15. 17; Ex. 20. 17; 21. 28.
SLAUGHTER,] as in 9. 2; Ge. 43. 16, &c.
FETTER,] as in Isa. 3. 18, &c.
CHASTISEMENT,] as in 1. 2, 3, 7, 8; 3. 11,&c.
FOOL,] as in 1. 7; 10. 8, 14, 21; 11. 29; 12. 15
23. ARROW,] as in 25. 18; 26. 18; Ge. 49. 23.
SPLIT,] as in 2 K. 4. 39; Job 16. 13; 39. 3.
LIVER,] as in Ex. 29. 3; Lev. 3. 4; 4. 9, &c.
BIRD,] as in 6. 5; 26. 2; 27. 8; Ge. 7. 14, &c.
HASTENED,] as in Ex. 12. 23; 1 Ch. 12. 8
Isa. 18. 1.
SNARE,] as in 22. 5; Ps. 11. 6; 69. 22; 91. 3.
LIFE,] as in 1. 18, 19; 2. 10; 3 22; 6. 16, &c.
24. GIVE ATTENTION,] as in 4. 1, 20; 5. 1.
SAYINGS OF MY MOUTH,] as in v. 1, 5; 5. 7.
25. TURN,] as in Nu. 5. 12, 19, 20, 29, &c.
WAYS,] as in v. 8, 9, 27, &c.
WANDER,] as in 14. 22; Ge. 21. 14, &c.
PATHS,] as in 1. 15; 3. 17; 4. 11; 12. 28.
26. WOUNDED,] as in Ge. 34. 27; Lev. 21. 7.
CAUSED TO FALL,] as in De. 25. 2; Jos. 23. 4.
MIGHTY,] as in 18. 18; 30. 26; Ge. 18. 18,&c.
SLAIN ONES,] as in Est. 9. 11; Isa. 10. 4, &c.
27. SHEOL,] the unseen world.
INNER CHAMBERS,] as in 18. 8; 20. 27, &c.

VIII. 1. WISDOM,] as in v. 11, 12; 1. 2, 7.
CALL,] as in v. 4; 1. 21, 28; 2. 3; 7. 4; 9. 3
UNDERSTANDING,] as in 2. 2; 3. 13; 5. 1, &c.
GIVE FORTH HER VOICE,] as in 1. 20, &c.
2. HEAD,] as in v. 23, 26; 1. 9, 21; 4. 9, &c.
HIGH PLACES,] as in 9. 3, 14; Jud. 5. 18, &c.
WAY,] as in v. 13, 22, 32; 1. 15, 31, &c.
PATHS,] as in v. 20; 1. 15; 3. 17; 12. 28, &c.
STOOD,] as in Ge. 37. 7; Ex. 7. 15; 15. 8, &c.
3. SIDE,] as in 1. 24; 3. 27; 6. 5; 7. 20, &c
GATES,] as in 1. 21; 14. 19; 22. 22; 24. 7, &c.
CITY,] as in 9. 3, 14; 11. 11; Job 29. 7.
ENTRANCE,] as in De. 11. 30; Jos. 1. 4, &c.
OPENINGS,] as in v. 34; 1. 21; 5. 8; 9. 14.
CRIETH ALOUD,] as in 1. 20; 29. 6; Lev. 9. 24.
4. CALL,] as in v. 1, &c.
SONS OF MEN,] as in v. 31; 15. 11; Ge. 11. 5

CRIETH,] as in 1. 21; 2. 3; 7. 4; 8. 1; 12. 23.
TOPS,] as in Ex. 21. 3, 4, &c.
HIGH PLACES,] as in v. 14; 8. 2; Jud. 5. 18.
CITY,] as in v. 14; 8. 3; 11. 11; Job 29. 7.
4. SIMPLE,] as in v. 6, 16; 1. 4, 22; 7. 7, &c.
TURN ASIDE.] as in v. 16; 5. 7; 22. 6, &c.
LACKETH HEART,] as in v. 16; 6. 32; 7. 7.
10. 13; 12. 11.
5. COME,] as in 1. 11; 3. 28; 6. 3, 6; 7. 18.
BREAD,] as in v. 17; 4. 17; 6. 8; 12. 9, &c
WINE,] as in v. 2, &c.
MINGLED,] as in v. 2, &c.
6. FORSAKE,] as in Ps. 37. 8; Jer. 48. 28, &c.
SIMPLE,] as in v. 4, 16, &c.
LIVE,] as in 4. 4; 7. 2; Ge. 20. 7; 42. 18, &c,
BE HAPPY,] as in 23. 19; Isa. 1. 17.
UNDERSTANDING,] as in v. 10; 1. 2; 2. 3, &c.
7. INSTRUCTOR,] as in Ps. 94. 10, &c.
SCORNER,] as in v. 8; 1. 22; 3. 34; 13. 1, &c.
SHAME,] as in 3. 35; 6. 33; 11. 2; 12. 16, &c.
REPROVER,] as in 24. 25; 25. 12; 28. 23, &c.
BLEMISH,] as in Lev. 21. 17; 22. 20, 21, 25.
8. SCORNER,] as in v. 7, &c.
WISE,] as in v. 9; 1. 5, 6; 3. 7, 25; 10. 1, &c.
9. MAKE KNOWN,] as in Ex. 33. 13; 1 Sa. 6. 2.
LEARNING,] as in 1. 5; 4. 2; 7. 21; 16. 21.
10. COMMENCEMENT,] as in Ge. 13. 3; 41. 21.
FEAR OF JEHOVAH,] as in 1. 7, 29; 2. 5, &c.
KNOWLEDGE,] as in 1. 4, 7, 22, 29; 2. 5, &c.
HOLY ONES.] as in Ex. 25. 33; 28. 2; 29. 37.
UNDERSTANDING,] as in v. 6, &c.
11. MULTIPLY,] as in 4. 10; 28. 28; 29. 16.
YEARS OF LIFE,] as in 3. 2; 4. 10; 5. 9, &c.
12. SCORNED,] as in v. 7, 8, &c.
BEAREST,] as in 6. 35; 18. 14; 19. 18, &c.
13. FOOLISH.] Original word is not found again.
NOISY,] as in 1. 21; 7. 11; 20. 1, &c.
SIMPLE,] as in v. 4, 6, &c.
14. SAT,] as in 1 K. 1. 35; 2. 12; 2 K. 7. 4.
OPENING,] as in 1. 21; 5. 8; 8. 3, 34; 17. 19.
THRONE,] as in 16. 12; 20. 8; 25. 5; 29. 14.
HIGH PLACES,] as in v. 3, &c.
CITY,] as in v. 3, &c.
15. PASSING BY,] as in 7. 8; 26. 10, 17, &c.
GOING STRAIGHT,] or 'making upright.'
16. SIMPLE,] as in v. 4, 6, &c.
TURN ASIDE,] as in v. 4, &c.
LACKETH HEART,] as in v. 4, &c.
17. STOLEN,] as in Ge. 30. 33; 31. 39, &c.
SWEET,] as in Ex. 15. 25; Job 21. 33; 24. 20.
HIDDEN,] as in 21. 14; 25. 23; De. 13. 6, &c.
PLEASANT,] as in 2. 10; 24. 25; Ge. 49. 15.
18. REPHAIM,] as in 2. 18; 21. 16; Job 26. 5.
DEEP PLACES,] as in Isa. 33. 19; Eze. 3. 5.
SHEOL,] as in 1. 12; 5. 5; 7. 27; 15. 11, &c.
INVITED ONES,] as in Nu. 1. 16; 26. 9; 1 Sa. 9. 13, &c. Sept. adds a long verse here not found elsewhere.

X. PROVERBS OF SOLOMON,] as in 1. 1; 25. 1. Sept. omits this inscription, which begins the Second Collection in this Book.
1. WISE SON,] as in 13. 1; 15. 20, &c.
REJOICE,] as in 12. 25; 15. 20, 30; 27. 9, &c.
FOOLISH SON,] as in 17. 25; 19. 13, &c.
AFFLICTION,] as in 14. 13; 17. 21; Ps. 119. 28.
2. TREASURES,] as in 8. 21; 15. 16; 21. 6, 20.
PROFIT,] as in 11. 4; 1 Sa. 12. 21, &c.
RIGHTEOUSNESS.] Sept. 'treasures shall not profit the lawless.'

DELIVERETH,] as in 11. 4, 6; 12. 6; 19. 19.
3. TO HUNGER,] as in De. 8. 3.
DESIRE,] not 'substance,' as in C. V.; Sept. 'life.'
THRUSTETH AWAY,] as in Nu. 35. 20, &c.
4. POOR,] as in 13. 8, 23; 14. 20; 17. 5, &c
WORKING,] or 'doing,' as in 11. 18; 12. 22
SLOTHFUL,] as in 12. 24, 27; 19. 15, &c.
DILIGENT,] as in 12. 24, 27; 13. 4; 21. 5.
MAKETH RICH,] as in v. 22; 21. 17; 23. 4.
5. GATHERING,] as in 6. 8; 26. 1; 30. 25; Ge. 8. 22.
SUMMER,] as in 6. 8; 26. 1; 30. 25; Ge. 8. 22.
SLEEPING,] as in Ps. 76. 6; Da. 10. 9, &c.
HARVEST,] as in 6. 8; 20. 4; 25. 13; 26. 1.
CAUSING SHAME,] as in 12. 4; 14. 35; 17. 2.
6. BLESSINGS,] as in v. 7, 22; 11. 11, 25, 26.
COVER,] as in v. 12.
VIOLENCE,] as in v. 11; 3. 31; 4. 17; 13. 2.
7. REMEMBRANCE,] as in Ex. 3. 15; 17. 14
BLESSING,] as in v. 6, 22.
ROT,] as in Isa. 40. 20.
8. ACCEPTETH,] or 'receiveth.'
TALKATIVE,] lit. 'fool of lips,' as in v. 10.
KICKETH,] as in Hos. 4. 14.
9. INTEGRITY,] as in v. 29; 2. 7; 13. 6, &c.
CONFIDENTLY,] not 'surely,' as in C. V.
PERVERTING,] as in Job 9. 20; Isa. 59. 8; Mic. 3. 9.
KNOWN,] as in 12. 16; 14. 33; Ge. 41. 31, &c.
10. WINKING,] as in 6. 13; 16. 30, &c.
GRIEF,] as in 15. 13; Job 9. 28; Ps. 16. 4; 147. 3.
FOOL,] as in v. 8, &c.
11. FOUNTAIN OF LIFE,] as in 13. 14; 14. 27; 16. 22; Ps. 36. 9.
MOUTH OF THE RIGHTEOUS,] as in v. 31, &c.
12. HATRED,] as in v. 18; 15. 17; 26. 26, &c.
AWAKETH,] as in Song 2. 7; 3. 5; 8. 4, &c.
CONTENTIONS,] as in 6. 14, 19.
TRANSGRESSIONS,] as in v. 19; 12. 13; 17. 9.
LOVE,] as in 5. 19; 15. 17; 17. 9; 27. 5, &c.
COVERETH,] as in v. 6.
13. INTELLIGENT,] as in 1. 5; 14. 6, 33, &c.
WISDOM,] as in v. 23, 31, &c.
ROD,] as in 13. 24; 22. 8, 15; 23. 13, 14, &c.
BACK,] as in 19. 29; 26. 3; Job 30. 5, &c.
UNDERSTANDING,] lit. 'heart.'
14. LAY UP,] as in 1. 11, 18; 2. 1, 7; 7. 1, &c.
RUIN,] or 'downfall,' as in v. 15, 29, &c.
15. WEALTH,] as in 1. 13; 3. 9; 6. 31; 8. 18, &c.
RICH,] as in 14. 20; 18. 11, 23; 22. 2, &c.
CITY,] as in 11. 10; 18. 11, 19; 29. 8, &c.
RUIN,] as in v. 14, 29, &c.
POOR,] or 'lean ones,' as in 14. 31, &c.
POVERTY,] as in 13. 18; 24. 34, &c.
16. WAGE,] as in 11. 18; Lev. 19. 13, &c.
LIFE,] as in v. 11, 17, &c.
INCREASE,] as in 3. 9, 14; 8. 19; 14. 4, &c.
SIN,] as in 5. 22; 20. 9; 21. 4; 24. 9, &c.
17. TRAVELLER,] as in 1. 19; 2. 8, 13, 15, &c
INSTRUCTION,] as in 1. 2, 3, 7, 8; 3. 11, &c.
FORSAKING,] as in 2. 13, 17; 15. 10; 28. 4, &c.
REBUKE,] as in 1. 23, 25, 30; 3. 11; 5. 12, &c.
CAUSING TO ERR,] as in Isa. 3. 12; 9. 16; 30. 28; Mic. 3. 5.
18. COVERING,] as in 11. 13; 17. 9; 28. 13, &c
HATRED,] as in v. 12, &c.
LYING LIPS,] as in 12. 22; 17. 7.
EVIL REPORT,] as in 25. 10; Ge. 37. 2, &c.
FOOL,] as in v. 1, 23, &c.
19. CEASETH,] as in Ge. 11. 8; Ex. 9. 29, &c

RESTRAINING,] as in 11. 24; 13. 24; 17. 27,&c.
20. CHOSEN,] as in 8. 10, 19; 16. 16; 21. 3, &c.
A LITTLE THING,] as in 5.14; 6. 10; 15. 16, &c.
21. DELIGHT,] or 'feed;' Vulg. 'instruct.'
LACK OF HEART,] as in 6. 32; 7. 7; 9. 4, &c.
22. BLESSING,] as in v. 6, 7, &c.
MAKETH RICH,] as in v. 4, &c.
GRIEF,] as in 5. 10; 14. 23; 15. 1, &c.
23. INVENTIONS,] not 'mischief,' as in C.V.
PLAY,] as in 14. 13; Job 8. 21; 12. 4, &c.
WISDOM,] as in v. 13, 31, &c.
24. FEARED THING,] as in Ps.34. 4; Isa. 66.4.
MEETETH,] or 'cometh' to him.
DESIRE,] as in 11. 23; 13. 12, 19; 18. 1, &c.
25. HURRICANE.] as in 1. 27; Job 21. 18, &c.
FOUNDATION,] as in Ex. 29. 12; Lev. 4. 7, &c.
26. VINEGAR,] as in 25. 20; Nu. 6. 3, &c.
TEETH,] as in 25. 19; 30. 14; Ge. 49. 12, &c.
SMOKE,] as in Ge. 15. 17; Ex. 19. 18, &c.
SLOTHFUL,] as in 6. 6, 9; 13. 4; 15. 19, &c.
27. FEAR OF JEHOVAH,] as in 1. 7, 29; 2. 5.
ADDETH,] as in v. 22; 1. 5; 3. 2; 9. 9, 11, &c.
SHORTENED,] as in Nu. 11. 23; 21. 4, &c.
28. HOPE,] as in 11. 7; 13. 12; Job 41. 9, &c.
JOYFUL,] as in 12. 20; 14. 10, 13; 15. 21, &c.
EXPECTATION,] as in 11. 7, 23; 19. 18, &c.
PERISHETH,] or ' is lost.'
29. WAY OF JEHOVAH,] that revealed by
him.
STRENGTH,] as in 2 Sa. 22. 33; Neh. 8. 10, &c.
PERFECT,] not ' upright,' as in C.V.; see
v. 29, &c.
RUIN,] as in v. 14, 15, &c.
WORKERS OF INIQUITY,] as in 21. 15, &c.
30. MOVED,] as in 12. 3; Ps. 10. 6; 13. 4, &c.
INHERIT,] as in 1. 33; 2. 21; 7. 11, &c.
31. UTTERETH,] as in Ps. 62. 10; 92. 14.
FROWARDNESS,] as in v. 32; 2. 12, 14, &c.
CUT OUT,] as in 2. 22; 23. 18; 24. 14, &c.
32. PLEASING THING,] as in 8.35; 11.1,20,&c.
FROWARDNESS,] as in v. 31, &c.

XI. 1. BALANCES OF DECEIT,] as in 20. 23;
Hos. 12. 7.
ABOMINATION,] as in v. 20; 3. 32; 6. 16, &c.
WEIGHT,] as in v. 20; 8. 35; 10. 31, &c.
DELIGHT,] as in v. 20; 8. 35; 10. 31, &c.
2. PRIDE,] as in 13. 10; 21. 24; De. 17. 12, &c.
SHAME,] or ' disesteem,' as in 3. 25, &c.
LOWLY.] Original word not found again.
3. INTEGRITY,] as in Job 2. 3, 9; 27. 5; 31. 6.
UPRIGHT,] as in v. 6, 11, &c.
LEADETH,] as in 6. 22; 18. 16; Nu. 23. 7, &c.
PERVERSENESS,] as in 15. 4.
TREACHEROUS,] not 'transgressors,' as in
2. V.
DESTROYETH,] as in 19. 26, &c.
4. WEALTH,] as in 1. 13; 3. 9; 6. 31, &c.
PROFITETH,] as in 2. 20; 1 Sa. 12. 21, &c.
DAY OF WRATH,] as in Job 21. 30; Eze. 7.
19; Zeph. 1. 15, 18.
DELIVERETH,] as in v. 6; 10. 2; 12. 6, &c.
5. PERFECT,] as in v. 20; 1. 12; 2. 21, &c.
MAKETH RIGHT,] as in 3. 6; 15. 21, &c.
WICKEDNESS,] as in 13. 6; De. 9. 4, 5, &c.
FALL,] as in v. 14, 28; 13. 17; 17. 20, &c.
6 DELIVERETH,] as in v. 4, &c.
MISCHIEF,] as in 10. 3; 17. 4; 19. 13, &c.
CAPTURED,] as in 6. 2; Jos. 7. 16, 17, 18, &c.
7. HOPE,] as in v. 23; 10. 27; 19. 18, &c.
PERISHETH,] or ' is lost,' as in 10. 28, &c.

EXPECTATION,] as in 10. 28; 13. 12; Job
41. 9; Ps. 39. 7; La. 3 18.
INIQUITOUS,] as in 6. 12, 18; 10. 29, &c.
LOST,] or 'hath perished.'
8. DISTRESS,] as in 1. 27; 12. 13; 17. 17, &c.
DRAWN OUT,] as in v. 9; Ps. 60. 5; 108. 6.
HYPOCRITE,] or 'profane one,' as in Job
8. 13, &c.
CORRUPTETH,] or marreth, not 'destroy-
eth.' as in C.V.
DRAWN OUT,] as in v. 8, &c.
10. CITY,] as in 10. 15; 18. 11, 19; 29. 8, &c.
EXULTETH,] as in 28. 12; 1 Sa. 2. 1, &c.
DESTRUCTION,] as in 28. 28, &c.
SINGING,] or 'cry,' as in 1 K. 8. 28; 22. 36
11. UPRIGHT,] as in v. 3, 6, &c.
EXALTED,] or 'high,' as in Ge. 7. 17, &c.
THROWN DOWN,] as in 24. 31; Ps. 11. 3, &c.
12. DESPISING,] as in 13. 13; 14. 21, &c.
LACKETH HEART,] as in 6. 32; 7 7; 9. 4, 16.
KEEPETH SILENCE,] as in Ex. 14. 14; 30. 14.
13. BUSYBODY,] as in 20. 19; Lev. 19. 16;
Jer. 6. 28; 9. 4; Eze. 22. 9.
REVEALING,] as in Job 12. 22.
SECRET COUNSEL,] as in 32; 15. 22, &c.
FAITHFUL,] as in 25. 13; 27. 6, &c.
COVERING,] as in 10. 18; 17. 9; 28. 13, &c.
14. COUNSELS,] as in 1. 5; 12. 5; 20. 18; 24.
6; Job 37. 12.
FALL,] as in v. 5, 28, &c.
DELIVERANCE,] as in 21. 31; 24. 6, &c.
COUNSELLORS,] as in 12. 20; 15. 22; 24. 6.
15. EVIL,] as in v. 19, 21, 27; 12. 12, 13, &c
SUFFERETH,] as in 13. 20.
SURETY,] as in 3. 24; 6. 1; 20. 16; 27. 13, &c
STRANGE,] as in 2, 6; 5. 3, 10, 17, 20, &c.
CONFIDENT,] as in v. 23; 14. 16; 16. 20, &c
16. GRACIOUS,] as in 1. 9; 3. 4, 22, 34; 4. 9
RETAINETH,] as in 4. 4; 5. 5; 28. 17; 29. 23.
HONOUR,] as in 3. 16, 35; 8. 18; 15. 33, &c.
TERRIBLE,] not 'strong,' as in C.V.; see
Job 6. 23, &c.
RICHES,] as in v. 28; 3. 16; 8. 18; 13. 8. &c.
17. KIND,] as in 3. 3; 14. 22, 34; 16. 6, &c.
REWARDING,] as in 2 Ch. 20. 11; Isa. 18. 5;
Joel 3. 4.
FIERCE,] as in 5. 9; 12. 10; 17. 11; Isa. 13.
9; Jer. 6. 23; 30. 14; 50. 42.
TROUBLING,] as in v. 15; 29. 27; Jud. 11. 35.
FLESH,] or 'kindred,' as in 5. 11; Ex. 21. 10
18. GETTING,] lit 'making.'
LYING,] as in 6. 17, 19; 10. 18; 12. 17; 19. 22.
SOWING,] as in 22. 8; Ge. 1. 29; Job 4. 8, &c.
REWARD,] as in Ge. 15. 1; 30. 18, 28, 32, &c.
19. RIGHTLY,] not 'as,' as in C.V.; Sept.
'a son of the righteous is born to life.'
PURSUING,] as in 12. 11; 15. 9; 19. 7; 28. 19.
20. ABOMINATION,] as in v. 1, &c.
PERVERSE,] as in v. 2; 15. 8; 17. 20, &c.
PERFECT,] not 'upright,' as in C.V.; see
v. 5, &c.
DELIGHT,] as in v. 27; 8. 35; 10. 32, &c.
21. HAND TO HAND,] united together; Ge-
senius 'through all generations.'
ACQUITTED,] not 'unpunished,' as in C.V.
SEED,] as in Ge. 1. 11, 12, 29; 3. 15; 4. 25.
ESCAPED,] not 'shall be delivered,' as in
C.V.
22. RING,] not 'jewel,' as in C.V.
NOSE,] as in 30. 33, &c.
SOW,] as in Lev. 11. 7; De. 14. 8; Ps. 80. 13.

FAIR,] as in Ge. 12. 11, 14; 29. 17; 39. 6, &c.
STUBBORN,] or 'turned aside,' as in 14. 16.
BEHAVIOUR,] lit. 'taste.'
23. DESIRE,] as in 10. 24; 13. 12, 19; 18. 1.
HOPE,] as in v. 23; 10. 28; 19. 18, &c.
TRANSGRESSION,] or 'wrath,' as in v. 4, &c.
24. SCATTERING,] as in Ps. 112. 9, &c.
INCREASED,] or 'added,' as in Isa. 15. 9.
KEEPING BACK,] as in 10. 19; 13. 24; 17. 27.
UPRIGHTNESS,] as in 2. 13; 4. 11; 14. 2, &c.
WANT,] as in 6. 11; 14. 23; 21. 5, 17, &c.
25. LIBERAL,] lit. 'a soul of blessing.'
FAT,] as in 13. 4; 15. 30; 28. 25, &c.
WATERING,] as in Isa. 43. 24; 55. 10, &c.
26. WITHHOLDING,] as in Jer. 48. 10, &c.
CORN,] as in Ge. 41. 35, 49; 42. 3, 25, &c.
EXECRATE,] as in 24. 24; Lev. 24. 11, &c.
SELLING,] lit. 'breaking.'
27. EARNESTLY SEEKING,] or 'seeking early.'
SEEKETH,] not 'procureth,' as in C.V.
PLEASING THING,] as in v. 20, &c.
EVIL,] as in v. 15, 19, 21, &c.
MEETETH,] or 'cometh' to him.
28. CONFIDENT,] as in v. 15, &c.
WEALTH,] as in v. 16, &c.
LEAF,] not 'branch,' as in C.V.
FLOURISH,] as in Ge. 40. 10; Ex. 9. 9, &c.
29. TROUBLING,] as in v. 17, &c.
INHERITETH,] as in 3. 35; 14. 18; 28. 10, &c.
FOOL,] as in 1. 7; 7. 22; 10. 8, 10, &c.
WISE OF HEART,] as in 10. 8; 16. 21, &c.
30. FRUIT,] as in 1. 31; 8. 19; 11. 30, &c.
TREE OF LIFE,] as in 3. 18; 13. 12; 15. 4, &c.
TAKING,] as in 9. 7; Ge. 19. 14, &c.
31. RECOMPENSED,] as in 13. 13; Ps. 65. 1; Jer. 18. 20.
SINNER,] lit. one 'missing' the mark.

XII. 1. INSTRUCTION,] as in 1. 2, 3, 7, 8, &c.
KNOWLEDGE,] as in v. 23; 1. 4, 7, 22, 29, &c.
REPROOF,] as in 1. 23, 25, 30; 3. 11; 5. 12.
BRUTISH,] as in 30. 2; Ps. 49. 10; 73. 22; 92. 6.

2. BRINGETH FORTH,] not 'obtaineth,' as in C.V.; see 3. 13; 8. 35; 18. 22; Ps. 140. 8; 144. 13; Isa. 58. 10.
WICKED DEVICES,] as in 3. 13; 8. 35; 18. 22.
CONDEMNETH,] as in Ex. 22. 9; De. 25. 1, &c.
3. ESTABLISHED,] as in v. 19; 4. 29; 16. 3.
ROOT,] as in v. 12; De. 29. 18; Jud. 5. 14, &c.
MOVED,] as in 10. 30; 1 Ch. 16. 30, &c.
4. VIRTUOUS,] as in 13. 22; 31. 3, 10, 29, &c. Vulg. 'diligent.'
CROWN,] as in 4. 9; 14. 24; 16. 31; 17. 6, &c.
HUSBAND,] as in 1. 17, 19; 3. 27; 16. 22, &c.
ROTTENNESS,] as in 14. 30; Job 13. 29; Hos. 5. 12; Hab. 3. 16. Sept. 'a worm.'
BONES,] as in 3. 8; 14. 30; 15. 30; 16. 24, &c. Sept. 'wood.'
CAUSING SHAME,] as in 10. 5; 14. 35; 17. 2.
5. THOUGHTS,] as in 6. 18; 15. 22, 26; 16. 3.
JUSTICE,] as in 1. 3; 2. 8, 9; 8. 20; 13. 23, &c. Sept. Vulg. 'judgments.'
COUNSELS,] as in 1. 5; 11. 14; 20. 18; 24. 6; Job 37. 12.
DECEIT,] as in v. 17, 20; 11. 1; 14. 8, 25, &c.
6. LAY WAIT,] as in 1. 11, 18; 7. 12; 23. 28; 24. 15, &c. Sept. 'are crafty.'
DELIVERETH,] as in 2. 12, 16; 10. 2; 11. 4, 6.
7. OVERTHROW,] as in Ge. 19. 21, 25, 29, &c.

STANDETH,] as in 25. 6; 27. 4; Ge. 18. 8, &c.
8. PRAISED,] as in 3. 4; 13. 15; 16. 22; 19. 11.
PERVERTED,] as in 1 Sa. 20. 30; Est. 1. 16.
DESPISED,] as in 18. 3; Ge. 38. 23, &c.
9. LIGHTLY ESTEEMED,] as in De. 25. 3; 1 Sa. 18. 23; Isa. 3. 5; 16. 14. Vulg. 'poor and sufficient to him.'
SELF-HONOURED,] as in Nah. 3. 15.
LACKETH,] as in v. 11; 6. 32; 7. 7; 9. 4, &c.
10. KNOWETH,] that is, 'regardeth,' as in 14. 10; 17. 27; 24. 22; 28. 2, &c.
BEAST,] as in 30. 30; Ge. 1. 24, 25, 26; 2. 20.
MERCIES,] as in Ge. 43. 14, 30; De. 13. 17 &c. Sept. Vulg. 'bowels.'
CRUEL,] as in 5. 9; 11. 17; 17. 11; Isa. 13. 9
11. TILLING,] as in 28. 19; Ge. 2. 5, 15, &c.
SATISFIED,] as in v. 14; 1. 31; 5. 10; 14. 14.
PURSUING,] as in 11. 19; 13. 21; 15. 9; 19. 7.
VANITIES,] as in 28. 19; Ge. 37. 24; 41. 27, &c. Vulg. 'ease.'
LACKING HEART,] as in 6. 32; 7. 7; 9. 4, 16; 10. 13, &c. Sept. Vulg. add, 'Whoso is sweet in wine-banquets in his own strong-holds, leaveth dishonour.'
12. DESIRED,] as in 1. 22; 6. 25; Ex. 20. 17.
NET,] as in Ecc. 7. 26; 9. 14.
EVIL-DOERS,] as in v. 13, 20, 21; 1. 16, 33.
ROOT,] as in v. 3; De. 29. 18; Jud. 5. 14.
13. TRANSGRESSION,] as in 10. 12, 19; 17. 9.
SNARE,] as in 13. 14; 14. 27; 18. 7; 20. 25.
DISTRESS,] as in 1. 27; 11. 8; 17. 17; 21. 23.
14. SATISFIED,] as in v. 11.
DEED,] as in 19. 17; Jud. 9. 16; 2 Ch. 32. 25.
RETURNETH,] as in 1. 23; 2. 19; 3. 28, &c.
15. FOOL,] as in 16; 1. 7; 7. 22; 10. 8, &c
RIGHT,] as in v. 6; 2. 7, 21; 3. 32; 8. 9, &c
COUNSEL,] as in 1. 25, 30; 8. 14; 19. 20, &c.
16. ANGER,] as in 17. 25; 21. 19; 27. 3, &c.
PRUDENT,] as in v. 23; 13. 16; 14. 8, 15, &c.
COVERING,] as in v. 23; Ps. 32. 1.
SHAME,] as in 3. 35; 6. 33; 8. 7; 11. 2, &c.
17. UTTERETH,] as in 6. 19; 14. 5, 25; 19. 5.
FAITHFULNESS,] as in v. 22; 28. 20, &c.
DECLARETH,] as in 29. 24; Ge. 3. 11; 9. 22.
FALSE,] as in v. 22; 19; 6. 17, 19; 10. 18, &c
WITNESS,] as in 6. 19; 14. 5, 25; 19. 5, 9, &c
DECEIT,] as in v. 5, &c.
18. RASH,] as in Lev. 5. 4; Ps. 106. 33.
PIERCINGS.] Original word not found again.
SWORD,] as in 5. 4; 25. 18; 30. 14; Ge. 3. 24.
HEALING,] as in 4. 22; 6. 15; 13. 17; 16. 24.
19. LIP OF TRUTH.] Phrase not found else-where.
ESTABLISHED,] as in v. 3.
FOR A MOMENT,] Ges. 'while I wink.'
FALSEHOOD,] as in v. 17.
20. DEVISING,] not 'imagining,' as in C.V.; see 6. 14, 18. 22; 1 K. 7. 14, &c.
COUNSELLING,] as in 11. 14; 15. 22; 24. 6. &c.
JOY,] as in 10. 28; 14. 10, 13; 15. 21, 23, &c.
21. INIQUITY,] as in 6. 12, 18; 10. 29; 11. 7.
DESIRED,] not 'shall happen,' as in C. V., see Ps. 91. 10, &c.
FULL, OF EVIL,] as in Ecc. 9. 3.
22. ABOMINATION,] as in 3. 22; 6. 16; 8. 7.
LYING LIPS,] as in 17. 7; Ps. 31. 18; 120. 2.
STEDFAST DOERS,] as in 2 K. 22. 7.
DELIGHT,] as in 2; 8. 35; 10. 32; 11. 1, &c.
23. PRUDENT,] as in v. 16.
CONCEALING,] as in v. 23.

2 H

PROCLAIMETH,] as in 1. 21, 24, 28; 2. 3, &c.
FOLLY,] as in 5. 23; 13. 16; 14. 1, 8, 17, &c.
24. DILIGENT,] as in v. 27; 10. 4; 13. 5; 21.
5. Sept. 'choice;' Vulg. 'strong.'
RULETH,] as in 17. 2; 22. 7; Ge. 3. 16, &c.
SLOTHFULNESS,] as in v. 27; 10. 4; 19. 15.
TRIBUTARY,] as in Ge. 49. 15; Ex. 1. 11, &c.
25. SORROW,] as in Jos. 22. 24; Jer. 49. 23.
BOWETH DOWN.] Original word not found elsewhere. Vulg. 'humbles.'
MAKETH GLAD,] as in 10. 1; 15. 20, 30; 27. 9.
26. SEARCHETH,] not 'is more excellent,' as in C.V.
ERR,] as in 10. 17; 2 K. 21. 9, &c.
27. SLOTHFUL,] as in v. 24. Sept. Vulg. 'fraudulent.'
ROASTETH,] as in Da. 3 .27. Sept. 'catcheth;' Vulg. 'findeth.'
HUNTING,] as in Ge. 10. 9; 25. 27, 28; 27. 3, &c. Vulg. 'gain.'
WEALTH,] as in 1. 13; 3. 9; 6. 31; 8. 18, &c.
DILIGENT,] as in v. 24.
PRECIOUS,] as in 1. 13; 3. 15; 6. 26; 17. 27.
28. PATH,] as in 1. 19; 2. 8, 13, 17, 19, 20, &c.

XIII. 1. WISE SON,] as in 10. 1; 15. 20; 1 K. 5. 7, &c. Sept. 'obedient son.'
INSTRUCTION,] as in v. 18, 24.
SCORNER,] as in 1. 22; 3. 34; 9. 7, 8; 14. 6, &c. Sept. 'disobedient son.'
REBUKE,] as in v. 8; 17. 10; 2 Sa. 22. 16, &c.
2. FRUIT,] as in 1. 31; 8. 19; 11. 30; 12. 14.
TREACHEROUS,] not 'transgressors,' as in C.V.; see v. 15; 2. 22; 11. 3, 6; 21. 18, &c.
VIOLENCE,] as in 3. 31; 4. 17; 10. 6, 11, &c.
3. KEEPING,] as in 16. 17; 24. 12; 27. 18, &c.
OPENING WIDE,] as in Eze. 16. 25.
RUIN,] or 'downfall,' as in 10. 14, 15, 29, &c.
4. SLOTHFUL,] as in 6. 6, 9; 10. 26; 15. 19.
DESIRING,] as in Nu. 11. 34; Amos 5. 18.
DILIGENT,] as in 10. 4; 12. 24, 27; 21. 5.
MADE FAT,] as in 11. 25; 28. 25; Isa 34. 7.
5. FALSE,] as in 6. 17, 19; 10. 18; 11. 34, &c.
HATETH,] as in 1. 22; 9. 8; 26. 28; 29. 10.
CAUSETH ABHORRENCE,] as in Ec. 10. 1, &c.
CONFOUNDED,] as in 19. 26; Isa. 33. 9; 54. 4.
6. PERFECT,] not 'upright,' as in C.V.; see 2. 7; 10. 9, 29; 13. 6; 19. 1; 20. 7, &c. Vat. MS. omits this verse.
OVERTHROWETH,] as in 19. 3; 21. 12; 22. 12.
SIN-OFFERING,] not 'sinner,' as in C.V.; see Ge. 4. 7; Ex. 29. 14, 36; 30. 10, &c.
7. RICH.] Original word not found again.
POOR.] Original word not found again.
WEALTH,] as in v. 11; 1. 13; 3. 9; 6. 31, &c.
8. RANSOM,] as in 6. 35; 21. 18; Ex. 21. 30.
RICHES,] as in 3. 16; 8. 18; 11. 16, 28, &c.
POOR,] as in v. 23; 10. 4; 14. 20; 17. 5, &c.
REBUKE,] as in v. 1.
9. LIGHT,] as in 4. 18; 6. 23; 16. 15; Ge. 1. 3.
REJOICETH,] as in 17. 21; 23. 15, 24, 25, &c.
LAMP,] as in 6. 23; 20. 20, 27; 24. 20; 31. 18.
EXTINGUISHED,] as in 20. 20; 24. 20; Job 18. 5, &c. Sept. adds, 'Crafty souls err in sins; but just ones pity and are merciful.'
10. A VAIN MAN,] not 'only,' as in C.V. So Sept.
PRIDE,] as in 11. 2; 21. 24; De. 17. 12, &c.
DEBATE,] as in 17. 19; Isa. 58. 4.
COUNSELLED,] as in 1 K. 12. 6, 9; 2 Ch. 10. 6, 9.

11. WEALTH,] as in v. 7.
VANITY,] as in 21. 6; 31. 30; De. 32. 21, &c
LITTLE,] as in Ex. 12. 4; Neh. 9. 32, &c.
GATHERING,] as in Eze. 22. 19; Neh. 5. 16
1 K. 20. 1, &c. Sept. adds, with 'godliness. the ? at is merciful and lends.'
12. HOPE,] as in 10. 28; 11. 7; Job 41. 9.
PROLONGED,] as in Isa. 18. 2, 7.
SICK,] as in Isa. 53..10; Hos. 7. 5; Mi. 6. 13.
TREE OF LIFE,] as in 3. 18; 11. 30; 15. 4, &c.
DESIRE,] as in v. 19; 10. 24; 11. 23; 18. 1.
13. DESPISING,] as in 11. 12; 14. 21.
DESTROYED,] as in Job 17. 1; Isa. 10. 27.
FEARING,] as in 2. 16; 31. 30; Ge. 22. 12.
REPAYED,] as in 11. 31; Ps. 65. 1; Jer. 18. 20; Isa. 42. 19. Sept. adds, 'To a crafty son there shall not be good, but a wise domestic shall have prosperous doings, and his way shall be directed aright.'
14. LAW,] as in 1. 8; 3. 1; 4. 2; 6. 20, &c.
FOUNTAIN OF LIFE,] as in 10. 11; 14. 27, &c.
TURN ASIDE,] as in v. 19; 14. 27; 15. 24, &c.
SNARES,] as in 12. 13; 14. 27; 18. 7; 20. 25.
15. UNDERSTANDING,] as in 3. 4; 12. 8, &c.
GRACE,] as in 1. 9; 3. 4, 22, 34; 4. 9; 5. 19, &c. Sept. adds, 'and to know the law is the part of a sound understanding.'
TREACHEROUS,] not 'transgressors,' as in C.V.; see v. 2.
HARD,] as in Ge. 49. 24; Ex. 14. 27, &c.
16. PRUDENT,] as in 12. 16, 23; 14. 8, 15, &c.
DEALETH,] or 'doeth, acteth.'
FOLLY,] as in v. 19, 20; 1. 22, 32; 3. 25, &c.
17. MESSENGER,] as in 16. 14; 17. 11, &c.
EVIL,] as in v. 19, 21; 1. 16, 33; 2. 12, &c.
STEDFAST,] lit. 'stedfastnesses;' as in 14. 5; 20. 6; De. 32. 20; Isa. 26. 2. Sept. 'rash king.'
AMBASSADOR,] as in 25. 13; 26. 14, &c.
HEALING,] as in 4. 22; 6. 15; 12. 18; 16. 24.
18. REFUSING,] as in 15. 32.
INSTRUCTION,] as in v. 1, 24.
POVERTY,] as in 10. 15; 24. 34; 28. 19; 31. 7.
SHAME,] lit. 'lightness:' as in 3. 35, &c.
REPROOF,] as in 1. 23, 30; 10. 17; 15. 31; 5. 12.
HONOURED,] as in 27. 18; Isa. 58. 13.
19. DESIRE,] as in v. 12, &c.
ACCOMPLISHED,] lit. that 'has been;' as in Ex. 11. 6; De. 4. 32; 27. 9; Jud. 19. 30.
IS SWEET,] as in 3. 24; 6. 1; 11. 15, &c.
ABOMINATION,] as in 3. 32; 6. 16; 8. 7, &c.
TURN,] as in v. 14, &c.
20. WALKETH,] as in 2. 7; 4. 18; 6. 12, &c.
COMPANION,] lit. 'friend;' as in 28. 7, &c.
SUFFERETH EVIL,] as in 11. 15. Sept. 'is known.'
21. PURSUETH,] as in 6. 31; 19. 17; 20. 22; 25. 22, &c. Sept. 'overtaketh.'
22. CAUSETH TO INHERIT,] as in 8. 21, &c.
WEALTH,] or 'strength;' as in 12. 4; 31. 3.
23. ABUNDANCE,] as in 5. 23; 7. 21; 10. 19.
FOOD,] lit. 'eating;' as in Ge. 14. 11; 41. 35.
TILLAGE,] as in Jer. 4. 3; Hos. 10. 12.
POOR,] as in v. 8, &c.
SUBSTANCE,] as in v. 7; 3. 28; 8. 21; 11. 24.
CONSUMED,] as in 1 Ch. 21. 12.
24. SPARING,] as in 10. 19; 11. 24; 17. 27.
ROD,] as in 10. 13; 22. 8, 15; 23. 13, 14, &c
HATING,] as in 11. 15; 12. 1; 15. 10, 27, &c
HASTENED,] as in 1. 28; Job 7. 21; 8. 5, &c

CHASTISEMENT,] as in v. 1, &c.
25. SATIETY,] as in Ex. 16. 3; Lev. 25. 19.
BELLY,] as in 18. 8, 20; 20. 27, 30; 22. 18.
LACKETH,] as in 31. 11; Ge. 3. 3; 18. 28, &c.

XIV. 1. EVERY WISE WOMAN,] *lit.* 'wise women.'
BUILDED,] as in 9. 1; 24. 27; Ge. 2. 22, &c.
FOOLISH,] as in v. 8, 17, 18, 24, 29; 5. 23, &c.
BREAKETH IT DOWN,] as in 29. 4; Ex. 15. 7.
2. WALKING,] as in 2. 7; 4. 18; 6. 12; 7. 22.
UPRIGHTNESS,] as in 2. 13; 4. 11; 11. 24, &c.
FEARING,] as in v. 16; 13. 13; 31. 30, &c.
PERVERTED,] as in 2. 15; 3. 32; Isa. 30. 12.
DESPISING,] as in 11. 12; 13. 13. Sept.
'shall be dishonoured.'
3. ROD,] as in Isa. 11. 1.
PRIDE,] as in 29. 23; De. 33. 26, 29, &c.
PRESERVE,] as in 2. 8, 11, 20; 3. 26; 4. 6, &c.
4. OXEN,] as in De. 7. 13; 28. 4; Ps. 8. 8.
STALL,] as in Job 39. 9; Isa. 1. 3.
CLEAN,] as in Job 11. 4; Ps. 19. 8; 24. 4, &c.
INCREASE,] as in 3. 9, 14; 8. 19; 10. 16, &c.
5. FAITHFUL,] as in 13. 17; 20. 6; De. 32. 20; Isa. 26. 2.
FALSE,] as in 6. 17, 19; 10. 18; 11. 18, &c.
LIES,] as in v. 25; 6. 19; 19. 5, 9, 22; 21. 28.
6. SCORNER,] as in 1. 22; 3. 34; 9. 7, 8, &c.
SOUGHT,] as in 2. 4; 11. 27; 15. 14; 17. 11.
INTELLIGENT,] as in v. 33; 1. 5; 10. 13; 15. 14.
EASY,] as in 1 Sa. 18. 23; 2 Sa. 6. 22, &c.
7. FOOLISH,] as in v. 8, 16, 24, 33; 1. 22, 32; 3. 35, &c. Sept. 'all things are adverse to a foolish man.'
LIPS OF KNOWLEDGE,] as in 20. 15.
8. PRUDENT,] as in v. 15, 18; 12. 16, 23, &c.
UNDERSTAND,] as in 1. 2, 6; 1 K. 3. 9, 11.
FOLLY,] as in v. 1, &c.
FOOLS,] as in v. 7, &c.
DECEIT,] as in v. 25; 11. 1; 12. 5, 17, 20, &c.
9. MOCK,] as in 3. 34; 19. 28; Ps. 119. 51.
Sept. 'The houses of transgressors owe purification, but the houses of the just are acceptable.'
GUILT-OFFERING,] not 'sin,' as in C.V.
UPRIGHT,] as in v. 11, 12; 2. 7, 21; 3. 32, &c.
PLEASING THING,] as in v. 35; 8. 35; 10. 32.
10. BITTERNESS,] as in Ge. 26. 35.
JOY,] as in v. 13; 10. 28; 12. 20; 15. 21, &c.
STRANGER,] as in 2. 16; 5. 3, 10, 17, 20, &c.
INTERMEDDLE,] as in 20. 19; 24. 21, &c.
11. DESTROYED,] as in De. 4. 26; 7. 23, &c.
TENT,] as in Ge. 4. 20; 9. 21, 27; 12. 8, &c.
UPRIGHT,] as in v. 9, 12.
FLOURISHETH,] as in Nu. 17. 5, 8; Ps. 72. 7.
12. RIGHT,] as in v. 9, 11.
LATTER END,] as in v. 13; 5. 4, 11; 16. 25.
WAYS OF DEATH,] as in 16. 25; Jer. 21. 8.
13. LAUGHTER,] as in 10. 23; Job 8. 21, &c.
PAINED,] as in Ge. 34. 25; Ps. 69. 29, &c.
JOY,] as in v. 10.
AFFLICTION,] as in 10. 1; 17. 21; Ps. 119. 28.
14. BACKSLIDER,] as in Ps. 53. 3; 80. 18.
FRUITS,] *lit.* 'leaves, or branches;' as in 11. 28. Sept. 'thoughts.'
15. SIMPLE,] as in v. 18; 1. 4, 22, 32, &c.
GIVETH EVIDENCE,] *or* 'remaineth stedfast;' as in 26. 25, &c.
PRUDENT,] as in v. 8, &c.
STEP,] as in Job 23. 11; Ps. 17. 5; 37. 31, &c.

16. FEARING,] as in v. 2, &c.
TURNING,] as in 11. 22; Job 1. 1, 8; 2. 3; Jer. 6. 28.
TRANSGRESSING,] not 'rageth,' as in C.V. as in 20. 2; 26. 17, &c.
CONFIDENT,] as in 11. 15, 28; 16. 20, &c.
17. SHORT OF TEMPER,] as in v. 29; 2 K. 19. 26; Job 41. 1; Isa. 37. 27.
FOLLY,] as in v. 1, &c.
WICKED DEVICES,] as in 1. 4; 2. 11; 3. 21.
18. INHERITED,] as in 3. 35; 11. 29; 28. 10.
FOLLY,] as in v. 1, &c.
PRUDENT,] as in v. 8, &c.
CROWNED,] as in Ps. 142. 7; Hab. 1. 4.
19. EVIL,] as in v. 16, 22, 32; 1. 16, 33, &c.
BOWED DOWN,] as in Job 9. 3; Ps. 35. 4, &c.
GATES,] as in 1. 21; 8. 3; 22. 22; 24. 7, &c.
20. POOR,] as in 10. 4; 13. 8, 23; 17. 5, &c.
RICH,] as in 10. 15; 18. 11, 23; 22. 2, &c.
21. DESPISING,] as in 11. 12; 13. 13.
NEIGHBOUR,] *or* 'friend;' as in v. 20; 3. 28.
FAVOURETH,] as in Ps. 102. 14, &c.
HUMBLE,] as in 3. 24; 15. 15; 16. 19; 22. 22.
HAPPINESS,] as in 3. 13; 8. 32, 34; 14. 21, &c.
22. ERR,] as in 7. 25; 21. 16; Ge. 21. 14, &c.
DEVISING,] as in 6. 14, 18; 12. 20, &c.
KINDNESS,] as in v. 34; 3. 3; 11. 17, &c.
TRUTH,] as in v. 25; 3. 3; 8. 7; 11. 18, &c.
Sept. adds, 'The framers of evil do not understand mercy and truth, but compassion and faithfulness are with the framers of good.'
23. LABOUR,] as in 5. 10; 10. 22; 15. 1, &c.
ADVANTAGE,] as in 21. 5; Ecc. 3. 19.
WANT,] as in 6. 11; 11. 24; 21. 5, 17, &c.
24. CROWN,] as in 4. 9; 12. 4; 16. 31; 17. 6.
WEALTH,] as in 3. 16; 8. 18; 11. 16, 28, &c.
FOLLY,] as in v. 1, &c.
FOOLS,] as in v. 7, 8, 16, 33; 1. 22, 32, &c.
25. WITNESS,] as in v. 5.
DELIVERING,] *lit.* 'snatching;' as in De 32. 39, &c.
DECEITFUL ONE,] as in v. 8, &c.
BREATHETH OUT,] as in v. 5.
LIES,] as in v. 5, &c.
26. FEAR OF JEHOVAH,] as in v. 27; 1. 7, 29; 2. 5; 8. 13, &c.
CONFIDENCE,] as in 21. 22; 22. 19; 25. 19, &c.
REFUGE,] as in Job 24. 8; Ps. 14. 6; 46. 1.
27. FOUNTAIN OF LIFE,] as in 10. 11; 13. 14.
TURN ASIDE,] as in 13. 14, 19; 15. 24, &c.
SNARES OF DEATH,] as in 12. 13; 13. 14, &c.
28. MULTITUDE,] *or* 'abundance;' as in v. 4.
HONOUR,] as in 1 Ch. 16. 29; 2 Ch. 20. 21; Ps. 29. 2; 96. 9.
LACK,] *or* 'want;' as in 26. 20; 30. 4, &c.
RUIN,] *or* 'downfall;' as in 10. 14, 15, 29.
PRINCE,] *lit.* a 'lean one;' not found elsewhere.
29. SLOW TO ANGER,] as in 15. 18; 16. 32, &c.
UNDERSTANDING,] as in 2. 2, 3, 6, 11, &c.
SHORT IN TEMPER.] Phrase not found elsewhere.
EXALTING,] as in 3. 35; Ex. 35. 24; Ps. 3. 3.
FOLLY,] as in v. 1, &c.
30. HEALED,] *or* 'healing;' as in 15. 4; Ecc. 10. 4. Sept. 'a meek man is a healer of the heart.'
FLESH,] as in 4. 22; 5. 11; 23. 20; Ge. 2. 21.
ROTTENNESS,] as in 12. 4; Job 13. 28; Hos 5. 12; Hab. 3. 16.

BONES,] as in 3. 8; 12. 4; 15 30; 16. 24, &c.
ENVY,] as in 6. 34; 27. 4; Nu. 5. 14, 15, &c.
31. OPPRESSOR,] as in 22. 16; 28. 3, &c.
POOR,] as in 10. 15; 19. 4, 17; 21. 31, &c.
MAKER,] as in 10. 4; 11. 18; 12. 22; 17. 5.
HONOURING,] as in 1 Sa. 2. 30; 2 Sa. 10. 3.
FAVOURING,] as in 19. 17; 28. 8; Ps. 37. 21.
NEEDY,] as in 30. 14; 31. 9, 20; Ex. 23. 6, &c.
32. WICKEDNESS,] as in v. 16, &c.
DRIVEN AWAY,] as in Jer. 23. 12.
TRUSTFUL,] as in 30. 5; 2 Sa. 22. 31, &c.
DEATH.] Sept. 'holiness.'
33. INTELLIGENT,] as in v. 6, &c.
REST,] as in 21. 16; Ge. 8. 4; Ex. 10. 14, &c.
FOOLS,] as in v. 7, 8, 16, 24.
34. EXALTETH,] as in 4. 8; Ex. 15. 2, &c.
GOODLINESS,] not 'reproach,' as in C.V.; see v. 22.
SIN-OFFERING,] not 'sin,' as in C.V.; as in 5. 22; 10. 16; 13. 6; 20. 9, &c.
35. OBJECT OF HIS WRATH,] as in 11. 4, &c.
CAUSING SHAME,] as in 10. 5; 12. 4; 17. 2.

XV. 1. SOFT,] as in 4. 3; 25. 15; Ge. 18. 7; 29. 17, &c. Sept. prefixes, 'Anger slays even wise men.'
FURY,] as in v. 18; 16. 14; 19. 19; 21. 14, &c.
GRIEVOUS,] as in 5. 10; 10. 22; 14. 23, &c.
ANGER,] as in v. 18; 14. 17, 29; 16. 32, &c.
2. MAKETH GOOD,] as in v. 13; 17. 22, &c.
UTTERETH,] as in v. 28; 1. 23; Ps. 19. 2, &c.
3. EYES OF JEHOVAH,] as in 5. 21; 22. 12.
WATCHING,] as in 31. 27; Nu. 23. 14, &c.
4. HEALED,] or 'healing;' as in 14. 30; Ecc. 10. 4. Sept. 'healing of the tongue.'
TREE OF LIFE,] as in 3. 18; 11. 30; 13. 12, &c.
PERVERSENESS,] as in 11. 3. Sept. 'he that keeps it.'
BREACH,] as in 16. 18; 17. 19; 18. 12, &c.
SPIRIT,] as in v. 13; 1. 23; 11. 13, 29, &c.
5. DESPISETH,] as in 1. 30; 5. 12, &c.
INSTRUCTION,] as in v. 10, 32, 33; 1. 2, 3, &c.
REGARDING,] lit. 'watching, keeping.'
REPROOF,] as in v. 10, 31, 32; 1. 23; 25. 30.
PRUDENT,] as in 19. 25; 1 Sa. 23. 22; Ps. 83. 3. Sept. adds, 'In abounding righteousness is great strength, but the ungodly shall be wholly rooted out of the land.'
6. STRENGTH,] as in 27. 24; Isa. 33. 6; Jer. 20. 5; Eze. 22. 25.
INCREASE,] as in 3. 9, 14; 8. 19; 10. 16, &c.
TROUBLE,] or 'it is troubled;' as in Ps. 39. 2. Sept. 'shall perish.'
7. SCATTER,] as in 20. 8, 26; Lev. 26. 28, &c. Sept. 'are bound.'
RIGHT,] as in 28. 2; Ge. 42. 11, 19, 31, &c.
8. SACRIFICE,] as in 7. 14; 17. 1; 21. 3, 27.
ABOMINATION,] as in v. 9, 26; 3. 32; 6. 16.
DELIGHT,] as in 8. 35; 10. 32; 11. 1, 20, &c.
UPRIGHT,] as in v. 19; 2. 7, 21; 3. 32, &c.
9. WAY OF THE WICKED,] as in 4. 19; 12. 26.
PURSUING,] as in 11. 19; 12. 11; 19. 7; 28. 19.
10. CHASTISEMENT,] or 'instruction;' as in v. 5, 32, 33.
GRIEVOUS,] or 'evil.'
FORSAKING,] as in 2. 13, 17; 10. 17; 28. 4, &c.
REPROOF,] as in v. 5, 31, 32.
11. SHEOL,] as in v. 24; 1. 12; 5. 5; 7. 27, &c.
DESTRUCTION,] as in 27. 20; Job 26. 6; 28. 22; 31. 12; Ps. 88. 11.
SONS OF MEN,] as in 8. 4 31, &c.

12. SCORNER,] as in 1. 22; 3. 24; 9. 7, 8; 13. 1, &c. Sept. 'uninstructed one.'
REPROVER,] lit. 'to reprove;' as in Lev 19. 17, &c.
13. JOYFUL,] as in 2. 14; 17. 5, 22; 29. 6, &c
MAKETH GLAD,] as in v. 2, &c.
GRIEF,] as in 10. 10.
SMITTEN,] not 'broken,' as in C.V.
14. INTELLIGENT,] as in 1. 5; 10. 13; 14. 6
ENJOYETH,] as in 13. 20; 28. 7; 29. 3, &c
Sept. 'experience.'
15. AFFLICTED,] or 'poor;' as in 3. 34, &c
GLADNESS,] lit. 'goodness.'
PERPETUAL,] as in 5. 19; 6. 21; 28. 14, &c.
BANQUET,] as in Ge. 19. 3; 21. 8; 26. 30, &c.
16. LITTLE,] as in 5. 14; 6. 10; 10. 20, &c.
FEAR OF JEHOVAH,] as in v. 33.
TREASURE,] as in 8. 21; 10. 2; 21. 6, 20, &c.
TUMULT,] not 'trouble,' as in C.V.; see De. 7. 23, &c.
17. ALLOWANCE,] not 'dinner,' as in C.V.; see 2 K. 25. 30; Jer. 40. 5; 52. 34.
GREEN HERBS,] as in De. 11. 10; 1 K. 21. 2; 2 K. 19. 26; Isa. 37. 27.
FATTED,] as in 1 K. 4. 23; or 'ox of the stall.'
OX,] as in 7. 22; 14. 4; Ge. 32. 5, &c.
HATRED,] as in 10. 12, 18; 26. 26; Nu. 35. 20.
18. MAN OF FURY,] as in 19. 19; 22. 24, &c.
STIRRETH UP,] as in 28. 25; 29. 22.
CONTENTION,] as in 6. 14; 16. 28; 17. 14, &c.
SLOW TO ANGER,] as in 14. 29; 16. 32, &c.
APPEASETH,] as in Job 34. 29; 16. 32, &c.
STRIFE,] as in 17. 1, 14; 18. 6, 17; 20. 3, &c.
Sept. adds, 'a man slow to anger will extinguish quarrels, but an ungodly man stirs them up.'
19. SLOTHFUL,] as in 6. 6, 9; 10. 26; 13. 4.
HEDGE,] as in Isa. 5. 5. Sept. 'strewn with thorns.'
BRIERS,] as in Mic. 7. 4.
UPRIGHT,] as in v. 8.
RAISED UP,] not 'made plain,' as in C.V.; see Jer. 18. 15.
20. REJOICETH,] as in v. 20; De. 24. 5, &c.
FOOLISH,] as in v. 2, 7, 14.
DESPISING,] as in 14. 2; 19. 16; 1 Sa. 2. 30.
21. FOLLY,] as in v. 2, 14; 5. 23; 12. 23, &c.
JOY,] as in v. 23; 10. 28; 12. 20; 14. 10, 13.
LACKING HEART,] as in 6. 32; 7. 7; 9. 4, 16.
INTELLIGENCE,] as in 2. 2, 3, 6, 11, &c.
DIRECTETH,] as in 3. 6; 11. 5; 2 Ch. 32. 30.
22. COUNSEL,] as in 3. 32; 11. 13; 20. 19, &c
MAKING VOID,] as in Lev. 26. 15, 44, &c.
PURPOSES,] as in v. 26; 6. 18; 12. 5; 16. 3.
MULTITUDES,] as in 5. 23; 7. 21; 10. 19, &c.
COUNSELLORS,] as in 11. 14; 12. 20; 24. 6.
ESTABLISHED,] as in 6. 9; 19. 21; 24. 22, &c.
23. JOY,] as in v. 21, &c.
ANSWER,] as in v. 1; 16. 1, 4; 29. 19, &c.
SEASON,] as in 5. 19; 6. 14; 8. 30; 17. 17, &c.
24. PATH OF LIFE,] as in 2. 19; 5. 6; Ps. 16. 11.
ON HIGH,] as in Ex. 25. 20; 37. 9; De. 28. 13.
SHEOL,] as in v. 11.
BENEATH,] as in Ex. 26. 24; 27. 5; 28. 27.
25. PROUD,] as in 16. 19; Job 40. 11, 12, &c.
PULLETH DOWN,] not 'destroyeth,' as in C.V.; see 2. 22; Ps. 52. 5.
SETTETH UP,] as in Ge. 21. 28; 33. 20, &c.
BORDER,] as in 22. 28; 23. 10; Ge. 10. 19, &c

WIDOW,] as in Ge. 38. 11; Ex. 22. 22, 24, &c.
26. THOUGHTS,] as in v. 22, &c.
PURE,] as in 22. 11; 30. 12; Ge. 7. 2, 8, &c.
PLEASANTNESS,] as in 3. 17; 16. 24; Ps. 27. 4.
27. DISHONEST GAINER,] not 'greedy of gain,' as in C.V.; see 1. 19; Jer. 6. 13; 8. 10; Hab. 2. 9.
TROUBLING,] as in 11. 17, 29; Jud. 11. 35.
HATING,] as in v. 10; 11. 15; 12. 1; 13. 24.
GIFTS,] as in Ge. 25. 6; Ex. 28. 38; Lev. 23. 38, &c. Sept. adds, 'By alms and faithful dealings sins are purged, but by the fear of the Lord every one departs from evil.'
28. MEDITATETH,] as in 8. 7; 24. 2; Jos. 1. 8.
TO ANSWER,] as in Ge. 45. 3; Ex. 32. 18, &c.
UTTERETH,] as in v. 2, &c. Sept. adds, 'The ways of the righteous are acceptable with the Lord, and through them even enemies become friends.'
29. FAR,] as in 7. 19; 27. 10; 31. 10, &c.
PRAYER,] as in v. 8; 28. 9; 2 Sa. 7. 27, &c. Sept. adds, 'Better are small receipts with righteousness than abundant fruits with unrighteousness.'
30. LIGHT,] as in Ge. 1. 14, 15, 16; Ex. 25. 6.
REJOICETH,] as in v. 20.
REPORT,] as in 25. 25; 1 Sa. 2. 24; 4. 19, &c.
MAKETH FAT,] as in Ps. 23. 5, &c.
BONE,] as in 3. 8; 12. 4; 14. 30; 16. 24, &c.
31. EAR,] as in 2. 2; 4. 20; 5. 1, 13; 18. 15.
REPROOF,] as in v. 5, 10, 32.
LODGE,] as in 19. 23; Ge. 19. 2; 24. 23, &c.
32. REFUSING,] as in 13. 28.
DESPISING,] as in Isa. 33. 15; Eze. 21. 10.
REPROOF,] as in v. 5, 10, 31.
UNDERSTANDING,] lit. 'heart;' as in v. 7.
33. FEAR OF JEHOVAH,] as in v. 16.
INSTRUCTION,] as in v. 5, 10, 32.
HONOUR,] as in 3. 16, 35; 8. 18; 11. 16, &c.
HUMILITY,] as in 18. 12; 22. 4; 2 Sa. 22. 36.

XVI. 1. ARRANGEMENTS,] as in Ex. 39. 37.
ANSWER,] as in v. 4; 15. 1, 23; 29. 19, &c.
2. PURE,] as in 20. 11; 21. 8; Ex. 27. 20, &c.
PONDERING,] as in 21. 2; 24. 12.
3. ROLL,] as in 26. 27; Jos. 10. 18, &c.
WORKS,] as in v. 11; 31. 31; Ge. 5. 29, &c.
ESTABLISHED,] as in v. 12; 4. 26; 12. 3, &c.
PURPOSES,] as in 6. 18; 12. 5; 15. 22, 26, &c.
4. WROUGHT,] in providence as well as in creation.
A DAY OF EVIL,] in which they may enjoy themselves.
5. ABOMINATION,] as in v. 12; 3. 32; 6. 16.
PROUD,] or 'high;' as in Ps. 101. 5; Ecc. 7. 8; Eze. 31. 3.
HAND TO HAND,] as in 11. 21.
ACQUITTED,] not 'unpunished,' as in C.V.; see 6. 29, &c.
6. KINDNESS,] as in 3. 3; 11. 17; 14. 22, &c.
TRUTH,] as in 3. 3; 8. 7; 11. 18; 12. 19, &c.
PARDONED,] lit. 'covered;' as in Ex. 29. 33.
FEAR OF JEHOVAH,] as in 1. 7, 29; 2. 5, &c.
TURN ASIDE,] as in v. 17; 3. 7; Ge. 19. 2, &c.
7. PLEASE,] as in 1 Ch. 29. 3; Job 34. 9, &c.
ENEMIES,] as in 24. 17; Ge. 22. 17; 49. 8, &c.
TO BE AT PEACE,] as in De. 20. 12, &c.
8. LITTLE,] as in 5. 14; 10. 20; 16. 10, &c.
INCREASE,] as in 3. 9, 14; 8. 19; 10. 16, &c.
JUSTICE,] as in v. 10, 11, 13; 1. 3; 2. 8, 9, &c.
9 DEVISETH,] as in 24. 8; Lev. 25. 2 7, 50, &c.

ESTABLISHETH,] or 'prepareth;' as in 6. 8; 21. 29, &c.
STEP,] as in 4. 12; 5. 5; 30. 20.
10. OATH,] not 'a divine sentence,' as in C.V.; see Nu. 22. 7, &c.
TRESPASSETH,] as in Lev. 5. 15; 6. 2, &c.
11. BEAM,] as in Isa. 40. 12.
BALANCES,] as in 11. 1; 20. 23; Lev. 19. 36.
WORKS,] as in v. 3.
STONES,] which anciently were used for weights.
BAG,] as in 1. 14; 23. 31; De. 25. 13, &c.
12. ABOMINATION,] as in v. 5.
THRONE,] as in 9. 14; 20. 8, 28; 25. 5, &c.
ESTABLISHED,] as in v. 3.
13. DELIGHT,] as in v. 15; 8. 35; 10. 32, &c.
UPRIGHTLY,] or 'upright things.'
14. FURY,] as in 6. 34; 15. 1, 18; 19. 19, &c.
MESSENGER OF DEATH.] A phrase not found again.
PACIFIETH,] lit. 'covereth;' as in Ge. 32. 20, &c.
15. LIFE,] lit. 'lives.'
GOOD WILL,] or ' delight;' as in v. 15.
THICK CLOUD,] as in Ex. 19. 9; Jud. 5. 4, &c.
LATTER RAIN,] lit. 'gathered' rain; as in De. 11. 14, &c.
16. GET,] as in 17. 16; Lev. 25. 14; Ru. 4. 5.
GOLD,] as in 3. 14; 8. 10, 19; Job 41. 30, &c.
UNDERSTANDING,] as in 1. 2; 2. 3; 3. 5, &c.
CHOSEN,] as in 8. 10, 19; 10. 20; 21. 3; 22. 1.
SILVER,] as in 2. 4; 3. 14; 7. 20; 8. 10, &c.
17. HIGHWAY,] as in Nu. 20. 19; Jud. 5. 20.
UPRIGHT,] as in v. 13, 25.
TURN,] as in v. 6. Sept. reads, 'Paths of life turn aside from evil, and length of life are ways of righteousness; he who receives instruction shall be in good, and he who is observing reproofs shall be made wise.'
PRESERVING,] as in 10. 17; 13. 3, 18; 15. 5.
WATCHING,] as in 13. 3; 24. 12; 27. 18; 28. 7, &c. Sept. adds, 'and he who is loving his life will spare his mouth.'
18. DESTRUCTION,] lit. a 'breach;' as in 15. 4, &c.
PRIDE,] as in 8. 13; Ex. 15. 7; Lev. 26. 19.
STUMBLING.] Original word not found again.
HAUGHTY SPIRIT,] lit. 'height of spirit.' Sept. 'folly.'
19. HUMILITY,] as in 29. 23; Lev. 13. 20, &c.
POOR,] as in 3. 34; 14. 21; 15. 15; 22. 22, &c. Sept. 'with lowliness.'
APPORTION,] as in Jos. 19. 51; Isa. 9. 3, &c.
SPOIL,] as in 1. 13; 31. 11; Ge. 49. 27, &c.
PROUD,] as in 15. 25; Job 40. 11, 12, &c.
20. WISE,] as in 5. 19; 14. 35; 15. 24, &c.
TRUSTING,] as in 11. 15, 28; 14. 16; 28. 25.
HAPPINESS,] as in 3. 13; 8. 32, 34; 14. 21.
21. INTELLIGENT,] as in 1. 5; 10. 13; 14. 6, 33; 15. 14, &c. Sept. 'evil.'
SWEETNESS,] as in 27. 9.
LEARNING,] lit. 'reception.'
22. FOUNTAIN OF LIFE,] as in 5. 18; 10. 11.
POSSESSORS,] lords or masters.
INSTRUCTION,] as in 1. 2, 3, 7, 8; 3. 11, &c.
FOLLY,] as in 5. 23; 12. 23; 13. 16; 14. 1, &c.
23. ACT WISELY,] as in 17. 8; De. 29. 9, &c.
INCREASETH,] as in v. 21.
24. PLEASANTNESS,] as in 3. 17; 15. 26, &c.
HONEY-COMB,] as in Ps. 19. 10.

BONE,] as in 25. 15; Ge. 49. 14; 2 K. 9. 13; Job 40. 18.
23. BRIBE,] as in v. 8; 6. 35; 21. 14, &c.
BOSOM,] as in 5. 20; 6. 27; 16. 33; 21. 14, &c.
TURN ASIDE,] as in 18. 5; Ex. 23. 2, &c.
PATHS OF JUDGMENT,] as in 2. 13, 15, &c.
24. INTELLIGENT,] as in v. 10; 8. 9; 28. 2, &c.
FOOL,] as in v. 10, 12, 16, 21, 25; 1. 22, 32.
END OF THE EARTH,] as in De. 13. 27, &c.
25. PROVOCATION,] as in 12. 16; 21. 19; 27. 3.
FOOLISH,] as in v. 10, 12, 16, 21, 24, &c.
26. FINE,] as in 21. 11; Ecc. 21. 22.
NOBLE,] as in v. 7; 8. 16; 19. 6; 25. 7, &c.
UPRIGHTNESS,] as in 2. 13; 4. 11; 11. 24, &c.
27. ACQUAINTED,] as in 12. 10; 14. 10, &c.
SPARING,] as in 10. 19; 11. 24; 13. 34.
COOL OF TEMPER,] as in 25. 25; Jer. 18. 14.
28. KEEPING SILENCE,] as in Ge. 24. 21; 1 Sa. 10. 27; 23. 9; 2 Sa. 19. 10.
RECKONED,] as in 27. 14; Lev. 7. 18; 17. 4.
SHUTTING,] as in 21. 13; 1 K. 6. 4; Isa. 30. 5.
INTELLIGENT,] as in 1. 5; 10. 13; 14. 6, 33.

XVIII. 1. DESIRE,] as in 10. 24; 11. 23, &c.
SEPARATED.] as in Jud. 4. 11; Neh. 4. 19.
INTERMEDDLETH,] as in 17. 14; 20. 3.
2. DELIGHT,] as in 21. 1; De. 25. 7; Ru. 3. 13.
UNDERSTANDING,] as in 2. 2, 5 6, 11, &c.
UNCOVERING,] as in Ge. 9. 21.
3. CONTEMPT,] as in 12. 8; Ge. 38. 23, &c.
SHAME,] as in 3. 35; 6. 33; 9. 7; 11. 2, &c.
REPROACH,] as in 6. 33; Ge. 30. 23; 34. 14.
4. DEEP WATERS,] as in 20. 5; 22. 14, &c.
FOUNTAIN,] as in 5. 18; 10. 11; 13. 14, &c.
5. ACCEPTANCE,] as in 30. 21; Ge. 4. 13, &c.
TO TURN ASIDE,] as in 17. 23; Ex. 23. 2, &c.
6. FOOL,] as in v. 2, 7; 1. 22, 32; 3. 35, &c.
STRIFE,] as in v. 17; 15. 18; 17. 1, 14, &c.
STRIPES,] as in 19. 29. Sept. 'death.'
7. RUIN,] as in 10. 14, 15, 29; 13. 3, &c.
SNARE,] as in 12. 13; 13. 14; 14. 27; 20. 25.
8. TALE-BEARER,] as in 16. 28; 26. 20, 22. Sept. reads, 'Fear casts down the slothful, and the souls of the effeminate shall hunger.'
SELF-INFLICTED WOUNDS,] as in 26. 22.
INNER PARTS,] as in 7. 27; 20. 27, 30, &c.
9. REMISS,] as in 24. 10; Jos. 18. 3.
DESTROYER,] as in 6. 32; 28. 24; Ge. 6. 13.
10. TOWER,] as in Ge. 11. 4, 5; 35. 21, &c.
STRENGTH,] as in v. 11, 19; 10. 15; 14. 26.
NAME OF JEHOVAH,] as in 10. 7; 21. 24, &c.
RUNNETH,] as in 1. 16; 4. 12; Ge. 18. 2, &c.
SET ON HIGH,] as in v. 11; Ps. 139. 6, &c.
11. WEALTH,] as in 1. 13; 3. 9; 6. 31; 8. 18.
RICH,] as in v. 23; 10. 15; 14. 20; 22. 2, &c.
CITY,] as in v. 19; 10. 15; 11. 10; 29. 8, &c.
STRENGTH,] as in v. 10, 19; 10. 15; 14. 26.
WALL,] as in 25. 28; Ex. 14. 22, 29, &c.
SET ON HIGH,] as in Ps. 148. 13; Isa. 12. 4.
IMAGINATION,] as in 25. 11; Lev. 26. 1; Nu. 33. 52; Ps. 73. 7; Eze. 8. 11.
12. DESTRUCTION,] as in 15. 4; 16. 18; 17. 19; Lev. 21. 19.
HIGH,] as in 1 Sa. 16. 7; 2 Ch. 17. 6; Job 36. 7.
HONOUR,] as in 15. 33; 3. 16, 35; 8. 18, &c.
HUMILITY,] as in 15. 33; 22. 4; 2 Sa. 22. 36; Zeph. 2. 3.
13. ANSWERING,] as in 17. 13; 24. 26; 26. 16.
FOLLY,] as in 5. 2, 3; 12. 23; 13. 16; 14. 1.
SHAME,] as in Job 20. 3; Ps. 4. 2; 35. 26, &c.

14. SUSTAINETH,] as in Ge. 47. 12; 50. 21; 2 Sa. 20. 3, &c.   Sept. 'a wise servant calms a man's anger.'
SICKNESS,] as in 2 Ch. 21. 15.
SMITTEN,] as in 15. 13; 17. 22.
BEAR,] as in 6. 35; 9. 12; 19. 18; Ge. 7. 17.
15. INTELLIGENT,] as in 1. 5; 10. 13, &c.
GETTETH,] as in 1. 5; Ge. 33. 19; 39. 1, &c.
SEEKETH,] as in v. 1; 2. 4; 11. 27; 15. 14, &c.
16. GIFT,] as in 19. 6; 21. 14; Ge. 34. 12; Nu. 18. 11.
MAKETH ROOM,] as in De. 12. 20; 19. 8, &c.
GREAT,] as in 19. 19; 25. 6; 27. 14; Ge. 1. 16.
LEADETH,] as in 6. 22; 11. 3; Nu. 23. 7, &c.
17. CAUSE,] as in v. 6; 15. 18; 17. 1, 14, &c.
NEIGHBOUR,] as in v. 24; 3. 28, 29; 6. 1, &c.
SEARCHED,] as in De. 13. 14; Job 5. 27; 28. 27; Ps. 139. 1.
18. LOT,] as in 1. 14; 16. 33; Lev. 16. 8, &c.
CONTENTIONS,] as in v. 19; 19. 13; 21. 9, 19; 23. 29; 25. 24; 26. 21; 27. 15.
TO CEASE,] as in Ex. 12. 15; Lev. 2. 13, &c.
MIGHTY,] as in 7. 26; 30. 26; Ge. 18. 18, &c.
SEPARATETH,] as in Ru. 1. 17; 2 K. 2. 11.
19. STRONG CITY,] as in v. 11; 10. 15, &c.
BAR,] as in Ex. 26, 26, 27, 28, 29; 35. 11, &c.
PALACE,] as in 1 K. 16. 18; 2 K. 15. 25, &c.
20. FRUIT,] as in v. 21; 1. 3; 8. 19; 11. 30.
SATISFIED,] as in 1. 31; 5. 10; 12. 11, 14, &c.
INCREASE,] as in 3. 9, 14; 8. 19; 10. 16, &c.
21. POWER,] as in 1. 24; 3. 27; 6. 5, 10, &c.
EAT,] as in 1. 31; 13. 2; 27. 18; 30. 17, &c.
22. FOUND,] as in 3. 13; 8. 35; 24. 14, &c.
BRINGETH OUT,] as in 3. 13; 8. 35; 12. 2, &c.
GOOD WILL,] as in 8. 35; 10. 32; 11. 1, 20, 27, &c.   Sept. adds, 'He that puts away a good wife puts away good things, and he that keeps an adulteress is foolish and ungodly.'
23. SUPPLICATIONS,] as in 2 Ch. 6. 21, &c.
POOR,] as in 10. 4; 13. 8, 23; 14. 20, &c.
RICH,] as in v. 11; 10. 15; 14. 20; 22. 2, &c.
ANSWERETH,] as in 1. 28; 20. 14; 18. 27.
FIERCE THINGS,] as in 21. 14; 30. 25, &c.
24. FRIENDS,] as in v. 17; 3. 28, 29; 6. 1, &c.
LOVER,] as in v. 21; 8. 17, 21; 12. 1, &c.
ADHERING,] as in De. 4. 4; 2 Ch. 3. 12.

XIX. 1. POOR,] as in v. 7, 22; 10. 4; 13. 8.
WALKING,] as in 2. 7; 4. 18; 6. 12; 7. 22, &c.
INTEGRITY,] as in 2. 7; 10. 9, 29; 13. 6, &c.
PERVERSE,] as in 2. 15; 8. 8; 11. 20, &c.
FOOL,] as in v. 10, 13, 29; 1. 22, 32; 3. 35, &c.
2. KNOWLEDGE,] as in v. 25, 27; 1. 4, 7, &c.
HASTY,] as in 21. 5; 28. 20; 29. 20.
SINNING,] as in 5. 36; 11. 31; 13. 22; 14. 21.
3. FOLLY,] as in 5. 23; 12. 23; 13. 16, &c.
PERVERTETH,] as in 13. 16; 22. 12, &c.
WROTH,] as in 2 Ch. 26. 19.
4. WEALTH,] as in v. 14; 1. 13; 3. 9; 6. 31.
FRIENDS,] as in v. 6; 3. 28, 29; 6. 1, 3, &c.
NEIGHBOUR,] as in v. 6; 3. 28, 29; 6. 1, &c.
SEPARATED,] as in Ge. 2. 10; 13. 11; 25. 23
5. FALSE WITNESS,] as in v. 9; 6. 17, &c.
ACQUITTED,] as in v. 9; 6. 29; 11. 21, &c.
BREATHETH OUT,] as in v. 9; 6. 19; 12. 17
LIES,] as in v. 9, 22; 6. 19; 14. 5, 25, &c.
DELIVERED,] as in 28. 26; Ge. 19. 20, &c.
6. ENTREAT,] as in Ex. 32. 11; De. 29. 22.
NOBLE,] as in 8. 16; 17. 7, 26; 25. 7, &c.
GIFTS,] as in 18. 16; 21. 14; Ge. 34. 12, &c

THRONE,] as in v. 28; 9. 14; 16. 12; 25. 5, &c.
SCATTERING,] as in v. 26; Jer. 31. 10.
9. PURIFIED,] as in Ps. 73. 13; 119. 9.
CLEANSED,] as in Lev. 11. 32; 12. 7, 8, &c.
10. STONE,] used anciently for weights, as in v. 23; 11. 1; 16. 11; 17. 8, &c.
EPHAH,] as in Ex. 16. 36; Lev. 5. 11; 6. 20.
ABOMINATION,] as in v. 23; 3. 32; 6. 16, &c.
11. ACTIONS,] as in De. 28. 20; Jud. 2. 19, &c.
MAKETH HIMSELF KNOWN,] as in Ge. 42. 7.
PURE,] as in 16. 2; 21. 8; Ex. 27. 20; 30. 34.
UPRIGHT,] as in 2. 7, 21; 3. 32; 8. 9; 11. 3.
12. HEARING,] as in 1. 33; 8. 34; 12. 15, &c.
SEEING,] as in Ge. 13. 15; 31. 5, 43; 39. 23.
13. SLEEP,] as in 3. 24; 4. 16; 6. 4, 9, 10, &c.
POOR,] as in 23. 21; 30. 9; Ge. 45. 11.
OPEN,] as in 2 K. 6. 17, 20; 19. 16, &c.
BREAD,] as in v. 17; 4. 17; 6. 8, 26; 9. 5, 17.
14. BAD,] as in v. 14, 22, 30; 1. 16, 33, &c.
BUYER,] as in 15. 32; 19. 8; 14. 19, 22, &c.
BOASTETH HIMSELF,] as in 27. 1; 30. 30, &c.
15. SUBSTANCE,] as in 3. 28; 8. 21; 11. 24.
GOLD,] as in 11. 22; 17. 3; 22. 1; 25. 11, &c.
RUBIES,] as in 3. 15; 8. 11; 31. 10; Lam. 4. 7.
PRECIOUS,] as in Est. 1. 4, 20; 6. 3, 6, 7, 9.
16. GARMENT,] as in 6. 27; 25. 20; 27. 13, &c.
STRANGER,] as in 2. 16; 5. 3, 10, 17, 20, &c.
SURETY,] as in 3. 24; 6. 1; 11. 15; 27. 13, &c.
PLEDGE,] as in 27. 13.
17. SWEET,] as in Song 2. 14.
FALSEHOOD,] as in 6. 17, 19; 10. 18; 11. 18.
GRAVEL,] as in Ps. 77. 17; Lam. 3. 16.
18. PURPOSES,] as in 6. 18; 12. 5; 15. 22, 26.
COUNSEL,] as in v. 5; 1. 25, 30; 8. 14, &c.
ESTABLISH,] as in 4. 26; 12. 3, 19; 16. 3, &c.
PLANS,] as in 1. 5; 11. 14; 12. 15; 24. 6; Job 37. 12.
19. REVEALER,] as in 1 Sa. 22. 8, &c.
SECRET COUNSELS,] as in 3. 32; 11. 13, &c.
BUSY-BODY,] as in 11. 13; Lev. 19. 16; Jer. 6. 28; 9. 4; Eze. 22. 9.
DECEIVER,] as in Job 5. 2.
SURETY,] as in 14. 10; 24. 21; Ezr. 9. 2; Ps. 106. 35.
VILIFYING,] as in Ge. 12. 3; Ex. 21. 17; Lev. 24. 14, 23, &c.
EXTINGUISHED,] as in 13. 9; 24. 20, &c.
BLACKNESS,] as in 7. 2, 9; De. 32. 10; Ps. 17. 8.
DARKNESS,] as in 2. 13; Ge. 1. 2, 4, 5, 18; Ex. 10. 21, 22.
21. INHERITANCE,] as in 17. 2; 19. 14, &c.
LATTER END,] as in 5. 4, 11; 14. 12, 13, &c.
22. RECOMPENSE,] as in 6. 31; 13. 21; 19. 17.
WAIT,] as in Ps. 27. 14; 37. 34; Hos. 12. 6.
DELIVERETH,] as in Jud. 2. 18; 6. 14; 7. 2.
23. ABOMINATION,] as in v. 10; 3. 32; 6. 16.
BALANCES,] as in v. 10.
DECEIT,] as in 11. 1; 12. 5, 17, 20; 14. 8, 25.
24. STEPS,] as in Ps. 37. 23; Da. 11. 43.
UNDERSTANDETH,] as in 2. 5, 9; 7. 7, &c.
25. SNARE,] as in 12. 13; 13. 14; 14. 27, &c.
VOWS,] as in 7. 14; 31. 2; Ge. 28. 20; 31. 13.
MAKE INQUIRY,] as in 2 K. 16. 15; Ps. 27. 4.
26. SCATTERED,] as in v. 8; Jer. 31. 10.
WHEEL,] as in 25. 11; Ex. 14. 15; 1 K. 7. 30.
27. BREATH,] as in Ge. 2. 7; 7. 22; De. 20. 16.
LAMP,] as in v. 20; 6. 23; 13. 9; 24. 20, &c.
INNER PARTS,] as in v. 30; 7. 27; 18. 8, &c.
28. KINDNESS,] as in v. 6; 3. 3; 11. 17, &c.
TRUTH,] as in 3. 3; 8. 7; 11. 18; 12. 19, &c.

SUPPORTED,] as in Ps. 18. 35; 20. 2; 41. 3. 94. 18; 104. 15.
THRONE,] as in v. 8; 9. 14; 16. 12; 25. 5, &c.
29. BEAUTY,] as in 4. 9; 16. 31; 17. 6; 19. 11.
YOUNG MEN,] as in De. 32. 25; Jud. 14. 10.
STRENGTH,] as in 5. 10; 14. 4; 24. 5, 10, &c.
HONOUR,] as in 31. 25; Lev. 23. 40; De. 33. 17.
OLD MEN,] as in 17. 6; 31. 23; Ge. 18. 11, &c.
GREY HAIRS,] as in 16. 31; Ge. 15. 15, &c.
30. WOUND,] as in 23. 29; 27. 6; Ge. 4. 23.
PLAGUES,] as in Lev. 26. 21; Nu. 11. 33, &c.
INNER PARTS,] as in v. 27; Ge. 43. 30, &c.

XXI. 1. RIVULETS,] as in 5. 16; Job 29. 6.
PLEASETH,] as in 18. 2; De. 25. 7; Ru. 3. 13.
INCLINETH,] as in 2. 2; 5. 13; 7. 21, &c.
2. RIGHT,] as in v. 8, 18, 29; 2. 7, 21; 3. 32.
PONDERING,] as in 16. 2; 24. 12.
3. CHOSEN,] as in 8. 10, 19; 10. 20; 16. 16; 22. 1.
SACRIFICE,] as in v. 27; 7. 14; 15. 8; 17. 1.
4. LOFTINESS,] as in 25. 3; Isa. 2. 11, 17; 10. 12; Jer. 48. 29.
BREADTH,] as in 28. 25; Ge. 34. 21; Ex. 3. 8.
5. PURPOSES,] as in 6. 18; 12. 5; 15. 22, 26.
DILIGENT,] as in 10. 4; 12. 24, 27; 13. 4.
ADVANTAGE,] as in 14. 23; Ecc. 3. 19.
HASTY ONE,] as in 19. 2; 28. 20; 29. 20.
WANT,] as in 17; 6. 11; 11. 24; 14. 23, &c.
6. TREASURES,] as in v. 20; 8. 21; 10. 2, &c.
LYING TONGUE,] as in v. 23; 6. 17, 24, &c.
VANITY,] as in 13. 11; 31. 30; De. 32. 21, &c.
DRIVEN AWAY,] as in Lev. 26. 36; Job 13. 25; Isa. 41. 2.
SEEKING,] as in 17. 9, 19; 28. 5; 29. 26, &c.
7. SPOIL,] as in 24. 2; Job 5. 21, 22; Ps. 12. 5.
8. PURE,] as in 16. 2; 20. 11; Ex. 27. 20, &c.
UPRIGHT,] as in v. 2; 2. 7, 21; 3. 32, &c.
9. CORNER,] as in 7. 12; 25. 24; Ex. 27. 2, &c.
ROOF,] as in 25. 24; Ex. 30. 3; 37. 26, &c.
CONTENTIONS,] as in v. 19; 6. 14; 15. 18, &c.
COMPANY,] as in 25. 24; Hos. 6. 9.
10. DESIRED,] as in Job 23. 13; Ps. 132. 13.
GRACIOUS,] as in Isa. 26. 10.
11. SCORNER,] as in v. 24; 1. 22; 3. 34; 9. 7, 8.
PUNISHED,] as in 17. 26; Ex. 21. 22.
SIMPLE,] as in 1. 4, 24, 32; 7. 7; 8. 5; 9. 4.
GIVING UNDERSTANDING,] as in v. 16; Ge. 3. 6; Neh. 8. 13, &c.
RECEIVETH,] as in 1. 19; 2. 1; 6. 25; 10. 8.
12. RIGHTEOUS ONE,] as in v. 15, 18, 26, &c.
ACTING WISELY,] as in 10. 5, 19; 14. 35, &c.
13. SHUTTING,] as in 17. 28; 1 K. 6. 4, &c.
CRY,] as in Ge. 18. 20; Neh. 5. 6; 9. 9, &c.
POOR,] as in 10. 15; 14. 31; 19. 4, 17; 22. 9.
ANSWERED,] as in Job 11. 2; 19. 7; Eze. 14. 4.
14. GIFT,] as in 18. 16; 19. 6; Ge. 34. 12; Nu. 18. 11.
SECRET,] as in 9. 17; 25. 23; De. 13. 6, &c.
BRIBE,] as in 36; 17. 8, 23; Ex. 23. 8, &c.
BOSOM,] as in 5. 20; 6. 27; 16. 33; 17. 23, &c.
STRONG FURY,] as in 6. 34; 15. 1, 18; 16. 14.
15. TO DO JUSTICE,] as in v. 3, 7; 1. 3, &c.
JOY,] as in v. 17; 10. 28; 12. 20, &c.
RUIN,] as in 10. 14, 15, 29; 13. 3; 14. 28, &c.
WORKERS OF INIQUITY,] as in 10. 29, &c.
16. WANDERING,] as in 37. 15; Ex. 23. 4.
REPHAIM,] as in 2. 18; 9. 18; Job 26. 5, &c.
RESTETH,] as in 14. 33; Ge. 8. 4; Ex. 10. 14

17. MIRTH,] as in v. 15; 10. 28; 12. 20, &c.
OIL,] as in v. 20; 5. 3; 27. 9, 16; Ge. 28. 18.
WEALTH,] as in 10. 4, 22; 1 Sa. 17. 25, &c.
18. ATONEMENT,] as in 6. 35; 13. 8, &c.
UPRIGHT,] as in v. 12, 15, 26; 2. 20; 3. 33.
TREACHEROUS DEALER,] as in 2. 22; 11. 3, 6.
19. WILDERNESS LAND,] as in Ge. 14. 6, &c.
CONTENTIONS,] as in v. 9.
20. TREASURE,] as in v. 6; 8. 21; 10. 2, &c.
DESIRED,] as in Ge. 2. 9; 3. 6; Ps. 19. 10.
FOOLISH MAN,] as in 1. 22, 32; 3. 35; 8. 5.
SWALLOWETH IT UP,] as in 19. 28, &c.
21. PURSUING,] as in 28. 1; Lev. 26. 17, &c.
22. MIGHTY,] as in 16. 32; 30. 30; Ge. 6. 4.
CONFIDENCE,] as in 14. 26; 22. 19; 25. 19.
23. ADVERSITIES,] as in 1. 27; 11. 8; 12. 13.
24. PROUD,] as in Ps. 19. 13; 86. 14; 119. 21.
PRIDE,] as in 11. 2; 13. 10; De. 17. 12, &c.
25. DESIRE,] as in v. 26; 10. 24; 11. 23, &c.
SLOTHFUL,] as in 6. 6, 9; 10. 26; 13. 4, &c.
REFUSED,] as in v. 7; Ex. 7. 14; 10. 3, &c.
26.DESIRING,] as in v. 25; 10. 24; 11. 23, &c.
DESIRED,] as in 23. 3, 6; 24. 1; Nu. 11. 4, &c.
WITHHOLDETH,] as in 20.6; 24. 11; Job 7. 11.
27. SACRIFICE,] as in v. 3; 7. 14; 15. 8, &c.
ABOMINATION,] as in 3. 32; 6. 16; 8. 7, &c.
28. FALSE,] as in 6. 19; 14. 5, 25; 19. 5, &c.
PERISH,] as in 10. 28; 11. 7; 19. 9; Nu. 16. 33.
ATTENTIVE MAN,] as in 1. 33; 8. 34; 12. 15.
29. HARDENED,] as in 7. 13.
UPRIGHT,] as in v. 2, 8, 18; 2. 7, 21, &c.
PREPARETH,] as in 6. 8; 16. 9; 30. 25, &c.
30. OVER-AGAINST,] as in 2 Sa. 22. 25; 2 K.
1. 13; Neh. 3. 28; 11. 22.
31. HORSE,] as in 26. 3; Ge. 47. 17; 49. 17.
PREPARED,] as in Eze. 40. 43.
DELIVERANCE,] as in 11. 14; 24. 6, &c.

XXII. 1. NAME,] as in 10. 7; 18. 10; 21. 24.
CHOSEN,] as in 8. 10, 19; 10. 20; 16. 16; 21. 3.
WEALTH,] as in v. 4; 3. 16; 8. 18; 11. 16, &c.
GRACE,] as in v. 11; 1. 9; 3. 4, 22, 34, &c.
2. MET TOGETHER,] as in 29. 13; Ps. 85. 10
MAKER,] as in 10. 4; 11. 18; 12. 22; 14. 31.
3. PRUDENT,] as in 12. 16, 23; 13. 16; 14. 8,
15, 18; 27. 12.
HIDDEN,] as in 27. 12; Nu. 5. 13; 1 Sa. 20. 5.
SIMPLE,] as in 1. 4, 22, 32; 7. 7; 8. 5, &c.
PUNISHED,] as in 27. 12; Ex. 21. 22.
4. HUMILITY,] as in 15. 33; 18. 12; Zeph. 2.3.
RICHES,] as in v. 1; 3. 16; 8. 18; 11. 16, &c.
5. THORNS,] as in Job 5. 5.
SNARES,] as in 7. 23; Ex. 39. 3; Nu. 16. 38;
Jos. 23. 13, &c.
PERVERSE,] as in 2. 15; 8. 8; 11. 20; 17. 20;
19. 1; 28. 6.
FAR,] as in Ex. 23. 7; De. 12. 21; 11. 24, &c.
6. YOUTH,] as in v. 15; 1. 4; 7. 7; 20. 11, &c.
OLD,] as in Job 14. 8.
7. RICH,] as in v. 2, 16; 10. 15; 14. 20, &c.
RULETH,] as in 12. 24; 17. 2; Ge. 3. 6, &c.
BORROWER,] as in Ps. 37. 21; Isa. 24. 2.
LENDER,] as in 19. 17; Ps. 37. 26; 112. 5;
Isa. 24. 2.
8. SOWING,] as in 11. 18; Ge. 1. 29, &c.
PERVERSENESS,] as in 2 Sa. 3. 34; 7. 10, &c.
REAPETH,] as in 10. 27; Lev. 25. 5, 11, &c.
SORROW,] as in 6. 12, 18; 10. 29; 11. 7, &c.
ROD,] as in v. 15; 10. 13; 13. 24; 23. 13, &c.
WEARETH OUT,] as in Ge. 21. 15; 41. 53;
Ex. 39. 32, &c. Sept. adds, 'God loves a

cheerful and liberal man, but he shall fully
prove the folly of his works.'
10. CAST OUT,] as in Ex. 11. 1; 1 Ch. 17. 21
2 Ch. 20. 11.
SCORNER,] as in 1. 22; 3. 34; 9. 7, 8, &c.
CONTENTION,] as in 6. 14; 15. 18; 16. 28, &c.
STRIFE,] as in 20. 8; 29. 7; 31. 5, 8, &c.
SHAME,] as in 3. 35; 6. 33; 9. 7; 11. 2, &c.
CEASE,] as in Ge. 2. 2, 3; 8. 22; Ex. 31. 17.
11. GRACE,] as in v. 1; 1. 9; 3. 4, 22, 34, &c.
FRIEND,] as in 3. 28, 29; 6. 1, 3, 29, &c.
12. EYES OF JEHOVAH,] as in Nu. 24. 1, &c
OVERTHROWETH,] as in 13. 6; 19. 3, &c.
TREACHROUS,] as in 2. 22; 11. 3, 6; 13. 2.
13. SLOTHFUL,] as in 6. 6, 9; 10. 26; 13. 4.
LION,] as in 26. 13; 28. 15; Ge. 49. 9, &c.
WITHOUT,] as in 1. 20; 5. 16; 7. 12; 8. 26, &c.
BROAD PLACES,] as in 1. 20; 5. 16; 7. 12, &c.
14. PIT,] as in 23. 27; Jer. 2. 6; 18. 20, 22.
STRANGE WOMEN,] as in 2. 6; 5. 3, 10, &c.
ABHORRED,] as in Mic. 6. 10.
15. FOLLY,] as in 5. 23; 12. 23; 13. 16, &c.
YOUTH,] as in v. 6; 1. 4; 7. 7; 20. 11, &c.
ROD,] as in v. 8; 10. 13; 13. 24; 23. 13, &c
CHASTISEMENT,] as in 1. 2, 3, 7, 8; 3. 11.
PUTTETH IT FAR,] as in Ex. 8. 28; Jos. 8. 4.
16. OPPRESSING,] as in 14. 31; 28. 3, &c.
MULTIPLY,] as in 25. 27; Ge. 3. 16; 15. 1, &c.
RICH,] as in v. 2, 7; 10. 15; 14. 20; 18. 11.
WANT,] as in 6. 11; 11. 24; 14. 23; 21. 5, &c.
17. INCLINE THINE EAR,] as in 2. 2; 4. 20;
5. 1, 13; 15. 31, &c. This is evidently the
beginning of a new Collection of Proverbs.
HEAR,] as in 1. 8; 4. 1, 10; 5. 7; 7. 24, &c.
SET,] as in 24. 32; 26. 24; Ge. 3. 15; 30. 40.
18. PLEASANT,] as in 23. 8; 24. 4; 2 Sa. 1. 23.
PREPARED TOGETHER,] as in 2. 8, 11, 20.
19. TRUST,] as in 14. 26; 21. 22; 25. 19, &c.
CAUSED TO KNOW,] as in Ex. 18. 16, 20, &c.
20. WRITTEN,] as in Ex. 24. 12; 32. 32, &c.
COUNSELS,] as in 1. 31; Ps. 5. 10; 81. 12, &c.
21. SENDING,] as in 10. 26; 25. 13; 26. 6, &c.
22. ROB,] as in Ge. 31. 31; Lev. 19. 13, &c.
POOR,] as in v. 9, 16; 10. 5; 14. 31; 19. 4, &c.
BRUISE,] as in Job 4. 19; 6. 9; 19. 2, &c.
AFFLICTED,] as in 3. 34; 14. 21; 15. 15, &c.
GATE,] as in 1. 21; 8. 3; 14. 19; 24. 7, &c.
23. PLEADETH,] as in 3. 30; 23. 11, &c.
CAUSE,] as in 15. 18; 17. 1, 14; 18. 6, &c.
SPOILED,] as in Mal. 3. 8, 9.
24. ANGRY MAN,] as in 11. 22; 14. 17, 29, &c.
MAN OF FURY,] as in 6. 34; 15. 1, 18, &c.
25. PATHS,] as in 1. 19; 2. 8, 13, 15, 19, &c.
SNARE,] as in 12. 13; 13. 14; 14. 27; 18. 7, &c.
26. STRIKING HANDS,] as in 11. 15; 17. 18.
SURETIES,] as in 17. 18; Neh. 5. 3; Eze.
27. 27.
BURDENS,] as in De. 24. 10.
27. TO PAY,] as in Ex. 21. 36; 22. 3, 6, 14, &c.
BED,] as in Ge. 49. 4; Ex. 8. 3; 21. 18, &c.
28. REMOVE,] as in 23. 10; Da. 19. 14; Mic.
6. 14.
BORDER,] as in 23. 10; Ge. 10. 19; 23. 17, &c.
OLDEN TIMES,] as in 8. 23; 10. 25, 30; 23.
10; 27. 24.
29. SPEEDY,] as in Ezra 7. 6; Ps. 45. 1
Isa. 16. 5.
BUSINESS,] as in 18. 9; 24. 27; Ge. 2. 2, &c
STATION HIMSELF,] as in Ex. 2. 4; 19. 17, &c

XXIII. 1. RULER,] as in 6. 7; 16. 32, &c.

CONSIDEREST DILIGENTLY,] as in 2. 5, 9; 7. 7; 14. 15; 19. 25, &c.
2. MAN OF APPETITE,] *lit.* 'of soul.'
3. HAVE DESIRE,] as in v. 6; 24. 1; Pe. 5. 21.
DAINTIES,] as in v. 6.
LYING,] as in 6. 19; 14. 5, 25; 19. 5, 9, &c.
4. LABOUR,] as in Job 9. 29; Isa. 40. 28, &c.
WEALTH,] as in 28. 20.
CEASE,] as in 19. 17; Ex. 14. 12; 2 Ch. 25. 16.
5. WINGS,] as in 1. 17; Ge. 1. 21; 7. 14, &c.
EAGLE,] as in 30. 17, 19; Ex. 19. 4, &c.
6. EVIL EYE,] as in v. 5, 26, 29, 31, 33, &c.
DAINTIES,] as in v. 3.
7. EAT,] as in 24. 13; 25. 16; Ge. 27. 19; 45. 18.
DRINK,] as in 5. 15; 9. 5; Ge. 24. 14, 18, &c.
8. MORSEL,] as in 17. 1; 28. 21; Ge. 18. 5, &c.
VOMIT UP,] as in Lev. 18. 25, 28; 20. 22, &c.
MARRED,] as in Ge. 38. 9; Ex. 21. 26, &c.
SWEET,] as in 22. 18; 24. 4; 2 Sa. 1. 23, &c.
9. FOOL,] as in 1. 22, 32; 3. 35; 8. 5, &c.
TREADETH,] as in v. 22; 6. 30; 30. 17; Song 8. 1, 7.
10. REMOVE,] as in 22. 28; De. 19. 14; Mic. 6. 14.
BORDER,] as in 15. 25; 22. 28; Ge. 10. 19, &c.
FIELDS,] as in 24. 27, 30; 27. 26; 31. 16, &c.
FATHERLESS,] as in Ex. 22. 22, 24; De.10.18.
11. REDEEMER,] as in Ge. 48. 16; Lev. 25. 25.
STRONG,] as in Ex. 3. 19; 6. 1; 10. 19, &c.
PLEAD,] as in 3. 30; 23. 11; 26. 20, 21, &c.
CAUSE,] as in 15. 18; 17. 1, 14; 18. 6, 17, &c.
12. INSTRUCTION,] as in v. 13, 23; 1. 2, &c.
13. WITHHOLD,] as in 3. 27; 30. 7, &c.
YOUTH,] as in 1. 4; 7. 7; 20. 11; 22. 6, &c.
CHASTISEMENT,] as in v. 12, 23; 1. 2, 3, &c.
ROD,] as in v. 14; 10. 13; 13. 24; 22. 8, &c.
14. SHEOL,] as in 1. 12; 5. 5; 7. 27; 9. 18, &c.
DELIVEREST,] as in 10. 2; 11. 4, 6, &c.
15. MY SON,] as in v. 19, 26; 1. 1, 8, 10, &c.
REJOICETH,] as in v. 24, 25; 13. 9; 17. 21.
16. EXULT,] as in 2 Sa. 1. 20; Ps. 28. 7, &c.
UPRIGHTLY,] as in v. 31; 1. 3; 2. 9; 8. 6, &c.
17. ENVIOUS,] as in 3. 31; 24. 1, 19, &c.
FEAR OF JEHOVAH,] as in 1. 7, 29; 2. 5, &c.
18. POSTERITY,] as in v. 32; 5. 4, 11, &c.
HOPE,] as in 10. 28; 11. 7, 23; 19. 18, &c.
CUT OFF,] as in 2. 22; 10. 31; 24. 14, &c.
19. HEAR,] as in v. 22; 1. 8; 4. 1, 10, &c.
MAKE HAPPY,] as in Isa. 1. 17.
20. QUAFFERS,] as in v. 21; De. 21. 20; Eze. 23. 42.
GLUTTONOUS ONES,] as in v. 21; 28. 7; De. 21. 20; Jer. 15. 19.
FLESH,] as in 4. 22; 5. 11; 14. 30; Isa. 64. 1, 3.
21. BECOME POOR,] as in 20. 13; 30. 9; Ge. 45. 11.
CLOTHETH,] as in Ge. 3. 21; 27. 15; 41. 42.
22. BEGAT,] as in Ge. 4. 18, 22; 6. 4; 10. 8.
DESPISE,] as in v. 9; 1. 7; 6. 30; 30. 17; Song 8. 1, 7; Zech. 4. 10.
23. TRUTH,] as in 3. 3; 8. 7; 11. 18; 12. 19.
BUY,] as in 4. 5, 7.
SELL,] as in 31. 24; Ge. 25. 33; 37. 27, &c.
24. REJOICETH,] as in v. 25; 2. 14; 24. 17, &c.
BEGETTER,] as in 17. 21.
25. JOYFUL,] as in 3. 12; Ge. 33. 10, &c.
27. HARLOT,] as in 6. 26; 7. 10; 29. 3, &c.
DITCH,] as in 22. 14; Jer 2. 6; 18. 20, 22.
STRANGE WOMAN,] as in 2. 16; 5. 10, 20, &c.
PIT,] as in 5. 15; Ge. 14. 10; 16. 14; 21. 19.
28. LIETH IN WAIT,] as in 1. 11, 18; 7. 12, &c.

TREACHEROUS,] as in 2. 22; 11. 3, 6, &c.
INCREASETH,] as in 1. 5: 3. 2; 9. 9, 11, &c.
29. WO,] as in Nu. 21. 29; 24. 23; 1 Sa. 4. 7.
CONTENTIONS,] as in 6. 14; 15. 18; 16. 28.
PLAINT,] as in 1 Sa. 1. 16; 1 K. 18. 27, &c.
WOUNDS,] as in 20. 30; 27. 6; Ge. 4. 23, &c.
WITHOUT CAUSE,] as in 1. 11, 17; 3. 30, &c.
30. TARRYING,] as in Ps. 127. 2; Isa. 5. 11.
WINE,] as in v. 20, 31; 4. 17; 9. 2, 5, &c.
SEARCH OUT,] as in 25. 2; Jud. 18. 2, &c.
MIXED WINE,] as in Isa. 65. 11.
31. CUP,] as in Ge. 40. 11, 13, 21; Lev. 11. 17.
COLOUR,] as in v. 5, 6, 26, 29, 33; 1. 17, &c.
GOETH UP AND DOWN,] as in Ge. 5. 22, 24.
UPRIGHT,] as in 1. 3; 2. 9; 8. 6; 23. 6, &c.
32. LATTER END,] as in v. 18; 5. 4, 11, &c.
SERPENT,] as in 30. 19; Ge. 3. 1, 2, 4, &c.
BITETH,] as in Nu. 21. 9; Ecc. 10. 8; Amos 5. 19; 9. 3.
BASILISK,] as in Isa. 11. 8; 59. 5; Jer. 8. 17.
33. STRANGE WOMEN,] as in 2. 16; 5. 3, &c.
PERVERSE THINGS,] as in 2. 12, 14; 6. 14; 8. 13; 10. 31, 32; 16. 28, 30.
34. LYING DOWN,] as in Ge. 28. 13; Ex. 22. 19.
HEART,] as in 2. 2, 10; 3. 1, &c.
MAST,] as in 1. 9, 21; 4. 9; 8. 2, 23, 26, &c.
35. SMOTE,] as in Ge. 19. 11; 32. 8, 11, &c.
SICK,] as in Jud. 16. 7, 11, 17; 1 Sa. 30. 13.
BEAT,] as in Jud. 5. 22, 26; Ps. 74. 6; 141. 5; Isa. 16. 18.
AWAKE,] as in 6. 22; Job 14. 12; Jer. 51. 39, 57; Da. 12. 2. Sept. 'when will it be morning, that I may go and seek those with whom I may go in company.'

XXIV. 1. ENVIOUS,] as in v. 19; 3. 31, &c.
DESIRE,] as in 23. 3, 6; Ecc. 6. 2.
2. DESTRUCTION,] as in 21. 7; Job 5. 21, &c.
MEDITATE,] as in 8. 7; 15. 28; Job 27. 4, &c.
PERVERSENESS,] as in 31. 7; Ge. 41. 51, &c.
3. BUILDED,] as in Ge. 16. 2; 30. 3, &c.
ESTABLISHETH,] as in Nu. 21. 27; Ps. 59. 4; Isa. 54. 14.
4. INNER PARTS,] as in 7. 27; 18. 8; 20. 27.
PRECIOUS,] as in 1. 13; 3. 15; 6. 26; 12. 27.
PLEASANT,] as in 22. 18; 23. 8; 2 Sa. 1. 23.
WEALTH,] as in 1. 13; 3. 9; 6. 18, 31, &c.
5. MIGHTY,] as in 10. 34; 20. 24; 28. 3, &c.
STRENGTH,] as in 10. 15; 14. 26; 18. 10, &c.
6. PLANS,] as in 1 5; 11. 14; 12. 5; 20. 18; Job 37. 12.
WAR,] as in 20. 18; 21. 31; Ge. 14. 2, 8, &c.
DELIVERANCE,] as in 11. 14; 21. 31, &c.
COUNSELLORS,] as in 11. 14; 12. 20; 15. 22.
7. HIGH,] as in Job 28. 18; Eze. 27. 16.
FOOL,] as in 1. 7; 7. 22; 10. 8, 14, 21, &c.
GATE,] as in 1. 21; 8; 14. 19; 22. 22, &c.
OPENETH,] as in 31. 26; Ge. 8. 6; 29. 31, &c.
8. MASTER,] as in 1. 17, 19; 3. 27; 12. 4; 16. 22.
WICKED DEVICES,] as in 1. 4; 3. 21.
9. DEVICE,] as in 10. 23; 21. 27; Lev. 18. 17.
FOLLY,] as in 5. 23; 12. 23; 13. 16; 14. 1, &c.
ABOMINATION,] as in 3. 32; 6. 16; 8. 7, &c.
SCORNER,] as in 1. 22; 3. 34; 9. 7, 8, &c.
10. POWER,] as in v. 5; Ge. 4. 12; 31. 6, &c.
11. DELIVERING,] as in Ge. 32. 11; Jud. 10.15.
SLIPPING,] as in 25. 20.
SLAUGHTER,] as in Est. 9. 5; Isa. 27. 7; 30. 25; Eze. 26. 15.
KEEPEST BACK,] as in 21. 26; Ge. 20. 6: Job 7. 11; 16. 5, &c. Sept. reads, 'But if

thou shouldst say, I know not this man,
know that the Lord knows the hearts of all,
and he that formed breath for all, he knows
all things, who renders to every man according to his works.'
12. PONDERER,] as in 2. 5, 9; 7. 7; 14. 15, &c.
KEEPER,] as in 13. 3; 16. 17; 27. 18; 28. 7.
RENDERED,] as in v. 18; Ge. 14. 16; 28. 15.
13. HONEY,] as in 16 24; 25. 16, 27, &c.
HONEYCOMB,] as in 5. 3; 27. 7; P's. 19. 10;
Song 4. 11.
SWEET,] as in 16. 24; 27. 7; Jud. 14. 14, &c.
PALATE,] as in 5. 3; 8. 7; Job 6. 30; 12. 11.
14. POSTERITY,] as in v. 20; 5. 4, 11, &c.
HOPE,] as in 10. 28; 11. 7, 23; 19. 18, &c.
CUT OFF,] as in 2. 22; 10. 31; 23. 18, &c.
15. LAY WAIT,] as in 1. 11, 18; 7. 12, &c.
HABITATION,] as in 3. 33; 21. 20; Ex. 15. 13.
RESTING-PLACE,] as in Isa. 35. 7; 65. 10;
Jer. 50. 6.
16. RISE,] as in 31. 28; Ge. 37. 7; 41. 30, &c.
STUMBLE,] as in 4. 12, 19; Ps. 9. 3; Isa. 40.,3.
17. ENEMY,] as in Ge. 22. 17; 49. 8; Ex. 23. 4.
REJOICE,] as in 13. 9; 17. 21; 23. 15, 24, &c.
STUMBLING,] as in Da. 11. 34.
JOYFUL,] as in 2. 14; 23. 24, 25; 1 Ch. 16. 31.
18. TURNED,] as in v. 12; Ge. 14. 16, &c.
ANGER,] as in 11. 22: 14. 17, 29; 15. 1, &c.
19. FRET THYSELF,] as in Ps. 37. 1, 7, 8.
EVIL DOERS,] as in 17. 4; Job 8. 20, &c.
ENVIOUS,] as in v. 1; 3. 31; 23. 17, &c.
20. POSTERITY,] as in v. 14; 5. 4, 11, &c.
LAMP,] as in 6. 23; 13. 9; 20. 20, 27, &c.
EXTINGUISHED,] as in 13. 9; 20. 20; Job
18. 5, 6; 21. 17.
21. FEAR,] as in 3. 7; Jos. 24. 14; 1 Sa. 12. 24.
CHANGERS,] as in 17. 9; 26. 11; Est. 1. 7; 3. 8.
MIX UP THYSELF,] as in 14. 10; 20. 19; Ps.
106. 35.
22. SUDDENLY,] as in 3. 25; 6. 15; 7. 22, &c.
CALAMITY,] as in 1. 26, 27; 6. 15; 17. 5, &c.
RUIN,] as in Job 30. 24; 31. 29.
23. THESE ALSO.] Compare 22. 17.
24. EXECRATE,] as in 11. 26; Lev. 24. 11, &c.
ABHOR,] as in Nu. 23. 8; Isa. 66. 14, &c.
25. REPROVING,] as in 9. 7; 25. 12; 28. 23.
PLEASANT,] as in 2. 10; 9. 17; Ge. 49. 15, &c.
26. KISSETH,] as in Ge. 27. 27; 29. 11, &c.
STRAIGHT-FORWARD,] as in 8. 9; 2 Sa. 15. 3.
27. PREPARE,] as in Ge. 43. 16; Nu. 23. 1.
OUT-PLACE,] as in 1. 20; 5. 16; 7. 12; 8. 26.
FIELD,] as in v. 30; 23. 10; 27. 26; 31. 16, &c.
AFTERWARDS,] as in 7. 22; 20. 7, 17, 25, &c.
28. WITNESS,] as in 6. 19; 12. 17; 14. 5, 27.
FOR NOUGHT,] as in 1. 11, 17; 3. 30; 23. 29.
ENTICED,] as in Jer. 20. 7; Eze. 14. 9.
29. RENDER,] as in 12. 14; 15. 1; 19. 24, &c.
30. SLOTHFUL MAN,] as in 6. 6, 9; 10. 26, &c.
PASSED BY,] as in 22. 3; 27. 12; Ge. 15. 17.
VINEYARD,] as in 31. 16; Ge. 9. 20, &c.
LACKING HEART,] as in 6. 32; 7. 7; 9. 4, &c.
31. COVERED,] as in Ps. 80. 10.
NETTLES,] as in Job 30. 7; Zeph. 2. 9.
WALL,] as in Eze. 42. 10.
BROKEN DOWN,] as in Jer. 50. 15; Eze. 30.
4; 38. 20; Joel 1. 17.
32. INSTRUCTION,] as in 1. 2, 3, 7, 8; 3. 11.
33. SLEEP,] as in 3. 24; 4. 16; 6. 4, 9, 10, &c.
SLUMBER,] as in 6. 4, 10; Job 33. 15; Ps.
132. 41.
FOLDING,] as in 6. 10.

LIE DOWN,] as in 6. 10, 22.
34. POVERTY,] as in 10. 15; 13. 18.
TRAVELLER,] as in 20. 7; Ge. 3. 8; De. 23. 14
WANT,] as in 6. 11; 11. 24; 14. 23; 21. 5, 17
22. 16; 28. 27.
ARMED MEN,] as in 6. 11; 30. 5.

XXV. 1. PROVERBS OF SOLOMON,] as in 1
1; 10. 1.
2. HONOUR,] as in v. 27; 3. 16, 35; 8. 18, &c
TO HIDE,] as in De. 31. 18; Isa. 29. 15; 57. 17.
SEARCH OUT,] as in 23. 30.
3. HEIGHT,] as in 21. 4; Isa. 2. 11, 17; 10
12; Jer. 48. 29.
UNSEARCHABLE,] as in v. 27; Job 5. 9, &c
4. TAKE AWAY,] as in v. 5.
DROSS,] as in 26. 23; Ps. 119. 119; Isa. 1.
22, 25; Eze. 22. 18, 19.
VESSEL,] as in 20. 15; Ge. 24. 53; 27. 3, &c.
REFINER,] as in Jud. 17. 4; Neh. 3. 8, 32.
5. TAKE AWAY,] as in v. 14.
ESTABLISHED,] as in 4. 26; 12. 3, 19, &c.
THRONE,] as in 9. 14; 16. 12; 20. 8, 28, &c.
6. GREAT,] as in 18. 16; 10. 19; 27. 14, &c.
7. HITHER,] as in Ge. 15. 16; 21. 23, 29, &c
HUMBLE,] as in Eze. 21. 26.
NOBLE,] as in 8. 16; 17. 7, 26; 19. 6, &c.
8. TO STRIVE,] as in Jud. 11. 25; 21. 22, &c
TURN,] as in Ge. 3. 3; 24. 6; 31. 31; 42. 4.
LATTER END,] as in 5. 4, 11; 14. 12, 13, &c.
TO BLUSH,] as in Jer. 6. 15.
9. CAUSE,] as in 15. 18; 17. 1, 14; 18. 6, 17.
PLEAD,] as in Ps. 35. 1; 43. 1; 74. 22, &c.
SECRET COUNSEL,] as in Prov. 3. 32; 11. 13.
REVEAL,] as in Lev. 18. 7, 8; 9. 10, 12, &c.
10. HEARER,] as in v. 12; 1. 33; 8. 34, &c.
EVIL REPORT,] as in 10. 18; Ge. 27. 2, &c.
11. APPLES,] as in Song 2. 3, 5; 7. 8; 8. 5;
Joel 1. 12.
IMAGERY,] as in 18. 11; Lev. 26. 1; Nu. 33.
52; Ps. 73. 7; Eze. 8. 12.
12. RING,] as in 11. 22; Ge. 24. 22, 30, 47, &c.
ORNAMENT,] as in Song 7. 1.
PURE GOLD,] as in Job 28. 16, 19; 31. 24, &c.
REPROVER,] as in 9. 7; 24. 25; 28. 23, &c.
ATTENTIONS,] as in v. 10; 1. 33; 8. 34, &c.
13. SNOW,] as in 26. 1; 31. 21; Ex. 4. 6, &c.
HARVEST,] as in 6. 8; 10. 5; 20. 4; 26. 1, &c.
FAITHFUL,] as in 27. 6; Nu. 12. 7, &c.
AMBASSADOR,] as in 13. 17; 26. 14, &c.
SENDING,] as in 10. 26; 22. 21; 26. 6, &c.
MASTERS,] as in 27. 18; 30. 10; Ge. 18. 12.
REFRESHETH,] as in 12. 14; 15. 1; 19. 24.
14. CLOUDS,] as in Ps. 135. 7; Jer. 10. 13;
51. 16.
WIND,] as in v. 23, 28; 1. 23; 11. 13, 29, &c.
RAIN,] as in v. 23; Ge. 7. 12; 8. 2, &c.
BOASTING HIMSELF,] as in Ps. 97. 7; Jer.
9. 24.
FALSE,] as in v. 18; 6. 17, 19; 10. 18, &c.
15. RULER,] as in 6. 7; Ge. 10. 24, &c.
PERSUADED.] as in Jer. 20. 10; Eze. 14. 9.
SOFT,] as in 4. 3; 15. 1; Ge. 18. 7; 29. 17.
BREAKETH,] as in Ex. 12. 46; Lev. 11. 33.
BONE,] as in 17. 22; Ge. 49. 14; 2 K. 9. 13;
Job 40. 18.
16. HONEY,] as in v. 27; 16. 24; 24. 13, &c.
SUFFICIENCY,] as in 27. 27; Ex. 36. 5, 7, &c.
SATIATED,] as in v. 17; 1. 31; 5. 10; 12 11.
17. HATED,] as in 1. 29; 5. 12; 6. 16; 8. 13.
18. SWORD,] as in 27. 40; 30. 14; 31. 26, &c

SHARP,] as in Ps. 45. 5; 120. 4; Isa. 5. 28.
ARROW,] as in 7. 23; 26. 18; Ge. 49. 23, &c.
TESTIFYING,] as in Ge. 35. 3; Jud. 19. 28.
TESTIMONY,] as in 6. 19; 12. 17; 14. 5, 25, &c.
19. TOOTH,] as in 10. 26; 13. 14; Ge. 49. 12.
CONFIDENCE,] as in 14. 26; 21. 22; 22. 19, &c.
TREACHEROUS,] as in 2. 22; 11. 3, 6, &c.
DAY OF ADVERSITY,] as in 24. 10; Ge. 35. 3.
20. GARMENT,] as in 6. 27; 20. 16; 27. 13, &c.
COLD,] as in Job 24. 7; 37. 9; Ps. 147. 7;
Nah. 3. 17.
VINEGAR,] as in 10. 26; Nu. 6. 3; Ru. 2. 14;
Ps. 69. 21.
NITRE,] as in Jer. 2. 20.
SINGER,] as in 2 Sa. 19. 35; 1 K. 10. 12, &c.
SONGS,] as in Ge. 21. 27; Jud. 5. 12, &c.
SAD,] as in Ge. 2. 9, 17; 3. 5, 22; 6. 5, &c.
21. HATING,] as in 11. 15; 12. 1; 13. 24, &c.
HUNGER,] as in 27. 7; 1 Sa. 2. 5; 2 Sa. 17. 29.
CAUSE TO EAT,] as in 1 K. 22. 27; 2 Ch.
18. 26.
THIRST,] as in De. 29. 19; 2 Sa. 17. 29, &c.
CAUSE TO DRINK,] as in Ge. 24. 43, 45; 29. 7.
22. COALS,] as in 6. 28; 26. 21; Lev. 16. 12.
GIVETH RECOMPENSE,] as in 6. 31; 13. 21.
23. RAIN,] as in Ge. 7. 12; 8. 2; Lev. 26. 4.
SECRET,] as in 9. 17; 21. 14; De. 13. 6, &c.
24. SIT,] as in 21. 9, 19; 31. 23; Ge. 13. 6, &c.
CORNER,] as in 7. 12; 21. 9; Ex. 27. 2, &c.
ROOF,] as in 21. 9; Ex. 30. 3; 37. 26, &c.
CONTENTIONS,] as in 6. 14; 15. 18; 16. 28, &c.
COMPANY,] as in 21. 9; De. 18. 11, &c.
25. COLD,] as in 17. 27; Jer. 18. 14.
WEARY,] as in Ge. 25. 29, 30; De. 25. 18, &c.
REPORT,] as in 15. 30; 1 Sa. 2. 24; 4. 19, &c.
FAR,] as in 31. 14; 2 Sa. 15. 17; Ps. 138. 6.
26. SPRING,] as in 5. 16; 8. 24; Ge. 7. 11, &c.
FOUNTAIN,] as in 5. 18; 10. 11; 13. 14, &c.
CORRUPT,] as in Mal. 1. 14.
FALLING,] as in 24. 11.
27. HONEY,] as in v. 16; 16. 24; 24. 13, &c.
SEARCHING OUT,] as in v. 3; Jud. 5. 16, &c.
HONOUR,] as in v. 2; 3. 16, 35; 8. 18, &c.
28. CITY,] as in 1. 21; 16. 32; 21. 22, &c.
BROKEN DOWN,] as in 2 Ch. 32. 5; Neh. 2.
13; 4. 7.
WALLS,] as in 18. 11; Ex. 14. 22, 29, &c.

XXVI. 1. SNOW,] as in 25. 13; 31. 21, &c.
SUMMER,] as in 6. 8; 10. 5; 20. 4; 25. 13, &c.
RAIN,] as in 28. 3; Ex. 9. 33, 34; De. 11. 11.
HARVEST,] as in 6. 8; 10. 5; 20. 4; 25. 13, &c.
HONOUR,] as in v. 8; 3. 16, 35; 8. 18, &c.
COMELY,] as in 17. 7; 19. 10; Ps. 33. 1, &c.
FOOL,] as in v. 3, 4, 5, 6, 7, 8, 9, 10, 11, 12.
2. BIRD,] as in 6. 5; 7. 23; 27. 8; Ge. 7. 14.
SWALLOW,] as in Ps. 84. 3.
FLYING,] as in Job 5. 7.
REVILING,] as in 27. 14; Ge. 27. 12, 13, &c.
WITHOUT CAUSE,] as in 1. 11, 17; 3. 30, &c.
3. WHIP,] as in 1 K. 12. 11, 14; 2 Ch. 10. 11.
HORSE,] as in 21. 31; Ge. 47. 17; 49. 17, &c.
BRIDLE,] as in 2 Sa. 8. 1; 2 K. 19. 28; Ps.
32. 9; Isa. 37. 29.
ASS,] as in Ge. 12. 16; 22. 3, 5; 24. 35, &c.
ROD,] as in 10. 13; 13. 24; 22. 8, 15; 23. 13.
BACK,] as in 10. 13; 19. 29; Job 30. 5; Isa.
38. 17; 50. 6; 51. 23.
4. ANSWER,] as in 1. 28; 18. 23; Ge. 18. 27.
FOLLY,] as in v. 1, 3, 5, 6, 7, 8, 9, 10, 11, 12.
6. DRINKING,] as in 1 Sa. 30. 16; 1 K. 1. 25.

INJURY,] as in 3. 31; 4. 17; 10. 6; 13. 2, &c.
SENDING,] as in 10. 26; 22. 21; 25. 13, &c.
7. WEAK,] as in Job 28. 4; Ps. 79. 8; 116. 6.
Isa. 19. 6; 38. 14.
LAME,] as in Lev. 21. 18; De. 15. 21, &c.
PARABLE,] as in v. 9; 1. 1, 6; 10. 1; 25. 1.
8. BINDING,] as in 7. 20; Ge. 42. 35, &c.
GIVING HONOUR,] as in 1 Sa. 16. 5, &c.
9. THORN,] as in 1 Sa. 13. 6; 2 K. 14. 9, &c.
GONE UP,] as in 21. 22; 24. 31; 30. 4; 31. 29.
10. TRANSGRESSORS,] as in Nu. 14. 41; 2 Ch.
24. 20; Est. 3. 3.
11. DOG,] as in v. 17; Ex. 11. 7; 22. 31, &c.
REPEATING,] as in 17. 9; 24. 21.
12. HOPE,] as in 10. 28; 11. 7, 23; 19. 18, &c.
13. SLOTHFUL,] as in v. 14, 15, 16; 6. 6, 9.
LION,] as in Job 4. 10; 10. 16; 28. 8, &c.
BROAD PLACES,] as in 1. 20; 5. 16; 7. 12, &c.
14. DOOR,] as in 8. 34; Ge. 19. 6, 9, 10, &c.
TURNETH ROUND,] as in Ge. 42. 24, &c.
BED,] as in Ge. 47. 31; 48. 2; 49. 33, &c.
15. HID,] as in 19. 24; Ps. 9. 15; 31. 4, &c.
DISH,] as in 19. 24; 2 K. 21. 13.
WEARY,] as in Ex. 7. 18; Ps. 68. 9, &c.
16. SLOTHFUL,] as in v. 13, 14, 15; 6. 6, &c.
SEVEN.] A perfect number.
REASON,] as in 11. 22; Job 12. 30; Ps
119. 66.
17. LAYING HOLD,] as in 3. 18; Ex. 9. 2, &c.
DOG,] as in v. 16; Ex. 11. 7; 22. 31, &c.
PASSER-BY,] as in v. 10; 7. 8; 9. 15, &c.
WROTH,] as in 14. 16; 20. 2.
STRIFE,] as in v. 21; 15. 18; 17. 1, 14, &c.
18. CASTING,] as in 1 Ch. 10. 3; 2 Ch. 35
23; Hos. 6. 3.
ARROWS,] as in 7. 23; 25. 18; Ge. 49. 23, &c.
19. DECEIVED,] as in Ge. 29. 25; Jos. 9. 22.
PLAYING,] as in Jer. 15. 17.
20. WOOD,] as in v. 21; 3. 18; 11. 30, &c.
FIRE,] as in v. 21; 6. 27; 16. 27; 30. 16, &c.
TALE-BEARER,] as in v. 22; 16. 28; 18. 8.
CONTENTION,] as in v. 21; 6. 14; 15. 18, &c.
CEASETH,] as in Ps. 107. 30; Jon. 1. 11, 12.
21. COAL,] as in Isa. 44. 12; 54. 16.
BURNING COALS,] as in 6. 28; 25. 22, &c.
CONTENTIONS,] as in v. 20; 6. 14; 15. 18, &c.
22. INNER PARTS,] as in 7. 27; 18. 8, &c.
23. DOORS,] as in 25. 4; Eze. 22. 18, 19, &c.
SPREAD,] as in Ex. 26. 32.
POTSHERD,] as in Lev. 6. 28; 11. 33, &c.
BURNING,] as in Ps. 7. 13.
24. HATER,] as in 11. 15; 12. 1; 13. 24, &c.
DECEIT,] as in 11. 1; 12. 5, 17, 20; 14. 8, &c.
25. GRACIOUS,] as in 2 Sa. 12. 22.
TRUST,] as in 14. 15; Ex. 4. 1, 5, 8, 9, 31, &c.
ABOMINATIONS,] as in 3. 32; 6. 16; 8. 7, &c.
26. HATRED,] as in 10. 12, 18; 15. 17, &c.
COVERED,] as in Ge. 24. 65; 2 K. 19. 1, &c.
REVEALED,] as in Ex. 20. 26; 1 Sa. 3. 7, &c.
ASSEMBLY,] as in 5. 14; 21. 16; Ge. 28. 3, &c.
27. DIGGING,] as in 16. 27.
PIT,] as in Job 9. 31; 17. 14; 33. 18, 22, &c.
TURNETH,] as in 1. 23; 2. 19; 12. 14; 25. 10.
28. LYING,] as in 6. 17, 19; 10. 18; 11. 18, &c
BRUISED ONES,] as in Ps. 9. 9; 10. 18; 74. 21
FLATTERING,] as in 5. 3; Ge. 27. 11; Jos
11. 17; 12. 7; Eze. 12. 24.

XXVII. 1. BOAST THYSELF,] as in 20. 14
31. 30; 1 K. 20. 11; Ps. 34. 2, &c.
TO-MORROW,] as in 3. 28; Ge. 30. 33, &c.

BRINGETH FORTH,] as in Ge. 4. 18, 22, &c.
2. PRAISE,] as in 28. 4; 31. 28, 31; Ge. 12. 15.
STRANGER,] as in v. 13; 2. 16; 5. 10, 20, &c.
3. HEAVY,] as in Isa. 21. 15; 30. 27; Nah.
3. 3.
SAND,] as in Ge. 22. 17; 32. 12; 41. 49, &c.
FOOL,] as in v. 22.
4. FURY,] as in 6. 34; 15. 1, 18; 16. 14, &c.
OVERFLOWING,] as in Job 38. 25; Ps. 32. 6.
JEALOUSY,] as in 6. 34; 14. 30; Nu. 5. 14, &c.
5. REPROOF,] as in 1. 23, 25, 30; 3. 11, &c.
6. FAITHFUL,] as in 25. 13; Nu. 12. 7, &c.
WOUNDS,] as in 20. 30; 23. 29; Ge. 4. 23, &c.
KISSES,] as in Song 1. 2.
7. SATIATED,] as in 19. 23; Ge. 25. 8, &c.
TREADETH DOWN,] as in Ps. 44. 5; 68. 12.
HONEY-COMB,] as in 5. 3; 24. 13; Ps. 19. 10;
Song 4. 11.
HUNGRY,] as in 25. 21; 1 Sa. 2. 5, &c.
BITTER,] as in 5. 4; 31. 6; Ge. 27. 34, &c.
SWEET,] as in 16. 24; 24. 13; Jud. 14. 14, &c.
8. BIRD,] as in 6. 5; 7. 23; 26. 2; Ge. 7. 14.
NEST,] as in Ge. 6. 14; Nu. 24. 21; De. 22. 6.
9. OINTMENT,] as in v. 16; 5. 3; 21. 17, &c.
PERFUME,] as in Ex. 25. 6; 30. 1, 7, 8, &c.
REJOICE,] as in 10. 1; 12. 25; 15. 20, 30, &c.
SWEETNESS,] as in 16. 21.
FRIEND,] as in v. 10, 14, 17; 3. 28, 29, &c.
COUNSEL,] as in 1. 25, 30; 8. 14; 12. 15, &c.
10. FRIEND,] as in v. 9, 14, 17; 3. 28, &c.
FORSAKE,] as in 3. 3; 4. 2, 6; Ge. 2. 24, &c.
CALAMITY,] as in 1. 26, 27; 6. 15; 17. 5, &c.
NEAR,] as in 10. 14; Ge. 19. 20; 45. 10, &c.
AFAR OFF,] as in 7. 19; 15. 29; 31. 10, &c.
11. BE WISE,] as in 6. 6; 8. 33; 23. 19.
REJOICE,] as in Ps. 86. 4; 90. 15.
REPROACHER,] as in Ps. 69. 9; 119. 42.
12. PRUDENT,] as in 12. 16, 23; 13. 16, &c.
HIDDEN,] as in 22. 3; Nu. 5. 13; 1 Sa. 20. 5.
SIMPLE,] as in 1. 4, 22, 32; 7. 7; 8. 5, &c.
PUNISHED,] as in 22. 3; Ex. 21. 22.
13. GARMENT,] as in 6. 27; 20. 16; 25. 20, &c.
STRANGER,] as in v. 2; 2. 16; 5. 3, 10, &c.
SURETY,] as in 3. 24; 6. 1; 11. 15; 20. 16, &c.
STRANGE WOMAN,] as in v. 2; 2. 16; 5. 10.
PLEDGE,] as in 20. 16.
14. SALUTING,] as in Ge. 12. 3; 27. 29; Nu.
24. 9; Isa. 66. 3.
FRIEND,] as in v. 9, 10, 17; 3. 28, 29, &c.
LOUD VOICE,] as in 18. 16; 19. 19; 25. 6, &c.
RISING EARLY,] as in 7. 18; Ge. 1. 5, 8, &c.
LIGHT THING,] as in 26. 2; Ge. 27. 12, &c.
RECKONED,] as in 17. 28; Lev. 7. 18, &c.
15. CONTINUAL,] as in 19. 13.
CONTENTIONS,] as in 6. 14; 15. 18; 16. 28, &c.
16. OINTMENT,] as in v. 9; 5. 3; 21. 17, 20.
CALLETH OUT,] as in 1. 21, 28; 2. 3; 7. 4, &c.
17. IRON,] as in Ge. 4. 22; Lev. 26. 19, &c.
18. FIG-TREE,] as in Ge. 3. 7; Nu. 13. 23, &c.
PRESERVER,] as in 10. 17; 13. 13, 18, &c.
HONOURED,] as in 13. 18.
20. SHEOL,] as in 1. 12; 5. 5; 7. 27; 9. 18, &c.
SATISFIED,] as in 1. 31; 5. 10; 12. 11, &c.
21. REFINING POT,] as in 17. 3.
FURNACE,] as in 17. 3; De. 4. 20: 1 K. 8. 51.
22. FOOLISH,] as in v. 3; 1. 7; 7. 22; 10. 8, &c.
MORTAR,] as in Jud. 15. 19.
WASHED THINGS,] as in 2 Sa. 17. 19.
TURNETH ASIDE,] as in 5. 7; 9. 4; 22. 6, &c.
23. KNOW,] as in v. 1; 5. 6; 10. 32; 24. 12, &c.
FLOCK,] as in Ge. 4. 2, 4; 12. 16; 13. 5, &c.

SET THY HEART,] as in Ps. 48. 13; Jer. 31. 21
DROVES,] as in Ge. 29. 2, 3, 8; 30. 40, &c.
24. RICHES,] as in 15. 6; Isa. 33. 6; Jer. 20
5; Eze. 22. 25.
CROWN,] as in Ex. 29. 6; 39. 30; Lev. 8. 9, &c.
GENERATION,] as in 30. 11, 12, 13, 14, &c.
25. REVEALED,] as in 1 Sa. 9. 15; 20. 12, &c
HAY,] as in 1 K. 18. 5; 2 K. 19. 26, &c.
TENDER GRASS,] as in Ge. 1. 11, 12, &c.
GATHERED,] as in Ge. 29. 3; 34. 30, &c.
HERBS,] as in 19. 12; Ge. 1. 11, 12, 29, &c.
26. LAMBS,] as in Ex. 12. 5; 29. 38, 39, &c.
CLOTHING,] as in 31. 22, 35; Ge. 49. 11, &c.
PRICE,] as in 17. 16; De. 23. 18; 2 Sa. 24. 24.
FIELD,] as in 23. 10; 24. 27, 30; 31. 16, &c.
HE-GOATS,] as in Ge. 31. 10, 12; Nu. 7. 17.
27. SUFFICIENCY,] as in 25. 16; Ex. 36. 5, &c.
DAMSELS,] as in 9. 3; 31. 15; Ge. 24. 14, &c.

XXVIII. 1. FLED,] as in Ge. 14. 10, &c.
PURSUER,] as in 21. 21; Ge. 14. 14, 15, &c.
2. TRANSGRESSION,] as in v. 13, 24; 10. 12.
HEADS,] as in 8. 16; 19. 10; Ge. 12. 15, &c.
INTELLIGENT MAN,] as in v. 7, 11, &c.
RIGHT,] as in Ge. 42. 11; Ex. 10. 29, &c.
PROLONGED,] as in v. 16; Ex. 20. 12, &c.
3. POOR,] as in 6. 27; 10. 4; 13. 8, 23, &c.
OPPRESSING,] as in 14. 31; 22. 16; Ps. 72. 4.
WEAK,] as in 8, 11, 15; 10. 15; 14. 31, &c.
RAIN,] as in 26. 1; Ex. 9. 33, 34; De. 11. 11.
4. FORSAKING,] as in v. 13; 2. 13, 17, &c.
PRAISE,] as in 27. 2; 31. 28, 31; Ge. 12. 15.
PLEAD,] as in 7. 5, 9, 10; 2 K. 14. 10;
2 Ch. 25. 19; Da. 11. 10, 25.
5. EVIL MEN,] as in Ps. 14. 4, 9.
UNDERSTAND,] as in 2. 5, 9; 7. 7; 14. 15, &c.
SEEKING JEHOVAH,] as in Ps. 105. 32, &c.
6. INTEGRITY,] as in 2. 7; 10. 9, 29; 13. 6, &c.
PERVERSE,] as in 2. 15; 8. 8; 11. 20; 17. 20;
19. 1; 22. 5.
RICH,] as in v. 11; 10. 15; 14. 20; 18. 11, &c.
7. FRIEND,] as in 13. 20; 29. 3; Ge. 4. 2, &c.
GLUTTONS,] as in 23. 20, 21; De. 21. 20.
TO BLUSH,] as in 1 Sa. 20. 34; 25. 7; Ruth
2. 15; Job 17. 3; Ps. 44. 9.
8. MULTIPLYING,] as in Ex. 16. 17, 18, &c.
WEALTH,] as in v. 22; 1. 13; 3. 9; 6. 31, &c.
BITING,] as in Ex. 22. 25; Lev. 25. 36, 37;
De. 23. 19; Ps. 15. 5; Eze. 18. 8, 13, 17; 22. 12.
USURY,] as in Lev. 25. 36; Eze. 18. 8, 13,
17; 22. 12.
FAVOURING,] as in 14. 31; 19. 17; Ps. 37.
21, 26; 109. 12; 112. 5.
GATHER,] as in De. 30. 3; Neh. 1. 9; 13. 11.
9. TURNING,] as in Job 12. 20, 24; Isa. 3. 1.
LAW,] as in v. 4, 7; 1. 8; 3. 1; 4. 2; 6. 20, &c.
PRAYER,] as in 15. 8, 29; 2 Sa. 7. 27, &c.
ABOMINATION,] as in 3. 32; 6. 16; 8. 7, &c.
10. CAUSING TO ERR,] as in De. 27. 18; Job
12. 16.
PERFECT,] as in v. 18; 1. 12; 2. 21; 11. 5, &c.
INHERIT,] as in 3. 35; 11. 29; 14. 18, &c.
11. RICH,] as in v. 6; 10. 15; 14. 20, &c.
SEARCHETH,] as in 18. 17; De. 13. 14, &c.
12. GLORY,] as in 4. 9; 16. 31; 17. 6, &c.
ABUNDANT,] as in v. 2, 16, 20, 27; 7. 26, &c.
RISING,] as in v. 28; Ge. 19. 33, 35, &c.
13. COVERING,] as in 10. 18; 11. 13, &c.
TRANSGRESSIONS,] as in v. 2, 24; 10. 12, &c
PROSPERETH,] as in De. 28. 29; Jos. 1. 8.
FORSAKING,] as in v. 4; 2. 13, 17; 10. 17.

MERCY,] as in Hos. 14. 3.

14. HAPPINESS,] as in 3. 13; 8. 32, 34, &c.
CONTINUALLY,] as in 5. 19; 6. 21; 15. 15, &c.
HARDENING,] as in 29. 1.
15. LION,] as in 22. 13; 26. 13; Ge. 49. 9, &c.
RANGING,] as in Ps. 107. 9.
BEAR,] as in 17. 12; 1 Sa. 17. 34, 36, 37, &c.
RULER,] as in 6. 7; 16. 32; 23. 1; 29. 12, &c.
16. LEADER,] as in 1 Sa. 9. 16; 10. 1, &c.
LACKING UNDERSTANDING,] as in 6. 32; 7.
7; 9. 4, 16; 10. 13, &c.
MULTIPLIETH,] as in v. 2, 12, 20, 27, &c.
OPPRESSIONS,] as in Isa. 33. 15.
DISHONEST GAIN,] as in 1. 19; 15. 27, &c.
PROLONGETH,] as in v. 2; Ex. 20. 12, &c.
17. OPPRESSED,] as in De. 28. 29, 33; Ps.
103. 6; 146. 7; Ecc. 4. 1; Jer. 50. 33; Hos. 5. 11.
PIT,] as in 1. 12; 5. 15; Ge. 37. 20, 22, &c.
FLEETH,] as in v. 25; 1. 18, 19; 2. 10, &c.
TAKETH HOLD,] as in 4. 4; 5. 5; 11. 16; 29.
23; Ge. 48. 17; Job 36. 17; Isa. 42. 1.
18. WALKING,] as in v. 6, 26; 2. 7; 4. 18, &c.
UPRIGHTLY,] as in v. 10; 1. 12; 2. 21, &c.
SAVED,] as in Nu. 10. 9; 2 Sa. 22. 4, &c.
AT ONCE,] as in Ps. 89. 35.
19. TILLING,] as in 12. 11; Ge. 4. 2; 49. 15.
SATISFIED,] as in 1. 31; 5. 10; 12. 11, 14, &c.
BREAD,] as in 3. 21; 4. 17; 6. 8, 26; 9. 5, &c.
PURSUING,] as in 11. 19; 12. 11; 15. 9; 19. 7.
VANITY,] as in 12. 11; Ge. 37. 24; 41. 27, &c.
POVERTY,] as in 31. 7.
20. STEDFAST,] as in Ex. 17. 12; De. 32. 4.
MULTIPLIED,] as in v. 2, 12, 16, 27; 7. 26.
BLESSINGS,] as in 10. 6, 7, 22; 11. 11, &c.
HASTING,] as in 19. 2; 21. 5; 29. 20; Ex. 5. 13.
RICH,] as in 23. 4.
ACQUITTED,] as in 6. 29; 11. 21; 16. 5; 17.
5; 19. 5, 9; Ge. 24. 41; Jer. 25. 29; 49. 12.
21. DISCERN FACES,] as in 24. 23.
PIECE OF BREAD,] as in 6. 26; Ge. 18. 5; 1
Sa. 2. 36; Eze. 13. 19.
TRANSGRESS,] as in 1 K. 8. 50; 2 K. 3. 7, &c.
22. TROUBLED,] as in Ps. 30. 7.
WEALTH,] as in v. 8; 1. 13; 3. 9; 6. 31, &c.
EVIL EYE,] as in 23. 6.
WANT,] as in Job 30. 3.
MEET,] as in 2. 10; 3. 25; 4. 14; 6. 15, &c.
23. REPROVING,] as in 9. 7; 24. 25; 25. 12.
GRACE,] as in 1. 9; 3. 4, 22, 34; 4. 9; 5. 19.
FLATTERER,] as in 29. 5.
24. ROBBING,] as in Ps. 35. 10; Mic. 3. 2.
TRANSGRESSION,] as in v. 2, 13; 10. 12, &c.
COMPANION,] as in Jud. 20. 11; Ps. 45. 7, &c.
DESTROYER,] as in 6. 32; 18. 9; Ge. 6. 13.
25. PROUD,] as in 21. 4; Ps. 101. 5.
STIRRETH UP,] as in 15. 18; 29. 22.
CONTENTION,] as in 6. 14; 15. 18; 16. 28, &c.
TRUSTING,] as in v. 26; 11. 15, 28; 14. 16.
MADE FAT,] as in 11. 25; 13. 4; Isa. 34. 7.
26. FOOL,] as in 1. 22, 32; 3. 35; 8. 5, &c.
WALKING,] as in v. 6, 18; 2. 7; 4. 18, &c.
DELIVERED,] as in 19. 5; Ge. 19. 20, &c.
27. LACK,] as in 6. 11; 11. 24; 14. 23; 21. 5,
17; 22. 16; 24. 34.
MULTIPLIED,] as in v. 2, 12, 16, 20; 7. 26.
CURSES,] as in 3. 33; De. 28. 20; Mal 2.
2; 3. 9.
28. RISING,] as in v. 12; Ge. 10. 33, 35, &c.
HIDDEN,] as in Ge. 4. 14; 31. 49; 1 Sa. 20. 24.
DESTRUCTION,] as in 11. 10; De. 4. 26, &c.
MULTIPLY,] as in 4. 10; 9. 11; 29. 16, &c.

XXIX. 1. OFTEN REPROVED,] lit. 'of re-
proofs,' as in v. 15; 1. 23, 25, 30, &c.
HARDENING THE NECK,] as in Ex. 32. 9;
33. 3, 5; 34. 9; De. 9. 6, &c.
BROKEN,] as in 6. 15; Lev. 6. 28; 15. 12, &c.
HEALING,] as in 4. 22; 6. 15; 12. 18; 13. 17;
16. 24; Jer. 8. 15; 14. 19; 33. 6; Mal. 4. 2.
2. MULTIPLYING,] as in v. 16; Ex 11. 9;
Ecc. 5. 11.
REJOICE,] as in 13. 9; 17. 21; 23. 15, &c.
RULING,] as in 19. 10; Ge. 1. 18; 37. 8, &c.
SIGH,] as in Ex. 2. 23; Isa. 24. 7, &c.
3. REJOICETH,] as in 10. 1; 12. 25; 15. 20.
FRIEND,] as in 13. 20; 28. 7.
HARLOTS,] as in 6. 26; 7. 10; 23. 27, &c.
DESTROYETH,] as in 1. 32; Nu. 33. 52, &c.
WEALTH,] as in 1. 13; 3. 9; 6. 31; 8. 18, &c.
4. ESTABLISHETH,] as in Ge. 47. 7, &c.
GIFTS,] as in Ex. 25. 2, 3; 20. 27, 28, &c.
THROWETH IT DOWN,] as in 14. 1; Ex. 15. 7.
5. PORTION,] as in 28. 23.
NEIGHBOUR,] as in 3. 28, 29; 6. 1, 3, 29, &c.
SPREADETH,] as in Ex. 25. 20; 37. 9, &c.
NET,] as in 1. 17; Ex. 27. 4, 5; 38. 4, &c.
STEPS,] as in 2 K. 19. 24; Ps. 17. 5, &c.
6. TRANSGRESSION,] as in v. 16, 22, &c.
SNARE,] as in v. 25; 12. 13; 13. 14, &c.
SING,] as in 1. 20; 8. 3; Ps. 35. 27, &c.
REJOICE,] as in 2. 14; 15. 13; 17. 5, 22, &c.
7. PLEA,] as in 20. 8; 22. 10; 31. 5, 8, &c.
UNDERSTANDETH NOT,] as in v. 19; 2. 5, 9.
8. MEN OF SCORNING,] as in 1. 22; Isa.
28. 14.
ENSNARE,] as in 6. 19; 12. 17; 14. 5, 25, &c.
CITY,] as in 10. 15; 11. 10; 18. 11, 19, &c.
ANGER,] as in v. 22; 11. 22; 14. 17, 29, &c.
9. JUDGED,] as in 1 Sa. 12. 7; Ps. 19. 9, &c.
FOOLISH,] as in 1. 7; 7. 22; 10. 8, 14, 21, &c.
ANGRY,] as in 30. 1.
LAUGHED,] as in 1. 26; 31. 25; Job 30. 1;
Lam. 1. 7.
REST,] as in Job 17. 16; 36. 16; Ecc. 4. 6;
6. 5; 9. 17; Isa. 30. 15, 30.
10. MEN OF BLOOD,] as in 1. 11, 16, 18, &c.
PERFECT,] as in Ge. 25. 27; Job 1. 1, 8, &c.
UPRIGHT,] as in v. 27; 2. 7, 21; 3. 32, &c.
11. MIND,] lit. 'heart,' as in v. 23; 1. 23, &c.
12. RULER,] as in v. 26; Ge. 24. 2; 45. 8, &c.
ATTENDING,] as in 1. 24; 17. 4; Song 8. 13.
LYING,] as in 6. 17, 19; 10. 18; 11. 18, &c.
MINISTERS,] as in Ex. 24. 13; 33. 11, &c.
WICKED,] as in v. 2, 7, 16, 27; 2. 22, &c.
13. POOR,] as in 10. 4; 13. 8, 23; 14. 20, &c.
MET TOGETHER,] as in 22. 2; Ps. 85. 10.
ENLIGHTENING,] as in Ps. 19. 8.
14. JUDGING,] as in 8. 16; Ge. 18. 25, &c.
THRONE,] as in 16. 12; 20. 8, 28; 25. 5, &c.
ESTABLISHED,] as in 4. 16; 12. 13, 19, &c.
15. ROD,] as in 10. 13; 13. 24; 22. 8, 15, &c.
REPROOF,] as in v. 1; 1. 23, 25, 30; 3. 11, &c.
YOUTH,] as in 1. 4; 7. 7; 20. 11; 22. 6, 15.
LET AWAY,] as in Isa. 16. 2; 27. 10.
SHAMING,] as in 10. 5; 12. 4; 14. 35; 17. 2;
19. 26.
16. MULTIPLYING,] as in 4. 10; 9. 11, &c.
TRANSGRESSION,] as in v. 6, 22; 10. 12, 19
LACK,] as in 7. 7; 23. 31, 33; 24. 18, &c.
17. CHASTISE,] as in 10. 18; Jer. 10. 24.
COMFORT,] as in Isa. 30. 32; 63. 14, &c.
DELIGHTS,] as in Ge. 49. 20.
18. VISION,] as in 1 Sa. 3. 1; 1 Ch. 17. 15, &c.

33. MILK,] as in 27. 27; Ge. 18. 8; 49. 12, &c.
BUTTER,] as in Ge. 18. 8; De. 32. 14, &c.
NOSE,] as in 11. 22; 14. 17, 29; 15. 1, 18, &c.
BLOOD,] as in 1. 11, 16, 18; 6. 17; 12. 6, &c.
STRIFE,] as in 11. 22; 14. 17, 29; 15. 1, 18.

XXXI. 1. LEMUEL,] i.e. 'for whom is a mighty one.'
KING,] as in v. 3, 4; 1. 1; 8. 15, &c.
DECLARATION,] as in 30. 1; Jer. 23. 36, &c.
TAUGHT HIM,] as in Isa. 28. 26.
2. MY SON,] *lit.* 'my pure *or* chosen one.'
WOMB,] as in Ge. 25. 23, 24; 30. 2; 38. 27.
VOWS,] as in Ge. 28. 20; 31. 13; Lev. 7. 16.
3. WOMEN,] as in 14. 1; Ge. 4. 19, 23, &c.
STRENGTH,] as in v. 10, 29; 12. 4; 13. 22, &c.
4. WINE,] as in v. 6; 4. 17; 9. 2, 5, &c.
PRINCES,] as in 8. 15; Jud. 5. 3; Ps. 2. 2, &c.
STRONG DRINK,] as in v. 6; 20. 1; Lev. 10. 9.
5. DRINK,] as in v. 7; 4. 17; Ge. 9. 21, &c.
FORGET,] as in v. 7; 3. 1; 4. 5: Ge. 40. 23.
CHANGE,] as in 1 Sa. 21. 13; Est. 2. 9, &c.
6. PERISHING,] as in De. 26. 5; Job 4. 11.
BITTER IN SOUL,] as in Jud. 18. 25, &c.
7. POVERTY,] as in 28. 19.
MISERY,] as in Ge. 41. 51; Jud. 10. 16, &c.
8. OPEN THY MOUTH,] as in v. 9.
DUMB,] as in Ex. 4. 11; Ps. 38. 13; Isa. 35. 6; 56. 10; Hab 2. 18.
RIGHT,] as in De. 17. 8; Est. 1. 13. &c.
9. RIGHTEOUSLY,] as in Lev 19. 15; De. 1. 16; Ps. 9. 4, &c.
CAUSE,] as in Jer. 21. 12.
POOR,] as in v. 20; 3. 34; 14. 21, &c.
NEEDY,] as in v. 20; 14. 31; 30. 14, &c.
10. WORTH,] as in v. 3, 29; 12. 4; 13. 22, &c.
FIND,] as in 1. 13, 28; 2. 5; 6. 33, &c.
RUBIES,] as in 3. 15; 8. 11; 20. 15; Job 28. 18; Lam. 4. 7.
PRICE,] as in Nu. 20. 19; Neh. 13. 16.
11. HUSBAND,] as in v 23, 28; 12. 4; 16. 22; Joel 1. 8.
TRUSTED,] as in Jud. 20. 36; 2 K. 18. 5, &c.
SPOIL,] as in 1. 13; 16. 19; Ge. 49. 27, &c.
LACKETH,] as in Ge. 8. 3; 18. 28; De. 8. 9.
13. SOUGHT,] as in Lev. 10. 16; De. 13. 14.
WOOL,] as in Lev. 13. 47, 48, 52, 59, &c.
FLAX,] as in Lev. 13. 47, 48, 52, 59, &c.
DELIGHT,] as in 3. 15; 8. 11; 1 Sa. 15. 22, &c.
14. SHIPS,] as in 30. 19; Ge. 49. 13.
MERCHANT,] as in Ge. 23. 16; 37. 28, &c.
15. NIGHT,] as in v. 18; 7. 9; Ge. 1. 5, &c.
FOOD,] as in Ge. 49. 9; Nu. 23. 24; Job 4. 11.

PORTION,] as in 30. 8; Ge. 47. 22; Job 23. 12.
DAMSELS,] as in 9. 3; 27. 27; Ge. 24. 14, &c.
16. CONSIDERED,] as in 30. 32; De. 19. 19.
FIELD,] as in 23. 10; 24. 27, 30; 27. 26, &c.
PLANTED,] as in Lev. 19. 23; Nu. 24. 6, &c.
VINEYARD,] as in 24. 30; Ge. 9. 20, &c.
17. GIRDED,] as in Ex. 29. 9; Isa. 15. 3, &c.
MIGHT,] as in v. 25; 10. 15; 14. 26; 18. 10.
LOINS,] as in 30. 31; Ge. 37. 34; Ex. 12. 11.
STRENGTHEN,] as in De. 15. 7; 2 Ch. 11. 17.
ARMS,] as in Ge. 49. 24; Ex. 6. 6; 15. 6.
18. MERCHANDIZE,] as in 3. 14; Isa. 23. 18.
LAMP,] as in 6. 23; 13. 19; 20. 20, 27, &c.
EXTINGUISHED,] as in 26. 20; Lev. 6. 12, 13
19. DISTAFF,] as 2 Sa. 3. 29.
20. SPREAD FORTH,] as in Nu. 4. 6, 8, &c.
POOR,] as in v. 9; 3. 34; 14. 21; 15. 15, &c.
NEEDY,] as in v. 9; 14. 31: 30. 14; Ex. 23. 6.
21. AFRAID,] as in 3. 25; Ge. 3. 10; 15. 1, &c.
SNOW,] as in 25. 13; 26. 1; Ex. 4. 6, &c.
CLOTHED,] as in 1 Sa. 17. 5; Eze. 9. 2, 3, &c.
SCARLET,] as in Ge. 38. 28, 30; Ex. 25. 4, &c.
22. ORNAMENTAL COVERINGS,] as in 7. 16.
SILK,] as in Ge. 41. 42; Ex. 25. 4, &c.
PURPLE,] as in Ex. 25. 4; 26. 1; 31. 36, &c.
CLOTHING,] as in v. 25; 27. 26; Ge. 49. 11.
23. KNOWN,] as in Ps. 76. 1; Ecc. 6. 10.
GATES,] as in 1. 21; 8. 3; 14. 9, &c.
ELDERS,] as in 17. 6; 20. 29; Ge. 18. 11, &c.
24. LINEN GARMENTS,] as in Jud. 14. 12, 13; Isa. 3. 23.
SELLETH,] as in 23. 23; Ge. 25. 33; 37. 27, 28.
GIRDLE,] as in 1 Sa. 18. 4; 2 Sa. 20. 8; Eze 23. 15.
MERCHANT,] as in Job 41. 6; Zec. 14. 21
25. STRENGTH,] as in v. 17; 10. 15; 14. 2., HONOUR,] as in 20. 29; De. 33. 17, &c.
REJOICETH,] as in 1. 26; 20. 5. 22; 29. 24.
LATTER DAY,] as in Ge. 33. 2; Ex. 4. 8, &c.
26. OPENED,] as in De. 20. 11; 2 K. 9. 3, &c.
27. WATCHING,] as in 15. 3; Nu. 23. 14, &c.
28. PRONOUNCE HER HAPPY,] as in 4. 14; Job 29. 11; Ps. 72. 17; Song 6. 9.
PRAISETH,] as in v. 31; 27. 2; 28. 4, &c.
29. WORTHILY,] as in v. 3, 10; 12. 4; 13. 22.
30. GRACE,] as in 1. 9; 3. 4, 22, 34; 4. 9, &c.
FALSE,] as in 6. 17, 19; 10. 18; 11. 18, &c.
BEAUTY,] as in 6. 25; Est. 1. 11; Ps 45. 11
VAIN,] as in 11. 21. 6; De. 32. 21, &c.
FEARING JEHOVAH,] as in 13. 13; 14. 2, 16
BOAST HERSELF,] as in 20. 14; 27. 1, &c.
31. PRAISE,] as in v. 28; 27. 2; 28. 4, &c.
GATES,] as in v. 23; 1. 21; 8. 3, &c.

ECCLESIASTES

THE BOOK OF ECCLESIASTES has been generally believed to be the work of king Solomon, though the book itself does not say so. It is professedly the "words of a preacher [in Hebrew *Koheleth*, i.e. one who calls an 'assembly' together] a son of David, king in Jerusalem." As Araunah is called a 'king' in 2 Sa. 24. 23, this *Koheleth* was doubtless a man of noble estate, and a 'son,' i.e. a descendant of David. The words in v. 1, 12, 'king in Jerusalem,' and 'king over Israel in Jerusalem,' seem to point to a period later than the breaking off of the ten tribes.

The whole style of the composition appears to indicate a much later date, and a greater deterioration of the Hebrew language, than any other portion of the Old Testament, yet as it has always formed a portion of the Jewish Scriptures, there is no valid reason to doubt its canonical authority. It has always formed a part also of the Septuagint Version, commenced B.C. 280.

I. 1. A PREACHER,] as in v. 2, 12; 7. 27; 12. 8, 9, 10.
SON OF DAVID,] as in 2 Ch. 35. 3; Prov. 1. 1.
KING IN JERUSALEM,] over the two tribes.
2. VANITY ! VANITIES!] not 'vanity of vanities,' which yields no real sense; as in 12. 8.
THE WHOLE,] as in Ge. 3. 17; 6. 17; 7. 4, &c.
3. ADVANTAGE,] as in 2. 11, 13; 3. 9; 5. 9, &c.
MAN,] as in v. 18; 2. 3, 8, 12, 18, 21, 22, &c.
LABOUR,] as in 2. 10, 11, 18—22, 24, &c.
LABOURETH AT,] as in 2. 11, 19—21; 5. 16, 18; 8. 17; Ps. 127. 1; Jon. 4. 10.
SUN,] as in v. 5, 9, 14; 2. 11, 17—20, 22, &c.
4. GENERATION,] as in Ge. 6. 9; 7. 1, &c.
IS GOING,] as in v. 6, 7; 2. 14; 3. 20, &c.
IS COMING,] as in v. 5; 5. 15, 16; 6. 4, &c.
IS STANDING,] as in Ge. 18. 8, 22; 24. 30, &c.
5. RISEN,] as in Ex. 22. 3; De. 33. 2, &c.
GONE IN,] not 'down,' as in C. V.: as in v. 4.
I ARISING,] as in Ps. 57. 3; Amos 2. 7; 8. 4.
6. SOUTH,] as in 11. 3; De. 33. 23; Job 37. 17.
TURNING ROUND,] as in Jos. 6. 3, 15; 1 Sa. 7. 16; 22. 22, &c.
NORTH,] as in 11. 3; Ge. 13. 14; 28. 14, &c.
WIND,] as in v. 14, 17; 2. 11, 17, 26, &c.
CIRCUITS,] as in Ge. 23. 17; 35. 5; 41. 48, &c.
RETURNED,] as in 3. 20; 4. 1, 7; 9. 11, &c.
7. STREAMS,] as in Ge. 26. 17, 19; 32. 23, &c.
SEA,] as in Ge. 1. 10, 22, 26; 9. 2, &c.
FULL,] as in 11. 5; Ge. 23. 9; 41. 7, 22, &c.
8. WEARYING,] as in De. 25. 18; 2 Sa. 17. 2.
TO SPEAK,] as in 3. 7; Ge. 17. 22; 18. 27, &c.
SATISFIED,] as in 4. 8; 5. 10; 6. 3; Ex. 16. 18.
SEEING,] as in 2. 12; 3. 18, 22; 5. 18, &c.
HEARING,] as in 5. 1; 7. 5; Ge. 24. 30, &c.

9. **HATH BEEN,**] in days past; as in Ge. 1. 2; 3. 1; 4. 14; 11. 3, &c.
WHICH IS] even now existing in the world; as in Ex. 9. 8.

DONE,] by the children of men; as in v. 13; 1. 14; 2. 17, &c.
IS DONE,] even now at the present time; as in Ge. 20. 9; 29. 6, &c.
ENTIRELY,] as in Ge. 3. 17; 6. 17; 7. 4, &c.
NEW THING,] as in v. 10; Ex. 1. 8, &c.
SUN,] as in v. 3, 5; 2. 11; 3. 16, &c.
10. ALREADY,] as in 2. 12, 16; 3. 15; 4. 2; 6. 10; 9. 6, 7.
AGES,] as in v. 4; Ezra 4. 15, 19; Da. 4. 3.
11. REMEMBRANCE,] as in 2. 16; Ex. 12. 14.
FORMER,] as in 7. 10; Ge. 8. 13; 13. 4, &c.
THE LAST,] as in 4. 16; Ge. 33. 2; Ex. 4. 8.
12. A PREACHER,] as in v. 1, 2; 7. 27; 12. 8, 9, 10.
KING,] as in v. 1; 2. 8, 12; 4. 13; 5. 9, &c.
13. GIVEN,] as in 2. 26; 3. 10, 11; 5. 18, &c.
HEART,] as in v. 16, 17; 2. 1, 3, 10, 15, &c.
SEEK,] as in Ge. 25. 22; Ex. 18. 15, &c.
SEARCH OUT,] as in 7. 25; Nu. 10. 33, &c.
UNDER THE HEAVENS,] as in 2. 3; 3. 1, &c.
SAD,] as in 2. 17, 21; 4. 3, 8, 5. 1, 13, &c.
TRAVAIL,] as in 2. 23, 26; 3. 10; 4. 8; 5. 3, 14; 8. 16.
SONS OF MAN,] as in v. 3; 2. 3, 8, 12, &c.
HUMBLED,] as in 3. 10.
14. SEEN,] as in v. 16; 2. 13, 24; 3. 10, &c.
WORKS,] as in 2. 4, 11, 17; 3. 11, 17, &c.
VEXATION OF SPIRIT,] as in 2. 11, 17, 26; 4. 4, 6; 6. 9.
16. MAGNIFIED,] as in Ps. 38. 16; 41. 9, &c.
ADDED,] as in 2. 9; 1 K. 10. 7; 2 K. 20. 6; 24. 7; Ps. 71. 14.
ABUNDANTLY,] as in 2. 7; 5. 7, 12, 17, &c.
KNOWLEDGE,] as in v. 18; 2. 21, 26, &c.
17. TO KNOW,] as in 2. 14; 3. 12, 14; 4. 13, &c.
MADNESS,] as in 2. 12; 7. 25; 9. 3.
VEXATION OF SPIRIT,] as in 4. 16.
18. SADNESS,] as in 2. 23; 7. 3, 9; 11. 10, &c.
PAIN,] as in 2. 23; Ex. 3. 7; 2 Ch. 6. 29, &c.

II. 1. PRAY,] as in Ge. 12. 11, 13; 18. 4, &c.
TRY,] as in Ex. 17. 2; Nu. 14. 22; De. 6. 16.
MIRTH,] as in v. 2, 10, 26; 5. 20; 7. 4, &c.
GLADNESS,] as in v. 3, 24; 26; 3. 12, &c.
VANITY,] as in v. 11, 15, 17, 19, 21, 23, &c.
2. LAUGHTER,] as in 7. 3, 6; 10. 19, &c.
FOOLISH,] as in Ps. 102. 8.
3. SOUGHT,] as in Nu. 13. 32; 14. 34; Eze. 20. 6.
WINE,] as in 9. 7; 10. 19; Ge. 9. 21, 24, &c.
APPETITE,] as in 4. 5; 5. 6; 11. 10, &c.
LEADING,] as in 2 Sa. 6. 3; 1 Ch. 13. 7; Ps. 80. 1; Isa. 11. 6.
TAKE HOLD,] as in 1 K. 6. 6; 1 Ch. 13. 9; Job 38. 13; Ps. 56. 1.
FOLLY,] as in v. 12, 13; 7. 25; 10. 1, 13.
SONS OF MAN,] as in v. 8, 12, 18, 21, 22, &c.
NUMBER,] as in 5. 18; 6. 12; Ge. 34. 30, &c.
4. MADE GREAT,] as in Ps. 38. 16; 55. 12, &c.

WORKS,] as in v. 11, 17; 3. 11, 17, 22, &c.
BUILDED,] as in 9. 14; Ge. 11. 5; Nu. 32. 37.
PLANTED,] as in v. 5; Lev. 19. 23; Nu. 24. 6.
VINEYARDS,] as in Ge. 9. 20; Ex. 22. 5, &c.

WROUGHT,] as in v. 11; 2. 5, 6, 8, 11, 12, &c.
FEAR,] as in 8. 12; 12. 5; Ge. 3. 10; 15. 1, &c.
15. HATH BEEN,] as in Ge. 1. 2; 3. 1; 4. 14.
ALREADY,] as in 1. 10; 2. 12; 4. 2; 6. 10;
9. 6, 7.
REQUIRETH,] as in Ge. 31. 39; 37. 15, &c.
16. UNDER THE SUN,] as in 1. 3, 5, 9, 14, &c.
PLACE OF JUDGMENT,] the courts of law.
WICKED,] as in 7. 25; 8. 8; De. 9. 27, &c.
PLACE OF RIGHTEOUSNESS,] occupied by
judge or witness.
17. IN MY HEART,] as in v. 18; 2. 1, 3, &c.
JUDGE,] as in Ge. 16. 5; 19. 9; 31. 53, &c.
MATTER,] as in v. 1; 5. 4, 8; 8. 6, &c.
WORK,] as in v. 11, 22; 1. 14; 2. 4, &c.
18. BEASTS,] as in v. 19. 21; Ge. 1. 24, &c.
19. EVENT,] as in 2. 14, 15; 9. 2, 3; Ru. 2.
3; 1 Sa. 6. 9; 20. 26.
DEATH,] as in 7. 1, 26; 8. 8; 10. 1; Ge. 21. 16.
SPIRIT,] as in v. 21; 1. 6, 14, 17; 2. 11, &c.
ADVANTAGE,] as in Prov. 14. 23; 21. 5.
VANITY,] as in 1. 2, 14; 21. 11, 15, 19, &c.
20. ONE PLACE,] as in 6. 6; Ge. 1. 9.
DUST,] as in 12. 7; Ge. 2. 7; 3. 14, 19, &c.
TURNING BACK,] as in 1. 6; 4. 1, 7; 9. 11,&c.
21. KNOWETH,] as in 2. 19; 5. 1; 6. 8, 12, &c.
SONS OF MAN,,] as in 1. 13; 2. 3, 8; 3. 10, &c.
GOING DOWN,] as in Ge. 28. 12; De. 9. 21, &c.
22. REJOICE,] as in 4. 16; 11. 8; Jud. 9. 19.
WORKS,] as in v. 4, 17; 1. 14; 2. 4, 11, &c.
PORTION,] as in 2. 10, 21; 5. 18, 19; 9. 6, &c.

IV. 1. TURNED,] as in v. 7; 1. 6; 3. 20, &c.
OPPRESSIONS,] as in 5. 8; 7. 7; Ps. 62. 10.
TEAR,] as in 2 K. 20. 5; Ps. 6. 6; 39. 12, &c.
OPPRESSED,] as in De. 28. 29, 33; Ps. 103.
6; 146. 7; Jer. 50. 33; Hos. 5. 11.
COMFORTER,] as in 2 Sa. 10. 3; 1 Ch. 19. 3.
POWER,] as in 9. 10; Ge. 4. 12; 31. 6; 49. 3.
2. DEAD,] as in 9. 3, 4, 5; Ge. 20. 2; 23. 3.
ALREADY,] as in 1. 10; 2. 12, 16; 3. 15; 6
10; 9. 6, 7.
LIVING,] as in v. 15; 2. 3, 17; 3. 12; 5. 18.
ALIVE,] as in v. 15; 2. 3, 17; 3. 12; 5. 18, &c.
3. YET,] as in v. 2.
EVIL WORK,] as in v. 4; 1. 14; 2. 4, 11, 17.
4. LABOUR,] as in v. 6, 8, 9; 1. 3; 2. 10, &c.
BENEFIT,] as in 2. 21; 5. 11.
ENVY,] as in 9. 6; Nu. 5. 14; 25. 11, &c.
NEIGHBOUR,] as in Ge. 11. 3, 7; 15. 10, &c
5. CLASPING,] as in 2 K. 4. 16.
EATING,] as in 5. 11; Ge. 39. 6; 40. 17, &c.
6. HANDFUL,] as in 1 K. 17. 12.
QUIETNESS,] as in 6. 5; 9. 17; Isa. 30. 15, 30.
LABOUR,] as in v. 4, 8, 9; 1. 3; 2. 10. &c.
SPIRIT,] as in v. 4, 8, 16; 1. 6, 14, 17; 3. 9, 21.
7. TURNED,] as in v. 1; 1. 6; 3. 20, &c.
VAIN THING,] as in v. 4, 8, 16; 1. 2, 14, &c.
8. ONE,] as in v. 9—12; 2. 14; 3. 19, 20, &c.
SECOND,] as in v. 3, 9, 11, 12; 11. 6.
END,] as in v. 16; 12. 12; Ge. 4. 3, &c.
SATISFIED,] as in v. 1, 8; 5. 10; 6. 3, &c.
RICHES,] as in 5. 13, 14, 19; 6. 2; 9. 11, &c.
LABOURING,] as in 2. 18, 22; 3. 9; 9. 9, &c.
SAD TRAVAIL,] as in 1. 13.
9. REWARD,] as in 9. 5; Ge. 15. 1; 30. 18, &c.
10. RAISETH UP,] as in Nu. 7. 1; 9. 15, &c.
COMPANION,] as in Jud. 20. 11; Ps. 45. 7, &c.
WO,] as in Nu. 21. 29; 24. 23; 1 Sa. 4. 7, 8.
11. LIE DOWN,] as in Ge. 19. 4, 32, 33, 35, &c.
HEAT,] as in Ex. 16. 21; 1 K. 1. 2, &c.

12. STRENGTHEN HIMSELF,] as in Job 14.
20; 15. 24.
THREEFOLD,] as in Ge. 15. 9; Eze. 42. 8
CORD,] as in Ge. 14. 23; Jos. 2. 18, &c.
HASTILY,] as in 8. 11; Nu. 16. 46; De. 11 17
13. POOR,] as in 9. 15, 16.
YOUTH,] as in v. 15; Ge. 4. 23; 21. 8, &c.
FOOLISH,] as in v. 5.
WARNED,] as in 12. 12.
14. PRISONERS,] as in Ge. 39. 20; 40. 3, 5.
REIGN,] as in Ge. 36. 31; 37. 8; 1 Sa. 8 7.
KINGDOM,] as in Nu. 24. 7; 1 Sa. 20. 31, &c
POOR,] as in 5. 8; 1 Sa. 18. 23; 2 Sa. 12. 1.
15. LIVING,] as in v. 2; 3. 3, 17; 3. 12, &c.
WALKING,] as in Ps. 104. 3; Prov. 6. 11.
PLACE,] as in Ge. 4. 25; 22. 13; Lev. 14. 42
LATTER,] as in 1. 11; Ge. 33. 2; Ex. 4. 8, &c.
REJOICE,] as in 3. 22; 11. 8; Ex. 4. 14, &c.
SPIRIT,] as in v. 4; Ge. 1. 2; 3. 8, &c.

V. 1. FOOL,] as in Ge. 8. 9; 18. 4; 19. 2, &c.
HOUSE OF GOD,] as in 2. 4, 7; 4. 14; 7. 2. 4.
DRAW NEAR,] as in Ge. 19. 20; 45. 10, &c.
TO HEAR,] as in 1. 8; 7. 5; Ge. 24. 30, &c.
FOOLS,] as in v. 3, 4; 2. 14—16; 4. 5, 13, &c.
SACRIFICE,] as in Ge. 31. 54; 46. 1, &c.
EVIL,] as in v. 13, 14, 16; 1. 13; 2. 17, 21.
2. TO HASTEN,] as in Ge. 18. 6, 7; 24. 18, &c
WORD,] as in v. 3, 7; 1. 1, 8, 10; 6. 11, &c.
HEAVENS,] as in 1. 13; 2. 3; 3. 1; 10. 20, &c.
EARTH,] as in v. 9; 1. 4; 3. 22; 7. 20, &c.
FEW,] as in v. 12; 9. 14; 10. 1; Ge. 18. 4, &c.
3. DREAM,] as in v. 7; Ge. 20. 3, 6; 31. 10.
ABUNDANCE,] as in v. 7; 1. 18; 11. 1, &c.
BUSINESS,] as in v. 14; 1. 13; 2. 13, 16, &c.
4. VOWEST,] as in v. 5; Ge. 31. 13, &c.
VOW,] as in Ge. 28. 20; 31. 13; Lev. 7. 16.
DELAY,] as Ge. 24. 56; Ex. 22. 29.
COMPLETE,] as in Ex. 21. 36; 22. 5, 6, &c.
PLEASURE,] as in v. 8; 3. 1, 17; 8. 6; 12. 1.
5. SUFFER,] as in 1. 17; 2. 21; 6. 2; 7. 2, 21.
CAUSE TO SIN,] as in 1. 16, 19; Jer. 32. 35.
MESSENGER,] of God, that is, the priest or
Levite.
ERROR,] as in 10. 5; Lev. 4. 2, 22, 27, &c.
WROTH,] as in Ge. 40. 2; Ex. 16. 20, &c.
VOICE,] as in v. 3; 7. 6; 10. 20; 12. 4, &c.
7. DREAMS,] as in v. 3; Ge. 20. 3, 6; 31. 10.
VANITIES,] as in v. 10; 1. 2, 14; 2. 1, 11, &c.
ABOUND,] as in v. 12, 17, 20; 1. 16; 2. 7, &c.
FEAR,] as in 12. 13; Jos. 24. 14; 1 Sa. 12. 24.
8. OPPRESSION,] as in 7. 7; Lev. 6. 4, &c
VIOLENT TAKING AWAY,] as in Eze. 18. 18.
PROVINCE,] as in 8; 1 K. 20. 14, 15, &c.
MARVEL,] as in Ge. 43. 33; Job 26. 11, &c.
HIGH,] as in Ge. 7. 19; De. 3. 5, &c.
OBSERVING,] as in 8. 5; 11. 4; 12. 3, &c.
9. ABUNDANCE,] as in v. 16; 1. 3; 2. 11, 13.
LAND,] as in v. 2; 1. 4; 3. 21; 7. 20, &c.
FIELD,] as in Ge. 2. 5, 19, 20; 3. 1, 14, &c.
10. LOVING,] as in Ge. 25. 28; Ex. 20. 6, &c.
SATISFIED,] as in 1. 8; 4. 8; 6. 3; Ex. 16. 12.
STORES,] as in Ge. 17. 4, 5; Jud. 4. 7, &c.
INCREASE,] as in Ge. 47. 24; Ex. 23. 10;
Lev. 19. 25.
11. CONSUMERS,] as in 4. 5; Ge. 39, 6, &c.
POSSESSOR,] as in v. 13; Ge. 14. 13; 37. 19.
12. SWEET,] as in 11. 7; Jud. 14. 14, 18. &c.
SLEEP,] as in 8. 16; Ge. 28. 16; 31. 40. &c.

LABOURER,] as in Ge. 4. 2; 49. 15, &c.
MUCH,] as in v. 7, 17, 20; 1. 16; 2. 7, &c.
SUFFICIENCY,] as in Ge. 41. 29, 30, 31, 34, 47, 53; Prov. 3. 10.
WEALTHY,] as in 10. 6, 20; Ex. 30. 15, &c.
13. PAINFUL,] as in v. 16; Ge. 48. 1, &c.
EVIL,] as in v. 1, 14, 16; 1. 13.
14. LOST,] as in 9. 6; Ex. 10. 7; Lev. 26. 38.
BUSINESS,] as in v. 3; 1. 13; 2. 23, 26; 3. 10; 4. 8; 8. 16.
BEGOTTEN,] as in Ge. 11. 27; 25. 19; 48. 6.
HAND,] as in v. 6, 15; 2. 11, 24; 4. 1, 5, &c.
15. BELLY,] as in 11. 5; 25. 23, 24; 30. 2.
NAKED,] as in Ge. 2. 25; 1 Sa. 19. 24, &c.
TURNETH BACK,] as in 12. 7; Ge. 3. 19, &c.
AS HE CAME,] as in v. 16.
ADVANTAGE,] as in v. 9; 1. 3; 2. 11, 13, &c.
LABOURETH,] as in v. 18; 1. 3; 2. 11, 19, &c.
WIND,] as in 1. 6, 14, 17; 2. 11; 3. 11, 19, &c.
17. DARKNESS,] as in 2. 13, 14; 6. 4; 11. 8.
CONSUMETH,] as in 2. 24, 25; 3. 13; 6. 2, &c.
SADNESS,] as in Ps. 112. 10.
WRATH,] as in Nu. 1. 53; 16. 46; 18. 5, &c.
SICKNESS,] as in 6. 2; De. 7. 15; 28. 59, 61.
ABOUND,] as in v. 7, 12, 20; 1. 16; 2. 7, &c.
18. BEAUTIFUL,] as in 3. 11; Ge. 12. 11, &c.
EAT,] as in v. 19; 6. 2; 8. 15; Ge. 2. 16, &c.
DRINK,] as in 8. 15; Ge. 24. 19, 22; 30. 38.
SEE GOOD,] as in Ps. 27. 13; 106. 5.
LIFE,] as in v. 20; 2. 3, 17; 3. 12, &c.
PORTION,] us in v. 19; 2. 10, 21; 3. 22, &c.
19. WEALTH,] as in v. 13, 14; 3. 16; 8. 18.
RICHES,] as in 6. 2; Jos. 22. 8; 2 Ch. 1. 11, 12.
PORTION,] as in v. 18; 2. 10, 21; 3. 22, &c.
REJOICE,] as in 3. 12; 8. 15; Ps. 106. 5; Eze. 35. 14.
LABOUR,] as in v. 15. 18; 1. 3; 2. 10, &c.
GIFT,] as in 3. 13; 1 K. 13. 7; Prov. 25. 14; Eze. 46. 5, 11.
20. REMEMBER,] as in 11. 8; Ge. 8. 1; 19. 29.
JOY,] as in 2. 1, 2, 10, 26; 7. 4; 8. 15, &c.

VI. 1. EVIL,] as in v. 2; 1. 13; 2. 17, 21, &c.
GREAT,] as in v. 3; 2. 21; 7. 22, 29, &c.
2. WEALTH,] as in 4. 8; 5. 13, 14, 19; 9. 11.
RICHES,] as in 5. 19; Jos. 22. 8; 2 Ch. 1. 11, 12.
HONOUR,] as in 10. 1; Ge. 31. 1; 45. 13, &c.
LACK,] as in 10. 3; 1 Sa. 21. 15; 2 Sa. 3. 29.
DESIRETH,] as in De. 5. 21; 2 Sa. 23. 15, &c.
POWER,] as in 5. 19; Ps. 119. 133.
STRANGER,] as in Ge. 31. 15; Ex. 2. 22, &c.
DISEASE,] as in 5. 17; De. 7. 15; 28. 59, 61.
3. BEGAT,] as in 5. 14; Ge. 11. 27; 25. 19, &c.
GREAT,] as in v. 1; 2. 21; 7. 22, 29, &c.
SATISFIED,] as in 1. 8; 4. 8; 5. 10, &c.
GRAVE] as in Ge. 35. 20; 47. 30; De. 34. 6.
UNTIMELY BIRTH,] as in Job 3. 16; Ps. 58. 8.
4. VANITY,] as in v. 2, 9, 11, 12; 1. 2, 14, &c.
DARKNESS,] as in 2. 13, 14; 5. 17; 11. 8, &c.
NAME,] as in v. 10; 7. 1; Ge. 2. 11, &c.
COVERED,] as in Ge. 7. 19, 20; Ps. 80. 10.
Prov. 24. 31.
5. SURE,] as in v. 1; 1. 3, 5, 9, 14; 2. 11, &c.
REST,] as in 4. 6; 9. 17; Job 17. 16; 36. 16, &c.
6. TWICE,] as in 7. 22; Ge. 2. 23; 18. 32, &c.
GOOD,] true, real, lasting good.
PLACE,] as in 1. 5, 7; 3. 16, 20; 8. 10, &c.
7. LABOUR,] as in 1. 3· 2. 10, 11, 18—22, 24; 3. 13, &c.

MOUTH,] to satisfy the cravings of nature; as in 5. 2, 6; 10. 12, 13; Ge. 4. 11; 8. 11, &c.
FILLED,] as in 1. 8; 11. 3; Ge. 6. 11, &c.
8. ADVANTAGE,] as in v. 11; 2. 15; 7. 11, 16; 12. 9, 12; Est. 6. 6.
LIVING,] as in v. 12; 2. 3, 17; 3. 12, &c.
9. SIGHT OF THE EYES,] that which one sees and possesses.
GOING,] up and down, on the going away to death.
10. ALREADY,] as in 1. 10; 2. 12, 16, &c.
MAN,] as in v. 1, 7, 11, 12; 1. 3, 13; 2. 3, &c.
CONTEND,] as in Ps. 50. 4; Isa. 3. 13.
11. MULTIPLYING,] as in Ex. 36. 5; Lev. 11. 42.
12. LIFE,] as in v. 8; 2. 3, 17; 3. 12, &c.
NUMBER,] as in 2. 3; 5. 18; Ge. 34. 30, &c.
SHADOW,] as in 7. 12; 8. 13; Ge. 19. 8, &c.
DECLARETH,] as in 8. 7; 10. 14, 20, &c.

VII. 1. NAME,] as in 6. 4, 10; Ge. 2. 11, &c.
PERFUME,] as in 9. 8; 10. 1; Ge. 28. 18, &c.
DEATH,] as in v. 26; 3. 19; 8. 8; 10. 1, &c.
BIRTH,] as in Ge. 21. 5; Hos. 2. 3.
2. MOURNING,] as in v. 4; Ge. 27. 41, &c.
BANQUETING,] as in Ge. 19. 3; 21. 8, &c.
END,] as in 3. 11; 12. 13; 2 Ch. 20. 16, Joel 2. 20.
LAYETH,] as in 1. 17; 2. 21; 5. 6, &c.
3. SORROW,] as in v. 9; 1. 18; 2. 23, &c.
LAUGHTER,] as in v. 6; 2. 2; 10. 19, &c.
SADNESS,] as in Ge. 41. 19; De. 28. 20, &c.
IS MADE BETTER,] as in Ge. 12. 13; 34. 18.
4. MOURNING,] as in v. 2; Ge. 27. 41; 50. 10
MIRTH,] as in 2. 10, 26; 5. 20; 8. 15, &c.
5. REBUKE,] as in Nah. 1. 4; Mal. 2. 3, &c.
SONG,] as in 12. 4; Ge. 31. 27; Jud. 5. 12, &c.
6. NOISE,] as in 5. 3, 6; 10. 20; 12. 4, &c.
THORNS,] as in Isa. 34. 13; Hos. 2. 6, &c.
POT,] as in Ex. 16. 3; 27. 3; 38. 3; 1 K. 7. 45
7. OPPRESSION,] as in 5 8; Lev. 6. 4, &c.
MAD,] as in Job 12. 17; Isa. 44. 25.
GIFT,] as in Ge. 25. 6; Ex. 28. 38; Lev. 23. 38.
DESTROYETH,] as in 9. 18; Nu. 33. 52, &c.
8. LATTER END,] as in 10. 13; Ge. 49. 1, &c.
BEGINNING,] as in Ge. 7. 1; 10. 10; 40. 3.
PATIENT,] as in Ex. 34. 6; Nu. 14. 18, &c.
HAUGHTY,] as in Ps. 101. 5; Prov. 16. 5;
Eze. 31. 3.
9. HASTY,] as in 5. 2; Est. 2. 9; Job 22. 10.
ANGRY,] as in v. 3; 1. 18; 2. 23; 11. 10, &c.
BOSOM,] as in Ge. 16. 5; Ex. 4. 6, 7, &c.
RESTETH,] as in Ge. 8. 4; Ex. 10. 14, &c.
10. ASKED,] as in 2. 10; Ge. 32. 17, &c.
11. INHERITANCE,] as in Ge. 31. 14, &c.
ADVANTAGE,] as in 1. 3; 2. 11, 13; 3. 9, &c.
12. MONEY,] as in 2. 8; 5. 10; 10. 19, &c.
REVIVETH,] as in Ge. 12. 12; 19. 32, 34, &c.
POSSESSORS,] as in 5. 11, 13; 8. 8; 10. 11, &c.
13. ABLE,] as in 1. 8, 15; 6. 10; 8. 17, &c.
14. GLADNESS,] as in 3. 3, 24, 26; 3. 12, &c.
CONSIDER,] as in v. 13, 27, 29; Ex. 33. 12.
OVER-AGAINST,] as in Ex. 25. 27; 28. 27, &c.
15. CONSIDERED,] as in 1. 14, 16; 2. 13, &c.
PERISHING,] as in De. 26. 5; 32. 28, &c.
WRONG-DOER,] as in 8. 10, 13, 14, &c.
WRONG,] as in 5. 1, 13, 16; 8. 3, 5, 9, 11, &c.
17. TIME,] as in 3. 1—8, 11, 17; 7. 17, &c.
LAY HOLD,] as in Ex. 15. 15; De. 32. 41, &c.
WITHDRAWEST,] as in 2. 18; 10. 4; 11. 6.
FEARING,] as in 8. 12, 13; 9. 2; Ge. 22. 12.
18. GIVE STRENGTH,] as in Jud. 3. 10, &c.

RULERS,] as in 8. 8; 10. 5; Ge. 42. 6.
CITY,] as in 8. 10; 9. 14, 15; 10. 15, &c.
20. SINNETH,] as in Ge. 42. 22; Ex. 20. 20.
21. REVILING,] as in Ge. 12. 3; Ex. 21. 17.
22. REVILED,] as in Lev. 20. 9; 2 Sa. 19. 21;
1 K. 2. 8; Isa. 8. 21.
23. TRIED,] as in Ge. 22. 1; Ex. 15. 25, &c.
WISE,] as in 1 K. 4. 31; Job 32. 9; Prov. 9. 9.
FAR,] as in v. 24; Ge. 22. 4; 37. 18, &c.
24. DEEP,] as in Lev. 13. 3, 4, 25, 30—32, &c.
25. TURNED ROUND,] as in 2. 20; 9. 14, &c.
SEARCH,] as in 1. 13; Nu. 10. 33; 13. 16, &c.
SEEK OUT,] as in 3. 6; 8. 7; 1 Sa. 10. 2, &c.
REASON,] as in v. 27; 9. 10.
WRONG,] as in 3. 16; 8. 8; De. 9. 27, &c.
FOOLISHNESS,] as in 2. 3, 12, 13; 10. 1, 13.
MADNESS,] as in 1. 17; 2. 12; 9. 3.
26. BITTER,] as in Ge. 27. 34; Ex. 15. 23, &c.
DEATH,] as in v. 1; 3. 19; 8. 8; 10. 1, &c.
SNARES,] as in Eze. 26. 5, 14; 32. 3, &c.
BANDS,] as in Jud. 15. 14; Jer. 37. 15.
ESCAPETH,] as in Ge. 19. 20; Jud. 3. 26, &c.
CAPTURED,] as in Jos. 7. 16—18; 1 Sa. 10. 20.
27. PREACHER,] as in 1. 1, 2, 12; 12. 8, 9, 10.
REASON,] as in v. 25; 9. 10.
28. SOUGHT,] as in v. 29; 12. 10; Nu. 16. 10.
29. ALONE,] as in Est. 4. 11; Zec. 12. 12.
UPRIGHT,] as in Ex. 15. 26; Nu. 23. 10, &c.
DEVICES,] as in 2 Ch. 26. 15.

VIII. 1. TO SHINE,] as in Ex. 14. 20, &c.
HARDNESS OF HIS FACE,] as in Ge. 49. 3, &c.
2. COMMANDMENT,] as in Ge. 45. 21, &c.
FOR THE SAKE OF,] as in Ge. 19. 17; 27. 41.
OATH,] as in 9. 2; Ge. 24. 8; 26. 3, &c.
3. TROUBLED,] as in Jud. 20. 41; Job 4. 5.
STAND,] as in 4. 12, 15; Ge. 19. 17; 24. 31.
PLEASETH,] as in De. 25. 7; Ruth 3. 13, &c.
4. POWER,] as in v. 8.
5. KEEPING,] as in 5. 8; 11. 4; 12. 3, &c.
TIME,] as in v. 6, 9; 3. 1—8, 11, 17; 7. 17.
6. DELIGHT,] as in 3. 1, 17; 5. 4, 8; 12. 1, &c.
MISFORTUNE,] as in v. 5, 9, 11, 12; 1. 13, &c.
GREAT,] as in 2. 21; 6. 1, 3; 7. 22, 29, &c.
7. DECLARETH,] as in 6. 12; 10. 14, 20, &c.
8. RULING,] as in 7. 19; 10. 5; Ge. 42. 6.
SPIRIT,] as in 1. 6, 14, 17; 2. 11; 3. 19, &c.
AUTHORITY,] as in v. 4.
DAY OF DEATH,] as in Ge. 27. 2; 1 Sa. 15. 35.
BATTLE,] as in 3. 8; 9. 11; Ge. 14. 2, 8, &c.
DELIVERETH,] as in 2 K. 23. 18; Job 20. 20.
POSSESSORS,] as in 5. 11, 13; 7. 12; 10. 11.
9. GIVE MY HEART,] as in 2. 26; 5. 1, &c.
SUN,] as in v. 15, 17; 1. 3, 5, 9, 14; 2. 11, &c.
RULED,] as in Neh. 5. 15.
EVIL,] as in v. 3, 5, 6, 11, 12; 1. 13; 2. 17.
10. WICKED,] as in v. 13, 14; 3. 17; 7. 15.
BURIED,] as in 1 K. 13. 31.
HOLY PLACE,] as in Ex. 29. 31; Lev. 6. 16.
CITY,] as in 7. 19; 9. 14, 15; 10. 15, &c.
VANITY,] as in v. 14; 1. 2, 14; 2. 1, 11, &c.
11. SENTENCE,] as in Est. 1. 20.
SPEEDILY,] as in 4. 12; Nu. 16. 46; De. 11.
17, &c.
SONS OF MAN,] as in 1. 13; 2. 3, 8; 3. 10, &c.
FULL,] as in 9. 3; Ge. 6. 13; 29. 21, &c.
12. SINNER,] as in 2. 26; 7. 26; 9. 2, 18, &c.
PROLONGING,] as in 7. 15.
FEARING GOD,] as in 7. 18; Ge. 22. 12, &c.
13. WICKED,] as in v. 10, 14; 3. 17; 7. 15.
PROLONG,] as in Ex. 20. 12; De. 4. 26, &c.

SHADOW,] as in 6. 12; 7. 12; Ge. 19. 8, &c.
14. EARTH,] or 'land,' as in v. 16; 1. 4, &c
RIGHTEOUS ONES,] as in 3. 17; 7. 15, 16, &c
COMING,] as in Ge. 28. 12; 2 Ch. 3. 11, &c.
15. MIRTH,] as in 2. 1, 2, 10, 26, &c.
EAT. . DRINK.] Compare 5. 18; Ex. 32. 6.
LABOUR,] as in 1. 3; 2. 10, 11, 18—22, 24.
DAYS OF HIS LIFE,] as in 5. 18; 1 K. 4. 15
16. BUSINESS,] as in 1. 13; 2. 23, 26, &c.
SPECTATOR,] as in 7. 11; 11. 14; 12. 3, &c.
SLEEP,] as in 5. 12; Ge. 28. 16; 31. 40, &c.
17. CONSIDERED,] as in 7. 11; 11. 4; 12. 3.
FIND OUT,] as in 7. 27; 12. 10; Ge. 19. 11.
TO SEEK,] as in 3. 6; 7. 25; 1 Sa. 10. 2, &c.
WISE MAN,] as in v. 1, 5; 2. 14, 16, 19, &c.

IX. 1. LAID,] as in 1. 13; 3. 11; Ps. 4. 7, &c.
LOVE,] as in v. 6; Ge. 29. 20; De. 7. 3, &c.
HATRED,] as in v. 6; Nu. 35. 20; De. 1. 27
2. EVENT,] as in v. 3; 2. 14, 15; 3. 19; Ru.
2. 3; 1 Sa. 6. 9; 20. 26.
CLEAN,] as in Ge. 7. 2, 8; 8. 20, &c.
UNCLEAN,] as in Lev. 5. 2; 7. 19, 21, &c.
SACRIFICING,] as in Ex. 13. 15; 22. 20, &c.
SWEARING,] as in Ps. 63. 11; Isa. 19. 18, &c.
OATH,] as in 8. 2; Ge. 24. 8; 26. 3, &c.
3. EVIL,] as in v. 12; 1. 13; 2. 17, 21, &c.
FULL,] as in 8. 11; Ge. 6. 13; 20. 21, &c.
MADNESS,] as in 1. 17; 2. 12; 7. 25.
LIFE,] as in v. 4, 5, 9; 2. 3, 17; 3. 12, &c.
DEAD,] as in v. 4, 5; 4. 2; Ge. 20 3, &c.
4. LIVING,] as in v. 3; 3. 7; 3. 17; 3. 12, &c.
CONFIDENCE,] as in 2 K. 18. 19; Isa. 36. 4.
DOG,] as in Ex. 11. 7; 22. 31; De. 23. 18, &c.
LION,] as in Ge. 49. 9; Nu. 23. 24; De. 4, &c
5. DIE,] as in 2. 16; 7. 17; Ge. 2. 17, &c.
DEAD,] as in v. 3, 4; 4. 2; Ge. 20 3, &c.
REWARD,] as in 4. 9; Ge. 15. 1; 30. 18, &c.
REMEMBRANCE,] as in Ex. 3. 15; 17. 14, &c.
FORGOTTEN,] as in 2. 16; Ge. 41. 30; Ps. 31.
12; Isa. 65. 16.
6. LOVE,] as in v. 1; Ge. 29. 20; De. 7. 8, &c.
HATRED,] as in v. 1; Nu. 35. 20; De. 1. 27.
ENVY,] as in 4. 4; Job 5. 2; Prov. 14. 30, &c.
PERISHED,] as in 5. 14; Ex. 10. 7, &c.
PORTION,] as in v. 9; 2. 10, 21; 3. 22, &c.
7. JOY,] as in 2. 1, 2, 10, 26; 5. 20; 7. 4, &c.
GLAD HEART,] as in 5. 9; 2 Ch. 7. 10.
WINE,] as in 2. 3; 10. 19; Ge. 9. 21, &c.
ALREADY,] as in v. 6; 1. 10; 2. 12, 16, &c.
PLEASED,] as in 1 Ch. 28. 4; 2 Ch. 10. 7, &c.
8. GARMENTS,] as in Ge. 24. 53; 27. 15, &c.
WHITE,] as in Ge. 30. 35, 37; Ex. 16. 31, &c.
PERFUME,] as in 7. 1; 10. 1; Ge. 28. 18, &c.
LACKING,] as in Ge. 8. 3; 18. 28; De. 8. 9.
9. SEE,] as in 1. 16; 2. 1; 7. 13, &c.
DAYS OF THE LIFE,] as in 2. 3; 5. 18, &c.
PORTION,] as in v. 6; 2. 10, 21; 3. 22, &c.
LABOUR,] as in v. 3; 2. 10; 3. 13, &c.
LABOURING,] as in 3. 11; 7. 14, 24; 8. 17.
10. FINDETH,] as in 3. 11; 7. 14, 24; 8. 17.
POWER,] as in 4. 1; Ge. 4. 12; 31. 6, &c.
WORK,] as in 7. 1. 14; 2. 4, 11, 17, &c.
DEVICE,] as in 7. 25, 27.
KNOWLEDGE,] as in 1. 16, 18; 2. 21, 26, &c
WISDOM,] as in v. 13, 15, 16, 18; 1. 13, &c
SHEOL,] as in Ge. 37. 35; 42. 38; 44. 29, &c
11. TURNED,] as in 1. 6; 3. 20; 4. 1, 7, &c.
SWIFT,] as in 2 Sa. 2. 18; Job 24. 18, &c.
MIGHTY,] as in Ge. 6. 4; 10. 8, 9; De. 10. 17
BATTLE,] as in 3. 8; 8. 8; Ge. 14. 2, 8, &c.

BREAD,] that is, food, as in v. 7; 10. 19, &c.
INTELLIGENT,] as in Ge. 41. 33, 39, &c.
WEALTH,] as in 3. 16; 8. 18; 11. 16, 28, &c.
SKILFUL,] as in v. 1, 5; 2. 19; 3. 21, &c.
GRACE,] as in 10. 12; Ge. 6. 8; 18. 3, &c.
HAPPEN,] as in 2. 14, 15; Nu. 11. 23, &c.
12. TIME,] as in v. 8, 11; 3. 1—8, 11, 17, &c.
FISH,] as in Ge. 9. 2; Nu. 11. 22, &c.
TAKEN HOLD OF,] as in Ge. 22. 13.
NET,] as in Eze. 19. 9.
BIRDS,] as in 12. 4; Ge. 7. 14; 15. 10, &c.
SNARE,] as in Jos. 23. 13; Job 18. 9, &c.
SONS OF MAN,] as in 1. 13; 2. 3; 3. 10, &c.
SUDDENLY,] as in Nu. 6. 9; 12. 4; Jos. 10. 9.
13. SEEN,] as in 1. 6, 14; 2. 13, 24; 3. 10, &c.
WISDOM,] as in v. 10, 15, 16, 18; 1. 13, &c.
GREAT,] as in v. 14; 10. 4; Ge. 1. 16, &c.
14. CITY,] as in v. 15; 7. 19; 8. 10; 10. 15.
FEW,] as in 5. 2, 12; 10. 1; Ge. 18. 4, &c.
KING,] as in 1. 1, 12; 2. 8, 12; 4. 13, &c.
SURROUNDED,] as in 2. 20; 7. 25; 12. 5, &c.
BUILT,] as in 2. 4; Ge. 11. 5; Nu. 32. 37, &c.
BULWARKS,] as in Prov. 12. 12.
15. POOR,] as in v. 16; 4. 13.
DELIVERED,] as in 2 Sa. 19. 9; Eze. 33. 5.
WISDOM,] as in v. 10, 13, 16, 18; 1. 13, &c.
REMEMBERED,] as in 5. 20; 11. 8; Ge. 9. 15.
16. MIGHT,] as in 10. 17; Ex. 32. 18, &c.
DESPISED,] as in Ps. 22. 6; Jer. 49. 15;
Obad. 2.
17. QUIET,] as in 4. 6; 6. 5; Job 17. 16, &c.
CRY,] as in Ge. 18. 20; Neh. 5. 6; 9. 9, &c.
RULER,] as in 10. 4; Ge. 24. 2; 45. 8, &c.
FOOLS,] as in 2. 14—16; 4. 5, 13; 5. 1, &c.
18. WEAPONS,] as in Ge. 27 3; Nu. 35. 16.
CONFLICT,] as in 2 Sa. 17. 11; Job 38. 23.
DESTROYETH,] as in 7. 7; Nu. 33. 52, &c.

X. 1. DEAD FLIES,] lit. 'flies of death.'
PERFUMER,] as in Ex. 30. 25, 35; 37. 29; 1
Ch. 9. 30.
PERFUME,] as in 7. 1; 9. 8; Ge. 28. 18, &c.
STINK,] as in Ex. 5. 21; 16. 24; 1 Sa. 27. 12.
PRECIOUS,] as in 1 Sa. 3. 1; 2 Sa. 12. 30, &c.
HONOUR,] as in 6. 2; 3. 1; 45. 13, &c.
FOLLY,] as in v. 13; 2. 3, 12, 13; 7. 25.
2. RIGHT HAND,] as in Ge. 13. 9; 24. 49, &c.
LEFT,] as in Ge. 13. 9; 14. 15; 24. 49, &c.
3. WALKING,] as in v. 7; 1. 4; 2. 14, &c.
LACKING,] as in 6. 2; 2 Sa. 3. 29, &c.
FOOL,] as in v. 14; 2. 19; 7. 17; Jer. 4. 22;
5. 21.
4. RULER,] as in 9. 17; Ge. 24. 2; 45. 8, &c.
LEAVE,] as in 2. 18; 7. 18; 11. 6; Ge. 2. 15.
5. EVIL,] as in v. 13; 1. 13; 2. 17, 21, &c.
ERROR,] as in 5. 6; Lev. 4. 2, 22, 27, &c.
6. SET,] as in 12. 11; Ge. 9. 2; 38. 14, &c.
HIGH PLACES,] as in Jud. 5. 18; 2 Sa. 22. 17.
RICH,] as in v. 20; 5. 12; Ex. 30. 15, &c.
LOW PLACE,] as in Ps. 136. 23.
7. HORSES,] as in Ge. 47. 17; 49. 17, &c.
PRINCES,] as in v. 16, 17; Ge. 12. 15, &c.
SERVANTS,] as in 2. 7; 7. 21; 9. 25, 26, &c.
BREAKING;] as in Mic. 2. 13.
HEDGE,] as in Ps. 80. 12; Eze. 13. 5; 22. 30.
SERPENT,] as in v. 11; Ge. 3. 1, 2, 4, 13, &c
BITETH,] as in v. 11; Prov. 23. 32.
9. STONES,] as in 3. 5; Ge. 2. 12; 11. 3.
GRIEVED,] as in Ge. 45. 5; 1 Sa. 20. 3; Neh
8. 10, 11.
CLEAVING,] as in Ps. 141. 7; Isa. 63. 12.

10. IRON,] as in Ge. 4. 22; Lev. 26. 19, &c.
SHARPENED,] as in Eze. 21. 21.
STRENGTH,] as in 12. 3; 1 Sa. 2. 4; 14. 48.
ADVANTAGEOUS,] as in v. 11; 1. 3; 2. 11, 13;
3. 9; 5. 9, 16; 7. 12.
11. ENCHANTMENT,] as in Isa. 3. 3; 26. 16;
Jer. 8. 17.
MASTER OF THE TONGUE,] that is, a man
of eloquence.
12. GRACIOUS,] as in 9. 11; Ge. 6. 8; 18. 3.
SWALLOW UP,] as in 2 Sa. 20. 19, 20, &c.
13. BEGINNING,] as as Ge. 13. 3; 41. 21, &c.
FOLLY,] as in v. 1; 2. 3, 12, 13; 7. 25.
LATTER END,] as in 7. 8; Ge. 49. 1, &c.
MISCHIEVOUS,] as in v. 5; 1. 13; 2. 17, 21.
14. MULTIPLIETH,] as in Ge. 3. 16; 16. 10
DECLARE,] as in v. 20; 6. 12; 8. 7, &c.
15. LABOUR,] as in 1. 3; 2. 10; 3. 13, &c.
WEARIETH,] as in Jos. 7. 3.
CITY,] as in v. 14; 7. 19; 8. 10, &c.
16. YOUTH,] as in Ge. 14. 24; 18. 7; 19. 4.
PRINCES,] as in v. 7. 17; Ge. 12. 15; 21. 22.
MORNING,] as in 11. 6; Ge. 1. 5; 19. 27, &c.
17. HAPPY,] as in De. 33. 29; 1 K. 10. 8, &c.
FREEMAN,] as in 1 K. 21. 8, 11; Neh. 2. 16.
DUE SEASON,] as in 3. 1—8, 11, 17; 7. 17, &c.
MIGHT,] as in 9. 16; Ex. 32. 18; De. 3. 24.
18. SLOTHFULNESS,] as in Prov. 19. 15.
DROP,] as in Job 16. 20; Ps. 119. 28.
19. MIRTH,] as in 2. 2; 7. 3, 6; Job 8. 21, &c.
FEAST,] as in 9. 7, 11; 11. 1; Ge. 3. 19.
WINE,] as in 2. 3; 9. 7; Ge. 9. 21, &c.
JOYFUL,] as in Ps. 46. 4; 104. 15; Prov. 10. 1.
20. MIND,] as in 2 Ch. 1. 10, 11, 12; Da. 1.
4, 17.
REVILE,] as in Ex. 22. 28; Lev. 19. 14, &c.
INNER PARTS,] as in Ge. 43. 30; Ex. 8. 3, &c.
BED-CHAMBER,] as in Ge. 49. 4; Ex. 8. 3.
RICH,] as in v. 6; 5. 12; Job 27. 19, &c.
FOWL,] as in Ge. 1. 20—22, 26, 30; 2. 19, 20.
TO GO,] as in 5. 15; Ex. 14. 21; Lev. 26. 13.
POSSESSOR,] as in v. 11; 5. 11, 13; 7. 12, &c.
DECLARETH,] as in v. 14; 6. 12; 8. 7, &c.

XI. 1. SEND FORTH,] as in Ge. 24. 54, 56, &c.
BREAD,] as in 9. 7, 11; 10. 19; Ge. 3. 19, &c.
MULTITUDE,] as in 9. 9; 2. 3, 16, 23, &c.
2. PORTION,] as in 2. 10, 21; 3. 22; 5. 18, &c.
EVIL,] as in v. 10; 1. 13; 2. 17, 21, &c.
3. THICK CLOUDS,] as in v. 4; 12. 2, &c.
RAIN,] as in 12. 2; Ge. 7. 12; 8. 2, &c.
EMPTY,] as in Ge. 14. 14; 15. 9; Ps. 18. 42.
SOUTH,] as in 1. 6; De. 33. 23; Job 37. 17.
NORTH,] as in 1. 6; Ge. 13. 14; 28. 14, &c.
4. OBSERVING,] as in 5. 8; 8. 5; 11. 4, &c.
SOWETH,] as in Ge. 26. 12; Ex. 23. 10, 16.
LOOKING,] as in 7. 11; 8. 16; 12. 3, &c.
REAPETH,] as in Lev. 25. 5, 11; Nu. 11. 23.
5. SPIRIT,] as in v. 1. 6, 14, 17; 11. 23, &c.
BONES,] as in Ge. 2. 23; 7. 13; 17. 23, 26, &c.
WOMB,] as in 5. 16; Ge. 25. 23, 24; 30. 2, &c.
FULL ONE,] as in 1. 7; Ge. 23. 9; 41. 7.
WORK OF GOD,] as in 7. 13; 8. 17; Ps. 64. 9.
6. MORNING,] as in 10. 16; Ge. 1. 5, 8, &c.
SOW,] as in 2 K. 19. 29; Isa. 37. 30; Hos.
10. 12.
SEED,] as in Ge. 1. 11, 12, 29; 3. 15, &c.
EVENING,] as in Ge. 1. 5, 8, 13, 19, 23, 31.
WITHDRAW,] as in 2. 18; 7. 18; 10. 4, &c.
7. SWEET,] as in 5. 12; Jud. 14. 14, 18, &c
LIGHT] as in 1. 8; 2. 12; 3. 18. 22, &c.

SUN,] as in 1. 3, 5, 9, 14; 2. 11, &c.
8. MANY YEARS,] as in 6. 3; Lev. 25. 51, &c.
REJOICE,] as in 3. 22; 4. 16; Jud. 9. 19, &c.
REMEMBER,] as in 5. 20; 8. 1; 19. 29, &c.
DARKNESS,] as in 2. 13, 14; 5. 17; 6. 4, &c.
COMING,] as in 1. 4, 5; 5. 15, 16; 6. 4, &c.
9. YOUNG MAN,] as in De. 32. 25; Jud. 14. 10.
CHILDHOOD,] as in Ps. 110. 3.
YOUTH,] as in 12. 1.
SIGHT OF THINE EYES,] as in De. 28. 34, 67.
KNOW,] as in Ge. 20. 7; Nu. 32. 23, &c.
BRING,] as in 3. 22; 12. 14; Ge. 2. 19, &c.
JUDGMENT,] as in 3. 16; 5. 8; 8. 5, 6, &c.
10. TURN ASIDE,] as in Ge. 35. 2; Jos. 24. 14.
ANGER,] as in 1. 18; 2. 3; 7. 3, 9, &c.
TO PASS,] as in 2 Sa. 24. 10; 1 Ch. 21. 8, &c.
FLESH,] as in 2 3; 4. 5; 5. 6; 12. 12, &c.
CHILDHOOD,] as in v. 9; Ps. 110. 3.

XII. 1. REMEMBER,] as in Ex .32. 13, &c.
CREATORS,] as in Isa. 40. 28; 42. 5; 43. 1, &c.
YOUTH,] as in 11. 9.
YEARS,] as in 6. 3, 6; 11. 8; Ge. 1. 14, &c.
ARRIVED,] as in Ex. 12. 22; 2 Ch. 28. 9, &c.
PLEASURE,] as in v. 10; 3. 1, 17; 5. 4, 8; 8. 6.
2. SUN,] as in 1. 3, 5, 9, 14; 2. 11, 17, &c.
DARKENED,] as in Ex. 10. 15; Job 3. 9; Ps.
69. 23.
LIGHT,] as in 2. 13; 11. 7; Ge. 1. 3—5, &c.
MOON,] as in Ge. 37. 9; De. 4. 19; 17. 3, &c.
STARS,] as in Ge. 1. 16; 15. 5; 22. 17, &c.
THICK CLOUDS,] as in 3. 4; Ex. 19. 9, &c.
RAIN,] as in 11. 3; Ge. 7. 12; 8. 2, &c.
3. KEEPERS,] as in 5. 8; 8. 5; 11. 4, &c.
STRENGTH,] as in 10. 10; Ge. 34. 29; 47. 6.
GRINDERS,] as in Jud. 16. 21.
WINDOWS,] as in Ge. 7. 11; 8. 2; 2 K. 7. 2.
DIM,] as in Job 18. 6; Isa. 5. 30; 13. 10, &c.
4. DOORS,] as in Ge. 19. 6, 9, 10; Ex. 21. 6.
SHUT,] as in Isa. 24. 10, 22; Jer. 13. 9, &c.
STREET,] as in v. 5; Prov. 7. 8; Song 3. 2.
NOISE,] as in 5. 3, 6; 7. 6; 10. 20. &c

LOW,] as in Lev. 13. 20; 2 Sa. 6. 22, &c.
BIRD,] as in 9. 12; Ge. 7. 14; 15. 10, &c.
BOWED DOWN,] as in Isa. 2. 9; 5. 15; 29. 4.
5. HIGH,] as in 5. 8; Ge. 7. 19; De. 3. 5, &c.
AFRAID,] as in 3. 14; 8. 12; Ge. 3. 10, &c.
GRASSHOPPER,] as in Lev. 11. 22; Nu. 13. 33.
MOURNERS,] as in Isa. 32. 12.
GONE ROUND,] as in 2. 20; 7. 25; 9. 14, &c.
STREET,] as in v. 4; Prov. 7. 8; Song 3. 2.
6. CORD,] as in 2 Sa. 8. 2; 17. 13; 22. 6, &c.
GOLDEN,] as in 2. 8; Ge. 2. 11, 12; 13. 2, &c.
BROKEN,] as in Isa. 42. 4.
PITCHER,] as in Ge. 24. 14—18, 20, 43, &c.
FOUNTAIN,] as in Isa. 35. 7; 49. 10.
WHEEL,] as in Ps. 83. 13; Isa. 5. 28, &c.
WELL,] as in Ge. 37. 20; 40. 15; 41. 14, &c.
7. DUST,] as in 3. 20; Ge. 2. 7; 3. 14, &c.
RETURNETH,] as in 3. 20; Ge. 3. 19, &c.
8. VANITIES,] as in 1. 2.
PREACHER,] as in v. 9, 10; 1. 1, 2, 12; 7. 27.
9. WISE,] as in v. 11; 2. 14, 16, 19; 4. 13.
TAUGHT,] as in De. 4. 5; 11. 19; Ps. 71. 17.
KNOWLEDGE,] as in 1. 16, 18; 2. 21, 26, &c.
SIMILIES,] as in Nu. 23. 7; De. 28. 37, &c.
10. PLEASING,] as in v. 1; 3. 1, 17; 5. 4, &c.
WRITTEN,] as in Ex. 31. 18; 32. 15, &c.
UPRIGHT,] as in De. 9. 5; 1 K. 9. 4, &c.
TRUTH,] as in Ge. 24. 47—49; 32. 10, &c.
11. PLANTED] as in 3. 2.
MASTERS,] as in 5. 11, 13; 7. 12; 8. 8, &c.
SHEPHERD,] as in Ge. 4. 2; 13. 7, 8, &c.
12. BOOK,] as in Ge. 5. 1; Ex. 17. 14, &c.
END,] as in 4. 8, 16; Ge. 4. 3; 6. 13, &c.
FLESH,] as in 3. 4; 4. 5; 5. 6, &c.
13. HEAR,] as in 7. 21; Ge. 3. 8; 11. 7, &c.
FEAR GOD,] as in 5. 7; Ge. 42. 18; Ex. 1. 17.
KEEP HIS COMMANDS,] as in De. 7. 9; 8.
2; 26. 18, &c.
14. BRING,] as in 3. 22; 11. 9; Ge. 2. 19, &c.
HIDDEN THING,] as in 1 K. 10. 3.
GOOD OR BAD,] as in Lev. 12. 14; Nu. 13
19; 24 13 &c

SONG OF SONGS

THE SONG OF SONGS has always formed a part of the Jewish Canon of Scripture, and has been universally received as canonical by the Jewish Synagogue and the Christian Church from the beginning; the title ascribes it to SOLOMON, either as its author or its subject, and though he would not himself have given it the title 'the Song of Songs,' i.e. the 'Short Excellent Song,' all existing Versions and MSS. have it so. Modern objections to its authorship and canonicity rest entirely on its meaning, for the Chaldaisms in it are similar to those found in the Song of Deborah and Barak, and allowable in poetical compositions, not to allude to the extensive intercourse of Solomon with other nations, east and west. It appears to be an *allegory* wherein under the image of maidenly and nuptial love the affection between the Saviour and his people are exhibited. The Chaldee Targum explains it as an allegorical history of God's dealings with Israel from the Exodus till the building of the third temple. The Canonicity of the Book is not at all affected by regarding it as relating to Solomon, rather than as written by him; compare the title to Ps. 72. &c.

I. 1. SONG OF SONGS,] that is, 'the chief song,' or 'one of the songs.'
SOLOMON'S,] *lit.* 'belonging to' him.
2. KISS,] as in 8. 1; Ge. 27. 27; 29. 11, &c.
KISSES,] as in Prov. 27. 6.
LOVES,] as in v. 4, 13, 14, 16; 2. 3, 8—10, &c.
WINE,] as in v. 4; 2. 4; 4. 10, &c.
3. FRAGRANCE,] as in v. 12; 2. 13; 4. 10, 11.
PERFUMES,] as in 4. 10; Ge. 28. 18; 35. 14.
NAME,] as in Ge. 2. 11, 13, 14, 19, 20; 3. 20.
VIRGINS,] as in 6. 8; Ge. 24. 43; Ex. 2. 8, &c.
LOVED,] as in v. 4, 7; 3. 1—4; Ge. 22. 2, &c.
4. DRAW,] as in Ex. 12. 21; Ps. 36. 10; Eze. 32. 20.
RUN,] as in Ge. 18. 2; 24. 17; 29. 12, &c.
KING,] as in v. 12; 3. 9, 11; 7. 5, &c.
BROUGHT,] as in 2. 4; 3. 4; Ge. 4. 4, &c.
INNER CHAMBERS,] as in 3. 4; Ge. 43. 30.
JOY,] as in 1 Ch. 16. 31; Ps. 9. 14; 13. 4, 5.
REJOICE,] as in Jud. 9. 19; 19. 3; 1 Sa. 6. 13.
MENTION,] as in Ex. 20. 24; 23. 13, &c.
LOVES .. WINE,] as in v. 2.
UPRIGHTLY,] as in 1 Ch. 29. 17; Ps. 9. 8, &c.
5. DARK,] as in 5. 11; Lev. 13. 31, 37; Zec. 6. 2, 6.
COMELY,] as in 2. 14; 4. 3; 6. 4, &c.
DAUGHTERS OF JERUSALEM,] as in 2. 7; 3. 5, 10; 5. 8, 16; 8. 4, &c.
TENTS,] as in Ge. 4. 20; 9. 21, 27; 12. 8, &c.
CURTAINS,] as in Ex. 26. 1—10. 12, 13, &c.
SOLOMON,] as in v. 1; Prov. 1. 1, &c.
6. FEAR,] as in Ge. 3. 10; 15. 1; 20. 8, &c.
SUN,] as in Ge. 15. 12, 17; 19. 23; 28. 11.
SCORCHED,] as in Job 20. 9; 28. 7.
WERE ANGRY,] or heated, as in Ps. 69. 3.

KEEPER,] as in 8. 11, 12.
VINEYARDS,] as in v. 14; 7. 12; 8. 11, 12, &c
7. DECLARE,] as in Ge. 24. 23, 49; 29. 15, &c
MY SOUL,] as in 3. 1—4; 5. 6; 6. 12, &c.
DELIGHTEST,] as in Ge. 30. 31; 41. 2, 18, &c.
LIEST DOWN,] as in Ps. 23. 2; Isa. 13. 20, &c
NOON,] as in Ge. 43. 16, 25; De. 28. 29, &c.
VEILED,] as in 1 Sa. 28. 14; Ps. 104. 2, &c.
RANKS,] as in 4. 1, 2; 6. 5, 6; Ge. 29. 2, &c.
COMPANIONS,] as in 8. 13; Jud. 20. 11, &c.
8. FAIR,] as in v. 15, 16; 2. 10, 13; 4. 1, 7.
GET FORTH,] as in 3. 11; Ge. 8. 16; 19. 14.
TRACES,] as in Ps. 56. 6; 77. 19; 89. 51.
FLOCK,] as in Ge. 4. 2, 4; 12. 16; 13. 5, &c.
FEED,] as in 2. 16; 4. 5; 6. 3; Ge. 4. 2, &c.
SHEPHERDS',] as in Ge. 4. 2; 13. 7, 8; 26. 20.
DWELLINGS,] as in Ex. 25. 9; 26. 1, 6, 7, &c.
9. CHARIOTS,] as in Ge. 50. 9; Ex. 14. 6. 7.
COMPARED,] as in Isa. 40. 18, 25; 46. 5, &c.
FRIEND,] as in 5. 1, 16; Ge. 38. 12. 20, &c.
10. COMELY,] as in Ps. 93. 5; Isa. 52. 7.
CHEEKS,] as in 5. 13; De. 18. 3; 1 K. 22. 24.
GARLANDS,] as in v. 11.
NECK,] as in 4. 4; 7. 4; Ge. 27. 16, 40, &c.
11. GARLANDS,] as in v. 10.
GOLD,] as in 3. 10; 5. 14; Ge. 2. 11, 12, &c.
MAKE,] as in 8. 8; Ge. 1. 7, 16, 25, 26, &c.
SILVER,] as in 3. 10; 8. 9, 11; Ge. 13. 2.
12. KING,] as in v. 4; 3. 9, 11; 7. 5, &c.
CIRCLE,] as in 1 K. 6. 29; 2 K. 23. 5, &c.
SPIKENARD,] as in 4. 13, 14.
GIVEN,] as in 2. 13; 7. 13; 8. 11, &c.
FRAGRANCE,] as in v. 3; 2. 13; 4. 10, 11, &c.
13. BUNDLE,] as in Ge. 42. 35; 1 Sa. 25. 29.
MYRRH,] as in 3. 6; 4. 6, 14; 5. 1, 5, 13, &c.
BELOVED,] as in v. 2, 4, 14, 16; 2. 3, 4, &c.
BREASTS,] as in 4. 5; 7. 3; 7, 8; 8. 1, &c.
IT LODGETH,] as in 7. 11; Ge. 19. 2; 24. 54.
14. CLUSTER,] as in 7. 7, 8; Ge. 40. 10, &c.
CYPRESS,] as in 4. 13.
VINEYARDS,] as in v. 6; 2. 15; 7. 12, &c.
15. FAIR,] as in v. 8, 16; 2. 10, 13; 4. 1, 7.
FRIEND,] as in 5. 1, 16; Ge. 38. 12, 20, &c.
DOVES,] as in 2. 14; 4. 1; 5. 2, 12, &c.
16. LOVE,] as in v. 2, 4, 13, 14; 2. 3, &c.
PLEASANT,] as in 2 Sa. 1. 23; 23. 1, &c.
COUCH,] as in De. 3. 11; Job 7. 13, &c.
GREEN,] as in De. 12. 2; 1 K. 14. 23, &c.
17. BEAMS,] as in Ge. 19. 8; 2 K. 6. 2, 5, &c.
CEDARS,] as in 5. 15; 8. 9; Lev. 14. 4, 49, &c.
ROSE,] as in Isa. 35. 1.
LILY,] as in 2. 1; 2 Ch. 4. 5; Hos. 14. 5.
VALLEYS,] as in Ge. 14. 3, 8, 10, 17; 37. 14

II. 1. LILY,] as in 1. 17; 2 Ch. 4. 5; Hos. 14. 5.
THORNS,] as in 1 Sa. 13. 6; 2 K. 14. 9, &c.
2. FRIEND,] as in 5. 1. 16; Ge. 38. 12, &c.
DAUGHTERS,] as in v. 7; 1. 5; 3. 5, 10, 11.
3. CITRON,] as in 5; 7. 8; 8. 5; Prov. 25. 11.
TREES OF THE FOREST,] as in Ps. 96. 12; Isa. 7. 2; Eze. 15. 2, &c.
BELOVED,] as in 1. 4, 16; 3. 8—10, 16, 17.
SONS,] as in 1. 6; Ge. 3. 16; 4. 17, &c.

SHADE,] as in Ge. 19. 8; Nu. 14. 9, &c.
SAT DOWN,] as in Ge. 13. 12; 19. 29; 27. 44.
FRUIT,] as in 4. 13, 16; 8. 11, 12; Ge. 1. 11.
PALATE,] as in 5. 16; 7. 9; Job 6. 30, &c.
4. BROUGHT,] as in 1. 4; 3. 4; Ge. 4. 4, &c.
BANNER,] as in Nu. 1. 52; 2. 2, 3, &c.
LOVE,] as in v. 5, 7; 3. 5, 10; 5. 8, &c.
5. GRAPE-CAKES,] as in 2 Sa. 6. 19; 1 Ch. 16. 3.
CITRONS,] as in 2. 3; 7. 8; 8. 5; Prov. 25. 11.
SICK,] as in 5. 8; Ge. 48. 1; 1 Sa. 19. 14, &c.
LOVE,] as in v. 4. 7; 3. 10; 5. 8, &c.
6. LEFT HAND,] as in 8. 3; Ge. 13. 9, &c.
HEAD,] as in 4. 8, 14; 5. 2, 11; 7. 5, &c.
RIGHT HAND,] as in 8. 3; Ge. 13. 9; 24. 49.
EMBRACE,] as in 8. 3.
7. ADJURED,] as in 3. 5; 5. 8; 8. 4, &c.
DAUGHTERS OF JERUSALEM,] as in v. 2;
1. 5; 3. 5, 10, 11, &c.
ROES,] as in v. 9, 17; 3. 5; 8. 14, &c.
HINDS,] as in 3. 5; Ge. 49. 21; 2 Sa. 22. 34.
FIELD,] as in 3. 5; 7. 11; Ge. 2. 5, 19. 20, &c.
STIR UP,] as in 3. 5; 8. 4; De. 32. 11, &c.
WAKE,] as in 8. 4; Prov. 10. 12; Isa. 15. 5.
THE LOVE,] as in v. 4, 5; 3. 10; 5. 8, &c.
SHE PLEASE,] as in 3. 5; 8. 4; De. 25. 7, &c.
8. VOICE,] as in v. 12, 14; 5. 2; 8. 13, &c.
BELOVED,] as in v. 3, 9, 10, 16, 17; 1. 2, &c.
LO,] as in Ge. 6. 17; 16. 11; Nu. 14. 40, &c.
COMING,] as in Ge. 7. 16; 18. 11, 21, &c.
MOUNTAINS,] as in v. 17; 4. 1, 6; 8. 14, &c.
HILLS,] as in 4. 6; Ge. 49. 26; Ex. 17. 9, 10.
9. BELOVED,] as in v. 3, 8, 10, 16, 17, &c.
ROE,] as in v. 7. 17; 3. 5; 8. 14, &c.
YOUNG ONE,] as in v. 17; 4. 5; 7. 3; 8. 14.
HARTS,] as in v. 17; 8. 14; De. 12. 13, 22.
STANDING,] as in Ge. 18. 8, 22; 24. 30, &c.
BEHIND,] as in 1. 4; Ge. 5. 4, 7; 6. 4, &c.
WINDOWS,] as in Ge. 8. 6; 26. 8; Jos. 2. 15.
10. BELOVED,] as in v. 3, 8, 9, 16, 17, &c.
ANSWERED,] as in 5. 6; Ge. 30. 33, &c.
RISE UP,] as in v. 13; Ge. 13. 17; 19. 14, &c.
FRIEND,] as in v. 2, 13; 1. 9, 15; 4. 1, 7, &c.
FAIR ONE,] as in v. 13; 1. 8, 15, 16; 4. 1, 7.
COME AWAY,] as in v. 13; 7. 11; Ge. 12. 1.
11. PASSED AWAY,] as in 3. 4; 5. 6, &c.
GONE,] as in 6. 1; Ge. 14. 24; 19. 2, &c.
12. APPEARED,] as in Ge. 8. 5; 9. 14; 48. 3.
EARTH,] as in Ge. 1. 1, 2, 10—12; 2. 1, &c.
TIME,] as in Ge. 8. 11; 18. 10; 21. 22, &c. ?
COME,] as in Ex. 12. 22; 2 Ch. 28. 9, &c.
TURTLE,] as in Ge. 15. 9; Lev. 1. 14; 5. 7.
HEARD,] as in Ge. 45. 16; Ex. 28. 35, &c.
LAND,] as in Ge. 1. 1, 2, 10—12; 2. 1, &c.
13. FIG TREE,] as in Ge. 3. 7; Nu. 13. 23, &c.
SWEET SMELLING VINE,] as in v. 15; 7. 12.
GIVEN FORTH,] as in 1. 12; 7. 13; 8. 11, &c.
FRAGRANCE,] as in 1. 3, 12; 2. 13; 4. 10, 11.
RISE,] as in v. 10; Ge. 37. 7; 41. 30, &c.
COME,] as in v. 10; 7. 11; Ge. 12. 1, 19, &c.
FRIEND . . FAIR ONE,] as in v. 10; 1. 15, &c.
COME AWAY,] as in v. 10; 7. 11; Ge. 12. 1.
14. DOVE,] as in 1. 15; 4. 1; 5. 2, 12, &c.
CLEFTS,] as in Jer. 49. 16; Obad. 3.
ROCK,] as in Nu. 20. 8, 10, 11; 24. 21, &c.
SECRET PLACE,] as in 13. 6; 27. 15, 24.
ASCENT,] as in Eze. 38. 20.
TO SEE,] as in Ex. 33. 18; Jud. 1. 24; Ps.
35. 7
APPEARANCE,] as in 5. 15; Ge. 2. 9; 12. 11.
CAUSE TO HEAR,] as in 8. 13; Ps. 66. 8, &c.
VOICE,] as in v. 8, 12; 5. 2; 8. 13, &c.

SWEET,] as in Prov. 20. 17.
COUNTENANCE,] as in 5. 15; Ge. 2. 9; 12. 11
COMELY,] as in 1. 5; 4. 3; 6. 4, &c.
15. SEIZE YE,] as in Ex. 4. 4; Lu. 3. 15, &c
FOXES,] as in Jud. 15. 4; Neh. 4. 3; Ps. 63.
10; Lam. 5. 18; Eze. 13. 4.
LITTLE,] as in 8. 8; Ge. 9. 24; 27. 15, 42, &c.
VINEYARDS,] as in 1. 6, 14; 7. 12; 8. 11, 12.
SWEET SMELLING VINE,] as in v. 13; 7. 12.
16. BELOVED,] as in v. 3, 8, 9, 10, 17, &c.
DELIGHTING,] as in 1. 8; 4. 5; 6. 3, &c.
LILIES,] as in 4. 5; 5. 13; 6. 2. 3; 7. 2, &c.
17. DAY,] the light of day; as in 3. 11; 4.
6; 8. 8, &c.
BREAK FORTH,] as in 4. 6.
SHADOWS,] as in 4. 6; Job 40. 22; Jer. 6. 4.
FLED AWAY,] as in 4. 6; Ge. 14. 10, &c.
TURN,] as in Jos. 6. 7; 1 Sa. 22. 17, 18, &c.
BE LIKE,] as in 8. 14.
ROE,] as in v. 7, 9; 3. 5; 8. 14, &c.
SEPARATION,] as in Ge. 15. 10; Jer. 34.
18, 19.

III. 1. COUCH,] as in Ge. 49. 1; Ex. 8. 3, &c.
BY NIGHT,] as in v. 8; 5. 2; Ge. 1. 5, &c.
SOUGHT,] as in v. 2; 5. 6; Nu. 16. 10, &c.
LOVED,] as in v. 2, 3, 4; 1. 3, 4, 7; Ge. 22. 2
FOUND NOT,] as in v. 3, 4; 5. 6, 7; Ge. 2. 22.
2. PRAY,] as in Ge. 12. 11, 13; 18. 4, 30, &c.
LET ME ARISE,] as in Ge. 4. 8; 18. 16; 19.
4, 35.
GO ROUND,] as in De. 32. 10; Ps. 7. 7.
CITY,] as in v. 3; 5. 7; Ge. 4. 17; 10. 11, 12.
STREETS,] as in Prov. 7. 8; Ecc. 12. 4, 5.
BROAD PLACES,] as in Ge. 19. 2; De. 13. 16.
3. WATCHMAN,] as in 5. 7; Ge. 4. 9, &c.
FOUND,] as in v. 1, 2, 4; 5. 6, 7; Ge. 2. 20.
SAW YE,] as in 6. 9; Ge. 7. 1; 9. 16, 23, &c.
4. LITTLE,] as in Ge. 18. 4; 24. 17, 43, &c.
PASSED ON,] as in 2. 11; 5. 6; Ge. 15. 17, &c.
SEIZED,] as in De. 4. 31; 31. 6, 8; Jos. 1. 5.
LET GO,] as in 2. 15; Ge. 8; Jos. 1. 5.
BROUGHT,] as in 1. 4; 2. 4; Ge. 4. 4, &c.
MOTHER,] as in v. 11; 1. 6; 6. 9, &c.
CHAMBER,] as in 1. 4; Ge. 43. 30; Ex. 8. 3.
CONCEIVED,] as in Ge. 49. 26; Hos. 2. 5.
5. ADJURED,] as in 2. 7; 5. 8, 9; 8. 4, &c.
SHE PLEASE,] as in 2. 7; 8. 4; De. 25. 7, &c.
6. WHO,] as in 8. 3. 11; 19. 12; 24. 23, &c.
COMING UP,] as in 8. 5; Ge. 14. 6; 16. 7.
WILDERNESS,] as in 8. 5; Ge. 14. 6; 16. 7.
PALM-TREES,] as in Joel 2. 30.
SMOKE,] as in Ge. 15. 17; Ex. 19. 18; Jos.
8. 20.
MYRRH,] as in 1. 13; 4. 6, 14; 5. 1, 5, 13, &c.
FRANKINCENSE,] as in 4. 6, 14; Ex. 30. 34.
MERCHANT,] as in 1 K. 10. 15; Neh. 3. 31.
7. COUCH,] as in Ge. 47. 31; 48. 2; 49. 33, &c
SIXTY,] as in 6. 8; Ge. 5. 15; 25. 26, &c.
MIGHTY ONES,] as in 4. 4; Ge. 6. 4; 10. 9, &c
8. HOLDING,] as in Nu. 31. 30, 47, &c.
SWORD,] as in Ge. 3. 24; 27. 40; 31. 26, &c
TAUGHT,] as in 1 Ch. 25. 7; Isa. 29. 13; Hos
10. 11.
BATTLE,] as in Ge. 14. 28; Nu. 1. 20, &c.
SWORD,] as in Ge. 3. 24; 27. 40; 31. 26, &c
THIGH,] as in 7. 1; Ge. 24. 2, 9; 32. 25, &c
FEAR,] as in Ge. 31. 42, 53; Ex. 15. 16, &c.
NIGHT,] as in v. 1; 5. 2; Ge. 1. 5, 14, &c.
9. KING SOLOMON,] as in v. 11; 2 Ch. 4. 16
WOOD,] as in 5. 4; 8. 14, &c.

CLEAR,] as in v. 9; Job 11. 4; Ps. 19. 8, &c.
SUN,] as in Job 30. 28; Ps. 19. 6; Isa. 24. 23.
AWE-INSPIRING,] as in v. 4; Hab. 1. 7.
BANNERED-HOSTS,] as in v. 4.
11. GARDEN,] as in Est. 1. 5; 7. 7, 8.
WENT DOWN,] as in v. 2; Ge. 43. 20, &c.
LOOK,] as in Ge. 2. 19; 8. 8; 11. 5, &c.
BUDS,] as in Job 8. 12.
VALLEY,] as in Ge. 26. 17, 19; 32. 23, &c.
SEE,] as in Ge. 2. 19; 8. 8; 11. 5, &c.
VINE,] as in 2. 13; Ge. 40. 9, 10; 49. 11, &c.
FLOURISHED,] as in 7. 12; Nu. 17. 18. &c.
POMEGRANATES,] as in v. 7; 4. 3, 13, &c.
BLOSSOMED,] as in 7. 12.
12. CHARIOTS,] as in Ge. 41. 43; 46. 29, &c.
13. RETURN,] as in Ge. 16. 9; 31. 3, 13, &c.
LOOK,] as in Ex. 24. 11; Nu. 24. 4, 16, &c.
SEE,] as in Ex. 24. 11; Nu. 24. 4, 16, &c.

VII. 1. CHORUS,] as in Ex. 15. 20; 32. 19.
BEAUTIFUL,] as in v. 6; 4. 1.
FEET,] as in Ps. 58. 10; 74. 3; Prov. 29. 5.
SANDALS,] as in Ge. 14. 23; Ex. 3. 5, &c.
NADIB,] as in 6. 12.
SIDES,] as in 3. 8; Ge. 24. 2, 9; 32. 25, &c.
ORNAMENTS,] as in Prov. 25. 12.
WORK,] as in Ge. 5. 29; 20. 9; 40, 17, &c.
2. BASON,] as in Ex. 24. 6; Isa. 22. 24.
LACKETH,] as in Ge. 8. 3; 18. 28; De. 8. 9.
BODY,] as in Ge. 25. 23, 24; 30. 2; 38. 27, &c.
HEAP,] as in Ru. 3. 7; 2 Ch. 31. 6—9, &c.
WHEAT,] as in 14; Ex. 9. 32, &c.
LILIES,] as in 2. 16; 4. 5; 5. 13; 6. 2, &c.
3. TWO BREASTS,] as in 4. 5.
YOUNG ONES,] as in 4. 5.
TWINS,] as in 4. 2.
ROE,] as in 4. 5.
4. NECK,] as in 1. 10; 4. 4, &c.
TOWER,] as in 4. 4; 5. 13; 8. 10, &c.
IVORY,] as in 4. 2; 5. 14; 6. 6, &c.
POOLS,] as in 2 Sa. 2. 13; 4. 12; 1 K. 22. 38.
GATE,] as in Ge. 19. 1; 22. 17; 23. 10, &c.
5. HEAD,] as in 2. 6; 4. 8, 14; 5. 2, 11, &c.
PURPLE,] as in 3. 10; Ex. 25. 4; 26. 1, &c.
KING,] as in 1. 4, 12; 3. 9, 11, &c.
BOUND,] as in Ge. 39. 26; 40. 3, 5, &c.
FLOWINGS,] as in Ge. 30. 38, 41; Ex. 2. 16.
6. FAIR,] as in 4. 10.
PLEASANT,] as in Ge. 49. 15; 2 Sa. 1. 26, &c.
LOVE,] as in 2. 4, 5, 7; 3. 10; 5. 8, &c.
DELIGHTS,] as in Prov. 19. 10; Ecc. 2. 8;
Mic. 1. 16; 2. 9.
7. STATURE,] as in Ge. 6. 15; Ex. 25. 10, &c.
LIKE,] as in Ps. 102. 6; 144. 4; Isa. 1. 9;
Eze. 31. 2, 8, 18.
PALM,] as in v. 8; Ex. 15. 27; Lev. 23. 40.
BREASTS,] as in v. 8; 1. 13; 4. 5; 7. 3, &c.
CLUSTERS,] as in v. 8; 1. 14; Ge. 40. 10, &c.
8. GO UP,] as in Ge. 12. 6; 13. 1; 17. 22, &c.
LAY HOLD,] as in Ex. 15. 15; De. 32. 41, &c.
PRAY THEE,] as in Ge. 12. 11, 13; 18. 4, &c.
CLUSTERS,] as in v. 7; 1. 14; Ge. 40. 10, &c.
VINE,] as in v. 12; Ge. 40. 9, 10; 49. 11, &c.
FRAGRANCE,] as in v. 13; Ge. 8. 21, &c.
CITRONS,] as in 2. 3, 5; 8. 5; Prov. 25. 11;
Joel 1. 12.
9. PALATE,] as in 2. 3; 5. 16; Job 6. 30, &c.
WINE,] as in 1. 2, 4; 2. 4; 4. 10, 5. 1, &c.
FLOWING,] as in Ge. 2. 4; 13. 5; 15. 2, &c.
BELOVED,] as in v. 10—13; 1. 2; 2. 3, &c.
UPRIGHTNESS,] as in 1. 4; 1 Ch. 29. 17, &c.

AGED,] as in 5. 2; 1 Sa. 26. 7, 12; 1 K. 3. 20.
10. DESIRE,] as in Ge. 3. 16; 4. 7.
11. COME,] as in 2. 10, 13; Ge. 12. 1, 19, &c.
FIELD,] as in 2. 7; 3. 5; Ge. 2. 5, 19, 20, &c.
12. LODGE,] as in 1. 13; Ge. 19. 2; 24. 54, &c.
VILLAGES,] as in Jos. 18. 24; 1 Ch. 27. 25.
GO EARLY,] as in Ge. 19. 27; 20. 8; 21. 14.
VINEYARDS,] as in 1. 6, 14; 2. 15; 8. 11, &c.
SEE,] as in 1. 6; Ge. 1. 4, 10, 31; 3. 6, &c.
VINE,] as in v. 8; 2. 13; 6. 11, &c.
FLOURISHED,] as in 6. 11; Nu. 17. 8, &c.
SWEET-SMELLING-FLOWER,] as in 2. 13, 15.
OPENED,] as in Job 12. 18; 30. 11; 39. 5, &c.
POMEGRANATES,] as in 2. 13, 15.
BLOSSOMED,] as in 6. 11.
LOVES,] as in 1. 2; 4. 10.
13. MANDRAKES,] as in Ge. 30. 14, 15, 16;
Jer. 24. 1.
FRAGRANCE,] as in v. 8; 4. 3, 12; 2. 13, &c.
OPENINGS,] as in Ge. 4. 7; 6. 16; 18. 1, &c.
PLEASANT THINGS,] as in 4. 13, 16; De. 33.
13—16.
NEW,] as in Ex. 1. 8; Lev. 23. 16; 26. 10.
OLD,] as in Lev. 25. 22; 26. 10; Neh. 3. 6, &c.
LAID UP,] as in Job 10. 13; 17. 4; 23. 12, &c.

VIII. 1. MAKE THEE,] as in v. 7; 7. 12, &c.
BROTHER,] as in Ge. 4. 2, 8—11, 21, &c.
SUCKING,] as in Nu. 11. 12; De. 32. 25, &c.
BREASTS,] as in v. 8; 1. 13; 4. 5, &c.
MY MOTHER,] as in v. 2; 1. 6; 3. 4, &c.
FIND,] as in 5. 8; Ge. 11. 2; 16. 7, &c.
KISS,] as in 1. 2; 2 Sa. 15. 5; 1 K. 19. 18, &c.
DESPISE,] as in v. 7; Prov. 6. 30; 23. 9, 22;
30. 17.
2. LEAD,] as in Ge. 31. 18; Ex. 3. 1, &c.
BRING,] as in v. 11; Ge. 2. 19, 22; 4. 3, &c.
HOUSE,] as in v. 7; 1. 17; 2. 4, &c.
TEACH,] as in De. 4. 10; 5. 31; 20. 18, &c.
TO DRINK,] as in Ge. 19. 32—35; 21. 19, &c.
WINE,] as in 1. 2, 4; 2. 4; 4. 10, &c.
POMEGRANATE,] as in 4. 3, 13; 6. 7, 11, &c.
3. LEFT HAND,] as in 2. 6; Ge. 13. 9, &c.
EMBRACE,] as in 2. 6; Ge. 29. 13; 33. 4, &c.
4. ADJURED,] as in 2. 7; 3. 5; 5. 8, 9, &c.
DAUGHTERS OF JERUSALEM,] as in 1. 5;
2. 7; 3. 5, 10, &c.
STIR UP,] as in 2. 7; 3. 5; Prov. 10. 12, &c.
WAKE,] as in 2. 7; 3. 5; De. 32. 11, &c.
LOVE,] as in v. 6, 7; 2. 4, 5, 7; 3. 5, &c.
SHE PLEASE,] as in 2. 7; 3. 5; De. 25. 7, &c.
5. WHO IS THIS,] as in Ge. 24. 65.
WILDERNESS,] as in 3. 6; Ge. 14. 6; 16. 7.
BELOVED,] as in v. 14; 1. 2, 4, 13, 14, &c.
CITRON-TREE,] as in 2. 3, 5; 7. 8; Prov. 25.
11; Joel 1. 12.
WAKED,] as in 2 Sa. 23. 18; 1 Ch. 11. 11, 20.
MOTHER,] as in v. 1, 2; 2. 6; 3. 4, 11, &c.
BARE,] as in Ge. 16. 1, 15; 19. 38; 21. 3, &c.
6. SET,] as in Ge. 24. 2; 31. 37; 43. 31, &c.
SEAL,] as in Ge. 38. 18; Ex. 28. 11, 21, &c.
HEART,] as in 3. 11; 5. 2; Ge. 6. 5, 6, &c.
ARM,] as in Ge. 49. 24; Ex. 6. 6; 15. 16, &c.
STRONG,] as in Ge. 49. 3, 7; Ex. 14. 21, &c.
DEATH,] as in Ge. 21. 16; 25. 11; 26. 18, &c.
LOVE,] as in v. 4, 6; 2. 4, 5, 7; 3. 5, 10, &c.
SHARP,] as in Ge. 42. 7, 30; Ex. 1. 14, &c.
SHEOL,] as in Ge. 37. 35; 42. 38; 44. 29, &c.
JEALOUSY,] as in Nu. 5. 14, 15; 25. 11, &c.
BURNINGS,] as in De. 32. 24; Job 5. 7, &c.
FIRE,] as in Ge. 15. 17; 19. 24; 22. 6, 7, &c.

7. MANY WATERS,] as in Ps. 93. 4.
QUENCH,] as in Eze. 32. 7.
LOVE,] as in v. 4, 6; 2. 4, 5, 7; 8. 10, &c.
FLOODS,] as in Ge. 2. 10, 13, 14; 15. 18, &c.
WASH IT AWAY,] as in Job 14. 19; Ps. 69. 15.
WEALTH,] as in Ps. 44. 12; 112. 3; 119. 14.
TREAD,] as in v. 1; Prov. 6. 30; 23. 9, 22.
8. SISTER,] as in 4. 9, 10, 12; 5. 1, 2, &c.
BREASTS,] as in v. 1, 10; 1. 3; 4. 5; 7. 3, &c.
9. WALL,] as in v. 10; 5. 7; Ex. 14. 22, &c.
BUILD,] as in Ge. 2. 22; 8. 20; 10. 11, &c.
PALACE,] as in Ge. 25. 16; Nu. 31. 10, &c.
DOOR,] as in Ge. 19. 6, 9, 10; Ex. 21. 6, &c.
FASHION,] as in Ex. 32. 4.
BOARD-WORK,] as in Ex. 27. 8; 38. 7; Eze.
27. 5.
CEDAR,] as in 1. 17; 5. 15; Lev. 14. 4, &c.
10. WALL,] as in v. 9; 5. 7; Ex. 14. 22, &c.
BREASTS,] as in v. 1, 8; 1. 3; 4. 5; 7. 3, &c.
TOWERS,] as in 4. 4; 5. 13; 7. 4, &c.

GRACE,] as in Ge. 15. 15; 26. 29, 31, &c.
11. VINEYARD,] as in v. 12; 1. 6, 14; 2. 15.
KEEPERS,] as in v. 12; 1. 6; Nah. 1. 2.
FRUIT,] as in v. 12; 2. 3; 4. 3, 16, &c.
SILVERLINGS,] as in v. 9; 1. 11: 3. 10, &c.
12. VINEYARD,] as in v. 11; 1. 6, 14; 2. 15.
THOUSAND,] silverlings; as in v. 11; 4. 4.
TWO HUNDRED,] as in Ge. 11. 19, 21, 23, &c.
FRUIT,] as in v. 11; 2. 3; 4. 13, 16, &c.
DWELLER,] as in Ge. 4. 20; 13. 7; 14. 7, &c.
GARDENS,] as in 4. 12, 15, 16; 5. 1; 6. 2, &c.
13. COMPANIONS,] as in 1. 7; Jud. 20. 11, &c.
ATTENDING,] as in Prov. 1. 24; 17. 4; 29. 12.
TO HEAR,] as in 2. 14; Ps. 66. 8; 143. 8, &c.
FLEE,] as in Ge. 27. 43; Nu. 24. 11, &c.
BELOVED,] as in v. 5; 1. 2, 4, 13, 14, 16, &c.
ROE,] as in 2. 7, 9, 17; 3. 5, &c.
14. YOUNG ONE,] as in 2. 9, 17; 4. 5; 7. 3.
HARTS,] as in 2. 9, 17; De. 12. 15, 22, &c.
SPICES,] as in 4. 10, 14, 16; Ex. 25. 6, &c.

VISIONS OF ISAIAH

THE VISIONS OF ISAIAH, son of Amotz, may be divided into two parts, the *first* comprising chapters i.—xxxix, and the *second* ch. xl.—lxvi. inclusive. The first part consists of 20 sections, viz.: i.; ii.—iv.; v.; vi.; vii. —xii.; xiii. xiv. 27; xiv. 28—32; xv. xvi.; xvii.; xviii.; xix.; xx.; xxi. 1—10; xxi. 11, 12, xxi. 13—17; xxii.; xxiii.; xxiv.—xxx. 5; xxx. 6—xxxv.; xxxvi.—xxxix. The second part (xl—lxvi.) may be divided into three, each consisting of nine chapters, viz.: xl.—xlviii.; xlix.—lvii.; lviii.—lxvi. There is no doubt a considerable difference of style in the original between the two great divisions, but there is nothing in this to prevent the whole from being the work of one and the same writer, as all history and tradition testify they are. There are about 58 quotations from the book in the New Testament, 34 of which are from the latter part alone. Isaiah was preceded by Jonah, Amos, Hosea, and Joel.

I. 1. VISIONS,] *lit.* 'vision,' the plural form never occurring. From the enumeration of the four kings, it seems to include the whole book.

ISAIAH,] i.e. 'safety of Jahu,' or 'a safety (is) Jahu.'

AMOTZ,] sometimes confounded with 'Amos,' the prophet.

SEEN,] in mental spiritual vision.

JUDAH,] the kingdom of the two tribes, with

JERUSALEM,] its capital city.

UZZIAH,] who reigned B.C. 806—758.

JOTHAM,] who reigned B.C. 758—740.

AHAZ,] who reigned B.C. 740—724.

HEZEKIAH,] who reigned B.C. 726—697.

2. JEHOVAH,] the Existing One, the God of Israel, not 'the Lord' merely, as in C.V.

HATH SPOKEN,] in vision to the prophet, not 'speaks,' as J. A. Alexander has it in his 'Commentary.'

SONS,] not 'children,' as in C.V.

NOURISHED,] *lit.* 'made great.'

BROUGHT UP,] *lit.* 'made high.'

TRANSGRESSED,] not 'rebelled,' as in C.V.; Sept. 'rejected;' Vulg. 'despised.'

3. OWNER,] *lit.* 'acquirer, purchaser.'

KNOWN,] not 'doth not know,' as in C.V.; the reference is to the past as well as to the present.

UNDERSTOOD.] Sept. Vulg. adds, 'me,' unnecessarily.

4. AH,] *or* 'ho!'; Vulg. and Arabic 'wo.'

SINNING,] not 'sinful,' as in C.V.; it expresses present and habitual action.

NATION.] This is one of the few instances where Israel is reckoned a *goy*, that is, a heathen.

HEAVY,] not 'laden,' as in C.V.

SEED,] i.e. generation, race.

CORRUPTERS,] of themselves and others.

DESPISED,] not 'provoked to anger,' as in C V.; so Sept. Aben Ezra, Kinchi, &c.

HOLY ONE OF ISRAEL,] whom they had 'set apart' as their God.

GONE AWAY,] *or* 'have separated.'

5. WHEREFORE,] *lit.* 'on or concerning what.'

APOSTACY,] *or* 'turning aside;' as in 14. 6; 31. 6; 59. 13, &c.

EVERY HEAD.] So Hitzig, Winer, &c.

EVERY HEART.] So Hitzig, Winer, &c.

6. SOLE OF THE FOOT,] as in De. 2. 5, &c.

SOUNDNESS,] *or* 'sound-place;' as in Ps. 38. 3, 7.

WOUND,] not 'wounds,' as in C.V.

FRESH SMITING,] not 'putrifying sores,' as in C.V.

CLOSED,] pressed, or squeezed.

OINTMENT,] *or* 'oil,' as in 5. 1; 10. 27, &c.

7. DESOLATION,] as in 6. 11; 17. 9; 62. 4, &c.

STRANGERS,] as in 25. 2, 5; 29. 5; 61. 5, &c.

STRANGERS.] Saadias, Doederlein, Lowth, 'an inundation.'

8. LEFT,] perhaps by the Syrians against Ahaz, or by the Assyrians against Hezekiah.

DAUGHTER OF ZION,] as in 3. 16, 17, &c.

BOOTH,] not 'cottage,' as in C.V.; as in 4. 6; Ge. 33. 17; Lev. 23. 34, &c.

VINEYARD,] *lit.* 'prepared place;' as in 3. 14; 5. 1, 3—5, 7, 10; 16. 10, &c.

BESEIGED,] *or* 'preserved,' or 'watched;' as in 48. 6; 49. 6; Eze. 6. 12, &c.

9. UNLESS,] as in 3. 6, 7; 22. 3; Jos. 10. 24.

LEFT,] as in v. 8, i.e. 'caused to remain over;' as in Nu. 21. 35; 24. 19; De. 2. 34, &c.

SHORTLY,] *or* 'as a little thing;' as in 7. 13; 10. 7, 25; 16. 14, &c.

10. HEAR,] as in v. 2; 6. 9; 7. 13, &c.

A LAW,] *lit.* 'direction;' as in 2. 3; 5. 24, &c.

11. ABUNDANCE,] not 'multitude,' as in C.V.; as in 7. 22; 24. 22; 37. 24, &c.

SATIATED,] not 'full,' as in C.V.; as in 9. 20; 66. 11; Jer. 36. 10, &c.

FATLINGS,] not 'fed beasts for the altar, as J. A. Alexander has it.

12. APPEAR.] Syr. 'to see my face.'

TRAMPLE,] not merely 'to tread,' as in C.V.

13. VAIN,] as in 5. 18; 30. 28; 59. 4, &c.

PRESENT,] not 'oblation,' as in C.V.; as in 19. 21; 39. 1; 43. 23, &c.

NEW MOON,] as in v. 14; 66. 23; Ge. 7. 11.

SABBATH,] as in 56. 2, 4, 6; 58. 13, &c.

CONVOCATION,] as in 4. 15.

RESTRAINT,] that is, a day of pretended humiliation and fasting.

14. NEW MOONS,] as in v. 13; 66. 23, &c.

HATED,] as in Ge. 26. 27; De. 12. 31, &c.

BURDEN,] not 'trouble,' as in C.V.; as in 10. 1; 29. 20; 31. 2, &c.

BEARING.] Sept. Targ. Sym. 'forgiving.'

15. SPREADING FORTH,] as in Ps. 68. 14.

HIDE,] as in Lev. 20. 4; 1 Sa. 12. 3, &c.

16. WASH,] as in Ge. 18. 4; 19. 2; 2 Sa. 11. 8; 2 K. 5. 13.

MAKE PURE,] Aben Ezra, 'purify your-
selves;' Hitzig, Henderson, &c. 'be ye
purified.'
DOINGS.] Sept. 'souls,' Vulg. 'thoughts.'
DO GOOD,] as in Ge. 32. 12; Ex. 30. 7, &c.
17. SEEK,] as in 8. 19; 34. 16; 55. 6, &c.
MAKE HAPPY,] not 'relieve,' as in C.V.;
as in Prov. 23. 19.
OPPRESSED.] Gesenius, Hitzig, Ewald, &c.
'oppressors.'
STRIVE,] or 'contend;' as in Ps. 35. 1, &c.
18. I PRAY YOU,] not 'now,' as in C.V.; as
in Ge. 12. 11, 13; 18. 4, 30; Ex. 33. 18, &c.
REASON,] lit. 'are cleared up.'
IF,] not 'though,' as in C.V.
SINS,] or 'errors;' as in 31. 7; 38. 17, &c.
MADE WHITE,] as in Ps. 51. 7.
WOOL,] as in 51. 8; Lev. 13. 47, 48, 52, &c.
19. WILLING,] or 'do will,' or 'desire;' as
in Ge. 24. 5, 8; Lev. 26. 21; De. 13. 8, &c.
HEARKENED.] Sept. adds, 'to me.'
20. REFUSE,] as in Ge. 37. 35; 39. 8, &c.
MOUTH OF JEHOVAH,] as in 40. 5; 58. 14, &c.
21. A FAITHFUL,] or 'stedfast,' not 'the
faithful.'
I HAVE FILLED,] or 'it is full;' as in Ge.
23. 9; 41. 7, 22; Nu. 7. 13, &c.
LODGETH,] lit. 'doth pass the night;' not
'lodged,' as in C.V.
MURDERERS,] as in 2 K. 6. 32.
22. DROSS,] as in v. 25; Ps. 119. 119, &c.
POLLUTED,] not merely 'mixed, 'as in C.V.
23. PRINCES,] as in 3. 4, 14; 9. 6; 10. 8, &c.
APOSTATES,] lit. 'turning aside,' not 're-
bellious,' as in C.V.; as in 30. 1; 65. 2, &c.
BRIBE,] not 'gifts,' as in C.V.; as in Ex.
23. 8; De. 10. 17; 16. 19, &c.
REWARDS,] or 'recompenses;' as in Sept.
PLEA,] or 'strife, contention;' as in 34. 8.
24. AFFIRMATION,] as in 3. 15; 14. 22, &c.
AH,] or 'ho!'; as in v. 4; 5. 8, 11, 18, &c.
EASED,] lit. 'comforted;' as in 57. 6, &c.
ENEMIES,] as in 9. 11; 42. 13; 59. 18, &c.
25. TURN BACK,] as in v. 26; 14. 27, &c.
UPON THEE,] or 'against thee;' as in Ge.
1. 2, 20; 6. 1; 8. 1, &c.
PURITY,] or 'potash;' as in 2 Sa. 22. 21,
25; Job 9. 30; 22. 30; Ps. 18. 20, 24.
TIN.] Targ. 'sin;' as in Nu. 31. 22; Eze.
22. 18, 20; 27. 12; Zech. 4. 10.
26. GIVE BACK,] as in v. 25; Ge. 14. 16, &c.
COUNSELLORS,] as in 3. 3; 9. 6; 19. 11, &c.
THOU ART CALLED,] lit. 'it is called to
thee.'
FAITHFUL,] or 'stedfast,' as in v. 21.
27. ZION,] as in 2. 3; 3. 16; 4. 3, &c.
RANSOMED,] as in Lev. 27. 29.
CAPTIVITY,] not 'converts,' as in C.V.
28. DESTRUCTION,] lit. 'breach, breaking.'
TRANSGRESSORS,] lit. those 'stepping' on
in evil; as in 46. 8; 48. 8; 53. 12, &c.
SINNERS,] lit. 'erring ones;' as in 13. 9, &c.
CONSUMED,] or 'ended;' as in 31. 3, &c.
29. ASHAMED,] as in 20. 11; 29. 22, &c.
OAKS,] or 'terebinths;' Sept. 'idols.'
CONFOUNDED,] as in Job 6. 20; Ps. 34. 5.
30. OAK,] as in 61. 3, Eze. 31. 14.
FADING,] as in 28. 1, 4; 34. 4.
31. STRONG,] lit. 'strength;' as in Am. 2. 9.
WORK,] not 'maker,' as in C.V.; so Sept.
Vulg. Targ.

QUENCHING,] as in Jer. 4. 4; 21. 12; Am. 5. 6

II. 1. THING,] or 'word;' as in v. 3; 1. 10.
ISAIAH, SON OF AMOZ,] as in 1. 1.
CONCERNING,] or 'against;' as in 1. 1.
2. HATH COME TO PASS,] not 'shall come
to pass,' as in C.V. Verses 2—4, are supposed to be taken from Micah 1. 1—3, which
see.
LATTER END OF THE DAYS] of the Jewish
dispensation, as the phrase everywhere
means in S.S.
ESTABLISHED,] or 'made ready,' or 'prepared,' so Vulg.
FLOWED,] in great numbers and joy.
3. PEOPLES,] as in v. 4, 6; 1. 3, 4, 10, &c.
TEACH,] lit. 'shew;' as in 28. 9, 26, &c.
OF HIS WAYS,] that is, 'out of his ways,'
or 'some of his ways.'
A LAW,] not 'the law,' as in C.V., nor
'law,' as in J. A. Alexander.
4. BETWEEN,] not 'among,' as in C. V.
GIVEN A DECISION,] or 'made a clearing
up;' as in 11. 4; 37. 4; Ge. 21. 25, &c.
SWORDS,] or 'wasting instruments;' as in
1. 20: 3. 25; 13. 15, &c.
PLOUGHSHARES,] hoes, mattocks, or cul-
ters; as in 1 Sa. 13. 20, 21; Joel 3. 10; Mic.
4. 3.
WAR,] or 'battle,' lit. an 'eating' of one
another.
5. HOUSE OF JACOB,] as in 8. 17; 48. 1, &c.
LIGHT OF JEHOVAH,] which he exhibits.
6. BECAUSE,] not 'therefore,' as in C.V.;
so Sept. Vulg., &c.
FILLED,] or 'full;' not 'replenished,' as in
C.V.
FROM THE EAST,] lit. 'Kedem;' Sept. Vulg.
'as of old.'
SORCERERS,] or 'observers of clouds;' as
in 57. 3; De. 18. 10, 14; Jud. 9. 37, &c.
PHILISTINES,] on the coast of the great sea.
STRIKE HANDS,] not 'please themselves.'
as in C.V.; so Ges. De Wette, &c.
7. IS FULL,] or 'is filled,' not 'has been
filled,' as J. A. Alexander has it.
HORSES,] which was contrary to De. 17. 16.
CHARIOTS,] which were of little use in the
hilly country of Canaan.
8. IDOLS,] lit. 'empty, vain things.' Sept.
'abominations.'
BOWETH ITSELF,] as in 36. 7; 44. 15, 17, &c.
9. LOW,] in Heb. 'Adam;' i.e. common man.
HIGH,] lit. a 'being, substance.'
ACCEPTEST,] lit. 'dost not lift up [thy
face] to them.' Vulg. and C.V. very unnaturally read it as a prayer.
10. ENTER,] as in 22. 15; 26. 20; 30. 8, &c.
BE HIDDEN,] not 'hide,' as in C.V.
FEAR OF JEHOVAH,] as in v. 19, 21; 1 Sa
11. 7; 2 Ch. 14. 14; 17. 10.
HONOUR,] as in v. 19, 21; 5. 14; 35. 2, &c.
HAUGHTY,] lit. 'eyes of height.'
BOWED DOWN,] as in v. 17; Job 9. 3; Ps.
35. 4; 38. 6; Prov. 14 ·19; Hab. 3. 6.
SET ON HIGH,] as in v. 17; Ps. 139 6;
Prov. 18. 10.
12. A DAY IS,] not 'the day .. shall be,' as
in C.V.
PROUD,] or 'gay; as in Job 40. 11, 12, &c
AND LOW ONE,] not, 'and he shall be

brought low,' as in C.V.; so Calvin, Coccheus, Michaelis, &c.
13. CEDARS,] as in 9. 10; 14. 8; 37. 24, &c.
LEBANON,] *lit.* 'the Lebanon,' the 'white' mountain.
EXALTED ONES,] *or* 'lifted up ones,' as in v. 2, 12, 14; 6. 1; 30. 25, &c.
BASHAN,] *lit.* 'the Bashan,' i.e. the 'fat' place.
14. HIGH MOUNTAINS,] as in 13. 2; 30. 25.
EXALTED,] *or* 'lifted up;' as in v. 2, 12, &c.
15. HIGH TOWER,] *lit.* 'great place;' as in Zeph. 1. 16.
FENCED WALL,] as in 25. 2; 27. 10; 36. 1, &c.
16. SHIPS OF TARSHISH,] perhaps, large sea-faring vessels in opposition to smaller ones.
17. BOWED DOWN,] as in v. 11; Job 9. 3, &c.
HUMBLED,] as in v. 11, 12; 5. 15; 10. 33, &c.
18. IDOLS,] *lit.* 'vain, empty things;' as in v. 8, 20; 10. 10, 11, &c.
PASS AWAY,] that is, each of them does so.
19. CAVERNS,] as in 32. 14; Ge. 19. 30, &c.
CAVES,] *lit.* 'pierced places.'
DUST,] not of 'earth,' as in C.V.
TERRIFY,] not 'shake terribly,' as in C.V.
20. CAST,] as in Lev. 1. 16; 14. 40; Nu. 19. 6.
VAIN THINGS OF HIS SILVER,] as in 31. 7.
VAIN THINGS OF HIS GOLD,] as in 31. 7.
WORSHIP,] *lit.* 'bow themselves to;' as in Ge. 37. 10; Lev. 26. 1; Jud. 2. 19, &c.
BATS,] as in Lev. 11. 19; De. 14. 18.
21. CAVITIES,] *or* 'holes;' as in Ex. 33. 22.
CLEFTS,] *lit.* 'boughs;' as in 17. 6; 27. 10; 57. 5.
TO TERRIFY,] as in Ps. 10. 18.
22. CEASE,] as in 1. 16; Ex. 14. 12, &c.
NOSTRILS,] *lit.* 'NOSE;' as in 3. 21; 37. 29.
ESTEEMED.] Sept. omits this verse.

III. 1. LORD,] as in 1. 24; 10. 16, 33, &c.
IS TURNING ASIDE,] as in Job 12. 20, 24; Prov. 28. 9.
STAY AND STAFF,] every kind of support.
EVERY STAY,] not 'the whole stay,' as in C.V.
2. HERO,] *lit.* 'mighty one;' as in 5. 22, &c.
MAN OF WAR,] *or* of 'battle;' as in v. 25; 41. 12; Ge. 15. 3, &c.
JUDGE,] *or* 'magistrate' perhaps, one who exercises merely an executive power.
PROPHET,] public announcer of the will of God, whether that relates to past, present, or future things.
DIVINER,] not 'prudent,' as in C.V.; Targ. 'scribe.'
ELDER,] *lit.* 'bearded one.'
3. HEAD OF FIFTY,] as in 2 K. 1. 9, 14.
ACCEPTED,] *lit.* 'lifted up' of faces.
WISE,] *or* 'skilful;' as in 5. 21; 19. 11, &c.
CHARMERS,] *or* 'whisperers.'
4. YOUTH,] not 'children,' as in C.V.
5. HATH EXACTED,] not 'shall be oppressed.'
MAN,] that is one on another.
NEIGHBOUR,] *lit.* 'friend;' as in 13. 8, &c.
ENLARGE THEMSELVES,] not 'behave himself proudly.'
AGED,] *or* 'elder,' *lit.* 'bearded;' as in v. 2.
LIGHTLY ESTEEMED,] not 'mean,' as J. A. Alexander has it.

HONOURED,] *lit.* the one 'become heavy,' with riches, fame, &c.; not 'noble,' as J. A. Alexander.
6. LAYETH HOLD,] as in 36. 1; Ge. 39. 12, &c
GARMENT,] as in v. 7; 4. 1; 9. 5; Ge. 9. 23
COME.] So Vitringa, Lowth, &c.
RUIN,] *lit.* 'stumbling place;' as in Zeph. 1. 3.
7. LIFTETH UP,] his hand to swear.
BINDER UP,] not 'healer,' as in C. V.
8. STUMBLED,] not 'is ruined,' as in C.V.
PROVOKE,] *or* 'make bitter;' as in Job 17. 2; Ps. 78. 17.
EYES,] Lowth, 'cloud;' as in v. 16; 1. 15.
9. WITNESSED,] *lit.* 'responded;' as in 59. 12.
AS SODOM,] boldly and unblushingly.
HIDDEN,] as in 1 Sa. 3. 18; Job 6. 10; 15. 18; Ps. 40. 10.
DONE,] not 'rewarded,' as in C.V.
10. RIGHTEOUS,] *or* 'just, right.'
EAT,] that is receive and enjoy.
11. WO,] as in Nu. 21. 29; 24. 23; 1 Sa. 4. 7.
WICKED,] *or* 'he who is in the wrong;' as in 5. 23; 11. 4; 13. 11, &c.
DEED,] not 'reward,' as in C.V.
12. PEOPLE,] as in v. 5, 7, 13—15; 1. 3, &c.
EXACTORS,] not 'oppressors,' as in C.V.
SUCKLINGS,] each of them.
EULOGISTS,] *lit.* 'those declaring thee happy,' not 'those which lead,' as in C.V.
CAUSING TO ERR,] *or* 'stray' from the path; not 'destroy,' as in C.V.
SWALLOWED,] as in 25. 7, 8; Ps. 35. 25; Lam. 2. 5, 16.
13. JEHOVAH,] the covenant God of Israel.
PLEAD,] *or* 'contend, strive.'
TO JUDGE,] as a legislator, the 'peoples.'
14. ELDERS,] *lit.* 'bearded ones.'
VINEYARD,] *or* 'prepared place;' as in. 1. 8; 5. 1, 3—5, 7, 10, &c.
POOR,] *or* 'afflicted;' as in v. 15; 10. 2, &c.
15. BRUISE,] as in Job 4. 19; 6. 9; 19. 2; Ps. 72. 4; 94. 5; Prov. 22. 22.
FACE OF THE POOR,] *or* 'afflicted.'
GRIND,] as in Ex. 32. 20; Nu. 11. 8; Job 31. 10.
16. DAUGHTERS OF ZION,] as in v. 17; 1. 8.
HAUGHTY,] as in 52. 13; 2 Ch. 26. 16, &c.
STRETCHING OUT,] as in 25; 9. 12, 17, &c.
DECEIVING,] *or* 'making falsehoods;' not 'wanton,' as in C.V.
17. LORD,] as in v. 17, 18; 4. 4; 6. 1, 8, &c.
SIMPLICITY,] *lit.* 'openness.'
EXPOSETH,] *lit.* 'maketh bare;' as in Ge. 24. 20; 2 Ch. 24. 11; Ps. 141. 8.
18. TURN ASIDE,] as in 1. 25; 5. 23; 10. 13.
EMBROIDERED WORKS,] *or* 'little suns.'
MOONS,] as in Jud. 8. 21, 26.
19. DROPS,] as in Jud. 8. 26.
20. BONNETS,] *or* 'fair things;' as in 61. 3, 10; Ex. 39. 28; Eze. 24. 17, 23; 44. 18.
ORNAMENTS,] *lit.* 'steppings;' as in 2 Sa. 5. 24; 1 Ch. 14. 15.
PERFUME BOXES,] *lit.* 'houses of the soul.'
21. SEALS,] as in Ge. 41. 42; Ex. 25. 12, &c.
NOSE-RINGS,] as in Ge. 24. 22, 30, 47, &c.
22. COSTLY-APPAREL,] as in Zec. 3. 4.
COVERINGS,] as in Ru. 3. 15.
PURSES,] as in 2 K. 4. 23.
23. MIRRORS,] *lit.* 'uncoverers, revealers.'
VAILS,] as in Song 5. 7.

2 K

24. SPICE,] or 'balsam;' as in Ex. 30. 23;
35. 28; 1 K. 10. 10; 2 Ch. 9. 9; Song 5. 13; 6.
2; Eze. 27. 22.
MUCK,]in Heb. 'maq;' Sept. Syr. Ar. 'dust.'
ROPE,]not 'rent,' as in C.V.; so Sept. Vulg.
BALDNESS,] as in 15. 2; 22. 12; Lev. 21. 5.
GIRDLE,] as in 32. 11; Ge. 3. 7; 2 Sa. 18. 11;
1 K. 2. 5; 2 K. 3. 21.
SACKCLOTH,] as in 15. 3; 20. 2; 22. 12, &c.
25. FOR.] So Sept. Vulg. Syr. Targ. &c.
GLORY,] lit. 'fairness,' or beauty.
MIGHT,] as in 11. 2; 28. 6; 30. 15, &c.
26. LAMENTED,] as in 19. 8.
SITTETH,] mourning and desolate.

IV. 1. TAKEN HOLD,] as in 41. 9; 45. 1, &c.
SEVEN,] an indefinite number of persons.
BREAD..RAIMENT,] provided by them-
selves.
REMOVE,] or 'to remove;' as in Nu. 11. 16.
REPROACH,]of barrenness and widowhood.
2. SHOOT,] or 'sprout;' as in 61. 11, &c.
DESIRE,] not 'beauty,' as in C.V.; nor
'honour,' as J. A. Alexander has it.
HONOUR,] lit. 'weight, heaviness;' as in v.
5; 3. 8; 5. 13, &c.
ESCAPED,] part of Israel; as in 10. 20, &c.
3. LEFT,] as a remnant; as in 37. 31, &c.
REMAINING,] over beyond a certain num-
ber.
HOLY,] that is, 'set apart;' as in 1. 4, &c.
FOR LIFE,] or 'for living ones.'
4. IF,] as in Ge. 4. 7; 14. 23; 24. 21, &c.
WASHED AWAY,] or 'bathed;' as in Ex. 29.
4, 17; 30. 19, 21, &c.
FILTH,] lit. 'out-going;' as in 28. 8; 36.
12; 2 K. 18. 27; Prov. 30. 12.
BLOOD,] lit. 'bloods;' as in 1. 11, 15; 9. 5.
PURGETH,] as in 2 Ch. 4. 6; Ex. 40. 38.
BURNING,] as in 5. 5; 40. 16; 44. 15; 2 Ch.
4. 20; 13. 11; Neh. 10. 34.
5. PREPARED,] as in Ge. 1. 1, &c.
EVERY FIXED PLACE,] or 'prepared place,
place made ready;' not 'the whole extent,'
as J. A. Alexander has it.
CONVOCATIONS,] lit. 'callings together;'
as in 1. 13; Ex. 12. 16; Lev. 23. 2, &c.
SMOKE,] as in 6. 4; 9. 18; 14. 31, &c.
FLAMING,] as in 5. 24; 10. 17; 43. 2; 47. 14.
SAFE-GUARD,] as in Ps. 19. 5; Joel 2. 16.
6. COVERING,] or 'booth;' as in 1. 8, &c.
DROUGHT,] or 'wasting;' as in 25. 4, 5; 61.
4; Ge. 31. 40.
RAIN,] as in 5. 6; 30. 23; Ex. 9. 33, &c.

V. 1. LET ME SING,] as in Ex. 15. 1, &c.
I PRAY YOU,] not 'now,' as in C.V.
FOR MY BELOVED,] not 'of my beloved,'
as in C.V., nor 'concerning' him, as J. A.
Alexander has it; as in Ge. 9. 5; Ps. 56. 10.
VINEYARD,] lit. 'prepared place;' as in v.
3, 4, 5, 7, 10; 16. 10, &c.
FRUITFUL HILL,] lit. 'horn, a son of oil.'
2. FENCETH.] So Sept.
CASTETH OUT ITS STONES,]as in 2 Sa.16.6,13.
TOWER,] lit. 'great place;' as in 2. 15, &c.
WAITETH,] as in v. 4, 7; so Sept.
YIELDING,] lit. 'doing, making.'
BAD,] lit. 'base ones;' Jerome, 'labrusca.'
3. INHABITANT,] lit. 'sitter, dweller.'
JUDGE,] according to law and custom.

4. STILL,] or 'any more.'
WAITED,] as in v. 2, 7; 8. 17; 25. 9, &c.
5. CAUSE TO KNOW,] as in Ge. 26. 27, &c.
CONSUMPTION,]or 'burning;' as in 4. 4, &c.
BREAK DOWN,] or 'break through;' as in
2 Ch. 31. 5; Ecc. 3. 3.
TREADING PLACE,] as in 7. 25; 10. 6; 28.
18; Eze. 34. 19; Da. 8. 13; Mic. 7. 10.
6. WASTE,] or 'empty place;' as in 15. 9;
Jer. 2. 15; 22. 6; 50. 3.
PRUNED,] or 'plucked.'
ARRANGED,] not 'digged,' as in C.V.; as
in 7. 25.
RAINING,] as in Job 38. 26.
7. HOUSE OF ISRAEL,] as in 8. 14; 14. 2, &c.
PLEASANT,] as in Ps. 119. 24, 77, 92, 143,
174; Prov. 8. 30, 31; Jer. 31. 20.
WAITETH,] as in v. 2, 4; 8. 17; 25. 9, &c.
CRY,] of distress and anguish; as in Ge. 18.
21; 19. 13; 27. 34, &c.
8. WO,] as in v. 11, 18, 20—22; 1. 4, &c.
JOINING,] lit. 'causing to touch;' as in
Ge. 28. 12; 2 Ch. 3. 11, 12, &c.
FIELD,] lit. a 'broken, cultivated' place;
as in 7. 3; 32. 12; 36. 2, &c.
BRING NEAR,] not 'lay,' as in C.V.
9. WEAPONS,] not 'in my ears,' as in C.V.
INHABITANT,] as in v. 3; 6. 1, 5, 11, &c.
10. ACRES,] lit. 'yokes.'
EPHAH,] as in Ex. 16. 36; Lev. 5. 11, &c.
11. WO,] or 'ho;' as in v. 8, 18, 20—22, &c.
RISING EARLY,] as in Ps. 127. 2; Hos. 6.
4; 13. 3.
STRONG DRINK,] or 'sweet drink;' as in v.
22; 24. 9; 28. 7, &c.
TARRYING,] as in Ps. 127. 2; Prov. 23. 30.
TWILIGHT,] not 'night,' as in C.V.; as in
21. 4; 59. 10; 1 Sa. 30. 17, &c.
12. HARP,] as in 16. 11; 23. 16; 24. 8, &c.
BANQUETS,] lit. 'drink;' as in 25. 6, &c.
BEHELD] attentively; as in 8. 22; 18. 4, &c.
SEEN,] not 'consider,' as in C.V.
13. REMOVED,] as in 24. 11; 1 Sa. 4. 21, &c.
HONOURABLE ONES,] lit. 'honour;' as in
3. 8; 4. 2, 5; 6. 3, &c.
FAMISHED,] lit. 'men of hunger.'
14. SHEOL,] the world of spirits.
ENLARGED HERSELF,] or 'made her soul
broad.'
LIMIT,] or 'statute;' as in 24. 5; Ge. 47. 26.
GONE DOWN,] as in 34. 7; 38. 8; 52. 4, &c.
NOISE,] as in 13. 4; 17. 12, 13; 24. 8, &c.
15. BOWED DOWN,] as in 2. 9; 29. 4; Ecc. 12. 4.
LOW,] lit. 'man, or Adam.'
HIGH,] lit. 'being, or substance.'
HAUGHTY,] or 'high.'
16. JEHOVAH OF HOSTS,] as in v. 7, 9, &c.
SANCTIFIED,] lit. 'separated or set apart.'
17. FED,] as in 14. 30; 61. 5; Jer. 3. 15.
LEADING,] not 'manner,' as in C.V.
WASTE PLACES,] lit. 'dry places;' as in 44.
26; 48. 21; 49. 19, &c.
SOJOURNERS,] not 'strangers;' as in C.V.
18. DRAWING OUT,] as in 66. 19; Jud. 5. 14;
Ps. 109. 12; Am. 9. 13.
VANITY,] or 'emptiness;' as in 1. 13, &c.
19. HURRY,] as in 32. 4; 59. 7; Ge. 18. 6, &c.
HASTEN,] as in 28. 16; 60. 22.
DRAW NEAR,] as in 8. 3; 41. 1; 54. 14, &c.
20. WO,] as in v. 8, 11, 18, 21, 22; 1. 4, &c
PUTTING,] lit. 'setting.'

SWEET,] as in Jud. 14. 14, 18; Ps. 19. 10.
21. INTELLIGENT,] as in 3. 3; 29. 14, &c.
22. MIGHTY,] as in 3. 2; 9. 6; 13. 3, &c.
DRINK,] as in 21. 5; 22. 13; 36. 12, &c.
STRONG DRINK,] as in v. 11; 24. 9; 28. 7, &c.
23. DECLARING RIGHTEOUS,] as in 50. 8;
Prov. 17. 15; Da. 12. 3.
TURN ASIDE,] as in 1. 25; 3. 18; 10. 13, &c.
24. TONGUE OF FIRE,] that is, a flame.
FLAMING,] as in 4. 5; 10. 17; 43. 2, &c.
FALLETH,] *lit.* 'becometh weak;' as in Ex.
4. 26: 2 Sa. 4. 1; 2 Ch. 15. 7, &c.
MUCK,] as in 3. 24.
GOETH UP,] as in 2. 3; 7. 6; 14. 8, 13, &c.
REJECTED,] as in 8. 6; 33. 8; 41. 9, &c.
LAW,] *or* 'direction;' as in 1. 10; 2. 3, &c.
DESPISED,] as in 1. 4; Nu. 16. 30, &c.
25. ANGER,] as in 7. 4; 9. 12, 17, 21, &c.
BURNED,] *or* 'been heated,' not 'kindled,'
as in C.V.
SMITETH,] as in 9. 12, 17, 21; 10. 4, &c.
CARCASE,] *lit.* 'fallen, faded thing;' as in
26. 19; Lev. 5. 2; 7. 24, &c.
TURN BACK,] as in 9. 12, 13, 17, 21, &c.
26. LIFTETH UP,] as in 10. 26; 11. 12, &c.
AFAR OFF,] *lit.* 'from afar.'
HISSED,] as in 1 K. 9. 8; Lam. 2. 15, &c.
SWIFT,] as in 18. 2; 19. 1; 30. 16, &c.
27. WEARY,] as in 28. 12; 29. 8; 32. 2, &c.
SLUMBER,] as in Ps. 76. 5; 121. 3, 4; Nah.
3. 18.
OPENED,] as in 24. 18; Ge. 7. 11; Eze. 1. 1;
Nah. 2. 6; 3. 13.
DRAWN AWAY,] as in Jos. 4. 18; Job 17. 11;
Jer. 6. 29; 10. 20.
SANDALS,] as in 11. 15; 20. 2; Ge. 14. 23, &c.
28. ARROWS,] as in 7. 24; 37. 33; 49. 2, &c.
BENT,] *or* 'trodden;' as in 21. 15.
FLINT,] *lit.* 'sharpness *or* rock.'
RECKONED,] as in 40. 15, 17; Ge. 31. 15, &c.
WHEELS,] *lit.* 'rolling things;' as in 17.
13: Ps. 77. 18; Ecc. 12. 6, &c.
HURRICANE,] ac in 17. 13; 21. 1; 29. 6, &c.
29. ITS ROARING,] *lit.* 'roaring is to it.'
LIONESS,] as in 30. 6; Ge. 49. 9; Nu. 23. 24.
HOWLETH,] as in v. 30; Prov. 5. 11; Eze.
24. 23.
PREY,] *lit.* a 'torn thing;' as in 13. 8, &c.
CARRIETH AWAY SAFELY,] *lit.* 'causeth to
escape;' as in Mic. 6. 14.
DELIVERING,] *lit.* 'snatching;' as in 42.
22; 43. 13; De. 32. 29, &c.
30. HOWLING,] as in v. 29; Prov. 5. 11;
Eze. 24. 23.
DISTRESS,] *lit.* 'straitness, sharpness;' as
in v. 30; 25. 4; 26. 16, &c.
ABUNDANCE,] *lit.* 'droppings.'

VI. 1. UZZIAH,] B.C. 760.
I SEE,] not 'I saw,' as in C.V.
THE LORD,] the 'basis *or* foundation' of
all things.
TRAIN,] *or* 'hem, skirt;' as in Ex. 28. 33,
34; 39. 24—26; Jer. 13. 22, 26; Lam. 1. 9;
Nah. 3. 5.
FILLING,] as in 1. 21; 22. 2; 51. 20, &c.
TEMPLE,] as in 44. 28; 66. 6; 1 Sa. 1. 9, &c.
2. SERAPHS,] *lit.* 'burning ones;' as in v. 6.
STANDING,] as in 3. 13; 11. 10; 21. 8, &c.
WINGS,] *lit.* 'six wings six wings are to one.'
FLIETH,] as in Ge. 1. 20.

3. HOLY,] that is, 'separate,' apart from
all.
FULNESS,] as in 8. 8; 31. 4; 34. 1; 42. 10, &c.
4. THRESHOLDS,] *lit.* 'extremities;' as in
Jud. 19. 27; 1 K. 14. 17; 2 K. 12. 9, &c.
CALLING,] as in v. 3.
HOUSE,] that is, the temple, as in v. 1.
SMOKE,] as in 4. 5; 9. 18; 14. 31; 34. 10, &c.
5. WO,] as in 1. 4, 24; 5. 8, 11, 18, 20, &c.
SILENT,] *or* 'cut off;' as in 15. 1, &c.
6. FLEE,] as in 60. 8; De. 4. 17; Jud. 4. 21.
BURNING,] not 'live,' as in C.V.
7. STRIKETH,] as in 16. 6; Ge. 26. 29, &c.
TURNED ASIDE,] as in 11. 13; 14. 25, &c.
COVERED,] not 'purged,' as in C.V.
8. THE LORD,] as in v. 1.
SEND,] as in 19. 20; 36. 2; 37. 2, 9, 21, &c.
FOR US.] Compare Ge. 1. 26; 3. 22, &c.
9. UNDERSTAND,] as in v. 10; 28. 9, &c.
10. DECLARE FAT,] not 'make fat,' as in
C.V.; the Hiphil conjugation in Hebrew is
permissive or *declarative*, as well as *causa-*
tive; see the Grammars of Gesenius, Lee, &c.
UNDERSTAND,] as in v. 9.
HEALTH,] *lit.* 'healing;' as in 19. 22; 57.
19; Jer. 33. 6.
11. WITHOUT,] *lit.* 'from want of.'
BE WASTED,] as in 17. 12, 13.
12. PUT FAR OFF,] as in 26. 15; 29. 13;
Eze. 43. 9.
13. TENTH,] as in Ge. 8. 5; Ex. 16..36.
BURNING,] not 'shall be eaten,' as in C.V.
IN FALLING,] *or* in 'casting.'

VII. 1. AHAZ,] B. C. 472.
JUDAH,] including Benjamin.
REZIN,] i.e. 'firm, stable, prince.'
ARAM,] i.e. a 'high place.'
PEKAH,] i.e. 'open.'
ISRAEL,] that is, the ten tribes.
JERUSALEM,] i.e. 'possession of peace.'
TO FIGHT,] *lit.* 'to be fought with.'
2. DECLARED,] *or* 'set before;' as in Ge. 22.
20: 27. 42; 31. 22, &c.
HOUSE OF DAVID,] ruling in Judah.
LED,] not 'is confederate,' as in C.V.
TOWARDS,] *or* 'along with.'
EPHRAIM,] that is, the ten tribes.
MOVED,] as in 6. 4; 24. 20; Ex. 20. 18, &c.
PRESENCE,] *lit.* 'from the face of.'
3. JEHOVAH,] the covenant God of Israel.
GO FORTH,] as in 22. 20; 36. 16; 48 20, &c.
I PRAY THEE,] not 'now,' as in C.V.
SHEAR-JASHUB,] i.e. a 'remnant return-
eth.'
CONDUIT,] *lit.* a 'thing causing to go up.'
POOL,] *lit.* 'blessing,' because of the value
of water.
HIGHWAY,] *lit.* 'a place raised up.'
FULLER,] *or* 'washerman;' as in 2 K. 18.
17; Isa. 36. 2.
4. TAKE HEED,] *or* 'be watchful.'
TIMID,] *lit.* 'tender;' as in De. 20. 3; Jer.
51. 46.
TAILS,] as in 9. 14, 15; 19. 15; Ex. 4. 4; De.
28. 13, 44; Jud. 15. 4; Job 40. 17.
SMOKING,] as in Ex. 20. 18.
BRANDS,] as in Am. 4. 11; Zech. 3. 2.
FIERCENESS,] *lit.* 'heat;' as in Ex 11. 8;
De. 29. 24; 1 Sa. 20. 34; 2 Ch. 25. 10; Lam
2. 3.

5. COUNSELLED,] as in 14. 24, 27; 19. 12, &c.
EPHRAIM,] that is, the ten tribes.
6. WE GO UP,] as in 2. 3; 5. 24; 14. 8, 13, &c.
VEX,] *lit.* 'disgust.'
REND,] *or* 'cleave.'
TABEAL,] i.e. 'goodness of God,' **or** 'good is God.'
7. LORD JEHOVAH,] as in 3. 15; 10. 23, 24.
STAND,] *or* 'rise;' as in 8. 10; 14. 21, 24, &c.
HEAD,] as in v. 9, 20; 1. 5, 6; 2. 2; 9. 14, 15.
BROKEN,] *or* 'brought down;' as in 30. 31.
9. REMAIN STEDFAST,] as in 43. 10; Ex. 4. 15
MADE STEDFAST,] as in 60. 4; Ge. 42. 20, &c.
10. ADDETH,] as in 1. 5, 13; 8. 5; 10. 20, &c.
11. ASK,] as in 45. 11; De. 4. 32; 32. 7, &c.
SIGN,] *or* 'token;' as in v. 14; 8. 18; 19. 20.
THY GOD,] whom he professed to worship.
REQUEST,] *or* 'asking.'
MAKE HIGH,] as in Eze. 21. 26.
12. TRY,] not 'tempt,' as in C.V.
13. I PRAY YOU,] not 'now,' as in C.V.
HOUSE OF DAVID,] not Ahaz merely.
MY GOD,] the God of Israel also.
14. SIGN,] *or* 'token;' as in v. 11; 8. 18, &c.
THE VIRGIN,] not 'a virgin,' as in C.V.; as in Ge. 24. 43; Ex. 2. 8; Ps. 68. 25; Prov. 30. 19; Song 1. 3; 6. 8.
CONCEIVING,] *or* 'bearing, yielding.'
IMMANUEL,] i.e. 'with us (he is) God.'
15. BUTTER,] as in v. 22; Ge. 18. 8; De. 32. 14; Jud. 5. 25; 2 Sa. 17. 29; Job 20. 17; Prov. 30. 33.
16. REFUSE,] as in v. 15; 30. 12; Jer. 14. 19; Lam. 3. 45; 5. 22; Am. 2. 4.
FIX ON,] as in v. 15; 1 Sa. 2. 28; Eze. 20. 5.
FORSAKEN,] *or* 'abandoned;' as in 18. 6; Lev. 26. 43; Job 18. 4.
VEXED,] *or* 'disgusted.'
BECAUSE OF,] *lit.* 'from the face of.'
17. BRINGETH,] as in 31. 2; 43. 5; 46. 11, &c.
KING OF ASSHUR,] through his instrumentality.
18. HISS,] as in Job 27. 23; Jer. 19. 8; 49. 17; 50. 13; Zeph. 2. 15; Zech. 10. 8.
BEE,] as in De. 1. 44; Jud. 14. 8; Ps. 118. 12.
19. RESTED,] as in v. 2; 11. 2; 14. 7, &c.
DESOLATE VALLEYS.] Sept. 'clefts of the land.'
HOLES OF THE ROCKS,] as in Jer. 13. 4; 16. 16.
THORNS.] Sept. 'caves.'
COMMENDABLE THINGS,] not 'bushes,' as in C.V.; Sept. 'ravines.'
20. SHAVE,] as in Ge. 41. 14; Lev. 13. 33, &c.
HIRED.] Aquila, Sym., Theod., read 'drunken.' So Alex. MS.
RIVER,] that is, the Euphrates.
HAIR OF THE FEET.] Not mentioned again.
CONSUMETH,] *or* 'endeth;' as in Ge. 18. 23, 24.
21. KEEPETH ALIVE,] as in Ge. 12. 12, &c.
22. ABUNDANCE,] as in 1. 11; 24. 22; 37. 24.
YIELDING,] *lit.* 'making;' as in 5. 2, 4, &c.
MILK,] *or* 'fat;' as in 28. 9; 55. 1; 60. 16.
BUTTER.] Gesenius reads 'curds.'
23. PLACE,] as in 5. 8; 13. 13; 14. 2, &c.
SILVERLINGS.] Sept. 'shekels.'
THORNS,] as in v. 24, 25; 5. 6; 9. 18, &c.
24. ARROWS,] as in 5. 28; 37. 33; 49. 2, &c.
25. HILLS,] as in 2. 2, 3, 14; 4. 5; 5. 25, &c.
MATTOCK,] *lit.* an 'arranger.'

KEPT IN ORDER,] *or* 'arranged;' as in 5. 6
SENDING FORTH,] as in Est. 9. 19, 22.
TREADING,] as in 5. 5; 10. 6; 28. 18, &c.

VIII. 1. ME,] that is, the prophet Isaiah.
TABLET,] *lit.* a 'revealer;' or a 'thing rolled up.'
GRAVING TOOL,] not 'pen,' as in C.V.
2. FAITHFUL,] *or* 'stedfast;' as in 1. 21, 26.
TESTIFY,] as in De. 31. 28; 1 Sa. 8. 9, &c.
URIAH,] i.e. 'light of Jah.'
ZECHARIAH,] i.e. 'remembered of Jah.'
JEBERECHIAH.] Sept. 'Barachias.'
3. DRAW NEAR,] as in Ge. 27. 41; 37. 18, &c.
PROPHETESS,] as in Ex. 15. 20; Jud. 4. 4; 2 K. 22. 14; 2 Ch. 34. 22; Neh. 6. 14.
MAHER-SHALAL-HASH-BAZ,] as explained in v. 1.
YOUTH,] not 'child,' as in C.V.
4. MY FATHER,] as in 37. 12; Ge. 24. 7, &c.
MY MOTHER,] as in 49. 1; Jos. 2. 13, &c.
TAKETH AWAY,] *or* 'lifteth up.'
5. ADDETH,] as in 1. 5, 13; 7. 10; 10. 20, &c.
6. REFUSED,] as in 5. 24. Sept. 'chose not.'
SHILOAH,] *lit.* 'thing sent.'
GO SOFTLY,] as in 2 Sa. 18. 5; 1 K. 21. 27; Job 15. 11.
7. BRINGING UP,] as in 63. 11; 66. 3, &c.
MIGHTY,] *lit.* 'bony;' as in 53. 12; 60. 22.
GREAT,] *or* 'numerous;' as in v. 15; 2. 3.
STREAMS,] as in 2 Sa. 22. 16. Sept. 'valley.'
BANKS,] *or* 'heaps;' as in Jos. 3. 15; 4. 18; 1 Ch. 12. 15. Sept. 'wall.'
PASSED ON,] as in 24. 5; Jud. 5. 26, &c.
OVERFLOW,] as in Lev. 15. 11; Ps. 69. 2; 124. 4; Da. 11. 10, 40.
PASSED OVER,] as in 21. 17; 10. 28, 29, &c.
COMETH,] as in 6. 7; 26. 5; 30. 4; Ex. 4. 25.
FULNESS,] as in 6. 3; 31. 4; 34. 1, &c.
IMMANUEL,] as in 7. 16.
9. FRIENDS,] *or* 'associated;' so Targ. Vulg.; Sept. 'know ye.'
BROKEN,] *or* 'brought down;' Sept. 'conquered.'
GIVE EAR,] as in 1. 2, 10; 28. 23; 32. 9, &c.
10. TAKE COUNSEL,] *lit.* 'counsel ye counsel.'
STAND,] *lit.* 'rise. '
11. INSTRUCTETH,] as in 28. 26; Job 4. 3, &c.
WALKING IN THE WAY,] as in Ge. 11. 31, &c.
12. CONFEDERACY,] *or* 'bond;' as in 2 Sa. 15. 12, &c.
DECLARE FEARFUL,] *or* 'terrible.'
13. JEHOVAH OF HOSTS,] as in v. 18; 1. 9, 24.
SANCTIFY,] *or* 'set apart.'
DREAD,] *or* 'terrible one;' as in v. 12, &c.
14. SANCTUARY,] *or* 'set apart place.'
ROCK OF FALLING,] as in 57. 14; Lev. 19. 14.
TWO HOUSES,] that is Judah and Ephraim.
15. STUMBLED,] as in Ex. 10. 7; 23. 33, &c.
BROKEN,] as in 14. 29; 24. 10; 28. 13, &c.
SNARED,] as in 28. 13; Prov. 6. 2.
CAPTURED,] as in 24. 18; 28. 13; 1 K. 16. 18.
SEAL,] as in Est. 8. 8; Da. 12. 4.
LAW,] *or* 'direction;' as in v. 20; 1. 10, &c.
DISCIPLES,] *lit.* 'taught ones;' as in 50. 4; 54. 13; Jer. 2. 24; 13. 23.
17. WAITED,] as in 5. 4; 25. 9; 26. 8, &c.
HIDING,] *lit.* 'making secret.'
18. CHILDREN,] as in 2. 6; 9. 6; 11. 7, &c.
SIGNS,] *or* 'tokens;' as in 7. 11, 14; 19. 20.

WONDERS,] *lit.* 'fair things;' as in 20. 3, &c.
ZION,] the 'dry or sunny' place.
19. SEEK,] as in 1. 17; 34. 16; 55. 6, &c.
FAMILIAR SPIRITS,] *lit.* 'bottles.'
WIZARDS,] *lit.* 'knowing ones.'
CHATTER,] as in 10. 14.
FOR,] in behalf of; as in 1 Sa. 7. 9, &c.
20. LAW,] *or* 'direction;' as in v. 16; 1. 10.
DAWN,] *lit.* 'darkness,' either of morning or of evening.
21. PASSED OVER,] as in v. 8; 10. 28, 29, &c.
HARDENED,] *or* 'sharpened.'
WROTH,] *or* 'shown itself wroth;' as in Lev. 20. 9; 2 Sa. 19. 21; Job 7. 6, &c.
GOD.] Sept. 'fathers' ordinances.'
LOOKED,] as in 53. 6; 56. 11; Lev. 26. 9, &c.
22. LOOKETH ATTENTIVELY,] as in 5. 12, &c.
ADVERSITY,] *or* 'straitness; as in 30. 6, &c.
DIMNESS,] *or* 'weariness.'

IX. 1. FORMER TIME,] as in De. 19. 14, &c.
MADE LIGHT OF,] as in 1 Sa. 6. 5; 2 Sa. 19. 43; Eze. 22. 7.
LATTER,,] as in Ge. 33. 2; Ex. 4. 8, &c.
MADE HONOURED,] *lit.* 'heavy.'
SEA,] of Galilee or Genneseret.
GALIL,] i.e. 'circuit' of the nations.
2. WALKING IN DARKNESS,] as in Ecc. 2. 14.
HAVE SEEN,] not 'shall see,' as in C.V.
DEATH-SHADE,] *or* 'deep darkness; as in Job 3. 5; 10. 21, 22; 12. 22, &c.
SHONE,] as in Job 22. 28.
3. MULTIPLIED,] as in Ge. 7 (. 20; 26. 4, &c.
ITS JOY,] *lit.* 'joy to it;' the Masoretic text for 'to it' reads 'not.'
JOYED,] as in 14. 8; Ex. 4. 14; Lev. 23. 40.
HARVEST,] *lit.* 'reaping' time.
REJOICE,] as in 25. 9; 29. 19; 35. 1, 2, &c.
APPORTIONING,] as in Jos. 19. 51; Prov. 16. 19.
4. YOKE,] as in 10. 27; 14. 25; 47. 6, &c.
STAFF,] *or* 'rod;' as in 10. 5, 15, 24, 26, &c.
ROD,] *or* 'sceptre;' as in 10. 5, 15, 24, &c.
BROKEN,] *or* 'brought down.'
5. FUEL,] *lit.* 'food;' as in v. 19.
6. CHILD,] *or* 'lad;' as in 6. 8. 18; 29. 23.
SON,] *lit.* a 'builder up;' as in 1. 1, 2, &c.
PRINCELY POWER,] *or* 'rule;' as in v. 7.
COUNSELLOR.] Sept. 'messenger of great counsel.'
MIGHTY GOD,] as in 10. 21.
FATHER OF ETERNITY,] or of the 'age,' or of 'duration.'
PRINCE OF PEACE,] *or* 'completeness.'
7. ESTABLISH,] *or* 'make ready, prepare.'
AGE,] *or* 'hidden indefinite time.'
ZEAL,] as in 37. 32; 59. 17; 63. 15, &c.
8. WORD,] *or* 'matter, thing.' Sept. 'pestilence.'
9. GREATNESS OF HEART,] as in 10. 12.
10. BUILD,] as in 5. 2; 45. 13; 65. 22, &c.
RENEW,] *or* 'cause to pass over;' as in 40. 31.
11. SET ON HIGH,] as in Ps. 20. 1; 59. 1; 69. 29; 91. 14; 107. 41.
ADVERSARIES,] *or* 'distressors;' as in 1. 24; 5. 28, 30; 25. 4, &c. Some MS. read 'princes.'
REZIN.] Sept. 'upon mount Sion.'
JOINETH TOGETHER,] *or* 'intertwineth;' as in 19. 2. Targum reads 'stirred up.'
12. PHILISTIA.] Sept. 'the Greeks.'

DEVOUR,] as in v. 18, 20; 11. 7; 26. 11, &c
TURNED BACK,] as in v. 13, 17; 19. 22, &c.
STRETCHED OUT,] as in v. 17. 21; 3. 16; 5. 25
13. SMITING,] as in 10. 20; 14. 6, 29; 27. 7.
SOUGHT,] as in 19. 3; 31. 1; 65. 10, &c.
14. OUTTETH OFF,] as in Nu. 4. 18; De. 12. 29.
BRANCH,] *or* 'bending bough;' as in 19. 15; Job 15. 32.
15. ELDER,] *lit.* 'bearded one.'
ACCEPTED,] *lit.* 'lifted up.'
PROPHET,] proclaimer of God's will, whether past, present, or future. Targ. 'scribe.'
TEACHER,] *lit.* 'shower;' as in 30. 20, &c.
16. EULOGISTS.] those 'declaring them happy;' as in 3. 12; Mal. 3. 15.
CAUSING TO ERR,] as in 3. 12; 30. 28; Mic. 3. 5.
EULOGISED ONES,] those 'declared happy.'
CONSUMED,] *lit.* 'swallowed up.'
17. YOUNG MEN,] *lit.* 'choice ones;' as in 23. 4, &c.
ORPHANS,] *or* 'fatherless ones;' as in 1. 17.
WIDOWS,] *or* 'solitary ones;' as in 1. 17, 23.
PITIETH,] as in 13. 18; 14. 1; 27. 11; 49. 13.
PROFANE,] not 'hypocritical,' as in C.V.; Sept. 'lawless.'
FOLLY,] *lit.* 'fading, falling thing.'
STRETCHED OUT,] as in v. 12, 21; 3. 16, &c.
18. BURNED,] as in 1. 31; 10. 17; Nu. 11. 3.
DEVOURETH,] *lit.* 'eateth;' as in 24. 6, &c.
KINDLETH,] as in 33. 12; Jer. 49. 2; 51. 58.
LIFT THEMSELVES UP.] So Aben Ezra, Kimchi, &c. Syr. 'roll together.'
EXALTATION,] as in 12. 5; 26. 10; 28. 1, &c.
SMOKE,] as in 4. 5; 6. 4; 14. 31; 34. 10, &c.
19. WRATH,] *lit.* 'passing over;' as in 19. 6.
CONSUMED,] *or* 'darkened;' Syr. 'tremble,' Vulg. 'disturbed,' Sept. Targ. 'burnt up.'
FUEL,] *lit.* 'food;' as in v. 5.
20. OUTTETH DOWN,] as in 2 K. 6. 4; Job 22. 28; Hab. 3. 17. Sept. Vulg. 'turn aside;' Targ. 'plunder.'
SATISFIED,] as in 1. 11; 66. 11; De. 6. 11, &c.
ARM.] Targ. 'neighbour.' Alexandrian MS. 'brother.'
21. STRETCHED OUT,] as in v. 12, 17; 3. 16.

X. 1. WO,] as in v. 5; 1. 4, 24; 5. 8, 11, &c.
DECREEING,] *lit.* 'engraving;' as in 22. 16; Jud. 5. 9.
DECREES,] *lit.* 'gravings;' as in Jud. 5. 15.
PRESCRIBED,] *lit.* 'written.'
2. TURN ASIDE,] *or* 'incline;' as in Ex. 23. 2.
AFFLICTED,] *or* 'meek;' as in v. 30; 3. 14.
FATHERLESS,] *or* 'orphans.'
3. INSPECTION,] as in 15. 7; 60. 17, &c.
LEAVE,] forsake or abandon.
4. WITHOUT ME,] as in Hos. 13. 4.
BOWED DOWN,] as in 46. 1, 2; Ge. 49. 9, &c.
STRETCHED OUT,] as in 3. 16; 5. 25; 9. 12, 17.
5. ROD,] *or* 'sceptre;' as in v. 15, 24; 9. 4.
STAFF,] *or* 'rod;' as in v. 15, 24, 26; 9. 4, &c.
6. PROFANE,] not 'hypocritical,' as in C.V.; Sept. 'sinful.'
WRATH.] Sept. omits.
TO SPOIL,] as in Ru. 2. 16; Eze. 38. 12, 13.
SEIZE,] as in 2 Ch. 20. 25; Est. 3. 13, &c.
7. RECKONETH,] as in 13. 17; Ge. 15. 6, &c.
DESTROY,] as in 14. 23; 23. 11; De. 1. 27, &c.
8. PRINCES,] *or* 'heads;' as in 1. 23; 3. 3, 4

9. CALNO,] on the east bank of the Tigris opposite Seleucia.
CARCHEMISH,] on an island in the Euphrates, at the mouth of the Chaboras.
HAMATH,] on the Orontes, Nu. 34. 8.
ARPAD,] near Hamath in Syria.
10. GOT,] *lit.* 'found;' as in 34. 14; 57. 10.
THE WORTHLESS THING,] *or* 'the nothing;' as in v. 11, &c.
11. GRIEVOUS THINGS,] as in 46. 1; 1 Sa. 31. 9.
12. FULFIL,] *or* 'cut off;' as in 38. 12; Job 6. 9; Eze 22. 12; Zech. 4. 9.
GLORY,] *or* 'beauty;' as in 3. 18; 4. 2, &c.
HEIGHT OF THE EYES,] as in Prov. 21. 4.
13. POWER OF MY HAND,] as in Ge. 31. 29.
WROUGHT,] as in v. 11; 2. 8, 20; 5. 4, &c.
REMOVE,] *lit.* 'turn aside;' as in 1. 25, &c.
CHIEF ONE,] *lit.* 'he-goats.'
PUT DOWN,] as in 63. 6; Ge. 24. 18, 46, &c.
14. NEST,] *lit.* 'prepared or established place.'
GETTETH,] *lit.* 'findeth;' as in v. 10; 34. 14.
WEALTH,] *lit.* 'strength;' as in 5. 22; 8. 4.
GATHERING,] as in 17. 5; Ex. 23. 16, &c.
FORSAKEN,] *or* 'abandoned.'
GATHERED,] as in 11. 12; Ge. 6. 21; 30. 23.
MOVING,] as in 16. 2, 3; 21. 14; Job 15. 23.
OPENING MOUTH,] as in Ps. 144. 10.
WHISPERING,] as in 8. 19.
15. AXE,] as in De. 19. 5; 20. 19; 1 K. 6. 7.
GLORIFY,] *or* 'beautify itself;' as in 44. 23; 49. 3; Jud. 7. 2.
HEWING,] as in 22. 16; 1 K. 5. 15, &c.
SHAKING,] as in 19. 16; Zech. 2. 9. Sept. Vulg. 'drawing.'
WARRING,] as in Ex. 35. 24; Ps. 3. 3; Prov. 3. 35; 14. 29; Hos. 11. 4.
THOSE LIFTED UP,] as in Ge. 39. 18, &c.
16. LORD,] as in v. 33; 1. 24; 3. 1; 19. 4, &c.
FAT,] *lit.* 'oily ones;' as in 17. 4, &c.
17. THE HOLY ONE,] the 'one set-apart.'
DEVOURED,] as in v. 12, 20; 1. 19; 3. 10, &c.
18. FOREST,] as in v. 19, 34.
FRUITFUL FIELD,] *or* 'prepared place;' as in 16. 10, &c.
CONSUME,] as in v. 1; 7. 2; 9. 18, &c.
19. YOUTH,] as in 3—5; 7. 16; 8. 4, &c.
20. REMNANT,] as in v. 19, 21, 22; 7. 3, &c.
ESCAPED,] as in 4. 2; 15. 9; 37. 31, 32, &c.
ADD,] as in 1. 5, 13; 7. 10; 8. 5, &c.
TO LEAN,] *or* 'be supported;' as in 2 Ch. 16. 7, 8; Eze. 29. 7.
21. RETURNETH,] as in v. 22; 7. 3; 12. 1, &c.
MIGHTY GOD,] as in 9. 6.
22. SAND,] as in 48. 19; Ge. 22. 17; 32. 12.
CONSUMPTION,] *or* 'completion;' as in Jer. 37. 4.
23. LAND,] of Israel and Judah.
24. AFRAID,] as in 7. 4; 8. 12; 25. 3; 35. 4.
ROD,] *or* 'sceptre;' as in v. 5, 15; 9. 4, &c.
SMITE,] as in 5. 25; 30. 31; 37. 36, &c.
STAFF,] *or* 'rod;' as in v. 5, 15, 26; 9. 4, &c.
25. VERY LITTLE,] as in v. 7; 1. 9; 7. 13, &c.
COMPLETED,] as in 15. 6; 16. 4; 21, 16, &c.
WEARING OUT,] *or* 'fading away.'
26. AWAKING,] *or* 'arousing;' as in 14. 9.
SCOURGE,] *or* 'whip;' as in 28. 15, 18, &c.
27. TURNED,] as in 14. 25; Ge. 19. 3, &c.
DESTROYED.] as in Job 17. 1.
BECAUSE OF PROSPERITY,] *lit.* 'from the face of oil.' Sept. 'from your shoulders.'

28. MIGRON,] as in 1 Sa. 14. 2.
MICHMASH,] north east of Jeba.
VESSELS,] *or* 'instruments;' as in 13. 5, &c.
29. PASSAGE,] as in 16. 2; Jer. 51. 32, &c.
GEBA,] between Benjamin and Judah, as in 1 K. 15. 22.
TREMBLED,] as in 19. 16; 1 Sa. 13. 7, &c.
RAMA,] six miles from Jerusalem.
FLED,] as in 17. 13; 20. 6; 31. 8, &c.
30. CRY ALOUD,] as in 12. 6; 54. 1; Jer. 31. 7.
GALLIM.] Targ. 'Bath-Gallim.'
GIVE ATTENTION,] as in 28. 23; 34. 1, &c.
ANATHOTH,] a priest's city in Benjamin.
31. FLED AWAY,] *or* 'moved off;' as in 21. 15; 22. 3, &c.
HARDENED THEMSELVES,] *or* 'made themselves strong.'
32. NOB,] a priest's city in Benjamin.
REMAIN,] *or* 'stand;' as in Ge. 41. 46, &c.
33. VIOLENCE,] *or* 'terribleness.'
CUT DOWN,] as in 15. 2.
34. GONE ROUND,] as in Job 19. 26.
MIGHTY,] *or* 'honourable one;' as in 33. 21, &c.

XI. 1. ROD,] as in Prov. 14. 3.
STOCK,] *or* 'stump,' as in 40. 24; Job 14. 8.
BRANCH.] Targ. 'king Messiah.'
FRUITFUL,] as in 45. 8; Ge. 47. 27; Ex. 23. 30.
2. RESTED,] as in 7. 2, 19; 14. 7; 2 K. 2. 15.
SPIRIT.] The seven-fold 'spirit' here has been compared with the 'seven' of the Revelation.
3. REFRESH,] *lit.* 'cause him to breathe.'
JUDGETH,] as in 1. 23; 51. 5; Ge. 16. 5, &c.
DECIDETH,] as in 2. 4. Sept. Vulg. 'convict.'
4. POOR,] as in 10. 2; 14. 30; 25. 4; 26. 6.
HUMBLE,] meek or poor; as in 29. 19, &c.
SMITTEN,] as in v. 15; 27. 7; 37. 37, &c.
ROD OF HIS MOUTH,] as in 9. 4; 10. 5, &c.
PUTTETH TO DEATH,] as in Ge. 38. 7, &c.
5. GIRDLE,] as in 5. 27; 2 K. 1. 8, &c.
THE STEDFASTNESS,] as in 25. 1; 33. 6, &c.
6. WOLF,] as in 65. 25; Ge. 49. 27; Jer. 5. 6.
SOJOURNED,] as in 33. 14; 54. 15, &c.
LEOPARD,] panther or tiger.
LIE DOWN,] as in v. 7; 13. 21; 14. 30, &c.
FATLINGS.] Sept. Syr. 'ox.'
LEADER,] as in 2 Sa. 6. 3; 1 Ch. 13. 7; Ps. 80. 1; Ecc. 2. 3.
7. COW,] as in Ge. 32. 15; 41. 2—4, 18—20.
FEED,] as in 27. 10; 30. 23; 40. 11, &c.
YOUNG ONES,] *lit.* 'children;' as in 2. 6, &c.
8. PLAYED,] as in Ps. 219. 70.
WEANED ONE,] as in 28. 9; Ps. 131. 2.
9. EVIL,] as in 41. 23; 65. 25; Ge. 19. 7, &c.
DESTROY,] mar or corrupt.
HOLY MOUNTAIN,] the one I have set apart for myself.
10. ROOT,] as in v. 1; 5. 24; 14. 29, 30, &c.
STANDING,] as in 3. 13; 6. 2; 21. 8, &c.
REST,] *or* 'place of rest;' as in 28. 12, &c.
11. ADDETH,] as in 1. 5, 13; 7. 10; 8. 5, &c
PATHROS,] Thebais or Upper Egypt.
CUSH,] both sides of Red Sea.
ELAM,] that is, Persia.
SHINAR,] the Babylonian plain.
HAMATH,] as in 9. 10.
ISLES OF THE SEA,] as in Est. 10. 1.

12. LIFTED UP,] as in 5. 26; 10. 26, &c.
DRIVEN AWAY,] as in 56. 8; Ps. 147. 2.
SCATTERED,] as in Jer. 22. 28.
ASSEMBLETH,] as in 22. 9; 40. 11; 43. 5, &c.
13. TURNED ASIDE,] as in 6. 7; 14. 25, &c.
ENVY,] or 'zeal;' as in 9. 7; 26. 11, &c.
ADVERSARIES,] or 'straiteners;' as in Ex.
23. 22; Nu. 10. 9; 25. 18.
CUT,] as in 48. 19; 55. 13; 56. 5, &c.
DISTRESS,] or 'straiten.'
14. FLOWN,] as in 6. 6; 60. 8.
WESTWARD,] lit. 'toward the sea.'
THE EAST,] or of ' Kedem.'
SENDING FORTH,] as in Est. 9. 19, 22.
OBEYING,] as in 1 Sa. 22. 14; 2 Sa. 23. 23;
1 Ch. 11. 25.
15. DEVOTED TO DESTRUCTION,] as in 34. 2.
TONGUE,] that is, 'bay;' as in 3. 8; 5. 24, &c.
SEA OF EGYPT,] perhaps the Red Sea.
WAVED HIS HAND,] as in Ex. 20. 25, &c.
SMITTEN,] as in v. 4; 27. 7; 37. 38; 60..10.
TO TREAD,] as in Jud. 20. 43; Job 28. 8;
Prov. 4. 11.
16. HIGHWAY,] or 'raised up place;' as in
7. 3; 19. 23, &c.
LEFT,] as in Ge. 7. 23; Ex. 8. 9, 11, &c.

XII. 1. THANK,] or ' confess;' as in 25. 1.
ANGRY,] as in 1 K. 8. 46; 2 Ch. 6. 36; Ps. 60.1.
TURN BACK,] as in 7. 3; 10. 21, 22; 35. 10, &c.
COMFORT,] as in 51. 19; 66. 13; 2 Sa. 10. 3.
2. SALVATION,] or 'safety;' as in v. 3, &c.
JAH JEHOVAH,] as in 26. 4.
3. DRAWN,] as in Ge. 24. 19, 20, 44, 45, &c.
4. GIVE PRAISE,] thanks or confession.
CALL IN,] not ' on,' as in C. V.
MAKE KNOWN,] as in Ex. 33. 13; 1 Sa. 6. 2.
ACTS,] or 'doings;' as in 1 Sa. 2. 3, &c.
MAKE MENTION,] or ' cause to remember;'
as in 43. 26; Jer. 4. 16.
SET ON HIGH,] as in 26. 5; 30. 13; 33. 5, &c.
5. EXCELLENCE,] as in 9. 18; 26. 10; Ps. 93.1.
6. CRY ALOUD,] as in 10. 30; 54. 1; Jer. 31. 7.
SING,] as in 1 Ch. 16. 9; Ps. 9. 11; 30. 4, &c.
HOLY ONE,] the one 'set apart.'

XIII. 1. BURDEN,] lit. 'thing lifted up;'
Vulg. ' vision.'
BABYLON,] i.e. 'confusion;' as in 13. 1, &c.
SEEN,] in vision.
2. HIGH,] or 'bare, bald.'
LIFT UP,] as in 40. 26; 49. 18; 51. 6, &c.
ENSIGN,] or 'banner;' as in 5. 26; 11. 10, &c.
RAISE,] as in 40. 9; 57. 14; 58. 1, &c.
NOBLES,] or ' liberal, willing ones;' as in
32. 5, 8, &c.
3. GIVEN CHARGE,] as in 23. 11; 34. 16, &c.
SANCTIFIED ONES,] those 'set apart' for
service.
REJOICING,] or 'exulting' ones; as in 22.
2; 23. 7, &c.
4. MULTITUDE,] as in 5. 13, 14; 16. 14, &c.
GATHERED,] as in 57. 1; Ge. 49. 29; 1 Sa.
13. 11.
INSPECTING,] or 'looking after.'
5. AFAR OFF,] lit. 'from afar;' as in 8. 9.
DESTROY,] mar or corrupt; as in 32. 7; 54. 16.
6. HOWL,] as in 14. 12.
NEAR,] as in v. 22; 33. 13; 50. 8, &c.
MIGHTY,] or 'sufficient one,' or 'destroyer.'
7. FAIL,] or ' are feeble.'

MELT,] as in 19. 1; De. 20. 8; Jos. 2. 11, &c.
8. TROUBLED,] as in 21. 3; Ge. 45. 3, &c.
PAINS,] or 'straitnesses;' as in 18. 2; 21. 3;
57. 9, &c. Sept. 'ambassadors.'
PANGS,] or 'cords;' as in 5. 18; 26. 17, &c.
TRAVAILING WOMAN,] as in 7. 14, &c.
PAINED,] as in 23. 5; 26. 17; 45. 10, &c.
MARVEL,] or 'are astonished;' as in Ge.
43. 33, &c.
APPEARANCE,] lit. 'faces;' as in 1. 12, &c.
9. LO,] as in 41. 27; Ge. 1. 29; 12. 11, &c.
DESTROYETH,] as in 26. 14; Nu. 33. 52, &c.
10. STARS,] as in 14. 13; 47. 13; Ge. 1. 16, &c.
CONSTELLATIONS,] as in Job 9. 9; Am. 5.
8. Sept. 'Orions.'
CAUSE TO SHINE,] as in 2 Sa. 22. 29; Ps.
18. 28.
DARKENED,] as in 5. 30; Job 18. 6, &c.
GOING FORTH,] as in 37. 28; Ge. 8. 7, &c.
COME FORTH,] as in 2 Sa. 22. 29; Ps. 18. 28.
11. APPOINTED,] as in 26. 14, 16.
WORLD,] the 'fruit-bearing' or inhabited
part.
TO CEASE,] as in 16. 10; 21. 2; Ex. 5. 5, &c.
MAKE LOW,] as in 25. 11, 12; 26. 5; 57. 9, &c.
12. MORE RARE,] or 'precious,' as in C. V.
13. TREMBLE,] or 'make angry;' as in 24. 18.
SHAKE,] as in 24. 18; 2 Sa. 22. 8, &c.
14. ROE,] as in De. 12. 15, 22; 14. 5, &c.
TURN,] the face, as the original word im-
plies.
FLEE,] as in 10. 3; 30. 16, 17; Ge. 14. 10, &c.
15. ADDED,] or 'admitted.'
16. SUCKLINGS,] as in 1 Sa. 15. 3; 22. 19, &c.
DASHED TO PIECES,] as in v. 18; Hos. 13.
16; Nah. 3. 10.
SPOILED,] as in Zech. 14. 2.
LAIN WITH,] as in Zech. 14. 2.
17. STIRRING,] or 'rousing;' as in Jer. 50. 9.
ESTEEM,] or 'think of;' as in 10. 7, &c.
18. DASH TO PIECES,] as in v. 16; Hos.
13. 16; Nah. 3. 10.
YOUNG MEN,] or ' youths;' as in 3. 4, 5, &c
WOMB,] or 'belly;' as in 44. 2, 24; 46. 3, &c
PITY,] as in 9. 17; 14. 1; 27. 11, &c.
19. BEAUTY,] or 'roe,' as in v. 14.
GLORY,] lit. 'beauty;' as in 3. 18; 4. 2, &c
OVERTHROWN,] as in 1. 7; De. 29. 23, &c.
20. SIT,] as in 3. 26; 14. 13; 30. 19, &c.
CONTINUETH,] lit. 'tabernacleth;' as in 33.
16; 34. 11, &c.
MANY GENERATIONS,] lit. 'generation and
generation.'
PITCH TENT,] as in Ge. 13. 12, 18.
LIE DOWN, 1 as in Ps. 23. 2; Song 1. 7; Eze.
34. 15.
22. RESPONDED,] as in 3. 9; 30. 19, &c.
FORSAKEN HABITATIONS,] lit. 'places of
widowhood.'
PALACES,] or 'temples.'
NEAR,] as in v. 6; 33. 13; 50. 8; 51. 5, &c.
DRAWN OUT,] as in Eze. 12. 25, 28.

XIV. 1. JEHOVAH,] the 'existing one,
God of Israel.
LOVETH,] as in Ex. 33. 19; De. 13. 17, &c.
FIXED,] as in 1. 29; 41. 8, 9; 43. 10, &c.
GIVEN REST,] as in 28. 2; 65. 15; Lev. 16. 23.
2. PLACE,] as in 5. 8; 7. 23; 13. 13, &c.
INHERITED,] as in Lev. 25. 46; Nu. 33. 54
CAPTORS,] as in 1 K. 8. 46, 47, 50, &c.

RULED,] as in Lev. 26. 17; Eze. 34. 4.
3. GIVING REST,] as in De. 25. 19; Eze. 24.
13; 44. 30.
TROUBLE,] or 'raging;' as in Job 3. 17, &c.
BONDAGE,] or 'service;' as in Ge. 29. 27, &c.
4. SIMILE,] or 'ruling' saying; as in Nu.
23. 7, 18, 24, &c.
CEASED,] as in 24. 8; 33. 8; Ge. 2. 3, &c.
5. BROKEN,] as in 30. 14; Lev. 26. 19, &c.
STAFF,] or 'rod;' as in 9. 4; 10. 5, 15, &c.
6. SMITING,] as in v. 29; 9. 13; 10. 20, &c.
INTERMISSION,] lit. 'turning aside;' as in
1. 5; 31. 6, &c.
RULING,] as in 1 K. 4. 24; 5. 16, &c.
PURSUING,] or 'is pursued.'
RESTRAINT,] lit. 'darkness;' as in Ge. 22.
12, 16, &c.
7. AT REST,] as in 7. 2, 19; 11. 2, &c.
QUIET,] as in Jos. 11. 23; 14. 15, &c.
8. FIRS,] as in 37. 24; 41. 19; 55. 13, &c.
REJOICED,] as in 9. 3; Ex. 4. 14, &c.
LAIN DOWN,] as in v. 18; 51. 20, &c.
9. SHEOL,] the unseen world.
TROUBLED,] as in De. 2. 25; Ps. 77. 18, &c.
WAKING UP,] or 'stirring up;' as in 10. 26.
REPHAIM,] as in 26. 14, 19; Job 26. 5, &c.
CHIEF ONES,] lit. 'he-goats;' as in 1. 11, &c.
RAISED UP,] as in 23. 13; 29. 3; Ge. 6. 18.
KINGS OF NATIONS,] as in v. 18; Ge. 14. 9;
Jer. 10. 7.
10. ANSWER,] as in v. 32; 21. 9; 25. 5, &c.
WEAK,] or 'pierced.'
LIKE,] or 'been compared;' as in Ps. 23. 1.
11. EXCELLENCY,] as in 2. 10; 4. 2; 13. 11.
SPREAD,] as in Est. 4. 3.
WORM,] as in Ex. 16. 24; Job 7. 5, &c.
COVERING,] as in 23. 18; Lev. 9. 19, &c.
WORM,] as in 41. 14; 66. 4; De. 28. 39, &c.
12. CUT DOWN,] as in 22. 25; Jud. 21. 6, &c.
13. HEART,] as in 1. 5; 6. 10; 7. 2, 4, &c.
I GO UP,] as in v. 8, 14; 2. 3; 5. 24; 7. 6, &c.
GOD,] lit. 'mighty one.'
RAISE,] as in 49. 22; Ge. 31. 45; 41. 44, &c.
SIT,] as in 3. 26; 13. 20; 30. 19, &c.
SIDES,] lit. 'thighs;' as in v. 15; 37. 24, &c.
14. LIKE,] or 'likened.'
15. SIDES,] lit. 'thighs;' as in v. 13, &c.
16. BEHOLDERS,] as in 28. 4; 29. 15, &c.
LOOK,] as in Ps. 33. 14.
ATTEND,] as in 43. 18; 1 K. 3. 21, &c.
TREMBLE,] as in Job 9. 6.
SHAKING,] as in Hag. 2. 6, 21.
17. WORLD,] the 'fruit-bearing or habitable'
earth.
WILDERNESS,] or 'pasture-land.'
BROKEN DOWN,] as in Jud. 6. 25; 1 K. 19. 10.
OPENED,] as in 22. 22; 50. 5; De. 20. 11, &c.
18. KINGS OF NATIONS,] as in v. 9; Ge. 14.
9; Jer. 10. 7.
19. CAST OUT,] as in Ps. 22. 10; Jer. 22. 28.
ABOMINABLE,] as in Job 15. 16.
SONS OF THE PIT,] those belonging to it;
not 'stones,' as in C.V.; compare the use of
the same word in Ge. 49. 24; Ex. 1. 16, &c.
20. UNITED,] or 'dost not rejoice;' as in
Ge. 49. 6.
DESTROYED,] or 'marred;' as in Ge. 38. 9.
NAMED,] as in 1. 26; 4. 1; 31. 4, &c.
21. PREPARE,] or 'make ready;' as in Ge.
43. 16, &c.
RISE,] as in v. 24; 7. 7; 8. 10, &c.

POSSESSED,] as in 34. 11; 63. 18; 65. 9, &c.
22. RISEN UP,] as in 31. 2; 49. 7; Ge. 37. 7.
AFFIRMATION,] as in v. 23; 1. 24; 3. 15, &c.
CUT OFF,] as in Lev. 17. 10; 20. 3, 5, 6, &c.
CONTINUATOR,] as in Ge. 21. 23; Job 18. 19.
SUCCESSOR,] as in Ge. 21. 23; Job 18. 19.
23. POSSESSION,] as in Job 17. 11; Obad. 17.
THE MIRE,] or 'a daubing.'
OF DESTRUCTION,] or 'to destroy;' as in
10. 7; 23. 11, &c.
24. SWORN,] lit. 'sworn hath been;' as in
19. 18, &c.
COUNSELLED,] as in v. 27; 7. 5; 19. 12, &c.
STANDETH,] as in v. 21; 26. 14, 19, &c.
25. BREAK,] as in Ge. 19. 9; Lev. 26. 26, &c.
TREAD DOWN,] as in 63. 6; Ps. 44. 5; 60.
12; Prov. 27. 7.
TURNED,] as in 6. 7; 11. 13; 59. 15, &c.
TURNETH ASIDE,] as in 10. 27; Ge. 19. 3, &c.
26. COUNSEL,] as in 5. 19; 8. 10; 11. 2, &c.
STRETCHED OUT,] as in v. 27; 3. 16, &c.
27. PURPOSED,] as in v. 24; 7. 5; 19. 12, &c.
MAKE VOID,] as in Ps. 33. 10; 89. 33; Eze.
17. 19.
TURN BACK,] as in 1. 25, 26; 36. 9, &c.
28. KING AHAZ,] B.C. 740—724.
BURDEN,] lit. 'lifted up thing;' as in 13.
1; 15. 1; 17. 1, &c.
29. REJOICE,] as in 9. 17; 25. 9; 39. 2, &c.
PHILISTIA,] as in v. 31; Ex. 15. 14.
BROKEN,] as in 8. 15; 24. 10; 28. 13, &c.
ROD,] or 'sceptre;' as in v. 5; 9. 4, &c.
FLYING,] as in 30. 6.
30. DELIGHTED,] as in 5. 17; 61. 5, &c.
FIRST-BORN,] as in Ge. 10. 15; 22. 21, &c.
LIE DOWN,] as in 11. 6, 7; 27. 10, &c.
PUT TO DEATH,] as in 65. 15; Lev. 1. 16, &c.
SLAYETH,] as in Ge. 4. 8, 14; 20. 4, &c.
31. HOWL,] as in v. 12; 13. 6.
MELTED,] as in Ex. 15. 15; Jos. 2. 9, 24, &c.
32. MESSENGERS,] as in 18. 2; 30. 4; 33. 7.
FOUNDED,] as in 28. 16; 1 K. 16. 34, &c.
TRUST,] or 'take refuge;' as in 2 Sa. 22. 3

XV. 1. BURDEN,] lit. 'thing lifted up.'
DESTROYED,] as in 23. 1, 14; Jer. 4. 13, &c.
CUT OFF,] or 'silent;' as in 6. 5; Jer. 47. 5.
2. WEEP,] as in v. 3, 5; 16. 9; 22. 4, 12, &c.
HOWLETH,] as in v. 3; 16. 7; 52. 5, &c.
CUT OFF,] as in 10. 33.
3 OUT-PLACES,] as in 5. 25; 10. 6; 24. 11, &c.
GIRDED,] as in Ex. 29. 9; Prov. 31. 17, &c.
PINNACLES,] or 'roofs;' as in 22. 1; 37. 27.
HOWLETH,] as in v. 2; 16. 7; 52. 5, &c.
4. CRY,] as in v. 5; 26. 17; Ex. 2. 23, &c.
ARMED,] or 'girded ones.'
LIFE,] lit. 'soul;' as in 1. 14; 3. 9, 20, &c.
5. CRY,] as in v. 8; 65. 19; Ge. 18. 20, &c.
FUGITIVES,] or 'bars;' as in 45. 2, &c.
THIRD YEAR,] as in 37. 30; Jer. 48. 34.
DESTRUCTION,] lit. 'breaking;' as in 1. 28;
30. 13, 14, &c.
WAKE UP,] as in Prov. 10. 12; Song 2. 7; 3.
5: 8. 4.
6. WATERS,] as in v. 9; 1. 22, 30; 3. 1, &c.
WITHERED,] or 'dried up;' as in 19. 5, &c
FINISHED,] as in 10. 25; 16. 4; 21. 16, &c.
7. ABUNDANCE,] as in Jer. 48. 36.
CARRY,] as in 8. 4; 30. 6; 37. 23.
8. GONE ROUND,] as in 2 K. 11. 8; 2 Ch. 23. 7.
9. ESCAPED,] as in 14. 30; 37. 4, 32; 44. 17

XVI. 1. SEND,] as in 6. 8; Ge. 42. 16; 43. 8.
LAMB,] *or* 'ram;' as in 30. 23; 34. 6, &c.
2. WANDERING,] as in v. 3; 10. 14; 21. 14.
CAST OUT,] as in 27. 10; Prov. 29. 15.
3. COUNSEL,] as in 5. 19; 8. 10; 11. 2, &c.
REVEAL,] as in 22. 8; Lev. 18. 7, 11, 15, &c.
4. SOJOURN,] as in 33. 14; 54. 15; Ge. 20. 1.
CEASED,] as in 29. 20; Ge. 47. 15, 16; Ps. 77. 8.
FINISHED,] 10. 25; 15. 6; 21. 16, &c.
CONSUMED,] as in Ge. 47. 18; Lev. 26. 20, &c.
5. ESTABLISHED,] *or* 'made ready;' as in 30. 33, &c.
TENT,] that is, 'dwelling.'
HASTING,] as in Ex. 7. 6; Ps. 45. 1; Prov. 22. 29.
6. PRIDE,] as in 13. 11; 14. 11; 23. 9, &c.
VERY PROUD,] *lit.* 'gay exceedingly.'
DEVICES,] *or* 'parts;' as in Job 11. 3, &c.
7. HOWL,] as in 15. 2, 3; 52. 5; 65. 14, &c.
MEDITATETH,] as in 33. 18; 38. 14; 59. 3, &c.
8. FIELDS,] as in De. 32. 32; 2 K. 23. 4, &c.
LANGUISH,] as in 19. 8; 24. 4, 7; 33. 9, &c.
BEAT,] as in Jud. 5. 22, 26; Prov. 23. 35.
WANDERED,] *or* 'gone astray;' as in 21. 4.
PLANTS,] *lit.* ' things sent forth.'
SPREAD THEMSELVES,] as in 33. 23; Am. 5. 2.
PASSED OVER,] as in 8. 8, 21; 10. 28, 29, &c.
9. WEEP,] as in 30. 19; 33. 7; 38. 3, &c.
10. REMOVED,] *lit.* ' gathered up;' as in 57. 1; Ge. 29. 3; 34. 30, &c.
FRUITFUL FIELD,] *or* 'prepared place.'
PRESSES,] as in 5. 2; Nu. 18. 27, 30, &c.
TREADETH,] as in 63. 3; De. 11. 24, 25, &c.
TO CEASE,] as in 13. 11; 21. 2; Ex. 5. 5, &c.
11. BOWELS,] as in 48. 19; 49. 1; 63. 15, &c.
SOUND,] as in 17. 12; 51. 15; 59. 11, &c.
12. WEARY,] as in 1. 14; 47. 13; Ex. 7. 18.
PRAY,] *lit.* 'judge himself;' as in 1 Sa. 1. 12, 26; 12. 23; 2 Sa. 7. 27.
ABLE,] as in 1. 13; 29. 11; 36. 8, 14, &c.
13. WORD,] *or* ' thing;' as in 1. 10; 2. 1, &c.
14. HIRELING,] as in 21. 16; Ex. 12. 45, &c.
LIGHTLY ESTEEMED,] as in De. 25. 3.
MIGHTY,] as in 10. 13; 17. 12; 28. 2, &c.

XVII. 1. BURDEN,] *lit.* 'thing lifted up;' as in 13. 1; 14. 28; 15. 1, &c.
DAMASCUS,] in *Heb.* 'Dammeseq.'
RUIN,] *lit.* a 'fallen thing.'
2. FORSAKEN,] as in v. 9; 10. 14; 54. 6, &c.
DROVES,] *or* 'herds;' as in 32. 14; 40. 11, &c.
LAIN DOWN,] as in 13. 21; Ge. 49. 9, &c.
TROUBLING,] *or* 'causing trembling;' as in Lev. 26. 6; 28. 26; Job 11. 19, &c.
3. CEASED,] as in Eze. 6. 6; 30. 18; 33. 28.
KINGDOM,] that is, the power of a kingdom.
AFFIRMATION,] as in v. 6;1. 24; 3. 15, &c.
4. WAX POOR,] as in Jud. 6. 6.
5. GATHERING,] as in 10. 14; Ex. 23. 16, &c.
GATHERING,] *or* 'collecting;' as in Jud. 1. 7; Jer. 7. 18.
VALLEY,] *or* 'deep place;' as in 22. 7, &c.
6. LEFT,] as in 24. 6, 12; 49. 21; Ge. 42. 38.
COMPASSING,] as in 24. 13.
GOD OF ISRAEL,] as in 21. 10, 17; 24. 15, &c.
7. MAKER,] as in 22. 11; 27. 11; 51. 13, &c.
HOLY ONE,] *or* 'separate one.'
8. ALTARS,] as in 6. 6; 19. 19; 27. 9, &c.
SHRINES.] *lit.* ' happy things;' as in 27. 9.

9. STRENGTH,] as in v. 10; 23. 4, 11, 14, &c.
LEFT,] *or* 'forsaken or abandoned.'
10. FORGOTTEN,] as in 49. 14; Ge. 27. 45, &c.
SALVATION,] *or* ' safety;' as in 45. 8; 51. 5.
REMEMBERED,] as in 47. 7; 57. 11, Ge. 9. 15.
PLANTEST,] as in 5. 2; 65. 22, Ge. 2. 8, &c.
SOWEST,] as in 30. 23; Ge. 26. 12; Ex. 23. 10.
11. FLOURISH,] as in 32. 12; Ge. 49. 22, &c.
OVERFLOWING,] *lit.* 'inheritance.'
12. MULTITUDES,] as in 5. 13, 14; 13. 4, &c.
SOUNDING,] as in 16. 11; 51. 15; 59. 11, &c.
WASTING,] as in v. 13; 24. 8, 25; 66. 6, &c.
WASTED,] as in v. 13; 6. 11.
15. PUSHED,] as in Ps. 9. 5; 119. 21, &c.
FLED,] as in 10. 29; 20. 6; 31. 8, &c.
14. EVEN TIME,] as in Ge. 1. 5, 8, 13, &c.
PLUNDERERS,] as in 42. 24; Jer. 30. 16; Eze. 39. 10.

XVIII. 1. HO,] as in 1. 4, 24; 5. 8, 11, &c.
AMBASSADORS,] as in 14. 32; 30. 4; 32. 7, &c.
IMPLEMENTS,] that is, 'pens,' not 'ships,' which the original word never means.
LIGHT,] as in 5. 26; 19. 1; 30. 16, &c.
DRAWN OUT,] as in v. 7; Prov. 13. 12.
PEELED,] as in v. 7; 1 K. 7. 45; Eze. 21. 10, 11.
FEARFUL,] as in v. 7; 21. 1; 64. 3, &c.
FROM ITS BEGINNING,] *lit.* 'from it—and farther;' as in v. 7.
BY LINE,] as in v. 7.
TREADING DOWN,] *or* 'trodden down;' as in v. 7.
FLOODS,] *or* ' rivers.'
SPOILED,] as in v. 7; 7. 20; 8. 7; 11. 15, &c.
3. INHABITANTS,] as in 5. 39; 6. 1, 5, &c.
WORLD,] the 'fruit-bearing or habitable earth.
DWELLERS,] *lit.* 'tabernaclers.'
LIFTING UP,] as in 1. 14; Ge. 4. 13; 36. 7, &c.
BLOWING,] *lit.* ' striking;' as in Jer. 6. 9, 13; Jud. 7. 20.
4. I REST,] as in 62. 1; Jud. 3. 11, 30, &c.
SETTLED PLACE,] *or* 'prepared place.'
5. HARVEST,] as in v. 4; 9. 3; 16. 9; 17. 5.
PERFECT,] as in Lev. 25. 29; De. 31. 24, &c.
CUT,] as in 28. 15; Ge. 15. 18; Ex. 24. 8, &c.
TURNED ASIDE,] as in 31. 2; 30. 7; Ex. 23. 25.
6. LEFT,] as in Lev. 26. 43; Job 18. 4.
7. PRESENT,] as in Ps. 68. 29; 76. 11.
DRAWN OUT,] as in v. 7; Prov. 13. 12.
MOUNT ZION,] as in 4. 5; 8. 18; 10. 12, &c.

XIX. 1. BURDEN,] *lit.* 'thing lifted up;' as in 13. 1; 14. 28; 15. 1, &c.
RIDING,] as in 36. 8; Ge. 49. 17; Ex. 15. 1.
ENTERED,] as in v. 23; 2. 19; 7. 17, 36, 10. 28.
MOVED,] as in 29. 9; Job 28. 4; Prov. 5. 6.
IDOLS,] *lit.* 'nothings;' as in v. 3; 2. 8, &c.
MELTETH,] as in 13. 7; De. 20. 8; Jos. 2. 11.
2. ARMED,] *or* 'intertwined.'
FOUGHT,] as in 30. 32; 63. 10; Ex. 1. 10, &c.
3. SWALLOW UP,] as in 2 Sa. 20. 19, 20, &c.
SOUGHT,] as in 9. 13; 31.1; 65. 10, &c.
IDOLS,] *lit.* 'nothings;' as in v 1; 2, 8, &c.
CHARMERS,] *lit.* 'soft ones.'
FAMILIAR SPIRITS,] *lit.* 'bottles;' as in 8 10; 29. 4, &c.
WIZARDS,] *lit.* 'knowing ones;' as in 8. 19

4. DELIVERED,] or 'made secure.'
HARD LORD,] lit. 'lords sharp.'
STRONG,] as in 25. 3; 43. 6; 56. 11, &c.
RULE,] as in 3. 4; Ge. 3. 16; 4. 7; 37. 8, &c.
5. WASTED,] as in v. 6; Ge. 8. 13; Job 16. 11.
DRIED UP,] as in 15. 6; 40. 7, 8; Ge. 8. 14.
6. TURNED AWAY,] as in 2 Ch. 11. 14; 29. 19.
FLOWINGS,] or 'rivers;' as in v. 5.
WEAK,] or 'poor, lean, thin.'
DRIED UP,] as in 40. 24; 1 K. 13. 4; 17. 7.
WITHERED,] as in 33. 9.
7. EDGE,] lit. 'mouth;' as in 5. 14; 6. 7, &c.
8. LAMENTED,] as in 3. 26.
MOURNED,] as in 3. 26; 24. 4, 7; 33. 9, &c.
CASTING,] as in Ps. 147. 17; Mic. 2. 5.
SPREADING,] as in Ex. 25. 20; 37. 9, &c.
LANGUISHED,] as in 16. 8; 24. 47; 33. 9, &c.
9. ASHAMED,] as in 20. 5; 24. 23; 37. 27, &c.
10. FOUNDATIONS,] as in Ps. 11. 3.
WAGES,] lit. 'hire, reward;' as in Prov.
11. 18.
AFFLICTED,] as in 53. 10.
11. FOOLS,] as in 35. 8; Job 5. 2, 3, &c.
ANTIQUITY,] or 'the east, or Kedem.'
12. WISE ONES,] as in v. 11; 3. 3; 5. 21, &c.
TELL,] as in 21. 6; 36. 22; 41. 22, &c.
I PRAY THEE,] as in Ge. 12. 11, 13, &c.
COUNSELLED,] as in 7. 5; 14. 24, 27; 23. 8.
13. FOOLISH,] as in v. 11.
PRINCES,] lit. 'heads;' as in v. 11.
CAUSED TO ERR,] as in v. 14; Ge. 20. 13, &c.
CHIEF,] or 'corner;' as in 28. 16; Ex. 27. 2.
14. MINGLED,] as in Ps. 102. 9; Prov. 9. 2, 5.
DRUNKARD,] or 'merry one;' as in 24. 20.
15. WORK,] as in v. 15, 25; 2. 8; 3. 24, &c.
16. WOMAN,] as in 3. 12; 4. 1; 13. 16, &c.
MOURNED,] as in 10. 29; 1 Sa. 13. 7; 14. 15.
AFRAID,] as in 33. 14; 60. 5; De. 28. 66, &c.
WAVING,] as in 30. 32; Ex. 29. 24, 26, &c.
17. MENTION,] or 'make remembrance.'
COUNSELLING,] as in v. 11; 1. 26; 3. 3, &c.
18. CITIES,] as in v. 2; 1. 7, 8, 26; 6. 11, &c.
SWEARING,] lit. 'sworn;' as in 48. 1, &c.
19. ALTAR,] as in 6. 6; 17. 8; 27. 9, &c.
20. SIGN,] or 'token;' as in 7. 11, 14; 8. 18.
CRY,] as in 42. 2; 46. 7; 65. 14, &c.
21 KNOWN,] as in 61. 9; 66. 14; Ge. 41. 21.
SACRIFICE,] as in 1. 11; 34. 6; 43. 23, &c.
VOWED,] as in Ge. 31. 13; Nu. 30. 10, &c.
COMPLETED,] as in Ge. 44. 4; Lev. 6. 5, &c.
22. SMITTEN,] as in Ex. 21. 22; 1 Sa. 4. 3;
2 Ch. 13. 15; 21. 18.
TURNED BACK,] as in 5. 25; 6. 13; 9. 12, &c.
HEALED,] as in 6. 10; 57. 19; Jer. 33. 6;
Hos. 11. 3.
23. HIGHWAY,] as in 7. 3; 11. 16; 33. 8, &c.
SERVED] Jehovah as their God.
25. BLESS.] as in 61. 9; Ge. 17. 16, 20, &c.
MY PEOPLE,] as in 1. 3; 3. 12, 15; 5. 13, &c.
WORK OF MY HANDS,] as in 29. 23; 45. 11;
60. 21.
MINE INHERITANCE,] as in 47. 6; Ru. 4. 6.

XX. 1. TARTAN,] as in 2 K. 18. 17.
ASHDOD,] as in Jos. 11. 22.
SARGON.] Not mentioned again.
FIGHTETH,] as in Ex. 14. 14; 17. 8, &c.
CAPTURETH,] as in Nu. 21. 32; 32. 39, &c.
2. BY THE HAND,] as in 37. 24; 64. 6, &c.
LOOSED,] or 'opened;' as in 48. 8; 60. 11, &c.
NAKED,] as in v. 3, 4; 58. 7; Ge. 2. 25.

BAREFOOT,] as in v. 3, 4; 2 Sa. 15. 30; Jer.
2. 25.
3. MY SERVANT,] as in 22. 20; 36. 9; 37. 35.
THREE YEARS,] as in 16. 14; 1 K. 2. 11, &c.
SIGN,] or 'token;' as in 7. 11, 14; 8. 18, &c.
WONDER,] lit. 'fair thing;' as in 8. 18, &c.
4. LEAD,] as in Ge. 31. 18; Ex. 3. 1, &c.
OLD,] lit. 'bearded;' as in 3. 2, 5, 14, &c.
UNCOVERED,] as in v. 2, 3; 58. 7, &c.
5. AFFRIGHTED,] or 'brought down;' as
in 31. 9; 37. 27, &c.
ASHAMED,] as in 19. 9; 24. 23; 37. 27, &c.
6. INHABITANT,] as in 5. 3, 9; 6. 1, 5, &c.
TRUST,] or 'confidence;' as in v. 5.
FLED,] as in 10. 29; 17. 13; 31. 8, &c.
DELIVERED,] or 'snatched;' as in Hab. 2. 9.
ESCAPE,] as in 49. 24, 25; Ge. 19. 20, &c.

XXI. 1. BURDEN,] lit. 'thing lifted up.'
WILDERNESS,] or 'pasture-land;' as in 14.
17; 16. 1, 8, &c.
FEARFUL,] as in 18. 2, 7; 64. 3, &c.
2. HARD,] or 'sharp;' as in 14. 3; 19. 4, &c.
DECLARED,] as in 40. 21; De. 17. 4, &c.
BESEIGE,] or 'straiten, distress.'
TO CEASE,] as in 13. 11; 16. 10; Ex. 5. 5, &c.
3. LOINS,] as in 11. 5; 20. 2; 45. 1, &c.
SEIZED,] as in 33. 14; Ex. 15. 14, &c.
BENT DOWN,] as in Ps. 38. 6.
TROUBLED,] as in 13. 8; Ge. 45. 3, &c.
4. WANDERED,] erred or 'gone astray.'
TERRIFIED,] as in 1 Sa. 16. 14; 2 Sa. 22. 5.
5. ARRANGE,] as in Jud. 20. 22; 1 Sa. 17. 8.
WATCH,] or 'look out.'
WATCH-TOWER,] as in v. 8.
EAT,] as in 5. 24; 22. 13; 23. 18, &c.
DRINK,] as in 5. 22; 22. 13; 51. 22, &c.
RISE,] as in 23. 12; 32. 9; 51. 17, &c.
ANOINT,] as in 1 Sa. 16. 12.
6. WATCHMAN,] or 'looker-out.'
DECLARE,] as in 19. 12; 36. 22; 41. 22, &c.
7. CHARIOT,] as in v. 9; 22. 6, 7; 31. 1, &c.
GIVEN ATTENTION,] lit. 'he hath attended
with attention.'
INCREASED ATTENTION,] lit. 'great of at-
tention.'
8. CALLETH,] as a lion, that is, powerfully.
WARD,] or 'charge;' as in Ge. 26. 5, &c.
STATIONED,] or 'set up;' as in 3. 13, &c.
9. CHARIOT,] as in v. 7; 22. 6, 7; 31. 1, &c.
FALLEN,] as in 3. 8; 8. 15; 9. 8, 10, &c.
BROKEN,] as in Ex. 9. 25; 34. 1, &c.
10. DECLARED,] as in 3. 9; 41. 26; 43. 12, &c.
11. BURDEN,] lit. 'thing lifted up;' as in
13. 1; 14. 28; 15. 1, &c.
DUMAH,] i.e. 'silence.'
SEIR,] as in Ge. 32. 3; 33. 14; 36. 20, &c.
WATCHMAN,] or 'keeper;' as in v. 12, &c.
12. MORNING.. NIGHT,] that is, all things
at present are as they were.
ENQUIRE.. ENQUIRE,] continue to make
enquiry.
TURN BACK,] unto me for future intima-
tions of coming events, do not remain in
ignorance.
13. BURDEN,] lit. 'thing lifted up.'
LODGE,] or 'pass the night;' as in 1. 21, &c.
TRAVELLERS,] or 'wayfarers;' as in Ge. 37.
25, &c.
14. THIRSTY,] as in 29. 8; 32. 6; 44. 3, &c.
TEMA,] or the 'south;' as in Ge. 25. 15, &c

FUGITIVE,] *lit.* one 'moving about.'
15. DESTRUCTIONS,] *lit.* 'wastes.'
FLED,] *or* 'moved away or about;' as in
10. 31; 22. 3, &c.
STRETCHED OUT,] as in 1 Sa. 30. 16.
GRIEVOUSNESS,] *lit.* 'heaviness, weight.'
16. LORD,] as in v. 6, 8; 3. 15, 17, 18, &c.
CONSUMED,] as in 10. 25; 15. 6; 16. 4, &c.
17. REMNANT,] as in 7. 3; 10. 19—22, &c.
MIGHTY,] as in 3. 2; 5. 22; 9. 6, &c.
SPOKEN,] and who can gainsay it?

XXII. 1. BURDEN,] *lit.* 'thing lifted up.'
GONE UP,] as in 5. 6; 7. 1; 8. 7, &c.
2. STIRS,] as in Job 36. 29; 39. 7; Zech. 4. 7.
NOISY,] as in 1 K. 1. 41; Prov. 1. 21, &c.
EXULTING,] as in 13. 3; 23. 7; 24. 8, &c.
PIERCED,] as in 34. 3; 66. 16; Ge. 34. 27.
3. RULERS,] as in 1. 10; 3. 6, 7; Jos. 10. 24.
FLED,] *or* 'moved away;' as in Ge. 31. 22.
4. LOOK,] as in Job 14. 6.
BITTER,] as in Ge. 49. 23; Ex. 1. 14.
HASTE NOT,] *or* 'be not urgent;' as in
Ge. 19. 15.
COMFORT,] as in 61. 2; Ge. 37. 35, &c.
5. NOISE,] as in De. 7. 23; 28. 20, &c.
PERPLEXITY,] *or* 'intermingling;' as in
Mic. 7. 4.
VALLEY OF VISION,] as in v. 1.
6. BORNE,] *or* 'lifted up;' as in 11. 11, &c.
KIR,] supposed to be a river in the Cau-
casus, emptying into the Caspian.
EXPOSED,] *or* 'made bare;' as in Zeph. 2.14.
7. CHOICE,] as in 37. 24; Ge. 23. 6; Ex. 15. 4.
8. REMOVETH,] *lit.* 'revealeth;' as in 16. 3.
COVERING,] as in Ex. 26. 36, 37; 27. 16, &c.
LOOKEST,] as in Ex. 33. 8; Nu. 21. 9, &c.
9. BREACHES,] *or* 'clefts;' as in Am. 6. 11.
GATHER,] as in 11. 12; 40. 11; 43. 5, &c.
LOWER POOL,] *lit.* 'blessing.'
10. NUMBER,] as in Lev. 15. 13, 28; 23. 15.
BREAK,] as in Ex. 34. 13; De. 7. 5, &c.
11. DITCH,] *lit.* 'place of gathering.'
12. LORD,] as in v. 5, 14; 3. 15, 17, 18, &c.
13. JOY,]*or* 'leaping;' as in 12. 3; 35. 10, &c.
SLAYING,] as in Ge. 4. 23, 25; 12. 12; 20. 11.
SLAUGHTERING,] as in Ge. 22. 10, &c.
SHEEP,] *or* a 'flock;' as in 7. 21; 13. 14, &c.
DIE,] as in v. 14, 18; 50. 2; 51. 6, &c.
14. REVEALED,] as in 23 1; 38. 12; 40. 5, &c.
PARDONED,] *lit.* 'covered;' as in 6. 7, &c.
15. JEHOVAH OF HOSTS,] as in v. 5, 12, &c.
STEWARD,] *lit.* 'useful one.'
THE HOUSE,] that is, the temple.
16. HEWN OUT,] as in 5. 2; De. 6, 11, &c.
SEPULCHRE,] *lit.* 'grave;' as in 14. 19, &c.
HEWING,] as in 10. 15; 1 K. 5. 15; 2 K. 12. 12.
DWELLING,] *lit.* 'tabernacle.'
18. COVERER,] as in Lev. 16. 4.
WRAPPETH ROUND,] as in 23. 9; Eze. 24. 5.
BABBLER,] as in 29. 3.
BROAD OF SIDES,] *lit.* 'of hands;' as in
33. 21.
SHAME,] *lit.* 'lightness;' as in Ps. 83. 16, &c.
19. THRUST,] as in Nu. 35. 22; Jer. 46. 15.
THROWETH DOWN,] as in Ex. 15. 17; 19. 21.
20. SERVANT,] as in 14. 2; 20. 3; 24. 2, &c.
21. CLOTHED,] as in 61. 10; Ge. 27. 16, &c.
STRENGTHEN,] as in 33. 23; 41. 7; Ex. 4. 21.
RULE,] as in 39. 2; Ge. 1. 16; 1 K. 9. 19, &c.
FATHER,] as in v. 23, 24; 3. 6; 7. 17, &c.

INHABITANT OF JERUSALEM,] as in 5. 3, &c.
HOUSE OF JUDAH,] as in 3. 7, 31; 2 Ch. 19. 11.
22. KEY,] *lit.* 'given the opener.'
SHOULDER,] as in 9. 4, 6; 10. 27; 14. 25, &c.
OPENED,] as in 14. 17; 50. 5; De. 20. 11, &c.
SHUTTING,] as in Jos. 6. 1.
SHUT,] as in Ge. 19. 6, 10; Ex. 14. 3, &c.
OPENING,] as in Jud. 3. 25; Ps. 145. 16, &c
23. FIXED,] *lit.* 'struck;' as in Ge. 31. 25.
NAIL,] *or* 'pin;' as in v. 25; 33. 20; 54. 2.
STEDFAST,] as in v. 25; 1. 21, 26; 8. 2, &c.
24. HANGED,] as in Ge. 40. 19, 22; 41. 13, &c
SMALL QUANTITY,] as in 36. 9; Ge. 9. 24, &c.
25. AFFIRMATION,] as in 30. 1, 31; 9. 37, &c.
MOVED,] as in 54. 10; 59. 21; Jos. 1. 8, &c.
FIXED,] as in v. 23; 1. 21, 26; 8. 2, &c.
CUT DOWN,] as in 14. 12; Jer. 48. 25, &c.
CUT OFF,] as in 29. 20; Ge. 17. 14; Ex. 12. 15
SPOKEN,] as in 1. 2, 20; 16. 13, 14; 20. 2, &c.

XXIII. 1. BURDEN,] as in 13. 1; 14. 28, &c.
TYRE,] i.e. 'rock, sharpness, straitness.'
HOWL,] as in v. 6; 13. 6; 14. 12, 31, &c.
SHIPS OF TARSHISH,] as in 2. 16; 60. 9, &c.
DESTROYED,] as in v. 14; 15. 1; Jer. 4. 13.
HOUSE,] or place of habitation.
ENTRANCE,] for ships as formerly.
REVEALED,] as in 22. 14; 38. 12; 40. 5, &c.
2. SILENT,] as in Jos. 10. 12; 1 Sa. 14. 9, &c.
PASSING,] as in 29. 5; 33; 8; 34. 10, &c.
FILLED,] as in 33. 5; Ex. 28. 3, 17, 41, &c.
3. MANY WATERS,] as in Ps. 29. 3; 32. 6, &c.
4. BE ASHAMED,] as in Eze. 16. 52; 36. 32.
PAINED,] as in 26. 18; 54. 1; 66. 8, &c.
BROUGHT FORTH,] as in 26. 18; 49. 21, &c.
NOURISHED,] as in 1. 2; 49. 21; 51. 18, &c.
YOUNG,] *or* 'choice men.'
BROUGHT UP,] as in 1. 2; Eze. 31. 4.
5. REPORT,] as in 66. 19; Ge. 29. 13, &c.
PAINED,] as in 13. 8; 26. 17; 66. 7, &c.
6. PASS OVER,] as in v. 10, 11; 47. 2; 62. 10.
HOWL,] as in v. 1; 13. 6; 14. 12, 31, &c.
7. EXULTING ONE,] as in 13. 3; 22. 2; 24. 8
CARRY,] as in Ps. 60. 9; 68. 29; 76. 11, &c.
SOJOURN,] that she might traffic.
8. COUNSELLED,] as in v. 9; 7. 5; 14. 24, &c.
HONOURED,] as in v. 9; Ge. 34. 19, &c.
9. JEHOVAH OF HOSTS,] as in 1. 9, 24, &c.
POLLUTE,] *or* 'pierce;' as in 56. 2, 6, &c.
MAKE LIGHT.] as in Jon. 1. 5.
10. PASS,] as in v. 6, 12; 47. 2; 62. 10, &c.
11. STRETCHED OUT,] as in 34. 11; 44. 13, &c.
TREMBLE,] as in 1 Sa. 28. 15; Jer. 50. 34.
CHARGED,] as in 13. 3; 34. 16; 45. 12, &c.
DESTROY,] as in 10. 7; 14. 23; De. 1. 27, &c.
12. ADD,] as in 1. 5, 13; 7. 10; 8. 5, &c.
CHITTIM,] as in v. 1.
13. CHALDEANS,] in *Heb.* 'Chasdim.'
FOUNDED,] as in 48. 13; 54. 11; Ps. 24. 2, &c.
RAISED,] as in 14. 9; 29. 3; Ge. 6. 18, &c.
LIFTED UP,] *lit.* 'waked up.'
PALACES,] *or* 'high places,' as in 25. 2, &c.
APPOINTED,] *lit.* 'set;' as in 14. 17, 23, &c.
RUIN,] *lit.* 'fallen place;' as in 25. 2.
14. HOWL,] as in v. 1; 15. 1; Jer. 4. 13, &c.
DESTROYED,] as in v. 1; 15. 1; Jer. 4. 13, &c.
15. FORGOTTEN,] as in v. 16; Job 28. 4.
HARLOT,] as in v. 16; 1. 21; Ge. 34. 31, &c.
16. TAKE,] as in 8. 1; 47. 2; Ge. 6. 21, &c.
GO ROUND,] as in Jos. 6. 7; 1 Sa. 22. 17, &c.
FORGOTTEN,] as in v. 15; Job 28. 4.

PLAY WELL,] *lit.* 'make good to play.'
MULTIPLY,] as in Ge. 34. 12; Jud. 20. 38, &c.
REMEMBERED,] as in 65. 17; Job 24. 20, &c.
17. INSPECTETH,] as in 10. 12; 24. 21, &c.
REPENTED,] *lit.* 'turned back;' as in 5. 25.
COMMITTED FORNICATION,] as in Ge. 38.
24; Ex. 34. 15, 16; De. 31. 16, &c.
18. MERCHANDIZE,] as in Prov. 3. 14; 31. 18.
HOLY,] that is, 'separate, set apart.'
STORED,] *lit.* 'strengthened.'
SITTING,] as in v. 2, 6; 5. 3, 9; 6. 1, 5, &c.
LASTING,] *lit.* 'ancient.'

XXIV. 1. EMPTYING,] as in Hos. 10. 1;
Nah. 2. 2.
SCATTERED,] as in 28. 25; Ge. 11. 9, &c.
2. PRIEST] is, with reference to the univer-
sal desolation of the land, not in moral
character, as is commonly supposed.
LIFTING,] as in Neh. 5. 7.
3. SPOKEN,] as in 1. 2, 20; 16. 13, 14; 20. 2.
4. MOURNED,] as in v. 7; 3. 26; 19. 8, &c.
FADED,] as in 40. 7, 8; Prov. 30. 32; Jer.
8. 13.
LANGUISHED,] as in v. 7; 16. 8; 19. 8, &c.
WORLD,] or 'fruit-bearing and habitable
earth.'
5. DEFILED,] or 'profaned;' as in Jer. 23. 11.
TRANSGRESSED,] as in 8. 8, 21; 10. 28, &c.
LAWS,] or 'directions;' as in 1. 10; 2. 3, &c.
CHARGED,] as in 8. 8; Jud. 5. 26; 1 Sa. 10. 3.
MADE VOID,] as in 33. 8; Ge. 17. 14, &c.
6. CURSE,] or 'oath;' as in Ge. 24. 41, &c.
CONSUMED,] or 'burned;' as in 10. 17, &c.
LEFT,] as in v. 12; 17. 6; 49. 21, &c.
7, MOURNED,] as in v. 7; 3. 26; 19. 8, &c.
SIGHED,] as in Lam. 1. 8.
8. CEASED,] as in 14. 4; 33. 8; Ge. 2. 3, &c.
JOY,] or 'leaping;' as in v. 11.
9. SONG,] as in 23. 16; 26. 1; 30. 29, &c.
DRINKING,] as in 29. 8; 1 Sa. 30. 16, &c.
10. BROKEN DOWN,] as in 8. 15; 14. 29, &c.
EMPTINESS,] or 'ruin;' as in 29. 21; 34. 11.
SHUT,] as in v. 22; Ecc. 12. 4; Jer. 13. 19.
11. CRY,] as in Ps. 144. 14; Jer. 14. 2; 46. 12.
REMOVED,] as in 5. 13; 1 Sa. 4. 21, 22, &c.
12. LEFT,] as in v. 6; 17. 6; 49. 21, &c.
SMITTEN,] as in Job 4. 20; Jer. 26. 5; Mic.
1. 7.
13. COMPASSING,] as in 17. 6.
FINISHED,] as in 10. 25; 15. 6; 16. 4, &c.
14. LIFT UP THE VOICE,] as in 2. 4, 9; 3. 7.
CRIED ALOUD,] as in Eze. 8. 15.
15. PROSPERITY,] or 'in lights;' as in 31.
9; 44. 16; 47. 14, &c.
HONOUR YE,] as in Ex. 20. 12; De. 5. 16, &c.
ISLES OF THE SEA,] as in 11. 11; Est. 10. 1.
16. SKIRT,] *lit.* 'wing.'
DESIRE,] 'beauty or glory;' as in 4. 2, &c.
DEALT TREACHEROUSLY,] as in 33. 1, &c.
17. FEAR,] as in v. 18; 2. 10; 19. 21, &c.
18. FLEEING,] as in Ex. 14. 27; Jos. 8. 6, &c.
CAPTURED,] as in Jos. 7. 16—18; 1 Sa. 10. 21.
OPENED,] as in 5. 27; Ge. 7. 11; Eze. 1. 1, &c.
SHAKEN,] as in 13. 13; 2 Sa. 22. 8; Ps. 18. 7.
19. MOVED,] as in Ps. 38. 16; 46. 2; 55. 22.
20. STAGGER,] as in 6. 4; 7. 2; Ps. 59. 15;
107. 27; 109. 10.
DRUNKARD,] or 'merry one;' as in 19. 14.
LODGE,] as in 1. 8.
HEAVY,] as in 59. 1; Ge. 13. 2; 18. 20, &c.

21. LAYETH A CHARGE,] as in 10. 12; 23. 17
22. GATHERED,] as in 33. 4; Hos. 10. 10,
Zech. 14. 14.
SHUT UP,] as in 10. 4; 42. 7.
INSPECTED,] as in 10. 12; 23. 17; 27. 1, &c.
23. CONFOUNDED,] as in Ps. 71. 24, &c.
ASHAMED,] as in 19. 9; 20. 5; 37. 27, &c.
MOON,] *lit.* 'the white one.'
SUN,] *lit.* 'the heat.'
REIGNED,] as in 52. 7; Ge. 36. 31, &c.
ELDERS,] aged or 'bearded' ones.

XXV. 1. JEHOVAH,] the 'existing one.'
MY GOD,] as in 7. 13; Ge. 31. 30; Ex. 15. 2
EXALT,] as in Ex. 15. 2; 2 Sa. 22. 49, &c.
CONFESS THY NAME,] as in 12. 1; 38. 18, &c.
STEDFASTNESS,] as in 11. 5; 33. 6; 59. 4, &c.
2. HEAP,] as in 10. 30; 37. 26; 48. 18, &c.
RUIN,] *lit.* 'fallen place;' as in 23. 13.
BUILT,] as in 44. 26, 28; Ge. 16. 2, &c.
3. HONOUR,] as in 43. 20; 60. 13; Nu. 22. 17.
STRONG,] as in 19. 4; 43. 16; 56. 11, &c.
TERRIBLE,] as in v. 4, 5; 13. 11; 29. 5, &c.
FEARETH,] as in 7. 4; 8. 12; 10. 24, &c.
4. STRONGHOLD,] as in 17. 9, 10; 23. 4, &c.
DISTRESS,] or 'straitness;' as in 1. 24, &c.
STORM,] or 'inundation;' as in 4. 6; 28. 2.
A WALL,] immovable and stedfast.
5. HEAT,] as in v. 4; 4. 6; Ge. 31. 40, &c.
HUMBLEST,] or 'causest to bend;' as in
De. 9. 3; Jud. 4. 23; 2 Sa. 8. 1, &c.
HUMBLED,] or 'answered;' as in 14. 10, &c.
6. MOUNT,] as in v. 7, 10; 2. 2, 3, 14; 4. 5, &c.
BANQUET,] *lit.* 'drinking;' as in 5. 12, &c.
FAT THINGS,] *lit.* 'oils;' as in 5. 1, &c.
PRESERVED THINGS,] as in Ps. 75. 8; Jer.
48. 11; Zeph. 1, 12.
REFINED,] as in 1 Ch. 28. 18; 29. 4; Ps. 12. 6
7. SWALLOWED UP,] as in v. 7; 3. 12; Ps.
35. 25; Lam. 2. 2, 5, 16.
SPREAD,] or 'poured out.'
8. DEATH,] as in 6. 1; 14. 28; 25. 15, 18, &c.
IN VICTORY,] or 'pre-eminently.'
WIPED,] as in 44. 22; Ge. 7. 4; Nu. 5. 23, &c.
TURNETH ASIDE,] as in 1. 25; 3. 18; 5. 23.
SPOKEN,] as in 1. 2, 20; 16. 13, 14; 20. 2, &c.
9. LO,] as in Ge. 1. 29; 12. 11; 19. 11, &c.
OUR GOD,] as in 1. 10; 35. 2; 36. 7, &c.
WAITED,] as in 5. 4; 8. 17; 26. 8, &c.
SAVETH,] or 'easeth;' as in 33. 22; 35. 4, &c.
JOY,] or 'leap for joy;' as in 3. 9; 29. 19, &c.
REJOICE,] as in 9. 17; 14. 29; 39. 2, &c.
10. REST,] as in 23. 12; 57. 2; Ge. 8. 4, &c.
11. SPREAD OUT,] as in Jer. 4. 31.
HUMBLED,] or 'made low;' as in v. 12, &c.
12. FORTRESS,] as in 7; 3. 34. 13; Nu. 13. 19.
BOWED DOWN,] as in v. 1; Job 22. 29; Eze.
17. 24.
MADE LOW,] or 'humbled;' as in Ps. 88. 3.

XXVI. 1. SUNG,] as in 23. 16; 24. 9; 30. 29
STRONG,] as in 12. 2; 45. 24; 49. 5, &c.
SALVATION,] or 'ease or safety.'
BULWARK,] or 'strength.'
2. OPEN,] as in Jos. 10. 22; 2 K. 13. 17, &c.
RIGHTEOUS NATION,] as in Ge. 20. 4.
PRESERVING,] or 'watching;' as in 21. 11.
STEDFASTNESS,] or 'stedfastly;' as in De.
32. 20; Prov. 13. 17, &c.
3. IMAGINATION,] *lit.* 'formation;' as in
29. 16; Ge. 6. 5; 8. 21, &c.

SUPPORTED,] as in Ps. 111. 8; 112. 8.
FORTIFIEST,] or 'straitenest, sharpenest.'
CONFIDENT,] or 'trustful.'
4. FOR EVER,] lit. 'unto duration.'
JAH JEHOVAH,] as in 12. 2.
ROCK OF AGES,] or 'rock age-during.'
5. BOWED DOWN,] as in 25. 12.
ON HIGH,] or 'of a high place.'
SET ON HIGH,] as in 12. 4; 30. 13; 33. 5;
Prov. 18. 11.
MAKETH LOW,] as in 13. 11; 57. 9, &c.
6. TREAD DOWN,] as in 41. 25; 63. 3, &c.
POOR,] or 'meek, afflicted;' as in 3. 14, 15.
WEAK,] lean or thin ones.
7. PATH,] or road for 'waggons.'
UPRIGHTNESS,] or 'upright things.'
PONDER,] as in Ps. 58. 2; 78. 50; Prov. 5. 6.
8. JUDGMENTS,] as in v. 9; 1. 17, 21, 27, &c
WAITED,] as in 5. 4; 8. 17; 25. 9, &c.
9. DESIRED,] as in Job 23. 13; Ps. 132. 13.
SEEK EARNESTLY,] or 'early or in the
dawn.'
WORLD,] the 'fruit-bearing and habitable
earth.'
10. FAVOUR,] as in Prov. 21. 10.
LEARNED,] as in v. 9; De. 5. 1; 31. 13; Prov.
30. 3.
STRAIGHTFORWARDNESS,] or 'straightfor-
ward things;' as in 30. 10; 57. 2; 59. 14, &c.
11. HIGH,] as in De. 8. 14; 32. 27, &c.
ASHAMED,] as in 1. 29; 29. 22; 41. 11, &c.
ADVERSARIES,] or 'straiteners;' as in v.
16; 1. 24; 5. 28, 30, &c.
CONSUMETH,] as in 1. 19; 3. 10; 4. 1, &c.
12. APPOINTEST,] or 'settest on;' as in Ps.
22. 15.
WROUGHT,] as in 41. 4; 44. 12; Ex. 15. 17.
13. OUR GOD,] as in 1. 10; 25. 9; 35. 2, &c.
RULED,] as in 45. 5, 21; 64. 4.
MAKE MENTION,] as in 19. 17; 48. 1; 63. 7.
14. DEAD,] as in v. 19; 8. 19; 22. 2, &c.
REPHAIM,] as in 17. 5; Ge. 14. 5; 15. 20, &c.
RISE,] as in 7. 7; 8. 10; 14. 21, 24, &c.
INSPECTED,] as in v. 16; 13. 11; 34. 16, &c.
DESTROYED,] as in 13. 9; Nu. 33. 52, &c.
15. ADDED,] as in 29. 19; 37. 31; Ge. 8. 12.
HONOURED,] lit. 'made heavy;' as in 43. 4.
PUT FAR OFF,] as in 6. 12; 29. 13.
16. DISTRESS,] or 'straitness, sharpness;'
as in v. 11; 1. 24; 5. 28, 30, &c.
MISSED,] or 'looked after;' as in v. 14, &c.
CHASTISEMENT,] or 'instruction;' as in 53.
5; De. 11. 2; Job 5. 17. &c.
17. PREGNANT,] as in 7. 14; Ge. 16. 11, &c.
TO BEAR,] as in 37. 3; Ge. 4. 2; 16. 2, &c.
PAINED,] as in 13. 8; 23. 5; 45. 10, &c.
CRIETH.] as in 15. 4, 5; Ex. 2. 23, &c.
PANG,] lit. 'cords;' as in 5. 18; 13. 8, &c.
18. CONCEIVED,] as in Ge. 16. 4, 5, &c.
PAINED,] as in 23. 4; 54. 1; 66. 8, &c.
BROUGHT FORTH,] as in 23. 4; 49. 21, &c.
WORLD,] as in v. 9.
19. DEAD,] as in v. 14; 8. 19; 22. 2, &c.
LIVE,] as in v. 14; 38. 1, 9, 16, 21, &c.
DEAD BODY,] or 'carcase, fallen thing.'
RISE,] as in 7. 7; 8. 10; 14. 21, &c.
AWAKE,] as in Ps. 35. 23; 44. 23; 59. 5, &c.
SING,] as in 52. 9; Ps. 33. 1; 98. 4.
DWELLERS,] lit. 'tabernacles.'
REPHAIM,] as in v. 14; Ge. 14. 5; 15. 20, &c.
20. MY PEOPLE,] as in 1. 3; 3. 12, 15; 5. 13.

SHUT,] lit. 'secure.'
BEHIND THEE,] or 'on thine own b ehalf.'
SHORTLY,] as in Job 24. 24; 32. 22, &c.
21. CHARGE,] as in Ps. 59. 5; Jer. 27. 22,&c.
REVEALED,] as in 57. 8; Lev. 20. 11, 17, &c.
COVER,] as in 6. 2; 60. 2, 6; Ge. 9. 23, &c.

XXVII. 1. LAY A CHARGE,] as in v. 3, &c.
LEVIATHAN,] as in Job 3. 8; 41. 1; Ps. 74.
14; 104. 26.
CROOKED SERPENT,] as in Job 26. 13.
SLAIN,] as in 14. 20; Ge. 4. 23, 25; 12. 12.
2. DESIRABLE,] as in 32. 12; Eze. 23. 6, 12,
23; Am. 5. 11.
RESPOND,] as in Nu. 21. 17; 1 Sa. 12. 3; 1
K. 18. 26, 27.
3. KEEPER,] as in 26. 3; 42. 6; 49. 8, &c.
EVERY MOMENT,] lit. 'at the moments;' as
in 26. 20; 47. 9; 54. 7, 8, &c.
KEEP,] or 'straiten;' as in 26. 3; 42. 6, &c.
4. FURY,] lit. 'heat;' as in 34. 2; 42. 25, &c.
STEP,] or 'transgress' against it.
BURN.] Original word not found again.
5. TAKE HOLD,] as in 42. 6; 56. 2; Ge. 19. 16.
MAKE PEACE,] as in 45. 7; Job 25. 2; Ps.
147. 14.
WITH ME,] lit. 'in reference to me.'
6. TO TAKE ROOT,] as in Ps. 80. 9.
FLOURISHED,] as in Nu. 17. 8; Ps. 72. 16.
WORLD,] the 'fruit-bearing and habitable
earth.'
7. SMITING,] as in 9. 13; 10. 20; 14. 6, &c.
SMITTEN,] as in 11. 4, 15; 37. 38; 60. 10, &c.
SLAYING,] as in 14. 19; 26. 21, &c.
SLAY,] as in Ps. 44. 22.
8. STRIVEST,] as in 49. 25; 50. 8; 51. 22, &c.
TAKEN AWAY,] not 'stayeth;' as in Prov.
25. 4, 5.
9. INIQUITY,] as in 1. 4; 5. 18; 6. 7, &c.
TO TAKE AWAY,] or 'turn aside.'
SETTING,] as in 10. 6; 13. 9; 44. 7; 61. 3, &c.
SHRINES,] or 'happy ones, or places.'
10. FENCED CITY,] as in 36. 1; 37. 26, &c.
HABITATION,] lit. 'comely place;' as in 32.
18; 33. 20; 34. 13, &c.
CAST OUT,] as in Prov. 29. 15; Isa. 16. 2.
FORSAKEN,] as in 62. 12; Ps. 37. 25; Eze.
36. 4.
LIETH DOWN,] as in 11. 6, 7; 14. 30, &c.
CONSUMED,] as in 49. 4; Ge. 18. 33; 24. 15.
11. WITHERING,] as in Ge. 8. 7; Eze. 17. 10;
Zech. 11. 17.
BRANCH,] or 'crop, harvest.'
BROKEN OFF,] as in Lev. 6. 28; 15. 12, &c.
SETTING ON FIRE,] as in Ps. 19. 8; Prov.
29. 13.
FAVOUR,] as in 30. 19; Ge. 43. 29, &c.
12. BEAT OUT,] as in De. 24. 20; Ru. 2. 17.
BRANCH,] lit. 'ear;' as in 17. 5; Ge. 41. 5—
7, 22—24, 26, 27,&c.
STREAM OF EGYPT,] as in Jos. 15. 4, 47, &c.
GATHERED,] or 'gleaned.'
13. BLOWN,] lit. 'struck;' as in Job 17. 3;
Am. 3. 6.
PERISHING,] as in De. 26. 5; 32. 28, &c.
CAST OUT,] as in 16. 3, 4; De. 22. 1; 30. 4.
BOWED THEMSELVES,] as in 60. 14; Ex. 11.
8; 24. 1.
HOLY,] or 'separate, set apart.'

XXVIII. 1. WO,] as in 1. 4, 24; 5. 8, 11, &c.

PROUD CROWN,] *or* 'crown of the pride;' as in v. 3.
DRUNKARDS,] *or* 'merry ones;' as in v. 3.
FADING,] as in v. 4; 1. 30; 34. 4.
FAT VALLEY,] *lit.* 'valley of oils.'
2. MIGHTY,] as in 27. 1; 40. 10; Ex. 3. 19, &c.
STORM,] *or* 'inundation;' as in 4. 6; 25. 4.
DESTRUCTIVE,] as in 10. 22; 15. 18; 30. 28.
CAST DOWN,] as in 14. 1; 65. 15; Lev. 16. 23.
3. PROUD CROWN,] as in v. 1.
4. FADING FLOWER,] as in v. 1.
SWALLOWETH,] as in Ge. 41. 7, 24, &c.
5. JEHOVAH OF HOSTS,] as in v. 22, 29, &c.
6. SPIRIT OF JUDGMENT,] as in 4. 4.
TURNING BACK,] as in 38. 8; 44. 25, &c.
7. WINE,] as in v. 1; 5. 11, 12, 22; 16. 10, &c.
ERRED,] as in Job 6. 24; 19. 4.
WANDERED,] as in 16. 8; 21. 4; 47. 15, &c.
SWALLOWED UP,] as in Hos. 8. 8.
JUDICIALLY,] *or* 'in the judgment of Jah, in acting as his servants.
8. TABLES,] as in 21. 6; 65. 11; Ex. 25. 23.
FILTH,] as in 4. 4; 36. 12; 2 K. 18. 27; Prov. 30. 12.
WITHOUT PLACE,] as in 5. 8.
9. BY WHOM,] *lit.* 'with whom;' compare Ge. 4. 1, &c.
TEACH,] *lit.* 'shew;' as in v. 26; 2. 3, &c.
TO UNDERSTAND,] as in 6. 9, 10; 32. 4, &c.
REPORT,] *lit.* 'hearing, a thing heard;' as in v. 19; 37. 7; 53. 1, &c.
WEANED,] as in 11. 8; Ps. 131. 2.
REMOVED,] *or* 'aged for breasts.'
10. RULE,] as in v. 13; Hos. 5. 11.
LINE,] as in v. 13, 17; 18. 2, 7; 34. 11, &c.
11. SCORNED LIP,] *lit.* 'scorned ones of lip.'
12. REST,] that is, resting place.
REFRESHING,] *or* 'quieting, or place of quieting.'
TO HEAR,] as in 6. 9; 21. 3; 30. 9, 19, &c.
13. STUMBLED,] as in 3. 8; 8. 15; 31. 3, &c.
BROKEN,] as in 8. 15; 14. 29; 24. 10, &c.
SNARED,] as in 8. 15; Prov. 6. 2.
CAPTURED,] as in 8. 15; 1 K. 16. 18, &c.
14. MEN OF SCORNING,] as in Prov. 1. 22; 29. 8.
RULING,] as in 14. 5; 16. 1; 40. 10, &c.
15. COVENANT,] as in v. 18; 24. 5; 33. 8, &c.
PROVISION,] *lit.* a 'seeing or fore-seeing;' as in 29. 10; 30. 10; 47. 13, &c.
OVERFLOWING,] as in v. 2, 15, 18; 10. 22, &c.
PASSETH OVER,] as in v. 18. 19; 26. 20, &c.
HIDDEN,] *or* 'kept, secret.'
16. LAYING A FOUNDATION,] *lit.* 'founding;' as in 14. 32; 1 K. 16. 34; 1 Ch. 9. 22, &c.
TRIED,] *or* 'trying, testing.'
PRECIOUS,] as in 1 Sa. 3. 1; 2 Sa. 12. 30, &c.
SETTLED FOUNDATION,] *lit.* 'a foundation, foundation.'
BELIEVING,] *lit.* 'remaining stedfast.'
MAKE HASTE.] Sept. and New Test. read is 'not ashamed,' by the change of one Hebrew letter.
17. PUT,] *or* 'set;' as in v. 15; 14. 17, &c.
REFUGE OF LIES,] as in v. 15.
OVERFLOW,] as in 43. 2; 1 K. 22. 38, &c.
18. DISANNULLED,] *lit.* 'covered, pardoned.'
COVENANT WITH DEATH,] as in v. 15.
STAND,] *lit.* 'rise;' as in v. 21; 7. 7; 8. 10.
19. FULNESS.] *lit.* 'sufficiency;' as in 40. 16.

PASSETH OVER,] as in v. 15, 18; 26. 20, &c.
REPORT,] *or* 'to understand the thing heard.'
20. SHORTER,] as in 50. 2; 59. 1; Lev. 23. 10.
BED,] *or* 'spread-out place.'
NARROWER,] *lit.* 'straiter;' as in Nu. 33. 55; Jud. 11. 7; 1 Sa. 13. 6, &c.
21. PERAZIM,] i.e. 'breaches;' as in 2 Sa. 5. 20; 1 Ch. 14. 11.
TROUBLED,] *or* 'angry;' as in 5. 25; 32. 10.
22. BANDS,] *or* 'chastisements, instructions;' as in 52. 2; Job 30. 5; Ps. 2. 3, &c.
DETERMINED,] as in 10. 23; Da. 9. 26, 27; 11. 36.
23. GIVE EAR,] as in 1. 2, 10; 8. 9; 32. 9, &c.
HEAR,] as in v. 14; 1. 2, 10; 6. 9, &c.
ATTEND,] as in 10. 30; 34. 1; 49. 1, &c.
24. PLOUGHETH,] as in De. 22. 10; Prov. 20. 4; Am. 6. 12.
OPENETH,] as in 45. 1; Ge. 24. 32; Ex. 28. 11.
HARROWETH,] *lit.* 'destroyeth;' as in Job 39. 10; Hos. 10. 11.
25. MADE LEVEL,] *or* 'equal;' as in 38. 13.
SCATTERED,] as in 24. 1; Ge. 11. 9, &c.
SPRINKLE,] as in Ex. 9. 10; 24. 8; Lev. 7. 2.
PLACED,] *or* 'set;' as in v. 15, 17; 21. 4, &c.
26. INSTRUCT,] as in 8. 11; Lev. 26. 28, &c.
DIRECT,] *lit.* 'show;' as in v. 9; 2. 3, &c.
27. SHARP-POINTED,] as in 41. 15; Job 41. 30; Am. 1. 3.
28. BREAD,] as in 3. 1, 7; 4. 1; 21. 14, &c.
THRESH,] as in 41. 15; Hab. 3. 12.
29. JEHOVAH OF HOSTS,] as in v. 5, 22, &c.
GONE FORTH,] as in 11. 1; 37. 9; 45. 23, &c.
MADE WONDERFUL,] as in De. 28. 59; 2 Ch. 26. 15; Ps. 31. 21.
MADE GREAT,] as 9. 3; 1 Sa. 12. 24; 20. 41.

XXIX. 1. WO,] as in v. 15; 1. 4, 24; 5. 8, &c.
ARIEL,] i.e. 'lion of God;' as in v. 2, 7; 2 Sa. 23. 20; Eze. 43. 15.
ADD,] as in Jer. 7. 21.
2. DISTRESS,] as in Jud. 14. 17; 16. 16; Job 32. 18.
3. ENCAMPED,] as in v. 1; Nu. 1. 52; 2. 34.
BABBLER,] as in 22. 18.
LAID SIEGE,] as in Ex. 23. 22; De. 14. 25, &c.
CAMP,] *lit.* a thing 'set up.'
BULWARKS,] *or* 'straitness;' as in 2 Ch. 11. 10, 11, 23, &c.
4. LOW,] as in 2. 11, 12, 17.
5. SMALL DUST,] as in 5. 24; Ex. 9. 9, &c.
SCATTERING,] as in 1. 7; 17. 10; 25. 2, &c.
PASSING ON,] as in 23. 2; 33. 8; 34. 10, &c.
SUDDENLY,] as in 30. 13; 47. 11; 48. 3, &c.
6. INSPECTED,] as in 24. 22; Nu. 16. 29, &c.
EARTHQUAKE,] *lit.* 'rushing;' as in 9. 5, &c.
7. DREAM,] as in 29. 3, 6; 31. 10, 11, &c.
WARRING,] *or* 'assembling themselves;' as in v. 3.
DISTRESSING,] as in 51. 13.
8. HUNGRY,] as in 8. 21; 9. 20; 32. 6, &c.
EATING,] as in v. 6; 1. 7; 30. 27, 30, &c.
WAKED,] as in 2 Sa. 4. 81; Ps. 3. 5; 139. 18.
DRINKING,] as in 24. 9; 1 Sa. 30. 16, &c.
LONGING,] as in 33. 4; Ps. 107. 9; Prov. 28. 15.
9. STAGGER,] as in 19. 1; Job 28. 4; Prov. 5. 6.
10. POURED OUT,] as in 40. 19; 44. 10
DEEP SLEEP,] as in Ge. 2. 21; 15. 12, &c
CLOSETH,] *or* 'shutteth.'

COVERED,] as in 51. 16; 58. 7; Ge. 37. 26, &c·
11. VISION,] as in 21. 2; 28. 18; Da. 8. 5, 8·
KNOWING,] as in v. 15· Ge. 3. 5; 25. 27, &c.
READ,] as in 34. 16; Jer. 36. 15.
NOT ABLE,] as in 1. 13; 16. 12; 56. 10, &c.
SEALED,] as in De. 32. 34; Neh. 9. 38, &c.
13. DRAWN NEAR,] as in Ge. 33. 7, &c.
HONOURED,] as in 43. 23; 58. 13; Jud. 13. 17.
PUT FAR OFF,] as in 6. 12; 26. 15.
TAUGHT,] as in 1 Ch. 25. 7; Song 3. 8; Hos.
10. 11.
14. WONDERFULLY,] as in 2 Ch. 2. 9; Joel
2. 26.
WONDER,] lit. 'to do wonderfully;' as in
9. 6; 25. 1; Ex. 15. 11, &c.
MARVEL,] or 'wonder;' as in 9. 6; 25. 1, &c.
PERISH,] as in 57. 1; Ex. 10. 7; Lev. 26. 38.
INTELLIGENT,] or 'understanding ones;'
as in 3. 3; 5. 21; Ge. 41. 33, &c.
15. HIDE,] or 'conceal, keep secret;' as in
57. 17; De. 31. 18; Prov. 25. 2.
SEEING,] as in 14. 16; 28. 4; 30. 10, 20, &c.
KNOWING,] as in v. 11; 51. 7; Ge. 3. 5, &c.
16. PERVERSION,] lit. 'overturn;' as in Ge.
19. 21, 29, &c.
POTTER,] lit. 'framer;' as in 22. 11; 27. 11.
ESTEEMED,] as in v. 17; 32. 15; Lev. 7. 18.
17. VERY LITTLE,] as in 10. 25; 16. 14; 24. 6.
TURNED,] as in 5. 25; 6. 13; 9. 12, &c.
FRUITFUL FIELD,] lit. 'prepared place.'
RECKONED,] as in v. 16; 32. 15; Lev. 7. 18.
18. DEAF,] as in 35. 5; 42. 18, 19; 43. 8, &c.
19. HUMBLE,] as in 11. 4; 32. 7; 61. 1, &c.
POOR,] lit. 'needy;' as in 14. 30; 25. 4, &c.
REJOICE,] as in 9. 3; 25. 9; 35. 1, 2, &c.
20. CEASED,] as in 16. 4; Ge. 47. 15, 16; Ps.
77. 8.
CONSUMED,] as in 10. 25; 15. 16; 16. 4, &c.
CUT OFF,] as in 22. 25; Ge. 17. 14; Ex. 12. 15.
21. CAUSING TO SIN,] lit. 'to miss' the mark.
REPROVER,] lit. 'one who makes manifest
or evident.'
TURN ASIDE,] lit. 'incline;' as in 31. 3; 54.
2; Ex. 23. 6.
EMPTINESS,] or 'ruin;' as in 24. 10; 34. 11.
22. JEHOVAH,] as in 12. 2; 26. 4; Ex. 6. 3.
RANSOMED,] as in Lev. 27. 27; De. 9. 26, &c.
ASHAMED,] as in 1. 29; 26. 11; 41. 11, &c.
PALE,] or 'white.'
CHILDREN,] as in 2. 6; 8. 18; 9. 6, &c.
23. WORK OF MY HANDS,] as in 19. 25; 45.
11; 60. 21.
SANCTIFY,] that is, 'set apart.'
DECLARE FEARFUL,] or 'terrible;' as in
8. 12.
24. ERRING,] those 'going astray;' as in
Ge. 37. 15; Ex. 23. 4; Ps. 95. 10; Prov. 21. 16.
DOCTRINE,] lit. a 'thing received.'

XXX. 1. WO,] as in 1. 4, 24; 5. 8, 11, &c.
APOSTATE,] lit. 'turning aside:' as in 1. 23.
COVERING,] or 'spreading;' as in v. 22, &c.
2. WALKING,] as in v. 29; 8. 6; 9. 2, &c.
ASKED,] as in 65. 1; Ge. 32. 17; 43. 7, &c.
TRUST,] lit. 'take refuge;' as in Ru. 2. 12;
Ps. 118. 8, 9.
3. SHAME,] as 45. 16; 59. 6; 61. 7, &c.
TRUST,] or 'taking refuge.'
4. PRINCES,] lit. 'heads;' as in 1. 23, &c.
REACH,] as in 6. 7; 8. 8; 26. 5, &c.
5. MADE ASHAMED,] as in 2 Sa. 19. 5, &c.

PROFIT NOT,] as in Ge. 2. 18, 20; Ex. 18. 4
PROFIT,] or 'not useful;' as in 44. 10, &c.
6. BURDEN,] lit. 'thing lifted up;' as in 13.
1; 14. 28; 15. 1, &c.
ADVERSITY,] or 'straitness, sharpness;' as
in 8. 22; 33. 2; 37. 3, &c.
CARRY,] or 'lift up;' as in 2. 4, 9; 3. 7, &c.
WEALTH,] lit. 'strength;' as in 5. 22, &c.
PROFITABLE,] or 'useful;' as in v. 5, &c.
7. VANITY,] as in 49. 4; 57. 3; De. 32. 21, &c.
SIT STILL,] as in Ex. 21. 19; Prov. 20. 3.
8. WRITE,] as in 8. 1; Ex. 17. 14; 34. 27, &c.
BOOK,] or 'scroll, roll;' as in 29. 11, 12, &c.
9. REBELLIOUS,] as in Nu. 17. 10, &c
NOT WILLING,] as in v. 15; 28. 12; 42. 24, &c.
LAW,] or 'direction;' as in 1. 10; 2. 3, &c.
10. SEERS,] as in v. 20; 1 Sa. 9. 9, 11, &c.
PROPHETS,] lit. 'visionists, or viewers.'
STRAIGHTFORWARD THINGS,] as in 26. 10.
11. TURN ASIDE,] as in 52. 11; Ge. 19. 2, &c.
FROM BEFORE US,] lit. 'from our face.'
12. KICKING,] as in 7. 15, 16; Jer. 14. 19, &c.
TRUST,] or 'are confident;' as in 12. 2, &c.
RELY,] or 'lean;' as in 31. 1; 50. 10, &c.
13. INIQUITY,] as in 1. 4; 5. 18; 6. 7, &c.
SWELLED OUT,] as in Ge. 15. 12; Nu. 24. 4.
SET ON HIGH,] as in 12. 4; 26. 5; 33. 5, &c.
SUDDENLY,] as in 29. 5; 47. 11; 48. 3, &c.
14. BROKEN,] as in 14. 5; Lev. 26. 19, &c.
BREAKING,] as in v. 13, 26; 1. 28; 15. 5, &c.
POTTERS,] lit. 'framers, fashioners;' as in
22. 11; 27. 11; 29. 16, &c.
SPARE,] as in 9. 19; Ex. 2. 6; Da. 13. 8, &c.
DRAW OUT,] as in Hag. 2. 16.
15. SAVED,] or 'eased;' as in 64. 5, &c.
KEEPING QUIET,] as in 32. 17; 57. 20, &c.
16. HORSE,] as in 2. 7; 5. 28; 30. 1, 3, &c.
FLEE,] as in v. 17; 10. 3; 13. 4, &c.
RIDE,] as in Ge. 24. 61; Lev. 15. 9, &c.
17. BECAUSE OF,] lit. 'from the face of.
LEFT,] as in 1. 8; Ex. 10. 15; Nu. 26. 65, &c.
18. WAIT,] as in 2 K. 9. 3.
FAVOUR,] as in v. 19; Ge. 33. 5, 11, &c.
EXALTED,] or 'high;' as in 49. 11; 52. 13.
PITY,] as in 49. 15; Ps. 103. 13, &c.
19. ZION,] as in 1. 27; 12. 6; 14. 32, &c.
WEEP,] as in 16. 9; 33. 7; 38. 3, &c.
CRY,] as in 57. 13; 1 Sa. 7. 8, &c.
ANSWERETH,] as in 3. 9; 18. 22; 36. 21, &c.
20. ADVERSITY,] or 'straitness;' as in 1. 24.
OPPRESSION,] as in Ex. 3. 9; Jud. 2. 18, &c.
ARE REMOVED,] lit. 'winged.'
DIRECTORS,] lit. 'shewers;' as in 9. 15, &c.
21. BEHIND,] lit. 'from behind;' as in 1.
26; 37. 22; 38. 17, &c.
22. DEFILED,] as in 34. 5, 13, 27; Lev. 13. 3.
SCATTEREST,] as in 41. 16; Ex. 32. 20; Jer.
15. 7; Eze. 5. 2.
23. GIVEN RAIN,] as in 4. 6; 5. 6; Ex. 9. 33.
SOW,] as in 17. 10; Ge. 26. 12; Ex. 23. 10, &c.
PLENTEOUS,] lit. 'oily;' as in Ge. 49. 20, &c.
ENJOY,] as in 11. 7; 27. 10; 40. 11, &c.
ENLARGED,] or 'broadened,'
24. OXEN,] as in 2 Ch. 7. 5; 15. 11; 29. 33.
SERVING,] as in 19. 9; Ge. 4. 2; 49. 15, &c.
WINNOWING,] as in Ru. 3. 2.
25. HIGH MOUNT,] as in 40. 9; 57. 7, &c.
TOWERS,] lit. 'great places;' as in 2. 15; 5.
2; 33. 18.
26. MOON,] lit. 'white one;' as in 24. 23;
Song 6. 10.

SUN,] *lit.* 'heat, or hot one;' as in 24. 23.
SEVENFOLD] its usual brilliance.
SEVEN DAYS,] concentrated into one.
BINDING UP,] as in 61. 1; Eze. 30. 21.
WOUND,] *lit.* 'smiting;' as in 1. 6; 10. 26.
HEALETH,] as in 57. 18; Ge. 20. 27, &c.
27. NAME,] as in 4. 1; 7. 14; 8. 3, &c.
FROM FAR,] as in 8. 9; 10. 3; 13. 5, &c.
GREAT,] *lit.* 'heavy;' as in 21. 15, &c.
FLAME,] *lit.* 'thing lifted up;' as in 13. 8.
28. BREATH,] *or* 'spirit;' as in v. 1; 4. 4, &c.
OVERFLOWING,] as in 10. 22; 28. 2, 15, &c.
DIVIDETH,] *lit.* 'halveth;' as in Ge. 32. 7.
SIFT,] *or* 'wave;' as in 10. 15; Lev. 7. 30, &c.
CAUSING TO ERR,] as in 3. 12; 9. 16, &c.
29. SINGING,] as in 23. 16; 24. 9; 26. 1, &c.
SANCTIFIED,] *or* 'set-apart;' as in 2 Ch. 29. 34.
30. CAUSED TO BE HEARD,] as in 43. 12, &c.
COMING DOWN,] as in v. 15; Job 17. 16, &c.
SHEW,] as in 39. 2; Ge. 12. 1; Nu. 13. 26, &c.
RAGING,] as in 2 Ch. 16. 10; 28. 9; Prov. 19. 12; Jon. 1. 15; Mic. 7. 9.
31. VOICE OF JEHOVAH,] as in 6. 8; 66. 6.
BROKEN DOWN,] *or* 'brought down;' as in 7. 8; 30. 31; 51. 6, 7, &c.
ROD,] *or* 'sceptre;' as in 9. 4; 10. 5, 15, &c.
SMITETH,] as in 5. 25; 10. 24; 37. 36, &c.
32. PASSAGE,] as in Ge. 32. 22; 1 Sa 13. 23.
SETTLED STAFF,] *or* 'founded rod;' as in 9. 4; 10. 5, 15, 24, 26; 14. 5, &c.
TO REST,] as in 63. 14; Prov. 29. 17; Eze. 37. 1; 40. 2.
SHAKING,] as in 19. 16; Ex. 29. 24—27, &c.
33. ARRANGED,] as in Jos. 2. 6; 2 Sa. 23. 5.
FORMER TIME,] *lit.* 'yesterday;' as in 1 Sa. 4 7; 10. 11; 14. 21, &c.
TOPHET,] *or* Tophteh, i. e. a 'spitting place.'
THE KING] of Asshur.
PREPARED,] *or* 'made ready;' as in 16. 5.
MADE LARGE,] *or* 'broad;' as in 5. 14, &c.

XXXI. 1. WO,] as in 1. 4, 24; 5. 8, 11, &c.
LEAN,] as in 18. 4, &c.
TRUST,] *or* 'are confident;' as in 12. 2, &c.
STRONG,] *or* 'bony;' as in Ge. 26. 16, &c.
HOLY ONE,] the one 'set-apart, separate.'
SOUGHT,] as in 9. 13; 19. 3; 65. 10, &c.
2. WISE,] as in 3. 3; 5. 21; 19. 11, 12, &c.
TURNED ASIDE,] as in 18. 5; 36. 7, &c.
RISEN,] as in 14. 22; 49. 7; Ge. 37. 7, &c.
3. GOD,] i.e. 'mighty;' as in 5. 16; 7. 14, &c.
STRETCHED OUT,] *or* 'inclineth;'
STUMBLED,] as in 3. 8; 8. 15; 28. 13, &c.
CONSUMED,] *or* 'ended, finished;' as in 1. 28; Ge. 21. 15; 41. 53, &c.
4. GROWL,] *lit.* 'meditate;' as in 16. 7, &c.
AFFRIGHTED,] *or* 'brought down;' as in 7. 8; 30. 31; 51. 6, 7, &c.
HUMBLED,] as in Ps. 119. 67; Zech. 10. 2.
TO WAR,] as in Nu. 4. 23; 8. 24.
5. BIRDS,] *or* 'sparrows;' as in Ge. 7. 44, &c.
FLYING,] as in Zech. 5. 1, 2.
DELIVERING,] *lit.* 'snatching;' as in 19. 20.
CAUSING TO ESCAPE,] as in 66. 7.
6. TURN BACK,] as in 21. 12; 44. 22; 63. 17.
DEEPENED,] as in 30. 33; Jer. 49. 8, 30, &c.
APOSTACY,] *lit.* 'a turning aside;' as in 1. 5; 14. 6; 59. 18, &c
7. DESPISE,] as in Lev. 26. 15; 1 Sa. 15. 23.
IDOLS,] *lit.* 'nothings;' as in 2. 8, 18, &c.

8. SWORD,] as in 1. 20; 2. 4; 3. 25, &c.
CONSUME,] as in 1. 19; 3. 10; 4. 1, &c.
FLED,] as in 10. 29; 17. 13; 20. 6, &c.
YOUNG MEN,] *or* 'choice ones;' as in 9. 17.
9. ROCK,] as in 2. 21; 7. 19; 16. 1, &c.
PASSETH ON,] as in 26. 20; 28. 15, 18, &c.
AFFRIGHTED,] *or* 'brought down;' as in 20. 5; 37. 27; 2 K. 19. 26, &c.

XXXII. 1. LO,] as in Ge. 1. 29; 12. 11, &c.
REIGN,] as in 37. 38; Ge. 36. 31; 37. 8, &c.
RULE,] as in Prov. 8. 16, &c.
2. EACH,] *lit.* a 'man;' as in 2. 9; 3. 2, &c.
4. HASTENED,] as in 35. 4; Job 5. 13, &c.
HASTETH,] as in 5. 19; 59. 7; Ge. 18. 6, 7.
5. FOOL,] as in v. 6; De. 32. 6, 21; 2 Sa. 3. 33.
NOBLE,] *or* 'willing.'
6. FOLLY,] as in 9. 17; Ge. 34. 7; De. 21. 22.
7. COUNSELLED,] as in v. 8; 7. 5; 14. 24, &c.
CORRUPT,] as in 13. 5; 54. 16.
POOR,] *or* 'meek;' as in 11. 4; 29. 19, &c.
LYING SAYINGS,] *or* 'sayings of falsehood.
JUSTLY,] *lit.* 'judgment;' as in v. 1, &c.
8. NOBLE,] *or* 'willing;' as in v. 5; Ex. 35. 5.
RISETH UP,] as in 21. 5; 23. 12; 51. 17, &c.
9. EASY ONES,] as in 11. 18; 33. 20; 37. 29.
HEAR,] as in 1. 2, 10; 6. 9; 7. 13, &c.
GIVE EAR,] as in 1. 2, 10; 8. 9; 28. 23, &c.
10. TROUBLED,] as in v. 11; Ps. 4. 4.
CONSUMED,] *or* 'ended;' as in 10. 25; 15. 6.
11. TROUBLED,] as in v. 10; Ps. 4. 4.
12. BREASTS,] as in 28. 9; Ge. 49. 25, &c.
LAMENTING,] as in Ecc. 12. 5.
13. THORN,] as in 33. 12; Ge. 3. 18; Ex. 22. 6.
EXULTING,] as in 13. 3; 22. 2; 23. 7; 24. 8.
14. PALACE,] *lit.* 'high place;' as in 23. 13.
FORSAKEN,] as in Jer. 49. 25, &c.
DENS,] *or* 'holes;' as in 2. 19; 19. 30; 23. 9.
15. EMPTIED OUT,] *or* 'made bare, or exposed.'
FRUITFUL FIELD,] *or* 'prepared place.'
RECKONED,] as in 29. 16, 17; Lev. 7. 18, &c.
16. DWELT,] *lit.* 'tabernacled.'
REMAINETH,] as in 13. 21; Ex. 35. 8, &c.
17. WORK,] as in 2. 8; 3. 24; 5. 12, 19, &c.
KEEPING QUIET,] as in 30. 15; 57. 20, &c.
18. DWELT,] as in 65. 21; Ge. 13. 12; 19. 29.
HABITATION,] *lit.* 'comely place.'
20. HAPPY,] as in 30. 18; 56. 2; De. 33. 29.
SOWING,] as in 55. 10; Ge. 1. 29; Job 4. 8.

XXXIII. 1. WO,] as in 1. 4, 24; 5. 8; 10. 1.
DEALT TREACHEROUSLY,] as in 24. 16, &c.
FINISH,] as in Eze. 24. 10; Da. 8. 23, &c.
2. FAVOUR,] as in Ge. 33. 5, 11; Ex. 33. 19.
WAITED,] as in 5. 4; 8. 17; 25. 9; 26. 8, &c.
TIME OF ADVERSITY,] *lit.* 'straitness.'
3. FLED,] *lit.* 'moved away;' as in 10. 31.
SCATTERED,] as in Ge. 9. 19; 1 Sa. 13. 11.
4. GATHERED,] as in 24. 22; Hos. 10. 10.
Zech. 14. 14.
SPOIL,] as in v. 23; 8. 1, 3, 4; 9. 3, &c.
RUNNING TO AND FRO,] as in 29. 8, &c.
5. SET ON HIGH,] as in 12. 4; 26. 5; 30. 13.
DWELLING,] *lit.* 'tabernacling.'
6. STEDFASTNESS,] as in 11. 5; 25. 1; 59. 4.
7. THEIR ARIEL,] as in 29. 1. Most ancient versions read, 'I will see to them.'
CRIED,] as in De. 22. 24, 27; 1 K. 20. 39, &c.
WEEP,] as in 16. 9; 30. 9, 38. 3, &c.
8. DESOLATED,] as in Lev. 26. 22; Job 18. 20.

CEASED,] or rested, *lit.* 'kept sabbath.'
PASSETH ALONG,] as in 23. 2; 29. 5; 34. 10.
DISPISED,] as in 5. 24; 8. 6; 41. 9, &c.
ENEMIES,] or 'cities;' as in 1. 7, 8, 26, &c.
ESTEEMED,] as in 53. 3, 4.
9. MOURNED,] as in 3. 26; 19. 8; 24. 4, 7, &c.
LANGUISHED,] as in 16. 8; 19. 8; 24. 4, &c.
WITHERED,] as in 19. 6.
10. ARISE,] as in 7. 7; 8. 10; 14. 21, 24, &c.
EXALTED,] as in Eze. 10. 15, 17, 19.
LIFTED UP,] as in 40. 4; 49. 22; 66. 12, &c.
11. CONCEIVE,] as in 8. 3; Hos. 1. 3, 6, 8.
BEAR,] as in 8. 3; 65. 23; Ge. 3. 16, &c.
DEVOURETH,] as in 1. 19; 3. 10; 4. 1, &c.
12. BURNINGS,] as in Jos. 11. 8; 13. 6; Jer. 34. 5.
BURN,] or 'art burnt;' as in Ps. 80. 16.
13. FAR OFF,] as in 5. 26; 22. 3; 23. 7, &c.
14. AFRAID,] as in 19. 16; 60. 5; De. 28. 66.
SINNERS,] *lit.* those 'missing the mark.'
SEIZED,] as in 21. 3; Ex. 15. 14; 2 Sa. 1. 9.
DWELL,] *lit.* 'sojourn;' as in 16. 4; 54. 15.
15. RIGHTEOUSLY,] *lit.* 'rightnesses;' as in 1 K. 3. 6.
UPRIGHTLY,] *lit.* 'upright things;' as in 26. 7; 45. 19; 1 Ch. 29. 17, &c.
KICKING,] as in Prov. 15. 32; Eze. 21. 10, 13.
TAKING HOLD,] as in Ps. 17. 5.
STOPPING,] as in Prov. 17. 28; 21. 13.
16. HIGH PLACES,] as in v. 5; 22. 16, &c.
INHABIT,] *lit.* 'tabernacle.'
GIVEN,] as in Ex. 5. 16; 2 K. 22. 7, &c.
17. BEAUTY,] or 'fairness;' as in 3. 24, &c.
18. HEART,] as in 6. 10; 15. 5; 24. 7, &c.
MEDITATE,] as in 16. 7; 31. 4; 38. 14, &c.
COUNTING,] as in 36. 3; 37. 2; Jud. 5. 14, &c.
WEIGHING,] as in 36. 3; 37. 2; Jud. 5. 14, &c.
TOWERS,] *lit.* 'great places;' as in 2. 15, &c.
19. UNDERSTOOD,] *lit.* 'heard;' as in v. 15.
20. MEETINGS,] as in 1. 14; 14. 33; Ex. 27. 21.
HABITATION,] or 'comely place;' as in 27. 10.
REMOVED,] *lit.* 'caused to journey.'
BROKEN,] or 'removed;' as in Jos. 8. 16, &c.
21. MIGHTY,] or 'honourable;' as in 10. 34.
BROAD OF SIDES,] *lit.* 'of hands.'
22. JUDGE,] as in 1. 26; 3. 2; 16. 5, &c.
SAVE,] as in 25. 9; 35. 4; 45. 20, &c.
23. LEFT,] as in 16. 8; Am. 5. 2.
STRENGTHEN,] as in 22. 21; 41. 7; Ex. 4. 21.
RIGHTLY,] as in Ex. 10. 29; Nu. 27. 7, &c.
SPREAD OUT,] as in Nu. 4. 6; De. 22. 17, &c.
SAIL,] or 'ensign;' as in 5. 26; 11. 10, &c.
APPORTIONED,] as in Zech. 14. 1.
LAME,] *lit.* 'leaping, limping ones.'
24. SICK,] or 'pained;' as in 38. 1; 39. 1, &c.
FORGIVEN,] *lit.* 'lifted up of iniquity.'

XXXIV. 1. COME NEAR,] as in 48. 16, &c.
GIVE ATTENTION,] as in 10. 30; 28. 23, &c.
WORLD,] the 'fruit-bearing or habitable earth.'
PRODUCTIONS,] *lit* out-goings;' as in 22. 24; 42. 5; 44; 3, &c.
2. WRATH,] as in 54. 8; 60. 10; Nu. 1. 53, &c.
FURY,] *lit* 'heat;' as in 27. 4; 42. 25, &c.
DEVOTED,] as in 3. 4; 8. 18; 22. 22, &c.
3. WOUNDED,] *lit* 'pierced ones;' as in 22. 2; 66. 16; Ge. 34. 27, &c.
CAST OUT,] as in Ex. 10. 5.
• MELTED,] as in Ex. 16. 21; 1 Sa. 15. 9, &c.
4. CONSUMED,] as in Ps. 38. 5; Eze. 4. 17.

BOOK,] or 'scroll, roll;' as in v. 16; 29. 11.
FADE,] as in 64. 6; Ex. 18. 18; 2 Sa. 22. 46.
OF A VINE,] *lit.* 'from a vine.'
OF A FIG-TREE,] *lit.* 'from a fig-tree.'
5. SOAKED,] or 'withered,' as in v. 7.
COMETH DOWN,] as in 31. 4; 55. 10; 63. 14.
MY CURSE,] *lit.* 'my devoted thing.'
6. FULL OF BLOOD,] as in 1. 15; 15. 9; Eze. 9. 9.
LAMBS,] or 'rams;' as in 1. 11; 14. 9, &c.
BOZRAH,] as in 63. 1; Ge. 36. 33; Jer. 48. 24.
7. REEMS,] as in Nu. 23. 22; 24. 8; De. 33. 17.
SOAKED,] as in v. 5.
8. DAY OF VENGEANCE,] as in 61. 2; 63. 4. Prov. 6. 34.
RECOMPENSES,] *lit.* 'completings;' as in Hos. 9. 7; Mic. 7. 3.
9. STREAMS,] as in 11. 15, 27. 12; 30. 28, &c.
10. QUENCHED,] as in 66. 24; Lev. 6. 12, &c.
11. POSSESS,] as in 14. 21; 63. 18; 65. 9, &c.
DWELL,] *lit.* 'tabernacle.'
VACANCY,] or 'ruin;' as in 24. 10; 29. 11, &c.
EMPTINESS,] as in Ge. 1. 2; Jer. 4. 23.
12. FREEMEN,] *lit.* 'white men.'
PRINCES,] *lit.* 'heads;' as in 1. 23; 3. 4, &c.
AT AN END,] or 'nothing.'
13. PALACES,] or 'high places.'
HABITATION,] *lit.* 'comely place.'
DAUGHTERS OF AN OSTRICH,] as in 13. 21.
14. GOAT,] *lit.* 'hairy one;' as in 13. 21, &c.
COMPANION,] or 'friend;' as in 3. 5; 13. 8.
RESTED,] momentarily, as the original word implies; as in Jer. 50. 34.
15. NEST,] as in Ps. 104. 17; Jer. 48. 28; Eze. 31. 6.
LAYETH,] *lit.* 'letteth escape;' as in 46. 4.
HATCHED,] *lit.* 'cleaved;' as in Neh. 9. 11.
GATHERED,] as in Jer. 17. 11.
EACH..COMPANION,] *lit.* 'a woman, her friend.'
16. SEEK,] as in 1. 17; 8. 19; 55. 16, &c.
BOOK,] roll or scroll; as in v. 4; 19. 11, &c.
READ,] *lit.* 'call,' for reading in the east is generally done aloud.
LACKING,] *lit.* 'arranged;' as in 40. 26, &c.
MISSED,] *lit.* 'inspected;' as in 13. 11. &c.
COMMANDED,] as in 13. 3; 23. 11; 45. 12, &c.
GATHERED,] as in 43. 9; 49. 18; 60. 4, &c.
17. CAST,] *lit.* 'caused to fall;' as in 3. 2.
APPORTIONED,] as in Lam. 4. 16; Eze. 5. 1; 47. 21; Joel 3. 2.
ALL GENERATIONS,] *lit.* 'generation of generation.'

XXXV. 1. JOY,] *lit.* 'leap for joy;' as in 61. 10; 62. 5; De. 28. 63, &c.
REJOICE,] as in v. 2; 9. 3; 25. 9, &c.
FLOURISH,] as in Lev. 13. 12; Nu. 17. 5, &c.
2. JOY,] as in 1. 9, 3; 25. 9, &c.
HONOUR,] *lit.* 'weight, heaviness.'
BEAUTY,] or 'majesty;' as in 2. 10; 5. 14.
3. STRENGTHEN,] as in 54. 2; De. 1. 38, &c.
FEEBLE HANDS,] as in 2 Sa. 17. 2; Job 4. 3.
STRENGTHEN,] as in De. 3. 28; Nah. 2. 1.
4. BE STRONG,] as in 41. 6; De. 31. 6, 7, &c.
FEAR NOT,] as in 7. 4; 8. 12; 10. 24, &c.
RECOMPENSE,] or 'deed;' as in 34. 8; 47. 3.
SAVE,] or 'ease;' as in 25. 9; 33. 45. 20.
5. OPENED,] as in Neh. 7. 3; Job 14, &c.
UNSTOPPED,] or 'opened;' as in Neh. 7. 3.
6. LEAP,] as in 2 Sa. 22. 30; Ps. 18. 29.

2 L

LAME,] *or* 'limping, leaping.'
SING,] as in 24. 14; 42. 11; 61. 7, &c.
BROKEN UP,] *or* 'cleft;' as in Ge. 7. 11, &c.
7. THIRSTY,] as in De. 8. 15; Ps 107. 33.
CROUCHING DOWN,] as in 65. 10; Prov. 24.
15; Jer. 50. 6.
8. HIGHWAY,] *or* 'raised up way.'
HOLINESS,] *or* 'separation.'
UNCLEAN,] as in 6. 5; 52. 1, 11; 64. 6, &c.
ERR,] *or* 'go astray;' as in Ge. 21. 14, &c.
9. LION,] as in 11. 7; 15. 9; 21. 8, &c.
DESTRUCTIVE,] *lit.* 'breaking forth or
through.'
10. RANSOMED,] as in 51. 11; Nu. 18. 16.
RETURN,] as in 7. 3; 10. 21, 22; 12. 1, &c.
ATTAIN,] *or* 'overtake;' as in 51. 11; 59. 9.
FLED AWAY,] as in 10. 29; 17. 13, 20. 6, &c.

XXXVI. 1. FOURTEENTH YEAR,] B.C.
SEIZETH,] as in 3. 6; Ge. 39. 12; De. 9. 17.
2. UPPER POOL,] *or* 'blessing;' as in 7. 3; 2
K. 18. 17.
FULLER,] *or* 'washerman;' as in 7. 3; 2
K. 18. 17.
3. THE HOUSE,] that is, 'the temple.'
SCRIBE,] *or* 'writer, counter, enumerator.'
REMEMBRANCER,] as in v. 22; 62. 6; 66. 3.
4. I PRAY YOU,] as in Ge. 12. 11, 13, &c.
CONFIDED,] as in v. 5, 6, 7; Jud. 20. 36, &c.
5. I HAVE SAID,] regarding this confi-
dence.
TRUSTED,] *or* ' confided;' as in v. 4, 6, &c.
REBELLED,] as in Ge. 14. 4; 2 K. 18. 20, &c.
6. STAFF,] as in Ex. 21. 19; Nu. 21. 18, &c.
LEANETH,] *or* ' is supported on;' as in Jud.
16. 29; 2 K. 18. 21, &c.
PIERCED,] as in 2 K. 18. 21; Hab. 3. 14.
7. ALTARS,] *lit.* ' places of sacrifice.'
TURNED ASIDE,] as in 18. 5; 31. 2, &c.
BOW YOURSELVES,] as in 2 K. 17. 3, 5.
8. NEGOTIATE,] *lit.* 'trade or mix yourselves up.'
HORSES,] in which Judah was deficient.
9. CAPTAIN,] as in 1 K. 10. 15; 20. 24, &c.
10. DESTROY,] *or* 'mar;' as in 51. 13; 65. 8.
11. UNDERSTANDING,] *lit.* ' hearing;' as in
1. 15; 32. 3; 41. 26, &c.
WALL,] listening to the conversation.
13. GREAT VOICE,] as in 1 Sa. 28. 12, &c.
14. LIFT YOU UP,] as in 37. 10; 2 K. 18. 29.
DELIVER,] *lit.* 'snatch;' as in v. 15; 50. 2.
15. MAKE YOR TRUST,] as in 2 K. 18. 30; Jer.
29. 31.
JEHOVAH,] the covenant God of Israel.
16. HEARKEN,] as in 6. 8, 10; 18. 3; 30. 21.
BLESSING,] as in 19. 24; 44. 3; 65. 8, &c.
17. WINE,] *or* ' new wine,' as in 24. 7; 62. 8.
VINEYARD,] *or* ' prepared place.'
PERSUADE,] as in De. 13. 16; Jos. 15. 18, &c.
18. GODS OF THE NATIONS,] as in 37. 12, &c.
21. KEEP SILENT,] *lit.* ' remain deaf;' as in
42. 14; Ex. 14. 14; Nu. 30. 14, &c.
COMMAND,] as in 29. 13; 48. 18; Ge. 26. 5.
ANSWER,] as in 14. 10, 32; 21. 9; 25. 5, &c.
22. WITH RENT GARMENTS,] *lit.* ' rent of
garments.'
DECLARE,] *or* 'set before him;' as in Ge.
26. 32; 42. 20; 43. 7, &c.

XXXVII. 1. HEARING] the report of Elea-
kim.

RENDETH,] as in Ge. 37. 29, 34; 44. 13, &c
COVERETH HIMSELF,] as in 59. 6; Ge. 24. 65
HOUSE OF JEHOVAH,] that is, the temple.
2. SENDETH,] as his ambassadors.
ELDERS OF THE PRIESTS,] as in 2 K. 19. 2
PROPHET,] the declarer of God's law
whether past, present, or future.
3. DISTRESS,] *lit.* 'straitness;' as in 8. 22.
REBUKE,]*lit.* 'making prominent, evident.
BIRTH,] *lit.* ' breaking;' as in 2. K. 19. 3.
TO BEAR,] as in 26. 17; Ge. 4. 2; 16. 2, &c.
4. IT MAY BE,] as in Ge. 16. 2; Ex. 32. 30.
THY GOD,] as in v. 10; 7. 11; 41. 10, &c.
DECIDED,] *or* ' made prominent, evident.'
LIFTED UP,] as in 5. 26; 10. 26; 11. 12, &c.
FOUND,] as in 13. 15; 22. 3; Ge. 19. 15, &c.
5. SERVANTS,] mentioned in v. 2.
6. AFRAID,] as in 7. 4; 8. 12; 10. 24, &c.
REVILED,] as in v. 23; 2 K. 19. 6, 22; Eze.
20. 27.
7. GIVING,] as in 40. 23, 29; 42. 5; 43. 16, &c.
IN HIM,] not 'against him,' as in C.V.
REPORT,] *lit.* a ' hearing;' as in 28. 9, &c.
TURNED BACK,] as in v. 34. 37; 7. 3, &c.
CAUSED TO FALL,] as in 34. 17; Ge. 15. 12.
8. FIGHTING,] as in Ex. 14. 25; De. 3. 22, &c.
JOURNEYED,] as in 33. 20; Ge. 12. 9; 13. 11.
10. LIFT THEE UP,] as in 36. 14; 2 K. 18. 29.
TRUSTING,] as in 32. 9—11; 36. 6; 42. 17, &c.
11. DEVOTE,] as in De. 3. 6; 7. 2; 20. 17, &c.
12. GODS OF THE NATIONS,] as in 36. 18, &c.
DESTROYED,] *or* 'marred;' as in Ge. 6. 12, &c.
14. LETTERS,] *lit.* ' scroll, rolls, or books.'
SPREADETH,] as in Ex. 9. 29, 33; 40. 19, &c.
15. PRAYETH,] as in 38. 2; 44. 17; 45. 14, &c.
16. JEHOVAH OF HOSTS,] as in v. 32; 1. 9.
INHABITING THE CHERUBS,] as in 2 K. 19.
15; 1 Ch. 13. 6; Ps. 80. 1; 99. 1, &c.
MADE,] as in v. 11, 26, 31; 2. 8, 20; 5. 4, &c.
17. INCLINE THINE EAR,] as in 30. 11, &c.
HEAR,] as in 1. 2, 10; 6. 9; 7. 13, &c.
SEE,] as in 6. 9; 40. 26; 49. 18, &c.
HEAR,] as in 1. 2, 10; 6. 9; 7. 13, &c.
18. TRULY,] as in 19. 17; Ru. 3. 12, &c.
LAID WASTE,] as in 2 K. 19. 17; Jer. 51. 36.
THEIR LAND,] their own land, that of
Asshur.
19. PUT,] *lit.* ' give;' as in 36. 8; 61. 3, &c.
DESTROY,] as in 26. 14; Nu. 33. 52; De. 11. 4.
20. SAVE,] as in Jos. 10. 6; 2 Sa. 14. 4, &c.
21. PRAYED,] as in 1 Sa. 1. 27; 1 K. 8. 33, &c.
22. TRAMPLED,] as in 2 K. 19. 21; Nu. 15.
31; 2 Sa. 12. 9, 10.
LAUGHED,] as in 2 K. 19. 21.
SHAKEN,] *or* 'moved;' as in 2 K. 19. 21, &c
23. REPROACHED,] as in v. 24; 2 K. 19. 6, &c.
REVILED,] as in v. 6, 24; 2 K. 19. 6, &c.
LIFTED UP,] as in Ge. 14. 22; 39. 15, &c.
HOLY ONE,] *or* ' separate one.'
24. REVILED,] as in v. 6, 23; 2 K. 19. 6, &c.
MULTITUDE,] *or* 'abundance;' as in 1. 11.
SIDES,] *lit.* ' thighs;' as in 14. 13, 15, &c.
CUT DOWN,] as in 55. 3; 57. 8; 61. 8, &c.
CARMEL,] *or* ' fruitful place;' as in 10. 18.
25. DUG,] as in 2 K. 19. 24.
DRY UP,] as in 44. 12; 51. 17; Ex. 17. 6, &c
26. AFAR,] as in 5. 26; 22. 3, 11; 23. 7, &c
OF OLD,] *or* ' of antiquity or former time.
FORMED,] as in v. 11, 16, 31; 2. 8, 20, &c.
MAKE DESOLATE,] as in 2 K. 19. 25.
27. FEEBLE-HANDED,] *lit.* ' short of hand.'

BROKEN DOWN,] as in 20. 5; 31. 9, &c.
DRIED UP,] as in 19. 9; 20. 5; 24. 23, &c.
RISEN UP,] as in 17. 5; Ex. 22. 6; De. 16. 9.
28. SITTING DOWN,] as in 40. 22; 44. 13, &c.
GOING OUT,] as in 13. 10; Ge. 8. 7; 12. 4, &c.
COMING IN,] as in 2. 21; 13. 22; 14. 9, &c.
THY ANGER,] *lit.* 'thy being angry.'
29. NOISE,] as in 2 K. 19. 28.
TO TURN BACK] to Asshur.
30. SIGN,] *or* 'token;' as in 7. 11, 14, &c.
SELF-SOWN GRAIN,] as in 2 K. 19. 29, &c.
SOW,] as in 2 K. 19. 29; Ecc. 11. 6, &c.
PLANT,] as in 2 K. 19. 29; Jer. 29. 5, 28.
31. CONTINUED,] as in 26. 15; 29. 19; &c.
LEFT,] as in 4. 3; Ge. 14. 10; 32. 8, &c.
32. REMNANT,] as in v. 4; 14. 30; 15. 7, &c.
33. CITY] of Jerusalem.
SHOOT,] as in 2. 3; 23. 9, 26; Ex. 15. 25, &c.
POUR OUT,] as in 42. 25.
MOUNT,] *or* 'raised up place;' as in 2 K.
19. 32; 2 Sa. 20. 15; Jer. 6. 6, &c.
34. TURNETH BACK,] as in 7. 3; 10. 21, &c.
35. COVERED,] as in 38. 6; 2 K. 19. 34; 20. 6.
SAVE,] as in 38. 20; 59. 1; 63. 1, &c.
36. MESSENGER OF JEHOVAH,] as in Ge. 16.
7, 9—11; 22. 11, 15; Ex. 3. 2, &c.
SMITETH,] as in 5. 25; 10. 24; 30. 31, &c.
FIVE THOUSAND.] The Hebrew order of
words is ambiguous, it may mean 185,000 or
85,000 or 5,180. The order of Eze. xlviii.
supports the latter computation; in either
case the judgment was direct and divine.
37. JOURNEY,] as in 33. 20; 2 K. 3. 27, &c.
38. BOWING HIMSELF,] as in 2 K. 19. 37, &c.

XXXVIII. 1. SICK,] *or* 'pained;' as in 33.
24; 39. 1; 57. 10, &c.
GIVE A CHARGE,] as in 2 K. 20. 1; Lev. 6. 9.
DYING,] as in 2 K. 20. 1; Ge. 20. 3, &c.
2. TURNETH ROUND HIS FACE,] as in 2 K.
20. 2; 1 K. 8. 14; 21. 4, &c.
PRAYETH,] as in 2 K. 20. 2; Isa. 37. 15, &c.
3. I PRAY THEE,] as in 2 K. 20. 3; Ge. 50. 17.
REMEMBER,] as in 44. 21; 46. 8, 9, &c.
WALKED HABITUALLY,] as in 6. 9; 24. 40.
WEEPETH,] as in 16. 9; 30. 19; 33. 7, &c.
4. WORD OF JEHOVAH,] as in 1. 10; 2. 3, &c.
5. GOD OF DAVID,] as in 2 K. 20. 5; 2 Ch.
21. 12.
ADDING,] as in 29. 14; De. 5. 25.
6. DELIVER,] *or* 'snatch;' as in 36. 15, &c.
COVERED,] as in 37. 35; 2 K. 19. 34; 20. 6.
7. SIGN,] as in 7. 11, 14; 8. 18; 19. 20, &c.
8. SHADOW,] as in 4. 6; 16. 3; 25. 4, 5, &c.
DEGREES,] as in 2 K. 20. 9, 10, 11, &c.
GONE DOWN,] as in 5. 14; 34. 7; 52. 4, &c.
9. WRITING,] as in Ex. 32. 16; 39. 30, &c.
BEING SICK,] as in Ps. 35. 15.
REVIVETH,] as in v. 1, 16, 21; 26. 14, &c.
10. NUMBERED,] as in Ex. 38. 21.
11. JAH JAH.] Probably a scribe's error for
'Yehovah.'
LAND OF THE LIVING,] as in 53. 8; Job
28. 13.
WORLD] of spirits, for the word is, *lit.* a
ceasing' or cessation.
12. SOJOURNING,] *or* 'circuit;' as in 13. 20.
DEPARTED,] *or* 'journeyed;' as in Job 4. 21.
REMOVED,] as in 22. 14; 23. 1; 40. 5, &c.
CUTTETH ME OFF,] as in 10. 12; Job 6. 9, &c.
END,] *or* 'complete;' as in v. 13; 44. 26, &c.

13. SET,] *or* 'equaled;' as in 28. 25, &c.
BONES,] as in 58. 11; 66. 14; Ge. 2. 23, &c.
14. CHATTER,] as in 29. 4.
MOURN,] as in 16. 7; 31. 4; 33. 18, &c.
DRAWN UP,] as in 19. 6; Job 28. 4, &c.
15. WROUGHT,] *or* 'done it.'
GO SOFTLY,] as in Ps. 42. 4.
16. LORD,] as in 3. 15, 17; 4. 4; 6. 1, 8, &c.
LIVE,] as in v. 1, 9, 21; 26. 14, 19; 55. 3, &c.
SAVEST,] *or* 'makest me fat.'
LIVE,] as in Nu. 31. 18.
17. CHANGED,] as in Ru. 1. 13; 1 Sa. 30. 6.
DELIGHTED,] as in Ge. 34. 8; De. 7. 7, &c.
CORRUPTION,] *or* 'marring.'
18. SHEOL,] as in v. 18; 5. 14; 14. 9, &c.
CONFESS,] as in v. 19; 12. 1; 25. 1, &c.
PRAISE,] as in Ge. 12. 15; Jud. 16. 24, &c.
HOPE,] as in Ru. 1. 13; Ps. 104. 27; 145. 15.
19. LIVING,] as in v. 11; 53. 8; Ge. 1. 20, &c.
20. MAKE KNOWN,] as in 5. 5; 40. 13, &c.
SAVE,] as in 37. 35; 59. 1; 63. 1, &c.
SONGS,] *or* 'stringed instruments;' as in
Job 30. 9; Ps. 4. 61. 67. 69. 12; 76. 77. 6, &c.
SING,] *or* 'play on, or use.'
HOUSE OF JEHOVAH,] that is, the temple.
21. BUNCH OF FIGS,] as in 1 Sa. 25. 18, &c.
SIGN,] *or* 'token;' as in v. 7; 7. 11, 14, &c.

XXXIX. 1. SICK,] *or* 'pained;' as in 33. 24.
2. REJOICETH,] as in 9. 17; 14. 29; 25. 9, &c.
SPICES,] *or* 'balsams.'
SHOWED,] as in v. 4; Ge. 41. 28; 48. 11, &c.
3. ISAIAH THE PROPHET,] as in 37. 2, &c.
4. TREASURES,] as in v. 2; 2. 7; 30. 6, &c.
5. JEHOVAH OF HOSTS,] as in 1. 9, 24, &c.
6. DAYS ARE COMING,] as in 1 Sa. 2. 31, &c.
BORNE,] as in 52. 13; Ex. 25. 28; 2 K. 20. 17.
TREASURED UP,] as in 2 K. 10. 17.
LEFT,] as in 32. 24; 44. 20; Ex. 29. 34.
7. BEGETTEST,] as in Ge. 5. 3, 4; 6. 10, &c.
PALACE,] *or* 'temple;' as in 6. 1; 13. 22, &c.
8. GOOD,] as in 3. 10; 5. 9, 20; 7. 15, 16, &c.
TRUTH,] as in 10. 20; 16. 5; 38. 3, &c.
Here ends the *first* great division of the
" Visions of Isaiah."

XL. 1. COMFORT.] Targ. 'prophesy com-
fort.'
2. SPEAK TO THE HEART,] as in Jud. 19. 8.
COMPLETED,] *lit.* 'full;' as in 1. 15; 2. 6, &c.
ACCEPTED,] *lit.* 'pleasing;' as in 6. 6, &c.
DOUBLE,] as in Job 11. 6; 41. 13.
3. CRYING,] *or* 'calling;' as in 6. 4; 21. 11.
WILDERNESS,] *or* 'pasture-land;' as in 14.
17; 16. 1, 8; 21. 1, &c.
PREPARE,] *lit.* 'face ye;' as in 57. 14;
62. 10.
MAKE STRAIGHT,] *or* 'right, upright.'
4. VALLEY,] as in 22. 1, 5; 28. 1, 4, &c.
RAISED UP,] *or* 'lifted up;' as in 33. 10, &c.
VALLEY,] *lit.* a 'cleft place;' as in 41. 18.
5. REVEALED,] as in 22. 14; 23. 1; 38. 12, &c.
6. CALL,] as in v. 2; 8. 3; 12. 4, &c.
GOODLINESS,] *lit.* 'kindness;' as in 16. 5, &c.
7. WITHERED,] as in v. 8; 15. 6; 19. 5, &c.
FADED,] as in v. 8; 24. 4; Prov. 30. 32, &c.
8. RISETH,] as in 7. 7; 8. 10; 14. 21, 24, &c.
9. HIGH MOUNT,] as in 2. 14; 13. 2; 30. 25.
PROCLAIMING TIDINGS,] as in 41. 27, &c.
LIFT UP,] as in 13. 2; 57. 14; 58. 1, &c.
10. LORD JEHOVAH,] as in 3. 15; 7. 7 &c.

RULING,] as in 14. 5; 16. 1; 28. 14, &c.
WAGE,] or ' work;' as in 62. 11; Ge. 15. 1, &c.
11. SHEPHERD,] as in 13. 20; 31. 4; 44. 20.
FLOCK,] lit. ' herd, drove;' as in 17. 2, &c.
FEEDETH,] as in 11. 7; 27. 10; 30. 23, &c.
GATHERETH,] as in 11. 12; 22. 9; 43. 5, &c.
CARRIETH,] as in 2. 4; 3. 7; 8. 4, &c.
LEADETH,] as in 49. 10; Ge. 47. 17, &c.
12. MEASURED,] as in 65. 7; Nu. 35. 5, &c.
METED,] as in v. 13; Job 28. 25.
WEIGHED,] as in 46. 6; 55. 2; 2 Sa. 14. 26.
13. SPIRIT OF JEHOVAH,] as in 11. 2, &c.
COUNSELLOR,] lit. ' and a man, his coun-
sellor.'
TEACH,] lit. ' cause him to know.'
14. CONSULTED,] as in Ps. 71. 10; 83. 5.
TEACHETH,] as in De. 4. 10; 5. 31; 20. 18, &c.
15. RECKONED,] as in v. 17; 5. 28; Ge. 31. 15.
SMALL THING,] or ' thin, lean thing;' as in
29. 5; Ge. 41. 3, 4, 6, 7, 23, 24; Ex. 16. 14, &c.
16. SUFFICIENT,] as in 28. 19; 66. 23, &c.
BURN,] as in 4. 4; 5. 5; 6. 13; 44. 15, &c.
BEASTS,] or ' living creatures;' as in 43.
20; 46. 1; 56. 9, &c.
17. NOTHING,] as in 5. 8; 34. 12; 41. 12, &c.
EMPTINESS,] or ' ruin;' as in v. 23.
RECKONED,] as in v. 15; 5. 28; Ge. 31. 15.
18. LIKEN,] as in v. 25; 10. 7; 46. 5, &c.
COMPARE,] or ' set in array;' as in 44. 7, &c.
19. GRAVEN IMAGE,] as in v. 20; 42. 17, &c.
FOUND OUT,] as in 29. 10; 44. 10.
ARTIZAN,] or ' worker;' as in v. 20.
REFINING,] as in 41. 7; 46. 6; Jud. 17. 4, &c.
20. ROTTEN,] as in Prov. 10. 7.
MOVED,] as in 41. 7; 1 Ch. 16. 30; Job 41. 23.
21. DECLARED,] as in 21. 2; De. 17. 4, &c.
22. CIRCLE,] as in Job 22. 14; Prov. 8. 27.
STRETCHING OUT,] as in 42. 5; 44. 24, &c.
23. MAKING,] lit. ' giving princes for no-
thing.'
EMPTINESS,] or ' ruin;' as in v. 17.
24. BLOWN,] as in Ex. 15. 10.
WITHER,] as in 19. 17; 1 K. 13. 4; 17. 7, &c.
25. LIKEN,] as in v. 18; 10. 7; 46. 5, &c.
EQUAL,] as in Prov. 3. 15; 8. 11; 26. 4.
HOLY ONE,] or ' separate one.'
26. LIFT UP,] as in 13. 2; 49. 18; 51. 6, &c.
PREPARED,] as in 4. 5; 41. 20; 43. 7, &c.
ABUNDANCE OF STRENGTH,] or ' strong
ones;' as in v. 29.
LACKING,] or ' arranged;' as in 34. 16, &c.
27. HID,] or ' kept secret;' as in 28. 15, &c.
PASSETH OVER,] as in 26. 20; 28. 15, 19, &c.
28. GOD OF THE AGE,] as in Ge. 21. 33.
PREPARER,] as in 42. 5; 43. 1, 15; 45. 7, &c.
WEARIED,] as in v. 30; 31; 44. 12; Jer. 2. 24.
FATIGUED,] as in v. 30, 31; 65. 23, &c.
29. WEARY,] as in 50. 4. Jud. 8. 15; 2 Sa.
16. 2.
INCREASETH,] or ' maketh abundant.'
30. YOUTHS,] as in 3. 4, 5; 7. 16; 8. 4, &c.
YOUNG MEN,] or ' choice ones.'
STUMBLE,] as in 63. 13; Ps. 9. 3; Prov. 4. 12.
31. EXPECTING,] as in 49. 23; Ps. 25. 3, &c.
PASS,] as in 9. 10; 41. 1; Ge. 31. 41, &c.
RAISE UP,] or ' rise upon.'
RUN,] as in 55. 5; 59. 7; Ge. 18. 2, &c.
GO ON,] as in 2. 3, 5; 3. 16; 6. 8, &c.

XLI. 1. KEEP SILENT,] as in Jud. 18. 19, &c.
COME NIGH,] as in 50. 8; 65. 5; Ge. 18. 53.

DRAW NEAR,] as in 5. 19; 8. 3; 54. 14, &c.
2. STIRRED UP,] or ' roused up;' as in v.
25; 45. 13; 2 Ch. 26. 22, &c.
EAST,] or ' sun-rising;' as in v. 25; 43. 5, &c.
RIGHTEOUS ONE,] or ' righteousness.'
FOOT,] to attend him as his servant, as in
Jud. 5. 15, &c.
GIVETH] up to his will.
3. PURSUETH,] as in 5. 11; Ge. 14. 14, &c.
SAFETY,] lit. ' peace or completeness.'
4. WROUGHT,] as in 26. 12; 44. 12, &c.
5. ISLES,] as in v. 1; 11. 11; 20. 6, &c.
FEAR,] as in v. 10, 13, 14; 7. 4; 8. 12, &c.
TREMBLE,] as in Ge. 27. 33; 42. 28, &c.
6. NEIGHBOUR,] or ' friend;' as in 3. 5, &c.
BE STRONG,] as in 35. 4; De. 12. 23, &c.
7. STRENGTHEN,] as in 22. 41; 33. 23, &c.
JOINING,] as in 22. 34; 2 Ch. 18. 33.
MOVED,] as in 40. 20; 1 Ch. 16. 30, &c.
8. MY SERVANT,] as in v. 9; 20. 3; 22. 20, &c.
9. TAKEN HOLD OF,] as in v. 8; 1. 29, &c.
REJECTED,] as in 5. 24; 8. 6; 33. 8, &c.
10. AFRAID,] as in v. 5, 13, 14; 7. 4; 8. 12.
LOOK AROUND,] as in v. 23.
STRENGTHENED,] as in De. 2. 30; Ps. 80.
15, 17.
HELPED,] as in v. 13, 14; 49. 8; Jos. 1. 14.
UPHOLD,] as in Ex. 17. 12; Ps. 41. 12, &c.
11. DISPLEASED,] as in 45. 24.
ASHAMED,] as in 45. 17; 54. 4; Nu. 12. 14, &c.
BLUSH,] as in 45. 17; 54. 4; Nu. 12. 14, &c.
PERISH,] as in 60. 12; Nu. 16. 33; De. 4. 26.
STRIVE,] lit. ' the men of thy strife;' as in
Job 31. 35.
12. DEBATE,] lit. ' men of thy debate.'
WAR,] lit. ' men of thy warfare.'
13. JEHOVAH THY GOD,] as in v. 10; 37. 4.
HELPED,] as in v. 10, 14; 49. 8; Jos. 1. 14.
14. WORM,] as in 14. 11; 66. 24; De. 28. 39.
HOLY ONE,] or ' separate one.'
15. SET,] as in 14. 17, 23; 21. 4; 23. 13, &c.
THRESHEST,] as in 28. 28; Hab. 3. 12.
BEATEST SMALL,] as in 28. 28.
MAKEST,] or ' settest.'
16. WINNOWEST,] as in Ge. 11. 8; 49. 7, &c.
LIFTETH UP,] as in 45. 25; 1 K. 20. 11, &c.
SCATTEREST,] as in 30. 22; Ex. 32. 20, &c.
REJOICEST,] or ' leapest for joy.'
BOAST,] lit. ' praise thyself.'
17. POOR,] or ' meek;' as in 3. 14, 15, &c.
FAILED,] as in Jer. 51. 30.
FORSAKE NOT,] as in 10. 3; 55. 7; Ge. 2. 24.
18. OPEN,] as in 45. 8; 53. 7; Ge. 8. 6, &c.
19. CEDAR,] as in 2. 13; 9. 10; 14. 8, &c.
20. REGARD,] as in v. 15, 18, 19, 22; 3. 7, &c.
ACT WISELY,] as in 52. 13; De. 29, 9, &c.
PREPARED,] as in v. 4; 2. 8, 20; 5. 4, &c.
21. BRING NEAR,] as in Eze. 37. 17.
CAUSE,] lit. ' strife, controversy.'
BRING NIGH,] as in 45. 25; Ge. 27. 25, &c.
22. DECLARE,] as in v. 23; 45. 21; 48. 20, &c.
HAPPEN,] as in Nu. 11. 23; Ru. 2. 3, &c.
23. HEREAFTER,] as in v. 17; Prov. 29. 11.
LOOK AROUND,] as in v. 10.
24. FIXETH,] as in 40. 20; 49. 7; 58. 5, &c.
25. STIRRED,] or ' awaked;' as in v. 2, &c.
IN MY NAME,] as in v. 14; 27. 15, &c.
POTTER,] lit. ' fashioner, former;' as in 22.
11; 27. 11; 29. 16, &c.
TREADETH DOWN,] as in 26. 6; 63. 3, &c.
26. FIRST,] as in v 4; 48. 16; Prov. 8. 23.

DECLARING,] as in 42. 9; 45. 19; 46. 10, &c.
PROCLAIMING,] or 'sounding, causing to be heard.'
28. MAN,] as in v. 6; 2. 9; 3. 2, &c.
29. VANITY,] as in 58. 9; Ps. 10. 7, &c.
EMPTINESS,] or 'ruin;' as in 24. 10, &c.

XLII. 1. SERVANT,] as in v. 19; 14. 2, &c.
TAKE HOLD,] as in Ge. 48. 17; Job 36. 17.
CHOSEN,] or 'choice one;' as in 43. 20, &c.
ACCEPTED,] as in 1 Ch. 28. 4; 2 Ch. 10. 7.
PUT,] lit. 'given.'
BRINGETH FORTH,] as in v. 3; 61. 11, &c.
2. CRY,] as in 19. 20; 46. 7; 65. 14, &c.
LIFT UP,] as in v. 11; 2. 4, 9; 3. 7, &c.
STREET,] lit. 'out-place;' as in 5. 25, &c.
3. BRUISED,] as in 36. 6; 58. 6; De. 28. 33.
BREAKETH,] as in Ex. 12. 46; Lev. 11. 33.
QUENCHETH,] as in 2 Sa. 21. 17; 2 Ch. 29. 7.
4. WEAK,] as in Ge. 27. 1; Job 17. 7; Zech. 11. 17.
BRUISED,] as in Ecc. 12. 6.
SETTETH,] as in v. 12, 16, 25; 3. 7, &c.
LAW,] or 'direction;' as in v. 21, 24, &c.
WAIT WITH HOPE,] as in 51. 5; Job 6. 11.
5. PREPARING,] as in 40. 28; 43. 1, 15, &c.
STRETCHING OUT,] as in 40. 22; 44. 24, &c.
SPREADING OUT,] as in 44. 24; Ps. 136. 6.
PRODUCTIONS,] or 'out-goings;' as in 22. 24; 34. 1; 44. 3, &c.
GIVING BREATH,] as in 2. 22; 30. 33, &c.
6. RIGHTEOUSNESS,] as in v. 17; 1. 21, &c.
LAY HOLD,] as in 27. 5; 56. 2; Ge. 19. 16.
KEEP,] as in 26. 3; 27. 3; 49. 8, &c.
7. OPEN THE EYES,] as in 37. 17.
8. NAME,] as in 4. 1; 7. 14; 8. 3, &c.
9. FORMER THINGS,] as in 1. 26; 9. 1, &c.
DECLARING,] as in 41. 26; 45. 19; 46. 10, &c.
SPRING UP,] as in 43. 19; 58. 8; Ge. 2. 5, &c.
10. SING TO JEHOVAH,] as in Ex. 15. 21, &c.
GOING DOWN,] as in 14. 19; 15. 3; 31. 1, &c.
11. WILDERNESS,] or 'pasture-land;' as in 14. 17; 16. 1, 8; 21. 1, &c.
LIFT UP,] as in v. 2; 2. 4, 9; 3. 7; 8. 4, &c.
VILLAGES,] or 'courts;' as in 1. 12, &c.
12. ASCRIBE,] lit. 'set;' as in v. 4, 16, &c.
DECLARE,] or 'set forward;' as in 19. 12.
13. MIGHTY ONE,] as in 3. 2; 5. 22; 9. 6, &c.
STIRRETH UP,] or 'arouseth, awaketh;' as in 50. 4; De. 32. 11; 1 Ch. 5. 26, &c.
CRIETH,] or 'shouteth;' as in 15. 4, &c.
SHOWETH HIMSELF MIGHTY,] as in Job 15. 25; 36. 9.
14. KEEP SILENT,] lit. 'deaf;' as in 36. 21; Ex. 14. 14; Nu. 30. 14, &c.
REFRAIN MYSELF,] or 'withdraw myself;' as in 1 Sa. 13. 12.
SWALLOW UP,] as in Job 7. 2; 36. 20; Ps. 119. 131.
15. MAKE WASTE,] as in 37. 25; 50. 2, &c.
DRY UP,] as in 44. 27.
16. BLIND,] as in v. 7, 18, 19; 29. 18, &c.
TO GO,] as in 48. 21; De. 8. 2; Ch. 24. 15, &c.
TO TREAD,] as in Ps. 25. 9; 107. 7; Hab. 3. 19.
UNLEVELLED,] or 'crooked.'
FORSAKEN,] as in 1. 4; 17. 9; 49. 14, &c.
17. REMOVED,] as in 50. 5; Ps. 44. 18; Jer. 38. 22.
ASHAMED,] as in 1. 29; 26. 11; 29. 22, &c.
TRUSTING,] as in 32. 9, 10, 11; 36. 6, &c.
18. DEAF,] as in v. 19; 29. 18; 35. 5, &c.

HEAR,] as in 1. 2, 10; 6. 9; 7. 13, &c.
19. MY SERVANT,] as in v. 1; 14. 2, &c.
MY MESSENGER,] as in Ex. 23. 23; 32. 34.
20. SEEING,] as in v. 18; 6. 9; 21. 3, &c.
OBSERVEST,] as in 56. 4; Ge. 17. 9, 10, &c.
21. DELIGHT,] as in 1. 11; 53. 10; 55. 11, &c.
MAGNIFIETH,] lit. 'maketh great;' as in Ge. 19. 19; Job 19. 5; Eze. 24. 9, &c.
22. DELIVERER,] lit. 'snatcher away;' as in 5. 29; 43. 13; De. 32. 39, &c.
RESTORE,] or 'send back.'
23. GIVETH EAR,] as in Job 9. 16; 32. 11; Ps. 135. 17.
ATTENDETH,] as in Ps. 10. 17; Jer. 6. 17, &c.
24. SINNED,] or 'missed' the mark.
WILLING,] as in 28. 12; 30. 9, 15, &c.
LAW,] or 'direction;' as in v. 4, 21, &c.
25. POURETH,] as in 37. 33; Ge. 37. 22, &c.
FURY,] lit. 'heat;' as in 27. 4; 34. 2, &c.
SETTETH ON FIRE,] as in De. 32. 22, &c.
BURNETH,] as in 43. 2; 62. 1; Ex. 3. 3, &c.
LAYETH TO HEART,] lit. 'setteth on heart.'

XLIII. 1. THUS SAITH JEHOVAH,] as in v. 14, 16; 7. 7; 10. 24, &c.
CREATOR,] i.e. he who 'prepared' thee to be to himself a people.
BE NOT AFRAID,] as in v. 5; 7. 4; 8. 12, &c.
2. PASSEST,] as in Ge. 31. 52; Nu. 20. 18.
FLOODS,] or 'rivers;' as in v. 19, 20, &c.
OVERFLOW,] as in 28. 17; 1 K. 22. 38, &c.
BURNT,] or 'scorched;' as in Prov. 6. 28.
BURN,] as in 42. 25; 62. 1; Ex. 3. 3, &c.
3. JEHOVAH THY GOD,] or 'am thy God;' as in 7. 11; 37. 4; 41. 10, 13, &c.
HOLY,] or 'separate one.'
SAVIOUR,] one who gives 'ease, safety;' as in v. 11; 19. 20; 45. 15, &c.
APPOINTED,] lit. 'given.'
ATONEMENT,] lit. 'covering;' as in Ex. 21. 30; Job 33. 24; 36. 18; Ps. 49. 7, &c.
STEAD,] lit. 'under thee;' as in Ge. 4. 25.
4. PRECIOUS,] or 'rare;' as in 1 Sa. 26. 21.
HONOURED,] lit. 'hast become heavy.'
5. AFRAID,] as in 7. 4; 8. 12; 10. 24, &c.
EAST,] lit. 'rising' of the sun.
GATHER,] as in 11. 12; 27. 12; 40. 11, &c.
6. NORTH,] as in 14. 13, 31; 41. 25, &c.
GIVE UP,] as in Ge. 14. 21; 23. 4; 30. 14, &c.
SOUTH,] lit. 'Teman;' as in Ex. 26. 18, &c.
RESTRAIN,] as in Ge. 23. 6; Ps. 40. 9, 11.
7. CALLED,] as in 48. 1; Est. 6. 1; Jer. 44. 26.
CREATED,] lit. 'prepared;' as in 4. 5, &c.
FORMED,] as in v. 21; 37. 26; 44. 10, &c.
MADE,] as in 2. 8, 21; 5. 4; 10. 11, 13, &c.
8. BLIND,] as in 29. 18; 35. 5; 42. 7, &c.
9. GATHERED,] as in 34. 15; 49. 18, &c.
ASSEMBLED,] as in 49. 5; 60. 20, &c.
DECLARETH,] as in 19. 12; 21. 6; 36. 22, &c.
DECLARED RIGHTEOUS,] as in v. 26, &c.
10. AFFIRMATION,] as in v. 12; 1. 24, &c.
GIVE CREDENCE,] or 'remain stedfast;' as in 7. 9; Ex. 4. 1, 5, 8, 9, 31; 14. 31, &c.
GOD,] lit. 'mighty one;' as in v. 12, &c.
11. SAVIOUR,] giving 'ease or safety.'
12. DECLARED,] or 'set forward.'
PROCLAIMED,] lit. 'caused to be heard;' as in 30. 30; 44. 8; 45. 21, &c.
GOD,] lit. 'a mighty one;' as in v. 10, &c.
13. DELIVERER,] lit. 'snatcher;' as in 5. 29; 42. 22; De. 32. 39, &c.

TURN BACK,] as in 1. 25. 26; 14. 27, &c.
14. REDEEMER,] as in 41. 14; 44. 6, 24, &c.
BABYLON,] the capital of the Chaldeans.
CAUSED TO DESCEND,] as in 39. 1; 42. 38, &c.
SONG,] or 'loud cry;' as in 14. 7; 35. 10, &c.
15. HOLY ONE,] as in v 3, 14; 1. 4; 4. 3, &c.
16. WAY,] as in v. 19; 2. 3; 3. 12, &c.
17. CHARIOT,] as in 21. 7, 9; 22. 6, 7, &c.
LIE DOWN,] as in 50. 11; Ge. 19. 4; 28. 11.
RISE NOT,] as in 7. 7; 8. 10; 14. 21, 24, &c.
18. REMEMBER NOT,] as in v 25; 54. 4, &c.
CONSIDER,] or 'understand;' as in 6. 9, &c.
19. SPRINGETH UP,] as in 42. 9; 58. 8, &c.
WILDERNESS,] or 'pasture-land;' as in v.
20; 14. 17; 16. 1, 8, &c.
FLOODS,] or 'rivers;' as in v. 2, 20, &c.
20. HONOUR,] as in 25. 3; 60. 13; Nu. 22. 17.
GIVE DRINK,] as in Ge. 2. 10; 24. 19, &c.
CHOSEN,] or 'choice one;' as in 42. 1, &c.
21. FORMED,] as in v. 7; 37. 26; 44. 10, &c.
RECOUNT,] as in Ge. 24. 66; 29. 13, &c.
22. NOT CALLED,] as in Jer. 2. 2; 10. 25, &c.
LAMB,] as in 7. 25; 53. 7; 66. 3, &c.
HONOURED,] as in 29. 13; 58. 13; Jud. 13 17.
24. BOUGHT,] or 'acquired;' as in Ge. 4.
1; 25. 10; 47. 22, 23, &c.
SWEET CANE,] as in Jer. 6. 20.
CAUSED TO SERVE,] as in v. 23; Jer. 17. 4.
25. TRANSGRESSIONS,] lit. 'steps;' as in
24. 20; 44. 22; 50. 1, &c.
REMEMBER,] as in v. 18; 54. 4; 63. 11, &c.
26. JUDGED,] as in 1 Sa. 12. 7; Ps. 9. 19, &c.
JUSTIFIED,] or 'declared right;' as in v.
9; 45. 25; Job 4. 17, &c.
27. INTERPRETERS,] lit. 'sweeteners;' as in
Ge. 42. 23; 2 Ch. 32. 31; Job 16. 20; 33. 23, &c.
TRANSGRESSED,] lit. 'stepped.'
28. POLLUTE,] as in Ex. 20. 25; Lev. 18. 21.
SANCTUARY,] or 'separate place.'

XLIV. 1. HEAR,] as in 1. 2, 10; 6. 9, &c.
FIXED ON,] as in v. 2; 1. 29; 14. 1, &c.
2. MAKER,] as in v. 24; 10. 23; 17. 7, &c.
WOMB,] lit. 'belly;' as in v. 24; 13. 18, &c.
FEAR NOT,] as in 7. 4; 8. 12; 10. 24, &c.
JESHURUN,] i.e. the 'little upright' one.
3. POUR,] or 'squeeze out;' as in Ge. 28.
18; 35. 14; Ex. 36. 36, &c.
FLOODS,] or 'flowings;' as in Ex. 15. 8, &c.
MY SPIRIT,] as in Ge. 6. 3; Job 21. 4, &c.
OFFSPRING,] or 'productions, issue;' as in
15. 7; Lev. 23. 40; Job 40. 22; Ps. 137. 2.
4. SPRING UP,] as in Lev. 13. 37.
5. CALLETH BY,] lit. 'in the name of
Jacob.'
WITH HIS HAND,] or 'his memorial.'
6. KING OF ISRAEL,] as in 1 Sa. 24. 14, &c.
NO GOD,] worthy of the name of gods.
7. DECLARE,] lit. 'set forward;' as in 19.
12; 21. 6, &c.
COMING,] as in 41. 23; 45. 11.
DO COME,] as in 1. 12, 23; 3. 14; 5. 19, &c.
8. FEAR NOT,] as in v. 12; 2. 19. 17, &c.
WITNESSES,] as in v. 9; 8. 2; 19. 20, &c.
ROCK,] as in 2. 10, 19, 21; 8. 14; 10. 26, &c.
9. FRAMERS,] formers or fashioners; as in
v. 2, 24; 22. 11; 27. 11, &c.
EMPTINESS,] lit. 'ruin;' as in 24. 10, &c.
ASHAMED,] as in v. 11; 1. 29; 26. 11, &c.
10. FORMED,] as in v. 21; 37. 26, &c.
PROFITABLE,] as in 30. 5; 47. 12, &c.

11. COMPANIONS,] as in 1. 23; Jud. 20. 11.
STAND UP,] as in 36. 2, 13; 46. 7, &c.
12. WROUGHT,] as in v. 19; 5. 2, 4, 10, &c.
AXE,] as in Jer. 10. 3.
COALS,] as in 54. 16; Prov. 26. 21.
POWERFUL ARM,] lit. 'arm of his power.'
WEARIED,] as in 40. 28, 30, 31; Jer. 2. 24.
13. WOOD,] lit. 'trees;' as in v. 14, 19, &c.
FORM,] or 'building,' as in Ex. 25. 9, &c.
BEAUTY,] as in 13. 19; 20. 5; 28. 1, &c.
14. CUTTING DOWN,] as in De. 19. 5, &c.
CYPRESS,] or 'holly.'
TREES OF A FOREST,] as in 7. 2; 10. 19, &c
NOURISH,] lit. 'make great;' as in Hos. 9. 12
15. TO BURN,] as in 4. 4; 5. 5; 6. 13, &c.
FALLETH DOWN,] as in v. 17, 19; 46. 6.
16. HALF OF IT,] as in v. 19; Ex. 24. 6, &c.
ENJOYED LIGHT,] lit. 'seen light.'
17. REMNANT,] as in 14. 30; 15. 9; 37. 4, &c.
PRAYETH,] or 'judgeth himself;' as in 37.
15; 38. 2; 45. 14, &c.
DELIVER,] lit. 'snatch;' as in Ge. 32. 11.
18. DAUBED,] as in Lev. 14. 42; Eze. 13.
12, 14; 22. 28.
ACTING WISELY,] as in Ge. 3. 6; Neh. 8. 13.
19. TURN BACK,] as in 1. 25, 26; 14. 17, &c.
20. FEEDING ON,] or 'enjoying;' as in 40.
11; Ge. 41. 2, 18; Ex. 34. 3, &c.
DELIVERETH,] lit. 'snatcheth;' as in 30.
15, 18, 20; 38. 6, &c.
LIE,] or 'falsehood;' as in 9. 15; 28. 15, &c.
21. REMEMBER,] as in 38. 3: 46. 8, 9, &c.
22. BLOTTED OUT,] or 'wiped away;' as in
25. 8; Ge. 7. 4; Nu. 5. 23, &c.
TRANSGRESSIONS,] lit. 'steps;' as in 24.
20; 43. 25; 50. 1, &c.
REDEEMED,] as in v. 23; 43. 1; 48. 20, &c.
23. SING,] as in 12. 6; 49. 13; 54. 1, &c.
BEAUTIFY HIMSELF,] or 'make himself
fair;' as in 10. 15; 49. 3; Jud. 7. 2.
24. REDEEMER,] as in v. 6; 41. 14, &c.
SPREADING OUT,] as in 42. 5; Ps. 136. 6.
25. MAKING VOID,] as in Job 5. 12.
MAKETH FOOLISH,] as in Job 12. 17;
Ecc. 7. 7.
26. CONFIRMING,] as in Ge. 9. 9; 1 Sa. 2. 8.
RAISE UP,] as in 58. 12; 61. 4; Mic. 2. 8, &c.
27. CAUSE TO DRY UP,] as in 42. 15.
28. CYRUS,] lit. a 'throne,' i.e. one who
fills it.

XLV. 1. JEHOVAH,] the 'existing one.'
ANOINTED,] lit. 'his Messiah;' as in Lev.
4. 3, 5, 16; 6. 22; 1 Sa. 2. 10, &c.
CYRUS,] king of Persia.
LOOSE,] or 'open;' as in 28. 24; Ge. 24. 32.
SHUT,] as in 60. 11; Nu. 12. 14, 15, &c.
2. CUT ASUNDER,] as in 38. 13; Ex. 23. 24.
3. GOD OF ISRAEL,] as in v. 15; 17. 6, &c.
4. MY SERVANT,] as in 20. 3; 22. 20, &c.
MY CHOSEN,] or 'choice one;' as in 42. 1.
5. NO GOD,] as in v. 14, 21; 44. 6; De. 32. 39.
GIRD,] as in 2 Sa. 22. 40; Ps. 18. 39, &c.
6. RISING OF THE SUN,] as in 41. 2, 25, &c.
7. FORMING LIGHT,] which Cyrus adored
as a fire worshipper.
PREPARING DARKNESS,] which he feared
as the work of an evil spirit.
EVIL,] as in 3. 9, 11; 5. 20; 7. 5, 15, 16, &c.
8. DROP,] lit. 'cause ye to drop '
PREPARED,] as in v. 12, 18, i. 9, 40. 26, &c.

9. WO,] as in v. 10; 1. 4, 24; 5. 8, &c.
STRIVING,] or 'contending;' as in Jer.51.36.
10. BRING FORTH,] lit. 'pain,' or 'suffer pain;' as in 13. 8; 23. 5; 26. 17; 66. 7, &c.
11. ASK,] as in 7. 11; De. 4. 32; 32. 7, &c.
WORK OF MY HANDS,] as in 60. 21.
COMMAND,] or 'give me a charge;' as in 5. 6; 10. 6; Ge. 2. 16, &c.
12. MADE,] as in 2. 8, 20; 5. 4; 10. 11, &c.
PREPARED,] as in v. 8, 18; 4. 5; 40. 26, &c.
STRETCHED OUT,] or 'inclined;' as in 23. 11; 34. 11; 44. 13, &c.
COMMANDED,] or 'charged.'
13. STIRRED UP,] or 'awaked;' as in 41. 2, &c.
MAKE STRAIGHT,] or 'upright;' as in v. 2.
MY CITY,] that is, Jerusalem.
14. LABOUR,] or 'fatigue;' as in 55. 2, &c.
SEBAIM,] as in Job 1. 15; Eze. 23. 42; Joel 3. 8.
MEN OF MEASURE,] as in Nu. 13. 32; 1 Ch. 11. 23; 20. 6.
PRAY,] lit. 'judge themselves.'
IS GOD,] lit. 'a mighty one;' as in Ex. 34. 14; De. 4. 31; 6. 15, &c.
15. HIDING THYSELF,] or 'keeping thyself secret.'
16. ASHAMED,] as in 19. 9; 20. 5; 24. 23, &c.
CONFUSION,] or 'blushing;' as in 30. 3, &c.
CARVING IMAGES,] lit. 'workers of forms;' as in 40. 19, 20.
17. SAVED,] as in Nu. 10. 9; Jer. 8. 20.
AGE-DURING,] lit. 'of the ages;' as in 9. 7.
AGES OF ETERNITY,] or 'of duration;' as in 9. 7; 14. 20; 30. 8, &c.
18. CREATOR,] lit. 'preparer;' as in v. 7, &c.
FORMERS,] framer or fashioner.
ESTABLISHED,] or 'made ready;' as in 51. 13; Ex. 15. 17; 2 Sa. 7. 13, &c.
EMPTY,] lit. 'ruin;' as in Ge. 1. 2, &c.
19. SECRET,] as in 16. 4; 28. 17; 32. 2, &c.
SEED OF JACOB,] as in I's. 22. 23; Jer. 33. 26.
VAIN,] or for 'ruin;' as in v. 18.
DECLARING,] lit. 'setting forward.'
UPRIGHTNESS,] or 'upright things.'
20. BE GATHERED,] as in 48. 14; Eze. 39. 17.
GOD,] lit. 'mighty one.'
21. PROCLAIMED,] lit. 'caused to bear.'
22. TURN,] lit. 'face ye unto me;' as in Nu. 14. 25; De. 1. 7, 40; 2. 3, &c.
ENDS OF EARTH,] as in 52. 10; De. 33. 17.
23. SWORN,] lit. 'been sworn;' as in 14. 24.
SWEAR,] lit. 'be sworn.'
24. RIGHTEOUSNESS, or 'righteous acts;' as in v. 8, 23; 1. 27; 5. 7, &c.
DISPLEASED,] lit. 'heated;' as in 41. 11.
25. SEED OF ISRAEL,] as in 2 K. 17. 20, &c.
JUSTIFIED,] or 'become right, just;' as in 43. 9, 26; Job 4. 17; 9. 2, 20, &c.

XLVI. 1. BOWED DOWN,] as in v. 2; 10. 4.
BEL,] i.e. 'lord, master,' the Baal of the Babylonians; as in Jer. 50. 2; 51. 44.
NEBO,] i.e. a 'prophet,' i.e. the Mercury of the Babylonians; as in 15. 2; Nu. 32. 3, 28.
IDOLS,] lit. 'grievous things;' as in 10. 11.
BURDENS,] lit. 'lifted up things.'
WEARY,] or 'faint;' as in 5. 27; 28. 12, &c.
2. STOOPED,] as in v. 1.
DELIVER,] lit. 'let escape;' as in Jer. 39. 18.
3. BORNE,] or 'loaded;' as in v. 1.
CARRIED,] lit. 'lifted up;' as in 3. 3; 9. 15.

4. OLD AGE,] lit. 'bearded state;' as in Ge. 24. 36; 2 K. 11. 4; 15. 23; Ps. 71. 9, 18, &c.
BEAR,] or 'lifted up;' as in v. 7; 2. 4, &c.
DELIVER,] or 'cause to escape;' as in v. 2.
6. BAG,] or 'cup;' as in De. 25. 13; Prov. 1. 14; 16. 11; 23. 31; Mic. 6. 11.
BEAM,] lit. 'reed, cane;' as in 19. 6; 35. 7.
HIRE,] lit. 'make sweet;' as in Jud. 9. 4.
7. CRIETH,] in distress; as in 19. 20, &c.
ADVERSITY,] or 'straitness;' as in 8. 22, &c.
8. TRANSGRESSORS,] lit. 'stepping ones;' as in 1. 28; 48. 8; 53. 12; 66. 24, &c.
10. DECLARING,] lit. 'setting forward.'
STAND,] lit. 'rise;' as in 7. 7; 8. 10; 14. 21.
DELIGHT,] or 'desire;' as in 44. 28; 48. 14.
11. EAST,] lit. 'rising' of the sun; as in 41. 2, 25; 43. 5; 45. 6, &c.
MAN OF MY COUNSEL,] as in Ps. 119. 24.
MIGHTY IN HEART,] as in Ps. 76. 5.
13. TARRY,] lit. 'it is not behind;' as in Ex. 22. 29; De. 7. 10; 23. 21, &c.
GLORY,] or 'beauty;' as in 3. 18. 4. 2, &c.

XLVII. 1. COME DOWN,] as in Ge. 42. 2, &c.
VIRGIN DAUGHTER,] as in Jer. 14. 17; Lam. 2. 13.
DAUGHTER OF THE CHALDEANS,] as in v. 5.
DELICATE ONE,] as in De. 28. 54, 56.
2. MILL-STONES,] as in De. 24. 6; Jer. 25. 10.
FLOUR,] or 'meal;' as in Ge. 18. 6, &c.
REMOVE,] or 'uncover;' as in Ps. 119. 18.
FLOODS,] or 'rivers;' as in 70; 8. 7, &c.
3. REVEALED,] or 'uncovered;' as in Ex. 20. 26; 1 Sa. 3. 7; 14. 11, &c.
MEET,] lit. 'kick or come' against any one.
4. REDEEMER,] as in 41. 14; 43. 41; 44. 6, &c.
SIT SILENT,] lit. 'dumb;' as in v. 1; 52. 2.
CRY,] as in v. 1.
MISTRESS,] lit. 'mighty one;' as in v. 7.
6. WROTH,] as in 57. 7; 64. 5; Ge. 41. 10, &c.
POLLUTED,] or 'pierced;' as in Ge. 49. 4, &c.
APPOINTED,] lit. 'set;' as in v. 7; 14. 17. &c.
HEAVY,] as in 9. 1; 1 K. 12. 10, 14, &c.
7. LAID TO HEART,] as in 57. 11; Mal. 2. 2.
8. BEREAVEMENT,] or 'childlessness;' as in v. 9; Ps. 35. 12.
9. MOMENT,] as in 26. 20; 27. 3; 45. 7, &c.
CHILDLESSNESS,] or 'bereavement;' as in v. 8.
PERFECTION,] or 'completeness;' as in Job 21. 23.
SORCERIES,] as in 2 K. 9. 22; Mic. 5. 12; Nah. 3. 4.
CHARMS,] as in v. 12; De. 18. 11; Ps. 58. 5.
10. CONFIDENT,] or 'trustful, learning;' as in 12. 2; 30. 12; 31. 1, &c.
TURNING BACK,] as in Jer. 8. 5; 50. 6, 19; Eze. 38. 4; 39. 2.
11. RISING,] lit. 'dawn;' as in 8. 20; 14. 12.
MISCHIEF,] or 'accident;' as in Eze. 7. 26.
PACIFY,] lit. 'cover;' as in Ex. 29. 36, &c.
DESOLATION,] as in 10. 3; Job 30. 3, 14, &c.
12. SORCERIES,] as in 2 K. 9. 22; Mic. 5. 12. Nah. 3. 4.
YOUTH,] lit. 'youthful periods.'
PROFIT,] or 'be useful;' as in 30. 5; 44. 10; 48. 17; Jer. 7. 8. 32.
TERRIFY,] as in De. 1. 29; 7. 21; 20. 3, &c.
13. WEARIED,] as in 1. 4; 16. 12; Ex. 7. 18.
MONTHS,] as in Ge. 7. 11; 8. 4; 29. 14, &c.
14. STUBBLE,] as in 5. 24; 33. 11; 40. 24, &c.

DELIVER,] *lit.* 'snatch;' as in 36. 15, 18, &c·
POWER,] *lit.* 'hand.'
15. LABOURED,] as in v. 12; 43. 22; 49. 4, &c.
WANDERED,] *or* 'gone astray;' as in 16. 8.

XLVIII. 1. HOUSE OF JACOB,] as in 2. 5, &c.
NAME OF ISRAEL,] as in Ps. 83. 4.
WATERS.] Compare Nu. 24. 7, &c
SWEARING,] *lit.* 'are sworn.'
TRUTH,] *lit.* 'stedfastness;' as in 10. 20, &c.
2. HOLY CITY,] as in 52. 1; Neh. 11. 18; De.
9. 24.
3. FORMER THINGS,] as in v. 12; 41. 22, &c.
DECLARED,] *or* 'set forth;' as in v. 14, &c.
4. OBSTINATE,] *lit.* 'sharp, hard;' as in 14.
3; 19. 4; 21. 2; 27. 1, 8, &c.
BRASS,] as in 45. 2; Lev. 26. 19; 2 Sa. 22. 35.
5. DECLARE,] as in v. 6; 10. 12; 21. 6, &c.
IDOL,] *lit.* 'grievous thing.'
6. NEW THINGS,] as in 42. 9.
THINGS RESERVED,] as in 49. 6.
7. PRODUCED,] *lit.* 'prepared;' as in Ex. 34.
10; Ps. 148. 5; Eze. 21. 30.
8. CRYING,] *or* 'calling; as in 58. 12; 61. 3;
62. 2; Eze. 10. 13.
DEFER,] *lit.* 'prolong;' as in 53. 10; 57. 4.
CUT OFF,] as in 10. 7; Ex. 8. 9; 1 Sa. 20. 15.
10. REFINED,] as in Ps. 17. 3; 66. 10; 105.
19; Jer. 6. 29; Zech. 13. 9.
AFFLICTION,] as in Ge. 16. 11; 29. 32, &c.
11. POLLUTED,] *or* 'pierced;' as in Lev. 21.
9; Eze. 22. 26.
12. HEARKEN,] as in v. 1, 14, 16; 1. 2, &c.
LAST,] as in 41. 4; 44. 6; Ge. 33. 2, &c.
13. FOUNDED,] as in 23. 13; 54. 11; Ps. 24. 2.
14. BE GATHERED,] as in 45. 20; Ge. 49. 2;
Eze. 39. 17.
PLEASURE,] *or* 'desire;' as in 44. 28, &c.
15. MADE PROSPEROUS,] as in 55. 11, &c.
16. COME NEAR,] as in 34. 1; 57. 3; 65. 5, &c.
LORD JEHOVAH,] as in 3. 15; 7. 7; 10. 23.
SPIRIT,] as in 11. 2; 26. 9; 32. 15, &c.
17. REDEEMER,] as in 41. 14; 43. 14; 44. 6.
18. ATTENDED,] as in 21. 17; 2 Ch. 33. 10.
19. SAND,] as in 10. 22; Ge. 22. 17; 32. 12, &c
DESTROYED,] as in De. 4. 26; Prov. 14. 11.
20. GO FORTH,] as in 7. 3; 30. 22; 36. 16, &c.
END OF THE EARTH,] *or* 'land;' as in 5. 26.
SERVANT JACOB,] as in 44. 1, 2; Ge. 32. 20.
21. THIRSTED,] as in Jud. 4. 19; Ru. 2. 9.
FLOW,] *or* 'issue;' as in Lev. 15. 25; Ps. 78.
20; 105. 41; Lam. 4. 9.
WICKED,] *lit.* 'those who are in the wrong.'

XLIX. 1. HEARKEN,] as in 1. 2, 10; 6. 9, &c.
MADE MENTION,] as in 40. 14.
2. SHARP,] as in Ps. 57. 4; Prov. 5. 4; Eze.
5. 1.
CLEAR,] *or* 'pure;' as in Job 33. 3; Zeph.
3. 9.
HID,] *or* 'made secret.'
3. BEAUTIFY MYSELF,] *or* 'make myself
fair.'
4. VAIN THING,] as in 30. 7; 65. 23, &c.
EMPTINESS,] *lit.* 'ruin;' as in 24. 10; 29. 21.
CONSUMED,] *or* 'completed;' as in 27. 10.
WAGE,] *or* 'work;' as in 40. 10; 61. 8, &c.
5. FORMING,] as in 22. 11; 27. 11; 29. 16, &c.
STRENGTH,] as in 12. 2; 26. 1; 45. 24, &c.
6. LIGHT THING,] as in 1 Sa. 18. 23, &c.
PRESERVED,] as in 1. 8; 48. 6.

LIGHT OF NATIONS,] as in 42. 6.
END OF THE EARTH,] as in 5. 26; 42. 10.
RISEN] in honour of him.
WORSHIP,] *lit.* 'bow themselves.'
FAITHFUL,] *or* 'stedfast;' as in 1. 21, &c.
CHOOSETH,] as in 40. 20; 41. 24; 58. 5, &c.
8. GOOD PLEASURE,] as in 56. 7; 58. 5, &c.
COVENANT OF THE PEOPLE,] as in 42. 6.
INHERITANCES,] as in 19. 25; 47. 6; 54. 17.
9. BOUND,] as in 61. 1; Ge. 39. 20; 40. 3, &c.
HIGH PLACES,] as in 41. 18; Nu. 23. 3, &c.
PASTURE,] as in Ps. 74. 1; 79. 13; 95. 7, &c.
10. HUNGER,] as in 8. 21; 65. 13; Ge. 41. 55.
MIRAGE,] as in 35. 7.
PITYING,] as in 54. 10; Ps. 116. 5.
11. MADE,] as in 14. 17, 23, &c.
LIFTED UP,] as in 30. 18; 52. 13; Ge. 7. 17.
12. AFAR,] as in 5. 26; 22. 3, 11; 23. 7, &c.
SEA,] that is, the west.
SINIM,] generally believed to be China.
13. SING,] as in 12. 6; 44. 23; 54. 1, &c.
PITY,] as in 9. 17; 13. 18; 14. 1; 27. 11, &c.
14. FORSAKEN,] as in 1. 4; 17. 9; 42. 16, &c.
FORGOTTEN,] as in 17. 10; Ge. 27. 45, &c.
15. SUCKLING,] as in 65. 20.
16. PALMS OF THE HAND,] as in 1 Sa. 5. 4.
WALLS,] as in 2. 15; 22. 10, 11; 25. 12, &c.
17. HASTENED,] as in 51. 14; Ge. 27. 20, &c.
LAYING WASTE,] as in Jud. 16. 24.
18. LIFT UP THINE EYES,] as in 37. 23, &c.
BRIDE,] as in 61. 10; 62. 5; Jer. 2. 32, &c.
19. WASTES,] as in 5. 17; 44. 26; 48. 21, &c.
CONSUMING,] *lit.* 'swallowing up.'
20. BEREAVEMENT,] *or* 'childlessness.'
COME NIGH,] not 'give place,' as in C.V.;
as in Ge. 19. 9; 27. 21, 26; 45. 4, &c.
DWELL,] *lit.* 'sit;' as in 3. 26; 13. 20, &c.
21. BEGOTTEN,] *or* 'born;' as in 23. 4, &c.
GLOOMY,] as in Job 3. 7; 15. 34; 30. 3.
TURNED ASIDE,] *or* 'apostate;' as in Jer.
17. 13.
NOURISHED,] *lit.* 'made great;' as in 1.
2; 23. 4; 51. 18, &c.
22. LIFT UP MY HAND,] as in 2. 4, 9, &c.
BOSOM,] as in Neh. 5. 13.
CARRIED,] *or* 'lifted up;' as in 2. 4, &c.
23. NURSING FATHERS,] *lit.* 'stedfast ones'
or 'supporters;' as in Nu. 11. 12; 2 K. 10. 15.
PRINCESSES,] *or* kings' daughters;' as in
1 K. 11. 3; Est. 1. 18; Lam. 1. 1, &c.
NURSING MOTHERS,] *lit.* 'suckling ones.'
LICK UP,] as in Nu. 22. 4; Ps. 72. 9; Mic. 7. 17.
EXPECTING,] as in 40. 31; Ps. 25. 3, &c.
24. PREY,] as in 49. 24, &c.
RIGHTEOUS,] *or* 'just' one; as in 3. 10, &c.
DELIVERED,] *lit.* 'let escape;' as in v. 25.
25. TERRIBLE,] as in 13. 11; 25. 3—5, &c.
OPPRESSORS,] as in Ps. 35. 1; Jer. 18. 19.
26. NEW WINE,] as in Song 8. 2; Joel 1. 5.
DRINK ABUNDANTLY,] *or* 'are merry;' as
in Ge. 9. 21; 43. 24; Lam. 4. 21; Nah. 3. 11.
ALL FLESH,] all the human race.
MIGHTY ONE OF JACOB,] as in 60. 16, &c.

L. 1. THUS SAID JEHOVAH,] as in 7. 7, &c.
BILL,] *lit.* 'scroll or roll;' as in 34. 4, &c.
DIVORCE,] *lit.* 'cutting off;' as in De. 24.
1, 3; Jer. 3. 8.
SENT AWAY,] as in Ge. 44. 3; Jud. 5. 15, &c
2. ANSWERING,] as in 66. 4; Ge. 35. 3, &c.

REDEMPTION,] or 'ransom;' as in Ex. 8. 23.
Ps. 111. 9; 130. 7.
  DELIVER,] lit. 'snatch away;' as in 36. 14.
  WILDERNESS,] or 'pasture-land;' as in 14.
17; 16. 1, 8; 21. 1, &c.
  3. CLOTHE,] as in Ge. 3. 21; 27. 15, &c.
  4. LORD JEHOVAH,] as in v. 5, 7, 9, &c.
  TAUGHT ONES,] as in 8. 16; 54. 13, &c.
  WEARY,] or 'faint;' as in 40. 29; Jud. 8. 15.
2 Sa. 16. 2.
  WAKETH,] or 'stirreth up;' as in 42. 13, &c.
  5. OPENED THE EAR,] as in 14. 17, &c.
  MOVED,] as in 42. 17; Ps. 44. 18; Jer. 38. 22.
  6. BACK,] or 'body;' as in 38. 17; 51. 23, &c.
  HID,] lit. 'made or kept secret.'
  SPITTING,] as in Job 7. 19; 30. 10.
  7. GIVETH HELP,] as in v. 9; 30. 7, &c.
  SET MY FACE,] as in Lev. 17. 10; 20. 3, &c.
  FLINT,] as in De. 8. 15; 32. 13; Job 28. 9;
Ps. 114. 8.
  8. JUSTIFYING,] as in 5. 23; Prov. 17. 15.
  OPPONENT,] lit. 'master of my judgment.'
  COME NIGH,] as in 41. 1; 65. 5; Ge. 18. 23.
  9. DECLARETH WICKED,] or 'wrong;' as in
54. 17; Ex. 22. 9; Job 9. 20, &c.
  WEAR OUT,] or 'fade;' as in 51. 6, &c.
  MOTH,] as in 5. 8; Job 4. 19; 13. 28, &c.
  10. FEARING JEHOVAH,] as in 1 K. 18. 3, &c.
  BRIGHTNESS,] as in 4. 5; 60. 3, 19; 62. 1, &c.
  TRUST,] or 'lean;' as in 12. 2; 30. 12, &c.
  LEAN,] or 'be supported;' as in 30. 12, &c.

LI. 1. PURSUING,] as in 1. 23; 30. 16, &c.
  SEEKING JEHOVAH,] as in 1 Ch. 16. 10, &c.
  LOOK ATTENTIVELY,] as in v. 2, 6; 63. 15.
  2. BRINGETH FORTH,] as in Job 26. 5, &c.
  CALLED HIM,] from Ur of the Chaldees.
  MULTIPLY,] lit. 'make many;' as in 1. 15.
  3. COMFORTED,] as in 49. 13; 52. 9, &c.
  WASTES,] lit. 'dry places;' as in 5. 17, &c.
  WILDERNESS,] or 'pasture-land;' as in 14.
17; 16. 1, 8; 21. 1, &c.
  EDEN,] lit. 'delight, pleasure.'
  GARDEN OF JEHOVAH,] as in Ge. 13. 10.
  VOICE OF SONG,] as in Ps. 98. 5.
  4. ATTEND,] as in 10. 30; 28. 23; 34. 1, &c.
  LAW,] or 'direction;' as in v. 7; 1. 10, &c.
  CAUSE TO REST,] as in De 28. 65, &c.
  5. WAIT WITH HOPE,] as in 5. 2, 7, &c.
  6. WEARETH,] or 'fadeth;' as in 50. 9, &c.
  GNATS,] as in Ex. 8. 16, 17, 18; Ps. 105. 31.
  BROKEN,] or 'cast down;' as in v. 7, &c.
  7. KNOWING,] as in 29. 11, 15; Ge. 3. 5, &c.
  AFFRIGHTED,] or 'cast down;' as in v. 12.
  8. MOTH,] as in 50. 9; Job 4. 19; 13. 28.
  ALL GENERATIONS,] lit. 'generation of
generations;' as in 13. 20; 34. 10, 17, &c.
  9. AWAKE,] as in 52. 1; Jud. 5. 12, &c.
  ARM OF JEHOVAH,] as in 53. 1.
  RAHAB,] i.e. the 'broad or proud one,'
Egypt; as in Ps. 87. 4; 89. 10, &c.
  DRAGON,] as in 27. 1; De. 32. 33; Neh. 2. 13.
  10. DEEP,] as in 63. 13; Ge. 1. 2, &c.
  DEEP PLACES,] or 'valleys' of the sea; as
in Ps. 69. 2, 14; 130. 1; Eze. 27. 34, &c.
  REDEEMED,] as in 35. 9; 62. 12; 63. 4, &c.
  11. RANSOMED,] as in 35. 10; Nu. 18. 16.
  JOY AGE-DURING,] as in 35. 10; 61. 7.
  ATTAIN,] or 'overtake;' as in 35. 10, &c.
  12. COMFORTER,] as in 2 Sa. 10. 3, &c.
  GRASS,] as in 15. 6; 35. 7; 37. 27, &c.

  13. STRETCHING,] as in 40. 22; 42. 5, &c.
  FOUNDING,] as in Zech. 12. 1.
  OPPRESSOR,] lit. 'squeezer out;' as in 29. 7.
  DESTROY,] or 'mar;' as in 36. 10; 65. 8, &c.
  FURY,] lit. 'heat;' as in v. 17, 20, 22, &c.
  14. LOOSED,] lit. 'opened.'
  PIT,] or 'at the marring;' as in 38. 17, &c.
  15. JEHOVAH THY GOD,] as in 7. 11, &c.
  QUIETING,] as in 34. 14.
  BILLOWS,] lit. 'heaps;' as in 10. 30, &c.
  NAME,] as in 4. 1; 7. 14; 8. 3, &c.
  16. PUT,] or 'set;' as in v. 3, 23; 3. 7. &c.
  TO PLANT,] as in Ecc. 3. 2; Jer. 1. 10, &c.
  TO FOUND,] as in 2 Ch. 31. 7; Eze. 3. 12, &c.
  17. GOBLET,] as in v. 22.
  TREMBLING,] as in v. 22.
  WRUNG OUT,] as in Eze. 23. 34.
  18. NOURISHED,] lit. 'made great;' as in
1. 2; 23. 4; 49. 21, &c.
  19. MOVED,] as in 14. 15; Job 42. 11.
  DESTRUCTION,] lit. 'breach.'
  20. FURY OF JEHOVAH,] as in 2 K. 22. 13.
  21. AFFLICTED,] as in 3. 14, 15; 10. 2, &c.
  22. CUP OF TREMBLING,] as in v. 17.
  CUP OF FURY,] as in v. 17.
  23. BODY,] as in 38. 17; 50. 6; Prov. 10. 13
  STREET,] lit. 'out-place.'

LII 1. AWAKE,] as in 51. 9; Jud. 5. 12, &c.
  HOLY CITY,] as in 48. 2.
  UNCLEAN,] as in v. 11; 6. 5; 35. 8; 64. 6, &c.
  2. DAUGHTER OF ZION,] as in 1. 8; 3. 16, &c.
  3. FOR NOUGHT,] as in v. 5; Ge. 29. 15, &c.
  REDEEMED,] as in Lev. 25. 30, 54, &c.
  4. TO SOJOURN,] as in 23. 7; 54. 15, &c.
  ASSHUR,] in the days of Hezekiah.
  5. AFFIRMATION,] as in 1. 24; 3. 15; 14. 22.
  CAUSE HOWLING,] as in 15. 2, 3; 16. 7, &c.
  7. COMELY,] as in Ps. 93. 5; Song 1. 10.
  PROCLAIMING TIDINGS,] as in 40. 9; 41. 27.
  SOUNDING,] lit. 'causing to be heard.'
  8. WATCHMEN,] as in 56. 10; 1 Sa. 1. 1, &c.
  TURNING BACK,] as in Ge. 3. 19; 8. 3, 7, &c.
  9. BREAK FORTH,] as in 44. 23; 49. 13, &c.
  WASTES,] lit. 'dry places;' as in 5. 17, &c.
  REDEEMED,] as in 43. 1; 44. 22, 23; 48. 20.
  10. MADE BARE,] as in Jer. 13. 26; 49. 10, &c.
  ENDS OF EARTH,] as in 45. 22; Jer. 16. 19.
  11. TURN ASIDE,] as in 30. 11; Ge. 19. 2, &c.
  UNCLEAN,] as in v. 1; 6. 5; 35. 8; 64. 6, &c.
  BEARING,] lit. 'lifting up;' as in 45. 20, &c.
  WEAPONS,] as in 13. 5; 18. 2; 22. 24, &c.
  12. HASTE,] as in Ex. 12. 11; De. 16. 2.
  GATHERING,] as in 62. 9; Nu. 10. 25, &c.
  GOD OF ISRAEL,] as in 17. 6; 21. 10, 17, &c.
  13. MY SERVANT,] Targ. adds 'Messiah;' as
in 20. 3; 37. 35; 41. 8, &c.
  ACT WISELY,] as in 41. 20; Jos. 1. 7, 8, &c.
  HIGH,] as in 30. 18; 49. 11; Ge. 7. 7, &c.
  LIFTED UP,] as in 39. 6; Ex. 25. 28, &c.
  14. ASTONISHED,] as in Lev. 26. 32, &c.
  APPEARANCE,] as in 11. 14; 53. 2; Ge. 2. 9.
  FORM,] as in 53. 2; Ge. 29. 17; 39. 6, &c.
  15. SPRINKLE,] an eastern token of welcome.
  SHUT,] as in De. 15. 7.
  UNDERSTOOD,] as in 1. 3; Job 38. 18, &c.

LII. 1. GIVEN CREDENCE,] lit. 'remained
stedfast;' as in Ge. 15. 6; 45. 26; Ex. 4. 8, &c.
  WE HEARD,] lit. 'to our hearing;' as in 28.
9, 19; 37. 7; 1 Sa. 2. 24, &c.

ARM OF JEHOVAH,] that by which he manifests his power; as in 51. 9, &c.
REVEALED.] or 'uncovered;' as in 22. 14.
2. COMETH UP,] as in 2. 3; 5. 24; 7. 6, &c.
ROOT,] as in 5. 24; 11. 1, 10; 14. 29, 30, &c.
DRY GROUND,] or 'land;' as in 35. 1, &c.
FORM,] as in 52. 14; Ge. 29. 17; 39. 6, &c.
HONOUR,] or 'majesty;' as in 2. 10; 5. 14.
APPEARANCE,] as in 11. 3; 52. 14.
DESIRE,] as in Ex. 20. 17; 34. 24; De. 5. 21.
3. DESPISED,] as in Ps. 15. 4; 119. 141, &c.
LEFT,] lit. 'ceased.'
PAINS,] as in v. 4.
ACQUAINTED,] lit. 'knowing;' as in De. 1. 13, 15. &c.
SICKNESS,] as in v. 4; 1. 5; 38. 9, &c.
HIDING THE FACE,] lit. 'making secret,' as if he were ashamed; as in 8. 17, &c.
ESTEEMED,] or 'thought of;' as in v. 4.
4. SICKNESSES,] as in v. 3; 1. 5; 38. 9, &c.
BORNE,] or 'lifted up;' as in v. 12; 5. 26, &c.
PAINS,] as in v. 3.
CARRIED,] as in Lam. 5. 17.
PLAGUED,] as in 73. 14.
SMITTEN,] as in Ex. 5. 16; Nu. 25. 14, &c.
5. TRANSGRESSIONS,] lit. 'steps;' as in v. 8.
BRUISED,] as in 19. 10.
INIQUITIES,] as in v. 6, 11; 1. 4; 5. 18, &c.
CHASTISEMENT,] as in 26. 16; De. 11. 2, &c.
BRUISE,] as in 1. 6; Ge. 4. 23; Ex. 21. 25, &c.
HEALING,] as in Lev. 13. 18, 37; 14. 3, &c.
6. SHEEP,] or a 'flock;' as in 7. 21; 13. 14.
WANDERED,] or 'gone astray.'
TURNED] the face; as in 8. 21; 56. 11, &c.
PUNISHMENT,] or 'iniquity;' as in v. 5, &c.
7. EXACTED,] as in 3. 5, 1 Sa. 13. 6; 14. 24.
ANSWERED,] as in 58. 10.
OPEN HIS MOUTH,] as in Ps. 38. 13; Prov. 24. 7.
LAMB,] as in 66. 3; Ge. 22. 7, 8; Ex. 12. 3.
SLAUGHTER,] as in 34. 2, 6; 65. 12, &c.
BROUGHT,] as in 18. 7; 55. 12; Job 10. 9, &c.
SHEEP,] as in Ge. 31. 38; 32. 14; Song 6. 5.
SHEARERS,] as in Ge. 38. 12; 1 Sa. 25. 4, &c.
DUMB,] as in Ps. 39. 2, 9; Eze. 3. 26, &c.
8. RESTRAINT,] as in Ps. 107. 39; Prov. 30. 16.
GENERATION,] his contemporaries.
MEDITATE,] as in Ps. 143. 5.
CUT OFF,] or 'decreed;' as in 2 Ch. 26. 21; Est. 2. 1; Ps. 88. 5; Lam. 3. 54; Eze. 37. 11.
LAND OF THE LIVING,] as in 38. 11, &c.
PLAGUED,] lit. 'plague is to him.'
9. APPOINTETH,] lit. 'giveth;' as in 7. 14.
WICKED,] or 'wrong ones;' as in 3. 11, &c.
GRAVE,] as in 14. 19; 22. 16; 65. 4, &c.
RICH,] as in Ex. 30. 15; Ru. 3. 10; 2 Sa. 12. 1.
HIGH PLACES,] or 'deaths;' i.e. 'most bitter death.'
VIOLENCE,] as in 59. 6; 60. 8; Ge. 6. 11, &c.
DECEIT,] as in Ge. 27. 35; 34. 13; 2 K. 9. 23.
10. DELIGHTED,] or 'wished, pleased;' as in 1. 11; 42. 21; 55. 11, &c.
BRUISE,] as in Lam. 3. 34.
SICK,] as in Hos. 7. 5; Mic. 6. 13.
OFFERING FOR GUILT,] as in Lev. 5. 6, &c.
SEED,] as in 1. 4; 5. 10; 6. 13, &c.
PROLONG DAYS,] as in 48. 9; 57. 4, &c.
PLEASURE,] or 'wish;' as in 44. 28; 46. 10.
PROSPER,] as in 54. 17; Nu. 14. 41, &c.
11. LABOUR,] as in Ge. 41. 51; De. 26. 7, &c.
SATISFIED,] as in 44. 16; Ex. 16. 12, &c.

HIS KNOWLEDGE,] or 'the knowledge of him.'
GIVE RIGHTEOUSNESS,] or 'declare righteous;' as in Ex. 23. 7; Job 27. 5, &c.
MY SERVANT,] as in 20. 3; 22. 20; 37. 35, &c.
TO MANY,] or 'to the multitude;' as in v. 10.
INIQUITIES,] as in v. 5, 6; 1. 4; 5. 18, &c.
BEAR,] as in 46. 4, 7.
12. GIVE A PORTION,] as in Ge. 49. 7.
MIGHTY,] lit. 'bony, strong;' as in 8. 7, &c.
APPORTION,] as in Ge. 49. 17; Ex. 15. 9, &c.
SPOIL,] as in 8. 4; 9. 3; 10. 2, &c.
MADE BARE,] as in Lev. 20. 18, 19.
TRANSGRESSORS,] as in 1. 28; 46. 8; 48. 8.
MANY,] or the 'multitude;' as in v. 11.
BORNE,] or 'lifted up.'

LIV. 1. SING,] as in 12. 6; 44. 23; 49. 13, &c.
BARREN,] as in Ge. 11. 30; 25. 21; 29. 31, &c.
BREAK FORTH,] as in 44. 23; 49. 13; 52. 9.
CRY ALOUD,] as in 10. 30; 12. 6; Jer 31. 7.
BROUGHT FORTH,] or 'been pained;' as in 23. 4; 26. 18; 66. 8, &c.
MARRIED ONE,] as in 62. 4; Ge. 20. 3, &c.
2. ENLARGE,] lit. 'make broad;' as in Ps. 81. 10; Mic. 1. 16, &c.
STRETCH OUT,] as in 29. 21; 31. 3; Ex. 23. 6.
RESTRAIN,] or 'kept back, or dark;' as in 58. 1; Ge. 20. 6; Job 7. 11, &c.
MAKE STRONG,] as in 35. 3; Ex. 4. 21, &c.
3. BREAKETH FORTH,] as in Ge. 30. 30, &c.
POSSESS,] as in 34. 17; 57. 13; 60. 21, &c.
4. DESOLATE,] as in Ge. 38. 11; 33. 10.
YOUTH,] as in Job 20. 11; 33. 25; Ps. 89. 45.
WIDOWHOOD,] as in Ge. 38. 14, 19, &c.
5. MAKER,] lit. 'makers;' as in 17. 7, &c.
HUSBAND,] lit. 'husbands.'
HOLY ONE OF ISRAEL,] as in 1. 4; 5. 19, &c.
CALLED,] by his believing people.
6. FORSAKEN,] as in 10. 14; 17. 2, 9; 60. 15.
YOUTHFUL WIFE,] lit. 'wife of youths;' as in Mal. 2. 14, 15, &c.
7. SMALL MOMENT,] as in v. 8; 26. 20, &c.
8. HID,] lit. 'made secret;' as in 49. 2, &c.
9. NOAH,] as in Ge. 6. 8—10, 13; 7. 1, 5, &c.
SWORN,] lit. 'been sworn.'
10. DEPART,] as in 22. 25; 59. 21; Jos. 1. 8.
REMOVE,] as in De. 32. 35.
KINDNESS,] not 'mercy,' as in C.V.
LOVING ONE,] as in 49. 10; Ps. 116. 5.
11. AFFLICTED,] as in 3. 14, 15; 10. 2, &c.
STORM-TOSSED,] as in Jon. 1. 11, 13.
LAYING,] as in Jer. 33. 12.
CEMENT,] as in 2 K. 9. 30; 1 Ch. 29. 2; Jer. 4. 30.
SAPPHIRES,] as in Ex. 24. 10; 28. 18, &c.
12. AGATE,] as in Eze. 27. 16.
PINNACLES,] as in 14. 31; 22. 7; 24. 12, &c.
DELIGHT,] or 'desire, pleasure;' as in 44. 28; 46. 10; 48. 14, &c.
13. TAUGHT,] as in 8. 16; 50. 4; Jer. 2. 24; 13. 23.
14. ESTABLISHEST,] or 'made ready.'
RUIN,] or 'downfall.'
15. FALLETH,] and is destroyed.
16. PREPARED,] as in Ge. 1. 1, &c.
DESTROYER,] lit. 'one marring.'
17. WEAPON,] or 'instrument,' as in v. 16.
CONDEMNEST,] or 'declarest wrong;' as in 50. 9; Ex. 22. 9; Job 9. 20, &c.
AFFIRMATION,] as in 1. 24; 3. 15; 14. 22, &c.

LV. 1. HO,] as in Zeph. 2. 6, &c.
MONEY,] *lit.* 'silver.'
BUY,] *lit.* 'break;' and perhaps there is an ellipsis, 'break [your fast] and eat.'
2. WEIGH,] as in 46. 6; Ge. 23. 16, &c.
LABOUR,] *or* 'fatigue;' as in 45. 14, &c.
FATNESS,] as in Jud. 9. 9; Job 36. 6, &c.
3. COVENANT AGE-DURING,] as in 24. 5, &c.
KIND ACTS,] as in 16. 5; 40. 6; 54. 8, &c.
STEDFAST,] as in 1. 21, 26; 8. 2; 22. 23, &c.
4. WITNESS,] as in 8. 2; 19. 20; 43. 9, &c.
LEADER,] as in 1 Sa. 9. 16; 10. 1; 13. 14, &c.
5. CALLEST,] to thy standard.
RUN,] for protection and defence.
BEAUTIFIED,] as in 60. 9.
6. SEEK YE JEHOVAH,] as in 1 Ch. 16. 11.
7. FORSAKE,] *or* 'abandon;' as in 10. 3, &c.
THOUGHTS,] as in v. 8.
TO PARDON,] as in De. 29. 20; 2 K. 24. 4.
8. THOUGHTS,] as in v. 7.
9. HIGH,] as in 3. 16; 52. 13; 2 Ch. 26. 16.
10. SHOWER,] as in 44. 14; Ge. 7. 12, &c.
WATERED,] as in 43. 24, &c.
EATER,] as in 1. 7; 29. 6, 8; 30. 27, 30, &c.
11. EMPTY,] as in Ge. 31. 42; Ex. 3. 21, &c.
DESIRED,] *or* 'wished;' as in 1. 11, &c.
12. PEACE,] *lit.* 'completeness.'
CLAP THE HAND,] as in Ps. 98. 8.
13. THORN,] as in 7. 19.
MYRTLE,] as in 41. 19; Neh. 8. 15; Zech. 1. 8, 10, 11.

LVI. 1. THUS SAID JEHOVAH,] as in v. 4.
SALVATION,] *or* 'safety;' as in 12. 2, 3, &c.
REVEALED,] *or* 'uncovered;' as in 1 Sa. 2. 27; 2 Sa. 6. 20; Eze. 21. 24, &c.
2. HAPPINESS,] as in 30. 18; 32. 20, &c.
SABBATH,] *lit.* 'cessation;' as in v. 4, 6, &c.
POLLUTING,] *lit.* 'piercing;' as in v. 6, &c.
3. SON OF THE STRANGER,] as in v. 6.
JOINED,] as in Est. 9. 27, &c.
EUNUCH,] as in v. 4; 39. 7; Ge. 37. 36, &c.
4. FIXED,] as in 1. 29; 14. 1; 41. 8, 9, &c.
DESIRED,] *or* 'wished;' as in 1. 11, &c.
5. WALLS,] as in 2. 15; 22. 10, 11; 25. 12, &c.
STATION,] *lit.* 'hand;' as in v. 2; 1. 12, &c.
NAME AGE-DURING,] as in 63. 12, &c.
6. SONS OF THE STRANGER,] as in v. 3.
SERVE,] *lit.* 'minister;' as in Ex. 28. 35.
LOVE THE NAME,] as in Ps. 5. 11; 69. 36, &c.
SERVANTS,] as in 14. 2; 20. 3; 22. 20, &c.
7. HOLY MOUNTAIN,] as in 11. 9; 27. 13, &c.
PEOPLES,] whether Jew or Gentile.
8. GATHERING,] as in 13. 14, &c.
OUT-CASTS,] as in 11. 12; Ps. 147. 2.
9. This verse evidently begins a new topic.
BEAST,] *lit.* 'living creature;' as in 35. 9.
10. WATCHMEN,] as in 52. 8; 1 Sa. 14. 16, &c.
DUMB,] as in 35. 6; Ex. 4. 11; Ps. 38. 13, &c.
11. UNDERSTANDING,] *lit.* 'to understand.'
TURN] the face; as in 8. 21; 53. 6; Lev. 26. 9.
QUARTER,] *lit.* 'extremity;' as in 5. 26, &c.
12. ABUNDANT,] as in 38. 10; 44. 19, &c.

LVII. 1. RIGHTEOUS,] *or* 'just one;' as in 3. 10; 5. 23; 24. 16, &c.
PERISHED.] *or* 'been lost;' as in 29. 14, &c.
LAYING TO HEART,] as in Jer. 12. 11, &c.
MAN OF KINDNESS,] as in Prov. 11. 17.
GATHERED] to their fathers.
2. PEACE,] *or* 'completeness;' as in 9. 6, 7.

STRAIGHTFORWARD,] as in 26. 10; 30. 10.
3. SORCERESS,] *lit.* 'observer of clouds;' as in 2. 6; De. 18. 10, 14; Jud. 9. 37; Jer. 27. 9.
ADULTERER,] as in Ps. 50. 18; Jer. 9. 2, &c.
COMMIT WHOREDOM,] as in Lev. 19. 29, &c.
4. ENLARGE,] *lit.* 'make broad;' as in De. 12. 20; 19. 8; 2 Sa. 22. 37; Ps. 18. 36, &c.
5. VALLEYS,] *or* 'brooks;' as in v. 6.
6. BROOK,] *or* 'valley;' as in v. 5.
COMFORTED,] as in 1. 24; Ge. 24. 67, &c.
7. EXALTED,] *lit.* 'lifted up;' as in v. 15, &c.
COUCH,] *lit.* 'place of lying down;' as in v. 2, 8; Ge. 49. 4; Ex. 8. 3, &c.
8. DOOR,] as in 26. 20; 45. 1, 2; Ge. 19. 6, &c.
POST.] as in Ex. 12. 7, 22, 23; 21. 6; De. 6. 9.
MEMORIAL,] as in Ex. 12. 14; 13. 9; 17. 14.
STATION,] *lit.* 'hand;' as in 56. 5.
9. AMBASSADORS,] as in 18. 2; Prov. 13. 17.
SHEOL,] the world of spirits; as in 5. 14, &c.
10. LABOURED,] as in 47. 12, 15; 49. 4, &c.
DESPERATE,] as in 1 Sa. 27. 1; Jer. 2. 25; 18. 12.
SICK,] *or* 'pained;' as in 33. 24; 38. 1, &c.
11. AFRAID,] as in 7. 4; 8. 12; 10. 24, &c.
LAID TO HEART,] as in v. 1; 42. 25; 47. 7
SILENT,] as in Jud. 18. 9; 1 K. 22. 3, &c
12. DECLARE,] *lit.* 'set forward.'
13. CRIEST] for help: as in 30. 19; 1 Sa. 7. 8
CARRY AWAY,] *lit.* 'lift up;' as in 2. 4, &c.
TRUSTING,] *lit.* 'taking refuge;' as in 2 Sa. 22. 31, &c.
14. RAISE UP,] as in 62. 10; Ps. 68. 4; 22. 31.
PREPARE A WAY,] as in 40. 3; 62. 10.
15. EXALTED,] *or* 'lifted up;' as in v. 7, &c.
ETERNITY,] *lit.* 'duration.'
HUMBLE OF SPIRIT,] as in Prov. 16. 19, &c.
REVIVE,] *lit.* 'cause to live;' as in 2 K. 5. 7; Eze. 13. 22, &c.
16. STRIVE,] *or* 'contend;' as in 27. 8, &c.
17. DISHONEST GAIN,] as in Eze. 22. 13, &c.
HIDING,] *lit.* 'making secret;' as in 29. 15.
18. LEAD,] as in 23. 7; De. 32. 12, &c.
RECOMPENSE,] *or* 'complete;' as in 59. 18.
19. PRODUCING,] *or* 'preparing;' as in 40. 28; 42. 5; 43. 1, 15, &c.
20. WICKED,] *or* 'those in the wrong;' as in v. 21; 3. 11; 5. 23; 11. 4, &c.
21. MY GOD,] the God of the prophet.

LVIII. 1. CALL,] as in 8. 3; 12. 4; 40. 2, &c.
RESTRAIN,] *lit.* 'darken;' as in 54. 2, &c.
LIFT UP THY VOICE,] as in 13. 2; 40. 9, &c.
SINS,] *or* 'errors;' as in 3. 9; 6. 7; 27. 9, &c.
2. SEEK,] as in 8. 19; 11. 10; Ge. 9. 5, &c.
DRAWING NEAR,] in answer to prayer.
3. FASTED,] as in 2 Sa. 12. 21, 22; Zech. 7. 5.
4. DEBATE,] as in Prov. 13. 10; 17. 19, &c.
FIST,] as in Ex. 21. 18.
TO SOUND,] *or* 'cause to hear;' as in 1 Ch. 15. 19; 2 Ch. 5. 13; Ps. 26. 7, &c.
5. ABASED,] as in 9. 14; 19. 15; Job 41. 2, &c.
SPREAD OUT,] as in Ps. 139. 8.
6. TO LOOSE,] *lit.* 'open;' as in 2 Ch. 2. 7.
BANDS,] as in Ps. 73. 4.
YOKE,] as in v. 9; Lev. 26. 13; Jer. 27. 2, &c
DRAW OFF,] as in Jud. 16. 9, 12; Ps. 2. 3.
7. FLESH,] that is, kindred.
HIDE THYSELF,] as in Ps. 55. 1, &c.
8. BROKEN UP,] *or* 'cleft;' as in 59. 5, &c.
HEALTH,] *lit.* 'prolongation;' as in Jer. 8. 22; 38. 17; 33. 6, &c.

GATHER,] as in Ge. 29. 22; 42. 17; 49. 33, &c.
9. CALLEST,] in prayer and supplication.
CRIEST,] as in v. 9; 9. 6; 21. 8, &c.
FINGER,] as in 2. 8; 17. 8; 59. 3, &c.
10. RISEN,] as in 60. 1; Ex. 22. 3; De. 33. 2.
NOON,] as in 16. 3; 59. 10; Ge. 43. 16, &c.
11. LEAD,] as in Ge. 24. 27; Ex. 13. 17, &c.
WATERED GARDEN,] as in Jer. 31. 12.
OUTLET OF WATERS,] as in 41. 18, &c.
LIE NOT,] nor deceive by drying up.
12. WASTES,] lit. 'dry places;' as in 5. 17.
REPAIRER,] as in 2 K. 12. 12; 22. 6, &c.
RESTORER,] lit. 'bringer back.'
TO REST,] or 'dwell in;' as in 37. 28, &c.
13. HOLY DAY,] as in Ex. 35. 2; Neh. 10. 31.
DELIGHT,] as in 13. 22.
WORD] of complaint or expostulation.
14. HIGH PLACES,] as in 14. 14; 15. 2, &c.
SPOKEN] and it cannot be reversed.

LIX. 1. HAND OF JEHOVAH,] as in 9. 16, &c.
SAVING,] or 'easing;' as in 37. 35; 38. 20.
2. SEPARATING,] as in Ge. 1. 6, &c.
HIDDEN,] lit. 'made secret;' as in 49. 2, &c.
PRESENCE,] lit. 'the face' of God.
3. POLLUTED,] lit. 'redeemed;' as in Lam.
4. 14.
INIQUITY,] or 'punishments of iniquity.'
MUTTER,] as in v. 11; 16. 7; 31. 4, &c.
4. CALLING,] that is, proclaiming, preach-
ing.
PLEADING,] lit. 'judged;' as in 66. 16, &c.
FAITHFULNESS,] or 'stedfastness;' as in
11. 5; 25. 1; 33. 6, &c.
TRUSTING,] or 'leaning;' as in Ps. 118. 8.
EMPTINESS,] or 'ruin;' as in 24. 10; 29. 21.
FALSEHOOD,] or 'vanity;' as in 1. 13, &c.
PERVERSENESS,]or 'labour;' as in 10. 1, &c.
5. EGGS,] as in 10. 14; De. 22. 6; Job 39. 14.
VIPER,] as in 11. 8; Prov. 23. 32; Jer. 8. 17.
HATCHED,] lit. 'cleaved;' as in 2 K. 15. 16.
WEBS,] as in v. 6.
SPIDER,] as in Job 8. 14.
VIPER,] as in Job 20. 16; 30. 6, &c.
7. SHED,] or 'pour out;' as in 1 Sa. 25. 31.
THOUGHTS,] as in 55. 7—9; 65. 2; 66. 18, &c.
DESTRUCTION,] lit. 'breaking;' as in 1. 28.
HIGHWAYS,] as in 7. 3; 11. 16; 19. 23, &c.
8. PATHS,] as in Ps. 17. 5; Prov. 2. 15, &c.
9. REACHETH,] lit. 'overtake;' as in 35. 10.
10. NOON,] as in 16. 3; 58. 10; Ge. 43. 16, &c.
11. MAKE A NOISE,] as in 16. 11; 17. 12, &c.
COO,] as in 16. 7; 31. 4; 38. 14, &c.
SALVATION,] or 'ease, safety;' as in 12. 2.
12. TESTIFIED,] lit. 'answered, responded.'
13. TRANSGRESSING,] as in Ezr. 10. 13, &c.
APOSTACY,] lit. 'turning aside;' as in 1. 5.
CONCEIVING,] as in Job 15. 35.
14. FEEBLE,] or 'stumbling;' as in v. 10, &c.
STRAIGHTFORWARDNESS,] as in 26. 10, &c.
15. TRUTH,] or 'stedfastness;' as in v. 14.
TURNING ASIDE FROM EVIL,] as in Job 1. 1.
16. ASTONISHED,] as in 52. 14, &c.
INTERCESSOR,] as in Job 36. 32.
SUSTAINED,] as in 63. 5; Ge. 37. 37, &c.
17. BREAST PLATE,] as in 1 K. 22. 34; 2 Ch.
18. 33.
HELMET,] as in 2 Sa. 17. 5; 2 Ch. 26. 14, &c.
COVERED,] as in Lev. 13. 45; Ps. 71. 13, &c.
18. DEEDS,] as in 2 Sa. 19. 36; Jer. 51. 56.
FURY,] lit. 'heat;' as in 27. 4; 34. 2, &c.

ISLES,] as in 11. 11; 20. 6; 23. 2, 6, &c.
19. WEST,] as in 43. 5; 1 Ch. 7. 28; 12. 15.
RISING OF THE SUN,] as in 41. 25; 45. 6, &c.
HONOUR,] lit. 'heaviness, weight.'
FLOOD,] or 'river;' as in 7. 20; 8. 7; 11. 15.
ADVERSARY,] lit. 'straitener;' as in v. 18.
SPIRIT OF JEHOVAH,] as in 11. 2; 40. 7, &c.
20. REDEEMER,] as in 41. 14; 43. 14; 44. 6.
21. COVENANT,] as in 24. 5; 28. 15, 18, &c.
SET IN THY MOUTH,] as in 51. 16; 59. 21, &c.
DEPART,] as in 22. 25; 54. 10; Jos. 1. 8, &c
AGE,] as in 9. 7; 14. 20; 25. 2, &c.

LX. 1. ARISE,] as in 21. 5; 23. 19; 32. 9, &c.
RISEN,] as in 58. 10; Ex. 22. 3; De. 33. 2, &c.
2. COVER,] as in v. 6; 6. 2; 26. 21, &c.
NATIONS,] or 'peoples;' as in v. 5, 11, &c.
3. BRIGHTNESS,] as in v. 19; 4. 5; 50. 10, &c.
4. LIFT UP THINE EYES,] as in 49. 18, &c.
SIDE,] as in 66. 12; Ge. 6. 16; Ex. 25. 32, &c.
SUPPORTED,] or 'kept stedfast;' as in 7. 9.
5. BRIGHT,] as in Ps. 34. 5, &c.
FORCES,] lit. 'strength;' as in v. 11; 5. 22.
6. COMPANY,] as in 2 K. 9. 17; Job 22. 11.
DROMEDARIES,] as in Jer. 2. 23.
PROCLAIM TIDINGS,] as in 2 Sa. 1. 20, &c.
7. RAMS,] lit. 'strong ones;' as in 1. 11, &c.
NEBAIOTH,] as in Ge. 25. 13, &c.
BEAUTY,] as in v. 19; 3. 18; 4. 2, &c.
BEAUTIFY,] as in Ps. 149. 4, &c.
8. FLY,] as in 6. 6; Nah. 3. 16; Hab. 1. 8, &c.
WINDOWS,] or 'net works;' as in 24. 18, &c.
9. WAIT,] as in 5. 2, 7; 51. 5; 59. 9, 11, &c.
SHIPS OF TARSHISH,] as in 2. 16; 23. 1, &c.
BEAUTIFIED,] as in 55. 5, &c.
10. SONS OF A STRANGER,] as in 56. 3, &c.
PITIED,] as in 54. 8; Ex. 33. 19; De. 13. 17.
11. SHUT,] lit. 'secured;' as in 45. 1, &c.
FORCE,] or 'strength;' as in v. 5; 5. 22, &c.
12. PERISH,] or 'be lost,' from among
nations.
WASTED,] or 'dried up;' as in 19. 5; 34. 10.
13. HONOUR OF LEBANON,] as in 35. 2.
PINE,] as in 41. 19.
BOX,] as in 41. 19.
SANCTUARY,] as in 8. 14; 16. 12; 63. 18, &c.
MAKE HONOURABLE,] as in 25. 3; 43. 20, &c.
14. SOLES,] as in 1. 6; De. 2. 5; Eze. 1. 7, &c.
CRIED,] or 'called;' as in v. 18; 6. 3; 7. 14.
15. FORSAKEN,] as in 10. 14; 17. 2, 9; 54. 6.
HATED,] as in 29. 31, 33; De. 21. 15—17, &c.
EXCELLENCY,] as in 2. 10, 19, 21; 4. 2, &c.
16. SUCKED,] as in 66. 11; De. 33. 19, &c.
MIGHTY ONE OF JACOB,] as in 49. 26; Ge.
49. 24; Ps. 132. 2, 5, &c.
17. INSPECTION,] as in 10. 3; 2 K. 11. 18, &c.
EXACTORS,] as in 3. 12; 9. 4; 14. 2, 4, &c.
18. DESTRUCTION,] lit. 'breaking;' as in 1.
28; 15. 5; 30. 13, 14, &c.
PRAISE,] as in v. 6; 42. 8, 10, 12; 43. 21, &c.
19. SUN,] as in v. 20; 13. 10; 38. 8, &c.
LIGHT AGE-DURING,] as in v. 20.
BEAUTY,] as in v. 7; 4. 2; 10. 12; 13. 19, &c.
20. GO IN,] not 'down,' as in C.V.
REMOVED,] lit. 'gathered.
21. BRANCH,] as in 11. 1; 14. 19; Da. 11. 7.
PLANTING,] as in 61. 3; Eze. 17. 7; 31. 4, &c.
BEAUTIFIED,] as in 61. 3.
22. CHIEF,] as in 7. 23; 30. 17, &c.
SMALL ONE,] as in Ge. 19. 31, 34, 35, 38, &c.
MIGHTY,] lit. 'bony, strong.'

HASTEN,] as in 5. 19; 28. 16; Ps. 55. 8.

LXI. 1. SPIRIT OF THE LORD,] as in 11. 2.
ANOINT,] as in Ge. 31. 13; Ex. 28. 41, &c.
PROCLAIM TIDINGS,] as in 1 Sa. 31. 9; 1 Ch. 10. 9.
HUMBLE,] or 'meek;' as in 11. 4; 29. 19, &c.
BROKEN OF HEART,] as in Ps. 34. 18, &c.
CAPTIVES,] as in Ge. 31. 26.
LIBERTY,] as in Lev. 25. 10; Jer. 34. 8, &c.
2. GOOD PLEASURE,] as in 49. 8; 56. 7, &c.
DAY OF VENGEANCE,] as in 34. 8; 63. 4, &c.
3. APPOINT,] lit. 'set.'
BEAUTIFIED,] as in 60. 21.
4. WASTES OF OLD,] as in 58. 12.
WASTE CITIES,] lit. 'cities of heat.'
5. SONS OF A FOREIGNER,] as in 56. 3, 6, &c.
6. PRIESTS OF JEHOVAH,] as in 1 Sa. 1. 3.
MINISTERS,] as in Ex. 24. 13; 33. 11, &c.
STRENGTH OF NATIONS,] as in 60. 5, 11, &c.
7. JOY AGE-DURING,] as in 35. 10, &c.
8. WAGE,] or 'work;' as in 40. 10; 49. 4, &c.
9. SEED,] that is, 'posterity.'
OFFSPRING,] as in 1. 4; 6. 13; 14. 20, &c.
ACKNOWLEDGE,] as in 19. 21; 66. 14, &c.
10. REJOICE,] lit. 'rejoicing I rejoice.'
PREPARETH,] as in Jer. 4. 30; 31. 4, &c.
ORNAMENTS,] or a 'bonnet;' as in 2 Ch. 32. 27; Job 28. 17; Eze. 16. 17, 39, &c.
JEWELS,] lit. 'vessels.'
11. SHOOTS,] as in 4. 2; Ge. 19. 25, &c.

LXII. 1. ZION,] the 'dry or sunny place.'
SILENT,] as in v. 6; 64. 12; 65. 6; Ps. 28. 1.
REST,] as in 18. 4; Jud. 3. 11, 30; 5. 31, &c.
TORCH,] as in Ge. 15. 17; Ex. 20. 18, &c.
2. HONOUR,] lit. 'weight, heaviness.'
3. CROWN OF BEAUTY,] as in 28. 5; Prov. 4. 9.
HAND OF JEHOVAH,] as in 9. 16; 25. 10, &c.
4. FORSAKEN,] as in 10. 14; 17. 2, 9; 54. 6.
MARRIED,] as in 54. 1; Ge. 20. 3; De. 22. 22.
5. YOUNG MAN,] or 'choice one;' as in 9. 17.
BUILDERS,] not 'sons,' as in C.V.
6. APPOINTED,] as in Ge. 39. 5; Lev. 26. 16.
SILENT,] as in v. 1; 64. 12; 65. 6; Ps. 28. 1.
REMEMBRANCERS,] as in 36. 3, 22; 66. 3, &c.
KEEP NOT SILENCE,] as in Ps. 83. 1.
7. ESTABLISH,] or 'make ready.'
8. SWORN,] lit. 'sworn hath been.'
ARM OF HIS STRENGTH,] as in 44. 12, &c.
SONS OF A STRANGER,] as in 56. 3, 6, &c.
9. GATHERING,] as in 52. 12; Nu. 10. 25, &c.
COLLECTING,] as in 13. 14; 56. 8; Jer. 32. 37.
10. PREPARE A WAY,] as in 40. 3; 57. 14, &c.
11. PROCLAIMED,] lit. 'caused to hear.'
DAUGHTER OF ZION,] as in 1. 8; 3. 16, &c.
SALVATION,] as in 17. 10; 45. 8; 51. 5, &c.
HIRE,] as in 40. 10; Ge. 15. 1; 30. 18, &c.
WAGE,] as in 40. 10; 49. 4; 61. 8; Lev. 19. 13.
12. REDEEMED OF JEHOVAH,] as in Ps. 107. 2, &c.
FORSAKEN,] as in 27. 10; Ps. 37. 25, &c.

LXIII. 1. EDOM,] the land of Esau.
BOZRAH,] as in 34. 6; Ge. 36. 33; Jer. 48. 24.
TRAVELLING,] as in 51. 14; Jer. 2. 20, &c.
2. RED,] as in Ge. 25. 30; Nu. 19. 2, &c.
WINE-VAT,] as in Jud. 6. 11; Neh. 13. 15.
3. WINE-PRESS,] as in Hag. 2. 16.
4. DAY OF VENGEANCE,] as in 34. 8; 61. 2.
REDEEMED,] as in 35. 9; 51. 10; 62. 12, &c.

5. ASTONISHED,] as in 59. 16; Da. 8. 27, &c.
WRATH,] lit. 'heat.'
6. DRUNK,] as in 2 Sa. 11. 13.
7. KIND ACTS,] as in Ps. 25. 6; 89. 49, &c.
8. LIE,] or 'speak falsely;' as in Lev. 19. 11; 1 Sa. 15. 29; Ps. 89. 33, &c.
9. ADVERSARY,] or 'distressor;' as in 1. 24.
10. REBELLED,] or 'been bitter;' as in 1. 20; 50. 5; Nu. 20. 24, &c.
11. DAYS OF OLD,] as in v. 9; Lam. 1. 7, &c.
BRINGING UP,] as in 8. 7; 66. 3; Lev. 11. 3.
HOLY SPIRIT,] as in v. 10.
12. LEADING,] lit. 'causing to go;' as in v 13; De. 8. 15; Job 12. 17, 19, &c.
CLEAVING,] lit. 'rending;' as in Ps. 141. 7.
13. DEPTHS,] as in 51. 10; Ge. 1. 2; 7. 11, &c.
14. VALLEY,] as in 40. 4; 41. 18; Ge. 11. 2.
LED,] as in Ex. 10. 13.
GLORIOUS NAME,] lit. 'name of beauty;' as in v. 12, 15; 3. 18; 4. 2, &c.
15. HABITATION,] as in 1 K. 8. 13; 2 Ch. 6. 2.
16. OUR FATHER,] that is, our Creator, the source or cause of our being, whether as individuals or as a community.
ABRAHAM.. ISRAEL,] fathers according to the flesh.
17. TO WANDER,] as in 2 K. 21. 9, &c.
HARDENEST,] i.e. 'sufferest to harden.'
SERVANTS' SAKE,] as in 37. 35; 45. 4, &c.
18. HOLY PEOPLE,] as in 62. 12; De. 7. 6, &c.
TRODDEN DOWN,] as in Jer. 12. 10.
19. FROM OF OLD,] as in Ps. 90. 2; 93. 2, &c.

LXIV. 1. REND,] as in Lev. 13. 56, &c.
COME DOWN,] as at Sinai.
FLOW,] as in v. 3.
2. TREMBLE,] or 'are moved;' as in 5. 25.
3. FEARFUL THINGS,] as in Ex. 34. 10, &c.
EXPECT,] as in 5. 2, 7; 51. 5; 59. 9, 11, &c.
4. ANTIQUITY,] or 'of old;' as in 46. 9, &c.
WAITING,] as in Job 3. 21; Da. 12. 12, &c.
5. MET,] as in 1 Sa. 2. 32; Am. 5. 19, &c.
DOER OF RIGHTEOUSNESS,] as in Ps. 106. 3.
IN THEM,] that is, in thy ways.
CONTINUANCE,] lit. 'hidden, indefinite time.'
6. UNCLEAN,] as in 6. 5; 35. 8; 52. 1, 11, &c.
TAKE US AWAY,] or 'lift us up.'
7. IN THY NAME,] as by thy authority.
HID,] lit. 'made secret.'
MELTEST,] as in Ps. 46. 6; Am. 9. 5, &c.
8. OUR FATHER,] the source and cause of our being.
CLAY,] as in 29. 16; 45. 9; Job 4. 9, &c.
FRAMER,] as in 22. 11; 27. 11; 29. 16, &c.
WORK OF THY HAND,] as in De. 16. 15, &c.
9. VERY SORE,] lit. 'unto might;' as in v. 12.
10. HOLY CITIES,] as in 52. 1.
11. PRAISE,] as in 62. 9; Ps. 119. 164, &c.
DESIRABLE THINGS,] as in Lam. 1. 10, &c.
12. VERY SORE,] as in v. 9.

LXV. 1. ENQUIRED OF,] as in Ge. 42. 22, &c.
2. SPREAD OUT,] as in 25. 11; Ps. 143. 6, &c.
APOSTATE,] lit. 'turning aside.'
3. TO ANGER,] as in 1 K. 14. 15; 2 K. 21. 15.
GARDENS,] as the heathen did.
MAKING PERFUME,] as in 1 K. 22. 43, &c.
4. RESERVED PLACES,] as in 49. 6.
5. KEEP TO THYSELF,] as in 34. 1; 48. 16.
COME NOT NIGH,] as in Ex. 19. 15; 24. 2, &c

DECLARED THEE HOLY,] *or* 'set thee a-part.'
6. WRITTEN,] as in 4. 3; Ex. 31. 18; 32. 15.
RECOMPENSED,] *or* 'completed;' as in Ge. 44. 4; Lev. 6. 5; 2 K. 9. 26, &c.
7. MADE PERFUME,] as in 1 K. 22. 43, &c.
REPROACHED,] as in 37. 23, 24; Jud. 5. 18.
8. NEW WINE,] as in 24. 7; 36. 17; 62. 8, &c.
DESTROY,] *lit.* 'mar;' as in v. 25; 11. 9, &c.
SERVANTS' SAKE,] as in 45. 4; Ge. 26. 24, &c.
9. POSSESSOR,] as in 14. 21; 34. 11; 63. 18.
CHOSEN,] *or* 'choice ones.'
10. SHARON,] *lit.* 'the Sharon;' as in 33. 9.
VALLEY OF ACHOR,] as in Jos. 7. 24. 26, &c.
11. FORSAKING JEHOVAH,] as in 1. 28.
HOLY MOUNTAIN,] as in v. 25; 11. 9; 29. 13.
SETTING IN ARRAY,] as in 1 Ch. 12. 33.
GAD,] *lit.* a 'troop' or fortune; as in Ge. 30. 11.
MENI,] *lit.* a 'number.'
12. BOW DOWN,] as in 45. 23; Jud. 7. 5, &c.
THE EVIL THING,] as in 3. 9, 11; 5. 20, &c.
13. LORD JEHOVAH,] as in 3. 15; 7. 7, &c.
14. JOY,] *lit.* 'goodness' of heart.
BREAKING OF SPIRIT,] as in Prov. 15. 4.
HOWL,] as in 15. 2, 3; 16. 7; 52. 5, &c.
15. LEFT,] as in 14. 1; 28. 2; Lev. 16. 23, &c.
CHOSEN,] *or* 'choice ones.'
16. FAITHFULNESS,] *or* 'stedfastness.'
SWEARING,] *lit.* 'being sworn;' as in 19. 18; 48. 1; Ps. 63. 11, &c.
17. CREATING,] *or* 'preparing;' as in v. 18.
ASCEND ON THE HEART,] as in Jer. 3. 16, &c.
18. REJOICE,] *or* 'leap for joy; as in 8. 6.
CREATOR,] *or* 'preparer;' as in v. 17, &c.
19. VOICE OF WEEPING,] as in Ps. 6. 8; Ezra 3. 13.
VOICE OF CRYING,] as in Jer. 51. 54, &c.
20. COMPLETE,] *lit.* 'fill up;' as in Ge. 21. 19; 24. 16; 26. 15, &c.
LIGHTLY ESTEEMED,] as in Job 24. 18.
21. BUILT,] as in 58. 12; 60. 10; 61. 4, &c.
22. WEAR OUT,] as in Job 21. 13, &c.
23. LABOUR,] as in 40. 28, 30, 31; Job 9. 29.
BLESSED OF JEHOVAH,] as in 19. 25, &c.
24. HEAR,] as in 22. 24; 34. 1; 42. 5; 44. 3.
25. WOLF,] as in 11. 6, Ge. 49. 27; Jer. 5. 6.
LAMB,] as in 1 Sa. 7. 9.
DUST IS ITS FOOD,] as in Ge. 3. 14.
DESTROY,] *or* 'mar;' as in v. 8; 11. 9, &c.
HOLY MOUNTAIN,] as in v. 11; 11. 9; 27. 12.

LXVI. 1. THUS SAID JEHOVAH,] as in v. 12; Ex. 4. 22; 5. 1, &c.
FOOTSTOOL,] as in 1 Ch. 28. 2; Ps. 99. 5, &c.
REST,] as in 11. 10; 28. 12; 32. 18, &c.
2. AFFIRMATION,] as in v. 17, 22; 1. 24, &c.
BRUISED IN SPIRIT.] Compare 57. 15, &c.
3. SLAUGHTERETH,] as in 57. 5, &c.

SMITETH,] as in 9. 13; 10. 20; 14. 6, &c.
MAKING MENTION,] as in 36. 3, 22; 62. 6, &c
BLESSING,] as in Ge. 12. 3; 27. 29; Nu. 24. 9
ABOMINATIONS,] as in De. 29. 17; 1 K. 11. 5
DELIGHTED,] as in v. 4; 1. 11; 42. 21, &c.
4. FEARS,] as in Ps. 34. 4.
EVIL THINGS,] as in 7. 15, 16; Prov. 15. 3.
FIXED,] as in v. 3; 1. 20; 14. 1, &c.
5. TREMBLING,] as in v. 2; Jud. 7. 3, &c.
DRIVING OUT,] as in Am. 6. 3.
6. VOICE OF NOISE,] as in 13. 4; Jer. 51. 55.
GIVING RECOMPENSE,] *or* 'completion;' as in Jer. 51. 6; Joel 3. 4, 7, &c.
7. PAINED,] as in 13. 8; 23. 5; 26. 17, &c.
PANG,] as in 13. 8; 26. 7; Job 21. 17, &c.
DELIVERED,] *lit.* 'let escape;' as in 31. 5.
8. AT ONCE,] *lit.* 'one step or blow.'
9. BIRTH,] *lit.* 'do I break.'
10. REJOICE,] as in De. 33. 18; Jud. 9. 19.
MOURNING,] as in 1 Sa. 16. 1; 2 Sa. 14. 2, &c.
11. SUCK,] as in 60. 16; De. 33. 19, &c.
WRING OUT,] as in 51. 17.
DELIGHTED YOURSELVES,] as in 37. 11. &c.
12. STRETCHING OUT,] as in 40. 22; 42. 5,&c.
OVERFLOWING STREAM,] as in 28. 2; 30.28.
SIDE,] as in 60. 4; Ge. 9. 16; Ex. 25. 32, &c.
CARRIED,] *or* 'lifted up;' as in 33. 10, &c.
13. COMFORTETH,] as in 12. 1; 51. 19, &c.
14. REJOICED,] as in 65. 19; De. 28. 63, &c.
TENDER GRASS,] as in 15. 6; 37. 27, &c.
HAND OF JEHOVAH,] as in 9. 16; 25. 10, &c.
INDIGNANT,] as in Da. 11. 30; Zech. 1. 12.
15. HURRICANE,] as in 5. 28; 17. 13; 21. 1.
REFRESH,] *lit.* 'bring back;' as in 49. 6, &c.
FLAMES OF FIRE,] as in 13. 8; 29. 6, &c.
16. DO JUDGMENT,] *or* 'is he judged;' as in 59. 4; Prov. 29. 9; Jer. 2. 35; 25. 31, &c.
FLESH,] all the human race.
PIERCED ONES,] as in 22. 2; 34. 3, &c.
17. SANCTIFYING,] as in 2 Sa. 11. 4.
CLEANSING THEMSELVES,] as in Lev. 14. 4.
AFTER ACHAD.] *lit.* 'after one.'
FLESH OF THE SOW,] as in 65. 4.
MOUSE,] as in Lev. 11. 29; 1 Sa. 6. 4, 5, 11, 18.
18. THOUGHTS,] as in 55. 7, 8, 9; 59. 7, &c.
TONGUES,] that is languages.
19. SIGN,] *or* 'token;' as in 7. 11, 14; 8. 18.
20. PRESENT,] as in v. 3; 1. 13; 19. 21, &c.
LITTERS,] as in Nu. 7. 3.
MULES,] as in 2 Sa. 13. 29; 18. 9, &c.
HOLY MOUNTAIN,] as in 11. 9; 27. 13, &c.
22. NEW HEAVENS,] as in 65. 17,
STANDING,] as in 8. 13; 6. 12. 11. 10, &c.
23. MONTH,] as in 1. 13, 14; 47. 13; Ge. 7. 11.
SABBATH,] *lit.* 'cessation;' as in 1. 13, &c.
24. CARCASES,] as in 14. 19; 34. 3; 37. 36,
QUENCHED,] as in 34. 10; Lev. 6. 12. 13, &c.
TO ALL FLESH,] to all the human race.

WORDS OF JEREMIAH

THE BOOK of the "Words of Jeremiah" is the longest in the Bible, with the exception of the Book of Psalms. The author prophecied between B.C. 638—578. Its contents may be divided into seven sections, viz. 1.) Ch. i—xxi.; 2.) xxii –xxv.; 3.) xxvi—xxviii.; 4.) xxix—xxxi.; 5.) xxxii—xliv.; 6.) xlvi–li.; 7.) lii. New Testament references to this book may be seen in Math. 2. 17, 18; 11. 29; 21. 13, 33; Mark 11. 17; 12. 1; Luke 19. 46; 20. 9; John 4. 14; Acts 7. 52; Rom. 9. 20; 1 Cor. 1. 29, 30, 31; 1 Tim. 2. 2; Heb. 8. 8, 9, 10; 10. 16, 17, &c.

I. 1. WORDS,] or 'matters,' relating to, and recorded by
ᴊEREMIAH,] i.e. 'high one of Jah.'
HILKIAH,] i.e. 'portion of Jah.'
ANATHOTH,] i.e. 'answers, responses.'
BENJAMIN,] in the kingdom of Judah.
2. A WORD OF JEHOVAH,] as in v. 4, 11, &c.
JOSIAH,] i.e. 'despaired of Jah.'
AMON,] i.e. 'stedfast one.'
JUDAH,] including the tribe of Benjamin. 13th YEAR,] B.C. 625.
3. JEHOIAKIM,] i.e. 'Jah raises up.'
ZEDEKIAH,] i.e. 'justice of Jah.'
REMOVAL,] to Babylon by Neouchadnezzar.
4. WORD OF JEHOVAH,] as in v. 2, 11, &c.
5. FORM,] or 'fashion, frame;' as in Ge. 2. 7, 19; Isa. 44, 12, &c.
SEPARATED,] or 'set apart;' as in Nu. 3. 13; 8. 17; Jud. 17. 3, &c.
PROPHET,] an announcer of God's will and glory.
NATIONS,] both Jews and Gentile.
MADE,] lit. 'given' thee.
6. AH LORD JEHOVAH,] as in 4. 18; 14. 13.
TO SPEAK,] lit. 'lead forth' words.
YOUTH,] as in 51. 22; Ge. 18. 7.
7. SEND,] messages of mercy or judgment.
COMMAND,] or 'charge;' as in v. 17; 7. 23.
8. AFRAID,] as in 5. 22, 24; 10. 5, 7; 23. 4.
DELIVER,] lit. 'snatch;' as in v. 19; 15. 20.
AFFIRMATION,] as in v. 15, 19; 2. 3, 9, &c.
9. PUTTETH FORTH HIS HAND,] as in 1 K. 13. 4; 2 K. 6. 7; Job 30. 24, &c.
STRIKETH], as in Ex. 4. 25; Lev. 5. 7, &c.
PUT,] lit. 'given.'
10. SEE,] or 'perceive;' as in 2. 10, 19, &c.
CHARGED,] or 'given thee a charge,' to declare or announce and foretell that all these things would come to pass; in virtue of this authority he is represented as doing them himself. Compare parallel passages in Ge. 41. 13; Ex. 7. 3; Isa. 6. 9, &c.
PLUCK UP,] as in 12. 15, 17; 18. 7; 31. 28, &c.
BREAK DOWN,] as in 18. 7; 31. 28; Ps. 58. 6.
DESTROY,] as in 18. 7; 31. 28, &c.
THROW DOWN,] as in 31. 28, &c.
BUILD,] as in 18. 9; 31. 28; 35. 9, &c.
PLANT,] as in 18. 9; 31. 28; Ecc. 3. 2, &c.
11. WORD OF JEHOVAH,] as in v. 2. 4, &c.
ROD,] as in 48. 17; Ge. 30. 37—39, 41, &c.

ALMOND-TREE,] in Ecc. 12. 5, &c.
12. WELL SEEN,] lit. 'thou hast done good to see.'
WATCHING,] as in 5. 6; 44. 27; Isa. 29. 20.
13. WORD OF JEHOVAH,] as in v. 2, 4, &c.
BLOWN,] as in Job 41. 20.
POT,] as in 52. 18, 19; Ex. 16. 3; 27. 3, &c.
NORTH,] as in v. 14, 15; 3. 12, 18; 4. 6, &c.
14. LOOSED,] as in Neh. 7. 3; Job 12. 14, &c.
LAND] of Judah and Benjamin.
15. FAMILIES,] as in 2. 4; 3. 14; 8. 3, &c.
AFFIRMATION,] as in v. 8, 15, 19, &c.
PUT,] lit. 'given;' as in v. 18, &c.
OPENING OF THE GATES,] as in Jos. 8. 29.
16. MAKE PERFUME,] as in 18. 15; 19. 4, &c.
WORKS OF THEIR OWN HANDS,] as in 25. 14.
17. GIRD UP THY LOINS,] as in 2 K. 4. 29, &c.
COMMAND,] as in v. 7; 7. 23; 11. 4, &c.
AFFRIGHTED, or 'brought down;' as in 10. 2; 17. 18; 23. 4, &c.
18. FENCED CITY,] as in 4. 5; 5. 17; 8. 14, &c.
BRAZEN WALLS,] as in 15. 20, &c.
PEOPLE OF THE LAND,] as in 34. 19, &c.
19. PREVAIL,] lit. 'are not able for thee;' as in 5. 22; 11. 11; 15. 20, &c.
AFFIRMATION,] as in v. 8, 15, 19, &c.
DELIVER,] lit. 'snatch;' as in 15. 20, &c.

II. 1. WORD OF JEHOVAH,] as in v. 4. 21, &c.
2. CALLED IN THE EARS,] as in Ex. 24. 7, &c.
THUS SAID JEHOVAH,] as in v. 5; 4. 3, &c.
YOUTH,] lit. 'youths;' as in 3. 4, 24, &c.
WILDERNESS,] or 'pasture-land;' as in v. 6, 24, 31; 3. 2; 4. 11, &c.
3. HOLY,] that is 'separate, set apart.'
INCREASE,] or 'incoming;' as in 13. 13, &c.
GUILTY,] as in 50. 7; Lev. 5. 5; Jud. 21. 22.
AFFIRMATION,] as in v. 9, 12, 19, 22, &c.
4. HOUSE OF JACOB,] as in 5. 20; Isa. 2. 5.
FAMILIES,] as in 1. 15; 3. 14; 8. 3, &c.
5. PERVERSITY, as in Lev. 19. 15, 35, &c.
VANITY,] as in 8. 19; 10. 3, 8, 15; 14. 22, &c.
BECOME VAIN,] as in 2 K. 17. 15; Job 27. 12.
6. JEHOVAH,] the Existing One, God of Israel.
BRINGETH UP,] as in 33. 6, 18; 48. 35, &c.
LEADETH,] lit. 'causing to go;' as in v. 17.
DESERTS,] as in 5. 6; 17. 6; 50. 12, &c.
PITS,] as in 18. 20, 22; Prov. 22. 14; 23. 27.
DEATH-SHADE,] as in 13. 16; Job 3. 5, &c.
7. BRING IN,] as in 13. 1; 28. 3; 35. 4, &c.
FRUITFUL FIELDS,] as in 4. 26; 48. 33, &c.
DEFILE,] as in Lev. 11. 44; 13. 44, &c.
8. PRIESTS,] professed servants of the Lord.
SHEPHERDS,] as in 3. 15; 6. 3; 10. 21, &c.
PROPHETS, as in v. 26, 30; 1. 5; 4. 9, &c.
BAAL,] the God of the Phenicians.
PROFIT,] as in v. 11, &c.
9. PLEAD,] strive, or contend; as in v. 29.
10. PASS,] as in Go. 32. 16; Ex. 17. 5; 32. 27.
ISLES OF CHITTIM,] as in Eze. 27. 6.
CONSIDER,] as in 9. 17; Job 37. 14.
12. WASTED,] or 'dry;' as in 50. 21, &c.
13. FOUNTAIN,] as in 9. 1; 17. 13; 51. 36, &c.

LIVING WATERS,] as in 17. 13 ; Ge. 26. 19.
CONTAIN,] as in 10. 10 ; 1 K. 7. 26, 38, &c.
14. CHILD OF THE HOUSE,] as in Ge. 14. 14.
15. ROAR,] as in 25. 30 ; 51. 38 ; Job 37. 4, &c.
GIVEN FORTH THEIR VOICE,] as in 4. 16, &c.
DESOLATION,] as in 22. 6 ; 50. 3 ; Isa. 5. 6, &c.
BURNT,] as in 9. 10, 12 ; Neh. 1. 3 ; 2. 17, &c.
16. NOPH,] as in 46. 14, 19 ; Isa. 19. 13, &c.
CROWN OF THE HEAD,] as in 48. 45, &c.
17. JEHOVAH THY GOD,] as in 40. 2 ; 42. 2.
LEADING,] *lit.* 'causing to go;' as in v. 6.
18. SIHOR,] as in Jos. 13. 3.
RIVER,] that is, the Euphrates.
19. INSTRUCT,] as in De. 8. 5 ; 1 K. 12. 11.
REPROVE,] as in Ge. 31. 37, 42 ; Lev. 19. 17.
KNOW AND SEE,] as in 1 Sa. 12. 17 ; 14. 38.
HOSTS,] as in 3. 19 ; 5. 14 ; 6. 6, &c.
20. OF OLD,] i.e. for a 'hidden, indefinite time.'
DRAWN AWAY,] as in 5. 5, &c.
SERVE.] The Qeri reads, 'pass over.'
HIGH HEIGHT,] as in 17. 2 ; 1 K. 14. 23, &c.
GREEN TREE,] as in 3. 6, 13 ; 17. 2 ; 2 K. 16. 4.
WANDERING,] as in 48. 12 ; Isa. 51. 14, &c.
21. CHOICE VINE,] as in Isa. 5. 2.
22. WASH,] as in Ex. 19. 14 ; Lev. 6. 27, &c.
SOAP,] as in Mal. 3. 2.
23. DEFILED,] as in Lev. 18. 24 ; Nu. 5. 13.
BAALIM,] *lit.* 'lords;' as in 9. 14 ; Jud. 8. 33.
VALLEY,] as in 7. 31, 32 ; 19. 2, 6 ; 32. 35.
SWIFT,] *lit.* 'light;' as in 46. 6 ; 2 Sa. 2. 18.
DROMEDARY,] as in Isa. 60. 6.
WINDING,] as in 3. 2, 13, &c.
24. WILD ASS,] as in 14. 6 ; Job 6. 5, &c.
ACCUSTOMED,] *lit.* 'taught of;' as in 13. 23.
SWALLOWED UP,] as in 14. 6 ; Job 5. 5, &c.
WEARY THEMSELVES,] as in Hab. 2. 13, &c.
25. WITHHOLD,] as in 31. 16 ; Prov. 1. 15.
UNSHOD,] as in 2 Sa. 15. 30 ; Isa. 20. 2—4.
INCURABLE,] as in 18. 12 ; Job. 6. 26.
26. SHAME,] as in 3. 24, 25 ; 7. 19 ; 11. 13, &c.
PUT TO SHAME,] as in 6. 15 ; 8. 9, 12, &c.
27. MY FATHER,] the cause of my being.
TURNED,] *lit.* 'faced;' as in 6. 4 ; Lev. 26. 9.
BACK,] *lit.* 'neck;' as in 7. 26 ; 17. 23, &c.
28. GODS,] of wood, stone, silver, and gold.
NUMBER,] as in v. 32 ; 11. 13 ; 44. 28, &c.
29. STRIVE,] as in v. 9 ; 12. 1 ; 50. 34, &c.
TRANSGRESSED,] as in v. 8 ; 3. 13 ; 33. 8, &c.
30. IN VAIN,] *lit.* 'for a vain, empty thing.'
INSTRUCTION,] as in 5. 3 ; 7. 28 ; 17. 23, &c.
DESTROYING,] *or* 'marring;' as in 4. 7, &c.
31. GENERATION,] as in 7. 29 ; 50. 39, &c.
MOURNED,] as in Hos. 11. 12, &c.
32. VIRGIN,] as in 14. 17 ; 18. 13 ; 31. 4, &c.
ORNAMENTS,] as in 4. 30 ; Ex. 33. 4—6, &c.
BRIDE,] as in 7. 34 ; 16. 19 ; 25. 10 ; 33. 11.
BANDS,] as in Isa. 3. 20.
33. MAKE PLEASING,] *lit.* 'make good.'
WICKED,] *or* 'evil ones;' as in 5. 28, 29, &c.
34. SKIRTS,] *lit.* 'wings;' as in 48. 40, &c.
DIGGING,] as in Ex. 22. 2.
35. TURNED BACK ANGER,] as in 4. 8, &c.
36. TO REPEAT,] as in Ps. 34 (title),
ASHAMED,] as a source of confidence.
37. HEAD,] in token of shame and sorrow.
KICKED,] as in 4. 30 ; 6. 30 ; 7. 29, &c.

III. 1. SENDETH AWAY,] as in 17. 8, &c.
TURN BACK,] to be her husband.
DEFILED,] as in v. 9 ; Ps. 106. 38 ; Mic. 4. 11.

LOVERS,] *lit.* 'friends;' as in v. 20 ; 5. 8, &c.
2. LIFT THINE EYES,] as in 13. 20, &c.
HIGH PLACES,] as in v. 21 ; 4. 11 ; 7. 29, &c.
ARAB,] *or* 'one lying in wait.'
DEFILEST,] as in Nu. 35. 33 ; De. 11. 32, &c.
3. SHOWERS,] as in 14. 22 ; De. 32. 2, &c.
GATHERED,] as in 5. 24 ; De. 11. 14, &c.
FOREHEAD,] as in Ex. 28. 38 ; 1 Sa. 17. 49.
ASHAMED,] as in 8. 12.
4. MY FATHER,] as in v. 19 ; Isa. 8. 4, &c.
LEADER,] as in 13. 21 ; Ge. 36. 15, 16, &c.
5. KEEP,] as in 5. 24 ; 35. 18 ; Ge. 17. 9, &c.
PREVAILEST,] *lit.* 'art able.'
6. JOSIAH,] B.C. 641.
BACKSLIDING,] as in v. 8, 11, 12, 22, &c
ISRAEL,] that is, the ten tribes.
HIGH MOUNTAIN,] as in 2. 20 ; 17. 2, &c.
GREEN TREE,] as in v. 13 ; 2. 20 ; 11. 16, &c.
7. TREACHEROUS,] as in v. 10, &c.
JUDAH,] including Benjamin.
8. CAUSES,] as in Ge. 21. 11, 25 ; Ex. 18. 8.
BILL,] *lit.* 'scroll, roll, book;' as in 25. 13.
DIVORCE,] *lit.* 'cutting off;' as in De. 24. 1, 3 ; Isa. 50, 1.
NOT FEARED,] incurring the same punishment.
9. VILENESS,] *lit.* 'lightness,' *or* 'voice.'
DEFILED,] as in v. 1 ; Ps. 106. 38 ; Mic. 4. 11.
STONE .. WOOD,] that is, idols made of these.
11. HERSELF,] *lit.* 'her soul;' as in 2. 24, &c.
BACKSLIDING ISRAEL,] as in v. 6, 8, 12.
TREACHEROUS JUDAH,] as in v. 8.
12. CAUSE TO FALL,] as in Ge. 2. 21, &c.
ANGER,] *lit.* 'faces;' as in 1. 8, 17 ; 44. 11.
KIND,] as in 2 Sa. 22. 26 ; 2 Ch. 6. 41, &c.
WATCH,] as in v. 5 ; Lev. 19. 18 ; Ps. 103. 9.
13. KNOW,] that is, fully realise it.
SCATTER,] as in Ps. 147. 16, &c.
14. BACKSLIDING SONS,] as in v. 22, &c.
RULED,] as in De. 21. 13 ; 24. 1 ; 1 Ch. 4. 22.
FAMILY,] as in 1. 15 ; 2. 4 ; 8. 3, &c.
15. KNOWLEDGE,] as in 1 Sa. 2. 3 ; Job 36. 4 ; Ps. 73. 11 ; Isa. 11. 9 ; 28. 9.
UNDERSTANDING,] as in 9. 24 ; Job. 34. 35.
16. ARK OF THE COVENANT,] as in Nu. 10. 33 ; 14. 44 ; De. 10. 8, &c.
GO UPON THE HEART,] as in 7. 31 ; 19. 5, &c.
INSPECT,] as in 5. 9 ; 9. 9 ; 29. 10, &c.
17. JERUSALEM,] i.e. 'the possession of peace.'
GATHERED,] as in Ge. 1. 9.
NAME OF JEHOVAH,] as in 26. 9, 16, 20, &c.
STUBBORNNESS,] as in 7. 24 ; 9. 14 ; 11. 8, &c.
18. HOUSE OF JUDAH,] as in 11. 17 ; 12. 14.
19. THE SONS,] who had already possession of the land.
DESIRABLE LAND,] as in Ps. 106. 24 ; Zech. 7. 14.
MY FATHER,] as in 2. 27 ; Isa. 8. 4, &c.
20. DECEIVED,] as in 5. 11 ; 12. 6 ; Isa. 24. 16.
FRIEND,] *or* 'companion;' as in v. 1 ; 5. 8.
DEALT TREACHEROUSLY,] as in 5. 11 ; 12. 6.
21. HIGH PLACES,] as in v. 2 ; 4. 11 ; 7. 29.
SUPPLICATION,] as in 31. 9 ; 2 Ch. 6. 21, &c.
MADE PERVERSE,] as in 2 Sa. 19. 90, &c.
22. BACKSLIDING SONS,] as in v. 14, &c.
CAUSE TO CEASE,] as in 30. 17 ; Ge. 20. 17.
JEHOVAH OUR GOD,] as in v. 23, 25, &c.
23. IN VAIN,] *lit.* 'for a falsehood ;' as in v. 10 ; 8. 8 ; 10. 14, &c.

24. SHAMEFUL THING,] as in 2. 26; 7. 19, &c.
25. LAIN DOWN,] as in Ge. 19. 4, 32, 33, &c.
COVER,] as in 46. 8; Ge. 9. 23; 38. 14, &c.
HEARKENED TO THE VOICE,] as in v. 13, &c.

IV. 1. TURN BACK,] as in v. 28; 3. 1, 7, &c.
BEMOAN,] as in 15. 5; 16. 5; 22. 10, &c.
2. SWORN,] *lit.* 'been sworn.'
JEHOVAH LIVETH,] as in 5. 2; 12. 16, &c.
BLESSED THEMSELVES,] as in Ge. 22. 18, &c.
BOAST THEMSELVES,] as in 9. 23, 24; 49. 4.
3. MAN OF JUDAH,] as in v. 4; 11. 2; 27. 25.
TILL,] as in Hos. 10. 12.
TILLAGE,] as in Prov. 13. 23; Hos. 10. 12.
4. FORESKINS,] as in 9. 25; Ge. 17. 11, &c.
INHABITANTS OF JERUSALEM,] as in 8. 1.
FURY,] *lit.* 'heat;' as in 6. 11; 7. 20; 10. 25.
QUENCHING,] as in 21. 12; Isa. 1. 31; Am.
5. 6.
EVIL OF YOUR DOINGS,] as in 21. 12; 23. 2.
5. SOUND,] *lit.* 'cause to be heard.;
BLOW,] *lit.* 'strike;' as in 6. 1; 51. 27, &c.
FENCED CITY,] as in 1. 18; 5. 17; 8. 14, &c.
6. LIFT UP AN ENSIGN,] as in 50. 2; 51. 12.
STRENGTHEN YOURSELVES,] as in 6. 1; Ex.
9. 19.
NORTH,] as in 1. 13—15; 3. 12, 18; 6. 1, &c.
DESTRUCTION,] *lit.* 'breaking;' as in v. 20.
7. DESTROYER,] *or* 'marrer;' as in 2. 30, &c.
LAID WASTE,] as in 10. 22; 18. 16; 51. 29.
8. GIRD ON SACKCLOTH,] as in 6. 26; 49. 3,&c.
LAMENT,] as in 49. 3; 2 Sa. 3. 31; Joel 1. 13
FIERCE,] *lit.* 'heat of anger;' as in v. 26, &c.
9. AFFIRMATION,] as in v. 1, 17; 5. 9, &c.
PERISH,] as in 10. 15; 18. 18; 51. 18, &c.
ASTONISHED,] as in 12. 11; Lev. 26. 22, &c.
WONDER,] as in Ge. 43. 33; Job 26. 11; Ex.
5. 8; Isa. 13. 8.
10. LORD JEHOVAH,] as in 7. 20; 14. 13, &c.
FORGOTTEN,] *or* 'lifted up;' as in 49. 16, &c.
STRUCK,] as in v. 18; 48. 32; 51. 9, &c.
11. HIGH PLACES,] as in 3. 2, 21; 7. 29, &c.
12. SPEAK JUDGMENTS,] as in 1. 16; 39. 5.
13. CLOUDS,] as in De. 4. 11; Joel 2. 2, &c.
SPOILED,] as in v. 20; 9. 19; 10. 20, &c.
14. WASH,] as in Ps. 51. 2.
STRENGTH,] *or* 'sorrow;' as in v. 15.
15. DECLARING,] *lit.* 'setting forward;' as
in Ge. 41. 24; Isa. 42. 9, &c.
SOUNDING,] *lit.* 'causing to hear;' as in 1
Ch. 15. 16, 28; 16. 5, &c.
16. MAKE MENTION,] as in Isa. 12. 4; 43. 26.
GIVE FORTH THEIR VOICE,] as in 10. 13, &c.
17. KEEPERS,] as in 35. 4; 51. 12; 52. 24, &c.
18. VEXATION,] *lit.* 'evil;' as in v. 6, &c.
STRUCK,] as in v. 10; 48. 32; 51. 9, &c.
19. BOWELS,] as in 31. 20; Ge. 15. 4; 25. 23.
PAINED,] as in 5. 22; 23. 19; 30. 23, &c.
SHOUT OF BATTLE,] as in v. 21; 6. 17, &c.
20. DESTRUCTION,] *lit.* 'breaking upon
breaking.'
MOMENT,] as in 18. 7, 9; Ex. 33. 5, &c.
CURTAINS,] as in 10. 20; 49. 29; Ex. 26. 1.
21. ENSIGN,] as in v. 6; 50. 2; 51. 12, &c.
22. FOOLISH,] as in Job 5. 2, 3; Ps. 107. 17.
INTELLIGENT,] *or* 'understanding;' as in
Ge. 41. 33, 39; De. 1. 13, &c.
23. WASTE,] *or* 'ruin;' as in Ge. 1. 2; De.
32. 10.
VOID,] *or* 'empty;' as in Ge. 1. 2; Isa. 34. 11.
25. FOWLS OF THE HEAVENS,] as in 9. 10.

FLED,] *lit.* 'moved away;' as in 9. 10, &c.
26. FRUITFUL PLACE,] as in 2. 7; 48. 33, &c.
BROKEN DOWN,] as in Neh. 1. 6.
27. THUS SAID JEHOVAH,] as in v. 3; 2. 2.
FIERCENESS OF HIS ANGER,] as in v. 8, &c.
COMPLETION,] as in 5. 10, 18; 30. 11, &c.
28. MOURN,] as in 12. 4; Job 14. 22, &c.
BLACK,] as in 8. 21; 14. 2; Joel 2. 10, &c.
PURPOSED,] as in 51. 12; De. 19. 19, &c.
REPENTED,] as in 18. 8, 10; 20. 16; 26. 3.
29. HORSEMAN,] as in 46. 4; Ge. 50. 9, &c.
SHOOTING,] as in Ps. 78. 9.
FLEEING,] as in Ge. 16. 8; 31. 20, &c.
CLIFFS,] as in Job 30. 6.
30. SPOILED ONE,] as in Jud. 5. 27, &c.
ADORNEST THYSELF,] as in 31. 4; Isa. 61.10;
Ez. 16. 11, 13; Hos. 2. 13.
ORNAMENTS,] as in 2. 32; Ex. 33, 4, 5, &c.
RENDEST,] as in 36. 23; Ge. 37. 29, 34, &c.
PAINT,] as in 2 K. 9. 30; 1 Ch. 29. 2, &c.
31. SICK,] *or* 'pained;' as in Ge. 48. 1, &c.
DISTRESS,] *lit.* 'straitness.'
SLAYERS,] as in Ge. 4. 15; Ex. 4. 23, &c.

V. 1. STREETS,] *or* 'out places;' as in 6. 11.
BROAD PLACES,] as in 9. 21; 48. 38, &c.
DOING JUDGMENT,] as in De. 5. 10, &c.
STEDFASTNESS,] as in v. 3
PROPITIOUS,] as in v. 7; 31. 34; 33. 8, &c.
2. JEHOVAH LIVETH,] as in 12. 16; 16. 14.
SWEAR,] *or* 'are sworn;' as in v. 7; 38. 16.
3. GRIEVED,] *lit.* 'pained;' as in De. 2. 25.
MADE HARDER,] as in 23. 14; Ex. 14. 4, &c.
4. POOR,] lean, or thin ones; as in 39. 10.
FOOLISH,] as in 50. 36; Nu. 12. 11; Isa. 19.13.
JUDGMENT,] as in v. 1, 5, 28; 1. 16, &c.
5. GREAT,] as in 4. 6; 6.1, 13, 22; 8. 10, &c
DRAWN AWAY,] as in Jer. 2. 20.
BANDS,] *or* 'instructions;' as in 2. 20, &c.
6. SMITTEN,] as in 2. 19; 3. 6, 8, 11, &c.
SPOIL,] as in Pro. 11. 3; Ps. 17. 9; Eze. 32. 12
LEOPARD,] as in 13. 23; Song 1. 8; Isa. 11. 6,
Hos. 13. 7; Hab. 1. 8.
WATCHING,] as in 1. 12; 44. 27; Isa. 29. 20.
BACKSLIDINGS,] as in 2. 19; 3. 6, 8, 11, &c.
7. PROPITIOUS,] as in v. 1; 31. 34; 50. 20.
GATHER THEMSELVES TOGETHER,] as in 16.
6; 47. 5; De. 14. 1, &c.
8. NEIGH,] as in 50. 11; Est. 8. 15; Isa. 24. 14.
9. LAY A CHARGE,] as in 3. 16; 9. 9, &c.
AVENGE ITSELF,] as in v. 29; 9. 9.
10. DESTROY,] *lit.* 'mar.'
BRANCHES,] as in 48. 32; Isa. 18. 5.
11. DEALT TREACHEROUSLY,] as in 3. 20.
12. LIED,] as in Lev. 6. 2, 3; Jos. 7. 11, &c.
SWORD AND FAMINE,] as in 14. 15; Eze. 14. 21.
15. STRONG,] as in 49. 19; 50. 44; Ge. 49. 24.
TONGUE,] *or* 'language;' as in 9. 3, &c.
16. QUIVER,] as in Job 39. 23; Ps. 127. 5.
SEPULCHRE,] *or* 'grave;' as in 8. 1, &c.
17. HARVEST,] as in v. 24; 8. 20; 50. 16,&c.
FENCED CITIES,] as in 1. 18; 4. 5; 6. 27, &c.
18. COMPLETION,] as in v. 10; 4. 27; 30. 11.
19. FOREIGNER,] as in 8. 19; Ge. 17. 12, &c.
20. SOUND,] *lit.* 'cause to be heard.'
FOOLISH,] as in 4. 22; Ecc. 2. 19; 7. 17, &c.
WITHOUT HEART,] as in 1 Ch. 12. 33, &c.
22. PAINED,] as in Job 39. 23; Ps. 13. 4, &c.
SAND,] as in 15. 8; 33. 22; Ge. 22. 17, &c.
BORDER OF THE SEA,] as in Nu. 34. 6.
LIMIT,] *or* 'statute;' as in 31. 36; 32. 11, &c
2 M

SHAKE THEMSELVES,] as in 46. 7; 2 Sa. 22. 8; Ps. 18. 7.
SOUNDED,] as in 31. 20; 51. 55; Ps. 46. 6, &c.
BILLOWS,] or 'heaps;' as in 9. 11; 31. 35, &c.
23. APOSTATE,] lit. 'turning aside;' as in 6. 28, &c.
REBELLIOUS,] as in Nu. 20. 10; De. 21. 18.
24. JEHOVAH OUR GOD,] as in v. 19, &c.
RAIN,] lit. a 'shower;' as in 14. 4, &c.
SPRINKLING,] as in De. 11. 14.
GATHERED,] as in 3. 3; De. 11. 14, &c.
APPOINTED,] lit. 'statutes;' as in 31. 36, &c.
WEEKS,] lit. 'sevens;' as in Ge. 29. 27, 28.
25. KEPT,] lit. 'withheld;' as in Ge. 30. 2.
26. LOOKETH,] as in Nu. 23. 9; 24. 17, &c.
COVERING,] as in Est. 2. 1.
SET UP,] as in Ge. 21. 28, 29; 33. 20, &c.
TRAP,] lit. 'marring or destroying thing;' as in 51. 25; Ex. 12, 13; 2 K. 23. 13, &c.
27. CAGE,] as in Am. 8. 1.
ARE RICH,] as in Ge. 14. 23; 1 Sa. 17. 25, &c.
28. FAT,] or 'oily;' as in De. 32. 15.
ACTS,] or 'words, matters.'
JUDGED,] as in Ge. 16. 5; 18. 16, 22, 26, &c.
FATHERLESS,] or 'orphan;' as in 7. 6, &c.
29. INSPECT,] as in v. 9; 3. 16; 9. 9; 13. 21.
AVENGE ITSELF,] as in v. 9; 9. 9.
30. ASTONISHING,] as in 2. 15; 4. 7; 8. 21.
HORRIBLE THING,] as in Hos. 6. 10.
31. BEAR RULE,] as in Neh. 9. 28; Ps. 49. 14; 72. 8; Lam. 1. 13.

VI. 1. STRENGTHEN YOURSELVES,] as in 4. 6.
TEKOA,] i.e. a 'blowing, striking.'
BLOW A TRUMPET,] as in 4. 5; 51. 27, &c.
BETH- HACCEREM,] i.e. 'house of the vineyard.'
FLAME,] lit. a 'thing lifted up; as in 40. 5.
BEEN SEEN,] as in Nu. 21. 20; Jud. 5. 28.
DESTRUCTION,] lit. 'breaking;' as in v. 14.
2. COMELY,] as in Job 8. 6; Ps. 68. 12; Zep. 2. 6.
CUT OFF,] as in 14. 17; Hos. 4. 5; Lam. 3. 49.
3. STRIKEN TENTS,] as in Ge. 31. 25.
STATION,] lit. 'hand;' as in v. 9, 12, 24, &c.
4. SANCTIFY,] lit. 'set apart.'
NOON,] as in 15. 8; 20. 16; 43. 16, 25, &c.
5. DESTROY,] or 'mar;' as in 11. 19; 13. 9.
PALACES,] lit. 'high places;' as in 9. 21, &c.
6. POUR OUT,] as in 10. 25; Jud. 6. 20, &c.
MOUNT,] lit. 'place raised up;' as in 32. 24.
INSPECTED,] as in Lev. 6. 4.
7. WELL,] as in 37. 16; 38. 6, 7—11, 13, &c.
SICKNESS,] lit. 'pain;' as in 10. 19, &c.
8. BE INSTRUCTED,] as in Ps. 2. 10.
ALIENATED,] as in 4. 27; 9. 11; 10. 22, &c.
9. PUT BACK THY HAND,] as in Ex. 4. 7.
GATHERER,] as in 8. 3; 11. 23; 15. 9, &c.
10. TESTIFY,] lit. 'cause to witness.'
REPROACH,] as in 15. 15; 20. 8; 23. 40, &c.
DELIGHT NOT,] as in De. 25. 7; Ru. 3. 13.
11. YOUTHS,] or 'choice ones;' as in 9. 21.
ELDER,] lit. 'bearded one;' as in 19. 1, &c.
FULL OF DAYS,] as in Ge. 35. 29, &c.
12. TURNED,] as in 31. 39; Ge. 19. 4, &c.
AFFIRMATION,] as in 1. 8, 15, 19; 2. 3, &c.
13. LEAST . . GREATEST,] as in 8. 10; 16. 6.
DEALING FALSELY,] as in 8. 10, &c.
14. SLIGHT,] as in 8. 11; 1 Sa. 18. 23, &c.
15. ASHAMED,] as in 8. 9, 12; 10. 14; 46. 24.
BLUSHING,] as in 2. 36; 8. 12; 17. 13, &c.

STUMBLE,] as in 8. 12; 20. 11; 31. 9, &c.
16. STAND,] as in 7. 2; 26. 2; 48. 19, &c.
PATHS OF OLD,] or 'of hidden, indefinite time.'
REST,] as in Ru. 1. 9; 1 Sa. 20. 21, 36; Prov. 3. 4.
17. WATCHMEN,] as in Nu. 23. 14; 1 Sa. 1. 1.
18. COMPANY,] as in 30. 20; Ex. 12. 3, &c.
19. DEVICES,] or 'thoughts;' as in 4. 14, &c.
LAW,] lit. 'direction.'
20. FRANKINCENSE,] as in 17. 26; 41. 5, &c.
SWEET CANE,] as in 43. 24; Song 4. 14, &c.
SWEET,] as in 30. 21; 31. 26; Ge. 44. 32, &c.
21. STUMBLING-BLOCKS,] as in Lev. 19. 14.
PERISH,] or 'are lost;' as in 7. 28; 9. 12, &c.
22. NORTH,] as in v. 1; 1. 13, 14, 15; 3. 12.
SIDES,] lit. 'thighs;' as in 25. 32; 31. 8. &c.
23. JAVELIN,] as in 50. 42; Jos. 8. 18, &c.
FIERCE,] as in 30. 14; 50. 42; Prov. 5. 9, &c.
SOUND,] as in v. 17; 2. 15; 3. 9, 13, 21, &c.
SET IN ARRAY,] as in 50. 42; Jos. 2. 6, &c.
DAUGHTER OF ZION.] as in v. 2; Ps. 9. 14.
24. SOUND,] lit. 'hearing, fame, report;' as in Jos. 6. 27; 9. 9, &c.
FEEBLE,] as in 49. 24; 50. 43; Jud. 8. 3, &c.
TRAVAILING,] lit. 'bearing;' as in 15. 9, &c.
25. FEAR,] as in 20. 3, 4, 10; 46. 5; 49 29.
26. GIRD ON SACKLOTH,] as in 4. 8; 49. 3; 2 Sa. 3. 31.
ROLL THYSELF,] as in 25. 34; Mic. 1. 10.
ONLY ONE,] as in Ge. 22. 2, 12, 16, &c.
MOST BITTER,] as in 31. 15; Hos. 12. 14.
27. TRIED,] or 'proved;' as in 9. 7; 12. 3.
28. APOSTATES,] lit. 'turners aside;' as in 5. 23; De. 11. 18, 20, &c.
SLANDEROUSLY,] as in 9. 4; Lev. 19. 16, &c.
CORRUPTERS,] as in 2. 30; 4. 7; 22. 7, &c.
29. BURNT,] or 'heated.'
REFINER,] as in Ps. 66. 10; Da. 11. 35; Zech. 13. 9.
DRAWN AWAY,] as in 10. 20; Jos. 4. 18; Job 17. 11; Isa. 5. 27.
30. REJECTED,] as in Ps. 15. 4.
KICKED,] as in 2. 37; 4. 30; 7. 29; 8. 9, &c.

VII. 1. WORD] of Jehovah, as in v. 2.
2. PROCLAIMED,] lit. 'called;' as in 2. 2, &c.
TO BOW,] as in 13. 10; 25. 6; 26. 2, &c.
3. JEHOVAH OF HOSTS,] as in v. 21; 2. 19.
AMEND,] lit. 'make good;' as in 18, 11, &c.
CAUSE TO DWELL,] or tabernacle; as in v. 7, 12; Ps. 78. 60.
4. TRUST,] or 'lean;' as in 9. 4; 13. 25, &c.
TEMPLE,] as in 24. 1; 50. 28; 51. 11, &c.
6. SOJOURNER,] as in 14. 8; 22. 3; Ge. 15.13.
INNOCENT BLOOD,] as in 19. 4; 22. 3, 17, &c.
WALK,] or 'go;' as in v. 24; 1. 7; 2. 5, &c.
7. AGE UNTO AGE,] as in 25. 9; Ex. 15. 18.
8. TRUSTING,] or 'leaning;' as in 9. 4, &c.
PROFIT,] as in 23. 32; Isa. 30. 5; 44. 10, &c.
9. STEALING,] as in Ex. 22. 12; Hos. 4. 2.
SWEARING,] lit. 'being sworn;' as in 12. 16; Nu. 30. 2.
OTHER GODS,] as in v. 6, 18; 11. 10; 13. 10.
10. STAND BEFORE ME,] as in 15. 1, 19, &c.
NAME IS CALLED,] as in v. 11, 14, 30, &c.
DELIVERED,] lit. 'snatched;' as in Ge. 32. 30; De. 23. 15, &c
DEN,] as in Ge. 19. 30; 23. 9, 11, 17, 19, &c.
BURGLERS,] lit. 'breakers forth or up;' as in Ps. 7. 4; Isa. 35. 9; Eze. 7. 22; 18. 10.

AFFIRMATION,] as in v. 13, 19, 30, 32, &c.
12. SHILOH,] in Ephraim, north of Bethel.
CAUSED TO DWELL,] or 'tabernacle.'
13. RISING EARLY,] as in v. 25; 11. 7; 25. 3.
14. TRUSTING,] or "leaning;' as in v. 8, &c.
16. PRAY,] as in 11. 14; 14. 11; 32. 16, &c.
INTERCEDE,] as in 27. 18, &c.
18. GATHERING,] as in Jud. 1. 7; Isa. 17. 5.
CAKES,] as in 44. 19.
QUEEN,] or 'workmanship.'
PROVOKE TO ANGER,] as in 11. 17; 25. 7, &c.
19. SHAME,] as in 2. 26; 3. 24, 25; 11. 13, &c.
20. LORD JEHOVAH,] as in 1. 6; 4. 10, &c.
FURY,] lit. 'heat;' as in 4. 4; 6. 11; 10. 25.
BURNED,] as in 4. 4; 21. 12; Nu. 11. 3, &c.
QUENCHED,] as in 17. 27; Lev. 6. 12, 13, &c.
21. ADD,] as in Isa. 29. 1.
22. COMMAND,] as in v. 23, 31; 11. 4, 8, &c.
BRINGING OUT,] as in 11. 4; 31. 32; 34. 13,
23. BUT,] lit. 'but rather;' as in 31. 37, &c.
WELL,] lit. 'good;' as in 38. 20; 40. 9, &c.
24. COUNSELS,] as in 5. 10; Ps. 81. 12; Prov.
l. 31; 22. 20; Hos. 11. 6; Mic. 6. 16.
STUBBORNNESS,] as in 3. 17; 9. 14; 11. 8, &c.
FORWARD,] lit. 'faces.'
25. RISING EARLY,] as in v. 13; 11. 7; 25. 3.
26. HARDEN THE NECK,] as in 17 23, &c.
27. SPOKEN,] in the name of the Lord.
CALLED,] with a loud voice, in earnest en-
treaty.
ANSWER,] or respond to the call.
28. NATION,] or collective 'body' of men.
ACCEPTED INSTRUCTION,] as in 2. 30, &c.
STEDFASTNESS,] as in 5. 1, 3; 9. 3; Ex. 17, 12.
29. CUT OFF,] as in Mic. 1. 16.
CROWN,] or 'separation;' as in Ex. 29. 6.
HIGH PLACES,] as in 3. 2, 21; 4. 11; 12. 12.
LAMENTATION,] as in 9. 10, 20; 2 Sa. 1.17.
REJECTED,] as in 2. 37; 4. 30; 6. 30, &c.
LEAVETH,] as in Nu. 11. 31; De. 32. 15, &c.
30. THE EVIL THING,] as in v.12, 24, 30, &c.
ABOMINATIONS,] as in 4. 1; 13. 27; 16. 18.
NAME IS CALLED,] as in v. 10. 14; 14. 9, &c.
DEFILE,] as in 32. 34; Lev. 13. 44, 50; 15. 31;
18. 28; 20. 3, 25.
31. HIGH PLACES,] as in 17. 3; 19. 5, &c.
THE TOPHET,] i.e. 'spittle, spitting.'
VALLEY OF HINNOM,] i.e. 'gratis.'
BURN,] as in 19. 5; 36. 25, 27; Jud. 9. 52;
2 Sa. 23. 7; Am. 2. 1.
32. DAYS ARE COMING,] as in 9. 25; 16. 14.
SLAUGHTER,] as in 12. 3; 19. 6; Zech. 11. 4, 7.
WITHOUT PLACE,] as in 19. 11.
33. CARCASE,] lit. 'faded or fallen thing.'
TROUBLING,] as in 30. 10; 46. 27; Lev. 26. 6.
34. CAUSED TO CEASE,] as in 36. 29; 48. 33.
VOICE OF JOY,] as in 16. 9; 25. 10; 33. 11,
VOICE OF GLADNESS,] as in 16. 9; 25. 10;
33. 11.
BRIDEGROOM,] as in 16. 9; 25. 10; 33. 11.
DESOLATION,] lit. 'dry place;' as in 22. 5.

VIII. 1. AFFIRMATION,] as in v. 3, 13, 17.
GRAVES,] as in 5. 16; 20. 17; 26. 23, &c.
2. HOST OF THE HEAVENS,] as in De. 4. 19.
GATHERED,] as in 25. 33; Ge. 25. 8, 17, &c.
DUNG,] as in 9. 22; 16. 4; 25. 33; 2 K. 9. 37.
3. DRIVEN,] as in 16. 15; 23. 3, 8; 27. 10.
4. THUS SAID JEHOVAH,] as in 2. 2, 5, &c.
5. BACKSLIDING,] as in 2. 19; 3. 6, 8, 11, 12.
6. RIGHT,] or 'so;' as in Ge. 1. 7; 42. 25, &c.

REPENTED,] as in Jud. 21. 15; Joel 2. 13;
Jon. 4. 2.
COURSES,] as in 22. 17; 23. 10; 2 Sa. 18. 27.
RUSHING,] as in 47. 2; 2 Ch. 32. 4; Isa. 10. 22.
7. STORK,] lit. 'kind one;' as in Lev. 11. 19;
De. 14. 18; Job 39. 13; Ps. 104. 17; Zech. 5. 9.
CRANE,] as in Isa. 38. 14.
8. LAW,] lit. 'direction.'
9. ASHAMED,] as in v. 12; 2. 26; 6. 15, &c.
AFFRIGHTED,] or 'brought down.'
KICKED,] as in 2. 37; 4. 30; 6. 30; 7. 29, &c.
10. DISPOSSESSORS,] as in 49. 1, 2; Ge. 15. 3.
LEAST.. GREATEST,] as in 6. 13; 31. 34; 42.
1, 8; 44. 12.
DEALING FALSELY,] as in 6. 13; Prov. 11. 18.
11. SLIGHTLY,] as in 6. 14; 1 Sa. 18. 23, &c.
12. ASHAMED,] as in 2. 36; 6. 15; 9. 19, &c.
FALLING ONES,] as in 6. 15; 37. 13, 14, &c.
STUMBLE,] as in 6. 15; 20. 11; 31. 9, &c.
13. CONSUME,] as in Ex. 23. 16; Lev. 23. 39.
GRAPES,] as in Ge. 40. 10, 11; 49. 11, &c.
STRENGTH,] as in 5. 15; 49. 19; 50. 44, &c.
14. BE GATHERED,] as in 4. 5; 47. 6; Ge. 49.
1; De. 32. 50; Eze. 39. 17; Am. 3. 9.
FENCED CITIES,] as in 1. 18; 4. 5; 5. 17, &c.
SILENT,] as in 48. 2; 49. 26; 50. 30; 51. 6; 1
Sa. 2. 9.
GALL,] as in 9. 15; 23. 15; De. 29. 18, &c.
15. LOOKING,] as in 14. 19; Ps. 40. 1.
HEALING,] as in 14. 19; 33. 6; 2 Ch. 21. 18.
16. DAN,] the northern limit of Palestine.
NEIGHINGS,] as in 13. 27.
TREMBLED,] as in 49. 21; Jud. 5. 4; Ps. 68.
8; Eze. 38. 20; Joel 2. 10; 3. 16; Nah. 1. 5.
17. VIPERS,] as in Prov. 23. 32; Isa. 11. 8;
50. 5.
CHARMER,] as in Ecc. 10. 11; Isa. 33. 20;
26. 16.
18. SICK,] as in Isa. 1. 5; Lam. 1. 22.
19. CRY,] as in Ex. 2. 23; 1 Sa. 5. 12, &c.
PROVOKED,] as in 1 K. 15. 30; 21. 20, &c.
20. HARVEST,] or 'reaping;' as in 5. 17, &c.
SUMMER,] as in 40. 10, 12; 48. 32; Ge. 8. 22.
SAVED,] or 'eased;' as in Nu. 10. 9; Isa.
45. 17.
21. BLACK,] as in 4. 28; 14. 2; Joel 2. 10; 3.
15; Mic. 3. 6.
22. BALM,] as in 46. 11; 51. 8; Ge. 37. 25;
43. 11; Eze. 27. 17.
GILEAD,] as in 22. 6; 46. 11; 50. 19, &c.
PHYSICIAN,] lit. 'healer;' as in Ge. 50. 2.
HEALTH,] lit. 'prolongation.'

IX. 1. WHO DOTH MAKE,] lit. 'give;' as
in v. 2.
WOUNDED,] lit. 'pierced;' as in 14. 18, &c.
2. WILDERNESS,] or 'pasture land.'
LEAVE,] forsake or abandon.
ASSEMBLY,] lit. 'restraint;' as in Lev.
23. 36, &c.
TREACHEROUS,] lit. 'covering with a gar-
ment;' as in 12. 1; 12. 1; Ps. 25. 3, &c.
3. BEND,] lit. 'cause to tread or walk;' as
in Ps. 25. 9; 107. 7; Isa. 42. 16; Hab. 3. 19, &c.
LIE,] or 'falsehood;' as in v. 3; 3. 10, &c.
STEDFASTNESS,] as in 5. 1, 3; 7. 28, &c.
MIGHTY,] as in Ge. 7. 19, 20; 49. 26, &c.
4. BEWARE,] or 'be guarded;' as in 17. 21.
TRUST,] or 'lean;' as in 7. 4; 13. 25; 17. 5
SUPPLANT,] lit. 'take the heel.'

SLANDEROUSLY,] as in 9. 4: Lev. 19. 16, &c.
5. MOCK,] as in Ge. 31. 7; Jud. 16. 10, &c.
TRUTH,] or 'stedfastness;' as in v. 3.
TAUGHT,] or 'accustomed;' as in v. 14, &c.
COMMIT INIQUITY,] as in 2 Sa. 7. 14.
LABOURED,] to 'weariness;' as in 6. 11, &c.
6. DECEIT,] lit. 'lifting up.'
7. REFINING,] as in 10. 9, 14; 51. 17, &c.
TRIED,] as in 6. 27; 12. 3; Job 23. 10, &c.
8. SLAUGHTERING,] as in Lev. 14. 6, 51, &c.
AMBUSH,] lit. 'lying in wait.'
9. AVENGE ITSELF,] as in 5. 9, 29.
10. WAILING,] as in v. 18—20; 31. 15; Am.
5. 16; Mic. 2. 4.
HABITATIONS,] lit. 'comely places;' as in
23. 10; 25. 37; Ps. 23. 2, &c.
LAMENTATION,] as in v. 20; 7. 29, &c.
BURNT UP,] as in v. 12; 2. 15; 46. 19, &c.
CATTLE,] lit. 'acquisition, gain, getting.'
FLED,] lit. 'moved away;' as in 4. 25, &c.
11. HEAPS,] as in 5. 22; 31. 35; 51. 37, &c.
WITHOUT,] or 'from want of;' as in Ge. 31.
20; Job 8. 11, &c.
12. DECLARE,] lit. 'set forward;' as in 16.
10; 20. 10; 33. 3, &c.
PERISHED,] or 'been lost;' as in 6. 21, &c.
14. STUBBORNNESS,] as in 3. 17; 7. 24, &c.
BAALIM,] i.e. 'the lords;' as in 2. 23; Jud.
8. 33; 1 Sa. 7. 4; 2 Ch. 17. 3; Hos. 2. 13, 17.
15. CAUSING TO EAT,] as in 23. 15; De. 8. 16.
GALL,] as in 8. 14; 23. 15; De. 29. 18, &c.
16. SCATTERED,] as in 23. 2; 30. 11, &c.
17. JEHOVAH OF HOSTS,] as in v. 7; 2. 19.
CONSIDER,] or 'understand;' as in 2. 10;
Job 37. 14.
18. HASTEN,] as in Ge. 18. 6; 19. 22; 45. 9.
FLOW,] as in 13. 17; 14. 17; 18. 3, &c.
19. WAILING,] as in v. 18.
SPOILED,] or 'destroyed; as in 4. 13, &c.
TABERNACLES,] as in 30. 18; 51. 30, &c.
20. TEACH,] or 'accustom;' as in De. 31. 19.
LAMENTATION,] as in v. 10, 18, 19; 31. 15;
Am. 5. 16; Mic. 2. 4.
21. WINDOWS,] lit. 'pierced places;' as in
22. 14; Ge. 8. 6; 26. 8, &c.
PALACES,] or 'high places;' as in 6. 5, &c.
SUCKING,] or infant.
22. CARCASE,] lit. 'faded or falling thing.'
DUNG,] as in 8. 2; 16. 4; 25. 33; 2 K. 9. 37;
Ps. 107. 29.
HANDFUL,] as in Am. 2. 13; Mic. 4. 12;
Zech. 12. 6.
GATHERING,] as in Nu. 10. 25; Jos. 6. 9, &c.
23. BOAST HIMSELF,] as in v. 24; 4. 2, &c.
RICHES,] as in 17. 11; Ge. 31. 16; 1 Sa. 17. 25.
24. BOASTER,] as in Ps. 97. 7; Prov. 25. 14.
DOING KINDNESS,] as in 5. 1; 6. 13; 7. 17.
25. DAYS ARE COMING,] as in 7. 32; 16. 14.
FORESKIN,] as in 4. 4; Ge. 17. 11, 14, 23, &c.
26. CUTTING THE CORNER,] as in 25. 23;
49. 32.
UNCIRCUMCISED IN HEART,] as in Lev. 26. 41.

X. 1. HEAR YE THE WORD,] as in 2. 4; 7. 2.
2. THUS SAID JEHOVAH,] as in v. 18; 2. 2.
ACCUSTOM NOT YOURSELVES,] as in 12. 16.
AFFRIGHTED,] or 'brought down;' as in 1.
17; 17. 18, &c.
3. STATUTES,] lit. 'engraved things;' as in
5. 24, &c.
ARTIFICER,] as in v. 9; 24. 1; 29. 2, &c.

AXE,] as in Isa. 44. 12.
4. BEAUTIFY,] or 'make it fair.'
NAILS,] as in 1 Ch. 22. 3; 2 Ch. 3. 9; Isa
41. 7.
HAMMERS,] as in 1 K. 6. 7; Isa. 44. 12.
STUMBLE or 'go forth;' Comp. Isa. 28. 7.
5. STEP,] as in Prov. 7. 8; Hab. 3. 12, &c.
7. BECOMING.] Original word not found a-
gain.
8. INSTRUCTION,] as in 2. 30; 5. 3; 7. 28, &c.
9. SPREAD OUT,] as in Ex. 29. 3; Nu. 16. 39.
SKILFUL,] as in v. 7; 4. 22; 8. 8, 9; 9. 12, &c.
10. GOD OF TRUTH,] or 'stedfastness.'
LIVING GOD,] as in 23. 36; 44. 26, &c.
INDIGNATION,] as in 15. 17; 50. 25, &c.
11. SAY.] This verse in the original is in
the Chaldee, not the Hebrew language.
PERISH,] or 'be lost;' as in v. 15, &c.
12. MAKER OF EARTH,] as in 51. 15, &c.
ESTABLISHER OF THE WORLD,] as in 51. 15.
STRETCHED FORTH,] or 'inclined;' as in
45. 12, &c.
13. VAPOURS,] lit. 'things lifted up;' as in
51. 16, &c.
TREASURES,] as in 15. 13; 17. 3; 20. 5, &c.
14. BRUTISH,] as in v. 21; 51. 17; Isa. 19. 11.
BY KNOWLEDGE,] lit. 'from knowledge.'
15. ERRING,] or 'going astray;' as in 51. 18.
16. PORTION OF JACOB,] as in 51. 19.
FRAMER,] former or fashioner; as in 18. 2.
ROD OF HIS INHERITANCE,] as in 51. 19;
Isa. 63. 17.
17. GATHER,] as in 12. 9; 40. 10; Nu. 11. 16.
BULWARK,] as in 19. 9; 52. 5; De. 20. 19, &c.
18. SLINGING OUT,] as in Jud. 20. 16.
19. GRIEVOUS,] or 'painful;' as in 44. 17,&c.
SICKNESS,] or 'pain;' as in 6. 7; De. 7. 15.
BEAR,] or 'lift up;' as in 7. 16; 9. 10, &c.
20. SPOILED,] or 'destroyed;' as in 4. 13, 20.
CORDS,] or 'pins;' as in Ex. 35. 18; 39. 40.
BROKEN,] as in 6. 29, &c.
CURTAINS,] as in 4. 20; 49. 29, &c.
21. BRUTISH,] as in v. 14.
ACTED WISELY,] as in 20. 11; 23. 5, &c.
22. REPORT,] lit. 'hearing;' as in 49. 14, 23.
SHAKING,] or 'rushing;' as in 47. 3, &c.
23. JEHOVAH,] who is, 'that which he is,'
i.e. unsearchable.
STEP,] as in 2 Sa. 6. 13; 22. 37; Job 14. 16.
24. CHASTISE,] or 'instruct;' as in Prov.
19. 18; 20. 17.
SMALL,] as in Ex. 30. 15; Lev. 25. 16, &c.
25. POUR OUT,] as in 6. 6; Jud. 6. 20, &c.

XI. 1. THE WORD,] of warning and rebuke;
as in 7. 1.
2. COVENANT,] lit. a 'eating;' as in v. 3, 6.
3. THUS SAID JEHOVAH,] as in v. 11, 12, 22.
CURSED,] lit. 'bitter;' as in 17. 5; 20. 14.
OBEY,] lit. 'hear;' as in v. 11, &c.
4. COMMANDED,] or 'charged;' as in v. 8
IRON FURNACE,] as in De. 4. 20; 1 K. 8. 51.
5. ESTABLISH,] lit. 'raise up;' as in 23. 20.
SWORN,] lit. 'been sworn;' as in 4. 2, &c.
AMEN,] lit. 'stedfast;' as in 28. 6, &c.
6. PROCLAIM,] lit. 'call;' as in 4. 5; 9. 17.
7. TESTIFIED,] as in Ge. 43. 3; 1 Sa. 8. 9, &c.
RISING EARLY,] as in 7. 13, 25; 25. 3, 4, &c.
8. INCLINED THEIR EAR,] as in 7. 24, &c.
STUBBORNNESS,] not 'imagination,' as
in C. V

9. CONSPIRACY,] *lit.* 'binding;' as in 2 Sa. 15. 12, &c.
10. FIRST FATHERS,] as in Isa. 43. 27, &c.
MADE VOID,] as in 31. 32; Ge. 17. 14, &c.
11. CRIED,] in anguish: as in v. 12; 43. 2.
12. CITIES OF JUDAH,] that is, those inhabiting them.
MAKING PERFUME,] as in 44. 15, 19, &c.
VEXATION,] *lit.* 'evil;' as in v. 8, 11, 14, &c.
13. NUMBER OF THY CITIES,] as in 2. 28, &c.
SHAMEFUL THING,] as in 2. 26; 3. 24, &c.
14. PRAY,] as in 7. 16; 14. 11, &c.
CRY,] as in 7. 16; 14. 12; 1 K. 8. 28, &c.
VEXATION,] *or* 'evil;' as in v. 12.
15. BELOVED,] as in De. 33. 12; Ps. 60. 5.
WICKEDNESS,] as in 23. 20; 30. 24; 51. 11.
HOLY FLESH,] as in Hag. 2. 12.
16. GREEN OLIVE,] as in Ps. 52. 8.
GOODLY FRUIT,] *lit.* 'fruit of form.'
TUMULT,] as in Eze. 1. 24.
KINDLED,] as in 17. 27; 21. 14; 32. 29, &c.
BROKEN,] as in 15. 20; 40. 4, &c.
BRANCHES,] as in Eze. 17. 6, 7, 23; 19. 11.
17. JEHOVAH OF HOSTS,] as in v. 20, 22, &c.
PLANTING,] as in 31. 5; Ps. 94. 9.
PROVOKE TO ANGER,] as in 7. 18; 25. 7, &c.
18. SHEWED,] *lit.* 'caused to see;' as in 24. 1; 38. 21, &c.
19. TRAINED,] as in 3. 4; 13. 21, &c.
BROUGHT TO SLAUGHTER,] as in Isa. 53. 7.
DEVISED,] *or* 'thought;' as in 18. 8; 48. 2.
DEVICES,] *or* 'thoughts;' as in 4. 14; 6. 19.
DESTROY,] *lit.* 'mar;' as in 6. 5; 13. 9, &c.
LAND OF THE LIVING,] as in Job 28. 13, &c.
20. JUDGING RIGHTEOUSNESS,] as in Ps. 9. 4.
TRYING REINS,] as in 17. 10; Ps. 7. 9.
REVEALED,] *or* 'uncovered, discovered;' as in 20. 12, &c.
21. ANATHOTH,] Jeremiah's birth-place; as in 1. 1.
PROPHESY,] *or* 'be not a prophet;' as in 25. 30, &c.
22. SEEING AFTER,] not 'punish,' as in C.V.
CHOSEN,] *or* 'choice' ones; as in 6. 11, &c.
FAMINE,] *lit.* 'hunger;' as in 5. 12; 14. 12.
23. INSPECTION,] as in 8. 12; 10. 15; 23. 12.

XII. 1. RIGHTEOUS,] *or* 'right, just;' as in 20. 12, &c.
PLEAD,] strive, or contend; as in 2. 9, &c.
2. PLANTED,] as in 2. 21; 24. 6; 31. 5, &c.
FAR OFF,] as in 23. 23; 25. 26; 30. 10, &c.
3. TRIED MY HEART,] as in Ps. 7. 9; 17. 3.
SEPARATE,] not 'prepare,' as in C.V.
SLAUGHTER,] as in 7. 32; 19. 6; Zech. 11. 4.
4. WITHER,] *or* 'dry up;' as in 23. 10, &c.
FOR,] *lit.* 'from, or because of.'
CONSUMED,] *or* 'ended;' as in Ge. 18. 23.
FOWL,] not 'birds,' as in C.V.
5. FOOTMEN,] as in Ex. 12. 37; Nu. 11. 21.
FRET THYSELF,] *or* 'burn or heat thyself;' not 'contend,' as in C.V.
RISING OF JORDAN,] overflowing its banks.
6. TRUST,] *lit.* 'stedfast;' as in 40. 14, &c.
7. FORSAKEN,] as in 1. 16; 2. 13; 5. 7, &c.
HAND,] *lit.* 'paw;' as in 4. 31; 15. 21, &c.
8. INHERITANCE,] as in v. 7, 9, 14, 15, &c.
9. SPECKLED.] Original word not found again.
BEAST,] *lit.* 'living creature;' as in v. 16.
10. SHEPHERDS,] not 'pastors,' as in C.V.

DESTROY,] *lit.* 'mar;' as in 48. 18, &c.
DESIRABLE,] not 'pleasant,' as in C.V.
WILDERNESS,] *or* 'pasture land;' as in v. 12
11. DESOLATION,] as in v. 10.
LAYING,] *or* 'setting;' as in Isa. 57. 1, &c.
12. PLAIN,] *or* 'pasture land;' as in v. 10.
SPOILERS,] *or* 'destroyers;' as in v. 10.
13. SOWED,] as in 4. 3; 31. 27; 35. 7, &c.
SICK,] *or* 'pained;' as in Da. 8. 27; Am. 6. 6.
FIERCENESS,] *lit.* 'heat;' as in 4. 8, 26, &c.
14. NEIGHBOURS,] *lit.* 'tabernaclers;' as in 6. 21.
STRIKING,] not 'touch' merely, as in C.V.
15. TURN BACK,] as in 3. 1, 7, 19; 4. 1, &c.
16 LEARN WELL,] *lit.* 'to learn they learn.'
TO SWEAR,] *lit.* 'to be sworn;' as in 7. 9.
17. HEAR,] not 'obey,' as in C.V.

XIII. 1. THUS SAID JEHOVAH,] as in v. 9.
GOT,] acquired, obtained, or purchased; as in v. 4; 19. 1, &c.
2. WORD OF JEHOVAH,] as in v. 3, 8, &c.
4. HIDE,] as in 40. 13, &c.
5. COMMANDED,] *or* 'charged me;' as in v. 6; 7. 22, &c.
6. MANY DAYS,] as in 35. 7; 37. 16, &c.
7. DIG,] as in Ge. 21. 30; 26. 15, 18, 19, &c.
MARRED,] as in 18. 4; Ge. 6. 12.
PROFITABLE,] *lit.* 'it does not prosper;' as in v. 10. &c.
9. MAR,] as in 6. 5; 11. 19; 15. 6, &c.
GREAT,] *or* 'abundant.'
10. STUBBORNNESS,] not 'imagination,' as in C.V.
11. CLEAVETH,] as in 42. 16; Ge. 2. 24, &c.
AFFIRMATION OF JEHOVAH,] as in v. 14. 25.
12. IS FULL,] *or* 'is filled;' as in Ge. 6 11.
13. FILLING,] as in 1 Ch. 12. 5; Job 3. 15, &c.
DRUNKENNESS,] *or* 'merriment;' as in Eze. 23. 33; 39. 19.
14. DASHED,] as in 50. 20, 21, 22, 23, &c.
DESTROY,] *or* 'mar;' as in 13. 5; 51. 11, &c.
15. HEAR,] as in 2. 4; 5. 21; 6. 18, 19, &c.
16. HONOUR,] *lit.* 'weight, heaviness;' as in 2. 11, &c.
STUMBLE,] *or* 'strike, smite.'
WAITED,] not 'look,' as in C.V.
DEATH-SHADE,] i.e. 'a very deep shade.'
17. SECRET PLACES,] as in 23. 24; 49. 10, &c.
FLOCK,] herd or drove; as in v. 20; 6. 3, &c.
18. MISTRESS,] *lit.* 'mighty' lady; as in 29. 2.
PRINCIPALITIES,] *lit.* 'first estates.'
19. CITIES OF THE SOUTH,] as in 32. 44, &c.
20. LIFT UP YOUR EYES,] as in 3. 2; Ge. 13. 14.
DROVE,] *or* 'herd;' not 'flock,' as in C.V.
21. LOOKETH AFTER,] not 'punish,' as in C.V.
TRAVAILING,] *lit.* 'bearing.'
22. MET,] as in 23; Ge. 42. 38, &c.
FOR,] *lit.* 'in or by.'
SUFFERED VIOLENCE,] not 'made bare;' as in C.V.
23. CUSHITE,] not 'Ethiopian,' as in C.V.
ACCUSTOMED,] *lit.* 'taught, learned,' as in 2. 24, &c.
24. SCATTER,] as in 9. 16; 18. 17; 23. 2, &c.
WILDERNESS,] *or* pasture land.
25. LOT,] as in Lev. 16. 8, 9, 10; Nu. 26. 55.
TRUST,] *or* 'lean;' as in 7. 4; 9. 4; 17. 5, &c.
26. MADE BARE,] not 'discover;' as in C.V
27. ADULTERIES,] as in Eze. 23. 43

CLEANSED,] as in Lev. 11. 32; 12. 7, 8, &c.

XIV. 1. WORD OF JEHOVAH,] as in 1. 2, 4.
DEARTHS,] or 'restraints;' as in 17. 8.
2. MOURNED,] as in 4. 28; 12. 4, 11; 23. 10.
CRY] of distress; as in 46. 12; Ps. 144. 41.
3. HONOURABLE ONES,] as in 25. 34, 35, &c.
COVERED,] as in v. 4; 2 Sa. 15. 30; Est. 7. 8.
4. BROKEN,] as in 8. 9; 48. 1, 20, 39, &c.
RAIN,] lit. a 'shower;' as in 5. 24, &c.
HUSBANDMEN,] not 'ploughmen,' as in C. V.
5. HIND,] as in Ps. 22. 1; Prov. 5. 19.
GRASS,] or 'tender grass;' as in Ge. 1. 11.
6. WILD ASSES,] as in 2. 24; Ge. 16. 12, &c.
SWALLOWED UP,] not 'snuffed up,' as in C. V.
HERB,] not 'grass,' as in C. V.; as in 12. 4.
7. SURELY,] lit. 'if;' or 'have not.'
SINNED,] lit. 'missed' the mark; as in 2. 35.
8. HOPE OF ISRAEL,] as in 17. 13; 50. 7.
TROUBLE,] lit. 'straitness;' as in 4. 31, &c.
SOJOURNER,] not 'stranger,' as in C. V.
TRAVELLER,] or 'way-farer;' as in 9. 2, &c.
9. DUMB,] or 'become dumb.'
LEAVE,] or 'let not alone;' as in 27. 11, &c.
10. WELL,] not 'thus,' as in C. V.
TO WANDER,] or 'move on;' as in Jud. 9. 9, 11, 13, &c.
INSPECT,] not 'visit,' as in C. V.
11. PRAY,] or 'judge thyself;' as in 7. 16.
12. CRY,] or 'shout;' as in 7. 16; 11. 14, &c.
PRESENT,] not 'oblation,' as in C. V.
FAMINE,] lit. 'hunger;' as in v. 13, 15, &c.
CONSUMING,] or 'ending;' as in Lev. 26. 16.
13. LORD JEHOVAH,] as in 1. 6; 4. 10, &c.
FAMINE,] or 'hunger;' as in v. 12.
TRUE PEACE,] lit. 'peace of truth' or stedfastness.
14. FALSEHOOD,] as in 3. 10, 23; 5. 2, 31, &c.
COMMAND,] or 'charge;' as in 7. 22, 23, &c.
FALSE VISION,] lit. 'vision of falsehood.'
VANITY,] lit. 'nothingness.'
FAMINE,] lit. 'hunger;' as in v. 12, &c.
15. CONSUMED,] or 'ended, finished;' as in 44. 12, &c.
16. BECAUSE,] lit. 'from the face of.'
OUT-PLACES,] not 'streets,' as in C. V.
17. TEARS,] as in 9. 1, 18; 13. 17; 31. 16, &c.
CEASE,] or 'are cut off;' as in La. 3. 49, &c.
BREACH,] or 'breaking;' as in 4. 6, 20, &c.
GRIEVOUS,] or 'painful;' as in 10. 19, &c.
STROKE,] or 'smiting;' as in 6. 7; 10. 19.
18. FIELD,] as in v. 5; 6. 12, 25; 7. 20, &c.
PIERCED,] not 'slain,' as in C. V.
DISEASED,] or 'pained,' of hunger.
GONE UP AND DOWN,] as in Ge. 34. 10, &c.
19. REJECTED,] as in 2. 37; 4. 30; 6. 19, &c.
LOOKING,] or 'waiting;' as in 8. 15, &c.
TERROR,] not 'trouble,' as in C. V.
20. SINNED,] lit. 'missed' the mark.
21. DESPISE,] not 'abhor,' as in C. V.
BREAK,] or 'make void.'
22. VANITIES,] as in 2. 5; 8. 19; 10. 3, &c.
CAUSING RAIN,] or 'showers.'
SHOWERS,] as in 3. 3; De. 32. 2; Ps. 65. 10.
WAIT,] as in v. 19.

XV. 1. THOUGH,] lit. 'if.'
SEND,] not 'cast,' as in C. V.; as in 7e 24. 54, &c.
2. GO FORTH,] as in v. 1; 2. 37; 4. 4; 6. 25.

FAMINE,] lit. 'hunger;' as in 5. 12; 11. 22
3. APPOINTED,] as in 6. 15; 9. 25; 21. 14, &c.
KINDS,] lit. 'families;' as in 1. 15; 2. 4, &c.
DRAG,] not 'tear,' as in C. V.; as in 22. 19
DESTROY,] lit. 'mar;' as in 13. 14; 51. 11.
4. TREMBLING,] not 'removal,' as in C. V.
5. PITY,] as in 13. 14; 21. 7; 50. 14; 51. 3.
BEMOAN,] lit. 'nod or move.'
WELFARE,] lit. 'peace, completeness.'
6. LEFT,] as in 7. 29; 12. 7; 23. 33, 39, &c.
DESTROY,] or 'mar;' as in v. 3.
7. SCATTER,] as in 4. 11; Ex. 32. 20, &c.
8. WIDOWS,] as in 7. 6; 18. 21; 22. 3, &c.
YOUNG MAN,] or 'choice one;' as in 6. 11.
SPOILER,] or 'destroyer;' as in 6. 26, &c.
9. LANGUISHED,] as in 14. 2; 1 Sa. 2. 5, &c.
SPIRIT,] lit. 'soul;' not 'ghost,' as in C. V.
10. WO,] as in 4. 31, 31; 6. 4; 10 19; 13. 27.
STRIFE,] or 'contention;' as in 11. 20, &c.
CONTENTION,] or 'judgment;' as in Ps. 80. 6.
LENT ON USURY,] or 'lifted up' a burden.
REVILING,] or 'making light;' as in Ge. 12. 3.
11. DIRECT,] as in Job 37. 3.
INTERCEDE,] lit. 'kick or strike;' as in 36. 25, &c.
ADVERSITY,] lit. 'straitness;' as in 4. 31.
12. BREAK,] as in 11. 16; 40. 4, &c.
NORTHERN IRON,] lit. 'iron from the north.'
BRASS,] not 'steel,' as in C. V.
13. STRENGTH,] as in 17. 3; 32. 2; 34. 1, &c.
BORDERS,] as in 5. 22; 17. 3; 31. 17, &c.
14. CAUSED TO PASS OVER,] as in 32. 35, &c.
15. REMEMBER,] as in 14. 21; 18. 20; 51. 50.
INSPECT,] not 'visit,' as in C. V.
TAKE VENGEANCE,] lit. 'be avenged;' as in 50. 15, &c.
PURSUERS,] not 'persecutors,' as in C. V.
LONG-SUFFERING,] lit. 'length of face, or anger.'
BORNE,] lit. 'my bearing or lifting up.'
REPROACH,] not 'rebuke,' as in C. V.
16. NAME IS CALLED,] not 'called by thy name.'
17. SAT] still or down.
ASSEMBLY,] or 'secret counsel;' as in 6. 19
18. PAIN,] as in Job 2. 13; 16. 6; Ps. 39. 2.
PERPETUAL,] or 'pre-eminent;' as in 3. 5.
WOUND,] lit. 'smiting;' as in 6. 7; 10. 19.
FAILING,] lit. 'lying;' as in Mic. 1. 14.
19. PRECIOUS,] as in 1 Sa. 3. 1; 2 Sa. 12. 30.
20. MADE,] lit. 'given;' as in v. 4; 1. 5, &c.
PERVAIL AGAINST,] lit. 'able for.'
DELIVER,] lit. 'snatch away;' as in 1. 8.
21. EVIL DOERS,] or 'evil ones.'
RANSOMED,] not 'redeem,' as in C. V.
HAND,] lit. 'paw;' as in 4. 31; 12. 7, &c.

XVI. 1. WORD OF JEHOVAH,] as in 1. 2, 4.
3. THUS SAID JEHOVAH,] as in v. 5, 9, &c
BEGETTING,] as in Isa. 66. 9.
4. PAINFUL,] not 'grievous,' as in C. V.
FAMINE,] lit. 'hunger.'
CONSUMED.] or 'ended, gathered.'
CARCASE,] lit. 'fallen thing;' as in v. 18.
EARTH,] or 'land.'
5. MOURNING-FEAST,] not 'house,' as in C. V
BEMOAN,] lit. 'nod or move' the head.
REMOVED,] lit. 'gathered;' as in 21. 4, &c
6. GREAT AND SMALL,] as in 6. 13; 31. 34.
CUT HIMSELF,] as in 5. 7; 41. 5; 47. 5, &c
7. DEAL,] as in Isa. 58. 7.

CONSOLATIONS,] as in Ps. 94. 19; Isa. 66. 11.
8.BANQUETING,] *lit.* 'drinking;' as in 51. 39.
9. GOD OF ISRAEL,] as in 9. 15; 11. 3, &c.
10. DECLAREST,] *or* 'settest forth,' not 'shew,' as in C.V.
11. FORSAKEN,] as in 1. 16; 2. 13; 5. 7, 19.
KEPT,] watched, or observed; as in 8. 7,&c.
12. DONE EVIL,] as in 7. 36; 10. 5; 25. 6, &c.
STUBBORNNESS,] not 'imagination,' as in C.V.
13. CAST,] as in 22. 26, 28; 1 Sa. 18. 11, &c.
WHERE,] *or* 'because, in that.'
14. DAYS ARE COMING,] as in 7. 32; 9. 25, &c.
15. NORTH,] as in 3. 18; 6. 22; 10. 22, &c.
16. SENDING,] as in 25. 9, 15, 16, 27; 26. 5.
HOLES OF THE ROCK,] as in 13. 4; Isa. 7. 19.
17. WAYS,] as in 2. 17, 18, 23, 33, 36; 3. 2.
18. RECOMPENSED,] as in 25. 14; 51. 24, &c.
POLLUTING,] *lit.* 'piercing;' as in Lev. 20.3.
CARCASE,] *lit.* 'fallen thing;' as in v. 4.
19. STRENGTH,] as in 48. 17; 51. 53, &c.
ADVERSITY,] *lit.* 'straitness.'
20. GODS,] that is, objects of worship.
21. TIME,] *lit.* 'stroke, step;' as in 10. 18.
JEHOVAH,] i.e. He who is, the ExistingOne.

XVII. 1. SIN,] as in v. 3; 5. 25; 14. 20, &c.
2. ALTARS,] *lit.* 'places for sacrifice.'
SHRINES,] *lit.* 'happy places;' as in Ex. 34. 13, &c.
3. MOUNTAIN,] as in Ge. 14. 6; Nu. 23. 7.
4. LET GO,] as in Ex. 23. 11; De. 15. 2, &c.
ANGER,] *or* 'nose;' as in 2. 25; 4. 8, 26, &c.
AGE,] i.e. a 'hidden,' indefinite time.
5. THUS SAID JEHOVAH,] as in v. 19, &c.
CURSED,] *lit.* 'bitter;' as in 11. 3; 20.14,&c.
TRUST,] *lit.* 'lean;' as in v. 7, &c.
FLESH,] that is, any of the human race.
HEART TURNETH] aside, as the original word implies.
6. NAKED THING,] not 'heath,' as in C.V.
INHABITED,] *lit.* 'tabernacled,' or set down.
WILDERNESS,] or place of 'leading forth' the cattle.
7. BLESSED,] *lit.* 'bent of knee.'
TRUSTETH,] *lit.* 'leaneth;' as in v. 5.
8. TREE,] as in v. 2; 2. 20, 27; 3. 6, 9, &c.
RIVULET,] not 'waters,' as in C.V.
SENDETH FORTH,] not 'spreadeth out,' as in C.V.
SORROWFUL,] not 'careful,' as in C.V.
CEASE,] *lit.* 'move;' as in Ex. 13. 22, &c.
9. CROOKED,] not 'deceitful,' as in C.V.
INCURABLE,] not 'desperately wicked,' as in C.V.
10. SEARCH,] as in Job 28. 3.
TRY THE REINS,] as in 11. 20.
11. PARTRIDGE,] *lit.* a 'caller.'
RIGHT,] *lit.* 'judgment, justice.'
MIDST,] *lit.* 'half;' as in Ex. 12. 29, &c.
12. THRONE OF HONOUR,] as in 14. 21, &c.
SANCTUARY,] *lit.* 'set apart place.'
13. HOPE OF ISRAEL,] as in 14. 8; 50. 7.
APOSTATES,] *lit.* 'turners aside.'
LIVING WATERS,] as in 2. 13; Ge. 26. 19, &c.
14. HEAL,] as in Nu. 12. 13; Ps. 6. 2; 41. 4; 60. 2.
PRAISE,] as in 13. 11; 33. 9; 48. 2, &c.
15. WORD OF JEHOVAH,] as in v. 20.
16. HASTENED,] as in Jos. 10. 13; 17. 15.
DESIRED] for myself; as in Nu. 11. 4, &c.

BEFORE,] *lit* 'over against.'
17. TERROR,] as in 48. 39; Ps. 89. 40. &c.
HOPE,] *or* 'place of refuge;' as in Job 14. 8
18. PURSUERS,] not 'persecutors,' as in C.V
AFFRIGHTED,] *or* 'brought down;' as in 1. 17; 10. 2, &c.
DESTRUCTION,] *lit.* 'breaking;' as in Eze. 21. 6.
DESTROY,] *or* 'break;' as in Ps. 10. 5.
19. GATE,] as in v. 20, 21, 24, 25, 27, &c.
SONS OF THE PEOPLE,] as in 26. 23, &c.
20. HEAR A WORD OF JEHOVAH,] as in 2. 4.
21. TAKE YE HEED,] *or* 'be ye watchful;' as in 9. 3; Ge. 24. 6, &c.
TO YOURSELVES,] *lit.* 'of your souls.'
22. BURDEN,] *lit.* a 'thing lifted up.'
SANCTIFIED,] *lit.* 'set apart;' as in 22. 7.
COMMANDED,] *or* 'charged;' as in 7. 22, &c.
23. INCLINED THEIR EAR,] as in 7. 24, &c.
TO RECEIVE,] take, or accept.
24. AFFIRMATION,] as in 1. 8, 15, 19; 2. 3.
25. PRINCES,] as in 1. 18; 2. 26; 4. 9, &c.
REMAINED,] *lit.* 'sat still or down.'
26. CITIES OF JUDAH,] as in 1. 15; 4. 16, &c.
PRAISE,] *lit.* 'confession' or thanksgiving; as in 30. 19, &c.
27. KINDLED A FIRE,] as in 11. 16; 21. 14.
TO BEAR,] *lit.* 'lift up.'
QUENCHED,] as in 7. 20; Lev. 6. 12, &c.

XVIII. 1. THE WORD,] as in 7. 1; 11. 1, &c.
2. POTTER,] *lit.* 'framer, fashioner;' as in v. 3, 4, 6, 11, &c.
3. WORK,] as in 17. 22, 24; 48. 10; 50. 25, &c.
STONES,] not 'wheels,' as in C.V.; which the word never means.
4. MARRED,] as in 13. 7; Ge. 6. 11, 12, &c.
5. WORD OF JEHOVAH,] as in 1. 2, 4, 11, &c.
7. MOMENT,] as in v. 9; 4. 20; Ge. 33. 5, &c.
8. REPENTED,] as in v. 10; 4. 28; 20. 16, &c
9. BUILD,] as in 1. 10; 31. 28; 35. 9, &c.
11. MEN,] *lit.* 'man of Judah.'
FRAMING,] forming, or fashioning.
DEVISING,] *or* 'thinking;' as in 23. 27, &c.
DEVICE,] *or* 'thought;' as in 49. 30.
AMEND,] *lit.* 'make good;' as in 7. 3; 26. 13.
12. IT IS INCURABLE,] as in 2. 25; Job 6. 26.
DEVICES,] *or* 'thoughts;' as in v. 18, &c.
13. ASK,] as in 6. 16; 30. 6; 48. 18, &c.
VIRGIN OF ISRAEL,] as in 31. 4, 21, &c.
14. SNOW,] as in Ex. 4. 6; Nu. 12. 10, &c.
FAILED,] not 'be forsaken,' as in C.V.; as in 31. 40, &c.
15. FORGOTTEN,] as in 2. 32; 3. 21; 13. 25.
16. MAKE,] *lit.* 'set.
BEMOANETH,] *lit.* 'noddeth or moveth.'
17. EAST WIND,] as in Ge. 41. 6, 23, 27, &c.
DAY OF THEIR CALAMITY,] as in 46. 21, &c.
18. LAW,] *lit.* 'direction;' as in 2. 8; 6. 19.
PRIEST,] the appointed expositor of the law.
A WORD] of Jehovah, revealing or explaining truth.
ATTEND,] as in 6. 17, 19; 8. 6; 23. 18, &c.
19. GIVE ATTENTION,] as in 6. 17; 2 Ch. 20. 15
20. RECOMPENSED,] as in Ps. 65. 1, &c.
DUG,] *or* 'prepared;' as in v. 22; Ge. 26. 25
WRATH,] *lit.* 'heat;' as in 4. 4; 6. 11, &c.
21. FAMINE,] *lit.* 'hunger.'
CAUSE TO RUN,] not 'pour out,' as in C V
SIDES,] *lit.* 'hands' of the sword.

YOUNG MEN,] *lit.* 'choice ones.'
SMITTEN,] not 'slain,' as in C.V.
22. CRY] of distress; as in 20. 16; 48. 4, &c.
DUG,] *or* 'prepared;' as in v. 20.
23. COUNSEL,] as in v. 18; 19. 7; 32. 19, &c.
COVER OVER,] *or* 'scrape upon,' i.e. erase.
BLOTTEST OUT,] *or* 'wipest away;' as in
Neh. 13. 14, &c.

XIX. 1. THUS SAID JEHOVAH,] as in v. 3.
GOT,] obtained, or purchased; as in 13. 1.
ELDERS OF THE PEOPLE,] the civil authorities.
ELDERS OF THE PRIESTS,] the ecclesiastical authorities.
2. SON OF HINNOM,] as in 7. 31, 32, &c.
POTTERY.] Original word not found again.
PROCLAIMED,] *lit.* 'call;' as in 2. 2; 3. 4, 12.
3. HEAR A WORD OF JEHOVAH,] as in 2. 4.
4. FORSAKEN,] as in 1. 16; 2. 13; 5. 7, &c.
MAKE KNOWN,] as in De. 32. 27; Job 21. 29.
INNOCENT BLOOD,] *lit.* 'blood of innocent
ones.'
5. OF BAAL,] *lit.* 'of the Baal.'
6. DAYS ARE COMING,] as in 7. 32; 9. 25, &c.
TOPHET,] *lit.* 'the Tophet,' i.e. 'spitting.'
7. MADE VOID,] *or* 'empty;' as in Na. 2. 2.
LIFE,] *lit.* 'soul;' as in v. 9, &c.
CARCASE,] *lit.* 'fallen thing;' as in 7. 33.
EARTH,] *or* 'land.'
8. MADE,] *lit.* 'set;' as in 2. 7; 5. 22, &c.
PLAGUES,] *lit.* 'smitings;' as in 6. 7; 10. 19.
9. CAUSED TO EAT,] as in Ex. 16. 32, &c.
LIFE,] *lit.* 'soul;' as in v. 7, &c.
10. BROKEN,] as in 2. 20; 5. 5; 28. 2, &c.
11. BREAK,] as in 28. 4, 10, 11; 30. 8, &c.
REPAIRED,] *lit.* 'healed;' as in 15. 18, &c.
12. MAKE,] *lit.* 'give;' as in 10. 13; 11. 5.
13. DEFILED,] as in Lev. 5. 2; 7. 19, 21, &c.
OBLATIONS,] as in 7. 18; 10. 14; 32. 29, &c.
14. PROPHESY,] *lit.* 'be a prophet;' as in
26. 12, &c.
15. GOD OF ISRAEL,] as in v. 3; 7. 3, 21, &c.
HARDENED THEIR NECK,] as in 7. 26; 17. 23.

XX. 1. PASHHUR,] i.e. 'prosperity round
about.'
IMMER,] i.e. a 'lamb' *or* a 'sayer.'
OVERSEER,] as in 29. 26; 52. 25; Ge. 41. 34.
2. PUTTETH,] *lit.* 'giveth;' as in v. 4, 5, &c.
STOCKS,] *lit.* 'place of turning;' as in v. 3;
29. 26; 2 Ch. 16. 10.
HIGH GATE,] leading to Benjamin.
3. MAGOR-MISSABIB,] i.e. 'fear is round
about;' as in v. 10.
4. THUS SAID JEHOVAH,] as in 2. 2, 5, &c.
MAKING,] *lit.* 'giving;' as in v. 2, 5, &c.
SMITTEN,] not 'slay,' as in C.V.
5. STRENGTH,] as in Prov. 15. 6; 27. 24; Isa.
33. 6; Eze. 22. 25.
SPOILED,] as in Nu. 31. 9, 32; 53, &c.
6. CAPTIVITY,] as in 15. 2; 22. 22; 30. 10, &c.
FALSELY,] *lit.* 'in or with a falsehood.'
7. PERSUADED,] as in Ex. 22. 16; 1 K. 22. 20.
HARDENED,] *or* 'strengthened;' as in v. 5.
PREVAIL,] *lit.* 'art able;' as in 1. 19; 3. 5.
8. CRY OUT,] as in 11. 11, 12; 30. 15; 47. 2.
CRY,] *lit.* 'call *or* proclaim.'
DERISION,] as in Ps. 44. 13; 79. 4, &c.
9. MENTION,] *or* 'remember;' as in 3. 16.
SHUT UP,] *or* 'restrained;' as in 33. 1, &c.

10. EVIL REPORT,] as in Ge. 37. 2, &c.
DECLARE,] *lit.* 'set forth;' as in 4. 5, &c.
ALLIES,] *lit.* 'men of my peace;' not 'fa
miliars,' as in C.V.
WATCHING,] *or* 'observing;' as in 4. 17, &c.
ENTICED,] *or* 'persuaded;' as in v. 7, &c.
PREVAIL,] *lit.* 'are able for him.'
TAKE,] *or* 'receive;' as in 9. 20; 13. 7, &c.
11. TERRIBLE,] as in 15. 21; Job 6. 23, &c.
PERSECUTORS,] *or* 'pursuers;' as in 15. 15.
STUMBLE,] *or* 'are stumbled;' as in 6. 15.
PREVAIL,] *lit.* 'are not able.'
ACTED WISELY,] not 'prosper,' as in C.V.
12. TRIER,] as in 11. 20; 17. 10; 1 Ch. 29. 17.
CAUSE,] *lit.* 'strife or contention.'
13. SING YE,] as in Ex. 15. 21; 1 Ch. 16. 9.
DELIVERED,] *lit.* 'snatched;' as in 15. 21.
14. CURSED IS THE DAY,] as in Job 3. 3.
15. BORE TIDINGS,] as in 2 Sa. 1. 20; 18. 19.
CHILD,] *lit.* 'a son.'
VERY GLAD,] *lit.* 'to gladden he made him
glad.'
16. OVERTHREW,] as in 13. 23; 23. 36, &c.
CRY] of distress; as in 18. 22; 48. 4, &c.
17. PUT TO DEATH,] not 'slew,' as in C.V.
PREGNANCY,] *or* 'conception;' as in 31. 8.
18. SORROW,] as in 8. 18; 31. 13; 45. 3, &c.

XXI. 1. THE WORD,] as in 7. 1; 11. 1, &c.
MAASEIAH,] i.e. 'work of Jah.'
2. INQUIRE,] as in 29. 7; 1 K. 22. 5, &c.
DOTH CAUSE HIM TO GO UP,] *or* 'he doth
go up.'
4. THUS SAID JEHOVAH,] as in v. 8. 12, &c.
TURNING ROUND,] not 'back,' as in C.V.
GATHERED,] as in 16. 5. 40. 12, &c.
5. FOUGHT,] *lit.* 'been fought with.'
FURY,] *lit.* 'heat.'
GREAT WRATH,] as in 32. 17, &c.
6. SMITTEN,] as in v. 7; 2. 20; 5. 3, &c.
7. AFFIRMATION,] as in v. 10, 13, 14, &c.
FAMINE,] *lit.* 'hunger;' as in v. 9; 5. 12, &c
LIFE,] *lit.* 'soul;' as in v. 9, &c.
MERCY,] as in 6. 23; 12. 15; 13. 14, &c.
8. SETTING,] *lit.* 'giving;' as in 5. 14, &c.
9. ABIDING,] as in v. 6. 13; 1. 14; 2. 15, &c.
FAMINE,] *lit.* 'hunger;' as in v. 7, &c.
LIFE,] *lit.* 'soul;' as in v. 7, &c.
10. SET MY FACE,] as in 42. 17; 44. 12, &c.
11. HOUSE,] that is, palace.
12. HOUSE OF DAVID,] as in 1 K. 12. 19, &c.
DECIDE,] *or* 'judge;' as in Prov. 31. 9.
DELIVER,] *lit.* 'snatch;' as in 22. 3, &c.
FURY,] *lit.* 'heat;' as in v. 5, &c.
EVIL OF YOUR DOINGS,] as in 4. 4; 23. 2, 22.
13. VALLEY,] *lit.* 'deep place.'
HABITATIONS,] as in De. 33. 27; Job 37. 8.
14. LAID A CHARGE,] not 'punish,' as in C.V.
SUBURBS,] as in 1. 15; 4. 7; 6. 3, &c.

XXII. 1. THUS SAID JEHOVAH,] as in v. 3.
HOUSE,] that is, palace; as in 21. 11, &c.
2. HEAR,] as in v. 29; 2. 4; 5. 21, &c.
THRONE OF DAVID,] as in v. 4, 30; 17. 25.
3. RIGHTEOUSNESS,] *or* 'justice;' as in v.
15; 4. 2, &c.
DELIVER,] *lit.* 'snatch;' as in 21. 12, &c.
SOJOURNER,] not 'stranger,' as in C.V.
WRONG,] *lit.* 'violate;' as in Job 15. 33, &c.
INNOCENT BLOOD,] *lit.* 'blood of an inno-
cent.'

SHED,] *lit.* 'pour out;' as in 7. 6; 14. 16, &c.
4. SITTING,] as in v. 2, 23, 30, &c.
5. SWORN,] *lit.* 'been sworn;' as in 4. 2, &c.
DESOLATION,] *or* 'waste;' as in 7. 34, &c.
6. WILDERNESS,] *or* 'pasture-land;' as in 2. 2, 6, &c.
7. SEPARATED,] that is, 'set apart;' as in 17. 22, &c.
DESTROYERS,] *lit.* 'marrers;' as in 2. 30.
CAST,] *lit.* 'caused to fall;' as in 15. 8, &c.
8. PASSED BY,] as in 2. 6; 5. 28; 8. 20, &c.
NEIGHBOUR,] *lit.* 'a man unto his friend.'
9. FORSAKEN,] as in 1. 16; 2. 13; 5. 7, &c.
10. WEEP,] as in 9. 1; 13. 17; 48. 32, &c.
BEMOAN,] *lit.* 'nod or move' the head.
TRAVELLER,] *lit.* 'goer;' as in 3. 6; 6. 28.
LAND OF HIS BIRTH,] as in 46. 16; Ge. 11. 28.
11. SHALLUM,] i.e. 'recompence, completion.'
JOSIAH,] killed at Megiddo.
GONE FORTH,] into captivity to Babylon.
12. REMOVED,] as in 20. 4; 29. 1, 4, 7, 14.
13. WO,] as in v. 18; 23.1; 30. 7; 34. 5, &c.
BY UNRIGHTEOUSNESS,] *or* 'without justice.'
BY INJUSTICE,] *or* 'without judgment.'
WAGE,] as in 25. 14; 50. 29; De. 32. 4, &c.
14. LARGE HOUSE,] *lit.* 'house of measures.'
WINDOWS,] *lit.* 'holes;' as in 9. 21; Ex. 8. 6.
PAINTED,] *lit.* to 'anoint;' as in Lev. 7. 36.
VERMILION,] as in Eze. 23. 14.
15. FRETTING,] *or* 'heating thyself,' not closest,' as in C.V.
EAT AND DRINK.] that is, enjoy life.
16. DECIDED,] *or* 'judged,' as in 5. 28, &c.
CAUSE,] *lit.* 'judgment, contention.'
POOR,] humble, or afflicted.
17. DISHONEST GAIN,] not 'covetousness,' as in C.V.
SHEDDING,] *lit.* 'pouring out;' as in 6. 11.
INNOCENT BLOOD,] *lit.* 'blood of the innocent.'
VIOLENCE,] as in 8. 6; 23. 10; 2 Sa. 18. 27.
18. JEHOIAKIM,] i.e. 'Jah raises up.'
HONOUR,] as in Nu. 27. 20; 1 Ch. 16. 27, &c.
19. BURIAL,] as in Ge. 35. 20; 47. 30, &c.
CAST FORTH,] as in 36. 23; 52. 3, &c.
20. CRY,] for anguish; as in 49. 3.
ABARIM,] *lit.* 'passages.'
21. EASE,] *or* 'quietness;' as in Ps. 122. 7.
YOUTH,] *lit.* 'youths,' i.e. youthful periods.
22. CONSUME,] as in 2. 16; 3. 15; 6. 3, &c.
WICKEDNESS,] as in 1. 14, 16; 2. 3, 13, &c.
23. MAKING A NEST,] *or* 'having a nest made.'
TRAVAILING WOMAN,] *lit.* 'bearing;' as in 6. 24, &c.
24. THOUGH,] *lit.* 'if.'
CONIAH,] i.e. 'made ready of Jah.'
DRAW AWAY,] as in Lev. 22. 24; Jud. 20. 32.
25. LIFE,] *lit.* 'soul.'
26. CAST,] as in 16. 13; 1 Sa. 18. 11, &c.
27. LIFTING UP THEIR SOUL,] as in 44. 14.
28. GRIEF,] not 'idol,' as in C.V.; as in Ge. 3. 16, &c.
CAST UP AND DOWN,] not 'cast out,' as in C.V.
30. WRITE,] as in 30. 2; 36. 28; Ex. 17. 14.
CHILDLESS,] *lit.* 'barren;' as in Ge. 15. 2; Lev. 20. 20, 21.
RULING,] as in 30. 21; 33. 26; 51. 46, &c.

XXIII. 1. WO,] *or* ho! as in 22. 13, 18, &c.
FLOCK,] not 'sheep,' as in C.V.
AFFIRMATION,] as in v. 2, 4, 5, 7, 11, 12, &c
2. THUS SAID JEHOVAH,] as in v. 15, 16, 38.
INSPECTED,] not 'visited,' as in C.V.
CHARGING,] not 'visit,' as in C.V.
3. GATHER,] as in 29. 14; 31. 10; 31. 8, &c.
DROVE,] *or* 'flock;' as in v. 1, 2; 3. 24, &c.
FOLD,] *lit.* 'comely place;' as in 10. 25, &c.
4. RAISED,] as in v. 5; 6. 17; 28. 6; 29. 10.
AFFRIGHTED,] *or* 'brought down;' as in 1. 17; 10. 2, &c.
LACKING,] *lit.* 'inspected;' as in Nu. 16. 29.
5. DAYS ARE COMING,] as in v. 7; 7. 32, &c.
SHOOT,] as in 33. 15; Ge. 19. 25, &c.
ACTED WISELY,] as in 10. 21; 20. 11, &c.
6. SAVED,] *or* 'eased;' as in 33. 16, &c.
DWELLEST,] *lit.* 'tabernacleth.'
CONFIDENTLY,] not 'safely,' as in C.V.
OUR RIGHTEOUSNESS,] as in 33. 16.
7. BROUGHT UP,] as in 16. 14, 15; 27. 22, &c.
8. JEHOVAH LIVETH,] as in v. 7; 4. 2; 5. 2.
9. IN REFERENCE TO.] A separate prophecy here commences.
FLUTTERED,] as in Ge. 1. 2; De. 32. 11.
DRUNKARD,] *or* 'merry one;' as in 1 Sa. 1. 13.
HOLY WORDS,] *lit.* 'words of his separation.'
10. ADULTERERS,] as in 7. 2; Ps. 50. 18, &c.
THESE,] *or* 'cursing.'
PLEASANT,] *or* 'comely places;' as in 9. 10.
WILDERNESS,] *or* 'pasture land.'
COURSE,] as in 8. 6; 22. 17; 2 Sa. 18. 27.
11. PROFANE,] as in 3. 1, 9; Ps. 106. 38, &c.
HOUSE,] that is, the temple.
12. SLIPPERY PLACES,] as in Ps. 35. 6, &c.
INSPECTION,] as in 11. 23; 48. 44, &c.
13. FOLLY,] as in Job 1. 22; 24. 12.
CAUSE TO ERR,] as in v. 32; 42. 20, &c.
14. HORRIBLE THING,] as in 5. 30.
FALSELY,] *lit.* 'in or with a falsehood.'
15. JEHOVAH OF HOSTS,] as in v. 16, 36, &c.
GALL,] as in 8. 14; 9. 15; De. 29. 18, &c.
16. VISION,] as in 14. 14; 1 Sa. 3. 1, &c.
MOUTH OF JEHOVAH,] as in 9. 12; Nu. 3. 16.
17. DESPISING,] as in Nu. 14. 23; Isa. 60. 14.
STUBBORNNESS,] not 'imagination,' as in C.V.
18. COUNSEL,] as in v. 22; 6. 11; 15. 17, &c.
19. WHIRLWIND,] as in 25. 32; 30. 23, &c.
FURY,] *lit.* 'heat;' as in 4. 4; 6. 11, &c.
20. ANGER OF JEHOVAH,] as in 4. 8; 12. 13.
ESTABLISHING,] *lit.* 'raising up;' as in 11.5.
UNDERSTANDING,] as in De. 4. 6; 1 Ch. 12.32.
21. NOT SENT,] as in v. 32; 14. 14, 15, &c.
22. STOOD,] as in v. 18, &c.
EVIL OF THEIR DOINGS,] as in v. 2.
23. A GOD,] as in 1. 16; 2. 11, 17, 19, 28, &c.
24. HIDDEN,] *or* 'kept secret;' as in 16. 17.
SECRET PLACES,] as in 13. 17; 49. 10, &c.
25. FALSEHOOD,] as in v. 14, 26, 32, &c.
26. DECEIT OF THEIR HEART,] as in 14. 14.
27. DEVISING,] *or* 'thinking;' as in 18. 11.
28. RECOUNT,] as in v. 32; 51. 10, &c.
TRULY,] *lit.* '(with) truth or stedfastness.'
CORN,] *lit.* 'pure corn;' as in Ge. 41. 35, &c
29. HAMMER,] as in 50. 23; Isa. 41. 7.
30. STEALING,] as in 2 Sa. 15. 6, &c.
31. MAKING SMOOTH,] *or* 'taking.'
32. RECOUNT,] as in v. 28, &c.
PROFITABLE,] as in 2. 8, 11; 12. 13, &c.
33. BURDEN OF JEHOVAH,] as in v. 34, &c

34. SEEN AFTER,] as in v. 2.
35. ANSWERED,] as in v. 37; 7. 13; 14. 7, &c.
36. MENTION,] as in 3. 16; 14. 10; 20. 9, &c.
LIVING GOD,] as in 10. 10; 44. 26, &c.
39. TAKEN AWAY,] or 'lifted up.'
40. PUT,] lit. 'given;' as in v. 39, &c.
FORGOTTEN,] as in 20. 11; 50. 5, &c.

XXIV. 1. SHEWED,] as in 11. 18; 38. 21, &c.
APPOINTED,] as in Eze. 21. 16.
ARTIZAN,] as in 10. 3, 9; 29. 2; Ex. 28. 11.
SMITH,] as in 29. 2; 2 K. 24. 14, &c.
2. FIRST RIPE,] as in Hos. 9. 10; Mic. 7. 1.
BADNESS,] as in v. 3, 8; 4. 4; 21. 21, &c.
4. WORD OF JEHOVAH,] as in 1. 2, 4, 11, &c.
5. THUS SAID JEHOVAH,] as in v. 8, &c.
6. SET MINE EYES,] as in 40. 4; Am. 9. 4.
THROW DOWN,] as in 12. 14, 17; 42. 10, &c.
7. TO KNOW,] as in 9. 6, 24; 13. 12; 24. 7, &c.
ALL THEIR HEART,] as in 3. 10; 32. 41, &c
8. FIGS,] as in v. 1, &c.
LEFT,] as in 8. 3; 21. 7; 38. 4; 39. 9, &c.
9. TREMBLING,] as in 15. 4; 29. 18; 34. 17.
DRIVE,] as in 8. 3; 16. 15; 23. 2, 3, 8, &c.
10. CONSUMPTION,] as in 1. 3; 27. 8; 36. 23.

XXV. 1. THE WORD,] of prophecy from
Jehovah.
2. JEREMIAH THE PROPHET,] as in 20. 2.
3. WORD OF JEHOVAH,] as in 1. 2, 4, 11, &c.
RISING EARLY AND SPEAKING,] as in 7. 13.
4. INCLINED YOUR EAR,] as in 7. 24, 26, &c.
5. EVIL WAY,] as in 18. 11; 23. 22.
AGE UNTO AGE,] as in 7. 7; Neh. 9. 5, &c.
6. TO SERVE,] as in 11. 10; 13. 10; 27. 6, &c.
7. PROVOKE TO ANGER,] as in 7. 13; 11. 17.
WORK OF YOUR HANDS,] as in v. 6. 14, &c.
8. OBEYED,] lit. 'heard.'
9. FAMILIES,] as in 1. 15; 2. 4; 3. 14, &c.
DEVOTED,] as in Lev. 27. 28, &c.
APPOINTED,] lit. 'set;' as in v. 12; 2. 7, &c.
WASTES,] lit. 'dried up places.'
10. DESTROYED,] not 'taken,' as in C.V.
A LAMP,] or 'light;' as in Ex. 27. 37, &c.
11. WASTES,] as in v 9, &c.
SEVENTY YEARS,] as in v. 12; 2 Ch. 36. 21.
12. FULNESS,] or 'filling up;' as in 29. 10.
CHARGE,] not 'punish,' as in C.V.
APPOINTED,] lit. 'set;' as in v. 9.
13. BROUGHT IN,] as in v. 13; 3. 14; 15. 8.
14. LAID SERVICE,] or 'done service.'
WORK OF THEIR HANDS,] as in v. 6, 7, &c.
15. FURY,] lit. 'heat;' as in v. 17, 28, &c.
16. DRUNK,] as in 22. 15; 35. 14; 51. 7, &c.
SHAKEN THEMSELVES,] not 'be moved,'
as in C.V.
SHEWN THEMSELVES FOOLISH,] not 'mad,'
as in C.V.
17. HAND OF JEHOVAH,] as in 51. 7, &c.
18. JERUSALEM,] the holy city itself.
WASTE,] or 'dried up place.'
REVILING,] lit. 'lightness or disesteem.'
19. PHARAOH,] the general name of the
kings of Egypt.
20. MIXED PEOPLE,] Heb. 'Ereb;' as in v.
24; 50. 37.
LAND OF UZ,] as in Job 1. 1.
21. EDOM,] elder brother of Jacob.
SONS OF AMMON,] younger son of Lot.
22. TYRE,] the chief city of Phenicia.
ISLE,] not 'isles,' as in C.V.

23. DEDAN,] a descendant of Keturah.
CUTTING THE CORNERS,] as in 9. 26; 49. 32
24. ARABIA,] i.e. 'mixture.'
MIXED PEOPLE,] as in v. 20.
25. ZIMRI,] i.e. 'celebrated.'
26. NORTH,] as in v. 9; 1. 13, 14, 15, &c.
SHESHACH,] another name of Babel.
27. DRINK,] as in 35. 5; Ge. 24. 14, &c.
DRINK ABUNDANTLY,] or 'be merry;' as in
Song 5. 1.
28. REFUSE,] as in 3. 3; 5. 3; 8. 5; 9. 6, &c.
TO RECEIVE,] take, or accept.
29. BEGINNING,] or 'commencing.'
ACQUITTED,] innocent or freed; as in 2. 35
PROCLAIMING,] or 'calling;' as in 4. 20, &c
30. HIGH PLACE,] as in 17. 12; 31. 12, &c.
HOLY HABITATION,] lit. 'of his separation.'
31. WASTING,] as in 46. 17; 48. 45; 51. 55.
EXECUTED JUDGMENT,] lit. 'he hath been
judged.'
WICKED,] those in the 'wrong.'
32. GOING FORTH,] as in 5. 6; 21. 9; 37. 4.
SIDES,] lit. 'thighs;' as in 6. 22, &c.
33. PIERCED,] not 'slain,' as in C.V.
END OF THE EARTH,] or 'land.'
DUNG,] as in 8. 2; 9. 22; 16. 4, &c.
34. HOWL,] as in 4. 8; 48. 20, 39; 49. 3, &c
CRY] for help; as in 48. 20; Jud. 10. 14, &c
DESIRABLE VESSEL,] as in 2 Ch. 32. 27, &c
35. PERISHED,] as in 6. 21; 7. 28; 9. 12, &c
REFUGE,] i.e. a place of refuge; as in 16. 19.
36. HOWLING,] as in Isa. 15. 8; Zeph. 1. 10;
Zech. 11. 3.
PASTURE,] lit. 'feeding-place;' as in 10. 21.
37. HABITATIONS,] lit. 'comely places of
peace.'
ANGER OF JEHOVAH,] as in 4. 8; 12. 13, &c
38. FORSAKEN,] as in 1. 16; 2. 13; 5. 7, &c
YOUNG LION,] not 'lion,' as in C.V.
COVERT,] or 'thicket;' as in Ps. 10. 9; 27.
5; 76. 2.
FIERCENESS,] lit. 'heat;' as in v. 37.

XXVI. 1. REIGN,] lit. 'kingdom.'
2. STAND,] as in 6. 16; 7. 2; 48. 19, &c.
DIMINISH,] or 'withdraw;' as in Ex. 5. 8.
3. HEARKEN,] or 'hear.'
DOINGS,] as in v. 13; 4. 4, 18, &c.
4. LAW,] or 'direction;' as in 2. 8; 6. 19, &c.
SET,] lit. 'given;' as in v. 6; 1. 5, 9, 15, &c.
5. MY SERVANTS,] as in 7. 25; 25. 4, &c.
RISING EARLY,] as in 7. 13, 25; 11. 7, &c.
6. SHILOH,] where the tabernacle had been.
REVILING,] lit. 'lightness or disesteem.'
7. HOUSE OF JEHOVAH,] that is, the temple.
8. COMPLETION,] as in 6. 19; 43. 1; 49. 37.
CATCH,] not 'take,' as in C.V.
9. PROPHESIED,] declared publicly or beforehand.
WASTED,] lit. 'dried up.'
ASSEMBLED,] or 'congregated;' as in Ex.
32. 1, &c.
10. HEADS OF JUDAH,] as in 24. 1; 34. 19.
SIT,] or 'abide;' as in 17. 6; 30. 18, &c.
11. DEATH,] not 'worthy to die,' as in C.V
12. SENT,] as in v. 2.
13. AMEND,] lit. 'make good;' as in 7. 3, &c.
14. IN YOUR HAND,] that is, in your
power.
RIGHT,] lit. 'upright;' as in 31. 9; 34. 15.
15. KNOW,] as in 9. 6, 24; 13. 12; 24. 7, &c

INNOCENT BLOOD,] *lit.* 'blood of an innocent one.'
16. JUDGMENT OF DEATH,] as in v. 11.
17. ELDERS OF THE LAND,] as in' Ge. 50. 7.
18. MICAH,] i.e. 'who is like Jah?'
PLOUGHED,] as in Mic. 3. 12.
FOREST,] as in 5. 6; 10. 3; 12. 8; 21. 14, &c.
19. PUT TO DEATH,] as in v. 21, 24; 38. 15.
APPEASETH,] *lit.* 'smootheth;' as in Ex. 32. 11, &c.
20. IN THE NAME OF JEHOVAH,] as in v. 16
21. JEHOIAKIM,] i.e. 'Jah raises up,'
22. ELNATHAN,] i.e. 'God hath given.'
23. SMITETH,] as in 18. 18; 20. 2; 40. 15, &c.
CORPSE,] *lit.* 'fallen thing;' as in 7. 33, &c.
24. AHIKAM,] i.e. 'my brother has risen.'
PUT TO DEATH,] as in v. 21.

XXVII. 1. BEGINNING OF THE REIGN,] as in Ge. 10. 10, &c.
2. BANDS,] not 'bonds,' as in C.V.
3. PUT,] *lit.* 'given;' as in v. 5, 6, &c.
TYRE,] *Heb.* 'Tsor,' i.e. a 'rock.'
4. LORDS,] as in 22. 18; 34. 5; 37. 20, &c.
5. CATTLE,] *or* 'beast;' as in 7. 20, 33, &c.
RIGHT,] *lit.* 'upright;' as in 27. 5, &c.
6. BEAST,] *or* 'living thing;' as in 12. 9, &c.
7. FOR HIM,] not 'of him,' as in C.V.
8. YOKE,] as in v. 2, 11, 12; 28 10, 11, &c
FAMINE,] *lit.* 'hunger;' as in v. 13, &c.
LAY A CHARGE,] not 'punish' as in C.V.
I CONSUME,] *lit.* 'my consuming.'
9. DIVINERS,] as in 29. 8; De. 18. 10, &c.
OBSERVERS OF CLOUDS,] as in De. 18. 10, 14.
10. FALSEHOOD,] as in v. 14, 15, 16.; 3. 10.
PERISHED,] *or* 'been lost;' as in v. 15, &c.
11. LEFT,] *lit.* 'caused to rest;' as in 14. 9.
TILLED,] *lit.* 'served;' as in v. 7, 11, &c.
DWELT,] *lit.* 'sat;' as in 2. 6; 3. 2; 15. 17.
12. CAUSE TO ENTER,] as in Ge. 27. 4, 7, &c.
LIVE,] as in v. 17; Ge. 20. 7; 42. 18, &c.
13. DIE,] as in 11. 21, 22; 16. 4; 20. 6, &c.
14. NOT HEARKEN,] as in v. 9, 16, 17; 5. 15.
15. FALSELY,] *lit.* 'to a falsehood.'
PERISHED,] *or* 'been lost;' as in v. 10, &c.
16. VESSELS,] made of gold, silver, &c.
17. WASTE,] *lit.* 'dried up place.'
18. INTERCEDE,] *lit.* 'kick;' as in 7. 16, &c.
LEFT,] *or* 'remaining over;' as in v. 19.
19. PILLARS,] as in 52. 17, 20, 21, 22, &c.
20. FREEMAN,] *lit.* 'white men;' as in 39. 6.
21. VESSELS,] as in v. 16, &c.
22. INSPECTING,] not 'visit,' as in C.V.

XXVIII. 1 BEGINNING OF THE REIGN,] as in 27. 1, &c.
ZEDEKIAH,] i.e. 'rightness of Jah '
FOURTH YEAR,] B.C. 596.
FIFTH MOUTH,] that is, Shebet.
HANANIAH,] i.e. 'grace of Jah.'
GOD OF ISRAEL,] as in v. 14.
2. BROKEN,] *lit.* 'shivered;' as in v. 4.
3. TWO YEARS OF DAYS,] as in v. 11, &c.
4. JECONIAH,] i.e. 'made ready by Jah.'
REMOVED OF JUDAH,] as in 24. 5; 29. 22, &c.
5. JEREMIAH THE PROPHET,] as in v. 6, &c.
6. AMEN,] as in 11. 5; Nu. 5. 22, &c.
ESTABLISH,] *lit* 'raise up;' as in 30. 9, &c.
7. HEAR] as in v. 15; 2. 4; 5. 21, &c.
8. FROM OF OLD,] *lit.* 'from hidden time.'
BATTLE,] *or* 'war;' as in 4. 19; 6. 4, 23, &c

9. TRULY,] *lit.* 'in truth.'
10. HANANIAH THE PROPHET,] as in v. 1, 5.
YOKE,] as in 27. 3, &c.
11. BREAK THE YOKE,] as in v. 4; 30. 8, &c.
12. WORD OF JEHOVAH,] as in 1. 2, 4, &c.
13. I HAVE MADE,] *or* 'thou hast made.'
14. BEAST,] *lit.* 'living thing;' as in 12. 9.
15. CAUSED TO TRUST,] *or* 'lean;' as in 19. 31.
16. CASTING,] *lit.* 'sending;' as in 8. 17, &c.
GROUND,] not 'earth,' as in C.V.
APOSTACY,] *or* 'a turning aside;' as in 29. 32.
SEVENTH MONTH,] that is, Abib or Nisan.

XXIX. 1. LETTER,] *lit.* 'roll or scroll.'
2. MISTRESS,] *lit.* 'mighty' lady; as in 13. 18
OFFICERS,] *lit.* ' eunuchs;' as in 34. 19, &c.
3. ELEASAH,] i.e. 'God has made.'
4. GOD OF ISRAEL,] as in v. 8, 21, 25, &c.
ABIDE,] *lit.* 'sit, dwell.'
6. TAKE WIVES,] as in Ge. 28. 2; Hos. 1. 2.
HUSBANDS,] *lit.* 'men;' as in 44. 19, &c.
FEW,] *or* 'little;' as in 30. 19, &c.
7. PEACE,] *or* 'completeness;' as in v. 11.
PRAY,] *or* 'judge yourselves;' as in 37. 3.
8. DIVINERS,] as in 27. 9; De. 18. 10, &c.
9. FALSEHOOD,] as in v. 21, 23, 31, &c.
10. FULNESS,] *lit.* 'mouth of the fulness.
ESTABLISHED,] *lit.* 'raised up.'
11. THOUGHT,] as in 4. 14; 6. 19; 18. 12, &c.
POSTERITY,] *lit.* a 'latter end;' as in 5. 31.
HOPE,] *or* 'line;' as in 31. 17; Jos. 2. 18, 21.
12. PRAYED,] as in 7. 16; 11. 14; 14. 11, &c.
13. SOUGHT,] as in 4. 30; 26. 21; 45. 5, &c.
14. FOUND,] as in 2. 34; 5. 26; 11. 9; 15. 16.
DRIVEN,] as in v. 18; 8. 3; 16. 5; 53. 3, &c.
15. RAISED UP,] as in v. 10; 6. 17; 23. 4, 5.
16. THRONE OF DAVID,] as in 17. 25; 22. 2.
17. SENDING,] as in 8. 17; 28. 16; Ge 43. 4.
18. PURSUED,] not 'persecute,' as in C.V.
TREMBLING,] as in 15. 4; 24. 9; 34. 17, &c.
CURSE,] *or* 'execration;' as in 23. 10, &c.
19. RISING EARLY,] as in 7. 13, 25; 11. 7, &c.
20. HEAR A WORD OF JEHOVAH,] as in 2. 4.
21. JEHOVAH OF HOSTS,] as in v. 4, 8, &c.
AHAB,] i.e. 'brother of father.'
SMITTEN,] not 'slay,' as in C.V.
22. REVILING,] *lit.* 'lightness or disesteem.
SET,] not 'make,' as in C.V.
ROASTED,] as in Lev. 2. 14; Jos. 5. 11.
23. FOLLY,] not 'villany;' as in Ge. 34. 7,&c.
NEIGHBOURS,] *lit.* 'friends;' as in 3. 1, 20.
WITNESS,] as in 32. 10, 12, 25, 44; 42. 5, &c.
24. SHEMAIAH,] i.e. 'heard of Jah.'
NEHELAMITE, i.e. ' dreamer.'
25. LETTERS,] rolls or scrolls; as in v. 1, 29.
26. MADE,] *lit.* 'given.'
INSPECTORS,] not 'officers,' as in C.V.
PUT,] *lit.* 'given;' as in v. 17. 18. &c.
TORTURE,] *lit.* 'a thing for turning over;
as in 20. 2. 3; 2 Ch. 16. 10.
STOCKS.] Original word not found again.
27. PUSHED,] as in Ge. 37. 10; Ruth 2. 16.
28. LONG,] as in 2 Sa. 3. 1; Job 11. 9.
ABIDE,] *lit.* 'sit, dwell.'
29. READETH,] *lit.* 'calleth;' as in 3. 17, &c.
30. JEHOVAH,] as in v. 20, &c.
31. SEND,] as in 2. 10; 9. 17; Ge. 42. 16, &c.
CAUSE TO TRUST,] *or* 'lean;' as in 2 K. 18. 30
32. SEEING AFTER,] not 'punish,' as in C.V.
APOSTACY,] *lit.* a 'turning aside;' not 're
bellion,' as in C.V.

XXX. 1. THE WORD,] as in 7. 1; 11. 1, &c.
2. WRITE,] as in 22. 30; 36. 28; Ex. 17. 14.
ON A BOOK,] or 'scroll;' not 'in it,' as in C.V.
3. DAYS ARE COMING,] as in 7. 32; 9. 25, &c.
4. SPOKEN,] by the mouth and pen of Jeremiah.
5. TREMBLING,] as in Ge. 27. 33, &c.
6. ASK,] as in 6. 16; 18. 13; 48. 19, &c.
TRAVAILING WOMAN,] as in 6. 24; 15. 9, &c.
FALENESS,] as in De. 28. 22; 1 K. 8. 37, &c.
7. WO,] as in 22. 13, 18; 23. 1; 34. 5, &c.
ADVERSITY,] lit. 'straitness.'
8. AFFIRMATION,] as in v. 3, 10, 11, 17, &c.
DRAW AWAY,] not 'burst,' as in C.V.
STRANGERS,] as in 2. 25; 3. 13; 5. 19, &c.
9. THEIR GOD,] by a special covenant.
DAVID,] the beloved of the Lord.
10. AFRAID,] as in 1. 8; 5. 22, 24; 10. 5, &c.
AFFRIGHTED,] or 'cast down;' as in 1. 17.
QUIET,] as in 46. 27; 48. 11; Job 3. 18; Prov. 1. 33.
TROUBLING.] as in 7. 33; 46. 27; Lev. 26. 6.
11. TO SAVE,] as in 11. 12; 14. 9; 15. 20, &c.
END,] or 'consummation;' as in 4. 27, &c.
CHASTISED,] or 'instructed;' as in 31. 18; 46. 26, &c.
ACQUIT,] or 'free or declare innocent.'
12. INCURABLE,] as in v. 15; 15. 18; 17. 9.
BREACH,] not 'bruise,' as in C.V.
GRIEVOUS,] or 'painful;' as in 10. 19, &c.
STROKE,] or 'smiting;' as in v. 14. 17, &c.
13. JUDGING,] as in Ge. 15. 14, &c.
CAUSE,] or 'judgment;' as in 5. 28; 22. 16.
HEALING,] as in 46. 11; 1 K. 18. 32, &c.
MEDICINES,] as in 46. 11; Eze. 30. 21.
14. LOVING,] as in 22. 20, 22; La. 1. 19, &c.
SMOTE.] not 'wounded,' as in C.V.
CHASTISEMENT,] or 'instruction;' as in 2. 30; 5. 3, &c.
15. CRIEST] for help; as in 20. 8; 48. 31, &c.
BREACH,] not 'affliction,' as in C.V.
16. CONSUMING,] as in 2. 3; 12. 12; 31. 30.
ADVERSARIES,] lit. 'distressers;' as in 46. 10; 48. 5, &c.
SPOILERS,] as in 50. 11; Jud. 2. 14, 16, &c.
SPOIL,] as in 2 K. 21. 14; Isa. 42. 22, &c.
PLUNDER,] as in 2. 14; 15. 13; 17. 2; 49. 32.
17. INCREASE HEALTH,] lit. 'cause a lengthening to go up.'
OUTCAST,] as in 49. 36; De. 22. 1; 30. 4, &c.
18. CAPTIVITY,] as in v. 3; 29. 14; 31. 23, &c.
DWELLING PLACES,] lit. 'tabernacles.'
ORDINANCE,] lit. 'judgment.'
19. THANKSGIVING,] or 'confession;' as in 17. 26; 33. 11, &c.
PLAYFUL,] or 'laughing' ones; as in 15. 17.
NOT SMALL,] as in Job 14. 21.
20. AFORETIME,] as in 46. 26; 49. 28, &c.
COMPANY,] as in 6. 18; Ex. 12. 3, 6, 19, &c.
ESTABLISHED,] or 'made ready.'
21. HONOURABLE ONE,] as in 14. 3; 25. 34.
PLEDGED,] or 'sweet;' as in 6. 20; 31. 26.
22. A PEOPLE .. A GOD,] as in 7. 23; 11. 4, &c.
23. WHIRLWIND,] as in 23. 19; 25. 32, &c.
FURY,] lit. 'heat.'
CUTTING,] not 'continual,' as in C.V.
STAYETH,] as in 23. 19, &c.
24. FIERCENESS,] lit. 'heat.'
DEVICES,] as in 11. 15; 23. 20; 51. 11, &c.
CONSIDER,] as in 23 20; 1 K. 7. 21, &c.

XXXI. 1. AFFIRMATION,] as in v. 14, &c.
2. FOUND GRACE,] as in Ge. 6. 8; 18. 3, &c.
3. APPEARED,] as in 13. 26, &c.
4. VIRGIN,] as in v. 13, 21; 2. 32, &c.
TABRETS,] as in Ge. 31. 27; Ex. 15. 20, &c.
CHORUS,] as in v. 13; Ps. 30. 11; 149. 3, &c.
PLAYFUL,] lit. 'laughing;' as in 15. 17, &c.
5. PLANT,] as in 2. 21; 12. 2; 24. 6, &c.
MADE COMMON,] lit. 'pierced;' as in 34. 16.
6. CRIED,] or 'called.'
7. SING,] as in Isa. 12. 6; 44. 23; 49. 13, &c.
CRY ALOUD,] as in Isa. 10. 30; 12. 6; 54. 1.
SOUND,] lit. 'cause to be heard.'
REMNANT,] as in 6. 9; 8. 3; 11. 23; 15. 9, &c.
8. COUNTRY,] or 'land of the north.'
SIDES,] lit. 'thighs;' as in 6. 22; 25. 32, &c.
LAME,] or limping; as in Lev. 21. 18, &c.
CONCEIVING,] as in 20. 17; Ge. 16. 11, &c.
9. SUPPLICATIONS,] as in 3. 21; 2 Ch. 6. 21.
STREAMS OF WATER,] as in De. 8. 7, &c.
STUMBLE,] or 'are not stumbled;' as in 6. 15, &c.
FIRST-BORN,] as in Ge. 10. 15; 22. 21, &c.
10. DECLARE,] lit. 'set forth.'
SCATTERING,] as in Prov. 20. 8, 26, &c.
FLOCK,] herd, or drove.
11. RANSOMED,] as in 15. 21; Ex. 13. 13, &c.
REDEEMED,] as in Ex. 6. 6; 15. 13, &c.
12. SUNG,] as in 51. 48; Lev. 9. 24, &c.
FLOWED,] or 'been bright;' as in 51. 44, &c.
YOUNG,] lit. 'sons' of the flock.
WATERED GARDEN,] as in Isa. 58. 11.
GRIEVE,] as in v. 25; Ps. 88. 9.
13. CHORUS,] as in v. 4.
YOUNG MEN,] or 'choice ones.'
SORROW,] as in 8. 18; 20. 18; 45. 3, &c.
14. SATISFIED,] as in 46. 10; Ps. 36. 8, &c.
15. RAMAH,] a city of Benjamin.
WAILING,] as in 5. 10, 18, 19, 20; Am. 5. 16; Mic. 2. 4.
WEEPING,] as in v. 9, 16; 3. 21; 9. 10, &c.
MOST BITTER,] as in 6. 26; Hos. 11. 14.
RACHEL,] the beloved wife of Jacob.
WEEPING,] as in Eze. 8. 14.
REFUSED,] as in 3. 3; 5. 3; 8. 5; 9 6, &c.
TO BE COMFORTED,] as in 15. 16; 1 Sa. 15. 29; Ps. 77. 2.
16. WITHHOLD,] as in 2. 25; Prov. 1. 15.
REWARD,] as in Ge. 15. 1; 30. 18, 28, &c.
17. HOPE,] as in 29. 11; Jos. 2. 18, 21, &c.
BORDER,] as in 5. 22; 15. 13; 17. 3, &c.
18. BEMOANING HIMSELF,] as in 48. 27; Isa. 24. 20.
CHASTISED,] or 'instructed;' as in 6. 8, &c.
NOT TAUGHT,] or 'accustomed, trained.'
19. BEING INSTRUCTED,] lit. 'made to know.'
STRUCK,] as in 48. 26; Nu. 24. 10, &c.
BORNE,] or 'lifted up.'
20. DELIGHTS,] as in Ps. 119. 24, 27, 92, &c.
21. SIGNS,] as in 2 K. 23. 17; Eze. 39. 15.
HIGHWAY,] as in Nu. 20. 19; Jud. 5. 20, &c.
22. BACKSLIDING,] as in 49. 4.
PREPARED,] as in Ge. 1. 1, 27; 2. 3, &c.
COMPASS,] as in De. 32. 10; Ps. 7. 7, &c.
23. HABITATION,] lit. 'comely place.'
HILL OF HOLINESS,] i.e. of 'separation.'
24. IN ORDER,] or 'with the herd.'
25. SATIATED,] as in Isa. 43. 24; 55. 10, &c.
26. AWAKED,] as in 51. 39, 57; 2 K. 4. 31, &c.
27. DAYS ARE COMING,] as in 7. 32; 9. 25, &c.
BEAST,] or 'cattle.'

28. WATCHED,] as in 31. 28; Job 21. 32, &c.
PLUCK UP,] as in 1. 10; 12. 5, 17; 18. 7, &c.
BREAK DOWN,] as in 1. 10; 18. 7; Ps. 58. 6.
THROW DOWN,] as in 1. 10.
AFFLICT,] *lit.* 'do evil;' as in 4. 22; 13. 23.
29. UNRIPE FRUIT,] as in v. 30; Isa. 18. 5.
BLUNTED,] as in v. 30; Eze. 18. 2; Ec. 10. 10.
31. COVENANT,] as in v. 32, 33; 3. 16, &c.
32. LAYING HOLD,] as in 2 K. 15. 19, &c.
RULED,] as in 3. 14; De. 21. 13; 24. 1, &c.
33. MY LAW,] *or* 'direction.'
34. TEACH,] as in 2. 33; 9. 5, 14; 12. 16, &c.
LEAST . . GREATEST,] as in 6. 13; 16. 6, &c.
PARDON,] as in 5. 1, 7; 50. 20, &c.
35. SUN,] as in 8. 2; 15. 9; 43. 13, &c.
STATUTES,] *lit.* 'engraved things.'
QUIETING,] as in Isa. 51. 15.
BILLOWS,] *lit.* 'heaps.'
36. DEPART,] *lit.* 'move;' as in Nu. 14. 44.
CEASE,] *lit.* 'keep sabbath.'
37. MEASURED,] as in 33. 22; Hos. 1. 10.
KICK,] as in 6. 19; 33. 24, 26, &c.
38. TOWER,]*lit.* 'great place;' as in Ge. 11. 4.
39. LINE,] as in 1 K. 7. 23; Zec. 1. 16.
40. VALLEY,] *lit.* 'deep place.'
EASTWARD.] *lit.* at the 'rising' of the sun.

XXXII. 1. THE WORD,] as in 7. 1; 11. 1, &c.
TENTH YEAR,] B. C. 590.
2. FORCES,] as in v. 7, 21; 15. 13; 17. 3, &c.
SHUT UP,] as in Ps. 88. 8.
COURT OF THE PRISON,] as in v. 8, 12; 33.
1; 37. 21, &c.
3. ZEDEKIAH,] i.e. 'rightness of Jah.'
CAPTURED,] as in v. 28; 34. 22; 37. 8, &c.
4. NOT ESCAPE,] as in 34. 3; 38. 18, 23, &c.
5. LEADETH,] *lit.* 'causeth to go;' as in
31. 9, &c.
7. UNCLE,] as in v. 8, 9, 12; Lev. 10. 4.
REDEMPTION,] as in v. 8; Lev. 25. 24, &c.
9. WEIGH,] as in v. 10; Ge. 23. 16, &c.
10. WRITE,] as in 31. 33; 36. 4, 32; 51. 60.
BOOK,] *or* 'scroll, or roll.'
BALANCES,] as in Lev. 19. 36; Job 6. 2, &c.
11. PURCHASE,] as in v. 12, 14, 16; Ge. 17. 12.
12. BARUCH,] i.e. 'bent of knee,' or
blessed.
NERIAH,] i.e. 'light of Jah.'
MAASEIAH,] i.e. 'refuge of Jah.'
SITTING,] dwelling, or abiding.
13. CHARGE,] as in 1. 7, 17; 7. 23; 11. 4, &c.
14. HOSTS,] as in v. 15, 18; 2. 19, &c.
EARTHEN VESSEL,] as in 19. 1; Lev. 6. 28.
15. BOUGHT,] as in v. 43.
16. PRAY,] as in 7. 16; 11. 14; 14. 11, &c.
17. AH,] as in 1. 6; 4. 10; 14. 13, &c.
GREAT POWER,] as in 27. 5, &c.
18. DOING KINDNESS,] as in 9. 24; Ge. 24. 49.
NAME,] as in 10. 16; 16. 21; 31. 35, &c.
19. COUNSEL,] as in 18. 18, 23; 19. 7; 49. 7.
FRUIT OF HIS DOINGS,] as in 17. 10; 21. 14.
20. SIGNS AND WONDERS,] as in Ex. 7. 3, &c.
21. BRINGEST FORTH,] as in 8. 1; 10. 13, &c.
GREAT FEAR,] as in De. 4. 34; 26. 8; 34. 12.
22. SWEAR,] as in 4. 2; 11. 5; 22. 5; 46. 26.
MILK AND HONEY,] as in 11. 5; Ex. 3. 8, 17.
23. POSSESS,] as in 30. 3; 49. 1, 2; Ge. 15. 4.
24. MOUNTS,] as in 6. 6; 33. 4; 2 Sa. 20. 15.
SEEING,] as in 1. 11, 13; 7. 17; 20. 4, &c.
25. CAUSE TO TESTIFY,] as in Ex. 19. 21;
Am. 3. 13.

CHALDEANS,] who ruled in Babylon.
26. WORD,] as in v. 6, 8, &c.
27. JEHOVAH,] the Existing One.
GOD OF ALL FLESH,] maker and ruler of
men.
WONDERFUL,] as in v. 17; 21. 2; Ge. 18. 14.
28. CAPTURED,] as in v. 3.
29. SET ON FIRE,] as in 11. 16; 17. 27, &c.
PROVOKE TO ANGER,] as in v. 32; 7. 18, &c.
30. ONLY,] as in 10. 19, &c.
AFFIRMATION,] as in v. 5, 44, &c.
31. ANGER,] as in v. 37; 2. 35; 4. 8, &c.
TURN IT ASIDE,] as in Ge. 30. 32; 48. 17, &c.
32. EVIL,] as in v. 23, 30, 42, &c.
JERUSALEM,] though a holy city of God.
33. TURN . . THE NECK,] indifferent to reproof.
RISING EARLY,] showing earnestness and
purpose.
INSTRUCTION,] in the way of duty and life.
34. SET,] openly and publicly, without
shame.
DEFILE,] and drive God out of it.
35. BUILD,] as in 22. 14; 31. 4; 35. 7; 52. 4.
CAUSE TO SIN,] a thing which is abhorrent
to God's nature and character.
36. JEHOVAH,] the Existing One, He who is.
PESTILENCE,] all of which are his servants.
37. GATHERING,] as in 49. 5; Isa. 13. 14, &c
CONFIDENTLY,] without fear of danger.
38. PEOPLE . . GOD,] affording mutual joy.
39. ONE HEART,] inclined to God's laws.
FEAR,] that is, 'reverence,' and adore.
40. AGE-DURING,] as long as the dispensation continues.
TURN ASIDE,] after other objects of worship.
41. REJOICED,] being the God of love.
TRUTH,] *or* 'stedfastness;' as in 2. 21, &c.
42. EVIL,] mentioned, in v. 36.
43. BOUGHT,] as in v. 15.
44. FIELDS,] that is, cultivated ones.
WITNESSES,] as in v. 10, 12, 25, &c.
CAPTIVITY,] from the land of the enemy.

XXXIII. 1. WORD,] announcing his will
to men.
PRISON,] into which he had been cast.
2. MAKER,] into a nation and kingdom.
NAME,] that by which he is known.
3. CALL,] in prayer and supplication.
FENCED THINGS,] hitherto unrevealed.
4. ISRAEL,] by covenant relationship.
TOOLS,] to use in defence of the city.
5. FIGHT,] as in 41. 12; 51. 30; Da. 10. 20.
EVIL,] in breaking law and covenant.
6. INCREASING,] *lit.* 'causing to go up.'
TRUTH,] *or* 'stedfastness;' as in 2. 21, &c.
7. TURNED BACK,] as in 12. 15; 16. 15, &c.
BUILT,] into a nation and people.
8. CLEANSED,]*or* 'purified;' as in 13. 27, &c.
TRANSGRESSED,] *lit.* 'stepped;' as in 2.
8, 29, &c.
9. JOY,] as in 7. 34; 15. 16; 16. 9, &c.
TREMBLED,] *or* 'been moved, agitated.'
10. WASTE,] *lit.* 'dried up; as in v. 12.
DESOLATED,] as in Ps. 69. 25; Isa. 54. 3, &c
11. GLADNESS,] as in 7. 34; 15. 16; 16. 9, &c
TO THE AGE,] that is, as long as life lasts.
CAPTIVITY,] as in v. 7, 26, &c.
12. WASTE,] as in v. 10, &c.

CAUSING TO LIE DOWN,] as in Isa. 54. 11.
13. HILL-COUNTRY,] as in 32. 44, &c.
NUMBERER,] as in Ps. 147. 4.
14. DAYS ARE COMING,] as in 7. 32; 9. 25.
15. CAUSE TO SHOOT UP,] as in Ge. 2. 9, &c.
DONE JUDGMENT,] *or* 'justice;' as in 5. 1.
16. SAVED,] from fears within and without.
OUR RIGHTEOUSNESS,] the promised Messiah.
17. CUT OFF,] as in v. 18; 7. 28; 35. 19, &c.
THRONE,] as in v. 21; 1. 15; 3. 17, &c.
18. PRIESTS,] as in v. 21; 1. 1, 18; 2. 8, &c.
SACRIFICE,] as in 6. 20; 7. 21, 22; 17. 26, &c.
19. WORD,] or intimation of God's will.
20. BREAK,] as in 11. 10; 14. 21; 31. 32, &c.
‹ MINISTERS,] adminstering God's blessings ‹to the people.
22. HOST OF THE HEAVENS,] that is, the stars.
MULTIPLY,] as in 2. 22; 30. 19; 46. 11, &c.
23. WORD OF JEHOVAH,] as in v. 1, 19, &c.
24. CONSIDERED,] *lit.* 'seen.'
DESPISE,] as weak and insignificant.
25. STATUTES,] *lit.* 'engraved things.'
APPOINTED,] *lit.* 'set, placed.'
26. SEED,] that is, 'posterity.'
PITIED,] so as to bring them back.

XXXIV. 1. THE WORD,] or declaration of God's will.
FIGHTING,] as in v. 7; 21. 2, 4; 32. 24, &c.
2. GOD OF ISRAEL,] its supreme ruler.
KING OF JUDAH,] vice-gerent only of God.
3. ESCAPE,] as in 32. 4; 38. 18, 23; 46. 6, &c.
ENTERED,] as a captive, never to return.
4. HEAR,] that is, attend and obey.
5. BURNINGS,] in honour of the dead.
AFFIRMATION,] an oracular declaration.
6. JEREMIAH THE PROPHET,] announcer of God's will.
7. FORCES,] as in v. 1, 21, &c.
CITIES OF FORTRESSES,] guarding the land.
8. THE WORD,] as in v. 1, &c.
COVENANT,] mutual agreement or bargain.
LIBERTY,] from servile work to which they had been reduced.
9. TO SEND FORTH,] to their own homes.
10. HEADS,] or chief men in Jerusalem.
11. TURN,] having repented of their vows.
12. WORD OF JEHOVAH,] suited for the occasion.
13. GOD OF ISRAEL,] to which they owed obedience.
14. SOLD,] for debt or otherwise.
INCLINED THEIR EAR,] to hear and obey the law.
15. TURN BACK,] from their evil ways.
CALLED,] that is, the temple.
16. POLLUTE,] *lit.* 'pierce.'
SUBDUE,] against their will and interest.
17. NOT HEARKENED,] as in v. 14; 3. 13, 25.
TREMBLING,] as in 15. 4; 24. 9; 29. 18, &c.
18. TRANSGRESSING,] *lit.* 'passing over.'
PIECES,] as in v. 19; Ge. 15. 10; Song 2. 17.
19. HEADS,] as in v. 10, 21; 1. 18; 2. 26, &c.
OFFICERS,] *lit.* 'eunuchs.'
20. ENEMIES,] as in v. 21; 6. 25; 12. 7, &c.
SOUL,] that is, life; as in 11. 21; 19. 7, &c.
EARTH,] as in v. 33; 9. 10; 15. 3, &c.
21. ZEDEKIAH,] i.e. 'justice of Jah.'
GOING UP,] as in 47. 2; 48. 44; Ge. 28. 12.

22. COMMANDING,] *or* 'charging.'
INHABITANT,] *lit.* sitter;' as in 2. 15, &c.

XXXV. 1. THE WORD,] of warning and instruction.
JEHOIAKIM,] i.e. 'Jah raises up.'
JOSIAH,] B.C. 642—611.
2. RECHABITES,] *lit.* 'riders.'
HOUSE OF JEHOVAH,] that is, the temple.
CHAMBERS,] *lit.* a 'place for throwing oneself down in.'
3. JAAZANIAH,] i.e. 'Jah gives ear.'
4. HANAN,] i.e. 'gracious.'
IGDALIAH,] i.e. 'Great is Jah.'
MAN OF GOD,] *lit.* of the God, i.e. the True One.
PRINCES,] *lit.* 'heads;' as in 1. 18; 2. 26, &c.
MAASEIAH,] i.e. 'works of Jah.'
SHALLUM,] i.e. 'recompensed.'
THRESHOLD,] *lit.* 'end, extremity.'
5. PUT,] *lit.* 'given;' as in 3. 8, 19, &c.
GOBLETS,] *lit.* 'high things; as in Ge. 44. 2.
6. JONADAB,] i.e. 'Jah is willing, liberal.'
AGE,] that is, during life.
7. HOUSE,] a settled habitation.
VINEYARD,] *lit.* 'prepared place;' as in v. 9.
TENTS,] *lit.* 'shining things;' as in v. 10, &c.
SOJOURNING,] as in Ex. 3. 22; 12. 49, &c. ‹
9. DWELLING,] *or* 'inhabiting;' as in 9. 6,&c.
11. COMING UP,] as in Ge. 32. 24; 26. 4, &c.
12. WORD,] *lit.* a 'leading forth.'
13. ISRAEL,] publicly avouched to be such.
RECEIVE,] accept or take.
14. PERFORMED,] *lit.* 'raised up;' as in Ex. 40. 17, &c.
RISING EARLY,] as in v. 15; 7. 13, 25; 11. 7.
15. AMEND,] *lit.* 'make good;' as in 7. 3, &c.
WALK,] *or* 'go on.'
INCLINED,] *or* 'stretched out;' as in 7. 24.
16. PERFORMED,] *lit.* 'raised up;' as in v. 15.
17. HOSTS,] in heaven and earth.
ANSWERED,] *or* 'responded.'
18. OBSERVE,] watch, keep or guard.
19. JEHOVAH,] the Existing One.
STANDING,] that is, remaining, continuing.

XXXVI. 1. FOURTH YEAR,] B.C. 607.
2. BOOK,] *or* 'scroll;' as in v. 4, &c.
WRITTEN,] for future use and preservation.
3. THINKING,] *or* 'devising;' as in 18. 11,&c.
PROPITIOUS,] *or* 'have sent away;' as in 33.8.
4. BARUCH,] i.e. 'bent of knee,' blessed.
NERIAH,] i.e. 'light of Jah.'
5. RESTRAINED,] *or* 'shut up;' as in 20. 9.
6. READ,] *lit.* 'called' aloud.
FAST,] *lit.* a 'being dumb.'
7. SUPPLICATION,] for 'grace;' as in 37. 20
FURY,] *lit.* 'heat;' as in 4. 4; 6. 11, &c.
9. FIFTH YEAR,] B.C. 606.
NINTH MONTH,] i.e. Sivan.
FAST,] as in v. 6, &c.
10. READETH,] *or* 'calleth, proclaimeth.'
GEMARIAH,] i.e. 'completeness of Jah.'
SCRIBE,] *lit.* 'cipherer, writer.'
NEW GATE,] as in 26. 10.
11. MICHAIAH,] i.e. 'who is like Jah.'
BOOK,] as in v. 2, 4, &c.
12. GOETH DOWN,] from the temple.
ELISHAMA,] i.e. 'my God has heard '
ELNATHAN,] i.e. 'God hath given.'
ACBOR,] i.e. 'mouse.'

HANANIAH,] i.e. 'grace of Jah.'
13. DECLARE,] *lit.* 'set forth;' as in v. 16.
14. BARUCH,] who was sitting in the temple.
JEDHUDI,] i.e. 'a Jew.'
NETHANIAH,] i.e. 'given of Jah.'
SHELEMIAH,] i.e. 'completeness of Jah.'
15. SIT DOWN,] *or* 'remain, abide;' as in 13. 18, &c.
17. ASKED,] *or* 'demanded.'
18. PRONOUNCETH,] *lit.* 'calleth;' as in v. 4.
WITH INK,] *or* 'its parts;' as in Job 17. 16.
19. BE HIDDEN,] *or* 'kept secret.'
20. KING,] that is, Jehoiakim.
LAID UP,] *or* 'looked after;' as in 37. 21, &c.
21. TAKE,] *or* 'receive;' as in v. 26; 5. 3, &c.
STANDING,] *or* 'remaining;' as in 28. 5, &c.
22. WINTER HOUSE,] as in Am. 3. 15.
STOVE,] as in v. 23.
23. LEAVES,] *or* 'pages;' *lit.* 'doors;' as in 49. 31, &c.
CUTTETH OUT,] *or* 'rendeth;' as in 4. 30,&c.
KNIFE,] razor or sheath; as in 47. 6, &c.
CONSUMPTION,] as in 1. 3; 24. 10; 27. 8, &c.
24. RENT,] as in Ge. 37. 29, 34; 44. 13, &c.
25. INTERCEDED,] as in 15. 11; Job 36. 32.
26. JERAHMEEL,] i.e. 'God is merciful.'
HAMMELECK,] *or* 'of the king.'
SERAIAH,] i.e. 'head of Jah.'
AZRIEL,] i.e. 'help of God.'
SHELEMIAH,] i.e. 'completeness of Jah.'
ABDEEL,] i.e. 'servant of God.'
HIDE,] *or* 'keep secret;' as in 33. 5; Ex. 3. 6.
27. BURNING,] as in v. 25, &c.
28. TURN,] *lit.* 'turn back;' as in 3. 12, 14.
ROLL,] as in v. 2, 4, 6, 14, 20, 21, 23, 25, &c.
29. DESTROYED,] *lit.* 'marred;' as in 49. 9.
CAUSED TO CEASE,] as in 7. 34; 48. 33, &c.
30. THRONE OF DAVID,] as in 17. 25; 22. 2.
CARCASE,] *lit.* 'falling thing;' as in 7. 33.
HEAT,] as in 49. 13; 50. 38; Ge. 31. 40, &c.
COLD,] as in Ge. 31. 40; Job 6. 16; 37. 10, &c.
31. CHARGED,] as in 6. 15; 9. 25; 15. 3, &c.
32. ROLL,] as in v. 2, 4, 6, 14, 20, 21, 23, &c.

XXXVII. 1. REIGN,] over Judah and Jerusalem.
ZEDEKIAH,] i.e. 'rightness of Jah.'
CONIAH,] i.e. 'prepared of Jah.'
CAUSED TO REIGN,] as his vice-gerent, and tributary.
2. HEARKENED,] *lit.* 'heard.'
3. SHELEMIAH,] i.e. 'completeness of Jah.'
ZEPHANIAH,] i.e. 'laid up of Jah.'
MAASEIAH,] i.e. 'works of Jah.'
PRAY,] *lit.* 'judge thyself;' as in 29. 7, &c.
4. PRISON,] *lit.* 'restraint;' as in 52. 31.
5. LAYING SEIGE,] *or* 'straitening;' as in 21. 4, 9, &c.
REPORT,] *lit.* 'hearing;' as in 50. 43, &c.
7. TO SEEK,] as in Ge. 25. 22; Ex. 18. 15, &c.
HELP,] as in Jud. 5. 23; 2 Ch. 28. 21, &c.
8. FOUGHT,] *lit.* 'been fought with.'
9. LIFT UP,] as in 22. 27; 44. 14, &c.
10. FIGHTING,] *lit.* 'having been fought.'
WOUNDED,] *lit.* 'pierced;' as in 51. 4, &c.
11. GOING UP,] *or* 'being taken up;' as in Ex. 40. 36, &c.
12. LAND OF BENJAMIN,] his native territory.
13. GATE OF BENJAMIN,] that is, leading towards it.

IRIJAH,] i.e. 'fear of Jah.'
SHELEMIAH,] i.e. 'completeness of Jah.'
HANANIAH,] i.e. 'grace of Jah.'
FALLING,] as in v. 14; 6. 15; 8. 12; 39. 9, &c.
14. FALSEHOOD,] as in 3. 10, 23; 5. 2, 31, &c.
LAYETH HOLD,] as in v. 13; 26. 8; 52. 9, &c.
15. PUT,] *lit.* given;' as in v. 4, 18, &c.
PRISON,] *lit.* 'bound one, or binding.'
PRISON HOUSE,] *lit.* 'house of restraint.'
16. DUNGEON,] *lit.* 'pit,' a dug place; as in 6. 7, &c.
CELLS.] Original word not found again.
17. SECRET,] as in 38. 16; 40. 15; De. 13. 6.
A WORD,] that is, a new revelation.
GIVEN,] as a captive and spoil.
18. SINNED,] *lit.* 'missed' the mark of duty.
PRISON HOUSE,] *lit.* 'house of restraint;' as in v. 15, &c.
20. SUPPLICATION,] for 'grace;' as in 36. 7.
FALL,] as in 36. 7; 42. 2, &c.
21. COMMIT,] as in 36. 20, &c.
PRISON,] as in 32. 2, 8, 12; 33. 1, &c.
CAKE,] as in Ex. 29. 23; Jud. 8. 5, &c.
CONSUMPTION,] as in 1. 3; 24. 10; 27. 8, &c.

XXXVIII. 1. SHEPHATIAH,] i.e. 'judged of Jah.'
MATTAN,] i.e. a 'gift.'
GEDALIAH,] i.e. 'greatness of Jah.'
PASHHUR,] i.e. 'prosperity everywhere.'
SHELEMIAH,] i.e. 'completeness of Jah.'
MALCHIAH,] i.e. 'king of Jah.'
2. REMAINING,] *lit.* 'sitting;' as in v. 7, &c.
PREY,] as in 21. 9; 39. 18; 45. 5; 49. 32, &c.
4. MAKING FEEBLE,] as in Ezra 4. 4.
5. IN YOUR HAND,] that is, power.
6. MALCHIAH,] i.e. 'my king is Jah.'
PRISON,] as in v. 13, 28; 32. 2, &c.
SEND DOWN,] to the bottom of the pit.
MIRE,] as in 2 Sa. 22. 43; Job 41. 30, &c.
SINKETH,] as in 1 Sa. 17. 49; Ps. 69. 14, &c.
7. EBED-MELECH,] i.e. 'servant of a king.'
EUNUCH,] as in 29. 2; 34. 19; 39. 3, &c.
GATE OF BENJAMIN,] as in 20. 2; 37. 13, &c.
9. MY LORD,] as in 22. 18; 27. 4; 34. 5, &c.
CAST INTO THE PIT,] as in v. 6.
10. WITH THEE,] *lit.* 'in thy hands;' as in v. 11.
11. TREASURY,] *or* 'treasure;' as in 10. 13, CLOUTS..RAGS,] as in v. 12.
12. ARM-HOLES,] *lit.* 'near places of the hands.'
13. DRAW OUT,] as in 31. 3; Ge. 37. 28, &c.
14. ENTRANCE,] as in De. 11. 30; Jos. 1. 4.
HIDE,] *lit.* 'cut off;' as in v. 25; 50. 2, &c.
15. DECLARE,] *lit.* 'set forth.'
COUNSEL,] as in Ex. 18. 19; Nu. 24. 14, &c.
16. SWEARETH,] *lit.* 'is sworn;' as in 5. 2.
IN SECRET,] as in 37. 17; 40. 15; De. 13. 6.
SOUL,] or breathing principle, in man or beast.
SOUL,] that is, 'life;' as in v. 2, 17, 20, &c.
18. ESCAPE,] *or* 'art let go;' as in v. 23, &c.
19. FEARING,] as in 42. 16.
INSULTED,] as in Nu. 22. 29; Jud. 19. 25, &c.
21. REFUSING,] as in Ex. 8. 2; 9. 2; 10. 4.
22. PERSUADED,] as in 1 Sa. 26. 19, &c.
ALLIES,] *lit.* 'men of thy peace.'
SUNK,] *or* 'been dipped;' as in Job 38. 6; Prov. 8. 25.

MIRE,] as in Job 8. 11; 40. 21; Eze. 47. 11.
TURNED,] as in Ps. 44. 18; Isa. 42. 17, &c.
25. HIDE,] as in v. 14; 50 2, &c.
26. CAUSING TO FALL,] as in Da. 9, 18, &c.
SUPPLICATION,] for 'grace;' as in 36. 7, &c.
27. KEEP SILENT,] as in 4. 19; Ge. 34. 5, &c.
28. PRISON,] as in v. 6, 13, &c.

XXXIX. 1. NINTH YEAR,] B.C. 602.
TENTH MONTH,] i.e. 'Tammuz.'
LAY SEIGE,] lit. 'straitened.'
2. ELEVENTH YEAR.] B.C. 600.
FOURTH MONTH,] i.e. Tebeth.
BROKEN UP,] or 'cleft.'
3.NERGAL SHAREZER,] i.e. 'prince of Mars.'
SHAMGAR-NEBO,] i.e. 'sword of Nebo.'
CHIEF OF THE EUNUCHS,] as in v. 13.
MAGES,] some of whom came to Christ.
4. TWO WALLS,] as in 52. 7.
PLAIN,] or 'wilderness;' as in v. 5; 2. 6, &c.
5. OVERTAKE,] as in 42. 16; 52. 8, &c.
PLAINS OF JERICHO,] as in 52. 8; Jos. 4. 13.
JUDGMENTS,] which they had resolved on.
6. SLAUGHTERETH,] as in 41. 7; 52. 10, &c.
FREEMEN,] as in 27. 20; 1 K. 21. 8, &c.
7. BLINDED,] as in 52. 11; 2 K. 25. 7, &c.
BRAZEN FETTERS,] or 'double pieces of
brass.'
8. HOUSE OF THE PEOPLE,] the public assembly hall.
BROKEN DOWN,] as in 52. 14; Ex. 24. 13, &c.
9. EXECUTIONERS,] lit. 'slaughterers, or
cooks.'
10. POOR,] lit. 'thin, lean;' as in 5. 4, &c.
12. PLACE THINE EYES,] that is, watch
carefully.
13. CHIEFS,] or 'great men.'
14. GEDALIAH,] i.e. 'greatness of Jah.'
AHIKAM,] i.e. 'my brother has risen.'
HOME,] lit. 'unto the house.'
15. DETAINED,] as in 20. 9; 33. 1; 39. 15, &c.
PRISON,] as in v. 14, &c.
16. EBED-MELEK,] i.e. 'servant of a king.'
17. DELIVERED,] lit. 'snatched.'
18. SPOIL,] as in 21. 9; 38. 2; 45. 5, &c.
TRUSTED,] or 'leant.'

XL. 1. THE WORD,] or communication from
God.
RAMAH,] i.e. 'the high place.'
PRISONER,] lit. 'bound one.'
CHAINS,] as in v. 4.
2. THY GOD,] the God of Israel.
3. SINNED,] erred or 'missed' the mark.
4. LOOSED,] lit. 'opened;' as in Ge. 24. 32.
CHAINS,] as in v. 1.
KEEP,] lit. 'set;' as in 24. 6; 39. 12, &c.
FORBEAR,] lit. 'cease.'
5. REPLY,] lit. 'turn back;' as in Ex. 14. 12.
APPOINTED,] as in v. 7, 11; 1. 10; 36. 20, &c.
FOR THE WAY,] as in 52. 34; 2 K. 5. 30, &c.
GIFT,] lit. a 'thing lifted up.'
6. MIZPAH,] i.e. a 'watch-tower.'
7. APPOINTED,] as in v. 5, 11; 1. 10; 36. 20.
INFANTS,] as in 41. 16; 43. 6; Ge. 34. 29, &c.
POOR,] lit. 'lean, thin;' as in 5. 4; Ex. 23. 3.
8. MIZPAH,] as in v. 6, 10.
ISHMAEL,] i.e. 'God hears.'
NETHANIAH,] i.e. 'given of God.'
JOHANAN,] i.e. 'Jah is gracious.'
JONATHAN,] i.e. 'Jah has given.'

KAREAH,] i.e. 'bald.'
SERAIAH,] i.e. 'head of Jah.'
TANHUMETH,] i.e. 'comfort, consolation'
9. SWEAR,] lit. 'is sworn;' as in 5. 2, 7, &c
ABIDE,] lit. 'sit, dwell;' as in v. 5, 10, &c
10. MIZPAH,] as in v. 6, 8, &c.
STAND,] as a leader and friend.
SUMMER-FRUIT,] as in v. 12; 8. 20; 48. 32.
TAKEN,] or 'received;' lit. 'captured.'
11. MOAB,] beyond the Jordan eastward.
12. DRIVEN,] as in 43. 5; 49. 5, &c.
SUMMER-FRUIT,] as in v. 10; 8 20; 48. 32.
14. BAALIS,] i.e. 'son of exultation.'
SMITE THY SOUL,] that is, life; as in v. 15.
15. IN SECRET,] as in 37. 17; 38. 16; De. 13. 6.
SCATTERED,] as in 10. 21; 52. 8, &c.
16. FALSEHOOD,] as in 3. 10, 23; 5. 2, 31, &c.

XLI. 1. SEVENTH MONTH,] i.e. Abib or
Nisan.
SEED ROYAL,] lit. 'seed of the kingdom.'
CHIEFS,] lit. 'great ones.'
2. APPOINTED,] as in v. 10, 18; 1. 10, &c.
5. SHECHEM,] i.e. a 'shoulder.'
SHILOH,] i.e. 'peace, tranquillity.
SAMARIA,] i.e. 'a guarded place.'
SHAVEN,] as in Jud. 16. 7, 22.
RENT,] as in 1 Sa. 4. 12; 2 Sa. 1. 2, &c.
CUTTING THEMSELVES,] as in 5. 7; 16. 6, &c.
HOUSE OF JEHOVAH,] which was lying in
ruins.
6. TO MEET,] as in 51. 31; Ge. 14. 7; 15. 10.
7. SLAUGHTER,] as in 39. 6; 52. 10, &c.
PIT,] as in v. 9; 6. 7; 37. 16; 38. 6, &c.
8. THINGS HIDDEN,] as in Ge. 43. 23, &c.
FORBEARETH,] lit. 'ceaseth;' as in 44. 18.
9. PIT,] as in v. 7; 6. 7; 37. 16, &c.
CARCASES,] as in 31. 40; 33. 5; Ge. 15. 11.
ASA,] i.e. a 'physician.'
PIERCED,] as in 9. 1; 14. 18; 25. 33, &c.
10. TAKETH CAPTIVE,] as in v. 14; 43. 12.
THE KING,] that is, Zedekiah.
COMMITTED,] as in v. 2, 18, &c.
PASS OVER,] the river Jordan eastward.
12. TO FIGHT,] lit. 'be fought;' as in 33. 5.
GREAT,] lit. 'many;' as in 51. 13, 55, &c.
GIBEON,] i.e. 'high place.'
14. TURN ROUND,] as in 52. 21; Ge. 37. 7, &c.
15. ESCAPED,] as in 32. 4; 34. 3; 38. 18, &c.
16. INFANTS,] as in 40. 7; 43. 6; Ge. 34. 29.
EUNUCHS,] as in 29. 2; 34. 19; 38. 7, &c.
17. EGYPT,] as Joseph and Mary did in
later days.
18. PRESENCE,] lit. 'face.'

XLII. 1. COME NIGH,] as in Ge. 18. 23, &c.
JOHANAN,] i.e. 'Jah is gracious.'
LEAST..GREATEST,] as in v. 8; 8. 10, &c.
2. SUPPLICATION,] for 'grace;' as in v. 9.
PRAY,] lit. 'judge thyself;' as in v. 20, &c.
FEW,] as in 51. 33; Ge. 18. 4; 24. 17, &c.
3. DECLARE,] lit. 'set forth;' as in v. 4, 21.
WALK,] or 'go on in.'
4. PRAYING,] as in 1 K. 8. 28; 2 Ch. 6. 19.
YOUR GOD,] as well as mine; see v. 2.
WITHHOLD,] as in 5. 25; Ge. 30. 2, &c.
5. JEHOVAH,] the Existing One.
FAITHFUL,] lit. 'stedfast;' as in Nu. 12. 7.
6. OUR GOD,] as well as that of the prophet.
7. TEN DAYS,] testing their patience.

JOHANAN,] i.e. 'Jah is gracious.'
8. LEAST..GREATEST,] as in v. 1; 8. 10, &c.
9. CAUSE TO FALL,] as in Nu. 5. 22, &c.
SUPPLICATION,] as in v. 2; 36. 7; 37. 20, &c.
10. THIS LAND] of Palestine, their own by God's gift.
THROW DOWN,] as in 24. 6; Ex. 15. 7, &c.
PLUCK UP,] as in 12. 14, 17; 24. 6, &c.
11. DELIVER,] *lit.* 'snatch;' as in 1. 8, &c.
12. MERCIES,] as in 16. 5; Ge. 43. 14, &c.
15. WORD,] in reference to this matter.
SET YOUR FACES,] as in v. 17; 21. 10, &c.
SOJOURN,] as in v. 17, 22; 43. 2, 5; 44. 8, &c.
16. OVERTAKE,] as in 39. 5; 52. 8, &c.
17. ESCAPED ONE,] as in 44. 14, 28, &c.
18. POURED OUT,] as in 44. 6; 2 Ch. 12. 7.
FURY,] *lit.* 'heat;' as in 4. 4; 6, 11; 7. 20.
EXECRATION,] as in 23. 10; 29. 18; 44. 12.
REPROACH,] as in 6.10; 15. 15; 20. 8; 23. 40.
19. REMNANT,] as in v. 15, &c.
EGYPT,] as if it were a place of safety.
TESTIFIED,] as in 6. 10; 11. 7; 32. 10, &c.
20. PRAY,] or 'judge yourself;' as in v. 2.
DECLARE,] *lit.* 'set forth;' as in 4. 5, &c.
22. DESIRED,] as in 6. 10; 9. 24; Ge. 34. 19.
SOJOURN,] as in v. 15, 17, &c.

XLIII. 1. FINISH TO SPEAK,] as in 26. 8, &c.
2. AZARIAH,] i.e. 'helped of Jah.'
JOHANAN,] i.e. 'Jah is gracious.'
PROUD MEN,] as in 19. 13; Ps. 86. 14; 119. 21.
3. MORNING,] as in 2 Ch. 32. 11.
REMOVE,] as in 24. 1; 27. 20; 1 Ch. 6. 15, &c.
5. DRIVEN,] as in 40. 12; 49. 5, &c.
6. INFANT,] as in 40. 7; 41. 16; Ge. 34. 27.
7. TAHPANHES,] as in 2. 16, &c.
9. HIDDEN,] as in v. 10; 13. 7; 18. 22, &c.
CLAY.] Original word not found again.
BRICK-KILN,] as in 2 Sa. 12. 31; Nah. 3. 14.
10. MY SERVANT,] though an unconscious one.
PAVILION.] Original word not found again.
12. KINDLED,] as in 11. 16; 17. 27; 21. 14.
COVERED HIMSELF,] as in Lev. 13. 45, &c.
13. STANDING-PILLARS,] as in 28. 18, &c.

XLIV. 1. WORD,] or communication.
MIGDOL,] i.e. a 'great place.'
TAHPANHES,] as in 2. 16, &c.
NOPH,] i.e. 'elevation.'
PATHROS,] as in v. 15; Eze. 29. 14; 30. 14.
2. WASTE,] *lit.* 'dried up' place.
3. PROVOKING,] as in v. 8; 7. 18; 11. 17, &c.
4. RISING EARLY,] as in 7. 13, 25; 11. 7, &c.
OTHER GODS,] as in v. 3, 8, 15; 1. 16, &c.
6. POURED OUT,] as in 42. 18; 2 Ch. 12. 7,
FURY,] *lit.* 'heat;' as in 4. 4; 6. 11; 7. 20,
7. CUT OFF,] as in v. 8. 11; 9. 21; 47. 4, &c.
INFANT,] as in 6. 11; 9. 21; 1 Sa. 15. 3, &c.
8. REVILING,] *lit.* 'lightness or disesteem.'
9. STREETS,] *lit.* 'out-places.'
10. HUMBLED,] as in Job 22. 9, &c.
SET,] *lit.* 'given;' as in v. 30; 1. 5, 9, &c.
11. SETTING MY FACE,] as in v. 12; 21. 10.
CUT OFF,] as in v. 7, &c.
12. SOJOURN,] as in v. 8, 14, 28, &c.
CONSUMED,] as in v. 18, 27, &c.
LEAST..GREATEST,] as in 8. 10; 42. 1, &c.
EXECRATION,] as in 23. 10; 29. 18; 42. 18, &c.
REPROACH,] as in v. 8; 6. 10; 15. 15; 20. 8.
13. SEEN AFTER,] as in 6. 15; 9. 25; 15. 3,&c.

14. ESCAPED,] as in v. 28; 42. 17; Ge. 14. 13.
LIFTING UP,] as in 22. 27; Est. 9. 3.
ESCAPING,] as in 50. 28; 51. 50.
15. REMAINING,] *lit.* 'standing; as in 28. 5.
PATHROS,] as in v. 1, &c.
17. QUEEN,] or 'workmanship;' as in v. 18.
LIBATIONS,] as in v. 19, 25; 7. 18; 10. 14, &c.
WELL,] *lit.* 'good.'
18. CEASED,] as in 41. 8; 51. 30, &c.
LACKED,] as in De. 2. 7; Neh. 9. 21, &c.
CONSUMED,] ended or completed.
19. HUSBANDS,] that is, apart from them.
CAKES,] as in 7. 18.
IDOLIZE,] 'make her a grievous thing.'
22. TO ACCEPT,] *lit.* 'lift up;' as in 10. 5, &c.
25. FULFILLED,] as in 15. 17; 31. 25; 41. 9.
QUEEN,] as in v. 17, 18, 19, &c.
ESTABLISH,] *lit.* 'raise up.'
26. SWORN,] *lit.* 'been sworn.'
PROCLAIMED,] as in Est. 6. 1; Isa. 43. 7, &c.
27. WATCHING,] as in 1. 12; 5. 6; Isa. 29. 20.
CONSUMPTION,] as in Ru. 2. 23; 1 Ch. 18. 20.
28. ESCAPED,] as in v. 14; 42. 17; Ge. 14. 13.
FEW,] *lit.* 'men of number.'
29. SIGN,] or 'token;' as in 10. 2; 32. 20, &c.
30. PHARAOH-HOPHRA,] grandson of Pharaoh-Necho.
SEEKING HIS LIFE,] *lit.* 'soul.'

XLV. 1. THE WORD,] or communication from God.
BARUCH,] i.e. 'bent of knee,' or 'blessed.'
ON A BOOK,] or 'scroll.'
FOURTH YEAR,] B.C. 607.
3. WO,] as in 4. 13, 31; 6. 4; 10. 19, &c.
SORROW,] as in 8. 18; 20. 18; 31. 13, &c.
PAIN,] as in 30. 15; 51. 8; Ex. 3. 7, &c.
WEARIED,] as in 51. 58; Jos. 28. 13, &c.
SIGHING,] as in Job 3. 24; 23. 2; 6. 6, &c.
REST,] as in 51. 59; Ge. 49. 15; Nu. 10. 33.
4. THROWING DOWN,] as in 24. 6; 42. 10, &c.
PLUCKING,] as in 12. 14.
5. SPOIL,] as in 21. 9; 38. 2; 39. 18, &c.

XLVI. 1. WORD,] as in 7. 1; 11. 1, &c.
2. EGYPT,] the ancient oppressor and stay of Israel.
PHARAOH-NECHO,] i.e. 'Pharaoh the lame' or smitten.
PHRAT,] i.e. 'fruitful, fructifier.'
FOURTH YEAR,] B.C. 607.
3. SET IN ARRAY,] or 'arrange;' as in 50. 14.
SHIELD,] *lit.* 'covering;' as in v. 9; Ge. 15.1·
BUCKLER,] *lit.* a 'thorn;' as in 1 Sa. 17. 7.
DRAW NIGH,] as in Ge. 19. 9; 27. 21, 26, &c.
4. GIRD,] or 'bind;' as in 1 K. 18. 44, &c.
STATION YOURSELVES,] or 'set yourselves up;' as in v. 14.
HELMETS,] i.e. 'high things;' as in 1 Sa. 17.5.
POLISH,] or 'brighten;' as in 2 Ch. 4. 16.
JAVELINS,] *lit.* things for 'casting;' as in Nu. 25. 7, &c.
COATS OF MAIL,] as in 51. 3.
5. DISMAYED,] *lit.* 'dreads;' as in Ge. 9. 2; 1 Sa. 2. 4; Job 31. 43.
BEATEN DOWN,] as in Job 4. 20; Isa. 24. 12; Mic. 1. 7.
6. SWIFT,] *lit.* 'light;' as in 2. 23; 2 Sa. 2. 18
ESCAPE,] or 'let go;' as in 32. 4; 34. 3, &c.
SIDE,] *lit.* 'hand;' as in v. 24, 26; 1. 9, &c.
7. FLOOD,] as in v. 8; Ge. 41. 1, 2, 3, 18, &c.

2 N

SHAKE THEMSELVES,] as in 25. 16.
9. BOAST YOURSELVES,] as in 25. 16.
CHARIOTS,] *lit.* things for 'riding' in.
HANDLING,] as in 2. 8; 49. 16; 50. 16, &c.
SHIELD,] *lit.* ' covering;' as in v. 3.
TREADING,] *or* ' directing;' as in 25. 30, &c.
10. LORD JEHOVAH,] as in 1. 6; 2. 19, &c.
ADVERSARIES,] *or* ' distressors;' as in 30.
16; 48. 5, &c.
WATERED,] as in Ps 36. 8; Prov. 7. 18, &c.
11. GILEAD,] i.e. ' heap of witness.'
BALM,] as in 8. 22; 51. 8; Ge. 37. 25, &c.
IN VAIN,] *lit.* ' for a vain thing;' as in 2.
30; 4. 30, &c.
MEDICINES,] *or* ' healing' things: as in 30.
13; Eze. 30. 21.
HEALING,] *lit.* a 'leading up;' as in 30. 13.
12. SHAME,] *lit.* ' lightness;' as in 13. 26, &c.
CRY,] as in 14. 2; Ps. 144. 14; Isa. 24. 11.
13. THE WORD,] or communication from
God.
14. DECLARE,] *lit.* ' set forward.'
MIGDOL,] i.e. a ' great place.'
NOPH,] i.e. an 'elevation.'
STATION THYSELF,] *or* ' set thyself up;' as
in v. 4.
PREPARE,] make ready, right, or set up.
15. BULLS,] as in 8. 16; 47. 3; 50. 11, &c.
16. NEIGHBOUR,] *lit.* ' friend;' as in 3. 1, 20.
BIRTH,] as in 22. 10; Ge. 11. 28; 12. 1, &c.
OPPRESSING,] as in 25. 38; 50. 16; Ps. 123.
4; Zeph. 3. 1.
17. CRIED,] *or* ' called.'
APPOINTED TIME,] as in 8. 7; Ge 1. 14, &c.
18. I LIVE,] as in 22. 24; 46. 18; Nu. 14. 21.
TABOR,] i.e. a ' broken place.'
CARMEL,] i.e. ' prepared place.'
19. NOPH,] i.e. ' elevation.'
20. HEIFER,] as in 48. 34; 50. 11; Ge. 15. 9.
RENDING.] Original word not found again.
21. HIRED ONES,] as in Ex. 12. 45; 22. 15.
STALL,] as in 1 Sa. 28. 24; Am. 6. 4; Mal.
4. 2.
CALAMITY,] as in 18. 17; 48. 16; 49. 8, &c.
INSPECTION,] as in 8. 12; 10. 15; 11. 23, &c.
23. CUT DOWN,] *or* ' cut off;' as in 8. 17, &c.
GRASSHOPPER,] *lit.* ' multiplier;' as in Ex.
10. 4, 12, 13, &c.
25. AMON OF NO,] where Jupiter Ham-
mon had a temple.
TRUSTING,] *or* ' leaning' as in 5. 17; 7. 8.
26. LIFE,] *lit.* ' soul.'
INHABITED,] *lit.* ' tabernacle;' as in 23. 6.
DAYS OF OLD,] *lit.* of ' former' time.
27. DISMAYED,] *or* ' brought down;' as in
1. 17; 10. 2, &c.
SAVING,] *lit.* ' easing;' as in 14. 8; 30. 10.
AT REST,] as in 30. 10; 47. 6, 7; Jos. 11. 23.
AT EASE,] as in 30. 10; 48. 11; Job 3. 18;
Prov. 1. 33.
DISTURBING,] as in 7. 33; 30. 10; Lev. 26. 6.
28. END,] *or* ' consummation.'
REPROVED,] instructed or chastised.
ACQUIT,] *or* ' declare innocent.'

XLVII. 1. THE WORD,] as in 7 1; 11. 1, &c.
PHILISTINES,] dwelling on the sea-shore.
GAZA,] i.e. a ' strong' place of the Philis-
tines.
2. WATERS,] a symbol of a multitude.
CRIED OUT] for help; as in 11. 11, 12, &c.

HOWLED,] as in 4. 8; 25. 34; 48. 20, 39, &c
3. STAMPING,] Original word not found a-
gain.
WHEELS,] *lit.* ' rolling things;' as in Ps.
83. 13, &c.
FEEBLENESS.] Original word not found a-
gain.
4. TYRE,] i.e. a ' rocky' place.
ZIDON,] a ' fishing' place.
ISLE OF CAPHTOR,] as in Ge. 10. 14; De.
2. 23.
5. BALDNESS,] as a sign of disgrace and
age.
GAZA,] as in v. 1.
CUT OFF,] *or* ' become silent.'
ASHKELON,] i.e. a ' weighing' place.
VALLEY,] *or* ' deep' place; as in 21. 13, &c.
CUT THYSELF,] as in 5. 7; 16. 6.
6. BE REMOVED,] *lit.* ' gathered;' as in 4. 5.
SHEATH,] as in 1 Sa. 17. 51; 2 Sa. 20. 8, &c.
REST,] *or* ' be quieted.'
CEASE,] *or* ' be dumb or silent.'
7. SEA-SHORE,] *or* ' haven of the sea;' as
in Ge. 49. 13, &c.
APPOINTED,] as in Ex. 21. 8; 2 Sa. 20. 5, &c.

XLVIII. 1. MOAB,] descendants of the son
of Lot.
NEBO,] i.e. ' prophet,' Mercury.
KIRIATHAIM,] i.e. ' two cities.'
HIGH TOWER,] as in 2 Sa. 22. 3; Ps. 9. 9, &c.
BROKEN DOWN,] *or* ' brought down;' as in
v. 20, 39, &c.
2. HESHBON,] i.e. a ' reckoning, thinking,
devising.'
MADMEN,] i.e. a ' place of dung.'
3. CRY] for help in distress.
HORONAIM,] i.e.' two holes,' i.e. caverns.
DESTRUCTION,] *lit.* ' breaking.'
4. LITTLE ONES,] as in 14. 3; 49. 20; 50. 45.
5. LUHITH,] i.e. ' tables, tablets.'
DESCENT,] as in Jos. 7. 5; 10. 11; 1 K. 7. 29
6. DELIVER YOURSELVES,] *or* ' escape;' as
in 51. 6, 45, &c.
NAKED THING,] as in 17. 6; Ps. 102. 17.
7. TRUSTING,] *lit.* ' leaning;' as in Ps. 118.
8, 9, &c.
REMOVAL,] as in v. 11; 28. 6; 29. 1, 4, &c.
8. VALLEY,] *lit.* ' deep' place; as in 21. 13.
PLAIN,] *lit.* ' straight' place; as in v. 21, &c.
9. WINGS,] *lit.* ' flower, blossom;' as in Ex.
28. 36, &c.
10. CURSED,] *lit.* ' bitter;' as in 11. 3, &c.
SLOTHFULLY,] *or* ' deceitfully;' as in Job
13. 7, &c.
11. YOUTH,] *lit.* ' youthful periods;' as in
2. 2; 3. 4, &c.
TASTE,] as in Ex. 16. 31; Nu. 11. 8, &c.
FRAGRANCE,] as in Ge. 8. 21; 27. 27, &c.
12. DAYS ARE COMING,] as in 7. 33; 9. 25.
WANDERERS,] as in 2. 20; Isa. 51. 14; 63. 1.
DASH IN PIECES,] as in 13. 14; 51. 20, &c.
13. CHEMOSH,] their great national deity.
CONFIDENCE,] *or* ' thing 'leant' on; as in
2. 37, &c.
15. CHOICE,] as in 22. 7; Ge. 23. 6, &c.
YOUNG,] *or* ' choice' ones; as in 6. 11, &c.
SLAUGHTER,] as in 50. 27; Ge. 43. 16, &c.
17. BEMOAN,] as in 49. 30; 50. 8; Ps. 11. 1.
ROD,] as in 1. 11; Ge. 30. 37, 38, 39, 41, &c
18. DIBON,] i.e. ' pining;' as in Nu. 21. 30.

FENCED PLACES,] as in 1. 18; 4. 5; 5. 17, &c.
19. WATCH,] as in Nah. 2. 1.
AROER,] i.e. a 'naked thing;' as in De. 2. 36.
20. BROKEN,] or 'brought down;' as in v.
1, 39, &c.
ARNON,] i.e. 'rushing, roaring, sounding.'
21. PLAIN,] lit. 'straight place;' as in v. 8.
HOLON,] i. e. 'sandy,' or 'delay.'
JAHAZAH,] i.e. 'he halves.'
MEPHAATH,] i.e. 'beauty.'
22. DIBON,] as in v. 18, &c.
NEBO,] as in v. 1, &c.
BETH- DIBLATHAIM,] i.e. 'house of two
cakes.'
KIRATHAIM,] i.e. 'two cities.'
23. BETH-GAMUL,] i.e. 'house of recompense.'
BETH-MEON,] i.e. 'house of habitation.'
24. KERIOTH,] i.e. 'cities;' as in v. 41.
BOZRAH,] i e. a 'fold' for flocks.
25. HORN,] a symbol of pride and power.
26. DECLARE HIM DRUNK,] or 'merry;' as
in 51. 39, 57.
MADE HIMSELF GREAT,] or 'done greatly.'
STRICKEN,] as in 31. 19; Nu. 24. 10, &c.
VOMIT,] as in Isa. 19. 14; 28. 8.
27. BEMOAN THYSELF,] as in 31. 18; Isa.
24. 20.
28. DWELL,] lit. 'tabernacle.'
MAKING A NEST.] as in Ps. 104. 17, &c.
PITS,] as in v. 43, 44; 2 Sa. 17. 9, &c.
29. ARROGANCE,] lit. 'gayness, gaiety;' as
in 12. 5, &c.
PROUD,] lit. 'gay;' as in Job 40. 11, 12, &c.
30. WRATH,] lit. a 'passing over;' as in 7. 29.
NOT RIGHT,] or 'so.'
DEVICES,] or 'parts;' as in 50. 36, &c.
31. HOWL,] as in v. 20, 39; 4. 18; 25. 34, &c.
KIR-HERES,] i.e. 'city of clay.'
MOURN,] or 'meditate;' as in Jos. 1. 8, &c.
32. JAZER,] i.e. 'he helps.'
SIBMAH,] i.e. 'cold, or sweet scent.'
BRANCHES,] as in 5. 10; Jer. 18. 5.
33. REMOVED,] lit. 'gathered;' as in 8. 2.
GLADNESS,] lit. 'leaping;' as in Job 3. 22.
FRUITFUL FIELD,] in Heb. 'Carmel.'
WINE- PRESSES,] as in Nu. 18. 27, 30, &c.
SHOUTING,] as in 25. 30; 51. 14; Isa. 16. 9.
34. HESHBON,] i.e. 'reckoning, devising,
thinking.'
ZOAR,] i.e. a 'little' one.
HORONAIM,] i.e. 'two holes' or caverns.
NIMRIM,] as in Isa. 15. 6.
35. CAUSED TO CEASE,] as in v. 33: 7. 34, &c.
36. PIPES,] lit. 'pierced' things, with holes.
KIR-HERES,] as in v. 31.
ABUNDANCE,] or 'superfluity;' as in Isa.
15. 7.
37. BALD,] lit. 'baldness;' as in 47. 5, &c.
SACKCLOTH,] lit. 'sacks.'
38. ROOFS,] as in 19. 13; 32. 39; Ex. 30. 3.
39. BROKEN,] or 'brought down;' as in v.
1, 20, &c.
NECK,] as in 2. 27; 7. 26; 17. 23, &c.
TERROR,] or 'downfall;' as in 17. 17, &c.
40. FLY,] as in 49. 22; De. 28. 49; Ps. 18. 10.
41. CAPTURED,] as in v. 1; 38. 28; 50. 2, &c.
DISTRESSED,] as in 49. 22.
42. EXERTED HIMSELF,] or 'did greatly.'
43. FEAR,] as in v. 44; 30. 5; 49. 7, &c.
JIN,] as in v. 44; 18. 22; Ex. 39. 3, &c.

44. INSPECTION,] as in 8. 12; 10. 15; 11. 23.
45. SHADOW,] as in Ge. 19. 8; Nu. 14. 9, &c.
HESHBON,] i.e. 'reckoning.'
POWERLESS,] lit. 'from power.'
SIHON,] i.e. 'sweeping away.'
46. SHAON,] i.e. 'wasting, desolation,
noise.'
47. HITHERTO.] This clause seems a marginal note by the scribes.

XLIX. 1. AMMON,] younger son of Lot.
HEIR,] that is, 'possessor;' as in v. 2, &c.
MALCAM,] i.e. 'their king' and god.
GAD,] i.e. 'troop, or fortune.'
2. SOUNDED,] lit. 'caused to be heard.'
RABBAH,] i.e. 'numerous,' or 'great.'
HEAP,] lit. a 'raised up' thing; as in 30. 18
3. HESHBON,] i.e. 'reckoning, device.'
AI,] i.e. a 'heap.'
SACKCLOTH,] lit. 'sacks;' as in 4. 8; 6. 26.
LAMENT,] lit. 'smite or beat' the breast.
4. BOAST THYSELF,] as in 4, 2; 9. 23, 24, &c.
VALLEYS,] lit. 'deep' places; as in 21. 13.
TRUSTING,] lit. 'leaning.'
TREASURES,] lit. 'things gathered or
bound' together.
5. WANDERING,] lit. 'noding, moving.'
7. EDOM,] i.e. 'red;' the elder brother of
Jacob.
TEMAN,] i.e. the 'south' country.
COUNSEL,] lit. a 'hard, fixed plan.'
VANISHED,] lit. 'stretched out.'
8. TURN] the face; as in Eze. 9. 2.
DEDAN,] i.e. 'going softly;' as in 25. 23, &c.
9. GATHERERS,] as in 6. 9; Obad. 5.
LEAVE,] lit. 'cause or suffer to leave or be
left.'
DESTROYED,] lit. 'marred.'
10. MADE BARE,] as in 13. 26; Ps. 29. 9, &c.
TO BE HIDDEN,] as in 1 K. 22. 25; 2. K. 7. 12.
11. LEAVE,] or 'forsake, abandon.'
KEEP ALIVE,] or 'give life;'as in Ge. 12. 12
TRUST,] lit. 'lean.'
12. ACQUITTED,] or 'set free.'
13. SWORN,] lit. 'been sworn.'
WASTE,] lit. 'dried up' place; as in 36. 30.
REVILING,] lit. 'lightness, disesteem;' as
in 24. 9, &c.
BOZRAH,] i.e. a 'fold.'
14. REPORT,] lit. 'hearing;' as in v. 23.
AMBASSADOR,] lit. a 'hinge,' for both
parties.
15. LITTLE,] as in 8. 10; 42. 1, 8; 44. 12, &c.
16. TERRIBLENESS.] Original word not
found again.
LIFTED THEE UP,] with pride and conceit.
CLEFTS OF THE ROCK,] as in Song 2. 14;
Obad. 3.
NEST,] lit. 'prepared or set-up' place; as
in Ge. 6. 14, &c.
17. PLAGUES,] lit. 'smitings;' as in 6. 7, &c
18. OVERTHROW,] as in 50. 14; De. 29. 23.
NEIGHBOURS,] lit. 'tabernaclers;' as in
v. 10.
19. RISING,] lit. 'gayness;' as in 12. 5, &c.
CAUSE TO REST,] as in 50. 34, 44; De. 28. 65.
CHOSEN,] or 'choice;' as in 50. 44, &c.
COVERETH,] as in 50. 19.
20. COUNSEL,] lit. 'hard or fixed' thing.
DEVICES,] or 'thoughts;' as in 4. 14; 6. 19
TEMAN,] lit. the 'south;' as in Ex. 26. 18.

DRAG OUT,] as in 15. 3; 22. 19; 50. 45.
HABITATION,] *lit.* 'comely place;' as in
v. 19, &c.
21. FALL,] *lit.* 'falling;' as in 51. 49, &c.
SEA OF SUPH,] i.e. the 'extremity' of
Egypt.
22. FLIETH,] as in 48. 40; De. 28. 49; Ps.
18. 10.
BOZRAH,] i.e. a 'fold *or* defence.'
DISTRESSED,] as in 48. 41.
23. DAMASCUS,] at the foot of Anti-lib-
anus.
HAMATH,] i.e. a 'walled' city.
ARPAD,] i.e. a 'support.'
24. FEEBLE,] as in 6. 24; 50. 43; Ex. 4. 26.
FEAR.] Original word not found again.
DISTRESS,] *lit.* 'straitness;' as in 4. 31, &c.
PANGS,] *lit,* 'cords, ropes;' as in 13. 21, &c.
TRAVAILING,] *lit.* 'yielding, bearing.'
25. LEFT,] forsaken, or abandoned.
26. YOUNG MEN,] *lit.* 'choice ones;' as in 6.
11; 9. 21, &c.
CUT OFF,] *or* 'silent, dumb;' as in 8. 14, &c.
27. PALACES,] *lit.* 'high places.'
BEN-HADAD,] i.e. 'son of shouting.'
28. KEDAR,] i.e. 'black;' as in Ge. 25. 13.
HAZOR,] i.e. a 'surrounded, enclosed'
place.
EAST,] *or* of 'Kedem.'
29. TENTS,] as in 4. 20; 6. 3; 10. 20, &c.
CURTAINS,] as in 4. 20; 10. 20; Ex. 26. 1.
FEAR,] as in 6. 25; 30. 2, 4, 10; 46. 5, &c.
30. BEMOAN,] *lit,* 'nod or move;' as in 48.
17; 50. 8, &c.
DEVICE,] *lit.* 'thought;' as in 18. 11.
31. AT REST,] as in 1 Ch. 4. 40; Job 16. 12.
TWO-LEAVED DOORS,] as in 36. 23; De. 3. 5.
32. CAMELS,] as in v. 29; Ge. 12. 16; 24. 10.
CATTLE,] *or* 'acquisitions;' as in 9. 10, &c.
CUT OFF,] as in 9. 26; 25. 23.
33. DRAGONS,] *lit.* 'extended' animals; as
in 9. 11, &c.
34. THE WORD,] as in 7. 1; 11. 1, &c.
ELAM,] i.e. 'hidden' country.
ZEDEKIAH,] i.e. 'rightness of Jah.'
35. BEGINNING OF THEIR MIGHT.]Compare
Ge. 49. 3; Ps. 78. 51; 105. 36.
36. FOUR WINDS,] *or* 'spirits.'
OUTCASTS,] *lit.* 'driven away' ones; as in
30. 17, &c.
37. AFFRIGHTED,] *or* 'brought down;' as
in 1. 17, &c.
SEEKING THEIR LIFE,] *lit.* 'soul.'
CONSUMED,] *lit.* 'finished, ended.'
38. SET MY THRONE,] as in 1. 15; 43. 10, &c.
CAPTIVITY,] as in 29. 14; Nu. 21. 29, &c.

L. 1. THE WORD,] as in 7. 1; 11. 1, &c.
BABYLON,] *lit.* 'Babel;' i.e. 'confusion.'
CHALDEANS,] i.e. 'kind ones.'
2. DECLARE,] *lit.* 'set forth or forward.'
SOUND,] *lit.* 'cause to hear *or* be heard.'
BEL,] i.e. 'lord, master, possessor.'
BROKEN,] *or* 'brought down;' as in v. 36.
GRIEVOUS THINGS,] as in 1 Sa. 31. 9, &c.
IDOLS,] *lit.* 'dungy' things; as in Lev. 26. 30.
3. MOVED,] as in 4. 1; 15. 5; 16. 5; 22. 10.
4. SEEK,] as in 4. 30; 26. 21; 45. 5, &c.
5. ZION,] i.e. the 'sunny' place.
JOINED, as in Ge. 29. 34; Nu. 18. 2, 4, &c.
6. SHEPHERDS,] *lit.* 'feeders;' or 'friends.'

CROUCHING-PLACE,] as in Prov. 24. 15, &c.
7. ADVERSARIES,] *lit.* 'distressors;' as in
30. 16; 46. 10, &c.
HABITATION,] *lit.* 'comely' place; as in v.
19; 44. 45.
8. MOVE,] as in v. 3.
9. STIRRING UP,] as in 51. 1; Isa. 13. 17, &c.
SKILFUL,] *lit.* one 'acting wisely'; as in 1
Sa. 18. 14, &c.
10. SPOIL,] as in 21. 9; 38. 2; 39. 18; 45. 5.
SATISFIED,] with their plunder.
11. REJOICEST,] as in 31. 13; 41. 13; 50. 11.
BULLS,] *lit.* 'mighty ones;' as in 8. 16, &c.
12. CONFOUNDED,] as in 15. 9; Job 6. 20, &c.
13. WRATH,] as in 10. 10; 21. 5; 32. 37, &c.
PLAGUES,] *lit.* 'smitings;' as in 6. 7; 10. 19.
14. SET YOURSELVES IN ARRAY,] as in 46. 3;
Job 33. 5.
15. SHOUT,] as in Jos. 6. 10, 16; Ps. 47. 1, &c.
16. CUT OFF,] as in 6. 6; Jos. 9. 6, 11, &c.
OPPRESSING,] as in 25. 38; 46. 16, &c.
17. SCATTERED FLOCK,] exposed to danger
on every hand.
ASSHUR,] i.e. a 'straight, happy' place.
18. SEEING AFTER,] as in 11. 22; 23. 2, &c.
19. HABITATION,] *lit.* 'comely' place; as in
v. 7, 44, 45, &c.
CARMEL,] i.e. a 'prepared' fertile place.
BASHAN,] i.e. the 'fat' place.
GILEAD,] i.e. 'heap of witness.'
20. SOUGHT,] as in Est. 2. 23; Eze. 26. 21.
PROPITIOUS,] *lit.* 'send away;' as in 5. 1.
LEAVE,] that is, suffer to remain.
21. MERATHAIM,] i.e. 'two rebellions,'
doubly rebellious.
PEKOD,] i.e. 'inspection.'
WASTE,] *lit.* 'dry up;' as in v. 27; 2. 12, &c.
TO DEVOTE,] *lit.* 'make flat;' as in De. 3. 6.
22. DESTRUCTION,] *lit.* 'breach *or* breaking.'
23. HAMMER,] as in 23. 29; Isa. 41. 7.
24. LAID A SNARE,] as in Ps. 149. 1.
STIRRED THYSELF UP,] as in De. 2. 5, 9, 19.
25. TREASURY,] *or* 'treasure;' as in v. 37.
WEAPONS,] *lit.* 'vessels;' as in 14. 3; 18. 4.
26. STORE HOUSES.] Original word not found
again.
RAIN,] as in Ps. 68. 4; Isa. 57. 14; 62. 10, &c.
27. SLAY,] as in v. 21.
28. FUGITIVES,] *or* 'fleers;' as in 48. 19, &c.
TEMPLE,] which had been destroyed.
29. SUMMON,] *lit.* 'cause to hear *or* be heard.'
ARCHERS,] as in Job 16. 13, &c.
30. YOUNG MEN,] *lit.* 'choice ones.'
CUT OFF,] *lit.* 'dumb or silent.'
31. PRIDE,] as in v. 32; 49. 16; De. 17. 12.
32. STUMBLED,] as in 6. 21; 46. 6, 12, &c.
33. OPPRESSED,] as in De. 28. 29, 33, &c.
34. REDEEMER,] as in Ge. 48. 16; Lev. 25. 25.
GIVEN TROUBLE,] as in 1 Sa. 28. 15; Job 6. 9.
35. SWORD,] *lit.* a 'wasting' weapon.
36. PRINCES,] *lit.* 'staves;' as in 48. 30, &c.
BROKEN DOWN,] *or* 'brought down;' as
in v. 2, &c.
37. RABBLE,] *lit.* 'mixture;' as in 25. 20, 24.
38. IDOLS,] *lit.* 'fearful things;' as in Ge.
15. 12; Ex. 15. 6, &c.
BOAST THEMSELVES,] as in 4. 2; 9. 23, &c.
39. TSIIM..IJIM,] inhabitants of 'dry and
island' places.
40. OVERTHROWN,] as in 49. 18; De. 29. 23.
41. SIDES,] *lit.* 'thighs;' as in 6. 22; 25. 32.

42. HALBERT,] as in 6. 23; Jos. 8. 18, 26, &c.
43. REPORT,] *lit.* 'hearing;' as in 37. 5, &c.
44. HABITATION,] *or* 'comely place of strength.'
CAUSE TO REST,] as in v. 34, &c.
CHOSEN,] *or* 'choice;' as in 49. 19; Ex. 14. 7.
CONVENE,] as in 49. 19; Job 9. 19.
45. DEVICES,] *or* 'thoughts;' as in 4 14, &c.
DRAG OUT,] as in 49. 20; 2 Sa. 17. 13.
46. CAPTURED,] *or* 'caught;' as in v. 24, &c.

LI. 1. STIRRING UP,] as in 50. 9; Isa. 13. 17.
LEB,] i.e. the 'heart.'
MY WITHSTANDERS,] those 'rising up' against me.
2. FANNERS,] *or* 'strangers;' as in v. 51, &c.
EMPTY,] as in 19. 7; Nah. 2. 2, &c.
3. TREAD,] *or* 'direct;' as in 48. 33; Ps. 7. 12.
COAT OF MAIL,] as in 46. 4.
DEVOTE,] *lit.* 'make flat;' as in 50. 26, &c.
4. PIERCED THROUGH,] as in 37. 10; La. 4. 9.
5. FORSAKEN,] *or* a 'widower.'
GUILT,] as in Ge. 26. 10; Lev. 5. 6, 7, &c.
6. DELIVER,] *or* 'let escape;' as in v. 45, &c.
CUT OFF,] *or* 'dumb or silent;' as in 8. 14.
7. MAKING DRUNK,] *or* 'merry;' as in 2 Sa.
11. 13, &c.
BOAST THEMSELVES,] as in 9. 24; 50. 38, &c.
8. BALM,] as in 8. 22; 46. 11; Ge. 37. 25, &c.
9. COME,] *or* 'touched;' as in 4. 10, 18, &c.
CLOUDS,] as in De. 33. 26; 2 Sa. 22. 12, &c.
10. RIGHTEOUSNESSES,] *or* 'right acts.'
11. CLEANSE,] as in 4. 11.
SHIELDS,] as in 2 Sa. 8. 7; 2 K. 11. 10, &c.
DEVICE,] as in 11. 15; 23. 20; 30. 24, &c.
12. WATCH,] as in Ge. 40. 3, 4, 7; 41. 10, &c.
DEVISED,] as in 4. 28; Ge. 11. 6; 19. 19, &c.
13. DWELLER,] *lit.* 'tabernacler.'
MEASURE,] *lit.* 'cubit;' as in 52. 21, &c.
14. CANKERWORM,] *lit.* 'green thing;' as in v. 27, &c.
SHOUTING,] as in 25. 30; 48. 33, &c.
15. WORLD,] *lit.* 'fruitbearing or habitable.'
16. VAPOURS,] *lit.* things 'lifted up;' as in 10. 13, &c.
17. BY KNOWLEDGE,] *lit.* 'from knowledge.'
BY A GRAVEN IMAGE,] *lit.* 'from' one.
18. ERRORS,] *lit.* 'goings astray;' as in 10. 15.
19. PORTION,] *lit.* 'smooth' thing; as in 10. 16, &c.
ROD,] *or* 'sceptre;' as in 10. 16, &c.
20. AXE,] *lit.* a 'breaker in pieces;' as in Eze. 9. 2.
DESTROYED,] *lit.* 'marred;' as in 36. 29, &c.
21. BROKEN IN PIECES,] as in v. 21, 22, &c.
22. YOUNG,] as in 1. 6, 7; Ge. 14. 24, &c.
23. TEAM,] *or* 'yoke, pair' of oxen; as in Ge. 19. 3, &c.
GOVERNORS,] as in v. 28, 57; 1 K. 10. 15. &c.
PREFECTS,] as in v. 28. 57; Ezra 9. 2, &c.
24. RECOMPENSED,] as in 56; 16. 18, &c.
25. DESTROYING,] *lit.* 'marring.'
26. CORNERS,] *lit.* 'face, front;' as in 31. 38.
27. BLOW,] *lit.* 'strike;' as in 4. 5; 6. 1, &c.
SANCTIFY,] *lit.* 'separate, set apart.'
ARARAT,] in 'the middle of Armenia.'
MINNI,] a tract in Armenia.
ASHKENAZ,] as in Ge. 10. 3. &c.
28. SANCTIFY,] *lit.* 'set apart,' as in v 27.
GOVERNORS AND PREFECTS,] as in v. 23.
29. PURPOSES,] *or* 'thoughts;' as in 4. 4. &c.

30. TO FIGHT,] *lit.* 'to be fought with.'
31. RUNNER,] as in 1 Sa. 20. 36; 22. 17, &c.
ANNOUNCER,] *lit.* 'setter forward.'
32. CAPTURED,] as in 48. 41; 50. 24, 46, &c.
33. THRESHING,] *lit.* 'treading.'
34. CRUSHED,] as in Ex. 14. 24; 23. 27, &c.
SET UP,] as in Ge. 30. 38; 33. 15; 43. 9, &c.
BELLY.] Original word not found again.
35. WRONG,] *or* 'violence;' as in v. 46, &c.
36. PLEADING,] as in Isa. 45. 7.
CAUSE,] *or* 'plea;' as in 11. 20; 15. 10, &c.
37. HEAPS,] as in v. 42. 55; 5. 22; 9. 11, &c.
HABITATION,] as in 9. 11; 10. 22; 25. 30, &c.
38. SHAKEN THEMSELVES,] as in Neh. 5. 13.
39. TO DRINK,] *or* 'be merry;' as in v. 57.
40 LAMBS,] as in De. 32. 14; 1 Sa. 15. 9, &c.
41. SHESHACH,] a poetical name of Babel.
42. BILLOWS,] *or* 'heaps;' as in v. 37, &c.
44. BEL,] i.e. 'lord, master.'
FLOW,] *or* 'bright;' as in 31. 12, &c.
45. DELIVER,] as in v. 6, &c.
46. BE TENDER,] as in De. 20. 3; Isa. 7. 4.
RULER,] as in 22. 30; 30. 21; 33. 26; 51. 46.
47. DAYS ARE COMING,] as in 7. 32; 9. 25.
48. CRIED ALOUD,] as in 31. 12; 1 Ch. 16. 33.
49. PIERCED,] as in v. 4, 47, 52, &c.
50. ESCAPED,] *lit.* 'let go;' as in 44. 14, &c.
51. ASHAMED,] as in 2. 36; 9. 19; 12. 13, &c.
SANCTUARIES,] *lit.* 'set apart places.'
52. GROAN,] as in Eze. 26. 15.
53. FENCETH,] as in Isa. 22. 10.
54. CRY] of distress; as in 18. 22; 20. 16, &c.
55. SPOILING,] as in v. 48. 53, 56, &c.
BILLOWS,] *lit.* 'heaps;' as in v. 37. 42, &c.
56. BROKEN,] *or* 'brought down;' as in Job 7. 14.
GOD,] *lit.* 'mighty one.'
57. TO DRINK,] *or* 'be merry;' as in v. 39.
GOVERNORS . . PREFECTS,] as in v. 23, 28, &c.
58. WALL,] *lit.* 'walls.'
MADE BARE,] *lit.* 'to be bare is made bare.'
WEARY,] as in v. 64; 2. 24, &c.
59. COMMANDED,] *or* 'charged.'
QUIET PRINCE,] *lit.* prince of 'rest.'
60. ON ONE BOOK,] *or* 'scroll.'
61. READ,] *lit.* 'called;' as in 2. 2; 3. 4, 12.
62. TO CUT IT OFF,] as in 9. 21; 44. 7, 8, &c.
63. BIND,] as in Ge. 38. 28; De. 6. 8, &c.
64. SINK,] as in Nu. 11, 2; Amos 9. 5.
WEARY,] as in v. 58; 2. 24, &c.
HITHERTO.] This last clause appears to be added by the writer of the next chapter, which contains a final account and recapitulation of the carrying away to Babylon of the treasures of the temple and the remnant of the people. See 2 K. xxiv. xxv.

LII. 1. ZEDEKIAH,] son of the good king Josiah.
2. JEHOIAKIM,] his elder brother.
3. REBEL,] as in Ge. 14. 4; Nu. 14. 9, &c.
4. TENTH MONTH,] that is, Thammuz.
FORTIFICATION,] as in 2 K. 25. 1; Eze. 4. 2.
5. COMETH INTO SIEGE,] as in 2 K. 24. 10.
6. SEVERE,] *or* 'strong;' as in Ge. 41. 56.
7. BROKEN,] *or* 'cleft up;' as in 2 K. 25. 4.
PLAIN,] as in v. 8; 2. 6; 5. 6; 17. 6; 39. 4.
8. SCATTERED,] as in 10. 21; 40. 15, &c.
9. CAPTURE,] *or* 'catch.'
HAMATH,] i.e. a 'walled' city.
JUDGMENTS,] as a rebel against his king.

10. SLAUGHTERETH,] as in 39. 6; 41. 7, &c.
11. BLINDED,] as in 39. 7; Ex. 23. 8, &c.
INSPECTION,] as in 8. 12; 10. 15; 11. 23, &c.
12. FIFTH MONTH,] that is, Shebat.
EXECUTIONERS,] or 'cooks;' as in v. 14, 15.
13. BURNETH,] as in 34. 5; 38. 23; 43. 13, &c.
14. BROKEN DOWN,] as in 39. 8; Ex. 34. 13.
15. POOR,] lit. 'lean, thin;' as in v. 16, &c.
16. VINE-DRESSERS,] as in 2 K. 25. 12, &c.
HUSBANDMEN,] as in 14. 4; 31. 24, &c.
17. PILLARS OF BRASS,] as in 1 K. 7. 15, &c.
SEA OF BRASS,] as in 2 K. 25. 13, &c.
18. POTS,] as in v. 19; 1. 13; Ex. 16. 2, &c.
19. BASINS,] as in Ex. 12. 12; 2 Sa. 17. 28.
20. BRAZEN OXEN,] as in 2 K. 16. 17, &c.
WEIGHING,] as in Ge. 24. 22; 43. 21, &c.
21. CUBITS,] of eighteen inches each.
HOLLOW,] as in Ex. 27. 8; 38. 7; Job 11. 12.
22. CHAPITER,] as in 1 K. 7. 16, 17, 18, &c.
POMEGRANATES,] as in v. 23; Ex. 28. 33, &c.
23. NET-WORK,] as in v. 22; 1 K. 7. 17, &c.

24. HEAD-PRIEST,] as in 2 K. 25. 18, &c.
SECOND PRIEST,] as in 2 K. 25. 18.
THRESHOLD,] lit. 'end, extremity.'
25. EUNUCH,] i.e. a 'root,' and nothing more.
SEEING THE KING'S FACE,] as in 2 K. 25. 19.
MUSTERETH,] as in 2 K. 25. 19.
27. GROUND,] to the city of Babylon.
28. REMOVED,] from Jerusalem to Babel.
SEVENTH YEAR] of Nebuchadnezzar's reign.
29. SOULS,] that is, 'persons.'
31. JEHOIACHIN,] i.e. 'Jah prepares or sets up.'
TWELFTH MONTH.] that is, Elul.
RESTRAINT,] as in 37. 4.
32. KINGS,] captives like himself.
33. CHANGED,] as in 1 Sa. 21. 13; Est. 2. 9.
34. ALLOWANCE,] as in 40. 5; 2 K. 25. 30, &c.
MATTER OF A DAY,] as in Ex. 5. 13, 19; 16. 4, &c.

LAMENTATIONS

THIS BOOK is anonymous, like many others of the writings contained in the Sacred Scriptures, but its composition is generally attributed to the 'weeping' prophet JERE-MIAH. As in OBADIAH the only enemy mentioned is EDOM (4. 21), though there is an incidental allusion to Egypt and Asshur in 5. 6. The Jews call it *Aikha*, i.e. 'How,' from its initial word. The Laments are five-fold, and each is arranged artificially, according to the letters of the alphabet, like Psalm cxix. xxv. xxxiv. xxxvii. cxi. cxii. cxlv. Prov. xxxi.

Chap. I. II. and IV. consist each of 22 verses, arranged alphabetically. Chap. III. contains 66 verses, each letter being repeated thrice. Chap. V. has 22 verses, but not artificially arranged.

The last chapter of 'Jeremiah' seems originally to have been the preface of the 'Lamentations.'

I. 1. HOW.] A particle of astonishment and enquiry.
ALONE,] *or* 'apart;' as in 3. 28, &c.
A WIDOW,] *lit.* a 'dumb, silent' one; as in 5. 3, &c.
PRINCESS,] one possessing principality.
PROVINCES,] *lit.* 'places of judgment;' as in 1 K. 20. 14, &c.
2. SORE,] *lit.* 'to weep she weepeth.'
DEALT TREACHEROUSLY,] *lit.* 'covered' themselves as with a 'garment.'
3. BECAUSE OF,] *lit.* 'from.'
REST,] *or* a 'place of rest;' as in Ge. 8. 9.
THE STRAITS,] as in Ps. 116. 3; 118. 5.
4. APPOINTED TIME,] *or* 'thing,' such as festivals, &c.
5. ADVERSARIES,] *lit.* 'distressors;' as in v. 7, 10, 17; 2. 4, &c.
TRANSGRESSIONS,] *lit.* 'steps;' as in v. 14.
6. HONOUR,] beauty or majesty; as in Lev. 23. 40, &c.
PASTURE,] *or* a 'place of feeding;' as in Ge. 47. 4, &c.
7. MOURNING,] as in 3. 19; Isa. 58. 7.
CESSATIONS.] Original word is not found again.
8. IMPURE.] See v. 17.
ESTEEMED HER LIGHTLY,] *or* 'vilely.'
9. WONDERFULLY,] *lit.* 'wonders;' as in Ex. 15. 11, &c.
EXERTED HIMSELF,] *or* 'done greatly.'
10. SANCTUARY,] *or* 'set-apart place.'
ASSEMBLY,] as in De. 23. 3, &c.
11. FOOD,] *lit.* 'eating.'
REFRESH THE BODY,] *lit.* 'bring back the soul.'
LIGHTLY ESTEEMED,] as in De. 21. 20, &c.
12. PAIN,] as in v. 18; Ex. 3. 7; 2 Ch. 6. 29.
ROLLING,] *or* 'doing.'
13. FROM ABOVE,] *lit.* 'from on high.'
SUBDUETH,] *or* 'goeth down into it.'

NET,] as in Ex. 27. 4, 5; 38. 4; Job 18. 8, &c.
SICK,] as in 5. 17; Lev. 15. 33; 20. 18, &c.
14. BOUND.] Sept. Syr. Vulg. 'watched;' Targ. 'made heavy.'
WRAPPED TOGETHER.] Comp. Job 40. 17.
15. TRODDEN DOWN,] as in Ps. 119. 118.
DESTROY,] *lit.* 'shiver.'
16. REFRESHING,] *lit.* 'bringing back;' as in Ge. 20. 7, &c.
17. NEIGHBOURS,] *lit.* 'those around about him.'
IMPURE,] as in Lev. 12. 2, 5; 15. 19, 20, &c.
18. PROVOKED,] *or* 'made bitter;' as in v. 20, &c.
19. LOVERS,] as in Jer. 22. 20, 22; 30 14, &c.
DECEIVED,] *or* 'cast down.'
EXPIRED,] *or* 'been heaped together.'
GAVE BACK] to God their maker.
20. DISTRESS,] *lit.* 'there has been straitness.'
TROUBLED,] as in 2. 11; Job 16. 16.
BEREAVED,] as in Ge. 31, 33; 42. 36, &c.
21. SIGHED,] as in v. 4, 11; Eze. 9. 4, &c.
CALAMITY,] *lit.* 'evil.'
22. DONE,] as in 2. 20; 3. 51, &c
SICK,] as in Isa. 1. 5; Jer. 8. 18.

II. 1. CLOUD,] *lit.* 'wrap round.'
BEAUTY,] *lit.* 'fairness;' as in Ex. 28. 2, &c.
FOOTSTOOL,] as in 1 Ch. 28. 2; Ps. 99. 5, &c.
2. SWALLOWED UP,] as in v. 5, 17, &c.
PLEASANT,] *or* 'comely' places; as in Ps. 23. 2, &c.
POLLUTED,] *lit.* 'pierced;' as in Ge. 49. 4.
3. CUT OFF,] as in 1 Sa. 2. 31; Zech. 11. 10.
FLAMING FIRE,] as in Ps. 105. 32; Isa. 4. 5.
4. TRODDEN HIS BOW,] as in 3. 12; Ps. 7. 12.
DESIRABLE ONES,] as in 1. 10, 11; 1 K. 20. 6.
5. SWALLOWED UP,] as in v. 2, 17, &c.
PALACES,] *or* 'high places;' as in v. 7, &c.
DESTROYED,] *lit.* 'marred;' as in v. 6, &c.
6. SHAKETH,] *lit.* 'violateth;' or 'useth violently.'
TABERNACLE,] booth or fence.
APPOINTED PLACE,] *or* 'thing,' as in v. 7.
DESPISETH,] as in De. 32. 19; Prov. 15. 15.
7. CAST OFF,] as in 3. 17, 31; Ps. 43. 2, &c
REJECTED,] as in Ps. 89. 39.
SHUT UP,] *lit.* 'made secure;' as in Lev 13. 4, &c.
NOISE,] *lit.* 'voice.'
APPOINTMENT,] as in v. 6, 22; 1. 4, 15, &c.
8. DEVISED,] *or* 'thought;' as in Ge. 15. 6.
DESTROY,] *or* 'mar;' as in De. 10. 10, &c.
TURNED,] *lit.* 'turned back;' as in v. 3, &c.
DESTROYING,] *lit.* 'swallowing up.'
9. SUNK,] as in 1 Sa. 17. 49; Ps. 9. 15, &c.
BARS,] as in Ex. 26. 26, 27, 28, 29; 35. 11.
LAW,] *lit.* 'direction.'
VISION,] as in 1 Sa. 3. 1; 1 Ch. 17. 15, &c.
10. KEEP SILENT,] *lit.* 'dumb;' as in v. 18.
SACKCLOTH,] *lit.* 'sacks.'
11. CONSUMED,] as in 3. 22; 4. 17, &c.
TROUBLED,] as in 1. 20; Job 16. 16.

LIVER,] *lit.* 'heaviness;' as in Ex. 29. 13.
SUCKLING,] as in 4. 4; Nu. 11. 12, &c.
12. CORN AND WINE,] as in Ge. 27. 28, &c.
POURING,] *or* 'sheding itself out.'
13. TESTIFY,] as in Ge. 43. 3: Ex. 19. 23, &c.
EQUAL,] as in Isa. 46. 5.
14. FALSE,] *lit.* 'empty' thing.
INSIPID THING,] as in Job 6. 6; Eze. 13.
10, 11, 14, 15; 22. 28.
INIQUITY,] *or* 'punishment.'
BURDENS,] as in Ge. 43. 34; Jud. 20. 38, &c.
15. CLAPPED,] as in Nu. 24. 10; Job 34. 26.
SHAKE,] *or* 'move;' as in Nu. 32. 13, &c.
LAND] of Israel, not the 'earth,' as in C.V.
16. OPENED,] as in 3. 46; Ge. 4. 11, &c.
GNASH,] as in Job 16. 9; Ps. 112. 10, &c.
LOOKED FOR,] *or* 'waited for;' as in Ge.
49. 18, &c.
17. DEVISED,] as in De. 19. 19; Ps. 31. 13.
FULFILLED.] *or* 'finished, cut off;' as in
Job 6. 9, &c.
18. CRIED,] for distress; as in Ge. 27. 34.
DAUGHTER OF THINE EYE,] as in Ps. 17. 8.
19. CRY ALOUD,] as in Isa. 12. 6; 44. 23.
WATCHES,] as in Ex. 14. 24; Jud. 7. 19, &c.
20. LOOK ATTENTIVELY,] as in 1. 11, &c.
HANDBREADTH,] *lit.* 'stretched out' things.
21. LAIN,] that is, 'lain down' for rest.
YOUNG MEN,] *or* 'choice' ones.
22. APPOINTMENT,] *or* 'meeting;' as in v.
6, 7, &c.
ESCAPED,] *lit.* 'let go;' as in Ge. 14. 13, &c.
STRETCHED OUT,] as in Isa. 48. 13.
NOURISHED,] *lit.* 'made great;' as in Ps.
44. 12, &c.

III. 1. MAN,] *lit.* 'mighty' one; as in v. 27.
WRATH,] *lit.* a 'passing over;' as in 2. 2, &c.
3. SURELY,] *or* 'only.'
4. WORN OUT,] as in Job 21. 13; Isa. 65. 22.
BROKEN,] *lit.* 'shivered.'
5. SETTETH ROUND,] as in Lev. 19. 27, &c.
6. DEAD,] *or* 'men' of antiquity.
7. FETTER,] *lit.* 'brazen' thing.
8. SHUT OUT,] *or* 'shut up.'
9. HEWN WORK,] *lit.* 'cut, shorn' thing; as
in Ex. 20. 25, &c.
11. PULLETH IN PIECES.] The original word
is not found again.
MADE,] *lit.* 'set.'
12. TRODDEN HIS BOW,] as in 2. 4; Ps. 7. 12.
13. SONS OF HIS QUIVER,] that is, his arrows.
14. DERISION,] *lit.* 'laughter;' as in Job 8.
21; 12. 4, &c.
SONG,] accompanied with 'stringed instruments.'
16. COVERED.] Targ. 'humbled'; Sept. Vulg.
'fed.'
17. PEACE,] *lit.* 'completeness.'
PROSPERITY.] *lit.* 'good.'
18. STRENGTH,] *or* 'pre-eminence;' as in
5. 20, &c.
20. WELL,] *lit.* 'to remember it doth remember.'
21. TURN,] *lit.* 'turn back;' as in v. 64, &c.
22. CONSUMED,] ended, or finished; as in 2.11.
ENDED,] as in 2. 11; 4. 17, &c.
23. EVERY MORNING,] *lit.* 'at the mornings.'
FAITHFULNESS,] *lit.* 'stedfastness;' as in
Ex. 17. 12; De. 32. 4, &c.
24. PORTION,] *or* 'share;' as in Ge. 14. 24.

25. WAITING,] as in Ps 25. 3; 37. 9; 69. 6.
26 STAY,] as in Ge. 8. 10; Jud. 3. 25, &c.
27. BEARETH,] *or* 'lifteth up.'
28. SILENT,] *lit.* 'dumb;' as in 2. 10, 18, &c
29. PUTTETH,] *lit.* 'giveth.'
30. FILLED,] *lit.* 'satisfied;' as in Ex. 16. 12.
31. CAST OFF,] as in v. 17; 2. 7; Ps. 43. 2.
32. AFFLICTED,] as in 1. 5, 12; Job 19. 2, &c.
33. AFFLICTED,] *or* 'removed.'
WITH,] *lit.* 'from his heart.'
34. BRUISE,] as in Isa 53. 10.
35. TURN ASIDE,] *or* 'incline;' as in Ex.
23 2, &c.
36. SUBVERT,] *or* 'pervert;' as in Am. 8. 5.
APPROVED,] *lit.* 'seen.'
37. THE LORD,] *lit.* 'my lord or lords.'
38. MOUTH,] *or* 'command;' as in 1. 18, &c.
39. SIGH HABITUALLY,] as in Nu. 11. 1.
40. SEARCH,] as in Ps. 64. 6; Prov. 2. 4.
41. ON THE HAND,] *lit.* 'unto the hands.'
IN,] *lit.* 'unto the heavens.'
42. TRANSGRESSED,] *lit.* 'stepped;' as in 1
K. 8. 50, &c.
REBELLED,] *or* 'been bitter.'
FORGIVEN,] *lit.* 'sent away;' as in Ex. 34.9.
43. COVERED,] as in v. 44; Ex. 40. 3, &c.
44. NOT PASS,] *lit.* 'from passing over.'
45. OFFSCOURING,] *or* 'scraping.'
MAKE,] *lit.* 'settest.'
46. OPENED,] as in 2. 16; Ge. 4. 11, &c.
47. DESOLATION,] *lit.* 'the desolation *or*
waste.'
48. RIVULETS,] *lit.* 'divisions;' as in Job
29. 6, &c.
DESTRUCTION,] *lit.* 'breach.'
49. POURED OUT,] as in Ps. 77. 2.
CEASE,] *lit.* 'is not dumb *or* silent.'
50. LOOKETH] out, as from a window.
51. AFFECTETH,] *or* 'is acting on.'
52. SORE,] *lit.* 'to hunt they have hunted me.'
53. CUT OFF,] *lit.* 'make silent, dumb.'
54. CUT OFF,] as in 2 Ch. 26. 21; Est. 2. 1.
55. LOWER PIT,] as in Ps. 88. 6.
56. HIDE,] as in Lev. 20. 4; 1 Sa. 12. 3, &c.
57. DRAWN NEAR,] *or* 'been near;' as in
4. 18, &c.
58. PLEADED,] *or* 'striven, contended;' as
in Ge. 26. 20, &c.
REDEEMED,] as in Ge. 48. 16; Ex. 6. 6, &c.
59. OVERTHROW,] *or* 'perverseness.'
JUDGE,] as a 'magistrate;' as in Ps. 7. 8.
60. VENGEANCE,] as in Nu. 31. 2, 3, &c.
THOUGHTS,] *or* 'purposes, devices.'
61. REPROACH,] as in v. 30; 5. 1; Ge. 30. 23.
62. WITHSTANDERS,] those 'rising up against me.'
MEDITATION,] *lit.* a 'moving to and fro' in
thought.
63. SITTING DOWN,] as in Ge. 13. 6; 16. 3.
BEHOLD ATTENTIVELY,] as in 2. 20; 1. 11.
SONG,] as accompanied with 'stringed' instruments.
64. DEED,] as in Jud. 9. 16; 2 Ch. 32. 25, &c.
65. COVERED,] like a 'garden.'
CURSE,] *or* 'execration.'
66. PURSUEST,] as in v. 43; Ge. 14. 14, &c.

IV. 1. BECOME DIM,] *or* 'concealed.'
PURE GOLD,] that is, 'sealed or treasured
up.'

POURED OUT,] *or* 'shed forth;' as in 2. 12.

2. PRECIOUS,] *lit.* 'rare.'

COMPARABLE,] *lit.* 'lifted or raised up.'

FINE GOLD,] that is, 'refined;' as in Job 28. 17, &c.

3. DRAGONS,] *lit.* 'extended' animals.

DRAWN OUT,] as in De. 25. 9; Hos. 5. 6, &c.

YOUNG ONES,] *lit.* 'sojourners;' because remaining with the old ones.

4. PALATE,] as in Job 6. 30; 12. 11; 20. 13.

5. DAINTIES,] as in Ge. 49. 20; 1 Sa. 15. 32; Prov. 29. 17.

6. INIQUITY,] *or* 'punishment for iniquity.'

7. NAZARITES,] *lit.* 'separate' ones; as in Ge. 49. 26, &c.

BODY,] *lit.* 'bone, substance;' as in v. 8, &c.

FORM,] *lit.* 'cutting' out or shape; as in Eze. 41. 12, &c.

8. VISAGE,] *lit.* 'form or outline;' as in Ge. 29. 17, &c.

9. FAMINE,] *lit.* 'hunger;' as in 2. 19, &c.

10. BOILED,] *or* 'cooked;' as in Ex. 16. 23.

DESTRUCTION,] *lit.* 'breach;' as in 2. 11, 13.

11. COMPLETED,] as in 2. 22; Ge. 2. 2, &c.

12. BELIEVE,] *lit.* 'remain stedfast;' as in Ge. 15. 6, &c.

13. BECAUSE OF,] *lit.* 'from.'

SHEDDING,] *or* 'pouring out;' as in Ge. 9. 6.

14. WANDERED,] *or* 'moved;' as in v. 15, &c.

TOUCH,] *or* 'come against;' as in v. 15, &c.

15. TURN ASIDE,] as in Ge. 19. 2; Nu. 16. 26.

16. DIVIDED,] as in Ge. 49. 7, 27; Ex. 15. 9.

TO BEHOLD] attentively; as in Ex. 3. 6, &c.

17. WHILE WE EXIST,] *lit.* 'yet we are.'

18. HUNTED,] as in 3. 52; Lev. 17. 13, &c.

19. SWIFTER,] *lit.* 'lighter;' as in 2 Sa. 2. 18; Job 24. 18, &c.

20. BREATH,] *lit.* 'spirit.'

ANOINTED,] *in Heb.* 'Meshiah'

21. EDOM,] the elder son of Isaac.

UZ,] i.e. 'counsel.' a 'hard,' settled plan.

DRUNK,] *or* 'merry;' as in Ge. 9. 21, &c

MAKEST THYSELF NAKED,] as in Ps. 37. 35

22. INIQUITY,] *or* 'punishment for iniquity.'

V. 1. REMEMBER,] *or* 'be mindful of;' as in 3. 19, &c.

2. TURNED,] as in v. 15; 1. 20; Ex. 7. 15, 20.

3. ORPHANS,] as in Ex. 22. 22, 24; De. 10. 18.

4. MONEY,] *lit.* 'silver;' as in Ge. 13. 2, &c.

5. FOR,] *or* 'because of.'

6. GIVEN A HAND,] as in 2 Ch. 30. 8, &c.

7. INIQUITIES,] *or* 'punishments for iniquity.'

8. DELIVERER,] *lit.* 'breaker off;' as in Ps. 7. 2.

9. LIVES,] *lit.* 'souls.'

10. BURNING,] as in Ge. 43. 30; 1 K. 3. 26; Hos. 11. 8.

11. HUMBLED,] *or* 'afflicted;' as in 3. 33, &c.

12. HANGED,] *lit.* 'made high.'

13. YOUNG MEN,] *lit.* 'choice' ones.

14. AGED,] *or* 'elders.'

CEASED,] *lit.* 'kept sabbath;' as in v 15.

SONG,] accompanied with musical instruments.

15. DANCING,] *or* 'chorus,' as in Ps. 30. 11.

16. CROWN,] as in 2 Sa. 12. 30; 1 Ch. 20. 2.

17. SICK,] as in 1. 13; Lev. 15. 33; 20. 18.

DIM,] *lit.* 'dark;' as in 4. 8; Job 18. 6, &c.

18. DESOLATE,] *or* 'has been desolate.'

19. REMAINETH,] *or* 'sittest.'

20. FOR EVER,] *or* 'to pre-eminence;' as in 3. 18, &c.

21. RENEW,] as in Ps. 51. 10.

22. FOR,] *or* 'except;' as in Ge. 32. 26; 39. 6, &c.

EZEKIEL

THE BOOK OF EZEKIEL is not directly quoted in the New Testament, but some of the latter chapters are obviously paralleled in that of the 'Revelation' made to John. It has *two* great divisions, viz. chap. i—xxiv, *before* the final destruction of Jerusalem, and ch. xxv—xlviii. after that event. More particularly, this Book—consisting of 'Visions, symbolical actions, similitudes, parables, proverbs, poems, allegories,' &c.—may be divided into nine sections, viz.
1. Ezekiel's call to be a prophet, i—iii. 15.
2. Carrying out of his commission, iii. 16—vii.
3. Rejection of the people for idolatry, viii—xi.
4. Special sins rebuked, xii—xix.
5. Nature of the Judgments, xx—xxiii.
6. Meaning of the Punishments, xxiv.
7. Punishments of Seven Heathen Nations, xxv—xxxii.
8. Future condition of the true Israel, xxxiii—xxxix.
9. Glorious Consummation, xl—xlviii.

I. 1. THIRTIETH YEAR,] B.C. 595.
FOURTH MONTH,] that is, Thammuz.
THE REMOVED,] from Judah to Babel.
CHEBAR,] i.e. the 'heavy, mighty' river.
OPENED,] in vision, as in Mat. 3. 16.
VISIONS,] *lit.* 'appearances;' as in 8. 3, &c.
2. JEHOIACHIN,] i.e. 'Jah makes ready or sets up.'
3. A WORD,] or communication from the God of Israel.
EZEKIEL,] i.e. a 'mighty one sees.'
BUZI,] i.e. 'despised one.'
PRIEST,] who 'makes ready' offerings to God.
CHALDEANS,] i.e. 'kind ones.'
HAND,] as a symbol of power.
4. LOOK,] *or* 'see;' as in v. 15, 27.
IS COMING,] as in 7. 5, 6, 7, 10; 9. 2; 16. 16.
CATCHING ITSELF,] *lit.* 'taking itself;' as in Ex. 9. 24.
BRIGHTNESS,] *or* 'shining;' as in v. 13, &c.
COLOUR,] *lit.* 'eye;' as in v. 5, 16, 22, &c.
COPPER,] *or* 'polished brass;' as in v. 27.
5. LIVING CREATURES,] as in v. 13, 14, &c.
6. FACES,] *or* 'fronts.'
EACH,] *lit.* 'to one.'
WINGS,] *or* 'pair of wings.'
7. STRAIGHT,] *or* 'upright;' as in v. 23, &c.
SOLE,] as in 6. 11; 21. 11, 14, 17, 24; 22. 13.
SPARKLING.] Original word not found again.
BRIGHT,] *lit.* 'light,' that is, not weighty.
8. SIDES,] *lit.* 'fours;' as in v. 17; 43. 17.
9. JOINING,] *or* 'companions;' as in v. 11.
ONE,] *lit.* a 'woman unto her sister;' as in v. 23, &c.
STRAIGHTFORWARD,] *lit.* 'unto over his face;' as in v. 12.
10. ON,] *lit.* 'from' the left.

12. SPIRIT,] *or* 'wind;' as in v. 4, 20, &c.
13. COALS,] as in 10. 2; 24. 11; Lev. 16. 12.
GOING UP AND DOWN,] as in Ge. 3. 8, &c.
14. RUNNING,] *lit.* 'are to run and to turn back.'
FLESH.] Original word not found again.
15. WHEEL,] as in v. 16. 19, 20, 21; 3. 13, &c.
16. WORKS,] *or* 'deeds.'
BERYL,] as in 10. 9; 28. 13; Ex. 28. 20, &c.
18. RINGS,] *lit.* 'curves;' as in 10. 12, &c.
19. BESIDE,] *or* 'near.'
20. SPIRIT,] *or* 'wind;' as in v. 4, 12, &c.
LIVING SPIRIT,] *or* 'wind of life;' as in v. 21, &c.
22. LIVING CREATURES,] *lit.* 'living creature.'
ICE,] *lit.* a 'bald, clear' thing; as in Ge. 31. 40, &c.
23. ON THIS..THAT SIDE,] *lit.* 'to these.. to these.'
24. NOISE,] *lit.* 'voice.'
MIGHTY ONE,] *or* 'He who is sufficient.'
LET FALL,] *lit.* 'enfeeble;' as in v. 25, &c.
26. SAPPHIRE,] *lit.* a 'scraped' thing; as in 10. 1, &c.
28. RAIN,] *lit.* 'shower;' as in 13. 11, &c.

II. 1. HONOUR,] *lit.* 'heaviness, weightiness;' as in 3. 12, 23; 8. 4. &c.
SPEAKING,] *lit.* a 'speaker;' as in 2. 8, &c.
SON OF MAN.] *or* 'of Adam;' i.e. a human being.
2. A SPIRIT,] as in 1. 4, 12, 20, 21, &c.
3. REBELS,] as in 20. 38; Neh. 2. 19; Job 24. 13.
TRANSGRESSED,] *lit.* 'stepped;' as in 18. 31.
THIS VERY,] *lit.* 'unto the bone *or* substance of this day.'
4. BRAZEN,] *lit.* 'hard or sharp' of face.
HARD,] *or* 'strong' of heart; as in 3. 7, &c.
LORD JEHOVAH,] the 'basis' *or* 'judge' of all.
5. WHETHER,] *lit.* 'if;' as in v. 7, &c.
FORBEAR,] *lit.* 'cease;' as in v. 7; 3. 11, &c.
REBELLIOUS,] *or* 'bitter;' as in v. 7, 8, &c.
PROPHET,] one declaring the will of God, whether relating to past, present, or future things.
6. WORDS,] *or* 'matters;' as in v. 7.
NEAR,] *lit.* 'unto.'
DWELLING,] *lit.* 'sitting.'
AFFRIGHTED,] *or* 'brought down;' as in 3. 9; De. 1. 21, &c.
8. OPEN,] as in Ps. 144. 7, 11.
9. ROLL OF A BOOK,] as in Ps. 40. 7, &c.
10. LAMENTATIONS,] as in 19. 1, 14; 26. 17.
MOURNING,] *or* 'meditation;' as in Job 37. 2; Ps. 90. 9.
WO.] Original word not found again.

III. 2. OPEN,] as in v. 27; 33. 22, &c.
3. FEED,] *lit.* 'cause to eat.'
5. DEEP OF LIP,] as in v. 6; Isa. 33. 19.
HEAVY OF TONGUE,] as in v. 6; Ex. 4. 10.

6. UNDERSTAND,] *lit.* 'hear;' as in v. 11, 12.
NOT SENT,] but he had gone in any other name.
7. UNTO ME,] whoseword the prophet spake.
BRAZEN-FACED,] *lit.* 'hard or strong forehead.'
STRONG-HEARTED,] *lit.* 'sharp or hard of heart.'
8. MADE,] *lit.* 'given;' as in v. 9, &c.
9. ADAMANT,] as in Éze. 7. 12.
AFFRIGHTED,] *lit.* 'brought down;' as in 2. 6, &c.
10. RECEIVE,] take, or accept.
11. REMOVED,] from Judah; as in v. 15.
WHETHER..FORBEAR,] *lit.* 'if..cease.'
12. A SPIRIT,] *or* 'wind;' as in v. 14, 24, &c.
NOISE,] *lit.* 'voice;' as in v. 13; 1. 24, &c.
BLESSED,] *lit.* 'bent of knee;' as in Ge. 9. 26.
13. TOUCHING,] *lit.* 'kissing, a woman unto her friend.'
14. TAKE ME AWAY,] *or* simply 'take me.'
15. TEL ABIB,] *lit.* 'heap or hill of budding.'
CHEBAR,] i.e. 'great;' in Aram Naharaim.
CAUSING ASTONISHMENT,] *or* 'desolation;' as in 14. 8, &c.
16. SEVEN DAYS,] probably the next sabbath.
17. WATCHMAN,] one 'looking out;' as in 33. 2, 6, 7, &c.
WARNED,] *lit.* 'giving brightness or shining;' as in v. 18.
18. WICKED,] one in the 'wrong;' as in v. 19; 7. 21, &c.
SURELY,] *lit.* 'to die thou dost die.'
INIQUITY,] *or* 'punishment;' as in v. 19,&c.
I REQUIRE,] *lit.* 'seek;' as in v. 20; 22. 30.
19. DELIVERED,] *lit.* 'snatched away;' as in v. 21, &c.
20. RIGHTEOUS,] *lit.* 'right or just' one; as in v. 21, &c.
RIGHTEOUSNESS,] *or* 'state of rightness;' as in 45. 10, &c.
PUT,] *lit.* 'given;' as in v. 8, 9, 17, 25, &c.
IN,] *or* 'because of' his sin.
21. SURELY,] *lit.* 'to live he liveth.'
22. VALLEY,] *lit.* 'cleft' place; as in v. 23.
24. A SPIRIT,] *or* simply 'spirit;' as in v. 12, 14, &c.
SHUT UP,] *lit.* 'made secure;' as in 46. 2.
25. PUT,] *lit.* 'given;' as in v. 8, 9, 17, &c.
26. BEEN DUMB,] *or* 'become dumb.'
REPROVER,] *lit.* 'a man making prominent.'
27. FORBEARING,] *lit.* 'ceasing doth cease.'

IV. 1. BRICK,] *lit.* a 'white' thing; as in Ge. 11. 3, &c.
PUT,] *lit.* 'given;' as in v. 3, 5, 6, 8, 9, &c.
2. PLACED,] *lit.* 'given;' as in v. 1, 3, 5, &c.
SIEGE,] as in v. 3, 7, 8; 5. 2; De. 20. 19, &c.
FORTIFICATION,] *lit.* 'dyke;' as in 17. 17.
POURED OUT,] by continual loads of material.
MOUNT,] *lit.* a 'raised up' thing.
3. PAN,] as in Lev. 2. 5; 6. 21; 7. 9; 1 Ch 23. 29.
MADE,] *lit.* 'given;' as in v. 1, 5, 6, 8, &c.
PREPARED,] made ready, or 'set up.'
AGAINST,] *lit.* 'unto.'
LAID SIEGE,] or sent 'straitness.'
SIGN,] *or* 'token;' as in 14. 8; 20. 12, &c.

4. PLACED,] *lit.* 'set;' as in 5. 5; 7. 20, &c.
INIQUITY,] *or* 'punishment;' as in v. 5, &c.
BEAREST,] *lit.* 'liftest up their punishment;' as in v. 5, 6.
5. LAID,] *lit.* 'given;' as in v. 1, 3, 6, 8, &c 390 DAYS,] or thirteen lunar months.'
6. 40 DAYS,] as in 29. 11, 12, 13, &c.
APPOINTED,] *lit.* 'given.' Very unreasonable is the theory that in prophetic language a 'day' means a 'year.' In all the *fulfilled* prophecies, without exception, a day, a month, or a year, mean exactly those periods, and that unfulfilled prophecies are to be explained differently, is a gratuitous assumption and a mockery of Scripture.
7. PREPARE,]make 'ready'or'set up;'asinv.3.
PROPHESIED,] that is, declared the will of God.
8. PUT,] *lit.* 'given;' as in v. 1, 3, 5, 6, &c
SIDE,] *lit.* 'thy side unto thy side.'
9. BARLEY,] *lit.* a 'hairy' thing; as in v. 12.
PUT,] *lit.* 'given;' as in v. 1, 3, 5, 6, 8, &c
11. HIN,] as in 45. 24; 46. 5, 7, 11. 14.
12. CAKE,] *lit.* a 'round' thing; as in Ge 18. 6, &c.
FILTH,] *lit.* 'outgoing;' as in De. 23. 13.
BAKE,] *or* 'make round' cakes.
14. CARCASE,] *lit.* a 'fallen' thing; as in 44. 31, &c.
TORN THING,] that is, torn by wild animals.
YOUTH,] *lit.* 'youths,' i.e. periods of youth.
15. DUNG,] *lit.* a thing 'expelled, thrust out.'
16. STAFF,] *lit.* a thing 'stretched out;' as in 5. 16, &c.
ASTONISHMENT,] *or* 'desolation;' as in 12. 19.
17. SO THAT,] *or* 'because that.'
ASTONISHED,] *or* 'desolated, a man and his brother.'
CONSUMED,] *or* 'corrupt or wasted.'
INIQUITY,] *or* 'punishment;' as in v. 4, 5.

V. 1. WEAPON,] *lit.* 'destroying or wasting' implement; as in v. 2.
BARBER,] *lit.* a 'scraper, shearer.'
BEARD,] a token of 'age.'
SCALES,] *lit.* a 'pair of ears.'
2. FIRE,] *lit.* 'light;' as in Isa. 24. 15, &c.
SCATTER,] *or* 'fan;' as in Ex. 32. 20, &c.
3. FEW,] *or* 'little;' as in 11. 16; 16. 20, 47.
BOUND,] *lit.* 'pressed;' as in 4. 3, &c.
SKIRTS,] *lit.* 'wings.'
6. STATUTES,] *lit.* 'graved' laws; as in v. 7; 11. 20, &c.
WALKED,] *or* 'gone on;' as in v. 7.
7. MULTIPLYING,] *or* 'raging;' original word not found again.
8. EVEN I,] *or* 'also I.'
9. ITS LIKE,] *lit.* 'like it.'
11. AFFIRMATION,] an oracular declaration; as in 11. 8, &c.
SANCTUARY,] *lit.* 'set-apart place;' as in 8. 6, &c.
12. FAMINE,] *lit.* 'hunger;' as in v. 16. 17.
13 FURY,] *lit.* 'heat;' as in v. 15; 3. 14, &c.
COMFORTED,] *or* 'repented of.'
14. WASTE,] *or* 'dried up' place; as in 13. 4; 25. 14, &c.

REPROACH,] *lit.* a 'plucking off.'
15. REVILING,] *lit.* 'cutting off.'
INSTRUCTION,] *or* 'band;' as in De. 11. 2.
FURIOUS REPROOFS,] *lit.* 'reasonings of heat.'
16. DESTRUCTION,] *lit.* a 'marring' thing.
DESTROY,] *lit.* 'mar;' as in 20. 17; 22. 30.
ADDING,] *or* 'gathering.'
17. BEASTS,] *lit.* 'living creature.'
ON,] *or* 'into thee.'

VI. 1. WORD,] *or* 'matter;' as in v. 3; 7. 1.
2. PROPHESY,] *lit.* 'be a prophet.'
4. ALTARS,] *lit.* 'places for sacrifice;' as in v. 6, &c.
IMAGES,] as in v. 6; Lev. 26. 30; 2 Ch. 14. 5.
WOUNDED,] *lit.* 'pierced' ones; as in v. 7.
IDOLS,] *lit.* 'dungy ones;' as in v. 5, 9, &c.
5. PUT,] *lit.* 'given;' as in v. 13, 14; 7. 3, &c.
CARCASES,] *lit.* 'faint' ones; as in 43. 7, 9.
6. LAID WASTE,] *lit.* 'dried up.'
BLOTTED OUT,] *or* 'wiped away;' as in Ge. 7. 23, &c.
8. TO REMAIN,] *or* 'be over;' as in 12. 16.
11. FOR ALL,] *or* 'unto all.'
FAMINE,] *lit.* 'hunger;' as in v. 12; 5. 12.
12. FURY,] *lit.* 'heat;' as in 3. 14; 5. 13, 15.
13. WOUNDED,] *lit.* 'pierced' ones.
TOPS,] *lit.* 'heads;' as in 1. 22, 25, 26, &c.
SWEET FRAGRANCE,] *or* 'fragrance of rest.'
14. MADE,] *lit.* 'given;' as in v. 5. 13, &c.
WILDERNESS,] *lit.* place of 'leading forth' the flock.

VII. 1. GROUND] *or* 'soil;' as in 11. 17, &c.
CORNERS,] *lit.* 'wings;' as in 1. 25; 3. 13,&c.
3. UNTO,] *or* 'upon thee.'
SET,] *lit.* 'given;' as in v. 4, 8, 20, 21, &c.
5. EVIL,] *or* misfortune; as in v. 24; 5. 16.
6. FOR THEE,] *lit.* 'unto thee.'
MORNING,] Ges. 'circle' of events; as in v. 10; Isa. 28. 5.
8. SHORTLY,] *lit.* 'from near.'
POUR OUT,] *or* 'shed forth;' as in 16. 15, &c.
FURY,] *lit.* 'heat;' as in 3. 14; 5. 13, &c.
9. PITY,] *lit.* 'haste or take refuge.'
10. ROD,] *lit.* 'extended or stretched out.'
FLOURISHED,] *lit.* 'broken forth.'
11. FOR THEM.] *or* 'among them.'
12. ARRIVED,] *or* 'touched, stricken;' as in 13. 14, &c.
BUYER,] *lit.* 'acquirer, gainer;' as in Ge. 14. 19, 22. &c.
BECOME A MOURNER,] *or* 'mourn for himself;' as in v. 27.
WRATH,] *lit.* 'heat;' as in v. 14.
13. BY,]*or* 'in' his iniquity or 'punishment.'
STRENGTHEN,] *or* 'himself strengthen *or* strengthen for himself.'
14. BLOW,] *lit.* 'struck;' as in 33. 3, 6, &c.
TRUMPET,] *lit.* as object for 'striking' with the mouth or breath.
15. FIELD,] *lit.* a broken down or 'level' place.
CITY,] a 'stirring' or bustling place.
16. ON,] *or* 'unto' the mountains.
FOR HIS INIQUITY,] *or* 'in his punishment.'
18. SACKCLOTH,] *lit.* 'sacks;' as in 27. 31.
19. BECOMETH,] *lit.* 'for impurity is.'
DELIVER,] *lit.* 'snatch' them away; as in Ge. 37. 22, &c.

WRATH,]*lit.* 'passing over;' as in 21. 31. &c.
20. ORNAMENT,] *or* 'desirable thing.'
EXCELLENCY,] *lit.* 'gaity, gayness;' as in v. 24, &c.
21. POLLUTED,] *lit.* 'pierced' it; as in v. 22.
22. TURNED,] *lit.* 'turned round.'
DESTROYERS,]*lit.* 'breakers up;' as in 18. 10.
24. WICKED,]*or* 'evil ones;' as in v. 5; 5. 16.
SANCTIFYING,] *lit.* 'setting apart.'
25. DESTRUCTION,]*or* a 'shrinking together.
26. MISCHIEF,] *or* 'accident;' as in Isa. 47. 11.
REPORT,] *lit.* 'hearing upon hearing.'
COUNSEL,] *lit.* 'direction is lost.'
27. PRINCE,] *lit.* a 'fixed, firm' plan.
PRINCE,] *lit.* 'lifted up' one in the opinion of others.

VIII. 1. SIXTH YEAR,] B.C. 593.
SIXTH MONTH,] that is, Elul.
ELDERS,] *lit.* 'bearded or aged' ones.
2. LOOK,] *or* 'see;' as in v. 6, 7, 10, 13, &c
DOWNWARD,] *lit.* 'beneath.'
COLOUR,] *lit.* 'eye;' as in v. 5. 18, &c.
3. FORM,] *lit.* 'building or framework;' as in v. 10.
VISIONS,] *lit.* 'appearances;' as in 1. 1, &c
4. HONOUR,] *lit.* 'weightiness.'
VALLEY,] *lit.* 'cleft' place; as in 3. 22, &c
5. ON,] *lit.* 'from the north.'
6. SANCTUARY,] *lit.* 'set apart' place.
7. COURT,] *lit.* 'enclosed or surrounded' place; as in v. 16. &c.
LOOK,] *or* 'see;' as in v. 10, &c.
A HOLE,] *lit.* 'one (certain) hole or white place.
8. THROUGH,] *or* 'in' the wall.
AN OPENING,] *or* 'one (certain) opening.'
10. BEAST,] quadruped or 'cattle;' as in 14. 13., &c.
IDOL,] *lit.* 'dungy' ones; as in 6. 4, 5, &c.
ALL,] *lit.* 'round about round about.'
11. JAAZANIAH,] i.e. 'Jah gives ear.'
SHAPHAN,] *lit.* one that 'covers' or hides.
ABUNDANCE,] *or* 'riches;' as in Zeph. 3. 10.
14. TAMMUZ,] the Greek Adonis, probably.
16. BACKS,] *lit.* 'hinder parts;' as in 2. 10.
17. PUTTING,] *or* 'sending forth.'
BRANCH,] *lit.* 'pruned thing;' as in Nu. 13. 23; Isa. 17. 10.
NOSE,] *or* 'anger;' as in 5. 13, 15; 7. 3, &c
18. FURY,] *lit.* 'heat;' as in 3. 14; 5. 13, 15.
CRIED,] *or* 'called.'

IX. 1. CRIETH,] *or* 'calleth;' as in v. 3, &c.
LOUD,] *lit.* 'great.'
2. DESTROYING WEAPON,] *lit.* 'vessel of marring.'
SLAUGHTER WEAPON,] *lit.* 'vessel of dashing in pieces.'
3. HONOUR,] *lit.* 'weightiness, heaviness.'
THRESHOLD,] as in 10. 4, 18; 46. 2; 47. 1.
4. MADE,] *lit.* 'marked a mark;' as in Ps 78. 41.
MARK,] *lit.* 'cross;' as in v. 6; Job 31. 35.
5. TO THE OTHERS,] *lit.* 'to them.'
PASS ON,] *or* 'pass over.'
6. AGED,] *lit.* 'bearded or elder,' as in v. 7.
YOUNG MAN,] *lit.* 'choice one;' as in 23. 6.
VIRGIN,] *lit.* 'separate one;' as in 44. 22, &c.
SANCTUARY,] *lit.* 'set apart' place.

BEGIN,] *or* 'pierce;' as in 39. 7, &c.
7. WOUNDED,] *lit.* 'pierced' ones; as in 6. 4, 7, 13, &c.
8. CRY,] in distress; as in 11. 13; 27. 30, &c.
DESTROYING,] *lit.* 'marring.'
POURING OUT,] *or* 'shedding forth;' as in 17. 17; 20. 8, &c.
WRATH,] *lit.* 'heat.'
9. INIQUITY,] *or* 'punishment;' as in 3. 18.
VERY VERY,] *lit.* 'great, with might,' might.'
10. PUT,] *lit.* 'given.'
11. COMMANDED,] charged or 'willed' me to do.

X. 1. LOOK,] *or* 'see;' as in v. 9; 1. 1, &c.
2. SPEAKETH,] *lit.* 'saith.'
WHEEL,] *lit.* 'rolling thing;' as in v. 6, 13.
3. ON,] *lit.* 'from the right side.'
4. HONOUR,] *lit.* 'weightiness, heaviness.'
BRIGHTNESS,] *or* 'shining;' as in 1. 4, &c.
5. NOISE,] *lit.* 'voice.'
MIGHTY,] *lit.* 'he who is sufficient.'
6. WHEEL,] as in v. 2, 6, 13, &c.
7. PUTTETH,] *lit.* 'sendeth forth.'
8. APPEARETH,] *lit.* 'there is seen;' as in 19. 11, &c.
IN,] *lit.* 'to the cherubs.'
9. COLOUR,] *lit.* 'eye;' as in v. 2, 12, 19, &c.
13. WHEELS,] *lit.* things 'turning round;' as in v. 6, 9, 10, &c.
WHEEL,] *lit.* 'rolling' thing; as in v. 2, 6.
14. TO EACH,] *lit.* 'to one;' as in v. 21.
15. LIFTED UP,] *or* 'high;' as in v. 17, 19.
16. ABOVE,] *lit.* 'from on' the land.
17. EXALTATION,] as in v. 16; De. 17. 20; s. 12. 8.
20. UNDER,] *or* 'the place of.'
STRAIGHTFORWARD,] *lit.* 'unto over his face' they go.

XI. 1. THE EAST,] *lit.* 'toward the east.'
AZZUR,] i.e. 'helped' one.
PELATIAH,] i.e. 'escaped of Jah.'
BENAIAH,] i.e. 'built up of Jah.'
2. DEVISING,] *or* 'thinking;' as in Ex. 26. 1, 31, &c.
GIVING,] *lit.* 'counselling.'
EVIL COUNSEL,] *lit.* a 'counsel of evil.'
3. NOT NEAR,] *lit.* 'not in nearness.'
4. PROPHESY,] *lit.* 'be a prophet;' as in 6. 2.
5. RIGHTLY,] *or* 'so.'
STEPS,] *lit.* 'goings up;' as in 40. 6, 22, &c.
6. WOUNDED,] *lit.* 'pierced' one; as in v. 7.
13. CRY] in distress; as in 9. 8; 27. 30, &c.
LOUD,] *lit.* 'great.'
END,] *or* 'consummation;' as in 13. 13, &c.
15. KINDRED,] *lit* 'redemption;' as in Lev. 25 24, &c.
KEEP,] *or* 'be far off.'
INHERITANCE,] *or* 'possession;' as in 25. 4, 10; 33. 24, &c.
17. GROUND,] *or* 'soil;' as in 7. 2; 12. 19, &c.
19. TURNED,] *lit.* 'turned aside.'
21. PUT,] *lit.* 'given.'
AFFIRMATION,] *or* 'affirmed thing;' as in v. 8; 5. 11, &c.
23. ON,] *lit.* 'from the east.'
24. TO,] *or* 'towards Chaldea.'
VISION,] *lit.* 'appearance;' as in 1. 5, &c.
25. MATTERS,] *or* 'things;' as in v. 14, &c.

XII. 2. DWELLING,] *lit.* 'sitting;' as in v. 19; 2. 6, &c.
3. CONSIDER,] *lit.* 'see;' as in v. 6, 12, &c.
6. BEAR,] *or* 'lift up;' as in v. 7, 10.
TYPE,] *lit.* 'fair' thing; as in v. 10.
10. PRINCE.] *lit.* 'lifted up' one; as in v. 12.
BURDEN,] *lit.* 'thing lifted up or borne.'
11. TYPE,] *or* 'fair, wonderful' thing; as in v. 6.
INTO,] *or* 'with or in.'
12. BEARETH,] *or* 'lifteth up;' as in v. 6. 7.
SURFACE,] *lit.* 'eye;' as in 1. 4, 7, 16, &c.
13. SNARE,] *lit.* a thing for 'hunting' with.
14. TO HELP,] *lit.* 'his helper.'
BANDS,] *or* 'wings;' as in 17. 21; 38. 6, &c.
DRAW OUT,] *or* 'make empty.'
16. LEFT] over; as in 6. 8; 39. 28, &c.
FEW,] *lit.* 'men of number.'
18. HASTE,] *lit.* 'rushing, shaking.'
19. ASTONISHMENT,] *or* 'desolation.'
20. LAID WASTE,] *or* 'dried up.'
22. SIMILE,] *lit.* 'ruling' thing; as in v. 23.
PERISHED,] *or* 'lost has been all vision.'
23. BUT,] *lit.* 'but rather.'
DRAWN NEAR,] *or* 'near have been.'
SPOKEN,] *or* 'and the word of' every vision.
24. VAIN,] *or* 'empty;' as in 13. 6, 7, 8, &c.
FLATTERING,] *lit.* 'smooth.'
25. PROLONGED,] *lit.* 'drawn out;' as in v. 28.
FOR,] *or* 'of about,' as in next clause.

XIII. 1. PROPHESY,] *lit.* 'be a prophet;' as in v. 17; 6. 2, &c.
CONCERNING,] *lit.* 'unto.'
3. WO UNTO,] *or* 'upon.'
4. WASTES,] *or* 'dry places;' as in 5. 14, &c
5. MAKE,] *lit.* 'fence a fence or hedge.'
6. VANITY,] *or* 'emptiness;' as in v. 7, &c.
HOPED,] *or* 'waited;' as in Job 6. 11, &c.
ESTABLISH,] *lit.* 'raise up;' as in Ru. 4. 7.
7. SPOKEN,] *lit.* 'said.'
LIE,] *or* 'deceiving thing;' as in v. 6, &c.
9. ASSEMBLY,] *or* 'secret counsel;' as in Ge. 49. 6, &c.
10. TO ERR,] *or* 'wander, stray.'
CHALK,] *lit.* an 'insipid' thing.
11. REND,] *or* 'cleave;' as in v. 13.
12. SAY,] *lit.* 'is it not said.'
13. FURY,] *lit.* 'heat;' as in v. 15; 3. 14, &c.
CONSUME,] end or finish; as in 5. 13, &c.
14. TO COME,] *lit.* 'touch or strike;' as in 7. 12, &c.
REVEALED,] *or* 'uncovered;' as in 16. 36.
16. CONCERNING,] *or* 'unto' Jerusalem.
17. AGAINST,] *or* 'unto.'
PROPHESYING,] *or* 'showing themselves prophets.'
PROPHIES,] *lit.* 'be a prophet;' as in v. 1.
18. PILLOWS,] *lit.* 'coverings;' as in v. 20.
STATURE,] *lit.* 'height;' as in 17. 16; 19. 11.
KEEP ALIVE,] *or* 'make alive;' as in 18. 27.
19. TO LIES,] *lit.* 'to a lie.'
20. FLOURISHING,] *lit.* 'breaking forth.'
21. KERCHIEFS,] *lit.* 'spread-out things.'
DELIVERED,] *lit.* 'snatched;' as in v. 22.
PREY,] *lit.* thing caught by 'hunting.'
22. PAINING,] *or* 'smiting.'
KEEP ALIVE,] *or* 'make live;' as in 3. 18.

XIV. 1. CERTAIN,] *lit.* 'men.'

3. IDOLS,] *lit.* 'dungy ones;' as in v. 4, &c.
PUT,] *lit.* 'given;' as in v. 8, &c.
AT ALL,] *lit.* 'am I inquired of, am I inquired of.'
4. EVERY ONE,] *lit.* 'a man a man;' as in v. 7.
ANSWER,] *lit.* 'have been answered or afflicted;' as in v. 7.
8. SIGN,] *or* 'token;' as in 4. 3; 20. 12, &c.
SIMILIES,] *lit.* 'ruling' sayings; as in 12. 22, 23, &c.
9. ENTICED,] *or* 'persuaded;' as in Prov. 25. 15; Jer. 20. 10.
ENTICED,] that is, suffered him to be persuaded.
10. BORNE,] *lit.* 'lifted up;' as in 3. 14, &c.
INIQUITY,] *or* 'punishment;' as in v. 3, 4.
11. WANDER,] *or* 'err, stray;' as in 44. 10.
TRANSGRESSIONS,] *lit.* 'steps;' as in 18. 22.
13. SINNETH,] *lit.* 'misseth' the mark.
COMMIT,] *lit.* 'trespass a trespass.'
STAFF,] *lit.* a thing 'stretched' out.
FAMINE,, *lit.* 'hunger;' as in v. 21; 5. 12.
14. DELIVER,] *lit.* 'snatch;' as in v. 16, &c.
15. BEAST,] *lit.* 'living creature;' as in v. 21, &c.
16. NEITHER,] *lit.* 'if sons, and if daughters;' as in v. 20.
ALONE,] *or* 'apart by themselves.'
17. BEAST,] *or* 'cattle;' as in v. 19, 21, &c.
19. POURED OUT,] *or* 'shed forth;' as in 4. 2; 21. 31, &c.
FURY,] *lit.* 'heat;' as in 3. 14; 5. 13, 15, &c.
21. 'ALTHOUGH,] *lit.* 'also because.'
SORE,] *lit.* 'evil, sad;' as in v. 15, 22, &c.
PESTILENCE,] *lit.* a thing 'led forth.'
22. LEFT] over, as in Ex. 10. 15; 29. 34, &c.

XV. 2. VINE-TREE,] *lit.* ' wood of the vine;' as in v. 6.
VINE-BRANCH,] *lit.* 'pruned thing.'
3. USE,] *lit.* 'make, do;' as in v. 5.
PIN,] as in Ex. 27. 19; 35. 18; 38. 20, 21, &c.
HANG] up or suspend; as in Est. 6. 4.
4. FUEL,] *lit.* 'food;' as in v. 6; 21. 32, &c.
SCORCHED,] *or* 'heated:' as in v. 5.
PROFITABLE,] *lit.* 'doth it prosper.'
7. SET,] *lit.* 'given;' as in v. 6, 8, &c.
8. MADE,] *lit.* 'given;' as in v. 6, 7.
COMMITTED,] *lit.* 'trespassed a trespass.'

XVI. 3. BIRTH,] *lit.* place of 'preparation or cutting out.'
NATIVITY,] *or* 'kindred;' as in v. 4, &c.
CANAANITE,] i.e 'one of a humbled land.'
AMORITE,] i.e. a 'mountaineer.'
HITTITE,] i.e. 'terror, downfall.'
AT ALL,] *lit.* 'and to salt thou hast not been salted.'
5. HATH HAD PITY,] *or* 'hastened upon thee.'
ANY,] *lit.* ' one of these.'
PERSON,] *lit.* 'soul;' as in v. 27; 3. 19, &c.
6. TRODDEN DOWN,] *lit.* 'being thyself trodden down.'
BLOOD,] *lit.* 'bloods;' as in v. 9.
7. MADE,] *lit.* 'given;' as in v. 17. 18, 19, &c.
EXCELLENT,] *lit.* 'adornment of adornments.'
FORMED,] prepared or 'set up.'
GROWN,] *lit.* 'sprouted.'

8. SKIRT,] *lit.* 'wing.'
I SWEAR,] *lit.* 'am sworn.'
9. PERFUME,] *lit.* ' oil;' as in v. 13.
13. GO PROSPEROUSLY,] *or* 'prosperest.'
14. THY NAME,] *lit.* ' for thee a name.
15. TRUST,] *lit.* 'lean.'
POUR OUT,] *or* 'shed forth.'
17. VESSELS,] *lit.* 'vessels of thy beauty.'
18. SET,] *lit.* 'given;' as in v. 17. 18, &c.
19. SWEET,] *lit.* 'a fragrance of rest.'
20. FOR FOOD,] *or* 'to eat;' as in 33. 27, &c.
22. YOUTH,] *lit.* 'youths,' i.e. youthful periods; as in v. 43, 60.
WHEN THOU WAST,] *lit.* 'in thy being.'
23. WICKEDNESS,] *or* 'evil;' as in v. 57, &c.
25. OPEN WIDE,] as in Prov. 13. 3.
26. EGYPT,] *Heb.* Mitsrayim, i.e. 'two strait places.'
NEIGHBOURS,] *lit.* 'settlers down;' as in Ex. 3. 22, &c.
APPETITE,] *lit.* 'flesh.'
27. DIMINISH,] *or* 'withdraw;' as in 5. 11.
PORTION,] *or* 'appointed statute' food and allowance.
DESIRE,] *lit.* 'soul;' as in v. 5, &c.
WICKED,] as in v. 43, 58; 22. 9, 11; 23. 21.
28. WITHOUT,] *or* 'from want of thy being satisfied.'
29. ON,] *lit.* 'unto.'
33. GIFT.] Original word not found again.
34. CONTRARY,] *lit.* 'turning.'
WOMEN,] *lit.* 'from the women.'
36. POURED,] *or* 'shed forth.'
REVEALED,]*or* 'uncovered;' as in v. 57, &c.
IDOLS,] *lit.* 'rolled or dungy ones;' as in 6 4, 5, 6, 9, 13, &c.
37. TO WHOM,] *lit.* 'on whom.'
BY THEE,] *or* 'against thee from round about.'
38. FURY,] *lit.* 'heat;' as in v. 42, &c.
JEALOUSY,] *or* 'zeal,' *lit.* 'set up, stiffness.'
39. VESSELS,] *lit.* 'vessels of thy beauty.'
LEFT,] *or* 'let thee rest;' as in 22. 20, &c.
41. IN,] *or* 'with thee.'
42. FURY,] *lit.* 'heat;' as in v. 38, &c.
43. THOUGHT,] as in v. 27, 58; 22. 9, 11, &c.
44. SIMILE,] *lit.* 'ruling' saying; as in 12. 23, &c.
45. HUSBAND,] *lit.* 'man;' as in v. 32, &c.
46. ELDER,] *lit.* 'greater;' as in v. 61, &c.
DWELLING,] *lit.* 'sitting;' as in 2. 6; 3. 15.
YOUNGER,] *lit.* 'lesser;' as in v. 61, &c.
48. NOT DONE,] *lit.* 'if she hath done.'
49. ANNOYANCE,[*lit.* 'gayness, gaiety;' as in v. 56, &c.
FULNESS,] *lit.* 'satiety;' as in 39. 19, &c.
QUIET EASE,] *lit.* 'ease of quietnesss.'
AFFLICTED,] *or* 'humble;' as in 18. 12, &c.
51. JUSTIFY,] that is, 'declare just *or* right.'
52. BEAR,] *lit.* 'lift up; as in v. 54, &c.
56. REPORT,] *lit.* 'hearing;' as in 7. 26, &c.
57. REVEALED,] *or* 'uncovered;' as in v. 36; 13. 14, &c.
NEIGHBOURS,] *lit.* 'those round about her.
58. BORNE,] *lit.* 'lifted up;' as in 3. 14, &c.
59. OATH,] *or* ' execration;' as in 17. 13, &c.
60. ESTABLISHED,] *lit.* 'raised up;' as in v. 62, &c.
61. WITH,] *lit.* 'unto the lesser ones than thee.'

BY,] *lit.* 'from' thy covenant.
63. BECAUSE OF,] *lit.* 'from the face of.'
RECEIVING ATONEMENT,] *lit.* 'covering or scraping away,' i.e. erasing.

XVII. 1. PUT FORTH,] *lit.* 'hide a hidden' thing, *or* 'sharpen a sharp thing,' *or* 'tie a tie.'
USE A SIMILE,] *lit.* 'rule (with) a ruling' thing.
3. FOLIAGE,] *lit.* 'pruned' thing; as in 8. 17; Nu. 13. 23, &c.
4. TOP,] *or* 'head.'
TENDER TWIGS,] *lit.* 'sucklings.'
MERCHANT,] *lit.* a ' pedlar,' one who 'goes about;' as in 27. 3, &c.
PLACED,] *or* 'set' it; as in v. 5, &c.
5. PUT,] *lit.* 'give;' as in 5. 14; 7. 4, 9, &c.
6. THIN SHOOTS,] *or* 'leaves;' as in v. 7, 23.
BOUGHS,] *lit.* 'parts or staves;' as in 19. 14.
7. ANOTHER,] *lit.* 'one,' a 'certain' one.
8. ON..BY,] *or* 'near..near.'
GOODLY,] *lit.* 'honourable;' as in v. 23, &c.
9. PROSPERETH,] *lit.* 'sends forth;' as in v. 10, 15, &c.
LEAVES,] *lit.* things 'torn off;' as in 19. 3.
STRENGTH,] *lit.* 'arm;' as in 4. 7; 13. 20, &c.
BY,] *lit.* 'from' its roots.
10. COME,] *lit.* 'strike;' as in Ge. 20. 6, &c.
13. MAKETH,] *lit.* 'prepareth, or cutteth.'
OATH,] *lit.* 'execration;' as in v. 16, 18, 19.
MIGHTY,] *or* 'oaks;' as in 31. 14; Ex. 15. 15.
15. ESCAPE,] *or* 'is he let go;' as in v. 18.
16. DOTH HE NOT,] *lit.* 'if not.'
17. MAINTAIN,] *lit.* 'make *or* do.'
MOUNT,] *lit.* 'raised up' place; as in 4. 2.
18. GIVEN HIS HAND,] in token of true allegiance.
19. HAVE I NOT,] *lit.* 'if not..I have put.'
20. NET,] *lit.* instrument for 'hunting' with.
PLEADED,] *lit.* 'been judged;' as in 20. 35.
21. BANDS,] *or* 'wings;' as in 12. 14, &c.
22. FOLIAGE,] *lit.* 'pruned' thing;' as in v. 3; 31. 3, 10, 14.
SET, *lit.* 'given;' as in v. 18, 19, &c.
23. YIELDED,] *lit.* 'made;' as in v. 18, 24.
DWELT,] *lit.* 'tabernacled' or settled.
24. TO FLOURISH,] *lit.* 'break forth.'

XVIII. 2. SIMILE,] *lit.* 'ruling (with) this ruling' saying; as in v. 3, 12, 23, &c.
BLUNTED,] *or* perhaps 'weakened;' as in [sa. 31. 29, 30; Ecc. 10.10.
3. NO MORE,] *lit.* 'if there is to you any more.'
6. IDOLS,] *lit.* 'rolled or dungy' ones; as in v. 12, 15, &c.
NEIGHBOUR,] *lit.* 'friend;' as in v. 11, 15.
7. TAKE AWAY,] that is 'violently;' as in v. 12, 16, &c.
8. WEARY,] *lit.* 'biting;' as in v. 13, 17, &c.
TRUE,] *lit.* 'judgment of truth,' or stedfastness.
9. DEAL TRULY,] *lit.* 'do truth' or stedfastness.
SURELY,] *lit.* 'to live he doth live;' as in v. 13, 17, 19, 21, 23, &c.
10. BURGLAR,] *lit.* 'breaker up ;' as in 7. 22.
16. BOUND,] *lit.* 'pledged.'
17. FOR,] *or* 'in' the punishment.

18. USED,] *lit.* 'oppressed (with) oppression.
IN,] *or* 'for' his punishment.
19. BORNE,] *lit.* 'lifted up of the punishment;' as in v. 20, &c.
22. TRANSGRESSIONS,] *lit.* 'steps;' as in v. 28, 31, &c.
23. AT ALL,] *lit.* 'to desire do I desire.'
24. FOR,] *or* 'in his sin..in them;' as in v. 26, &c.
25. PONDERED,] *lit.* 'ready, right, straight.'
30. EACH,] *lit.* 'a man.'
31. MAKE TO YOU,] by using the proper means, in reflection on the duty and privilege of obedience, and the danger of delay.

XIX. 1. LAMENTATION,] *lit.* 'conning;' as in v. 14, &c.
PRINCES,] *lit.* 'lifted up' ones.
AMONG,] *lit.* 'between.'
YOUNG LIONS,] *lit.* 'scraping' ones; as in v. 3, 5, 6, &c.
WHELPS,] *lit.* 'sojourners,' those 'abiding' with her.
3. PREY,] *lit.* 'torn' food; as in v. 6, &c.
4. PIT,] thing for 'marring' or 'destroying; as in v. 8, &c.
5. MADE,] *lit.* 'set;' as in 4. 4; 5. 5; 7. 20.
7. FORSAKEN,] *lit.* 'widowed,' i.e. silent, dumb.
BECAUSE OF,] *lit.* 'from;' as in v. 10, &c.
8. SET,] *lit.* 'give;' as in v. 9; 5. 14; 7. 4, 9.
PROVINCES,] *lit.* places of 'judgment.'
9. PUT,] *lit.* 'give;' as in v. 8; 5. 14; 7. 4, 9.
PRISON,] *lit.* a 'secured' place.
BULWARKS,] *lit.* 'hunting' places; as in Ecc. 9. 12; Isa. 29. 7.
10. VINE,] *lit.* a 'high, curved or bent' thing.
11. RODS,] *lit.* 'extended, stretched out' objects.
APPEARETH,] *or* 'is seen;' as in 10. 1, &c.
THIN SHOOTS,] *or* 'leaves;' as in 17. 6, &c.
12. FURY,] *lit.* 'heat;' as in 3. 14; 5. 13, &c.
13. WILDERNESS,] *lit.* place of 'leading forth' a flock.
14. BOUGHS,] *lit.* 'parts, staves;' as in 17. 6.

XX. 1. SEVENTH YEAR,] B.C. 594.
FIFTH MONTH,] that is, Ab.
CERTAIN,] *lit.* 'men.'
3. I AM NOT,] *lit.* 'if I am sought.'
5. I AM,] *or* 'I, Jehovah, am your God;' as in v. 18, 20, &c.
6. SPIED OUT,] *lit.* 'went round about.'
MILK,] *lit.* 'fat;' as in v. 15, &c.
BEAUTY,] *lit.* 'desirable' thing; as in v. 15.
7. EACH,] *lit.* a 'man;' as in v. 8, &c.
IDOLS,] *lit.* 'dungy' things; as in v. 16.
8. REBEL,] *or* 'are bitter;' as in v. 13, 21.
POUR OUT,] *or* 'shed forth;' as in v. 13, &c
FURY,] *lit.* 'heat;' as in v. 13, &c.
9. POLLUTE,] *or* 'pierce;' as in v. 13, &c.
10. WILDERNESS,] *lit.* place of 'leading forth' a flock.
11. STATUTES,] *or* 'appointed, limited' things.
12. SABBATHS,] *or* periods of 'cessations.'
SIGN,] *or* 'token;' as in 4. 3; 20. 12, 20, &c.
SANCTIFIER,] that is 'setting them apart.'
13. CONSUME,] complete or 'end' them.

14. NAME,] that is, renown and character, as in v. 22, &c.

17. HATH PITY,] or 'fleeth upon them.'

DESTROYING,] corrupting or 'marring' them.

END,] or 'consummation, finish;' as in 11. 13; 13. 13, &c.

23. SPREAD,] or 'scatter;' as in Ps. 106. 27.

26. DESOLATE,] or 'astonished;' as in 14. 8.

27. COMMITTING,] lit. 'trespassing.'

28. OFFERING,] lit. a thing 'brought near.'

MAKE,] lit. 'set;' as in 14. 4, 7; 21. 20, &c.

SWEET,] lit. 'fragrance of their rest.'

LIBATIONS,] lit. 'pourings out;' as in 45. 17.

31. OFFERING,] lit. 'lifting up;' as in 16. 16.

NOT SOUGHT,] lit. 'if I am sought.'

32. MIND,] lit. 'spirit.'

33. DO NOT,] lit. 'if not.'

FURY,] lit. 'heat shed forth.'

34. PEOPLES,] lit. those 'associated' together.

ASSEMBLED,] lit. 'pressed, shut or closed' together.

37. ROD,] or 'sceptre;' as in 19. 11, 14, &c.

38. TRANSGRESSING,] lit. 'stepping;' as in Ps. 37. 38, &c.

39. EACH,] lit. a 'man.'

40. GIFTS,] lit. things 'lifted up;' as in Ge. 43. 34, &c.

41. SWEET,] lit. 'fragrance of rest.'

44. CORRUPT,] or 'marred.'

46. TEMAN,] lit. the 'south,' or 'right' hand.

PROPHESY,] lit. 'drop,' or 'cause to drop.'

PROPHESY,] lit. 'be a prophet;' as in 6. 2.

THE SOUTH,] in Heb. 'Negeb;' as in v. 47.

47. KINDLING,] lit. 'causing to go forth.'

49. USING,] lit. 'ruling (with) ruling' sayings.

XXI. 2. PROPHESY,] lit. 'cause to drop;' as in 20. 46.

PROPHESY,] lit. 'be a prophet;' as in v. 9.

7. REPORT,] lit. 'hearing, thing heard.'

10. BRIGHTNESS,] lit. 'lightning;' as in v. 15, &c.

REJOICED,] lit. 'made to leap;' as in De. 28. 63, &c.

11. HAND,] lit. 'palm, paw;' as in v. 14, &c.

12. PRINCES,] lit. 'lifted up' ones; as in v. 25, &c.

14. WOUNDED,] lit. 'pierced;' as in v. 25, 15. RUINS,] lit. 'stumbling blocks;' as in 3. 20; 7. 19, &c.

SET,] lit. 'given;' as in v. 27, 31; 3. 8, &c.

POINT,] or 'slaughter;' as in Sept. and Targum.

16. TAKE POSSESSION,] or 'be thyself united.'

PLACE,] or 'set.'

17. FURY,] lit. 'heat;' as in 3. 14; 5. 13, &c.

19. APPOINT,] lit. 'set;' as in v. 2; 4. 2, &c.

A STATION,] lit. 'hand.'

PREPARE,] not 'choose,' as in C.V.; as in 23. 47; Jos. 17. 15, 18, &c.

TOP,] lit. 'head;' as in v. 21.

20. APPOINT,] lit. 'thou dost set;' as in v. 27; 14. 4, 7, &c.

21. TO USE,] lit. 'to divine (with) a divination.'

TERAPHIM,] lit. 'tearing,' or 'burning' ones.

22. AT,] lit. 'in his right hand.'

PLACE,] lit. 'set;' as in 15. 7; 30. 21, &c.

SLAUGHTER,] lit. 'murder;' as in Ps. 42. 10.

FORTIFICATION,] lit. 'wall or dyke;' as in 4. 2; 17. 17, &c.

23. FALSE,] or 'vain, empty;' as in v. 29.

24. REVEALED,] or 'uncovered;' as in 1 Sa. 2. 27; 2 Sa. 6. 20, &c.

TRANSGRESSIONS,] lit. 'steps;' as in 14. 11.

25. WOUNDED,] lit. 'pierced;' as in v. 14.

INIQUITY,] or 'punishment.'

26. MITRE,] or 'diadem;' as in Ex. 28. 4, 29.

27. MAKE,] lit. 'set;' as in v. 20; 14. 4, 7.

28. PROPHESY,] lit. 'be a prophet.'

CONCERNING,] or 'unto.'

TO THE UTMOST,] lit. 'to contain;' as in 1 K. 8. 64, &c.

BRIGHTNESS,] lit. 'lightning;' as in v. 10.

29. PUT,] lit. 'give;' as in v. 11; 16. 34, &c.

WOUNDED,] lit. 'pierced;' as in v. 14, 25.

30. PRODUCED,] 'prepared, made, created;' as in 28. 13, 15, &c.

BIRTH,] lit. 'cutting out;' as in 16. 3; 29. 14.

31. WRATH,] lit. a 'passing over;' as in v. 21; 7. 19, &c.

DESTRUCTION,] or 'marring.'

32. FUEL,] lit. 'food;' as in 15, 4, 6; 23. 27.

XXII. 3. IDOLS,] lit. 'rolled or dungy' objects.

4. BY,] or 'in thy blood..in thine idols.'

5. SCOFF,] or 'shew themselves scoffers.'

6. PRINCES,] lit. 'lifted up' ones; as in 7. 27, &c.

EACH,] lit. a 'man;' as in v. 11.

ARM,] that is, 'power, strength;' as in 4. 7

7. OPPRESSIVELY,] lit. 'in oppression.'

WIDOW,] lit. 'silent one;' as in v. 25; 44. 22.

8. POLLUTED,] lit. 'pierced;' as in 7. 21, 22.

9. SLANDER,] lit. a 'walking up and down.

10. HUMBLED,] or 'afflicted' in thee; as in v. 11, &c.

11. NEIGHBOUR,] lit. 'friend;' as in v. 12.

12. BRIBE,] lit. a 'marring, corrupting thing.'

USURY,] lit. 'biting;' as in 18. 8, 13, 17, &c.

13. HAND,] lit. 'palm, paw;' as in 1. 7, &c.

GAINED,] lit. 'made;' as in v. 3, 4, 7, 9, &c.

15. NATIONS,] that is, political 'bodies;' as in v. 4. 16, &c.

SPREAD,] or 'scattered;' as in 5. 18; 6. 5.

CONSUMED,] lit. 'ended, finished;' as in 2 Sa. 20. 18, &c.

16. POLLUTED,] lit. 'pierced;' as in 7. 24.

18. DROSS,] or 'refuse;' as in v. 18. 19, &c.

19. GATHERING,] lit. 'pressing, shutting;' as in Prov. 13. 11.

21. WRATH,] lit. 'passing over.'

22. FURY,] lit. 'heat;' as in v. 31; 7. 19, &c

24. RAINED,] lit. 'showered on.'

25. CONSPIRACY,] lit. 'bond or binding;' as in 2 Sa. 15. 12, &c.

PREY,] lit. 'torn' food; as in v. 27, &c.

WIDOWS,] lit. 'dumb, silent' ones; as in v. 7.

26. WRONGED,] or 'violated;' as in Zeph. 3. 4, &c.

POLLUTE,] lit. 'pierce;' as in 13. 19; 20. 39.

COMMON,] or 'profane,' i.e. 'pierced;' as in v. 16, &c.

27. PRINCES,] lit. 'heads;' as in 11. 1, &c.

28. CHALK,] *lit.* an 'insipid' thing; as in 13. 10, 11, 14, 15, &c.
30. DESTROY,] *lit.* 'mar;' as in 5. 16, &c.
31. PUT,] *lit.* 'given;' as in v. 4; 3. 8, &c.

XXIII. 3. EGYPT,] *in Heb.* 'Mitsrayim.'
YOUTH,] *lit.* 'youths;' as in v. 8, 19, 21, &c.
4. AHOLAH,] i.e. 'her tent.'
AHOLIBAH,] i.e. 'my tent is in her.'
ELDER,] *lit.* 'greater.'
5. UNDER ME,] that is, while under my protection.
6. PREFECTS,] perhaps 'seconds' in rank.
DESIRABLE,] *lit.* 'choice ones of desire;' as in v. 12, &c.
7. IDOLS,] *lit.* 'rolled or dungy' objects.
9. ASSHUR,] *lit.* 'straight, happy.'
11. CORRUPT,] *lit.* 'marred;' as in 16. 47.
14. GRAVED,] *lit.* 'men of graving.'
PICTURES,] *lit.* 'images;' as in 7. 20, &c.
15. SPREAD OUT,] *lit.* 'spread out ones of dyed' things.
RULERS,] *lit.* ones of the 'third' rank.
17. BED,] *lit.* place of 'lying down.'
ALIENATED,] *lit.* 'disjointed;' as in v. 18.
18. REVEALETH,] *lit.* 'uncovereth;' as in 16. 37; 22. 10; 23. 10, &c.
20. PARAMOUR,] *lit.* a 'divided' wife; as in Ge. 22. 24, &c.
23. AND OF ALL,] *or* 'and (even) all Chaldeans.'
PEKOD,] i.e. 'inspection.'
SHOA,] i.e. 'rich, safe, easy.'
KOA,] i.e. 'disjointed, stricken;' perhaps 'poor.'
PROCLAIMED,] *or* 'called,' i.e. invited.
24. WHEEL,] *lit.* 'rolling' thing;' as in 10. 2.
TARGET,] *lit.* 'thorn,' because studded with nails or points.
SHIELD,] *lit.* a 'protecting covering;' as in 27. 10; 28. 4, &c.
HELMET,] *lit.* a 'high' thing; as in 1 Sa. 17. 38.
SET,] *lit.* 'given;' as in v. 9, 25, 31, 49, &c.
IN,] *or* 'with' their judgment.
25. SET,] *lit.* 'given;' as in v. 9, 24, 31, &c.
JEALOUSY,] *or* 'zeal;' as in 5. 13; 8. 3, &c.
POSTERITY,] *lit.* 'latter end;' as in 38. 8.
26. STRIPPED,] *or* 'pushed off thee' thy garments.
JEWELS,] *lit.* 'vessels of thy beauty.'
28. HATED,] *lit.* 'hast been sharp' towards.
29. LABOUR,] the produce of 'striking' an object.
32. WIDE,] *or* 'broad' one; as in Ge. 34. 21.
33. DRUNKENNESS,] *lit.* 'merriment;' as in 39. 19; Jer. 13. 13.
34. DRAINED,] *lit.* 'squeezed, pressed;' as in Jud. 6. 38; Ps. 75. 8, &c.
GNAW,] *lit.* 'gnaw the bone;' as in Nu. 24. 8; Zeph. 3. 3.
35. BEAR,] *or* 'lift up;' as in 8. 5; 16. 52, &c.
36. DECLARE,] *lit.* 'set forth, or forward.'
38. SANCTUARY,] *lit.* place 'set apart.'
40. PAINTED,] *lit.* 'blackened as coal,' perhaps.
41. COUCH,] *lit.* a thing 'stretched out.'
TABLE,] *lit.* a thing 'sent forth;' i.e. extended.
42. COMMON PEOPLE,] *lit.* 'of the multitude of man.'

WILDERNESS,] *lit.* place of 'leading forth' cattle.
PUT,] *lit.* 'give;' as in v. 7; 5. 14; 7. 4, &c.
43. WORN OUT,] *or* 'faded' one; as in Jos. 9. 4, 5, &c.
47. CUT THEM,] *or* 'prepared them,' that is, the stones with their 'weapons.'
SONS..DAUGHTERS,] those of the 'assembly,' not of the 'women.'
HOUSES,] those of the 'women.'
49. PUT,] *lit.* 'given;' as in v. 9, 24, 25, &c.

XXIV. 1. NINTH YEAR,] B.C. 593.
TENTH MONTH,] that is, Thebet.
2. SELF-SAME,] *lit.* the 'bone or substance' of this day.
LEANED,] *or* 'supported was;' as in Ge. 27. 37; Ex. 29. 10, &c.
3. USE,] *lit.* 'rule (with) a ruling' saying.
POUR OUT,] as in 1 K. 18. 33; 2 K. 4. 41.
4. THIGH,] so called from its 'tenderness;' as in 21. 12, &c.
BONES,] *lit.* 'strong' parts; as in v. 5, &c.
5. PILE] round; *lit.* 'go in a circle.'
THROUGHLY,] *lit.* 'boil its boilings.'
6. CITY,] *lit.* 'stirring,' noisy place.
SCUM,] *lit.* 'painful, sick or diseased' part.
8. FURY,] *lit.* 'heat;' as in v. 13, &c.
PUT,] *lit.* 'given;' as in 3. 8, 9, 17, 20, &c.
9. PILE,] *lit.* place 'gone round.'
10. CONSUME,] *lit.* 'end, finish.'
MAKE,] *lit.* 'compound the compound.'
BURNT,] *or* 'heated;' as in Job 30. 10; Isa. 24. 6.
11. BURNING,] *lit.* 'heated.'
14. REPENT,] *or* 'am I comforted.'
16. MOURN,] *lit.* 'smite' the breast; as in v. 23, &c.
17. BONNET,] *lit.* 'fair, beautiful' thing.
PUT,] *lit.* 'set;' as in 14. 4, 7; 20. 28, &c.
18. MORNING,] *lit.* 'breaking forth;' as in 12. 8; 33. 22, &c.
EVENING,] *lit.* 'mixture;' as in 12. 4, &c.
19. DECLARE,] *lit.* 'set forward;' as in 37. 18, &c.
21. POLLUTING,] *lit.* 'piercing my setapart' place.
EXCELLENCY,] *lit.* 'gaiety or gayness.'
23. INIQUITIES,] *or* 'in your punishment.
ONE,] *lit.* 'a man unto his brother.'
24. TYPE,] *lit.* 'fair or wonderful' thing.
25. SONG,] *lit.* 'thing lifted up;' as in 12. 10.
27. SILENT,] *or* 'dumb;' as in 3. 26; 33. 22.

XXV. 2. SONS OF AMMON,] descendants of Lot.
PROPHESY,] *lit.* 'be a prophet;' i.e. declare God's will.
3. SANCTUARY,] *lit.* a place 'set-apart.'
POLLUTED,] *lit.* 'pierced;' as in 7. 24, &c.
4. THE EAST,] *lit.* 'of Kedem.'
SET,] *lit.* 'cause to dwell, remain.'
PLACED,] *lit.* 'given;' as in v. 5, 7, 10, &c.
5. HABITATION,] *lit.* 'comely place;' as in 34. 14, &c.
6. CLAPPING,] *or* 'smiting;' as in Ps. 98. 8; Isa. 55. 12.
8. MOAB,] i.e. 'waters of a father;' as in Ge. 19. 37, &c.
SEIR,] i.e. 'hairy'

2 o

9. FRONTIER,] *lit.* 'extremity, end;' as in
8. 16; 33. 2, &c.
BETH-JESHIMOTH,] i.e. 'house of the
desolations.'
BAAL-MEON,] i.e. 'lord of a habitation.'
KIRATHAIM,] i.e. 'two cities.'
12. EDOM,] i.e. 'red;' as in Ge. 25. 30, &c.
VERY GUILTY,] *lit.* 'guilty to be guilty.'
13. BEAST,] *or* 'cattle;' as in 8. 10; 14. 13.
14. FURY,] *lit.* 'heat;' as in v. 17; 3 14, &c.
15. DESTROY,] *lit.* 'mar;' as in 5. 16; 9. 6.
16. CHERETHIM,] *lit.* 'cutters off;' as in 2
Sa. 8. 18, &c.
17. REPROOFS,] *or* 'reasonings of heat.'

XXVI. 1. ELEVENTH YEAR,] B.C. 588.
2. TYRE,] *in Heb.* Tsor, i.e. a 'rock.'
3. BILLOWS,] *lit.* 'heaps;' as in Ge. 31. 46.
4. DESTROYED,] *lit.* 'marred;' as in 28. 17.
TOWERS,] *lit.* 'great places;' as in v. 9, &c.
MADE,] *lit.* 'given;' as in v. 8, 14, 17, &c.
ROCK,] so called from its 'height.'
5. NETS,] *lit.* 'flat things;' as in v. 14, &c.
8. MADE,] *lit.* 'given;' as in v. 4, 14, &c.
FORT,] *or* 'wall, dyke;' as in 4. 2; 17. 17, &c.
MOUNT,] *or* 'raised up' place.
BUCKLER,] *lit.* 'thorn;' as in 23. 24, &c.
9. BATTERING RAM,] *lit.* 'smiting' object.
PLACETH,] *lit.* 'giveth;' as in v. 21; 5. 14.
WEAPONS,] *or* 'swords;' *lit.* 'wasters,' as
in v. 6, 8, 11, &c.
10. WHEEL,] *lit.* 'rolling' thing; as in 10. 2.
BROKEN UP,] *or* 'cleft.'
11. PILLARS,] *lit.* 'set-up' things; as in Ge.
28. 18, 22; 31. 13. &c.
12. WEALTH,] *or* 'strength;' as in 17. 17, &c.
DESIRABLE,] *lit.* 'houses of thy desire.'
15. WOUNDED,] *lit.* 'pierced;' as in 6. 4, &c.
ISLES,] *or* 'islanders;' as in v. 18, &c.
16. PRINCES,] *lit.* 'lifted up' ones; as in 7.
27; 12. 10, &c.
ROBES,] *lit.* 'upper' ones; as in Ex. 28. 4.
EVERY MOMENT,] *lit.* 'at the moments.'
17. LAMENTATION,] *or* 'conning;' as in 2. 10.
PUT,] *lit.* 'give;' as in v. 4, 14, 20, &c.
19. MAKING,] *lit.* 'giving;' as in 16. 34, &c.
WASTED,] *or* 'dried up;' as in 30. 17, &c.
21. WASTES,] *lit.* 'faded, worn out' places;
as in 27. 36; 28. 19, &c.

XXVII. 2. CONCERNING,] *or* 'against.'
LAMENTATION,] *lit.* 'conning;' as in 2. 10.
3. MERCHANT,] *lit.* 'pedlar, trafficker;' one
who 'goes up and down.'
SENIR,] another name of mount Hermon.
6. IVORY,] *lit.* 'tooth;' as in v. 15, &c.
BRANCH,] *lit.* 'daughter.'
ASHURIM,] *lit.* 'happy' ones.
7. SAIL,] *lit.* a thing 'spread out;' as in
Job 36. 29.
ELISHAH,] Ellis or Hellas: as in Ge. 10. 4.
8. ZIDON,] i.e. place for 'hunting' fish.
ARVAD,] now called Ruwad by the Arabs.
GEBAL,] from the dead sea to Petra.
9. MARINERS,] *lit.* 'salt' men; as in v. 27.
29; Jon. 1. 5.
11. TOWERS,] *lit.* 'great' places; as in 26. 4.
12. FOR,] in *or* with.
REMNANTS,] *lit.* things left or 'abandoned.'
13. JAVAN,] as in Ge. 10. 2; Isa. 66. 19, &c.

MESHECH,] i.e. 'drawing out;' the Moshi.
PERSONS,] *lit.* 'souls.'
15. DEDAN,] as in Ge. 10. 7.
MART,] *or* 'merchandize,' or 'merchant.
REWARD,] *or* 'hire;' as in Ps. 72. 10.
16. FOR,] *lit.* 'in or with.'
17. MINNITH,] near Ammon; as in Jud
11. 33.
PANNAG.] Ges. a 'kind of sweet pastry.'
18. DAMASCUS,] at the foot of Antilibanus.
HELBON,] i.e. 'fat, fertile.'
19. VEDAN.] Some suppose 'Aden' to be
meant.
20. DEDAN,] as in v. 15.
21. ARABIA,] *lit.* 'mixed' country.
KEDAR,] i.e. 'black;' as in Ge. 25. 13.
22. SHEBA,] in Arabia Felix.
RAAMAH,] a city of Cush; as in Ge. 10. 7.
23. HARAN,] a city of Aram Naharaim.
CANNEH.] One Heb. MS. reads ' Kalneh.'
EDEN,] as in 2 K. 19. 12; Isa. 37. 12.
CHILMAD.] Not mentioned elsewhere in
the Sacred Writings.
24. MERCHANDIZE,] *or* 'market.'
25. HONOURED,] *lit.* 'become heavy,
weighty.'
26. GREAT,] *lit.* 'many.'
27. MARINERS,] *lit.* 'salt men;' as in v. 9.
PILOTS,] *lit.* 'rope or cable' men.
28. SUBURBS,] *lit.* places for 'driving out
cattle into.'
31. MADE,] *lit.* 'made baldness baldness.'
SACKCLOTH,] *lit.* 'sacks;' as in 7. 18, &c.
32. CUT OFF,] *or* 'dumb' one.
33. FILLED,] *lit.* 'satisfied;' as in 32. 4, &c.
34. BY,] *lit.* 'from the seas.'
36. WASTES,] *lit.* 'faded or worn out'
things or places.

XXVIII. 1. LEADER,] *lit.* one who is 'before' others.
2. A GOD,] *lit.* 'mighty one;' as in v. 9.
HABITATION,] *or* 'seat.'
NOT GOD,] *lit.* 'not a mighty one;' as in v. 9.
3. DANIEL,] i.e. 'judge of God;' as in Da.
1. 6, &c.
4. WEALTH,] *lit.* 'strength;' as in v. 5, &c.
IN,] *or* 'among thy treasuries.'
7. DRAWN OUT,] *lit.* 'made empty;' as in
30. 11, &c
9. REALLY,] *lit.* 'to say dost thou say.'
NOT GOD,] *lit.* not a 'mighty one;' as in v. 2.
12. LAMENTATION,] as in 2. 10; 19. 1, &c.
13. GARDEN,] *lit.* 'covered, protected'
place; as in 31. 8, 9, &c.
PRECIOUS,] *or* 'rare;' as in 27. 22, &c.
PIPES,] *lit.* things 'pierced' with holes.
PRODUCED,] *or* 'prepared;' as in v. 15, &c.
PREPARED,] *lit.* 'made ready' or set up.
14. CHERUB,] *lit.* perhaps 'one near' to
God.
COVERING] the ark; as in Ex. 25. 20; 37. 9.
SET,] *lit.* 'given;' as in v. 17. 25. &c.
GOD,] *or* 'a god,' in his own thoughts.
15. PERFECT,] *or* 'complete, simple;' as in
15. 5, &c.
16. IN,] *or* 'by' the abundance.
THRUST,] *lit.* 'pierce;' as in 13. 19; 20. 39.
17. BECAUSE OF,] *or* 'in' thy beauty.
SET,] *lit.* 'given;' as in v. 14, 25, &c.
18. SANCTUARIES,] *or* places 'set-apart.'

19. WASTES,] *lit.* 'faded or worn out' things.
21. ZIDON,] *lit.* a place for 'hunting' fish.
PROPHESY,] *lit.* 'be a prophet;' as in 6. 2.
22. HONOURED,] *lit.* 'become weighty, heavy.'
23. WOUNDED,] *lit.* 'pierced;' as in v. 8, &c.
SWORD,] *or* 'destroying' weapon.
24. PRICKING,] *lit.* 'making bitter;' as in Lev. 13. 51, &c.
DESPISING,] *lit.* perhaps 'lashing, whiping;' as in v. 26.
25. GATHERING,] *lit.* 'pressing' together; as in Isa. 66. 18, &c.
26. CONFIDENTLY,] *lit.* 'leaningly.'

XXIX. 1. TENTH YEAR,] B.C. 589.
TENTH MONTH,] that is, Thebet.
2. PHARAOH,] i.e. the 'head' of the nation.
PROPHESY,] *lit.* 'be a prophet;' as in 6. 2.
3. SPEAK,] *lit.* 'lead forth' words.
DRAGON,] *lit.* long 'extended' animal.
FLOODS,] a 'bright, shining' thing.
4. PUT,] *lit.* 'given;' as in v. 5, 10, 12, &c.
HOOKS,] *lit.* 'thorns, pressing' things.
5. WILDERNESS,] *lit.* place of 'leading forth' the flock.
FIELD,] *lit.* 'broken,' or cultivated place.
BEAST,] *lit.* 'living creature;' as in 1. 5, &c.
FOWL,] *lit.* 'flying things;' as in 31. 6, &c.
EGYPT,] *in Heb.* 'Mitsrayim.'
6. STAFF] for 'leaning on;' as in Ex. 21. 19.
7. HAND,] *lit.* 'palm;' as in 1. 7, &c.
RENT,] *lit.* 'broken up, cleft;' as in Jud. 15. 19, &c.
LEANING,] *or* 'being supported;' as in 2 Ch. 16. 7, &c.
8. BEAST,] *lit.* 'cattle;' as in v. 11.
9. WASTE,] *or* 'dried up' place; as in v. 10.
10. MIGDOL,] *lit.* a 'great place.'
SYENE,] i.e. 'opening;' in south of Egypt.
CUSH,] the south side of the Red Sea.
11. FORTY YEARS,] as long as Israel was in the wilderness.
12. MADE,] *lit.* 'given;' as in v. 4, 5, &c.
13. AT,] *lit.* 'from' the end.
14. PATHROS,] that is, Upper Egypt.
BIRTH,] *lit.* 'place of cutting out *or* preparation.'
LOW,] *or* 'humble;' as in v. 15; 17. 6, &c.
15. FEW,] *or* 'little;' as in Ex. 30. 15, &c.
16. CONFIDENCE,] *or* thing for 'leaning on.'
TURNING] the 'face;' as in 17. 6; 43. 17, &c.
19. TAKEN AWAY,] *or* 'lifted up;' as in 3. 14.
STORE,] *or* 'multitude;' as in 7. 11, 12, &c.
TAKEN..TAKEN,] *lit.* 'spoiled..preyed.'
20. WAGE,] *or* 'work;' as in Lev. 19. 13, &c.
WROUGHT,] *lit.* 'did.'

XXX. 2. PROPHESY,] *lit.* 'be a prophet;' as in 6. 2; 11. 4, &c.
3. CLOUDS,] *lit.* 'cloud.'
4. WOUNDED,] *lit.* 'pierced;' as in v. 11, 24.
STORE,] *or* 'multitude;' as in 7. 11, 12, &c.
6. ARROGANCE,] *lit.* 'gayness, gaiety;' as in v. 18; 7. 20, 24, &c.
MIGDOL,] *lit.* a 'great place.'
7. WASTED,] *lit.* 'dried up;' as in 26. 19.
9. SHIPS,] *lit.* 'dry or set up' objects; as in Nu. 24. 24, &c.
11. DESTROY,] *or* 'mar;' as in 5. 16; 20. 17.

DRAWN,] *lit.* 'made empty;' as in 28. 7, &c.
12. MADE,] *lit.* 'given;' as in v. 13, 14, &c.
EVIL DOERS,] *or* 'evil ones;' as in 5. 16, &c.
13. IDOLS,] *lit.* things 'rolled *or* dungy;' as in 6. 4, &c.
VAIN THINGS,] *lit.* 'nothings;' as in Lev. 19. 4; 26. 1, &c.
15. POURED OUT,] *or* 'shed forth;' as in 4. 2.
FURY,] *lit.* 'heat;' as in 3. 14; 5. 13, &c.
16. RENT,] *or* 'cleft.'
17. YOUTHS,] *lit.* 'choice ones;' as in 9. 6.
18. YOKES,] *or* 'rods;' as in 34. 27, &c.
20. ELEVENTH YEAR,] B.C. 588.
FIRST MONTH,] that is, Nisan.
21. PUT,] *lit.* 'set;' as in 15. 7; 21. 22, &c.

XXXI. 1. THIRD MONTH,] that is, Sivan.
3. ASSHUR,] i.e. 'a step, or happy.'
4. FLOWINGS,] *or* 'rivers;' as in v. 15, &c.
CONDUITS,] *lit.* things for 'lifting or carrying up.'
5. BOUGHS.] Original word not found again.
BRANCHES,] *lit.* 'fair or fruitful' things.'
BECAUSE OF,] *lit.* 'from.'
SHOOTING,] *lit.* 'sending forth;' as in 5. 16.
6. BOUGHS,] *lit.* 'divisions;' as in v. 8.
FOWL,] *lit.* 'flying' thing; as in v. 13, &c.
BEAST,] *lit.* 'living creature;' as in v. 13.
DWELL,] *lit.* 'sit;' as in 2. 6; 3. 15; 7. 7, &c.
7. THIN SHOOTS,] *or* leaves; as in v. 9, &c.
GREAT,] *lit.* 'many waters.'
8. GARDEN,] *lit.* a 'protected, covered place.
CHESNUT,] *or* 'plane tree;' as in Ge. 30. 37
9. ENVY,] *or* 'jealous (for) him.'
10. YIELDETH,] *lit.* 'giveth;' as in v. 11, &c.
11. A GOD,] *lit.* 'mighty' one.
SORELY,] *lit.* 'to deal he dealeth.'
12. STREAMS,] *lit.* things 'going forth;' as in 6. 3, &c.
13. RUIN,] *lit.* 'fallen thing;' as in v. 16.
DWELL,] *or* 'tabernacle,' i.e. settle down.
15. SHEOL,] the place or world of spirits
FLOWINGS,] *or* 'rivers;' as in v. 4.
16. SOUND,] *lit.* 'voice;' as in 1. 24, 25, &c.
PIT,] *or* 'prepared' place; as in v. 14, &c.
18. HONOUR,] *lit.* 'weightiness, heaviness.

XXXII. 1. TWELFTH YEAR,] B.C. 587.
TWELFTH MONTH,] that is, Adar.
2. LAMENTATION,] *lit.* 'conning;' as in v. 16.
YOUNG LION,] *lit.* a 'scraper;' as in 19. 2.
DRAGON,] *lit.* long 'extended' object; as in Job 30. 29, &c.
FLOWINGS,] *or* 'rivers;' as in v. 14; 1. 1, 3.
3. FOR,] *or* 'over' thee.
4. DWELL,] *lit.* 'tabernacle;' as in Ge. 3. 24.
BEASTS,] *lit.* 'living' things; as in v. 23, &c.
5. PUT,] *lit.* 'given;' as in v. 8, 23. 24, &c.
6. WATERED,] *lit.* 'caused to drink;' as in Ge. 2. 6; 24. 46, &c.
STREAMS,] *lit.* 'goings forth;' as in 6. 3, &c.
7. SUN,] *lit.* 'minister;' as in 8. 16, &c.
9. VEXED,] *or* 'provoked;' as in De. 32. 16.
10. BRANDISHING,] *lit.* 'causing to fly; as in Ge. 1. 20, &c.
EVERY,] *lit.* 'at the moments.'
LIFE,] *lit.* 'soul.'
12. EXCELLENCE,] *lit.* 'gaiety, gayness;' as in 7. 20, &c.

BEASTS,] or 'cattle;' as in 8. 10; 14. 13, &c.
15. MAKING,] lit. 'giving;' as in 16. 34, &c.
17. TWELFTH YEAR,] B.C. 587.
18. WAIL,] as in Mic. 2. 4; 1 Sa. 7. 2.
21. SPEAK,] lit. 'lead forth' words.
GODS,] lit. 'mighty ones;' as in 10. 5, &c.
22. ASSHUR,] lit. 'happy or upright' one.
23. APPOINTED,] lit. 'given;' as in v. 5, 8.
SIDES,] lit. 'thighs;' as in 38. 6, 15; 39. 2.
WOUNDED,] lit. 'pierced;' as in v. 20, &c.
TERROR,] or 'downfall;' as in v. 24, 25, 26,
27, 30, 32; 26. 17.
24. ELAM,] i.e. 'hidden or concealed.'
BEAR,] lit. 'lift up;' as in v. 25, 30; 3. 12.
25. BED,] lit. place of 'lying down.'
PUT,] lit. 'given;' as in v. 5, 8, 23, 24, &c.
26.MESHECH,] i.e. a 'drawing out;' between
Armenia, Iberia, and Colchis.
TUBAL,] on the west of the Moschi.
WAR,] lit. 'with weapons of their war.'
27. PUT,] lit. 'give;' as in 5. 14; 7. 4, &c.
INIQUITIES,] or 'punishments for iniquity.'
29. EDOM,] i.e. 'red;' as in Ge. 25. 30, &c.
PRINCES,] lit. 'lifted up' ones; as in 7. 27,&c.
30. PRINCES,] those upon whom oil is
poured out.'
31. PHARAOH,] the general name of the
rulers of Egypt.
32. TERROR,] or 'downfall;' as in v. 23, &c.

XXXIII. 2. BORDERS,] lit. 'ends, extremity;' as in 3. 16; 25. 9, &c.
MADE,] lit. 'given;' as in v. 7, 27, 28, &c.
WATCHMAN,] lit. a 'looker out;' as in v. 6.
3. BLOWN,] lit. 'struck;' as in v. 6, 7, 14.
WARNED,] lit. 'made clear;' as in v. 7, &c.
5. DELIVERED,] or 'let escape;' as in 2 K.
19. 9, &c.
8. SURELY,] lit. 'to die thou diest.'
9. OF,] lit. 'from his way.'
DELIVERED,] lit. 'snatched away;' as in
3. 19, 21; 13. 21, &c.
10. SURELY,] or 'because.'
TRANSGRESSIONS,]lit.'steppings;' as inv.12.
SINS,] lit. 'missings' of the mark.
11. NOT,] lit. 'if I delight.'
TURNING] back, as the word always
means.
12. RIGHTEOUSNESS,] or 'rightness;' as in
v. 13, 14, 16, 18, 19, &c.
STUMBLE,] lit. 'he is not stumbled.'
13. SURELY,] lit. 'to live he liveth.'
TRUSTED IN,] lit. 'leant on;' as in 16. 15.
14. SURELY,] lit. 'to die thou diest.'
17. PONDERED,] or 'weighed, set up;' as in
v. 20, &c.
18. FOR IT,] lit. 'for or in them.'
20. EACH,] lit. a 'man.'
21. TWELFTH YEAR,] B.C. 587.
TENTH MONTH,] that is, Thebet.
22. SILENT,] or 'dumb;' as in 3. 26; Ps. 31. 18.
24. WASTES,] lit. 'dry places;' as in v. 27.
ALONE,] lit. 'one;' as in v. 2, 30; 1. 6, &c.
25. WITH,] lit. 'upon, above, along with.'
IDOLS,] lit. 'rolling or dungy things;' as
in 6. 4, 5, &c.
26. ON,] or 'by' your sword.
NEIGHBOUR,] lit. 'friend;' as in 18. 6, 11.
27. DO NOT,] lit. 'if not.'
BEAST,] lit. 'living' thing; as in 1. 5, 13, 14.
FOR FOOD,] lit. 'for its food.'

28. MADE,] lit. 'given;' as in v. 2, 7, &c.
30. BY,] or 'near' the walls.
ANOTHER,] lit. 'one with one.'
32. SINGER,] or 'song;' as in 26. 13, &c.
PLEASANT.] lit. 'fair of voice.'
33. PROPHET,] one announcing the will of
God.

XXXIV. 2. PROPHESY,] lit. 'be a prophet;'
as in 6. 2; 11. 4, &c.
CONCERNING,] or 'against.'
3. FED,] or 'fat, fattened one;' as in Ge. 41.2.
SLAUGHTER,]lit. 'sacrifice;' as in 16. 20, &c.
4. WEAK,] or 'pierced;' as in v. 21, &c.
MIGHT,] or 'strength;' as in Jud. 4. 3, &c.
VIGOUR,] or 'breaking;' as in Ex. 1. 13, 14.
5. SHEPHERD,] lit. 'feeder, friend;' as in
v. 2, 7, 8, 9, 10, &c.
BEAST,] lit. 'living thing;' as in v. 8, &c.
10. DELIVERED,] lit. 'snatched;' as in v. 12.
IT,] lit. 'sought them out.'
12. DROVE, or 'herd;' as in Ge. 29. 2, &c.
DELIVERED,] lit. 'snatched;' as in v. 10.
13. STREAMS,] lit. 'goings out;' as in 6. 3.
14. PASTURE,] or 'in a good feeding place;'
as in v. 18, &c.
HABITATION,]lit. 'comely' place; as in 25.5.
LIE,] lit. 'crouch down;' as in 19. 2, &c.
FAT,] lit. 'pasture of oil;' as in v. 16, &c.
16. SICK,] or 'pierced;' as in v. 4; Ge. 48. 1.
18. FOR,] lit. 'from you.'
DEPTH,] lit. a 'sunk' place.
19. CONSUMETH,]lit. 'feedeth or enjoyeth.'
21. DISEASED,] or 'pierced;' as in v. 4, &c.
22. SAFETY,] or 'ease;' as in 36. 29; 37. 23.
24. PRINCE,] lit. 'lifted up one;' as in 7. 27.
25. MADE,] or 'prepared;' as in 17. 13, &c.
BEASTS,] lit. 'living' beings; as in v. 8, 28.
CONFIDENTLY,] or 'leaningly;' as in v. 27.
27. BANDS,] or 'rods;' as in 30. 18, &c.
28. TROUBLING,] or 'causing to tremble;'
as in 39. 26, &c.
29. RENOWN,] lit. 'name.'
CONSUMED,] or 'gathered ones.'
BEAR,] lit. 'lift up;' as in 3. 12; 4. 4, &c.
31. MEN,] lit. 'man.'

XXXV. 2. SEIR,] i.e. 'hairy.'
PROPHESY,] lit. 'be a prophet;' as in 6. 2.
3. MADE,] lit. 'given;' as in v. 7; 3. 8, &c.
4. WASTE,] or 'dry place;' as in 5. 14, &c.
5. HAVING,] lit. 'there being to thee.'
6. SURELY,] or 'because, that.'
APPOINT,] lit. 'make;' as in v. 11, 14, &c.
8. WOUNDED,] lit. 'pierced;' as in 6. 4, &c.
11. ENVY,] or 'zeal;' as in 5. 13; 8. 3, &c.
15. EDOM,] between the Salt and the Red
Seas.

XXXVI. 1. PROPHESY,]lit. 'be a prophet;
as in 6. 2; 11. 4, &c.
3. TIP,] lit. 'lip;' as in 3. 5, 6; 36. 3, &c.
4. STREAMS,] lit. 'goings out;' as in 6. 3.
WASTES,] or 'dried up' places; as in v. 10.
PREY,] lit. a thing 'trampled on;' as in
v. 5; 7. 21, &c.
ROUND,] lit. 'from round about.'
5. HAVE I NOT,] lit. 'if not.'
JEALOUSY,] or 'zeal;' as in v. 6; 5. 13, &c.
6. FURY,] lit. 'heat;' as in v. 18; 3.14; 5. 13.
BORNE,] or 'lifted up;' as in v. 7; 3. 14, &c

7. WITH,] *lit.* 'to you.'
8. DRAWN,] *or* 'been near;' as in Job 31. 37.
9. TURNED] the face; as in 10. 11; Ge. 18,22.
TILLED,] *lit.* 'served;' as in v. 34; De. 21. 4.
11. BEAST,] *or* 'cattle;' as in 8. 10; 14. 13.
DONE BETTER,] *or* 'done good more than.'
15. PROCLAIM,] *lit.* 'cause to be heard;' as in 27. 30, &c.
18. POUR OUT,] *or* 'shed;' as in 7. 8, &c.
IDOLS,] *lit.* 'rolled or dungy' objects; as in v. 25, &c.
19 SPREAD,] *or* 'strewn;' as in 6. 8.
20. POLLUTE,] *lit.* 'pierce;' as is 13. 19, &c.
22. WORKING,] *or* 'doing;' as in v. 32, &c.
23. SANCTIFIED,] that is, 'set apart;' as in 44. 19, 24, &c.
PROFANED,] *lit.* 'pierced;' as in 32. 26.
25. IDOLS,] *lit.* 'rolled or dungy' objects; as in v. 18, &c.
29. PUT,] *lit.* 'not given..hunger.'
32. BECAUSE OF,] *lit.* 'from' your ways.
33. WASTES,] *or* 'dried up' places; as in v. 4.
34. TILLED,] *lit.* 'served;' as in v. 9, &c.
35. GARDEN,] *lit.* 'covered, protected' place; as in 28. 13, &c.

XXXVII. 1. A HAND,] that is, a powerful influence.
VALLEY,] *lit.* 'cleft or rent' place; as in v. 2.
2. ALL,] *lit.* 'round about round about.'
4. PROPHECY,] *lit.* 'be a prophet;' as in v. 9, 12; 6. 2, &c.
6. COVERED,] as in v. 8.
7. COMMANDED,] *or* 'wished;' as in 12. 7.
NOISE,] *lit.* 'voice;' as in 1. 24, 25, 28, &c.
9. WINDS,] *lit.* 'spirits;' as in v. 1, 5, 6, &c.
12. GRAVES,] *lit.* things 'heaped' up.
16. STICK,] *or* 'tree;' *lit.* 'hard' thing.
17. ANOTHER,] *lit.* 'one unto one.'
18. SPEAK,] *lit.* 'say.'
DECLARE,] *lit.* 'set forth;' as in 24. 19, &c.
19. TRIBES,] *lit.* 'rods, or sceptres;' as in 19. 11, 14, &c.
21. AMONG,] *lit.* 'from between.'
22. AS,] *lit.* 'for two nations.'
DIVIDED,] *lit.* 'halved;' as in 2 K. 2. 8, 14.
23. IDOLS,] *lit.* 'rolled or dungy' things.
TRANSGRESSIONS,] *lit.* 'steps;' as in 6. 4, 5.
25. JACOB,] i.e. 'one who takes by the heel.'
PRINCE,] *lit.* 'lifted up' one; as in 7. 27, &c.
26. MADE,] *or* 'prepared;' as in 17, 13, &c.
PLACED,] *lit.* 'given;' as in v. 6, 14, 19, &c.
27. TABERNACLE,] *or* place of 'settling down.'
28. SANCTIFYING,] *lit.* 'he who is setting apart.'

XXXVIII. 2. GOG,] i.e. 'high;' as in v. 2.
MAGOG,] i. e. 'place of height;' as in Ge. 10. 2.
PRINCE,] *lit.* 'lifted up' one; as in v. 3, &c.
ROSH,] i.e. 'head;' the Russians.
MESHECH,] i.e. a 'drawing out;' the Muscovites.
TUBAL,] i.e. 'overflowing;' the Tibareni.
PROPHESY,] *lit.* 'be a prophet.'
4. PUT,] *lit.* 'given;' as in v. 9, 12; 6. 2, &c.
BUCKLER,] *lit.* 'thorn' or prickling thing.
SHIELD,] *lit.* 'covering, protecting' object.
5. PERSIAN,] i.e. 'dividing.'
CUSH,] on both sides of the Red Sea.

PHUT,] perhaps 'Libyia.'
HELMET,] *lit.* a 'high thing;' as in 37. 10.
6. GOMER,] the Cimerii, near the Don and Danube.
BANDS,] *lit.* 'wings;' as in v. 9, 22; 12. 14.
TOGARMAH,] perhaps Armenia.
SIDES,] *lit.* 'thighs;' as in v. 15; 32. 23, &c.
7. PREPARED,] *or* 'ready;' as in 2 Ch. 35. 4; Am. 4. 12.
8. AFTER,] *lit.* 'from.'
APPOINTED,] *or* 'inspected;' as in Nu. 16. 29.
SAFELY,] *lit.* 'leaningly;' as in v. 11. 14, &c.
10. THOUGHT,] *or* 'devised..a device.'
UNWALLED VILLAGES,] *lit.* places 'spread out or separated.'
BAR,] *lit.* a thing 'fleeing' through another.
12. TAKE..TAKE,] *lit.* 'spoil..prey.'
CATTLE,] *lit.* an 'acquisition;' as in v. 13.
HIGH PART,] as in Jud. 9. 37.
13. SHEBA,] in Arabia Felix.
TARSHISH,] or Tartessus, a city in Spain.
BEAR AWAY,] *or* 'lift up;' as in 10. 16, &c
18. FURY,] *lit.* 'heat;' as in v. 6; 3. 14, &c.
19. WRATH,] *lit.* a 'passing over;' as in 7. 19; 21. 31; 22. 21, 31, &c.
IS THERE NOT,] *lit.* 'if not.'
20. FOWL,] *lit.* 'flying' thing; as in 29. 5.
BEAST,] *lit.* 'living' creature; as in 1. 5, &c
ASCENTS,] as in Song 2. 14.
21. EACH,] *lit.* a 'man.'
22. RAIN,] *or* 'shower;' as in 1. 28; 13. 11.

XXXIX. 1. PROPHESY,] *lit.* 'be a prophet;' as in 6. 2, &c.
2. ENTICED.] Original word not found again.
SIDES,] [*lit.* 'thighs;' as in 32. 23; 38. 6, &c.
4. BANDS,] *lit.* 'wings;' as in 12. 14, &c.
BEAST,] *lit.* 'living' thing; as in v. 17, &c
6. CONFIDENT,] *lit.* 'leaning;' as in v. 26.
7. POLLUTE,] *lit.* 'pierce; as in 9. 6, &c.
9. SHIELD,] *lit.* 'thorn;' as in 23. 24, &c.
BUCKLER,] *lit.* 'covering, or protecting' object.
JAVELINS,] *lit.* weapons for 'casting, throwing.'
10. TAKE,] *lit.* 'lift up;' as in 3. 12; 4. 4, &c.
12. MONTHS,] *lit.* 'new' things, phases of the moon.
13. HONOURED,] *lit.* 'becoming weighty or heavy.'
14. CONTINUAL,] *lit.* 'men of continuity.'
AT,] *lit.* 'from' the end of seven months.
15. BONE,] *lit.* 'substance, hardness.'
CONSTRUCTED,] *lit.* 'built up;' as in 4. 2.
18. PRINCES,] *lit.* 'lifted up' ones; as in v. 1, &c.
BASHAN,] i.e. 'fat, fertile' place.
19. DRUNKENNESS,] *lit.* 'merriment;' as in 23. 33, &c.
21. HONOUR,] *lit.* 'weightiness, heaviness.'
LAID,] *lit.* 'set;' as in 4. 4; 5. 5; 7. 20, &c.
23. INIQUITY,] *or* 'in their punishment.'
HIDE,] *or* 'secrete;' as in v. 24, 29, &c.
ADVERSARIES,] *lit.* 'distressors;' as in 30. 16; Ge. 14. 20, &c.
24. TRANSGRESSIONS,] *lit.* 'steps;' as in 14. 11; 18. 22, &c.
26. FORGOTTEN,] *or* 'lifted up or away;' as in 3. 14, &c.

27. SANCTIFIED,] *lit.* 'set apart;' as in 20. 41; 28. 22, &c.
29. POURED OUT,] *or* 'shed forth;' as in 4. 2.

XL. 1. 25th YEAR,] B.C. 587.
SELF-SAME,] *lit.* 'the substance of this day.'
2. VISIONS,] *or* 'appearances;' as in 1. 1.
FRAME,] *lit.* 'building.'
ON,] *lit.* 'from the south.'
3. REED,] *or* 'cane;' as in v. 5, 6, 7, 8, &c.
4. DECLARE,] *lit.* 'set forth;' as in 23. 36.
5. ON,] *lit.* 'from' the outside of the temple.
ALL,] *lit.* 'round about round about.'
6. STEPS,] *lit.* 'ascents;' as in v. 22, 26, &c.
THRESHOLD,] *lit.* 'extremity;' as in v. 7.
7. LITTLE CHAMBER,] as in v. 10, 12, &c.
THE SIDE OF,] *lit.* 'from near.'
10. ON THIS SIDE,] *lit.* 'from here..from here;' as in v. 12, 21, 26, 34, 37, 39, 41, &c.
12. BEFORE,] *lit.* 'at the face of.'
13. ROOF OF ANOTHER,] *lit.* 'its roof.'
14. ALL,] *lit.* 'round about round about.'
16. NARROW,] *lit.* 'shut;' as in 41. 16, &c.
WINDOWS,] *lit.* 'pierced' places; as in v. 22.
17. PAVEMENT,] as in v. 18; 42. 3, &c.
18. SIDE,] *lit.* 'shoulder;' as in v. 40, &c.
19. ON,] *lit.* 'from' the outside.
38. CHAMBER,] as in v. 17, 44, 45, 46, &c.
PURGE,] *lit.* 'cast out, force away.'
BURNT OFFERING,] *lit.* that which is 'going up' on the altar.
29. TABLES,] *lit.* things 'sent or stretched forth.'
40. SIDE,] *lit.* 'shoulder;' as in v. 18, &c
42. HEWN-STONE,] *lit.* 'stones of hewn-work.'
PLACE,] *lit.* 'cause to rest;' as in 42. 13, &c.
43. BOUNDARIES,] as in Ps. 68. 13.
PREPARED,] *or* 'made ready, set up.'
OFFERING,] *lit.* thing 'brought near;' as in 20. 38, &c.
44. ON,] *lit.* 'from' the outside.
SINGERS,] as in 2 Sa. 19. 35; 1 K. 10. 12, &c.
46. ALTAR,] *lit.* 'place of sacrifice;' as in v. 47; 6. 4, 5, &c.
ZADOK,] i.e. 'just.'
48. POST,] as in v. 7, 8, 9, 15, 39, 40, 49, &c.
49. STEPS,] *or* 'ascents;' as in v. 6, 22, &c.
PILLARS,] *lit.* things 'standing' still; as in 42. 6, &c.

XLI. 1. TEMPLE,] as in v. 4, 15, 20, 21, &c.
2. SIDES,] *lit.* 'shoulders,' as in v. 26, &c.
3. INWARD,] *or* 'to the inner part.'
5. WALL,] as in v. 6, 9, 12, 13, 17, 20, &c.
SIDE-CHAMBER,] *lit.* 'rib;' as in v. 6, 7, &c.
ALL,] *lit.* 'round about round about.'
6. TIMES,] *lit.* 'steps, strokes;' as in Ge. 2. 23; 18. 32, &c.
7. STILL,] *lit.* 'upward upwards.'
8. REED,] *or* 'cane;' as in 27. 19; 29, 6, &c.
9. LEFT,] *lit.* 'let rest;' as in v. 11.
PLACE,] *lit.* 'house.'
12. SEPARATE PLACE,] *lit.* 'place cut off;' as in v. 13, 14, 15; 42. 1, 10, 13; Lam. 4. 7.
WESTWARD,] *lit.* 'way of the sea.'
15. GALLERIES,] as in v. 16; 42. 3, 5.
16. THRESHOLDS,] *lit.* 'ends, extremities;' as in 40. 6, &c.

NARROW,] as in v. 26; 40. 16; 1 K. 6. 4, &c.
CEILING.] Original word not found again.
17. ALL,] *lit.* 'round about round about;' as in v. 5, 7, 8, 10, 12, 16, 19, &c.
MEASURE,] *lit.* 'measures.'
19. THIS..THAT SIDE,] *lit.* 'from here. from here;' as in v. 1, 2, 15, 19, 26, &c.
21. SQUARE,] *lit.* 'four;' as in 43. 16, &c.
22. WOOD,] *lit.* 'hard' thing.
CORNERS,] as in 46. 21, 22; Ex. 26. 24, &c.
TABLE,] *lit.* a thing 'sent or spread forth.
23. DOORS,] *lit.* 'leaves;' as in v. 24.
25. ON,] *lit.* 'from the outside.'
26. SIDES,] *lit.* 'shoulders;' as in v. 2, &c.
SIDE-CHAMBERS,] *lit.* 'ribs;' as in v. 5, &c.

XLII. 1. CHAMBER,] as in v. 4, 5, 7, 8, &c.
SEPARATE,] *or* 'cut off' place; as in v. 10.
3. PAVEMENT,] as in 40. 17, 18; 2 Ch. 7. 3.
GALLERY,] *lit.* a 'going forth;' as in v. 5.
6. THREE-FOLD,] as in Ecc. 4. 12.
7. WALL,] *or* 'fence;' as in 13. 5; 22. 30, &c.
9. UNDER,] *lit.* 'from under.'
11. FASHIONS,] *lit.* 'judgments;' as in 5. 6.
12. DIRECTLY.] Original word not found again.
13. PLACE,] *or* 'cause to rest;' as in v. 14.
15. ALL,] *lit.* 'round about round about;' as in v. 20.
16. SIDE,] *lit.* 'wind;' as in v. 17, 18, &c.
20. PROFANE,] *lit.* 'pierced;' as in 22. 26.

XLIII. 1. LOOKING,] *lit.* 'facing;' as in 8. 3; 11. 1, &c.
2. HONOUR,] *lit.* 'weightiness, heaviness;' as in v. 4,,5, &c
SHONE,] *or* 'given light; as in 33. 7, &c.
3. TO DESTROY,] that is, to foretell or announce it, as often elsewhere.
5. TAKE,] *or* 'lift me up.'
THE,] or simply perhaps 'a spirit.'
7. DWELL,] *lit.* 'tabernacle,' that is, 'settle down.'
8. THEM,] *lit.* 'and between them.'
CONSUME,] *or* 'end, finish.'
19. SHEW,] *lit.* 'set forth or forward.'
OF,] *lit.* 'from.'
MEASUREMENT,] as in 28. 12.
11. SINCE,] *lit.* 'if.'
FORM,] as in Ps. 49. 5.
LAWS,] *or* 'directions;' as in v. 12; 7. 26.
12. TOP,] *or* 'head;' as in 1. 22, 25, 26, &c.
ALL,] *lit.* 'round about round about.'
13. HAND-BREADTH,] as in 40. 5, 43; Ex. 25. 25; 37. 12.
EDGE,] *lit.* 'lip;' as in 3. 5, 6; 36. 3; 47. 6.
14. GROUND,] *lit.* 'land.'
BORDER,] as in v. 17, 20; 45. 19; 2 Ch. 4. 9; 6. 13.
17. STEPS,] *lit.* 'goings up *or* ascents;' as in 11. 5, &c.
20. PUT,] *lit.* 'given;' as in v. 19; 3, 8, &c.
21. PURIFIED,] *lit.* 'covered or scraped it.'
APPOINTED PLACE,] *or* 'place of inspection.'
22. KID,] *lit.* 'hairy one;' as in v. 25, &c.
SIN-OFFERING,] *or* sacrifice 'declaring the missing of the mark.'
CLEANSED,] *lit.* 'declared sinful;' as in v. 20.
FOR,] *lit.* 'in or by' the bullock.
23. CLEANSING,] *lit.* 'from' doing so.
25. PREPARE,] *lit.* 'make;' as in v. 27, &c.

26. FILLED,] *or* 'made full' their hand.
27. BURNT-OFFERINGS,] that 'go up' on the altar.
PEACE-OFFERINGS,] thus 'completing' their gifts.
ACCEPTED,] *or* 'been pleased with you.'

XLIV. 1. LOOKING,] *lit.* 'facing;' as in 8. 3.
SHUT,] *or* 'secure;' as in v. 2; 46. 1, &c.
2. NONE,] *lit.* 'a man doth not.'
3. PRINCE.] *lit.* one 'lifted up;' as in 7. 27.
BY..BY,] *lit.* 'from..from the way.'
4. LOOK,] *or* 'see;' as in 1. 1, 4, 15, 27, &c.
6. ENOUGH,] *or* 'abundant; as in 1. 24, &c.
OF,] *lit.* 'from' all your abominations.'
7. POLLUTE,] *lit.* 'pierce;' as in 23. 39, &c.
FAT,] *or* 'milk;' as in v. 15; 34. 3, &c.
9. NO,] *lit.* 'every son..doth not come in.'
10. BUT,] *or* 'except.'
GONE,] *or* 'been far from being on me.'
WANDERING,] *or* 'going astray;' as in v. 15; 48. 11.
IDOLS,] *lit.* 'rolled or dungy' objects.
11. OVERSEERS,] *or* 'inspectors;' as in 9. 1.
SLAY,] *lit.* 'slaughter;' as in 16. 21; 40. 41.
12. BORNE,] *or* 'lifted up' their punishment.
13. ACT AS PRIEST,] *lit.* 'make ready.'
14. MADE,] *lit.* 'given;' as in 3. 8, 9, 17, 20.
15. FROM OFF,] *lit.* 'from (being) on me.'
FAT,] *or* 'milk;' as in v. 7; 34. 3, &c.
18. TROUSERS,] as in Ex. 28. 42; 39. 28; Lev. 6. 10; 16. 4.
RESTRAINED,] *lit.* 'girded;' as in Ex. 29. 9.
SWEAT.] Original word not found again.
19. STRIP,] *lit.* 'push off;' as in 26. 16, &c.
PLACED,] *lit.* 'caused to rest;' as in 16. 39.
20. LOCK,] *or* 'top' turf of hair.
CERTAINLY,] *lit.* 'to poll they poll.'
22. WIDOW,] *lit.* 'dumb, silent' one.
DIVORCED,] *lit.* 'driven forth' one.
BUT,] *lit.* 'but rather.'
23. COMMON,] *lit.* 'pierced;' as in 22. 26. &c.
DISCERN,] *lit.* 'know;' as in 20. 11; 22. 2.
24. CONTROVERSY,] *lit.* 'strife, contention.'
25. DEAD MAN,] *lit.* 'dead of man.'
BUT,] *or* 'except.'
28. POSSESSION,] *lit.* a thing to be 'laid hold of.'
29. DEVOTED,] *lit.* thing made or laid 'flat.'
30. FIRST,] *lit.* 'beginning;' as in 20. 40, &c.
HEAVE-OFFERING,] *lit.* thing raised up or made 'high.'
DOUGH,] *lit.* 'doughts;' as in Nu. 15. 20, 21; Neh. 10. 37.
31. CARCASE,] *lit* 'fallen' thing; as in 4. 14.
BEASTS,] *or* 'cattle;' as in 8. 10; 14. 13, &c.

XLV. 1. CAUSING TO FALL,] that is, by lot.
HOLY,] *lit.* 'separation from the land;' as in v. 4.
2. SQUARE,] *lit.* 'four;' as in 40. 47, &c.
SUBURB,] *lit.* place for 'driving out' cattle into.
4. SANCTUARY,] *or* 'for the holy place.'
6. OVER-AGAINST.] *or* 'near to ;' as in v. 7.
7. PRINCE,] who is 'lifted up' in the eyes of the community.
SIDE,] *lit.* 'from this, and from this.'
8. OPPRESS,] as in 18. 7, 12, 16; 22. 7, &c.
9. SPOIL,] *or* 'destruction;' as in Job 5. 21.

EXACTIONS,] *lit.* 'drivings out.'
10. BALANCES,] *lit.* 'balances of justness.'
11. MEASURE,] *or* 'measurement;' as in Ex. 5. 18.
TO BEAR,] *lit.* 'lift up;' as in 10. 16, &c.
12. GERAH,] *lit.* 'a grain, bean;' as in Ex. 30. 13, &c.
MANCH,] as in 1 K. 10. 17; Ezra 2. 68; Neh. 7. 71, 72.
14. PORTION,] *or* 'allotted, limited, statute portion.'
15. LAMB,] *or* 'sheep;' as in 34. 17, 20, &c.
WATERED COUNTRY,] as in Ge. 13. 10, &c.
17. LIBATION,] *or* 'pouring out;' as in 20. 28.
FEASTS,] *or* 'festivals;' periods of 'dancing.'
FOR,] that is, 'in behalf of.'
18. FIRST MONTH,] that is, Nisan.
19. CLEANSED,] *or* rather 'declared sinful.'
20. ERRING,] as in Ps.119. 21,118; Prov. 20.1.
SIMPLE,] perhaps 'persuaded, seduced' one.
PURIFIED,] *lit.* 'scraped;' as in 43. 20, &c.
21. PASSOVER,] *lit.* a 'leaping or passing over.'
22. PREPARED,] *lit.* 'made;' as in 3. 20, &c.
23. KID,] *lit.* 'hairy one;' as in 43. 22, &c.
25. SEVENTH] month, that is, Tisri.

XLVI. 1. LOOKING,] *lit.* 'facing;' as in v. 12.
SHUT,] *lit* 'secure; as in 44. 1, 2; 1 K. 6. 20.
2. AT,] *lit.* 'from' the outside.
SHUT,] *or* 'secured;' as in Nu. 12. 14, &c.
6. PERFECT ONE,] *lit.* 'perfect ones.'
7. PREPARETH,] *lit.* 'maketh;' as in v. 12.
9. HE,] *or* 'they go forth;' as in v. 10.
12. SHUT,] *or* 'made secure;' as in Ge. 2. 21.
13. A YEAR,] *lit.* 'son of his year.'
MORNING,] *lit.* 'in morning in morning.'
14. FOR,] *lit.* 'on,' i.e. in addition to it.
TEMPER,] *lit.* 'to break, dissolve.'
A STATUTE,] *lit.* 'statutes.'
15. PREPARE,] *lit.* 'make;' as in v. 7, &c.
16. ANY OF,] *lit.* 'a man, out of.'
17. FREEDOM,] *lit.* 'the freedom;' as in Lev 25. 10, &c.
18. EACH,] *lit.* 'a man.'
19. SIDE,] *lit.* 'shoulder;' as in 12. 6, 7, &c.
LOOKING,] *lit.* 'facing;' as in v. 1, 12, &c.
SIDES,] *lit.* 'thighs;' as in 32. 22; 38. 6, &c.
21. CORNERS,] as in v. 22; 41. 22; Ex. 26. 24.
24. HOUSES,] *lit.* 'house.'

XLVII. 1. WATER,] *lit.* 'waters.'
SIDE,] *lit.* 'shoulder;' as in v. 2; 12. 6, &c.
2. LOOKING,] *lit.* 'facing;' as in 8. 3, &c.
3. WATER TO,] *lit.* 'waters of the ancles.'
4. WATER TO,] *lit.* 'waters of the loins.'
5. RISEN,] *lit.* 'gay, proud;' as in Ex. 15. 1.
6. LEADETH,] *lit.* 'causeth to go on.'
EDGE,] *lit.* 'lips;' as in v. 7, 12; 3. 5, 6, &c.
7. ON..SIDE,] *lit.* 'from this and from this.'
8. UNTO,] *lit.* 'over' the Arabah.
10. EN-GEDI,] i.e. 'fountain of a kid.'
EN-EGLAIM,] i.e. 'fountain of two calves.'
NETS,] *lit.* 'flat' objects;' as in 26. 5, &c.
12. CONSUMED,] *or* 'ended, finished.'
13. INHERIT] for yourselves; as in Lev. 25. 46, &c.
14. ANOTHER,] *lit.* a 'man like his brother.'
15. QUARTER,] *lit.* 'corner;' as in v. 17, &c

21. DIVIDED,] *or* 'apportioned;' as in 5. 1.
22. SEPARATE,] *or* 'cause it to fall;' as in 32. 12, &c.
NATIVE,] *lit.* one 'rising' from the soil.

XLVIII. 1. SIDE,] *lit.* 'hand;' as in 1. 3, 8.
SIDE,] *lit.* 'corner;' as in v. 2—8, 16, &c.
8. PARTS,] *lit.* 'shares or portions;' as in v. 21; 45. 7, &c.
11. ERR,] *or* 'go astray;' as in 14. 11, &c.
13. OVER-AGAINST,] *or* 'near to;' as in v. 18, 21; 1. 20, &c.
15. COMMON,] *lit.* 'pierced;' as in 22. 26,&c.
SUBURB,] *lit.* place for 'driving out' cattle to.
16. SIDE,] *lit.* 'corner;' as in v. 1—7, &c.
18. INCREASE,] *lit.* 'income;' as in Ge. 47. 24, &c.
20. WITH,] *lit.* 'unto' the possession.

21. ON..SIDE,] *lit.* 'from this and from this.'
23. SIDE,] *lit.* 'corner;' as in v. 1—8, 16, 24—28, &c.
29. SEPARATE,] *lit.* 'cause to fall.'
30. FIVE HUNDRED, AND FOUR THOUSAND.] This might be read, as if it were 504,000; but v. 35 shows distinctly that it can only be 4,500. Many of the enormous numbers in the Old Testament are caused by mistaken translations, e.g. Isa. 37. 36, where a 'hundred and eighty and five thousand, should be 'a hundred, and eighty, and five thousand,' i.e. 5,180.
35. 18,000,] measures or reeds, which, according to Cornelius a Lapide, is 32,000 miles, for which Millenarians find difficulty in finding room in the 'holy land' of Israel of old.

DANIEL

1HE BOOK OF DANIEL consists of two great divisions, the former (i—vi) partly historical and partly prophetical, and the latter (vii—xii) entirely prophetical. Daniel lived between B.C. 600—500, and his writings were, according to Josephus, shewn to Alexander the Great, B.C. 333; they were also referred to by Mattathias (1 Macc. 2. 49—68), B.C. 170, and formed a part of the Septuagint Version, commenced B.C. 280, and have always been included in the Jewish Canon of Scripture, and as such are quoted by the Saviour in Matt. 24. 15; Mark 13. 14. Porphyry, in the third century after Christ, was the first gratuitously to question their genuineness and authenticity, in which he was followed by Spinoza, &c. Its contents are:—

Chap. I. Early training of Daniel and his three Companions.

II. His interpretation of Nebuchadnezzar's Dream.

III. His three Companions and the Golden Image.

IV. His interpretation of Nebuchadnezzar's Second Dream.

V. His interpretation of Belshazzar's Vision, B.C. 538.

VI. Darius' Decree and Daniel's Trial, B.C. 537.

VII. Daniel's first Vision, B.C. 555.

VIII. Daniel's second Vision, B.C. 553.

IX. Daniel's prayer and its response, B.C. 557.

X. XI. Daniel's third Vision, B.C. 533.

XII. Conclusion of the 'Revelation.'

I. 1. THIRD YEAR,].B.C. 607.
LAYETH SEIGE,] *lit.* 'straitens, distresses, binds.'
2. SOME,] *lit.* 'from the extremity.'
SHINAR,] a region around Babel.
2. ASHPENAZ.] Etymology unknown.
EUNUCHS,] *lit.* 'roots,' and nothing more.
SEED-ROYAL,] *lit.* 'seed of the kingdom.'
CHIEFS,] *Heb.* Partemim, from Sanscrit *prathamas* first; as in Est. 1. 3; 6. 9.
4. LADS,] of from 7 to 14 years of age.
SKILFUL,] *or* 'acting wisely;' as in 11. 33.
POSSESSING,] *lit.* 'knowers of knowledge.'
PALACE,] *or* 'temple;' as in 4. 4, 29; 5. 2.
LITERATURE,] *or* 'writing;' as in v. 17, &c.
CHALDEANS,] *Heb.* Chasdim, i.e. 'kind ones.'
5. RATE,] *lit.* 'thing;' as in v. 14, 20, &c.
PORTION OF FOOD,] *lit.* 'of prey;' as in v. 8.
NOURISH,] *lit.* 'make great;' as in Nu. 6. 5.
6. DANIEL,] i.e. a 'judge of God,' or 'my judge is mighty.'
HANANIAH,] i.e. 'grace of Jah.'
MISHAEL,] i.e. 'who (is) what God (is)?'
AZARIAH,] i.e. 'helped of Jah.'
7. BELTESHAZZAR,] i.e. 'prince of Bel,' or Baal.

SHADRACH,] i.e. 'rejoicing in the way.
MESHACH,] i.e. 'guest of the king.'
ABED-NEGO,] i.e. 'servant of Nego,' or Nebo, i.e. Mercury, the 'prophet.'
8. PURPOSETH,] *lit.* 'setteth;' as in v. 7, &c.
POLLUTE HIMSELF.] Original word not found again in this form.
9. GOD,] *lit.* 'the God.'
10. SADDER,] as in Ge. 40. 6.
CIRCLE,] *lit.* 'leaping, revolving;' as in Job 3. 22, &c.
ENDEBTED.] Original verb not found again.
11. MELTZAR,] i.e. 'chief over the wine or treasury.'
12. VEGETABLES,] *lit.* 'seeds;' as in v. 16.
13. DEAL,] *lit.* 'do;' as in 9. 19; Ge. 6. 14.
15. AT,] *lit.* 'from' the end of ten days.
FATTER,] *or* 'firmer;' as in Ge. 41. 2, 4, &c.
16. TAKING AWAY,] *lit.* 'lifting up;' as in Ge. 37. 25, &c.
17. KNOWLEDGE,] as in v. 4; 2 Ch. 1. 10, 11, 12; Ecc. 10. 20.
20. SOUGHT OF,] *lit.* 'from them.'
SCRIBES,] as in 2. 2; Ge. 41. 8, 24; Ex. 7. 11.
ENCHANTERS,] as in 2. 2.
21. FIRST YEAR,] B.C. 536.
CYRUS,] i.e. 'one who sits on a chair' or 'throne.'

II. 1. SECOND YEAR,] B.C. 603.
DOTH MOVE ITSELF,] *lit.* 'make steps for itself.'
2. SORCERERS,] as in Ex. 7. 11; 22. 18; De. 18. 10; Mal. 3. 5.
DECLARE,] *lit.* 'set or put forth or before.'
3. MOVED,] as in Ge. 41. 8; Ps. 77. 4; Jud. 13. 25.
4. ARAMAEAN,] the language of Eastern Aram, otherwise called *Chaldee*, while that of Western Aram is called *Syriac*. The remainder of this verse and chapter, and up to the end of chapter vii., is not in Hebrew, but in this eastern Aramaean tongue.
KING,] that is, 'counsellor or leader.'
TELL,] *lit.* 'say;' as in v. 9; 4. 9, 18.
SHEW,] *or* 'indicate;' as in v. 11, 24; 7. 5.
5. ANSWERED,] *or* 'responded;' as in v. 8.
THING,] *or* 'word;' as in v. 8, 9, 10, 11, &c.
DUNGHILLS,] as in 3. 29.
8. TRUTH,] as in v. 45; 3. 24; 6. 12; 7. 16.
GAINING,] *or* 'buying;' original word not found again.
9. SENTENCE,] *lit.* 'law, or judgment;' as in v. 13, 15, &c.
CORRUPT,] *or* 'marred;' as in 6. 4.
PREPARED.] Original verb not found again.
10. EARTH,] *lit.* 'dry land.'
11. PRECIOUS,] *or* 'rare;' as in Ezra 4. 10.
13. SLAIN,] *or* 'killed.'
COMPANIONS,] *lit.* those 'joined together
14. REPLIED,] *or* 'turned back counsel.'
DISCRETION,] *lit.* 'taste;' as in 5. 2, &c.
ARIOCH,] i.e. 'lion-like.'

EXECUTIONERS,] *lit.* 'slaughterers,' or 'cooks.'
15. URGENT,] as in 3. 22.
16. GONE UP,] to the king's palace, no doubt.
18. SECRET,] *lit.* 'lean' thing; as in v. 19.
19. REVEALED,] *or* 'uncovered;' as in v. 30.
BLESSED,] that is, 'declared blessed;' as in 4. 34, &c.
20. THEY ARE,] *lit.* 'it is,' each of them is so.
21. POSSESSING,] *lit.* 'knowers of understanding.'
22. REVEALING,] *or* 'uncovering;' as in v. 27, 28, 29.
HIDDEN,] *or* 'secret.'
DWELT,] *or* 'hath begun;' as in Ezra 5. 2.
23. THANKING,] *or* 'confessing, avowing;' as in 6. 10.
27. SOOTHSAYERS,] *lit.* 'deciders, determinators;' as in 4. 4; 5. 7, 11.
28. BED,] *lit.* 'place of lying down;' as in v. 29; 4. 5, 10, 13; 7. 1.
31. EXCELLENT,] *lit.* 'over-abundant;' as in 3. 22; 4. 36; 5. 12, 14; 6. 3; 7. 7, 19.
32. BELLY,] *lit.* 'bowels.'
33. CLAY,] *or* 'earthen-ware;' as in v. 34, 35, 41, 42, 43.
35. CARRIED AWAY,] *lit.* 'lifted up.'
36. TELL,] *lit.* 'say;' as in v. 7.
38. FIELD,] *lit.* 'bare, clean, pure place.'
39. ANOTHER KINGDOM,] that of the Medes and Persians, and followed by the Greek, Roman, and Christian.
41. STANDING,] Vulg. 'planting.'
43. ADHERING,] *or* 'clearing.'
44. DESTROYED,] *or* 'corrupted, or bound;' as in 6. 26; 7. 14.
46. SWEET THINGS,] as in Ezra 6. 10.
48. PROVINCE,] *lit.* 'place of judgment;' as in v. 49, &c.
PREFECTS,] *or* 'seconds;' as in 3 2, 3, 27 ;6. 7.
49. GATE] of the king; as in Ge. 23. 10, &c.

III. 1. GOLD,] that is, overlaid with it.
HEIGHT,] inclusive of the pillar on which it probably stood.
VALLEY,] not 'plain' of Dura, in Aram Naharaim.
2. SATRAPS,] governors of *great* provinces.
PREFECTS,] *or* 'seconds,' i.e. substitutes; as in v. 3, 27; 2. 48; 6. 7.
GOVERNORS,] as in v. 3, 27; 6. 8; Ezra 5.3, 14; 6. 7.
HONOURABLE JUDGES,] as in v. 3.
TREASURERS,] as in v. 3; Ezra 7. 21.
COUNSELLORS,] as in v. 3.
SHERIFFS,] *or* 'lawyers, pleaders;' as in v.3.
4. THEY ARE SAYING.] Plural form used for singular.
5. CORNET,] *lit.* 'horn;' as in v. 7, 10, 15; . 7—24.
FLUTE,] *or* 'pipe;' as in v. 7, 10, 15.
HARP,] as in v. 7; from *Gr.* 'kitharis.'
SACKBUT,] as in v. 7, 10, 15; from *Gr.* 'sambuke.'
PSALTERY,] as in v. 7, 10, 15; from *Gr.* 'psalterion.'
SYMPHONY,] as in v. 10, 14; from *Gr.* 'sumphonia.'
8. CERTAIN,] *lit.* 'men;' as in v. 12.

ACCUSED,] *lit.* 'eat the pieces of' the Jews.
12. MADE OF THEE,] *lit.* 'set on thee.'
REGARD,] *lit.* 'taste;' as in v. 10, 29, &c.
13. FURY,] *lit.* 'heat;' as in v. 19.
14. LAID PLAN.] Compare Nu. 35. 20, 22.
15. LO,] as in v. 17, 18; 2. 5, 6, 9; 4. 27, &c
19. EXPRESSION,] *lit.* 'image;' as in v. 1, 2.
21. COATS,] as in v. 27: perhaps 'mantles.
TUNICS,] or under garments.
TURBANS.] Gesenius says 'cloaks.'
24. COUNSELLORS,] *lit.* those 'leading forth words; as in 4. 33; 6. 8.
27. SMELL,] *lit.* 'breath, wind, fragrance.'
29. BY ME,] *lit.* 'from me.'
MADE,] *lit.* 'set;' as in 4. 6; 6. 17, 26, &c.
ERRONEOUSLY,] *or* 'say error.'
DUNGHILL,] as in 2. 5.

IV. 1. PEACE,] *or* 'completeness;' as in 6. 25; Ezra 4. 17; 5. 7.
2. SIGNS,] *or* 'tokens;' as in v. 3; 6. 27.
GOOD,] *lit.* 'fair;' as in 6. 1, &c.
3. GREAT,] *or* 'numerous;' as in 2. 48; 7. 3, 7, 8, 11, 17, 20.
4. PALACE,] *or* 'temple;' as in v. 29; 5. 2.
6. BY ME,] *lit.* 'from me.'
7. TOLD,] *lit.* 'said;' as in v. 14, 19, 23, 31.
8. COME UP,] not 'come in,' as in C.V.
9. SCRIBES,] not 'magicians,' as in C.V.
PRESS,] not 'trouble,' as in C.V.
10. TREE,] an emblem of a man, a king, &c. as in Ex. 31. 3, 9.
12: BUDDING,] not 'fruit,' as in C.V.
13. SIFTER,] *lit.* 'stirrer up, awakener;' as in v. 17, 23.
15. STUMP,] *lit* 'barren thing;' as in v. 23.
WET,] *lit.* 'dipped or baptized;' as in v. 23, 33; 5. 21.
17. SENTENCE,] *or* 'word. thing;' as in 3.16.
18. TELL,] *lit.* 'say;' as in v. 9; 2.4, 9, &c.
19. ABOUT,] not 'for,' as in C.V.
21. BUDDING,] not 'fruit,' as in C.V.
SIT,] *lit.* 'tabernacle,' i.e. settle down.
BIRDS,] not 'fowls,' as in C.V.
23. SIFTER,] *lit.* 'stirrer up, awakener;' as in v. 13.
24. DECREE,] *lit.* a thing 'cut out.'
25. TO EAT,] *lit.* 'to taste;' as in v. 32; 5. 21.
26. ABIDETH,] *lit.* 'riseth up.'
27. ACCEPTABLE,] *lit.* 'fair;' as in v. 2; 6. 1.
PITYING,] *or* doing 'kindness.'
29. ON THE PALACE] *or* 'temple,' not 'in it, as in C.V.
31. THEY ARE SAYING,] as in 3. 4.
33. HOUR,] *lit.* 'look or glance;' as in v. 16; 3. 6, 15; 5. 5.
FULFILLED,] *lit.* 'ended.'
HERB,] not 'grass,' as in C. V.
BY,] *lit.* 'from or because of.'
35. DWELLING ON,] *lit.* 'dwellers of.'
CLAP WITH,] as an eastern master does when calling his servant, not 'stay,' as in C.V.
36. MADE RIGHT,] *or* 'set up.'

V. 1. GREAT FEAST,] *lit.* 'abundant bread.'
WINE,] as in v. 2, 4, 23; Ezra 6. 9; 7, 22.
TAKEN,] *or* 'brought out of' the temple: as in v. 3.
WIVES AND CONCUBINES,] as in v. 3, 23.
5. CANDLESTICK,] So in Syriac and Arabic.

EXTREMITY,] not 'part,' as in C. V.; as in **v. 24; comp. Ge. 37. 3, 23; 2 Sa. 13. 18, 19.
7. BRING UP,] not 'in,' as in C. V.; as in 4. 6.
PURPLE,] as in v. 16, 29.
THIRD,] after the king and the vizier.
9. PERPLEXED,] not 'astonished,' as in C.V.
11. FATHER,] or grandfather; as in v. 13, 18.
ENIGMAS,] or 'acute sayings.'
KNOTS,] not 'doubts,' as in C.V.
16. GIVE,] lit. 'interpret.'
17. FEE,] as in 2. 6.
19. BECAUSE OF,] lit. 'from.'
21. LIKE,] or 'equal.'
HERB,] not 'grass,' as in C.V; as in 4. 15, 25, 32, 33.
BY,] lit. 'from.'
RAISETH UP,] not 'appointeth,' as in C.V.
23. ARE DRINKING,] not 'have drunk,' as in C.V.
24. NOTED DOWN,] as in v. 25; 6. 10.
25. NUMBERED,] as in Ge. 13. 16; Nu. 23. 10.
WEIGHED,] as in Ge. 23. 16; Ex. 22. 17.
DIVIDED,] or 'dealt out;' as in Isa. 58. 7.
26. THING,] or 'word,' that is, of God.
30. DARIUS,] i.e. Cyaxares II. B.C. 567—536.

VI. 1. GOOD,] lit. 'fair;' as in 4. 2, 27.
SATRAPS,] as in v. 2, 3, 4, 6, 7; 3. 2, 3, 27.
2. PRESIDENTS,] lit. 'dear or little princes.'
AN ACCOUNT,] lit. 'taste;' as in Ezra 4. 21. 5. 5; 6. 14; 7. 23.
3. OVERSEER,] or 'prominent one.'
4. CAUSE OF COMPLAINT,] as in v. 5.
CONCERNING,] lit. 'from the side of.'
FAITHFUL,] or 'stedfast' in his duties.
IN HIM,] lit. 'upon or against him.
6. ASSEMBLED] tumultuously;' as in v. 11, 15; Ps. 2. 1.
7. ESTABLISH,] or 'raise up.'
10. GONE UP,] not 'in' merely, as in C.V.
WINDOW,] lit. 'hollowed' place.
12. CERTAIN,] or 'set up;' as in 2. 8, 45; 3. 24; 7. 16.
13. REGARD,] lit. 'taste;' as in v. 26.
SEEKING,] as in v. 4, 11.
14. DELIVER,] or 'free;' as in v. 20; 3. 17.
GOING UP,] not 'going down,' as in C.V.
DELIVER,] lit. 'snatch;' as in 3. 29.
17. AT,] lit. 'on' the mouth of the DEN,] or 'pit;' as in v. 7, 16, 19, 20, 23, 24.
PURPOSE,] lit. 'will.'
18. PALACE,] lit. 'temple;' as in 4. 4, &c.
DAHAVAN.] Syr. and Theod. 'food;' Ges. 'concubines.'
20. COMING NEAR,] not 'come' merely, as in C.V.
22. SHUT,] lit. 'secured.'
23. COMMANDED,] lit. 'said;' as in v. 16, 24.
BELIEVED,] lit. 'remained stedfast.'
24. ACCUSED,] lit. 'eat the pieces;' as in 3. 8.
26. MADE,] lit. 'set;' as in v. 17; 3. 29, &c.
ABIDING,] lit. 'rising;' as in 4. 26.
27. RESCUER,] lit. 'snatcher away.'
SIGNS,] lit. 'tokens;' as in 4. 2, 3.
PAW,] lit. 'hand;' as in 2. 34, 38, 45; 3. 15.
CYRUS,] as in 1. 21; 10. 1, &c.

VII. 1. FIRST YEAR,] B.C 555.

WRITTEN,] as in 6. 25; Ezra 4. 8, &c.
SAID,] as in v. 16, 23; 2. 12, 24, 25, 46, &c.
2. BY,] lit. 'with.'
COMING FORTH,] or 'bursting, breaking forth.'
3. BEASTS,] lit. 'living' creatures; as in v. 5, 6, 7, 11, 12, &c.
ONE FROM ANOTHER,] lit. 'this from this.'
4. LION,] corresponding to the head of gold in 2. 38.
5. BEAR,] equal to the 'silver' breasts and arms of 2. 32.
SAME AUTHORITY.] Junius and Tremellius read, 'raised up one government.'
6. LEOPARD,] lit. one 'spotted;' corresponding to the belly and thighs of brass.
7. TEN HORNS,] corresponding to the 'ten toes.'
9. THRONES,] or 'seats' of kings; as in 5. 20.
THROW DOWN,] as in 3. 21.
ANCIENT,] as in v. 13, 22.
PURE,] lit. 'clean, innocent.'
WHEELS,] lit. 'rolling things.'
10. FLOOD,] or 'river;' as in Ezra 4. 10, &c.
RISE UP,] not 'stand,' as in C.V.
11. BECAUSE OF,] lit. 'from.'
SLAIN,] lit. 'killed;' as in 5. 30.
12. IN LIFE,] or 'among the living.
13. A SON OF MAN,] that is, a human being.
14. DESTROYED,] or 'corrupted;' as in 2. 44; 6. 26.
15. SHEATH,] as in 1 Ch. 21. 27.
16. CERTAINTY,] as in 2. 8, 45; 3. 24; 6. 12; 7. 16.
17. BEASTS,] lit. 'living creatures.'
18. MOST HIGH] Ones, the word being plural; as in v. 22, &c.
STRENGTHEN,] as in v. 22.
21. WAR,] lit. a 'drawing near.'
22. COME,] as in v. 13; 4. 11, 20, 22, 24, 28; 6. 24.
23. TREADETH DOWN,] or 'thresheth' it.
25. AS AN ADVERSARY,] as in 6. 4.
26. JUDGE,] as in v. 10, 22; 4. 34; Ezra 7. 26.
TO CUT OFF,] or 'lay waste.'
27. OBEY,] lit. 'hear.'

VIII. 1. THIRD YEAR,] B.C. 553—2.
2. SHUSHAN,] i.e. a 'lily;' capital of Susiana.
PALACE,] or fortress, castle; as in 1 Ch. 29. 1, &c.
ELAM,] i.e. a 'hidden, concealed' place.
ULAI,] now called 'Kerah.'
3. OTHER,] lit. 'the second.'
4. DELIVERING,] lit. 'snatching;' as in v. 7.
PLEASURE,] or 'good-will;' as in 11. 3, &c.
EXERTED ITSELF,] or 'done greatly.'
5. YOUNG HE-GOAT,] lit. a 'leaping one' of the goats.
WEST,] lit. place of 'evening;' as in 1 Ch. 17. 28, &c.
CONSPICUOUS,] lit. 'horn of vision.'
6. POSSESSING,] lit. 'master of the two horns.'
FURY,] lit. 'heat;' as in 9. 16; Ge. 27. 44.
7. EMBITTERED,] or 'sheweth itself bitter.'
POWER,] lit. 'hand;' as in v. 4, 25, &c.
9. SOUTH,] lit. 'the 'Negeb;' as in v. 4, &c.
EAST,] lit. 'place of the 'rising' of the sun.
11. BY IT,] or 'from him.'

CONTINUED,] being offered daily; as in v. 12, 13, &c.
BASE,] as in Ex. 15. 17; 1 K. 8. 13, 39, &c.
12. WITH,] along with, in addition to.
TRUTH,] lit. 'stedfastness;' as in v. 26, &c.
13. WONDERFUL NUMBERER.] So Junius and Tremellius. Original word not found again.
MAKE,] lit. 'give;' as in 12. 11; Ge. 4. 12.
14. 2,300,] or 6 lunar years, 4 months, and 20 days; ending 13th Adar 151 B.C.
DECLARED RIGHT,] not 'cleansed;' as in C.V.
15. REQUIRE,] or 'seek;' as in 1. 8, &c.
16. GABRIEL,] i.e. 'man of God;' whom some suppose to be Moses, who is the first called 'a man of God,' as De. 33. 1.
17. STATION,] as in v. 18; 10. 11; 11. 1. &c.
18. POSSESSING,] lit. 'master of;' as in v. 6.
21. YOUNG HE-GOAT,] as in v. 5, 8; 2 Ch. 29. 21; Ezr. 8. 35.
HAIRY ONE,] not necessarily 'rough,' as in C.V.
FIRST KING,] that is, Alexander the Great.
23. HIDDEN THINGS,] or 'enigmas;' as in Nu. 12. 8, &c.
24. MIGHTY,] lit. 'bony;' as in 11. 23, &c.
DESTROYETH,] or 'marreth;' as in v. 25.
25. UNDERSTANDING,] not 'policy,' as in C.V.
WITHOUT HAND,] or 'for want of hand.'
26. TOLD,] lit. 'said;' as in Ge. 10. 9, &c.
AFTER,] or 'for.'
27. SICK,] lit. 'pained;' as in Jer. 12. 13.

IX. 1. FIRST YEAR,] B.C. 537—538.
AHASUERUS,] i.e. 'lion-king,' or Xerxes.
2. BOOKS,] or 'letters, writings' of the prophets.
FULFILLING,] or 'filling out;' as in Ex. 29. 29, 33, &c.
3. SET,] lit. 'give;' as in 1. 2, 9, 12; 11. 17.
COMMANDS,] or 'precepts, desires;' as in v. 5, &c.
MEN,] lit. 'man.'
10. HEARKENED,] not merely 'obeyed,' as in C.V.
SET,] lit. 'given;' as in 1. 17; 10. 12, 15, &c.
11. EXECRATION,] as in Ge. 24. 41; 26. 28.
12. CONFIRMETH,] lit. 'raised up;' as in Ge. 17. 21, &c.
13. APPEASED,] lit. 'smoothed;' as in Ex. 32. 11, &c.
14. WATCH,] as in Job 21. 32; Jer. 31. 28.
16. NEIGHBOURS,] those 'round about' us.
19. FORGIVE,] lit. 'send away;' as in Nu. 14, 19, &c.
ATTEND,] as in 2 Ch. 20. 15; Job 13. 6, &c.
21. THAT ONE,] lit. 'the man,' the individual.
23. THE WORD,] lit. 'a word' of command or information.
FOR,] or 'that.'
MATTER,] or 'word.'
24. WEEKS,] lit. 'seventy sevens,' that is, of years; as in v. 25, 26, 27.
SHUT UP,] or 'restrain;' as in Ge. 23. 6, &c.
SEAL UP,] not 'make an end,' as in C.V.
COVER,] or 'scrape out,' that is, erase; as in Ex. 29. 36, &c.
AGE-DURING,] lit. 'of the ages.'

25. RESTORE,] lit. 'give, send, cause to come back.'
LEADER,] one in the 'fore-ground.'
26. CUT OFF] by a violent or judicial sentence, as the word generally implies.
NOT HIS,] not 'for himself,' as in C.V.; they are no longer his place of abode and love—but are 'rejected.'
LEADER,] even Messiah; the Romans were only instruments in his hands of accomplishing his will.
DETERMINED,] or a 'determined thing;' as in v. 27; 11. 36, &c.
27. STRENGTHENED,] lit. 'made mighty;' as in Ps. 12. 4.
ONE WEEK,] or 'one seven' years; as in v. 24, &c.
MIDST OF THE WEEK,] or 'seven' years, i.e. at his crucifixion.

X. 1. THIRD YEAR,] B.C. 534.
REVEALED,] lit. 'uncovered;' as in Ge. 35. 7, &c.
WARFARE,] lit. 'host;' as in 8. 10, 11, &c.
3. THREE WEEKS,] or 'three sevens' of days, these words being added to prevent 'years' being understood, as in 9. 24, &c.
DESIRABLE,] lit. 'bread of desires.'
AT ALL,] lit. 'to anoint I have not anointed myself.'
COMPLETION,] lit. 'fulness;' as in Lev. 8. 33; 12. 4, &c.
4. FIRST MONTH,] that is, Nisan.
SIDE,] lit. 'hand;' as in v. 10; 1. 2, 20, &c.
HIDDEKEL,] i.e. 'sharp and light,' the Tigris.
UPHAZ,] perhaps the same as Ophir; see Jer. 10. 9.
6. ASPECT,] lit. 'eye;' as in v. 5; 8. 3, &c.
BRIGHT,] lit. 'light;' as in Eze. 1. 7.
8. IN ME,] lit. 'on or against me.'
10. SHAKETH,] or 'moveth;' as in Nu. 32. 13, &c.
11. GREATLY DESIRED,] as in v. 19.
12. HUMBLE,] or 'afflict thyself;' as in Eze. 8. 21.
13. MICHAEL,] i.e. 'who is as God?'
FIRST,] lit. 'one' of the first princes.
14. AFTER,] lit. 'for.'
15. WHEN HE SPEAKETH,] lit. 'in his speaking.'
SET,] lit. 'given;' as in v. 10; 1. 17; 9. 10.
SILENT,] or 'dumb;' as in Ps. 31. 18, &c.
16. MANNER,] lit. 'likeness;' as in Ge. 1. 16.
17. HENCEFORTH,] lit. 'from now.'
20. TO FIGHT,] lit. 'to be fought with;' as in Ex. 17. 10, &c.
STRENGTHENING HIMSELF,] as in 2 Sa 3. 6; 1 Ch. 11. 10.

XI. 1. FIRST YEAR,] B.C. 539—8. This verse ought probably to have closed Ch. X.
2. FOURTH,] probably Xerxes.
3. WILL,] or 'good-pleasure;' as in v. 16, 36.
4. DIVIDED,] lit. 'halved;' as in 2 K. 2. 8, 14; Eze. 37. 22.
5. PRINCES,] or 'heads;' as in 1. 7—11, &c.
AGAINST HIM,] or 'over him.'
6. UPRIGHT THINGS,] as in 1 Ch. 29. 17, &c.
CHILD,] not 'he that begat her,' as in C.V.
7. BRANCH,] as in Isa. 11. 1; 14. 19; 60. 21.

8. PRINCES,] *lit.* those on whom oil is 'poured out.'

10. CERTAINLY,] *lit.* 'to come in;' as in v. 13.

11. EMBITTERED,] *or* 'sheweth himself bitter.'

13. SUBSTANCE,] *or* 'gathering;' as in v. 24.

14. DESTROYERS,] *lit.* 'breakers forth;' as in Pa. 17. 4, &c.

16. WHOLLY,] *lit.* 'consummation;' as in 9. 27, &c.

18. ISLES,] *or* 'islanders:' as in Ge. 10. 5. PRINCE,] *lit.* 'a cutter off, decider.'

20. EXACTOR,] as in Ex. 3. 7; 5. 6, 10, &c. FEW,] *or* 'some.' DESTROYED,] *lit.* 'broken;' as in v. 4, &c.

21. DESPICABLE,] *or* 'despised' one; as in Ps. 15. 4, &c. QUIETLY,] *lit.* 'with ease;' as in v. 24, &c. STRENGTHENED,] not 'obtain,' as in C.V. FLATTERIES,] *or* 'smooth things;' as in v. 34, &c.

23. AFTER THEY JOIN,] *lit.* 'from their being companions.'

24. FERTILE,] *lit.* 'fat;' as in Ge. 27. 28, 39. SUBSTANCE,] as in v. 13, 28; Ge. 12. 5, &c.

25. HEART,] 'not 'courage,' as in C.V.

26. PORTION OF FOOD,] as in 1. 5, 8, 13. DESTROY,] *lit.* 'break;' as in Ex. 12. 46, &c. WOUNDED,] *lit.* 'pierced;' as in Ge. 34. 27.

27. AT,] *lit.* 'on or by.' LIES,] *lit.* a 'lie.'

29. AGAINST,] *or* 'into.'

30. INSOLENT,] as in Nu. 23. 8; Prov. 24. 24.

31. POLLUTED,] *lit.* 'pierced;' as in Ge. 49. 4, &c. APPOINTED,] *lit.* 'given;' as in v. 21; 1. 17.

32. ACTING WICKEDLY,] *or* 'the wrong-doers of the covenant.' FLATTERIES.] *lit.* 'smooth things.'

33. TEACHERS,] *lit.* 'causing to act wisely;' as in v. 35, &c.

STUMBLED,] *lit.* 'been stumbled;' as in v .14, 19, &c.

34. STUMBLING,] *lit.* 'being stumbled;' as in Prov. 24. 17.

36. GOD OF GODS,] *lit.* 'mighty one of mighty ones.'

39. IN,] *or* 'in reference to.' AT A PRICE,] as in De. 23. 18; 2 Sa. 24. 24.

41. ESCAPE,] *or* 'are let go;' as in 12. 1, &c.

44. EAST,] *lit.* the 'rising' of the sun. FURY,] *lit.* 'heat;' as in 8. 6; 9. 16, &c. DEVOTE TO DESTRUCTION,] *lit.* 'lay flat;' as in De. 3. 6, &c.

45. AND,] *lit.* 'to.'

XII. 1. BOOK,] *or* 'muster-roll' of the inhabitants of a city; as in Ge. 5. 1; Ex 17. 14.

2. THE MULTITUDE,] *or* 'many,' as in C.V.; the passage has no reference whatever to the last judgment, but to the spiritual awakening introduced by Christianity, and the rejection of Judaism and its followers, as in 9. 26. SOME,] *lit.* 'these.'

3. SHINE,] *lit.* 'make clear;' as in Ex. 18. 20. JUSTIFYING,] i.e. 'making *or* declaring right.' FOR EVER,] *lit.* 'and duration,' i.e. onwards.

4. THINGS,] *or* 'words.' KNOWLEDGE,] *lit.* 'the knowledge.'

5. EDGE..EDGE,] *lit.* 'lip..lip.'

7. SWEARETH,] *lit.* 'is sworn by the Living One of the age.' AFTER,] *lit.* 'for.' POWER,] *lit.* 'hand;' as in 1. 2, 20; 8. 4, &c.

11. PERPETUAL,] as in 8. 11, 12, 13; 11. 31. DAYS 1290,] *or* 43 lunar months.

12. BLESSEDNESS,] *or* 'happiness;' as in De. 33. 29, &c. DAYS 1335,] or 44½ lunar months.

13. IN,] *lit.* 'at or for.'

HOSEA

THE WORDS OF HOSEA were delivered, according to some Jewish writers, between 807—720 B.C. They may be divided into *two* parts, the first containing chap. I—III. and the second containing chap. IV—XIV. This latter part has been subdivided by Wells into *five*, and by Eichhorn into *sixteen* poems.
Hosea is quoted in Mat. 9. 13; 12. 7, (Hos. 6. 6); Luke 23. 30; Rev. 6. 16, (Hos. 10. 8); Mat. 2. 15, (Hos. 11. 1); Rom. 9. 25, 26; 1 Pet. 2. 10, (Hos. 1. 10; 2. 23); Heb. 13. 15, (Hos. 14. 2); 1 Cor. 15. 45, (Hos. 13. 14), &c.
Hosea was contemporary with Isaiah, Amos, Joel, Micah, and Nahum.

I. 1. A WORD,] or communication from JEHOVAH,] the Existing One, God of Israel unto
HOSEA,] i.e. 'he hath eased or saved.'
BEERI,] i.e. 'my well or pit,' or the 'well-man.'
UZZIAH,] i.e. 'strength of Jah.' B.C. 810 —758.
JOTHAM,] i.e. 'Jo (or Jah) is perfect.' B.C. 758—742.
AHAZ,] i.e. 'he has laid hold of.' B.C. 742 —726.
HEZEKIAH,] i.e. 'strong is Jah.' B.C. 726 —698.
2. BY,] or 'in.'
WOMAN,] not necessarily a 'wife,' as in C.V.
CHILDREN,] *lit.* 'begotten ones;' as in Ge. 4. 23, &c.
UTTERLY,] *lit.* 'to go a-whoring go a-whoring.'
3. GOMER,] i.e. 'He will complete;' as in Ge. 10. 2, &c.
DIBLAIM,] i.e. 'two-cakes' of dried figs.
BEARETH,] *lit.* 'yieldeth;' as in v. 6, 8, &c.
4. JEZREEL,] i.e. 'a mighty one sows.'
CHARGED,] not 'visited,' as in C.V.
JEHU,] i.e. 'Jah is he;' as in 2 K. 10. 11.
5. VALLEY,] *lit.* 'deep place;' as in 2. 15.
6. LO-RUHAMAH,] i.e. 'not pitied.'
UTTERLY,] or 'ceased;' as in 13. 10; 14. 3.
7. SAVED,] or 'eased;' as in 13. 10; 14. 3.
BATTLE,] *lit.* 'an eating;' as in 2. 18, &c.
8. WEANETH,] *lit.* 'cherisheth, ripeneth.'
9. LO-AMMI,] i.e. 'not my people.'
FOR YOU,] not 'your God,' as in C.V.
10. IS NOT,] not 'cannot,' as in C.V.
LIVING GOD,] or 'mighty one.'

II. 1. AMMI,] i.e. 'my people.'
RUHAMAH,] i.e. 'pitied.'
2. PLEAD,] or 'strive, contend;' as in Ps. 35. 1; 43. 1, &c.
HUSBAND,] *lit.* 'man.'
TURNETH] aside; as in v. 17, &c.
3. BIRTH,] *lit.* 'being born;' as in Ge. 21. 5; Ecc. 7. 1.
MADE,] *lit.* 'set.'
WILDERNESS.] *or* 'pasture-land;' as in v. 4.

6. MADE,] *lit.* 'walled her wall.'
7. BETTER,] *lit.* 'good.'
8. NEW WINE,] *lit.* 'that which takes possession.'
OIL,] *lit.* 'shining, clear thing;' as in v. 22.
SILVER.] *lit.* 'desirable thing.'
PREPARED,] *lit.* 'made;' as in 6. 9; 8. 4, &c.
9. TAKEN AWAY,] *lit.* 'snatched;' as in v. 10, &c.
NAKEDNESS,] or 'bareness.'
10. REVEAL,] *lit.* 'uncover.'
DELIVER,] *lit.* 'snatch;' as in v. 9, &c.
11. FESTIVAL,] *lit.* 'reeling, staggering, dancing;' as in 9. 5, &c.
APPOINTED TIMES,] not 'solemn feasts,' as in C.V.
12. MADE DESOLATE,] as in Lev. 26. 31, &c.
MADE,] *lit.* 'set;' as in v. 3; 1. 11, &c.
BEAST,] *lit.* 'living creature;' as in v. 18.
13. CHARGED,] not ' visited,' as in C.V.
RING] for the 'nose;' as in Ge. 24. 22, &c.
ORNAMENT,] *lit.* 'smooth thing;' as in Prov. 25. 12, &c.
AFFIRMATION,] or oracular announcement; as in v. 16, 21, &c.
14. ENTICING,] *lit.* 'persuading;' as in Ex 22. 16, &c.
UNTO,] *lit.* 'on' her heart.
15. VINEYARDS,] *lit.* 'prepared places;' as in Ge. 9. 20, &c.
VALLEY,] *lit.* 'deep place;' as in 1. 5, &c.
YOUTH,] *lit.* 'youths,' i.e. youthful years.
RESPONDED,] not 'sung,' as in C.V.
EGYPT,] in *Heb.* Mitsrayim.
16. MY HUSBAND,] *lit.* 'my man.'
MY LORD,] *lit.* 'my possessor.'
18. MADE,] *lit.* 'cut or prepared;' as in 12. 1.
BEAST,] *lit.* 'living creature;' as in v. 12.
FOWL,] or 'flying thing;' as in 4.3; 7. 12,&c.
CONFIDENTLY,] or 'leaningly.'
IN RIGHTEOUSNESS,] or 'rightness.'
20. FAITHFULNESS,] or 'stedfastness.'
21. ANSWER,] not 'hear;' as in C.V.
23. SOWED,] that is, 'scattered, spread abroad.'

III. 1. A WOMAN,] or 'a wife.'
TURNING] the face; as in De. 29. 18, &c.
2. BUY,] or 'prepare..with fifteen.'
HOMER,] a dry measure containing ten baths; elsewhere called a 'Kor.'
LETECH.] Original word not found again.
3. REMAIN,] *lit.* 'sit.'
4. KING,] that is, 'leader or counsellor.'
PRINCE,] *lit.* 'head;' as in 5. 10; 7. 3, 5, &c.
STANDING-PILLAR,] *lit.* 'image,' as in C.V.
EPHOD,] girding a 'priest' of Jehovah.
TERAPHIM,] or 'healers, tearers, or burning' ones.
5. DAVID,] i.e. the 'beloved' of the Lord.
HASTENED,] *lit.* 'feared,' i.e. came tremblingly.

IV.1. A WORD,] or communication; as in 1.1.

STRIFE,] or 'contention, controversy;' as in 12. 3, &c.
TRUTH,] lit. 'stedfastness;' as in Ge. 24. 27.
2. SWEARING,] lit. 'to execrate;' as in 10. 4.
INCREASED,] lit. 'broken forth;' as in v. 10.
TOUCHED,] lit. 'struck;' as in Ge. 3. 3, &c.
3. BEAST,] lit. 'living thing;' as in 2. 12.
FOWL,] lit. 'flying' thing; as in 2. 18, &c.
REMOVED,] lit. gathered;' as in Ge. 29. 3.
4. REPROVE,] lit. 'make manifest or prominent.'
STUMBLED,] not 'fallen,' as in C.V.
PROPHET,] or public preacher; as in 6. 5.
CUT OFF,] or 'silenced;' as in Jer. 6. 2, &c.
6. CUT OFF,] or 'become silenced;' as in 10. 7, 15, &c.
KNOWLEDGE,] lit. 'the knowledge.'
LAW,] lit. 'direction;' as in 8. 1, 12, &c.
7. SINNED,] or 'missed the mark.'
HONOUR,] lit. 'weightiness, heaviness.'
SHAME,] lit. 'lightness;' as in v. 18, &c.
8. SOUL,] that is, their 'desire, or breathing.'
9. CHARGED,] not 'visited,' as in C.V.
10. INCREASE,] lit. 'break forth;' as in v. 2, &c.
11. NEW WINE,] as in 2. 8, 9, 22; 7. 14, &c.
12. STAFF,] lit. 'wood;' as in Ge. 1. 11, 12.
DECLARETH,] or 'setteth forth or forward.'
ERR,] or 'go astray, wander;' as in Ge. 20. 13, &c.
13. TOPS,] or 'heads;' as in 1. 11; Ge. 2. 10.
HILLS,] or 'heights;' as in 10. 8; Ge. 49. 36.
POPLAR,] as in Ge. 30. 37.
TEREBINTH,] as in Ge. 35. 4; Jud. 6. 11, &c.
14. SPOUSES,] as in v. 13; Ge. 11. 31, &c.
SEE AFTER,] as in 1. 4; 2. 23; 8. 13; 9. 9, &c.
WHEN,] or 'because.'
KICKETH,] as in Prov. 10. 8, 10.
15. THOUGH,] lit. 'if a whoremonger.'
GUILTY,] or 'desolate;' as in 5. 15; 10. 2.
GILGAL,] i.e. a 'rolling;' between Jericho and the Jordan.
SWARE,] lit. 'be sworn;' as in Ge. 21. 24.
16. REFRACTORY HEIFER,] or 'cow turning aside.'
LARGE,] or 'broad' place; as in 2 Sa. 22. 20.
17. IDOLS,] lit. 'grievous things;' as in 8. 4.
SOUR,] or 'turned aside;' as in 7. 14, &c.
DILIGENTLY,] lit. 'to go a-whoring.'
PROTECTORS,] or 'shields;' as in Ge. 15. 1.
SHAME,] lit. 'lightness;' as in v. 7, &c.
19. DISTRESSED,] or 'straitened, pressed.'

V. 1. ATTEND,] as in 2 Ch. 20. 15; Job 13. 6.
SNARE,] lit. a thing 'spread out;' as in 9. 8, &c.
MIZPAH,] i.e. a 'place of looking out.'
TABOR,] between Zebulun and Naphtali.
2. SINNERS,] those 'turning aside;' as in Ps. 40. 4.
FETTER,] lit. 'band, instruction;' as in De. 11. 2, &c.
4. MIDST,] lit. 'heart;' as in 11. 9; Ge. 18. 12.
5. HUMBLED..TO,] or 'afflicted..in' his face.
STUMBLE..BY,] or 'are stumbled in.'
6. WITHDRAWN,] as in De. 25. 9; Lam. 4. 3.
7. AGAINST,] or 'with..Jehovah.'
3. BLOW,] lit. 'strike a trumpet.'

9. REPROOF,] a 'making prominent or manifest.'
SURE,] lit. 'stedfast' thing; as in 11. 12.
10. PRINCES,] lit. 'heads;' as in 3. 4, &c.
POUR OUT,] or 'shed forth;' as in Ge. 37. 22.
WRATH,] lit. 'passing over;' as in 13. 11.
13. SICKNESS,] or 'pain;' as in De. 7. 15, &c.
WOUND,] as in Jer. 30. 13.
WARLIKE,] lit. 'striving, contending;' as in 4. 4; 10. 6, &c.
REMOVE,] as in 2 Sa. 20. 13.
14. LION,] perhaps 'a black' one; as in 13. 7, &c.
YOUNG LION,] lit. a 'scraper;' as in Jud. 14. 5, &c.
BEAR AWAY,] or 'lift up;' as in 1. 6, &c.
DELIVERER,] lit. 'snatcher away;' as in De. 32. 39, &c.
15. DESOLATE,] as in 4. 15; 10. 2; 13. 1, &c.
SPEEDILY,] or 'earnestly, early;' as in Job 8. 5, &c.

VI. 2. AFTER,] lit. 'from.'
3. PREPARED,] made ready or 'set up.'
5. MY,] not 'thy,' as in C.V.; so Sept., &c.
6. ABOVE,] or 'more than.
7. ADAM,] or 'a man,' a human being.
TRANSGRESSED,] lit. 'passed over;' as in 8. 1; 10. 11, &c.
8. GILEAD,] i.e. a 'heap of witness.'
SLIPPERY,] as in Isa. 40. 4; Jer. 17. 9.
9. WICKEDNESS,] or 'device;' as in Lev 18. 17, &c.
SHECHEM,] i.e. a 'shoulder.'
11. APPOINTED,] lit. 'set;' as in 2. 3, &c.

VII.1. WHEN,] or 'at, according to.'
REVEALED,] lit. 'uncovered;' as in Ge 35. 7, &c.
WICKEDNESS,] lit. 'evils;' as in v. 2, 3, &c
STREET,] lit. 'out-place;' as in Ge. 6. 14.
3. WICKEDNESS,] or 'evil;' as in v. 1, &c.
4. OF,] lit. 'from, by.'
AFTER,] lit. 'from' kneading.
5. POISON,] lit. 'heat;' as in Ge. 27. 44, &c
7. JUDGES,] or 'executive' rulers; as in 13. 10, &c.
8. MIXETH HIMSELF,] or 'confoundeth himself.'
UNTURNED,] lit. 'without a turning.'
10. EXCELLENCE,] lit. 'gaiety, gayness;' as in 5. 5, &c.
FOR,] or 'in.'
11. EGYPT,] in Heb. 'Mitsrayim.'
12. FOWL,] lit. 'flying thing;' as in 2. 18,&c.
CHASTISE,] or 'instruct, correct.'
COMPANY,] as in Ex. 12. 3. 6, 19, 47; 16. 1.
13. WANDERED,] or 'moved;' as in Ge 31. 40, &c.
TRANSGRESSED,] lit. 'stepped;' as in 8. 1.
14. BEDS,] lit. 'places for lying down '
ASSEMBLE,] or 'drag themselves,' or 'sojourn.'
15. THINK,] or 'devise, or reckon;' as in Lev. 25. 27, &c.
16. PRINCES,] or 'heads;' as in v. 3, 5, &c.

VIII. 1. MOUTH,] lit. 'palate;' as in Job 6. 30, &c.
TRANSGRESSED,] lit. 'passed over;' as in 6. 7; 10. 11, &c.

LAW,] or 'direction;' as in v. 12; 4. 6, &c.
REBELLED,] lit. 'passed over or stepped.'
4. BY,] lit. 'from me.'
IDOLS,] lit. 'grievous things;' as in 4. 7.
5. CALF,] or 'heifer;' as in v. 6; 13. 2, &c.
BURNED,] or 'been hot;' as in Ge. 4, 5, &c.
PURITY,] as in Ge. 20. 5; Ps. 26. 6; 73. 13;
Am. 4. 6.
7. YIELDING,] lit. 'making;' as in 6. 4, &c.
10. THOUGH,] or 'when,' or 'because.'
14. PALACES,] or 'high places;' as in 1 K.
16. 18; 2 K. 15. 25, &c.

IX. 1. JOYFUL,] or 'leaping;' as in Ps. 2. 11.
FROM,] lit. 'from on or near.'
2. DELIGHT,] or 'feed;' as in 4. 16; Ge. 30. 31.
FAIL,] lit. 'lie;' as in Ge. 18. 15; Lev. 6. 2.
5. APPOINTED,] or 'of appointment.'
FESTIVAL,] a period of 'moving to and fro.'
6. BECAUSE OF,] or 'from.'
MOPH,] also called 'Noph', i.e. Memphis.
7. MAD,] as in De. 28. 34; 1 Sa. 21. 15, &c.
HATRED,] as in v. 8.
9. GIBEAH,] i.e. a 'height,' in tribe of
Benjamin.
10. WILDERNESS,] or place for 'leading
forth' cattle.
BAAL-PEOR,] i e. 'lord or possessor of
gaping.'
11. FOWL,] lit. 'flying thing;' as in 2. 18, &c.
12. THOUGH,] lit. 'if they make great.'
CHILDLESS,] or 'bereaved them;' as in Ge.
31. 38, &c.
13. COMELINESS,] or a 'comely place;' as in
Ex. 15. 13, &c.
14. MISCARRYING,] lit. 'bereaving;' as in
Jer. 50. 9.
15. APOSTATES.] lit. 'turners aside;' as in
4. 16, &c.
17. WANDERERS,] lit. 'moving about;' as in
Job 15. 23, &c.

X. 1. EMPTY,] as in Isa. 24. 1; Neh. 2. 2.
LIKE,] or 'equal to himself.'
2. BREAK DOWN,] lit. 'behead;' as in Ex.
13. 13; 34. 20, &c.
STANDING-PILLARS,] as in v. 1; 3. 4, &c.
4. FALSEHOOD,] lit. a 'vain, empty' thing.
MAKING,] or 'cutting, preparing.'
FLOURISHED,] or 'broken forth;' as in 14. 5.
5. FEAR,] or 'sojourn;' as in Ge. 20. 1, &c.
PRIESTS,] as in 2 K. 23. 5; Zeph. 1. 4.
6. WARLIKE,] or 'striving;' as in 4. 4, &c.
OF,] lit. 'from, because of.'
7 CUT OFF,] or 'become silent or dumb.'
11. TRAINED,] lit. 'taught, accustomed.'
12. IN,] or 'with a view to, in reference to.'
SHEW,] as in Ex. 4. 12, 15; 15. 15; De. 17. 10.
13. TRUSTED,] lit. 'leant;' as in Jud. 9. 26.
14. SHALMAN,] or Shalmanezar, as in 2 K.
17. 3, &c.
BETH-ABEL,] i.e. 'house of the ambush of
God.'
AGAINST,] or 'with, in addition to.'
15. WICKEDNESS,] lit. 'evil of your evil.'
CUT OFF,] lit. 'to become dumb become
dumb.'

XI. 1. BECAUSE,] not 'when,' as in C.V.
2. RIGHTLY,] as in Ex. 10. 29; Nu. 27. 7, &c.
BEFORE THEM,] lit. 'from their faces.'

3. STRENGTHENED,] or 'healed;' as in 6. 1.
6. GRIEVOUS,] or 'painful;' as in De. 2. 25.
BARS,] or 'parts;' as in Ex. 25. 13, 14, &c.
8. MAKE,] lit. 'give;' as in 5. ;4; 9. 14, &c.
IN,] lit. 'on or against me.
9. FIERCENESS,] lit. 'heat;' as in Ex. 15. 7.
DESTROY,] mar, or 'corrupt;' as in Ge. 6. 17.
ENMITY,] or 'city;' as in v. 6; 8. 14; 13. 10.
10. WEST,] lit. 'the sea,' the Mediterranean.
12. FEIGNING,] lit. 'lying;' as in 7. 3, &c.
FAITHFUL,] or 'stedfast;' as in 5. 9, &c.

XII. 1. EPHRAIM,] that is, the ten tribes.
ENJOYING,] as in Ge. 4. 2; 13. 7, 8; 26. 20.
MAKE,] prepare, or 'cut;' as in 2. 18, &c.
2. CONTROVERSY,] or 'strife, contention;'
as in 4. 1, &c.
4. WITH US,] or 'with him.'
6. THROUGH,] or 'in.'
8. WEALTH,] or 'strength;' as in v. 3, &c
AGAINST,] or 'in reference to me.'
10. UNTO,] or 'by' their instrumentality.
USE SIMILIES,] or 'make likenesses.'
11. SURELY,] lit. 'if.'

XIII. 1. WHEN,] lit. 'and.'
2. OF,] lit. 'from.'
IDOLS,] lit. 'grievous things;' as in 4. 17
4. SAVIOUR,] one who 'gives ease;' as in
Ge. 22. 27, &c.
5. WILDERNESS,] or 'pasture-land;' as in
v. 15, &c.
6. SATIATED,] or 'satisfied;' as in 4. 10, &c.
LIFTED UP,] or 'is high;' as in Ge. 7. 17, &c.
7. LION,] probably a 'black' one; as in 5. 14.
LEOPARD,] a 'spotted one;' as in Song 4. 8.
3. MEET,] or 'come or kick against' them.
ENCLOSURE,] or 'shut, secured' part.
9. BEAST,] lit. 'living' creature; as in 2. 12.
REND,] or 'cleave;' as in Ge. 22. 3, &c.
10. DESTROYED,] marred or 'corrupted;'
as in 9. 9, &c.
11. WRATH,] or 'passing over;' as in 5. 10.
13. REMAINETH,] lit. 'standeth still;' as
in 10. 9, &c.
14. HID,] or 'kept secret;' at in Ge. 4. 14.
15. THOUGH..AMONG,] or 'when..between.'
16. REBELLED,] or 'been bitter;' as in Nu.
20. 24, &c.
RIPPED UP,] or 'cleft;' as in Jos. 9. 4; Ex.
26. 10, &c.

XIV. 1. BY,] or 'in.'
2. TURN] back; as in v. 1; Ge. 16. 9, &c.
TAKE AWAY,] lit. 'thou dost lift up.'
GIVE,] as in Ps. 68. 18.
RENDER,] or 'complete, recompense.'
3. SAVE,] or 'ease;' as in 1. 7; 13. 10, &c.
FATHERLESS,] or 'orphan;' as in Ex. 22.
22, 24, &c.
5. FLOURISHETH,] lit. 'breaketh forth;' as
in v. 7; 10. 4, &c.
6. BEAUTY,] or 'honour, majesty;' as in
Nu. 27. 20, &c.
7. UNDER,] or 'in.'
8. IDOLS,] lit. 'grievous things;' as in 4. 17.
GREEN,] or 'flourishing;' as in De. 12. 2, &c.
9. PRUDENT,] or 'intelligent, understanding.'
STUMBLE,] or 'are stumbled.'

JOEL

THE WORDS OF JOEL have no date affixed to them; the Septuagint Version places them after Amos and Micah, and some Rabbis make him contemporary with Elisha (B.C. 906—838), others as late as Manasseh (B.C. 698—643). New Testament references or allusions are Mat. 24. 29; Acts 2. 16—21; Rom. 10. 13—16; Rev. 21. 27; 22. 1.

I. 1. A WORD,] or communication from JEHOVAH,] the Existing One, unto JOEL,] i.e. 'Jo is a mighty one;' son of PETHUEL,] i.e. 'persuaded of a mightyone.'
2. AGED ONES,] 'elders,' lit. 'bearded ones.' OR,] lit. 'and.'
3. TALK,] or 'recount, rehearse;' as in Ge. 40 8, &c.
4. LEFT] over; as in Ge. 49. 3; Ex. 10. 5, &c. PALMER-WORM,] lit. 'shearing, cutting, cropping' one.
LOCUST,] lit. 'multiplier;' as in 2. 25, &c. CANKER-WORM,] lit. 'yellow' one; as in 2. 25; Ps. 105. 34, &c.
CATERPILLAR,] as in 1 K. 8. 37; 2 Ch. 6. 28.
5. DRUNKARDS,] or 'merry ones;' as in 1 Sa. 1. 13, &c.
6. ON,] or 'against.'
STRONG,] lit. 'bony;' as in 2. 2, 5, 11, &c. LIONESS,] or 'old lion;' as in Ge. 49. 9, &c.
7. MADE,] lit. 'set;' as in Ge. 2. 8; 4. 15, &c. CHIP,] lit. thing 'cut off.'
THROUGHLY,] lit. 'to make bare it made bare.'
8. VIRGIN,] lit. 'separated' from others. YOUTH,] lit. 'youths, youthful days.'
10. NEW WINE,] as in 2. 19, 24; Ge. 27. 28. OIL,] lit. 'shining or clear' thing.
11. VINE-DRESSERS,] as in 2 K. 25. 12, &c.
12. WITHERED,] or 'dried up;' as in Ge.
13. LAMENT,] or 'smite' the breast; as in 2 Sa. 3. 31, &c.
14. SANCTIFY,] that is, 'set apart.'
15. CRY] for help; as in Jud. 10. 14, &c. MIGHTY,] as in Ge. 17. 1; 28. 3; 35. 11, &c.
16. REJOICING,] lit. 'leaping;' as in Job 3. 22, &c.
18. DROVES,] or 'herds;' as in Ge. 29. 2, 3. PASTURE,] or 'feeding-place;' as in Ge. 47. 4; 1 Ch. 4. 39, &c.
20. STREAMS,] lit. 'goings forth;' as in 3.18.

II. 1. BLOW,] lit. 'strike;' as in v. 15, &c.
2. MIGHTY,] lit. 'bony;' as in v. 5, 11, &c. OF OLD,] lit. 'from the hidden time.'
3. EDEN,] i.e. 'delight;' as in Ge. 2. 8, &c.
5. NOISE,] lit. 'voice.'
BATTLE,] lit. an 'eating;' as in v. 7; 3. 9, &c.
7. EACH,] lit. a 'man.'
8. WAY,] lit. 'high-way;' as in Nu. 20. 19. MISSILE,] lit. a 'thing sent;' as in 2 Ch. 23. 10; 32. 5, &c.
9. RUN TO AND FRO.] lit. 'leg,' use the legs, that is, they run up and down. ON,] or 'in within.'

BY,] or 'though.'
10. SUN,] lit. a 'minister;' as in v. 31, &c. MOON,] lit. 'yellow or pale one;' as in v. 31.
11. BEAR,] or 'contain;' as in 1 K. 7. 26.
12. LAMENTATION,] lit. 'beating' of the breast; as in Ge. 50. 10, &c.
15. BLOW,] lit. 'strike;' as in v. 1, &c. PROCLAIM,] lit. 'call;' as in 1. 14; 3. 9, &c.
16. AGED,] or 'elders;' as in v. 28; 1. 2, &c. CLOSET,] or 'covering;' as in Ps. 19. 5; Isa. 4. 5.
17. HAVE PITY,] or 'flee or haste unto.'
20. FROM YOU,] lit. 'from on you.'
EASTERN,] that is, the Salt Sea.
WESTERN,] that is, the Mediterranean.
TO WORK,] or 'to do it.'
21. JOY,] lit. 'leap;' as in v. 23; Ps. 2. 11.
22. SPRING FORTH,] or 'become tender.' PASTURES,] lit. 'comely-places;' as in 1. 19.
BORNE,] lit. 'lifted up;' as in Ge. 7. 17, &c.
23. JOY,] lit. 'leap;' as in v. 21, &c. TEACHER,] lit. one 'shewing' the path; as in Ps. 84. 6.
SPRINKLING,] lit. 'casting, shooting;' as in Prov. 26. 18, &c.
GATHERED,] as in De. 11. 14; Job 29. 23.
26. EATING,] lit. 'to eat;' as in Ge. 2. 16,&c.
28. OLD MEN,] lit. 'bearded ones,' elders. YOUNG MEN,] lit. 'choice ones;' as in De. 32. 25, &c.
30. WONDERS,] lit. 'fair things;' as in Ex. 4. 21; 7. 3, 9, &c.
COLUMNS,] lit. 'palm-trees;' as in Ex. 15. 27, &c.
32. IN,] not 'on,' as in C.V.

III. 2. VALLEY,] lit. 'deep place;' as in v. 12, 14, &c.
3. YOUNG MAN,] lit. 'lad;' as in Ge. 4. 23. YOUNG WOMAN,] lit. 'lass;' as in Ge. 34. 4; Zec. 8. 5.
THAT,] lit. 'and.'
4. TYRE,] i.e. a 'rock.'
ZIDON,] i.e. place of 'hunting' fish.
SWIFTLY,] lit. 'light;' as in 2 Sa. 2. 18, &c.
6. FROM,] lit. 'from (being) on.'
8. SHABEANS,] in Arabia Felix.
9. WAR,] or 'of the battle.'
10. SWORDS,] lit. 'wasting' instruments. JAVELINS,] for 'throwing;' as in Nu. 25. 7.
11. ROUND,] lit. 'from around.'
JEHOSHAPHAT,] i.e. 'Jah has judged.'
13. HARVEST,] the time of 'reaping;' as in 1. 11, &c.
GREAT,] or 'abundant.'
14. DECISION,] lit. 'the determined thing.'
15. SUN,] i.e. 'minister;' as in Nu. 2. 10, 31.
17. DWELLING,] tabernacling or 'settling down.'
HOLY,] that is, 'set apart.'
18. FLOW,] lit. 'go;' as in 2. 7, 8, &c. VALLEY,] as in Ge. 32. 23; Lev. 11. 9, &c.
19. FOR,] lit. 'from, because of.'
21. DWELLING,] lit. 'settling-down.'

2 P

AMOS

THE WORDS OF AMOS were delivered during the reigns of Uzziah (B.C.810) and of Jeroboam (B.C.825). New Testament references are Acts 7. 42, 43; 15. 15—17. They may be divided into four sections, *first*, ch. 1.1—2. 3; *second*, ch. 2. 4—6. 14; *third*, ch. 7. 1—9. 10; *fourth*, ch. 9. 11—15. There are many allusions to pastoral life, natural to the author as a herdsman, e.g. 1. 3; 2. 13; 3. 4, 5; 4. 2, 7, 9; 5. 8, 19; 6. 12; 7. 1; 9. 3, 9, 13, 14. The author is not to be confounded with Amos (*pr.* Amots), father of Isaiah, as has been done by some.'

I. 1. WORDS,] *or* 'matters' recorded by AMOS,] i.e. a 'burden,' who was among the HERDSMEN,] as in 2 K. 3. 4.
TEKOA,] i.e. a 'striking or blowing,' a city six miles south of Beth-Lehem, whence he went to Samaria.
SEEN] in mental, prophetic vision concerning
ISRAEL,] the kingdom of the ten tribes.
UZZIAH,] i.e. 'strength of Jah.' B.C. 810 —758.
JEROBOAM,] i.e. a 'people pleads;' B.C. 825—784.
JOASH,] i.e. 'Jo is a foundation;' B.C. 841 —825.
SHAKING,] noticed also in Zech. 14. 5; Isa. 5. 25.
2. JEHOVAH,] the Existing One, God of Israel.
ZION,] i.e. 'dry or sunny place.'
ROAR] as a lion; as in 3. 4, 8; Job 37. 4, &c.
PASTURES,] *or* 'comely places;' as in Ps. 23. 2; 65. 12, &c.
CARMEL,] i.e. a 'prepared place.'
3. THUS SAID,] as in v. 5, 6, 8, 9, 11, &c.
THREE TRANSGRESSIONS,] *or* 'steps' in the way of evil.
DAMASCUS,] the capital city of Syria.
REVERSE,] *or* 'turn back' the judgment.
GILEAD,] i.e. 'heap of witness.'
4. HAZAEL,] i.e. 'God has seen.'
PALACES,] *or* 'high places;' as in v. 7, &c.
BEN-HADAD,] i.e. 'son of shouting.'
5. BAR] *lit.* a thing 'fleeing' through another.
BIQAT-AVEN,] i.e. 'cleft place of iniquity.'
BETH-EDEN,] i.e. a 'house of delight.'
KIR,] i.e. a 'wall.'
6. GAZA,] i.e. 'strength.'
CAPTIVITY,] *lit.* 'removal;' as in v. 9, &c.
DELIVER UP,] *or* 'make secure;' as in v. 9; 1 Sa. 23. 20.
8. ASHDOD,] in N.T. called 'Azotus.'
ASHKELON,] i.e. a 'little weighing' machine.
EKRON,] i.e. a 'little root.'
PHILISTINES,] by the Mediterranean sea.
9. TYRE,] i.e. a 'rock.'
BROTHERLY,] *lit.* 'covenant of brothers.'
11. EDOM,] i.e. 'red;' as in v. 6.

DESTROYED,] marred, or corrupted; as in Ge. 38. 9, &c.
WRATH,] *lit.* a 'passing over;' as in Ge. 49.7.
FOR EVER,] *or* 'pre-eminently;' as in 8. 7.
12. TEMAN,] i.e. 'south.'
BOZRAH,] i.e. 'fold.'
13. AMMON,] i.e. a 'little' people
RIPPING UP,] *lit.* 'cleaving;' as in 2 Ch. 32. 1.
GILEAD,] i.e. 'heap of witness.'
14. RABBAH,, i.e. the 'populous' one.
15. THEIR KING,] *or* 'Malcom,' the national idol.

II. 1. MOAB,] i.e. 'waters of a father.'
LIME,] as in De. 27. 2, 4; Isa. 33. 12.
2. KERIOTH,] i.e. 'cities or walled ones.'
4. JUDAH,] i.e. 'praise, confession.'
LOATHING,] as in Isa. 7. 15, 16; 30. 12, &c
LAW,] *lit.* 'direction;' as in Ge. 26. 5, &c.
LIES,] *or* 'lying things;' as in Jud. 16. 10.
ERR,] wander or 'go astray;' as in Ge. 20. 13.
5. JERUSALEM,] i.e. 'possession of peace.'
6. ISRAEL,] i.e. 'he is a prince with God.'
7. FOR,] *or* 'concerning.'
POOR,] *lit.* 'lean, thin' ones; as in 4. 1, &c.
POLLUTE,] *lit.* 'pierce;' as in Lev. 20. 3, &c.
9. AMORITE,] i.e. 'mountaineer.'
STRONG,] as in Isa. 1. 31.
10. EGYPT,] in *Heb.* Mitsrayim.
11. NAZARITES,] *lit.* 'separated ones.'
13. PRESSING YOU UNDER,] *or* 'your under parts.'
SHEAF,] *or* 'bundle;' as in Jer. 9. 22; Mic. 4. 12; Zec. 12. 6.
14. SWIFT,] *lit.* 'light;' as in v. 15; 2 Sa. 2.18.
16. COURAGEOUS,] *or* 'strong;' as in 2 Sa. 12. 15, &c.

III. 1. CONCERNING,] *or* 'against.'
FAMILY,]*lit.* a 'spreading' abroad; as in v. 2.
2. LAND,] *lit.* 'ground;' as in v.5; 5. 2, &c.
3. MET,] as in Ex. 25. 22; 29. 42, &c.
4. YOUNG LION,] *lit.* a 'scraper;' as in Jud. 14. 5, &c.
CAUGHT,] *or* 'captured;' as in v. 5; Nu. 21. 32
5. INTO,] *lit.* 'on or by means of.'
PREY,] *lit.* 'to capture;' as in Jer. 18. 22; 32. 24.
6. BLOWN,] *or* 'struck;' as in Job. 17. 3; Isa. 27. 13.
AFFLICTION,] *or* 'evil,' misfortune of any kind.
7. NOTHING,] *lit.* 'doth not do a thing.'
REVEALED,] *or* 'uncovered;' as in 1. 5, &c.
COUNSEL,] as in Ge. 49. 6; Job 15. 8, &c.
9. SOUND,] *lit.* 'cause to be heard;' as in 4. 5.
PALACES,] *or* 'high places;' as in v. 10, 11.
ASHDOD,] called in N.T. 'Azotus;' as in 1.8.
TROUBLES,] as in De. 7. 23; 28. 20; 1 Sa. 5. 9.
10. ACT,] *lit.* 'do;' as in Ge. 2. 3, 4; 11. 6.
11. SPOILED,] despoiled as 'prey;' as in Isa. 24. 3, &c.
12. DELIVERETH,] *lit.* 'snatcheth;' as in Ge. 31. 16, &c.

BED,] *lit.* 'extended' thing; as in 6. 4, &c.
13. TO,] *or* 'against, with.'
14. BETH-EL,] i.e. 'house of God.'
15. WITH,] that is, 'in addition to.'
IVORY,] *lit.* 'teeth;' as in 4. 6; 6. 4, &c.
CONSUMED,] *or* ' ended;' as in Est. 9. 23; Ps. 73. 19, &c.

IV. 1. BASHAN,] i.e. 'fat or fertile place.'
POOR,] *lit.* 'lean, thin' ones; as in 2. 7, &c.
2. SWORN HATH,] *lit.* 'sworn hath been.'
j HOLINESS,] *or* 'state of separation.'
TAKEN AWAY,] *lit.* 'lifted up;' as in Ezra 1. 4, &c.
POSTERITY,] *lit.* 'latter end;' as in 8. 10, &c.
3. WOMAN,] that is, 'each one.'
4. GILGAL,] i.e. a 'rolling away.'
EVERY MORNING,] *lit.* 'at the morning.'
EVERY THIRD,] *lit.* 'at the third.'
5. THANK-OFFERING,] *or* 'confession;' as in Lev. 7. 12, &c.
SOUND,] *lit.* 'cause to be heard;' as in 3. 9.
7. RAIN,] *lit.* 'shower;' as in Ge. 7. 12, &c.
HARVEST,]*or* 'reaping, crop;' as in Ge. 8. 22.
ANOTHER,] *lit.* 'one.'
WITHERETH,] *or* 'drieth up;' as in 1. 2, &c.
8. THE SAME,] *lit.* 'one.'
9. MILDEW,]*lit.* 'greenness;' as in De. 28. 22.
GARDENS,] that is, 'covered or protected places.'
VINEYARDS,] *lit.* 'prepared places.'
PALMER-WORM,] *lit.* 'shearer, cropper.'
10. BY,] *or* 'in.'
CAPTIVE,] *or* a 'captivity of your horses.'
11. DELIVERED,] *lit.* 'snatched;' as in Zec. 3. 3.
12. PREPARE,]*or* 'be ready;' as in 2 Ch. 35. 4.
THOUGHT.] Original word not found again.

V. 1. BEARING,] *lit.* 'lifted up;' as in Ge. 37. 25, &c.
2. NOT AGAIN,] *lit.* 'she doth not add.'
3. LEAVE] over, as a remnant.
5. BEER-SHEBA,] i.e. 'well of an oath.'
KIMAH,] as in Job 9. 9; 38. 31.
KESIL,] i.e. a 'fool;' as in Job 9. 9; 38. 31.
DEATH-SHADE,] that is, a deep shade; as in Job 3. 5, &c.
10. REPROVER,] one 'making prominent' or evident.
PLAIN,] *or* 'perfect;' as in Ge. 6. 9; 17. 1.
11. POOR,] *lit.* 'lean, thin' one; as in 2. 7.
TRIBUTE,] *lit.* 'thing lifted up;' as in Ge. 43. 34, &c.
CORN,] *lit.* 'pure;' as in 8. 5, 6; Ge. 41. 35.
DESIRABLE,] *lit.* 'vineyards of desire.'
12. MIGHTY,] *lit.* 'bony;' as in Ge. 18. 18.
RANSOMS,] *lit.* a 'scraping,' i.e. erasure.
13. WISE,] *or* 'acting wisely;' as in 1 Sa. 18. 14, &c.
SILENT,] *lit.* 'dumb;' as in Ex. 15. 16, &c.
15. PITY,] *or* 'is gracious' to; as in Ge. 33. 5, 11, &c.
16. LAMENTATION,] *or* 'beating' of the breast.
ALAS.] *Heb.* 'ho! ho!'
SKILFUL,] *lit.* 'knowers of;' as in Ge. 3. 5.
17. FOR,] *or* 'in.'
18. DESIRING,] as in Nu. 11. 34; Prov. 13. 4.
19. ONE,] *lit.* a 'man.'
LEANT,] *or* 'supported;' as in Ge. 27. 37.

20. BRIGHTNESS,] *or* 'shining;' as in 2 Sa. 22. 13, &c.
21. LOATHED,] as in Lev. 26. 15, 43, 44, &c.
FESTIVALS,] *lit.* 'reels, dances;' as in 8. 10.
REFRESHED,] *or* 'draw breath;' as in Ge. 8. 21, &c.
RESTRAINTS,] as in Lev. 23. 36; Nu. 29. 35.
22. BEHOLD] attentively; as in Ge. 19. 17.
23. FROM ME,] *lit.* 'from (being) on me.'
26. BARE,] *lit.* 'lifted up;' as in 6. 10, &c.
CHIUN,] i.e. Raiphan or Saturn.

VI. 1. SECURE,] as in 2 K. 19. 28, &c.
CONFIDENT,] *lit.* 'leaning;' as in De. 28. 52
CALNEH,] as in Ge. 10. 10; Isa. 10. 9.
HAMATH,] i.e. 'walled;' on the Orontes.
GATH,] i.e. a 'wine-fat,' birth-place of Goliath.
3. PUTTING AWAY,] as in Isa. 66. 5.
4. IVORY,] *lit.* 'tooth;' as in 3. 15; 4. 6, &c.
LAMBS,] as in De. 32. 14; 1 Sa. 15. 9, &c.
5. ACCORDING,] *or* ' on the mouth.'
7. CAPTIVES,]*or* ' removing' ones; as in 2 Sa. 15. 19, &c.
8. SWORN,] *lit.* 'sworn hath been.'
HIMSELF,] *lit.* 'by his soul.'
EXCELLENCE,] *lit.* 'gayness, gaiety;' as in 8. 7, &c.
DELIVERED,] *or* 'shut up, made secure.'
9. LEFT] over; as in Ge. 32. 24; 44. 20, &c.
LOVED ONE,]*or* 'uncle;' as in Lev. 10. 4, &c.
SIDES,] *lit.* 'thighs;' as in Ge. 49. 13, &c.
HUSH,] as in 8. 3; Jud. 3. 19; Neh. 8. 11.
11. COMMANDING,] *or* ' wishing;' as in 9. 9.
BREACHES,] *or* 'droppings;' as in Song 5. 2.
14. DESERT,] *or* ' Arabah;' as in Nu. 22. 1.

VII. 1. LATTER GROWTH,] *lit.* 'gathered' thing.
MOWINGS,] *or* 'shearings, cuttings;' as in De. 18. 4, &c.
2. WHEN,] *lit.* 'if.'
FORGIVE,] *lit.* 'send away;' as in Nu. 14.19.
HOW,] *lit.* 'who.'
3. REPENTED OF,] *or* 'been comforted;' as in v. 6, &c.
4. GREAT DEEP,] as in Ge. 7. 11; Ps. 36. 6.
PORTION] of Jehovah, that is, Israel.
7. STANDING,] *or* 'set up;' as in 9. 1, &c.
9. SANCTUARIES,] *lit.* 'set-apart places.'
WASTED,] *or* 'dried up;' as in Ge. 8. 13, &c.
10. AMAZIAH,] i.e. 'Jah strengthens.'
CONSPIRED,] *lit.* 'bound;' as in Ge. 38. 28.
BEAR,] *or* 'contain;' as in 1 K. 8. 64, &c.
11. CERTAINLY,] *lit.* 'to remove doth remove.'
12. JUDAH,] i.e. 'confession, praise.'
13. SANCTUARY,] as in v. 6.
14. PROPHET,] *or* preacher of God's will.
SON,] that is, a pupil of one.
HERDSMAN.] Original word not found again.
CULTIVATOR.] Original word not found again.
15. PROPHESY,] *lit.* 'be a prophet;' as in Eze. 6. 2, &c.
16. DROP,] as in 9. 13; Mic. 2. 6, 11, &c.

VIII. 1. BASKET,] as in Jer. 7. 27.
3. SONGSTRESSES,]*or* 'songs;' as in Ex. 15. 1
PALACE,] *lit.* 'temple;' as in 1 Sa. 1. 9, &c.

HUSH,] as in 6. 10; Jud. 3. 19; Neh. 8. 11.
4. POOR,] or 'afflicted, humble;' as in Ex.
22. 25, &c.
5. GROUND,] lit. 'broken' corn; as in Ge.
42. 1, &c.
PURE CORN,] as in v. 6; 5. 11; Ge. 41. 35, &c.
USE PERVERSELY,] as in Lam. 3. 36.
6. PURCHASE,] or 'acquire;' as in Lev.
25. 14, &c.
MONEY,] lit. 'silver.'
POOR,] lit. 'lean or thin' ones; as in 2. 7.
7. SWORN HATH,] lit. 'sworn hath been.'
NOT FOR EVER,] lit. 'if to pre-eminence.'
8. A FLOOD,] or 'a light.'
9. AT NOON,] lit. 'in the bright' times.
10. FESTIVALS,] as in 5. 21; Ex. 10. 9, &c.
MADE,] lit. 'set;' as in 9. 4; Ge. 2. 8, &c.
11. BUT,] lit. 'but rather.'
12. EAST,] the place of sun-'rising.'
GO TO AND FRO,] as in Da. 12. 4, &c.
13. FAINT,] lit. 'wrap themselves up;' as
in Ge. 38. 14; Jon. 4. 8.
YOUNG MEN,] lit. 'choice ones;' as in 2. 11.

14. SWEARING,] lit. 'been sworn.'

IX. 1. THRESHOLDS,] as in Ex. 12. 22, &c.
FUGITIVE,] as in Ge. 14. 13; Jos. 8. 22, &c.
2. SHEOL,] the state of departed spirits.
3. CARMEL,] i.e. 'prepared place.'
HID,] or 'kept secret;' as in Ge. 4. 14, &c.
4. ON,] or 'against.'
5. FLOOD,] as in 8. 8; Ge. 41. 1, 2, 3, 17, &c.
SUNK,] as in Nu. 11. 2; Jer. 51. 64.
7. CUSHIM,] residing on both sides of Red
Sea.
KIR,] i.e. a 'wall or walled city.'
CAPHTOR,] Crete, Cyprus, or Cappadocia.
8. UTTERLY,] lit. 'to destroy I destroy.'
9. GRAIN,] lit. 'bundle;' as in Ge. 42. 35.
10. EVIL,] lit. 'the evil.'
11. TABERNACLE,] or 'booth;' as in Ge.
33. 17, &c.
13. TO,] lit. 'with.'
SCATTERER,] lit. 'drawer out;' as in Jud.
5. 14, &c.
MELT,] as in Ps. 107. 26.

OBADIAH

THE VISION OF OBADIAH was delivered according to most critics about B.C. 585, in the reign of Jehoiakim, but its position in the Jewish Canon points to a much earlier date, and OBADIAH is conjectured to have been the prince of that name commissioned by Jehoshaphat (2 Ch. 17. 7), to teach in Judah, B.C. 913. Verse 11 may refer to the capture of Jerusalem mentioned in 2 Ch. 12. 2, or in 21. 16, or in 25. 22, the Edomites being inveterate enemies of Judah, see Joel 3. 19; Amos 1. 11; Eze. 25. 35; Lam. 4. 21; Ps. 137. The VISION naturally divides itself into three parts, v. 1—11, (almost copied by Jeremiah, ch. 49. 7—17); v. 12—15, and v. 16—21, the first, proclaiming Edom's doom, the second, Edom's disappointment, and the third, Israel's complete victory.

. 1. OBADIAH,] i.e. 'servant of Jah.'
EDOM,] i.e. 'red;' as in Ge. 25. 30, &c.
REPORT,] lit. 'hearing;' as in 1 Sa. 2. 24.
2. MADE,] lit. 'given.'
3. LIFTED UP,] or 'caused thee to forget;'
as in v. 7, &c.
DWELLER,] settler down or tabernacler.
ROCK.] Heb. Sela; as in 2 K. 14. 7, &c.
5. CUT OFF,] lit. 'become dumb;' as in Isa.
6. 5, &c.
GATHERERS,] as in Jer. 6. 9; 49. 9.

GLEANINGS,] as in Jud. 8. 2; Isa. 17. 6, &c.
6. ESAU,] i.e. 'made.'
HIDDEN,] or 'treasured up' things. '
7. ALLIES,] lit. 'men of thy covenant.
FORGOTTEN,] or 'lifted thee up;' as in v. 3
FRIENDS,] lit. 'men of thy peace.'
MAKE,] lit. 'set.'
9. BROKEN DOWN,] or 'brought down;' as
in 2 K. 19. 26, &c.
TEMAN,] i.e. the 'south.'
10. FOR,] lit. 'from, because of.'
11. OVER-AGAINST,] lit. 'from over-against.
FOREIGNERS,] or 'strangers;' as in Ge.
31. 15, &c.
12. SHALT,] not 'shouldst not have,' as in
C.V.; it is simply a prophecy.
13. EVEN,] or 'also.'
MISFORTUNE,] lit. 'evil;' as in Ge. 2. 9, &c.
14. DELIVER,] lit. 'secure or make secure.'
16. SWALLOWED,] as in Job 6. 3.
19. SOUTH.] Heb. 'Negeb;' as in v. 20, &c.
PHILISTINES,] on the coast of the great sea.
GILEAD,] i.e. 'the heap of witness.'
20. ZAREPHAT,] i.e. 'a ' refining;' as in 1
K. 17. 9, 10.
SEPHARAD.] Supposed by the rabbis to
be Spain, or Sippharah on the Euphrates.
21. SAVIOURS,] those 'giving ease or
safety.'
ON,] lit. 'into.'

JONAH

THE BOOK OF JONAH was written probably B.C. 850, and we learn from 2 K. 14. 25, that he was of Gath-hepher, a town of Lower Galilee, in the tribe of Zebulun. He was thus the earliest of the prophets whose works have come down to us, and as his mission was to a Gentile nation, it may have led many of the ancient believers to think of the time when the 'nations' should rejoice with Israel as 'His People.' He is specially referred to in Mat. 12. 39, 41; 16. 4; Luke 11. 29. Its contents are:—

Chap. I. Jonah's commission and his attempt to evade it.

II. His Song of Thanksgiving after his Deliverance.

III. The Execution of his Commission and its result.

IV. His Impatience and Reproof.

I. 1. WORD,] or communication from JEHOVAH,] the 'Existing' One, God of Israel, unto

JONAH,] i.e. a 'dove' or 'oppressor,' the son of

AMITTAI,] i.e. a 'stedfast' one.

2. NINEVEH,] on the eastern bank of the Tigris, now called Mosul.

THAT,] or 'because.'

3. TARSHISH,] in Spain or in Cilicia.

JOPPA,] i.e. a 'fair' place, now called Japha.

FARE,] lit. 'hire or reward;' as in Ge. 15. 1; 30. 18, &c.

4. ON,] lit. 'unto.'

RECKONED,] or 'thought;' as in Lev. 25. 27.

5. MARINERS.] lit. 'salt-men;' as in Eze. 27. 9, 27, 29.

EACH,] lit. a 'man.'

GOODS,] lit. 'vessels, instruments;' as in Ge. 24. 53, &c.

SIDES,] lit. 'thighs;' as in Ge. 49. 13, &c.

6. COMPANY,] or 'rope;' as in Eze. 27. 8, &c.

BETHINK HIMSELF,] or 'shine.'

PERISH,] or 'art lost;' as in v. 14; 3. 9, &c.

7. EACH,] lit. a 'man.'

NEIGHBOUR,] lit. 'friend;' as in Ge. 11. 3.

ON,] lit. 'to us.'

8. DECLARE,] lit. 'set forward;' as in Ge. 24. 23, &c.

OCCUPATION,] lit. 'work,' as in Ge. 2. 2, &c.

9. HEBREW,] i.e. a 'passer over;' or a descendant of Eber; as in Ge. 14. 13, &c.

10. TOLD,] lit. 'set forward;' as in Ge. 3.11.

11. CEASE,] as in v. 12; Ps. 107. 30; Prov. 26. 30.

MORE AND MORE,] lit. 'going and tempestuous.'

14. CRY,] or 'call.'

PERISH,] or 'be lost;' as in v. 6; 3. 9, &c.

LIFE,] lit. 'soul.'

LAY,] lit. 'give;' as in v. 3.

15. CEASETH,] lit. 'standeth;' as in Ge. 19.17.

17. APPOINTETH,] as in 4. 6, 7, 8; Job 7. 3.

II. 1. PRAYETH,] lit. 'judgeth himself;' as in 4. 2, &c.

FROM,] or 'out of, because of.'

2. SAITH] after his deliverance, for this song that follows cannot possibly be the prayer of humiliation and confession of sin that one would expect from a penitent prophet in danger of his life; v. 4, 5, 6, appear to have been fragments of the prayer that was offered.

3. DEEP,] or 'shady place;' as in Job 41. 31; Ps. 68. 22; 69. 2, 15; 107. 24, &c.

FLOOD,] or 'river;' as in Ge. 2. 10, 13, &c.

BILLOWS,] lit. 'heaps' as in Ge. 31. 46, 47, 48, 51, 52; Jos. 7. 26; 8. 29, &c.

4. YET,] lit. 'and.'

LOOK] attentively; as in Ex. 3. 6, &c.

6. PIT,] or 'corruption, marring;' as in Job 9. 31, &c.

7. WITHIN ME,] lit. 'on me.'

8. LYING VANITIES,] or 'vanities of emptiness.'

MERCY,] or 'kindness;' as in 4. 2, &c.

9. THANKSGIVING,] or 'confession;' as in Lev. 7. 12, &c.

COMPLETE,] as in Ge. 44. 4; Ex. 21. 34, &c.

SALVATION,] ease or 'safety;' as in Ge. 49.18; Ex. 14. 13; 15. 2; De. 32. 15, &c.

III. 3. BEFORE,] lit. 'to God,' in his estimation.

JOURNEY,] lit. 'walk;' as in v. 4; Neh. 2. 6; Eze. 42. 4.

5. BELIEVE,] lit. 'remain stedfast;' as in Ge. 15. 6, &c.

6. COME,] lit. 'striketh;' as in Ge. 3. 3, &c.

REMOVETH,] lit. 'causeth to pass over or away.'

SPREADETH OUT,] or 'covereth himself.'

7. BY A DECREE,] lit. 'taste;' as in Ex. 16. 31; Nu. 11. 8; 1 Sa. 21. 13, &c.

8. MIGHTILY,] lit. 'with strength.'

EACH,] lit. a 'man.'

HANDS,] lit. 'palms;' as in Ge. 8. 9; 20. 5.

9. PERISH.] or 'art not lost;' as in 1. 6, 14.

IV. 1. GRIEVOUS,] lit. 'evil;' as in Ge. 21. 11, 12; 38. 10; 48. 17; De. 15. 10, &c.

DISPLEASED,] lit. 'there is heat to him, or at it.'

2. PRAYETH,] or 'judgeth himself;' as in 2. 1, &c.

SLOW TO ANGER,] lit. 'long of faces;' as in Ex. 34. 6, &c.

5. ON,] lit. 'from.'

6. GOURD.] Sept. 'cucumber;' Jerome, 'ricinus.'

AFFLICTION,] lit. 'evil, misfortune.'

7. WORM,] as in Job 26. 5; Ps. 22. 6; Isa. 14. 11; 41. 14; 66. 24.

8. CUTTING,] or 'silent.'

10. HAD PITY,] lit. 'hast hastened upon.'

NOURISH,] lit. 'make great;' as in Ge. 12. 2

11. HUMAN BEINGS,] lit 'man.'

597

MICAH

THE WORDS OF MICAH were delivered between B.C. 756—697, during the reigns of three kings, and are placed in the Septuagint after those of Hosea and Amos. They naturally divide themselves into three sections, the *first* containing chap. I. II. the *second*, ch. III. IV. V. and the *third*, ch. VI. VII. each commencing with a 'Hear!' accompanied with rebukes and threatenings, and closing with gracious promises. Ch. 1. 6—8, is supposed to relate to the invasion of Shalmanescr (2 K. 17. 4, 6); ch. 1. 9—16, to that of Sennacherib (2 K. 18. 13); ch. 3. 12; 7. 13, to the destruction of Jerusalem; ch. 4. 10, to the captivity in Babylon; ch. 4. 1—8; 7. 11, to the return; ch. 5. 2, to the Ruler from Beth-Lehem; ch. 5. 5, 6; 7. 8, 10, to the destruction of Assyria and Babylon. New Testament quotations are in Mat. 2. 5, 6, 10, 35, 36; Mark 13. 12; Luke 12. 53; John 7. 42.

I. 1. WORD,] or communication from MICAH,] i.e. 'who is like Jah?'
MORASHITE,] as in Jer. 26. 18.
2. HEAR,] as in 3. 1; 6. 1, &c.
AGAINST,] or 'among.'
WHAT,] *lit.* 'who?'
7. MAKE,] *lit.* 'set;' as in 2. 12; 4. 13; 7. 16.
HIRE,] *lit.* 'gift;' as in De. 23. 18, &c.
9. WOUNDS,] *lit.* 'smitings;' as in Lev. 26.21.
COME,] *lit.* 'struck;' as in Ge. 3. 3; 26. 29.
10. GATH,] i.e. a 'wine-vat.'
IN ACOO,] or 'to weep do not weep.'
12. STAYED,] or 'pained;' as in Ge. 8. 10.
13. LACHISH,] i.e. 'captured;' in Judah.
14. MORESHETH GATH,] birth-place of Micah.
ACHZIB,] i.e. a 'lying one;' as in Jos. 15. 44.
15. POSSESSOR,] as in Ge. 15. 3; Nu. 36. 8.
MARESHAH,] in the plain of Judah.
ADULLAM,] i.e. 'hiding-place.'

II. 1. DEVISING,] or 'thinking;' as in v. 3.
4. TAKE,] or 'lift up;' as in 4. 3; 6. 16, &c.
SIMILE,] or 'ruling' saying; as in Nu. 23. 7.
6. SHAME,] or 'shames;' as in Job 20. 3, &c.
7. BENEFIT,] *lit.* 'do good;' as in Ge. 4. 7.
8. YESTERDAY,] as in 1 Sa. 4. 7; 10. 11, &c.
FROM WAR,] *lit.* 'turners back of battle.'
9. SUCKLINGS,] as in 1 Sa. 15. 3; 22. 19, &c.
10. REST,] that is, 'resting place.'
11. PROPHESY,] *lit.* 'drop;' as in Ge. 49. 15.
PROPHET,] *lit.* 'one causing to drop.'
12. SURELY,] *lit.* 'to gather I gather.'
BOZRAH,] i.e. a 'fold.'
DROVE.] or 'herd;' as in 4. 8; 5. 8, &c

III. 1. JUDGES,] *lit.* 'deciders;' as in v. 9.
3. BROKEN,] *lit.* 'opened.'
CALDRON,] as in 1 Sa. 2. 14.
UNTO,] *lit.* 'on.'
SANCTIFIED,] *lit.* 'set apart;' as in Ge. 2. 3.
6. DIVINATION,] as in De. 18. 10, 14, &c.
9. JUDGES,] *lit.* 'deciders;' as in v. 1, &c.

10. BLOOD,] *lit.* 'bloods;' as in Ge. 4, 10, &c
11. TEACH,] or 'shew' the law; as in 4. 2.
LEAN,] or 'are supported;' as in Jud. 16. 26
12. PLOUGHED,] as in Jer. 26. 18.

IV. 2. LAW,] *lit.* 'direction;' as in Ge. 26. 5.
7. MIGHTY,] *lit.* 'bony;' as in v. 3, &c.
8. EDAR,] i.e. 'herd, drove.'
9. TRAVAILING,] *lit.* 'yielding;' as in v. 10.
10. DWELT,] *lit.* 'settled down, tabernacled.
13. MAKE,] *lit.* 'set.'
DEVOTED,] *lit.* 'laid flat;' as in Lev. 27. 28.

V. 1. LAID,] *lit.* 'set;' as in 1. 6, 7; 4. 7, 13.
2. BETH-LEHEM,] i.e. 'house of bread.'
EPHRATAH,] i.e. 'fruitful place.'
CHIEFS,] as in Mat. 2. 6.
ANTIQUITY,] or 'hidden time;' as in 2. 9.
3. TO,] or 'with, in addition to.'
4. DELIGHTED,] or 'fed;' as in v. 6; 7. 14.
5. ASSHUR,] a general name for an enemy.
PALACES,] or 'high places;' as in 1 K. 16. 18.
6. NIMROD,] as in Ge. 10. 8, 9.
8. YOUNG LION,] *lit.* a 'scraper,' or eraser.
9. ABOVE,] or 'on, over.'
13. STANDING PILLARS,] as in Ge. 28. 18, 22.
FURY,] *lit.* 'heat;' as in Ge. 27. 44; Lev. 26. 28.

VI. 1. HEAR,] as in 3. 1, 13; 4. 1; 7. 16, &c.
2. REASON,] or 'show himself prominent.'
5. BALAK,] i.e. 'empty, void;' as in Nu. 22. 5.
BEOR,] i.e. 'torch, lamp.'
SHITTIM,] i.e. 'accacia wood;' as in Nu. 25.1.
GILGAL,] i.e. a 'rolling' away.
6. BOW,] or 'be bent down.'
MOST HIGH,] *lit.* 'God of the high place.'
7. STREAMS,] as in Job 6. 15, &c.
TRANSGRESSIONS,] *lit.* 'steps;' as in 1. 5. 13.
BODY,] *lit.* 'belly;' as in Ge. 25. 23, 24, &c.
8. MAN,] *in Heb.* 'Adam.'
9. WISDOM,] as in Job 5. 12; 6. 13; 11. 6, &c.
APPOINTED,] as in Ex. 21. 8, 9; 2 Sa. 20. 5.
10. SCANTY,] *lit.* 'lean;' as in Ps. 116. 15.
14. PIT.] Original word not found again.
15. REAP,] as in 2. 7; Lev. 23. 10, &c.
16. OMRI,] i.e. 'my sheaf.'
AHAB,] i.e. 'brother of father.'
BEAR,] or 'lift up;' as in 2. 4; 4. 3; 7. 9, &c.

VII. 1. MY WO,] as in Job 10. 15.
2. KIND] one; as in De. 23. 8; 1 Sa. 2. 9.
NET,] *lit.* thing 'laid flat;' as in Lev. 27. 21.
5. TRUST,] *lit.* 'lean;' as in Jud. 9. 26, &c.
6. DISHONOURING,] as in De. 32.15; Jer. 14.21
7. WATCH,] or 'look out;' as in Ps. 5. 3, &c
9. BEAR,] or 'lift up;' as in 2. 4; 4. 3, &c.
EXECUTED,] *lit.* 'done;' as in 5. 15; 6. 3, &c.
12. FORTRESS,] as in 5. 1; De. 20. 19, &c.
13. BECAUSE OF,] *lit.* 'from.'
14. RULE,] or 'feed;' as in Ge. 29. 7, &c.
16. LAY,] *lit.* 'set;' as in 1. 7; 2. 11; 4. 13.
17. FEARFUL THINGS,] as in De. 32. 24.
18. TAKING AWAY,] *lit.* 'lifting up.'
FOR EVER,] *lit.* 'to duration;' as in 4. 5

598

NAHUM

THE VISION OF NAHUM was probably delivered about B.C. 712, and Elkosh, his birthplace, is supposed to have been afterwards called by his name CAPERNAUM, (i.e. 'village of Nahum'), and is famous in the Gospels. Nineveh was finally taken by the Medes and Chaldeans, B.C. 625. New Testament allusions to Nahum are found in Rom. 10. 5; Rev. 18. 2, 3.

I. 1. BURDEN,] *lit.* 'thing lifted up;' as in Ex. 23. 5, &c.
NINEVEH,] on the eastern bank of the Tigris.
BOOK,] *or* 'scroll, roll;' as in Ge. 5. 1, &c.
NAHUM,] i.e. 'comforted.'
ELKOSHITE,] from a town in Galilee.
2. GOD,] *lit.* 'mighty one;' as in Ge. 14. 18.
ZEALOUS,] as in Jos. 24. 19.
AVENGING,] as in Lev. 26. 25; Ps. 99. 8.
POSSESSING,] *or* 'owner of heat.'
3. SLOW,] *lit.* 'long of faces;' as in Ex. 34. 6.
ENTIRELY,] *lit.* 'to acquit doth not acquit.'
4. PUSHING,] as in Mal. 2. 3.
FLOODS,] *or* 'rivers;' as in 2. 6; Ge. 2. 10.
BASHAN,] i.e. a 'fat, fertile place.'
CARMEL,] in the tribe of Asher.
LEBANON,] i.e. the 'white' mountain.
5. MELTED,] *or* 'melt themselves;' as in Ps. 107. 39; Amos 9. 13.
WORLD,] the habitable or fruit bearing earth.
6. STAND,] *or* 'stand still;' as in Ge. 19. 17.
FURY,] *lit.* 'heat;' as in v. 2; Ge. 27. 44, &c.
BY,] *lit.* 'from *or* because of him *or* it.'
7. TRUSTING,] *or* 'taking refuge;' as in 2. Sa. 22. 31, &c.
8. END,] *lit.* 'consummation;' as in v. 9, &c.
9. DEVISE,] *or* 'think, or reckon;' as in Lev. 25. 27, &c.
10. PRINCES,] *lit.* 'thorns;' as in Ecc. 7. 6.
PERPLEXED,] *or* 'entangled.'
WITH,] *or* 'as.'
11. DEVISER,] *or* 'thinker;' as in Ex. 26. 1.
12. THOUGH,] *lit.* 'if.'
14. COMMANDED,] *or* 'willed;' as in Ge. 2. 16; 3. 11, &c.
APPOINT,] *lit.* 'set;' as in 3. 6; Ge. 2. 8, &c.
15. PROCLAIMING TIDINGS,] as in 1 Sa. 4. 27; 2 Sa. 4. 10, &c.
SOUNDING,] *lit.* 'causing to be heard;' as in 1 Ch. 15. 16, &c.
COMPLETELY,] *or* 'all of him.'

II. 1. SCATTERER,] as in Jer. 23. 1.
2. EXCELLENCY,] *lit.* 'gaiety, gayness.'
BRANCHES,] *or* 'pruned, praised things.'
3. SHIELD,] *lit.* 'protector;' as in Ge. 15. 1.
SCARLET.] Original word not found again.
PREPARATION,] *or* 'setting up;' as in Jos. 3. 17, &c.
4. SHINE,] *or* 'shew themselves foolish;' as in 1 Sa. 21 13, &c.
GO TO AND FRO,] *lit.* 'use the legs.'

5. STUMBLE,] *lit.* 'are stumbled;' as in 3. 8
COVERING,] as in Ex. 25. 20; 37. 9, &c.
6. PALACE,] *or* 'temple;' as in 1 Sa. 1. 9, &c.
7. TABERING,] as in Ps. 68. 25.
8. OF OLD,] *lit.* 'from days of (old) it is.'
TURNING] the face; *or* 'causing to turn.'
9. PREPARED THINGS,] *or* 'things set up;' as in Eze. 23. 11, &c.
ABUNDANCE,] *lit.* 'weight, heaviness.'
10. PALENESS,] as in Joel 2. 6.
11. LIONESSES,] *or* 'lions;' as in v. 12, &c
OLD LION,] as in Ge. 49. 9; Nu. 23. 24, &c
12. RAPINE,] *lit.* 'torn' food; as in Ge. 31. 39.
13. AFFIRMATION,] as in 3. 5; Ge. 22. 16, &c
HOSTS,] of the heavens and earth.
MESSENGERS,] announcing peace or war.

III. 1. WO,] *or* 'alas!' as in 1 K. 13. 30, &c.
BLOOD,] *lit.* 'bloods.'
2. WHEEL,] as in Ex. 14. 25; 1 K. 7. 30, &c.
BOUNDING,] as in 1 Ch. 15. 29.
3. WOUNDED,] *lit.* 'pierced;' as in Ge. 34. 27.
OVER,] *or* 'among.'
4. BECAUSE OF,] *lit.* 'from.'
5. SKIRTS,] as in Ex. 28. 33, 34; 39. 24, &c.
SHEWED,] *or* 'caused to see;' as in Ge. 12. 1.
SHAME,] *lit.* 'lightness;' as in Job 10. 15.
6. DISHONOURED,] as in De. 32. 15; Jer. 14. 21.
MADE,] *lit.* 'set;' as in 1. 14; Ge. 2. 8, &c.
7. FLEETH,] *or* 'moveth away;' as in Ge. 31. 40, &c.
8. NO-AMMON,] Thebes or Diospolis.
BROOKS] of Egypt; as in Ge. 41. 1, 2, 3, &c.
9. CUSH,] on both sides of Red Sea.
EGYPT,] in *Heb.* Mitsrayim.
PUT,] as in Ge. 10. 6; Jer. 46. 9, &c.
LABIM,] as in 2 Ch. 12. 3; 16. 8; Da. 11. 43.
FOR,] *or* 'in.'
10. SUCKLINGS,] as in 1 Sa. 15. 3; 22. 9, &c.
11. DRUNKEN,] *or* 'merry;' as in Ge. 9. 21.
12. SHAKEN,] as in Amos 9. 9.
INTO,] *lit.* 'on.'
13. THROUGHLY,] *lit.* 'to open they have been open.'
14. ON,] *or* 'among.'
15. CANKER-WORM,] as in v. 16; Ps. 105. 34.
LOCUST,] as in v. 17; Ex. 10. 4, 12, 13, &c.
16. MERCHANTS,] *lit.* those 'going up and down.'
STRIPPED,] *or* 'pushed off;' as in Lev. 6. 11.
17. PRINCES,] *or* 'crowned ones.'
GREAT,] *lit.* 'grasshopper or grasshoppers.'
FLEE,] *or* 'move away.'
18. FRIENDS,] *or* 'feeders, shepherds;' as in Ge. 4. 2, &c.
ASSHUR,] ruling in Nineveh.
REST,] *lit.* 'settle down, or tabernacle.'
19. DESTRUCTION,] *lit.* 'breaking;' as in Lev. 21. 19, &c.
GRIEVOUS,] *lit.* 'pierced;' as in Isa. 17. 11
CLAPPED,] *or* 'struck the palm.'
AT,] *or* 'over, against.'
WICKEDNESS,] *lit.* 'evil.'

HABAKKUK

THE BURDEN OF HABAKKUK was probably delivered about the year 630 B.C., and is quoted or referred to in Acts 2. 4; 13. 41; Rom. 1. 17; Heb. 10 37, 38. It seems to divide into *three* sections, corresponding to its three chapters.

I. 1. BURDEN,] *lit.* 'thing lifted up;' as in Ex. 23. 5, &c.
HABAKKUK,] i.e. 'embracing, clasping.'
SEEN,] in prophetic vision from the Lord.
2. JEHOVAH,] the 'Existing' One, God of Israel.
CRIED] for help in distress.
SAVE,] *or* 'ease;' as in Ex. 2. 17; 14. 30, &c.
3. SHEW,] *or* 'cause me to see;' as in Ge. 12. 1, &c.
BEHOLD] attentively; as in v. 13; Ge. 19. 17.
4. CEASE,] as in Ge. 45. 26; Ps. 77. 2.
FOR EVER,] *or* 'to pre-eminence;' as in 2 Sa. 2. 26, &c.
WRONG,] *or* 'perverted.'
5. GREATLY,] *lit.* 'marvel ye, marvel ye.'
BELIEVE,] *or* 'remain stedfast;' as in Ge. 15. 6, &c.
DECLARED,] *or* 'recounted, rehearsed;' as in Job 37. 20, &c.
6. CHALDEANS,] *lit.* 'pious ones.'
HASTY,] *or* 'hastened;' as in Job. 15. 13.
OCCUPY,] *or* 'possess;' as in Ge. 15. 7, &c.
TABERNACLES,] as in Ex. 25. 9; 26. 1—35.
7. EXCELLENCE,] *or* 'uplifting;' as in Ge. 4. 7; 49. 3, &c.
8. SWIFTER,] *lit.* 'lighter;' as in Ge. 8. 8.
9. SWALLOWING UP.] The original word is not found again.
10. SCOFF,] *lit.* 'shew itself a scoffer.'
11. TRANSGRESS,] *lit.* 'passeth over;' as in 3. 10, &c.
DOTH ASCRIBE.] Sept. 'make atonement.'
12. OF OLD,] *lit.* 'from before or the east.'
APPOINTED,] *lit.* 'set;' as in 3. 19; Ge. 2. 8.
13. LOOK] attentively; as in v. 3; Ge. 19. 17.
TREACHEROUS,] as in 2. 5; Ps. 25. 3, &c.
SILENT,] *or* 'deaf;' as in Ge. 34. 5, &c.
15. NET,] *lit.* a 'flat' thing; as in v. 16, 17.
DRAG,] as in v. 16.
16. FERTILE,] *lit.* 'oily or fat;' as in Ge. 49. 20, &c.
FAT,] *or* 'firm;' as in Ge. 41. 2, 4, 5, 7, &c.

II. 1. STAND] still; as in 3. 6, 11, &c.
WATCH,] *lit.* 'look out;' as in Ps. 5. 3, &c.
AGAINST,] *or* 'with *or* in me.'
REPLY,] *lit.* 'turn back;' as in Ge. 14. 16.
2. EXPLAIN,] *or* 'dig;' as in De. 1. 5; 27. 8.
3. SEASON,] *or* 'appointed time;' as in Ge. 14; 17. 21, &c.
TARRY,] as in Ge. 19. 16; 43. 10; Jud. 19. 8.
SURELY,] *lit.* 'to come it cometh.'
LATE,] *or* 'behind;' as in Ge. 24. 56; 32. 4,

4. PRESUMPTUOUS,] *or* 'one lifted up.'
BY,] *or* 'in, during.'
5. ENLARGED,] *lit.* 'made broad;' as in Ge. 26. 22, &c.
6. SIMILE,] *or* 'ruling' saying; as in Nu. 23. 7, &c.
MORAL,] *or* 'sweet thing;' as in Prov. 1. 6,
ACUTE SAYINGS,] as in Nu. 12. 8; Jud. 14. 12.
MULTIPLYING,] as in Ex. 16. 17, 18; 36. 5.
7. USURERS,] *lit.* 'biters;' as in Ge. 49. 17.
9. GAIN,] as in Ge. 37. 26; Ex. 18. 21, &c.
DELIVERED,] *lit.* 'snatched;' as in Isa. 20. 6.
HAND,] *or* 'palm, paw;' as in Ge. 8. 9, &c.
10. SHAMEFUL THING,] *or* 'shame;' as in 1 Sa. 20. 30, &c.
12. ESTABLISHING,] *or* 'making ready, setting up.'
13. FOR,] *or* 'in sufficiency of.'
15. NEIGHBOUR,] *lit.* 'friend;' as in Ge. 11. 3.
BOTTLE,] as in Ge. 21. 14, 15, 19.
MAKING DRUNK,] *or* 'to make merry.'
16. SHAME,] *lit.* 'lightness;' as in Job 16. 15.
17. BEASTS,] *or* 'cattle;' as in Ge. 1. 24, &c.
18. TEACHER,] *lit.* 'shower or thrower;' as in 1 Sa. 20. 26, &c.
TRUSTED,] *or* 'leant;' as in Jud. 9. 26, &c.
19. TEACHER,] *or* 'doth teach;' as in Ex. 4. 12.
20. BE SILENT,] *or* 'hush;' as in Jud. 3. 19.

III. 1. PRAYER,] *or* 'judgment;' as in 2 Sa. 7. 27, &c.
ERRING ONES,] as in Ps. 7. 1.
2. REPORT,] *lit.* 'hearing;' as in Ge. 29. 13.
REVIVE,] *or* 'give it life, cause it to live.'
3. TEMAN,] i.e. the 'South,' east of Edom.
PARAN,] between Edom, Arabia Petraea, and Palestine.
PAUSE,] as in v. 9, 13; Ps. 3. 2, 4, 8; 4. 2.
4. BRIGHTNESS,] *or* 'shining;' as in v. 11.
RAYS,] *lit.* 'horns; as in Ge. 22. 13; Ex. 27. 2.
5. PESTILENCE,] as in Ex. 5. 3; 9. 3, 15, &c.
CUSHAN,] another form of 'Cush.'
8. WROTH,] *or* 'hot;' as in Ge. 4. 5, 6, &c.
9. UTTERLY,] *lit.* 'nakedness thou makest naked.'
TRIBES,] *lit.* 'rods;' as in v. 14; Ge. 38. 18.
11. BRIGHTNESS,] *or* 'shining;' as in v. 4.
OF,] *lit.* 'from.'
14. STAVES,] as in v. 9; Ge. 38. 18, 25, &c.
SECRET,] as in Ps. 10. 8, 9; 17. 12; 64. 4, &c.
15. PROCEEDED,] *or* 'trodden;' as in Nu. 24. 17.
CLAY,] as in Ge. 11. 3; Ex. 1. 14; 8. 14, &c.
16. NOISE,] *lit.* 'voice;' as in v. 10.
IN MY PLACE,] *lit.* 'under me.'
OVERCOMETH,] *or* 'cutteth;' as in Ge. 49. 19.
17. FAILED,] *lit.* 'lied; as in Ge. 18. 15, &c.
YIELDED,] *lit.* 'made;' as in 1. 14; Ge. 1. 31.
HERD,] *or* 'oxen;' as in Ge. 12. 16; 13. 5,
18. JOY,] *lit.* 'leap;' as in 1. 15; 1 Ch. 16. 31
19. OVERSEER,] as in Ps. 4. 5. 6. 8. 9, &c.
STRINGED INSTRUMENTS,] as in Job 30. 9.

ZEPHANIAH

THE WORDS OF ZEPHANIAH were delivered between 642—611 B.C., and are directed against Judah (1. 1—2. 3); the Philistines '2. 4—7); Moabites and Ammonites (2. 8—;1); Cush (2. 12); Nineveh (2. 13—15); Jewish Captivity is foretold (3. 1—7); and restoration (3. 8—9). New Testament references are John 4. 21; Heb. 12. 12; Jas. 2. 5; 5. 1; Rev. 19. 17—19.

I. 1. A WORD,] or communication from JEHOVAH,]the Existing One, God of Israel.
ZEPHANIAH,] i.e. 'treasured up of Jah.'
CUSHI,] probably a convert to Judaism.
GEDALIAH,] i.e. 'greatness of Jah.'
AMARIAH,] i.e. 'saying of Jah.'
HEZIKIAH,] i.e. 'my strength is Jah.'
JOSIAH,] i.e. 'healed by Jah.'
AMON,] i.e. 'stedfast, supported.'
2. UTTERLY,] lit. 'to gather I gather.'
AFFIRMATION,] as in v. 3, 10; 2. 9; 3. 8, &c.
BEAST,] or 'cattle;' as in Ge. 1. 24, 25, &c.
4. AGAINST,] or 'on, over.'
REMNANT,] as in 1 Ch. 11. 8; 16. 41, &c.
IDOLATROUS PRIESTS,] as in 2 K. 23. 5; Hos. 10. 5.
5.ROOFS]of houses, as common in the east.
SWEARING,] lit. 'been sworn;' as in Ps. 63. 11; Ecc. 9. 2, &c.
MALCHAM,] i.e. 'their king;' the national idol of Ammon.
6. REMOVING,] as in Jer. 46. 5.
7. PREPARED,] made ready or 'set up.'
SANCTIFIED,] lit. 'set apart;' as in Nu.3. 13.
9. LEAPING,] as in Song 2. 8.
THRESHOLD,] as in 1 Sa. 5. 4, 5; Eze. 9. 3.
10. NOISE,] lit. 'voice;' as in v. 14; 2. 14.
DESTRUCTION,] lit. 'breaking;' as in Lev. 21. 19; 24. 20, &c.
11. CUT OFF,] or 'become silent or dumb.'
MERCHANT,] in Heb. 'Kenaan.'
12. HARDENED,] lit. 'congealed.'
13. WEALTH,]or 'strength;' as in Ge. 34. 29.
VINEYARDS,] or 'prepared places;' as in Ge. 9. 20, &c.
15. WRATH,] lit. 'passing over;' as in v. 18.
17. DUNG,] or 'rolling things;' as in Job 20. 7, &c.
18. DELIVER,] lit. 'snatch them away.'
END,] or 'consummation;' as in Ge. 18. 21.

II. 1. DESIRED] as 'silver;' as in Ge. 31. 30.
BRINGING FORTH,] as in Ge. 4. 2; 16. 2, 16.
STATUTE,] or 'engraved' thing, as in Ge. 47. 22, 26, &c.
3. HUMBLE,] as in 2 Sa. 22. 36; Prov. 15. 33.
DONE,] or 'wrought;' as in Ge. 4. 14.
HIDDEN,] or 'kept secret;' as in Ge. 4. 14.
4. GAZA,] i.e. a 'strong place.'
ASHKELON,] i.e. a 'weighing place.'
ASHDOD,] i.e. a 'castle or fortress.'
AT NOON,] lit. 'in the clear shining' times.
EKRON,] i.e. a 'root.'
5. CHERETHITES,] i.e. 'cutters.'

CANAAN,] i.e. 'humble one.'
6. HABITATIONS,] lit. 'comely places;' as in Job 8. 6, &c.
COTTAGES,] or 'prepared places.
FOLDS,]lit. 'walled, fenced, hedged' places.
7. BY,] or 'on, upon them.'
PLEASURE,] or 'they feed;' as in 3. 13, &c.
LIE,] or 'crouch down;' as in v. 14; 3. 13.
8. MOAB,] the descendants of Lot.
AMMON,] the younger brother of Moab.
9. SURELY,] or 'that, because.'
SODOM,] i.e. 'burnt' place.
GOMORRAH,] i.e. a 'binding or heaping up.
OVER-RUNNING,] or 'possession.'
NETTLES,] as in Job 30. 7; Prov. 24. 31.
PITS.] Original word not found again.
SEIZE] them as 'prey, spoil.'
10. ARROGANCE] or 'gaiety; 'as in Ex. 15.7.
11. MADE BARE,] or 'lean;' as in Isa. 17. 4.
EACH,] lit. a 'man.'
12. CUSHIM,] dwellers on both sides of Red Sea.
13. ASSHUR,] the greatest empire.
NINEVEH,] capital of Asshur.
14. DROVES,] or 'herds;' as in Ge. 29. 2, &c.
BEAST,]or 'living creature;' as in v. 15, &c.
PELICAN,] as in Lev. 11. 18; De. 14. 17, &c.
HEDGE-HOG,] as in Isa. 14. 23; 34. 11.
LODGE,] or 'remain, pass the night.'
EXPOSED,] or 'made bare;' as in Ge. 24. 20.
15. CONFIDENTLY,] or 'leaningly;' as in Ge. 34. 25, &c.
BEASTS,] lit. 'living creature;' as in v. 14.
SHAKE,] as in Nu. 32. 13; 2 Sa. 15. 20, &c.

III. WO,] as in 2. 5; 1 K. 13. 30; Isa. 1. 4.
2. INSTRUCTION,] or 'a band;' as in v. 7.
TRUSTED,] or 'leant;' as in Jud. 9. 26, &c.
3. GNAWN THN BONE,] as in Nu. 24. 8, &c.
4. UNSTABLE,] as in Jud. 9. 4.
SANCTUARY,] or 'set apart place.'
LAW,] or 'direction;' as in Ge. 26. 5, &c.
5. PERVERSENESS,] as in v. 13; 2 Sa. 3. 34.
MORNING,] lit. 'in morning in morning.'
LACKING,] or 'arranged;' as in 1 Sa. 30. 19.
6. CHIEF ONES,] lit. 'corners;' as in 1. 16.
7. HABITATION,] as in De. 26. 15; 1 Sa. 2. 29
RISEN EARLY,] or 'given the shoulder.'
CORRUPTED,] or 'marred;' as in Ge. 6. 12.
8. PREY,] as in Ge. 49. 27; Isa. 33. 23.
POUR OUT,] or 'shed forth;' as in 1 Sa. 25. 31, &c.
EARTH,] 'land' of Israel.
9. PURE,] as in 1 Ch. 7. 40; 9. 22; 16. 41, &c.
BY,] or 'in' the name of Jehovah.
11. ACTIONS,] as in v. 7; De. 22. 14, &c.
TRANSGRESSED,] lit. 'stepped;' as in 1 K. 8. 50; 12. 19, &c.
EXCELLENCE,] or 'gaiety;' as in De. 33. 26
12. POOR,] or 'lean, thin;' as in Ex. 23. 3.
TRUSTED,] or 'taken refuge in;' as in De. 32. 37, &c.
13. DELIGHT,] or 'feed;' as in 2. 7, &c.
LAIN,] lit. 'crouched down;' as in 2. 7, 14.

15. FACED,] as in Ge. 24. 31; Lev. 14. 36, &c.
SEEST,] as in Ge. 1. 4, 10, 12, 18, 21, &c.
16. ZION,] i.e. 'sunny or dry place.'
17. SAVE,] or 'ease;' as in v. 19; Ex. 2. 17.
JOYETH,] as in De. 28. 63; 30. 9; Job 3. 22.

18. BEARING,] or 'lifting up.'
19. SAVED,] or 'given ease;' as in v. 17.
HALTING ONE,] as in Ge. 32. 31; Mic. 4. 6, 7.
20. CAPTIVITY,] or 'captivities,' i.e. captive bands.

HAGGAI

THE WORDS OF HAGGAI were delivered during the 6th, 7th, 8th, and 9th months of B.C. 520, to the captives who had returned from Babel, and who for 14 years had been interrupted in building the temple. In 1. 1—12 he reproves them, and in 1. 13—15 encourages them. In 2. 1—19 he encourages them, and in 2. 20—23 fortells the establishment of the church of God. New Testament references are found in Mat. 28. 20; Rom. 8. 31; Heb. 12. 26, &c.

I. 1. SECOND YEAR,] B.C. 520.
DARIUS] Hystaspis, of Persia.
SIXTH MONTH,] that is, Elul.
A WORD,] or communication from JEHOVAH,] the Existing One, God of Israel.
BY,] or 'in' the hand or instrumentality of HAGGAI,] i.e. 'my festive one;' the PROPHET,] or announcer of Jehovah's will to
ZERUBBABEL,] i.e. 'scattered to Babel.'
SHEALTIEL,] i.e. 'I have asked God.'
GOVERNOR,] as in v. 14: 2. 2, 21; 1 K. 10. 15.
JOSHUA,] i.e. 'Jah saves.'
JOSEDECH,] i.e. 'Jah is just or right.'
HIGH,] lit. 'the great' one.
2. HOSTS] of the heavens and the earth.
HOUSE,] that is, the 'temple' for sacrifices.
3. BY,] or 'in' the hand of Haggai.
4. COVERED,] as in De. 33. 21; 1 K. 7. 3, &c.
LIE WASTE,] or 'be dried up;' as in v. 9, &c.
5. TO,] lit. 'on your ways.'
6. MUCH,] or 'to multiply;' as in v. 9, &c.
BROUGHT IN,] or 'and to bring in' little.
DRUNKENNESS,] or 'be merry.'
HEAT,] or 'there is not to heat.'
HIRING HIMSELF OUT,] or 'making himself sweet.'
8. THE MOUNT,] the hill-country of Judah, or Lebanon.
9. LOOKING,] lit. 'to face;' as in Ge. 24. 63.
HOME,] lit. 'to the house.'
AFFIRMATION,] as in v. 13; 2. 4, 8, 9, &c.
10. REFRAINED,] as in Ge. 23. 6; 1 Sa. 6. 10.
INCREASE,] as in Lev. 26. 4, 20; De. 11. 17.
11. BEAST,] or 'cattle;' as in Ge. 1. 24, &c.
LABOUR,] as in Ge. 31. 42; De. 28. 33, &c.
HANDS,] or 'palms;' as in Ge. 8. 9; 20. 5.

12. REMNANT,] as in v. 14; 2. 2; Ge. 45. 7.
THEIR GOD,] by creation and preservation
13. MESSENGER,] or 'worker;' as in Ge. 16.7.
MESSAGES,] or 'works.'
14. STIR UP,] as in De. 32. 11; 1 Ch. 5. 26.
15. THE KING] of Persia; as in v. 1.

II. 1. SEVENTH] month, that is, Tisri.
BY,] or 'in the hand of Haggai.'
2. I PRAY THEE,] not 'now,' as in C.V.
3. FORMER,] lit. 'first' honour, before its destruction.
4. STRONG,] as in De. 12. 23; 31. 6, 7, &c.
5. THING,] or 'word,' of mutual obligation.
EGYPT,] B.C. 1491.
6. SHAKING,] as in v. 21; Isa. 14. 16.
7. SHAKEN,] as in Ps. 60. 2; Eze. 31. 16.
THEY HAVE COME,] that is, the nations have come to the
DESIRE,] or desired thing, either Jerusalem or Messiah.
HONOUR,] lit. 'weightiness, heaviness.'
8. MINE,] lit. 'to me.'
9. PEACE,] or 'completeness;' as in Ge. 15. 15; 26. 29, &c.
10. NINTH] month, that is, Chisleu.
12. ONE,] lit. a 'man.'
HOLY FLESH,] lit. 'flesh of a set-apart thing.'
NO,] that is, mere contact with holy things does not make a thing holy.
13. UNCLEAN] of soul, lit. 'of soul.'
UNCLEAN,] pollution coming by contact.
15. LAY,] lit. 'set;' as in v. 8; 1. 5, 7, &c.
ONWARDS,] lit. 'upwards.'
LAYING,] lit. 'setting;' as in Ge. 45. 7, &c.
16. HEAP,] as in Ruth 3. 7; 2 Ch. 31. 6, &c.
WINE-VAT,] as in Nu. 18. 27, 30; Da. 15. 14.
PURAH,] as in Isa. 63. 3.
17. BLASTING,] as in De. 28. 22; 1 K. 8. 37.
MILDEW,] lit. 'yellowness;' as in De. 28. 22.
18. NINTH] month, that is, Chisleu.
FOUNDED,] as in 1 K. 6. 37; Ezra 3. 6, &c.
19. BARN,] lit. 'place of gathering.'
BORNE,] lit. 'lifted up;' as in v. 12, &c.
21. SPEAK,] lit. 'say;' as in v. 2; Ge. 12. 13.
22. EACH,] lit. a 'man.'
23. SERVANT,] as in Jos. 1. 1, 2, &c.
SIGNET,] as in Ge. 38. 18; Ex. 28. 11, &c.
FIXED,] as in Ge. 6. 2; 13. 11, &c.

ZECHARIAH

THE WORDS OF ZECHARIAH were delivered B.C. 520—518, and may be divided into two parts, the *first*, containing chap. i—vi. and the *second*, chap. vii—xiv. New Testament quotations are Mat. 16. 18; 21. 4, 5; 26. 31; 27. 3, 10; Mark 14. 27; John 1. 14, 45; 12. 14, 15; 19. 34—37; Rom. 8. 33; Eph. 2. 19—22; Heb. 3. 1—3; 13. 20; Rev. 1. 7; 5. 6; 6. 2—4.

I. 1. EIGHTH] month, Bul or Marshevan.
SECOND] year, B.C. 520.
DARIUS,] *or* 'Daryavesh,' king of Persia.
A WORD,] *or* 'communication,' from
JEHOVAH,] the Existing One, God of Israel.
ZECHARIAH,] i.e. 'remembered of Jah.'
BERACHIAH,] i.e. 'blessed of Jah.'
IDDO,] i.e. 'seasonable.'
PROPHET,] or proclaimer of God's will.
2. WROTH,] as in v. 15; Ge. 40. 2; 41. 10, &c.
3. HOSTS] of the heavens and earth.
AFFIRMATION,] as in v. 4, 16; 2. 5, 6, &c.
4. FORMER,] such as, Elijah, Elisha, &c.
I PRAY YOU.] not 'now,' as in C.V.
HEARKEN,] *lit.* 'hear;' as in 6. 15; 7. 13.
5. PROPHETS,] as in v. 1, 4, 6, 7; 7. 3, 7, &c.
6. STATUTES,] *lit.* 'engraved things;' as in Ge. 47. 22, &c.
OVERTAKEN,] as in Ge. 31. 45; 44. 4, 6, &c.
DESIGNED,] as in 8. 14, 15; Ge. 11. 6, &c.
7. ELEVENTH] month, that is, Shebat.
SHEBAT,] part of February and March.
8. BY NIGHT,] *lit.* 'the night.'
ONE,] *lit.* a 'man.'
STANDING,] *or* 'standing still;' as in v. 10.
MYRTLES,] as in v. 10, 11; Neh. 8. 15, &c.
SHADE.] Original word not found again.
BAY,] *or* 'tawny.'
9. WITH,] *or* 'in me.'
10. ONE,] *lit.* 'man.'
WALK UP AND DOWN,] *or* 'habitually;' as in 6. 7, &c.
11. AT REST,] as in Jud. 18. 7, 27; 1 Ch. 4. 40.
12. PITY,] as in 10. 6; Ex. 33. 19; De. 13. 17.
ABHORRED,] as in Nu. 23. 8; Prov. 24. 24, &c.
13. WORDS,] *or* 'things, matters.'
14. ZEALOUS,] as in 8. 2; Ge. 26. 14; 30. 1.
15. WRATH,] as in v. 2; 7. 12; Nu. 1. 53, &c.
EASE,] as in 2 K. 19. 28; Job 12. 5, &c.
16. WITH,] *or* 'in' mercies.
LINE,] as in 1 K. 7. 23; Jer. 31. 39.
17. OVERFLOW,] *or* 'break forth;' as in 13. 7; Ge. 11. 4, &c.
18. LOOK,] *or* 'see.'
HORNS,] as in v. 19, 21; Ge. 22. 13, &c.
19. SCATTERED,] as in v. 21; Lev. 26. 33, &c.
20. ARTIZANS,] as in Ex. 28. 11; 35. 35, &c.
21. SPEAKETH,] *lit.* 'saith.'
SO THAT,] *lit.* 'according to the mouth.'
TROUBLE,] as in Eze. 30. 9.
CAST DOWN,] or forth; as in Lam. 3. 53.
AGAINST,] *lit.* 'unto.'

II. 1. LOOK,] *or* 'see.'
LINE,] *or* 'cord;' as in De. 3. 4, 12, 14, &c.

4. YOUNG MAN,] *or* 'youth;' as in 11. 16, &c.
UNWALLED VILLAGES,] as in Est. 9. 19; Eze. 38. 11.
5. BEAST,] *or* 'cattle;' as in 8. 10; 14. 15.
6. HONOUR,] *lit.* 'heaviness, weightiness.'
7. BE DELIVERED,] as in Ge. 19. 19, 22.
8. SPOILING,] as in Jer. 50. 10; Eze. 39. 10.
COMING,] *or* 'striking;' as in Ge. 26. 11, &c.
DAUGHTER.] Original word not found a-gain.
9. WAVING,] as in Isa. 10. 15; 19. 16, &c.
10. SING,] as in Isa. 12. 6; 44. 23; 49. 13, &c.
DWELT,] tabernacled or 'settled down.'
13. BECAUSE OF,] *or* 'from the face of.'

III. 1. JOSHUA,] i.e. 'Jo has saved.'
HIGH PRIEST,] *lit.* 'great priest.'
STANDING,] as in v. 3, 4, 5, 7; 1. 8, 10, &c.
THE ADVERSARY,] *or* 'accusor;' as in v. 2; Nu. 22. 22, 32; 1 Sa. 29. 4; 2 Sa. 19. 22; 1 K. 5. 4, &c.
AT,] *lit.* 'on.'
2. PUSH,] as in Ge. 37. 10; Ruth 2. 16, &c.
BRAND,] as in Isa. 7. 4; Amos 4. 11.
DELIVERED,] *lit.* 'snatched;' as in Amos 4. 11.
3. FILTHY,] as in v. 4.
4. SPEAKETH,] *lit.* 'saith.'
FROM OFF,] *lit.* 'from (being) on him.'
COSTLY APPAREL,] as in Isa. 3. 22.
5. HE ALSO SAID,] *or* 'and I say.'
DIADEM,] as in Job 29. 14; Isa. 3. 23; 62. 3.
6. PROTEST TO,] *or* 'testifyeth against.'
7. JUDGE,] as in Ge. 30. 9; 49. 6, &c.
CONDUCTORS,] *lit.* 'causers to go.'
8. COMPANIONS,] *or* 'friends;' as in v. 10.
TYPE,] *or* 'wonder;' as in Ex. 4. 21; 7. 3, 9.
SHEOL,] as in Ge. 19. 25; Ps. 65. 10.
9. PUT,] *lit.* 'given;' as in v. 7.
GRAVING,] *lit.* 'opening its opening.'
10. EACH,] *lit.* a 'man unto his friend.'

IV. 1. TURN BACK,] from speaking to the messenger, as in 2. 3.
STIR UP,] as in De. 32. 11; 1 Ch. 5. 26, &c.
2. CANDLESTICK,] as in v. 11; Ex. 25. 31, &c.
BOWL,] *or* 'spring;' as in Jos. 15. 19, &c.
LAMPS,] as in Ex. 25. 37; 27. 20; 30. 7, &c.
TWICE,] *lit.* 'seven and seven.'
3. ON,] *lit.* 'from the right.'
6. SPEAKETH,] *lit.* 'saith.'
A FORCE,] as in 9. 4; 14. 14; Ge. 34. 29, &c.
7. PLAIN,] as in De. 3. 10; 4. 43; Jos. 13. 9.
CRIES,] as in Job 36. 29; 39. 7; Isa. 22. 2.
9. FOUND,] as in Jos. 6. 26; 1 K. 16. 34, &c.
FINISH,] as in Job 6. 9; Isa. 10. 12, &c.
10. TRAMPLED,] *or* 'despised;' as in Prov. 1. 7; 6. 30, &c.
TIN WEIGHT,] *lit.* 'tin-stone.'
GOING TO AND FRO,] as in 2 Ch. 16. 9.
12. BRANCHES,] *or* 'ears;' as in Ge. 41. 5, 6.
BY MEANS OF,] *lit.* 'by the hand of.'
OIL,] *lit.* the shining thing;' as in v. 2, &c
14. BY,] *lit.* 'on, near.'

663

V. 1. FLYING,] as in v. 2; Isa. 31. 5.
ROLL,] as in v. 2; Ps. 40. 7; Jer. 36. 2, &c.
2. BY,] or 'with the cubit.'
3. EXECRATION,] as in Ge. 24. 41; 26. 28, &c.
ON THE ONE SIDE,] lit. 'from this.'
4. SWORN,] or 'been sworn.'
REMAINED,] or 'lodged;' as in Ge. 19. 2, &c.
CONSUMED,] or 'ended;' as in Ge. 2. 2, &c.
6. THE EPHAH,] a measure containing 3
seahs or 10 omers; Ex. 16. 36, &c.
ASPECT,] lit. 'eye;' as in v. 1, 5, 9; 1. 18, &c.
7. CAKE,] as in Ex. 29. 23, &c.
LEAD,] as in 1. 8; Ge. 25. 30; Nu. 19. 2, &c.
8. WEIGHT,] lit. 'stone;' as in v. 4; 3. 9, &c.
9. STORK,] as in Lev. 11. 19; De. 14. 18, &c.
11. SHINAR,] a district round Babel.
PREPARED,] made ready, or 'set up.'
PLACED,] lit 'caused to rest.'
BASE,] or 'prepared, set up place.'

VI. 1. CHARIOTS,] as in v. 2, 3; Ge. 41. 43.
BRASS,] as in Ge. 4. 22; Ex. 25. 3; 26. 11. 37.
2. RED,] as in 1. 8; Ge. 25. 30; Nu. 19. 2, &c.
BROWN,] as in v. 6; Lev. 13. 31, 37; Song
1. 5.
3. WHITE,] as in v. 6; 1. 8; Ge. 30. 35, &c.
GRISLED,] as in v. 6: Ge. 31. 10, 12.
5. SPIRITS,] lit. 'winds.'
PRESENTING,] lit. 'setting themselves up.'
6. NORTH,] as in v. 8; 2. 6; 14. 4, &c.
SOUTH,] or 'of Teman;' as in 9. 14; Hab. 3. 3.
7. STRONG ONES,] as in v. 3.
WALK UP AND DOWN,] as in 1. 18; Job 1. 7.
EARTH,] or 'land.'
8. CALLETH,] or 'crieth,' i.e. summoneth.
REST,] as in Ex. 17. 11; 33. 14; De. 3. 20.
9. WORD,] or divine communication.
10. CAPTIVITY,] or 'removal;' as in 14. 2.
HELDAI,] in v. 14 it is 'Helem.'
TOBIJAH,] i.e. 'goodness of Jah.'
JEDAIAH,] i.e. 'known of Jah.'
JOSIAH,] i.e. 'healed of Jah.'
ZEPHANIAH,] i.e. 'concealed of Jah.'
11. A CROWN,] lit. 'crowns.'
PLACED,] lit. 'set;' as in 7. 12; 9. 13; 10. 3.
12. SPAKE,] lit. 'said.'
A SHOOT,] as in 3. 8; Ge. 19. 25; Ps. 65. 10.
FROM HIS PLACE,] or 'from beneath him.'
13. BEAR AWAY,] or 'lift up;' as in v. 1, &c.
HONOUR,] as in 10. 3; Nu. 27. 20, &c.
14. HEN,] i.e. 'grace.'
15. CERTAINLY,] lit. 'to hear ye do hear.'

VII. 1. FOURTH] year, B.C. 518.
NINTH] month, that is, Chisleu.
3. BETH-EL,] the village of that name.
SHEREZER,] i.e. 'prince of fire.'
REGEM-MELECH,] i.e. 'friend of the king.'
APPEASE,] lit. 'smooth;' as in 8. 21, &c.
3. SEPARATED,] lit. 'to be separated.'
5. FIFTH] month, that is, Ab.
SEVENTH] month, that is, Tisri.
7. FORMER,] such as Moses, Elijah, &c.
BEING INHABITED,] as in 1. 11; 2. 7, &c.
8. WORD,] or divine communication.
9. SPAKE,] lit. 'said.'
TRUE,] lit. 'judgment of stedfastness.'
MERCY,] lit. 'mercies;' as in v. 9, &c.
ONE,] lit. 'a man with his brother.'
10. WIDCW,] lit. 'dumb, silent, solitary
one.'

CALAMITY,] lit. 'evil;' as in 1. 4, 15; 8. 17.
11, REFRACTORY,] lit. 'turning aside;' as
in De. 21, 18, &c.
12. MADE,] lit. 'set;' as in 6. 11; 9. 13, &c.
BY,] or 'with or in' his spirit.
14. TOSS,] as in Hab. 3. 14; Hos. 3. 3, &c.
DESIRABLE,] lit. 'land of desire.'

VIII. 1. WORD,] or 'leading forth' of
Jehovah.
2. ZEALOUS,] as in 1. 14; Ge. 26. 14, &c.
3. DWELT,] 'tabernacled or settled down.'
TRUTH,] lit. 'stedfastness;' as in v. 8, &c.
4. EACH,] lit. 'a man.'
BECAUSE OF,] lit. 'from.'
5. PLAYING,] lit. 'laughing; as in 1 Sa. 18. 7.
6. WONDERFUL,] as in Ge. 18. 14; De. 17. 4.
7. SAVING,] or 'easing;' as in De. 22. 27, &c.
SUN,] lit. 'minister;' as in Ge. 15. 12, &c.
8. DWELT,] 'tabernacled or settled down.
TRUTH,] or 'stedfastness;' as in v. 3, &c.
10. HIRING,] as in 11. 12; Ge. 15. 1; 30. 18.
ADVERSARY,] as in Ge. 14. 20; Nu. 10. 9, &c.
EACH,] lit. a 'man against his friend.'
12. INCREASE,] as in Lev. 26. 4, 20, &c.
13. REVILING,] or 'disesteem, lightness.'
14. PURPOSE,] as in v. 15; 1. 6; Ge. 11. 6.
REPENT,] or 'was not comforted.'
16. TRUTH,] or 'stedfastness;' as in v. 3.
EACH,] lit. a 'man with his friend.'
17. NEIGHBOUR,] or 'friend;' as in v. 10, 16.
DEVISE,] or 'think;' as in v. 14; 1. 6, &c.
18. WORD,] or divine communication.
19. FOURTH] month, that is, Thammuz.
FIFTH] month, that is, Ab.
SEVENTH] month, that is, Tisri.
TENTH] month, that is, Tebet.
PLEASANT,] lit. 'good;' as in 1. 13. 17, &c.
TRUTH,] as in v. 3, 8, 16, 19, &c.
21. ANOTHER,] lit. 'one unto one.'
DILIGENTLY,] lit. 'we go to go.'
APPEASE,] lit. 'smooth;' as in v. 22, &c.
22. MIGHTY,] lit. 'bony;' as in Ge. 18. 18.
23. SKIRT,] lit. 'wing;' as in 5. 9; Ge. 1. 21.
A JEW,] a name applied to any Israelite.

IX. 1. BURDEN,] lit. 'thing lifted up;' as
in 12. 1, &c.
HADROCH,] i.e. 'dwelling.'
DAMASCUS,] Dammeseq or Darmeseq.
2. HAMATH,] i.e. 'walled.'
TYRE,] i.e. a 'rock or sharpness.'
ZIDON,] i.e. place for 'hunting' fish.
3. BULWARK,] as in 12. 2; De. 20. 19, &c
HEAP,] as in Ge. 41. 35, 49; Ex. 8. 14, &c.
GOLD,] as in 2 Ch. 9. Ps. 68. 13, &c.
4. FORCE,] as in 4. 6; 14. 14; Ge. 34. 29, &c.
5. ASHKELON,] i.e. a place of 'weighing.'
GAZA,] i.e. a 'strong place.'
EKRON,] i.e. a 'root.'
EXPECTATION,] as in Isa. 20. 5, 6.
6. FOREIGNER,] as in De. 23. 2.
ASHDOD,] in N.T. called 'Azotus.'
EXCELLENCE,] lit. 'gayness;' as in 10. 11.
7. REMAINED,] or 'been left;' as in Ge. 14.
10; 32. 8, &c.
LEADER,] guide or chief; as in 12. 5, 6, &c.
JEBUSITE,] ancient inhabitants of Jerusalem.
8. CAMP,] lit. 'set-up' place; as in 1 Sa.
14. 12, &c.

EXACTOR,] as in 10. 4; Ex. 3. 7; 5. 6, &c.
9. REJOICE,] *lit.* 'leap;' as in Ps. 2. 11, &c.
KING,] counsellor or leader; as in v. 5, &c.
RIGHTEOUS,] *or* 'just, right;' as in Ge. 6. 9.
SAVED,] in that which he feared, not
'having salvation,' as in C.V.
AFFLICTED,] *or* 'poor;' as in 7. 10; 11. 7.
ASS,] as in 14, 15; Ge. 12. 16; 22. 3, 5, &c.
COLT,] as in Ge. 32. 15; 49. 11; Jud. 10. 4.
SHE-ASSES,] as in Ge. 12. 16; 32. 15; 45. 23.
10. RULE,] as in Da. 11. 4.
THE RIVER,] that is, the Euphrates.
11. BY,] *or* 'in, with.'
PRISONERS,] *lit.* 'bound ones;' as in v. 12.
12. SECOND,] as in Ge. 41. 43; 43. 12, &c.
13. FILLED,] as in Ge. 21. 19; 24. 16, &c.
STIRRED UP,] as in 2 Sa. 23. 18; 1 Ch. 11. 11.
JAVAN,] that is, Ionia or Greece.
HERO,] *or* 'mighty one;' as in 10. 5, 7, &c.
14. FOR,] *or* 'over.'
BLOWETH,] *lit.* 'striketh;' as in Ge. 31. 25.
SOUTH,] *or* 'of Teman;' as in 6. 6, &c.
15. CORNERS,] as in Ps. 144. 12.
16. DISPLAYING THEMSELVES,] *or* 'ensigns.'
17. BEAUTY,] as in Est. 1. 11; Ps. 45. 11, &c.
YOUNG MEN,] *or* 'choice ones;' as in De.
32. 25, &c.
MAKE FRUITFUL,] *or* 'cause to bring forth'
words.

X. 1. LIGHTNINGS,] as in Job 28. 26, &c.
LATTER RAIN,] *lit.* 'gathered' rain; as in
De. 11. 14, &c.
EACH,] *lit.* a 'man.'
2. TERAPHIM,] i.e. 'tearers, burners, heal-
ers.'
DIVINERS,] as in De. 18. 10, 14; Jos. 13. 22.
VANITY,] as in De. 32. 21; 1 K. 16. 13, &c.
3. BURN,] *or* 'was hot;' as in Ge. 4. 5, &c.
FLOCK,] *or* 'drove, herd;' as in Ge. 29. 2.
4. CORNER-STONE,] as in Ex. 27. 2; 38. 2, &c.
NAIL,] *or* 'pin' for fixing a tent.
5. HEROES,] *or* 'mighty ones;' as in v. 7.
FOUGHT,] *or* 'been fought with.'
6. LOVED,] as in 1. 12; Ex. 33. 19; De 13. 17.
ANSWER,] as in 1. 10—13; 3. 4; 4. 4, &c.
7. REJOICE,] as in 4. 10; Ex. 4. 14, &c.
8. HIST,] as in 1 K. 9. 8; Job 27. 23, &c.
REDEEM,] *or* 'ransomed;' as in Ex. 13. 13.
MULTIPLY,] in former days in Egypt.
10. EGYPT,] in *Heb.* 'Mitsrayim.'
ASSHUR,] *or* Nimrod.
GILEAD,] i.e. 'heap of witness.'
LEBANON,] i.e. the 'white' mountain.
11. BILLOWS,] *or* 'heaps;' as in Ge. 31. 46.
FLOOD,] as in Ge. 41. 1, 2, 3, 17, 18, &c.
EXCELLENCE,] *or* 'gayness;' as in 9. 6, &c.
ROD,] *or* 'sceptre;' as in 9. 1; Ge. 49. 10, &c.
12. WALK UP AND DOWN,] *or* 'habitually;'
as in 6. 7, &c.

XI. 1. OPEN,] as in Jos. 10. 22; 2 K. 13. 17.
2. HOWL,] as in Isa. 13. 6; 14. 12, 31, &c.
FOR,] *or* 'in that.'
4. JORDAN,] the chief river of Palestine.
5. BUYERS,] *or* 'acquirers;' as in Lev. 25. 28.
6. EACH,] *lit.* 'a man.'
NEIGHBOUR,] *or* 'friend;' as in 3. 8, &c.
BEATEN DOWN,] as in 2 K. 18. 4; 2 Ch. 34. 7.
DELIVER OUT,] *or* 'snatch away;' as in Ge.
31. 9, 16, &c.

7. SLAUGHTER,] *lit.* 'the slaughter.'
STAVES,] as in v. 10, 14; Ge. 30. 37, &c.
8. CUT OFF,] *or* 'conceal;' as in Ex. 23. 23.
IS GRIEVED,] *lit.* 'shortened;' as in Lev.
23. 10; 25. 5, &c.
ABHORRED.] Original word not found a-
gain.
10. CUT ASUNDER,] as in v. 14; 1 Sa. 2. 31.
MADE,] *lit.* 'prepared, cut;' as in Ge. 15. 18.
11. BROKEN,] as in Isa. 8. 10; Jer. 33. 21. '
12. HIRE,] *or* 'reward;' as in 8. 10, &c.
FORBEAR,] *lit.* 'cease;' as in Ex. 14. 12, &c.
WEIGH OUT,] money being weighed, not
counted, in those days.
THIRTY,] the value of a servant; as in Ex.
21. 32, &c.
13. GOODLY PRICE.] Ges. 'magnificence of
the price.'
PRIZED AT,] as in 1 Sa. 18. 20; 26. 21, &c.
14. BREAK,] *or* 'make void;' as in v. 10, &c.
15. FOOLISH.] Original word not found a-
gain.
16. SHAKEN OFF,] Noldius 'wanderer.'
FAT,] *or* 'firm;' as in Ge. 41. 2, 4, 5, 7, &c.
17. WORTHLESS,] *or* 'nothing;' as in Lev.
19. 4; 26. 1, &c.
VERY,] *lit.* 'to be dim is dim.'

XII. 1. BURDEN,] as in Zech. 9. 1, &c.
2. MAKING,] *lit.* 'setting;' as in Ps. 66. 9.
3. MAKE,] *lit.* 'set;' as in v. 6; 3. 5; 7. 14.
COMPLETELY,] *lit.* 'to press down is pressed down.'
4. MADNESS,] as in De. 28. 28; 2 K. 9. 20.
5. LEADERS,] guides, or chiefs; as in v. 6.
6. MAKE,] *lit.* 'set;' as in v. 3; 3. 5. &c.
7. SAVE!] *or* 'eased;' as in 8. 13; 9. 16, &c.
8. STUMBLING,] *or* 'stumbled one;' as in 1
Sa. 2. 4.
GOD,] *or* 'as a god,' or divine being.
10. POURED OUT,] *or* 'shed forth;' as in
Ge. 37. 22, &c.
PIERCED,] as in 13. 3; Nu. 25. 8, &c.
MOURNED,] *or* 'beat' the breast; as in v. 12.
FIRST-BORN,] as in Ex. 12. 29, &c.
11. HADAD-RIMMON.] Not mentioned elsewhere.
MEGEDDON,] where Josiah was killed.
12. FAMILY,] as in v. 13, 14; 14. 17, 18, &c.
DAVID,] the 'beloved' king of Israel.
NATHAN,] the prophet who rebuked David.
13. LEVI,] the tribe chosen for priests.
SHEMEI,] grandson of Levi, 1 Ch. 3. 5, but
Sept. Syr. Arab. read 'Simeon,' second son
of Jacob.
14. LEFT,] as in 11. 9; Ge. 14. 10; 32. 8, &c.

XIII. 1. FOUNTAIN,] as in Lev. 12. 7, &c.
IMPURITY,] as in Lev. 12. 2, 5; 15. 19, &c.
2. IDOLS,] *lit.* 'grievous things;' as in 1 Sa.
31. 9, &c.
3. ONE,] *lit.* a 'man.'
PARENTS,] *lit.* 'begetters;' as in Ge. 16. 11.
PIERCED,] as in 12. 10; Nu. 25. 8, &c.
4. EACH,] *lit.* a 'man.'
HAIRY ROBE,] *or* 'honourable robe of hair.'
DECEIVE,] *lit.* 'He;' as in Isa. 59. 13; Hos.
4. 2.
5. TILLER,] *lit.* 'serving;' as in 2. 9, &c.
GROUND,] *or* 'man possessed me,' as in C.V.
YOUTH,] *or* 'youthful days.'

6. WOUNDS,] *lit.* 'smitings;' as in Lev. 26. 21.
IN,] *lit.* 'between.'
7. HERO,] *or* 'man;' as in Ex. 10. 11, &c.
FELLOW,] belonging to the same 'people;'
as in Lev. 6. 2; 18. 20; 19. 11, 15, 17, &c.
8. TWO PARTS,] *lit.* 'mouth of two.'
EXPIRE,] *or* 'are heaped up;' as in Ge. 6. 17.
LEFT] over; as in Ge. 32. 24; 44. 20, &c.
9. REFINING,] as in Ps. 66. 10; Jer. 6. 29.
TRYING,] *or* 'testing, proving.'
MY GOD,] or object of worship.

XIV. 1. DIVIDED,] *or* 'apportioned;' as in
Isa. 33. 23, &c.
2. LAIN WITH,] as in Isa. 13. 6.
3. FOUGHT,] *lit.* 'been fought with.'
FIGHTING,] *lit.* 'being fought with.'
CONFLICT,] *lit.* 'drawing near;' as in 2 Sa.
17. 11, &c.
4. OLIVES,] *lit.* 'the olives.'
AT ITS MIDST,] *lit.* 'from its half.'
VALLEY,] as in v. 5; Nu. 21. 20; De. 3. 29.
5. JOIN,] *lit.* 'strike or touch;' as in Ex.
4. 25, &c.
AZAL.] Not mentioned elsewhere.
SHAKING,] *or* 'rushing;' as in 1 K. 19. 11.
UZZIAH,] B.C. 810—758; Amos 1. 1.
6. PRECIOUS,] *lit.* 'light of precious or
rare' things.

8. EASTERN,] either the Salt or Red Sea.
WESTERN,] or the Mediterranean sea.
9. ONE JEHOVAH,] that is, 'One Existing
One.'
NAME,] *or* 'renown,' that is, character.
10. CHANGED,] *lit.* 'turned round;' as in
Ge. 19. 4, &c.
GEBO,] in the north of Benjamin, to
RIMMON,] in the south of Judah.
TOWER,] *lit.* 'great place;' as in Ge. 11. 4.
HANANEEL,] i.e. 'grace of a mighty one.'
11. DESTRUCTION,] *lit.* a 'laying flat;' as in
Lev. 27. 21, &c.
CONFIDENTLY,] *or* 'leaningly;' as in Ge
34. 25, &c.
12. PLAGUE,] as in v. 15, 18; Ex. 9. 14, &c.
CONSUMED AWAY,] as in Lev. 26. 39, &c.
13. DESTRUCTION,] as in De. 7. 23; 28. 20.
EACH,] *lit.* a 'man.'
NEIGHBOUR,] *lit.* 'friend;' as in 3. 8, &c.
16. OF,] *lit.* 'from, out of.'
FROM YEAR,] *lit.* 'from sufficiency of year
with year.'
CELEBRATE,] *lit.* 'feast;' as in v. 18, &c.
18. BOOTHS,] as in v. 16, 18, 19; Ge. 33. 17.
19. PUNISHMENT,] *or* 'sin-offering;' as in
13. 1, &c.
20. BELLS,] for warning passers by.
21. MERCHANT.] *Heb.* 'Canaanite.'

MALACHI

THE BURDEN OF MALACHI is generally supposed to have been delivered between B.C. 420—380. It may be divided into two parts, the *first*, containing ch. i—ii, and the *second*, ch. iii. iv. New Testament references are Mat. 11. 10; 17. 12; Mark 1. 2; 9. 11, 12; Luke 1. 17; 7. 27; Rom. 9. 13; 2 Pet. 1. 19.

I. 1. BURDEN,] *lit.* 'thing lifted up;' as in Ex. 23. 5, &c.

A WORD,] *or* divine communication from JEHOVAH,] the 'Existing One,' God of ISRAEL,] that is, the returned two tribes. MALACHI,] i.e. 'my messenger or worker.'
3. ESAU,] i.e 'made;' the elder brother of JACOB,] the father of the patriarchs.
AFFIRMATION,]*or* oracular announcement.
HATED,] that is, loved less than the other; compare Ge. 29. 31, 33, &c.
MAKE,] *lit.* 'set;' as in 2. 2; Ge. 2. 8, &c.
WILDERNESS,] *or* place for 'leading forth' flocks.
4. EDOM,] i.e. 'red;' as in Ge. 25. 30, &c.
MADE POOR,] as in Jer. 5. 17.
DESTROY,] as in Ex. 15. 7; 19. 21, 24, &c.
DEFIED,] as in Nu. 23. 7, 8; Prov. 24. 24.
6. HONOURETH,] *lit.* 'maketh heavy or weighty.'
DESPISING,] as in 1 Sa. 2. 30; 2 Ch. 36. 16.
7. POLLUTED,] as in v. 12.
TABLE,] as in v. 12; Ex. 25. 23; 27. 28, &c.
DESPICABLE,] *or* 'despised;' as in v. 12, &c.
8. LAME,] *or* 'limping;' as in v. 13, &c.
SICK,] *lit.* 'pierced;' as in v. 13; Ge. 48. 1.
GOVERNOR,] as in 1 K. 10. 15; 20. 24, &c.
9. APPEASE,] *lit.* 'smooth;' as in 1 K. 13. 8.
APPEARANCES,] *lit.* 'faces;' as in v. 8, &c.
10. SHUTTETH,] *or* 'maketh secure;' as in Ge. 2. 21, &c.
PLEASURE,] as in 2. 12; 1 Sa. 15. 22, &c.
12. POLLUTING,] *lit.* 'piercing;' as in Ex. 31. 14, &c.
FRUIT,] as in Isa. 57. 19.
13. PUFFED,] as in Job 31. 39.
PLUNDER,] a thing 'taken violently away.'
LAME,] *or* 'limping;' as in v. 13, &c.
14. CURSED,] *or* 'made bitter;' as in Ge. 3. 14.
DROVE,] *or* 'herd;' as in Ge. 29. 2, 3, &c.
REVERED,] *or* 'fearful;' as in 4, 5, &c.

II. 1. PRIESTS,] those 'making ready' the sacrifices.
2. LAY,] *lit.* 'set;' as in 1, 3; Ge. 2. 8, &c.
3. PUSHING AWAY,] as in Nah. 1. 4.
DUNG,] as in Ex. 29. 14; Lev. 4. 11; 8. 17.
FESTIVALS,] as in Ex. 10. 9; 12. 14; 13. 6.
TAKE AWAY,] *lit.* 'lifted up;' as in 1. 8, 9.
5. MAKE,] *lit.* 'give;' as in v. 9; Ge. 1. 17.
6. TRUTH,] *or* 'stedfastness;' as in Ge. 24. 27.
7. LAW,] *or* 'direction' in time of difficulty.
MESSENGER,] *or* 'worker;' as in 3.
8. TURNED] aside; as in 3. 7; Ge. 19. 2, &c.
CORRUPTED,] *or* 'marred;' as in Ge. 38. 9.
9. MADE,] *lit.* 'given;' as in v. 5.
BECAUSE,] *or* 'according as.'

ACCEPTING,] *or* 'lifting up faces;' as in 2 K. 3. 14, &c.
10. PREPARED,] as in Ge. 1. 1, 21, 27, &c.
POLLUTE,] *lit.* 'pierce;' as in v. 11.
11. STRANGE GOD,] *or* 'mighty one of a stranger.'
12. TEMPTER,] *lit.* 'waker up;' as in Song 5. 2.
TEMPTED,] *lit.* 'responder;' as in Ge. 35. 3.
14. WHEREFORE,] *lit.* 'for what?'
AGAINST,] *or* 'with' her.
WIFE,] *or* 'woman of thy covenant.'
15. SEED,] *lit.* a 'seed of God.'
OVER,] *or* 'with.'
YOUTH,] *lit.* 'youths;' as in v. 14, &c.
16. WITH,] *or* 'by.'
17. WEARIED,] as in Isa. 43. 23, 24.

III. 1. MESSENGER,] *or* 'worker;' as in 2. 7.
PREPARED,] *lit.* 'faced;' as in Ge. 24. 31.
BEFORE ME,] *or* 'before him;' dividing the Hebrew words differently.
THE LORD,] *lit.* 'basis or judge.'
COVENANT,] the new one; as in Jer. 31. 31.
2. BEARING,] *or* 'sustaining.'
APPEARING,] *lit.* 'being seen.'
SOAP,]*or* 'purifying matter;' as in Jer. 2. 22.
3. REFINED,] as in Job 28. 1; 36. 27.
4. SWEET,] *or* a 'surety;' as in Ge. 43. 9, &c.
5. SWEARERS,] *or* 'those sworn;' as in Ps 63. 11, &c.
6. CONSUMED,] *or* 'ended;' as in Ge. 21. 15
8. DECEIVE,] as in v. 9; Prov. 22. 23.
HEAVE-OFFERING,] as in Ex. 25. 2, 3, &c.
9. CURSE,] as in 2. 2; De. 28. 20; Prov. 3. 33; 28. 27.
10. FOOD,] *lit.* 'torn thing;' as in Ge. 49. 9.
TRIED,] *or* 'proved, tested;' as in Ps. 26. 2.
DO NOT,] *lit.* 'if not.'
WINDOWS,] as in Ge. 7. 11; 8. 2; 2 K. 7. 2.
11. DESTROY,] *lit.* 'mar;' as in Ge. 6. 12, &c.
MISCARRY,] *lit.* 'bereave;' as in Ge. 31. 38.
12. HAPPY,] not 'blessed;' as in v. 15.
13. SPOKEN,] *lit.* 'been spoken to;' as in v. 16.
14. VAIN THING,] as in Ex. 20. 7; 23. 1, &c.
GAIN,] as in Ge. 37. 26; Ex. 18. 21, &c.
IN BLACK,] as in Isa. 50. 3.
BECAUSE OF,] *lit.* 'from the face of.'
15. HAPPY,] as in v. 13.
16. SPOKEN,] as in v. 13.
BOOK OF MEMORIAL,] as in Est. 6. 1.
ESTEEMING,] as in Ex. 26. 1, 31; 28. 6, &c.
17. IN,] *or* 'at, or for.'
APPOINTING,] *lit.* 'making;' as in v. 15, &c.
ONE,] *lit.* a 'man.'
18. CONSIDERED,] *lit.* 'seen;' as in 1. 5, &c.

IV. 2. RISEN,] as in Ge. 32. 31; Lx. 22. 8.
STALL,] as in 1 Sa. 28. 24; Jer. 46. 21; Am. 6. 4.
3. APPOINTING,] *lit.* 'making;' as in 2. 17.
4. LAW,] *or* 'direction;' as in 2. 6, 7, &c.
HOREB,] i.e. 'dry place;' as in Ex. 3. 1, &c.
5. ALIJAH,] i.e. 'my God is Jah.'
6. TO,] *lit.* 'on, upon, with, in addition to.'
BEFORE,] *or* 'lest;' *lit.* 'facing.'
UTTERLY,] *lit.* 'smitten the land flat.'

607

Chronology from Adam to Christ.

4004 Creation of Adam and Eve.
3998 Births of Cain and Abel.
3876 Cain kills Abel.
3874 Birth of Seth to Eve.
3769 Birth of Enos to Seth.
3679 Birth of Cainan to Enos.
3609 Birth of Mahalaleel to Cainan.
3544 Birth of Jared to Mahalaleel.
3382 Birth of Enoch to Jared.
3317 Birth of Methusalah to Enoch.
3130 Birth of Lamech to Methuselah.
3074 Death of Adam, aged 930.
3017 Departure of Enoch, aged 365.
2962 Death of Seth, aged 912.
2948 Birth of Noah to Lamech.
2864 Death of Enos, aged 905.
2769 Death of Cainan, aged 910.
2714 Death of Mahalaleel, aged 895.
2582 Death of Jared, aged 962.
2468 First Intimation of Deluge.
2353 Death of Lamech, aged 777.
2349 Death of Methuselah, aged 969.
2347 Noah and family quit the ark.
2346 Birth of Arphaxad to Shem.
2311 Birth of Salah to Arphaxad.
2281 Birth of Heber to Salah.
2247 Birth of Phaleg to Heber.
2234 Building of Tower of Babel.
2233 Nimrod in Asshur, & Ham in Egypt.
2217 Birth of Reu to Phaleg.
2185 Birth of Serug to Reu.
2155 Birth of Nahor to Serug.
2126 Birth of Terah to Nahor.
2056 Birth of Harah to Terah.
1998 Death of Noah, aged 950.
1996 Birth of Abraham to Terah.
1986 Birth of Sarai, Abraham's wife.
1937 Call of Abraham from Ur.
1921 Second Call from Haran.
1913 Abram rescues Lot.
1910 Birth of Ishmael to Hagar.
1897 Second Covenant with Abraham.
1896 Birth of Isaac to Sarah.
1871 Command to offer up Isaac.
1858 Isaac marries Rebecca.
1836 Birth of Esau and Jacob.
1818 Death of Abraham, aged 175.
1759 Jacob flees to Padan-Aram to Laban.
1728 Joseph sold into Egypt.
1715 Joseph made governor of Egypt.
1706 Jacob goes down to Egypt.
1571 Birth of Moses to Amram.
1531 Kills Egyptian, and flees to Midian.
1491 Israel delivered from Egypt.
1451 Israel enters Canaan under Joshua.
1443 Death of Joshua, aged 110 years.
1212 Birth of Samson.
1171 Birth of Samuel.
1095 Saul anointed king of Israel.
1053 David succeeds Saul over Israel.
1023 Absalom's Rebellion and Death.
1017 Solomon crowned by David's order.
1003 Dedication of Solomon's Temple.
971 Revolt of Ten Tribes under Jeroboam.
954 Rehoboam succeeded by Abijam.
951 Asa reigns, and represses idolatry.
950 Jeroboam succeeded by Nadab.
946 Nadab dies; Baasha succeeds.
926 Baasha dies and Elah succeeds him.
921 Omri builds Samaria.

910 Jehoshaphat reigns over Judah.
885 Jehoram reigns; Homer flourishes.
884 Ahaziah reigns but one year.
878 Jehoash reigns and Athaliah dies.
836 He kills Zechariah son of Jehoiada.
835 Fined by Hazael; Jehoahaz dies.
822 Amaziah and Benhadad reign.
810 Uzziah reigns; Isaiah and Amos.
754 Jotham reigns; Hosea prophesies.
736 Ahaz reigns; Rezin invades him.
735 Hoshea slays Pekah, and reigns.
722 Hezekiah reigns.
712 Sennacherib invades Judah.
706 Hezekiah's miraculous cure.
705 Esar-haddon succeeds Sennacherib.
694 Manasseh reigns.
677 Esar-haddon unites Asshur and Babel
671 Manasseh carried to Babylon.
653 Holofernes slain by Judith.
639 Amon reigns for two years.
637 Josiah reigns, Jeremiah prophecies.
606 Jehoahaz and Eliakim reign.
602 Nebuchadnezzar takes away Daniel.
598 His first dream explained.
596 Jehoiakim revolts against him.
595 Birth of Cyrus to Cambyses.
590 Ezekiel prophesies to the Jews.
588 Jerusalem taken; temple burnt.
587 Gedaliah made governor of Judah.
553 Darius the Mede reigns.
551 Cyrus the Persian succeeds him.
536 Babylon taken; Joshua high priest.
535 Second Temple begun to be rebuilt.
529 Cambysis reigns over Persia.
521 Darius Hystaspis succeeds him.
516 Temple finished to be built.
485 Xerxes reigns over Persia.
483 Jehoiakim made high priest.
464 Artaxerxes reigns over Persia.
463 Rebuilding of Jerusalem stopped.
460 Esther married to Artaxerxes.
457 Ezra sent by him to Jerusalem.
453 Eliashib made high priest.
423 Darius Nothus succeeds Artaxerxes.
420 Nehemiah's reformation in Jerusalem
413 Joiada made high priest.
373 Jonathan (or John) succeeds him.
341 Jaddua (or Jaddus), high priest.
321 Onias I. becomes high priest.
300 Simon the just succeeds him.
291 Eleazar.
276 Manasses.
250 Onias II.
217 Simon II.
195 Onias III.
175 Jason (or Jesus).
172 Onias (or Menelaus).
163 Judas Maccabaeus becomes prince
160 Jachim (or Alcimus) high priest.
153 Jonathan appointed high priest.
143 Simon his brother succeeds
136 John Hyrcanus.
106 Aristobulus and Antigonus.
105 Alexander Jannae_s.
78 Queen Alexandra reigns.
69 Hyrcanus II. (and Aristobulus II.)
63 Pompey captures Jerusalem.
40 Antigonus high priest.
37 Herod the Great becomes king.
4 John and Jesus born, A.M. 4004—5411